American Literature

VOLUME TWO

American Literature
A Prentice Hall Anthology

EMORY ELLIOTT, General Editor
University of California, Riverside

LINDA K. KERBER
University of Iowa

A. WALTON LITZ
Princeton University

TERENCE MARTIN
Indiana University

 PRENTICE HALL, ENGLEWOOD CLIFFS, NEW JERSEY 07632

Library of Congress Cataloging-in-Publication Data
(Revised for vol. 2)
American literature.

Includes bibliographical references and indexes.
1. American literature. I. Elliott, Emory (date)
PS507.A5757 1990   810.8   90-7875
ISBN 0-13-027244-2 (v. 1)
ISBN 0-13-027269-8 (v. 2)

Acquisition editor: Kate Morgan
*Editorial/production supervision and
   interior design:* Hilda Tauber
Development editor: Karen S. Karlin
Prepress buyer: Herb Klein
Manufacturing buyer: Dave Dickey
Photo research: Barbara Schultz
Photo editor: Lorinda Morris-Nantz
Design director: Florence Dara Silverman
Art preparation: Carol Hyland
Cover design: Lydia Gershey
Cover art: The Montclair Quilt (detail), 1976.
Pieced and appliqued quilt in honor of
the 1976 Bicentennial. 84 × 96".
© Montclair Craft Guild 1976, Montclair, N.J.

Printed in the United States of America
10 9 8 7 6 5 4 3 2 1

ISBN   0-13-027269-8

Prentice-Hall International (UK) Limited, *London*
Prentice-Hall of Australia Pty. Limited, *Sydney*
Prentice-Hall Canada Inc., *Toronto*
Prentice-Hall Hispanoamericana, S.A., *Mexico*
Prentice-Hall of India Private Limited, *New Delhi*
Prentice-Hall of Japan, Inc., *Tokyo*
Simon & Schuster Asia Pte. Ltd., *Singapore*
Editora Prentice-Hall do Brasil, Ltda., *Rio de Janeiro*

Contents

Emily Dickinson (1830–1886)   **150**

= PART TWO =

America in the World Community: The Early 20th Century   907

EARLY 20TH-CENTURY POETRY   *916*

Edwin Arlington Robinson (1869–1935)   **921**

Hilda Doolittle (H. D.) (1886–1961)   **1014**

Ezra Pound (1885–1972)   **1022**

Marianne Moore (1887–1972)   **1061**

Louise Bogan (1897–1970)   **1141**

Yvor Winters (1900–1968)   **1149**

Allen Tate (1899–1979)   **1157**

Langston Hughes (1902–1967)   **1167**

EARLY 20TH-CENTURY FICTION   *1193*

PART THREE

*Diversity, Technology, and Social Change: The Middle
to Late 20th Century*   **1391**

MIDDLE TO LATE 20TH-CENTURY DRAMA   *1400*

Preface

During the past twenty years, the field of American literature has been going through one of the most exciting periods in its development as a discipline. Of the many changes in literary theory and in critical methods, the most significant advance affecting the teaching of American writing—and thereby anthologies of American literature—has been the discovery and rediscovery of important works that had received little critical attention in the past. For the most part, these newly valued texts are by women writers and members of ethnic and racial minority groups whose works had been misunderstood, overlooked, or consciously rejected by the professors who were in positions to make such decisions, most of whom were themselves male and primarily interested in the English heritage of American literature. Thus, for example, anthologies always used to begin with the writings of the English Puritans who came to what was referred to as a "new world." One recent shift has been the recognition that long before the English arrived in the land now called America, that land had been inhabited for centuries by peoples who possessed rich and complex literary cultures that form part of American literature. Before the English arrived, explorers from Spain, Italy, and other parts of the world had also left a literary record of their encounters with this land and its peoples. Today's literature courses and anthologies present these earlier writings as more accurate beginnings of American literature.

Whereas the list of writers and texts in American literature has grown substantially as a result of these new attitudes, the number of weeks in each semester and the number of courses in college curricula allotted for the teaching of the subject have not expanded. Teachers in the field would like more time to do justice to the established writers such as Emerson, Melville, James, and Faulkner, whose works have long been studied. Concurrently, they want to introduce students to the many rewarding texts by writers such as Kate Chopin, Charlotte Perkins Gilman, Constance Fenimore Woolson, Mary E. Wilkins Freeman, Emma Lazarus, Charles W. Chesnutt, Paul Laurence Dunbar, Booker T. Washington, and W. E. B. Du Bois, to note a few examples from the 1880s and 1890s alone. To accommodate these desires, anthology editors have been producing longer and longer texts. In 1974 a standard collection of this kind was about 1700 pages per volume; the most recent anthologies have been approaching 3000 pages per volume. Teachers lament that they are overwhelmed by the huge number of choices to be made and frustrated by the hundreds of pages to be covered in a given year. The large physical size of the books has even become an inconvenience, and in some cases the efforts of publishers to produce smaller books has led to the use of very thin paper and a reduced typeface that makes reading the texts difficult.

Balancing the Canon

Before beginning this anthology, Prentice Hall conducted an extensive survey of American literature teachers at a wide range of institutions of higher learning. The results demonstrated that most teachers want an anthology that is more concise and, at the same time, provides a balance of works by the long-established authors and by those receiving recognition and attention long overdue. Therefore, the editors of *American Literature: A Prentice Hall Anthology* have attempted to produce a text that is complete and contemporary in its inclusion of the widest representation of American writing and yet is more concise than other available texts. In every decision about the table of contents, the format, and the critical apparatus of this anthology, we have kept the needs of teachers and students in the forefront. By making the difficult decision to exclude some texts by established authors that are not frequently taught, we have been able to make room for ample selections by writers excluded in the past. We believe that this anthology provides teachers and students with a practical and useable text that fully reflects the cultural diversity of our national literature.

Indeed, teachers will find many authors and selections that either have not been included in previous anthologies or have only very recently been acknowledged as part of the canon. Robert Calef is placed next to Cotton Mather to demonstrate a rationalist Puritan response to the Salem witchcraft trials. Judith Sargent Murray is included with Mercy Otis Warren, Hannah Webster Foster, and Susanna Haswell Rowson, thus expanding the coverage of female authors of the late eighteenth century. Henry Clay Lewis appears with Augustus Baldwin Longstreet, George Washington Harris, and Thomas Bangs Thorpe as increased interest in regionalism has led to new attention to the Southwest Humorists. Fanny Fern joins Lydia Maria Child, Margaret Fuller, Louisa May Alcott, Rebecca Harding Davis, and Frances E. W. Harper in the antebellum period, and the Declaration of Sentiments, issued at the Seneca Falls Women's Rights Convention, provides readers with a chorus of voices for women's rights in the 1840s. In the twentieth-century sections, Maya Angelou, Paula Gunn Allen, Lawson Inada, Maxine Kumin, Yvor Winters, and Stanley Kunitz are included with T. S. Eliot, William Faulkner, and Flannery O'Connor. In addition to offering the complete texts of *The Contrast*, *The Scarlet Letter*, "Benito Cereno," *Billy Budd*, *Nature*, *Walden*, *Huckleberry Finn*, *The Awakening*, *Daisy Miller*, *Maggie*, "Red Wind," "Hugh Selwyn Mauberley," "The Waste Land," and *Seize the Day*, we have included in their entirety the *Narrative of the Life of Frederick Douglass*, Lorraine Hansberry's *A Raisin in the Sun* and N. Scott Momaday's *The Way to Rainy Mountain*. These are only a few examples of the newly recognized and established authors and texts that readers will find here. Because some survey courses cover Whitman in the first term and others cover him in the second, we duplicate the entire Whitman section in each volume. In addition, we are proud of our extraordinarily full list of complete plays. The limited number of selections by Hemingway, Fitzgerald, and Faulkner are the result of restrictions their publishers have placed upon reprinting their works.

Placing Works in Contexts

This anthology focuses strongly upon the connections between American literature and its various contexts: historical, political, economic, religious, intellectual, and international. Because teachers report that students are often daunted by extremely long period introductions that attempt to cover too much history and literature at once, we have provided shorter introductory background segments and placed them closer to the appropriate texts. We have avoided overly long introductions and designed a combination of historical background essays by editor-historian Linda K. Kerber and essays on the various literary genres. This separation enables readers to perceive the literary matters in relation to—but separate from—the political and social contexts at the time of writing. The repeated juxtaposition of literary text with historical material reminds the readers of the connections between them as well. The historical introductions engage controversial issues of American history and examine the conflicts and failures as well as the victories of America's past. Genre introductions discuss the development and complexities of the literary forms and styles in relation to the intellectual movements of the time periods.

Along with the emphasis upon linking texts and contexts more closely, we have placed in each section several "Contexts" boxes, which present relevant historical and critical statements or examples of other pertinent literature. In some cases, the "Contexts" boxes present special developments: a series of boxes in the twentieth-century sections traces the chronological development of different schools of literary criticism and theory. Throughout both volumes, boxes help to define and illustrate key terms such as "neoclassicism," "romanticism," and "modernism." Significant nonliterary documents also appear, including portions of the "I Have a Dream" speech by Dr. Martin Luther King, Jr.

Adding the Visual Element

With the strong emphasis upon the visual in our society, it is surprising how few illustrations appear in literature anthologies. The Prentice Hall anthology has portraits of one hundred authors and one hundred additional illustrations that capture the feel of the historical periods, the action and events that surrounded the writing of the literature, and the associations between writing and other arts. For example, students using this text will be able to see the domes and columns of neoclassical architecture and thus better grasp the relationship between the balance and form of eighteenth-century writing and the style of neoclassical buildings. The illustrations add an exciting feature to the Prentice Hall anthology that distinguishes it sharply from others.

With the daily experiences of teachers and students in mind, we have sought to make an anthology that people will truly enjoy using. Avoiding overly long biographical essays, we have made the headnotes more concise. In addition to historical period introductions, we have provided illustrated, eye-catching time lines that integrate key historical and literary events and their dates. Readers will obtain a clear picture of the chronology and the interconnection of texts and contexts. A glossary at the end of each volume serves to underscore and define literary terms that arise in the historical and genre introductions and headnotes as well as those that naturally come up in classroom discussions. An appendix, "Writing About Literature," discusses the student's special problems involved in writing an essay about literature and outlines procedures for meeting the challenge successfully. We have tried to annotate the texts sensibly in order to provide in a concise form the essential information students need. Dates for the initial publication of works are listed at the end of each selection; when known, dates of composition precede the publication dates. Whenever possible, we have used the approved, definitive editions of the texts. For ease of reading we have modernized archaic punctuation and spelling of some works in the early period. Readers should note that within excerpts of works, three centered asterisks indicate an omission of a paragraph or more, whereas run-in ellipses marks indicate the omission of less than a paragraph. Finally, each volume is accompanied by an instructor's manual with questions for study and discussion, suggested topics for student papers, and guidelines for teaching American literature.

ACKNOWLEDGMENTS

Many scholars provided various forms of assistance in the preparation of this anthology. We are grateful to Anne Agee, Anne Arundel Community College; Steven Gould Axelrod, University of California, Riverside; David Arnold, University of California, Riverside; David Austin; Lea Baechler, Columbia University; Rosemarie Battaglia, Michigan State University; Ronald Bosco, State University of New York, Albany; Jack Branscomb, East Tennessee State University; Brian Bremen, University of Texas; Mark Busby, Texas A & M University; James Buzzard, Harvard University; Bruce Coad, Mountain View College; Joan Corcoran, Columbia University; Gwen Crane, Princeton University; Keith Cushman, University of North Carolina, Greensboro; Allan Emery, Bowling Green State University; Joseph Essid, Indiana University; Virginia Feury-Gagnon; Thomas Fick, Southeastern Louisiana University; Joan Frederick, James Madison University; Sam Girgus, Vanderbilt University; Sonja Froiland, Indiana University; Maureen Goldman, Bentley College; Consuela Golden; Janet Gray, Princeton University; Jennifer M. Ginn, North Carolina State University; June Chase Hankins, Southwest Texas State University; Joseph Heininger, University of Michigan; Wendy Hirsh, Columbia University; Anne Hiemstra, Columbia University; Michael J. Hoffman, University of California, Davis; Joonok Huh, Northern Colorado University; Mary Hunter, University of California, Riverside; Claudia Johnson, University of Alabama; Emory D. Jones, Northeast Mississippi Community College; Alan Kaufman, Bergen Community College; Margot Kelley, Indiana University; Katherine Kinney, University of California, Riverside; James A. Levernier, University of Arkansas, Little Rock; Ina Lipkowitz, Columbia University; Michael Lofaro, University of Tennessee; Mason Lowance, University of Massachusetts; Robert Lynch, University of Nebraska; John McCammon, Indiana University; John H. McElroy, University of Arizona; June J. McManus, San Antonio College; Marilyn Miller; Randall Moon, University of California, Riverside; Nancy A. Mower, University of Hawaii; Anne C. Myers, DeVry Institute of Technology, Phoenix; Louis Owens, University of New Mexico; Jay Parini, Middlebury College; Mark Patterson, University of Washington; Timothy Redman, Ohio State University; Mary Margaret Richards, University of Texas, Permian Basin; Judith M. Riggin, Northern Virginia Community College; Michael Robertson, Lafayette College; James K. Ruppert, University of Alaska; Ramón Saldivar, University of Texas, Austin; Rosalind Sackoff; William J. Scheick, University of Texas; James Scrimgeour; Thomas E. Shields, East Carolina University; Frank Shuffelton, Rochester University; William Shurr, University of Tennessee; Nancy Craig Simmons, Virginia Polytechnic Institute and State University; Pat Skantze, Columbia University; Diane Stevens, Indiana University; Gordon Tapper, Columbia University; John Timmerman, Calvin College; David Van Leer, University of California, Davis; Edward Watts, Indiana University; Lori J. Williams, Indiana University; Ann Woodlief, Virginia Commonwealth University; and David Wyatt, University of Maryland. We also thank Josephine Koster Tarvers of Rutgers University, New Brunswick, for composing the essay "Writing About Literature."

Several students, secretaries, family members, and friends have provided various forms of editorial assistance. We wish to thank Deborah Barker, Sara Lynn Bowers, Marcia Hack, Bruce Hagood, Carla Latteri, Kandi Leonard, Barbara Burke Martin, Elizabeth Patton, Marsha Rosh, Maggi Schuman, Estelle Shapiro-Childers, and Holly Witten. The staffs of the following libraries have been quite helpful: the University of California, Riverside; the University of California, Los Angeles; the Huntington Library; Princeton University; the University of Iowa; and Indiana University, especially Anthony Shipps.

Finally, we wish to thank the following people at Prentice Hall who worked closely with us: our development editor, Karen Karlin, whose endurance, patience, and editorial skills have been remarkable; Hilda Tauber, our production editor and designer, for her imaginative work and flexible planning; and editor in chief Phil Miller and senior English editor Kate Morgan for directing the project with wisdom and good cheer. Others who contributed in important ways are supplements editor Ann Knitel, photo editor Lorinda Morris-Nantz, design director Florence Silverman, permissions researcher Mary Helen Fitzgerald, marketing managers Tracy Augustine and Gina Sluss, and assistants Fran Falk, Heidi Moore, Page Poore, and Kathy Hursch.

EMORY ELLIOTT
General Editor

PART ONE

Expansion and National Redefinition

The Late 19th Century

The assassination of Abraham Lincoln only five days after General Robert E. Lee's surrender in Appomattox Court House, Virginia, in 1865 was an eerie precursor of the violence and profound disruption that continued to characterize American life even after the Civil War had officially ended. The meaning of the Civil War remained contested. To many northerners the war had increasingly come to have a moral component. Victory seemed to validate the increased power of the central government, which had directed the war, and also to commit the nation to a revolution in race relations. For many white southerners, defeat in war signified simply an end to claims of southern independence and to the system of slavery. Many thought they could return to life as it had been before the guns fired on Fort Sumter in Charleston: that is, to a system of race relations in which whites were dominant and blacks were submissive, and to a political system in which the white men who had controlled politics would resume their seats in Congress and in state legislatures as though nothing had happened.

Reconstruction

National politics were poisoned by a struggle among former Unionists about what ought to be done to "reconstruct" the defeated South. This was especially true after the former Confederate states passed "Black Codes," laws ostensibly intended to grant freedpeople civil rights—to marry, to testify in court, to hold property, to sue and be sued—but that in fact created second-class citizenships. The Black Codes generally forbade African Americans to marry whites, to bear arms, to possess alcoholic beverages, to be on the streets after dark, and to claim seats on public conveyances. As the level of violence in the South rose, the distance between President Andrew Johnson and Congress also grew. Congress had to override presidential vetoes in order to establish its most important Reconstruction legislation, notably the Freedmen's Bureau, the Civil Rights Act of 1866, and the Reconstruction Act of 1867. The Freedmen's Bureau was empowered to establish courts to protect the lives of freedpeople, to feed and clothe refugees, and to

1

supervise the renting of land confiscated from Confederates to loyal refugees and freedpeople. The Civil Rights Act of 1866 guaranteed ex-slaves the right to own property, to make contracts, and to enforce their claims in court. The Reconstruction Act of 1867 divided the South into five military districts in which military officers would maintain order, register voters, and supervise the creation of new state constitutions that guaranteed suffrage to African-American men. The struggle between Congress and the President ended with the impeachment and trial of Andrew Johnson in 1868; one vote short of the required two-thirds majority, he was not convicted, but the stigma of being the first president to be impeached made him politically helpless for the rest of his term.

To make change permanent, Congress amended the Constitution in 1868. The Fourteenth Amendment was the most significant single act of the postwar years. It defines as citizens "all persons born or naturalized in the United States" and guarantees all Americans "equal protection of the laws." The Fourteenth Amendment in effect requires the states as well as the federal government to enforce the provisions of the Bill of Rights and has remained central to American civil liberties since its passage.

The second section of the Fourteenth Amendment canceled the "three-fifths" clause of the Constitution, set up by the Three-Fifths Compromise, and guaranteed suffrage to African-American men by penalizing states that did not permit all adult men to vote by cutting their representation in Congress. In framing the guarantee clause this way, however, Congress for the first time introduced the word "male" into the Constitution and explicitly made gender a limiting factor in interpreting constitutional rights. This was done despite the bitter protest of women's suffrage organizations; ironically, it was never enforced to protect the rights of African-American male voters. The Fifteenth Amendment, passed in 1870, straightforwardly prohibits states from denying the right to vote on the basis of race, color, or previous condition of servitude. It does not guarantee suffrage to women, who began to urge a separate constitutional amendment on their own behalf. Northerners were much more willing to insist on suffrage for African-American men in the South than in the North: in referendums held in nine northern states between 1865 and 1869, suffrage for African-American men was voted down in all except Iowa and Minnesota.

In areas where the Union had been in control during the war, such as the Sea Islands off Georgia, some freedpeople had worked forty-acre plots of confiscated land. Many African Americans expected that this policy would be extended and that, with the defeat of slavery, each former slave would receive "forty acres and a mule." But although Congress was reluctantly willing to offer citizenship rights to African-Americans, it was not prepared to offer them either the education or the economic security that would transform the dependent relations of slavery into authentic independence. Education was left to the states and to voluntary organizations. Federal troops were used to enforce traditional property relations, and in the years after the war former slaves became tenant farmers bound to their former masters by a series of contractual arrangements. Through sharecropping, freedpeople used landlords' land and supplies and in return gave up one-half to two-thirds of what was produced. By making the ex-slaves indebted to country stores and dependent on landowners for seed for the following year's crop, share-cropping maintained the hierarchy of race relations within the structure of political freedom.

A decade after Appomattox, a special electoral commission, voting along party lines, awarded contested electoral votes to Rutherford B. Hayes, the Republican presidential candidate. Democratic resentment at the "stolen" election was soothed by a "compromise" in which Hayes and the Republicans promised to support federal economic aid to railroad development in the South and to let white southerners handle local race relations. The few troops still in the South were withdrawn.

In the absence of northern control, a "New South" developed, characterized by the exclusion of African Americans from both voting and officeholding and by the erasure of the reforms Reconstruction legislatures had undertaken, notably in support for public education. Mass media throughout the South stereotyped African Americans as childlike fools or degenerates, and state legislation disfranchised African Americans by imposing poll taxes and manipulative literacy tests. In the 1890s a new wave of legislation excluded African Americans from public places, inventing a new system of segregation in which railroads, libraries, restaurants, schools, hospitals, cemetaries, and prisons were different for blacks and whites. According to the Supreme Court ruling *Plessy* v. *Ferguson* of 1896, segregation with roughly equal though separate facilities was not a denial of equal protection under the law. Subsequent courts made no effort to ensure actual "equality" of public accomodations. Systematically excluded from the skilled trades, southern African Americans were pushed into marginal jobs even more extensively than they had been under slavery; it has been estimated that at the end of the Civil War, at least fifty percent of all skilled craftsmen in the South were African Americans, but by the 1890s that figure had dropped below ten percent. The new system was maintained by intimidation and violence: 1400 African-American men were hanged, shot, or burned alive in lynchings during the 1890s alone.

Expansion

The Civil War was succeeded by an undeclared civil war against the Native Americans of the Great Plains. The violence intensified with the completion of the transcontinental railway and the coming of more white settlers. Native Americans watched with dismay the near-extermination of the buffalo; some 13 million were killed by 1883. When the federal government allowed gold prospectors to enter the Black Hills of South Dakota and of Wyoming, the Sioux fought back to protect their land and their holy places. Although they were victorious over General George Custer at the Battle of the Little Bighorn in 1876, they were defeated elsewhere, and their hero, Chief Crazy Horse, was killed. Congress ceased to treat the tribes as independent nations. The Dawes Severalty Act of 1887 entitled each head of household to only 160 acres of land, thus forcing the Native Americans into agriculture rather than hunting and transforming relationships within the tribes as well as the relationship of the tribes to the federal government.

Some works of literature and art, such as The Spirit of the Frontier *(1872), by John Dost, helped transform the harsh realities of frontier life into a myth of limitless opportunity.*

The expansionist vision that haunted relationships with Native Americans also affected foreign policy. On overseas expansion, however, there was considerably more ambivalence: "We want no unwilling citizens to enter our Union," Theodore Roosevelt wrote in 1886. But as American economic interests overseas increased, as exports grew (more than three hundred percent between 1870 and 1900), and as European imperialism closed major markets off to American trade, overseas expansion seemed increasingly attractive to more people. American planters and the American ambassador to Hawaii supported a successful coup against Queen Liliuokalani, who had challenged American domination of the sugar market in 1893; five years later the Hawaiian islands were annexed. The United States intervened to assist the Cuban resistance to Spain in 1898 but quickly transformed an act of assistance to a claim for empire. After the battleship *Maine* blew up in Havana harbor, President William McKinley declared war on Spain, although no one knows if Spain was responsible for the explosion. The fighting, which lasted only ten weeks, was distinctly one-sided. The result of the Spanish-American War was not only the establishment of Cuban independence but also the achievement of a stable environment for American sugar producers and exporters and the annexation of other Spanish possessions: the Philippines, Puerto Rico, and Guam. In the Philippines American expansion faced intense resistance from the native people, who maintained a bloody and bitter guerilla war for three years.

===CONTEXTS===

The Westward Expansion After 1865

By the late 1860s, exploitation of the last frontier in North America, the Great Plains/Rocky Mountain region, was well under way. The scarcity of cheap, fertile land in the East and Far West spurred westward migration, as did the passage of the Homestead Act of 1862, by which Congress gave 160 acres of land to each permanent settler in exchange for a small fee. The British historian James Bryce (1838–1922) twice visited the American West in the 1880s. In his book on American custom and culture, *The American Commonwealth* (1893), he attempted to define the western character and in so doing perpetuates old myths that seem to honor white mercantile expansionism.

The American Commonwealth

It is the most enterprising and unsettled Americans that come West; and when they have left their old haunts, broken their old ties, resigned the comforts and pleasures of their former homes, they are resolved to obtain the wealth and success for which they have come. They throw themselves into work with a feverish yet sustained intensity. They rise early, they work all day, they have few pleasures, few opportunities for relaxation. I remember in the young city of Seattle on Puget Sound to have found business in full swing at seven o'clock A.M.: the shops open, the streets full of people. Everything is speculative, land (or, as it is usually called, "real estate") most so, the value of lots of ground rising or falling perhaps two or three hundred per cent in the year. No one has any fixed occupation; he is a storekeeper to-day, a ranchman to-morrow, a miner next week. . . . Few men stay in one of the newer cities more than a few weeks or months; to have been there a whole year is to be an old inhabitant, an oracle if you have succeeded, a by-word if you have not, for to prosper in the West you must be able to turn your hand to anything, and seize the chance to-day which everyone else will have seen to-morrow.

* * *

These people are intoxicated by the majestic scale of the nature in which their lot is cast, enormous mineral deposits, boundless prairies, forests which, even squandered—wickedly squandered—as they now are, will supply timber to the United States for centuries; a soil which, with the rudest cultivation, yields the most abundant crops, a populous continent for their market. They see all round them railways being built, telegraph wires laid, steamboat lines across the Pacific projected, cities springing up in the solitudes, and settlers making the wilderness to blossom like the rose. Their imagination revels in these sights and signs of progress, and they gild their own struggles for fortune with the belief that they are the missionaries of civilization and the instruments of Providence in the greatest work the world has seen. . . .

                                                                James Bryce, 1893

Industrialization and Immigration

One of the most striking exhibits of the Great Centennial Exposition in Philadelphia in 1876 was the Corliss engine. Like the rest of its companions in Machinery Hall, the Corliss engine would have been inconceivable in 1776. It was an emblem of "smokestack America" and the extraordinary productivity of an economy dependent on heavy industry. In addition to the consumer goods—textiles, clothing, processed grains—turned out by pre-Civil War factories, the new industry emphasized mining, metal processing, and the manufacture of machinery. Vast sums of capital sustained a phenomenal output of the basic metals: iron, steel, and copper. A new technology of steel—iron refined in a Bessemer converter—cut the cost in half and revolutionized the production of rails, engines, and bridges. A new technology of brake and gear design transformed railcars. The result was a change in the scale of economic activity: with a national transportation system, the entire nation could be treated as a single market. And even that market was to broaden after Orville and Wilbur Wright made the first sustained airplane flight in Kitty Hawk, North Carolina, in 1903.

The industrial economy had what seemed like an insatiable demand for workers, as the number of jobs increased some four hundred percent during the second half of the nineteenth century. But factory owners rarely hired African Americans, for whom factory work would have represented a major improvement in situation. Instead employers recruited what seemed like a limitless supply of Europeans. Fourteen million immigrants entered between 1860 and 1900, nearly three times as many as in the forty years before the Civil War. Some of the Europeans—notably Jews—were forced from their native lands by religious and political persecution; most others left because of overpopulation, by the consolidation of land, and by desperate poverty. They were attracted to the United States by economic opportunity, commonly in the form of advertisements for labor.

In 1890 Ellis Island, New York, was opened as a receiving depot for immigration. American law welcomed immigrants: through the process of naturalization, virtually unknown elsewhere, foreigners could become citizens with exactly the same legal status as the native-born. In this sense America really was a "Promised Land." Other new countries—Canada, Australia, Argentina—also were populated by European immigrants, but from only a few nationalities: eighty percent of Argentina's immigrants came from Italy and Spain, and seventy-five percent of Canadian immigrants were from English-speaking countries. But immigration to the United States was characterized by many language groups and nationalities: British, German, Irish, Italian, Polish, Hungarian, Russian, and Scandinavian. The Chinese, however, met great hostility: race riots in San Francisco in 1877 marked the beginning of a campaign that culminated in the Chinese Exclusion Act of 1882, which prohibited the immigration of both skilled and unskilled Chinese workers.

The work immigrants found was hard and often precarious. Working-class families relied upon the work of adult women as well as adult men. By 1900 twenty percent of adult women were in the paid labor force, and many more earned money by taking in boarders or laundry at home. Working-class families also relied on the labor of their children, who were generally in their early teens when they left school. The immigrants entered an erratic economy, highly vulnerable to boom and bust business cycles. Particularly severe depressions occurred between 1873 and 1878 and again between 1893 and 1897. It is estimated that between one-quarter and one-third of the work force was unemployed at some time every year during the late nineteenth century, when there was no unemployment insurance in the United States. Still, perhaps one-fifth of the immigrants managed to climb into the middle class, and many children of immigrants improved on the situation of their parents.

The last quarter of the nineteenth century was a time of major working-class protest, in which railroad workers played a leading part. In 1888 1 out of 357 railroad workers in the United States was killed on the job, and 1 out of 35 injured. (In England, by comparison, railroad work killed 1 out of 875 and injured 1 out of 158 [Nell Painter, *Standing at Armageddon*, 1987].) In 1877 railroad workers staged the first national industrial strike, and for the first time on a national scale, the military was called out to break it. Fourteen hundred strikes, involving nearly half a million workers, were called in 1886 alone, and all the major ones failed. With virtually no evidence, eight anarchists were convicted of planting a bomb at the Haymarket Square protest against the McCormick Reaper Company in Chicago. The defeat of strikes gradually demoralized the Knights of Labor, which had sought to represent the interests of labor as a whole. In the 1890s the American Federation of Labor, which stressed the interests of skilled workers, replaced it as the leading voice of organized workers.

Social Change

Changes in industry were accompanied by changes in bureaucracy, in the family, and in education. Like industrial changes, bureaucratic changes had begun almost unnoticed during the Civil War. The invention of the typewriter in 1876 provided a technical tool by which to record business transactions—as well as to write literary works more efficiently—and was part of a great explosion of paperwork that accompanied the transformed economy. During the Civil War government agencies facing a shortage of men became the first workplaces in America in which men and women worked side by side doing similar jobs. By the end of the century many middle-class men and women worked in large hierarchical bureaucracies, their reward security rather than Horatio Alger's dream of fortune.

At the urging of Anthony Comstock, the head of the New York Society for the Suppression of Vice, Congress provided severe penalties for the transportation by mail not only of pornographic materials but of all materials "for the prevention of conception." However, birth rates continued to decline in the late nineteenth century. In 1860 each American woman bore on average 5.2 children, but in 1900 the figure had dropped to 3.6. The decline was even sharper among the business and professional classes, in which families with only 2 children were increasingly common. Middle-class families believed that they could provide their children with more advantages, such as higher education, if the children were fewer in

The Chicago Riots

One of the most intense labor struggles in American history was the nationwide crusade for the eight-hour workday. At its 1884 national convention in Chicago, the Federation of Organized Trades and Labor Unions of the United States and Canada (the forerunner of the American Federation of Labor) delivered an ultimatum: on May 1, 1886, an eight-hour system would go into effect nationally, or strikes and demonstrations would be held to convince rebellious employers to comply.

At the McCormick Reaper Company on May 3, 1886, Chicago police opened fire on a crowd of strikers, killing and wounding several men. When workers held a protest meeting near Chicago's Haymarket Square the following evening, a bomb was thrown into the ranks of the police, trying to stop the meeting. The officers in turn opened fire on the crowd. Seventy people were wounded, and seven police officers died. Eight anarchists were blamed for the bombing and convicted of murder—although the bombthrower was never apprehended. The trial became the *cause célèbre* for liberals, including the novelist William Dean Howells. Four of the defendants were hanged, a fifth killed himself in his cell, and the others received lengthy prison terms. In 1893 the latter were pardoned by the reform governor of Illinois, John Peter Altgeld, who decided that the evidence failed to link them to the bombing.

The night before the Haymarket Riot, anarchists distributed to striking workers a circular, introduced as evidence in the trial:

REVENGE!
—■—
Workingmen, to Arms!!!

Your masters sent out their bloodhounds — the police --; they killed six of your brothers at McCormicks this afternoon. They killed the poor wretches, because they, like you, had the courage to disobey the supreme will of your bosses. They killed them, because they dared ask for the shortenin of the hours of toil. They killed them to show you, ' Free American Citizens'', that you must be satisfied and contended with whatever your bosses condescend to allow you, or you will get killed!

You have for years endured the most abject humiliations; you have for years suffered unmeasurable iniquities; you have worked yourself to death; you have endured the pangs of want and hunger; your Children you have sacrificed to the factory-lords — in short: You have been miserable and obedient slave all these years: Why? To satisfy the insatiable greed, to fill the coffers of your lazy thieving master? When you ask them now to lessen your burden, he sends his bloodhounds out to shoot you, kill you!

If you are men, if you are the sons of your grand sires, who have shed their blood to free you, then you will rise in your might, Hercules, and destroy the hideous monster that seeks to destroy you. To arms we call you, to arms!

Your Brothers.

Anonymous circular, 1886

Author, educator, reformer, and 1931 Nobel Peace Prize winner, Jane Addams experimented with new teaching methods at her famous community center, Hull House, which she founded in Chicago in 1889.

number. Between 1870 and 1900 the number of public high schools increased from 160 to 6,000, and in 1900 nearly two-thirds of the states had laws for compulsory schooling. The number of students in colleges and universities rose sharply as new institutions were founded, and the impact was particularly great for women. Between 1890 and 1900 the proportion of female college graduates rose from thirteen to twenty percent. Many members of this first sizable generation of women graduates emerged with a strong sense of civic obligation, and many—notably Jane Addams of Chicago's Hull House—were stimulated to found settlement houses and social-service agencies and to address the major social problems of the new industrial society.

LATE 19TH-CENTURY POETRY

The publication of Walt Whitman's *Leaves of Grass* in 1855 signaled the coming of age of poetry in the United States. In his essay "The Poet" (1844), Ralph Waldo Emerson had announced that "America is a poem in our eyes" and called for a writer, as yet unknown, who could exalt the dazzling geography of national life. A decade later Whitman embraced the task of writing this vibrant poem. With egocentric generosity he remarked to the journalist J. T. Trowbridge, "I had been simmering, simmering, simmering; Emerson brought me to a boil."

At the time of Whitman's dramatic accomplishment American poetry was characterized to a large extent by the work of such writers as Henry Wadsworth Longfellow, John Greenleaf Whittier, Oliver Wendell Holmes, and James Russell Lowell. To be sure, other poets had developed and were developing noteworthy perspectives on art and on society, as evidenced by the gnostic reflections of Emerson, the craftmanship of Edgar Allan Poe, the southern voices of Henry Timrod and Paul Hamilton Hayne, and the eloquence of Frances E. W. Harper in her portrayals of human oppression. But the most popular and ubiquitous poetry at the time Whitman began to write was that of the so-called Fireside Poets: Longfellow, Whittier, Holmes, and Lowell, whose work provided instruction for the classroom and piety for the home. These writers incorporated American topics into their poetry through the lens of a temperate romanticism. In a variety of ways they affirmed traditional values and championed moral causes with idealistic passion. Whitter's devotion to the abolitionist movement, for example, brought Frederick Douglass to call him the "slave's poet" in Douglass's autobiographical *Narrative* (1845). Yet in *Snowbound* (1866), Whittier produced the classic memory poem of the nineteenth century, a nostalgic tribute to the values of home and hearth. Content with established forms, the Fireside Poets were public figures, writers available for political discourse or for ceremonial occasions. In a fundamental way they were part of the grateful society for which they wrote.

Radically different in form and content from previous or contemporary poetry, Whitman's *Leaves of Grass* celebrates the grandeur of the democratic "self," body and soul, male and female: no longer is it necessary to forge an epic from history and legend, as Whitman makes clear in the remarkable preface to the 1855 edition of *Leaves* and in "Song of Myself"; the human being is epic in potential, deserving of epic treatment in a land of epic proportions. Undaunted by the poor sales of his book, Whitman published a second edition in 1856 and a much enlarged edition in 1860; there were nine editions in all, the final one completed in the year of his death, 1892. As different as Whitman's poetic credo was from that of Ezra Pound in the early decades of the twentieth century, the imperious Pound (with his passion for a poetry fresh and uncompromised by habit) found it necessary to treat Whitman's achievement with grudging respect. In a poem first entitled "A Truce" and then "A Pact" (1916), Pound addresses Whitman as a reluctant "grown child" coming to a "pig-headed father." Then comes a significant admission: "It was you that broke the new wood, / Now is a time for carving." Among nineteenth-century American poets only Whitman elicits this kind of concession from Pound; only Whitman brings Pound to say "We have one sap and one root— / Let there be commerce between us."

From Pound's perspective, the persistent influence of the Fireside Poets throughout the final decades of the nineteenth century put a damper on poetic initiative and innovation. With his interest in history, he had no concern for the way Whittier and Longfellow came to be revered as guardians of virtue who made society's way of wanting poetry their way of writing it. For a different reason it was not possible for him (or for nineteenth-century readers) to appreciate the distinctive achievement of Emily Dickinson, who saw only a dozen of her 1,776 poems published during her lifetime—and those with misgivings.

Like Whitman, Dickinson was a poet of striking originality. Whereas his poetic impulse led to stylistic expansiveness and discursiveness, however, hers yielded spareness and a determined lack of excess. Whereas he reached out to include the world in his utterance, she looked within to define a world bright with surprise, startling in its scope. Definition is an integral part of Dickinson's poetic mode: in defining such virtues as faith and hope and such emotions as elysium (happiness) and remorse, she translates them into a personal idiom in which we meet and know them afresh. "Renunciation is a piercing virtue," she asserts in a poem that enacts a central paradox of her work, the idea that one knows best by not having: thus "Success is counted sweetest," as she writes, "By those who ne'er succeed."

In her personal life Dickinson rejected the standard nineteenth-century roles for women, preferring an unfettered existence that left her the necessary time for thinking and writing; similarly, throughout her career as a poet in the 1860s and 1870s, she often moved beyond conventional usage in matters of syntax, capitalization, and punctuation. Perhaps her most-remarked stylistic idiosyncracy is her use of the dash as a principal mark of punctuation. Her preference for the dash (sometimes tilting up, sometimes slightly down) over the period may be a private way of directing the reading of her poems; it may also suggest a rejection of finality in experience, a belief that conventional signs in human discourse oversimplify reality.

The work of other poets in the second half of the nineteenth century suggests that the period was not given over to revolutionary breakthroughs of form and idiom but was also a time of applying traditional modes of expression to a postbellum world and of perfecting established poetic techniques. The reclusive Henry Goddard Tuckerman and the politically active Emma Lazarus, for example, extended the resources of the sonnet in markedly different ways: the former in three inner-directed sonnet sequences written around 1870 but not published until 1931, the latter in protests against mistreatment of Jews in Europe and in the very public "The New Colossus" (1883), the sonnet carved on the pedestal of the Statue of Liberty. That poem includes words that are better known than the poet herself: "Give me your tired, your poor, / Your huddled masses yearning to breathe free." It was an ideal to which Lazarus dedicated herself wholeheartedly.

The rhythms of African-American folk speech and those of nature transposed to metrical patterns are registered, respectively and with mixed success, in the poetry of Paul Laurence Dunbar and of Sidney Lanier. Dunbar cultivated a poetic voice rooted in present realities yet aware of the past and of rich folk traditions. Praised by the novelist and editor William Dean Howells in a preface to *Lyrics of Lowly Life* (1896), Dunbar's dialect poems give a popular version of speech patterns from plantation life infused with a romantic combination of pathos and humor. In other poems of the 1890s ("We Wear the Mask" [1896], for example), Dunbar demonstrates an ironic understanding of what it is to be an African American in a race-conscious United States.

Much of Sidney Lanier's poetry portrays nature in the American South. But

=CONTEXTS=

The Completion of the Transcontinental Railway

The building of the transcontinental railway in the 1860s linked the West with eastern markets, encouraged settlement of the Great Plains, and brought about the extermination of the buffalo and the massacre of the Plains Indians. The government-created Union Pacific and the California-chartered Central Pacific railroads competed for government land grants and loans based on the miles of track laid. Their race across deserts and through mountains ended 1,776 miles of rails later on May 10, 1869, when the westbound tracks of the Union Pacific met the eastbound tracks of the Central Pacific in Promontory, Utah. Amidst cheers, a golden spike was driven into one of the ties, signaling completion of the line.

Chinese, African-American, Irish, and Mormon laborers had successfully hauled engines, rails, and other supplies across mountains, negotiated swamps, spanned gorges, blasted through granite walls in the Sierras (marking the first use of nitroglycerine in America), and built towns along the railroad's path virtually overnight. With a rapidity never before dreamed of, the tracks were laid by an assembly-line method, described in the *Cincinnati Gazette* in June 1867:

The trucks, each drawn by two horses, ply between the track-layers and their supplies. One of these trucks takes on a load of rails, about forty, with the proper proportion of spikes and chairs, making a load, when the horses are started off on a full gallop for the track-layers. On each side of these trucks are rollers to facilitate running off the iron.

The rails within reach, parties of five men stand on either side. One in the rear throws a rail upon the rollers, three in advance seize it, and run out with it to the proper distance. The chairs have, meantime, been set under the last rails placed.

The two men in the rear, with a single swing, force the end of the rail into the chair, and the chief of the squad calls out "Down," in a tone that equals the "Forward" to an army. Every thirty seconds there came that brave "Down," "Down," on either side of the track. They were the pendulum beats of a mighty era; they marked the time of the march and its regulation beat.

Cincinnati Gazette, 1867

there is a difference between the work of Lanier and that of his southern colleagues Henry Timrod and Paul Hamilton Hayne: for Lanier was not only a musician (at one time a flutist in the Peabody Orchestra in Baltimore); he was a theorist deeply concerned with the relationship of music and the cadences of poetry. In "The Symphony" (1875) he adapts words to the various instruments of an orchestra to construct a symphonic dialogue about economic and aesthetic matters. And in such poems as "The Marshes of Glynn" (1878) and "March Song—at Sunset" (1882), he captures in fascinating if somewhat ponderous detail the diurnal rhythms of marsh and seacoast in Glynn County, Georgia.

Julia A. Moore, the Sweet Singer of Michigan, by common consent the worst poet the nation has ever produced, should not be overlooked in this discussion. There has always been bad poetry, verse that makes us wince, in every nation and time. Moore's *The Sweet Singer of Michigan Salutes the Public* (1876) takes its place with the most fatuous and maudlin. Unconscious of her parodic talent and

Crowded and unsanitary conditions created hardships for the thousands of urban poor, as shown here on Hester Street in New York City in 1890. Such a setting was used by Stephen Crane in Maggie.

startling grammatical lapses, Moore specialized in obituary poems, saccharine verses on death: "Little Henry" died as an infant; "Little Andrew" drowned at the age of two; "Little Minnie" passed away suddenly when she was four; little "Hattie House" (age six) died "at play" after falling into "a fit"; in the most tragic case of all, "Little Libbie," a "dear little child of ten," choked to death "on a piece of beef." Poems such as these may have inspired the hilarious "Ode to Stephen Dowling Bots, Dec'd" in Mark Twain's *Adventures of Huckleberry Finn* (1884). In *Following the Equator* (1897), Mark Twain notes that the Sweet Singer of Michigan had brought joy to his heart for twenty years.

Caustic and filled with self-awareness, the poetry of Stephen Crane thrives on cosmic irony. At first glance some of his poems (all written in the 1890s) might seem to resemble those of Emily Dickinson. But Crane's poems lack Dickinson's specificity and verbal texture; for the most part they are bitter parables of human destiny played out in an uncaring universe. Properly disciplined and expressed, however, the ironic vision that pervades Crane's fiction can generate a poem such as "Do not weep, maiden, for war is kind" (1899), in which the experience of loss is magnified by the muted and sardonic tone.

Set in a context of interesting poetry of uneven quality, the work of Whitman and of Dickinson constitutes the major poetic achievement of the late nineteenth century. More than that, it exercised a lasting influence on the accomplishments of such early twentiety-century modernists as Ezra Pound, T. S. Eliot, Hilda Doolittle, William Carlos Williams, and Hart Crane. In many ways it continues to affect the writing of poetry in a postmodern era searching for fresh ways of visualizing our common humanity.

Walt Whitman
(1819–1892)

Walt Whitman owes his considerable prominence in American literary history to a single volume of poetry, *Leaves of Grass,* which he first published in 1855 and continued to rework through eight subsequent editions until his death in 1892. Whitman's poetry is marked by startling innovations in style and content that not only reflect the contemporary transition from romanticism to realism, but that signal the liberation of American literature from its European parentage and from the domination of the New England intellectual establishment. A politicized and self-conscious writer, Whitman adapted the romantic concept of the poet as national bard, developing and enacting the role of the American poet as a personification of the democratic ideal: the preeminently common man. In his poetry he celebrates his own vigor as a poet and a man and the dynamic diversity that characterized mid-nineteenth-century America.

Walter Whitman, Jr., the second of eight surviving children, was born on May 31, 1819, in rural West Hills, Long Island. His mother, Louisa Van Velsor, was an energetic woman of Dutch extraction to whom he was devoted. His father had farmed a share of the large tract of land on eastern Long Island that had been owned by the Whitmans since the seventeenth century, but he moved his family to Brooklyn to work as a carpenter when Walt was just four. A noticeable strain of instability ran through the family: Whitman's father was probably an alcoholic; a feeble-minded brother required lifelong care; another died, syphilitic, in a mental institution; and a sister suffered from neurologic problems and depression. A penchant for solitude earned young Walt a reputation for eccentricity.

Whitman's father was a friend of Thomas Paine and an avid reader of political literature. Discourse in the Whitman household was thus imbued with eighteenth-century liberalism, and the individualistic and egalitarian premise of the senior Whitman's politics remained a permanent influence. The family also supported the views of the Scottish feminist Fanny Wright and subscribed to her radical newspaper, *The Free Enquirer.* As a youth Walt looked to the leaders of the American Revolution, especially George Washington, as heroes, and one of Whitman's most important childhood memories centered on seeing the Marquis de Lafayette at an Independence Day ceremony.

Whitman's liberal political beliefs were matched by a nonsectarian religious outlook, an outlook associated with the tolerance that had historically characterized the Dutch of his maternal ancestry. His family was familiar with eighteenth-century deism and was much influenced by the Quaker preacher Elias Hicks, whose earthbound religious philosophy bore some resemblance to Ralph Waldo Emerson's. Throughout his life Whitman valued the quiet introspection and the humanitarianism that are fundamental to Quaker belief.

Despite the senior Whitman's political and philosophical interests, the family did not represent the learned tradition of, say, a Henry Adams; nevertheless, Whitman was well read, and many of the classics of western literature were available to him. In addition to his father's political pamphlets, he read at an early age the novels of Sir Walter Scott, Charles Dickens, and George Sand. Whitman knew the Bible well and had read Greek drama and the writings of Homer, Epicurus, and Lucretius, as well as the work of Shakespeare, Dante, John Milton, and the English romantic poets. The thread of mysticism running through Whitman's poetry may owe something to his reading of Indian literature, especially the Hindu *Bhagavad-Gita* and the Vedic Upanishads.

One of the most important elements of Whitman's thought is his glorification of the experiences of the common man. His own life was composed of such experiences. He left school when he was twelve to become a printer's apprentice, and by nineteen he was editing the weekly *Long Islander*. He taught school in rural Long Island from 1836 to 1841 and then took up his journalistic career once again, editing and writing for newspapers in Brooklyn, New York City, and New Orleans. In 1842 he published *Franklin Evans: Or, the Inebriate,* a formula-ridden and forgettable temperance novel. During these years Whitman developed a camaraderie with stagecoach drivers and with other working-class men, thus demonstrating an egalitarian politics even in his social life. He also became an avid theatergoer and enthusiast of Italian opera. He continued doing newspaper work into the 1850s, writing political editorials and sentimental poems and stories.

In 1855 Whitman published (at his own expense) *Leaves of Grass,* a curious, slim volume of twelve untitled poems prefaced by nine pages of rambling prose and an engraved daguerreotype of the anonymous author. This portrait of the artist as a relaxed young man, casually clothed, one hand resting on his hip, conveys the essence of Whitman's concept of himself as poet: "one of the roughs," he called himself, a man of the quotidian world, curious, confident, and aware. Whitman sent a gift copy of *Leaves of Grass* to Ralph Waldo Emerson, who responded in a now-famous letter greeting the author "at the beginning of a great career" and congratulating him on having produced "the most extraordinary bit of wit and wisdom that America has yet contributed." Despite Emerson's acclaim, this first edition of Whitman's poetry knew little critical success, except for some anonymous and positive reviews written by Whitman himself.

The 1855 preface, which did not appear in subsequent editions of *Leaves of Grass,* is now regarded as an American literary manifesto on the order of Emerson's *American Scholar* (1837) and "The Poet" (1844), to which it is indebted. In it Whitman foreshadows a countercultural poetics that neglects ordinary conventions of versification to exploit the "brawny" richness of Americanized English, "the dialect of common sense." He defines "the greatest poet" as one who "says to the past, Rise and walk before me that I may realize you," as someone connected realistically with his own time and place yet transcending it to "glow for a moment on the extremist verge." The style of the preface is eccentric, punctuated by numerous ellipses and characterized by the declamatory tone of a voice crying in the wilderness; it is the sound of a new voice calling attention to itself. Whitman sings of the beauty of America that coexists with the spiritual beauty of the American people. He hails his country as the ultimate democracy in which citizens can enjoy "the President's taking off his hat to them not they to him."

"Song of Myself" (untitled until 1881) is probably the best known and most significant of the twelve poems in this first edition. In this poem of 1346 lines, the poet celebrates his individuality, the authenticity of his own experiences in nature and in American society, and the diversity of the American population with whom he identifies. Whitman's style here reflects his rejection of nineteenth-century poetic convention and draws its strength from structural and rhythmic patterns similar to the language of biblical texts. Much critical notice has been given to the "chanting" voice of "Song of Myself"; the primitive power of the poem originates partly in the cumulative effect of Whitman's descriptive catalogues, which build in force to a mythic authority.

During the year following the first edition of *Leaves of Grass,* Whitman continued to do

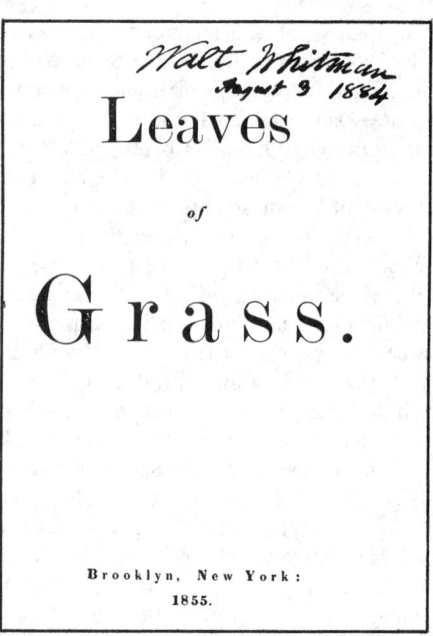

The frontispiece and title page of the first edition of Walt Whitman's Leaves of Grass.

newspaper work and promoted the sale of his book. He flaunted Emerson's personal letter of congratulation in newspaper advertisements and on the spine of the second edition, a bit of self-promotion that many (but apparently not Emerson) found offensive. Whitman's preoccupation with personal image (evident even in the studied insouciance of the first edition daguerreotype), is part of his chosen subject, the dignity of the individual human being; yet, there remains a quality of self-interest in his search for identity that allows some to dismiss him as insincere and affected. Certainly, it can be said that one literary tradition in which Whitman participated fully was the age-old quest for fame. He seemed to have achieved some measure of it in 1855 and 1856, when he was visited by Emerson, Henry David Thoreau, and Bronson Alcott. In 1856 Whitman published a second edition of *Leaves of Grass,* which contains the important addition of the "Sun-Down Poem" (later called "Crossing Brooklyn Ferry"). At this time he worked as an editor at the Brooklyn *Times* and began working on the group of homoerotic poems known as the "Calamus" poems. In 1860 he published a third edition of *Leaves of Grass,* which includes the sexually frank "Enfans d'Adam" (later titled "Children of Adam") and "Calamus" poems as well as the important metaphorical account of the poet's assumption of his vocation, "A Word Out of the Sea" (later titled "Out of the Cradle Endlessly Rocking"). Whitman was always concerned about the sexually explicit nature of some of his work, and Emerson had tried, to no avail, to persuade him not to publish "Enfans d'Adam." Upon the publication of this third edition, the doors of Boston's literary elite were slammed in Whitman's face, in smarting contrast to the effusive reception that had earlier greeted him. The 1860 edition is considered critically important, however, because it marks the conclusion of Whitman's interest in the creative and procreative aspect of his poetic role; henceforth, Whitman's poetry would convey an emphasis on the poet as cultural prophet.

In 1862 Whitman traveled to Washington, D.C., to care for his brother George, who had been wounded in the Civil War. Whitman had always visited the sick among his Brooklyn acquaintances, and he now found himself performing that same humanitarian service among his brother's many wounded comrades. He was greatly appreciated as a cheering presence and worked arduously as a hospital attendant, sometimes assisting during medical procedures. These experiences and his general political interest in Abraham Lincoln's presidential election and in the Civil War provide the subject for *Drum-Taps*, a group of poems published in 1865. The volume was subsequently issued as a "sequel" with the addition of the magnificent elegy of Lincoln, "When Lilacs Last in the Dooryard Bloom'd," and was incorporated, with the *Passage to India* (1871) poems, in the 1872 edition of *Leaves of Grass*.

In Washington in 1865 Whitman worked for six months in the Army Paymaster's Office but lost his job when the supervisor discovered the erotic nature of his poetry. Whitman was given a new job in the Attorney General's office, however, by William O'Connor, a friend who wrote the appreciative biography *The Good Gray Poet* (1866). In 1871 Whitman published *Democratic Vistas*, a prose pamphlet that explores the cultural possibilities of democracy. In 1873 he suffered a paralytic stroke, after which he was moved to the Camden, New Jersey, home of his brother George to recuperate.

Whitman's poetic power, many feel, diminished after the 1860 edition of *Leaves of Grass*. When he had recovered physically from the events of 1873, he did not produce anything of substance, with the exception of *Specimen Days*, a volume of prose published in 1882. But his popular reputation grew in these later years, and he came to be lionized in Camden in much the same way Emerson had been in Concord. Whitman issued subsequent editions of *Leaves of Grass* in 1876, 1881, and 1891 to 1892 despite continuing threats of suppression because of the candid quality of his poetry. He died in Camden on March 26, 1892. A century later Whitman's celebration of democracy, diversity, and his own vitality remains for us the quintessential expression of the American artist.

Suggested Readings: *Leaves of Grass*, 1860 edition, ed. R. H. Pearce, 1961. *Walt Whitman: The Correspondence*, 6 vols., ed. E. H. Miller, 1961–1977. *The Collected Writings of Walt Whitman*, ed. G. W. Allen and S. Bradley, 1961– . H. Traubel, *With Walt Whitman in Camden*, 6 vols., 1906. G. W. Allen, *The Solitary Singer: A Critical Biography of Walt Whitman*, 1955, rpt. 1985. R. Asselineau, *The Evolution of Walt Whitman*, 1962. J. C. Smuts, *Walt Whitman: A Study in the Evolution of a Personality*, 1973. J. Woodress, ed., *Critical Essays on Walt Whitman*, 1983. G. W. Allen, *The New Walt Whitman Handbook*, 1986. G. Hutchinson, *The Ecstatic Whitman: Literary Shamanism and the Crisis of the Union*, 1986. M. W. Thomas, *The Lunar Light of Whitman's Poetry*, 1987. K. C. Larson, *Whitman's Drama of Consensus*, 1988. B. Erkkila, *Whitman the Political Poet*, 1989. E. H. Miller, *Walt Whitman's "Song of Myself": A Mosaic of Interpretations*, 1989. K. M. Price, *Whitman and Tradition*, 1990.

Texts Used: "Preface," poems, and "A Backward Glance O'er Travel'd Roads": *Leaves of Grass*, ed. H. W. Blodgett and S. Bradley, 1965. "My Tribute to Four Poets" and "Boston Common": *The Complete Prose Works of Walt Whitman*, Vol. II, 1902. All else: *The Complete Prose Works*, Vol. I.

from   *LEAVES OF GRASS*

Preface to the 1855 Edition*

America does not repel the past or what it has produced under its forms or amid other politics or the idea of castes or the old religions. . . . accepts the lesson with calmness . . . is not so impatient as has been supposed that the slough[1] still sticks

---

* Omitted from later editions, although much of the preface material is retained in the poems added to those editions. The ellipses and idiosyncratic spellings are Whitman's.

[1] The outer, discarded skin of a snake.

to opinions and manners and literature while the life which served its requirements has passed into the new life of the new forms . . . perceives that the corpse is slowly borne from the eating and sleeping rooms of the house . . . perceives that it waits a little while in the door . . . that it was fittest for its days . . . that its action has descended to the stalwart and wellshaped heir who approaches . . . and that he shall be fittest for his days.

The Americans of all nations at any time upon the earth have probably the fullest poetical nature. The United States themselves are essentially the greatest poem. In the history of the earth hitherto the largest and most stirring appear tame and orderly to their ampler largeness and stir. Here at last is something in the doings of man that corresponds with the broadcast doings of the day and night. Here is not merely a nation but a teeming nation of nations. Here is action untied from strings necessarily blind to particulars and details magnificently moving in vast masses. Here is the hospitality which forever indicates heroes. . . . Here are the roughs and beards and space and ruggedness and nonchalance that the soul loves. Here the performance disdaining the trivial unapproached in the tremendous audacity of its crowds and groupings and the push of its perspective spreads with crampless and flowing breadth and showers its prolific and splendid extravagance. One sees it must indeed own the riches of the summer and winter, and need never be bankrupt while corn grows from the ground or the orchards drop apples or the bays contain fish or men beget children upon women.

Other states indicate themselves in their deputies. . . . but the genius of the United States is not best or most in its executives or legislatures, nor in its ambassadors or authors or colleges or churches or parlors, nor even in its newspapers or inventors . . . but always most in the common people. Their manners speech dress friendships—the freshness and candor of their physiognomy—the picturesque looseness of their carriage . . . their deathless attachment to freedom—their aversion to anything indecorous or soft or mean—the practical acknowledgment of the citizens of one state by the citizens of all other states—the fierceness of their roused resentment—their curiosity and welcome of novelty—their self-esteem and wonderful sympathy—their susceptibility to a slight—the air they have of persons who never knew how it felt to stand in the presence of superiors—the fluency of their speech—their delight in music, the sure symptom of manly tenderness and native elegance of soul . . . their good temper and openhandedness—the terrible significance of their elections—the President's taking off his hat to them not they to him—these too are unrhymed poetry. It awaits the gigantic and generous treatment worthy of it.

The largeness of nature or the nation were monstrous without a corresponding largeness and generosity of the spirit of the citizen. Not nature nor swarming states nor streets and steamships nor prosperous business nor farms nor capital nor learning may suffice for the ideal of man . . . nor suffice the poet. No reminiscences may suffice either. A live nation can always cut a deep mark and can have the best authority the cheapest . . . namely from its own soul. This is the sum of the profitable uses of individuals or states and of present action and grandeur and of the subjects of poets.—As if it were necessary to trot back generation after generation to the eastern records! As if the beauty and sacredness of the demonstrable must fall behind that of the mythical! As if men do not make their mark out of any times! As if the opening of the western continent by discovery and what has transpired since in North and South America were less than the small theatre of the antique or the aimless sleep-walking of the middle ages! The pride of the United

States leaves the wealth and finesse of the cities and all returns of commerce and agriculture and all the magnitude of geography or shows of exterior victory to enjoy the breed of fullsized men or one fullsized man unconquerable and simple.

The American poets are to enclose old and new for America is the race of races. Of them a bard[2] is to be commensurate with a people. To him the other continents arrive as contributions . . . he gives them reception for their sake and his own sake. His spirit responds to his country's spirit. . . . he incarnates its geography and natural life and rivers and lakes. Mississippi with annual freshets and changing chutes, Missouri and Columbia and Ohio and Saint Lawrence with the falls and beautiful masculine Hudson, do not embouchure[3] where they spend themselves more than they embouchure into him. The blue breadth over the inland sea of Virginia and Maryland and the sea off Massachusetts and Maine and over Manhattan bay and over Champlain and Erie and over Ontario and Huron and Michigan and Superior, and over the Texan and Mexican and Floridian and Cuban seas and over the seas off California and Oregon, is not tallied by the blue breadth of the waters below more than the breadth of above and below is tallied by him. When the long Atlantic coast stretches longer and the Pacific coast stretches longer he easily stretches with them north or south. He spans between them also from east to west and reflects what is between them. On him rise solid growths that offset the growths of pine and cedar and hemlock and liveoak and locust and chestnut and cypress and hickory and limetree and cottonwood and tuliptree and cactus and wildvine and tamarind and persimmon. . . . and tangles as tangled as any canebrake or swamp. . . . and forests coated with transparent ice and icicles hanging from the boughs and crackling in the wind. . . . and sides and peaks of mountains. . . . and pasturage sweet and free as savannah or upland or prairie. . . . with flights and songs and screams that answer those of the wildpigeon and highhold[4] and orchard oriole and coot and surf-duck and redshouldered-hawk and fish-hawk and white-ibis and indian-hen and cat-owl and water-pheasant and qua-bird and pied-sheldrake and blackbird and mockingbird and buzzard and condor and night-heron and eagle. To him the hereditary countenance descends both mother's and father's. To him enter the essences of the real things and past and present events—of the enormous diversity of temperature and agriculture and mines—the tribes of red aborigines—the weatherbeaten vessels entering new ports or making landings on rocky coasts—the first settlements north or south—the rapid stature and muscle—the haughty defiance of '76,[5] and the war and peace and formation of the constitution. . . . the union always surrounded by blatherers and always calm and impregnable—the perpetual coming of immigrants—the wharf hem'd cities and superior marine[6]—the unsurveyed interior—the loghouses and clearings and wild animals and hunters and trappers. . . . the free commerce—the fisheries and whaling and golddigging—the endless gestation of new states—the convening of Congress every December,[7] the members duly coming up from all climates and the uttermost parts. . . . the noble character of the young mechanics[8] and of all free American workmen and workwomen. . . . the general ardor and friendliness and enterprise—the perfect equality of the female with the male. . . . the large amativeness[9]—the fluid movement of the population—the

---

[2] A national or tribal poet, traditionally in the epic or heroic vein; one who sustained and continued the oral tradition of the people.
[3] Pour out.   [4] Woodpecker.   [5] The Declaration of Independence.
[6] Maritime industry.   [7] Before 1933 Congress convened on the first Monday in December.
[8] Manual laborers.   [9] Amorousness.

factories and mercantile life and laborsaving machinery—the Yankee swap[10]—the New-York firemen and the target excursion[11]—the southern plantation life—the character of the northeast and of the northwest and southwest—slavery and the tremulous spreading of hands to protect it, and the stern opposition to it which shall never cease till it ceases or the speaking of tongues and the moving of lips cease. For such the expression of the American poet is to be transcendant and new. It is to be indirect and not direct or descriptive or epic. Its quality goes through these to much more. Let the age and wars of other nations be chanted and their eras and characters be illustrated and that finish the verse. Not so the great psalm of the republic. Here the theme is creative and has vista. Here comes one among the wellbeloved stonecutters and plans with decision and science and sees the solid and beautiful forms of the future where there are now no solid forms.

Of all nations the United States with veins full of poetical stuff most need poets and will doubtless have the greatest and use them the greatest. Their Presidents shall not be their common referee so much as their poets shall. Of all mankind the great poet is the equable man. Not in him but off from him things are grotesque or eccentric or fail of their sanity. Nothing out of its place is good and nothing in its place is bad. He bestows on every object or quality its fit proportions neither more nor less. He is the arbiter of the diverse and he is the key. He is the equalizer of his age and land. . . . he supplies what wants supplying and checks what wants checking. If peace is the routine out of him speaks the spirit of peace, large, rich, thrifty, building vast and populous cities, encouraging agriculture and the arts and commerce—lighting the study of man, the soul, immortality—federal, state or municipal government, marriage, health, freetrade, intertravel by land and sea. . . . nothing too close, nothing too far off . . . the stars not too far off. In war he is the most deadly force of the war. Who recruits him recruits horse and foot[12] . . . he fetches parks of artillery[13] the best that engineer ever knew. If the time becomes slothful and heavy he knows how to arouse it . . . he can make every word he speaks draw blood. Whatever stagnates in the flat[14] of custom or obedience or legislation he never stagnates. Obedience does not master him, he masters it. High up out of reach he stands turning a concentrated light . . . he turns the pivot with his finger . . . he baffles the swiftest runners as he stands and easily overtakes and envelops them. The time straying toward infidelity and confections and persiflage he withholds by his steady faith . . . he spreads out his dishes . . . he offers the sweet firmfibred meat that grows men and women. His brain is the ultimate brain. He is no arguer . . . he is judgment. He judges not as the judge judges but as the sun falling around a helpless thing. As he sees the farthest he has the most faith. His thoughts are the hymns of the praise of things. In the talk on the soul and eternity and God off of his equal plane he is silent. He sees eternity less like a play with a prologue and denouement. . . . he sees eternity in men and women . . . he does not see men and women as dreams or dots. Faith is the antiseptic of the soul . . . it pervades the common people and preserves them . . . they never give up believing and expecting and trusting. There is that indescribable freshness and unconsciousness about an illiterate person that humbles and mocks the power of the noblest expressive genius. The poet sees for

---

[10] A shrewd deal, from the reputation of New Englanders (Yankees) for hard bargaining.
[11] The outing to a shooting match.   [12] Cavalry and infantry.
[13] Local militias commonly drilled in city parks, which in times of need became supply depots.
[14] Low, marshy land.

a certainty how one not a great artist may be just as sacred and perfect as the greatest artist. . . . The power to destroy or remould is freely used by him but never the power of attack. What is past is past. If he does not expose superior models and prove himself by every step he takes he is not what is wanted. The presence of the greatest poet conquers . . . not parleying or struggling or any prepared attempts. Now he has passed that way see after him! there is not left any vestige of despair or misanthropy or cunning or exclusiveness or the ignominy of a nativity or color or delusion of hell or the necessity of hell. . . . and no man thenceforward shall be degraded for ignorance or weakness or sin.

The greatest poet hardly knows pettiness or triviality. If he breathes into any thing that was before thought small it dilates with the grandeur and life of the universe. He is a seer. . . . he is individual . . . he is complete in himself. . . . the others are as good as he, only he sees it and they do not. He is not one of the chorus. . . . he does not stop for any regulation . . . he is the president of regulation. What the eyesight does to the rest he does to the rest. Who knows the curious mystery of the eyesight? The other senses corroborate themselves, but this is removed from any proof but its own and foreruns the identities of the spiritual world. A single glance of it mocks all the investigations of man and all the instruments and books of the earth and all reasoning. What is marvellous? what is unlikely? what is impossible or baseless or vague? after you have once just opened the space of a peachpit and given audience to far and near and to the sunset and had all things enter with electric swiftness softly and duly without confusion or jostling or jam.

The land and sea, the animals fishes and birds, the sky of heaven and the orbs, the forests mountains and rivers, are not small themes . . . but folks expect of the poet to indicate more than the beauty and dignity which always attach to dumb real objects . . . . they expect him to indicate the path between reality and their souls. Men and women perceive the beauty well enough. .probably as well as he. The passionate tenacity of hunters, woodmen, early risers, cultivators of gardens and orchards and fields, the love of healthy women for the manly form, seafaring persons, drivers of horses, the passion for light and the open air, all is an old varied sign of the unfailing perception of beauty and of a residence of the poetic in outdoor people. They can never be assisted by poets to perceive . . . some may but they never can. The poetic quality is not marshalled in rhyme or uniformity or abstract addresses to things nor in melancholy complaints or good precepts, but is the life of these and much else and is in the soul. The profit of rhyme is that it drops seeds of a sweeter and more luxuriant rhyme, and of uniformity that it conveys itself into its own roots in the ground out of sight. The rhyme and uniformity of perfect poems show the free growth of metrical laws and bud from them as unerringly and loosely as lilacs or roses on a bush, and take shapes as compact as the shapes of chestnuts and oranges and melons and pears, and shed the perfume impalpable to form. The fluency and ornaments of the finest poems or music or orations or recitations are not independent but dependent. All beauty comes from beautiful blood and a beautiful brain. If the greatnesses are in conjunction in a man or woman it is enough . . . . the fact will prevail through the universe . . . . but the gaggery[15] and gilt of a million years will not prevail. Who troubles himself about his ornaments or fluency is lost. This is what you shall do: Love the earth and sun and the animals, despise riches, give alms to every one that

---

[15] Falseness.

asks, stand up for the stupid and crazy, devote your income and labor to others, hate tyrants, argue not concerning God, have patience and indulgence toward the people, take off your hat to nothing known or unknown or to any man or number of men, go freely with powerful uneducated persons and with the young and with the mothers of families, read these leaves in the open air every season of every year of your life, re-examine all you have been told at school or church or in any book, dismiss whatever insults your own soul, and your very flesh shall be a great poem and have the richest fluency not only in its words but in the silent lines of its lips and face and between the lashes of your eyes and in every motion and joint of your body. . . . . The poet shall not spend his time in unneeded work. He shall know that the ground is always ready ploughed and manured . . . . others may not know it but he shall. He shall go directly to the creation. His trust shall master the trust of everything he touches . . . . and shall master all attachment.

The known universe has one complete lover and that is the greatest poet. He consumes an eternal passion and is indifferent which chance happens and which possible contingency of fortune or misfortune and persuades daily and hourly his delicious pay. What balks or breaks others is fuel for his burning progress to contact and amorous joy. Other proportions of the reception of pleasure dwindle to nothing to his proportions. All expected from heaven or from the highest he is rapport with in the sight of the daybreak or a scene of the winter woods or the presence of children playing or with his arm round the neck of a man or woman. His love above all love has leisure and expanse . . . . he leaves room ahead of himself. He is no irresolute or suspicious lover . . . he is sure . . . he scorns intervals. His experience and the showers and thrills are not for nothing. Nothing can jar him . . . . suffering and darkness cannot—death and fear cannot. To him complaint and jealousy and envy are corpses buried and rotten in the earth . . . . he saw them buried. The sea is not surer of the shore or the shore of the sea than he is of the fruition of his love and of all perfection and beauty.

The fruition of beauty is no chance of hit or miss . . . it is inevitable as life . . . . it is exact and plumb as gravitation. From the eyesight proceeds another eyesight and from the hearing proceeds another hearing and from the voice proceeds another voice eternally curious of the harmony of things with man. To these respond perfections not only in the committees that were supposed to stand for the rest but in the rest themselves just the same. These understand the law of perfection in masses and floods . . . that its finish is to each for itself and onward from itself . . . that it is profuse and impartial . . . that there is not a minute of the light or dark nor an acre of the earth or sea without it—nor any direction of the sky nor any trade or employment nor any turn of events. This is the reason that about the proper expression of beauty there is precision and balance . . . one part does not need to be thrust above another. The best singer is not the one who has the most lithe and powerful organ . . . the pleasure of poems is not in them that take the handsomest measure and similes and sound.

Without effort and without exposing in the least how it is done the greatest poet brings the spirit of any or all events and passions and scenes and persons some more and some less to bear on your individual character as you hear or read. To do this well is to compete with the laws that pursue and follow time. What is the purpose must surely be there and the clue of it must be there . . . . and the faintest indication is the indication of the best and then becomes the clearest indication. Past and present and future are not disjoined but joined. The greatest poet forms the consistence of what is to be from what has been and is. He drags the dead out of their coffins and stands them again on their feet . . . . he says to the past, Rise and walk before me that I may realize you. He learns the lesson. . . . he places himself where the future becomes present. The greatest poet does not only dazzle his rays over character and scenes and passions . . . he finally ascends and finishes all . . . he exhibits the pinnacles that no man can tell what they are for or what is beyond . . . . he glows a moment on the extremest verge. He is most wonderful in his last half-hidden smile or frown . . . by that flash of the moment of parting the one that sees it shall be encouraged or terrified afterward for many years. The greatest poet does not moralize or make applications of morals . . . he knows the soul. The soul has that measureless pride which consists in never acknowledging any lessons but its own. But it has sympathy as measureless as its pride and the one balances the other and neither can stretch too far while it stretches in company with the other. The inmost secrets of art sleep with the twain. The greatest poet has lain close betwixt both and they are vital in his style and thoughts.

The art of art, the glory of expression and the sunshine of the light of letters is simplicity. Nothing is better than simplicity . . . . nothing can make up for excess or for the lack of definiteness. To carry on the heave of impulse and pierce intellectual depths and give all subjects their articulations are powers neither common nor very uncommon. But to speak in literature with the perfect rectitude and insousiance[16] of the movements of animals and the unimpeachableness of the sentiment of trees in the woods and grass by the roadside is the flawless triumph of art. If you have looked on him who has achieved it you have looked on one of the masters of the artists of all nations and times. You shall not contemplate the flight of the graygull over the bay or the mettlesome action of the blood horse or the tall leaning of sunflowers on their stalk or the appearance of the sun journeying through heaven or the appearance of the moon afterward with any more satisfaction than you shall contemplate him. The greatest poet has less a marked style and is more the channel of thoughts and things without increase or diminution, and is the free channel of himself. He swears to his art, I will not be meddlesome, I will not have in my writing any elegance or effect or originality to hang in the way between me and the rest like curtains. I will have nothing hang in the way, not the richest curtains. What I tell I tell for precisely what it is. Let who may exalt or startle or fascinate or sooth I will have purposes as health or heat or snow has and be as regardless of observation. What I experience or portray shall go from my composition without a shred of my composition. You shall stand by my side and look in the mirror with me.

The old red blood and stainless gentility of great poets will be proved by their unconstraint. A heroic person walks at his ease through and out of that custom or precedent or authority that suits him not. Of the traits of the brotherhood of writers savans[17] musicians inventors and artists nothing is finer than silent defiance advancing from new free forms. In the need of poems philosophy politics mechanism science behaviour, the craft of art, an appropriate native grand-opera, shipcraft, or any craft, he is greatest forever and forever who contributes the greatest original practical example. The cleanest expression is that which finds no sphere worthy of itself and makes one.

The messages of great poets to each man and woman are, Come to us on equal terms, Only then can you understand us, We are no better than you, What we

---

[16] Indifference.   [17] Savants, or learned men.

enclose you enclose, What we enjoy you may enjoy. Did you suppose there could be only one Supreme? We affirm there can be unnumbered Supremes, and that one does not countervail another any more than one eyesight countervails another . . and that men can be good orgrand only of the consciousness of their supremacy within them. What do you think is the grandeur of storms and dismemberments and the deadliest battles and wrecks and the wildest fury of the elements and the power of the sea and the motion of nature and of the throes of human desires and dignity and hate and love? It is that something in the soul which says, Rage on, Whirl on, I tread master here and everywhere, Master of the spasms of the sky and of the shatter of the sea, Master of nature and passion and death, And of all terror and all pain.

The American bards shall be marked for generosity and affection and for encouraging competitors . . They shall be kosmos . . without monopoly or secresy . . glad to pass any thing to any one . . hungry for equals night and day. They shall not be careful of riches and privilege . . . . they shall be riches and privilege . . . . they shall perceive who the most affluent man is. The most affluent man is he that confronts all the shows he sees by equivalents out of the stronger wealth of himself. The American bard shall delineate no class of persons nor one or two out of the strata of interests nor love most nor truth most nor the soul most nor the body most . . . . and not be for the eastern states more than the western or the northern states more than the southern.

Exact science and its practical movements are no checks on the greatest poet but always his encouragement and support. The outset and remembrance are there . . there the arms that lifted him first and brace him best. . . . there he returns after all his goings and comings. The sailor and traveler . . the anatomist, chemist, astronomer, geologist, phrenologist, spiritualist, mathematician, historian and lexicographer are not poets, but they are the lawgivers of poets and their construction underlies the structure of every perfect poem. No matter what rises or is uttered they sent the seed of the conception of it . . . . of them and by them stand the visible proofs of souls . . . . . always of their fatherstuff must be begotten the sinewy races of bards. If there shall be love and content between the father and the son and if the greatness of the son is the exuding of the greatness of the father there shall be love between the poet and the man of demonstrable science. In the beauty of poems are the tuft and final applause of science.

Great is the faith of the flush of knowledge and of the investigation of the depths of qualities and things. Cleaving and circling here swells the soul of the poet yet it president of itself always. The depths are fathomless and therefore calm. The innocence and nakedness are resumed . . . they are neither modest nor immodest. The whole theory of the special and supernatural and all that was twined with it or educed[18] out of it departs as a dream. What has ever happened . . . . what happens and whatever may or shall happen, the vital laws enclose all . . . . they are sufficent for any case and for all cases . . . none to be hurried or retarded . . . . any miracle of affairs or persons inadmissible in the vast clear scheme where every motion and every spear of grass and the frames and spirits of men and women and all that concerns them are unspeakably perfect miracles all referring to all and each distinct and in its place. It is also not consistent with the reality of the soul to admit that there is anything in the known universe more divine than men and women.

---

[18] Drawn forth.

Men and women and the earth and all upon it are simply to be taken as they are, and the investigation of their past and present and future shall be unintermitted and shall be done with perfect candor. Upon this basis philosophy speculates ever looking toward the poet, ever regarding the eternal tendencies of all toward happiness never inconsistent with what is clear to the senses and to the soul. For the eternal tendencies of all toward happiness make the only point of sane philosophy. Whatever comprehends less than that . . . whatever is less than the laws of light and of astronomical motion . . . or less than the laws that follow the thief the liar the glutton and the drunkard through this life and doubtless afterward . . . . . . or less than vast stretches of time or the slow formation of density or the patient upheaving of strata—is of no account. Whatever would put God in a poem or system of philosophy as contending against some being or influence is also of no account. Sanity and ensemble characterise the great master . . . spoilt in one principle all is spoilt. The great master has nothing to do with miracles. He sees health for himself in being one of the mass . . . . he sees the hiatus in singular eminence. To the perfect shape comes common ground. To be under the general law is great for that is to correspond with it. The master knows that he is unspeakably great and that all are unspeakably great. . . . that nothing for instance is greater than to conceive children and bring them up well . . . that to be is just as great as to perceive or tell.

In the make of the great masters the idea of political liberty is indispensible. Liberty takes the adherence of heroes wherever men and women exist . . . . but never takes any adherence or welcome from the rest more than from poets. They are the voice and exposition of liberty. They out of ages are worthy the grand idea . . . . to them it is confided and they must sustain it. Nothing has precedence of it and nothing can warp or degrade it. The attitude of great poets is to cheer up slaves and horrify despots. The turn of their necks, the sound of their feet, the motions of their wrists, are full of hazard to the one and hope to the other. Come nigh them awhile and though they neither speak or advise you shall learn the faithful American lesson. Liberty is poorly served by men whose good intent is quelled from one failure or two failures or any number of failures, or from the casual indifference or ingratitude of the people, or from the sharp show of the tushes[19] of power, or the bringing to bear soldiers and cannon or any penal statutes. Liberty relies upon itself, invites no one, promises nothing, sits in calmness and light, is positive and composed, and knows no discouragement. The battle rages with many a loud alarm and frequent advance and retreat . . . . the enemy triumphs . . . . the prison, the handcuffs, the iron necklace and anklet, the scaffold, garrote and leadballs do their work . . . . the cause is asleep . . . . the strong throats are choked with their own blood . . . . the young men drop their eyelashes toward the ground when they pass each other . . . . and is liberty gone out of that place? No never. When liberty goes it is not the first to go nor the second or third to go . . it waits for all the rest to go . . it is the last. . . When the memories of the old martyrs are faded utterly away . . . . when the large names of patriots are laughed at in the public halls from the lips of the orators . . . . when the boys are no more christened after the same but christened after tyrants and traitors instead . . . . when the laws of the free are grudgingly permitted and laws for informers and bloodmoney are sweet to the taste of the people . . . . when I and you walk abroad upon the earth stung with compassion at the sight of

---

[19] Tusks.

numberless brothers answering our equal friendship and calling no man master—and when we are elated with noble joy at the sight of slaves . . . . when the soul retires in the cool communion of the night and surveys its experience and has much extasy over the word and deed that put back a helpless innocent person into the gripe of the gripers or into any cruel inferiority . . . . when those in all parts of these states who could easier realize the true American character but do not yet—when the swarms of cringers, suckers, doughfaces,[20] lice of politics, planners of sly involutions for their own preferment to city offices or state legislatures or the judiciary or congress or the presidency, obtain a response of love and natural deference from the people whether they get the offices or no . . . . when it is better to be a bound booby[21] and rogue in office at a high salary than the poorest free mechanic or farmer with his hat unmoved from his head and firm eyes and a candid and generous heart . . . . and when servility by town or state or the federal government or any oppression on a large scale or small scale can be tried on without its own punishment following duly after in exact proportion against the smallest chance of escape . . . . or rather when all life and all the souls of men and women are discharged from any part of the earth—then only shall the instinct of liberty be discharged from that part of the earth.

As the attributes of the poets of the kosmos concentre in the real body and soul and in the pleasure of things they possess the superiority of genuineness over all fiction and romance. As they emit themselves facts are showered over with light . . . . the daylight is lit with more volatile light . . . . also the deep between the setting and rising sun goes deeper many fold. Each precise object or condition or combination or process exhibits a beauty . . . . the multiplication table its—old age its—the carpenter's trade its—the grand-opera its . . . . the hugehulled clean-shaped New-York clipper at sea under steam or full sail gleams with unmatched beauty . . . . the American circles and large harmonies of government gleam with theirs . . . . and the commonest definite intentions and actions with theirs. The poets of the kosmos advance through all interpositions and coverings and turmoils and stratagems to first principles. They are of use . . . . they dissolve poverty from its need and riches from its conceit. You large proprietor they say shall not realize or perceive more than any one else. The owner of the library is not he who holds a legal title to it having bought and paid for it. Any one and every one is owner of the library who can read the same through all the varieties of tongues and subjects and styles, and in whom they enter with ease and take residence and force toward paternity and maternity, and make supple and powerful and rich and large. . . . . These American states strong and healthy and accomplished shall receive no pleasure from violations of natural models and must not permit them. In paintings or mouldings or carvings in mineral or wood, or in the illustrations of books or newspapers, or in any comic or tragic prints, or in the patterns of woven stuffs or any thing to beautify rooms or furniture or costumes, or to put upon cornices or monuments or on the prows of sterns of ships, or to put anywhere before the human eye indoors or out, that which distorts honest shapes or which creates unearthly beings or places or contingencies is a nuisance and revolt. Of the human form especially it is so great it must never be made ridiculous. Of ornaments to a work nothing outre[22] can be allowed . . but those ornaments can be allowed that conform to the perfect facts of the open air and that flow out of the

---

[20] Swindlers; changeable, unscrupulous people.   [21] A political fool who owes favors.
[22] Extravagant, improper.

nature of the work and come irrepressibly from it and are necessary to the completion of the work. Most works are most beautiful without ornament. . . Exaggerations will be revenged in human physiology. Clean and vigorous children are jetted[23] and conceived only in those communities where the models of natural forms are public every day. . . . . Great genius and the people of these states must never be demeaned to romances. As soon as histories are properly told there is no more need of romances.

The great poets are also to be known by the absence in them of tricks and by the justification of perfect personal candor. Then folks echo a new cheap joy and a divine voice leaping from their brains: How beautiful is candor! All faults may be forgiven of him who has perfect candor. Henceforth let no man of us lie, for we have seen that openness wins the inner and outer world and that there is no single exception, and that never since our earth gathered itself in a mass have deceit or subterfuge or prevarication attracted its smallest particle or the faintest tinge of a shade—and that through the enveloping wealth and rank of a state or the whole republic of states a sneak or sly person shall be discovered and despised . . . . and that the soul has never been once fooled and never can be fooled . . . . and thrift without the loving nod of the soul is only a fœtid puff . . . . and there never grew up in any of the continents of the globe nor upon any planet or satellite or star, nor upon the asteroids, nor in any part of ethereal space, nor in the midst of density, nor under the fluid wet of the sea, nor in that condition which precedes the birth of babes, nor at any time during the changes of life, nor in that condition that follows what we term death, nor in any stretch of abeyance or action afterward of vitality, nor in any process of formation or reformation anywhere, a being whose instinct hated the truth.

Extreme caution or prudence, the soundest organic health, large hope and comparison and fondness for women and children, large alimentiveness[24] and destructiveness and causality, with a perfect sense of the oneness of nature and the propriety of the same spirit applied to human affairs . . these are called up of the float[25] of the brain of the world to be parts of the greatest poet from his birth out of his mother's womb and from her birth out of her mother's. Caution seldom goes far enough. It has been thought that the prudent citizen was the citizen who applied himself to solid gains and did well for himself and his family and completed a lawful life without debt or crime. The greatest poet sees and admits these economies as he sees the economies of food and sleep, but has higher notions of prudence than to think he gives much when he gives a few slight attentions at the latch of the gate. The premises of the prudence of life are not the hospitality of it or the ripeness and harvest of it. Beyond the independence of a little sum laid aside for burial-money, and of a few clapboards around and shingles overhead on a lot of American soil owned, and the easy dollars that supply the year's plain clothing and meals, the melancholy prudence of the abandonment of such a great being as a man is to the toss and pallor of years of moneymaking with all their scorching days and icy nights and all their stifling deceits and underhanded dodgings, or infinitessimals of parlors, or shameless stuffing while others starve . . and all the loss of the bloom and odor of the earth and of the flowers and atmosphere and of the sea and of the true taste of the women and men you pass or have to do with in youth or middle age, and the issuing sickness and desperate revolt at the close of a life without elevation or naivete, and the ghastly chatter of a death

[23] Ejaculated.   [24] Love of food.   [25] Buoyancy.

without serenity or majesty, is the great fraud upon modern civilization and fore-thought, blotching the surface and system which civilization undeniably drafts, and moistening with tears the immense features it spreads and spreads with such velocity before the reached kisses of the soul. . . Still the right explanation re-mains to be made about prudence. The prudence of the mere wealth and respecta-bility of the most esteemed life appears too faint for the eye to observe at all when little and large alike drop quietly aside at the thought of the prudence suitable for immortality. What is wisdom that fills the thinness of a year or seventy or eighty years to wisdom spaced out by ages and coming back at a certain time with strong reinforcements and rich presents and the clear faces of wedding-guests as far as you can look in every direction running gaily toward you? Only the soul is of itself . . . . all else has reference to what ensues. All that a person does or thinks is of consequence. Not a move can a man or woman make that affects him or her in a day or a month or any part of the direct lifetime or the hour of death but the same affects him or her onward afterward through the indirect lifetime. The indi-rect is always as great and real as the direct. The spirit receives from the body just as much as it gives to the body. Not one name of word or deed . . not of venereal sores or discolorations . . not the privacy of the onanist[26] . . not of the putrid veins of gluttons or rumdrinkers . . . not peculation[27] or cunning or betrayal or murder . . no serpentine poison of those that seduce women . . not the foolish yielding of women . . not prostitution . . not of any depravity of young men . . not of the attainment of gain by discreditable means . . not any nastiness of appetite . . not any harshness of officers to men or judges to prisoners or fa-thers to sons or sons to fathers or of husbands to wives or bosses to their boys . . not of greedy looks or malignant wishes . . . nor any of the wiles prac-tised by people upon themselves . . . ever is or ever can be stamped on the pro-gramme but it is duly realized and returned, and that returned in further perform-ances . . . and they returned again. Nor can the push of charity or personal force ever be any thing else than the profoundest reason, whether it bring arguments to hand or no. No specification is necessary . . to add or subtract or divide is in vain. Little or big, learned or unlearned, white or black, legal or illegal, sick or well, from the first inspiration down the windpipe to the last expiration out of it, all that a male or female does that is vigorous and benevolent and clean is so much sure profit to him or her in the unshakable order of the universe and through the whole scope of it forever. If the savage or felon is wise it is well. . . . if the greatest poet or savan is wise it is simply the same . . if the President or chief justice is wise it is the same . . if the young mechanic or farmer is wise it is no more or less . . if the prostitute is wise it is no more nor less. The interest will come round . . all will come round. All the best actions of war and peace . . . all help given to relatives and strangers and the poor and old and sorrowful and young children and widows and the sick, and to all shunned persons . . all furtherance of fugitives and of the escape of slaves . . all the self-denial that stood steady and aloof on wrecks and saw others take the seats of the boats . . . all offering of substance or life for the good old cause, or for a friend's sake or opinion's sake . . . all pains of enthusiasts scoffed at by their neighbors . . all the vast sweet love and precious suffering of mothers . . . all honest men baffled in strifes recorded or unre-corded . . . . all the grandeur and good of the few ancient nations whose frag-

---

[26] Masturbator, after Onan, the son of Judah, in Genesis 38:9.   [27] Embezzlement.

ments of annals we inherit . . and all the good of the hundreds of far mightier and more ancient nations unknown to us by name or date or location. . . . . all that was ever manfully begun, whether it succeeded or no. . . . all that has at any time been well suggested out of the divine heart of man or by the divinity of his mouth or by the shaping of his great hands . . and all that is well thought or done this day on any part of the surface of the globe . . or on any of the wandering stars or fixed stars by those there as we are here . . or that is henceforth to be well thought or done by you whoever you are, or by any one—these singly and wholly inured at their time and inure now and will inure always to the identities from which they sprung or shall spring . . . Did you guess any of them lived only its moment? The world does not so exist . . no parts palpable or impalpable so exist . . . no result exists now without being from its long antecedent result, and that from its antecedent, and so backward without the farthest mentionable spot coming a bit nearer the beginning than any other spot. . . . . Whatever satisfies the soul is truth. The prudence of the greatest poet answers at last the craving and glut of the soul, is not contemptuous of less ways of prudence if they conform to its ways, puts off nothing, permits no let-up for its own case or any case, has no particular sabbath or judgment-day, divides not the living from the dead or the righteous from the unrighteous, is satisfied with the present, matches every thought or act by its correlative, knows no possible forgiveness or deputed atonement . . knows that the young man who composedly periled his life and lost it has done exceeding well for himself, while the man who has not periled his life and retains it to old age in riches and ease has perhaps achieved nothing for himself worth mentioning . . and that only that person has no great prudence to learn who has learnt to prefer real longlived things, and favors body and soul the same, and perceives the indirect assuredly following the direct, and what evil or good he does leaping onward and waiting to meet him again—and who in his spirit in any emergency whatever neither hurries or avoids death.

The direct trial of him who would be the greatest poet is today. If he does not flood himself with the immediate age as with vast oceanic tides . . . . . and if he does not attract his own land body and soul to himself and hang on its neck with incomparable love and plunge his semitic muscle[28] into its merits and demerits . . . and if he be not himself the age transfigured . . . . and if to him is not opened the eternity which gives similitude to all periods and locations and processes and animate and inanimate forms, and which is the bond of time, and rises up from its inconceivable vagueness and infiniteness in the swimming shape of today, and is held by the ductile anchors of life, and makes the present spot the passage from what was to what shall be, and commits itself to the representation of this wave of an hour and this one of the sixty beautiful children of the wave— let him merge in the general run and wait his development. . . . . . . Still the final test of poems or any character or work remains. The prescient poet projects himself centuries ahead and judges performer or performance after the changes of time. Does it live through them? Does it still hold on untired? Will the same style and the direction of genius to similar points be satisfactory now? Has no new discovery in science or arrival at superior planes of thought and judgment and behaviour fixed him or his so that either can be looked down upon? Have the marches of tens and hundreds and thousands of years made willing detours to the

[28] Whitman's euphemism for penis.

right hand and the left hand for his sake? Is he beloved long and long after he is buried? Does the young man think often of him? and the young woman think often of him? and do the middleaged and the old think of him?

A great poem is for ages and ages in common and for all degrees and complexions and all departments and sects and for a woman as much as a man and a man as much as a woman. A great poem is no finish to a man or woman but rather a beginning. Has any one fancied he could sit at last under some due authority and rest satisfied with explanations and realize and be content and full? To no such terminus does the greatest poet bring . . . he brings neither cessation or sheltered fatness and ease. The touch of him tells in action. Whom he takes he takes with firm sure grasp into live regions previously unattained . . . . thenceforward is no rest . . . . they see the space and ineffable sheen that turn the old spots and lights into dead vacuums. The companion of him beholds the birth and progress of stars and learns one of the meanings. Now there shall be a man cohered out of tumult and chaos . . . . the elder encourages the younger and shows him how . . . they two shall launch off fearlessly together till the new world fits an orbit for itself and looks unabashed on the lesser orbits of the stars and sweeps through the ceaseless rings and shall never be quiet again.

There will soon be no more priests. Their work is done. They may wait awhile . . perhaps a generation or two . . dropping off by degrees. A superior breed shall take their place. . . . the gangs of kosmos and prophets en masse shall take their place. A new order shall arise and they shall be the priests of man, and every man shall be his own priest. The churches built under their umbrage[29] shall be the churches of men and women. Through the divinity of themselves shall the kosmos and the new breed of poets be interpreters of men and women and of all events and things. They shall find their inspiration in real objects today, symptoms of the past and future . . . . They shall not deign to defend immortality or God or the perfection of things or liberty or the exquisite beauty and reality of the soul. They shall arise in America and be responded to from the remainder of the earth.

The English language befriends the grand American expression. . . . it is brawny enough and limber and full enough. On the tough stock of a race who through all change of circumstance was never without the idea of political liberty, which is the animus of all liberty, it has attracted the terms of daintier and gayer and subtler and more elegant tongues. It is the powerful language of resistance . . . it is the dialect of common sense. It is the speech of the proud and melancholy races and of all who aspire. It is the chosen tongue to express growth faith self-esteem freedom justice equality friendliness amplitude prudence decision and courage. It is the medium that shall well nigh express the inexpressible.

No great literature nor any like style of behaviour or oratory or social intercourse or household arrangements or public institutions or the treatment by bosses of employed people, nor executive detail of the army or navy, nor spirit of legislation or courts or police or tuition or architecture or songs or amusements or the costumes of young men, can long elude the jealous and passionate instinct of American standards. Whether or no the sign appears from the mouths of the people, it throbs a live interrogation in every freeman's and freewoman's heart after that which passes by, or this built to remain. Is it uniform with my country? Are its disposals without ignominious distinctions? Is it for the evergrowing communes of brothers and lovers, large, well-united, proud beyond the old models,

[29] Shade, shelter.

generous beyond all models? Is it something grown fresh out of the fields or drawn from the sea for use to me today here? I know that what answers for me an American must answer for any individual or nation that serves for a part of my materials. Does this answer? or is it without reference to universal needs? or sprung of the needs of the less developed society of special ranks? or old needs of pleasure overlaid by modern science and form? Does this acknowledge liberty with audible and absolute acknowledgment, and set slavery at nought for life and death? Will it help breed one goodshaped and wellhung man, and a woman to be his perfect and independent mate? Does it improve manners? Is it for the nursing of the young of the republic? Does it solve[30] readily with the sweet milk of the nipples of the breasts of the mother of many children? Has it too the old ever-fresh forbearance and impartiality? Does it look with the same love on the last born and on those hardening toward stature, and on the errant, and on those who disdain all strength of assault outside of their own?

The poems distilled from other poems will probably pass away. The coward will surely pass away. The expectation of the vital and great can only be satisfied by the demeanor of the vital and great. The swarms of the polished deprecating and reflectors and the polite float off and leave no remembrance. America prepares with composure and goodwill for the visitors that have sent word. It is not intellect that is to be their warrant and welcome. The talented, the artist, the ingenious, the editor, the statesman, the erudite . . they are not unappreciated . . they fall in their place and do their work. The soul of the nation also does its work. No disguise can pass on it . . no disguise can conceal from it. It rejects none, it permits all. Only toward as good as itself and toward the like of itself will it advance half-way. An individual is as superb as a nation when he has the qualities which make a superb nation. The soul of the largest and wealthiest and proudest nation may well go half-way to meet that of its poets. The signs are effectual. There is no fear of mistake. If the one is true the other is true. The proof of a poet is that his country absorbs him as affectionately as he has absorbed it.

1855

ONE'S-SELF I SING

One's-Self I sing, a simple separate person,
Yet utter the word Democratic, the word En-Masse.

Of physiology from top to toe I sing,
Not physiognomy[1] alone nor brain alone is worthy for the Muse, I say the
  Form complete is worthier far,
The Female equally with the Male I sing.

---

[30] Dissolve.

* Group title for the opening nine poems of the 1871 edition of *Leaves of Grass*, increased to include twenty-four poems in 1881.

[1] The art of judging human character from physical characteristics, especially facial features.

Of Life immense in passion, pulse, and power,
Cheerful, for freest action form'd under the laws divine,
The Modern Man I sing.

1867

BEGINNING MY STUDIES*

Beginning my studies the first step pleas'd me so much,
The mere fact consciousness, these forms, the power of motion,
The least insect or animal, the senses, eyesight, love,
The first step I say awed me and pleas'd me so much,
I have hardly gone and hardly wish'd to go any farther,
But stop and loiter all the time to sing it in ecstatic songs.

1865

SHUT NOT YOUR DOORS**

Shut not your doors to me proud libraries,
For that which was lacking on all your well-fill'd shelves, yet needed most,
    I bring,
Forth from the war emerging, a book I have made,
The words of my book nothing, the drift of it every thing,
A book separate, not link'd with the rest nor felt by the intellect,
But you ye untold latencies will thrill to every page.

1865

POETS TO COME†

Poets to come! orators, singers, musicians to come!
Not to-day is to justify me and answer what I am for,
But you, a new brood, native, athletic, continental, greater than before known,
Arouse! for you must justify me.

I myself but write one or two indicative words for the future,
I but advance a moment only to wheel and hurry back in the darkness.

I am a man who, sauntering along without fully stopping, turns a casual look upon
    you and then averts his face,

* First appeared in *Drum-Taps* (1865) and added to "Inscriptions" in 1871.
** First appeared in *Drum-Taps* (1865), revised, and added to "Inscriptions" in 1881.
† First appeared in "Chants Democratic" of the 1860 edition of *Leaves of Grass*, revised, and eventually added to "Inscriptions" in 1881.

Leaving it to you to prove and define it,
Expecting the main things from you.

1860

SONG OF MYSELF*

1

I celebrate myself, and sing myself,
And what I assume you shall assume,
For every atom belonging to me as good belongs to you.

I loafe and invite my soul,
I lean and loafe at my ease observing a spear of summer grass.
My tongue, every atom of my blood, form'd from this soil, this air,
Born here of parents born here from parents the same, and their parents
    the same,
I, now thirty-seven years old in perfect health begin,
Hoping to cease not till death.

Creeds and schools in abeyance,   10
Retiring back a while sufficed at what they are, but never forgotten,
I harbor for good or bad, I permit to speak at every hazard,
Nature without check with original energy.

2

Houses and rooms are full of perfumes, the shelves are crowded with
    perfumes,
I breathe the fragrance myself and know it and like it,
The distillation would intoxicate me also, but I shall not let it.

The atmosphere is not a perfume, it has no taste of the distillation, it is
    odorless,
It is for my mouth forever, I am in love with it,
I will go to the bank by the wood and become undisguised and naked,
I am mad for it to be in contact with me.   20
The smoke of my own breath,
Echoes, ripples, buzz'd whispers, love-root, silk-thread, crotch and vine,
My respiration and inspiration, the beating of my heart, the passing of
    blood and air through my lungs,
The sniff of green leaves and dry leaves, and of the shore and dark-color'd
    sea-rocks, and of hay in the barn,
The sound of the belch'd words of my voice loos'd to the eddies of the wind,
A few light kisses, a few embraces, a reaching around of arms,
The play of shine and shade on the trees as the supple boughs wag,

---

* Appeared in the 1855 edition of *Leaves of Grass* untitled and without subdivisions. In the 1856
edition it was titled "Poem of Walt Whitman, an American," and in 1860 and later editions, "Walt
Whitman." Not until 1881 did it appear as "Song of Myself."

The delight alone or in the rush of the streets, or along the fields and
    hill-sides,
The feeling of health, the full-noon trill, the song of me rising from bed
    and meeting the sun.

Have you reckon'd a thousand acres much? have you reckon'd the
    earth much?   30
Have you practis'd so long to learn to read?
Have you felt so proud to get at the meaning of poems?

Stop this day and night with me and you shall possess the origin of
    all poems,
You shall possess the good of the earth and sun, (there are millions of suns
    left,)
You shall no longer take things at second or third hand, nor look through
    the eyes of the dead, nor feed on the spectres in books,
You shall not look through my eyes either, nor take things from me,
You shall listen to all sides and filter them from yourself.

3

I have heard what the talkers were talking, the talk of the beginning
    and the end,
But I do not talk of the beginning or the end.

There was never any more inception than there is now,   40
Nor any more youth or age than there is now,
And will never be any more perfection than there is now,
Nor any more heaven or hell than there is now.

Urge and urge and urge,
Always the procreant urge of the world.

Out of the dimness opposite equals advance, always substance and
    increase, always sex,
Always a knit of identity, always distinction, always a breed of life.

To elaborate is no avail, learn'd and unlearn'd feel that it is so.

Sure as the most certain sure, plumb in the uprights, well entretied,[1]
    braced in the beams,
Stout as a horse, affectionate, haughty, electrical,
I and this mystery here we stand.   50

Clear and sweet is my soul, and clear and sweet is all that is not my soul.

Lack one lacks both, and the unseen is proved by the seen,
Till that becomes unseen and receives proof in its turn.

[1] Cross-braced or supported.

Showing the best and dividing it from the worst, age vexes age,
Knowing the perfect fitness and equanimity of things, while they discuss
 I am silent, and go bathe and admire myself.

Welcome is every organ and attribute of me, and of any man hearty
 and clean,
Not an inch nor a particle of an inch is vile, and none shall be less familiar
 than the rest.

I am satisfied—I see, dance, laugh, sing;
As the hugging and loving bed-fellow[2] sleeps at my side through the
 night, and withdraws at the peep of the day with stealthy tread,   60
Leaving me baskets cover'd with white towels swelling the house with
 their plenty,
Shall I postpone my acceptation and realization and scream at my eyes,
That they turn from gazing after and down the road,
And forthwith cipher[3] and show me to a cent,
Exactly the value of one and exactly the value of two, and which
 is ahead?

4

Trippers and askers[4] surround me,
People I meet, the effect upon me of my early life or the ward and city I
 live in, or the nation,
The latest dates, discoveries, inventions, societies, authors old and new,
My dinner, dress, associates, looks, compliments, dues,
The real or fancied indifference of some man or woman I love,   70
The sickness of one of my folks or of myself, or ill-doing or loss or lack
 of money, or depressions or exaltations,
Battles, the horrors of fratricidal war, the fever of doubtful news, the
 fitful events;
These come to me days and nights and go from me again,
But they are not the Me myself.

Apart from the pulling and hauling stands what I am,
Stands amused, complacent, compassionating, idle, unitary,
Looks down, is erect, or bends an arm on an impalpable certain rest,
Looking with side-curved head curious what will come next,
Both in and out of the game and watching and wondering at it.

Backward I see in my own days where I sweated through fog with
 linguists and contenders,   80
I have no mockings or arguments, I witness and wait.

5

I believe in you my soul, the other I am must not abase itself to you,
And you must not be abased to the other.

---

[2] In the 1855 version, God is the "loving bed-fellow."   [3] Calculate.   [4] Travelers and solicitors.

Loafe with me on the grass, loose the stop from your throat,
Not words, not music or rhyme I want, not custom or lecture, not even
  the best,
Only the lull I like, the hum of your valvèd voice.

I mind how once we lay such a transparent summer morning,
How you settled your head athwart my hips and gently turn'd over
  upon me,
And parted the shirt from my bosom-bone, and plunged your tongue to
  my bare-stript heart,
And reach'd till you felt my beard, and reach'd till you held my feet.   90

Swiftly arose and spread around me the peace and knowledge that pass
  all the argument of the earth,
And I know that the hand of God is the promise of my own,
And I know that the spirit of God is the brother of my own,
And that all the men ever born are also my brothers, and the women my
  sisters and lovers,
And that a kelson[5] of the creation is love,
And limitless are leaves stiff or drooping in the fields,
And brown ants in the little wells beneath them,
And mossy scabs of the worm fence,[6] heap'd stones, elder, mullein and
  poke-weed.

6

A child said *What is the grass?* fetching it to me with full hands;
How could I answer the child? I do not know what it is any more
  than he.   100

I guess it must be the flag of my disposition, out of hopeful green
  stuff woven.

Or I guess it is the handkerchief of the Lord,
A scented gift and remembrancer designedly dropt,
Bearing the owner's name someway in the corners, that we may see and
  remark, and say *Whose?*

Or I guess the grass is itself a child, the produced babe of the vegetation.

Or I guess it is a uniform hieroglyphic,
And it means, Sprouting alike in broad zones and narrow zones,
Growing among black folks as among white,
Kanuck, Tuckahoe,[7] Congressman, Cuff,[8] I give them the same, I
  receive them the same.

And now it seems to me the beautiful uncut hair of graves.   110

---

[5] Keelson, or timbers that brace a ship's keel.   [6] An undulating or zigzag fence of split rails.
[7] A French-Canadian; a native of Tidewater Virginia.   [8] An African American.

Tenderly will I use you curling grass,
It may be you transpire from the breasts of young men,
It may be if I had known them I would have loved them,
It may be you are from old people, or from offspring taken soon out of
   their mothers' laps,
And here you are the mothers' laps.

This grass is very dark to be from the white heads of old mothers,
Darker than the colorless beards of old men,
Dark to come from under the faint red roofs of mouths.

O I perceive after all so many uttering tongues,
And I perceive they do not come from the roofs of mouths for nothing.   120

I wish I could translate the hints about the dead young men and women,
And the hints about old men and mothers, and the offspring taken soon
   out of their laps.

What do you think has become of the young and old men?
And what do you think has become of the women and children?

They are alive and well somewhere,
The smallest sprout shows there is really no death,
And if ever there was it led forward life, and does not wait at the end to
   arrest it,
And ceas'd the moment life appear'd.

All goes onward and outward, nothing collapses,
And to die is different from what any one supposed, and luckier.   130

7
Has any one supposed it lucky to be born?
I hasten to inform him or her it is just as lucky to die, and I know it.

I pass death with the dying and birth with the new-wash'd babe, and am
   not contain'd between my hat and boots,
And peruse manifold objects, no two alike and every one good,
The earth good and the stars good, and their adjuncts all good.

I am not an earth nor an adjunct of an earth,
I am the mate and companion of people, all just as immortal and
   fathomless as myself,
(They do not know how immortal, but I know.)

Every kind for itself and its own, for me mine male and female,
For me those that have been boys and that love women,   140
For me the man that is proud and feels how it stings to be slighted,
For me the sweet-heart and the old maid, for me mothers and the mothers
   of mothers,

For me lips that have smiled, eyes that have shed tears,
For me children and the begetters of children.

Undrape! you are not guilty to me, nor stale nor discarded,
I see through the broadcloth and gingham whether or no,
And am around, tenacious, acquisitive, tireless, and cannot be
    shaken away.

                                    8

The little one sleeps in its cradle,
I lift the gauze and look a long time, and silently brush away flies with
    my hand.

The youngster and the red-faced girl turn aside up the busy hill,   150
I peeringly view them from the top.

The suicide sprawls on the bloody floor of the bedroom,
I witness the corpse with its dabbled hair, I note where the pistol
    has fallen.

The blab of the pave,[9] tires of carts, sluff of boot-soles, talk of
    the promenaders,
The heavy omnibus, the driver with his interrogating thumb, the clank of
    the shod horses on the granite floor,
The snow-sleighs, clinking, shouted jokes, pelts of snow-balls,
The hurrahs for popular favorites, the fury of rous'd mobs,
The flap of the curtain'd litter, a sick man inside borne to the hospital,
The meeting of enemies, the sudden oath, the blows and fall,
The excited crowd, the policeman with his star quickly working his
    passage to the centre of the crowd,   160
The impassive stones that receive and return so many echoes,
What groans of over-fed or half-starv'd who fall sunstruck or in fits,
What exclamations of women taken suddenly who hurry home and give
    birth to babes,
What living and buried speech is always vibrating here, what howls
    restrain'd by decorum,
Arrests of criminals, slights, adulterous offers made, acceptances,
    rejections with convex lips,
I mind them or the show or resonance of them—I come and I depart.

                                    9

The big doors of the country barn stand open and ready,
The dried grass of the harvest-time loads the slow-drawn wagon,
The clear light plays on the brown gray and green intertinged,
The armfuls are pack'd to the sagging mow.   170

I am there, I help, I came stretch'd atop of the load,
I felt its soft jolts, one leg reclined on the other,

---

[9] Street talk.

I jump from the cross-beams and seize the clover and timothy,
And roll head over heels and tangle my hair full of wisps.

10

Alone far in the wilds and mountains I hunt,
Wandering amazed at my own lightness and glee,
In the late afternoon choosing a safe spot to pass the night,
Kindling a fire and broiling the fresh-kill'd game,
Falling asleep on the gather'd leaves with my dog and gun by my side.

The Yankee clipper is under her sky-sails,[10] she cuts the sparkle
    and scud,   180
My eyes settle the land, I bend at her prow or shout joyously from
    the deck.

The boatmen and clam-diggers arose early and stopt for me,
I tuck'd my trowser-ends in my boots and went and had a good time;
You should have been with us that day round the chowder-kettle.

I saw the marriage of the trapper in the open air in the far west, the bride
    was a red girl,
Her father and his friends sat near cross-legged and dumbly smoking,
    they had moccasins to their feet and large thick blankets hanging from
    their shoulders,
On a bank lounged the trapper, he was drest mostly in skins, his
luxuriant beard and curls protected his neck, he held his bride by
the hand,
She had long eyelashes, her head was bare, her coarse straight locks
    descended upon her voluptuous limbs and reach'd to her feet.[11]

The runaway slave came to my house and stopt outside,
I heard his motions crackling the twigs of the woodpile,   190
Through the swung half-door of the kitchen I saw him limpsy and weak,
And went where he sat on a log and led him in and assured him,
And brought water and fill'd a tub for his sweated body and bruis'd feet,
And gave him a room that enter'd from my own, and gave him some
    coarse clean clothes,
And remember perfectly well his revolving eyes and his awkwardness,
And remember putting plasters on the galls of his neck and ankles;
He staid with me a week before he was recuperated and pass'd north,
I had him sit next me at table, my fire-lock[12] lean'd in the corner.

11

Twenty-eight young men bathe by the shore,
Twenty-eight young men and all so friendly;   200
Twenty-eight years of womanly life and all so lonesome.

[10] Top sails; scud is sea foam.
[11] This stanza is based on the painting *The Trapper's Bride,* by Alfred Jacob Miller (1810–1874).
[12] Gun.

She owns the fine house by the rise of the bank,
She hides handsome and richly drest aft the blinds of the window.

Which of the young men does she like the best?
Ah the homeliest of them is beautiful to her.

Where are you off to, lady? for I see you,
You splash in the water there, yet stay stock still in your room.

Dancing and laughing along the beach came the twenty-ninth bather,
The rest did not see her, but she saw them and loved them.

The beards of the young men glisten'd with wet, it ran from their
    long hair,   210
Little streams pass'd all over their bodies.

An unseen hand also pass'd over their bodies,
It descended tremblingly from their temples and ribs.

The young men float on their backs, their white bellies bulge to the sun,
    they do not ask who seizes fast to them,
They do not know who puffs and declines with pendant and
    bending arch,
They do not think whom they souse with spray.

12

The butcher-boy puts off his killing-clothes, or sharpens his knife at the
    stall in the market,
I loiter enjoying his repartee and his shuffle and break-down.[13]

Blacksmiths with grimed and hairy chests environ the anvil,
Each has his main-sledge, they are all out, there is a great heat in
    the fire.   220

From the cinder-strew'd threshold I follow their movements,
The lithe sheer[14] of their waists plays even with their massive arms,
Overhand the hammers swing, overhand so slow, overhand so sure,
They do no hasten, each man hits in his place.

13

The negro holds firmly the reins of his four horses, the block swags
    underneath on its tied-over chain,
The negro that drives the long dray[15] of the stone-yard, steady and tall he
    stands pois'd on one leg on the string piece,[16]

---

[13] Two popular minstrel-show steps: the shuffle, a sliding, slow step; the break-down, faster and uninhibited.
   [14] Upward curve.   [15] A low, heavy cart for haulage.
   [16] A heavy timber used to shore up construction or to brace a load.

His blue shirt exposes his ample neck and breast and loosens over his
    hip-band,
His glance is calm and commanding, he tosses the slouch of his hat away
    from his forehead,
The sun falls on his crispy hair and mustache, falls on the black of his
    polish'd and perfect limbs.

I behold the picturesque giant and love him, and I do not stop there,   230
I go with the team also.

In me the caresser of life wherever moving, backward as well as
    forward sluing,[17]
To niches aside and junior[18] bending, not a person or object missing,
Absorbing all to myself and for this song.

Oxen that rattle the yoke and chain or halt in the leafy shade, what is that
    you express in your eyes?
It seems to me more than all the print I have read in my life.

My tread scares the wood-drake and wood-duck on my distant and day-
    long ramble,
They rise together, they slowly circle around.

I believe in those wing'd purposes,
And acknowledge red, yellow, white, playing within me,   240
And consider green and violet and the tufted crown intentional,
And do not call the tortoise unworthy because she is not something else,
And the jay in the woods never studied the gamut,[19] yet trills pretty
    well to me,
And the look of the bay mare shames silliness out of me.

14

The wild gander leads his flock through the cool night,
Ya-honk he says, and sounds it down to me like an invitation,
The pert[20] may suppose it meaningless, but I listening close,
Find its purpose and place up there toward the wintry sky.

The sharp-hoof'd moose of the north, the cat on the house-sill, the
    chickadee, the prairie dog,
The litter of the grunting sow as they tug at her teats,   250
The brood of the turkey-hen and she with her half-spread wings,
I see in them and myself the same old law.

The press of my foot to the earth springs a hundred affections,
They scorn the best I can do to relate them.
I am enamour'd of growing out-doors,
Of men that live among cattle or taste of the ocean or woods,

---

[17] Twisting.   [18] Lesser.   [19] Never practiced musical scales.   [20] The bold.

Of the builders and steerers of ships and the wielders of axes and mauls,
    and the drivers of horses,
I can eat and sleep with them week in and week out.

What is commonest, cheapest, nearest, easiest, is Me,
Me going in for my chances, spending for vast returns,   260
Adorning myself to bestow myself on the first that will take me,
Not asking the sky to come down to my good will,
Scattering it freely forever.

15

The pure contralto sings in the organ loft,
The carpenter dresses his plank, the tongue of his foreplane whistles its
    wild ascending lisp,
The married and unmarried children ride home to their Thanksgiving
    dinner,
The pilot seizes the king-pin,[21] he heaves down with a strong arm,
The mate stands braced in the whale-boat, lance and harpoon are ready,
The duck-shooter walks by silent and cautious stretches,
The deacons are ordain'd with cross'd hands at the altar,   270
The spinning-girl retreats and advances to the hum of the big wheel,
The farmer stops by the bars[22] as he walks on a First-day loafe[23] and
    looks at the oats and rye,
The lunatic is carried at last to the asylum a confirm'd case,
(He will never sleep any more as he did in the cot in his mother's
    bed-room;)
The jour printer[24] with gray head and gaunt jaws works at his case,
He turns his quid of tobacco while his eyes blurr with the manuscript;
The malform'd limbs are tied to the surgeon's table,
What is removed drops horribly in a pail;
The quadroon[25] girl is sold at the auction-stand, the drunkard nods by the
    bar-room stove,
The machinist rolls up his sleeves, the policeman travels his beat, the
    gate-keeper marks who pass,   280
The young fellow drives the express-wagon, (I love him, though I do not
    know him;)
The half-breed straps on his light boots to compete in the race,
The western turkey-shooting draws old and young, some lean on their
    rifles, some sit on logs,
Out from the crowd steps the marksman, takes his position, levels
    his piece;
The groups of newly-come immigrants cover the wharf or levee,
As the woolly-pates[26] hoe in the sugar-field, the overseer views them
    from his saddle,
The bugle calls in the ball-room, the gentlemen run for their partners, the
    dancers bow to each other,

---

[21] The extended spoke of the pilot wheel.   [22] Fence rails.
[23] The Quaker designation for the first day of the week: Sunday, a day of leisure.
[24] Journeyman printer, working out his case of typefaces.
[25] One-quarter black (with one black grandparent).   [26] African-American slaves.

The youth lies awake in the cedar-roof'd garret and harks to the
    musical rain,
The Wolverine[27] sets traps on the creek that helps fill the Huron,
The squaw wrapt in her yellow-hemm'd cloth is offering moccasins and
    bead-bags for sale,   290
The connoisseur peers along the exhibition-gallery with half-shut eyes
    bent sideways,
As the deck-hands make fast the steamboat the plank is thrown for the
    shore-going passengers,
The young sister holds out the skein while the elder sister winds it off in
    a ball, and stops now and then for the knots,
The one-year wife is recovering and happy having a week ago borne her
    first child,
The clean-hair'd Yankee girl works with her sewing-machine or in the
    factory or mill,
The paving-man leans on his two-handed rammer, the reporter's lead
    flies swiftly over the note-book, the sign-painter is lettering with blue
    and gold,
The canal boy trots on the tow-path,[28] the book-keeper counts at his
    desk, the shoemaker waxes his thread,
The conductor beats time for the band and all the performers follow him,
The child is baptized, the convert is making his first professions,
The regatta is spread on the bay, the race is begun, (how the white
    sails sparkle!)   300
The drover watching his drove sings out to them that would stray,
The pedler sweats with his pack on his back, (the purchaser higgling
    about the odd cent;)
The bride unrumples her white dress, the minute-hand of the clock
    moves slowly,
The opium-eater reclines with rigid head and just-open'd lips,
The prostitute draggles her shawl, her bonnet bobs on her tipsy and
    pimpled neck,
The crowd laugh at her blackguard oaths, the men jeer and wink to
    each other,
(Miserable! I do not laugh at your oaths nor jeer you;)
The President holding a cabinet council is surrounded by the
    great Secretaries,
On the piazza walk three matrons stately and friendly with
    twined arms,
The crew of the fish-smack pack repeated layers of halibut in the hold,   310
The Missourian crosses the plains toting his wares and his cattle,
As the fare-collector goes through the train he gives notice by the
    jingling of loose change,
The floor-men are laying the floor, the tinners are tinning[29] the roof, the
    masons are calling for mortar,
In single file each shouldering his nod pass onward the laborers;
Seasons pursuing each other the indescribable crowd is gather'd, it is the
    fourth of Seventh-month,[30] (what salutes of cannon and small arms!)

---

[27] Michigan resident.   [28] A path along which draft animals tow canal barges.
[29] Repairing a sheet-metal roof.   [30] The Quaker designation for the Fourth of July.

Seasons pursuing each other the plougher ploughs, the mower mows,
    and the winter-grain falls in the ground;
Off on the lakes the pike-fisher watches and waits by the hole in the
    frozen surface,
The stumps stand thick round the clearing, the squatter strikes deep with
    his axe,
Flatboatmen make fast towards dusk near the cotton-wood or
    pecan-trees,
Coon-seekers[31] go through the regions of the Red river or through those
    drain'd by the Tennessee, or through those of the Arkansas,   320
Torches shine in the dark that hangs on the Chattahooche
    or Altamahaw,[32]
Patriarchs sit at supper with sons and grandsons and great-grandsons
    around them,
In walls of adobie, in canvas tents, rest hunters and trappers after their
    day's sport,
The city sleeps and the country sleeps,
The living sleep for their time, the dead sleep for their time,
The old husband sleeps by his wife and the young husband sleeps by
    his wife;
And these tend inward to me, and I tend outward to them,
And such as it is to be of these more or less I am,
And of these one and all I weave the song of myself.

16

I am of old and young, of the foolish as much as the wise,   330
Regardless of others, ever regardful of others,
Maternal as well as paternal, a child as well as a man,
Stuff'd with the stuff that is coarse and stuff'd with the stuff that is fine,
One of the Nation of many nations, the smallest the same and the largest
    the same,
A Southerner soon as a Northerner, a planter nonchalant and hospitable
    down by the Oconee[33] I live,
A Yankee bound my own way ready for trade, my joints the limberest
    joints on earth and the sternest joints on earth,
A Kentuckian walking the vale of the Elkhorn[34] in my deer-skin leggings,
    a Louisianian or Georgian,
A boatman over lakes or bays or along coasts, a Hoosier, Badger,
    Buckeye;[35]
At home on Kanadian snow-shoes or up in the bush, or with fishermen
    off Newfoundland,
At home in the fleet of ice-boats, sailing with the rest and tacking,   340
At home on the hills of Vermont or in the woods of Maine, or the
    Texan ranch,
Comrade of Californians, comrade of free North-Westerners, (loving
    their big proportions,)

[31] Racoon hunters; the Red River borders Texas and Oklahoma.
[32] Rivers in Alabama and Louisiana.   [33] A river in Georgia.   [34] A river in Nebraska.
[35] An inhabitant of Indiana, Wisconsin, and Ohio, respectively.

Comrade of raftsmen and coalmen, comrade of all who shake hands and
    welcome to drink and meat,
A learner with the simplest, a teacher of the thoughtfullest,
A novice beginning yet experient of myriads of seasons,
Of every hue and caste am I, of every rank and religion,
A farmer, mechanic, artist, gentleman, sailor, quaker,
Prisoner, fancy-man,[36] rowdy, lawyer, physician, priest.

I resist any thing better than my own diversity,
Breathe the air but leave plenty after me,   350
And am not stuck up, and am in my place.

(The moth and the fish-eggs are in their place,
The bright suns I see and the dark suns I cannot see are in their place,
The palpable is in its place and the impalpable is in its place.)

17

These are really the thoughts of all men in all ages and lands, they are
    not original with me,
If they are not yours as much as mine they are nothing, or next to nothing,
If they are not the riddle and the untying of the riddle they are nothing,
If they are not just as close as they are distant they are nothing.

This is the grass that grows wherever the land is and the water is,
This the common air that bathes the globe.   360

18

With music strong I come, with my cornets and my drums,
I play not marches for accepted victors only, I play marches for
    conquer'd and slain persons.

Have you heard that it was good to gain the day?
I also say it is good to fall, battles are lost in the same spirit in which
    they are won.

I beat and pound for the dead,
I blow through my embouchures[37] my loudest and gayest for them.

Vivas to those who have fail'd!
And to those whose war-vessels sank in the sea!
And to those themselves who sank in the sea!
And to all generals that lost engagements, and all overcome heroes!   370
And the numberless unknown heroes equal to the greatest heroes known!

19

This is the meal equally set, this the meat for natural hunger,
It is for the wicked just the same as the righteous, I make appointments
    with all,
I will not have a single person slighted or left away,

---

[36] A pimp.   [37] Mouthpieces of wind and brass instruments.

The kept-woman, sponger, thief, are hereby invited,
The heavy-lipp'd slave is invited, the venerealee[38] is invited;
There shall be no difference between them and the rest.

This is the press of a bashful hand, this the float and odor of hair,
This the touch of my lips to yours, this the murmur of yearning,
This the far-off depth and height reflecting my own face,   380
This the thoughtful merge of myself, and the outlet again.

Do you guess I have some intricate purpose?
Well I have, for the Fourth-month[39] showers have, and the mica on the
    side of a rock has.

Do you take it I would astonish?
Does the daylight astonish? does the early redstart twittering through
    the woods?
Do I astonish more than they?

This hour I tell things in confidence,
I might not tell everybody, but I will tell you.

                              20
Who goes there? hankering, gross, mystical, nude;
How is it I extract strength from the beef I eat?   390

What is a man anyhow? what am I? what are you?

All I mark as my own you shall offset it with your own,
Else it were time lost listening to me.

I do not snivel that snivel the world over,
That months are vacuums and the ground but wallow and filth.

Whimpering and truckling fold with powders for invalids,[40] conformity,
    goes to the fourth-remov'd,[41]
I wear my hat as I please indoors or out.

Why should I pray? why should I venerate and be ceremonious?

Having pried through the strata, analyzed to a hair, counsel'd with
    doctors and calculated close,
I find no sweeter fat than sticks to my own bones.   400

In all people I see myself, none more and not one a barley-corn less,
And the good or bad I say of myself I say of them.

---

[38] One infected with a venereal disease or obsessed with sexual desire.   [39] April.
[40] Whimpering and yielding are appropriate medicines to be combined with the other powders administered to invalids.
[41] Those removed from society.

I know I am solid and sound,
To me the converging objects of the universe perpetually flow,
All are written to me, and I must get what the writing means.

I know I am deathless,
I know this orbit of mine cannot be swept by a carpenter's compass,
I know I shall not pass like a child's carlacue[42] cut with a burnt stick
    at night.

I know I am august,
I do not trouble my spirit to vindicate itself or be understood,   410
I see that the elementary laws never apologize,
(I reckon I behave no prouder than the level I plant my house by,
    after all.)

I exist as I am, that is enough,
If no other in the world be aware I sit content,
And if each and all be aware I sit content.

One world is aware and by far the largest to me, and that is myself,
And whether I come to my own to-day or in ten thousand or ten
    million years,
I can cheerfully take it now, or with equal cheerfulness I can wait.
My foothold is tenon'd and mortis'd[43] in granite,
I laugh at what you call dissolution,   420
And I know the amplitude of time.

21

I am the poet of the Body and I am the poet of the Soul,
The pleasures of heaven are with me and the pains of hell are with me,
The first I graft and increase upon myself, the latter I translate into a
    new tongue.

I am the poet of the woman the same as the man,
And I say it is as great to be a woman as to be a man,
And I say there is nothing greater than the mother of men.

I chant the chant of dilation or pride,
We have had ducking and deprecating about enough,
I show that size is only development.   430

Have you outstript the rest? are you the President?
It is a trifle, they will more than arrive there every one, and still pass on.

I am he that walks with the tender and growing night,
I call to the earth and sea half-held by the night.

---

[42] A curlicue, here a brief pattern of light "cut" in the darkness by the glowing end of a burning stick.
[43] Joined with interlocking pieces.

Press close bare-bosom'd night—press close magnetic nourishing night!
Night of south winds—night of the large few stars!
Still nodding night—mad naked summer night.

Smile O voluptuous cool-breath'd earth!
Earth of the slumbering and liquid trees!
Earth of departed sunset—earth of the mountains misty-topt!   440
Earth of the vitreous[44] pour of the full moon just tinged with blue!
Earth of shine and dark mottling the tide of the river!
Earth of the limpid gray of clouds brighter and clearer for my sake!
Far-swooping elbow'd earth—rich apple blossom'd earth!
Smile, for your lover comes.

Prodigal, you have given me love—therefore I to you give love!
O unspeakable passionate love.

                                    22
You sea! I resign myself to you also—I guess what you mean,
I behold from the beach your crooked inviting fingers,
I believe you refuse to go back without feeling of me,   450
We must have a turn together, I undress, hurry me out of sight of
    the land,
Cushion me soft, rock me in billowy drowse,
Dash me with amorous wet, I can repay you.

Sea of stretch'd ground-swells,
Sea breathing broad and convulsive breaths,
Sea of the brine of life and of unshovell'd yet always-ready graves,
Howler and scooper of storms, capricious and dainty sea,
I am integral with you, I too am of one phase and of all phases.

Partaker of influx and efflux, I, extoller of hate and conciliation,
Extoller of amies[45] and those that sleep in each others' arms.   460

I am he attesting sympathy,
(Shall I make my list of things in the house and skip the house that
    supports them?)

I am not the poet of goodness only, I do not decline to be the poet of
    wickedness also.

What blurt is this about virtue and about vice?
Evil propels me and reform of evil propels me, I stand indifferent,
My gait is no fault-finder's or rejecter's gait,
I moisten the roots of all that has grown.

---

[44] Glasslike.   [45] "Friends" or "lovers" (French).

Did you fear some scrofula[46] out of the unflagging pregnancy?
Did you guess the celestial laws are yet to be work'd over and rectified?

I find one side a balance and the antipodal side a balance,   470
Soft doctrine as steady help as stable doctrine,
Thoughts and deeds of the present our rouse and early start.

This minute that comes to me over the past decillions,[47]
There is no better than it and now.

What behaved well in the past or behaves well to-day is not such
    a wonder,
The wonder is always and always how there can be a mean man or
    an infidel.

23

Endless unfolding of words of ages!
And mine a word of the modern, the word En-Masse.

A word of the faith that never balks,
Here or henceforward it is all the same to me, I accept Time
    absolutely.   480

It alone is without flaw, it alone rounds and completes all,
That mystic baffling wonder alone completes all.

I accept Reality and dare not question it,
Materialism first and last imbuing.

Hurrah for positive science! long live exact demonstration!
Fetch stonecrop[48] mixt with cedar and branches of lilac,
This is the lexicographer, this the chemist, this made a grammar of the
    old cartouches,[49]
These mariners put the ship through dangerous unknown seas,
This is the geologist, this works with the scalpel, and this is a
    mathematician.

Gentlemen, to you the first honors always!   490
Your facts are useful, and yet they are not my dwelling,
I but enter by them to an area of my dwelling.

Less the reminders of properties told my words,
And more the reminders they of life untold, and of freedom and
    extrication,

---

[46] A form of tuberculosis involving swelling of the lymph glands and inflammation of the joints;
"scrofulous" carries a connotation of moral degeneracy.
[47] Many years: one followed by thirty-three zeros.   [48] A plant used as a medicinal herb.
[49] Deciphered the Egyptian hieroglyphs carved in oblong or oval figures.

And make short account of neuters and geldings, and favor men and
    women fully equipt,
And beat the gong of revolt, and stop with fugitives and them that plot
    and conspire.

24

Walt Whitman, a kosmos, of Manhattan the son,
Turbulent, fleshy, sensual, eating, drinking and breeding,
No sentimentalist, no stander above men and women or apart
    from them,
No more modest than immodest.   500

Unscrew the locks from the doors!
Unscrew the doors themselves from their jambs!

Whoever degrades another degrades me,
And whatever is done or said returns at last to me.

Through me the afflatus[50] surging and surging, through me the current
    and index.

I speak the pass-word primeval, I give the sign of democracy,
By God! I will accept nothing which all cannot have their counterpart
    of on the same terms.

Through me many long dumb voices,
Voices of the interminable generations of prisoners and slaves,
Voices of the diseas'd and despairing and of thieves and dwarfs,   510
Voices of cycles of preparation and accretion,
And of the threads that connect the stars, and of wombs and of the
    father-stuff,
And of the rights of them the others are down upon,
Of the deform'd, trivial, flat, foolish, despised,
Fog in the air, beetles rolling balls of dung.

Through me forbidden voices,
Voices of sexes and lusts, voices veil'd and I remove the veil,
Voices indecent by me clarified and transfigur'd.

I do not press my fingers across my mouth,
I keep as delicate around the bowels as around the head and heart,   520
Copulation is no more rank to me than death is.

I believe in the flesh and the appetites,
Seeing, hearing, feeling, are miracles, and each part and tag of me is a
    miracle.

[50] A divine wind, communicating knowledge or inspiration.

Divine am I inside and out, and I make holy whatever I touch or am
  touch'd from,
The scent of these arm-pits aroma finer than prayer,
This head more than churches, bibles, and all the creeds.

If I worship one thing more than another it shall be the spread of my
  own body, or any part of it,
Translucent mould of me it shall be you!
Shaded ledges and rests it shall be you!
Firm masculine colter[51] it shall be you!   530
Whatever goes to the tilth[52] of me it shall be you!
You my rich blood! your milky stream pale strippings of my life!
Breast that presses against other breasts it shall be you!
My brain it shall be your occult convolutions!
Root of wash'd sweet-flag![53] timorous pond-snipe! nest of guarded
  duplicate eggs! it shall be you!
Mix'd tussled hay of head, beard, brawn, it shall be you!
Trickling sap of maple, fibre of manly wheat, it shall be you!
Sun so generous it shall be you!
Vapors lighting and shading my face it shall be you!
You sweaty brooks and dews it shall be you!   540
Winds whose soft-tickling genitals rub against me it shall be you!
Broad muscular fields, branches of live oak, loving lounger in my
  winding paths, it shall be you!
Hands I have taken, face I have kiss'd, mortal I have ever touch'd, it
  shall be you.

I dote on myself, there is that lot of me and all so luscious,
Each moment and whatever happens thrills me with joy,
I cannot tell how my ankles bend, nor whence the cause of my
  faintest wish,
Nor the cause of the friendship I emit, nor the cause of the friendship I
  take again.

That I walk up my stoop, I pause to consider if it really be,
A morning-glory at my window satisfies me more than the
  metaphysics of books.

To behold the day-break!   550
The little light fades the immense and diaphanous shadows,
The air tastes good to my palate.

Hefts[54] of the moving world at innocent gambols silently rising freshly
  exuding,
Scooting obliquely high and low.

---

[51] A sharp blade that cuts the ground in front of a plowshare.   [52] Cultivation.
[53] The aromatic root of the calamus plant.   [54] The most massive parts.

Something I cannot see puts upward libidinous prongs,
Seas of bright juice suffuse heaven.

The earth by the sky staid with, the daily close of their junction,
The heav'd challenge from the east that moment over my head,
The mocking taunt, See then whether you shall be master!

25

Dazzling and tremendous how quick the sun-rise would kill me,   560
If I could not now and always send sun-rise out of me.

We also ascend dazzling and tremendous as the sun,
We found our own O my soul in the calm and cool of the daybreak.

My voice goes after what my eyes cannot reach,
With the twirl of my tongue I encompass worlds and volumes of worlds.

Speech is the twin of my vision, it is unequal to measure itself,
It provokes me forever, it says sarcastically,
Walt you contain enough, why don't you let it out then?

Come now I will not be tantalized, you conceive too much of
    articulation,
Do you not know O speech how the buds beneath you are folded?   570
Waiting in gloom, protected by frost,
The dirt receding before my prophetical screams,
I underlying causes to balance them at last,
My knowledge my live parts, it keeping tally with the meaning of all
    things,
Happiness, (which whoever hears me let him or her set out in search of
    this day.)

My final merit I refuse you, I refuse putting from me what I really am,
Encompass worlds, but never try to encompass me,
I crowd your sleekest and best by simply looking toward you.

Writing and talk do not prove me,
I carry the plenum[55] of proof and every thing else in my face,   580
With the hush of my lips I wholly confound the skeptic.

26

Now I will do nothing but listen,
To accrue what I hear into this song, to let sounds contribute toward it.

I hear bravuras of birds, bustle of growing wheat, gossip of flames, clack
    of sticks cooking my meals,

[55] Fullness.

I hear the sound I love, the sound of the human voice,
I hear all sounds running together, combined, fused or following,
Sounds of the city and sounds out of the city, sounds of the day and night,
Talkative young ones to those that like them, the loud laugh of work-
    people at their meals,
The angry base[56] of disjointed friendship, the faint tones of the sick,
The judge with hands tight to the desk, his pallid lips pronouncing a
    death-sentence,   590
The heave'e'yo of stevedores unlading ships by the wharves, the refrain
    of the anchor-lifters,
The ring of alarm-bells, the cry of fire, the whirr of swift-streaking
    engines and hose-carts with premonitory tinkles and color'd lights,
The steam-whistle, the solid roll of the train of approaching cars,
The slow march play'd at the head of the association marching two
    and two,
(They go to guard some corpse, the flag-tops are draped with black
    muslin.)

I hear the violoncello, ('tis the young man's heart's complaint,)
I hear the key'd cornet, it glides quickly in through my ears,
It shakes mad-sweet pangs through my belly and breast.

I hear the chorus, it is a grand opera,
Ah this indeed is music—this suits me.   600

A tenor large and fresh as the creation fills me,
The orbic flex of his mouth is pouring and filling me full.

I hear the train'd soprano (what work with hers is this?)
The orchestra whirls me wider than Uranus[57] flies,
It wrenches such ardors from me I did not know I possess'd them,
It sails me, I dab with bare feet, they are lick'd by the indolent waves,
I am cut by bitter and angry hail, I lose my breath,
Steep'd amid honey'd morphine, my windpipe throttled in fakes[58]
    of death,
At length let up again to feel the puzzle of puzzles,
And that we call Being.   610

27

To be in any form, what is that?
(Round and round we go, all of us, and ever come back thither,)
If nothing lay more develop'd the quahaug[59] in its callous shell were
    enough.

---

[56] Bass.
[57] Then thought to be the most remote planet; it orbits the sun at a mean distance of nearly 2 million
miles.
[58] Coils of rope.   [59] Quahog, an edible Atlantic clam.

Mine is no callous shell,
I have instant conductors all over me whether I pass or stop,
They seize every object and lead it harmlessly through me.

I merely stir, press, feel with my fingers, and am happy,
To touch my person to some one else's is about as much as I can stand.

28

Is this then a touch? quivering me to a new identity,
Flames and ether making a rush for my veins,   620
Treacherous tip of me reaching and crowing to help them,
My flesh and blood playing out lightning to strike what is hardly
    different from myself,
On all sides prurient provokers stiffening my limbs,
Straining the udder of my heart for its withheld drip,
Behaving licentious toward me, taking no denial,
Depriving me of my best as for a purpose,
Unbuttoning my clothes, holding me by the bare waist,
Deluding my confusion with the calm of the sunlight and pasture-fields,
Immodestly sliding the fellow-senses away,
They bribed to swap off with touch and go and graze at the edges of me,   630
No consideration, no regard for my draining strength or my anger,
Fetching the rest of the herd around to enjoy them a while,
Then all uniting to stand on a headland and worry me.

The sentries desert every other part of me,
They have left me helpless to a red marauder,
They all come to the headland to witness and assist against me.

I am given up by traitors,
I talk wildly, I have lost my wits, I and nobody else am the greatest
    traitor,
I went myself first to the headland, my own hands carried me there.

You villain touch! what are you doing? my breath is tight in its throat,   640
Unclench your floodgates, you are too much for me.

29

Blind loving wrestling touch, sheath'd hooded sharp-tooth'd touch!
Did it make you ache so, leaving me?

Parting track'd by arriving, perpetual payment of perpetual loan,
Rich showering rain, and recompense richer afterward.

Sprouts take and accumulate, stand by the curb prolific and vital,
Landscapes projected masculine, full-sized and golden.

30

All truths wait in all things,
They neither hasten their own delivery nor resist it,

They do not need the obstetric forceps of the surgeon,   650
The insignificant is as big to me as any,
(What is less or more than a touch?)

Logic and sermons never convince,
The damp of the night drives deeper into my soul.

(Only what proves itself to every man and woman is so,
Only what nobody denies is so.)

A minute and a drop of me settle my brain,
I believe the soggy clods shall become lovers and lamps,
And a compend[60] of compends is the meat of a man or woman,
And a summit and flower there is the feeling they have for each other,   660
And they are to branch boundlessly out of that lesson until it becomes
    omnific,
And until one and all shall delight us, and we them.

31

I believe a leaf of grass is no less than the journey-work of the stars,
And the pismire[61] is equally perfect, and a grain of sand, and the egg of
    the wren,
And the tree-toad is a chef-d'œuvre[62] for the highest,
And the running blackberry would adorn the parlors of heaven,
And the narrowest hinge in my hand puts to scorn all machinery,
And the cow crunching with depress'd head surpasses any statue,
And a mouse is miracle enough to stagger sextillions[63] of infidels.

I find I incorporate gneiss,[64] coal, long-threaded moss, fruits, grains,
    esculent roots,   670
And am stucco'd with quadrupeds and birds all over,
And have distanced what is behind me for good reasons,
But call any thing back again when I desire it.

In vain the speeding or shyness,
In vain the plutonic rocks[65] send their old heat against my approach,
In vain the mastodon retreats beneath its own powder'd bones,
In vain objects stand leagues off and assume manifold shapes,
In vain the ocean settling in hollows and the great monsters lying low,
In vain the buzzard houses herself with the sky,
In vain the snake slides through the creepers and logs,   680
In vain the elk takes to the inner passes of the woods,
In vain the razor-bill'd auk sails far north to Labrador,
I follow quickly, I ascend to the nest in the fissure of the cliff.

---

[60] A compendium or short summary, especially of a very broad subject.   [61] Ant.
[62] A masterpiece (French).   [63] A large number: one followed by twenty-one zeros.
[64] Layered, coarse-grained metamorphic rock.
[65] Rock formed from molten material beneath the earth's crust; from the Roman god Pluto, the ruler of the Underworld.

32

I think I could turn and live with animals, they are so placid and self-
  contain'd,
I stand and look at them long and long.

They do not sweat and whine about their condition,
They do not lie awake in the dark and weep for their sins,
They do not make me sick discussing their duty to God,
Not one is dissatisfied, not one is demented with the mania of owning
  things,
Not one kneels to another, nor to his kind that lived thousands of
  years ago,   690
Not one is respectable or unhappy over the whole earth.

So they show their relations to me and I accept them,
They bring me tokens of myself, they evince them plainly in their
  possession.

I wonder where they get those tokens,
Did I pass that way huge times ago and negligently drop them?

Myself moving forward then and now and forever,
Gathering and showing more always and with velocity,
Infinite and omnigenous,[66] and the like of these among them,
Not too exclusive toward the reachers of my remembrancers,
Picking out here one that I love, and now go with him on brotherly
  terms.   700

A gigantic beauty of a stallion, fresh and responsive to my caresses,
Head high in the forehead, wide between the ears,
Limbs glossy and supple, tail dusting the ground,
Eyes full of sparkling wickedness, ears finely cut, flexibly moving.

His nostrils dilate as my heels embrace him,
His well-built limbs tremble with pleasure as we race around and return.

I but use you a minute, then I resign you, stallion,
Why do I need your paces when I myself out-gallop them?
Even as I stand or sit passing faster than you.

33

Space and Time! now I see it is true, what I guess'd at,   710
What I guess'd when I loaf'd on the grass,
What I guess'd while I lay alone in my bed,
And again as I walk'd the beach under the paling stars of the morning.

My ties and ballasts leave me, my elbows rest in sea-gaps,[67]
I skirt sierras, my palms cover continents,
I am afoot with my vision.

---

[66] Of all forms.   [67] Estuaries, inlets.

By the city's quadrangular houses—in log huts, camping with
    lumbermen,
Along the ruts of the turnpike, along the dry gulch and rivulet bed,
Weeding my onion-patch or hoeing rows of carrots and parsnips,
    crossing savannas, trailing in forests,
Prospecting, gold-digging, girdling the trees of a new purchase,   720
Scorch'd ankle-deep by the hot sand, hauling by boat down the shallow
    river,
Where the panther walks to and fro on a limb overhead, where the buck
    turns furiously at the hunter,
Where the rattlesnake suns his flabby length on a rock, where the otter is
    feeding on fish,
Where the alligator in his tough pimples sleeps by the bayou,
Where the black bear is searching for roots or honey, where the beaver
    pats the mud with his paddle-shaped tail;
Over the growing sugar, over the yellow-flower'd cotton plant, over the
    rice in its low moist field,
Over the sharp-peak'd farm house, with its scallop'd scum and slender
    shoots from the gutters,[68]
Over the western persimmon, over the long-leav'd corn, over the
    delicate blue-flower flax,
Over the white and brown buckwheat, a hummer and buzzer[69] there with
    the rest,
Over the dusky green of the rye as it ripples and shades in the breeze;   730
Scaling mountains, pulling myself cautiously up, holding on by low
    scragged[70] limbs,
Walking the path worn in the grass and beat through the leaves of the
    brush,
Where the quail is whistling betwixt the woods and the wheat-lot,
Where the bat flies in the Seventh-month eve, where the great goldbug[71]
    drops through the dark,
Where the brook puts out of the roots of the old tree and flows to the
    meadow,
Where cattle stand and shake away flies with the tremulous shuddering
    of their hides,
Where the cheese-cloth hangs in the kitchen, where andirons straddle the
    hearth-slab, where cobwebs fall in festoons from the rafters;
Where trip-hammers crash, where the press is whirling its cylinders,
Wherever the human heart beats with terrible throes under its ribs,
Where the pear-shaped balloon is floating aloft, (floating in it myself
    and looking composedly down,)   740
Where the life-car[72] is drawn on the slip-noose, where the heat hatches
    pale-green eggs in the dented sand,
Where the she-whale swims with her calf and never forsakes it,
Where the steam-ship trails hind-ways its long pennant of smoke,
Where the fin of the shark cuts like a black chip out of the water,

---

[68] Patterns of sediment washed down from the roof peaks, and shoots of plants that have colonized
the sediment deposited in the rain-gutters.
[69] A hummingbird and a bee.   [70] Low-growing.   [71] A beetle.
[72] A watertight "car" that moves on ropes, used to evacuate ships.

Where the half-burn'd brig[73] is riding on unknown currents,
Where shells grow to her slimy deck, where the dead are corrupting
   below;
Where the dense-starr'd flag is borne at the head of the regiments,
Approaching Manhattan up by the long-stretching island,
Under Niagara, the cataract[74] falling like a veil over my countenance,
Upon a door-step, upon the horse-block[75] of hard wood outside,   750
Upon the race-course, or enjoying picnics or jibs or a good game of
   baseball,
At he-festivals, with blackguard gibes, ironical license, bull-dances,[76]
   drinking, laughter,
At the cider-mill tasting the sweets of the brown mash, sucking the
   juice through a straw,
At apple-peelings wanting kisses for all the red fruit I find,
At musters,[77] beach-parties, friendly bees, huskings,[78] house-raisings;
Where the mocking-bird sounds his delicious gurgles, cackles, screams,
   weeps,
Where the hay-rick[79] stands in the barn-yard, where the dry-stalks are
   scatter'd, where the brood-cow waits in the hovel,
Where the bull advances to do his masculine work, where the stud to the
   mare, where the cock is treading the hen,
Where the heifers browse, where geese nip their food with short jerks,
Where sun-down shadows lengthen over the limitless and lonesome
   prairie,   760
Where herds of buffalo make a crawling spread of the square miles far
   and near,
Where the humming-bird shimmers, where the neck of the long-lived
   swan is curving and winding,
Where the laughing-gull scoots by the shore, where she laughs her near-
   human laugh,
Where bee-hives range on a gray bench in the garden half hid by the high
   weeds,
Where band-neck'd partridges roost in a ring on the ground with their
   heads out,
Where burial coaches enter the arch'd gates of a cemetery,
Where winter wolves bark amid wastes of snow and icicled trees,
Where the yellow-crown'd heron comes to the edge of the marsh at night
   and feeds upon small crabs,
Where the splash of swimmers and divers cools the warm noon,
Where the katy-did works her chromatic reed[80] on the walnut-tree over
   the well,   770
Through patches of citrons[81] and cucumbers with silver-wired leaves,
Through the salt-lick or orange glade, or under conical firs,

---

[73] A brigantine, or two-masted ship.   [74] Large waterfall.   [75] A step to aid in mounting horses.
[76] Country dances in which men danced with men, due to a shortage of women.
[77] Military assemblies or community gatherings.
[78] Social events for the completion of a labor-intensive task such as quilting or preserving; corn-husking.
[79] Hayracks, from which livestock eat hay.   [80] Colorful harmony.
[81] An edible type of watermelon.

Through the gymnasium, through the curtain'd saloon, through the
    office or public hall;
Pleas'd with the native and pleas'd with the foreign, pleas'd with the
    new and old,
Pleas'd with the homely woman as well as the handsome,
Pleas'd with the quakeress as she puts off her bonnet and talks
    melodiously,
Pleas'd with the tune of the choir of the whitewash'd church,
Pleas'd with the earnest words of the sweating Methodist preacher,
    impress'd seriously at the camp-meeting;
Looking in at the shop windows of Broadway the whole forenoon,
    flatting the flesh of my nose on the thick plate glass,
Wandering the same afternoon with my face turn'd up to the clouds, or
    down a lane or along the beach,   780
My right and left arms round the sides of two friends, and I in the
    middle;
Coming home with the silent and dark-cheek'd bush-boy, (behind me he
    rides at the drape[82] of the day,)
Far from the settlements studying the print of animals' feet, or the
    moccasin print,
By the cot in the hospital reaching lemonade to a feverish patient,
Nigh the coffin'd corpse when all is still, examining with a candle;
Voyaging to every port to dicker and adventure,
Hurrying with the modern crowd as eager and fickle as any,
Hot toward one I hate, ready in my madness to knife him,
Solitary at midnight in my back yard, my thoughts gone from me a
    long while,
Walking the old hills of Judæa with the beautiful gentle God by
    my side,   790
Speeding through space, speeding through heaven and the stars,
Speeding amid the seven satellites and the broad ring,[83] and the
    diameter of eighty thousand miles,
Speeding with tail'd meteors, throwing fire-balls like the rest,
Carrying the crescent child that carries its own full mother in its belly,[84]
Storming, enjoying, planning, loving, cautioning,
Backing and filling, appearing and disappearing,
I tread day and night such roads.

I visit the orchards of spheres and look at the product,
And look at quintillions[85] ripen'd and look at quintillions green.

I fly those flights of a fluid and swallowing soul,   800
My course runs below the soundings of plummets.

I help myself to material and immaterial,
No guard can shut me off, no law prevent me.

---

[82] Close.   [83] The seven planets then known and the rings of Saturn.
[84] A crescent moon, with the full moon palely visible.   [85] Many: one followed by eighteen zeros.

I anchor my ship for a little while only,
My messengers continually cruise away or bring their returns to me.

I go hunting polar furs and the seal, leaping chasms with a pike-pointed
   staff, clinging to topples[86] of brittle and blue.

I ascend to the foretruck,[87]
I take my place late at night in the crow's-nest,
We sail the arctic sea, it is plenty light enough,
Through the clear atmosphere I stretch around on the wonderful beauty,   810
The enormous masses of ice pass me and I pass them, the scenery is
   plain in all directions,
The white-topt mountains show in the distance, I fling out my fancies
   toward them,
We are approaching some great battle-field in which we are soon to be
   engaged,
We pass the colossal outposts of the encampment, we pass with still feet
   and caution,
Or we are entering by the suburbs some vast and ruin'd city,
The blocks and fallen architecture more than all the living cities of
   the globe.

I am a free companion, I bivouac by invading watchfires,
I turn the bridegroom out of bed and stay with the bride myself,
I tighten her all night to my thighs and lips.

My voice is the wife's voice, the screech by the rail of the stairs,   820
They fetch my man's body up dripping and drown'd.

I understand the large hearts of heroes,
The courage of present times and all times,
How the skipper saw the crowded and rudderless wreck of the steam-
   ship, and Death chasing it up and down the storm,
How he knuckled tight and gave not back an inch, and was faithful of
   days and faithful of nights,
And chalk'd in large letters on a board, *Be of good cheer, we will not
   desert you;*
How he follow'd with them and tack'd with them three days and would
   not give it up,
How he saved the drifting company at last,
How the lank loose-gown'd women look'd when boated from the side of
   their prepared graves,
How the silent old-faced infants and the lifted sick, and the sharp-lipp'd
   unshaved men;   830
All this I swallow, it tastes good, I like it well, it becomes mine,
I am the man, I suffer'd, I was there.[88]

---

[86] Fallen, or "toppled" chunks of ice.   [87] The platform of a foremast.
[88] At the wreck of the *San Francisco*, caught in a storm only one day out from New York. The ship
drifted in high seas from December 23, 1853 to January 5, 1854.

The disdain and calmness of martyrs,
The mother of old, condemn'd for a witch, burnt with dry wood, her
    children gazing on,
The hounded slave that flags in the race, leans by the fence, blowing,
    cover'd with sweat,
The twinges that sting like needles his legs and neck, the murderous
    buckshot and the bullets,
All these I feel or am.

I am the hounded slave, I wince at the bite of the dogs,
Hell and despair are upon me, crack and again crack the marksmen,
I clutch the rails of the fence, my gore dribs,[89] thinn'd with the ooze of
    my skin,   840
I fall on the weeds and stones,
The riders spur their unwilling horses, haul close,
Taunt my dizzy ears and beat me violently over the head with whip-
    stocks.

Agonies are one of my changes of garments,
I do not ask the wounded person how he feels, I myself become the
    wounded person,
My hurts turn livid upon me as I lean on a cane and observe.

I am the mash'd fireman with breast-bone broken,
Tumbling walls buried me in their debris,
Heat and smoke I inspired,[90] I heard the yelling shouts of my comrades,
I heard the distant click of their picks and shovels,   850
They have clear'd the beams away, they tenderly lift me forth.

I lie in the night air in my red shirt, the pervading hush is for my sake,
Painless after all I lie exhausted but not so unhappy,
White and beautiful are the faces around me, the heads are bared of
    their fire-caps,
The kneeling crowd fades with the light of the torches.

Distant and dead resuscitate,
They show as the dial or move as the hands of me, I am the
    clock myself.

I am an old artillerist, I tell of my fort's bombardment,
I am there again.

Again the long roll of the drummers,   860
Again the attacking cannon, mortars,
Again to my listening ears the cannon responsive.

I take part, I see and hear the whole,
The cries, curses, roar, the plaudits for well-aim'd shots,

---

[89] Drips.   [90] Inhaled.

The ambulanza slowly passing trailing its red drip,
Workmen searching after damages, making indispensable repairs,
The fall of grenades through the rent roof, the fan-shaped explosion,
The whizz of limbs, heads, stone, wood, iron, high in the air.

Again gurgles the mouth of my dying general, he furiously waves with
    his hand,
He gasps through the clot *Mind not me—mind—the entrenchments.*   870

34

Now I tell what I knew in Texas in my early youth,
(I tell not the fall of Alamo,
Not one escaped to tell the fall of Alamo,
The hundred and fifty are dumb yet at Alamo,)
'Tis the tale of the murder in cold blood of four hundred and twelve
    young men.[91]

Retreating they had form'd in a hollow square with their baggage for
    breastworks,
Nine hundred lives out of the surrounding enemy's, nine times their
    number, was the price they took in advance,
Their colonel was wounded and their ammunition gone,
They treated for an honorable capitulation, receiv'd writing and seal,
    gave up their arms and march'd back prisoners of war.

They were the glory of the race of rangers,   880
Matchless with horse, rifle, song, supper, courtship,
Large, turbulent generous, handsome, proud, and affectionate,
Bearded, sunburnt, drest in the free costume of hunters,
Not a single one over thirty years of age.

The second First-day morning they were brought out in squads and
    massacred, it was beautiful early summer,
The work commenced about five o'clock and was over by eight.

None obey'd the command to kneel,
Some made a mad and helpless rush, some stood stark and straight,
A few fell at once, shot in the temple or heart, the living and dead lay
    together,
The maim'd and mangled dug in the dirt, the new-comers saw
    them there,   890
Some half-kill'd attempted to crawl away,
These were despatch'd with bayonets or batter'd with the blunts of
    muskets,
A youth not seventeen years old seiz'd his assassin till two more came to
    release him,
The three were all torn and cover'd with the boy's blood.

[91] A massacre near what is now Goliad, Texas, in March 1836; Whitman had never been in Texas.

At eleven o'clock began the burning of the bodies;
That is the tale of the murder of the four hundred and twelve young men.

35
Would you hear of an old-time-sea-fight?[92]
Would you learn who won by the light of the moon and stars?
List to the yarn, as my grandmother's father the sailor told it to me.

Our foe was no skulk in his ship I tell you, (said he,)   900
His was the surly English pluck, and there is no tougher or truer, and
    never was, and never will be;
Along the lower'd eve he came horribly raking[93] us.

We closed with him, the yards entangled, the cannon touch'd,
My captain lash'd fast[94] with his own hands.

We had receiv'd some eighteen pound shots under the water,
On our lower-gun-deck two large pieces had burst at the first fire, killing
    all around and blowing up overhead.

Fighting at sun-down, fighting at dark,
Ten o'clock at night, the full moon well up, our leaks on the gain, and
    five feet of water reported,[95]
The master-at-arms loosing the prisoners confined in the after-hold to
    give them a chance for themselves.

The transit to and from the magazine[96] is now stopt by the sentinels,   910
They see so many strange faces they do not know whom to trust.

Our frigate takes fire,
The other asks if we demand quarter[97]?
If our colors are struck and the fighting done?[98]

Now I laugh content, for I hear the voice of my little captain,
We have not struck, he composedly cries, *we have just begun our
    part of the fighting.*

Only three guns are in use,
One is directed by the captain himself against the enemy's mainmast,
Two well serv'd with grape and canister[99] silence his musketry and
    clear his decks.

---

[92] The sea battle between the American ship *Bonhomme Richard,* commanded by John Paul Jones, and the British ship *Serapis* on September 23, 1779; in this battle Jones uttered the famous words, "I have not yet begun to fight."
[93] Aiming heavy gunfire along the length of.   [94] Lashed the two ships fast to one another.
[95] Jones reported that the *Bonhomme Richard* took on five feet of water during the battle.
[96] Ammunition storeroom.   [97] Mercy.
[98] The British thought the Americans, whose flag had been shot away, were surrendering.
[99] Grape-size and smaller iron balls fired from the cannon.

The tops[100] alone second the fire of this little battery, especially the
    main-top,   920
The hold out bravely during the whole of the action.

Not a moment's cease,
The leaks gain fast on the pumps, the fire eats toward the powder-
    magazine.

One of the pumps has been shot away, it is generally thought we are
    sinking.

Serene stands the little captain,
He is not hurried, his voice is neither high nor low,
His eyes give more light to us than our battle-lanterns.

Toward twelve there in the beams of the moon they surrender to us.

36

Stretch'd and still lies the midnight,
Two great hulls motionless on the breast of the darkness,   930
Our vessel riddled and slowly sinking, preparations to pass to the one
    we have conquer'd,
The captain on the quarter-deck coldly giving his orders through a
    countenance white as a sheet,
Near by the corpse of the child that serv'd in the cabin,
The dead face of an old salt with long white hair and carefully curl'd
    whiskers,
The flames spite of all that can be done flickering aloft and below,
The husky voices of the two or three officers yet fit for duty,
Formless stacks of bodies and bodies by themselves, dabs of flesh upon
    the masts and spars,
Cut of cordage, dangle of rigging, slight shock of the soothe of waves,
Black and impassive guns, litter of powder-parcels, strong scent,
A few large stars overhead, silent and mournful shining,   940
Delicate sniffs of sea-breeze, smells of sedgy grass and fields by the
    shore, death-messages given in charge to survivors,
The hiss of the surgeon's knife, the gnawing teeth of this saw,
Wheeze, cluck, swash of falling blood, short wild scream, and long,
    dull, tapering groan,
These so, these irretrievable.

37

You laggards there on guard! look to your arms!
In at the conquer'd doors they crowd! I am possess'd!
Embody all presences outlaw'd or suffering,
See myself in prison shaped like another man,
And feel the dull unintermitted pain.

---

[100] Marksmen firing from platforms on the ship's masts.

For me the keepers of convicts shoulder their carbines and keep watch,   950
It is I let out in the morning and barr'd at night.

Not a mutineer walks handcuff'd to jail but I am handcuff'd to him and
     walk by his side,
(I am less the jolly one there, and more the silent one with sweat on my
     twitching lips.)

Not a youngster is taken for larceny but I go up too, and am tried and
     sentenced.

Not a cholera patient lies at the last gasp but I also lie at the last gasp,
My face is ash-color'd, my sinews gnarl, away from me people retreat.

Askers embody themselves in me and I am embodied in them,
I project my hat,[101] sit shame-faced, and beg.

38

Enough! enough! enough!
Somehow I have been stunn'd. Stand back!   960
Give me a little time beyond my cuff'd head, slumbers, dreams, gaping,
I discover myself on the verge of a usual mistake.

That I could forget the mockers and insults!
That I could forget the trickling tears and the blows of the bludgeons
     and hammers!
That I could look with a separate look on my own crucifixion and bloody
     crowning.

I remember now,
I resume the overstaid fraction,
The grave of rock multiplies what has been confided to it, or to any
     graves,
Corpses rise, gashes heal, fastenings roll from me.

I troop forth replenish'd with supreme power, one of an average
     unending procession,   970
Inland and sea-coast we go, and pass all boundary lines,
Our swift ordinances on their way over the whole earth,
The blossoms we wear in our hats the growth of thousands of years.

Eleves,[102] I salute you! come forward!
Continue your annotations, continue your questionings.

39

The friendly and flowing savage, who is he?
Is he waiting for civilization, or past it and mastering it?

[101] Extend my hat (as though to beg for money).   [102] "Students" or "disciples" (French).

Is he some Southwesterner rais'd out-doors? is he Kanadian?
Is he from the Mississippi country? Iowa, Oregon, California?
The mountains? prairie-life, bush-life? or sailor from the sea?   980

Wherever he goes men and women accept and desire him,
They desire he should like them, touch them, speak to them, stay
    with them.

Behavior lawless as snow-flakes, words simple as grass, uncomb'd head,
    laughter, and naiveté,
Slow-stepping feet, common features, common modes and emanations,
They descend in new forms from the tips of his fingers,
They are wafted with the odor of his body or breath, they fly out of the
    glance of his eyes.

40

Flaunt of the sunshine I need not your bask—lie over!
You light surfaces only, I force surfaces and depths also.

Earth! you seem to look for something at my hands,
Say, old top-knot,[103] what do you want?   990

Man or woman, I might tell how I like you, but cannot,
And might tell what it is in me and what it is in you, but cannot,
And might tell that pining I have, that pulse of my nights and days.

Behold, I do not give lectures or a little charity,
When I give I give myself.

You there, impotent, loose in the knees,
Open your scarf'd chops[104] till I blow grit[105] within you,
Spread your palms and lift the flaps of your pockets,
I am not to be denied, I compel, I have stores plenty and to spare,
And any thing I have I bestow.   1000

I do not ask who you are, that is not important to me,
You can do nothing and be nothing but what I will infold you.

To cotton-field drudge or cleaner of privies I lean,
On his right cheek I put the family kiss,
And in my soul I swear I never will deny him.

On women fit for conception I start bigger and nimbler babes,
(This day I am jetting the stuff of far more arrogant republics.)

---

[103] "Indian": Certain tribes of Native Americans wore an ornament or tuft of hair on the top of the
head.
    [104] Lined and weathered jaws.   [105] Breathe courage.

To any one dying, thither I speed and twist the knob of the door,
Turn the bed-clothes toward the foot of the bed,
Let the physician and the priest go home.   1010

I seize the descending man and raise him with resistless will,
O despairer, here is my neck,
By God, you shall not go down! hang your whole weight upon me.

I dilate you with tremendous breath, I buoy you up,
Every room of the house do I fill with an arm'd force,
Lovers of me, bafflers of graves.

Sleep—I and they keep guard all night,
Not doubt, not decease shall dare to lay finger upon you,
I have embraced you, and henceforth possess you to myself,
And when you rise in the morning you will find what I tell you is so.   1020

4I

I am he bringing help for the sick as they pant on their backs,
And for strong upright men I bring yet more needed help.

I heard what was said of the universe,
Heard it and heard it of several thousand years;
It is middling well as far as it goes—but is that all?

Magnifying and applying come I,
Outbidding at the start the old cautious hucksters,
Taking myself the exact dimensions of Jehovah,[106]
Lithographing Kronos, Zeus his son, and Hercules his grandson,
Buying drafts of Osiris, Isis, Belus, Brahma, Buddha,   1030
In my portfolio placing Manito loose, Allah on a leaf, the crucifix
   engraved,
With Odin and the hideous-faced Mexitli[107] and every idol and image,
Taking them all for what they are worth and not a cent more,
Admitting they were alive and did the work of their days,
(They bore mites as for unfledg'd birds who have now to rise and fly and
   sing for themselves,)
Accepting the rough deific sketches to fill out better in myself,
   bestowing them freely on each man and woman I see,
Discovering as much or more in a framer framing a house,

---

[106] The Judeo-Christian God.
[107] The Titan, or giant god, Kronos (or Cronus) was the supreme god in Greek myth until he was overthrown by his son Zeus; Hercules, the son of Zeus and Alcmene, was known for his strength; Osiris and Isis, the Egyptian god and goddess of fertility; Belus, an Assyrian god-king; Brahma, the supreme Hindu god; Buddha, Siddhartha Gautama (6th century B.C.), founder of Buddhism; Manito, the Algonquian Indian god of nature; Allah, the Muslim God; Odin, the supreme Norse god; Mexitli, an Aztec war god.

Putting higher claims for him there with his roll'd-up sleeves driving the
    mallet and chisel,
Not objecting to special revelations, considering a curl of smoke or a
    hair on the back of my hand just as curious as any revelation,
Lads ahold of fire-engines and hook-and-ladder ropes no less to me than
    the gods of the antique wars,   1040
Minding their voices peal through the crash of destruction,
Their brawny limbs passing safe over charr'd laths, their white foreheads
    whole and unhurt out of the flames;
By the mechanic's wife with her babe at her nipple interceding for every
    person born,
Three scythes at harvest whizzing in a row from three lusty angels with
    shirts bagg'd out at their waists,
The snag-tooth'd hostler[108] with red hair redeeming sins past and to
    come,
Selling all he possesses, traveling on foot to fee lawyers for his brother
    and sit by him while he is tried for forgery;
What was strewn in the amplest strewing the square rod about me, and
    not filling the square rod then,
The bull and the bug[109] never worshipp'd half enough,
Dung and dirt more admirable than was dream'd,
The supernatural of no account, myself waiting my time to be one of
    the supremes,   1050
The day getting ready for me when I shall do as much good as the best,
    and be as prodigious;
By my life-lumps![110] becoming already a creator,
Putting myself here and now to the ambush'd womb of the shadows.

42

A call in the midst of the crowd,
My own voice, orotund sweeping and final.

Come my children,
Come my boys and girls, my women, household and intimates,
Now the performer launches his nerve, he has pass'd his prelude on the
    reeds within.

Easily written loose-finger'd chords—I feel the thrum of your climax
    and close.

My head slues round on my neck,   1060
Music rolls, but not from the organ,
Folks are around me, but they are no household of mind.

---

[108] Stableman.
[109] The bull was worshipped by Greeks, Egyptians, and Moslems; the beetle, by Egyptians.
[110] Testicles.

Ever the hard unsunk ground,
Ever the eaters and drinkers, ever the upward and downward sun, ever
    the air and the ceaseless tides,
Ever myself and my neighbors, refreshing, wicked, real,
Ever the old inexplicable query, ever that thorn'd thumb, that breath of
    itches and thirsts,
Ever the vexer's *hoot! hoot!* till we find where the sly one hides and
    bring him forth,
Ever love, ever the sobbing liquid of life,
Ever the bandage under the chin, ever the trestles[111] of death.

Here and there with dimes on the eyes walking,[112]   1070
To feed the greed of the belly the brains liberally spooning,
Tickets buying, taking, selling, but in to the feast never once going,
Many sweating, ploughing, thrashing, and then the chaff for payment
    receiving,
A few idly owning, and they the wheat continually claiming.

This is the city and I am one of the citizens,
Whatever interests the rest interests me, politics, wars, markets,
    newspapers, schools,
The mayor and councils, banks, tariffs, steamships, factories, stocks,
    stores, real estate and personal estate.

The little plentiful manikins skipping around in collars and tail'd coats,
I am aware who they are, (they are positively not worms or fleas,)
I acknowledge the duplicates of myself, the weakest and shallowest is
    deathless with me,   1080
What I do and say the same waits for them,
Every thought that flounders in me the same flounders in them.

I know perfectly well my own egotism,
Know my omnivorous lines and must not write any less,
And would fetch you whoever you are flush with myself.

Not words of routine this song of mine,
But abruptly to question, to leap beyond yet nearer bring;
This printed and bound book—but the printer and the printing-office
    boy?
The well-taken photographs—but your wife or friend close and solid in
    your arms?
The black ship mail'd with iron, her mighty guns in her turrets—but the
    pluck of the captain and engineers?   1090
In the houses the dishes and fare and furniture—but the host and hostess,
    and the look out of their eyes?

---

[111] Sawhorses or other supports for a coffin.
[112] Coins placed on the eyes of the dead; also, the greedy.

The sky up there—yet here or next door, or across the way?
The saints and sages in history—but you yourself?
Sermons, creeds, theology—but the fathomless human brain,
And what is reason? and what is love? and what is life?

43

I do not despise you priests, all time, the world over,
My faith is the greatest of faiths and the least of faiths,
Enclosing worship ancient and modern and all between ancient and
　　modern,
Believing I shall come again upon the earth after five thousand years,
Waiting responses from oracles, honoring the gods, saluting the sun,　　　　1100
Making a fetich[113] of the first rock or stump, powowing with sticks in the
　　circle of obis,[114]
Helping the llama or brahmin[115] as he trims the lamps of the idols,
Dancing yet through the streets in a phallic procession, rapt and austere
　　in the woods a gymnosophist,[116]
Drinking mead[117] from the skull-cup, to Shastas and Vedas[118] admirant,
　　minding the Koran,
Walking the teokallis,[119] spotted with gore from the stone and knife,
　　beating the serpent-skin drum,
Accepting the Gospels, accepting him that was crucified, knowing
　　assuredly that he is divine,
To the mass kneeling or the puritan's prayer rising, or sitting patiently in
　　a pew,
Ranting and frothing in my insane crisis, or waiting dead-like till my
　　spirit arouses me,
Looking forth on pavement and land, or outside of pavement and land,
Belonging to the winders of the circuit of circuits.　　　　　　　　　　　　1110

One of that centripetal and centrifugal gang I turn and talk like a man
　　leaving charges before a journey.

Down-hearted doubters dull and excluded,
Frivolous, sullen, moping, angry, affected, dishearten'd, atheistical,
I know every one of you, I know the sea of torment, doubt, despair and
　　unbelief.

How the flukes splash!
How they contort rapid as lightning, with spasms and spouts of blood!

Be at peace bloody flukes[120] of doubters and sullen mopers,
I take my place among you as much as among any,

---

[113] A fetish, or primitive object of worship.　　[114] Charms used in sorcery, of African origin.
[115] Lama (or Tibetan high priest) or member of the highest Hindu caste.
[116] Member of an ascetic Hindu sect.
[117] An alcoholic beverage made from fermented honey and water.
[118] Books of Hindu law (Shastas) and Hindu sacred writings, respectively.
[119] An Aztec temple where human sacrifice was conducted.　　[120] The tail fins of stricken whales.

The past is the push of you, me, all, precisely the same,
And what is yet untried and afterward is for you, me, all, precisely
    the same.   1120

I do not know what is untried and afterward,
But I know it will in its turn prove sufficient, and cannot fail.

Each who passes is consider'd, each who stops is consider'd, not a single
    one can it fail.

It cannot fail the young man who died and was buried,
Nor the young woman who died and was put by his side,
Nor the little child that peep'd in at the door, and then drew back and
    was never seen again,
Nor the old man who has lived without purpose, and feels it with
    bitterness worse than gall,
Nor him in the poor house tubercled by rum and the bad disorder,[121]
Nor the numberless slaughter'd and wreck'd, nor the brutish koboo
    call'd the ordure[122] of humanity,
Nor the sacs merely floating with open mouths for food to slip in,   1130
Nor any thing in the earth, or down in the oldest graves of the earth,
Nor any thing in the myriads of spheres, nor the myriads of myriads that
    inhabit them,
Nor the present, nor the least wisp that is known.

44

It is time to explain myself—let us stand up.

What is known I strip away,
I launch all men and women forward with me into the Unknown.

The clock indicates the moment—but what does eternity indicate?

We have thus far exhausted trillions of winters and summers,
There are trillions ahead, and trillions ahead of them.

Births have brought us richness and variety,   1140
And other births will bring us richness and variety.

I do not call one greater and one smaller,
That which fills its period and place is equal to any.

Were mankind murderous or jealous upon you, my brother, my sister?
I am sorry for you, they are not murderous or jealous upon me,
All has been gentle with me, I keep no account with lamentation,
(What have I to do with lamentation?)

I am an acme of things accomplish'd, and I am encloser of things to be.

---

[121] Syphilis.   [122] Native of Sumatra; excrement.

My feet strike an apex of the apices of the stairs,
On every step bunches of ages, and larger bunches between the steps,   1150
All below duly travel'd, and still I mount and mount.

Rise after rise bow the phantoms behind me,
Afar down I see the huge first Nothing, I know I was even there,
I waited unseen and always, and slept through the lethargic mist,
And took my time, and took no hurt from the fetid carbon.

Long I was hugg'd close—long and long.

Immense have been the preparations for me,
Faithful and friendly the arms that have help'd me.

Cycles ferried my cradle, rowing and rowing like cheerful boatmen,
For room to me stars kept aside in their own rings,   1160
They sent influences to look after what was to hold me.

Before I was born out of my mother generations guided me,
My embryo has never been torpid, nothing could overlay it.

For it the nebula cohered to an orb,
The long slow strata piled to rest it on,
Vast vegetables gave it sustenance,
Monstrous sauroids[123] transported it in their mouths and deposited it
    with care.

All forces have been steadily employ'd to complete and delight me,
Now on this spot I stand with my robust soul.

45

O span of youth! ever-push'd elasticity!
O manhood, balanced, florid and full.   1170

My lovers suffocate me,
Crowding my lips, thick in the pores of my skin,
Jostling me through streets and public halls, coming naked to me at
    night,
Crying by day *Ahoy!* from the rocks of the river, swinging and chirping
    over my head,
Calling my name from flower-beds, vines, tangled underbrush,
Lighting on every moment of my life,
Bussing[124] my body with soft balsamic busses,
Noiselessly passing handfuls out of their hearts and giving them to
    be mine.

Old age superbly rising! O welcome, ineffable grace of dying days!   1180

---

[123] Lizardlike reptiles; here, dinosaurs.   [124] Kissing.

Every condition promulges[125] not only itself, it promulges what grows
    after and out of itself,
And the dark hush promulges as much as any.

I open my scuttle[126] at night and see the far-sprinkled systems,
And all I see multiplied as high as I can cipher edge but the rim of the
    farther systems.

Wider and wider they spread, expanding, always expanding,
Outward and outward and forever outward.

My sun has his sun and round him obediently wheels,
He joins with his partners a group of superior circuit,
And greater sets follow, making specks of the greatest inside them.

There is no stoppage and never can be stoppage,   1190
If I, you, and the worlds, and all beneath or upon their surfaces, were
    this moment reduced back to a pallid float,[127] it would not avail in
    the long run,
We should surely bring up again where we now stand,
And surely go as much farther, and then farther and farther.

A few quadrillions of eras, a few octillions[128] of cubic leagues, do not
    hazard the span or make it impatient,
They are but parts, any thing is but a part.

See ever so far, there is limitless space outside of that,
Count ever so much, there is limitless time around that.

My rendezvous is appointed, it is certain,
The Lord will be there and wait till I come on perfect terms,
The great Camerado,[129] the lover true for whom I pine will be there.   1200

46

I know I have the best of time and space, and was never measured and
    never will be measured.

I tramp a perpetual journey, (come listen all!)
My signs are a rain-proof coat, good shoes, and a staff cut from the
    woods,
No friend of mine takes his ease in my chair,
I have no chair, no church, no philosophy,
I lead no man to a dinner-table, library, exchange,[130]
But each man and each woman of you I lead upon a knoll,
My left hand hooking you round the waist,
My right hand pointing to landscapes of continents and the public road.

---

[125] Promulgates or publicly advocates.   [126] Roof hatch.   [127] Returned to a primordial soup.
[128] One followed by twenty-seven zeros.   [129] Comrade.   [130] Stock exchange.

Not I, not any one else can travel that road for you,   1210
You must travel it for yourself.
It is not far, it is within reach,
Perhaps you have been on it since you were born and did not know,
Perhaps it is everywhere on water and on land.

Shoulder your duds dear son, and I will mine, and let us hasten forth,
Wonderful cities and free nations we shall fetch[131] as we go.

If you tire, give me both burdens, and rest the chuff[132] of your hand on
    my hip,
And in due time you shall repay the same service to me,
For after we start we never lie by again.

This day before dawn I ascended a hill and look'd at the crowded
    heaven,   1220
And I said to my spirit *When we become the enfolders of those orbs,*
    and the pleasure and knowledge of every thing in them, shall we be
    fill'd and satisfied then?
And my spirit said *No, we but level that lift[133] to pass and continue*
    beyond.

You are also asking me questions and I hear you,
I answer that I cannot answer, you must find out for yourself.

Sit a while dear son,
Here are biscuits to eat and here is milk to drink,
But as soon as you sleep and renew yourself in sweet clothes, I kiss you
    with a good-by kiss and open the gate for your egress hence.

Long enough have you dream'd contemptible dreams,
Now I wash the gum from your eyes,
You must habit yourself to the dazzle of the light and of every moment
    of your life.   1230

Long have you timidly waded holding a plank by the shore,
Now I will you to be a bold swimmer,
To jump off in the midst of the sea, rise again, nod to me, shout, and
    laughingly dash with your hair.

47

I am the teacher of athletes,
He that by me spreads a wider breast than my own proves the width of
    my own,
He most honors my style who learns under it to destroy the teacher.

The boy I love, the same becomes a man not through derived power, but
    in his own right,

---

[131] Reach.   [132] The fleshy part of the palm.   [133] Elevation.

Wicked rather than virtuous out of conformity or fear,
Fond of his sweetheart, relishing well his steak,
Unrequited love or a slight cutting him worse than sharp steel cuts,   1240
First-rate to ride, to fight, to hit the bull's eye, to sail a skiff, to sing a
     song or play on the banjo,
Preferring scars and the beard and faces pitted with small-pox over all
     latherers,
And those well-tann'd to those that keep out of the sun.

I teach straying from me, yet who can stray from me?
I follow you whoever you are from the present hour,
My words itch at your ears till you understand them.

I do not say these things for a dollar or to fill up the time while I wait
     for a boat,
(It is you talking just as much as myself, I act as the tongue of you,
Tied in your mouth, in mine it begins to be loosen'd.)

I swear I will never again mention love or death inside a house,   1250
And I swear I will never translate myself at all, only to him or her who
     privately stays with me in the open air.

If you would understand me go to the heights or water-shore,
The nearest gnat is an explanation, and a drop or motion of waves a key,
The maul, the oar, the hand-saw, second my words.

No shutter'd room or school can commune with me,
But roughs and little children better than they.

The young mechanic is closest to me, he knows me well,
The woodman that takes his axe and jug with him shall take me with him
     all day,
The farm-boy ploughing in the field feels good at the sound of my voice,
In vessels that sail my words sail, I go with fishermen and seamen and
     love them.   1260

The soldier camp'd or upon the march is mine,
On the night ere the pending battle many seek me, and I do not fail them,
On that solemn night (it may be their last) those that know me seek me.

My face rubs to the hunter's face when he lies down alone in his blanket,
The driver thinking of me does not mind the jolt of his wagon,
The young mother and old mother comprehend me,
The girl and the wife rest the needle a moment and forget where they are,
They and all would resume what I have told them.

48

I have said that the soul is not more than the body,
And I have said that the body is not more than the soul,   1270
And nothing, not God, is greater to one than one's self is,

And whoever walks a furlong without sympathy walks to his own funeral
    drest in his shroud,
And I or you pocketless of a dime may purchase the pick of the earth,
And to glance with an eye or show a bean in its pod confounds the
    learning of all times,
And there is no trade or employment but the young man following it
    may become a hero,
And there is no object so soft but it makes a hub for the wheel'd
    universe,
And I say to any man or woman, Let your soul stand cool and composed
    before a million universes.

And I say to mankind, Be not curious about God,
For I who am curious about each am not curious about God,
(No array of terms can say how much I am at peace about God
    and about death.)   1280

I hear and behold God in every object, yet understand God not in the
    least,
Nor do I understand who there can be more wonderful than myself.

Why should I wish to see God better than this day?
I see something of God each hour of the twenty-four, and each moment
    then,
In the faces of men and women I see God, and in my own face in the
    glass,
I find letters from God dropt in the street, and every one is sign'd by
    God's name,
And I leave them where they are, for I know that wheresoe'er I go,
Others will punctually come for ever and ever.

49

And as to you Death, and you bitter hug of mortality, it is idle to try to
    alarm me.

To his work without flinching the accoucheur[134] comes,   1290
I see the elder-hand pressing receiving supporting,
I recline by the sills of the exquisite flexible doors,
And mark the outlet, and mark the relief and escape.

And as to you Corpse I think you are good manure, but that does not
    offend me,
I smell the white roses sweet-scented and growing,
I reach to the leafy lips, I reach to the polish'd breasts of melons.

And as to you Life I reckon you are the leavings of many deaths,
(No doubt I have died myself ten thousand times before.)

---

[134] Midwife or obstetrician.

I hear you whispering there O stars of heaven,
O suns—O grass of graves—O perpetual transfers and promotions,   1300
If you do not say any thing how can I say any thing?

Of the turbid pool that lies in the autumn forest,
Of the moon that descends the steeps of the soughing[135] twilight,
Toss, sparkles of day and dusk—toss on the black stems that decay in
    the muck,
Toss to the moaning gibberish of the dry limbs.

I ascend from the moon, I ascend from the night,
I perceive that the ghastly glimmer is noonday sunbeams reflected,
And debouch[136] to the steady and central from the offspring great
    or small.

50

There is that in me—I do not know what it is—but I know it is in me.

Wrench'd and sweaty—calm and cool then my body becomes,   1310
I sleep—I sleep long.

I do not know it—it is without name—it is a word unsaid,
It is not in any dictionary, utterance, symbol.

Something it swings on more than the earth I swing on,
To it the creation is the friend whose embracing awakes me.

Perhaps I might tell more. Outlines! I plead for my brothers and sisters.

Do you see O my brothers and sisters?
It is not chaos or death—it is form, union, plan—it is eternal life—it
    is Happiness.

51

The past and present wilt—I have fill'd them, emptied them,
And proceed to fill my next fold of the future.   1320

Listener up there! what have you to confide to me?
Look in my face while I snuff the sidle of evening,[137]
(Talk honestly, no one else hears you, and I stay only a minute longer.)

Do I contradict myself?
Very well then I contradict myself,
(I am large, I contain multitudes.)

I concentrate toward them that are nigh, I wait on the door-slab.

---

[135] Murmuring.   [136] Emerge, or flow outward from a narrow place into open country.
[137] The fading twilight.

Who has done his day's work? who will soonest be through with his
   supper?
Who wishes to walk with me?

Will you speak before I am gone? will you prove already too late?   1330

52

The spotten hawk swoops by and accuses me, he complains of my gab
   and my loitering.

I too am not a bit tamed, I too am untranslatable,
I sound my barbaric yawp over the roofs of the world.

The last scud[138] of day holds back for me,
It flings my likeness after the rest and true as any on the
   shadow'd wilds,
It coaxes me to the vapor and the dusk.

I depart as air, I shake my white locks at the runaway sun,
I effuse[139] my flesh in eddies, and drift it in lacy jags.

I bequeath myself to the dirt to grow from the grass I love,
If you want me again look for me under your boot-soles.   1340

You will hardly know who I am or what I mean,
But I shall be good health to you nevertheless,
And filter and fibre your blood.

Failing to fetch me at first keep encouraged,
Missing me one place search another,
I stop somewhere waiting for you.

1855

from   CHILDREN OF ADAM*

FROM PENT-UP ACHING RIVERS[1]

From pent-up aching rivers,
From that of myself without which I were nothing,
From what I am determin'd to make illustrious, even if I stand
   sole among men,

---

[138] Mist.   [139] Pour forth.
   * Fifteen poems were included in the group "Enfans d'Adam" in the 1860 edition of *Leaves of Grass;*
by 1871 sixteen poems comprised "Children of Adam."
   [1] Originally untitled; first appeared with this title in the 1867 edition of *Leaves of Grass.*

From my own voice resonant, singing the phallus,
Singing the song of procreation,
Singing the need of superb children and therein superb grown people,
Singing the muscular urge and the blending,
Singing the bedfellow's song, (O resistless yearning!
O for any and each the body correlative attracting!
O for you whoever you are your correlative body! O it, more than
    all else, you delighting!)   10
From the hungry gnaw that eats me night and day,
From native moments, from bashful pains, singing them,
Seeking something yet unfound though I have diligently sought it
    many a long year,
Singing the true song of the soul fitful at random,
Renascent with grossest Nature or among animals,
Of that, of them and what goes with them my poems informing,
Of the smell of apples and lemons, of the pairing of birds,
Of the wet of woods, of the lapping of waves,
Of the mad pushes of waves upon the land, I them chanting,
The overture lighty sounding, the strain anticipating,   20
The welcome nearness, the sight of the perfect body,
The swimmer swimming naked in the bath, or motionless on his
    back lying and floating,
The female form approaching, I pensive, love-flesh tremulous aching,
The divine list for myself or you or for any one making,
The face, the limbs, the index from head to foot, and what it arouses,
The mystic deliria, the madness amourous, the utter abandonment,
(Hark close and still what I now whisper to you,
I love you, O you entirely possess me,
O that you and I escape from the rest and go utterly off, free and lawless,
Two hawks in the air, two fishes swimming in the sea not more
    lawless than we;)   30
The furious storm through me careering, I passionately trembling,
The oath of the inseparableness of two together, of the woman that
    loves me and whom I love more than my life, that oath swearing,
(O I willingly stake all for you,
O let me be lost if it must be so!
O you and I! what is it to us what the rest do or think?
What is all else to us? only that we enjoy each other and exhaust
    each other if it must be so;)
From the master, the pilot I yield the vessel to,
The general commanding me, commanding all, from him permission
    taking,
From time the programme hastening, (I have loiter'd too long as it is,)
From sex, from the warp and from the woof,[2]   40
From privacy, from frequent repinings alone,
From plenty of persons near and yet the right person not near,
From the soft sliding of hands over me and thrusting of fingers
    through my hair and beard,

---

[2] From the lengthwise threads in fabric and from the threads woven horizontally between them.

From the long sustain'd kiss upon the mouth or bosom,
From the close pressure that makes me or any man drunk, fainting
    with excess,
From what the divine husband knows, from the work of fatherhood,
From exultation, victory and relief, from the bedfellow's embrace
    in the night,
From the act-poems of eyes, hands, hips and bosoms,
From the cling of the trembling arm,
From the bending curve and the clinch,   50
From side by side the pliant coverlet off-throwing,
From the one so unwilling to have me leave, and me just as unwilling
    to leave,
(Yet a moment O tender waiter, and I return,)
From the hour of shining stars and dropping dews,
From the night a moment I emerging flitting out,
Celebrate you act divine and you children prepared for,
And you stalwart loins.

                                                                1860

ONCE I PASS'D THROUGH A POPULOUS CITY

Once I pass'd through a populous city imprinting my brain for future
    use with its shows, architecture, customs, traditions,
Yet now of all that city I remember only a woman I casually met
    there who detain'd me for love of me,
Day by day and night by night we were together—all else has
    long been forgotten by me,
I remember I say only that woman who passionately clung to me,
Again we wander, we love, we separate again,
Again she holds me by the hand, I must not go.
I see her close beside me with silent lips sad and tremulous.

                                                                1860

FACING WEST FROM CALIFORNIA'S SHORES*

Facing west from California's shores,
Inquiring, tireless, seeking what is yet unfound.
I, a child, very old, over waves, towards the house of maternity,[1]
    the land of migrations, look afar,
Look off the shores of my Western sea, the circle almost circled;
For starting westward from Hindustan,[2] from the vales of Kashmere,[3]
From Asia, from the north, from the God, the sage, and the hero,

---

* Originally untitled; first appeared with this title in the 1867 edition of *Leaves of Grass*.
[1] Asia, believed to be the birthplace of civilization.   [2] India.
[3] Kashmire, a mountainous region adjacent to India, Pakistan, and Tibet.

From the south, from the flowery peninsulas and the spice islands,[4]
Long having wander'd since, round the earth having wander'd
Now I face home again, very pleas'd and joyous,
(But where is what I started for so long ago?
And why is it yet unfound?)

1860

AS ADAM EARLY IN THE MORNING

As Adam early in the morning,
Walking forth from the bower refresh'd with sleep,
Behold me where I pass, hear my voice, approach,
Touch me, touch the palm of your hand to my body as I pass,
Be not afraid of my body.

1861

from   CALAMUS*

IN PATHS UNTRODDEN[1]

In paths untrodden,
In the growth by margins of pond-waters,
Escaped from the life that exhibits itself,
From all the standards hitherto publish'd, from the pleasure,
    profits, conformities,
Which too long I was offering to feed my soul,
Clear to me now standards not yet publish'd, clear to me that my soul,
That the soul of the man I speak for rejoices in comrades,
Here by myself away from the clank of the world,
Tallying and talk'd to here by tongues aromatic,
No longer abash'd, (for in this secluded spot I can respond as I
    would not dare elsewhere,)   10
Strong upon me the life that does not exhibit itself, yet contains
    all the rest,
Resolv'd to sing no songs to-day but those of manly attachment,
Projecting them along that substantial life,
Bequeathing hence types of athletic love,
Afternoon this delicious Ninth-month in my forty-first year,[2]

---

[4] Indonesia.
   * Forty-five poems were included in this group in the 1860 edition of *Leaves of Grass;* by the 1881 edition, there were thirty-nine. Whitman defined calamus as "the very large & aromatic grass, or rush, growing about water-ponds in the valleys—spears about three feet high—often called 'sweet flag'—grows all over the Northern and Middle States. . . . "
   [1] First appeared with this title in the 1867 edition of *Leaves of Grass.*
   [2] September 1859, from the Quaker numerical designations for months.

I proceed for all who are or have been young men,
To tell the secret of my nights and days,
To celebrate the need of comrades.

1860

RECORDERS AGES HENCE*

Recorders ages hence,
Come, I will take you down underneath this impassive[1] exterior, I
    will tell you what to say to me,
Publish my name and hang up my picture as that of the tenderest lover,
The friend the lover's portrait, of whom his friend his lover was fondest,
Who was not proud of his songs, but of the measureless ocean of
    love within him, and freely pour'd it forth,
Who often walk'd lonesome walks thinking of his dear friends,
    his lovers,
Who pensive away from one he lov'd often lay sleepless and
    dissatisfied at night,
Who knew too well the sick, sick dread lest the one he lov'd
    might secretly be indifferent to him,
Whose happiest days were far away through fields, in woods, on
    hills, he and another wandering hand in hand, they twain
    apart from other men,
Who oft as he saunter'd the streets curv'd with his arm the shoulder
    of his friend, while the arm of his friend rested upon him also.   10

1860

I SAW IN LOUISIANA A LIVE-OAK GROWING†

I saw in Louisiana a live-oak growing,
All alone stood it and the moss hung down from the branches,
Without any companion it grew there uttering joyous leaves of
    dark greed,
And its look, rude, unbending, lusty, made me think of myself,
But I wonder'd how it could utter joyous leaves standing alone
    there without its friend near, for I knew I could not,
And I broke off a twig with a certain number of leaves upon it,
    and twined around it a little moss,
And brought it away, and I have placed it in sight in my room,
It is not needed to remind me as of my own dear friends,
(For I believe lately I think of little else than of them,)

---

* First appeared with this title in 1867.   [1] Unemotional.
† First appeared with this title in the 1867 edition of *Leaves of Grass*.

Yet it remains to me a curious token, it makes me think of manly love; 10
For all that, and though the live-oak glistens there in Louisiana
   solitary in a wide flat space,
Uttering joyous leaves all its life without a friend a lover near,
I know very well I could not.

1860

I HEAR IT WAS CHARGED AGAINST ME*

I hear it was charged against me that I sought to destroy institutions,
But really I am neither for nor against institutions,
(What indeed have I in common with them? or what with the
   destruction of them?)
Only I will establish in the Mannahatta and in every city of these
   States inland and seaboard,
And in the fields and woods, and above every keel little or large
   that dents the water,
Without edifices or rules or trustees or any argument,
The institution of the dear love of comrades.

1860

HERE THE FRAILEST LEAVES OF ME**

Here the frailest leaves of me and yet my strongest lasting,
Here I shade and hide my thoughts, I myself do not expose them,
And yet they expose me more than all my other poems.

1860

FULL OF LIFE NOW†

Full of life now, compact, visible,
I, forty years old the eighty-third year of the States,
To one a century hence or any number of centuries hence,
To you yet unborn these, seeking you.

When you read these I that was visible am become invisible,
Now it is you, compact, visible, realizing my poems, seeking me,

* First appeared with this title in the 1867 edition of *Leaves of Grass*.
** First appeared with this title in the 1867 edition of *Leaves of Grass*.
† First appeared with this title in the 1867 edition of *Leaves of Grass*.

Fancying how happy you were if I could be with you and become
   your comrade;
Be it as if I were with you. (Be not too certain but I am now with you.)

1857, 1860

CROSSING BROOKLYN FERRY*

I

Flood-tide below me! I see you face to face!
Clouds of the west—sun there half an hour high—I see you
   also face to face.

Crowds of men and women attired in the usual costumes, how
   curious you are to me!
On the ferry-boats the hundreds and hundreds that cross, returning
   home, are more curious to me than you suppose,
And you that shall cross from shore to shore years hence are more
   to me, and more in my meditations, than you might suppose.

2

The impalpable sustenance of me from all things at all hours of
   the day,
The simple, compact, well-join'd scheme, myself disintegrated,
   every one disintegrated yet part of the scheme,
The similitudes of the past and those of the future,
The glories strung like beads on my smallest sights and hearings,
   on the walk in the street and the passage over the river,
The current rushing so swiftly and swimming with me far away,   10
The others that are to follow me, the ties between me and them,
The certainty of others, the life, love, sight, hearing of others.

Others will enter the gates of the ferry and cross from shore to shore,
Others will watch the run of the flood-tide,
Others will see the shipping of Manhattan north and west, and the
   heights of Brooklyn to the south and east,
Others will see the islands large and small;
Fifty years hence, others will see them as they cross, the sun half
   an hour high,
A hundred years hence, or ever so many hundred years hence,
   others will see them,
Will enjoy the sunset, the pouring-in of the flood-tide, the falling-
   back to the sea of the ebb-tide.

---

* Titled "Sun-Down Poem" in the 1856 edition of *Leaves of Grass;* first appeared with this title in the
1860 edition.

3

It avails not, time nor place—distance avails not,   20
I am with you, you men and women of a generation, or ever so
    many generations hence,
Just as you feel when you look on the river and sky, so I felt,
Just as any of you is one of a living crowd, I was one of a crowd,
Just as you are refresh'd by the gladness of the river and the bright
    flow, I was refresh'd,
Just as you stand and lean on the rail, yet hurry with the swift
    current, I stood yet was hurried,
Just as you look on the numberless masts of ships and the thick-
    stemm'd pipes of steamboats, I look'd.

I too many and many a time cross'd the river of old,
Watched the Twelfth-month[1] sea-gulls, saw them high in the air
    floating with motionless wings, oscillating their bodies,
Saw how the glistening yellow lit up parts of their bodies and left the
    rest in strong shadow,
Saw the slow-wheeling circles and the gradual edging toward the south,   30
Saw the reflection of the summer sky in the water,
Had my eyes dazzled by the shimmering track of beams,
Look'd at the fine centrifugal spokes of light round the shape of my
    head in the sunlit water,
Look'd on the haze on the hills southward and south-westward,
Look'd on the vapor as it flew in fleeces tinged with violet,
Look'd toward the lower bay to notice the vessels arriving,
Saw their approach, saw aboard those that were near me,
Saw the white sails of schooners and sloops, saw the ships at anchor,
The sailors at work in the rigging or out astride the spars,
The round masts, the swinging motion of the hulls, the slender
    serpentine pennants,   40
The large and small steamers in motion, the pilots in their pilot-
    houses,
The white wake left by the passage, the quick tremulous whirl of
    the wheels,
The flags of all nations, the falling of them at sunset,
The scallop-edged waves in the twilight, the ladled cups, the
    frolicsome crests and glistening,
The stretch afar growing dimmer and dimmer, the gray walls of
    the granite storehouses by the docks,
On the river the shadowy group, the big steam-tug closely flank'd
    on each side by the barges, the hay-boat, the belated lighter,[2]
On the neighboring shore the fires from the foundry chimneys
    burning high and glaringly into the night,
Casting their flicker of black contrasted with wild red and yellow light
    over the tops of houses, and down into the clefts of streets.

[1] December, from the Quaker numerical designations for months.
[2] A barge used to load or to lighten (unload) cargo ships.

4

These and all else were to me the same as they are to you,
I loved well those cities, loved well the stately and rapid river,   50
The men and women I saw were all near to me,
Others the same—others who look back on me because I look'd
    forward to them,
(The time will come, though I stop here to-day and to-night.)

5

What is it then between us?
What is the count of the scores or hundreds of years between us?

Whatever it is, it avails not—distance avails not, and place avails not,
I too lived, Brooklyn of ample hills was mine,
I too walk'd the streets of Manhattan island, and bathed in the waters
    around it,
I too felt the curious abrupt questionings stir within me,
In the day among crowds of people sometimes they came upon me,   60
In my walks home late at night or as I lay in my bed they came upon me,
I too had been struck from the float forever held in solution,
I too had receiv'd identity by my body,
That I was I knew was of my body, and what I should be I knew I
    should be of my body.

6

It is not upon you alone the dark patches fall,
The dark threw its patches down upon me also,
The best I had done seem'd to me blank and suspicious,
My great thoughts as I supposed them, were they not in reality meagre?
Nor is it you alone who know what it is to be evil,
I am he who knew what it was to be evil,   70
I too knitted the old knot of contrariety,
Blabb'd, blush'd, resented, lied, stole, grudg'd,
Had guile, anger, lust, hot wishes I dared not speak,
Was wayward, vain, greedy, shallow, sly, cowardly, malignant,
The wolf, the snake, the hog, not wanting[3] in me,
The cheating look, the frivolous word, the adulterous wish, not
    wanting,
Refusals, hates, postponements, meanness, laziness, none of these
    wanting,
Was one with the rest, the days, and haps[4] of the rest,
Was call'd by my nighest[5] name by clear loud voices of young men
    as they saw me approaching or passing,
Felt their arms on my neck as I stood, or the negligent leaning of
    their flesh against me as I sat,   80
Saw many I loved in the street or ferry-boat or public assembly, yet
    never told them a word,
Lived the same life with the rest, the same old laughing, gnawing,
    sleeping,

---

[3] Lacking.   [4] Chance happenings.   [5] Nearest, most familiar.

Play'd the part that still looks back on the actor or actress,
The same old role, the role that is what we make it, as great as we like,
Or as small as we like, or both great and small.

7

Closer yet I approach you,
What thought you have of me now, I had as much of you—I laid in
   my stores in advance,
I consider'd long and seriously of you before you were born.

Who was to know what should come home to me?
Who knows but I am enjoying this?   90
Who knows, for all the distance, but I am as good as looking at
   you now, for all you cannot see me?

8

Ah, what can ever be more stately and admirable to me than mast-
   hemm'd Manhattan?
River and sunset and scallop-edg'd waves of flood-tide?
The sea-gulls oscillating their bodies, the hay-boat in the twilight,
   and the belated lighter?
What gods can exceed these that clasp me by the hand, and with
   voices I love call me promptly and loudly by my nighest
   name as I approach?
What is more subtle than this which ties me to the woman or man that
   looks in my face?
Which fuses me into you now, and pours my meaning into you?

We understand then do we not?
What I promis'd without mentioning it, have you not accepted?
What the study could not teach—what the preaching could not
   accomplish is accomplish'd, is it not?   100

9

Flow on, river! flow with the flood-tide, and ebb with the ebb-tide!
Frolic on, crested and scallop-edg'd waves!
Gorgeous clouds of the sunset! drench with your splendor me, or the
   men and women generations after me!
Cross from shore to shore, countless crowds of passengers!
Stand up, tall masts of Mannahatta! stand up, beautiful hills of Brooklyn!
Throb, baffled and curious brain! throw out questions and answers!
Suspend here and everywhere, eternal float of solution!
Gaze, loving and thirsting eyes, in the house or street or public
   assembly!
Sound out, voices of young men! loudly and musically call me by
   my nighest name!
Live, old life! play the part that looks back on the actor or actress!   110
Play the old role, the role that is great or small according as one
   makes it!
Consider, you who peruse me, whether I may not in unknown ways
   be looking upon you;

Be firm, rail over the river, to support those who lean idly, yet
    haste with the hasting current;
Fly on, sea-birds! fly sideways, or wheel in large circles high in
    the air;
Receive the summer sky, you water, and faithfully hold it till all
    downcast eyes have time to take it from you!
Diverge, fine spokes of light, from the shape of my head, or any
    one's head, in the sunlit water!
Come on, ships from the lower bay! pass up or down, white-sail'd
    schooners, sloops, lighters!
Flaunt away, flags of all nations! be duly lower'd at sunset!
Burn high your fires, foundry chimneys! cast black shadows at
    nightfall! cast red and yellow light over the tops of the
    houses!
Appearances, now or henceforth, indicate what you are,   120
You necessary film, continue to envelop the soul,
About my body for me, and your body for you, be hung our
    divinest aromas,
Thrive, cities—bring your freight, bring your shows, ample and
    sufficient rivers,
Expand, being than which none else is perhaps more spiritual,
Keep your places, objects than which none else is more lasting.

You have waited, you always wait, you dumb, beautiful ministers,
We receive you with free sense at last, and are insatiate henceforward,
Not you any more shall be able to foil us, or withhold yourselves from us,
We use you, and do not cast you aside—we plant you permanently
    within us,
We fathom you not—we love you—there is perfection in you also,   130
You furnish your parts toward eternity,
Great or small, you furnish your parts toward the soul.

1856

from   Sea-Drift*

OUT OF THE CRADLE ENDLESSLY ROCKING[1]

Out of the cradle endlessly rocking,
Out of the mocking-bird's throat, the musical shuttle,
Out of the Ninth-month[2] midnight,

---

   * Eleven poems compiled in the 1881 edition of *Leaves of Grass*.
   [1] First appeared as "A Child's Reminiscence" in the December 24, 1859 issue of the New York *Saturday Press* and with this title in the 1871 edition of *Leaves of Grass*.
   [2] September, from the Quaker numerical designations for months; perhaps reflective of the nine-month-long human gestational cycle.

Over the sterile sands and the fields beyond, where the child leaving
    his bed wander'd alone, bareheaded, barefoot,
Down from the shower'd halo,
Up from the mystic play of shadows twining and twisting as if they
    were alive,
Out from the patches of briers and blackberries,
From the memories of the bird that chanted to me,
From your memories sad brother, from the fitful risings and fallings
    I heard,
From under that yellow half-moon late-risen and swollen as if with tears,   10
From those beginning notes of yearning and love there in the mist,
From the thousand responses of my heart never to cease,
From the myriad thence-arous'd words,
From the word stronger and more delicious than any,
From such as now they start the scene revisiting,
As a flock, twittering, rising, or overhead passing,
Borne hither, ere all eludes me, hurriedly,
A man, yet by these tears a little boy again,
Throwing myself on the sand, confronting the waves,
I, chanter of pains and joys, uniter of here and hereafter,   20
Taking all hints to use them, but swiftly leaping beyond them,
A reminiscence sing.

Once Paumanok,[3]
When the lilac-scent was in the air and Fifth-month[4] grass was
    growing,
Up this seashore in some briers,
Two feather'd guests from Alabama, two together,
And their nest, and four light-green eggs spotted with brown,
And every day the he-bird to and fro near at hand,
And every day the she-bird crouch'd on her nest, silent, with
    bright eyes,
And every day I, a curious boy, never too close, never disturbing
    them,   30
Cautiously peering, absorbing, translating.

Shine! shine! shine!
Pour down your warmth, great sun!
While we bask, we two together.

Two together!
Winds blow south, or winds blow north,
Day come white, or night come black,
Home, or rivers and mountains from home,
Singing all time, minding no time,
While we two keep together.   40

Till of a sudden,
May-be kill'd, unknown to her mate,

---

[3] A Native-American name for Long Island.   [4] May.

One forenoon the she-bird crouch'd not on the nest,
Nor return'd that afternoon, nor the next,
Nor ever appear'd again.

And thenceforward all summer in the sound of the sea,
And at night under the full of the moon in calmer weather,
Over the hoarse surging of the sea,
Or flitting from brier to brier by day,
I saw, I heard at intervals the remaining one, the he-bird,   50
The solitary guest from Alabama.

Blow! blow! blow!
Blow up sea-winds along Paumanok's shore;
I wait and I wait till you blow my mate to me.

Yes, when the stars glisten'd,
All night long on the prong of a moss-scallop'd stake,
Down almost amid the slapping waves,
Sat the lone singer wonderful causing tears.

He call'd on his mate,
He pour'd forth the meanings which I of all men know.   60

Yes my brother I know,
The rest might not, but I have treasur'd every note,
For more than once dimly down to the beach gliding,
Silent, avoiding the moonbeams, blending myself with the shadow,
Recalling now the obscure shapes, the echoes, the sounds and
    sights after their sorts,
The white arms out in the breakers tirelessly tossing,
I, with bare feet, a child, the wind wafting my hair,
Listen'd long and long.

Listen'd to keep, to sing, now translating the notes,
Following you my brother,   70

Soothe! soothe! soothe!
Close on its wave soothes the wave behind,
And again another behind embracing and lapping, every one close,
But my love soothes not me, not me.

Low hangs the moon, it rose late,
It is lagging—O I think it is heavy with love, with love.

O madly the sea pushes upon the land,
With love, with love.

O night! do I not see my love fluttering out among the breakers?
What is that little black thing I see there in the white?   80

Loud! loud! loud!
Loud I call to you, my love!

High and clear I shoot my voice over the waves,
Surely you must know who is here, is here,
You must know who I am, my love.

Low-hanging moon!
What is that dusky spot in your brown yellow?
O it is the shape, the shape of my mate!
O moon do not keep her from me any longer.

Land! land! O land!   90
Whichever way I turn, O I think you could give me my mate back
  again if you only would,
For I am almost sure I see her dimly whichever way I look.

O rising stars!
Perhaps the one I want so much will rise, will rise with some of you.

O throat! O trembling throat!
Sound clearer through the atmosphere!
Pierce the woods, the earth,
Somewhere listening to catch you must be the one I want.

Shake out carols!
Solitary here, the night's carols!   100
Carols of lonesome love! death's carols!
Carols under that lagging, yellow, waning moon!
O under that moon where she droops almost down into the sea!
O reckless despairing carols.

But soft! sink low!
Soft! let me just murmur,
And do you wait a moment you husky-nois'd sea,
For somewhere I believe I heard my mate responding to me,
So faint, I must be still, be still to listen,
But not altogether still, for then she might not come immediately
  to me.   110

Hither my love!
Here I am! here!
With this just-sustain'd note I announce myself to you,
This gentle call is for you my love, for you.

Do not be decoy'd elsewhere,
That is the whistle of the wind, it is not my voice,
That is the fluttering, the fluttering of the spray,
Those are the shadows of leaves.

O darkness! O in vain!
O I am very sick and sorrowful.   120

O brown halo in the sky near the moon, drooping upon the sea!
O troubled reflection in the sea!
O throat! O throbbing heart!
And I singing uselessly, uselessly all the night.

O past! O happy life! O songs of joy!
In the air, in the woods, over fields,
Loved! loved! loved! loved! loved!
But my mate no more, no more with me!
We two together no more.

The aria sinking,   130
All else continuing, the stars shining,
The winds blowing, the notes of the bird continuous echoing,
With angry moans the fierce old mother incessantly moaning,
On the sands of Paumanok's shore gray and rustling,
The yellow half-moon enlarged, sagging down, drooping, the face
    of the sea almost touching,
The boy ecstatic, with his bare feet the waves, with his hair the
    atmosphere dallying,
The love in the heart long pent, now loose, now at last tumultuously
    bursting,
The aria's meaning, the ears, the soul, swiftly depositing,
The strange tears down the cheeks coursing,
The colloquy there, the trio, each uttering,   140
The undertone, the savage old mother incessantly crying,
To the boy's soul's questions sullenly timing, some drown'd secret
    hissing,
To the outsetting bard.

Demon or bird! (said the boy's soul,)
Is it indeed toward your mate you sing? or is it really to me?
For I, that was a child, my tongue's use sleeping, now I have
    heard you,
Now in a moment I know what I am for, I awake,
And already a thousand singers, a thousand songs, clearer, louder
    and more sorrowful than yours,
A thousand warbling echoes have started to life within me, never
    to die.

O you singer solitary, singing by yourself, projecting me,   150
O solitary me listening, never more shall I cease perpetuating you,
Never more shall I escape, never more the reverberations,
Never more the cries of unsatisfied love be absent from me,
Never again leave me to be the peaceful child I was before what there
    in the night,
By the sea under the yellow and sagging moon,

The messenger there arous'd, the fire, the sweet hell within,
The unknown want, the destiny of me.

O give me the clew! (it lurks in the night here somewhere,)
O if I am to have so much, let me have more!

A word then, (for I will conquer it,)   160
The word final, superior to all,
Subtle, sent up—what is it?—I listen;
Are you whispering it, and have been all the time, you sea-waves?
Is that it from your liquid rims, and wet sands?

Whereto answering, the sea,
Delaying not, hurrying not,
Whisper'd me through the night, and very plainly before day-break,
Lisp'd to me the low and delicious word death,
And again death, death, death, death,
Hissing melodious, neither like the bird nor like my arous'd child's
    heart,   170
But edging near as privately for me rustling at my feet,
Creeping thence steadily up to my ears and laving me softly all over,
Death, death, death, death, death.

Which I do not forget,
But fuse the song of my dusky demon and brother,
That he sang to me in the moonlight on Paumanok's gray beach,
With the thousand responsive songs at random,
My own songs awaked from that hour,
And with them the key, the word up from the waves,
The word of the sweetest song and all songs,   180
That strong and delicious word which, creeping to my feet,
(Or like some old crone rocking the cradle, swathed in sweet
    garments, bending aside,)
The sea whisper'd me.

1859

AS I EBB'D WITH THE OCEAN OF LIFE*

As I ebb'd with the ocean of life,
As I wended the shores I know,
As I walk'd where the ripples continually wash you Paumanok,[1]
Where they rustle up hoarse and sibilant,

* First published as "Bardic Symbols" in the April 1860 issue of the *Atlantic Monthly* and with this
title in the 1881 edition of *Leaves of Grass*.
[1] A Native-American name for Long Island.

Where the fierce old mother endlessly cries for her castaways,
I musing late in the autumn day, gazing off southward,
Held by this electric self out of the pride of which I utter poems,
Was seiz'd by the spirit that trails in the lines underfoot,
The rim, the sediment that stands for all the water and all the land
   of the globe.

Fascinated, my eyes reverting from the south, dropt, to follow those
   slender windrows,[2]   10
Chaff, straw, splinters of wood, weeds, and the sea-gluten,
Scum, scales from shining rocks, leaves of salt-lettuce, left by the tide,
Miles walking, the sound of breaking waves the other side of me,
Paumanok there and then as I thought the old thought of likenesses,[3]
These you presented to me you fish-shaped island,
As I wended the shores I know,
As I walk'd with that electric self seeking types.

2

As I wend to the shores I know not,
As I list to the dirge, the voices of men and women wreck'd,
As I inhale the impalpable breezes that set in upon me,   20
As the ocean so mysterious rolls toward me closer and closer,
I too but signify at the utmost a little wash'd-up drift.
A few sands and dead leaves to gather,
Gather, and merge myself as part of the sands and drift.

O baffled, balk'd, bent to the very earth,
Oppress'd with myself that I have dared to open my mouth,
Aware now that amid all that blab whose echoes recoil upon me I
   have not once had the least idea who or what I am,
But that before all my arrogant poems the real Me stands yet
   untouch'd, untold, altogether unreach'd,
Withdrawn far, mocking me with mock-congratulatory signs and bows,
With peals of distant ironical laughter at every word I have written,   30
Pointing in silence to these songs, and then to the sand beneath.

I perceive I have not really understood any thing, not a single
   object, and that no man ever can,
Nature here in sight of the sea taking advantage of me to dart
   upon me and sting me,
Because I have dared to open my mouth to sing at all.

3

You oceans both, I close with you,
We murmur alike reproachfully rolling sands and drift, knowing
   not why,
These little shreds indeed standing for you and me and all.

---

[2] Rows of waves formed by the wind.
[3] In transcendental terms, the correspondence between the "wash'd-up drift" and the poet.

You friable[4] shore with trails of debris,
You fish-shaped island, I take what is underfoot,
What is yours is mine my father.   40

I too Paumanok,
I too have bubbled up, floated the measureless float, and been
   wash'd on your shores,
I too am but a trail of drift and debris,
I too leave little wrecks upon you, you fish-shaped island.

I throw myself upon your breast my father,[5]
I cling to you so that you cannot unloose me,
I hold you so firm till you answer me something.

Kiss me my father,
Touch me with your lips as I touch those I love,
Breathe to me while I hold you close the secret of the murmuring
   I envy.   50

4
Ebb, ocean of life, (the flow will return,)
Cease not your moaning you fierce old mother,
Endlessly cry for your castaways, but fear not, deny not me,
Rustle not up so hoarse and angry against my feet as I touch you
   or gather from you.

I mean tenderly by you and all,
I gather for myself and for this phantom looking down where we
   lead, and following me and mine.
Me and mine, loose windrows, little corpses,
Froth, snowy white, and bubbles,
(See, from my dead lips the ooze exuding at last,
See, the prismatic colors glistening and rolling,)   60
Tufts of straw, sands, fragments,
Buoy'd hither from many moods, one contradicting another,
From the storm, the long calm, the darkness, the swell,
Musing, pondering, a breath, a briny tear, a dab of liquid or soil,
Up just as much out of fathomless workings fermented and thrown,
A limp blossom or two, torn, just as much over waves floating, drifted
   at random,
Just as much for us that sobbing dirge of Nature,
Just as much whence we come that blare of the cloud-trumpets,
We, capricious, brought hither we know not whence, spread out
   before you,
You up there walking or sitting,   70
Whoever you are, we too lie in drifts at your feet.

1859?, 1860

---

[4] Crumbling.   [5] Paumanok, his native land; the ocean is his "fierce old mother."

from   BY THE ROADSIDE*

A HAND-MIRROR[1]

Hold it up sternly—see this it sends back, (who is it? is it you?)
Outside fair costume, within ashes and filth,
No more a flashing eye, no more a sonorous voice or springy step,
Now some slave's eye, voice, hands, step,
A drunkard's breath, unwholesome eater's face, venerealee's flesh,
Lungs rotting away piecemeal, stomach sour and cankerous,
Joints rheumatic, bowels clogged with abomination,
Blood circulating dark and poisonous streams,
Words babble, hearing and touch callous,
No brain, no heart left, no magnetism of sex;   10
Such from one look in this looking-glass ere you go hence,
Such a result so soon—and from such a beginning!

                                                                        1860

WHEN I HEARD THE LEARN'D ASTRONOMER**

When I heard the learn'd astronomer,
When the proofs, the figures, were ranged in columns before me,
When I was shown the charts and diagrams, to add, divide, and
    measure them,
When I sitting heard the astronomer where he lectured with much
    applause in the lecture-room,
How soon unaccountable I became tired and sick,
Till rising and gliding out I wander'd off by myself,
In the mystical moist night-air, and from time to time,
Look'd up in perfect silence at the stars.

                                                                        1865

TO A PRESIDENT†

All you are doing and saying is to America dangled mirages,
You have not learn'd of Nature—of the politics of Nature you
    have not learn'd the great amplitude, rectitude, impartiality,

---

* Twenty-nine poems that appeared in various sections of *Leaves of Grass* and *Drum-Taps* (1865) until grouped with this title in the 1881 edition of *Leaves*.
[1] First appeared with this title in the 1860 edition of *Leaves*.
** First published in *Drum-Taps* (1865) and eventually added to "By the Roadside" in the 1881 edition of *Leaves of Grass*.
† Whitman's criticism is aimed at James Buchanan (1791–1868), the fifteenth U.S. president (1857–1861), who failed to take a firm stand against slavery.

You have not seen that only such as they are for these States,
And that what is less than they must sooner or later lift off from
 these States.

1860

THE DALLIANCE OF THE EAGLES*

Skirting the river road, (my forenoon walk, my rest,)
Skyward in air a sudden muffled sound, the dalliance of the eagles,
The rushing amorous contact high in space together,
The clinching interlocking claws, a living, fierce, gyrating wheel,
Four beating wings, two beaks, a swirling mass tight grappling,
In tumbling turning clustering loops, straight downward falling,
Till o'er the river pois'd, the twain yet one, a moment's lull,
A motionless still balance in the air, then parting, talons loosing,
Upward again on slow-firm pinions slanting, their separate diverse flight,
She hers, he his, pursuing.   10

1880

THE RUNNER

On a flat road runs the well-train'd runner,
He is lean and sinewy with muscular legs,
He is thinly clothed, he leans forward as he runs,
With lightly closed fists and arms partially rais'd.

1867

from   DRUM-TAPS†

BEAT! BEAT! DRUMS!¹

Beat! beat! drums!—blow! bugles! blow!
Through the windows—through doors—burst like a ruthless force,
Into the solemn church, and scatter the congregation,
Into the school where the scholar is studying;

---

 * First appeared in *Cope's Tobacco Plant* in November 1880; added to the 1881 edition of *Leaves of Grass*. Here, "dalliance" refers to mating.
 † First published separately with fifty-three poems in 1865; revised with eighteen new poems as "Sequel to Drum-Taps" (1865–1866)—a volume that received unenthusiastic reviews—and added to the 1867 edition of *Leaves of Grass*, ultimately as a group of forty-three poems in the 1881 edition.
 ¹ First published simultaneously in *Harper's Weekly* and the New York *Ledger* on September 28, 1861.

Leave not the bridegroom quiet—no happiness must he have now
    with his bride,
Nor the peaceful farmer any peace, ploughing his field or gathering
    his grain,
So fierce you whirr and pound you drums—so shrill you bugles blow.

Beat! beat! drums!—blow! bugles! blow!
Over the traffic of cities—over the rumble of wheels in the streets;
Are beds prepared for sleepers at night in the houses? no sleepers
    must sleep in those beds,   10
No bargainers' bargains by day—no brokers or speculators—would
    they continue?
Would the talkers be talking? would the singer attempt to sing?
Would the lawyer rise in the court to state his case before the judge?
Beat! beat! drums!—blow! bugles! blow!
Then rattle quicker, heavier drums—you bugles wilder blow.
Make no parley—stop for no expostulation,
Mind not the timid—mind not the weeper or prayer,
Mind not the old man beseeching the young man,
Let not the child's voice be heard, nor the mother's entreaties,
Make even the trestles to shake the dead where they lie awaiting
    the hearses,   20
So strong you thump O terrible drums—so loud you bugles blow.

1861

CAVALRY CROSSING A FORD

A line in long array where they wind betwixt green islands,
They take a serpentine course, their arms flash in the sun—hark
    to the musical clank,
Behold the silvery river, in it the splashing horses loitering stop to drink,
Behold the brown-faced men, each group, each person a picture, the
    negligent rest on the saddles,
Some emerge on the opposite bank, others are just entering the
    ford—while,
Scarlet and blue and snowy white,
The guidon flags[1] flutter gayly in the wind.

1865

VIGIL STRANGE I KEPT ON THE FIELD ONE NIGHT

Vigil strange I kept on the field one night;
When you my son and my comrade dropt at my side that day,
One look I but gave which your dear eyes return'd with a look I
    shall never forget,

---

[1] Military flags or pennants for identification and signaling.

One touch of your hand to mine O boy, reach'd up as you lay
  on the ground,
Then onward I sped in the battle, the even-contested battle,
Till late in the night reliev'd to the place at last again I made my way,
Found you in death so cold dear comrade, found your body son
  of responding kisses, (never again on earth responding,)
Bared your face in the starlight, curious the scene, cool blew the
  moderate night-wind,
Long there and then in vigil I stood, dimly around me the battle-
  field spreading,
Vigil wondrous and vigil sweet there in the fragrant silent night,   10
But not a tear fell, not even a long-drawn sigh, long, long I gazed,
Then on the earth partially reclining sat by your side leaning my chin
  in my hands,
Passing sweet hours, immortal and mystic hours with you dearest
  comrade—not a tear, not a word,
Vigil of silence, love and death, vigil for you my son and my soldier,
As onward silently stars aloft, eastward new ones upward stole,
Vigil final for you brave boy, (I could not save you, swift was your
  death,
I faithfully loved you and cared for you living, I think we shall surely
  meet again,)
Till at latest lingering of the night, indeed just as the dawn appear'd,
My comrade I wrapt in his blanket, envelop'd well his form,
Folded the blanket well, tucking it carefully over head and carefully
  under feet,   20
And there and then and bathed by the rising sun, my son in his
  grave, in his rude-dug grave I deposited,
Ending my vigil strange with that, vigil of night and battle-field dim,
Vigil for boy of responding kisses, (never again on earth responding,)
Vigil for comrade swiftly slain, vigil I never forget, how as day
  brighten'd,
I rose from the chill ground and folded my soldier well in his blanket,
And buried him where he fell.

1865

A MARCH IN THE RANKS HARD-PREST, AND
THE ROAD UNKNOWN

A march in the ranks hard-prest, and the road unknown,
A route through a heavy wood with muffled steps in the darkness,
Our army foil'd with loss severe, and the sullen remnant retreating,
Till after midnight glimmer upon us the lights of a dim-lighted building,
We come to an open space in the woods, and halt by the dim-lighted
  building,
'Tis a large old church at the crossing roads, now an impromptu hospital,
Entering but for a minute I see a sight beyond all the pictures and
  poems ever made,
Shadows of deepest, deepest black, just lit by moving candles and lamps,

And by one great pitchy torch stationary with wild red flame and clouds
    of smoke,
By these, crowds, groups of forms vaguely I see on the floor, some
    in the pews laid down,   10
At my feet more distinctly a soldier, a mere lad, in danger of bleeding
    to death, (he is shot in the abdomen,)
I stanch the blood temporarily, (the youngster's face is white as a lily,)
Then before I depart I sweep my eyes o'er the scene fain to absorb it all,
Faces, varieties, postures beyond description, most in obscurity,
    some of them dead,
Surgeons operating, attendants holding lights, the smell of ether,
    the odor of blood,
The crowd, O the crowd of the bloody forms, the yard outside also fill'd,
Some on the bare ground, some on planks or stretchers, some in the
    death-spasm sweating,
An occasional scream or cry, the doctor's shouted orders or calls,
The glisten of the little steel instruments catching the glint of the
    torches,
These I resume as I chant, I see again the forms, I smell the odor,   20
Then hear outside the orders given, *Fall in, my men, fall in;*
But first I bend to the dying lad, his eyes open, a half-smile gives
    he me,
Then the eyes close, calmly close, and I speed forth to the darkness,
Resuming, marching, ever in darkness marching, on in the ranks,
The unknown road still marching.

                    1865

A SIGHT IN CAMP IN THE DAYBREAK
GRAY AND DIM

A sight in camp in the daybreak gray and dim,
As from my tent I emerge so early sleepless,
As slow I walk in the cool fresh air the path near by the hospital tent,
Three forms I see on stretchers lying, brought out there untended lying,
Over each the blanket spread, ample brownish woolen blanket,
Gray and heavy blanket, folding, covering all.

Curious I halt and silent stand,
Then with light fingers I from the face of the nearest the first just lift
    the blanket;
Who are you elderly man so gaunt and grim, with well-gray'd hair,
    and flesh all sunken about the eyes?
Who are you my dear comrade?   10
Then to the second I step—and who are you my child and darling?
Who are you sweet boy with cheeks yet blooming?

Then to the third—a face nor child nor old, very calm, as of beautiful
    yellow-white ivory;

Young man I think I know you—I think this face is the face of the
  Christ himself,
Dead and divine and brother of all, and here again he lies.

1865

THE WOUND-DRESSER*

1

An old man bending I come among new faces,
Years looking backward resuming in answer to children,
Come tell us old man, as from young men and maidens that love me,
(Arous'd and angry, I'd thought to beat the alarum, and urge
  relentless war,
But soon my fingers fail'd me, my face droop'd and I resign'd myself,
To sit by the wounded and soothe them, or silently watch the dead;)
Years hence of these scenes, of these furious passions, these chances,
Of unsurpass'd heroes, (was one side so brave? the other was
  equally brave;)
Now be witness again, paint the mightiest armies of earth,
Of those armies so rapid so wondrous what saw you to tell us?   10
What stays with you latest and deepest? of curious panics,
Of hard-fought engagements or sieges tremendous what deepest
  remains?

2

O maidens and young men I love and that love me,
What you ask of my days those the strangest and sudden your
  talking recalls,
Soldier alert I arrive after a long march covr'd with sweat and dust,
In the nick of time I come, plunge in the fight, loudly shout in the
  rush of successful charge,
Enter the captur'd works[1]—yet lo, like a swift-running river they fade,
Pass and are gone they fade—I dwell not on soldiers' perils or
  soldiers' joys,
(Both I remember well—many the hardships, few the joys, yet I
  was content.)

But in silence, in dreams' projections,   20
While the world of gain and appearance and mirth goes on,
So soon what is over forgotten, and waves wash the imprints off
  the sand,
With hinged knees returning I enter the doors, (while for you up there,
Whoever you are, follow without noise and be of strong heart.)

---

* First appeared as "The Dresser" in the 1865 edition of *Leaves of Grass* and with this title in the
1876 edition.
[1] Breastworks, fortifications.

Bearing the bandages, water and sponge,
Straight and swift to my wounded I go,
Where they lie on the ground after the battle brought in,
Where their priceless blood reddens the grass the ground,
Or to the rows of the hospital tent, or under the roof'd hospital,
To the long rows of cots up and down each side I return,   30
To each and all one after another I draw near, not one do I miss,
An attendant follows holding a tray, he carries a refuse pail,
Soon to be fill'd with clotted rags and blood, emptied, and fill'd again.

I onward go, I stop,
With hinged knees and steady hand to dress wounds,
I am firm with each, the pangs are sharp yet unavoidable,
One turns to me his appealing eyes—poor boy! I never knew you,
Yet I think I could not refuse this moment to die for you, if that
    would save you.

3
On, on I go, (open doors of time! open hospital doors!)
The crush'd head I dress, (poor crazed hand tear not the bandage away,)   40
The neck of the cavalry-man with the bullet through and through
    I examine,
Hard the breathing rattles, quite glazed already the eye, yet life
    struggles hard,
(Come sweet death! be persuaded O beautiful death!
In mercy come quickly.)

From the stump of the arm, the amputated hand,
I undo the clotted lint, remove the slough, wash off the matter
    and blood,
Back on his pillow the soldier bends with curv'd neck and side-
    falling head,
His eyes are closed, his face is pale, he dares not look on the
    bloody stump,
And has not yet look'd on it.

I dress a wound in the side, deep, deep,   50
But a day or two more, for see the frame all wasted and sinking,
And the yellow-blue countenance see.

I dress the perforated shoulder, the foot with the bullet-wound,
Cleanse the one with a gnawing and putrid gangrene, so sickening,
    so offensive,
While the attendant stands behind aside me holding the tray and pail.

I am faithful, I do not give out,
The fractur'd thigh, the knee, the wound in the abdomen,
These and more I dress with impassive hand, (yet deep in my
    breast a fire, a burning flame.)

4

Thus in silence in dreams' projections,
Returning, resuming, I thread my way through the hospitals,   60
The hurt and wounded I pacify with soothing hand,
I sit by the restless all the dark night, some are so young,
Some suffer so much, I recall the experience sweet and sad,
(Many a soldier's loving arms about this neck have cross'd and rested,
Many a soldier's kiss dwells on these bearded lips.)

1865

DIRGE FOR TWO VETERANS*

The last sunbeam
Lightly falls from the finish'd Sabbath,
On the pavement here, and there beyond it is looking,
    Down a new-made double grave.

Lo, the moon ascending,
Up from the east the silvery round moon,
Beautiful over the house-tops, ghastly, phantom moon,
    Immense and silent moon.

I see a sad procession,
And I hear the sound of coming full-key'd bugles,   10
All the channels of the city streets they're flooding,
    As with voices and with tears.

I hear the great drums pounding,
And the small drums steady whirring,
And every blow of the great convulsive drums,
    Strikes me through and through.

For the son is brought with the father,
(In the foremost ranks of the fierce assault they fell,
Two veterans son and father dropt together,
    And the double grave awaits them.)   20

Now nearer blow the bugles,
And the drums strike more convulsive,
And the daylight o'er the pavement quite has faded,
    And the strong dead-march enwraps me.

In the eastern sky up-buoying,
The sorrowful vast phantom moves illumin'd,

---

* First appeared in the "Sequel to Drum-Taps" (1865–1866).

    ('Tis some mother's large transparent face,
      In heaven brighter growing.)

    O strong dead-march you please me!
    O moon immense with your silvery face you soothe me!   30
    O my soldiers twain! O my veterans passing to burial!
      What I have I also give you.

    The moon gives you light,
    And the bugles and the drums give you music,
    And my heart, O my soldiers, my veterans,
      My heart gives you love.

                                            1865–1866

THE ARTILLERYMAN'S VISION*

While my wife at my side lies slumbering, and the wars are over long,
And my head on the pillow rests at home, and the vacant midnight passes,
And through the stillness, through the dark, I hear, just hear, the
    breath of my infant,
There in the room as I wake from sleep this vision presses upon me;
The engagement opens there and then in fantasy unreal,
The skirmishers begin, they crawl cautiously ahead, I hear the
    irregular snap! snap!
I hear the sounds of the different missiles, the short *t-h-t! t-h-t!* of
    the rifle-balls,
I see the shells exploding leaving small white clouds, I hear the great
    shells shrieking as they pass,
The grape like the hum and whirr of wind through the trees,
    (tumultuous now the contest rages,)
All the scenes at the batteries rise in detail before me again,   10
The crashing and smoking, the pride of the men in their pieces,
The chief-gunner ranges and sights his piece and selects a fuse of the
    right time,
After firing I see him lean aside and look eagerly off to note the effect;
Elsewhere I hear the cry of a regiment charging, (the young colonel
    leads himself this time with brandish'd sword,)
I see the gaps cut by the enemy's volleys, (quickly fill'd up, no delay,)
I breathe the suffocating smoke, then the flat clouds hover low
    concealing all;
Now a strange lull for a few seconds, not a shot fired on either side,
Then resumed the chaos louder than ever, with eager calls and orders
    of officers,

---

* First published as "The Veteran's Vision" in the 1865 edition of *Leaves of Grass* and with this title
in the 1871 edition.

While from some distant part of the field the wind wafts to my ears
　a shout of applause, (some special success,)
And ever the sound of the cannon far or near, (rousing even in
　dreams a devilish exultation and all the old mad joy
　in the depths of my soul,)　　　　　　　　　　　　　　　　20
And ever the hastening of infantry shifting positions, batteries,
　cavalry, moving hither and thither,
(The falling, dying, I heed not, the wounded dripping and red I heed
　not, some to the rear are hobbling,)
Grime, heat, rush, aide-de-camps galloping by or on a full run,
With the patter of small arms, the warning *s-s-t* of the rifles, (these in
　my vision I hear or see,)
And bombs bursting in air, and at night the vari-color'd rockets.

1865

RECONCILIATION*

Word over all, beautiful as the sky,
Beautiful that war and all its deeds of carnage must in time be utterly lost,
That the hands of the sisters Death and Night incessantly softly wash again,
　and ever again, this soil'd world;
For my enemy is dead, a man divine as myself is dead,
I look where he lies white-faced and still in the coffin—I draw near,
Bend down and touch lightly with my lips the white face in the coffin.

1865–1866

from　MEMORIES OF PRESIDENT LINCOLN†

WHEN LILACS LAST IN THE DOORYARD BLOOM'D¹

I

When lilacs last in the dooryard bloom'd,
And the great star² early droop'd in the western sky in the night,
I mourn'd, and yet shall mourn with ever-returning spring.

Ever-returning spring, trinity sure to me you bring,
Lilac blooming perennial and drooping star in the west,
And thought of him I love.

---

　* First appeared in the "Sequel to Drum-Taps" (1865–1866).
　† Four poems first grouped as "President Lincoln's Burial Hymn" in the 1871 edition of *Leaves of Grass* and with this title in the 1881 edition.
　¹ First appeared in the "Sequel to Drum-Taps"(1865–1866).　　² Venus.

2
O powerful western fallen star!
O shades of night—O moody, tearful night!
O great star disappear'd—O the black murk that hides the star!
O cruel hands that hold me powerless—O helpless soul of me!   10
O harsh surrounding cloud that will not free my soul.

3
In the dooryard fronting an old farm-house near the white-wash'd palings,
Stands the lilac-bush tall-growing with heart-shaped leaves of rich green,
With many a pointed blossom rising delicate, with the perfume strong
    I love,
With every leaf a miracle—and from this bush in the dooryard,
With delicate-color'd blossoms and heart-shaped leaves of rich green,
A sprig with its flower I break.

4
In the swamp in secluded recesses,
A shy and hidden bird is warbling a song.

Solitary the thrush,   20
The hermit withdrawn to himself, avoiding the settlements,
Sings by himself a song.

Song of the bleeding throat,
Death's outlet song of life, (for well dear brother I know,
If thou wast not granted to sing thou would'st surely die.)

5
Over the breast of the spring, the land, amid cities,
Amid lanes and through old woods, where lately the violets peep'd
    from the ground, spotting the gray debris,
Amid the grass in the fields each side of the lanes, passing the endless
    grass,
Passing the yellow-spear'd wheat, every grain from its shroud in the
    dark-brown fields uprisen,
Passing the apple-tree blows[3] of white and pink in the orchards,   30
Carrying a corpse to where it shall rest in the grave,
Night and day journeys a coffin.[4]

6
Coffin that passes through lanes and streets,
Through day and night with the great cloud darkening the land,
With the pomp of the inloop'd flags with the cities draped in black,
With the show of the States themselves as of crape-veil'd women standing,

[3] Blossoms.
[4] Lincoln's body was transported by train from Washington, D.C., to Springfield, Illinois, for burial after he was assassinated in April 1865.

With processions long and winding and the flambeaus[5] of the night,
With the countless torches lit, with the silent sea of faces and the
    unbared heads,
With the waiting depot, the arriving coffin, and the sombre faces,
With dirges through the night, with the thousand voices rising strong
    and solemn,   40
With all the mournful voices of the dirges pour'd around the coffin,
The dim-lit churches and the shuddering organs—where amid these
    you journey,
With the tolling tolling bells' perpetual clang,
Here, coffin that slowly passes,
I give you my sprig of lilac.

7

(Nor for you, for one alone,
Blossoms and branches green to coffins all I bring,
For fresh as the morning, thus would I chant a song for you O sane
    and sacred death.

All over bouquets of roses,
O death, I cover you over with roses and early lilies,   50
But mostly and now the lilac that blooms the first,
Copious I break, I break the sprigs from the bushes,
With loaded arms I come, pouring for you,
For you and the coffins all of you O death.)

8

O western orb sailing the heaven,
Now I know what you must have meant as a month since I walk'd,
As I walk'd in silence the transparent shadowy night,
As I saw you had something to tell as you bent to me night after night,
As you droop'd from the sky low down as if to my side, (while the
    other stars all look'd on,)
As we wander'd together the solemn night, (for something I know not
    what kept me from sleep,)   60
As the night advanced, and I saw on the rim of the west how full you
    were of woe,
As I stood on the rising ground in the breeze in the cool transparent night,
As I watch'd where you pass'd and was lost in the netherward black of
    the night,
As my soul in its trouble dissatisfied sank, as where you sad orb,
Concluded, dropt in the night, and was gone.

9

Sing on there in the swamp,
O singer bashful and tender, I hear your notes, I hear your call,
I hear, I come presently, I understand you,

[5] Torches or candles.

But a moment I linger, for the lustrous star has detain'd me,
The star my departing comrade holds and detains me.   70

10

O how shall I warble myself for the dead one there I loved?
And how shall I deck my song for the large sweet soul that has gone?
And what shall my perfume be for the grave of him I love?

Sea-winds blown from east and west,
Blown from the Eastern sea and blown from the Western sea, till
    there on the prairies meeting,
These and with these and the breath of my chant,
I'll perfume the grave of him I love.

11

O what shall I hang on the chamber walls?
And what shall the pictures be that I hang on the walls,
To adorn the burial-house of him I love?   80

Pictures of growing spring and farms and homes,
With the Fourth-month[6] eve at sundown, and the gray smoke lucid
    and bright,
With floods of the yellow gold of the gorgeous, indolent, sinking
    sun, burning, expanding the air,
With the fresh sweet herbage under foot, and the pale green leaves of
    the trees prolific,
In the distance the flowing glaze, the breast of the river, with a
    wind-dapple here and there,
With ranging hills on the banks, with many a line against the sky, and
    shadows,
And the city at hand with dwellings so dense, and stacks of chimneys,
And all the scenes of life and the workshops, and the workmen homeward
    returning.

12

Lo, body and soul—this land,
My own Manhattan with spires, and the sparkling and hurrying tides,
    and the ships,   90
The varied and ample land, the South and the North in the light, Ohio's
    shores and flashing Missouri,
And ever the far-spreading prairies cover'd with grass and corn.

Lo, the most excellent sun so calm and haughty,
The violet and purple morn with just-felt breezes,
The gentle soft-born measureless light
The miracle spreading bathing all, the fulfill'd noon,

---

[6] April, from the Quaker numerical designations for months.

The coming eve delicious, the welcome night and the stars,
Over my cities shining all, enveloping man and land.

13

Sing on, sing on you gray-brown bird,
Sing from the swamps, the recesses, pour your chant from the bushes,   100
Limitless out of the dusk, out of the cedars and pines.

Sing on dearest brother, warble your reedy song,
Loud human song, with voice of uttermost woe.

O liquid and free and tender!
O wild and loose to my soul—O wondrous singer!
You only I hear—yet the star holds me, (but will soon depart,)
Yet the lilac with mastering odor holds me.

14

Now while I sat in the day and look'd forth,
In the close of the day with its light and the fields of spring, and
    the farmers preparing their crops,
In the large unconscious scenery of my land with its lakes and forests,   110
In the heavenly aerial beauty, (after the perturb'd winds and the storms,)
Under the arching heavens of the afternoon swift passing, and the voices
    of children and women,
The many-moving sea-tides, and I saw the ships how they sail'd,
And the summer approaching with richness, and the fields all busy
    with labor,
And the infinite separate houses, how they all went on, each with
    its meals and minutia of daily usages,
And the streets how their throbbings throbb'd, and the cities pent—lo,
    then and there,
Falling upon them all and among them all, enveloping me with the rest,
Appear'd the cloud, appear'd the long black trail,
And I knew death, its thought, and the sacred knowledge of death.

Then with the knowledge of death as walking one side of me,   120
And the thought of death close-walking the other side of me,
And I in the middle as with companions, and as holding the hands
    of companions,
I fled forth to the hiding receiving night that talks not,
Down to the shores of the water, the path by the swamp in the dimness,
To the solemn shadowy cedars and ghostly pines so still.

And the singer so shy to the rest receiv'd me,
The gray-brown bird I know receiv'd us comrades three,
And he sang the carol of death, and a verse for him I love.

From deep secluded recesses,
From the fragrant cedars and the ghostly pines so still,   130
Came the carol of the bird.

And the charm of the carol rapt me,
As I held as if by their hands my comrades in the night,
And the voice of my spirit tallied the song of the bird.

Come lovely and soothing death,
Undulate round the world, serenely arriving, arriving,
In the day, in the night, to all, to each,
Sooner or later delicate death.

Prais'd be the fathomless universe,
For life and joy, and for objects and knowledge curious,   140
And for love, sweet love—but praise! praise! praise!
For the sure-enwinding arms of cool-enfolding death.

Dark mother always gliding near with soft feet,
Have none chanted for thee a chant of fullest welcome?
Then I chant it for thee, I glorify thee above all,
I bring thee a song that when thou must indeed come, come unfalteringly.

Approach strong deliveress,
When it is so, when thou hast taken them I joyously sing the dead,
Lost in the loving floating ocean of thee,
Laved in the flood of thy bliss O death.   150

From me to thee glad serenades,
Dances for thee I propose saluting thee, adornments and feastings
*   for thee,*
And the sights of the open landscape and the high-spread sky are fitting,
And life and the fields, and the huge and thoughtful night.

The night in silence under many a star,
The ocean shore and the husky whispering wave whose voice I know,
And the soul turning to thee O vast and well-veil'd death,
And the body gratefully nestling close to thee.

Over the tree-tops I float thee a song,
Over the rising and sinking waves, over the myriad fields and the
*   prairies wide,*   160
Over the dense-pack'd cities all and the teeming wharves and ways,
I float this carol with joy, with joy to thee O death.

15

To the tally of my soul,
Loud and strong kept up the gray-brown bird,
With pure deliberate notes spreading filling the night.

Loud in the pines and cedars dim,
Clear in the freshness moist and the swamp-perfume,
And I with my comrades there in the night.

While my sight that was bound in my eyes unclosed,
As to long panoramas of visions. 170

And I saw askant[7] the armies,
I saw as in noiseless dreams hundreds of battle-flags,
Borne through the smoke of the battles and pierc'd with missiles I
　saw them,
And carried hither and yon through the smoke, and torn and bloody,
And at last but a few shreds left on the staffs, (and all in silence,)
And the staffs all splinter'd and broken.

I saw battle-corpses, myriads of them,
And the white skeletons of young men, I saw them,
I saw the debris and debris of all the slain soldiers of the war,
But I saw they were not as was thought, 180
They themselves were fully at rest, they suffer'd not,
The living remain'd and suffer'd, the mother suffer'd,
And the wife and the child and the musing comrade suffer'd,
And the armies that remain'd suffer'd.

16

Passing the visions, passing the night,
Passing, unloosing the hold of my comrades' hands,
Passing the song of the hermit bird and the tallying song of my soul,
Victorious song, death's outlet song, yet varying ever-altering song,
As low and wailing, yet clear the notes, rising and falling, flooding
　the night,
Sadly sinking and fainting, as warning and warning, and yet again
　bursting with joy, 190
Covering the earth and filling the spread of the heaven,
As that powerful psalm in the night I heard from recesses,
Passing, I leave thee lilac with heart-shaped leaves,
I leave thee there in the door-yard, blooming, returning with spring.

I cease from my song for thee,
From my gaze on thee in the west, fronting the west, communing with thee,
O comrade lustrous with silver face in the night.

Yet each to keep and all, retrievements out of the night,
The song, the wondrous chant of the gray-brown bird,
And the tallying chant, the echo arous'd in my soul, 200
With the lustrous and drooping star with the countenance full of woe,
With the holders holding my hand nearing the call of the bird,
Comrades mine and I in the midst, and their memory ever to keep,
　for the dead I loved so well,
For the sweetest, wisest soul of all my days and lands—and this for his
　dear sake,

[7] From the corner of the eye, obliquely.

Lilac and star and bird twined with the chant of my soul,
There in the fragrant pines and the cedars dusk and dim.

1865–1866

from   AUTUMN RIVULETS*

THERE WAS A CHILD WENT FORTH[1]

There was a child went forth every day,
And the first object he look'd upon, that object he became,
And that object became part of him for the day or a certain part of
    the day,
Or for many years or stretching cycles of years.

The early lilacs became part of this child,
And grass and white and red morning-glories, and white and red clover,
    and the song of the phœbe-bird,
And the Third-month lambs and the sow's pink-faint litter, and the
    mare's foal and the cow's calf,
And the noisy brood of the barnyard or by the mire of the pond-side,
And the fish suspending themselves so curiously below there, and the
    beautiful curious liquid,
And the water-plants with their graceful flat heads, all became part
    of him.   10

The field-sprouts of Fourth-month and Fifth-month became part of him,
Winter-grain sprouts and those of the light-yellow corn, and the
    esculent roots of the garden,
And the apple-trees cover'd with blossoms and the fruit afterward,
    and wood-berries, and the commonest weeds by the road,
And the old drunkard staggering home from the outhouse of the tavern
    whence he had lately risen,
And the schoolmistress that pass'd on her way to the school,
And the friendly boys that pass'd, and the quarrelsome boys,
And the tidy and fresh-cheek'd girls, and the barefoot negro boy and girl,
And all the changes of city and country wherever he went.

His own parents, he that had father'd him and she that had conceiv'd
    him in her womb and birth'd him,
They gave this child more of themselves than that,   20
They gave him afterward every day, they became part of him.

---

* Thirty-eight poems first grouped with this title in the 1881 edition of *Leaves of Grass*.
[1] Originally untitled, published as "Poem of the Child That Went Forth, and Always Goes Forth,
Forever and Forever" in the 1856 edition of *Leaves* and ultimately with this title in the 1871 edition.

The mother at home quietly placing the dishes on the supper-table,
The mother with mild words, clean her cap and gown, a wholesome
  odor falling off her person and clothes as she walks by,
The father, strong, self-sufficient, manly, mean, anger'd, unjust,
The blow, the quick loud word, the tight bargain, the crafty lure,
The family usages, the language, the company, the furniture, the
  yearning and swelling heart,
Affection that will not be gainsay'd, the sense of what is real, the
  thought if after all it should prove unreal,
The doubts of day-time and the doubts of night-time, the curious
  whether and how,
Whether that which appears so is so, or is it all flashes and specks?
Men and women crowding fast in the streets, if they are not flashes
  and specks what are they?   30
The streets themselves and the façades of houses, and goods in the
  windows,
Vehicles, teams, the heavy-plank'd wharves, the huge crossing at
  the ferries,
The village on the highland seen from afar at sunset, the river between,
Shadows, aureola and mist, the light falling on roofs and gables of
  white or brown two miles off,
The schooner near by sleepily dropping down the tide, the little boat
  slack-tow'd astern,
The hurrying tumbling waves, quick-broken crests, slapping,
The strata of color'd clouds, the long bar of maroon-tint away solitary
  by itself, the spread of purity it lies motionless in,
The horizon's edge, the flying sea-crow, the fragrance of salt marsh
  and shore mud,
These became part of that child who went forth every day, and who
  now goes, and will always go forth every day.

1855

TO A COMMON PROSTITUTE

Be composed—be at ease with me—I am Walt Whitman, liberal
  and lusty as Nature,
Not till the sun excludes you do I exclude you,
Not till the waters refuse to glisten for you and the leaves to rustle
  for you, do my words refuse to glisten and rustle for you.

My girl I appoint with you an appointment, and I charge you that
  you make preparation to be worthy to meet me,
And I charge you that you be patient and perfect till I come.

Till then I salute you with a significant look that you do not forget me.

1860

PASSAGE TO INDIA*

I

Singing my days,
Singing the great achievements of the present,
Singing the strong light works of engineers,
Our modern wonders, (the antique ponderous Seven[1] outvied,)
In the Old World the east the Suez canal,[2]
The New by its mighty railroad spann'd,[3]
The seas inlaid with eloquent gentle wires;[4]
Yet first to sound, and ever sound, the cry with thee O soul,
The Past! the Past! the Past!

The Past—the dark unfathom'd retrospect!   10
The teeming gulf—the sleepers and the shadows!
The past—the infinite greatness of the past!
For what is the present after all but a growth out of the past?
(As a projectile form'd, impell'd, passing a certain line, still keeps on,
So the present, utterly form'd, impell'd by the past.)

2

Passage O soul to India!
Eclaircise[5] the myths Asiatic, the primitive fables.

Not you alone proud truths of the world,
Nor you alone ye facts of modern science,
But myths and fables of eld,[6] Asia's, Africa's fables,   20
The far-darting beams of the spirit, the unloos'd dreams,
The deep diving bibles and legends,
The daring plots of the poets, the elder religions;
O you temples fairer than lilies pour'd over by the rising sun!
O you fables spurning the known, eluding the hold of the known,
    mounting to heaven!
You lofty and dazzling towers, pinnacled, red as roses, burnish'd with
    gold!
Towers of fables immortal fashion'd from mortal dreams!
You too I welcome and fully the same as the rest!
You too with joy I sing.

---

* First published as the title poem of a volume of seventy-five poems in 1871 and in the 1871 edition of *Leaves of Grass*.
[1] The Seven Wonders of the Ancient World: the pyramids of Egypt; the Temple of Artemis at Ephesus, in Asia Minor; the hanging gardens of Babylon; the Mausoleum at Halicarnassus, in Asia Minor; the Pharos, or lighthouse, at Alexandria, Egypt; the statue of Zeus at Olympia, Greece; and the Colossus of Rhodes.
[2] Begun in April 1859 and completed in November 1869.
[3] The Union Pacific and Central Pacific railroads, joined at Promontory, Utah, in May 1869.
[4] The Trans-Atlantic cable, completed in 1866.
[5] Make clear, explain; from *éclair*, "a flash of illumination" (French).　　[6] Old, or antiquity.

Passage to India!   30
Lo, soul, seest thou not God's purpose from the first?
The earth to be spann'd, connected by network,
The races, neighbors, to marry and be given in marriage,
The oceans to be cross'd, the distant brought near,
The lands to be welded together.

A worship new I sing,
You captains, voyagers, explorers, yours,
You engineers, you architects, machinists, yours,
You, not for trade or transportation only,
But in God's name, and for thy sake O soul.   40

3

Passage to India!
Lo soul for thee of tableaus twain,
I see in one the Suez canal initiated, open'd,
I see the procession of steamships, the Empress Eugenie's[7] leading
    the van,
I mark from on deck the strange landscape, the pure sky, the level
    sand in the distance,
I pass swiftly the picturesque groups, the workmen gather'd,
The gigantic dredging machines.

In one again, different, (yet thine, all thine, O soul, the same,)
I see over my own continent the Pacific railroad surmounting every
    barrier,[8]
I see continual trains of cars winding along the Platte carrying freight
    and passengers,   50
I hear the locomotives rushing and roaring, and the shrill steam-whistle,
I hear the echoes reverberate through the grandest scenery in the world,
I cross the Laramie plains, I note the rocks in grotesque shapes, the buttes,
I see the plentiful larkspur and wild onions, the barren, colorless,
    sage-deserts,
I see in glimpses afar or towering immediately above me the great
    mountains, I see the Wind river and the Wahsatch mountains,
I see the Monument mountain and the Eagle's Nest, I pass the
    Promontory, I ascend the Nevadas,
I scan the noble Elk mountain and wind around its base,
I see the Humboldt range, I thread the valley and cross the river,
I see the clear waters of Lake Tahoe, I see forests of majestic pines,
Or crossing the great desert, the alkaline plains, I behold enchanting
    mirages of waters and meadows,   60
Marking through these and after all, in duplicate slender lines,

---

[7] Eugénie de Guzmán (1853–1920), wife of Napoleon III and empress of France (1853–1871).
[8] Along the route from Omaha to San Francisco.

Bridging the three or four thousand miles of land travel,
Tying the Eastern to the Western sea,
The road between Europe and Asia.

(Ah Genoese[9] thy dream! thy dream!
Centuries after thou art laid in thy grave,
The shore thou foundest verifies thy dream.)

4

Passage to India!
Struggles of many a captain, tales of many a sailor dead,
Over my mood stealing and spreading they come,   70
Like clouds and cloudlets in the unreach'd sky.

Along all history, down the slopes,
As a rivulet running, sinking now, and now again to the surface rising,
A ceaseless thought, a varied train—lo, soul, to thee, thy sight, they rise,
The plans, the voyages again, the expeditions;
Again Vasco de Gama[10] sails forth,
Again the knowledge gain'd, the mariner's compass,
Lands found and nations born, thou born America,
For purpose vast, man's long probation fill'd,
Thou rondure[11] of the world at last accomplish'd.   80

5

O vast Rondure, swimming in space,
Cover'd all over with visible power and beauty,
Alternate light and day and the teeming spiritual darkness,
Unspeakable high processions of sun and moon and countless stars above,
Below, the manifold grass and waters, animals, mountains, trees,
With inscrutable purpose, some hidden prophetic intention,
Now first it seems my thought begins to span thee.

Down from the gardens of Asia descending radiating,
Adam and Eve appear, then their myriad progeny after them,
Wandering, yearning, curious, with restless explorations,   90
With questionings, baffled, formless, feverish, with never-happy hearts,
With that sad incessant refrain, *Wherefore unsatisfied soul?* and *Whither
    O mocking life?*

Ah who shall soothe these feverish children?
Who justify these restless explorations?
Who speak the secret of impassive earth?
Who bind it to us? what is this separate Nature so unnatural?

[9] Christopher Columbus, a native of Genoa, Italy.
[10] Da Gama (1469?–1524), a Portuguese navigator, was the first European to sail around southern Africa to India.
[11] Encirclement.

What is this earth to our affections? (unloving earth, without a throb
    to answer ours,
Cold earth, the place of graves.)

Yet soul be sure the first intent remains, and shall be carried out,
Perhaps even how the time has arrived.   100

After the seas are all cross'd, (as they seem already cross'd,)
After the great captains and engineers have accomplish'd their work,
After the noble inventors, after the scientists, the chemist, the
    geologist, ethnologist,
Finally shall come the poet worthy that name,
The true son of God shall come singing his songs.

Then not your deeds only O voyagers, O scientists and inventors, shall
    be justified,
All these hearts as of fretted children shall be sooth'd,
All affection shall be fully responded to, the secret shall be told,
All these separations and gaps shall be taken up and hook'd and link'd
    together,
The whole earth, this cold, impassive, voiceless earth, shall be
    completely justified,   110
Trinitas[12] divine shall be gloriously accomplish'd and compacted by
    the true son of God, the poet,
(He shall indeed pass the straits and conquer the mountains,
He shall double the cape of Good Hope to some purpose,)
Nature and Man shall be disjoin'd and diffused no more,
The true son of God shall absolutely fuse them.

6

Year at whose wide-flung door I sing!
Year of the purpose accomplish'd!
Year of the marriage of continents, climates and oceans!
(No mere doge of Venice[13] now wedding the Adriatic,)
I see O year in you the vast terraqueous globe given and giving all,   120
Europe to Asia, Africa join'd, and they to the New World,
The lands, geographies, dancing before you, holding a festival garland,
As brides and bridegrooms hand in hand.

Passage to India!
Cooling airs from Caucasus[14] far, soothing cradle of man,
The river Euphrates[15] flowing, the past lit up again.

---

[12] The Holy Trinity (an attempt at Spanish).

[13] The doge, or chief magistrate, each year cast a ring into the sea to symbolize the marriage of the Adriatic Sea and the city-state of Venice.

[14] The mountainous region in Russia between the Black and Caspian Seas.

[15] A river originating in Turkey and flowing into the Persian Gulf, one of four rivers said to flow from the Garden of Eden; the Euphrates Valley was considered the cradle of Western civilization.

Lo soul, the retrospect brought forward,
The old, most populous, wealthiest of earth's lands,
The streams of the Indus and the Ganges[16] and their many affluents,
(I my shores of America walking to-day behold, resuming all,)   130
The tale of Alexander[17] on his warlike marches suddenly dying,
On one side China and on the other side Persia and Arabia,
To the south the great seas and the bay of Bengal,
The flowing literatures, tremendous epics, religions, castes,
Old occult Brahma interminably far back, the tender and junior Buddha,[18]
Central and southern empires and all their belongings, possessors,
The wars of Tamerlane, the reign of Aurungzebe,[19]
The traders, rulers, explorers, Moslems, Venetians, Byzantium, the
    Arabs, Portuguese,
The first travelers famous yet, Marco Polo, Batouta the Moor,[20]
Doubts to be solv'd, the map incognita,[21] blanks to be fill'd,   140
The foot of man unstay'd, the hands never at rest,
Thyself O soul that will not brook a challenge.

The mediæval navigators rise before me,
The world of 1492, with its awaken'd enterprise,
Something swelling in humanity now like the sap of the earth in spring,
The sunset splendor of chivalry declining.

And who art thou sad shade?
Gigantic, visionary, thyself a visionary,
With majestic limbs and pious beaming eyes,
Spreading around with every look of thine a golden world,   150
Enhuing it with gorgeous hues.

As the chief histrion,[22]
Down to the footlights walks in some great scena,
Dominating the rest I see the Admiral[23] himself,
(History's type of courage, action, faith,)
Behold him sail from Palos[24] leading his little fleet,
His voyage behold, his return, his great fame,
His misfortunes, calumniators, behold him a prisoner, chain'd,
Behold his dejection, poverty, death.

(Curious in time I stand, noting the efforts of heroes,   160
Is the deferment long? bitter the slander, poverty, death?

[16] Great rivers of India.
    [17] Alexander III (356–323 B.C.), or Alexander the Great, king of Macedon (336–323 B.C.), who extended his empire as far as the Indus River and died on his return from an invasion of India.
    [18] Brahma was the supreme Hindu god; Buddha, or Siddhartha Gautama (6th century B.C.) founder of Buddhism.
    [19] Tamerlane (1336?–1405) was the Mongol conqueror of southern and western Asia; Aurungzebe (1618–1707) was the self-proclaimed "Conquerer of the World."
    [20] Polo (1254–1324), the famed Venetian traveler, was in China from 1271 to 1295; Batouta (1303–1377) was an explorer of Asia and Africa.
    [21] Unknown.   [22] Actor.   [23] Columbus.
    [24] The Spanish port from which Columbus sailed in August 1492.

Lies the seed unreck'd[25] for centuries in the ground? lo, to God's
　　due occasion,
Uprising in the night, its sprouts, blooms,
And fills the earth with use and beauty.)

7

Passage indeed O soul to primal thought,
Not lands and seas alone, thy own clear freshness,
The young maturity of brood and bloom,
To realms of budding bibles.

O soul, repressless, I with thee and thou with me,
Thy circumnavigation of the world begin,　　　　　　　　　　170
Of man, the voyage of his mind's return,
To reason's early paradise,
Back, back to wisdom's birth, to innocent intuitions,
Again with fair creation.

8

O we can wait no longer,
We too take ship O soul,
Joyous we too launch out on trackless seas,
Fearless for unknown shores on waves of ecstasy to sail,
Amid the wafting winds, (thou pressing me to thee, I thee to me, O soul,)
Caroling free, singing our song of God,　　　　　　　　　　180
Chanting our chant of pleasant exploration.

With laugh and many a kiss,
(Let others deprecate, let others weep for sin, remorse, humiliation,)
O soul thou pleasest me, I thee.

Ah more than any priest O soul we too believe in God,
But with the mystery of God we dare not dally.

O soul thou pleasest me, I thee,
Sailing these seas or on the hills, or waking in the night,
Thoughts, silent thoughts, of Time and Space and Death, like waters
　　flowing,
Bear me indeed as through the regions infinite,　　　　　　　190
Whose air I breathe, whose ripples hear, lave me all over,
Bathe me O God in thee, mounting to thee,
I and my soul to range in range of thee.

O Thou transcendent,
Nameless, the fibre and the breath,
Light of the the light, shedding forth universes, thou centre of them,
Thou mightier centre of the true, the good, the loving,
Thou moral, spiritual fountain—affection's source—thou reservoir,

---

[25] Unnoticed or disregarded.

(O pensive soul of me—O thirst unsatisfied—waitest not there?
Waitest not haply for us somewhere there the Comrade perfect?)   200
Thou pulse—thou motive of the stars, suns, systems,
That, circling, move in order, safe, harmonious,
Athwart the shapeless vastnesses of space,
How should I think, how breathe a single breath, how speak, if, out
   of myself,
I could not launch, to those, superior universes?

Swiftly I shrivel at the thought of God,
At Nature and its wonders, Time and Space and Death,
But that I, turning, call to thee O soul, thou actual Me,
And lo, thou gently masterest the orbs,
Thou matest Time, smilest content at Death,
And fillest, swellest full the vastnesses of Space.   210

Greater than stars or suns,
Bounding O soul thou journeyest forth;
What love than thine and ours could wider amplify?
What aspirations, wishes, outvie thine and ours O soul?
What dreams of the ideal? what plans of purity, perfection, strength?
What cheerful willingness for others' sake to give up all?
For others' sake to suffer all?

Reckoning ahead O soul, when thou, the time achiev'd,
The seas all cross'd, weather'd the capes, the voyage done,   220
Surrounded, copest, frontest God, yieldest, the aim attain'd,
As fill'd with friendship, love complete, the Elder Brother found,
The Younger melts in fondness in his arms.

9

Passage to more than India!
Are thy wings plumed indeed for such far flights?
O soul, voyagest thou indeed on voyages like those?
Disportest thou on waters such as those?
Soundest below the Sanscrit and the Vedas?[26]
Then have thy bent[27] unleash'd.

Passage to you, your shores, ye aged fierce enigmas!   230
Passage to you, to mastership of you, ye strangling problems!
You, strew'd with the wrecks of skeletons, that, living, never
   reach'd you.

Passage to more than India!
O secret of the earth and sky!
Of you O waters of the sea! O winding creeks and rivers!
Of you O woods and fields! of you strong mountains of my land!
Of you O prairies! of you gray rocks!

[26] Ancient Hindu scriptures written in Sanskrit.   [27] Energy.

O morning red! O clouds! O rain and snows!
O day and night, passage to you!

O sun and moon and all your stars! Sirius and Jupiter!   240
Passage to you!

Passage, immediate passage! the blood burns in my veins!
Away O soul! hoist instantly the anchor!
Cut the hawsers—haul out—shake out every sail!
Have we not stood here like trees in the ground long enough?
Have we not grovel'd here long enough, eating and drinking like
    mere brutes?
Have we not darken'd and dazed ourselves with books long enough?

Sail forth—steer for the deep waters only,
Reckless O soul, exploring, I with thee, and thou with me,
For we are bound where mariner has not yet dared to go,   250
And we will risk the ship, ourselves and all.

O my brave soul!
O farther farther sail!
O daring joy, but safe! are they not all the seas of God?
O farther, farther, farther sail!

                                                                    1871

THE SLEEPERS*

I

I wander all night in my vision,
Stepping with light feet, swiftly and noiselessly stepping and stopping,
Bending with open eyes over the shut eyes of sleepers,
Wandering and confused, lost to myself, ill-assorted, contradictory,
Pausing, gazing, bending, and stopping.

How solemnly they look there, stretch'd and still,
How quiet they breathe, the little children in their cradles.

The wretched features of ennuyés,[1] the white features of corpses, the
    livid faces of drunkards, the sick-gray faces of onanists,[2]
The gash'd bodies on battle-fields, the insane in their strong-door'd
    rooms, the sacred idiots, the new-born emerging from gates,
    and the dying emerging from gates,
The night pervades them and infolds them.   10

---

* Originally untitled; published as "Night Poem" in the 1856 edition of *Leaves of Grass*, as "Sleep-Chasings" in the 1860 edition, and with this title in the 1871 edition.
[1] Bored people, from *ennui*, "boredom" (French).
[2] Masturbators, after Onan, the son of Judah, in Genesis 38:9.

The married couple sleep calmly in their bed, he with his palm on the
    hip of the wife, and she with her palm on the hip of the husband,
The sisters sleep lovingly side by side in their bed,
The men sleep lovingly side by side in theirs,
And the mother sleeps with her little child carefully wrapt.

The blind sleep, and the deaf and dumb sleep,
The prisoner sleeps well in the prison, the runaway son sleeps,
The murderer that is to be hung next day, how does he sleep?
And the murder'd person, how does he sleep?

The female that loves unrequited sleeps,
And the male that loves unrequited sleeps,   20
The head of the money-maker that plotted all day sleeps,
And the enraged and treacherous dispositions, all, all sleep.

I stand in the dark with drooping eyes by the worst-suffering and the
    most restless,
I pass my hands soothingly to and fro a few inches from them,
The restless sink in their beds, they fitfully sleep.

Now I pierce the darkness, new beings appear,
The earth recedes from me into the night,
I saw that it was beautiful, and I see that what is not the earth is beautiful.

I go from bedside to bedside, I sleep close with the other sleepers each
    in turn,
I dream in my dream all the dreams of the other dreamers,   30
And I become the other dreamers.

I am a dance—play up there! the fit is whirling me fast!

I am the ever-laughing—it is new moon and twilight,
I see the hiding of douceurs,[3] I see nimble ghosts whichever way I look,
Cache[4] and cache again deep in the ground and sea, and where it is
    neither ground nor sea.

Well do they do their jobs those journeymen divine,
Only from me can they hide nothing, and would not if they could,
I reckon I am their boss and they make me a pet besides,
And surround me and lead me and run ahead when I walk,
To lift their cunning covers to signify[5] me with stretch'd arms, and
    resume the way;   40
Onward we move, a gay gang of blackguards! with mirth-shouting
    music and wild-flapping pennants of joy!

I am the actor, the actress, the voter, the politician,
The emigrant and the exile, the criminal that stood in the box,[6]

---

[3] "Delights" or "pleasures" (French).   [4] Hide.
[5] Their knowing covers to signal.   [6] The courtroom box in which the accused stands.

He who has been famous and he who shall be famous after to-day,
The stammerer, the well-form'd person, the wasted or feeble person.

I am she who adorn'd herself and folded her hair expectantly,
My truant lover has come, and it is dark.

Double yourself and receive me darkness,
Receive me and my lover too, he will not let me go without him.

I roll myself upon you as upon a bed, I resign myself to the dusk.   50

He whom I call answers me and takes the place of my lover,
He rises with me silently from the bed.

Darkness, you are gentler than my lover, his flesh was sweaty and panting,
I feel the hot moisture yet that he left me.

My hands are spread forth, I pass them in all directions,
I would sound up the shadowy shore to which you are journeying.

Be careful darkness! already what was it touch'd me?
I thought my lover had gone, else darkness and he are one,
I hear the heart-beat, I follow, I fade away.

2

I descend my western course,[7] my sinews are flaccid,   60
Perfume and youth course through me and I am their wake.

It is my face yellow and wrinkled instead of the old woman's,
I sit low in a straw-bottom chair and carefully darn my grandson's
    stockings.

It is I too, the sleepless widow looking out on the winter midnight,
I see the sparkles of starshine on the icy and pallid earth.

A shroud I see and I am the shroud, I wrap a body and lie in the coffin,
It is dark here under ground, it is not evil or pain here, it is blank here,
    for reasons.

(It seems to me that every thing in the light and air ought to be happy,
Whoever is not in his coffin and the dark grave let him know he
    has enough.)

3

I see a beautiful gigantic swimmer swimming naked through the eddies
    of the sea,   70
His brown hair lies close and even to his head, he strikes out with
    courageous arms, he urges himself with his legs,
I see his white body, I see his undaunted eyes,

[7] Age.

I hate the swift-running eddies that would dash him head-foremost on
   the rocks.

What are you doing you ruffianly red-trickled waves?
Will you kill the courageous giant? will you kill him in the prime of his
   middle age?

Steady and long he struggles,
He is baffled, bang'd, bruis'd, he holds out while his strength holds out,
The slapping eddies are spotted with his blood, they bear him away,
   they roll him, swing him, turn him,
His beautiful body is borne in the circling eddies, it is continually
   bruis'd on rocks,
Swiftly and out of sight is borne the brave corpse.   80

4

I turn but do not extricate myself,
Confused, a past-reading, another, but with darkness yet.

The beach is cut by the razory ice-wind, the wreck-guns[8] sound,
The tempest lulls, the moon comes floundering through the drifts.

I look where the ship helplessly heads end on, I hear the burst as she
   strikes, I hear the howls of dismay, they grow fainter and fainter.

I cannot aid with my wringing fingers,
I can but rush to the surf and let it drench me and freeze upon me.

I search with the crowd, not one of the company is wash'd to us alive,
In the morning I help pick up the dead and lay them in rows in a barn.

5

Now of the older war-days, the defeat at Brooklyn,[9]   90
Washington stands inside the lines, he stands on the intrench'd hills amid
   a crowd of officers,
His face is cold and damp, he cannot repress the weeping drops,
He lifts the glass perpetually to his eye, the color is blanch'd from
   his cheeks,
He sees the slaughter of the southern braves confided to him by
   their parents.

The same at last and at last when peace is declared,
He stands in the room of the old tavern, the well-belov'd soldiers all pass
   through,
The officers speechless and slow draw near in their turns,

---

[8] Guns that fire a life line to ships in distress.
[9] The British defeated American forces at the Battle of Brooklyn Heights on August 27; 1776.
Washington was able to ferry his troops to New York City.

The chief encircles their necks with his arm and kisses them on the
    cheek,
He kisses lightly the wet cheeks one after another, he shakes hands and
    bids good-by to the army.

6

Now what my mother told me one day as we sat at dinner together,   100
Of when she was a nearly grown girl living home with her parents
    on the old homestead.

A red squaw came one breakfast-time to the old homestead,
On her back she carried a bundle of rushes for rush-bottoming chairs,
Her hair, straight, shiny, coarse, black, profuse, half-envelop'd her face,
Her step was free and elastic, and her voice sounded exquisitely as
    she spoke.

My mother look'd in delight and amazement at the stranger,
She look'd at the freshness of her tall-borne face and full and pliant limbs,
The more she look'd upon her she loved her,
Never before had she seen such wonderful beauty and purity,
She made her sit on a bench by the jamb of the fireplace, she cook'd
    food for her,   110
She had no work to give her, but she gave her remembrance and fondness.

The red squaw staid all the forenoon, and toward the middle of the
    afternoon she went away,
O my mother was loth to have her go away,
All the week she thought of her, she watch'd for her many a month,
She remember'd her many a winter and many a summer,
But the red squaw never came nor was heard of there again.

7

A show of the summer softness—a contact of something unseen—an
    amour of the light and air,
I am jealous and overwhelm'd with friendliness,
And will go gallivant with the light and air myself.

O love and summer, you are in the dreams and in me,   120
Autumn and winter are in the dreams, the farmer goes with his thrift,
The droves[10] and crops increase, the barns are well-fill'd.

Elements merge in the night, ships make tacks in the dreams,
The sailor sails, the exile returns home,
The fugitive returns unharm'd, the immigrant is back beyond months
    and years,
The poor Irishman lives in the simple house of his childhood with the
    well-known neighbors and faces,
They warmly welcome him, he is barefoot again, he forgets he is well off,

---

[10] Of animals.

The Dutchman voyages home, and the Scotchman and Welshman
  voyage home, and the native of the Mediterranean voyages home,
To every port of England, France, Spain, enter well-fill'd ships,
The Swiss foots it toward his hills, the Prussian goes his way, the
  Hungarian his way, and the Pole his way,   130
The Swede returns, and the Dane and Norwegian return.

The homeward bound and the outward bound,
The beautiful lost swimmer, the ennuyé, the onanist, the female that
  loves unrequited, the money-maker,
The actor and actress, those through with their parts and those waiting
  to commence,
The affectionate boy, the husband and wife, the voter, the nominee that
  is chosen and the nominee that has fail'd,
The great already known and the great any time after to-day,
The stammerer, the sick, the perfect-form'd, the homely,
The criminal that stood in the box, the judge that sat and sentenced him,
  the fluent lawyers, the jury, the audience,
The laugher and weeper, the dancer, the midnight widow, the red squaw,
The consumptive, the erysipalite,[11] the idiot, he that is wrong'd,   140
The antipodes,[12] and every one between this and them in the dark,
I swear they are averaged now—one is no better than the other,
The night and sleep have liken'd them and restored them.

I swear they are all beautiful,
Every one that sleeps is beautiful, every thing in the dim light is
  beautiful,
The wildest and bloodiest is over, and all is peace.

Peace is always beautiful,
The myth of heaven indicates peace and night.

The myth of heaven indicates the soul,
The soul is always beautiful, it appears more or it appears less, it comes
  or it lags behind,   150
It comes from its embower'd garden and looks pleasantly on itself
  and encloses the world,
Perfect and clean the genitals previously jetting, and perfect and clean
  the womb cohering,
The head well-grown proportion'd and plumb, and the bowels and joints
  proportion'd and plumb.

The soul is always beautiful,
The universe is duly in order, every thing is in its place,
What has arrived is in its place and what waits shall be in its place,
The twisted skull waits, the watery or rotten blood waits,

---

[11] One who suffers from erysipelas, a bacterial infection of the skin.
[12] Points on opposite sides of the earth; here, those who live on the other side of the earth.

The child of the glutton or venerealee waits long, and the child
    of the drunkard waits long, and the drunkard himself waits long,
The sleepers that lived and died wait, the far advanced are to go on in
    their turns, and the far behind are to come on in their turns,
The diverse shall be no less diverse, but they shall flow and unite—
    hey unite now.   160

8

The sleepers are very beautiful as they lie unclothed,
They flow hand in hand over the whole earth from east to west as
    they lie unclothed,
The Asiatic and African are hand in hand, the European and American
    are hand in hand,
Learn'd and unlearn'd are hand in hand, and male and female are hand
    in hand,
The bare arm of the girl crosses the bare breast of her lover, they
    press close without lust, his lips press her neck,
The father holds his grown or ungrown son in his arms with measureless
    love, and the son holds the father in his arms with measureless love,
The white hair of the mother shines on the white wrist of the daughter,
The breath of the boy goes with the breath of the man, friend is inarm'd
    by friend,
The scholar kisses the teacher and the teacher kisses the scholar, the
    wrong'd is made right,
The call of the slave is one with the master's call, and the master
    salutes the slave,   170
The felon steps forth from the prison, the insane becomes sane, the
    suffering of sick persons is reliev'd,
The sweatings and fevers stop, the throat that was unsound is sound, the
    lungs of the consumptive are resumed, the poor distress'd head is free,
The joints of the rheumatic move as smoothly as ever, and smoother
    than ever,
Stiflings and passages open, the paralyzed become supple,
The swell'd and convuls'd and congested awake to themselves in
    condition,
They pass the invigoration of the night and the chemistry of the night,
    and awake.

I too pass from the night,
I stay a while away O night, but I return to you again and love you.

Why should I be afraid to trust myself to you?
I am not afraid, I have been well brought forward by you,   180
I love the rich running day, but I do not desert her in whom I lay so long,
I know not how I came of you and I know not where I go with you, but
    I know I came well and shall go well.

I will stop only a time with the night, and rise betimes,
I will duly pass the day O my mother, and duly return to you.

1855

from   WHISPERS OF HEAVENLY DEATH*

CHANTING THE SQUARE DEIFIC[1]

I

Chanting the square deific, out of the One advancing, out of the sides,
Out of the old and new, out of the square entirely divine,
Solid, four-sided, (all the sides needed,) from this side Jehovah[2] am I,
Old Brahm I, and I Saturnius[3] am;
Not Time affects me—I am Time, old, modern as any,
Unpersuadable, relentless, executing righteous judgments,
As the Earth, the Father, the brown old Kronos,[4] with laws,
Aged beyond computation, yet ever new, ever with those mighty laws
    rolling,
Relentless I forgive no man—whoever sins dies—I will have that
    man's life;
Therefore let none expect mercy—have the seasons, gravitation, the
    appointed days, mercy? no more have I,   10
But as the seasons and gravitation, and as all the appointed days that
    forgive not,
I dispense from this side judgments inexorable without the least remorse.

2

Consolator most mild, the promis'd one advancing,
With gentle hand extended, the mightier God am I,
Foretold by prophets and poets in their most rapt prophecies and poems,
From this side, lo! the Lord Christ gazes—lo! Hermes[5] I—lo! mine is
    Hercules'[6] face,
All sorrow, labor, suffering, I, tallying it, absorb in myself,
Many times have I been rejected, taunted, put in prison, and crucified,
    and many times shall be again,
All the world have I given up for my dear brothers' and sisters' sake,
    for the soul's sake,
Wending my way through the homes of men, rich or poor, with the kiss
    of affection,   20
For I am affection, I am the cheer-bringing God, with hope and
    all-enclosing charity,
With indulgent words as to children, with fresh and sane words,
    mine only,

---

* Thirteen poems that first appeared in *Passage to India* (1871); published as a group of eighteen poems in the 1881 edition of *Leaves of Grass*.
[1] First printed in "Sequel to Drum-Taps" (1856–1866), then in *Passage to India* (1871); added to the 1881 edition of *Leaves*.
[2] The Judeo-Christian God.
[3] Brahma, the supreme god of Hindu theology; Saturn, the Titan, or giant god, who preceded Jupiter as the supreme god of Roman myth.
[4] The equivalent of Saturn; Chronus, associated with time.
[5] According to Greek myth, the winged messenger of the gods.
[6] According to Greek myth, a hero known for his strength.

Young and strong I pass knowing well I am destin'd myself to an
  early death;
But my charity has no death—my wisdom dies not, neither early nor late,
And my sweet love bequeath'd here and elsewhere never dies.

3

Aloof, dissatisfied, plotting revolt,
Comrade of criminals, brother of slaves,
Crafty, despised, a drudge, ignorant,
With sudra[7] face and worn brow, black, but in the depths of my heart,
  proud as any,
Lifted now and always against whoever scorning assumes to rule me,   30
Morose, full of guile, full of reminiscences, brooding, with many wiles,
(Though it was thought I was baffled and dispel'd, and my wiles done,
  but that will never be,)
Defiant, I, Satan, still live, still utter words, in new lands duly appearing,
  (and old ones also,)
Permanent here from my side, warlike, equal with any, real as any,
Nor time nor change shall ever change me or my words.

4

Santa Spirita,[8] breather, life,
Beyond the light, lighter than light,
Beyond the flames of hell, joyous, leaping easily above hell,
Beyond Paradise, perfumed solely with mine own perfume,
Including all life on earth, touching, including God, including Saviour
  and Satan,   40
Ethereal, pervading all, (for without me what were all? what were God?)
Essence of forms, life of the real identities, permanent, positive,
  (namely the unseen,)
Life of the great round world, the sun and stars, and of man, I, the
  general soul,
Here the square finishing, the solid, I the most solid,
Breathe my breath also through these songs.

1865–1866

A NOISELESS PATIENT SPIDER*

A noiseless patient spider,
I mark'd where on a little promontory it stood isolated,
Mark'd how to explore the vacant vast surrounding,
It launch'd forth filament, filament, filament, out of itself,
Ever unreeling them, ever tirelessly speeding them.

---

[7] The lowest Hindu caste.   [8] The Holy Spirit.
* First appeared in London's *Broadway Magazine* in October 1868.

And you O my soul where you stand,
Surrounded, detached, in measureless oceans of space,
Ceaselessly musing, venturing, throwing, seeking the spheres to
    connect them,
Till the bridge you will need be form'd, till the ductile anchor hold,
Till the gossamer thread you fling catch somewhere, O my soul.   10

1868

from   FROM NOON TO STARRY NIGHT*

TO A LOCOMOTIVE IN WINTER[1]

Thee for my recitative,[2]
Thee in the driving storm even as now, the snow, the winter-day declining,
Thee in thy panoply,[3] thy measur'd dual throbbing and thy beat convulsive,
Thy black cylindric body, golden brass and silvery steel,
Thy ponderous side-bars, parallel and connecting rods, gyrating, shuttling
    at thy sides,
Thy metrical, now swelling pant and roar, now tapering in the distance,
Thy great protruding head-light fix'd in front,
Thy long, pale, floating vapor-pennants, tinged with delicate purple,
The dense and murky clouds out-belching from thy smoke-stack,
Thy knitted frame, thy springs and valves, the tremulous twinkle of
    thy wheels,   10
Thy train of cars behind, obedient, merrily following,
Through gale or calm, now swift, now slack, yet steadily careering;
Type of the modern—emblem of motion and power—pulse of the
    continent,
For once come serve the Muse and merge in verse, even as here I see thee,
With storm and buffeting gusts of wind and falling snow,
By day thy warning ringing bell to sound its notes,
By night thy silent signal lamps to swing.

Fierce-throated beauty!
Roll through my chant with all thy lawless music, thy swinging lamps
    at night,
Thy madly-whistled laughter, echoing, rumbling like an earthquake,
    rousing all,   20
Law of thyself complete, thine own track firmly holding,
(No sweetness debonair of tearful harp or glib piano thine,)

---

* Twenty-two poems that first appeared in the 1881 edition of *Leaves of Grass*.
[1] First published in the New York *Daily Tribune* on February 19, 1876.
[2] In musical terminology, an intermediate form between speaking and singing: a particularly apt mode of address for Whitman, who is both conversational and celebratory.
[3] Armor.

Thy trills of shrieks by rocks and hills return'd,
Launch'd o'er the prairies wide, across the lakes,
To the free skies unpent and glad and strong.

1876

from   SONGS OF PARTING*

CAMPS OF GREEN[1]

Not alone those camps of white, old comrades of the wars,
When as order'd forward, after a long march,
Footsore and weary, soon as the light lessens we halt for the night,
Some of us so fatigued carrying the gun and knapsack, dropping asleep
   in our tracks,
Others pitching the little tents, and the fires lit up begin to sparkle,
Outposts of pickets posted surrounding alert through the dark,
And a word provided for countersign, careful for safety,
Till to the call of the drummers at daybreak loudly beating the drums,
We rise up refresh'd, the night and sleep pass'd over, and resume our
   journey,
Or proceed to battle.   10

Lo, the camps of the tents of green,
Which the days of peace keep filling, and the days of war keep filling,
With a mystic army, (is it too order'd forward? is it too only halting awhile,
Till night and sleep pass over?)

Now in those camps of green, in their tents dotting the world,
In the parents, children, husbands, wives, in them, in the old and young,
Sleeping under the sunlight, sleeping under the moonlight, content and
   silent there at last,
Behold the mighty bivouac-field and waiting-camp of all,
Of the corps and generals all, and the President over the corps and
   generals all,
And of each of us O soldiers, and of each and all in the ranks we fought,   20
(There without hatred we all, all meet.)

For presently O soldiers, we too camp in our place in the bivouac-
   camps of green,
But we need not provide for outposts, nor word for the countersign,
Nor drummer to beat the morning drum.

1865

---

* Seventeen poems from five different editions, first collected with this title in the 1881 edition of
Leaves of Grass.
[1] First appeared in *Drum-Taps* (1865); added to the 1867 edition of *Leaves*.

AS THEY DRAW TO A CLOSE*

As they draw to a close,
Of what underlies the precedent songs—of my aims in them,
Of the seed I have sought to plant in them,
Of joy, sweet joy, through many a year, in them,
(For them, for them have I lived, in them my work is done,)
Of many an aspiration fond, of many a dream and plan;
Through Space and Time fused in a chant, and the flowing eternal identity,
To Nature encompassing these, encompassing God—to the joyous,
    electric all,
To the sense of Death, and accepting exulting in Death in its turn the
    same as life,
The entrance of man to sing;   10
To compact you, ye parted, diverse lives,
To put rapport the mountains and rocks and streams,
And the winds of the north, and the forests of oak and pine,
With you O soul.

1871

from   FIRST ANNEX: SANDS AT SEVENTY†

DEATH OF GENERAL GRANT[1]

As one by one withdraw the lofty actors,
From that great play on history's stage eterne,
That lurid, partial act of war and peace—of old and new contending,
Fought out through wrath, fears, dark dismays, and many a long suspense;
All past—and since, in countless graves receding, mellowing,
Victor's and vanquish'd—Lincoln's and Lee's[2]—now thou with them,
Man of the mighty days—and equal to the days!
Thou from the prairies!—tangled and many-vein'd and hard has been
    thy part,
To admiration has it been enacted!

1885

---

  * First published in *Passage to India* (1871) as "Thought" and with this title in the 1881 edition of *Leaves of Grass*.
  † First published with prose pieces in *November Boughs* (1888); added to the 1884 reprint of *Leaves of Grass*.
  [1] First appeared in *Harper's Weekly* on May 16, 1885, although Ulysses S. Grant (1822–1885), eighteenth U.S. president (1869–1877), did not die until July 23, 1885.
  [2] Abraham Lincoln and Robert E. Lee.

from   SECOND ANNEX: GOOD-BYE MY FANCY*

OSCEOLA[1]

[When I was nearly grown to manhood in Brooklyn, New York, (middle of 1838,) I met one of the return'd U. S. Marines from Fort Moultrie, S. C., and had long talks with him—learn'd the occurrence below described—death of Osceola. The latter was a young, brave, leading Seminole in the Florida war of that time—was surrender'd to our troops, imprison'd and literally died of "a broken heart," at Fort Moultrie. He sicken'd of his confinement—the doctor and officers made every allowance and kindness possible for him; then the close:]

When his hour for death had come,
He slowly rais'd himself from the bed on the floor,
Drew on his war-dress, shirt, leggings, and girdled the belt around his waist,
Call'd for vermilion paint (his looking-glass was held before him,)
Painted half his face and neck, his wrists, and back-hands.
Put the scalp-knife carefully in his belt—then lying down, resting a moment,
Rose again, half sitting, smiled, gave in silence his extended hand to each
    and all,
Sank faintly low to the floor (tightly grasping the tomahawk handle,)
Fix'd his look on wife and little children—the last:

(And here a line in memory of his name and death.)

1890

L. OF G.'S PURPORT†

Not to exclude or demarcate, or pick out evils from their formidable
    masses (even to expose them,)
But add, fuse, complete, extend—and celebrate the immortal and
    the good.

Haughty this song, its words and scope,
To span vast realms of space and time,
Evolution—the cumulative—growths and generations.
Begun in ripen'd youth and steadily pursued,

---

* Thirty-one poems and prose pieces added to the 1891–1892 edition of *Leaves of Grass*.
[1] First published in *Monson's Illustrated World* in April 1890. Osceola (?–1838) was a brave leader in the second Seminole War (1835–1837) who was seized and imprisoned while working toward a truce; he died after four months in captivity. The bracketed note is Whitman's.
† A statement of Whitman's intent in writing *Leaves of Grass*.

Wandering, peering, dallying with all—war, peace, day, and night
   absorbing,
Never even for one brief hour abandoning my task,
I end it here in sickness, poverty, and old age.

I sing of life, yet mind me well of death: 10
To-day shadowy Death dogs my steps, my seated shape, and has for years—
Draws sometimes close to me, as face to face.

1891

GOOD-BYE MY FANCY!

Good-bye my Fancy!
Farewell dear mate, dear love!
I'm going away, I know not where,
Or to what fortune, or whether I may ever see you again,
So Good-bye my Fancy.
Now for my last—let me look back a moment;
The slower fainter ticking of the clock is in me,
Exit, nightfall, and soon the heart-thud stopping.

Long have we lived, joy'd, caress'd together;
Delightful!—now separation—Good-bye my Fancy.   10

Yet let me not be too hasty,
Long indeed have we lived, slept, filter'd, become really blended
   into one;
Then if we die we die together, (yes, we'll remain one,)
If we go anywhere we'll go together to meet what happens,
May-be we'll be better off and blither, and learn something,
May-be it is yourself now really ushering me to the true songs,
   (who knows?)
May-be it is you the mortal knob really undoing, turning—so now
   finally,
Good-bye—and hail! my Fancy.

1891

from   A BACKWARD GLANCE O'ER TRAVEL'D ROADS*

Perhaps the best of songs heard, or of any and all true love, or life's fairest episodes, or sailors', soldiers' trying scenes on land or sea, is the *résumé* of them, or
any of them, long afterwards, looking at the actualities away back past, with all

---

   * First appeared as the introduction to *November Boughs* (1888) and added to the 1889 edition of
Leaves of Grass.

their practical excitations gone. How the soul loves to float amid such reminiscences!

So here I sit gossiping in the early candle-light of old age—I and my book—casting backward glances over our travel'd road. After completing, as it were, the journey—(a varied jaunt of years, with many halts and gaps of intervals—or some lengthen'd ship-voyage, where in more than once the last hour had apparently arrived, and we seem'd certainly going down—yet reaching port in a sufficient way through all discomfitures at last)—After completing my poems, I am curious to review them in the light of their own (at the time unconscious, or mostly unconscious) intentions, with certain unfoldings of the thirty years they seek to embody. These lines, therefore, will probably blend the weft of first purposes and speculations, with the warp of that experience afterwards, always bringing strange developments.

Result of seven or eight stages and struggles extending through nearly thirty years, (as I nigh my three-score-and-ten[1] I live largely on memory,) I look upon "Leaves of Grass," now finish'd to the end of its opportunities and powers, as my definitive *carte visite*[2] to the coming generations of the New World,[3] if I may assume to say so. That I have not gain'd the acceptance of my own time, but have fallen back on fond dreams of the future—anticipations—("still lives the song, though Regnar dies"[4])—That from a worldly and business point of view "Leaves of Grass" has been worse than a failure—that public criticism on the book and myself as author of it yet shows mark'd anger and contempt more than anything else—("I find a solid line of enemies to you everywhere,"—letter from W. S. K.,[5] Boston, May 28, 1884)—And that solely for publishing it I have been the object of two or three pretty serious special official buffetings—is all probably no more than I ought to have expected.[6] I had my choice when I commmenc'd. I bid neither for soft eulogies, big money returns, nor the approbation of existing schools and conventions. As fulfill'd, or partially fulfill'd, the best comfort of the whole business (after a small band of the dearest friends and upholders ever vouchsafed to man or cause—doubtless all the more faithful and uncompromising—this little phalanx!—for being so few) is that, unstopp'd and unwarp'd by any influence outside the soul within me, I have had my say entirely my own way, and put it unerringly on record—the value thereof to be decided by time.

In calculating that decision, William O'Connor and Dr. Bucke[7] are far more peremptory than I am. Behind all else that can be said, I consider "Leaves of Grass" and its theory experimental—as, in the deepest sense, I consider our American republic itself to be, with its theory. (I think I have at least enough philosophy not to be too absolutely certain of any thing, or any results.) In the second place, the volume is a *sortie*—whether to prove triumphant, and conquer

---

[1] The biblical "allotment" of years for human life, in Psalm 89:10.   [2] "Calling card" (French).

[3] From the ballad "Alfred the Harper" (14.1.3), by John Sterling (1806–1844); Regnar was a British hero slaughtered by the Danes.

[4] Whitman's note: "When Champollion, on his death-bed, handed to the printer the revised proof of his 'Egyptian Grammer,' he said gayly, 'Be careful of this—it is my *carte de visite* to posterity.' " Jean François Champollion (1790–1832) was a French Egyptologist.

[5] William Sloane Kennedy (1850–1929), a critic and Whitman biographer.

[6] Whitman was in fact fired from his Department of the Interior post in 1865.

[7] O'Connor (1832–1929), a journalist, wrote a vindication of Whitman (*The Good Gray Poet* [1866]); Richard Maurice Bucke (1837–1902), a Canadian physician, wrote a biographical study of the poet (*Walt Whitman* [1883]). Both men were close friends and disciples of Whitman.

its field of aim and escape and construction, nothing less than a hundred years from now can fully answer. I consider the point that I have positively gain'd a hearing, to far more than make up for any and all other lacks and withholdings. Essentially, *that* was from the first, and has remain'd throughout, the main object. Now it seems to be achiev'd, I am certainly contented to waive any otherwise momentous drawbacks, as of little account. Candidly and dispassionately reviewing all my intentions, I feel that they were creditable—and I accept the result, whatever it may be.

After continued personal ambition and effort, as a young fellow, to enter with the rest into competition for the usual rewards, business, political, literary, etc.— to take part in the great *mêlée,* both for victory's prize itself and to do some good—After years of those aims and pursuits, I found myself remaining possess'd, at the age of thirty-one to thirty-three, with a special desire and conviction. Or rather, to be quite exact, a desire that had been flitting through my previous life, or hovering on the flanks, mostly indefinite hitherto, had steadily advanced to the front, defined itself, and finally dominated everything else. This was a feeling or ambition to articulate and faithfully express in literary or poetic form, and uncompromisingly, my own physical, emotional, moral, intellectual, and æsthetic Personality, in the midst of, and tallying, the momentous spirit and facts of its immediate days, and of current America—and to exploit that Personality, identified with place and date, in a far more candid and comprehensive sense than any hitherto poem or book.

Perhaps this is in brief, or suggests, all I have sought to do. Given the Nineteenth Century, with the United States, and what they furnish as area and points of view, "Leaves of Grass" is, or seeks to be, simply a faithful and doubtless self-will'd record. In the midst of all, it gives one man's—the author's—identity, ardors, observations, faiths, and thoughts, color'd hardly at all with any decided coloring from other faiths or other identities. Plenty of songs had been sung— beautiful, matchless songs—adjusted to other lands than these—another spirit and stage of evolution; but I would sing, and leave out or put in, quite solely with reference to America and to-day. Modern science and democracy seem'd to be throwing out their challenge to poetry to put them in its statements in contradistinction to the songs and myths of the past. As I see it now (perhaps too late,) I have unwittingly taken up that challenge and made an attempt at such statements—which I certainly would not assume to do now, knowing more clearly what it means.

For grounds for "Leaves of Grass," as a poem, I abandon'd the conventional themes, which do not appear in it: none of the stock ornamentation, or choice plots of love or war, or high, exceptional personages of Old-World song; nothing, as I may say, for beauty's sake—no legend, or myth, or romance, nor euphemism, nor rhyme. But the broadest average of humanity and its identities in the now ripening Nineteenth Century, and especially in each of their countless examples and practical occupations in the United States to-day.

One main contrast of the ideas behind every page of my verses, compared with establish'd poems, is their different relative attitude towards God, towards the objective universe, and still more (by reflection, confession, assumption, etc.) the quite changed attitude of the ego, the one chanting or talking, towards himself and towards his fellow-humanity. It is certainly time for America, above all, to begin this readjustment in the scope and basic point of view of verse; for everything else has changed. As I write, I see in an article on Wordsworth, in one of the current English magazines, the lines, "A few weeks ago an eminent French critic said that, owing to the special tendency to science and to its all-devouring force, poetry would cease to be read in fifty years." But I anticipate the very contrary. Only a firmer, vastly broader, new area begins to exist—nay, is already form'd—to which the poetic genius must emigrate. Whatever may have been the case in years gone by, the true use for the imaginative faculty of modern times is to give ultimate vivification to facts, to science, and to common lives, endowing them with the glows and glories and final illustriousness which belong to every real thing, and to real things only. Without that ultimate vivification—which the poet or other artist alone can give—reality would seem incomplete, and science, democracy, and life itself, finally in vain.

Few appreciate the moral revolutions, our age, which have been profounder far than the material or inventive or war-produced ones. The Nineteenth Century, now well towards its close (and ripening into fruit the seeds of the two preceding centuries[8])—the uprisings of national masses and shiftings of boundary-lines—the historical and other prominent facts of the United States—the war of attempted Secession—the stormy rush and haste of nebulous forces—never can future years witness more excitement and din of action—never completer change of army front along the whole line, the whole civilized world. For all these new and evolutionary facts, meanings, purposes, new poetic messages, new forms and expressions, are inevitable.

My Book and I—what a period we have presumed to span! those thirty years from 1850 to '80—and America in them! Proud, proud indeed may we be, if we have cull'd enough of that period in its own spirit to worthily waft a few live breaths of it to the future!

Let me not dare, here or anywhere, for my own purposes, or any purposes, to attempt the definition of Poetry, nor answer the question what it is. Like Religion, Love, Nature, while those terms are indispensable, and we all give a sufficiently accurate meaning to them, in my opinion no definition that has ever been made sufficiently encloses the name Poetry; nor can any rule or convention ever so absolutely obtain but some great exception may arise and disregard and overturn it.

Also it must be carefully remember'd that first-class literature does not shine by any luminosity of its own; nor do its poems. They grow of circumstances, and are evolutionary. The actual living light is always curiously from elsewhere—follows unaccountable sources, and is lunar and relative at the best. There are, I know, certain controling themes that seem endlessly appropriated to the poets—as war, in the past—in the Bible, religious rapture and adoration—always love, beauty, some fine plot, or pensive or other emotion. But, strange as it may sound at first, I will say there is something striking far deeper and towering far higher than those themes for the best elements of modern song.

Just as all the old imaginative works rest, after their kind, on long trains of presuppositions, often entirely unmention'd by themselves, yet supplying the most important bases of them, and without which they could have had no reason

---

[8] Whitman's note: "The ferment and germination even of the United States to-day, dating back to, and in my opinion mainly founded on, the Elizabethan age in English history, the age of Francis Bacon and Shakspere. Indeed, when we pursue it, what growth or advent is there that does not date back, back, until lost—perhaps its most tantalizing clues lost—in the receded horizons of the past?"

for being, so "Leaves of Grass," before a line was written, presupposed something different from any other, and, as it stands, is the result of such presupposition. I should say, indeed, it were useless to attempt reading the book without first carefully tallying that preparatory background and quality in the mind. Think of the United States to-day—the facts of these thirty-eight or forty empires solder'd in one—sixty or seventy millions of equals, with their lives, their passions, their future—these incalculable, modern, American, seething multitudes around us, of which we are inseparable parts! Think, in comparison, of the petty environage and limited area of the poets of past or present Europe, no matter how great their genius. Think of the absence and ignorance, in all cases hitherto, of the multitudinousness, vitality, and the unprecedented stimulants of to-day and here. It almost seems as if a poetry with cosmic and dynamic features of magnitude and limitlessness suitable to the human soul, were never possible before. It is certain that a poetry of absolute faith and equality for the use of the democratic masses never was.

In estimating first-class song, a sufficient Nationality, or, on the other hand, what may be call'd the negative and lack of it, (as in Goethe's case, it sometimes seems to me,) is often, if not always, the first element. One needs only a little penetration to see, at more or less removes, the material facts of their country and radius, with the coloring of the moods of humanity at the time, and its gloomy or hopeful prospects, behind all poets and each poet, and forming their birth-marks. I know very well that my "Leaves" could not possibly have emerged or been fashion'd or completed, from any other era than the latter half of the Nineteenth Century, nor any other land than democratic America, and from the absolute triumph of the National Union arms.

And whether my friend claim it for me or not, I know well enough, too, that in respect to pictorial talent, dramatic situations, and especially in verbal melody and all the conventional technique of poetry, not only the divine works that to-day stand ahead in the world's reading, but dozens more, transcend (some of them immeasurably transcend) all I have done, or could do. But it seem'd to me, as the objects in Nature, the themes of æstheticism, and all special exploitations of the mind and soul, involve not only their own inherent quality, but the quality, just as inherent and important, of *their point of view,*[9] the time had come to reflect all themes and things, old and new, in the lights thrown on them by the advent of America and democracy—to chant those themes through the utterance of one, not only the grateful and reverent legatee of the past, but the born child of the New World—to illustrate all through the genesis and ensemble of to-day; and that such illustration and ensemble are the chief demands of America's prospective imaginative literature. Not to carry out, in the approved style, some choice plot of fortune or misfortune, or fancy, or fine thoughts, or incidents, or courtesies—all of which has been done overwhelmingly and well, probably never to be excell'd—but that while in such æsthetic presentation of objects, passions, plots, thoughts, etc., our lands and days do not want, and probably will never have, anything better than they already possess from the bequests of the past, it still remains to be said that there is even towards all those a subjective and contemporary point of view appro-

---

[9] Whitman's note:"According to Immanuel Kant, the last essential reality, giving shape and significance to all the rest." Kant (1724–1804) was a German metaphysician and transcendental philosopher.

priate to ourselves alone, and to our new genius and environments, different from anything hitherto; and that such conception of current or gone-by life and art is for us the only means of their assimilation consistent with the Western world.

Indeed, and anyhow, to put it specifically, has not the time arrived when, (if it must be plainly said, for democratic America's sake, if for no other) there must imperatively come a readjustment of the whole theory and nature of Poetry? The question is important, and I may turn the argument over and repeat it: Does not the best thought of our day and Republic conceive of a birth and spirit of song superior to anything past or present? To the effectual and moral consolidation of our lands (already, as materially establish'd, the greatest factors in known history, and far, far greater through what they prelude and necessitate, and are to be in future)—to conform with and build on the concrete realities and theories of the universe furnish'd by science, and henceforth the only irrefragable basis for anything, verse included—to root both influences in the emotional and imaginative action of the modern time, and dominate all that precedes or opposes them—is not either a radical advance and step forward, or a new verteber[10] of the best song indispensable?

The New World receives with joy the poems of the antique, with European feudalism's rich fund of epics, plays, ballads—seeks not in the least to deaden or displace those voices from our ear and area—holds them indeed as indispensable studies, influences, records, comparisons. But though the dawn-dazzle of the sun of literature is in those poems for us of to-day—though perhaps the best parts of current character in nations, social groups, or any man's or woman's individuality, Old World or New, are from them—and though if I were ask'd to name the most precious bequest to current American civilization from all the hitherto ages, I am not sure but I would name those old and less old songs ferried hither from east and west—some serious words and debits remain; some acrid considerations demand a hearing. Of the great poems receiv'd from abroad and from the ages, and to-day enveloping and penetrating America, is there one that is consistent with these United States, or essentially applicable to them as they are and are to be? Is there one whose underlying basis is not a denial and insult to democracy? What a comment it forms, anyhow, on this era of literary fulfilment, with the splendid day-rise of science and resuscitation of history, that our chief religious and poetical works are not our own, nor adapted to our light, but have been furnish'd by far-back ages out of their arriere[11] and darkness, or, at most, twilight dimness! What is there in those works that so imperiously and scornfully dominates all our advanced civilization, and culture?

Even Shakespere, who so suffuses current letters and art (which indeed have in most degrees grown out of him,) belongs essentially to the buried past. Only he holds the proud distinction for certain important phases of that past, of being the loftiest of the singers life has yet given voice to. All, however, relate to and rest upon conditions, standards, politics, sociologies, ranges of belief, that have been quite eliminated from the Eastern hemisphere, and never existed at all in the Western. As authoritative types of song they belong in America just about as much as the persons and institutes they depict. True, it may be said, the emotional, moral, and æsthetic natures of humanity have not radically changed—that in these the old poems apply to our times and all times, irrespective of date; and that they are of

[10] Vertebra.   [11] "Backward," "behind the times" (French).

incalculable value as pictures of the past. I willingly make those admissions, and to their fullest extent; then advance the points herewith as of serious, even paramount importance.

I have indeed put on record elsewhere my reverence and eulogy for those never-to-be-excell'd poetic bequests, and their indescribable preciousness as heirlooms for America. Another and separate point must now be candidly stated. If I had not stood before those poems with uncover'd head, fully aware of their colossal grandeur and beauty of form and spirit, I could not have written "Leaves of Grass." My verdict and conclusions as illustrated in its pages are arrived at through the temper and inculcation of the old works as much as through anything else—perhaps more than through anything else. As America fully and fairly construed is the legitimate result and evolutionary outcome of the past, so I would dare to claim for my verse. Without stopping to qualify the averment, the Old World has had the poems of myths, fictions, feudalism, conquest, caste, dynastic wars, and splendid exceptional characters and affairs, which have been great; but the New World needs the poems of realities and science and of the democratic average and basic equality, which shall be greater. In the centre of all, and object of all, stands the Human Being, towards whose heroic and spiritual evolution poems and everything directly or indirectly tend, Old World or New.

Continuing the subject, my friends have more than once suggested—or may be the garrulity of advancing age is possessing me—some further embryonic facts of "Leaves of Grass," and especially how I enter'd upon them. Dr. Bucke has, in his volume, already fully and fairly described the preparation of my poetic field, with the particular and general plowing, planting, seeding, and occupation of the ground, till everything was fertilized, rooted, and ready to start its own way for good or bad. Not till after all this, did I attempt any serious acquaintance with poetic literature. Along in my sixteenth year I had become possessor of a stout, well-cramm'd one thousand page octavo volume (I have it yet,) containing Walter Scott's poetry entire—an inexhaustible mine and treasury of poetic forage (especially the endless forests and jungles of notes)—has been so to me for fifty years, and remains so to this day.[12]

Later, at intervals, summers and falls, I used to go off, sometimes for a week at a stretch, down in the country, or to Long Island's seashores—there, in the presence of outdoor influences, I went over thoroughly the Old and New Testaments, and absorb'd (probably to better advantage for me than in any library or indoor room—it makes such difference *where* you read,) Shakespere, Ossian,[13] the best

---

[12] Whitman's note: "Sir Walter Scott's COMPLETE POEMS; especially including BORDER MINSTRELSY; then Sir Tristrem; Lay of the Last Minstrel; Ballads from the German; Marmion; Lady of the Lake; Vision of Don Roderick; Lord of the Isles; Rokeby; Bridal of Triermain; Field of Waterloo; Harold the Dauntless; all the Dramas; various Introductions, endless interesting Notes, and Essays on Poetry, Romance, etc.

Lockhart's 1833 (or '34) edition with Scott's latest and copious revisions and annotations. (All the poems were thoroughly read by me, but the ballads of the Border Minstrelsy over and over again.)"

[13] A third-century Gaelic poet whose epic poems were translated by James Macpherson (1736–1796), a Scottish poet; many of the poems presented by Macpherson as close translations from the Gaelic were largely Macpherson's own work. Even after the hoax was exposed, the poems remained very popular.

translated versions I could get of Homer, Eschylus, Sophocles,[14] the old German Nibelungen,[15] the ancient Hindoo poems, and one or two other masterpieces, Dante's[16] among them. As it happen'd, I read the latter mostly in an old wood. The Iliad (Buckley's prose version,) I read first thoroughly on the peninsula of Orient, northeast end of Long Island, in a shelter'd hollow of rocks and sand, with the sea on each side. (I have wonder'd since why I was not overwhelm'd by those mighty masters. Likely because I read them, as described, in the full presence of Nature, under the sun, with the far-spreading landscape and vistas, or the sea rolling in.)

Toward the last I had among much else look'd over Edgar Poe's poems—of which I was not an admirer, tho' I always saw that beyond their limited range of melody (like perpetual chimes of music bells, ringing from lower *b* flat up to *g*) they were melodious expressions, and perhaps never excell'd ones, of certain pronounc'd phases of human morbidity. (The Poetic area is very spacious—has room for all—has so many mansions!) But I was repaid in Poe's prose by the idea that (at any rate for our occasions, our day) there can be no such thing as a long poem. The same thought had been haunting my mind before, but Poe's argument, though short, work'd the sum out and proved it to me.

Another point had an early settlement, clearing the ground greatly. I saw from the time my enterprise and questionings positively shaped themselves (how best can I express my own distinctive era and surroundings, America, Democracy?) that the trunk and centre whence the answer was to radiate, and to which all should return from straying however far a distance, must be an identical body and soul, a personality—which personality, after many considerations and ponderings I deliberately settled should be myself—indeed could not be any other. I also felt strongly (whether I have shown it or not) that to the true and full estimate of the Present both the Past and the Future are main considerations.

These, however, and much more might have gone on and come to naught (almost positively would have come to naught,) if a sudden, vast, terrible, direct and indirect stimulus for new and national declamatory expression had not been given to me. It is certain, I say, that, although I had made a start before, only from the occurrence of the Secession War, and what it show'd me as by flashes of lightning, with the emotional depths it sounded and arous'd (of course, I don't mean in my heart only, I saw it just as plainly in others, in millions)—that only from the strong flare and provocation of that war's sights and scenes the final reasons-for-being of an autochthonic[17] and passionate song definitely came forth.

I went down to the war fields in Virginia (end of 1862), lived thenceforward in camp—saw great battles and the days and nights afterward—partook of all the fluctuations, gloom, despair, hopes again arous'd, courage evoked—death readily risk'd—*the cause,* too—along and filling those agonistic and lurid following years, 1863–'64–'65—the real parturition years (more than 1776–'83) of this

[14] The eighth-century B.C. Greek epic poet, author of the *Iliad* and the *Odyssey*; Aeschylus (525–456 B.C.) and Sophocles (496?–406 B.C.) were Greek tragic dramatists who wrote *Oedipus the King* and *Agamemnon,* respectively.

[15] The *Nibelungen,* or *Nibelungenlied* (early 13th century) is the German epic about the legendary Siegfried, and is the subject of Richard Wagner's four-part opera, *Der Ring des Nibelungen* (1876).

[16] Dante Alighieri (1265–1321), the Italian poet whose masterpiece was *The Divine Comedy.*

[17] Indigenous; here, a peculiarly American song.

henceforth homogeneous Union. Without those three or four years and the experiences they gave, "Leaves of Grass" would not now be existing.

1888

from   DEMOCRATIC VISTAS*

[American Literature]

America, filling the present with greatest deeds and problems, cheerfully accepting the past, including feudalism (as, indeed, the present is but the legitimate birth of the past, including feudalism), counts, as I reckon, for her justification and success (for who, as yet, dare claim success?) almost entirely on the future. Nor is that hope unwarranted. To-day, ahead, though dimly yet, we see, in vistas, a copious, sane, gigantic offspring. For our New World I consider far less important for what it has done, or what it is, than for results to come. Sole among nationalities, these States have assumed the task to put in forms of lasting power and practicality, on areas of amplitude rivaling the operations of the physical kosmos, the moral political speculations of ages, long, long deferr'd, the democratic republican principle, and the theory of development and perfection by voluntary standards, and self-reliance. Who else, indeed, except the United States, in history, so far, have accepted in unwitting faith, and, as we now see, stand, act upon, and go security for, these things?

* * *

Before proceeding further, it were perhaps well to discriminate on certain points. Literature tills its crops in many fields, and some may flourish, while others lag. What I say in these Vistas has its main bearing on imaginative literature, especially poetry, the stock of all. In the department of science, and the specialty of journalism, there appear, in these States, promises, perhaps fulfilments, of highest earnestness, reality, and life. These, of course, are modern. But in the region of imaginative, spinal and essential attributes, something equivalent to creation is, for our age and lands, imperatively demanded. For not only is it not enough that the new blood, new frame of democracy shall be vivified[1] and held together merely by political means, superficial suffrage, legislation, etc., but it is clear to me that, unless it goes deeper, gets at least as firm and as warm a hold in men's hearts, emotions and belief, as, in their days, feudalism or ecclesiasticism, and inaugurates its own perennial sources, welling from the centre forever, its strength will be defective, its growth doubtful, and its main charm wanting. I suggest, therefore, the possibility, should some two or three really original American poets (perhaps artists or lecturers), arise, mounting the horizon like planets,

---

* First appeared in the *Galaxy* in December 1867 as "Democracy"; incorporated in *Democratic Vistas* with the essays "Personalism" and "Literature" in 1871. In 1867 Thomas Carlyle (1795–1881) published the essay "Shooting Niagara," in which he offered a scathing critique of American democracy. *Democratic Vistas* is Whitman's response.

[1] Brought to life.

stars of the first magnitude, that, from their eminence, fusing contributions, races, far localities, etc., together, they would give more compaction and more moral identity (the quality to-day most needed), to these States, than all its Constitutions, legislative and judicial ties, and all its hitherto political, warlike, or materialistic experiences.

* * *

It may be claim'd (and I admit the weight of the claim) that common and general worldly prosperity and a populace well to do, and with all life's material comforts, is the main thing, and is enough. It may be argued that our republic is, in performance, really enacting to-day the grandest arts, poems, etc., by beating up the wilderness into fertile farms, and in her railroads, ships, machinery, etc. And it may be ask'd, Are these not better, indeed, for America, than any utterances even of greatest rhapsode,[2] artist, or literatus?

I too hail those achievements with pride and joy: then answer that the soul of man will not with such only—nay, not with such at all—be finally satisfied; but needs what (standing on these and on all things, as the feet stand on the ground) is address'd to the loftiest, to itself alone.

Out of such considerations, such truths, arises for treatment in these Vistas the important question of character, of an American stock-personality, with literatures and arts for outlets and return-expressions, and, of course, to correspond, within outlines common to all. To these, the main affair, the thinkers of the United States, in general so acute, have either given feeblest attention, or have remain'd, and remain, in a state of somnolence.[3]

For my part, I would alarm and caution even the political and business reader, and to the utmost extent, against the prevailing delusion that the establishment of free political institutions, and plentiful intellectual smartness, with general good order, physical plenty, industry, etc. (desirable and precious advantages as they all are), do, of themselves, determine and yield to our experiment of democracy the fruitage of success. With such advantages at present fully, or almost fully, possess'd—the Union just issued, victorious, from the struggle[4] with the only foes it need ever fear (namely, those within itself, the interior ones), and with unprecedented materialistic advancement—society, in these States, is canker'd, crude, superstitious, and rotten. Political, or law-made society is, and private, or voluntary society, is also. In any vigor, the element of the moral conscience, the most important, the verteber[5] to State or man, seems to me either entirely lacking, or seriously enfeebled or ungrown.

I say we had best look our times and lands searchingly in the face, like a physician diagnosing some deep disease. Never was there, perhaps, more hollowness at heart than at present, and here in the United States. Genuine belief seems to have left us. The underlying principles of the States are not honestly believ'd in (for all this hectic glow, and these melodramatic screamings), nor is humanity itself believ'd in. What penetrating eye does not everywhere see through the mask? The spectacle is appaling.[6] We live in an atmosphere of hypocrisy throughout. The men believe not in the women, nor the women in the men. A scornful superciliousness rules in literature. The aim of all the *littérateurs*[7] is to find something to

---

[2] Rhapsodist: in ancient Greece, a traveling singer of heroic songs.
[3] Sleep.   [4] The Civil War.   [5] Vertebrae.
[6] Appalling: literally, causing a person to turn pale.   [7] "Literary men" (French).

make fun of. A lot of churches, sects, etc., the most dismal phantasms I know, usurp the name of religion. Conversation is a mass of badinage.

* * *

. . . Today, in books, in the rivalry of writers, especially novelists, success (so-call'd), is for him or her who strikes the mean flat, average, the sensational appetite for stimulus, incident, persiflage,[8] etc., and depicts, to the common calibre, sensual, exterior life. To such, or the luckiest of them, as we see the audiences are limitless and profitable; but they cease presently. While this day, or any day, to workmen portraying interior or spiritual life, the audiences were limited, and often laggard—but they last forever.

Compared with the past, our modern science soars, and our journals serve— but ideal and even ordinary romantic literature, does not, I think, substantially advance. Behold the prolific brood of the contemporary novel, magazine-tale, theatre-play, etc. The same endless thread of tangled and superlative love-story, inherited, apparently from the Amadises and Palmerins[9] of the 13th, 14th, and 15th centuries over there in Europe. The costumes and associations brought down to date, the seasoning hotter and more varied, the dragons and ogres left out—but the *thing*, I should say, has not advanced—is just as sensational, just as strain'd— remains about the same, nor more, nor less.

* * *

. . . America demands a poetry that is bold, modern, and all-surrounding and kosmical, as she is herself. It must in no respect ignore science or the modern, but inspire itself with sciennce and the modern. It must bend its vision toward the future, more than the past. Like America, it must extricate itself from even the greatest models of the past, and, while courteous to them, must have entire faith in itself, and the products of its own democratic spirit only. Like her, it must place in the van, and hold up at all hazards, the banner of the divine pride of man in himself (the radical foundation of the new religion). Long enough have the People been listening to poems in which common humanity, deferential, bends low, humiliated, acknowledging superiors. But America listens to no such poems. Erect, inflated, and fully self-esteeming be the chant; and then America will listen with pleased ears.

1867

from   *SPECIMEN DAYS**

ABRAHAM LINCOLN

August 12th.[1863]—I see the President almost every day, as I happen to live where he passes to or from his lodgings out of town. He never sleeps at the White House during the hot season, but has quarters at a healthy location some three

---

[8] Playful banter.   [9] Amadis de Gaul and Palmerin were heroes of chivalric romance.

* *Specimen Days and Collect* (1882) is Whitman's autobiographical narrative consisting of prefaces and essays.

miles north of the city, the Soldiers' Home, a United States military establishment. I saw him this morning about 8 $^1/_2$ coming in to business, riding on Vermont Avenue, near L Street. He always has a company of twenty-five or thirty cavalry, with sabres drawn and held upright over their shoulders. They say this guard was against his personal wish, but he let his counselors have their way. The party makes no great show in uniform or horses. Mr. Lincoln on the saddle generally rides a good-sized, easy-going gray horse, is dress'd in plain black, somewhat rusty and dusty, wears a black stiff hat, and looks about as ordinary in attire, etc., as the commonest man. A lieutenant, with yellow straps, rides at his left, and following behind, two by two, come the cavalry men, in their yellow-striped jackets. They are generally going at a slow trot, as that is the pace set them by the one they wait upon. The sabres and accoutrements[1] clank, and the entirely unornamental *cortège*[2] as it trots towards Lafayette Square arouses no sensation, only some curious stranger stops and gazes. I see very plainly Abraham Lincoln's dark brown face, with the deep-cut lines, the eyes, always to me with a deep latent sadness in the expression. We have got so that we exchange bows, and very cordial ones. Sometimes the President goes and comes in an open barouche.[3] The cavalry always accompany him, with drawn sabres. Often I notice as he goes out evenings—and sometimes in the morning, when he returns early—he turns off and halts at the large and handsome residence of the Secretary of War, on K Street, and holds conference there. If in his barouche, I can see from my window he does not alight, but sits in his vehicle, and Mr. Stanton[4] comes out to attend him. Sometimes one of his sons, a boy of ten or twelve, accompanies him, riding at his right on a pony. Earlier in the summer I occasionally saw the President and his wife, toward the latter part of the afternoon, out in a barouche, on a pleasure ride through the city. Mrs. Lincoln was dress'd in complete black, with a long crape veil. The equipage is of the plainest kind, only two horses, and they nothing extra. They pass'd me once very close, and I saw the President in the face fully, as they were moving slowly, and his look, though abstracted, happen'd to be directed steadily in my eye. He bow'd and smiled, but far beneath his smile I noticed well the expression I have alluded to. None of the artists or pictures has caught the deep, though subtle and indirect expression of this man's face. There is something else there. One of the great portrait painters of two or three centuries ago is needed.

TWO BROTHERS, ONE SOUTH, ONE NORTH

May 28–9. [1865]—I staid to-night a long time by the bedside of a new patient, a young Baltimorean, aged about 19 years, W. S. P., (2d Maryland, southern,) very feeble, right leg amputated, can't sleep hardly at all—has taken a great deal of morphine, which, as usual, is costing more than it comes to. Evidently very intelligent and well bred—very affectionate—held on to my hand, and put it by

---

[1] Miscellaneous equipment of a soldier.

[2] "Retinue" (French) ceremonial procession.

[3] A four-wheeled carriage with an outside seat for the driver and a top that could be raised to cover the back seat.

[4] Edwin Masters Stanton (1814–1869), U.S. secretary of war from 1862 to 1868.

his face, not willing to let me leave. As I was lingering, soothing him in his pain, he says to me suddenly, "I hardly think you know who I am—I don't wish to impose upon you—I am a rebel soldier." I said I did not know that, but it made no difference. Visiting him daily for about two weeks after that, while he lived, (death had mark'd him, and he was quite alone,) I loved him much, always kiss'd him, and he did me. In an adjoining ward I found his brother, an officer of rank, a Union soldier, a brave and religious man, (Col. Clifton K. Prentiss, sixth Maryland infantry, Sixth corps, wounded in one of the engagements at Petersburg, April 2—linger'd, suffer'd much, died in Brooklyn, Aug. 20, '65).[1] It was in the same battle both were hit. One was a strong Unionist, the other Secesh;[2] both fought on their respective sides, both badly wounded, and both brought together here after a separation of four years. Each died for his cause.

THE MILLION DEAD, TOO, SUMM'D UP

The dead in this war—there they lie, strewing the fields and woods and valleys and battle-fields of the South—Virginia, the Peninsula—Malvern Hill and Fair Oaks—the banks of the Chickahominy—the terraces of Fredericksburg—Antietam bridge—the grisly ravines of Manassas—the bloody promenade of the Wilderness[1]—the varieties of the *strayed* dead, (the estimate of the War Department is 25,000 national soldiers kill'd in battle and never buried at all, 5,000 drown'd—15,000 inhumed[2] by strangers, or on the march in haste, in hitherto unfound localities—2,000 graves cover'd by sand and mud by Mississippi freshets,[3] 3,000 carried away by caving-in of banks, etc.,)—Gettysburg, the West, Southwest—Vicksburg—Chattanooga—the trenches of Petersburg[4]—the numberless battles, camps, hospitals everywhere—the crop reap'd by the mighty reapers, typhoid, dysentery, inflammations—and blackest and loathsomest of all, the dead and living burial-pits, the prison-pens of Andersonville, Salisbury, Belle Isle, etc., (not Dante's pictured hell[5] and all its woes, its degradations, filthy torments, excell'd those prisons)—the dead, the dead, the dead—*our* dead—or South or North, ours all, (all, all, all, finally dear to me)—or East or West—Atlantic coast or Mississippi valley—somewhere they crawl'd to die, alone, in bushes, low gullies, or on the sides of hills—(there, in secluded spots, their skeletons, bleach'd bones, tufts of hair, buttons, fragments of clothing, are occasionally found yet)— our young men once so handsome and so joyous, taken from us—the son from the mother, the husband from the wife, the dear friend from the dear friend—the clusters of camp graves, in Georgia, the Carolinas, and in Tennessee—the single graves left in the woods or by the roadside, (hundreds, thousands, obliterated)— the corpses floated down the rivers, and caught and lodged, (dozens, scores, floated down the upper Potomac, after the cavalry engagements, the pursuit of Lee, following Gettysburg)—some lie at the bottom of the sea—the general million, and the special cemeteries in almost all the States—the infinite dead—(the

[1] This information was added after the essay was first written.   [2] A secessionist.
[1] The scenes of Civil War battles in Virginia.   [2] Buried.
[3] A rush of fresh water flowing into a salt sea.
[4] The scenes of Civil War battles in Pennsylvania, Mississippi, Tennessee, and Virginia.
[5] In *The Divine Comedy* by Dante Alighieri (1265–1321).

land entire saturated, perfumed with their impalpable ashes' exhalation in Nature's chemistry distill'd, and shall be so forever, in every future grain of wheat and ear of corn, and every flower that grows, and every breath we draw)—not only Northern dead leavening[6] Southern soil—thousands, aye tens of thousands, of Southerners, crumble to-day in Northern earth.

And everywhere among those countless graves—everywhere in the many soldier Cemeteries of the Nation, (there are now, I believe, over seventy of them)—as at the time in the vast trenches, the depositories of the slain, Northern and Southern, after the great battles—not only where the scathing trail passed those years, but radiating since in all the peaceful quarters of the land—we see, and ages yet may see, on monuments and gravestones, singly or in masses, to thousands or tens of thousands, the significant word *Unknown*.

(In some of the cemeteries nearly *all* the dead are unknown. At Salisbury, N. C., for instance, the known are only 85, while the unknown are 12,027, and 11,700 of these are buried in trenches. A national monument has been put up here, by order of Congress, to mark the spot—but what visible, material monument can ever fittingly commemorate that spot?)

MY TRIBUTE TO FOUR POETS*

April 16. [1881]—A short but pleasant visit to Longfellow. I am not one of the calling kind, but as the author of *Evangeline* kindly took the trouble to come and see me three years ago in Camden,[1] where I was ill, I felt not only the impulse of my own pleasure on that occasion, but a duty. He was the only particular eminence I called on in Boston, and I shall not soon forget his lit-up face and glowing warmth and courtesy, in the modes of what is called the old school.

And now just here I feel the impulse to interpolate something about the mighty four who stamp this first American century with its birth-marks of poetic literature. In a late magazine one of my reviewers, who ought to know better, speaks of my "attitude of contempt and scorn and intolerance" toward the leading poets—of my "deriding" them, and preaching their "uselessness." If anybody cares to know what I think—and have long thought and avow'd—about them, I am entirely willing to propound. I can't imagine any better luck befalling these States for a poetical beginning and initiation than has come from Emerson, Longfellow, Bryant, and Whittier. Emerson, to me, stands unmistakably at the head, but for the others I am at a loss where to give any precedence. Each illustrious, each rounded, each distinctive. Emerson for his sweet, vital-tasting melody, rhym'd philosophy, and poems as amber-clear as the honey of the wild bee he loves to sing. Longfellow for rich color, graceful forms and incidents—all that makes life beautiful and love refined—competing with the singers of Europe on their own ground, and, with one exception,[2] better and finer work than that of any of them. Bryant puls-

---

[6] Fermenting; permeating with an influence that changes the original material. This image complements that of "Nature's chemistry distill'd."

* Ralph Waldo Emerson (1803–1882), Henry Wadsworth Longfellow (1807–1882), William Cullen Bryant (1794–1878), and John Greenleaf Whittier (1819–1892).

[1] Camden, New Jersey, where Whitman spent his last nineteen years.

[2] Alfred, Lord Tennyson (1809–1892), the British poet laureate from 1850 to 1892, is the obvious choice.

ing the first interior verse-throbs of a mighty world—bard of the river and the wood, ever conveying a taste of open air, with scents as from hayfields, grapes, birch-borders—always lurkingly fond of threnodies[3]—beginning and ending his long career with chants of death, with here and there through all, poems, or passages of poems, touching the highest universal truths, enthusiasms, duties—morals as grim and eternal, if not as stormy and fateful, as anything in Eschylus.[4] While in Whittier, with his special themes—(his outcropping love of heroism and war, for all his Quakerdom, his verses at times like the measur'd step of Cromwell's old vererans[5])—in Whittier lives the zeal, the moral energy, that founded New England—the splendid rectitude and ardor of Luther, Milton, George Fox[6]—I must not, dare not, say the wilfulness and narrowness—though doubtless the world needs now, and always will need, almost above all, just such narrowness and wilfulness.[7]

BOSTON COMMON—MORE OF EMERSON*

Oct. 10–13. [1881]—I spend a good deal of time on the Common, these delicious days and nights—every mid-day from 11.30 to about 1—and almost every sunset another hour. I know all the big trees, especially the old elms along Tremont and Beacon streets,[1] and have come to a sociable-silent understanding with most of them, in the sunlit air (yet crispy-cool enough), as I saunter along the wide unpaved walks. Up and down this breadth by Beacon Street, between these same old elms, I walk'd for two hours, of a bright sharp February mid-day twenty-one years ago, with Emerson, then in his prime, keen, physically and morally magnetic, arm'd at every point, and when he chose, wielding the emotional just as well as the intellectual. During those two hours he was the talker and I the listener. It was an argument-statement, reconnoitring, review, attack, and pressing home (like an army corps in order, artillery, cavalry, infantry), of all that could be said against that part (and a main part) in the construction of my poems, "Children of Adam."[2] More precious than gold to me that dissertion—it afforded me, ever

[3] Funereal songs or poems.

[4] Aeschylus (525–456 B.C.), a Greek tragedian.

[5] Veterans; Oliver Cromwell (1599–1658), revolutionary leader and Lord protector of England from 1653 to 1658, known for imposing strict discipline on his troops.

[6] Martin Luther (1483–1546), German leader of the Protestant Reformation; the English poet John Milton (1608–1674), author of *Paradise Lost* (1667); Fox (1624–1691), the English founder of the Society of Friends, or Quakers. Whitman had a profound respect for the Quakers, as is evident in this comparison of Fox to a great reformer and a great poet.

[7] The "narrowness and wilfulness" of Luther, Milton, and Fox would be narrowness of concentration and wilfulness of purpose; while Whitman offers tribute to the artistic talents of the four poets, he stops just short of crediting them with the attributes of the three great men just named.

* The Common is a public park in central Boston; Ralph Waldo Emerson (1803–1882). In this more personal form of writing, Whitman does not employ the Quaker numerical designations for days and months that he uses in his poems.

[1] Boston streets.

[2] A group of poems first published in the 1860 edition of *Leaves of Grass* as "Enfans d'Adam" and in the 1867 edition with this title.

after, this strange and paradoxical lesson: each point of E.'s statement was unanswerable, no judge's charge ever more complete or convincing, I could never hear the points better put—and then I felt down in my soul the clear and unmistakable conviction to disobey all, and pursue my own way. "What have you to say then to such things?" said E., pausing in conclusion. "Only that while I can't answer them at all, I feel more settled than ever to adhere to my own theory, and exemplify it," was my candid response. Whereupon we went and had a good dinner at the American House. And thenceforward I never waver'd or was touch'd with qualms (as I confess I had been two or three times before).

1863–1882, 1882

=CONTEXTS=

The Move to the Cities

Post-Civil War America was characterized by the national drive to develop the material resources of the West. Towns and cities grew at a spectacular rate as miners, cattlemen, cowboys, farmers, and indigent immigrants traveled the railways, looking for land and work. William Fraser Rae (1835–1905), a correspondent for the London *Daily News,* was one of the first to take the trip by rail from New York to San Francisco. In his book *Westward by Rail: The New Route to the East* (1871), he describes Omaha, whose rapid growth was typical of American cities in the post-Civil War era:

Over the Rocky Mountains

Omaha is one of those American cities which seem to spring up, flourish, and wax great in the twinkling of an eye. Its history dates from 1854. In that year a few squatters fixed their residence in this section of what was then the Territory of Nebraska, which was regarded as in the heart of the Far West. Situated on the bank of the Missouri River, at a point almost equidistant between the Atlantic and Pacific Oceans, Omaha had many natural advantages, and these have been turned to profitable account since the Pacific Railway has furnished the opportunity. Certain it is that the city's prospects are bright. In 1860 the population did not exceed 1,883; now the number of inhabitants is estimated at 20,000. There are many manufactories within its bounds, one distillery, and several breweries. In the year 1868–9 the sales of the merchants were upwards of a million and a quarter sterling. Like most American cities it possesses two daily newspapers, the one the Republican the other the Democratic organ. Four other journals are published at longer intervals. Of schools, both public and private, there is abundance. The churches are fifteen in number. There are eleven hotels, of which one or two are first-class establishments. That this progress should have been made within the space of a few short years is not only marvellous, but inspires hope that the city's future will be a great and an enviable one. . . .

William Fraser Rae, 1871

Emily Dickinson
(1830–1886)

"The Banquet of Abstemiousness / Defaces that of wine": that line from a poem by Emily Dickinson sets forth a perspective that permeates both her life and her poetic vision. Dickinson cared little for quantity, for multitude, for aggregating things or experiences. Outwardly her life was quiet, uncluttered by the public activities that customarily measure development or success. She died in the village of Amherst, Massachusetts, in 1886 in the same house in which she had been born in 1830. She traveled outside Massachusetts only once, in 1855, when she accompanied her father to Philadelphia and to Washington, D.C. During the last fifteen years of her life in Amherst she restricted her movements severely, rarely leaving her house and garden. In no way, however, was this election of privacy an abandonment of life; as the documents in the biographer Jay Leyda's *The Years and Hours of Emily Dickinson* (1960) testify, Dickinson's steady focus on an inner world was deliberate, purposeful, the condition of creativity. To prefer the "banquet of abstemiousness" means to find more in less, to nourish oneself on the quality of experience rather than on the plentiful menu of social convention. Making such a perspective possible for Dickinson was her extreme sensitivity to the outside world, her inclination not to let the obligations and institutions of society regulate her life; in later years simply receiving a letter or conversing with a visitor was an overpowering experience for her, at once intense, animating, and threatening.

The second child of Edward and Emily Norcross Dickinson, the poet-to-be had a devoted brother, Austin, one year her senior, and a protective younger sister, Lavinia. The family lived quietly, secure financially: Dickinson's imposing father was a lawyer and at one time a member of Congress, her mother, a woman of retiring habit, apparently remote from her children. In this family, genuinely supportive yet with no insistent habits of sociality, Dickinson could be herself, could play the games of childhood as a young girl, could withdraw to think and write as her imagination cultivated privacy. When she was seventeen she attended Amherst Academy and the nearby Mount Holyoke Female Seminary for one year. But she returned home the following year, willingly and with the ready assent of her parents.

Dickinson's attachment not only to members of her family but to those she knew well constituted a meaningful dimension of her life. Among her friends was Helen Hunt Jackson, also from Amherst, who began publishing poetry in the 1860s (when Dickinson was writing a poem almost every day) and repeatedly urged her friend to bring her work before the public. Jackson's novel *Mercy Philbrick's Choice* (1876) is thought to be a portrait of Dickinson; the forceful and romantic figure of Rev. Charles Wadsworth, doubtless the subject of eloquent poems of separation, made a deep imprint on her emotions and her imagination. The family friend Judge Otis P. Lord was a treasured part of Dickinson's life; apparently Judge Lord suggested marriage when Dickinson was fifty years old and accepted her refusal with an understanding that matched his longtime admiration. And the sympathetic critic Thomas Wentworth Higginson was for years her confidante about mat-

An 1858 lithograph of the Dickinson homestead on Main Street, Amherst, Massachusetts, where Emily Dickinson spent most of her life.

ters of poetry. Above all, Dickinson's sister-in-law, Susan Gilbert Dickinson, who lived next door ("a hedge away," as an early poem says), was a person whom Dickinson regarded with a unique love and openness throughout her adult life.

Domestic tension was far from unknown in the Dickinson household: the thirteen-year love affair between Austin Dickinson and Mabel Loomis Todd, the wife of David Peck Todd, a professor of astronomy at Amherst, brought increasing stress into the environment. We can only surmise what Dickinson thought of this affair (which became common knowledge in the family) and the swirling emotions it must have caused her. For a while at least it seems to have bonded her all the more closely to her sister-in-law, Susan, not out of a knowing pity but out of a glorification of their role as sisters.

In a letter to her vacationing sister-in-law in 1871, Dickinson adopted the same perspective that informs her statement about the "Banquet of Abstemiousness": "To miss you, Sue, is power. The stimulus of Loss makes most Possession mean." A virtual signature of her way of expressing emotion, this idea of feeding on emptiness has profound implications for Dickinson's poetry. "Success is counted sweetest," she writes, "By those who ne'er succeed." Similarly, "Water, is taught by thirst." In "I had been hungry, all the Years," the poet finds that hunger is a way "Of Persons outside Windows / The Entering— takes away." What such poems confidently assert amounts to a paradoxical theory of knowledge, the idea that a person knows something best, most keenly, by not having it. In fashioning this perspective Dickinson's poems formulate a poetics of deprivation that has its roots in the stern moral dictates of the Puritans of an earlier Massachusetts. Dickinson secularizes Puritan "thou shalt nots" and makes the injunctions part of her mode of expression. Additionally, with the announcement that "My business is circumference," she encircles her world, makes it her own with a startling range of definitions (of hope, exultation, remorse), describes its citizens (crickets, robins, hummingbirds), and presides over its parade of death and celebration with a "self," an "I," that is whimsical, ironic, insistent, and terribly aware of loss, both individual and universal.

What Dickinson says and how she says it are finally inseparable; they come together in a remarkable idiom that consists of the elliptical quality of her lines, her use of syntax, slant (imperfect) rhyme, punctuation, and capitalization, and even the unconventional use of articles: when she writes in "A Bird came down the Walk" that the bird drank "A Dew / from a convenient Grass," the reader sees that her way of using language extends originality to minute detail. Few writers succeed in creating a genuine idiom in which the world is transformed by language into something original, fresh with discovery. Along with Walt Whitman and Mark Twain in nineteenth-century American literature, Dickinson is one of the few, and the only one whose idiom was fully arrayed from the beginning of her career. Although she liked to read a number of nineteenth-century British writers, among them John Keats, Charlotte and Emily Brönte, Robert and Elizabeth Barrett Browning, and George Eliot, Dickinson's reading had no discernable effect on the style of her poetry. She knew the Bible well, as evidenced by her numerous allusions to biblical events. But even these episodes are made part of the idiom that serves as Dickinson's way of apprehending the world: thus, in the early poem "A little East of Jordan," the story of Jacob wrestling with an angel becomes "A Gymnast and an Angel / Did wrestle long and hard."

Dickinson's concern with herself as the center of her world is reminiscent of Henry David Thoreau, who advocates self-exploration as the only worthy kind of travel. In her assumptions about the individual's access to the infinite, she enacts even more distinctively the precepts of Ralph Waldo Emerson's brand of self-reliance. And, to borrow a term from Emerson's essay "The Poet" (1844), we may say that she rules over the world of her poetry with the "tyrannous eye" Emerson thought so necessary. In so doing, she comes to a triumphant sense of her importance as a woman: "I'm 'wife'—I've finished that . . . / I'm Czar—I'm 'Woman' now," she writes in one poem; "Title divine—is mine!" she begins another; and although "Sages" might think her life small, it "Swelled—like Horizons—in my breast." Without the benefit of committees and organizations, Dickinson celebrated her autonomy as an individual and as a woman.

Like any aspiring poet, even one desirous of maintaining privacy, Dickinson wanted to have some outside estimate of her work. Accordingly, in April 1862 she wrote to Higginson, enclosing four poems, to ask if her work was "alive." By this time Dickinson had a developing sense of herself as a poet, which Higginson encouraged without understanding the full range of its passion and depth or the poems it generated. Nonetheless, Higginson's liberal attention over the years was a boon to Dickinson, something deeply appreciated, as her letters show.

As we have learned from the invaluable *Manuscript Books of Emily Dickinson* (1981), edited by the critic Ralph Franklin, Dickinson assembled her poems privately and systematically over a period of years. Her method of composition was to write out a draft of a poem on a sheet of paper or whatever was at hand—the back of a used envelope, at some times, a scrap of paper at others. She would assemble a number of such drafts, then, at a later time, copy them onto folded sheets of unlined paper, frequently adding alternative choices for words of which she was unsure. Arranging these folded sheets in a pile, she would punch two holes on the left-hand side and tie them together with string, thus making packets of sixteen or more pages, called "fascicles," with about twenty poems in each packet. Franklin prints these fascicles in *The Manuscript Books,* supplies lists of the poems in each fascicle, and adds photostats so that it is possible to see Dickinson's handwriting, her alternate words, idiosyncratic punctuation, and capitalization, as well as the unconventional line breaks she sometimes made.

Only a dozen of Dickinson's poems were published during her lifetime, and she seems neither to have sought nor welcomed their publication. As she said in an 1862 letter to Higginson, publication was "foreign" to her thought. After her death recognition of her achievement came slowly because of the circumstances of publication. When Lavinia found over a thousand poems loose or bound in fascicles, she gave them to Susan with an apparent intention of seeing them in print. After two years she retrieved the poems and asked Higginson and Mabel Loomis Todd (herself a writer and poet) to edit them for publication. Accordingly, Higginson and Todd selected poems for a volume published in 1890 (*Poems*) and another in 1891 (*Poems: Second Series*), and in 1896 Todd edited a third selection of Dickinson's poems (*Poems: Third Series*). Although these editions attracted considerable interest, they performed a disservice to the poems Dickinson actually wrote: for they made Dickinson's poetry as conventional as possible by assigning titles, adjusting syntax, inserting regular punctuation, altering the text in some cases to make lines more "readable," and arranging the poems in such categories as Nature, Death, Love, and Friendship. Not until Thomas Johnson's three-volume edition of the poems appeared in 1955 were adequate texts of Dickinson's poems made public. Johnson not only edited the poems with scrupulous care but studied Dickinson's handwriting and the evidence in letters so that he could number them according to their approximate dates of composition. Thus, the numbers given to Dickinson's poems in all recent collections are those assigned by Johnson. Together with fellow editor Theodora Ward, Johnson also brought out three volumes of Dickinson's letters in 1958. Frequently, Dickinson included poems as part of these striking documents; at other times the cadences of her poetry emerge from her prose so that poems seem to evolve in the context of a letter. And in many of her letters the singular idiom of the poetry takes impressionistic form: "Friday I tasted life," she wrote to her close friend Mrs. J. G. Holland in 1866: "A circus passed the house—still I feel the red in my mind though the drums are out."

Dickinson's poetry has attracted the attention of musicians and composers in the twentieth century. Aaron Copland's "Twelve Poems by Emily Dickinson" (1950), written for solo voice and piano, includes "I felt a Funeral, in my Brain" and "There came a Wind like a Bugle." John Adams's "Harmonium" (1981) features a chorus singing the words of "Wild Nights—Wild Nights!" and "Because I Could Not Stop for Death." These notable compositions evidence more than a fashionable interest in the work of a major poet. For, as a number of scholars have pointed out, Dickinson's metrical patterns derive primarily from the prosody of hymns to which she was exposed in her early life. The poetry specialist Mary Favret has observed that many of Dickinson's poems can be sung to the melody of "Amazing Grace" and to the far different beat of "Battle Hymn of the Republic." The critic Susan Gubar adds "The Yellow Rose of Texas" to this list and makes a point of having students who might yawn at an introduction to "prosody" sing Dickinson poems to all three melodies in order to discover how music and words do and do not fit.

Dickinson has also been honored by the practice and testimony of poets in the twentieth century. A number of American poets, among them William Carlos Williams, Hart Crane, Richard Wilbur, and Adrienne Rich, have looked to her work for a renewed sense of the possibilities of more recent poetry. In selecting the "Banquet of Abstemiousness" as the surest way of knowing the intensity of life and the dimensions of modern consciousness, Dickinson has left a legacy of abundance to poets and readers alike.

Suggested Readings: *The Years and Hours of Emily Dickinson,* 2 vols., ed. J. Leyda, 1960. *A Concordance to the Poems of Emily Dickinson,* ed. S. P. Rosenbaum, 1964. *The Manuscript Books of Emily Dickinson,* 2 vols., ed. R. W. Franklin, 1981. T. H. Johnson, *Emily Dickinson: An Interpretive Biography,* 1955. C. R. Anderson, *Emily Dickinson's Poetry,* 1960. A. J. Gelpi, *Emily Dickinson: The Mind of the Poet,* 1965. J. Cody, *After Great Pain: The Inner Life of Emily Dickinson,* 1971. I. N. Kher, *The Landscape of Absence: Emily Dickinson's Poetry,* 1974. R. B. Sewall, *The Life of Emily Dickinson,* 2 vols., 1974. S. Cameron, *Lyric Time: Dickinson and the Limits of Genre,* 1979. A. Rich, "Vesuvius at Home: The Power of Emily Dickinson," 1976, rpt. in *On Lies, Secrets and Silence: Selected Prose 1966–1978,* 1979. M. Homan, *Women Writers and Poetic Identity,* 1980. B. A. Clarke Mossberg, *Emily Dickinson: When a Writer Is a Daughter,* 1982. S. Juhasz, ed., *Feminist Critics Read Emily Dickinson,* 1983. P. Longsworth, *Austin and Mabel: The Amherst Affair,* 1983. V. R. Pollak, *Dickinson: The Anxiety of Gender,* 1984. J. Loving, *Emily Dickinson: The Poet on the Second Story,* 1986. C. G. Wolff, *Emily Dickinson,* 1986. J. Dobson, *Dickinson and the Strategies of Reticence: The Woman Writer in Nineteenth-Century America,* 1989.

Texts Used: *The Poems of Emily Dickinson,* 3 vols., ed. T. H. Johnson, 1951, 1955. *The Letters of Emily Dickinson,* 3 vols., ed. T. H. Johnson and T. Ward, 1958.

49*

I never lost as much but twice,
And that was in the sod.[1]
Twice have I stood a beggar
Before the door of God!

Angels – twice descending
Reimbursed my store –
Burglar! Banker – Father!
I am poor once more!

1858?, 1890

59

A little East of Jordan,
Evangelists record,
A Gymnast and an Angel[1]
Did wrestle long and hard –

* Dickinson titled few of her poems; they were numbered by Thomas Johnson in his *Poems of Emily Dickinson* (1955).
[1] In the ground (the grave).
[1] In Genesis 32, the biblical patriarch Jacob (here a "Gymnast") wrestles with an angel.

Till morning touching mountain –
And Jacob, waxing strong,
The Angel begged permission
To Breakfast – to return –

Not so, said cunning Jacob!
"I will not let thee go   10
Except thou bless me" – Stranger![2]
The which acceded to –

Light swung the silver fleeces
"Peniel" Hills[3] beyond,
And the bewildered Gymnast
Found he had worsted God!

1858?, 1890

67

Success is counted sweetest
By those who ne'er succeed.
To comprehend a nectar[1]
Requires sorest need.

Not one of all the purple Host
Who took the Flag[2] today
Can tell the definition
So clear of Victory

As he defeated – dying –
On whose forbidden ear   10
The distant strains of triumph
Burst agonized and clear!

1859?, 1878

76

Exultation is the going
Of an inland soul to sea

---

[2] According to Thomas Johnson, Dickinson later penciled in the alternative word "Signor."
[3] "And Jacob called the name of the place Peniel: for I have seen God face to face, and my life is preserved," from Genesis 32:30.
[1] According to classical myth, the drink of the gods; here, any celebratory beverage.
[2] Who captured the enemy flag in battle.

Past the houses – past the headlands –
Into deep Eternity –

Bred as we, among the mountains,
Can the sailor understand
The divine intoxication
Of the first league out from land?

1859?, 1890

125

For each extatic[1] instant
We must an anguish pay
In keen and quivering ratio
To the extasy.

For each beloved hour
Sharp pittances of years –
Bitter contested farthings[2] –
And Coffers[3] heaped with Tears!

1859?, 1891

130

These are the days when Birds come back –
A very few – a Bird or two –
To take a backward look.

These are the days when skies resume
The old – old sophistries[1] of June –
A blue and gold mistake.

Oh fraud that cannot cheat the Bee –
Almost thy plausibility
Induces my belief.

Till ranks of seeds their witness bear –   10
And softly thro' the altered air
Hurries a timid leaf.

---

[1] Ecstatic.   [2] British coins of little value.   [3] Trunks or chests for holding valuables.
[1] Deceptive reasonings in subtle form.

Oh Sacrament of summer days,
Oh Last Communion[2] in the Haze –
Permit a child to join.

Thy sacred emblems to partake –
Thy consecrated bread to take
And thine immortal wine!

1859?, 1890

Water, is taught by thirst.[1]
Land – by the Oceans passed.
Transport – by throe[2] –
Peace – by it's battles told –
Love, by Memorial Mold[3] –
Birds, by the Snow.

1859?, 1896

166

I met a King this afternoon!
He had not on a Crown indeed,
A little Palmleaf Hat was all,
And he was barefoot, I'm afraid!

But sure I am he Ermine wore
Beneath his faded Jacket's blue –
And sure I am, the crest he bore
Within that Jacket's pocket too![1]

For 'twas too stately for an Earl –
A Marquis would not go so grand!   10

---

[2] Dickinson compares the death of nature in autumn to the death of Christ commemorated in the sacrament of communion. The metaphors of the final stanza extend the comparison.
   [1] We learn the value of water by being thirsty. Each line of the poem offers another instance of what we know or learn by not having it.
   [2] We learn rapture by experiencing anguish.
   [3] A memorial photograph or pictorial representation.
   [1] The speaker of the poem surmises that this little king's riches are hidden beneath an appearance of poverty.

'Twas possibly a Czar petite –
A Pope, or something of that kind!

If I must tell you, of a Horse
My freckled Monarch held the rein –
Doubtless an estimable Beast,
But not at all disposed to run!

And such a wagon![2] While I live
Dare I presume to see
Another such a vehicle
As then transported me!   20

1860?, 1893

185

"Faith" is a fine invention
When Gentlemen can *see* –
But *Microscopes* are prudent
In an Emergency.

1860?, 1891

199

I'm "wife" – I've finished that –[1]
That other state –
I'm Czar – I'm "Woman" now –
It's safer so –

How odd the Girl's life looks
Behind this soft Eclipse –
I think that Earth feels so
To folks in Heaven – now –

This being comfort – then
That other kind – was pain –   10
But why compare?
I'm "Wife"! Stop there!

1860?, 1890

[2] Apparently in a run-down condition: again, the appearance is one of dilapidation; the reality, one of royalty.

[1] Although Dickinson never married, this poem announces a triumphant sense of having graduated from the life of a girl to that of a woman; her feeling of being a "wife" was possibly brought about by her love for Rev. Charles Wadsworth.

214*

I taste a liquor never brewed –
From Tankards scooped in Pearl –
Not all the Frankfort Berries[1]
Yield such an Alcohol!

Inebriate of Air – am I –
And Debauchee of Dew –
Reeling – thro endless summer days –
From inns of Molten Blue –

When "Landlords" turn the drunken Bee
Out of the Foxglove's door –   10
When Butterflies – renounce their "drams" –
I shall but drink the more!

Till Seraphs swing their snowy Hats[2] –
And Saints – to windows run –
To see the little Tippler
From Manzanilla come![3]

                                          1860?, 1861

216†

Safe in their Alabaster Chambers –
Untouched by Morning
And untouched by Noon –
Sleep the meek members of the Resurrection[1] –
Rafter of satin,
And Roof of stone.

Light laughs the breeze
In her Castle above them –
Babbles the Bee in a stolid Ear,
Pipe the Sweet Birds in ignorant cadence –   10
Ah, what sagacity perished here!

                                          1859, 1862

---

* Published anonymously as "The May-Wine" in the *Springfield Daily Republican* on May 4, 1861.
[1] Dickinson's manuscript offers "Vats upon the Rhine" as an alternative for "Frankfort Berries."
[2] Till angels swing their halos.
[3] Dickinson apparently associated Manzanilla, Cuba, with rum; she supplied the alternative final line, "Leaning against the – Sun."
† Published as "The Sleeping" in the *Springfield Daily Republican* on March 1, 1862.
[1] Those who have died (and joined the Resurrection) are unaware of the passage of time.

216*

Safe in their Alabaster Chambers –
Untouched by Morning –
And untouched by Noon –
Lie the meek members of the Resurrection –
Rafter of Satin – and Roof of Stone!

Grand go the Years – in the Crescent – above them –
Worlds scoop their Arcs –
And Firmaments – row –
Diadems – drop – and Doges[1] – surrender –
Soundless as dots – on a Disc of Snow –   10

1861, 1890

241

I like a look of Agony,
Because I know it's true –
Men do not sham Convulsion,
Nor simulate, a Throe[1] –

The Eyes glaze once – and that is Death –
Impossible to feign
The Beads upon the Forehead
By homely Anguish strung.

1861?, 1890

249†

Wild Nights – Wild Nights!
Were I with thee
Wild Nights should be
Our luxury!

---

* A later version of the previous poem; here, the passage of time is registered on a much larger scale.
  [1] Chief magistrates in the Italian republics of Venice and Genoa from the twelfth to the sixteenth centuries.
  [1] Pain or anguish.
  † According to Thomas Johnson, Thomas Wentworth Higginson (1823–1911) admitted to Mabel Loomis Todd (1856–1932) that in selecting poems for their 1891 volume *Poems: Second Series*, he was somewhat reluctant to include this poem "lest the malignant read into it more than that virgin recluse ever dreamed of putting there." The poem does suggest the depth and intensity of Dickinson's feelings.

Futile – the Winds –
To a Heart in port –
Done with the Compass –
Done with the Chart!

Rowing in Eden –
Ah, the Sea!   10
Might I but moor – Tonight –
In Thee!

                                        1861?, 1891

254

"Hope" is the thing with feathers –
That perches in the soul –
And sings the tune without the words –
And never stops – at all –

And sweetest – in the Gale – is heard –
And sore must be the storm –
That could abash the little Bird
That kept so many warm –

I've heard it in the chillest land –
And on the strangest Sea –   10
Yet, never, in Extremity,
It asked a crumb – of Me.

                                        1861?, 1891

258

There's a certain Slant of light,
Winter Afternoons –
That oppresses, like the Heft[1]
Of Cathedral Tunes –

Heavenly Hurt, it gives us –
We can find no scar,
But internal difference,
Where the Meanings, are –

None may teach it – Any[2] –
'Tis the Seal Despair –   10

---

[1] Weight, bulk.   [2] Anything: Dickinson's personal idiom here compresses "anything" to "any."

An imperial affliction
Sent us of the Air –

When it comes, the Landscape listens –
Shadows – hold their breath –
When it goes, 'tis like the Distance
On the look of Death –

1861?, 1890

271

A solemn thing – it was – I said –
A Woman – white[1] – to be –
And wear – if God should count me fit –
Her blameless mystery –

A timid thing – to drop a life
Into the mystic well –
Too plummetless[2] – that it come back –
Eternity – until –

I pondered how the bliss would look –
And would it feel as big –   10
When I could take it in my hand –
As hovering – seen – through fog –

And then – the size of this "small" life –
The Sages – call it small –
Swelled – like Horizons – in my breast[3] –
And I sneered – softly – "small"![4]

1861?, 1896

274

The only Ghost I ever saw
Was dressed in Mechlin[1] – so –
He had no sandal on his foot –
And stepped like flakes of snow –

[1] Pure, virginal.   [2] Too deep to fathom.
[3] Dickinson suggested "vest" as an alternative for "breast."
[4] In this final stanza Dickinson sneers ironically at the supposed wise people who would call her life small; she has found it to be as large as the horizon.
[1] A dainty bobbin lace made in Malines (Mechlin), Belgium.

His Mien,[2] was soundless, like the Bird –
But rapid – like the Roe –
His fashions, quaint, Mosaic –
Or haply, Mistletoe –

His conversation – seldom –
His laughter, like the Breeze   10
That dies away in Dimples
Among the pensive Trees –

Our interview – was transient –
Of me, himself was shy –
And God forbid I look behind –
Since that appalling Day!

                                                    1861?, 1891

280

I felt a Funeral, in my Brain,
And Mourners to and fro
Kept treading – treading – till it seemed
That Sense was breaking through[1] –

And when they all were seated,
A Service, like a Drum –
Kept beating – beating – till I thought
My Mind was going numb –

And then I heard them lift a Box
And creak across my Soul   10
With those same Boots of Lead, again,
Then Space – began to toll,

As[2] all the Heavens were a Bell,
And Being, but an Ear,
And I, and Silence, some strange Race
Wrecked, solitary, here –

And then a Plank in Reason, broke,
And I dropped down, and down –
And hit a World, at every plunge,
And Finished knowing – then –   20

                                                    1861?, 1896

---

[2] Demeanor, manner.
[1] Breaking down, giving way; the poem continues to develop the idea of the faculties disintegrating and concludes with the climactic breaking of "Reason."
[2] As if: Dickinson's personal idiom uses the elliptical substitution of "As" for "As if."

285

The Robin's my Criterion for Tune –
Because I grow – where Robins do –
But, were I Cuckoo born[1] –
I'd swear by him –
The ode familiar – rules the Noon –
The Buttercup's, my Whim for Bloom –
Because, we're Orchard sprung –
But, were I Britain born,
I'd Daisies spurn –
None but the Nut – October fit –   10
Because, through dropping it,
The seasons flit – I'm taught –
Without the Snow's Tableau
Winter, were lie – to me –
Because I see – New Englandly –
The Queen, discerns like me –
Provincially –

1861?, 1929

293

I got so I could hear his name –
Without – Tremendous gain –
That Stop-sensation – on my Soul –
And Thunder – in the Room –

I got so I could walk across
That Angle in the floor,
Where he turned so, and I turned – how –
And all our Sinew tore –

I got so I could stir the Box –
In which his letters grew[1]   10
Without that forcing, in my breath –
As Staples – driven through –

Could dimly recollect a Grace –
I think, they call it "God" –
Renowned to ease Extremity –
When Formula, had failed –

---

[1] If I had been born where the cuckoo is a common bird, I'd take his song as "normal."
[1] I could look through the box in which the number of his letters grew. Dickinson's elliptical style is evident.

And shape my Hands –
Petition's way,
Tho' ignorant of a word
That Ordination[2] – utters –   20

My Business, with the Cloud,
If any Power behind it, be,
Not subject to Despair –
It care, in some remoter way,
For so minute affair
As Misery –
Itself, too great, for interrupting – more –

1861?, 1929

315

He fumbles at your Soul
As Players at the Keys
Before they drop[1] full Music on –
He stuns you by degrees –
Prepares your brittle Nature
For the Etherial Blow
By fainter Hammers – further heard –
Then nearer – Then so slow
Your Breath has time to straighten –
Your Brain – to bubble Cool –   10
Deals – One – imperial – Thunderbolt –
That scalps your naked Soul –

When Winds take Forests in their Paws –
The Universe – is still –

1862?, 1896

326

I cannot dance upon my Toes –
No Man instructed me –
But oftentimes, among my mind,
A Glee possesseth me,

That had I Ballet knowledge –
Would put itself abroad

---

[2] To the ministry.
[1] Turn: before piano players begin to play the full composition.

In Pirouette to blanch a Troupe[1] –
Or lay a Prima, mad,

And though I had no Gown of Gauze –
No Ringlet, to my Hair,   10
Nor hopped for Audiences – like Birds,
One Claw upon the Air,

Nor tossed my shape in Eider Balls,[2]
Nor rolled on wheels of snow
Till I was out of sight, in sound,
The House encore me so –

Nor any know I know the Art
I mention – easy – Here –
Nor any Placard boast me –
It's full as Opera –   20

                                                    1862?, 1929

328

A bird came down the Walk –
He did not know I saw –
He bit an Angleworm in halves
And ate the fellow, raw,

And then he drank a Dew
From a convenient Grass –
And then hopped sidewise to the Wall
To let a Beetle pass –

He glanced with rapid eyes
That hurried all around –   10
They looked like frightened Beads, I thought –
He stirred his Velvet Head

Like one in danger, Cautious,
I offered him a Crumb
And he unrolled his feathers
And rowed him softer home –

Than Oars divide the Ocean,
Too silver for a seam –

---

[1] The speaker imagines dancing that would make a ballet troupe turn white in amazement or drive a primadonna mad.
[2] Very soft balls of down from the eider duck.

Or Butterflies, off Banks of Noon
Leap, plashless[1] as they swim.   20

1862?, 1891

336

The face I carry with me – last –
When I go out of Time –
To take my Rank – by – in the West –
That face – will just be thine –

I'll hand it to the Angel –
That – Sir – was my Degree –
In Kingdoms – you have heard the Raised[1] –
Refer to – possibly.

He'll take it – scan it – step aside –
Return – with such a crown   10
As Gabriel – never capered at –
And beg me put it on –

And then – he'll turn me round and round –
To an admiring sky –
As one that bore her Master's name –
Sufficient Royalty!

1862?, 1945

341

After great pain, a formal feeling comes –
The Nerves sit ceremonious, like Tombs –
The stiff Heart questions was it He, that bore,
And Yesterday, or Centuries before?

The Feet, mechanical, go round –
Of ground, or Air, or Ought[1] –
A Wooden way
Regardless grown,
A Quartz contentment, like a stone –

---

[1] Splashless.
[1] Those who have died and been resurrected to glory in Heaven.
[1] A double meaning: anything (from Dickinson's spelling of "aught"), and obligation (the feet simply do what they are obliged to do, mechanically, without thought).

This is the Hour of Lead –   10
Remembered, if outlived,
As Freezing persons, recollect the Snow –
First – Chill – then Stupor – then the letting go –

1862?, 1929

348

I dreaded that first Robin, so,
But He is mastered, now,
I'm some accustomed to Him grown,
He hurts a little, though –

I thought if I could only live
Till that first Shout got by –
Not all Pianos in the Woods
Had power to mangle me –

I dared not meet the Daffodils –
For fear their Yellow Gown   10
Would pierce me with a fashion
So foreign to my own –

I wished the Grass would hurry –
So – when 'twas time to see –
He'd be too tall, the tallest one
Could stretch – to look at me –

I could not bear the Bees should come,
I wished they'd stay away
In those dim countries where they go,
What word had they, for me?   20

They're here, though; not a creature failed –
No Blossom stayed away
In gentle deference to me –
The Queen of Calvary[1] –

Each one salutes me, as he goes,
And I, my childish Plumes,
Lift, in bereaved acknowledgement
Of their unthinking Drums –

1862?, 1891

---

[1] The hill near Jerusalem on which Christ was crucified. The idea of the poem is that spring arrives
with all its new life despite the suffering of the speaker.

401

What Soft – Cherubic Creatures –
These Gentlewomen are –
One would as soon assault a Plush[1] –
Or violate a Star –

Such Dimity[2] Convictions –
A Horror so refined
Of freckled Human Nature[3] –
Of Deity – ashamed[4] –

It's such a common – Glory –
A Fisherman's – Degree[5] –   10
Redemption – Brittle Lady –
Be so – ashamed of Thee –

1862?, 1896

435

Much Madness is divinest Sense –
To a discerning Eye –
Much Sense – the starkest Madness –
'Tis the Majority
In this, as All, prevail –
Assent – and you are sane –
Demur – you're straightway dangerous –
And handled with a Chain –

1862?, 1890

441*

This is my letter to the World
That never wrote to Me –

---

[1] A cloth with long, soft pile.   [2] A thin, sheer cotton fabric.
[3] Ordinary human nature, with spots or imperfections.
[4] "For whosoever shall be ashamed of me and of my words, of him shall the Son of man be ashamed, when he shall come in his own glory," from Luke 9:26.
[5] To be like the Apostles (who were fishermen) is common and ordinary, according to the "Gentlewomen."
* Although Thomas Wentworth Higginson (1823–1911) and Mabel Loomis Todd (1856–1932) inserted this poem just after the table of contents and before the selections in *Poems* (1890), there is no evidence that Dickinson thought of it as an introduction to her poetry. Higginson also published it as one of fourteen poems in an article he wrote for the *Christian Union* in September 1890.

The simple News that Nature told –
With tender Majesty

Her Message is committed
To Hands I cannot see –
For love of Her – Sweet – countrymen –
Judge tenderly – of Me

1862?, 1890

448

This was a Poet – It is That[1]
Distills amazing sense
From ordinary Meanings –
And Attar[2] so immense

From the familiar species
That perished by the Door –
We wonder it was not Ourselves
Arrested it – before –

Of Pictures, the Discloser –
The Poet – it is He –   10
Entitles Us – by Contrast –
To ceaseless Poverty –

Of Portion – so unconscious –
The Robbing – could not harm –
Himself – to Him – a Fortune –
Exterior – to Time –

1862?, 1929

449

I died for Beauty – but was scarce
Adjusted in the Tomb
When One who died for Truth, was lain
In an adjoining Room –

He questioned softly "Why I failed"?[1]
"For Beauty", I replied –

---

[1] The poet is that person who distills amazing sense from ordinary meanings; an instance of Dickinson's elliptical style.
[2] Perfume made from crushed flower petals.
[1] Died.

"And I – for Truth – Themself are One –
We Bretheren, are", He said –

And so, as Kinsmen, met a Night –
We talked between the Rooms –   10
Until the Moss had reached our lips –
And covered up – our names –

1862?, 1890

465

I heard a Fly buzz – when I died –
The Stillness in the Room
Was like the Stillness in the Air –
Between the Heaves of Storm –

The Eyes around – had wrung them dry –
And Breaths were gathering firm
For that last Onset – when the King
Be witnessed – in the Room –

I willed my Keepsakes – Signed away
What portion of me be   10
Assignable – and then it was
There interposed a Fly –

With Blue – uncertain stumbling Buzz –
Between the light – and me –
And then the Windows failed – and then
I could not see to see –

1862?, 1896

511

If you were coming in the Fall,
I'd brush the Summer by
With half a smile, and half a spurn,
As Housewives do, a Fly.

If I could see you in a year,
I'd wind the months in balls –
And put them each in separate Drawers,
For fear the numbers fuse[1] –

---

[1] Would melt together.

If only Centuries, delayed,
I'd count them on my Hand,   10
Subtracting, till my fingers dropped
Into Van Dieman's Land.[2]

If certain, when this life was out –
That your's and mine, should be
I'd toss it yonder, like a Rind,
And take Eternity –

But, now, uncertain of the length
Of this, that is between,
It goads me, like the Goblin Bee –
That will not state – it's sting.   20

1862?, 1890

512

The Soul has Bandaged moments –
When too appalled to stir –
She feels some ghastly Fright come up
And stop to look at her –

Salute her – with long fingers –
Caress her freezing hair –
Sip, Goblin, from the very lips
The Lover – hovered – o'er –
Unworthy, that a thought so mean
Accost a Theme – so – fair –   10

The soul has moments of Escape –
When bursting all the doors –
She dances like a Bomb, abroad,
And swings upon the Hours,

As do the Bee – delirious borne –
Long Dungeoned from his Rose –
Touch Liberty – then know no more,
But Noon, and Paradise –

The Soul's retaken moments –
When, Felon led along,   20
With shackles on the plumed feet,
And staples,[1] in the Song,

---

[2] An early name for Tasmania.
[1] Rivets.

The Horror welcomes her, again,
These, are not brayed of Tongue –

1862?, 1945

526

To hear an Oriole sing
May be a common thing –
Or only a divine.

It is not of the Bird
Who sings the same, unheard,
As unto Crowd –

The Fashion of the Ear
Attireth that it hear
In Dun,[1] or fair –

So whether it be Rune,[2]   10
Or whether it be none
Is of within.

The "Tune is in the Tree – "
The Skeptic – showeth me –
"No Sir! In Thee!"

1862?, 1891

569

I reckon – when I count at all –
First – Poets – Then the Sun –
Then Summer – Then the Heaven of God –
And then – the List is done –

But, looking back – the First so seems
To Comprehend the Whole –
The Others look a needless Show –
So I write – Poets – All –

Their Summer – lasts a Solid Year –
They can afford a Sun   10
The East – would deem extravagant –
And if the Further Heaven –

---

[1] A color of low brilliance and saturation.
[2] A character of the alphabet used by Teutonic peoples from approximately the third century A.D.

Be Beautiful as they prepare
For Those who worship Them –
It is too difficult a Grace –
To justify the Dream –

1862?, 1929

579

I had been hungry, all the Years –
My Noon had Come – to dine –
I trembling drew the Table near –
And touched the Curious Wine –

'Twas this on Tables I had seen –
When turning, hungry, Home
I looked in Windows, for the Wealth
I could not hope – for Mine –

I did not know the ample Bread –
'Twas so unlike the Crumb   10
The Birds and I, had often shared
In Nature's – Dining Room –

The Plenty hurt me – 'twas so new –
Myself felt ill – and odd –
As Berry – of a Mountain Bush –
Transplanted – to the Road –

Nor was I hungry – so I found
That Hunger – was a way
Of Persons outside Windows –
The Entering – takes away –   20

1862?, 1891

585

I like to see it lap the Miles –
And lick the Valleys up –
And stop to feed itself at Tanks –
And then – prodigious step

Around a Pile of Mountains –
And supercilious peer
In Shanties – by the sides of Roads –
And then a Quarry pare

To fit it's sides
And crawl between   10
Complaining all the while
In horrid – hooting stanza –
Then chase itself down Hill –

And neigh like Boanerges[1] –
Then – prompter than a Star
Stop – docile and omnipotent
At it's[2] own stable door –

1862?, 1891

636

The Way I read a Letter's – this –
'Tis first – I lock the Door –
And push it with my fingers – next –
For transport it be sure –[1]

And then I go the furthest off
To counteract a knock –
Then draw my little Letter forth
And slowly pick the lock[2] –

Then – glancing narrow, at the Wall –
And narrow at the floor   10
For firm Conviction of a Mouse
Not exorcised before –

Peruse how infinite I am
To no one that You – know –
And sigh for lack of Heaven – but not
The Heaven God bestow –

1862?, 1891

640

I cannot live with You –
It would be Life –

---

[1] "Sons of Thunder" (Greek): originally a term describing the active evangelizing of the Apostles John and James; here, any loud preacher or orator.
[2] Dickinson consistently makes the error of using this contraction for a possessive.
[1] A line rich in ambiguity: on the most literal level, "to make sure the letter has been transported to her"; on an emotional level, "to be sure of the happiness contained inside."
[2] Open the letter very carefully.

And Life is over there –
Behind the Shelf

The Sexton[1] keeps the Key to –
Putting up
Our Life – His Porcelain –
Like a Cup –

Discarded of the Housewife –
Quaint – or Broke –   10
A newer Sevres[2] pleases –
Old Ones crack –

I could not die – with You –
For One must wait
To shut the Other's Gaze down –
You – could not –

And I – Could I stand by –
And see You – freeze –
Without my Right of Frost –
Death's privilege?   20

Nor could I rise – with You –
Because Your Face
Would put out Jesus' –
That New Grace

Glow plain – and foreign
On my homesick Eye –
Except that You than He
Shone closer by –

They'd judge Us – How –
For You – served Heaven[3] – You know,   30
Or sought to –
I could not –

Because You saturated Sight –
And I had no more Eyes
For sordid excellence
As Paradise

And were You lost, I would be –
Though My Name

---

[1] A church caretaker, bellringer, and gravedigger.   [2] Fine porcelain china made in Sèvres, France.
[3] The poem supposedly registers Dickinson's feelings about Rev. Charles Wadsworth, who had moved to California.

Rang loudest
On the Heavenly fame –   40

And were You – saved –
And I – condemned to be
Where You were not –
That self – were Hell to Me –

So We must meet apart –
You there – I – here –
With just the Door ajar
That Oceans are – and Prayer –
And that White Sustenance –
Despair –   50

1862?, 1890

650

Pain – has an Element of Blank –
It cannot recollect
When it begun – or if there were
A time when it was not –

It has no Future – but itself –
It's Infinite contain[1]
It's Past – enlightened to perceive
New Periods – of Pain.

1862?, 1890

657

I dwell in Possibility –
A fairer House than Prose –
More numerous of Windows –
Superior – for Doors –

Of Chambers as the Cedars –
Impregnable of Eye[1] –
And for an Everlasting Roof
The Gambrels[2] of the Sky –

---

[1] To make this line more conventional, Thomas Wentworth Higginson (1823–1911) and Mabel Loomis Todd (1856–1932) altered it in *Poems* (1890) to "Its infinite realms contain."
[1] Impenetrable to the eye.   [2] Angled roofs.

Of Visiters – the fairest –
For Occupation – This –
The spreading wide my narrow Hands
To gather Paradise –

1862?, 1929

712

Because I could not stop for Death –
He kindly stopped for me –
The Carriage held but just Ourselves –
And Immortality.

We slowly drove – He knew no haste
And I had put away
My labor and my leisure too,
For His Civility –

We passed the School, where Children strove
At Recess – in the Ring –
We passed the Fields of Gazing Grain –
We passed the Setting Sun –

Or rather – He passed Us –
The Dews drew quivering and chill –
For only Gossamer, my Gown –
My Tippet – only Tulle[1] –

We paused before a House that seemed
A Swelling of the Ground –
The Roof was scarcely visible –
The Cornice[2] – in the Ground –

Since then – 'tis Centuries – and yet
Feels shorter than the Day
I first surmised the Horses Heads
Were toward Eternity –

1863?, 1890

725

Where Thou art – that – is Home –
Cashmere – or Calvary[1] – the same –

---

[1] My cape or scarf, made only of a thin netlike fabric.   [2] Decorative molding just below a roof.
[1] A fine wool from goats in Kashmir and Tibet; the hill near Jerusalem where Christ was crucified.
Being with her lover is so paramount that these things and everything else become the same to the
speaker.

Degree – or Shame –
I scarce esteem Location's Name –
So I may Come –

What Thou dost – is Delight –
Bondage as Play – be sweet –
Imprisonment – Content –
And Sentence – Sacrament –
Just We two – meet –

Where Thou art not – is Wo –
Tho' Bands of Spices – row –
What Thou dost not – Despair –
Tho' Gabriel – praise me – Sir –

1863?, 1929

732

She rose to His Requirement – dropt
The Playthings of Her Life
To take the honorable Work
Of Woman, and of Wife –

If ought[1] She missed in Her new Day,
Of Amplitude, or Awe –
Or first Prospective – Or the Gold
In using, wear away,

It lay unmentioned – as the Sea
Develope Pearl, and Weed,
But only to Himself – be known
The Fathoms they abide[2] –

1863?, 1890

744

Remorse – is Memory – awake –
Her Parties all astir –
A Presence of Departed Acts –
At window – and at Door –

It's Past – set down before the Soul
And lighted with a Match –

---

[1] Aught, anything.   [2] Only the sea knows how deep its creatures live.

Perusal – to facilitate –
And help Belief to stretch –

Remorse is cureless – the Disease
Not even God – can heal –   10
For 'tis His institution – and
The Adequate of Hell –

1863?, 1891

745

Renunciation – is a piercing Virtue –
The letting go
A Presence – for an Expectation –
Not now –
The putting out of Eyes –
Just Sunrise –
Lest Day –
Day's Great Progenitor[1] –
Outvie
Renunciation – is the Choosing   10
Against itself –
Itself to justify
Unto itself –
When larger function –
Make that appear –
Smaller – that Covered Vision – Here –

1863?, 1929

754

My Life had stood – a Loaded Gun –
In Corners – till a Day
The Owner passed – identified –
And carried Me away –

And now We roam in Sovreign Woods –
And now We hunt the Doe –
And every time I speak for Him –
The Mountains straight reply –

And do I smile, such cordial light
Upon the Valley glow –   10

---

[1] One (or something) that brings forth; "Sunrise" is the day's "Great Progenitor."

It is as a Vesuvian face[1]
Had let it's pleasure through –

And when at Night – Our good Day done –
I guard My Master's Head –
'Tis better than the Eider-Duck's
Deep[2] Pillow – to have shared –

To foe of His – I'm deadly foe –
None stir the second time –
On whom I lay a Yellow Eye[3] –
Or an emphatic Thumb –   20

Though I than He – may longer live
He longer must – than I –
For I have but the power to kill,
Without – the power to die –

1863?, 1929

765

You constituted Time –
I deemed Eternity
A Revelation of Yourself –
'Twas therefore Deity

The Absolute – removed
The Relative away –
That I unto Himself adjust
My slow idolatry –

1863?, 1945

771

None can experience stint
Who Bounty – have not known –
The fact of Famine – could not be
Except for Fact of Corn –

Want – is a meagre Art
Acquired by Reverse –

[1] Capable of erupting like Italy's Mt. Vesuvius.   [2] Downy.
[3] A metaphor for a hunter's deadly eye; similarly, an "emphatic Thumb" rubs things out.

The Poverty that was not Wealth –
Cannot be Indigence

1863?, 1945

870

Finding is the first Act
The second, loss,
Third, Expedition for
The "Golden Fleece"[1]

Fourth, no Discovery –
Fifth, no Crew –
Finally, no Golden Fleece –
Jason – sham – too.

1864?, 1945

986*

A narrow Fellow in the Grass
Occasionally rides –
You may have met Him – did you not
His notice sudden is –

The Grass divides as with a Comb –
A spotted shaft is seen –
And then it closes at your feet –
And opens further on –

He likes a Boggy Acre –
A Floor too cool for Corn –   10
Yet when a Boy, and Barefoot –
I more than once at Noon
Have passed, I thought, a Whip lash
Unbraiding in the Sun
When stooping to secure it
It wrinkled, and was gone –

Several of Nature's People
I know, and they know me –

[1] According to Greek myth, the Argonaut Jason was sent in quest of the Golden Fleece, which was placed by the king of Colchis in a sacred grove and guarded by a dragon. The poem reports an escalating series of let-downs until, finally, there is no Golden Fleece and the noble Jason is termed a sham.

* Published as "The Snake" in the *Springfield Daily Republican* on February 14, 1866.

I feel for them a transport
Of cordiality –   20

But never met this Fellow
Attended, or alone
Without a tighter breathing
And Zero at the Bone –

1865?, 1866

997

Crumbling is not an instant's Act
A fundamental pause
Delapidation's processes
Are organized Decays.

'Tis first a Cobweb on the Soul
A Cuticle[1] of Dust
A Borer in the Axis[2]
An Elemental Rust –

Ruin is formal – Devils work
Consecutive and slow –   10
Fail in an instant, no man did
Slipping – is Crashe's law.[3]

1865?, 1945

1068

Further in Summer than the Birds
Pathetic from the Grass
A minor Nation celebrates
It's unobtrusive Mass.

No Ordinance[1] be seen
So gradual the Grace
A pensive Custom it becomes
Enlarging Loneliness.

---

[1] A thin, dead covering.   [2] Something that makes a small hole at the center.
[3] According to the critic Charles Anderson, Dickinson may have made up a person named Crashe, and thus "Crashe's law" (like Newton's law), to give mock authority to her point about "Crumbling" being a slow process. If so, "Crashe" is ironic for a process so prolonged and "formal."
[1] A prescribed practice that, in the context of "Mass" and "Grace," takes on the connotation of religious ritual.

Antiquest[2] felt at Noon
When August burning low   10
Arise this spectral Canticle[3]
Repose to typify

Remit as yet no Grace
No Furrow on the Glow
Yet a Druidic[4] Difference
Enhances Nature now

1866?, 1891

1072

Title divine – is mine!
The Wife – without the Sign!
Acute Degree – conferred on me –
Empress of Calvary![1]
Royal – all but the Crown!
Betrothed – without the swoon
God sends us Women –
When you – hold – Garnet to Garnet –
Gold – to Gold –
Born – Bridalled – Shrouded –   10
In a Day –
"My Husband" – women say –
Stroking the Melody –
Is *this* – the way?

1862?, 1924

1078

The Bustle in a House
The Morning after Death
Is solemnest of industries
Enacted upon Earth –

The Sweeping up the Heart
And putting Love away
We shall not want to use again
Until Eternity.

1866?, 1890

---

[2] Most antique; in one version of the poem Dickinson had "antiquer."
[3] A song or hymn; a biblical song of praise.
[4] The Druids were pre-Christian, Celtic nature worshipers.
[1] The hill near Jerusalem on which Christ was crucified. Dickinson evokes the idea of suffering in a situation that yields the closeness but not the fact of marriage.

1082

Revolution is the Pod
Systems rattle from
When the Winds of Will are stirred
Excellent is Bloom

But except it's Russet Base[1]
Every Summer be
The Entomber of itself,
So of Liberty –

Left inactive on the Stalk
All it's Purple[2] fled   10
Revolution shakes it for
Test if it be dead.

1866?, 1929

1100*

The last Night that She lived
It was a Common Night
Except the Dying – this to Us
Made Nature different

We noticed smallest things –
Things overlooked before
By this great light upon our Minds
Italicized – as 'twere.

As We went out and in
Between Her final Room   10
And Rooms where Those to be alive
Tomorrow were, a Blame

That Others could exist
While She must finish quite
A Jealousy for Her arose
So nearly infinite –

We waited while She passed –
It was a narrow time –

---

[1] Except for its red-brown base (associated with pods and seeds and hence the possibility of renewed life).
[2] The traditional color of royalty, nobility.
* Written about the daughter of Mr. and Mrs. L. M. Hills, Laura Dickey, who died at her parents' home in Amherst on May 3, 1866. The Hills were the Dickinsons' neighbors.

Too jostled were Our Souls to speak
At length the notice came.   20

She mentioned, and forgot –
Then lightly as a Reed
Bent to the Water, struggled scarce –
Consented, and was dead –

And We – We placed the Hair –
And drew the Head erect –
And then as awful leisure was
Belief to regulate –

1866?, 1890

1129

Tell all the Truth but tell it slant –
Success in Circuit lies
Too bright for our infirm Delight
The Truth's superb surprise
As Lightning to the Children eased
With explanation kind
The Truth must dazzle gradually
Or every man be blind –

1868?, 1945

1271

September's Baccalaureate[1]
A combination is
Of Crickets – Crows – and Retrospects
And a dissembling Breeze

That hints without assuming –
An Innuendo sear[2]
That makes the Heart put up it's Fun
And turn Philosopher.

1873?, 1892

---

[1] College degree.
[2] Withered, dried up. Although in early printings of the poem the spelling was changed to "sere," according to Thomas Johnson, Dickinson's spelling is correct.

1317*

Abraham to kill him
Was distinctly told –
Isaac was an Urchin –
Abraham was old –

Not a hesitation –
Abraham complied –
Flattered by Obeisance
Tyranny[1] demurred –

Isaac – to his children
Lived to tell the tale –   10
Moral – with a Mastiff[2]
Manners may prevail.

                                        1874?, 1945

1331

Wonder – is not precisely Knowing
And not precisely Knowing not –
A beautiful but bleak condition
He has not lived who has not felt –

Suspense – is his maturer Sister –
Whether Adult Delight is Pain
Or of itself a new misgiving –
This is the Gnat that mangles men[1] –

                                        1874?, 1945

1333

A little Madness in the Spring
Is wholesome even for the King,
But God be with the Clown –

---

* A stylized narrative based on the story of the biblical patriarchs Abraham and Isaac in Genesis 22, in which God tests Abraham's faith by asking him to sacrifice his only son, Isaac.
[1] God.   [2] A large, powerful breed of dog.
[1] The tiny question or consideration that confuses human beings.

Who ponders this tremendous scene –
This whole Experiment of Green –
As if it were his own!

1875?, 1914

1463

A Route of Evanescence[1]
With a revolving Wheel –
A Resonance of Emerald –
A Rush of Cochineal[2] –
And every Blossom on the Bush
Adjusts it's tumbled Head –
The mail from Tunis,[3] probably,
An easy Morning's Ride –

1879?, 1891

1540

As imperceptibly as Grief
The Summer lapsed away –
Too imperceptible at last
To seem like Perfidy[1] –
A Quietness distilled
As Twilight long begun,
Or Nature spending with herself
Sequestered Afternoon –
The Dusk drew earlier in –
The Morning foreign shone –   10
A courteous, yet harrowing Grace,
As Guest, that would be gone –
And thus, without a Wing
Or service of a Keel[2]
Our Summer made her light escape
Into the Beautiful.

1865 – 1882, 1891

1624

Apparently with no surprise
To any happy Flower

---

[1] Vanishing from sight. This poem describes a hummingbird.   [2] A red dye.   [3] A city in Tunisia.
[1] A violation of faith.   [2] Without the use of a ship.

The Frost beheads it at it's play –
In accidental power –
The blonde Assassin passes on –
The Sun proceeds unmoved
To measure off another Day
For an Approving God.

1884?, 1890

1670

In Winter in my Room
I came upon a Worm
Pink lank and warm
But as he was a worm
And worms presume
Not quite with him at home
Secured him by a string
To something neighboring
And went along.

A Trifle afterward   10
A thing occurred
I'd not believe it if I heard
But state with creeping blood
A snake with mottles rare
Surveyed my chamber floor
In feature as the worm before
But ringed with power
The very string with which
I tied him – too
When he was mean and new   20
That string was there –

I shrank – "How fair you are"!
Propitiation's claw[1] –
"Afraid he hissed
Of me"?
"No cordiality" –
He fathomed me –
Then to a Rhythm *Slim*[2]
Secreted in his Form
As Patterns swim   30
Projected him.[3]

That time I flew
Both eyes his way

---

[1] The above statement was meant to propitiate, or appease, the snake.   [2] Cunning, sly.
[3] He projected himself, glided toward me.

Lest he pursue
Nor ever ceased to run
Till in a distant Town
Towns on from mine
I set me down
This was a dream –

1914

1732

My life closed twice before its close;
It yet remains to see
If Immortality unveil
A third event to me,

So huge, so hopeless to conceive
As these that twice befel.
Parting is all we know of heaven,
And all we need of hell.

1896

1755

To make a prairie it takes a clover and one bee,
One clover, and a bee,
And revery.
The revery alone will do,
If bees are few.

1896

1760

Elysium[1] is as far as to
The very nearest Room
If in that Room a Friend await
Felicity or Doom –

What fortitude the Soul contains,
That it can so endure
The accent of a coming Foot –
The opening of a Door –

1882?, 1890

---

[1] According to Greek myth, the home of the virtuous after death; here, Paradise or happiness.

LETTER TO THOMAS WENTWORTH HIGGINSON*

25 April 1862

Mr. Higginson,

Your kindness claimed earlier gratitude – but I was ill – and write today, from my pillow.

Thank you for the surgery[1] – it was not so painful as I supposed. I bring you others[2] – as you ask – though they might not differ –

While my thought is undressed – I can make the distinction, but when I put them in the Gown – they look alike, and numb.

You asked how old I was? I made no verse – but one or two – until this winter – Sir –

I had a terror – since September – I could tell to none – and so I sing, as the Boy does by the Burying Ground – because I am afraid – You inquire my Books – For Poets – I have Keats – and Mr and Mrs Browning. For Prose – Mr Ruskin –Sir Thomas Browne – and the Revelations.[3] I went to school – but in your manner of the phrase – had no education. When a little Girl, I had a friend, who taught me Immortality – but venturing too near, himself – he never returned – Soon after, my Tutor,[4] died – and for several years, my Lexicon – was my only companion –Then I found one more – but he was not contented I be his scholar – so he left the Land.[5]

You ask of my Companions Hills – Sir – and the Sundown – and a Dog – large as myself, that my Father bought me – They are better than Beings – because they know – but do not tell – and the noise in the Pool, at Noon – excels my Piano. I have a Brother and Sister – My Mother does not care for thought – and Father, too busy with his Briefs[6] – to notice what we do – He buys me many Books – but begs me not to read them – because he fears they joggle the Mind. They are religious – except me – and address an Eclipse, every morning – whom they call their "Father." But I fear my story fatigues you – I would like to learn – Could you tell me how to grow – or is it unconveyed – like Melody – or Witchcraft?

You speak of Mr Whitman – I never read his Book[7] – but was told that he was disgraceful –

I read Miss Prescott's "Circumstance,"[8] but it followed me, in the Dark – so I avoided her –

---

* Dickinson wrote a letter to the editor Thomas Wentworth Higginson (1823–1911) on April 15, 1862, after reading the practical advice to beginning writers offered in his "Letter to a Young Contributor" in the April 1862 issue of the *Atlantic Monthly*. She enclosed a card with her signature along with four poems she asked him to judge. After Higginson replied, Dickinson wrote this letter; the two became close friends.

[1] Probably "surgery" on her poems, suggested revisions.   [2] I send you additional poems.

[3] The English romantic poet John Keats (1795–1821); the English poets Elizabeth Barrett Browning (1806–1861) and Robert Browning (1812–1889); John Ruskin (1819–1900), an English essayist and art critic; Browne (1606–1682), an English physician and notable author; the final book of the New Testament.

[4] Dickinson's "friend" and "Tutor" may have been Benjamin Franklin Newton (1821–1853), who studied law in her father's office in the 1840s and died of consumption.

[5] Probably Rev. Charles Wadsworth, who left Philadelphia in April 1862 to be pastor of a church in California.

[6] His legal work.

[7] Walt Whitman's *Leaves of Grass* (1855), which was criticized because of the sexual frankness of some of its poems.

[8] A story of bloodshed and atrocity by Harriet Prescott Spofford (1835–1921) that appeared in the *Atlantic Monthly* in May 1860; Dickinson says that because it haunted her imagination, she avoided that author.

Two Editors[9] of Journals came to my Father's House, this winter – and asked me for my Mind – and when I asked them "Why," they said I was penurious – and they, would use it for the World –

I could not weigh myself – Myself –

My size felt small – to me – I read your Chapters in the Atlantic – and experienced honor for you – I was sure you would not reject a confiding question –

Is this – Sir – what you asked me to tell you?

Your friend,
E – Dickinson.
1862, 1958

LETTER TO SUSAN GILBERT DICKINSON*

early October 1883

Dear Sue –

The Vision of Immortal Life has been fulfilled –[1]

How simply at the last the Fathom comes! The Passenger and not the Sea, we find surprises us –

Gilbert rejoiced in Secrets –

His Life was panting with them – With what menace of Light he cried "Dont tell, Aunt Emily"! Now my ascended Playmate must instruct *me*. Show us, prattling Preceptor, but the way to thee!

He knew no niggard moment – His Life was full of Boon – The Playthings of the Dervish were not so wild as his –

No crescent was this Creature[2] – He traveled from the Full –

Such soar, but never set –

I see him in the Star, and meet his sweet velocity in everything that flies – His Life was like the Bugle, which winds itself away, his Elegy an echo – his Requiem ecstasy –

Dawn and Meridian in one.[3]

Wherefore would he wait, wronged only of Night, which he left for us –

Without a speculation, our little Ajax[4] spans the whole –

Pass to thy Rendezvous of Light,
Pangless except for us –

---

[9] Probably Dr. Joseph Gilbert Holland (1819–1881) and Samuel Bowles (1826–1878), both associated with the *Springfield Daily Republican,* which had published a few of Dickinson's poems anonymously.

* Emily Dickinson's sister-in-law and friend, the wife of Austin Dickinson.

[1] Gilbert, the youngest child of Susan and Austin Dickinson, died of typhoid fever on October 5, 1883. According to Thomas Johnson and Theodora Ward, no death "shocked and grieved" Dickinson more than that of her young nephew.

[2] There was nothing partial (like the crescent of a new moon) about Gilbert; his life was "Full."

[3] He was like dawn and noon rolled into one.

[4] According to Greek myth, a hero known for his bravery and strength.

Who slowly ford the Mystery
Which thou hast leaped across!

Emily.
1883, 1958

Sidney Lanier
(1842–1881)

Studies of Sidney Lanier have tended to neglect his writing to focus on his life as a poet, perhaps because he fits the role of tragic artist so well. He fought as a Confederate soldier, endured imprisonment as a prisoner of war, and became ill with tuberculosis while in prison. With a series of jobs during Reconstruction, he strove to support a wife and four children, wrote feverishly at night, and died young of tuberculosis in 1881 with his projected works unfinished. In the midst of his struggles, Lanier drove himself to work at his two passions, music and poetry.

Lanier's early life gives no hint of his later struggles. Born in Macon, Georgia, in 1842, he grew up in an affluent home, studied the flute, and entered Oglethorpe University in nearby Milledgeville in 1857. The outbreak of the Civil War ended his leisurely life. After arduous years of battle and a four-month imprisonment, Lanier returned home, walking the entire distance to Macon from the Union prison camp Point Lookout, Maryland. He worked in his father's law office and in 1867 married Mary Day and published his only novel, *Tiger-Lilies,* which drew on his war experiences and confirmed his idea of being a writer.

In 1873 Lanier settled with his wife and three young children in Baltimore, where he played first flute for the Peabody Orchestra. He also lectured on English dramatists (the two-volume *Shakespeare and His Forerunners* was published posthumously in 1902) and taught briefly at Johns Hopkins University, but much of his energy went into a series of jobs that were necessary to support his family. Despite his difficulties, however, Lanier worked diligently at his poetry. Encouraged by the reception of his first published poem, "Corn," in *Lippincott's Magazine* in 1875, he wrote "Cantata" for the Philadelphia centennial in 1876, and his volume *Poems* was published the following year. In addition to writing poetry Lanier developed an elaborate theory to unite poetic form and musical notation, which was published as *The Science of English Verse* in 1880. Although his efforts to imitate musical patterns with the repetition of words and refrains could be awkward, the effectiveness of such poems as "The Song of the Chattahoochee" (1877) and "The Marshes of Glynn" (1878) comes from Lanier's conviction that music and poetry follow deep and identical rules of order.

Responses to Lanier's work have ranged from the enthusiasm of Walt Whitman and the measured approval of Harriet Monroe, the founder of *Poetry* magazine, to the virtual hostility of the poet and critic Allen Tate, who overlooked the agrarian vision in Lanier's verse out of disapproval for its frequent sentimentality and pathos. Despite the focus of such judgments on Lanier's poetry, the vicissitudes of his career still enthrall the imagination, as evidenced by Andrew Hudgins's *After the Lost War* (1988), a book of poems that tells the story of Lanier's life in his own voice. Hudgins's biographical meditation bears out the suggestion of one early critic that Lanier's greatest contribution to American letters might be the way in which he embodied "the poetic temperament."

Suggested Readings: *Tiger-Lilies: A Novel,* 1867, rpt. 1969. *The English Novel,* 1897. *The Centennial Edition of the Works of Sidney Lanier,* 10 vols., ed. C. R. Anderson, 1945. *Sidney Lanier: Poems and Letters,* ed. Charles R. Anderson, 1969. A. H. Stark, *Sidney Lanier: A Biographical and Critical Study,* 1933, rpt. 1964. E. W. Parks, *Sidney Lanier: The Man, The Poet, The Critic,* 1968. J. De Bellis, *Sidney Lanier,* 1972. J. S. Gabin, *A Living Minstrelsy: The Poetry and Music of Sidney Lanier,* 1985.

Text Used: *Poems of Sidney Lanier, Edited by His Wife,* ed. M. D. Lanier, 1896.

THE RAVEN DAYS*

Our hearths are gone out and our hearts are broken,
  And but the ghosts of homes to us remain,
And ghastly eyes and hollow sighs give token
  From friend to friend of an unspoken pain.

O Raven days, dark Raven days of sorrow,[1]
  Bring to us in your whetted ivory beaks
Some sign out of the far land of To-morrow,
  Some strip of sea-green dawn, some orange streaks.

Yet float in dusky files, forever croaking.
  Ye chill our manhood with your dreary shade.   10
Dumb in the dark, not even God invoking,
  We lie in chains, too weak to be afraid.

O Raven days, dark Raven days of sorrow,
  Will ever any warm light come again?
Will ever the lit mountains of To-morrow
  Begin to gleam athwart the mournful plain?

1868

SONG OF THE CHATTAHOOCHEE†

Out of the hills of Habersham,[1]
Down the valleys of Hall,[2]

---

* First published in *Scott's Monthly* (1868).   [1] The Reconstruction period, following the Civil War.
  † Some evidence suggests that this poem was first published in *Scott's Magazine* (1877), but according to Lanier scholar Charles R. Anderson, no such periodical has been found for that year; the first verified publication was in the *Independent* (1883). The Chattahoochee River is in Northeast Georgia.
  [1] Habersham County, Georgia, the source of the Chattahoochee River.
  [2] A county in Georgia through which the river flows.

I hurry amain³ to reach the plain,
Run the rapid and leap the fall,
Split at the rock and together again,
Accept my bed, or narrow or wide,
And flee from folly on every side
With a lover's pain to attain the plain
    Far from the hills of Habersham,
    Far from the valleys of Hall.   10

All down the hills of Habersham,
    All through the valleys of Hall,
The rushes cried *Abide, abide,*
The willful waterweeds held me thrall,
The laving laurel turned my tide,
The ferns and the fondling grass said *Stay,*
The dewberry dipped for to work delay,
And the little reeds sighed *Abide, abide,*
    Here in the hills of Habersham,
    Here in the valleys of Hall.   20

High o'er the hills of Habersham,
    Veiling the valleys of Hall,
The hickory told me manifold
Fair tales of shade, the poplar tall
Wrought me her shadowy self to hold,
The chestnut, the oak, the walnut, the pine,
Overleaning, with flickering meaning and sign,
Said *Pass not, so cold, these manifold*
    Deep shades of the hills of Habersham,
    These glades in the valleys of Hall.   30

And oft in the hills of Habersham,
    And oft in the valleys of Hall,
The white quartz shone, and the smooth brook-stone
Did bar me of passage with friendly brawl,⁴
And many a luminous jewel lone
—Crystals clear or a-cloud with mist,
Ruby, garnet and amethyst—
Made lures with the lights of streaming stone
    In the clefts of the hills of Habersham,
    In the beds of the valleys of Hall.   40

But oh, not the hills of Habersham,
    And oh, not the valleys of Hall
Avail: I am fain⁵ for to water the plain.
Downward the voices of Duty call—
Downward, to toil and be mixed with the main,⁶

---

³ At full speed; the voice in the poem is that of the Chattahoochee River, which seeks to water the crops and flowers of the plain.
⁴ The river does not have smooth passage but must churn its way through rocks and colorful stones.
⁵ Ready.   ⁶ The sea.

The dry fields burn, and the mills are to turn,
And a myriad flowers mortally yearn,
And the lordly main from beyond the plain
   Calls o'er the hills of Habersham,
   Calls through the valleys of Hall.   50

                                             1877?, 1883

MARSH SONG—AT SUNSET*

Over the monstrous shambling sea,
   Over the Caliban sea,[1]
Bright Ariel-cloud,[2] thou lingerest:
Oh wait, oh wait, in the warm red West,—
   Thy Prospero[3] I'll be.

Over the humped and fishy sea,
   Over the Caliban sea
O cloud in the West, like a thought in the heart
Of pardon, loose thy wing, and start,
   And do a grace for me.   10

Over the huge and huddling sea,
   Over the Caliban sea,
Bring hither my brother Antonio,[4]—Man,—
My injurer: night breaks the ban:
   Brother, I pardon thee.

                                             1880?, 1882

Emma Lazarus
(1849–1887)

Many readers who have never heard of Emma Lazarus are familiar with two lines of her most famous poem, "The New Colossus" (1883): "Give me your tired, your poor, / Your huddled masses yearning to breathe free." Inscribed on the base of the Statue of Liberty,

---

* First published posthumously in *Our Continent* (1882); apparently intended for inclusion in Lanier's projected volume, "Hymns of the Marshes."

[1] A monstrous sea: in Shakespeare's *The Tempest,* Caliban is a monster, son of the witch Sycorax. All the allusions here are to *The Tempest.*

[2] A good spirit: Ariel, formerly imprisoned by Sycorax, was now released by the magic of Prospero, the duke of Milan.

[3] Ousted from his throne by his brother, Antonio, Prospero lives on a lonely island with his daughter, Miranda. His magical powers help bring the play to a compassionate and happy ending.

[4] Antonio is here equated with humankind, and the poem concludes with the speaker offering both individual and general forgiveness.

this sonnet epitomizes the spirit of Lazarus's writing. Her most important work consistently supports the dignity of the poor and downtrodden. Specifically, her strongest and most passionate poetry protests the mistreatment of her people, the Jews.

Born to a cultured and cosmopolitan New York family in 1849, Lazarus showed in her teens a talent for languages, learning German, French, and Italian with enviable skill. She read voraciously the work of such English writers as Shakespeare, Keats, Shelley, and Tennyson and that of the Americans Ralph Waldo Emerson and Henry Wadsworth Longfellow. She soon began writing poetry and published her first book of verse, *Poems and Translations* (1860), when she was seventeen. Most of these early poems cultivate a popular romantic spirit, using conventional poetic forms and diction. Lazarus sent a copy of her first book to Emerson, and despite the flowery quality of some of the poems, he became a friend and occasional mentor. In 1871 she published a second volume, *Admetus and Other Poems,* which she dedicated to Emerson. She turned to fiction in 1874 with the novel *Alide,* based on the life of the German writer Johann Wolfgang von Goethe. Lazarus's interest in German romantic literature is also attested by her excellent translation of the *Poems and Ballads* of Heinrich Heine in 1881.

Lazarus's discovery of her need to write about Jewish themes came about when she became indignantly aware of the Russian pogroms of the early 1880s and the persecution of Jews in Europe. The critic E. C. Stedman helped Lazarus discover her voice at this time by urging her to write about her Jewish heritage. Once she realized the extent of anti-Semitic purges in Germany and Russia, she became a poet with a sacred cause and wrote both poetry and prose about the injustices meted out to her people. An advocate of the establishment of a Jewish state in Palestine, she organized relief work for the persecuted Jews. *Songs of a Semite,* published in 1882, reflects Lazarus's Jewish themes in poems such as "The Banner of the Jew" and in the verse drama "The Dance to Death," which is based on the hysterical accusation that Jews had poisoned wells and brought on the Black Death in Thuringia, in central Germany, during the twelfth century.

Although she wrote eloquently about the mistreatment of Jews, Lazarus worked with other subjects and forms as well. Not only did she translate the work of Heine but also that of the German dramatist and poet Friedrich von Schiller, the French writers Victor Hugo and Alexandre Dumas père, and several medieval Hebrew poets. She also wrote essays on American writers and on socialism. A few months before her death in 1887, she published "By the Waters of Babylon," a series of prose poems, in the *Century Illustrated Monthly Magazine.* In short, Lazarus's work reflects the broad interests of an intelligent student of languages and of history who found her most powerful voice in championing her own rich heritage.

Suggested Readings: *Songs of a Semite,* 1882, rpt. 1966. *Poems,* 1889. H. E. Jacobs, *The World of Emma Lazarus,* 1949. E. Merriam, *Emma Lazarus: Woman With a Torch,* 1956. C. Angoff, *Emma Lazarus: Poet, Jewish Activist, Pioneer Zionist,* 1979. D. Vogel, *Emma Lazarus,* 1980.

Text Used: "In the Jewish Synagogue at Newport": *Emma Lazarus: Selections From Her Poetry and Prose,* ed. M. U. Schappes, 1967. "The New Colossus": *The Poems of Emma Lazarus,* Vol. I, 1888. "1492": *The Poems of Emma Lazarus,* Vol. II, 1888.

IN THE JEWISH SYNAGOGUE AT NEWPORT*

Here, where the noises of the busy town,
The ocean's plunge and roar can enter not,

---

* First published in *Poems and Translations* (1867). The poem has interesting similarities to "The Jewish Cemetery at Newport" (1854), by Henry Wadsworth Longfellow, a poet Lazarus admired.

We stand and gaze around with tearful awe,
　　And muse upon the consecrated spot.

No signs of life are here: the very prayers
　　Inscribed around are in a language dead;[1]
The light of the "perpetual lamp" is spent
　　That an undying radiance was to shed.

What prayers were in this temple offered up,
　　Wrung from sad hearts that knew no joy on earth,　　　　10
By these lone exiles of a thousand years,
　　From the fair sunrise land that gave them birth!

Now as we gaze, in this new world of light,
　　Upon this relic of the days of old,
The present vanishes, and tropic bloom
　　And Eastern towns and temples we behold.

Again we see the patriarch with his flocks,
　　The purple seas, the hot blue sky o'erhead,
The slaves of Egypt,—omens, mysteries,—
　　Dark fleeing hosts by flaming angels led.　　　　20

A wondrous light upon a sky-kissed mount,
　　A man[2] who reads Jehovah's written law,
'Midst blinding glory and effulgence rare,
　　Unto a people prone with reverent awe.

The pride of luxury's barbaric pomp,
　　In the rich court of royal Solomon[3]—
Alas! we wake: one scene alone remains,—
　　The exiles by the streams of Babylon.[4]

Our softened voices send us back again
　　But mournful echoes through the empty hall;　　　　30
Our footsteps have a strange, unnatural sound,
　　And with unwonted gentleness they fall.

The weary ones, the sad, the suffering,
　　All found their comfort in the holy place,
And children's gladness and men's gratitude
　　Took voice and mingled in the chant of praise.

The funeral and the marriage, now, alas!
　　We know not which is sadder to recall;
For youth and happiness have followed age,
　　And green grass lieth gently over all.　　　　40

[1] Hebrew.　　[2] Moses.
[3] The proverbial wise king of ancient Israel, son and successor of King David.
[4] An ancient city of Mesopotamia, on the Euphrates River, where the Hebrews were exiled.

And still the sacred shrine is holy yet,
  With its lone floors where reverent feet once trod.
Take off your shoes as by the burning bush,
  Before the mystery of death and God.

1867

THE NEW COLOSSUS*

Not like the brazen giant of Greek fame,[1]
With conquering limbs astride from land to land;
Here at our sea-washed, sunset gates shall stand
A mighty woman with a torch, whose flame
Is the imprisoned lightning, and her name
Mother of Exiles. From her beacon-hand
Glows world-wide welcome; her mild eyes command
The air-bridged harbor that twin cities[2] frame.
"Keep, ancient lands, your storied pomp!" cries she
With silent lips. "Give me your tired, your poor,   10
Your huddled masses yearning to breathe free,
The wretched refuse of your teeming shore.
Send these, the homeless, tempest-tost to me,
I lift my lamp beside the golden door!"

1883

1492

Thou two-faced year,[1] Mother of Change and Fate,
Didst weep when Spain cast forth with flaming sword,
The children of the prophets of the Lord,
Prince, priest, and people, spurned by zealot hate.
Hounded from sea to sea, from state to state,
The West refused them, and the East abhorred.
No anchorage the known world could afford,
Close-locked was every port, barred every gate.

---

* This sonnet is inscribed on the base of the Statue of Liberty in New York harbor. The "old" Colossus, the Colossus of Rhodes, was a gigantic statue of the Greek god Apollo erected at the entrance to the harbor at Rhodes about 280 B.C. to celebrate a military victory.

[1] In these opening lines Lazarus establishes the difference between the Colossus at Rhodes and the Statue of Liberty, the "new" Colossus, designed by the French sculptor Frederic Auguste Bartholdi (1834–1904) and originally named "Liberty Enlightening the World." It was presented to the United States by the Franco-American Union to commemorate the American Revolution; formally dedicated in 1886, it became a national monument in 1924.

[2] The closest cities to Liberty Island, where the statue is located, are New York City (specifically Brooklyn), on the New York side, and Jersey City, on the New Jersey side.

[1] The "two-faced" year 1492 wept at the persecution of Jews in Spain, then smiled at the unveiling of a "virgin world," America, in which ancient prejudice had no reality.

Then smiling, thou unveil'dst, O two-faced year,
A virgin world where doors of sunset part,   10
Saying, "Ho, all who weary, enter here!
There falls each ancient barrier that the art
Of race or creed or rank devised, to rear
Grim bulwarked hatred between heart and heart!"

1883

Typically fleeing near-starvation in Europe, immigrants spent their last funds to book passage on the decks of ships like the S.S. Pennland, *photographed in 1893.*

Paul Laurence Dunbar
(1872–1906)

Paul Laurence Dunbar was born in Dayton, Ohio, in 1872 to parents who had been slaves in Kentucky. The only African American in his class, he excelled as a student in the Dayton public schools and went on to become the editor of his high school student magazine and to write the school song for his graduation. After finishing high school, however, Dunbar found his opportunities severely limited. Financially unable to attend college, he worked at a number of menial positions. He became an elevator operator for several months, then took a temporary job, arranged for him by Frederick Douglass, in the Haiti building at the 1894 Chicago World's Fair. During this period of instability Dunbar began to write poetry.

Oak and Ivy (1893) and *Majors and Minors* (1895)—both published at his own expense—were Dunbar's first collections of verse. William Dean Howells's favorable full-page review of *Majors and Minors* in *Harper's Weekly* gave Dunbar sudden recognition and launched his career as a writer. He became very popular, in demand for readings of his work as well as for lectures. In 1896 he published *Lyrics of Lowly Life,* a compilation of the best pieces from his first two books along with some newer poems. This collection helped to secure his growing reputation, and he traveled as far as England in 1897 to read his poetry. Upon Dunbar's return from England in 1898, he married Alice Ruth Moore and accepted a position as an assistant in the Library of Congress.

Unfortunately, the hectic lifestyle that accompanied Dunbar's success took its toll on the young writer. By 1899 he had contracted tuberculosis; he spent one winter in Colorado in the hope that his health would improve, but it began to fail rapidly. No longer able to make public appearances, he returned to Dayton and made a stubborn effort to go on writing. His marriage also deteriorated at this time; after only four years Dunbar and his wife separated. He died at the age of thirty-three in 1906.

Although Dunbar has achieved some recognition for his work in standard, or "literary," English (a recognition he definitely wanted), he has been more highly acclaimed for his dialect verse. He was popular during a time when literary regionalism and the use of dialect were much in fashion, and his acquaintance with African-American speech patterns and customs helped him to depict aspects of African-American life with a grace that appealed to many readers. Because such writers as Thomas Nelson Page, Robert Burns, and James Whitcomb Riley influenced Dunbar's work, some of his poetry has a sentimental flavor. Dunbar also wrote some conventional short fiction and four novels, the most interesting of which, *The Sport of the Gods* (1902), concerns a southern African-American family in Harlem. His primary gift, however, was lyric, not narrative: in the rhythms of his dialect poems and in the more intense rhetoric of his sonnets is heard a voice both playful and serious, both popular and filled with the anguish of our history.

Suggested Readings: *Oak and Ivy,* 1893. *Lyrics of Lowly Life,* 1896. *The Uncalled: A Novel,* 1898, rpt. 1972. *Lyrics of the Hearthside,* 1899, rpt. 1988. *Complete Poems,* 1980. L. K. Wiggins, *The Life and Works of Paul Laurence Dunbar,* 1907, rpt. 1971. A. D. Nelson, *Paul Laurence Dunbar: Poet Laureate of the Negro Race,* 1914. V. Lawson, *Dunbar Critically Examined,* 1941. V. Cunningham, *Paul Laurence Dunbar and His Song,* 1947. A. Gayle, Jr., *Oak and Ivy: A Biography of Paul Laurence Dunbar,* 1971. J. Martin, ed., *A Singer in the Rain: Reinterpretations of Paul Laurence Dunbar,* 1975. P. Revell, *Paul Laurence Dunbar,* 1979.

Text Used: *The Complete Poems of Paul Laurence Dunbar,* 1913.

AN ANTE-BELLUM SERMON*

We is gathahed hyeah, my brothahs,
    In dis howlin' wildaness,

* Included in *Lyrics of Lowly Life* (1896).

Fu' to speak some words of comfo't
    To each othah in distress.
An' we chooses fu' ouah[1] subjic'
    Dis—we'll 'splain it by an' by;
"An' de Lawd said, 'Moses, Moses,'
    An' de man said, 'Hyeah am I.' "

Now ole Pher'oh,[2] down in Egypt,
    Was de wuss man evah bo'n,   10
An' he had de Hebrew chillun
    Down dah wukin' in his co'n;
'Twell de Lawd got tiahed o' his foolin',
    An' sez he: "I'll let him know—
Look hyeah, Moses, go tell Pher'oh
    Fu' to let dem chillun go."

"An' ef he refuse to do it,
    I will make him rue de houah,[3]
Fu' I'll empty down on Egypt
    All de vials of my powah."   20
Yes, he did—an' Pher'oh's ahmy
    Wasn't wuth a ha'f a dime;
Fu' de Lawd will he'p his chillun,
    You kin trust him evah time.

An' yo' enemies may 'sail[4] you
    In de back an' in de front;
But de Lawd is all aroun' you,
    Fu' to ba'[5] de battle's brunt.
Dey kin fo'ge yo' chains an' shackles
    F'om de mountains to de sea;   30
But de Lawd will sen' some Moses
    Fu' to set his chillun free.

An' de lan' shall hyeah his thundah,
    Lak a blas' f'om Gab'el's ho'n,[6]
Fu' de Lawd of hosts is mighty
    When he girds his ahmor on.
But fu' feah[7] some one mistakes me,
    I will pause right hyeah to say,
Dat I'm still a-preachin' ancient,
    I ain't talkin' 'bout to-day.   40

But I tell you, fellah christuns,
    Things'll happen mighty strange;
Now, de Lawd done dis fu' Isrul,

---

[1] Our.   [2] Pharaoh, a ruler of ancient Egypt.   [3] Hour.   [4] Assail.   [5] For to bear.
    [6] Gabriel's horn: the archangel Gabriel heralded good news by blowing his horn (see Daniel 8:16,
Luke 1:26).
    [7] For fear.

An' his ways don't nevah change,
An' de love he showed to Isrul
   Wasn't all on Isrul spent;
Now don't run an' tell yo' mastahs
   Dat I's preachin' discontent.

'Cause I isn't; I'se a-judgin'
   Bible people by deir ac's;[8]   50
I'se a-givn' you de Scriptuah,
   I'se a-handin' you de fac's.
Cose[9] ole Pher'oh b'lieved in slav'ry,
   But de Lawd he let him see,
Dat de people he put bref in,—
   Evah mothah's son was free.

An' dah's othahs thinks lak Pher'oh,
   But dey calls de Scriptuah liar,
Fu' de Bible says "a servant
   Is a-worthy of his hire."   60
An' you cain't git roun' nor thoo[10] dat,
   An' you cain't git ovah it,
Fu' whatevah place you git in,
   Dis hyeah Bible too'll fit.

So you see de Lawd's intention,
   Evah sence de worl' began,
Was dat His almighty freedom
   Should belong to evah man,
But I think it would be bettah,
   Ef I'd pause agin to say,   70
Dat I'm talkin' 'bout ouah freedom
   In a Bibleistic way.

But de Moses is a-comin',
   An he's comin', suah[11] and fas'
We kin hyeah his feet a-trompin',
   We kin hyeah his trumpit blas'.
But I want to wa'n you people,
   Don't you git too brigity;
An' don't you git to braggin'
   'Bout dese things, you wait an' see.   80

But when Moses wif his powah
   Comes an' sets us chillun free,
We will praise de gracious Mastah
   Dat has gin us liberty;
An' we'll shout ouah halleluyahs,

---

[8] Their acts.   [9] Because.   [10] Through.   [11] Sure.

On dat mighty reck'nin' day,
When we'se reco'nised ez citiz'[12]—
Huh uh! Chillun, let us pray!

1896

WE WEAR THE MASK*

We wear the mask that grins and lies,
It hides our cheeks and shades our eyes,—
This debt we pay to human guile;
With torn and bleeding hearts we smile,
And mouth with myriad subtleties.

Why should the world be overwise,
In counting all our tears and sighs?
Nay, let them only see us, while
   We wear the mask.

We smile, but, O great Christ, our cries   10
To thee from tortured souls arise.
We sing, but oh the clay is vile
Beneath our feet, and long the mile;
But let the world dream otherwise,
   We wear the mask!

1896

THEOLOGY**

There is a heaven, for ever, day by day,
The upward longing of my soul doth tell me so.
There is a hell, I'm quite as sure; for pray,
If there were not, where would my neighbours go?

1899

HARRIET BEECHER STOWE†

She told the story,[1] and the whole world wept
At wrongs and cruelties it had not known

[12] The preacher starts to say "citizens," then breaks off with the concluding line. Throughout the poem, the preacher's strategy has been to talk about slavery in "a Bibleistic way" so that he will not be accused of "preachin' discontent"; here at the end the true subject emerges.
* Included in *Lyrics of Lowly Life* (1896).
** Included in *Lyrics of the Hearthside* (1899).
† Included in *Lyrics of the Hearthside* (1899); Stowe (1811–1896) was influenced by abolitionists at the theological seminary run by her father, Lyman Beecher (1775–1863).
[1] *Uncle Tom's Cabin: Or, Life Among the Lowly* (1852), Stowe's famous novel that sold more than 300,000 copies in its first year of publication and kindled widespread opposition to slavery in the United States.

But for this fearless woman's voice alone.
She spoke to consciences that long had slept:
Her message, Freedom's clear reveille, swept
From heedless hovel to complacent throne.
Command and prophecy were in the tone
And from its sheath the sword of justice leapt.
Around two peoples swelled a fiery wave,
    But both came forth transfigured from the flame.   10
Blest be the hand that dared be strong to save,
    And blest be she who in our weakness came—
Prophet and priestess! At one stroke she gave
A race to freedom and herself to fame.

1899

DOUGLASS*

Ah, Douglass, we have fall'n on evil days,
    Such days as thou, not even thou didst know,
    When thee, the eyes of that harsh long ago
Saw, salient, at the cross of devious ways,
And all the country heard thee with amaze.
    Not ended then, the passionate ebb and flow,
    The awful tide that battled to and fro;
We ride amid a tempest of dispraise.

Now, when the waves of swift dissension swarm,
    And Honor, the strong pilot, lieth stark,   10
Oh, for thy voice high-sounding o'er the storm,
    For thy strong arm to guide the shivering bark,
The blast-defying power of thy form,
    To give us comfort through the lonely dark.

1903

BOOKER T. WASHINGTON†

The word is writ that he who runs may read.
What is the passing breath of earthly fame?
But to snatch glory from the hands of blame—
That is to be, to live, to strive indeed.

---

  * Included in *Lyrics of Love and Laughter* (1903); Frederick Douglass (1818–1895), who escaped from slavery in 1838 and thereafter lectured to antislavery societies. His autobiographical *Narrative of the Life of Frederick Douglass* (1845) is an eloquent account of his experiences as a slave and of his escape to the North.
  † Included in *Lyrics of Love and Laughter* (1903); Washington (1856–1915), an African-American educational leader who was hailed by many, black and white, in the United States. He continued his work despite criticism by those who disapproved of his position on the separation of the races. His books include an autobiography, *Up From Slavery* (1901).

A poor Virginia cabin gave the seed,
And from its dark and lowly door there came
A peer of princes in the world's acclaim,
A master spirit for the nation's need.
Strong, silent, purposeful beyond his kind,
    The mark of rugged force on brow and lip,   10
Straight on he goes, nor turns to look behind
    Where hot the hounds come baying at his hip;
With one idea foremost in his mind,
    Like the keen prow of some on-forging ship.

1903

LATE 19TH-CENTURY NONFICTION PROSE

At the time of the American Revolution nonfiction prose served primarily a political purpose. In the first half of the nineteenth century it functioned in the climate of an American romanticism to assert the significance of the democratic self. And in the late nineteenth century it evolved again in style and substance to express the situation of different groups within the nation—African Americans striving to define their freedom, immigrants confronting the issue of identity in a new land, and others exploring the resources of journalism, literary theory, travel writing, and historical inquiry. The genre of nonfiction prose remained vibrant precisely because it was so changeable in form, so responsive to personal and social issues.

During the final decades of the nineteenth century, substantial contributions to the genre were made in the area of autobiography. Earlier writers such as Mary Rowlandson, Benjamin Franklin, Harriet Jacobs, and Frederick Douglass had used forms of autobiography to illustrate their travails or to offer to the public their personal visions of Americanness. The autobiographical impulse continued unabated as the nineteenth century drew to a close. In different ways William Dean Howells, Henry James, and Mark Twain described their lives in volumes that remain of great importance to students of their work; yet, despite their manifest narrative skills, none of these writers fashioned autobiographies with the social and historical significance of Booker T. Washington's *Up From Slavery* (1901), W. E. B. Du Bois's *The Souls of Black Folk* (1903), or Henry Adams's *The Education of Henry Adams* (1907).

In *Up From Slavery* the acclaimed educator Washington encouraged members of his own race and soothed nervous white readers with the story of his Horatio Alger-like rise to success. By telling so optimistic a story, however, excusing white cruelty that he knew first-hand, encouraging blacks to take up practical and vocational training, and celebrating the virtues of hard work and selflessness, Washington (as he was aware) drew criticism for what seemed a conciliatory vision. Du Bois, for one, advocated an alternative, more assertive role for African Americans with his contributions to the founding of the National Association for the Advancement of Colored People, his work as editor of *The Crisis* magazine, and his collection of essays and meditations, *The Souls of Black Folk*. With a quiet audacity that enlarges our sense of what autobiography can be, that prophetic book reaches beyond the story of an individual life to offer the collective story of a race articulated by a writer who (as he says) is "bone of the bone and flesh of the flesh" of those for whom he speaks.

The use of an unconventional narrative technique likewise distinguishes *The Education of Henry Adams*. Adams, a historian and direct descendant of two of America's early presidents, intended his autobiography for selected friends only. Privately printed in 1907, it was published for the public at large in 1918, after Adams's death. By choosing to write of himself in the third person (a technique Norman Mailer would later adopt in such works as *The Armies of the Night* [1968]), Adams managed to distance himself from his own experience. The perspective he adopted allowed him at least implicitly to criticize the romantic insistence on the self that had informed the nonfiction work of his predecessors. It also allowed him to pass over portions of his life that he wished not to discuss—his wife's suicide in 1885, for example, an event with lasting repercussions that resulted in his "posthumous existence" and introduced a despondent tone to *The Education*. Adams's preoccupation with the impersonal forces of the modern world and with the superior virtues of centuries past are vividly documented in his autobiography. In a nation that was reeling from rapid change and in part recoiling from the sheer numbers of new immigrants, his passion for order along with his

The grandeur of the buildings and monuments of The World's Columbian Exposition, Chicago, 1893 (shown in this 1894 painting by Theodore Robinson), demonstrated America's technological and industrial innovations and its new wealth and power.

=CONTEXTS=

The Birth of Labor Unions

Between 1870 and 1890 America experienced a wave of industrial growth. Older industries such as beef packing and garment making were expanding; giant industries such as steel making and oil refining were developing due to technological inventions and new techniques. The resulting rapid rise of urban industrial centers across America occurred without systematic planning or control. During this chaotic period, as the populations of America's cities doubled (or tripled), Americans were faced with the new urban problems of fire protection, garbage collection, waste elimination, street paving, clean water supplies, and even organized crime. The American city, celebrated by America's great writers before the Civil War, was now descried by them in its commercial greed and industrial heartlessness as a force of anticivilization.

New ways of running factories and managing offices (corporations, trusts, holding companies, and monopolies among them) were started, and the trend toward "bigness" in business was born. As factories grew, communication between owners and workers stopped: employment conditions worsened, and the need for organized labor arose. By 1884, worsening factory conditions had caused over seven hundred thousand frustrated workers to join the Knights of Labor, then the most important labor union. Before the Civil War three out of five Americans worked on a farm; by 1880 more worked in factories than in farms; after 1880 immigrants from eastern and southern Europe (who so needed work that they accepted low wages and long hours) displaced many Americans from their factory jobs. For the first time, workers in America faced long bouts of unemployment. In an April 1885 editorial published in the *North American Review*, Terence V. Powderly (1849–1924), a leading spokesman for the Knights of Labor and champion of the eight-hour workday, shows why labor unions were needed:

The Army of the Discontented

. . . When the President of the United States issued his Thanksgiving proclamation in 1884, there were millions of men and women in want of bread, notwithstanding "the abundant harvests and continued prosperity which God hath vouchsafed to this nation," and the cry, not of thanksgiving, went up from millions of farmers of "Too much wheat!" Doubting as to the exact meaning of the Creator in growing so much wheat, they invoked the aid of such institutions as the Chicago Board of Trade, in the hope of thwarting the will of God by cornering wheat. These men invoked blessings on their Thanksgiving dinners, and thanked God for the turkey, while they hoarded the wheat away from those who asked for bread.

Give men shorter hours in which to labor, and you give them more time to study and learn why bread is so scarce while wheat is so plenty. . . .

Terence V. Powderly, 1885

---

undeniable anti-Semitism must have appealed to some readers. The lasting reputation of *The Education,* however, is a consequence of a narrative voice that is at once nostalgic and intelligent, scrupulous in its search for values in history, and prescient in its ability to identify forces that have dominated life in the twentieth century.

As a tidal wave of immigration brought millions to America's shores in the 1880s and 1890s, Michel-Guillaume Jean de Crèvecoeur's old question, "What is an American?" took on a new and sometimes heated relevance. The subject of immigration was debated in magazines; it was even considered by the U.S. Congress. No one handled the subject with greater enthusiasm and passion than did immigrants themselves, men and women who used autobiographical forms to point to their distinctive place in the American mainstream. Such figures as the Danish-born journalist Jacob Riis and the Polish-born writer Mary Antin, both nineteenth-century arrivals who lived well into the twentieth century, described in memorable self-portraits immigrant life and the achievement of becoming "American": Riis in *The Making of an American* (1901) and Antin in *The Promised Land* (1912). The latter is an extended version of *From Plotzk to Boston*, which Antin wrote in Yiddish as a young girl and translated into English for publication in 1899.

While immigrants explored the difficult experience of coming to a new home, a number of prominent American writers described the fashionable experience of visiting Europe in the decades following the Civil War. Among Mark Twain's numerous books of travels, *The Innocents Abroad* (1869) stands out for its irreverent (and self-deprecating) account of a journey to Europe and the Middle East. His *A Tramp Abroad* (1880) and *Following the Equator* (1897) are erratic in form and lumpy with detail; their episodes of genuine humor tend to give way to observations that seem strained and grim. Nonetheless, these books do suggest that the market for travel à la Twain remained steady. William Dean Howells had the opportunity to gather material for *Venetian Life* (1866) and *Italian Journeys* (1867), volumes richly appreciative of art and culture, during his four years at the U.S. consulate in Venice in the early 1860s. Henry James's travel writing includes the accomplished sketches of Italy, France, and England that he collected in *Portraits of Places* (1883), the cosmopolitan perspectives of *Essays in London and Elsewhere* (1893), and the revealing (and self-revelatory) assessments of American society that make up *The American Scene* (1907), written after his many years of residence in England.

To note that Howells and James also wrote impressive volumes of literary criticism and biography—*Criticism and Fiction* (1891) and *My Mark Twain* (1910) by Howells, for example; *Hawthorne* (1879) and *Partial Portraits* (1888) by James—is to understand that these novelists contributed significantly to the achievement of nonfiction prose. A series of essays written at the turn of the century made another novelist, Frank Norris, a leading exponent of naturalism. In "A Plea for Romantic Fiction" (1901), Norris admits that realism can be "respectable as a church and proper as a deacon," such as "the novels of Mr. Howells"; but his preference was for fiction that plumbs the extraordinary secrets of the heart and soul. That kind of fiction Norris labels "Romance" or, in its contemporary form, "naturalism." Despite his reservations about realism, Norris echoed the appreciation of Howells sounded by many writers and critics. During his years of writing the "Editor's Study" column in *Harper's Monthly*, Howells promoted the cause of various types of fiction: he praised the work of established European realists and championed that of new American writers, among them Stephen Crane, Hamlin Garland, Sarah Orne Jewett, Paul Laurence Dunbar, and Abraham Cahan.

Both Howells and Twain came to their literary endeavors by way of newspaper work. The anecdotal quality of a volume such as Howells's *Literary Friends and Acquaintance* (1900) suggests the manner in which reporting and editorial-writing affected the pace and style of his writing. With Twain the case is even more obvious. In *Roughing It* (1872), for example, Twain interspersed the realistic account of his trip westward with set pieces similar to the humorous feature articles that often appeared in the newspapers of the time (a straightforward tribute to pony express riders, the account of a buffalo that climbed a tree, the story of Jim Blaine's grandfather's ram). What results is a book that is realistic yet hyperbolic, fact spiced with the oral traditions of the tall tale.

In his own distinctive way, Stephen Crane extended the range of journalism in the 1890s to achieve a remarkable blending of forms. Crane wrote *The Red Badge of Courage* (1895), his classic account of a youth maturing in the context of the Civil War, at a time when he had not seen war; yet, as a consequence of that novel and his previous experience in journalism, he became a correspondent in the Greco-Turkish war and the Spanish-American War in Cuba in the late 1890s. His war dispatches, like his other newspaper stories, bring an impressionistic prose to bear on the material he reports. Whether Crane is writing of a night spent with the homeless men of the Bowery in New York City ("An Experiment in Misery" [1894]), giving his personal account of survival in a lifeboat between Cuba and Florida ("Stephen Crane's Own Story" [1897]), or supplying an explanation of how a child may have been brainwashed after witnessing a murder ("An Illusion in Red and White" [1900]), his laconic prose, ironic posture, and introduction of dialogue into newspaper articles (as these were) leads to a point at which fact and fiction become indistinguishable parts of a new form, immersed in the event. Crane's journalistic prose courts a world in which language must take on new burdens because reality, increasingly bizarre, threatens to outstrip the imagination; his work anticipates such varied twentieth-century experiments in form as Truman Capote's *In Cold Blood* (1966), subtitled "A Non-Fiction Novel," and Carl Bernstein and Bob Woodward's *All the President's Men* (1974). Crane's achievement, along with that of Du Bois, Adams, Antin, and others, demonstrates that the essential thrust of nonfiction prose in the late nineteenth century was to forge an awareness of what America had become, and out of that awareness to point unblinkingly to the problems and opportunities that would be part of a new century.

Henry Adams
(1838–1918)

The achievement of Henry Adams is inseparable from his personal and family history, making it appropriate that his reputation should rest largely on his searching and ironic autobiography, *The Education of Henry Adams* (1907). Henry Brooks Adams was born in

1838 in Boston and raised there and in nearby Quincy. Two strains of American culture were available to young Henry: one, the heritage of public service embodied by his great-grandfather John Adams (second president of the United States), his grandfather John Quincy Adams (sixth president of the United States), and his father, the diplomat Charles Francis Adams; another, the path of State Street commerce set forth by his wealthy maternal grandfather. The latter path Adams rejected when he was a boy of age ten. The issue at stake in that choice—the divorce of practical power and social ideals—would lead Adams through a lifetime of study.

After graduating from Harvard University in 1858, Adams traveled to Berlin to study law but left his studies to make a grand tour of Europe, with the help of the Adams name. Back in the United States he became his father's private secretary, first in Washington and then in England during the Civil War. With some misgivings, he returned to Harvard in 1870 to teach medieval history. Although Adams was not a trained medievalist and later deprecated his teaching, his courses were well received, and he remained at Harvard for seven years. During this period he accepted the editorship of the *North American Review* and, in perceptive essays that had little tangible effect, criticized political corruption and individual abuses of wealth.

In 1877 Adams moved to Washington, D.C., to him the center of power, and directed his interest in national politics into his work in American history. Not only does his *Documents Relating to New England Federalism, 1800–1815* (1877) vindicate the principled politics of John Quincy Adams; his biography *The Life of Albert Gallatin* (1879) shows Gallatin, a contemporary of John Adams and Thomas Jefferson, to be, like them, an embodiment of eighteenth-century integrity. Adams next began work on the nine-volume *History of the United States of America During the Administrations of Thomas Jefferson and James Madison* (1889–1891). As he had done before, he relied on historical documents to tell the story, attempting to write "scientific" history by stating the facts severely and with minimal comment, "in such order as seemed rigorously consequent," as he put it in *The Education*. The result, a major study of the period, remains valuable today.

In 1872 Adams had married Marian Hooper, the daughter of a wealthy Boston surgeon. She and Adams became prominent members of Washington society, forming close ties with the diplomat John Hay and the geologist Clarence King and friendships with such well-known persons as Henry James, who sketched them as the Bonnycastles in "Pandora" (1884). The protagonists of Adams's two novels may have been modeled on his wife, although many readers detect as much of Henry Adams as of Marian Adams in the characters. In *Democracy* (1880), an anonymously written satire of political corruption, Madeline Lee goes to Washington to find the springs of power in government but discovers only low conniving in high places. In *Esther* (1884), published under the pseudonym Frances Snow Compton, young Esther Dudley is sent on a search for a principle of order that will give meaning and purpose to life. Esther owes her name to the protagonist of Nathaniel Hawthorne's tale "Old Esther Dudley" (1839), about a forlorn American Loyalist who believes that "Heaven's cause and the King's are one." Adams's Esther, searching for an analogous connection in a scientific age, finds nothing that can fulfill both her mind and her heart.

Marian Adams committed suicide in December 1885—undoubtedly depressed over the death of her father and perhaps driven by her position as a thoughtful woman fettered by masculine society. Adams commissioned a memorial from a friend, the sculptor Augustus Saint-Gaudens, and referred to the enigmatic figure as "The Peace of God." (From another perspective, Mark Twain called it "Grief.") Marian's suicide shattered Adams's life. He finished the projects that he had begun in her lifetime and withdrew with the feeling that life was over, that, according to *The Education*, "the rest mattered so little."

Yet, it is the "rest" of Adams's work that has come to matter so much. In 1894 he was elected president of the American Historical Association; his inaugural address, "The Ten-dency of History," articulated the "dynamic theory of history" that would inform his best work, most notably *Mont-Saint-Michel and Chartres* (1904) and *The Education*. In these studies Adams undertakes to determine the place of human beings as a force in a world of forces. Force, for Adams, is both philosophical and physical, mental and material: "any-thing that does, or helps to do work," be it man, the sun, or a mathematical point, he asserts in *The Education*. Adams now pursued knowledge from different premises than fact and sequence. Starting from "the point of history when man held the highest idea of himself as a unit in a unified universe" (the thirteenth century, as manifested in "Amiens Cathedral and the works of Thomas Aquinas"), Adams proposed to "measure motion down to his own time, without assuming anything as true or untrue, except relation."

Mont-Saint-Michel and Chartres is Adams's compelling "Study of Thirteenth-Century Unity" in the great cathedrals of northwestern France. Here disparate forces—wealth and knowledge, skill and faith—had been marshalled by the power of the Virgin to attract the mind: with arches and buttresses human beings had elevated stone, dissipated strain, and opened room for art and instruction. In *The Education,* subtitled "A Study of Twentieth-Century Multiplicity," Adams traces the proliferation of forces in the modern world; such things as democracy, capitalism, electricity, and radium attract the mind, he feels, but to

Extraordinary in size and power, late nineteenth-century industrial machines were objects of awe and secular worship. "The Dynamo and the Virgin" is based on the machines Henry Adams saw at the 1900 Universal Exposition in Paris.

no discernible purpose. Alleging that his own education had failed to prepare him to be a force among twentieth-century forces, Adams nevertheless tenuously hoped that education is still possible, that the mind can respond with a necessary "jump." *The Education* was first published in a 1907 private edition of one hundred copies, which a few privileged readers were to correct and return. Not until October 1918, six months after Adams's death, did the book reach the public. It was awarded a Pulitzer Prize in 1919.

Suggested Readings: *The Education of Henry Adams*, ed. E. Samuels, 1973. *The Letters of Henry Adams*, 6 vols., ed. J. C. Levenson et al., 1982–1988. *Novels, Mont-Saint-Michel, The Education*, 1983. E. Samuels, *The Young Henry Adams*, 1948. W. H. Jordy, *Henry Adams: Scientific Historian*, 1952. J. C. Levenson, *The Mind and Art of Henry Adams*, 1957. E. Samuels, *Henry Adams: The Middle Years*, 1958. G. Hochfield, *Henry Adams: An Introduction and Interpretation*, 1962. *Henry Adams: The Major Phase*, 1964. J. C. Rowe, *Henry Adams and Henry James: The Emergence of a Modern Consciousness*, 1976. E. N. Harbert, *The Force So Much Closer Home: Henry Adams and the Adams Family*, 1977. R. P. Blackmur, *Henry Adams*, 1980. W. Dusinberre, *Henry Adams: The Myth of Failure*, 1980. J. F. Byrnes, *The Virgin of Chartres: An Intellectual and Psychological History of Henry Adams*, 1981. W. Wasserstrom, *The Ironies of Progress*, 1984. C. Tichi, "Dynamo, Virgin, Engineer," in *Shifting Gears: Technology, Literature, Culture in Modernist America*, 1987.

Text Used: *The Education of Henry Adams: An Autobiography*, 1927.

from **THE EDUCATION OF HENRY ADAMS***

CHAPTER XXV: THE DYNAMO AND THE VIRGIN (1900)[1]

Until the Great Exposition of 1900 closed its doors in November,[2] Adams haunted it, aching to absorb knowledge, and helpless to find it. He would have liked to know how much of it could have been grasped by the best-informed man in the world. While he was thus meditating chaos, Langley[3] came by, and showed it to him. At Langley's behest, the Exhibition dropped its superfluous rags and stripped itself to the skin, for Langley knew what to study, and why, and how; while Adams might as well have stood outside in the night, staring at the Milky Way. Yet Langley said nothing new, and taught nothing that one might not have learned from Lord Bacon, three hundred years before; but though one should have known the "Advancement of Science" as well as one knew the "Comedy of Errors,"[4] the literary knowledge counted for nothing until some teacher should show how to apply it. Bacon took a vast deal of trouble in teaching King James I[5] and

---

* Adams assesses the contemporary world through selected facts from his own life and study, although he insistently distances personal experience by writing of himself in the third person.

[1] Adams's attempt to find order and value in the present as well as in the past leads him to contemplate the development of impersonal "forces" in the modern world; these he juxtaposes with the harmony of previous centuries and other cultures, once experienced as "force," now regarded as symbol. Here, the "Dynamo" represents the forces of the modern world, the "Virgin" that of a world gone by.

[2] The Universal Exposition, or World's Fair, held in Paris from April to November 1900.

[3] Samuel Pierpont Langley (1834–1906), an American scientist, inventor of the bolometer for recording variations in solar radiation, founder of the Smithsonian Astrophysical Observatory (1890), and designer of the first airplane to fly successfully (1896).

[4] Actually, the *Advancement of Learning* (1605), by the English natural philosopher Sir Francis Bacon (1561–1626); an early Shakespearean comedy.

[5] James I (1566–1625) was king of England from 1603 to 1625.

his subjects, American or other, towards the year 1620, that true science was the development or economy of forces; yet an elderly American in 1900 knew neither the formula nor the forces; or even so much as to say to himself that his historical business in the Exposition concerned only the economies or developments of force since 1893, when he began the study at Chicago.[6]

Nothing in education is so astonishing as the amount of ignorance it accumulates in the form of inert facts. Adams had looked at most of the accumulations of art in the storehouses called Art Museums; yet he did not know how to look at the art exhibits of 1900. He had studied Karl Marx[7] and his doctrines of history with profound attention, yet he could not apply them at Paris. Langley, with the ease of a great master of experiment, threw out of the field every exhibit that did not reveal a new application of force, and naturally threw out, to begin with, almost the whole art exhibit. Equally, he ignored almost the whole industrial exhibit. He led his pupil directly to the forces. His chief interest was in new motors to make his airship feasible, and he taught Adams the astonishing complexities of the new Daimler[8] motor, and of the automobile, which, since 1893, had become a nightmare at a hundred kilometres an hour, almost as destructive as the electric tram which was only ten years older; and threatening to become as terrible as the locomotive steam-engine itself, which was almost exactly Adams's own age.

Then he showed his scholar the great hall of dynamos, and explained how little he knew about electricity or force of any kind, even of his own special sun, which spouted heat in inconceivable volume, but which, as far as he knew, might spout less or more, at any time, for all the certainty he felt in it. To him, the dynamo itself was but an ingenious channel for conveying somewhere the heat latent in a few tons of poor coal hidden in a dirty engine-house carefully kept out of sight; but to Adams the dynamo became a symbol of infinity. As he grew accustomed to the great gallery of machines, he began to feel the forty-foot dynamos as a moral force much as the early Christians felt the Cross. The planet itself seemed less impressive, in its old-fashioned, deliberate, annual or daily revolution, than this huge wheel, revolving within arm's length at some vertiginous speed, and barely murmuring—scarcely humming an audible warning to stand a hair's-breadth further for respect of power—while it would not wake the baby lying close against its frame. Before the end, one began to pray to it; inherited instinct taught the natural expression of man before silent and infinite force. Among the thousand symbols of ultimate energy, the dynamo was not so human as some, but it was the most expressive.

Yet the dynamo, next to the steam-engine, was the most familiar of exhibits. For Adams's objects its value lay chiefly in its occult mechanism. Between the dynamo in the gallery of machines and the engine-house outside, the break of continuity amounted to abysmal fracture for a historian's objects. No more relation could he discover between the steam and the electric current than between the

---

[6] The Columbian Exposition held at Chicago in 1893; in Ch. XXII of *The Education*, Adams tells how the exhibits kindled his interest in the "economy of forces."

[7] Marx (1818–1883), a German social philosopher, founder (with Friedrich Engels) of modern socialism and communism, and author of *Das Kapital* (3 vols., 1867–1894), in which he uses the concept of dialectical materialism to analyze economic and social history.

[8] Gottlieb Daimler (1834–1900), a German engineer, inventor, and pioneer automobile manufacturer who constructed the first high-speed internal combustion engine in 1885.

Cross and the cathedral. The forces were interchangeable if not reversible, but he could see only an absolute *fiat* in electricity as in faith. Langley could not help him. Indeed, Langley seemed to be worried by the same trouble, for he constantly repeated that the new forces were anarchical, and specially that he was not responsible for the new rays, that were little short of parricidal in their wicked spirit towards science. His own rays, with which he had doubled the solar spectrum, were altogether harmless and beneficent; but Radium denied its God—or, what was to Langley the same thing, denied the truths of his Science.[9] The force was wholly new.

A historian who asked only to learn enough to be as futile as Langley or Kelvin,[10] made rapid progress under this teaching, and mixed himself up in the tangle of ideas until he achieved a sort of Paradise of ignorance vastly consoling to his fatigued senses. He wrapped himself in vibrations and rays which were new, and he would have hugged Marconi and Branly[11] had he met them, as he hugged the dynamo; while he lost his arithmetic in trying to figure out the equation between the discoveries and the economies of force. The economies, like the discoveries, were absolute, supersensual, occult; incapable of expression in horse-power. What mathematical equivalent could he suggest as the value of a Branly coherer? Frozen air, or the electric furnace, had some scale of measurement, no doubt, if somebody could invent a thermometer adequate to the purpose; but X-rays[12] had played no part whatever in man's consciousness, and the atom itself had figured only as a fiction of thought. In these seven years man had translated himself into a new universe which had no common scale of measurement with the old. He had entered a supersensual world, in which he could measure nothing except by chance collisions of movements imperceptible to his senses, perhaps even imperceptible to his instruments, but perceptible to each other, and so to some known ray at the end of the scale. Langley seemed prepared for anything, even for an indeterminable number of universes interfused—physics stark mad in metaphysics.

Historians undertake to arrange sequences,—called stories, or histories—assuming in silence a relation of cause and effect. These assumptions, hidden in the depths of dusty libraries, have been astounding, but commonly unconscious and childlike; so much so, that if any captious critic were to drag them to light, historians would probably reply, with one voice, that they had never supposed themselves required to know what they were talking about. Adams, for one, had toiled in vain to find out what he meant. He had even published a dozen volumes of American history for no other purpose than to satisfy himself whether, by the severest process of stating, with the least possible comment, such facts as seemed sure, in such order as seemed rigorously consequent, he could fix for a familiar

[9] The spontaneous transformation of radium through radioactive emission could not be explained by the existing paradigm that distinguished between matter and energy; hence, radium seemed to deny the "truths" of science.

[10] William Thomson (1824–1907), Baron Kelvin, a British mathematician and physicist, whose work in thermodynamics established the law of the conservation of energy.

[11] Guglielmo Marconi (1874–1937), an Italian physicist and inventor of wireless telegraphy in 1905, who (with Karl Braun) received the Nobel Prize for physics in 1909; Édouard Branly (1844–1940), a French physicist and inventor of the Branly "coherer" for distinguishing radio waves.

[12] Discovered by the German physicist Wilhelm Conrad Roentgen (1845–1923), who received the first Nobel Prize in physics (1901).

moment a necessary sequence of human movement. The result had satisfied him as little as at Harvard College. Where he saw sequence, other men saw something quite different, and no one saw the same unit of measure. He cared little about his experiments and less about his statesmen, who seemed to him quite as ignorant as himself and, as a rule, no more honest; but he insisted on a relation of sequence, and if he could not reach it by one method, he would try as many methods as science knew. Satisfied that the sequence of men led to nothing and that the sequence of their society could lead no further, while the mere sequence of time was artificial, and the sequence of thought was chaos, he turned at last to the sequence of force; and thus it happened that, after ten years' pursuit, he found himself lying in the Gallery of Machines at the Great Exposition of 1900, his historical neck broken by the sudden irruption of forces totally new.

Since no one else showed much concern, an elderly person without other cares had no need to betray alarm. The year 1900 was not the first to upset schoolmasters. Copernicus and Galileo[13] had broken many professorial necks about 1600; Columbus had stood the world on its head towards 1500; but the nearest approach to the revolution of 1900 was that of 310, when Constantine set up the Cross.[14] The rays that Langley disowned, as well as those which he fathered, were occult, supersensual, irrational; they were a revelation of mysterious energy like that of the Cross; they were what, in terms of mediæval science, were called immediate modes of the divine substance.

The historian was thus reduced to his last resources. Clearly if he was bound to reduce all these forces to a common value, this common value could have no measure but that of their attraction on his own mind. He must treat them as they had been felt; as convertible, reversible, interchangeable attractions on thought. He made up his mind to venture it; he would risk translating rays into faith. Such a reversible process would vastly amuse a chemist, but the chemist could not deny that he, or some of his fellow physicists, could feel the force of both. When Adams was a boy in Boston, the best chemist in the place had probably never heard of Venus except by way of scandal, or of the Virgin except as idolatry;[15] neither had he heard of dynamos or automobiles or radium; yet his mind was ready to feel the force of all, though the rays were unborn and the women were dead.

Here opened another totally new education, which promised to be by far the most hazardous of all. The knife-edge along which he must crawl, like Sir Lancelot[16] in the twelfth century, divided two kingdoms of force which had nothing in

---

[13] Nicholaus Copernicus (1473–1543), a Polish astronomer who determined the movements of the solar system; Galileo Galilei (1564–1642), an Italian astronomer and physicist who supported Copernican ideas rather than the classical Ptolemaic theory that the earth is the center of the universe.

[14] The Roman Emperor Constantine the Great (A.D. 288?–337) introduced Christianity to the Roman Empire after the battle at Mulvian Bridge in A.D. 312. Adams dates the introduction at A.D. 310, when Constantine began his reign.

[15] The "chemist," or druggist, would know of Venus (the Roman goddess of love) only from dispensing medicine for venereal disease, and as a Bostonian descended from the Puritans would think of the Virgin Mary as an object of idolatry.

[16] The heroic knight in *Lancelot*, by the French poet Chrétien de Troyes (12th century); Lancelot was once obliged to crawl across a bridge consisting of a long knife in order to rescue Queen Guinevere.

common but attraction. They were as different as a magnet is from gravitation, supposing one knew what a magnet was, or gravitation, or love. The force of the Virgin was still felt at Lourdes,[17] and seemed to be as potent as X-rays; but in America neither Venus nor Virgin ever had value as force—at most as sentiment. No American had ever been truly afraid of either.

This problem in dynamics gravely perplexed an American historian. The Woman had once been supreme; in France she still seemed potent, not merely as a sentiment, but as a force. Why was she unknown in America? For evidently America was ashamed of her, and she was ashamed of herself, otherwise they would not have strewn fig-leaves so profusely all over her. When she was a true force, she was ignorant of fig-leaves, but the monthly-magazine-made American female had not a feature that would have been recognized by Adam.[18] The trait was notorious, and often humorous, but any one brought up among Puritans knew that sex was sin. In any previous age, sex was strength. Neither art nor beauty needed. Every one, even among Puritans, knew that neither Diana of the Ephesians[19] nor any of the Oriental goddesses was worshipped for her beauty. She was goddess because of her force; she was the animated dynamo; she was reproduction—the greatest and most mysterious of all energies; all she needed was to be fecund. Singularly enough, not one of Adams's many schools of education had ever drawn his attention to the opening lines of Lucretius, though they were perhaps the finest in all Latin literature, where the poet invoked Venus exactly as Dante invoked the Virgin:—

"Quae quoniam rerum naturam *sola* gubernas."[20]

The Venus of Epicurean philosophy survived in the Virgin of the Schools:[21]—

"Donna, sei tanto grande, e tanto vali,
Che qual vuol grazia, e a te non ricorre,
Sua disianza vuol volar senz' ali."[22]

All this was to American thought as though it had never existed. The true American knew something of the facts, but nothing of the feelings; he read the letter, but

---

[17] The famous shrine in southwestern France where the Virgin Mary is reported to have appeared to St. Bernadette in 1858; since then the shrine has been known for miraculous cures.

[18] The Woman, originally a "true force" in her nakedness and sensuality, has been turned into the stylishly-clad "American female" that the biblical Adam would not recognize by the popular monthly magazines.

[19] According to Greek myth, the ancient city of Ephesus in Asia Minor was sacred to Artemis (Diana to the Romans), a virgin huntress but also a goddess of maternity.

[20] "Since you alone govern the nature of things" (Latin), from *On the Nature of Things,* by the Roman philosophical poet Lucretius (99?–55? B.C.), addressed to Venus.

[21] In the following lines from Dante Alighieri (1265–1321), the magnetism of the pagan Venus survived the adjustments made by medieval scholastic philosophers in presenting the figure of the Virgin Mary.

[22] "Lady, thou art so great and so triumphant, / that if there be one who would have grace and does not turn to thee, / his longing seeks to fly without wings" (Italian), from Dante's *Paradiso* (XXXIII 13–15).

he never felt the law. Before this historical chasm, a mind like that of Adams felt itself helpless; he turned from the Virgin to the Dynamo as though he were a Branly coherer. On one side, at the Louvre and at Chartres,[23] as he knew by the record of work actually done and still before his eyes, was the highest energy ever known to man, the creator of four-fifths of his noblest art, exercising vastly more attraction over the human mind than all the steam-engines and dynamos ever dreamed of; and yet this energy was unknown to the American mind. An American Virgin would never dare command; an American Venus would never dare exist.

The question, which to any plain American of the nineteenth century seemed as remote as it did to Adams, drew him almost violently to study, once it was posed; and on this point Langleys were as useless as though they were Herbert Spencers[24] or dynamos. The idea survived only as art. There one turned as naturally as though the artist were himself a woman. Adams began to ponder, asking himself whether he knew of any American artist who had ever insisted on the power of sex, as every classic had always done; but he could think only of Walt Whitman; Bret Harte,[25] as far as the magazines would let him venture; and one or two painters, for the flesh-tones. All the rest had used sex for sentiment, never for force; to them, Eve was a tender flower, and Herodias[26] an unfeminine horror. American art, like the American language and American education, was as far as possible sexless. Society regarded this victory over sex as its greatest triumph, and the historian readily admitted it, since the moral issue, for the moment, did not concern one who was studying the relations of unmoral force. He cared nothing for the sex of the dynamo until he could measure its energy.

Vaguely seeking a clue, he wandered through the art exhibit, and, in his stroll, stopped almost every day before St. Gaudens's General Sherman,[27] which had been given the central post of honor. St. Gaudens himself was in Paris, putting on the work his usual interminable last touches, and listening to the usual contradictory suggestions of brother sculptors. Of all the American artists who gave to American art whatever life it breathed in the seventies, St. Gaudens was perhaps the most sympathetic, but certainly the most inarticulate. General Grant or Don Cameron[28] had scarcely less instinct of rhetoric than he. All the others—the

---

[23] Formerly a palace, the Louvre is a renowned museum of art in Paris; the medieval cathedral of Chartres, France, is praised for its Gothic spires. Adams treated the importance of this cathedral in *Mont-Saint-Michel and Chartres: A Study of Thirteenth-Century Unity* (1904, 1913). *The Education*, in contrast, is designed to be "A Study of Twentieth-Century Multiplicity."

[24] Spencer (1820–1893) was an English popularizer of Charles Darwin's evolutionary theories; Adams suggests that Spencer's interpretations were flimsy.

[25] Whitman's *Leaves of Grass* (1855) treats sex prominently as a major force in human life; Bret Harte (1836–1902) portrayed prostitutes sentimentally in such stories as "The Outcasts of Poker Flat" (1869). Adams may be the only writer who ever saw similarities in the work of Whitman and of Harte.

[26] King Herod's wife, who instructed her daughter to ask for the head of John the Baptist as a reward for her dancing (see Matthew 14:8).

[27] A statue of William Tecumseh Sherman (1820–1891), a Union general in the Civil War, by the American sculptor Augustus St. Gaudens (1848–1907); then situated in Paris, the statue is now in Central Park, New York City.

[28] James Donald Cameron (1833–1918), U.S. Senator and secretary of war under the eighteenth president, Ulysses S. Grant (1822–1885).

Hunts, Richardson, John La Farge, Stanford White[29]—were exuberant; only St. Gaudens could never discuss or dilate on an emotion, or suggest artistic arguments for giving to his work the forms that he felt. He never laid down the law, or affected the despot, or became brutalized like Whistler[30] by the brutalities of his world. He required no incense; he was no egoist; his simplicity of thought was excessive; he could not imitate, or give any form but his own to the creations of his hand. No one felt more strongly than he the strength of other men, but the idea that they could affect him never stirred an image in his mind.

This summer his health was poor and his spirits were low. For such a temper, Adams was not the best companion, since his own gaiety was not *folle;*[31] but he risked going now and then to the studio on Mont Parnasse[32] to draw him out for a stroll in the Bois de Boulogne, or dinner as pleased his moods, and in return St. Gaudens sometimes let Adams go about in his company.

Once St. Gaudens took him down to Amiens, with a party of Frenchmen, to see the cathedral. Not until they found themselves actually studying the sculpture of the western portal, did it dawn on Adams's mind that, for his purposes, St. Gaudens on that spot had more interest to him than the cathedral itself. Great men before great monuments express great truths, provided they are not taken too solemnly. Adams never tired of quoting the supreme phrase of his idol Gibbon,[33] before the Gothic cathedrals: "I darted a contemptuous look on the stately monuments of superstition." Even in the footnotes of his history, Gibbon had never inserted a bit of humor more human than this, and one would have paid largely for a photograph of the fat little historian, on the background of Notre Dame of Amiens, trying to persuade his readers—perhaps himself—that he was darting a contemptuous look on the stately monument, for which he felt in fact the respect which every man of his vast study and active mind always feels before objects worthy of it; but besides the humor, one felt also the relation. Gibbon ignored the Virgin, because in 1789 religious monuments were out of fashion. In 1900 his remark sounded fresh and simple as the green fields to ears that had heard a hundred years of other remarks, mostly no more fresh and certainly less simple. Without malice, one might find it more instructive than a whole lecture of Ruskin.[34] One sees what one brings, and at that moment Gibbon brought the French Revolution. Ruskin brought reaction against the Revolution. St. Gaudens had passed beyond all. He liked the stately monuments much more than he liked Gibbon or

---

[29] The brothers William Morris Hunt (1824–1879), an eminent painter, and Richard Morris Hunt (1828–1895), an architect and founder of an architectural studio in New York City; Henry Hobson Richardson (1838–1886), an architect noted for his "Richardson Romanesque" style, as seen in Trinity Church, Boston (1872–1877); La Farge (1835–1910), a mural painter and designer of stained glass; White (1853–1906), an architect famous for the Washington Arch and the Century Club in New York City.

[30] James Abbott McNeill Whistler (1834–1903), a painter and lithographer who acquired a reputation as a dandy and publicity seeker when he lived in London in the 1860s.

[31] "Wild" (French).

[32] A Left Bank section of Paris frequented by writers and artists; the Bois de Boulogne is a wooded park on the outskirts of Paris.

[33] Edward Gibbon (1737–1794), an English historian and author of *The Decline and Fall of the Roman Empire* (6 vols., 1776–1788) and the autobiographical *Memoirs of His Life and Writings* (1796); Adams apparently paraphrases from a February 1763 entry in Gibbon's journal.

[34] John Ruskin (1819–1900), an English critic of art and architecture, especially that of the Italian Renaissance.

Ruskin; he loved their dignity; their unity; their scale; their lines; their lights and shadows; their decorative sculpture; but he was even less conscious than they of the force that created it all—the Virgin, the Woman—by whose genius "the stately monuments of superstition" were built, through which she was expressed. He would have seen more meaning in Isis[35] with the cow's horns, at Edfoo, who expressed the same thought. The art remained, but the energy was lost even upon the artist.

Yet in mind and person St. Gaudens was a survival of the 1500; he bore the stamp of the Renaissance, and should have carried an image of the Virgin round his neck, or stuck in his hat, like Louis XI.[36] In mere time he was a lost soul that had strayed by chance into the twentieth century, and forgotten where it came from. He writhed and cursed at his ignorance, much as Adams did at his own, but in the opposite sense. St. Gaudens was a child of Benvenuto Cellini,[37] smothered in an American cradle. Adams was a quintessence of Boston, devoured by curiosity to think like Benvenuto. St. Gaudens's art was starved from birth, and Adams's instinct was blighted from babyhood. Each had but half of a nature, and when they came together before the Virgin of Amiens they ought both to have felt in her the force that made them one; but it was not so. To Adams she became more than ever a channel of force; to St. Gaudens she remained as before a channel of taste.

For a symbol of power, St. Gaudens instinctively preferred the horse, as was plain in his horse and Victory of the Sherman monument. Doubtless Sherman also felt it so. The attitude was so American that, for at least forty years, Adams had never realized that any other could be in sound taste. How many years had he taken to admit a notion of what Michael Angelo and Rubens[38] were driving at? He could not say; but he knew that only since 1895 had he begun to feel the Virgin or Venus as force, and not everywhere even so. At Chartres—perhaps at Lourdes— possibly at Cnidos if one could still find there the divinely naked Aphrodite of Praxiteles[39]—but otherwise one must look for force to the goddesses of Indian mythology. The idea died out long ago in the German and English stock. St. Gaudens at Amiens was hardly less sensitive to the force of the female energy than Matthew Arnold at the Grande Chartreuse.[40] Neither of them felt goddesses as power—only as reflected emotion, human expression, beauty, purity, taste, scarcely even as sympathy. They felt a railway train as power; yet they, and all other artists, constantly complained that the power embodied in a railway train could never be embodied in art. All the steam in the world could not, like the Virgin, build Chartres.

[35] Adams saw a statue of the Egyptian goddess Isis at Edfu ("Edfoo") on the Nile River in 1873 and again in 1893.

[36] Louis XI (1423–1483) was a politically and militarily active king of France (1461–1483); fearing assassination in his later days, he frequently disguised himself as a holy pilgrim.

[37] Cellini (1500–1571), an Italian sculptor and metalsmith and author of a picaresque autobiography, a major document of the sixteenth century.

[38] Michelangelo (1475–1564), an Italian artist and sculptor and chief architect of St. Peter's Cathedral in Rome. Peter Paul Rubens (1577–1640), an eminent Flemish painter; "Venus and Adonis" is among his principal works.

[39] A famous fourth-century B.C. Greek sculptor whose renowned "Aphrodite of Cnidus" (a city in Asia Minor) exists only in a copy at the Vatican in Rome.

[40] Arnold (1822–1888) was a British poet whose "Stanzas From the Grande Chartreuse" (a monastery of the Carthusian monks, an order founded in 1086) laments the loss of medieval religious faith.

Yet in mechanics, whatever the mechanicians might think, both energies acted as interchangeable forces on man, and by action on man all known force may be measured. Indeed, few men of science measured force in any other way. After once admitting that a straight line was the shortest distance between two points, no serious mathematician cared to deny anything that suited his convenience, and rejected no symbol, unproved or unproveable, that helped him to accomplish work. The symbol was force, as a compass-needle or a triangle was force, as the mechanist might prove by losing it, and nothing could be gained by ignoring their value. Symbol or energy, the Virgin had acted as the greatest force the Western world ever felt, and had drawn man's activities to herself more strongly than any other power, natural or supernatural, had ever done; the historian's business was to follow the track of the energy; to find where it came from and where it went to; its complex source and shifting channels; its values, equivalents, conversions. It could scarcely be more complex than radium; it could hardly be deflected, diverted, polarized, absorbed more perplexingly than other radiant matter. Adams knew nothing about any of them, but as a mathematical problem of influence on human progress, though all were occult, all reacted on his mind, and he rather inclined to think the Virgin easiest to handle.

The pursuit turned out to be long and tortuous, leading at last into the vast forests of scholastic science. From Zeno to Descartes, hand in hand with Thomas Aquinas, Montaigne, and Pascal,[41] one stumbled as stupidly as though one were still a German student of 1860. Only with the instinct of despair could one force one's self into this old thicket of ignorance after having been repulsed at a score of entrances more promising and more popular. Thus far, no path had led anywhere, unless perhaps to an exceedingly modest living. Forty-five years of study had proved to be quite futile for the pursuit of power; one controlled no more force in 1900 than in 1850, although the amount of force controlled by society had enormously increased. The secret of education still hid itself somewhere behind ignorance, and one fumbled over it as feebly as ever. In such labyrinths, the staff is a force almost more necessary than the legs; the pen becomes a sort of blind-man's dog, to keep him from falling into the gutters. The pen works for itself, and acts like a hand, modelling the plastic material over and over again to the form that suits it best. The form is never arbitrary, but is a sort of growth like crystallization, as any artist knows too well; for often the pencil or pen runs into side-paths and shapelessness, loses its relations, stops or is bogged. Then it has to return on its trail, and recover, if it can, its line of force. The result of a year's work depends more on what is struck out than on what is left in; on the sequence of the main lines of thought, than on their play or variety. Compelled once more to lean heavily on this support, Adams covered more thousands of pages with figures as formal as though they were algebra, laboriously striking out, altering, burning, experimenting, until the year had expired, the Exposition had long been closed, and winter drawing to its end, before he sailed from Cherbourg,[42] on January 19, 1901, for home.

1907

---

[41] Adams refers to studies that took him from one philosopher to another: from the Greek Zeno (366?–264 B.C.) to the French René Descartes (1596–1650) and the unlikely trio of the theologically oriented Thomas Aquinas (1225?–1274), the French skeptic Michel de Montaigne (1533–1592), and the French scientist and religious thinker Blaise Pascal (1623–1662).

[42] A port in France.

=CONTEXTS=

The World's Columbian Exposition of 1893

The World's Columbian Exposition, held in Chicago in 1893 to commemorate the four hundredth anniversary of Christopher Columbus's discovery of America, marked the first time that machines were used for fun at a fair. (The fact that Chicago won the right to house the fair illustrates the rising status of the West in national affairs.) On the Midway, spectators sampled a range of amusements, including George Ferris's wheel, hot-air balloon rides, artificial ice for warm-weather skating, an electrified house demonstrating the practical applications of electricity, Buffalo Bill's Wild West Show, Scott Joplin's ragtime piano-playing, and the hootchy-kootchy dancing of Little Egypt. In the numerous exhibition halls, spectators heard the pianist Ignace Paderewski play Chopin, attended intellectual congresses on such hotly debated topics as the Victorian stereotyping of women, and saw demonstrations of the latest inventions—the phonograph and Linotype. The Pullman car, a railroad car with folding upper berths, was displayed in the Transportation Building, the uncluttered lines of which clashed with the ornate, gilded facades of the exhibition halls. The waters of nearby Lake Michigan fed a network of manmade lagoons within the fair itself and served as an exotic backdrop to the 65,000 exhibits from 47 different countries, displayed on the 686-acre fairground.

An observer of the fair, Charles Eliot Norton (1827–1908), co-editor of the *North American Review* with James Russell Lowell, offered this view:

The Great American Fair

The great Fair was indeed a superb and appropriate symbol of our great nation, in its noble general design and in the inequalities of its execution; in its unexampled display of industrial energy and practical capacity; in the absence of the higher works of the creative imagination; in its incongruities, its mingling of noble realities and ignoble pretences, in its refinements cheek-by-jowl with vulgarities, in its order and its confusion—in its heterogeneousness and in its unity.

Charles Eliot Norton, 1894?

Booker T. Washington
(1856–1915)

The son of a black woman named Jane and an anonymous white plantation owner, Booker T. Washington was born into slavery in 1856. After the Civil War ended, he and his mother moved to Malden, West Virginia. There he worked as a salt packer, a coal miner, and a house servant and, when he could, attended the local school out of a desire to read and write. In 1872 he made his famous five-hundred-mile journey, partly on foot, to enroll in the Hampton Institute in Virginia, a school established by the American Missionary Association to train African-American teachers and to promote the study of agriculture and trade.

After graduating from Hampton in 1875, Washington moved back to Malden to become an itinerant teacher; he established, among other things, a library and a night school. Several years later he accepted an invitation from the founder of the Hampton Institute, Samuel Chapman Armstrong, to return there to teach and to conduct an experimental program for the instruction of Native-American students. In 1881 Washington, helped by Armstrong's recommendation, was invited to become the principal of an industrial school for ex-slaves in Tuskegee, Alabama. Through hard work and perseverance he built it up from a $2,000 legislative appropriation to a college with 2500 students, 111 buildings, and 3500 acres of land by the time of his death in 1915. He used the system at Hampton Institute as his primary model in creating the Tuskegee Institute, with one major difference: instead of using a predominately white faculty, Washington employed black teachers.

Both his "Atlanta Exposition Address" (an 1895 speech given at the Cotton States and International Exposition) and his autobiography, *Up From Slavery* (1901), demonstrate the manner in which Washington's skills as orator and writer brought him to national attention. Popularly known as the "Atlanta Compromise," Washington's influential speech set a practical and conciliatory agenda for African Americans in society: let African Americans, he counseled, be given the opportunity to improve their economic condition; let them (as a trade-off) overlook matters of human and political rights. Given the racial tumult in the South in the late nineteenth century, the tenor of this speech brought many blacks and whites alike to see Washington as a welcome and uniquely qualified peacemaker, the leading African-American spokesman. His position was enhanced by the publication of *Up From Slavery*, a compelling autobiography that both appropriated and validated Franklinesque virtues of diligence and hard work. Further honors came from an appreciative white world when Washington received an honorary degree from Harvard University and dined at the White House with President Theodore Roosevelt.

For his many accomplishments Washington was hailed as the "Moses of his race." Even W. E. B. Du Bois admitted Washington's predominance as a spokesman for African Americans. But to Du Bois and to an increasing number of blacks, especially those who came of age after World War I, Washington's ideas seemed to accept racial inequality, to bargain for the doctrine of "separate but unequal," to play the white man's game. Washington remains a significant figure—significant to some for the limitations of his vision.

Suggested Readings: *The Future of the American Negro,* 1899. *Working With the Hands,* 1904. *The Booker T. Washington Papers,* ed. L. R. Harlan, 1972– . B. Matthews, *Booker T. Washington: Educator and Interracial Interpreter,* 1948. A. Meier, *Negro Thought in America, 1880–1915,* 1963. E. L. Thornborough, *Booker T. Washington,* 1969. Louis R. Harlan, *Booker T. Washington: The Making of a Black Leader, 1865–1901,* 1972. R. B. Stepto, *From Behind the Veil: A Study of Afro-American Narrative,* 1979. L. R. Harlan, *Booker T. Washington: The Wizard of Tuskegee, 1901–1915,* 1983. R. Smock, ed., *Booker T. Washington in Perspective: Essays of Louis R. Harlan,* 1988.

Text Used: *Up From Slavery,* 1901.

from   UP FROM SLAVERY*

CHAPTER XIV: THE ATLANTA EXPOSITION ADDRESS[1]

The Atlanta Exposition, at which I had been asked to make an address as a representative of the Negro race, as stated in the last chapter, was opened with a short address from Governor Bullock. After other interesting exercises, including an invocation from Bishop Nelson,[2] of Georgia, a dedicatory ode by Albert Howell, Jr., and addresses by the President of the Exposition and Mrs. Joseph Thompson, the President of the Woman's Board, Governor Bullock introduced me with the words, "We have with us to-day a representative of Negro enterprise and Negro civilization."

When I arose to speak, there was considerable cheering, especially from the coloured people. As I remember it now, the thing that was uppermost in my mind was the desire to say something that would cement the friendship of the races and bring about hearty cooperation between them. So far as my outward surroundings were concerned, the only thing that I recall distinctly now is that when I got up, I saw thousands of eyes looking intently into my face. The following is the address which I delivered:—

MR. PRESIDENT AND GENTLEMEN OF THE BOARD OF DIRECTORS AND CITIZENS.

One-third of the population of the South is of the Negro race. No enterprise seeking the material, civil, or moral welfare of this section can disregard this element of our population and reach the highest success. I but convey to you, Mr. President and Directors, the sentiment of the masses of my race when I say that in no way have the value and manhood of the American Negro been more fittingly and generously recognized than by the managers of this magnificent Exposition at every stage of its progress. It is a recognition that will do more to cement the friendship of the two races than any occurrence since the dawn of our freedom.

Not only this, but the opportunity here afforded will awaken among us a new era of industrial progress. Ignorant and inexperienced, it is not strange that in the first years of our new life we began at the top instead of at the bottom; that a seat in Congress or the state legislature was more sought than real estate or industrial skill; that the political convention of stump speaking had more attractions than starting a dairy farm or truck garden.

A ship lost at sea for many days suddenly sighted a friendly vessel. From the mast of the unfortunate vessel was seen a signal, "Water, water; we die of thirst!" The answer from the friendly vessel at once came back, "Cast down your bucket where you are." A second time the signal, "Water, water; send us water!" ran up from the distressed vessel, and was answered, "Cast down your bucket where you are." And a third and fourth signal for water was answered, "Cast down your bucket where you are." The captain of the distressed vessel, at last heeding the injunction, cast down his bucket, and it came up full of fresh, sparkling water from the mouth of the Amazon River. To those of my race who depend on bettering their condition in a foreign land or who underestimate the importance of culti-

---

* First published serially in *The Outlook* from November 3, 1900, to February 23, 1901, and in book form in 1901.
[1] Washington delivered this address at the opening ceremonies of the Cotton States and International Exposition in Atlanta, September 18, 1895.
[2] Cleland Kinlock Nelson (1852–1917), Episcopal bishop of Atlanta (1907–1917).

vating friendly relations with the Southern white man, who is their next-door neighbour, I would say: "Cast down your bucket where you are"—cast it down in making friends in every manly way of the people of all races by whom we are surrounded.

Cast it down in agriculture, mechanics, in commerce, in domestic service, and in the professions. And in this connection it is well to bear in mind that whatever other sins the South may be called to bear, when it comes to business, pure and simple, it is in the South that the Negro is given a man's chance in the commercial world, and in nothing is this Exposition more eloquent than in emphasizing this chance. Our greatest danger is that in the great leap from slavery to freedom we may overlook the fact that the masses of us are to live by the productions of our hands, and fail to keep in mind that we shall prosper in proportion as we learn to dignify and glorify common labour and put brains and skill into the common occupations of life; shall prosper in proportion as we learn to draw the line between the superficial and the substantial, the ornamental gewgaws of life and the useful. No race can prosper till it learns that there is as much dignity in tilling a field as in writing a poem. It is at the bottom of life we must begin, and not at the top. Nor should we permit our grievances to overshadow our opportunities.

To those of the white race who look to the incoming of those of foreign birth and strange tongue and habits for the prosperity of the South, were I permitted I would repeat what I say to my own race, "Cast down your bucket where you are." Cast it down among the eight millions of Negroes whose habits you know, whose fidelity and love you have tested in days when to have proved treacherous meant the ruin of your firesides. Cast down your bucket among these people who have, without strikes and labour wars, tilled your fields, cleared your forests, builded your railroads and cities, and brought forth treasures from the bowels of the earth, and helped make possible this magnificent representation of the progress of the South. Casting down your bucket among my people, helping and encouraging them as you are doing on these grounds, and to education of head, hand, and heart, you will find that they will buy your surplus land, make blossom the waste places in your fields, and run your factories. While doing this, you can be sure in the future, as in the past, that you and your families will be surrounded by the most patient, faithful, law-abiding, and unresentful people that the world has seen. As we have proved our loyalty to you in the past, in nursing your children, watching by the sick-bed of your mothers and fathers, and often following them with tear-dimmed eyes to their graves, so in the future, in our humble way, we shall stand by you with a devotion that no foreigner can approach, ready to lay down our lives, if need be, in defence of yours, interlacing our industrial, commercial, civil, and religious life with yours in a way that shall make the interests of both races one. In all things that are purely social we can be as separate as the fingers, yet one as the hand in all things essential to mutual progress.

There is no defence or security for any of us except in the highest intelligence and development of all. If anywhere there are efforts tending to curtail the fullest growth of the Negro, let these efforts be turned into stimulating, encouraging, and making him the most useful and intelligent citizen. Effort or means so invested will pay a thousand per cent interest. These efforts will be twice blessed—"blessing him that gives and him that takes."[3]

There is no escape through law of man or God from the inevitable:—

[3] From Shakespeare's *Merchant of Venice* (IV.1.1670): "It blesseth him that gives and him that takes."

> The laws of changeless justice bind
> Oppressor with oppressed;
> And close as sin and suffering joined
> We march to fate abreast.[4]

Nearly sixteen millions of hands will aid you in pulling the load upward, or they will pull against you the load downward. We shall constitute one-third and more of the ignorance and crime of the South, or one-third its intelligence and progress; we shall contribute one-third to the business and industrial prosperity of the South, or we shall prove a veritable body of death, stagnating, depressing, retarding every effort to advance the body politic.

Gentlemen of the Exposition, as we present to you our humble effort at an exhibition of our progress, you must not expect overmuch. Starting thirty years ago with ownership here and there in a few quilts and pumpkins and chickens (gathered from miscellaneous sources), remember the path that has led from these to the inventions and production of agricultural implements, buggies, steam-engines, newspapers, books, statuary, carving, paintings, the management of drugstores and banks, has not been trodden without contact with thorns and thistles. While we take pride in what we exhibit as a result of our independent efforts, we do not for a moment forget that our part in this exhibition would fall far short of your expectations but for the constant help that has come to our educational life, not only from the Southern states, but especially from Northern philanthropists, who have made their gifts a constant stream of blessing and encouragement.

The wisest among my race understand that the agitation of questions of social equality is the extremest folly, and that progress in the enjoyment of all the privileges that will come to us must be the result of severe and constant struggle rather than of artificial forcing. No race that has anything to contribute to the markets of the world is long in any degree ostracized. It is important and right that all privileges of the law be ours, but it is vastly more important that we be prepared for the exercises of these privileges. The opportunity to earn a dollar in a factory just now is worth infinitely more than the opportunity to spend a dollar in an opera-house.

In conclusion, may I repeat that nothing in thirty years has given us more hope and encouragement, and drawn us so near to you of the white race, as this opportunity offered by the Exposition; and here bending, as it were, over the altar that represents the results of the struggles of your race and mine, both starting practically empty-handed three decades ago, I pledge that in your effort to work out the great and intricate problem which God has laid at the doors of the South, you shall have at all times the patient, sympathetic help of my race; only let this be constantly in mind, that, while from representations in these buildings of the product of field, of forest, of mine, of factory, letters, and art, much good will come, yet far above and beyond material benefits will be that higher good, that, let us pray God, will come, in a blotting out of sectional differences and racial animosities and suspicions, in a determination to administer absolute justice, in a willing obedience among all classes to the mandates of law. This, this, coupled with our material prosperity, will bring into our beloved South a new heaven and a new earth.

The first thing that I remember, after I had finished speaking, was that Governor Bullock rushed across the platform and took me by the hand, and that others did the same. I received so many and such hearty congratulations that I found it

---

[4] From "Song of the Negro Boatman," by the poet John Greenleaf Whittier (1807–1892).

difficult to get out of the building. I did not appreciate to any degree, however, the impression which my address seemed to have made, until the next morning, when I went into the business part of the city. As soon as I was recognized, I was surprised to find myself pointed out and surrounded by a crowd of men who wished to shake hands with me. This was kept up on every street on to which I went, to an extent which embarrassed me so much that I went back to my boarding-place. The next morning I returned to Tuskegee.[5] At the station in Atlanta, and at almost all of the stations at which the train stopped between that city and Tuskegee, I found a crowd of people anxious to shake hands with me.

The papers in all parts of the United States published the address in full, and for months afterward there were complimentary editorial references to it. Mr. Clark Howell, the editor of the Atlanta *Constitution*, telegraphed to a New York paper, among other words, the following, "I do not exaggerate when I say that Professor Booker T. Washington's address yesterday was one of the most notable speeches, both as to character and as to the warmth of its reception, ever delivered to a Southern audience. The address was a revelation. The whole speech is a platform upon which blacks and whites can stand with full justice to each other."

The Boston *Transcript* said editorially: "The speech of Booker T. Washington at the Atlanta Exposition, this week, seems to have dwarfed all the other proceedings and the Exposition itself. The sensation that it has caused in the press has never been equalled."

I very soon began receiving all kinds of propositions from lecture bureaus, and editors of magazines and papers, to take the lecture platform, and to write articles. One lecture bureau offered me fifty thousand dollars, or two hundred dollars a night and expenses, if I would place my services at its disposal for a given period. To all these communications I replied that my life-work was at Tuskegee; and that whenever I spoke it must be in the interests of the Tuskegee school and my race, and that I would enter into no arrangements that seemed to place a mere commercial value upon my services.

Some days after its delivery I sent a copy of my address to the President of the United States, the Hon. Grover Cleveland.[6] I received from him the following autograph reply:—

> Gray Gables, Buzzard's Bay, Mass.,
> October 6, 1895.
>
> BOOKER T. WASHINGTON, ESQ.:
>
> My Dear Sir: I thank you for sending me a copy of your address delivered at the Atlanta Exposition.
>
> I thank you with much enthusiasm for making the address. I have read it with intense interest, and I think the Exposition would be fully justified if it did not do more than furnish the opportunity for its delivery. Your words cannot fail to delight and encourage all who wish well for your race; and if our coloured fellow-citizens do not from your utterances gather new hope and form new determinations to gain every valuable advantage offered them by their citizenship, it will be strange indeed.
>
> Yours very truly,
> GROVER CLEVELAND.

[5] Tuskegee, Alabama, where Washington had founded the Tuskegee Institute, a school for training African-American teachers, in 1881.

[6] Cleveland (1837–1908) was the twenty-second (1885–1889) and twenty-fourth (1893–1897) U.S. president.

Later I met Mr. Cleveland, for the first time, when, as President, he visited the Atlanta Exposition. At the request of myself and others he consented to spend an hour in the Negro Building, for the purpose of inspecting the Negro exhibit and of giving the coloured people in attendance an opportunity to shake hands with him. As soon as I met Mr. Cleveland I became impressed with his simplicity, greatness, and rugged honesty. I have met him many times since then, both at public functions and at his private residence in Princeton, and the more I see of him the more I admire him. When he visited the Negro Building in Atlanta he seemed to give himself up wholly, for that hour, to the coloured people. He seemed to be as careful to shake hands with some old coloured "auntie" clad partially in rags, and to take as much pleasure in doing so, as if he were greeting some millionnaire. Many of the coloured people took advantage of the occasion to get him to write his name in a book or on a slip of paper. He was as careful and patient in doing this as if he were putting his signature to some great state document.

Mr. Cleveland has not only shown his friendship for me in many personal ways, but has always consented to do anything I have asked of him for our school. This he has done, whether it was to make a personal donation or to use his influence in securing the donations of others. Judging from my personal acquaintance with Mr. Cleveland, I do not believe that he is conscious of possessing any colour prejudice. He is too great for that. In my contact with people I find that, as a rule, it is only the little, narrow people who live for themselves, who never read good books, who do not travel, who never open up their souls in a way to permit them to come into contact with other souls—with the great outside world. No man whose vision is bounded by colour can come into contact with what is highest and best in the world. In meeting men, in many places, I have found that the happiest people are those who do the most for others; the most miserable are those who do the least. I have also found that few things, if any, are capable of making one so blind and narrow as race prejudice. I often say to our students, in the course of my talks to them on Sunday evenings in the chapel, that the longer I live and the more experience I have of the world, the more I am convinced that, after all, the one thing that is most worth living for—and dying for, if need be—is the opportunity of making some one else more happy and more useful.

The coloured people and the coloured newspapers at first seemed to be greatly pleased with the character of my Atlanta address, as well as with its reception. But after the first burst of enthusiasm began to die away, and the coloured people began reading the speech in cold type, some of them seemed to feel that they had been hypnotized. They seemed to feel that I had been too liberal in my remarks toward the Southern whites, and that I had not spoken out strongly enough for what they termed the "rights" of the race. For a while there was a reaction, so far as a certain element of my own race was concerned, but later these reactionary ones seemed to have been won over to my way of believing and acting.

While speaking of changes in public sentiment, I recall that about ten years after the school at Tuskegee was established, I had an experience that I shall never forget. Dr. Lyman Abbott,[7] then the pastor of Plymouth Church, and also editor of the *Outlook* (then the *Christian Union*), asked me to write a letter for his paper giving my opinion of the exact condition, mental and moral, of the coloured ministers in the South, as based upon my observations. I wrote the letter, giving the

---

[7] Abbott (1835–1922) was a Congregationalist minister, pastor of Plymouth Church in Brooklyn, New York, and editor of *The Christian Examiner* (1870–1893) and of its successor, *The Outlook* (1893–1935).

exact facts as I conceived them to be. The picture painted was a rather black one—or, since I am black, shall I say "white"? It could not be otherwise with a race but a few years out of slavery, a race which had not had time or opportunity to produce a competent ministry.

What I said soon reached every Negro minister in the country, I think, and the letters of condemnation which I received from them were not few. I think that for a year after the publication of this article every association and every conference or religious body of any kind, of my race, that met, did not fail before adjourning to pass a resolution condemning me, or calling upon me to retract or modify what I had said. Many of these organizations went so far in their resolutions as to advise parents to cease sending their children to Tuskegee. One association even appointed a "missionary" whose duty it was to warn the people against sending their children to Tuskegee. This missionary had a son in the school, and I noticed that, whatever the "missionary" might have said or done with regard to others, he was careful not to take his son away from the institution. Many of the coloured papers, especially those that were the organs of religious bodies, joined in the general chorus of condemnation or demands for retraction.

During the whole time of the excitement, and through all the criticism, I did not utter a word of explanation or retraction. I knew that I was right, and that time and the sober second thought of the people would vindicate me. It was not long before the bishops and other church leaders began to make a careful investigation of the conditions of the ministry, and they found out that I was right. In fact, the oldest and most influential bishop in one branch of the Methodist Church said that my words were far too mild. Very soon public sentiment began making itself felt, in demanding a purifying of the ministry. While this is not yet complete by any means, I think I may say, without egotism, and I have been told by many of our most influential ministers, that my words had much to do with starting a demand for the placing of a higher type of men in the pulpit. I have had the satisfaction of having many who once condemned me thank me heartily for my frank words.

The change of the attitude of the Negro ministry, so far as regards myself, is so complete that at the present time I have no warmer friends among any class than I have among the clergymen. The improvement in the character and life of the Negro ministers is one of the most gratifying evidences of the progress of the race. My experience with them, as well as other events in my life, convince me that the thing to do, when one feels sure that he has said or done the right thing, and is condemned, is to stand still and keep quiet. If he is right, time will show it.

In the midst of the discussion which was going on concerning my Atlanta speech, I received the letter which I give below, from Dr. Gilman,[8] the President of Johns Hopkins University, who had been made chairman of the judges of award in connection with the Atlanta Exposition:—

> Johns Hopkins University, Baltimore,
> President's Office, September 30, 1895.

> Dear Mr. Washington: Would it be agreeable to you to be one of the Judges of Award in the Department of Education at Atlanta? If so, I shall be glad to place your name upon the list. A line by telegraph will be welcomed.
>
> Yours very truly,
> D. C. GILMAN.

[8] Daniel Coit Gilman (1831–1908), president of the University of California (1872–1875), and first president of Johns Hopkins University (1876–1901) and of the Carnegie Institution (1901–1904).

I think I was even more surprised to receive this invitation than I had been to receive the invitation to speak at the opening of the Exposition. It was to be a part of my duty, as one of the jurors, to pass not only upon the exhibits of the coloured schools, but also upon those of the white schools. I accepted the position, and spent a month in Atlanta in performance of the duties which it entailed. The board of jurors was a large one, consisting in all of sixty members. It was about equally divided between Southern white people and Northern white people. Among them were college presidents, leading scientists and men of letters, and specialists in many subjects. When the group of jurors to which I was assigned met for organization, Mr. Thomas Nelson Page,[9] who was one of the number, moved that I be made secretary of that division, and the motion was unanimously adopted. Nearly half of our division were Southern people. In performing my duties in the inspection of the exhibits of white schools I was in every case treated with respect, and at the close of our labours I parted from my associates with regret.

I am often asked to express myself more freely than I do upon the political condition and the political future of my race. These recollections of my experience in Atlanta give me the opportunity to do so briefly. My own belief is, although I have never before said so in so many words, that the time will come when the Negro in the South will be accorded all the political rights which his ability, character, and material possessions entitle him to. I think, though, that the opportunity to freely exercise such political rights will not come in any large degree through outside or artificial forcing, but will be accorded to the Negro by the Southern white people themselves, and that they will protect him in the exercise of those rights. Just as soon as the South gets over the old feeling that it is being forced by "foreigners," or "aliens," to do something which it does not want to do, I believe that the change in the direction that I have indicated is going to begin. In fact, there are indications that it is already beginning in a slight degree.

Let me illustrate my meaning. Suppose that some months before the opening of the Atlanta Exposition there had been a general demand from the press and public platform outside the South that a Negro be given a place on the opening programme, and that a Negro be placed upon the board of jurors of award. Would any such recognition of the race have taken place? I do not think so. The Atlanta officials went so far as they did because they felt it to be a pleasure, as well as a duty, to reward what they considered merit in the Negro race. Say what we will, there is something in human nature which we cannot blot out, which makes one man, in the end, recognize and reward merit in another, regardless of colour or race.

I believe it is the duty of the Negro—as the greater part of the race is already doing—to deport himself modestly in regard to political claims, depending upon the slow but sure influences that proceed from the possession of property, intelligence, and high character for the full recognition of his political rights. I think that the according of the full exercise of political rights is going to be a matter of natural, slow growth, not an over-night, gourd-vine affair. I do not believe that the Negro should cease voting, for a man cannot learn the exercise of self-government by ceasing to vote, any more than a boy can learn to swim by keeping out of the water, but I do believe that in his voting he should more and more be influenced by those of intelligence and character who are his next-door neighbours.

I know coloured men who, through the encouragement, help, and advice of

---

[9] Page (1853–1922) was a Virginia-born author of novels set in the old South and during Reconstruction and served as U.S. ambassador to Italy (1913–1919).

Southern white people, have accumulated thousands of dollars' worth of property, but who, at the same time, would never think of going to those same persons for advice concerning the casting of their ballots. This, it seems to me, is unwise and unreasonable, and should cease. In saying this I do not mean that the Negro should truckle, or not vote from principle, for the instant he ceases to vote from principle he loses the confidence and respect of the Southern white man even.

I do not believe that any state should make a law that permits an ignorant and poverty-stricken white man vote, and prevents a black man in the same condition from voting. Such a law is not only unjust, but it will react, as all unjust laws do, in time; for the effect of such a law is to encourage the Negro to secure education and property, and at the same time it encourages the white man to remain in ignorance and poverty. I believe that in time, through the operation of intelligence and friendly race relations, all cheating at the ballot-box in the South will cease. It will become apparent that the white man who begins by cheating a Negro out of his ballot soon learns to cheat a white man out of his, and that the man who does this ends his career of dishonesty by the theft of property or by some equally serious crime. In my opinion, the time will come when the South will encourage all of its citizens to vote. It will see that it pays better, from every standpoint, to have healthy, vigorous life than to have that political stagnation which always results when one-half of the population has no share and no interest in the Government.

As a rule, I believe in universal, free suffrage, but I believe that in the South we are confronted with peculiar conditions that justify the protection of the ballot in many of the states, for a while at least, either by an educational test, a property test, or by both combined; but whatever tests are required, they should be made to apply with equal and exact justice to both races.

1900–1901

W. E. B. Du Bois
(1868–1963)

In the "Forethought" to *The Souls of Black Folk* (1903), William Edward Burghardt Du Bois made the following provocative statement: "Herein lie buried many things which if read with patience may show the strange meaning of being black here in the dawning of the twentieth century." Near the end of the twentieth century, the import of these words and of the experiences out of which they came has become clearer than ever before. We have begun to see that anyone who hopes to understand the meaning of black experience in American society must pay attention to Du Bois and to his ideas about racial diversity and conflict in the United States.

Born in 1868 in Great Barrington, Massachusetts, Du Bois was educated at Fisk University in Nashville, Harvard University, and the University of Berlin. He dedicated his intellectual energies to the then new discipline of sociology. If his education differed from that of other African Americans, his life experiences were distinct from those of most sociologists. During his summers as an undergraduate at Fisk, for example, he taught at African-American schools in rural Tennessee and thus came to know chronic racial oppression in a deeply personal way. As a young sociologist living in the North, however, Du Bois began his professional career as the product of his scholarly training. His study *The Philadelphia Negro* (1899) manifests an objective approach to its subject, a detached marshaling of evidence.

When Du Bois settled in Atlanta in 1897, an environment of racist violence brought him to realize that his race and his professional training could no longer be separated. On his way to visit the folk writer Joel Chandler Harris (creator of the Uncle Remus stories), he saw a lynched African-American man hanging in a storefront window. The brutality of such spectacles led Du Bois to write *The Souls of Black Folk,* a compelling mélange of exhortation, sociological survey, folk study, autobiography, and realist narrative. In this volume he sets himself in vehement opposition to the doctrine of acceptance and compromise articulated by Booker T. Washington at the Atlanta Exposition in 1895. Du Bois argues that blacks will never be a part of white America, that they should educate themselves not as members of a white industrial society but rather as members of a black and ancient race. In *The Souls of Black Folk* Du Bois also found the idiom that would characterize his expanding career as champion of black dignity. He extended his ideas to include black experience globally, until his death in Ghana in 1963.

Du Bois fashioned a voice of resistance and a mode of perception that have become beacons for black writers in the twentieth century. As different as they are, such writers as James Weldon Johnson and Jean Toomer, Langston Hughes and Malcolm X, Ralph Ellison and Toni Morrison have described "the strange meaning of being black" in America as unique in its complexity and in the resonance of its pain. In doing so, they—like Du Bois before them—have converted suppression to achievement, "invisibility" to a determined quest for self-affirming identity.

Suggested Readings: *The Philadelphia Negro: A Social Study,* 1899. *W. E. B. Du Bois Speaks: Speeches and Addresses,* ed. P. S. Foner, 1970. *The Emerging Thought of W. E. B. Du Bois: Essays and Editorials From the "Crisis",* ed. H. L. Moon, 1972. *The Correspondence of W. E. B. Du Bois,* 3 vols., ed. H. Aptheker, 1973–1978. F. L. Broderick, *W. E. B. DuBois: Negro Leader in a Time of Crisis,* 1959. E. M. Rudwick, *W. E. B. Du Bois: A Study in Minority Group Leadership,* 1961. J. H. Franklin, *From Slavery to Freedom: A History of American Negroes,* 1967. A. Rampersad, *The Art and Imagination of W. E. B. Du Bois,* 1976. J. B. Moore, *W. E. B. Du Bois,* 1981. J. P. De Marco, *The Social Thought of W. E. B. Du Bois,* 1983. W. L. Andrews, *Critical Essays on W. E. B. Du Bois,* 1985.

Text Used: *The Souls of Black Folk: Essays and Sketches,* 1903.

from THE SOULS OF BLACK FOLK*

THE FORETHOUGHT[1]

Herein lie buried many things which if read with patience may show the strange meaning of being black here in the dawning of the Twentieth Century. This meaning is not without interest to you, Gentle Reader; for the problem of the Twentieth Century is the problem of the color-line.

---

* This collection of fourteen essays on the social and spiritual world in which African Americans lived at the beginning of the twentieth century was first published in 1903.

[1] A brief preface written to introduce the essays in *The Souls of Black Folk* and to explain the book's mission.

I pray you, then, receive my little book in all charity, studying my words with me, forgiving mistake and foible for sake of the faith and passion that is in me, and seeking the grain of truth hidden there.

I have sought here to sketch, in vague, uncertain outline, the spiritual world in which ten thousand thousand Americans live and strive. First, in two chapters I have tried to show what Emancipation meant to them, and what was its aftermath. In a third chapter I have pointed out the slow rise of personal leadership, and criticised candidly the leader who bears the chief burden of his race to-day. Then, in two other chapters I have sketched in swift outline the two worlds within and without the Veil, and thus have come to the central problem of training men for life. Venturing now into deeper detail, I have in two chapters studied the struggles of the massed millions of the black peasantry, and in another have sought to make clear the present relations of the sons of master and man.

Leaving, then, the world of the white man, I have stepped within the Veil, raising it that you may view faintly its deeper recesses,—the meaning of its religion, the passion of its human sorrow, and the struggle of its greater souls. All this I have ended with a tale twice told but seldom written.

Some of these thoughts of mine have seen the light before in other guise. For kindly consenting to their republication here, in altered and extended form, I must thank the publishers of *The Atlantic Monthly, The World's Work, The Dial, The New World,* and the *Annals of the American Academy of Political and Social Science.*

Before each chapter, as now printed, stands a bar of the Sorrow Songs,—some echo of haunting melody from the only American music which welled up from black souls in the dark past. And, finally, need I add that I who speak here am bone of the bone and flesh of the flesh of them that live within the Veil?

W. E. B. Du B.

Atlanta, Ga., Feb. 1, 1903.

III: Of Mr. Booker T. Washington and Others*

From birth till death enslaved; in word, in deed, unmanned!

Hereditary bondsmen! Know ye not
Who would be free themselves must strike the blow?

Byron.[1]

* An essay first published in the *Guardian,* July 27, 1902.
[1] From *Childe Harold's Pilgrimage* (11. 74.710, 11.76.720–721), by the English romantic poet George Gordon (1788–1824), Lord Byron. The music that follows is from the refrain of a spiritual, what Du Bois calls a "Sorrow Song," entitled "A Great Camp-Meeting in de Promised Land." The words are "Going to mourn and never tire, / Mourn and never tire, mourn and never tire."

Easily the most striking thing in the history of the American Negro since 1876[2] is the ascendancy of Mr. Booker T. Washington.[3] It began at the time when war memories and ideals were rapidly passing; a day of astonishing commercial development was dawning; a sense of doubt and hesitation overtook the freedmen's sons,—then it was that his leading began. Mr. Washington came, with a simple definite programme, at the psychological moment when the nation was a little ashamed of having bestowed so much sentiment on Negroes, and was concentrating its energies on Dollars. His programme of industrial education, conciliation of the South, and submission and silence as to civil and political rights, was not wholly original; the Free Negroes from 1830 up to war-time had striven to build industrial schools, and the American Missionary Association had from the first taught various trades; and Price[4] and others had sought a way of honorable alliance with the best of the Southerners. But Mr. Washington first indissolubly linked these things; he put enthusiasm, unlimited energy, and perfect faith into this programme, and changed it from a by-path into a veritable Way of Life. And the tale of the methods by which he did this is a fascinating study of human life.

It startled the nation to hear a Negro advocating such a programme after many decades of bitter complaint; it startled and won the applause of the South, it interested and won the admiration of the North; and after a confused murmur of protest, it silenced if it did not convert the Negroes themselves.

To gain the sympathy and cooperation of the various elements comprising the white South was Mr. Washington's first task; and this, at the time Tuskegee was founded, seemed, for a black man, well-nigh impossible. And yet ten years later it was done in the word spoken at Atlanta: "In all things purely social we can be as separate as the five fingers, and yet one as the hand in all things essential to mutual progress." This "Atlanta Compromise"[5] is by all odds the most notable thing in Mr. Washington's career. The South interpreted it in different ways: the radicals received it as a complete surrender of the demand for civil and political equality; the conservatives, as a generously conceived working basis for mutual understanding. So both approved it, and to-day its author is certainly the most distinguished Southerner since Jefferson Davis,[6] and the one with the largest personal following.

Next to this achievement comes Mr. Washington's work in gaining place and consideration in the North. Others less shrewd and tactful had formerly essayed to sit on these two stools and had fallen between them; but as Mr. Washington knew the heart of the South from birth and training, so by singular insight he intuitively grasped the spirit of the age which was dominating the North. And so thoroughly did he learn the speech and thought of triumphant commercialism, and the ideals

[2] The year marking the end of Reconstruction in the South.

[3] Washington (1856?–1915), the renowned African-American educator who founded Tuskegee Institute in Alabama and was an influential spokesman for African Americans; his address at the Atlanta Exposition in 1895 brought him to national prominence.

[4] Thomas Frederick Price (1860–1919), a Roman Catholic priest who was a founder of the American Missionary Association.

[5] "Compromise" is Du Bois's term for what Washington proposed in his Atlanta address: an emphasis on vocational training for African Americans rather than an insistence on civil and social rights. Washington intended to promote racial harmony and to prepare young men and women for employment.

[6] Davis (1809–1889) was a U.S. senator from Mississippi (1847–1851, 1857–1861) and secretary of war (1853–1857) under the fourteenth President, Franklin Pierce (1804–1869); Davis became president of the Confederacy during the Civil War.

of material prosperity, that the picture of a lone black boy poring over a French grammar amid the weeds and dirt of a neglected home soon seemed to him the acme of absurdities.[7] One wonders what Socrates and St. Francis of Assisi would say to this.

And yet this very singleness of vision and thorough oneness with his age is a mark of the successful man. It is as though Nature must needs make men narrow in order to give them force. So Mr. Washington's cult has gained unquestioning followers, his work has wonderfully prospered, his friends are legion, and his enemies are confounded. To-day he stands as the one recognized spokesman of his ten million fellows, and one of the most notable figures in a nation of seventy millions. One hesitates, therefore, to criticize a life which, beginning with so little, has done so much. And yet the time is come when one may speak in all sincerity and utter courtesy of the mistakes and shortcomings of Mr. Washington's career, as well as of his triumphs, without being thought captious or envious, and without forgetting that it is easier to do ill than well in the world.

The criticism that has hitherto met Mr. Washington has not always been of this broad character. In the South especially has he had to walk warily to avoid the harshest judgments,—and naturally so, for he is dealing with the one subject of deepest sensitiveness to that section. Twice—once when at the Chicago celebration of the Spanish-American War he alluded to the color-prejudice that is "eating away the vitals of the South," and once when he dined with President Roosevelt[8]—has the resulting Southern criticism been violent enough to threaten seriously his popularity. In the North the feeling has several times forced itself into words, that Mr. Washington's counsels of submission overlooked certain elements of true manhood, and that his educational programme was unnecessarily narrow. Usually, however, such criticism has not found open expression, although, too, the spiritual sons of the Abolitionists have not been prepared to acknowledge that the schools founded before Tuskegee, by men of broad ideals and self-sacrificing spirit, were wholly failures or worthy of ridicule. While, then, criticism has not failed to follow Mr. Washington, yet the prevailing public opinion of the land has been but too willing to deliver the solution of a wearisome problem into his hands, and say, "If that is all you and your race ask, take it."

Among his own people, however, Mr. Washington has encountered the strongest and most lasting opposition, amounting at times to bitterness, and even to-day continuing strong and insistent even though largely silenced in outward expression by the public opinion of the nation. Some of this opposition is, of course, mere envy; the disappointment of displaced demagogues and the spite of narrow minds. But aside from this, there is among educated and thoughtful colored men in all parts of the land a feeling of deep regret, sorrow, and apprehension at the wide currency and ascendancy which some of Mr. Washington's theories have gained. These same men admire his sincerity of purpose, and are willing to forgive much to honest endeavor which is doing something worth the doing. They cooperate with Mr. Washington as far as they conscientiously can; and, indeed, it is no ordinary tribute to this man's tact and power that, steering as he must between so many diverse interests and opinions, he so largely retains the respect of all.

[7] Washington encountered this situation during his travels in the South and lamented the futility of such study when practical skills seemed so necessary (in *Up From Slavery* [1901], Ch. VIII).

[8] Theodore Roosevelt (1858–1919), twenty-sixth U.S. president (1901–1909). Different groups in different parts of the country criticized Washington for attending this dinner in 1901.

But the hushing of the criticism of honest opponents is a dangerous thing. It leads some of the best of the critics to unfortunate silence and paralysis of effort, and others to burst into speech so passionately and intemperately as to lose listeners. Honest and earnest criticism from those whose interests are most nearly touched,—criticism of writers by readers, of government by those governed, of leaders by those led,—this is the soul of democracy and the safeguard of modern society. If the best of the American Negroes receive by outer pressure a leader whom they had not recognized before, manifestly there is here a certain palpable gain. Yet there is also irreparable loss,—a loss of that peculiarly valuable education which a group receives when by search and criticism it finds and commissions its own leaders. The way in which this is done is at once the most elementary and the nicest problem of social growth. History is but the record of such group-leadership; and yet how infinitely changeful is its type and character! And of all types and kinds, what can be more instructive than the leadership of a group within a group?—that curious double movement where real progress may be negative and actual advance be relative retrogression. All this is the social student's inspiration and despair.

Now in the past the American Negro has had instructive experience in the choosing of group leaders, founding thus a peculiar dynasty which in the light of present conditions is worth while studying. When sticks and stones and beasts form the sole environment of a people, their attitude is largely one of determined opposition to and conquest of natural forces. But when to earth and brute is added an environment of men and ideas, then the attitude of the imprisoned group may take three main forms,—a feeling of revolt and revenge; an attempt to adjust all thought and action to the will of the greater group; or, finally, a determined effort at self-realization and self-development despite environing opinion. The influence of all of these attitudes at various times can be traced in the history of the American Negro, and in the evolution of his successive leaders.

Before 1750, while the fire of African freedom still burned in the veins of the slaves, there was in all leadership or attempted leadership but the one motive of revolt and revenge,—typified in the terrible Maroons, the Danish blacks, and Cato of Stono,[9] and veiling all the Americas in fear of insurrection. The liberalizing tendencies of the latter half of the eighteenth century brought, along with kindlier relations between black and white, thoughts of ultimate adjustment and assimilation. Such aspiration was especially voiced in the earnest songs of Phyllis, in the martyrdom of Attucks, the fighting of Salem and Poor, the intellectual accomplishments of Banneker and Derham, and the political demands of the Cuffes.[10]

Stern financial and social stress after the war cooled much of the previous hu-

---

[9] Fugitive slaves from the West Indies and Guiana in the seventeenth and eighteenth centuries, or their descendants; slaves in the Danish West Indies, who revolted in 1733 because of food shortages; Cato of Stono, North Carolina, who led a slave insurrection in 1739 during which twenty-five whites were killed.

[10] Notable eighteenth-century African Americans: the poet Phillis Wheatley (1753?–1784); Crispus Attucks (1723?–1770), the leader of colonists killed by British troops in the "Boston Massacre"; Peter Salem (?–1816), the patriot who shot Major Pitcairn in the Battle of Bunker Hill during the Revolutionary War; Salem Poor (1747–?), a soldier who fought at Bunker Hill and Valley Forge; Benjamin Banneker (1731–1806), a Maryland mathematician who published his astronomical calculations from 1791 to 1797 in his *Almanack and Ephemeris;* James Derham (1762–?), an eminent New Orleans physician who bought his freedom in 1783; Paul Cuffe (1759–1817), a Massachusetts organizer of a movement to settle free blacks in African colonies.

manitarian ardor. The disappointment and impatience of the Negroes at the persistence of slavery and serfdom voiced itself in two movements. The slaves in the South, aroused undoubtedly by vague rumors of the Haytian revolt, made three fierce attempts at insurrection,—in 1800 under Gabriel in Virginia, in 1822 under Vesey in Carolina, and in 1831 again in Virginia under the terrible Nat Turner.[11] In the Free States, on the other hand, a new and curious attempt at self-development was made. In Philadelphia and New York color-prescription led to a withdrawal of Negro communicants from white churches and the formation of a peculiar socio-religious institution among the Negroes known as the African Church,—an organization still living and controlling in its various branches over a million of men.

Walker's[12] wild appeal against the trend of the times showed how the world was changing after the coming of the cotton-gin. By 1830 slavery seemed hopelessly fastened on the South, and the slaves thoroughly cowed into submission. The free Negroes of the North, inspired by the mulatto immigrants from the West Indies, began to change the basis of their demands; they recognized the slavery of slaves, but insisted that they themselves were freemen, and sought assimilation and amalgamation with the nation on the same terms with other men. Thus, Forten and Purvis of Philadelphia, Shad of Wilmington, Du Bois of New Haven, Barbadoes of Boston,[13] and others, strove singly and together as men, they said, not as slaves; as "people of color," not as "Negroes." The trend of the times, however, refused them recognition save in individual and exceptional cases, considered them as one with all the despised blacks, and they soon found themselves striving to keep even the rights they formerly had of voting and working and moving as freemen. Schemes of migration and colonization arose among them; but these they refused to entertain, and they eventually turned to the Abolition movement as a final refuge.

Here, led by Remond, Nell, Wells-Brown, and Douglass,[14] a new period of self-assertion and self-development dawned. To be sure, ultimate freedom and assimilation was the ideal before the leaders, but the assertion of the manhood

---

[11] Gabriel (1775?–1800) was hanged after his aborted attempt to attack Richmond, Virginia, with a thousand slaves; Denmark Vesey (1767?–1822), after purchasing his freedom in 1800, was hanged for leading a slave uprising in North Carolina; Turner (1800–1831) was hanged for commanding approximately sixty slaves in an insurrection in Southampton County, Virginia.

[12] David Walker (1785?–1830), a free-born African American, who urged blacks to unite against slavery in his pamphlet, *Walker's Appeal,* in Boston in 1831.

[13] James Forten (1766–1842), a drummer-boy during the American Revolution, later a prosperous manufacturer of sailboat equipment in Philadelphia; Robert Purvis (1810–1898), president of the Underground Railroad and co-founder of the American Anti-Slavery Society in 1833; Abraham Shadd (?–1860?), a Delaware delegate to the first National Negro Convention in 1830 and president of the third Convention in 1833; Alexander Du Bois (1803–1887), active in the Negro Episcopal church in Massachusetts and grandfather of W. E. B. Du Bois; James G. Barbadoes, a Massachusetts delegate to the first National Negro Convention.

[14] African-American leaders whose careers spanned the Civil War: Charles Lenox Remond (1810–1873), an abolitionist and powerful orator from Salem, Massachusetts, who served as recruiting officer for the Massachusetts militia during the Civil War; William Cooper Nell (1816–1874), an abolitionist and the first African American to secure a U.S. government appointment (as postal clerk), instrumental in extending equal opportunities to all schoolchildren in Boston; William Wells Brown (1816?–1884), a writer whose works included an autobiographical *Narrative* (1847) and *Clotel: Or, The President's Daughter* (1853), the first published novel by an African American; Frederick Douglass (1817–1895), author of the *Narrative of the Life of Frederick Douglass* (1845), later U.S. minister to Haiti and U.S. marshal of the District of Columbia.

rights of the Negro by himself was the main reliance, and John Brown's raid[15] was the extreme of its logic. After the war and emancipation, the great form of Frederick Douglass, the greatest of American Negro leaders, still led the host. Self-assertion, especially in political lines, was the main programme, and behind Douglass came Elliot, Bruce, and Langston, and the Reconstruction politicians, and, less conspicuous but of greater social significance Alexander Crummell and Bishop Daniel Payne.[16]

Then came the Revolution of 1876, the suppression of the Negro votes, the changing and shifting of ideals, and the seeking of new lights in the great night. Douglass, in his old age, still bravely stood for the ideals of his early manhood,—ultimate assimilation *through* self-assertion, and on no other terms. For a time Price arose as a new leader, destined, it seemed, not to give up, but to re-state the old ideals in a form less repugnant to the white South. But he passed away in his prime. Then came the new leader. Nearly all the former ones had become leaders by the silent suffrage of their fellows, had sought to lead their own people alone, and were usually, save Douglass, little known outside their race. But Booker T. Washington arose as essentially the leader not of one race but of two,—a compromiser between the South, the North, and the Negro. Naturally the Negroes resented, at first bitterly, signs of compromise which surrendered their civil and political rights, even though this was to be exchanged for larger chances of economic development. The rich and dominating North, however, was not only weary of the race problem, but was investing largely in Southern enterprises, and welcomed any method of peaceful cooperation. Thus, by national opinion, the Negroes began to recognize Mr. Washington's leadership; and the voice of criticism was hushed.

Mr. Washington represents in Negro thought the old attitude of adjustment and submission; but adjustment at such a peculiar time as to make his programme unique. This is an age of unusual economic development, and Mr. Washington's programme naturally takes an economic cast, becoming a gospel of Work and Money to such an extent as apparently almost completely to overshadow the higher aims of life. Moreover, this is an age when the more advanced races are coming in closer contact with the less developed races, and the race-feeling is therefore intensified; and Mr. Washington's programme practically accepts the alleged inferiority of the Negro races. Again, in our own land, the reaction from the sentiment of war time has given impetus to race-prejudice against Negroes, and Mr. Washington withdraws many of the high demands of Negroes as men and American citizens. In other periods of intensified prejudice all the Negro's tendency to self-assertion has been called forth; at this period a policy of submission is advocated. In the history of nearly all other races and peoples the doctrine

[15] Brown (1800–1859) was a white abolitionist who led a raid on the U.S. armory in Harper's Ferry, Virginia, in October 1859. He was captured, tried, and hanged in December 1859.

[16] African Americans whose careers flourished in the latter half of the nineteenth century: Robert Brown Elliot (1842–1884), a graduate of Eton in England and U.S. congressman from South Carolina; Blanche K. Bruce (1841–1898), a Virginia-born slave educated at Oberlin College in Ohio, U.S. Senator from Mississippi (1875–1881); John Mercer Langston (1829–1897), an educator, lawyer, president of the Virginia Normal and Collegiate Institute (1885–1888), and U.S. congressman from Virginia (1888–1890); Crummell (1819–1898) was an Episcopal missionary in Liberia for twenty years after being educated at Cambridge University in England; Payne (1811–1893) was bishop of the African Methodist Episcopal church and president of Wilberforce University (1863–1870).

preached at such crises has been that manly self-respect is worth more than lands and houses, and that a people who voluntarily surrender such respect, or cease striving for it, are not worth civilizing.

In answer to this, it has been claimed that the Negro can survive only through submission. Mr. Washington distinctly asks that black people give up, at least for the present, three things,—

First, political power,

Second, insistence on civil rights,

Third, higher education of Negro youth,—

and concentrate all their energies on industrial education, the accumulation of wealth, and the conciliation of the South. This policy has been courageously and insistently advocated for over fifteen years, and has been triumphant for perhaps ten years. As a result of this tender of the palm-branch, what has been the return? In these years there have occurred:

1. The disfranchisement of the Negro.

2. The legal creation of a distinct status of civil inferiority for the Negro.

3. The steady withdrawal of aid from institutions for the higher training of the Negro.

These movements are not, to be sure, direct results of Mr. Washington's teachings; but his propaganda has, without a shadow of doubt, helped their speedier accomplishment. The question then comes: Is it possible, and probable, that nine millions of men can make effective progress in economic lines if they are deprived of political rights, made a servile caste, and allowed only the most meagre chance for developing their exceptional men? If history and reason give any distinct answer to these questions, it is an emphatic *No*. And Mr. Washington thus faces the triple paradox of his career:

1. He is striving nobly to make Negro artisans business men and property-owners; but it is utterly impossible, under modern competitive methods, for workingmen and property-owners to defend their rights and exist without the right of suffrage.

2. He insists on thrift and self-respect, but at the same time counsels a silent submission to civic inferiority such as is bound to sap the manhood of any race in the long run.

3. He advocates common-school[17] and industrial training, and depreciates institutions of higher learning; but neither the Negro common-schools, nor Tuskegee itself, could remain open a day were it not for teachers trained in Negro colleges, or trained by their graduates.

This triple paradox in Mr. Washington's position is the object of criticism by two classes of colored Americans. One class is spiritually descended from Toussaint the Savior,[18] through Gabriel, Vesey, and Turner, and they represent the attitude of revolt and revenge; they hate the white South blindly and distrust the white race generally, and so far as they agree on definite action, think that the Negro's only hope lies in emigration beyond the borders of the United States. And yet, by the irony of fate, nothing has more effectually made this programme seem

---

[17] Free public schools.

[18] François Dominique Toussaint L'Ouverture (1774?–1803), a self-educated freed slave, leader of the 1791 slave rebellion in Haiti that led to Haitian independence; treacherously seized by the French in 1802, he died in a dungeon in France, a symbol of the fight for individual freedom and national independence.

hopeless than the recent course of the United States toward weaker and darker peoples in the West Indies, Hawaii, and the Philippines,—for where in the world may we go and be safe from lying and brute force?

The other class of Negroes who cannot agree with Mr. Washington has hitherto said little aloud. They deprecate the sight of scattered counsels, of internal disagreement; and especially they dislike making their just criticism of a useful and earnest man an excuse for a general discharge of venom from small-minded opponents. Nevertheless, the questions involved are so fundamental and serious that it is difficult to see how men like the Grimkes, Kelly Miller, J. W. E. Bowen,[19] and other representatives of this group, can much longer be silent. Such men feel in conscience bound to ask of this nation three things:

1. The right to vote.
2. Civic equality.
3. The education of youth according to ability.

They acknowledge Mr. Washington's invaluable service in counselling patience and courtesy in such demands; they do not ask that ignorant black men vote when ignorant whites are debarred, or that any reasonable restrictions in the suffrage should not be applied; they know that the low social level of the mass of the race is responsible for much discrimination against it, but they also know, and the nation knows, that relentless color-prejudice is more often a cause than a result of the Negro's degradation; they seek the abatement of this relic of barbarism, and not its systematic encouragement and pampering by all agencies of social power from the Associated Press to the Church of Christ. They advocate, with Mr. Washington, a broad system of Negro common schools supplemented by thorough industrial training; but they are surprised that a man of Mr. Washington's insight cannot see that no such educational system ever has rested or can rest on any other basis than that of the well-equipped college and university, and they insist that there is a demand for a few such institutions throughout the South to train the best of the Negro youth as teachers, professional men, and leaders.

This group of men honor Mr. Washington for his attitude of conciliation toward the white South; they accept the "Atlanta Compromise" in its broadest interpretation; they recognize, with him, many signs of promise, many men of high purpose and fair judgment, in this section; they know that no easy task has been laid upon a region already tottering under heavy burdens. But, nevertheless, they insist that the way to truth and right lies in straightforward honesty, not in indiscriminate flattery; in praising those of the South who do well and criticising uncompromisingly those who do ill; in taking advantage of the opportunities at hand and urging their fellows to do the same, but at the same time in remembering that only a firm adherence to their higher ideals and aspirations will ever keep those ideals within the realm of possibility. They do not expect that the free right to vote, to enjoy civic rights, and to be educated, will come in a moment; they do not expect to see the bias and prejudices of years disappear at the blast of a trumpet; but they are absolutely certain that the way for a people to gain their reasonable

---

[19] The brothers Archibald (1849–1930) and Francis (1850–1937) Grimké, who demonstrated a concern for African-American affairs after the Civil War; Miller (1863–1939) was dean of Howard University in the 1890s; John Wesley Edward Bowen (1855–?), a Methodist clergyman and then president of Gammon Theological Seminary in Atlanta.

rights is not by voluntarily throwing them away and insisting that they do not want them; that the way for a people to gain respect is not by continually belittling and ridiculing themselves; that, on the contrary, Negroes must insist continually, in season and out of season, that voting is necessary to modern manhood, that color discrimination is barbarism, and that black boys need education as well as white boys.

In failing thus to state plainly and unequivocally the legitimate demands of their people, even at the cost of opposing an honored leader, the thinking classes of American Negroes would shirk a heavy responsibility,—a responsibility to themselves, a responsibility to the struggling masses, a responsibility to the darker races of men whose future depends so largely on this American experiment, but especially a responsibility to this nation,—this common Fatherland. It is wrong to encourage a man or a people in evil-doing; it is wrong to aid and abet a national crime simply because it is unpopular not to do so. The growing spirit of kindliness and reconciliation between the North and South after the frightful differences of a generation ago ought to be a source of deep congratulation to all, and especially to those whose mistreatment caused the war; but if that reconciliation is to be marked by the industrial slavery and civic death of those same black men, with permanent legislation into a position of inferiority, then those black men, if they are really men, are called upon by every consideration of patriotism and loyalty to oppose such a course by all civilized methods, even though such opposition involves disagreement with Mr. Booker T. Washington. We have no right to sit silently by while the inevitable seeds are sown for a harvest of disaster to our children, black and white.

First, it is the duty of black men to judge the South discriminatingly. The present generation of Southerners are not responsible for the past, and they should not be blindly hated or blamed for it. Furthermore, to no class is the indiscriminate endorsement of the recent course of the South toward Negroes more nauseating than to the best thought of the South. The South is not "solid"; it is a land in the ferment of social change, wherein forces of all kinds are fighting for supremacy; and to praise the ill the South is to-day perpetrating is just as wrong as to condemn the good. Discriminating and broad-minded criticism is what the South needs,— needs it for the sake of her own white sons and daughters, and for the insurance of robust, healthy mental and moral development.

To-day even the attitude of the Southern whites toward the blacks is not, as so many assume, in all cases the same; the ignorant Southerner hates the Negro, the workingmen fear his competition, the money-makers wish to use him as a laborer, some of the educated see a menace in his upward development, while others— usually the sons of the masters—wish to help him to rise. National opinion has enabled this last class to maintain the Negro common schools, and to protect the Negro partially in property, life, and limb. Through the pressure of the money-makers, the Negro is in danger of being reduced to semi-slavery, especially in the country districts; the workingmen, and those of the educated who fear the Negro, have united to disfranchise him, and some have urged his deportation; while the passions of the ignorant are easily aroused to lynch and abuse any black man. To praise this intricate whirl of thought and prejudice is nonsense; to inveigh indiscriminately against "the South" is unjust; but to use the same breath in praising Governor Aycock, exposing Senator Morgan, arguing with Mr. Thomas Nelson

Page, and denouncing Senator Ben Tillman,[20] is not only sane, but the imperative duty of thinking black men.

It would be unjust to Mr. Washington not to acknowledge that in several instances he has opposed movements in the South which were unjust to the Negro; he sent memorials to the Louisiana and Alabama constitutional conventions, he has spoken against lynching, and in other ways has openly or silently set his influence against sinister schemes and unfortunate happenings. Notwithstanding this, it is equally true to assert that on the whole the distinct impression left by Mr. Washington's propaganda is, first, that the South is justified in its present attitude toward the Negro because of the Negro's degradation; secondly, that the prime cause of the Negro's failure to rise more quickly is his wrong education in the past; and, thirdly, that his future rise depends primarily on his own efforts. Each of these propositions is a dangerous half-truth. The supplementary truths must never be lost sight of: first, slavery and race-prejudice are potent if not sufficient causes of the Negro's position; second, industrial and common-school training were necessarily slow in planting because they had to await the black teachers trained by higher institutions,—it being extremely doubtful if any essentially different development was possible, and certainly a Tuskegee was unthinkable before 1880; and, third, while it is a great truth to say that the Negro must strive and strive mightily to help himself, it is equally true that unless his striving be not simply seconded, but rather aroused and encouraged, by the initiative of the richer and wiser environing group, he cannot hope for great success.

In his failure to realize and impress this last point, Mr. Washington is especially to be criticised. His doctrine has tended to make the whites, North and South, shift the burden of the Negro problem to the Negro's shoulders and stand aside as critical and rather pessimistic spectators; when in fact the burden belongs to the nation, and the hands of none of us are clean if we bend not our energies to righting these great wrongs.

The South ought to be led, by candid and honest criticism, to assert her better self and do her full duty to the race she has cruelly wronged and is still wronging. The North—her co-partner in guilt—cannot salve her conscience by plastering it with gold. We cannot settle this problem by diplomacy and suaveness, by "policy" alone. If worse come to worst, can the moral fibre of this country survive the slow throttling and murder of nine millions of men?

The black men of America have a duty to perform, a duty stern and delicate,— a forward movement to oppose a part of the work of their greatest leader. So far as Mr. Washington preaches Thrift, Patience, and Industrial Training for the masses, we must hold up his hands and strive with him, rejoicing in his honors and glorying in the strength of this Joshua[21] called of God and of man to lead the headless

---

[20] Charles Brantley Aycock (1859–1912), governor of North Carolina (1901–1905); Edward Denison Morgan (1811–1883), governor of New York (1859–1863) and U.S. senator (1863–1869), who voted with the minority in President Andrew Johnson's veto of the Freedman's Bureau bill and later to try Johnson for impeachment; Page (1853–1922) was a Virginia-born writer and diplomat whose novels contributed to romantic legends of life in the South before the Civil War; Benjamin Ryan Tillman (1847–1918), governor of South Carolina (1890–1894) and U.S. senator (1895–1918), who designed the article requiring literacy and property qualifications for voting during the South Carolina constitutional conventional, making it virtually impossible for freed slaves to vote, and advocated the repeal of the Fifteenth Amendment (ratified in 1870), which gave all (male) U.S. citizens the right to vote regardless of race, color, or "previous condition of servitude."

[21] The Old Testament successor of Moses who led the Israelites into Canaan.

host. But so far as Mr. Washington apologizes for injustice, North or South, does not rightly value the privilege and duty of voting, belittles the emasculating effects of caste distinctions, and opposes the higher training and ambition of our brighter minds,—so far as he, the South, or the Nation, does this,—we must unceasingly and firmly oppose them. By every civilized and peaceful method we must strive for the rights which the world accords to men, clinging unwaveringly to those great words which the sons of the Fathers would fain forget: "We hold these truths to be self-evident: That all men are created equal; that they are endowed by their Creator with certain unalienable rights; that among these are life, liberty, and the pursuit of happiness."

1903

Frank Norris
(1870–1902)

Frank Norris proclaims in "Zola as a Romantic Writer" ([1896], about the French novelist Émile Zola), that "terrible things must happen to the characters of the naturalistic tale." Along with the work of other American naturalists, his fiction helped shatter taboos that limited novelists' subject matter. With a painter's eye for detail, Norris, born Benjamin Franklin Norris, Jr., in 1870, found his subjects in the back rooms as well as the front parlors of San Francisco, where he moved with his parents from his native Chicago in 1884. After studying painting in Paris in the late 1880s, he turned his talents to writing, publishing *Yvernelle*, a verse narrative about medieval France, in 1891.

Norris was accepted as a "special student" at Harvard University for the 1894 to 1895 school year, after which he traveled to South Africa and worked as a correspondent covering the Boer War. Expelled from the country by the Boers, he returned to San Francisco and began to write for the San Francisco *Wave*. His first novel, *Moran of the Lady Letty*, was published in 1898. Next came *McTeague* (1899), his best known work and one of the milestones of American naturalism. At the turn of the century, however, the American reading public was still too genteel to accept *McTeague*'s brutal portrayal of life. Subtitled "A Story of San Francisco," the novel presents a cast of characters caught in the grips of lust, greed, or revenge. Its tone borders on black comedy as primitive McTeague, "jaw salient, like that of the carnivora," stumbles through a life that is beyond the capacity of his brain to understand. Norris's next major work was *The Octopus* (1901), the first part of a projected trilogy, "The Epic of the Wheat." Norris lived to complete only the second part of the trilogy, *The Pit*, published posthumously in 1903. He and his wife since 1900, Jeanette Black, were planning a trip to Europe to do research for the third part, *The Wolf*, when he died of peritonitis following a burst appendix in 1902. The novelist's brother Charles arranged for the publication of *Vandover and the Brute*, which appeared in 1914.

In the essays "A Plea for Romantic Fiction" (1901) and "Zola as a Romantic Writer" Norris states that naturalism is a form of romance, quite separate from William Dean Howells's brand of realism. According to Norris, naturalism deals not with the ordinary but with the extraordinary events that make and frequently break characters' lives. Thus, the bewildered and stupid McTeague, the decadent socialite Vandover, and the doomed ranchers from *The Octopus* all experience an array of elemental passions that work themselves out in senseless violence and dissipation. On the basis of *McTeague* and *Vandover*, Norris has often been viewed as "the boy Zola," a characterization that ignores other aspects of his career: he produced the light-hearted *Blix* (1899) the same year as *McTeague,* for example, and *The Octopus* includes several subplots, romantic as well as naturalistic. Naturalistic works and theories of fiction, however, remain Norris's greatest legacy to American literature. The aftershocks of Norris's fiction are felt in the lives of F. Scott Fitzgerald's doomed heroes and in the tone of Nathanael West's grotesque satires of American culture. And the curious transformations of Norris's critical ideas are evident in the larger-than-life characters of Ken Kesey's fables and the grotesque strategies of postmodern narrative.

Suggested Readings: *McTeague,* 1899. *The Octopus,* 1901. *The Pit,* 1903. *The Complete Edition of Frank Norris,* 10 vols., 1928. *The Letters of Frank Norris,* ed. F. Walker, 1956. *The Literary Criticism of Frank Norris,* ed. D. Pizer, 1964. *Collected Letters,* ed. J. S. Crisler, 1986. F. Walker, *Frank Norris: A Biography,* 1932. E. Marchand, *Frank Norris: A Study,* 1942. W. French, *Frank Norris,* 1962. D. Pizer, *The Novels of Frank Norris,* 1966. W. B. Dillingham, *Frank Norris: Instinct and Art,* 1969. D. Graham, *The Fiction of Frank Norris: The Aesthetic Context,* 1978. B. Hochman, *The Art of Frank Norris, Storyteller,* 1988. D. H. Borus, *Howells, James, and Norris in the Mass Market,* 1989.

Text Used: *The Complete Edition of Frank Norris: (I) The Responsibilities of the Novelist,* Vol. VII, 1928.

from   THE "VOLUNTEER MANUSCRIPT"*

At a conservative estimate there are 70,000,000 people in the United States. At a liberal estimate 100,000 of these have lost the use of both arms; remain then 69,900,000 who write novels. Indeed, many are called, but few—oh, what a scanty, skimped handful that few represent—are chosen.

The work of choosing these few, or rather of rejecting these many, devolves upon the manuscript readers for the baker's dozen of important New York publishing houses, and a strange work it is, and strange are the contributions that pass under their inspection.

As one not unfamiliar with the work of "reading," the present writer may offer a little seasonable advice.

1. First have your manuscript typewritten.[1] The number of manuscripts is too great and the time too short to expect the reader to decipher script; and, besides, ideas presented or scenes described in type are infinitely more persuasive, more plausible than those set down in script. A good story typewritten will appear to better advantage; a poor one similarly treated seems less poverty stricken.

2. Do not, by any manner of means, announce in a prefatory note that you "lay

---

* First published in the *Boston Evening Transcript* on December 11, 1901, and collected in *The Responsibilities of the Novelist* (1903).

[1] Having manuscripts typewritten became standard only toward the end of the nineteenth century; apparently, some handwritten manuscripts were still being submitted.

no claim to literary excellence," with the intention thereby of ingratiating yourself with regard to the "reader," winning him over by a parade of modesty. Invariably the statement is prejudicial, producing an effect exactly contrary to the one desired. It will make the mildest of "readers" angry. If you have no claims upon literary excellence, why in Heaven's name are you bothering him to read your work?

3. Enclose a forwarding address in case of rejection. This, seemingly, is superfluous advice. But it is astonishing how many manuscripts come in innocent even of the author's name, with never a scrap nor clue as to their proper destination.

4. Don't ask for criticism. The reader is not a critic. He passes only upon the availability of the manuscript for the uses of the publisher who employs him. And a manuscript of paramount literary quality may be rejected for any number of reasons, none of which have anything to do with its literary worth—or accepted for causes equally outside the domain of letters. Criticism is one thing, professional "reading" quite another.

5. Don't bother about "enclosing stamps for return." The manuscript will go back to you by c.o.d. express.[2]

6. Don't submit a part of a manuscript. It is hard enough sometimes to judge the story as a whole, and no matter how discouraging the initial chapter may be the publisher will always ask to see the remaining portions before deciding.

7. Don't write to the publisher beforehand asking him if he will consider your manuscript. If it is a novel he will invariably express his willingness to consider it. How can he tell whether he wants it or not until he, through his "reader," has seen it?

8. Don't expect to get an answer much before a month. Especially if your story has merit, it must pass through many hands and be considered by many persons before judgment is rendered. The better it is the longer you will wait before getting a report.

9. Don't, in Heaven's name, enclose commendatory letters written by your friends, favourable reviews by your pastor or by the president of the local college. The story will speak for itself more distinctly than any of your acquaintances.

10. Don't say you will revise or shorten to suit the tastes or judgment of the publisher. At best that's a servile humility that in itself is a confession of weakness and that will make you no friends at court.

11. Don't forward a letter of introduction, no matter from how near a friend of the publisher. The publisher will only turn the MS. over to his "readers," and with them the letter from a stranger carries no weight.

12. Don't write a Colonial novel.

13. Don't write a Down East [3] novel.

14. Don't write a *Prisoner of Zenda*[4] novel.

15. Don't write a novel.

16. Try to keep your friends from writing novels.

1901

---

[2] Today a publisher would expect a "volunteer" manuscript to be accompanied by a stamped, self-addressed envelope.

[3] New England, especially Maine.

[4] *The Prisoner of Zenda* (1894), a swashbuckling romantic adventure that inspired many imitations, by the British novelist Anthony Hope (Sir Anthony Hope Hawkins [1863–1933]).

A PLEA FOR ROMANTIC FICTION*

Let us at the start make a distinction. Observe that one speaks of Romanticism and not Sentimentalism. One claims that the latter is as distinct from the former as is that other form of art which is called Realism. Romance has been often put upon and overburdened by being forced to bear the onus of abuse that by right should fall to sentiment; but the two should be kept very distinct, for a very high and illustrious place will be claimed for Romance, while Sentiment will be handed down the scullery stairs.

Many people to-day are composing mere sentimentalism, and calling it and causing it to be called Romance; so with those who are too busy to think much upon these subjects, but who none the less love honest literature, Romance, too, has fallen into disrepute. Consider now the cut-and-thrust stories.[1] They are all labelled Romances, and it is very easy to get the impression that Romance must be an affair of cloaks and daggers, or moonlight and golden hair. But this is not so at all. The true Romance is a more serious business than this. It is not merely a conjurer's trick box, full of flimsy quackeries, tinsel, and claptraps, meant only to amuse, and relying upon deception to do even that. Is it not something better than this? Can we not see in it an instrument keen, finely tempered, flawless—an instrument with which we may go straight through the clothes and tissues and wrapping of flesh down deep into the red, living heart of things?

Is all this too subtle, too merely speculative and intrinsic, too *précieuse*[2] and nice and "literary"? Devoutly one hopes the contrary. So much is made of so-called Romanticism in present-day fiction that the subject seems worthy of discussion, and a protest against the misuse of a really noble and honest formula of literature appears to be timely—misuse, that is, in the sense of limited use. Let us suppose for the moment that a romance can be made out of a cut-and-thrust business. Good heavens, are there no other things that are romantic, even in this—falsely, falsely called—humdrum world of to-day? Why should it be that so soon as the novelist addresses himself—seriously—to the consideration of contemporary life he must abandon Romance and take up that harsh, loveless, colourless, blunt tool called Realism?

Now, let us understand at once what is meant by Romance and what by Realism. Romance, I take it, is the kind of fiction that takes cognizance of variations from the type of normal life. Realism is the kind of fiction that confines itself to the type of normal life. According to this definition, then, Romance may even treat of the sordid, the unlovely—as, for instance, the novels of M. Zola.[3] (Zola has been dubbed a Realist, but he is, on the contrary, the very head of the Romanticists.) Also, Realism, used as it sometimes is as a term of reproach, need not be in the remotest sense or degree offensive, but on the other hand respectable as a church and proper as a deacon—as, for instance, the novels of Mr. Howells.[4]

The reason why one claims so much for Romance, and quarrels so pointedly

---

* First published in the *Boston Evening Transcript* on December 18, 1901, and collected in *The Responsibilities of the Novelist* (1903).

[1] Stories featuring swordplay and adventure, such as *The Prisoner of Zenda* (1894) by Anthony Hope (1863–1933).

[2] "Precious" (French).

[3] Émile Zola (1840–1902), a French novelist and leading exemplar of naturalism (one kind of "Romance," according to Norris).

[4] The American novelist, critic, and editor William Dean Howells (1837–1920), a notable advocate of realism in fiction.

with Realism, is that Realism stultifies itself. It notes only the surface of things. For it, Beauty is not even skin deep, but only a geometrical plane, without dimensions and depth, a mere outside. Realism is very excellent so far as it goes, but it goes no further than the Realist himself can actually see, or actually hear. Realism is minute; it is the drama of a broken teacup, the tragedy of a walk down the block, the excitement of an afternoon call, the adventure of an invitation to dinner. It is the visit to my neighbour's house, a formal visit, from which I may draw no conclusions. I see my neighbour and his friends—very, oh, such very! probable people—and that is all. Realism bows upon the doormat and goes away and says to me, as we link arms on the sidewalk: "That is life." And I say it is not. It is not, as you would very well see if you took Romance with you to call upon your neighbour.

Lately you have been taking Romance a weary journey across the water—ages and the flood of years—and haling her into the fusty, musty, worm-eaten, moth-riddled, rust-corroded Grandes Salles[5] of the Middle Ages and the Renaissance, and she has found the drama of a bygone age for you there. But would you take her across the street to your neighbour's front parlour (with the bisque fisher boy on the mantel and the photograph of Niagara Falls on glass hanging in the front window); would you introduce her there? Not you. Would you take a walk with her on Fifth Avenue, or Beacon Street, or Michigan Avenue?[6] No, indeed. Would you choose her for a companion of a morning spent in Wall Street, or an afternoon in the Waldorf-Astoria?[7] You just guess you would not.

She would be out of place, you say—inappropriate. She might be awkward in my neighbour's front parlour, and knock over the little bisque fisher boy. Well, she might. If she did, you might find underneath the base of the statuette, hidden away, tucked away—what? God knows. But something that would be a complete revelation of my neighbour's secretest life.

So you think Romance would stop in the front parlour and discuss medicated flannels and mineral waters with the ladies? Not for more than five minutes. She would be off upstairs with you, prying, peeping, peering into the closets of the bedroom, into the nursery, into the sitting room; yes, and into that little iron box screwed to the lower shelf of the closet in the library; and into those compartments and pigeonholes of the *secrétaire* in the study. She would find a heartache (maybe) between the pillows of the mistress bed, and a memory carefully secreted in the master's deed box. She would come upon a great hope amid the books and papers of the study table of the young man's room, and—perhaps—who knows—an affair, or, great heavens, an intrigue, in the scented ribbons and gloves and hair-pins of the young lady's bureau. And she would pick here a little and there a little, making up a bag of hopes and fears and a package of joys and sorrows—great ones, mind you—and then come down to the front door, and, stepping out into the street, hand you the bags and package and say to you, "That is Life!"

Romance does very well in the castles of the Middle Ages and the Renaissance châteaux,[8] and she has the entrée there and is very well received. That is all well and good. But let us protest against limiting her to such places and such times. You will find her, I grant you, in the chatelaine's[9] chamber and the dungeon of the man-at-arms; but, if you choose to look for her, you will find her equally at home

[5] "Great halls" (French).
[6] Fashionable streets in New York City, Boston, and Chicago, respectively.
[7] A luxury hotel in New York City.   [8] "Castles" (French).
[9] A warden or governor of a castle or fort (French).

in the brownstone house on the corner and in the office building downtown. And this very day, in this very hour, she is sitting among the rags and wretchedness, the dirt and despair of the tenements of the East Side of New York.

"What?" I hear you say. "Look for Romance—the lady of the silken robes and golden crown, our beautiful, chaste maiden of soft voice and gentle eyes—look for her among the vicious ruffians male and female, of Allen Street and Mulberry Bend?" I tell you she is there, and to your shame be it said you will not know her in those surroundings. You, the aristocrats, who demand the fine linen and the purple in your fiction; you, the sensitive, the delicate, who will associate with your Romance only so long as she wears a silken gown. You will not follow her to the slums, for you believe that Romance should only amuse and entertain you, singing you sweet songs and touching the harp of silver strings with rosy-tipped fingers. If haply she should call to you from the squalor of a dive, or the awful degradation of a disorderly house, crying: "Look! Listen! This, too, is life. These, too, are my children! Look at them, know them, and knowing, help!" Should she call thus you would stop your ears; you would avert your eyes and you would answer, "Come from there, Romance. Your place is not there!" And you would make of her a harlequin, a tumbler, a sword-dancer, when, as a matter of fact, she should be by right divine a teacher sent from God.

She will not often wear the robe of silk, the gold crown, the jewelled shoon; will not always sweep the silver harp. An iron note is hers if so she choose, and coarse garments, and stained hands; and, meeting her thus, it is for you to know her as she passes—know her for the same young queen of the blue mantle and lilies. She can teach you if you will be humble to learn—teach you by showing. God help you if at last you take from Romance her mission of teaching; if you do not believe that she has a purpose—a noble purpose and a mightier than mere amusement, mere entertainment. Let Realism do the entertaining with its meticulous presentation of teacups, rag carpets, wall paper and hair-cloth sofas, stopping with these, going no deeper than it sees, choosing the ordinary, the untroubled, the commonplace.

But to Romance belongs the wide world for range, and the unplumbed depths of the human heart, and the mystery of sex, and the problems of life, and the black, unsearched penetralia[10] of the soul of man. You, the indolent, must not always be amused. What matter the silken clothes, what matter the prince's houses? Romance, too, is a teacher, and if—throwing aside the purple—she wears the camel's-hair and feeds upon the locusts, it is to cry aloud unto the people, "Prepare ye the way of the Lord; make straight his path."

1901

from SALT AND SINCERITY*

Where are the Books for Girls? Adults' books there are and books for boys by the carload, but where is the book for the young girls? Something has already been said about literature for the amiable young woman, but this, now, is a very different person. One means the girl of fourteen to eighteen. The boy passing through this most trying formative period finds his literature ready to hand. Boys' books,

[10] Innermost parts.
* First published as a series of articles in *The Critic* from May to October 1902 and collected in *The*

tales of hunting, adventure and sport abound. They are good books, too, sane, "healthy," full of fine spirit and life. But the girl, where does she read? Surely the years between fourteen and eighteen are even more trying to a young girl than to a boy. She is not an active animal. When the boy is out of doors, pitching curves or "running the ends," the girl (even yet in the day and age of "athletics for women") is in the house, and, as like as not, reading. And reading what, if you please? The feeblest, thinnest, most colourless lucubrations that it is given to the mind of mis- guided man to conceive or to perpetuate. It must be this or else the literature of the adult; and surely the novels written for mature minds, for men and women who have some knowledge of the world and powers of discrimination, are not good reading, in any sense of the word, for a sixteen-year-old girl in the formative period of her life.

Besides Alcott,[1] no one has ever written intelligently for girls. Surely there is a field here. Surely a Public, untried and unexplored, is wailing for its author; nor is it a public wanting in enthusiasm, loyalty, or intelligence.

But for all this great parade and prating of emancipated women it nevertheless remains a fact that the great majority of twentieth-century opinion is virtually Ori- ental[2] in its conception of the young girl. The world to-day is a world for boys, men, and women. Of all humans, the young girl, the sixteen-year-old, is the least important—or, at least, is so deemed. Wanted: a Champion. Wanted: the Discov- erer and Poet of the Very Young Girl. Unimportant she may now appear to you, who may yet call her by her first name without fear and without reproach. But remember this, you who believe only in a world of men and boys and women; the Very Young Girl of to-day is the woman of to-morrow, the wife of the day after, and the mother of next week. She only needs to put up her hair and let down her frocks to become a very important person indeed. Meanwhile, she has no litera- ture; meanwhile, *faute de mieux*,[3] she is trying to read Ouida[4] and many other books intended for maturer minds; or, worse than all, she is enfeebling her mind by the very thin gruel purveyed by the mild-mannered gentlemen and ladies who write for the Sunday-school libraries. Here is a bad business; here is a field that needs cultivation. All very well to tend and train the saplings, the oaks, and the vines. The flowers—they have not bloomed yet—are to be thought about, too.

All the more so that the young girl takes a book to heart infinitely more than a boy. The boy—*his* story once read—votes it "bully," takes down his cap, and there's an end. But the average Very Young Girl does not read her story: she lives it, lingers over it, weeps over it, lies awake nights over it. So long as she lives she will never quite forget the books she read when she was sixteen. It is not too much to say that the "favourite" books of a girl at this age become a part of her life. They influence her character more than any of us, I imagine, would suspect or admit. All the more reason, then, that there should not only be good books for girls, but plenty of good books.

1902

Responsibilities of the Novelist (1903). In these articles Norris surveys the current American literary scene and the strengths and weaknesses of American fiction, and comes to the question with which he begins in this excerpt.
    [1] Louisa May Alcott (1832–1888), author of such well-known books as *Little Women* (1868–1869), *Work* (1873), and *Rose in Bloom* (1876).
    [2] Distanced, out-of-touch.   [3] "For want of anything better" (French).
    [4] Pseudonym of the British novelist Marie Louise de la Ramee (1839–1908), derived from a childish mispronunciation of "Louise"; she wrote forty-five novels dealing chiefly with fashionable life and romantic situations.

LATE 19TH-CENTURY FICTION

The central movement in American fiction in the last half of the nineteenth century was the development of realism. The realistic novel had been a salient feature of the literary landscape in Europe for several decades before realism took hold in America. Through his reviews and columns in the *Atlantic Monthly* and *Harper's*, William Dean Howells introduced French and Russian novelists to the reading public. He also recognized the promise of America's new and innovative writers, among them Charles W. Chesnutt, Sarah Orne Jewett, and Stephen Crane. As a practicing novelist Howells avoided the bizarre and the heroic out of a conviction that the proper task of the serious American writer is to delineate the details of everyday existence. To portray life realistically, he felt, is to portray it as most readers know it. In his more than two dozen novels, Howells examined a broad range of middle-class life in late nineteenth-century American settings, affirming its values and criticizing with a sometimes withering touch its moral shortcomings. He wrote of weakness, self-indulgence, and divorce in *A Modern Instance* (1882); the amorality of the business world in *The Rise of Silas Lapham* (1885); and the complex issues of workers' rights and socialist goals in *A Hazard of New Fortunes* (1890).

As a novelist Howells displayed considerable insight into the motives and convictions of his characters. Yet, his sensitivity to character serves large social concerns: for Howells's great subject is life in society, the analysis of ethical conduct in a world devoid of absolutes. Conversely, his friend Henry James was absorbed with what we might call the inner life. Throughout a lengthy career, in such early works as *The American* (1877) and *Daisy Miller* (1879) and in such accomplished late novels as *The Wings of the Dove* (1902), *The Ambassadors* (1903), and *The Golden Bowl* (1904), James explored with increasing sophistication and acuity the contrast between American "innocence" and European "experience." His Gothic dramas of the mind, chief among them "The Turn of the Screw" (1898) and "The Jolly Corner" (1908), manipulate ghostly conventions with a similar concern for character and for psychological validity. James's evocative stories of artists and writers, often wry and always compassionate, as shown by "The Real Thing" (1892) and "The Death of the Lion" (1894), reveal still another aspect of his achievement in fiction. So do *The Bostonians* (1886), a provocative portrait of human relationships in the context of the feminist movement, and *What Maisie Knew* (1897), a novel of adult misunderstandings told through the medium of a little girl's mind. Whatever his subject, James's concern for psychological realism remained constant.

Unlike Howells or James, Mark Twain had roots in the fiction of the pre-Civil War Southwest Humorists, whose use of the oral tale and vernacular speech left a rich legacy for later writers. Twain did write a number of novels that make little or no use of such a tradition: *The Prince and the Pauper* (1882), *A Connecticut Yankee in King Arthur's Court* (1889), and *The Tragedy of Pudd'nhead Wilson* (1894) suggest his interest in a variety of locales and themes. First and foremost, however, Twain's achievement was one of language and place. In *The Adventures of Tom Sawyer* (1876) he deals with the setting he knew best to tell a boy's story from a perspective at once good-natured, satirical, and nostalgic; in the anecdotal

The image of the locomotive on the western plains—"the machine in the garden"—depicted in this 1871 engraving of a Kansas-Pacific Railroad train, symbolized human intrusion into the wilderness.

Life on the Mississippi (1883) he joyfully recalls his boyhood years on the river and bemoans the manner in which commerce had converted adventure to matters of dollars and cents; and in *Adventures of Huckleberry Finn* (1884) he brings language and place together to create an idiom as vital to American prose fiction as the achievement of Walt Whitman and Emily Dickinson is to American poetry. In *Huckleberry Finn* Twain's use of the vernacular is vibrant, metaphorically fresh. It allows him to describe customs and attitudes with precision, to give a rambunctious scrutiny of small-town river life in its generosity and cruelty, and yet to preserve the innocence of the narrator, Huckleberry Finn, throughout what the critic James M. Cox (in *Mark Twain: The Fate of Humor* [1978]) has called a sad and inevitable initiation into the moral dimensions of life. With its unique blending of naïvete and knowledge, the language of Huckleberry Finn is a notable contribution to the development of realism in American fiction.

A native-born impulse toward realism, nourished by authors who sought to portray the manner in which lives are conditioned by regional environments, was also evident in the late nineteenth century. The term "local-color writing" conventionally applied to the fiction of those authors has long had the unintentional effect of measuring the quality of such work according to quantitative standards. The cameolike achievement of the best regional fiction evokes condescending praise if we assume that excellence comes only on a grand scale, that the scope of Harriet

Beecher Stowe's *Uncle Tom's Cabin* (1851–1852) or Henry James's *Portrait of a Lady* (1881) takes precedence over the focus of stories such as Constance Fenimore Woolson's "King David" (1878) and Mary E. Wilkins Freeman's "A Village Singer" (1891). Just as music criticism assesses the quality of a sonata without measuring it against the dimensions of a symphony, so literary criticism stands in need of perspectives to describe achievement in regional writing.

With their expert use of dialect and their dispassionate observation of characters needing to feel important or at least useful in their restrictive environments, the stories of Woolson and of Freeman put us inside the worlds of which they write, that of the South during Reconstruction in Woolson's *Rodman the Keeper* (1880), that of New England village life in Freeman's *A New England Nun* (1891). The work of Sarah Orne Jewett enlarges this tradition of unpretentious distinction with stories set in her native state of Maine; from the promise of *Deephaven* (1877) to the achievement of *Country of the Pointed Firs* (1896), Jewett's work demonstrates how character and locale interact. To appreciate her stories is to understand why Jewett exercised so important an influence on the fiction of Willa Cather (as Cather gracefully acknowledges in *Not Under Forty* [1936]).

The most popular books in the second half of the nineteenth century were those published in the Dime Novel series, originated by Erastus F. Beadle, and those that made up the various series written by Horatio Alger, Jr. Paperback dime novels (which actually sold for a nickel) were immensely popular with soldiers during the Civil War and with the general public until the 1890s. Melodramatic and ridden with formula, they were written (generally for $75) by various authors under a baffling array of pseudonyms and deal chiefly with the American Revolution and with episodes of frontier fighting. By 1865 the publishing firm of Beadle & Adams had sold more than four million dime novels, among them Ann Sophia Stephens's *Malaeska: The Indian Wife of the White Hunter* (1860), which sold 300,000 copies.

Moralistic critics objected to the extravagance of dime novels the way some people objected to comic books a century later. But no moralist could find fault with the 119 books written by Horatio Alger, Jr., an estimated twenty million copies of which were sold in the late nineteenth century. Among the most popular were those in the Ragged Dick Series (begun in 1867), the Luck and Pluck Series (begun in 1869), and the Tattered Tom Series (begun in 1871). Invariably, Alger's young (and poor) heroes shine shoes or sell newspapers; just as invariably, they discover that working hard and being good lead to fame and fortune. Life is that simple in Alger novels, which deplore liquor and idleness and show that virtue leads to financial rewards.

Understandably, readers were also drawn to fiction that portrays, in different ways, the complexities of human life. In her stories of Cajun society in Louisiana, Kate Chopin employed both realistic techniques and the emphasis on rootedness that is an essential part of regional writing. Similarly, she brought a strong sense of the French-Catholic ambience of New Orleans to *The Awakening* (1899), her memorable account of Edna Pontellier's futile attempt to balance her role as a wife and her existence as a woman. Told in the first person (and based on her own experience), Charlotte Perkins Gilman's landmark story "The Yellow Wallpaper" (1892) moves disjointedly from realistic awareness to visions of fantasy and terror

═CONTEXTS═

Regionalism

Regionalistic literature deals with the conditions and environment of a specific geographic area. Authors in this tradition make use of a region's folklore and history and show how they affect the lives of the inhabitants. Bret Harte (1836–1902), a noted regional author, gained fame as an adept observer of character and conditions in middle nineteenth-century northern California. Though best known for his colorful portraits of California frontier life, Harte subordinates local-color interests to the more universal issues of personal courage and moral ambiguity. His most widely acclaimed work, "The Luck of Roaring Camp" (1868), has served as a model for many tales of the Old West. The opening paragraph typifies life in the gold fields and mining camps of California's gold-rush days:

The Luck of Roaring Camp

There was a commotion in Roaring Camp. It could not have been a fight, for in 1850 that was not novel enough to have called together the entire settlement. The ditches and claims were not only deserted, but "Tuttle's grocery" had contributed its gamblers, who, it will be remembered, calmly continued their game the day that French Pete and Kanaka Joe shot each other to death over the bar in the front room. The whole camp was collected before a rude cabin on the outer edge of the clearing. Conversation was carried on in a low tone, but the name of a woman was frequently repeated. It was a name familiar enough in the camp,—"Cherokee Sal."

Perhaps the less said of her the better. She was a coarse, and it is to be feared, a very sinful woman. But at that time she was the only woman in Roaring Camp. . . .

Regional authors typically use peculiar dialects to convey regional color. Harte uses this technique in the miner Stumpy's speech to the Roaring Camp crowd at the christening of the child of the dead Cherokee Sal:

"It ain't my style to spoil fun, boys," said the little man, stoutly eying the faces around him, "but it strikes me that this thing ain't exactly on the squar. It's playing it pretty low down on this yer baby to ring in fun on him that he ain't goin' to understand. And ef there's goin' to be any godfathers 'round, I'd like to see who's got any better rights than me."

Bret Harte, 1868

as it portrays the mind of a woman virtually suffocating from her physician-husband's efforts to restore her to health. The different and distinctive worlds of Charles W. Chesnutt can be seen in the stories that make up *The Conjure Woman* (1899) and those collected in *The Wife of His Youth* (1899), the first a series of dialect tales, the second a set of realistic fictions centering on conflicts of loyalties. The surface joviality of *The Conjure Woman* and the role of coincidence in parts of *The Wife of His Youth* do not obscure the books' underlying tone. What Howells said in reviewing Chesnutt's novel *The Marrow of Tradition* (1901) for the *North American Review* applies to both collections of stories: "bitter, bitter," but "powerful."

Realism prizes accuracy, as Frank Norris correctly observes in his 1896 essay on the French novelist Émile Zola. But naturalism, according to Norris, distorts, probes, and caricatures in its efforts to get at the truths of human life that lie beneath the drama of the commonplace. As a literary movement arriving with force at the end of the nineteenth century, naturalism was a way of seeing human beings "twisted from the ordinary" (in Norris's words), "wrenched" from the uneventful. In novels such as *Vandover and the Brute* (published posthumously in 1914) and *McTeague* (1899), Norris enacts his ideas with characteristic energy: beneath the socialized exterior of life lie elemental forces that erupt into the lives of Vandover and McTeague and plunge them into worlds deformed with pain and tragedy.

Whereas Norris's fiction stresses elemental forces at odds with social constraints, the work of other naturalists tends to portray human beings overwhelmed by environmental forces. In many of Jack London's stories and novels, the struggle to stay alive in settings desolate and threatening is the focus of the narrative; setting becomes the adversary in these tales, mighty in its power to erase life. More complex is the work of Stephen Crane. Crane emphasized the grinding and overwhelming power of environment, social and economic, in *Maggie: A Girl of the Streets* (1893) and in *George's Mother* (1896) but developed a prose both supple and impressionistic to tell the ironic story of Henry Fleming's maturation in *The Red Badge of Courage* (1895), in which the sun mirrors emotional states, and the struggle for survival in "The Open Boat" (1898), in which nature is flatly indifferent to human hopes and prayers. Likewise ironic is "The Bride Comes to Yellow Sky" (1898), a western comedy of manners that punctures the glamor of a gunfighter era Crane would deny ever existed. Naturalism was significant in shaping Crane's fiction. But anyone who writes of women working "in various shades of yellow discontent" or a character living through the "red years" of his youth (as Crane does in *Maggie*) is cultivating an impressionistic style that resists a rigid adherence to naturalism. The work of Theodore Dreiser in the twentieth century would give naturalism its fullest place in American fiction. That work would take its place beside the fiction of Edith Wharton, Willa Cather, and other writers who invoked new strategies of expression to explore the human condition.

Mark Twain (Samuel Clemens)
(1835–1910)

Born in the hamlet of Florida, Missouri, in 1835, Samuel Langhorne Clemens grew up in the Mississippi River town of Hannibal that he later fictionalized as St. Petersburg in *The Adventures of Tom Sawyer* (1876) and *Adventures of Huckleberry Finn* (1884). His father, John Marshall Clemens, was a hopeful but struggling lawyer, postmaster, justice of the peace, and storekeeper. John Clemens had failed in a move westward after he married the vivacious Jane Lampton in Adair Country, Kentucky, in 1823; the couple wound up in Missouri, where John, ever dignified, strove toward success until his death in 1847. From Jane Lampton Clemens, blessed with a good sense of humor to go with her hard life, Samuel Clemens may have learned at least the rudiments of the deadpan humor he later perfected. As his friend and biographer Albert Bigelow Paine notes, Clemens remembered his mother's way of saying something humorous with the air of not seeing its humor at all. He admired that type of delivery.

After the death of his father, twelve-year-old Samuel was apprenticed to a local printer; four years later, having learned the trade, he went to work for his older brother Orion, who had become a publisher in Hannibal. But in 1853 young Clemens decided to roam: he traveled to St. Louis, Cincinnati, Philadelphia, New York, and other cities, working in printing establishments often on a daily basis to earn his way. During this time he also visited and worked in Keokuk, Iowa, and it was in the Keokuk *Saturday Post* in the late 1850s that he published three humorous accounts of his experiences on the Mississippi River under the unlikely pseudonym of Thomas Jefferson Snodgrass. He likewise reached back to his days on the river when he adopted his enduring pseudonym from the riverboat cry of "Mark Twain" (signifying "two fathoms deep," and therefore a safe channel) for the sketches of mining life and western adventure he wrote for newspapers in Nevada and California in 1863 and 1864.

At age twenty-one Clemens signed on with the experienced Horace Bixby to serve an apprenticeship of eighteen months as a cub riverboat pilot, after which he fulfilled a child-hood ambition and became a licensed pilot on the Mississippi River. Not only did the job give him status among those connected with riverboat commerce; it also gave him deep inner satisfaction, the product of a way of life that he saw as authentic, without sham. Writing as Mark Twain almost two decades later, he looked back on those pre-Civil War days with reverent pleasure in *Old Times on the Mississippi* (1875), a series of seven articles written for the *Atlantic Monthly,* then edited by his friend William Dean Howells.

When the Civil War brought an end to commercial traffic on the Mississippi River, Clemens spent several weeks in an irregular unit of the Confederate Army, an experience he recalled in "The Private History of a Campaign That Failed," published in the *Century Magazine* in 1885. Typically, he exaggerated his military misadventures with an ever-developing sense of language and pace and the effects to be gained by reprise and auda-cious changes in tone. "The Private History" is comic with sudden interludes of serious-ness, humorous at the expense of fellow-soldiers with boomerang thrusts reserved for the soldier-writer, who concludes his account of an inglorious career by saying, "I knew more about retreating than the man that invented retreating." One of Mark Twain's most endear-ing traits as a humorist was his willingness to make a target of himself: "I am a great and sublime fool," he once wrote to his friend Howells; "but then I am God's fool, & all His works must be contemplated with respect."

Late in 1861, Clemens, no longer part of the amateur militia, accompanied his brother Orion to the Nevada Territory: an official trip for Orion, who had been appointed secretary of the territory by President Abraham Lincoln; an adventure for Samuel, who hoped to get rich mining silver but wound up mining his experiences for sketches in the Virginia City *Territorial Enterprise*. Clemens was officially known as Mark Twain by 1865, when he published his version of a well-known tall tale, "Jim Smiley and His Jumping Frog" (later called "The Notorious Jumping Frog of Calaveras County") in the New York *Saturday Press*. The story brought an appreciative national audience to Mark Twain at his unbuckled best.

After traveling east in 1866, Twain sailed the following year on the excursion ship *Quaker City,* touring Mediterranean countries and the Holy Land as a correspondent for the New York *Tribune* and the San Francisco *Alta California*. His letters to these newspapers were shaped into his first book, *The Innocents Abroad* (1869); both the letters and the book were immensely popular for their satire of "Old World" institutions and manners and for their good-natured account of provincial attitudes among the American "pilgrims." Although it thrives on stereotypes, Twain's narrative voice in *The Innocents Abroad* sets the conditions for humor, from his observations on the gradual demise of the diaries-of-the-trip begun by many passengers to his wide-eyed report that the legendary Sea of Galilee was really no bigger than Lake Tahoe.

The success of his first book gave Twain some remunerative years as a writer and lecturer. During this period he met, courted, and married (in 1870) Olivia Langdon, the daughter of a wealthy coal merchant in Elmira, New York. If part of Mark Twain remained irreverent and wild, another part now yearned for social solidity; the couple built a mansion in Hartford, Connecticut, and became established members of the community. And almost because they were opposites in temperament and background—with her refinement and his roughneck ways—their relationship was mutually rewarding, despite the tendency of some recent critics to see Olivia as one who stifled her husband's lusty imagination. Twain could contrive an elaborate letter to Howells claiming that Howells had called someone "a quadrilateral, astronomical, incandescent sonuvabitch"; at the same time he could play "Youth" to Olivia's "Angel" and depend on a gentility as authentic as the riverboat experiences that had made him Mark Twain.

The pace of Twain's career accelerated in the 1870s. In 1872 he published *Roughing It*, an unbridled account of his adventures in Nevada and California, complete with outlandish tall tales and satirical broadsides. The following year, in collaboration with the journalist Charles Dudley Warner, he brought out *The Gilded Age*, a flimsy attempt at a novel, which nonetheless gave a name to an era of rampant capitalism in nineteenth-century American history. And in 1876 he returned to the surer ground of childhood memories in Hannibal with *Tom Sawyer*, a book filled with nostalgia for a simple world of good and bad and dominated by a narrative voice that mocks both patent medicines and the romantic pretensions of its young protagonist. In *Tom Sawyer* we first see Tom and Huckleberry Finn operating as a pair: Tom as society's hero, the entrepreneur who gets other boys to whitewash the family fence; Huck as the asocial sidekick who enjoys an unschooled and unwashed life and sleeps in discarded barrels. Whereas it is evident from the very beginning of *Tom Sawyer* that Tom has complete (and sometimes tiresome) authority over Huck in all matters referring to society and to books, it is also evident that he knows the power of Huck's reputation: asked why he arrived late for school, Tom replies, "I stopped to talk with Huckleberry Finn." Characteristically, Tom knows how to unload a bombshell in the schoolroom; he is a master at gauging "effects."

Perhaps because the figure of Huckleberry Finn had a latent energy that could not be realized in the tidy world of *Tom Sawyer*, in which fate metes out punishment and society dispenses rewards, Twain began writing *Adventures of Huckleberry Finn* in 1876. Working on it intermittently, struggling with elements of plot, and taking time to write *The Prince and the Pauper* in 1882, he did not finish the new novel until 1883, and even then took seven additional months for revision. The master step in the book that became his classic was to make Huckleberry Finn the narrator. Twain thereby relied not only on his knowledge of the river and of small-town life in the antebellum South but on all he had assimilated about the vibrancy and freshness of vernacular speech—extending its resources far beyond what other writers had done, sacrificing nothing by way of description and character portrayal, converting the world Huckleberry Finn sees and hears and smells into an idiom that has remained vital for more than a century. First and foremost, *Huckleberry Finn* is a triumph of language. "All modern American literature comes from one

An illustration by E. W. Kemble from the first edition of Mark Twain's Adventures of Huckleberry Finn.

book by Mark Twain called *Huckleberry Finn,*" writes Ernest Hemingway in *The Green Hills of Africa* (1935), a resounding tribute even when adjusted for exaggeration. Such was not the opinion of genteel readers who greeted the book in the 1880s, however; many thought the book vulgar and trashy, and the public library in Concord, Massachusetts, banned the novel from its shelves. One hundred years later *Huckleberry Finn* still offends some readers, who view its racial epithets out of context and overlook the education that rubs off on the unsuspecting Huck from his association with the runaway slave Jim. It is not surprising that Twain's novel continues to trouble readers; for it makes us confront in unrelenting terms the pain, and shame, of our history.

By 1885 fame and fortune had come to Mark Twain, and the future appeared even brighter. His large investment in the Charles R. Webster and Company publishing firm looked like a stroke of genius when the company brought out the remarkably successful *Personal Memoirs of U. S. Grant* (1885). And the automatic typesetting machine of James W. Paige, heavily underwritten by Twain for more than a dozen years, seemed like an invention that would secure the future for those wise enough to read it. But Webster's firm, unable to repeat its commercial success, foundered and eventually failed after the financial panic of 1893. And Paige's typesetter became a total loss because of unforeseen competition from the superior Linotype machine. Before the final collapse of these two ventures, which sent Twain into bankruptcy, *A Connecticut Yankee in King Arthur's Court* (1889) suggested his frustration: ostensibly a comic satire on medieval superstition and cant, the novel becomes a scathing indictment of nineteenth-century "progress," astonishing in its violence, disturbing in its vision. *The Tragedy of Pudd'nhead Wilson* (1894) extends that vision, spinning out its contrived plot on issues of slavery and nurture with little to offset a tone of disdain. To protect some property from creditors, the bankrupt Twain went so far as to copyright *Pudd'nhead* in Olivia's name.

With some hope and little inspiration Twain turned back to his best-known characters in *Tom Sawyer Abroad* (1894) and *Tom Sawyer, Detective* (1896), both narrated by Huckleberry Finn, and embarked on a round-the-world lecture trip—out of which came *Following the Equator* (1897), a travel book that understandably lacks the buoyancy of his earlier work. Although he finished paying off his debts in 1898, personal tragedy followed him at this time: his oldest daughter, Susy, died of meningitis while he and Olivia were abroad, and Olivia's health began a gradual decline that made her an invalid until her death in

1904. Emotionally and psychologically battered, unable to recover the perspective on himself that had made his humor possible, Twain's work began to evince a general pessimism. His love affair with language had never faltered: *Connecticut Yankee* and *Puddn'head Wilson* contain admirable cadences of style, remarkable juxtapositions of word and event, and Huckleberry Finn's voice has moments of genuine vigor in the later novels he narrates. But *what* Twain said in works such as *The Man That Corrupted Hadleyburg* (1900), *What Is Man?* (1906), the "The Mysterious Stranger" manuscripts (arranged into one narrative by Paine in 1916, published in their entirety in 1969), and the posthumously published *The War Prayer* (1923) and *Letters From the Earth* (1963) reveals an increasing despair about the "awful human race."

In the years before his death in 1910, Twain was a renowned and highly respected public figure despite his disillusionment with the human race. The acclaim was richly deserved. For this writer, "the Lincoln of our literature," according to Howells in *My Mark Twain* (1910), raised the act of storytelling to high art. Twain's special talent was to introduce the flavor of oral speech, its vernacular rhythms and turns of phrase, into prose of lasting appeal. At his best, in *Huckleberry Finn*, he turns that prose into an instrument that measures the moral dimensions of our humanity.

Suggested Readings: *The Writings of Mark Twain*, 37 vols., ed. A. B. Paine, 1922–1925. *The Correspondence of Samuel L. Clemens and William Dean Howells, 1872–1910*, ed. H. N. Smith and W. Gibson, 1960. *The Mark Twain Papers*, ed. F. Anderson et al., 1967– . *The Works of Mark Twain*, ed. J. Gerber et al., 1972– . W. D. Howells, *My Mark Twain*, 1910. A. B. Paine, *Mark Twain: A Biography*, 3 vols., 1912. B. DeVoto, *The Ordeal of Mark Twain*, 1932. W. Blair, *Mark Twain and Huck Finn*, 1960. P. Fatout, *Mark Twain on the Lecture Circuit*, 1960. R. Salomon, *Twain and the Image of History*, 1961. H. N. Smith, *Mark Twain: The Development of a Writer*, 1962. J. M. Cox, *Mark Twain: The Fate of Humor*, 1966. J. Kaplan, *Mr. Clemens and Mark Twain*, 1966. H. Hill, *Mark Twain, God's Fool*, 1973. W. Gibson, *The Art of Mark Twain*, 1976. D. Sloane, *Mark Twain as a Literary Comedian*, 1979. L. J. Budd, *Our Mark Twain: The Making of His Public Personality*, 1983. E. Emerson, *The Authentic Mark Twain: A Literary Biography of Samuel Clemens*, 1984. E. Long, *The New Mark Twain Handbook*, 1985. F. G. Robinson, *In Bad Faith: The Dynamics of Deception in Mark Twain's America*, 1986. S. Gillman, *Dark Twins: Imposture and Identity in Mark Twain's America*, 1989. J. Lauber, *The Inventions of Mark Twain*, 1990.

Texts Used: "The Notorious Jumping Frog of Calaveras County" and "The Late Benjamin Franklin": *Sketches: New and Old*, 1917. "The Private History of a Campaign That Failed": *The American Claimant and Other Stories and Sketches*, 1924. "Fenimore Cooper's Literary Offenses": *In Defense of Harriet Shelley and Other Essays*, 1925. "The Man That Corrupted Hadleyburg": *The Man That Corrupted Hadleyburg and Other Essays and Stories*, 1928. *Adventures of Huckleberry Finn*, 1885 (some spelling from first edition corrected).

THE NOTORIOUS JUMPING FROG
OF CALAVERAS COUNTY*

In compliance with the request of a friend of mine, who wrote me from the East, I called on good-natured, garrulous old Simon Wheeler, and inquired after my friend's friend, Leonidas W. Smiley, as requested to do, and I hereunto append the result. I have a lurking suspicion that *Leonidas W.* Smiley is a myth; that my friend never knew such a personage; and that he only conjectured that if I asked old Wheeler about him, it would remind him of his infamous *Jim* Smiley, and he would go to work and bore me to death with some exasperating reminiscence of

* First published in the New York *Saturday Press* on November 18, 1865, as "Jim Smiley and His Jumping Frog," revised as "The Celebrated Jumping Frog of Calaveras County," and revised again with the title here. Mark Twain's note: "pronounced Cal-e-*va*-ras."

him as long and as tedious as it should be useless to me. If that was the design, it succeeded.

I found Simon Wheeler dozing comfortably by the bar-room stove of the dilapidated tavern in the decayed mining camp of Angel's,[1] and I noticed that he was fat and bald-headed, and had an expression of winning gentleness and simplicity upon his tranquil countenance. He roused up, and gave me good day. I told him that a friend of mine had commissioned me to make some inquiries about a cherished companion of his boyhood named *Leonidas W.* Smiley—*Rev. Leonidas W.* Smiley, a young minister of the Gospel, who he had heard was at one time a resident of Angel's Camp. I added that if Mr. Wheeler could tell me anything about this Rev. Leonidas W. Smiley, I would feel under many obligations to him.

Simon Wheeler backed me into a corner and blockaded me there with his chair, and then sat down and reeled off the monotonous narrative which follows this paragraph. He never smiled, he never frowned, he never changed his voice from the gentle-flowing key to which he tuned his initial sentence, he never betrayed the slightest suspicion of enthusiasm; but all through the interminable narrative there ran a vein of impressive earnestness and sincerity, which showed me plainly that, so far from his imagining that there was anything ridiculous or funny about his story, he regarded it as a really important matter, and admired its two heroes as men of transcendent genius in *finesse*. I let him go on in his own way, and never interrupted him once.

"Rev. Leonidas W. H'm, Reverend Le—well, there was a feller here once by the name of *Jim* Smiley, in the winter of '49—or maybe it was the spring of '50—I don't recollect exactly, somehow, though what makes me think it was one or the other is because I remember the big flume[2] warn't finished when he first come to the camp; but anyway, he was the curiousest man about always betting on anything that turned up you ever see, if he could get anybody to bet on the other side; and if he couldn't he'd change sides. Any way that suited the other man would suit *him*—any way just so's he got a bet, *he* was satisfied. But still he was lucky, uncommon lucky; he most always come out winner. He was always ready and laying for a chance; there couldn't be no solit'ry thing mentioned but that feller'd offer to bet on it, and take ary side you please, as I was just telling you. If there was a horse-race, you'd find him flush or you'd find him busted at the end of it; if there was a dog-fight, he'd bet on it; if there was a cat-fight, he'd bet on it; if there was a chicken-fight, he'd bet on it; why, if there was two birds setting on a fence, he would bet you which one would fly first; or if there was a camp-meeting, he would be there reg'lar to bet on Parson Walker, which he judged to be the best exhorter about here, and so he was too, and a good man. If he even see a straddle-bug[3] start to go anywheres, he would bet you how long it would take him to get to—to wherever he was going to, and if you took him up, he would foller that straddle-bug to Mexico but what he would find out where he was bound for and how long he was on the road. Lots of the boys here has seen that Smiley, and can tell you about him. Why, it never made no difference to *him*—he'd bet on *any* thing—the dangdest feller. Parson Walker's wife laid very sick once, for a good while, and it seemed as if they warn't going to save her; but one morning he come in, and Smiley up and asked him how she was, and he said she was considerable better—thank the Lord for his inf'nite mercy—and coming on so smart that with

---

[1] In Calaveras County, California.

[2] A ravine with a stream running through it; in mining, an inclined channel made of wood, through which water is brought to the site.

[3] A type of beetle, also called tumble-bug or tumble-dung.

the blessing of Prov'dence she'd get well yet; and Smiley, before he thought, says, 'Well, I'll resk two-and-a-half she don't anyway.'

"Thish-yer Smiley had a mare—the boys called her the fifteen-minute nag, but that was only in fun, you know, because of course she was faster than that—and he used to win money on that horse, for all she was so slow and always had the asthma, or the distemper, or the consumption, or something of that kind. They used to give her two or three hundred yards' start, and then pass her under way; but always at the fag end of the race she'd get excited and desperate like, and come cavorting and straddling up, and scattering her legs around limber, sometimes in the air, and sometimes out to one side among the fences, and kicking up m-o-r-e dust and raising m-o-r-e racket with her coughing and sneezing and blowing her nose—and *always* fetch up at the stand just about a neck ahead, as near as you could cipher it down.

"And he had a little small bull-pup, that to look at him you'd think he warn't worth a cent but to set around and look ornery and lay for a chance to steal something. But as soon as money was up on him he was a different dog; his underjaw'd begin to stick out like the fo'castle of a steamboat, and his teeth would uncover and shine like the furnaces. And a dog might tackle him and bully-rag him, and bite him, and throw him over his shoulder two or three times, and Andrew Jackson—which was the name of the pup—Andrew Jackson would never let on but what *he* was satisfied, and hadn't expected nothing else—and the bets being doubled and doubled on the other side all the time, till the money was all up; and then all of a sudden he would grab that other dog jest by the j'int of his hind leg and freeze to it—not chaw, you understand, but only just grip and hang on till they throwed up the sponge, if it was a year. Smiley always come out winner on that pup, till he harnessed a dog once that didn't have no hind legs, because they'd been sawed off in a circular saw, and when the thing had gone along far enough, and the money was all up, and he come to make a snatch for his pet holt, he see in a minute how he'd been imposed on, and how the other dog had him in the door, so to speak, and he 'peared surprised, and then he looked sorter discouraged-like, and didn't try no more to win the fight, and so he got shucked out bad. He give Smiley a look, as much as to say his heart was broke, and it was *his* fault, for putting up a dog that hadn't no hind legs for him to take holt of, which was his main dependence in a fight, and then he limped off a piece and laid down and died. It was a good pup, was that Andrew Jackson, and would have made a name for hisself if he'd lived, for the stuff was in him and he had genius—I know it, because he hadn't no opportunities to speak of, and it don't stand to reason that a dog could make such a fight as he could under them circumstances if he hadn't no talent. It always makes me feel sorry when I think of that last fight of his'n, and the way it turned out.

"Well, thish-yer Smiley had rat-tarriers, and chicken cocks, and tomcats and all them kind of things, till you couldn't rest, and you couldn't fetch nothing for him to bet on but he'd match you. He ketched a frog one day, and took him home, and said he cal'lated to educate him; and so he never done nothing for three months but set in his back yard and learn that frog to jump. And you bet you he *did* learn him too. He'd give him a little punch behind, and the next minute you'd see that frog whirling in the air like a doughnut—see him turn one summerset,[4] or maybe a couple, if he got a good start, and come down flat-footed and all right, like a cat.

___
[4] Somersault.

He got him up so in the matter of ketching flies, and kep' him in practice so constant, that he'd nail a fly every time as fur as he could see him. Smiley said all a frog wanted was education, and he could do 'most anything—and I believe him. Why, I've seen him set Dan'l Webster down here on this floor—Dan'l Webster was the name of the frog—and sing out, 'Flies, Dan'l, flies!' and quicker'n you could wink he'd spring straight up and snake a fly off'n the counter there, and flop down on the floor ag'in as solid as a gob of mud, and fall to scratching the side of his head with his hind foot as indifferent as if he hadn't no idea he'd been doin' any more'n any frog might do. You never see a frog so modest and straight-for'ard as he was, for all he was so gifted. And when it come to fair and square jumping on a dead level, he could get over more ground at one straddle than any animal of his breed you ever see. Jumping on a dead level was his strong suit, you understand; and when it come to that, Smiley would ante up money on him as long as he had a red.[5] Smiley was monstrous proud of his frog, and well he might be, for fellers that had traveled and been everywheres all said he laid over any frog that ever *they* see.

"Well, Smiley kep' the beast in a little lattice box, and he used to fetch him down-town sometimes and lay for a bet. One day a feller—a stranger in the camp, he was—come acrost him with his box, and says:

"'What might it be that you've got in the box?'

"And Smiley says, sorter indifferent-like, 'It might be a parrot, or it might be a canary, maybe, but it ain't—it's only just a frog.'

"And the feller took it, and looked at it careful, and turned it round this way and that, and says, 'H'm—so 'tis. Well, what's *he* good for?'

"'Well,' Smiley says, easy and careless, 'he's good enough for *one* thing, I should judge—he can outjump any frog in Calaveras County.'

"The feller took the box again, and took another long, particular look, and give it back to Smiley, and says, very deliberate, 'Well,' he says, 'I don't see no p'ints about that frog that's any better'n any other frog.'

"'Maybe you don't,' Smiley says. 'Maybe you understand frogs and maybe you don't understand 'em; maybe you've had experience, and maybe you ain't only a amature, as it were. Anyways, I've got *my* opinion and I'll resk forty dollars that he can outjump any frog in Calaveras County.'

"And the feller studied a minute, and then says, kinder sadlike, 'Well, I'm only a stranger here, and I ain't got no frog; but if I had a frog, I'd bet you.'

"And then Smiley says, 'That's all right—that's all right—if you'll hold my box a minute, I'll go and get you a frog.' And so the feller took the box, and put up his forty dollars along with Smiley's, and set down to wait.

"So he set there a good while thinking and thinking to himself, and then he got the frog out and prized his mouth open and took a teaspoon and filled him full of quail-shot—filled him pretty near up to his chin—and set him on the floor. Smiley he went to the swamp and slopped around in the mud for a long time, and finally he ketched a frog, and fetched him in, and give him to this feller, and says:

"'Now, if you're ready, set him alongside of Dan'l, with his fore paws just even with Dan'l's, and I'll give the word.' Then he says, 'One—two—three—*git!*' and him and the feller touched up the frogs from behind, and the new frog hopped off lively, but Dan'l give a heave, and hysted up his shoulders—so—like a Frenchman, but it warn't no use—he couldn't budge; he was planted as solid as

---

[5] A red cent, a penny.

a church, and he couldn't no more stir than if he was anchored out. Smiley was a good deal surprised, and he was disgusted too, but he didn't have no idea what the matter was, of course.

"The feller took the money and started away; and when he was going out at the door, he sorter jerked his thumb over his shoulder—so—at Dan'l, and says again, very deliberate, 'Well,' he says, '*I* don't see no p'ints about that frog that's any better'n any other frog.'

"Smiley he stood scratching his head and looking down at Dan'l a long time, and at last he says, 'I do wonder what in the nation that frog throw'd off for—I wonder if there ain't something the matter with him—he 'pears to look mighty baggy, somehow.' And he ketched Dan'l by the nap of the neck, and hefted him, and says, 'Why blame my cats if he don't weigh five pound!' and turned him upside down and he belched out a double handful of shot. And then he see how it was, and he was the maddest man—he set the frog down and took out after that feller, but he never ketched him. And—"

[Here Simon Wheeler heard his name called from the front yard, and got up to see what was wanted.] And turning to me as he moved away, he said: "Just set where you are stranger, and rest easy—I ain't going to be gone a second."

But, by your leave, I did not think that a continuation of the history of the enterprising vagabond *Jim* Smiley would be likely to afford me much information concerning the Rev. *Leonidas W.* Smiley, and so I started away.

At the door I met the sociable Wheeler returning, and he buttonholed me and recommenced:

"Well, thish-yer Smiley had a yailer one-eyed cow that didn't have no tail, only just a short stump like a bannanner, and—"

However, lacking both time and inclination, I did not wait to hear about the afflicted cow, but took my leave.

1865

THE LATE BENJAMIN FRANKLIN*

"Never put off till to-morrow what you can do day after to-morrow just as well."—B. F.[1]

This party was one of those persons whom they call Philosophers. He was twins,[2] being born simultaneously in two different houses in the city of Boston. These houses remain unto this day, and have signs upon them worded in accordance with the facts. The signs are considered well enough to have, though not necessary, because the inhabitants point out the two birthplaces to the stranger anyhow, and sometimes as often as several times in the same day. The subject of this memoir was of a vicious disposition, and early prostituted his talents to the invention of maxims and aphorisms calculated to inflict suffering upon the rising generation of all subsequent ages. His simplest acts, also, were contrived with a view to their being held up for the emulation of boys forever—boys who might otherwise have

---

* First published in *Sketches New and Old* (1870). Twain's biographers have long noted his interest in and admiration for Benjamin Franklin, whom he parodies in this tongue-in-cheek sketch.

[1] An inversion of Franklin's maxim "Never put off till tomorrow what you can do today."

[2] Franklin was born in Boston and achieved much of his fame as a citizen of Philadelphia; because both cities claim him as a native and show a house in which he lived, Mark Twain concludes that Franklin was twins.

been happy. It was in this spirit that he became the son of a soap-boiler,[3] and probably for no other reason than that the efforts of all future boys who tried to be anything might be looked upon with suspicion unless they were the sons of soap-boilers. With a malevolence which is without parallel in history, he would work all day, and then sit up nights, and let on to be studying algebra by the light of a smoldering fire, so that all other boys might have to do that also, or else have Benjamin Franklin thrown up to them. Not satisfied with these proceedings he had a fashion of living wholly on bread and water, and studying astronomy at meal-time—a thing which has brought affliction to millions of boys since, whose fathers had read Franklin's pernicious biography.[4]

His maxims were full of animosity toward boys. Nowadays a boy cannot follow out a single natural instinct without tumbling over some of those everlasting aphorisms[5] and hearing from Franklin on the spot. If he buys two cents' worth of peanuts, his father says, "Remember what Franklin has said, my son—'A groat a day's a penny a year'"; and the comfort is all gone out of those peanuts. If he wants to spin his top when he has done work, his father quotes, "Procrastination is the thief of time." If he does a virtuous action, he never gets anything for it, because "Virtue is its own reward." And that boy is hounded to death and robbed of his natural rest, because Franklin said once, in one of his inspired flights of malignity:

> Early to bed and early to rise
> Makes a man healthy and wealthy and wise.

As if it were any object to a boy to be healthy and wealthy and wise on such terms. The sorrow that that maxim has cost me, through my parents, experimenting on me with it, tongue cannot tell. The legitimate result is my present state of general debility, indigence, and mental aberration. My parents used to have me up before nine o'clock in the morning sometimes when I was a boy. If they had let me take my natural rest where would I have been now? Keeping store, no doubt, and respected by all.

And what an adroit old adventurer the subject of this memoir was! In order to get a chance to fly his kite[6] on Sunday he used to hang a key on the string and let on to be fishing for lightning. And a guileless public would go home chirping about the "wisdom" and the "genius" of the hoary Sabbath-breaker. If anybody caught him playing "mumble-peg" by himself, after the age of sixty, he would immediately appear to be ciphering out how the grass grew—as if it was any of his business. My grandfather knew him well, and he says Franklin was always fixed—always ready. If a body, during his old age, happened on him unexpectedly when he was catching flies, or making mud-pies, or sliding on a cellar door, he would immediately look wise, and rip out a maxim, and walk off with his nose in the air and his cap turned wrong side before, trying to appear absent-minded and eccentric. He was a hard lot.

He invented a stove that would smoke your head off in four hours by the clock.

---

[3] Franklin's father, Josiah Franklin, was a candlemaker and a soap-boiler.

[4] Franklin's *Autobiography* (1791) is regarded as one of the classics of the genre.

[5] The maxims Twain cites are among the many expressions of proverbial wisdom Franklin inserted in *Poor Richard's Almanack,* which he published annually from 1733 to 1758.

[6] Franklin's experiments with electricity, including the famous kite-flying episode, took place in the 1740s; his *Experiments and Observations in Electricity* was first published in 1741. The Sabbath-breaking story is Twain's invention.

One can see the almost devilish satisfaction he took in it by his giving it his name.[7]

He was always proud of telling how he entered Philadelphia for the first time, with nothing in the world but two shillings in his pocket and four rolls of bread under his arm. But really, when you come to examine it critically, it was nothing. Anybody could have done it.

To the subject of this memoir belongs the honor of recommending the army to go back to bows and arrows in place of bayonets and muskets. He observed, with his customary force, that the bayonet was very well under some circumstances, but that he doubted whether it could be used with accuracy at a long range.

Benjamin Franklin did a great many notable things for his country, and made her young name to be honored in many lands as the mother of such a son. It is not the idea of this memoir to ignore that or cover it up. No; the simple idea of it is to snub those pretentious maxims of his, which he worked up with a great show of originality out of truisms that had become wearisome platitudes as early as the dispersion from Babel;[8] and also to snub his stove, and his military inspirations, his unseemly endeavor to make himself conspicuous when he entered Philadelphia, and his flying his kite and fooling away his time in all sorts of such ways when he ought to have been foraging for soap-fat, or constructing candles. I merely desired to do away with somewhat of the prevalent calamitous idea among heads of families that Franklin *acquired* his great genius by working for nothing, studying by moonlight, and getting up in the night instead of waiting till morning like a Christian; and that this program, rigidly inflicted, will make a Franklin of every father's fool. It is time these gentlemen were finding out that these execrable eccentricities of instinct and conduct are only the *evidence* of genius, not the *creators* of it. I wish I had been the father of my parents long enough to make them comprehend this truth, and thus prepare them to let their son have an easier time of it. When I was a child I had to boil soap, notwithstanding my father was wealthy, and I had to get up early and study geometry at breakfast, and peddle my own poetry, and do everything just as Franklin did, in the solemn hope that I would be a Franklin some day. And here I am.

1870

THE PRIVATE HISTORY OF A CAMPAIGN THAT FAILED*

You have heard from a great many people who did something in the war;[1] is it not fair and right that you listen a little moment to one who started out to do something in it, but didn't? Thousands entered the war, got just a taste of it, and then stepped out again permanently. These, by their very numbers, are respectable, and are therefore entitled to a sort of voice—not a loud one, but a modest one; not a boastful one, but an apologetic one. They ought not to be allowed much space among better people—people who did something. I grant that; but they ought at

---

[7] The Franklin Stove, orginally called a "fireplace" in Franklin's *Account of the New Invented Pennsylvania Fireplace* (1744); by all reports it worked well.

[8] In Genesis 11:9, a city and tower in the ancient land of Shinar, the scene of the confusion of languages.

* First published in the *Century Magazine*, December 1885.   [1] The Civil War (1861–1865).

least to be allowed to state why they didn't do anything, and also to explain the process by which they didn't do anything. Surely this kind of light must have a sort of value. *[any different perspective is worthy of notice]*

Out West[2] there was a good deal of confusion in men's minds during the first months of the great trouble—a good deal of unsettledness, of leaning first this way, then that, then the other way. It was hard for us to get our bearings. I call to mind an instance of this. I was piloting on the Mississippi when the news came that South Carolina had gone out of the Union on the 20th of December, 1860. My pilot mate was a New-Yorker. He was strong for the Union; so was I. But he would not listen to me with any patience; my loyalty was smirched, to his eye, because my father had owned slaves. *[judged by history]* I said, in palliation of this dark fact, that I had heard my father say, some years before he died, that slavery was a great wrong, and that he would free the solitary negro he then owned if he could think it right to give away the property of the family when he was so straitened in means. My mate retorted that a mere impulse was nothing—anybody could pretend to a good impulse; and went on decrying my Unionism and libeling my ancestry. A month later the secession atmosphere had considerably thickened on the Lower Mississippi, and I became a rebel; so did he. We were together in New Orleans the 26th of January, when Louisiana went out of the Union. He did his full share of the rebel shouting, but was bitterly opposed to letting me do mine. He said that I came of bad stock—of a father who had been willing to set slaves free. In the *[turns it around & uses history against him again]* following summer he was piloting a Federal gunboat and shouting for the Union again, and I was in the Confederate army. I held his note for some borrowed money. He was one of the most upright men I ever knew, but he repudiated that note without hesitation because I was a rebel and the son of a man who owned slaves.

In that summer—of 1861—the first wash of the wave of war broke upon the shores of Missouri. Our state was invaded by the Union forces. They took possession of St. Louis, Jefferson Barracks,[3] and some other points. The Governor, Calib Jackson, issued his proclamation calling out fifty thousand militia to repel the invader.

I was visiting in the small town where my boyhood had been spent—Hannibal, Marion County. Several of us got together in a secret place by night and formed ourselves into a military company. One Tom Lyman, a young fellow of a good deal of spirit but of no military experience, was made captain; I was made second lieutenant. We had no first lieutenant; I do not know why; it was long ago. There were fifteen of us. By the advice of an innocent connected with the organization we called ourselves the Marion Rangers. I do not remember that any one found fault with the name. I did not; I thought it sounded quite well. The young fellow who proposed this title was perhaps a fair sample of the kind of stuff we were made of. He was young, ignorant, good-natured, well-meaning, trivial, full of romance, and given to reading chivalric novels and singing forlorn love-ditties. He had some pathetic little nickel-plated aristocratic instincts, and detested his name, which was Dunlap; detested it, partly because it was nearly as common in that region as Smith, but mainly because it had a plebeian sound to his ear. So he tried to ennoble it by writing it in this way: *d'Unlap*. That contented his eye, but left his ear unsatisfied, for people gave the new name the same old pronunciation—emphasis on the front end of it. He then did the bravest thing that can be imagined—a thing to make one shiver when one remembers how the world is

---

[2] In Missouri, where Twain lived.   [3] An army camp near St. Louis.

given to resenting shams and affectations; he began to write his name so: *d'Un Lap*. And he waited patiently through the long storm of mud that was flung at this work of art, and he had his reward at last; for he lived to see that name accepted, and the emphasis put where he wanted it by people who had known him all his life, and to whom the tribe of Dunlaps had been as familiar as the rain and the sunshine for forty years. So sure of victory at last is the courage that can wait. He said he had found, by consulting some ancient French chronicles, that the name was rightly and originally written d'Un Lap; and said that if it were translated into English it would mean Peterson: *Lap,* Latin or Greek, he said, for stone or rock, same as the French *pierre,* that is to say, Peter: *d',* of or from; *un,* a or one; hence, d'Un Lap, of or from a stone or a Peter; that is to say, one who is the son of a stone, the son of a Peter—Peterson. Our militia company were not learned, and the explanation confused them; so they called him Peterson Dunlap. He proved useful to us in his way; he named our camps for us, and he generally struck a name that was "no slouch," as the boys said.

That is one sample of us. Another was Ed Stevens, son of the town jeweler—trim-built, handsome, graceful, neat as a cat; bright, educated, but given over entirely to fun. There was nothing serious in life to him. As far as he was concerned, this military expedition of ours was simply a holiday. I should say that about half of us looked upon it in the same way; not consciously, perhaps, but unconsciously. We did not think; we were not capable of it. As for myself, I was full of unreasoning joy to be done with turning out of bed at midnight and four in the morning for a while;[4] grateful to have a change, new scenes, new occupations, a new interest. In my thoughts that was as far as I went; I did not go into the details; as a rule, one doesn't at twenty-four.

Another sample was Smith, the blacksmith's apprentice. This vast donkey had some pluck, of a slow and sluggish nature, but a soft heart; at one time he would knock a horse down for some impropriety and at another he would get homesick and cry. However, he had one ultimate credit to his account which some of us hadn't; he stuck to the war, and was killed in battle at last.

Jo Bowers, another sample, was a huge, good-natured, flax-headed lubber; lazy, sentimental, full of harmless brag, a grumbler by nature; an experienced, industrious, ambitious, and often quite picturesque liar, and yet not a successful one, for he had had no intelligent training, but was allowed to come up just any way. This life was serious enough to him, and seldom satisfactory. But he was a good fellow, anyway, and the boys all liked him. He was made orderly sergeant; Stevens was made corporal.

These samples will answer—and they are quite fair ones. Well, this herd of cattle started for the war. What could you expect of them? They did as well as they knew how; but, really, what was justly to be expected of them? Nothing, I should say. That is what they did.

We waited for a dark night, for caution and secrecy were necessary; then, toward midnight, we stole in couples and from various directions to the Griffith place, beyond the town; from that point we set out together on foot. Hannibal lies at the extreme southeastern corner of Marion County, on the Mississippi River; our objective point was the hamlet of New London, ten miles away, in Ralls County.

The first hour was all fun, all idle nonsense and laughter. But that could not be kept up. The steady trudging came to be like work; the play had somehow oozed

---

[4] As a riverboat pilot on the Mississippi, Twain would have watches at these and other hours.

out of it; the stillness of the woods and the somberness of the night began to throw a depressing influence over the spirits of the boys, and presently the talking died out and each person shut himself up in his own thoughts. During the last half of the second hour nobody said a word.

Now we approached a log farm-house where, according to report, there was a guard of five Union soldiers. Lyman called a halt; and there, in the deep gloom of the overhanging branches, he began to whisper a plan of assault upon that house, which made the gloom more depressing than it was before. It was a crucial moment; we realized, with a cold suddenness, that here was no jest—we were standing face to face with actual war. We were equal to the occasion. In our response there was no hesitation, no indecision: we said that if Lyman wanted to meddle with those soldiers, he could go ahead and do it; but if he waited for us to follow him, he would wait a long time.

Lyman urged, pleaded, tried to shame us, but it had no effect. Our course was plain, our minds were made up: we would flank the farm-house—go out around. And that was what we did.

We struck into the woods and entered upon a rough time, stumbling over roots, getting tangled in vines, and torn by briers. At last we reached an open place in a safe region, and sat down, blown and hot, to cool off and nurse our scratches and bruises. Lyman was annoyed, but the rest of us were cheerful; we had flanked the farm-house, we had made our first military movement, and it was a success; we had nothing to fret about, we were feeling just the other way. Horse-play and laughing began again; the expedition was become a holiday frolic once more.

Then we had two more hours of dull trudging and ultimate silence and depression; then, about dawn, we straggled into New London, soiled, heel-blistered, fagged with our little march, and all of us except Stevens in a sour and raspy humor and privately down on the war. We stacked our shabby old shotguns in Colonel Ralls's barn, and then went in a body and breakfasted with that veteran of the Mexican War.[5] Afterward he took us to a distant meadow, and there in the shade of a tree we listened to an old-fashioned speech from him, full of gunpowder and glory, full of that adjective-piling, mixed metaphor and windy declamation which were regarded as eloquence in that ancient time and that remote region; and then he swore us on the Bible to be faithful to the State of Missouri and drive all invaders from her soil, no matter whence they might come or under what flag they might march. This mixed us considerably, and we could not make out just what service we were embarked in; but Colonel Ralls, the practised politician and phrase-juggler, was not similarly in doubt; he knew quite clearly that he had invested us in the cause of the Southern Confederacy. He closed the solemnities by belting around me the sword which his neighbor, Colonel Brown, had worn at Buena Vista and Molino del Rey;[6] and he accompanied this act with another impressive blast.

Then we formed in line of battle and marched four miles to a shady and pleasant piece of woods on the border of the far-reaching expanses of a flowery prairie. It was an enchanting region for war—our kind of war.

We pierced the forest about half a mile, and took up a strong position, with some low, rocky, and wooded hills behind us, and a purling, limpid creek in front. Straightway half the command were in swimming and the other half fishing. The ass with the French name gave this position a romantic title, but it was too long, so the boys shortened and simplified it to Camp Ralls. *doesn't coincide w/ his character description*

---

[5] The war between Mexico and the United States (1846–1848).   [6] Mexican War battles.

We occupied an old maple-sugar camp, whose half-rotted troughs were still propped against the trees. A long corn-crib served for sleeping-quarters for the battalion. On our left, half a mile away, were Mason's farm and house; and he was a friend to the cause. Shortly after noon the farmers began to arrive from several directions, with mules and horses for our use, and these they lent us for as long as the war might last, which they judged would be about three months. The animals were of all sizes, all colors, and all breeds. They were mainly young and frisky, and nobody in the command could stay on them long at a time; for we were town boys, and ignorant of horsemanship. The creature that fell to my share was a very small mule, and yet so quick and active that it could throw me without difficulty; and it did this whenever I got on it. Then it would bray—stretching its neck out, laying its ear back, and spreading its jaws till you could see down to its works. It was a disagreeable animal in every way. If I took it by the bridle and tried to lead it off the grounds, it would sit down and brace back, and no one could budge it. However, I was not entirely destitute of military resources, and I did presently manage to spoil this game; for I had seen many a steamboat aground in my time, and knew a trick or two which even a grounded mule would be obliged to respect. There was a well by the corn-crib; so I substituted thirty fathom of rope for the bridle, and fetched him home with the windlass.[7]

I will anticipate here sufficiently to say that we did learn to ride, after some days' practice, but never well. We could not learn to like our animals; they were not choice ones, and most of them had annoying peculiarities of one kind or another. Stevens's horse would carry him, when he was not noticing, under the huge excrescences which form on the trunks of oak-trees, and wipe him out of the saddle; in this way Stevens got several bad hurts. Sergeant Bowers's horse was very large and tall, with slim, long legs, and looked like a railroad bridge. His size enabled him to reach all about, and as far as he wanted to, with his head; so he was always biting Bowers's legs. On the march, in the sun, Bowers slept a good deal; and as soon as the horse recognized that he was asleep he would reach around and bite him on the leg. His legs were black and blue with bites. This was the only thing that could ever make him swear, but this always did; whenever his horse bit him he always swore, and of course Stevens, who laughed at everything, laughed at this, and would even get into such convulsions over it as to lose his balance and fall off his horse; and then Bowers, already irritated by the pain of the horse-bite, would resent the laughter with hard language, and there would be a quarrel; so that horse made no end of trouble and bad blood in the command.

However, I will get back to where I was—our first afternoon in the sugar-camp. The sugar-troughs came very handy as horse-troughs, and we had plenty of corn to fill them with. I ordered Sergeant Bowers to feed my mule; but he said that if I reckoned he went to war to be a dry-nurse to a mule it wouldn't take me very long to find out my mistake. I believed that this was insubordination, but I was full of uncertainties about everything military, and so I let the thing pass, and went and ordered Smith, the blacksmith's apprentice, to feed the mule; but he merely gave me a large, cold, sarcastic grin, such as an ostensibly seven-year-old horse gives you when you lift his lip and find he is fourteen, and turned his back on me. I then went to the captain, and asked if it were not right and proper and military for me to have an orderly. He said it was, but as there was only one orderly in the corps, it was but right that he himself should have Bowers on his staff. Bowers said he wouldn't serve on anybody's staff; and if anybody thought he could make

---

[7] Any machine for hoisting or hauling; here a homemade means of winding the mule in with the rope.

him, let him try it. So, of course, the thing had to be dropped; there was no other way.

Next, nobody would cook; it was considered a degradation; so we had no dinner. We lazied the rest of the pleasant afternoon away, some dozing under the trees, some smoking cob-pipes and talking sweethearts and war, some playing games. By late supper-time all hands were famished; and to meet the difficulty all hands turned to, on an equal footing, and gathered wood, built fires, and cooked the meal. Afterward everything was smooth for a while; then trouble broke out between the corporal and the sergeant, each claiming to rank the other. Nobody knew which was the higher office; so Lyman had to settle the matter by making the rank of both officers equal. The commander of an ignorant crew like that has many troubles and vexations which probably do not occur in the regular army at all. However, with the song-singing and yarn-spinning around the camp-fire, everything presently became serene again; and by and by we raked the corn down level in one end of the crib, and all went to bed on it, tying a horse to the door, so that he would neigh if any one tried to get in.[8]

We had some horsemanship drill every forenoon; then, afternoons, we rode off here and there in squads a few miles, and visited the farmers' girls, and had a youthful good time, and got an honest good dinner or supper, and then home again to camp, happy and content.

For a time life was idly delicious, it was perfect; there was nothing to mar it. Then came some farmers with an alarm one day. They said it was rumored that the enemy were advancing in our direction from over Hyde's prairie. The result was a sharp stir among us, and general consternation. It was a rude awakening from our pleasant trance. The rumor was but a rumor—nothing definite about it; so, in the confusion, we did not know which way to retreat. Lyman was for not retreating at all in these uncertain circumstances; but he found that if he tried to maintain that attitude he would fare badly, for the command were in no humor to put up with insubordination. So he yielded the point and called a council of war—to consist of himself and the three other officers; but the privates made such a fuss about being left out that we had to allow them to remain, for they were already present, and doing the most of the talking too. The question was, which way to retreat; but all were so flurried that nobody seemed to have even a guess to offer. Except Lyman. He explained in a few calm words that, inasmuch as the enemy were approaching from over Hyde's prairie, our course was simple: all we had to do was not to retreat *toward* him; any other direction would answer our needs perfectly. Everybody saw in a moment how true this was, and how wise; so Lyman got a great many compliments. It was now decided that we should fall back on Mason's farm.

It was after dark by this time, and as we could not know how soon the enemy might arrive, it did not seem best to try to take the horses and things with us; so we only took the guns and ammunition, and started at once. The route was very rough and hilly and rocky, and presently the night grew very black and rain began to fall; so we had a troublesome time of it, struggling and stumbling along in the dark; and soon some person slipped and fell, and then the next person behind

---

[8] Twain's note: "It was always my impression that that was what the horse was there for, and I know that it was also the impression of at least one other of the command, for we talked about it at the time, and admired the military ingenuity of the device; but when I was out West, three years ago, I was told by Mr. A. G. Fuqua, a member of our company, that the horse was his; that the leaving him tied at the door was a matter of mere forgetfulness, and that to attribute it to intelligent invention was to give him quite too much credit. In support of his position he called my attention to the suggestive fact that the artifice was not employed again. I had not thought of that before."

stumbled over him and fell, and so did the rest, one after the other; and then Bowers came, with a keg of powder in his arms, while the command were all mixed together, arms and legs, on the muddy slope; and so he fell, of course, with the keg, and this started the whole detachment down the hill in a body, and they landed in the brook at the bottom in a pile, and each that was undermost pulling the hair and scratching and biting those that were on top of him; and those that were being scratched and bitten scratching and biting the rest in their turn, and all saying they would die before they would ever go to war again if they ever got out of this brook this time, and the invader might rot for all they cared, and the country along with him—and all such talk as that, which was dismal to hear and take part in, in such smothered, low voices, and such a grisly dark place and so wet, and the enemy, maybe, coming any moment.

The keg of powder was lost, and the guns, too; so the growling and complaining continued straight along while the brigade pawed around the pasty hillside and slopped around in the brook hunting for these things; consequently we lost considerable time at this; and then we heard a sound, and held our breath and listened, and it seemed to be the enemy coming, though it could have been a cow, for it had a cough like a cow; but we did not wait, but left a couple of guns behind and struck out for Mason's again as briskly as we could scramble along in the dark. But we got lost presently among the rugged little ravines, and wasted a deal of time finding the way again, so it was after nine when we reached Mason's stile at last; and then before we could open our mouths to give the countersign several dogs came bounding over the fence, with great riot and noise, and each of them took a soldier by the slack of his trousers and began to back away with him. We could not shoot the dogs without endangering the persons they were attached to; so we had to look on helpless at what was perhaps the most mortifying spectacle of the Civil War. There was light enough, and to spare, for the Masons had now run out on the porch with candles in their hands. The old man and his son came and undid the dogs without difficulty, all but Bowers's; but they couldn't undo his dog, they didn't know his combination; he was of the bull kind, and seemed to be set with a Yale time-lock; but they got him loose at last with some scalding water, of which Bowers got his share and returned thanks. Peterson Dunlap afterward made up a fine name for this engagement, and also for the night march which preceded it, but both have long ago faded out of my memory.

We now went into the house, and they began to ask us a world of questions, whereby it presently came out that we did not know anything concerning who or what we were running from; so the old gentleman made himself very frank, and said we were a curious breed of soldiers, and guessed we could be depended on to end up the war in time, because no government could stand the expense of the shoe-leather we should cost it trying to follow us around. "Marion *Rangers!* good name, b'gosh!" said he. And wanted to know why we hadn't had a picket-guard at the place where the road entered the prairie, and why we hadn't sent out a scouting party to spy out the enemy and bring us an account of his strength, and so on, before jumping up and stampeding out of a strong position upon a mere vague rumor—and so on, and so forth, till he made us all feel shabbier than the dogs had done, not half so enthusiastically welcome. So we went to bed shamed and low-spirited; except Stevens. Soon Stevens began to devise a garment for Bowers which could be made to automatically display his battle-scars to the grateful, or conceal them from the envious, according to his occasions; but Bowers was in no humor for this, so there was a fight, and when it was over Stevens had some battle-scars of his own to think about.

Then we got a little sleep. But after all we had gone through, our activities were not over for the night; for about two o'clock in the morning we heard a shout of warning from down the lane, accompanied by a chorus from all the dogs, and in a moment everybody was up and flying around to find out what the alarm was about. The alarmist was a horseman who gave notice that a detachment of Union soldiers was on its way from Hannibal with orders to capture and hang any bands like ours which it could find, and said we had no time to lose. Farmer Mason was in a flurry this time himself. He hurried us out of the house with all haste, and sent one of his negroes with us to show us where to hide ourselves and our telltale guns among the ravines half a mile away. It was raining heavily.

We struck down the lane, then across some rocky pasture-land which offered good advantages for stumbling; consequently we were down in the mud most of the time, and every time a man went down he blackguarded the war, and the people that started it, and everybody connected with it, and gave himself the master dose of all for being so foolish as to go into it. At last we reached the wooded mouth of a ravine, and there we huddled ourselves under the streaming trees, and sent the negro back home. It was a dismal and heart-breaking time. We were like to be drowned with the rain, deafened with the howling wind and the booming thunder, and blinded by the lighting. It was, indeed, a wild night. The drenching we were getting was misery enough, but a deeper misery still was the reflection that the halter might end us before we were a day older. A death of this shameful sort had not occurred to us as being among the possibilities of war. It took the romance all out of the campaign, and turned our dreams of glory into a repulsive nightmare. As for doubting that so barbarous an order had been given, not one of us did that.

The long night wore itself out at last, and then the negro came to us with the news that the alarm had manifestly been a false one, and that breakfast would soon be ready. Straightway we were light-hearted again, and the world was bright, and life as full of hope and promise as ever—for we were young then. How long ago that was! Twenty-four years.

The mongrel child of philology[9] named the night's refuge Camp Devastation, and no soul objected. The Masons gave us a Missouri country breakfast, in Missourian abundance, and we needed it: hot biscuits; hot "wheat bread," prettily criss-crossed in a lattice pattern on top; hot corn-pone; fried chicken; bacon, coffee, eggs, milk, buttermilk, etc.; and the world may be confidently challenged to furnish the equal of such a breakfast, as it is cooked in the South.

We stayed several days at Mason's; and after all these years the memory of the dullness, and stillness, and lifelessness of that slumberous farm-house still oppresses my spirit as with a sense of the presence of death and mourning. There was nothing to do, nothing to think about; there was no interest in life. The male part of the household were away in the fields all day, the women were busy and out of our sight; there was no sound but the plaintive wailing of a spinning-wheel, forever moaning out from some distant room—the most lonesome sound in nature, a sound steeped and sodden with homesickness and the emptiness of life. The family went to bed about dark every night, and as we were not invited to intrude any new customs we naturally followed theirs. Those nights were a hundred years long to youths accustomed to being up till twelve. We lay awake and miserable till that hour every time, and grew old, and decrepit waiting through the still eternities for the clock-strikes. This was no place for town boys. So at last it

---

[9] Peterson Dunlap; philology means scholarship, the love of learning and literature.

was with something very like joy that we received news that the enemy were on our track again. With a new birth of the old warrior spirit we sprang to our places in line of battle and fell back on Camp Ralls.

Captain Lyman had taken a hint from Mason's talk, and he now gave orders that our camp should be guarded against surprise by the posting of pickets. I was ordered to place a picket at the forks of the road in Hyde's prairie. Night shut down black and threatening. I told Sergeant Bowers to go out to that place and stay till midnight; and, just as I was expecting, he said he wouldn't do it. I tried to get others to go, but all refused. Some excused themselves on account of the weather; but the rest were frank enough to say they wouldn't go in any kind of weather. This kind of thing sounds odd now, and impossible, but there was no surprise in it at the time. On the contrary, it seemed a perfectly natural thing to do. There were scores of little camps scattered over Missouri where the same thing was happening. These camps were composed of young men who had been born and reared to a sturdy independence, and who did not know what it meant to be ordered around by Tom, Dick, and Harry, whom they had known familiarly all their lives, in the village or on the farm. It is quite within the probabilities that this same thing was happening all over the South. James Redpath[10] recognized the justice of this assumption, and furnished the following instance in support of it. During a short stay in East Tennessee he was in a citizen colonel's tent one day talking, when a big private appeared at the door, and, without salute or other circumlocution, said to the colonel:

"Say, Jim, I'm a-goin' home for a few days."

"What for?"

"Well, I hain't b'en there for a right smart while, and I'd like to see how things is comin' on."

"How long are you going to be gone?"

"'Bout two weeks."

"Well, don't be gone longer than that; and get back sooner if you can."

That was all, and the citizen officer resumed his conversation where the private had broken it off. This was in the first months of the war, of course. The camps in our part of Missouri were under Brigadier-General Thomas H. Harris. He was a townsman of ours, a first-rate fellow, and well liked; but we had all familiarly known him as the sole and modest-salaried operator in our telegraph-office, where he had to send about one despatch a week in ordinary times, and two when there was a rush of business; consequently, when he appeared in our midst one day, on the wing, and delivered a military command of some sort, in a large military fashion, nobody was surprised at the response which he got from the assembled soldiery:

"Oh, now, what'll you take to *don't,* Tom Harris?"

It was quite the natural thing. One might justly imagine that we were hopeless material for war. And so we seemed, in our ignorant state; but there were those among us who afterward learned the grim trade; learned to obey like machines; became valuable soldiers; fought all through the war, and came out at the end with excellent records. One of the very boys who refused to go out on picket duty that night, and called me an ass for thinking he would expose himself to danger in such a foolhardy way, had become distinguished for intrepidity before he was a year older. *His characters change often.*

---

[10] Redpath (1833–1891), a Scottish-born journalist, was a correspondent for the New York *Tribune.*

I did secure my picket that night—not by authority, but by diplomacy. I got Bowers to go by agreeing to exchange ranks with him for the time being, and go along and stand the watch with him as his subordinate. We stayed out there a couple of dreary hours in the pitchy darkness and the rain, with nothing to modify the dreariness but Bowers's monotonous growlings at the war and the weather; then we began to nod, and presently found it next to impossible to stay in the saddle; so we gave up the tedious job, and went back to the camp without waiting for the relief guard. We rode into camp without interruption or objection from anybody, and the enemy could have done the same, for there were no sentries. Everybody was asleep; at midnight there was nobody to send out another picket, so none was sent. We never tried to establish a watch at night again, as far as I remember, but we generally kept a picket out in the daytime.

In that camp the whole command slept on the corn in the big corn-crib; and there was usually a general row before morning, for the place was full of rats, and they would scramble over the boys' bodies and faces, annoying and irritating everybody; and now and then they would bite some one's toe, and the person who owned the toe would start up and magnify his English and begin to throw corn in the dark. The ears were half as heavy as bricks, and when they struck they hurt. The persons struck would respond, and inside of five minutes every man would be locked in a death-grip with his neighbor. There was a grievous deal of blood shed in the corn-crib, but this was all that was spilt while I was in the war. No, that is not quite true. But for one circumstance it would have been all. I will come to that now.

Our scares were frequent. Every few days rumors would come that the enemy were approaching. In these cases we always fell back on some other camp of ours; we never stayed where we were. But the rumors always turned out to be false; so at last even we began to grow indifferent to them. One night a negro was sent to our corn-crib with the same old warning: the enemy was hovering in our neighborhood. We all said let him hover. We resolved to stay still and be comfortable. It was a fine warlike resolution, and no doubt we all felt the stir of it in our veins—for a moment. We had been having a very jolly time, that was full of horse-play and school-boy hilarity; but that cooled down now, and presently the fast-waning fire of forced jokes and forced laughs died out altogether, and the company became silent. Silent and nervous. And soon uneasy—worried—apprehensive. We had said we would stay, and we were committed. We could have been persuaded to go, but there was nobody brave enough to suggest it. An almost noiseless movement presently began in the dark by a general but unvoiced impulse. When the movement was completed each man knew that he was not the only person who had crept to the front wall and had his eye at a crack between the logs. No, we were all there; all there with our hearts in our throats, and staring out toward the sugar-troughs where the forest footpath came through. It was late, and there was a deep woodsy stillness everywhere. There was a veiled moonlight, which was only just strong enough to enable us to mark the general shape of objects. Presently a muffled sound caught our ears, and we recognized it as the hoof-beats of a horse or horses. And right away a figure appeared in the forest path; it could have been made of smoke, its mass had so little sharpness of outline. It was a man on horseback, and it seemed to me that there were others behind him. I got hold of a gun in the dark, and pushed it through a crack between the logs, hardly knowing what I was doing, I was so dazed with fright. Somebody said "Fire!" I pulled the trigger. I seemed to see a hundred flashes and hear a hundred reports; then I saw the man fall down out of the saddle. My first feeling was of surprised gratification; my first impulse was an apprentice-sportsman's impulse to run and pick up his game. Somebody said, hardly audibly, "Good—we've got him!—wait for the rest." But the rest did not come. We waited—listened—still no more came. There was not a sound, not the whisper of a leaf; just perfect stillness; an uncanny kind of stillness, which was all the more uncanny on account of the damp, earthy, late-night smells now rising and pervading it. Then, wondering, we crept stealthily out, and approached the man. When we got to him the moon revealed him distinctly. He was lying on his back, with his arms abroad; his mouth was open and his chest heaving with long gasps, and his white shirt-front was all splashed with blood. The thought shot through me that I was a murderer; that I had killed a man—a man who had never done me any harm. That was the coldest sensation that ever went through my marrow. I was down by him in a moment, helplessly stroking his forehead; and I would have given anything then—my own life freely—to make him again what he had been five minutes before. And all the boys seemed to be feeling in the same way; they hung over him, full of pitying interest, and tried all they could to help him, and said all sorts of regretful things. They had forgotten all about the enemy; they thought only of this one forlorn unit of the foe. Once my imagination persuaded me that the dying man gave me a reproachful look out of his shadowy eyes, and it seemed to me that I could rather he had stabbed me than done that. He muttered and mumbled like a dreamer in his sleep about his wife and his child; and I thought with a new despair, "This thing that I have done does not end with him; it falls upon *them* too, and they never did me any harm, any more than he."

In a little while the man was dead. He was killed in war; killed in fair and legitimate war; killed in battle, as you may say; and yet he was as sincerely mourned by the opposing force as if he had been their brother. The boys stood there a half-hour sorrowing over him, and recalling the details of the tragedy, and wondering who he might be, and if he were a spy, and saying that if it were to do over again they would not hurt him unless he attacked them first. It soon came out that mine was not the only shot fired; there were five others—a division of the guilt which was a great relief to me, since it in some degree lightened and diminished the burden I was carrying. There were six shots fired at once; but I was not in my right mind at the time, and my heated imagination had magnified my one shot into a volley.

The man was not in uniform, and was not armed. He was a stranger in the country; that was all we ever found out about him. The thought of him got to preying upon me every night; I could not get rid of it. I could not drive it away, the taking of that unoffending life seemed such a wanton thing. And it seemed an epitome of war; that all war must be just that—the killing of strangers against whom you feel no personal animosity; strangers whom, in other circumstances, you would help if you found them in trouble, and who would help you if you needed it.[11] My campaign was spoiled. It seemed to me that I was not rightly equipped for this awful business; that war was intended for men, and I for a child's nurse. I resolved to retire from this avocation of sham soldiership while I could save some remnant of my self-respect. These morbid thoughts clung to me against reason; for at bottom I did not believe I had touched that man. The law of probabilities decreed me guiltless of his blood; for in all my small experience with

[11] A memorable definition of war from a very serious Twain.

guns I had never hit anything I had tried to hit, and I knew I had done my best to hit him. Yet there was no solace in the thought. Against a diseased imagination demonstration goes for nothing.

The rest of my war experience was of a piece with what I have already told of it. We kept monotonously falling back upon one camp or another, and eating up the farmers and their families. They ought to have shot us; on the contrary, they were as hospitably kind and courteous to us as if we had deserved it. In one of these camps we found Ab Grimes, an Upper Mississippi pilot,[12] who afterward became famous as a dare-devil rebel spy, whose career bristled with desperate adventures. The look and style of his comrades suggested that they had not come into the war to play, and their deeds made good the conjecture later. They were fine horsemen and good revolver shots; but their favorite arm was the lasso. Each had one at his pommel, and could snatch a man out of the saddle with it every time, on a full gallop, at any reasonable distance.

In another camp the chief was a fierce and profane old blacksmith of sixty, and he had furnished his twenty recruits with gigantic home-made bowie-knives, to be swung with two hands, like the *machetes* of the Isthmus. It was a grisly spectacle to see that earnest band practising their murderous cuts and slashes under the eye of that remorseless old fanatic.

The last camp which we fell back upon was in a hollow near the village of Florida, where I was born—in Monroe County. Here we were warned one day that a Union colonel was sweeping down on us with a whole regiment at his heel. This looked decidedly serious. Our boys went apart and consulted; then we went back and told the other companies present that the war was a disappointment to us, and we were going to disband. They were getting ready themselves to fall back on some place or other, and we were only waiting for General Tom Harris, who was expected to arrive at any moment; so they tried to persuade us to wait a little while, but the majority of us said no, we were accustomed to falling back, and didn't need any of Tom Harris's help; we could get along perfectly well without him—and save time, too. So about half of our fifteen, including myself, mounted and left on the instant; the others yielded to persuasion and stayed—stayed through the war.

An hour later we met General Harris on the road, with two or three people in his company—his staff, probably, but we could not tell; none of them were in uniform; uniforms had not come into vogue among us yet. Harris ordered us back; but we told him there was a Union colonel coming with a whole regiment in his wake, and it looked as if there was going to be a disturbance; so we had concluded to go home. He raged a little, but it was of no use; our minds were made up. We had done our share; had killed one man, exterminated one army, such as it was; let him go and kill the rest, and that would end the war. I did not see that brisk young general again until last year; then he was wearing white hair and whiskers.

In time I came to know that Union colonel whose coming frightened me out of the war and crippled the Southern cause to that extent—General Grant. I came within a few hours of seeing him when he was as unknown as I was myself; at a time when anybody could have said, "Grant?—Ulysses S. Grant?[13] I do not remember hearing the name before." It seems difficult to realize that there was once

---

[12] A riverboat pilot.

[13] Grant (1822–1885) became commander in chief of the Union Armies and later the eighteenth U.S. president (1869–1877).

a time when such a remark could be rationally made; but there *was,* and I was within a few miles of the place and the occasion, too, though proceeding in the other direction.

The thoughtful will not throw this war paper of mine lightly aside as being valueless. It has this value: it is a not unfair picture of what went on in many and many a militia camp in the first months of the rebellion, when the green recruits were without discipline, without the steadying and heartening influence of trained leaders; when all their circumstances were new and strange, and charged with exaggerated terrors, and before the invaluable experience of actual collision in the field had turned them from rabbits into soldiers. If this side of the picture of that early day has not before been put into history, then history has been to that degree incomplete, for it had and has its rightful place there. There was more Bull Run[14] material scattered through the early camps of this country than exhibited itself at Bull Run. And yet it learned its trade presently, and helped to fight the great battles later. I could have become a soldier myself if I had waited. I had got part of it learned; I knew more about retreating than the man that invented retreating.

1885

FENIMORE COOPER'S LITERARY OFFENSES*

The Pathfinder and *The Deerslayer*[1] stand at the head of Cooper's novels as artistic creations. There are others of his works which contain parts as perfect as are to be found in these, and scenes even more thrilling. Not one can be compared with either of them as a finished whole.

The defects in both of these tales are comparatively slight. They were pure works of art.—PROF. LOUNSBURY[2]

The five tales reveal an extraordinary fullness of invention.

. . . One of the very greatest characters in fiction, Natty Bumppo. . . .

The craft of the woodsman, the tricks of the trapper, all the delicate art of the forest, were familiar to Cooper from his youth up.—PROF. BRANDER MATTHEWS[3]

Cooper is the greatest artist in the domain of romantic fiction yet produced by America.—WILKIE COLLINS[4]

It seems to me that it was far from right for the Professor of English Literature in Yale, the Professor of English Literature in Columbia, and Wilkie Collins to deliver opinions on Cooper's literature without having read some of it. It would have

[14] A small stream in Northeast Virginia, the site of two Union defeats during the Civil War: in the first Battle of Bull Run (or Manassas), July 21, 1861, General Stonewall Jackson and other Confederate forces routed the inexperienced Union troops; in the second Battle of Bull Run, August 29–30, 1862, Confederate forces under Jackson and General James Longstreet twice repulsed Union troops under General John Pope.

* First published in the *North American Review,* July 1895. The American novelist James Fenimore Cooper (1789–1851) wrote the five Leather-Stocking Tales that Twain discusses. Twain indulges his talent for humorous exaggeration in detailing Cooper's "literary offenses," but other evidence makes it clear that he liked neither the type of adventure story Cooper wrote nor Cooper's wordy style.

[1] Published in 1840 and 1841, respectively. *The Deerslayer,* the final novel in the Leather-Stocking series, presents Cooper's protagonist, Natty Bumppo, at his youngest and most innocent.

[2] Thomas R. Lounsbury (1838–1915), a noted scholar and author of *James Fenimore Cooper* (1882).

[3] Matthews (1852–1929) had written an appreciative essay on Cooper in 1889, the centennial of Cooper's birth.

[4] William Wilkie Collins (1824–1889), an English novelist, author of *The Woman in White* (1860) and *The Moonstone* (1868).

been much more decorous to keep silent and let persons talk who have read Cooper.

Cooper's art has some defects. In one place in *Deerslayer,* and in the restricted space of two-thirds of a page, Cooper has scored 114 offenses against literary art out of a possible 115. It breaks the record.

There are nineteen rules governing literary art in the domain of romantic fiction—some say twenty-two. In *Deerslayer* Cooper violated eighteen of them. These eighteen require:

1. That a tale shall accomplish something and arrive somewhere. But the *Deerslayer* tale accomplishes nothing and arrives in the air.

2. They require that the episodes of a tale shall be necessary parts of the tale, and shall help to develop it. But as the *Deerslayer* tale is not a tale, and accomplishes nothing and arrives nowhere, the episodes have no rightful place in the work, since there was nothing for them to develop.

3. They require that the personages in a tale shall be alive, except in the case of corpses, and that always the reader shall be able to tell the corpses from the others. But this detail has often been overlooked in the *Deerslayer* tale.

4. They require that the personages in a tale, both dead and alive, shall exhibit a sufficient excuse for being there. But this detail also has been overlooked in the *Deerslayer* tale.

5. They require that when the personages of a tale deal in conversation, the talk shall sound like human talk, and be talk such as human beings would be likely to talk in the given circumstances, and have a discoverable meaning, also a discoverable purpose, and a show of relevancy, and remain in the neighborhood of the subject in hand, and be interesting to the reader, and help out the tale, and stop when the people cannot think of anything more to say. But this requirement has been ignored from the beginning of the *Deerslayer* tale to the end of it.

6. They require that when the author describes the character of a personage in his tale, the conduct and conversation of that personage shall justify said description. But this law gets little or no attention in the *Deerslayer* tale, as Natty Bumppo's case will amply prove.

7. They require that when a personage talks like an illustrated, gilt-edged, tree-calf, hand-tooled, seven-dollar Friendship's Offering[5] in the beginning of a paragraph, he shall not talk like a negro minstrel in the end of it. But this rule is flung down and danced upon in the *Deerslayer* tale.

8. They require that crass stupidities shall not be played upon the reader as "the craft of the woodsman, the delicate art of the forest," by either the author or the people in the tale. But this rule is persistently violated in the *Deerslayer* tale.

9. They require that the personages of a tale shall confine themselves to possibilities and let miracles alone; or, if they venture a miracle, the author must so plausibly set it forth as to make it look possible and reasonable. But these rules are not respected in the *Deerslayer* tale.

10. They require that the author shall make the reader feel a deep interest in the personages of his tale and in their fate; and that he shall make the reader love the good people in the tale and hate the bad ones. But the reader of the *Deerslayer* tale dislikes the good people in it, is indifferent to the others, and wishes they would all get drowned together.

11. They require that the characters in a tale shall be so clearly defined that the

---

[5] An invented name for the type of gift book typically filled with sentimental verse and flowery language; "gilt-edged, tree-calf, hand-tooled," are terms for an expensive, elegantly bound book.

reader can tell beforehand what each will do in a given emergency. But in the *Deerslayer* tale this rule is vacated.

In addition to these large rules there are some little ones. These require that the author shall

12. *Say* what he is proposing to say, not merely come near it.
13. Use the right word, not its second cousin.
14. Eschew surplusage.
15. Not omit necessary details.
16. Avoid slovenliness of form.
17. Use good grammar.
18. Employ a simple and straightforward style.

Even these seven are coldly and persistently violated in the *Deerslayer* tale.

Cooper's gift in the way of invention was not a rich endowment; but such as it was he liked to work it, he was pleased with the effects, and indeed he did some quite sweet things with it. In his little box of stage-properties he kept six or eight cunning devices, tricks, artifices for his savages and woodsmen to deceive and circumvent each other with, and he was never so happy as when he was working these innocent things and seeing them go. A favorite one was to make a mocca-sined person tread in the tracks of the moccasined enemy, and thus hide his own trail. Cooper wore out barrels and barrels of moccasins in working that trick. Another stage-property that he pulled out of his box pretty frequently was his broken twig. He prized his broken twig above all the rest of his effects, and worked it the hardest. It is a restful chapter in any book of his when somebody doesn't step on a dry twig and alarm all the reds and whites for two hundred yards around. Every time a Cooper person is in peril, and absolute silence is worth four dollars a minute, he is sure to step on a dry twig. There may be a hundred handier things to step on, but that wouldn't satisfy Cooper. Cooper requires him to turn out and find a dry twig; and if he can't do it, go and borrow one. In fact, the Leatherstocking Series ought to have been called the Broken Twig Series.

I am sorry there is not room to put in a few dozen instances of the delicate art of the forest, as practised by Natty Bumppo and some of the other Cooperian ex-perts. Perhaps we may venture two or three samples. Cooper was a sailor—a naval officer; yet he gravely tells us how a vessel, driving toward a lee shore[6] in a gale, is steered for a particular spot by her skipper because he knows of an *under-tow* there which will hold her back against the gale and save her. For just pure woodcraft, or sailorcraft, or whatever it is, isn't that neat? For several years Cooper was daily in the society of artillery, and he ought to have noticed that when a cannon-ball strikes the ground it either buries itself or skips a hundred feet or so; skips again a hundred feet or so—and so on, till finally it gets tired and rolls. Now in one place he loses some "females"—as he always calls women—in the edge of a wood near a plain at night in a fog, on purpose to give Bumppo a chance to show off the delicate art of the forest before the reader. These mislaid people are hunting for a fort. They hear a cannon-blast, and a cannon-ball pres-ently comes rolling into the wood and stops at their feet. To the females this suggests nothing. The case is very different with the admirable Bumppo. I wish I may never know peace again if he doesn't strike out promptly and *follow the track*

---

[6] The shore protected from the wind. Cooper wrote a number of sea novels, among them *The Pilot* (1823) and *The Two Admirals* (1842); one of the Leather-Stocking Tales, *The Pathfinder* (1840), has a lengthy section that takes place on Lake Huron.

of that cannon-ball across the plain through the dense fog and find the fort. Isn't it a daisy? If Cooper had any real knowledge of Nature's ways of doing things, he had a most delicate art in concealing the fact. For instance: one of his acute Indian experts, Chingachgook[7] (pronounced Chicago, I think), has lost the trail of a person he is tracking through the forest. Apparently that trail is hopelessly lost. Neither you nor I could ever have guessed out the way to find it. It was very different with Chicago. Chicago was not stumped for long. He turned a running stream out of its course, and there, in the slush in its old bed, were that person's moccasin tracks.[8] The current did not wash them away, as it would have done in all other like cases—no, even the eternal laws of Nature have to vacate when Cooper wants to put up a delicate job of woodcraft on the reader.

We must be a little wary when Brander Matthews tell us that Cooper's books "reveal an extraordinary fullness of invention." As a rule, I am quite willing to accept Brander Matthews's literary judgments and applaud his lucid and graceful phrasing of them; but that particular statement needs to be taken with a few tons of salt. Bless your heart, Cooper hadn't any more invention than a horse; and I don't mean a high-class horse, either; I mean a clothes-horse. It would be very difficult to find a really clever "situation" in Cooper's books, and still more difficult to find one of any kind which he has failed to render absurd by his handling of it. Look at the episodes of "the caves"; and at the celebrated scuffle between Maqua[9] and those others on the table-land a few days later; and at Hurry Harry's[10] queer water-transit from the castle to the ark; and at Deerslayer's half-hour with his first corpse;[11] and at the quarrel between Hurry Harry and Deerslayer later; and at—but choose for yourself; you can't go amiss.

If Cooper had been an observer his inventive faculty would have worked better; not more interestingly, but more rationally, more plausibly. Cooper's proudest creations in the way of "situations" suffer noticeably from the absence of the observer's protecting gift. Cooper's eye was splendidly inaccurate. Cooper seldom saw anything correctly. He saw nearly all things as through a glass eye, darkly. Of course a man who cannot see the commonest little every-day matters accurately is working at a disadvantage when he is constructing a "situation." In the *Deerslayer* tale Cooper has a stream which is fifty feet wide where it flows out of a lake; it presently narrows to twenty as it meanders along for no given reason, and yet when a stream acts like that it ought to be required to explain itself. Fourteen pages later the width of the brook's outlet from the lake has suddenly shrunk thirty feet, and become "the narrowest part of the stream." This shrinkage is not accounted for. The stream has bends in it, a sure indication that it has alluvial banks and cuts them; yet these bends are only thirty and fifty feet long. If Cooper had been a nice and punctilious observer he would have noticed that the bends were oftener nine hundred feet long than short of it.

Cooper made the exit of that stream fifty feet wide, in the first place, for no

---

[7] A Mohican chief, Natty Bumppo's friend and companion in four of the Leather-Stocking Tales (Chingachgook dies in *The Pioneers* [1823], well before the time covered in *The Prairie* [1827]).

[8] An incident in *The Last of the Mohicans* (1826); actually, Uncas, Chingachgook's son, performs this wondrous feat of tracking.

[9] An evil Huron chief in *The Last of the Mohicans*.

[10] Hurry Harry March, an amoral white hunter in *The Deerslayer*.

[11] In a memorable scene in *The Deerslayer*, young Natty Bumppo ("Deerslayer") kills his first human being in single combat and remains with his dying foe until the end. This Huron Indian names Natty "Hawkeye" in tribute to his marksmanship.

particular reason; in the second place, he narrowed it to less than twenty to accommodate some Indians. He bends a "sapling" to the form of an arch over this narrow passage, and conceals six Indians in its foliage. They are "laying" for a settler's scow or ark which is coming up the stream on its way to the lake; it is being hauled against the stiff current by a rope whose stationary end is anchored in the lake; its rate of progress cannot be more than a mile an hour. Cooper describes the ark, but pretty obscurely. In the matter of dimensions "it was little more than a modern canal-boat." Let us guess, then, that it was about one hundred and forty feet long. It was of "greater breadth than common." Let us guess, then, that it was about sixteen feet wide. This leviathan had been prowling down bends which were but a third as long as itself, and scraping between banks where it had only two feet of space to spare on each side. We cannot too much admire this miracle. A low-roofed log dwelling occupies "two-thirds of the ark's length"—a dwelling ninety feet long and sixteen feet wide, let us say—a kind of vestibule train. The dwelling has two rooms—each forty-five feet long and sixteen feet wide, let us guess. One of them is the bedroom of the Hutter girls, Judith and Hetty; the other is the parlor in the daytime, at night it is papa's bedchamber. The ark is arriving at the stream's exit now, whose width has been reduced to less than twenty feet to accommodate the Indians—say to eighteen. There is a foot to spare on each side of the boat. Did the Indians notice that there was going to be a tight squeeze there? Did they notice that they could make money by climbing down out of that arched sapling and just stepping aboard when the ark scraped by? No, other Indians would have noticed these things, but Cooper's Indians never notice anything. Cooper thinks they are marvelous creatures for noticing, but he was almost always in error about his Indians. There was seldom a sane one among them.

The ark is one hundred and forty-feet long; the dwelling is ninety feet long. The idea of the Indians is to drop softly and secretly from the arched sapling to the dwelling as the ark creeps along under it at the rate of a mile an hour, and butcher the family. It will take the ark a minute and a half to pass under. It will take the ninety-foot dwelling a minute to pass under. Now, then, what did the six Indians do? It would take you thirty years to guess, and even then you would have to give it up, I believe. Therefore, I will tell you what the Indians did. Their chief, a person of quite extraordinary intellect for a Cooper Indian, warily watched the canal-boat as it squeezed along under him, and when he had got his calculations fined down to exactly the right shade, as he judged, he let go and dropped. And *missed the house!* That is actually what he did. He missed the house, and landed in the stern of the scow. It was not much of a fall, yet it knocked him silly. He lay there unconscious. If the house had been ninety-seven feet long he would have made the trip. The fault was Cooper's, not his. The error lay in the construction of the house. Cooper was no architect.

There still remained in the roost five Indians. The boat has passed under and is now out of their reach. Let me explain what the five did—you would not be able to reason it out for yourself. No. 1 jumped for the boat, but fell in the water astern of it. Then No. 2 jumped for the boat, but fell in the water still farther astern of it. Then No. 3 jumped for the boat, and fell a good way astern of it. Then No. 4 jumped for the boat, and fell in the water *away* astern. Then even No. 5 made a jump for the boat—for he was a Cooper Indian. In the matter of intellect, the difference between a Cooper Indian and the Indian that stands in front of the cigar-shop is not spacious. The scow episode is really a sublime burst of invention; but it does not thrill, because the inaccuracy of the details throws a sort of air of fictitiousness and general improbability over it. This comes of Cooper's inadequacy as an observer.

The reader will find some examples of Cooper's high talent for inaccurate observation in the account of the shooting-match in *The Pathfinder*.

> A common wrought nail was driven lightly into the target, its head having been first touched with paint.

The color of the paint is not stated—an important omission, but Cooper deals freely in important omissions. No, after all, it was not an important omission; for this nail-head is a *hundred yards from* the marksmen, and could not be seen by them at that distance, no matter what its color might be. How far can the best eyes see a common house-fly? A hundred yards? It is quite impossible. Very well; eyes that cannot see a house-fly that is a hundred yards away cannot see an ordinary nail-head at that distance, for the size of the two objects is the same. It takes a keen eye to see a fly or a nail-head at fifty yards—one hundred and fifty feet. Can the reader do it?

The nail was lightly driven, its head painted, and game called. Then the Cooper miracles began. The bullet of the first marksman chipped an edge of the nail-head; the next man's bullet drove the nail a little way into the target—and removed all the paint. Haven't the miracles gone far enough now? Not to suit Cooper; for the purpose of this whole scheme is to show off his prodigy, Deerslayer-Hawkeye-Long-Rifle-Leatherstocking-Pathfinder-Bumppo[12] before the ladies.

> "Be all ready to clench it, boys!" cried out Pathfinder, stepping into his friend's tracks the instant they were vacant. "Never mind a new nail; I can see that, though the paint is gone, and what I can see I can hit at a hundred yards, though it were only a mosquito's eye. Be ready to clench!"
>
> The rifle cracked, the bullet sped its way, and the head of the nail was buried in the wood, covered by the piece of flattened lead.

There, you see, is a man who could hunt flies with a rifle, and command a ducal salary in a Wild West show to-day if we had him back with us.

The recorded feat is certainly surprising just as it stands; but it is not surprising enough for Cooper. Cooper adds a touch. He has made Pathfinder do this miracle with another man's rifle; and not only that, but Pathfinder did not have even the advantage of loading it himself. He had everything against him, and yet he made that impossible shot; and not only made it, but did it with absolute confidence, saying, "Be ready to clench." Now a person like that would have undertaken that same feat with a brickbat, and with Cooper to help he would have achieved it, too.

Pathfinder showed off handsomely that day before the ladies. His very first feat was a thing which no Wild West show can touch. He was standing with the group of marksmen, observing—a hundred yards from the target, mind; one Jasper raised his rifle and drove the center of the bull's-eye. Then the Quartermaster fired. The target exhibited no result this time. There was a laugh. "It's a dead miss," said Major Lundie. Pathfinder waited an impressive moment or two; then

---

[12] Various names Natty Bumppo earns in the Leather-Stocking Tales.

said, in that calm, indifferent, know-it-all way of his, "No, Major, he has covered Jasper's bullet, as will be seen if any one will take the trouble to examine the target."

Wasn't it remarkable! How *could* he see that little pellet fly through the air and enter that distant bullet-hole? Yet that is what he did; for nothing is impossible to a Cooper person. Did any of those people have any deep-seated doubts about this thing? No; for that would imply sanity, and these were all Cooper people.

> The respect for Pathfinder's skill and for his *quickness and accuracy of sight* [the italics are mine] was so profound and general, that the instant he made this declaration the spectators began to distrust their own opinions, and a dozen rushed to the target in order to ascertain the fact. There, sure enough, it was found that the Quartermaster's bullet had gone through the hole made by Jasper's, and that, too, so accurately as to require a minute examination to be certain of the circumstance, which, however, was soon clearly established by discovering one bullet over the other in the stump against which the target was placed.

They made a "minute" examination; but never mind, how could they know that there were two bullets in that hole without digging the latest one out? for neither probe nor eyesight could prove the presence of any more than one bullet. Did they dig? No; as we shall see. It is the Pathfinder's turn now; he steps out before the ladies, takes aim, and fires.

But, alas! here is a disappointment; an incredible, an unimaginable disappointment—for the target's aspect is unchanged; there is nothing there but that same old bullet-hole!

> "If one dared to hint at such a thing," cried Major Duncan, "I should say that the Pathfinder has also missed the target!"

As nobody had missed it yet, the "also" was not necessary; but never mind about that, for the Pathfinder is going to speak.

> "No, no, Major," said he, confidently, "that *would* be a risky declaration. I didn't load the piece, and can't say what was in it, but if it was lead, you will find the bullet driving down those of the Quartermaster and Jasper, else is not my name Pathfinder."
>
> A shout from the target announced the truth of this assertion.

Is the miracle sufficient as it stands? Not for Cooper. The Pathfinder speaks again, as he "now slowly advances toward the stage occupied by the females":

> "That's not all, boys, that's not all; if you find the target touched at all, I'll own to a miss. The Quartermaster cut the wood, but you'll find no wood cut by that last messenger."

The miracle is at last complete. He knew—doubtless *saw*—at the distance of a hundred yards—that his bullet had passed into the hole *without fraying the edges*. There were now three bullets in that one hole—three bullets embedded proces-sionally in the body of the stump back of the target. Everybody knew this—somehow or other—and yet nobody had dug any of them out to make sure.[13] Cooper is not a close observer, but he is interesting. He is certainly always that, no matter what happens. And he is more interesting when he is not noticing what he is about than when he is. This is a considerable merit.

The conversations in the Cooper books have a curious sound in our modern ears. To believe that such talk really ever came out of people's mouths would be to believe that there was a time when time was of no value to a person who thought he had something to say; when it was the custom to spread a two-minute remark out to ten; when a man's mouth was a rolling-mill, and busied itself all day long in turning four-foot pigs[14] of thought into thirty-foot bars of conversational railroad iron by attenuation; when subjects were seldom faithfully stuck to, but the talk wandered all around and arrived nowhere; when conversations consisted mainly of irrelevancies, with here and there a relevancy, a relevancy with an embarrassed look, as not being able to explain how it got there.

Cooper was certainly not a master in the construction of dialogue. Inaccurate observation defeated him here as it defeated him in so many other enterprises of his. He even failed to notice that the man who talks corrupt English six days in the week must and will talk it on the seventh, and can't help himself. In the *Deerslayer* story he lets Deerslayer talk the showiest kind of book-talk sometimes, and at other times the basest of base dialects. For instance, when some one asks him if he has a sweetheart, and if so, where she abides, this is his majestic answer:

> "She's in the forest—hanging from the boughs of the trees, in a soft rain—in the dew on the open grass—the clouds that float about in the blue heavens—the birds that sing in the woods—the sweet springs where I slake my thirst—and in all the other glorious gifts that come from God's Providence!"

And he preceded that, a little before, with this:

> "It consarns me as all things that touches a fri'nd consarns a fri'nd."

And this is another of his remarks:

> "If I was Injin born, now, I might tell of this, or carry in the scalp and boast of the expl'ite afore the whole tribe; or if my inimy had only been a bear"—[and so on].

We cannot imagine such a thing as a veteran Scotch Commander-in-Chief comporting himself in the field like a windy melodramatic actor, but Cooper could. On one occasion Alice and Cora were being chased by the French through a fog in the neighborhood of their father's fort:[15]

> "*Point de quartier aux coquins!*"[16] cried an eager pursuer, who seemed to direct the operations of the enemy.

---

[13] This episode takes place pretty much as Twain recounts it.
[14] Ingots of metal rolled into railroad tracks.
[15] The British Fort William Henry in *The Last of the Mohicans*.
[16] "Show no mercy to the rascals!" (French).

"Stand firm and be ready, my gallant 6oths!" suddenly exclaimed a voice above them; "wait to see the enemy; fire low, and sweep the glacis."[17]

"Father! father" exclaimed a piercing cry from out the mist; "it is I! Alice! thy own Elsie! O! save your daughters!"

"Hold!" shouted the former speaker, in the awful tones of parental agony, the sound reaching even to the woods, and rolling back in solemn echo. "'Tis she! God has restored me my children! Throw open the sally-port;[18] to the field, 6oths, to the field! pull not a trigger, lest ye kill my lambs! Drive off these dogs of France with your steel!"

Cooper's word-sense was singularly dull. When a person has a poor ear for music he will flat and sharp right along without knowing it. He keeps near the tune, but it is *not* the tune. When a person has a poor ear for words, the result is a literary flatting and sharping; you perceive what he is intending to say, but you also perceive that he doesn't *say* it. This is Cooper. He was not a word-musician. His ear was satisfied with the *approximate* word. I will furnish some circumstantial evidence in support of this charge. My instances are gathered from half a dozen pages of the tale called *Deerslayer*. He uses "verbal" for "oral"; "precision" for "facility"; "phenomena" for "marvels"; "necessary" for "predetermined"; "unsophisticated" for "primitive"; "preparation" for "expectancy"; "rebuked" for "subdued"; "dependent on" for "resulting from"; "fact" for "condition"; "fact" for "conjecture"; "precaution" for "caution"; "explain" for "determine"; "mortified" for "disappointed"; "meretricious" for "factitious"; "materially" for "considerably"; "decreasing" for "deepening"; "increasing" for "disappearing"; "embedded" for "inclosed"; "treacherous" for "hostile"; "stood" for "stooped"; "softened" for "replaced"; "rejoined" for "remarked"; "situation" for "condition"; "different" for "differing"; "insensible" for "unsentient"; "brevity" for "celerity"; "distrusted" for "suspicious"; "mental imbecility" for "imbecility"; "eyes" for "sight"; "counteracting" for "opposing"; "funeral obsequies" for "obsequies."

There have been daring people in the world who claimed that Cooper could write English, but they are all dead now—all dead but Lounsbury. I don't remember that Lounsbury makes the claim in so many words, still he makes it, for he says that *Deerslayer* is a "pure work of art." Pure, in that connection, means faultless—faultless in all details—and language is a detail. If Mr. Lounsbury had only compared Cooper's English with the English which he writes himself—but it is plain that he didn't; and so it is likely that he imagines until this day that Cooper's is as clean and compact as his own. Now I feel sure, deep down in my heart, that Cooper wrote about the poorest English that exists in our language, and that the English of *Deerslayer* is the very worst that even Cooper ever wrote.

I may be mistaken, but it does seem to me that *Deerslayer* is not a work of art in any sense; it does seem to me that it is destitute of every detail that goes to the making of a work of art; in truth, it seems to me that *Deerslayer* is just simply a literary *delirium tremens*.[19]

A work of art? It has no invention; it has no order, system, sequence, or result; it has no lifelikeness, no thrill, no stir, no seeming of reality; its characters are

---

[17] Clear the field in front of the wall of the fort.

[18] A door in the wall of a fort through which troops can rush out.

[19] "Trembling delirium" (Latin): a violent delirium, induced by excessive and prolonged use of alcohol.

confusedly drawn, and by their acts and words they prove that they are not the sort of people the author claims that they are; its humor is pathetic; its pathos is funny; its conversations are—oh! indescribable; its love-scenes odious; its English a crime against the language.

Counting these out, what is left is Art. I think we must all admit that.

1893, 1895

THE MAN THAT CORRUPTED HADLEYBURG*

I

It was many years ago. Hadleyburg was the most honest and upright town in all the region around about. It had kept that reputation unsmirched during three generations, and was prouder of it than of any other of its possessions. It was so proud of it, and so anxious to insure its perpetuation, that it began to teach the principles of honest dealing to its babies in the cradle, and made the like teachings the staple of their culture thenceforward through all the years devoted to their education. Also, throughout the formative years temptations were kept out of the way of the young people, so that their honesty could have every chance to harden and solidify, and become a part of their very bone. The neighboring towns were jealous of this honorable supremacy, and affected to sneer at Hadleyburg's pride in it and call it vanity; but all the same they were obliged to acknowledge that Hadleyburg was in reality an incorruptible town; and if pressed they would also acknowledge that the mere fact that a young man hailed from Hadleyburg was all the recommendation he needed when he went forth from his natal town to seek for responsible employment.

But at last, in the drift of time, Hadleyburg had the ill luck to offend a passing stranger—possibly without knowing it, certainly without caring, for Hadleyburg was sufficient unto itself, and cared not a rap for strangers or their opinions. Still, it would have been well to make an exception in this one's case, for he was a bitter man and revengeful. All through his wanderings during a whole year he kept his injury in mind, and gave all his leisure moments to trying to invent a compensating satisfaction for it. He contrived many plans, and all of them were good, but none of them was quite sweeping enough; the poorest of them would hurt a great many individuals, but what he wanted was a plan which would comprehend the entire town, and not let so much as one person escape unhurt. At last he had a fortunate idea, and when it fell into his brain it lit up his whole head with an evil joy. He began to form a plan at once, saying to himself, "That is the thing to do—I will corrupt the town."

Six months later he went to Hadleyburg, and arrived in a buggy at the house of the old cashier of the bank about ten at night. He got a sack out of the buggy, shouldered it, and staggered with it through the cottage yard, and knocked at the door. A woman's voice said "Come in," and he entered, and set his sack behind

---

* First published in *Harper's Magazine* in December 1899. The ellipses and brackets are Mark Twain's.

the stove in the parlor, saying politely to the old lady who sat reading the *Mission-ary Herald* by the lamp:

"Pray keep your seat, madam, I will not disturb you. There—now it is pretty well concealed; one would hardly know it was there. Can I see your husband a moment, madam?"

No, he was gone to Brixton, and might not return before morning.

"Very well, madam, it is no matter. I merely wanted to leave that sack in his care, to be delivered to the rightful owner when he shall be found. I am a stranger; he does not know me; I am merely passing through the town to-night to discharge a matter which has been long in my mind. My errand is now completed, and I go pleased and a little proud, and you will never see me again. There is a paper attached to the sack which will explain everything. Good night, madam."

The old lady was afraid of the mysterious big stranger, and was glad to see him go. But her curiosity was roused, and she went straight to the sack and brought away the paper. It began as follows:

TO BE PUBLISHED; or, the right man sought out by private inquiry—either will answer. This sack contains gold coin weighing a hundred and sixty pounds four ounces—

"Mercy on us, and the door not locked!"

Mrs. Richards flew to it all in a tremble and locked it, then pulled down the window-shades and stood frightened, worried, and wondering if there was any-thing else she could do toward making herself and the money more safe. She listened awhile for burglars, then surrendered to curiosity and went back to the lamp and finished reading the paper:

I am a foreigner, and am presently going back to my own country, to remain there permanently. I am grateful to America for what I have received at her hands during my long stay under her flag; and to one of her citizens—a citizen of Hadleyburg—I am especially grateful for a great kindness done me a year or two ago. Two great kindnesses, in fact. I will explain. I was a gambler. I say I was. I was a ruined gambler. I arrived in this village at night, hungry and without a penny. I asked for help—in the dark; I was ashamed to beg in the light. I begged of the right man. He gave me twenty dollars—that is to say, he gave me life, as I considered it. He also gave me fortune; for out of that money I have made myself rich at the gaming-table. And finally, a remark which he made to me has remained with me to this day, and has at last conquered me; and in conquering has saved the remnant of my morals; I shall gamble no more. Now I have no idea who that man was, but I want him found, and I want him to have this money, to give away, throw away, or keep, as he pleases. It is merely my way of testifying my gratitude to him. If I could stay, I would find him myself; but no matter, he will be found. This is an honest town, an incorruptible town, and I know I can trust it without fear. This man can be identified by the remark which he made to me; I feel persuaded that he will remember it.

And now my plan is this: If you prefer to conduct the inquiry privately, do so. Tell the contents of this present writing to any one who is likely to be the right man. If he shall answer, 'I am the man; the remark I made was so-and-so,' apply the test—to wit: open the sack, and in it you will find a sealed envelope containing that remark. If the remark mentioned by the candidate tallies with it, give him the money, and ask no further questions, for he is certainly the right man.

But if you shall prefer a public inquiry, then publish this present writing in the local paper—with these instructions added, to wit: Thirty days from now, let the candidate appear at the town-hall at eight in the evening (Friday), and hand his remark, in a sealed envelope, to the Rev. Mr. Burgess (if he will be kind enough to act); and let Mr. Burgess there and then destroy the seals of the sack, open it, and see if the remark is correct; if correct, let the money be delivered, with my sincere gratitude, to my benefactor thus identified.

Mrs. Richards sat down, gently quivering with excitement, and was soon lost in thinkings—after this pattern: "What a strange thing it is! . . . And what a fortune for that kind man who set his bread afloat upon the waters! . . . If it had only been my husband that did it!—for we are so poor, so old and poor! . . . " Then, with a sigh—"But it was not my Edward; no, it was not he that gave a stranger twenty dollars. It is a pity, too; I see it now. . . . " Then, with a shudder—"But it is *gambler's* money! the wages of sin: we couldn't take it; we couldn't touch it. I don't like to be near it; it seems a defilement." She moved to a farther chair. . . . "I wish Edward would come and take it to the bank; a burglar might come at any moment; it is dreadful to be here all alone with it."

At eleven Mr. Richards arrived, and while his wife was saying, "I am *so* glad you've come!" he was saying, "I'm so tired—tired clear out; it is dreadful to be poor, and have to make these dismal journeys at my time of life. Always at the grind, grind, grind, on a salary—another man's slave, and he sitting at home in his slippers, rich and comfortable."

"I am so sorry for you, Edward, you know that; but be comforted: we have our livelihood; we have our good name—"

"Yes, Mary, and that is everything. Don't mind my talk—it's just a moment's irritation and doesn't mean anything. Kiss me—there, it's all gone now, and I am not complaining any more. What have you been getting? What's in the sack?"

Then his wife told him the great secret. It dazed him for a moment; then he said:

"It weighs a hundred and sixty pounds? Why, Mary, it's for-ty thou-sand dol-lars—think of it—a whole fortune! Not ten men in this village are worth that much. Give me the paper."

He skimmed through it and said:

"Isn't it an adventure! Why, it's a romance; it's like the impossible things one reads about in books, and never sees in life." He was well stirred up now; cheerful, even gleeful. He tapped his old wife on the cheek, and said, humorously, "Why we're rich, Mary, rich; all we've got to do is to bury the money and burn the papers. If the gambler ever comes to inquire, we'll merely look coldly upon him and say: 'What is this nonsense you are talking? We have never heard of you and your sack of gold before'; and then he would look foolish, and—"

"And in the mean time, while you are running on with your jokes, the money is still here, and it is fast getting along toward burglar-time."

"True. Very well, what shall we do—make the inquiry private? No, not that: it would spoil the romance. The public method is better. Think what a noise it will make! And it will make all the other towns jealous; for no stranger would trust such a thing to any town but Hadleyburg, and they know it. It's a great card for us. I must get to the printing-office now, or I shall be too late."

"But stop—stop—don't leave me here alone with it, Edward!"

But he was gone. For only a little while, however. Not far from his own house he met the editor-proprietor of the paper, and gave him the document, and said, "Here is a good thing for you, Cox—put it in."

"It may be too late, Mr. Richards, but I'll see."

At home again he and his wife sat down to talk the charming mystery over; they were in no condition for sleep. The first question was, Who could the citizen have been who gave the stranger the twenty dollars? It seemed a simple one; both answered it in the same breath:

"Barclay Goodson."

"Yes," said Richards, "he could have done it, and it would have been like him, but there's not another in the town."

"Everybody will grant that, Edward—grant it privately, anyway. For six months, now, the village has been its own proper self once more—honest, narrow, self-righteous, and stingy."

"It is what he always called it, to the day of his death—said it right out publicly, too."

"Yes, and he was hated for it."

"Oh, of course; but he didn't care. I reckon he was the best-hated man among us, except the Reverend Burgess."

"Well, Burgess deserves it—he will never get another congregation here. Mean as the town is, it knows how to estimate *him*. Edward, doesn't it seem odd that the stranger should appoint Burgess to deliver the money?"

"Well, yes—it does. That is—that is—"

"Why so much that-*is*-ing? Would *you* select him?"

"Mary, maybe the stranger knows him better than this village does."

"Much *that* would help Burgess!"

The husband seemed perplexed for an answer; the wife kept a steady eye upon him, and waited. Finally Richards said, with the hesitancy of one who is making a statement which is likely to encounter doubt:

"Mary, Burgess is not a bad man."

His wife was certainly surprised.

"Nonsense!" she exclaimed.

"He is not a bad man. I know. The whole of his unpopularity had its foundation in that one thing—the thing that made so much noise."

"That 'one thing,' indeed! As if that 'one thing' wasn't enough, all by itself."

"Plenty. Plenty. Only he wasn't guilty of it."

"How you talk! Not guilty of it! Everybody knows he *was* guilty."

"Mary, I give you my word—he was innocent."

"I can't believe it, and I don't. How do you know?"

"It is a confession. I am ashamed, but I will make it. I was the only man who knew he was innocent. I could have saved him, and—and—well, you know how the town was wrought up—I hadn't the pluck to do it. It would have turned everybody against me. I felt mean, ever so mean; but I didn't dare; I hadn't the manliness to face that."

Mary looked troubled, and for a while was silent. Then she said, stammeringly:

"I—I don't think it would have done for you to—to—One mustn't—er—public opinion—one has to be so careful—so—" It was a difficult road, and she got mired; but after a little she got started again. "It was a great pity, but—Why, we couldn't afford it, Edward—we couldn't indeed. Oh, I wouldn't have had you do it for anything!"

"It would have lost us the good will of so many people, Mary; and then—and then—"

"What troubles me now is, what *he* thinks of us, Edward."

"He? *He* doesn't suspect that I could have saved him."

"Oh," exclaimed the wife, in a tone of relief, "I am glad of that! As long as he doesn't know that you could have saved him, he—he—well, that makes it a great deal better. Why, I might have known he didn't know, because he is always trying to be friendly with us, as little encouragement as we give him. More than once people have twitted me with it. There's the Wilsons, and the Wilcoxes, and the Harknesses, they take a mean pleasure in saying, '*Your friend* Burgess,' because they know it pesters me. I wish he wouldn't persist in liking us so; I can't think why he keeps it up."

"I can explain it. It's another confession. When the thing was new and hot, and the town made a plan to ride him on a rail, my conscience hurt me so that I couldn't stand it, and I went privately and gave him notice, and he got out of the town and staid out till it was safe to come back."

"Edward! If the town had found it out—"

"*Don't!* It scares me yet, to think of it. I repented of it the minute it was done; and I was even afraid to tell you, lest your face might betray it to somebody. I didn't sleep any that night, for worrying. But after a few days I saw that no one was going to suspect me, and after that I got to feeling glad I did it. And I feel glad yet, Mary—glad through and through."

"So do I, now, for it would have been a dreadful way to treat him. Yes, I'm glad; for really you did owe him that, you know. But, Edward, suppose it should come out yet, some day!"

"It won't."

"Why?"

"Because everybody thinks it was Goodson."

"Of course they would!"

"Certainly. And of course he didn't care. They persuaded poor old Sawlsberry to go and charge it on him, and he went blustering over there and did it. Goodson looked him over, like as if he was hunting for a place on him that he could despise the most, then he says, 'So you are the Committee of Inquiry, are you?' Sawlsberry said that was about what he was. 'Hm. Do they require particulars, or do you reckon a kind of a *general* answer will do?' 'If they require particulars, I will come back, Mr. Goodson; I will take the general answer first.' 'Very well, then, tell them to go to hell—I reckon that's general enough. And I'll give you some advice, Sawlsberry; when you come back for the particulars, fetch a basket to carry the relics of yourself home in.'"

"Just like Goodson; it's got all the marks. He had only one vanity: he thought he could give advice better than any other person."

"It settled the business, and saved us, Mary. The subject was dropped."

"Bless you, I'm not doubting *that*."

Then they took up the gold-sack mystery again, with strong interest. Soon the conversation began to suffer breaks—interruptions caused by absorbed thinkings. The breaks grew more and more frequent. At last Richards lost himself wholly in thought. He sat long, gazing vacantly at the floor, and by and by he began to punctuate his thoughts with little nervous movements of his hands that seemed to indicate vexation. Meantime his wife too had relapsed into a thoughtful silence, and her movements were beginning to show a troubled discomfort. Finally Richards got up and strode aimlessly about the room, plowing his hands through his hair, much as a somnambulist might do who was having a bad dream. Then he seemed to arrive at a definite purpose; and without a word he put on his hat and passed quickly out of the house. His wife sat brooding, with a drawn face, and did not seem to be aware that she was alone. Now and then she murmured, "Lead us not into t— . . . but—but—we are so poor, so poor! . . . Lead us not into . . . Ah, who would be hurt by it?—and no one would ever know. . . . Lead us . . . " The voice died out in mumblings. After a little she glanced up and muttered in a half-frightened, half-glad way:

"He is gone! But, oh dear, he may be too late—too late. . . . Maybe not— maybe there is still time." She rose and stood thinking, nervously clasping and unclasping her hands. A slight shudder shook her frame, and she said, out of a dry throat, "God forgive me—it's awful to think such things—but . . . Lord, how we are made—how strangely we are made!"

She turned the light low, and slipped stealthily over and kneeled down by the sack and felt of its ridgy sides with her hands, and fondled them lovingly; and there was a gloating light in her poor old eyes. She fell into fits of absence; and came half out of them at times to mutter, "If we had only waited!—oh, if we had only waited a little, and not been in such a hurry!"

Meantime Cox had gone home from his office and told his wife all about the strange thing that had happened, and they had talked it over eagerly, and guessed that the late Goodson was the only man in the town who could have helped a suffering stranger with so noble a sum as twenty dollars. Then there was a pause, and the two became thoughtful and silent. And by and by nervous and fidgety. At last the wife said, as if to herself:

"Nobody knows this secret but the Richardses . . . and us . . . nobody."

The husband came out of his thinkings with a slight start, and gazed wistfully at his wife, whose face was become very pale; then he hesitatingly rose, and glanced furtively at his hat, then at his wife—a sort of mute inquiry. Mrs. Cox swallowed once or twice, with her hand at her throat, then in place of speech she nodded her head. In a moment she was alone, and mumbling to herself.

And now Richards and Cox were hurrying through the deserted streets, from opposite directions. They met, panting, at the foot of the printing-office stairs; by the night light there they read each other's face. Cox whispered:

"Nobody knows about this but us?"

The whispered answer was,

"Not a soul—on honor, not a soul!"

"If it isn't too late to—"

The men were starting up-stairs; at this moment they were overtaken by a boy, and Cox asked:

"Is that you, Johnny?"

"Yes, sir."

"You needn't ship the early mail—nor *any* mail; wait till I tell you."

"It's already gone, sir."

"*Gone?*" It had the sound of an unspeakable disappointment in it.

"Yes, sir. Time-table for Bixton and all the towns beyond changed to-day, sir—had to get the papers in twenty minutes earlier than common. I had to rush; if I had been two minutes later—"

The men turned and walked slowly away, not waiting to hear the rest. Neither of them spoke during ten minutes; then Cox said, in a vexed tone:

"What possessed you to be in such a hurry, *I* can't make out."

The answer was humble enough:

"I see it now, but somehow I never thought, you know, until it was too late. But the next time—"

"Next time be hanged! It won't come in a thousand years."

Then the friends separated without a good night, and dragged themselves home with the gait of mortally stricken men. At their homes their wives sprang up with an eager "Well?"—then saw the answer with their eyes and sank down sorrowing, without waiting for it to come in words. In both houses a discussion followed of a heated sort—a new thing; there had been discussions before, but not heated ones, not ungentle ones. The discussions to-night were a sort of seeming plagiarisms of each other. Mrs. Richards said,

"If you had only waited, Edward—if you had only stopped to think; but no, you must run straight to the printing-office and spread it all over the world."

"It *said* publish it."

"That is nothing; it also said do it privately, if you liked. There, now—is that true, or not?"

"Why, yes—yes, it is true; but when I thought what a stir it would make, and what a compliment it was to Hadleyburg that a stranger should trust it so—"

"Oh, certainly, I know all that; but if you had only stopped to think, you would have seen that you *couldn't* find the right man, because he is in his grave, and hasn't left chick nor child nor relation behind him; and as long as the money went to somebody that awfully needed it, and nobody would be hurt by it, and—and—"

She broke down, crying. Her husband tried to think of some comforting thing to say, and presently came out with this:

"But after all, Mary, it must be for the best—it *must* be; we know that. And we must remember that it was so ordered—"

"Ordered! Oh, everything's *ordered,* when a person has to find some way out when he has been stupid. Just the same, it was *ordered* that the money should come to us in this special way, and it was you that must take it on yourself to go meddling with the designs of Providence—and who gave you the right? It was wicked, that is what it was—just blasphemous presumption, and no more becoming to a meek and humble professor of—"

"But, Mary, you know how we have been trained all our lives long, like the whole village, till it is absolutely second nature to us to stop not a single moment to think when there's an honest thing to be done—"

"Oh, I know it, I know it—it's been one everlasting training and training and training in honesty—honesty shielded, from the very cradle, against every possible temptation, and so it's *artificial* honesty, and weak as water when temptation comes, as we have seen this night. God knows I never had shade nor shadow of a doubt of my petrified and indestructible honesty until now—and now, under the very first big and real temptation, I—Edward, it is my belief that this town's honesty is as rotten as mine is; as rotten as yours is. It is a mean town, a hard, stingy town, and hasn't a virtue in the world but this honesty it is so celebrated for and so conceited about; and so help me, I do believe that if ever the day comes that its honesty falls under great temptation, its grand reputation will go to ruin like a house of cards. There, now, I've made confession, and I feel better; I am a humbug, and I've been one all my life, without knowing it. Let no man call me honest again—I will not have it."

"I—well, Mary, I feel a good deal as you do; I certainly do. It seems strange, too, so strange. I never could have believe it—never."

A long silence followed; both were sunk in thought. At last the wife looked up and said:

"I know what you are thinking, Edward."

Richards had the embarrassed look of a person who is caught.

"I am ashamed to confess it, Mary, but—"

"It's no matter, Edward, I was thinking the same question myself."

"I hope so. State it."

"You were thinking, if a body could only guess out *what the remark was* that Goodson made to the stranger."

"It's perfectly true. I feel guilty and ashamed. And you?"

"I'm past it. Let us make a pallet[1] here; we've got to stand watch till the bank vault opens in the morning and admits the sack. . . . Oh dear, oh dear—if we hadn't made the mistake!"

The pallet was made, and Mary said:

"The open sesame—what could it have been? I do wonder what that remark could have been? But come; we will get to bed now."

"And sleep?"

"No: think."

"Yes, think."

By this time the Coxes too had completed their spat and their reconciliation, and were turning in—to think, to think, and toss, and fret, and worry over what the remark could possibly have been which Goodson made to the stranded dere-lict; that golden remark; that remark worth forty thousand dollars, cash.

The reason that the village telegraph-office was open later than usual that night was this: The foreman of Cox's paper was the local representative of the Associated Press. One might say its honorary representative, for it wasn't four times a year that he could furnish thirty words that would be accepted. But this time it was different. His despatch stating what he had caught got an instant answer:

Send the whole thing—all the details—twelve hundred words.

A colossal order! The foreman filled the bill; and he was the proudest man in the State. By breakfast-time the next morning the name of Hadleyburg the Incor-ruptible was on every lip in America, from Montreal to the Gulf, from the glaciers of Alaska to the orange-groves of Florida; and millions and millions of people were discussing the stranger and his money-sack, and wondering if the right man would be found, and hoping some more news about the matter would come soon—right away.

II

Hadleyburg village woke up world-celebrated—astonished—happy—vain. Vain beyond imagination. Its nineteen principal citizens and their wives went about shaking hands with each other, and beaming, and smiling, and congratulating,

---

[1] A small bed put together with cushions, pillows, blankets.

and saying *this* thing adds a new word to the dictionary—*Hadleyburg*, synonym for *incorruptible*—destined to live in dictionaries forever! And the minor and un-important citizens and their wives went around acting in much the same way. Everybody ran to the bank to see the gold-sack; and before noon grieved and envious crowds began to flock in from Brixton and all neighboring towns; and that afternoon and next day reporters began to arrive from everywhere to verify the sack and its history and write the whole thing up anew, and make dashing free-hand pictures of the sack, and of Richards's house, and the bank, and the Presby-terian church, and the Baptist church, and the public square, and the town-hall where the test would be applied and the money delivered; and damnable portraits of the Richardses, and Pinkerton the banker, and Cox, and the foreman, and Rev-erend Burgess, and the postmaster—and even of Jack Halliday, who was the loaf-ing, good-natured, no-account, irreverent fisherman, hunter, boys' friend, stray-dogs' friend, typical "Sam Lawson"[2] of the town. The little mean, smirking, oily Pinkerton showed the sack to all comers, and rubbed his sleek palms together pleasantly, and enlarged upon the town's fine old reputation for honesty and upon this wonderful indorsement of it, and hoped and believed that the example would now spread far and wide over the American world, and be epoch-making in the matter of moral regeneration. And so on, and so on.

By the end of a week things had quieted down again; the wild intoxication of pride and joy had sobered to a soft, sweet, silent delight—a sort of deep, name-less, unutterable content. All faces bore a look of peaceful, holy happiness.

Then a change came. It was a gradual change: so gradual that its beginnings were hardly noticed; maybe were not noticed at all, except by Jack Halliday, who always noticed everything; and always made fun of it, too, no matter what it was. He began to throw out chaffing remarks about people not looking quite so happy as they did a day or two ago; and next he claimed that the new aspect was deepen-ing to positive sadness; next, that it was taking on a sick look; and finally he said that everybody was become so moody, thoughtful, and absent-minded that he could rob the meanest man in town of a cent out of the bottom of his breeches pocket and not disturb his revery.

At this stage—or at about this stage—a saying like this was dropped at bed-time—with a sigh, usually—by the head of each of the nineteen principal house-holds: "Ah, what *could* have been the remark that Goodson made?"

And straightway—with a shudder—came this, from the man's wife:

"Oh, *don't!* What horrible thing are you mulling in your mind? Put it away from you, for God's sake!"

But that question was wrung from those men again the next night—and got the same retort. But weaker.

And the third night the men uttered the question yet again—with anguish, and absently. This time—and the following night—the wives fidgeted feebly, and tried to say something. But didn't.

And the night after that they found their tongues and responded—longingly:

"Oh, if we *could* only guess!"

Halliday's comments grew daily more and more sparklingly disagreeable and disparaging. He went diligently about, laughing at the town, individually and in mass. But his laugh was the only one left in the village: it fell upon a hollow and mournful vacancy and emptiness. Not even a smile was findable anywhere. Halli-

---

[2] A shiftless character in *Oldtown Folks* (1869) and its sequel, *Sam Lawson's Oldtown Fireside Sto-ries* (1872), by Harriet Beecher Stowe (1811–1896).

day carried a cigar-box around on a tripod, playing that it was a camera, and halted all passers and aimed the thing and said, "Ready!—now look pleasant, please," but not even this capital joke could surprise the dreary faces into any softening.

So three weeks passed—one week was left. It was Saturday evening—after supper. Instead of the aforetime Saturday-evening flutter and bustle and shopping and larking, the streets were empty and desolate. Richards and his old wife sat apart in their little parlor—miserable and thinking. This was become their evening habit now: the lifelong habit which had preceded it, of reading, knitting, and contented chat, or receiving or paying neighborly calls, was dead and gone and forgotten, ages ago—two or three weeks ago; nobody talked now, nobody read, nobody visited—the whole village sat at home, sighing, worrying, silent. Trying to guess out that remark.

The postman left a letter. Richards glanced listlessly at the superscription and the postmark—unfamiliar, both—and tossed the letter on the table and resumed his might-have-beens and his hopeless dull miseries where he had left them off. Two or three hours later his wife got wearily up and was going away to bed without a good night—custom now—but she stopped near the letter and eyed it awhile with a dead interest, then broke it open, and began to skim it over. Richards, sitting there with his chair tilted back against the wall and his chin between his knees, heard something fall. It was his wife. He sprang to her side, but she cried out:

"Leave me alone, I am too happy. Read the letter—read it!"

He did. He devoured it, his brain reeling. The letter was from a distant state, and it said:

> *I am a stranger to you, but no matter: I have something to tell. I have just arrived home from Mexico, and learned about that episode. Of course you do not know who made that remark, but I know, and I am the only person living who does know. It was* GOODSON. *I knew him well, many years ago. I passed through your village that very night, and was his guest till the midnight train came along. I overheard him make that remark to the stranger in the dark—it was in Hale Alley. He and I talked of it the rest of the way home, and while smoking in his house. He mentioned many of your villagers in the course of his talk—most of them in a very uncomplimentary way, but two or three favorably; among these latter yourself. I say "favorably"— nothing stronger. I remember his saying he did not actually* LIKE *any person in the town—not one; but that you—I* THINK *he said you—am almost sure—had done him a very great service once, possibly without knowing the full value of it, and he wished he had a fortune, he would leave it to you when he died, and a curse apiece for the rest of the citizens. Now, then, if it was you that did him that service, you are his legitimate heir, and entitled to the sack of gold. I know that I can trust to your honor and honesty, for in a citizen of Hadleyburg these virtues are an unfailing inheritance, and so I am going to reveal to you the remark, well satisfied that if you are not the right man you will seek and find the right one and see that poor Goodson's debt of gratitude for the service referred to is paid. This is the remark: "*YOU ARE FAR FROM BEING A BAD MAN: GO, AND REFORM.*"*
>
> HOWARD L. STEPHENSON.

"Oh, Edward, the money is ours, and I am so grateful, *oh*, so grateful—kiss me, dear, it's forever since we kissed—and we needed it so—the money—and now you are free of Pinkerton and his bank, and nobody's slave any more; it seems to me I could fly for joy."

It was a happy half-hour that the couple spent there on the settee caressing each other; it was the old days come again—days that had begun with their courtship and lasted without a break till the stranger brought the deadly money. By and by the wife said:

"Oh, Edward, how lucky it was you did him that grand service, poor Goodson! I never liked him, but I love him now. And it was fine and beautiful of you never to mention it or brag about it." Then, with a touch of reproach, "But you ought to have told *me,* Edward, you ought to have told your wife, you know."

"Well, I—er—well, Mary, you see—"

"Now stop hemming and hawing, and tell me about it, Edward. I always loved you, and now I'm proud of you. Everybody believes there was only one good generous soul in this village, and now it turns out that you—Edward, why don't you tell me?"

"Well—er—er— Why, Mary, I can't!"

"You *can't? Why* can't you?"

"You see, he—well, he—he made me promise I wouldn't."

The wife looked him over, and said, very slowly:

"Made—you—promise? Edward, what do you tell me that for?"

"Mary, do you think I would lie?"

She was troubled and silent for a moment, then she laid her hand within his and said:

"No . . . no. We have wandered far enough from our bearings—God spare us that! In all your life you have never uttered a lie. But now—now that the foundations of things seem to be crumbling from under us, we—we—" She lost her voice for a moment, then said, brokenly, "Lead us not into temptation. . . . I think you made the promise, Edward. Let it rest so. Let us keep away from that ground. Now—that is all gone by; let us be happy again; it is no time for clouds."

Edward found it something of an effort to comply, for his mind kept wandering—trying to remember what the service was that he had done Goodson.

The couple lay awake the most of the night, Mary happy and busy, Edward busy but not so happy. Mary was planning what she would do with the money. Edward was trying to recall that service. At first his conscience was sore on account of the lie he had told Mary—if it was a lie. After much reflection—suppose it *was* a lie? What then? Was it such a great matter? Aren't we always *acting* lies? Then why not *tell* them? Look at Mary—look what she had done. While he was hurrying off on his honest errand, what was she doing? Lamenting because the papers hadn't been destroyed and the money kept! Is theft better than lying?

That point lost its sting—the lie dropped into the background and left comfort behind it. The next point came to the front: *Had* he rendered that service? Well, here was Goodson's own evidence as reported in Stephenson's letter; there could be no better evidence than that—it was even *proof* that he had rendered it. Of course. So that point was settled. . . . No, not quite. He recalled with a wince that this unknown Mr. Stephenson was just a trifle unsure as to whether the performer of it was Richards or some other—and, oh dear, he had put Richards on his honor! He must himself decide whither that money must go—and Mr. Stephenson was not doubting that if he was the wrong man he would go honorably and find the right one. Oh, it was odious to put a man in such a situation—ah, why couldn't Stephenson have left out that doubt! What did he want to intrude that for?

Further reflection. How did it happen that *Richards's* name remained in Stephenson's mind as indicating the right man, and not some other man's name? That looked good. Yes, that looked very good. In fact, it went on looking better and better, straight along—until by and by it grew into positive *proof*. And then Richards put the matter at once out of his mind, for he had a private instinct that a proof once established is better left so.

He was feeling reasonably comfortable now, but there was still one other detail that kept pushing itself on his notice: of course he had done that service—that was settled; but what *was* that service? He must recall it—he would not go to sleep till he had recalled it; it would make his peace of mind perfect. And so he thought and thought. He thought of a dozen things—possible services, even probable services—but none of them seemed adequate, none of them seemed large enough, none of them seemed worth the money—worth the fortune Goodson had wished he could leave in his will. And besides, he couldn't remember having done them, anyway. Now, then—now, then—what *kind* of a service would it be that would make a man so inordinately grateful? Ah—the saving of his soul! That must be it. Yes, he could remember, now, how he once set himself the task of converting Goodson, and labored at it as much as—he was going to say three months; but upon closer examination it shrunk to a month, then to a week, then to a day, then to nothing. Yes, he remembered now, and with unwelcome vividness, that Goodson had told him to go to thunder and mind his own business—*he* wasn't hankering to follow Hadleyburg to heaven!

So that solution was a failure—he hadn't saved Goodson's soul. Richards was discouraged. Then after a little came another idea: had he saved Goodson's property? No, that wouldn't do—he hadn't any. His life? That is it! Of course. Why, he might have thought of it before. This time he was on the right track, sure. His imagination-mill was hard at work in a minute, now.

Thereafter during a stretch of two exhausting hours he was busy saving Goodson's life. He saved it in all kinds of difficult and perilous ways. In every case he got it saved satisfactorily up to a certain point; then, just as he was beginning to get well persuaded that it had really happened, a troublesome detail would turn up which made the whole thing impossible. As in the matter of drowning, for instance. In that case he had swum out and tugged Goodson ashore in an unconscious state with a great crowd looking on and applauding, but when he had got it all thought out and was just beginning to remember all about it, a whole swarm of disqualifying details arrived on the ground; the town would have known of the circumstance, Mary would have known of it, it would glare like a limelight in his own memory instead of being an inconspicuous service which he had possibly rendered "without knowing its full value." And at this point he remembered that he couldn't swim, anyway.

Ah—*there* was a point which he had been overlooking from the start: it had to be a service which he had rendered "possibly without knowing the full value of it." Why, really, that ought to be an easy hunt—much easier than those others. And sure enough, by and by he found it. Goodson, years and years ago, came near marrying a very sweet and pretty girl, named Nancy Hewitt, but in some way or other the match had been broken off; the girl died, Goodson remained a bachelor, and by and by became a soured one and a frank despiser of the human species. Soon after the girl's death the village found out, or thought it had found out, that she carried a spoonful of negro blood in her veins. Richards worked at these details a good while, and in the end he thought he remembered things concerning them which must have gotten mislaid in his memory through long neglect. He seemed to dimly remember that it was *he* that found out about the negro blood; that it was he that told the village; that the village told Goodson where they got it; that he thus saved Goodson from marrying the tainted girl; that he had done him this great service "without knowing the full value of it," in fact without knowing that he *was* doing it; but that Goodson knew the value of it, and what a narrow escape he had had, and so went to his grave grateful to his benefactor and wishing he had a fortune to leave him. It was all clear and simple now, and the more he went over it the more luminous and certain it grew; and at last, when he nestled to sleep satisfied and happy, he remembered the whole thing just as if it had been yesterday. In fact, he dimly remembered Goodson's *telling* him his gratitude once. Meantime Mary had spent six thousand dollars on a new house for herself and a pair of slippers for her pastor, and then had fallen peacefully to rest.

That same Saturday evening the postman had delivered a letter to each of the other principal citizens—nineteen letters in all. No two of the envelopes were alike, and no two of the superscriptions were in the same hand, but the letters inside were just like each other in every detail but one. They were exact copies of the letter received by Richards—handwriting and all—and were all signed by Stephenson, but in place of Richards's name each receiver's own name appeared.

All night long eighteen principal citizens did what their caste-brother Richards was doing at the same time—they put in their energies trying to remember what notable service it was that they had unconsciously done Barclay Goodson. In no case was it a holiday job; still they succeeded.

And while they were at this work, which was difficult, their wives put in the night spending the money, which was easy. During that one night the nineteen wives spent an average of seven thousand dollars each out of the forty thousand in the sack—a hundred and thirty-three thousand altogether.

Next day there was a surprise for Jack Halliday. He noticed that the faces of the nineteen chief citizens and their wives bore that expression of peaceful and holy happiness again. He could not understand it, neither was he able to invent any remarks about it that could damage it or disturb it. And so it was his turn to be dissatisfied with life. His private guesses at the reasons for the happiness failed in all instances, upon examination. When he met Mrs. Wilcox and noticed the placid ecstasy in her face, he said to himself, "Her cat has had kittens"—and went and asked the cook: it was not so; the cook had detected the happiness, but did not know the cause. When Halliday found the duplicate ecstasy in the face of "Shadbelly" Billson (village nickname), he was sure some neighbor of Billson's had broken his leg, but inquiry showed that this had not happened. The subdued ecstasy in Gregory Yates's face could mean but one thing—he was a mother-in-law short: it was another mistake. "And Pinkerton—Pinkerton—he has collected ten cents that he thought he was going to lose." And so on, and so on. In some cases the guesses had to remain in doubt, in the others they proved distinct errors. In the end Halliday said to himself, "Anyway it foots up that there's nineteen Hadleyburg families temporarily in heaven: I don't know how it happened; I only know Providence is off duty to-day."

An architect and builder from the next state had lately ventured to set up a small business in this unpromising village, and his sign had now been hanging out a week. Not a customer yet; he was a discouraged man, and sorry he had come. But his weather changed suddenly now. First one and then another chief citizen's wife said to him privately:

"Come to my house Monday week—but say nothing about it for the present. We think of building."

He got eleven invitations that day. That night he wrote his daughter and broke off her match with her student. He said she could marry a mile higher than that.

Pinkerton the banker and two or three other well-to-do men planned country-seats—but waited. That kind don't count their chickens until they are hatched.

The Wilsons devised a grand new thing—a fancy-dress ball. They made no actual promises, but told all their acquaintanceship in confidence that they were thinking the matter over and thought they should give it—"and if we do, you will be invited, of course." People were surprised, and said, one to another, "Why, they are crazy, those poor Wilsons, they can't afford it." Several among the nineteen said privately to their husbands, "It is a good idea: we will keep still till their cheap thing is over, then *we* will give one that will make it sick."

The days drifted along, and the bill of future squanderings rose higher and higher, wilder and wilder, more and more foolish and reckless. It began to look as if every member of the nineteen would not only spend his whole forty thousand dollars before receiving-day, but be actually in debt by the time he got the money. In some cases light-headed people did not stop with planning to spend, they really spent—on credit. They bought land, mortgages, farms, speculative stocks, fine clothes, horses, and various other things, paid down the bonus, and made themselves liable for the rest—at ten days. Presently the sober second thought came, and Halliday noticed that a ghastly anxiety was beginning to show up in a good many faces. Again he was puzzled, and didn't know what to make of it. "The Wilcox kittens aren't dead, for they weren't born; nobody's broken a leg; there's no shrinkage in mother-in-laws; *nothing* has happened—it is an unsolvable mystery."

There was another puzzled man, too—the Rev. Mr. Burgess. For days, wherever he went, people seemed to follow him or to be watching out for him; and if he ever found himself in a retired spot, a member of the nineteen would be sure to appear, thrust an envelope privately into his hand, whisper "To be opened at the town-hall Friday evening," then vanish away like a guilty thing. He was expecting that there might be one claimant for the sack—doubtful, however, Goodson being dead—but it never occurred to him that all this crowd might be claimants. When the great Friday came at last, he found that he had nineteen envelopes.

III

The town hall had never looked finer. The platform at the end of it was backed by a showy draping of flags; at intervals along the walls were festoons of flags; the gallery fronts were clothed in flags; the supporting columns were swathed in flags; all this was to impress the stranger, for he would be there in considerable force, and in a large degree he would be connected with the press. The house was full. The 412 fixed seats were occupied; also the 68 extra chairs which had been packed into the aisles; the steps of the platform were occupied; some distinguished strangers were given seats on the platform; at the horseshoe of tables which fenced the front and sides of the platform sat a strong force of special correspondents who had come from everywhere. It was the best-dressed house the town had ever produced. There were some tolerably expensive toilets[3] there, and in several cases the ladies who wore them had the look of being unfamiliar with that kind of clothes. At least the town thought they had that look, but the notion could have arisen from the town's knowledge of the fact that these ladies had never inhabited such clothes before.

The gold-sack stood on a little table at the front of the platform where all the house could see it. The bulk of the house gazed at it with a burning interest, a mouth-watering interest, a wistful and pathetic interest; a minority of nineteen couples gazed at it tenderly, lovingly, proprietarily, and the male half of this minority kept saying over to themselves the moving little impromptu speeches of thankfulness for the audience's applause and congratulations which they were presently going to get up and deliver. Every now and then one of these got a piece of paper out of his vest pocket and privately glanced at it to refresh his memory.

Of course there was a buzz of conversation going on—there always is; but at last when the Rev. Mr. Burgess rose and laid his hand on the sack he could hear his microbes gnaw, the place was so still. He related the curious history of the sack, then went on to speak in warm terms of Hadleyburg's old and well-earned reputation for spotless honesty, and of the town's just pride in this reputation. He said that this reputation was a treasure of priceless value; that under Providence its value had now become inestimably enhanced, for the recent episode had spread this fame far and wide, and thus had focused the eyes of the American world upon this village, and made its name for all time, as he hoped and believed, a synonym for commercial incorruptibility. [*Applause.*] "And who is to be the guardian of this noble treasure—the community as a whole? No! The responsibility is individual, not communal. From this day forth each and every one of you is in his own person its special guardian, and individually responsible that no harm shall come to it. Do you—does each of you—accept this great trust? [*Tumultuous assent.*] Then all is well. Transmit it to your children and to your children's children. To-day your purity is beyond reproach—see to it that it shall remain so. To-day there is not a person in your community who could be beguiled to touch a penny not his own—see to it that you abide in this grace [*"We will! we will!"*] This is not the place to make comparisons between ourselves and other communities—some of them ungracious toward us; they have their ways, we have ours; let us be content. [*Applause.*] I am done. Under my hand, my friends, rests a stranger's eloquent recognition of what we are; through him the world will always henceforth know what we are. We do not know who he is, but in your name I utter your gratitude, and ask you to raise your voices in indorsement."

The house rose in a body and made the walls quake with the thunders of its thankfulness for the space of a long minute. Then it sat down, and Mr. Burgess took an envelope out of his pocket. The house held its breath while he slit the envelope open and took from it a slip of paper. He read its contents—slowly and impressively—the audience listening with tranced attention to this magic document, each of whose words stood for an ingot of gold:

"*The remark which I made to the distressed stranger was this: "You are very far from being a bad man: go, and reform."*" Then he continued:

"We shall know in a moment now whether the remark here quoted corresponds with the one concealed in the sack; and if that shall prove to be so—and it undoubtedly will—this sack of gold belongs to a fellow-citizen who will henceforth

---

[3] Clothing and accessories that made up expensive outfits.

stand before the nation as the symbol of the special virtue which has made our town famous throughout the land—Mr. Billson!"

The house had gotten itself all ready to burst into the proper tornado of applause; but instead of doing it, it seemed stricken with a paralysis; there was a deep hush for a moment or two, then a wave of whispered murmurs swept the place—of about this tenor: "*Billson!* oh, come, this is *too* thin! Twenty dollars to a stranger—or *anybody—Billson!* tell it to the marines!" And now at this point the house caught its breath all of a sudden in a new access of astonishment, for it discovered that whereas in one part of the hall Deacon Billson was standing up with his head meekly bowed, in another part of it Lawyer Wilson was doing the same. There was a wondering silence now for a while.

Everybody was puzzled, and nineteen couples were surprised and indignant.

Billson and Wilson turned and stared at each other. Billson asked, bitingly:

"Why do *you* rise, Mr. Wilson?"

"Because I have a right to. Perhaps you will be good enough to explain to the house why *you* rise?"

"With great pleasure. Because I wrote that paper."

"It is an impudent falsity! I wrote it myself."

It was Burgess's turn to be paralyzed. He stood looking vacantly at first one of the men and then the other, and did not seem to know what to do. The house was stupefied. Lawyer Wilson spoke up, now, and said,

"I ask the Chair to read the name signed to that paper."

That brought the Chair to itself, and it read out the name:

"'John Wharton *Billson*.'"

"There!" shouted Billson, "what have you got to say for yourself now? And what kind of apology are you going to make to me and to this insulted house for the imposture which you have attempted to play here?"

"No apologies are due, sir; and as for the rest of it, I publicly charge you with pilfering my note from Mr. Burgess and substituting a copy of it signed with your own name. There is no other way by which you could have gotten hold of the test-remark; I alone, of living men, possessed the secret of its wording."

There was likely to be a scandalous state of things if this went on; everybody noticed with distress that the short-hand scribes were scribbling like mad; many people were crying "Chair, Chair! Order! order!" Burgess rapped with his gavel, and said:

"Let us not forget the proprieties due. There has evidently been a mistake somewhere, but surely that is all. If Mr. Wilson gave me an envelope—and I remember now that he did—I still have it."

He took one out of his pocket, opened it, glanced at it, looked surprised and worried, and stood silent a few moments. Then he waved his hand in a wandering and mechanical way, and made an effort or two to say something, then gave it up, despondently. Several voices cried out:

"Read it! read it! What is it!"

So he began in a dazed and sleep-walker fashion:

"'*The remark which I made to the unhappy stranger was this: "You are far from being a bad man.* [The house gazed at him, marveling.] *Go, and reform."* [*Murmurs:* "Amazing! what can this mean?"] This one," said the Chair, "is signed Thurlow G. Wilson."

"There!" cried Wilson. "I reckon that settles it! I knew perfectly well my note was purloined."

"Purloined!" retorted Billson. "I'll let you know that neither you nor any man of your kidney must venture to—"

The Chair. "Order, gentlemen, order! Take your seats, both of you, please."

They obeyed, shaking their heads and grumbling angrily. The house was profoundly puzzled; it did not know what to do with this curious emergency. Presently Thompson got up. Thompson was the hatter. He would have liked to be a Nineteener;[4] but such was not for him: his stock of hats was not considerable enough for the position. He said:

"Mr. Chairman, if I may be permitted to make a suggestion, can both of these gentlemen be right? I put it to you, sir, can both have happened to say the very same words to the stranger? It seems to me—"

The tanner[5] got up and interrupted him. The tanner was a disgruntled man; he believed himself entitled to be a Nineteener, but he couldn't get recognition. It made him a little unpleasant in his ways and speech. Said he:

"Sho, *that's* not the point! *That* could happen—twice in a hundred years—but not the other thing. *Neither* of them gave the twenty dollars!"

[*A ripple of applause.*]

Billson. "I did!"

Wilson. "I did!"

Then each accused the other of pilfering.

The Chair. "Order! Sit down, if you please—both of you. Neither of the notes has been out of my possession at any moment."

A Voice. "Good—that settles *that!*"

The Tanner. "Mr. Chairman, one thing is now plain: one of these men has been eavesdropping under the other one's bed, and filching family secrets. If it is not unparliamentary to suggest it, I will remark that both are equal to it. [*The Chair.* "Order! order!"] I withdraw the remark, sir, and will confine myself to suggesting that *if* one of them has overheard the other reveal the test-remark to his wife, we shall catch him now."

A Voice. "How?"

The Tanner. "Easily. The two have not quoted the remark in exactly the same words. You would have noticed that, if there hadn't been a considerable stretch of time and an exciting quarrel inserted between the two readings."

A Voice. "Name the difference."

The Tanner. "The word *very* is in Billson's note, and not in the other."

Many voices. "That's so—he's right!"

The Tanner. "And so, if the Chair will examine the test-remark in the sack, we shall know which of these two frauds—[*The Chair.* "Order!"]—which of these two adventurers—[*The Chair.* "Order! order!"]—which of these two gentlemen—[*laughter and applause*]—is entitled to wear the belt as being the first dishonest blatherskite ever bred in this town—which he has dishonored, and which will be a sultry place for him from now out!" [*Vigorous applause.*]

Many Voices. "Open it!—open the sack!"

Mr. Burgess made a slit in the sack, slid his hand in and brought out an envelope. In it were a couple of folded notes. He said:

"One of these is marked, 'Not to be examined until all written communications which have been addressed to the Chair—if any—shall have been read.' The other is marked '*The Test.*' Allow me. It is worded—to wit:

---

[4] One of the nineteen principal citizens of the town.   [5] A person who cures and tans animal hides.

" 'I do not require that the first half of the remark which was made to me by my benefactor shall be quoted with exactness, for it was not striking, and could be forgotten; but its closing fifteen words are quite striking, and I think easily rememberable; unless *these* shall be accurately reproduced, let the applicant be regarded as an impostor. My benefactor began by saying he seldom gave advice to any one, but that it always bore the hall-mark[6] of high value when he did give it. Then he said this—and it has never faded from my memory: *"You are far from being a bad man—"* ' "

Fifty Voices. "That settles it—the money's Wilson's! Wilson! Wilson! Speech! Speech!"

People jumped up and crowded around Wilson, wringing his hand and congratulating fervently—meantime the Chair was hammering with the gavel and shouting:

"Order, gentlemen! Order! Order! Let me finish reading, please." When quiet was restored, the reading was resumed—as follows:

" ' *"Go, and reform—or, mark my words—some day, for your sins, you will die and go to hell or Hadleyburg—*TRY AND MAKE IT THE FORMER." ' "

A ghastly silence followed. First an angry cloud began to settle darkly upon the faces of the citizenship; after a pause the cloud began to rise, and a tickled expression tried to take its place; tried so hard that it was only kept under with great and painful difficulty; the reporters, the Brixtonites, and other strangers bent their heads down and shielded their faces with their hands, and managed to hold in by main strength and heroic courtesy. At this most inopportune time burst upon the stillness the roar of a solitary voice—Jack Halliday's:

"That's got the hall-mark on it!"

Then the house let go, strangers and all. Even Mr. Burgess's gravity broke down presently, then the audience considered itself officially absolved from all restraint, and it made the most of its privilege. It was a good long laugh, and a tempestuously whole-hearted one, but it ceased at last—long enough for Mr. Burgess to try to resume, and for the people to get their eyes partially wiped; then it broke out again; and afterward yet again; then at last Burgess was able to get out these serious words:

"It is useless to try to disguise the fact—we find ourselves in the presence of a matter of grave import. It involves the honor of your town, it strikes at the town's good name. The difference of a single word between the test-remarks offered by Mr. Wilson and Mr. Billson was itself a serious thing, since it indicated that one or the other of these gentlemen had committed a theft—"

The two men were sitting limp, nerveless, crushed; but at these words both were electrified into movement, and started to get up—

"Sit down!" said the Chair, sharply, and they obeyed. "That, as I have said, was a serious thing. And it was—but for only one of them. But the matter has become graver; for the honor of *both* is now in formidable peril. Shall I go even further, and say in inextricable peril? *Both* left out the crucial fifteen words." He paused. During several moments he allowed the pervading stillness to gather and

---

[6] A stamp or mark to ensure authenticity.

deepen its impressive effects, then added: "There would seem to be but one way whereby this could happen. I ask these gentlemen—Was there *collusion?—agreement?*"

A low murmur sifted through the house; its import was, "He's got them both."

Billson was not used to emergencies; he sat in a helpless collapse. But Wilson was a lawyer. He struggled to his feet, pale and worried, and said:

"I ask the indulgence of the house while I explain this most painful matter. I am sorry to say what I am about to say, since it must inflict irreparable injury upon Mr. Billson, whom I have always esteemed and respected until now, and in whose invulnerability to temptation I entirely believed—as did you all. But for the preservation of my own honor I must speak—and with frankness. I confess with shame—and I now beseech your pardon for it—that I said to the ruined stranger all of the words contained in the test-remark, including the disparaging fifteen. [*Sensation.*] When the late publication was made I recalled them, and I resolved to claim the sack of coin, for by every right I was entitled to it. Now I will ask you to consider this point, and weigh it well: that stranger's gratitude to me that night knew no bounds; he said himself that he could find no words for it that were adequate, and that if he should ever be able he would repay me a thousand-fold. Now, then, I ask you this: Could I expect—could I believe—could I even remotely imagine—that, feeling as he did, he would do so ungrateful a thing as to add those quite unnecessary fifteen words to his test?—set a trap for me?—expose me as a slanderer of my own town before my own people assembled in a public hall? It was preposterous; it was impossible. His test would contain only the kindly opening clause of my remark. Of that I had no shadow of doubt. You would have thought as I did. You would not have expected a base betrayal from one whom you had befriended and against whom you had committed no offense. And so, with perfect confidence, perfect trust, I wrote on a piece of paper the opening words—ending with 'Go, and reform,'—and signed it. When I was about to put it in an envelope I was called into my back office, and without thinking I left the paper lying open on my desk." He stopped, turned his head slowly toward Billson, waited a moment, then added: "I ask you to note this: when I returned, a little later, Mr. Billson was retiring by my street door." [*Sensation.*]

In a moment Billson was on his feet and shouting: "It's a lie! It's an infamous lie!"

The Chair. "Be seated, sir! Mr. Wilson has the floor."

Billson's friends pulled him into his seat and quieted him, and Wilson went on:

"Those are the simple facts. My note was now lying in a different place on the table from where I had left it. I noticed that, but attached no importance to it, thinking a draught had blown it there. That Mr. Billson would read a private paper was a thing which could not occur to me; he was an honorable man, and he would be above that. If you will allow me to say it, I think his extra word '*very*' stands explained; it is attributable to a defect of memory. I was the only man in the world who could furnish here any detail of the test-remark—by *honorable* means. I have finished."

There is nothing in the world like a persuasive speech to fuddle the mental apparatus and upset the convictions and debauch the emotions of an audience not practised in the tricks and delusions of oratory. Wilson sat down victorious. The house submerged him in tides of approving applause; friends swarmed to him and shook him by the hand and congratulated him, and Billson was shouted down and not allowed to say a word. The Chair hammered and hammered with its gavel, and kept shouting:

"But let us proceed, gentlemen, let us proceed!"

At last there was a measurable degree of quiet, and the hatter said:

"But what is there to proceed with, sir, but to deliver the money?"

Voices. "That's it! That's it! Come forward, Wilson!"

The Hatter. "I move three cheers for Mr. Wilson, Symbol of the special virtue which—"

The cheers burst forth before he could finish; and in the midst of them—and in the midst of the clamor of the gavel also—some enthusiasts mounted Wilson on a big friend's shoulder and were going to fetch him in triumph to the platform. The Chair's voice now rose above the noise—

"Order! To your places! You forget that there is still a document to be read." When quiet had been restored he took up the document and was going to read it, but laid it down again, saying, "I forgot; this is not to be read until all written communications received by me have first been read." He took an envelope out of his pocket, removed its inclosure, glanced at it—seemed astonished—held it out and gazed at it—stared at it.

Twenty or thirty voices cried out:

"What is it? Read it! read it!"

And he did—slowly, and wondering:

" 'The remark which I made to the stranger—[*Voices.* "Hello! how's this?"]—was this: "You are far from being a bad man. [*Voices.* "Great Scott!"] Go, and reform." ' [*Voice.* "Oh, saw my leg off!"] Signed by Mr. Pinkerton, the banker."

The pandemonium of delight which turned itself loose now was of a sort to make the judicious weep. Those whose withers were unwrung[7] laughed till the tears ran down; the reporters, in throes of laughter, set down disordered pot-hooks which would never in the world be decipherable; and a sleeping dog jumped up, scared out of its wits, and barked itself crazy at the turmoil. All manner of cries were scattered through the din: "We're getting rich—*two* Symbols of Incorruptibility!—without counting Billson!" "*Three!*—count Shadbelly in—we can't have too many!" "All right—Billson's elected!" "Alas, poor Wilson—victim of *two* thieves!"

A Powerful Voice. "Silence! The Chair's fished up something more out of its pocket."

Voices. "Hurrah! Is it something fresh? Read it! read! read!"

The Chair [reading]. " 'The remark which I made,' etc.: ' "You are far from being a bad man. Go,' " etc. Signed, 'Gregory Yates.' "

Tornado of Voices. "Four Symbols!" " 'Rah for Yates!" "Fish again!"

The house was in a roaring humor now, and ready to get all the fun out of the occasion that might be in it. Several Nineteeners, looking pale and distressed, got up and began to work their way toward the aisles, but a score of shouts went up:

---

[7] Those who had not laughed before.

"The doors, the doors—close the doors; no Incorruptible shall leave this place! Sit down, everybody!"

The mandate was obeyed.

"Fish again! Read! read!"

The Chair fished again, and once more the familiar words began to fall from its lips—" 'You are far from being a bad man' "

"Name! name! What's his name?"

" 'L. Ingoldsby Sargent.' "

"Five elected! Pile up the Symbols! Go on, go on!"

" 'You are far from being a bad—' "

"Name! name!"

" 'Nicholas Whitworth.' "

"Hooray! hooray! it's a symbolical day!"

Somebody wailed in, and began to sing this rhyme (leaving out "it's") to the lovely "Mikado" tune of "When a man's afraid, a beautiful maid—";[8] the audience joined in, with joy; then, just in time, somebody contributed another line—

> And don't you this forget—

The house roared it out. A third line was at once furnished—

> Corruptibles far from Hadleyburg are—

The house roared that one too. As the last note died, Jack Halliday's voice rose high and clear, freighted with a final line—

> But the Symbols are here, you bet!

That was sung, with booming enthusiasm. Then the happy house started in at the beginning and sang the four lines through twice, with immense swing and dash, and finished up with a crashing three-times-three and a tiger for "Hadleyburg the Incorruptible and all Symbols of it which we shall find worthy to receive the hall-mark to-night."

Then the shoutings at the Chair began again, all over the place:

"Go on! go on! Read! read some more! Read all you've got!"

"That's it—go on! We are winning eternal celebrity!"

A dozen men got up now and began to protest. They said that this farce was the work of some abandoned joker, and was an insult to the whole community. Without a doubt these signatures were all forgeries—

"Sit down! sit down! Shut up! You are confessing. We'll find *your* names in the lot."

"Mr. Chairman, how many of those envelopes have you got?"

The Chair counted.

"Together with those that have been already examined, there are nineteen."

A storm of derisive applause broke out.

"Perhaps they all contain the secret. I move that you open them all and read

---

[8] From *The Mikado* (1885), an opera by Sir William S. Gilbert (1836–1911) and Sir Arthur S. Sullivan (1842–1900): "When a man's afraid, a beautiful maid is a cheering sight to see."

every signature that is attached to a note of that sort—and read also the first eight words of the note."

"Second the motion!"

It was put and carried—uproariously. Then poor old Richards got up, and his wife rose and stood at his side. Her head was bent down, so that none might see that she was crying. Her husband gave her his arm, and so supporting her, he began to speak in a quavering voice:

"My friends, you have known us two—Mary and me—all our lives, and I think you have liked us and respected us—"

The Chair interrupted him:

"Allow me. It is quite true—that which you are saying, Mr. Richards: this town *does* know you two; it *does* like you; it *does* respect you; more—it honors you and *loves* you—'"

Halliday's voice rang out:

"That's the hall-marked truth, too! If the Chair is right, let the house speak up and say it. Rise! Now, then—hip! hip! hip!—all together!"

The house rose in mass, faced toward the old couple eagerly, filled the air with a snow-storm of waving handkerchiefs, and delivered the cheers with all its affectionate heart.

The Chair then continued:

"What I was going to say is this: We know your good heart, Mr. Richards, but this is not a time for the exercise of charity toward offenders. [*Shouts of "Right! right!"*] I see your generous purpose in your face, but I cannot allow you to plead for these men—"

"But I was going to—"

"Please take your seat, Mr. Richards. We must examine the rest of these notes—simple fairness to the men who have already been exposed requires this. As soon as that has been done—I give you my word for this—you shall be heard."

Many Voices. "Right!—the Chair is right—no interruption can be permitted at this stage! Go on!—the names! the names!—according to the terms of the motion!"

The old couple sat reluctantly down, and the husband whispered to the wife, "It is pitifully hard to have to wait; the shame will be greater than ever when they find we were only going to plead for *ourselves*."

Straightway the jollity broke loose again with the reading of the names.

" 'You are far from being a bad man—'Signature, 'Robert J. Titmarsh.' "

" 'You are far from being a bad man—' Signature 'Eliphalet Weeks.' "

" 'You are far from being a bad man—' Signature, 'Oscar B. Wilder.' "

At this point the house lit upon the idea of taking the eight words out of the Chairman's hands. He was not unthankful for that. Thenceforward he held up each note in its turn, and waited. The house droned out the eight words in a massed and measured and musical deep volume of sound (with a daringly close resemblance to a well-known church chant)—" 'You are f-a-r from being a b-a-a-a-d man.' " Then the Chair said, "Signature, 'Archibald Wilcox.' " And so on, and so on, name after name, and everybody had an increasingly and gloriously good time except the wretched Nineteen. Now and then, when a particularly shining name was called, the house made the Chair wait while it chanted the whole of the test-remark from the beginning to the closing words, "And go to hell or Hadleyburg—try and make it the for-or-m-e-r!" and in these special cases they added a grand and agonized and imposing "A-a-a-a-*men!*"

The list dwindled, dwindled, dwindled, poor old Richards keeping tally of the count, wincing when a name resembling his own was pronounced, and waiting in miserable suspense for the time to come when it would be his humiliating privilege to rise with Mary and finish his plea, which he was intending to word thus: " . . . for until now we have never done any wrong thing, but have gone our humble way unreproached. We are very poor, we are old, and have no chick nor child to help us; we were sorely tempted, and we fell. It was my purpose when I got up before to make confession and beg that my name might not be read out in this public place, for it seemed to us that we could not bear it; but I was prevented. It was just; it was our place to suffer with the rest. It has been hard for us. It is the first time we have ever heard our name fall from any one's lips—sullied. Be merciful—for the sake of the better days; make our shame as light to bear as in your charity you can." At this point in his revery Mary nudged him, perceiving that his mind was absent. The house was chanting, "You are f-a-r," etc.

"Be ready," Mary whispered. "Your name comes now; he has read eighteen."

The chant ended.

"Next! next! next!" came volleying from all over the house.

Burgess put his hand into his pocket. The old couple, trembling, began to rise. Burgess fumbled a moment, then said,

"I find I have read them all."

Faint with joy and surprise, the couple sank into their seats, and Mary whispered:

"Oh, bless God, we are saved!—he has lost ours—I wouldn't give this for a hundred of those sacks!"

The house burst out with its "Mikado" travesty, and sang it three times with ever-increasing enthusiasm, rising to its feet when it reached for the third time the closing line—

But the Symbols are here, you bet!

and finishing up with cheers and a tiger for "Hadleyburg purity and our eighteen immortal representatives of it."

Then Wingate, the saddler, got up and proposed cheers "for the cleanest man in town, the one solitary important citizen in it who didn't try to steal that money—Edward Richards."

They were given with great and moving heartiness; then somebody proposed that Richards be elected sole guardian and Symbol of the now Sacred Hadleyburg Tradition, with power and right to stand up and look the whole sarcastic world in the face.

Passed, by acclamation; then they sang the "Mikado" again, and ended it with:

And there's *one* Symbol left, you bet!

There was a pause; then—

A Voice. "Now, then, who's to get the sack?"

The Tanner (with bitter sarcasm). "That's easy. The money has to be divided among the eighteen Incorruptibles. They gave the suffering stranger twenty dollars apiece—and that remark—each in his turn—it took twenty-two minutes for the procession to move past. Staked the stranger—total contribution, $360. All they want is just the loan back—and interest—forty thousand dollars altogether."

Many Voices [derisively]. "That's it! Divvy! divvy! Be kind to the poor—don't keep them waiting!"

The Chair. "Order! I now offer the stranger's remaining document. It says: 'If no claimant shall appear [*grand chorus of groans*] I desire that you open the sack and count out the money to the principal citizens of your town, they to take it in trust [*cries of "Oh! Oh! Oh!"*], and use it in such ways as to them shall seem best for the propagation and preservation of your community's noble reputation for incorruptible honesty [*more cries*]—a reputation to which their names and their efforts will add a new and far-reaching luster.' [*Enthusiastic outburst of sarcastic applause.*] That seems to be all. No—here is a postscript:

" 'P. S.—CITIZENS OF HADLEYBURG: There *is* no test-remark—nobody made one. [*Great sensation.*] There wasn't any pauper stranger, nor any twenty-dollar contribution, nor any accompanying benediction and compliment—these are all inventions. [*General buzz and hum of astonishment and delight.*] Allow me to tell my story—it will take but a word or two. I passed through your town at a certain time, and received a deep offense which I had not earned. Any other man would have been content to kill one or two of you and call it square, but to me that would have been a trivial revenge, and inadequate; for the dead do not *suffer*. Besides, I could not kill you all—and, anyway, made as I am, even that would not have satisfied me. I wanted to damage every man in the place, and every woman—and not in their bodies or in their estate, but in their vanity—the place where feeble and foolish people are most vulnerable. So I disguised myself and came back and studied you. You were easy game. You had an old and lofty reputation for honesty, and naturally you were proud of it—it was your treasure of treasures, the very apple of your eye. As soon as I found out that you carefully and vigilantly kept yourselves and your children *out of temptation,* I knew how to proceed. Why, you simple creatures, the weakest of all weak things is a virtue which has not been tested in the fire. I laid a plan, and gathered a list of names. My project was to corrupt Hadleyburg the Incorruptible. My idea was to make liars and thieves of nearly half a hundred smirchless men and women who had never in their lives uttered a lie or stolen a penny. I was afraid of Goodson. He was neither born nor reared in Hadleyburg. I was afraid that if I started to operate my scheme by getting my letter laid before you, you would say to yourselves, "Goodson is the only man among us who would give away twenty dollars to a poor devil"—and then you might not bite at my bait. But Heaven took Goodson; then I knew I was safe, and I set my trap and baited it. It may be that I shall not catch all the men to whom I mailed the pretended test secret, but I shall catch the most of them, if I know Hadleyburg nature. [*Voices.* "Right—he got every last one of them."] I believe they will even steal ostensible *gamble*-money, rather than miss, poor, tempted, and mistrained fellows. I am hoping to eternally and everlastingly squelch your vanity and give Hadleyburg a new renown—one that will *stick*—and spread far. If I have succeeded, open the sack and summon the Committee on Propagation and Preservation of the Hadleyburg Reputation.' "

A Cyclone of Voices. "Open it! Open it! The Eighteen to the front! Committee on Propagation of the Tradition! Forward—the Incorruptibles!"

The Chair ripped the sack wide, and gathered up a handful of bright, broad, yellow coins, shook them together, then examined them—

"Friends, they are only gilded disks of lead!"

There was a crashing outbreak of delight over this news, and when the noise had subsided, the tanner called out:

"By right of apparent seniority in this business, Mr. Wilson is Chairman of the Committee on Propagation of the Tradition. I suggest that he step forward on behalf of his pals, and receive in trust the money."

A Hundred Voices. "Wilson! Wilson! Wilson! Speech! Speech!"

Wilson [in a voice trembling with anger.] "You will allow me to say, and without apologies for my language, *damn* the money!"

A Voice. "Oh, and him a Baptist!"

A Voice. "Seventeen Symbols left! Step up, gentlemen, and assume your trust!"

There was a pause—no response.

The Saddler. "Mr. Chairman, we've got *one* clean man left, anyway, out of the late aristocracy; and he needs money, and deserves it. I move that you appoint Jack Halliday to get up there and auction off that sack of gilt twenty-dollar pieces, and give the result to the right man—the man whom Hadleyburg delights to honor—Edward Richards."

This was received with great enthusiasm, the dog taking a hand again; the saddler started the bids at a dollar, the Bixton folk and Barnum's[9] representative fought hard for it, the people cheered every jump that the bids made, the excitement climbed moment by moment higher and higher, the bidders got on their mettle and grew steadily more and more daring, more and more determined, the jumps went from a dollar up to five, then to ten, then to twenty, then fifty, then to a hundred, then—

At the beginning of the auction Richards whispered in distress to his wife: "O Mary, can we allow it? It—it—you see, it is an honor-reward, a testimonial to purity of character, and—and—can we allow it? Hadn't I better get up and—O Mary, what ought we to do?—what do you think we—*[Halliday's voice. "Fifteen I'm bid!—fifteen for the sack!—twenty!—ah, thanks!—thirty—thanks again! Thirty, thirty, thirty!—do I hear forty?—forty it is! Keep the ball rolling, gentlemen, keep it rolling!—fifty! thanks, noble Roman! going at fifty, fifty, fifty!—seventy!—ninety!—splendid!—a hundred!—pile it up, pile it up!—hundred and twenty—forty!—just in time!—hundred and fifty!—*two *hundred!—superb! Do I hear two h—thanks! two hundred and fifty!—"]*

"It is another temptation, Edward—I'm all in a tremble—but, oh, we've escaped *one* temptation, and that ought to warn us to—[*"Six did I hear?—thanks!—six-fifty, six-f—*seven *hundred!"*] And yet, Edward, when you think— nobody susp—[*"Eight hundred dollars!—hurrah!—make it nine!—Mr. Parsons, did I hear you say—thanks—nine!—this noble sack of virgin lead going at only nine hundred dollars, gilding and all—come! do I hear—a thousand!—gratefully yours!—did some one say eleven?—a sack which is going to be the most celebrated in the whole Uni—"*] O Edward" (beginning to sob), "we are *so* poor!— but—but—do as you think best—do as you think best."

Edward fell—that is, he sat still; sat with a conscience which was not satisfied, but which was overpowered by circumstances.

Meantime a stranger, who looked like an amateur detective gotten up as an impossible English earl, had been watching the evening's proceedings with manifest interest, and with a contented expression on his face; and he had been privately commenting to himself. He was now soliloquizing somewhat like this:

---

[9] P. T. Barnum (1810–1891), the showman famous for exhibiting freaks and curiosities in his American Museum.

"None of the Eighteen are bidding; that is not satisfactory; I must change that—the dramatic unities require it; they must buy the sack they tried to steal; they must pay a heavy price, too—some of them are rich. And another thing, when I make a mistake in Hadleyburg nature the man that puts that error upon me is entitled to a high honorarium, and some one must pay it. This poor old Richards has brought my judgment to shame; he is an honest man:—I don't understand it, but I acknowledge it. Yes, he saw my deuces *and* with a straight flush, and by rights the pot is his. And it shall be a jack-pot, too, if I can manage it. He disappointed me, but let that pass."

He was watching the bidding. At a thousand, the market broke; the prices tumbled swiftly. He waited—and still watched. One competitor dropped out; then another, and another. He put in a bid or two, now. When the bids had sunk to ten dollars, he added a five; some one raised him a three; he waited a moment, then flung in a fifty-dollar jump, and the sack was his—at $1,282. The house broke out in cheers—then stopped; for he was on his feet, and had lifted his hand. He began to speak.

"I desire to say a word, and ask a favor. I am a speculator in rarities, and I have dealings with persons interested in numismatics all over the world. I can make a profit on this purchase, just as it stands; but there is a way, if I can get your approval, whereby I can make every one of these leaden twenty-dollar pieces worth its face in gold, and perhaps more. Grant me that approval, and I will give part of my gains to your Mr. Richards, whose invulnerable probity you have so justly and so cordially recognized to-night; his share shall be ten thousand dollars, and I will hand him the money to-morrow. [*Great applause from the house.* But the "invulnerable probity" made the Richardses blush prettily; however, it went for modesty, and did no harm.] If you will pass my proposition by a good majority—I would like a two-thirds vote—I will regard that as the town's consent, and that is all I ask. Rarities are always helped by any device which will rouse curiosity and compel remark. Now if I may have your permission to stamp upon the faces of each of these ostensible coins the names of the eighteen gentlemen who—"

Nine-tenths of the audience were on their feet in a moment—dog and all—and the proposition was carried with a whirlwind of approving applause and laughter.

They sat down, and all the Symbols except "Dr." Clay Harkness got up, violently protesting against the proposed outrage, and threatening to—

"I beg you not to threaten me," said the stranger, calmly. "I know my legal rights, and am not accustomed to being frightened at bluster." [*Applause.*] He sat down. "Dr." Harkness saw an opportunity here. He was one of the two very rich men of the place, and Pinkerton was the other. Harkness was proprietor of a mint; that is to say, a popular patent medicine. He was running for the legislature on one ticket, and Pinkerton on the other. It was a close race and a hot one, and getting hotter every day. Both had strong appetites for money; each had bought a great tract of land, with a purpose; there was going to be a new railway, and each wanted to be in the legislature and help locate the route to his own advantage; a single vote might make the decision, and with it two or three fortunes. The stake was large, and Harkness was a daring speculator. He was sitting close to the stranger. He leaned over while one or another of the Symbols was entertaining the house with protests and appeals, and asked, in a whisper.

"What is your price for the sack?"

"Forty thousand dollars."

"I'll give you twenty."

"No."

"Twenty-five."

"No."

"Say thirty."

"The price is forty thousand dollars; not a penny less."

"All right, I'll give it. I will come to the hotel at ten in the morning. I don't want it known: will see you privately."

"Very good." Then the stranger got up and said to the house:

"I find it late. The speeches of these gentlemen are not without merit, not without interest, not without grace; yet if I may be excused I will take my leave. I thank you for the great favor which you have shown me in granting my petition. I ask the Chair to keep the sack for me until to-morrow, and to hand these three five-hundred-dollar notes to Mr. Richards." They were passed up to the Chair. "At nine I will call for the sack, and at eleven will deliver the rest of the ten thousand to Mr. Richards in person, at his home. Good night."

Then he slipped out, and left the audience making a vast noise, which was composed of a mixture of cheers, the "Mikado" song, dog-disapproval, and the chant, "You are f-a-r from being a b-a-a-d man—a-a-a-a-men!"

IV

At home the Richardses had to endure congratulations and compliments until midnight. Then they were left to themselves. They looked a little sad, and they sat silent and thinking. Finally Mary sighed and said,

"Do you think we are to blame, Edward—*much* to blame?" and her eyes wandered to the accusing triplet of big bank-notes lying on the table, where the congratulators had been gloating over them and reverently fingering them. Edward did not answer at once; then he brought out a sigh and said, hesitatingly:

"We—we couldn't help it, Mary. It—well, it was ordered. *All* things are."

Mary glanced up and looked at him steadily, but he didn't return the look. Presently she said:

"I thought congratulations and praises always tasted good. But—it seems to me, now—Edward?"

"Well?"

"Are you going to stay in the bank?"

"N-no."

"Resign?"

"In the morning—by note."

"It does seem best."

Richards bowed his head in his hands and muttered:

"Before, I was not afraid to let oceans of people's money pour through my hands, but—Mary, I am so tired, so tired—"

"We will go to bed."

At nine in the morning the stranger called for the sack and took it to the hotel in a cab. At ten Harkness had a talk with him privately. The stranger asked for and got five checks on a metropolitan bank—drawn to "Bearer"—four for $1,500 each, and one for $34,000. He put one of the former in his pocketbook, and the remainder, representing $38,500, he put in an envelope, and with these he added a note, which he wrote after Harkness was gone. At eleven he called at the Richards house and knocked. Mrs. Richards peeped through the shutters, then went and received the envelope, and the stranger disappeared without a word. She came back flushed and a little unsteady on her legs, and gasped out:

"I am sure I recognized him! Last night it seemed to me that maybe I had seen him somewhere before."

"He is the man that brought the sack here?"

"I am almost sure of it."

"Then he is the ostensible Stephenson, too, and sold every important citizen in this town with his bogus secret. Now if he has sent checks instead of money, we are sold, too, after we thought we had escaped. I was beginning to feel fairly comfortable once more, after my night's rest, but the look of that envelope makes me sick. It isn't fat enough; $8,500 in even the largest bank-notes makes more bulk than that."

"Edward, why do you object to checks?"

"Checks signed by Stephenson! I am resigned to take the $8,500 if it could come in bank-notes—for it does seem that it was so ordered, Mary—but I have never had much courage, and I have not the pluck to try to market a check signed with that disastrous name. It would be a trap. That man tried to catch me; we escaped somehow or other; and now he is trying a new way. If it is checks—"

"Oh, Edward, it is *too* bad!" and she held up the checks and began to cry.

"Put them in the fire! quick! we mustn't be tempted. It is a trick to make the world laugh at *us*, along with the rest, and—Give them to *me*, since you can't do it!" He snatched them and tried to hold his grip till he could get to the stove; but he was human, he was a cashier, and he stopped a moment to make sure of the signature. Then he came near to fainting.

"Fan me, Mary, fan me! They are the same as gold!"

"Oh, how lovely, Edward! Why?"

"Signed by Harkness. What can the mystery of that be, Mary?"

"Edward, do you think—"

"Look here—look at this! Fifteen—fifteen—fifteen—thirty-four. Thirty-eight thousand five hundred! Mary, the sack isn't worth twelve dollars, and Harkness— apparently—has paid about par for it."

"And does it all come to us, do you think—instead of the ten thousand?"

"Why, it looks like it. And the checks are made to 'Bearer,' too."

"Is that good, Edward? What is it for?"

"A hint to collect them at some distant bank, I reckon. Perhaps Harkness doesn't want the matter known. What is that—a note?"

"Yes. It was with the checks."

It was in the "Stephenson" handwriting, but there was no signature. It said:

"I am a disappointed man. Your honesty is beyond the reach of temptation. I had a different idea about it, but I wronged you in that, and I beg pardon, and do it sincerely. I honor you—and that is sincere too. This town is not worthy to kiss the hem of your garment. Dear sir, I made a square bet with myself that there were nineteen debauchable men in your self-righteous community. I have lost. Take the whole pot, you are entitled to it."

Richards drew a deep sigh, and said:

"It seems written with fire—it burns so. Mary—I am miserable again."

"I, too. Ah, dear, I wish—"

"To think, Mary—he *believes* in me."

"Oh, don't, Edward—I can't bear it."

"If those beautiful words were deserved, Mary—and God knows I believed I deserved them once—I think I could give the forty thousand dollars for them. And I would put that paper away, as representing more than gold and jewels, and keep it always. But now—We could not live in the shadow of its accusing presence, Mary."

He put it in the fire.

A messenger arrived and delivered an envelope.

Richards took from it a note and read it; it was from Burgess.

"You saved me, in a difficult time. I saved you last night. It was at cost of a lie, but I made the sacrifice freely, and out of a grateful heart. None in this village knows so well as I know how brave and good and noble you are. At bottom you cannot respect me, knowing as you do of that matter of which I am accused, and by the general voice condemned; but I beg that you will at least believe that I am a grateful man; it will help me to bear my burden.

[Signed] "BURGESS."

"Saved, once more. And on such terms!" He put the note in the fire. "I—I wish I were dead, Mary, I wish I were out of it all."

"Oh, these are bitter, bitter days, Edward. The stabs, through their very generosity, are so deep—and they come so fast!"

Three days before the election each of two thousand voters suddenly found himself in possession of a prized momento—one of the renowned bogus double-eagles. Around one of its faces was stamped these words: "THE REMARK I MADE TO THE POOR STRANGER WAS—"Around the other face was stamped these: "GO, AND RE-FORM. [SIGNED] PINKERTON." Thus the entire remaining refuse of the renowned joke was emptied upon a single head, and with calamitous effect. It revived the recent vast laugh and concentrated it upon Pinkerton; and Harkness's election was a walkover.

Within twenty-four hours after the Richardses had received their checks their consciences were quieting down, discouraged; the old couple were learning to reconcile themselves to the sin which they had committed. But they were to learn, now, that a sin takes on new and real terrors when there seems a chance that it is going to be found out. This gives it a fresh and most substantial and important aspect. At church the morning sermon was of the usual pattern; it was the same old things said in the same old way; they had heard them a thousand times and found them innocuous, next to meaningless, and easy to sleep under; but now it was different: the sermon seemed to bristle with accusations; it seemed aimed straight and specially at people who were concealing deadly sins. After church they got away from the mob of congratulators as soon as they could, and hurried homeward, chilled to the bone at they did not know what—vague, shadowy, indefinite fears. And by chance they caught a glimpse of Mr. Burgess as he turned a corner. He paid no attention to their nod of recognition! He hadn't seen it; but they did not know that. What could his conduct mean? It might mean—it might mean—oh, a dozen dreadful things. Was it possible that he knew that Richards could have cleared him of guilt in that bygone time, and had been silently waiting for a chance to even up accounts? At home, in their distress they got to imagining that their servant might have been in the next room listening when Richards revealed the secret to his wife that he knew of Burgess's innocence; next, Richards began to imagine that he had heard the swish of a gown in there at that time; next, he was sure he *had* heard it. They would call Sarah in, on a pretext, and watch her face: if she had been betraying them to Mr. Burgess, it would show in her manner. They asked her some questions—questions which were so random and incoherent and seemingly purposeless that the girl felt sure that the old people's minds had been affected by their sudden good fortune; the sharp and watchful gaze which they bent upon her frightened her, and that completed the business. She blushed, she became nervous and confused, and to the old people these were plain signs of guilt—guilt of some fearful sort or other—without doubt she was a spy and a traitor. When they were alone again they began to piece many unrelated things together and get horrible results out of the combination. When things had got about to the worst, Richards was delivered of a sudden gasp, and his wife asked:

"Oh, what is it?—what is it?"

"The note—Burgess's note! Its language was sarcastic, I see it now." He quoted: " 'At bottom you cannot respect me, *knowing,* as you do, of *that matter* of which I am accused'—oh, it is perfectly plain, now, God help me! He knows that I know! You see the ingenuity of the phrasing. It was a trap—and like a fool, I walked into it. And Mary—?"

"Oh, it is dreadful—I know what you are going to say—he didn't return your transcript of the pretended test-remark."

"No—kept it to destroy us with. Mary, he has exposed us to some already. I know it—I know it well. I saw it in a dozen faces after church. Ah, he wouldn't answer our nod of recognition—*he* knew what he had been doing!"

In the night the doctor was called. The news went around in the morning that the old couple were rather seriously ill—prostrated by the exhausting excitement growing out of their great windfall, the congratulations, and the late hours, the doctor said. The town was sincerely distressed; for these old people were about all it had left to be proud of, now.

Two days later the news was worse. The old couple were delirious, and were doing strange things. By witness of the nurses, Richards had exhibited checks—for $8,500? No—for an amazing sum—$38,500! What could be the explanation of this gigantic piece of luck?

The following day the nurses had more news—and wonderful. They had concluded to hide the checks, lest harm come to them; but when they searched they were gone from under the patient's pillow—vanished away. The patient said:

"Let the pillow alone; what do you want?"

"We thought it best that the checks—"

"You will never see them again—they are destroyed. They came from Satan. I saw the hellbrand on them, and I knew they were sent to betray me to sin." Then he fell to gabbling strange and dreadful things which were not clearly understandable, and which the doctor admonished them to keep to themselves.

Richards was right; the checks were never seen again.

A nurse must have talked in her sleep, for within two days the forbidden gabblings were the property of the town; and they were of a surprising sort. They seemed to indicate that Richards had been a claimant for the sack himself, and that Burgess had concealed that fact and then maliciously betrayed it.

Burgess was taxed with this and stoutly denied it. And he said it was not fair to attach weight to the chatter of a sick old man who was out of his mind. Still, suspicion was in the air, and there was much talk.

After a day or two it was reported that Mrs. Richards's delirious deliveries were getting to be duplicates of her husband's. Suspicion flamed up into conviction, now, and the town's pride in the purity of its one undiscredited important citizen began to dim down and flicker toward extinction.

Six days passed, then came more news. The old couple were dying. Richards's mind cleared in his latest hour, and he sent for Burgess. Burgess said:

"Let the room be cleared. I think he wishes to say something in privacy."

"No!" said Richards: "I want witnesses. I want you all to hear my confession, so that I may die a man, and not a dog. I was clean—artificially—like the rest; and like the rest I fell when temptation came. I signed a lie, and claimed the miserable sack. Mr. Burgess remembered that I had done him a service, and in gratitude (and ignorance) he suppressed my claim and saved me. You know the thing that was charged against Burgess years ago. My testimony, and mine alone, could have cleared him, and I was a coward, and left him to suffer disgrace—"

"No—no—Mr. Richards, you—"

"My servant betrayed my secret to him—"

"No one has betrayed anything to me—"

—"and then he did a natural and justifiable thing, he repented of the saving kindness which he had done me, and he *exposed* me—as I deserved—"

"Never!—I make oath—"

"Out of my heart I forgive him."

Burgess's impassioned protestations fell upon deaf ears; the dying man passed away without knowing that once more he had done poor Burgess a wrong. The old wife died that night.

The last of the sacred Nineteen had fallen a prey to the fiendish sack; the town was stripped of the last rag of its ancient glory. Its mourning was not showy, but it was deep.

By act of the Legislature—upon prayer and petition—Hadleyburg was allowed to change its name to (never mind that—I will not give it away), and leave one word out of the motto that for many generations had graced the town's official seal.

It is an honest town once more, and the man will have to rise early that catches it napping again.

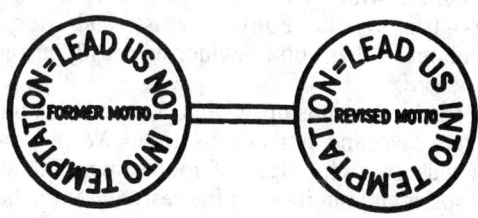

1898, 1899

ADVENTURES OF HUCKLEBERRY FINN*

(*Tom Sawyer's Comrade*[1]).

SCENE: THE MISSISSIPPI VALLEY.
TIME: FORTY TO FIFTY YEARS AGO.[2]

NOTICE.

Persons attempting to find a motive in this narrative will be prosecuted; persons attempting to find a moral in it will be banished; persons attempting to find a plot in it will be shot.

BY ORDER OF THE AUTHOR
PER G. G., CHIEF OF ORDNANCE.

EXPLANATORY.

In this book a number of dialects are used, to wit: the Missouri negro dialect; the extremest form of the backwoods South-Western dialect; the ordinary "Pike-County"[3] dialect; and four modified varieties of this last. The shadings have not been done in a hap-hazard fashion or by guess-work; but pains-takingly, and with the trustworthy guidance and support of personal familiarity with these several forms of speech.

I make this explanation for the reason that without it many readers would suppose that all these characters were trying to talk alike and not succeeding.

THE AUTHOR.

CHAPTER I

You don't know about me, without you have read a book by the name of "The Adventures of Tom Sawyer," but that ain't no matter. That book was made by Mr. Mark Twain, and he told the truth, mainly. There was things which he stretched, but mainly he told the truth. That is nothing. I never seen anybody but lied, one time or another, without it was Aunt Polly, or the widow, or maybe Mary.[4] Aunt Polly—Tom's Aunt Polly, she is—and Mary, and the Widow Douglas, is all told about in that book—which is mostly a true book; with some stretchers, as I said before.

Now the way that the book winds up, is this: Tom and me found the money that the robbers hid in the cave and it made us rich. We got six thousand dollars apiece—all gold. It was an awful sight of money when it was piled up. Well, Judge Thatcher, he took it and put it out at interest, and it fetched us a dollar a day

---

* First published in England in 1884; the first American edition was in 1885.
[1] Twain had already published *The Adventures of Tom Sawyer* in 1876.
[2] That would put the setting between 1835 and 1845.   [3] In Missouri.
[4] Tom Sawyer's cousin.

apiece, all the year round—more than a body could tell what to do with. The Widow Douglas, she took me for her son, and allowed she would sivilize me; but it was rough living in the house all the time, considering how dismal regular and decent the widow was in all her ways; and so when I couldn't stand it no longer, I lit out. I got into my old rags, and my sugar-hogshead⁵ again, and was free and satisfied. But Tom Sawyer, he hunted me up and said he was going to start a band of robbers, and I might join if I would go back to the widow and be respectable. So I went back.

The widow she cried over me, and called me a poor lost lamb, and she called me a lot of other names, too, but she never meant no harm by it. She put me in them new clothes again, and I couldn't do nothing but sweat and sweat, and feel all cramped up. Well, then, the old thing commenced again. The widow rung a bell for supper, and you had to come on time. When you got to the table you couldn't go right to eating, but you had to wait for the widow to tuck down her head and grumble a little over the victuals, though there warn't really anything the matter with them. That is, nothing only everything was cooked by itself. In a barrel of odds and ends it is different; things get mixed up, and the juice kind of swaps around, and the things go better.

After supper she got out her book and learned me about Moses and the Bulrushers;⁶ and I was in a sweat to find out all about him; but by-and-by she let it out that Moses had been dead a considerable long time; so then I didn't care no more about him; because I don't take no stock in dead people.

Pretty soon I wanted to smoke, and asked the widow to let me. But she wouldn't. She said it was a mean practice and wasn't clean, and I must try to not do it any more. That is just the way with some people. They get down on a thing when they don't know nothing about it. Here she was a bothering about Moses, which was no kin to her, and no use to anybody, being gone, you see, yet finding a power of fault with me for doing a thing that had some good in it. And she took snuff too; of course that was all right, because she done it herself.

Her sister, Miss Watson, a tolerable slim old maid, with goggles on, had just come to live with her, and took a set at me now, with a spelling-book. She worked me middling hard for about an hour, and then the widow made her ease up. I couldn't stood it much longer. Then for an hour it was deadly dull, and I was fidgety. Miss Watson would say, "Don't put your feet up there, Huckleberry;" and "don't scrunch up like that, Huckleberry—set up straight;" and pretty soon she would say, "Don't gap⁷ and stretch like that, Huckleberry—why don't you try to behave?" Then she told me all about the bad place, and I said I wished I was there. She got mad, then, but I didn't mean no harm. All I wanted was to go somewheres; all I wanted was a change, I warn't particular. She said it was wicked to say what I said; said she wouldn't say it for the whole world; *she* was going to live so as to go to the good place. Well, I couldn't see no advantage in going where she was going, so I made up my mind I wouldn't try for it. But I never said so, because it would only make trouble, and wouldn't do no good.

Now she had got a start, and she went on and told me all about the good place. She said all a body would have to do there was to go around all day long with a harp and sing, forever and ever. So I didn't think much of it. But I never said so. I asked her if she reckoned Tom Sawyer would go there, and, she said, not by a

---

⁵ A large barrel.
⁶ In Exodus 2:1–10 the pharaoh's daughter finds the infant Moses in a basket made of bulrushes.
⁷ Yawn.

considerable sight. I was glad about that, because I wanted him and me to be together.

Miss Watson she kept pecking at me, and it got tiresome and lonesome. By-and-by they fetched the niggers[8] in and had prayers, and then everybody was off to bed. I went up to my room with a piece of candle and put it on the table. Then I set down in a chair by the window and tried to think of something cheerful, but it warn't no use. I felt so lonesome I most wished I was dead. The stars was shining, and the leaves rustled in the woods ever so mournful; and I heard an owl, away off, who-whooing about somebody that was dead, and a whippowill and a dog crying about somebody that was going to die; and the wind was trying to whisper something to me and I couldn't make out what it was, and so it made the cold shivers run over me. Then away out in the woods I heard that kind of a sound that a ghost makes when it wants to tell about something that's on its mind and can't make itself understood, and so can't rest easy in its grave and has to go about that way every night grieving. I got so down-hearted and scared, I did wish I had some company. Pretty soon a spider went crawling up my shoulder, and I flipped it off and it lit in the candle; and before I could budge it was all shriveled up. I didn't need anybody to tell me that that was an awful bad sign and would fetch me some bad luck, so I was scared and most shook the clothes off of me. I got up and turned around in my tracks three times and crossed my breast every time; and then I tied up a little lock of my hair with a thread to keep witches away. But I hadn't no confidence. You do that when you've lost a horse-shoe that you've found, instead of nailing it up over the door, but I hadn't ever heard anybody say it was any way to keep off bad luck when you'd killed a spider.

I set down again, a shaking all over, and got out my pipe for a smoke; for the house was all as still as death, now, and so the widow wouldn't know. Well, after a long time I heard the clock away off in the town go boom—boom—boom—twelve licks—and all still again—stiller than ever. Pretty soon I heard a twig snap, down in the dark amongst the trees—something was a stirring. I set still and listened. Directly I could just barely hear a "*me-you! me-yow!*" down there. That was good! Says I, "*me-yow! me-yow!*" as soft as I could, and then I put out the light and scrambled out of the window onto the shed. Then I slipped down to the ground and crawled in amongst the trees, and sure enough there was Tom Sawyer waiting for me.

Chapter II

We went tip-toeing along a path amongst the trees back towards the end of the widow's garden, stooping down so as the branches wouldn't scrape our heads. When we was passing by the kitchen I fell over a root and made a noise. We scrouched down and laid still. Miss Watson's big nigger, named Jim, was setting in the kitchen door; we could see him pretty clear, because there was a light behind him. He got up and stretched his neck out about a minute, listening. Then he says,

---

[8] This term, a corruption of "Negro," has long been the most highly charged and offensive word in American English. Prior to the Civil War it was frequently used as a synonym for "slave," and Huckleberry Finn uses it descriptively, without personal derision, even when he decides to go to Hell rather than let his friend Jim remain in captivity. The use of the term here is part of Twain's effort to reproduce with social realism the speech of this particular time and place. Twain makes us wince by touching the raw nerve of our history.

"Who dah?"

He listened some more; then he come tip-toeing down and stood right between us; we could a touched him, nearly. Well, likely it was minutes and minutes that there warn't a sound, and we all there so close together. There was a place on my ankle that got to itching; but I dasn't scratch it; and then my ear begun to itch; and next my back, right between my shoulders. Seemed like I'd die if I couldn't scratch. Well, I've noticed that thing plenty of times since. If you are with the quality, or at a funeral, or trying to go to sleep when you ain't sleepy—if you are anywheres where it won't do for you to scratch, why you will itch all over in upwards of a thousand places. Pretty soon Jim says:

"Say—who is you? Whar is you? Dog my cats ef I didn' hear sumf'n. Well, I knows what I's gwyne to do. I's gwyne to set down here and listen tell I hears it agin."

So he set down on the ground betwixt me and Tom. He leaned his back up against a tree, and stretched his legs out till one of them most touched one of mine. My nose begun to itch. It itched till the tears come into my eyes. But I dasn't scratch. Then it begun to itch on the inside. Next I got to itching underneath. I didn't know how I was going to set still. This miserableness went on as much as six or seven minutes; but it seemed a sight longer than that. I was itching in eleven different places now. I reckoned I couldn't stand it more'n a minute longer, but I set my teeth hard and got ready to try. Just then Jim begun to breathe heavy; next he begun to snore—and then I was pretty soon comfortable again.

Tom he made a sign to me—kind of a little noise with his mouth—and we went creeping away on our hands and knees. When we was ten foot off, Tom whispered to me and wanted to tie Jim to the tree for fun; but I said no; he might wake and make a disturbance, and then they'd find out I warn't in. Then Tom said he hadn't got candles enough, and he would slip in the kitchen and get some more. I didn't want him to try. I said Jim might wake up and come. But Tom wanted to resk it; so we slid in there and got three candles, and Tom laid five cents on the table for pay. Then we got out, and I was in a sweat to get away; but nothing would do Tom but he must crawl to where Jim was, on his hands and knees, and play something on him. I waited, and it seemed a good while, everything was so still and lonesome.

As soon as Tom was back, we cut along the path, around the garden fence, and by-and-by fetched up on the steep top of the hill the other side of the house. Tom said he slipped Jim's hat off of his head and hung it on a limb right over him, and Jim stirred a little, but he didn't wake. Afterwards Jim said the witches bewitched him and put him in a trance, and rode him all over the State, and then set him under the trees again and hung his hat on a limb to show who done it. And next time Jim told it he said they rode him down to New Orleans: and after that, every time he told it he spread it more and more, till by-and-by he said they rode him all over the world, and tired him most to death, and his back was all over saddle-boils. Jim was monstrous proud about it, and he got so he wouldn't hardly notice the other niggers. Niggers would come miles to hear Jim tell about it, and he was more looked up to than any nigger in that country. Strange niggers[1] would stand with their mouths open and look him all over, same as if he was a wonder. Niggers is always talking about witches in the dark by the kitchen fire; but whenever one was talking and letting on to know all about such things, Jim would happen in and say, "Hm! What you know 'bout witches?" and that nigger was corked up and

---

[1] Who do not live in the area.

had to take a back seat. Jim always kept that five-center piece around his neck with a string and said it was a charm the devil give to him with his own hands and told him he could cure anybody with it and fetch witches whenever he wanted to, just by saying something to it; but he never told what it was he said to it. Niggers would come from all around there and give Jim anything they had, just for a sight of that five-center piece; but they wouldn't touch it, because the devil had had his hands on it. Jim was most ruined, for a servant, because he got so stuck up on account of having seen the devil and been rode by witches.

Well, when Tom and me got to the edge of the hill-top, we looked away down into the village[2] and could see three or four lights twinkling, where there was sick folks, may be; and the stars over us was sparkling ever so fine; and down by the village was the river, a whole mile broad, and awful still and grand. We went down the hill and found Jo Harper, and Ben Rogers, and two or three more of the boys, hid in the old tanyard. So we unhitched a skiff[3] and pulled down the river two mile and a half, to the big scar on the hillside, and went ashore.

We went to a clump of bushes, and Tom made everybody swear to keep the secret, and then showed them a hole in the hill, right in the thickest part of the bushes. Then we lit the candles and crawled in on our hands and knees. We went about two hundred yards, and then the cave opened up. Tom poked about amongst the passages and pretty soon ducked under a wall where you wouldn't a noticed that there was a hole. We went along a narrow place and got into a kind of room, all damp and sweaty and cold, and there we stopped. Tom says:

"Now we'll start this band of robbers and call it Tom Sawyer's Gang. Everybody that wants to join has got to take an oath, and write his name in blood."

Everybody was willing. So Tom got out a sheet of paper that he had wrote the oath on, and read it. It swore every boy to stick to the band, and never tell any of the secrets; and if anybody done anything to any boy in the band, whichever boy was ordered to kill that person and his family must do it, and he mustn't eat and he mustn't sleep till he had killed them and hacked a cross in their breasts, which was the sign of the band. And nobody that didn't belong to the band could use that mark, and if he did he must be sued; and if he done it again he must be killed. And if anybody that belonged to the band told the secrets, he must have his throat cut, and then have his carcass burnt up and the ashes scattered all around, and his name blotted off of the list with blood and never mentioned again by the gang, but have a curse put on it and be forgot, forever.

Everybody said it was a real beautiful oath, and asked Tom if he got it out of his own head. He said, some of it, but the rest was out of pirate books, and robber books, and every gang that was high-toned had it.

Some thought it would be good to kill the *families* of boys that told the secrets. Tom said it was a good idea, so he took a pencil and wrote it in. Then Ben Rogers says:

"Here's Huck Finn, he hain't got no family—what you going to do 'bout him?"

"Well, hain't he got a father?" says Tom Sawyer.

"Yes, he's got a father, but you can't never find him, these days. He used to lay drunk with the hogs in the tanyard, but he hain't been seen in these parts for a year or more."

They talked it over, and they was going to rule me out, because they said every

---

[2] St. Petersburg (here and in *Tom Sawyer*), a fictionalized version of Hannibal, Missouri, where Twain grew up.

[3] A light rowboat.

boy must have a family or somebody to kill, or else it wouldn't be fair and square for the others. Well, nobody could think of anything to do—everybody was stumped, and set still. I was most ready to cry; but all at once I thought of a way, and so I offered them Miss Watson—they could kill her. Everybody said:

"Oh, she'll do, she'll do. That's all right. Huck can come in."

Then they all stuck a pin in their fingers to get blood to sign with, and I made my mark on the paper.

"Now," says Ben Rogers, "what's the line of business of this Gang?"

"Nothing only robbery and murder," Tom said.

"But who are we going to rob? houses—or cattle—or—"

"Stuff! stealing cattle and such things ain't robbery, it's burglary," says Tom Sawyer. "We ain't burglars. That ain't no sort of style. We are highwaymen. We stop stages and carriages on the road, with masks on and kill the people and take their watches and money."

"Must we always kill the people?"

"Oh, certainly. It's best. Some authorities think different, but mostly it's considered best to kill them. Except some that you bring to the cave here and keep them till they're ransomed."

"Ransomed? What's that?"

"I don't know. But that's what they do. I've seen it in books; and so of course that's what we've got to do."

"But how can we do it if we don't know what it is?"

"Why blame it all, we've *got* to do it. Don't I tell you it's in the books? Do you want to go to doing different from what's in the books, and get things all muddled up?"

"Oh, that's all very fine to *say,* Tom Sawyer, but how in the nation[4] are these fellows going to be ransomed if we don't know how to do it to them? that's the thing *I* want to get at. Now what do you *reckon* it is?"

"Well I don't know. But per'aps if we keep them till they're ransomed, it means that we keep them till they're dead."

"Now, that's something *like.* That'll answer. Why couldn't you said that before? We'll keep them till they're ransomed to death—and a bothersome lot they'll be, too, eating up everything and always trying to get loose."

"How you talk, Ben Rogers. How can they get loose when there's a guard over them, ready to shoot them down if they move a peg?"

"A guard. Well, that *is* good. So somebody's got to set up all night and never get any sleep, just so as to watch them. I think that's foolishness. Why can't a body take a club and ransom them as soon as they get here?"

"Because it ain't in the books so—that's why. Now Ben Rogers, do you want to do things regular, or don't you?—that's the idea. Don't you reckon that the people that made the books knows what's the correct thing to do? Do you reckon *you* can learn 'em anything? Not by a good deal. No sir, we'll just go on and ransom them in the regular way."

"All right. I don't mind; but I say it's a fool way, anyhow. Say—do we kill the women, too?"

"Well, Ben Rogers, if I was as ignorant as you I wouldn't let on. Kill the women? No—nobody ever saw anything in the books like that. You fetch them to the cave, and you're always as polite as pie to them; and by-and-by they fall in love with you and never want to go home any more."

---

[4] Damnation.

"Well, if that's the way, I'm agreed, but I don't take no stock in it. Mighty soon we'll have the cave so cluttered up with women, and fellows waiting to be ransomed, that there won't be no place for the robbers. But go ahead, I ain't got nothing to say."

Little Tommy Barnes was asleep, now, and when they waked him up he was scared, and cried, and said he wanted to go home to his ma, and didn't want to be a robber any more.

So they all made fun of him, and called him cry-baby, and that made him mad, and he said he would go straight and tell all the secrets. But Tom give him five cents to keep quiet, and said we would all go home and meet next week and rob somebody and kill some people.

Ben Rogers said he couldn't get out much, only Sundays, and so he wanted to begin next Sunday; but all the boys said it would be wicked to do it on Sunday, and that settled the thing. They agreed to get together and fix a day as soon as they could, and then we elected Tom Sawyer first captain and Jo Harper second captain of the Gang, and so started home.

I clumb up the shed and crept into my window just before day was breaking. My new clothes was all greased up and clayey, and I was dog-tired.

Chapter III

Well, I got a good going-over in the morning, from old Miss Watson, on account of my clothes; but the widow she didn't scold, but only cleaned off the grease and clay and looked so sorry that I thought I would behave a while if I could. Then Miss Watson she took me in the closet[1] and prayed, but nothing come of it. She told me to pray every day, and whatever I asked for I would get it. But it warn't so. I tried it. Once I got a fish-line, but no hooks. It warn't any good to me without hooks. I tried for the hooks three or four times, but somehow I couldn't make it work. By-and-by, one day, I asked Miss Watson to try for me, but she said I was a fool. She never told me why, and I couldn't make it out no way.

I set down, one time, back in the woods, and had a long think about it. I says to myself, if a body can get anything they pray for, why don't Deacon Winn get back the money he lost on pork? Why can't the widow get back her silver snuff-box that was stole? Why can't Miss Watson fat up? No, says I to myself, there ain't nothing in it. I went and told the widow about it, and she said the thing a body could get by praying for it was "spiritual gifts." This was too many for me, but she told me what she meant—I must help other people, and do everything I could for other people, and look out for them all the time, and never think about myself. This was including Miss Watson, as I took it. I went out in the woods and turned it over in my mind a long time, but I couldn't see no advantage about it—except for the other people—so at last I reckoned I wouldn't worry about it any more, but just let it go. Sometimes the widow would take me one side and talk about Providence in a way to make a body's mouth water; but maybe next day Miss Watson would take hold and knock it all down again. I judged I could see that there was two Providences, and a poor chap would stand considerable show with the

[1] Small, private room for prayer or meditation.

widow's Providence, but if Miss Watson's got him there warn't no help for him any more. I thought it all out, and reckoned I would belong to the widow's, if he wanted me, though I couldn't make out how he was agoing to be any better off then than what he was before, seeing I was so ignorant and so kind of low-down and ornery.

Pap he hadn't been seen for more than a year, and that was comfortable for me; I didn't want to see him no more. He used to always whale me when he was sober and could get his hands on me; though I used to take to the woods most of the time when he was around. Well, about this time he was found in the river drowned, about twelve mile above town, so people said. They judged it was him, anyway; said this drowned man was just his size, and was ragged, and had uncommon long hair—which was all like pap—but they couldn't make nothing out of the face, because it had been in the water so long it warn't much like a face at all. They said he was floating on his back in the water. They took him and buried him on the bank. But I warn't comfortable long, because I happened to think of something. I knowed mighty well that a drownded man don't float on his back, but on his face. So I knowed, then, that this warn't pap, but a woman dressed up in a man's clothes. So I was uncomfortable again. I judged the old man would turn up again by-and-by, though I wished he wouldn't.

We played robber now and then about a month, and then I resigned. All the boys did. We hadn't robbed nobody, we hadn't killed any people, but only just pretended. We used to hop out of the woods and go charging down on hog-drovers and women in carts taking garden stuff to market, but we never hived[2] any of them. Tom Sawyer called the hogs "ingots," and he called the turnips and stuff "julery" and we would go to the cave and pow-wow[3] over what we had done and how many people we had killed and marked. But I couldn't see no profit in it. One time Tom sent a boy to run about town with a blazing stick, which he called a slogan (which was the sign for the Gang to get together), and then he said he had got secret news by his spies that next day a whole parcel of Spanish merchants and rich A-rabs was going to camp in Cave Hollow with two hundred elephants, and six hundred camels, and over a thousand "sumter" mules,[4] all loaded down with di'monds, and they didn't have only a guard of four hundred soldiers, and so we would lay in ambuscade, as he called it, and kill the lot and scoop the things. He said we must slick up our swords and guns, and get ready. He never could go after even a turnip-cart but he must have the swords and guns all scoured up for it; though they was only lath and broom-sticks, and you might scour at them till you rotted and then they warn't worth a mouthful of ashes more than what they was before. I didn't believe we could lick such a crowd of Spaniards and A-rabs, but I wanted to see the camels and elephants, so I was on hand next day, Saturday, in the ambuscade; and when we got the word, we rushed out of the woods and down the hill. But there warn't no Spaniards and A-rabs, and there warn't no camels nor no elephants. It warn't anything but a Sunday-school picnic, and only a primer-class at that. We busted it up, and chased the children up the hollow; but we never got anything but some doughnuts and jam, though Ben Rogers got a rag doll, and Jo Harper got a hymn-book and a tract; and then the teacher charged in and made us drop everything and cut. I didn't see no di'monds, and I told Tom Sawyer so. He said there was loads of them there, anyway; and he said there was A-rabs

---

[2] Captured.   [3] Talk.   [4] Pack mules.

there, too, and elephants and things. I said, why couldn't we see them, then? He said if I warn't so ignorant, but had read a book called "Don Quixote,"[5] I would know without asking. He said it was all done by enchantment. He said there was hundreds of soldiers there, and elephants and treasure, and so on, but we had enemies which he called magicians, and they had turned the whole thing into an infant Sunday school, just out of spite. I said, all right, then the thing for us to do was to go for the magicians. Tom Sawyer said I was a numskull.

"Why," says he, "a magician could call up a lot of genies, and they would hash you up like nothing before you could say Jack Robinson. They are as tall as a tree and as big around as a church."

"Well," I says, "s'pose we got some genies to help *us*—can't we lick the other crowd then?"

"How you going to get them?"

"I don't know. How do *they* get them?"

"Why they rub an old tin lamp or an iron ring, and then the genies come tearing in, with the thunder and lightning a-ripping around and the smoke a-rolling, and everything they're told to do they up and do it. They don't think nothing of pulling a shot tower[6] up by the roots, and belting a Sunday-school superintendent over the head with it—or any other man."

"Who makes them tear around so?"

"Why, whoever rubs the lamp or the ring. They belong to whoever rubs the lamp or the ring, and they've got to do whatever he says. If he tells them to build a palace forty miles long, out of di'monds, and fill it full of chewing gum, or whatever you want, and fetch an emperor's daughter from China for you to marry, they've got to do it—and they've got to do it before sun-up next morning, too. And more—they've got to waltz that palace around over the country wherever you want it, you understand."

"Well," says I, "I think they are a pack of flatheads for not keeping the palace themselves 'stead of fooling them away like that. And what's more—if I was one of them I would see a man in Jericho[7] before I would drop my business and come to him for the rubbing of an old tin lamp."

"How you talk, Huck Finn. Why, you'd *have* to come when he rubbed it, whether you wanted to or not."

"What, and I as high as a tree and as big as a church? All right, then; I *would* come; but I lay I'd make that man climb the highest tree there was in the country."

"Shucks, it ain't no use to talk to you, Huck Finn. You don't seem to know anything, somehow—perfect sap-head."

I thought all this over for two or three days, and then I reckoned I would see if there was anything in it. I got an old tin lamp and an iron ring and went out in the woods and rubbed and rubbed till I sweat like an Injun, calculating to build a palace and sell it; but it warn't no use, none of the genies come. So then I judged

---

[5] The picaresque novel (1605) by Miguel de Cervantes (1547–1616), in which Don Quixote attacks a flock of sheep and explains that they were knights transformed by the spell of a magician.

[6] A small "tower" or device filled with water into which molten lead is poured to make pellets. Tom refers here to *The Arabian Nights* (1838–1841), a collection of ancient eastern tales; he gets many of his ideas from books.

[7] An ancient Canaanite city with fortified walls (that were miraculously destroyed at the sound of trumpets, according to Joshua 6).

that all that stuff was only just one of Tom Sawyer's lies. I reckoned he believed in the A-rabs and the elephants, but as for me I think different. It had all the marks of a Sunday school.

Chapter IV

Well, three or four months run along, and it was well into the winter, now. I had been to school most all the time, and could spell, and read, and write just a little, and could say the multiplication table up to six times seven is thirty-five, and I don't reckon I could ever get any further than that if I was to live forever. I don't take no stock in mathematics, anyway.

At first I hated the school, but by-and-by I got so I could stand it. Whenever I got uncommon tired I played hookey, and the hiding I got next day done me good and cheered me up. So the longer I went to school the easier it got to be. I was getting sort of used to the widow's ways, too, and they warn't so raspy on me. Living in a house, and sleeping in a bed, pulled on me pretty tight, mostly, but before the cold weather I used to slide out and sleep in the woods, sometimes, and so that was a rest to me. I liked the old ways best, but I was getting so I liked the new ones, too, a little bit. The widow said I was coming along slow but sure, and doing very satisfactory. She said she warn't ashamed of me.

One morning I happened to turn over the salt-cellar at breakfast. I reached for some of it as quick as I could, to throw over my left shoulder and keep off the bad luck, but Miss Watson was in ahead of me, and crossed me off. She says, "Take your hands away, Huckleberry—what a mess you are always making." The widow put in a good word for me, but that warn't going to keep off the bad luck, I knowed that well enough. I started out, after breakfast, feeling worried and shaky, and wondering where it was going to fall on me, and what it was going to be. There is ways to keep off some kinds of bad luck, but this wasn't one of them kind; so I never tried to do anything, but just poked along low-spirited and on the watch-out.

I went down the front garden and clumb over the stile,[1] where you go through the high board fence. There was an inch of new snow on the ground, and I seen somebody's tracks. They had come up from the quarry and stood around the stile a while, and then went on around the garden fence. It was funny they hadn't come in, after standing around so. I couldn't make it out. It was very curious, somehow. I was going to follow around, but I stooped down to look at the tracks first. I didn't notice anything at first, but next I did. There was a cross in the left boot-heel made with big nails, to keep off the devil.

I was up in a second and shinning down the hill. I looked over my shoulder every now and then, but I didn't see nobody. I was at Judge Thatcher's as quick as I could get there. He said:

"Why, my boy, you are all out of breath. Did you come for your interest?"

"No sir," I says; "is there some for me?"

"Oh, yes, a half-yearly is in, last night. Over a hundred and fifty dollars. Quite a fortune for you. You better let me invest it along with your six thousand, because if you take it you'll spend it."

---

[1]Steps ascending and descending a fence.

"No sir," I says, "I don't want to spend it. I don't want it at all—nor the six thousand, nuther. I want you to take it; I want to give it to you—the six thousand and all."

He looked surprised. He couldn't seem to make it out. He says:

"Why, what can you mean, my boy?"

I says, "Don't you ask me no questions about it, please. You'll take it—won't you?"

He says:

"Well I'm puzzled. Is something the matter?"

"Please take it," says I, "and don't ask me nothing—then I won't have to tell no lies."

He studied a while, and then he says:

"Oho-o. I think I see. You want to *sell* all your property to me—not give it. That's the correct idea."

Then he wrote something on a paper and read it over, and says:

"There—you see it says 'for a consideration.' That means I have bought it of you and paid you for it. Here's a dollar for you. Now, you sign it."

So I signed it, and left.

Miss Watson's nigger, Jim, had a hair-ball as big as your fist, which had been took out of the fourth stomach of an ox, and he used to do magic with it. He said there was a spirit inside of it, and it knowed everything. So I went to him that night and told him pap was here again, for I found his tracks in the snow. What I wanted to know, was, what he was going to do, and was he going to stay? Jim got out his hair-ball, and said something over it, and then he held it up and dropped it on the floor. It fell pretty solid, and only rolled about an inch. Jim tried it again, and then another time, and it acted just the same. Jim got down on his knees and put his ear against it and listened. But it warn't no use; he said it wouldn't talk. He said sometimes it wouldn't talk without money. I told him I had an old slick counterfeit quarter that warn't no good because the brass showed through the silver a little, and it wouldn't pass nohow, even if the brass didn't show, because it was so slick it felt greasy, and so that would tell on it every time. (I reckoned I wouldn't say nothing about the dollar I got from the judge.) I said it was pretty bad money, but maybe the hair-ball would take it, because maybe it wouldn't know the difference. Jim smelt it, and bit it, and rubbed it, and said he would manage so the hair-ball would think it was good. He said he would split open a raw Irish potato and stick the quarter in between and keep it there all night, and next morning you couldn't see no brass, and it wouldn't feel greasy no more, and so anybody in town would take it in a minute, let alone a hair-ball. Well, I knowed a potato would do that, before, but I had forgot it.

Jim put the quarter under the hair-ball and got down and listened again. This time he said the hair-ball was all right. He said it would tell my whole fortune if I wanted it to. I says, go on. So the hair-ball talked to Jim, and Jim told it to me. He says:

"Yo' ole father doan' know, yit, what he's a-gwyne to do. Sometimes he spec he'll go 'way, en den agin he spec he'll stay. De bes' way is to res' easy en let de ole man take his own way. Dey's two angels hoverin' roun' 'bout him. One uv 'em is white en shiny, en 'tother one is black. De white one gits him to go right, a little while, den de black one sail in en bust it all up. A body can't tell, yit, which one gwyne to fetch him at de las'. But you is all right. You gwyne to have considable trouble in yo' life, en considable joy. Sometimes you gwyne to git hurt, en sometimes you gwyne to git sick; but every time you's gwyne to git well agin. Dey's two gals flying' 'bout you in yo' life. One uv 'em's light en 'tother one is dark. One is rich en 'tother is po'. You's gwyne to marry de po' one fust en de rich one by-en-by. You wants to keep 'way fum de water as much as you kin, en don't run no resk, 'kase it's down in de bills[2] dat you's gwyne to git hung."

When I lit my candle and went up to my room that night, there set pap, his own self!

CHAPTER V

I had shut the door to. Then I turned around, and there he was. I used to be scared of him all the time, he tanned me so much. I reckoned I was scared now, too; but in a minute I see I was mistaken. That is, after the first jolt, as you may say, when my breath sort of hitched—he being so unexpected; but right away after, I see I warn't scared of him worth bothering about.

He was most fifty, and he looked it. His hair was long and tangled and greasy, and hung down, and you could see his eyes shining through like he was behind vines. It was all black, no gray; so was his long, mixed-up whiskers. There warn't no color in his face, where his face showed; it was white; not like another man's white, but a white to make a body sick, a white to make a body's flesh crawl—a tree-toad white, a fish-belly white. As for his clothes—just rags, that was all. He had one ankle resting on 'tother knee; the boot on that foot was busted, and two of his toes stuck through, and he worked them now and then. His hat was laying on the floor; an old black slouch with the top caved in, like a lid.

I stood a-looking at him; he set there a-looking at me, with his chair tilted back a little. I set the candle down. I noticed the window was up; so he had clumb in by the shed. He kept a-looking me all over. By-and-by he says:

"Starchy clothes—very. You think you're a good deal of a big-bug, *don't* you?"

"Maybe I am, maybe I ain't," I says.

"Don't you give me none o' your lip," says he. "You've put on considerble many frills since I been away. I'll take you down a peg before I get done with you. You're educated, too, they say; can read and write. You think you're better'n your father, now, don't you, because he can't? *I'll* take it out of you. Who told you you might meddle with such hifalut'n foolishness, hey?—who told you you could?"

"The widow. She told me."

"The widow, hey?—and who told the widow she could put in her shovel about a thing that ain't none of her business?"

"Nobody never told her."

"Well, I'll learn her how to meddle. And looky here—you drop that school, you hear? I'll learn people to bring up a boy to put on airs over his own father and let on to be better'n what *he* is. You lemme catch you fooling around that school again, you hear? Your mother couldn't read, and she couldn't write, nuther, before she died. None of the family couldn't, before *they* died. *I* can't; and here you're a-swelling yourself up like this. I ain't the man to stand it—you hear? Say—lemme hear you read."

---

[2] Written in the books of fate; decreed.

I took up a book and begun something about General Washington and the wars.[1] When I'd read about a half a minute, he fetched the book a whack with his hand and knocked it across the house. He says:

"It's so. You can do it. I had my doubts when you told me. Now looky here; you stop that putting on frills. I won't have it. I'll lay for you, my smarty; and if I catch you about that school I'll tan you good. First you know you'll get religion, too. I never see such a son."

He took up a little blue and yaller picture of some cows and a boy, and says: "What's this?"

"It's something they give me for learning my lessons good."

He tore it up, and says—

"I'll give you something better—I'll give you a cowhide."[2]

He set there a-mumbling and a-growling a minute, and then he says—

"*Ain't* you a sweet-scented dandy, though? A bed; and bedclothes; and a look'n-glass; and a piece of carpet on the floor—and your own father got to sleep with the hogs in the tanyard. I never see such a son. I bet I'll take some o' these frills out o' you before I'm done with you. Why there ain't no end to your airs—they say you're rich. Hey?—how's that?"

"They lie—that's how."

"Looky here—mind how you talk to me; I'm a-standing about all I can stand, now—so don't gimme no sass. I've been in town two days and I hain't heard nothing but about you bein' rich. I heard about it away down the river, too. That's why I come. You git me that money to-morrow—I want it."

"I hain't got no money."

"It's a lie. Judge Thatcher's got it. You git it. I want it."

"I hain't got no money, I tell you. You ask Judge Thatcher; he'll tell you the same."

"All right. I'll ask him; and I'll make him pungle,[3] too, or I'll know the reason why. Say—how much you got in your pocket? I want it."

"I hain't got only a dollar, and I want that to—"

"It don't make no difference what you want it for—you just shell it out."

He took it and bit it to see if it was good, and then he said he was going down town to get some whisky; said he hadn't had a drink all day. When he had got out on the shed, he put his head in again, and cussed me for putting on frills and trying to be better than him; and when I reckoned he was gone, he come back and put his head in again, and told me to mind about that school, because he was going to lay for me and lick me if I didn't drop that.

Next day he was drunk, and he went to Judge Thatcher's and bullyragged[4] him and tried to make him give up the money, but he couldn't, and then he swore he'd make the law force him.

The judge and the widow went to law to get the court to take me away from him and let one of them be my guardian; but it was a new judge that had just come, and he didn't know the old man, so he said courts mustn't interfere and separate families if they could help it; said he'd druther not take a child away from its father. So Judge Thatcher and the widow had to quit on the business.

---

[1] George Washington (1732–1799), first U.S. president (1789–1797), served in the French and Indian War (1754–1763) as well as in the Revolutionary War (1775–1785).
[2] A whipping with a cowhide whip.   [3] Turn over the money.   [4] Threatened, scolded.

That pleased the old man till he couldn't rest. He said he'd cowhide me till I was black and blue if I didn't raise some money for him. I borrowed three dollars from Judge Thatcher, and pap took it and got drunk and went a-blowing around and cussing and whooping and carrying on; and he kept it up all over town, with a tin pan, till most midnight; then they jailed him, and next day they had him before court, and jailed him again for a week. But he said *he* was satisfied; said he was boss of his son, and he'd make it warm for *him*.

When he got out the new judge said he was agoing to make a man of him. So he took him to his own house, and dressed him up clean and nice, and had him to breakfast and dinner and supper with the family, and was just old pie to him, so to speak. And after supper he talked to him about temperance and such things till the old man cried, and said he'd been a fool, and fooled away his life; but now he was agoing to turn over a new leaf and be a man nobody wouldn't be ashamed of, and he hoped the judge would help him and not look down on him. The judge said he could hug him for them words, so *he* cried, and his wife she cried again; pap said he'd been a man that had always been misunderstood before, and the judge said he believed it. The old man said that what a man wanted that was down, was sympathy; and the judge said it was so; so they cried again. And when it was bedtime, the old man rose up and held out his hand, and says:

"Look at it gentlemen, and ladies all; take ahold of it; shake it. There's a hand that was the hand of a hog; but it ain't so no more; it's the hand of a man that's started in on a new life, and 'll die before he'll go back. You mark them words— don't forget I said them. It's a clean hand now; shake it—don't be afeard."

So they shook it, one after the other, all around, and cried. The judge's wife she kissed it. Then the old man he signed a pledge—made his mark.[5] The judge said it was the holiest time on record, or something like that. Then they tucked the old man into a beautiful room, which was the spare room, and in the night sometime he got powerful thirsty and clumb out onto the porch-roof and slid down a stanchion and traded his new coat for a jug of forty-rod,[6] and clumb back again and had a good old time; and towards daylight he crawled out again, drunk as a fiddler, and rolled off the porch and broke his left arm in two places and was most froze to death when somebody found him after sun-up. And when they come to look at that spare room, they had to take soundings before they could navigate it.

The judge he felt kind of sore. He said he reckoned a body could reform the ole man with a shot-gun, maybe, but he didn't know no other way.

Chapter VI

Well, pretty soon the old man was up and around again, and then he went for Judge Thatcher in the courts to make him give up that money, and he went for me, too, for not stopping school. He catched me a couple of times and thrashed me, but I went to school just the same, and dodged him or out-run him most of the time. I didn't want to go to school much, before, but I reckoned I'd go now to spite pap. That law trial was a slow business; appeared like they warn't ever going to get started on it; so every now and then I'd borrow two or three dollars off of

---

[5] Pap can't write his name, so he signs his mark (an "X") to a pledge that he will drink no more.
[6] Homemade whiskey powerful enough to knock a man 40 rods, or 220 yards.

the judge for him, to keep from getting a cowhiding. Every time he got money he got drunk; and every time he got drunk he raised Cain[1] around town; and every time he raised Cain he got jailed. He was just suited—this kind of thing was right in his line.

He got to hanging around the widow's too much, and so she told him at last, that if he didn't quit using[2] around there she would make trouble for him. Well, *wasn't* he mad? He said he would show who was Huck Finn's boss. So he watched out for me one day in the spring, and catched me, and took me up the river about three mile, in a skiff, and crossed over to the Illinois shore where it was woody and there warn't no houses but an old log hut in a place where the timber was so thick you couldn't find it if you didn't know where it was.

He kept me with him all the time, and I never got a chance to run off. We lived in that old cabin, and he always locked the door and put the key under his head, nights. He had a gun which he had stole, I reckon, and we fished and hunted, and that was what we lived on. Every little while he locked me in and went down to the store, three miles, to the ferry, and traded fish and game for whisky and fetched it home and got drunk and had a good time, and licked me. The widow she found out where I was, by-and-by, and she sent a man over to try to get hold of me, but pap drove him off with the gun, and it warn't long after that till I was used to being where I was, and liked it, all but the cowhide part.

It was kind of lazy and jolly, laying off comfortable all day, smoking and fishing, and no books nor study. Two months or more run along, and my clothes got to be all rags and dirt, and I didn't see how I'd ever got to like it so well at the widow's, where you had to wash, and eat on a plate, and comb up, and go to bed and get up regular, and be forever bothering over a book and have old Miss Watson pecking at you all the time. I didn't want to go back no more. I had stopped cussing, because the widow didn't like it; but now I took to it again because pap hadn't no objections. It was pretty good times up in the woods there, take it all around.

But by-and-by pap got too handy with his hick'ry, and I couldn't stand it. I was all over welts. He got to going away so much, too, and locking me in. Once he locked me in and was gone three days. It was dreadful lonesome. I judged he had got drowned and I wasn't ever going to get out any more. I was scared. I made up my mind I would fix up some way to leave there. I had tried to get out of that cabin many a time, but I couldn't find no way. There warn't a window to it big enough for a dog to get through. I couldn't get up the chimbly, it was too narrow. The door was thick solid oak slabs. Pap was pretty careful not to leave a knife or anything in the cabin when he was away; I reckon I had hunted the place over as much as a hundred times; well, I was 'most all the time at it, because it was about the only way to put in the time. But this time I found something at last; I found an old rusty wood-saw without any handle; it was laid in between a rafter and the clapboards of the roof. I greased it up and went to work. There was an old horse-blanket nailed against the logs at the far end of the cabin behind the table, to keep the wind from blowing through the chinks and putting the candle out. I got under the table and raised the blanket and went to work to saw a section of the big bottom log out, big enough to let me through. Well, it was a good long job, but I was getting towards the end of it when I heard pap's gun in the woods. I got rid of

---

[1] Created a great commotion; after the oldest son of Adam and Eve in Genesis 4: Cain killed his brother, Abel.

[2] Making a habit of loitering.

the signs of my work, and dropped the blanket and hid my saw, and pretty soon pap come in.

Pap warn't in a good humor—so he was his natural self. He said he was down to town, and everything was going wrong. His lawyer said he reckoned he would win his lawsuit and get the money, if they ever got started on the trial; but then there was ways to put it off a long time, and Judge Thatcher knowed how to do it. And he said people allowed there'd be another trial to get me away from him and give me to the widow for my guardian, and they guessed it would win, this time. This shook me up considerable, because I didn't want to go back to the widow's any more and be so cramped up and sivilized, as they called it. Then the old man got to cussing, and cussed everything and everybody he could think of, and then cussed them all over again to make sure he hadn't skipped any, and after that he polished off with a kind of a general cuss all around, including a considerable parcel which he didn't know the names of, and so called them what's-his-name, when he got to them, and went right along with his cussing.

He said he would like to see the widow get me. He said he would watch out, and if they tried to come any such game on him he knowed of a place six or seven mile off, to stow me in, where they might hunt till they dropped and they couldn't find me. That made me pretty uneasy again, but only for a minute; I reckoned I wouldn't stay on hand till he got that chance.

The old man made me go to the skiff and fetch the things he had got. There was a fifty-pound sack of corn meal, and a side of bacon, ammunition, and a four-gallon jug of whisky, and an old book and two newspapers for wadding, besides some tow.[3] I toted up a load, and went back and set down on the bow of the skiff to rest. I thought it all over, and I reckoned I would walk off with the gun and some lines, and take to the woods when I run away. I guessed I wouldn't stay in one place, but just tramp right across the country, mostly night times, and hunt and fish to keep alive, and so get so far away that the old man nor the widow couldn't ever find me any more. I judged I would saw out and leave that night if pap got drunk enough, and I reckoned he would. I got so full of it I didn't notice how long I was staying, till the old man hollered and asked me whether I was asleep or drownded.

I got the things all up to the cabin, and then it was about dark. While I was cooking supper the old man took a swig or two and got sort of warmed up, and went to ripping again. He had been drunk over in town, and laid in the gutter all night, and he was a sight to look at. A body would a thought he was Adam, he was just all mud.[4] Whenever his liquor begun to work, he most always went for the govment. This time he says:

"Call this a govment! why, just look at it and see what it's like. Here's the law a-standing ready to take a man's son away from him—a man's own son, which he has had all the trouble and all the anxiety and all the expense of raising. Yes, just as that man has got that son raised at last, and ready to go to work and begin to do suthin' for *him* and give him a rest, the law up and goes for him. And they call *that* govment! That ain't all, nuther. The law backs that old Judge Thatcher up and helps him to keep me out o' my property. Here's what the law does. The law takes a man worth six thousand dollars and upards, and jams him into an old trap of a cabin like this, and lets him go round in clothes that ain't fitten for a hog. They

---

[3] Material for packing gunpowder in a rifle; besides some cheap rope.

[4] A vernacular form of Genesis 2:7: "And the Lord God formed man of the dust of the ground."

call that govment! A man can't get his rights in a govment like this. Sometimes I've a mighty notion to just leave the country for good and all. Yes, and I *told* 'em so; I told old Thatcher so to his face. Lots of 'em heard me, and can tell what I said. Says I, for two cents I'd leave the blamed country and never come anear it agin. Them's the very words. I says, look at my hat—if you call it a hat—but the lid raises up and the rest of it goes down till it's below my chin, and then it ain't rightly a hat at all, but more like my head was shoved up through a jint o' stove-pipe. Look at it, says I—such a hat for me to wear—one of the wealthiest men in this town, if I could git my rights.

"Oh, yes, this is a wonderful govment, wonderful. Why, looky here. There was a free nigger there, from Ohio; a mulatter,[5] most as white as a white man. He had the whitest shirt on you ever see, too, and the shiniest hat; and there ain't a man in that town that's got as fine clothes as what he had; and he had a gold watch and chain, and a silver-headed cane—the awfulest old gray-headed nabob[6] in the State. And what do you think? they said he was a p'fessor in a college, and could talk all kinds of languages, and knowed everything. And that ain't the wust. They said he could *vote*, when he was at home. Well, that let me out. Thinks I, what is the country a-coming to? It was 'lection day, and I was just about to go and vote, myself, if I warn't too drunk to get there; but when they told me there was a State in this country where they'd let that nigger vote, I drawed out. I says I'll never vote agin. Them's the very words I said; they all heard me; and the country may rot for all me—I'll never vote agin as long as I live. And to see the cool way of that nigger—why, he wouldn't a give me the road if I hadn't shoved him out o' the way. I says to the people, why ain't this nigger put up at auction and sold?— that's what I want to know. And what do you reckon they said? Why, they said he couldn't be sold till he'd been in the State six months, and he hadn't been there that long yet. There, now—that's a specimen. They call that a govment that can't sell a free nigger till he's been in the State six months. Here's a govment that calls itself a govment, and lets on to be a govment, and thinks it is a govment, and yet's got to set stock-still for six whole months before it can take ahold of a prowling, thieving, infernal, white-shirted free nigger, and—"[7]

Pap was agoing on so, he never noticed where his old limber legs was taking him to, so he went head over heels over the tub of salt pork, and barked both shins, and the rest of his speech was all the hottest kind of language—mostly hove at the nigger and the govment, though he give the tub some, too, all along, here and there. He hopped around the cabin considerable, first on one leg and then on the other, holding first one shin and then the other one, and at last he let out with his left foot all of a sudden and fetched the tub a rattling kick. But it warn't good judgment, because that was the boot that had a couple of his toes leaking out of the front end of it; so now he raised a howl that fairly made a body's hair raise, and down he went in the dirt, and rolled there, and held his toes; and the cussing he done then laid over anything he had ever done previous. He said so his own self, afterwards. He had heard old Sowberry Hagan in his best days, and he said it laid over him, too; but I reckon that was sort of piling it on, maybe.

After supper pap took the jug, and said he had enough whisky there for two drunks and one delirium tremens. That was always his word. I judged he would be

---

[5] A mulatto, or person of mixed racial ancestry; Ohio was not a slave state.

[6] Originally, a native viceroy in India; here, a man of wealth and position.

[7] The Missouri laws concerning freed slaves became stricter between 1835 and 1845; Pap's under-standing of the law is that after six months even a free Negro can be sold into slavery; what he objects to is the waiting period.

blind drunk in about an hour, and then I would steal the key, or saw myself out, one or 'tother. He drank, and drank, and tumbled down on his blankets, by-and-by; but luck didn't run my way. He didn't go sound asleep, but was uneasy. He groaned, and moaned, and thrashed around this way and that, for a long time. At last I got so sleepy I couldn't keep my eyes open, all I could do, and so before I knowed what I was about I was sound asleep, and the candle burning.

I don't know how long I was asleep, but all of a sudden there was an awful scream and I was up. There was pap, looking wild and skipping around every which way and yelling about snakes. He said they was crawling up his legs; and then he would give a jump and scream, and say one had bit him on the cheek—but I couldn't see no snakes. He started and run round and round the cabin, hollering "take him off! take him off! he's biting me on the neck!" I never see a man look so wild in the eyes. Pretty soon he was all fagged out, and fell down panting; then he rolled over and over, wonderful fast, kicking things every which way, and striking and grabbing at the air with his hands, and screaming, and saying there was devils ahold of him. He wore out, by-and-by, and laid still a while, moaning. Then he laid stiller, and didn't make a sound. I could hear the owls and the wolves, away off in the woods, and it seemed terrible still. He was laying over by the corner. By-and-by he raised up, part way, and listened, with his head to one side. He says very low:

"Tramp—tramp—tramp; that's the dead; tramp—tramp—tramp; they're coming after me; but I won't go—Oh, they're here! don't touch me—don't! hands off—they're cold; let go—Oh, let a poor devil alone!"

Then he went down on all fours and crawled off begging them to let him alone, and he rolled himself up in his blanket and wallowed in under the old pine table, still a-begging; and then he went to crying. I could hear him through the blanket.

By-and-by he rolled out and jumped up on his feet looking wild and he see me and went for me. He chased me round and round the place, with a clasp-knife, calling me the Angel of Death and saying he would kill me and then I couldn't come for him no more. I begged, and told him I was only Huck, but he laughed *such* a screechy laugh, and roared and cussed, and kept on chasing me up. Once when I turned short and dodged under his arm he made a grab and got me by the jacket between my shoulders, and I thought I was gone; but I slid out of the jacket quick as lightning, and saved myself. Pretty soon he was all tired out, and dropped down with his back against the door, and said he would rest a minute and then kill me. He put his knife under him, and said he would sleep and get strong, and then he would see who was who.

So he dozed off, pretty soon. By-and-by I got the old split-bottom chair[8] and clumb up, as easy as I could, not to make any noise, and got down the gun. I slipped the ramrod down it to make sure it was loaded, and then I laid it across the turnip barrel, pointing towards pap, and set down behind it to wait for him to stir. And how slow and still the time did drag along.

CHAPTER VII

"Git up! what you 'bout!"

I opened my eyes and looked around, trying to make out where I was. It was after sun-up, and I had been sound asleep. Pap was standing over me, looking sour—and sick, too. He says—

---

[8] With a seat made by interweaving strips of wood.

"What you doin' with this gun?"

I judged he didn't know nothing about what he had been doing, so I says:

"Somebody tried to get in, so I was laying for him."

"Why didn't you roust me out?"

"Well I tried to, but I couldn't; I couldn't budge you."

"Well, all right. Don't stand there palavering[1] all day, but out with you and see if there's a fish on the lines for breakfast. I'll be along in a minute.

He unlocked the door and I cleared out, up the river bank. I noticed some pieces of limbs and such things floating down, and a sprinkling of bark; so I knowed the river had begun to rise. I reckoned I would have great times, now, if I was over at the town. The June rise used to be always luck for me; because as soon as that rise begins, here comes cord-wood[2] floating down, and pieces of log rafts—sometimes a dozen logs together; so all you have to do is to catch them and sell them to the wood yards and the sawmill.

I went along up the bank with one eye out for pap and 'tother one out for what the rise might fetch along. Well, all at once, here comes a canoe; just a beauty, too, about thirteen or fourteen foot long, riding high like a duck. I shot head first off of the bank, like a frog, clothes and all on, and struck out for the canoe. I just expected there'd be somebody laying down in it, because people often done that to fool folks, and when a chap had pulled a skiff out most to it they'd raise up and laugh at him. But it warn't so this time. It was a drift-canoe, sure enough, and I clumb in and paddled her ashore. Thinks I, the old man will be glad when he sees this—she's worth ten dollars. But when I got to shore pap wasn't in sight yet, and as I was running her into a little creek like a gully, all hung over with vines and willows, I struck another idea; I judged I'd hide her good, and then, stead of taking to the woods when I run off, I'd go down the river about fifty mile and camp in one place for good, and not have such a rough time tramping on foot.

It was pretty close to the shanty, and I thought I heard the old man coming, all the time; but I got her hid; and then I out and looked around a bunch of willows, and there was the old man down the path apiece just drawing a bead on a bird with his gun. So he hadn't seen anything.

When he got along, I was hard at it taking up a "trot" line.[3] He abused me a little for being so slow, but I told him I fell in the river and that was what made me so long. I knowed he would see I was wet, and then he would be asking questions. We got five cat-fish off of the lines and went home.

While we laid off, after breakfast, to sleep up, both of us being about wore out, I got to thinking that if I could fix up some way to keep pap and the widow from trying to follow me, it would be a certainer thing than trusting to luck to get far enough off before they missed me; you see, all kinds of things might happen. Well, I didn't see no way for a while, but by-and-by pap raised up a minute, to drink another barrel of water, and he says:

"Another time a man comes a-prowling round here, you roust me out, you hear? That man warn't here for no good. I'd a shot him. Next time, you roust me out, you hear?"

Then he dropped down and went to sleep again—but what he had been saying give me the very idea I wanted. I says to myself, I can fix it now so nobody won't think of following me.

---

[1] Jabbering.   [2] Wood cut into four-foot lengths.

[3] A fishing line strung across a stream from which hooks are attached at intervals.

About twelve o'clock we turned out and went along up the bank. The river was coming up pretty fast, and lots of drift-wood going by on the rise. By-and-by, along comes part of a log raft—nine logs fast together. We went out with the skiff and towed it ashore. Then we had dinner. Anybody but pap would a waited and seen the day through, so as to catch more stuff; but that warn't pap's style. Nine logs was enough for one time; he must shove right over to town and sell. So he locked me in and took the skiff and started off towing the raft about half-past three. I judged he wouldn't come back that night. I waited till I reckoned he had got a good start, then I out with my saw and went to work on that log again. Before he was 'tother side of the river I was out of the hole; him and his raft was just a speck on the water away off yonder.

I took the sack of corn meal and took it to where the canoe was hid, and shoved the vines and branches apart and put it in; then I done the same with the side of bacon; then the whisky jug; I took all the coffee and sugar there was, and all the ammunition; I took the wadding; I took the bucket and gourd, I took a dipper and a tin cup, and my old saw and two blankets, and the skillet and the coffee-pot. I took fish-lines and matches and other things—everything that was worth a cent. I cleaned out the place. I wanted an axe, but there wasn't any, only the one out at the wood pile, and I knowed why I was going to leave that. I fetched out the gun, and now I was done.

I had wore the ground a good deal, crawling out of the hole and dragging out so many things. So I fixed that as good as I could from the outside by scattering dust on the place, which covered up the smoothness and the sawdust. Then I fixed the piece of log back into its place, and put two rocks under it and one against it to hold it there,—for it was bent up at that place, and didn't quite touch ground. If you stood four or five foot away and didn't know it was sawed, you wouldn't ever notice it; and besides, this was the back of the cabin and it warn't likely anybody would go fooling around there.

It was all grass clear to the canoe; so I hadn't left a track. I followed around to see. I stood on the bank and looked out over the river. All safe. So I took the gun and went up a piece into the woods and was hunting around for some birds, when I see a wild pig; hogs soon went wild in them bottoms after they had got away from the prairie farms. I shot this fellow and took him into camp.

I took the axe and smashed in the door—I beat it and hacked it considerable, a-doing it. I fetched the pig in and took him back nearly to the table and hacked into his throat with the ax, and laid him down on the ground to bleed—I say ground, because it *was* ground—hard packed, and no boards. Well, next I took an old sack and put a lot of big rocks in it,—all I could drag—and I started it from the pig and dragged it to the door and through the woods down to the river and dumped it in, and down it sunk, out of sight. You could easy see that something had been dragged over the ground. I did wish Tom Sawyer was there, I knowed he would take an interest in this kind of business, and throw in the fancy touches. Nobody could spread himself like Tom Sawyer in such a thing as that.

Well, last I pulled out some of my hair, and bloodied the ax good, and stuck it on the back side, and slung the ax in the corner. Then I took up the pig and held him to my breast with my jacket (so he couldn't drip) till I got a good piece below the house and then dumped him into the river. Now I thought of something else. So I went and got the bag of meal and my old saw out of the canoe and fetched them to the house. I took the bag to where it used to stand, and ripped a hole in the bottom of it with the saw, for there warn't no knives and forks on the place—pap done everything with his clasp-knife, about the cooking. Then I carried the sack about a hundred yards across the grass and through the willows east of the house, to a shallow lake that was five mile wide and full of rushes—and ducks too, you might say, in the season. There was a slough or a creek leading out of it on the other side, that went miles away, I don't know where, but it didn't go to the river. The meal sifted out and made a little track all the way to the lake. I dropped pap's whetstone there too, so as to look like it had been done by accident. Then I tied up the rip in the meal sack with a string, so it wouldn't leak no more, and took it and my saw to the canoe again.

It was about dark, now; so I dropped the canoe down the river under some willows that hung over the bank, and waited for the moon to rise. I made fast to a willow; then I took a bite to eat, and by-and-by laid down in the canoe to smoke a pipe and lay out a plan. I says to myself, they'll follow the track of that sackful of rocks to the shore and then drag the river for me. And they'll follow that meal track to the lake and go browsing down the creek that leads out of it to find the robbers that killed me and took the things. They won't ever hunt the river for anything but my dead carcass. They'll soon get tired of that, and won't bother no more about me. All right; I can stop anywhere I want to. Jackson's Island[4] is good enough for me; I know that island pretty well, and nobody ever comes there. And then I can paddle over to town, nights, and slink around and pick up things I want. Jackson's Island's the place.

I was pretty tired, and the first thing I knowed, I was asleep. When I woke up I didn't know where I was, for a minute. I set up and looked around, a little scared. Then I remembered. The river looked miles and miles across. The moon was so bright I could a counted the drift logs that went a slipping along, black and still, hundreds of yards out from shore. Everything was dead quiet, and it looked late, and *smelt* late. You know what I mean—I don't know the words to put it in.

I took a good gap and a stretch, and was just going to unhitch and start, when I heard a sound away over the water. I listened. Pretty soon I made it out. It was that dull kind of a regular sound that comes from oars working in rowlocks when it's a still night. I peeped out through the willow branches, and there it was—a skiff, away across the water. I couldn't tell how many was in it. It kept a-coming, and when it was abreast of me I see there warn't but one man in it. Thinks I, maybe it's pap, though I warn't expecting him. He dropped below me, with the current, and by-and-by he come a-swinging up shore in the easy water,[5] and he went by so close I could a reached out the gun and touched him. Well, it *was* pap, sure enough—and sober, too, by the way he laid to his oars.

I didn't lose no time. The next minute I was a-spinning down stream soft but quick in the shade of the bank. I made two mile and a half, and then struck out a quarter of a mile or more towards the middle of the river, because pretty soon I would be passing the ferry landing and people might see me and hail me. I got out amongst the drift-wood and then laid down in the bottom of the canoe and let her float. I laid there and had a good rest and a smoke out of my pipe, looking away into the sky, not a cloud in it. The sky looks ever so deep when you lay down on your back in the moonshine; I never knowed it before. And how far a body can hear on the water such nights! I heard people talking at the ferry landing. I heard what they said, too, every word of it. One man said it was getting towards the

---

[4] An island to which Tom Sawyer, Joe Harper, and Huck sneak away in *Tom Sawyer*.
[5] With little current, hence easy for rowing.

long days and the short nights, now. 'Tother one said *this* warn't one of the short ones, he reckoned—and then they laughed, and he said it over again and they laughed again; then they waked up another fellow and told him, and laughed, but he didn't laugh; he ripped out something brisk and said let him alone. The first fellow said he 'lowed to tell it to his old woman—she would think it was pretty good; but he said that warn't nothing to some things he had said in his time. I heard one man say it was nearly three o'clock, and he hoped daylight wouldn't wait more than about a week longer. After that, the talk got further and further away, and I couldn't make out the words any more, but I could hear the mumble; and now and then a laugh, too, but it seemed a long ways off.

I was away below the ferry now. I rose up and there was Jackson's Island, about two mile and a half down stream, heavy-timbered and standing up out of the middle of the river, big and dark and solid, like a steamboat without any lights. There warn't any signs of the bar at the head—it was all under water, now.

It didn't take me long to get there. I shot past the head at a ripping rate, the current was so swift, and then I got into the dead water[6] and landed on the side towards the Illinois shore. I run the canoe into a deep dent in the bank that I knowed about; I had to part the willow branches to get in; and when I made fast nobody could a seen the canoe from the outside.

I went up and set down on a log at the head of the island and looked out on the big river and the black driftwood, and away over to the town, three mile away, where there was three or four lights twinkling. A monstrous big lumber raft was about a mile up stream, coming along down, with a lantern in the middle of it. I watched it come creeping down, and when it was most abreast of where I stood I heard a man say, "Stern oars, there! heave her head to stabboard!"[7] I heard that just as plain as if the man was by my side.

There was a little gray in the sky, now; so I stepped into the woods and laid down for a nap before breakfast.

Chapter VIII

The sun was up so high when I waked, that I judged it was after eight o'clock. I laid there in the grass and the cool shade, thinking about things and feeling rested and ruther comfortable and satisfied. I could see the sun out at one or two holes, but mostly it was big trees all about, and gloomy in there amongst them. There was freckled places on the ground where the light sifted down through the leaves, and the freckled places swapped about a little, showing there was a little breeze up there. A couple of squirrels set on a limb and jabbered at me very friendly.

I was powerful lazy and comfortable—didn't want to get up and cook breakfast. Well, I was dozing off again, when I thinks I hears a deep sound of "boom!" away up the river. I rouses up and rests on my elbow and listens; pretty soon I hears it again. I hopped up and went and looked out at a hole in the leaves, and I see a bunch of smoke laying on the water a long ways up—about abreast the ferry. And there was the ferry-boat full of people, floating along down. I knowed what was the matter, now. "Boom!" I see the white smoke squirt out of the ferry-boat's side. You see, they was firing cannon over the water, trying to make my carcass come to the top.

---

[6] With no current. Huck knows the river well.
[7] Starboard, the right-hand side when facing forward.

I was pretty hungry, but it warn't going to do for me to start a fire, because they might see the smoke. So I set there and watched the cannon-smoke and listened to the boom. The river was a mile wide, there, and it always looks pretty on a summer morning—so I was having a good enough time seeing them hunt for my remainders, if I only had a bite to eat. Well, then I happened to think how they always put quicksilver in loaves of bread and float them off because they always go right to the drownded carcass and stop there. So says I, I'll keep a lookout, and if any of them's floating around after me, I'll give them a show. I changed to the Illinois edge of the island to see what luck I could have, and I warn't disappointed. A big double loaf come along, and I most got it, with a long stick, but my foot slipped and she floated out further. Of course I was where the current set in the closest to the shore—I knowed enough for that. But by-and-by along comes another one, and this time I won. I took out the plug and shook out the little dab of quicksilver, and set my teeth in. It was "baker's bread"[1]—what the quality eat— none of your low-down corn-pone.

I got a good place amongst the leaves, and set there on a log, munching the bread and watching the ferry-boat, and very well satisfied. And then something struck me. I says, now I reckon the widow or the parson or somebody prayed that this bread would find me, and here it has gone and done it. So there ain't no doubt but there is something in that thing. That is, there's something in it when a body like the widow or the parson prays, but it don't work for me, and I reckon it don't work for only just the right kind.

I lit a pipe and had a good long smoke and went on watching. The ferry-boat was floating with the current, and I allowed I'd have a chance to see who was aboard when she come along, because she would come in close, where the bread did. When she'd got pretty well along down towards me, I put out my pipe and went to where I fished out the bread, and laid down behind a log on the bank in a little open place. Where the log forked I could peep through.

By-and-by she come along, and she drifted in so close that they could a run out a plank and walked ashore. Most everybody was on the boat. Pap, and Judge Thatcher, and Bessie Thatcher, and Jo Harper, and Tom Sawyer, and his old Aunt Polly, and Sid and Mary, and plenty more. Everybody was talking about the murder, but the captain broke in and says:

"Look sharp, now; the current sets in the closest here, and maybe he's washed ashore and got tangled amongst the brush at the water's edge. I hope so, anyway."

I didn't hope so. They all crowded up and leaned over the rails, nearly in my face, and kept still, watching with all their might. I could see them first-rate, but they couldn't see me. Then the captain sung out:

"Stand away!" and the cannon let off such a blast right before me that it made me deef with the noise and pretty near blind with the smoke, and I judged I was gone. If they'd a had some bullets in, I reckon they'd a got the corpse they was after. Well, I see I warn't hurt, thanks to goodness. The boat floated on and went out of sight around the shoulder of the island. I could hear the booming, now and then, further and further off, and by-and-by after an hour, I didn't hear it no more. The island was three mile long. I judged they had got to the foot, and was giving it up. But they didn't yet a while. They turned around the foot of the island and started up the channel on the Missouri side, under steam, and booming once in a

---

[1] White bread made from wheat flour, not corn bread.

while as they went. I crossed over to that side and watched them. When they got abreast the head of the island they quit shooting and dropped over to the Missouri shore and went home to the town.

I knowed I was all right now. Nobody else would come a-hunting after me. I got my traps out of the canoe and made me a nice camp in the thick woods. I made a kind of a tent out of my blankets to put my things under so the rain couldn't get at them. I catched a cat-fish and haggled him open with my saw, and towards sundown I started my camp fire and had supper. Then I set out a line to catch some fish for breakfast.

When it was dark I set by my camp fire smoking, and feeling pretty satisfied; but by-and-by it got sort of lonesome, and so I went and set on the bank and listened to the currents washing along, and counted the stars and drift-logs and rafts that come down, and then went to bed; there ain't no better way to put in time when you are lonesome; you can't stay so, you soon get over it.

And so for three days and nights. No difference—just the same thing. But the next day I went exploring around down through the island. I was boss of it; it all belonged to me, so to say, and I wanted to know all about it; but mainly I wanted to put in the time. I found plenty strawberries, ripe and prime; and green summer-grapes, and green razberries; and the green blackberries was just beginning to show. They would all come handy by-and-by, I judged.

Well, I went fooling along in the deep woods till I judged I warn't far from the foot of the island. I had my gun along, but I hadn't shot nothing; it was for protection; thought I would kill some game nigh home. About this time I mighty near stepped on a good sized snake, and it went sliding off through the grass and flowers, and I after it, trying to get a shot at it. I clipped along, and all of a sudden I bounded right on to the ashes of a camp fire that was still smoking.

My heart jumped up amongst my lungs. I never waited for to look further, but uncocked my gun and went sneaking back on my tip-toes as fast as ever I could. Every now and then I stopped a second, amongst the thick leaves, and listened; but my breath come so hard I couldn't hear nothing else. I slunk along another piece further, then listened again; and so on, and so on; if I see a stump, I took it for a man; if I trod on a stick and broke it, it made me feel like a person had cut one of my breaths in two and I only got half, and the short half, too.

When I got to camp I warn't feeling very brash, there warn't much sand in my craw;[2] but I says, this ain't no time to be fooling around. So I got all my traps into my canoe again so as to have them out of sight, and I put out the fire and scattered the ashes around to look like an old last year's camp, and then clumb a tree.

I reckon I was up in the tree two hours; but I didn't see nothing, I didn't hear nothing—I only *thought* I heard and seen as much as a thousand things. Well, I couldn't stay up there forever; so at last I got down, but I kept in the thick woods and on the lookout all the time. All I could get to eat was berries and what was left over from breakfast.

By the time it was night I was pretty hungry. So when it was good and dark, I slid out from shore before moonrise and paddled over to the Illinois bank—about a quarter of a mile. I went out in the woods and cooked a supper, and I had about made up my mind I would stay there all night, when I hear a *plunkety-plunk, plunkety-plunk,* and says to myself, horses coming; and next I hear people's

---

[2] Not much courage in my heart.

voices. I got everything into the canoe as quick as I could, and then went creeping through the woods to see what I could find out. I hadn't got far when I hear a man say:

"We better camp here, if we can find a good place; the horses is about beat out. Let's look around."

I didn't wait, but shoved out and paddled away easy. I tied up in the old place, and reckoned I would sleep in the canoe.

I didn't sleep much. I couldn't, somehow, for thinking. And every time I waked up I thought somebody had me by the neck. So the sleep didn't do me no good. By-and-by I says to myself, I can't live this way; I'm agoing to find out who it is that's here on the island with me; I'll find it out or bust. Well, I felt better, right off.

So I took my paddle and slid out from shore just a step or two, and then let the canoe drop along down amongst the shadows. The moon was shining, and outside of the shadows it made it most as light as day. I poked along well onto an hour, everything still as rocks and sound asleep. Well by this time I was most down to the foot of the island. A little ripply, cool breeze begun to blow, and that was as good as saying the night was about done. I give her a turn with the paddle and brung her nose to shore; then I got my gun and slipped out and into the edge of the woods. I set down there on a log and looked out through the leaves. I see the moon go off watch and the darkness begin to blanket the river. But in a little while I see a pale streak over the tree-tops, and knowed the day was coming. So I took my gun and slipped off towards where I had run across that camp fire, stopping every minute or two to listen. But I hadn't no luck, somehow; I couldn't seem to find the place. But by-and-by sure enough, I catched a glimpse of fire, away through the trees. I went for it, cautious and slow. By-and-by I was close enough to have a look, and there laid a man on the ground. It most give me the fan-tods.[3] He had a blanket around his head, and his head was nearly in the fire. I set there behind a clump of bushes, in about six foot of him, and kept my eyes on him steady. It was getting gray daylight, now. Pretty soon he gapped, and stretched himself, and hove off the blanket, and it was Miss Watson's Jim! I bet I was glad to see him. I says:

"Hello, Jim!" and skipped out.

He bounced up and stared at me wild. Then he drops down on his knees, and puts his hands together and says:

"Doan' hurt me—don't! I hain't ever done no harm to a ghos'. I awluz liked dead people, en done all I could for 'em. You go en git in de river agin, whah you b'longs, en doan' do nuffn to Ole Jim, 'at 'uz awluz yo' fren'."

Well, I warn't long making him understand I warn't dead. I was ever so glad to see Jim. I warn't lonesome, now. I told him I warn't afraid of *him* telling the people where I was. I talked along, but he only set there and looked at me; never said nothing. Then I says:

"It's good daylight. Le's get breakfast. Make up your camp fire good."

"What's de use er makin' up de camp fire to cook strawbries en sich truck? But you got a gun, hain't you? Den we kin git sumfn better den strawbries."

"Strawberries and such truck," I says. "Is that what you live on?"

"I couldn' git nuffn else," he says.

---

[3] The willies, the nervous fidgets.

"Why, how long you been on the island, Jim?"

"I come heah de night arter you's killed."

"What, all that time?"

"Yes-indeedy."

"And ain't you had nothing but that kind of rubbage to eat?"

"No, sah—nuffn else."

"Well, you must be most starved, ain't you?"

"I reck'n I could eat a hoss. I think I could. How long you ben on de islan'?"

"Since the night I got killed."

"No! W'y, what has you lived on? But you got a gun. Oh, yes, you got a gun. Dat's good. Now you kill sumfn en I'll make up de fire."

So we went over to where the canoe was, and while he built a fire in a grassy open place amongst the trees, I fetched meal and bacon and coffee, and coffee-pot and frying-pan, and sugar and tin cups, and the nigger was set back considerable, because he reckoned it was all done with witchcraft. I catched a good big cat-fish, too, and Jim cleaned him with his knife, and fried him.

When breakfast was ready, we lolled on the grass and eat it smoking hot. Jim laid it in with all his might, for he was most about starved. Then when we had got pretty well stuffed, we laid off and lazied.

By-and-by Jim says:

"But looky here, Huck, who wuz it dat 'uz killed in dat shanty, ef it warn't you?"

Then I told him the whole thing, and he said it was smart. He said Tom Sawyer couldn't get up no better plan than what I had. Then I says:

"How do you come to be here, Jim, and how'd you get here?"

He looked pretty uneasy, and didn't say nothing for a minute. Then he says:

"Maybe I better not tell."

"Why, Jim?"

"Well, dey's reasons. But you wouldn' tell on me ef I 'uz to tell you, would you, Huck?"

"Blamed if I would, Jim."

"Well, I b'lieve you, Huck. I—I *run off*."

"Jim!"

"But mind, you said you wouldn't tell—you know you said you wouldn't tell, Huck."

"Well, I did. I said I wouldn't, and I'll stick to it. Honest *injun* I will. People would call me a low down Ablitionist[4] and despise me for keeping mum—but that don't make no difference. I ain't agoing to tell, and I ain't agoing back there anyways. So now, le's know all about it."

"Well, you see, it 'uz dis way. Ole Missus—dat's Miss Watson—she pecks on me all de time, en treats me pooty rough, but she awluz said she wouldn' sell me down to Orleans. But I noticed dey wuz a nigger trader roun' de place considable, lately, en I begin to git oneasy. Well, one night I creeps to de do', pooty late, en de do' warn't quite shet, en I hear ole missus tell de widder she gwyne to sell me down to Orleans,[5] but she didn' want to, but she could git eight hund'd dollars for me, en it 'uz sich a big stack o' money she couldn' resis'. De widder she try to git

---

[4] Abolitionist.

[5] New Orleans; to be "sold down the river," separated from family, and sent to work as a field hand on a large plantation was a fate understandably feared by slaves.

her to say she wouldn' do it, but I never waited to hear de res'. I lit out mighty quick, I tell you.

"I tuck out en shin down de hill en 'spec to steal a skift 'long de sho' som'ers 'bove de town, but dey wuz people a-stirrin' yit, so I hid in de ole tumble-down cooper shop[6] on de bank to wait for everybody to go 'way. Well, I wuz dah all night. Dey wuz somebody roun' all de time. 'Long 'bout six in de mawnin', skifts begin to go by, en 'bout eight er nine every skift dat went 'long wuz talkin' 'bout how yo' pap come over to de town en say you's killed. Dese las' skifts wuz full o' ladies en genlmen agoin' over for to see de place. Sometimes dey'd pull up at de sho' en take a res' b'fo' dey started acrost, so by de talk I got to know all 'bout de killin'. I 'uz powerful sorry you's killed, Huck, but I ain't no mo', now.

"I laid dah under de shavins all day. I 'uz hungry, but I warn't afeard; bekase I knowed ole missus en de widder wuz goin' to start to de camp-meetn' right arter breakfas' en be gone all day, en dey knows I goes off wid de cattle 'bout daylight, so dey wouldn' 'spec to see me roun' de place, en so dey wouldn' miss me tell arter dark in de evenin'. De yuther servants wouldn' miss me, kase dey'd shin out en take holiday, soon as de ole folks 'uz out'n de way.

"Well, when it come dark I tuck out up de river road, en went 'bout two mile er more to whah dey warn't no houses. I'd made up my mine 'bout what I's agwyne to do. You see ef I kep' on tryin' to git away afoot, de dogs 'ud track me; ef I stole a skift to cross over, dey'd miss dat skift, you see, en dey'd know 'bout whah I'd lan' on de yuther side en whah to pick up my track. So I says, a raff is what I's arter; it doan' *make* no track.

"I see a light a-comin' roun' de p'int, bymeby, so I wade' in en shove' a log ahead o' me, en swum more'n half-way acrost de river, en got in 'mongst de drift-wood, en kep' my head down low, en kinder swum agin de current tell de raff come along. Den I swum to de stern uv it, en tuck aholt. It clouded up en 'uz pooty dark for a little while. So I clumb up en laid down on de planks. De men 'uz all 'way yonder in de middle, whah de lantern wuz. De river wuz arisin' en dey wuz a good current; so I reck'n'd 'at by fo' in de mawnin' I'd be twenty-five mile down de river, en den I'd slip in, jis' b'fo' daylight, en swim asho' en take to de woods on de Illinoi side.

"But I didn' have no luck. When we 'uz mos' down to de head er de islan', a man begin to come aft wid de lantern. I see it warn't no use fer to wait, so I slid overboard, en struck out fer de islan'. Well, I had a notion I could lan' mos' anywhers, but I couldn't—bank too bluff. I'uz mos' to de foot er de islan' b'fo' I foun' a good place. I went into de woods en jedged I wouldn' fool wid raffs no mo', long as dey move de lantern roun' so. I had my pipe en a plug er dog-leg,[7] en some matches in my cap, en dey warn't wet, so I 'uz all right."

"And so you ain't had no meat nor bread to eat all this time? Why didn't you get mud-turkles?"

"How you gwyne to git'm? You can't slip up on um en grab um; en how's a body gwyne to hit um wid a rock? How could a body do it in de night? en I warn't gwyne to show mysef on de bank in de daytime."

"Well, that's so. You've had to keep in the woods all the time, of course. Did you hear 'em shooting the cannon?"

---

[6] Barrel-maker's shop.
[7] Cheap leaf chewing tobacco, twisted into the shape of a dog's hind leg.

"Oh, yes. I knowed dey was arter you. I see um go by heah; watched um thoo de bushes."

Some young birds come along, flying a yard or two at a time and lighting. Jim said it was a sign it was going to rain. He said it was a sign when young chickens flew that way, and so he reckoned it was the same way when young birds done it. I was going to catch some of them, but Jim wouldn't let me. He said it was death. He said his father laid mighty sick once, and some of them catched a bird, and his old granny said his father would die, and he did.

And Jim said you musn't count the things you are going to cook for dinner, because that would bring bad luck. The same if you shook the table-cloth after sundown. And he said if a man owned a bee-hive, and that man died, the bees must be told about it before sun-up next morning, or else the bees would all weaken down and quit work and die. Jim said bees wouldn't sting idiots; but I didn't believe that, because I had tried them lots of times myself, and they wouldn't sting me.

I had heard about some of these things before, but not all of them. Jim knowed all kinds of signs. He said he knowed most everything. I said it looked to me like all the signs was about bad luck, and so I asked him if there warn't any good-luck signs. He says:

"Mighty few—an' *dey* ain' no use to a body. What you want to know when good luck's a-comin for? want to keep it off?" And he said: "Ef you's got hairy arms en a hairy breas', it's a sign dat you's agwyne to be rich. Well, dey's some use in a sign like dat, 'kase it's so fur ahead. You see, maybe you's got to be po' a long time fust, en so you might git discourage' en kill yo'sef 'f you didn' know by de sign dat you gwyne to be rich bymeby."

"Have you got hairy arms and a hairy breast, Jim?"

"What's de use to ax dat question? don' you see I has?"

"Well, are you rich?"

"No, but I ben rich wunst, and gwyne to be rich agin. Wunst I had foteen dollars, but I tuck to specalat'n', en got busted out."

"What did you speculate in, Jim?"

"Well, fust I tackled stock."

"What kind of stock?"

"Why, live stock. Cattle, you know. I put ten dollars in a cow. But I ain' gwyne to resk no mo' money in stock. De cow up 'n' died on my han's."

"So you lost the ten dollars."

"No, I didn' lose it all. I on'y los' 'bout nine of it. I sole de hide en taller[8] for a dollar en ten cents."

"You had five dollars and ten cents left. Did you speculate any more?"

"Yes. You know dat one-laigged nigger dat b'longs to old Misto Bradish? well, he sot up a bank, en say anybody dat put in a dollar would git fo' dollars mo' at de en' er de year. Well, all de niggers went in, but dey didn' have much. I wuz de on'y one dat had much. So I stuck out for mo' dan fo' dollars, en I said 'f I didn't git it I'd start a bank mysef. Well o' course dat nigger want' to keep me out er de business, bekase he say dey warn't business 'nough for two banks, so he say I could put in my five dollars en he pay me thirty-five at de en' er de year.

"So I done it. Den I reck'n'd I'd inves' de thirty-five dollars right off en keep

---

[8] Tallow.

things a-movin'. Dey wuz a nigger name' Bob, dat had ketched a wood-flat,[9] en his marster didn' know it; en I bought it off'n him en told him to take de thirty-five dollars when de en' er de year come; but somebody stole de wood-flat dat night, en nex' day de one-laigged nigger say de bank's busted. So dey didn' none uv us git no money."

"What did you do with the ten cents, Jim?"

"Well, I'uz gwyne to spen' it, but I had a dream, en de dream tole me to give it to a nigger name' Balum—Balum's Ass[10] dey call him for short, he's one er dem chuckle-heads, you know. But he's lucky, dey say, en I see I warn't lucky. De dream say let Balum inves' de ten cents en he'd make a raise for me. Well, Balum he tuck de money, en when he wuz in church he hear de preacher say dat whoever give to de po' len' to de Lord, en boun' to git his money back a hund'd times. So Balum he tuck en give de ten cents to de po,' en laid low to see what wuz gwyne to come of it."

"Well, what did come of it, Jim?"

"Nuffn' never come of it. I couldn' manage to k'leck dat money no way; en Balum he couldn'. I ain' gwyne to len' no mo' money 'dout I see de security. Boun' to git yo' money back a hund'd times, de preacher says! Ef I could git de ten *cents* back, I'd call it squah, en be glad er de chanst."

"Well, it's all right, anyway, Jim, long as you're going to be rich again some time or other."

"Yes—en I's rich now, come to look at it. I owns mysef, en I's wuth eight hund'd dollars. I wisht I had de money, I wouldn' want no mo'."

Chapter IX

I wanted to go and look at a place right about the middle of the island, that I'd found when I was exploring; so we started, and soon got to it, because the island was only three miles long and a quarter of a mile wide.

This place was a tolerable long steep hill or ridge, about forty foot high. We had a rough time getting to the top, the sides was so steep and the bushes so thick. We tramped and clumb around all over it, and by-and-by found a good big cavern in the rock, most up to the top on the side towards Illinois. The cavern was as big as two or three rooms bunched together, and Jim could stand up straight in it. It was cool in there. Jim was for putting our traps in there, right away, but I said we didn't want to be climbing up and down there all the time.

Jim said if we had the canoe hid in a good place, and had all the traps in the cavern, we could rush there if anybody was to come to the island, and they would never find us without dogs. And besides, he said them little birds had said it was going to rain, and did I want the things to get wet?

So we went back and got the canoe and paddled up abreast the cavern, and lugged all the traps up there. Then we hunted up a place close by to hide the canoe in, amongst the thick willows. We took some fish off of the lines and set them again, and begun to get ready for dinner.

---

[9] A flat-bottomed boat used for carrying wood. Jim makes a point that Bob's "marster didn' know it" because slaves were forbidden to own property; the ⟨m⟩arster" would have taken the boat.

[10] In Numbers 22:21–34 the biblical Balaam, bl⟨in⟩d ⟨t⟩o an angel's presence, was saved from destruction by the ass upon which he rode; here, Balaam is blin⟨d⟩ to anything but literal meaning.

The door of the cavern was big enough to roll a hogshead in, and on one side of the door the floor stuck out a little bit and was flat and a good place to build a fire on. So we built it there and cooked dinner.

We spread the blankets inside for a carpet, and eat our dinner in there. We put all the other things handy at the back of the cavern. Pretty soon it darkened up and begun to thunder and lighten; so the birds was right about it. Directly it begun to rain, and it rained like all fury, too, and I never see the wind blow so. It was one of these regular summer storms. It would get so dark that it looked all blue-black outside, and lovely; and the rain would thrash along by so thick that the trees off a little ways looked dim and spider-webby; and here would come a blast of wind that would bend the trees down and turn up the pale underside of the leaves; and then a perfect ripper of a gust would follow along and set the branches to tossing their arms as if they was just wild; and next, when it was just about the bluest and blackest—*fst!* it was as bright as glory and you'd have a little glimpse of tree-tops a-plunging about, away off yonder in the storm, hundreds of yards further than you could see before; dark as sin again in a second, and now you'd hear the thunder let go with an awful crash and then go rumbling, grumbling, tumbling down the sky towards the under side of the world, like rolling empty barrels down stairs, where it's long stairs and they bounce a good deal, you know.

"Jim, this is nice," I says. "I wouldn't want to be nowhere else but here. Pass me along another hunk of fish and some hot cornbread."

"Well, you wouldn't a ben here, 'f it hadn't a ben for Jim. You'd a ben down dah in de woods widout any dinner, en gittin' mos' drownded, too, dat you would, honey. Chickens knows when its gwyne to rain, en so do de birds, chile."

The river went on raising and raising for ten or twelve days, till at last it was over the banks. The water was three or four foot deep on the island in the low places and on the Illinois bottom. On that side it was a good many miles wide; but on the Missouri side it was the same old distance across—a half a mile—because the Missouri shore was just a wall of high bluffs.

Daytimes we paddled all over the island in the canoe. It was mighty cool and shady in the deep woods even if the sun was blazing outside. We went winding in and out amongst the trees; and sometimes the vines hung so thick we had to back away and go some other way. Well, on every old broken-down tree, you could see rabbits, and snakes, and such things; and when the island had been overflowed a day or two, they got so tame, on account of being hungry, that you could paddle right up and put your hand on them if you wanted to; but not the snakes and turtles—they would slide off in the water. The ridge our cavern was in, was full of them. We could a had pets enough if we'd wanted them.

One night we catched a little section of a lumber raft—nice pine planks. It was twelve foot wide and about fifteen or sixteen foot long, and the top stood above water six or seven inches, a solid level floor. We could see saw-logs[1] go by in the daylight, sometimes, but we let them go; we didn't show ourselves in daylight.

Another night, when we was up at the head of the island, just before daylight, here comes a frame house down, on the west side. She was a two-story, and tilted over, considerable. We paddled out and got aboard—clumb in at an up-stairs window. But it was too dark to see yet, so we made the canoe fast and set in her to wait for daylight.

---

[1] Logs that are split in preparation for sawing.

The light begun to come before we got to the foot of the island. Then we looked in at the window. We could make out a bed, and a table, and two old chairs, and lots of things around about on the floor; and there was clothes hanging against the wall. There was something laying on the floor in the far corner that looked like a man. So Jim says:

"Hello, you!"

But it didn't budge. So I hollered again, and then Jim says:

"De man ain't asleep—he's dead. You hold still—I'll go en see."

He went and bent down and looked, and says:

"It's a dead man. Yes, indeedy; naked, too. He's ben shot in de back. I reck'n he's ben dead two er three days. Come in, Huck, but doan' look at his face—it's too gashly."

I didn't look at him at all. Jim throwed some old rags over him, but he needn't done it; I didn't want to see him. There was heaps of old greasy cards scattered around over the floor, and old whisky bottles, and a couple of masks made out of black cloth; and all over the walls was the ignorantest kind of words and pictures, made with charcoal. There was two old dirty calico dresses, and a sun-bonnet, and some women's underclothes, hanging against the wall, and some men's clothing, too. We put the lot into the canoe; it might come good. There was a boy's old speckled straw hat on the floor; I took that too. And there was a bottle that had had milk in it; and it had a rag stopper for a baby to suck. We would a took the bottle, but it was broke. There was a seedy old chest, and an old hair trunk[2] with the hinges broke. They stood open, but there warn't nothing left in them that was any account. The way things was scattered about, we reckoned the people left in a hurry and warn't fixed so as to carry off most of their stuff.

We got an old tin lantern, and a butcher knife without any handle, and a bran-new Barlow knife[3] worth two bits in any store, and a lot of tallow candles, and a tin candlestick, and a gourd, and a tin cup, and a ratty old bed-quilt off the bed, and a reticule[4] with needles and pins and beeswax and buttons and thread and all such truck in it, and a hatchet and some nails, and a fish-line as thick as my little finger, with some monstrous hooks on it, and a roll of buckskin, and a leather dog-collar, and a horse-shoe, and some vials of medicine that didn't have no label on them; and just as we was leaving I found a tolerable good curry-comb,[5] and Jim he found a ratty old fiddle-bow, and a wooden leg. The straps was broke off of it, but barring that, it was good enough for Jim, and we couldn't find the other one, though we hunted all around.

And so, take it all around, we made a good haul. When we was ready to shove off, we was a quarter of a mile below the island, and it was pretty broad day; so I made Jim lay down in the canoe and cover up with the quilt, because if he set up, people could tell he was a nigger a good ways off. I paddled over to the Illinois shore, and drifted down most a half a mile doing it. I crept up the dead water under the bank, and hadn't no accidents and didn't see nobody. We got home all safe.

---

[2] A trunk covered with hides from which the hair has not been removed.
[3] An inexpensive jacknife named for its inventor, the eighteenth-century English knife-maker Russell Barlow.
[4] A woman's small handbag.
[5] A circular comb with rows of teeth, for grooming a horse's coat.

CHAPTER X

After breakfast I wanted to talk about the dead man and guess out how he come to be killed, but Jim didn't want to. He said it would fetch bad luck; and besides, he said, he might come and ha'nt us; he said a man that warn't buried was more likely to go a-ha'nting around than one that was planted and comfortable. That sounded pretty reasonable, so I didn't say no more; but I couldn't keep from studying over it and wishing I knowed who shot the man, and what they done it for.

We rummaged the clothes we'd got, and found eight dollars in silver sewed up in the lining of an old blanket overcoat. Jim said he reckoned the people in that house stole the coat, because if they'd a knowed the money was there they wouldn't a left it. I said I reckoned they killed him, too; but Jim didn't want to talk about that. I says:

"Now you think it's bad luck; but what did you say when I fetched in the snake-skin that I found on the top of the ridge day before yesterday? You said it was the worst bad luck in the world to touch a snake-skin with my hands. Well, here's your bad luck! We've raked in all this truck and eight dollars besides. I wish we could have some bad luck like this every day, Jim."

"Never you mind, honey, never you mind. Dont' you git too peart.[1] It's a-comin'. Mind I tell you, it's a-comin'."

It did come, too. It was a Tuesday that we had that talk. Well, after dinner Friday, we was laying around in the grass at the upper end of the ridge, and got out of tobacco. I went to the cavern to get some, and found a rattlesnake in there. I killed him, and curled him up on the foot of Jim's blanket, ever so natural, thinking there'd be some fun when Jim found him there. Well, by night I forgot all about the snake, and when Jim flung himself down on the blanket while I struck a light, the snake's mate was there, and bit him.

He jumped up yelling, and the first thing the light showed was the varmint curled up and ready for another spring. I laid him out in a second with a stick, and Jim grabbed pap's whisky jug and begun to pour it down.

He was barefooted, and the snake bit him right on the heel. That all comes of my being such a fool as to not remember that wherever you leave a dead snake its mate always comes there and curls around it. Jim told me to chop off the snake's head and throw it away, and then skin the body and roast a piece of it. I done it, and he eat it and said it would help cure him.[2] He made me take off the rattles and tie them around his wrist, too. He said that that would help. Then I slid out quiet and throwed the snakes clear away amongst the bushes; for I warn't going to let Jim find out it was all my fault, not if I could help it.

Jim sucked and sucked at the jug, and now and then he got out of his head and pitched around and yelled; but every time he come to himself he went to sucking at the jug again. His foot swelled up pretty big, and so did his leg; but by-and-by the drunk begun to come, and so I judged he was all right; but I'd druther been bit with a snake than pap's whisky.

Jim was laid up for four days and nights. Then the swelling was all gone and he was around again. I made up my mind I wouldn't ever take aholt of a snake-skin again with my hands, now that I see what had come of it. Jim said he reckoned I

---

[1] Smart.   [2] A traditional remedy in folk medicine.

would believe him next time. And he said that handling a snake-skin was such awful bad luck that maybe we hadn't got to the end of it yet. He said he druther see the new moon over his left shoulder as much as a thousand times than take up a snake-skin in his hand. Well, I was getting to feel that way myself, though I've always reckoned that looking at the new moon over your left shoulder is one of the carelessest and foolishest things a body can do. Old Hank Bunker done it once, and bragged about it; and in less than two years he got drunk and fell off of the shot tower and spread himself out so that he was just a kind of a layer, as you may say; and they slid him edgeways between two barn doors for a coffin, and buried him so, so they say, but I didn't see it. Pap told me. But anyway, it all come of looking at the moon that way, like a fool.

Well, the days went along, and the river went down between its banks again; and about the first thing we done was to bait one of the big hooks with a skinned rabbit and set it and catch a cat-fish that was as big as a man, being six foot two inches long, and weighed over two hundred pounds. We couldn't handle him, of course; he would a flung us into Illinois. We just set there and watched him rip and tear around till he drownded. We found a brass button in his stomach, and a round ball, and lots of rubbage. We split the ball open with the hatchet, and there was a spool in it. Jim said he'd had it there a long time, to coat it over so and make a ball of it. It was as big a fish as was ever catched in the Mississippi, I reckon. Jim said he hadn't ever seen a bigger one. He would a been worth a good deal over at the village. They peddle out such a fish as that by the pound in the market house there; everybody buys some of him; his meat's as white as snow and makes a good fry.

Next morning I said it was getting slow and dull, and I wanted to get a stirring up, some way. I said I reckoned I would slip over the river and find out what was going on. Jim liked that notion; but he said I must go in the dark and look sharp. Then he studied it over and said, couldn't I put on some of them old things and dress up like a girl? That was a good notion, too. So we shortened up one of the calico gowns and I turned up my trowser-legs to my knees and got into it. Jim hitched it behind with the hooks, and it was a fair fit. I put on the sun-bonnet and tied it under my chin, and then for a body to look in and see my face was like looking down a joint of stove-pipe. Jim said nobody would know me, even in the day-time, hardly. I practiced around all day to get the hang of things, and by-and-by I could do pretty well in them, only Jim said I didn't walk like a girl; and he said I must quit pulling up my gown to get at my britches pocket. I took notice, and done better.

I started up the Illinois shore in the canoe just after dark.

I started across to the town from a little below the ferry landing, and the drift of the current fetched me in at the bottom of the town. I tied up and started along the bank. There was a light burning in a little shanty that hadn't been lived in for a long time, and I wondered who had took up quarters there. I slipped up and peeped in at the window. There was a woman about forty year old in there, knitting by a candle that was on a pine table. I didn't know her face; she was a stranger, for you couldn't start[3] a face in that town that I didn't know. Now this was lucky, because I was weakening; I was getting afraid I had come; people might know my voice and find me out. But if this woman had been in such a little town two days she could tell me all I wanted to know; so I knocked at the door, and made up my mind I wouldn't forget I was a girl.

---

[3] Come across, find.

CHAPTER XI

"Come in," says the woman, and I did. She says:

"Take a cheer."

I done it. She looked me all over with her little shiny eyes, and says:

"What might your name be?"

"Sarah Williams."

"Where 'bouts do you live? In this neighborhood?"

"No'm. In Hookerville, seven mile below. I've walked all the way and I'm all tired out."

"Hungry, too, I reckon. I'll find you something."

"No'm, I ain't hungry. I was so hungry I had to stop two mile below here at a farm; so I ain't hungry no more. It's what makes me so late. My mother's down sick, and out of money and everything, and I come to tell my uncle Abner Moore. He lives at the upper end of the town, she says. I hain't ever been here before. Do you know him?"

"No; but I don't know everybody yet. I haven't lived here quite two weeks. It's a considerable ways to the upper end of the town. You better stay here all night. Take off your bonnet."

"No," I says, "I'll rest a while, I reckon, and go on. I ain't afeard of the dark."

She said she wouldn't let me go by myself, but her husband would be in by-and-by, maybe in a hour and a half, and she'd send him along with me. Then she got to talking about her husband, and about her relations up the river, and her relations down the river, and about how much better off they used to was, and how they didn't know but they'd made a mistake coming to our town, instead of letting well alone—and so on and so on, till I was afeard *I* had made a mistake coming to her to find out what was going on in the town; but by-and-by she dropped onto pap and the murder, and then I was pretty willing to let her clatter right along. She told about me and Tom Sawyer finding the six thousand dollars[1] (only she got it ten) and all about pap and what a hard lot he was, and what a hard lot I was, and at last she got down to where I was murdered. I says:

"Who done it? We've heard considerable about these goings on, down in Hookerville, but we don't know who 'twas that killed Huck Finn."

"Well, I reckon there's a right smart chance of[2] people *here* that'd like to know who killed him. Some thinks old Finn done it himself."

"No—is that so?"

"Most everybody thought it at first. He'll never know how nigh he come to getting lynched. But before night they changed around and judged it was done by a runaway nigger named Jim."

"Why *he*—"

I stopped. I reckoned I better keep still. She run on, and never noticed I had put in at all.

"The nigger run off the very night Huck Finn was killed. So there's a reward out for him—three hundred dollars. And there's a reward out for old Finn too—two hundred dollars. You see, he come to town the morning after the murder, and told about it, and was out with 'em on the ferry-boat hunt, and right away after he up and left. Before night they wanted to lynch him, but he was gone, you see.

---

[1] The money found by Tom and Huck in *Tom Sawyer* actually totaled $12,000, or $6,000 apiece.

[2] A good many.

Well, next day they found out the nigger was gone; they found out he hadn't ben seen sence ten o'clock the night the murder was done. So then they put it on him, you see, and while they was full of it, next day back comes old Finn and went boo-hooing to Judge Thatcher to get money to hunt for the nigger all over Illinois with. The judge give him some, and that evening he got drunk and was around till after midnight with a couple of mighty hard looking strangers, and then went off with them. Well, he hain't come back sence, and they ain't looking for him back till this thing blows over a little, for people thinks now that he killed his boy and fixed things so folks would think robbers done it, and then he'd get Huck's money without having to bother a long time with a lawsuit. People do say he warn't any too good to do it. Oh, he's sly, I reckon. If he don't come back for a year, he'll be all right. You can't prove anything on him, you know; everything will be quieted down then, and he'll walk into Huck's money as easy as nothing."

"Yes, I reckon so, 'm. I don't see nothing in the way of it. Has everybody quit thinking the nigger done it?"

"Oh, no, not everybody. A good many thinks he done it. But they'll get the nigger pretty soon, now, and maybe they can scare it out of him."

"Why, are they after him yet?"

"Well, you're innocent, ain't you! Does three hundred dollars lay round every day for people to pick up? Some folks thinks the nigger ain't far from here. I'm one of them—but I hain't talked it around. A few days ago I was talking with an old couple that lives next door in the log shanty, and they happened to say hardly anybody ever goes to that island over yonder that they call Jackson's Island. Don't anybody live there? says I. No, nobody, says they. I didn't say any more, but I done some thinking. I was pretty near certain I'd seen smoke over there, about the head of the island, a day or two before that, so I says to myself, like as not that nigger's hiding over there; anyway, says I, it's worth the trouble to give the place a hunt. I hain't seen any smoke sence, so I reckon maybe he's gone, if it was him; but husband's going over to see—him and another man. He was gone up the river; but he got back to-day and I told him as soon as he got here two hours ago."

I had got so uneasy I couldn't set still. I had to do something with my hands; so I took up a needle off of the table and went to threading it. My hands shook, and I was making a bad job of it. When the woman stopped talking, I looked up, and she was looking at me pretty curious, and smiling a little. I put down the needle and thread and let on to be interested—and I was, too—and says:

"Three hundred dollars is a power of money. I wish my mother could get it. Is your husband going over there to-night?"

"Oh, yes. He went up town with the man I was telling you of, to get a boat and see if they could borrow another gun. They'll go over after midnight."

"Couldn't they see better if they was to wait till daytime?"

"Yes. And couldn't the nigger see better, too? After midnight he'll likely be asleep, and they can slip around through the woods and hunt up his camp fire all the better for the dark, if he's got one."

"I didn't think of that."

The woman kept looking at me pretty curious, and I didn't feel a bit comfortable. Pretty soon she says:

"What did you say your name was, honey?"

"M—Mary Williams."

Somehow it didn't seem to me that I said it was Mary before, so I didn't look up; seemed to me I said it was Sarah; so I felt sort of cornered, and was afeared maybe I was looking it, too. I wished the woman would say something more; the longer she set still, the uneasier I was. But now she says:

"Honey, I thought you said it was Sarah when you first come in?"

"Oh, yes'm, I did. Sarah Mary Williams. Sarah's my first name. Some calls me Sarah, some calls me Mary."

"Oh, that's the way of it?"

"Yes'm."

I was feeling better, then, but I wished I was out of there, anyway. I couldn't look up yet.

Well, the woman fell to talking about how hard times was, and how poor they had to live, and how the rats was as free as if they owned the place, and so forth, and so on, and then I got easy again. She was right about the rats. You'd see one stick his nose out of a hole in the corner every little while. She said she had to have things handy to throw at them when she was alone, or they wouldn't give her no peace. She showed me a bar of lead, twisted up into a knot, and said she was a good shot with it generly, but she'd wrenched her arm a day or two ago, and didn't know whether she could throw true, now. But she watched for a chance, and directly she banged away at a rat, but she missed him wide, and said "Ouch!" it hurt her arm so. Then she told me to try for the next one. I wanted to be getting away before the old man got back, but of course I didn't let on. I got the thing, and the first rat that showed his nose I let drive, and if he'd a stayed where he was he'd a been a tolerable sick rat. She said that that was first-rate, and she reckoned I would hive[3] the next one. She went and got the lump of lead and fetched it back and brought along a hank of yarn, which she wanted me to help her with. I held up my two hands and she put the hank over them and went on talking about her and her husband's matters. But she broke off to say:

"Keep your eye on the rats. You better have the lead in your lap, handy."

So she dropped the lump into my lap, just at that moment, and I clapped my legs together on it and she went on talking. But only about a minute. Then she took off the hank and looked me straight in the face, but very pleasant, and says:

"Come, now—what's your real name?"

"Wh-what, mum?"

"What's your real name? Is it Bill, or Tom, or Bob?—or what is it?"

I reckon I shook like a leaf, and I didn't know hardly what to do. But I says:

"Please to don't poke fun at a poor girl like me, mum. If I'm in the way, here, I'll—"

"No, you won't. Set down and stay where you are. I ain't going to hurt you, and I ain't going to tell on you, nuther. You just tell me your secret, and trust me. I'll keep it; and what's more, I'll help you. So'll my old man, if you want him to. You see, you're a runaway 'prentice—that's all. It ain't anything. There ain't any harm in it. You've been treated bad, and you made up your mind to cut. Bless you, child, I wouldn't tell on you. Tell me all about it, now—that's a good boy."

So I said it wouldn't be no use to try to play it any longer, and I would just make a clean breast and tell her everything, but she mustn't go back on her promise. Then I told her my father and mother was dead, and the law had bound me out to[4] a mean old farmer in the country thirty mile back from the river, and he treated me so bad I couldn't stand it no longer; he went away to be gone a couple of days, and so I took my chance and stole some of his daughter's old clothes, and cleared

---

[3] Hit.   [4] Put me in the legal custody of.

out, and I had been three nights coming the thirty miles; I traveled nights, and hid day-times and slept, and the bag of bread and meat I carried from home lasted me all the way and I had a plenty. I said I believed my uncle Abner Moore would take care of me, and so that was why I struck out for this town of Goshen."

"Goshen, child? This ain't Goshen. This is St. Petersburg. Goshen's ten mile further up the river. Who told you this was Goshen?"

"Why, a man I met at day-break this morning, just as I was going to turn into the woods for my regular sleep. He told me when the roads forked I must take the right hand, and five mile would fetch me to Goshen."

"He was drunk I reckon. He told you just exactly wrong."

"Well, he did act like he was drunk, but it ain't no matter now. I got to be moving along. I'll fetch Goshen before daylight."

"Hold on a minute. I'll put you up a snack to eat. You might want it."

So she put me up a snack, and says:

"Say—when a cow's laying down, which end of her gets up first? Answer up prompt, now—don't stop to study over it. Which end gets up first?"

"The hind end, mum."

"Well, then, a horse?"

"The for'rard end, mum."

"Which side of a tree does the most moss grow on?"

"North side."

"If fifteen cows is browsing on a hillside, how many of them eats with their heads pointed the same direction?"

"The whole fifteen, mum."

"Well, I reckon you *have* lived in the country. I thought maybe you was trying to hocus me again. What's your real name, now?"

"George Peters, mum."

"Well, try to remember it, George. Don't forget and tell me it's Elexander before you go, and then get out by saying it's George-Elexander when I catch you. And don't go about women in that old calico. You do a girl tolerable poor, but you might fool men, maybe. Bless you, child, when you set out to thread a needle, don't hold the thread still and fetch the needle up to it; hold the needle still and poke the thread at it—that's the way a woman most always does; but a man always does 'tother way. And when you throw at a rat or anything, hitch yourself up a tip-toe, and fetch your hand up over your head as awkard as you can, and miss your rat about six or seven foot. Throw stiff-armed from the shoulder, like there was a pivot there for it to turn on—like a girl; not from the wrist and elbow, with your arm out to one side, like a boy. And mind you, when a girl tries to catch anything in her lap, she throws her knees apart: she don't clap them together, the way you did when you catched the lump of lead. Why, I spotted you for a boy when you was threading the needle; and I contrived the other things just to make certain. Now trot along to your uncle, Sarah Mary Williams George Elexander Peters, and if you get into trouble you send word to Mrs. Judith Loftus, which is me, and I'll do what I can to get you out of it. Keep the river road, all the way, and next time you tramp, take shoes and socks with you. The river road's a rocky one, and your feet'll be in a condition when you get to Goshen, I reckon."

I went up the bank about fifty yards, and then I doubled on my tracks and slipped back to where my canoe was, a good piece below the house. I jumped in and was off in a hurry. I went up stream far enough to make the head of the island, and then started across. I took off the sun-bonnet, for I didn't want no blinders on, then. When I was about the middle, I hear the clock begin to strike; so I stops and listens; the sound come faint over the water, but clear—eleven. When I struck the head of the island I never waited to blow, though I was most winded, but I shoved right into the timber where my old camp used to be, and started a good fire there on a high-and-dry spot.

Then I jumped in the canoe and dug out for our place a mile and a half below, as hard as I could go. I landed, and slopped through the timber and up the ridge and into the cavern. There Jim laid, sound asleep on the ground. I roused him out and says:

"Git up and hump yourself, Jim! There ain't a minute to lose. They're after us!"

Jim never asked no questions, he never said a word; but the way he worked for the next half an hour showed about how he was scared. By that time everything we had in the world was on our raft and she was ready to be shoved out from the willow cove where she was hid. We put out the camp fire at the cavern the first thing, and didn't show a candle outside after that.

I took the canoe out from shore a little piece and took a look, but if there was a boat around I couldn't see it, for stars and shadows ain't good to see by. Then we got out the raft and slipped along down in the shade, past the foot of the island dead still, never saying a word.

CHAPTER XII

It must a been close onto one o'clock when we got below the island at last, and the raft did seem to go mighty slow. If a boat was to come along, we was going to take to the canoe and break for the Illinois shore; and it was well a boat didn't come, for we hadn't ever thought to put the gun into the canoe, or a fishing-line or anything to eat. We was in ruther too much of a sweat to think of so many things. It warn't good judgment to put *everything* on the raft.

If the men went to the island, I just expect they found the camp fire I built, and watched it all night for Jim to come. Anyways, they stayed away from us, and if my building the fire never fooled them it warn't no fault of mine. I played it as low-down on them as I could.

When the first streak of day begun to show, we tied up to a tow-head in a big bend on the Illinois side, and hacked off cotton-wood branches with the hatchet and covered up the raft with them so she looked like there had been a cave-in in the bank there. A tow-head is a sand-bar that has cotton-woods on it as thick as harrow-teeth.[1]

We had mountains on the Missouri shore and heavy timber on the Illinois side, and the channel was down the Missouri shore at that place, so we warn't afraid of anybody running across us. We laid there all day and watched the rafts and steamboats spin down the Missouri shore, and up-bound steamboats fight the big river in the middle. I told Jim all about the time I had jabbering with that woman; and Jim said she was a smart one, and if she was to start after us herself *she* wouldn't set down and watch a camp fire—no sir, she'd fetch a dog. Well, then, I said, why couldn't she tell her husband to fetch a dog? Jim said he bet she did think of it by the time the men was ready to start, and he believed they must a gone up town

---

[1] As teeth on a rake.

to get a dog and so they lost all that time, or else we wouldn't be here on a tow-head sixteen or seventeen mile below the village—no, indeedy, we would be in that same old town again. So I said I didn't care what was the reason they didn't get us, as long as they didn't.

When it was beginning to come on dark, we poked our heads out of the cotton-wood thicket and looked up, and down, and across; nothing in sight; so Jim took up some of the top planks of the raft and built a snug wigwam to get under in blazing weather and rainy, and to keep the things dry. Jim made a floor for the wigwam, and raised it a foot or more above the level of the raft, so now the blankets and all the traps was out of the reach of steamboat waves. Right in the middle of the wigwam we made a layer of dirt about five or six inches deep with a frame around it for to hold it to its place; this was to build a fire on in sloppy weather or chilly; the wigwam would keep it from being seen. We made an extra steering oar, too, because one of the others might get broke, on a snag or something. We fixed up a short forked stick to hang the old lantern on; because we must always light the lantern whenever we see a steamboat coming down stream, to keep from getting run over; but we wouldn't have to light it for up-stream boats unless we see we was in what they call a "crossing;" for the river was pretty high yet, very low banks being still a little under water; so up-bound boats didn't always run the channel, but hunted easy water.

This second night we run between seven and eight hours, with a current that was making over four mile an hour. We catched fish, and talked, and we took a swim now and then to keep off sleepiness. It was kind of solemn, drifting down the big still river, laying on our backs looking up at the stars, and we didn't ever feel like talking out loud, and it warn't often that we laughed, only a little kind of a low chuckle. We had mighty good weather, as a general thing, and nothing ever happened to us at all, that night, nor the next, nor the next.

Every night we passed towns, some of them away up on black hillsides, nothing but just a shiny bed of lights, not a house could you see. The fifth night we passed St. Louis,[2] and it was like the whole world lit up. In St. Petersburg they used to say there was twenty or thirty thousand people in St. Louis, but I never believed it till I see that wonderful spread of lights at two o'clock that still night. There warn't a sound there; everybody was asleep.

Every night, now, I used to slip ashore, towards ten o'clock, at some little village, and buy ten or fifteen cents' worth of meal or bacon or other stuff to eat; and sometimes I lifted a chicken that warn't roosting comfortable, and took him along. Pap always said, take a chicken when you get a chance, because if you don't want him yourself you can easy find somebody that does, and a good deed ain't ever forgot. I never see pap when he didn't want the chicken himself, but that is what he used to say, anyway.

Mornings, before daylight, I slipped into corn fields and borrowed a water-melon, or a mushmelon, or a punkin, or some new corn, or things of that kind. Pap always said it warn't no harm to borrow things, if you was meaning to pay them back, sometime; but the widow said it warn't anything but a soft name for stealing, and no decent body would do it. Jim said he reckoned the widow was partly right and pap was partly right; so the best way would be for us to pick out two or three things from the list and say we wouldn't borrow them any more—

---

[2] Almost one hundred and seventy miles down river from where they began their journey.

then he reckoned it wouldn't be no harm to borrow the others. So we talked it over all one night, drifting along down the river, trying to make up our minds whether to drop the watermelons, or the cantelopes, or the mushmelons, or what. But towards daylight we got it all settled satisfactory, and concluded to drop crab-apples and p'simmons. We warn't feeling just right, before that, but it was all comfortable now. I was glad the way it come out, too, because crabapples ain't ever good, and the p'simmons wouldn't be ripe for two or three months yet.

We shot a water-fowl, now and then, that got up too early in the morning or didn't go to bed early enough in the evening. Take it all around, we lived pretty high.

The fifth night below St. Louis we had a big storm after midnight, with a power of thunder and lightning, and the rain poured down in a solid sheet. We stayed in the wigwam and let the raft take care of itself. When the lightning glared out we could see a big straight river ahead, and high rocky bluffs on both sides. By-and-by says I, "Hel-*lo*, Jim, looky yonder!" It was a steamboat that had killed herself on a rock. We was drifting straight down for her. The lightning showed her very distinct. She was leaning over, with part of her upper deck above water, and you could see every little chimbly-guy[3] clean and clear, and a chair by the big bell, with an old slouch hat hanging on the back of it when the flashes come.

Well, it being away in the night, and stormy, and all so mysterious-like, I felt just the way any other boy would a felt when I see that wreck laying there so mournful and lonesome in the middle of the river. I wanted to get aboard of her and slink around a little, and see what there was there. So I says:

"Le's land on her, Jim."

But Jim was dead against it, at first. He says:

"I doan' want to go fool'n 'long er no wrack. We's doin' blame' well, en we better let blame' well alone, as de good book says. Like as not dey's a watchman on dat wrack."

"Watchman your grandmother," I says; "there ain't nothing to watch but the texas[4] and the pilot-house; and do you reckon anybody's going to resk his life for a texas and a pilot-house such a night as this, when it's likely to break up and wash off down the river any minute?" Jim couldn't say nothing to that, so he didn't try. "And besides," I says, "we might borrow something worth having, out of the captain's stateroom. Seegars, *I* bet you—and cost five cents apiece, solid cash. Steamboat captains is always rich, and get sixty dollars a month, and *they* don't care a cent what a thing costs, you know, long as they want it. Stick a candle in your pocket; I can't rest, Jim, till we give her a rummaging. Do you reckon Tom Sawyer would ever go by this thing? Not for pie, he wouldn't. He'd call it an adventure—that's what he'd call it; and he'd land on that wreck if it was his last act. And wouldn't he throw style into it?—wouldn't he spread himself, nor nothing? Why, you'd think it was Christopher C'lumbus discovering Kingdom-Come. I wish Tom Sawyer *was* here."

Jim he grumbled a little, but give in. He said we mustn't talk any more than we could help, and then talk mighty low. The lightning showed us the wreck again, just in time, and we fetched the starboard derrick,[5] and made fast there.

---

[3] Wires that brace smoke stacks.
[4] The largest cabin on the top deck of a steamboat, which serves as the officers' quarters.
[5] A beam for loading and unloading cargo.

The deck was high out, here. We went sneaking down the slope of it to lab-board,[6] in the dark, towards the texas, feeling our way slow with our feet, and spreading our hands out to fend off the guys, for it was so dark we couldn't see no sign of them. Pretty soon we struck the forward end of the skylight, and clumb onto it; and the next step fetched us in front of the captain's door, which was open, and by Jimminy, away down through the texas-hall we see a light! and all in the same second we seem to hear low voices in yonder!

Jim whispered and said he was feeling powerful sick, and told me to come along. I says, all right; and was going to start for the raft; but just then I heard a voice wail out and say:

"Oh, please don't, boys; I swear I won't ever tell!"

Another voice said, pretty loud:

"It's a lie, Jim Turner. You've acted this way before. You always want more'n your share of the truck, and you've always got it, too, because you've swore 't if you didn't you'd tell. But this time you've said it jest one time too many. You're the meanest, treacherousest hound in this country."

By this time Jim was gone for the raft. I was just a-biling with curiosity; and I says to myself, Tom Sawyer wouldn't back out now, and so I won't either; I'm agoing to see what's going on here. So I dropped on my hands and knees, in the little passage, and crept aft in the dark, till there warn't but about one stateroom betwixt me and the cross-hall of the texas. Then, in there I see a man stretched on the floor and tied hand and foot, and two men standing over him, and one of them had a dim lantern in his hand, and the other one had a pistol. This one kept point-ing the pistol at the man's head on the floor and saying—

"I'd *like* to! And I order, too, a mean skunk!"

The man on the floor would shrivel up, and say: "Oh, please don't, Bill—I hain't ever goin' to tell."

And every time he said that, the man with the lantern would laugh, and say:

"'Deed you *ain't!* You never said no truer thing 'n that, you bet you." And once he said: "Hear him beg! and yit if we hadn't got the best of him and tied him, he'd a killed us both. And what *for*? Jist for noth'n. Jist because we stood on our *rights*—that's what for. But I lay you ain't agoin' to threaten nobody any more, Jim Turner. Put *up* that pistol, Bill."

Bill says:

"I don't want to, Jake Packard. I'm for killin' him—and didn't he kill old Hatfield jist the same way—and don't he deserve it?"

"But I don't *want* him killed, and I've got my reasons for it."

"Bless yo' heart for them words, Jake Packard! I'll never forget you, long's I live!" says the man on the floor, sort of blubbering.

Packard didn't take no notice of that, but hung up his lantern on a nail, and started towards where I was, there in the dark, and motioned Bill to come. I craw-fished[7] as fast as I could, about two yards, but the boat slanted so that I couldn't make very good time; so to keep from getting run over and catched I crawled into a stateroom on the upper side. The man come a-pawing along in the dark, and when Packard got to my stateroom, he says:

"Here—come in here."

And in he come, and Bill after him. But before they got in, I was up in the upper berth, cornered, and sorry I come. Then they stood there, with their hands

---

[6] Larboard, the left side of a boat when facing forward.   [7] Crawled backward on all fours.

on the ledge of the berth, and talked. I couldn't see them, but I could tell where they was, by the whisky they'd been having. I was glad I didn't drink whisky; but it wouldn't made much difference, anyway, because most of the time they couldn't a treed me because I didn't breathe. I was too scared. And besides, a body *couldn't* breathe, and hear such talk. They talked low and earnest. Bill wanted to kill Turner. He says:

"He's said he'll tell, and he will. If we was to give both our shares to him *now,* it wouldn't make no difference after the row, and the way we've served him. Shore's you're born, he'll turn State's evidence; now you hear *me.* I'm for putting him out of his troubles."

"So'm I," says Packard, very quiet.

"Blame it, I'd sorter begun to think you wasn't. Well, then, that's all right. Les' go and do it."

"Hold on a minute; I hain't had my say yit. You listen to me. Shooting's good, but there's quieter ways if the thing's *got* to be done. But what *I* say, is this; it ain't good sense to go court'n around after a halter,[8] if you can git at what you're up to in some way that's jist as good and at the same time don't bring you into no resks. Ain't that so?"

"You bet it is. But how you goin' to manage it this time?"

"Well, my idea is this: we'll rustle around and gether up whatever pickins we've overlooked in the staterooms, and shove for shore and hide the truck. Then we'll wait. Now I say it ain't agoin' to be more 'n two hours befo' this wrack breaks up and washes off down the river. See? He'll be drownded, and won't have nobody to blame for it but his own self. I reckon that's a considerble sight better'n killin' of him. I'm unfavorable to killin' a man as long as you can git around it; it ain't good sense, it ain't good morals. Ain't I right?"

"Yes—I reck'n you are. But s'pose she *don't* break up and wash off?"

"Well, we can wait the two hours anyway, and see, can't we?"

"All right, then; come along."

So they started, and I lit out, all in a cold sweat, and scrambled forward. It was dark as pitch there; but I said in a kind of a coarse whisper, "Jim!" and he answered up, right at my elbow, with a sort of a moan, and I says:

"Quick, Jim, it ain't no time for fooling around and moaning; there's a gang of murderers in yonder, and if we don't hunt up their boat and set her drifting down the river so these fellows can't get away from the wreck, there's one of 'em going to be in a bad fix. But if we find their boat we can put *all* of 'em in a bad fix—for the Sheriff 'll get 'em. Quick—hurry! I'll hunt the labboard side, you hunt the stabboard. You start at the raft, and—"

"Oh, my lordy, lordy! *Raf'?* Dey ain' no raf' no mo', she done broke loose en gone!—'en here we is!"

CHAPTER XIII

Well, I catched my breath and most fainted. Shut up on a wreck with such a gang as that! But it warn't no time to be sentimentering. We'd *got* to find that boat, now—had to have it for ourselves. So we went a-quaking and shaking down the stabboard side, and slow work it was, too—seemed a week before we got to the

---

[8] A hangman's noose.

stern. No sign of a boat. Jim said he didn't believe he could go any further—so scared he hadn't hardly any strength left, he said. But I said come on, if we get left on this wreck, we are in a fix, sure. So on we prowled, again. We struck for the stern of the texas, and found it, and then scrabbled along forwards on the skylight, hanging on from shutter to shutter, for the edge of the skylight was in the water. When we got pretty close to the cross-hall door, there was the skiff, sure enough! I could just barely see her. I felt ever so thankful. In another second I would a been aboard of her; but just then the door opened. One of the men stuck his head out, only about a couple of foot from me, and I thought I was gone; but he jerked it in again, and says:

"Heave that blame lantern out o' sight, Bill!"

He flung a bag of something into the boat, and then got in himself, and set down. It was Packard. Then Bill *he* come out and got in. Packard says, in a low voice:

"All ready—shove off!"

I couldn't hardly hang onto the shutters, I was so weak. But Bill says:

"Hold on—'d you go through him?"

"No. Didn't you?"

"No. So he's got his share o' the cash, yet."

"Well, then, come along—no use to take truck and leave money."

"Say—won't he suspicion what we're up to?"

"Maybe he won't. But we got to have it anyway. Come along."

So they got out and went in.

The door slammed to, because it was on the careened side; and in a half second I was in the boat, and Jim come a tumbling after me. I out with my knife and cut the rope, and away we went!

We didn't touch an oar, and we didn' speak nor whisper, nor hardly even breathe. We went gliding swift along, dead silent, past the tip of the paddle-box, and past the stern; then in a second or two more we was a hundred yards below the wreck, and the darkness soaked her up, every last sign of her, and we was safe, and knowed it.

When we was three or four hundred yards down stream, we see the lantern show like a little spark at the texas door, for a second, and we knowed by that that the rascals had missed their boat, and was beginning to understand that they was in just as much trouble, now, as Jim Turner was.

Then Jim manned the oars, and we took out after our raft. Now was the first time that I begun to worry about the men—I reckon I hadn't had time to before. I begun to think how dreadful it was, even for murderers, to be in such a fix. I says to myself, there ain't no telling but I might come to be a murderer myself, yet, and then how would *I* like it? So says I to Jim:

"The first light we see, we'll land a hundred yards below it or above it, in a place where it's a good hiding-place for you and the skiff, and then I'll go and fix up some kind of a yarn, and get somebody to go for that gang and get them out of their scrape, so they can be hung when their time comes."

But that idea was a failure; for pretty soon it begun to storm again, and this time worse than ever. The rain poured down, and never a light showed; everybody in bed, I reckon. We boomed along down the river, watching for lights and watching for our raft. After a long time the rain let up, but the clouds staid, and the lightning kept whimpering, and by-and-by a flash showed us a black thing ahead, floating, and we made for it.

It was the raft, and mighty glad was we to get aboard of it again. We seen a light, now, away down to the right, on shore. So I said I would go for it. The skiff was half full of plunder which that gang had stole, there on the wreck. We hustled it onto the raft in a pile, and I told Jim to float along down, and show a light when he judged he had gone about two mile, and keep it burning till I come; then I manned my oars and shoved for the light. As I got down towards it, three or four more showed—up on a hillside. It was a village. I closed in above the shore-light, and laid on my oars and floated. As I went by, I see it was a lantern hanging on the jackstaff of a double-hull ferry-boat. I skimmed around for the watchman, a-wondering whereabouts he slept; and by-and-by I found him roosting on the bitts,[1] forward, with his head down between his knees. I give his shoulder two or three little shoves, and begun to cry.

He stirred up, in a kind of a startlish way; when he see it was only me, he took a good gap and stretch, and then he says:

"Hello, what's up? Don't cry, bub. What's the trouble?"

I says:

"Pap, and mam, and sis, and—"

Then I broke down. He says:

"Oh, dang it, now, *don't* take on so, we all has to have our troubles and this'n'll come out all right. What's the matter with 'em?"

"They're—they're—are you the watchman of the boat?"

"Yes," he says, kind of pretty-well-satisfied like. "I'm the captain and the owner, and the mate, and the pilot, and watchman, and head deck-hand; and sometimes I'm the freight and passengers. I ain't as rich as old Jim Hornback, and I can't be so blame' generous and good to Tom, Dick and Harry as what he is, and slam around money the way he does; but I've told him a many a time 't I wouldn't trade places with him; for, says I, a sailor's life's the life for me, and I'm derned if *I'd* live two mile out o' town, where there ain't nothing ever goin' on, not for all his spondulicks[2] and as much more on top of it. Says I—"

I broke in and says:

"They're in an awful peck of trouble, and—"

"*Who* is?"

"Why, pap, and mam, and sis, and Miss Hooker; and if you'd take your ferry-boat and go up there—"

"Up where? Where are they?"

"On the wreck."

"What wreck?"

"Why, there ain't but one."

"What, you don't mean the *Walter Scott?*"[3]

"Yes."

"Good land! what are they doin' *there,* for gracious sakes?"

"Well, they didn't go there a-purpose."

"I bet they didn't. Why, great goodness, there ain't no chance for 'em if they

---

[1] Posts, attached to a deck, to which lines can be secured.   [2] Wealth, riches.
[3] The wrecked steamboat is named after Sir Walter Scott (1771–1832), a British novelist and poet whose work Twain disliked even more than he disliked that of James Fenimore Cooper. Twain felt that Scott's romances set in feudal England helped to feed beguiling notions of chivalry that were harmful to the American South. "The Sir Walter disease," he wrote in Ch. XLVI of *Life on the Mississippi* (1883) "was in a great measure responsible" for the Civil War.

don't git off mighty quick! Why, how in the nation did they ever git into such a scrape?"

"Easy enough. Miss Hooker was a-visiting, up there to the town—"

"Yes, Booth's Landing—go on."

"She was a-visiting, there at Booth's Landing, and just in the edge of the evening she started over with her nigger woman in the horse-ferry,[4] to stay all night at her friend's house, Miss What-you-may-call-her, I disremember her name, and they lost their steering-oar, and swung around and went a-floating down, stern-first, about two mile, and saddle-baggsed[5] on the wreck, and the ferry man and the nigger woman and the horses was all lost, but Miss Hooker she made a grab and got aboard the wreck. Well, about an hour after dark, we come along down in our trading-scow,[6] and it was so dark we didn't notice the wreck till we was right on it; and so *we* saddle-baggsed; but all of us was saved but Bill Whipple—and oh, he *was* the best cretur!—I most wish't it had been me, I do."

"My George! It's the beatenest thing I ever struck. And *then* what did you all do?"

"Well, we hollered and took on, but it's so wide there, we couldn't make nobody hear. So pap said somebody got to get ashore and get help somehow. I was the only one that could swim, so I made a dash for it, and Miss Hooker she said if I didn't strike help sooner, come here and hunt up her uncle, and he'd fix the thing. I made the land about a mile below, and been fooling along ever since, trying to get people to do something, but they said, 'What, in such a night and such a current? there ain't no sense in it; go for the steam-ferry.' Now if you'll go, and—"

"By Jackson, I'd *like* to, and blame it I don't know but I will; but who in the dingnation's agoin' to *pay* for it? Do you reckon your pap—"

"Why *that's* all right. Miss Hooker she told me, *particular,* that her uncle Hornback—"

"Great guns! is *he* her uncle? Looky here, you break for that light over yonder-way, and turn out west when you git there, and about a quarter of a mile out you'll come to the tavern; tell 'em to dart you out to Jim Hornback's and he'll foot the bill. And don't you fool around any, because he'll want to know the news. Tell him I'll have his niece all safe before he can get to town. Hump yourself, now; I'm agoing up around the corner here, to roust out my engineer."

I struck for the light, but as soon as he turned the corner I went back and got into my skiff and bailed her out and then pulled up shore in the easy water about six hundred yards, and tucked myself in among some woodboats; for I couldn't rest easy till I could see the ferry-boat start. But take it all around, I was feeling ruther comfortable on accounts of taking all this trouble for that gang, for not many would a done it. I wished the widow knowed about it. I judged she would be proud of me for helping these rapscallions, because rapscallions and dead beats is the kind the widow and good people takes the most interest in.

Well, before long, here comes the wreck, dim and dusky, sliding along down! A kind of cold shiver went through me, and then I struck out for her. She was very deep, and I see in a minute there warn't much chance for anybody being alive in

---

[4] A ferry large enough to carry horses and wagons.

[5] Wrapped around the wreck, like saddlebags on a horse.

[6] A flat-bottomed cargo boat. Huck continues to invent detailed stories to save lives—his own, Jim's, and here those of the men on the *Walter Scott.*

her. I pulled all around her and hollered a little, but there wasn't any answer; all dead still. I felt a little bit heavy-hearted about the gang, but not much, for I reckoned if they could stand it, I could.

Then here comes the ferry-boat; so I shoved for the middle of the river on a long down-stream slant; and when I judged I was out of eye-reach, I laid on my oars, and looked back and see her go and smell around the wreck for Miss Hooker's remainders, because the captain would know her uncle Hornback would want them; and then pretty soon the ferry-boat give it up and went for shore, and I laid into my work and went a-booming down the river.

It did seem a powerful long time before Jim's light showed up; and when it did show, it looked like it was a thousand mile off. By the time I got there the sky was beginning to get a little gray in the east; so we struck for an island, and hid the raft, and sunk the skiff, and turned in and slept like dead people.

CHAPTER XIV

By-and-by, when we got up, we turned over the truck the gang had stole off of the wreck, and found boots, and blankets, and clothes, and all sorts of other things, and a lot of books, and a spyglass, and three boxes of seegars. We hadn't ever been this rich before, in neither of our lives. The seegars was prime. We laid off all the afternoon in the woods talking, and me reading the books, and having a general good time. I told Jim all about what happened inside the wreck, and at the ferry-boat; and I said these kinds of things was adventures; but he said he didn't want no more adventures. He said that when I went in the texas and he crawled back to get on the raft and found her gone, he nearly died; because he judged it was all up with *him*, anyway it could be fixed; for if he didn't get saved he would get drownded; and if he did get saved, whoever saved him would send him back home so as to get the reward, and then Miss Watson would sell him South, sure. Well, he was right; he was most always right; he had an uncommon level head, for a nigger.

I read considerable to Jim about kings, and dukes, and earls, and such, and how gaudy they dressed, and how much style they put on, and called each other your majesty, and your grace, and your lordship, and so on, 'stead of mister; and Jim's eyes bugged out, and he was interested. He says:

"I didn' know dey was so many un um. I hain't hearn 'bout none un um, skasely, but ole King Sollermun, onless you counts dem kings dat's in a pack er k'yards. How much do a king git?"

"Get?" I says; "why, they get a thousand dollars a month if they want it; they can have just as much as they want; everything belongs to them."

"*Ain'* dat gay? En what dey got to do, Huck?"

"*They* don't do nothing! Why how you talk. They just set around."

"No—is dat so?"

"Of course it is. They just set around. Except maybe when there's a war; then they go to the war. But other times they just lazy around; or go hawking—just hawking and sp—Sh!—d' you hear a noise?"

We skipped out and looked; but it warn't nothing but the flutter of a steamboat's wheel, away down coming around the point; so we come back.

"Yes," says I, "and other times, when things is dull, they fuss with the parlyment; and if everybody don't go just so he whacks their heads off. But mostly they hang round the harem."

"Roun' de which?"

"Harem."

"What's de harem?"

"The place where he keep his wives. Don't you know about the harem? Solomon had one; he had about a million wives."

"Why, yes, dat's so; I—I'd done forgot it. A harem's a bo'd'n-house, I reck'n. Mos' likely dey has rackety times in de nussery. En I reck'n de wives quarrels considable; en dat 'crease de racket. Yit dey say Sollermun de wises' man dat ever live'. I doan' take no stock in dat. Bekase why: would a wise man want to live in de mids' er sich a blimblammin' all de time? No—'deed he wouldn't. A wise man 'ud take en buil' a biler-factry; en den he could shet *down* de biler-factry when he want to res'."

"Well, but he *was* the wisest man, anyway; because the widow she told me so, her own self."

"I doan k'yer what de widder say, he *warn't* no wise man, nuther. He had some er de dad-fetchedes' ways I ever see. Does you know 'bout dat chile dat he 'uz gwyne to chop in two?"[1]

"Yes, the widow told me all about it."

"*Well,* den! Warn' dat de beatenes' notion in de worl'? You jes' take en look at it a minute. Dah's de stump, dah—dat's one er de women; heah's you—dat's de yuther one; I's Sollermun; en dish-yer dollar bill's de chile. Bofe un you claims it. What does I do? Does I shin aroun' mongs' de neighbors en fine out which un you de bill *do* b'long to, en han' it over to de right one, all safe en soun', de way dat anybody dat had any gumption would? No—I take en whack de bill in *two,* en give half un it to you, en de yuther half to de yuther woman. Dat's de way Sollermun was gwyne to do wid de chile. Now I want to ast you: waht's de use er dat half a bill?—can't buy noth'n wid it. En what use is a half a chile? I would'n give a dern for a million un um."

"But hang it, Jim, you've clean missed the point—blame it, you've missed it a thousand mile."

"Who? Me? Go 'long. Doan' talk to *me* 'bout yo' pints. I reck'n I knows sense when I sees it; en dey ain' no sense in sich doin's as dat. De 'spute warn't 'bout a half a chile, de 'spute was 'bout a whole chile; en de man dat think he kin settle a 'spute 'bout a whole child wid a half a chile, doan' know enough to come in out'n de rain. Doan' talk to me 'bout Sollermun, Huck, I knows him by de back."

"But I tell you you don't get the point."

"Blame de pint! I reck'n I knows what I knows. En mine you, de *real* pint is down furder—it's down deeper. It lays in de way Sollermun was raised. You take a man dat's got on'y one er two chillen; is dat man gwyne to be waseful o'chillen? No, he ain't; he can't 'ford it. *He* know how to value 'em. But you take a man dat's got 'bout five million chillen runnin' roun' de house, en it's diffunt. *He* as soon chop a chile in two as a cat. Dey's plenty mo'. A chile er two, mo' er less, warn't no consekens to Sollermun, dad fetch him!"

---

[1] In I Kings 3:16–28, to discover the true mother of a child that two women claimed as their own, Solomon ordered the child divided in two, expecting the real mother to surrender it in order to save its life. The story exemplifies Solomon's wisdom.

I never see such a nigger. If he got a notion in his head once, there warn't no getting it out again. He was the most down on Solomon of any nigger I ever see. So I went to talking about other kings, and let Solomon slide. I told about Louis Sixteenth that got his head cut off in France long time ago; and about his little boy the dolphin,[2] that would a been a king, but they took and shut him up in jail, and some say he died there.

"Po' little chap."

"But some says he got out and got away, and come to America."

"Dat's good! But he'll be pooty lonesome—dey ain' no kings here, is dey, Huck?"

"No."

"Den he cain't git no situation. What he gwyne to do?"

"Well, I don't know. Some of them gets on the police, and some of them learns people how to talk French."

"Why, Huck, doan' de French people talk de same way we does?"

"*No*, Jim; you couldn't understand a word they said—not a single word."

"Well, now, I be ding-busted! How do dat come?"

"*I* don't know; but it's so. I got some of their jabber out of a book. Spose a man was to come to you and say *Polly-voo-franzy*—what would you think?"

"I wouldn't think nuff'n; I'd take en bust him over de head. Dat is, if he warn't white. I wouldn't 'low no nigger to call me dat."

"Shucks, it ain't calling you anything. It's only saying do you know how to talk French."

"Well, den, why couldn't he *say* it?"

"Why, he *is* a-saying it. That's a Frenchman's *way* of saying it."

"Well, it's a blame' ridicklous way, en I doan' want to hear no mo' 'bout it. Dey ain' no sense in it."

"Looky here, Jim; does a cat talk like we do?"

"No, a cat don't."

"Well, does a cow?"

"No, a cow don't, nuther."

"Does a cat talk like a cow, or a cow talk like a cat?"

"No, dey don't."

"It's natural and right for 'em to talk different from each other, ain't it?"

"'Course."

"And ain't it natural and right for a cat and a cow to talk different from *us*?"

"Why, mos' sholy it is."

"Well, then, why ain't it natural and right for a *Frenchman* to talk different from us? You answer me that."

"Is a cat a man, Huck?"

"No."

"Well, den, dey ain't no sense in a cat talkin' like a man. Is a cow a man?—er is a cow a cat?"

[2] The dauphin (eldest son of a French king), Louis Charles (1785–1795), was eight years old when his father, Louis XVI, was beheaded in 1793 during the French Revolution; the boy, whose mother, Marie Antoinette (1755–1793), was herself guillotined, died in prison two years later. Legends of his escape abounded, and numerous impostors in America and Europe claimed to be Louis XVII. Twain owned a then-recent book that discusses the subject, Horace W. Fuller's *Impostors and Adventurers, Noted French Trials* (1882).

"No, she ain't either of them."

"Well, den, she ain' got no business to talk like either one er the yuther of 'em. Is a Frenchman a man?"

"Yes."

"*Well,* den! Dad blame it, why doan' he *talk* like a man? You answer me *dat!*"

I see it warn't no use wasting words—you can't learn a nigger to argue. So I quit.

Chapter XV

We judged that three nights more would fetch us to Cairo,[1] at the bottom of Illinois, where the Ohio River comes in, and that was what we was after. We would sell the raft and get on a steamboat and go way up the Ohio amongst the free States, and then be out of trouble.

Well, the second night a fog begun to come on, and we made for a tow-head to tie to, for it wouldn't do to try to run in fog; but when I paddled ahead in the canoe, with the line, to make fast, there warn't anything but little saplings to tie to. I passed the line around one of them right on the edge of the cut bank,[2] but there was a stiff current, and the raft come booming down so lively she tore it out by the roots and away she went. I see the fog closing down, and it made me so sick and scared I couldn't budge for most a half a minute it seemed to me—and then there warn't no raft in sight; you couldn't see twenty yards. I jumped into the canoe and run back to the stern and grabbed the paddle and set her back a stroke. But she didn't come. I was in such a hurry I hadn't untied her. I got up and tried to untie her, but I was so excited my hands shook so I couldn't hardly do anything with them.

As soon as I got started I took out after the raft, hot and heavy, right down the tow-head. That was all right as far as it went, but the tow-head warn't sixty yards long, and the minute I flew by the foot of it I shot out into the solid white fog, and hadn't no more idea which way I was going than a dead man.

Thinks I, it won't do to paddle; first I know I'll run into the bank or a tow-head or something; I got to set still and float, and yet it's mighty fidgety business to have to hold your hands still at such a time. I whooped and listened. Away down there, somewheres, I hears a small whoop, and up comes my spirits. I went tearing after it, listening sharp to hear it again. The next time it come, I see I warn't heading for it but heading away to the right of it. And the next time, I was heading away to the left of it—and not gaining on it much, either, for I was flying around, this way and that and 'tother, but it was going straight ahead all the time.

I did wish the fool would think to beat a tin pan, and beat it all the time, but he never did, and it was the still places between the whoops that was making the trouble for me. Well, I fought along, and directly I hears the whoop *behind* me. I was tangled good, now. That was somebody else's whoop, or else I was turned around.

---

[1] Pronounced KAY-ro. Because southern Illinois was heavily proslavery in sentiment in the 1840s, Jim would stand a better chance of reaching freedom if he could get farther North, up the Ohio River. Huck does not consider the possible difficulties of a boy selling a raft and then buying steamboat tickets for himself and for Jim; what he proposes is more a hope than a realistic plan.

[2] A steep river bank shaped ("cut") by the force of the current.

I throwed the paddle down. I heard the whoop again; it was behind me yet, but in a different place; it kept coming, and kept changing its place, and I kept answering, till by-and-by it was in front of me again and I knowed the current had swung the canoe's head down stream and I was all right, if that was Jim and not some other raftsman hollering. I couldn't tell nothing about voices in a fog, for nothing don't look natural nor sound natural in a fog.

The whooping went on, and in about a minute I come a booming down on a cut bank with smoky ghosts of big trees on it, and the current throwed me off to the left and shot by, amongst a lot of snags that fairly roared, the current was tearing by them so swift.

In another second or two it was solid white and still again. I set perfectly still, then, listening to my heart thump, and I reckon I didn't draw a breath while it thumped a hundred.

I just give up, then. I knowed what the matter was. That cut bank was an island, and Jim had gone down 'tother side of it. It warn't no tow-head, that you could float by in ten minutes. It had the big timber of a regular island; it might be five or six mile long and more than a half a mile wide.

I kept quiet, with my ears cocked, about fifteen minutes, I reckon. I was floating along, of course, four or five mile an hour; but you don't ever think of that. No, you *feel* like you are laying dead still on the water; and if a little glimpse of a snag slips by, you don't think to yourself how fast *you're* going, but you catch your breath and think, my! how that snag's tearing along. If you think it ain't dismal and lonesome out in a fog that way, by yourself, in the night, you try it once—you'll see.

Next, for about a half an hour, I whoops now and then; at last I hears the answer a long ways off, and tries to follow it, but I couldn't do it, and directly I judged I'd got into a nest of tow-heads, for I had little dim glimpses of them on both sides of me, sometimes just a narrow channel between; and some that I couldn't see, I knowed was there, because I'd hear the wash of the current against the old dead brush and trash that hung over the banks. Well, I warn't long losing the whoops, down amongst the tow-heads; and I only tried to chase them a little while, anyway, because it was worse than chasing a Jack-o-lantern.[3] You never knowed a sound dodge around so, and swap places so quick and so much.

I had to claw away from the bank pretty lively, four or five times, to keep from knocking the islands out of the river; and so I judged the raft must be butting into the bank every now and then, or else it would get further ahead and clear out of hearing—it was floating a little faster than what I was.

Well, I seemed to be in the open river again, by-and-by, but I couldn't hear no sign of a whoop nowheres. I reckoned Jim had fetched up on a snag, maybe, and it was all up with him. I was good and tired, so I laid down in the canoe and said I wouldn't bother no more. I didn't want to go to sleep, of course; but I was so sleepy I couldn't help it; so I thought I would take just one little cat-nap.

But I reckon it was more than a cat-nap, for when I waked up the stars was shining bright, the fog was all gone, and I was spinning down a big bend stern first. First I didn't know where I was; I thought I was dreaming; and when things begun to come back to me, they seemed to come up dim out of last week.

It was a monstrous big river here, with the tallest and the thickest kind of tim-

---

[3] An elusive light that appears over marshy grounds at night, supposedly caused by the combustion of marsh gas; popularly called will-o'-the-wisp.

ber on both banks; just a solid wall, as well as I could see, by the stars. I looked away down stream, and seen a black speck on the water. I took out after it; but when I got to it it warn't nothing but a couple of saw-logs made fast together. Then I see another speck, and chased that; then another, and this time I was right. It was the raft.

When I got to it Jim was setting there with his head down between his knees, asleep, with his right arm hanging over the steering oar. The other oar was smashed off, and the raft was littered up with leaves and branches and dirt. So she'd had a rough time.

I made fast and laid down under Jim's nose on the raft, and begun to gap, and stretch my fists out against Jim, and says:

"Hello, Jim, have I been asleep? Why didn't you stir me up?"

"Goodness gracious, is dat you, Huck? En you ain' dead—you ain' drownded—you's back agin? It's too good for true, honey, it's too good for true. Lemme look at you, chile, lemme feel o' you. No, you ain' dead! you's back agin, 'live en soun', jis de same ole Huck—de same ole Huck, thanks to goodness!"

"What's the matter with you, Jim? You been a drinking?"

"Drinkin'? Has I ben a drinkin'? Has I had a chance to be a drinkin'?"

"Well, then, what makes you talk so wild?"

"How does I talk wild?"

"*How?* why, hain't you been talking about my coming back, and all that stuff, as if I'd been gone away?"

"Huck—Huck Finn, you look me in de eye; look me in de eye. *Hain't* you ben gone away?"

"Gone away? Why, what in the nation do you mean? *I* hain't been gone any-wheres. Where would I go to?"

"Well, looky here, boss, dey's sumf'n wrong, dey is. Is I *me,* or who *is* I? Is I heah, or whah *is* I? Now dat's what I wants to know?"

"Well, I think you're here, plain enough, but I think you're a tangle-headed old fool, Jim."

"I is, is I? Well you answer me dis. Didn't you tote out de line in de canoe, fer to make fas' to de tow-head?"

"No, I didn't. What tow-head? I hain't seen no tow-head."

"You hain't seen no tow-head? Looky here—didn't de line pull loose en de raf' go a hummin' down de river, en leave you en de canoe behine in de fog?"

"What fog?"

"Why *de* fog. De fog dat's ben aroun' all night. En didn't you whoop, en didn't I whoop, tell we got mix' up in de islands en one un us got los' en 'tother one was jis' as good as los', 'kase he didn't know whah he wuz? En didn't I bust up agin a lot er dem islands en have a turrible time en mos' git drownded? Now ain' dat so, boss—ain't it so? You answer me dat."

"Well, this is too many for me, Jim. I hain't seen no fog, nor no islands, nor no troubles, nor nothing. I been setting here talking with you all night till you went to sleep about ten minutes ago, and I reckon I done the same. You couldn't a got drunk in that time, so of course you've been dreaming."

"Dad fetch it, how is I gwyne to dream all dat in ten minutes?"

"Well, hang it all, you did dream it, because there didn't any of it happen."

"But Huck, it's all jis' as plain to me as—"

"It don't make no difference how plain it is, there ain't nothing in it. I know, because I've been here all the time."

Jim didn't say nothing for about five minutes, but set there studying over it. Then he says:

"Well, den, I reck'n I did dream it, Huck; but dog my cats ef it ain't de powerfullest dream I ever see. En I hain't ever had no dream b'fo' dat's tired me like dis one."

"Oh, well, that's all right, because a dream does tire a body like everything, sometimes. But this one was a staving[4] dream—tell me all about it, Jim."

So Jim went to work and told me the whole thing right through, just as it happened, only he painted it up considerable. Then he said he must start in and "'terpret" it, because it was sent for a warning. He said the first tow-head stood for a man that would try to do us some good, but the current was another man that would get us away from him. The whoops was warnings that would come to us every now and then, and if we didn't try hard to make out to understand them they'd just take us into bad luck, 'stead of keeping us out of it. The lot of tow-heads was troubles we was going to get into with quarrelsome people and all kinds of mean folks, but if we minded our business and didn't talk back and aggravate them, we would pull through and get out of the fog and into the big clear river,[5] which was the free States, and wouldn't have no more trouble.

It had clouded up pretty dark just after I got onto the raft, but it was clearing up again, now.

"Oh, well, that's all interpreted well enough, as far as it goes, Jim," I says; "but what does *these* things stand for?"

It was the leaves and rubbish on the raft, and the smashed oar. You could see them first rate, now.

Jim looked at the trash, and then looked at me, and back at the trash again. He had got the dream fixed so strong in his head that he couldn't seem to shake it loose and get the facts back into its place again, right away. But when he did get the thing straightened around, he looked at me steady, without ever smiling, and says:

"What do dey stan' for? I's gwyne to tell you. When I got all wore out wid work, en wid de callin' for you, en went to sleep, my heart wuz mos' broke bekase you wuz los', en I didn' k'yer no mo' what become er me en de raf'. En when I wake up en fine you back agin', all safe en soun', de tears come en I could a got down on my knees en kiss' yo' foot I's so thankful. En all you wuz thinkin 'bout wuz how you could make a fool uv ole Jim wid a lie. Dat truck dah is *trash;* en trash is what people is dat puts dirt on de head er dey fren's en makes 'em ashamed."

Then he got up slow, and walked to the wigwam, and went in there, without saying anything but that. But that was enough. It made me feel so mean I could almost kissed *his* foot to get him to take it back.

It was fifteen minutes before I could work myself up to go and humble myself to a nigger—but I done it, and I warn't ever sorry for it afterwards, neither. I didn't do him no more mean tricks, and I wouldn't done that one if I'd a knowed it would make him feel that way.

---

[4] Graphic and involved.   [5] The Ohio River.

Chapter XVI

We slept most all day, and started out at night, a little ways behind a monstrous long raft that was as long going by as a procession. She had four long sweeps[1] at each end, so we judged she carried as many as thirty men, likely. She had five big wigwams aboard, wide apart, and an open camp fire in the middle, and a tall flag-pole at each end. There was a power of style about her. It *amounted* to something being a raftsman on such a craft as that.

We went drifting down into a big bend, and the night clouded up and got hot. The river was very wide, and was walled with solid timber on both sides; you couldn't see a break in it hardly ever, or a light. We talked about Cairo, and wondered whether we would know it when we got to it. I said likely we wouldn't, because I had heard say there warn't but about a dozen houses there, and if they didn't happen to have them lit up, how was we going to know we was passing a town? Jim said if the two big rivers joined together there, that would show. But I said maybe we might think we was passing the foot of an island and coming into the same old river again. That disturbed Jim—and me too. So the question was, what to do? I said, paddle ashore the first time a light showed, and tell them pap was behind, coming along with a trading-scow, and was a green hand at the business, and wanted to know how far it was to Cairo. Jim thought it was a good idea, so we took a smoke on it and waited.

There warn't nothing to do, now, but to look out sharp for the town, and not pass it without seeing it. He said he'd be mighty sure to see it, because he'd be a free man the minute he seen it, but if he missed it he'd be in the slave country again and no more show[2] for freedom. Every little while he jumps up and says:

"Dah she is!"

But it warn't. It was Jack-o-lanterns, or lightning-bugs; so he set down again, and went to watching, same as before. Jim said it made him all over trembly and feverish to be so close to freedom. Well, I can tell you it made me all over trembly and feverish, too, to hear him, because I begun to get it through my head that he *was* most free—and who was to blame for it? Why, *me*. I couldn't get that out of my conscience, no how nor no way. It got to troubling me so I couldn't rest; I couldn't stay still in one place. It hadn't ever come home to me before, what this thing was that I was doing. But now it did; and it staid with me, and scorched me more and more. I tried to make out to myself that *I* warn't to blame, because *I* didn't run Jim off from his rightful owner; but it warn't no use, conscience up and says, every time, "But you knowed he was running for his freedom, and you could a paddled ashore and told somebody." That was so—I couldn't get around that, noway. That was where it pinched. Conscience says to me, "What had poor Miss Watson done to you, that you could see her nigger go off right under your eyes and never say one single word? What did that poor old woman do to you, that you could treat her so mean? Why, she tried to learn you your book, she tried to learn you your manners, she tried to be good to you every way she knowed how. *That's* what she done."

I got to feeling so mean and so miserable I most wished I was dead. I fidgeted up and down the raft, abusing myself to myself, and Jim was fidgeting up and down past me. We neither of us could keep still. Every time he danced around and

---

[1] Long oars used for steering rafts of this sort.   [2] Chance.

says, "Dah's Cairo!" it went through me like a shot, and I thought if it *was* Cairo I reckoned I would die of miserableness.

Jim talked out loud all the time while I was talking to myself. He was saying how the first thing he would do when he got to a free State he would go to saving up money and never spend a single cent, and when he got enough he would buy his wife, which was owned on a farm close to where Miss Watson lived; and then they would both work to buy the two children, and if their master wouldn't sell them, they'd get an Ab'litionist to go and steal them.

It most froze me to hear such talk. He wouldn't ever dared to talk such talk in his life before. Just see what a difference it made in him the minute he judged he was about free. It was according to the old saying, "give a nigger an inch and he'll take an ell." Thinks I, this is what comes of my not thinking. Here was this nigger which I had as good as helped to run away, coming right out flat-footed and saying he would steal his children—children that belonged to a man I didn't even know; a man that hadn't ever done me no harm.

I was sorry to hear Jim say that, it was such a lowering of him. My conscience got to stirring me up hotter than ever, until at last I says to it, "Let up on me—it ain't too late, yet—I'll paddle ashore at the first light, and tell." I felt easy, and happy, and light as a feather, right off. All my troubles was gone. I went to looking out sharp for a light, and sort of singing to myself. By-and-by one showed. Jim sings out:

"We's safe, Huck, we's safe! Jump up and crack yo' heels, dat's de good ole Cairo at las', I jis knows it!"

I says:

"I'll take the canoe and go see, Jim. It mightn't be, you know."

He jumped and got the canoe ready, and put his old coat in the bottom for me to set on, and give me the paddle; and as I shoved off, he says:

"Pooty soon I'll be a-shout'n for joy, en I'll say, it's all on accounts o' Huck; I's a free man, en I couldn't ever ben free ef it hadn' ben for Huck; Huck done it. Jim won't ever forgit you, Huck; you's de bes' fren' Jim's ever had; en you's de *only* fren' ole Jim's got now."

I was paddling off, all in a sweat to tell on him; but when he says this, it seemed to kind of take the tuck all out of me. I went along slow then, and I warn't right down certain whether I was glad I started or whether I warn't. When I was fifty yards off, Jim says:

"Dah you goes, de ole true Huck; de on'y white genlman dat ever kep' his promise to ole Jim."

Well, I just felt sick. But I says, I *got* to do it—I can't get *out* of it. Right then, along comes a skiff with two men in it, with guns, and they stopped and I stopped. One of them says:

"What's that, yonder?"

"A piece of a raft," I says.

"Do you belong on it?"

"Yes, sir."

"Any men on it?"

"Only one, sir."

"Well, there's five niggers run off to-night, up yonder above the head of the bend. Is your man white or black?"

I didn't answer up prompt. I tried to, but the words wouldn't come. I tried, for a second or two, to brace up and out with it, but I warn't man enough—hadn't the spunk of a rabbit. I see I was weakening; so I just give up trying, and up and says—

"He's white."

"I reckon we'll go and see for ourselves."

"I wish you would," says I, "because it's pap that's there, and maybe you'd help me tow the raft ashore where the light is. He's sick—and so is mam and Mary Ann."

"Oh, the devil! we're in a hurry, boy. But I s'pose we've got to. Come—buckle to your paddle, and let's get along."

I buckled to my paddle and they laid to their oars. When we had made a stroke or two, I says:

"Pap'll be mighty much obleeged to you, I can tell you. Everybody goes away when I want them to help me tow the raft ashore, and I can't do it by myself."

"Well, that's infernal mean. Odd, too. Say, boy, what's the matter with your father?"

"It's the—a—the—well, it ain't anything, much."

They stopped pulling. It warn't but a mighty little ways to the raft, now. One says:

"Boy, that's a lie. What *is* the matter with your pap? Answer up square, now, and it'll be the better for you."

"I will sir, I will, honest—but don't leave us, please. It's the—the—gentle-men, if you'll only pull ahead, and let me heave you the head-line, you won't have to come a-near the raft—please do."

"Set her back, John, set her back!" says one. They backed water. "Keep away, boy—keep to looard.[3] Confound it, I just expect the wind has blowed it to us. Your pap's got the small-pox,[4] and you know it precious well. Why didn't you come out and say so? Do you want to spread it all over?"

"Well," says I, a-blubbering, "I've told everybody before, and then they just went away and left us."

"Poor devil, there's something in that. We are right down sorry for you, but we—well, hang it, we don't want the small-pox, you see. Look here, I'll tell you what to do. Don't you try to land by yourself, or you'll smash everything to pieces. You float along down about twenty miles and you'll come to a town on the left-hand side of the river. It will be long after sun-up, then, and when you ask for help, you tell them your folks are all down with chills and fever. Don't be a fool again, and let people guess what is the matter. Now we're trying to do you a kindness; so you just put twenty miles between us, that's a good boy. It wouldn't do any good to land yonder where the light is—it's only a wood-yard. Say—I reckon your father's poor, and I'm bound to say he's in pretty hard luck. Here—I'll put a twenty dollar gold piece on this board, and you get it when it floats by. I feel mighty mean to leave you, but my kingdom! it won't do to fool with small-pox, don't you see?"

"Hold on, Parker," says the other man, "here's a twenty to put on the board for me. Good-bye, boy, you do as Mr. Parker told you, and you'll be all right."

"That's so, my boy—good-bye, good-bye. If you see any runaway niggers, you get help and nab them, and you can make some money by it."

---

[3] Leeward, away from the wind.

[4] Huck allows the men to name a disease they fear; smallpox was highly infectious and often fatal at the time.

"Good-bye, sir," says I, "I won't let no runaway niggers get by me if I can help it."

They went off, and I got aboard the raft, feeling bad and low, because I knowed very well I had done wrong, and I see it warn't no use for me to try to learn to do right; a body that don't get *started* right when he's little, ain't got no show—when the pinch comes there ain't nothing to back him up and keep him to his work, and so he gets beat. Then I thought a minute, and says to myself, hold on—s'pose you'd a done right and give Jim up; would you felt better than what you do now? No, says I, I'd feel bad—I'd feel just the same way I do now. Well, then, says I, what's the use you learning to do right, when it's troublesome to do right and ain't no trouble to do wrong, and the wages is just the same? I was stuck. I couldn't answer that. So I reckoned I wouldn't bother no more about it, but after this always do whichever come handiest at the time.

I went into the wigwam; Jim warn't there. I looked all around; he warn't any-where. I says:

"Jim!"

"Here I is, Huck. Is dey out o' sight yit? Don't talk loud."

He was in the river, under the stern oar, with just his nose out. I told him they was out of sight, so he come aboard. He says:

"I was a-listening' to all de talk, en I slips into de river en was gwyne to shove for sho' if dey come aboard. Den I was gwyne to swim to de raf' agin when dey was gone. But lawsy, how you did fool 'em, Huck! Dat *wuz* de smartes' dodge! I tell you, chile, I 'speck it save' old Jim—ole Jim ain't gwyne to forgit you for dat, honey."

Then we talked about the money. It was a pretty good raise, twenty dollars apiece. Jim said we could take deck passage[5] on a steamboat now, and the money would last us as far as we wanted to go in the free States. He said twenty mile more warn't far for the raft to go, but he wished we was already there.

Towards daybreak we tied up, and Jim was mighty particular about hiding the raft good. Then he worked all day fixing things in bundles, and getting all ready to quit rafting.

That night about ten we hove in sight of the lights of a town away down in a left-hand bend.

I went off in the canoe, to ask about it. Pretty soon I found a man out in the river with a skiff, setting a trot-line. I ranged up and says:

"Mister, is that town Cairo?"

"Cairo? no. You must be a blame' fool."

"What town is it mister?"

"If you want to know, go and find out. If you stay here botherin' around me for about a half a minute longer, you'll get something you don't want."

I paddled to the raft. Jim was awful disappointed, but I said never mind, Cairo would be the next place, I reckoned.

We passed another town before daylight, and I was going out again; but it was high ground, so I didn't go. No high ground about Cairo, Jim said. I had forgot it. We laid up for the day, on a tow-head tolerable close to the left-hand bank. I begun to suspicion something. So did Jim. I says:

"Maybe we went by Cairo in the fog that night."

---

[5] Without a cabin, the cheapest way to travel; the forty dollars makes the hope of steamboating to freedom seem more feasible.

He says:

"Doan' less' talk about it, Huck. Po' niggers can't have no luck. I awluz 'spected dat rattle-snake skin warn't done wid it's work."

"I wish I'd never seen that snake-skin, Jim—I do wish I'd never laid eyes on it."

"It ain't yo' fault, Huck; you didn' know. Don't you blame yo'self 'bout it."

When it was daylight, here was the clear Ohio water in shore, sure enough, and outside was the old regular Muddy! So it was all up with Cairo.[6]

We talked it all over. It wouldn't do to take to the shore; we couldn't take the raft up the stream, of course. There warn't no way but to wait for dark, and start back in the canoe and take the chances. So we slept all day amongst the cotton-wood thicket, so as to be fresh for the work, and when we went back to the raft about dark the canoe was gone!

We didn't say a word for a good while. There warn't anything to say. We both knowed well enough it was some more work of the rattle-snake skin; so what was the use to talk about it? It would only look like we was finding fault, and that would be bound to fetch more bad luck—and keep on fetching it, too, till we knowed enough to keep still.

By-and-by we talked about what we better do, and found there warn't no way but just to go along down with the raft till we got a chance to buy a canoe to go back in. We warn't going to borrow it when there warn't anybody around, the way pap would do, for that might set people after us.

So we shoved out, after dark, on the raft.

Anybody that don't believe yet, that it's foolishness to handle a snake-skin, after all that that snake-skin done for us, will believe it now, if they read on and see what more it done for us.

The place to buy canoes is off of rafts laying up at shore. But we didn't see no rafts laying up; so we went along during three hours and more. Well, the night got gray, and ruther thick, which is the next meanest thing to fog. You can't tell the shape of the river, and you can't see no distance. It got to be very late and still, and then along comes a steamboat up the river. We lit the lantern, and judged she would see it. Up-stream boats didn't generly come close to us; they go out and follow the bars and hunt for easy water under the reefs; but nights like this they bull right up the channel against the whole river.

We could hear her pounding along, but we didn't see her good till she was close. She aimed right for us. Often they do that and try to see how close they can come without touching; sometimes the wheel bites off a sweep, and then the pilot sticks his head out and laughs, and thinks he's mighty smart. Well, here she comes, and we said she was going to try to shave us; but she didn't seem to be sheering off a bit. She was a big one, and she was coming in a hurry, too, looking like a black cloud with rows of glow-worms around it; but all of a sudden she bulged out, big and scary, with a long row of wide-open furnace doors shining like red-hot teeth, and her monstrous bows and guards hanging right over us. There was a yell at us, and a jingling of bells to stop the engines, a pow-wow of cussing, and whistling of steam—and as Jim went overboard on one side and I on the other, she come smashing straight through the raft.

I dived—and I aimed to find the bottom, too, for a thirty-foot wheel had got to go over me, and I wanted it to have plenty of room. I could always stay under

---

[6] The relatively clear water of the Ohio River flowing near the eastern shore of the Mississippi tells Jim and Huck that they have passed the confluence of the two rivers at Cairo.

water a minute; this time I reckon I staid under water a minute and a half. Then I bounced for the top in a hurry, for I was nearly busting. I popped out to my arm-pits and blowed the water out of my nose, and puffed a bit. Of course there was a booming current; and of course that boat started her engines again ten seconds after she stopped them, for they never cared much for raftsmen; so now she was churning along up the river, out of sight in the thick weather, though I could hear her.

I sung out for Jim about a dozen times, but I didn't get any answer; so I grabbed a plank that touched me while I was "treading water," and struck out for shore, shoving it ahead of me. But I made out to see that the drift of the current was towards the left-hand shore,[7] which meant that I was in a crossing; so I changed off and went that way.

It was one of these long, slanting, two-mile crossings; so I was a good long time in getting over. I made a safe landing, and clum up the bank. I couldn't see but a little ways, but I went poking along over rough ground for a quarter of a mile or more, and then I run across a big old-fashioned double log house before I noticed it. I was going to rush by and get away, but a lot of dogs jumped out and went to howling and barking at me, and I knowed better than to move another peg.

Chapter XVII

In about half a minute somebody spoke out of a window, without putting his head out, and says:

"Be done, boys! Who's there?"

I says:

"It's me."

"Who's me?"

"George Jackson, sir."

"What do you want?"

"I don't want nothing, sir. I only want to go along by, but the dogs won't let me."

"What are you prowling around here this time of night, for—hey?"

"I warn't prowling around, sir; I fell overboard off of the steam-boat."

"Oh you did, did you? Strike a light there, somebody. What did you say your name was?"

"George Jackson, sir, I'm only a boy."

"Look here; if you're telling the truth, you needn't be afraid—nobody 'll hurt you. But don't try to budge; stand right where you are. Rouse out Bob and Tom, some of you, and fetch the guns. George Jackson, is there anybody with you?"

"No sir, nobody."

I heard the people stirring around in the house, now, and see a light. The man sung out:

"Snatch that light away, Betsy, you old fool—aint's you got any sense? Put it on the floor behind the front door. Bob, if you and Tom are ready, take your places."

"All ready."

"Now, George Jackson, do you know the Shepherdsons?"

---

[7] Kentucky, where the following two chapters are set.

"No, sir—I never heard of them."

"Well, that may be so, and it mayn't. Now, all ready. Step forward, George Jackson. And mind, don't you hurry—come mighty slow. If there's anybody with you, let him keep back—if he shows himself he'll be shot. Come along, now. Come slow; push the door open, yourself—just enough to squeeze in, d' you hear?"

I didn't hurry, I couldn't if I'd a wanted to. I took one slow step at a time, and there warn't a sound, only I thought I could hear my heart. The dogs were as still as the humans, but they followed a little behind me. When I got to the three log door-steps, I heard them unlocking and unbarring and unbolting. I put my hand on the door and pushed it a little and a little more, till somebody said, "There, that's enough—put your head in." I done it, but I judged they would take it off.

The candle was on the floor, and there they all was, looking at me, and me at them, for about a quarter of a minute. Three big men with guns pointed at me, which made me wince, I tell you; the oldest, gray and about sixty, the other two thirty or more—all of them fine and handsome—and the sweetest old gray-headed lady, and back of her two young women which I couldn't see right well. The old gentleman says:

"There—I reckon it's all right. Come in."

As soon as I was in, the old gentleman he locked the door and barred it and bolted it, and told the young men to come in with their guns, and they all went in a big parlor that had a new rag carpet on the floor, and got together in a corner that was out of range of the front windows—there warn't none on the side. They held the candle, and took a good look at me, and all said "Why *he* ain't a Shepherdson—no, there ain't any Shepherdson about him." Then the old man said he hoped I wouldn't mind being searched for arms, because he didn't mean no harm by it—it was only to make sure. So he didn't pry into my pockets, but only felt outside with his hands, and said it was all right. He told me to make myself easy and at home, and tell all about myself; but the old lady says:

"Why bless you, Saul, the poor thing's as wet as he can be; and don't you reckon it may be he's hungry?"

"True for you, Rachel—I forgot."

So the old lady says:

"Betsy" (this was a nigger woman), "you fly around and get him something to eat, as quick as you can, poor thing; and one of you girls go and wake up Buck and tell him—Oh, here he is himself. Buck, take this little stranger and get the wet clothes off from him and dress him up in some of yours that's dry."

Buck looked about as old as me—thirteen or fourteen[1] or along there, though he was a little bigger than me. He hadn't on anything but a shirt, and he was very frowsy-headed. He come in gaping and digging one fist into his eyes, and he was dragging a gun along with the other one. He says:

"Ain't they no Shepherdsons around?"

They said, no, 'twas a false alarm.

"Well," he says, "if they'd a ben some, I reckon I'd a got one."

They all laughed, and Bob says:

"Why, Buck, they might have scalped us all, you've been so slow in coming."

"Well, nobody come after me, and it ain't right. I'm always kep' down; I don't get no show."

---

[1] In a notebook entry Twain characterizes Huck as "a boy of 14."

"Never mind, Buck, my boy," says the old man, "you'll have show enough, all in good time, don't you fret about that. Go 'long with you now, and do as your mother told you."

When we got up stairs to his room, he got me a coarse shirt and a roundabout[2] and pants of his, and I put them on. While I was at it he asked me what my name was, but before I could tell him, he started to telling me about a blue jay and a young rabbit he had catched in the woods day before yesterday, and he asked me where Moses was when the candle went out. I said I didn't know; I hadn't heard about it before, no way.

"Well, guess," he says.

"How'm I going to guess," says I, "when I never heard tell about it before?"

"But you can guess, can't you? It's just as easy."

"*Which* candle?" I says.

"Why, any candle," he says.

"I don't know where he was," says I; "where was he?"

"Why he was in the *dark!* That's where he was!"

"Well, if you knowed where he was, what did you ask me for?"

"Why, blame it, it's a riddle, don't you see? Say, how long are you going to stay here? You got to stay always. We can just have booming times—they don't have no school now. Do you own a dog? I've got a dog—and he'll go in the river and bring out chips that you throw in. Do you like to comb up, Sundays, and all that kind of foolishness? You bet I don't, but ma she makes me. Confound these ole britches, I reckon I'd better put 'em on, but I'd ruther not, it's so warm. Are you all ready? All right—come along, old hoss."

Cold corn-pone, cold corn-beef, butter and butter-milk—that is what they had for me down there, and there ain't nothing better that ever I've come across yet. Buck and his ma and all of them smoked cob pipes, except the nigger woman, which was gone, and the two young women. They all smoked and talked, and I eat and talked. The young women had quilts around them, and their hair down their backs. They all asked me questions, and I told them how pap and me and all the family was living on a little farm down at the bottom of Arkansaw, and my sister Mary Ann run off and got married and never was heard of no more, and Bill went to hunt them and he warn't heard of no more, and Tom and Mort died, and then there warn't nobody but just me and pap left, and he was just trimmed down to nothing, on account of his troubles; so when he died I took what there was left, because the farm didn't belong to us, and started up the river, deck passage, and fell overboard; and that was how I come to be here. So they said I could have a home there as long as I wanted it. Then it was most daylight, and everybody went to bed, and I went to bed with Buck, and when I waked up in the morning, drat it all, I had forgot what my name was. So I laid there about an hour trying to think, and when Buck waked up, I says:

"Can you spell, Buck?"

"Yes," he says.

"I bet you can't spell my name," says I.

"I bet you what you dare I can," says he.

"All right," says I, "go ahead."

"G-o-r-g-e J-a-x-o-n—there now," he says.

---

[2] A short jacket.

"Well," says I, "you done it, but I didn't think you could. It ain't no slouch of a name to spell—right off without studying."

I set it down, private, because somebody might want *me* to spell it, next, and so I wanted to be handy with it and rattle it off like I was used to it.

It was a mighty nice family, and a mighty nice house, too. I hadn't seen no house out in the country before that was so nice and had so much style. It didn't have an iron latch on the front door, nor a wooden one with a buckskin string, but a brass knob to turn, the same as houses in a town. There warn't no bed in the parlor, not a sign of a bed; but heaps of parlors in towns has beds in them. There was a big fireplace that was bricked on the bottom, and the bricks were kept clean and red by pouring water on them and scrubbing them with another brick; sometimes they washed them over with red water-paint that they call Spanish-brown, same as they do in town. They had big brass dog-irons that could hold up a sawlog.[3] There was a clock on the middle of the mantel-piece, with a picture of a town painted on the bottom half of the glass front, and a round place in the middle of it for the sun, and you could see the pendulum swing behind it. It was beautiful to hear that clock tick; and sometimes when one of these peddlers had been along and scoured her up and got her in good shape, she would start in and strike a hundred and fifty before she got tuckered out. They wouldn't took any money for her.

Well, there was a big outlandish parrot on each side of the clock, made out of something like chalk, and painted up gaudy. By one of the parrots was a cat made of crockery, and a crockery dog by the other; and when you pressed down on them they squeaked, but didn't open their mouths nor look different nor interested. They squeaked through underneath. There was a couple of big wild-turkey-wing fans spread out behind those things. On a table in the middle of the room was a kind of a lovely crockery basket that had apples and oranges and peaches and grapes piled up in it which was much redder and yellower amd prettier than real ones is, but they warn't real because you could see where pieces had got chipped off and showed the white chalk or whatever it was, underneath.

This table had a cover made out of beautiful oil-cloth, with a red and blue spread-eagle painted on it, and a painted border all around. It come all the way from Philadelphia, they said. There was some books too, piled up perfectly exact, on each corner of the table. One was a big family Bible, full of pictures. One was "Pilgrim's Progress," about a man that left his family it didn't say why. I read considerable in it now and then. The statements was interesting, but tough. Another was "Friendship's Offering," full of beautiful stuff and poetry; but I didn't read the poetry. Another was Henry Clay's Speeches, and another was Dr. Gunn's Family Medicine,[4] which told you all about what to do if a body was sick or dead. There was a Hymn Book, and a lot of other books. And there was nice split-bottom chairs, and perfectly sound, too—not bagged down in the middle and busted, like an old basket.

[3] Andirons that could hold a log large enough to be sawed into planks.

[4] The Grangerford library consists of a Bible; *The Pilgrim's Progress* (1678), a dream allegory by the English preacher and writer John Bunyan (1628–1688); *Friendship's Offering*, a popular gift book containing sentimental verse and pious prose; the "Speeches" of Henry Clay (1777–1852), a noted politician and orator from Kentucky; and Dr. Gunn's *Domestic Medicine* (1830). The furnishings of this household clearly give the impressionable Huck a sense of class and dignity; the irony is that this "cultured" family is involved in a blood feud.

They had pictures hung on the walls—mainly Washingtons and Lafayettes, and battles, and Highland Marys,[5] and one called "Signing the Declaration." There was some that they called crayons, which one of the daughters which was dead made her own self when she was only fifteen years old. They was different from any pictures I ever see before; blacker, mostly, than is common. One was a woman in a slim black dress, belted small under the arm-pits, with bulges like a cabbage in the middle of the sleeves, and a large black scoop-shovel bonnet with a black veil, and white slim ankles crossed about with black tape, and very wee black slippers, like a chisel, and she was leaning pensive on a tombstone on her right elbow, under a weeping willow, and her other hand hanging down her side holding a white handkerchief and a reticule, and underneath the picture it said "Shall I Never See Thee More Alas." Another one was a young lady with her hair all combed up straight to the top of her head, and knotted there in front of a comb like a chair-back, and she was crying into a handkerchief and had a dead bird laying on its back in her other hand with its heels up, and underneath the picture it said "I Shall Never Hear Thy Sweet Chirrup More Alas." There was one where a young lady was at a window looking up at the moon, and tears running down her cheeks; and she had an open letter in one hand with black sealing-wax showing on one edge of it, and she was mashing a locket with a chain to it against her mouth, and underneath the picture it said "And Art Thou Gone Yes Thou Art Gone Alas." These was all nice pictures, I reckon, but I didn't somehow seem to take to them, because if ever I was down a little, they always give me the fan-tods. Everybody was sorry she died, because she had laid out a lot more of these pictures to do, and a body could see by what she had done what they had lost. But I reckoned, that with her disposition, she was having a better time in the graveyard. She was at work on what they said was her greatest picture when she took sick, and every day and every night it was her prayer to be allowed to live till she got it done, but she never got the chance. It was a picture of a young woman in a long white gown, standing on the rail of a bridge all ready to jump off, with her hair all down her back, and looking up to the moon, with the tears running down her face, and she had two arms folded across her breast, and two arms stretched out in front, and two more reaching up towards the moon—and the idea was, to see which pair would look best and then scratch out all the other arms; but, as I was saying, she died before she got her mind made up, and now they kept this picture over the head of the bed in her room, and every time her birthday come they hung flowers on it. Other times it was hid with a little curtain. The young woman in the picture had a kind of a nice sweet face, but there was so many arms it made her look too spidery, seemed to me.

This young girl kept a scrap-book when she was alive, and used to paste obituaries and accidents and cases of patient suffering in it out of the *Presbyterian Observer,* and write poetry after them out of her own head. It was very good poetry. This is what she wrote about a boy by the name of Stephen Dowling Bots that fell down a well and was drownded:

---

[5] Marquis de Lafayette (1757–1834) was a French general and statesman who served in the Continental army during the American Revolution. The pictures are selected to suggest the taste of the region at this time: "Highland Mary" is Mary Campbell, an early love of the Scottish poet Robert Burns (1759–1796), who wrote several elegies in her honor, among them "To Mary in Heaven."

ODE TO STEPHEN DOWLING BOTS, DEC'D.[6]

And did young Stephen sicken,
   And did young Stephen die?
And did the sad hearts thicken,
   And did the mourners cry?

No; such was not the fate of
   Young Stephen Dowling Bots;
Though sad hearts round him thickened,
   'Twas not from sickness' shots.

No whooping-cough did rack his frame,
   Nor measles drear, with spots;
Not these impaired the sacred name
   Of Stephen Dowling Bots.

Despised love struck not with woe
   That head of curly knots,
Nor stomach troubles laid him low,
   Young Stephen Dowling Bots.

O no. Then list with tearful eye,
   Whilst I his fate do tell.
His soul did from this cold world fly,
   By falling down a well.

They got him out and emptied him;
   Alas it was too late;
His spirit was gone for to sport aloft
   In the realms of the good and great.

If Emmeline Grangerford could make poetry like that before she was fourteen, there ain't no telling what she could a done by-and-by. Buck said she could rattle off poetry like nothing. She didn't ever have to stop to think. He said she would slap down a line, and if she couldn't find anything to rhyme with it she would just scratch it out and slap down another one, and go ahead. She warn't particular, she could write about anything you choose to give her to write about, just so it was sadful. Every time a man died, or a woman died, or a child died, she would be on hand with her "tribute" before he was cold. She called them tributes. The neighbors said it was the doctor first, then Emmeline, then the undertaker—the undertaker never got in ahead of Emmeline but once, and then she hung fire on a rhyme for the dead person's name, which was Whistler. She warn't ever the same, after that; she never complained, but she kind of pined away and did not live long. Poor

---

[6] Deceased. This parodic poem was probably occasioned by the work of Julia A. Moore (1847–1920), whose book of sentimental verse *The Sweet Singer of Michigan Salutes the Public* appeared in 1876. Moore specialized in "obituary" poems evoked by the death of children. In *Following the Equator* (1897), Twain said that *The Sweet Singer of Michigan* had brought joy to his heart for twenty years.

thing, many's the time I made myself go up to the little room that used to be hers and get out her poor old scrapbook and read in it when her pictures had been aggravating me and I had soured on her a little. I liked all that family, dead ones and all, and warn't going to let anything come between us. Poor Emmeline made poetry about all the dead people when she was alive, and it didn't seem right that there warn't nobody to make some about her, now she was gone; so I tried to sweat out a verse or two myself, but I couldn't seem to make it go, somehow. They kept Emmeline's room trim and nice and all the things fixed in it just the way she liked to have them when she was alive, and nobody ever slept there. The old lady took care of the room herself, though there was plenty of niggers, and she sewed there a good deal and read her Bible there, mostly.

Well, as I was saying about the parlor, there was beautiful curtains on the windows: white, with pictures painted on them, of castles with vines all down the walls, and cattle coming down to drink. There was a little old piano, too, that had tin pans in it,[7] I reckon, and nothing was ever so lovely as to hear the young ladies sing, "The Last Link is Broken" and play "The Battle of Prague"[8] on it. The walls of all the rooms was plastered, and most had carpets on the floors, and the whole house was whitewashed on the outside.

It was a double house, and the big open place betwixt them was roofed and floored, and sometimes the table was set there in the middle of the day, and it was a cool, comfortable place. Nothing couldn't be better. And warn't the cooking good, and just bushels of it too!

Chapter XVIII

Col. Grangerford was a gentleman, you see. He was a gentleman all over; and so was his family. He was well born, as the saying is, and that's worth as much in a man as it is in a horse, so the Widow Douglas said, and nobody ever denied that she was of the first aristocracy in our town; and pap he always said it, too, though he warn't no more quality than a mud-cat,[1] himself. Col. Grangerford was very tall and very slim, and had a darkish-paly complexion, not a sign of red in it anywheres; he was clean-shaved every morning, all over his thin face, and he had the thinnest kind of lips, and the thinnest kind of nostrils, and a high nose, and heavy eyebrows, and the blackest kind of eyes, sunk so deep back that they seemed like they was looking out of caverns at you, as you may say. His forehead was high, and his hair was black and straight, and hung to his shoulders. His hands was long and thin, and every day of his life he put on a clean shirt and a full suit from head to foot made out of linen so white it hurt your eyes to look at it; and on Sundays he wore a blue tail-coat with brass buttons on it. He carried a mahogany cane with a silver head to it. There warn't no frivolishness about him, not a bit, and he warn't ever loud. He was as kind as he could be—you could feel that, you know, and so you had confidence. Sometimes he smiled, and it was good to see; but when he straightened himself up like a liberty-pole,[2] and the lightning

---

[7] Some pianos in the nineteenth century were equipped with cymbals and other percussion devices that responded to foot pedals.

[8] "The Last Link Is Broken" (1840?) is a sentimental song by William Clifton; "The Battle of Prague" (1788) is a flamboyant piano piece by the Czech composer Franz Kotzwara that attempts to recreate the sounds of a military battle.

[1] A catfish.   [2] A flagpole.

begun to flicker out from under his eyebrows you wanted to climb a tree first, and find out what the matter was afterwards. He didn't ever have to tell anybody to mind their manners—everybody was always good mannered where he was. Everybody loved to have him around, too; he was sunshine most always—I mean he made it seem like good weather. When he turned into a cloud-bank it was awful dark for a half a minute and that was enough; there wouldn't nothing go wrong again for a week.

When him and the old lady come down in the morning, all the family got up out of their chairs and give them good-day, and didn't set down again till they had set down. Then Tom and Bob went to the sideboard where the decanters was, and mixed a glass of bitters and handed it to him, and he held it in his hand and waited till Tom's and Bob's was mixed, and then they bowed and said "Our duty to you, sir and madam;" and *they* bowed the least bit in the world and said thank you, and so they drank, all three, and Bob and Tom poured a spoonful of water on the sugar and the mite of whisky or apple brandy in the bottom of their tumblers, and give it to me and Buck, and we drank to the old people too.

Bob was the oldest, and Tom was next. Tall, beautiful men with very broad shoulders and brown faces, and long black hair and black eyes. They dressed in white linen from head to foot, like the old gentleman, and wore broad Panama hats.

Then there was Miss Charlotte, she was twenty-five, and tall and proud and grand, but as good as she could be, when she warn't stirred up; but when she was, she had a look that would make you wilt in your tracks, like her father. She was beautiful.

So was her sister, Miss Sophia, but it was a different kind. She was gentle and sweet, like a dove, and she was only twenty.

Each person had their own nigger to wait on them—Buck, too. My nigger had a monstrous easy time, because I warn't used to having anybody do anything for me, but Buck's was on the jump most of the time.

This was all there was of the family, now; but there used to be more—three sons; they got killed; and Emmeline that died.

The old gentleman owned a lot of farms, and over a hundred niggers. Sometimes a stack of people would come there, horseback, from ten or fifteen mile around, and stay five or six days, and have such junketings round about and on the river, and dances and picnics in the woods, day-times, and balls at the house, nights. These people was mostly kin-folks of the family. The men brought their guns with them. It was a handsome lot of quality, I tell you.

There was another clan of aristocracy around there—five or six families— mostly of the name of Shepherdson. They was as high-toned, and well born, and rich and grand, as the tribe of Grangerfords. The Shepherdsons and the Grangerfords used the same steamboat landing, which was about two mile above our house; so sometimes when I went up there with a lot of our folks I used to see a lot of the Shepherdsons there, on their fine horses.

One day Buck and me was away out in the woods, hunting, and heard a horse coming. We was crossing the road. Buck says:

"Quick! Jump for the woods!"

We done it, and then peeped down the woods through the leaves. Pretty soon a splendid young man come galloping down the road, setting his horse easy and looking like a soldier. He had his gun across his pommel. I had seen him before. It was young Harney Shepherdson. I heard Buck's gun go off at my ear, and Harney's hat tumbled off from his head. He grabbed his gun and rode straight to the place where we was hid. But we didn't wait. We started through the woods on a run. The woods warn't thick, so I looked over my shoulder, to dodge the bullet, and twice I seen Harney cover Buck with his gun; and then he rode away the way he come—to get his hat, I reckon, but I couldn't see. We never stopped running till we got home. The old gentleman's eyes blazed a minute—'twas pleasure, mainly, I judged—then his face sort of smoothed down, and he says, kind of gentle:

"I don't like that shooting from behind a bush. Why didn't you step into the road, my boy?"

"The Shepherdsons don't, father. They always take advantage."

Miss Charlotte she held her head up like a queen while Buck was telling his tale, and her nostrils spread and her eyes snapped. The two young men looked dark, but never said nothing. Miss Sophia she turned pale, but the color come back when she found the man warn't hurt.

Soon as I could get Buck down by the corn-cribs under the trees by ourselves, I says:

"Did you want to kill him, Buck?"

"Well, I bet I did."

"What did he do to you?"

"Him? He never done nothing to me."

"Well, then, what did you want to kill him for?"

"Why nothing—only it's on account of the feud."

"What's a feud?"

"Why, where was you raised? Don't you know what a feud is?"

"Never heard of it before—tell me about it."

"Well," says Buck, "a feud is this way. A man has a quarrel with another man, and kills him; then that other man's brother kills *him;* then the other brothers, on both sides, goes for one another; then the *cousins* chip in—and by-and-by everybody's killed off, and there ain't no more feud. But it's kind of slow, and takes a long time."

"Has this one been going on long, Buck?"

"Well, I should *reckon!* it started thirty year ago, or som'ers along there. There was trouble 'bout something and then a lawsuit to settle it; and the suit went agin one of the men, and so he up and shot the man that won the suit—which he would naturally do, of course. Anybody would."

"What was the trouble about, Buck?—land?"

"I reckon maybe—I don't know."

"Well, who done the shooting?—was it a Grangerford or a Shepherdson?"

"Laws, how do *I* know? it was so long ago."

"Don't anybody know?"

"Oh, yes, pa knows, I reckon, and some of the other old folks; but they don't know, now, what the row was about in the first place."

"Has there been many killed, Buck?"

"Yes—right smart chance of funerals. But they don't always kill. Pa's got a few buck-shot in him; but he don't mind it 'cuz he don't weigh much anyway. Bob's been carved up some with a bowie, and Tom's been hurt once or twice."

"Has anybody been killed this year, Buck?"

"Yes, we got one and they got one. 'Bout three months ago my cousin Bud, fourteen year old, was riding through the woods on t'other side of the river, and didn't have no weapon with him, which was blame' foolishness, and in a lonesome place he hears a horse a-coming behind him, and sees old Baldy Shepherdson a-linkin' after him with his gun in his hand and his white hair a-flying in the wind; and 'stead of jumping off and taking to the brush, Bud 'lowed he could outrun him; so they had it, nip and tuck, for five mile or more, the old man a-gaining all the time; so at last Bud seen it warn't any use, so he stopped and faced around so as to have the bullet holes in front, you know, and the old man he rode up and shot him down. But he didn't git much chance to enjoy his luck, for inside of a week our folks laid *him* out."

"I reckon that old man was a coward, Buck."

"I reckon he *warn't* a coward. Not by a blame' sight. There ain't a coward amongst them Shepherdsons—not a one. And there ain't no cowards amongst the Grangerfords, either. Why, that old man kep' up his end in a fight one day, for a half an hour, against three Grangerfords, and come out winner. They was all a-horseback; he lit off of his horse and got behind a little wood-pile, and kep' his horse before him to stop the bullets; but the Grangerfords staid on their horses and capered around the old man, and peppered away at him, and he peppered away at them. Him and his horse both went home pretty leaky and crippled, but the Grangerfords had to be *fetched* home—and one of 'em was dead, and another died the next day. No, sir, if a body's out hunting for cowards, he don't want to fool away any time amongst them Shepherdsons, becuz they don't breed any of that *kind*."

Next Sunday we all went to church, about three mile, everybody a-horseback. The men took their guns along, so did Buck, and kept them betweeen their knees or stood them handy against the wall. The Shepherdsons done the same. It was pretty ornery preaching—all about brotherly love, and such-like tiresomeness; but everybody said it was a good sermon, and they all talked it over going home, and had such a powerful lot to say about faith, and good works, and free grace, and preforeordestination,[3] and I don't know what all, that it did seem to me to be one of the roughest Sundays I had run across yet.

About an hour after dinner everybody was dozing around, some in their chairs and some in their rooms, and it got to be pretty dull. Buck and a dog was stretched out on the grass in the sun, sound asleep. I went up to our room, and judged I would take a nap myself. I found that sweet Miss Sophia standing in her door, which was next to ours, and she took me in her room and shut the door very soft, and asked me if I liked her, and I said I did; and she asked me if I would do something for her and not tell anybody, and I said I would. Then she said she'd forgot her Testament, and left it in the seat at church, between two other books and would I slip out quiet and go there and fetch it to her, and not say nothing to nobody. I said I would. So I slid out and slipped off up the road, and there warn't anybody at the church, except maybe a hog or two, for there warn't any lock on the door, and hogs likes a puncheon floor[4] in summer-time because it's cool. If you notice, most folks don't go to church only when they've got to; but a hog is different.

Says I to myself something's up—it ain't natural for a girl to be in such a sweat about a Testament; so I give it a shake, and out drops a little piece of paper with "*Half-past two*" wrote on it with a pencil. I ransacked it, but couldn't find any-

---

[3] Huck combines the terms "predestination" and "foreordination" to make this jawbreaking word.
[4] A floor of log slabs set into the ground.

thing else. I couldn't make anything out of that, so I put the paper in the book again, and when I got home and up stairs, there was Miss Sophia in her door waiting for me. She pulled me in and shut the door; then she looked in the Testament till she found the paper, and as soon as she read it she looked glad; and before a body could think, she grabbed me and give me a squeeze, and said I was the best boy in the world, and not to tell anybody. She was mighty red in the face, for a minute, and her eyes lighted up and it made her powerful pretty. I was a good deal astonished, but when I got my breath I asked her what the paper was about, and she asked me if I had read it, and I said no, and she asked me if I could read writing, and I told her "no, only coarse-hand,"[5] and then she said the paper warn't anything but a book-mark to keep her place, and I might go and play now.

I went off down to the river, studying over this thing, and pretty soon I noticed that my nigger was following along behind. When we was out of sight of the house, he looked back and around a second, and then comes a-running, and says:

"Mars Jawge, if you'll come down into de swamp, I'll show you a whole stack o' water-moccasins."

Thinks I, that's mighty curious; he said that yesterday. He oughter know a body don't love water-moccasins enough to go around hunting for them. What is he up to anyway? So I says—

"All right, trot ahead."

I followed a half a mile, then he struck out over the swamp and waded ankle deep as much as another half mile. We come to a little flat piece of land which was dry and very thick with trees and bushes and vines, and he says—

"You shove right in dah, jist a few steps, Mars Jawge, dah's whah dey is. I's seed 'm befo', I don't k'yer to see 'em no mo'. "

Then he slopped right along and went away, and pretty soon the trees hid him. I poked into the place a-ways, and come to a little open patch as big as a bedroom, all hung around with vines, and found a man laying there asleep—and by jings it was my old Jim!

I waked him up, and I reckoned it was going to be a grand surprise to him to see me again, but it warn't. He nearly cried, he was so glad, but he warn't surprised. He said he swum along behind me, that night, and heard me yell every time, but dasn't answer, because he didn't want nobody to pick *him* up, and take him into slavery again. Says he—

"I got hurt a little, en couldn't swim fas', so I wuz a considable ways behine you, towards de las'; when you landed I reck'ned I could ketch up wid you on de lan' 'dout havin' to shout at you, but when I see dat house I begin to go slow. I 'uz off too fur to hear what dey say to you—I wuz 'fraid o' de dogs—but when it 'uz all quiet agin, I knowed you's in de house, so I struck out for de woods to wait for day. Early in de mawnin' some er de niggers come along, gwyne to de fields, en dey tuck me en showed me dis place, whah de dogs can't track me on accounts o' de water, en dey brings me truck to eat every night, en tells me how you's a gitt'n along."

"Why didn't you tell my Jack to fetch me here sooner, Jim?"

"Well, 'twarn't no use to 'sturb you, Huck, tell we could do sumfn—but we's all right now. I ben a-buyin' pots en pans en vittles, as I got a chanst, en a patching' up de raf' nights, when—"

"*What* raft, Jim?"

---

[5] Block printing by hand.

"Our ole raf'."

"You mean to say our old raft warn't smashed all to flinders?"

"No, she warn't. She was tore up a good deal—one en' of her was—but dey warn't no great harm done, on'y our traps was mos' all los'. Ef we hadn' dive' so deep en swum so fur under water, en de night hadn' ben so dark, en we warn't so sk'yerd, en ben sich punkin-heads, as de sayin' is, we'd a seed de raf'. But it's jis' as well we didn't, 'kase now she's all fixed up agin mos' as good as new, en we's got a new lot o'stuff, too, in de place o' what 'uz los'. "

"Why, how did you get hold of the raft again, Jim—did you catch her?"

"How I gwyne to ketch her, en I out in de woods? No, some er de niggers foun' her ketched on a snag, along heah in de ben', en dey hid her in a crick, 'mongst de willows, en dey wuz so much jawin' 'bout which un 'um she b'long to de mos', dat I come to heah 'bout it pooty soon, so I ups en settles de trouble by tellin' 'um she don't b'long to none uv um, but to you en me; en I ast 'm if dey gwyne to grab a young white genlman's propaty, en git a hid'n for it? Den I gin 'm ten cents apiece, en dey 'uz mighty well satisfied, en wisht some mo' raf's 'ud come along en make 'm rich agin. Dey's mighty good to me, dese niggers is, en whatever I wants 'm to do fur me, I doan't have to ast 'm twice, honey. Dat Jack's a good nigger, en pooty smart."

"Yes, he is. He ain't ever told me you was here; told me to come, and he'd show me a lot of water-moccasins. If anything happens, *he* ain't mixed up in it. He can say he never seen us together, and it'll be the truth."

I don't want to talk much about the next day. I reckon I'll cut it pretty short. I waked up about dawn, and was agoing to turn over and go to sleep again, when I noticed how still it was—didn't seem to be anybody stirring. That warn't usual. Next I noticed that Buck was up and gone. Well, I gets up, a-wondering, and goes down stairs—nobody around; everything as still as a mouse. Just the same outside; thinks I, what does it mean? Down by the wood-pile I comes across my Jack, and says:

"What's it all about?"

Says he:

"Don't you know, Mars Jawge?"

"No," says I, "I don't."

"Well, den, Miss Sophia's run off! 'deed she has. She run off in de night, sometime—nobody don't know jis' when—run off to git married to dat young Harney Shepherdson, you know—leastways, so dey 'spec. De fambly foun' it out, 'bout half an hour ago—maybe a little mo'—en' I *tell* you dey warn't no time los'. Sich another hurryin' up guns en hosses *you* never see! De women folks has gone for to stir up relations, en ole Mars Saul en de boys tuck dey guns en rode up de river road for to try to ketch dat young man en kill him 'fo' he kin git acrost de river wid Mis Sophia. I reck'n dey's gwyne to be mighty rough times."

"Buck went off 'thout waking me up."

"Well I reck'n he *did!* Dey warn't gwyne to mix you up in it. Mars Buck he loaded up his gun en 'lowed he's gwyne to fetch home a Shepherdson or bust. Well, dey'll be plenty un 'm dah, I reck'n, en you bet you he'll fetch one ef he gits a chanst."

I took up the river road as hard as I could put. By-and-by I begin to hear guns a good ways off. When I come in sight of the log store and the wood-pile where the steamboats lands, I worked along under the trees and brush till I got to a good place, and then I clumb up into the forks of a cotton-wood that was out of reach, and watched. There was a wood-rank[6] four foot high, a little ways in front of the tree, and first I was going to hide behind that; but maybe it was luckier I didn't.

There was four or five men cavorting around on their horses in the open place before the log store, cussing and yelling, and trying to get at a couple of young chaps that was behind the wood-rank alongside of the steamboat landing—but they couldn't come it. Every time one of them showed himself on the river side of the wood-pile he got shot at. The two boys was squatting back to back behind the pile, so they could watch both ways.

By-and-by the men stopped cavorting around and yelling. They started riding towards the store; then up gets one of the boys, draws a steady bead over the wood-rank, and drops one of them out of his saddle. All the men jumped off of their horses and grabbed the hurt one and started to carry him to the store; and that minute the two boys started on the run. They got half-way to the tree I was in before the men noticed. Then the men see them, and jumped on their horses and took out after them. They gained on the boys, but it didn't do no good, the boys had too good a start; they got to the wood-pile that was in front of my tree, and slipped in behind it, and so they had the bulge[7] on the men again. One of the boys was Buck, and the other was a slim young chap about nineteen years old.

The men ripped around awhile, and then rode away. As soon as they was out of sight, I sung out to Buck and told him. He didn't know what to make of my voice coming out of the tree, at first. He was awful surprised. He told me to watch out sharp and let him know when the men come in sight again; said they was up to some devilment or other—wouldn't be gone long. I wished I was out of that tree, but I dasn't come down. Buck begun to cry and rip, and 'lowed that him and his cousin Joe (that was the other young chap) would make up for this day, yet. He said his father and his two brothers was killed, and two or three of the enemy. Said the Shepherdsons laid for them, in ambush. Buck said his father and brothers ought to waited for their relations—the Shepherdsons was too strong for them. I asked him what was become of young Harney and Miss Sophia. He said they'd got across the river and was safe. I was glad of that; but the way Buck did take on because he didn't manage to kill Harney that day he shot at him—I hain't ever heard anything like it.

All of a sudden, bang! bang! bang! goes three or four guns— the men had slipped around through the woods and come in from behind without their horses! The boys jumped for the river—both of them hurt—and as they swum down the current the men run along the bank shooting at them and singing out, "Kill them, kill them!" It made me so sick I most fell out of the tree. I ain't agoing to tell *all* that happened—it would make me sick again if I was to do that. I wished I hadn't ever come ashore that night, to see such things. I ain't ever going to get shut of them—lots of times I dream about them.

I staid in the tree till it begun to get dark, afraid to come down. Sometimes I heard guns away off in the woods; and twice I seen little gangs of men gallop past the log store with guns; so I reckoned the trouble was still agoing on. I was mighty down-hearted; so I made up my mind I wouldn't ever go anear that house again, because I reckoned I was to blame, somehow. I judged that that piece of paper meant that Miss Sophia was to meet Harney somewheres at half-past two and run off; and I judged I ought to told her father about that paper and the curious way

[6] A stack of firewood.   [7] The edge, the advantage.

she acted, and then maybe he would a locked her up and this awful mess wouldn't ever happened.

When I got down out of the tree, I crept along down the river bank a piece, and found the two bodies laying in the edge of the water, and tugged at them till I got them ashore; then I covered up their faces, and got away as quick as I could. I cried a little when I was covering up Buck's face, for he was mighty good to me.

It was just dark, now. I never went near the house, but struck through the woods and made for the swamp. Jim warn't on his island, so I tramped off in a hurry for the crick, and crowded through the willows, red-hot to jump aboard and get out of that awful country—the raft was gone! My souls, but I was scared! I couldn't get my breath for most a minute. Then I raised a yell. A voice not twenty-five foot from me, says—

"Good lan'! is dat you, honey? Doan' make no noise."

It was Jim's voice—nothing ever sounded so good before. I run along the bank a piece and got aboard, and Jim he grabbed me and hugged me, he was so glad to see me. He says—

"Laws bless you, chile, I 'uz right down sho' you's dead agin. Jack's been heah, he say he reck'n you's ben shot, kase you didn' come home no mo'; so I's jes' dis minute a startin' de raf' down towards de mouf er de crick, so's to be all ready for to shove out en leave soon as Jack comes agin en tells me for certain you *is* dead. Lawsy, I's mighty glad to git you back agin, honey."

I says—

"All right—that's mighty good; they won't find me, and they'll think I've been killed, and floated down the river—there's something up there that'll help them to think so—so don't you lose no time, Jim, but just shove off for the big water as fast as ever you can."

I never felt easy till the raft was two mile below there and out in the middle of the Mississippi. Then we hung up our signal lantern, and judged that we was free and safe once more. I hadn't had a bite to eat since yesterday; so Jim he got out some corn-dodgers[8] and buttermilk, and pork and cabbage, and greens—there ain't nothing in the world so good, when it's cooked right—and whilst I eat my supper we talked, and had a good time. I was powerful glad to get away from the feuds, and so was Jim to get away from the swamp. We said there warn't no home like a raft, after all. Other places do seem so cramped up and smothery, but a raft don't. You feel mighty free and easy and comfortable on a raft.

Chapter XIX

Two or three days and nights went by; I reckon I might say they swum by, they slid along so quiet and smooth and lovely. Here is the way we put in the time. It was a monstrous big river down there—sometimes a mile and a half wide; we run nights, and laid up and hid day-times; soon as night was most gone, we stopped navigating and tied up—nearly always in the dead water under a tow-head; and then cut young cotton-woods and willows and hid the raft with them. Then we set out the lines. Next we slid into the river and had a swim, so as to freshen up and cool off; then we set down on the sandy bottom where the water was about knee deep, and watched the daylight come. Not a sound, anywheres—perfectly still—

[8] Hard-baked cornmeal cakes.

just like the whole world was asleep, only sometimes the bull-frogs a-cluttering, maybe. The first thing to see, looking away over the water, was a kind of dull line—that was the woods on t'other side—you couldn't make nothing else out; then a pale place in the sky; then more paleness, spreading around; then the river softened up, away off, and warn't black any more, but gray; you could see little dark spots drifting along, ever so far away—trading scows, and such things; and long black streaks—rafts; sometimes you could hear a sweep screaking; or jumbled up voices, it was so still, and sounds come so far; and by-and-by you could see a streak on the water which you know by the look of the streak that there's a snag there in a swift current which breaks on it and makes that streak look that way; and you see the mist curl up off the water, and the east reddens up, and the river, and you make out a log cabin in the edge of the woods, away on the bank on t'other side of the river, being a wood-yard, likely, and piled by them cheats so you can throw a dog through it anywheres;[1] then the nice breeze springs up, and comes fanning you from over there, so cool and fresh, and sweet to smell, on account of the woods and the flowers; but sometimes not that way, because they've left dead fish laying around, gars,[2] and such, and they do get pretty rank; and next you've got the full day, and everything smiling in the sun, and the song-birds just going it!

A little smoke couldn't be noticed, now, so we would take some fish off of the lines, and cook up a hot breakfast. And afterwards we would watch the lonesome-ness of the river, and kind of lazy along, and by-and-by lazy off to sleep. Wake up, by-and-by, and look to see what done it, and maybe see a steamboat, cough-ing along up stream, so far off towards the other side you couldn't tell nothing about her only whether she was stern-wheel or side-wheel; then for about an hour there wouldn't be nothing to hear nor nothing to see—just solid lonesomeness. Next you'd see a raft sliding by, away off yonder, and maybe a galoot[3] on it chopping, because they're most always doing it on a raft; you'd see the ax flash, and come down—you don't hear nothing; you see that ax go up again, and by the time it's above the man's head, then you hear the *k'chunk!*—it had took all that time to come over the water. So we would put in the day, lazying around, listen-ing to the stillness. Once there was a thick fog, and the rafts and things that went by was beating tin pans so the steamboats wouldn't run over them. A scow or a raft went by so close we could hear them talking and cussing and laughing—heard them plain; but we couldn't see no sign of them; it made you feel crawly, it was like spirits carrying on that way in the air. Jim said he believed it was spirits; but I says:

"No, spirits wouldn't say, 'dern the dern fog.' "

Soon as it was night, out we shoved; when we got her out to about the middle, we let her alone, and let her float wherever the current wanted her to; then we lit the pipes, and dangled our legs in the water and talked about all kinds of things—we was always naked, day and night, whenever the mosquitoes would let us—the new clothes Buck's folks made for me was too good to be comfortable, and be-sides I didn't go much on clothes, nohow.

Sometimes we'd have that whole river all to ourselves for the longest time. Yonder was the banks and the islands, across the water; and maybe a spark—

---

[1] Stacks of wood were sold by measurement (height and width) to passing steamboats; by stacking the wood with large gaps, the owners tried to have less wood in a standard measurement.

[2] A seldom-eaten variety of pike.   [3] A bumpkin or oaf.

which was a candle in a cabin window—and sometimes on the water you could see a spark or two—on a raft or a scow, you know; and maybe you could hear a fiddle or a song coming over from one of them crafts. It's lovely to live on a raft. We had the sky, up there, all speckled with stars, and we used to lay on our backs and look up at them, and discuss about whether they was made, or only just happened—Jim he allowed they was made, but I allowed they happened; I judged it would have took too long to *make* so many. Jim said the moon could a *laid* them; well, that looked kind of reasonable, so I didn't say nothing against it, because I've seen a frog lay most as many, so of course it could be done. We used to watch the stars that fell, too, and see them streak down. Jim allowed they'd got spoiled and was hove out of the nest.

Once or twice of a night we would see a steamboat slipping along in the dark, and now and then she would belch a whole world of sparks up out of her chimbleys, and they would rain down in the river and look awful pretty; then she would turn a corner and her lights would wink out and her pow-wow[4] shut off and leave the river still again; and by-and-by her waves would get to us, a long time after she was gone, and joggle the raft a bit, and after that you wouldn't hear nothing for you couldn't tell how long, except maybe frogs or something.

After midnight the people on shore went to bed, and then for two or three hours the shores was black—no more sparks in the cabin windows. These sparks was our clock—the first one that showed again meant morning was coming, so we hunted a place to hide and tie up, right away.

One morning about day-break, I found a canoe[5] and crossed over a chute[6] to the main shore—it was only two hundred yards—and paddled about a mile up a crick amongst the cypress woods, to see if I couldn't get some berries. Just as I was passing a place where a kind of a cow-path crossed the crick, here comes a couple of men tearing up the path as tight as they could foot it. I thought I was a goner, for whenever anybody was after anybody I judged it was *me*—or maybe Jim. I was about to dig out from there in a hurry, but they was pretty close to me then, and sung out and begged me to save their lives—said they hadn't been doing nothing, and was being chased for it—said there was men and dogs a-coming. They wanted to jump right in, but I says—

"Don't you do it. I don't hear the dogs and horses yet; you've got time to crowd through the brush and get up the crick a little ways; then you take to the water and wade down to me and get in—that'll throw the dogs off the scent."

They done it, and soon as they was aboard I lit out for our tow-head, and in about five or ten minutes we heard the dogs and the men away off, shouting. We heard them come along towards the crick, but couldn't see them; they seemed to stop and fool around a while; then, as we got further and further away all the time, we couldn't hardly hear them at all; by the time we had left a mile of woods behind us and struck the river, everything was quiet, and we paddled over to the tow-head and hid in the cotton-woods and was safe.

One of these fellows was about seventy, or upwards, and had a bald head and very gray whiskers. He had an old battered-up slouch hat on, and a greasy blue woolen shirt, and ragged old blue jeans britches stuffed into his boot tops, and home-knit galluses[7]—no, he only had one. He had an old long-tailed blue jeans

---

[4] Engine noise.

[5] Twain had originally written "I took the canoe"; when a sharp-eyed proofreader pointed out on page 160 of the proofs that the canoe had been lost on page 129, Twain simply changed the wording.

[6] A narrow channel with a rapidly flowing current.   [7] Suspenders.

coat with slick brass buttons, flung over his arm, and both of them had big fat ratty-looking carpet-bags.

The other fellow was about thirty and dressed about as ornery. After breakfast we all laid off and talked, and the first thing that come out was that these chaps didn't know one another.

"What got you into trouble?" says the baldhead to t'other chap.

"Well, I'd been selling an article to take the tartar off the teeth—and it does take it off, too, and generly the enamel along with it—but I staid about one night longer than I ought to, and was just in the act of sliding out when I ran across you on the trail this side of town, and you told me they were coming, and begged me to help you to get off. So I told you I was expecting trouble myself and would scatter out *with* you. That's the whole yarn—what's yourn?"

"Well, I'd ben a-runnin' a little temperance revival thar, 'bout a week, and was the pet of the women-folks, big and little, for I was makin' it mighty warm for the rummies, I *tell* you, and takin' as much as five or six dollars a night—ten cents a head, children and niggers free—and business a growin' all the time; when somehow or another a little report got around, last night, that I had a way of puttin' in my time with a private jug, on the sly. A nigger rousted me out this mornin', and told me the people was getherin' on the quiet, with their dogs and horses, and they'd be along pretty soon and give me 'bout half an hour's start, and then run me down, if they could; and if they got me they'd tar and feather me and ride me on a rail, sure. I didn't wait for no breakfast—I warn't hungry."

"Old man," says the young one, "I reckon we might double-team it together; what do you think?"

"I ain't undisposed. What's your line—mainly?"

"Jour printer,[8] by trade; do a little in patent medicines; theatre-actor—tragedy, you know; take a turn at mesmerism and phrenology,[9] when there's a chance; teach singing-geography school for a change; sling a lecture, sometimes—oh, I do lots of things—most anything that comes handy, so it ain't work. What's your lay?"[10]

"I've done considerable in the doctoring way in my time. Layin' on o' hands[11] is my best holt—for cancer, and paralysis, and sich things; and I k'n tell a fortune pretty good, when I've got somebody along to find out the facts for me. Preachin's my line, too: and workin' camp-meetin's;[12] and missionaryin around."

Nobody never said anything for a while; then the young man hove a sigh and says—

"Alas!"

"What're you alassin' about?" says the baldhead.

"To think I should have lived to be leading such a life, and be degraded down into such company." And he begun to wipe the corner of his eye with a rag.

"Dern your skin, ain't the company good enough for you?" says the baldhead, pretty pert and uppish.

"Yes, it *is* good enough for me; it's as good as I deserve; for who fetched me so low, when I was so high? *I* did myself. I don't blame *you*, gentlemen—far from it; I don't blame anybody. I deserve it all. Let the cold world do its worst; one thing

---

[8] Journeyman-printer who worked by the day.

[9] Hypnotism and the pseudoscience of reading character from contours of the skull.

[10] Racket, game.   [11] Faith healing, to cure such things as "cancer" and "paralysis."

[12] Evangelical revivals held outdoors, typically for several days.

I know—there's a grave somewhere for me. The world may go on just as its always done, and take everything from me—loved ones, property, everything—but it can't take that. Some day I'll lie down in it and forget it all, and my poor broken heart will be at rest." He went on a-wiping.

"Drot your pore broken heart," says the baldhead; "what are you heaving your pore broken heart at *us* f'r? *We* hain't done nothing."

"No, I know you haven't. I ain't blaming you, gentlemen. I brought myself down—yes, I did it myself. It's right I should suffer—perfectly right—I don't make any moan."

"Brought you down from whar? Whar was you brought down from?"

"Ah, you would not believe me; the world never believes—let it pass—'tis no matter. The secret of my birth—"

"The secret of your birth? Do you mean to say—"

"Gentlemen," says the young man, very solemn, "I will reveal it to you, for I feel I may have confidence in you. By rights I am a duke!"

Jim's eyes bugged out when he heard that; and I reckon mine did, too. Then the baldhead says: "No! you can't mean it?"

"Yes. My great-grandfather, eldest son of the Duke of Bridgewater, fled to this country about the end of the last century, to breathe the pure air of freedom; married here, and died, leaving a son, his own father dying about the same time. The second son of the late duke seized the title and estates—the infant real duke was ignored. I am the lineal descendant of that infant—I am the rightful Duke of Bridgewater; and here am I, forlorn, torn from my high estate, hunted of men, despised by the cold world, ragged, worn, heart-broken, and degraded to the companionship of felons on a raft!"

Jim pitied him ever so much, and so did I. We tried to comfort him, but he said it warn't much use, he couldn't be much comforted; said if we was a mind to acknowledge him, that would do him more good than most anything else; so we said we would, if he would tell us how. He said we ought to bow, when we spoke to him, and say "Your Grace," or "My Lord," or "Your Lordship"—and he wouldn't mind it if we called him plain "Bridgewater," which he said was a title, anyway, and not a name; and one of us ought to wait on him at dinner, and do any little thing for him he wanted done.

Well, that was all easy, so we done it. All through dinner Jim stood around and waited on him, and says, "Will yo' Grace have some o' dis, or some o' dat?" and so on, and a body could see it was mighty pleasing to him.

But the old man got pretty silent, by-and-by—didn't have much to say, and didn't look pretty comfortable over all that petting that was going on around that duke. He seemed to have something on his mind. So, along in the afternoon, he says:

"Looky here, Bilgewater," he says, "I'm nation sorry for you, but you ain't the only person that's had troubles like that."

"No?"

"No, you ain't. You ain't the only person that's ben snaked down wrongfully out'n a high place.'

"Alas!"

"No, you ain't the only person that's had a secret of his birth." And by jing, *he* begins to cry.

"Hold! What do you mean?"

"Bilgewater, kin I trust you?" says the old man, still sort of sobbing.

"To bitter death!" He took the old man by the hand and squeezed it, and says, "The secret of your being: speak!"

"Bilgewater, I am the late Dauphin!"[13]

You bet you Jim and me stared, this time. Then the duke says:

"You are what?"

"Yes, my friend, it is too true—your eyes is lookin' at this very moment on the pore disappeared Dauphin, Looy the Seventeen, son of Looy the Sixteen and Marry Antonette."

"You! At your age! No! You mean you're the late Charlemagne;[14] you must be six or seven hundred years old, at the very least."

"Trouble has done it, Bilgewater, trouble has done it; trouble has brung these gray hairs and this premature balditude. Yes, gentlemen, you see before you, in blue jeans and misery, the wanderin', exiled, trampled-on and sufferin' rightful King of France."

Well, he cried and took on so, that me and Jim didn't know hardly what to do, we was so sorry—and so glad and proud we'd got him with us, too. So we set in, like we done before with the duke, and tried to comfort *him*. But he said it warn't no use, nothing but to be dead and done with it all could do him any good; though he said it often made him feel easier and better for a while if people treated him according to his rights, and got down on one knee to speak to him, and always called him "Your Majesty," and waited on him first at meals, and didn't set down in his presence till he asked them. So Jim and me set to majestying him, and doing this and that and t'other for him, and standing up till he told us we might set down. This done him heaps of good, and so he got cheerful and comfortable. But the duke kind of soured on him, and didn't look a bit satisfied with the way things was going; still, the king acted real friendly towards him, and said the duke's great-grandfather and all the other Dukes of Bilgewater was a good deal thought of by *his* father and was allowed to come to the palace considerable; but the duke staid huffy a good while, till by-and-by the king says:

"Like as not we got to be together a blamed long time, on this h-yer raft, Bilgewater, and so what's the use o' your bein' sour? It'll only make things on-comfortable. It ain't my fault I warn't born a duke, it ain't your fault you warn't born a king—so what's the use to worry? Make the best o' things the way you find 'em, says I—that's my motto. This ain't no bad thing that we've struck here—plenty grub and an easy life—come, give us your hand, Duke, and less all be friends."

The duke done it, and Jim and me was pretty glad to see it. It took away all the uncomfortableness, and we felt mighty good over it, because it would a been a miserable business to have any unfriendliness on the raft; for what you want, above all things, on a raft, is for everybody to be satisfied, and feel right and kind towards the others.

It didn't take me long to make up my mind that these liars warn't no kings nor dukes, at all, but just low-down humbugs and frauds. But I never said nothing, never let on; kept it to myself; it's the best way; then you don't have no quarrels,

---

[13] Had he survived, the dauphin would have been in his fifties.

[14] Charles the Great (742?–814), crowned emperor by Pope Leo III on Christmas Day, 800, thus laying the foundation for the Holy Roman Empire.

and don't get into no trouble. If they wanted us to call them kings and dukes, I hadn't no objections, 'long as it would keep peace in the family; and it warn't no use to tell Jim, so I didn't tell him. If I never learnt nothing else out of pap, I learnt that the best way to get along with his kind of people is to let them have their own way.

Chapter XX

They asked us considerable many questions; wanted to know what we covered up the raft that way for, and laid by in the day-time instead of running—was Jim a runaway nigger? Says I—

"Goodness sakes, would a runaway nigger run *south?*"

No, they allowed he wouldn't. I had to account for things some way, so I says:

"My folks was living in Pike County, in Missouri, where I was born, and they all died off but me and pa and my brother Ike. Pa, he 'lowed he'd break up and go down and live with Uncle Ben, who's got a little one-horse place on the river, forty-four mile below Orleans. Pa was pretty poor, and had some debts; so when he'd squared up there warn't nothing left but sixteen dollars and our nigger, Jim. That warn't enough to take us fourteen hundred mile, deck passage nor no other way. Well, when the river rose, pa had a streak of luck one day; he ketched this piece of a raft; so we reckoned we'd go down to Orleans on it. Pa's luck didn't hold out; a steamboat run over the forrard corner of the raft, one night, and we all went overboard and dove under the wheel; Jim and me come up, all right, but pa was drunk, and Ike was only four years old, so they never come up no more. Well, for the next day or two we had considerable trouble, because people was always coming out in skiffs and trying to take Jim away from me, saying they believed he was a runaway nigger. We don't run day-times no more, now; nights they don't bother us."

The duke says—

"Leave me alone to cipher out a way so we can run in the day-time if we want to. I'll think the thing over—I'll invent a plan that'll fix it. We'll let it alone for to-day, because of course we don't want to go by that town yonder in daylight—it mightn't be healthy."

Towards night it begun to darken up and look like rain; the heat lightning was squirting around, low down in the sky, and the leaves was beginning to shiver—it was going to be pretty ugly, it was easy to see that. So the duke and the king went to overhauling our wigwam, to see what the beds was like. My bed was a straw tick[1]—better than Jim's, which was a corn-shuck tick; there's always cobs around about in a shuck tick, and they poke into you and hurt; and when you roll over, the dry shucks sound like you was rolling over in a pile of dead leaves; it makes such a rustling that you wake up. Well, the duke allowed he would take my bed; but the king allowed he wouldn't. He says—

"I should a reckoned the difference in rank would a sejested to you that a corn-shuck bed warn't just fitten for me to sleep on. Your Grace'll take the shuck bed yourself."

[1] A mattress.

Jim and me was in a sweat again, for a minute, being afraid there was going to be some more trouble amongst them; so we was pretty glad when the duke says—

" 'Tis my fate to be always ground into the mire under the iron heel of oppression. Misfortune has broken my once haughty spirit; I yield, I submit; 'tis my fate. I am alone in the world—let me suffer; I can bear it."

We got away as soon as it was good and dark. The king told us to stand well out towards the middle of the river, and not show a light till we got a long ways below the town. We come in sight of the little bunch of lights by-and-by—that was the town, you know—and slid by, about a half a mile out, all right. When we was three-quarters of a mile below, we hoisted up our signal lantern; and about ten o'clock it come on to rain and blow and thunder and lighten like everything; so the king told us to both stay on watch till the weather got better; then him and the duke crawled into the wigwam and turned in for the night. It was my watch below, till twelve, but I wouldn't a turned in, anyway, if I'd had a bed; because a body don't see such a storm as that every day in the week, not by a long sight. My souls, how the wind did scream along! And every second or two there'd come a glare that lit up the white-caps for a half a mile around, and you'd see the islands looking dusty through the rain, and the trees thrashing around in the wind; then comes a *h-wack!*—bum! bum! bumble-umble-um-bum-bum-bum-bum—and the thunder would go rumbling and grumbling away, and quit–and then *rip* comes another flash and another sockdolager.[2] The waves most washed me off the raft, sometimes, but I hadn't any clothes on, and didn't mind. We didn't have no trouble about snags; the lightning was glaring and flittering around so constant that we could see them plenty soon enough to throw her head this way or that and miss them.

I had the middle watch,[3] you know, but I was pretty sleepy by that time, so Jim he said he would stand the first half of it for me; he was always mighty good, that way, Jim was. I crawled into the wigwam, but the king and the duke had their legs sprawled around so there warn't no show for me; so I laid outside—I didn't mind the rain, because it was warm, and the waves warn't running so high, now. About two they come up again, though, and Jim was going to call me, but he changed his mind because he reckoned they warn't high enough yet to do any harm; but he was mistaken about that, for pretty soon all of a sudden along comes a regular ripper, and washed me overboard. It most killed Jim a-laughing. He was the easiest nigger to laugh that ever was, anyway.

I took the watch, and Jim he laid down and snored away; and by-and-by the storm let up for good and all; and the first cabin-light that showed, I rousted him out and we slid the raft into hiding-quarters for the day.

The king got out an old ratty deck of cards, after breakfast, and him and the duke played seven-up a while, five cents a game. Then they got tired of it, and allowed they would "lay out a campaign," as they called it. The duke went down into his carpet-bag and fetched up a lot of little printed bills, and read them out loud. One bill said "The celebrated Dr. Armand de Montalban of Paris," would "lecture on the Science of Phrenology" at such and such a place, on the blank day of blank, at ten cents admission, and "furnish charts of character at twenty-five cents apiece." The duke said that was *him*. In another bill he was the "world

---

[2] A tremendous clap of thunder.   [3] Midnight to 4 A.M.

renowned Shaksperean tragedian, Garrick the Younger,[4] of Drury Lane, London." In other bills he had a lot of other names and done other wonderful things, like finding water and gold with a "divining rod,"[5] "dissipating witch-spells," and so on. By-and-by he says—

"But the histrionic muse is the darling. Have you ever trod the boards,[6] Royalty?"

"No," says the king.

"You shall, then, before you're three days older, Fallen Grandeur," says the duke. "The first good town we come to, we'll hire a hall and do the sword-fight in Richard III. and the balcony scene in Romeo and Juliet. How does that strike you?"

"I'm in, up to the hub, for anything that will pay, Bilgewater, but you see I don't know nothing about play-actn', and hain't ever seen much of it. I was too small when pap used to have 'em at the palace. Do you reckon you can learn me?"

"Easy!"

"All right. I'm jist a-freezn' for something fresh, anyway. Less commence, right away."

So the duke he told him all about who Romeo was, and who Juliet was, and said he was used to being Romeo, so the king could be Juliet.

"But if Juliet's such a young gal, Duke, my peeled head and my white whiskers is goin' to look oncommon odd on her, maybe."

"No, don't you worry—these country jakes won't ever think of that. Besides, you know, you'll be in costume, and that makes all the difference in the world; Juliet's in a balcony, enjoying the moonlight before she goes to bed, and she's got on her night-gown and her ruffled night-cap. Here are the costumes for the parts."

He got out two or three curtain-calico suits, which he said was meedyevil armor for Richard III. and t'other chap,[7] and a long white cotton night-shirt and a ruffled night-cap to match. The king was satisfied; so the duke got out his book and read the parts over in the most splendid spread-eagle way, prancing around and acting at the same time, to show how it had got to be done; then he give the book to the king and told him to get his part by heart.

There was a little one-horse town about three mile down the bend, and after dinner the duke said he had ciphered out his idea about how to run in daylight without it being dangersome for Jim; so he allowed he would go down to the town and fix that thing. The king allowed he would go too, and see if he couldn't strike something. We was out of coffee, so Jim said I better go along with them in the canoe and get some.

When we go there, there warn't nobody stirring; streets empty, and perfectly dead and still, like Sunday. We found a sick nigger sunning himself in a back yard, and he said everybody that warn't too young or too sick or too old, was gone to camp-meeting, about two mile back in the woods. The king got the directions, and allowed he'd go and work that camp-meeting for all it was worth, and I might go, too.

The duke said what he was after was a printing office. We found it; a little bit of a concern, up over a carpenter shop—carpenters and printers all gone to the meeting, and no doors locked. It was a dirty, littered-up place, and had ink marks,

---

[4] David Garrick (1717–1779), a famous tragedian at the Royal Theatre in Drury Lane, London. There was no Garrick the Younger.

[5] A forked stick that supposedly points (by divination) to water, gold, or other treasure in the earth.

[6] Acted on the stage.   [7] The earl of Richmond, in Shakespeare's *Richard III.*

and handbills with pictures of horses and runaway niggers on them, all over the walls. The duke shed his coat and said he was all right, now. So me and the king lit out for the camp-meeting.

We got there in about a half an hour, fairly dripping, for it was a most awful hot day. There was as much as a thousand people there, from twenty mile around. The woods was full of teams and wagons, hitched everywheres, feeding out of the wagon troughs and stomping to keep off the flies. There was sheds made out of poles and roofed over with branches, where they had lemonade and gingerbread to sell, and piles of watermelons and green corn and such-like truck.

The preaching was going on under the same kinds of sheds, only they was bigger and held crowds of people. The benches was made out of outside slabs of logs, with holes bored in the round side to drive sticks into for legs. They didn't have no backs. The preachers had high platforms to stand on, at one end of the sheds. The women had on sun-bonnets; and some had linsey-woolsey[8] frocks, some gingham ones, and a few of the young ones had on calico. Some of the young men was barefooted, and some of the children didn't have on any clothes but just a tow-linen[9] shirt. Some of the old women was knitting, and some of the young folks was courting on the sly.

The first shed we come to, the preacher was lining out a hymn.[10] He lined out two lines, everybody sung it, and it was kind of grand to hear it, there was so many of them and they done it in such a rousing way; then he lined out two more for them to sing—and so on. The people woke up more and more, and sung louder and louder; and towards the end, some begun to groan, and some begun to shout. Then the preacher begun to preach; and begun in earnest, too; and went weaving first to one side of the platform and then the other, and then a leaning down over the front of it, with his arms and his body going all the time, and shouting his words out with all his might; and every now and then he would hold up his Bible and spread it open, and kind of pass it around this way and that, shouting, "It's the brazen serpent in the wilderness! Look upon it and live!" And people would shout out, "Glory!—A-a-*men!*" And so he went on, and the people groaning and crying and saying amen:

"Oh, come to the mourners' bench![11] come, black with sin! (*amen!*) come, sick and sore! (*amen!*) come, lame and halt, and blind! (*amen!*) come, pore and needy, sunk in shame! (*a-a-men!*) come all that's worn, and soiled, and suffering!— come with a broken spirit! come with a contrite heart! come in your rags and sin and dirt! the waters that cleanse is free, the door of heaven stands open—oh, enter in and be at rest!" (*a-a-men! glory, glory hallelujah!*)

And so on. You couldn't make out what the preacher said, any more, on account of the shouting and crying. Folks got up, everywheres in the crowd, and worked their way, just by main strength, to the mourners' bench, with the tears running down their faces; and when all the mourners had got up there to the front benches in a crowd, they sung, and shouted, and flung themselves down on the straw, just crazy and wild.

Well, the first I knowed, the king got agoing; and you could hear him over

---

[8] Cheap homespun cloth of cotton, or wool, or flax.   [9] Coarse linen cloth.

[10] Because the people are too poor to have hymnals, the preacher is reading a hymn aloud, line by line, so the congregation can follow in song. Twain makes a point that these are people of humble means before he shows us the "king" conning them.

[11] The front-row bench to be filled with those who come forward and repent.

everybody; and next he went a-charging up on to the platform and the preacher he begged him to speak to the people, and he done it. He told them he was a pirate—been a pirate for thirty years, out in the Indian Ocean, and his crew was thinned out considerable, last spring, in a fight, and he was home now, to take out some fresh men, and thanks to goodness he'd been robbed last night, and put ashore off of a steamboat without a cent, and he was glad of it, it was the blessedest thing that ever happened to him, because he was a changed man now, and happy for the first time in his life; and poor as he was, he was going to start right off and work his way back to the Indian Ocean and put in the rest of his life trying to turn the pirates into the true path; for he could do it better than anybody else, being acquainted with all the pirate crews in that ocean; and though it would take him a long time to get there, without money, he would get there anyway, and every time he convinced a pirate he would say to him, "Don't you thank me, don't you give me no credit, it all belongs to them dear people in Pokeville camp-meeting, natural brothers and benefactors of the race—and that dear preacher there, the truest friend a pirate ever had!"

And then he busted into tears, and so did everybody. Then somebody sings out, "Take up a collection for him, take up a collection!" Well, a half a dozen made a jump to do it, but somebody sings out, "Let *him* pass the hat around!" Then everybody said it, the preacher too.

So the king went all through the crowd with his hat, swabbing his eyes, and blessing the people and praising them and thanking them for being so good to the poor pirates away off there; and every little while the prettiest kind of girls, with the tears running down their cheeks, would up and ask him would he let them kiss him, for to remember him by; and he always done it; and some of them he hugged and kissed as many as five or six times—and he was invited to stay a week; and everybody wanted him to live in their houses, and said they'd think it was an honor; but he said as this was the last day of the camp-meeting he couldn't do no good, and besides he was in a sweat to get to the Indian Ocean right off and go to work on the pirates.

When we got back to the raft and he come to count up, he found he had collected eighty-seven dollars and seventy-five cents. And then he had fetched away a three-gallon jug of whisky, too, that he found under a wagon when we was starting home through the woods. The king said, take it all around, it laid over any day he'd ever put in in the missionarying line. He said it warn't no use talking, heathens don't amount to shucks, alongside of pirates, to work a camp-meeting with.

The duke was thinking *he'd* been doing pretty well, till the king come to show up, but after that he didn't think so so much. He had set up and printed off two little jobs for farmers, in that printing office—horse bills—and took the money, four dollars. And he had got in ten dollars worth of advertisements for the paper, which he said he would put in for four dollars if they would pay in advance—so they done it. The price of the paper was two dollars a year, but he took in three subscriptions for half a dollar apiece on condition of them paying him in advance; they were going to pay in cord-wood and onions, as usual, but he said he had just bought the concern and knocked down the price as low as he could afford it, and was going to run it for cash. He set up a little piece of poetry, which he made, himself, out of his own head—three verses—kind of sweet and saddish—the name of it was, "Yes, crush, cold world, this breaking heart"—and he left that all set up and ready to print in the paper and didn't charge nothing for it. Well, he took in nine dollars and a half, and said he'd done a pretty square day's work for it.

Then he showed us another little job he'd printed and hadn't charged for, because it was for us. It had a picture of a runaway nigger, with a bundle on a stick, over his shoulder, and "$200 reward" under it. The reading was all about Jim, and just described him to a dot. It said he run away from St. Jacques' plantation, forty mile below New Orleans, last winter, and likely went north, and whoever would catch him and send him back, he could have the reward and expenses.

"Now," says the duke, "after to-night we can run in the day-time if we want to. Whenever we see anybody coming, we can tie Jim hand and foot with a rope, and lay him in the wigwam and show this handbill and say we captured him up the river, and were too poor to travel on a steamboat, so we got this little raft on credit from our friends and are going down to get the reward. Handcuffs and chains would look still better on Jim, but it wouldn't go well with the story of us being so poor. Too much like jewelry. Ropes are the correct thing—we must preserve the unities,[12] as we say on the boards."

We all said the duke was pretty smart, and there couldn't be no trouble about running daytimes. We judged we could make miles enough that night to get out of the reach of the pow-wow we reckoned the duke's work in the printing office was going to make in that little town—then we could boom right along, if we wanted to.

We laid low and kept still, and never shoved out till nearly ten o'clock; then we slid by, pretty wide away from the town, and didn't hoist our lantern till we was clear out of sight of it.

When Jim called me to take the watch at four in the morning, he says—

"Huck, does you reck'n we gwyne to run acrost any mo' kings on dis trip?"

"No," I says, "I reckon not."

"Well," says he, "dat's all right, den. I doan' mine one er two kings, but dat's enough. Dis one's powerful drunk, en de duke ain' much better."

I found Jim had been trying to get him to talk French, so he could hear what it was like; but he said he had been in this country so long, and had so much trouble, he'd forgot it.

Chapter XXI

It was after sun-up, now, but we went right on, and didn't tie up. The king and the duke turned out, by-and-by, looking pretty rusty; but after they'd jumped overboard and took a swim, it chippered them up a good deal. After breakfast the king he took a seat on a corner of the raft, and pulled off his boots and rolled up his britches, and let his legs dangle in the water, so as to be comfortable, and lit his pipe, and went to getting his Romeo and Juliet by heart. When he had got it pretty good, him and the duke begun to practice it together. The duke had to learn him over and over again, how to say every speech; and he made him sigh, and put his hand on his heart, and after while he said he done it pretty well; "only," he says, "you mustn't bellow out *Romeo!* that way, like a bull—you must say it soft, and

---

[12] The unities of time, place, and action in classical drama; the duke means that their con games must be consistent, unified.

sick, and languishy, so—R-o-o-meo! that is the idea; for Juliet's a dear sweet mere child of a girl, you know, and she don't bray like a jackass."

Well, next they got out a couple of long swords that the duke made out of oak laths, and begun to practice the sword-fight—the duke called himself Richard III.; and the way they laid on, and pranced around the raft was grand to see. But by-and-by the king tripped and fell overboard, and after that they took a rest, and had a talk about all kinds of adventures they'd had in other times along the river.

After dinner, the duke says:

"Well, Capet,[1] we'll want to make this a first-class show, you know, so I guess we'll add a little more to it. We want a little something to answer encores with, anyway."

"What's onkores, Bilgewater?"

The duke told him, and then says:

"I'll answer by doing the Highland fling or the sailor's hornpipe;[2] and you— well, let me see—oh, I've got it—you can do Hamlet's soliloquy."

"Hamlet's which?"

"Hamlet's soliloquy, you know; the most celebrated thing in Shakespeare. Ah, it's sublime, sublime! Always fetches the house. I haven't got it in the book—I've only got one volume—but I reckon I can piece it out from memory. I'll just walk up and down a minute, and see if I can call it back from recollection's vaults."

So he went to marching up and down, thinking, and frowning horrible every now and then; then he would hoist up his eyebrows; next he would squeeze his hand on his forehead and stagger back and kind of moan; next he would sigh, and next he'd let on to drop a tear. It was beautiful to see him. By-and-by he got it. He told us to give attention. Then he strikes a most noble attitude, with one leg shoved forwards, and his arms stretched away up, and his head tilted back, look-ing up at the sky; and then he begins to rip and rave and grit his teeth; and after that, all through his speech he howled, and spread around, and swelled up his chest, and just knocked the spots out of any acting ever *I* see before. This is the speech[3]—I learned it, easy enough, while he was learning it to the king:

> To be, or not to be; that is the bare bodkin
> That makes calamity of so long life;
> For who would fardels bear, till Birnam Wood do come to Dunsinane,
> But that the fear of something after death
> Murders the innocent sleep,
> Great nature's second course,
> And makes us rather sling the arrows of outrageous fortune
> Than fly to others that we know not of.
> There's the respect must give us pause:
> Wake Duncan with thy knocking! I would thou couldst;
> For who would bear the whips and scorns of time,
> The oppressor's wrong, the proud man's contumely,
> The law's delay, and the quietus which his pangs might take,
> In the dead waste and middle of the night, when churchyards yawn

[1] The family name of King Louis XVI of France.
[2] Dances: the "Highland fling" from Scotland, the "sailor's hornpipe" from Wales.
[3] A hodgepodge of Shakespeare quotations that come principally from *Hamlet* and *Macbeth* but also from *Richard III*.

In customary suits of solemn black,
But that the undiscovered country from whose bourne no traveler returns,
Breathes forth contagion on the world,
And thus the native hue of resolution, like the poor cat i' the adage,
Is sicklied o'er with care,
And all the clouds that lowered o'er our housetops,
With this regard their currents turn awry,
And lose the name of action.
'Tis a consummation devoutly to be wished. But soft you, the fair Ophelia:
Ope not thy ponderous and marble jaws,
But get thee to a nunnery—go!

Well, the old man he liked that speech, and he mighty soon got it so for he could do it first rate. It seemed like he was just born for it; and when he had his hand in and was excited, it was perfectly lovely the way he would rip and tear and rair up behind when he was getting it off.

The first chance we got, the duke he had some show bills printed; and after that, for two or three days as we floated along, the raft was a most uncommon lively place, for there warn't nothing but sword-fighting and rehearsing—as the duke called it—going on all the time. One morning, when we was pretty well down the State of Arkansaw, we come in sight of a little one-horse town in a big bend; so we tied up about three-quarters of a mile above it, in the mouth of a crick which was shut in like a tunnel by the cypress trees, and all of us but Jim took the canoe and went down there to see if there was any chance in that place for our show.

We struck it mighty lucky; there was going to be a circus there that afternoon, and the country people was already beginning to come in, in all kinds of old shackly wagons, and on horses. The circus would leave before night, so our show would have a pretty good chance. The duke he hired the court house, and we went around and stuck up our bills. They read like this:

Shaksperean Revival ! ! !
Wonderful Attraction!
For One Night Only!
The world renowned tragedians,
David Garrick the younger, of Drury Lane Theatre, London,
and
Edmund Kean the elder,[4] of the Royal Haymarket Theatre, White-
chapel, Pudding Lane, Piccadilly, London, and the
Royal Continental Theatres, in their sublime
Shaksperean Spectacle entitled
The Balcony Scene
in
Romeo and Juliet ! ! !

Romeo. . . . . .Mr.   Garrick.
Juliet. . . . . .Mr.   Kean.

---

[4] Kean (1787–1833), a famous tragedian, acted at the Royal Theatre in Drury Lane, London, not at the theaters advertised by the duke.

Assisted by the whole strength of the company!
New costumes, new scenery, new appointments!
Also:
The thrilling, masterly, and blood-curdling
Broad-sword conflict
In Richard III. ! ! !

Richard III. . . . . .Mr. Garrick.
Richmond. . . . . .Mr. Kean.

also:
(by special request,)
Hamlet's Immortal Soliloquy! !
By the Illustrious Kean!
Done by him 300 consecutive nights in Paris!
For One Night Only,
On account of imperative European engagements!
Admission 25 cents; children and servants, 10 cents.

Then we went loafing around the town. The stores and houses was most all old shackly dried-up frame concerns that hadn't ever been painted; they was set up three or four foot above ground on stilts, so as to be out of reach of the water when the river was overflowed. The houses had little gardens around them, but they didn't seem to raise hardly anything in them but jimpson weeds, and sun-flowers, and ash-piles, and old curled-up boots and shoes, and pieces of bottles, and rags, and played-out tin-ware. The fences was made of different kinds of boards, nailed on at different times; and they leaned every which-way, and had gates that didn't generly have but one hinge—a leather one. Some of the fences had been white-washed, some time or another, but the duke said it was in Clumbus's time, like enough. There was generly hogs in the garden, and people driving them out.

All the stores was along one street. They had white-domestic[5] awnings in front, and the country people hitched their horses to the awning-posts. There was empty dry-goods boxes under the awnings, and loafers roosting on them all day long, whittling them with their Barlow knives; and chawing tobacco, and gaping and yawning and stretching—a mighty ornery lot. They generly had on yellow straw hats most as wide as an umbrella, but didn't wear no coats nor waistcoats; they called one another Bill, and Buck, and Hank, and Joe, and Andy, and talked lazy and drawly, and used considerable many cuss-words. There was as many as one loafer leaning up against every awning-post, and he most always had his hands in his britches pockets, except when he fetched them out to lend a chaw of tobacco or scratch. What a body was hearing amongst them, all the time was—

"Gimme a chaw 'v tobacker, Hank."

"Cain't—I hain't got but one chaw left. Ask Bill."

Maybe Bill he gives him a chaw; maybe he lies and says he ain't got none. Some of them kinds of loafers never has a cent in the world, nor a chaw of to-bacco of their own. They get all their chawing by borrowing—they say to a fel-low, "I wisht you'd len' me a chaw, Jack, I jist this minute give Ben Thompson the last chaw I had"—which is a lie, pretty much every time; it don't fool nobody but a stranger; but Jack ain't no stranger, so he says—

---

[5] Made of coarse canvas.

"*You* give him a chaw, did you? so did your sister's cat's grandmother. You pay me back the chaws you've awready borry'd off'n me, Lafe Buckner, then I'll loan you one or two ton of it, and won't charge you no back intrust, nuther."

"Well, I *did* pay you back some of it wunst."

"Yes, you did—'bout six chaws. You borry'd store tobacker and paid back nigger-head."[6]

Store tobacco is flat black plug, but these fellows mostly chaws the natural leaf twisted. When they borrow a chaw, they don't generly cut it off with a knife, but they set the plug in between their teeth, and gnaw with their teeth and tug at the plug with their hands till they get it in two—then sometimes the one that owns the tobacco looks mournful at it when it's handed back, and says, sarcastic—

"Here, gimme the *chaw*, and you take the *plug*."

All the streets and lanes was just mud, they warn't nothing else *but* mud—mud as black as tar, and nigh about a foot deep in some places; and two or three inches deep in *all* the places. The hogs loafed and grunted around, everywheres. You'd see a muddy sow and a litter of pigs come lazying along the street and whollop herself right down in the way, where folks had to walk around her, and she'd stretch out, and shut her eyes, and wave her ears, whilst the pigs was milking her, and look as happy as if she was on salary. And pretty soon you'd hear a loafer sing out, "Hi! *so* boy! sick him, Tige!" and away the sow would go, squealing most horrible, with a dog or two swinging to each ear, and three or four dozen more a-coming; and then you would see all the loafers get up and watch the thing out of sight, and laugh at the fun and look grateful for the noise. Then they'd settle back again till there was a dog-fight. There couldn't anything wake them up all over, and make them happy all over, like a dog-fight—unless it might be putting turpentine on a stray dog and setting fire to him, or tying a tin pan to his tail and see him run himself to death.

On the river front some of the houses was sticking out over the bank, and they was bowed and bent, and about ready to tumble in. The people had moved out of them. The bank was caved away under one corner of some others, and that corner was hanging over. People lived in them yet, but it was dangersome, because sometimes a strip of land as wide as a house caves in at a time. Sometimes a belt of land a quarter of a mile deep will start in and cave along and cave along till it all caves into the river in one summer. Such a town as that has to be always moving back, and back, and back, because the river's always gnawing at it.

The nearer it got to noon that day, the thicker and thicker was the wagons and horses in the streets, and more coming all the time. Families fetched their dinners with them, from the country, and eat them in the wagons. There was considerable whiskey drinking going on, and I seen three fights. By-and-by somebody sings out—

"Here comes old Boggs!—in from the country for his little old monthly drunk—here he comes, boys!"

All the loafers looked glad—I reckoned they was used to having fun out of Boggs. One of them says—

"Wonder who he's a gwyne to chaw up this time. If he'd a chawed up all the men he's ben a gwyne to chaw up in the last twenty year, he'd have a considerble ruputation, now."

Another one says, "I wisht old Boggs 'd threaten me, 'cuz then I'd know I warn't gwyne to die for a thousan' year."

[6] Cheap leaf tobacco rolled into a plug for chewing.

Boggs comes a-tearing along on his horse, whooping and yelling like an Injun, and singing out—

"Cler the track, thar. I'm on the waw-path, and the price uv coffins is a gwyne to raise."

He was drunk, and weaving about in his saddle; he was over fifty year old, and had a very red face. Everybody yelled at him, and laughed at him, and sassed him, and he sassed back, and said he'd attend to them and lay them out in their regular turns, but he couldn't wait now, because he'd come to town to kill old Colonel Sherburn, and his motto was "meat first, and spoon vittles to top off on."

He see me, and rode up and says—

"Whar'd you come f'm, boy? You prepared to die?"

Then he rode on. I was scared; but a man says—

"He don't mean nothing; he's always a carryin' on like that, when he's drunk. He's the best-naturedest old fool in Arkansaw—never hurt nobody, drunk or sober."

Boggs rode up before the biggest store in town and bent his head down so he could see under the curtain of the awning, and yells—

"Come out here, Sherburn! Come out and meet the man you've swindled. You're the houn' I'm after, and I'm a gwyne to have you, too!"

And so he went on, calling Sherburn everything he could lay his tongue to, and the whole street packed with people listening and laughing and going on. By-and-by a proud-looking man about fifty-five—and he was a heap the best dressed man in that town, too—steps out of the store, and the crowd drops back on each side to let him come. He says to Boggs, mighty ca'm and slow—he says:

"I'm tired of this; but I'll endure it till one o'clock. Till one o'clock, mind—no longer. If you open your mouth against me only once, after that time, you can't travel so far but I will find you."

Then he turns and goes in. The crowd looked mighty sober; nobody stirred, and there warn't no more laughing. Boggs rode off blackguarding Sherburn as loud as he could yell, all down the street; and pretty soon back he comes and stops before the store, still keeping it up. Some men crowded around him and tried to get him to shut up, but he wouldn't; they told him it would be one o'clock in about fifteen minutes, and so he *must* go home—he must go right away. But it didn't do no good. He cussed away, with all his might, and thowed his hat down in the mud and rode over it, and pretty soon away he went a-raging down the street again, with his gray hair a-flying. Everybody that could get a chance at him tried their best to coax him off of his horse so they could lock him up and get him sober; but it warn't no use—up the street he would tear again, and give Sherburn another cussing. By-and-by somebody says—

"Go for his daughter!—quick, go for his daughter; sometimes he'll listen to her. If anybody can persuade him, she can."

So somebody started on a run. I walked down street a ways, and stopped. In about five or ten minutes, here comes Boggs again—but not on his horse. He was a-reeling across the street towards me, bareheaded, with a friend on both sides of him aholt of his arms and hurrying him along. He was quiet, and looked uneasy; and he warn't hanging back any, but was doing some of the hurrying himself. Somebody sings out—

"Boggs!"

I looked over there to see who said it, and it was that Colonel Sherburn. He was standing perfectly still, in the street, and had a pistol raised in his right hand—not aiming it, but holding it out with the barrel tilted up towards the sky. The same second I see a young girl coming on the run, and two men with her. Boggs and the men turned round, to see who called him, and when they see the pistol the men jumped to one side, and the pistol barrel come down slow and steady to a level—both barrels cocked. Boggs throws up both of his hands, and says, "O Lord, don't shoot!" Bang! goes the first shot, and he staggers back clawing at the air—bang! goes the second one, and he tumbles backwards onto the ground, heavy and solid, with his arms spread out. That young girl screamed out, and comes rushing, and down she throws herself on her father, crying and saying, "Oh, he's killed him, he's killed him!" The crowd closed up around them, and shouldered and jammed one another, with their necks stretched, trying to see, and people on the inside trying to shove them back, and shouting, "Back, back! give him air, give him air!"

Colonel Sherburn he tossed his pistol onto the ground, and turned around on his heels and walked off.

They took Boggs to a little drug store, the crowd pressing around, just the same, and the whole town following, and I rushed and got a good place at the window, where I was close to him and could see in. They laid him on the floor, and put one large Bible under his head, and opened another one and spread it on his breast—but they tore open his shirt first, and I seen where one of the bullets went in. He made about a dozen long gasps, his breast lifting the Bible up when he drawed in his breath, and letting it down again when he breathed it out—and after that he laid still; he was dead.[7] Then they pulled his daughter away from him, screaming and crying, and took her off. She was about sixteen, and very sweet and gentle-looking, but awful pale and scared.

Well, pretty soon the whole town was there, squirming and scrouging and pushing and shoving to get at the window and have a look, but people that had the places wouldn't give them up, and folks behind them was saying all the time, "Say, now, you've looked enough, you fellows; 'taint right and 'taint fair, for you to stay thar all the time, and never give nobody a chance; other folks has their rights as well as you."

There was considerable jawing back, so I slid out, thinking maybe there was going to be trouble. The streets was full, and everybody was excited. Everybody that seen the shooting was telling how it happened, and there was a big crowd packed around each one of these fellows, stretching their necks and listening. One long lanky man, with long hair and a big white fur stove-pipe hat on the back of his head, and a crooked-handled cane, marked out the places on the ground where Boggs stood, and where Sherburn stood, and the people following him around from one place to t'other and watching everything he done, and bobbing their heads to show they understood, and stooping a little and resting their hands on their thighs to watch him mark the places on the ground with his cane; and then he stood up straight and stiff where Sherburn had stood, frowning and having his hat-brim down over his eyes, and sung out, "Boggs!" and then fetched his cane down slow to a level, and says "Bang!" staggered backwards, says "Bang!" again, and fell down flat on his back. The people that had seen the thing said he done it perfect; said it was just exactly the way it all happened. Then as much as a dozen people got their bottles and treated him.

---

[7] This description of the shooting of Boggs resembles the details of a shooting Twain had witnessed in Hannibal in 1845. His father was judge at the ensuing trial, which resulted in acquittal.

Well, by-and-by somebody said Sherburn ought to be lynched. In about a minute everybody was saying it; so away they went, mad and yelling, and snatching down every clothes-line they come to, to do the hanging with.

Chapter XXII

They swarmed up the street towards Sherburn's house, a-whooping and yelling and raging like Injuns, and everything had to clear the way or get run over and tromped to mush, and it was awful to see. Children was heeling it ahead of the mob, screaming and trying to get out of the way; and every window along the road was full of women's heads, and there was nigger boys in every tree, and bucks and wenches[1] looking over every fence; and as soon as the mob would get nearly to them they would break and skaddle back out of reach. Lots of the women and girls was crying and taking on, scared most to death.

They swarmed up in front of Sherburn's palings as thick as they could jam together, and you couldn't hear yourself think for the noise. It was a little twenty-foot yard. Some sung out "Tear down the fence! tear down the fence!" Then there was a racket of ripping and tearing and smashing, and down she goes, and the front wall of the crowd begins to roll in like a wave.

Just then Sherburn steps out on to the roof of his little front porch, with a double-barrel gun in his hand, and takes his stand, perfectly ca'm and deliberate, not saying a word. The racket stopped, and the wave sucked back.

Sherburn never said a word—just stood there, looking down. The stillness was awful creepy and uncomfortable. Sherburn run his eye slow along the crowd; and wherever it struck, the people tried a little to outgaze him, but they couldn't; they dropped their eyes and looked sneaky. Then pretty soon Sherburn sort of laughed; not the pleasant kind, but the kind that makes you feel like when you are eating bread that's got sand in it.

Then he says, slow and scornful:

"The idea of *you* lynching anybody! It's amusing. The idea of you thinking you had pluck enough to lynch a *man!* Because you're brave enough to tar and feather poor friendless cast-out women that come along here, did that make you think you had grit enough to lay your hands on a *man?* Why, a *man's* safe in the hands of ten thousand of your kind—as long as it's day-time and you're not behind him.

"Do I know you? I know you clear through. I was born and raised in the South, and I've lived in the North; so I know the average all around. The average man's a coward. In the North he lets anybody walk over him that wants to, and goes home and prays for a humble spirit to bear it. In the South one man, all by himself, has stopped a stage full of men, in the day-time, and robbed the lot. Your newspapers call you a brave people so much that you think you *are* braver than any other people—whereas you're just *as* brave, and no braver. Why don't your juries hang murderers? Because they're afraid the man's friends will shoot them in the back, in the dark—and it's just what they *would* do.

"So they always acquit; and then a *man* goes in the night, with a hundred masked cowards at his back, and lynches the rascal. Your mistake is, that you didn't bring a man with you; that's one mistake, and the other is that you didn't

[1] Youthful male and female slaves.

come in the dark, and fetch your masks. You brought *part* of a man—Buck Harkness, there—and if you hadn't had him to start you, you'd a taken it out in blowing.

"You didn't want to come. The average man don't like trouble and danger. *You*
don't like trouble and danger. But if only *half* a man—like Buck Harkness,
there—shouts 'Lynch him, lynch him!' you're afraid to back down—afraid you'll
be found out to be what you are—*cowards*—and so you raise a yell, and hang
yourselves onto that half-a-man's coat tail, and come raging up here, swearing
what big things you're going to do. The pitifulest thing out is a mob; that's what
an army is—a mob; they don't fight with courage that's born in them, but with
courage that's borrowed from their mass, and from their officers. But a mob without any *man* at the head of it, is *beneath* pitifulness. Now the thing for *you* to do,
is to droop your tails and go home and crawl in a hole. If any real lynching's
going to be done, it will be done in the dark, Southern fashion; and when they
come they'll bring their masks, and fetch a *man* along. Now *leave*—and take your
half-a-man with you"—tossing his gun up across his left arm and cocking it, when
he says this.

The crowd washed back sudden, and then broke all apart and went tearing off
every which way, and Buck Harkness he heeled it after them, looking tolerable
cheap. I could a staid, if I'd a wanted to, but I didn't want to.

I went to the circus, and loafed around the back side till the watchman went by,
and then dived in under the tent. I had my twenty-dollar gold piece and some other
money, but I reckoned I better save it, because there ain't no telling how soon you
are going to need it, away from home and amongst strangers, that way. You can't
be too careful. I ain't opposed to spending money on circuses, when there ain't no
other way, but there ain't no use in *wasting* it on them.

It was a real bully circus. It was the splendidest sight that ever was, when they
all come riding in, two and two, a gentleman and lady, side by side, the men just
in their drawers and undershirts, and no shoes nor stirrups, and resting their hands
on their thighs, easy and comfortable—there must a' been twenty of them—and
every lady with a lovely complexion, and perfectly beautiful, and looking just like
a gang of real sure-enough queens, and dressed in clothes that cost millions of
dollars, and just littered with diamonds. It was a powerful fine sight; I never see
anything so lovely. And then one by one they got up and stood, and went a-
weaving around the ring so gentle and wavy and graceful, the men looking ever so
tall and airy and straight, with their heads bobbing and skimming along, away up
there under the tent-roof, and every lady's rose-leafy dress flapping soft and silky
around her hips, and she looking like the most loveliest parasol.

And then faster and faster they went, all of them dancing, first one foot stuck
out in the air and then the other, the horses leaning more and more, and the ring-
master going round and round the centre-pole, cracking his whip and shouting
"hi!—hi!" and the clown cracking jokes behind him; and by-and-by all hands
dropped the reins, and every lady put her knuckles on her hips and every gentleman folded his arms, and then how the horses did lean over and hump themselves!
And so, one after the other they all skipped off into the ring, and made the sweetest bow I ever see, and then scampered out, and everybody clapped their hands
and went just about wild.

Well, all through the circus they done the most astonishing things; and all the
time that clown carried on so it most killed the people. The ring-master couldn't

ever say a word to him but he was back at him quick as a wink with the funniest things a body ever said; and how he ever *could* think of so many of them, and so sudden and so pat, was what I couldn't noway understand. Why, I couldn't a thought of them in a year. And by-and-by a drunk man tried to get into the ring— said he wanted to ride; said he could ride as well as anybody that ever was. They argued and tried to keep him out, but he wouldn't listen, and the whole show come to a standstill. Then the people begun to holler at him and make fun of him, and that made him mad, and he began to rip and tear; so that stirred up the people, and a lot of men begun to pile down off of the benches and swarm towards the ring, saying, "Knock him down! throw him out!" and one or two women begun to scream. So, then, the ring-master he made a little speech, and said he hoped there wouldn't be no disturbance, and if the man would promise he wouldn't make no more trouble, he would let him ride, if he thought he could stay on the horse. So everybody laughed and said all right, and the man got on. The minute he was on, the horse begun to rip and tear and jump and cavort around, with two circus men hanging onto his bridle trying to hold him, and the drunk man hanging onto his neck, and his heels flying in the air every jump, and the whole crowd of people standing up shouting and laughing till the tears rolled down. And at last, sure enough, all the circus men could do, the horse broke loose, and away he went like the very nation, round and round the ring, with that sot laying down on him and hanging to his neck, with first one leg hanging most to the ground on one side, and then t'other one on t'other side, and the people just crazy. It warn't funny to me, though; I was all of a tremble to see his danger. But pretty soon he struggled up astraddle and grabbed the bridle, a-reeling this way and that; and the next minute he sprung up and dropped the bridle and stood! and the horse agoing like a house afire too. He just stood up there, a-sailing around as easy and comfortable as if he warn't ever drunk in his life—and then he begun to pull off his clothes and sling them. He shed them so thick they kind of clogged up the air, and altogether he shed seventeen suits. And then, there he was, slim and handsome, and dressed the gaudiest and prettiest you ever saw, and he lit into that horse with his whip and made him fairly hum—and finally skipped off, and made his bow and danced off to the dressing-room, and everybody just a-howling with pleasure and astonishment.

Then the ring-master he see how he had been fooled, and he *was* the sickest ring-master you ever see, I reckon. Why, it was one of his own men! He had got up that joke all out of his own head, and never let on to nobody. Well, I felt sheepish enough, to be took in so, but I wouldn't a been in that ring-master's place, not for a thousand dollars. I don't know; there may be bullier circuses than what that one was, but I never struck them yet. Anyways it was plenty good enough for *me;* and wherever I run across it, it can have all of *my* custom, every time.

Well, that night we had *our* show; but there warn't only about twelve people there; just enough to pay expenses. And they laughed all the time, and that made the duke mad; and everybody left, anyway, before the show was over, but one boy which was asleep. So the duke said these Arkansaw lunkheads couldn't come up to Shakspeare; what they wanted was low comedy—and may be something ruther worse than low comedy, he reckoned. He said he could size their style. So next morning he got some big sheets of wrapping-paper and some black paint, and drawed off some handbills and stuck them up all over the village. The bills said:

AT THE COURT HOUSE!
FOR 3 NIGHTS ONLY!
The World-Renowned Tragedians
DAVID GARRICK THE YOUNGER!
AND
EDMUND KEAN THE ELDER!
Of the London and Continental
Theatres,
In their Thrilling Tragedy of
THE KING'S CAMELOPARD[2]
OR
THE ROYAL NONESUCH! ! !
Admission 50 cents.

Then at the bottom was the biggest line of all—which said:

LADIES AND CHILDREN NOT ADMITTED.

"There," says he, "if that line don't fetch them, I don't know Arkansaw!"

Chapter XXIII

Well, all day him and the king was hard at it, rigging up a stage, and a curtain, and a row of candles for footlights; and that night the house was jam full of men in no time. When the place couldn't hold no more, the duke he quit tending door and went around the back way and come onto the stage and stood up before the curtain, and made a little speech, and praised up this tragedy, and said it was the most thrillingest one that ever was; and so he went on a-bragging about the tragedy and about Edmund Kean the Elder, which was to play the main principal part in it; and at last when he'd got everybody's expectations up high enough, he rolled up the curtain, and the next minute the king come a-prancing out on all fours, naked; and he was painted all over, ring-streaked-and-striped, all sorts of colors, as splendid as a rainbow. And—but never mind the rest of his outfit, it was just wild, but it was awful funny. The people most killed themselves laughing; and when the king got done capering, and capered off behind the scenes, they roared and clapped and stormed and haw-hawed till he come back and done it over again; and after that, they made him do it another time. Well, it would a made a cow laugh to see the shines that old idiot cut.

Then the duke he lets the curtain down, and bows to the people, and says the great tragedy will be performed only two nights more, on accounts of pressing London engagements, where the seats is all sold aready for it in Drury Lane; and then he makes them another bow, and says if he has succeeded in pleasing them and instructing them, he will be deeply obleeged if they will mention it to their friends and get them to come and see it.

Twenty people sings out:

"What, is it over? Is that *all?*"

---

[2] An archaic word for giraffe, from a Greek word meaning "camel" plus "pard" (leopard).

The duke says yes. Then there was a fine time. Everybody sings out "sold,"[1] and rose up mad, and was agoing for that stage and them tragedians. But a big fine-looking man jumps up on a bench, and shouts:

"Hold on! Just a word, gentlemen." They stopped to listen. "We are sold—mighty badly sold. But we don't want to be the laughing-stock of this whole town, I reckon, and never hear the last of this thing as long as we live. *No.* What we want, is to go out of here quiet, and talk this show up, and sell the *rest* of the town! Then we'll all be in the same boat. Ain't that sensible?" ("You bet it is!—the jedge is right!" everybody sings out.) "All right, then—not a word about any sell. Go along home, and advise everybody to come and see the tragedy."

Next day you couldn't hear nothing around that town but how splendid that show was. House was jammed again, that night, and we sold this crowd the same way. When me and the king and the duke got home to the raft, we all had a supper; and by-and-by, about midnight, they made Jim and me back her out and float her down the middle of the river and fetch her in and hide her about two mile below town.

The third night the house was crammed again—and they warn't new-comers, this time, but people that was at the show the other two nights. I stood by the duke at the door, and I see that every man that went in had his pockets bulging, or something muffled up under his coat—and I see it warn't no perfumery neither, not by a long sight. I smelt sickly eggs by the barrel, and rotten cabbages, and such things; and if I know the signs of a dead cat being around, and I bet I do, there was sixty-four of them went in. I shoved in there for a minute, but it was too various for me, I couldn't stand it. Well, when the place couldn't hold no more people, the duke he give a fellow a quarter and told him to tend door for him a minute, and then he started around for the stage door, I after him; but the minute we turned the corner and was in the dark, he says:

"Walk fast, now, till you get away from the houses, and then shin for the raft like the dickens was after you!"

I done it, and he done the same. We struck the raft at the same time, and in less than two seconds we was gliding down stream, all dark and still, and edging towards the middle of the river, nobody saying a word. I reckoned the poor king was in for a gaudy time of it with the audience; but nothing of the sort; pretty soon he crawls out from under the wigwam, and says:

"Well, how'd the old thing pan out this time, duke?"

He hadn't been up town at all.

We never showed a light till we was about ten mile below that village. Then we lit up and had a supper, and the king and the duke fairly laughed their bones loose over the way they'd served them people. The duke says:

"Greenhorns, flatheads! *I* knew the first house would keep mum and let the rest of the town get roped in; and I knew they'd lay for us the third night, and consider it was *their* turn now. Well, it *is* their turn, and I'd give something to know how much they'd take for it. I *would* just like to know how they're putting in their opportunity. They can turn it into a picnic, if they want to—they brought plenty provisions."

Them rapscallions took in four hundred and sixty-five dollars in that three nights. I never see money hauled in by the wagon-load like that, before.

By-and-by, when they was asleep and snoring, Jim says:

---

[1] Robbed, cheated.

"Don't it 'sprise you, de way dem kings carries on, Huck?"

"No," I says, "it don't."

"Why don't it, Huck?"

"Well, it don't, because it's in the breed. I reckon they're all alike."

"But, Huck, dese kings o' ourn is regular rapscallions; dat's jist what dey is; dey's reglar rapscallions."

"Well, that's what I'm a-saying; all kings is mostly rapscallions, as fur as I can make out."

"Is dat so?"

"You read about them once—you'll see. Look at Henry the Eight; this'n 's a Sunday-School Superintendent to *him*. And look at Charles Second, and Louis Fourteen, and Louis Fifteen, and James Second, and Edward Second, and Richard Third, and forty more; besides all them Saxon heptarchies[2] that used to rip around so in old times and raise Cain. My, you ought to seen old Henry the Eight when he was in bloom. He *was* a blossom. He used to marry a new wife every day, and chop off her head next morning. And he would do it just as indifferent as if he was ordering up eggs. 'Fetch up Nell Gwynn,' he says. They fetch her up. Next morning, 'Chop off her head!' And they chop it off. 'Fetch up Jane Shore,' he says; and up she comes. Next morning 'Chop off her head'—and they chop it off. 'Ring up Fair Rosamun.' Fair Rosamun answers the bell. Next morning, 'Chop off her head.' And he made every one of them tell him a tale every night; and he kept that up till he had hogged a thousand and one tales that way, and then he put them all in a book, and called it Domesday Book[3]—which was a good name and stated the case. You don't know kings, Jim, but I know them; and this old rip of ourn is one of the cleanest I've struck in history. Well, Henry he takes a notion he wants to get up some trouble with this country. How does he go at it—give notice?—give the country a show? No. All of a sudden he heaves all the tea in Boston Harbor overboard, and whacks out a declaration of independence,[4] and dares them to come on. That was *his* style—he never give anybody a chance. He had suspicions of his father, the Duke of Wellington. Well, what did he do?—ask him to show up? No—drownded him in a butt of mamsey,[5] like a cat. Spose people left money laying around where he was—what did he do? He collared it. Spose he contracted to do a thing; and you paid him, and didn't set down there and see that he done it—what did he do? He always done the other thing. Spose

---

[2] This mishmash of history is a tour de force on Twain's part; from the little time Huck has spent in school he would hardly be able to garble so many facts. Henry VIII (1491–1547), king of England (1509–1547), executed two of his wives and divorced two others, but the women Huck mentions were the mistresses of other kings: Nell Gwynn (1650–1687) of Charles II (1630–1685), king of England, Scotland, and Ireland (1660–1685); Jane Shore (1445?–1527?) of Edward IV (1442–1483), king of England (1461–1470, 1471–1483); Rosamund Clifford (?–1176?) of Henry II (1133–1189), king of England (1154–1189). The seven Anglo-Saxon kingdoms (the heptarchy: East Anglia, Essex, Kent, Mercia, Northumbria, Sussex, and Wessex) ruled England from the fifth to the ninth centuries.

[3] Huck mixes in a reference to the Arabian Nights, ancient eastern tales far removed from the time and the culture of Henry VIII, then has those tales recorded in the Domesday Book, which tallies the landowners in England in 1086 under the guidance of William the Conqueror, or William I (1027?–1087), king of England (1066–1087).

[4] Events from American history, the Boston Tea Party (1773) and the Declaration of Independence (signed in 1776), have no connection with Henry VIII.

[5] Arthur Wellesley (1769–1852), the first duke of Wellington, defeated Napoleon at the Battle of Waterloo in 1815; it was William IV (1765–1837), the duke of Clarence, who reportedly drowned in a butt of mamsey, or barrel of wine.

he opened his mouth—what then? If he didn't shut it up powerful quick, he'd lose a lie, every time. That's the kind of a bug Henry was; and if we'd a had him along 'stead of our kings, he'd a fooled that town a heap worse than ourn done. I don't say that ourn is lambs, because they ain't, when you come right down to the cold facts; but they ain't nothing to *that* old ram, anyway. All I say is, kings is kings, and you got to make allowances. Take them all around, they're a mighty ornery lot. It's the way they're raised."

"But dis one do *smell* so like de nation, Huck."

"Well, they all do, Jim. *We* can't help the way a king smells; history don't tell no way."

"Now de duke, he's a tolerble likely man, in some ways."

"Yes, a duke's different. But not very different. This one's a middling hard lot, for a duke. When he's drunk, there ain't no near-sighted man could tell him from a king."

"Well, anyways, I doan' hanker for no mo' un um, Huck. Dese is all I kin stan'."

"It's the way I feel, too, Jim. But we've got them on our hands, and we got to remember what they are, and make allowances. Sometimes I wish we could hear of a country that's out of kings."

What was the use to tell Jim these warn't real kings and dukes? It wouldn't a done no good; and besides, it was just as I said; you couldn't tell them from the real kind.

I went to sleep, and Jim didn't call me when it was my turn. He often done that. When I waked up, just at day-break, he was setting there with his head down betwixt his knees, moaning and mourning to himself. I didn't take notice, nor let on. I knowed what it was about. He was thinking about his wife and his children, away up yonder, and he was low and homesick; because he hadn't ever been away from home before in his life; and I do believe he cared just as much for his people as white folks does for their'n. It don't seem natural, but I reckon it's so. He was often moaning and mourning that way, nights, when he judged I was asleep, and saying, "Po' little 'Lizabeth! po' little Johnny! Its mighty hard; I spec' I ain't ever gwyne to see you no mo', no mo'!" He was a mighty good nigger, Jim was.

But this time I somehow got to talking to him about his wife and young ones; and by-and-by he says:

"What makes me feel so bad dis time, 'uz bekase I hear sumpn over yonder on de bank like a whack, er a slam, while ago, en it mine me er de time I treat my little 'Lizabeth so ornery. She warn't on'y 'bout fo' year ole, en she tuck de sk'yarlet-fever, en had a powful rough spell; but she got well, en one day she was a-stannin' aroun', en I says to her, I says:

"Shet de do'."

"She never done it; jis' stood dah, kiner smilin' up at me. It make me mad; en I says agin, mighty loud, I says:

" 'Doan' you hear me?—shet de do'!'

"She jis' stood de same way, kiner smilin' up. I was a-bilin'! I says:

" 'I lay I *make* you mine!'

"En wid dat I fetch' her a slap side de head dat sont her a-sprawlin'. Den I went into de yuther room, en 'uz gone 'bout ten minutes; en when I come back, dah was dat do' a-stannin' open *yit*, en dat chile stannin' mos' right in it, a-lookin' down and mournin', en de tears runnin' down. My, but I *wuz* mad, I was agwyne for de chile, but jis' den—it was a do' dat open innerds—jis' den, 'long come de wind en slam it to, behine de chile, ker-*blam!*—en my lan', de chile never move'! My breff mos' hop outer me; en I feel so—so—I doan' know *how* I feel. I crope out, all a-tremblin', en crope aroun' en open de do' easy en slow, en poke my head in behine de chile, sof' en still, en all uv a sudden, I says *pow!* jis' as loud as I could yell: *She never budge!* Oh, Huck, I bust out a-cryin' en grab her up in my arms, en say, 'Oh, de po' little thing! de Lord God Almighty fogive po' ole Jim, kaze he never gwyne to fogive hisself as long's he live!' Oh, she was plumb deef en dumb, Huck, plumb deef en dumb—en I'd ben a-treat'n her so!"

CHAPTER XXIV

Next day, towards night, we laid up under a little willow tow-head out in the middle, where there was a village on each side of the river, and the duke and the king begun to lay out a plan for working them towns. Jim he spoke to the duke, and said he hoped it wouldn't take but a few hours, because it got mighty heavy and tiresome to him when he had to lay all day in the wigwam tied with the rope. You see, when we left him all alone we had to tie him, because if anybody happened on him all by himself and not tied, it wouldn't look much like he was a runaway nigger, you know. So the duke said it *was* kind of hard to have to lay roped all day, and he'd cipher out some way to get around it.

He was uncommon bright, the duke was, and he soon struck it. He dressed Jim up in King Lear's outfit—it was a long curtain-calico gown, and a white horse-hair wig and whiskers; and then he took his theatre-paint and painted Jim's face and hands and ears and neck all over a dead dull solid blue, like a man that's been drownded nine days. Blamed if he warn't the horriblest looking outrage I ever see. Then the duke took and wrote out a sign on a shingle so—

Sick Arab—but harmless when not out of his head.

And he nailed that shingle to a lath, and stood the lath up four or five foot in front of the wigwam. Jim was satisfied. He said it was a sight better than laying tied a couple of years every day and trembling all over every time there was a sound. The duke told him to make himself free and easy, and if anybody ever come meddling around, he must hop out of the wigwam, and carry on a little, and fetch a howl or two like a wild beast, and he reckoned they would light out and leave him alone. Which was sound enough judgment; but you take the average man, and he wouldn't wait for him to howl. Why, he didn't only look like he was dead, he looked considerable more than that.

These rapscallions wanted to try the Nonesuch again, because there was so much money in it, but they judged it wouldn't be safe, because maybe the news might a worked along down by this time. They couldn't hit no project that suited, exactly; so at last the duke said he reckoned he'd lay off and work his brains an hour or two and see if he couldn't put up something on the Arkansaw village; and the king he allowed he would drop over to t'other village, without any plan, but just trust in Providence to lead him the profitable way—meaning the devil, I reckon. We had all bought store clothes where we stopped last; and now the king put his'n on, and he told me to put mine on. I done it, of course. The king's duds was all black, and he did look real swell and starchy. I never knowed how clothes could change a body before. Why, before, he looked like the orneriest old rip that ever was; but now, when he'd take off his new white beaver[1] and make a bow and do a smile, he looked that grand and good and pious that you'd say he had walked right out of the ark, and maybe was old Leviticus[2] himself. Jim cleaned up the canoe, and I got my paddle ready. There was a big steamboat laying at the shore away up under the point, about three mile above town—been there a couple of hours, taking on freight. Says the king:

"Seein' how I'm dressed, I reckon maybe I better arrive down from St. Louis or Cincinnati, or some other big place. Go for the steamboat, Huckleberry; we'll come down to the village on her."

I didn't have to be ordered twice, to go and take a steamboat ride. I fetched the shore a half a mile above the village, and then went scooting along the bluff bank in the easy water. Pretty soon we come to a nice innocent-looking young country jake setting on a log swabbing the sweat off of his face, for it was powerful warm weather; and he had a couple of big carpet-bags by him.

"Run her nose in shore," says the king. I done it. "Wher' you bound for, young man?"

"For the steamboat; going to Orleans."

"Git aboard," says the king. "Hold on a minute, my servant 'll he'p you with them bags. Jump out and he'p the gentleman, Adolphus"—meaning me, I see.

I done so, and then we all three started on again. The young chap was mighty thankful; said it was tough work toting his baggage such weather. He asked the king where he was going, and the king told him he'd come down the river and landed at the other village this morning, and now he was going up a few mile to see an old friend on a farm up there. The young fellow says:

"When I first see you, I says to myself, 'It's Mr. Wilks, sure, and he come mighty near getting here in time.' But then I says again, 'No, I reckon it ain't him, or else he wouldn't be paddling up the river.' You *ain't* him, are you?"

"No, my name's Blodgett—Elexander Blodgett—*Reverend* Elexander Blodgett, I spose I must say, as I'm one o' the Lord's poor servants. But still I'm jist as able to be sorry for Mr. Wilks for not arriving in time, all the same, if he's missed anything by it—which I hope he hasn't."

"Well, he don't miss any property by it, because he'll get that all right; but he's missed seeing his brother Peter die—which he mayn't mind, nobody can tell as to that—but his brother would a give anything in this world to see *him* before he died; never talked about nothing else all these three weeks; hadn't seen him since they was boys together—and hadn't ever seen his brother William at all—that's the deef and dumb one—William ain't more than thirty or thirty-five. Peter and George was the only ones that come out here; George was the married brother; him and his wife both died last year. Harvey and William's the only ones that's left now; and, as I was saying, they haven't got here in time."

"Did anybody send 'em word?"

"Oh, yes; a month or two ago, when Peter was first took; because Peter said then that he sorter felt like he warn't going to get well this time. You see, he was pretty old, and George's g'yirls was too young to be much company for him, except Mary Jane the red-headed one; and so he was kinder lonesome after George and his wife died, and didn't seem to care much to live. He most desperately

---

[1] Hat.
[2] Huck mistakes Leviticus, a book of the Old Testament, with Noah, who built the ark and thereby survived the biblical flood (see Genesis).

wanted to see Harvey—and William too, for that matter—because he was one of them kind that can't bear to make a will. He left a letter behind for Harvey, and said he'd told in it where his money was hid, and how he wanted the rest of the property divided up so George's g'yirls would be all right—for George didn't leave nothing. And that letter was all they could get him to put a pen to."

"Why do you reckon Harvey don't come? Wher' does he live?"

"Oh, he lives in England—Sheffield—preaches there—hasn't ever been in this country. He hasn't had any too much time—and besides he mightn't a got the letter at all, you know."

"Too bad, too bad he couldn't a lived to see his brothers, poor soul. You going to Orleans, you say?"

"Yes, but that ain't only a part of it. I'm going in a ship, next Wednesday, for Ryo Janeero,[3] where my uncle lives."

"It's a pretty long journey. But it'll be lovely; I wisht I was agoing. Is Mary Jane the oldest? How old is the others?"

"Mary Jane's nineteen, Susan's fifteen, and Joanna's about fourteen—that's the one that gives herself to good works and has a hare-lip."

"Poor things! to be left alone in the cold world so."

"Well, they could be worse off. Old Peter had friends, and they ain't going to let them come to no harm. There's Hobson, the Babtis' preacher; and Deacon Lot Hovey, and Ben Rucker, and Abner Shackleford, and Levi Bell, the lawyer; and Dr. Robinson, and their wives, and the widow Bartley, and—well, there's a lot of them; but these are the ones that Peter was thickest with, and used to write about sometimes, when he wrote home; so Harvey 'll know where to look for friends when he gets here."

Well, the old man he went on asking questions till he just fairly emptied that young fellow. Blamed if he didn't inquire about everybody and everything in that blessed town, and all about all the Wilkses; and about Peter's business—which was a tanner; and about George's—which was a carpenter; and about Harvey's—which was a dissentering[4] minister; and so on, and so on. Then he says:

"What did you want to walk all the way up to the steamboat for?"

"Because she's a big Orleans boat, and I was afeard she mightn't stop there. When they're deep they won't stop for a hail. A Cincinnati boat will, but this is a St. Louis one."

"Was Peter Wilks well off?"

"Oh, yes, pretty well off. He had houses and land, and it's reckoned he left three or four thousand in cash hid up som'ers."

"When did you say he died?"

"I didn't say, but it was last night."

"Funeral to-morrow, likely?"

"Yes, 'bout the middle of the day."

"Well, it's all terrible sad; but we've all got to go, one time or another. So what we want to do is to be prepared; then we're all right."

"Yes, sir, it's the best way. Ma used to always say that."

When we struck the boat, she was about done loading, and pretty soon she got off. The king never said nothing about going aboard, so I lost my ride, after all. When the boat was gone, the king made me paddle up another mile to a lonesome place, and then he got ashore, and says:

[3] Rio de Janeiro, Brazil.   [4] Dissenting.

"Now hustle back, right off, and fetch the duke up here, and the new carpet-bags. And if he's gone over to t'other side, go over there and git him. And tell him to git himself up regardless. Shove along, now."

I see what *he* was up to; but I never said nothing, of course. When I got back with the duke, we hid the canoe and then they set down on a log, and the king told him everything, just like the young fellow had said it—every last word of it. And all the time he was a doing it, he tried to talk like an Englishman; and he done it pretty well too, for a slouch. I can't imitate him, and so I ain't agoing to try to; but he really done it pretty good. Then he says:

"How are you on the deef and dumb, Bilgewater?"

The duke said, leave him alone for that; said he had played a deef and dumb person on the histrionic boards. So then they waited for a steamboat.

About the middle of the afternoon a couple of little boats come along, but they didn't come from high enough up the river; but at last there was a big one, and they hailed her. She sent out her yawl, and we went aboard, and she was from Cincinnati; and when they found we only wanted to go four or five mile, they was booming mad, and give us a cussing, and said they wouldn't land us. But the king was ca'm. He says:

"If gentlemen kin afford to pay a dollar a mile apiece, to be took on and put off in a yawl, a steamboat kin afford to carry 'em, can't it?"

So they softened down and said it was all right; and when we got to the village, they yawled us ashore. About two dozen men flocked down, when they see the yawl a coming; and when the king says—

"Kin any of you gentlemen tell me wher' Mr. Peter Wilks lives?" they give a glance at one another, and nodded their heads, as much as to say, "What d' I tell you?" Then one of them says, kind of soft and gentle:

"I'm sorry, sir, but the best we can do is to tell you where he *did* live yesterday evening."

Sudden as winking, the ornery old cretur went all to smash, and fell up against the man, and put his chin on his shoulder, and cried down his back, and says:

"Alas, alas, our poor brother—gone, and we never got to see him; oh, it's too, *too* hard!"

Then he turns around, blubbering, and makes a lot of idiotic signs to the duke on his hands, and blamed if *he* didn't drop a carpet-bag and bust out a-crying. If they warn't the beatenest lot, them two frauds, that ever I struck.

Well, the men gethered around, and sympathized with them, and said all sorts of kind things to them, and carried their carpet-bags up the hill for them, and let them lean on them and cry, and told the king all about his brother's last moments, and the king he told it all over again on his hands to the duke, and both of them took on about that dead tanner like they'd lost the twelve disciples. Well, if ever I struck anything like it, I'm a nigger. It was enough to make a body ashamed of the human race.

Chapter XXV

The news was all over town in two minutes, and you could see the people tearing down on the run, from every which way, some of them putting on their coats as they come. Pretty soon we was in the middle of a crowd, and the noise of the tramping was like a soldier-march. The windows and dooryards was full; and every minute somebody would say, over a fence:

"Is it *them?*"

And somebody trotting along with the gang would answer back and say, "You bet it is."

When we got to the house, the street in front of it was packed, and the three girls was standing in the door. Mary Jane *was* red-headed, but that don't make no difference, she was most awful beautiful, and her face and her eyes was all lit up like glory, she was so glad her uncles was come. The king he spread his arms, and Mary Jane she jumped for them, and the hare-lip jumped for the duke, and there they *had* it! Everybody most, leastways women, cried for joy to see them meet again at last and have such good times.

Then the king he hunched the duke, private—I see him do it—and then he looked around and see the coffin, over in the corner on two chairs; so then, him and the duke, with a hand across each other's shoulder, and t'other hand to their eyes, walked slow and solemn over there, everybody dropping back to give them room, and all the talk and noise stopping, people saying "Sh!" and all the men taking their hats off and drooping their heads, so you could a heard a pin fall. And when they got there, they bent over and looked in the coffin, and took one sight, and then they bust out a crying so you could a heard them to Orleans, most; and then they put their arms around each other's necks, and hung their chins over each other's shoulders; and then for three minutes, or maybe four, I never see two men leak the way they done. And mind you, everybody was doing the same; and the place was that damp I never see anything like it. Then one of them got on one side of the coffin, and t'other on t'other side, and they kneeled down and rested their foreheads on the coffin, and let on to pray all to theirselves. Well, when it come to that, it worked the crowd like you never see anything like it, and so everybody broke down and went to sobbing right out loud—the poor girls, too; and every woman, nearly, went up to the girls, without saying a word, and kissed them, solemn, on the forehead, and then put their hand on their head, and looked up towards the sky, with the tears running down, and then busted out and went off sobbing and swabbing, and give the next woman a show. I never see anything so disgusting.

Well, by-and-by the king he gets up and comes forward a little, and works himself up and slobbers out a speech, all full of tears and flapdoodle about its being a sore trial for him and his poor brother to lose the diseased, and to miss seeing diseased alive, after the long journey of four thousand mile, but its a trial that's sweetened and sanctified to us by this dear sympathy and these holy tears, and so he thanks them out of his heart and out of his brother's heart, because out of their mouths they can't, words being too weak and cold, and all that kind of rot and slush, till it was just sickening; and then he blubbers out a pious goody-goody Amen, and turns himself loose and goes to crying fit to bust.

And the minute the words was out of his mouth somebody over in the crowd struck up the doxolojer,[1] and everybody joined in with all their might, and it just warmed you up and made you feel as good as church letting out. Music *is* a good thing; and after all that soul-butter and hogwash, I never see it freshen up things so, and sound so honest and bully.

Then the king begins to work his jaw again, and says how him and his nieces would be glad if a few of the main principal friends of the family would take supper here with them this evening, and help set up with the ashes of the diseased;

---

[1] Doxology, a hymn or chant praising God.

and says if his poor brother laying yonder could speak, he knows who he would name, for they was names that was very dear to him, and mentioned often in his letters; and so he will name the same, to-wit, as follows, vizz:—Rev. Mr. Hobson, and Deacon Lot Hovey, and Mr. Ben Rucker, and Abner Shackleford, and Levi Bell, and Dr. Robinson, and their wives, and the widow Bartley.

Rev. Hobson and Dr. Robinson was down to the end of the town, a-hunting together; that is, I mean the doctor was shipping a sick man to t'other world, and the preacher was pinting him right. Lawyer Bell was away up to Louisville on some business. But the rest was on hand, and so they all come and shook hands with the king and thanked him and talked to him; and then they shook hands with the duke, and didn't say nothing but just kept a-smiling and bobbing their heads like a passel of sapheads whilst he made all sorts of signs with his hands and said "Goo-goo—goo-goo-goo," all the time, like a baby that can't talk.

So the king he blatted along, and managed to inquire about pretty much everybody and dog in town, by his name, and mentioned all sorts of little things that happened one time or another in the town, or to George's family, or to Peter; and he always let on that Peter wrote him the things, but that was a lie, he got every blessed one of them out of that young flathead that we canoed up to the steamboat.

Then Mary Jane she fetched the letter her father left behind, and the king he read it out loud and cried over it. It give the dwelling-house and three thousand dollars, gold, to the girls; and it give the tanyard (which was doing a good business), along with some other houses and land (worth about seven thousand), and three thousand dollars in gold to Harvey and William, and told where the six thousand cash was hid, down cellar. So these two frauds said they'd go and fetch it up, and have everything square and above-board; and told me to come with a candle. We shut the cellar door behind us, and when they found the bag they spilt it out on the floor, and it was a lovely sight, all them yaller-boys.[2] My, the way the king's eyes did shine! He slaps the duke on the shoulder, and says:

"Oh, *this* ain't bully, nor noth'n! Oh, no, I reckon not! Why, Biljy, it beats the Nonesuch, *don't* it!"

The duke allowed it did. They pawed the yaller-boys, and sifted them through their fingers and let them jingle down on the floor; and the king says:

"It ain't no use talkin'; bein' brothers to a rich dead man, and representatives of furrin heirs that's got left, is the line for you and me, Bilge. Thish-yer comes of trust'n to Providence. It's the best way, in the long run. I've tried 'em all, and ther' ain't no better way."

Most everybody would a been satisfied with the pile, and took it on trust; but no, they must count it. So they counts it, and it comes out four hundred and fifteen dollars short. Says the king:

"Dern him, I wonder what he done with that four hundred and fifteen dollars?"

They worried over that a while, and ransacked all around for it. Then the duke says:

"Well, he was a pretty sick man, and likely he made a mistake—I reckon that's the way of it. The best way's to let it go, and keep still about it. We can spare it."

"Oh, shucks, yes, we can *spare* it. I don't k'yer noth'n 'bout that—it's the *count* I'm thinkin' about. We want to be awful square and open and above-board, here, you know. We want to lug this h-yer money up stairs and count it before everybody—then ther' ain't noth'n suspicious. But when the dead man says ther's six thous'n dollars, you know, we don't want to—"

---

[2] Gold coins.

"Hold on," says the duke. "Less make up the deffisit"—and he begun to haul out yaller-boys out of his pocket.

"It's a most amaz'n' good idea, duke—you *have* got a rattlin' clever head on you," says the king. "Blest if the old Nonesuch ain't a heppin' us out agin"—and *he* begun to haul out yallerjackets and stack them up.

It most busted them, but they made up the six thousand clean and clear.

"Say," says the duke, "I got another idea. Le's go up stairs and count this money, and then take and *give it to the girls.*"

"Good land, duke, lemme hug you! It's the most dazzling idea 'at ever a man struck. You have cert'nly got the most astonishin' head I ever see. Oh, this is the boss dodge,[3] ther' ain't no mistake 'bout it. Let 'em fetch along their suspicions now, if they want to—this'll lay 'em out."

When we got up stairs, everybody gethered around the table, and the king he counted it and stacked it up, three hundred dollars in a pile—twenty elegant little piles. Everybody looked hungry at it, and licked their chops. Then they raked it into the bag again, and I see the king begin to swell himself up for another speech. He says:

"Friends all, my poor brother that lays yonder, has done generous by them that's left behind in the vale of sorrers. He has done generous by these-'yer poor little lambs that he loved and sheltered, and that's left fatherless and motherless. Yes, and we that knowed him, knows that he would a done *more* generous by 'em if he hadn't ben afeard o' woundin' his dear William and me. Now, *wouldn't* he? Ther' ain't no question 'bout it, in *my* mind. Well, then—what kind o'brothers would it be, that 'd stand in his way at sech a time? And what kind o' uncles would it be that 'd rob—yes, *rob*—sech poor sweet lambs as these 'at he loved so, at sech a time? If I know William—and I *think* I do—he—well, I'll jest ask him." He turns around and begins to make a lot of signs to the duke with his hands; and the duke he looks at him stupid and leather-headed a while, then all of a sudden he seems to catch his meaning, and jumps for the king, goo-gooing with all his might for joy, and hugs him about fifteen times before he lets up. Then the king says, "I knowed it; I reckon *that*'ll convince anybody the way *he* feels about it. Here, Mary Jane, Susan, Joanner, take the money—take it *all.* It's the gift of him that lays yonder, cold but joyful."

Mary Jane she went for him, Susan and the hare-lip went for the duke, and then such another hugging and kissing I never see yet. And everybody crowded up with the tears in their eyes, and most shook the hands off of them frauds, saying all the time:

"You *dear* good souls!—how *lovely!*—how *could* you!"

Well, then, pretty soon all hands got to talking about the diseased again, and how good he was, and what a loss he was, and all that; and before long a big iron-jawed man worked himself in there from outside, and stood a listening and looking, and not saying anything; and nobody saying anything to him either, because the king was talking and they was all busy listening. The king was saying—in the middle of something he'd started in on—

"—they bein' partickler friends o' the diseased. That's why they're invited here this evenin'; but to-morrow we want *all* to come—everybody; for he respected everybody, he liked everybody, and so it's fitten that his funeral orgies sh'd be public."

And so he went a-mooning on and on, liking to hear himself talk, and every

---

[3] The major confidence trick.

little while he fetched in his funeral orgies again, till the duke he couldn't stand it no more; so he writes on a little scrap of paper, "*obsequies,* you old fool," and folds it up and goes to goo-gooing and reaching it over people's heads to him. The king he reads it, and puts it in his pocket, and says:

"Poor William, afflicted as he is, his *heart's* aluz right. Asks me to invite everybody to come to the funeral—wants me to make 'em all welcome. But he needn't a worried—it was jest what I was at."

Then he weaves along again, perfectly ca'm, and goes to dropping in his funeral orgies again every now and then, just like he done before. And when he done it the third time, he says:

"I say orgies, not because it's the common term, because it ain't—obsequies bein' the common term—but because orgies is the right term. Obsequies ain't used in England no more, now—it's gone out. We say orgies now, in England. Orgies is better, because it means the thing you're after, more exact. It's a word that's made up out'n the Greek *orgo,* outside, open, abroad; and the Hebrew *jeesum,* to plant, cover up; hence in*ter*.[4] So, you see, funeral orgies is an open er public funeral."

He was the *worst* I ever struck. Well, the iron-jawed man he laughed right in his face. Everybody was shocked. Everybody says, "Why *doctor!*" and Abner Shackleford says:

"Why, Robinson, hain't you heard the news? This is Harvey Wilks."

The king he smiled eager, and shoved out his flapper, and says:

"*Is* it my poor brother's dear good friend and physician? I—"

"Keep your hands off of me!" says the doctor. "*You* talk like an Englishman— *don't* you? It's the worse imitation I ever heard. *You* Peter Wilks's brother. You're a fraud, that's what you are!"

Well, how they all took on! They crowded around the doctor, and tried to quiet him down, and tried to explain to him, and tell him how Harvey'd showed in forty ways that he *was* Harvey, and knowed everybody by name, and the names of the very dogs, and begged and *begged* him not to hurt Harvey's feelings and the poor girls' feelings, and all that; but it warn't no use, he stormed right along, and said any man that pretended to be an Englishman and couldn't imitate the lingo no better than what he did, was a fraud and a liar. The poor girls was hanging to the king and crying; and all of a sudden the doctor ups and turns on *them.* He says:

"I was your father's friend, and I'm your friend; and I warn you *as* a friend, and an honest one, that wants to protect you and keep you out of harm and trouble, to turn your backs on that scoundrel, and have nothing to do with him, the ignorant tramp, with his idiotic Greek and Hebrew as he calls it. He is the thinnest kind of an impostor—has come here with a lot of empty names and facts which he has picked up somewheres, and you take them for *proofs,* and are helped to fool yourselves by these foolish friends here, who ought to know better. Mary Jane Wilks, you know me for your friend, and for your unselfish friend, too. Now listen to me; turn this pitiful rascal out—I *beg* you to do it. Will you?"

Mary Jane straightened herself up, and my, but she was handsome! She says:

"*Here* is my answer." She hove up the bag of money and put it in the king's hands, and says, "Take this six thousand dollars, and invest it for me and my sisters any way you want to, and don't give us no receipt for it."

---

[4] A standard comedy routine based on mock etymologies.

Then she put her arm around the king on one side, and Susan and the hare-lip done the same on the other. Everybody clapped their hands and stomped on the floor like a perfect storm, whilst the king held up his head and smiled proud. The doctor says:

"All right, I wash *my* hands of the matter. But I warn you all that a time's coming when you're going to feel sick whenever you think of this day"—and away he went.

"All right, doctor," says the king, kinder mocking him, "we'll try and get 'em to send for you"—which made them all laugh, and they said it was a prime good hit.

Chapter XXVI

Well, when they was all gone, the king he asks Mary Jane how they was off for spare rooms, and she said she had one spare room, which would do for Uncle William, and she'd give her own room to Uncle Harvey, which was a little bigger, and she would turn into the room with her sisters and sleep on a cot; and up garret was a little cubby, with a pallet in it. The king said the cubby would do for his valley—meaning me.

So Mary Jane took us up, and she showed them their rooms, which was plain but nice. She said she'd have her frocks and a lot of other traps took out of her room if they was in Uncle Harvey's way, but he said they warn't. The frocks was hung along the wall, and before them was a curtain made out of calico that hung down to the floor. There was an old hair trunk in one corner, and a guitar box in another, and all sorts of little knick-knacks and jimcracks around, like girls brisken up a room with. The king said it was all the more homely and more pleasanter for these fixings, and so don't disturb them. The duke's room was pretty small, but plenty good enough, and so was my cubby.

That night they had a big supper, and all them men and women was there, and I stood behind the king and the duke's chairs and waited on them, and the niggers waited on the rest. Mary Jane she set at the head of the table, with Susan along side of her, and said how bad the biscuits was, and how mean the preserves was, and how ornery and tough the fried chickens was—and all that kind of rot, the way women always do for to force out compliments; and the people all knowed everything was tip-top, and said so—said "How *do* you get biscuits to brown so nice?" and "Where, for the land's sake *did* you get these amaz'n pickles?" and all that kind of humbug talky-talk, just the way people always does at a supper, you know.

And when it was all done, me and the hare-lip had supper in the kitchen off of the leavings, whilst the others was helping the niggers clean up the things. The hare-lip she got to pumping me about England, and blest if I didn't think the ice was getting mighty thin, sometimes. She says:

"Did you ever see the king?"

"Who? William Fourth?[1] Well, I bet I have—he goes to our church." I knowed he was dead years ago, but I never let on. So when I says he goes to our church, she says:

[1] William IV (1765–1837), king of Great Britain and Ireland (1830–1837).

"What—regular?"

"Yes—regular. His pew's right over opposite ourn—on 'tother side the pulpit."

"I thought he lived in London?"

"Well, he does. Where *would* he live?"

"But I thought *you* lived in Sheffield?"[2]

I see I was up a stump. I had to let on to get choked with a chicken bone, so as to get time to think how to get down again. Then I says:

"I mean he goes to our church regular when he's in Sheffield. That's only in the summer-time, when he comes there to take the sea baths."

"Why, how you talk—Sheffield ain't on the sea."

"Well, who said it was?"

"Why, you did."

"I *didn't* nuther."

"You did!"

"I didn't."

"You did."

"I never said nothing of the kind."

"Well, what *did* you say, then?"

"Said he come to take the sea *baths*—that's what I said."

"Well, then! how's he going to take the sea baths if it ain't on the sea?"

"Looky here," I says; "did you ever see any Congress water?"[3]

"Yes."

"Well, did you have to go to Congress to get it?"

"Why, no."

"Well, neither does William Fourth have to go to the sea to get a sea bath."

"How does he get it, then?"

"Gets it the way people down here gets Congress-water—in barrels. There in the palace at Sheffield they've got furnaces, and he wants his water hot. They can't bile that amount of water away off there at the sea. They haven't got no conveniences for it."

"Oh, I see, now. You might a said that in the first place and saved time."

When she said that, I see I was out of the woods again, and so I was comfortable and glad. Next, she says:

"Do you go to church, too?"

"Yes—regular."

"Where do you set?"

"Why, in our pew."

"*Whose* pew?"

"Why, *ourn*—your Uncle Harvey's."

"His'n? What does *he* want with a pew?"

"Wants it to set in. What did you *reckon* he wanted with it?"

"Why, I thought he'd be in the pulpit."

Rot him, I forgot he was a preacher. I see I was up a stump again, so I played another chicken bone and got another think. Then I says:

"Blame it, do you suppose there ain't but one preacher to a church?"

"Why, what do they want with more?"

---

[2] A city north of London.   [3] Mineral water from the Congress Spring in Saratoga, New York.

"What!—to preach before a king? I never see such a girl as you. They don't have no less than seventeen."

"Seventeen! My land! Why, I wouldn't set out such a string as that, not if I *never* got to glory. It must take 'em a week."

"Shucks, they don't *all* of 'em preach the same day—only *one* of 'em."

"Well, then, what does the rest of 'em do?"

"Oh, nothing much. Loll around, pass the plate—and one thing or another. But mainly they don't do nothing."

"Well, then, what are they *for?*"

"Why, they're for *style*. Don't you know nothing?"

"Well, I don't *want* to know no such foolishness as that. How is servants treated in England? Do they treat 'em better 'n we treat our niggers?"

"*No!* A servant ain't nobody there. They treat them worse than dogs."

"Don't they give 'em holidays, the way we do, Christmas and New Year's week, and Fourth of July?"

"Oh, just listen! A body could tell *you* hain't ever been to England, by that. Why, Hare-l—why, Joanna, they never see a holiday from year's end to year's end; never go to the circus, nor theatre, nor nigger shows,[4] nor nowheres."

"Nor church?"

"Nor church."

"But *you* always went to church."

Well, I was gone up again. I forgot I was the old man's servant. But next minute I whirled in on a kind of an explanation how a valley was different from a common servant, and *had* to go to church whether he wanted to or not, and set with the family, on account of it's being the law. But I didn't do it pretty good, and when I got done I see she warn't satisfied. She says:

"Honest injun, now, hain't you been telling me a lot of lies?"

"Honest injun," says I.

"None of it at all?"

"None of it at all. Not a lie in it," says I.

"Lay your hand on this book and say it."

I see it warn't nothing but a dictionary, so I laid my hand on it and said it. So then she looked a little better satisfied, and says:

"Well, then, I'll believe some of it; but I hope to gracious if I'll believe the rest."

"What is it you won't believe, Joe?" says Mary Jane, stepping in with Susan behind her. "It ain't right nor kind for you to talk so to him, and him a stranger and so far from his people. How would you like to be treated so?"

"That's always your way, Maim—always sailing in to help somebody before they're hurt. I hain't done nothing to him. He's told some stretchers, I reckon; and I said I wouldn't swallow it all; and that's every bit and grain I *did* say. I reckon he can stand a little thing like that, can't he?"

"I don't care whether 'twas little or whether 'twas big, he's here in our house and a stranger, and it wasn't good of you to say it. If you was in his place, it would make you feel ashamed; and so you oughtn't to say a thing to another person that will make *them* feel ashamed."

"Why, Maim, he said—"

"It don't make no difference what he *said*—that ain't the thing. The thing is for

---

[4] Minstrel shows.

you to treat him *kind,* and not be saying things to make him remember he ain't in his own country and amongst his own folks."

I says to myself, *this* is a girl that I'm letting that old reptile rob her of her money!

Then Susan *she* waltzed in; and if you'll believe me, she did give Hare-lip hark from the tomb![5]

Says I to myself, And this is *another* one that I'm letting him rob her of her money!

Then Mary Jane she took another inning, and went in sweet and lovely again—which was her way—but when she got done there warn't hardly anything left o' poor Hare-lip. So she hollered.

"All right, then," says the other girls, "you just ask his pardon."

She done it, too. And she done it beautiful. She done it so beautiful it was good to hear; and I wished I could tell her a thousand lies, so she could do it again.

I says to myself, this is *another* one that I'm letting him rob her of her money. And when she got through, they all jest laid theirselves out to make me feel at home and know I was amongst friends. I felt so ornery and low down and mean, that I says to myself, My mind's made up; I'll hive[6] that money for them or bust.

So then I lit out—for bed, I said, meaning some time or another. When I got by myself, I went to thinking the thing over. I says to myself, shall I go to that doctor, private, and blow on these frauds? No—that won't do. He might tell who told him; then the king and the duke would make it warm for me. Shall I go, private, and tell Mary Jane? No—I dasn't do it. Her face would give them a hint, sure; they've got the money, and they'd slide right out and get away with it. If she was to fetch in help, I'd get mixed up in the business, before it was done with, I judge. No, there ain't no good way but one. I got to steal that money, somehow; and I got to steal it some way that they won't suspicion that I done it. They've got a good thing, here; and they ain't agoing to leave till they've played this family and this town for all they're worth, so I'll find a chance time enough. I'll steal it, and hide it; and by-and-by, when I'm away down the river, I'll write a letter and tell Mary Jane where it's hid. But I better hive it to-night, if I can, because the doctor maybe hasn't let up as much as he lets on he has; he might scare them out of here, yet.

So, thinks I, I'll go and search them rooms. Up stairs the hall was dark, but I found the duke's room, and started to paw around it with my hands; but I recollected it wouldn't be much like the king to let anybody else take care of that money but his own self; so then I went to his room and begun to paw around there. But I see I couldn't do nothing without a candle, and I dasn't light one, of course. So I judged I'd got to do the other thing—lay for them, and eavesdrop. About that time, I hears their footsteps coming, and was going to skip under the bed; I reached for it, but it wasn't where I thought it would be; but I touched the curtain that hid Mary Jane's frocks, so I jumped in behind that and snuggled in amongst the gowns, and stood there perfectly still.

They come in and shut the door; and the first thing the duke done was to get down and look under the bed. Then I was glad I hadn't found the bed when I wanted it. And yet, you know, it's kind of natural to hide under the bed when you are up to anything private. They sets down, then, and the king says:

"Well, what is it? and cut it middlin' short, because it's better for us to be down

---

[5] A scolding that would wake the dead.   [6] Get and keep.

there a whoopin'-up the mournin', than up here givin' 'em a chance to talk us over."

"Well, this is it, Capet. I ain't easy; I ain't comfortable. That doctor lays on my mind. I wanted to know your plans. I've got a notion, and I think it's a sound one."

"What is it, duke?"

"That we better glide out of this, before three in the morning, and clip it down the river with what we've got. Specially, seeing we got it so easy—*given* back to us, flung at our heads, as you may say, when of course we allowed to have to steal it back. I'm for knocking off and lighting out."

That made me feel pretty bad. About an hour or two ago, it would a been a little different, but now it made me feel bad and disappointed. The king rips out and says:

"What! And not sell out the rest o' the property? March off like a passel 'o fools and leave eight or nine thous'n' dollars' worth o' property layin' around jest sufferin' to be scooped in?—and all good salable stuff, too."

The duke he grumbled; said the bag of gold was enough, and he didn't want to go no deeper—didn't want to rob a lot of orphans of *everything* they had.

"Why, how you talk!" says the king. "We shan't rob 'em of nothing at all but jest this money. The people that *buys* the property is the suff'rers; because as soon's it's found out 'at we didn't own it—which won't be long after we've slid—the sale won't be valid, and it'll all go back to the estate. These-yer orphans 'll git their house back agin, and that's enough for *them;* they're young and spry, and k'n easy earn a livin'. *They* ain't agoing to suffer. Why, jest think—there's thous'n's and thous'n's that ain't nigh so well off. Bless you, *they* ain't got noth'n to complain of."

Well, the king he talked him blind; so at last he give in, and said all right, but said he believed it was blame foolishness to stay, and that doctor hanging over them. But the king says:

"Cuss the doctor! What do we k'yer for *him?* Hain't we got all the fools in town on our side? and ain't that a big enough majority in any town?"

So they got ready to go down stairs again. The duke says:

"I don't think we put that money in a good place."

That cheered me up. I'd begun to think I warn't going to get a hint of no kind to help me. The king says:

"Why?"

"Because Mary Jane 'll be in mourning from this out; and first you know the nigger that does up the rooms will get an order to box these duds up and put 'em away; and do you reckon a nigger can run across money and not borrow some of it?"

"Your head's level, agin, duke," says the king; and he come a fumbling under the curtain two or three foot from where I was. I stuck tight to the wall, and kept mighty still, though quivery; and I wondered what them fellows would say to me if they catched me; and I tried to think what I'd better do if they did catch me. But the king he got the bag before I could think more than about a half a thought, and he never suspicioned I was around. They took and shoved the bag through a rip in the straw tick that was under the feather bed, and crammed it in a foot or two amongst the straw and said it was all right, now, because a nigger only makes up the feather bed, and don't turn over the straw tick only about twice a year, and so it warn't in no danger of getting stole, now.

But I knowed better. I had it out of there before they was half-way down stairs. I groped along up to my cubby, and hid it there till I could get a chance to do better. I judged I better hide it outside of the house somewheres, because if they missed it they would give the house a good ransacking. I knowed that very well. Then I turned in, with my clothes all on; but I couldn't a gone to sleep, if I'd a wanted to, I was in such a sweat to get through with the business. By-and-by I heard the king and the duke come up; so I rolled off of my pallet and laid with my chin at the top of my ladder and waited to see if anything was going to happen. But nothing did.

So I held on till all the late sounds had quit and the early ones hadn't begun, yet; and then I slipped down the ladder.

CHAPTER XXVII

I crept to their doors and listened; they was snoring, so I tip-toed along, and got down stairs all right. There warn't a sound anywheres. I peeped through a crack of the dining-room door, and see the men that was watching the corpse all sound asleep on their chairs. The door was open into the parlor, where the corpse was laying, and there was a candle in both rooms. I passed along, and the parlor door was open; but I see there warn't nobody in there but the remainders of Peter; so I shoved on by; but the front door was locked, and the key wasn't there. Just then I heard somebody coming down the stairs, back behind me. I run in the parlor, and took a swift look around, and the only place I see to hide the bag was in the coffin. The lid was shoved along about a foot, showing the dead man's face down in there, with a wet cloth over it, and his shroud on. I tucked the money-bag in under the lid, just down beyond where his hands was crossed, which made me creep, they was so cold, and then I run back across the room and in behind the door.

The person coming was Mary Jane. She went to the coffin, very soft, and kneeled down and looked in; then she put up her handkerchief and I see she begun to cry, though I couldn't hear her, and her back was to me. I slid out, and as I passed the dining-room I thought I'd make sure them watchers hadn't seen me; so I looked through the crack and everything was all right. They hadn't stirred.

I slipped up to bed, feeling ruther blue, on accounts of the thing playing out that way after I had took so much trouble and run so much resk about it. Says I, if it could stay where it is, all right; because when we get down the river a hundred mile or two, I could write back to Mary Jane, and she could dig him up again and get it; but that ain't the thing that's going to happen; the thing that's going to happen is, the money 'll be found when they come to screw on the lid. Then the king 'll get it again, and it 'll be a long day before he gives anybody another chance to smouch[1] it from him. Of course I *wanted* to slide down and get it out of there, but I dasn't try it. Every minute it was getting earlier, now, and pretty soon some of them watchers would begin to stir, and I might get catched—catched with six thousand dollars in my hands that nobody hadn't hired me to take care of. I don't wish to be mixed up in no such business as that, I says to myself.

When I got down stairs in the morning, the parlor was shut up, and the watchers was gone. There warn't nobody around but the family and the widow Bartley

---

[1] Get it away, steal.

and our tribe. I watched their faces to see if anything had been happening, but I couldn't tell.

Towards the middle of the day the undertaker come, with his man, and they set the coffin in the middle of the room on a couple of chairs, and then set all our chairs in rows, and borrowed more from the neighbors till the hall and the parlor and the dining-room was full. I see the coffin lid was the way it was before, but I dasn't go to look in under it, with folks around.

Then the people begun to flock in, and the beats[2] and the girls took seats in the front row at the head of the coffin, and for a half an hour the people filed around slow, in single rank, and looked down at the dead man's face a minute, and some dropped in a tear, and it was all very still and solemn, only the girls and the beats holding handkerchiefs to their eyes and keeping their heads bent, and sobbing a little. There warn't no other sound but the scraping of the feet on the floor, and blowing noses—because people always blows them more at a funeral than they do at other places except church.

When the place was packed full, the undertaker he slid around in his black gloves with his softy soothering ways, putting on the last touches, and getting people and things all shipshape and comfortable, and making no more sound than a cat. He never spoke; he moved people around, he squeezed in late ones, he opened up passage-ways, and done it all with nods, and signs with his hands. Then he took his place over against the wall. He was the softest, glidingest, stealthiest man I ever see; and there warn't no more smile to him than there is to a ham.

They had borrowed a melodeum[3]—a sick one; and when everything was ready, a young woman set down and worked it, and it was pretty skreeky and colicky, and everybody joined in and sung, and Peter was the only one that had a good thing, according to my notion. Then the Reverend Hobson opened up, slow and solemn, and begun to talk; and straight off the most outrageous row busted out in the cellar a body ever heard; it was only one dog, but he made a most powerful racket, and he kept it up, right along; the parson he had to stand there, over the coffin, and wait—you couldn't hear yourself think. It was right down awkward, and nobody didn't seem to know what to do. But pretty soon they see that long-legged undertaker make a sign to the preacher as much as to say, "Don't you worry—just depend on me." Then he stooped down and begun to glide along the wall, just his shoulders showing over the people's heads. So he glided along, and the pow-wow and racket getting more and more outrageous all the time; and at last, when he had gone around two sides of the room, he disappears down cellar. Then, in about two seconds we heard a whack, and the dog he finished up with a most amazing howl or two, and then everything was dead still, and the parson begun his solemn talk where he left off. In a minute or two here comes this under-taker's back and shoulders gliding along the wall again; and so he glided, and glided, around three sides of the room, and then rose up, and shaded his mouth with his hands, and stretched his neck out towards the preacher, over the people's heads, and says, in a kind of a coarse whisper, "*He had a rat!*" Then he drooped down and glided along the wall again to his place. You could see it was great satisfaction to the people, because naturally they wanted to know. A little thing like that don't cost nothing, and it's just the little things that makes a man to be

---

[2] Deadbeats.

[3] Melodeon, a small reed organ in which a suction bellows draws air inward through the reeds.

looked up to and liked. There warn't no more popular man in town than what that undertaker was.

Well, the funeral sermon was very good, but pison long and tiresome; and then the king he shoved in and got off some of his usual rubbage, and at last the job was through, and the undertaker begun to sneak up on the coffin with his screwdriver. I was in a sweat then, and watched him pretty keen. But he never meddled at all; just slid the lid along, as soft as mush, and screwed it down tight and fast. So there I was! I didn't know whether the money was in there, or not. So, says I, spose somebody has hogged that bag on the sly?—now how do *I* know whether to write to Mary Jane or not? 'Spose she dug him up and didn't find nothing—what would she think of me? Blame it, I says, I might get hunted up and jailed; I'd better lay low and keep dark, and not write at all; the thing's awful mixed, now; trying to better it, I've worsened it a hundred times, and I wish to goodness I'd just let it alone, dad fetch the whole business!

They buried him, and we come back home, and I went to watching faces again—I couldn't help it, and I couldn't rest easy. But nothing come of it; the faces didn't tell me nothing.

The king he visited around, in the evening, and sweetened every body up, and made himself ever so friendly; and he give out the idea that his congregation over in England would be in a sweat about him, so he must hurry and settle up the estate right away, and leave for home. He was very sorry he was so pushed, and so was everybody; they wished he could stay longer, but they said they could see it couldn't be done. And he said of course him and William would take the girls home with them; and that pleased everybody too, because then the girls would be well fixed, and amongst their own relations; and it pleased the girls, too—tickled them so they clean forgot they ever had a trouble in the world; and told him to sell out as quick as he wanted to, they would be ready. Them poor things was that glad and happy it made my heart ache to see them getting fooled and lied to so, but I didn't see no safe way for me to chip in and change the general tune.

Well, blamed if the king didn't bill[4] the house and the niggers and all the property for auction straight off—sale two days after the funeral; but anybody could buy private beforehand if they wanted to.

So the next day after the funeral, along about noontime, the girls' joy got the first jolt; a couple of nigger traders come along, and the king sold them the niggers reasonable, for three-day drafts[5] as they called it, and away they went, the two sons up the river to Memphis, and their mother down the river to Orleans. I thought them poor girls and them niggers would break their hearts for grief; they cried around each other, and took on so it most made me down sick to see it. The girls said they hadn't ever dreamed of seeing the family separated or sold away from the town. I can't ever get it out of my memory, the sight of them poor miserable girls and niggers hanging around each other's necks and crying; and I reckon I couldn't a stood it all but would a had to bust out and tell on our gang if I hadn't knowed the sale warn't no account and the niggers would be back home in a week or two.

The thing made a big stir in the town, too, and a good many come out flatfooted and said it was scandalous to separate the mother and the children that way.

---

[4] Advertise with handbills.   [5] Bank drafts or checks made payable in three days.

It injured the frauds some; but the old fool he bulled right along, spite of all the duke could say or do, and I tell you the duke was powerful uneasy.

Next day was auction day. About broad-day in the morning, the king and the duke come up in the garret and woke me up, and I see by their look that there was trouble. The king says:

"Was you in my room night before last?"

"No, your majesty"—which was the way I always called him when nobody but our gang warn't around.

"Was you in there yisterday er last night?"

"No, your majesty."

"Honor bright, now—no lies."

"Honor bright, your majesty, I'm telling you the truth. I hain't been anear your room since Miss Mary Jane took you and the duke and showed it to you."

The duke says:

"Have you seen anybody else go in there?"

"No, your grace, not as I remember, I believe."

"Stop and think."

I studied a while, and see my chance, then I says:

"Well, I see the niggers go in there several times."

Both of them give a little jump; and looked like they hadn't ever expected it, and then like they *had*. Then the duke says:

"What, *all* of them?"

"No—leastways not all at once. That is, I don't think I ever see them all come *out* at once but just one time."

"Hello—when was that?"

"It was the day we had the funeral. In the morning. It warn't early, because I overslept. I was just starting down the ladder, and I see them."

"Well, go on, *go* on—what did they do? How'd they act?"

"They didn't do nothing. And they didn't act anyway, much, as fur as I see. They tip-toed away; so I seen, easy enough, that they'd shoved in there to do up your majesty's room, or something, sposing you was up; and found you *warn't* up, and so they was hoping to slide out of the way of trouble without waking you up, if they hadn't already waked you up."

"Great guns, *this* is a go!" says the king; and both of them looked pretty sick, and tolerable silly. They stood there a thinking and scratching their heads, a minute, and then the duke he bust into a kind of a little raspy chuckle, and says:

"It does beat all, how neat the niggers played their hand. They let on to be *sorry* they was going out of this region! and I believed they *was* sorry. And so did you, and so did everybody. Don't ever tell *me* any more that a nigger ain't got any histrionic talent. Why, the way they played that thing, it would fool *anybody*. In my opinion there's a fortune in 'em. If I had capital and a theatre, I wouldn't want a better lay out than that—and here we've gone and sold 'em for a song. Yes, and ain't privileged to sing the song, yet. Say, where *is* that song?—that draft."

"In the bank for to be collected. Where *would* it be?"

"Well, *that's* all right then, thank goodness."

Says I, kind of timid-like:

"Is something gone wrong?"

The king whirls on me and rips out:

"None o' your business! You keep your head shet, and mind y'r own affairs—

if you got any. Long as you're in this town, don't you forgit *that,* you hear?" Then he says to the duke, "We got to jest swaller it, and say noth'n: mum's the word for *us*."

As they was starting down the ladder, the duke he chuckles again, and says:

"Quick sales *and* small profits! It's a good business—yes."

The king snarls around on him and says,

"I was trying to do for the best, in sellin' 'm out so quick. If the profits has turned out to be none, lackin' considable, and none to carry, is it my fault any more'n it's yourn?"

"Well, *they'd* be in this house yet, and we *wouldn't* if I could a got my advice listened to."

The king sassed back, as much as was safe for him, and then swapped around and lit into *me* again. He give me down the banks[6] for not coming and *telling* him I see the niggers come out of his room acting that way—said any fool would a *knowed* something was up. And then waltzed in and cussed *himself* a while; and said it all come of him not laying late and taking his natural rest that morning, and he'd be blamed if he'd ever do it again. So they went off a jawing; and I felt dreadful glad I'd worked it all off onto the niggers and yet hadn't done the niggers no harm by it.

CHAPTER XXVIII

By-and-by it was getting-up time; so I come down the ladder and started for down stairs, but as I come to the girls' room, the door was open, and I see Mary Jane setting by her old hair trunk, which was open and she'd been packing things in it—getting ready to go to England. But she had stopped now, with a folded gown in her lap, and had her face in her hands, crying. I felt awful bad to see it; of course anybody would. I went in there, and says:

"Miss Mary Jane, you can't abear to see people in trouble, and *I* can't—most always. Tell me about it."

So she done it. And it was the niggers—I just expected it. She said the beautiful trip to England was most about spoiled for her; she didn't know *how* she was ever going to be happy there, knowing the mother and the children warn't ever going to see each other no more—and then busted out bitterer than ever, and flung up her hands, and says:

"Oh, dear, dear, to think they ain't *ever* going to see each other any more!"

"But they *will*—and inside of two weeks—and I *know* it!" says I.

Laws it was out before I could think!—and before I could budge, she throws her arms around my neck, and told me to say it *again,* say it *again,* say it *again!*

I see I had spoke too sudden, and said too much, and was in a close place. I asked her to let me think a minute; and she set there, very impatient and excited, and handsome, but looking kind of happy and eased-up, like a person that's had a tooth pulled out. So I went to studying it out. I says to myself, I reckon a body that ups and tells the truth when he is in a tight place, is taking considerable many resks, though I ain't had no experience, and can't say for certain; but it looks so to me, anyway; and yet here's a case where I'm blest if it don't look to me like the truth is better, and actuly *safer,* than a lie. I must lay it by in my mind, and think it

---

[6] A real cussing out.

over some time or other, it's so kind of strange and unregular. I never see nothing like it. Well, I says to myself at last, I'm agoing to chance it; I'll up and tell the truth this time, though it does seem most like setting down on a kag of powder and touching it off just to see where you'll go to. Then I says:

"Miss Mary Jane, is there any place out of town a little ways, where you could go and stay three or four days?"

"Yes—Mr. Lothrop's. Why?"

"Never mind why, yet. If I'll tell you how I know the niggers will see each other again—inside of two weeks—here in this house—and *prove* how I know it—will you go to Mr. Lothrop's and stay four days?"

"Four days!" she says: "I'll stay a year!"

"All right," I says, "I don't want nothing more out of *you* than just your word—I druther have it than another man's kiss-the-Bible."[1] She smiled, and reddened up very sweet, and I says, "If you don't mind it, I'll shut the door—and bolt it."

Then I come back and set down again, and says:

"Don't you holler. Just set still, and take it like a man. I got to tell the truth, and you want to brace up, Miss Mary, because it's a bad kind, and going to be hard to take, but there ain't no help for it. These uncles of yourn ain't no uncles at all—they're a couple of frauds—regular dead-beats. There, now we're over the worst of it—you can stand the rest middling easy."

It jolted her up like everything, of course; but I was over the shoal water[2] now, so I went right along, her eyes a blazing higher and higher all the time, and told her every blame thing, from where we first struck that young fool going up to the steamboat, clear through to where she flung herself onto the king's breast at the front door and he kissed her sixteen or seventeen times—and then up she jumps, with her face afire like sunset, and says:

"The brute! Come—don't waste a minute—not a *second*—we'll have them tarred and feathered, and flung in the river!"

Says I:

"Cert'nly. But do you mean, *before* you go to Mr. Lothrop's, or—"

"Oh," she says, "what am I *thinking* about!" she says, and set right down again. "Don't mind what I said—please don't—you *won't*, now, *will* you?" Laying her silky hand on mind in that kind of a way that I said I would die first. "I never thought, I was so stirred up," she says; "now go on, and I won't do so any more. You tell me what to do, and whatever you say, I'll do it."

"Well," I says, "it's a rough gang, them two frauds, and I'm fixed so I got to travel with them a while longer, whether I want to or not—I druther not tell you why—and if you was to blow on them this town would get me out of their claws, and *I'd* be all right, but there'd be another person that you don't know about who'd be in big trouble. Well, we got to save *him*, hain't we? Of course. Well, then, we won't blow on them."

Saying them words put a good idea in my head. I see how maybe I could get me and Jim rid of the frauds; get them jailed here, and then leave. But I didn't want to run the raft in daytime, without anybody aboard to answer questions but me; so I didn't want the plan to begin working till pretty late to-night. I says:

"Miss Mary Jane, I'll tell you what we'll do—and you won't have to stay at Mr. Lothrop's so long, nuther. How fur is it?"

---

[1] A sworn oath.   [2] Over the rough part.

"A little short of four miles—right out in the country, back here."

"Well, that'll answer. Now you go along out there, and lay low till nine or half-past, to-night, and then get them to fetch you home again—tell them you've thought of something. If you get here before eleven, put a candle in this window, and if I don't turn up, wait *till* eleven, and *then* if I don't turn up it means I'm gone, and out of the way, and safe. Then you come out and spread the news around, and get these beats jailed."

"Good," she says, "I'll do it."

"And if it just happens so that I don't get away, but get took up along with them, you must up and say I told you the whole thing beforehand, and you must stand by me all you can."

"Stand by you, indeed I will. They sha'n't touch a hair of your head!" she says, and I see her nostrils spread and her eyes snap when she said it, too.

"If I get away, I sha'n't be here," I says, "to prove these rapscallions ain't your uncles, and I couldn't do it if I *was* here. I could swear they was beats and bummers, that's all; though that's worth something. Well, there's others can do that better than what I can—and they're people that ain't going to be doubted as quick as I'd be. I'll tell you how to find them. Gimme a pencil and a piece of paper. There—'*Royal Nonesuch, Bricksville.*' Put it away, and don't lose it. When the court wants to find out something about these two, let them send up to Bricksville and say they've got the men that played the Royal Nonesuch, and ask for some witnesses—why, you'll have that entire town down here before you can hardly wink, Miss Mary. And they'll come a-biling, too."

I judged we had got everything fixed about right, now. So I says:

"Just let the auction go right along, and don't worry. Nobody don't have to pay for the things they buy till a whole day after the auction, on accounts of the short notice, and they ain't going out of this till they get that money—and the way we've fixed it the sale ain't going to count, and they ain't going to *get* no money. It's just like the way it was with the niggers—it warn't no sale, and the niggers will be back before long. Why, they can't collect the money for the *niggers,* yet—they're in the worst kind of a fix, Miss Mary."

"Well," she says, "I'll run down to breakfast now, and then I'll start straight for Mr. Lothrop's."

" 'Deed, *that* ain't the ticket, Miss Mary Jane," I says, "by no manner of means; go *before* breakfast."

"Why?"

"What did you reckon I wanted you to go at all for, Miss Mary?"

"Well, I never thought—and come to think, I don't know. What was it?"

"Why, it's because you ain't one of these leather-face people. I don't want no better book than what your face is. A body can set down and read it off like coarse print. Do you reckon you can go and face your uncles, when they come to kiss you good-morning, and never————"

"There, there, don't! Yes, I'll go before breakfast—I'll be glad to. And leave my sisters with them?"

"Yes—never mind about them. They've got to stand it yet a while. They might suspicion something if all of you was to go. I don't want you to see them, nor your sisters, nor nobody in this town—if a neighbor was to ask how is your uncles this morning, your face would tell something. No, you go right along, Miss Mary Jane, and I'll fix it with all of them. I'll tell Miss Susan to give your love to your uncles and say you've went away for a few hours for to get a little rest and change, or to see a friend, and you'll be back to-night or early in the morning."

"Gone to see a friend is all right, but I won't have my love given to them."

"Well, then, it sha'n't be." It was well enough to tell *her* so—no harm in it. It was only a little thing to do, and no trouble; and it's the little things that smoothes people's roads the most, down here below; it would make Mary Jane comfortable, and it wouldn't cost nothing. Then I says: "There's one more thing—that bag of money."

"Well, they've got that; and it makes me feel pretty silly to think *how* they got it."

"No, you're out, there. They hain't got it."

"Why, who's got it?"

"I wish I knowed, but I don't. I *had* it, because I stole it from them: and I stole it to give to you; and I know where I hid it, but I'm afraid it ain't there no more. I'm awful sorry, Miss Mary Jane, I'm just as sorry as I can be; but I done the best I could; I did, honest. I come nigh getting caught, and I had to shove it into the first place I come to, and run—and it warn't a good place."

"Oh, stop blaming yourself—it's too bad to do it, and I won't allow it—you couldn't help it; it wasn't your fault. Where did you hide it?"

I didn't want to set her to thinking about her troubles again; and I couldn't seem to get my mouth to tell her what would make her see that corpse laying in the coffin with that bag of money on his stomach. So for a minute I didn't say nothing—then I says:

"I'd ruther not *tell* you where I put it, Miss Mary Jane, if you don't mind letting me off; but I'll write it for you on a piece of paper, and you can read it along the road to Mr. Lothrop's, if you want to. Do you reckon that'll do?"

"Oh, yes."

So I wrote: "I put it in the coffin. It was in there when you was crying there, away in the night. I was behind the door, and I was mighty sorry for you, Miss Mary Jane."

It made my eyes water a little, to remember her crying there all by herself in the night, and them devils laying there right under her own roof, shaming her and robbing her; and when I folded it up and give it to her, I see the water come into her eyes, too; and she shook me by the hand, hard, and says:

"*Good*-bye—I'm going to do everything just as you've told me; and if I don't ever see you again, I sha'n't ever forget you, and I'll think of you a many and a many a time, and I'll *pray* for you, too!"—and she was gone.

Pray for me! I reckoned if she knowed me she'd take a job that was more nearer her size. But I bet she done it, just the same—she was just that kind. She had the grit to pray for Judus[3] if she took the notion—there warn't no back-down to her, I judge. You may say what you want to, but in my opinion she had more sand[4] in her than any girl I ever see; in my opinion she was just full of sand. It sounds like flattery, but it ain't no flattery. And when it comes to beauty—and goodness too—she lays over them all. I hain't ever seen her since that time that I see her go out of that door; no, I hain't even seen her since, but I reckon I've thought of her a many and a many a million times, and of her saying she would pray for me; and

---

[3] Judas Iscariot, the betrayer of Christ.   [4] Courage, backbone.

if ever I'd a thought it would do any good for me to pray for *her,* blamed if I wouldn't a done it or bust.

Well, Mary Jane she lit out the back way, I reckon; because nobody see her go. When I struck Susan and the hare-lip, I says:

"What's the name of them people over on t'other side of the river that you all goes to see sometimes?"

They says:

"There's several; but it's the Proctors, mainly."

"That's the name," I says; "I most forgot it. Well, Miss Mary Jane she told me to tell you she's gone over there in a dreadful hurry—one of them's sick."

"Which one?"

"I don't know; leastways I kinder forget; but I think it's————"

"Sakes alive, I hope it ain't *Hanner?*"

"I'm sorry to say it," I says, "but Hanner's the very one."

"My goodness—and she so well only last week! Is she took bad?"

"It ain't no name for it. They set up with her all night, Miss Mary Jane said, and they don't think she'll last many hours."

"Only think of that, now! What's the matter with her!"

I couldn't think of anything reasonable, right off that way, so I says:

"Mumps."

"Mumps your granny! They don't set up with people that's got the mumps."

"They don't, don't they? You better bet they do with *these* mumps. These mumps is different. It's a new kind, Miss Mary Jane said."

"How's it a new kind?"

"Because it's mixed up with other things."

"What other things?"

"Well, measles, and whooping-cough, and erysiplas, and consumption, and yaller janders,[5] and brain fever, and I don't know what all."

"My land! And they call it the *mumps?*"

"That's what Miss Mary Jane said."

"Well, what in the nation do they call it the *mumps* for?"

"Why, because it *is* the mumps. That's what it starts with."

"Well, ther' ain't no sense in it. A body might stump his toe, and take pison, and fall down the well, and break his neck, and bust his brains out, and somebody come along and ask what killed him, and some numskull up and say, 'Why, he stumped his *toe.'* Would ther' be any sense in that? *No.* And ther' ain't no sense in *this,* nuther. Is it ketching?"

"Is it *ketching?* Why, how you talk. Is a *harrow* catching?— in the dark? If you don't hitch onto one tooth, you're bound to on another, ain't you? And you can't get away with that tooth without fetching the whole harrow along, can you? Well, these kind of mumps is a kind of a harrow, as you may say—and it ain't no slouch of a harrow, nuther, you come to get it hitched on good."

"Well, it's awful, *I* think," says the hare-lip. "I'll go to Uncle Harvey and——"

"Oh, yes," I says, "I *would.* Of *course* I would. I wouldn't lose no time."

"Well, why wouldn't you?"

"Just look at it a minute, and maybe you can see. Hain't your uncles obleeged to get along home to England as fast as they can? And do you reckon they'd be

[5] Erysipelas is a skin disease with severe inflammation; consumption, tuberculosis; and yaller janders, yellow jaundice.

mean enough to go off and leave you to go all that journey by yourselves? *You* know they'll wait for you. So fur, so good. Your uncle Harvey's a preacher, ain't he? Very well, then; is a *preacher* going to deceive a steamboat clerk? is he going to deceive a *ship clerk?*— so as to get them to let Miss Mary Jane go aboard? Now *you* know he ain't. What *will* he do, then? Why, he'll say, 'It's a great pity, but my church matters has got to get along the best way they can; for my niece has been exposed to the dreadful pluribus-unum mumps,[6] and so it's my bounden duty to set down here and wait the three months it takes to show on her if she's got it.' But never mind, if you think it's best to tell your uncle Harvey————"

"Shucks, and stay fooling around here when we could all be having good times in England whilst we was waiting to find out whether Mary Jane's got it or not? Why, you talk like a muggins."[7]

"Well, anyway, maybe you better tell some of the neighbors."

"Listen at that, now. You do beat all, for natural stupidity. Can't you *see* that *they'd* go and tell? Ther' ain't no way but just to not tell anybody at *all.*"

"Well, maybe you're right—yes, I judge you *are* right."

"But I reckon we ought to tell Uncle Harvey she's gone out a while, anyway, so he wont be uneasy about her?"

"Yes, Miss Mary Jane she wanted you to do that. She says, 'Tell them to give Uncle Harvey and William my love and a kiss, and say I've run over the river to see Mr.—Mr.—what *is* the name of that rich family your uncle Peter used to think so much of?—I mean the one that————"

"Why, you must mean the Apthorps, ain't it?"

"Of course; bother them kind of names, a body can't ever seem to remember them, half the time, somehow. Yes, she said, say she has run over for to ask the Apthorps to be sure and come to the auction and buy this house, because she allowed her uncle Peter would ruther they had it than anybody else; and she's going to stick to them till they say they'll come, and then, if she ain't too tired, she's coming home; and if she is, she'll be home in the morning anyway. She said, don't say nothing about the Proctors, but only about the Apthorps—which'll be perfectly true, because she *is* going there to speak about their buying the house; I know it, because she told me so, herself."

"All right," they said, and cleared out to lay for their uncles, and give them the love and the kisses, and tell them the message.

Everything was all right now. The girls wouldn't say nothing because they wanted to go to England; and the king and the duke would ruther Mary Jane was off working for the auction than around in reach of Doctor Robinson. I felt very good; I judged I had done it pretty neat—I reckoned Tom Sawyer couldn't a done it no neater himself. Of course he would a throwed more style into it, but I can't do that very handy, not being brung up to it.

Well, they held the auction in the public square, along towards the end of the afternoon, and it strung along, and strung along, and the old man he was on hand and looking his level piousest, up there longside of the auctioneer, and chipping in a little Scripture, now and then, or a little goody-goody saying, of some kind, and the duke he was around goo-gooing for sympathy all he knowed how, and just spreading himself generly.

---

[6] Reaching for anything he can to make these "mumps" sound bad, Huck comes up with part of the Latin motto stamped on U.S. coins: "E Pluribus Unum": "out of many, one."

[7] A fool.

But by-and-by the thing dragged through, and everything was sold. Everything but a little old trifling lot in the graveyard. So they'd got to work *that* off—I never see such a giraff as the king was for wanting to swallow *everything*. Well, whilst they was at it, a steamboat landed, and in about two minutes up comes a crowd a whooping and yelling and laughing and carrying on, and singing out:

"*Here's* your opposition line! here's your two sets o' heirs to old Peter Wilks— and you pays your money and you takes your choice!"

Chapter XXIX

They was fetching a very nice looking old gentleman along, and a nice looking younger one, with his right arm in a sling. And my souls, how the people yelled, and laughed, and kept it up. But I didn't see no joke about it, and I judged it would strain the duke and the king some to see any. I reckoned they'd turn pale. But no, nary a pale did *they* turn. The duke he never let on he suspicioned what was up, but just went a goo-gooing around, happy and satisfied, like a jug that's googling out buttermilk; and as for the king, he just gazed and gazed down sorrowful on them newcomers like it give him the stomach-ache in his very heart to think there could be such frauds and rascals in the world. Oh, he done it admirable. Lots of the principal people gethered around the king, to let him see they was on his side. That old gentleman that had just come looked all puzzled to death. Pretty soon he begun to speak, and I see, straight off, he pronounced *like* an Englishman, not the king's way, though the king's *was* pretty good, for an imitation. I can't give the old gent's words, nor I can't imitate him; but he turned around to the crowd, and says, about like this:

"This is a surprise to me which I wasn't looking for; and I'll acknowledge, candid and frank, I ain't very well fixed to meet it and answer it; for my brother and me has had misfortunes, he's broke his arm, and our baggage got put off at a town above here, last night in the night by a mistake. I am Peter Wilks's brother Harvey, and this is his brother William, which can't hear nor speak—and can't even make signs to amount to much, now 't he's only got one hand to work them with. We are who we say we are; and in a day or two, when I get the baggage, I can prove it. But, up till then, I won't say nothing more, but go to the hotel and wait."

So him and the new dummy[1] started off; and the king he laughs, and blethers out:

"Broke his arm—*very* likely *ain't* it?—and very convenient, too, for a fraud that's got to make signs, and hain't learnt how. Lost their baggage! That's *mighty* good!—and mighty ingenious—under the *circumstances!*"

So he laughed again; and so did everybody else, except three or four, or maybe half a dozen. One of these was that doctor; another one was a sharp looking gentleman, with a carpet-bag of the old-fashioned kind made out of carpet-stuff, that had just come off of the steamboat and was talking to him in a low voice, and glancing towards the king now and then and nodding their heads—it was Levi Bell, the lawyer that was gone up to Louisville; and another one was a big rough husky that come along and listened to all the old gentleman said, and was listening to the king now. And when the king got done, this husky up and says:

[1] Deaf mute.

"Say, looky here; if you are Harvey Wilks, when'd you come to this town?"

"The day before the funeral, friend," says the king.

"But what time o' day?"

"In the evenin'—'bout an hour er two before sundown."

"*How'd* you come?"

"I come down on the *Susan Powell,* from Cincinnati."

"Well, then how'd you come to be up at the Pint in the *mornin'*—in a canoe?"

"I warn't up at the Pint in the mornin'."

"It's a lie."

Several of them jumped for him and begged him not to talk that way to an old man and a preacher.

"Preacher be hanged, he's a fraud and a liar. He was up at the Pint that mornin'. I live up there, don't I? Well, I was up there, and he was up there. I *see* him there. He come in a canoe, along with Tim Collins and a boy."

The doctor he up and says: "Would you know the boy again if you was to see him, Hines?"

"I reckon I would, but I don't know. Why, yonder he is, now. I know him perfectly easy."

It was me he pointed at. The doctor says:

"Neighbors, I don't know whether the new couple is frauds or not; but if *these* two ain't frauds, I am an idiot, that's all. I think it's our duty to see that they don't get away from here till we've looked into this thing. Come along, Hines; come along, the rest of you. We'll take these fellows to the tavern and affront them with t'other couple, and I reckon we'll find out *something* before we get through."

It was nuts for the crowd, though maybe not for the king's friends; so we all started. It was about sundown. The doctor he led me along by the hand, and was plenty kind enough, but he never let *go* my hand.

We all got in a big room in the hotel, and lit up some candles, and fetched in the new couple. First, the doctor says:

"I don't wish to be too hard on these two men, but *I* think they're frauds, and they may have complices that we don't know nothing about. If they have, won't the complices get away with that bag of gold Peter Wilks left? It ain't unlikely. If these men ain't frauds; they won't object to sending for that money and letting us keep it till they prove they're all right—ain't that so?"

Everybody agreed to that. So I judged they had our gang in a pretty tight place, right at the outstart. But the king he only looked sorrowful, and says:

"Gentlemen, I wish the money was there, for I ain't got no disposition to throw anything in the way of a fair, open, out-and-out investigation o' this misable business; but alas, the money ain't there; you k'n send and see, if you want to."

"Where is it, then?"

"Well, when my niece give it to me to keep for her, I took and hid it inside o' the straw tick o' my bed, not wishin' to bank it for the few days we'd be here, and considerin' the bed a safe place, we not bein' used to niggers, and suppos'n' 'em honest, like servants in England. The niggers stole it the very next mornin' after I had went down stairs; and when I sold 'em, I hadn't missed the money yit, so they got clean away with it. My servant here k'n tell you 'bout it gentlemen."

The doctor and several said "Shucks!" and I see nobody didn't altogether believe him. One man asked me if I see the niggers steal it. I said no, but I see them sneaking out of the room and hustling away, and I never thought nothing, only I reckoned they was afraid they had waked up my master and was trying to get away before he made trouble with them. That was all they asked me. Then the doctor whirls on me and says:

"Are *you* English too?"

I says yes; and him and some others laughed, and said, "Stuff!"

Well, then they sailed in on the general investigation, and there we had it, up and down, hour in, hour out, and nobody never said a word about supper, nor ever seemed to think about it—and so they kept it up, and kept it up; and it *was* the worst mixed-up thing you ever see. They made the king tell his yarn, and they made the old gentleman tell his'n; and anybody but a lot of prejudiced chuckle-heads would a *seen* that the old gentleman was spinning truth and t'other one lies. And by-and-by they had me up to tell what I knowed. The king he give me a left-handed look out of the corner of his eye, and so I knowed enough to talk on the right side. I begun to tell about Sheffield, and how we lived there, and all about the English Wilkses, and so on; but I didn't get pretty fur till the doctor begun to laugh; and Levi Bell, the lawyer, says:

"Set down, my boy, I wouldn't strain myself, if I was you. I reckon you ain't used to lying, it don't seem to come handy; what you want is practice. You do it pretty awkward."

I didn't care nothing for the compliment, but I was glad to be let off, anyway.

The doctor he started to say something, and turns and says:

"If you'd been in town at first, Levi Bell————"

The king broke in and reached out his hand, and says:

"Why, is this my poor dead brother's old friend that he's wrote so often about?"

The lawyer and him shook hands, and the lawyer smiled and looked pleased, and they talked right along a while, and then got to one side and talked low; and at last the lawyer speaks up and says:

"That'll fix it. I'll take the order and send it, along with your brother's, and then they'll know it's all right."

So they got some paper and a pen, and the king he set down and twisted his head to one side, and chawed his tongue, and scrawled off something; and then they give the pen to the duke—and then for the first time, the duke looked sick. But he took the pen and wrote. So then the lawyer turns to the new old gentleman and says:

"You and your brother please write a line or two and sign your names."

The old gentleman wrote, but nobody couldn't read it. The lawyer looked powerful astonished, and says:

"Well, it beats *me*"—and snaked a lot of old letters out of his pocket, and examined them, and then examined the old man's writing, and then *them* again; and then says: "These old letters is from Harvey Wilks; and here's *these* two's handwritings, and anybody can see *they* didn't write them" (the king and the duke looked sold and foolish, I tell you, to see how the lawyer had took them in), "and here's *this* old gentleman's handwriting, and anybody can tell, easy enough, *he* didn't write them—fact is, the scratches he makes ain't properly *writing,* at all. Now here's some letters from————"

The new old gentleman says:

"If you please, let me explain. Nobody can read my hand but my brother there—so he copies for me. It's *his* hand you've get there, not mine."

"*Well!*" says the lawyer, "this *is* a state of things. I've got some of William's letters too; so if you'll get him to write a line or so we can com————"

"He *can't* write with his left hand," says the old gentleman. "If he could use his right hand, you would see that he wrote his own letters and mine too. Look at both, please—they're by the same hand."

The lawyer done it, and says:

"I believe it's so—and if it ain't so, there's a heap stronger resemblance than I'd noticed before, anyway. Well, well, well! I thought we was right on the track of a slution, but it's gone to grass, partly. But anyway, *one* thing is proved—*these* two ain't either of 'em Wilkses"—and he wagged his head towards the king and the duke.

Well, what do you think?—that muleheaded old fool wouldn't give in *then!* Indeed he wouldn't. Said it warn't no fair test. Said his brother William was the cussedest joker in the world, and hadn't *tried* to write—he see William was going to play one of his jokes the minute he put the pen to paper. And so he warmed up and went warbling and warbling right along, till he was actuly beginning to believe what he was saying, *himself*—but pretty soon the new old gentleman broke in, and says:

"I've thought of something. Is there anybody here that helped to lay out my br—helped to lay out the late Peter Wilks for burying?"

"Yes," says somebody, "me and Ab Turner done it. We're both here."

Then the old man turns towards the king, and says:

"Peraps this gentleman can tell me what was tatooed on his breast?"

Blamed if the king didn't have to brace up mighty quick, or he'd a squshed down like a bluff bank that the river has cut under, it took him so sudden—and mind you, it was a thing that was calculated to make most *anybody* sqush to get fetched such a solid one as that without any notice—because how was *he* going to know what was tatooed on the man? He whitened a little; he couldn't help it; and it was mighty still in there, and everybody bending a little forwards and gazing at him. Says I to myself, *Now* he'll throw up the sponge—there ain't no more use. Well, did he? A body can't believe it, but he didn't. I reckon he thought he'd keep the thing up till he tired them people out, so they'd thin out, and him and the duke could break loose and get away. Anyway, he set there, and pretty soon he begun to smile, and says:

"Mf! It's a *very* tough question, *ain't* it! *Yes,* sir, I k'n tell you what's tatooed on his breast. It's jest a small, thin, blue arrow—that's what it is; and if you don't look clost, you can't see it. *Now* what do you say—hey?"

Well, *I* never see anything like that old blister for clean out-and-out cheek.

The new old gentleman turns brisk towards Ab Turner and his pard, and his eye lights up like he judged he'd got the king *this* time, and says:

"There—you've heard what he said! Was there any such mark on Peter Wilks's breast?"

Both of them spoke up and says:

"We didn't see no such mark."

"Good!" says the old gentleman. "Now, what you *did* see on his breast was a small dim P, and a B (which is an initial he dropped when he was young), and a W, with dashes between them, so: P—B—W"—and he marked them that way on a piece of paper. "Come—ain't that what you saw?"

Both of them spoke up again, and says:

"No, we *didn't.* We never seen any marks at all."

Well, everybody *was* in a state of mind, now; and they sings out:

"The whole *bilin'* of 'm 's frauds! Le's duck 'em! le's drown 'em! le's ride 'em on a rail!" and everybody was whooping at once, and there was a rattling pow-wow. But the lawyer he jumps on the table and yells, and says:

"Gentlemen—gentle*men!* Hear me just a word—just a *single* word—if you PLEASE! There's one way yet—let's go and dig up the corpse and look."

That took them.

"Hooray!" they all shouted, and was starting right off; but the lawyer and the doctor sung out:

"Hold on, hold on! Collar all these four men and the boy, and fetch *them* along, too!"

"We'll do it!" they all shouted: "and if we don't find them marks we'll lynch the whole gang."

I *was* scared, now, I tell you. But there warn't no getting away, you know. They gripped us all, and marched us right along, straight for the graveyard, which was a mile and half down the river, and the whole town at our heels, for we made noise enough, and it was only nine in the evening.

As we went by our house I wished I hadn't sent Mary Jane out of town; because now if I could tip her the wink, she'd light out and save me, and blow on our dead-beats.

Well, we swarmed along down the river road, just carrying on like wild-cats; and to make it more scary, the sky was darking up, and the lightning beginning to wink and flitter, and the wind to shiver amongst the leaves. This was the most awful trouble and most dangersome I ever was in; and I was kinder stunned; everything was going so different from what I had allowed for; stead of being fixed so I could take my own time, if I wanted to, and see all the fun, and have Mary Jane at my back to save me and set me free when the close-fit come, here was nothing in the world betwixt me and sudden death but just them tatoo-marks. If they didn't find them—

I couldn't bear to think about it; and yet, somehow, I couldn't think about nothing else. It got darker and darker, and it was a beautiful time to give the crowd the slip; but that big husky had me by the wrist—Hines—and a body might as well try to give Goliar[2] the slip. He dragged me right along, he was so excited; and I had to run to keep up.

When they got there they swarmed into the graveyard and washed over it like an overflow. And when they got to the grave, they found they had about a hundred times as many shovels as they wanted, but nobody hadn't thought to fetch a lantern. But they sailed into digging, anyway, by the flicker of the lightning, and sent a man to the nearest house a half a mile off, to borrow one.

So they dug and dug, like everything; and it got awful dark, and the rain started, and the wind swished and swushed along, and the lightning come brisker and brisker, and the thunder boomed; but them people never took no notice of it, they was so full of this business; and one minute you could see everything and every face in that big crowd, and the shovelfuls of dirt sailing up out of the grave, and the next second the dark wiped it all out, and you couldn't see nothing at all.

At last they got out the coffin, and begun to unscrew the lid, and then such another crowding, and shouldering, and shoving as there was, to scrouge in and get a sight, you never see; and in the dark, that way, it was awful. Hines he hurt

---

[2] Goliath, the Philistine giant who challenged the Israelites and was slain by a stone hurled from David's sling (see I Samuel 17:4, 49).

my wrist dreadful, pulling and tugging so, and I reckon he clean forgot I was in the world, he was so excited and panting.

All of a sudden the lightning let go a perfect sluice of white glare, and some-body sings out:

"By the living jingo, here's the bag of gold on his breast!"

Hines let out a whoop, like everybody else, and dropped my wrist and give a big surge to bust his way in and get a look, and the way I lit out and shinned for the road in the dark, there ain't nobody can tell.

I had the road all to myself, and I fairly flew—leastways I had it all to myself except the solid dark, and the now-and-then glares, and the buzzing of the rain, and the thrashing of the wind, and the splitting of the thunder; and sure as you are born I did clip it along!

When I struck the town, I see there warn't nobody out in the storm, so I never hunted for no back streets, but humped it straight through the main one; and when I begun to get towards our house I aimed my eye and set it. No light there; the house all dark—which made me feel sorry and disappointed, I didn't know why. But at last, just as I was sailing by, *flash* comes the light in Mary Jane's window! and my heart swelled up sudden, like to bust; and the same second the house and all was behind me in the dark, and wasn't ever going to be before me no more in this world. She *was* the best girl I ever see, and had the most sand.

The minute I was far enough above the town to see I could make the towhead, I begun to look sharp for a boat to borrow; and the first time the lightning showed me one that wasn't chained, I snatched it and shoved. It was a canoe, and warn't fastened with nothing but a rope. The towhead was a rattling big distance off, away out there in the middle of the river, but I didn't lose no time; and when I struck the raft at last, I was so fagged I would a just laid down to blow and gasp if I could afforded it. But I didn't. As I sprung aboard I sung out:

"Out with you Jim, and set her loose! Glory be to goodness, we're shut of them!"

Jim lit out, and was a coming for me with both arms spread, he was so full of joy; but when I glimpsed him in the lightning, my heart shot up in my mouth, and I went overboard backwards; for I forgot he was old King Lear and a drownded A-rab all in one, and it most scared the livers and lights out of me. But Jim fished me out, and was going to hug me and bless me, and so on, he was so glad I was back and we was shut of the king and the duke, but I says:

"Not now—have it for breakfast, have it for breakfast![3] Cut loose and let her slide!"

So, in two seconds, away we went, a sliding down the river, and it *did* seem so good to be free again and all by ourselves on the big river and nobody to bother us. I had to skip around a bit, and jump up and crack my heels a few times, I couldn't help it; but about the third crack, I noticed a sound that I knowed mighty well—and held my breath and listened and waited—and sure enough, when the next flash busted out over the water, here they come!—and just a laying to their oars and making their skiff hum! It was the king and the duke.

So I wilted right down onto the planks, then, and give up; and it was all I could do to keep from crying.

---

[3] Wait until later, wait until tomorrow.

CHAPTER XXX

When they got aboard, the king went for me, and shook me by the collar, and says;

"Tryin' to give us the slip, was ye, you pup! Tired of our company—hey?"

I says:

"No, your majesty, we warn't—*please* don't, your majesty!"

"Quick, then, and tell us what *was* your idea, or I'll shake the insides out o' you!"

"Honest, I'll tell you everything, just as it happened, your majesty. The man that had aholt of me was very good to me, and kept saying he had a boy about as big as me that died last year, and he was sorry to see a boy in such a dangerous fix, and when they was all took by surprise by the finding the gold, and made a rush for the coffin, he lets go of me and whispers, 'Heel it, now, or they'll hang ye, sure!' and I lit out. It didn't seem no good for *me* to stay—*I* couldn't do nothing, and I didn't want to be hung if I could get away. So I never stopped running till I found the canoe; and when I got here I told Jim to hurry, or they'd catch me and hang me yet, and said I was afeard you and the duke wasn't alive, now, and I was awful sorry, and so was Jim, and was awful glad when we see you coming, you may ask Jim if I didn't."

Jim said it was so; and the king told him to shut up, and said, "Oh, yes, it's *mighty* likely!" and shook me up again, and said he reckoned he'd drownd me. But the duke says:

"Leggo the boy, you old idiot! Would *you* a done any different? Did you inquire around for *him,* when you got loose? *I* don't remember it."

So the king let go of me, and begun to cuss that town and everybody in it. But the duke says:

"You better a blame sight give *yourself* a good cussing, for you're the one that's entitled to it most. You hain't done a thing, from the start, that had any sense in it, except coming out so cool and cheeky with that imaginary blue-arrow mark. That *was* bright—it was right down bully; and it was the thing that saved us. For if it hadn't been for that, they'd a jailed us till them Englishmen's baggage come—and then—the penitentiary, you bet! But that trick took 'em to the graveyard, and the gold done us a still bigger kindness; for if the excited fools hadn't let go all holts and made that rush to get a look, we'd a slept in our cravats[1] tonight—cravats warranted to *wear,* too—longer than *we'd* need 'em."

They was still a minute—thinking—then the king says, kind of absent-minded like:

"Mf! And we reckoned the *niggers* stole it!"

That made me squirm!

"Yes," says the duke, kinder slow, and deliberate, and sarcastic, "*We* did."

After about a half a minute, the king drawls out:

"Leastways—*I* did."

The duke says, the same way:

"On the contrary—*I* did."

The king kind of ruffles up, and says:

"Looky here, Bilgewater, what'r you referrin' to?"

The duke says, pretty brisk:

---

[1] Neckties; here, nooses: "we'd have been hanged."

"When it comes to that, maybe you'll let me ask, what was *you* referring to?"

"Shucks!" says the king, very sarcastic; "but *I* don't know—maybe you was asleep, and didn't know what you was about."

The duke bristles right up, now, and says:

"Oh, let *up* on this cussed nonsense—do you take me for a blame' fool? Don't you reckon *I* know who hid that money in that coffin?"

"*Yes,* sir! I know you *do* know—because you done it yourself!"

"It's a lie!"—and the duke went for him. The king sings out:

"Take y'r hands off!—leggo my throat!—I take it all back!"

The duke says:

"Well, you just own up, first, that you *did* hide that money there, intending to give me the slip one of these days, and come back and dig it up, and have it all to yourself."

"Wait jest a minute, duke—answer me this one question, honest and fair; if you didn't put the money there, say it, and I'll b'lieve you, and take back everything I said."

"You old scoundrel, I didn't, and you know I didn't. There, now!"

"Well, then, I b'lieve you. But answer me only jest this one more—now *don't* git mad; didn't you have it in your *mind* to hook the money and hide it?"

The duke never said nothing for a little bit; then he says:

"Well—I don't care if I *did,* I didn't *do* it, anyway. But you not only had it in mind to do it, but you *done* it."

"I wisht I may never die if I done it, duke, and that's honest. I won't say I warn't *goin'* to do it, because I *was;* but you—I mean somebody—got in ahead o' me."

"It's a lie! You done it, and you got to *say* you done it, or—"

The king begun to gurgle, and then he gasps out:

"'Nough!—I *own up!*"

I was very glad to hear him say that, it made me feel much more easier than what I was feeling before. So the duke took his hands off, and says:

"If you ever deny it again, I'll drown you. It's *well* for you to set there and blubber like a baby—it's fitten for you, after the way you've acted. I never see such an old ostrich for wanting to gobble everything—and I a trusting you all the time, like you was my own father. You ought to been ashamed of yourself to stand by and hear it saddled onto a lot of poor niggers and you never say a word for 'em. It makes me feel ridiculous to think I was soft enough to *believe* that rubbage. Cuss you, I can see, now, why you was so anxious to make up the deffesit—you wanted to get what money I'd got out of the Nonesuch and one thing or another, and scoop it *all!*"

The king says, timid, and still a snuffling:

"Why, duke, it was you that said make up the deffersit, it warn't me."

"Dry up! I don't want to hear no more *out* of you!" Says the duke. "And *now* you see what you *got* by it. They've got all their own money back, and all of *ourn* but a shekel[2] or two, *besides.* G'long to bed—and don't you deffersit *me* no more deffersits, long 's *you* live!"

So the king sneaked into the wigwam, and took to his bottle for comfort; and before long the duke tackled *his* bottle; and so in about a half an hour they was as thick as thieves again, and the tighter they got, the lovinger they got; and went off

---

[2] A coin of ancient Babylonia and the Near East; here, a coin of small value.

a snoring in each other's arms. They both got powerful mellow, but I noticed the king didn't get mellow enough to forget to remember to not deny about hiding the money-bag again. That made me feel easy and satisfied. Of course when they got to snoring, we had a long gabble, and I told Jim everything.

Chapter XXXI

We dasn't stop again at any town, for days and days; kept right along down the river. We was down south in the warm weather, now, and a mighty long ways from home. We begun to come to trees with Spanish moss on them, hanging down from the limbs like long gray beards. It was the first I ever see it growing, and it made the woods look solemn and dismal. So now the frauds reckoned they was out of danger, and they begun to work the villages again.

First they done a lecture on temperance; but they didn't make enough for them both to get drunk on. Then in another village they started a dancing school; but they didn't know no more how to dance than a kangaroo does; so the first prance they made, the general public jumped in and pranced them out of town. Another time they tried a go at yellocution; but they didn't yellocute long till the audience got up and give them a solid good cussing and made them skip out. They tackled missionarying, and mesmerizering, and doctoring, and telling fortunes, and a little of everything; but they couldn't seem to have no luck. So at last they got just about dead broke, and laid around the raft, as she floated along, thinking, and thinking, and never saying nothing, by the half a day at a time, and dreadful blue and desperate.

And at last they took a change, and begun to lay their heads together in the wigwam and talk low and confidential two or three hours at a time. Jim and me got uneasy. We didn't like the look of it. We judged they was studying up some kind of worse deviltry than ever. We turned it over and over, and at last we made up our minds they was going to break into somebody's house or store, or was going into the counterfeit-money business, or something. So then we was pretty scared, and made up an agreement that we wouldn't have nothing in the world to do with such actions, and if we ever got the least show we would give them the cold shake, and clear out and leave them behind. Well, early one morning we hid the raft in a good safe place about two mile below a little bit of a shabby village, named Pikesville, and the king he went ashore, and told us all to stay hid whilst he went up to town and smelt around to see if anybody had got any wind of the Royal Nonesuch there yet. ("House to rob, you *mean*," says I to myself; "and when you get through robbing it you'll come back here and wonder what's become of me and Jim and the raft—and you'll have to take it out in wondering.") And he said if he warn't back by midday, the duke and me would know it was all right, and we was to come along.

So we staid where was was. The duke he fretted and sweated around, and was in a mighty sour way. He scolded us for everything, and we couldn't seem to do nothing right; he found fault with every little thing. Something was a-brewing, sure. I was good and glad when midday come and no king; we could have a change, anyway—and maybe a chance for *the* change, on top of it. So me and the duke went up to the village, and hunted around there for the king, and by-and-by we found him in the back room of a little low doggery,[1] very tight, and a lot of

---

[1] Cheap saloon.

loafers bullyragging him for sport, and he a cussing and threatening with all his might, and so tight he couldn't walk, and couldn't do nothing to them. The duke he began to abuse him for an old fool, and the king begun to sass back; and the minute they was fairly at it, I lit out, and shook the reefs out of[2] my hind legs, and spun down the river road like a deer—for I see our chance; and I made up my mind that it would be a long day before they ever see me and Jim again. I got down there all out of breath but loaded up with joy, and sung out—

"Set her loose, Jim, we're all right, now!"

But there warn't no answer, and nobody come out of the wigwam. Jim was gone! I set up a shout—and then another—and then another one; and run this way and that in the woods, whooping and screeching; but it warn't no use—old Jim was gone. Then I set down and cried; I couldn't help it. But I couldn't set still long. Pretty soon I went out on the road, trying to think what I better do, and I run across a boy walking, and asked him if he'd seen a strange nigger, dressed so and so, and he says:

"Yes."

"Whereabouts?" says I.

"Down to Silas Phelps's place, two mile below here. He's a runaway nigger, and they've got him. Was you looking for him?"

"You bet I ain't! I run across him in the woods about an hour or two ago, and he said if I hollered he'd cut my livers out—and told me to lay down and stay where I was; and I done it. Been there ever since; afeard to come out."

"Well," he says, "you needn't be afeard no more, becuz they've got him. He run off f'm down South, som'ers."

"It's a good job they got him."

"Well, I *reckon!* There's two hunderd dollars reward on him. It's like picking up money out'n the road."

"Yes, it is—and *I* could a had it if I'd been big enough; I see him *first.* Who nailed him?"

"It was an old fellow—a stranger—and he sold out his chance in him for forty dollars, becuz he's got to go up the river and can't wait. Think o' that, now! You bet *I'd* wait, if it was seven year."

"That's me, every time," says I. "But maybe his chance ain't worth no more than that, if he'll sell it so cheap. Maybe there's something ain't straight about it."

"But it *is,* though—straight as a string. I see the handbill myself. It tells all about him, to a dot—paints him like a picture, and tells the plantation he's frum, below Newr*leans.* No-sirree-*bob,* they ain't no trouble 'bout *that* speculation, you bet you. Say, gimme a chaw tobacker, won't ye?"

I didn't have none, so he left. I went to the raft, and set down in the wigwam to think. But I couldn't come to nothing. I thought till I wore my head sore, but I couldn't see no way out of the trouble. After all this long journey, and after all we'd done for them scoundrels, here was it all come to nothing, everything all busted up and ruined, because they could have the heart to serve Jim such a trick as that, and make him a slave again all his life, and amongst strangers, too, for forty dirty dollars.

Once I said to myself it would be a thousand times better for Jim to be a slave at home where his family was, as long as he'd *got* to be a slave, and so I'd better write a letter to Tom Sawyer and tell him to tell Miss Watson where he was. But I soon give up that notion, for two things: she'd be mad and disgusted at his rascal-

---

[2] Stretched out.

ity and ungratefulness for leaving her, and so she'd sell him straight down the river again; and if she didn't, everybody naturally despises an ungrateful nigger, and they'd make Jim feel it all the time, and so he'd feel ornery and disgraced. And then think of *me!* It would get all around, that Huck Finn helped a nigger to get his freedom; and if I was to ever see anybody from that town again, I'd be ready to get down and lick his boots for shame. That's just the way: a person does a low-down thing, and then he don't want to take no consequences of it. Thinks as long as he can hide it, it ain't no disgrace. That was my fix exactly. The more I studied about this, the more my conscience went to grinding me, and the more wicked and low-down and ornery I got to feeling. And at last, when it hit me all of a sudden that here was the plain hand of Providence slapping me in the face and letting me know my wickedness was being watched all the time from up there in heaven, whilst I was stealing a poor old woman's nigger that hadn't ever done me no harm, and now was showing me there's One that's always on the lookout, and ain't agoing to allow no such miserable doings to go only just so fur and no further, I most dropped in my tracks I was so scared. Well, I tried the best I could to kinder soften it up somehow for myself, by saying I was brung up wicked, and so I warn't so much to blame; but something inside of me kept saying, "There was the Sunday school, you could a gone to it; and if you'd a done it they'd a learnt you, there, that people that acts as I'd been acting about that nigger goes to everlasting fire."

It made me shiver. And I about made up my mind to pray; and see if I couldn't try to quit being the kind of a boy I was, and be better. So I kneeled down. But the words wouldn't come. Why wouldn't they? It warn't no use to try and hide it from Him. Nor from *me,* neither. I knowed very well why they wouldn't come. It was because my heart warn't right; it was because I warn't square; it was because I was playing double. I was letting *on* to give up sin, but away inside of me I was holding on to the biggest one of all. I was trying to make my mouth *say* I would do the right thing and the clean thing, and go and write to that nigger's owner and tell where he was; but deep down in me I knowed it was a lie—and He knowed it. You can't pray a lie—I found that out.

So I was full of trouble, full as I could be; and didn't know what to do. At last I had an idea; and I says, I'll go and write the letter—and *then* see if I can pray. Why, it was astonishing, the way I felt as light as a feather, right straight off, and my troubles all gone. So I got a piece of paper and a pencil, all glad and excited, and set down and wrote:

> Miss Watson your runaway nigger Jim is down here two mile below Pikesville and Mr. Phelps has got him and he will give him up for the reward if you send.
>
> HUCK FINN.

I felt good and all washed clean of sin for the first time I had ever felt so in my life, and I knowed I could pray now. But I didn't do it straight off, but laid the paper down and set there thinking—thinking how good it was all this happened so, and how near I come to being lost and going to hell. And went on thinking. And got thinking over our trip down the river; and I see Jim before me, all the time, in the day, and in the night-time, sometimes moonlight, sometimes storms, and we a floating along, talking, and singing, and laughing. But somehow I couldn't seem to strike no places to harden me against him, but only the other kind. I'd see him standing my watch on top of his'n, stead of calling me, so I could go on sleeping; and see him how glad he was when I come back out of the fog; and when I come to him again in the swamp, up there where the feud was; and such-like times; and would always call me honey, and pet me, and do everything he could think of for me, and how good he always was; and at last I struck the time I saved him by telling the men we had small-pox aboard, and he was so grateful, and said I was the best friend old Jim ever had in the world, and the *only* one he's got now; and then I happened to look around, and see that paper.

It was a close place. I took it up, and held it in my hand. I was a trembling, because I'd got to decide, forever, betwixt two things, and I knowed it. I studied a minute, sort of holding my breath, and then says to myself:

"All right, then, I'll *go* to hell"—and tore it up.[3]

It was awful thoughts, and awful words, but they was said. And I let them stay said; and never thought no more about reforming. I shoved the whole thing out of my head; and said I would take up wickedness again, which was in my line, being brung up to it, and the other warn't. And for a starter I would go to work and steal Jim out of slavery again; and if I could think up anything worse, I would do that, too; because as long as I was in, and in for good, I might as well go the whole hog.

Then I set to thinking over how to get at it, and turned over considerable many ways in my mind; and at last fixed up a plan that suited me. So then I took the bearings of a woody island that was down the river a piece, and as soon as it was fairly dark I crept out with my raft and went for it, and hid it there, and then turned in. I slept the night through, and got up before it was light, and had my breakfast, and put on my store clothes, and tied up some others and one thing or another in a bundle, and took the canoe and cleared for shore. I landed below where I judged was Phelps's place, and hid my bundle in the woods, and then filled up the canoe with water, and loaded rocks into her and sunk her where I could find her again when I wanted her, about a quarter of a mile below a little steam sawmill that was on the bank.

Then I struck up the road, and when I passed the mill I see a sign on it, "Phelps's Sawmill," and when I come to the farmhouses, two or three hundred yards further along, I kept my eyes peeled, but didn't see nobody around, though it was good daylight, now. But I didn't mind, because I didn't want to see nobody just yet—I only wanted to get the lay of the land. According to my plan, I was going to turn up there from the village, not from below. So I just took a look, and shoved along, straight for town. Well, the very first man I see, when I got there, was the duke. He was sticking up a bill for the Royal Nonesuch—three-night performance—like that other time. *They* had the cheek, them frauds! I was right on him, before I could shirk. He looked astonished, and says:

"Hel-*lo!* Where'd *you* come from?" Then he says, kind of glad and eager, "Where's the raft?—got her in a good place?"

I says:

"Why, that's just what I was a going to ask your grace."

Then he didn't look so joyful—and says:

"What was your idea for asking *me?*" he says.

"Well," I says, "when I see the king in that doggery yesterday, I says to my-

---

[3] Twain once said that Huckleberry Finn was a boy "with a stout heart and a deformed conscience," Huck's heart being human and his conscience social. Here Huck's heart wins out; he becomes morally heroic at the moment he thinks he will go to Hell.

self, we can't get him home for hours, till he's soberer; so I went a loafing around town to put in the time, and wait. A man up and offered me ten cents to help him pull a skiff over the river and back to fetch a sheep, and so I went along; but when we was dragging him to the boat, and the man left me aholt of the rope and went behind him to shove him along, he was too strong for me, and jerked loose and run, and we after him. We didn't have no dog, and so we had to chase him all over the country till we tired him out. We never got him till dark, then we fetched him over, and I started down for the raft. When I got there and see it was gone, I says to myself, 'they've got into trouble and had to leave; and they've took my nigger, which is the only nigger I've got in the world, and now I'm in a strange country, and ain't got no property no more, nor nothing, and no way to make my living;' so I set down and cried. I slept in the woods all night. But what *did* become of the raft then?—and Jim, poor Jim!"

"Blamed if *I* know—that is, what's become of the raft. That old fool had made a trade and got forty dollars, and when we found him in the doggery the loafers had matched half dollars with him and got every cent but what he'd spent for whisky; and when I got him home late last night and found the raft gone, we said, 'That little rascal has stole our raft and shook us, and run off down the river.'"

"I wouldn't shake my *nigger,* would I?—the only nigger I had in the world, and the only property."

"We never thought of that. Fact is, I reckon we'd come to consider him *our* nigger; yes, we did consider him so—goodness knows we had trouble enough for him. So when we see the raft was gone, and we flat broke, there warn't anything for it but to try the Royal Nonesuch another shake. And I've pegged along ever since, dry as a powderhorn. Where's that ten cents? Give it here."

I had considerable money, so I give him ten cents, but begged him to spend it for something to eat, and give me some, because it was all the money I had, and I hadn't had nothing to eat since yesterday. He never said nothing. The next minute he whirls on me and says:

"Do you reckon that nigger would blow on us? We'd skin him if he done that!"

"How can he blow? Hain't he run off?"

"No! That old fool sold him, and never divided with me, and the money's gone."

"*Sold* him?" I says, and begun to cry; "why, he was *my* nigger, and that was my money. Where is he?—I want my nigger."

"Well, you can't *get* your nigger, that's all—so dry up your blubbering. Looky here—do you think *you'd* venture to blow on us? Blamed if I think I'd trust you. Why, if you *was* to blow on us—"

He stopped, but I never see the duke look so ugly out of his eyes before. I went on a-whimpering, and says:

"I don't want to blow on nobody; and I ain't got no time to blow, nohow. I got to turn out and find my nigger."

He looked kinder bothered, and stood there with his bills fluttering on his arm, thinking, and wrinkling up his forehead. At last he says:

"I'll tell you something. We got to be here three days. If you'll promise you won't blow, and won't let the nigger blow, I'll tell you where to find him."

So I promised, and he says:

"A farmer by the name of Silas Ph—" and then he stopped. You see he started to tell me the truth; but when he stopped, that way, and begun to study and think again, I reckoned he was changing his mind. And so he was. He wouldn't trust me; he wanted to make sure of having me out of the way the whole three days. So pretty soon he says: "The man that bought him is named Abram Foster—Abram G. Foster—and he lives forty mile back here in the country, on the road to Lafayette."

"All right," I says, "I can walk it in three days. And I'll start this very afternoon."

"No, you won't, you'll start *now;* and don't you lose any time about it, neither, nor do any gabbling by the way. Just keep a tight tongue in your head and move right along, and then you won't get into trouble with *us,* d'ye hear?"

That was the order I wanted, and that was the one I played for. I wanted to be left free to work my plans.

"So clear out," he says; "and you can tell Mr. Foster whatever you want to. Maybe you can get him to believe that Jim *is* your nigger—some idiots don't require documents—leastways I've heard there's such down South here. And when you tell him the handbill and the reward's bogus, maybe he'll believe you when you explain to him what the idea was for getting 'em out. Go 'long, now, and tell him anything you want to; but mind you don't work your jaw any *between* here and there."

So I left, and struck for the back country. I didn't look around, but I kinder felt like he was watching me. But I knowed I could tire him out at that. I went straight out in the country as much as a mile, before I stopped; then I doubled back through the woods towards Phelps's. I reckoned I better start in on my plan straight off, without fooling around, because I wanted to stop Jim's mouth till these fellows could get away. I didn't want no trouble with their kind. I'd seen all I wanted to of them, and wanted to get entirely shut of them.

Chapter XXXII

When I got there it was all still and Sunday-like, and hot and sunshiny—the hands was gone to the fields; and there was them kind of faint dronings of bugs and flies in the air that makes it seem so lonesome and like everybody's dead and gone; and if a breeze fans along and quivers the leaves, it makes you feel mournful, because you feel like it's spirits whispering—spirits that's been dead ever so many years— and you always think they're talking about *you.* As a general thing it makes a body wish *he* was dead, too, and done with it all.

Phelps's was one of these little one-horse cotton plantations; and they all look alike. A rail fence round a two-acre yard; a stile, made out of logs sawed off and up-ended, in steps, like barrels of a different length, to climb over the fence with, and for the women to stand on when they are going to jump onto a horse; some sickly grass-patches in the big yard, but mostly it was bare and smooth, like an old hat with the nap rubbed off; big double log house for the white folks—hewed logs, with the chinks stopped up with mud or mortar, and these mud-stripes been whitewashed some time or another; round-log kitchen, with a big broad, open but roofed passage joining it to the house; log smoke-house back of the kitchen; three little log nigger-cabins in a row t'other side the smoke-house; one little hut all by itself away down against the back fence, and some out-buildings down a piece the other side; ash-hopper,[1] and big kettle to bile soap in, by the little hut; bench by

---

[1] A hopper, or container, for fireplace ashes, which are leached to make lye (used in making soap).

the kitchen door, with bucket of water and a gourd; hound asleep there, in the sun; more hounds asleep, round about; about three shade-trees away off in a corner; some currant bushes and gooseberry bushes in one place by the fence; outside of the fence a garden and a water-melon patch; then the cotton fields begins; and after the fields, the woods.

I went around and clumb over the back stile by the ash-hopper, and started for the kitchen. When I got a little ways, I heard the dim hum of a spinning-wheel wailing along up and sinking along down again; and then I knowed for certain I wished I was dead—for that *is* the lonesomest sound in the whole world.

I went right along, not fixing up any particular plan, but just trusting to Providence to put the right words in my mouth when the time come; for I'd noticed that Providence always did put the right words in my mouth, if I left it alone.

When I got half-way, first one hound and then another got up and went for me, and of course I stopped and faced them, and kept still. And such another pow-wow as they made! In a quarter of a minute I was a kind of a hub of a wheel, as you may say—spokes made out of dogs—circle of fifteen of them packed together around me, with their necks and noses stretched up towards me, a barking and howling; and more a coming; you could see them sailing over fences and around corners from everywheres.

A nigger woman come tearing out of the kitchen with a rolling-pin in her hand, singing out, "Begone! *you* Tige! you Spot! begone, sah!" and she fetched first one and then another of them a clip and sent him howling, and then the rest followed; and the next second, half of them come back, wagging their tails around me and making friends with me. There ain't no harm in a hound, nohow.

And behind the woman comes a little nigger girl and two little nigger boys, without anything on but tow-linen shirts, and they hung onto their mother's gown, and peeped out from behind her at me, bashful, the way they always do. And here comes the white woman running from the house, about forty-five or fifty year old, bareheaded, and her spinning-stick in her hand; and behind her comes her little white children, acting the same way the little niggers was doing. She was smiling all over so she could hardly stand—and says:

"It's *you*, at last!—*ain't* it?"

I out with a "Yes'm," before I thought.

She grabbed me and hugged me tight; and then gripped me by both hands and shook and shook; and the tears come in her eyes, and run down over; and she couldn't seem to hug and shake enough, and kept saying, "You don't look as much like your mother as I reckoned you would; but law sakes, I don't care for that, I'm *so* glad to see you! Dear, dear, it does seem like I could eat you up! Childern, it's your cousin Tom!—tell him howdy."

But they ducked their heads, and put their fingers in theirs mouths, and hid behind her. So she run on:

"Lize, hurry up and get him a hot breakfast, right away—or did you get your breakfast on the boat?"

I said I had got it on the boat. So then she started for the house, leading me by the hand, and the children tagging after. When we got there, she set me down in a split-bottomed chair, and set herself down on a little low stool in front of me, holding both of my hands, and says:

"Now I can have a *good* look at you; and laws-a-me, I've been hungry for it a many and a many a time, all these long years, and it's come at last! We been expecting you a couple of days and more. What's kep' you?—boat get aground?"

"Yes'm—she—"

"Don't say yes'm—say Aunt Sally. Where'd she get aground?"

I didn't rightly know what to say, because I didn't know whether the boat would be coming up the river or down. But I go a good deal on instinct; and my instinct said she would be coming up—from down towards Orleans. That didn't help me much, though; for I didn't know the names of bars down that way. I see I'd got to invent a bar, or forget the name of the one we got aground on—or— Now I struck an idea, and fetched it out:

"It warn't the grounding—that didn't keep us back but a little. We blowed out a cylinder-head."

"Good gracious! Anybody hurt?"

"No'm. Killed a nigger."

"Well, it's lucky; because sometimes people do get hurt. Two years ago last Christmas, your uncle Silas was coming up from Newrleans on the old *Lally Rook*,[2] and she blowed out a cylinder-head and crippled a man. And I think he died afterwards. He was a Babtist. Your uncle Silas knowed a family in Baton Rouge that knowed his people very well. Yes, I remember, now he *did* die. Mortification[3] set in, and they had to amputate him. But it didn't save him. Yes, it was mortification—that was it. He turned blue all over, and died in the hope of a glorious resurrection. They say he was a sight to look at. Your uncle's been up to the town every day to fetch you. And he's gone again, not more'n an hour ago; he'll be back any minute, now. You must a met him on the road, didn't you?— oldish man, with a—"

"No, I didn't see nobody, Aunt Sally. The boat landed just at daylight, and I left my baggage on the wharf-boat[4] and went looking around the town and out a piece in the country, to put in the time and not get here too soon; and so I come down the back way."

"Who'd you give the baggage to?"

"Nobody."

"Why, child, it'll be stole!"

"Not where *I* hid it I reckon it won't," I says.

"How'd you get your breakfast so early on the boat?"

It was kinder thin ice, but I says:

"The captain see me standing around, and told me I better have something to eat before I went ashore; so he took me in the texas to the officers' lunch,[5] and give me all I wanted."

I was getting so uneasy I couldn't listen good. I had my mind on the children all the time; I wanted to get them out to one side, and pump them a little, and find out who I was. But I couldn't get no show, Mrs. Phelps kept it up and run on so. Pretty soon she made the cold chills streak all down my back, because she says:

"But here we're a running on this way, and you hain't told me a word about Sis, nor any of them. Now I'll rest my works a little, and you start up yourn; just tell me *everything*—tell me all about 'm all—every one of 'm; and how they are, and what they're doing, and what they told you to tell me; and every last thing you can think of."

Well, I see I was up a stump—and up it good. Providence had stood by me this

---

[2] Named for the princess in *Lalla Rookh* (1817), a series of oriental tales in verse that are connected by a story in prose, by the English writer Thomas Moore (1779-1852).
[3] Gangrene.   [4] Landing dock.   [5] Officer's mess, or dining room.

fur, all right, but I was hard and tight aground, now. I see it warn't a bit of use to try to go ahead—I'd *got* to throw up my hand. So I says to myself, here's another place where I got to resk the truth. I opened my mouth to begin; but she grabbed me and hustled me in behind the bed, and says:

"Here he comes! stick your head down lower—there, that'll do; you can't be seen, now. Don't you let on you're here. I'll play a joke on him. Childern, don't you say a word."

I see I was in a fix, now. But it warn't no use to worry; there warn't nothing to do but just hold still, and try and be ready to stand from under when the lightning struck.

I had just one little glimpse of the old gentleman when he come in, then the bed hid him. Mrs. Phelps she jumps for him and says:

"Has he come?"

"No," says her husband.

"Good-*ness* gracious!" she says, "what in the world *can* have become of him?"

"I can't imagine," says the old gentleman; "and I must say, it makes me dreadful uneasy."

"Uneasy!" she says, "I'm ready to go distracted! He *must* a come; and you've missed him along the road. I *know* it's so—something *tells* me so."

"Why Sally, I *couldn't* miss him along the road—*you* know that."

"But oh, dear, dear, what *will* Sis say? He must a come! You must a missed him. He—"

"Oh, don't distress me any more'n I'm already distressed. I don't know what in the world to make of it. I'm at my wit's end, and I don't mind acknowledging 't I'm right down scared. But there's no hope that he's come; for he *couldn't* come and me miss him. Sally, it's terrible—just terrible—something's happened to the boat, sure!"

"Why, Silas! Look yonder!—up the road!—ain't that somebody coming?"

He sprung to the window at the head of the bed, and that give Mrs. Phelps the chance she wanted. She stooped down quick, at the foot of the bed, and give me a pull, and out I come; and when he turned back from the window, there she stood, a-beaming and a-smiling like a house afire, and I standing pretty meek and sweaty alongside. The old gentleman stared, and says:

"Why, who's that?"

"Who do you reckon 't is?"

"I hain't no idea. Who *is* it?"

"It's *Tom Sawyer!*"

By jings, I most slumped through the floor. But there warn't no time to swap knives;[6] the old man grabbed me by the hand and shook, and kept on shaking; and all the time, how the woman did dance around and laugh and cry; and then how they both did fire off questions about Sid, and Mary, and the rest of the tribe.

But if they was joyful, it warn't nothing to what I was; for it was like being born again, I was so glad to find out who I was. Well, they froze to me for two hours; and at last when my chin was so tired it couldn't hardly go, any more, I had told them more about my family—I mean the Sawyer family—than ever happened to any six Sawyer families. And I explained all about how we blowed out a cylinder-head at the mouth of White River and it took us three days to fix it.

---

[6] Change plans.

Which was all right, and worked first rate; because *they* didn't know but what it would take three days to fix it. If I'd a called it a bolt-head it would a done just as well.

Now I was feeling pretty comfortable all down one side, and pretty uncomfortable all up the other. Being Tom Sawyer was easy and comfortable; and it stayed easy and comfortable till by-and-by I hear a steamboat coughing along down the river—then I says to myself, spose Tom Sawyer come down on that boat?—and spose he steps in here, any minute, and sings out my name before I can throw him a wink to keep quiet? Well, I couldn't *have* it that way—it wouldn't do at all. I must go up the road and waylay him. So I told the folks I reckoned I would go up to the town and fetch down my baggage. The old gentleman was for going along with me, but I said no, I could drive the horse myself, and I druther he wouldn't take no trouble about me.

CHAPTER XXXIII

So I started for town, in the wagon, and when I was half-way I see a wagon coming, and sure enough it was Tom Sawyer, and I stopped and waited till he come along. I says "Hold on!" and it stopped alongside, and his mouth opened up like a trunk, and staid so; and he swallowed two or three times like a person that's got a dry throat, and then says:

"I hain't ever done you no harm. You know that. So then, what you want to come back and ha'nt *me* for?"

I says:

"I hain't come back—I hain't been *gone*."

When he heard my voice, it righted him up some, but he warn't quite satisfied yet. He says:

"Don't you play nothing on me, because I wouldn't on you. Honest injun, now, you ain't a ghost?"

"Honest injun, I ain't," I says.

"Well—I—I—well, that ought to settle it, of course; but I can't somehow seem to understand it, no way. Looky here, warn't you ever murdered *at all?*"

"No. I warn't ever murdered at all—I played it on them. You come in here and feel of me if you don't believe me."

So he done it; and it satisfied him; and he was that glad to see me again, he didn't know what to do. And he wanted to know all about it right off; because it was a grand adventure, and mysterious, and so it hit him where he lived. But I said, leave it alone till by-and-by; and told his driver to wait, and we drove off a little piece, and I told him the kind of fix I was in, and what did he reckon we better do? He said, let him alone a minute, and don't disturb him. So he thought and thought, and pretty soon he says:

"It's all right, I've got it. Take my trunk in your wagon, and let on it's your'n; and you turn back and fool along slow, so as to get to the house about the time you ought to; and I'll go towards town a piece, and take a fresh start, and get there a quarter or a half an hour after you; and you needn't let on to know me, at first."

I says:

"All right; but wait a minute. There's one more thing—a thing that *nobody* don't know but me. And that is, there's a nigger here that I'm a trying to steal out of slavery—and his name is *Jim*—old Miss Watson's Jim."

He says:

"What! Why Jim is—"

He stopped and went to studying. I says:

"*I* know what you'll say. You'll say it's dirty low-down business; but what if it is?—*I*'m low down; and I'm agoing to steal him, and I want you to keep mum and not let on. Will you?"

His eye lit up, and he says:

"I'll *help* you steal him!"

Well, I let go all holts then, like I was shot. It was the most astonishing speech I ever heard—and I'm bound to say Tom Sawyer fell, considerable, in my estimation. Only I couldn't believe it. Tom Sawyer a *nigger stealer!*

"Oh, shucks," I says, "you're joking."

"I ain't joking, either."

"Well, then," I says, "joking or no joking, if you hear anything said about a runaway nigger, don't forget to remember that *you* don't know nothing about him, and *I* don't know nothing about him."

Then we took the trunk and put it in my wagon, and he drove off his way, and I drove mine. But of course I forgot all about driving slow, on accounts of being glad and full of thinking; so I got home a heap too quick for that length of a trip. The old gentleman was at the door, and he says:

"Why, this is wonderful. Who ever would a thought it was in that mare to do it. I wish we'd a timed her. And she hain't sweated a hair—not a hair. It's wonderful. Why, I wouldn't take a hunderd dollars for that horse now; I wouldn't, honest; and yet I'd a sold her for fifteen before, and thought 'twas all she was worth."

That's all he said. He was the innocentest, best old soul I ever see. But it warn't surprising; because he warn't only just a farmer, he was a preacher, too, and had a little one-horse log church down back of the plantation, which he built it himself at his own expense, for a church and school-house, and never charged nothing for his preaching, and it was worth it, too. There was plenty other farmer-preachers like that, and done the same way, down South.

In about half an hour Tom's wagon drove up to the front stile, and Aunt Sally she see it through the window because it was only about fifty yards, and says:

"Why, there's somebody come! I wonder who 'tis? Why, I do believe it's a stranger. Jimmy" (that's one of the children), "run and tell Lize to put on another plate for dinner."

Everybody made a rush for the front door, because, of course, a stranger don't come *every* year, and so he lays over the yaller fever, for interest, when he does come. Tom was over the stile and starting for the house; the wagon was spinning up the road for the village, and we was all bunched in the front door. Tom had his store clothes on, and an audience—and that was always nuts for Tom Sawyer. In them circumstances it warn't no trouble to him to throw in an amount of style that was suitable. He warn't a boy to meeky along[1] up that yard like a sheep; no, he come ca'm and important, like the ram. When he got afront of us, he lifts his hat ever so gracious and dainty, like it was the lid of a box that had butterflies asleep in it and he didn't want to disturb them, and says:

"Mr. Archibald Nichols, I presume?"

"No, my boy," says the old gentleman, "I'm sorry to say 't your driver has deceived you; Nichol's place is down a matter of three mile more. Come in, come in."

---

[1] To approach meekly.

Tom he took a look back over his shoulder, and says, "Too late—he's out of sight."

"Yes, he's gone, my son, and you must come in and eat your dinner with us; and then we'll hitch up and take you down to Nichols's."

"Oh, I *can't* make you so much trouble; I couldn't think of it. I'll walk—I don't mind the distance."

"But we won't *let* you walk—it wouldn't be Southern hospitality to do it. Come right in."

"Oh, *do*," says Aunt Sally; "it ain't a bit of trouble to us, not a bit in the world. You *must* stay. It's a long dusty three mile, and we *can't* let you walk. And besides, I've already told 'em to put on another plate, when I see you coming; so you mustn't disappoint us. Come right in, and make yourself at home."

So Tom he thanked them very hearty and handsome, and let himself be persuaded, and come in; and when he was in, he said he was a stranger from Hicksville, Ohio, and his name was William Thompson—and he made another bow.

Well, he run on, and on, and on, making up stuff about Hicksville and everybody in it he could invent, and I getting a little nervous, and wondering how this was going to help me out of my scrape; and at last, still talking along, he reached over and kissed Aunt Sally right on the mouth, and then settled back again in his chair, comfortable, and was going on talking; but she jumped up and wiped it off with the back of her hand and says:

"You owdacious puppy!"

He looked kind of hurt, and says:

"I'm surprised at you, m'am."

"You're s'rp—Why, what do you reckon *I* am? I've a good notion to take and—say, what do you mean by kissing me?"

He looked kind of humble, and says:

"I didn't mean nothing, m'am. I didn't mean no harm. I—I—thought you'd like it."

"Why, you born fool!" She took up the spinning-stick, and it looked like it was all she could do to keep from giving him a crack with it. "What made you think I'd like it?"

"Well, I don't know. Only, they—they—told me you would."

"*They* told you I would. Whoever told you's *another* lunatic. I never heard the beat of it. Who's *they?*"

"Why—everybody. They all said so, m'am."

It was all she could do to hold in; and her eyes snapped, and her fingers worked like she wanted to scratch him; and she says:

"Who's 'everybody?' Out with their names—or ther'll be an idiot short."

He got up and looked distressed, and fumbled his hat, and says:

"I'm sorry, and I warn't expecting it. They told me to. They all told me to. They all said kiss her; and said she'll like it. They all said it—every one of them. But I'm sorry, m'am, and I won't do it no more—I won't, honest."

"You won't, won't you? Well, I sh'd *reckon* you won't!"

"No'm, I'm honest about it; I won't ever do it again. Till you ask me."

"Till I *ask* you! Well, I never see the beat of it in my born days! I lay you'll be the Methusalem-numskull of creation[2] before ever *I* ask you—or the likes of you."

"Well," he says, "it does surprise me so. I can't make it out, somehow. They

---

[2] The oldest numbskull in creation: Methuselah was the biblical patriarch said to have lived 969 years (see Genesis 5:27).

said you would, and I thought you would. But—" He stopped and looked around slow, like he wished he could run across a friendly eye, somewhere's; and fetched up on the old gentleman's, and says, "Didn't *you* think she'd like me to kiss her, sir?"

"Why, no, I—I—well, no, I b'lieve I didn't."

Then he looks on around, the same way, to me—and says:

"Tom, didn't *you* think Aunt Sally 'd open out her arms and say, 'Sid Sawyer—'"

"My land!" she says, breaking in and jumping for him, "you impudent young rascal, to fool a body so—" and was going to hug him, but he fended her off, and says:

"No, not till you've asked me, first."

So she didn't lose no time, but asked him; and hugged him and kissed him, over and over again, and then turned him over to the old man, and he took what was left. And after they got a little quiet again, she says:

"Why, dear me, I never see such a surprise. We warn't looking for *you,* at all, but only Tom. Sis never wrote to me about anybody coming but him."

"It's because it warn't *intended* for any of us to come but Tom," he says; "but I begged and begged, and at the last minute she let me come, too; so, coming down the river, me and Tom thought it would be a first-rate surprise for him to come here to the house first, and for me to by-and-by tag along and drop in and let on to be a stranger. But it was a mistake, Aunt Sally. This ain't no healthy place for a stranger to come."

"No—not impudent whelps, Sid. You ought to had your jaws boxed; I hain't been so put out since I don't know when. But I don't care, I don't mind the terms—I'd be willing to stand a thousand such jokes to have you here. Well, to think of that performance! I don't deny it, I was most putrified[3] with astonishment when you give me that smack."

We had dinner out in that broad open passage betwixt the house and the kitchen; and there was things enough on that table for seven families—and all hot, too; none of your flabby tough meat that's laid in a cupboard in a damp cellar all night and tastes like a hunk of old cold cannibal in the morning. Uncle Silas he asked a pretty long blessing over it, but it was worth it; and it didn't cool it a bit, neither, the way I've seen them kind of interruptions do, lots of times.

There was a considerable good deal of talk, all the afternoon, and me and Tom was on the lookout all the time, but it warn't no use, they didn't happen to say nothing about any runaway nigger, and we was afraid to try to work up to it. But at supper, at night, one of the little boys says:

"Pa, mayn't Tom and Sid and me go to the show?"

"No," says the old man, "I reckon there ain't going to be any; and you couldn't go if there was; because the runaway nigger told Burton and me all about that scandalous show, and Burton said he would tell the people; so I reckon they've drove the owdacious loafers out of town before this time."

So there it was!—but *I* couldn't help it. Tom and me was to sleep in the same room and bed; so, being tired, we bid good-night and went up to bed, right after supper, and clumb out of the window and down the lightning-rod, and shoved for the town; for I didn't believe anybody was going to give the king and the duke a hint, and so, if I didn't hurry up and give them one they'd get into trouble sure.

---

[3] Petrified.

On the road Tom he told me all about how it was reckoned I was murdered, and how pap disappeared, pretty soon, and didn't come back no more, and what a stir there was when Jim run away; and I told Tom all about our Royal Nonesuch rapscallions, and as much of the raft-voyage as I had time to; and as we struck into the town and up through the middle of it—it was as much as half-after eight, then—here comes a raging rush of people, with torches, and an awful whooping and yelling, and banging tin pans and blowing horns; and we jumped to one side to let them go by; and as they went by, I see they had the king and the duke astraddle of a rail—that is, I knowed it *was* the king and the duke, though they was all over tar and feathers, and didn't look like nothing in the world that was human—just looked like a couple of monstrous big soldier-plumes.[4] Well, it made me sick to see it; and I was sorry for them poor pitiful rascals, it seemed like I couldn't ever feel any hardness against them any more in the world. It was a dreadful thing to see. Human beings *can* be awful cruel to one another.

We see we was too late—couldn't do no good. We asked some stragglers about it, and they said everybody went to the show looking very innocent; and laid low and kept dark till the poor old king was in the middle of his cavortings on the stage; then somebody give a signal, and the house rose up and went for them.

So we poked along back home, and I warn't feeling so brash as I was before, but kind of ornery, and humble, and to blame, somehow—though *I* hadn't done nothing. But that's always the way; it don't make no difference whether you do right or wrong, a person's conscience ain't got no sense, and just goes for him *anyway*. If I had a yaller dog that didn't know no more than a person's conscience does, I would pison him. It takes up more room than all the rest of a person's insides, and yet ain't no good, nohow. Tom Sawyer he says the same.

Chapter XXXIV

We stopped talking, and got to thinking.

By-and-by Tom says:

"Looky here, Huck, what fools we are, to not think of it before! I bet I know where Jim is."

"No! Where?"

"In that hut down by the ash-hopper. Why, looky here. When we was at dinner, didn't you see a nigger man go in there with some vittles?"

"Yes."

"What did you think the vittles was for?"

"For a dog."

"So'd I. Well, it wasn't for a dog."

"Why?"

"Because part of it was watermelon."

"So it was—I noticed it. Well, it does beat all, that I never thought about a dog not eating watermelon. It shows how a body can see and don't see at the same time."

"Well, the nigger unlocked the padlock when he went in, and he locked it again when he come out. He fetched uncle a key, about the time we got up from table—same key, I bet. Watermelon shows man, lock shows prisoner; and it ain't likely

---

[4] Feathers adorning military hats.

there's two prisoners on such a little plantation, and where the people's all so kind and good. Jim's the prisoner. All right—I'm glad we found it out detective fashion; I wouldn't give shucks for any other way. Now you work your mind and study out a plan to steal Jim, and I will study out one, too; and we'll take the one we like the best."

What a head for just a boy to have! If I had Tom Sawyer's head, I wouldn't trade it off to be a duke, nor mate of a steamboat, nor clown in a circus, nor nothing I can think of. I went to thinking out a plan, but only just to be doing something. I knowed very well where the right plan was going to come from. Pretty soon, Tom says:

"Ready?"

"Yes," I says.

"All right—bring it out."

"My plan is this," I says, "We can easy find out if it's Jim in there. Then get up my canoe to-morrow night, and fetch my raft over from the island. Then the first dark night that comes, steal the key out of the old man's britches, after he goes to bed, and shove off down the river on the raft, with Jim, hiding daytimes and running nights, the way me and Jim used to do before. Wouldn't that plan work?"

"*Work?* Why cert'nly, it would work, like rats a fighting. But it's too blame' simple; there ain't nothing *to* it. What's the good of a plan that ain't no more trouble than that? It's as mild as goose-milk. Why, Huck, it wouldn't make no more talk than breaking into a soap factory."

I never said nothing, because I warn't expecting nothing different; but I knowed mighty well that whenever he got *his* plan ready it wouldn't have none of them objections to it.

And it didn't. He told me what it was, and I see in a minute it was worth fifteen of mine, for style, and would make Jim just as free a man as mine would, and maybe get us all killed besides. So I was satisfied, and said we would waltz in on it. I needn't tell what it was, here, because I knowed it wouldn't stay the way it was. I knowed he would be changing it around, every which way, as we went along, and heaving in new bullinesses wherever he got a chance. And that is what he done.

Well, one thing was dead sure; and that was, that Tom Sawyer was in earnest and was actly going to help steal that nigger out of slavery. That was the thing that was too many for me. Here was a boy that was respectable, and well brung up; and had a character to lose; and folks at home that had characters; and he was bright and not leather-headed; and knowing and not ignorant; and not mean, but kind; and yet here he was, without any more pride, or rightness, or feeling, than to stoop to this business, and make himself a shame, and his family a shame, before everybody. I *couldn't* understand it, no way at all. It was outrageous, and I knowed I ought to just up and tell him so; and so be his true friend, and let him quit the thing right where he was, and save himself. And I *did* start to tell him; but he shut me up, and says:

"Don't you reckon I know what I'm about? Don't I generly know what I'm about?"

"Yes."

"Didn't I *say* I was going to help steal the nigger?"

"Yes."

"*Well* then."

That's all he said, and that's all I said. It warn't no use to say any more; because when he said he'd do a thing, he always done it. But *I* couldn't make out how he was willing to go into this thing; so I just let it go, and never bothered no more about it. If he was bound to have it so, *I* couldn't help it.

When we got home, the house was all dark and still; so we went on down to the hut by the ash-hopper, for to examine it. We went through the yard, so as to see what the hounds would do. They knowed us, and didn't make no more noise than country dogs is always doing when anything comes by in the night. When we got to the cabin, we took a look at the front and the two sides; and on the side I warn't acquainted with—which was the north side—we found a square window-hole, up tolerable high, with just one stout board nailed across it. I says:

"Here's the ticket. This hole's big enough for Jim to get through, if we wrench off the board."

Tom says:

"It's as simple as tit-tat-toe, three-in-a-row, and as easy as playing hooky. I should *hope* we can find a way that's a little more complicated than *that*, Huck Finn."

"Well then," I says, "how'll it do to saw him out, the way I done before I was murdered, that time?"

"That's more *like*," he says. "It's real mysterious, and troublesome, and good," he says; "but I bet we can find a way that's twice as long. There ain't no hurry; le's keep on looking around."

Betwixt the hut and the fence, on the back side, was a lean-to, that joined the hut at the eaves, and was made out of plank. It was as long as the hut, but narrow—only about six foot wide. The door to it was at the south end, and was padlocked. Tom he went to the soap kettle, and searched around and fetched back the iron thing they lift the lid with; so he took it and prized out one of the staples. The chain fell down, and we opened the door and went in, and shut it, and struck a match, and see the shed was only built against the cabin and hadn't no connection with it; and there warn't no floor to the shed, nor nothing in it but some old rusty played-out hoes, and spades, and picks, and a crippled plow. The match went out, and so did we, and shoved in the staple again, and the door was locked as good as ever. Tom was joyful. He says:

"Now we're all right. We'll *dig* him out. It'll take about a week!"

Then we started for the house, and I went in the back door—you only have to pull a buckskin latch-string, they don't fasten the doors—but that warn't romantical enough for Tom Sawyer: no way would do him but he must climb up the lightning rod. But after he got up half-way about three times, and missed fire and fell every time, and the last time most busted his brains out, he thought he'd got to give it up; but after he was rested, he allowed he would give her one more turn for luck, and this time he made the trip.

In the morning we was up at break of day, and down to the nigger cabins to pet the dogs and make friends with the nigger that fed Jim—if it *was* Jim that was being fed. The niggers was just getting through breakfast and starting for the fields; and Jim's nigger was piling up a tin pan with bread and meat and things; and whilst the others was leaving, the key come from the house.

This nigger had a good-natured, chuckle-headed face, and his wool was all tied up in little bunches with thread. That was to keep witches off. He said the witches was pestering him awful, these nights, and making him see all kinds of strange things, and hear all kinds of strange words and noises, and he didn't believe he was ever witched so long, before, in his life. He got so worked up, and got to running on so about his troubles, he forgot all about what he'd been agoing to do. So Tom says:

"What's the vittles for? Going to feed the dogs?"

The nigger kind of smiled around gradualy over his face, like when you heave a brickbat[1] in a mud puddle, and he says:

"Yes, Mars Sid, *a* dog. Cur'us dog, too. Does you want to go en look at 'im?"

"Yes."

I hunched Tom, and whispers:

"You going, right here in the day-break? *That* warn't the plan."

"No, it warn't—but it's the plan *now*."

So, drat him, we went along, but I didn't like it much. When we got in, we couldn't hardly see anything, it was so dark; but Jim was there, sure enough, and could see us; and he sings out:

"Why, *Huck!* En good *lan'!* ain' dat Misto Tom?"

I just knowed how it would be; I just expected it. *I* didn't know nothing to do; and if I had, I couldn't a done it; because that nigger busted in and says:

"Why, de gracious sakes! do he know you genlmen?"

We could see pretty well, now. Tom he looked at the nigger, steady and kind of wondering, and says:

"Does *who* know us?"

"Why, dish-yer runaway nigger."

"I don't reckon he does; but what put that into your head?"

"What *put* it dar? Didn' he jis' dis minute sing out like he knowed you?"

Tom says, in a puzzled-up kind of way:

"Well, that's mighty curious. *Who* sung out? *When* did he sing out? *What* did he sing out?" And turns to me, perfectly ca'm, and says, "Did *you* hear anybody sing out?"

Of course there warn't nothing to be said but the one thing; so I says:

"No; *I* ain't heard nobody say nothing."

Then he turns to Jim, and looks him over like he never see him before; and says:

"Did you sing out?"

"No, sah," says Jim; "*I* hain't said nothing, sah."

"Not a word?"

"No, sah, I hain't said a word."

"Did you ever see us before?"

"No, sah; not as *I* knows on."

So Tom turns to the nigger, which was looking wild and distressed, and says, kind of severe:

"What do you reckon's the matter with you, anyway? What made you think somebody sung out?"

"Oh, it's de dad-blame' witches, sah, en I wisht I was dead, I do. Dey's awluz at it, sah, en dey do mos' kill me, dey sk'yers me so. Please to don't tell nobody 'bout it sah, er ole Mars Silas he'll scole me; 'kase he say dey *ain't* no witches. I jis' wish to goodness he was heah now—*den* what would he say! I jis' bet he

---

[1] A piece of brick that is thrown.

couldn' fine no way to git aroun' it *dis* time. But it's awluz jis' so; people dat's *sot,* stays sot; dey won't look into nothn' en fine it out f'r deyselves, en when *you* fine it out en tell um 'bout it, dey doan' b'lieve you."

Tom give him a dime, and said we wouldn't tell nobody; and told him to buy some more thread to tie up his wool with; and then looks at Jim, and says:

"I wonder if Uncle Silas is going to hang this nigger. If I was to catch a nigger that was ungrateful enough to run away, *I* wouldn't give him up, I'd hang him." And whilst the nigger stepped to the door to look at the dime and bite it to see if it was good, he whispers to Jim, and says:

"Don't ever let on to know us. And if you hear any digging going on nights, it's us: we're going to set you free."

Jim only had time to grab us by the hand and squeeze it, then the nigger come back, and we said we'd come again some time if the nigger wanted us to; and he said he would, more particular if it was dark, because the witches went for him mostly in the dark, and it was good to have folks around then.

CHAPTER XXXV

It would be most an hour, yet, till breakfast, so we left, and struck down into the woods; because Tom said we got to have *some* light to see how to dig by, and a lantern makes too much, and might get us into trouble; what we must have was a lot of them rotten chunks that's called fox-fire[1] and just makes a soft kind of a glow when you lay them in a dark place. We fetched an armful and hid it in the weeds, and set down to rest, and Tom says, kind of dissatisfied:

"Blame it, this whole thing is just as easy and awkard as it can be. And so it makes it so rotten difficult to get up a difficult plan. There ain't no watchman to be drugged—now there *ought* to be a watchman. There ain't even a dog to give a sleeping-mixture to. And there's Jim chained by one leg, with a ten-foot chain, to the leg of his bed: why, all you got to do is to lift up the bedstead and slip off the chain. And Uncle Silas he trusts everybody; sends the key to the punkin-headed nigger, and don't send nobody to watch the nigger. Jim could a got out of that window hole before this, only there wouldn't be no use trying to travel with a ten-foot chain on his leg. Why, drat it, Huck, it's the stupidest arrangement I ever see. You got to invent *all* the difficulties. Well, we can't help it, we got to do the best we can with the materials we've got. Anyhow, there's one thing—there's more honor in getting him out through a lot of difficulties and dangers, where there warn't one of them furnished to you by the people who it was their duty to furnish them, and you had to contrive them all out of your own head. Now look at just that one thing of the lantern. When you come down to the cold facts, we simply got to *let on* that a lantern's resky. Why, we could work with a torchlight procession if we wanted to, *I* believe. Now, whilst I think of it, we got to hunt up something to make a saw out of, the first chance we get."

"What do we want of a saw?"

"What do we *want* of it? Hain't we got to saw the leg of Jim's bed off, so as to get the chain loose?"

"Why, you just said a body could lift up the bedstead and slip the chain off."

---

[1] The phosphorescent glow of fungus on rotting wood.

"Well, if that ain't just like you, Huck Finn. You *can* get up the infant-schooliest ways of going at a thing. Why, hain't you ever read any books at all?— Baron Trenck, nor Casanova, nor Benvenuto Chelleeny, nor Henri IV.,[2] nor none of them heroes? Whoever heard of getting a prisoner loose in such an old-maidy way as that? No; the way all the best authorities does, is to saw the bed-leg in two, and leave it just so, and swallow the sawdust, so it can't be found, and put some dirt and grease around the sawed place so the very keenest seneskal[3] can't see no sign of it's being sawed, and thinks the bed-leg is perfectly sound. Then, the night you're ready, fetch the leg a kick, down she goes; slip off your chain, and there you are. Nothing to do but hitch your rope-ladder to the battlements, shin down it, break your leg in the moat—because a rope-ladder is nineteen foot too short, you know—and there's your horses and your trusty vassles, and they scoop you up and fling you across a saddle and away you go, to your native Langudoc, or Navarre,[4] or wherever it is. It's gaudy, Huck. I wish there was a moat to this cabin. If we get time, the night of the escape, we'll dig one."

I says:

"What do we want of a moat, when we're going to snake him out from under the cabin?"

But he never heard me. He had forgot me and everything else. He had his chin in his hand, thinking. Pretty soon, he sighs, and shakes his head; then sighs again, and says:

"No, it wouldn't do—there ain't necessity enough for it."

"For what?" I says.

"Why, to saw Jim's leg off," he says.

"Good land!" I says, "why, there ain't *no* necessity for it. And what would you want to saw his leg off for, anyway?"

"Well, some of the best authorities has done it. They couldn't get the chain off, so they just cut their hand off, and shoved. And a leg would be better still. But we got to let that go. There ain't necessity enough in this case; and besides, Jim's a nigger and wouldn't understand the reasons for it, and how it's the custom in Europe; so we'll let it go. But there's one thing—he can have a rope-ladder; we can tear up our sheets and make him a rope-ladder easy enough. And we can send it to him in a pie; it's mostly done that way. And I've et worse pies."

"Why, Tom Sawyer, how you talk," I says; "Jim ain't got no use for a rope-ladder."

"He *has* got use for it. How *you* talk, you better say; you don't know nothing about it. He's *got* to have a rope ladder; they all do."

"What in the nation can he *do* with it?"

"*Do* with it? He can hide it in his bed, can't he? That's what they all do; and *he's* got to, too. Huck, you don't ever seem to want to do anything that's regular; you want to be starting something fresh all the time. Spose he *don't* do nothing with it? ain't it there in his bed, for a clew, after he's gone? and don't you reckon they'll want clews? Of course they will. And you wouldn't leave them any? That would be a *pretty* howdy-do, *wouldn't* it! I never heard of such a thing."

---

[2] Baron Friedrich von Trenck (1726–1794), an Austrian soldier; the Italian lover Giovanni Giacomo Casanova (1725–1798); Benvenuto Cellini (1500–1571), an Italian artist; and Henry IV (1553–1610), king of France (1589–1610): all attempted daring escapes.

[3] Seneschal, a high-ranking official in important medieval households.

[4] Provinces in southern France and in the Pyrenees (between France and Spain), respectively.

"Well," I says, "if it's in the regulations, and he's got to have it, all right, let him have it; because I don't wish to go back on no regulations; but there's one thing, Tom Sawyer—if we go to tearing up our sheets to make Jim a rope-ladder, we're going to get into trouble with Aunt Sally, just as sure as you're born. Now, the way I look at it, a hickry-bark ladder don't cost nothing, and don't waste nothing, and is just as good to load up a pie with, and hide in a straw tick, as any rag ladder you can start; and as for Jim, he ain't had no experience, and so *he* don't care what kind of a——"

"Oh, shucks, Huck Finn, if I was as ignorant as you, I'd keep still—that's what *I'd* do. Who ever heard of a state prisoner escaping by a hickry-bark ladder? Why, it's perfectly ridiculous."

"Well, all right, Tom, fix it your own way; but if you'll take my advice, you'll let me borrow a sheet off of the clothes-line."

He said that would do. And that give him another idea, and he says:

"Borrow a shirt, too."

"What do we want of a shirt, Tom?"

"Want it for Jim to keep a journal on."

"Journal your granny—*Jim* can't write."

"Spose he *can't* write—he can make marks on the shirt, can't he, if we make him a pen out of an old pewter spoon or a piece of an old iron barrel-hoop?"

"Why, Tom, we can pull a feather out of a goose and make him a better one; and quicker, too."

"*Prisoners* don't have geese running around the donjon-keep to pull pens out of, you muggins. They *always* make their pens out of the hardest, toughest, troublesomest piece of old brass candlestick or something like that they can get their hands on; and it takes them weeks and weeks, and months and months to file it out, too, because they've got to do it by rubbing it on the wall. *They* wouldn't use a goose-quill if they had it. It ain't regular."

"Well, then, what'll we make him the ink out of?"

"Many makes it out of iron-rust and tears; but that's the common sort and women; the best authorities uses their own blood. Jim can do that; and when he wants to send any little common ordinary mysterious message to let the world know where he's captivated, he can write it on the bottom of a tin plate with a fork and throw it out of the window. The Iron Mask[5] always done that, and it's a blame' good way, too."

"Jim ain't got no tin plates. They feed him in a pan."

"That ain't anything; we can get him some."

"Can't nobody *read* his plates."

"That ain't got nothing to *do* with it, Huck Finn. All *he's* got to do is to write on the plate and throw it out. You don't *have* to be able to read it. Why, half the time you can't read anything a prisoner writes on a tin plate, or anywhere else."

"Well, then, what's the sense in wasting the plates?"

"Why, blame it all, it ain't the *prisoner's* plates."

"But it's *somebody's* plates, ain't it?"

"Well, spos'n it is? What does the *prisoner* care whose——"

---

[5] The protagonist in the romantic novel *Le Vicomte de Bragelonne* (1848–1850), or *"The Viscount of Bragelonne"* (French), by Alexandre Dumas (1802–1870); part of it was translated in the 1850s as *The Man in the Iron Mask*.

He broke off there, because we heard the breakfast-horn blowing. So we cleared out for the house.

Along during that morning I borrowed a sheet and a white shirt off of the clothes-line; and I found an old sack and put them in it, and we went down and got the fox-fire, and put that in too. I called it borrowing, because that was what pap always called it; but Tom said it warn't borrowing, it was stealing. He said we was representing prisoners; and prisoners don't care how they get a thing so they get it, and nobody don't blame them for it, either. It ain't no crime in a prisoner to steal the thing he needs to get away with, Tom said; it's his right; and so, as long as we was representing a prisoner, we had a perfect right to steal anything on this place we had the least use for, to get ourselves out of prison with. He said if we warn't prisoners it would be a very different thing, and nobody but a mean ornery person would steal when he warn't a prisoner. So we allowed we would steal everything there was that come handy. And yet he made a mighty fuss, one day, after that, when I stole a watermelon out of the nigger patch[6] and eat it; and he made me go and give the niggers a dime, without telling them what it was for. Tom said that what he meant was, we could steal anything we *needed*. Well, I says, I needed the watermelon. But he said I didn't need it to get out of prison with, there's where the difference was. He said if I'd a wanted it to hide a knife in, and smuggle it to Jim to kill the seneskal with, it would a been all right. So I let it go at that, though I couldn't see no advantage in my representing a prisoner, if I got to set down and chaw over a lot of gold-leaf[7] distinctions like that, every time I see a chance to hog a watermelon.

Well, as I was saying, we waited that morning till everybody was settled down to business, and nobody in sight around the yard; then Tom he carried the sack into the lean-to whilst I stood off a piece to keep watch. By-and-by he come out, and we went and set down on the wood-pile, to talk. He says:

"Everything's all right, now, except tools; and that's easy fixed."

"Tools?" I says.

"Yes."

"Tools for what?"

"Why, to dig with. We ain't agoing to *gnaw* him out, are we?"

"Ain't them old crippled picks and things in there good enough to dig a nigger out with?" I says.

He turns on me looking pitying enough to make a body cry, and says:

"Huck Finn, did you *ever* hear of a prisoner having picks and shovels, and all the modern conveniences in his wardrobe to dig himself out with? Now I want to ask you—if you got any reasonableness in you at all—what kind of a show would *that* give him to be a hero? Why, they might as well lend him the key, and done with it. Picks and shovels—why they wouldn't furnish 'em to a king."

"Well, then," I says, "if we don't want the picks and shovels, what do we want?"

"A couple of case-knives."[8]

"To dig the foundations out from under that cabin with?"

"Yes."

"Confound it, it's foolish, Tom."

"It don't make no difference how foolish it is, it's the *right* way—and it's the regular way. And there ain't no *other* way, that ever *I* heard of, and I've read all

---

[6] A slave's garden for growing fruits and vegetables.   [7] Flimsy, thin as gold leaf.
[8] Kitchen knives.

the books that gives any information about these things. They always dig out with a case-knife—and not through dirt, mind you; generly it's through solid rock. And it takes them weeks and weeks and weeks, and for ever and ever. Why, look at one of them prisoners in the bottom dungeon of the Castle Deef,[9] in the harbor of Marseilles, that dug himself out that way; how long was *he* at it, you reckon?"

"I don't know."

"Well, guess."

"I don't know. A month and a half?"

"*Thirty-seven year*—and he come out in China. *That's* the kind. I wish the bottom of *this* fortress was solid rock."

"*Jim* don't know nobody in China."

"What's *that* got to do with it? Neither did that other fellow. But you're always a-wandering off on a side issue. Why can't you stick to the main point?"

"All right—*I* don't care where he comes out, so he *comes* out; and Jim don't, either, I reckon. But there's one thing, anyway—Jim's too old to be dug out with a case-knife. He won't last."

"Yes he will *last,* too. You don't reckon it's going to take thirty-seven years to dig out through a *dirt* foundation, do you?"

"How long will it take, Tom?"

"Well, we can't resk being as long as we ought to, because it mayn't take very long for Uncle Silas to hear from down there by New Orleans. He'll hear Jim ain't from there. Then his next move will be to advertise Jim, or something like that. So we can't resk being as long digging him out as we ought to. By rights I reckon we ought to be a couple of years; but we can't. Things being so uncertain, what I recommend is this: that we really dig right in, as quick as we can; and after that, we can *let on,* to ourselves, that we was at it thirty-seven years. Then we can snatch him out and rush him away the first time there's an alarm. Yes, I reckon that'll be the best way."

"Now, there's *sense* in that," I says. "Letting on don't cost nothing; letting on ain't no trouble; and if it's any object, I don't mind letting on we was at it a hundred and fifty year. It wouldn't strain me none, after I got my hand in. So I'll mosey along now, and smouch a couple of case-knives."

"Smouch three," he says; "we want one to make a saw out of."

"Tom, if it ain't unregular and irreligious to sejest it," I says, "there's an old rusty saw-blade around yonder sticking under the weatherboarding behind the smoke-house."

He looked kind of weary and discouraged-like, and says:

"It ain't no use to try to learn you nothing, Huck. Run along and smouch the knives—three of them." So I done it.

CHAPTER XXXVI

As soon as we reckoned everybody was asleep, that night, we went down the lightning rod, and shut ourselves up in the lean-to, and got our pile of fox-fire, and went to work. We cleared everything out of the way, about four or five foot along the middle of the bottom log. Tom said he was right behind Jim's bed now, and we'd dig in under it, and when we got through there couldn't nobody in the

[9] The Chateau d'If, the prison in Dumas's *Count of Monte Cristo* (1845).

cabin ever know there was any hole there, because Jim's counterpin[1] hung down most to the ground, and you'd have to raise it up and look under to see the hole. So we dug and dug, with the case-knives, till most midnight; and then we was dog-tired, and our hands were blistered, and yet you couldn't see we'd done anything, hardly. At last I says:

"This ain't no thirty-seven year job, this is a thirty-eight year job, Tom Sawyer."

He never said nothing. But he sighed, and pretty soon he stopped digging, and then for a good little while I knowed he was thinking. Then he says:

"It ain't no use, Huck, it ain't agoing to work. If we was prisoners it would, because then we'd have as many years as we wanted, and no hurry; and we wouldn't get but a few minutes to dig, every day, while they was changing watches, and so our hands wouldn't get blistered, and we could keep it up right along, year in and year out, and do it right, and the way it ought to be done. But *we* can't fool along, we got to rush; we ain't got no time to spare. If we was to put in another night this way, we'd have to knock off for a week to let our hands get well—couldn't touch a case-knife with them sooner."

"Well, then, what we going to do, Tom?"

"I'll tell you. It ain't right, and it ain't moral, and I wouldn't like it to get out—but there ain't only just the one way; we got to dig him out with the picks, and *let on* it's case knives."

"*Now* you're *talking!*" I says: "your head gets leveler and leveler all the time, Tom Sawyer," I says. "Picks is the thing, moral or no moral; and as for me, I don't care shucks for the morality of it, nohow. When I start in to steal a nigger, or a watermelon, or a Sunday-school book, I ain't no ways particular how it's done so it's done. What I want is my nigger; or what I want is my watermelon; or what I want is my Sunday-school book; and if a pick's the handiest thing, that's the thing I'm agoing to dig that nigger or that watermelon or that Sunday-school book out with; and I don't give a dead rat what the authorities thinks about it nuther."

"Well," he says, "there's excuse for picks and letting-on in a case like this; if it warn't so, I wouldn't approve of it, nor I wouldn't stand by and see the rules broke—because right is right, and wrong is wrong, and a body ain't got no business doing wrong when he ain't ignorant and knows better. It might answer for *you* to dig Jim out with a pick, *without* any letting-on, because you don't know no better; but it wouldn't for me, because I do know better. Gimme a case-knife."

He had his own by him, but I handed him mine. He flung it down, and says:

"Gimme a *case-knife*."

I didn't know just what to do—but then I thought. I scratched around amongst the old tools, and got a pick-ax and give it to him, and he took it and went to work, and never said a word.

He was always just that particular. Full of principle.

So then I got a shovel, and then we picked and shoveled, turn about, and made the fur fly. We stuck to it about a half an hour, which was as long as we could stand up; but we had a good deal of a hole to show for it. When I got up stairs, I looked out of the window and see Tom doing his level best with the lightning-rod, but he couldn't come it, his hands was so sore. At last he says:

---

[1] Counterpane, bedspread.

"It ain't no use, it can't be done. What you reckon I better do? Can't you think up no way?"

"Yes," I says, "but I reckon it ain't regular. Come up the stairs, and let on it's a lightning rod."

So he done it.

Next day Tom stole a pewter spoon and a brass candlestick in the house, for to make some pens for Jim out of, and six tallow candles; and I hung around the nigger cabins, and laid for a chance, and stole three tin plates. Tom said it wasn't enough; but I said nobody wouldn't ever see the plates that Jim throwed out, because they'd fall in the dog-fennel and jimpson weeds under the window-hole—then we could tote them back and he could use them over again. So Tom was satisfied. Then he says:

"Now, the thing to study out is, how to get the things to Jim."

"Take them in through the hole," I says, "when we get it done."

He only just looked scornful, and said something about nobody ever heard of such an idiotic idea, and then he went to studying. By-and-by he said he had ciphered out two or three ways, but there warn't no need to decide on any of them yet. Said we'd got to post Jim first.

That night we went down the lightning-rod a little after ten, and took one of the candles along, and listened under the window-hole, and heard Jim snoring; so we pitched it in, and it didn't wake him. Then we whirled in with the pick and shovel, and in about two hours and a half the job was done. We crept in under Jim's bed and into the cabin, and pawed around and found the candle and lit it, and stood over Jim a while, and found him looking hearty and healthy, and then we woke him up gentle and gradual. He was so glad to see us he most cried; and called us honey, and all the pet names he could think of; and was for having us hunt up a cold chisel to cut the chain off of his leg with, right away, and clearing out without losing any time. But Tom he showed him how unregular it would be, and set down and told him all about our plans, and how we could alter them in a minute any time there was an alarm; and not to be the least afraid, because we would see he got away, *sure*. So Jim he said it was all right, and we set there and talked over old times a while, and then Tom asked a lot of questions, and when Jim told him Uncle Silas come in every day or two to pray with him, and Aunt Sally come in to see if he was comfortable and had plenty to eat, and both of them was kind as they could be, Tom says:

"*Now* I know how to fix it. We'll send you some things by them."

I said, "Don't do nothing of the kind; it's one of the most jackass ideas I ever struck;" but he never paid no attention to me; went right on. It was his way when he'd got his plans set.

So he told Jim how we'd have to smuggle in the rope-ladder pie, and other large things, by Nat, the nigger that fed him, and he must be on the lookout, and not be surprised, and not let Nat see him open them; and we would put small things in uncle's coat pockets and he must steal them out; and we would tie things to aunt's apron strings or put them in her apron pocket, if we got a chance; and told him what they would be and what they was for. And told him how to keep a journal on the shirt with his blood, and all that. He told him everything. Jim he couldn't see no sense in the most of it, but he allowed we was white folks and knowed better than him; so he was satisfied, and said he would do it all just as Tom said.

Jim had plenty corn-cob pipes and tobacco; so we had a right down good sociable time; then we crawled out through the hole, and so home to bed, with hands that looked like they'd been chawed. Tom was in high spirits. He said it was the best fun he ever had in his life, and the most intellectural; and said if he only could see his way to it we would keep it up all the rest of our lives and leave Jim to our children to get out; for he believed Jim would come to like it better and better the more he got used to it. He said that in that way it could be strung out to as much as eighty year, and would be the best time on record. And he said it would make us all celebrated that had a hand in it.

In the morning we went out to the wood-pile and chopped up the brass candle-stick into handy sizes, and Tom put them and the pewter spoon in his pocket. Then we went to the nigger cabins, and while I got Nat's notice off, Tom shoved a piece of candlestick into the middle of a corn-pone that was in Jim's pan, and we went along with Nat to see how it would work, and it just worked noble; when Jim bit into it it most mashed all his teeth out; and there warn't ever anything could a worked better. Tom said so himself. Jim he never let on but what it was only just a piece of rock or something like that that's always getting into bread, you know; but after that he never bit into nothing but what he jabbed his fork into it in three or four places, first.

And whilst we was a standing there in the dimmish light, here comes a couple of the hounds bulging in, from under Jim's bed; and they kept on piling in till there was eleven of them, and there warn't hardly room in there to get your breath. By jings, we forgot to fasten that lean-to door. The nigger Nat he only just hollered "witches!" once, and keeled over onto the floor amongst the dogs, and begun to groan like he was dying. Tom jerked the door open and flung out a slab of Jim's meat, and the dogs went for it, and in two seconds he was out himself and back again and shut the door, and I knowed he'd fixed the other door too. Then he went to work on the nigger, coaxing him and petting him, and asking him if he'd been imagining he saw something again. He raised up, and blinked his eyes around, and says:

"Mars Sid, you'll say I's a fool, but if I didn't b'lieve I see most a million dogs, er devils, er some'n, I wisht I may die right heah in dese tracks. I did, mos' sholy. Mars Sid, I *felt* um—I *felt* um, sah; dey was all over me. Dad fetch it, I jis' wisht I could git my han's on one er dem witches jis' wunst—on'y jis' wunst—it's all *I*'d ast. But mos'ly I wisht dey'd lemme 'lone, I does."

Tom says:

"Well, I tell you what *I* think. What makes them come here just at this runaway nigger's breakfast-time? It's because they're hungry; that's the reason. You make them a witch pie; that's the thing for *you* to do."

"But my lan', Mars Sid, how's *I* gwyne to make 'm a witch pie? I doan' know how to make it. I hain't ever hearn er sich a thing b'fo'."

"Well, then, I'll have to make it myself."

"Will you do it, honey?—will you? I'll wusshup de groun' und' yo' foot, I will!"

"All right, I'll do it, seeing it's you, and you've been good to us and showed us the runaway nigger. But you got to be mighty careful. When we come around, you turn your back; and then whatever we've put in the pan, don't you let on you see it at all. And don't you look, when Jim unloads the pan—something might happen, I don't know what. And above all, don't you *handle* the witch-things."

"*Hannel* 'm Mars Sid? What *is* you a talkin' 'bout? I wouldn' lay de weight er my finger on um, not f'r ten hund'd thous'n' billion dollars, I wouldn't."

CHAPTER **XXXVII**

That was all fixed. So then we went away and went to the rubbage-pile in the back yard where they keep the old boots, and rags, and pieces of bottles, and wore-out tin things, and all such truck, and scratched around and found an old tin washpan and stopped up the holes as well as we could, to bake the pie in, and took it down cellar and stole it full of flour, and started for breakfast and found a couple of shingle-nails that Tom said would be handy for a prisoner to scrabble his name and sorrows on the dungeon walls with, and dropped one of them in Aunt Sally's apron pocket which was hanging on a chair, and t'other we stuck in the band of Uncle Silas's hat, which was on the bureau, because we heard the children say their pa and ma was going to the runaway nigger's house this morning, and then went to breakfast, and Tom dropped the pewter spoon in Uncle Silas's coat pocket, and Aunt Sally wasn't come yet, so we had to wait a little while.

And when she come she was hot, and red, and cross, and couldn't hardly wait for the blessing; and then she went to sluicing out coffee with one hand and cracking the handiest child's head with her thimble with the other, and says:

"I've hunted high, and I've hunted low, and it does beat all, what *has* become of your other shirt."

My heart fell down amongst my lungs and livers and things, and a hard piece of corn-crust started down my throat after it and got met on the road with a cough and was shot across the table and took one of the children in the eye and curled him up like a fishing-worm, and let a cry out of him the size of a war-whoop, and Tom he turned kinder blue around the gills, and it all amounted to a considerable state of things for about a quarter of a minute or as much as that, and I would a sold out for half price if there was a bidder. But after that we was all right again— it was the sudden surprise of it that knocked us so kind of cold. Uncle Silas he says:

"It's most uncommon curious, I can't understand it. I know perfectly well I took it *off*, because—"

"Because you hain't got but one *on*. Just *listen* at the man! *I* know you took it off, and know it by a better way than your wool-gethering memory, too, because it was on the clo'es-line yesterday—I see it there myself. But it's gone—that's the long and the short of it, and you'll just have to change to a red flann'l one till I can get time to make a new one. And it'll be the third I've made in two years; it just keeps a body on the jump to keep you in shirts; and whatever you do manage to *do* with 'm all, is more'n *I* can make out. A body'd think you *would* learn to take some sort of care of 'em, at your time of life."

"I know it, Sally, and I do try all I can. But it oughtn't to be altogether my fault, because you know I don't see them nor have nothing to do with them except when they're on me; and I don't believe I've ever lost one of them *off* of me."

"Well, it ain't *your* fault if you haven't, Silas—you'd a done it if you could, I reckon. And the shirt ain't all that's gone, nuther. Ther's a spoon gone; and *that* ain't all. There was ten, and now ther's only nine. The calf got the shirt I reckon, but the calf never took the spoon, *that's* certain."

"Why, what else is gone, Sally?"

"Ther's six *candles* gone—that's what. The rats could a got the candles, and I reckon they did; I wonder they don't walk off with the whole place, the way you're always going to stop their holes and don't do it; and if they warn't fools they'd sleep in your hair, Silas—*you'd* never find it out; but you can't lay the *spoon* on the rats, and that I *know*."

"Well, Sally, I'm in fault, and I acknowledge it; I've been remiss; but I won't let to-morrow go by without stopping up them holes."

"Oh, I wouldn't hurry, next year'll do. Matilda Angelina Araminta *Phelps!*"

Whack comes the thimble, and the child snatches her claws out of the sugar-bowl without fooling around any. Just then, the nigger woman steps onto the passage, and says:

"Missus, dey's a sheet gone."

"A *sheet* gone! Well, for the land's sake!"

"I'll stop up them holes *to-day*," says Uncle Silas, looking sorrowful.

"Oh, *do* shet up!—spose the rats took the *sheet? Where's* it gone, Lize?"

"Clah to goodness I hain't no notion, Miss Sally. She wuz on de clo's-line yistiddy, but she done gone; she ain' dah no mo', now."

"I reckon the world *is* coming to an end. I *never* see the beat of it, in all my born days. A shirt, and a sheet, and a spoon, and six can————"

"Missus," comes a young yaller wench, "dey's a brass cannel-stick miss'n."

"Cler out from here, you hussy, er I'll take a skillet to ye!"

Well, she was just a biling. I begun to lay for a chance; I reckoned I would sneak out and go for the woods till the weather moderated. She kept a raging right along, running her insurrection all by herself, and everybody else mighty meek and quiet; and at last Uncle Silas, looking kind of foolish, fishes up that spoon out of his pocket. She stopped, with her mouth open and her hands up; and as for me, I wished I was in Jeruslem or somewheres. But not long; because she says:

"It's *just* as I expected. So you had it in your pocket all the time; and like as not you've got the other things there, too. How'd it get there?"

"I reely don't know, Sally," he says, kind of apologizing, "or you know I would tell. I was a-studying over my text in Acts Seventeen,[1] before breakfast, and I reckon I put it in there, not noticing, meaning to put my Testament in, and it must be so, because my Testament ain't in, but I'll go and see, and if the Testament is where I had it, I'll know I didn't put it in, and that will show that I laid the Testament down and took up the spoon, and————"

"Oh, for the land's sake! Give a body a rest! Go 'long now, the whole kit and biling of ye; and don't come nigh me again till I've got back my peace of mind."

I'd a heard her, if she'd a said it to herself, let alone speaking it out; and I'd a got up and obeyed her, if I'd a been dead. As we was passing through the setting-room, the old man he took up his hat, and the shingle-nail fell out on the floor, and he just merely picked it up and laid it on the mantel-shelf, and never said nothing, and went out. Tom see him do it, and remembered about the spoon, and says:

"Well, it ain't no use to send things by *him* no more, he ain't reliable." Then he says: "But he done us a good turn with the spoon, anyway, without knowing it, and so we'll go and do him one without *him* knowing it—stop up his rat-holes."

There was a noble good lot of them, down cellar, and it took us a whole hour, but we done the job tight and good, and ship-shape. Then we heard steps on the stairs, and blowed out our light, and hid; and here comes the old man, with a candle in one hand and a bundle of stuff in t'other, looking as absent-minded as

---

[1] Uncle Silas has been reading about the biblical Silas in the New Testament, Acts 17.

year before last. He went a mooning around, first to one rat-hole and then another, till he'd been to them all. Then he stood about five minutes, picking tallow-drip off of his candle and thinking. Then he turns off slow and dreamy towards the stairs, saying:

"Well, for the life of me I can't remember when I done it. I could show her now that I warn't to blame on account of the rats. But never mind—let it go. I reckon it wouldn't do no good."

And so he went on a mumbling up stairs, and then we left. He was a mighty nice old man. And always is.

Tom was a good deal bothered about what to do for a spoon, but he said we'd got to have it; so he took a think. When he had ciphered it out, he told me how we was to do; then we went and waited around the spoon-basket till we see Aunt Sally coming, and then Tom went to counting the spoons and laying them out to one side, and I slid one of them up my sleeve, and Tom says:

"Why, Aunt Sally, there ain't but nine spoons, *yet*."

She says:

"Go 'long to your play, and don't bother me. I know better, I counted 'm myself."

"Well, I've counted them twice, Aunty, and *I* can't make but nine."

She looked out of all patience, but of course she come to count—anybody would.

"I declare to gracious ther' *ain't* but nine!" she says. "Why, what in the world—plague *take* the things, I'll count 'm again."

So I slipped back the one I had, and when she got done counting, she says:

"Hang the troublesome rubbage, ther's *ten* now!" and she looked huffy and bothered both. But Tom says:

"Why, Aunty, *I* don't think there's ten."

"You numskull, didn't you see me *count* 'm?"

"I know, but———"

"Well, I'll count 'm *again*."

So I smouched one, and they come out nine same as the other time. Well, she *was* in a tearing way—just a trembling all over, she was so mad. But she counted and counted, till she got that addled she'd start to count-in the *basket* for a spoon, sometimes; and so, three times they come out right, and three times they come out wrong. Then she grabbed up the basket and slammed it across the house and knocked the cat galley-west;[2] and she said cle'r out and let her have some peace, and if we come bothering around her again betwixt that and dinner, she'd skin us. So we had the odd spoon; and dropped in in her apron pocket whilst she was giving us our sailing-orders, and Jim got it all right, along with her shingle-nail, before noon. We was very well satisfied with this business, and Tom allowed it was worth twice the trouble it took, because he said *now* she couldn't ever count them spoons twice alike again to save her life; and wouldn't believe she'd counted them right, if she *did;* and said that after she'd about counted her head off, for the next three days, he judged she'd give it up and offer to kill anybody that wanted her to ever count them any more.

So we put the sheet back on the line, that night, and stole one out of her closet; and kept on putting it back and stealing it again, for a couple of days, till she

---

[2] For a loop.

didn't know how many sheets she had, any more, and said she didn't *care,* and warn't agoing to bullyrag the rest of her soul out about it, and wouldn't count them again not to save her life, she druther die first.

So we was all right now, as to the shirt and the sheet and the spoon and the candles, by the help of the calf and the rats and the mixed-up counting; and as to the candlestick, it warn't no consequence, it would blow over by-and-by.

But that pie was a job; we had no end of trouble with that pie. We fixed it up away down in the woods, and cooked it there; and we got it done at last, and very satisfactory, too; but not all in one day; and we had to use up three washpans full of flour, before we got through, and we got burnt pretty much all over, in places, and eyes put out with the smoke; because, you see, we didn't want nothing but a crust, and we wouldn't prop it up right, and she would always cave in. But of course we thought of the right way at last; which was to cook the ladder, too, in the pie. So then we laid in with Jim, the second night, and tore up the sheet all in little strings, and twisted them together, and long before daylight we had a lovely rope, that you could a hung a person with. We let on it took nine months to make it.

And in the forenoon we took it down to the woods, but it wouldn't go in the pie. Being made of a whole sheet, that way, there was rope enough for forty pies, if we'd a wanted them, and plenty left over for soup, or sausage, or anything you choose. We could a had a whole dinner.

But we didn't need it. All we needed was just enough for the pie, and so we throwed the rest away. We didn't cook none of the pies in the washpan, afraid the solder would melt; but Uncle Silas he had a noble brass warming-pan[3] which he thought considerable of, because it belonged to one of his ancestors with a long wooden handle that come over from England with William the Conqueror in the *Mayflower*[4] or one of them early ships and was hid away up garret with a lot of other old pots and things that was valuable, not on account of being any account because they warn't, but on account of them being relicts, you know, and we snaked her out, private, and took her down there, but she failed on the first pies, because we didn't know how, but she come up smiling on the last one. We took and lined her with dough, and set her in the coals, and loaded her up with rag-rope, and put on a dough roof, and shut down the lid, and put hot embers on top, and stood off five foot, with the long handle, cool and comfortable, and in fifteen minutes she turned out a pie that was a satisfaction to look at. But the person that et it would want to fetch a couple of kags of toothpicks along, for if that rope-ladder wouldn't cramp him down to business, I don't know nothing what I'm talking about, and lay him in enough stomach-ache to last him till next time, too.

Nat didn't look, when we put the witch-pie in Jim's pan; and we put the three tin plates in the bottom of the pan under the vittles; and so Jim got everything all right, as soon as he was by himself he busted into the pie and hid the rope-ladder inside of his straw tick, and scratched some marks on a tin plate and throwed it out of the window-hole.

---

[3] A long-handled, lidded pan filled with hot coals and put under the covers to warm a bed. Huck's word order adds to the humor of the sentence: suddenly we are told of an ancestor "with a long wooden handle."

[4] Another instance of Huck's uncertain hold on history: William the Conqueror lived from 1027 to 1087, whereas the *Mayflower* brought the Pilgrims to America in 1620.

CHAPTER XXXVIII

Making them pens was a distressid-tough job, and so was the saw; and Jim allowed the inscription was going to be the toughest of all. That's the one which the prisoner has to scrabble on the wall. But we had to have it; Tom said we'd *got* to; there warn't no case of a state prisoner not scrabbling his inscription to leave behind, and his coat of arms.

"Look at Lady Jane Grey," he says; "look at Gilford Dudley; look at old Northumberland![1] Why, Huck, spose it *is* considerble trouble?—what you going to do?—how you going to get around it? Jim's *got* to do his inscription and coat of arms. They all do."

Jim says:

"Why, Mars Tom, I hain't got no coat o' arms; I hain't got nuffn but dish-yer ole shirt, en you knows I got to keep de journal on dat."

"Oh, you don't understand, Jim; a coat of arms is very different."

"Well," I says, "Jim's right, anyway, when he says he hain't got no coat of arms, because he hain't."

"I reckon *I* knowed that," Tom says, "but you bet he'll have one before he goes out of this—because he's going out *right,* and there ain't going to be no flaws in his record."

So whilst me and Jim filed away at the pens on a brickbat apiece, Jim a making his'n out of the brass and I making mine out of the spoon, Tom set to work to think out the coat of arms. By-and-by he said he'd struck so many good ones he didn't hardly know which to take, but there was one which he reckoned he'd decide on. He says:

"On the scutcheon[2] we'll have a bend *or* in the dexter base, a saltire *murrey* in the fess, with a dog, couchant, for common charge, and under his foot a chain embattled, for slavery, with a chevron *vert* in a chief engrailed, and three invected lines on a field *azure,* with the nombril points rampant on a dancette indented; crest, a runaway nigger, *sable,* with his bundle over his shoulder on a bar sinister: and a couple of gules for supporters, which is you and me; motto, *Maggiore fretta, minore atto.* Got it out of a book—means, the more haste, the less speed."[3]

"Geewhillikins," I says, "but what does the rest of it mean?"

"We ain't got no time to bother over that," he says, "we got to dig in like all git-out."

"Well, anyway," I says, "what's *some* of it? What's a fess?"

"A fess—a fess is—*you* don't need to know what a fess is. I'll show him how to make it when he gets to it."

"Shucks, Tom," I says, "I think you might tell a person. What's a bar sinister?"

"Oh, *I* don't know. But he's got to have it. All the nobility does."

---

[1] John Dudley (1502?–1553), the duke of Northumberland, made his daughter-in-law, Lady Jane Grey (1537–1554), queen of England in 1553; after a fierce political rebellion, Northumberland, Grey (a grandneice of Henry VIII), and her husband, Lord Guildford Dudley (?–1554), were imprisoned nine days later and executed. A romantic version of this grim story is related in W. H. Ainsworth's *The Tower of London* (1840).

[2] A shield with a coat-of-arms. Tom throws in an assortment of heraldic terms (with Twain's satire at feudal pretension lurking underneath) to describe how the shield should look.

[3] The Italian phrase actually means "the more fretting, the less action."

That was just his way. If it didn't suit him to explain a thing to you, he wouldn't do it. You might pump at him a week, it wouldn't make no difference.

He'd got all that coat of arms business fixed, so now he started in to finish up the rest of that part of the work, which was to plan out a mournful inscription—said Jim got to have one, like they all done. He made up a lot, and wrote them out on a paper, and read them off, so:

   1. *Here a captive heart busted.*
   2. *Here a poor prisoner, forsook by the world and friends, fretted out his sorrowful life.*
   3. *Here a lonely heart broke, and a worn spirit went to its rest, after thirty-seven years of solitary captivity.*
   4. *Here, homeless and friendless, after thirty-seven years of bitter captivity, perished a noble stranger, natural son of Louis XIV.*

Tom's voice trembled, whilst he was reading them, and he most broke down. When he got done, he couldn't no way make up his mind which one for Jim to scrabble onto the wall, they was all so good; but at last he allowed he would let him scrabble them all on. Jim said it would take him a year to scrabble such a lot of truck onto the logs with a nail, and he didn't know how to make letters, besides; but Tom said he would block them out for him, and then he wouldn't have nothing to do but just follow the lines. Then pretty soon he says:

"Come to think, the logs ain't agoing to do; they don't have log walls in a dungeon: we got to dig the inscriptions into a rock. We'll fetch a rock."

Jim said the rock was worse than the logs; he said it would take him such a pison long time to dig them into a rock, he wouldn't ever get out. But Tom said he would let me help him do it. Then he took a look to see how me and Jim was getting along with the pens. It was most pesky tedious hard work and slow, and didn't give my hands no show to get well of the sores, and we didn't seem to make no headway, hardly. So Tom says:

"I know how to fix it. We got to have a rock for the coat of arms and mournful inscriptions, and we can kill two birds with that same rock. There's a gaudy big grindstone down at the mill, and we'll smouch it, and carve the things on it, and file out the pens and the saw on it, too."

It warn't no slouch of an idea; and it warn't no slouch of a grindstone nuther; but we allowed we'd tackle it. It warn't quite midnight, yet, so we cleared out for the mill, leaving Jim at work. We smouched the grindstone, and set out to roll her home, but it was a most nation tough job. Sometimes, do what we could, we coudn't keep her from falling over, and she come mighty near mashing us, every time. Tom said she was going to get one of us, sure, before we got through. We got her half way; and then we was plumb played out, and most drownded with sweat. We see it warn't no use, we got to go and fetch Jim. So he raised up his bed and slid the chain off of the bed-leg, and wrapt it round and round his neck, and we crawled out through our hole and down there, and Jim and me laid into that grindstone and walked her along like nothing; and Tom superintended. He could out-superintend any boy I ever see. He knowed how to do everything.

Our hole was pretty big, but it warn't big enough to get the grindstone through; but Jim he took the pick and soon made it big enough. Then Tom marked out them things on it with the nail, and set Jim to work on them, with the nail for a chisel and an iron bolt from the rubbage in the lean-to for a hammer, and told him to work till the rest of his candle quit on him, and then he could go to bed, and hide the grindstone under his straw tick and sleep on it. Then we helped him fix his chain back on the bed-leg, and was ready for bed ourselves. But Tom thought of something, and says:

"You got any spiders in here, Jim?"

"No, sah, thanks to goodness I hain't, Mars Tom."

"All right, we'll get you some."

"But bless you, honey, I doan' *want* none. I's afeared un um. I jis' 's soon have rattlesnakes aroun'."

Tom thought a minute or two, and says:

"It's a good idea. And I reckon it's been done. It *must* a been done; it stands to reason. Yes, it's a prime good idea. Where could you keep it?"

"Keep what, Mars Tom?"

"Why, a rattlesnake."

"De goodness gracious alive, Mars Tom! Why, if dey was a rattlesnake to come in heah, I'd take en bust right out thoo dat log wall, I would, wid my head."

"Why, Jim, you wouldn't be afraid of it, after a little. You could tame it."

"*Tame* it!"

"Yes—easy enough. Every animal is grateful for kindness and petting, and they wouldn't *think* of hurting a person that pets them. Any book will tell you that. You try—that's all I ask; just try for two or three days. Why, you can get him so, in a little while, that he'll love you; and sleep with you; and won't stay away from you a minute; and will let you wrap him round your neck and put his head in your mouth."

"*Please*, Mars Tom—*doan'* talk so! I can't *stan'* it! He'd *let* me shove his head in my mouf—fer a favor, hain't it? I lay he'd wait a pow'ful long time 'fo' I *ast* him. En mo' en dat, I doan' *want* him to sleep wid me."

"Jim, don't act so foolish. A prisoner's *got* to have some kind of a dumb pet, and if a rattlesnake hain't ever been tried, why, there's more glory to be gained in your being the first to ever try it than any other way you could ever think of to save your life."

"Why, Mars Tom, I doan' *want* not sich glory. Snake take 'n bite Jim's chin off, den *whah* is de glory? No, sah, I doan' want no sich doin's."

"Blame it, can't you *try?* I only *want* you to try—you needn't keep it up if it don't work."

"But de trouble all *done*, ef de snake bite me while I's a tryin' him. Mars Tom, I's willin' to tackle mos' anything 'at ain't onreasonable, but ef you en Huck fetches a rattlesnake in heah for me to tame, I's gwyne to *leave*, dat's *shore*."

"Well then, let it go, let it go, if you're so bullheaded about it. We can get you some garter-snakes and you can tie some buttons on their tails, and let on they're rattlesnakes, and I reckon that'll have to do."

"I k'n stan' *dem*, Mars Tom, but blame' 'f I couldn't get along widout um, I tell you dat. I never knowed b'fo', 't was so much bother and trouble to be a prisoner."

"Well, it *always* is, when it's done right. You got any rats around here?"

"No, sah, I hain't seed none."

"Well, we'll get you some rats."

"Why, Mars Tom, I doan' *want* no rats. Dey's de dad-blamedest creturs to

sturb a body, en rustle roun' over 'im, en bite his feet, when he's tryin' to sleep, I
ever see. No, sah, gimme g'yarter-snakes, 'f I's got to have 'm, but doan' gimme
no rats, I ain' got no use f'r um, skasely."

"But Jim, you *got* to have 'em—they all do. So don't make no more fuss about
it. Prisoners ain't ever without rats. There ain't no instance of it. And they train
them, and pet them, and learn them tricks, and they get to be as sociable as flies.
But you got to play music to them. You got anything to play music on?"

"I ain' got nuffn but a coase comb en a piece o' paper, en a juice-harp; but I
reck'n dey wouldn't take no stock in a juice-harp."

"Yes they would. *They* don't care what kind of music 'tis. A jews-harp's plenty
good enough for a rat. All animals likes music—in a prison they dote on it. Specially, painful music; and you can't get no other kind out of a jews-harp. It always
interests them; they come out to see what's the matter with you. Yes, you're all
right; you're fixed very well. You want to set on your bed, nights, before you go
to sleep, and early in the mornings, and play your jews-harp; play The Last Link
is Broken—that's the thing that'll scoop a rat, quicker'n anything else: and when
you've played about two minutes, you'll see all the rats, and the snakes, and
spiders, and things begin to feel worried about you, and come. And they'll just
fairly swarm over you, and have a noble good time."

"Yes, *dey* will, I reck'n, Mars Tom, but what kine er time is *Jim* havin'? Blest
if I kin see de pint. But I'll do it ef I got to. I reck'n I better keep de animals
satisfied, en not have no trouble in de house."

Tom waited to think over, and see if there wasn't nothing else; and pretty soon
he says:

"Oh—there's one thing I forgot. Could you raise a flower here, do you
reckon?"

"I doan' know but maybe I could, Mars Tom; but it's tolable dark in heah, en I
ain' got no use f'r no flower, nohow, en she'd be a pow'ful sight o' trouble."

"Well, you try it, anyway. Some other prisoners has done it."

"One er dem big cat-tail-lookin' mullen-stalks would grow in heah, Mars Tom,
I reck'n, but she wouldn't be wuth half de trouble she'd coss."

"Don't you believe it. We'll fetch you a little one, and you plant it in the corner, over there, and raise it. And don't call it mullen, call it Pitchiola[4]—that's its
right name, when it's in a prison. And you want to water it with your tears."

"Why, I got plenty spring water, Mars Tom."

"You don't *want* spring water; you want to water it with your tears. It's the way
they always do."

"Why, Mars Tom, I lay I kin raise one er dem mullen-stalks twyste wid spring
water whiles another man's a *start'n* one wid tears."

"That ain't the idea. You *got* to do it with tears."

"She'll die on my han's, Mars Tom, she sholy will; kase I doan' skasely ever
cry."

So Tom was stumped. But he studied it over, and then said Jim would have to
worry along the best he could with an onion. He promised he would go to the
nigger cabins and drop one, private, in Jim's coffee-pot, in the morning. Jim said
he would "jis' 's soon have tobacker in his coffee;" and found so much fault with
it, and with the work and bother of raising the mullen, and jews-harping the rats,

---

[4] In *Picciola* (1836), a romantic tale by Joseph Xavier Boniface (1798–1865), a plant nourishes a
prisoner's wish to live.

and petting and flattering up the snakes and spiders and things, on top of all the other work he had to do on pens, and inscriptions, and journals, and things, which made it more trouble and worry and responsibility to be a prisoner than anything he ever undertook, that Tom most lost all patience with him; and said he was just loadened down with more gaudier chances than a prisoner ever had in the world to make a name for himself, and yet he didn't know enough to appreciate them, and they was just about wasted on him. So Jim he was sorry, and said he wouldn't behave so no more, and then me and Tom shoved for bed.

CHAPTER XXXIX

In the morning we went up to the village and bought a wire rat trap and fetched it down, and unstopped the best rat hole, and in about an hour we had fifteen of the bulliest kind of ones; and then we took it and put it in a safe place under Aunt Sally's bed. But while we was gone for spiders, little Thomas Franklin Benjamin Jefferson Elexander Phelps found it there, and opened the door of it to see if the rats would come out, and they did; and Aunt Sally she come in, and when we got back she was a standing on top of the bed raising Cain, and the rats was doing what they could to keep off the dull times for her. So she took and dusted us both with the hickry, and we was as much as two hours catching another fifteen or sixteen, drat that meddlesome cub, and they warn't the likeliest, nuther, because the first haul was the pick of the flock. I never see a likelier lot of rats than what that first haul was.

We got a splendid stock of sorted spiders, and bugs, and frogs, and caterpillars, and one thing or another; and we like-to got a hornet's nest, but we didn't. The family was at home. We didn't give it right up, but staid with them as long as we could; because we allowed we'd tire them out or they'd got to tire us out, and they done it. Then we got allycumpain[1] and rubbed on the places, and was pretty near all right again, but couldn't set down convenient. And so we went for the snakes, and grabbed a couple of dozen garters and house-snakes, and put them in a bag, and put it in our room, and by that time it was supper time, and a rattling good honest day's work; and hungry?—oh, no, I reckon not! And there warn't a blessed snake up there, when we went back—we didn't half tie the sack, and they worked out, somehow, and left. But it didn't matter much, because they was still on the premises somewheres. So we judged we could get some of them again. No, there warn't no real scarcity of snakes about the house for a considerble spell. You'd see them dripping from the rafters and places, every now and then; and they generly landed in your plate, or down the back of your neck, and most of the time where you didn't want them. Well, they was handsome, and striped, and there warn't no harm in a million of them; but that never made no difference to Aunt Sally, she despised snakes, be the breed what they might, and she couldn't stand them no way you could fix it; and every time one of them flopped down on her, it didn't make no difference what she was doing, she would just lay that work down and light out. I never see such a woman. And you could hear her whoop to Jericho. You couldn't get her to take aholt of one of them with the tongs. And if she turned over and found one in bed, she would scramble out and lift a howl that you would think the house was afire. She disturbed the old man, so that he said he

---

[1] Elecampane, an herb to relieve pain: the boys got stung by the hornets.

could most wish there hadn't ever been no snakes created. Why, after every last snake had been gone clear out of the house for as much as a week, Aunt Sally warn't over it yet; she warn't near over it; when she was setting thinking about something, you could touch her on the back of her neck with a feather and she would jump right out of her stockings. It was very curious. But Tom said all women was just so. He said they was made that way; for some reason or other.

We got a licking every time one of our snakes come in her way; and she allowed these lickings warn't nothing to what she would do if we ever loaded up the place again with them. I didn't mind the lickings, because they didn't amount to nothing; but I minded the trouble we had, to lay in another lot. But we got them laid in, and all the other things; and you never see a cabin as blithesome as Jim's was when they'd all swarm out for music and go for him. Jim didn't like the spiders, and the spiders didn't like Jim; and so they'd lay for him and make it mighty warm for him. And he said that between the rats, and the snakes, and the grindstone, there warn't no room in bed for him, skasely; and when there was, a body couldn't sleep, it was so lively, and it was always lively, he said, because *they* never all slept at one time, but took turn about, so when the snakes was asleep the rats was on deck, and when the rats turned in the snakes come on watch, so he always had one gang under him, in his way, and t'other gang having a circus over him, and if he got up to hunt a new place, the spiders would take a chance at him as he crossed over. He said if he ever got out, this time, he wouldn't ever be a prisoner again, not for a salary.

Well, by the end of three weeks, everything was in pretty good shape. The shirt was sent in early, in a pie, and every time a rat bit Jim he would get up and write a little in his journal whilst the ink was fresh; the pens was made, the inscriptions and so on was all carved on the grindstone; the bed-leg was sawed in two, and we had et up the sawdust, and it give us a most amazing stomach-ache. We reckoned we was all going to die, but didn't. It was the most undigestible sawdust I ever see; and Tom said the same. But as I was saying, we'd got all the work done, now, at last; and we was all pretty much fagged out, too, but mainly Jim. The old man had wrote a couple of times to the plantation below Orleans to come and get their runaway nigger, but hadn't got no answer, because there warn't no such plantation; so he allowed he would advertise Jim in the St. Louis and New Orleans papers; and when he mentioned the St. Louis ones, it give me the cold shivers, and I see we hadn't no time to lose. So Tom said, now for the nonnamous letters.

"What's them?" I says.

"Warnings to the people that something is up. Sometimes it's done one way, sometimes another. But there's always somebody spying around, that gives notice to the governor of the castle. When Louis XVI. was going to light out of the Tooleries,[2] a servant girl done it. It's a very good way, and so is the nonnamous letters. We'll use them both. And it's usual for the prisoner's mother to change clothes with him, and she stays in, and he slides out in her clothes. We'll do that too."

"But looky here, Tom, what do we want to *warn* anybody for, that something's up? Let them find it out for themselves—it's their lookout."

---

[2] The Tuileries, the Parisian residence of King Louis XVI of France. In *The French Revolution* (1837) the Scottish historian and essayist Thomas Carlyle (1795–1881) mentions the episode of a chambermaid reporting the king's plan to escape; the king was subsequently beheaded.

"Yes, I know; but you can't depend on them. It's the way they've acted from the very start—left us to do *everything*. They're so confiding and mullet-headed[3] they don't take notice of nothing at all. So if we don't *give* them notice, there won't be nobody nor nothing to interfere with us, and so after all our hard work and trouble this escape 'll go off perfectly flat: won't amount to nothing—won't be nothing *to* it."

"Well, as for me, Tom, that's the way I'd like."

"Shucks," he says, and looked disgusted. So I says:

"But I ain't going to make no complaint. Anyway that suits you suits me. What you going to do about the servant-girl?"

"You'll be her. You slide in, in the middle of the night, and hook that yaller girl's frock."

"Why, Tom, that'll make trouble next morning; because of course she prob'bly hain't got any but that one."

"I know; but you don't want it but fifteen minutes, to carry the nonnamous letter and shove it under the front door."

"All right, then, I'll do it; but I could carry it just as handy in my own togs."

"You wouldn't look like a servant-girl *then*, would you?"

"No, but there won't be nobody to see what I look like, *anyway*."

"That ain't got nothing to do with it. The thing for us to do, is just to do our *duty*, and not worry about whether anybody *sees* us do it or not. Hain't you got no principle at all?"

"All right, I ain't saying nothing; I'm the servant-girl. Who's Jim's mother?"

"I'm his mother. I'll hook a gown from Aunt Sally."

"Well, then, you'll have to stay in the cabin when me and Jim leaves."

"Not much. I'll stuff Jim's clothes full of straw and lay it on his bed to represent his mother in disguise, and Jim 'll take the nigger woman's gown[4] off of me and wear it, and we'll all evade together. When a prisoner of style escapes, it's called an evasion. It's always called so when a king escapes, f'rinstance. And the same with a king's son; it don't make no difference whether he's a natural one or an unnatural one."

So Tom he wrote the nonnamous letter, and I smouched the yaller wench's frock, that night, and put it on, and shoved it under the front door, the way Tom told me to. It said:

Beware. Trouble is brewing. Keep a sharp lookout.
UNKNOWN FRIEND.

Next night we stuck a picture which Tom drawed in blood, of a skull and crossbones, on the front door; and next night another one of a coffin, on the back door. I never see a family in such a sweat. They couldn't a been worse scared if the place had a been full of ghosts laying for them behind everything and under the beds and shivering through the air. If a door banged, Aunt Sally she jumped, and said "ouch!" if anything fell, she jumped and said "ouch!" if you happened to touch her, when she warn't noticing, she done the same; she couldn't face noway and be satisfied, because she allowed there was something behind her every

---

[3] Absent-minded.   [4] Some editors have changed this to "Aunt Sally's gown."

time—so she was always a whirling around, sudden, and saying "ouch," and before she'd get two-thirds around, she'd whirl back again, and say it again; and she was afraid to go to bed, but she dasn't set up. So the thing was working very well, Tom said; he said he never see a thing work more satisfactory. He said it showed it was done right.

So he said, now for the grand bulge! So the very next morning at the streak of dawn we got another letter ready, and was wondering what we better do with it, because we heard them say at supper they was going to have a nigger on watch at both doors all night. Tom he went down the lightning-rod to spy around; and the nigger at the back door was asleep, and he stuck it in the back of his neck and come back. This letter said:

> Don't betray me, I wish to be your friend. There is a desprate gang of cutthroats from over in the Ingean Territory⁵ going to steal your runaway nigger to-night, and they have been trying to scare you so as you will stay in the house and not bother them. I am one of the gang, but have got relliggion and wish to quit it and lead a honest life again, and will betray the helish design. They will sneak down from northards, along the fence, at midnight exact, with a false key, and go in the nigger's cabin to get him. I am to be off a piece and blow a tin horn if I see any danger; but stead of that, I will BA like a sheep soon as they get in and not blow at all; then whilst they are getting his chains loose, you slip there and lock them in, and can kill them at your leasure. Don't do anything but just the way I am telling you, if you do they will suspicion something and raise whoopjamboreehoo. I do not wish any reward but to know I have done the right thing.
>
> UNKNOWN FRIEND.

Chapter XL

We was feeling pretty good, after breakfast, and took my canoe and went over the river a fishing, with a lunch, and had a good time, and took a look at the raft and found her all right, and got home late to supper, and found them in such a sweat and worry they didn't know which end they was standing on, and made us go right off to bed the minute we was done supper, and wouldn't tell us what the trouble was, and never let on a word about the new letter, but didn't need to, because we knowed as much about it as anybody did, and as soon as we was half up stairs and her back was turned, we slid for the cellar cubboard and loaded up a good lunch and took it up to our room and went to bed, and got up about half-past eleven, and Tom put on Aunt Sally's dress that he stole and was going to start with the lunch, but says:

"Where's the butter?"

"I laid out a hunk of it," I says, "on a piece of a corn-pone."

"Well, you *left* it laid out, then—it ain't here."

"We can get along without it," I says.

"We can get along *with* it too," he says; "just you slide down cellar and fetch it. And then mosey right down the lightning-rod and come along. I'll go and stuff the

---

⁵ Indian Territory: what is now Oklahoma was considered "Indian Territory" in 1834; it became a refuge for outlaws throughout the nineteenth century.

straw into Jim's clothes to represent his mother in disguise, and be ready to *ba* like a sheep and shove soon as you get there."

So out he went, and down cellar went I. The hunk of butter, big as a person's fist, was where I had left it, so I took up the slab of corn-pone with it on, and blowed out my light, and started up stairs, very stealthy, and got up to the main floor all right, but here comes Aunt Sally with a candle, and I clapped the truck in my hat, and clapped my hat on my head, and the next second she see me; and she says:

"You been down cellar?"

"Yes'm."

"What you been doing down there?"

"Noth'n."

"*Noth'n!*"

"No'm."

"Well, then, what possessed you to go down there, this time of night?"

"I don't know'm."

"You don't *know*? Don't answer me that way, Tom, I want to know what you been *doing* down there?"

"I hain't been doing a single thing, Aunt Sally, I hope to gracious if I have."

I reckoned she'd let me go, now, and as a generl thing she would; but I spose there was so many strange things going on she was just in a sweat about every little thing that warn't yard-stick straight; so she says, very decided:

"You just march into that setting-room and stay there till I come. You been up to something you no business to, and I lay I'll find out what it is before *I'm* done with you."

So she went away as I opened the door and walked into the setting-room. My, but there was a crowd there! Fifteen farmers, and every one of them had a gun. I was most powerful sick, and slunk to a chair and set down. They was setting around, some of them talking a little, in a low voice, and all of them fidgety and uneasy, but trying to look like they warn't; but I knowed they was, because they was always taking off their hats, and putting them on, and scratching their heads, and changing their seats, and fumbling with their buttons. I warn't easy myself, but I didn't take my hat off, all the same.

I did wish Aunt Sally would come, and get done with me, and lick me, if she wanted to, and let me get away and tell Tom how we'd overdone this thing, and what a thundering hornet's nest we'd got ourselves into, so we could stop fooling around, straight off, and clear out with Jim before these rips got out of patience and come for us.

At last she come, and begun to ask me questions, but I *couldn't* answer them straight, I didn't know which end of me was up; because these men was in such a fidget now, that some was wanting to start right *now* and lay for them despera-does, and saying it warn't but a few minutes to midnight; and others was trying to get them to hold on and wait for the sheep-signal; and here was aunty pegging away at the questions, and me a shaking all over and ready to sink down in my tracks I was that scared; and the place getting hotter and hotter, and the butter beginning to melt and run down my neck and behind my ears: and pretty soon, when one of them says, "*I'm* for going and getting in the cabin *first*, and right *now,* and catching them when they come," I most dropped; and a streak of butter come a trickling down my forehead, and Aunt Sally she see it, and turns white as a sheet, and says:

"For the land's sake what *is* the matter with the child!—he's got the brain fever as shore as you're born, and they're oozing out!"

And everybody runs to see, and she snatches off my hat, and out comes the bread and what was left of the butter, and she grabbed me, and hugged me, and says:

"Oh, what a turn you did give me! and how glad and grateful I am it ain't no worse; for luck's against us, and it never rains but it pours, and when I see that truck I thought we'd lost you, for I knowed by the color and all, it was just like your brains would be if—Dear, dear, whyd'nt you *tell* me that was what you'd been down there for, *I* wouldn't a cared. Now cler out to bed, and don't lemme see no more of you till morning!"

I was up stairs in a second, and down the lightning-rod in another one, and shinning through the dark for the lean-to. I couldn't hardly get my words out, I was so anxious; but I told Tom as quick as I could, we must jump for it, now, and not a minute to lose—the house full of men, yonder, with guns!

His eyes just blazed; and he says:

"No!—is that so? *Ain't* it bully! Why, Huck, if it was to do over again, I bet I could fetch two hundred! If we could put it off till——"

"Hurry! *hurry!*" I says. "Where's Jim?"

"Right at your elbow; if you reach out your arm you can touch him. He's dressed, and everything's ready. Now we'll slide out and give the sheep-signal."

But then we heard the tramp of men, coming to the door, and heard them begin to fumble with the padlock; and heard a man say:

"I *told* you we'd be too soon; they haven't come—the door is locked. Here' I'll lock some of you into the cabin and you lay for 'em in the dark and kill 'em when they come; and the rest scatter around a piece, and listen if you can hear 'em coming."

So in they come, but couldn't see us in the dark, and most trod on us whilst we was hustling to get under the bed. But we got under all right, and out through the hole, swift but soft—Jim first, me next, and Tom last, which was according to Tom's orders. Now we was in the lean-to, and heard trampings close by outside. So we crept to the door, and Tom stopped us there and put his eye to the crack, but couldn't make out nothing, it was so dark; and whispered and said he would listen for the steps to get further, and when he nudged us Jim must glide out first, and him last. So he set his ear to the crack and listened, and listened, and listened, and the steps a scraping around, out there, all the time; and at last he nudged us, and we slid out, and stooped down, not breathing, and not making the least noise, and slipped stealthy towards the fence, in Injun file,[1] and got to it, all right, and me and Jim over it; but Tom's britches catched fast on a splinter on the top rail, and then he hear the steps coming, so he had to pull loose, which snapped the splinter and made a noise; and as he dropped in our tracks and started, somebody sings out:

"Who's that? Answer, or I'll shoot!"

But we didn't answer; we just unfurled our heels and shoved. Then there was a rush, and a *bang, bang, bang!* and the bullets fairly whizzed around us! We heard them sing out:

"Here they are! They've broke for the river! after 'em, boys! And turn loose the dogs!"

---

[1] Single file.

So here they come, full tilt. We could hear them, because they wore boots, and yelled, but we didn't wear no boots, and didn't yell. We was in the path to the mill; and when they got pretty close onto us, we dodged into the bush and let them go by, and then dropped in behind them. They'd had all the dogs shut up, so they wouldn't scare off the robbers; but by this time somebody had let them loose, and here they come, making pow-wow enough for a million; but they was our dogs; so we stopped in our tracks till they catched up; and when they see it warn't nobody but us, and no excitement to offer them, they only just said howdy, and tore right ahead towards the shouting and clattering; and then we up steam again and whizzed along after them till we was nearly to the mill, and then struck up through the bush to where my canoe was tied, and hopped in and pulled for dear life towards the middle of the river, but didn't make no more noise than we was obleeged to. Then we struck out, easy and comfortable, for the island where my raft was; and we could hear them yelling and barking at each other all up and down the bank, till we was so far away the sounds got dim and died out. And when we stepped onto the raft, I says:

"*Now,* old Jim, you're a free man *again,* and I bet you won't ever be a slave no more."

"En a mighty good job it wuz, too, Huck. It 'uz planned beautiful, en it 'uz *done* beautiful; en dey ain't *nobody* kin git up a plan dat's mo' mixed-up en splendid den what dat one wuz."

We was all as glad as we could be, but Tom was the gladdest of all, because he had a bullet in the calf of his leg.

When me and Jim heard that, we didn't feel so brash as what we did before. It was hurting him considerble, and bleeding; so we laid him in the wigwam and tore up one of the duke's shirts for to bandage him, but he says:

"Gimme the rags, I can do it myself. Don't stop, now; don't fool around here, and the evasion booming along so handsome; man the sweeps, and set her loose! Boys, we done it elegant!—'deed we did. I wish *we'd* a had the handling of Louis XVI., there wouldn't a been no 'Son of Saint Louis, ascend to heaven!'[2] wrote down in *his* biography: no, sir, we'd a whooped him over the *border*—that's what we'd a done with *him*—and done it just as slick as nothing at all, too. Man the sweeps—man the sweeps!"

But me and Jim was consulting—and thinking. And after we'd thought a minute, I says:

"Say it, Jim."

So he says:

"Well, den, dis is de way it look to me, Huck. Ef it wuz *him* dat 'uz bein' sot free, en one er de boys wuz to git shot, would he say, 'Go on en save me, nemmine 'bout a doctor f'r to save dis one?' Is dat like Mars Tom Sawyer? Would he say dat? You *bet* he wouldn't! *Well,* den, is *Jim* gwyne to say it? No, sah—I doan' budge a step out'n dis place, 'dout a *doctor;* not if it's forty year!"

I knowed he was white inside, and I reckoned he'd say what he did say—so it was all right, now, and I told Tom I was agoing for a doctor. He raised considerble row about it, but me and Jim stuck to it and wouldn't budge; so he was for crawling out and setting the raft loose himself; but we wouldn't let him. Then he give us a piece of his mind—but it didn't do no good.

So when he see me getting the canoe ready, he says:

---

[2] From Carlyle's account of the king's execution in *The French Revolution.*

"Well, then, if you're bound to go, I'll tell you the way to do, when you get to the village. Shut the door, and blindfold the doctor tight and fast, and make him swear to be silent as the grave, and put a purse full of gold in his hand, and then take and lead him all around the back alleys and everywheres, in the dark, and then fetch him here in the canoe, in a roundabout way amongst the islands, and search him and take his chalk away from him, and don't give it back to him till you get him back to the village, or else he will chalk this raft so he can find it again. It's the way they all do."

So I said I would, and left, and Jim was to hide in the woods when he see the doctor coming, till he was gone again.

Chapter XLI

The doctor was an old man; a very nice, kind-looking old man, when I got him up. I told him me and my brother was over on Spanish Island hunting, yesterday afternoon, and camped on a piece of a raft we found, and about midnight he must a kicked his gun in his dreams, for it went off and shot him in the leg, and we wanted him to go over there and fix it and not say nothing about it, nor let anybody know, because we wanted to come home this evening, and surprise the folks.

"Who is your folks?" he says.

"The Phelpses, down yonder."

"Oh," he says. And after a minute, he says: "How'd you say he got shot?"

"He had a dream," I says, "and it shot him."

"Singular dream," he says.

So he lit up his lantern, and got his saddle-bags, and we started. But when he see the canoe, he didn't like the look of her—said she was big enough for one, but didn't look pretty safe for two. I says:

"Oh, you needn't be afeard, sir, she carried the three of us, easy enough."

"What three?"

"Why, me and Sid, and—and—and *the guns;* that's what I mean."

"Oh," he says.

But he put his foot on the gunnel, and rocked her; and shook his head, and said he reckoned he'd look around for a bigger one. But they was all locked and chained; so he took my canoe, and said for me to wait till he come back, or I could hunt around further, or maybe I better go down home and get them ready for the surprise, if I wanted to. But I said I didn't; so I told him just how to find the raft, and then he started.

I struck an idea, pretty soon. I says to myself, spos'n he can't fix that leg just in three shakes of a sheep's tail, as the saying is? spos'n it takes him three or four days? What are we going to do?—lay around there till he lets the cat out of the bag? No, sir, I know what *I'll* do. I'll wait, and when he comes back, if he says he's got to go any more, I'll get down there, too, if I swim; and we'll take and tie him, and keep him, and shove out down the river; and when Tom's done with him, we'll give him what it's worth, or all we got, and then let him get shore.

So then I crept into a lumber pile to get some sleep; and next time I waked up the sun was away up over my head! I shot out and went for the doctor's house, but they told me he'd gone away in the night, some time or other, and warn't back yet. Well, thinks I, that looks powerful bad for Tom, and I'll dig out for the island, right off. So away I shoved, and turned the corner, and nearly rammed my head into Uncle Silas's stomach! He says:

"Why, *Tom!* Where you been, all this time, you rascal?"

"*I* hain't been nowheres," I says, "only just hunting for the runaway nigger— me and Sid."

"Why, where ever did you go?" he says. "Your aunt's been mighty uneasy."

"She needn't," I says, "because we was all right. We followed the men and the dogs, but they out-run us, and we lost them; but we thought we heard them on the water, so we got a canoe and took out after them, and crossed over but couldn't find nothing of them; so we cruised along up-shore till we got kind of tired and beat out; and tied up the canoe and went to sleep, and never waked up till about an hour ago, then we paddled over here to hear the news, and Sid's at the post-office to see what he can hear, and I'm a branching out to get something to eat for us, and then we're going home."

So then we went to the post-office to get "Sid"; but just as I suspicioned, he warn't there; so the old man he got a letter out of the office, and we waited a while longer but Sid didn't come; so the old man said come along, let Sid foot it home, or canoe-it, when he got done fooling around—but we would ride. I couldn't get him to let me stay and wait for Sid; and he said there warn't no use in it, and I must come along, and let Aunt Sally see we was all right.

When we got home, Aunt Sally was that glad to see me she laughed and cried both, and hugged me, and give me one of them lickings of hern that don't amount to shucks, and said she'd serve Sid the same when he come.

And the place was plumb full of farmers and farmers' wives, to dinner; and such another clack a body never heard. Old Mrs. Hotchkiss was the worst; her tongue was agoing all the time. She says:

"Well, Sister Phelps, I've ransacked that-air cabin over an' I b'lieve the nigger was crazy. I says so to Sister Damrell—didn't I, Sister Damrell?—s'I, he's crazy, s'I—them's the very words I said. You all hearn me: he's crazy, s'I; everything shows it, s'I. Look at that-air grindstone, s'I; want to tell *me*'t any cretur 'ts in his right mind 's agoin' to scrabble all them crazy things onto a grindstone, s'I? Here sich 'n' sich a person busted his heart; 'n' here so 'n' so pegged along for thirty-seven year, 'n' all that—nacherl son o' Louis somebody, 'n' sich everlast'n rub-bage. He's plumb crazy, s'I; it's what I says in the fust place, it's what I says in the middle, 'n' it's what I says last 'n' all the time—the nigger's crazy—crazy 's Nebokoodneezer,[1] s'I."

"An' look at that-air ladder made out'n rags, Sister Hotchkiss," says old Mrs. Damrell, "what in the name o' goodness *could* he ever want of——"

"The very words I was a-sayin' no longer ago th'n this minute to Sister Utter-back, 'n' she'll tell you so herself. Sh-she, look at that-air rag ladder, sh-she; 'n' s'I, yes, *look* at it, s'I—what *could* he a wanted of it, s'I. Sh-she, Sister Hotchkiss, sh-she ——"

"But how in the nation'd they ever *git* that grindstone *in* there, *any*-way? 'n' who dug that-air *hole?* 'n' who ——"

"My very *words*, Brer Penrod! I was a-sayin'—pass that-air sasser o' m'lasses, won't ye?—I was a-sayin' to Sister Dunlap, jist this minute, how *did* they git that

---

[1] Nebuchadnezzar II (?–562 B.C.), king of Babylon (605–562 B.C.) who, according to Daniel 4:29–37, went mad and ate grass.

grindstone in there, s'I. Without *help,* mind you—'thout *help! Thar's* wher' 'tis. Don't tell *me,* s'I; there *wuz* help, s'I; 'n' ther' wuz a *plenty* help, too, s'I; ther's ben a *dozen* a helpin' that nigger, 'n I lay I'd skin every last nigger on this place, but *I'd* find out who done it, s'I; 'n' moreover, s'I ——"

"A *dozen* says you!—*forty* couldn't a done everything that's been done. Look at them case-knife saws and things, how tedious they've been made; look at the bed-leg sawed off with 'm, a week's work for six men; look at that nigger made out'n straw on the bed; and look at ——"

"You may *well* say it, Brer Hightower! It's jist as I was a-sayin' to Brer Phelps, his own self. S'e, what do *you* think of it, Sister Hotchkiss, s'e? think o' what, Brer Phelps, s'I? think o' that bed-leg sawed off that a way, s'e? *think* of it, s'I? I lay it never sawed *itself* off, s'I—somebody *sawed* it, s'I; that's my opinion, take it or leave it, it mayn't be no 'count, s'I, but sich as 't is, it's my opinion, s'I, 'n' if anybody k'n start a better one, s'I, let him *do* it, s'I, that's all. I says to Sister Dunlap, s'I ——"

"Why, dog my cats, they must a ben a house-full o' niggers in there every night for four weeks, to a done all that work, Sister Phelps. Look at that shirt—every last inch of it kivered over with secret African writ'n done with blood! Must a ben a raft uv 'm at it right along, all the time, amost. Why, I'd give two dollars to have it read to me; 'n' as for the niggers that wrote it, I 'low I'd take 'n' lash 'm t'll ——"

"People to *help* him, Brother Marples! Well, I reckon you'd *think* so, if you'd a been in this house for a while back. Why, they've stole everything they could lay their hands on—and we a watching, all the time, mind you. They stole that shirt right off o' the line! and as for that sheet they made the rag ladder out of ther' ain't no telling how many times they *didn't* steal that; and flour, and candles, and candlesticks, and spoons, and the old warming-pan, and most a thousand things that I disremember, now, and my new calico dress; and me, and Silas, and my Sid and Tom on the constant watch day *and* night, as I was a telling you, and not a one of us could catch hide nor hair, nor sight nor sound of them; and here at the last minute, lo and behold you, they slides right in under our noses, and fools us, and not only fools *us* but the Injun Territory robbers too, and actuly gets *away* with that nigger, safe and sound, and that with sixteen men and twenty-two dogs right on their very heels at that very time! I tell you, it just bangs anything I ever *heard* of. Why, *sperits* couldn't a done better, and been no smarter. And I reckon they must a *been* sperits—because, *you* know our dogs, and ther' ain't no better; well, them dogs never even got on the *track* of 'm, once! You explain *that* to me, if you can!—*any* of you!"

"Well, it does beat ——"

"Laws alive, I never ——"

"So help me, I wouldn't a be ——"

"*House*-thieves as well as ——"

"Goodnessgracioussakes, I'd a ben afeard to *live* in sich a ——"

"'Fraid to *live!*—why, I was that scared I dasn't hardly go to bed, or get up, or lay down, or *set* down, Sister Ridgeway. Why, they'd steal the very—why, goodness sakes, you can guess what kind of a fluster *I* was in by the time midnight come, last night. I hope to gracious if I warn't afraid they'd steal some o' the family! I was just to that pass, I didn't have no reasoning faculties no more. It looks foolish enough, *now,* in the day-time; but I says to myself, there's my two poor boys asleep, 'way up stairs in that lonesome room, and I declare to goodness I was that uneasy 't I crep' up there and locked 'em in! I *did*. And anybody would. Because, you know, when you get scared, that way, and it keeps running on, and getting worse and worse, all the time, and your wits gets to addling, and you get to doing all sorts o' wild things, and by-and-by you think to yourself, spos'n I was a boy, and was away up there, and the door ain't locked, and you—" She stopped, looking kind of wondering, and then she turned her head around slow, and when her eye lit on me—I got up and took a walk.

Says I to myself, I can explain better how we come to not be in that room this morning, if I go out to one side and study over it a little. So I done it. But I dasn't go fur, or she'd a sent for me. And when it was late in the day, the people all went, and then I come in and told her the noise and shooting waked up me and "Sid," and the door was locked, and we wanted to see the fun, so we went down the lightning-rod, and both of us got hurt a little, and we didn't never want to try *that* no more. And then I went on and told her all what I told Uncle Silas before: and then she said she'd forgive us, and maybe it was all right enough anyway, and about what a body might expect of boys, for all boys was a pretty harum-scarum lot, as fur as she could see; and so, as long as no harm hadn't come of it, she judged she better put in her time being grateful we was alive and well and she had us still, stead of fretting over what was past and done. So then she kissed me, and patted me on the head, and dropped into a kind of a brown study; and pretty soon jumps up, and says:

"Why, lawsamercy, it's most night, and Sid not come yet! What *has* become of that boy?"

I see my chance; so I skips up and says:

"I'll run right up to town and get him," I says.

"No you won't," she says. "You'll stay right wher' you are; one's enough to be lost at a time. If he ain't here to supper, your uncle 'll go."

Well, he warn't there to supper; so right after supper uncle went.

He come back about ten, a little bit uneasy; hadn't run across Tom's track. Aunt Sally was a good *deal* uneasy; but Uncle Silas he said there warn't no occasion to be—boys will be boys, he said, and you'll see this one turn up in the morning, all sound and right. So she had to be satisfied. But she said she'd set up for him a while, anyway, and keep a light burning, so he could see it.

And then when I went up to bed she come up with me and fetched her candle, and tucked me in, and mothered me so good I felt mean, and like I couldn't look her in the face; and she set down on the bed and talked with me a long time, and said what a splendid boy Sid was, and didn't seem to want to ever stop talking about him; and kept asking me every now and then, if I reckoned he could a got lost, or hurt, or maybe drownded, and might be laying at this minute, somewheres, suffering or dead, and she not by him to help him, and so the tears would drip down, silent, and I would tell her that Sid was all right, and would be home in the morning, sure; and she would squeeze my hand, or maybe kiss me, and tell me to say it again, and keep on saying it, because it done her good, and she was in so much trouble. And when she was going away, she looked down in my eyes, so steady and gentle, and says:

"The door ain't going to be locked, Tom; and there's the window and the rod; but you'll be good, *won't* you? And you won't go? For *my* sake?"

Laws knows I *wanted* to go, bad enough, to see about Tom, and was all intending to go; but after that, I wouldn't a went, not for kingdoms.

But she was on my mind, and Tom was on my mind; so I slept very restless. And twice I went down the rod, away in the night, and slipped around front, and see her setting there by her candle in the window with her eyes towards the road and the tears in them; and I wished I could do something for her, but I couldn't, only to swear that I wouldn't never do nothing to grieve her any more. And the third time, I waked up at dawn, and slid down, and she was there yet, and her candle was most out, and her old gray head was resting on her hand, and she was asleep.

Chapter XLII

The old man was up town again, before breakfast, but couldn't get no track of Tom; and both of them set at the table, thinking, and not saying nothing, and looking mournful, and their coffee getting cold, and not eating anything. And by-and-by the old man says:

"Did I give you the letter?"

"What letter?"

"The one I got yesterday out of the post-office."

"No, you didn't give me no letter."

"Well, I must a forgot it."

So he rummaged his pockets, and then went off somewheres where he had laid it down, and fetched it, and give it to her. She says:

"Why, it's from St. Petersburg—it's from Sis."

I allowed another walk would do me good; but I couldn't stir. But before she could break it open, she dropped it and run—for she see something. And so did I. It was Tom Sawyer on a mattress; and that old doctor; and Jim, in *her* calico dress, with his hands tied behind him; and a lot of people. I hid the letter behind the first thing that come handy, and rushed. She flung herself at Tom, crying, and says:

"Oh, he's dead, he's dead, I know he's dead!"

And Tom he turned his head a little, and muttered something or other, which showed he warn't in his right mind; then she flung up her hands, and says:

"He's alive, thank God! And that's enough!" and she snatched a kiss of him, and flew for the house to get the bed ready, and scattering orders right and left at the niggers and everybody else, as fast as her tongue could go, every jump of the way.

I followed the men to see what they was going to do with Jim; and the old doctor and Uncle Silas followed after Tom into the house. The men was very huffy, and some of them wanted to hang Jim, for an example to all the other niggers around there, so they wouldn't be trying to run away, like Jim done, and making such a raft of trouble, and keeping a whole family scared most to death for days and nights. But the others said, don't do it, it wouldn't answer at all, he ain't our nigger, and his owner would turn up and make us pay for him, sure. So that cooled them down a little, because the people that's always the most anxious for to hang a nigger that hain't done just right, is always the very ones that ain't the most anxious to pay for him when they've got their satisfaction out of him.

They cussed Jim considerble, though, and give him a cuff or two, side the head, once in a while, but Jim never said nothing, and he never let on to know me, and they took him to the same cabin, and put his own clothes on him, and chained him again, and not to no bed-leg, this time, but to a big staple drove into the bottom log, and chained his hands, too, and both legs, and said he warn't to have nothing but bread and water to eat, after this, till his owner come or he was sold at auction, because he didn't come in a certain length of time, and filled up our hole, and said a couple of farmers with guns must stand watch around about the cabin every night, and a bull-dog tied to the door in the day-time; and about this time they was through with the job and was tapering off with a kind of generl good-bye cussing, and then the old doctor comes and takes a look, and says:

"Don't be no rougher on him than you're obleeged to, because he ain't a bad nigger. When I got to where I found the boy, I see I couldn't cut the bullet out without some help, and he warn't in no condition for me to leave, to go and get help; and he got a little worse and a little worse, and after a long time he went out of his head, and wouldn't let me come enigh him, any more, and said if I chalked his raft he'd kill me, and no end of wild foolishness like that, and I see I couldn't do anything at all with him; so I says, I got to have *help,* somehow; and the minute I says it, out crawls this nigger from somewheres, and says he'll help, and he done it, too, and done it very well. Of course I judged he must be a runaway nigger, and there I *was!* and there I had to stick, right straight along all the rest of the day, and all night. It was a fix, I tell you! I had a couple of patients with the chills, and of course I'd of liked to run up to town and see them, but I dasn't, because the nigger might get away, and then I'd be to blame; and yet never a skiff come close enough for me to hail. So there I had to stick, plumb till daylight this morning; and I never see a nigger that was a better nuss or faithfuller, and yet he was resking his freedom to do it, and was all tired out, too, and I see plain enough he'd been worked main hard, lately. I liked the nigger for that; I tell you, gentlemen, a nigger like that is worth a thousand dollars—and kind treatment, too. I had everything I needed, and the boy was doing as well there as he would a done at home—better, maybe, because it was so quiet; but there I *was,* with both of 'm on my hands; and there I had to stick, till about dawn this morning; then some men in a skiff come by, and as good luck would have it, the nigger was setting by the pallet with his head propped on his knees, sound asleep; so I motioned them in, quiet, and they slipped up on him and grabbed him and tied him before he knowed what he was about, and we never had no trouble. And the boy being in a kind of a flighty sleep, too, we muffled the oars and hitched the raft on, and towed her over very nice and quiet, and the nigger never made the least row nor said a word, from the start. He ain't no bad nigger, gentlemen; that's what I think about him."

Somebody says:

"Well, it sounds very good, doctor, I'm obleeged to say."

Then the others softened up a little, too, and I was mighty thankful to that old doctor for doing Jim that good turn; and I was glad it was according to my judgment of him, too; because I thought he had a good heart in him and was a good man, the first time I see him. Then they all agreed that Jim had acted very well, and was deserving to have some notice took of it, and reward. So every one of them promised, right out and hearty, that they wouldn't cuss him no more.

Then they come out and locked him up. I hoped they was going to say he could have one or two of the chains took off, because they was rotten heavy, or could have meat and greens with his bread and water, but they didn't think of it, and I reckoned it warn't best for me to mix in, but I judged I'd get the doctor's yarn to Aunt Sally, somehow or other, as soon as I'd got through the breakers that was laying just ahead of me. Explanations, I mean, of how I forgot to mention about Sid being shot, when I was telling how him and me put in that dratted night paddling around hunting the runaway nigger.

But I had plenty time. Aunt Sally she stuck to the sick-room all day and all night; and every time I see Uncle Silas mooning around, I dodged him.

Next morning I heard Tom was a good deal better, and they said Aunt Sally was gone to get a nap. So I slips to the sick-room, and if I found him awake I reckoned we could put up a yarn for the family that would wash. But he was sleeping, and sleeping very peaceful, too; and pale, not fire-faced the way he was when he come. So I set down and laid for him to wake. In about a half an hour, Aunt Sally comes gliding in, and there I was, up a stump again! She motioned me to be still, and set down by me, and begun to whisper, and said we could all be joyful now, because all the symptoms was first rate, and he'd been sleeping like that for ever so long, and looking better and peacefuller all the time, and ten to one he'd wake up in his right mind.

So we set there watching, and by-and-by he stirs a bit, and opened his eyes very natural, and takes a look, and says:

"Hello, why I'm at *home!* How's that? Where's the raft?"

"It's all right," I says.

"And *Jim?*"

"The same," I says, but couldn't say it pretty brash. But he never noticed, but says:

"Good! Splendid! *Now* we're all right and safe! Did you tell Aunty?"

I was going to say yes; but she chipped in and says:

"About what, Sid?"

"Why, about the way the whole thing was done."

"What whole thing?"

"Why, *the* whole thing. There ain't but one; how we set the runaway nigger free—me and Tom."

"Good land! Set the run—What *is* the child talking about! Dear, dear, out of his head again!"

"*No,* I ain't out of my HEAD; I know all what I'm talking about. We *did* set him free—me and Tom. We laid out to do it, and we *done* it. And we done it elegant, too." He'd got a start, and she never checked him up, just set and stared and stared, and let him clip along, and I see it warn't no use for *me* to put in. "Why, Aunty, it cost us a power of work—weeks of it—hours and hours, every night whilst you was all asleep. And we had to steal candles, and the sheet, and the shirt, and your dress, and spoons, and tin plates, and case-knives, and the warming-pan, and the grindstone, and flour, and just no end of things, and you can't think what work it was to make the saws, and pens, and inscriptions, and one thing or another, and you can't think *half* the fun it was. And we had to make up the pictures of coffins and things, and nonnamous letters from the robbers, and get up and down the lightning-rod, and dig the hole into the cabin, and make the rope-ladder and send it in cooked up in a pie, and send in spoons and things to work with, in your apron pocket"———

"Mercy sakes!"

———"and load up the cabin with rats and snakes and so on, for company for Jim; and then you kept Tom here so long with the butter in his hat that you come near spiling the whole business, because the men come before we was out of the cabin, and we had to rush, and they heard us and let drive at us, and I got my share, and we dodged out of the path and let them go by, and when the dogs come they warn't interested in us, but went for the most noise, and we got our canoe, and made for the raft, and was all safe, and Jim was a free man, and we done it all by ourselves, and *wasn't* it bully, Aunty!"

"Well, I never heard the likes of it in all my born days! So it was *you,* you little rapscallions, that's been making all this trouble, and turned everybody's wits clean inside out and scared us all most to death. I've as good a notion as ever I had in my life, to take it out o' you this very minute. To think, here I've been, night after night, a—*you* just get well once, you young scamp, and I lay I'll tan the Old Harry[1] out o' both o' ye!"

But Tom, he *was* so proud and joyful, he just *couldn't* hold in, and his tongue just *went* it—she a-chipping in, and spitting fire all along, and both of them going it at once, like a cat-convention; and she says:

"*Well,* you get all the enjoyment you can out of it *now,* for mind I tell you if I catch you meddling with him again ———"

"Meddling with *who?*" Tom says, dropping his smile and looking surprised.

"With *who?* Why, the runaway nigger, of course, Who'd you reckon?"

Tom looks at me very grave, and says:

"Tom, didn't you just tell me he was all right? Hasn't he got away?"

"*Him?*" says Aunt Sally; "the runaway nigger? 'Deed he hasn't. They've got him back, safe and sound, and he's in that cabin again, on bread and water, and loaded down with chains, till he's claimed or sold!"

Tom rose square up in bed, with his eye hot, and his nostrils opening and shutting like gills, and sings out to me:

"They hain't no *right* to shut him up! *Shove!*—and don't you lose a minute, Turn him loose! he ain't no slave; he's as free as any cretur that walks this earth!"

"What *does* the child mean?"

"I mean every word I *say,* Aunt Sally, and if somebody don't go, *I'll* go. I've knowed him all his life, and so has Tom, there. Old Miss Watson died two months ago, and she was ashamed she ever was going to sell him down the river, and *said* so; and she set him free in her will."

"Then what on earth did *you* want to set him free for, seeing he was already free?"

"Well, that *is* a question, I must say; and *just* like women! Why, I wanted the *adventure* of it; and I'd a waded neck-deep in blood to—goodness alive, AUNT POLLY!"

If she warn't standing right there, just inside the door, looking as sweet and contented as an angel half-full of pie, I wish I may never!

Aunt Sally jumped for her, and most hugged the head off of her, and cried over her, and I found a good enough place for me under the bed, for it was getting pretty sultry for *us,* seemed to me. And I peeped out, and in a little while Tom's

---

[1] The Devil.

Aunt Polly shook herself loose and stood there looking across at Tom over her spectacles—kind of grinding him into the earth, you know. And then she says:

"Yes, you *better* turn y'r head away—I would if I was you, Tom."

"Oh, deary me!" says Aunt Sally; "*is* he changed so? Why, that ain't *Tom* it's Sid; Tom's—Tom's—why, where is Tom? He was here a minute ago."

"You mean where's Huck *Finn*—that's what you mean! I reckon I hain't raised such a scamp as my Tom all these years, not to know him when I *see* him. That *would* be a pretty howdy-do. Come out from under that bed, Huck Finn."

So I done it. But not feeling brash.

Aunt Sally she was one of the mixed-upest looking persons I ever see; except one, and that was Uncle Silas, when he come in, and they told it all to him. It kind of made him drunk, as you may say, and he didn't know nothing at all the rest of the day, and preached a prayer-meeting sermon that night that give him a rattling ruputation, because the oldest man in the world couldn't a understood it. So Tom's Aunt Polly, she told all about who I was, and what; and I had to up and tell how I was in such a tight place that when Mrs. Phelps took me for Tom Sawyer— she chipped in and says, "Oh, go on and call me Aunt Sally, I'm used to it, now, and 'tain't no need to change"—that when Aunt Sally took me for Tom Sawyer, I had to stand it—there warn't no other way, and I knowed he wouldn't mind, because it would be nuts for him, being a mystery, and he'd make an adventure out of it and be perfectly satisfied. And so it turned out, and he let on to be Sid, and made things as soft as he could for me.

And his Aunt Polly she said Tom was right about old Miss Watson setting Jim free in her will; and so, sure enough, Tom Sawyer had gone and took all that trouble and bother to set a free nigger free! and I couldn't ever understand, before, until that minute and that talk, how he *could* help a body set a nigger free, with his bringing-up.

Well, Aunt Polly she said that when Aunt Sally wrote to her that Tom and *Sid* had come, all right and safe, she says to herself:

"Look at that, now! I might have expected it, letting him go off that way without anybody to watch him. So now I got to go and trapse all the way down the river, eleven hundred mile, and find out what that creetur's up to, *this* time; as long as I couldn't seem to get any answer out of you about it."

"Why, I never heard nothing from you," says Aunt Sally.

"Well, I wonder! Why, I wrote to you twice, to ask you what you could mean by Sid being here."

"Well, I never got 'em, Sis."

Aunt Polly, she turns around slow and severe, and says:

"You, Tom!"

"Well—*what?*" he says, kind of pettish.

"Don't you what *me,* you impudent thing—hand out them letters."

"What letters?"

"*Them* letters. I be bound, if I have to take aholt of you I'll————"

"They're in the trunk. There, now. And they're just the same as they was when I got them out of the office. I hain't looked into them, I hain't touched them. But I knowed they'd make trouble, and I thought if you warn't in no hurry, I'd————"

"Well, you *do* need skinning, there ain't no mistake about it. And I wrote another one to tell you I was coming; and I spose he————"

"No, it come yesterday; I hain't read it yet, but *it's* all right, I've got that one."

I wanted to offer to bet two dollars she hadn't, but I reckoned maybe it was just as safe to not to. So I never said nothing.

CHAPTER THE LAST

The first time I catched Tom, private, I asked him what was his idea, time of the evasion?—what it was he'd planned to do if the evasion worked all right and he managed to set a nigger free that was already free before? And he said, what he had planned in his head, from the start, if we got Jim out all safe, was for us to run him down the river, on the raft, and have adventures plumb to the mouth of the river, and then tell him about his being free, and take him back up home on a steamboat, in style, and pay him for his lost time, and write word ahead and get out all the niggers around, and have them waltz him into town with a torchlight procession and a brass band, and then he would be a hero, and so would we. But I reckened it was about as well the way it was.

We had Jim out of the chains in no time, and when Aunt Polly and Uncle Silas and Aunt Sally found out how good he helped the doctor nurse Tom, they made a heap of fuss over him, and fixed him up prime, and give him all he wanted to eat, and a good time, and nothing to do. And we had him up to the sick-room; and had a high talk; and Tom give Jim forty dollars for being prisoner for us so patient, and doing it up so good, and Jim was pleased most to death, and busted out, and says:

"*Dah*, now, Huck, what I tell you?—what I tell you up dah on Jackson islan'? I *tole* you I got a hairy breas', en what's de sign un it; en I *tole* you I ben rich wunst, en gwineter to be rich *agin;* en it's come true; en heah she *is! Dah*, now! doan' talk to *me*—signs is *signs*, mine I tell you; en I knowed jis' 's well 'at I 'uz gwineter be rich agin as I's a stannin' heah dis minute!"

And then Tom he talked along, and talked along, and says, le's all three slide out of here, one of these nights, and get an outfit, and go for howling adventures amongst the Injuns, over in the Territory, for a couple of weeks or two; and I says, all right, that suits me, but I ain't got no money for to buy the outfit, and I reckon I couldn't get none from home, because it's likely pap's been back before now, and got it all away from Judge Thatcher and drunk it up.

"No he hain't," Tom says; "it's all there, yet—six thousand dollars and more; and your pap hain't ever been back since. Hadn't when I come away, anyhow."

Jim says, kind of solemn:

"He ain't a comin' back no mo', Huck."

I says:

"Why, Jim?"

"Nemmine why, Huck—but he ain't comin' back no mo'."

But I kept at him; so at last he says:

"Doan' you 'member de house dat was float'n down de river, en dey wuz a man in dah, kivered up, en I went in en unkivered him and didn' let you come in? Well, den, you k'n git yo' money when you wants it; kase dat wuz him."

Tom's most well, now, and got his bullet around his neck on a watch-guard for a watch, and is always seeing what time it is, and so there ain't nothing more to

write about, and I am rotten glad of it, because if I'd a knowed what a trouble it was to make a book I wouldn't a tackled it and ain't agoing to no more. But I reckon I got to light out for the Territory ahead of the rest, because Aunt Sally she's going to adopt me and sivilize me and I can't stand it. I been there before.
THE END. YOURS TRULY, HUCK FINN.

Constance Fenimore Woolson
(1840–1894)

Constance Fenimore Woolson not only traveled widely but resided in a number of distinctively different places. Born in 1840 in Claremont, New Hampshire, the grandniece of James Fenimore Cooper, she moved with her family a short time later to Cleveland and grew up there, spending her summers on Mackinac Island in Lake Michigan. From 1873 to 1879 she lived with her mother in the Carolinas and in Florida and closely observed the effects of Reconstruction. Following the death of her mother in 1879, Woolson traveled to England and to Europe, finally settling in Italy for the remaining years of her life. She died tragically in Venice in 1894 during a severe attack of influenza, when delirium caused her either to jump or to fall from a window.

Woolson wrote about all the places in which she lived. In *Castle Nowhere: Lake Country Sketches* (1875) she portrays the lives of French settlers in the Great Lakes region; in *Rodman the Keeper: Southern Sketches* (1880) she examines the effects of Reconstruction on former slaves, southern whites, and visitors from the North. Two posthumous collections of stories, *The Front Yard* (1895) and *Dorothy* (1896), focus on the foibles of Americans in Italy. And *Mentone, Cairo, and Corfu* (1895) describes in compelling detail scenes of Woolson's frequent tours. Yet, Woolson's five novels, written during her years abroad, all have American settings; notable among them are *For the Major* (1883), the story of a woman's efforts to preserve her husband's illusions of the Old South, and *Horace Chase* (1894), in which the protagonist forgives his wife for her love of another man.

Given the range and the quality of her work, it seems anomalous that Woolson has been labelled a "local colorist"—a term conventionally reserved for writers of limited achievement who portray the peculiarities of regional life. The term seems almost an excuse for the neglect her work has suffered since her death. During her lifetime, however, Woolson's fiction was widely read in magazines such as *Harper's, Lippincott's,* and the *Atlantic Monthly*. William Dean Howells and Henry James praised her work for its acute insight into character. As the story "King David" (1878) reveals, Woolson had a special talent for probing the relationship between well-meaning northerners and former slaves during the years of Reconstruction. Unflinchingly, with a psychological realism that matches her precision of detail, she confronts David King's failure—despite his noble motives.

Woolson's friendship with Henry James has also tended to blur her achievement as a writer. In his biography of James, Leon Edel has characterized Woolson as a "provincial, middle-aged, deaf woman" who, filled with loneliness and a need for love, clung to James "in a kind of pathetic dependency." The words seem as unjust as they are unkind, and Edel gives no convincing evidence for them. But his view of Woolson as a mere irritant to James underscores the need for an enlightened reassessment of her work. For her writing suggests how a developing realism affected the tendency toward melodrama in American literature, even as that writing explores fundamental human emotions in the context of American history.

Suggested Readings: *Anne,* 1882, rpt. 1977. *"For the Major" and Selected Other Short Stories,* ed. R. S. Moore, 1967. *Castle Nowhere: Lake-Country Sketches,* 1971. *Women Artists, Women Exiles: "Miss Grief" and Other Stories,* ed. J. M. Weimer, 1988. R. S. Moore, *Constance Fenimore Woolson,* 1963. C. B. Torsney, *Constance Fenimore Woolson: The Grief of Artistry,* 1989.

Text Used: *Rodman the Keeper: Southern Sketches,* 1886.

KING DAVID*

I met a traveler on the road;
His face was wan, his feet were weary;
Yet he unresting went with such
A strange, still, patient mien—a look
Set forward in the empty air,
As he were reading an unseen book.
RICHARD WATSON GILDER[1]

The scholars were dismissed. Out they trooped—big boys, little boys, and full-grown men. Then what antics—what linked lines of scuffling; what double shuffles, leaps, and somersaults; what rolling laughter, interspersed with short yelps and guttural cries, as wild and free as the sounds the mustangs make, gamboling on the plains! For King David's scholars were black—black as the ace of spades. He did not say that; he knew very little about the ace. He said simply that his scholars were "colored"; and sometimes he called them "the Children of Ham."[2] But so many mistakes were made over this title, in spite of his careful explanations (the Children having an undoubted taste for bacon), that he finally abandoned it, and fell back upon the national name of "freedmen," a title both good and true. He even tried to make it noble, speaking to them often of their wonderful lot as the emancipated teachers and helpers of their race; laying before them their mission in the future, which was to go over to Africa, and wake out of their long sloth and slumber the thousands of souls there. But Cassius and Pompey had only a mythic idea of Africa; they looked at the globe as it was turned around, they saw it there on the other side, and then their attention wandered off to an adventurous ant who was making the tour of Soodan and crossing the mountains of Kong[3] as though they were nothing.

Lessons over, the scholars went home. The schoolmaster went home too, wiping his forehead as he went. He was a grave young man, tall and thin, somewhat narrow-chested, with the diffident air of a country student. And yet this country

* First published in *Scribner's Monthly* in March 1878. In the Old Testament David was the second king of Israel and Judah.
   [1] Gilder (1844–1909) was a writer and an assistant editor of *Scribner's Monthly* and editor of *The Century*.
   [2] In Genesis 6:10, Noah's second son.   [3] In the Ivory Coast.

student was here, far down in the South, hundreds of miles away from the New Hampshire village where he had thought to spend his life as teacher of the district school. Extreme near-sightedness and an inherited delicacy of constitution which he bore silently had kept him out of the field during the days of the war.[4] "I should be only an encumbrance," he thought. But, when the war was over, the fire which had burned within burst forth in the thought, "The freedmen!" There was work fitted to his hand: that one thing he could do. "My turn has come at last," he said. "I feel the call to go." Nobody cared much because he was leaving. "Going down to teach the blacks?" said the farmers. "I don't see as you're called, David. We've paid dear enough to set 'em free, goodness knows, and now they ought to look out for themselves."

"But they must first be taught," said the schoolmaster. "Our responsibility is great; our task is only just begun."

"Stuff!" said the farmers. What with the graves down in the South, and the taxes up in the North, they were not prepared to hear any talk about beginning. Beginning, indeed! They called it ending. The slaves were freed, and it was right they should be freed; but Ethan and Abner were gone, and their households were left unto them desolate. Let the blacks take care of themselves.

So, all alone, down came David King, with such aid and instruction as the Freedman's Bureau[5] could give him, to this little settlement among the pines, where the freedmen had built some cabins in a careless way, and then seated themselves to wait for fortune. Freedmen! Yes; a glorious idea! But how will it work its way out into practical life? What are you going to do with tens of thousands of ignorant, childish, irresponsible souls thrown suddenly upon your hands; souls that will not long stay childish, and that have in them also all the capacities for evil that you yourselves have—you with your safeguards of generations of conscious responsibility and self-government, and yet—so many lapses! This is what David King thought. He did not see his way exactly; no, nor the nation's way. But he said to himself: "I can at least begin; if I am wrong, I shall find it out in time. But now it seems to me that our first duty is to educate them." So he began at "a, b, and c"; "You must not steal"; "You must not fight"; "You must wash your faces"; which may be called, I think, the first working out of the emancipation problem.

Jubilee Town was the name of the settlement; and when the schoolmaster announced his own, David King, the title struck the imitative minds of the scholars, and, turning it around, they made "King David" of it, and kept it so. Delighted with the novelty, the Jubilee freedmen came to school in such numbers that the master was obliged to classify them; boys and men in the mornings and afternoons; the old people in the evenings; the young women and girls by themselves for an hour in the early morning. "I can not do full justice to all," he thought, "and in the men lies the danger, in the boys the hope; the women can not vote. Would to God the men could not either, until they have learned to read and to write, and to maintain themselves respectably!" For, abolitionist as he was, David King would have given years of his life for the power to restrict the suffrage. Not having this power, however, he worked at the problem in the only way left open:

---

[4] The Civil War (1861–1865).

[5] The Freedmen's Bureau, set up in March 1865 to aid freed slaves in the transition from slavery to freedom—by means of supplies, education, and assistance in land settlement.

"Take two apples from four apples, Julius—how many will be left?" "What is this I hear, Cæsar, about stolen bacon?"

On this day the master went home, tired and dispirited; the novelty was over on both sides. He had been five months at Jubilee, and his scholars were more of a puzzle to him than ever. They learned, some of them, readily; but they forgot as readily. They had a vast capacity for parrot-like repetition, and caught his long words so quickly, and repeated them so volubly, with but slight comprehension of their meaning, that his sensitive conscience shrank from using them, and he was forced back upon a rude plainness of speech which was a pain to his pedagogic ears. Where he had once said, "Demean yourselves with sobriety," he now said, "Don't get drunk." He would have fared better if he had learned to say "uncle" and "aunty," or "maumer," in the familiar Southern fashion. But he had no knowledge of the customs; how could he have? He could only blunder on in his slow Northern way.

His cabin stood in the pine forest, at a little distance from the settlement; he had allowed himself that grace. There was a garden around it, where Northern flowers came up after a while—a little pale, perhaps, like English ladies in India, but doubly beautiful and dear to exiled eyes. The schoolmaster had cherished from the first a wish for a cotton-field—a cotton-field of his own. To him a cotton-field represented the South—a cotton-field in the hot sunshine, with a gang of slaves toiling under the lash of an overseer. This might have been a fancy picture, and it might not. At any rate, it was real to him. There was, however, no overseer now, and no lash; no slaves and very little toil. The negroes would work only when they pleased, and that was generally not at all. There was no doubt but that they were almost hopelessly improvident and lazy. "Entirely so," said the planters. "Not quite," said the Northern schoolmaster. And therein lay the difference between them.

David lighted his fire of pitch-pine, spread his little table, and began to cook his supper carefully. When it was nearly ready, he heard a knock at his gate. Two representative specimens of his scholars were waiting without—Jim, a field-hand, and a woman named Esther, who had been a house-servant in a planter's family. Jim had come "to borry an axe," and Esther to ask for medicine for a sick child.

"Where is your own axe, Jim?" said the schoolmaster.

"Somehow et's rusty, sah. Dey gets rusty mighty quick."

"Of course, because you always leave them out in the rain. When will you learn to take care of your axes?"

"Don' know, mars."

"I have told you not to call me master," said David. "I am not your master."

"You's schoolmars, I reckon," answered Jim, grinning at his repartee.

"Well, Jim," said the schoolmaster, relaxing into a smile, "you have the best of it this time; but you know quite well what I mean. You can take the axe; but bring it back to-night. And you must see about getting a new one immediately; there is something to begin with.—Now, Esther, what is it? Your boy sick? Probably it is because you let him drink the water out of that swampy pool. I warned you."

"Yes, sah," said the woman impassively.

She was a slow, dull-witted creature, who had executed her tasks marvelously well in the planter's family, never varying by a hair's breadth either in time or method during long years. Freed, she was lost at once; if she had not been swept along by her companions, she would have sat down dumbly by the wayside, and died. The schoolmaster offered supper to both of his guests. Jim took a seat at the table at once, nothing loath, and ate and drank, talking all the time with occasional flashes of wit, and an unconscious suggestion of ferocity in the way he hacked and tore the meat with his clasp-knife and his strong white teeth. Esther stood; nothing could induce her to sit in the master's presence. She ate and drank quietly, and dropped a courtesy whenever he spoke to her, not from any especial respect or gratitude, however, but from habit. "I may possibly teach the man something," thought the schoolmaster; "but what a terrible creature to turn loose in the world, with power in his hand! Hundreds of these men will die, nay, must die violent deaths before their people can learn what freedom means, and what it does not mean. As for the woman, it is hopeless; she can not learn. But her child can. In truth, our hope is in the children."

And then he threw away every atom of the food, washed his dishes, made up the fire, and went back to the beginning again and cooked a second supper. For he still shrank from personal contact with the other race. A Southerner would have found it impossible to comprehend the fortitude it required for the New-Englander to go through his daily rounds among them. He did his best; but it was duty, not liking. Supper over, he went to the schoolhouse again: in the evenings he taught the old people. It was an odd sight to note them as they followed the letters with a big, crooked forefinger, slowly spelling out words of three letters. They spelled with their whole bodies, stooping over the books which lay before them until their old grizzled heads and gay turbans looked as if they were set on the table by the chins in a long row. Patiently the master taught them; they had gone no further than "cat" in five long months. He made the letters for them on the blackboard again and again, but the treat of the evening was the making of these letters on the board by the different scholars in turn. "Now, Dinah—B." And old Dinah would hobble up proudly, and, with much screwing of her mouth and tongue, and many long hesitations, produce something which looked like a figure eight gone mad. Joe had his turn next, and he would make, perhaps, an H for a D. The master would go back and explain to him carefully the difference, only to find at the end of ten minutes that the whole class was hopelessly confused; Joe's mistake had routed them all. There was one pair of spectacles among the old people: these were passed from hand to hand as the turn came, not from necessity always, but as an adjunct to the dignity of reading.

"Never mind the glasses, Tom. Surely you can spell 'bag' without them."

"Dey helps, Mars King David," replied old Tom with solemn importance. He then adorned himself with the spectacles, and spelled it—"g, a, b."

But the old people enjoyed their lesson immensely; no laughter, no joking broke the solemnity of the scene, and they never failed to make an especial toilet[6]—much shirt-collar for the old men, and clean turbans for the old women. They seemed to be generally half-crippled, poor old creatures; slow in their movements as tortoises, and often unwieldy; their shoes were curiosities of patches, rags, strings, and carpeting. But sometimes a fine old black face was lifted from the slow-moving bulk, and from under wrinkled eyelids keen sharp eyes met the master's, as intelligent as his own.

There was no church proper in Jubilee. On Sundays, the people, who were generally Baptists, assembled in the schoolroom, where services were conducted

---

[6] Attire.

by a brother who had "de gif' ob preachin'," and who poured forth a flood of Scripture phrases with a volubility, incoherence, and earnestness alike extraordinary. Presbyterian David attended these services, not only for the sake of example, but also because he steadfastly believed in "the public assembling of ourselves together for the worship of Almighty God."

"Perhaps they understand him," he thought, noting the rapt black faces, "and I, at least, have no right to judge them—I, who, with all the lights I have had, still find myself unable to grasp the great doctrine of Election."[7] For David had been bred in Calvinism,[8] and many a night, when younger and more hopeful of arriving at finalities, had he wrestled with its problems. He was not so sure, now, of arriving at finalities either in belief or in daily life; but he thought the fault lay with himself, and deplored it.

The Yankee schoolmaster was, of course, debarred from intercourse with those of his own color in the neighborhood. There were no "poor whites" there; he was spared the sight of their long, clay-colored faces, lank yellow hair, and half-open mouths; he was not brought into contact with the ignorance and dense self-conceit of this singular class. The whites of the neighborhood were planters, and they regarded the schoolmaster as an interloper, a fanatic, a knave, or a fool, according to their various degrees of bitterness. The phantom of a cotton-field still haunted the master, and he often walked by the abandoned fields of these planters, and noted them carefully. In addition to his fancy, there was now another motive. Things were not going well at Jubilee, and he was anxious to try whether the men would not work for good wages, paid regularly, and for their Northern teacher and friend. Thus it happened that Harnett Ammerton, retired planter, one afternoon perceived a stranger walking up the avenue that led to his dilapidated mansion; and as he was near-sighted, and as any visitor was, besides, a welcome interruption in his dull day, he went out upon the piazza to meet him; and not until he had offered a chair did he recognize his guest. He said nothing; for he was in his own house; but a gentleman can freeze the atmosphere around him even in his own house, and this he did. The schoolmaster stated his errand simply: he wished to rent one of the abandoned cotton-fields for a year. The planter could have answered with satisfaction that his fields might lie for ever untilled before Yankee hands should touch them; but he was a poor man now, and money was money. He endured his visitor, and he rented his field; and, with the perplexed feelings of his class, he asked himself how it was, how it could be, that a man like that—yes, like that—had money, while he himself had none! David had but little money—a mere handful to throw away in a day, the planter would have thought in the lavish old times; but David had the New England thrift.

"I am hoping that the unemployed hands over at Jubilee will cultivate this field for me," he said—"for fair wages, of course. I know nothing of cotton myself."

"You will be disappointed," said the planter.

"But they must live; they must lay up something for the winter."

"They do not know enough to live. They might exist, perhaps, in Africa, as the rest of their race exists; but here, in this colder climate, they must be taken care of, worked, and fed, as we work and feed our horses—precisely in the same way."

---

[7] According to Calvinist theology, God selects certain people, the elect, for salvation.

[8] The religious doctrine of the Protestant reformer John Calvin (1509–1564); based on predestination and associated with a stern moral code.

"I can not agree with you," replied David, a color rising in his thin face. "They are idle and shiftless, I acknowledge that; but is it not the natural result of generations of servitude and ignorance?"

"They have not capacity for anything save ignorance."

"You do not know then, perhaps, that I—that I am trying to educate those who are over at Jubilee," said David. There was no aggressive confidence in his voice; he knew that he had accomplished little as yet. He looked wistfully at his host as he spoke.

Harnett Ammerton was a born patrician. Poor, homely, awkward David felt this in every nerve as he sat there; for he loved beauty in spite of himself, and in spite of his belief that it was a tendency of the old Adam. (Old Adam has such nice things to bother his descendants with; almost a monopoly, if we are to believe some creeds.) So now David tried not to be influenced by the fine face before him, and steadfastly went on to sow a little seed, if possible, even upon this prejudiced ground.

"I have a school over there," he said.

"I have heard something of the kind, I believe," replied the old planter, as though Jubilee Town were a thousand miles away, instead of a blot upon his own border. "May I ask how you are succeeding?"

There was a fine irony in the question. David felt it, but replied courageously that success, he hoped, would come in time.

"And I, young man, hope that it will never come! The negro with power in his hand, which you have given him, with a little smattering of knowledge in his shallow, crafty brain—a knowledge which you and your kind are now striving to give him—will become an element of more danger in this land than it has ever known before. You Northerners do not understand the blacks. They are an inferior race by nature; God made them so. And God forgive those (although I never can) who have placed them over us—yes, virtually over us, their former masters— poor ignorant creatures!"

At this instant an old negro came up the steps with an armful of wood, and the eye of the Northerner noted (was forced to note) the contrast. There sat the planter, his head crowned with silver hair, his finely chiseled face glowing with the warmth of his indignant words; and there passed the old slave, bent and black, his low forehead and broad animal features seeming to typify scarcely more intelligence than that of the dog that followed him. The planter spoke to the servant in his kindly way as he passed, and the old black face lighted with pleasure. This, too, the schoolmaster's sensitive mind noted: none of his pupils looked at him with anything like that affection. "But it *is* right they should be freed—it *is* right," he said to himself as he walked back to Jubilee; "and to that belief will I cling as long as I have my being. It *is* right." And then he came into Jubilee, and found three of his freedmen drunk and quarreling in the street.

Heretofore the settlement, poor and forlorn as it was, had escaped the curse of drunkenness. No liquor was sold in the vicinity, and David had succeeded in keeping his scholars from wandering aimlessly about the country from place to place—often the first use the blacks made of their freedom. Jubilee did not go to the liquor; but, at last, the liquor had come to Jubilee. Shall they not have all rights and privileges, these new-born citizens of ours? The bringer of these doctrines, and of the fluids to moisten them, was a white man, one of that class which has gone down on the page of American history, knighted with the initials C. B.[9] "The Captain" the negroes called him; and he was highly popular already, three hours of the Captain being worth three weeks of David, as far as familiarity went. The man was a glib-tongued, smartly dressed fellow, well supplied with money; and his errand was, of course, to influence the votes at the next election. David, meanwhile, had so carefully kept all talk of politics from his scholars that they hardly knew that an election was near. It became now a contest between the two higher intelligences. If the schoolmaster had but won the easily won and strong affections of his pupils! But, in all those months, he had gained only a dutiful attention. They did not even respect him as they had respected their old masters, and the cause (poor David!) was that very thrift and industry which he relied upon as an example.

"Ole Mars Ammerton wouldn't wash his dishes ef dey was nebber washed," confided Maum June to Elsy, as they caught sight of David's shining pans.

The schoolmaster could have had a retinue of servants for a small price, or no price at all; but, to tell a truth which he never told, he could not endure them about him.

"I must have one spot to myself," he said feverishly, after he had labored all day among them, teaching, correcting untidy ways, administering simple medicines, or binding up a bruised foot. But he never dreamed that this very isolation of his personality, this very thrift, were daily robbing him of the influence which he so earnestly longed to possess. In New England every man's house was his castle, and every man's hands were thrifty. He forgot the easy familiarity, the lordly ways, the crowded households, and the royal carelessness to which the slaves had always been accustomed in their old masters' homes.

At first the Captain attempted intimacy.

"No reason why you and me shouldn't work together," he said with a confidential wink. "This thing's being done all over the South, and easy done, too. Now's the time for smart chaps like us—'transition,' you know. The old Southerners are mad, and won't come forward, so we'll just sail in and have a few years of it. When they're ready to come back—why, we'll give 'em up the place again, of course, if our pockets are well lined. Come, now, just acknowledge that the negroes have got to have somebody to lead 'em."

"It shall not be such as you," said David indignantly. "See those two men quarreling; that is the work of the liquor you have given them!"

"They've as good a right to their liquor as other men have," replied the Captain carelessly; "and that's what I tell 'em; they ain't slaves now—they're free. Well, boss, sorry you don't like my idees, but can't help it; must go ahead. Remember, I offered you a chance, and you would not take it. Morning."

The five months had grown into six and seven, and Jubilee Town was known far and wide as a dangerous and disorderly neighborhood. The old people and the children still came to school, but the young men and boys had deserted in a body. The schoolmaster's cotton-field was neglected; he did a little there himself every day, but the work was novel, and his attempts were awkward and slow. One

---

[9] Carpetbaggers, opportunistic northerners who came south during the Reconstruction, carrying their belongings in carpetbags and taking advantage of the unsettled condition of the South after the Civil War.

afternoon Harnett Ammerton rode by on horseback; the road passed near the angle of the field where the schoolmaster was at work.

"How is your experiment succeeding?" said the planter, with a little smile of amused scorn as he saw the lonely figure.

"Not very well," replied David.

He paused and looked up earnestly into the planter's face. Here was a man who had lived among the blacks all his life, and knew them: if he would but give honest advice! The schoolmaster was sorely troubled that afternoon. Should he speak? He would at least try.

"Mr. Ammerton," he said, "do you intend to vote at the approaching election?"

"No," replied the planter; "nor any person of my acquaintance."

"Then incompetent, and, I fear, evil-minded men will be put into office."

"Of course—the certain result of negro voting."

"But if you, sir, and the class to which you belong, would exert yourselves, I am inclined to think much might be done. The breach will only grow broader every year; act now, while you have still influence left."

"Then you think that we have influence?" said the planter.

He was curious concerning the ideas of this man, who, although not like the typical Yankee exactly, was yet plainly a fanatic; while as to dress and air—why, Zip, his old valet, had more polish.

"I know at least that I have none," said David. Then he came a step nearer. "Do you think, sir," he began slowly, "that I have gone to work in the wrong way? Would it have been wiser to have obtained some post of authority over them—the office of justice of the peace, for instance, with power of arrest?"

"I know nothing about it," said the planter curtly, touching his horse with his whip and riding on. He had no intention of stopping to discuss ways and means with an abolition schoolmaster!

Things grew from bad to worse at Jubilee. Most of the men had been field-hands; there was but little intelligence among them. The few bright minds among David's pupils caught the specious arguments of the Captain, and repeated them to the others. The Captain explained how much power they held; the Captain laid before them glittering plans; the Captain said that by good rights each family ought to have a plantation to repay them for their years of enforced labor; the Captain promised them a four-story brick college for their boys, which was more than King David had ever promised, teacher though he was. They found out that they were tired of King David and his narrow talk; and they went over to Hildore Corners, where a new store had been opened, which contained, among other novelties, a bar. This was one of the Captain's benefactions. "If you pay your money for it, you've as good a right to your liquor as any one, I guess," he observed. "Not that it's anything to me, of course; but I allow I like to see fair play!"

It was something to him, however: the new store had a silent partner; and this was but one of many small and silent enterprises in which he was engaged throughout the neighborhood.

The women of Jubilee, more faithful than the men, still sent their children to school; but they did it with discouraged hearts, poor things! Often now they were seen with bandaged heads and bruised bodies, the result of drunken blows from husband or brother; and, left alone, they were obliged to labor all day to get the poor food they ate, and to keep clothes on their children. Patient by nature, they lived along as best they could, and toiled in their small fields like horses; but the little prides, the vague, grotesque aspirations and hopes that had come to them with their freedom, gradually faded away. "A blue-painted front do'," "a black-silk apron with red ribbons," "to make a minister of little Job," and "a real crock'ry pitcher," were wishes unspoken now. The thing was only how to live from day to day, and keep the patched clothes together. In the mean while trashy finery was sold at the new store, and the younger girls wore gilt ear-rings.

The master, toiling on at his vain task, was at his wit's end. "They will not work; before long they must steal," he said. He brooded and thought, and at last one morning he came to a decision. The same day in the afternoon he set out for Hildore Corners. He had thought of a plan. As he was walking rapidly through the pine-woods Harnett Ammerton on horseback passed him. This time the Northerner had no questions to ask—nay, he almost hung his head, so ashamed was he of the reputation that had attached itself to the field of his labors. But the planter reined in his horse when he saw who it was: he was the questioner now.

"Schoolmaster," he began, "in the name of all the white families about here, I really must ask if you can do nothing to keep in order those miserable, drinking, ruffianly negroes of yours over at Jubilee? Why, we shall all be murdered in our beds before long! Are you aware of the dangerous spirit they have manifested lately?"

"Only too well," said David.

"What are you going to do? How will it end?"

"God knows."

"God knows! Is that all you have to say? Of course he knows; but the question is, Do you know? You have brought the whole trouble down upon our heads by your confounded insurrectionary school! Just as I told you, your negroes, with the little smattering of knowledge you have given them, are now the most dangerous, riotous, thieving, murdering rascals in the district."

"They are bad; but it is not the work of the school, I hope."

"Yes, it is," said the planter angrily.

"They have been led astray lately, Mr. Ammerton; a person has come among them—"

"Another Northerner?"

"Yes," said David, a flush rising in his cheek; "but not all Northerners are like this man, I trust."

"Pretty much all we see are. Look at the State."

"Yes, I know it; I suppose time alone can help matters," said the troubled teacher.

"Give up your school, and come and join us," said the planter abruptly. "You, at least, are honest in your mistakes. We are going to form an association[10] for our own protection; join with us. You can teach my grandsons if you like, provided you do not put any of your—your fanaticism into them."

This was an enormous concession for Harnett Ammerton to make; something in the schoolmaster's worn face had drawn it out.

"Thank you," said David slowly; "it is kindly meant, sir. But I can not give up my work. I came down to help the freedmen, and—"

"Then stay with them," said the planter, doubly angry for the very kindness of

---

[10] The Ku Klux Klan, one of several secret societies formed after the Civil War that used terrorism to subdue the newly freed slaves.

the moment before. "I thought you were a decent-living white man, according to your fashion, but I see I was mistaken. Dark days are coming, and you turn your back upon those of your own color and side with the slaves! Go and herd with your negroes. But, look you, sir, we are prepared. We will shoot down anyone found upon our premises after dark—shoot him down like a dog. It has come to that, and, by Heaven! we shall protect ourselves."

He rode on. David sat down on a fallen tree for a moment, and leaned his head upon his hand. Dark days were coming, as the planter had said; nay, were already there. Was he in any way responsible for them? He tried to think. "I know not," he said at last; "but I must still go on and do the best I can. I must carry out my plan." He rose and went forward to the Corners.

A number of Jubilee men were lounging near the new store, and one of them was reading aloud from a newspaper which the Captain had given him. He had been David's brightest scholar, and he could read readily; but what he read was inflammable matter of the worst kind, a speech which had been written for just such purposes, and which was now being circulated through the district. Mephistopheles in the form of Harnett Ammerton seemed to whisper in the schoolmaster's ears, "Do you take pride to yourself that you taught that man to read?"

The reader stopped; he had discovered the new auditor. The men stared; they had never seen the master at the Corners before. They drew together and waited. He approached them, and paused for a moment; then he began to speak.

"I have come, friends," he said, "to make a proposition to you. You, on your side, have nothing laid up for the winter, and I, on my side, am anxious to have your work. I have a field, you know, a cotton-field; what do you say to going to work there, all of you, for a month? I will agree to pay you more than any man about here pays, and you shall have the cash every Monday morning regularly. We will hold a meeting over at Jubilee, and you shall choose your own overseer; for I am very ignorant about cotton-fields; I must trust to you. What do you say?"

The men looked at each other, but no one spoke.

"Think of your little children without clothes."

Still silence.

"I have not succeeded among you," continued the teacher, "as well as I hoped to succeed. You do not come to school any more, and I suppose it is because you do not like me."

Something like a murmur of dissent came from the group. The voice went on:

"I have thought of something I can do, however. I can write to the North for another teacher to take my place, and he shall be a man of your own race; one who is educated, and, if possible, also a clergyman of your own faith. You can have a little church then, and Sabbath services. As soon as he comes, I will yield my place to him; but, in the mean time, will you not cultivate that field for me? I ask it as a favor. It will be but for a little while, for, when the new teacher comes, I shall go—unless, indeed," he added, looking around with a smile that was almost pathetic in its appeal, "you should wish me to stay."

There was no answer. He had thrown out this last little test question suddenly. It had failed.

"I am sorry I have not succeeded better at Jubilee," he said after a short pause—and his voice had altered in spite of his self-control—"but at least you will believe, I hope, that I have tried."

"Dat's so '; "Dat's de trouf," said one or two; the rest stood irresolute. But at

this moment a new speaker came forward; it was the Captain, who had been listening in ambush.

"All gammon,[11] boys, all gammon," he began, seating himself familiarly
among them on the fence-rail. "The season for planting's over, and your work
would be thrown away in that field of his. He knows it, too; he only wants to see
you marching around to his whistling. And he pays you double wages, does he?
Double wages for perfectly useless work! Doesn't that show, clear as daylight,
what he's up to? If he hankers so after your future—your next winter, and all
that—why don't he give yer the money right out, if he's so flush? But no; he
wants to put you to work, and that's all there is of it. He can't deny a word I've
said, either."

"I do not deny that I wish you to work, friends," began David—

"There! he tells yer so himself," said the Captain; "he wants yer back in yer old
places again. *I* seen him talking to old Ammerton the other day. Give 'em a
chance, them two classes, and they'll have you slaves a second time before you
know it."

"Never!" cried David. "Friends, it is not possible that you can believe this man!
We have given our lives to make you free," he added passionately; "we came
down among you, bearing your freedom in your hands—"

"Come, now—I'm a Northerner too, ain't I?" interrupted the Captain. "There's
two kinds of Northerners, boys. *I* was in the army, and that's more than he can
say. Much freedom *he* brought down in *his* hands, safe at home in his narrer-
minded, penny-scraping village! He wasn't in the army at all, boys, and he can't
tell you he was."

This was true; the schoolmaster could not. Neither could he tell them what was
also true, namely, that the Captain had been an *attaché* of a sutler's[12] tent, and
nothing more. But the sharp-witted Captain had the whole history of his opponent
at his fingers' ends.

"Come along, boys," said this jovial leader; "we'll have suthin' to drink the
health of this tremenjous soldier in—this fellow as fought so hard for you and for
your freedom. I always thought he looked like a fighting man, with them fine
broad shoulders of his!" He laughed loudly, and the men trooped into the store
after him. The schoolmaster, alone outside, knew that his chance was gone. He
turned away and took the homeward road. One of his plans had failed; there remained now nothing save to carry out the other.

Prompt as usual, he wrote his letter as soon as he reached his cabin, asking that
another teacher, a colored man if possible, should be sent down to take his place.

"I fear I am not fitted for the work," he wrote. "I take shame to myself that this
is so; yet, being so, I must not hinder by any disappointed strivings the progress of
the great mission. I will go back among my own kind; it may be that some whom
I shall teach may yet succeed where I have failed." The letter could not go until
the next morning. He went out and walked up and down in the forest. A sudden
impulse came to him; he crossed over to the schoolhouse and rang the little tinkling belfry-bell. His evening class had disbanded some time before; the poor old
aunties and uncles crept off to bed very early now, in order to be safely out of the
way when their disorderly sons and grandsons came home. But something moved
the master to see them all together once more. They came across the green, won-

---

[11] Nonsense, humbug.   [12] A merchant who followed the army, selling supplies to the fighting men.

dering, and entered the schoolroom; some of the younger wives came too, and the children. The master waited, letter in hand. When they were all seated—

"Friends," he said, "I have called you together to speak to you of a matter which lies very near my own heart. Things are not going on well at Jubilee. The men drink; the children go in rags. Is this true?"

Groans and slow assenting nods answered him. One old woman shrieked out shrilly, "It is de Lord's will," and rocked her body to and fro.

"No, it is not the Lord's will," answered the schoolmaster gently; "you must not think so. You must strive to reclaim those who have gone astray; you must endeavor to inspire them with renewed aspirations toward a higher plane of life; you must—I mean," he said, correcting himself, "you must try to keep the men from going over to the Corners and getting drunk."

"But dey will do it, sah; what can we do?" said Uncle Scipio, who sat leaning his chin upon his crutch and peering at the teacher with sharp intelligence in his old eyes. "If dey won't stay fo' you, sah, will dey stay fo' us?"

"That is what I was coming to," said the master. (They had opened the subject even before he could get to it! They saw it too, then—his utter lack of influence.) "I have not succeeded here as I hoped to succeed, friends; I have not the influence I ought to have." Then he paused. "Perhaps the best thing I can do will be to go away," he added, looking quickly from face to face to catch the expression. But there was nothing visible. The children stared stolidly back, and the old people sat unmoved; he even fancied that he could detect relief in the eyes of one or two, quickly suppressed, however, by the innate politeness of the race. A sudden mist came over his eyes; he had thought that perhaps some of them would care a little. He hurried on: "I have written to the North for a new teacher for you, a man of your own people, who will not only teach you, but also, as a minister, hold services on the Sabbath; you can have a little church of your own then. Such a man will do better for you than I have done, and I hope you will like him"—he was going to say, "better than you have liked me," but putting down all thought of self, he added, "and that his work among you will be abundantly blessed."

"Glory! glory!" cried an old aunty. "A color'd preacher ob our own! Glory! glory!"

Then Uncle Scipio rose slowly, with the aid of his crutches, and, as orator of the occasion, addressed the master.

"You see, sah, how it is; you see, Mars King David," he said, waving his hand apologetically, "a color'd man will unnerstan us, 'specially ef he hab lib'd at de Souf; we don't want no Nordern free niggahs hyar. But a 'spectable color'd preacher, now, would be de makin' ob Jubilee, fo' dis worl' an' de nex'."

"Fo' dis worl' and de nex'," echoed the old woman.

"Our service to you, sah, all de same," continued Scipio, with a grand bow of ceremony; "but you hab nebber *quite* unnerstan us, sah, nebber quite; an' you can nebber do much fo' us, sah, on 'count ob dat fack—ef you'll scuse my saying so. But it is de trouf. We give you our t'anks and our congratturrurlations, an' we hopes you'll go j'yful back to your own people, an' be a shining light to 'em for ebbermore."

"A shinin' light for ebbermore," echoed the rest. One old woman, inspired apparently by the similarity of words, began a hymn about "the shining shore," and the whole assembly, thinking no doubt that it was an appropriate and complimentary termination to the proceedings, joined in with all their might, and sang the whole six verses through with fervor.

"I should like to shake hands with you all as you go out," said the master, when at last the song was ended, "and—and I wish, my friends, that you would all remember me in your prayers to-night before you sleep."

What a sight was that when the pale Caucasian, with the intelligence of generations on his brow, asked for the prayers of these sons of Africa, and gently, nay, almost humbly, received the pressure of their black, toil-hardened hands as they passed out! They had taught him a great lesson, the lesson of a failure.

The schoolmaster went home, and sat far into the night, with his head bowed upon his hands. "Poor worm!" he thought—"poor worm! who even went so far as to dream of saying, 'Here am I, Lord, and these brethren whom thou hast given me!'"

The day came for him to go; he shouldered his bag and started away. At a turn in the road, some one was waiting for him; it was dull-faced Esther with a bunch of flowers, the common flowers of her small garden-bed. "Good-by, Esther," said the master, touched almost to tears by the sight of the solitary little offering.

"Good-by, mars," said Esther. But she was not moved; she had come out into the woods from a sort of instinct, as a dog follows a little way down the road to look after a departing carriage.

"David King has come back home again, and taken the district school," said one village gossip to another.

"Has he, now? Didn't find the blacks what he expected, I guess."

1878

Sarah Orne Jewett
(1849–1909)

In the short story "A White Heron" (1886), Sylvia wavers between directing a handsome ornithologist to the elusive heron's nest and saving the bird, eventually choosing silence and the green world of nature over the money and approval the young man from "the great world" offers. Her silence admits Sylvia into Sarah Orne Jewett's coterie of strong, independent females who choose the best lives they can with the meager resources that small, late nineteenth-century New England towns provided. Born the second daughter of Theodore Herman Jewett, a physician, and the former Caroline Frances Perry in 1849, Theodora Sarah Orne Jewett—who quickly dropped her first name—grew up in South Berwick, Maine, an inland port past its heyday, a place of remembered grandeur and romance. Because she suffered from arthritis as a child, and because her father doted on her, she often accompanied him on his rounds rather than going to school. During these visits, Jewett grew to appreciate both the people and the landscape of her region.

Jewett's father also encouraged her interest in literature; later, he urged her to "tell things *just as they are*," as stated in *Sarah Orne Jewett's Letters* (1967). Jewett followed this admonition in depicting the idiom, ideals, and environments of the elderly women whose strength and courage she admired. Influenced by the example of Harriet Beecher

Stowe's narrative of the Maine coast, *The Pearl of Orr's Island* (1862), Jewett began her literary career while still in her teens, publishing short fiction in magazines including the *Atlantic Monthly*, then edited by William Dean Howells. With his encouragement, she collected her sketches into the volume *Deephaven* (1877), named for one of her fictional Maine towns. Over the next twenty-five years Jewett published thirteen volumes of fiction, including *A Country Doctor* (1884)—in which a New England girl refuses an offer of marriage so that she might become a doctor—and *A Marsh Island* (1885).

Jewett is ranked highly among New England local-color writers, particularly for *The Country of the Pointed Firs* (1896), a work Willa Cather considered one of the three greatest American masterpieces (along with Nathaniel Hawthorne's *Scarlet Letter* [1850] and Mark Twain's *Adventures of Huckleberry Finn* [1884]). Despite this high praise, Jewett's novel-in-sketches is not well known; in *Short Fiction* (1979) the critic Barbara Solomon ascribes its neglect to its being "so thoroughly a woman's book about the world of women," a world of visiting and reminiscing, of quiet contemplation. With unerring pictorial detail, Jewett presents the limited world of Dunnet Landing as a place of few men and many strong women who live in close relationships to the land and sea, an economically declining and yet restorative, psychologically vivifying place.

Like many of her characters, Jewett did not marry; her closest relationships were with women, particularly her publisher's wife, Annie Adams Fields. After James Fields died in 1881 Jewett and Fields began living together platonically in a "Boston marriage." Although Jewett's career ended prematurely (after an injury in a carriage accident), she had already preserved the flavor of a New England soon to vanish under the pressures of industrialization. Several months after suffering a crippling stroke in 1909, she died in South Berwick in the house in which she was born.

Suggested Readings: *The Country of the Pointed Firs*, 1896. *The Best Short Stories of Sarah Orne Jewett*, intro. W. Cather, 1927, rpt. 1965. *Deephaven and Other Stories*, ed. R. Cary, 1966. *The Uncollected Short Stories of Sarah Orne Jewett*, ed. R. Cary, 1971. R. Cary, *Sarah Orne Jewett*, 1962. F. O. Mattiessen, *Sarah Orne Jewett*, 1965. R. Cary, ed., *Appreciation of Sarah Orne Jewett: 29 Interpretive Essays*, 1973. G. L. Nagel, *Critical Essays on Sarah Orne Jewett*, 1984. S. W. Sherman, *Sarah Orne Jewett, An American Persephone*, 1989.

Text Used: *Tales of New England*, 1890.

A WHITE HERON*

I

The woods were already filled with shadows one June evening, just before eight o'clock, though a bright sunset still glimmered faintly among the trunks of the trees. A little girl was driving home her cow, a plodding, dilatory, provoking creature in her behavior, but a valued companion for all that. They were going away from the western light, and striking deep into the dark woods, but their feet were familiar with the path, and it was no matter whether their eyes could see it or not.

* First published in Jewett's collection *A White Heron and Other Stories* (1886).

There was hardly a night the summer through when the old cow could be found waiting at the pasture bars; on the contrary, it was her greatest pleasure to hide herself away among the high huckleberry bushes, and though she wore a loud bell she had made the discovery that if one stood perfectly still it would not ring. So Sylvia had to hunt for her until she found her, and call Co'! Co'! with never an answering Moo, until her childish patience was quite spent. If the creature had not given good milk and plenty of it, the case would have seemed very different to her owners. Besides, Sylvia had all the time there was, and very little use to make of it. Sometimes in pleasant weather it was a consolation to look upon the cow's pranks as an intelligent attempt to play hide and seek, and as the child had no playmates she lent herself to this amusement with a good deal of zest. Though this chase had been so long that the wary animal herself had given an unusual signal of her whereabouts, Sylvia had only laughed when she came upon Mistress Moolly at the swamp-side, and urged her affectionately homeward with a twig of birch leaves. The old cow was not inclined to wander farther, she even turned in the right direction for once as they left the pasture, and stepped along the road at a good pace. She was quite ready to be milked now, and seldom stopped to browse. Sylvia wondered what her grandmother would say because they were so late. It was a great while since she had left home at half past five o'clock, but everybody knew the difficulty of making this errand a short one. Mrs. Tilley had chased the hornéd torment too many summer evenings herself to blame any one else for lingering, and was only thankful as she waited that she had Sylvia, nowadays, to give such valuable assistance. The good woman suspected that Sylvia loitered occasionally on her own account; there never was such a child for straying about out-of-doors since the world was made! Everybody said that it was a good change for a little maid who had tried to grow for eight years in a crowded manufacturing town, but, as for Sylvia herself, it seemed as if she never had been alive at all before she came to live at the farm. She thought often with wistful compassion of a wretched dry geranium that belonged to a town neighbor.

"'Afraid of folks,'" old Mrs. Tilley said to herself, with a smile, after she had made the unlikely choice of Sylvia from her daughter's houseful of children, and was returning to the farm. "'Afraid of folks,' they said! I guess she won't be troubled no great with 'em up to the old place!" When they reached the door of the lonely house and stopped to unlock it, the cat came to purr loudly, and rub against them, a deserted pussy, indeed, but fat with young robins, Sylvia whispered that this was a beautiful place to live in, and she never should wish to go home.

The companions followed the shady wood-road, the cow taking slow steps, and the child very fast ones. The cow stopped long at the brook to drink, as if the pasture were not half a swamp, and Sylvia stood still and waited, letting her bare feet cool themselves in the shoal water, while the great twilight moths struck softly against her. She waded on through the brook as the cow moved away, and listened to the thrushes with a heart that beat fast with pleasure. There was a stirring in the great boughs overhead. They were full of little birds and beasts that seemed to be wide-awake, and going about their world, or else saying good-night to each other in sleepy twitters. Sylvia herself felt sleepy as she walked along. However, it was not much farther to the house, and the air was soft and sweet. She was not often in the woods so late as this, and it made her feel as if she were a part of the gray shadows and the moving leaves. She was just thinking how long it seemed since she first came to the farm a year ago, and wondering if everything went on in the noisy town just the same as when she was there; the thought of the great red-faced boy who used to chase and frighten her made her hurry along the path to escape from the shadow of the trees.

Suddenly this little woods-girl is horror-stricken to hear a clear whistle not very far away. Not a bird's whistle, which would have a sort of friendliness, but a boy's whistle, determined, and somewhat aggressive. Sylvia left the cow to whatever sad fate might await her, and stepped discreetly aside into the bushes, but she was just too late. The enemy had discovered her, and called out in a very cheerful and persuasive tone, "Halloa, little girl, how far is it to the road?" and trembling Sylvia answered almost inaudibly, "A good ways."

She did not dare to look boldly at the tall young man, who carried a gun over his shoulder, but she came out of her bush and again followed the cow, while he walked alongside.

"I have been hunting for some birds," the stranger said kindly, "and I have lost my way, and need a friend very much. Don't be afraid," he added gallantly. "Speak up and tell me what your name is, and whether you think I can spend the night at your house, and go out gunning early in the morning."

Sylvia was more alarmed than before. Would not her grandmother consider her much to blame? But who could have foreseen such an accident as this? It did not appear to be her fault, and she hung her head as if the stem of it were broken, but managed to answer "Sylvy," with much effort when her companion again asked her name.

Mrs. Tilley was standing in the doorway when the trio came into view. The cow gave a loud moo by way of explanation.

"Yes, you'd better speak up for yourself, you old trial! Where'd she tucked herself away this time, Sylvy?" Sylvia kept an awed silence; she knew by instinct that her grandmother did not comprehend the gravity of the situation. She must be mistaking the stranger for one of the farmer-lads of the region.

The young man stood his gun beside the door, and dropped a heavy game-bag beside it; then he bade Mrs. Tilley good-evening, and repeated his wayfarer's story, and asked if he could have a night's lodging.

"Put me anywhere you like," he said. "I must be off early in the morning, before day; but I am very hungry, indeed. You can give me some milk at any rate, that's plain."

"Dear sakes, yes," responded the hostess, whose long slumbering hospitality seemed to be easily awakened. "You might fare better if you went out on the main road a mile or so, but you're welcome to what we've got. I'll milk right off, and you make yourself at home. You can sleep on husks or feathers," she proffered graciously. "I raised them all myself. There's good pasturing for geese just below here towards the ma'sh. Now step round and set a plate for the gentleman, Sylvy!" And Sylvia promptly stepped. She was glad to have something to do, and she was hungry herself.

It was a surprise to find so clean and comfortable a little dwelling in this New England wilderness. The young man had known the horrors of its most primitive housekeeping, and the dreary squalor of that level of society which does not rebel at the companionship of hens. This was the best thrift of an old-fashioned farmstead, though on such a small scale that it seemed like a hermitage. He listened eagerly to the old woman's quaint talk, he watched Sylvia's pale face and shining gray eyes with ever growing enthusiasm, and insisted that this was the best supper he had eaten for a month; then, afterward, the new-made friends sat down in the doorway together while the moon came up.

Soon it would be berry-time, and Sylvia was a great help at picking. The cow was a good milker, though a plaguy[1] thing to keep track of, the hostess gossiped frankly, adding presently that she had buried four children, so that Sylvia's mother, and a son (who might be dead) in California were all the children she had left. "Dan, my boy, was a great hand to go gunning," she explained sadly. "I never wanted for pa'tridges or gray squer'ls while he was to home. He's been a great wand'rer, I expect, and he's no hand to write letters. There, I don't blame him, I'd ha' seen the world myself if it had been so I could.

"Sylvia takes after him," the grandmother continued affectionately, after a minute's pause. "There ain't a foot o' ground she don't know her way over, and the wild creatur's counts her one o' themselves. Squer'ls she'll tame to come an' feed right out o' her hands, and all sorts o' birds. Last winter she got the jay-birds to bangeing[2] here, and I believe she'd 'a' scanted herself of her own meals to have plenty to throw out amongst 'em, if I had n't kep' watch. Anything but crows, I tell her, I'm willin' to help support,—though Dan he went an' tamed one o' them that did seem to have reason same as folks. It was round here a good spell after he went away. Dan an' his father they did n't hitch,—but he never held up his head ag'in after Dan had dared him an' gone off."

The guest did not notice this hint of family sorrows in his eager interest in something else.

"So Sylvy knows all about birds, does she?" he exclaimed, as he looked round at the little girl who sat, very demure but increasingly sleepy, in the moonlight. "I am making a collection of birds myself. I have been at it ever since I was a boy." (Mrs. Tilley smiled.) "There are two or three very rare ones I have been hunting for these five years. I mean to get them on my own ground if they can be found."

"Do you cage 'em up?" asked Mrs. Tilley doubtfully, in response to this enthusiastic announcement.

"Oh, no, they're stuffed and preserved, dozens and dozens of them," said the ornithologist, "and I have shot or snared every one myself. I caught a glimpse of a white heron three miles from here on Saturday, and I have followed it in this direction. They have never been found in this district at all. The little white heron, it is," and he turned again to look at Sylvia with the hope of discovering that the rare bird was one of her acquaintances.

But Sylvia was watching a hop-toad in the narrow footpath.

"You would know the heron if you saw it," the stranger continued eagerly. "A queer tall white bird with soft feathers and long thin legs. And it would have a nest perhaps in the top of a high tree, made of sticks, something like a hawk's nest."

Sylvia's heart gave a wild beat; she knew that strange white bird, and had once stolen softly near where it stood in some bright green swamp grass, away over at the other side of the woods. There was an open place where the sunshine always seemed strangely yellow and hot, where tall, nodding rushes grew, and her grandmother had warned her that she might sink in the soft black mud underneath and never be heard of more. Not far beyond were the salt marshes and beyond those was the sea, the sea which Sylvia wondered and dreamed about, but never had looked upon, though its great voice could often be heard above the noise of the woods on stormy nights.

---

[1] Annoying.   [2] Gathering or hanging around leisurely, a New England term.

"I can't think of anything I should like so much as to find that heron's nest," the handsome stranger was saying. "I would give ten dollars to anybody who could show it to me," he added desperately, "and I mean to spend my whole vacation hunting for it if need be. Perhaps it was only migrating, or had been chased out of its own region by some bird of prey."

Mrs. Tilley gave amazed attention to all this, but Sylvia still watched the toad, not divining, as she might have done at some calmer time, that the creature wished to get to its hole under the doorstep, and was much hindered by the unusual spectators at that hour of the evening. No amount of thought, that night, could decide how many wished-for treasures the ten dollars, so lightly spoken of, would buy.

The next day the young sportsman hovered about the woods, and Sylvia kept him company, having lost her first fear of the friendly lad, who proved to be most kind and sympathetic. He told her many things about the birds and what they knew and where they lived and what they did with themselves. And he gave her a jack-knife, which she thought as great a treasure as if she were a desert-islander. All day long he did not once make her troubled or afraid except when he brought down some unsuspecting singing creature from its bough. Sylvia would have liked him vastly better without his gun; she could not understand why he killed the very birds he seemed to like so much. But as the day waned, Sylvia still watched the young man with loving admiration. She had never seen anybody so charming and delightful; the woman's heart, asleep in the child, was vaguely thrilled by a dream of love. Some premonition of that great power stirred and swayed these young foresters who traversed the woodlands with soft-footed silent care. They stopped to listen to a bird's song; they pressed forward again eagerly, parting the branches,—speaking to each other rarely and in whispers; the young man going first and Sylvia following, fascinated, a few steps behind, with her gray eyes dark with excitement.

She grieved because the longed-for white heron was elusive, but she did not lead the guest, she only followed, and there was no such thing as speaking first. The sound of her own unquestioned voice would have terrified her,—it was hard enough to answer yes or no when there was need of that. At last evening began to fall, and they drove the cow home together, and Sylvia smiled with pleasure when they came to the place where she heard the whistle and was afraid only the night before.

II

Half a mile from home, at the farther edge of the woods, where the land was highest, a great pine-tree stood, the last of its generation. Whether it was left for a boundary mark, or for what reason, no one could say; the woodchoppers who had felled its mates were dead and gone long ago, and a whole forest of sturdy trees, pines and oaks and maples, had grown again. But the stately head of this old pine towered above them all and made a landmark for sea and shore miles and miles away. Sylvia knew it well. She had always believed that whoever climbed to the top of it could see the ocean; and the little girl had often laid her hand on the great rough trunk and looked up wistfully at those dark boughs that the wind always stirred, no matter how hot and still the air might be below. Now she thought of the tree with a new excitement, for why, if one climbed it at break of day, could not one see all the world, and easily discover whence the white heron flew, and mark the place, and find the hidden nest?

What a spirit of adventure, what wild ambition! What fancied triumph and delight and glory for the later morning when she could make known the secret! It was almost too real and too great for the childish heart to bear.

All night the door of the little house stood open, and the whippoorwills came and sang upon the very step. The young sportsman and his old hostess were sound asleep, but Sylvia's great design kept her broad awake and watching. She forgot to think of sleep. The short summer night seemed as long as the winter darkness, and at last when the whippoorwills ceased, and she was afraid the morning would after all come too soon, she stole out of the house and followed the pasture path through the woods, hastening toward the open ground beyond, listening with a sense of comfort and companionship to the drowsy twitter of a half-awakened bird, whose perch she had jarred in passing. Alas, if the great wave of human interest which flooded for the first time this dull little life should sweep away the satisfactions of an existence heart to heart with nature and the dumb life of the forest!

There was the huge tree asleep yet in the paling moonlight, and small and hopeful Sylvia began with utmost bravery to mount to the top of it, with tingling, eager blood coursing the channels of her whole frame, with her bare feet and fingers, that pinched and held like bird's claws to the monstrous ladder reaching up, up, almost to the sky itself. First she must mount the white oak tree that grew alongside, where she was almost lost among the dark branches and the green leaves heavy and wet with dew; a bird fluttered off its nest, and a red squirrel ran to and fro and scolded pettishly at the harmless housebreaker. Sylvia felt her way easily. She had often climbed there, and knew that higher still one of the oak's upper branches chafed against the pine trunk, just where its lower boughs were set close together. There, when she made the dangerous pass from one tree to the other, the great enterprise would really begin.

She crept out along the swaying oak limb at last, and took the daring step across into the old pine-tree. The way was harder than she thought; she must reach far and hold fast, the sharp dry twigs caught and held her and scratched her like angry talons, the pitch made her thin little fingers clumsy and stiff as she went round and round the tree's great stem, higher and higher upward. The sparrows and robins in the woods below were beginning to wake and twitter to the dawn, yet it seemed much lighter there aloft in the pine-tree, and the child knew that she must hurry if her project were to be of any use.

The tree seemed to lengthen itself out as she went up, and to reach farther and farther upward. It was like a great main-mast to the voyaging earth; it must truly have been amazed that morning through all its ponderous frame as it felt this determined spark of human spirit creeping and climbing from higher branch to branch. Who knows how steadily the least twigs held themselves to advantage this light, weak creature on her way! The old pine must have loved his new dependent. More than all the hawks, and bats, and moths, and even the sweet-voiced thrushes, was the brave, beating heart of the solitary gray-eyed child. And the tree stood still and held away the winds that June morning while the dawn grew bright in the east.

Sylvia's face was like a pale star, if one had seen it from the ground, when the last thorny bough was past, and she stood trembling and tired but wholly triumphant, high in the tree-top. Yes, there was the sea with the dawning sun making a golden dazzle over it, and toward that glorious east flew two hawks with slow-moving pinions.[3] How low they looked in the air from that height when before one had only seen them far up, and dark against the blue sky. Their gray feathers were as soft as moths; they seemed only a little way from the tree, and Sylvia felt as if she too could go flying away among the clouds. Westward, the woodlands and farms reached miles and miles into the distance; here and there were church steeples, and white villages; truly it was a vast and awesome world.

The birds sang louder and louder. At last the sun came up bewilderingly bright. Sylvia could see the white sails of ships out at sea, and the clouds that were purple and rose-colored and yellow at first began to fade away. Where was the white heron's nest in the sea of green branches, and was this wonderful sight and pageant of the world the only reward for having climbed to such a giddy height? Now look down again, Sylvia, where the green marsh is set among the shining birches and dark hemlocks; there where you saw the white heron once you will see him again; look, look! a white spot of him like a single floating feather comes up from the dead hemlock and grows larger, and rises, and comes close at last, and goes by the landmark pine with steady sweep of wing and outstretched slender neck and crested head. And wait! wait! do not move a foot or a finger, little girl, do not send an arrow of light and consciousness from your two eager eyes, for the heron has perched on a pine bough not far beyond yours, and cries back to his mate on the nest, and plumes his feathers for the new day!

The child gives a long sigh a minute later when a company of shouting catbirds comes also to the tree, and vexed by their fluttering and lawlessness the solemn heron goes away. She knows his secret now, the wild, light, slender bird that floats and wavers, and goes back like an arrow presently to his home in the green world beneath. Then Sylvia, well satisfied, makes her perilous way down again, not daring to look far below the branch she stands on, ready to cry sometimes because her fingers ache and her lamed feet slip. Wondering over and over again what the stranger would say to her, and what he would think when she told him how to find his way straight to the heron's nest.

"Sylvy, Sylvy!" called the busy old grandmother again and again, but nobody answered, and the small husk bed was empty, and Sylvia had disappeared.

The guest waked from a dream, and remembering his day's pleasure hurried to dress himself that it might sooner begin. He was sure from the way the shy little girl looked once or twice yesterday that she had at least seen the white heron, and now she must really be persuaded to tell. Here she comes now, paler than ever, and her worn old frock is torn and tattered, and smeared with pine pitch. The grandmother and the sportsman stand in the door together and question her, and the splendid moment has come to speak of the dead hemlock-tree by the green marsh.

But Sylvia does not speak after all, though the old grandmother fretfully rebukes her, and the young man's kind appealing eyes are looking straight in her own. He can make them rich with money; he has promised it, and they are poor now. He is so well worth making happy, and he waits to hear the story she can tell.

No, she must keep silence! What is it that suddenly forbids her and makes her dumb? Has she been nine years growing, and now, when the great world for the

---

[3] Wings or wing feathers.

first time puts out a hand to her, must she thrust it aside for a bird's sake? The murmur of the pine's green branches is in her ears, she remembers how the white heron came flying through the golden air and how they watched the sea and the morning together, and Sylvia cannot speak; she cannot tell the heron's secret and give its life away.

Dear loyalty, that suffered a sharp pang as the guest went away disappointed later in the day, that could have served and followed him and loved him as a dog loves! Many a night Sylvia heard the echo of his whistle haunting the pasture path as she came home with the loitering cow. She forgot even her sorrow at the sharp report of his gun and the piteous sight of thrushes and sparrows dropping silent to the ground, their songs hushed and their pretty feathers stained and wet with blood. Were the birds better friends than their hunter might have been,—who can tell? Whatever treasures were lost to her, woodlands and summer-time, remember! Bring your gifts and graces and tell your secrets to this lonely country child!

1886

MISS TEMPY'S WATCHERS*

The time of year was April; the place was a small farming town in New Hampshire, remote from any railroad. One by one the lights had been blown out in the scattered houses near Miss Tempy Dent's; but as her neighbors took a last look out-of-doors, their eyes turned with instinctive curiosity toward the old house, where a lamp burned steadily. They gave a little sigh. "Poor Miss Tempy!" said more than one bereft acquaintance; for the good woman lay dead in her north chamber, and the light was a watcher's light. The funeral was set for the next day, at one o'clock.

The watchers were two of the oldest friends, Mrs. Crowe and Sarah Ann Binson. They were sitting in the kitchen, because it seemed less awesome than the unused best room, and they beguiled the long hours by steady conversation. One would think that neither topics nor opinions would hold out, at that rate, all through the long spring night; but there was a certain degree of excitement just then, and the two women had risen to an unusual level of expressiveness and confidence. Each had already told the other more than one fact that she had determined to keep secret; they were again and again tempted into statements that either would have found impossible by daylight. Mrs. Crowe was knitting a blue yarn stocking for her husband; the foot was already so long that it seemed as if she must have forgotten to narrow it at the proper time. Mrs. Crowe knew exactly what she was about, however; she was of a much cooler disposition than Sister Binson, who made futile attempts at some sewing, only to drop her work into her lap whenever the talk was most engaging.

Their faces were interesting,—of the dry, shrewd, quick-witted New England type, with thin hair twisted neatly back out of the way. Mrs. Crowe could look vague and benignant, and Miss Binson was, to quote her neighbors, a little too

---

* First published in the *Atlantic Monthly* in March 1888. A watcher is a person who keeps watch over the dead or the sick.

sharp-set; but the world knew that she had need to be, with the load she must carry of supporting an inefficient widowed sister and six unpromising and unwilling nieces and nephews. The eldest boy was at last placed with a good man to learn the mason's trade. Sarah Ann Binson, for all her sharp, anxious aspect, never defended herself, when her sister whined and fretted. She was told every week of her life that the poor children never would have had to lift a finger if their father had lived, and yet she had kept her steadfast way with the little farm, and patiently taught the young people many useful things, for which, as everybody said, they would live to thank her. However pleasureless her life appeared to outward view, it was brimful of pleasure to herself.

Mrs. Crowe, on the contrary, was well to do, her husband being a rich farmer and an easy-going man. She was a stingy woman, but for all that she looked kindly; and when she gave away anything, or lifted a finger to help anybody, it was thought a great piece of beneficence, and a compliment, indeed, which the recipient accepted with twice as much gratitude as double the gift that came from a poorer and more generous acquaintance. Everybody liked to be on good terms with Mrs. Crowe. Socially she stood much higher than Sarah Ann Binson. They were both old schoolmates and friends of Temperance Dent, who had asked them, one day, not long before she died, if they would not come together and look after the house, and manage everything, when she was gone. She may have had some hope that they might become closer friends in this period of intimate partnership, and that the richer woman might better understand the burdens of the poorer. They had not kept the house the night before; they were too weary with the care of their old friend, whom they had not left until all was over.

There was a brook which ran down the hillside very near the house, and the sound of it was much louder than usual. When there was silence in the kitchen, the busy stream had a strange insistence in its wild voice, as if it tried to make the watchers understand something that related to the past.

"I declare, I can't begin to sorrow for Tempy yet. I am so glad to have her at rest," whispered Mrs. Crowe. "It is strange to set here without her, but I can't make it clear that she has gone. I feel as if she had got easy and dropped off to sleep, and I'm more scared about waking her up than knowing any other feeling."

"Yes," said Sarah Ann, "it's just like that, ain't it? But I tell you we are goin' to miss her worse than we expect. She's helped me through with many a trial, has Temperance. I ain't the only one who says the same, neither."

These words were spoken as if there were a third person listening; somebody beside Mrs. Crowe. The watchers could not rid their minds of the feeling that they were being watched themselves. The spring wind whistled in the window crack, now and then, and buffeted the little house in a gusty way that had a sort of companionable effect. Yet, on the whole, it was a very still night, and the watchers spoke in a half-whisper.

"She was the freest-handed woman that ever I knew," said Mrs. Crowe, decidedly. "According to her means, she gave away more than anybody. I used to tell her 't wa'n't right. I used really to be afraid that she went without too much, for we have a duty to ourselves."

Sister Binson looked up in a half-amused, unconscious way, and then recollected herself.

Mrs. Crowe met her look with a serious face. "It ain't so easy for me to give as it is for some," she said simply, but with an effort which was made possible only by the occasion. "I should like to say, while Tempy is laying here yet in her own house, that she has been a constant lesson to me. Folks are too kind, and shame me with thanks for what I do. I ain't such a generous woman as poor Tempy was, for all she had nothin' to do with, as one may say."

Sarah Binson was much moved at this confession, and was even pained and touched by the unexpected humility. "You have a good many calls on you"—she began, and then left her kind little compliment half finished.

"Yes, yes, but I've got means enough. My disposition's more of a cross to me as I grow older, and I made up my mind this morning that Tempy's example should be my pattern henceforth." She began to knit faster than ever.

"'T ain't no use to get morbid: that's what Tempy used to say herself," said Sarah Ann, after a minute's silence. "Ain't it strange to say 'used to say'?" and her own voice choked a little. "She never did like to hear folks git goin' about themselves."

"'T was only because they're apt to do it so as other folks will say 't was n't so, an' praise 'em up," humbly replied Mrs. Crowe, "and that ain't my object. There wa'n't a child but what Tempy set herself to work to see what she could do to please it. One time my brother's folks had been stopping here in the summer, from Massachusetts. The children was all little, and they broke up a sight of toys, and left 'em when they were going away. Tempy come right up after they rode by, to see if she could n't help me set the house to rights, and she caught me just as I was going to fling some of the clutter into the stove. I was kind of tired out, starting 'em off in season. 'Oh, give me them!' says she, real pleading; and she wropped 'em up and took 'em home with her when she went, and she mended 'em up and stuck 'em together, and made some young one or other happy with every blessed one. You'd thought I'd done her the biggest favor. 'No thanks to me. I should ha' burnt 'em, Tempy,' says I."

"Some of 'em came to our house, I know," said Miss Binson. "She'd take a lot o' trouble to please a child, 'stead o' shoving of it out o' the way, like the rest of us when we're drove."

"I can tell you the biggest thing she ever done, and I don't know there's anybody left but me to tell it. I don't want it forgot," Sarah Binson went on, looking up at the clock to see how the night was going. "It was that pretty-looking Trevor girl, who taught the Corners school, and married so well afterwards, out in New York State. You remember her, I dare say?"

"Certain," said Mrs. Crowe, with an air of interest.

"She was a splendid scholar, folks said, and give the school a great start; but she'd overdone herself getting her education, and working to pay for it, and she all broke down one spring, and Tempy made her come and stop with her a while,—you remember that? Well, she had an uncle, her mother's brother, out in Chicago, who was well off and friendly, and used to write to Lizzie Trevor, and I dare say make her some presents; but he was a lively, driving man, and did n't take time to stop and think about his folks. He had n't seen her since she was a little girl. Poor Lizzie was so pale and weakly that she just got through the term o' school. She looked as if she was just going straight off in a decline. Tempy, she cosseted[1] her up a while, and then, next thing folks knew, she was tellin' round

---

[1] Pampered.

how Miss Trevor had gone to see her uncle, and meant to visit Niagary Falls on the way, and stop over night. Now I happened to know, in ways I won't dwell on to explain, that the poor girl was in debt for her schoolin' when she come here, and her last quarter's pay had just squared it off at last, and left her without a cent ahead, hardly; but it had fretted her thinking of it, so she paid it all; those might have dunned her that she owed it to. An' I taxed Tempy about the girl's goin' off on such a journey till she owned up, rather 'n have Lizzie blamed, that she'd given her sixty dollars, same 's if she was rolling in riches, and sent her off to have a good rest and vacation."

"Sixty dollars!" exclaimed Mrs. Crowe. "Tempy only had ninety dollars a year that came in to her; rest of her livin' she got by helpin' about, with what she raised off this little piece o' ground, sand one side an' clay the other. An' how often I've heard her tell, years ago, that she'd rather see Niagary than any other sight in the world!"

The women looked at each other in silence; the magnitude of the generous sacrifice was almost too great for their comprehension.

"She was just poor enough to do that!" declared Mrs. Crowe at last, in an abandonment of feeling. "Say what you may, I feel humbled to the dust," and her companion ventured to say nothing. She never had given away sixty dollars at once, but it was simply because she never had it to give. It came to her very lips to say in explanation, "Tempy was so situated;" but she checked herself in time, for she would not betray her own loyal guarding of a dependent household.

"Folks say a great deal of generosity, and this one's being public-sperited, and that one free-handed about giving," said Mrs. Crowe, who was a little nervous in the silence. "I suppose we can't tell the sorrow it would be to some folks not to give, same 's 't would be to me not to save. I seem kind of made for that, as if 't was what I'd got to do. I should feel sights better about it if I could make it evident what I was savin' for. If I had a child, now, Sarah Ann," and her voice was a little husky,—"if I had a child, I should think I was heapin' of it up because he was the one trained by the Lord to scatter it again for good. But here's Mr. Crowe and me, we can't do anything with money, and both of us like to keep things same 's they 've always been. Now Priscilla Dance was talking away like a mill-clapper,[2] week before last. She'd think I would go right off and get one o' them new-fashioned gilt-and-white papers for the best room, and some new furniture, an' a marble-top table. And I looked at her, all struck up. 'Why,' says I, 'Priscilla, that nice old velvet paper ain't hurt a mite. I should n't feel 't was my best room without it. Dan'el says 't is the first thing he can remember rubbin' his little baby fingers on to it, and how splendid he thought them red roses was.' I maintain," continued Mrs. Crowe stoutly, "that folks wastes sights o' good money doin' just such foolish things. Tearin' out the insides o' meetin'-houses, and fixin' the pews different; 't was good enough as 't was with mendin'; then times come, an' they want to put it all back same 's 't was before."

This touched upon an exciting subject to active members of the parish. Miss Binson and Mrs. Crowe belonged to opposite parties, and had at one time come as near hard feelings as they could, and yet escape them. Each hastened to speak of other things and to show her untouched friendliness.

"I do agree with you," said Sister Binson, "that few of us know what use to

2 A person who talks a lot in a rapid, mechanical way.

make of money, beyond every-day necessities. You've seen more o' the world than I have, and know what's expected. When it comes to taste and judgment about such things, I ought to defer to others;" and with this modest avowal the critical moment passed when there might have been an improper discussion.

In the silence that followed, the fact of their presence in a house of death grew more clear than before. There was something disturbing in the noise of a mouse gnawing at the dry boards of a closet wall near by. Both the watchers looked up anxiously at the clock; it was almost the middle of the night, and the whole world seemed to have left them alone with their solemn duty. Only the brook was awake.

"Perhaps we might give a look up-stairs now," whispered Mrs. Crowe, as if she hoped to hear some reason against their going just then to the chamber of death; but Sister Binson rose, with a serious and yet satisfied countenance, and lifted the small lamp from the table. She was much more used to watching than Mrs. Crowe, and much less affected by it. They opened the door into a small entry with a steep stairway; they climbed the creaking stairs, and entered the cold upper room on tiptoe. Mrs. Crowe's heart began to beat very fast as the lamp was put on a high bureau, and made long, fixed shadows about the walls. She went hesitatingly toward the solemn shape under its white drapery, and felt a sense of remonstrance as Sarah Ann gently, but in a business-like way, turned back the thin sheet.

"Seems to me she looks pleasanter and pleasanter," whispered Sarah Ann Binson impulsively, as they gazed at the white face with its wonderful smile. "Tomorrow 't will all have faded out. I do believe they kind of wake up a day or two after they die, and it's then they go." She replaced the light covering, and they both turned quickly away; there was a chill in this upper room.

"'T is a great thing for anybody to have got through, ain't it?" said Mrs. Crowe softly, as she began to go down the stairs on tiptoe. The warm air from the kitchen beneath met them with a sense of welcome and shelter.

"I don' know why it is, but I feel as near again to Tempy down here as I do up there," replied Sister Binson. "I feel as if the air was full of her, kind of. I can sense things, now and then, that she seems to say. Now I never was one to take up with no nonsense of sperits and such, but I declare I felt as if she told me just now to put some more wood into the stove."

Mrs. Crowe preserved a gloomy silence. She had suspected before this that her companion was of a weaker and more credulous disposition than herself. "'T is a great thing to have got through," she repeated, ignoring definitely all that had last been said. "I suppose you know as well as I that Tempy was one that always feared death. Well, it's all put behind her now; she knows what 't is." Mrs. Crowe gave a little sigh, and Sister Binson's quick sympathies were stirred toward this other old friend, who also dreaded the great change.

"I'd never like to forgit almost those last words Tempy spoke plain to me," she said gently, like the comforter she truly was. "She looked up at me once or twice, that last afternoon after I come to set by her, and let Mis' Owen go home; and I says, 'Can I do anything to ease you, Tempy?' and the tears come into my eyes so I could n't see what kind of a nod she give me. 'No, Sarah Ann, you can't, dear,' says she; and then she got her breath again, and says she, looking at me real meanin', 'I'm only a-gettin' sleepier and sleepier; that's all there is,' says she, and smiled up at me kind of wishful, and shut her eyes. I knew well enough all she meant. She'd been lookin' out for a chance to tell me, and I don' know's she ever said much afterwards."

Mrs. Crowe was not knitting; she had been listening too eagerly. "Yes, 't will be a comfort to think of that sometimes," she said, in acknowledgment.

"I know that old Dr. Prince said once, in evenin' meetin', that he'd watched by many a dyin' bed, as we well knew, and enough o' his sick folks had been scared o' dyin' their whole lives through; but when they come to the last, he'd never seen one but was willin', and most were glad, to go. ''T is as natural as bein' born or livin' on,' he said. I don't know what had moved him to speak that night. You know he wa'n't in the habit of it, and 't was the monthly concert of prayer for foreign missions anyways," said Sarah Ann; "but 't was a great stay to the mind to listen to his words of experience."

"There never was a better man," responded Mrs. Crowe, in a really cheerful tone. She had recovered from her feeling of nervous dread, the kitchen was so comfortable with lamplight and firelight; and just then the old clock began to tell the hour of twelve with leisurely whirring strokes.

Sister Binson laid aside her work, and rose quickly and went to the cupboard. "We'd better take a little to eat," she explained. "The night will go fast after this. I want to know if you went and made some o' your nice cupcake, while you was home to-day?" she asked, in a pleased tone; and Mrs. Crowe acknowledged such a gratifying piece of thoughtfulness for this humble friend who denied herself all luxuries. Sarah Ann brewed a generous cup of tea, and the watchers drew their chairs up to the table presently, and quelled their hunger with good country appetites. Sister Binson put a spoon into a small, old-fashioned glass of preserved quince, and passed it to her friend. She was most familiar with the house, and played the part of hostess. "Spread some o' this on your bread and butter," she said to Mrs. Crowe. "Tempy wanted me to use some three or four times, but I never felt to. I know she'd like to have us comfortable now, and would urge us to make a good supper, poor dear."

"What excellent preserves she did make!" mourned Mrs. Crowe. "None of us has got her light hand at doin' things tasty. She made the most o' everything, too. Now, she only had that one old quince-tree down in the far corner of the piece, but she'd go out in the spring and tend to it, and look at it so pleasant, and kind of expect the old thorny thing into bloomin'."

"She was just the same with folks," said Sarah Ann. "And she'd never git more 'n a little apernful o' quinces, but she'd have every mite o' goodness out o' those, and set the glasses up onto her best-room closet shelf, *so* pleased. 'T wa'n't but a week ago to-morrow mornin' I fetched her a little taste o' jelly in a teaspoon; and she says, 'Thank ye,' and took it, an' the minute she tasted it she looked up at me as worried as could be. 'Oh, I don't want to eat that,' says she. 'I always keep that in case o' sickness.' 'You're goin' to have the good o' one tumbler yourself,' says I. 'I'd just like to know who's sick now, if you ain't!' An' she could n't help laughin', I spoke up so smart. Oh, dear me, how I shall miss talkin' over things with her! She always sensed things, and got just the p'int you meant."

"She didn't begin to age until two or three years ago, did she?" asked Mrs. Crowe. "I never saw anybody keep her looks as Tempy did. She looked young long after I begun to feel like an old woman. The doctor used to say 't was her young heart, and I don't know but what he was right. How she did do for other folks! There was one spell she was n't at home a day to a fortnight. She got most of her livin' so, and that made her own potatoes and things last her through. None o' the young folks could get married without her, and all the old ones was disappointed if she wa'n't round when they was down with sickness and had to go. An' cleanin', or tailorin' for boys, or rug-hookin',—there was nothin' but what she could do as handy as most. 'I do love to work,'—ain't you heard her say that twenty times a week?"

Sarah Ann Binson nodded, and began to clear away the empty plates. "We may want a taste o' somethin' more towards mornin'," she said. "There's plenty in the closet here; and in case some comes from a distance to the funeral, we'll have a little table spread after we get back to the house."

"Yes, I was busy all the mornin'. I've cooked up a sight o' things to bring over," said Mrs. Crowe. "I felt 't was the last I could do for her."

They drew their chairs near the stove again, and took up their work. Sister Binson's rocking-chair creaked as she rocked; the brook sounded louder than ever. It was more lonely when nobody spoke, and presently Mrs. Crowe returned to her thoughts of growing old.

"Yes, Tempy aged all of a sudden. I remember I asked her if she felt as well as common, one day, and she laughed at me good. There, when Mr. Crowe begun to look old, I could n't help feeling as if somethin' ailed him, and like as not 't was somethin' he was goin' to git right over, and I dosed him for it stiddy, half of one summer."

"How many things we shall be wanting to ask Tempy!" exclaimed Sarah Ann Binson, after a long pause. "I can't make up my mind to doin' without her. I wish folks could come back just once, and tell us how 'tis where they 've gone. Seems then we could do without 'em better."

The brook hurried on, the wind blew about the house now and then; the house itself was a silent place, and the supper, the warm fire, and an absence of any new topics for conversation made the watchers drowsy. Sister Binson closed her eyes first, to rest them for a minute; and Mrs. Crowe glanced at her compassionately, with a new sympathy for the hard-worked little woman. She made up her mind to let Sarah Ann have a good rest, while she kept watch alone; but in a few minutes her own knitting was dropped, and she, too, fell asleep. Overhead, the pale shape of Tempy Dent, the outworn body of that generous, loving-hearted, simple soul, slept on also in its white raiment. Perhaps Tempy herself stood near, and saw her own life and its surroundings with new understanding. Perhaps she herself was the only watcher.

Later, by some hours, Sarah Ann Binson woke with a start. There was a pale light of dawn outside the small windows. Inside the kitchen, the lamp burned dim. Mrs. Crowe awoke, too.

"I think Tempy 'd be the first to say 't was just as well we both had some rest," she said, not without a guilty feeling.

Her companion went to the outer door, and opened it wide. The fresh air was none too cold, and the brook's voice was not nearly so loud as it had been in the midnight darkness. She could see the shapes of the hills, and the great shadows that lay across the lower country. The east was fast growing bright.

"'T will be a beautiful day for the funeral," she said, and turned again, with a sigh, to follow Mrs. Crowe up the stairs.

1888

Mary E. Wilkins Freeman
(1852–1930)

Like many of her female characters, Mary Eleanor Wilkins grew up in small, cottage-industry towns—first Randolph, Massachusetts, where she was born in 1852, and later Brattleboro, Vermont, where her family moved when she was fifteen. These small towns were a rich source of regional material for her fiction, as South Berwick, Maine, was for Sarah Orne Jewett. The Wilkins family, however, struggled economically and personally. By the time Mary was thirty-one years old, her siblings and parents had died, leaving her alone and financially bereft. In the midst of this misfortune, she slowly began to achieve literary success, writing children's poetry and some adult fiction. She won a prize of fifty dollars in a short-story contest in 1882 and was soon published in such prominent magazines as *Harper's Bazar* (now spelled *"Bazaar"*).

Nevertheless, Wilkins returned to Randolph for comfort and security. She spent the next twenty years there with her childhood friend Mary John Wales. While Wales cared for her, Wilkins wrote *A Humble Romance and Other Stories* (1887) and *A New England Nun and Other Stories* (1891), two of her best works. Soon after the latter was published, Wilkins confronted a dilemma akin to that of Louisa Ellis in "A New England Nun." She met Dr. Charles Freeman in 1892; after deliberating whether or not ever to marry (and once breaking their engagement), she married him when she was forty-nine. The newlyweds moved to New Jersey. But Dr. Freeman suffered from alcoholism and was institutionalized several times. This "dismal" marriage ended with a legal separation in 1922, a year before his death; Mary Freeman herself died in 1930.

Recognized as a premier local-color writer, praised by Henry James for her grasp of character, and awarded the W. D. Howells Medal for Fiction in 1926, Freeman published six volumes of children's stories and twenty volumes of fiction, both novels and short stories, for adults. Her best stories—among them "A Village Singer," "The Revolt of Mother," and "A New England Nun," all from *A New England Nun*—chronicle the efforts of older women to maintain their independence and their convictions (commonly in the face of community scorn) in rural New England towns where partriarchal standards remained a powerful force even after the Civil War had considerably reduced the male population.

If many of Freeman's characters emerge from the sharp angles of New England life, they also seem spun out of the cloth of Freeman's resolute self-awareness: impoverished women determined to maintain their own identities, insistent upon their dignity and independence, at once heroic and ridiculous in their steadfast concern for diminutive issues. Typically, their victories are small, earned by a stubbornness Freeman controls with a disciplined and dispassionate perspective—and a laconic style that blocks sentimentality and courts ironic humor. Freeman is a a special type of realist, one who—at her best— explores the ruins of the romantic spirit and thereby shows in compelling detail the high cost of remaining human in a world unmindful of the individual spirit.

Suggested Readings: *The Shoulders of Atlas,* 1908, rpt. 1977. *A New England Nun and Other Stories,* 1920. *The Best Stories of Mary Wilkins Freeman,* ed. H. Lanier, 1927. B. L. Kendrick, ed., *The Infant Sphinx: Collected Letters of Mary E. Wilkins Freeman,* 1985. E. Foster, *Mary E. Wilkins Freeman,* 1956. P. D. Westbrook, *Mary Wilkins Freeman,* 1967.

Text Used: *A New England Nun and Other Stories,* 1891.

A VILLAGE SINGER*

The trees were in full leaf, a heavy south wind was blowing, and there was a loud murmur among the new leaves. The people noticed it, for it was the first time that year that the trees had so murmured in the wind. The spring had come with a rush during the last few days.

The murmur of the trees sounded loud in the village church, where the people sat waiting for the service to begin. The windows were open; it was a very warm Sunday for May.

The church was already filled with this soft sylvan music—the tender harmony of the leaves and the south wind, and the sweet, desultory whistles of birds—when the choir arose and began to sing.

In the centre of the row of women singers stood Alma Way. All the people stared at her, and turned their ears critically. She was the new leading soprano. Candace Whitcomb, the old one, who had sung in the choir for forty years, had lately been given her dismissal. The audience considered that her voice had grown too cracked and uncertain on the upper notes. There had been much complaint, and after long deliberation the church-officers had made known their decision as mildly as possible to the old singer. She had sung for the last time the Sunday before, and Alma Way had been engaged to take her place. With the exception of the organist, the leading soprano was the only paid musician in the large choir. The salary was very modest, still the village people considered it large for a young woman. Alma was from the adjoining village of East Derby; she had quite a local reputation as a singer.

Now she fixed her large solemn blue eyes; her long, delicate face, which had been pretty, turned paler; the blue flowers on her bonnet trembled; her little thin gloved hands, clutching the singing-book, shook perceptibly; but she sang out bravely. That most formidable mountain-height of the world, self-distrust and timidity, arose before her, but her nerves were braced for its ascent. In the midst of the hymn she had a solo; her voice rang out piercingly sweet; the people nodded admiringly at each other; but suddenly there was a stir; all the faces turned toward the windows on the south side of the church. Above the din of the wind and the birds, above Alma Way's sweetly straining tones, arose another female voice, singing another hymn to another tune.

"It's her," the women whispered to each other; they were half aghast, half smiling.

Candace Whitcomb's cottage stood close to the south side of the church. She was playing on her parlor organ, and singing, to drown out the voice of her rival.

Alma caught her breath; she almost stopped; the hymn-book waved like a fan; then she went on. But the long husky drone of the parlor organ and the shrill clamor of the other voice seemed louder than anything else.

When the hymn was finished, Alma sat down. She felt faint; the woman next her slipped a peppermint into her hand. "It ain't worth minding," she whispered, vigorously. Alma tried to smile; down in the audience a young man was watching her with a kind of fierce pity.

In the last hymn Alma had another solo. Again the parlor organ droned above

---

* Collected in Freeman's *A New England Nun and Other Stories* (1891).

the carefully delicate accompaniment of the church organ, and again Candace Whitcomb's voice clamored forth in another tune.

After the benediction, the other singers pressed around Alma. She did not say much in return for their expressions of indignation and sympathy. She wiped her eyes furtively once or twice, and tried to smile. William Emmons, the choir leader, elderly, stout, and smooth-faced, stood over her, and raised his voice. He was the old musical dignitary of the village, the leader of the choral club and the singing-schools. "A most outrageous proceeding," he said. People had coupled his name with Candace Whitcomb's. The old bachelor tenor and old maiden soprano had been wont to walk together to her home next door after the Saturday night rehearsals, and they had sung duets to the parlor organ. People had watched sharply her old face, on which the blushes of youth sat pitifully, when William Emmons entered the singing-seats. They wondered if he would ever ask her to marry him.

And now he said further to Alma Way that Candace Whitcomb's voice had failed utterly of late, that she sang shockingly, and ought to have had sense enough to know it.

When Alma went down into the audience-room, in the midst of the chattering singers, who seemed to have descended, like birds, from song flights to chirps, the minister approached her. He had been waiting to speak to her. He was a steady-faced, fleshy old man, who had preached from that one pulpit over forty years. He told Alma, in his slow way, how much he regretted the annoyance to which she had been subjected, and intimated that he would endeavor to prevent a recurrence of it. "Miss Whitcomb—must be—reasoned with," said he; he had a slight hesitation of speech, not an impediment. It was as if his thoughts did not slide readily into his words, although both were present. He walked down the aisle with Alma, and bade her good-morning when he saw Wilson Ford waiting for her in the doorway. Everybody knew that Wilson Ford and Alma were lovers; they had been for the last ten years.

Alma colored softly, and made a little imperceptible motion with her head; her silk dress and the lace on her mantle fluttered, but she did not speak. Neither did Wilson, although they had not met before that day. They did not look at each other's faces—they seemed to see each other without that—and they walked along side by side.

They reached the gate before Candace Whitcomb's little house. Wilson looked past the front yard, full of pink and white spikes on flowering bushes, at the lace-curtained windows; a thin white profile, stiffly inclined, apparently over a book, was visible at one of them. Wilson gave his head a shake. He was a stout man, with features so strong that they overcame his flesh. "I'm going up home with you, Alma," said he, "and then—I'm just coming back, to give Aunt Candace one blowing up."

"Oh, don't, Wilson."

"Yes, I shall. If you want to stand this kind of a thing you may; I sha'n't."

"There's no need of your talking to her. Mr. Pollard's going to."

"Did he say he was?"

"Yes. I think he's going in before the afternoon meeting, from what he said."

"Well, there's one thing about it, if she does that thing again this afternoon, I'll go in there and break that old organ up into kindling-wood." Wilson set his mouth hard, and shook his head again.

Alma gave little side glances up at him, her tone was deprecatory, but her face was full of soft smiles. "I suppose she does feel dreadfully about it," said she. "I can't help feeling kind of guilty, taking her place."

"I don't see how you're to blame. It's outrageous, her acting so."

"The choir gave her a photograph album last week, didn't they?"

"Yes. They went there last Thursday night, and gave her an album and a surprise-party. She ought to behave herself."

"Well, she's sung there so long, I suppose it must be dreadful hard for her to give it up."

Other people going home from church were very near Wilson and Alma. She spoke softly that they might not hear; he did not lower his voice in the least. Presently Alma stopped before a gate.

"What are you stopping here for?" asked Wilson.

"Minnie Lansing wanted me to come and stay with her this noon."

"You're going home with me."

"I'm afraid I'll put your mother out."

"Put mother out! I told her you were coming, this morning. She's got all ready for you. Come along; don't stand here."

He did not tell Alma of the pugnacious spirit with which his mother had received the announcement of her coming, and how she had stayed at home to prepare the dinner, and make a parade of her hard work and her injury.

Wilson's mother was the reason why he did not marry Alma. He would not take his wife home to live with her, and was unable to support separate establishments. Alma was willing enough to be married and put up with Wilson's mother, but she did not complain of his decision. Her delicate blond features grew sharper, and her blue eyes more hollow. She had had a certain fine prettiness, but now she was losing it, and beginning to look old, and there was a prim, angular, old maiden carriage about her narrow shoulders.

Wilson never noticed it, and never thought of Alma as not possessed of eternal youth, or capable of losing or regretting it.

"Come along, Alma," said he; and she followed meekly after him down the street.

Soon after they passed Candace Whitcomb's house, the minister went up the front walk and rang the bell. The pale profile at the window had never stirred as he opened the gate and came up the walk. However, the door was promptly opened, in response to his ring. "Good-morning, Miss Whitcomb," said the minister.

"*Good*-morning." Candace gave a sweeping toss of her head as she spoke. There was a fierce upward curl to her thin nostrils and her lips, as if she scented an adversary. Her black eyes had two tiny cold sparks of fury in them, like an enraged bird's. She did not ask the minister to enter, but he stepped lumberingly into the entry, and she retreated rather than led the way into her little parlor. He settled into the great rocking-chair and wiped his face. Candace sat down again in her old place by the window. She was a tall woman, but very slender and full of pliable motions, like a blade of grass.

"It's a—very pleasant day," said the minister.

Candace made no reply. She sat still, with her head drooping. The wind stirred the looped lace-curtains; a tall rose-tree outside the window waved; soft shadows floated through the room. Candace's parlor organ stood in front of an open window that faced the church; on the corner was a pitcher with a bunch of white lilacs. The whole room was scented with them. Presently the minister looked over at them and sniffed pleasantly.

"You have—some beautiful—lilacs there."

Candace did not speak. Every line of her slender figure looked flexible, but it was a flexibility more resistant than rigor.

The minister looked at her. He filled up the great rocking-chair; his arms in his shiny black coat-sleeves rested squarely and comfortably upon the hair-cloth arms of the chair.

"Well, Miss Whitcomb, I suppose I—may as well come to—the point. There was—a little—matter I wished to speak to you about. I don't suppose you were— at least I can't suppose you were—aware of it, but—this morning, during the singing by the choir, you played and—sung a little too—loud. That is, with—the windows open. It—disturbed us—a little. I hope you won't feel hurt—my dear Miss Candace, but I knew you would rather I would speak of it, for I knew—you would be more disturbed than anybody else at the idea of such a thing."

Candace did not raise her eyes; she looked as if his words might sway her through the window. "I ain't disturbed at it," said she. "I did it on purpose; I meant to."

The minister looked at her.

"You needn't look at me. I know jest what I'm about. I sung the way I did on purpose, an' I'm goin' to do it again, an' I'd like to see you stop me. I guess I've got a right to set down to my own organ, an' sing a psalm tune on a Sabbath day, 'f I want to; an' there ain't no amount of talkin' an' palaverin' a-goin' to stop me. See there!" Candace swung aside her skirts a little. "Look at that!"

The minister looked. Candace's feet were resting on a large red-plush photograph album.

"Makes a nice footstool, don't it?" said she.

The minister looked at the album, then at her; there was a slowly gathering alarm in his face; he began to think she was losing her reason.

Candace had her eyes full upon him now, and her head up. She laughed, and her laugh was almost a snarl. "Yes; I thought it would make a beautiful footstool," said she. "I've been wantin' one for some time." Her tone was full of vicious irony.

"Why miss—" began the minister; but she interrupted him:

"I know what you're a-goin' to say, Mr. Pollard, an' now I'm goin' to have my say; I'm a-goin' to speak. I want to know what you think of folks that pretend to be Christians treatin' anybody the way they've treated me? Here I've sung in those singin'-seats forty year. I 'ain't never missed a Sunday, except when I've been sick, an' I've gone an' sung a good many times when I'd better been in bed, an' now I'm turned out without a word of warnin'. My voice is jest as good as ever 'twas; there can't anybody say it ain't. It wa'n't ever quite so high-pitched as that Way girl's, mebbe; but she flats the whole durin' time. My voice is as good n' high to-day as it was twenty year ago; an' if it wa'n't, I'd like to know where the Christianity comes in. I'd like to know if it wouldn't be more to the credit of folks in a church to keep an old singer an' an old minister, if they didn't sing an' hold forth quite so smart as they used to, ruther than turn 'em off an' hurt their feelin's. I guess it would be full as much to the glory of God. S'pose the singin' an' the preachin' wa'n't quite so good, what difference would it make? Salvation don't hang on anybody's hittin' a high note, that I ever heard of. Folks are gettin' as high-steppin' an' fussy in a meetin'-house as they are in a tavern, nowadays. S'pose they should turn you off, Mr. Pollard, come an' give you a photograph album, an' tell you to clear out, how'd you like it? I ain't findin' any fault with your preachin'; it was always good enough to suit me; but it don't stand to reason folks'll be as took up with your sermons as when you was a young man. You can't expect it. S'pose they should turn you out in your old age, an' call in some young bob squirt, how'd you feel? There's William Emmons, too; he's three years older'n I am, if he does lead the choir an' run all the singin' in town. If my voice has gi'en out, it stan's to reason his has. It ain't, though. William Emmons sings jest as well as he ever did. Why don't they turn him out the way they have me, an' give him a photograph album? I dun know but it would be a good idea to send everybody, as soon as they get a little old an' gone by, an' young folks begin to push, onto some desert island, an' give 'em each a photograph album. Then they can sit down an' look at pictures the rest of their days. Mebbe government 'll take it up.

"There they come here last week Thursday, all the choir, jest about eight o'clock in the evenin', an' pretended they'd come to give me a nice little surprise. Surprise! h'm! Brought cake an' oranges, an' was jest as nice as they could be, an' I was real tickled. I never had a surprise-party before in my life. Jenny Carr she played, an' they wanted me to sing alone, an' I never suspected a thing. I've been made ever since to think what a fool I was, an' how they must have laughed in their sleeves.

"When they'd gone I found this photograph album on the table, all done up as nice as you please, an' directed to Miss Candace Whitcomb from her many friends, an' I opened it, an' there was the letter inside givin' me notice to quit.

"If they'd gone about it any decent way, told me right out honest that they'd got tired of me, an' wanted Alma Way to sing instead of me, I wouldn't minded so much; I should have been hurt 'nough, for I'd felt as if some that had pretended to be my friends wa'n't; but it wouldn't have been as bad as this. They said in the letter that they'd always set great value on my services, an' it wa'n't from any lack of appreciation that they turned me off, but they thought the duty was gettin' a little too arduous for me. H'm! I hadn't complained. If they'd turned me right out fair an' square, showed me the door, an' said, 'Here, you get out,' but to go an' spill molasses, as it were, all over the threshold, trying' to make me think it's all nice an' sweet—

"I'd sent that photograph album back quick's I could pack it, but I didn't know who started it, so I've used it for a footstool. It's all it's good for, 'cordin' to my way of thinkin'. An' I ain't been particular to get the dust off my shoes before I used it neither."

Mr. Pollard, the minister, sat staring. He did not look at Candace; his eyes were fastened upon a point straight ahead. He had a look of helpless solidity, like a block of granite. This country minister, with his steady, even temperament, treading with heavy precision his one track for over forty years, having nothing new in his life except the new sameness of the seasons, and desiring nothing new, was incapable of understanding a woman like this, who had lived as quietly as he, and all the time held within herself the elements of revolution. He could not account for such violence, such extremes, except in a loss of reason. He had a conviction that Candace was getting beyond herself. He himself was not a typical New-Englander; the national elements of character were not pronounced in him. He was aghast and bewildered at this outbreak, which was tropical, and more than tropical, for a New England nature has a floodgate, and the power which it releases is an accumulation. Candace Whitcomb had been a quiet woman, so delicately resolute that the quality had been scarcely noticed in her, and her ambition had been unsuspected. Now the resolution and the ambition appeared raging over her whole self.

[handwritten margin note: small segments to represent bigger things]

She began to talk again. "I've made up my mind that I'm goin' to sing Sundays the way I did this mornin', an' I don't care what folks say," said she. "I've made up my mind that I'm goin' to take matters into my own hands. I'm goin' to let folks see that I ain't trod down quite flat, that there's a little rise left in me. I ain't goin' to give up beat yet a while; an' I'd like to see anybody stop me. If I ain't got a right to play a psalm tune on my organ an' sing, I'd like to know. If you don't like it, you can move the meetin'-house."

Candace had had an inborn reverence for clergymen. She had always treated Mr. Pollard with the utmost deference. Indeed, her manner toward all men had been marked by a certain delicate stiffness and dignity. Now she was talking to the old minister with the homely freedom with which she might have addressed a female gossip over the back fence. He could not say much in return. He did not feel competent to make headway against any such tide of passion; all he could do was to let it beat against him. He made a few expostulations, which increased Candace's vehemence; he expressed his regret over the whole affair, and suggested that they should kneel and ask the guidance of the Lord in the matter, that she might be led to see it all in a different light.

Candace refused flatly. "I don't see any use prayin' about it," said she. "I don't think the Lord's got much to do with it, anyhow."

It was almost time for the afternoon service when the minister left. He had missed his comfortable noontide rest, through this encounter with his revolutionary parishioner. After the minister had gone, Candace sat by the window and waited. The bell rang, and she watched the people file past. When her nephew Wilson Ford with Alma appeared, she grunted to herself. "She's thin as a rail," said she; "guess there won't be much left of her by the time Wilson gets her. Little soft-spoken nippin' thing, she wouldn't make him no kind of a wife, anyway. Guess it's jest as well."

When the bell had stopped tolling, and all the people entered the church, Candace went over to her organ and seated herself. She arranged a singing-book before her, and sat still, waiting. Her thin, colorless neck and temples were full of beating pulses; her black eyes were bright and eager; she leaned stiffly over toward the music-rack, to hear better. When the church organ sounded out she straightened herself; her long skinny fingers pressed her own organ-keys with nervous energy. She worked the pedals with all her strength; all her slender body was in motion. When the first notes of Alma's solo began, Candace sang. She had really possessed a fine voice, and it was wonderful how little she had lost it. Straining her throat with jealous fury, her notes were still for the main part true. Her voice filled the whole room; she sang with wonderful fire and expression. That, at least, mild little Alma Way could never emulate. She was full of steadfastness and unquestioning constancy, but there were in her no smouldering fires of ambition and resolution. Music was not to her what it had been to her older rival. To this obscure woman, kept relentlessly by circumstances in a narrow track, singing in the village choir had been as much as Italy was to Napoleon[1]— and now on her island of exile she was still showing fight.

After the church service was done, Candace left the organ and went over to her old chair by the window. Her knees felt weak, and shook under her. She sat down, and leaned back her head. There were red spots on her cheeks. Pretty soon she heard a quick slam of her gate, and an impetuous tread on the gravel-walk.

---

[1] The French emperor Napoleon Bonaparte (1769–1821) conquered Italy and declared himself its king in 1805; in 1814 he was deposed and exiled to the Italian island of Elba.

She looked up, and there was her nephew Wilson Ford hurrying up to the door. She cringed a little, then she settled herself more firmly in her chair.

Wilson came into the room with a rush. He left the door open, and the wind slammed it to after him.

"Aunt Candace, where are you?" he called out, in a loud voice.

She made no reply. He looked around fiercely, and his eyes seemed to pounce upon her.

"Look here, Aunt Candace," said he, "are you crazy?" Candace said nothing. "Aunt Candace!" She did not seem to see him. "If you don't answer me," said Wilson, "I'll just go over there and pitch that old organ out of the window!"

"Wilson Ford!" said Candace, in a voice that was almost a scream.

"Well, what say! What have you got to say for yourself, acting the way you have? I tell you what 'tis, Aunt Candace, I won't stand it."

"I'd like to see you help yourself."

"I will help myself. I'll pitch that old organ out of the window, and then I'll board up the window on that side of your house. Then we'll see."

"It ain't your house, and it won't never be."

"Who said it was my house? You're my aunt, and I've got a little lookout for the credit of the family. Aunt Candace, what are you doing this for?"

"It don't make no odds what I'm doin' so for. I ain't bound to give my reasons to a young fellar like you, if you do act so mighty toppin'. But I'll tell you one thing, Wilson Ford, after the way you've spoke to-day, you sha'n't never have one cent of my money, an' you can't never marry that Way girl if you don't have it. You can't never take her home to live with your mother, an' this house would have been mighty nice an' convenient for you some day. Now you won't get it. I'm goin' to make another will. I'd made one, if you did but know it. Now you won't get a cent of my money, you nor your mother neither. An' I ain't goin' to live a dreadful while longer, neither. Now I wish you'd go home; I want to lay down. I'm 'bout sick."

Wilson could not get another word from his aunt. His indignation had not in the least cooled. Her threat of disinheriting him did not cow him at all; he had too much rough independence, and indeed his aunt Candace's house had always been too much of an air-castle for him to contemplate seriously. Wilson, with his burly frame and his headlong common-sense, could have little to do with aircastles, had he been hard enough to build them over graves. Still, he had not admitted that he never could marry Alma. All his hopes were based upon a rise in his own fortunes, not by some sudden convulsion, but by his own long and steady labor. Some time, he thought, he should have saved enough for the two homes.

He went out of his aunt's house still storming. She arose after the door had shut behind him, and got out into the kitchen. She thought that she would start a fire and make a cup of tea. She had not eaten anything all day. She put some kindling-wood into the stove and touched a match to it; then she went back to the sitting-room, and settled down again into the chair by the window. The fire in the kitchen-stove roared, and the light wood was soon burned out. She thought no more about it. She had not put on the teakettle. Her head ached, and once in a while she shivered. She sat at the window while the afternoon waned and the dusk came on. At seven o'clock the meeting bell rang again, and the people flocked by. This time she did not stir. She had shut her parlor organ. She did not need to out-sing her rival this evening; there was only congregational singing at the Sunday-night prayer-meeting.

She sat still until it was nearly time for meeting to be done; her head ached harder and harder, and she shivered more. Finally she arose. "Guess I'll go to bed," she muttered. She went about the house, bent over and shaking, to lock the doors. She stood a minute in the back door, looking over the fields to the woods. There was a red light over there. "The woods are on fire," said Candace. She watched with a dull interest the flames roll up, withering and destroying the tender green spring foliage. The air was full of smoke, although the fire was half a mile away.

Candace locked the door and went in. The trees with their delicate garlands of new leaves, with the new nests of song birds, might fall, she was in the roar of an intenser fire; the growths of all her springs and the delicate wontedness of her whole life were going down in it. Candace went to bed in her little room off the parlor, but she could not sleep. She lay awake all night. In the morning she crawled to the door and hailed a little boy who was passing. She bade him go for the doctor as quickly as he could, then to Mrs. Ford's, and ask her to come over. She held on to the door while she was talking. The boy stood staring wonderingly at her. The spring wind fanned her face. She had drawn on a dress skirt and put her shawl over her shoulders, and her gray hair was blowing over her red cheeks.

She shut the door and went back to her bed. She never arose from it again. The doctor and Mrs. Ford came and looked after her, and she lived a week. Nobody but herself thought until the very last that she would die; the doctor called her illness merely a light run of fever; she had her senses fully.

But Candace gave up at the first. "It's my last sickness," she said to Mrs. Ford that morning when she first entered; and Mrs. Ford had laughed at the notion; but the sick woman held to it. She did not seem to suffer much physical pain; she only grew weaker and weaker, but she was distressed mentally. She did not talk much, but her eyes followed everybody with an agonized expression.

On Wednesday William Emmons came to inquire for her. Candace heard him out in the parlor. She tried to raise herself on one elbow that she might listen better to his voice.

"William Emmons come in to ask how you was," Mrs. Ford said, after he was gone.

"I—heard him," replied Candace. Presently she spoke again. "Nancy," said she, "where's that photograph album?"

"On the table," replied her sister, hesitatingly.

"Mebbe—you'd better—brush it up a little."

"Well."

Sunday morning Candace wished that the minister should be asked to come in at the noon intermission. She had refused to see him before. He came and prayed with her, and she asked his forgiveness for the way she had spoken the Sunday before. "I—hadn't ought to—spoke so," said she. "I was—dreadful wrought up."

"Perhaps it was your sickness coming on," said the minister, soothingly.

Candace shook her head. "No—it wa'n't. I hope the Lord will—forgive me."

After the minister had gone, Candace still appeared unhappy. Her pitiful eyes followed her sister everywhere with the mechanical persistency of a portrait.

"What is it you want, Candace?" Mrs. Ford said at last. She had nursed her sister faithfully, but once in a while her impatience showed itself.

"Nancy!"

"What say?"

"I wish—you'd go out when—meetin's done, an'—head off Alma an' Wilson, an'—ask 'em to come in. I feel as if—I'd like to—hear her sing."

Mrs. Ford stared. "Well," said she.

The meeting was now in session. The windows were all open, for it was another warm Sunday. Candace lay listening to the music when it began, and a look of peace came over her face. Her sister had smoothed her hair back, and put on a clean cap. The white curtain in the bedroom window waved in the wind like a white sail. Candace almost felt as if she were better, but the thought of death seemed easy.

Mrs. Ford at the parlor window watched for the meeting to be out. When the people appeared, she ran down the walk and waited for Alma and Wilson. When they came she told them what Candace wanted, and they all went in together.

"Here's Alma an' Wilson, Candace," said Mrs. Ford, leading them to the bedroom door.

Candace smiled. "Come in," she said, feebly. And Alma and Wilson entered and stood beside the bed. Candace continued to look at them, the smile straining her lips.

"Wilson!"

"What is it, Aunt Candace?"

"I ain't altered that—will. You an' Alma can—come here an'—live—when I'm—gone. Your mother won't mind livin' alone. Alma can have—all—my things."

"Don't, Aunt Candace." Tears were running over Wilson's cheeks, and Alma's delicate face was all of a quiver.

"I thought—maybe—Alma'd be willin' to—sing for me," said Candace.

"What do you want me to sing?" Alma asked, in a trembling voice.

"'Jesus, lover of my soul,'"[2]

Alma, standing there beside Wilson, began to sing. At first she could hardly control her voice, then she sang sweetly and clearly.

Candace lay and listened. Her face had a holy and radiant expression. When Alma stopped singing it did not disappear, but she looked up and spoke, and it was like a secondary glimpse of the old shape of a forest tree through the smoke and flame of the transfiguring fire the instant before it falls. "You flatted[3] a little on—soul," said Candace.

1891

Kate Chopin
(1851–1904)

The publication of *The Awakening* in 1899 shocked readers who were accustomed to thinking of Kate Chopin's stories as "agreeable" sketches of Creole and Cajun life. Along with the theme of infidelity, the manifest sensuality of the novel evoked condemnation from many quarters. Recalling that "Miss Chopin" had created "sweet and lovable characters," an unidentified admonitory reviewer said it was wrong for this writer of "great refinement

---

[2] A popular hymn (1740) attributed to the English clergyman Charles Wesley (1707–1788).
[3] Sang flat.

and poetic grace to enter the overworked field of sex fiction." To examine *The Awakening* in the context of Chopin's earlier fiction, however, is to see that it entered no field, over- worked or not; rather, it extended the borders of an area in which Chopin had long been working. Nor were the gender issues that the work raises new to her writings. As Chopin biographer Per Seyersted has noted, the heroines of Chopin's three earliest stories could be labeled as "feminine," "emancipated," and "modern," respectively, in the existentialist writer Simone de Beauvoir's sense of these terms—suggesting that Chopin was long pre- occupied with female characters who sought to establish and maintain their identities in a partriarchal society.

Katherine O'Flaherty was born in St. Louis in 1851 to Thomas O'Flaherty, a wealthy merchant, and Eliza Faris, a French Creole aristocrat. After losing her father in a train wreck in 1855, young Kate spent much of her time listening to her great-grandmother, Mme. Charleville, describe Natchitoches (pronounced Nack-uh-tush) Parish in Louisiana and embellish the already racy histories of the settlers of St. Louis. Later, Kate received a Catholic convent-school education before entering St. Louis society as one of the promi- nent belles of 1868. Although she complained to her diary that St. Louis party life was "a nuisance," she participated fully before marrying Oscar Chopin, a Louisiana native, in 1870 and moving to New Orleans. The two had six children, for whom Kate Chopin cared dutifully; the Chopins ran a cotton plantation and a general store. In 1879 the young family moved to Cloutierville in Natchitoches Parish, where they remained until Oscar's death from swamp fever in 1883. The grief-stricken widow continued her husband's business for a year before returning to St. Louis, where she again faced the death of a loved one when her mother died suddenly in 1885.

Hoping to dispel some of her despair, Chopin's physician and close friend, Frederick Kolbenheyer, encouraged her to read more widely and to begin writing fiction. Chopin attempted poetry as well as short stories; in fact, her first printed work is a short poem, "If It Might Be," which appeared in the magazine *America* in January 1889. Quickly recog- nizing that her work was "crude and unformed," Chopin studied "to better her style," emulating the New England local-color writers Sarah Orne Jewett and Mary E. Wilkins Freeman as well as the French naturalists Gustave Flaubert, Émile Zola, and Guy de Maupassant. At the same time, Kolbenheyer encouraged her to read the work of the biolo- gists Charles Darwin and Thomas H. Huxley and of the philosopher Herbert Spencer; their work contributed to her own version of naturalism.

Chopin's novel from this period, *At Fault* (1890), received far less acclaim than did the short stories she wrote for *Vogue, Century, Harper's Young People,* and similar maga- zines. In 1894 she published twenty-three of these stories under the title *Bayou Folk,* a collection one critic termed "the best literary work that has come out of the Southland in a long time" (although another praised it more faintly as a group of "clever and charming" vignettes of Creole life). Both this collection and the subsequent *A Night in Acadie* (1897) were generally well received; yet, laudatory as most of Chopin's contemporaries were, they seem to have regarded her fiction as limited in scope and regional in achievement. Perhaps they overlooked what we see as fundamental human issues because of precon- ceived ideas about the work of local-color writers and because Chopin rarely loaded her fiction with moral judgments. However, even in her early stories she addresses problems of race and class tensions, of racially mixed marriage, of women choosing between mar- riage and career, of people considering divorce, and of couples seeking to have "modern" marriages in which the woman is not a subjugated figure. This range of concerns (sug- gested in such stories as "Désirée's Baby" [1893] and "The Storm" [1898]) demonstrates Chopin's continued interest in confronting the problems that exist both for women who accept conventional roles and women who seek to reject them. Her emphasis on women's

The cover of the first edition of Kate Chopin's Awakening.

struggles becomes still more obvious: within weeks of receiving the preliminary reviews of *Bayou Folk,* Chopin wrote "The Story of an Hour" (1894), the startling sketch of Louise Mallard's reaction to her husband's supposed death, and an eloquent example of how Chopin conflated issues of freedom, personal identity, and marital status.

Issues of female identity and autonomy are most apparent in Chopin's masterpiece, *The Awakening.* Set on Grand Isle (a resort island off the Louisiana coast) and in New Orleans, the novel contrasts Edna Pontellier with the perfect "mother-woman" and the eccentric artist, one readily accepted by society, the other tolerated—and implies that this same society cannot imagine the kind of autonomy Edna seeks. Although she is similar to Flaubert's Emma Bovary in enjoying her sexual liberation, Edna is less concerned with the erotic than with the close connections she perceives between sexual and social independence. The story of Edna's growth toward personal, emotional, and sexual liberation concludes, however, not only with the heroine's suicide, but in effect with the author's artistic death. Within months after its publication, *The Awakening* was banned by St. Louis libraries, Chopin's third collection of stories was refused by her publisher, and former friends lost interest in her company. That combination of events prompted her to cease writing almost entirely; she died soon afterward in 1904. Virtually dismissed from the literary scene, Chopin was not rediscovered and reassessed as a writer until the 1950s. In the decades since, scholars have come to value her work as a link between local-color writing and naturalism and to praise her insight into the profound relation between the quest for female autonomy and social attitudes toward sexuality and motherhood.

Suggested Readings: *Bayou Folk*, ed. W. Berthoff, 1970. *Portraits: Short Stories by Kate Chopin*, ed. H. Taylor, 1979. *The Awakening and Selected Stories*, ed. S. M. Gilbert, 1984. D. Rankin, *Kate Chopin and Her Creole Stories*, 1932. M. Springer, *Edith Wharton and Kate Chopin: A Reference Guide*, 1976. P. Seyersted, *Kate Chopin: A Critical Biography*, 1980. H. Bloom, ed., *Kate Chopin*, 1987. T. Bonner, *The Kate Chopin Companion: With Chopin's Translations From French Fiction*, 1988. W. Martin, ed., *New Essays on The Awakening*, 1988. A. S. Elfenbien, *Women on the Color Line: Evolving Stereotypes and the Writings of George Washington Cable, Grace King, and Kate Chopin*, 1989. H. Taylor, *Gender, Race, and Region in the Writings of Grace King, Ruth McEnery Stuart, and Kate Chopin*, 1989.

Texts Used: "Désirée's Baby," "The Story of an Hour," and "A Pair of Silk Stockings": *The Complete Works of Kate Chopin*, Vol. I, ed. P. Seyersted, 1969. All else: *The Complete Works*, Vol. II.

DÉSIRÉE'S BABY*

As the day was pleasant, Madame Valmondé drove over to L'Abri[1] to see Désirée and the baby.

It made her laugh to think of Désirée with a baby. Why, it seemed but yesterday that Désirée was little more than a baby herself; when Monsieur in riding through the gateway of Valmondé had found her lying asleep in the shadow of the big stone pillar.

The little one awoke in his arms and began to cry for "Dada." That was as much as she could do or say. Some people thought she might have strayed there of her own accord, for she was of the toddling age. The prevailing belief was that she had been purposely left by a party of Texans, whose canvas-covered wagon, late in the day, had crossed the ferry that Coton Maïs kept, just below the plantation. In time Madame Valmondé abandoned every speculation but the one that Désirée had been sent to her by a beneficent Providence to be the child of her affection, seeing that she was without child of the flesh. For the girl grew to be beautiful and gentle, affectionate and sincere,—the idol of Valmondé.

It was no wonder, when she stood one day against the stone pillar in whose shadow she had lain asleep, eighteen years before, that Armand Aubigny riding by and seeing her there, had fallen in love with her. That was the way all the Aubignys fell in love, as if struck by a pistol shot. The wonder was that he had not loved her before; for he had known her since his father brought him home from Paris, a boy of eight, after his mother died there. The passion that awoke in him that day, when he saw her at the gate, swept along like an avalanche, or like a prairie fire, or like anything that drives headlong over all obstacles.

Monsieur Valmondé grew practical and wanted things well considered: that is, the girl's obscure origin. Armand looked into her eyes and did not care. He was reminded that she was nameless. What did it matter about a name when he could give her one of the oldest and proudest in Louisiana? He ordered the *corbeille*[2]

---

* First published in *Vogue* in 1893.   [1] "Refuge" (French), an ironic name for a plantation.
[2] Wedding presents given by a bridegroom (French).

from Paris, and contained himself with what patience he could until it arrived; then they were married.

Madame Valmondé had not seen Désirée and the baby for four weeks. When she reached L'Abri she shuddered at the first sight of it, as she always did. It was a sad looking place, which for many years had not known the gentle presence of a mistress, old Monsieur Aubigny having married and buried his wife in France, and she having loved her own land too well ever to leave it. The roof came down steep and black like a cowl, reaching out beyond the wide galleries that encircled the yellow stuccoed house. Big, solemn oaks grew close to it, and their thick-leaved, far-reaching branches shadowed it like a pall. Young Aubigny's rule was a strict one, too, and under it his negroes had forgotten how to be gay, as they had been during the old master's easy-going and indulgent lifetime.

The young mother was recovering slowly, and lay full length, in her soft white muslins and laces, upon a couch. The baby was beside her, upon her arm, where he had fallen asleep, at her breast. The yellow nurse woman sat beside a window fanning herself.

Madame Valmondé bent her portly figure over Désirée and kissed her, holding her an instant tenderly in her arms. Then she turned to the child.

"This is not the baby!" she exclaimed, in startled tones. French was the language spoken at Valmondé in those days.

"I knew you would be astonished," laughed Désirée, "at the way he has grown. The little *cochon de lait!*[3] Look at his legs, mamma, and his hands and finger-nails,—real finger-nails. Zandrine had to cut them this morning. Isn't it true, Zandrine?"

The woman bowed her turbaned head majestically, "Mais si,[4] Madame."

"And the way he cries," went on Désirée, "is deafening. Armand heard him the other day as far away as La Blanche's cabin."

Madame Valmondé had never removed her eyes from the child. She lifted it and walked with it over to the window that was lightest. She scanned the baby narrowly, then looked as searchingly at Zandrine, whose face was turned to gaze across the fields.

"Yes, the child has grown, has changed," said Madame Valmondé, slowly, as she replaced it beside its mother. "What does Armand say?"

Désirée's face became suffused with a glow that was happiness itself.

"Oh, Armand is the proudest father in the parish, I believe, chiefly because it is a boy, to bear his name; though he says not,—that he would have loved a girl as well. But I know it isn't true. I know he says that to please me. And mamma," she added, drawing Madame Valmondé's head down to her, and speaking in a whisper, "he hasn't punished one of them—not one of them—since baby is born. Even Négrillon, who pretended to have burnt his leg that he might rest from work—he only laughed, and said Négrillon was a great scamp. Oh, mamma, I'm so happy; it frightens me."

What Désirée said was true. Marriage, and later the birth of his son had softened Armand Aubigny's imperious and exacting nature greatly. This was what made the gentle Désirée so happy, for she loved him desperately. When he frowned she trembled, but loved him. When he smiled, she asked no greater blessing of God. But Armand's dark, handsome face had not often been disfigured by frowns since the day he fell in love with her.

---

[3] "Suckling-pig" (French), used as an endearment. [4] "But yes" (French).

When the baby was about three months old, Désirée awoke one day to the conviction that there was something in the air menacing her peace. It was at first too subtle to grasp. It had only been a disquieting suggestion; an air of mystery among the blacks; unexpected visits from far-off neighbors who could hardly account for their coming. Then a strange, an awful change in her husband's manner, which she dared not ask him to explain. When he spoke to her, it was with averted eyes, from which the old love-light seemed to have gone out. He absented himself from home; and when there, avoided her presence and that of her child, without excuse. And the very spirit of Satan seemed suddenly to take hold of him in his dealings with the slaves. Désirée was miserable enough to die.

She sat in her room, one hot afternoon, in her *peignoir*,[5] listlessly drawing through her fingers the strands of her long, silky brown hair that hung about her shoulders. The baby, half naked, lay asleep upon her own great mahogany bed, that was like a sumptuous throne, with its satin-lined half-canopy. One of La Blanche's little quadroon[6] boys—half naked too—stood fanning the child slowly with a fan of peacock feathers. Désirée's eyes had been fixed absently and sadly upon the baby, while she was striving to penetrate the threatening mist that she felt closing about her. She looked from her child to the boy who stood beside him, and back again; over and over. "Ah!" It was a cry that she could not help; which she was not conscious of having uttered. The blood turned like ice in her veins, and a clammy moisture gathered upon her face.

She tried to speak to the little quadroon boy; but no sound would come, at first. When he heard his name uttered, he looked up, and his mistress was pointing to the door. He laid aside the great, soft fan, and obediently stole away, over the polished floor, on his bare tiptoes.

She stayed motionless, with gaze riveted upon her child, and her face the picture of fright.

Presently her husband entered the room, and without noticing her, went to a table and began to search among some papers which covered it.

"Armand," she called to him, in a voice which must have stabbed him, if he was human. But he did not notice. "Armand," she said again. Then she rose and tottered towards him. "Armand," she panted once more, clutching his arm, "look at our child. What does it mean? tell me."

He coldly but gently loosened her fingers from about his arm and thrust the hand away from him. "Tell me what it means!" she cried despairingly.

"It means," he answered lightly, "that the child is not white; it means that you are not white."

A quick conception of all that this accusation meant for her nerved her with unwonted courage to deny it. "It is a lie; it is not true, I am white! Look at my hair, it is brown; and my eyes are gray, Armand, you know they are gray. And my skin is fair," seizing his wrist. "Look at my hand; whiter than yours, Armand," she laughed hysterically.

"As white as La Blanche's," he returned cruelly; and went away leaving her alone with their child.

When she could hold a pen in her hand, she sent a despairing letter to Madame Valmondé.

"My mother, they tell me I am not white. Armand has told me I am not white. For God's sake tell them it is not true. You must know it is not true. I shall die. I must die. I cannot be so unhappy, and live."

---

[5] A loose dressing gown (French).   [6] Of one-quarter African ancestry.

The answer that came was as brief:

"My own Désirée: Come home to Valmondé; back to your mother who loves you. Come with your child."

When the letter reached Désirée she went with it to her husband's study, and laid it open upon the desk before which he sat. She was like a stone image: silent, white, motionless after she placed it there.

In silence he ran his cold eyes over the written words. He said nothing. "Shall I go, Armand?" she asked in tones sharp with agonized suspense.

"Yes, go."

"Do you want me to go?"

"Yes, I want you to go."

He thought Almighty God had dealt cruelly and unjustly with him; and felt, somehow, that he was paying Him back in kind when he stabbed thus into his wife's soul. Moreover he no longer loved her, because of the unconscious injury she had brought upon his home and his name.

She turned away like one stunned by a blow, and walked slowly towards the door, hoping he would call her back.

"Good-by, Armand," she moaned.

He did not answer her. That was his last blow at fate.

Désirée went in search of her child. Zandrine was pacing the sombre gallery with it. She took the little one from the nurse's arms with no word of explanation, and descending the steps, walked away, under the live-oak branches.

It was an October afternoon; the sun was just sinking. Out in the still fields the negroes were picking cotton.

Désirée had not changed the thin white garment nor the slippers which she wore. Her hair was uncovered and the sun's rays brought a golden gleam from its brown meshes. She did not take the broad, beaten road which led to the far-off plantation of Valmondé. She walked across a deserted field, where the stubble bruised her tender feet, so delicately shod, and tore her thin gown to shreds.

She disappeared among the reeds and willows that grew thick along the banks of the deep, sluggish bayou; and she did not come back again.

Some weeks later there was a curious scene enacted at L'Abri. In the centre of the smoothly swept back yard was a great bonfire. Armand Aubigny sat in the wide hallway that commanded a view of the spectacle; and it was he who dealt out to a half dozen negroes the material which kept this fire ablaze.

A graceful cradle of willow, with all its dainty furbishings, was laid upon the pyre, which had already been fed with the richness of a priceless *layette*.[7] Then there were silk gowns, and velvet and satin ones added to these; laces, too, and embroideries; bonnets and gloves; for the *corbeille* had been of rare quality.

The last thing to go was a tiny bundle of letters; innocent little scriblings that Désirée had sent to him during the days of their espousal. There was the remnant of one back in the drawer from which he took them. But it was not Désirée's; it was part of an old letter from his mother to his father. He read it. She was thanking God for the blessing of her husband's love:—

"But, above all," she wrote, "night and day, I thank the good God for having so arranged our lives that our dear Armand will never know that his mother, who adores him, belongs to the race that is cursed with the brand of slavery."

1892, 1893

---

[7] Clothes and linens for a baby (French).

THE STORY OF AN HOUR*

Knowing that Mrs. Mallard was afflicted with a heart trouble, great care was taken to break to her as gently as possible the news of her husband's death.

It was her sister Josephine who told her, in broken sentences; veiled hints that revealed in half concealing. Her husband's friend Richards was there, too, near her. It was he who had been in the newspaper office when intelligence of the railroad disaster was received, with Brently Mallard's name leading the list of "killed." He had only taken the time to assure himself of its truth by a second telegram, and had hastened to forestall any less careful, less tender friend in bearing the sad message.

She did not hear the story as many women have heard the same, with a paralyzed inability to accept its significance. She wept at once, with sudden, wild abandonment, in her sister's arms. When the storm of grief had spent itself she went away to her room alone. She would have no one follow her.

There stood, facing the open window, a comfortable, roomy armchair. Into this she sank, pressed down by a physical exhaustion that haunted her body and seemed to reach into her soul.

She could see in the open square before her house the tops of trees that were all aquiver with the new spring life. The delicious breath of rain was in the air. In the street below a peddler was crying his wares. The notes of a distant song which some one was singing reached her faintly, and countless sparrows were twittering in the eaves.

There were patches of blue sky showing here and there through the clouds that had met and piled one above the other in the west facing her window.

She sat with her head thrown back upon the cushion of the chair, quite motionless, except when a sob came up into her throat and shook her, as a child who has cried itself to sleep continues to sob in its dreams.

She was young, with a fair, calm face, whose lines bespoke repression and even a certain strength. But now there was a dull stare in her eyes, whose gaze was fixed away off yonder on one of those patches of blue sky. It was not a glance of reflection, but rather indicated a suspension of intelligent thought.

There was something coming to her and she was waiting for it, fearfully. What was it? She did not know; it was too subtle and elusive to name. But she felt it, creeping out of the sky, reaching toward her through the sounds, the scents, the color that filled the air.

Now her bosom rose and fell tumultuously. She was beginning to recognize this thing that was approaching to possess her, and she was striving to beat it back with her will—as powerless as her two white slender hands would have been.

When she abandoned herself a little whispered word escaped her slightly parted lips. She said it over and over under her breath: "free, free, free!" The vacant stare and the look of terror that had followed it went from her eyes. They stayed keen and bright. Her pulses beat fast, and the coursing blood warmed and relaxed every inch of her body.

She did not stop to ask if it were or were not a monstrous joy that held her. A clear and exalted perception enabled her to dismiss the suggestion as trivial.

She knew that she would weep again when she saw the kind, tender hands folded in death; the face that had never looked save with love upon her, fixed and

---

* First published in *Vogue* in 1894 as "The Dream of an Hour."

gray and dead. But she saw beyond that bitter moment a long procession of years to come that would belong to her absolutely. And she opened and spread her arms out to them in welcome.

There would be no one to live for her during those coming years: she would live for herself. There would be no powerful will bending hers in that blind persistence with which men and women believe they have a right to impose a private will upon a fellow-creature. A kind intention or a cruel intention made the act seem no less a crime as she looked upon it in that brief moment of illumination.

And yet she had loved him—sometimes. Often she had not. What did it matter! What could love, the unsolved mystery, count for in face of this possession of self-assertion which she suddenly recognized as the strongest impulse of her being!

"Free! Body and soul free!" she kept whispering.

Josephine was kneeling before the closed door with her lips to the keyhole, imploring for admission, "Louise, open the door! I beg; open the door—you will make yourself ill. What are you doing, Louise? For heaven's sake open the door."

"Go away. I am not making myself ill." No; she was drinking in a very elixir of life through that open window.

Her fancy was running riot along those days ahead of her. Spring days, and summer days, and all sorts of days that would be her own. She breathed a quick prayer that life might be long. It was only yesterday she had thought with a shudder that life might be long.

She arose at length and opened the door to her sister's importunities. There was a feverish triumph in her eyes, and she carried herself unwittingly like a goddess of Victory. She clasped her sister's waist, and together they descended the stairs. Richards stood waiting for them at the bottom.

Some one was opening the front door with a latchkey. It was Brently Mallard who entered, a little travel-stained, composedly carrying his grip-sack and umbrella. He had been far from the scene of accident, and did not even know there had been one. He stood amazed at Josephine's piercing cry; at Richards' quick motion to screen him from the view of his wife.

But Richards was too late.

When the doctors came they said she had died of heart disease—of joy that kills.

1894

A PAIR OF SILK STOCKINGS*

Little Mrs. Sommers one day found herself the unexpected possessor of fifteen dollars. It seemed to her a very large amount of money, and the way in which it stuffed and bulged her worn old *porte-monnaie*[1] gave her a feeling of importance such as she had not enjoyed for years.

The question of investment was one that occupied her greatly. For a day or two she walked about apparently in a dreamy state, but really absorbed in speculation and calculation. She did not wish to act hastily, to do anything she might after-

---

* First published in *Vogue* in 1897.   [1] "Purse" (French).

ward regret. But it was during the still hours of the night when she lay awake revolving plans in her mind that she seemed to see her way clearly toward a proper and judicious use of the money.

A dollar or two should be added to the price usually paid for Janie's shoes, which would insure their lasting an appreciable time longer than they usually did. She would buy so and so many yards of percale for new shirt waists for the boys and Janie and Mag. She had intended to make the old ones do by skilful patching. Mag should have another gown. She had seen some beautiful patterns, veritable bargains in the shop windows. And still there would be left enough for new stockings—two pairs apiece—and what darning that would save for a while! She would get caps for the boys and sailor-hats for the girls. The vision of her little brood looking fresh and dainty and new for once in their lives excited her and made her restless and wakeful with anticipation.

The neighbors sometimes talked of certain "better days" that little Mrs. Sommers had known before she had ever thought of being Mrs. Sommers. She herself indulged in no such morbid retrospection. She had no time—no second of time to devote to the past. The needs of the present absorbed her every faculty. A vision of the future like some dim, gaunt monster sometimes appalled her, but luckily to-morrow never comes.

Mrs. Sommers was one who knew the value of bargains; who could stand for hours making her way inch by inch toward the desired object that was selling below cost. She could elbow her way if need be; she had learned to clutch a piece of goods and hold it and stick to it with persistence and determination till her turn came to be served, no matter when it came.

But that day she was a little faint and tired. She had swallowed a light luncheon—no! when she came to think of it, between getting the children fed and the place righted, and preparing herself for the shopping bout, she had actually forgotten to eat any luncheon at all!

She sat herself upon a revolving stool before a counter that was comparatively deserted, trying to gather strength and courage to charge through an eager multitude that was besieging breast-works of shirting and figured lawn. An all-gone limp feeling had come over her and she rested her hand aimlessly upon the counter. She wore no gloves. By degrees she grew aware that her hand had encountered something very soothing, very pleasant to touch. She looked down to see that her hand lay upon a pile of silk stockings. A placard near by announced that they had been reduced in price from two dollars and fifty cents to one dollar and ninety-eight cents; and a young girl who stood behind the counter asked her if she wished to examine their line of silk hosiery. She smiled, just as if she had been asked to inspect a tiara of diamonds with the ultimate view of purchasing it. But she went on feeling the soft, sheeny luxurious things—with both hands now, holding them up to see them glisten, and to feel them glide serpent-like through her fingers.

Two hectic blotches came suddenly into her pale cheeks. She looked up at the girl.

"Do you think there are any eights-and-a-half among these?"

There were any number of eights-and-a-half. In fact, there were more of that size than any other. Here was a light-blue pair; there were some lavender, some all black and various shades of tan and gray. Mrs. Sommers selected a black pair and looked at them very long and closely. She pretended to be examining their texture, which the clerk assured her was excellent.

"A dollar and ninety-eight cents," she mused aloud. "Well, I'll take this pair." She handed the girl a five-dollar bill and waited for her change and for her parcel. What a very small parcel it was! It seemed lost in the depths of her shabby old shopping-bag.

Mrs. Sommers after that did not move in the direction of the bargain counter. She took the elevator, which carried her to an upper floor into the region of the ladies' waiting-rooms. Here, in a retired corner, she exchanged her cotton stockings for the new silk ones which she had just bought. She was not going through any acute mental process or reasoning with herself, nor was she striving to explain to her satisfaction the motive of her action. She was not thinking at all. She seemed for the time to be taking a rest from that laborious and fatiguing function and to have abandoned herself to some mechanical impulse that directed her actions and freed her of responsibility.

How good was the touch of the raw silk to her flesh! She felt like lying back in the cushioned chair and reveling for a while in the luxury of it. She did for a little while. Then she replaced her shoes, rolled the cotton stockings together and thrust them into her bag. After doing this she crossed straight over to the shoe department and took her seat to be fitted.

She was fastidious. The clerk could not make her out; he could not reconcile her shoes with her stockings, and she was not too easily pleased. She held back her skirts and turned her feet one way and her head another way as she glanced down at the polished, pointed-tipped boots. Her foot and ankle looked very pretty. She could not realize that they belonged to her and were a part of herself. She wanted an excellent and stylish fit, she told the young fellow who served her, and she did not mind the difference of a dollar or two more in the price so long as she got what she desired.

It was a long time since Mrs. Sommers had been fitted with gloves. On rare occasions when she had bought a pair they were always "bargains," so cheap that it would have been preposterous and unreasonable to have expected them to be fitted to the hand.

Now she rested her elbow on the cushion of the glove counter, and a pretty, pleasant young creature, delicate and deft of touch, drew a long-wristed "kid"[2] over Mrs. Sommer's hand. She smoothed it down over the wrist and buttoned it neatly, and both lost themselves for a second or two in admiring contemplation of the little symmetrical gloved hand. But there were other places where money might be spent.

There were books and magazines piled up in the window of a stall a few paces down the street. Mrs. Sommers bought two high-priced magazines such as she had been accustomed to read in the days when she had been accustomed to other pleasant things. She carried them without wrapping. As well as she could she lifted her skirts at the crossings. Her stockings and boots and well fitting gloves had worked marvels in her bearing—had given her a feeling of assurance, a sense of belonging to the well-dressed multitude.

She was very hungry. Another time she would have stilled the cravings for food until reaching her own home, where she would have brewed herself a cup of tea and taken a snack of anything that was available. But the impulse that was guiding her would not suffer her to entertain any such thought.

---

[2] A glove made of kidskin leather.

There was a restaurant at the corner. She had never entered its doors; from the outside she had sometimes caught glimpses of spotless damask and shining crystal, and soft-stepping waiters serving people of fashion.

When she entered her appearance created no surprise, no consternation, as she had half feared it might. She seated herself at a small table alone, and an attentive waiter at once approached to take her order. She did not want a profusion; she craved a nice and tasty bite—a half dozen blue-points,[3] a plump chop with cress, a something sweet—a crème-frappée,[4] for instance; a glass of Rhine wine, and after all a small cup of black coffee.

While waiting to be served she removed her gloves very leisurely and laid them beside her. Then she picked up a magazine and glanced through it, cutting the pages with a blunt edge of her knife.[5] It was all very agreeable. The damask was even more spotless than it had seemed through the window, and the crystal more sparkling. There were quiet ladies and gentlemen, who did not notice her, lunching at the small tables like her own. A soft, pleasing strain of music could be heard, and a gentle breeze was blowing through the window. She tasted a bite, and she read a word or two, and she sipped the amber wine and wiggled her toes in the silk stockings. The price of it made no difference. She counted the money out to the waiter and left an extra coin on his tray, whereupon he bowed before her as before a princess of royal blood.

There was still money in her purse, and her next temptation presented itself in the shape of a matinée poster.

It was a little later when she entered the theatre, the play had begun and the house seemed to her to be packed. But there were vacant seats here and there, and into one of them she was ushered, between brilliantly dressed women who had gone there to kill time and eat candy and display their gaudy attire. There were many others who were there solely for the play and acting. It is safe to say there was no one present who bore quite the attitude which Mrs. Sommers did to her surroundings. She gathered in the whole—stage and players and people in one wide impression, and absorbed it and enjoyed it. She laughed at the comedy and wept—she and the gaudy woman next to her wept over the tragedy. And they talked a little together over it. And the gaudy woman wiped her eyes and sniffled on a tiny square of filmy, perfumed lace and passed little Mrs. Sommers her box of candy.

The play was over, the music ceased, the crowd filed out. It was like a dream ended. People scattered in all directions. Mrs. Sommers went to the corner and waited for the cable car.

A man with keen eyes, who sat opposite to her, seemed to like the study of her small, pale face. It puzzled him to decipher what he saw there. In truth, he saw nothing—unless he were wizard enough to detect a poignant wish, a powerful longing that the cable car would never stop anywhere, but go on and on with her forever.

1896, 1897

---

[3] Oysters.   [4] An iced dessert drink made with cream.
[5] In manufacturing magazines or books, printers joined gatherings of pages in folds; the reader had to cut them apart before reading.

THE STORM*

A Sequel to "The 'Cadian Ball"[1]

I

The leaves were so still that even Bibi thought it was going to rain. Bobinôt, who was accustomed to converse on terms of perfect equality with his little son, called the child's attention to certain sombre clouds that were rolling with sinister intention from the west, accompanied by a sullen, threatening roar. They were at Friedheimer's store and decided to remain there till the storm had passed. They sat within the door on two empty kegs. Bibi was four years old and looked very wise.

"Mama'll be 'fraid, yes," he suggested with blinking eyes.

"She'll shut the house. Maybe she got Sylvie helpin' her this evenin'," Bobinôt responded reassuringly.

"No; she ent got Sylvie. Sylvie was helpin' her yistiday," piped Bibi.

Bobinôt arose and going across to the counter purchased a can of shrimps, of which Calixta was very fond. Then he returned to his perch on the keg and sat stolidly holding the can of shrimps while the storm burst. It shook the wooden store and seemed to be ripping great furrows in the distant field. Bibi laid his little hand on his father's knee and was not afraid.

II

Calixta, at home, felt no uneasiness for their safety. She sat at a side window sewing furiously on a sewing machine. She was greatly occupied and did not notice the approaching storm. But she felt very warm and often stopped to mop her face on which the perspiration gathered in beads. She unfastened her white sacque[2] at the throat. It began to grow dark, and suddenly realizing the situation she got up hurriedly and went about closing windows and doors.

Out on the small front gallery she had hung Bobinôt's Sunday clothes to air and she hastened out to gather them before the rain fell. As she stepped outside, Alcée Laballière rode in at the gate. She had not seen him very often since her marriage, and never alone. She stood there with Bobinôt's coat in her hands, and the big rain drops began to fall. Alcée rode his horse under the shelter of a side projection where the chickens had huddled and there were plows and a harrow piled up in the corner.

"May I come and wait on your gallery till the storm is over, Calixta?" he asked.

"Come 'long in, M'sieur Alcée."

---

* First published in *The Complete Works of Kate Chopin* in 1969. The story's frank treatment of unpunished adultery could be the reason it was not published during Chopin's lifetime.

[1] An 1892 Chopin story in which Alcée Laballière and Calixta, although mutually attracted, picked spouses within their own disparate social classes.

[2] A loose jacket.

His voice and her own startled her as if from a trance, and she seized Bobinôt's vest. Alcée, mounting to the porch, grabbed the trousers and snatched Bibi's braided jacket that was about to be carried away by a sudden gust of wind. He expressed an intention to remain outside, but it was soon apparent that he might as well have been out in the open: the water beat in upon the boards in driving sheets, and he went inside, closing the door after him. It was even necessary to put something beneath the door to keep the water out.

"My! what a rain! It's good two years sence it rain' like that," exclaimed Calixta as she rolled up a piece of bagging and Alcée helped her to thrust it beneath the crack.

She was a little fuller of figure than five years before when she married; but she had lost nothing of her vivacity. Her blue eyes still retained their melting quality; and her yellow hair, dishevelled by the wind and rain, kinked more stubbornly than ever about her ears and temples.

The rain beat upon the low, shingled roof with a force and clatter that threatened to break an entrance and deluge them there. They were in the dining room— the sitting room—the general utility room. Adjoining was her bed room, with Bibi's couch along side her own. The door stood open, and the room with its white, monumental bed, its closed shutters, looked dim and mysterious.

Alcée flung himself into a rocker and Calixta nervously began to gather up from the floor the lengths of a cotton sheet which she had been sewing.

"If this keeps up, *Dieu sait*[3] if the levees[4] goin' to stan' it!" she exclaimed.

"What have you got to do with the levees?"

"I got enough to do! An' there's Bobinôt with Bibi out in that storm—if he only didn' left Friedheimer's!"

"Let us hope, Calixta, that Bobinôt's got sense enough to come in out of a cyclone."

She went and stood at the window with a greatly disturbed look on her face. She wiped the frame that was clouded with moisture. It was stiflingly hot. Alcée got up and joined her at the window, looking over her shoulder. The rain was coming down in sheets obscuring the view of far-off cabins and enveloping the distant wood in a gray mist. The playing of the lightning was incessant. A bolt struck a tall chinaberry tree at the edge of the field. It filled all visible space with a blinding glare and the crash seemed to invade the very boards they stood upon.

Calixta put her hands to her eyes, and with a cry, staggered backward. Alcée's arm encircled her, and for an instant he drew her close and spasmodically to him.

"*Bonté!*"[5] she cried, releasing herself from his encircling arm and retreating from the window, "the house'll go next! If I only knew w'ere Bibi was!" She would not compose herself; she would not be seated. Alcée clasped her shoulders and looked into her face. The contact of her warm, palpitating body when he had unthinkingly drawn her into his arms, had aroused all the old-time infatuation and desire for her flesh.

"Calixta," he said, "don't be frightened. Nothing can happen. The house is too low to be struck, with so many tall trees standing about. There! aren't you going to be quiet? say, aren't you?" He pushed her hair back from her face that was warm and steaming. Her lips were as red and moist as pomegranate seed. Her white neck and a glimpse of her full, firm bosom disturbed him powerfully. As

---

[3] "God knows" (French).   [4] Embankments built to prevent floods.   [5] "Goodness!" (French).

she glanced up at him the fear in her liquid blue eyes had given place to a drowsy gleam that unconsciously betrayed a sensuous desire. He looked down into her eyes and there was nothing for him to do but to gather her lips in a kiss. It reminded him of Assumption.[6]

"Do you remember—in Assumption, Calixta?" he asked in a low voice broken by passion. Oh! she remembered; for in Assumption he had kissed her and kissed and kissed her; until his senses would well nigh fail, and to save her he would resort to a desperate flight. If she was not an immaculate dove in those days, she was still inviolate; a passionate creature whose very defenselessness had made her defense, against which his honor forbade him to prevail. Now—well, now—her lips seemed in a manner free to be tasted, as well as her round, white throat and her whiter breasts.

They did not heed the crashing torrents, and the roar of the elements made her laugh as she lay in his arms. She was a revelation in that dim, mysterious chamber; as white as the couch she lay upon. Her firm, elastic flesh that was knowing for the first time its birthright, was like a creamy lily that the sun invites to contribute its breath and perfume to the undying life of the world.

The generous abundance of her passion, without guile or trickery, was like a white flame which penetrated and found response in depths of his own sensuous nature that had never yet been reached.

When he touched her breasts they gave themselves up in quivering ecstasy, inviting his lips. Her mouth was a fountain of delight. And when he possessed her, they seemed to swoon together at the very borderland of life's mystery.

He stayed cushioned upon her, breathless, dazed, enervated, with his heart beating like a hammer upon her. With one hand she clasped his head, her lips lightly touching his forehead. The other hand stroked with a soothing rhythm his muscular shoulders.

The growl of the thunder was distant and passing away. The rain beat softly upon the shingles, inviting them to drowsiness and sleep. But they dared not yield.

The rain was over; and the sun was turning the glistening green world into a palace of gems. Calixta, on the gallery, watched Alcée ride away. He turned and smiled at her with a beaming face; and she lifted her pretty chin in the air and laughed aloud.

III

Bobinôt and Bibi, trudging home, stopped without at the cistern to make themselves presentable.

"My! Bibi, w'at will yo' mama say! You ought to be ashame'. You oughtn' put on those good pants. Look at 'em! An' that mud on yo' collar! How you got that mud on yo' collar, Bibi? I never saw such a boy!" Bibi was the picture of pathetic resignation. Bobinôt was the embodiment of serious solicitude as he strove to remove from his own person and his son's the signs of their tramp over heavy roads and through wet fields. He scraped the mud off Bibi's bare legs and feet with a stick and carefully removed all traces from his heavy brogans. Then, pre-

---

[6] A Roman Catholic festival honoring the Virgin Mary's ascent into Heaven.

pared for the worst—the meeting with an over-scrupulous housewife, they entered cautiously at the back door.

Calixta was preparing supper. She had set the table and was dripping coffee at the hearth. She sprang up as they came in.

"Oh, Bobinôt! You back! My! but I was uneasy. W'ere you been during the rain? An' Bibi? he ain't wet? he ain't hurt?" She had clasped Bibi and was kissing him effusively. Bobinôt's explanations and apologies which he had been composing all along the way, died on his lips as Calixta felt him to see if he were dry, and seemed to express nothing but satisfaction at their safe return.

"I brought you some shrimps, Calixta," offered Bobinôt, hauling the can from his ample side pocket and laying it on the table.

"Shrimps! Oh, Bobinôt! you too good fo' anything! and she gave him a smacking kiss on the cheek that resounded. "*J'vous réponds,*[7] we'll have a feas' to night– umph-umph!"

Bobinôt and Bibi began to relax and enjoy themselves, and when the three seated themselves at table they laughed much and so loud that anyone might have heard them as far away as Laballière's.

IV

Alcée Laballière wrote to his wife, Clarisse, that night. It was a loving letter, full of tender solicitude. He told her not to hurry back, but if she and the babies liked it at Biloxi, to stay a month longer. He was getting on nicely; and though he missed them, he was willing to bear the separation a while longer—realizing that their health and pleasure were the first things to be considered.

V

As for Clarisse, she was charmed upon receiving her husband's letter. She and the babies were doing well. The society was agreeable; many of her old friends and acquaintances were at the bay. And the first free breath since her marriage seemed to restore the pleasant liberty of her maiden days. Devoted as she was to her husband, their intimate conjugal life was something which she was more than willing to forego for a while.

So the storm passed and every one was happy.

1898, 1969

THE AWAKENING*

A green and yellow parrot, which hung in a cage outside the door, kept repeating over and over:

"*Allez vous-en! Allez vous-en! Sapristi!*[1] That's all right!"

He could speak a little Spanish, and also a language which nobody understood,

---

[7] "I assure you" (French).
* First published in 1899 as "A Solitary Soul."   [1] "Go away! Go away! For God's sake!" (French).

unless it was the mocking-bird that hung on the other side of the door, whistling his fluty notes out upon the breeze with maddening persistence.

Mr. Pontellier, unable to read his newspaper with any degree of comfort, arose with an expression and an exclamation of disgust. He walked down the gallery and across the narrow "bridges" which connected the Lebrun cottages one with the other. He had been seated before the door of the main house. The parrot and the mocking-bird were the property of Madame Lebrun, and they had the right to make all the noise they wished. Mr. Pontellier had the privilege of quitting their society when they ceased to be entertaining.

He stopped before the door of his own cottage, which was the fourth one from the main building and next to the last. Seating himself in a wicker rocker which was there, he once more applied himself to the task of reading the newspaper. The day was Sunday; the paper was a day old. The Sunday papers had not yet reached Grand Isle.[2] He was already acquainted with the market reports, and he glanced restlessly over the editorials and bits of news which he had not had time to read before quitting New Orleans the day before.

Mr. Pontellier wore eye-glasses. He was a man of forty, of medium height and rather slender build; he stooped a little. His hair was brown and straight, parted on one side. His beard was neatly and closely trimmed.

Once in a while he withdrew his glance from the newspaper and looked about him. There was more noise than ever over at the house. The main building was called "the house," to distinguish it from the cottages. The chattering and whistling birds were still at it. Two young girls, the Farival twins, were playing a duet from "Zampa"[3] upon the piano. Madame Lebrun was bustling in and out, giving orders in a high key to a yard-boy whenever she got inside the house, and directions in an equally high voice to a dining-room servant whenever she got outside. She was a fresh, pretty woman, clad always in white with elbow sleeves. Her starched skirts crinkled as she came and went. Farther down, before one of the cottages, a lady in black was walking demurely up and down, telling her beads.[4] A good many persons of the *pension*[5] had gone over to the Chênière Caminada in Beaudelet's lugger[6] to hear mass. Some young people were out under the water-oaks playing croquet. Mr. Pontellier's two children were there—sturdy little fellows of four and five. A quadroon[7] nurse followed them about with a far-away, meditative air.

Mr. Pontellier finally lit a cigar and began to smoke, letting the paper drag idly from his hand. He fixed his gaze upon a white sunshade[8] that was advancing at snail's pace from the beach. He could see it plainly between the gaunt trunks of the water-oaks and across the stretch of yellow camomile. The gulf looked far away, melting hazily into the blue of the horizon. The sunshade continued to approach slowly. Beneath its pink-lined shelter were his wife, Mrs. Pontellier, and young Robert Lebrun. When they reached the cottage, the two seated themselves with some appearance of fatigue upon the upper step of the porch, facing each other, each leaning against a supporting post.

"What folly! to bathe at such an hour in such heat!" exclaimed Mr. Pontellier.

---

[2] A resort island south of New Orleans in the Gulf of Mexico.
[3] A romantic opera (1831) by Louis Hérold (1791–1833).
[4] Using rosary beads to count prayers.   [5] A small hotel (French).
[6] To an island near Grand Isle in Beaudelet's small boat.   [7] Of one-quarter black ancestry.
[8] Parasol.

He himself had taken a plunge at daylight. That was why the morning seemed long to him.

"You are burnt beyond recognition," he added, looking at his wife as one looks at a valuable piece of personal property which has suffered some damage. She held up her hands, strong, shapely hands, and surveyed them critically, drawing up her lawn[9] sleeves above the wrists. Looking at them reminded her of her rings, which she had given to her husband before leaving for the beach. She silently reached out to him, and he, understanding, took the rings from his vest pocket and dropped them into her open palm. She slipped them upon her fingers; then clasping her knees, she looked across at Robert and began to laugh. The rings sparkled upon her fingers. He sent back an answering smile.

"What is it?" asked Pontellier, looking lazily and amused from one to the other. It was some utter nonsense; some adventure out there in the water, and they both tried to relate it at once. It did not seem half so amusing when told. They realized this, and so did Mr. Pontellier. He yawned and stretched himself. Then he got up, saying he had half a mind to go over to Klein's hotel and play a game of billiards.

"Come go along, Lebrun," he proposed to Robert. But Robert admitted quite frankly that he preferred to stay where he was and talk to Mrs. Pontellier.

"Well, send him about his business when he bores you, Edna," instructed her husband as he prepared to leave.

"Here, take the umbrella," she exclaimed, holding it out to him. He accepted the sunshade, and lifting it over his head descended the steps and walked away.

"Coming back to dinner?" his wife called after him. He halted a moment and shrugged his shoulders. He felt in his vest pocket; there was a ten-dollar bill there. He did not know; perhaps he would return for the early dinner and perhaps he would not. It all depended upon the company which he found over at Klein's and the size of "the game." He did not say this, but she understood it, and laughed, nodding good-by to him.

Both children wanted to follow their father when they saw him starting out. He kissed them and promised to bring them back bonbons and peanuts.

II

Mrs. Pontellier's eyes were quick and bright; they were a yellowish brown, about the color of her hair. She had a way of turning them swiftly upon an object and holding them there as if lost in some inward maze of contemplation or thought.

Her eyebrows were a shade darker than her hair. They were thick and almost horizontal, emphasizing the depth of her eyes. She was rather handsome than beautiful. Her face was captivating by reason of a certain frankness of expression and a contradictory subtle play of features. Her manner was engaging.

Robert rolled a cigarette. He smoked cigarettes because he could not afford cigars, he said. He had a cigar in his pocket which Mr. Pontellier had presented him with, and he was saving it for his after-dinner smoke.

This seemed quite proper and natural on his part. In coloring he was not unlike his companion. A clean-shaven face made the resemblance more pronounced than it would otherwise have been. There rested no shadow of care upon his open

---

[9] Fine linen or cotton cloth.

countenance. His eyes gathered in and reflected the light and languor of the summer day.

Mrs. Pontellier reached over for a palm-leaf fan that lay on the porch and began to fan herself, while Robert sent between his lips light puffs from his cigarette. They chatted incessantly: about the things around them; their amusing adventure out in the water—it had again assumed its entertaining aspect; about the wind, the trees, the people who had gone to the *Chênière;* about the children playing croquet under the oaks, and the Farival twins, who were now performing the overture to "The Poet and the Peasant."[1]

Robert talked a good deal about himself. He was very young, and did not know any better. Mrs. Pontellier talked a little about herself for the same reason. Each was interested in what the other said. Robert spoke of his intention to go to Mexico in the autumn, where fortune awaited him. He was always intending to go to Mexico, but some way never got there. Meanwhile he held on to his modest position in a mercantile house in New Orleans, where an equal familiarity with English, French and Spanish gave him no small value as a clerk and correspondent.

He was spending his summer vacation, as he always did, with his mother at Grand Isle. In former times, before Robert could remember, "the house" had been a summer luxury of the Lebruns. Now, flanked by its dozen or more cottages, which were always filled with exclusive visitors from the *"Quartier Français,"*[2] it enabled Madame Lebrun to maintain the easy and comfortable existence which appeared to be her birthright.

Mrs. Pontellier talked about her father's Mississippi plantation and her girlhood home in the old Kentucky blue-grass country. She was an American woman, with a small infusion of French which seemed to have been lost in dilution. She read a letter from her sister, who was away in the East, and who had engaged herself to be married. Robert was interested, and wanted to know what manner of girls the sisters were, what the father was like, and how long the mother had been dead.

When Mrs. Pontellier folded the letter it was time for her to dress for the early dinner.

"I see Léonce isn't coming back," she said, with a glance in the direction whence her husband had disappeared. Robert supposed he was not, as there were a good many New Orleans club men over at Klein's.

When Mrs. Pontellier left him to enter her room, the young man descended the steps and strolled over toward the croquet players, where, during the half-hour before dinner, he amused himself with the little Pontellier children, who were very fond of him.

III

It was eleven o'clock that night when Mr. Pontellier returned from Klein's hotel. He was in an excellent humor, in high spirits, and very talkative. His entrance awoke his wife, who was in bed and fast alseep when he came in. He talked to her while he undressed, telling her anecdotes and bits of news and gossip that he had gathered during the day. From his trousers pockets he took a fistful of crumpled

[1] A light opera (1846) by Franz von Suppé (1819–1895).

[2] "French Quarter" (French), the oldest part of New Orleans, where wealthy families lived at the time.

bank notes and a good deal of silver coin, which he piled on the bureau indiscriminately with keys, knife, handkerchief, and whatever else happened to be in his pockets. She was overcome with sleep, and answered him with little half utterances.

He thought it very discouraging that his wife, who was the sole object of his existence, evinced so little interest in things which concerned him, and valued so little his conversation.

Mr. Pontellier had forgotten the bonbons and peanuts for the boys. Notwithstanding he loved them very much, and went into the adjoining room where they slept to take a look at them and make sure that they were resting comfortably. The result of his investigation was far from satisfactory. He turned and shifted the youngsters about in bed. One of them began to kick and talk about a basket full of crabs.

Mr. Pontellier returned to his wife with the information that Raoul had a high fever and needed looking after. Then he lit a cigar and went and sat near the open door to smoke it.

Mrs. Pontellier was quite sure Raoul had no fever. He had gone to bed perfectly well, she said, and nothing had ailed him all day. Mr. Pontellier was too well acquainted with fever symptoms to be mistaken. He assured her the child was consuming[1] at that moment in the room.

He reproached his wife with her inattention, her habitual neglect of the children. If it was not a mother's place to look after children, whose on earth was it? He himself had his hands full with his brokerage business. He could not be in two places at once; making a living for his family on the street, and staying at home to see that no harm befell them. He talked in a monotonous, insistent way.

Mrs. Pontellier sprang out of bed and went into the next room. She soon came back and sat on the edge of the bed, leaning her head down on the pillow. She said nothing, and refused to answer her husband when he questioned her. When his cigar was smoked out he went to bed, and in half a minute he was fast asleep.

Mrs. Pontellier was by that time thoroughly awake. She began to cry a little, and wiped her eyes on the sleeve of her *peignoir*.[2] Blowing out the candle, which her husband had left burning, she slipped her bare feet into a pair of satin *mules*[3] at the foot of the bed and went out on the porch, where she sat down in the wicker chair and began to rock gently to and fro.

It was then past midnight. The cottages were all dark. A single faint light gleamed out from the hallway of the house. There was no sound abroad except the hooting of an old owl in the top of a water-oak, and the everlasting voice of the sea, that was not uplifted at that soft hour. It broke like a mournful lullaby upon the night.

The tears came so fast to Mrs. Pontellier's eyes that the damp sleeve of her *peignoir* no longer served to dry them. She was holding the back of her chair with one hand; her loose sleeve had slipped almost to the shoulder of her uplifted arm. Turning, she thrust her face, steaming and wet, into the bend of her arm, and she went on crying there, not caring any longer to dry her face, her eyes, her arms. She could not have told why she was crying. Such experiences as the foregoing were not uncommon in her married life. They seemed never before to have weighed much against the abundance of her husband's kindness and a uniform devotion which had come to be tacit and self-understood.

---

[1] Feverish.   [2] Loose dressing gown (French).   [3] Slippers.

An indescribable oppression, which seemed to generate in some unfamiliar part of her consciousness, filled her whole being with a vague anguish. It was like a shadow, like a mist passing across her soul's summer day. It was strange and unfamiliar; it was a mood. She did not sit there inwardly upbraiding her husband, lamenting at Fate, which had directed her footsteps to the path which they had taken. She was just having a good cry all to herself. The mosquitoes made merry over her, biting her firm, round arms and nipping at her bare insteps.

The little stinging, buzzing imps succeeded in dispelling a mood which might have held her there in the darkness half a night longer.

The following morning Mr. Pontellier was up in good time to take the rocka-way[4] which was to convey him to the steamer at the wharf. He was returning to the city to his business, and they would not see him again at the Island till the coming Saturday. He had regained his composure, which seemed to have been somewhat impaired the night before. He was eager to be gone, as he looked forward to a lively week in Carondelet Street.[5]

Mr. Pontellier gave his wife half of the money which he had brought away from Klein's hotel the evening before. She liked money as well as most women, and accepted it with no little satisfaction.

"It will buy a handsome wedding present for Sister Janet!" she exclaimed, smoothing out the bills as she counted them one by one.

"Oh! we'll treat Sister Janet better than that, my dear," he laughed, as he prepared to kiss her good-by.

The boys were tumbling about, clinging to his legs, imploring that numerous things he brought back to them. Mr. Pontellier was a great favorite, and ladies, men, children, even nurses, were always on hand to say good-by to him. His wife stood smiling and waving, the boys shouting, as he disappeared in the old rocka-way down the sandy road.

A few days later a box arrived for Mrs. Pontellier from New Orleans. It was from her husband. It was filled with *friandises,*[6] with luscious and toothsome bits—the finest of fruits, *patés,*[7] a rare bottle or two, delicious syrups, and bon-bons in abundance.

Mrs. Pontellier was always very generous with the contents of such a box; she was quite used to receiving them when away from home. The *patés* and fruit were brought to the dining-room; the bonbons were passed around. And the ladies, selecting with dainty and discriminating fingers and a little greedily, all declared that Mr. Pontellier was the best husband in the world. Mrs. Pontellier was forced to admit that she knew of none better.

IV

It would have been a difficult matter for Mr. Pontellier to define to his own satisfaction or any one else's wherein his wife failed in her duty toward their children. It was something which he felt rather than perceived, and he never voiced the feeling without subsequent regret and ample atonement.

If one of the little Pontellier boys took a tumble whilst at play, he was not apt to

---

[4] A four-wheeled carriage manufactured in Rockaway, New Jersey.
[5] The financial and commercial center of New Orleans.   [6] "Delicacies" (French).
[7] Meat spreads (French).

rush crying to his mother's arms for comfort; he would more likely pick himself up, wipe the water out of his eyes and the sand out of his mouth, and go on playing. Tots as they were, they pulled together and stood their ground in childish battles with doubled fists and uplifted voices, which usually prevailed against the other mother-tots. The quadroon nurse was looked upon as a huge encumbrance, only good to button up waists and panties and to brush and part hair; since it seemed to be a law of society that hair must be parted and brushed.

In short, Mrs. Pontellier was not a mother-woman. The mother-women seemed to prevail that summer at Grand Isle. It was easy to know them, fluttering about with extended, protecting wings when any harm, real or imaginary, threatened their precious brood. They were women who idolized their children, worshiped their husbands, and esteemed it a holy privilege to efface themselves as individuals and grow wings as ministering angels.

Many of them were delicious in the rôle; one of them was the embodiment of every womanly grace and charm. If her husband did not adore her, he was a brute, deserving of death by slow torture. Her name was Adèle Ratignolle. There are no words to describe her save the old ones that have served so often to picture the bygone heroine of romance and the fair lady of our dreams. There was nothing subtle or hidden about her charms; her beauty was all there, flaming and apparent: the spun-gold hair that comb nor confining pin could restrain; the blue eyes that were like nothing but sapphires; two lips that pouted, that were so red one could only think of cherries or some other delicious crimson fruit in looking at them. She was growing a little stout, but it did not seem to detract an iota from the grace of every step, pose, gesture. One would not have wanted her white neck[1] a mite less full or her beautiful arms more slender. Never were hands more exquisite than hers, and it was a joy to look at them when she threaded her needle or adjusted her gold thimble to her taper[2] middle finger as she sewed away on the little night-drawers or fashioned a bodice or a bib.

Madame Ratignolle was very fond of Mrs. Pontellier, and often she took her sewing and went over to sit with her in the afternoons. She was sitting there the afternoon of the day the box arrived from New Orleans. She had possession of the rocker, and she was busily engaged in sewing upon a diminutive pair of night-drawers.

She had bought the pattern of the drawers for Mrs. Pontellier to cut out—a marvel of construction, fashioned to enclose a baby's body so effectually that only two small eyes might look out from the garment, like an Eskimo's. They were designed for winter wear, when treacherous drafts came down chimneys and insidious currents of deadly cold found their way through key-holes.

Mrs. Pontellier's mind was quite at rest concerning the present material needs of her children, and she could not see the use of anticipating and making winter night garments the subject of her summer meditations. But she did not want to appear unamiable and uninterested, so she had brought forth newspapers, which she spread upon the floor of the gallery, and under Madame Ratignolle's directions she had cut a pattern of the impervious garment.

Robert was there, seated as he had been the Sunday before, and Mrs. Pontellier also occupied her former position on the upper step, leaning listlessly against the

---

[1] Bosom: a nineteenth-century euphemism.   [2] Tapered.

post. Beside her was a box of bonbons, which she held out at intervals to Madame Ratignolle.

That lady seemed at a loss to make a selection, but finally settled upon a stick of nougat, wondering if it were not too rich; whether it could possibly hurt her. Madame Ratignolle had been married seven years. About every two years she had a baby. At that time she had three babies, and was beginning to think of a fourth one. She was always talking about her "condition." Her "condition" was in no way apparent, and no one would have known a thing about it but for her persistence in making it the subject of conversation.

Robert started to reassure her, asserting that he had known a lady who had subsisted upon nougat during the entire—but seeing the color mount into Mrs. Pontellier's face he checked himself and changed the subject.

Mrs. Pontellier, though she had married a Creole,[3] was not thoroughly at home in the society of Creoles; never before had she been thrown so intimately among them. There were only Creoles that summer at Lebrun's. They all knew each other, and felt like one large family, among whom existed the most amicable relations. A characteristic which distinguished them and which impressed Mrs. Pontellier most forcibly was their entire absence of prudery. Their freedom of expression was at first incomprehensible to her, though she had no difficulty in reconciling it with a lofty chastity which in the Creole woman seems to be inborn and unmistakable.

Never would Edna Pontellier forget the shock with which she heard Madame Ratignolle relating to old Monsieur Farival the harrowing story of one of her *accouchements*,[4] withholding no intimate detail. She was growing accustomed to like shocks, but she could not keep the mounting color back from her cheeks. Oftener than once her coming had interrupted the droll story with which Robert was entertaining some amused group of married women.

A book had gone the rounds of the *pension*. When it came her turn to read it, she did so with profound astonishment. She felt moved to read the book in secret and solitude, though none of the others had done so—to hide it from view at the sound of approaching footsteps. It was openly criticised and freely discussed at table. Mrs. Pontellier gave over being astonished, and concluded that wonders would never cease.

V

They formed a congenial group sitting there that summer afternoon—Madame Ratignolle sewing away, often stopping to relate a story or incident with much expressive gesture of her perfect hands; Robert and Mrs. Pontellier sitting idle, exchanging occasional words, glances or smiles which indicated a certain advanced stage of intimacy and *camaraderie*.

He had lived in her shadow during the past month. No one thought anything of it. Many had predicted that Robert would devote himself to Mrs. Pontellier when

[3] A native-born Louisianan descendant of early French and Spanish settlers; then the upper class.

[4] "Childbirths" (French). Most upper-class American women in 1899 considered it shocking to speak of childbirth in front of a man, but in Creole society, more freedom of expression was allowed to women, who, as Edna perceives it, have an innate "chastity."

he arrived. Since the age of fifteen, which was eleven years before, Robert each summer at Grand Isle had constituted himself the devoted attendant of some fair dame or damsel. Sometimes it was a young girl, again a widow; but as often as not it was some interesting married woman.

For two consecutive seasons he lived in the sunlight of Mademoiselle Duvigné's presence. But she died between summers; then Robert posed as an inconsolable, prostrating himself at the feet of Madame Ratignolle for whatever crumbs of sympathy and comfort she might be pleased to vouchsafe.

Mrs. Pontellier liked to sit and gaze at her fair companion as she might look upon a faultless Madonna.

"Could any one fathom the cruelty beneath that fair exterior?" murmured Robert. "She knew that I adored her once, and she let me adore her. It was 'Robert, come; go; stand up; sit down; do this; do that; see if the baby sleeps; my thimble, please, that I left God knows where. Come and read Daudet[1] to me while I sew.' "

"*Par example!*[2] I never had to ask. You were always there under my feet, like a troublesome cat."

"You mean like an adoring dog. And just as soon as Ratignolle appeared on the scene, then it *was* like a dog. '*Passez! Adieu! Allez vous-en!*' "[3]

"Perhaps I feared to make Alphonse jealous," she interjoined, with excessive naïveté. That made them all laugh. The right hand jealous of the left! The heart jealous of the soul! But for that matter, the Creole husband is never jealous; with him the gangrene passion is one which has become dwarfed by disuse.

Meanwhile Robert, addressing Mrs. Pontellier, continued to tell of his one time hopeless passion for Madame Ratignolle; of sleepless nights, of consuming flames till the very sea sizzled when he took his daily plunge. While the lady at the needle kept up a little running, contemptuous comment:

"*Blagueur—farceur—gros bête, va!*"[4]

He never assumed this serio-comic tone when alone with Mrs. Pontellier. She never knew precisely what to make of it; at that moment it was impossible for her to guess how much of it was jest and what proportion was earnest. It was understood that he had often spoken words of love to Madame Ratignolle, without any thought of being taken seriously. Mrs. Pontellier was glad he had not assumed a similar rôle toward herself. It would have been unacceptable and annoying.

Mrs. Pontellier had brought her sketching materials, which she sometimes dabbled with in an unprofessional way. She liked the dabbling. She felt in it satisfaction of a kind which no other employment afforded her.

She had long wished to try herself on Madame Ratignolle. Never had that lady seemed a more tempting subject than at that moment, seated there like some sensuous Madonna, with the gleam of the fading day enriching her splendid color.

Robert crossed over and seated himself upon the step below Mrs. Pontellier, that he might watch her work. She handled her brushes with a certain ease and freedom which came, not from long and close acquaintance with them, but from a natural aptitude. Robert followed her work with close attention, giving forth little ejaculatory expressions of appreciation in French, which he addressed to Madame Ratignolle.

---

[1] Alphonse Daudet (1840–1897), a French novelist.   [2] "For heaven's sake!" (French).
[3] "Go on! Goodbye! Go away!" (French).   [4] "Joker—comic—fool, go!" (French).

"Mais ce n'est pas mal! Elle s'y connait, elle a de la force, oui."[5]

During his oblivious attention he once quietly rested his head against Mrs. Pontellier's arm. As gently she repulsed him. Once again he repeated the offense. She could not but believe it to be thoughtlessness on his part; yet that was no reason she should submit to it. She did not remonstrate, except again to repulse him quietly but firmly. He offered no apology.

The picture completed bore no resemblance to Madame Ratignolle. She was greatly disappointed to find that it did not look like her. But it was a fair enough piece of work, and in many respects satisfying.

Mrs. Pontellier evidently did not think so. After surveying the sketch critically she drew a broad smudge of paint across its surface, and crumpled the paper between her hands.

The youngsters came tumbling up the steps, the quadroon following at the respectful distance which they required her to observe. Mrs. Pontellier made them carry her paints and things into the house. She sought to detain them for a little talk and some pleasantry. But they were greatly in earnest. They had only come to investigate the contents of the bonbon box. They accepted without murmuring what she chose to give them, each holding out two chubby hands scoop-like, in the vain hope that they might be filled; and then away they went.

The sun was low in the west, and the breeze soft and languorous that came up from the south, charged with the seductive odor of the sea. Children, freshly befurbelowed,[6] were gathering for their games under the oaks. Their voices were high and penetrating.

Madame Ratignolle folded her sewing, placing thimble, scissors and thread all neatly together in the roll, which she pinned securely. She complained of faintness. Mrs. Pontellier flew for the cologne water and a fan. She bathed Madame Ratignolle's face with cologne, while Robert plied the fan with unnecessary vigor.

The spell was soon over, and Mrs. Pontellier could not help wondering if there were not a little imagination responsible for its origin, for the rose tint had never faded from her friend's face.

She stood watching the fair woman walk down the long line of galleries with the grace and majesty which queens are sometimes supposed to possess. Her little ones ran to meet her. Two of them clung about her white skirts, the third she took from its nurse and with a thousand endearments bore it along in her own fond, encircling arms. Though, as everybody well knew, the doctor had forbidden her to lift so much as a pin!

"Are you going bathing?" asked Robert of Mrs. Pontellier. It was not so much a question as a reminder.

"Oh, no," she answered, with a tone of indecision. "I'm tired; I think not." Her glance wandered from his face away toward the Gulf, whose sonorous murmur reached her like a loving but imperative entreaty.

"Oh, come!" he insisted. "You mustn't miss your bath. Come on. The water must be delicious; it will not hurt you. Come."

He reached up for her big, rough straw hat that hung on a peg outside the door, and put it on her head. They descended the steps, and walked away together toward the beach. The sun was low in the west and the breeze was soft and warm.

---

[5] "Not bad! She knows what she's doing, she has skill, yes." (French).   [6] Dressed elaborately.

VI

Edna Pontellier could not have told why, wishing to go to the beach with Robert, she should in the first place have declined, and in the second place have followed in obedience to one of the two contradictory impulses which impelled her.

A certain light was beginning to dawn dimly within her,—the light which, showing the way, forbids it.

At that early period it served but to bewilder her. It moved her to dreams, to thoughtfulness, to the shadowy anguish which had overcome her the midnight when she had abandoned herself to tears.

In short, Mrs. Pontellier was beginning to realize her position in the universe as a human being, and to recognize her relations as an individual to the world within and about her. This may seem like a ponderous weight of wisdom to descend upon the soul of a young woman of twenty-eight—perhaps more wisdom than the Holy Ghost is usually pleased to vouchsafe to any woman.

But the beginning of things, of a world especially, is necessarily vague, tangled, chaotic, and exceedingly disturbing. How few of us ever emerge from such beginning! How many souls perish in its tumult!

The voice of the sea is seductive; never ceasing, whispering, clamoring, murmuring, inviting the soul to wander for a spell in abysses of solitude; to lose itself in mazes of inward contemplation.

The voice of the sea speaks to the soul. The touch of the sea is sensuous, enfolding the body in its soft, close embrace.

VII

Mrs. Pontellier was not a woman given to confidences, a characteristic hitherto contrary to her nature. Even as a child she had lived her own small life all within herself. At a very early period she had apprehended instinctively the dual life— that outward existence which conforms, the inward life which questions.

That summer at Grand Isle she began to loosen a little the mantle of reserve that had always enveloped her. There may have been—there must have been—influences, both subtle and apparent, working in their several ways to induce her to do this; but the most obvious was the influence of Adèle Ratignolle. The excessive physical charm of the Creole had first attracted her, for Edna had a sensuous susceptibility to beauty. Then the candor of the woman's whole existence, which every one might read, and which formed so striking a contrast to her own habitual reserve—this might have furnished a link. Who can tell what metals the gods use in forging the subtle bond which we call sympathy, which we might as well call love.

The two women went away one morning to the beach together, arm in arm, under the huge white sunshade. Edna had prevailed upon Madame Ratignolle to leave the children behind, though she could not induce her to relinquish a diminutive roll of needlework, which Adèle begged to be allowed to slip into the depths of her pocket. In some unaccountable way they had escaped from Robert.

The walk to the beach was no inconsiderable one, consisting as it did of a long, sandy path, upon which a sporadic and tangled growth that bordered it on either side made frequent and unexpected inroads. There were acres of yellow camomile reaching out on either hand. Further away still, vegetable gardens abounded, with frequent small plantations of orange or lemon trees intervening. The dark green clusters glistened from afar in the sun.

The women were both of goodly height, Madame Ratignolle possessing the more feminine and matronly figure. The charm of Edna Pontellier's physique stole insensibly upon you. The lines of her body were long, clean and symmetrical; it was a body which occasionally fell into splendid poses; there was no suggestion of the trim, stereotyped fashion-plate about it. A casual and indiscriminating observer, in passing, might not cast a second glance upon the figure. But with more feeling and discernment he would have recognized the noble beauty of its modeling, and the graceful severity of poise and movement, which made Edna Pontellier different from the crowd.

She wore a cool muslin that morning—white, with a waving vertical line of brown running through it; also a white linen collar and the big straw hat which she had taken from the peg outside the door. The hat rested any way on her yellow-brown hair, that waved a little, was heavy, and clung close to her head.

Madame Ratignolle, more careful of her complexion, had twined a gauze veil about her head. She wore dogskin gloves, with gauntlets that protected her wrists. She was dressed in pure white, with a fluffiness of ruffles that became her. The draperies and fluttering things which she wore suited her rich, luxuriant beauty as a greater severity of line could not have done.

There were a number of bath-houses along the beach, of rough but solid construction, built with small, protecting galleries facing the water. Each house consisted of two compartments, and each family at Lebrun's possessed a compartment for itself, fitted out with all the essential paraphernalia of the bath and whatever other conveniences the owners might desire. The two women had no intention of bathing; they had just strolled down to the beach for a walk and to be alone and near the water. The Pontellier and Ratignolle compartments adjoined one another under the same roof.

Mrs. Pontellier had brought down her key through force of habit. Unlocking the door of her bath-room she went inside, and soon emerged, bringing a rug, which she spread upon the floor of the gallery, and two huge hair pillows covered with crash,[1] which she placed against the front of the building.

The two seated themselves there in the shade of the porch, side by side, with their backs against the pillows and their feet extended. Madame Ratignolle removed her veil, wiped her face with a rather delicate handkerchief, and fanned herself with the fan which she always carried suspended somewhere about her person by a long, narrow ribbon. Edna removed her collar and opened her dress at the throat. She took the fan from Madame Ratignolle and began to fan both herself and her companion. It was very warm, and for a while they did nothing but exchange remarks about the heat, the sun, the glare. But there was a breeze blowing, a choppy, stiff wind that whipped the water into froth. It fluttered the skirts of the two women and kept them for a while engaged in adjusting, readjusting, tucking in, securing hair-pins and hat-pins. A few persons were sporting some distance away in the water. The beach was very still of human sound at that hour. The lady in black was reading her morning devotions on the porch of a neighboring bath-

[1] Heavy linen fabric.

house. Two young lovers were exchanging their hearts' yearnings beneath the children's tent, which they had found unoccupied.

Edna Pontellier, casting her eyes about, had finally kept them at rest upon the sea. The day was clear and carried the gaze out as far as the blue sky went; there were a few white clouds suspended idly over the horizon. A lateen sail[2] was visible in the direction of Cat Island, and others to the south seemed almost motionless in the far distance.

"Of whom—of what are you thinking?" asked Adèle of her companion, whose countenance she had been watching with a little amused attention, arrested by the absorbed expression which seemed to have seized and fixed every feature into a statuesque repose.

"Nothing," returned Mrs. Pontellier, with a start, adding at once: "How stupid! But it seems to me it is the reply we make instinctively to such a question. Let me see," she went on, throwing back her head and narrowing her fine eyes till they shone like two vivid points of light. "Let me see. I was really not conscious of thinking of anything; but perhaps I can retrace my thoughts."

"Oh! never mind!" laughed Madame Ratignolle. "I am not quite so exacting. I will let you off this time. It is really too hot to think, especially to think about thinking."

"But for the fun of it," persisted Edna. "First of all, the sight of the water stretching so far away, those motionless sails against the blue sky, made a delicious picture that I just wanted to sit and look at. The hot wind beating in my face made me think—without any connection that I can trace—of a summer day in Kentucky, of a meadow that seemed as big as the ocean to the very little girl walking through the grass, which was higher than her waist. She threw out her arms as if swimming when she walked, beating the tall grass as one strikes out in the water. Oh, I see the connection now!"

"Where were you going that day in Kentucky, walking through the grass?"

"I don't remember now. I was just walking diagonally across a big field. My sun-bonnet obstructed the view. I could see only the stretch of green before me, and I felt as if I must walk on forever, without coming to the end of it. I don't remember whether I was frightened or pleased. I must have been entertained.

"Likely as not it was Sunday," she laughed; "and I was running away from prayers, from the Presbyterian service, read in a spirit of gloom by my father that chills me yet to think of."

"And have you been running away from prayers ever since, *ma chère?*"[3] asked Madame Ratignolle, amused.

"No! oh, no!" Edna hastened to say. "I was a little unthinking child in those days, just following a misleading impulse without question. On the contrary, during one period of my life religion took a firm hold upon me; after I was twelve and until—until—why, I suppose until now, though I never thought much about it—just driven along by habit. But do you know," she broke off, turning her quick eyes upon Madame Ratignolle and leaning forward a little so as to bring her face quite close to that of her companion, "sometimes I feel this summer as if I were walking through the green meadow again; idly, aimlessly, unthinking and unguided."

Madame Ratignolle laid her hand over that of Mrs. Pontellier, which was near

---

[2] The triangular sail of a lugger.   [3] "My dear?" (French).

her. Seeing that the hand was not withdrawn, she clasped it firmly and warmly. She even stroked it a little, fondly, with the other hand, murmuring in an under-tone, "*Pauvre chérie.*"[4]

The action was at first a little confusing to Edna, but she soon lent herself readily to the Creole's gentle caress. She was not accustomed to an outward and spoken expression of affection, either in herself or in others. She and her younger sister, Janet, had quarreled a good deal through force of unfortunate habit. Her older sister, Margaret, was matronly and dignified, probably from having assumed matronly and housewifely responsibilities too early in life, their mother having died when they were quite young. Margaret was not effusive; she was practical. Edna had had an occasional girl friend, but whether accidentally or not, they seemed to have been all of one type—the self-contained. She never realized that the reserve of her own character had much, perhaps everything, to do with this. Her most intimate friend at school had been one of rather exceptional intellectual gifts, who wrote fine-sounding essays, which Edna admired and strove to imitate; and with her she talked and glowed over the English classics, and sometimes held religious and political controversies.

Edna often wondered at one propensity which sometimes had inwardly disturbed her without causing any outward show or manifestation on her part. At a very early age—perhaps it was when she traversed the ocean of waving grass—she remembered that she had been passionately enamored of a dignified and sad-eyed cavalry officer who visited her father in Kentucky. She could not leave his presence when he was there, nor remove her eyes from his face, which was something like Napoleon's, with a lock of black hair falling across the forehead. But the cavalry officer melted imperceptibly out of her existence.

At another time her affections were deeply engaged by a young gentleman who visited a lady on a neighboring plantation. It was after they went to Mississippi to live. The young man was engaged to be married to the young lady, and they sometimes called upon Margaret, driving over of afternoons in a buggy. Edna was a little miss, just merging into her teens; and the realization that she herself was nothing, nothing, nothing to the engaged young man was a bitter affliction to her. But he, too, went the way of dreams.

She was a grown young woman when she was overtaken by what she supposed to be the climax of her fate. It was when the face and figure of a great tragedian began to haunt her imagination and stir her senses. The persistence of the infatuation lent it an aspect of genuineness. The hopelessness of it colored it with the lofty tones of a great passion.

The picture of the tragedian stood enframed upon her desk. Any one may possess the portrait of a tragedian without exciting suspicion or comment. (This was a sinister reflection which she cherished.) In the presence of others she expressed admiration for his exalted gifts, as she handed the photograph around and dwelt upon the fidelity of the likeness. When alone she sometimes picked it up and kissed the cold glass passionately.

Her marriage to Léonce Pontellier was purely an accident, in this respect resembling many other marriages which masquerade as the decrees of Fate. It was in the midst of her secret great passion that she met him. He fell in love, as men are in the habit of doing, and pressed his suit with an earnestness and an ardor

---

[4] "Poor darling" (French).

which left nothing to be desired. He pleased her; his absolute devotion flattered her. She fancied there was a sympathy of thought and taste between them, in which fancy she was mistaken. Add to this the violent opposition of her father and her sister Margaret to her marriage with a Catholic, and we need seek no further for the motives which led her to accept Monsieur Pontellier for her husband.

The acme of bliss, which would have been a marriage with the tragedian, was not for her in this world. As the devoted wife of a man who worshiped her, she felt she would take her place with a certain dignity in the world of reality, closing the portals forever behind her upon the realm of romance and dreams.

But it was not long before the tragedian had gone to join the cavalry officer and the engaged young man and a few others; and Edna found herself face to face with the realities. She grew fond of her husband, realizing with some unaccountable satisfaction that no trace of passion or excessive and fictitious warmth colored her affection, thereby threatening its dissolution.

She was fond of her children in an uneven, impulsive way. She would sometimes gather them passionately to her heart; she would sometimes forget them. The year before they had spent part of the summer with their grandmother Pontellier in Iberville. Feeling secure regarding their happiness and welfare, she did not miss them except with an occasional intense longing. Their absence was a sort of relief, though she did not admit this, even to herself. It seemed to free her of a responsibility which she had blindly assumed and for which Fate had not fitted her.

Edna did not reveal so much as all this to Madame Ratignolle that summer day when they sat with faces turned to the sea. But a good part of it escaped her. She had put her head down on Madame Ratignolle's shoulder. She was flushed and felt intoxicated with the sound of her own voice and the unaccustomed taste of candor. It muddled her like wine, or like a first breath of freedom.

There was the sound of approaching voices. It was Robert, surrounded by a troop of children, searching for them. The two little Pontelliers were with him, and he carried Madame Ratignolle's little girl in his arms. There were other children beside, and two nurse-maids followed, looking disagreeable and resigned.

The women at once rose and began to shake out their draperies and relax their muscles. Mrs. Pontellier threw the cushions and rug into the bath-house. The children all scampered off to the awning, and they stood there in a line, gazing upon the intruding lovers, still exchanging their vows and sighs. The lovers got up, with only a silent protest, and walked slowly away somewhere else.

The children possessed themselves of the tent, and Mrs. Pontellier went over to join them.

Madame Ratignolle begged Robert to accompany her to the house; she complained of cramp in her limbs and stiffness of the joints. She leaned draggingly upon his arm as they walked.

VIII

"Do me a favor, Robert," spoke the pretty woman at his side, almost as soon as she and Robert had started on their slow, homeward way. She looked up in his face, leaning on his arm beneath the encircling shadow of the umbrella which he had lifted.

"Granted; as many as you like," he returned, glancing down into her eyes that were full of thoughtfulness and some speculation.

"I only ask for one; let Mrs. Pontellier alone."

"*Tiens!*" he exclaimed, with a sudden, boyish laugh. "*Voilà que Madame Ratignolle est jalouse!*"[1]

"Nonsense! I'm in earnest; I mean what I say. Let Mrs. Pontellier alone."

"Why?" he asked; himself growing serious at his companion's solicitation.

"She is not one of us; she is not like us. She might make the unfortunate blunder of taking you seriously."

His face flushed with annoyance, and taking off his soft hat he began to beat it impatiently against his leg as he walked. "Why shouldn't she take me seriously?" he demanded sharply. "Am I a comedian, a clown, a jack-in-the-box? Why shouldn't she? You Creoles! I have no patience with you! Am I always to be regarded as a feature of an amusing programme? I hope Mrs. Pontellier does take me seriously. I hope she has discernment enough to find in me something besides the *blagueur*. If I thought there was any doubt—"

"Oh, enough, Robert!" she broke into his heated outburst. "You are not thinking of what you are saying. You speak with about as little reflection as we might expect from one of those children down there playing in the sand. If your attentions to any married women here were ever offered with any intention of being convincing, you would not be the gentleman we all know you to be, and you would be unfit to associate with the wives and daughters of the people who trust you."

Madame Ratignolle had spoken what she believed to be the law and the gospel. The young man shrugged his shoulders impatiently.

"Oh! well! That isn't it," slamming his had down vehemently upon his head. "You ought to feel that such things are not flattering to say to a fellow."

"Should our whole intercourse consist of an exchange of compliments? *Ma foi!*"[2]

"It isn't pleasant to have a woman tell you—" he went on, unheedingly, but breaking off suddenly: "Now if I were like Arobin—you remember Alcée Arobin and that story of the consul's wife at Biloxi?"[3] And he related the story of Alcée Arobin and the consul's wife; and another about the tenor of the French Opera,[4] who received letters which should never have been written; and still other stories, grave and gay, till Mrs. Pontellier and her possible propensity for taking young men seriously was apparently forgotten.

Madame Ratignolle, when they had regained her cottage, went in to take the hour's rest which she considered helpful. Before leaving her, Robert begged her pardon for the impatience—he called it rudeness—with which he had received her well-meant caution.

"You made one mistake, Adèle," he said, with a light smile; "there is no earthly possibility of Mrs. Pontellier ever taking me seriously. You should have warned me against taking myself seriously. Your advice might then have carried some weight and given me subject for some reflection. *Au revoir.* But you look tired," he added, solicitously. "Would you like a cup of bouillon? Shall I stir you a toddy?[5] Let me mix you a toddy with a drop of Angostura."

She acceded to the suggestion of bouillon, which was grateful and acceptable. He went himself to the kitchen, which was a building apart from the cottages and

---

[1] "So, Madame Ratignolle is jealous!" (French).   [2] "Really!" (French).   [3] Biloxi, Mississippi.
[4] Then a New Orleans opera company.
[5] A hot alcoholic drink; Angostura is a type of aromatic bitters.

lying to the rear of the house. And he himself brought her the golden-brown bouillon, in a dainty Sèvres cup,[6] with a flaky cracker or two on the saucer.

She thrust a bare, white arm from the curtain which shielded her open door, and received the cup from his hands. She told him he was a *bon garçon,*[7] and she meant it. Robert thanked her and turned away toward "the house."

The lovers were just entering the grounds of the *pension*. They were leaning toward each other as the water-oaks bent from the sea. There was not a particle of earth beneath their feet. Their heads might have been turned upside-down, so absolutely did they tread upon blue ether. The lady in black, creeping behind them, looked a trifle paler and more jaded than usual. There was no sign of Mrs. Pontellier and the children. Robert scanned the distance for any such apparition. They would doubtless remain away till the dinner hour. The young man ascended to his mother's room. It was situated at the top of the house, made up of odd angles and a queer, sloping ceiling. Two broad dormer windows looked out toward the Gulf, and as far across it as a man's eye might reach. The furnishings of the room were light, cool, and practical.

Madame Lebrun was busily engaged at the sewing-machine. A little black girl sat on the floor, and with her hands worked the treadle of the machine. The Creole woman does not take any chances which may be avoided of imperiling her health.

Robert went over and seated himself on the broad sill of one of the dormer windows. He took a book from his pocket and began energetically to read it, judging by the precision and frequency with which he turned the leaves. The sewing-machine made a resounding clatter in the room; it was of a ponderous, bygone make. In the lulls, Robert and his mother exchanged bits of desultory conversation.

"Where is Mrs. Pontellier?"

"Down at the beach with the children."

"I promised to lend her the Goncourt.[8] Don't forget to take it down when you go; it's there on the bookshelf over the small table." Clatter, clatter, clatter, bang! for the next five or eight minutes.

"Where is Victor going with the rockaway?"

"The rockaway? Victor?"

"Yes; down there in front. He seems to be getting ready to drive away somewhere."

"Call him." Clatter, clatter!

Robert uttered a shrill, piercing whistle which might have been heard back at the wharf.

"He won't look up."

Madame Lebrun flew to the window. She called "Victor!" She waved a handkerchief and called again. The young fellow below got into the vehicle and started the horse off at a gallop.

Madame Lebrun went back to machine, crimson with annoyance. Victor was the younger son and brother—a *tête montée,*[9] with a temper which invited violence and a will which no ax could break.

"Whenever you say the word I'm ready to thrash any amount of reason into him that he's able to hold."

---

[6] Fine porcelain made in Sèvres, France.   [7] "Good boy" (French).

[8] A novel by the French writers Edmond (1822–1896) and Jules (1839–1870) Goncourt.

[9] "Impulsive character" (French).

"If your father had only lived!" Clatter, clatter, clatter, clatter, bang! It was a fixed belief with Madame Lebrun that the conduct of the universe and all things pertaining thereto would have been manifestly of a more intelligent and higher order had not Monsieur Lebrun been removed to other spheres during the early years of their married life.

"What do you hear from Montel?" Montel was a middle-aged gentleman whose vain ambition and desire for the past twenty years had been to fill the void which Monsieur Lebrun's taking off had left in the Lebrun household. Clatter, clatter, bang, clatter!

"I have a letter somewhere," looking in the machine drawer and finding the letter in the bottom of the work-basket. "He says to tell you he will be in Vera Cruz[10] the beginning of next month"—clatter, clatter!—"and if you still have the intention of joining him"—bang! clatter, clatter, bang!

"Why didn't you tell me so before, mother? You know I wanted—" Clatter, clatter, clatter!

"Do you see Mrs. Pontellier starting back with the children? She will be in late to luncheon again. She never starts to get ready for luncheon till the last minute." Clatter, clatter! "Where are you going?"

"Where did you say the Goncourt was?"

IX

Every light in the hall was ablaze; every lamp turned as high as it could be without smoking the chimney or threatening explosion. The lamps were fixed at intervals against the wall, encircling the whole room. Some one had gathered orange and lemon branches, and with these fashioned graceful festoons between. The dark green of the branches stood out and glistened against the white muslin curtains which draped the windows, and which puffed, floated, and flapped at the capricious will of a stiff breeze that swept up from the Gulf.

It was Saturday night a few weeks after the intimate conversation held between Robert and Madame Ratignolle on their way from the beach. An unusual number of husbands, fathers, and friends had come down to stay over Sunday; and they were being suitably entertained by their families, with the material help of Madame Lebrun. The dining tables had all been removed to one end of the hall, and the chairs ranged about in rows and in clusters. Each little family group had had its say and exchanged its domestic gossip earlier in the evening. There was now an apparent disposition to relax; to widen the circle of confidences and give a more general tone to the conversation.

Many of the children had been permitted to sit up beyond their usual bedtime. A small band of them were lying on their stomachs on the floor looking at the colored sheets of the comic papers which Mr. Pontellier had brought down. The little Pontellier boys were permitting them to do so, and making their authority felt.

Music, dancing, and a recitation or two were the entertainments furnished, or rather, offered. But there was nothing systematic about the programme, no appearance of prearrangement nor even premeditation.

---

[10] A Mexican city on the Gulf of Mexico.

At an early hour in the evening the Farival twins were prevailed upon to play the piano. They were girls of fourteen, always clad in the Virgin's colors, blue and white, having been dedicated to the Blessed Virgin at their baptism. They played a duet from "Zampa," and at the earnest solicitation of every one present followed it with the overture to "The Poet and the Peasant."

"*Allez vous-en! Sapristi!*" shrieked the parrot outside the door. He was the only being present who possessed sufficient candor to admit that he was not listening to these gracious performances for the first time that summer. Old Monsieur Farival, grandfather of the twins, grew indignant over the interruption, and insisted upon having the bird removed and consigned to regions of darkness. Victor Lebrun objected; and his decrees were as immutable of those of Fate. The parrot fortunately offered no further interruption to the entertainment, the whole venom of his nature apparently having been cherished up and hurled against the twins in that one impetuous outburst.

Later a young brother and sister gave recitations, which every one present had heard many times at winter evening entertainments in the city.

A little girl performed a skirt dance in the center of the floor. The mother played her accompaniments and at the same time watched her daughter with greedy admiration and nervous apprehension. She need have had no apprehension. The child was mistress of the situation. She had been properly dressed for the occasion in black tulle[1] and black silk tights. Her little neck and arms were bare, and her hair, artificially crimped, stood out like fluffy black plumes over her head. Her poses were full of grace, and her little black-shod toes twinkled as they shot out and upward with a rapidity and suddenness which were bewildering.

But there was no reason why every one should not dance. Madame Ratignolle could not, so it was she who gaily consented to play for the others. She played very well, keeping excellent waltz time and infusing an expression into the strains which was indeed inspiring. She was keeping up her music on account of the children, she said; because she and her husband both considered it a means of brightening the home and making it attractive.

Almost every one danced but the twins, who could not be induced to separate during the brief period when one or the other should be whirling around the room in the arms of a man. They might have danced together, but they did not think of it.

The children were sent to bed. Some went submissively; others with shrieks and protests as they were dragged away. They had been permitted to sit up till after the ice-cream, which naturally marked the limit of human indulgence.

The ice-cream was passed around with cake—gold and silver cake arranged on platters in alternate slices; it had been made and frozen during the afternoon back of the kitchen by two black women, under the supervision of Victor. It was pronounced a great success—excellent if it had only contained a little less vanilla or a little more sugar, if it had been frozen a degree harder, and if the salt might have been kept out of portions of it. Victor was proud of his achievement, and went about recommending it and urging every one to partake of it to excess.

After Mrs. Pontellier had danced twice with her husband, once with Robert, and once with Monsieur Ratignolle, who was thin and tall and swayed like a reed in the wind when he danced, she went out on the gallery and seated herself on the

---

[1] Thin silk netting.

low window-sill, where she commanded a view of all that went on in the hall and could look out toward the Gulf. There was a soft effulgence in the east. The moon was coming up, and its mystic shimmer was casting a million lights across the distant, restless water.

"Would you like to hear Mademoiselle Reisz play?" asked Robert, coming out on the porch where she was. Of course Edna would like to hear Mademoiselle Reisz play; but she feared it would be useless to entreat her.

"I'll ask her," he said. "I'll tell her that you want to hear her. She likes you. She will come." He turned and hurried away to one of the far cottages, where Mademoiselle Reisz was shuffling away. She was dragging a chair in and out of her room, and at intervals objecting to the crying of a baby, which a nurse in the adjoining cottage was endeavoring to put to sleep. She was a disagreeable little woman, no longer young, who had quarreled with almost every one, owing to a temper which was self-assertive and a disposition to trample upon the rights of others. Robert prevailed upon her without any too great difficulty.

She entered the hall with him during a lull in the dance. She made an awkward, imperious little bow as she went in. She was a homely woman, with a small weazened[2] face and body and eyes that glowed. She had absolutely no taste in dress, and wore a batch of rusty black lace with a bunch of artificial violets pinned to the side of her hair.

"Ask Mrs. Pontellier what she would like to hear me play," she requested of Robert. She sat perfectly still before the piano, not touching the keys, while Robert carried her message to Edna at the window. A general air of surprise and genuine satisfaction fell upon every one as they saw the pianist enter. There was a settling down, and a prevailing air of expectancy everywhere. Edna was a trifle embarrassed at being thus signaled out for the imperious little woman's favor. She would not dare to choose, and begged that Mademoiselle Reisz would please herself in her selections.

Edna was what she herself called very fond of music. Musical strains, well rendered, had a way of evoking pictures in her mind. She sometimes liked to sit in the room of mornings when Madame Ratignolle played or practiced. One piece which that lady played Edna had entitled "Solitude." It was a short, plaintive, minor strain. The name of the piece was something else, but she called it "Solitude." When she heard it there came before her imagination the figure of a man standing beside a desolate rock on the seashore. He was naked. His attitude was one of hopeless resignation as he looked toward a distant bird winging its flight away from him.

Another piece called to her mind a dainty young woman clad in an Empire gown,[3] taking mincing dancing steps as she came down a long avenue between tall hedges. Again, another reminded her of children at play, and still another of nothing on earth but a demure lady stroking a cat.

The very first chords which Mademoiselle Reisz struck upon the piano sent a keen tremor down Mrs. Pontellier's spinal column. It was not the first time she had heard an artist at the piano. Perhaps it was the first time she was ready, perhaps the first time her being was tempered to take an impress of the abiding truth.

She waited for the material pictures which she thought would gather and blaze

---

[2] Wizened, withered.   [3] A high-waisted dress popularized at the time of the Napoleonic Empire.

before her imagination. She waited in vain. She saw no pictures of solitude, of hope, of longing, or of despair. But the very passions themselves were aroused within her soul, swaying it, lashing it, as the waves daily beat upon her splendid body. She trembled, she was choking, and the tears blinded her.

Mademoiselle had finished. She arose, and bowing her stiff, lofty bow, she went away, stopping for neither thanks nor applause. As she passed along the gallery she patted Edna upon the shoulder.

"Well, how did you like my music?" she asked. The young woman was unable to answer; she pressed the hand of the pianist convulsively. Mademoiselle Reisz perceived her agitation and even her tears. She patted her again upon the shoulder as she said:

"You are the only one worth playing for. Those others? Bah!" and she went shuffling and sidling on down the gallery toward her room.

But she was mistaken about "those others." Her playing had aroused a fever of enthusiasm. "What passion!" "What an artist!" "I have always said no one could play Chopin[4] like Mademoiselle Reisz!" "That last prelude! Bon Dieu![5] It shakes a man!"

It was growing late, and there was a general disposition to disband. But some one, perhaps it was Robert, thought of a bath[6] at that mystic hour and under that mystic moon.

X

At all events Robert proposed it, and there was not a dissenting voice. There was not one but was ready to follow when he led the way. He did not lead the way, however, he directed the way; and he himself loitered behind with the lovers, who had betrayed a disposition to linger and hold themselves apart. He walked between them, whether with malicious or mischievous intent was not wholly clear, even to himself.

The Pontelliers and Ratignolles walked ahead; the women leaning upon the arms of their husbands. Edna could hear Robert's voice behind them, and could sometimes hear what he said. She wondered why he did not join them. It was unlike him not to. Of late he had sometimes held away from her for an entire day, redoubling his devotion upon the next and the next, as though to make up for hours that had been lost. She missed him the days when some pretext served to take him away from her, just as one misses the sun on a cloudy day without having thought much about the sun when it was shining.

The people walked in little groups toward the beach. They talked and laughed; some of them sang. There was a band playing down at Klein's hotel, and the strains reached them faintly, tempered by the distance. There were strange, rare odors abroad—a tangle of the sea smell and of weeds and damp, new-plowed earth, mingled with the heavy perfume of a field of white blossoms somewhere near. But the night sat lightly upon the sea and the land. There was no weight of darkness; there were no shadows. The white light of the moon had fallen upon the world like the mystery and the softness of sleep.

---

[4] The Polish composer Frederic Chopin (1810–1849).   [5] "Good God!" (French).   [6] A swim.

Most of them walked into the water as though into a native element. The sea was quiet now, and swelled lazily in broad billows that melted into one another and did not break except upon the beach in little foamy crests that coiled back like slow, white serpents.

Edna had attempted all summer to learn to swim. She had received instructions from both the men and women; in some instances from the children. Robert had pursued a system of lessons almost daily; and he was nearly at the point of discouragement in realizing the futility of his efforts. A certain ungovernable dread hung about her when in the water, unless there was a hand near by that might reach out and reassure her.

But that night she was like the little tottering, stumbling, clutching child, who of a sudden realizes its powers, and walks for the first time alone, boldly and with over-confidence. She could have shouted for joy. She did shout for joy, as with a sweeping stroke or two she lifted her body to the surface of the water.

A feeling of exultation overtook her, as if some power of significant import had been given her to control the working of her body and her soul. She grew daring and reckless, overestimating her strength. She wanted to swim far out, where no woman had swum before.

Her unlooked-for achievement was the subject of wonder, applause, and admiration. Each one congratulated himself that his special teachings had accomplished this desired end.

"How easy it is!" she thought. "It is nothing," she said aloud; "why did I not discover before that it was nothing. Think of the time I have lost splashing about like a baby!" She would not join the groups in their sports and bouts, but intoxicated with her newly conquered power, she swam out alone.

She turned her face seaward to gather in an impression of space and solitude, which the vast expanse of water, meeting and melting with the moonlit sky, conveyed to her excited fancy. As she swam she seemed to be reaching out for the unlimited in which to lose herself.

Once she turned and looked toward the shore, toward the people she had left there. She had not gone any great distance—that is, what would have a great distance for an experienced swimmer. But to her unaccustomed vision the stretch of water behind her assumed the aspect of a barrier which her unaided strength would never be able to overcome.

A quick vision of death smote her soul, and for a second time appalled and enfeebled her senses. But by an effort she rallied her staggering faculties and managed to regain the land.

She made no mention of her encounter with death and her flash of terror, except to say to her husband, "I thought I should have perished out there alone."

"You were not so very far, my dear; I was watching you," he told her.

Edna went at once to the bath-house, and she had put on her dry clothes and was ready to return home before the others had left the water. She started to walk away alone. They all called to her and shouted to her. She waved a dissenting hand, and went on, paying no further heed to their renewed cries which sought to detain her.

"Sometimes I am tempted to think that Mrs. Pontellier is capricious," said Madame Lebrun, who was amusing herself immensely and feared that Edna's abrupt departure might put an end to the pleasure.

"I know she is," assented Mr. Pontellier; "sometimes, not often."

Edna had not traversed a quarter of the distance on her way home before she was overtaken by Robert.

"Did you think I was afraid?" she asked him, without a shade of annoyance.

"No; I knew you weren't afraid."

"Then why did you come? Why didn't you stay out there with the others?"

"I never thought of it."

"Thought of what?"

"Of anything. What difference does it make?"

"I'm very tired," she uttered, complainingly.

"I know you are."

"You don't know anything about it. Why should you know? I never was so exhausted in my life. But it isn't unpleasant. A thousand emotions have swept through me to-night. I don't comprehend half of them. Don't mind what I'm saying; I am just thinking aloud. I wonder if I shall ever be stirred again as Mademoiselle Reisz's playing moved me to-night. I wonder if any night on earth will ever again be like this one. It is like a night in a dream. The people about me are like some uncanny, half-human beings. There must be spirits abroad to-night."

"There are," whispered Robert. "Didn't you know this was the twenty-eighth of August?"

"The twenty-eighth of August?"

"Yes. On the twenty-eighth of August, at the hour of midnight, and if the moon is shining—the moon must be shining—a spirit that has haunted these shores for ages rises up from the Gulf. With its own penetrating vision the spirit seeks some one mortal worthy to hold him company, worthy of being exalted for a few hours into realms of the semi-celestials. His search has always hitherto been fruitless, and he has sunk back, disheartened, into the sea. But to-night he found Mrs. Pontellier. Perhaps he will never wholly release her from the spell. Perhaps she will never again suffer a poor, unworthy earthling to walk in the shadow of her divine presence."

"Don't banter me," she said, wounded at what appeared to be his flippancy. He did not mind the entreaty, but the tone with its delicate note of pathos was like a reproach. He could not explain; he could not tell her that he had penetrated her mood and understood. He said nothing except to offer her his arm, for, by her own admission, she was exhausted. She had been walking alone with her arms hanging limp, letting her white skirts trail along the dewy path. She took his arm, but she did not lean upon it. She let her hand lie listlessly, as though her thoughts were elsewhere—somewhere in advance of her body, and she was striving to overtake them.

Robert assisted her into the hammock which swung from the post before her door out to the trunk of a tree.

"Will you stay out here and wait for Mr. Pontellier?" he asked.

"I'll stay out here. Good-night."

"Shall I get you a pillow?"

"There's one here," she said, feeling about, for they were in the shadow.

"It must be soiled; the children have been tumbling it about."

"No matter." And having discovered the pillow, she adjusted it beneath her head. She extended herself in the hammock with a deep breath of relief. She was not a supercilious or an over-dainty woman. She was not much given to reclining in the hammock, and when she did so it was with no cat-like suggestion of voluptuous ease, but with a beneficent repose which seemed to invade her whole body.

"Shall I stay with you till Mr. Pontellier comes?" asked Robert, seating himself on the outer edge of one of the steps and taking hold of the hammock rope which was fastened to the post.

"If you wish. Don't swing the hammock. Will you get my white shawl which I left on the window-sill over at the house?"

"Are you chilly?"

"No; but I shall be presently."

"Presently?" he laughed. "Do you know what time it is? How long are you going to stay out here?"

"I don't know. Will you get the shawl?"

"Of course I will," he said, rising. He went over to the house, walking along the grass. She watched his figure pass in and out of the strips of moonlight. It was past midnight. It was very quiet.

When he returned with the shawl she took it and kept it in her hand. She did not put it around her.

"Did you say I should stay till Mr. Pontellier came back?"

"I said you might if you wished to."

He seated himself again and rolled a cigarette, which he smoked in silence. Neither did Mrs. Pontellier speak. No multitude of words could have been more significant than those moments of silence, or more pregnant with the first-felt throbbings of desire.

When the voices of the bathers were heard approaching, Robert said goodnight. She did not answer him. He thought she was asleep. Again she watched his figure pass in and out of the strips of moonlight as he walked away.

XI

"What are you doing out here, Edna? I thought I should find you in bed," said her husband, when he discovered her lying there. He had walked up with Madame Lebrun and left her at the house. His wife did not reply.

"Are you asleep?" he asked, bending down close to look at her.

"No." Her eyes gleamed bright and intense, with no sleepy shadows, as they looked into his.

"Do you know it is past one o'clock? Come on," and he mounted the steps and went into their room.

"Edna!" called Mr. Pontellier from within, after a few moments had gone by.

"Don't wait for me," she answered. He thrust his head through the door.

"You will take cold out there," he said, irritably. "What folly is this? Why don't you come in?"

"It isn't cold; I have my shawl."

"The mosquitoes will devour you."

"There are no mosquitoes."

She heard him moving about the room; every sound indicating impatience and irritation. Another time she would have gone in at his request. She would, through habit, have yielded to his desire; not with any sense of submission or obedience to his compelling wishes, but unthinkingly, as we walk, move, sit, stand, go through the daily treadmill of the life which has been portioned out to us.

"Edna, dear, are you not coming in soon?" he asked again, this time fondly, with a note of entreaty.

"No, I am going to stay out here."

"This is more than folly," he blurted out. "I can't permit you to stay out there all night. You must come in the house instantly."

With a writhing motion she settled herself more securely in the hammock. She perceived that her will had blazed up, stubborn and resistant. She could not at that moment have done other than denied and resisted. She wondered if her husband had ever spoken to her like that before, and if she had submitted to his command. Of course she had; she remembered that she had. But she could not realize why or how she should have yielded, feeling as she then did.

"Léonce, go to bed," she said. "I mean to stay out here. I don't wish to go in, and I don't intend to. Don't speak to me like that again; I shall not answer you."

Mr. Pontellier had prepared for bed, but he slipped on an extra garment. He opened a bottle of wine, of which he kept a small and select supply in a buffet of his own. He drank a glass of the wine and went out on the gallery and offered a glass to his wife. She did not wish any. He drew up the rocker, hoisted his slippered feet on the rail, and proceeded to smoke a cigar. He smoked two cigars; then he went inside and drank another glass of wine. Mrs. Pontellier again declined to accept a glass when it was offered to her. Mr. Pontellier once more seated himself with elevated feet, and after a reasonable interval of time smoked some more cigars.

Edna began to feel like one who awakens gradually out of a dream, a delicious, grotesque, impossible dream, to feel again the realities pressing into her soul. The physical need for sleep began to overtake her; the exuberance which had sustained and exalted her spirit left her helpless and yielding to the conditions which crowded her in.

The stillest hour of the night had come, the hour before dawn, when the world seems to hold its breath. The moon hung low, and had turned from silver to copper in the sleeping sky. The old owl no longer hooted, and the water-oaks had ceased to moan as they bent their heads.

Edna arose, cramped from lying so long and still in the hammock. She tottered up the steps, clutching feebly at the post before passing into the house.

"Are you coming in, Léonce?" she asked, turning her face toward her husband.

"Yes, dear," he answered, with a glance following a misty puff of smoke. "Just as soon as I have finished my cigar."

XII

She slept but a few hours. They were troubled and feverish hours, disturbed with dreams that were intangible, that eluded her, leaving only an impression upon her half-awakened senses of something unattainable. She was up and dressed in the cool of the early morning. The air was invigorating and steadied somewhat her faculties. However, she was not seeking refreshment or help from any source, either external or from within. She was blindly following whatever impulse moved her, as if she had placed herself in alien hands for direction, and freed her soul of responsibility.

Most of the people at that early hour were still in bed and asleep. A few, who intended to go over to the *Chênière* for mass, were moving about. The lovers, who had laid their plans the night before, were already strolling toward the wharf. The lady in black, with her Sunday prayer-book, velvet and gold-clasped, and her Sunday silver beads, was following them at no great distance. Old Monsieur Farival was up, and was more than half inclined to do anything that suggested itself. He put on his big straw hat, and taking his umbrella from the stand in the hall, followed the lady in black, never overtaking her.

The little negro girl who worked Madame Lebrun's sewing-machine was sweeping the galleries with long, absent-minded strokes of the broom. Edna sent her up into the house to awaken Robert.

"Tell him I am going to the *Chênière*. The boat is ready; tell him to hurry."

He had soon joined her. She had never sent for him before. She had never asked for him. She had never seemed to want him before. She did not appear conscious that she had done anything unusual in commanding his presence. He was apparently equally unconscious of anything extraordinary in the situation. But his face was suffused with a quiet glow when he met her.

They went together back to the kitchen to drink coffee. There was no time to wait for any nicety of service. They stood outside the window and the cook passed them their coffee and a roll, which they drank and ate from the window-sill. Edna said it tasted good. She had not thought of coffee nor of anything. He told her he had often noticed that she lacked forethought.

"Wasn't it enough to think of going to the *Chênière* and waking you up?" she laughed. "Do I have to think of everything?—as Léonce says when he's in a bad humor. I don't blame him; he'd never be in a bad humor if it weren't for me."

They took a short cut across the sands. At a distance they could see the curious procession moving toward the wharf—the lovers, shoulder to shoulder, creeping; the lady in black, gaining steadily upon them; old Monsieur Farival, losing ground inch by inch, and a young barefooted Spanish girl, with a red kerchief on her head and a basket on her arm, bringing up the rear.

Robert knew the girl, and he talked to her a little in the boat. No one present understood what they said. Her name was Mariequita. She had a round, sly, piquant face and pretty black eyes. Her hands were small, and she kept them folded over the handle of her basket. Her feet were broad and coarse. She did not strive to hide them. Edna looked at her feet, and noticed the sand and slime between her brown toes.

Beaudelet grumbled because Mariequita was there, taking up so much room. In reality he was annoyed at having old Monsieur Farival, who considered himself the better sailor of the two. But he would not quarrel with so old a man as Monsieur Farival, so he quarreled with Mariequita. The girl was deprecatory at one moment, appealing to Robert. She was saucy the next, moving her head up and down, making "eyes" at Robert and making "mouths" at Beaudelet.

The lovers were all alone. They saw nothing, they heard nothing. The lady in black was counting her beads for the third time. Old Monsieur Farival talked incessantly of what he knew about handling a boat, and of what Beaudelet did not know on the same subject.

Edna liked it all. She looked Mariequita up and down, from her ugly brown toes to her pretty black eyes, and back again.

"Why does she look at me like that?" inquired the girl of Robert.

"Maybe she thinks you are pretty. Shall I ask her?"

"No. Is she your sweetheart?"

"She's a married lady, and has two children."

"Oh! well! Francisco ran away with Sylvano's wife, who had four children. They took all his money and one of the children and stole his boat."

"Shut up!"

"Does she understand?"

"Oh, hush!"

"Are those two married over there—leaning on each other?"

"Of course not," laughed Robert.

"Of course not," echoed Mariequita, with a serious, confirmatory bob of the head.

The sun was high up and beginning to bite. The swift breeze seemed to Edna to bury the sting of it into the pores of her face and hands. Robert held his umbrella over her.

As they went cutting sidewise through the water, the sails bellied taut, with the wind filling and overflowing them. Old Monsieur Farival laughed sardonically at something as he looked at the sails, and Beaudelet swore at the old man under his breath.

Sailing across the bay to the *Chênière Caminada,* Edna felt as if she were being borne away from some anchorage which had held her fast, whose chains had been loosening—had snapped the night before when the mystic spirit was abroad, leaving her free to drift whithersoever she chose to set her sails. Robert spoke to her incessantly; he no longer noticed Mariequita. The girl had shrimps in her bamboo basket. They were covered with Spanish moss. She beat the moss down impatiently, and muttered to herself sullenly.

"Let us go to Grande Terre[1] to-morrow?" said Robert in a low voice.

"What shall we do there?"

"Climb up the hill to the old fort and look at the little wriggling gold snakes, and watch the lizards sun themselves."

She gazed away toward Grande Terre and thought she would like to be alone there with Robert, in the sun, listening to the ocean's roar and watching the slimy lizards writhe in and out among the ruins of the old fort.

"And the next day or the next we can sail to the Bayou Brulow,"[2] he went on.

"What shall we do there?"

"Anything—cast bait for fish."

"No; we'll go back to Grande Terre. Let the fish alone."

"We'll go wherever you like," he said. "I'll have Tonie come over and help me patch and trim my boat. We shall not need Beaudelet nor any one. Are you afraid of the pirogue?"[3]

"Oh, no."

"Then I'll take you some night in the pirogue when the moon shines. Maybe your Gulf spirit will whisper to you in which of these islands the treasures are hidden—direct you to the very spot, perhaps."

"And in a day we should be rich!" she laughed. "I'd give it all to you, the pirate gold and every bit of treasure we could dig up. I think you would know how to spend it. Pirate gold isn't a thing to be hoarded or utilized. It is something to squander and throw to the four winds, for the fun of seeing the golden specks fly."

"We'd share it, and scatter it together," he said. His face flushed.

They all went together up to the quaint little Gothic church of Our Lady of Lourdes, gleaming all brown and yellow with paint in the sun's glare.

Only Beaudelet remained behind, tinkering at his boat, and Mariequita walked away with her basket of shrimps, casting a look of childish ill-humor and reproach at Robert from the corner of her eye.

---

[1] An island near Grand Isle.

[2] A village in the marshlands of the Gulf Coast, built on stilts or platforms.   [3] Canoe.

XIII

A feeling of oppression and drowsiness overcame Edna during the service. Her head began to ache, and the lights on the altar swayed before her eyes. Another time she might have made an effort to regain her composure; but her one thought was to quit the stifling atmosphere of the church and reach the open air. She arose, climbing over Robert's feet with a muttered apology. Old Monsieur Farival, flurried, curious, stood up, but upon seeing that Robert had followed Mrs. Pontellier, he sank back into his seat. He whispered an anxious inquiry of the lady in black, who did not notice him or reply, but kept her eyes fastened upon the pages of her velvet prayer-book.

"I felt giddy and almost overcome," Edna said, lifting her hands instinctively to her head and pushing her straw hat up from her forehead. "I couldn't have stayed through the service." They were outside in the shadow of the church. Robert was full of solicitude.

"It was folly to have thought of going in the first place, let alone staying. Come over to Madame Antoine's; you can rest there." He took her arm and led her away, looking anxiously and continuously down into her face.

How still it was, with only the voice of the sea whispering through the reeds that grew in the salt-water pools! The long line of little gray, weather-beaten houses nestled peacefully among the orange trees. It must always have been God's day on that low, drowsy island, Edna thought. They stopped, leaning over a jagged fence made of sea-drift, to ask for water. A youth, a mild-faced Acadian,[1] was drawing water from the cistern, which was nothing more than a rusty buoy, with an opening on one side, sunk in the ground. The water which the youth handed to them in a tin pail was not cold to taste, but it was cool to her heated face, and it greatly revived and refreshed her.

Madame Antoine's cot[2] was at the far end of the village. She welcomed them with all the native hospitality, as she would have opened her door to let the sunlight in. She was fat, and walked heavily and clumsily across the floor. She could speak no English, but when Robert made her understand that the lady who accompanied him was ill and desired to rest, she was all eagerness to make Edna feel at home and to dispose of her comfortably.

The whole place was immaculately clean, and the big, four-posted bed, snow-white, invited one to repose. It stood in a small side room which looked out across a narrow grass plot toward the shed, where there was a disabled boat lying keel upward.

Madame Antoine had not gone to mass. Her son Tonie had, but she supposed he would soon be back, and she invited Robert to be seated and wait for him. But he went and sat outside the door and smoked. Madame Antoine busied herself in the large front room preparing dinner. She was boiling mullets[3] over a few red coals in the huge fireplace.

Edna, left alone in the little side room, loosened her clothes, removing the greater part of them. She bathed her face, her neck and arms in the basin that stood between the windows. She took off her shoes and stockings and stretched herself in the very center of the high, white bed. How luxurious it felt to rest thus

---

[1] A descendant of French-Canadians expelled from Acadia (Nova Scotia) in 1755.
[2] Cottage.   [3] Fish.

in a strange, quaint bed, with its sweet country odor of laurel lingering about the sheets and mattress! She stretched her strong limbs that ached a little. She ran her fingers through her loosened hair for a while. She looked at her round arms as she held them straight up and rubbed them one after the other, observing closely, as if it were something she saw for the first time, the fine, firm quality and texture of her flesh. She clasped her hands easily above her head, and it was thus she fell asleep.

She slept lightly at first, half awake and drowsily attentive to the things about her. She could hear Madame Antoine's heavy, scraping tread as she walked back and forth on the sanded floor. Some chickens were clucking outside the windows, scratching for bits of gravel in the grass. Later she half heard the voices of Robert and Tonie talking under the shed. She did not stir. Even her eyelids rested numb and heavily over her sleepy eyes. The voices went on—Tonie's slow, Acadian drawl, Robert's quick, soft, smooth French. She understood French imperfectly unless directly addressed, and the voices were only part of the other drowsy, muffled sounds lulling her senses.

When Edna awoke it was with the conviction that she had slept long and soundly. The voices were hushed under the shed. Madame Antoine's step was no longer to be heard in the adjoining room. Even the chickens had gone elsewhere to scratch and cluck. The mosquito bar was drawn over her; the old woman had come in while she slept and let down the bar. Edna arose quietly from the bed, and looking between the curtains of the window, she saw by the slanting rays of the sun that the afternoon was far advanced. Robert was out there under the shed, reclining in the shade against the sloping keel of the overturned boat. He was reading from a book. Tonie was no longer with him. She wondered what had become of the rest of the party. She peeped out at him two or three times as she stood washing herself in the little basin between the windows.

Madame Antoine had laid some coarse, clean towels upon a chair, and had placed a box of *poudre de riz*[4] within easy reach. Edna dabbed the powder upon her nose and cheeks as she looked at herself closely in the little distorted mirror which hung on the wall above the basin. Her eyes were bright and wide awake and her face glowed.

When she had completed her toilet she walked into the adjoining room. She was very hungry. No one was there. But there was a cloth spread upon the table that stood against the wall, and a cover was laid for one, with a crusty brown loaf and a bottle of wine beside the plate. Edna bit a piece from the brown loaf, tearing it with her strong, white teeth. She poured some of the wine into the glass and drank it down. Then she went softly out of doors, and plucking an orange from the low-hanging bough of a tree, threw it at Robert, who did not know she was awake and up.

An illumination broke over his whole face when he saw her and joined her under the orange tree.

"How many years have I slept?" she inquired. "The whole island seems changed. A new race of beings must have sprung up, leaving only you and me as past relics. How many ages ago did Madame Antoine and Tonie die? and when did our people from Grand Isle disappear from the earth?"

---

[4] "Rice powder" (French), used on the face.

He familiarly adjusted a ruffle upon her shoulder.

"You have slept precisely one hundred years. I was left here to guard your slumbers; and for one hundred years I have been out under the shed reading a book. The only evil I couldn't prevent was to keep a broiled fowl from drying up."

"If it has turned to stone, still will I eat it," said Edna, moving with him into the house. "But really, what has become of Monsieur Farival and the others?"

"Gone hours ago. When they found that you were sleeping they thought it best not to awake you. Any way, I wouldn't have let them. What was I here for?"

"I wonder if Léonce will be uneasy!" she speculated, as she seated herself at table.

"Of course not; he knows you are with me," Robert replied, as he busied himself among sundry pans and covered dishes which had been left standing on the hearth.

"Where are Madame Antoine and her son?" asked Edna.

"Gone to Vespers,[5] and to visit some friends, I believe. I am to take you back in Tonie's boat whenever you are ready to go."

He stirred the smoldering ashes till the broiled fowl began to sizzle afresh. He served her with no mean repast, dripping[6] the coffee anew and sharing it with her. Madame Antoine had cooked little else than the mullets, but while Edna slept Robert had foraged the island. He was childishly gratified to discover her appetite, and to see the relish with which she ate the food which he had procured for her.

"Shall we go right away?" she asked, after draining her glass and brushing together the crumbs of the crusty loaf.

"The sun isn't as low as it will be in two hours," he answered.

"The sun will be gone in two hours."

"Well, let it go; who cares!"

They waited a good while under the orange trees, till Madame Antoine came back, panting, waddling, with a thousand apologies to explain her absence. Tonie did not dare to return. He was shy, and would not willingly face any woman except his mother.

It was very pleasant to stay there under the orange trees, while the sun dipped lower and lower, turning the western sky to flaming copper and gold. The shadows lengthened and crept out like stealthy, grotesque monsters across the grass.

Edna and Robert both sat upon the ground—that is, he lay upon the ground beside her, occasionally picking at the hem of her muslin gown.

Madame Antoine seated her fat body, broad and squat, upon a bench beside the door. She had been talking all the afternoon, and had wound herself up to the story-telling pitch.

And what stories she told them! But twice in her life she had left the *Chênière Caminada,* and then for the briefest span. All her years she had squatted and waddled there upon the island, gathering legends of the Baratarians[7] and the sea. The night came on, with the moon to lighten it. Edna could hear the whispering voices of dead men and the click of muffled gold.

When she and Robert stepped into Tonie's boat, with the red lateen sail, misty

---

[5] Evening church service.   [6] Brewing.

[7] Inhabitants of Barataria Bay, a refuge near the mouth of the Mississippi for smugglers and pirates.

spirit forms were prowling in the shadows and among the reeds, and upon the water were phantom ships, speeding to cover.

XIV

The youngest boy, Etienne, had been very naughty, Madame Ratignolle said, as she delivered him into the hands of his mother. He had been unwilling to go to bed and had made a scene; whereupon she had taken charge of him and pacified him as well as she could. Raoul had been in bed and asleep for two hours.

The youngster was in his long white nightgown, that kept tripping him up as Madame Ratignolle led him along by the hand. With the other chubby fist he rubbed his eyes, which were heavy with sleep and ill humor. Edna took him in her arms, and seating herself in the rocker, began to coddle and caress him, calling him all manner of tender names, soothing him to sleep.

It was not more than nine o'clock. No one had yet gone to bed but the children.

Léonce had been very uneasy at first, Madame Ratignolle said, and had wanted to start at once for the *Chênière*. But Monsieur Farival had assured him that his wife was only overcome with sleep and fatigue, that Tonie would bring her safely back later in the day; and he had thus been dissuaded from crossing the bay. He had gone over to Klein's, looking up some cotton broker whom he wished to see in regard to securities, exchanges, stocks, bonds, or something of the sort, Madame Ratignolle did not remember what. He said he would not remain away late. She herself was suffering from heat and oppression, she said. She carried a bottle of salts[1] and a large fan. She would not consent to remain with Edna, for Monsieur Ratignolle was alone, and he detested above all things to be left alone.

When Etienne had fallen asleep Edna bore him into the back room, and Robert went and lifted the mosquito bar that she might lay the child comfortably in his bed. The quadroon had vanished. When they emerged from the cottage Robert bade Edna good-night.

"Do you know we have been together the whole livelong day, Robert—since early this morning?" she said at parting.

"All but the hundred years when you were sleeping. Good-night."

He pressed her hand and went away in the direction of the beach. He did not join any of the others, but walked alone toward the Gulf.

Edna stayed outside, awaiting her husband's return. She had no desire to sleep or to retire; nor did she feel like going over to sit with the Ratignolles, or to join Madame Lebrun and a group whose animated voices reached her as they sat in conversation before the house. She let her mind wander back over her stay at Grand Isle; and she tried to discover wherein this summer had been different from any and every other summer of her life. She could only realize that she herself—her present self—was in some way different from the other self. That she was seeing with different eyes and making the acquaintance of new conditions in herself that colored and changed her environment, she did not yet suspect.

She wondered why Robert had gone away and left her. It did not occur to her to think he might have grown tired of being with her the livelong day. She was not

---

[1] Smelling salts, used to revive a person who is dizzy or faint.

tired, and she felt that he was not. She regretted that he had gone. It was so much more natural to have him stay when he was not absolutely required to leave her.

As Edna waited for her husband she sang low a little song that Robert had sung as they crossed the bay. It began with "Ah! *Si tu savais*,"[2] and every verse ended with "*si tu savais*."

Robert's voice was not pretentious. It was musical and true. The voice, the notes, the whole refrain haunted her memory.

XV

When Edna entered the dining-room one evening a little late, as was her habit, an unusually animated conversation seemed to be going on. Several persons were talking at once, and Victor's voice was predominating, even over that of his mother. Edna had returned late from her bath, had dressed in some haste, and her face was flushed. Her head, set off by her dainty white gown, suggested a rich, rare blossom. She took her seat at table between old Monsieur Farival and Madame Ratignolle.

As she seated herself and was about to begin to eat her soup, which had been served when she entered the room, several persons informed her simultaneously that Robert was going to Mexico. She laid her spoon down and looked about her bewildered. He had been with her, reading to her all the morning, and had never even mentioned such a place as Mexico. She had not seen him during the afternoon; she had heard some one say he was at the house, upstairs with his mother. This she had thought nothing of, though she was surprised when he did not join her later in the afternoon, when she went down to the beach.

"To-night!" "This very evening!" "Did you ever!" "What possesses him!" were some of the replies she gathered, uttered simultaneously in French and English.

"Impossible!" she exclaimed. "How can a person start off from Grand Isle to Mexico at a moment's notice, as if he were going over to Klein's or to the wharf or down to the beach?"

"I said all along I was going to Mexico; I've been saying so for years!" cried Robert, in an excited and irritable tone, with the air of a man defending himself against a swarm of stinging insects.

Madame Lebrun knocked on the table with her knife handle.

"Please let Robert explain why he is going, and why he is going to-night," she called out. "Really, this table is getting to be more and more like Bedlam[1] every day, with everybody talking at once. Sometimes—I hope God will forgive me— but positively, sometimes I wish Victor would lose the power of speech."

Victor laughed sardonically as he thanked his mother for her holy wish, of which he failed to see the benefit to anybody, except that it might afford her a more ample opportunity and license to talk herself.

Monsieur Farival thought that Victor should have been taken out in mid-ocean

---

[2] "Couldst Thou But Know" (French), a song by the Irish composer Michael Balfe (1808–1870). The song reflects both Edna's longing for self-knowledge and the other characters' lack of knowledge about what she needs or wants.

[1] A London insane asylum.

in his earliest youth and drowned. Victor thought there would be more logic in thus disposing of old people with an established claim for making themselves universally obnoxious. Madame Lebrun grew a trifle hysterical; Robert called his brother some sharp, hard names.

"There's nothing much to explain, mother," he said; though he explained, nevertheless—looking chiefly at Edna—that he could only meet the gentleman whom he intended to join at Vera Cruz by taking such and such a steamer, which left New Orleans on such a day; that Beaudelet was going out with his lugger-load of vegetables that night, which gave him an opportunity of reaching the city and making his vessel in time.

"But when did you make up your mind to all this?" demanded Monsieur Farival.

"This afternoon," returned Robert, with a shade of annoyance.

"At what time this afternoon?" persisted the old gentleman, with nagging determination, as if he were cross-questioning a criminal in a court of justice.

"At four o'clock this afternoon, Monsieur Farival," Robert replied, in a high voice and with a lofty air, which reminded Edna of some gentleman on the stage.

She had forced herself to eat most of her soup, and now she was picking the flaky bits of a *court bouillon*[2] with her fork.

The lovers were profiting by the general conversation on Mexico to speak in whispers of matters which they rightly considered were interesting to no one but themselves. The lady in black had once received a pair of prayer-beads of curious workmanship from Mexico, with very special indulgence[3] attached to them, but she had never been able to ascertain whether the indulgence extended outside the Mexican border. Father Fochel of the Cathedral had attempted to explain it; but he had not done so to her satisfaction. And she begged that Robert would interest himself, and discover, if possible, whether she was entitled to the indulgence accompanying the remarkably curious Mexican prayer-beads.

Madame Ratignolle hoped that Robert would exercise extreme caution in dealing with the Mexicans, who, she considered, were a treacherous people, unscrupulous and revengeful. She trusted she did them no injustice in thus condemning them as a race. She had known personally but one Mexican, who made and sold excellent tamales, and whom she would have trusted implicitly, so soft-spoken was he. One day he was arrested for stabbing his wife. She never knew whether he had been hanged or not.

Victor had grown hilarious, and was attempting to tell an anecdote about a Mexican girl who served chocolate one winter in a restaurant in Dauphine Street. No one would listen to him but old Monsieur Farival, who went into convulsions over the droll story.

Edna wondered if they had all gone mad, to be talking and clamoring at that rate. She herself could think of nothing to say about Mexico or the Mexicans.

"At what time do you leave?" she asked Robert.

"At ten," he told her. "Beaudelet wants to wait for the moon."

"Are you all ready to go?"

---

[2] Fish cooked in seasoned sauce (French).
[3] A Roman Catholic practice of allowing remission of punishment due for a sin.

"Quite ready. I shall only take a hand-bag, and shall pack my trunk in the city."

He turned to answer some question put to him by his mother, and Edna, having finished her black coffee, left the table.

She went directly to her room. The little cottage was close and stuffy after leaving the outer air. But she did not mind; there appeared to be a hundred different things demanding her 'attention indoors. She began to set the toilet-stand to rights, grumbling at the negligence of the quadroon, who was in the adjoining room putting the children to bed. She gathered together stray garments that were hanging on the backs of chairs, and put each where it belonged in closet or bureau drawer. She changed her gown for a more comfortable and commodious wrapper. She rearranged her hair, combing and brushing it with unusual energy. Then she went in and assisted the quadroon in getting the boys to bed.

They were very playful and inclined to talk—to do anything but lie quiet and go to sleep. Edna sent the quadroon away to her supper and told her she need not return. Then she sat and told the children a story. Instead of soothing it excited them, and added to their wakefulness. She left them in heated argument, speculating about the conclusion of the tale which their mother promised to finish the following night.

The little black girl came in to say that Madame Lebrun would like to have Mrs. Pontellier go and sit with them over at the house till Mr. Robert went away. Edna returned answer that she had already undressed, that she did not feel quite well, but perhaps she would go over to the house later. She started to dress again, and got as far advanced as to remove her *peignoir*. But changing her mind once more she resumed the *peignoir*, and went outside and sat down before her door. She was overheated and irritable, and fanned herself energetically for a while. Madame Ratignolle came down to discover what was the matter.

"All that noise and confusion at the table must have upset me," replied Edna, "and moreover, I hate shocks and surprises. The idea of Robert starting off in such a ridiculously sudden and dramatic way! As if it were a matter of life and death! Never saying a word about it all morning when he was with me."

"Yes," agreed Madame Ratignolle. "I think it was showing us all—you especially—very little consideration. It wouldn't have surprised me in any of the others; those Lebruns are all given to heroics. But I must say I should never have expected such a thing from Robert. Are you not coming down? Come on, dear; it doesn't look friendly."

"No," said Edna, a little sullenly. "I can't go to the trouble of dressing again, I don't feel like it."

"You needn't dress; you look all right; fasten a belt around your waist. Just look at me!"

"No," persisted Edna; "but you go on. Madame Lebrun might be offended if we both stayed away."

Madame Ratignolle kissed Edna good-night, and went away, being in truth rather desirous of joining in the general and animated conversation which was still in progress concerning Mexico and the Mexicans.

Somewhat later Robert came up, carrying his hand-bag.

"Aren't you feeling well?" he asked.

"Oh, well enough. Are you going right away?"

He lit a match and looked at his watch. "In twenty minutes," he said. The sudden and brief flare of the match emphasized the darkness for a while. He sat down upon a stool which the children had left out on the porch.

"Get a chair," said Edna.

"This will do," he replied. He put on his soft hat and nervously took it off again, and wiping his face with his handkerchief, complained of the heat.

"Take the fan," said Edna, offering it to him.

"Oh, no! Thank you. It does no good; you have to stop fanning some time, and feel all the more uncomfortable afterward."

"That's one of the ridiculous things which men always say. I have never known one to speak otherwise of fanning. How long will you be gone?"

"Forever, perhaps. I don't know. It depends upon a good many things."

"Well, in case it shouldn't be forever, how long will it be?"

"I don't know."

"This seems to me perfectly preposterous and uncalled for. I don't like it. I don't understand your motive for silence and mystery, never saying a word to me about it this morning." He remained silent, not offering to defend himself. He only said, after a moment:

"Don't part from me in an ill-humor. I never knew you to be out of patience with me before."

"I don't want to part in any ill-humor," she said. "But can't you understand? I've grown used to seeing you, to having you with me all the time, and your action seems unfriendly, even unkind. You don't even offer an excuse for it. Why, I was planning to be together, thinking of how pleasant it would be to see you in the city next winter."

"So was I," he blurted. "Perhaps that's the—" He stood up suddenly and held out his hand. "Good-by, my dear Mrs. Pontellier; good-by. You won't—I hope you won't completely forget me." She clung to his hand, striving to detain him.

"Write to me when you get there, won't you, Robert?" she entreated.

"I will, thank you. Good-by."

How unlike Robert! the merest acquaintance would have said something more emphatic than "I will, thank you; good-by," to such a request.

He had evidently already taken leave of the people over at the house, for he descended the steps and went to join Beaudelet, who was out there with an oar across his shoulder waiting for Robert. They walked away in the darkness. She could only hear Beaudelet's voice; Robert had apparently not even spoken a word of greeting to his companion.

Edna bit her handkerchief convulsively; striving to hold back and to hide, even from herself as she would have hidden from another, the emotion which was troubling—tearing—her. Her eyes were brimming with tears.

For the first time she recognized anew the symptoms of infatuation which she had felt incipiently as a child, as a girl in her earliest teens, and later as a young woman. The recognition did not lessen the reality, the poignancy of the revelation by any suggestion or promise of instability. The past was nothing to her; offered no lesson which she was willing to heed. The future was a mystery which she never attempted to penetrate. The present alone was significant; was hers, to torture her as it was doing then with the biting conviction that she had lost that which she had held, that she had been denied that which her impassioned, newly awakened being demanded.

XVI

"Do you miss your friend greatly?" asked Mademoiselle Reisz one morning as she came creeping up behind Edna, who had just left her cottage on her way to the beach. She spent much of her time in the water since she had acquired finally the art of swimming. As their stay at Grand Isle drew near its close, she felt that she could not give too much time to a diversion which afforded her the only real pleasurable moments that she knew. When Mademoiselle Reisz came and touched her upon the shoulder and spoke to her, the woman seemed to echo the thought which was ever in Edna's mind; or, better, the feeling which constantly possessed her.

Robert's going had some way taken the brightness, the color, the meaning out of everything. The conditions of her life were in no way changed, but her whole existence was dulled, like a faded garment which seems to be no longer worth wearing. She sought him everywhere—in others whom she induced to talk about him. She went up in the mornings to Madame Lebrun's room, braving the clatter of the old sewing-machine. She sat there and chatted at intervals as Robert had done. She gazed around the room at the pictures and photographs hanging upon the wall, and discovered in some corner an old family album, which she examined with the keenest interest, appealing to Madame Lebrun for enlightenment concerning the many figures and faces which she discovered between its pages.

There was a picture of Madame Lebrun with Robert as a baby, seated in her lap, a round-faced infant with a fist in his mouth. The eyes alone in the baby suggested the man. And that was he also in kilts, at the age of five, wearing long curls and holding a whip in his hand. It made Edna laugh, and she laughed, too, at the portrait in his first long trousers; while another interested her, taken when he left for college, looking thin, long-faced, with eyes full of fire, ambition and great intentions. But there was no recent picture, none which suggested the Robert who had gone away five days ago, leaving a void and wilderness behind him.

"Oh, Robert stopped having his pictures taken when he had to pay for them himself! He found wiser use for his money, he says," explained Madame Lebrun. She had a letter from him, written before he left New Orleans. Edna wished to see the letter, and Madame Lebrun told her to look for it either on the table or the dresser, or perhaps it was on the mantelpiece.

The letter was on the bookshelf. It possessed the greatest interest and attraction for Edna; the envelope, its size and shape, the post-mark, the handwriting. She examined every detail of the outside before opening it. There were only a few lines, setting forth that he would leave the city that afternoon, that he had packed his trunk in good shape, that he was well, and sent her his love and begged to be affectionately remembered to all. There was no special message to Edna except a postscript saying that if Mrs. Pontellier desired to finish the book which he had been reading to her, his mother would find it in his room, among other books there on the table. Edna experienced a pang of jealousy because he had written to his mother rather than to her.

Every one seemed to take for granted that she missed him. Even her husband, when he came down the Saturday following Robert's departure, expressed regret that he had gone.

"How do you get on without him, Edna?" he asked.

"It's very dull without him," she admitted. Mr. Pontellier had seen Robert in the city, and Edna asked him a dozen questions or more. Where had they met? On Carondelet Street, in the morning. They had gone "in" and had a drink and a cigar together. What had they talked about? Chiefly about his prospects in Mexico, which Mr. Pontellier thought were promising. How did he look? How did he seem—grave, or gay, or how? Quite cheerful, and wholly taken up with the idea of his trip, which Mr. Pontellier found altogether natural in a young fellow about to seek fortune and adventure in a strange, queer country.

Edna tapped her foot impatiently, and wondered why the children persisted in playing in the sun when they might be under the trees. She went down and led them out of the sun, scolding the quadroon for not being more attentive.

It did not strike her as in the least grotesque that she should be making of Robert the object of conversation and leading her husband to speak of him. The sentiment which she entertained for Robert in no way resembled that which she felt for her husband, or had ever felt, or ever expected to feel. She had all her life long been accustomed to harbor thoughts and emotions which never voiced themselves. They had never taken the form of struggles. They belonged to her and were her own, and she entertained the conviction that she had a right to them and that they concerned no one but herself. Edna has once told Madame Ratignolle that she would never sacrifice herself for her children, or for any one. Then had followed a rather heated argument; the two women did not appear to understand each other or to be talking the same language. Edna tried to appease her friend, to explain.

"I would give up the unessential; I would give my money, I would give my life for my children; but I wouldn't give myself. I can't make it more clear; it's only something which I am beginning to comprehend, which is revealing itself to me."

"I don't know what you would call the essential, or what you mean by the unessential," said Madame Ratignolle, cheerfully; "but a woman who would give her life for her children could do no more than that—your Bible tells you so. I'm sure I couldn't do more than that."

"Oh, yes you could!" laughed Edna.

She was not surprised at Mademoiselle Reisz's question the morning that lady, following her to the beach, tapped her on the shoulder and asked if she did not greatly miss her young friend.

"Oh, good morning, Mademoiselle; is it you? Why, of course I miss Robert. Are you going down to bathe?"

"Why should I go down to bathe at the very end of the season when I haven't been in the surf all summer," replied the woman, disagreeably.

"I beg your pardon," offered Edna, in some embarrassment, for she should have remembered that Mademoiselle Reisz's avoidance of the water had furnished a theme for much pleasantry. Some among them thought it was on account of her false hair, or the dread of getting the violets wet, while others attributed it to the natural aversion for water sometimes believed to accompany the artistic temperament. Mademoiselle offered Edna some chocolates in a paper bag, which she took from her pocket, by way of showing that she bore no ill feeling. She habitually ate chocolates for their sustaining quality; they contained much nutriment in small compass, she said. They saved her from starvation, as Madame Lebrun's table was utterly impossible; and no one save so impertinent a woman as Madame Lebrun could think of offering such food to people and requiring them to pay for it.

"She must feel very lonely without her son," said Edna, desiring to change the subject. "Her favorite son, too. It must have been quite hard to let him go."

Mademoiselle laughed maliciously.

"Her favorite son! Oh, dear! Who could have been imposing such a tale upon you? Aline Lebrun lives for Victor, and for Victor alone. She has spoiled him into the worthless creature he is. She worships him and the ground he walks on. Robert is very well in a way, to give up all the money he can earn to the family, and keep the barest pittance for himself. Favorite son, indeed! I miss the poor fellow myself, my dear. I liked to see and to hear him about the place—the only Lebrun who is worth a pinch of salt. He comes to see me often in the city. I like to play to him. That Victor! hanging would be too good for him. It's a wonder Robert hasn't beaten him to death long ago."

"I thought he had great patience with his brother," offered Edna, glad to be talking about Robert, no matter what was said.

"Oh! he thrashed him well enough a year or two ago," said Mademoiselle. "It was about a Spanish girl, whom Victor considered that he had some sort of claim upon. He met Robert one day talking to the girl, or walking with her, or bathing with her, or carrying her basket—I don't remember what;—and he became so insulting and abusive that Robert gave him a thrashing on the spot that has kept him comparatively in order for a good while. It's about time he was getting another."

"Was her name Mariequita?" asked Edna.

"Mariequita—yes, that was it; Mariequita. I had forgotten. Oh, she's a sly one, and a bad one, that Mariequita!"

Edna looked down at Mademoiselle Reisz and wondered how she could have listened to her venom so long. For some reason she felt depressed, almost unhappy. She had not intended to go into the water; but she donned her bathing suit, and left Mademoiselle alone, seated under the shade of the children's tent. The water was growing cooler as the season advanced. Edna plunged and swam about with an abandon that thrilled and invigorated her. She remained a long time in the water, half hoping that Mademoiselle Reisz would not wait for her.

But Mademoiselle waited. She was very amiable during the walk back, and raved much over Edna's appearance in her bathing suit. She talked about music. She hoped that Edna would go to see her in the city, and wrote her address with the stub of a pencil on a piece of card which she found in her pocket.

"When do you leave?" asked Edna.

"Next Monday; and you?"

"The following week," answered Edna, adding, "It has been a pleasant summer, hasn't it, Mademoiselle?"

"Well," agreed Mademoiselle Reisz, with a shrug, "rather pleasant, if it hadn't been for the mosquitoes and the Farival twins."

XVII

The Pontelliers possessed a very charming home on Esplanade Street[1] in New Orleans. It was a large, double cottage, with a broad front veranda, whose round,

---

[1] A fashionable street where the rich lived.

fluted columns supported the sloping roof. The house was painted a dazzling white; the outside shutters, or jalousies, were green. In the yard, which was kept scrupulously neat, were flowers and plants of every description which flourishes in South Louisiana. Within doors the appointments were perfect after the conventional type. The softest carpets and rugs covered the floors; rich and tasteful draperies hung at doors and windows. There were paintings, selected with judgment and discrimination, upon the walls. The cut glass, the silver, the heavy damask[2] which daily appeared upon the table were the envy of many women whose husbands were less generous than Mr. Pontellier.

Mr. Pontellier was very fond of walking about his house examining its various appointments and details, to see that nothing was amiss. He greatly valued his possessions, chiefly because they were his, and derived genuine pleasure from contemplating a painting, a statuette, a rare lace curtain—no matter what—after he had bought it and placed it among his household gods.

On Tuesday afternoons—Tuesday being Mrs. Pontellier's reception day[3]—there was a constant stream of callers—women who came in carriages or in the street cars, or walked when the air was soft and distance permitted. A light-colored mulatto boy, in dress coat and bearing a diminutive silver tray for the reception of cards, admitted them. A maid, in white fluted cap, offered the callers liqueur, coffee, or chocolate, as they might desire. Mrs. Pontellier, attired in a handsome reception gown, remained in the drawing-room the entire afternoon receiving her visitors. Men sometimes called in the evening with their wives.

This had been the programme which Mrs. Pontellier had religiously followed since her marriage six years before. Certain evenings during the week she and her husband attended the opera or sometimes the play.

Mr. Pontellier left his home in the mornings between nine and ten o'clock, and rarely returned before half-past six or seven in the evening—dinner being served at half-past seven.

He and his wife seated themselves at table one Tuesday evening, a few weeks after their return from Grand Isle. They were alone together. The boys were being put to bed; the patter of their bare, escaping feet could be heard occasionally, as well as the pursuing voice of the quadroon, lifted in mild protest and entreaty. Mrs. Pontellier did not wear her usual Tuesday reception gown; she was in ordinary house dress. Mr. Pontellier, who was observant about such things, noticed it, as he served the soup and handed it to the boy in waiting.

"Tired out, Edna? Whom did you have? Many callers?" he asked. He tasted his soup and began to season it with pepper, salt, vinegar, mustard—everything within reach.

"There were a good many," replied Edna, who was eating her soup with evident satisfaction. "I found their cards when I got home; I was out."

"Out!" exclaimed her husband, with something like genuine consternation in his voice as he laid down the vinegar cruet and looked at her through his glasses. "Why, what could have taken you out on Tuesday? What did you have to do?"

"Nothing. I simply felt like going out, and I went out."

"Why, my dear, I should think you'd understand by this time that people don't

---

[2] Richly patterned table linen.
[3] A day when a woman stayed home to receive callers. A caller, told that the woman of the house was out, would be insulted.

do such things; we've got to observe *les convenances*[4] if we ever expect to get on and keep up with the procession. If you felt that you had to leave home this afternoon, you should have left some suitable explanation for your absence."

"This soup is really impossible; it's strange that woman hasn't learned yet to make a decent soup. Any free-lunch stand in town serves a better one. Was Mrs. Belthrop here?"

"Bring the tray with the cards, Joe. I don't remember who was here."

The boy retired and returned after a moment, bringing the tiny silver tray, which was covered with ladies' visiting cards. He handed it to Mrs. Pontellier.

"Give it to Mr. Pontellier," she said.

Joe offered the tray to Mr. Pontellier, and removed the soup.

Mr. Pontellier scanned the names of his wife's callers, reading some of them aloud, with comments as he read.

"'The Misses Delasidas.' I worked a big deal in futures[5] for their father this morning; nice girls; it's time they were getting married. 'Mrs. Belthrop.' I tell you what it is, Edna; you can't afford to snub Mrs. Belthrop. Why, Belthrop could buy and sell us ten times over. His business is worth a good, round sum to me. You'd better write her a note. 'Mrs. James Highcamp.' Hugh! the less you have to do with Mrs. Highcamp, the better. 'Madame Laforcé.' Came all the way from Carrolton,[6] too, poor old soul. 'Miss Wiggs,' 'Mrs. Eleanor Boltons.'" He pushed the cards aside.

"Mercy!" exclaimed Edna, who had been fuming. "Why are you taking the thing so seriously and making such a fuss over it?"

"I'm not making any fuss over it. But it's just such seeming trifles that we've got to take seriously; such things count."

The fish was scorched. Mr. Pontellier would not touch it. Edna said she did not mind a little scorched taste. The roast was in some way not to his fancy, and he did not like the manner in which the vegetables were served.

"It seems to me," he said, "we spend money enough in this house to procure at least one meal a day which a man could eat and retain his self-respect."

"You used to think the cook was a treasure," returned Edna, indifferently.

"Perhaps she was when she first came; but cooks are only human. They need looking after, like any other class of persons that you employ. Suppose I didn't look after the clerks in my office, just let them run things their own way; they'd soon make a nice mess of me and my business."

"Where are you going?" asked Edna, seeing that her husband arose from the table without having eaten a morsel except a taste of the highly-seasoned soup.

"I'm going to get my dinner at the club. Good night." He went into the hall, took his hat and stick from the stand, and left the house.

She was somewhat familiar with such scenes. They had often made her very unhappy. On a few previous occasions she had been completely deprived of any desire to finish her dinner. Sometimes she had gone into the kitchen to administer a tardy rebuke to the cook. Once she went to her room and studied the cookbook

---

[4] "The social conventions" (French). For women of Edna's class at the time, these rules were strictly followed, for fear of ostracism.

[5] Speculated in stocks or commodities by buying them for future delivery, in hopes their value will rise by then.

[6] A western sector of New Orleans.

during an entire evening, finally writing out a menu for the week, which left her harassed with a feeling that, after all, she had accomplished no good that was worth the name.

But that evening Edna finished her dinner alone, with forced deliberation. Her face was flushed and her eyes flamed with some inward fire that lighted them. After finishing her dinner she went to her room, having instructed the boy to tell any other callers that she was indisposed.

It was a large, beautiful room, rich and picturesque in the soft, dim light which the maid had turned low. She went and stood at an open window and looked out upon the deep tangle of the garden below. All the mystery and witchery of the night seemed to have gathered there amid the perfumes and the dusky and tortuous outlines of flowers and foliage. She was seeking herself and finding herself in just such sweet, half-darkness which met her moods. But the voices were not soothing that came to her from the darkness and the sky above and the stars. They jeered and sounded mournful notes with promise, devoid even of hope. She turned back into the room and began to walk to and fro down its whole length, without stopping, without resting. She carried in her hands a thin handkerchief, which she tore into ribbons, rolled into a ball, and flung from her. Once she stopped, and taking off her wedding ring, flung it upon the carpet. When she saw it lying there, she stamped her heel upon it, striving to crush it. But her small boot heel did not make an indenture, not a mark upon the little glittering circlet.

In a sweeping passion she seized a glass vase from the table and flung it upon the tiles of the hearth. She wanted to destroy something. The crash and clatter were what she wanted to hear.

A maid, alarmed at the din of breaking glass, entered the room to discover what was the matter.

"A vase fell upon the hearth," said Edna. "Never mind; leave it till morning."

"Oh! you might get some of the glass in your feet, ma'am," insisted the young woman, picking up bits of the broken vase that were scattered upon the carpet. "And here's your ring, ma'am, under the chair."

Edna held out her hand, and taking the ring, slipped it upon her finger.

XVIII

The following morning Mr. Pontellier, upon leaving for his office, asked Edna if she would not meet him in town in order to look at some new fixtures for the library.

"I hardly think we need new fixtures, Léonce. Don't let us get anything new; you are too extravagant. I don't believe you ever think of saving or putting by."

"The way to become rich is to make money, my dear Edna, not to save it," he said. He regretted that she did not feel inclined to go with him and select new fixtures. He kissed her good-by, and told her she was not looking well and must take care of herself. She was unusually pale and very quiet.

She stood on the front veranda as he quitted the house, and absently picked a few sprays of jessamine[1] that grew upon a trellis near by. She inhaled the odor of the blossoms and thrust them into the bosom of her white morning gown. The

---

[1] Jasmine.

boys were dragging along the banquette[2] a small "express wagon," which they had filled with blocks and sticks. The quadroon was following them with little quick steps, having assumed a fictitious animation and alacrity for the occasion. A fruit vender was crying his wares in the street.

Edna looked straight before her with a self-absorbed expression upon her face. She felt no interest in anything about her. The street, the children, the fruit vender, the flowers growing there under her eyes, were all part and parcel of an alien world which had suddenly become antagonistic.

She went back into the house. She had thought of speaking to the cook concerning her blunders of the previous night; but Mr. Pontellier had saved her that disagreeable mission, for which she was so poorly fitted. Mr. Pontellier's arguments were usually convincing with those whom he employed. He left home feeling quite sure that he and Edna would sit down that evening, and possibly a few subsequent evenings, to a dinner deserving of the name.

Edna spent an hour or two in looking over some of her old sketches. She could see their shortcomings and defects, which were glaring in her eyes. She tried to work a little, but found she was not in the humor. Finally she gathered together a few of the sketches—those which she considered the least discreditable; and she carried them with her when, a little later, she dressed and left the house. She looked handsome and distinguished in her street gown. The tan of the seashore had left her face, and her forehead was smooth, white, and polished beneath her heavy, yellow-brown hair. There were a few freckles on her face, and a small, dark mole near the under lip and one on the temple, half-hidden in her hair.

As Edna walked along the street she was thinking of Robert. She was still under the spell of her infatuation. She had tried to forget him, realizing the inutility of remembering. But the thought of him was like an obsession, ever pressing itself upon her. It was not that she dwelt upon details of their acquaintance, or recalled in any special or peculiar way his personality; it was his being, his existence, which dominated her thought, fading sometimes as if it would melt into the mist of the forgotten, reviving again with an intensity which filled her with an incomprehensible longing.

Edna was on her way to Madame Ratignolle's. Their intimacy, begun at Grand Isle, had not declined, and they had seen each other with some frequency since their return to the city. The Ratignolles lived at no great distance from Edna's home, on the corner of a side street, where Monsieur Ratignolle owned and conducted a drug store which enjoyed a steady and prosperous trade. His father had been in the business before him, and Monsieur Ratignolle stood well in the community and bore an enviable reputation for integrity and clear-headedness. His family lived in commodious apartments over the store, having an entrance on the side within the *porte cochère*.[3] There was something which Edna thought very French, very foreign, about their whole manner of living. In the large and pleasant salon which extended across the width of the house, the Ratignolles entertained their friends once a fortnight with a *soirée musicale*,[4] sometimes diversified by card-playing. There was a friend who played upon the 'cello. One brought his flute and another his violin, while there were some who sang and a number who performed upon the piano with various degrees of taste and agility. The Ratignol-

---

[2] Sidewalk.

[3] An entrance porch for carriages, where passengers can be protected from rain (French).

[4] An evening of musical entertainment (French).

les' *soirées musicales* were widely known, and it was considered a privilege to be invited to them.

Edna found her friend engaged in assorting the clothes which had returned that morning from the laundry. She at once abandoned her occupation upon seeing Edna, who had been ushered without ceremony into her presence.

"'Cité can do it as well as I; it is really her business," she explained to Edna, who apologized for interrupting her. And she summoned a young black woman, whom she instructed, in French, to be very careful in checking off the list which she handed her. She told her to notice particularly if a fine linen handkerchief of Monsieur Ratignolle's, which was missing last week, had been returned; and to be sure to set to one side such pieces as required mending and darning.

Then placing an arm around Edna's waist, she led her to the front of the house, to the salon, where it was cool and sweet with the odor of great roses that stood upon the hearth in jars.

Madame Ratignolle looked more beautiful than ever there at home, in a negligé which left her arms almost wholly bare and exposed the rich, melting curves of her white throat.

"Perhaps I shall be able to paint your picture some day," said Edna with a smile when they were seated. She produced the roll of sketches and started to unfold them. "I believe I ought to work again. I feel as if I wanted to be doing something. What do you think of them? Do you think it worth while to take it up again and study some more? I might study for a while with Laidpore."

She knew that Madame Ratignolle's opinion in such a matter would be next to valueless, that she herself had not alone decided, but determined; but she sought the words of praise and encouragement that would help her to put heart into her venture.

"Your talent is immense, dear!"

"Nonsense!" protested Edna, well pleased.

"Immense, I tell you," persisted Madame Ratignolle, surveying the sketches one by one, at close range, then holding them at arm's length, narrowing her eyes, and dropping her head on one side. "Surely, this Bavarian peasant is worthy of framing; and this basket of apples! never have I seen anything more lifelike. One might almost be tempted to reach out a hand and take one."

Edna could not control a feeling which bordered upon complacency at her friend's praise, even realizing, as she did, its true worth. She retained a few of the sketches, and gave all the rest to Madame Ratignolle, who appreciated the gift far beyond its value and proudly exhibited the pictures to her husband when he came up from the store a little later for his midday dinner.

Mr. Ratignolle was one of those men who are called the salt of the earth. His cheerfulness was unbounded, and it was matched by his goodness of heart, his broad charity, and common sense. He and his wife spoke English with an accent which was only discernible through its un-English emphasis and a certain carefulness and deliberation. Edna's husband spoke English with no accent whatever. The Ratignolles understood each other perfectly. If ever the fusion of two human beings into one has been accomplished on this sphere it was surely in their union.

As Edna seated herself at table with them she thought, "Better a dinner of herbs,"[5] though it did not take her long to discover that it was no dinner of herbs, but a delicious repast, simple, choice, and in every way satisfying.

---

[5] "Better is a dinner of herbs where love is, than a stalled ox and hatred therewith," from Proverbs 15:17.

Monsieur Ratignolle was delighted to see her, though he found her looking not so well as at Grand Isle, and he advised a tonic. He talked a good deal on various topics, a little politics, some city news and neighborhood gossip. He spoke with an animation and earnestness that gave an exaggerated importance to every syllable he uttered. His wife was keenly interested in everything he said, laying down her fork the better to listen, chiming in, taking the words out of his mouth.

Edna felt depressed rather than soothed after leaving them. The little glimpse of domestic harmony which had been offered her, gave her no regret, no longing. It was not a condition of life which fitted her, and she could see in it but an appalling and hopeless ennui.[6] She was moved by a kind of commiseration for Madame Ratignolle,—a pity for that colorless existence which never uplifted its possessor beyond the region of blind contentment, in which no moment of anguish ever visited her soul, in which she would never have the taste of life's delirium. Edna vaguely wondered what she meant by "life's delirium." It had crossed her thought like some unsought, extraneous impression.

XIX

Edna could not help but think that it was very foolish, very childish, to have stamped upon her wedding ring and smashed the crystal vase upon the tiles. She was visited by no more outbursts, moving her to such futile expedients. She began to do as she liked and to feel as she liked. She completely abandoned her Tuesdays at home, and did not return the visits of those who had called upon her. She made no ineffectual efforts to conduct her household *en bonne ménagère,*[1] going and coming as it suited her fancy, and, so far as she was able, lending herself to any passing caprice.

Mr. Pontellier had been a rather courteous husband so long as he met a certain tacit submissiveness in his wife. But her new and unexpected line of conduct completely bewildered him. It shocked him. Then her absolute disregard for her duties as a wife angered him. When Mr. Pontellier became rude, Edna grew insolent. She had resolved never to take another step backward.

"It seems to me the utmost folly for a woman at the head of a household, and the mother of children, to spend in an atelier[2] days which would be better employed contriving for the comfort of her family."

"I feel like painting," answered Edna. "Perhaps I shan't always feel like it."

"Then in God's name paint! but don't let the family go to the devil. There's Madame Ratignolle; because she keeps up her music, she doesn't let everything else go to chaos. And she's more of a musician than you are a painter."

"She isn't a musician, and I'm not a painter. It isn't on account of painting that I let things go."

"On account of what, then?"

"Oh! I don't know. Let me alone; you bother me."

It sometimes entered Mr. Pontellier's mind to wonder if his wife were not growing a little unbalanced mentally. He could see plainly that she was not herself. That is, he could not see that she was becoming herself and daily casting aside that fictitious self which we assume like a garment with which to appear before the world.

---

[6] "Boredom" (French).

[1] "As a good housekeeper" (French).   [2] "Studio" or "workshop" (French).

Her husband let her alone as she requested, and went away to his office. Edna went up to her atelier—a bright room in the top of the house. She was working with great energy and interest, without accomplishing anything, however, which satisfied her even in the smallest degree. For a time she had the whole household enrolled in the service of art. The boys posed for her. They thought it amusing at first, but the occupation soon lost its attractiveness when they discovered that it was not a game arranged especially for their entertainment. The quadroon sat for hours before Edna's palette, patient as a savage, while the house-maid took charge of the children, and the drawing-room went undusted. But the house-maid, too, served her term as model when Edna perceived that the young woman's back and shoulders were molded on classic lines, and that her hair, loosened from its confining cap, became an inspiration. While Edna worked she sometimes sang low the little air, *"Ah! si tu savais!"*

It moved her with recollections. She could hear again the ripple of the water, the flapping sail. She could see the glint of the moon upon the bay, and could feel the soft, gusty beating of the hot south wind. A subtle current of desire passed through her body, weakening her hold upon the brushes and making her eyes burn.

There were days when she was very happy without knowing why. She was happy to be alive and breathing, when her whole being seemed to be one with the sunlight, the color, the odors, the luxuriant warmth of some perfect Southern day. She liked then to wander alone into strange and unfamiliar places. She discovered many a sunny, sleepy corner, fashioned to dream in. And she found it good to dream and to be alone and unmolested.

There were days when she was unhappy, she did not know why,—when it did not seem worth while to be glad or sorry, to be alive or dead; when life appeared to her like a grotesque pandemonium and humanity like worms struggling blindly toward inevitable annihilation. She could not work on such a day, nor weave fancies to stir her pulses and warm her blood.

XX

It was during such a mood that Edna hunted up Mademoiselle Reisz. She had not forgotten the rather disagreeable impression left upon her by their last interview; but she nevertheless felt a desire to see her—above all, to listen while she played upon the piano. Quite early in the afternoon she started upon her quest for the pianist. Unfortunately she had mislaid or lost Mademoiselle Reisz's card, and looking up her address in the city directory, she found that the woman lived on Bienville Street, some distance away. The directory which fell into her hands was a year or more old, however, and upon reaching the number indicated, Edna discovered that the house was occupied by a respectable family of mulattoes who had *chambres garnies*[1] to let. They had been living there for six months, and knew absolutely nothing of a Mademoiselle Reisz. In fact, they knew nothing of any of their neighbors; their lodgers were all people of the highest distinction, they assured Edna. She did not linger to discuss class distinctions with Madame Pouponne, but hastened to a neighboring grocery store, feeling sure that Mademoiselle would have left her address with the proprietor.

---

[1] "Furnished rooms" (French).

He knew Mademoiselle Reisz a good deal better than he wanted to know her, he informed his questioner. In truth, he did not want to know her at all, or anything concerning her—the most disagreeable and unpopular woman who ever lived in Bienville Street. He thanked heaven she had left the neighborhood, and was equally thankful that he did not know where she had gone.

Edna's desire to see Mademoiselle Reisz had increased tenfold since these unlooked-for obstacles had arisen to thwart it. She was wondering who could give her the information she sought, when it suddenly occurred to her that Madame Lebrun would be the one most likely to do so. She knew it was useless to ask Madame Ratignolle, who was on the most distant terms with the musician, and preferred to know nothing concerning her. She had once been almost as emphatic in expressing herself upon the subject as the corner grocer.

Edna knew that Madame Lebrun had returned to the city, for it was the middle of November. And she also knew where the Lebruns lived, on Chartres Street.

Their home from the outside looked like a prison, with iron bars before the door and lower windows. The iron bars were a relic of the old *régime*,[2] and no one had ever thought of dislodging them. At the side was a high fence enclosing the garden. A gate or door opening upon the street was locked. Edna rang the bell at this side garden gate, and stood upon the banquette, waiting to be admitted.

It was Victor who opened the gate for her. A black woman, wiping her hands upon her apron, was close at this heels. Before she saw them Edna could hear them in altercation, the woman—plainly an anomaly—claiming the right to be allowed to perform her duties, one of which was to answer the bell.

Victor was surprised and delighted to see Mrs. Pontellier, and he made no attempt to conceal either his astonishment or his delight. He was a dark-browed, good-looking youngster of nineteen, greatly resembling his mother, but with ten times her impetuosity. He instructed the black woman to go at once and inform Madame Lebrun that Mrs. Pontellier desired to see her. The woman grumbled a refusal to do part of her duty when she had not been permitted to do it all, and started back to her interrupted task of weeding the garden. Whereupon Victor administered a rebuke in the form of a volley of abuse, which, owing to its rapidity and incoherence, was all but incomprehensible to Edna. Whatever it was, the rebuke was convincing, for the woman dropped her hoe and went mumbling into the house.

Edna did not wish to enter. It was very pleasant there on the side porch, where there were chairs, a wicker lounge, and a small table. She seated herself, for she was tired from her long tramp; and she began to rock gently and smooth out the folds of her silk parasol. Victor drew up his chair beside her. He at once explained that the black woman's offensive conduct was all due to imperfect training, as he was not there to take her in hand. He had only come up from the island the morning before, and expected to return next day. He stayed all winter at the island; he lived there, and kept the place in order and got things ready for the summer visitors.

But a man needed occasional relaxation, he informed Mrs. Pontellier, and every now and again he drummed up a pretext to bring him to the city. My! but he had had a time of it the evening before! He wouldn't want his mother to know, and he began to talk in a whisper. He was scintillant with recollections. Of course, he couldn't think of telling Mrs. Pontellier all about it, she being a woman and not

[2] The period from 1766 to 1803, when New Orleans was under the rule of Spanish governors.

comprehending such things. But it all began with a girl peeping and smiling at him through the shutters as he passed by. Oh! but she was a beauty! Certainly he smiled back, and went up and talked to her. Mrs. Pontellier did not know him if she supposed he was one to let an opportunity like that escape him. Despite herself, the youngster amused her. She must have betrayed in her look some degree of interest or entertainment. The boy grew more daring, and Mrs. Pontellier might have found herself, in a little while, listening to a highly colored story but for the timely appearance of Madame Lebrun.

That lady was still clad in white, according to her custom of the summer. Her eyes beamed an effusive welcome. Would not Mrs. Pontellier go inside? Would she partake of some refreshment? Why had she not been there before? How was that dear Mr. Pontellier and how were those sweet children? Had Mrs. Pontellier ever known such a warm November?

Victor went and reclined on the wicker lounge behind his mother's chair, where he commanded a view of Edna's face. He had taken her parasol from her hands while he spoke to her, and he now lifted it and twirled it above him as he lay on his back. When Madame Lebrun complained that it was *so* dull coming back to the city; that she saw *so* few people now; that even Victor, when he came up from the island for a day or two, had *so* much to occupy him and engage his time; then it was that the youth went into contortions on the lounge and winked mischievously at Edna. She somehow felt like a confederate in crime, and tried to look severe and disapproving.

There had been but two letters from Robert, with little in them, they told her. Victor said it was really not worth while to go inside for the letters, when his mother entreated him to go in search of them. He remembered the contents, which in truth he rattled off very glibly when put to the test.

One letter was written from Vera Cruz and the other from the City of Mexico. He had met Montel, who was doing everything toward his advancement. So far, the financial situation was no improvement over the one he had left in New Orleans, but of course the prospects were vastly better. He wrote of the City of Mexico, the buildings, the people and their habits, the conditions of life which he found there. He sent his love to the family. He inclosed a check to his mother, and hoped she would affectionately remember him to all his friends. That was about the substance of the two letters. Edna felt that if there had been a message for her, she would have received it. The despondent frame of mind in which she had left home began again to overtake her, and she remembered that she wished to find Mademoiselle Reisz.

Madame Lebrun knew where Mademoiselle Reisz lived. She gave Edna the address, regretting that she would not consent to stay and spend the remainder of the afternoon, and pay a visit to Mademoiselle Reisz some other day. The afternoon was already well advanced.

Victor escorted her out upon the banquette, lifted her parasol, and held it over her while he walked to the car[3] with her. He entreated her to bear in mind that the disclosures of the afternoon were strictly confidential. She laughed and bantered him a little, remembering too late that she should have been dignified and reserved.

---

[3] Streetcar.

"How handsome Mrs. Pontellier looked!" said Madame Lebrun to her son.

"Ravishing!" he admitted. "The city atmosphere has improved her. Some way she doesn't seem like the same woman."

XXI

Some people contended that the reason Mademoiselle Reisz always chose apartments up under the roof was to discourage the approach of beggars, peddlars and callers. There were plenty of windows in her little front room. They were for the most part dingy, but as they were nearly always open it did not make so much difference. They often admitted into the room a good deal of smoke and soot; but at the same time all the light and air that there was came through them. From her windows could be seen the crescent of the river, the masts of ships and the big chimneys of the Mississippi steamers. A magnificent piano crowded the apartment. In the next room she slept, and in the third and last she harbored a gasoline stove on which she cooked her meals when disinclined to descend to the neighboring restaurant. It was there also that she ate, keeping her belongings in a rare old buffet, dingy and battered from a hundred years of use.

When Edna knocked at Mademoiselle Reisz's front room door and entered, she discovered that person standing beside the window, engaged in mending or patching an old prunella gaiter.[1] The little musician laughed all over when she saw Edna. Her laugh consisted of a contortion of the face and all the muscles of the body. She seemed strikingly homely, standing there in the afternoon light. She still wore the shabby lace and the artificial bunch of violets on the side of her head.

"So you remembered me at last," said Mademoiselle. "I had said to myself, 'Ah, bah! she will never come.'"

"Did you want me to come?" asked Edna with a smile.

"I had not thought much about it," answered Mademoiselle. The two had seated themselves on a little bumpy sofa which stood against the wall. "I am glad, however, that you came. I have the water boiling back there, and was just about to make some coffee. You will drink a cup with me. And how is *la belle dame?*[2] Always handsome! always healthy! always contented!" She took Edna's hand between her strong wiry fingers, holding it loosely without warmth, and executing a sort of double theme upon the back and palm.

"Yes," she went on; "I sometimes thought: 'She will never come. She promised as those women in society always do, without meaning it. She will not come.' For I really don't believe you like me, Mrs. Pontellier."

"I don't know whether I like you or not," replied Edna, gazing down at the little woman with a quizzical look.

The candor of Mrs. Pontellier's admission greatly pleased Mademoiselle Reisz. She expressed her gratification by repairing forthwith to the region of the gasoline stove and rewarding her guest with the promised cup of coffee. The coffee and the biscuit accompanying it proved very acceptable to Edna, who had declined refreshment at Madame Lebrun's and was now beginning to feel hungry. Mademoi-

---

[1] A high-button shoe with a cloth upper.   [2] "The beautiful lady?" (French).

selle set the tray which she brought in upon a small table near at hand, and seated herself once again on the lumpy sofa.

"I have had a letter from your friend," she remarked, as she poured a little cream into Edna's cup and handed it to her.

"My friend?"

"Yes, your friend Robert. He wrote to me from the City of Mexico."

"Wrote to *you?*" repeated Edna in amazement, stirring her coffee absently.

"Yes, to me. Why not? Don't stir all the warmth out of your coffee; drink it. Though the letter might as well have been sent to you; it was nothing but Mrs. Pontellier from beginning to end."

"Let me see it," requested the young woman, entreatingly.

"No; a letter concerns no one but the person who writes it and the one to whom it is written."

"Haven't you just said it concerned me from beginning to end?"

"It was written about you, not to you. 'Have you seen Mrs. Pontellier? How is she looking?' he asks. 'As Mrs. Pontellier says,' or 'as Mrs. Pontellier once said.' 'If Mrs. Pontellier should call upon you, play for her that Impromptu of Chopin's,[3] my favorite. I heard it here a day or two ago, but not as you play it. I should like to know how it affects her,' and so on, as if he supposed we were constantly in each other's society."

"Let me see the letter."

"Oh, no."

"Have you answered it?"

"No."

"Let me see the letter."

"No, and again, no."

"Then play the Impromptu for me."

"It is growing late; what time do you have to be home?"

"Time doesn't concern me. Your question seems a little rude. Play the Impromptu."

"But you have told me nothing of yourself. What are you doing?"

"Painting!" laughed Edna. "I am becoming an artist. Think of it!"

"Ah! an artist! You have pretensions, Madame."

"Why pretensions? Do you think I could not become an artist?"

"I do not know you well enough to say. I do not know your talent or your temperament. To be an artist includes much; one must possess many gifts—absolute gifts—which have not been acquired by one's own effort. And, moreover, to succeed, the artist must possess the courageous soul."

"What do you mean by the courageous soul?"

"Courageous, *ma foi!*[4] The brave soul. The soul that dares and defies."

"Show me the letter and play for me the Impromptu. You see that I have persistence. Does that quality count for anthing in art?"

"It counts with a foolish old woman whom you have captivated," replied Mademoiselle, with her wriggling laugh.

The letter was right there at hand in the drawer of the little table upon which

[3] "Fantaisie-Impromptu in C-Sharp Minor," the melody of which is used in the song "I'm Always Chasing Rainbows."
[4] "To be sure!" (French).

Edna had just placed her coffee cup. Mademoiselle opened the drawer and drew forth the letter, the topmost one. She placed it in Edna's hands, and without further comment arose and went to the piano.

Mademoiselle played a soft interlude. It was an improvisation. She sat low at the instrument, and the lines of her body settled into ungraceful curves and angles that gave it an appearance of deformity. Gradually and imperceptibly the interlude melted into the soft opening minor chords of the Chopin Impromptu.

Edna did not know when the Impromptu began or ended. She sat in the sofa corner reading Robert's letter by the fading light. Mademoiselle had glided from the Chopin into the quivering love-notes of Isolde's song,[5] and back again to the Impromptu with its soulful and poignant longing.

The shadows deepened in the little room. The music grew strange and fantastic—turbulent, insistent, plaintive and soft with entreaty. The shadows grew deeper. The music filled the room. It floated out upon the night, over the house-tops, the crescent of the river, losing itself in the silence of the upper air.

Edna was sobbing, just as she had wept one midnight at Grand Isle when strange, new voices awoke in her. She arose in some agitation to take her departure. "May I come again, Mademoiselle?" she asked at the threshold.

"Come whenever you feel like it. Be careful; the stairs and landings are dark; don't stumble."

Mademoiselle reëntered and lit a candle. Robert's letter was on the floor. She stooped and picked it up. It was crumpled and damp with tears. Mademoiselle smoothed the letter out, restored it to the envelope, and replaced it in the table drawer.

XXII

One morning on his way into town Mr. Pontellier stopped at the house of his old friend and family physician, Doctor Mandelet. The Doctor was a semi-retired physician, resting, as the saying is, upon his laurels. He bore a reputation for wisdom rather than skill—leaving the active practice of medicine to his assistants and younger contemporaries—and was much sought for in matters of consultation. A few families, united to him by bonds of friendship, he still attended when they required the services of a physician. The Pontelliers were among these.

Mr. Pontellier found the Doctor reading at the open window of his study. His house stood rather far back from the street, in the center of a delightful garden, so that it was quiet and peaceful at the old gentleman's study window. He was a great reader. He stared up disapprovingly over his eye-glasses as Mr. Pontellier entered, wondering who had the temerity to disturb him at that hour of the morning.

"Ah, Pontellier! Not sick, I hope. Come and have a seat. What news do you bring this morning?" He was quite portly, with a profusion of gray hair, and small blue eyes which age had robbed of much of their brightness but none of their penetration.

"Oh! I'm never sick, Doctor. You know that I come of tough fiber—of that old Creole race of Pontelliers that dry up and finally blow away. I came to consult—

---

[5] A tragic love song from the opera *Tristan and Isolde* (1857–1859), by Richard Wagner (1813–1883).

no, not precisely to consult—to talk to you about Edna. I don't know what ails her."

"Madame Pontellier not well?" marveled the Doctor. "Why, I saw her—I think it was a week ago—walking along Canal Street, the picture of health, it seemed to me."

"Yes, yes; she seems quite well," said Mr. Pontellier, leaning forward and whirling his stick between his two hands; "but she doesn't act well. She's odd, she's not like herself. I can't make her out, and I thought perhaps you'd help me."

"How does she act?" inquired the doctor.

"Well, it isn't easy to explain," said Mr. Pontellier, throwing himself back in his chair. "She lets the housekeeping go to the dickens."

"Well, well; women are not all alike, my dear Pontellier. We've got to consider—"

"I know that; I told you I couldn't explain. Her whole attitude—toward me and everybody and everything—has changed. You know I have a quick temper, but I don't want to quarrel or be rude to a woman, especially my wife; yet I'm driven to it, and feel like ten thousand devils after I've made a fool of myself. She's making it devilishly uncomfortable for me," he went on nervously. "She's got some sort of notion in her head concerning the eternal rights of women; and—you understand—we meet in the morning at the breakfast table."

The old gentleman lifted his shaggy eyebrows, protruded his thick nether lip, and tapped the arms of his chair with his cushioned fingertips.

"What have you been doing to her, Pontellier?"

"Doing! *Parbleu!*"[1]

"Has she," asked the Doctor, with a smile, "Has she been associating of late with a circle of pseudo-intellectual women—super-spiritual superior beings? My wife has been telling me about them."

"That's the trouble," broke in Mr. Pontellier, "She hasn't been associating with any one. She has abandoned her Tuesdays at home, has thrown over all her acquaintances, and goes tramping about by herself, moping in the street-cars, getting in after dark. I tell you she's peculiar. I don't like it; I feel a little worried over it."

This was a new aspect for the Doctor. "Nothing hereditary?" he asked, seriously. "Nothing peculiar about her family antecedents, is there?"

"Oh, no, indeed! She comes of sound old Presbyterian Kentucky stock. The old gentleman, her father, I have heard, used to atone for his weekday sins with his Sunday devotions. I know for a fact, that his race horses literally ran away with the prettiest bit of Kentucky farming land I ever laid eyes upon. Margaret—you know Margaret—she has all the Presbyterianism undiluted. And the youngest is something of a vixen. By the way, she gets married in a couple of weeks from now."

"Send your wife up to the wedding," exclaimed the Doctor, foreseeing a happy solution. "Let her stay among her own people for a while; it will do her good."

"That's what I want her to do. She won't go to the marriage. She says a wedding is one of the most lamentable spectacles on earth. Nice thing for a woman to say to her husband!" exclaimed Mr. Pontellier, fuming anew at the recollection.

"Pontellier," said the Doctor, after a moment's reflection, "let your wife alone

---

[1] "Good heavens!" (French).

for a while. Don't bother her, and don't let her bother you. Woman, my dear friend, is a very peculiar and delicate organism—a sensitive and highly organized woman, such as I know Mrs. Pontellier to be, is especially peculiar. It would require an inspired psychologist to deal successfully with them. And when ordinary fellows like you and me attempt to cope with their idiosyncrasies the result is bungling. Most women are moody and whimsical. This is some passing whim of your wife, due to some cause or causes which you and I needn't try to fathom. But it will pass happily over, especially if you let her alone. Send her around to see me."

"Oh! I couldn't do that; there'd be no reason for it," objected Mr. Pontellier.

"Then I'll go around and see her," said the Doctor. "I'll drop in to dinner some evening *en bon ami*."[2]

"Do! by all means," urged Mr. Pontellier. "What evening will you come? Say Thursday. Will you come Thursday?" he asked, rising to take his leave.

"Very well; Thursday. My wife may possibly have some engagement for me Thursday. In case she has, I shall let you know. Otherwise, you may expect me."

Mr. Pontellier turned before leaving to say:

"I am going to New York on business very soon. I have a big scheme on hand, and want to be on the field proper to pull the ropes and handle the ribbons.[3] We'll let you in on the inside if you say so, Doctor," he laughed.

"No, I thank you, my dear sir," returned the Doctor. "I leave such ventures to you younger men with the fever of life still in your blood."

"What I wanted to say," continued Mr. Pontellier, with his hand on the knob; "I may have to be absent a good while. Would you advise me to take Edna along?"

"By all means, if she wishes to go. If not, leave her here. Don't contradict her. The mood will pass, I assure you. It may take a month, two, three months— possibly longer, but it will pass; have patience."

"Well, good-by, *à jeudi*,"[4] said Mr. Pontellier, as he let himself out. The Doctor would have liked during the course of conversation to ask, "Is there any man in the case?" but he knew his Creole too well to make such a blunder as that.

He did not resume his book immediately, but sat for a while meditatively looking out into the garden.

XXIII

Edna's father was in the city, and had been with them several days. She was not very warmly or deeply attached to him, but they had certain tastes in common, and when together they were companionable. His coming was in the nature of a welcome disturbance; it seemed to furnish a new direction for her emotions.

He had come to purchase a wedding gift for his daughter, Janet, and an outfit for himself in which he might make a creditable appearance at her marriage. Mr. Pontellier had selected the bridal gift, as every one immediately connected with him always deferred to his taste in such matters. And his suggestions on the question of dress—which too often assumes the nature of a problem—were of inestimable value to his father-in-law. But for the past few days the old gentleman had

---

[2] "As a good friend" (French).   [3] Reins.   [4] "Until Thursday" (French).

been upon Edna's hands, and in his society she was becoming acquainted with a new set of sensations. He had been a colonel in the Confederate army, and still maintained, with the title, the military bearing which had always accompanied it. His hair and mustache were white and silky, emphasizing the rugged bronze of his face. He was tall and thin, and wore his coats padded, which gave a fictitious breadth and depth to his shoulders and chest. Edna and her father looked very distinguished together, and excited a good deal of notice during their perambulations. Upon his arrival she began by introducing him to her atelier and making a sketch of him. He took the whole matter very seriously. If her talent had been ten-fold greater than it was, it would not have surprised him, convinced as he was that he had bequeathed to all of his daughters the germs of a masterful capability, which only depended upon their own efforts to be directed toward successful achievement.

Before her pencil he sat rigid and unflinching, as he had faced the cannon's mouth in days gone by. He resented the intrusion of the children, who gaped with wondering eyes at him, sitting so stiff up there in their mother's bright atelier. When they drew near he motioned them away with an expressive action of the foot, loath to disturb the fixed lines of his countenance, his arms, or his rigid shoulders.

Edna, anxious to entertain him, invited Mademoiselle Reisz to meet him, having promised him a treat in her piano playing; but Mademoiselle declined the invitation. So together they attended a *soirée musicale* at the Ratignolle's. Monsieur and Madame Ratignolle made much of the Colonel, installing him as the guest of honor and engaging him at once to dine with them the following Sunday, or any day which he might select. Madame coquetted with him in the most captivating and naïve manner, with eyes, gestures, and a profusion of compliments, till the Colonel's old head felt thirty years younger on his padded shoulders. Edna marveled, not comprehending. She herself was almost devoid of coquetry.

There were one or two men whom she observed at the *soirée musicale;* but she would never have felt moved to any kittenish display to attract their notice—to any feline or feminine wiles to express herself toward them. Their personality attracted her in an agreeable way. Her fancy selected them, and she was glad when a lull in the music gave them an opportunity to meet her and talk with her. Often on the street the glance of strange eyes had lingered in her memory, and sometimes had disturbed her.

Mr. Pontellier did not attend these *soirées musicales*. He considered them *bourgeois*,[1] and found more diversion at the club. To Madame Ratignolle he said the music dispensed at her *soirées* was too "heavy," too far beyond his untrained comprehension. His excuse flattered her. But she disapproved of Mr. Pontellier's club, and she was frank enough to tell Edna so.

"It's a pity Mr. Pontellier doesn't stay home more in the evenings. I think you would be more—well, if you don't mind my saying it—more united, if he did."

"Oh! dear no!" said Edna, with a blank look in her eyes. "What should I do if he stayed home? We wouldn't have anything to say to each other."

She had not much of anything to say to her father, for that matter; but he did not antagonize her. She discovered that he interested her, though she realized that he might not interest her long; and for the first time in her life she felt as if she

---

[1] "Middle class" (French), meant here as complacent, dull, and common.

were thoroughly acquainted with him. He kept her busy serving him and ministering to his wants. It amused her to do so. She would not permit a servant or one of the children to do anything for him which she might do herself. Her husband noticed, and thought it was the expression of a deep filial attachment which he had never suspected.

The Colonel drank numerous "toddies" during the course of the day, which left him, however, imperturbed. He was an expert on concocting strong drinks. He had even invented some, to which he had given fantastic names, and for whose manufacture he required diverse ingredients that it devolved upon Edna to procure for him.

When Doctor Mandelet dined with the Pontelliers on Thursday he could discern in Mrs. Pontellier no trace of that morbid condition which her husband had reported to him. She was excited and in a manner radiant. She and her father had been to the race course, and their thoughts when they seated themselves at table were still occupied with the events of the afternoon, and their talk was still of the track. The Doctor had not kept pace with turf affairs. He had certain recollections of racing in what he called "the good old times" when the Lecompte stables flourished, and he drew upon this fund of memories so that he might not be left out and seem wholly devoid of the modern spirit. But he failed to impose upon the Colonel, and was even far from impressing him with this trumped-up knowledge of bygone days. Edna had staked her father on his last venture, with the most gratifying results to both of them. Besides, they had met some very charming people, according to the Colonel's impressions. Mrs. Mortimer Merriman and Mrs. James Highcamp, who were there with Alcée Arobin, had joined them and had enlivened the hours in a fashion that warmed him to think of.

Mr. Pontellier himself had no particular leaning toward horse-racing, and was even rather inclined to discourage it as a pastime, especially when he considered the fate of that blue-grass farm in Kentucky. He endeavored, in a general way, to express a particular disapproval, and only succeeded in arousing the ire and opposition of his father-in-law. A pretty dispute followed, in which Edna warmly espoused her father's cause and the Doctor remained neutral.

He observed his hostess attentively from under his shaggy brows, and noted a subtle change which had transformed her from the listless woman he had known into a being who, for the moment, seemed palpitant with the forces of life. Her speech was warm and energetic. There was no repression in her glance or gesture. She reminded him of some beautiful, sleek animal waking up in the sun.

The dinner was excellent. The claret was warm and the champagne was cold, and under their beneficent influence the threatened unpleasantness melted and vanished with the fumes of the wine.

Mr. Pontellier warmed up and grew reminiscent. He told some amusing plantation experiences, recollections of old Iberville and his youth, when he hunted 'possum in company with some friendly darky; thrashed the pecan trees, shot the grosbec,[2] and roamed the woods and fields in mischievous idleness.

The Colonel, with little sense of humor and of the fitness of things, related a somber episode of those dark and bitter days, in which he had acted a conspicuous part and always formed a central figure. Nor was the Doctor happier in his selection, when he told the old, ever new and curious story of the waning of a woman's

---

[2] Grosbeak, a finchlike bird with a short, stout beak.

love, seeking strange, new channels, only to return to its legitimate source after days of fierce unrest. It was one of the many little human documents which had been unfolded to him during his long career as a physician. The story did not seem especially to impress Edna. She had one of her own to tell, of a woman who paddled away with her lover one night in a pirogue and never came back. They were lost amid the Baratarian Islands, and no one ever heard of them or found trace of them from that day to this. It was a pure invention. She said that Madame Antoine had related it to her. That, also, was an invention. Perhaps it was a dream she had had. But every glowing word seemed real to those who listened. They could feel the hot breath of the Southern night; they could hear the long sweep of the pirogue through the glistening moonlit water, the beating of birds' wings, rising startled from among the reeds in the salt-water pools; they could see the faces of the lovers, pale, close together, rapt in oblivious forgetfulness, drifting into the unknown.

The champagne was cold, and its subtle fumes played fantastic tricks with Edna's memory that night.

Outside, away from the glow of the fire and the soft lamplight, the night was chill and murky. The Doctor doubled his old-fashioned cloak across his breast as he strode home through the darkness. He knew his fellow-creatures better than most men; knew that inner life which so seldom unfolds itself to unannointed eyes. He was sorry he had accepted Pontellier's invitation. He was growing old, and beginning to need rest and an imperturbed spirit. He did not want the secrets of other lives thrust upon him.

"I hope it isn't Arobin," he muttered to himself as he walked. "I hope to heaven it isn't Alcée Arobin."

XXIV

Edna and her father had a warm, and almost violent dispute upon the subject of her refusal to attend her sister's wedding. Mr. Pontellier declined to interfere, to interpose either his influence or his authority. He was following Doctor Mandelet's advice, and letting her do as she liked. The Colonel reproached his daughter for her lack of filial kindness and respect, her want of sisterly affection and womanly consideration. His arguments were labored and unconvincing. He doubted if Janet would accept any excuse—forgetting that Edna had offered none. He doubted if Janet would ever speak to her again, and he was sure Margaret would not.

Edna was glad to be rid of her father when he finally took himself off with his wedding garments and his bridal gifts, with his padded shoulders, his Bible reading, his "toddies" and ponderous oaths.

Mr. Pontellier followed him closely. He meant to stop at the wedding on his way to New York and endeavor by every means which money and love could devise to atone somewhat for Edna's incomprehensible action.

"You are too lenient, too lenient by far, Léonce," asserted the Colonel. "Authority, coercion are what is needed. Put your foot down good and hard; the only way to manage a wife. Take my word for it."

The Colonel was perhaps unaware that he had coerced his own wife into her grave. Mr. Pontellier had a vague suspicion of it which he thought it needless to mention at that late day.

Edna was not so consciously gratified at her husband's leaving home as she had been over the departure of her father. As the day approached when he was to leave her for a comparatively long stay, she grew melting and affectionate, remembering his many acts of consideration and his repeated expressions of an ardent attachment. She was solicitous about his health and his welfare. She bustled around, looking after his clothing, thinking about heavy underwear, quite as Madame Ratignolle would have done under similar circumstances. She cried when he went away, calling him her dear, good friend, and she was quite certain she would grow lonely before very long and go to join him in New York.

But after all, a radiant peace settled upon her when she at last found herself alone. Even the children were gone. Old Madame Pontellier had come herself and carried them off to Iberville with their quadroon. The old madame did not venture to say she was afraid they would be neglected during Léonce's absence; she hardly ventured to think so. She was hungry for them—even a little fierce in her attachment. She did not want them to be wholly "children of the pavement," she always said when begging to have them for a space. She wished them to know the country, with its streams, its fields, its woods, its freedom, so delicious to the young. She wished them to taste something of the life their father had lived and known and loved when he, too, was a little child.

When Edna was at last alone, she breathed a big, genuine sigh of relief. A feeling that was unfamiliar but very delicious came over her. She walked all through the house, from one room to another, as if inspecting it for the first time. She tried the various chairs and lounges, as if she had never sat and reclined upon them before. And she perambulated around the outside of the house, investigating, looking to see if windows and shutters were secure and in order. The flowers were like new acquaintances; she approached them in a familiar spirit, and made herself at home among them. The garden walks were damp, and Edna called to the maid to bring out her rubber sandals. And there she stayed, and stooped, digging around the plants, trimming, picking dead, dry leaves. The children's little dog came out, interfering, getting in her way. She scolded him, laughed at him, played with him. The garden smelled so good and looked so pretty in the afternoon sunlight. Edna plucked all the bright flowers she could find, and went into the house with them, she and the little dog.

Even the kitchen assumed a sudden interesting character which she had never before perceived. She went in to give directions to the cook, to say that the butcher would have to bring much less meat, that they would require only half their usual quantity of bread, of milk and groceries. She told the cook that she herself would be greatly occupied during Mr. Pontellier's absence, and she begged her to take all thought and responsibility of the larder upon her own shoulders.

That night Edna dined alone. The candelabra, with a few candles in the center of the table, gave all the light she needed. Outside the circle of light in which she sat, the large dining-room looked solemn and shadowy. The cook, placed upon her mettle, served a delicious repast—a luscious tenderloin broiled *à point*.[1] The wine tasted good; the *marron glacé*[2] seemed to be just what she wanted. It was so pleasant, too, to dine in a comfortable *peignoir*.

---

[1] "Medium-broiled" (French).   [2] "Candied chestnuts" (French).

She thought a little sentimentally about Léonce and the children, and wondered what they were doing. As she gave a dainty scrap or two to the doggie, she talked intimately to him about Etienne and Raoul. He was beside himself with astonishment and delight over these companionable advances, and showed his appreciation by his little quick, snappy barks and a lively agitation.

Then Edna sat in the library after dinner and read Emerson[3] until she grew sleepy. She realized that she had neglected her reading, and determined to start anew upon a course of improving studies, now that her time was completely her own to do with as she liked.

After a refreshing bath, Edna went to bed. And as she snuggled comfortably beneath the eiderdown a sense of restfulness invaded her, such as she had not known before.

XXV

When the weather was dark and cloudy Edna could not work. She needed the sun to mellow and temper her mood to the sticking point. She had reached a stage when she seemed to be no longer feeling her way, working, when in the humor, with sureness and ease. And being devoid of ambition, and striving not toward accomplishment, she drew satisfaction from the work in itself.

On rainy or melancholy days Edna went out and sought the society of the friends she had made at Grand Isle. Or else she stayed indoors and nursed a mood with which she was becoming too familiar for her own comfort and peace of mind. It was not despair; but it seemed to her as if life were passing by, leaving its promise broken and unfulfilled. Yet there were other days when she listened, was led on and deceived by fresh promises which her youth held out to her.

She went again to the races, and again. Alcée Arobin and Mrs. Highcamp called for her one bright afternoon in Arobin's drag.[1] Mrs. Highcamp was a worldly but unaffected, intelligent, slim, tall blonde woman in the forties, with an indifferent manner and blue eyes that stared. She had a daughter who served her as a pretext for cultivating the society of young men of fashion. Alcée Arobin was one of them. He was a familiar figure at the race course, the opera, the fashionable clubs. There was a perpetual smile in his eyes, which seldom failed to awaken a corresponding cheerfulness in any one who looked into them and listened to his good-humored voice. His manner was quiet, and at times a little insolent. He possessed a good figure, a pleasing face, not overburdened with depth of thought or feeling; and his dress was that of the conventional man of fashion.

He admired Edna extravagantly, after meeting her at the races with her father. He had met her before on other occasions, but she had seemed to him unapproachable until that day. It was at his instigation that Mrs. Highcamp called to ask her to go with them to the Jockey Club[2] to witness the turf event of the season.

There were possibly a few track men out there who knew the race horse as well as Edna, but there was certainly none who knew it better. She sat between her two companions as one having authority to speak. She laughed at Arobin's pretensions, and deplored Mrs. Highcamp's ignorance. The race horse was a friend and

---

[3] Ralph Waldo Emerson (1803–1882), whose writings championed self-reliance and independence.
[1] A coach, generally drawn by four horses, with seats inside and on top.
[2] A social club for the wealthy.

intimate associate of her childhood. The atmosphere of the stables and the breath of the blue grass paddock revived in her memory and lingered in her nostrils. She did not perceive that she was talking like her father as the sleek geldings ambled in review before them. She played for very high stakes, and fortune favored her. The fever of the game flamed in her cheeks and eyes, and it got into her blood and into her brain like an intoxicant. People turned their heads to look at her, and more than one lent an attentive ear to her utterances, hoping thereby to secure the elusive but ever-desired "tip." Arobin caught the contagion of excitement which drew him to Edna like a magnet. Mrs. Highcamp remained, as usual, unmoved, with her indifferent stare and uplifted eyebrows.

Edna stayed and dined with Mrs. Highcamp upon being urged to do so. Arobin also remained and sent away his drag.

The dinner was quiet and uninteresting, save for the cheerful efforts of Arobin to enliven things. Mrs. Highcamp deplored the absence of her daughter from the races, and tried to convey to her what she had missed by going to the "Dante reading"[3] instead of joining them. The girl held a geranium leaf up to her nose and said nothing, but looked knowing and noncommittal. Mr. Highcamp was a plain, bald-headed man, who only talked under compulsion. He was unresponsive. Mrs. Highcamp was full of delicate courtesy and consideration toward her husband. She addressed most of her conversation to him at table. They sat in the library after dinner and read the evening papers together under the droplight;[4] while the younger people went into the drawing-room near by and talked. Miss Highcamp played some selections from Grieg[5] upon the piano. She seemed to have apprehended all of the composer's coldness and none of his poetry. While Edna listened she could not help wondering if she had lost her taste for music.

When the time came for her to go home, Mr. Highcamp grunted a lame offer to escort her, looking down at his slippered feet with tactless concern. It was Arobin who took her home. The car ride was long, and it was late when they reached Esplanade Street. Arobin asked permission to enter for a second to light his cigarette—his match safe[6] was empty. He filled his match safe, but did not light his cigarette until he left her, after she had expressed her willingness to go to the races with him again.

Edna was neither tired nor sleepy. She was hungry again, for the Highcamp dinner, though of excellent quality, had lacked abundance. She rummaged in the larder and brought forth a slice of Gruyère[7] and some crackers. She opened a bottle of beer which she found in the icebox. Edna felt extremely restless and excited. She vacantly hummed a fantastic tune as she poked at the wood embers on the hearth and munched a cracker.

She wanted something to happen—something, anything; she did not know what. She regretted that she had not made Arobin stay a half hour to talk over the horses with her. She counted the money she had won. But there was nothing else to do, so she went to bed, and tossed there for hours in a sort of monotonous agitation.

In the middle of the night she remembered that she had forgotten to write her regular letter to her husband; and she decided to do so next day and tell him about

---

[3] A group reading of the work of the Italian poet Dante Alighieri (1265–1321), author of *The Divine Comedy*.   [4] A lamp that can be adjusted in height.   [5] Edvard Grieg (1843–1907), a Norwegian composer.   [6] A fireproof container for storing matches.   [7] Cheese made in Gruyère, Switzerland.

her afternoon at the Jockey Club. She lay wide awake composing a letter which was nothing like the one which she wrote next day. When the maid awoke her in the morning Edna was dreaming of Mr. Highcamp playing the piano at the entrance of a music store on Canal Street, while his wife was saying to Alcée Arobin, as they boarded an Esplanade Street car:

"What a pity that so much talent has been neglected! but I must go."

When, a few days later, Alcée Arobin again called for Edna in his drag, Mrs. Highcamp was not with him. He said they would pick her up. But as that lady had not been apprised of his intention of picking her up, she was not at home. The daughter was just leaving the house to attend the meeting of a branch Folk Lore Society, and regretted that she could not accompany them. Arobin appeared nonplused, and asked Edna if there were any one else she cared to ask.

She did not deem it worth while to go in search of any of the fashionable acquaintances from whom she had withdrawn herself. She thought of Madame Ratignolle, but knew that her fair friend did not leave the house, except to take a languid walk around the block with her husband after nightfall. Mademoiselle Reisz would have laughed at such a request from Edna. Madame Lebrun might have enjoyed the outing, but for some reason Edna did not want her. So they went alone, she and Arobin.

The afternoon was intensely interesting to her. The excitement came back upon her like a remittent fever. Her talk grew familiar and confidential. It was no labor to become intimate with Arobin. His manner invited easy confidence. The preliminary stage of becoming acquainted was one which he always endeavored to ignore when a pretty and engaging woman was concerned.

He stayed and dined with Edna. He stayed and sat beside the wood fire. They laughed and talked; and before it was time to go he was telling her how different life might have been if he had known her years before. With ingenuous frankness he spoke of what a wicked, ill-disciplined boy he had been, and impulsively drew up his cuff to exhibit upon his wrist the scar from a saber cut which he had received in a duel outside of Paris when he was nineteen. She touched his hand as she scanned the red cicatrice[8] on the inside of his white wrist. A quick impulse that was somewhat spasmodic impelled her fingers to close in a sort of clutch upon his hand. He felt the pressure of her pointed nails in the flesh of his palm.

She arose hastily and walked toward the mantel.

"The sight of a wound or scar always agitates and sickens me," she said. "I shouldn't have looked at it."

"I beg your pardon," he entreated, following her; "it never occurred to me that it might be repulsive."

He stood close to her, and the effrontery in his eyes repelled the old, vanishing self in her, yet drew all her awakening sensuousness. He saw enough in her face to impel him to take her hand and hold it while he said his lingering good night.

"Will you go to the races again?" he asked.

"No," she said. "I've had enough of the races. I don't want to lose all the money I've won, and I've got to work when the weather is bright, instead of—"

"Yes; work; to be sure. You promised to show me your work. What morning may I come up to your atelier? To-morrow?"

"No!"

"Day after?"

---

[8] Scar.

"No, no."

"Oh, please don't refuse me! I know something of such things. I might help you with a stray suggestion or two."

"No, Good night. Why don't you go after you have said good night? I don't like you," she went on in a high, excited pitch, attempting to draw away her hand. She felt that her words lacked dignity and sincerity, and she knew that he felt it.

"I'm sorry you don't like me. I'm sorry I offended you. How have I offended you? What have I done? Can't you forgive me?" And he bent and pressed his lips upon her hand as if he wished never more to withdraw them.

"Mr. Arobin," she complained, "I'm greatly upset by the excitement of the afternoon; I'm not myself. My manner must have misled you in some way. I wish you to go, please." She spoke in a monotonous, dull tone. He took his hat from the table, and stood with eyes turned from her, looking into the dying fire. For a moment or two he kept an impressive silence.

"Your manner has not misled me, Mrs. Pontellier," he said finally. "My own emotions have done that. I couldn't help it. When I'm near you, how could I help it? Don't think anything of it, don't bother, please. You see, I go when you command me. If you wish me to stay away, I shall do so. If you let me come back, I—oh! you will let me come back?"

He cast one appealing glance at her, to which she made no response. Alcée Arobin's manner was so genuine that it often deceived even himself.

Edna did not care or think whether it were genuine or not. When she was alone she looked mechanically at the back of her hand which he had kissed so warmly. Then she leaned her head down on the mantelpiece. She felt somewhat like a woman who in a moment of passion is betrayed into an act of infidelity, and realizes the significance of the act without being wholly awakened from its glamour. The thought was passing vaguely through her mind, "What would he think?"

She did not mean her husband; she was thinking of Robert Lebrun. Her husband seemed to her now like a person whom she had married without love as an excuse.

She lit a candle and went up to her room. Alcée Arobin was absolutely nothing to her. Yet his presence, his manners, the warmth of his glances, and above all the touch of his lips upon her hand had acted like a narcotic upon her.

She slept a languorous sleep, interwoven with vanishing dreams.

XXVI

Alcée Arobin wrote Edna an elaborate note of apology, palpitant with sincerity. It embarrassed her; for in a cooler, quieter moment it appeared to her absurd that she should have taken his action so seriously, so dramatically. She felt sure that the significance of the whole occurrence had lain in her own self-consciousness. If she ignored his note it would give undue importance to a trivial affair. If she replied to it in a serious spirit it would still leave in his mind the impression that she had in a susceptible moment yielded to his influence. After all, it was no great matter to have one's hand kissed. She was provoked at his having written the apology. She answered in as light and bantering a spirit as she fancied it deserved, and said she would be glad to have him look in upon her at work whenever he felt the inclination and his business gave him the opportunity.

He responded at once by presenting himself at her home with all his disarming naïveté. And then there was scarcely a day which followed that she did not see him or was not reminded of him. He was prolific in pretexts. His attitude became one of good-humored subservience and tacit adoration. He was ready at all times to submit to her moods, which were as often kind as they were cold. She grew accustomed to him. They became intimate and friendly by imperceptible degrees, and then by leaps. He sometimes talked in a way that astonished her at first and brought the crimson into her face; in a way that pleased her at last, appealing to the animalism that stirred impatiently within her.

There was nothing which so quieted the turmoil of Edna's senses as a visit to Mademoiselle Reisz. It was then, in the presence of that personality which was offensive to her, that the woman, by her divine art, seemed to reach Edna's spirit and set it free.

It was misty, with heavy, lowering atmosphere, one afternoon, when Edna climbed the stairs to the pianist's apartments under the roof. Her clothes were dripping with moisture. She felt chilled and pinched as she entered the room. Mademoiselle was poking at a rusty stove that smoked a little and warmed the room indifferently. She was endeavoring to heat a pot of chocolate on the stove. The room looked cheerless and dingy to Edna as she entered. A bust of Beethoven,[1] covered with a hood of dust, scowled at her from the mantelpiece.

"Ah! here comes the sunlight!" exclaimed Mademoiselle, rising from her knees before the stove. "Now it will be warm and bright enough; I can let the fire alone."

She closed the stove door with a bang, and approaching, assisted in removing Edna's dripping mackintosh.

"You are cold; you look miserable. The chocolate will soon be hot. But would you rather have a taste of brandy? I have scarcely touched the bottle which you brought me for my cold." A piece of red flannel was wrapped around Mademoiselle's throat; a stiff neck compelled her to hold her head on one side.

"I will take some brandy," said Edna, shivering as she removed her gloves and overshoes. She drank the liquor from the glass as a man would have done. Then flinging herself upon the uncomfortable sofa she said, "Mademoiselle, I am going to move away from my house on Esplanade Street."

"Ah!" ejaculated the musician, neither surprised nor especially interested. Nothing ever seemed to astonish her very much. She was endeavoring to adjust the bunch of violets which had become loose from its fastening in her hair. Edna drew her down upon the sofa, and taking a pin from her own hair, secured the shabby artificial flowers in their accustomed place.

"Aren't you astonished?"

"Passably. Where are you going? to New York? to Iberville? to your father in Mississippi? where?"

"Just two steps away," laughed Edna, "in a little four-room house around the corner. It looks so cozy, so inviting and restful, whenever I pass by; and it's for rent. I'm tired looking after that big house. It never seemed like mine, anyway— like home. It's too much trouble. I have to keep too many servants. I am tired bothering with them."

"That is not your true reason, *ma belle*.[2] There is no use in telling me lies. I don't know your reason, but you have not told me the truth." Edna did not protest or endeavor to justify herself.

---

[1] The German composer Ludwig van Beethoven (1770–1827). [2] "My pretty one" (French).

"The house, the money that provides for it, are not mine. Isn't that enough reason?"

"They are your husband's," returned Mademoiselle, with a shrug and a malicious elevation of the eyebrows.

"Oh! I see there is no deceiving you. Then let me tell you: It is a caprice. I have a little money of my own from my mother's estate, which my father sends me by driblets. I won a large sum this winter on the races, and I am beginning to sell my sketches. Laidpore is more and more pleased with my work; he says it grows in force and individuality. I cannot judge of that myself, but I feel that I have gained in ease and confidence. However, as I said, I have sold a good many through Laidpore. I can live in the tiny house for little or nothing, with one servant. Old Celestine, who works occasionally for me, says she will come stay with me and do my work. I know I shall like it, like the feeling of freedom and independence."

"What does you husband say?"

"I have not told him yet. I only thought of it this morning. He will think I am demented, no doubt. Perhaps you think so."

Mademoiselle shook her head slowly. "Your reason is not yet clear to me," she said.

Neither was it quite clear to Edna herself; but it unfolded itself as she sat for a while in silence. Instinct had prompted her to put away her husband's bounty in casting off her allegiance. She did not know how it would be when he returned. There would have to be an understanding, an explanation. Conditions would some way adjust themselves, she felt; but whatever came, she had resolved never again to belong to another than herself.

"I shall give a grand dinner before I leave the old house!" Edna exclaimed. "You will have to come to it, Mademoiselle. I will give you everything that you like to eat and to drink. We shall sing and laugh and be merry for once." And she uttered a sigh that came from the very depths of her being.

If Mademoiselle happened to have received a letter from Robert during the interval of Edna's visits, she would give her the letter unsolicited. And she would seat herself at the piano and play as her humor prompted her while the young woman read the letter.

The little stove was roaring; it was red-hot, and the chocolate in the tin sizzled and sputtered. Edna went forward and opened the stove door, and Mademoiselle rising, took a letter from under the bust of Beethoven and handed it to Edna.

"Another! so soon!" she exclaimed, her eyes filled with delight. "Tell me, Mademoiselle, does he know that I see his letters?"

"Never in the world! He would be angry and would never write to me again if he thought so. Does he write to you? Never a line. Does he send you a message? Never a word. It is because he loves you, poor fool, and is trying to forget you, since you are not free to listen to him or to belong to him."

"Why do you show me his letters, then?"

"Haven't you begged for them? Can I refuse you anything? Oh! you cannot deceive me," and Mademoiselle approached her beloved instrument and began to play. Edna did not at once read the letter. She sat holding it in her hand, while the music penetrated her whole being like an effulgence, warming and brightening the dark places of her soul. It prepared her for joy and exultation.

"Oh!" she exclaimed, letting the letter fall to the floor. "Why did you not tell me?" She went and grasped Mademoiselle's hands up from the keys. "Oh! unkind! malicious! Why did you not tell me?"

"That he was coming back? No great news, *ma foi*. I wonder he did not come long ago."

"But when, when?" cried Edna, impatiently. "He does not say when."

"He says 'very soon.' You know as much about it as I do; it is all in the letter."

"But why? Why is he coming? Oh, if I thought—" and she snatched the letter from the floor and turned the pages this way and that way, looking for the reason, which was left untold.

"If I were young and in love with a man," said Mademoiselle, turning on the stool and pressing her wiry hands between her knees as she looked down at Edna, who sat on the floor holding the letter, "it seems to me he would have to be some *grand esprit;*[3] a man with lofty aims and ability to reach them; one who stood high enough to attract the notice of his fellow-men. It seems to me if I were young and in love I should never deem a man of ordinary caliber worthy of my devotion."

"Now it is you who are telling lies and seeking to deceive me, Mademoiselle; or else you have never been in love, and know nothing about it. Why," went on Edna, clasping her knees and looking up into Mademoiselle's twisted face, "do you suppose a woman knows why she loves? Does she select? Does she say to herself: 'Go to! Here is a distinguished statesman with presidential possibilities: I shall proceed to fall in love with him.' Or, 'I shall set my heart upon this musician, whose fame is on every tongue?' Or, 'This financier, who controls the world's money markets?'"

"You are purposely misunderstanding me, *ma reine*.[4] Are you in love with Robert?"

"Yes," said Edna. It was the first time she had admitted it, and a glow overspread her face, blotching it with red spots.

"Why?" asked her companion. "Why do you love him when you ought not to?"

Edna, with a motion or two, dragged herself on her knees before Mademoiselle Reisz, who took the glowing face between her two hands.

"Why? Because his hair is brown and grows away from his temples; because he opens and shuts his eyes, and his nose is a little out of drawing; because he has two lips and a square chin, and a little finger which he can't straighten from having played baseball too energetically in his youth. Because—"

"Because you do, in short," laughed Mademoiselle. "What will you do when he comes back?" she asked.

"Do? Nothing, except feel glad and happy to be alive."

She was already glad and happy to be alive at the mere thought of his return. The murky, lowering sky, which had depressed her a few hours before, seemed bracing and invigorating as she splashed through the streets on her way home.

She stopped at a confectioner's and ordered a huge box of bonbons for the children in Iberville. She slipped a card in the box, on which she scribbled a tender message and sent an abundance of kisses.

Before dinner in the evening Edna wrote a charming letter to her husband, telling him of her intention to move for a while into the little house around the block, and to give a farewell dinner before leaving, regretting that he was not there to share it, to help her out with the menu and assist her in entertaining the guests. Her letter was brilliant and brimming with cheerfulness.

---

[3] "Great soul" (French).   [4] "My queen" or "my dear" (French).

XXVII

"What is the matter with you?" asked Arobin that evening. "I never found you in such a happy mood." Edna was tired by that time, and was reclining on the lounge before the fire.

"Don't you know the weather prophet has told us we shall see the sun pretty soon?"

"Well, that ought to be reason enough," he acquiesced. "You wouldn't give me another if I sat here all night imploring you." He sat close to her on a low tabouret,[1] and as he spoke his fingers lightly touched the hair that fell a little over her forehead. She liked the touch of his fingers through her hair, and closed her eyes sensitively.

"One of these days," she said, "I'm going to pull myself together for a while and think—try to determine what character of a woman I am; for, candidly, I don't know. By all the codes which I am acquainted with, I am a devilishly wicked specimen of the sex. But some way I can't convince myself that I am. I must think about it."

"Don't. What's the use? Why should you bother thinking about it when I can tell you what manner of woman you are." His fingers strayed occasionally down to her warm, smooth cheeks and firm chin, which was growing a little full and double.

"Oh, yes! You will tell me that I am adorable; everything that is captivating. Spare yourself the effort."

"No; I shan't tell you anything of the sort, though I shouldn't be lying if I did."

"Do you know Mademoiselle Reisz?" she asked irrelevantly.

"The pianist? I know her by sight. I've heard her play."

"She says queer things sometimes in a bantering way that you don't notice at the time and you find yourself thinking about afterward."

"For instance?"

"Well, for instance, when I left her to-day, she put her arms around me and felt my shoulder blades, to see if my wings were strong, she said. 'The bird that would soar above the level plain of tradition and prejudice must have strong wings. It is a sad spectacle to see the weaklings bruised, exhausted, fluttering back to earth.'"

"Whither would you soar?"

"I'm not thinking of any extraordinary flights. I only half comprehend her."

"I've heard she's partially demented," said Arobin.

"She seems to me wonderfully sane," Edna replied.

"I'm told she's extremely disagreeable and unpleasant. Why have you introduced her at a moment when I desired to talk of you?"

"Oh! talk of me if you like," cried Edna, clasping her hands beneath her head; "but let me think of something else while you do."

"I'm jealous of your thoughts to-night. They're making you a little kinder than usual; but some way I feel as if they were wandering, as if they were not here with me." She only looked at him and smiled. His eyes were very near. He leaned upon the lounge with an arm extended across her, while the other hand still rested upon

---

[1] A stool or small seat, generally without arms or a back.

her hair. They continued silently to look into each other's eyes. When he leaned forward and kissed her, she clasped his head, holding his lips to hers.

It was the first kiss of her life to which her nature had really responded. It was a flaming torch that kindled desire.

XXVIII

Edna cried a little that night after Arobin left her. It was only one phase of the multitudinous emotions which had assailed her. There was with her an overwhelming feeling of irresponsibility. There was the shock of the unexpected and the unaccustomed. There was her husband's reproach looking at her from the external things around her which he had provided for her external existence. There was Robert's reproach making itself felt by a quicker, fiercer, more overpowering love, which had awakened within her toward him. Above all, there was understanding. She felt as if a mist had been lifted from her eyes, enabling her to look upon and comprehend the significance of life, that monster made up of beauty and brutality. But among the conflicting sensations which assailed her, there was neither shame nor remorse. There was a dull pang of regret because it was not the kiss of love which had inflamed her, because it was not love which had held this cup of life to her lips.

XXIX

Without even waiting for an answer from her husband regarding his opinion or wishes in the matter, Edna hastened her preparations for quitting her home on Esplanade Street and moving into the little house around the block. A feverish anxiety attended her every action in that direction. There was no moment of deliberation, no interval of repose between the thought and its fulfillment. Early upon the morning following those hours passed in Arobin's society, Edna set about securing her new abode and hurrying her arrangements for occupying it. Within the precincts of her home she felt like one who has entered and lingered within the portals of some forbidden temple in which a thousand muffled voices bade her begone.

Whatever was her own in the house, everything which she had acquired aside from her husband's bounty, she caused to be transported to the other house, supplying simple and meager deficiencies from her own resources.

Arobin found her with rolled sleeves, working in company with the house-maid when he looked in during the afternoon. She was splendid and robust, and had never appeared handsomer than in the old blue gown, with a red silk handkerchief knotted at random around her head to protect her hair from the dust. She was mounted upon a high step-ladder, unhooking a picture from the wall when he entered. He had found the front door open, and had followed his ring by walking in unceremoniously.

"Come down!" he said. "Do you want to kill yourself?" She greeted him with affected carelessness, and appeared absorbed in her occupation.

If he had expected to find her languishing, reproachful, or indulging in sentimental tears, he must have been greatly surprised.

He was no doubt prepared for any emergency, ready for any one of the foregoing attitudes, just as he bent himself easily and naturally to the situation which
confronted him.

"Please come down," he insisted, holding the ladder and looking up at her.

"No," she answered; "Ellen is afraid to mount the ladder. Joe is working over
at the 'pigeon house'—that's the name Ellen gives it, because it's so small and
looks like a pigeon house—and some one has to do this."

Arobin pulled off his coat, and expressed himself ready and willing to tempt
fate in her place. Ellen brought him one of her dust-caps, and went into contortions of mirth, which she found it impossible to control, when she saw him put it
on before the mirror as grotesquely as he could. Edna herself could not refrain
from smiling when she fastened it at his request. So it was he who in turn mounted
the ladder, unhooking pictures and curtains, and dislodging ornaments as Edna
directed. When he had finished he took off his dust-cap and went out to wash his
hands.

Edna was sitting on the tabouret, idly brushing the tips of a feather duster along
the carpet when he came in again.

"Is there anything more you will let me do?" he asked.

"That is all," she answered. "Ellen can manage the rest." She kept the young
woman occupied in the drawing-room, unwilling to be left alone with Arobin.

"What about the dinner?" he asked; "the grand event, the *coup d'état?*"[1]

"It will be day after to-morrow. Why do you call it the '*coup d'état?*' Oh! it
will be very fine; all my best of everything—crystal, silver and gold, Sèvres,
flowers, music, and champagne to swim in. I'll let Léonce pay the bills. I wonder
what he'll say when he sees the bills."

"And you ask me why I call it a *coup d'état?*" Arobin had put on his coat, and
he stood before her and asked if his cravat was plumb. She told him it was, looking no higher than the tip of his collar.

"When do you go to the 'pigeon house?'—with all due acknowledgment to
Ellen."

"Day after to-morrow, after the dinner. I shall sleep there."

"Ellen, will you very kindly get me a glass of water?" asked Arobin. "The dust
in the curtains, if you will pardon me for hinting such a thing, has parched my
throat to a crisp."

"While Ellen gets the water," said Edna, rising, "I will say good-by and let you
go. I must get rid of this grime, and I have a million things to do and think of."

"When shall I see you?" asked Arobin, seeking to detain her, the maid having
left the room.

"At the dinner, of course. You are invited."

"Not before?—not to-night or to-morrow morning or to-morrow noon or night?
or the day after morning or noon? Can't you see yourself, without my telling you,
what an eternity it is?"

He had followed her into the hall and to the foot of the stairway, looking up at
her as she mounted with her face half turned to him.

"Not an instant sooner," she said. But she laughed and looked at him with eyes
that at once gave him courage to wait and made it torture to wait.

---

[1] "Stroke of state" (French): an unexpected stroke of policy, or more particularly, a sudden seizure of
government.

XXX

Though Edna had spoken of the dinner as a very grand affair, it was in truth a very small affair and very select, in so much as the guests invited were few and were selected with discrimination. She had counted upon an even dozen seating themselves at her round mahogany board, forgetting for the moment that Madame Ratignolle was to the last degree *souffrante*[1] and unpresentable, and not foreseeing that Madame Lebrun would send a thousand regrets at the last moment. So there were only ten, after all, which made a cozy, comfortable number.

There were Mr. and Mrs. Merriman, a pretty, vivacious little woman in the thirties; her husband, a jovial fellow, something of a shallow-pate,[2] who laughed a good deal at other people's witticisms, and had thereby made himself extremely popular. Mrs. Highcamp had accompanied them. Of course, there was Alcée Arobin; and Mademoiselle Reisz had consented to come. Edna had sent her a fresh bunch of violets with black lace trimmings for her hair. Monsieur Ratignolle brought himself and his wife's excuses. Victor Lebrun, who happened to be in the city, bent upon relaxation, had accepted with alacrity. There was a Miss Mayblunt, no longer in her teens, who looked at the world through lorgnettes[3] and with the keenest interest. It was thought and said that she was intellectual; it was suspected of her that she wrote under a *nom de guerre*.[4] She had come with a gentleman by the name of Gouvernail, connected with one of the daily papers, of whom nothing special could be said, except that he was observant and seemed quiet and inoffensive. Edna herself made the tenth, and at half-past eight they seated themselves at table, Arobin and Monsieur Ratignolle on either side of their hostess.

Mrs. Highcamp sat between Arobin and Victor Lebrun. Then came Mrs. Merriman, Mr. Gouvernail, Miss Mayblunt, Mr. Merriman, and Mademoiselle Reisz next to Monsieur Ratignolle.

There was something extremely gorgeous about the appearance of the table, an effect of splendor conveyed by a cover of pale yellow satin under strips of lacework. There were wax candles in massive brass candelabra, burning softly under yellow silk shades; full, fragrant roses, yellow and red, abounded. There were silver and gold, as she had said there would be, and crystal which glittered like the gems which the women wore.

The ordinary stiff dining chairs had been discarded for the occasion and replaced by the most commodious and luxurious which could be collected throughout the house. Mademoiselle Reisz, being exceedingly diminutive, was elevated upon cushions, as small children are sometimes hoisted at table upon bulky volumes.

"Something new, Edna?" exclaimed Miss Mayblunt, with lorgnette directed toward a magnificent cluster of diamonds that sparkled, that almost sputtered, in Edna's hair, just over the center of her forehead.

"Quite new; 'brand' new, in fact; a present from my husband. It arrived this morning from New York. I may as well admit that this is my birthday, and that I am twenty-nine. In good time I expect you to drink my health. Meanwhile, I shall ask you to begin with this cocktail, composed—would you say 'composed?' "

---

[1] "Ill" (French).   [2] Lacking in intellectual depth.
[3] Eyeglasses with an ornamental handle.   [4] "War name" (French): pseudonym.

with an appeal to Miss Mayblunt—"composed by my father in honor of Sister Janet's wedding."

Before each guest stood a tiny glass that looked and sparkled like a garnet gem.

"Then, all things considered," spoke Arobin, "it might not be amiss to start out by drinking the Colonel's health in the cocktail which he composed, on the birthday of the most charming of women—the daughter whom he invented."

Mr. Merriman's laugh at this sally was such a genuine outburst and so contagious that it started the dinner with an agreeable swing that never slackened.

Miss Mayblunt begged to be allowed to keep her cocktail untouched before her, just to look at. The color was marvelous! She could compare it to nothing she had ever seen, and the garnet lights which it emitted were unspeakably rare. She pronounced the Colonel an artist, and stuck to it.

Monsieur Ratignolle was prepared to take things seriously: the *mets,* the *entre-mets,*[5] the service, the decorations, even the people. He looked up from his pompano[6] and inquired of Arobin if he were related to the gentleman of that name who formed one of the firm of Laitner and Arobin, lawyers. The young man admitted that Laitner was a warm personal friend, who permitted Arobin's name to decorate the firm's letterheads and to appear upon a shingle that graced Perdido Street.

"There are so many inquisitive people and institutions abounding," said Arobin, "that one is really forced as a matter of convenience these days to assume the virtue of an occupation if he has it not."

Monsieur Ratignolle stared a little, and turned to ask Mademoiselle Reisz if she considered the symphony concerts up to the standard which had been set the previous winter. Mademoiselle Reisz answered Monsieur Ratignolle in French, which Edna thought a little rude, under the circumstances, but characteristic. Mademoiselle had only disagreeable things to say of the symphony concerts, and insulting remarks to make of all the musicians of New Orleans, singly and collectively. All her interest seemed to be centered upon the delicacies placed before her.

Mr. Merriman said that Mr. Arobin's remark about inquisitive people reminded him of a man from Waco[7] the other day at the St. Charles Hotel—but as Mr. Merriman's stories were always lame and lacking point, his wife seldom permitted him to complete them. She interrupted him to ask if he remembered the name of the author whose book she had bought the week before to send to a friend in Geneva. She was talking "books" with Mr. Gouvernail and trying to draw from him his opinion upon current literary topics. Her husband told the story of the Waco man privately to Miss Mayblunt, who pretended to be greatly amused and to think it extremely clever.

Mrs. Highcamp hung with languid but unaffected interest upon the warm and impetuous volubility of her left-hand neighbor, Victor Lebrun. Her attention was never for a moment withdrawn from him after seating herself at table; and when he turned to Mrs. Merriman, who was prettier and more vivacious than Mrs. Highcamp, she waited with easy indifference for an opportunity to reclaim his attention. There was the occasional sound of music, of mandolins, sufficiently removed to be an agreeable accompaniment rather than an interruption to the conversation. Outside the soft, monotonous splash of a fountain could be heard; the sound penetrated into the room with the heavy odor of jessamine that came through the open windows.

---

[5] "Main dish" and "side dishes" (French).   [6] An edible variety of fish.   [7] Waco, Texas.

The golden shimmer of Edna's satin gown spread in rich folds on either side of her. There was a soft fall of lace encircling her shoulders. It was the color of her skin, without the glow, the myriad living tints that one may sometimes discover in vibrant flesh. There was something in her attitude, in her whole appearance when she leaned her head against the high-backed chair and spread her arms, which suggested the regal woman, the one who rules, who looks on, who stands alone.

But as she sat there amid her guests, she felt the old ennui overtaking her; the hopelessness which so often assailed her, which came upon her like an obsession, like something extraneous, independent of volition. It was something which announced itself; a chill breath that seemed to issue from some vast cavern wherein discords wailed. There came over her the acute longing which always summoned into her spiritual vision the presence of the beloved one, overpowering her at once with a sense of the unattainable.

The moments glided on, while a feeling of good fellowship passed around the circle like a mystic cord, holding and binding these people together with jest and laughter. Monsieur Ratignolle was the first to break the pleasant charm. At ten o'clock he excused himself. Madame Ratignolle was waiting for him at home. She was *bien souffrante*,[8] and she was filled with vague dread, which only her husband's presence could allay.

Mademoiselle Reisz arose with Monsieur Ratignolle, who offered to escort her to the car. She had eaten well; she had tasted the good, rich wines, and they must have turned her head, for she bowed pleasantly to all as she withdrew from table. She kissed Edna upon the shoulder, and whispered: *"Bonne nuit, ma reine; soyez sage."*[9] She had been a little bewildered upon rising, or rather, descending from her cushions, and Monsieur Ratignolle gallantly took her arm and led her away.

Mrs. Highcamp was weaving a garland of roses, yellow and red. When she had finished the garland, she laid it lightly upon Victor's black curls. He was reclining far back in the luxurious chair, holding a glass of champagne to the light.

As if a magician's wand had touched him, the garland of roses transformed him into a vision of Oriental beauty. His cheeks were the color of crushed grapes, and his dusky eyes glowed with a languishing fire.

"Sapristi!" exclaimed Arobin.

But Mrs. Highcamp had one more touch to add to the picture. She took from the back of her chair a white silken scarf, with which she had covered her shoulders in the early part of the evening. She draped it across the boy in graceful folds, and in a way to conceal his black, conventional evening dress. He did not seem to mind what she did to him, only smiled, showing a faint gleam of white teeth, while he continued to gaze with narrowing eyes at the light through his glass of champagne.

"Oh! to be able to paint in color rather than in words!" exclaimed Miss Mayblunt, losing herself in a rhapsodic dream as she looked at him.

> " 'There was a graven image of Desire
> Painted with red blood on a ground of gold.' "[10]

murmured Gouvernail, under his breath.

---

[8] "Quite ill" (French).   [9] "Good night, my queen; be good" (French).
[10] From the sonnet "A Cameo," by the English poet Algernon Charles Swinburne (1837–1909).

The effect of the wine upon Victor was to change his accustomed volubility into silence. He seemed to have abandoned himself to a reverie, and to be seeing pleasing visions in the amber bead.

"Sing," entreated Mrs. Highcamp. "Won't you sing to us?"

"Let him alone," said Arobin.

"He's posing," offered Mr. Merriman; "let him have it out."

"I believe he's paralyzed," laughed Mrs. Merriman. And leaning over the youth's chair, she took the glass from his hand and held it to his lips. He sipped the wine slowly, and when he had drained the glass she laid it upon the table and wiped his lips with her little filmy handkerchief.

"Yes, I'll sing for you," he said, turning in his chair toward Mrs. Highcamp. He clasped his hands behind his head, and looking up at the ceiling began to hum a little, trying his voice like a musician tuning an instrument. Then, looking at Edna, he began to sing:

"Ah! si tu savais!"

"Stop! she cried, "don't sing that. I don't want you to sing it," and she laid her glass so impetuously and blindly upon the table as to shatter it against a caraffe. The wine spilled over Arobin's legs and some of it trickled down upon Mrs. Highcamp's black gauze gown. Victor had lost all idea of courtesy, or else he thought his hostess was not in earnest, for he laughed and went on:

"Ah! si tu savais
Ce que tes yeux me disent"[11]—

"Oh! you mustn't! you mustn't," exclaimed Edna, and pushing back her chair she got up, and going behind him placed her hand over his mouth. He kissed the soft palm that pressed upon his lips.

"No, no, I won't, Mrs. Pontellier. I didn't know you meant it," looking up at her with caressing eyes. The touch of his lips was like a pleasing sting to her hand. She lifted the garland of roses from his head and flung it across the room.

"Come, Victor; you've posed long enough. Give Mrs. Highcamp her scarf."

Mrs. Highcamp undraped the scarf from about him with her own hands. Miss Mayblunt and Mr. Gouvernail suddenly conceived the notion that it was time to say good night. And Mr. and Mrs. Merriman wondered how it could be so late.

Before parting from Victor, Mrs. Highcamp invited him to call upon her daughter, who she knew would be charmed to meet him and talk French and sing French songs with him. Victor expressed his desire and intention to call upon Miss Highcamp at the first opportunity which presented itself. He asked if Arobin were going his way. Arobin was not.

The mandolin players had long since stolen away. A profound stillness had fallen upon the broad, beautiful street. The voices of Edna's disbanding guests jarred like a discordant note upon the quiet harmony of the night.

---

[11] "Ah, couldst thou but know / What thine eyes tell me" (French).

XXXI

"Well?" questioned Arobin, who had remained with Edna after the others had departed.

"Well," she reiterated, and stood up, stretching her arms, and feeling the need to relax her muscles after having been so long seated.

"What next?" he asked.

"The servants are all gone. They left when the musicians did. I have dismissed them. The house has to be closed and locked, and I shall trot around to the pigeon house, and shall send Celestine over in the morning to straighten things up."

He looked around, and began to turn out some of the lights.

"What about upstairs?" he inquired.

"I think it is all right; but there may be a window or two unlatched. We had better look; you might take a candle and see. And bring me my wrap and hat on the foot of the bed in the middle room."

He went up with the light, and Edna began closing doors and windows. She hated to shut in the smoke and the fumes of the wine. Arobin found her cape and hat, which he brought down and helped her to put on.

When everything was secured and the lights put out, they left through the front door, Arobin locking it and taking the key, which he carried for Edna. He helped her down the steps.

"Will you have a spray of jessamine?" he asked, breaking off a few blossoms as he passed.

"No; I don't want anything."

She seemed disheartened, and had nothing to say. She took his arm, which he offered her, holding up the weight of her satin train with the other hand. She looked down, noticing the black line of his leg moving in and out so close to her against the yellow shimmer of her gown. There was the whistle of a railway train somewhere in the distance, and the midnight bells were ringing. They met no one in their short walk.

The "pigeon-house" stood behind a locked gate, and a shallow *parterre*[1] that had been somewhat neglected. There was a small front porch, upon which a long window and the front door opened. The door opened directly into the parlor; there was no side entry. Back in the yard was a room for servants, in which old Celestine had been ensconced.

Edna had left a lamp burning low upon the table. She had succeeded in making the room look habitable and homelike. There were some books on the table and a lounge near at hand. On the floor was a fresh matting, covered with a rug or two; and on the walls hung a few tasteful pictures. But the room was filled with flowers. These were a surprise to her. Arobin had sent them, and had had Celestine distribute them during Edna's absence. Her bedroom was adjoining, and across a small passage were the dining-room and kitchen.

Edna seated herself with every appearance of discomfort.

"Are you tired?" he asked.

"Yes, and chilled, and miserable. I feel as if I had been wound up to a certain pitch—too tight—and something inside of me had snapped." She rested her head against the table upon her bare arm.

---

[1] "Flower-bed" (French).

"You want to rest," he said, "and to be quiet. I'll go; I'll leave you and let you rest."

"Yes," she replied.

He stood up beside her and smoothed her hair with his soft, magnetic hand. His touch conveyed to her a certain physical comfort. She could have fallen quietly asleep there if he had continued to pass his hand over her hair. He brushed the hair upward from the nape of her neck.

"I hope you will feel better and happier in the morning," he said. "You have tried to do too much in the past few days. The dinner was the last straw; you might have dispensed with it."

"Yes," she admitted; "it was stupid."

"No, it was delightful; but it has worn you out." His hand had strayed to her beautiful shoulders, and he could feel the response of her flesh to his touch. He seated himself beside her and kissed her lightly upon the shoulder.

"I thought you were going away," she said, in an uneven voice.

"I am, after I have said good night."

"Good night," she murmured.

He did not answer, except to continue to caress her. He did not say good night until she had become supple to his gentle, seductive entreaties.

XXXII

When Mr. Pontellier learned of his wife's intention to abandon her home and take up her residence elsewhere, he immediately wrote her a letter of unqualified disapproval and remonstrance. She had given reasons which he was unwilling to acknowledge as adequate. He hoped she had not acted upon her rash impulse; and he begged her to consider first, foremost, and above all else, what people would say. He was not dreaming of scandal when he uttered this warning; that was a thing which would never have entered into his mind to consider in connection with his wife's name or his own. He was simply thinking of his financial integrity. It might get noised about that the Pontelliers had met with reverses, and were forced to conduct their *ménage*[1] on a humbler scale than heretofore. It might do incalculable mischief to his business prospects.

But remembering Edna's whimsical turn of mind of late, and foreseeing that she had immediately acted upon her impetuous determination, he grasped the situation with his usual promptness and handled it with his well-known business tact and cleverness.

The same mail which brought to Edna his letter of disapproval carried instructions—the most minute instructions—to a well-known architect concerning the remodeling of his home, changes which he had long contemplated, and which he desired carried forward during his temporary absence.

Expert and reliable packers and movers were engaged to convey the furniture, carpets, pictures—everything movable, in short—to places of security. And in an incredibly short time the Pontellier house was turned over to the artisans. There was to be an addition—a small snuggery;[2] there was to be frescoing, and hardwood flooring was to be put into such rooms as had not yet been subjected to this improvement.

[1] "Household" (French).   [2] A cosy or comfortable place.

Furthermore, in one of the daily papers appeared a brief notice to the effect that Mr. and Mrs. Pontellier were contemplating a summer sojourn abroad, and that their handsome residence on Esplanade Street was undergoing sumptuous alterations, and would not be ready for occupancy until their return. Mr. Pontellier had saved appearances!

Edna admired the skill of his maneuver, and avoided any occasion to balk his intentions. When the situation as set forth by Mr. Pontellier was accepted and taken for granted, she was apparently satisfied that it should be so.

The pigeon-house pleased her. It at once assumed the intimate character of a home, while she herself invested it with a charm which it reflected like a warm glow. There was with her a feeling of having descended in the social scale, with a corresponding sense of having risen in the spiritual. Every step which she took toward relieving herself from obligations added to her strength and expansion as an individual. She began to look with her own eyes; to see and to apprehend the deeper undercurrents of life. No longer was she content to "feed upon opinion" when her own soul had invited her.

After a little while, a few days, in fact, Edna went up and spent a week with her children in Iberville. They were delicious February days, with all the summer's promise hovering in the air.

How glad she was to see the children! She wept for very pleasure when she felt their little arms clasping her; their hard, ruddy cheeks pressed against her own glowing cheeks. She looked into their faces with hungry eyes that could not be satisfied with looking. And what stories they had to tell their mother! About the pigs, the cows, the mules! About riding to the mill behind Gluglu; fishing back in the lake with their Uncle Jasper; picking pecans with Lidie's little black brood, and hauling chips in their express wagon. It was a thousand times more fun to haul real chips for old lame Susie's real fire than to drag painted blocks along the banquette on Esplanade Street!

She went with them herself to see the pigs and the cows, to look at the darkies laying the cane, to thrash the pecan trees, and catch fish in the back lake. She lived with them a whole week long, giving them all of herself, and gathering and filling herself with their young existence. They listened, breathless, when she told them the house in Esplanade Street was crowded with workmen, hammering, nailing, sawing, and filling the place with clatter. They wanted to know where their bed was; what had been done with their rocking-horse; and where did Joe sleep, and where had Ellen gone, and the cook? But, above all, they were fired with a desire to see the little house around the block. Was there any place to play? Were there any boys next door? Raoul, with pessimistic foreboding, was convinced that there were only girls next door. Where would they sleep, and where would papa sleep? She told them the fairies would fix it all right.

The old Madame was charmed with Edna's visit, and showered all manner of delicate attentions upon her. She was delighted to know that the Esplanade Street house was in a dismantled condition. It gave her the promise and pretext to keep the children indefinitely.

It was with a wrench and a pang that Edna left her children. She carried away with her the sound of their voices and the touch of their cheeks. All along the journey homeward their presence lingered with her like the memory of a delicious song. But by the time she had regained the city the song no longer echoed in her soul. She was again alone.

XXXIII

It happened sometimes when Edna went to see Mademoiselle Reisz that the little musician was absent, giving a lesson or making some small necessary household purchase. The key was always left in a secret hiding-place in the entry, which Edna knew. If Mademoiselle happened to be away, Edna would usually enter and wait for her return.

When she knocked at Mademoiselle Reisz's door one afternoon there was no response; so unlocking the door, as usual, she entered and found the apartment deserted, as she had expected. Her day had been quite filled up, and it was for a rest, for a refuge, and to talk about Robert, that she sought out her friend.

She had worked at her canvas—a young Italian character study—all the morning, completing the work without the model; but there had been many interruptions, some incident to her modest housekeeping, and others of a social nature.

Madame Ratignolle had dragged herself over, avoiding the too public thoroughfares, she said. She complained that Edna had neglected her much of late. Besides, she was consumed with curiosity to see the little house and the manner in which it was conducted. She wanted to hear all about the dinner party; Monsieur Ratignolle had left *so* early. What had happened after he left? The champagne and grapes which Edna sent over were *too* delicious. She had so little appetite; they had refreshed and toned her stomach. Where on earth was she going to put Mr. Pontellier in that little house, and the boys? And then she made Edna promise to go to her when her hour of trial overtook her.[1]

"At any time—any time of the day or night, dear," Edna assured her.

Before leaving Madame Ratignolle said:

"In some way you seem to me like a child, Edna. You seem to act without a certain amount of reflection which is necessary in this life. That is the reason I want to say you mustn't mind if I advise you to be a little careful while you are living here alone. Why don't you have some one come and stay with you? Wouldn't Mademoiselle Reisz come?"

"No; she wouldn't wish to come, and I shouldn't want her always with me."

"Well, the reason—you know how evil-minded the world is—some one was talking of Alcée Arobin visiting you. Of course, it wouldn't matter if Mr. Arobin had not such a dreadful reputation. Monsieur Ratignolle was telling me that his attentions alone are considered enough to ruin a woman's name."

"Does he boast of his successes?" asked Edna, indifferently, squinting at her picture.

"No, I think not. I believe he is a decent fellow as far as that goes. But his character is so well known among the men. I shan't be able to come back and see you; it was very, very imprudent to-day."

"Mind the step!" cried Edna.

"Don't neglect me," entreated Madame Ratignolle; "and don't mind what I said about Arobin, or having some one to stay with you."

"Of course not," Edna laughed. "You may say anything you like to me." They kissed each other good-by. Madame Ratignolle had not far to go, and Edna stood on the porch a while watching her walk down the street.

---

[1] When she went into labor before giving birth.

Then in the afternoon Mrs. Merriman and Mrs. Highcamp had made their "party call." Edna felt that they might have dispensed with the formality. They had also come to invite her to play *vingt-et-un*[2] one evening at Mrs. Merriman's. She was asked to go early, to dinner, and Mr. Merriman or Mr. Arobin would take her home. Edna accepted in a half-hearted way. She sometimes felt very tired of Mrs. Highcamp and Mrs. Merriman.

Late in the afternoon she sought refuge with Mademoiselle Reisz, and stayed there alone, waiting for her, feeling a kind of repose invade her with the very atmosphere of the shabby, unpretentious little room.

Edna sat at the window, which looked out over the house-tops and across the river. The window frame was filled with pots of flowers, and she sat and picked the dry leaves from a rose geranium. The day was warm, and the breeze which blew from the river was very pleasant. She removed her hat and laid it on the piano. She went on picking the leaves and digging around the plants with her hat pin. Once she thought she heard Mademoiselle Reisz approaching. But it was a young black girl, who came in, bringing a small bundle of laundry, which she deposited in the adjoining room, and went away.

Edna seated herself at the piano, and softly picked out with one hand the bars of a piece of music which lay open before her. A half-hour went by. There was the occasional sound of people going and coming in the lower hall. She was growing interested in her occupation of picking out the aria, when there was a second rap at the door. She vaguely wondered what these people did when they found Mademoiselle's door locked.

"Come in," she called, turning her face toward the door. And this time it was Robert Labrun who presented himself. She attempted to rise; she could not have done so without betraying the agitation which mastered her at sight of him, so she fell back upon the stool, only exclaiming, "Why, Robert!"

He came and clasped her hand, seemingly without knowing what he was saying or doing.

"Mrs. Pontellier! How do you happen—oh! how well you look! Is Mademoiselle Reisz not here? I never expected to see you."

"When did you come back?" asked Edna in an unsteady voice, wiping her face with her handkerchief. She seemed ill at ease on the piano stool, and he begged her to take the chair by the window. She did so, mechanically, while he seated himself on the stool.

"I returned day before yesterday," he answered, while he leaned his arm on the keys, bringing forth a crash of discordant sound.

"Day before yesterday!" she repeated, aloud; and went on thinking to herself, "day before yesterday," in a sort of an uncomprehending way. She had pictured him seeking her at the very first hour, and he had lived under the same sky since day before yesterday; while only by accident had he stumbled upon her. Mademoiselle must have lied when she said, "Poor fool, he loves you."

"Day before yesterday," she repeated, breaking off a spray of Mademoiselle's geranium; "then if you had not met me here to-day you wouldn't—when—that is, didn't you mean to come and see me?"

"Of course, I should have gone to see you. There have been so many things—" he turned the leaves of Mademoiselle's music nervously. "I started in at once yesterday with the old firm. After all there is as much chance for me here as there

---

[2] "Twenty-one" (French), or blackjack, a card game.

was there—that is, I might find it profitable some day. The Mexicans were not very congenial."

So he had come back because the Mexicans were not congenial; because business was as profitable here as there; because of any reason, and not because he cared to be near her. She remembered the day she sat on the floor, turning the pages of his letter, seeking the reason which was left untold.

She had not noticed how he looked—only feeling his presence; but she turned deliberately and observed him. After all, he had been absent but a few months, and was not changed. His hair—the color of hers—waved back from his temples in the same way as before. His skin was not more burned that it had been at Grand Isle. She found in his eyes, when he looked at her for one silent moment, the same tender caress, with an added warmth and entreaty which had not been there before—the same glance which had penetrated to the sleeping places of her soul and awakened them.

A hundred times Edna had pictured Robert's return, and imagined their first meeting. It was usually at her home, whither he had sought her out at once. She always fancied him expressing or betraying in some way his love for her. And here, the reality was that they sat ten feet apart, she at the window, crushing geranium leaves in her hand and smelling them, he twirling around on the piano stool, saying:

"I was very much surprised to hear of Mr. Pontellier's absence; it's a wonder Mademoiselle Reisz did not tell me; and your moving—mother told me yesterday. I should think you would have gone to New York with him, or to Iberville with the children, rather than be bothered here with housekeeping. And you are going abroad, too, I hear. We shan't have you at Grand Isle next summer; it won't seem—do you see much of Mademoiselle Reisz? She often spoke of you in the few letters she wrote."

"Do you remember that you promised to write to me when you went away?" A flush overspread his whole face.

"I couldn't believe that my letters would be of any interest to you."

"That is an excuse; it isn't the truth." Edna reached for her hat on the piano. She adjusted it, sticking the hat pin through the heavy coil of hair with some deliberation.

"Are you not going to wait for Mademoiselle Reisz?" asked Robert.

"No; I have found when she is absent this long, she is liable not to come back till late." She drew on her gloves, and Robert picked up his hat.

"Won't you wait for her?" asked Edna.

"Not if you think she will not be back till late," adding, as if suddenly aware of some discourtesy in his speech, "and I should miss the pleasure of walking home with you." Edna locked the door and put the key back in its hiding-place.

They went together, picking their way across muddy streets and sidewalks encumbered with the cheap display of small tradesmen. Part of the distance they rode in the car, and after disembarking, passed the Pontellier mansion, which looked broken and half torn asunder. Robert had never known the house, and looked at it with interest.

"I never knew you in your home," he remarked.

"I am glad you did not."

"Why?" She did not answer. They went on around the corner, and it seemed as if her dreams were coming true after all, when he followed her into the little house.

"You must stay and dine with me, Robert. You see I am all alone, and it is so long since I have seen you. There is so much I want to ask you."

She took off her hat and gloves. He stood irresolute, making some excuse about his mother who expected him; he even muttered something about an engagement. She struck a match and lit the lamp on the table; it was growing dusk. When he saw her face in the lamp-light, looking pained, with all the soft lines gone out of it, he threw his hat aside and seated himself.

"Oh! you know I want to stay if you will let me!" he exclaimed. All the softness came back. She laughed, and went and put her hand on his shoulder.

"This is the first moment you have seemed like the old Robert. I'll go tell Celestine." She hurried away to tell Celestine to set an extra place. She even sent her off in search of some added delicacy which she had not thought of for herself. And she recommended great care in dripping the coffee and having the omelet done to a proper turn.

When she reëntered, Robert was turning over magazines, sketches, and things that lay upon the table in great disorder. He picked up a photograph, and exclaimed:

"Alcée Arobin! What on earth is his picture doing here?"

"I tried to make a sketch of his head one day," answered Edna, "and he thought the photograph might help me. It was at the other house. I thought it had been left there. I must have packed it up with my drawing materials."

"I should think you would give it back to him if you have finished with it."

"Oh! I have a great many such photographs. I never think of returning them. They don't amount to anything." Robert kept looking at the picture.

"It seems to me—do you think his head worth drawing? Is he a friend of Mr. Pontellier's? You never said you knew him."

"He isn't a friend of Mr. Pontellier's; he's a friend of mine. I always knew him—that is, it is only of late that I know him pretty well. But I'd rather talk about you, and know what you have been seeing and doing and feeling out there in Mexico." Robert threw aside the picture.

"I've been seeing the waves and the white beach of Grand Isle; the quiet, grassy street of the *Chénière;* the old fort at Grande Terre. I've been working like a machine, and feeling like a lost soul. There was nothing interesting."

She leaned her head upon her hand to shade her eyes from the light.

"And what have you been seeing and doing and feeling all these days?" he asked.

"I've been seeing the waves and the white beach of Grand Isle; the quiet, grassy street of the *Chénière Caminada;* the old sunny fort at Grande Terre. I've been working with a little more comprehension than a machine, and still feeling like a lost soul. There was nothing interesting."

"Mrs. Pontellier, you are cruel," he said, with feeling, closing his eyes and resting his head back in his chair. They remained in silence till old Celestine announced dinner.

XXXIV

The dining-room was very small. Edna's round mahogany would have almost filled it. As it was there was but a step or two from the little table to the kitchen, to the mantel, the small buffet, and the side door that opened out on the narrow brick-paved yard.

A certain degree of ceremony settled upon them with the announcement of dinner. There was no return to personalities. Robert related incidents of his sojourn in Mexico, and Edna talked of events likely to interest him, which had occurred during his absence. The dinner was of ordinary quality, except for the few delicacies which she had sent out to purchase. Old Celestine, with a bandana *tignon*[1] twisted about her head, hobbled in and out, taking a personal interest in everything; and she lingered occasionally to talk patois[2] with Robert, whom she had known as a boy.

He went out to a neighboring cigar stand to purchase cigarette papers, and when he came back he found that Celestine had served the black coffee in the parlor.

"Perhaps I shouldn't have come back." he said. "When you are tired of me, tell me to go."

"You never tire me. You must have forgotten the hours and hours at Grand Isle in which we grew accustomed to each other and used to being together."

"I have forgotten nothing at Grand Isle," he said, not looking at her, but rolling a cigarette. His tobacco pouch, which he laid upon the table, was a fantastic embroidered silk affair, evidently the handiwork of a woman.

"You used to carry your tobacco in a rubber pouch," said Edna, picking up the pouch and examining the needlework.

"Yes; it was lost."

"Where did you buy this one? In Mexico?"

"It was given to me by a Vera Cruz girl; they are very generous," he replied, striking a match and lighting his cigarette.

"They are very handsome, I suppose, those Mexican women; very picturesque, with their black eyes and their lace scarfs."

"Some are; others are hideous. Just as you find women everywhere."

"What was she like—the one who gave you the pouch? You must have known her very well."

"She was very ordinary. She wasn't of the slightest importance. I knew her well enough."

"Did you visit at her house? Was it interesting? I should like to know and hear about the people you met, and the impressions they made on you."

"There are some people who leave impressions not so lasting as the imprint of an oar upon the water."

"Was she such a one?"

"It would be ungenerous for me to admit that she was of that order and kind." He thrust the pouch back in his pocket, as if to put away the subject with the trifle which had brought it up.

Arobin dropped in with a message from Mrs. Merriman, to say that the card party was postponed on account of the illness of one of her children.

"How do you do, Arobin?" said Robert, rising from the obscurity.

"Oh! Lebrun. To be sure! I heard yesterday you were back. How did they treat you down in Mexique?"

"Fairly well."

"But not well enough to keep you there. Stunning girls, though, in Mexico. I

[1] A turban made from a scarf.
[2] A local dialect reflecting the mixed ethnic groups of the area, such as French, Spanish, and English.

thought I should never get away from Vera Cruz when I was down there a couple of years ago."

"Did they embroider slippers and tobacco pouches and hat-bands and things for you?" asked Edna.

"Oh! my! no! I didn't get so deep in their regard. I fear they made more impression on me than I made on them."

"You were less fortunate than Robert, then."

"I am always less fortunate than Robert. Has he been imparting tender confidences?"

"I've been imposing myself long enough," said Robert, rising, and shaking hands with Edna. "Please convey my regards to Mr. Pontellier when you write."

He shook hands with Arobin and went away.

"Fine fellow, that Lebrun," said Arobin when Robert had gone. "I never heard you speak of him."

"I knew him last summer at Grand Isle," she replied. "Here is that photograph of yours. Don't you want it?"

"What do I want with it? Throw it away." She threw it back on the table.

"I'm not going to Mrs. Merriman's," she said. "If you see her, tell her so. But perhaps I had better write. I think I shall write now, and say that I am sorry her child is sick, and tell her not to count on me."

"It would be a good scheme," acquiesced Arobin. "I don't blame you; stupid lot!"

Edna opened the blotter, and having procured paper and pen, began to write the note. Arobin lit a cigar and read the evening paper, which he had in his pocket.

"What is the date?" she asked. He told her.

"Will you mail this for me when you go out?"

"Certainly." He read to her little bits out of the newspaper, while she straightened things on the table.

"What do you want to do?" he asked, throwing aside the paper. "Do you want to go out for a walk or a drive or anything? It would be a fine night to drive."

"No; I don't want to do anything but just be quiet. You go away and amuse yourself. Don't stay."

"I'll go away if I must; but I shan't amuse myself. You know that I only live when I am near you."

He stood up to bid her good night.

"Is that one of the things you always say to women?"

"I have said it before, but I don't think I ever came so near meaning it," he answered with a smile. There were no warm lights in her eyes; only a dreamy, absent look.

"Good night. I adore you. Sleep well," he said, and he kissed her hand and went away.

She stayed alone in a kind of reverie—a sort of stupor. Step by step she lived over every instant of the time she had been with Robert after he had entered Mademoiselle Reisz's door. She recalled his words, his looks. How few and meager they had been for her hungry heart! A vision—a transcendently seductive vision of a Mexican girl arose before her. She writhed with a jealous pang. She wondered when he would come back. He had not said he would come back. She had been with him, had heard his voice and touched his hand. But some way he had seemed nearer to her off there in Mexico.

XXXV

The morning was full of sunlight and hope. Edna could see before her no denial—
only the promise of excessive joy. She lay in bed awake, with bright eyes full of
speculation. "He loves you, poor fool." If she could but get that conviction firmly
fixed in her mind, what mattered about the rest? She felt she had been childish and
unwise the night before in giving herself over to despondency. She recapitulated
the motives which no doubt explained Robert's reserve. They were not insurmountable; they would not hold if he really loved her; they could not hold against
her own passion, which he must come to realize in time. She pictured him going
to his business that morning. She even saw how he was dressed; how he walked
down one street, and turned the corner of another; saw him bending over his desk,
talking to people who entered the office, going to his lunch, and perhaps watching
for her on the street. He would come to her in the afternoon or evening, sit and
roll his cigarette, talk a little, and go away as he had done the night before. But
how delicious it would be to have him there with her! She would have no regrets,
nor seek to penetrate his reserve if he still chose to wear it.

Edna ate her breakfast only half dressed. The maid brought her a delicious
printed scrawl from Raoul, expressing his love, asking her to send him some bonbons, and telling her they had found that morning ten tiny white pigs all lying in a
row beside Lidie's big white pig.

A letter also came from her husband, saying he hoped to be back early in
March, and then they would get ready for that journey abroad which he had promised her so long, which he felt now fully able to afford; he felt able to travel as
people should, without any thought of small economies—thanks to his recent
speculations in Wall Street.

Much to her surprise she received a note from Arobin, written at midnight from
the club. It was to say good morning to her, to hope she had slept well, to assure
her of his devotion, which he trusted she in some faintest manner returned.

All these letters were pleasing to her. She answered the children in a cheerful
frame of mind, promising them bonbons, and congratulating them upon their
happy find of the little pigs.

She answered her husband with friendly evasiveness,—not with any fixed design to mislead him, only because all sense of reality had gone out of her life; she
had abandoned herself to Fate, and awaited the consequences with indifference.

To Arobin's note she made no reply. She put it under Celestine's stove-lid.

Edna worked several hours with much spirit. She saw no one but a picture
dealer, who asked her if it were true that she was going abroad to study in Paris.

She said possibly she might, and he negotiated with her for some Parisian studies to reach him in time for the holiday trade in December.

Robert did not come that day. She was keenly disappointed. He did not come
the following day, nor the next. Each morning she awoke with hope, and each
night she was a prey to despondency. She was tempted to seek him out. But far
from yielding to the impulse, she avoided any occasion which might throw her in
his way. She did not go to Mademoiselle Reisz's nor pass by Madame Lebrun's,
as she might have done if he had still been in Mexico.

When Arobin, one night, urged her to drive with him, she went—out to the
lake, on the Shell Road. His horses were full of mettle, and even a little unmanageable. She liked the rapid gait at which they spun along, and the quick, sharp

sound of the horses' hoofs on the hard road. They did not stop anywhere to eat or to drink. Arobin was not needlessly imprudent. But they ate and they drank when they regained Edna's little dining-room—which was comparatively early in the evening.

It was late when he left her. It was getting to be more than a passing whim with Arobin to see her and be with her. He had detected the latent sensuality, which unfolded under his delicate sense of her nature's requirements like a torpid, torrid, sensitive blossom.

There was no despondency when she fell asleep that night; nor was there hope when she awoke in the morning.

XXXVI

There was a garden out in the suburbs; a small, leafy corner, with a few green tables under the orange trees. An old cat slept all day on the stone step in the sun, and an old *mulatresse*[1] slept her idle hours away in her chair at the open window, till some one happened to knock on one of the green tables. She had milk and cream cheese to sell, and bread and butter. There was no one who could make such excellent coffee or fry a chicken so golden brown as she.

The place was too modest to attract the attention of people of fashion, and so quiet as to have escaped the notice of those in search of pleasure and dissipation. Edna had discovered it accidentally one day when the high-board gate stood ajar. She caught sight of a little green table, blotched with the checkered sunlight that filtered through the quivering leaves overhead. Within she had found the slumbering *mulatresse*, the drowsy cat, and a glass of milk which reminded her of the milk she had tasted in Iberville.

She often stopped there during her perambulations; sometimes taking a book with her, and sitting an hour or two under the trees when she found the place deserted. Once or twice she took a quiet dinner there alone, having instructed Celestine beforehand to prepare no dinner at home. It was the last place in the city where she would have expected to meet any one she knew.

Still she was not astonished when, as she was partaking of a modest dinner late in the afternoon, looking into an open book, stroking the cat, which had made friends with her—she was not greatly astonished to see Robert come in at the tall garden gate.

"I am destined to see you only by accident," she said, shoving the cat off the chair beside her. He was surprised, ill at ease, almost embarrassed at meeting her thus so unexpectedly.

"Do you come here often?" he asked.

"I almost live here," she said.

"I used to drop in very often for a cup of Catiche's good coffee. This is the first time since I came back."

"She'll bring you a plate, and you will share my dinner. There's always enough for two—even three." Edna had intended to be indifferent and as reserved as he when she met him; she had reached the determination by a laborious train of reasoning, incident to one of her despondent moods. But her resolve melted when

[1] A female mulatto, a woman of mixed black and white ancestry (French).

she saw him before her, seated there beside her in the little garden, as if a design-ing Providence had led him into her path.

"Why have you kept away from me, Robert?" she asked, closing the book that lay open upon the table.

"Why are you so personal, Mrs. Pontellier? Why do you force me to idiotic subterfuges?" he exclaimed with sudden warmth. "I suppose there's no use telling you I've been very busy, or that I've been sick, or that I've been to see you and not found you at home. Please let me off with any one of these excuses."

"You are the embodiment of selfishness," she said. "You save yourself some-thing—I don't know what—but there is some selfish motive, and in sparing your-self you never consider for a moment what I think, or how I feel your neglect and indifference. I suppose this is what you would call unwomanly; but I have got into a habit of expressing myself. It doesn't matter to me, and you may think me unwomanly if you like."

"No; I only think you cruel, as I said the other day. Maybe not intentionally cruel; but you seem to be forcing me into disclosures which can result in nothing; as if you would have me bare a wound for the pleasure of looking at it, without the intention or power of healing it."

"I'm spoiling your dinner, Robert; never mind what I say. You haven't eaten a morsel."

"I only came in for a cup of coffee." His sensitive face was all disfigured with excitement.

"Isn't this a delightful place?" she remarked. "I am so glad it has never actually been discovered. It is so quiet, so sweet, here. Do you notice there is scarcely a sound to be heard? It's so out of the way; and a good walk from the car. However, I don't mind walking. I always feel so sorry for women who don't like to walk; they miss so much—so many rare little glimpses of life; and we women learn so little of life on the whole.

"Catiche's coffee is always hot. I don't know how she manages it, here in the open air. Celestine's coffee gets cold bringing it from the kitchen to the dining-room. Three lumps! How can you drink it so sweet? Take some of the cress with your chop; it's so biting and crisp. Then there's the advantage of being able to smoke with your coffee out here. Now, in the city—aren't you going to smoke?"

"After a while," he said, laying a cigar on the table.

"Who gave it to you?" she laughed.

"I bought it. I suppose I'm getting reckless; I bought a whole box." She was determined not to be personal again and make him uncomfortable.

The cat made friends with him, and climbed into his lap when he smoked his cigar. He stroked her silky fur, and talked a little about her. He looked at Edna's book, which he had read; and he told her the end, to save her the trouble of wading through it, he said.

Again he accompanied her back to her home; and it was after dusk when they reached the little "pigeon-house." She did not ask him to remain, which he was grateful for, as it permitted him to stay without the discomfort of blundering through an excuse which he had no intention of considering. He helped her to light the lamp; then she went into her room to take off her hat and to bathe her face and hands.

When she came back Robert was not examining the pictures and magazines as before; he sat off in the shadow, leaning his head back on the chair as if in a reverie. Edna lingered a moment beside the table, arranging the books there. Then she went across the room to where he sat. She bent over the arm of his chair and called his name.

"Robert," she said, "are you asleep?"

"No," he answered, looking up at her.

She leaned over and kissed him—a soft, cool, delicate kiss, whose voluptuous sting penetrated his whole being—then she moved away from him. He followed, and took her in his arms, just holding her close to him. She put her hand up to his face and pressed his cheek against her own. The action was full of love and tenderness. He sought her lips again. Then he drew her down upon the sofa beside him and held her hand in both of his.

"Now you know," he said, "now you know what I have been fighting against since last summer at Grand Isle; what drove me away and drove me back again."

"Why have you been fighting against it?" she asked. Her face glowed with soft lights.

"Why? Because you were not free; you were Léonce Pontellier's wife. I couldn't help loving you if you were ten times his wife; but so long as I went away from you and kept away I could help telling you so." She put her free hand up to his shoulder, and then against his cheek, rubbing it softly. He kissed her again. His face was warm and flushed.

"There in Mexico I was thinking of you all the time, and longing for you."

"But not writing to me," she interrupted.

"Something put into my head that you cared for me; and I lost my senses. I forgot everything but a wild dream of your some way becoming my wife."

"Your wife!"

"Religion, loyalty, everything would give way if only you cared."

"Then you must have forgotten that I was Léonce Pontellier's wife."

"Oh! I was demented, dreaming of wild, impossible things, recalling men who had set their wives free, we have heard of such things."

"Yes, we have heard of such things."

"I came back full of vague, mad intentions. And when I got here—"

"When you got here you never came near me!" She was still caressing his cheek.

"I realized what a cur I was to dream of such a thing, even if you had been willing."

She took his face between her hands and looked into it as if she would never withdraw her eyes more. She kissed him on the forehead, the eyes, the cheeks, and the lips.

"You have been a very, very foolish boy, wasting your time dreaming of impossible things when you speak of Mr. Pontellier setting me free! I am no longer one of Mr. Pontellier's possessions to dispose of or not. I give myself where I choose. If he were to say, 'Here, Robert, take her and be happy; she is yours,' I should laugh at you both."

His face grew a little white. "What do you mean?" he asked.

There was a knock at the door. Old Celestine came in to say that Madame Ratignolle's servant had come around the back way with a message that Madame had been taken sick and begged Mrs. Pontellier to go to her immediately.

"Yes, yes," said Edna, rising, "I promised. Tell her yes—to wait for me. I'll go back with her."

"Let me walk over with you," offered Robert.

"No," she said; "I will go with the servant." She went into her room to put on her hat, and when she came in again she sat once more upon the sofa beside him. He had not stirred. She put her arms about his neck.

"Good-by, my sweet Robert. Tell me good-by." He kissed her with a degree of passion which had not before entered into his caress, and strained her to him.

"I love you," she whispered, "only you; no one but you. It was you who awoke me last summer out of a life-long, stupid dream. Oh! you have made me so unhappy with your indifference. Oh! I have suffered, suffered! Now you are here we shall love each other, my Robert. We shall be everything to each other. Nothing else in the world is of any consequence. I must go to my friend; but you will wait for me? No matter how late; you will wait for me, Robert?"

"Don't go; don't go! Oh! Edna, stay with me," he pleaded. "Why should you go? Stay with me, stay with me."

"I shall come back as soon as I can; I shall find you here." She buried her face in his neck, and said good-by again. Her seductive voice, together with his great love for her, had enthralled his senses, had deprived him of every impulse but the longing to hold her and keep her.

XXXVII

Edna looked in at the drug store. Monsieur Ratignolle was putting up a mixture himself, very carefully, dropping a red liquid into a tiny glass. He was grateful to Edna for having come; her presence would be a comfort to his wife. Madame Ratignolle's sister, who had always been with her at such trying times, had not been able to come up from the plantation, and Adèle had been inconsolable until Mrs. Pontellier so kindly promised to come to her. The nurse had been with them at night for the past week, as she lived a great distance away. And Dr. Mandelet had been coming and going all the afternoon. They were then looking for him any moment.

Edna hastened upstairs by a private stairway that led from the rear of the store to the apartments above. The children were all sleeping in a back room. Madame Ratignolle was in the salon, whither she had strayed in her suffering impatience. She sat on the sofa, clad in an ample white *peignoir*, holding a handkerchief tight in her hand with a nervous clutch. Her face was drawn and pinched, her sweet blue eyes haggard and unnatural. All her beautiful hair had been drawn back and plaited. It lay in a long braid on the sofa pillow, coiled like a golden serpent. The nurse, a comfortable looking *Griffe*[1] woman in white apron and cap, was urging her to return to her bedroom.

"There is no use, there is no use," she said at once to Edna. "We must get rid of Mandelet; he is getting too old and careless. He said he would be here at half-past seven; now it must be eight. See what time it is, Joséphine."

The woman was possessed of a cheerful nature, and refused to take any situation too seriously, especially a situation with which she was so familiar. She urged Madame to have courage and patience. But Madame only set her teeth hard into her under lip, and Edna saw the sweat gather in beads on her white forehead. After a moment or two she uttered a profound sigh and wiped her face with the

---

[1] A person with mixed black and mulatto or black and Native-American ancestry.

handkerchief rolled in a ball. She appeared exhausted. The nurse gave her a fresh handkerchief, sprinkled with cologne water.

"This is too much!" she cried. "Mandelet ought to be killed! Where is Alphonse? Is it possible I am to be abandoned like this—neglected by every one?"

"Neglected, indeed!" exclaimed the nurse. Wasn't she there? And here was Mrs. Pontellier leaving, no doubt, a pleasant evening at home to devote to her? And wasn't Monsieur Ratignolle coming that very instant through the hall? And Joséphine was quite sure she had heard Doctor Mandelet's coupé. Yes, there it was, down at the door.

Adèle consented to go back to her room. She sat on the edge of a little low couch next to her bed.

Doctor Mandelet paid no attention to Madame Ratignolle's upbraidings. He was accustomed to them at such times, and was too well convinced of her loyalty to doubt it.

He was glad to see Edna, and wanted her to go with him into the salon and entertain him. But Madame Ratignolle would not consent that Edna should leave her for an instant. Between agonizing moments, she chatted a little, and said it took her mind off her sufferings.

Edna began to feel uneasy. She was seized with a vague dread. Her own like experiences seemed far away, unreal, and only half remembered. She recalled faintly an ecstasy of pain, the heavy odor of chloroform, a stupor which had deadened sensation, and an awakening to find a little new life to which she had given being, added to the great unnumbered multitude of souls that come and go.

She began to wish she had not come; her presence was not necessary. She might have invented a pretext for staying away; she might even invent a pretext now for going. But Edna did not go. With an inward agony, with a flaming, outspoken revolt against the ways of Nature, she witnessed the scene of torture.

She was still stunned and speechless with emotion when later she leaned over her friend to kiss her and softly say good-by. Adèle, pressing her cheek, whispered in an exhausted voice: "Think of the children, Edna. Oh think of the children! Remember them!"

XXXVIII

Edna still felt dazed when she got outside in the open air. The Doctor's coupé had returned for him and stood before the *porte cochère*. She did not wish to enter the coupé, and told Doctor Mandelet she would walk; she was not afraid, and would go alone. He directed his carriage to meet him at Mrs. Pontellier's, and he started to walk home with her.

Up—away up, over the narrow street between the tall houses, the stars were blazing. The air was mild and caressing, but cool with the breath of spring and the night. They walked slowly, the Doctor with a heavy, measured tread and his hands behind him; Edna, in an absent-minded way, as she had walked one night at Grand Isle, as if her thoughts had gone ahead of her and she was striving to overtake them.

"You shouldn't have been there, Mrs. Pontellier," he said. "That was no place for you. Adèle is full of whims at such times. There were a dozen women she might have had with her, unimpressionable women. I felt that it was cruel, cruel. You shouldn't have gone."

"Oh, well!" she answered, indifferently. "I don't know that it matters after all.

One has to think of the children some time or other; the sooner the better."

"When is Léonce coming back?"

"Quite soon. Some time in March?"

"And you are going abroad?"

"Perhaps—no, I am not going. I'm not going to be forced into doing things. I don't want to go abroad. I want to be let alone. Nobody has any right—except children, perhaps—and even then, it seems to me—or it did seem—" She felt that her speech was voicing the incoherency of her thoughts, and stopped abruptly.

"The trouble is," sighed the Doctor, grasping her meaning intuitively, "that youth is given up to illusions. It seems to be a provision of Nature; a decoy to secure mothers for the race. And Nature takes no account of moral consequences, or arbitrary conditions which we create, and which we feel obliged to maintain at any cost."

"Yes," she said. "The years that are gone seem like dreams—if one might go on sleeping and dreaming—but to wake up and find—oh! well! perhaps it is better to wake up after all, even to suffer, rather than to remain a dupe to illusions all one's life."

"It seems to me, my dear child," said the Doctor at parting, holding her hand, "you seem to me to be in trouble. I am not going to ask for your confidence. I will only say that if ever you feel moved to give it to me, perhaps I might help you. I know I would understand, and I tell you there are not many who would—not many, my dear."

"Some way I don't feel moved to speak of things that trouble me. Don't think I am ungrateful or that I don't appreciate your sympathy. There are periods of despondency and suffering which take possession of me. But I don't want anything but my own way. That is wanting a good deal, of course, when you have to trample upon the lives, the hearts, the prejudices of others—but no matter—still, I shouldn't want to trample upon the little lives. Oh! I don't know what I'm saying, Doctor. Good night. Don't blame me for anything."

"Yes, I will blame you if you don't come and see me soon. We will talk of things you never have dreamt of talking about before. It will do us both good. I don't want you to blame yourself, whatever comes. Good night, my child."

She let herself in at the gate, but instead of entering she sat upon the step of the porch. The night was quiet and soothing. All the tearing emotion of the last few hours seemed to fall away from her like a somber, uncomfortable garment, which she had but to loosen to be rid of. She went back to that hour before Adèle had sent for her; and her senses kindled afresh in thinking of Robert's words, the pressure of his arms, and the feeling of his lips upon her own. She could picture at that moment no greater bliss on earth than possession of the beloved one. His expression of love had already given him to her in part. When she thought that he was there at hand, waiting for her, she grew numb with the intoxication of expectancy. It was so late; he would be asleep perhaps. She would awaken him with a kiss. She hoped he would be asleep that she might arouse him with her caresses.

Still, she remembered Adèle's voice whispering, "Think of the children; think of them." She meant to think of them; that determination had driven into her soul like a death wound—but not to-night. To-morrow would be time to think of everything.

Robert was not waiting for her in the little parlor. He was nowhere at hand. The house was empty. But he had scrawled on a piece of paper that lay in the lamp-light:

"I love you. Good-by—because I love you."

Edna grew faint when she read the words. She went and sat on the sofa. Then she stretched herself out there, never uttering a sound. She did not sleep. She did not go to bed. The lamp sputtered and went out. She was still awake in the morning, when Celestine unlocked the kitchen door and came in to light the fire.

XXXIX

Victor, with hammer and nails and scraps of scantling,[1] was patching a corner of one of the galleries. Mariequita sat near by, dangling her legs, watching him work, and handing him nails from the tool-box. The sun was beating down upon them. The girl had covered her head with her apron folded into a square pad. They had been talking for an hour or more. She was never tired of hearing Victor describe the dinner at Mrs. Pontellier's. He exaggerated every detail, making it appear a veritable Lucullean[2] feast. The flowers were in tubs, he said. The champagne was quaffed from huge golden goblets. Venus[3] rising from the foam could have presented no more entrancing a spectacle than Mrs. Pontellier, blazing with beauty and diamonds at the head of the board, while the other women were all of them youthful houris,[4] possessed of incomparable charms.

She got it into her head that Victor was in love with Mrs. Pontellier, and he gave her evasive answers, framed so as to confirm her belief. She grew sullen and cried a little, threatening to go off and leave him to his fine ladies. There were a dozen men crazy about her at the *Chênière;* and since it was the fashion to be in love with married people, why, she could run away any time she liked to New Orleans with Célina's husband.

Célina's husband was a fool, a coward, and a pig, and to prove it to her, Victor intended to hammer his head into a jelly the next time he encountered him. This assurance was very consoling to Mariequita. She dried her eyes, and grew cheerful at the prospect.

They were still talking of the dinner and the allurements of city life when Mrs. Pontellier herself slipped around the corner of the house. The two youngsters stayed dumb with amazement before what they considered to be an apparition. But it was really she in flesh and blood, looking tired and a little travel-stained.

"I walked up from the wharf," she said, "and heard the hammering. I supposed it was you, mending the porch. It's a good thing. I was always tripping over those loose planks last summer. How dreary and deserted everything looks!"

It took Victor some little time to comprehend that she had come in Beaudelet's lugger, that she had come alone, and for no purpose but to rest.

"There's nothing fixed up yet, you see. I'll give you my room; it's the only place."

"Any corner will do," she assured him.

"And if you can stand Philomel's cooking," he went on, "though I might try to get her mother while you are here. Do you think she would come?" turning to Mariequita.

Mariequita thought that perhaps Philomel's mother might come for a few days, and money enough.

---

[1] Lumber.

[2] Like Lucius Licinius Lucullus (110?–57? B.C.), a wealthy Roman general and consul famous for his extravagant banquets.

[3] According to Roman myth, the goddess of love and beauty, who was created out of sea foam.

[4] According to Moslem belief, the beautiful virgins allotted to those who attain Paradise.

Beholding Mrs. Pontellier make her appearance, the girl had at once suspected a lovers' rendezvous. But Victor's astonishment was so genuine, and Mrs. Pontellier's indifference so apparent, that the disturbing notion did not lodge long in her brain. She contemplated with the greatest interest this woman who gave the most sumptuous dinners in America, and who had all the men in New Orleans at her feet.

"What time will you have dinner?" asked Edna. "I'm very hungry; but don't get anything extra."

"I'll have it ready in little or no time," he said, bustling and packing away his tools. "You may go to my room to brush up and rest yourself. Mariequita will show you."

"Thank you," said Edna. "But, do you know, I have a notion to go down to the beach and take a good wash and even a little swim, before dinner?"

"The water is too cold!" they both exclaimed. "Don't think of it."

"Well, I might go down and try—dip my toes in. Why, it seems to me the sun is hot enough to have warmed the very depths of the ocean. Could you get me a couple of towels? I'd better go right away, so as to be back in time. It would be a little too chilly if I waited till this afternoon."

Mariequita ran over to Victor's room, and returned with some towels, which she gave to Edna.

"I hope you have fish for dinner," said Edna, as she started to walk away; "but don't do anything extra if you haven't."

"Run and find Philomel's mother," Victor instructed the girl. "I'll go the kitchen and see what I can do. By Gimminy! Women have no consideration! She might have sent me word."

Edna walked on down to the beach rather mechanically, not noticing anything special except that the sun was hot. She was not dwelling upon any particular train of thought. She had done all the thinking which was necessary after Robert went away, when she lay awake upon the sofa till morning.

She had said over and over to herself: "To-day it is Arobin; to-morrow it will be some one else. It makes no difference to me, it doesn't matter about Léonce Pontellier—but Raoul and Etienne!" She understood now clearly what she had meant long ago when she said to Adèle Ratignolle that she would give up the unessential, but she would never sacrifice herself for her children.

Despondency had come upon her there in the wakeful night, and had never lifted. There was no one thing in the world that she desired. There was no human being whom she wanted near her except Robert; and she even realized that the day would come when he, too, and the thought of him would melt out of her existence, leaving her alone. The children appeared before her like antagonists who had overcome her; who had overpowered and sought to drag her into the soul's slavery for the rest of her days. But she knew a way to elude them. She was not thinking of these things when she walked down to the beach.

The water of the Gulf stretched out before her, gleaming with the million lights of the sun. The voice of the sea is seductive, never ceasing, whispering, clamoring, murmuring, inviting the soul to wander in abysses of solitude. All along the white beach, up and down, there was no living thing in sight. A bird with a broken wing was beating the air above, reeling, fluttering, circling disabled down, down to the water.

Edna had found her old bathing suit still hanging, faded, upon its accustomed peg.

She put it on, leaving her clothing in the bath-house. But when she was there beside the sea, absolutely alone, she cast the unpleasant, pricking garments from her, and for the first time in her life she stood naked in the open air, at the mercy of the sun, the breeze that beat upon her, and the waves that invited her.

How strange and awful it seemed to stand naked under the sky! how delicious! She felt like some new-born creature, opening its eyes in a familiar world that it had never known.

The foamy wavelets curled up to her white feet, and coiled like serpents about her ankles. She walked out. The water was chill, but she walked on. The water was deep, but she lifted her white body and reached out with a long, sweeping stroke. The touch of the sea is sensuous, enfolding the body in its soft, close embrace.

She went on and on. She remembered the night she swam far out, and recalled the terror that seized her at the fear of being unable to regain the shore. She did not look back now, but went on and on, thinking of the blue-grass meadow that she had traversed when a little child, believing that it had no beginning and no end.

Her arms and legs were growing tired.

She thought of Léonce and the children. They were a part of her life. But they need not have thought that they could possess her, body and soul. How Mademoiselle Reisz would have laughed, perhaps sneered, if she knew! "And you call yourself an artist! What pretensions, Madame! The artist must possess the courageous soul that dares and defies."

Exhaustion was pressing upon and overpowering her.

"Good-by—because I love you." He did not know; he did not understand. He would never understand. Perhaps Doctor Mandelet would have understood if she had seen him—but it was too late; the shore was far behind her, and her strength was gone.

She looked into the distance, and the old terror flamed up for an instant, then sank again. Edna heard her father's voice and her sister Margaret's. She heard the barking of an old dog that was chained to the sycamore tree. The spurs of the cavalry officer clanged as he walked across the porch. There was the hum of bees, and the musky odor of pinks filled the air.

1897–1898, 1899

Charles W. Chesnutt
(1858–1932)

Although he was born in 1858 in Cleveland, Ohio, and spent much of his childhood and adult life in that area, Charles Waddell Chesnutt set most of his fiction in the South. When he was eight his parents moved the family back to Fayetteville, North Carolina (which they had fled during the Civil War), and Chesnutt remained there until he was twenty-five. During these formative years he married Susan Perry from Fayetteville (in 1878) and developed an interest in the regional folkways that later became an integral part of his fiction.

Chesnutt was a light-skinned African American who could probably have "passed" for white had he desired to do so. However, he chose to live and work as a black, a choice that limited his career opportunities but did not stop him from achieving success. Largely self-educated, he became a teacher and by age twenty-two was the principal of the State Colored Normal School in Fayetteville. Hoping for greater opportunity, he went to New York City in 1883 and became a legal stenographer. Six months later he and his wife moved to Cleveland, where he passed the Ohio bar exam with high marks and established a successful legal-stenography firm. Chesnutt remained a court reporter until his death in 1932.

Chesnutt's first nationally recognized publication, "The Goophered Grapevine," appeared in the August 1887 issue of the *Atlantic Monthly*. This piece combined dialect with Chesnutt's awareness of southern folk customs. In 1899 his first collection of short stories, *The Conjure Woman*, was published. The narrator of these tales, an ex-slave named Uncle Julius McAdoo, was influenced in part by Joel Chandler Harris's figure Uncle Remus, although the powerful irony of such stories as "Sis' Becky's Pickaninny" comes directly from Chesnutt's personal vision. Later in 1899 Chesnutt published a biography of Frederick Douglass, *Life of Frederick Douglass*, and a second volume of short stories, *The Wife of His Youth and Other Stories of the Color Line*. Following these works came three novels more explicit in their criticism of American society: *The House Behind the Cedars* (1900), *The Marrow of Tradition* (1901), and *The Colonel's Dream* (1905).

Throughout his work Chesnutt was concerned with the racial situation in the post-Civil War South. Many of his stories deal with light-skinned blacks passing for white, with racial intermarriage, and with racial tensions arising from economic and social conditions. His belief that African Americans should be assimilated into the American mainstream was tempered by his perception of racial injustice. As a conservative Chesnutt believed that assimilation can best occur when African Americans are educated for careers that match their abilities. As a realist he deplored the manner in which the evils of prejudice choked off such possibilities.

Chesnutt wrote six novels after 1905, none of them published. But he remained active in civic and professional affairs in Cleveland. In 1928 the National Association for the Advancement of Colored People awarded him the Spingarn Medal for his "pioneer work as a literary artist depicting the life and struggles of Americans of Negro descent, and for his long and useful career as scholar, worker, and freeman of one of America's greatest cities."

Suggested Readings: *The Marrow of Tradition*, 1901. *The Colonel's Dream*, 1905. *The Short Fiction of Charles W. Chesnutt*, ed. S. L. Render, 1980. H. M. Chesnutt, *Charles Waddell Chesnutt, Pioneer of the Color Line*, 1952. J. N. Heermance, *Charles W. Chesnutt: America's First Great Black Novelist*, 1974. C. W. Ellison and E. W. Metcalf, Jr., *Charles W. Chesnutt: A Reference Guide*, 1977. F. R. Keller, *An American Crusade: The Life of Charles Waddell Chesnutt*, 1978. W. L. Andrews, *The Literary Career of Charles W. Chesnutt*, 1980. S. L. Render, *Charles W. Chesnutt*, 1980.

Texts Used: "The Passing of Grandison": *The Wife of His Youth and Other Stories of the Color Line*, 1899. "Sis' Becky's Pickaninny": *The Conjure Woman*, 1899.

THE PASSING OF GRANDISON*

I

When it is said that it was done to please a woman, there ought perhaps to be enough said to explain anything; for what a man will not do to please a woman is yet to be discovered. Nevertheless, it might be well to state a few preliminary

* First published in the *Atlantic Monthly* in July 1898.

facts to make it clear why young Dick Owens tried to run one of his father's negro men off to Canada.

In the early fifties,[1] when the growth of anti-slavery sentiment and the constant drain of fugitive slaves into the North had so alarmed the slaveholders of the border States as to lead to the passage of the Fugitive Slave Law,[2] a young white man from Ohio, moved by compassion for the sufferings of a certain bondman who happened to have a "hard master," essayed to help the slave to freedom. The attempt was discovered and frustrated; the abductor was tried and convicted for slave-stealing, and sentenced to a term of imprisonment in the penitentiary. His death, after the expiration of only a small part of the sentence, from cholera contracted while nursing stricken fellow prisoners, lent to the case a melancholy interest that made it famous in anti-slavery annals.

Dick Owens had attended the trial. He was a youth of about twenty-two, intelligent, handsome, and amiable, but extremely indolent, in a graceful and gentlemanly way; or, as old Judge Fenderson put it more than once, he was lazy as the Devil,—a mere figure of speech, of course, and not one that did justice to the Enemy of Mankind. When asked why he never did anything serious, Dick would good-naturedly reply, with a well-modulated drawl, that he didn't have to. His father was rich; there was but one other child, an unmarried daughter, who because of poor health would probably never marry, and Dick was therefore heir presumptive to a large estate. Wealth or social position he did not need to seek, for he was born to both. Charity Lomax had shamed him into studying law, but notwithstanding an hour or so a day spent at old Judge Fenderson's office, he did not make remarkable headway in his legal studies.

"What Dick needs," said the judge, who was fond of tropes,[3] as became a scholar, and of horses, as was befitting a Kentuckian, "is the whip of necessity, or the spur of ambition. If he had either, he would soon need the snaffle to hold him back."

But all Dick required, in fact, to prompt him to the most remarkable thing he accomplished before he was twenty-five, was a mere suggestion from Charity Lomax. The story was never really known to but two persons until after the war, when it came out because it was a good story and there was no particular reason for its concealment.

Young Owens had attended the trial of this slave-stealer, or martyr,—either or both,—and, when it was over, had gone to call on Charity Lomax, and, while they sat on the veranda after sundown, had told her all about the trial. He was a good talker, as his career in later years disclosed, and described the proceedings very graphically.

"I confess," he admitted, "that while my principles were against the prisoner, my sympathies were on his side. It appeared that he was of good family, and that he had an old father and mother, respectable people, dependent upon him for support and comfort in their declining years. He had been led into the matter by pity for a negro whose master ought to have been run out of the county long ago for abusing his slaves. If it had been merely a question of old Sam Briggs's negro, nobody would have cared anything about it. But father and the rest of them stood on the principle of the thing, and told the judge so, and the fellow was sentenced to three years in the penitentiary."

---

[1] The 1850s.

[2] Enacted in 1850, it allowed slaves who had escaped to free states to be recaptured and returned to their owners and made aiding an escaping slave illegal.

[3] Figures of speech; a rhetorical device, as in the metaphor "whip of necessity."

Miss Lomax had listened with lively interest.

"I've always hated old Sam Briggs," she said emphatically, "ever since the time he broke a negro's leg with a piece of cordwood.[4] When I hear of a cruel deed it makes the Quaker blood that came from my grandmother assert itself. Personally I wish that all Sam Briggs's negroes would run away. As for the young man, I regard him as a hero. He dared something for humanity. I could love a man who would take such chances for the sake of others."

"Could you love me, Charity, if I did something heroic?"

"You never will, Dick. You're too lazy for any use. You'll never do anything harder than playing cards or fox-hunting."

"Oh, come now, sweetheart! I've been courting you for a year, and it's the hardest work imaginable. Are you never going to love me?" he pleaded.

His hand sought hers, but she drew it back beyond his reach.

"I'll never love you, Dick Owens, until you have done something. When that time comes, I'll think about it."

"But it takes so long to do anything worth mentioning, and I don't want to wait. One must read two years to become a lawyer, and work five more to make a reputation. We shall both be gray by then."

"Oh, I don't know," she rejoined. "It doesn't require a lifetime for a man to prove that he is a man. This one did something, or at least tried to."

"Well, I'm willing to attempt as much as any other man. What do you want me to do, sweetheart? Give me a test."

"Oh, dear me!" said Charity, "I don't care what you *do,* so you do *something*. Really, come to think of it, why should I care whether you do anything or not?"

"I'm sure I don't know why you should, Charity," rejoined Dick humbly, "for I'm aware that I'm not worthy of it."

"Except that I do hate," she added, relenting slightly, "to see a really clever man so utterly lazy and good for nothing."

"Thank you, my dear; a word of praise from you has sharpened my wits already. I have an idea! Will you love me if *I* run a negro off to Canada?"

"What nonsense!" said Charity scornfully. "You must be losing your wits. Steal another man's slave, indeed, while your father owns a hundred!"

"Oh, there'll be no trouble about that," responded Dick lightly; "I'll run off one of the old man's; we've got too many anyway. It may not be quite as difficult as the other man found it, but it will be just as unlawful, and will demonstrate what I am capable of."

"Seeing's believing," replied Charity. "Of course, what you are talking about now is merely absurd. I'm going away for three weeks, to visit my aunt in Tennessee. If you're able to tell me, when I return, that you've done something to prove your quality, I'll—well, you may come and tell me about it."

II

Young Owens got up about nine o'clock next morning, and while making his toilet put some questions to his personal attendant, a rather bright looking young mulatto[5] of about his own age.

---

[4] Wood stacked in a cord, a pile of a specific size.

[5] A person with one black and one white parent.

"Tom," said Dick.

"Yas, Mars Dick," responded the servant.

"I'm going on a trip North. Would you like to go with me?"

Now, if there was anything that Tom would have liked to make, it was a trip North. It was something he had long contemplated in the abstract, but had never been able to muster up sufficient courage to attempt in the concrete. He was prudent enough, however, to dissemble his feelings.

"I wouldn't min' it, Mars Dick, ez long ez you'd take keer er me an' fetch me home all right."

Tom's eyes belied his words, however, and his young master felt well assured that Tom needed only a good opportunity to make him run away. Having a comfortable home, and a dismal prospect in case of failure, Tom was not likely to take any desperate chances; but young Owens was satisfied that in a free State but little persuasion would be required to lead Tom astray. With a very logical and characteristic desire to gain his end with the least necessary expenditure of effort, he decided to take Tom with him, if his father did not object.

Colonel Owens had left the house when Dick went to breakfast, so Dick did not see his father till luncheon.

"Father," he remarked casually to the colonel, over the fried chicken, "I'm feeling a trifle run down. I imagine my health would be improved somewhat by a little travel and change of scene."

"Why don't you take a trip North?" suggested his father. The colonel added to paternal affection a considerable respect for his son as the heir of a large estate. He himself had been "raised" in comparative poverty, and had laid the foundations of his fortune by hard work; and while he despised the ladder by which he had climbed, he could not entirely forget it, and unconsciously manifested, in his intercourse with his son, some of the poor man's deference toward the wealthy and well-born.

"I think I'll adopt your suggestion, sir," replied the son, "and run up to New York; and after I've been there awhile I may go on to Boston for a week or so. I've never been there, you know."

"There are some matters you can talk over with my factor[6] in New York," rejoined the colonel, "and while you are up there among the Yankees, I hope you'll keep your eyes and ears open to find out what the rascally abolitionists are saying and doing. They're becoming altogether too active for our comfort, and entirely too many ungrateful niggers are running away. I hope the conviction of that fellow yesterday may discourage the rest of the breed. I'd just like to catch any one trying to run off one of my darkeys. He'd get short shrift; I don't think any Court would have a chance to try him."

"They are a pestiferous lot," assented Dick, "and dangerous to our institutions. But say, father, if I go North I shall want to take Tom with me."

Now, the colonel, while a very indulgent father, had pronounced views on the subject of negroes, having studied them, as he often said, for a great many years, and, as he asserted oftener still, understanding them perfectly. It is scarcely worth while to say, either, that he valued more highly than if he had inherited them the slaves he had toiled and schemed for.

"I don't think it safe to take Tom up North," he declared, with promptness and decision. "He's a good enough boy, but too smart to trust among those low-down

---

[6] Business agent.

abolitionists. I strongly suspect him of having learned to read, though I can't imagine how. I saw him with a newspaper the other day, and while he pretended to be looking at a woodcut, I'm almost sure he was reading the paper. I think it by no means safe to take him."

Dick did not insist, because he knew it was useless. The colonel would have obliged his son in any other matter, but his negroes were the outward and visible sign of his wealth and station, and therefore sacred to him.

"Whom do you think it safe to take?" asked Dick. "I suppose I'll have to have a body-servant."

"What's the matter with Grandison?" suggested the colonel. "He's handy enough, and I reckon we can trust him. He's too fond of good eating, to risk losing his regular meals; besides, he's sweet on your mother's maid, Betty, and I've promised to let 'em get married before long. I'll have Grandison up, and we'll talk to him. Here, you boy Jack," called the colonel to a yellow youth in the next room who was catching flies and pulling their wings off to pass the time, "go down to the barn and tell Grandison to come here."

"Grandison," said the colonel, when the negro stood before him, hat in hand.

"Yas, marster."

"Haven't I always treated you right?"

"Yas, marster."

"Haven't you always got all you wanted to eat?"

"Yas, marster."

"And as much whiskey and tobacco as was good for you, Grandison?"

"Y-a-s, marster."

"I should just like to know, Grandison, whether you don't think yourself a great deal better off than those poor free negroes down by the plank road, with no kind master to look after them and no mistress to give them medicine when they're sick and—and"—

"Well, I sh'd jes' reckon I is better off, suh, dan dem low-down free niggers, suh! Ef anybody ax 'em who dey b'long ter, dey has ter say nobody, er e'se lie erbout it. Anybody ax me who I b'longs ter, I ain' got no 'casion ter be shame' ter tell 'em, no, suh, 'deed I ain', suh!"

The colonel was beaming. This was true gratitude, and his feudal heart thrilled at such appreciative homage. What cold-blooded, heartless monsters they were who would break up this blissful relationship of kindly protection on the one hand, of wise subordination and loyal dependence on the other! The colonel always became indignant at the mere thought of such wickedness.

"Grandison," the colonel continued, "your young master Dick is going North for a few weeks, and I am thinking of letting him take you along. I shall send you on this trip, Grandison, in order that you may take care of your young master. He will need some one to wait on him, and no one can ever do it so well as one of the boys brought up with him on the old plantation. I am going to trust him in your hands, and I'm sure you'll do your duty faithfully, and bring him back home safe and sound—to old Kentucky."

Grandison grinned. "Oh yas, marster, I'll take keer er young Mars Dick."

"I want to warn you, though, Grandison," continued the colonel impressively, "against these cussed abolitionists, who try to entice servants from their comfortable homes and their indulgent masters, from the blue skies, the green fields, and the warm sunlight of their southern home, and send them away off yonder to Canada, a dreary country, where the woods are full of wildcats and wolves and bears, where the snow lies up to the eaves of the houses for six months of the year, and the cold is so severe that it freezes your breath and curdles your blood; and where, when runaway niggers get sick and can't work, they are turned out to starve and die, unloved and uncared for. I reckon, Grandison, that you have too much sense to permit yourself to be led astray by any such foolish and wicked people."

"'Deed, suh, I would n' low none er dem cussed, low-down abolitioners ter come nigh me, suh. I'd—I'd—would I be 'lowed ter hit 'em, suh?"

"Certainly, Grandison," replied the colonel, chuckling, "hit 'em as hard as you can. I reckon they'd rather like it. Begad, I believe they would! It would serve 'em right to be hit by a nigger!"

"Er ef I didn't hit 'em, suh," continued Grandison reflectively, "I'd tell Mars Dick, en *he'd* fix 'em. He'd smash de face off'n 'em, suh, I jes' knows he would."

"Oh yes, Grandison, your young master will protect you. You need fear no harm while he is near."

"Dey won't try ter steal me, will dey, marster?" asked the negro, with sudden alarm.

"I don't know, Grandison," replied the colonel, lighting a fresh cigar. "They're a desperate set of lunatics, and there's no telling what they may resort to. But if you stick close to your young master, and remember always that he is your best friend, and understands your real needs, and has your true interests at heart, and if you will be careful to avoid strangers who try to talk to you, you'll stand a fair chance of getting back to your home and your friends. And if you please your master Dick, he'll buy you a present, and a string of beads for Betty to wear when you and she get married in the fall."

"Thanky, marster, thanky, suh," replied Grandison, oozing gratitude at every pore; "you is a good marster, to be sho', suh; yas, 'deed you is. You kin jes' bet me and Mars Dick gwine git 'long jes' lack I wuz own boy ter Mars Dick. En it won't be my fault ef he don' want me fer his boy all de time, w'en we come back home ag'in."

"All right, Grandison, you may go now. You needn't work any more to-day, and here's a piece of tobacco for you off my own plug."

"Thanky, marster, thanky, marster! You is de bes' marster any nigger ever had in dis worl'." And Grandison bowed and scraped and disappeared round the corner, his jaws closing around a large section of the colonel's best tobacco.

"You may take Grandison," said the colonel to his son. "I allow he's abolitionist-proof."

III

Richard Owens, Esq., and servant, from Kentucky, registered at the fashionable New York hostelry for Southerners in those days, a hotel where an atmosphere congenial to Southern institutions was sedulously maintained. But there were negro waiters in the dining-room, and mulatto bell-boys, and Dick had no doubt that Grandison, with the native gregariousness and garrulousness of his race, would foregather and palaver with them sooner or later, and Dick hoped that they would speedily inoculate him with the virus of freedom. For it was not Dick's intention to say anything to his servant about his plan to free him, for obvious reasons. To mention one of them, if Grandison should go away, and by legal process be recaptured, his young master's part in the matter would doubtless become known, which would be embarrassing to Dick, to say the least. If, on the other hand, he should merely give Grandison sufficient latitude, he had no doubt he would eventually lose him. For while not exactly skeptical about Grandison's perfervid loyalty, Dick had been a somewhat keen observer of human nature, in his own indolent way, and based his expectations upon the force of the example and argument that his servant could scarcely fail to encounter. Grandison should have a fair chance to become free by his own initiative; if it should become necessary to adopt other measures to get rid of him, it would be time enough to act when the necessity arose; and Dick Owens was not the youth to take needless trouble.

The young master renewed some acquaintances and made others, and spent a week or two very pleasantly in the best society of the metropolis, easily accessible to a wealthy, well-bred young Southerner, with proper introductions. Young women smiled on him, and young men of convivial habits pressed their hospitalities; but the memory of Charity's sweet, strong face and clear blue eyes made him proof against the blandishments of the one sex and the persuasions of the other. Meanwhile he kept Grandison supplied with pocket-money, and left him mainly to his own devices. Every night when Dick came in he hoped he might have to wait upon himself, and every morning he looked forward with pleasure to the prospect of making his toilet[7] unaided. His hopes, however, were doomed to disappointment, for every night when he came in Grandison was on hand with a bootjack, and a nightcap mixed for his young master as the colonel had taught him to mix it, and every morning Grandison appeared with his master's boots blacked and his clothes brushed, and laid his linen out for the day.

"Grandison," said Dick one morning, after finishing his toilet, "this is a chance of your life to go around among your own people and see how they live. Have you met any of them?"

"Yas, suh, I's seen some of 'em. But I don' keer nuffin fer 'em, suh. Dey're diffe'nt f'm de niggers down ou' way. Dey 'lows dey're free, but dey ain' got sense 'nuff ter know dey ain' half as well off as dey would be down Souf, whar dey'd be 'preciated."

When two weeks had passed without any apparent effect of evil example upon Grandison, Dick resolved to go on to Boston, where he thought the atmosphere might prove more favorable to his ends. After he had been at the Revere House for a day or two without losing Grandison, he decided upon slightly different tactics.

Having ascertained from a city directory the addresses of several well-known abolitionists, he wrote them each a letter something like this:—

DEAR FRIEND AND BROTHER:—

A wicked slaveholder from Kentucky, stopping at the Revere House, has dared to insult the liberty-loving people of Boston by bringing his slave into their midst. Shall this be tolerated? Or shall steps be taken in the name of liberty to rescue a fellow-man from bondage? For obvious reasons I can only sign myself,

A FRIEND OF HUMANITY.

[7] Dressing himself.

That his letter might have an opportunity to prove effective, Dick made it a point to send Grandison away from the hotel on various errands. On one of these occasions Dick watched him for quite a distance down the street. Grandison had scarcely left the hotel when a long-haired, sharp-featured man came out behind him, followed him, soon overtook him, and kept along beside him until they turned the next corner. Dick's hopes were roused by this spectacle, but sank correspondingly when Grandison returned to the hotel. As Grandison said nothing about the encounter, Dick hoped there might be some self-consciousness behind this unexpected reticence, the results of which might develop later on.

But Grandison was on hand again when his master came back to the hotel at night, and was in attendance again in the morning, with hot water, to assist at his master's toilet. Dick sent him on further errands from day to day, and upon one occasion came squarely up to him—inadvertently of course—while Grandison was engaged in conversation with a young white man in clerical garb. When Grandison saw Dick approaching, he edged away from the preacher and hastened toward his master, with a very evident expression of relief upon his countenance.

"Mars Dick," he said, "dese yer abolitioners is jes' pesterin' de life out er me tryin' ter git me ter run away. I don' pay no 'tention ter 'em, but dey riles me so sometimes dat I'm feared I'll hit some of 'em some er dese days, an' dat mought git me inter trouble. I ain' said nuffin' ter you 'bout it, Mars Dick, fer I did n' wanter 'sturb yo' min'; but I don' like it, suh; no, suh, I don'! Is we gwine back home 'fo' long, Mars Dick?"

"We'll be going back soon enough," replied Dick somewhat shortly, while he inwardly cursed the stupidity of a slave who could be free and would not, and registered a secret vow that if he were unable to get rid of Grandison without assassinating him, and were therefore compelled to take him back to Kentucky, he would see that Grandison got a taste of an article of slavery that would make him regret his wasted opportunities. Meanwhile he determined to tempt his servant yet more strongly.

"Grandison," he said next morning, "I'm going away for a day or two, but I shall leave you here. I shall lock up a hundred dollars in this drawer and give you the key. If you need any of it, use it and enjoy yourself,—spend it all if you like,—for this is probably the last chance you'll have for some time to be in a free State, and you'd better enjoy your liberty while you may."

When he came back a couple of days later and found the faithful Grandison at his post, and the hundred dollars intact, Dick felt seriously annoyed. His vexation was increased by the fact that he could not express his feelings adequately. He did not even scold Grandison; how could he, indeed, find fault with one who so sensibly recognized his true place in the economy of civilization, and kept it with such touching fidelity?

"I can't say a thing to him," groaned Dick. "He deserves a leather medal, made out of his own hide tanned. I reckon I'll write to father and let him know what a model servant he has given me."

He wrote his father a letter which made the colonel swell with pride and pleasure. "I really think," the colonel observed to one of his friends, "that Dick ought to have the nigger interviewed by the Boston papers, so that they may see how contented and happy our darkeys really are."

Dick also wrote a long letter to Charity Lomax, in which he said, among other things, that if she knew how hard he was working, and under what difficulties, to accomplish something serious for her sake, she would no longer keep him in suspense, but overwhelm him with love and admiration.

Having thus exhausted without result the more obvious methods of getting rid of Grandison, and diplomacy having also proved a failure, Dick was forced to consider more radical measures. Of course he might run away himself, and abandon Grandison, but this would be merely to leave him in the United States, where he was still a slave, and where, with his notions of loyalty, he would speedily be reclaimed. It was necessary, in order to accomplish the purpose of his trip to the North, to leave Grandison permanently in Canada, where he would be legally free.

"I might extend my trip to Canada," he reflected, "but that would be too palpable. I have it! I'll visit Niagara Falls on the way home, and lose him on the Canada side. When he once realizes that he is actually free, I'll warrant that he'll stay."

So the next day saw them westward bound, and in due course of time, by the somewhat slow conveyances of the period, they found themselves at Niagara. Dick walked and drove about the Falls for several days, taking Grandison along with him on most occasions. One morning they stood on the Canadian side, watching the wild whirl of the waters below them.

"Grandison," said Dick, raising his voice above the roar of the cataract,[8] "do you know where you are now?"

"I's wid you, Mars Dick; dat's all I keers."

"You're now in Canada, Grandison, where your people go when they run away from their masters. If you wished Grandison, you might walk away from me this very minute, and I could not lay my hand upon you to take you back."

Grandison looked around uneasily.

"Let's go back ober de ribber, Mars Dick. I's feared I'll lose you ovuh heah, an' den I won' hab no marster, an' won't nebber be able to git back home no mo'."

Discouraged, but not yet hopeless, Dick said, a few minutes later,—

"Grandison, I'm going up the road a bit, to the inn over yonder. You stay here until I return. I'll not be gone a great while."

Grandison's eyes opened wide and he looked somewhat fearful.

"Is dey any er dem dadblasted abolitioners roun' heah, Mars Dick?"

"I don't imagine that there are," replied his master, hoping there might be. "But I'm not afraid of *your* running away, Grandison. I only wish I were," he added to himself.

Dick walked leisurely down the road to where the whitewashed inn, built of stone, with true British solidity, loomed up through the trees by the roadside. Arrived there he ordered a glass of ale and a sandwich, and took a seat at a table by a window, from which he could see Grandison in the distance. For a while he hoped that the seed he had sown might have fallen on fertile ground, and that Grandison, relieved from the restraining power of a master's eye, and finding himself in a free country, might get up and walk away; but the hope was vain, for Grandison remained faithfully at his post, awaiting his master's return. He had seated himself on a broad flat stone, and turning his eyes away from the grand and

---

[8] Large waterfall.

Symbolic

awe-inspiring spectacle that lay close at hand, was looking anxiously toward the inn where his master sat cursing his ill-timed fidelity.

By and by a girl came into the room to serve his order, and Dick very naturally glanced at her; and as she was young and pretty and remained in attendance, it was some minutes before he looked for Grandison. When he did so his faithful servant had disappeared.

To pay his reckoning and go away without the change was a matter quickly accomplished. Retracing his footsteps toward the Falls, he saw, to his great disgust, as he approached the spot where he had left Grandison, the familiar form of his servant stretched out on the ground, his face to the sun, his mouth open, sleeping the time away, oblivious alike to the grandeur of the scenery, the thunderous roar of the cataract, or the insidious voice of sentiment.

"Grandison," soliloquized his master, as he stood gazing down at his ebony encumbrance, "I do not deserve to be an American citizen; I ought not to have the advantages I possess over you; and I certainly am not worthy of Charity Lomax, if I am not smart enough to get rid of you. I have an idea! You shall yet be free, and I will be the instrument of your deliverance. Sleep on, faithful and affectionate servitor, and dream of the blue grass and the bright skies of old Kentucky, for it is only in your dreams that you will ever see them again!"

Dick retraced his footsteps towards the inn. The young woman chanced to look out of the window and saw the handsome young gentleman she had waited on a few minutes before, standing in the road a short distance away, apparently engaged in earnest conversation with a colored man employed as a hostler[9] for the inn. She thought she saw something pass from the white man to the other, but at that moment her duties called her away from the window, and when she looked out again the young gentleman had disappeared, and the hostler, with two other young men of the neighborhood, one white and one colored, were walking rapidly towards the Falls.

IV

Dick made the journey homeward alone, and as rapidly as the conveyances of the day would permit. As he drew near home his conduct in going back without Grandison took on a more serious aspect than it had borne at any previous time, and although he had prepared the colonel by a letter sent several days ahead, there was still the prospect of a bad quarter of an hour with him; not, indeed, that his father would upbraid him, but he was likely to make searching inquiries. And notwithstanding the vein of quiet recklessness that had carried Dick through his preposterous scheme, he was a very poor liar, having rarely had occasion or inclination to tell anything but the truth. Any reluctance to meet his father was more than offset, however, by a stronger force drawing him homeward, for Charity Lomax must long since have returned from her visit to her aunt in Tennessee.

Dick got off easier than he had expected. He told a straight story, and a truthful one, so far as it went.

The colonel raged at first, but rage soon subsided into anger, and anger moderated into a sort of garrulous sense of injury. The colonel thought he had been hardly used; he had trusted this negro, and he had

---

[9] Innkeeper.

broken faith. Yet, after all, he did not blame Grandison so much as he did the abolitionists, who were undoubtedly at the bottom of it.

As for Charity Lomax, Dick told her, privately of course, that he had run his father's man, Grandison, off to Canada, and left him there.

"Oh, Dick," she had said with shuddering alarm, "what have you done? If they knew it they'd send you to the penitentiary, like they did that Yankee."

"But they don't know it," he had replied seriously; adding, with an injured tone, "you don't seem to appreciate my heroism like you did that of the Yankee; perhaps it's because I wasn't caught and sent to the penitentiary. I thought you wanted me to do it."

"Why, Dick Owens!" she exclaimed. "You know I never dreamed of any such outrageous proceeding.

"But I presume I'll have to marry you," she concluded, after some insistence on Dick's part, "if only to take care of you. You are too reckless for anything; and a man who goes chasing all over the North, being entertained by New York and Boston society and having negroes to throw away, needs some one to look after him."

"It's a most remarkable thing," replied Dick fervently, "that your views correspond exactly with my profoundest convictions. It proves beyond question that we were made for one another."

They were married three weeks later. As each of them had just returned from a journey, they spent their honeymoon at home.

A week after the wedding they were seated one afternoon, on the piazza of the colonel's house, where Dick had taken his bride, when a negro from the yard ran down the land and threw open the big gate for the colonel's buggy to enter. The colonel was not alone. Beside him, ragged and travel-stained, bowed with weariness, and upon his face a haggard look that told of hardship and privation, sat the lost Grandison.

The colonel alighted at the steps.

"Take the lines, Tom," he said to the man who had opened the gate, "and drive round to the barn. Help Grandison down,—poor devil, he's so stiff he can hardly move!—and get a tub of water and wash him and rub him down, and feed him, and give him a big drink of whiskey, and then let him come round and see his young master and his new mistress."

The colonel's face wore an expression compounded of joy and indignation,— joy at the restoration of a valuable piece of property; indignation for reasons he proceeded to state.

"It's astounding, the depths of depravity the human heart is capable of! I was coming along the road three miles away, when I heard some one call me from the roadside. I pulled up the mare, and who should come out of the woods but Grandison. The poor nigger could hardly crawl along, with the help of a broken limb. I was never more astonished in my life. You could have knocked me down with a feather. He seemed pretty far gone,—he could hardly talk above a whisper,—and I had to give him a mouthful of whiskey to brace him up so he could tell his story. It's just as I thought from the beginning, Dick; Grandison had no notion of running away; he knew when he was well off, and where his friends were. All the persuasions of abolition liars and runaway niggers did not move him. But the desperation of those fanatics knew no bounds; their guilty consciences gave them no rest. They got the notion somehow that Grandison belongs to a nigger-catcher, and had been brought North as a spy to help capture ungrateful runaway servants. They actually kidnaped him—just think of it!—and gagged him and bound him and threw him rudely into a wagon, and carried him into the gloomy depths of a Canadian forest, and locked him in a lonely hut, and fed him on bread and water for three weeks. One of the scoundrels wanted to kill him, and persuaded the others that it ought to be done; but they got to quarreling about how they should do it, and before they had their minds made up Grandison escaped, and, keeping his back steadily to the North Star, made his way, after suffering incredible hardships, back to the old plantation, back to his master, his friends, and his home. Why, it's as good as one of Scott's novels! Mr. Simms[10] or some other one of our Southern authors ought to write it up."

"Don't you think, sir," suggested Dick, who had calmly smoked his cigar throughout the colonel's animated recital, "that that kidnaping yarn sounds a little improbable? Isn't there some more likely explanation?"

"Nonsense, Dick; it's the gospel truth! Those infernal abolitionists are capable of anything—everything! Just think of their locking the poor, faithful nigger up, beating him, kicking him, depriving him of his liberty, keeping him on bread and water for three long, lonesome weeks, and he all the time pining for the old plantation!"

There were almost tears in the colonel's eyes at the picture of Grandison's sufferings that he conjured up. Dick still professed to be slightly skeptical, and met Charity's severely questioning eye with bland unconsciousness.

The colonel killed the fatted calf for Grandison, and for two or three weeks the returned wanderer's life was a slave's dream of pleasure. His fame spread throughout the county, and the colonel gave him a permanent place among the house servants, where he could always have him conveniently at hand to relate his adventures to admiring visitors.

About three weeks after Grandison's return the colonel's faith in sable humanity was rudely shaken, and its foundations almost broken up. He came near losing his belief in the fidelity of the negro to his master,—the servile virtue most highly prized and most sedulously cultivated by the colonel and his kind. One Monday morning Grandison was missing. And not only Grandison, but his wife, Betty the maid; his mother, aunt Eunice; his father, uncle Ike; his brothers, Tom and John, and his little sister Elsie, were likewise absent from the plantation; and a hurried search and inquiry in the neighborhood resulted in no information as to their whereabouts. So much valuable property could not be lost without an effort to recover it, and the wholesale nature of the transaction carried consternation to the hearts of those whose ledgers were chiefly bound in black. Extremely energetic measures were taken by the colonel and his friends. The fugitives were traced, and followed from point to point, on their northward run through Ohio. Several times the hunters were close upon their heels, but the magnitude of the escaping party begot unusual vigilance on the part of those who sympathized with the fugitives, and strangely enough, the underground railroad[11] seemed to have had its tracks

---

[10] The Scottish poet and novelist Sir Walter Scott (1771–1832), author of such famous historical romances as *Lady of the Lake* (1810) and *Ivanhoe* (1819); William Gilmore Simms (1806–1870), of Charleston, South Carolina, author of historical romances set in the American South, among them *Guy Rivers* (1834) and *The Partisan* (1835).

[11] A pre-Civil War system of helping fugitive slaves move North to freedom.

cleared and signals set for this particular train. Once, twice, the colonel thought he had them, but they slipped through his fingers.

One last glimpse he caught of his vanishing property, as he stood, accompanied by a United States marshal, on a wharf at a port on the south shore of Lake Erie. On the stern of a small steamboat which was receding rapidly from the wharf, with her nose pointing toward Canada, there stood a group of familiar dark faces, and the look they cast backward was not one of longing for the fleshpots of Egypt. The colonel saw Grandison point him out to one of the crew of the vessel, who waved his hand derisively toward the colonel. The latter shook his fist impotently—and the incident was closed.

1898

SIS' BECKY'S PICKANINNY*

We had not lived in North Carolina very long before I was able to note a marked improvement in my wife's health. The ozone-laden air of the surrounding piney woods, the mild and equable climate, the peaceful leisure of country life, had brought about in hopeful measure the cure we had anticipated. Toward the end of our second year, however, her ailment took an unexpected turn for the worse. She became the victim of a settled melancholy, attended with vague forebodings of impending misfortune.

"You must keep up her spirits," said our physician, the best in the neighboring town. "This melancholy lowers her tone too much, tends to lessen her strength, and, if it continue too long, may be fraught with grave consequences."

I tried various expedients to cheer her up. I read novels to her. I had the hands on the place come up in the evening and serenade her with plantation songs. Friends came in sometimes and talked, and frequent letters from the North kept her in touch with her former home. But nothing seemed to rouse her from the depression into which she had fallen.

One pleasant afternoon in spring, I placed an armchair in a shaded portion of the front piazza, and filling it with pillows led my wife out of the house and seated her where she would have the pleasantest view of a somewhat monotonous scenery. She was scarcely placed when old Julius came through the yard, and, taking off his tattered straw hat, inquired, somewhat anxiously:—

"How is you feelin' dis afternoon, ma'm?"

"She is not very cheerful, Julius," I said. My wife was apparently without energy enough to speak for herself.

The old man did not seem inclined to go away, so I asked him to sit down. I had noticed, as he came up, that he held some small object in his hand. When he had taken his seat on the top step, he kept fingering this object,—what it was I could not quite make out.

"What is that you have there, Julius?" I asked, with mild curiosity.

"Dis is my rabbit foot, suh."

This was at a time before this curious superstition had attained its present jocu-

---

* First published in Chesnutt's collection *The Conjure Woman* in 1899. A pickaninny is a black child.

lar popularity among white people, and while I had heard of it before, it had not yet outgrown the charm of novelty.

"What do you do with it?"

"I kyars it wid me fer luck, suh."

"Julius," I observed, half to him and half to my wife, "your people will never rise in the world until they throw off these childish superstitions and learn to live by the light of reason and common sense. How absurd to imagine that the fore-foot of a poor dead rabbit, with which he timorously felt his way along through a life surrounded by snares and pitfalls, beset by enemies on every hand, can pro-mote happiness or success, or ward off failure of misfortune!"

"It is ridiculous," assented my wife, with faint interest.

"Dat's w'at I tells dese niggers roun' heah," said Julius. "De fo'-foot ain' got no power. It has ter be de hin'-foot, suh,—de lef' hin'-foot er a grabe-ya'd rabbit, killt by a cross-eyed nigger on a da'k night in de full er de moon."

"They must be very rare and valuable," I said.

"Dey is kinder ska'ce, suh, en dey ain' no 'mount er money could buy mine, suh. I mought len' it ter anybody I sot sto' by, but I wouldn' sell it, no indeed, suh, I wouldn'."

"How do you know it brings good luck?" I asked.

"'Ca'se I ain' had no bad luck sence I had it, suh, en I's had dis rabbit foot fer fo'ty yeahs. I had a good marster befo' de wah, en I wa'n't sol' erway, en I wuz sot free; en dat 'uz all good luck."

"But that doesn't prove anything," I rejoined. "Many other people have gone through a similar experience, and probably more than one of them had no rabbit's foot."

"Law, suh! you doan hafter prove 'bout de rabbit foot! Eve'ybody knows dat; leas'ways eve'ybody roun' heah knows it. But ef it has ter be prove' ter folks w'at wa'n't bawn en raise' in dis naberhood, dey is a' easy way ter prove it. Is I eber tol' you de tale er Sis' Becky en her pickaninny?"

"No," I said, "let us hear it." I thought perhaps the story might interest my wife as much or more than the novel I had meant to read from.

"Dis yer Becky," Julius began, "useter b'long ter ole Kunnel Pen'leton, who owned a plantation down on de Wim'l'-ton Road, 'bout ten miles fum heah, des befo' you gits ter Black Swamp. Dis yer Becky wuz a fiel'-han', en a monst'us good 'un. She had a husban' oncet, a nigger w'at b'longed on de nex' plantation, but de man w'at owned her husban' died, en his lan' en his niggers had to be sol' fer ter pay his debts. Kunnel Pen'leton 'lowed he'd 'a' bought dis nigger, but he had be'n bettin' on hoss races, en didn' hab no money, en so Becky's husban' wuz sol' erway ter Fuhginny.[1]

"Co'se Becky went on some 'bout losin' her man, but she couldn' he'p herse'f; en 'sides dat, she had her pickaninny fer ter comfo't her. Dis yer little Mose wuz de cutes', blackes', shiny-eyedes' little nigger you eber laid eyes on, en he wuz ez fon' er his mammy ez his mammy wuz er him. Co'se Becky had ter wuk en didn' hab much time ter was'e wid her baby. Ole Aun' Nancy, de plantation nuss down at de qua'ters, useter take keer er little Mose in de daytime, en atter de niggers come in fum de cotton-fiel' Becky 'ud git her chile en kiss 'im en nuss 'im, en keep 'im 'tel mawnin'; en on Sundays she'd hab 'im in her cabin wid her all day long.

---

[1] Virginia.

"Sis' Becky had got sorter useter gittin' 'long widout her husban', w'en one day Kunnel Pen'leton went ter de races. Co'se w'en he went ter de races, he tuk his hosses, en co'se he bet on 'is own hosses, en co'se he los' his money; fer Kunnel Pen'leton didn' nebber hab no luck wid his hosses, ef he did keep hisse'f po' projeckin'[2] wid 'em. But dis time dey wuz a hoss name' Lightnin' Bug, w'at b'longed ter ernudder man, en dis hoss won de sweep-stakes; en Kunnel Pen'leton tuk a lackin' ter dat hoss, en ax' his owner w'at he wuz willin' ter take fer 'im.

" 'I'll take a thousan' dollahs fer dat hoss,' sez dis yer man, who had a big plantation dow to'ds Wim'l'ton, whar he raise' hosses fer ter race en ter sell.

"Well, Kunnel Pen'leton scratch' 'is head, en wonder whar he wuz gwine ter raise a thousan' dollahs; en he didn' see des how he could do it, fer he owed ez much ez he could borry a'ready on de skyo'ity he could gib. But he wuz des boun' ter hab dat hoss, so sezee:—

" 'I'll gib you my note fer 'leven hund'ed dollahs fer dat hoss.'

"De yuther man shuck 'is head, en sezee:—

" 'Yo' note, suh, is better 'n gol', I doan doubt; but I is made it a rule in my bizness not ter take no notes fum nobody. Howsomeber, suh, ef you is kinder sho't er fun's, mos' lackly we kin make some kin' er bahg'in. En w'iles we is talkin', I mought 's well say dat I needs ernudder good nigger down on my place. Ef you is got a good one ter spar', I mought trade wid you.'

"Now, Kunnell Pen'leton didn' r'ally hab no niggers fer ter spar', but he 'lowed ter hisse'f he wuz des bleedzd[3] ter hab dat hoss, en so he sez, sezee:—

" 'Well, I doan lack ter, but I reckon I'll haf ter. You come out ter my planta-tion ter-morrer en look ober my niggers, en pick out de one you wants.'

"So sho' 'nuff nex' day dis yer man come out ter Kunnel Pen'leton's place en rid roun' de plantation en glanshed at de niggers, en who sh'd he pick out fum 'em all but Sis' Becky.

" 'I needs a noo nigger 'oman down ter my place,' sezee, 'fer ter cook en wash, en so on; en dat young 'oman 'll des fill de bill. You gimme her, en you kin hab Lightnin' Bug.' "

"Now, Kunnel Pen'leton didn' lack ter trade Sis' Becky, 'ca'se she wuz nigh 'bout de bes' fiel'-han' he had; en 'sides, Mars Kunnel didn' keer ter take de mammies 'way fum dey chillun w'iles de chillun wuz little. But dis man say he want Becky, er e'se Kunnel Pen'leton couldn' hab de race hoss.

" 'Well,' sez de kunnel, 'you kin hab de 'oman. But I doan lack ter sen' her 'way fum her baby. W'at'll you gimme for dat nigger baby?'

" 'I doan want de baby,' sez de yuther man. 'I ain' got no use fer de baby.'

" 'I tell yer w'at I'll do,' 'lows Kunnel Pen'leton, 'I'll th'ow dat pickaninny in fer good measure.'

"But de yuther man shuck his head. 'No,' sezee, 'I's much erbleedzd, but I doan raise niggers; I raises hosses, en I doan wanter be both'rin' wid no nigger babies. Nemmine de baby. I'll keep dat 'oman so busy she'll fergit de baby; fer niggers is made ter wuk, en dey ain' got no time fer no sich foolis'-ness ez ba-bies.'

"Kunnel Pen'leton didn' wanter hu't Becky's feelin's,—fer Kunnel Pen'leton wuz a kin'-hea'ted man, en nebber lack' ter make no trouble fer nobody,—en so he tol' Becky he wuz gwine sen' her down ter Robeson County fer a day er so, ter

---

[2] Projecting, either gambling on his horses or making a project of them.
[3] 'Bliged, from obliged ("erbleedzd").

he'p out his son-in-law in his wuk; en bein' ez dis yuther man wuz gwine dat way, he had ax' 'im ter take her 'long in his buggy.

" 'Kin I kyar little Mose wid me, marster?' ax' Sis' Becky.

" 'N-o,' sez de kunnel, ez ef he wuz studyin' whuther ter let her take 'im er no; 'I reckon you better let Aun' Nancy look atter yo' baby fer de day er two you'll be gone, en she'll see dat he gits ernuff ter eat 'tel you gits back.'

"So Sis' Becky hug' en kiss' little Mose, en tol' 'im ter be a good little pickaninny, en take keer er hisse'f, en not fergit his mammy w'iles she wuz gone. En little Mose put his arms roun' his mammy en lafft en crowed des lack it wuz monst'us fine fun fer his mammy ter go 'way en leabe 'im.

"Well, dis yer hoss trader sta'ted out wid Becky, en bimeby,[4] atter dey'd gone down de Lumbe'ton Road fer a few miles er so, dis man tu'nt roun' in a diffe'nt d'rection, en kep' goin' dat erway, 'tel bimeby Sis' Becky up 'n ax' 'im ef he wuz gwine ter Robeson County by a noo road.

" 'No, nigger,' sezee, 'I ain' gwine ter Robeson County at all. I's gwine ter Bladen County, whar my plantation is, en whar I raises all my hosses.'

" 'But how is I gwine ter git ter Mis' Laura's plantation down in Robeson County?' sez Becky, wid her hea't in her mouf, fer she 'mence' ter git skeered all er a sudden.

"'You ain' gwine ter git dere at all,' sez de man. 'You b'longs ter me now, fer I done traded by bes' race hoss fer you, wid yo' ole marster. Ef you is a good gal, I'll treat you right, en ef you doan behabe yo'se'f,—w'y, w'at e'se happens 'll be yo' own fault.'

"Co'se Sis' Becky cried en went on 'bout her pickaninny, but co'se it didn' do no good, en bimeby dey got down ter dis yer man's place, en he put Sis' Becky ter wuk, en fergot all 'bout her habin' a pickaninny.

"Meanw'iles, w'en ebenin' come, de day Sis' Becky wuz tuk 'way, little Mose 'mence' ter git res'less, en bimeby, w'en his mammy didn' come, he sta'ted ter cry fer 'er. Aun' Nancy fed 'im en rocked 'im en rocked 'im, en fin'lly he des cried en cried 'tel he cried hisse'f ter sleep.

"De nex' day he didn' 'pear ter be as peart ez yushal,[5] en w'en night come he fretted en went on wuss'n he did de night befo'. De nex' day his little eyes 'mence' ter lose dey shine, en he wouldn' eat nuffin, en he 'mence' ter look so peaked dat Aun' Nancy tuk'n kyared 'im up ter de big house, en showed 'im ter her ole missis, en her ole missis gun her some med'cine fer 'im, en 'lowed ef he didn' git no better she sh'd fetch 'im up ter de big house ag'in, en dey'd hab a doctor, en nuss little Mose up dere. Fer Aun' Nancy's ole missis 'lowed he wuz a lackly little nigger en wu'th raisin'.

"But Aun' Nancy had l'arn' ter lack little Mose, en she didn' wanter hab 'im tuck up ter de big house. En so w'en he didn' git no better, she gethered a mess er green peas, and tuk de peas en de baby, en went ter see ole Aun' Peggy, de cunjuh 'oman[6] down by de Wim'l'ton Road. She gun Aun' Peggy de mess er peas, en tol' her all 'bout Sis' Becky en little Mose.

" 'Dat is a monst'us small mess er peas you is fotch' me,' sez Aun' Peggy, sez she.

" 'Yas, I knows,' 'lowed Aun' Nancy, 'but dis yere is a monst'us small pickaninny.'

---

[4] By and by.   [5] Lively as usual.   [6] Conjure woman: voodooist or sorceress.

" 'You'll hafter fetch me sump'n mo',' sez Aun' Peggy, 'fer you can't 'spec' me ter was'e my time diggin' roots en wukkin' cunj'ation fer nuffin.' "

" 'All right,' sez Aun' Nancy, 'I'll fetch you sump'n mo' nex' time.' "

" 'You bettah,' sez Aun' Peggy, 'er e'se dey'll be trouble. W'at dis yer little pickaninny needs is ter see his mammy. You leabe 'im heah 'tel ebenin' en I'll show 'im his mammy.' "

"So w'en Aun' Nancy had gone 'way, Aun' Peggy tuk'n wukked her roots, en tu'nt little Mose ter a hummin'-bird, en sont 'im off fer ter fin' his mammy.

"So little Mose flewed, en flewed, en flewed away, 'tel bimeby he got ter de place whar Sis' Becky b'longed. He seed his mammy wukkin' roun' de ya'd, en he could tell fum lookin' at her dat she wuz trouble' in her min' 'bout sump'n, en feelin' kin' er po'ly. Sis' Becky heared sump'n hummin' roun' en roun' her, sweet en low. Fus' she 'lowed it wuz a hummin'-bird; den she thought it sounded lack her little Mose croonin' on her breas' way back yander on de ole plantation. En she des 'magine' it wuz her little Mose, en it made her feel bettah, en she went on 'bout her wuk pearter'n she'd done sence she'd be'n down dere. Little Mose stayed roun' 'tel late in de ebenin', en den flewed back ez hard ez he could ter Aun' Peggy. Ez fer Sis' Becky, she dremp all dat night dat she wuz holdin' her pickaninny in her arms, en kissin' him, en nussin' him, des lack she useter do back on de ole plantation whar he wuz bawn. En fer th'ee er fo' days Sis' Becky went 'bout her wuk wid mo' sperrit dan she'd showed sence she'd be'n down dere ter dis man's plantation.

"De nex' day atter he come back, little Mose wuz mo' pearter en better'n he had be'n fer a long time. But to'ds de een' er de week he 'mence' ter git res'less ag'in, en stop' eatin', en Aun' Nancy kyared 'im down ter Aun' Peggy once mo', en she tu'nt 'im ter a mawkin'-bird dis time, en sont 'im off ter see his mammy ag'in.

"It didn' take him long fer ter git dere, en w'en he did, he seed his mammy standin' in de kitchen, lookin' back in de d'rection little Mose wuz comin' fum. En dey wuz tears in her eyes, en she look' mo' po'ly en peaked 'n she had w'en he wuz down dere befo'. So little Mose sot on a tree in de ya'd en sung, en sung, en sung, des fittin' ter split his th'oat. Fus' Sis' Becky didn' notice 'im much, but dis mawkin'-bird kep' stayin' roun' de house all day, en bimeby Sis' Becky des 'magine' dat mawkin'-bird wuz her little Mose crowin' en crowin', des lack he useter do w'en his mammy would come home at night fum de cotton-fiel'. De mawkin'-bird stayed roun' dere 'mos' all day, en w'en Sis' Becky went out in de ya'd one time, dis yer mawkin'-bird lit on her shoulder en peck' at de piece er bread she wuz eatin', en fluttered his wings so dey rub' up again de side er her head. En w'en he flewed away 'long late in de ebenin', des 'fo' sundown, Sis' Becky felt mo' better 'n she had sence she had heared dat hummin'-bird a week er so pas'. En dat night she dremp 'bout ole times ag'in, des lack she did befo'.

"But dis yer totin' little Mose down ter ole Aun' Peggy, en dis yer gittin' things fer ter pay de cunjuh 'oman, use' up a lot er Aun' Nancy's time, en she begun ter git kinder ti'ed. 'Sides dat, w'en Sis' Becky had be'n on de plantation, she had useter he'p Aun' Nancy wid de young uns ebenin's en Sundays; en Aun' Nancy 'mence' ter miss 'er monst'us, 'speshly sence she got a tech er de rheumatiz herse'f, en so she 'lows ter ole Aun' Peggy one day:—

" 'Aun' Peggy, ain' dey no way you kin fetch Sis' Becky back home?'

" 'Huh!' sez Aun' Peggy, 'I dunno 'bout dat. I'll hafter wuk my roots en fin' out whuther I kin er no. But it'll take a monst'us heap er wuk, en I can't was'e my time fer nuffin. Ef you'll fetch me sump'n ter pay me fer my trouble, I reckon we kin fix it.'

"So nex' day Aun' Nancy went down ter see Aun' Peggy ag'in.

" 'Aun' Peggy,' sez she, 'I is fotch' you my bes' Sunday head-hankercher. Will dat do?'

"Aun' Peggy look' at de head-hankerchef, en run her han' ober it, en sez she:—

" 'Yas, dat'll do fus'-rate. I's be'n wukkin' my roots sence you be'n gone, en I 'lows mos' lackly I kin git Sis' Becky back, but it's gwine take fig'rin' en studyin' ez well ez cunj'in'. De fus' thing ter do'll be ter stop fetchin' dat pickaninny down heah, en not sen' 'im ter see his mammy no mo'. Ef he gits too po'ly, you lemme know, en I'll gib you some kin' er mixtry fer ter make 'im fergit Sis' Becky fer a week er so. So 'less'n you comes fer dat, you neenter come back ter see me no mo' 'tel I sen's fer you.'

"So Aun' Peggy sont Aun' Nancy erway, en de fus' thing she done wuz ter call a hawnet fum a nes' unner her eaves.

" 'You go up ter Kunnel Pen'leton's stable, hawnet,' sez she, 'en sting de knees er de race hoss name' Lightnin' Bug. Be sho' en git de right one.'

"So de hawnet flewed up ter Kunnel Pen'leton's stable en stung Lightnin' Bug roun' de laigs, en de nex' mawnin' Lightnin' Bug's knees wuz all swoll' up, twice't ez big ez dey oughter be. W'en Kunnel Pen'leton went out ter de stable en see de hoss's laigs, hit would 'a' des made you trimble lack a leaf fer ter heah him cuss dat hoss trader. How-someber, he cool' off bimeby en tol' de stable boy fer ter rub Lightnin' Bug's laigs wid some linimum. De boy done ez his marster tol' 'im, en by de nex' day de swellin' had gone down consid'able. Aun' Peggy had sont a sparrer, w'at had a nes' in one er de trees close ter her cabin, fer ter watch w'at wuz gwine on 'roun' de big house, en w'en dis yer sparrer tol' 'er de hoss wuz gittin' ober de swellin', she sont de hawnet back fer ter sting 'is knees some mo', en de nex' mawnin' Lightnin' Bug's laigs wuz swoll' up wuss'n befo'.

"Well, dis time Kunnel Pen'leton wuz mad th'oo en th'oo, en all de way 'roun', en he cusst dat hoss trader up en down, fum *A* ter *Izzard*.[7] He cusst so ha'd dat de stable boy got mos' skeered ter def, en went off en hid hisse'f in de hay.

"Ez fer Kunnel Pen'leton, he went right up ter de house en got out his pen en ink, en tuk off his coat en roll' up his sleeves, en writ a letter ter dis yer hoss trader, en sezee:—

" 'You is sol' me a hoss w'at is got a ringbone er a spavin[8] er sump'n, en w'at I paid you fer wuz a soun' hoss. I wants you ter sen' my nigger 'oman back en take yo' ole hoss, er e'se I'll sue you, sho's you bawn.'

"But dis yer man wa'n't skeered a bit, en he writ back ter Kunnel Pen'leton dat a bahg'in wuz a bahg'in; dat Lightnin' Bug wuz soun' w'en he sol' 'im, en ef Kunnel Pen'leton didn' knowed ernuff 'bout hosses ter take keer er a fine racer, dat wuz his own fune'al. En he say Kunnel Pen'leton kin sue en be cusst fer all he keer, but he ain' gwine ter gib up de nigger he bought en paid fer.

"W'en Kunnell Pen'leton got dis letter he wuz madder'n he wuz befo', 'speshly 'ca'se dis man 'lowed he didn' know how ter take keer er fine hosses. But he couldn' do nuffin but fetch a lawsuit, en he knowed, by his own 'spe-'ience, dat lawsuits wuz slow ez de seben-yeah eetch and cos' mo' d'n dey come ter, en he 'lowed he better go slow en wait awhile.

---

[7] The letter *z*.

[8] A bony growth on a horse's foot; bone or lymph that develops in a horse's hock joint: both cause lameness.

"Aun' Peggy knowed w'at wuz gwine on all dis time, en she fix' up a little bag wid some roots en one thing en ernudder in it, en gun it ter dis sparrer er her'n, en tol' 'im ter take it 'way down yander whar Sis' Becky wuz, en drap it right befo' de do' er her cabin, so she'd be sho' en fin' it de fus' time she come out'n de do'.

"One night Sis' Becky dremp' her pickaninny wuz dead, en de nex' day she wuz mo'nin' en groanin' all day. She dremp' de same dream th'ee nights runnin', en den, de nex' mawnin' atter de las' night, she foun' dis yer little bag de sparrer had drap' in front her do'; en she 'lowed she'd be'n cunju'd, en wuz gwine ter die, en ez long ez her pickaninny wuz dead dey wa'n't no use tryin' ter do nuffin nohow. En so she tuk 'n went ter bed, en tol' her marster she'd be'n cunju'd en wuz gwine ter die.

"Her marster lafft at her, en argyed wid her, en tried ter 'suade her out'n dis yer fool notion, ez he called it,—fer he wuz one er dese yer w'ite folks w'at purten' dey doan b'liebe in cunj'in,—but hit wa'n't no use. Sis' Becky kep' gittin wusser en wusser, 'tel fin'lly dis yer man 'lowed Sis' Becky wuz gwine ter die, sho' 'nuff. En ez he knowed dey hadn' be'n nuffin de matter wid Lightnin' Bug w'en he traded 'im, he 'lowed mebee he could kyo' 'im en fetch 'im roun' all right, leas'ways good 'nuff ter sell ag'in. En anyhow, a lame hoss wuz better 'n a dead nigger. So he sot down en writ Kunnel Pen'leton a letter.

" 'My conscience,' sezee, 'has be'n troublin' me 'bout dat ringbone' hoss I sol' you. Some folks 'lows a hoss trader ain' got no conscience, but dey doan know me, fer dat is my weak spot, en de reason I ain' made no mo' money hoss tradin'. Fac' is,' sezee, 'I is got so I can't sleep nights fum studyin' 'bout dat spavin' hoss; en I is made up my min' dat, w'iles a bahg'in is a bahg'in, en you seed Lightnin' Bug befo' you traded fer 'im, principle is wuth mo' d'n money er hosses er niggers. So ef you'll sen' Lightnin' Bug down heah, I'll sen' yo' nigger 'oman back, en we'll call de trade off, en be ez good frien's ez we eber wuz, en no ha'd feelin's.'

"So sho' 'nuff, Kunnel Pen'leton sont de hoss back. En w'en de man w'at come ter bring Lightnin' Bug tol' Sis' Becky her pickaninny wa'n't dead, Sis' Becky wuz so glad dat she 'lowed she wuz gwine ter try ter lib 'tel she got back whar she could see little Mose once mo'. En w'en she retch' de ole plantation en seed her baby kickin' en crowin' en holdin' out his little arms to'ds her, she wush' she wuzn' cunju'd en didn' hafter die. En w'en Aun' Nancy tol' 'er all 'bout Aun' Peggy, Sis' Becky went down ter see de cunjuh 'oman, en Aun' Peggy tol' her she had cunju'd her. En den Aun' Peggy tuk de goopher,[9] off'n her, en she got well, en stayed on de plantation, en raise' her pickaninny. En w'en little Mose growed up, he could sing en whistle des lack a mawkin'-bird, so dat de w'ite folks useter hab 'im come up ter de big house at night, en whistle en sing fer 'em, en dey useter gib 'im money en vittles en one thing er ernudder, w'ich he alluz tuk home ter his mammy; fer he knowed all 'bout w'at she had gone th'oo. He tu'nt out ter be a sma't man, en l'arnt de blacksmif trade; en Kunnel Pen'leton let 'im hire his time. En bimeby he bought his mammy en sot her free, en den he bought hisse'f, en tuk keer er Sis' Becky ez long ez dey bofe libbed."

My wife had listened to this story with greater interest than she had manifested in any subject for several days. I had watched her furtively from time to time during the recital, and had observed the play of her countenance. It had expressed in turn sympathy, indignation, pity, and at the end lively satisfaction.

---

[9] Curse.

"That is a very ingenious fairy tale, Julius," I said, "and we are much obliged to you."

"Why, John!" said my wife severely, "the story bears the stamp of truth, if ever a story did."

"Yes," I replied, "especially the humming-bird episode, and the mocking-bird digression, to say nothing of the doings of the hornet and the sparrow."

"Oh, well, I don't care," she rejoined, with delightful animation; "those are mere ornamental details and not at all essential. The story is true to nature, and might have happened half a hundred times, and no doubt did happen, in those horrid days before the war."

"By the way, Julius," I remarked, "your story doesn't establish what you started out to prove,—that a rabbit's foot brings good luck."

"Hit's plain 'nuff ter me, suh," replied Julius. "I bet young missis dere king 'splain it herse'f."

"I rather suspect," replied my wife promptly, "that Sis' Becky had no rabbit's foot."

"You is hit de bull's-eye de fus' fire, ma'm," assented Julius. "Ef Sis' Becky had had a rabbit foot, she nebber would 'a' went th'oo all dis trouble."

I went into the house for some purpose, and left Julius talking to my wife. When I came back a moment later, he was gone.

My wife's condition took a turn for the better from this very day, and she was soon on the way to ultimate recovery. Several weeks later, after she had resumed her afternoon drives, which had been interrupted by her illness, Julius brought the rockaway[10] round to the front door one day, and I assisted my wife into the carriage.

"John," she said, before I had taken my seat, "I wish you would look in my room, and bring me my handkerchief. You will find it in the pocket of my blue dress."

I went to execute the commission. When I pulled the handkerchief out of her pocket, something else came with it and fell on the floor. I picked up the object and looked at it. It was Julius's rabbit's foot.

1899

Charlotte Perkins Gilman
(1860–1935)

At age twenty Charlotte Perkins composed a brief note "to gather strength from" and put it on her dresser mirror. "If I live, (as I do,) for others," the note began, "if all my high desires for self-improvement are solely with a view to the elevation of the race—if my mission is to lead a self-sacrificing life . . . to teach and guide, to love, protect and care for—then it behooves me to crush all personal sorrow and drop the whole ground of self-interest forever. Neither is this Quixotic or impossible." Perkins's rigorous self-discipline and unyielding commitment to social improvement enabled her to become one of the

---

[10] A horse-drawn carriage with four wheels and open sides.

strongest turn-of-the-century feminist voices despite a debilitating "nerve-ruin" that grievously impaired her ability to read and frequent periods of despair, during which nearly all activity was impossible.

The second child of Fredric Beecher Perkins and Mary Fitch, Charlotte Anna Perkins was born in Hartford, Connecticut, in 1860. Her father abandoned the family shortly after her birth, and although she later beseeched him to write more frequently, he remained remote. She did, however, know his family and proudly claimed her relation to her great-aunt Harriet Beecher Stowe. Family background notwithstanding, Mary Perkins and her son and daughter suffered poverty so severe that they were forced to move nineteen times in eighteen years. More distressing to Charlotte was her mother's response to hardship and disappointment: determined never to have her children suffer because of unfulfilled hopes and expectations, Mary Perkins withheld outward shows of affection, motherly hugs and kisses, and forbade Charlotte to enjoy such pleasures as reading novels or cultivating an "inner world" of imagination.

After briefly attending the Rhode Island School of Design, Charlotte enjoyed some success painting flowers and teaching art. In 1882 she met Charles Walter Stetson, a painter from Providence, who soon proposed marriage. Declining immediately, she subsequently reconsidered; after two years of wavering, uncertain whether marriage would fit into her plans for a life of service to society, she married Stetson in May 1884. Although the two were happy together, she noted in her autobiography, first published in 1935, that "something was going wrong from the start," like a "gray fog [that] drifted across my mind, a cloud that grew and darkened." This cloud of depression did not abate after the birth of their daughter in 1885, nor was it alleviated by the "rest-cure" prescribed by the noted physician S. Weir Mitchell. On the contrary, following his advice she "came perilously near to losing [her] mind."

In 1887, realizing the inherent dangers of remaining married, the Stetsons agreed to divorce, and Charlotte Perkins and her daughter moved to Pasadena the next autumn, aided by the writer Grace Channing. Although Perkins's four years in California were the hardest of her life, her feeling of being "finally free" (though a "wreck") in 1890 resulted in the production of some of her best work. Her acclaimed story "The Yellow Wallpaper," written at that time, chronicles the breakdown and progressive decline of a patient who follows the "rest-cure" (she sent a copy of this story to Dr. Mitchell and later heard that he changed his treatment of nervous prostration after reading it). At about this time she began lecturing professionally, most often to women's and labor groups. However, her efforts netted barely enough money for survival. Given her poor health and scanty income, Perkins reluctantly decided that her daughter should live with Charles Stetson and his new wife, Grace Channing, a decision for which Perkins was publicly condemned.

On her own in California, Perkins supported herself through writing, lecturing, teaching, and editing. "The Yellow Wallpaper" appeared in *The New England Magazine* in 1892 (later William Dean Howells included it in a collection of great American stories). Written in only fifty-eight days, her most influential book, *Women and Economics* (1898), argues that women's economic dependence on men is detrimental to both genders because it limits the ability of women to exercise their creativity in nondomestic fields. In this and later works (*Concerning Children* [1900], *The Home* [1904], and *Human Work* [1904]), she advanced her ideas for child-care centers, kitchenless homes, and professional housekeeping as ways to give women more usable time and children more effective supervision.

In 1900 Perkins married her cousin George Houghton Gilman, with whom she had had a long epistolary courtship. They remained together, happily, until his sudden death in 1934. He provided much support while she wrote, edited, published, and distributed *Forerunner,* a one-woman journal that appeared from 1909 to 1916, as well as *Man-Made World* (1911), *Herland* (serialized in *Forerunner* in 1915), *With Her in Ourland* (1916), and *His Religion and Hers* (1923). These late works maintain that women's nurturing, life-sustaining efforts are preferable to the bellicose tendencies of men, that a feminine influence is needed in national and international affairs as well as in religion, and that the female is "the primary type of the human species" (a claim she discussed with Lester Ward, a noted sociologist).

Gilman was influential as a public speaker, lecturing to a variety of audiences, including women's clubs, church groups, and college students. She traveled both nationally and internationally as a delegate to suffrage conventions and spoke at the International Suffrage Convention in Budapest in 1913. In the 1920s, however, her constituency waned. And in 1935, suffering from breast cancer, she ended her life with chloroform because of her conviction that "when all usefulness is over, when one is assured of unavoidable and imminent death, it is the simplest of human rights to choose a quick and easy death in place of a slow and horrible one." Gilman's works were largely forgotten for almost fifty years after her death, but now, as the era Gilman referred to as the "woman's century" comes to a close, they are being reclaimed as significant early contributions to the feminist tradition in America.

Suggested Readings: *His Religion and Hers: A Study of the Faith of Our Fathers and the Work of Our Mothers*, 1923, rpt. 1976. *The Living of Charlotte Perkins Gilman: An Autobiography*, 1935, rpt. 1972. *Herland*, 1979. *The Charlotte Perkins Gilman Reader: The Yellow Wallpaper and Other Fiction*, ed. A. J. Lane, 1980. M. A. Hill, *Charlotte Perkins Gilman: The Making of a Radical Feminist, 1860–1896*, 1980. G. Scharnhorst, *Charlotte Perkins Gilman*, 1985. P. W. Allen, *Building Domestic Liberty: Charlotte Perkins Gilman's Architectural Feminism*, 1988. S. L. Meyering, ed., *Charlotte Perkins Gilman: The Woman and Her Work*, 1989. A. J. Lane, *To "Herland" and Beyond: The Life and Work of Charlotte Perkins Gilman*, 1990.

Text Used: *The New England Magazine*, V (5):647–656, January 1892.

THE YELLOW WALL-PAPER*

It is very seldom that mere ordinary people like John and myself secure ancestral halls for the summer.

A colonial mansion, a hereditary estate, I would say a haunted house, and reach the height of romantic felicity—but that would be asking too much of fate!

Still I will proudly declare that there is something queer about it.

Else, why should it be let so cheaply? And why have stood so long untenanted?

John laughs at me, of course, but one expects that in marriage.

John is practical in the extreme. He has no patience with faith, an intense horror of superstition, and he scoffs openly at any talk of things not to be felt and seen and put down in figures.

John is a physician, and *perhaps*—(I would not say it to a living soul, of course, but this is dead paper and a great relief to my mind—) *perhaps* that is one reason I do not get well faster.

You see he does not believe I am sick!

And what can one do?

If a physician of high standing, and one's own husband, assures friends and

---

* First published in *The New England Magazine* in January 1892.

They treat her for "nothing" with nothing

relatives that there is really nothing the matter with one but temporary nervous depression—a slight hysterical tendency[1]—what is one to do?

My brother is also a physician, and also of high standing, and he says the same thing.

So I take phosphates or phosphites[2]—whichever it is, and tonics, and journeys, and air, and exercise, and am absolutely forbidden to "work" until I am well again. *inconsistancy*

Personally, I disagree with their ideas.

Personally, I believe that congenial work, with excitement and change, would do me good. *→ she's BORED*

But what is one to do?

I did write for a while in spite of them; but it *does* exhaust me a good deal—having to be so sly about it, or else meet with heavy opposition.

I sometimes fancy that in my condition if I had less opposition and more society and stimulus—but John says the very worst thing I can do is to think about my condition, and I confess it always makes me feel bad.

So I will let it alone and talk about the house.

The most beautiful place! It is quite alone, standing well back from the road, quite three miles from the village. It makes me think of English places that you read about, for there are hedges and walls and gates that lock, and lots of separate little houses for the gardeners and people.

There is a *delicious* garden! I never saw such a garden—large and shady, full of box-bordered paths, and lined with long grape-covered arbors with seats under them.

There were greenhouses, too, but they are all broken now.

There was some legal trouble, I believe, something about the heirs and co-heirs; anyhow, the place has been empty for years.

That spoils my ghostliness, I am afraid, but I don't care—there is something strange about the house—I can feel it.

I even said so to John one moonlight evening, but he said what I felt was a *draught,* and shut the window.

I get unreasonably angry with John sometimes. I'm sure I never used to be so sensitive. I think it is due to this nervous condition.

But John says if I feel so, I shall neglect proper self-control; so I take pains to control myself—before him, at least, and that makes me very tired.

I don't like our room a bit. I wanted one downstairs that opened on the piazza and had roses all over the window, and such pretty old-fashioned chintz hangings! but John would not hear of it.

He said there was only one window and not room for two beds, and no near room for him if he took another.

He is very careful and loving, and hardly lets me stir without special direction.

I have a schedule prescription for each hour in the day; he takes all care from me, and so I feel basely ungrateful not to value it more.

He said we came here solely on my account, that I was to have perfect rest and all the air I could get. "Your exercise depends on your strength, my dear," said he, "and your food somewhat on your appetite; but air you can absorb all the time." So we took the nursery at the top of the house.

It is a big, airy room, the whole floor nearly, with windows that look all ways,

[1] In the late nineteenth century the term "hysteria" was used to describe a number of emotional problems to which women were supposedly liable, among them anxiety, depression, and stress.

[2] Carbonated water with a small amount of acid phosphate, flavored with a fruit syrup.

and air and sunshine galore. It was nursery first and then playroom and gymnasium, I should judge; for the windows are barred for little children, and there are rings and things in the walls.

The paint and paper look as if a boys' school had used it. It is stripped off—the paper—in great patches all around the head of my bed, about as far as I can reach, and in a great place on the other side of the room low down. I never saw a worse paper in my life.

One of those sprawling flamboyant patterns committing every artistic sin.

It is dull enough to confuse the eye in following, pronounced enough to constantly irritate and provoke study, and when you follow the lame uncertain curves for a little distance they suddenly commit suicide—plunge off at outrageous angles, destroy themselves in unheard of contradictions.

The color is repellant, almost revolting; a smouldering unclean yellow, strangely faded by the slow-turning sunlight.

It is a dull yet lurid orange in some places, a sickly sulphur tint in others.

No wonder the children hated it! I should hate it myself if I had to live in this room long.

There comes John, and I must put this away,—he hates to have me write a word.

We have been here two weeks, and I haven't felt like writing before, since that first day.

I am sitting by the window now, up in this atrocious nursery, and there is nothing to hinder my writing as much as I please, save lack of strength.

John is away all day, and even some nights when his cases are serious.

I am glad my case is not serious!

But these nervous troubles are dreadfully depressing.

John does not know how much I really suffer. He knows there is no *reason* to suffer, and that satisfies him.

Of course it is only nervousness. It does weigh on me so not to do my duty in any way!

I meant to be such a help to John, such a real rest and comfort, and here I am a comparative burden already!

Nobody would believe what an effort it is to do what little I am able,—to dress and entertain, and order things.

It is fortunate Mary is so good with the baby. Such a dear baby!

And yet I *cannot* be with him, it makes me so nervous.

I suppose John never was nervous in his life. He laughs at me so about this wall-paper!

At first he meant to repaper the room, but afterwards he said that I was letting it get the better of me, and that nothing was worse for a nervous patient than to give way to such fancies.

He said that after the wall-paper was changed it would be the heavy bedstead, and then the barred windows, and then that gate at the head of the stairs, and so on.

"You know the place is doing you good," he said, "and really, dear, I don't care to renovate the house just for a three months' rental."

"Then do let us go downstairs," I said, "there are such pretty rooms there."

Then he took me in his arms and called me a blessed little goose, and said he would go down cellar, if I wished, and have it whitewashed into the bargain.

But he is right enough about the beds and windows and things.

It is an airy and comfortable room as any one need wish, and, of course, I would not be so silly as to make him uncomfortable just for a whim.

I'm really getting quite fond of the big room, all but that horrid paper.

Out of one window I can see the garden, those mysterious deep-shaded arbors, the riotous old-fashioned flowers, and bushes and gnarly trees.

Out of another I get a lovely view of the bay and a little private wharf belonging to the estate. There is a beautiful shaded lane that runs down there from the house. I always fancy I see people walking in these numerous paths and arbors, but John has cautioned me not to give way to fancy in the least. He says that with my imaginative power and habit of story-making, a nervous weakness like mine is sure to lead to all manner of excited fancies, and that I ought to use my will and good sense to check the tendency. So I try.

I think sometimes that if I were only well enough to write a little it would relieve the press of ideas and rest me.

But I find I get pretty tired when I try.

It is so discouraging not to have any advice and companionship about my work. When I get really well, John says we will ask Cousin Henry and Julia down for a long visit; but he says he would as soon put fireworks in my pillow-case as to let me have those stimulating people about now.

I wish I could get well faster.

But I must not think about that. This paper looks to me as if it *knew* what a vicious influence it had!

There is a recurrent spot where the pattern lolls like a broken neck and two bulbous eyes stare at you upside down.

I get positively angry with the impertinence of it and the everlastingness. Up and down and sideways they crawl, and those absurd, unblinking eyes are everywhere. There is one place where two breaths didn't match, and the eyes go all up and down the line, one a little higher than the other.

I never saw so much expression in an inanimate thing before, and we all know how much expression they have! I used to lie awake as a child and get more entertainment and terror out of blank walls and plain furniture than most children could find in a toy-store.

I remember what a kindly wink the knobs of our big, old bureau used to have, and there was one chair that always seemed like a strong friend.

I used to feel that if any of the other things looked too fierce I could always hop into that chair and be safe.

The furniture in this room is no worse than inharmonious, however, for we had to bring it all from downstairs. I suppose when this was used as a playroom they had to take the nursery things out, and no wonder! I never saw such ravages as the children have made here.

The wall-paper, as I said before, is torn off in spots, and it sticketh closer than a brother[3]—they must have had perserverance as well as hatred.

Then the floor is scratched and gouged and splintered, the plaster itself is dug out here and there, and this great heavy bed which is all we found in the room, looks as if it had been through the wars.

---

[3] A biblical maxim suddenly springs to the narrator's mind: "There is a friend that sticketh closer than a brother," from Proverbs 18:24.

"But I don't mind it a bit—only the paper.

There comes John's sister. Such a dear girl as she is, and so careful of me! I must not let her find me writing.

She is a perfect and enthusiastic housekeeper, and hopes for no better profession. I verily believe she thinks it is the writing which made me sick!

But I can write when she is out, and see her a long way off from these windows.

There is one that commands the road, a lovely shaded winding road, and one that just looks off over the country. A lovely country, too, full of great elms and velvet meadows.

This wallpaper has a kind of sub-pattern in a different shade, a particularly irritating one, for you can only see it in certain lights, and not clearly then.

But in the places where it isn't faded and where the sun is just so—I can see a strange, provoking, formless sort of figure, that seems to skulk about behind that silly and conspicuous front design.

There's sister on the stair!

Well, the Fourth of July is over! The people are all gone and I am tired out. John thought it might do me good to see a little company, so we just had mother and Nellie and the children down for a week.

Of course I didn't do a thing. Jennie sees to everything now.

But it tired me all the same.

John says if I don't pick up faster he shall send me to Weir Mitchell[4] in the fall.

But I don't want to go there at all. I had a friend who was in his hands once, and she says he is just like John and my brother, only more so!

Besides, it is such an undertaking to go so far.

I don't feel as if it was worth while to turn my hand over for anything, and I'm getting dreadfully fretful and querulous.

I cry at nothing, and cry most of the time.

Of course I don't when John is here, or anybody else, but when I am alone.

And I am alone a good deal just now. John is kept in town very often by serious cases, and Jennie is good and lets me alone when I want her to.

So I walk a little in the garden or down that lovely lane, sit on the porch under the roses, and lie down up here a good deal.

I'm getting really fond of the room in spite of the wallpaper. Perhaps *because* of the wallpaper.

It dwells in my mind so!

I lie here on this great immovable bed—it is nailed down, I believe—and follow that pattern about by the hour. It it as good as gymnastics, I assure you. I start, we'll say, at the bottom, down in the corner over there where it has not been touched, and I determine for the thousandth time that I *will* follow that pattern to some sort of a conclusion.

I know a little of the principle of design, and I know this thing was not arranged on any laws of radiation, or alternation, or repetition, or symmetry, or anything else that I ever heard of.

---

[4] S. Weir Mitchell (1829–1914), an American physician, a specialist in nervous disorders, whose "rest-cure" for "hysteria" Gilman had undergone. Mitchell was supposedly the model for the nerve specialist in William Dean Howells's *The Shadow of a Dream* (1890); he later became a novelist.

It is repeated, of course, by the breadths, but not otherwise.

Looked at in one way each breadth stands alone, the bloated curves and flourishes—a kind of "debased Romanesque" with *delirium tremens*[5]—go waddling up and down in isolated columns of fatuity.

But, on the other hand, they connect diagonally, and the sprawling outlines run off in great slanting waves of optic horror, like a lot of wallowing seaweeds in full chase.

The whole thing goes horizontally, too, at least it seems so, and I exhaust myself in trying to distinguish the order of its going in that direction.

They have used a horizontal breadth for a frieze,[6] and that adds wonderfully to the confusion.

There is one end of the room where it is almost intact, and there, when the crosslights fade and the low sun shines directly upon it, I can almost fancy radiation after all,—the interminable grotesque seem to form around a common centre and rush off in headlong plunges of equal distraction.

It makes me tired to follow it. I will take a nap I guess.

I don't know why I should write this.

I don't want to.

I don't feel able.

And I know John would think it absurd. But I *must* say what I feel and think in some way—it is such a relief!

But the effort is getting to be greater than the relief.

Half the time now I am awfully lazy, and lie down ever so much.

John says I mustn't lose my strength, and has me take cod liver oil and lots of tonics and things, to say nothing of ale and wine and rare meat.

Dear John! He loves me very dearly, and hates to have me sick. I tried to have a real earnest reasonable talk with him the other day, and tell him how I wish he would let me go and make a visit to Cousin Henry and Julia.

But he said I wasn't able to go, nor able to stand it after I got there; and I did not make out a very good case for myself, for I was crying before I had finished.

It is getting to be a great effort for me to think straight. Just this nervous weakness I suppose.

And dear John gathered me up in his arms, and just carried me upstairs and laid me on the bed, and sat by me and read to me till it tired my head.

He said I was his darling and his comfort and all he had, and that I must take care of myself for his sake, and keep well.

He says no one but myself can help me out of it, that I must use my will and self-control and not let any silly fancies run away with me.

There's one comfort, the baby is well and happy, and does not have to occupy this nursery with the horrid wallpaper.

If we had not used it, that blessed child would have! What a fortunate escape! Why, I wouldn't have a child of mine, an impressionable little thing, live in such a room for worlds.

---

[5] Romanesque architecture is elaborately ornamented; the narrator now sees the wallpaper designs not only as elaborate but as "debased" and afflicted with a violent and trembling delirium.
[6] An ornamental band that serves as a border where a wall meets the ceiling.

I never thought of it before, but it is lucky that John kept me here after all, I can stand it so much easier than a baby, you see.

Of course I never mention it to them any more—I am too wise,—but I keep watch of it all the same.

There are things in that paper that nobody knows but me, or ever will.

Behind that outside pattern the dim shapes get clearer every day.

It is always the same shape, only very numerous.

And it is like a woman stooping down and creeping about behind that pattern. I don't like it a bit. I wonder—I begin to think—I wish John would take me away from here!

It is so hard to talk with John about my case, because he is so wise, and because he loves me so.

But I tried last night.

It was moonlight. The moon shines in all around just as the sun does.

I hate to see it sometimes, it creeps so slowly, and always comes in by one window or another.

John was asleep and I hated to waken him, so I kept still and watched the moonlight on that undulating wallpaper till I felt creepy.

The faint figure behind seemed to shake the pattern, just as if she wanted to get out.

I got up softly and went to feel and see if the paper *did* move, and when I came back John was awake.

"What is it, little girl?" he said. "Don't go walking about like that—you'll get cold."

I thought it was a good time to talk, so I told him that I really was not gaining here, and that I wished he would take me away.

"Why, darling!" said he, "our lease will be up in three weeks, and I can't see how to leave before.

"The repairs are not done at home, and I cannot possibly leave town just now. Of course if you were in any danger, I could and would, but you really are better, dear, whether you can see it or not. I am a doctor, dear, and I know. You are gaining flesh and color, your appetite is better, I feel really much easier about you."

"I don't weigh a bit more," said I, "nor as much; and my appetite may be better in the evening when you are here, but it is worse in the morning when you are away!"

"Bless her little heart!" said he with a big hug, "she shall be as sick as she pleases! But now let's improve the shining hours[7] by going to sleep, and talk about it in the morning!"

"And you won't go away?" I asked gloomily.

"Why, how can I, dear? It is only three weeks more and then we will take a nice little trip of a few days while Jennie is getting the house ready. Really dear you are better!"

"Better in body perhaps—" I began, and stopped short, for he sat up straight

---

[7] "How doth the little busy bee / Improve each shining hour," from the poem "Against Idleness and Mischief" in *Divine Songs for Children*, by Isaac Watts (1674–1748). The smug superiority of Watts's lines matches that of John's demeanor toward his wife.

and looked at me with such a stern, reproachful look that I could not say another word.

"My darling," said he, "I beg of you, for my sake and for our child's sake, as well as for your own, that you will never for one instant let that idea enter your mind! There is nothing so dangerous, so fascinating, to a temperament like yours. It is a false and foolish fancy. Can you not trust me as a physician when I tell you so?"

So of course I said no more on that score, and we went to sleep before long. He thought I was asleep first, but I wasn't, and lay there for hours trying to decide whether that front pattern and the back pattern really did more together or separately.

On a pattern like this, by daylight, there is a lack of sequence, a defiance of law, that is a constant irritant to a normal mind.

The color is hideous enough, and unreliable enough, and infuriating enough, but the pattern is torturing.

You think you have mastered it, but just as you get well underway in following, it turns a back-somersault and there you are. It slaps you in the face, knocks you down, and tramples upon you. It is like a bad dream.

The outside pattern is a florid arabesque, reminding one of a fungus. If you can imagine a toadstool in joints, an interminable string of toadstools, budding and sprouting in endless convolutions—why, that is something like it.

That is, sometimes!

There is one marked peculiarity about this paper, a thing nobody seems to notice but myself, and that is that it changes as the light changes.

When the sun shoots in through the east window—I always watch for that first long, straight ray—it changes so quickly that I never can quite believe it.

That is why I watch it always.

By moonlight—the moon shines in all night when there is a moon—I wouldn't know it was the same paper.

At night in any kind of light, in twilight, candlelight, lamplight, and worst of all by moonlight, it becomes bars! The outside pattern I mean, and the woman behind it is as plain as can be.

I didn't realize for a long time what the thing was that showed behind, that dim sub-pattern, but now I am quite sure it is a woman.

By daylight she is subdued, quiet. I fancy it is the pattern that keeps her so still. It is so puzzling. It keeps me quiet by the hour.

I lie down ever so much now. John says it is good for me, and to sleep all I can.

Indeed he started the habit by making me lie down for an hour after each meal.

It is a very bad habit I am convinced, for you see I don't sleep.

And that cultivates deceit, for I don't tell them I'm awake—O no!

The fact is I am getting a little afraid of John.

He seems very queer sometimes, and even Jennie has an inexplicable look.

It strikes me occasionally, just as a scientific hypothesis,—that perhaps it is the paper!

I have watched John when he did not know I was looking, and come into the room suddenly on the most innocent excuses, and I've caught him several times *looking at the paper!* And Jennie too. I caught Jennie with her hand on it once.

She didn't know I was in the room, and when I asked her in a quiet, a very quiet voice, with the most restrained manner possible, what she was doing with the paper—she turned around as if she had been caught stealing, and looked quite angry—asked me why I should frighten her so!

Then she said that the paper stained everything it touched, that she had found yellow smooches on all my clothes and John's, and she wished we would be more careful!

Did not that sound innocent? But I know she was studying that pattern, and I am determined that nobody shall find it out but myself!

Life is very much more exciting now than it used to be. You see I have something more to expect, to look forward to, to watch. I really do eat better, and am more quiet than I was.

John is so pleased to see me improve! He laughed a little the other day, and said I seemed to be flourishing in spite of my wall-paper.

I turned it off with a laugh. I had no intention of telling him it was *because* of the wall-paper—he would make fun of me. He might even want to take me away.

I don't want to leave now until I have found it out. There is a week more, and I think that will be enough.

I'm feeling ever so much better! I don't sleep much at night, for it is so interesting to watch developments; but I sleep a good deal in the daytime.

In the daytime it is tiresome and perplexing.

There are always new shoots on the fungus, and new shades of yellow all over it. I cannot keep count of them, though I have tried conscientiously.

It is the strangest yellow, that wall-paper! It makes me think of all the yellow things I ever saw—not beautiful ones like buttercups, but old foul, bad yellow things.

But there is something else about that paper—the smell! I noticed it the moment we came into the room, but with so much air and sun it was not bad. Now we have had a week of fog and rain, and whether the windows are open or not, the smell is here.

It creeps all over the house.

I find it hovering in the dining-room, skulking in the parlor, hiding in the hall, lying in wait for me on the stairs.

It gets into my hair.

Even when I go to ride, if I turn my head suddenly and surprise it—there is that smell!

Such a peculiar odor, too! I have spent hours in trying to analyze it, to find what it smelled like.

It is not bad—at first, and very gentle, but quite the subtlest, most enduring odor I ever met.

In this damp weather it is awful, I wake up in the night and find it hanging over me.

It used to disturb me at first. I thought seriously of burning the house—to reach the smell.

But now I am used to it. The only thing I can think of that it is like is the *color* of the paper! A yellow smell.

There is a very funny mark on this wall, low down, near the mopboard. A streak that runs round the room. It goes behind every piece of furniture, except the bed, a long, straight, even *smooch,* as if it had been rubbed over and over.

I wonder how it was done and who did it, and what they did it for. Round and round and round—round and round and round—it makes me dizzy!

I really have discovered something at last.

Through watching so much at night, when it changes so, I have finally found out.

The front pattern *does* move—and no wonder! The woman behind shakes it!

Sometimes I think there are a great many women behind, and sometimes only one, and she crawls around fast, and her crawling shakes it all over.

Then in the very bright spots she keeps still, and in the very shady spots she just takes hold of the bars and shakes them hard.

And she is all the time trying to climb through. But nobody could climb through that pattern—it strangles so; I think that is why it has so many heads.

They get through, and then the pattern strangles them off and turns them upside down, and makes their eyes white!

If those heads were covered or taken off it would not be half so bad.

I think that woman gets out in the daytime!

And I'll tell you why—privately—I've seen her!

I can see her out of every one of my windows!

It is the same woman, I know, for she is always creeping, and most women do not creep by daylight.

I see her in that long shaded lane, creeping up and down. I see her in those dark grape arbors, creeping all around the garden.

I see her on that long road under the trees, creeping along, and when a carriage comes she hides under the blackberry vines.

I don't blame her a bit. It must be very humiliating to be caught creeping by daylight!

I always lock the door when I creep by daylight. I can't do it at night, for I know John would suspect something at once.

And John is so queer now, that I don't want to irritate him. I wish he would take another room! Besides, I don't want anybody to get that woman out at night but myself.

I often wonder if I could see her out of all the windows at once.

But, turn as fast as I can, I can only see out of one at one time.

And though I always see her, she *may* be able to creep faster than I can turn!

I have watched her sometimes away off in the open country, creeping as fast as a cloud shadow in a high wind.

If only that top pattern could be gotten off from the under one! I mean to try it, little by little.

I have found out another funny thing, but I shan't tell it this time! It does not do to trust people too much.

There are only two more days to get this paper off, and I believe John is beginning to notice. I don't like the look in his eyes.

And I heard him ask Jennie a lot of professional questions about me. She had a very good report to give.

She said I slept a good deal in the daytime.

John knows I don't sleep very well at night, for all I'm so quiet!

He asked me all sorts of questions, too, and pretended to be very loving and kind.

As if I couldn't see through him!

Still, I don't wonder he acts so, sleeping under this paper for three months.

It only interests me, but I feel sure John and Jennie are secretly affected by it.

Hurrah! This is the last day, but it is enough. John to stay in town over night, and won't be out until this evening.

Jennie wanted to sleep with me—the sly thing! but I told her I should undoubtedly rest better for a night all alone.

That was clever, for really I wasn't alone a bit! As soon as it was moonlight and that poor thing began to crawl and shake the pattern, I got up and ran to help her.

I pulled and she shook, I shook and she pulled, and before morning we had peeled off yards of that paper.

A strip about as high as my head and half around the room.

And then when the sun came and that awful pattern began to laugh at me, I declared I would finish it to-day!

We go away to-morrow, and they are moving all my furniture down again to leave things as they were before.

Jennie looked at the wall in amazement, but I told her merrily that I did it out of pure spite at the vicious thing.

She laughed and said she wouldn't mind doing it herself, but I must not get tired.

How she betrayed herself that time!

But I am here, and no person touches this paper but me,—not *alive!*

She tried to get me out of the room—it was too patent! But I said it was so quiet and empty and clean now that I believed I would lie down again and sleep all I could; and not to wake me even for dinner—I would call when I woke.

So now she is gone, and the servants are gone, and the things are gone, and there is nothing left but that great bedstead nailed down, with the canvas mattress we found on it.

We shall sleep downstairs to-night, and take the boat home to-morrow.

I quite enjoy the room, now it is bare again.

How those children did tear about here!

This bedstead is fairly gnawed!

But I must get to work.

I have locked the door and thrown the key down into the front path.

I don't want to go out, and I don't want to have anybody come in, till John comes.

I want to astonish him.

I've got a rope up here than even Jennie did not find. If that woman does get out, and tries to get away, I can tie her!

But I forgot I could not reach far without anything to stand on!

This bed will *not* move!

I tried to lift and push it until I was lame, and then I got so angry I bit off a little piece at one corner—but it hurt my teeth.

Then I peeled off all the paper I could reach standing on the floor. It sticks horribly and the pattern just enjoys it! All those strangled heads and bulbous eyes and waddling fungus growths just shriek with derision!

I am getting angry enough to do something desperate. To jump out of the window would be admirable exercise, but the bars are too strong even to try.

Besides I wouldn't do it. Of course not. I know well enough that a step like that is improper and might be misconstrued.

I don't like to *look* out of the windows even—there are so many of these creeping women, and they creep so fast.

I wonder if they all come out of that wall-paper as I did?

But I am securely fastened now by my well-hidden rope—you don't get *me* out in the road there!

I suppose I shall have to get back behind the pattern when it comes night, and that is hard!

It is so pleasant to be out in this great room and creep around as I please!

I don't want to go outside. I won't, even if Jennie asks me to.

For outside you have to creep on the ground, and everything is green instead of yellow.

But here I can creep smoothly on the floor, and my shoulder just fits in that long smooch around the wall, so I cannot lose my way.

Why there's John at the door!

It is no use, young man, you can't open it!

How he does call and pound!

Now he's crying for an axe.

It would be a shame to break down that beautiful door!

"John dear!" said I in the gentlest voice, "the key is down by the front steps, under a plantain leaf!"

That silenced him for a few moments.

Then he said—very quietly indeed, "Open the door, my darling!"

"I can't," said I. "The key is down by the front door under a plantain leaf!"

And then I said it again, several times, very gently and slowly, and said it so often that he had to go and see, and he got it of course, and came in. He stopped short by the door.

"What is the matter?" he cried. "For God's sake, what are you doing!"

I kept on creeping just the same, but I looked at him over my shoulder.

"I've got out at last," said I, "in spite of you and Jane? And I've pulled off most of the paper, so you can't put me back!"

Now why should that man have fainted? But he did, and right across my path by the wall, so that I had to creep over him every time!

1892

Henry James
(1843–1916)

According to Edith Wharton, Henry James "was greater than his works, much greater—and that is saying a good deal." The statement is generous, the tribute to the man heightened by an acknowledgment of the quality of his work. But the generosity of Wharton's appraisal has not found easy consensus in the twentieth century. Indeed, few writers have aroused admiration and antagonism in such measure as has Henry James. At times his monolithic presence has diverted attention from his work and converted his importance into the appearance of stuffy self-importance. Some readers attending to the work have been critical of James's frequent portrayal of naïve, even coarse, Americans among culti- vated Europeans, especially in the light of his own expatriation; others claim to have stum- bled through his dense fiction as they would through a cluttered Victorian parlor; still others have detected a studied and dogmatic quality in the nonfictional prose that makes a condescending fussbudget of the *doyen* of American fiction. Despite the difficulties James poses, however, he remains a formidable novelist and theoretician with a substantial claim to having revolutionized the novel in English.

Henry James, Jr., was born in New York City in 1843 into a family that enjoyed upper middle-class prosperity as the result of shrewd land purchases by Henry's paternal grandfa- ther, an Irish immigrant. James's father, Henry, Sr., was an energetic thinker and writer with a cork leg, whose eccentricity was to some extent balanced by the quiet stability of Mary Walsh James, the novelist's mother. The restlessness of Henry, Sr., led him to pro- mote the theology of the Swedish mystic Emanuel Swedenborg without ever bringing the recognition Henry, Sr., sought through his writing. And his roving spirit and independent pedagogical interests led him to move his family frequently between Europe and various homes in the United states in search of educational opportunities for his children. Young James thus developed an early familiarity with European society and the American com- munity in Europe. His older brother, William, was to attain prominence as a psychologist and become the leading exponent of pragmatism as an ethical and philosophical position. James also had two younger brothers, Wilkinson and Robertson, whose adult lives were adventurous but undistinguished; and a sister, Alice, a highly intelligent woman best known for her lifelong neurasthenia, a type of neurosis Henry and, to an even greater degree, William seem to have shared.

James's reminiscences, published as *A Small Boy and Others* (1913) and *Notes of a Son and Brother* (1914), describe a socially secure childhood, rich in privileged associations. He remembers, for example, the guest bedroom referred to as "Mr. Emerson's room," an avuncular William Thackeray admiring the buttons on his jacket, and an occasion when Washington Irving delivered the news that Margaret Fuller had just drowned. As a young boy, James demonstrated a consuming interest in the family library, especially in the works of Charles Dickens and in books of engravings.

James was always interested in art, and he and William took painting lessons together, but Henry soon recognized that his own gifts lay elsewhere. It is likely, however, that his concern for the visual affected his characteristically detailed depiction of fictional scenes, commonly transmitted by highly observant narrators. One of his most important early friendships was that of the American painter, John LaFarge, who encouraged James to write. The James family spent time in Newport, Rhode Island, and eventually settled in Cambridge, Massachusetts. Henry spent a year at a Swiss engineering school and a year at Harvard Law School, half-heartedly conceding to parental attempts to direct him toward a career, while he grew in the conviction that writing was his intended profession. His first published pieces, an anonymous tale in the *Continental Monthly* and a book review for *The North American Review* (edited by Charles Eliot Norton and James Russell Lowell), both appeared in 1864. He began to write travel articles as well as reviews and short fiction, publishing frequently in the *Atlantic Monthly*. He enjoyed a lifelong friendship with the editor of the *Atlantic*, William Dean Howells. Although he would come to see Howells as a novelist of limited power and scope, James continued to respect Howells for his generous encouragement of new writers. Together, James and Howells are now viewed as leading figures of American realism.

James spent a year alone in Europe from 1869 to 1870. He toured England and stayed for a time in London, where family connections permitted him access to pleasant society. He traveled to the continent, where he found France and Italy, especially Florence, particularly congenial. Indeed, his enthusiasm for Italy marked the beginning of a permanent affection for that country. While abroad he was devastated to hear of the death of his cousin, Minny Temple, to whom he may have been romantically attracted and for whom he felt tremendous admiration. Even in his immediate grief, he recognized that Minny would survive in his imagination. The later characterizations of Isabel Archer in *The Portrait of a Lady* (1881) and especially Millie Theale in *The Wings of the Dove* (1902) owe much to James's perception of Minny as a prototypical American girl—bright, sensitive, and refined yet irrepressibly spirited and gay.

James's awareness of himself as an author developed during this early stay in Europe: he quite consciously realized that he was gathering material for future writing, and he expressed a commitment to earning an income from his pen. When he came back to his family in Cambridge, he spent two years writing articles and short fiction for magazines— a period he afterward referred to as "brooding exile," marking time until he could return to Europe. That opportunity came when he was asked to accompany his sister and their aunt on a European tour in 1872. He traveled as a working writer, submitting travel sketches to the *Nation* during his stay. James remained in Europe after the tour ended, and he continued to write for the *Atlantic* and *Galaxy*. In 1875 he published *Transatlantic Sketches* and the short novel *A Passionate Pilgrim* before returning to Cambridge, Massachusetts, in July of that year. In October he set sail once again for Europe and stayed for a time in Paris, where he frequently visited with his fellow novelists Ivan Turgenev, Gustave Flaubert, Alphonse Daudet, and Émile Zola. James moved on to London and, with rare interruptions, made England his home for the rest of his life.

James's fiction is usually divided into three periods, the first inaugurated with the publication of *Roderick Hudson* in 1876. During this early period James wrote *The American* (1877), *The Europeans* (1878), *Daisy Miller* (1879), *Washington Square* (1881), and *The Portrait of a Lady*. The promising note struck by *Roderick Hudson*, the story of an American sculptor in Italy, would sound throughout James's career: the situation of the American in Europe and the contrast between American and European temperaments and moral codes recur in his fiction. On the basis of this contrast, some readers have imputed to James a snobbish rejection of a native land he regarded as provincial and a wish to acquire the sophistication and culture he identified with Europeans; others note that the strength and innocence exhibited by his American characters emerge as the ultimate values of his fiction.

Like Honoré de Balzac—whom he regarded as his most important model—James was an astute social chronicler. Although E. M. Forster, an English novelist, has argued that the refined detail of James's social observations becomes trivial in the absence of more profound concerns, it is these very details that yield characters such as Madame Merle in *The Portrait of a Lady* and Lambert Strether in *The Ambassadors* and ultimately such themes as the unlived life and the negating power of self-absorbtion. Except for *Daisy Miller,* which attracted international attention to its author, James was never a bestselling writer, but he developed a devoted audience among critics and readers and was able to earn a living from his writing. He also enjoyed the society of the artistic and intellectual circles of his day.

James is as important a theoretician of fiction as he is a novelist. In addition to an appreciative critical biography of Nathaniel Hawthorne (1879) and *French Poets and Novelists* (1878), his essay "The Art of Fiction" (1888) is a highly significant statement of fictional principles. He wrote unique prefaces to the New York edition of his works, in each providing information about the "germ" of a novel and compelling insight into its

*The frontispiece of the first
edition of Henry James's*
Daisy Miller.

composition. Selections from his voluminous notebooks have been edited and published since his death, and many of his sketches, reviews, and other essays have been published in various collections. James is considered a master of psychological realism and is always concerned with nuance of character and the subtleties of motivation and perception. For their mastery of these aspects of fiction writing, he admired George Eliot and, above all, the French and Russian realists Balzac, Flaubert, Zola, and Turgenev. It was his aim to refine and order the form of fiction to accommodate the exact and plenteous detail of these writers.

James's middle period is marked by *The Bostonians* (1886), *The Princess Casamassima* (1886), and *The Tragic Muse* (1889). At this time he put off novel-writing to write for the theater but found virtually no success. In 1895 he returned to fiction, writing tales and novellas, such as *What Maisie Knew* (1897), *The Spoils of Poynton* (1897), and the psychological thriller "The Turn of the Screw" (1898). Critics generally point out that the scenic techniques of the fiction he wrote at this time are informed by the dramatic method he had studied in the previous five years. The poet Stephen Spender claims that James revolutionized the modern novel with his manner of relating "scene" to the emotional development of the characters. In 1898 James purchased Lamb House in Rye, Sussex, and continued to enjoy an active social life as the intimate of such prominent figures as the American painter John Singer Sargent and Edith Wharton.

Out of the final period of James's writing came such accomplished tales as "The Beast in the Jungle" (1903) and "The Jolly Corner" (1906) as well as the novels *The Wings of the Dove*, *The Ambassadors* (1903), and *The Golden Bowl* (1904). (He left unfinished at his death in 1916 *The Ivory Tower* and *The Sense of the Past,* both published a year later.) His most significant technical innovations in these later novels have to do with narrative point of view; the editor Percy Lubbock has noted the consummate craftsmanship of *The Ambassadors,* for example, which enables James to convey the details of the story through the perspective of a single character while depicting the expanding perceptions of that character. James's technical progress in this direction served as a model for James Joyce, Virginia Woolf, and other writers who would go on to employ the stream-of-consciousness method of narration. The waggish observation that "Henry James chewed more than he could bite off" is a recurrent criticism of this late fiction, which is known for its fulsome prose, its difficult, sometimes obscure, grammatical constructions, and its meticulous detail. But James's attention to language derives from a profound concern that the reader know his characters in all their complexity and experience his fictional world in the fullest possible way.

When Great Britain was drawn into World War I, James became a British citizen as a gesture of loyalty to his adopted country and in despair over what he perceived as America's failure to support Britain's defense. He was granted the Royal Order of Merit on New Year's Day, 1916—the only novelist beside George Meredith and Thomas Hardy to have been so honored. Henry James remains one of the most productive and influential writers in the history of the novel. Like Balzac and Dickens, he has left a valuable record of an age that has since disappeared. Just as importantly, he has directed writers of fiction to a closer scrutiny of their craft and has clarified the critical reader's assessment of how social and psychological reality can be presented in fiction. To judge by the quality of his achievement as theoretician and writer of fiction, his claims as an artist rest secure.

Suggested Readings: *The Novels and Tales of Henry James* (New York edition), 26 vols., 1907–1917, rpt. 1962–1965. *The Art of the Novel: Critical Prefaces,* ed. R. Blackmur, 1943. *The Notebooks of Henry James,* ed. F. O. Matthiessen and K. Murdock, 1947. *Stories of the Supernatural,* ed. L. Edel, 1949. *Autobiography,* 3 vols., ed. F. W. Dupee, 1956. *The Complete Tales of Henry James,* 12 vols., ed. L. Edel, 1962–1965. *The Letters of Henry James,* 4 vols., ed L. Edel, 1975–1984. L. Edel, *Henry James,* 5 vols., 1953–1972. Q. Anderson, *The American Henry James,* 1957. C. Wegelin, *The Image of Europe in Henry James,* 1958. R. Poirer, *The Comic Sense of Henry James: A Study of the Early Novels,* 1960. J. Ward, *The Imagination of Disaster: Evil in the Fiction of Henry James,* 1961. D. Krook, *The Ordeal of Consciousness in Henry James,* 1962. L. Holland, *The Expense of Vision: Essays on the Craft of Henry James,* 1964. M. Banta, *Henry James and the Occult,* 1972. O. Cargill, *The Novels of Henry James,* 1975. W. R. Veeder, *The Lesson of the Master,* 1975. J. Rowe, *Henry Adams and Henry James,* 1976. R. Yeazell, *Language and Knowledge in the Late Novels of Henry James,* 1976. D. Fogel, *Henry James and the Structure of the Romantic Imagination,* 1981. M. E. Jacobson, *Henry James and the Mass Market,* 1983. M. Seltzer, *Henry James and the Art of Power,* 1984. L. Edel, *Henry James: A Life,* 1985. D. McWhirter, *Desire and Love in Henry James: A Study of the Late Novels,* 1989.

Texts Used: *Daisy Miller* and "The Real Thing": *The Novels and Tales of Henry James* (New York edition), Vol. XVIII, 1909. "The Beast in the Jungle" and "The Jolly Corner": *The Novels and Tales,* Vol. XVII, 1909. "The Art of Fiction": *Partial Portraits,* 1911.

DAISY MILLER*

I

At the little town of Vevey, in Switzerland, there is a particularly comfortable hotel; there are indeed many hotels, since the entertainment of tourists is the busi-

* First published in *Cornhill Magazine* in 1878 and revised by James to this version in 1909.

ness of the place, which, as many travellers will remember, is seated upon the edge of a remarkably blue lake[1]—a lake that it behoves every tourist to visit. The shore of the lake presents an unbroken array of establishments of this order, of every category, from the "grand hotel" of the newest fashion, with a chalk-white front, a hundred balconies, and a dozen flags flying from its roof, to the small Swiss pension[2] of an elder day, with its name inscribed in German-looking lettering upon a pink or yellow wall and an awkward summer-house in the angle of the garden. One of the hotels at Vevey, however, is famous, even classical, being distinguished from many of its upstart neighbours by an air both of luxury and of maturity. In this region, through the month of June, American travellers are extremely numerous; it may be said indeed that Vevey assumes at that time some of the characteristics of an American watering-place. There are sights and sounds that evoke a vision, an echo, of Newport and Saratoga.[3] There is a flitting hither and thither of "stylish" young girls, a rustling of muslin flounces, a rattle of dance-music in the morning hours, a sound of high-pitched voices at all times. You receive an impression of these things at the excellent inn of the "Trois Couronnes,"[4] and are transported in fancy to the Ocean House or to Congress Hall.[5] But at the "Trois Couronnes," it must be added, there are other features much at variance with these suggestions: neat German waiters who look like secretaries of legation; Russian princesses sitting in the garden; little Polish boys walking about, held by the hand, with their governors; a view of the snowy crest of the Dent du Midi and the picturesque towers of the Castle of Chillon.[6]

I hardly know whether it was the analogies or the differences that were uppermost in the mind of a young American, who, two or three years ago, sat in the garden of the "Trois Couronnes," looking about him rather idly at some of the graceful objects I have mentioned. It was a beautiful summer morning, and in whatever fashion the young American looked at things they must have seemed to him charming. He had come from Geneva the day before, by the little steamer, to see his aunt, who was staying at the hotel—Geneva having been for a long time his place of residence. But his aunt had a headache—his aunt had almost always a headache—and she was now shut up in her room smelling camphor,[7] so that he was at liberty to wander about. He was some seven-and-twenty years of age; when his friends spoke of him they usually said that he was at Geneva "studying." When his enemies spoke of him they said—but after all he had no enemies: he was extremely amiable and generally liked. What I should say is simply that when certain persons spoke of him they conveyed that the reason of his spending so much time at Geneva was that he was extremely devoted to a lady who lived there—a foreign lady, a person older than himself. Very few Americans—truly I think none—had ever seen this lady, about whom there were some singular stories. But Winterbourne had an old attachment for the little capital of Calvinism;[8] he had been put to school there as a boy and had afterwards even gone, on trial—trial of the grey old "Academy" on the steep and stony hillside—to college there; circumstances which had led to his forming a great many youthful friendships. Many of these he had kept, and they were a source of great satisfaction to him.

---

[1] Lake Geneva.   [2] A small residential hotel.
[3] Fashionable nineteenth-century resorts in Rhode Island and New York, respectively.
[4] "Three Crowns" (French).   [5] Hotels at Newport and Saratoga.
[6] A peak of Mont Blanc, in the Swiss Alps; a medieval castle on Lake Geneva.
[7] A fragrant compound used as a mild analgesic.
[8] The religious doctrine of the Protestant reformer John Calvin (1509–1564), who lived in Geneva from 1541 to 1564.

After knocking at his aunt's door and learning that she was indisposed he had taken a walk about the town and then he had come in to his breakfast. He had now finished that repast, but was enjoying a small cup of coffee which had been served him on a little table in the garden by one of the waiters who looked like *attachés*.[9] At last he finished his coffee and lit a cigarette. Presently a small boy came walking along the path—an urchin of nine or ten. The child, who was diminutive for his years, had an aged expression of countenance, a pale complexion and sharp little features. He was dressed in knickerbockers and had red stockings that displayed his poor little spindle-shanks;[10] he also wore a brilliant red cravat. He carried in his hand a long alpenstock,[11] the sharp point of which he thrust into everything he approached—the flower-beds, the garden-benches, the trains of the ladies' dresses. In front of Winterbourne he paused, looking at him with a pair of bright and penetrating little eyes.

"Will you give me a lump of sugar?" he asked in a small sharp hard voice—a voice immature and yet somehow not young.

Winterbourne glanced at the light table near him, on which his coffee-service rested, and saw that several morsels of sugar remained. "Yes, you may take one," he answered; "but I don't think too much sugar good for little boys."

This little boy stepped forward and carefully selected three of the coveted fragments, two of which he buried in the pocket of his knickerbockers, depositing the other as promptly in another place. He poked his alpenstock, lance-fashion, into Winterbourne's bench and tried to crack the lump of sugar with his teeth.

"Oh blazes; it's har-r-d!" he exclaimed, divesting vowel and consonants, pertinently enough, of any taint of softness.

Winterbourne had immediately gathered that he might have the honour of claiming him as a countryman. "Take care you don't hurt your teeth," he said paternally.

"I haven't got any teeth to hurt. They've all come out. I've only got seven teeth. Mother counted them last night, and one came out right afterwards. She said she'd slap me if any more came out. I can't help it. It's this old Europe. It's the climate that makes them come out. In America they didn't come out. It's these hotels."

Winterbourne was much amused. "If you eat three lumps of sugar your mother will certainly slap you," he ventured.

"She's got to give me some candy then," rejoined his young interlocutor. "I can't get any candy here—any American candy. American candy's the best candy."

"And are American little boys the best little boys?" Winterbourne asked.

"I don't know. *I'm* an American boy," said the child.

"I see you're one of the best!" the young man laughed.

"Are you an American man?" pursued this vivacious infant. And then on his friend's affirmative reply, "American men are the best," he declared with assurance.

His companion thanked him for the compliment, and the child, who had now got astride of his alpenstock, stood looking about him while he attacked another lump of sugar. Winterbourne wondered if he himself had been like this in his infancy, for he had been brought to Europe at about the same age.

---

[9] Minor embassy officials (French).   [10] Skinny legs; a cravat is a tie.
[11] A pointed staff used in mountain climbing.

"Here comes my sister!" cried his young compatriot. "She's an American girl, you bet!"

Winterbourne looked along the path and saw a beautiful young lady advancing. "American girls are the best girls," he thereupon cheerfully remarked to his visitor.

"My sister ain't the best!" the child promptly returned. "She's always blowing[12] at me."

"I imagine that's your fault, not hers," said Winterbourne. The young lady meanwhile had drawn near. She was dressed in white muslin, with a hundred frills and flounces and knots of pale-coloured ribbon. Bareheaded, she balanced in her hand a large parasol with a deep border of embroidery; and she was strikingly, admirably pretty. "How pretty they are!" thought our friend, who straightened himself in his seat as if he were ready to rise.

The young lady paused in front of his bench, near the parapet of the garden, which overlooked the lake. The small boy had now converted his alpenstock into a vaulting-pole, by the aid of which he was springing about in the gravel and kicking it up not a little. "Why Randolph," she freely began, "what *are* you doing?"

"I'm going up the Alps!" cried Randolph. "This is the way!" And he gave another extravagant jump, scattering the pebbles about Winterbourne's ears.

"That's the way they come down," said Winterbourne.

"He's an American man!" proclaimed Randolph in his harsh little voice.

The young lady gave no heed to this circumstance, but looked straight at her brother. "Well, I guess you'd better be quiet," she simply observed.

It seemed to Winterbourne that he had been in a manner presented. He got up and stepped slowly toward the charming creature, throwing away his cigarette. "This little boy and I have made acquaintance," he said with great civility. In Geneva, as he had been perfectly aware, a young man wasn't at liberty to speak to a young unmarried lady save under certain rarely-occurring conditions; but here at Vevey what conditions could be better than these?—a pretty American girl coming to stand in front of you in a garden with all the confidence in life. This pretty American girl, whatever that might prove, on hearing Winterbourne's observation simply glanced at him; she then turned her head and looked over the parapet, at the lake and the opposite mountains. He wondered whether he had gone too far, but decided that he must gallantly advance rather than retreat. While he was thinking of something else to say the young lady turned again to the little boy, whom she addressed quite as if they were alone together. "I should like to know where you got that pole."

"I bought it!" Randolph shouted.

"You don't mean to say you're going to take it to Italy!"

"Yes, I'm going to take it t' Italy!" the child rang out.

She glanced over the front of her dress and smoothed out a knot or two of ribbon. Then she gave her sweet eyes to the prospect again. "Well, I guess you'd better leave it somewhere," she dropped after a moment.

"Are you going to Italy?" Winterbourne now decided very respectfully to enquire.

She glanced at him with lovely remoteness. "Yes, sir," she then replied. And she said nothing more.

"And are you—a—thinking of the Simplon?"[13] he pursued with a slight drop of assurance.

---

[12] Screaming.   [13] A mountain pass between Switzerland and Italy.

"I don't know," she said. "I suppose it's some mountain. Randolph, what mountain are we thinking of?"

"Thinking of?"—the boy stared.

"Why going right over."

"Going to where?" he demanded.

"Why right down to Italy"—Winterbourne felt vague emulations.

"I don't know," said Randolph. "I don't want to go t' Italy. I want to go to America."

"Oh Italy's a beautiful place!" the young man laughed.

"Can you get candy there?" Randolph asked of all the echoes.

"I hope not," said his sister. "I guess you've had enough candy, and mother thinks so too."

"I haven't had any for ever so long—for a hundred weeks!" cried the boy, still jumping about.

The young lady inspected her flounces and smoothed her ribbons again; and Winterbourne presently risked an observation on the beauty of the view. He was ceasing to be in doubt, for he had begun to perceive that she was really not in the least embarrassed. She might be cold, she might be austere, she might even be prim; for that was apparently—he had already so generalised—what the most "distant" American girls did: they came and planted themselves straight in front of you to show how rigidly unapproachable they were. There hadn't been the slightest flush in her fresh fairness however; so that she was clearly neither offended nor fluttered. Only she was composed—he had seen that before too—of charming little parts that didn't match and that made no *ensemble*;[14] and if she looked another way when he spoke to her, and seemed not particularly to hear him, this was simply her habit, her manner, the result of her having no idea whatever of "form" (with such a tell-tale appendage as Randolph where in the world would she have got it?) in any such connexion. As he talked a little more and pointed out some of the objects of interest in the view, with which she appeared wholly unacquainted, she gradually, none the less, gave him more of the benefit of her attention; and then he saw that act unqualified by the faintest shadow of reserve. It wasn't however what would have been called a "bold" front that she presented, for her expression was as decently limpid as the very cleanest water. Her eyes were the very prettiest conceivable, and indeed Winterbourne hadn't for a long time seen anything prettier than his fair countrywoman's various features—her complexion, her nose, her ears, her teeth. He took a great interest generally in that range of effects and was addicted to noting and, as it were, recording them; so that in regard to this young lady's face he made several observations. It wasn't at all insipid, yet at the same time wasn't pointedly—what point, on earth, could she ever make?—expressive; and though it offered such a collection of small finenesses and neatnesses he mentally accused it—very forgivingly—of a want of finish. He thought nothing more likely than that its wearer would have had her own experience of the action of her charms, as she would certainly have acquired a resulting confidence; but even should she depend on this for her main amusement her bright sweet superficial little visage gave out neither mockery nor irony. Before long it became clear that, however these things might be, she was much disposed to conversation. She remarked to Winterbourne that they were going to Rome for the winter—she and her mother and Randolph. She asked him if he was a "real American"; she wouldn't have taken him for one; he seemed more like a German—this flower was

[marginal handwritten note: beauty of the environment adds to her beauty]

---

[14] Complementary parts that make up a whole, producing a single effect (French).

gathered as from a large field of comparison—especially when he spoke. Winterbourne, laughing, answered that he had met Germans who spoke like Americans, but not, so far as he remembered, any American with the resemblance she noted. Then he asked her if she mightn't be more at ease should she occupy the bench he had just quitted. She answered that she liked hanging round, but she none the less resignedly, after a little, dropped to the bench. She told him she was from New York State—"if you know where that is"; but our friend really quickened this current by catching hold of her small slippery brother and making him stand a few minutes by his side.

"Tell me your honest name, my boy." So he artfully proceeded.

In response to which the child was indeed unvarnished truth. "Randolph C. Miller. And I'll tell you hers." With which he levelled his alpenstock at his sister.

"You had better wait till you're asked!" said this young lady quite at her leisure.

"I should like very much to know *your* name," Winterbourne made free to reply.

"Her name's Daisy Miller!" cried the urchin.

"But that ain't her real name; that ain't her name on her cards."[15]

"It's a pity you haven't got one of my cards!" Miss Miller quite as naturally remarked.

"Her real name's Annie P. Miller," the boy went on.

It seemed, all amazingly, to do her good. "Ask him *his* now"—and she indicated their friend.

But to this point Randolph seemed perfectly indifferent; he continued to supply information with regard to his own family. "My father's name is Ezra B. Miller. My father ain't in Europe—he's in a better place than Europe." Winterbourne for a moment supposed this the manner in which the child had been taught to intimate that Mr. Miller had been removed to the sphere of celestial rewards. But Randolph immediately added: "My father's in Schenectady. He's got a big business. My father's rich, you bet."

"Well!" ejaculated Miss Miller, lowering her parasol and looking at the embroidered border. Winterbourne presently released the child, who departed, dragging his alpenstock along the path. "He don't like Europe," said the girl as with an artless instinct for historic truth. "He wants to go back."

"To Schenectady, you mean?"

"Yes, he wants to go right home. He hasn't got any boys here. There's one boy here, but he always goes round with a teacher. They won't let him play."

"And your brother hasn't any teacher?" Winterbourne enquired.

It tapped, at a touch, the spring of confidence. "Mother thought of getting him one—to travel round with us. There was a lady told her of a very good teacher; an American lady—perhaps you know her—Mrs. Sanders. I think she came from Boston. She told her of this teacher, and we thought of getting him to travel round with us. But Randolph said he didn't want a teacher travelling round with us. He said he wouldn't have lessons when he was in the cars.[16] And we *are* in the cars about half the time. There was an English lady we met in the cars—I think her name was Miss Featherstone; perhaps you know her. She wanted to know why I didn't give Randolph lessons—give him 'instruction,' she called it. I guess he could give me more instruction than I could give him. He's very smart."

"Yes," said Winterbourne; "he seems very smart."

---

[15] Calling cards, much like today's business cards.   [16] Railroad cars.

"Mother's going to get a teacher for him as soon as we get t' Italy. Can you get good teachers in Italy?"

"Very good, I should think," Winterbourne hastened to reply.

"Or else she's going to find some school. He ought to learn some more. He's only nine. He's going to college." And in this way Miss Miller continued to converse upon the affairs of her family and upon other topics. She sat there with her extremely pretty hands, ornamented with very brilliant rings, folded in her lap, and with her pretty eyes now resting upon those of Winterbourne, now wandering over the garden, the people who passed before her and the beautiful view. She addressed her new acquaintance as if she had known him a long time. He found it very pleasant. It was many years since he had heard a young girl talk so much. It might have been said of this wandering maiden who had come and sat down beside him upon a bench that she chattered. She was very quiet, she sat in a charming tranquil attitude; but her lips and her eyes were constantly moving. She had a soft slender agreeable voice, and her tone was distinctly sociable. She gave Winterbourne a report of her movements and intentions, and those of her mother and brother, in Europe, and enumerated in particular the various hotels at which they had stopped. "That English lady in the cars," she said—"Miss Featherstone—asked me if we didn't all live in hotels in America. I told her I had never been in so many hotels in my life as since I came to Europe. I've never seen so many—it's nothing but hotels." But Miss Miller made this remark with no querulous accent; she appeared to be in the best humour with everything. She declared that the hotels were very good when once you got used to their ways and that Europe was perfectly entrancing. She wasn't disappointed—not a bit. Perhaps it was because she had heard so much about it before. She had ever so many intimate friends who had been there ever so many times, and that way she had got thoroughly posted. And then she had had ever so many dresses and things from Paris. Whenever she put on a Paris dress she felt as if she were in Europe.

"It was a kind of a wishing-cap," Winterbourne smiled.

"Yes," said Miss Miller at once and without examining this analogy; "it always made me wish I was here. But I needn't have done that for dresses. I'm sure they send all the pretty ones to America; you see the most frightful things here. The only thing I don't like," she proceeded, "is the society. There ain't any society— or if there is I don't know where it keeps itself. Do you? I suppose there's some society somewhere, but I haven't seen anything of it. I'm very fond of society and I've always had plenty of it. I don't mean only in Schenectady, but in New York. I used to go to New York every winter. In New York I had lots of society. Last winter I had seventeen dinners given me, and three of them were by gentlemen," added Daisy Miller. "I've more friends in New York than in Schenectady—more gentlemen friends; and more young lady friends too," she resumed in a moment. She paused again for an instant; she was looking at Winterbourne with all her prettiness in her frank gay eyes and in her clear rather uniform smile. "I've always had," she said, "a great deal of gentlemen's society."

Poor Winterbourne was amused and perplexed—above all he was charmed. He had never yet heard a young girl express herself in just this fashion; never at least save in cases where to say such things was to have at the same time some rather complicated consciousness about them. And yet was he to accuse Miss Daisy Miller of an actual or a potential *arrière-pensée*,[17] as they said at Geneva? He felt he had lived at Geneva so long as to have got morally muddled; he had lost the

---

[17] "Ulterior motive" (French).

right sense for the young American tone. Never indeed since he had grown old enough to appreciate things had he encountered a young compatriot of so "strong" a type as this. Certainly she was very charming, but how extraordinarily communicative and how tremendously easy! Was she simply a pretty girl from New York State—were they all like that, the pretty girls who had had a good deal of gentlemen's society? Or was she also a designing, an audacious, in short an expert young person? Yes, his instinct for such a question had ceased to serve him, and his reason could but mislead. Miss Daisy Miller looked extremely innocent. Some people had told him that after all American girls *were* exceedingly innocent, and others had told him that after all they weren't. He must on the whole take Miss Daisy Miller for a flirt—a pretty American flirt. He had never as yet had relations with representatives of that class. He had known here in Europe two or three women—persons older than Miss Daisy Miller and provided, for respectability's sake, with husbands—who were great coquettes; dangerous terrible women with whom one's light commerce might indeed take a serious turn. But this charming apparition wasn't a coquette in that sense; she was very unsophisticated; she was only a pretty American flirt. Winterbourne was almost grateful for having found the formula that applied to Miss Daisy Miller. He leaned back in his seat; he remarked to himself that she had the finest little nose he had ever seen; he wondered what were the regular conditions and limitations of one's intercourse with a pretty American flirt. It presently became apparent that he was on the way to learn.

"Have you been to that old castle?" the girl soon asked, pointing with her parasol to the far-shining walls of the Château de Chillon.

"Yes, formerly, more than once," said Winterbourne. "You too, I suppose, have seen it?"

"No, we haven't been there. I want to go there dreadfully. Of course I mean to go there. I wouldn't go away from here without having seen that old castle."

"It's a very pretty excursion," the young man returned, "and very easy to make. You can drive, you know, or you can go by the little steamer."

"You can go in the cars," said Miss Miller.

"Yes, you can go in the cars," Winterbourne assented.

"Our courier says they take you right up to the castle," she continued. "We were going last week, but mother gave out. She suffers dreadfully from dyspepsia. She said she couldn't any more go—!" But this sketch of Mrs. Miller's plea remained unfinished. "Randolph wouldn't go either; he says he don't think much of old castles. But I guess we'll go this week if we can get Randolph."

"Your brother isn't interested in ancient monuments?" Winterbourne indulgently asked.

He now drew her, as he guessed she would herself have said, every time. "Why no, he says he don't care much about old castles. He's only nine. He wants to stay at the hotel. Mother's afraid to leave him alone, and the courier won't stay with him; so we haven't been to many places. But it will be too bad if we don't go up there." And Miss Miller pointed again at the Château de Chillon.

"I should think it might be arranged," Winterbourne was thus emboldened to reply. "Couldn't you get some one to stay—for the afternoon—with Randolph?"

Miss Miller looked at him a moment, and then with all serenity, "I wish *you'd* stay with him!" she said.

He pretended to consider it. "I'd much rather go to Chillon with you."

"With me?" she asked without a shadow of emotion.

She didn't rise blushing, as a young person at Geneva would have done; and yet, conscious that he had gone very far, he thought it possible she had drawn back. "And with your mother," he answered very respectfully.

But it seemed that both his audacity and his respect were lost on Miss Daisy Miller. "I guess mother wouldn't go—for *you*," she smiled. "And she ain't much *bent* on going, anyway. She don't like to ride round in the afternoon." After which she familiarly proceeded: "But did you really mean what you said just now—that you'd like to go up there?"

"Most earnestly I meant it," Winterbourne declared.

"Then we may arrange it. If mother will stay with Randolph I guess Eugenio will."

"Eugenio?" the young man echoed.

"Eugenio's our courier.[18] He doesn't like to stay with Randolph—he's the most fastidious man I ever saw. But he's a splendid courier. I guess he'll stay at home with Randolph if mother does, and then we can go to the castle."

Winterbourne reflected for an instant as lucidly as possible: "we" could only mean Miss Miller and himself. This prospect seemed almost too good to believe; he felt as if he ought to kiss the young lady's hand. Possibly he would have done so,—and quite spoiled his chance; but at this moment another person—presumably Eugenio—appeared. A tall handsome man, with superb whiskers and wearing a velvet morning-coat and a voluminous watch-guard, approached the young lady, looking sharply at her companion. "Oh Eugenio!" she said with the friendliest accent.

Eugenio had eyed Winterbourne from head to foot; he now bowed gravely to Miss Miller. "I have the honour to inform Mademoiselle that luncheon's on table."

Mademoiselle slowly rose. "See here, Eugenio, I'm going to that old castle anyway."

"To the Château de Chillon, Mademoiselle?" the courier enquired. "Mademoiselle has made arrangements?" he added in a tone that struck Winterbourne as impertinent.

Eugenio's tone apparently threw, even to Miss Miller's own apprehension, a slightly ironical light on her position. She turned to Winterbourne with the slightest blush. "You won't back out?"

"I shall not be happy till we go!" he protested.

"And you're staying in this hotel?" she went on. "And you're really American?"

The courier still stood there with an effect of offence for the young man so far as the latter saw in it a tacit reflexion on Miss Miller's behaviour and an insinuation that she "picked up" acquaintances. "I shall have the honour of presenting to you a person who'll tell you all about me," he said, smiling, and referring to his aunt.

"Oh well, we'll go some day," she beautifully answered; with which she gave him a smile and turned away. She put up her parasol and walked back to the inn beside Eugenio. Winterbourne stood watching her, and as she moved away, drawing her muslin furbelows[19] over the walk, he spoke to himself of her natural elegance.

---

[18] A traveler's paid attendant.   [19] Ruffles.

II

He had, however, engaged to do more than proved feasible in promising to present his aunt, Mrs. Costello, to Miss Daisy Miller. As soon as that lady had got better of her headache he waited on her in her apartment and, after a show of the proper solicitude about her health, asked if she had noticed in the hotel an American family—a mamma, a daughter and an obstreperous little boy.

"An obstreperous little boy and a preposterous big courier?" said Mrs. Costello. "Oh yes, I've noticed them. Seen them, heard them and kept out of their way." Mrs. Costello was a widow of fortune, a person of much distinction and who frequently intimated that if she hadn't been so dreadfully liable to sick-headaches she would probably have left a deeper impress on her time. She had a long pale face, a high nose and a great deal of very striking white hair, which she wore in large puffs and over the top of her head. She had two sons married in New York and another who was now in Europe. This young man was amusing himself at Homburg[20] and, though guided by his taste, was rarely observed to visit any particular city at the moment selected by his mother for her appearance there. Her nephew, who had come to Vevey expressly to see her, was therefore more attentive than, as she said, her very own. He had imbibed at Geneva the idea that one must be irreproachable in all such forms. Mrs. Costello hadn't seen him for many years and was now greatly pleased with him, manifesting her approbation by initiating him into many of the secrets of that social sway which, as he could see she would like him to think, she exerted from her stronghold in Forty-Second Street. She admitted that she was very exclusive, but if he had been better acquainted with New York he would see that one had to be. And her picture of the minutely hierarchical constitution of the society of that city, which she presented to him in many different lights, was, to Winterbourne's imagination, almost oppressively striking.

He at once recognised from her tone that Miss Daisy Miller's place in the social scale was low. "I'm afraid you don't approve of them," he pursued in reference to his new friends.

"They're horribly common"—it was perfectly simple. "They're the sort of Americans that one does one's duty by just ignoring."

"Ah you just ignore them?"—the young man took it in.

"I can't *not,* my dear Frederick. I wouldn't if I hadn't to, but I have to."

"The little girl's very pretty," he went on in a moment.

"Of course she's very pretty. But she's of the last crudity."

"I see what you mean of course," he allowed after another pause.

"She has that charming look they all have," his aunt resumed. "I can't think where they pick it up; and she dresses in perfection—no, you don't know how well she dresses. I can't think where they get their taste."

"But, my dear aunt, she's not, after all, a Comanche savage."

"She's a young lady," said Mrs. Costello, "who has an intimacy with her mamma's courier?"

"An 'intimacy' with him?" Ah there it was!

"There's no other name for such a relation. But the skinny little mother's just as bad! They treat the courier as a familiar friend—as a gentleman and a scholar. I shouldn't wonder if he dines with them. Very likely they've never seen a man with such good manners, such fine clothes, so *like* a gentleman—or a scholar. He

---

[20] A German resort.

probably corresponds to the young lady's idea of a count. He sits with them in the garden of an evening. I think he smokes in their faces."

Winterbourne listened with interest to these disclosures; they helped him to make up his mind about Miss Daisy. Evidently she was rather wild. "Well," he said, "I'm not a courier and I didn't smoke in her face, and yet she was very charming to me."

"You had better have mentioned at first," Mrs. Costello returned with dignity, "that you had made her valuable acquaintance."

"We simply met in the garden and talked a bit."

"By appointment—no? Ah that's still to come! Pray what did you say?"

"I said I should take the liberty of introducing her to my admirable aunt."

"Your admirable aunt's a thousand times obliged to you."

"It was to guarantee my respectability."

"And pray who's to guarantee hers?"

"Ah you're cruel!" said the young man. "She's a very innocent girl."

"You don't say that as if you believed it," Mrs. Costello returned.

"She's completely uneducated," Winterbourne acknowledged, "but she's wonderfully pretty, and in short she's very nice. To prove I believe it I'm going to take her to the Château de Chillon."

Mrs. Costello made a wondrous face. "You two are going off there together? I should say it proved just the contrary. How long had you known her, may I ask, when this interesting project was formed? You haven't been twenty-four hours in the house."

"I had known her half an hour!" Winterbourne smiled.

"Then she's just what I supposed."

"And what do you suppose?"

"Why that she's a horror."

Our youth was silent for some moments. "You really think then," he presently began, and with a desire for trustworthy information, "you really think that—" But he paused again while his aunt waited.

"Think what, sir?"

"That she's the sort of young lady who expects a man sooner or later to—well, we'll call it carry her off?"

"I haven't the least idea what such young ladies expect a man to do. But I really consider you had better not meddle with little American girls who are uneducated, as you mildly put it. You've lived too long out of the country. You'll be sure to make some great mistake. You're too innocent."

"My dear aunt, not so much as that comes to!" he protested with a laugh and a curl of his moustache.

"You're too guilty then!"

He continued all thoughtfully to finger the ornament in question. "You won't let the poor girl know you then?" he asked at last.

"Is it literally true that she's going to the Château de Chillon with you?"

"I've no doubt she fully intends it."

"Then, my dear Frederick," said Mrs. Costello, "I must decline the honour of her acquaintance. I'm an old woman, but I'm not too old—thank heaven—to be honestly shocked!"

"But don't they all do these things—the little American girls at home?" Winterbourne enquired.

Mrs. Costello stared a moment. "I should like to see my granddaughters do them!" she then grimly returned.

This seemed to throw some light on the matter, for Winterbourne remembered to have heard his pretty cousins in New York, the daughters of this lady's two daughters, called "tremendous flirts." If therefore Miss Daisy Miller exceeded the liberal license allowed to these young women it was probable she did go even by the American allowance rather far. Winterbourne was impatient to see her again, and it vexed, it even a little humiliated him, that he shouldn't by instinct appreciate her justly.

Though so impatient to see her again he hardly knew what ground he should give for his aunt's refusal to become aquainted with her; but he discovered promptly enough that with Miss Daisy Miller there was no great need of walking on tiptoe. He found her that evening in the garden, wandering about in the warm starlight after the manner of an indolent sylph and swinging to and fro the largest fan he had ever beheld. It was ten o'clock. He had dined with his aunt, had been sitting with her since dinner, and had just taken leave of her till the morrow. His young friend frankly rejoiced to renew their intercourse; she pronounced it the stupidest evening she had ever passed.

"Have you been all alone?" he asked with no intention of an epigram and no effect of her perceiving one.

"I've been walking round with mother. But mother gets tired walking round," Miss Miller explained.

"Has she gone to bed?"

"No, she doesn't like to go to bed. She doesn't sleep scarcely any—not three hours. She says she doesn't know how she lives. She's dreadfully nervous. I guess she sleeps more than she thinks. She's gone somewhere after Randolph; she wants to try to get him to go to bed. He doesn't like to go to bed."

The soft impartiality of her *constatations,*[21] as Winterbourne would have termed them, was a thing by itself—exquisite little fatalist as they seemed to make her. "Let us hope she'll persuade him," he encouragingly said.

"Well, she'll talk to him all she can—but he doesn't like her to talk to him": with which Miss Daisy opened and closed her fan. "She's going to try to get Eugenio to talk to him. But Randolph ain't afraid of Eugenio. Eugenio's a splended courier, but he can't make much impression on Randolph! I don't believe he'll go to bed before eleven." Her detachment from any invidious judgement of this was, to her companion's sense, inimitable; and it appeared that Randolph's vigil was in fact triumphantly prolonged, for Winterbourne attended her in her stroll for some time without meeting her mother. "I've been looking round for that lady you want to introduce me to," she resumed—"I guess she's your aunt." Then on his admitting the fact and expressing some curiosity as to how she had learned it, she said she had heard all about Mrs. Costello from the chambermaid. She was very quiet and very *comme il faut;*[22] she wore white puffs; she spoke to no one and she never dined at the common table. Every two days she had a headache. "I think that's a lovely description, headache and all!" said Miss Daisy, chattering along in her thin gay voice. "I want to know her ever so much. I know just what *your* aunt would be; I know I'd like her. She'd be very exclusive. I like a lady to be exclusive; I'm dying to be exclusive myself. Well, I guess we *are* exclusive, mother and I. We don't speak to any one—or they don't speak to us. I suppose it's about the same thing. Anyway, I shall be ever so glad to meet your aunt."

Winterbourne was embarrassed—he could but trump up some evasion. "She'd be most happy, but I'm afraid those tiresome headaches are always to be reckoned with."

The girl looked at him through the fine dusk.

"Well, I suppose she doesn't have a headache every day."

He had to make the best of it. "She tells me she wonderfully does." He didn't know what else to say.

Miss Miller stopped and stood looking at him. Her prettiness was still visible in the darkness; she kept flapping to and fro her enormous fan. "She doesn't want to know me!" she then lightly broke out. "Why don't you say so? You needn't be afraid. *I'm* not afraid!" And she quite crowed for the fun of it.

Winterbourne distinguished however a wee false note in this: he was touched, shocked, mortified by it. "My dear young lady, she knows no one. She goes through life immured. It's her wretched health."

The young girl walked on a few steps in the glee of the thing. "You needn't be afraid," she repeated. "Why should she want to know me?" Then she paused again; she was close to the parapet of the garden, and in front of her was the starlit lake. There was a vague sheen on its surface, and in the distance were dimly-seen mountain forms. Daisy Miller looked out at these great lights and shades and again proclaimed a gay indifference—"Gracious! she *is* exclusive!" Winterbourne wondered if she were seriously wounded and for a moment almost wished her sense of injury might be such as to make it becoming in him to reassure and comfort her. He had a pleasant sense that she would be all accessible to a respectful tenderness at that moment. He felt quite ready to sacrifice his aunt—conversationally; to acknowledge she was a proud rude woman and to make the point that they needn't mind her. But before he had time to commit himself to this questionable mixture of gallantry and impiety, the young lady, resuming her walk, gave an exclamation in quite another tone. "Well, here's mother! I guess she *hasn't* got Randolph to go to bed." The figure of a lady appeared, at a distance, very indistinct in the darkness; it advanced with a slow and wavering step and then suddenly seemed to pause.

"Are you sure it's your mother? Can you make her out in this thick dusk?" Winterbourne asked.

"Well," the girl laughed, "I guess I know my own mother! And when she has got on my shawl too. She's always wearing my things."

The lady in question, ceasing now to approach, hovered vaguely about the spot at which she had checked her steps.

"I'm afraid your mother doesn't see you," said Winterbourne. "Or perhaps," he added—thinking, with Miss Miller, the joke permissible—"perhaps she feels guilty about your shawl."

"Oh it's a fearful old thing!" his companion placidly answered. "I told her she could wear it if she didn't mind looking like a fright. She won't come here because she sees you."

"Ah then," said Winterbourne, "I had better leave you."

"Oh no—come on!" the girl insisted.

"I'm afraid your mother doesn't approve of my walking with you."

She gave him, he thought, the oddest glance. "It isn't for me; it's for you—that is it's for *her*. Well, I don't know who it's for! But mother doesn't like any of my gentlemen friends. She's right down timid. She always makes a fuss if I introduce a gentleman. But I *do* introduce them—almost always. If I didn't introduce my gentlemen friends to mother," Miss Miller added, in her small flat monotone, "I shouldn't think I was natural."

"Well, to introduce me," Winterbourne remarked, "you must know my name." And he proceeded to pronounce it.

"Oh my—I can't say all that!" cried his companion, much amused. But by this time they had come up to Mrs. Miller, who, as they drew near, walked to the parapet of the garden and leaned on it, looking intently at the lake and presenting her back to them. "Mother!" said the girl in a tone of decision—upon which the elder lady turned round. "Mr. Frederick Forsyth Winterbourne," said the latter's young friend, repeating his lesson of a moment before and introducing him very frankly and prettily. "Common" she might be, as Mrs. Costello had pronounced her; yet what provision was made by that epithet for her queer little native grace?

Her mother was a small spare light person, with a wandering eye, a scarce perceptible nose, and, as to make up for it, an unmistakeable forehead, decorated—but too far back, as Winterbourne mentally described it—with thin much-frizzled hair. Like her daughter Mrs. Miller was dressed with extreme elegance; she had enormous diamonds in her ears. So far as the young man could observe, she gave him no greeting—she certainly wasn't looking at him. Daisy was near her, pulling her shawl straight. "What are you doing, poking round here?" this young lady enquired—yet by no means with the harshness of accent her choice of words might have implied.

"Well, I don't know"—and the new-comer turned to the lake again.

"I shouldn't think you'd want that shawl!" Daisy familiarly proceeded.

"Well—I do!" her mother answered with a sound that partook for Winterbourne of an odd strain between mirth and woe.

"Did you get Randolph to go to bed?" Daisy asked.

"No, I couldn't induce him"—and Mrs. Miller seemed to confess to the same mild fatalism as her daughter. "He wants to talk to the waiter. He *likes* to talk to that waiter."

"I was just telling Mr. Winterbourne," the girl went on; and to the young man's ear her tone might have indicated that she had been uttering his name all her life.

"Oh yes!" he concurred—"I've the pleasure of knowing your son."

Randolph's mamma was silent; she kept her attention on the lake. But at last a sigh broke from her. "Well, I don't see how he lives!"

"Anyhow, it isn't so bad as it was at Dover,"[23] Daisy at least opined.

"And what occurred at Dover?" Winterbourne desired to know.

"He wouldn't go to bed at all. I guess he sat up all night—in the public parlour. He wasn't in bed at twelve o'clock: it seemed as if he couldn't budge."

"It was half-past twelve when *I* gave up," Mrs. Miller recorded with passion-less accuracy.

It was of great interest to Winterbourne. "Does he sleep much during the day?"

"I guess he doesn't sleep *very* much," Daisy rejoined.

"I wish he just *would!*" said her mother. "It seems as if he *must* make it up somehow."

"Well, I guess it's we that make it up. I think he's real tiresome," Daisy pursued.

After which, for some moments, there was silence. "Well, Daisy Miller," the elder lady then unexpectedly broke out, "I shouldn't think you'd want to talk against your own brother!"

"Well, he *is* tiresome, mother," said the girl, but with no sharpness of insistence.

---

[23] An English town.

"Well, he's only nine," Mrs. Miller lucidly urged.

"Well, he wouldn't go up to that castle, anyway," her daughter replied as for accommodation. "I'm going up there with Mr. Winterbourne."

To this announcement, very placidly made, Daisy's parent offered no response. Winterbourne took for granted on this that she opposed such a course; but he said to himself at the same time that she was a simple easily-managed person and that a few deferential protestations would modify her attitude. "Yes," he therefore interposed, "your daughter has kindly allowed me the honour of being her guide."

Mrs. Miller's wandering eyes attached themselves with an appealing air to her other companion, who, however, strolled a few steps further, gently humming to herself. "I presume you'll go in the cars," she then quite colourlessly remarked.

"Yes, or in the boat," said Winterbourne.

"Well, of course I don't know," Mrs. Miller returned. "I've never been up to that castle."

"It is a pity you shouldn't go," he observed, beginning to feel reassured as to her opposition. And yet he was quite prepared to find that as a matter of course she meant to accompany her daughter.

It was on this view accordingly that light was projected for him. "We've been thinking ever so much about going, but it seems as if we couldn't. Of course Daisy—she wants to go round everywhere. But there's a lady here—I don't know her name—she says she shouldn't think we'd want to go to see castles *here;* she should think we'd want to wait till we got t' Italy. It seems as if there would be so many there," continued Mrs. Miller with an air of increasing confidence. "Of course we only want to see the principal ones. We visited several in England," she presently added.

"Ah yes, in England there are beautiful castles," said Winterbourne. "But Chillon here is very well worth seeing."

"Well, if Daisy feels up to it—" said Mrs. Miller in a tone that seemed to break under the burden of such conceptions. "It seems as if there's nothing she won't undertake."

"Oh I'm pretty sure she'll enjoy it!" Winterbourne declared. And he desired more and more to make it a certainty that he was to have the privilege of a tête-à-tête[24] with the young lady who was still strolling along in front of them and softly vocalising. "You're not disposed, madam," he enquired, "to make the so interesting excursion yourself?"

So addressed Daisy's mother looked at him an instant with a certain scared obliquity and then walked forward in silence. Then, "I guess she had better go alone," she said simply.

It gave him occasion to note that this was a very different type of maternity from that of the vigilant matrons who massed themselves in the forefront of social intercourse in the dark old city at the other end of the lake. But his meditations were interrupted by hearing his name very distinctly pronounced by Mrs. Miller's unprotected daughter. "Mr. Winterbourne!" she piped from a considerable distance.

"Mademoiselle!" said the young man.

"Don't you want to take me out in a boat?"

"At present?" he asked.

"Why of course!" she gaily returned.

"Well, Annie Miller!" exclaimed her mother.

---

[24] A private conversation (French).

"I beg you, madam, to let her go," he hereupon eagerly pleaded; so instantly had he been struck with the romantic side of this chance to guide through the summer starlight a skiff freighted with a fresh and beautiful young girl.

"I shouldn't think she'd want to," said her mother. "I should think she'd rather go indoors."

"I'm sure Mr. Winterbourne wants to *take* me," Daisy declared. "He's so awfully devoted!"

"I'll row you over to Chillon under the stars."

"I don't believe it!" Daisy laughed.

"Well!" the elder lady again gasped, as in rebuke of this freedom.

"You haven't spoken to me for half an hour," her daughter went on.

"I've been having some very pleasant conversation with your mother," Winterbourne replied.

"Oh pshaw! I want you to take me out in a boat!" Daisy went on as if nothing else had been said. They had all stopped and she had turned round and was looking at her friend. Her face wore a charming smile, her pretty eyes gleamed in the darkness, she swung her great fan about. No, he felt, it was impossible to be prettier than that.

"There are half a dozen boats moored at that landing-place," and he pointed to a range of steps that descended from the garden to the lake. "If you'll do me the honour to accept my arm we'll go and select one of them."

She stood there smiling; she threw back her head; she laughed as for the drollery of this. "I like a gentleman to be formal!"

"I assure you it's a formal offer."

"I was bound I'd make you say something," Daisy agreeably mocked.

"You see it's not very difficult," said Winterbourne. "But I'm afraid you're chaffing[25] me."

"I think not, sir," Mrs. Miller shyly pleaded.

"Do then let me give you a row," he persisted to Daisy.

"It's quite lovely, the way you say that!" she cried in reward.

"It will be still more lovely to do it."

"Yes, it would be lovely!" But she made no movement to accompany him; she only remained an elegant image of free light irony.

"I guess you'd better find out what time it is," her mother impartially contributed.

"It's eleven o'clock, Madam," said a voice with a foreign accent out of the neighbouring darkness; and Winterbourne, turning, recognised the florid personage he had already seen in attendance. He had apparently just approached.

"Oh Eugenio," said Daisy, "I'm going out with Mr. Winterbourne in a boat!"

Eugenio bowed. "At this hour of the night, Mademoiselle?"

"I'm going with Mr. Winterbourne," she repeated with her shining smile. "I'm going this very minute."

"Do tell her she can't, Eugenio," Mrs. Miller said to the courier.

"I think you had better not go out in a boat, Mademoiselle," the man declared.

Winterbourne wished to goodness this pretty girl were not on such familiar terms with her courier; but he said nothing, and she meanwhile added to his ground. "I suppose you don't think it's proper! My!" she wailed; "Eugenio doesn't think anything's proper."

---

[25] Teasing.

"I'm nevertheless quite at your service," Winterbourne hastened to remark.

"Does Mademoiselle propose to go alone?" Eugenio asked of Mrs. Miller.

"Oh no, with this gentleman!" cried Daisy's mamma for reassurance.

"I *meant* alone with the gentleman." The courier looked for a moment at Winterbourne—the latter seemed to make out in his face a vague presumptuous intelligence as at the expense of their companions—and then solemnly and with a bow, "As Mademoiselle pleases!" he said.

But Daisy broke off at this. "Oh I hoped you'd make a fuss! I don't care to go now."

"Ah but I myself shall make a fuss if you don't go," Winterbourne declared with spirit.

"That's all I want—a little fuss!" With which she began to laugh again.

"Mr. Randolph has retired for the night!" the courier hereupon importantly announced.

"Oh Daisy, now we can go then!" cried Mrs. Miller.

Her daughter turned away from their friend, all lighted with her odd perversity. "Good-night—I hope you're disappointed or disgusted or something!"

He looked at her gravely, taking her by the hand she offered. "I'm puzzled, if you want to know!" he answered.

"Well, I hope it won't keep you awake!" she said very smartly; and, under the escort of the privileged Eugenio, the two ladies passed toward the house.

Winterbourne's eyes followed them; he was indeed quite mystified. He lingered beside the lake a quarter of an hour, baffled by the question of the girl's sudden familiarities and caprices. But the only very definite conclusion he came to was that he should enjoy deucedly "going off" with her somewhere.

Two days later he went off with her to the Castle of Chillon. He waited for her in the large hall of the hotel, where the couriers, the servants, the foreign tourists were lounging about and staring. It wasn't the place he would have chosen for a tryst, but she had placidly appointed it. She came tripping downstairs, buttoning her long gloves, squeezing her folded parasol against her pretty figure, dressed exactly in the way that consorted best, to his fancy, with their adventure. He was a man of imagination and, as our ancestors used to say, of sensibility; as he took in her charming air and caught from the great staircase her impatient confiding step the note of some small sweet strain of romance, not intense but clear and sweet, seemed to sound for their start. He could have believed he was *really* going "off" with her. He led her out through all the idle people assembled—they all looked at her straight and hard: she had begun to chatter as soon as she joined him. His preference had been that they should be conveyed to Chillon in a carriage, but she expressed a lively wish to go in the little steamer—there would be such a lovely breeze upon the water and they should see such lots of people. The sail wasn't long, but Winterbourne's companion found time for many characteristic remarks and other demonstrations, not a few of which were, from the extremity of their candour, slightly disconcerting. To the young man himself their small excursion showed so for delightfully irregular and incongruously intimate that, even allowing for her habitual sense of freedom, he had some expectation of seeing her appear to find in it the same savour. But it must be confessed that he was in this particular rather disappointed. Miss Miller was highly animated, she was in the brightest spirits; but she was clearly not at all in a nervous flutter—as she should have been to match *his* tension; she avoided neither his eyes nor those of any one else; she neither coloured from an awkward consciousness when she looked at him nor when she saw that people were looking at herself. People continued to look at her a great deal, and Winterbourne could at least take pleasure in his pretty companion's distinguished air. He had been privately afraid she would talk loud, laugh overmuch, and even perhaps desire to move extravagantly about the boat. But he quite forgot his fears; he sat smiling with his eyes on her face while, without stirring from her place, she delivered herself of a great number of original reflexions. It was the most charming innocent prattle he had ever heard, for, by his own experience hitherto, when young persons were so ingenuous they were less articulate and when they were so confident were more sophisticated. If he had assented to the idea that she was "common," at any rate, *was she proving* so, after all, or was he simply getting used to her commonness? Her discourse was for the most part of what immediately and superficially surrounded them, but there were moments when it threw out a longer look or took a sudden straight plunge.

"What on *earth* are you so solemn about?" she suddenly demanded, fixing her agreeable eyes on her friend's.

"*Am* I solemn?" he asked. "I had an idea I was grinning from ear to ear."

"You look as if you were taking me to a prayer-meeting or a funeral. If that's a grin your ears are very near together."

"Should you like me to dance a hornpipe[26] on the deck?"

"Pray do, and I'll carry round your hat. It will pay the expenses of our journey."

"I never was better pleased in my life," Winterbourne returned.

She looked at him a moment, then let it renew her amusement. "I like to make you say those things. You're a queer mixture!"

In the castle, after they had landed, nothing could exceed the light independence of her humour. She tripped about the vaulted chambers, rustled her skirts in the corkscrew staircases, flirted back with a pretty little cry and a shudder from the edge of the oubliettes[27] and turned a singularly well-shaped ear to everything Winterbourne told her about the place. But he saw she cared little for mediæval history and that the grim ghosts of Chillon loomed but faintly before her. They had the good fortune to have been able to wander without other society than that of their guide; and Winterbourne arranged with this companion that they shouldn't be hurried—that they should linger and pause wherever they chose. He intepreted the bargain generously—Winterbourne on his side had been generous—and ended by leaving them quite to themselves. Miss Miller's observations were marked by no logical consistency; for anything she wanted to say she was sure to find a pretext. She found a great many, in the tortuous passages and rugged embrasures of the place, for asking her young man sudden questions about himself, his family, his previous history, his tastes, his habits, his designs, and for supplying information on corresponding points in her own situation. Of her own tastes, habits and designs the charming creature was prepared to give the most definite and indeed the most favourable account.

"Well, I hope you know enough!" she exclaimed after Winterbourne had sketched for her something of the story of the unhappy Bonnivard.[28] "I never saw a man that knew so much!" The history of Bonnivard had evidently, as they say, gone into one ear and out of the other. But this easy erudition struck her none the less as wonderful, and she was soon quite sure she wished Winterbourne would

---

[26] A lively folk dance.   [27] Dungeons with openings only at the top.

[28] François de Bonivard (1496?–1570), a Swiss patriot imprisoned in the Castle of Chillon; hero of the poem "The Prisoner of Chillon" (1816), by George Gordon (1788–1824), Lord Byron.

travel with them and "go round" with them: they too in that case might learn something about something. "Don't you want to come and teach Randolph?" she asked; "I guess he'd improve with a gentleman teacher." Winterbourne was certain that nothing could possibly please him so much, but that he had unfortunately other occupations. "Other occupations? I don't believe a speck of it!" she protested. "What do you mean now? You're not in business." The young man allowed that he was not in business, but he had engagements which even within a day or two would necessitate his return to Geneva. "Oh bother!" she panted, "I don't believe it!" and she began to talk about something else. But a few moments later, when he was pointing out to her the interesting design of an antique fireplace, she broke out irrelevantly: "You don't mean to say you're going back to Geneva?"

"It is a melancholy fact that I shall have to report myself there to-morrow."

She met it with a vivacity that could only flatter him. "Well, Mr. Winterbourne, I think you're horrid!"

"Oh don't say such dreadful things!" he quite sincerely pleaded—"just at the last."

"The last?" the girl cried; "I call it the very first! I've half a mind to leave you here and go straight back to the hotel alone." And for the next ten minutes she did nothing but call him horrid. Poor Winterbourne was fairly bewildered; no young lady had as yet done him the honour to be so agitated by the mention of his personal plans. His companion, after this, ceased to pay any attention to the curiosities of Chillon or the beauties of the lake; she opened fire on the special charmer in Geneva whom she appeared to have instantly taken it for granted that he was hurrying back to see. How did Miss Daisy Miller know of that agent of his fate in Geneva? Winterbourne, who denied the existence of such a person, was quite unable to discover; and he was divided between amazement at the rapidity of her induction and amusement at the directness of her criticism. She struck him afresh, in all this, as an extraordinary mixture of innocence and crudity. "Does she never allow you more than three days at a time?" Miss Miller wished ironically to know. "Doesn't she give you a vacation in summer? there's no one so hard-worked but they can get leave to go off somewhere at this season. I suppose if you stay another day she'll come right after you in the boat. Do wait over till Friday and I'll go down to the landing to see her arrive!" He began at last even to feel he had been wrong to be disappointed in the temper in which his young lady had embarked. If he had missed the personal accent, the personal accent was now making its appearance. It sounded very distinctly, toward the end, in her telling him she'd stop "teasing" him if he'd promise her solemnly to come down to Rome that winter.

"That's not a difficult promise to make," he hastened to acknowledge. "My aunt has taken an apartment in Rome from January and has already asked me to come and see her."

"I don't want you to come for your aunt," said Daisy; "I want you just to come for me." And this was the only allusion he was ever to hear her make again to his invidious kinswoman. He promised her that at any rate he would certainly come, and after this she forbore from teasing. Winterbourne took a carriage and they drove back to Vevey in the dusk; the girl at his side, her animation a little spent, was now quite distractingly passive.

In the evening he mentioned to Mrs. Costello that he had spent the afternoon at Chillon with Miss Daisy Miller.

"The Americans—of the courier?" asked this lady.

"Ah happily the courier stayed at home."

"She went with you all alone?"

"All alone."

Mrs. Costello sniffed a little at her smelling-bottle.[29] "And that," she exclaimed, "is the little abomination you wanted me to know!"

III

Winterbourne, who had returned to Geneva the day after his excursion to Chillon, went to Rome toward the end of January. His aunt had been established there a considerable time and he had received from her a couple of characteristic letters. "Those people you were so devoted to last summer at Vevey have turned up here, courier and all," she wrote. "They seem to have made several acquaintances, but the courier continues to be the most *intime*.[30] The young lady, however, is also very intimate with various third-rate Italians, with whom she rackets about in a way that makes much talk. Bring me that pretty novel of Cherbuliez's—'Paule Méré'[31]—and don't come later than the 23d."

Our friend would in the natural course of events, on arriving in Rome, have presently ascertained Mrs. Miller's address at the American banker's and gone to pay his compliments to Miss Daisy. "After what happened at Vevey I certainly think I may call upon them," he said to Mrs. Costello.

"If after what happens—at Vevey and everywhere—you desire to keep up the acquaintance, you're very welcome. Of course you're not squeamish—a man may know every one.[32] Men are welcome to the privilege!" *indicates a little jealousy*

Free spirits

"Pray what is it then that 'happens'—here for instance?" Winterbourne asked.

"Well, the girl tears about alone with her unmistakeably low foreigners. As to what happens further you must apply elsewhere for information. She has picked up half a dozen of the regular Roman fortune-hunters of the inferior sort and she takes them about to such houses as she may put *her* nose into. When she comes to a party—such a party as she can come to— she brings with her a gentleman with a good deal of manner and a wonderful moustache."

"And where's the mother?"

"I haven't the least idea. They're very dreadful people."

Winterbourne thought them over in these new lights. "They're very ignorant—very innocent only, and utterly uncivilised. Depend on it they're not 'bad.'"

"They're hopelessly vulgar," said Mrs. Costello. "Whether or no being hopelessly vulgar is being 'bad' is a question for the metaphysicians. They're bad enough to blush for, at any rate; and for this short life that's quite enough."

The news that his little friend the child of nature of the Swiss lakeside was now surrounded by half a dozen wonderful moustaches checked Winterbourne's impulse to go straightway to see her. He had perhaps not definitely flattered himself that he had made an ineffaceable impression upon her heart, but he was annoyed at hearing of a state of affairs so little in harmony with an image that had lately flitted in and out of his own meditations; the image of a very pretty girl looking out of an old Roman window and asking herself urgently when Mr. Winterbourne would arrive. If, however, he determined to wait a little before reminding this

---

[29] Bottle of smelling salts, used as a stimulant or to prevent fainting.

[30] "Intimate" (French).

[31] An 1864 novel by the French author Charles Victor Cherbuliez (1829–1899).

[32] Women had to worry about damaging their reputations if they befriended people who refused to follow social conventions, but a man could befriend anyone without worrying about his reputation.

young lady of his claim to her faithful remembrance, he called with more promptitude on two or three other friends. One of these friends was an American lady who had spent several winters at Geneva, where she had placed her children at school. She was a very accomplished woman and she lived in Via Gregoriana. Winterbourne found her in a little crimson drawing-room on a third floor; the room was filled with southern sunshine. He hadn't been there ten minutes when the servant, appearing in the doorway, announced complacently "Madame Mila!" This announcement was presently followed by the entrance of little Randolph Miller, who stopped in the middle of the room and stood staring at Winterbourne. An instant later his pretty sister crossed the threshold; and then, after a considerable interval, the parent of the pair slowly advanced.

"I guess I know you!" Randolph broke ground without delay.

"I'm sure you know a great many things"—and his old friend clutched him all interestedly by the arm. "How's your education coming on?"

Daisy was engaged in some pretty babble with her hostess, but when she heard Winterbourne's voice she quickly turned her head with a "Well, I declare!" which he met smiling. "I told you I should come, you know."

"Well, I didn't believe it," she answered.

"I'm much obliged to you for that," laughed the young man.

"You might have come to see me then," Daisy went on as if they had parted the week before.

"I arrived only yesterday."

"I don't believe any such thing!" the girl declared afresh.

Winterbourne turned with a protesting smile to her mother, but this lady evaded his glance and, seating herself, fixed her eyes on her son. "We've got a bigger place than this," Randolph hereupon broke out. "It's all gold on the walls."

Mrs. Miller, more of a fatalist apparently than ever, turned uneasily in her chair. "I told you if I was to bring you you'd say something!" she stated as for the benefit of such of the company as might hear it.

"I told *you!*" Randolph retorted. "I tell *you,* sir!" he added jocosely, giving Winterbourne a thump on the knee. "It *is* bigger too!"

As Daisy's conversation with her hostess still occupied her Winterbourne judged it becoming to address a few words to her mother—such as "I hope you've been well since we parted at Vevey."

Mrs. Miller now certainly looked at him—at his chin. "Not very well, sir," she answered.

"She's got the dyspepsia,"[33] said Randolph. "I've got it too. Father's got it bad. But I've got it worst!"

This proclamation, instead of embarrassing Mrs. Miller, seemed to soothe her by reconstituting the environment to which she was most accustomed. "I suffer from the liver," she amiably whined to Winterbourne. "I think it's this climate; it's less bracing than Schenectady,[34] especially in the winter season. I don't know whether you know we reside at Schenectady. I was saying to Daisy that I certainly hadn't found any one like Dr. Davis and I didn't believe I *would.* Oh up in Schenectady, he stands first; they think everything of Dr. Davis. He has so much to do, and yet there was nothing he wouldn't do for *me.* He said he never saw anything like my dyspepsia, but he was bound to get at it. I'm sure there was nothing he wouldn't try, and I didn't care what he did to me if he only brought me relief. He was just going to try something new, and I just longed for it, when we came right

---

[33] Indigestion.   [34] Schenectady, New York.

off. Mr. Miller felt as if he wanted Daisy to see Europe for herself. But I couldn't help writing the other day that I supposed it was all right for Daisy, but that I didn't know as I *could* get on much longer without Dr. Davis. At Schenectady he stands at the very top; and there's a great deal of sickness there too. It affects my sleep."

Winterbourne had a good deal of pathological gossip with Dr. Davis's patient, during which Daisy chattered unremittingly to her own companion. The young man asked Mrs. Miller how she was pleased with Rome. "Well, I must say I'm disappointed," she confessed. "We had heard so much about it—I suppose we had heard too much. But we couldn't help that. We had been led to expect something different."

Winterbourne, however, abounded in reassurance. "Ah wait a little, and you'll grow very fond of it."

"I hate it worse and worse every day!" cried Randolph.

"You're like the infant Hannibal,"[35] his friend laughed.

"No I ain't—like any infant!" Randolph declared at a venture.

"Well, that's so—and you never *were!*" his mother concurred. "But we've seen places," she resumed, "that I'd put a long way ahead of Rome." And in reply to Winterbourne's interrogation, "There's Zürich—up there in the mountains," she instanced; "I think Zürich's real lovely, and we hadn't heard half so much about it."

"The best place we've seen's the *City of Richmond!*" said Randolph.

"He means the ship," Mrs. Miller explained. "We crossed in that ship. Randolph had a good time on the *City of Richmond*."

"It's the best place *I've* struck," the child repeated. "Only it was turned the wrong way."

"Well, we've got to turn the right way sometime," said Mrs. Miller with strained but weak optimism. Winterbourne expressed the hope that her daughter at least appreciated the so various interest of Rome, and she declared with some spirit that Daisy was quite carried away. "It's on account of the society—the society's splendid. She goes round everywhere; she has made a great number of acquaintances. Of course she goes round more than I do. I must say they've all been very sweet—they've taken her right in. And then she knows a great many gentlemen. Oh she thinks there's nothing like Rome. Of course it's a great deal pleasanter for a young lady if she knows plenty of gentlemen."

By this time Daisy had turned her attention again to Winterbourne, but in quite the same free form. "I've been telling Mrs. Walker how mean you were!"

"And what's the evidence you've offered?" he asked, a trifle disconcerted, for all his superior gallantry, by her inadequate measure of the zeal of an admirer who on his way down to Rome had stopped neither at Bologna nor at Florence, simply because of a certain sweet appeal to his fond fancy, not to say to his finest curiosity. He remembered how a cynical compatriot had once told him that American women—the pretty ones, and this gave a largeness to the axiom—were at once the most exacting in the world and the least endowed with a sense of indebtedness.

"Why you were awfully mean up at Vevey," Daisy said. "You wouldn't do most anything. You wouldn't stay there when I asked you."

"Dearest young lady," cried Winterbourne, with generous passion, "have I come all the way to Rome only to be riddled by your silver shafts?"

---

[35] Hannibal (247–183? B.C.) was a Carthaginian general sworn at birth to eternal hatred of Rome; he invaded Italy in 218 B.C.

"Just hear him say that!"—and she gave an affectionate twist to a bow on her hostess's dress. "Did you ever hear anything so quaint?"

"So 'quaint,' my dear?" echoed Mrs. Walker more critically—quite in the tone of a partisan of Winterbourne.

"Well, I don't know"—and the girl continued to finger her ribbons. "Mrs. Walker, I want to tell you something."

"Say, mother-r," broke in Randolph with his rough ends to his words, "I tell you you've got to go. Eugenio'll raise something!"

"I'm not afraid of Eugenio," said Daisy with a toss of her head. "Look here, Mrs. Walker," she went on, "you know I'm coming to your party."

"I'm delighted to hear it."

"I've got a lovely dress."

"I'm very sure of that."

"But I want to ask a favour—permission to bring a friend."

"I shall be happy to see any of your friends," said Mrs. Walker, who turned with a smile to Mrs. Miller.

"Oh they're not my friends," cried that lady, squirming in shy repudiation. "It seems as if they didn't take to *me*—I never spoke to one of them!"

"It's an intimate friend of mine, Mr. Giovanelli," Daisy pursued without a tremor in her young clearness or a shadow on her shining bloom.

Mrs. Walker had a pause and gave a rapid glance at Winterbourne. "I shall be glad to see Mr. Giovanelli," she then returned.

"He's just the finest kind of Italian," Daisy pursued with the prettiest serenity. "He's a great friend of mine and the handsomest man in the world—except Mr. Winterbourne! He knows plenty of Italians, but he wants to know some Americans. It seems as if he was crazy about Americans. He's tremendously bright. He's perfectly lovely!"

It was settled that this paragon should be brought to Mrs. Walker's party, and then Mrs. Miller prepared to take her leave. "I guess we'll go right back to the hotel," she remarked with a confessed failure of the larger imagination.

"You may go back to the hotel, mother," Daisy replied, "but I'm just going to walk round."

"She's going to go it with Mr. Giovanelli," Randolph unscrupulously commented.

"I'm going to go it on the Pincio,"[36] Daisy peaceably smiled, while the way that she "condoned" these things almost melted Winterbourne's heart.

"Alone, my dear—at this hour?" Mrs. Walker asked. The afternoon was drawing to a close—it was the hour for the throng of carriages and of contemplative pedestrians. "I don't consider it's safe, Daisy," her hostess firmly asserted.

"Neither do I then," Mrs. Miller thus borrowed confidence to add. "You'll catch the fever[37] as sure as you live. Remember what Dr. Davis told you!"

"Give her some of that medicine before she starts in," Randolph suggested.

The company had risen to its feet; Daisy, still showing her pretty teeth, bent over and kissed her hostess. "Mrs. Walker, you're too perfect," she simply said. "I'm not going alone; I'm going to meet a friend."

"Your friend won't keep you from catching the fever even if it *is* his own second nature," Mrs. Miller observed.

---

[36] A hill overlooking the city of Rome.

[37] Roman fever, or malaria, then thought to be transmitted by the night air rather than by mosquitoes.

"Is it Mr. Giovanelli that's the dangerous attraction?" Mrs. Walker asked without mercy.

Winterbourne was watching the challenged girl; at this question his attention quickened. She stood there smiling and smoothing her bonnet-ribbons; she glanced at Winterbourne. Then, while she glanced and smiled, she brought out all affirmatively and without a shade of hesitation: "Mr. Giovanelli—the beautiful Giovanelli."

"My dear young friend"—and, taking her hand, Mrs. Walker turned to pleading—"don't prowl off to the Pincio at this hour to meet a beautiful Italian."

"Well, he speaks first-rate English," Mrs. Miller incoherently mentioned.

"Gracious me," Daisy piped up, "I don't want to do anything that's going to affect my health—or my character either! There's an easy way to settle it." Her eyes continued to play over Winterbourne. "The Pincio's only a hundred yards off, and if Mr. Winterbourne were as polite as he pretends he'd offer to walk right in with me!"

Winterbourne's politeness hastened to proclaim itself, and the girl gave him gracious leave to accompany her. They passed downstairs before her mother, and at the door he saw Mrs. Miller's carriage drawn up, with the ornamental courier whose acquaintance he had made at Vevey seated within. "Good-bye, Eugenio," cried Daisy; "I'm going to take a walk!" The distance from Via Gregoriana[38] to the beautiful garden at the other end of the Pincian Hill is in fact rapidly traversed. As the day was splendid, however, and the concourse of vehicles, walkers and loungers numerous, the young Americans found their progress much delayed. This fact was highly agreeable to Winterbourne, in spite of his consciousness of his singular situation. The slow-moving, idly-gazing Roman crowd bestowed much attention on the extremely pretty young woman of English race who passed through it, with some difficulty, on his arm; and he wondered what on earth had been in Daisy's mind when she proposed to exhibit herself unattended to its appreciation. His own mission, to her sense, was apparently to consign her to the hands of Mr. Giovanelli; but, at once annoyed and gratified, he resolved that he would do no such thing.

"Why haven't you been to see me?" she meanwhile asked. "You can't get out of that."

"I've had the honour of telling you that I've only just stepped out of the train."

"You must have stayed in the train a good while after it stopped!" she derisively cried. "I suppose you were asleep. You've had time to go to see Mrs. Walker."

"I knew Mrs. Walker—" Winterbourne began to explain.

"I know where you knew her. You knew her at Geneva. She told me so. Well, you knew me at Vevey. That's just as good. So you ought to have come." She asked him no other question than this; she began to prattle about her own affairs. "We've got splendid rooms at the hotel; Eugenio says they're the best rooms in Rome. We're going to stay all winter—if we don't die of the fever; and I guess we'll stay then! It's a great deal nicer than I thought; I thought it would be fearfully quiet—in fact I was sure it would be deadly pokey. I foresaw we should be going round all the time with one of those dreadful old men who explain about the pictures and things. But we only had about a week of that, and now I'm enjoying myself. I know ever so many people, and they're all so charming. The society's

---

[38] A street in Rome.

extremely select. There are all kinds—English and Germans and Italians. I think I like the English best. I like their style of conversation. But there are some lovely Americans. I never saw anything so hospitable. There's something or other every day. There's not much dancing—but I must say I never thought dancing was everything. I was always fond of conversation. I guess I'll have plenty at Mrs. Walker's—her rooms are so small." When they had passed the gate of the Pincian Gardens Miss Miller began to wonder where Mr. Giovanelli might be. "We had better go straight to that place in front, where you look at the view."

Winterbourne at this took a stand. "I certainly shan't help you to find him."

"Then I shall find him without you," Daisy said with spirit.

"You certainly won't leave me!" he protested.

She burst into her familiar little laugh. "Are you afraid you'll get lost—or run over? But there's Giovanelli leaning against that tree. He's staring at the women in the carriages: did you ever see anything so cool?"

Winterbourne descried hereupon at some distance a little figure that stood with folded arms and nursing its cane. It had a handsome face, a hat artfully poised, a glass in one eye and a nosegay in its buttonhole. Daisy's friend looked at it a moment and then said: "Do you mean to speak to that thing?"

"Do I mean to speak to him? Why you don't suppose I mean to communicate by signs!"

"Pray understand then," the young man returned, "that I intend to remain with you."

Daisy stopped and looked at him without a sign of troubled consciousness, with nothing in her face but her charming eyes, her charming teeth and her happy dimples. "Well, she's a cool one!" he thought.

"I don't like the way you say that," she declared. "It's too imperious."

"I beg your pardon if I say it wrong. The main point's to give you an idea of my meaning."

The girl looked at him more gravely, but with eyes that were prettier than ever. "I've never allowed a gentleman to dictate to me or to interfere with anything I do."

"I think that's just where your mistake has come in," he retorted. "You should sometimes listen to a gentleman—the right one."

At this she began to laugh again. "I do nothing but listen to gentleman! Tell me if Mr. Giovanelli is the right one."

The gentleman with the nosegay in his bosom had now made out our two friends and was approaching Miss Miller with obsequious rapidity. He bowed to Winterbourne as well as to the latter's compatriot; he seemed to shine, in his coxcombical way,[39] with the desire to please and the fact of his own intelligent joy, though Winterbourne thought him not a bad-looking fellow. But he nevertheless said to Daisy: "No, he's not the right one."

She had clearly a natural turn for free introductions; she mentioned with the easiest grace the name of each of her companions to the other. She strolled forward with one of them on either hand; Mr. Giovanelli, who spoke English very cleverly—Winterbourne afterwards learned that he had practised the idiom upon a great many American heiresses—addressed her a great deal of very polite nonsense. He had the best possible manners, and the young American, who said nothing, reflected on that depth of Italian subtlety, so strangely opposed to Anglo-

---

[39] Acting foolishly.

Saxon simplicity, which enables people to show a smoother surface in proportion as they're more acutely displeased. Giovanelli of course had counted upon something more intimate—he had not bargained for a party of three; but he kept his temper in a manner that suggested far-stretching intentions. Winterbourne flattered himself he had taken his measure. "He's anything but a gentleman," said the young American; "he isn't even a very plausible imitation of one. He's a music-master or a penny-a-liner[40] or a third-rate artist. He's awfully on his good behaviour, but damn his fine eyes!" Mr. Giovanelli had indeed great advantages; but it was deeply disgusting to Daisy's other friend that something in her shouldn't have instinctively discriminated against such a type. Giovanelli chattered and jested and made himself agreeable according to his honest Roman lights. It was true that if he was an imitation the imitation was studied. "Nevertheless," Winterbourne said to himself, "a nice girl ought to know!" And then he came back to the dreadful question of whether this *was* in fact a nice girl. Would a nice girl—even allowing for her being a little American flirt—make a rendezvous with a presumably low-lived foreigner? The rendezvous in this case indeed had been in broad daylight and in the most crowded corner of Rome; but wasn't it possible to regard the choice of these very circumstances as a proof more of vulgarity than of anything else? Singular though it may seem, Winterbourne was vexed that the girl, in joining her *amoroso*,[41] shouldn't appear more impatient of his own company, and he was vexed precisely because of his inclination. It was impossible to regard her as a wholly unspotted flower—she lacked a certain indispensable fineness; and it would therefore much simplify the situation to be able to treat her as the subject of one of the visitations known to romancers as "lawless passions." That she should seem to wish to get rid of him would have helped him to think more lightly of her, just as to be able to think more lightly of her would have made her less perplexing. Daisy at any rate continued on this occasion to present herself as an inscrutable combination of audacity and innocence.

She had been walking some quarter of an hour, attended by her two cavaliers and responding in a tone of very childish gaiety, as it after all struck one of them, to the pretty speeches of the other, when a carriage that had detached itself from the revolving train drew up beside the path. At the same moment Winterbourne noticed that his friend Mrs. Walker—the lady whose house he had lately left—was seated in the vehicle and was beckoning to him. Leaving Miss Miller's side, he hastened to obey her summons—and all to find her flushed, excited, scandalised. "It's really too dreadful"—she earnestly appealed to him. "That crazy girl mustn't do this sort of thing. She mustn't walk here with you two men. Fifty people have remarked her."

Winterbourne—suddenly and rather oddly rubbed the wrong way by this—raised his grave eyebrows.

"I think it's a pity to make too much fuss about it."

"It's a pity to let the girl ruin herself!"

"She's very innocent," he reasoned in his own troubled interest.

"She's very reckless," cried Mrs. Walker, "and goodness knows how far—left to itself—it may go. Did you ever," she proceeded to enquire, "see anything so blatantly imbecile as the mother? After you had all left me just now I couldn't sit still for thinking of it. It seemed too pitiful not even to attempt to save them. I ordered the carriage and put on my bonnet and came here as quickly as possible. Thank heaven I've found you!"

---

[40] A hack writer working for a penny per line.   [41] "Lover," "admirer" (Italian).

"What do you propose to do with us?" Winterbourne uncomfortably smiled.

"To ask her to get in, to drive her about here for half an hour—so that the world may see she's not running absolutely wild—and then take her safely home."

"I don't think it's a very happy thought," he said after reflexion, "but you're at liberty to try."

Mrs. Walker accordingly tried. The young man went in pursuit of their young lady who had simply nodded and smiled, from her distance, at her recent patroness in the carriage and then had gone her way with her own companion. On learning, in the event, that Mrs. Walker had followed her, she retraced her steps, however, with a perfect good grace and with Mr. Giovanelli at her side. She professed herself "enchanted" to have a chance to present this gentleman to her good friend, and immediately achieved the introduction; declaring with it, and as if it were of as little importance, that she had never in her life seen anything so lovely as that lady's carriage-rug.

[margin annotation: She just wanders off]

[margin annotation: loopy]

[margin annotation: the girl is oblivious]

"I'm glad you admire it," said her poor pursuer, smiling sweetly. "Will you get in and let me put it over you?"

"Oh no, thank you!"—Daisy knew her mind. "I'll admire it ever so much more as I see you driving round with it."

"Do get in and drive round *with* me," Mrs. Walker pleaded.

"That would be charming, but it's so fascinating just as I am!"—with which the girl radiantly took in the gentlemen on either side of her.

"It may be fascinating, dear child, but it's not the custom here," urged the lady of the victoria,[42] leaning forward in this vehicle with her hands devoutly clasped.

"Well, it ought to be then!" Daisy imperturbably laughed. "If I didn't walk I'd expire."

"You should walk with your mother, dear," cried Mrs. Walker with a loss of patience.

"With my mother dear?" the girl amusedly echoed. Winterbourne saw she scented interference. "My mother never walked ten steps in her life. And then, you know," she blandly added, "I'm more than five years old."

"You're old enough to be more reasonable. You're old enough, dear Miss Miller, to be talked about."

Daisy wondered to extravagance. "Talked about? What do you mean?"

"Come into my carriage and I'll tell you."

Daisy turned shining eyes again from one of the gentlemen beside her to the other. Mr. Giovanelli was bowing to and fro, rubbing down his gloves and laughing irresponsibly; Winterbourne thought the scene the most unpleasant possible. "I don't think I want to know what you mean," the girl presently said. "I don't think I should like it."

Winterbourne only wished Mrs. Walker would tuck up her carriage-rug and drive away; but this lady, as she afterwards told him, didn't feel she could "rest there." "Should you prefer being thought a very reckless girl?" she accordingly asked.

"Gracious me!" exclaimed Daisy. She looked again at Mr. Giovanelli, then she turned to her other companion. There was a small pink flush in her cheek; she was tremendously pretty. "Does Mr. Winterbourne think," she put to him with a wonderful bright intensity of appeal, "that—to save my reputation—I ought to get into the carriage?"

---

[42] Horse-drawn carriage.

It really embarrassed him; for an instant he cast about—so strange was it to hear her speak that way of her "reputation." But he himself in fact had to speak in accordance with gallantry. The finest gallantry here was surely just to tell her the truth; and the truth, for our young man, as the few indications I have been able to give have made him known to the reader, was that his charming friend should listen to the voice of civilised society. He took in again her exquisite prettiness and then said the more distinctly: "I think you should get into the carriage."

Daisy gave the rein to her amusement. "I never heard anything so stiff! If this is improper, Mrs. Walker," she pursued, "then I'm *all* improper, and you had better give me right up. Good-bye; I hope you'll have a lovely ride!"—and with Mr. Giovanelli, who made a triumphantly obsequious salute, she turned away.

Mrs. Walker sat looking after her, and there were tears in Mrs. Walker's eyes. "Get in here, sir," she said to Winterbourne, indicating the place beside her. The young man answered that he felt bound to accompany Miss Miller; whereupon the lady of the victoria declared that if he refused her this favour she would never speak to him again. She was evidently wound up. He accordingly hastened to overtake Daisy and her more faithful ally, and, offering her his hand, told her that Mrs. Walker had made a stringent claim on his presence. He had expected her to answer with something rather free, something still more significant of the perversity from which the voice of society, through the lips of their distressed friend, had so earnestly endeavoured to dissuade her. But she only let her hand slip, as she scarce looked at him, through his slightly awkward grasp; while Mr. Giovanelli, to make it worse, bade him farewell with too emphatic a flourish of the hat.

Winterbourne was not in the best possible humour as he took his seat beside the author of his sacrifice. "That was not clever of you," he said candidly, as the vehicle mingled again with the throng of carriages.

"In such a case," his companion answered, "I don't want to be clever—I only want to be *true!*"

"Well, your truth has only offended the strange little creature—it has only put her off."

"It has happened very well"—Mrs. Walker accepted her work. "If she's so perfectly determined to compromise herself the sooner one knows it the better— one can act accordingly."

"I suspect she meant no great harm, you know," Winterbourne maturely opined.

"So I thought a month ago. But she has been going too far."

"What has she been doing?"

"Everything that's not done here. Flirting with any man she can pick up; sitting in corners with mysterious Italians; dancing all the evening with the same partners; receiving visits at eleven o'clock at night. Her mother melts away when the visitors come."

"But her brother," laughed Winterbourne, "sits up till two in the morning."

"He must be edified by what he sees. I'm told that at their hotel every one's talking about her and that a smile goes round among the servants when a gentleman comes and asks for Miss Miller."

"Ah we needn't mind the servants!" Winterbourne compassionately signified. "The poor girl's only fault," he presently added, "is her complete lack of education."

"She's naturally indelicate," Mrs. Walker, on her side, reasoned. "Take that example this morning. How long had you known her at Vevey?"

"A couple of days."

"Imagine then the taste of her making it a personal matter that you should have left the place!" (etiquette)

He agreed that taste wasn't the strong point of the Millers—after which he was silent for some moments; but only at last to add: "I suspect, Mrs. Walker, that you and I have lived too long at Geneva!" And he further noted that he should be glad to learn with what particular design she had made him enter her carriage.

"I wanted to enjoin on you the importance of your ceasing your relations with Miss Miller; that of your not appearing to flirt with her; that of your giving her no further opportunity to expose herself; that of your in short letting her alone."

"I'm afraid I can't do anything quite so enlightened as *that,* he returned. "I like her awfully, you know."

"All the more reason you shouldn't help her to make a scandal."

"Well, there shall be nothing scandalous in my attentions to her," he was willing to promise.

"There certainly will be in the way she takes them. But I've said what I had on my conscience," Mrs. Walker pursued. "If you wish to rejoin the young lady I'll put you down. Here, by the way, you have a chance."

The carriage was engaged in that part of the Pincian drive which overhangs the wall of Rome and overlooks the beautiful Villa Borghese.[43] It is bordered by a large parapet, near which are several seats. One of these, at a distance, was occupied by a gentleman and a lady, toward whom Mrs. Walker gave a toss of her head. At the same moment these persons rose and walked to the parapet. Winterbourne had asked the coachman to stop; he now descended from the carriage. His companion looked at him a moment in silence and then, while he raised his hat, drove majestically away. He stood where he had alighted; he had turned his eyes toward Daisy and her cavalier. They evidently saw no one; they were too deeply occupied with each other. When they reached the low garden-wall they remained a little looking off at the great flat-topped pine-clusters of Villa Borghese; then the girl's attendant admirer seated himself familiarly on the broad ledge of the wall. The western sun in the opposite sky sent out a brilliant shaft through a couple of cloud-bars; whereupon the gallant Giovanelli took her parasol out of her hands and opened it. She came a little nearer and he held the parasol over her; then, still holding it, he let is so rest on her shoulder that both of their heads were hidden from Winterbourne. This young man stayed but a moment longer; then he began to walk. But he walked—not toward the couple united beneath the parasol, rather toward the residence of his aunt Mrs. Costello.

IV

He flattered himself on the following day that there was no smiling among the servants when he at least asked for Mrs. Miller at her hotel. This lady and her daughter, however, were not at home; and on the next day after, repeating his visit, Winterbourne again was met by a denial. Mrs. Walker's party took place on the evening of the third day, and in spite of the final reserves that had marked his last interview with that social critic our young man was among the guests. Mrs.

---

[43] The former summer palace of the Borghese family of Italian noblemen; now a public park and museum.

Walker was one of those pilgrims from the younger world who, while in contact with the elder, make a point, in their own phrase, of studying European society; and she had on this occasion collected several specimens of diversely-born humanity to serve, as might be, for text-books. When Winterbourne arrived the little person he desired most to find wasn't there; but in a few moments he saw Mrs. Miller come in alone, very shyly and ruefully. This lady's hair, above the dead waste of her temples, was more frizzled than ever. As she approached their hostess Winterbourne also drew near.

"You see I've come all alone," said Daisy's unsupported parent. "I'm so frightened I don't know what to do; it's the first time I've ever been to a party alone—especially in this country. I wanted to bring Randolph or Eugenio or some one, but Daisy just pushed me off by myself. I ain't used to going round alone."

"And doesn't your daughter intend to favour us with her society?" Mrs. Walker impressively enquired.

"Well, Daisy's all dressed," Mrs. Miller testified with that accent of the dispassionate, if not of the philosophic, historian with which she always recorded the current incidents of her daughter's career. "She got dressed on purpose before dinner. But she has a friend of hers there; that gentleman—the handsomest of the Italians—that she wanted to bring. They've got going at the piano—it seems as if they couldn't leave off. Mr. Giovanelli does sing splendidly. But I guess they'll come before very long," Mrs. Miller hopefully concluded.

"I'm sorry she should come—in that particular way," Mrs. Walker permitted herself to observe.

"Well, I told her there was no use in her getting dressed before dinner if she was going to wait three hours," returned Daisy's mamma. "I didn't see the use of her putting on such a dress as that to sit round with Mr. Giovanelli."

"This is most horrible!" said Mrs. Walker, turning away and addressing herself to Winterbourne. "*Elle s'affiche, la malheureuse.*[44] It's her revenge for my having ventured to remonstrate with her. When she comes I shan't speak to her."

Daisy came after eleven o'clock, but she wasn't, on such an occasion, a young lady to wait to be spoken to. She rustled forward in radiant loveliness, smiling and chattering, carrying a large bouquet and attended by Mr. Giovanelli. Every one stopped talking and turned and looked at her while she floated up to Mrs. Walker, "I'm afraid you thought I never was coming, so I sent mother off to tell you. I wanted to make Mr. Giovanelli practise some things before he came; you know he sings beautifully, and I want you to ask him to sing. This is Mr. Giovanelli; you know I introduced him to you; he's got the most lovely voice and he knows the most charming set of songs. I made him go over them this evening on purpose; we had the greatest time at the hotel." Of all this Daisy delivered herself with the sweetest brightest loudest confidence, looking now at her hostess and now at all the room, while she gave a series of little pats, round her very white shoulders, to the edges of her dress. "Is there any one I know?" she as undiscourageably asked.

"I think every one knows you!" said Mrs. Walker as with a grand intention; and she gave a very cursory greeting to Mr. Giovanelli. This gentleman bore himself gallantly; he smiled and bowed and showed his white teeth, he curled his moustaches and rolled his eyes and performed all the proper functions of a handsome Italian at an evening party. He sang, very prettily, half a dozen songs, though Mrs. Walker afterwards declared that she had been quite unable to find out who

[44] "She flaunts herself, the poor wretch" (French).

asked him. It was apparently not Daisy who had set him in motion—this young lady being seated a distance from the piano and though she had publicly, as it were, professed herself his musical patroness or guarantor, giving herself to gay and audible discourse while he warbled.

"It's a pity these rooms are so small; we can't dance," she remarked to Winterbourne as if she had seen him five minutes before.

"I'm not sorry we can't dance," he candidly returned. "I'm incapable of a step."

"Of course you're incapable of a step," the girl assented. "I should think your legs *would* be stiff cooped in there so much of the time in that victoria."

"Well, they were very restless there three days ago," he amicably laughed; "all they really wanted was to dance attendance on you."

"Oh my other friend—my friend in need—stuck to me; he seems more at one with his limbs than you are—I'll say that for him. But did you ever hear anything so cool," Daisy demanded, "as Mrs. Walker's wanting me to get into her carriage and drop poor Mr. Giovanelli, and under the pretext that it was proper? People have different ideas! It would have been most unkind; he had been talking about that walk for ten days."

"He shouldn't have talked about it at all," Winterbourne decided to make answer on this: "he would never have proposed to a young lady of this country to walk about the streets of Rome with him."

"About the streets?" she cried with her pretty stare. "Where then would he have proposed to her to walk? The Pincio ain't the streets either, I guess; and I besides, thank goodness, am not a young lady of this country. The young ladies of this country have a dreadfully pokey time of it, by what I can discover; I don't see why I should change my habits for *such* stupids."

"I'm afraid your habits are those of a ruthless flirt," said Winterbourne with studied severity.

"Of course they are!"—and she hoped, evidently, by the manner of it, to take his breath away. "I'm a fearful frightful flirt! Did you ever hear of a nice girl that wasn't? But I suppose you'll tell me now I'm not a nice girl."

He remained grave indeed under the shock of her cynical profession. "You're a very nice girl, but I wish you'd flirt with me, and me only."

"Ah thank you, thank you very much: you're the last man I should think of flirting with. As I've had the pleasure of informing you, you're too stiff."

"You say that too often," he resentfully remarked.

Daisy gave a delighted laugh. "If I could have the sweet hope of making you angry I'd say it again."

"Don't do that—when I'm angry I'm stiffer than ever. But if you won't flirt with me do cease at least to flirt with your friend at the piano. They don't," he declared as in full sympathy with "them," "understand that sort of thing here."

"I thought they understood nothing else!" Daisy cried with startling world-knowledge.   *flirting*

"Not in young unmarried women."

"It seems to me much more proper in young unmarried than in old married ones," she retorted.

"Well," said Winterbourne, "when you deal with natives you must go by the custom of the country. American flirting is a purely American silliness; it has—in its ineptitude of innocence—no place in *this* system. So when you show yourself in public with Mr. Giovanelli and without your mother—"

"Gracious, poor mother!"—and she made it beautifully unspeakable.

Winterbourne had a touched sense for this, but it didn't alter his attitude. "Though *you* may be flirting Mr. Giovanelli isn't—he means something else."

"He isn't preaching at any rate," she returned. "And if you want very much to know, we're neither of us flirting—not a little speck. We're too good friends for that. We're real intimate friends."

He was to continue to find her thus at moments inimitable. "Ah," he then judged, "if you're in love with each other it's another affair altogether!"

She had allowed him up to this point to speak so frankly that he had no thought of shocking her by the force of his logic; yet she now none the less immediately rose, blushing visibly and leaving him mentally to exclaim that the name of little American flirts was incoherence. "Mr. Giovanelli at least," she answered, sparing but a single small queer glance for it, a queerer small glance, he felt, than he had ever yet had from her—"Mr. Giovanelli never says to me such very disagreeable things."

It had an effect on him—he stood staring. The subject of their contention had finished singing; he left the piano, and his recognition of what—a little awkwardly—didn't take place in celebration of this might nevertheless have been an acclaimed operatic tenor's series of repeated ducks before the curtain. So he bowed himself over to Daisy. "Won't you come to the other room and have some tea?" he asked—offering Mrs. Walker's slightly thin refreshment as he might have done all the kingdoms of the earth.

Daisy at last turned on Winterbourne a more natural and calculable light. He was but the more muddled by it, however, since so inconsequent a smile made nothing clear—it seemed at the most to prove in her a sweetness and softness that reverted instinctively to the pardon of offences. "It has never occurred to Mr. Winterbourne to offer me any tea," she said with her finest little intention of torment and triumph.

"I've offered you excellent advice," the young man permitted himself to growl.

"I prefer weak tea!" cried Daisy, and she went off with the brilliant Giovanelli. She sat with him in the adjoining room, in the embrasure of the window, for the rest of the evening. There was an interesting performance at the piano, but neither of these conversers gave heed to it. When Daisy came to take leave of Mrs. Walker this lady conscientiously repaired the weakness of which she had been guilty at the moment of the girl's arrival—she turned her back straight on Miss Miller and left her to depart with what grace she might.[45] Winterbourne happened to be near the door; he saw it all. Daisy turned very pale and looked at her mother, but Mrs. Miller was humbly unconscious of any rupture of any law or of any deviation from any custom. She appeared indeed to have felt an incongruous impulse to draw attention to her own striking conformity. "Good-night, Mrs. Walker," she said; "we've had a beautiful evening. You see if I let Daisy come to parties without me I don't want her to go away without me." Daisy turned away, looking with a small white prettiness, a blighted grace, at the circle near the door: Winterbourne saw that for the first moment she was too much shocked and puzzled even for indignation. He on his side was greatly touched.

"That was very cruel," he promptly remarked to Mrs. Walker.

---

[45] Mrs. Walker, in refusing to speak to Daisy, has administered what was considered a crushing insult, a "cut" or "cut direct."

But this lady's face was also as a stone. "She never enters my drawing-room again."

Since Winterbourne then, hereupon, was not to meet her in Mrs. Walker's drawing-room he went as often as possible to Mrs. Miller's hotel. The ladies were rarely at home, but when he found them the devoted Giovanelli was always present. Very often the glossy little Roman, serene in success, but not unduly presumptuous, occupied with Daisy alone the florid salon enjoyed by Eugenio's care, Mrs. Miller being apparently ever of the opinion that discretion is the better part of solicitude. Winterbourne noted, at first with surprise, that Daisy on these occasions was neither embarrassed nor annoyed by his own entrance; but he presently began to feel that she had no more surprises for him and that he really liked, after all, not making out what she was "up to." She showed no displeasure for the interruption of her *tête-à-tête* with Giovanelli; she could chatter as freshly and freely with two gentlemen as with one, and this easy flow had ever the same anomaly for her earlier friend that it was so free without availing itself of its freedom. Winterbourne reflected that if she was seriously interested in the Italian it was odd she shouldn't take more trouble to preserve the sanctity of their interviews, and he liked her the better for her innocent-looking indifference and her inexhaustible gaiety. He could hardly have said why, but she struck him as a young person not formed for a troublesome jealousy. Smile at such a betrayal though the reader may, it was a fact with regard to the women who had hitherto interested him that, given certain contingencies, Winterbourne could see himself afraid—literally afraid—of these ladies. It pleased him to believe that even were twenty other things different and Daisy should love him and he should know it and like it, he would still never be afraid of Daisy. It must be added that this conviction was not altogether flattering to her: it represented that she was nothing every way if not light.

But she was evidently very much interested in Giovanelli. She looked at him whenever he spoke; she was perpetually telling him to do this and to do that; she was constantly chaffing and abusing him. She appeared completely to have forgotten that her other friend had said anything to displease her at Mrs. Walker's entertainment. One Sunday afternoon, having gone to Saint Peter's with his aunt, Winterbourne became aware that the young woman held in horror by that lady was strolling about the great church under escort of her coxcomb of the Corso.[46] It amused him, after a debate, to point out the exemplary pair—even at the cost, as it proved, of Mrs. Costello's saying when she had taken them in through her eye-glass: "That's what makes you so pensive in these days, eh?"

"I hadn't the least idea I was pensive," he pleaded.

"You're very much preoccupied; you're always thinking of something."

"And what is it," he asked, "that you accuse me of thinking of?"

"Of that young lady's, Miss Baker's, Miss Chandler's—what's her name?—Miss Miller's intrigue with that little barber's block."

"Do you call it an intrigue," he asked—"an affair that goes on with such peculiar publicity?"

"That's their folly," said Mrs. Costello, "it's not their merit."

"No," he insisted with a hint perhaps of the preoccupation to which his aunt had alluded—"I don't believe there's anything to be called an intrigue."

---

[46] Dandy of this Roman street.

"Well"—and Mrs. Costello dropped her glass—"I've heard a dozen people speak of it: they say she's quite carried away by him."

"They're certainly as thick as thieves," our embarrassed young man allowed.

Mrs. Costello came back to them, however, after a little; and Winterbourne recognised in this a further illustration—than that supplied by his own condition—of the spell projected by the case. "He's certainly very handsome. One easily sees how it is. She thinks him the most elegant man in the world, the finest gentleman possible. She has never seen anything like him—he's better even than the courier. It was the courier probably who introduced him, and if he succeeds in marrying the young lady the courier will come in for a magnificent commission."

"I don't believe she thinks of marrying him," Winterbourne reasoned, "and I don't believe he hopes to marry her."

"You may be very sure she thinks of nothing at all. She romps on from day to day, from hour to hour, as they did in the Golden Age.[47] I can imagine nothing more vulgar," said Mrs. Costello, whose figure of speech scarcely went on all fours. "And at the same time," she added, "depend upon it she may tell you any moment that she is 'engaged.'"

"I think that's more than Giovanelli really expects," said Winterbourne.

"And who is Giovanelli?"

"The shiny—but, to do him justice, not greasy—little Roman. I've asked questions about him and learned something. He's apparently a perfectly respectable little man. I believe he's in a small way a *cavaliere avvocato*.[48] But he doesn't move in what are called the first circles. I think it really not absolutely impossible the courier introduced him. He's evidently immensely charmed with Miss Miller. If she thinks him the finest gentleman in the world, he, on his side, has never found himself in personal contact with such splendour, such opulence, such personal daintiness, as this young lady's. And then she must seem to him wonderfully pretty and interesting. Yes, he can't really hope to pull it off. That must appear to him too impossible a piece of luck. He has nothing but his handsome face to offer, and there's a substantial, a possibly explosive Mr. Miller in that mysterious land of dollars and six-shooters. Giovanelli's but too conscious that he hasn't a title to offer. If he were only a count or a *marchese!*[49] What on earth can he make of the way they've taken him up?"

"He accounts for it by his handsome face and thinks Miss Miller a young lady *qui se passe ses fantaisies!*"[50]

"It's very true," Winterbourne pursued. "that Daisy and her mamma haven't yet risen to that stage of—what shall I call it?—of culture, at which the idea of catching a count or a *marchese* begins. I believe them intellectually incapable of that conception."

"Ah but the *cavaliere avvocato* doesn't believe them!" cried Mrs. Costello.

Of the observation excited by Daisy's "intrigue" Winterbourne gathered that day at Saint Peter's[51] sufficient evidence. A dozen of the American colonists in Rome came to talk with his relative, who sat on a small portable stool at the base of one of the great pilasters.[52] The vesper-service was going forward in splendid

---

[47] According to classical myth, the first age of the world, marked by happiness, prosperity, and innocence.

[48] "Gentleman lawyer" (Italian).   [49] "Marquis" (Italian), a nobleman.

[50] "Who indulges her whims" (French).   [51] Saint Peter's Cathedral in Rome.

[52] Rectangular supports connected to a wall.

chants and organ-tones in the adjacent choir, and meanwhile, between Mrs. Costello and her friends, much was said about poor little Miss Miller's going really "too far." Winterbourne was not pleased with what he heard; but when, coming out upon the great steps of the church, he saw Daisy, who had emerged before him, get into an open cab with her accomplice and roll away through the cynical streets of Rome, the measure of her course struck him as simply there to take. He felt very sorry for her—not exactly that he believed she had completely lost her wits, but because it was painful to see so much that was pretty and undefended and natural sink so low in human estimation. He made an attempt after this to give a hint to Mrs. Miller. He met one day in the Corso a friend—a tourist like himself—who had just come out of the Doria Palace,[53] where he had been walking through the beautiful gallery. His friend "went on" for some moments about the great portrait of Innocent X, by Velasquez,[54] suspended in one of the cabinets of the palace, and then said: "And in the same cabinet, by the way, I enjoyed sight of an image of a different kind; that little American who's so much more a work of nature than of art and whom you pointed out to me last week." In answer to Winterbourne's enquiries his friend narrated that the little American—prettier now than ever—was seated with a companion in the secluded nook in which the papal presence is enshrined.

"All alone?" the young man heard himself disingenuously ask.

"Alone with a little Italian who sports in his button-hole a stack of flowers. The girl's a charming beauty, but I thought I understood from you the other day that she's a young lady *du meilleur monde*."[55]

"So she is!" said Winterbourne; and having assured himself that his informant had seen the interesting pair but ten minutes before, he jumped into a cab and went to call on Mrs. Miller. She was at home, but she apologised for receiving him in Daisy's absence.

"She's gone out somewhere with Mr. Giovanelli. She's always going round with Mr. Giovanelli."

"I've noticed they're intimate indeed," Winterbourne concurred.

"Oh it seems as if they couldn't live without each other!" said Mrs. Miller. "Well, he's a real gentleman anyhow. I guess I have the joke on Daisy—that she *must* be engaged!"

"And how does your daughter *take* the joke?"

"Oh she just says she ain't. But she might as *well* be!" this philosophic parent resumed. "She goes on as if she was. But I've made Mr. Giovanelli promise to tell me if Daisy don't. I'd want to write to Mr. Miller about it—wouldn't you?"

Winterbourne replied that he certainly should; and the state of mind of Daisy's mamma struck him as so unprecedented in the annals of parental vigilance that he recoiled before the attempt to educate at a single interview either her conscience or her wit.

After this Daisy was never at home and he ceased to meet her at the houses of their common acquaintance, because, as he perceived, these shrewd people had quite made up their minds as to the length she must have gone. They ceased to invite her, intimating that they wished to make, and make strongly, for the benefit of observant Europeans, the point that though Miss Daisy Miller was a pretty

[53] A Roman baroque palace.
[54] The Spanish painter Diego Rodríguez de Silva y Velásquez (1599–1660); his 1649 portrait of Pope Innocent X, Giovanni Battista Panfili (1574–1655) hangs in Rome's Doria Gallery.
[55] "Of the best society" (French).

American girl all right, her behaviour wasn't pretty at all—was in fact regarded by her compatriots as quite monstrous. Winterbourne wondered how she felt about all the cold shoulders that were turned upon her, and sometimes found himself suspecting with impatience that she simply didn't feel and didn't know. He set her down as hopelessly childish and shallow, as such mere giddiness and ignorance incarnate as was powerless either to heed or to suffer. Then at other moments he couldn't doubt that she carried about in her elegant and irresponsible little organism a defiant, passionate, perfectly observant consciousness of the impression she produced. He asked himself whether the defiance would come from the consciousness of innocence or from her being essentially a young person of the reckless class. Then it had to be admitted, he felt, that holding fast to a belief in her "innocence" was more and more but a matter of gallantry too fine-spun for use. As I have already had occasion to relate, he was reduced without pleasure to this chopping of logic and vexed at his poor fallibility, his want of instinctive certitude as to how far her extravagance was generic and national and how far it was crudely personal. Whatever it was he had helplessly missed her, and now it was too late. She was "carried away" by Mr. Giovanelli.

A few days after his brief interview with her mother he came across her at that supreme seat of flowering desolation know as the Palace of the Cæsars.[56] The early Roman spring had filled the air with bloom and perfume, and the rugged surface of the Palatine was muffled with tender verdure. Daisy moved at her ease over the great mounds of ruin that are embanked with mossy marble and paved with monumental inscriptions. It seemed to him he had never known Rome so lovely as just then. He looked off at the enchanting harmony of line and colour that remotely encircles the city—he inhaled the softly humid odours and felt the freshness of the year and the antiquity of the place reaffirm themselves in deep interfusion. It struck him also that Daisy had never showed to the eye for so utterly charming; but this had been his conviction on every occasion of their meeting. Giovanelli was of course at her side, and Giovanelli too glowed as never before with something of the glory of his race.

"Well," she broke out upon the friend it would have been such mockery to designate as the latter's rival, "I should think you'd be quite lonesome!"

"Lonesome?" Winterbourne resignedly echoed.

"You're always going round by yourself. Can't you get any one to walk with you?"

"I'm not so fortunate," he answered, "as your gallant companion."

Giovanelli had from the first treated him with distinguished politeness; he listened with a deferential air to his remarks; he laughed punctiliously at his pleasantries; he attached such importance as he could find terms for to Miss Miller's cold compatriot. He carried himself in no degree like a jealous wooer; he had obviously a great deal of tact; he had no objection to any one's expecting a little humility of him. It even struck Winterbourne that he almost yearned at times for some private communication in the interest of his character for common sense; a chance to remark to him as another intelligent man that, bless him, *he* knew how extraordinary was their young lady and didn't flatter himself with confident—at least *too* confident and too delusive—hopes of matrimony and dollars. On this occasion he strolled away from his charming charge to pluck a sprig of almond-blossom which he carefully arranged in his button-hole.

---

[56] A Roman palace, erected by the Caesars, on the Palatine Hill.

"I know why you say that," Daisy meanwhile observed. "Because you think I go round too much with *him!*" And she nodded at her discreet attendant.

"Every one thinks so—if you care to know," was all Winterbourne found to reply.

"Of course I care to know!"—she made this point with much expression. "But I don't believe a word of it. They're only pretending to be shocked. They don't really care a straw what I do. Besides, I don't go round so much."   *why should they?*

"I think you'll find they do care. They'll show it—disagreeably," he took on himself to state.

Daisy weighed the importance of that idea. "How—disagreeably?"

"Haven't you noticed anything?" he compassionately asked.

"I've noticed *you*. But I noticed you've no more 'give' than a ramrod the first time ever I saw you."

"You'll find at least that I've more 'give' than several others," he patiently smiled.

"How shall I find it?"

"By going to see the others."

"What will they do to me?"

"They'll show you the cold shoulder. Do you know what that means?"

Daisy was looking at him intently; she began to colour. "Do you mean as Mrs. Walker did the other night?"

"Exactly as Mrs. Walker did the other night."

She looked away at Giovanelli, still titivating with his almond-blossom. Then with her attention again on the important subject: "I shouldn't think you'd let people be so unkind!"

"How can I help it?"

"I should think you'd want to say something."

"I do want to say something"—and Winterbourne paused a moment. "I want to say that your mother tells me she believes you engaged."

"Well, I guess she does," said Daisy very simply.

The young man began to laugh. "And does Randolph believe it?"

"I guess Randolph doesn't believe anything." This testimony to Randolph's scepticism excited Winterbourne to further mirth, and he noticed that Giovanelli was coming back to them. Daisy, observing it as well, addressed herself again to her countryman. "Since you've mentioned it," she said, "I *am* engaged." He looked at her hard—he had stopped laughing. "You don't believe it!" she added.

He asked himself, and it was for a moment like testing a heart-beat; after which, "Yes, I believe it!" he said.

"Oh no, you don't," she answered. "But *if* you possibly do," she still more perversely pursued—"well, I ain't!"

Miss Miller and her constant guide were on their way to the gate of the enclosure, so that Winterbourne, who had but lately entered, presently took leave of them. A week later on he went to dine at a beautiful villa on the Cælian Hill,[57] and, on arriving, dismissed his hired vehicle. The evening was perfect and he promised himself the satisfaction of walking home beneath the Arch of Constantine and past the vaguely-lighted monuments of the Forum.[58] Above was a

---

[57] One of the hills surrounding Rome.

[58] A memorial in Rome built in A.D. 315 by Constantine I (A.D. 280?–337), or Constantine the Great, emperor of Rome from 306 to 337; the ruins of the administrative center of ancient Rome.

moon half-developed, whose radiance was not brilliant but veiled in a thin cloud-curtain that seemed to diffuse and equalise it. When on his return from the villa at eleven o'clock he approached the dusky circle of the Colosseum[59] the sense of the romantic in him easily suggested that the interior, in such an atmosphere, would well repay a glance. He turned aside and walked to one of the empty arches, near which, as he observed, an open carriage—one of the little Roman street-cabs— was stationed. Then he passed in among the cavernous shadows of the great structure and emerged upon the clear and silent arena. The place had never seemed to him more impressive. One half of the gigantic circus was in deep shade while the other slept in the luminous dusk. As he stood there he began to murmur Byron's famous lines out of "Manfred";[60] but before he had finished his quotation he remembered that if nocturnal meditation thereabouts was the fruit of a rich literary culture it was none the less deprecated by medical science. The air of other ages surrounded one; but the air of other ages, coldly analysed, was no better than a villainous miasma. Winterbourne sought, however, toward the middle of the arena, a further reach of vision, intending the next moment a hasty retreat. The great cross in the centre was almost obscured; only as he drew near did he make it out distinctly. He thus also distinguished two persons stationed on the low steps that formed its base. One of these was a woman seated; her companion hovered before her.

Presently the sound of the woman's voice came to him distinctly in the warm night-air. "Well, he looks at us as one of the old lions or tigers may have looked at the Christian martyrs!" These words were winged with their accent, so that they fluttered and settled about him in the darkness like vague white doves. It was Miss Daisy Miller who had released them for flight.

"Let us hope he's not very hungry"—the bland Giovanelli fell in with her humour. "He'll have to take *me* first; you'll serve for dessert."

Winterbourne felt himself pulled up with final horror now—and, it must be added, with final relief. It was as if a sudden clearance had taken place in the ambiguity of the poor girl's appearances and the whole riddle of her contradictions had grown easy to read. She was a young lady about the *shades* of whose perversity a foolish puzzled gentleman need no longer trouble his head or his heart. That once questionable quantity *had* no shades—it was a mere black little blot. He stood there looking at her, looking at her companion too, and not reflecting that though he saw them vaguely he himself must have been more brightly presented. He felt angry at all his shiftings of view—he felt ashamed of all his tender little scruples and his witless little mercies. He was about to advance again, and then again checked himself; not from the fear of doing her injustice, but from a sense of the danger of showing undue exhilaration for this disburdenment of cautious criticism. He turned away toward the entrance of the place; but as he did so he heard Daisy speak again.

"Why it was Mr. Winterbourne! He saw me and he cuts me dead!"

What a clever little reprobate she was, he was amply able to reflect at this, and how smartly she feigned, how promptly she sought to play off on him, a surprised and injured innocence! But nothing would induce him to cut her either "dead" or

---

[59] The ruins of an amphitheater, or arena, built in Rome (A.D. 75?–80?).

[60] "I do remember me, that in my youth, / When I was wandering,—upon such a night— / I stood within the Coliseum's wall, / Midst the chief relics of almighty Rome" (III. iv. 8–11), from the verse drama *Manfred* (1817), by Lord Byron.

to within any measurable distance even of the famous "inch" of her life. He came forward again and went toward the great cross. Daisy had got up and Giovanelli lifted his hat. Winterbourne had now begun to think simply of the madness, on the ground of exposure and infection, of a frail young creature's lounging away such hours in a nest of malaria. What if she *were* the most plausible of little reprobates? That was no reason for her dying of the *perniciosa*.[61] "How long have you been 'fooling round' here?" he asked with conscious roughness.

Daisy, lovely in the sinister silver radiance, appraised him a moment, roughness and all. "Well, I guess all evening." She answered with spirit and, he could see even then, with exaggeration. "I never saw anything so quaint."

"I'm afraid," he returned, "you'll not think a bad attack of Roman fever very quaint. This is the way people catch it. I wonder," he added to Giovanelli, "that you, a native Roman, should countenance such extraordinary rashness."

"Ah," said this seasoned subject, "for myself I have no fear."

"Neither have I—for you!" Winterbourne retorted in French. "I'm speaking for this young lady."

[handwritten margin note: just like he doesn't care about her reputation]

Giovanelli raised his well-shaped eyebrows and showed his shining teeth, but took his critic's rebuke with docility. "I assured Mademoiselle it was a grave indiscretion, but when was Mademoiselle ever prudent?"

"I never was sick, and I don't mean to be!" Mademoiselle declared. "I don't look like much, but I'm healthy! I was bound to see the Colosseum by moonlight—I wouldn't have wanted to go home without *that;* and we've had the most beautiful time, haven't we, Mr. Giovanelli? If there has been any danger Eugenio can give me some pills. Eugenio has got some splendid pills."

"*I* should advise you then," said Winterbourne, "to drive home as fast as possible and take one!"

Giovanelli smiled as for the striking happy thought.

"What you say is very wise. I'll go and make sure the carriage is at hand." And he went forward rapidly.

Daisy followed with Winterbourne. He tried to deny himself the small fine anguish of looking at her, but his eyes themselves refused to spare him, and she seemed moreover not in the least embarrassed. He spoke no word; Daisy chattered over the beauty of the place: "Well, I *have* seen the Colosseum by moonlight—that's one thing I can rave about!" Then noticing her companion's silence she asked him why he was so stiff—it had always been her great word. He made no answer, but he felt his laugh an immense negation of stiffness. They passed under one of the dark archways; Giovanelli was in front with the carriage. Here Daisy stopped a moment, looking at her compatriot. "*Did* you believe I was engaged the other day?"

"It doesn't matter now what I believed the other day!" he replied with infinite point.

It was a wonder how she didn't wince for it. "Well, what do you believe now?"

"I believe it makes very little difference whether you're engaged or not!"

He felt her lighted eyes fairly penetrate the thick gloom of the vaulted passage—as if to seek some access to him she hadn't yet compassed. But Giovanelli, with a graceful inconsequence, was at present all for retreat. "Quick, quick; if we get in by midnight we're quite safe!"

---

[61] "Pernicious malaria" (Italian).

Daisy took her seat in the carriage and the fortunate Italian placed himself beside her. "Don't forget Eugenio's pills!" said Winterbourne as he lifted his hat.

"I don't care," she unexpectedly cried out for this, "whether I have Roman fever or not!" On which the cab-driver cracked his whip and they rolled across the desultory patches of antique pavement.

Winterbourne—to do him justice, as it were—mentioned to no one that he had encountered Miss Miller at midnight in the Colosseum with a gentleman; in spite of which deep discretion, however, the fact of the scandalous adventure was known a couple of days later, with a dozen vivid details, to every member of the little American circle, and was commented accordingly. Winterbourne judged that the people about the hotel had been thoroughly empowered to testify, and that after Daisy's return there would have been an exchange of jokes between the porter and the cab-driver. But the young man became aware at the same moment of how thoroughly it had ceased to ruffle him that the little American flirt should be "talked about" by low-minded menials. These sources of current criticism a day or two later abounded still further: the little American flirt was alarmingly ill and the doctors now in possession of the scene. Winterbourne, when the rumour came to him, immediately went to the hotel for more news. He found that two or three charitable friends had preceded him and that they were being entertained in Mrs. Miller's salon by the all-efficient Randolph.

"It's going round at night that way, you bet—that's what has made her so sick. She's always going round at night. I shouldn't think she'd want to—it's so plaguey dark over here. You can't see anything over here without the moon's right up. In America they don't go round by the moon!" Mrs. Miller meanwhile wholly surrendered to her genius for unapparent uses; her salon knew her less than ever, and she was presumably now at least giving her daughter the advantage of her society. It was clear that Daisy was dangerously ill.

Winterboune constantly attended for news from the sick-room, which reached him, however, but with worrying indirectness, though he once had speech, for a moment, of the poor girl's physician and once saw Mrs. Miller, who, sharply alarmed, struck him as thereby more happily inspired than he could have conceived and indeed as the most noiseless and light-handed of nurses. She invoked a good deal the remote shade of Dr. Davis, but Winterbourne paid her the compliment of taking her after all for less monstrous a goose. To this indulgence indeed something she further said perhaps even more insidiously disposed him. "Daisy spoke of you the other day quite pleasantly. Half the time she doesn't know what she's saying, but that time I think she did. She gave me a message—she told me to tell you. She wanted you to know she never was engaged to that handsome Italian who was always round. I'm sure I'm very glad; Mr. Giovanelli hasn't been near us since she was taken ill. I thought he was so much of a gentleman, but I don't call that very polite! A lady told me he was afraid I hadn't approved of his being round with her so much evenings. Of course it ain't as if their evenings were as pleasant as ours—since *we* don't seem to feel that way about the poison. I guess I *don't* see the point now; but I suppose he knows I'm a lady and I'd scorn to raise a fuss. Anyway, she wants you to realise she ain't engaged. I don't know why she makes so much of it, but she said to me three times 'Mind you tell Mr. Winterbourne.' And then she told me to ask if you remembered the time you went up to that castle in Switzerland. But I said I wouldn't give any such message as *that*. Only if she ain't engaged I guess I'm glad to realise it too."

But, as Winterbourne had originally judged, the truth on this question had small actual relevance. A week after this poor girl died; it had been indeed a terrible case of the *perniciosa*. A grave was found for her in the little Protestant cemetery, by an angle of the wall of imperial Rome, beneath the cypresses and the thick spring-flowers. Winterbourne stood there beside it with a number of other mourners; a number larger than the scandal excited by the young lady's career might have made probable. Near him stood Giovanelli, who came nearer still before Winterbourne turned away. Giovanelli, in decorous mourning, showed but a whiter face; his button-hole lacked its nosegay and he had visibly something urgent—and even to distress—to say, which he scarce knew how to "place." He decided at last to confide it with a pale convulsion to Winterbourne. "She was the most beautiful young lady I ever saw, and the most amiable." To which he added in a moment: "Also—naturally!—the most innocent."

Winterbourne sounded him with hard dry eyes, but presently repeated his words, "The most innocent?"

"The most innocent!"

It came somehow so much too late that our friend could only glare at its having come at all. "Why the devil," he asked, "did you take her to that fatal place?"

Giovanelli raised his neat shoulders and eyebrows to within suspicion of a shrug. "For myself I had no fear; and *she* —she did what she liked!"

Winterbourne's eyes attached themselves to the ground. "She did what she liked!"

It determined on the part of poor Giovanelli a further pious, a further candid, confidence. "If she had lived I should have got nothing. She never would have married me."

It had been spoken as if to attest, in all sincerity, his disinterestedness, but Winterbourne scarce knew what welcome to give it. He said, however, with a grace inferior to his friend's: "I dare say not."

The latter was even by this not discouraged. "For a moment I hoped so. But no, I'm convinced."

Winterbourne took it in; he stood staring at the raw protuberance among the April daisies. When he turned round again his fellow mourner had stepped back.

He almost immediately left Rome, but the following summer he again met his aunt Mrs. Costello at Vevey. Mrs. Costello extracted from the charming old hotel there a value that the Miller family hadn't mastered the secret of. In the interval Winterbourne had often thought of the most interesting member of that trio—of her mystifying manners and her queer adventure. One day he spoke of her to his aunt—said it was on his conscience he had done her injustice.

"I'm sure I don't know"—that lady showed caution. "How did your injustice affect her?"

"She sent me a message before her death which I didn't understand at the time. But I've understood it since. She would have appreciated one's esteem."

"She took an odd way to gain it! But do you mean by what you say," Mrs. Costello asked, "that she would have reciprocated one's affection?"

As he made no answer to this she after a little looked round at him—he hadn't been directly within sight; but the effect of that wasn't to make her repeat her question. He spoke, however, after a while. "You were right in that remark that you made last summer. I was booked to make a mistake. I've lived too long in foreign parts." And this time she herself said nothing.

Nevertheless he soon went back to live at Geneva, whence there continue to come the most contradictory accounts of his motives of sojourn: a report that he's "studying" hard—an intimation that he's much interested in a very clever foreign lady.

1878

THE REAL THING*

I

When the porter's wife, who used to answer the house-bell, announced "A gentleman and a lady, sir," I had, as I often had in those days—the wish being father to the thought—an immediate vision of sitters. Sitters my visitors in this case proved to be; but not in the sense I should have preferred. There was nothing at first however to indicate that they mightn't have come for a portrait. The gentleman, a man of fifty, very high and very straight, with a moustache slightly grizzled and a dark grey walking-coat admirably fitted, both of which I noted professionally—I don't mean as a barber or yet as a tailor—would have struck me as a celebrity if celebrities often were striking. It was a truth of which I had for some time been conscious that a figure with a good deal of frontage[1] was, as one might say, almost never a public institution. A glance at the lady helped to remind me of this paradoxical law: she also looked too distinguished to be a "personality." Moreover one would scarcely come across two variations together.

Neither of the pair immediately spoke—they only prolonged the preliminary gaze suggesting that each wished to give the other a chance. They were visibly shy; they stood there letting me take them in—which, as I afterwards perceived, was the most practical thing they could have done. In this way their embarrassment served their cause. I had seen people painfully reluctant to mention that they desired anything so gross as to be represented on canvas; but the scruples of my new friends appeared almost insurmountable. Yet the gentleman might have said "I should like a portrait of my wife," and the lady might have said "I should like a portrait of my husband." Perhaps they weren't husband and wife—this naturally would make the matter more delicate. Perhaps they wished to be done together— in which case they ought to have brought a third person to break the news.

"We come from Mr. Rivet," the lady finally said with a dim smile that had the effect of a moist sponge passed over a "sunk"[2] piece of painting, as well as a vague allusion to vanished beauty. She was as tall and straight, in her degree, as her companion, and with ten years less to carry. She looked as sad as a woman could look whose face was not charged with expression; that is her tinted oval mask showed waste as an exposed surface shows friction. The hand of time had played over her freely, but to an effect of elimination. She was slim and stiff, and so well-dressed, in dark blue cloth, with lappets[3] and pockets and buttons, that it was clear she employed the same tailor as her husband. The couple had an indefin-

---

* First published in *Black and White* (1892).   [1] An imposing figure.   [2] Faded or dull.
[3] Folds or flaps.

able air of prosperous thrift—they evidently got a good deal of luxury for their money. If I was to be one of their luxuries it would behove me to consider my terms.

"Ah Claude Rivet recommended me?" I echoed; and I added that it was very kind of him, though I could reflect that, as he only painted landscape, this wasn't a sacrifice.

The lady looked very hard at the gentleman, and the gentleman looked round the room. Then staring at the floor a moment and stroking his moustache, he rested his pleasant eyes on me with the remark: "He said you were the right one."

"I try to be, when people want to sit."

"Yes, we should like to," said the lady anxiously.

"Do you mean together?"

My visitors exchanged a glance. "If you could do anything with *me* I suppose it would be double," the gentleman stammered.

"Oh yes, there's naturally a higher charge for two figures than for one."

"We should like to make it pay," the husband confessed.

"That's very good of you," I returned, appreciating so unwonted a sympathy—for I supposed he meant pay the artist.

A sense of strangeness seemed to dawn on the lady.

"We mean for the illustrations—Mr. Rivet said you might put one in."

"Put in—an illustration?" I was equally confused.

"Sketch her off, you know," said the gentleman, colouring.

It was only then that I understood the service Claude Rivet had rendered me; he had told them how I worked in black-and-white, for magazines, for story-books, for sketches of contemporary life, and consequently had copious employment for models. These things were true, but it was not less true—I may confess it now; whether because the aspiration was to lead to everything or to nothing I leave the reader to guess—that I couldn't get the honours, to say nothing of the emoluments,[4] of a great painter of portraits out of my head. My "illustrations" were my pot-boilers; I looked to a different branch of art—far and away the most interesting it had always seemed to me—to perpetuate my fame. There was no shame in looking to it also to make my fortune; but that fortune was by so much further from being made from the moment my visitors wished to be "done" for nothing. I was disappointed; for in the pictorial sense I had immediately *seen* them. I had seized their type—I had already settled what I would do with it. Something that wouldn't absolutely have pleased them, I afterwards reflected.

"Ah you're—you're—a—?" I began as soon as I had mastered my surprise. I couldn't bring out the dingy word "models": it seemed so little to fit the case.

"We haven't had much practice," said the lady.

"We've got to *do* something, and we've thought that an artist in your line might perhaps make something of us," her husband threw off. He further mentioned that they didn't know many artists and that they had gone first, on the off-chance—he painted views of course, but sometimes put in figures; perhaps I remembered—to Mr. Rivet, whom they had met a few years before at a place in Norfolk where he was sketching.

"We used to sketch a little ourselves," the lady hinted.

"It's very awkward, but we absolutely *must* do something," her husband went on.

---

[4] Profits.

"Of course we're not so *very* young," she admitted with a wan smile.

With the remark that I might as well know something more about them the husband had handed me a card extracted from a neat new pocket-book—their appurtenances[5] were all of the freshest—and inscribed with the words "Major Monarch." Impressive as these words were they didn't carry my knowledge much further; but my visitor presently added: "I've left the army and we've had the misfortune to lose our money. In fact our means are dreadfully small."

"It's awfully trying—a regular strain," said Mrs. Monarch.

They evidently wished to be discreet—to take care not to swagger because they were gentlefolk. I felt them willing to recognise this as something of a drawback, at the same time that I guessed at an underlying sense—their consolation in adversity—that they *had* their points. They certainly had; but these advantages struck me as preponderantly social; such for instance as would help to make a drawing-room look well. However, a drawing-room was always, or ought to be, a picture.

In consequence of his wife's allusion to their age Major Monarch observed: "Naturally it's more for the figure that we thought of going in. We can still hold ourselves up." On the instant I saw that the figure was indeed their strong point. His "naturally" didn't sound vain, but it lighted up the question. "*She* has the best one," he continued, nodding at his wife with a pleasant after-dinner absence of circumlocution. I could only reply, as if we were in fact sitting over our wine, that this didn't prevent his own from being very good; which led him in turn to make answer: "We thought that if you ever had to do people like us we might be something like it. *She* particularly—for a lady in a book, you know."

I was so amused by them that, to get more of it, I did my best to take their point of view; and though it was an embarrassment to find myself appraising physically, as if they were animals on hire or useful blacks, a pair whom I should have expected to meet only in one of the relations in which criticism is tacit, I looked at Mrs. Monarch judicially enough to be able to exclaim after a moment with conviction: "Oh yes, a lady in a book!" She was singularly like a bad illustration.

"We'll stand up, if you like," said the Major; and he raised himself before me with a really grand air.

I could take his measure at a glance—he was six feet two and a perfect gentleman. It would have paid any club in process of formation and in want of a stamp to engage him at a salary to stand in the principal window. What struck me at once was that in coming to me they had rather missed their vocation; they could surely have been turned to better account for advertising purposes. I couldn't of course see the thing in detail, but I could see them make somebody's fortune—I don't mean their own. There was something in them for a waistcoat-maker, an hotel-keeper or a soap-vendor. I could imagine "We always use it" pinned on their bosoms with the greatest effect; I had a vision of the brilliancy with which they would launch a table d'hôte.[6]

Mrs. Monarch sat still, not from pride but from shyness, and presently her husband said to her: "Get up, my dear, and show how smart you are." She obeyed, but she had no need to get up to show it. She walked to the end of the studio and then came back blushing, her fluttered eyes on the partner of her appeal. I was reminded of an incident I had accidentally had a glimpse of in Paris—being with a friend there, a dramatist about to produce a play, when an actress

---

[5] Belongings, accessories.   [6] A common table for guests at a hotel or restaurant.

came to him to ask to be entrusted with a part. She went through her paces before him, walked up and down as Mrs. Monarch was doing. Mrs. Monarch did it quite well, but I abstained from applauding. It was very odd to see such people apply for such poor pay. She looked as if she had ten thousand a year. Her husband had used the word that described her: she was in the London current jargon essentially and typically "smart." Her figure was, in the same order of ideas, conspicuously and irreproachably "good." For a woman of her age her waist was surprisingly small; her elbow moreover had the orthodox crook. She held her head at the conventional angle, but why did she come to *me?* She ought to have tried on jackets at a big shop. I feared my visitors were not only destitute but "artistic"—which would be a great complication. When she sat down again I thanked her, observing that what a draughtsman most valued in his model was the faculty of keeping quiet.

"Oh, *she* can keep quiet," said Major Monarch. Then he added jocosely: "I've always kept her quiet."

"I'm not a nasty fidget, am I?" It was going to wring tears from me, I felt, the way she hid her head, ostrich-like, in the other broad bosom.

The owner of this expanse addressed his answer to me. "Perhaps it isn't out of place to mention—because we ought to be quite business-like, oughtn't we?—that when I married her she was known as the Beautiful Statue."

"Oh dear!" said Mrs. Monarch ruefully.

"Of course I should want a certain amount of expression," I rejoined.

"Of *course!*"—and I had never heard such unanimity.

"And then I suppose you know that you'll get awfully tired."

"Oh we *never* get tired!" they eagerly cried.

"Have you had any kind of practice?"

They hesitated—they looked at each other. "We've been photographed—*immensely,*" said Mrs. Monarch.

"She means the fellows have asked us themselves," added the Major.

"I see—because you're so good-looking."

"I don't know what they thought, but they were always after us."

"We always got our photographs for nothing," smiled Mrs. Monarch.

"We might have brought some, my dear," her husband remarked.

"I'm not sure we have any left. We've given quantities away," she explained to me.

"With our autographs and that sort of thing," said the Major.

"Are they to be got in the shops?" I enquired as a harmless pleasantry.

"Oh yes, *hers*—they used to be."

"Not now," said Mrs. Monarch with her eyes on the floor.

II

I could fancy the "sort of thing" they put on the presentation copies of their photographs, and I was sure they wrote a beautiful hand. It was odd how quickly I was sure of everything that concerned them. If they were now so poor as to have to earn shillings and pence they could never have had much of a margin. Their good looks had been their capital, and they had good-humouredly made the most of the career that this resource marked out for them. It was in their faces, the blankness, the deep intellectual repose of the twenty years of country-house[7] visiting that had given them pleasant intonations. I could see the sunny drawing-rooms, sprinkled with periodicals she didn't read, in which Mrs. Monarch had continuously sat; I could see the wet shrubberies in which she had walked, equipped to admiration for either exercise. I could see the rich covers[8] the Major had helped to shoot and the wonderful garments in which, late at night, he repaired to the smoking-room to talk about them. I could imagine their leggings and waterproofs, their knowing tweeds and rugs, their rolls of sticks and cases of tackle and neat umbrellas; and I could evoke the exact appearance of their servants and the compact variety of their luggage on the platforms of country stations.

They gave small tips, but they were liked; they didn't do anything themselves, but they were welcome. They looked so well everywhere; they gratified the general relish for stature, complexion and "form." They knew it without fatuity or vulgarity, and they respected themselves in consequence. They weren't superficial; they were thorough and kept themselves up—it had been their line. People with such a taste for activity had to have some line. I could feel how even in a dull house they could have been counted on for the joy of life. At present something had happened—it didn't matter what, their little income had grown less, it had grown least—and they had to do something for pocket-money. Their friends could like them, I made out, without liking to support them. There was something about them that represented credit—their clothes, their manners, their type; but if credit is a large empty pocket in which an occasional chink reverberates, the chink at least must be audible. What they wanted of me was to help to make it so. Fortunately they had no children—I soon divined that. They would also perhaps wish our relations to be kept secret: this was why it was "for the figure"—the reproduction of the face would betray them.

I liked them—I felt, quite as their friends must have done—they were so simple; and I had no objection to them if they would suit. But somehow with all their perfections I didn't easily believe in them. After all they were amateurs, and the ruling passion of my life was the detestation of the amateur. Combined with this was another perversity—an innate preference for the represented subject over the real one: the defect of the real one was so apt to be a lack of representation. I liked things that appeared; then one was sure. Whether they *were* or not was a subordinate and almost always a profitless question. There were other considerations, the first of which was that I already had two or three recruits in use, notably a young person with big feet, in alpaca,[9] from Kilburn, who for a couple of years had come to me regularly for my illustrations and with whom I was still—perhaps ignobly—satisfied. I frankly explained to my visitors how the case stood, but they had taken more precautions than I supposed. They had reasoned out their opportunity, for Claude Rivet had told them of the projected *édition de luxe* of one of the writers of our day—the rarest of the novelists—who, long neglected by the multitudinous vulgar and dearly prized by the attentive (need I mention Philip Vincent?) had had the happy fortune of seeing, late in life, the dawn and then the full light of a higher criticism; an estimate in which on the part of the public there was something really of expiation. The edition preparing, planned by a publisher of taste, was practically an act of high reparation; the wood-cuts with which it was to be enriched were the homage of English art to one of the most independent repre-

[7] A country estate of the well-to-do.   [8] Game birds taken out of hiding places.
[9] Dressed in alpaca wool.

sentatives of English letters. Major and Mrs. Monarch confessed to me they had hoped I might be able to work *them* into my branch of the enterprise. They knew I was to do the first of the books, "Rutland Ramsay," but I had to make clear to them that my participation in the rest of the affair—this first book was to be a test—must depend on the satisfaction I should give. If this should be limited my employers would drop me with scarce common forms. It was therefore a crisis for me, and naturally I was making special preparations, looking about for new people, should they be necessary, and securing the best types. I admitted however that I should like to settle down to two or three good models who would do for everything.

"Should we have often to—a—put on special clothes?" Mrs. Monarch timidly demanded.

"Dear yes—that's half the business."

"And should we be expected to supply our own costumes?"

"Oh no; I've got a lot of things. A painter's models put on—or put off—anything he likes."

"And you mean—a—the same?"

"The same?"

Mrs. Monarch looked at her husband again.

"Oh she was just wondering," he explained, "if the costumes are in *general* use." I had to confess that they were, and I mentioned further that some of them— I had a lot of genuine greasy last-century things—had served their time, a hundred years ago, on living world-stained men and women; on figures not perhaps so far removed, in that vanished world, from *their* type, the Monarchs', *quoi!*[10] of a breeched and bewigged age. "We'll put on anything that *fits*," said the Major.

"Oh I arrange that—they fit in the pictures."

"I'm afraid I should do better for the modern books. I'd come as you like," said Mrs. Monarch.

"She has got a lot of clothes at home: they might do for contemporary life," her husband continued.

"Oh I can fancy scenes in which you'd be quite natural." And indeed I could see the slipshod rearrangements of stale properties—the stories I tried to produce pictures for without the exasperation of reading them—whose sandy tracts the good lady might help to people. But I had to return to the fact that for this sort of work—the daily mechanical grind—I was already equipped: the people I was working with were fully adequate.

"We only thought we might be more like *some* characters," said Mrs. Monarch mildly, getting up.

Her husband also rose; he stood looking at me with a dim wistfulness that was touching in so fine a man. "Wouldn't it be rather a pull sometimes to have—a—to have—?" He hung fire;[11] he wanted me to help him by phrasing what he meant. But I couldn't—I didn't know. So he brought it out awkwardly: "The *real* thing; a gentleman, you know, or a lady." I was quite ready to give a general assent—I admitted that there was a great deal in that. This encouraged Major Monarch to say, following up his appeal with an unacted gulp: "It's awfully hard—we've tried everything." The gulp was communicative; it proved too much for his wife. Before I knew it Mrs. Monarch had dropped again upon a divan[12] and burst into tears. Her husband sat down beside her, holding one of her hands; whereupon she

---

[10] "What!" (French).   [11] Delayed expressing himself.   [12] A long, backless couch.

quickly dried her eyes with the other, while I felt embarrassed as she looked up at me. "There isn't a confounded job I haven't applied for—waited for—prayed for. You can fancy we'd be pretty bad first. Secretaryships and that sort of thing? You might as well ask for a peerage. I'd be *anything*—I'm strong; a messenger or a coalheaver. I'd put on a gold-laced cap and open carriage-doors in front of the haberdasher's; I'd hang about a station to carry portmanteaux;[13] I'd be a postman. But they won't *look* at you; there are thousands as good as yourself already on the ground. *Gentlemen,* poor beggars, who've drunk their wine, who've kept their hunters!"

I was as reassuring as I knew how to be, and my visitors were presently on their feet again while, for the experiment, we agreed on an hour. We were discussing it when the door opened and Miss Churm came in with a wet umbrella. Miss Churm had to take the omnibus to Maida Vale and then walk half a mile. She looked a trifle blowsy and slightly splashed. I scarcely ever saw her come in without thinking afresh how odd it was that, being so little in herself, she should yet be so much in others. She was a meagre little Miss Churm, but was such an ample heroine of romance. She was only a freckled cockney, but she could represent everything, from a fine lady to a shepherdess; she had the faculty as she might have had a fine voice or long hair. She couldn't spell and she loved beer, but she had two or three "points," and practice, and a knack, and mother-wit, and a whimsical sensibility, and a love of the theatre, and seven sisters, and not an ounce of respect, especially for the *h*.[14] The first thing my visitors saw was that her umbrella was wet, and in their spotless perfection they visibly winced at it. The rain had come on since their arrival.

"I'm all in a soak; there *was* a mess of people in the 'bus. I wish you lived near a stytion," said Miss Churm. I requested her to get ready as quickly as possible, and she passed into the room in which she always changed her dress. But before going out she asked me what she was to get into this time.

"It's the Russian princess, don't you know?" I answered; "the one with the 'golden eyes,' in black velvet, for the long thing in the *Cheapside*."[15]

"Golden eyes? I *say!*" cried Miss Churm, while my companions watched her with intensity as she withdrew. She always arranged herself, when she was late, before I could turn round; and I kept my visitors a little on purpose, so that they might get an idea, from seeing her, what would be expected of themselves. I mentioned that she was quite my notion of an excellent model—she was really very clever.

"Do you think she looks like a Russian princess?" Major Monarch asked with lurking alarm.

"When I make her, yes."

"Oh if you have to *make* her—!" he reasoned, not without point.

"That's the most you can ask. There are so many who are not makeable."

"Well now, *here's* a lady"—and with a persuasive smile he passed his arm into his wife's—"who's already made!"

"Oh I'm not a Russian princess," Mrs. Monarch protested a little coldly. I could see she had known some and didn't like them. There at once was a complication of a kind I never had to fear with Miss Churm.

[13] Large leather suitcases with two hinged compartments.
[14] In the cockney dialect of London's East End, the *h*'s are dropped from words.
[15] An imaginary magazine named after a London business street.

This young lady came back in black velvet—the gown was rather rusty and very low on her lean shoulders—and with a Japanese fan in her red hands. I reminded her that in the scene I was doing she had to look over some one's head. "I forget whose it is; but it doesn't matter. Just look over a head."

"I'd rather look over a stove," said Miss Churm; and she took her station near the fire. She fell into position, settled herself into a tall attitude, gave a certain backward inclination to her head and a certain forward droop to her fan, and looked, at least to my prejudiced sense, distinguished and charming, foreign and dangerous. We left her looking so while I went downstairs with Major and Mrs. Monarch.

"I believe I could come about as near it as that," said Mrs. Monarch.

"Oh you think she's shabby, but you must allow for the alchemy of art."

However, they went off with an evident increase of comfort founded on their demonstrable advantage in being the real thing. I could fancy them shuddering over Miss Churm. She was very droll about them when I went back, for I told her what they wanted.

"Well, if *she* can sit I'll tyke to bookkeeping," said my model.

"She's very ladylike," I replied as an innocent form of aggravation.

"So much the worse for *you.* That means she can't turn round."

"She'll do for the fashionable novels."

"Oh yes, she'll *do* for them!" my model humorously declared. "Ain't they bad enough without her?" I had often sociably denounced them to Miss Churm.

III

It was for the elucidation of a mystery in one of these works that I first tried Mrs. Monarch. Her husband came with her, to be useful if necessary—it was sufficiently clear that as a general thing he would prefer to come with her. At first I wondered if this were for "propriety's" sake—if he were going to be jealous and meddling. The idea was too tiresome, and if it had been confirmed it would speedily have brought our acquaintance to a close. But I soon saw there was nothing in it and that if he accompanied Mrs. Monarch it was—in addition to the chance of being wanted—simply because he had nothing else to do. When they were separate his occupation was gone and they never *had* been separate. I judged rightly that in their awkward situation their close union was their main comfort and that this union had no weak spot. It was a real marriage, an encouragement to the hesitating, a nut for pessimists to crack. Their address was humble—I remember afterwards thinking it had been the only thing about them that was really professional—and I could fancy the lamentable lodgings in which the Major would have been left alone. He could sit there more or less grimly with his wife—he couldn't sit there anyhow without her.

He had too much tact to try and make himself agreeable when he couldn't be useful; so when I was too absorbed in my work to talk he simply sat and waited. But I liked to hear him talk—it made my work, when not interrupting it, less mechanical, less special. To listen to him was to combine the excitement of going out with the economy of staying at home. There was only one hindrance—that I seemed not to know any of the people this brilliant couple had known. I think he wondered extremely, during the term of our intercourse, whom the deuce I *did* know. He hadn't a stray sixpence of an idea to fumble for, so we didn't spin it very fine; we confined ourselves to questions of leather and even of liquor—saddlers and breeches-makers and how to get excellent claret cheap—and matters like "good trains" and the habits of small game. His lore on these last subjects was astonishing—he managed to interweave the station-master with the ornithologist. When he couldn't talk about greater things he could talk cheerfully about smaller, and since I couldn't accompany him into reminiscences of the fashionable world he could lower the conversation without a visible effort to my level.

So earnest a desire to please was touching in a man who could so easily have knocked one down. He looked after the fire and had an opinion on the draught of the stove without my asking him, and I could see that he thought many of my arrangements not half knowing. I remember telling him that if I were only rich I'd offer him a salary to come and teach me how to live. Sometimes he gave a random sigh of which the essence might have been: "Give me even such a bare old barrack as *this,* and I'd do something with it!" When I wanted to use him he came alone; which was an illustration of the superior courage of women. His wife could bear her solitary second floor, and she was in general more discreet; showing by various small reserves that she was alive to the propriety of keeping our relations markedly professional—not letting them slide into sociability. She wished it to remain clear that she and the Major were employed, not cultivated, and if she approved of me as a superior, who could be kept in his place, she never thought me quite good enough for an equal.

She sat with great intensity, giving the whole of her mind to it, and was capable of remaining for an hour almost as motionless as before a photographer's lens. I could see she had been photographed often, but somehow the very habit that made her good for that purpose unfitted her for mine. At first I was extremely pleased with her ladylike air, and it was a satisfaction, on coming to follow her lines, to see how good they were and how far they could lead the pencil. But after a little skirmishing I began to find her too insurmountably stiff; do what I would with it my drawing looked like a photograph or a copy of a photograph. Her figure had no variety of expression—she herself had no sense of variety. You may say that this was my business and was only a question of placing her. Yet I placed her in every conceivable position and she managed to obliterate their differences. She was always a lady certainly and into the bargain was always the same lady. She was the real thing, but always the same thing. There were moments when I rather writhed under the serenity of her confidence that she *was* the real thing. All her dealings with me and all her husband's were an implication that this was lucky for *me.* Meanwhile I found myself trying to invent types that approached her own, instead of making her own transform itself—in the clever way that was not impossible for instance to poor Miss Churm. Arrange as I would and take the precautions as I would, she always came out, in my pictures, too tall—landing me in the dilemma of having represented a fascinating woman as seven feet high, which (out of respect perhaps to my own very much scantier inches) was far from my idea of such a personage.

The case was worse with the Major—nothing I could do would keep *him* down, so that he became useful only for the representation of brawny giants. I adored variety and range, I cherished human accidents, the illustrative note; I wanted to characterise closely, and the thing in the world I most hated was the danger of being ridden by a type. I had quarrelled with some of my friends about it; I had parted company with them for maintaining that one *had* to be, and that if the type was beautiful—witness Raphael and Leonardo[16]—the servitude was only a gain. I was neither Leonardo nor Raphael—I might only be a presumptuous young modern searcher; but I held that everything was to be sacrificed sooner than character. When they claimed that the obsessional form could easily *be* character I retorted, perhaps superficially, "Whose?" It couldn't be everybody's—it might end in being nobody's.

After I had drawn Mrs. Monarch a dozen times I felt surer even than before that the value of such a model as Miss Churm resided precisely in the fact that she had no positive stamp, combined of course with the other fact that what she did have was a curious and inexplicable talent for imitation. Her usual appearance was like a curtain which she could draw up at request for a capital performance. This performance was simply suggestive; but it was a word to the wise—it was vivid and pretty. Sometimes even I thought it, though she was plain herself, too insipidly pretty; I made it a reproach to her that the figures drawn from her were monotonously (*bêtement,*[17] as we used to say) graceful. Nothing made her more angry: it was so much her pride to feel she could sit for characters that had nothing in common with each other. She would accuse me at such moments of taking away her "reputytion."

It suffered a certain shrinkage, this queer quantity, from the repeated visits of my new friends. Miss Churm was greatly in demand, never in want of employment, so I had no scruple in putting her off occasionally, to try them more at my ease. It was certainly amusing at first to do the real thing—it was amusing to do Major Monarch's trousers. They *were* the real thing, even if he did come out colossal. It was amusing to do his wife's back hair—it was so mathematically neat—and the particular "smart" tension of her tight stays.[18] She lent herself especially to positions in which the face was somewhat averted or blurred; she abounded in ladylike back views and *profils perdus.*[19] When she stood erect she took naturally one of the attitudes in which court-painters represent queens and princesses; so that I found myself wondering whether, to draw out this accomplishment, I couldn't get the editor of the *Cheapside* to publish a really royal romance, "A Tale of Buckingham Palace." Sometimes however the real thing and the make-believe came into contact; by which I mean that Miss Churm, keeping an appointment or coming to make one on days when I had much work in hand, encountered her invidious rivals. The encounter was not on their part, for they noticed her no more than if she had been the housemaid; not from intentional loftiness, but simply because as yet, professionally, they didn't know how to fraternise, as I could imagine they would have liked—or at least that the Major would. They couldn't talk about the omnibus—they always walked; and they didn't know what else to try—she wasn't interested in good trains or cheap claret. Besides, they must have felt—in the air—that she was amused at them, secretly derisive of their ever knowing how. She wasn't a person to conceal the limits of her faith if she had had a chance to show them. On the other hand Mrs. Monarch didn't think her tidy; for why else did she take pains to say to me—it was going out of the way, for Mrs. Monarch—that she didn't like dirty women?

One day when my young lady happened to be present with my other sitters—

---

[16] The famous Italian painters Raffaelo Sanzio (1483–1520) and Leonardo da Vinci (1452–1519).
[17] "Stupidly" (French).   [18] Stiffenings in a corset.
[19] "Lost profiles" (French), or poses that show a face looking back over the shoulder.

and she even dropped in, when it was convenient, for a chat—I asked her to be so good as to lend a hand in getting tea, a service with which she was familiar and which was one of a class that, living as I did in a small way, with slender domestic resources, I often appealed to my models to render. They liked to lay hands on my property, to break the sitting, and sometimes the china—it made them feel Bohemian.[20] The next time I saw Miss Churm after this incident she surprised me greatly by making a scene about it—she accused me of having wished to humiliate her. She hadn't resented the outrage at the time, but had seemed obliging and amused, enjoying the comedy of asking Mrs. Monarch, who sat vague and silent, whether she would have cream and sugar, and putting an exaggerated simper into the question. She had tried intonations—as if she too wished to pass for the real thing—till I was afraid my other visitors would take offence.

Oh they were determined not to do this, and their touching patience was the measure of their great need. They would sit by the hour, uncomplaining, till I was ready to use them; they would come back on the chance of being wanted and would walk away cheerfully if it failed. I used to go to the door with them to see in what magnificent order they retreated. I tried to find other employment for them—I introduced them to several artists. But they didn't "take," for reasons I could appreciate, and I became rather anxiously aware that after such disappointments they fell back upon me with a heavier weight. They did me the honour to think me most *their* form. They weren't romantic enough for the painters, and in those days there were few serious workers in black-and-white. Besides, they had an eye to the great job I had mentioned to them—they had secretly set their hearts on supplying the right essence for my pictorial vindication of our fine novelist. They knew that for this undertaking I should want no costume-effects, none of the frippery[21] of past ages—that it was a case in which everything would be contemporary and satirical and presumably genteel. If I could work them into it their future would be assured, for the labour would of course be long and the occupation steady.

One day Mrs. Monarch came without her husband—she explained his absence by his having had to go to the City.[22] While she sat there in her usual relaxed majesty there came at the door a knock which I immediately recognised as the subdued appeal of a model out of work. It was followed by the entrance of a young man whom I at once saw to be a foreigner and who proved in fact an Italian acquainted with no English word but my name, which he uttered in a way that made it seem to include all others. I hadn't then visited his country, nor was I proficient in his tongue; but as he was not so meanly constituted—what Italian is?—as to depend only on that member for expression he conveyed to me, in familiar but graceful mimicry, that he was in search of exactly the employment in which the lady before me was engaged. I was not struck with him at first, and while I continued to draw I dropped few signs of interest or encouragement. He stood his ground however—not importunately, but with a dumb dog-like fidelity in his eyes that amounted to innocent impudence, the manner of a devoted servant—he might have been in the house for years—unjustly suspected. Suddenly it struck me that this very attitude and expression made a picture; whereupon I told him to sit down and wait till I should be free. There was another picture in the way he obeyed me, and I observed as I worked that there were others still in the way he

---

[20] Artistic or unconventional.   [21] Cheap, gaudy clothes.
[22] London's financial and commercial district.

looked wonderingly, with his head thrown back, about the high studio. He might have been crossing himself in Saint Peter's.[23] Before I finished I said to myself "The fellow's a bankrupt orange-monger, but a treasure."

When Mrs. Monarch withdrew he passed across the room like a flash to open the door for her, standing there with the rapt pure gaze of the young Dante spellbound by the young Beatrice.[24] As I never insisted, in such situations, on the blankness of the British domestic, I reflected that he had the making of a servant—and I needed one, but couldn't pay him to be only that—as well as of a model; in short I resolved to adopt my bright adventurer if he would agree to officiate in the double capacity. He jumped at my offer, and in the event my rashness—for I had really known nothing about him—wasn't brought home to me. He proved a sympathetic though a desultory ministrant, and had in a wonderful degree the *sentiment de la pose*.[25] It was uncultivated, instinctive, a part of the happy instinct that had guided him to my door and helped him to spell out my name on the card nailed to it. He had had no other introduction to me than a guess, from the shape of my high north window, seen outside, that my place was a studio and that as a studio it would contain an artist. He had wandered to England in search of fortune, like other itinerants, and had embarked, with a partner and a small green hand-cart, on the sale of penny ices. The ices had melted away and the partner has dissolved in their train. My young man wore tight yellow trousers with reddish stripes and his name was Oronte. He was sallow but fair, and when I put him into some old clothes of my own he looked like an Englishman. He was as good as Miss Churm, who could look, when requested, like an Italian.

IV

I thought Mrs. Monarch's face slightly convulsed when, on her coming back with her husband, she found Oronte installed. It was strange to have to recognise in a scrap of a lazzarone[26] a competitor to her magnificent Major. It was she who scented danger first, for the Major was anecdotically unconscious. But Oronte gave us tea, with a hundred eager confusions—he had never been concerned in so queer a process—and I think she thought better of me for having at last an "establishment." They saw a couple of drawings that I had made of the establishment, and Mrs. Monarch hinted that it never would have struck her he had sat for them. "Now the drawings you make from *us,* they look exactly like us," she reminded me, smiling in triumph; and I recognised that this was indeed just their defect. When I drew the Monarchs I couldn't anyhow get away from them—get into the character I wanted to represent; and I hadn't the least desire my model should be discoverable in my picture. Miss Churm never was, and Mrs. Monarch thought I hid her, very properly, because she was vulgar; whereas if she was lost it was only as the dead who go to heaven are lost—in the gain of an angel the more.

By this time I had got a certain start with "Rutland Ramsay," the first novel in the great projected series; that is I had produced a dozen drawings, several with the help of the Major and his wife, and I had sent them in for approval. My understanding with the publishers, as I have already hinted, had been that I was to

[23] Saint Peters Cathedral in Rome.
[24] Beatrice Portinari (1266–1290), the inspiration for the Italian poet Dante Alighieri (1265–1321), and a character in his *Divine Comedy*.
[25] Instinct for posing (French).   [26] A beggar or cad (Italian).

be left to do my work, in this particular case, as I liked, with the whole book committed to me; but my connexion with the rest of the series was only contingent. There were moments when, frankly, it *was* a comfort to have the real thing under one's hand; for there were characters in "Rutland Ramsay" that were very much like it. There were people presumably as erect as the Major and women of as good a fashion as Mrs. Monarch. There was a great deal of country-house life—treated, it is true, in a fine fanciful ironical generalised way—and there was a considerable implication of knickerbockers and kilts. There were certain things I had to settle at the outset; such things for instance as the exact appearance of the hero and the particular bloom and figure of the heroine. The author of course gave me a lead, but there was margin for interpretation. I took the Monarchs into my confidence, I told them frankly what I was about, I mentioned my embarrassments and alternatives. "Oh take *him!* Mrs. Monarch murmured sweetly, looking at her husband; and "What could you want better than my wife?" the Major enquired with the comfortable candour that now prevailed between us.

I wasn't obliged to answer these remarks—I was only obliged to place my sitters. I wasn't easy in mind, and I postponed a little timidly perhaps the solving of my question. The book was a large canvas, the other figures were numerous, and I worked off at first some of the episodes in which the hero and the heroine were not concerned. When once I had set *them* up I should have to stick to them— I couldn't make my young man seven feet high in one place and five feet nine in another. I inclined on the whole to the latter measurement, though the Major more than once reminded me that *he* looked about as young as any one. It was indeed quite possible to arrange him, for the figure, so that it would have been difficult to detect his age. After the spontaneous Oronte had been with me a month, and after I had given him to understand several times over that his native exuberance would presently constitute an insurmountable barrier to our further intercourse, I waked to a sense of his heroic capacity. He was only five feet seven, but the remaining inches were latent. I tried him almost secretly at first, for I was really rather afraid of the judgement my other models would pass on such a choice. If they regarded Miss Churm as little better than a snare what would they think of the representation by a person so little the real thing as an Italian street-vendor of a protagonist formed by a public school?

If I went a little in fear of them it wasn't because they bullied me, because they had got an oppressive foothold, but because in their really pathetic decorum and mysteriously permanent newness they counted on me so intensely. I was therefore very glad when Jack Hawley came home: he was always of such good counsel. He painted badly himself, but there was no one like him for putting his finger on the place. He had been absent from England for a year; he had been somewhere—I don't remember where—to get a fresh eye. I was in a good deal of dread of any such organ, but we were old friends; he had been away for months and a sense of emptiness was creeping into my life. I hadn't dodged a missile for a year.

He came back with a fresh eye, but with the same old black velvet blouse, and the first evening he spent in my studio we smoked cigarettes till the small hours. He had done no work himself, he had only got the eye; so the field was clear for the production of my little things. He wanted to see what I had produced for the *Cheapside,* but he was disappointed in the exhibition. That at least seemed the meaning of two or three comprehensive groans which, as he lounged on my big divan, his leg folded under him, looking at my latest drawings, issued from his lips with the smoke of the cigarette.

"What's the matter with you?" I asked.

"What's the matter with *you?*"

"Nothing save that I'm mystified."

"You are indeed. You're quite off the hinge. What's the meaning of this new fad?" And he tossed me, with visible irreverence, a drawing in which I happened to have depicted both my elegant models. I asked if he didn't think it good, and he replied that it struck him as execrable, given the sort of thing I had always represented myself to him as wishing to arrive at; but I let that pass—I was so anxious to see exactly what he meant. The two figures in the picture looked colossal, but I supposed this was *not* what he meant, inasmuch as, for aught he knew to the contrary, I might have been trying for some such effect. I maintained that I was working exactly in the same way as when he last had done me the honour to tell me I might do something some day. "Well, there's a screw loose somewhere," he answered; "wait a bit and I'll discover it." I depended upon him to do so: where else was the fresh eye? But he produced at last nothing more luminous than "I don't know—I don't like your types." This was lame for a critic who had never consented to discuss with me anything but the question of execution, the direction of strokes and the mystery of values.

"In the drawings you've been looking at I think my types are very handsome."

"Oh they won't do!"

"I've been working with new models."

"I see you have. *They* won't do."

"Are you very sure of that?"

"Absolutely—they're stupid."

"You mean *I* am—for I ought to get round that."

"You *can't*—with such people. Who are they?"

I told him, so far as was necessary, and he concluded heartlessly: "Ce sont des gens qu'il faut mettre à la porte."[27]

"You've never seen them; they're awfully good"—I flew to their defence.

"Not seen them? Why all this recent work of yours drops to pieces with them. It's all I want to see of them."

"No one else has said anything against it—the *Cheapside* people are pleased."

"Every one else is an ass, and the *Cheapside* people the biggest asses of all. Come, don't pretend at this time of day to have pretty illusions about the public, especially about publishers and editors. It's not for *such* animals you work—it's for those who know, *coloro che sanno;*[28] so keep straight for *me* if you can't keep straight for yourself. There was a certain sort of thing you used to try for—and a very good thing it was. But this twaddle isn't *in* it." When I talked with Hawley later about "Rutland Ramsay" and its possible successors he declared that I must get back into my boat again or I should go to the bottom. His voice in short was the voice of warning.

I noted the warning, but I didn't turn my friends out of doors. They bored me a good deal; but the very fact that they bored me admonished me not to sacrifice them—if there was anything to be done with them—simply to irritation. As I look back at this phase they seem to me to have pervaded my life not a little. I have a vision of them as most of the time in my studio, seated against the wall on an old velvet bench to be out of the way, and resembling the while a pair of patient

---

[27] "They are people who should be shown the door" (French).

[28] "Those who know" (Italian): from Dante's *Inferno* (IV. 131).

courtiers in a royal ante-chamber. I'm convinced that during the coldest weeks of the winter they held their ground because it saved them fire. Their newness was losing its gloss, and it was impossible not to feel them objects of charity. Whenever Miss Churm arrived they went away, and after I was fairly launched in "Rutland Ramsay" Miss Churm arrived pretty often. They managed to express to me tacitly that they supposed I wanted her for the low life of the book, and I let them suppose it, since they had attempted to study the work—it was lying about the studio—without discovering that it dealt only with the highest circles. They had dipped into the most brilliant of our novelists without deciphering many passages. I still took an hour from them, now and again, in spite of Jack Hawley's warning: it would be time enough to dismiss them, if dismissal should be necessary, when the rigour of the season was over. Hawley had made their acquaintance—he had met them at my fireside—and thought them a ridiculous pair. Learning that he was a painter they tried to approach him, to show him too that they were the real thing; but he looked at them, across the big room, as if they were miles away; they were a compendium of everything he most objected to in the social system of his country. Such people as that, all convention and patent-leather, with ejaculations that stopped conversation, had no business in a studio. A studio was a place to learn to see, and how could you see through a pair of feather-beds?

The main inconvenience I suffered at their hands was that at first I was shy of letting it break upon them that my artful little servant had begun to sit to me for "Rutland Ramsay." They knew I had been odd enough—they were prepared by this time to allow oddity to artists—to pick a foreign vagabond out of the streets when I might have had a person with whiskers and credentials; but it was some time before they learned how high I rated his accomplishments. They found him in an attitude more than once, but they never doubted I was doing him as an organ-grinder. There were several things they never guessed, and one of them was that for a striking scene in the novel, in which a footman briefly figured, it occurred to me to make use of Major Monarch as the menial. I kept putting this off, I didn't like to ask him to don the livery—besides the difficulty of finding a livery to fit him. At last, one day late in the winter, when I was at work on the despised Oronte, who caught one's idea on the wing, and was in the glow of feeling myself go very straight, they came in, the Major and his wife, with their society laugh about nothing (there was less and less to laugh at); came in like country-callers— they always reminded me of that—who have walked across the park after church and are presently persuaded to stay to luncheon. Luncheon was over, but they could stay to tea—I knew they wanted it. The fit was on me, however, and I couldn't let my ardour cool and my work wait, with the fading daylight, while my model prepared it. So I asked Mrs. Monarch if she would mind laying it out—a request which for an instant brought all the blood to her face. Her eyes were on her husband's for a second, and some mute telegraphy passed between them. Their folly was over the next instant; his cheerful shrewdness put an end to it. So far from pitying their wounded pride, I must add, I was moved to give it as complete a lesson as I could. They bustled about together and got out the cups and saucers and made the kettle boil. I know they felt as if they were waiting on my servant, and when the tea was prepared I said: "He'll have a cup, please—he's tired." Mrs. Monarch brought him one where he stood, and he took it from her as if he had been a gentleman at a party squeezing a crush-hat with an elbow.

Then it came over me that she had made a great effort for me—made it with a kind of nobleness—and that I owed her a compensation. Each time I saw her after this I wondered what the compensation could be. I couldn't go on doing the wrong thing to oblige them. Oh it *was* the wrong thing, the stamp of the work for which they sat—Hawley was not the only person to say it now. I sent in a large number of the drawings I had made for "Rutland Ramsay," and I received a warning that was more to the point than Hawley's. The artistic adviser of the house for which I was working was of opinion that many of my illustrations were not what had been looked for. Most of these illustrations were the subjects in which the Monarchs had figured. Without going into the question of what *had* been looked for, I had to face the fact that at this rate I shouldn't get the other books to do. I hurled myself in despair on Miss Churm—I put her through all her paces. I not only adopted Oronte publicly as my hero, but one morning when the Major looked in to see if I didn't require him to finish a *Cheapside* figure for which he had begun to sit the week before, I told him I had changed my mind—I'd do the drawing from my man. At this my visitor turned pale and stood looking at me. "Is *he* your idea of an English gentleman?" he asked.

I was disappointed, I was nervous, I wanted to get on with my work; so I replied with irritation: "Oh my dear Major—I can't be ruined for *you!*"

It was a horrid speech, but he stood another moment—after which, without a word, he quitted the studio. I drew a long breath, for I said to myself that I shouldn't see him again. I hadn't told him definitely that I was in danger of having my work rejected, but I was vexed at his not having felt the catastrophe in the air, read with me the moral of our fruitless collaboration, the lesson that in the deceptive atmosphere of art even the highest respectability may fail of being plastic.[29]

I didn't owe my friends money, but I did see them again. They reappeared together three days later, and, given all the other facts, there was something tragic in that one. It was a clear proof they could find nothing else in life to do. They had threshed the matter out in a dismal conference—they had digested the bad news that they were not in for the series. If they weren't useful to me even for the *Cheapside* their function seemed difficult to determine, and I could only judge at first that they had come, forgivingly, decorously, to take a last leave. This made me rejoice in secret that I had little leisure for a scene; for I had placed both my other models in position together and I was pegging away at a drawing from which I hoped to derive glory. It had been suggested by the passage in which Rutland Ramsay, drawing up a chair to Artemisia's piano-stool, says extraordinary things to her while she ostensibly fingers out a difficult piece of music. I had done Miss Churm at the piano before—it was an attitude in which she knew how to take on an absolutely poetic grace. I wished the two figures to "compose" together with intensity, and my little Italian had entered perfectly into my conception. The pair were vividly before me, the piano had been pulled out; it was a charming show of blended youth and murmured love, which I had only to catch and keep. My visitors stood and looked at it, and I was friendly to them over my shoulder.

They made no response, but I was used to silent company and went on with my work, only a little disconcerted—even though exhilarated by the sense that *this* was at least the ideal thing—at not having got rid of them after all. Presently I heard Mrs. Monarch's sweet voice beside or rather above me: "I wish her hair were a little better done." I looked up and she was staring with a strange fixedness at Miss Churm, whose back was turned to her. "Do you mind my just touching it?" she went on—a question which made me spring up for an instant as with the instinctive fear that she might do the young lady a harm. But she quieted me with

---

[29] May be too stiff for artistic expression.

a glance I shall never forget—I confess I should like to have been able to paint *that*—and went for a moment to my model. She spoke to her softly, laying a hand on her shoulder and bending over her; and as the girl, understanding, gratefully assented, she disposed her rough curls, with a few quick passes, in such a way as to make Miss Churm's head twice as charming. It was one of the most heroic personal services I've ever seen rendered. Then Mrs. Monarch turned away with a low sigh and, looking about her as if for something to do, stooped to the floor with a noble humility and picked up a dirty rag that had dropped out of my paint-box.

The Major meanwhile had also been looking for something to do, and, wandering to the other end of the studio, saw before him my breakfast-things neglected, unremoved. "I say, can't I be useful *here?*" he called out to me with an irrepressible quaver. I assented with a laugh that I fear was awkward, and for the next ten minutes, while I worked, I heard the light clatter of china and the tinkle of spoons and glass. Mrs. Monarch assisted her husband—they washed up my crockery, they put it away. They wandered off into my little scullery, and I afterwards found that they had cleaned my knives and that my slender stock of plate had an unprecedented surface. When it came over me, the latent eloquence of what they were doing, I confess that my drawing was blurred for a moment—the picture swam. They had accepted their failure, but they couldn't accept their fate. They had bowed their heads in bewilderment to the perverse and cruel law in virtue of which the real thing could be so much less precious than the unreal; but they didn't want to starve. If my servants were my models, then my models might be my servants. They would reverse the parts—the others would sit for the ladies and gentlemen and *they* would do the work. They would still be in the studio—it was an intense dumb appeal to me not to turn them out. "Take us on," they wanted to say—"we'll do *anything*."

My pencil dropped from my hand; my sitting was spoiled and I got rid of my sitters, who were also evidently rather mystified and awestruck. Then, alone with the Major and his wife I had a most uncomfortable moment. He put their prayer into a single sentence: "I say, you know—just let *us* do for you, can't you?" I couldn't—it was dreadful to see them emptying my slops; but I pretended I could, to oblige them, for about a week. Then I gave them a sum of money to go away, and I never saw them again. I obtained the remaining books, but my friend Hawley repeats that Major and Mrs. Monarch did me a permanent harm, got me into false ways. If it be true I'm content to have paid the price—for the memory.

1892

THE BEAST IN THE JUNGLE*

I

What determined the speech that startled him in the course of their encounter scarcely matters, being probably but some words spoken by himself quite without intention—spoken as they lingered and slowly moved together after their renewal of acquaintance. He had been conveyed by friends an hour or two before to the

---

* First published in *The Better Sort* (1903) and revised by James to this version in 1909.

house at which she was staying; the party of visitors at the other house, of whom
he was one, and thanks to whom it was his theory, as always, that he was lost in
the crowd, had been invited over to luncheon. There had been after luncheon
much dispersal, all in the interest of the original motive, a view of Weatherend
itself and the fine things, intrinsic features, pictures, heirlooms, treasures of all the
arts, that made the place almost famous; and the great rooms were so numerous
that guests could wander at their will, hang back from the principal group and in
cases where they took such matters with the last seriousness give themselves up to
mysterious appreciations and measurements. There were persons to be observed,
singly or in couples, bending toward objects in out-of-the-way corners with their
hands on their knees and their heads nodding quite as with the emphasis of an
excited sense of smell. When they were two they either mingled their sounds of
ecstasy or melted into silences of even deeper import, so that there were aspects of
the occasion that gave it for Marcher much the air of the "look round," previous to
a sale highly advertised, that excites or quenches, as may be, the dream of acquisition. The dream of acquisition at Weatherend would have had to be wild indeed,
and John Marcher found himself, among such suggestions, disconcerted almost
equally by the presence of those who knew too much and by that of those who
knew nothing. The great rooms caused so much poetry and history to press upon
him that he needed some straying apart to feel in a proper relation with them,
though this impulse was not, as happened, like the gloating of some of his companions, to be compared to the movements of a dog sniffing a cupboard. It had an
issue promptly enough in a direction that was not to have been calculated.

It led, briefly, in the course of the October afternoon, to his closer meeting with
May Bartram, whose face, a reminder, yet not quite a remembrance, as they sat
much separated at a very long table, had begun merely by troubling him rather
pleasantly. It affected him as the sequel of something of which he had lost the
beginning. He knew it, and for the time quite welcomed it, as a continuation, but
didn't know what it continued, which was an interest or an amusement the greater
as he was also somehow aware—yet without a direct sign from her—that the
young woman herself hadn't lost the thread. She hadn't lost it, but she wouldn't
give it back to him, he saw, without some putting forth of his hand for it; and he
not only saw that, but saw several things more, things odd enough in the light of
the fact that at the moment some accident of grouping brought them face to face he
was still merely fumbling with the idea that any contact between them in the past
would have had no importance. If it had had no importance he scarcely knew why
his actual impression of her should so seem to have so much; the answer to which,
however, was that in such a life as they all appeared to be leading for the moment
one could but take things as they came. He was satisfied, without in the least
being able to say why, that this young lady might roughly have ranked in the
house as a poor relation; satisfied also that she was not there on a brief visit, but
was more or less a part of the establishment—almost a working, a remunerated
part. Didn't she enjoy at periods a protection that she paid for by helping, among
other services, to show the place and explain it, deal with the tiresome people,
answer questions about the dates of the building, the styles of the furniture, the
authorship of the pictures, the favourite haunts of the ghost? It wasn't that she
looked as if you could have given her shillings—it was impossible to look less so.
Yet when she finally drifted toward him, distinctly handsome, though ever so
much older—older than when he had seen her before—it might have been as an
effect of her guessing that he had, within the couple of hours, devoted more imagination to her than to all the others put together, and had thereby penetrated to a

kind of truth that the others were too stupid for. She *was* there on harder terms than any one; she was there as a consequence of things suffered, one way and another, in the interval of years; and she remembered him very much as she was remembered—only a good deal better.

By the time they at last thus came to speech they were alone in one of the rooms—remarkable for a fine portrait over the chimney-place—out of which their friends had passed, and the charm of it was that even before they had spoken they had practically arranged with each other to stay behind for talk. The charm, happily, was in other things too—partly in there being scarce a spot at Weatherend without something to stay behind for. It was in the way the autumn day looked into the high windows as it waned; the way the red light, breaking at the close from under a low sombre sky, reached out in a long shaft and played over old wainscots,[1] old tapestry, old gold, old colour. It was most of all perhaps in the way she came to him as if, since she had been turned on to deal with the simpler sort, he might, should he choose to keep the whole thing down, just take her mild attention for a part of her general business. As soon as he heard her voice, however, the gap was filled up and the missing link supplied; the slight irony he divined in her attitude lost its advantage. He almost jumped at it to get there before her. "I met you years and years ago in Rome. I remember all about it." She confessed to disappointment—she had been so sure he didn't; and to prove how well he did he began to pour forth the particular recollections that popped up as he called for them. Her face and her voice, all at his service now, worked the miracle—the impression operating like the torch of a lamplighter who touches into flame, one by one, a long row of gas-jets. Marcher flattered himself the illumination was brilliant, yet he was really still more pleased on her showing him, with amusement, that in his haste to make everything right he had got most things rather wrong. It hadn't been at Rome—it had been at Naples; and it hadn't been eight years before—it had been more nearly ten. She hadn't been, either, with her uncle and aunt, but with her mother and her brother; in addition to which it was not with the Pembles *he* had been, but with the Boyers, coming down in their company from Rome—a point on which she insisted, a little to his confusion, and as to which she had her evidence in hand. The Boyers she had known, but didn't know the Pembles, though she had heard of them, and it was the people he was with who had made them acquainted. The incident of the thunderstorm that had raged round them with such violence as to drive them for refuge into an excavation—this incident had not occurred at the Palace of the Cæsars, but at Pompeii,[2] on an occasion when they had been present there at an important find.

He accepted her amendments, he enjoyed her corrections, though the moral of them was, she pointed out, that he *really* didn't remember the least thing about her; and he only felt it as a drawback that when all was made strictly historic there didn't appear much of anything left. They lingered together still, she neglecting her office—for from the moment he was so clever she had no proper right to him—and both neglecting the house, just waiting as to see if a memory or two more wouldn't again breathe on them. It hadn't taken them many minutes, after all, to put down on the table, like the cards of a pack, those that constituted their respective hands; only what came out was that the pack was unfortunately not

---

[1] Wood lining or paneling on a wall.
[2] Not at the Palace of the Caesars in Rome but at the ancient ruined city of Pompeii, near Naples, entombed by a lava flow in A.D. 79.

perfect—that the past, invoked, invited, encouraged, could give them, naturally, no more than it had. It had made them anciently meet—her at twenty, him at twenty-five; but nothing was so strange, they seemed to say to each other, as that, while so occupied, it hadn't done a little more for them. They looked at each other as with the feeling of an occasion missed; the present would have been so much better if the other, in the far distance, in the foreign land, hadn't been so stupidly meagre. There weren't apparently, all counted, more than a dozen little old things that had succeeded in coming to pass between them; trivialities of youth, simplicities of freshness, stupidities of ignorance, small possible germs, but too deeply buried—too deeply (didn't it seem?) to sprout after so many years. Marcher could only feel he ought to have rendered her some service—saved her from a capsized boat in the Bay or at least recovered her dressing-bag, filched from her cab in the streets of Naples by a lazzarone with a stiletto.[3] Or it would have been nice if he could have been taken with fever all alone at his hotel, and she could have come to look after him, to write to his people, to drive him out in convalescence. *Then* they would be in possession of the something or other that their actual show seemed to lack. It yet somehow presented itself, this show, as too good to be spoiled; so that they were reduced for a few minutes more to wondering a little helplessly why—since they seemed to know a certain number of the same people—their reunion had been so long averted. They didn't use that name for it, but their delay from minute to minute to join the others was a kind of confession that they didn't quite want it to be a failure. Their attempted supposition of reasons for their not having met but showed how little they knew of each other. There came in fact a moment when Marcher felt a positive pang. It was vain to pretend she was an old friend, for all the communities were wanting, in spite of which it was as an old friend that he saw she would have suited him. He had new ones enough—was surrounded with them for instance on the stage of the other house; as a new one he probably wouldn't have so much as noticed her. He would have liked to invent something, get her to make-believe with him that some passage of a romantic or critical kind *had* originally occurred. He was really almost reaching out in imagination—as against time—for something that would do, and saying to himself that if it didn't come this sketch of a fresh start would show for quite awkwardly bungled. They would separate, and now for no second or no third chance. They would have tried and not succeeded. Then it was, just at the turn, as he afterwards made it out to himself, that, everything else failing, she herself decided to take up the case and, as it were, save the situation. He felt as soon as she spoke that she had been consciously keeping back what she said and hoping to get on without it; a scruple in her that immensely touched him when, by the end of three or four minutes more, he was able to measure it. What she brought out, at any rate, quite cleared the air and supplied the link—the link it was so odd he should frivolously have managed to lose.

"You know you told me something I've never forgotten and that again and again has made me think of you since; it was that tremendously hot day when we went to Sorrento,[4] across the bay, for the breeze. What I allude to was what you said to me, on the way back, as we sat under the awning of the boat enjoying the cool. Have you forgotten?"

He had forgotten and was even more surprised than ashamed. But the great thing was that he saw in this no vulgar reminder of any "sweet" speech. The

---

[3] A beggar with a stiletto knife.   [4] An Italian resort town on the Bay of Naples.

vanity of women had long memories, but she was making no claim on him of a compliment or a mistake. With another woman, a totally different one, he might have feared the recall possibly even some imbecile "offer."[5] So, in having to say that he had indeed forgotten, he was conscious rather of a loss than of a gain; he already saw an interest in the matter of her mention. "I try to think—but I give it up. Yet I remember the Sorrento day."

"I'm not very sure you do," May Bartram after a moment said; "and I'm not very sure I ought to want you to. It's dreadful to bring a person back at any time to what he was ten years before. If you've lived away from it," she smiled, "so much the better."

"Ah if *you* haven't why should I?" he asked.

"Lived away, you mean, from what I myself was?"

"From what *I* was. I was of course an ass," Marcher went on; "but I would rather know from you just the sort of ass I was than—from the moment you have something in your mind—not know anything."

Still, however, she hesitated. "But if you've completely ceased to be that sort—?"

"Why I can then all the more bear to know. Besides, perhaps I haven't."

"Perhaps. Yet if you haven't," she added. "I should suppose you'd remember. Not indeed that *I* in the least connect with my impression the invidious name you use. If I had only thought you foolish," she explained, "the thing I speak of wouldn't so have remained with me. It was about yourself." She waited as if it might come to him; but as, only meeting her eyes in wonder, he gave no sign, she burnt her ships. "Has it ever happened?"

Then it was that, while he continued to stare, a light broke for him and the blood slowly came to his face, which began to burn with recognition. "Do you mean I told you—?" But he faltered, lest what came to him shouldn't be right, lest he should only give himself away.

"It was something about yourself that it was natural one shouldn't forget—that is if one remembered you at all. That's why I ask you," she smiled, "if the thing you then spoke of has ever come to pass?"

Oh then he saw, but he was lost in wonder and found himself embarrassed. This, he also saw, made her sorry for him, as if her allusion had been a mistake. It took him but a moment, however, to feel it hadn't been, much as it had been a surprise. After the first little shock of it her knowledge on the contrary began, even if rather strangely, to taste sweet to him. She was the only other person in the world then who would have it, and she had had it all these years, while the fact of his having so breathed his secret had unaccountably faded from him. No wonder they couldn't have met as if nothing had happened. "I judge," he finally said, "that I know what you mean. Only I had strangely enough lost any sense of having taken you so far into my confidence."

"Is it because you've taken so many others as well?"

"I've taken nobody. Not a creature since then."

"So that I'm the only person who knows?"

"The only person in the world."

"Well," she quickly replied, "I myself have never spoken. I've never, never repeated of you what you told me." She looked at him so that he perfectly be-

[5] An offer of marriage.

lieved her. Their eyes met over it in such a way that he was without a doubt. "And I never will."

She spoke with an earnestness that, as if almost excessive, put him at ease about her possible derision. Somehow the whole question was a new luxury to him—that is from the moment she was in possession. If she didn't take the sarcastic view she clearly took the sympathetic, and that was what he had had, in all the long time, from no one whomsoever. What he felt was that he couldn't at present have begun to tell her, and yet could profit perhaps exquisitely by the accident of having done so of old. "Please don't then. We're just right as it is."

"Oh I am," she laughed, "if you are!" To which she added: "Then you do still feel in the same way?"

It was impossible he shouldn't take to himself that she was really interested, though it all kept coming as perfect surprise. He had thought of himself so long as abominably alone, and lo he wasn't alone a bit. He hadn't been, it appeared, for an hour—since those moments on the Sorrento boat. It was *she* who had been, he seemed to see as he looked at her—she who had been made so by the graceless fact of his lapse of fidelity. To tell her what he had told her—what had it been but to ask something of her? something that she had given, in her charity, without his having, by a remembrance, by a return of the spirit, failing another encounter, so much as thanked her. What he had asked of her had been simply at first not to laugh at him. She had beautifully not done so for ten years, and she was not doing so now. So he had endless gratitude to make up. Only for that he must see just how he had figured to her. "What, exactly, was the account I gave—?"

"Of the way you did feel? Well, it was very simple. You said you had had from your earliest time, as the deepest thing within you, the sense of being kept for something rare and strange, possibly prodigious and terrible, that was sooner or later to happen to you, that you had in your bones the foreboding and the conviction of, and that would perhaps overwhelm you."

"Do you call that very simple?" John Marcher asked.

She thought a moment. "It was perhaps because I seemed, as you spoke, to understand it."

"You do understand it?" he eagerly asked.

Again she kept her kind eyes on him. "You still have the belief?"

"Oh!" he exclaimed helplessly. There was too much to say.

"Whatever it's to be," she clearly made out, "it hasn't yet come."

He shook his head in complete surrender now. "It hasn't yet come. Only, you know, it isn't anything I'm to *do,* to achieve in the world, to be distinguished or admired for. I'm not such an ass as *that.* It would be much better, no doubt, if I were."

"It's to be something you're merely to suffer?"

"Well, say to wait for—to have to meet, to face, to see suddenly break out in my life; possibly destroying all further consciousness, possibly annihilating me; possibly, on the other hand, only altering everything, striking at the root of all my world and leaving me to the consequences, however they shape themselves."

She took this in, but the light in her eyes continued for him not to be that of mockery. "Isn't what you describe perhaps but the expectation—or at any rate the sense of danger, familiar to so many people—of falling in love?"

John Marcher wondered. "Did you ask me that before?"

"No—I wasn't so free-and-easy then. But it's what strikes me now."

"Of course," he said after a moment, "it strikes you. Of course it strikes *me*. Of course what's in store for me may be no more than that. The only thing is," he went on, "that I think if it had been that I should by this time know."

"Do you mean because you've *been* in love?" And then as he but looked at her in silence: "You've been in love, and it hasn't meant such a cataclysm, hasn't proved the great affair?"

"Here I am, you see. It hasn't been overwhelming."

"Then it hasn't been love," said May Bartram.

"Well, I at least thought it was. I took it for that—I've taken it till now. It was agreeable, it was delightful, it was miserable," he explained. "But it wasn't strange. It wasn't what *my* affair's to be."

"You want something all to yourself—that nobody else knows or *has* known?"

"It isn't a question of what I 'want'—God knows I don't want anything. It's only a queston of the apprehension that haunts me—that I live with day by day."

He said this so lucidly and consistently that he could see it further impose itself. If she hadn't been interested before she'd have been interested now. "Is it a sense of coming violence?"

Evidently now too again he liked to talk of it. "I don't think of it as—when it does come—necessarily violent. I only think of it as natural and as of course above all unmistakeable. I think of it simply as *the* thing. *The* thing will of itself appear natural."

"Then how will it appear strange?"

Marcher bethought himself. "It won't—to *me*."

"To whom then?"

"Well," he replied, smiling at last, "say to you."

"Oh then I'm to be present?"

"Why you *are* present—since you know."

"I see." She turned it over. "But I mean at the catastrophe."

At this, for a minute, their lightness gave way to their gravity; it was as if the long look they exchanged held them together. "It will only depend on yourself—if you'll watch with me."

"Are you afraid?" she asked.

"Don't leave me *now*," he went on.

"Are you afraid?" she repeated.

"Do you think me simply out of my mind?" he pursued instead of answering. "Do I merely strike you as a harmless lunatic?"

"No," said May Bartram. "I understand you. I believe you."

"You mean you feel how my obsession—poor old thing!—may correspond to some possible reality?"

"To some possible reality."

"Then you *will* watch with me?"

She hesitated, then for the third time put her question. "Are you afraid?"

"Did I tell you I was—at Naples?"

"No, you said nothing about it."

"Then I don't know. And I should *like* to know," said John Marcher. "You'll tell me yourself whether you think so. If you'll watch with me you'll see."

"Very good then." They had been moving by this time across the room, and at the door, before passing out, they paused as for the full wind-up of their understanding. "I'll watch with you," said May Bartram.

II

The fact that she "knew"—knew and yet neither chaffed[6] him nor betrayed him—
had in a short time begun to constitute between them a goodly bond, which became more marked when, within the year that followed their afternoon at Weatherend, the opportunities for meeting multiplied. The event that thus promoted
these occasions was the death of the ancient lady her great-aunt, under whose
wing, since losing her mother, she had to such an extent found shelter, and who,
though but the widowed mother of the new successor to the property, had succeeded—thanks to a high tone and a high temper—in not forfeiting the supreme
position at the great house. The deposition of this personage arrived but with her
death, which, followed by many changes, made in particular a difference for the
young woman in whom Marcher's expert attention had recognised from the first a
dependent with a pride that might ache though it didn't bristle. Nothing for a long
time had made him easier than the thought that the aching must have been much
soothed by Miss Bartram's now finding herself able to set up a small home in
London. She had acquired property, to an amount that made that luxury just possible, under her aunt's extremely complicated will, and when the whole matter
began to be straightened out, which indeed took time, she let him know that the
happy issue was at last in view. He had seen her again before that day, both
because she had more than once accompanied the ancient lady to town and because he had paid another visit to the friends who so conveniently made of Weatherend one of the charms of their own hospitality. These friends had taken him
back there; he had achieved there again with Miss Bartram some quiet detachment; and he had in London succeeded in persuading her to more than one brief
absence from her aunt. They went together, on these latter occasions, to the National Gallery and the South Kensington Museum, where, among vivid reminders,
they talked of Italy at large—not now attempting to recover, as at first, the taste of
their youth and their ignorance. That recovery, the first day at Weatherend, had
served its purpose well, had given them quite enough; so that they were, to
Marcher's sense, no longer hovering about the headwaters of their stream, but had
felt their boat pushed sharply off and down the current.

They were literally afloat together; for our gentleman this was marked, quite as
marked as that the fortunate cause of it was just the buried treasure of her knowledge. He had with his own hands dug up this little hoard, brought to light—that is
to within reach of the dim day constituted by their discretions and privacies—the
object of value the hiding-place of which he had, after putting it into the ground
himself, so strangely, so long forgotten. The rare luck of his having again just
stumbled on the spot made him indifferent to any other question; he would doubtless have devoted more time to the odd accident of his lapse of memory if he
hadn't been moved to devote so much to the sweetness, the comfort, as he felt, for
the future, that this accident itself had helped to keep fresh. It had never entered
into his plan that any one should "know," and mainly for the reason that it wasn't
in him to tell any one. That would have been impossible, for nothing but the
amusement of a cold world would have waited on it. Since, however, a mysterious fate had opened his mouth betimes, in spite of him, he would count that a
compensation and profit by it to the utmost. That the right person *should* know

[6] Teased.

tempered the asperity of his secret more even than his shyness had permitted him to imagine; and May Bartram was clearly right, because—well, because there she was. Her knowledge simple settled it; he would have been sure enough by this time had she been wrong. There was that in his situation, no doubt, that disposed him too much to see her as a mere confidant, taking all her light for him from the fact—the fact only—of her interest in his predicament; from her mercy, sympathy, seriousness, her consent not to regard him as the funniest of the funny. Aware, in fine, that her price for him was just in her giving him this constant sense of his being admirably spared, he was careful to remember that she had also a life of her own, with things that might happen to *her,* things that in friendship one should likewise take account of. Something fairly remarkable came to pass with him, for that matter, in this connexion—something represented by a certain passage of his consciousness, in the suddenest way, from one extreme to the other.

He had thought himself, so long as nobody knew, the most disinterested person in the world, carrying his concentrated burden, his perpetual suspense, ever so quietly, holding his tongue about it, giving others no glimpse of it nor of its effect upon his life, asking of them no allowance and only making on his side all those that were asked. He hadn't disturbed people with the queerness of their having to know a haunted man, though he had had moments of rather special temptation on hearing them say they were forsooth "unsettled." If they were as unsettled as he was—he who had never been settled for an hour in his life—they would know what it meant. Yet it wasn't, all the same, for him to make them, and he listened to them civilly enough. This was why he had such good—though possibly such rather colourless—manners; this was why, above all, he could regard himself, in a greedy world, as decently—as in fact perhaps even a little sublimely—unselfish. Our point is accordingly that he valued this character quite sufficiently to measure his present danger of letting it lapse, against which he promised himself to be much on his guard. He was quite ready, none the less, to be selfish just a little, since surely no more charming occasion for it had come to him. "Just a little," in a word, was just as much as Miss Bartram, taking one day with another, would let him. He never would be in the least coercive, and would keep well before him the lines on which consideration for her—the very highest—ought to proceed. He would thoroughly establish the heads under which her affairs, her requirements, her peculiarities—he went so far as to give them the latitude of that name—would come into their intercourse. All this naturally was a sign of how much he took the intercourse itself for granted. There was nothing more to be done about *that.* It simply existed; had sprung into being with her first penetrating question to him in the autumn light there at Weatherend. The real form it should have taken on the basis that stood out large was the form of their marrying. But the devil in this was that the very basis itself put marrying out of the question. His conviction, his apprehension, his obsession, in short, wasn't a privilege he could invite a woman to share; and that consequence of it was precisely what was the matter with him. Something or other lay in wait for him, amid the twists and the turns of the months and the years, like a crouching beast in the jungle. It signified little whether the crouching beast were destined to slay him or to be slain. The definite point was the inevitable spring of the creature; and the definite lesson from that was that a man of feeling didn't cause himself to be accompanied by a lady on a tiger-hunt. Such was the image under which he had ended by figuring his life.

They had at first, none the less, in the scattered hours spent together, made no allusion to that view of it; which was a sign he was handsomely alert to give that he didn't expect, that he in fact didn't care, always to be talking about it. Such a feature in one's outlook was really like a hump on one's back. The difference it made every minute of the day existed quite independently of discussion. One discussed of course *like* a hunchback, for there was always, if nothing else, the hunchback face. That remained, and she was watching him; but people watched best, as a general thing, in silence, so that such would be predominantly the manner of their vigil. Yet he didn't want, at the same time, to be tense and solemn; tense and solemn was what he imagined he too much showed for with other people. The thing to be, with the one person who knew, was easy and natural—to make the reference rather than be seeming to avoid it, to avoid it rather than be seeming to make it, and to keep it, in any case, familiar, facetious even, rather than pedantic and portentous. Some such consideration as the latter was doubtless in his mind for instance when he wrote pleasantly to Miss Bartram that perhaps the great thing he had so long felt as in the lap of the gods was no more than this circumstance, which touched him so nearly, of her acquiring a house in London. It was the first allusion they had yet again made, needing any other hitherto so little; but when she replied, after having given him the news, that she was by no means satisfied with such a trifle as the climax to so special a suspense, she almost set him wondering if she hadn't even a larger conception of singularity for him than he had for himself. He was at all events destined to become aware little by little, as time went by, that she was all the while looking at his life, judging it, measuring it, in the light of the thing she knew, which grew to be at last, with the consecration of the years, never mentioned between them save as "the real truth" about him. That had always been his own form of reference to it, but she adopted the form so quietly that, looking back at the end of a period, he knew there was no moment at which it was traceable that she had, as he might say, got inside his idea, or exchanged the attitude of beautifully indulging for that of still more beautifully believing him.

It was always open to him to accuse her of seeing him but as the most harmless of maniacs, and this, in the long run—since it covered so much ground—was his easiest description of their friendship. He had a screw loose for her, but she liked him in spite of it and was practically, against the rest of the world, his kind wise keeper, unremunerated but fairly amused and, in the absence of other near ties, not disreputably occupied. The rest of the world of course thought him queer, but she, she only, knew how, and above all why, queer; which was precisely what enabled her to dispose the concealing veil in the right folds. She took his gaiety from him—since it had to pass with them for gaiety—as she took everything else; but she certainly so far justified by her unerring touch his finer sense of the degree to which he had ended by convincing her. *She* at least never spoke of the secret of his life except as "the real truth about you," and she had in fact a wonderful way of making it seem, as such, the secret of her own life too. That was in fine how he so constantly felt her as allowing for him; he couldn't on the whole call it anything else. He allowed for himself, but she, exactly, allowed still more; partly because, better placed for a sight of the matter, she traced his unhappy perversion through reaches of its course into which he could scarce follow it. He knew how he felt, but, besides knowing that, she knew how he *looked* as well; he knew each of the things of importance he was insidiously kept from doing, but she could add up the amount they made, understand how much, with a lighter weight on his spirit, he might have done, and thereby establish how, clever as he was, he fell short.

Above all she was in the secret of the difference between the forms he went through—those of his little office under Government, those of caring for his modest patrimony, for his library, for his garden in the country, for the people in London whose invitations he accepted and repaid—and the detachment that reigned beneath them and that made of all behaviour, all that could in the least be called behaviour, a long act of dissimulation. What it had come to was that he wore a mask painted with the social simper, out of the eye-holes of which there looked eyes of an expression not in the least matching the other features. This the stupid world, even after years, had never more than half-discovered. It was only May Bartram who had, and she achieved, by an art indescribable, the feat of at once—or perhaps it was only alternately—meeting the eyes from in front and mingling her own vision, as from over his shoulder, with their peep through the apertures.

So while they grew older together she did watch with him, and so she let this association give shape and colour to her own existence. Beneath *her* forms as well detachment had learned to sit, and behaviour had become for her, in the social sense, a false account of herself. There was but one account of her that would have been true all the while and that she could give straight to nobody, least of all to John Marcher. Her whole attitude was a virtual statement, but the perception of that only seemed called to take its place for him as one of the many things necessarily crowded out of his consciousness. If she had moreover, like himself, to make sacrifices to their real truth, it was to be granted that her compensation might have affected her as more prompt and more natural. They had long periods, in this London time, during which, when they were together, a stranger might have listened to them without in the least pricking up his ears; on the other hand the real truth was equally liable at any moment to rise to the surface, and the auditor would then have wondered indeed what they were talking about. They had from an early hour made up their mind that society was, luckily, unintelligent, and the margin allowed them by this had fairly become one of their commonplaces. Yet there were still moments when the situation turned almost fresh—usually under the effect of some expression drawn from herself. Her expressions doubtless repeated themselves, but her intervals were generous. "What saves us, you know, is that we answer so completely to so usual an appearance: that of the man and woman whose friendship has become such a daily habit—or almost—as to be at last indispensable." That for instance was a remark she had frequently enough had occasion to make, though she had given it at different times different developments. What we are especially concerned with is the turn it happened to take from her one afternoon when he had come to see her in honour of her birthday. This anniversary had fallen on a Sunday, at a season of thick fog and general outward gloom; but he had brought her his customary offering, having known her now long enough to have established a hundred small traditions. It was one of his proofs to himself, the present he made her on her birthday, that he hadn't sunk into real selfishness. It was mostly nothing more than a small trinket, but it was always fine of its kind, and he was regularly careful to pay for it more than he thought he could afford. "Our habit saves you at least, don't you see? because it makes you, after all, for the vulgar, indistinguishable from other men. What's the most inveterate mark of men in general? Why the capacity to spend endless time with dull women—to spend it I won't say without being bored, but without minding that they are, without being driven off at a tangent by it; which comes to the same thing. I'm your dull woman, a part of the daily bread for which you pray at church. That covers your tracks more than anything."

"And what covers yours?" asked Marcher, whom his dull woman could mostly to this extent amuse. "I see of course what you mean by your saving me, in this way and that, so far as other people are concerned—I've seen it all along. Only what is it that saves *you?* I often think, you know, of that."

She looked as if she sometimes thought of that too, but rather in a different way. "Where other people, you mean, are concerned?"

"Well, you're really so in with me, you know—as a sort of result of my being so in with yourself. I mean of my having such an immense regard for you, being so tremendously mindful of all you've done for me. I sometimes ask myself if it's quite fair. Fair I mean to have so involved and—since one may say it—interested you. I almost feel as if you hadn't really had time to do anything else."

"Anything else but be interested?" she asked. "Ah what else does one ever want to be? If I've been 'watching' with you, as we long ago agreed I was to do, watching's always in itself an absorption."

"Oh certainly," John Marcher said, "if you hadn't had your curiosity—! Only doesn't it sometimes come to you as time goes on that your curiosity isn't being particularly repaid?"

May Bartram had a pause. "Do you ask that, by any chance, because you feel at all that yours isn't? I mean because you have to wait so long."

Oh he understood what she meant! "For the thing to happen that never does happen? For the beast to jump out? No, I'm just where I was about it. It isn't a matter as to which I can *choose,* I can decide for a change. It isn't one as to which there *can* be a change. It's in the lap of the gods. One's in the hands of one's law—there one is. As to the form the law will take, the way it will operate, that's its own affair."

"Yes," Miss Bartram replied; "of course one's fate's coming, of course it *has* come in its own form and its own way, all the while. Only, you know, the form and the way in your case were to have been—well, something so exceptional and, as one may say, so particularly *your* own."

Something in this made him look at her with suspicion. "You say 'were to *have* been,' as if in your heart you had begun to doubt."

"Oh!" she vaguely protested.

"As if you believed," he went on, "that nothing will now take place."

She shook her head slowly but rather inscrutably. "You're far from my thought."

He continued to look at her. "What then is the matter with you?"

"Well," she said after another wait, "the matter with me is simply that I'm more sure than ever my curiosity, as you call it, will be but too well repaid."

They were frankly grave now; he had got up from his seat, had turned once more about the little drawing-room to which, year after year, he brought his inevitable topic; in which he had, as he might have said, tasted their intimate community with every sauce, where every object was as familiar to him as the things of his own house and the very carpets were worn with his fitful walk very much as the desks in old counting-houses are worn by the elbows of generations of clerks. The generations of his nervous moods had been at work there, and the place was the written history of his whole middle life. Under the impression of what his friend had just said he knew himself, for some reason, more aware of these things; which made him, after a moment, stop again before her. "Is it possibly that you've grown afraid?"

"Afraid?" He thought, as she repeated the word that his question had made her, a little, change colour; so that, lest he should have touched on a truth, he explained very kindly: "You remember that that was what you asked *me* long ago—that first day at Weatherend."

"Oh yes, and you told me you didn't know—that I was to see for myself. We've said little about it since, even in so long a time."

"Precisely," Marcher interposed—"quite as if it were too delicate a matter for us to make free with. Quite as if we might find, on pressure, that I *am* afraid. For then," he said, "we shouldn't, should we? quite know what to do."

She had for the time no answer to this question. "There have been days when I thought you were. Only, of course," she added, "there have been days when we have thought almost anything."

"Everything. Oh!" Marcher softly groaned as with a gasp, half-spent, at the face, more uncovered just then than it had been for a long while, of the imagination always with them. It had always had its incalculable moments of glaring out, quite as with the very eyes of the very Beast, and, used as he was to them, they could still draw from him the tribute of a sigh that rose from the depths of his being. All they had thought, first and last, rolled over him; the past seemed to have been reduced to mere barren speculation. This in fact was what the place had just struck him as so full of—the simplification of everything but the state of suspense. That remained only by seeming to hang in the void surrounding it. Even his original fear, if fear it had been, had lost itself in the desert. "I judge, however," he continued, "that you see I'm not afraid now."

"What I see, as I make it out, is that you've achieved something almost unprecedented in the way of getting used to danger. Living with it so long and so closely you've lost your sense of it; you know it's there, but you're indifferent, and you cease even, as of old, to have to whistle in the dark. Considering what the danger is," May Bartram wound up, "I'm bound to say I don't think your attitude could well be surpassed."

John Marcher faintly smiled. "It's heroic?"

"Certainly—call it that."

It was what he would have liked indeed to call it. "I *am* then a man of courage?"

"That's what you were to show me."

He still, however, wondered. "But doesn't the man of courage know what he's afraid of—or *not* afraid of? I don't know *that*, you see. I don't focus it. I can't name it. I only know I'm exposed."

"Yes, but exposed—how shall I say?—so directly. So intimately. That's surely enough."

"Enough to make you feel then—as what we may call the end and the upshot of our watch—that I'm not afraid?"

"You're not afraid. But it isn't," she said, "the end of our watch. That is it isn't the end of yours. You've everything still to see."

"Then why haven't *you?*" he asked. He had had, all along, to-day, the sense of her keeping something back, and he still had it. As this was his first impression of that it quite made a date. The case was the more marked as she didn't at first answer; which in turn made him go on. "You know something I don't." Then his voice, for that of a man of courage, trembled a little. "You know what's to happen." Her silence, with the face she showed, was almost a confession—it made him sure. "You know, and you're afraid to tell me. It's so bad that you're afraid I'll find out."

All this might be true, for she did look as if, unexpectedly to her, he had crossed some mystic line that she had secretly drawn round her. Yet she might, after all, not have worried; and the real climax was that he himself, at all events, needn't. "You'll never find out."

III

It was all to have made, none the less, as I have said, a date; which came out in the fact that again and again, even after long intervals, other things that passed between them wore in relation to this hour but the character of recalls and results. Its immediate effect had been indeed rather to lighten insistence—almost to provoke a reaction; as if their topic had dropped by its own weight and as if moreover, for that matter, Marcher had been visited by one of his occasional warnings against egotism. He had kept up, he felt, and very decently on the whole, his consciousness of the importance of not being selfish, and it was true that he had never sinned in that direction without promptly enough trying to press the scales the other way. He often repaired his fault, the season permitting, by inviting his friend to accompany him to the opera; and it not infrequently thus happened that, to show he didn't wish her to have but one sort of food for her mind, he was the cause of her appearing there with him a dozen nights in the month. It even happened that, seeing her home at such times, he occasionally went in with her to finish, as he called it, the evening, and, the better to make his point, sat down to the frugal but always careful little supper that awaited his pleasure. His point was made, he thought, by his not eternally insisting with her on himself; made for instance, at such hours, when it befell that, her piano at hand and each of them familiar with it, they went over passages of the opera together. It chanced to be on one of these occasions, however, that he reminded her of her not having answered a certain question he had put to her during the talk that had taken place between them on her last birthday. "What is it that saves *you*?"—saved her, he meant, from that appearance of variation from the usual human type. If he had practically escaped remark, as she pretended, by doing, in the most important particular, what most men do—find the answer to life in patching up an alliance of a sort with a woman no better than himself—how had she escaped it, and how could the alliance, such as it was, since they must suppose it had been more or less noticed, have failed to make her rather positively talked about?

"I never said," May Bartram replied, "that it hadn't made me a good deal talked about."

"Ah well then you're not 'saved.'"

"It hasn't been a question for me. If you've had your woman I've had," she said, "my man."

"And you mean that makes you all right?"

Oh it was always as if there were so much to say! "I don't know why it shouldn't make me—humanly, which is what we're speaking of—as right as it makes you."

"I see," Marcher returned. " 'Humanly,' no doubt, as showing that you're living for something. Not, that is, just for me and my secret."

May Bartram smiled. "I don't pretend it exactly shows that I'm not living for you. It's my intimacy with you that's in question."

He laughed as he saw what she meant. "Yes, but since, as you say, I'm only, so far as people make out, ordinary, you're—aren't you?—no more than ordinary either. You help me to pass for a man like another. So if I *am,* as I understand you, you're not compromised. Is that it?"

She had another of her waits, but she spoke clearly enough. "That's it. It's all that concerns me—to help you to pass for a man like another."

He was careful to acknowledge the remark handsomely. "How kind, how beautiful, you are to me! How shall I ever repay you?"

She had her last grave pause, as if there might be a choice of ways. But she chose. "By going on as you are."

It was into this going on as he was that they relapsed, and really for so long a time that the day inevitably came for a further sounding of their depths. These depths, constantly bridged over by a structure firm enough in spite of its lightness and of its occasional oscillation in the somewhat vertiginous[7] air, invited on occasion, in the interest of their nerves, a dropping of the plummet and a measurement of the abyss. A difference had been made moreover, once for all, by the fact that she had all the while not appeared to feel the need of rebutting his charge of an idea within her that she didn't dare to express—a charge uttered just before one of the fullest of their later discussions ended. It had come up for him then that she "knew" something and that what she knew was bad—too bad to tell him. When he had spoken of it as visibly so bad that she was afraid he might find it out, her reply had left the matter too equivocal to be let alone and yet, for Marcher's special sensibility, almost too formidable again to touch. He circled about it at a distance that alternately narrowed and widened and that still wasn't much affected by the consciousness in him that there was nothing she could "know," after all, any better than he did. She had no source of knowledge he hadn't equally—except of course that she might have finer nerves. That was what women had where they were interested; they made out things, where people were concerned, that the people often couldn't have made out for themselves. Their nerves, their sensibility, their imagination, were conductors and revealers, and the beauty of May Bartram was in particular that she had given herself so to his case. He felt in these days what, oddly enough, he had never felt before, the growth of a dread of losing her by some catastrophe—some catastrophe that yet wouldn't at all be *the* catastrophe: partly because she had almost of a sudden begun to strike him as more useful to him than ever yet, and partly by reason of an appearance of uncertainty in her health, coincident and equally new. It was characteristic of the inner detachment he had hitherto so successfully cultivated and to which our whole account of him is a reference, it was characteristic that his complications, such as they were, had never yet seemed so as at this crisis to thicken about him, even to the point of making him ask himself if he were, by any chance, of a truth, within sight or sound, within touch or reach, within the immediate jurisdiction, of the thing that waited.

When the day came, as come it had to, that his friend confessed to him her fear of a deep disorder in her blood, he felt somehow the shadow of a change and the chill of a shock. He immediately began to imagine aggravations and disasters, and above all to think of her peril as the direct menace for himself of personal privation. This indeed gave him one of those partial recoveries of equanimity that were agreeable to him—it showed him that what was still first in his mind was the loss she herself might suffer. "What if she should have to die before knowing, before seeing—?" It would have been brutal, in the early stages of her trouble, to put that

---

[7] Whirling, spinning.

question to her; but it had immediately sounded for him to his own concern, and the possibility was what most made him sorry for her. If she did "know," moreover, in the sense of her having had some—what should he think?—mystical irresistible light, this would make the matter not better, but worse, inasmuch as her original adoption of his own curiosity had quite become the basis of her life. She had been living to see what would *be* to be seen, and it would quite lacerate her to have to give up before the accomplishment of the vision. These reflexions, as I say, quickened his generosity; yet, make them as he might, he saw himself, with the lapse of the period, more and more disconcerted. It lapsed for him with a strange steady sweep, and the oddest oddity was that it gave him, independently of the threat of much inconvenience, almost the only positive surprise his career, if career it could be called, had yet offered him. She kept the house as she had never done; he had to go to her to see her—she could meet him nowhere now, though there was scarce a corner of their loved old London in which she hadn't in the past, at one time or another, done so; and he found her always seated by her fire in the deep old-fashioned chair she was less and less able to leave. He had been struck one day, after an absence exceeding his usual measure, with her suddenly looking much older to him that he had ever thought of her being; then he recognised that the suddenness was all on his side—he had just simply and suddenly noticed. She looked older because inevitably, after so many years, she *was* old, or almost; which was of course true in still greater measure of her companion. If she was old, or almost, John Marcher assuredly was, and yet it was her showing of the lesson, not his own, that brought the truth home to him. His surprises began here; when once they had begun they multiplied; they came rather with a rush: it was as if, in the oddest way in the world, they had all been kept back, sown in a thick cluster, for the late afternoon of life, the time at which for people in general the unexpected has died out.

One of them was that he should have caught himself—for he *had* so done—*really* wondering if the great accident would take form now as nothing more than his being condemned to see this charming woman, this admirable friend, pass away from him. He had never so unreservedly qualified her as while confronted in thought with such a possibility; in spite of which there was small doubt for him that as an answer to his long riddle the mere effacement of even so fine a feature of his situation would be an abject anticlimax. It would represent, as connected with his past attitude, a drop of dignity under the shadow of which his existence could only become the most grotesque of failures. He had been far from holding it a failure—long as he had waited for the appearance that was to make it a success. He had waited for quite another thing, not for such a thing as that. The breath of his good faith came short, however, as he recognised how long he had waited, or how long at least his companion had. That she, at all events, might be recorded as having waited in vain—this affected him sharply, and all the more because of his at first having done little more than amuse himself with the idea. It grew more grave as the gravity of her condition grew, and the state of mind it produced in him, which he himself ended by watching as if it had been some definite disfigurement of his outer person, may pass for another of his surprises. This conjoined itself still with another, the really stupefying consciousness of a question that he would have allowed to shape itself had he dared. What did everything mean— what, that is, did *she* mean, she and her vain waiting and her probable death and the soundless admonition of it all—unless that, at this time of day, it was simply, it was overwhelmingly too late? He had never at any stage of his queer consciousness admitted the whisper of such a correction; he had never till within these last few months been so false to his conviction as not to hold that what was to come to him had time, whether *he* struck himself as having it or not. That at last, at last, he certainly hadn't it, to speak of, or had it but in the scantiest measure—such, soon enough, as things went with him, became the inference with which his old obsession had to reckon: and this it was not helped to do by the more and more confirmed appearance that the great vagueness casting the long shadow in which he had lived had, to attest itself, almost no margin left. Since it was in Time that he was to have met his fate, so it was in Time that his fate was to have acted; and as he waked up to the sense of no longer being young, which was exactly the sense of being stale, just as that, in turn, was the sense of being weak, he waked up to another matter beside. It all hung together; they were subject, he and the great vagueness, to an equal and indivisible law. When the possibilities themselves had accordingly turned stale, when the secret of the gods had grown faint, had perhaps even quite evaporated, that, and that only, was failure. It wouldn't have been failure to be bankrupt, dishonoured, pilloried, hanged; it was failure not to be anything. And so, in the dark valley into which his path had taken its unlooked-for twist, he wondered not a little as he groped. He didn't care what awful crash might overtake him, with what ignominy or what monstrosity he might yet be associated—since he wasn't after all too utterly old to suffer—if it would only be decently proportionate to the posture he had kept, all his life, in the threatened presence of it. He had but one desire left—that he shouldn't have been "sold."

IV

Then it was that, one afternoon, while the spring of the year was young and new she met all in her own way his frankest betrayal of these alarms. He had gone in late to see her, but evening hadn't settled and she was presented to him in that long fresh light of waning April days which affects us often with a sadness sharper than the greyest hours of autumn. The week had been warm, the spring was supposed to have begun early, and May Bartram sat, for the first time in the year, without a fire; a fact that, to Marcher's sense, gave the scene of which she formed part a smooth and ultimate look, an air of knowing, in its immaculate order and cold meaningless cheer, that it would never see a fire again. Her own aspect—he could scarce have said why—intensified this note. Almost as white as wax, with the marks and signs in her face as numerous and as fine as if they had been etched by a needle, with soft white draperies relieved by a faded green scarf on the delicate tone of which the years had further refined, she was the picture of a serene and exquisite but impenetrable sphinx, whose head, or indeed all whose person, might have been powdered with silver. She was a sphinx,[8] yet with her white petals and green fronds she might have been a lily too—only an artificial lily, wonderfully imitated and constantly kept, without dust or stain, though not exempt from a slight droop and a complexity of faint creases, under some clear glass bell. The perfection of household care, of high polish and finish, always reigned in her rooms, but they now looked most as if everything had been wound up, tucked in, put away, so that she might sit with folded hands and with nothing

[8] Mysterious or inscrutable like the mythic sphinx, a beast with a lion's body and a human head.

more to do. She was "out of it," to Marcher's vision; her work was over; she communicated with him as across some gulf or from some island of rest that she had already reached, and it made him feel strangely abandoned. Was it—or rather wasn't it—that if for so long she had been watching with him the answer to their question must have swum into her ken and taken on its name, so that her occupation was verily gone? He had as much as charged her with this in saying to her, many months before, that she even then knew something she was keeping from him. It was a point he had never since ventured to press, vaguely fearing as he did that it might become a difference, perhaps a disagreement, between them. He had in this later time turned nervous, which was what he in all the other years had never been; and the oddity was that his nervousness should have waited till he had begun to doubt, should have held off so long as he was sure. There was something, it seemed to him, that the wrong word would bring down on his head, something that would so at least ease off his tension. But he wanted not to speak the wrong word; that would make everything ugly. He wanted the knowledge he lacked to drop on him, if drop it could, by its own august weight. If she was to forsake him it was surely for her to take leave. This was why he didn't directly ask her again what she knew; but it was also why, approaching the matter from another side, he said to her in the course of his visit: "What do you regard as the very worst that at this time of day *can* happen to me?"

He had asked her that in the past often enough; they had, with the odd irregular rhythm of their intensities and avoidances, exchanged ideas about it and then had seen the ideas washed away by cool intervals, washed like figures traced in seasand. It had ever been the mark of their talk that the oldest allusions in it required but a little dismissal and reaction to come out again, sounding for the hour as new. She could thus at present meet his enquiry quite freshly and patiently. "Oh yes, I've repeatedly thought, only it always seemed to me of old that I couldn't quite make up my mind. I thought of dreadful things, between which it was difficult to choose; and so must you have done."

"Rather! I feel now as if I had scarce done anything else. I appear to myself to have spent my life in thinking of nothing *but* dreadful things. A great many of them I've at different times named to you, but there were others I couldn't name."

"They were too, too dreadful?"

"Too, too dreadful—some of them."

She looked at him a minute, and there came to him as he met it an inconsequent sense that her eyes, when one got their full clearness, were still as beautiful as they had been in youth, only beautiful with a strange cold light—a light that somehow was a part of the effect, if it wasn't rather a part of the cause, of the pale hard sweetness of the season and the hour. "And yet," she said at last, "there are horrors we've mentioned."

It deepened the strangeness to see her, as such a figure in such a picture, talk of "horrors," but she was to do in a few minutes something stranger yet—though even of this he was to take the full measure but afterwards—and the note of it already trembled. It was, for the matter of that, one of the signs that her eyes were having again the high flicker of their prime. He had to admit, however, what she said. "Oh yes, there were times when we did go far." He caught himself in the act of speaking as if it all were over. Well, he wished it were; and the consummation depended for him clearly more and more on his friend.

But she had now a soft smile. "Oh far—!"

It was oddly ironic. "Do you mean you're prepared to go further?"

She was frail and ancient and charming as she continued to look at him, yet it was rather as if she had lost the thread. "Do you consider that we went far?"

"Why I thought it the point you were just making—that we *had* looked most things in the face."

"Including each other?" She still smiled. "But you're quite right. We've had together great imaginations, often great fears; but some of them have been unspoken."

"Then the worst—we haven't faced that. I *could* face it, I believe, if I knew what you think it. I feel," he explained, "as if I had lost my power to conceive such things." And he wondered if he looked as blank as he sounded. "It's spent."

"Then why do you assume," she asked, "that mine isn't?"

"Because you've given me signs to the contrary. It isn't a question for you of conceiving, imagining, comparing. It isn't a question now of choosing." At last he came out with it. "You know something I don't. You've shown me that before."

These last words had affected her, he made out in a moment, exceedingly, and she spoke with firmness. "I've shown you, my dear, nothing."

He shook his head. "You can't hide it."

"Oh, oh!" May Bartram sounded over what she couldn't hide. It was almost a smothered groan.

"You admitted it months ago, when I spoke of it to you as of something you were afraid I should find out. Your answer was that I couldn't, that I wouldn't, and I don't pretend I have. But you had something therefore in mind, and I now see how it must have been, how it still is, the possibility that, of all possibilities, has settled itself for you as the worst. This," he went on, "is why I appeal to you. I'm only afraid of ignorance to-day—I'm not afraid of knowledge." And then as for a while she said nothing: "What makes me sure is that I see in your face and feel here, in this air and amid these appearances, that you're out of it. You've done. You've had your experience. You leave me to my fate."

Well, she listened, motionless and white in her chair, as on a decision to be made, so that her manner was fairly an avowal, though still, with a small fine inner stiffness, an imperfect surrender. "It *would* be the worst," she finally let herself say. "I mean the thing I've never said."

It hushed him a moment. "More monstrous than all the monstrosities we've named?"

"More monstrous. Isn't that what you sufficiently express," she asked, "in calling it the worst?"

Marcher thought. "Assuredly—if you mean, as I do, something that includes all the loss and all the shame that are thinkable."

"It would if it *should* happen," said May Bartram. "What we're speaking of, remember, is only my idea."

"It's your belief," Marcher returned. "That's enough for me. I feel your beliefs are right. Therefore if, having this one, you give me no more light on it, you abandon me."

"No, no!" she repeated. "I'm with you—don't you see?—still." And as to make it more vivid to him she rose from her chair—a movement she seldom risked in these days—and showed herself, all draped and all soft, in her fairness and slimness. "I haven't forsaken you."

It was really, in its effort against weakness, a generous assurance, and had the success of the impulse not, happily, been great, it would have touched him to pain more than to pleasure. But the cold charm in her eyes had spread, as she hovered before him, to all the rest of her person, so that it was for the minute almost a recovery of youth. He couldn't pity her for that; he could only take her as she showed—as capable even yet of helping him. It was as if, at the same time, her light might at any instant go out; wherefore he must make the most of it. There passed before him with intensity the three or four things he wanted most to know; but the question that came of itself to his lips really covered the others. "Then tell me if I shall consciously suffer."

She promptly shook her head. "Never!"

It confirmed the authority he imputed to her, and it produced on him an extraordinary effect. "Well, what's better than that? Do you call that the worst?"

"You think nothing is better?" she asked.

She seemed to mean something so special that he again sharply wondered, though still with the dawn of a prospect of relief. "Why not, if one doesn't *know?*" After which, as their eyes, over his question, met in a silence, the dawn deepened and something to his purpose came prodigiously out of her very face. His own, as he took it in, suddenly flushed to the forehead, and he gasped with the force of a perception to which, on the instant, everything fitted. The sound of his gasp filled the air; then he became articulate. "I see—if I don't suffer!"

In her own look, however, was doubt. "You see what?"

"Why what you mean—what you've always meant."

She again shook her head. "What I mean isn't what I've always meant. It's different."

"It's something new?"

She hung back from it a little. "Something new. It's not what you think. I see what you think."

His divination drew breath then; only her correction might be wrong. "It isn't that I *am* a blockhead?" he asked between faintness and grimness. "It isn't that it's all a mistake?"

"A mistake?" she pityingly echoed. *That* possibility, for her, he saw, would be monstrous; and if she guaranteed him the immunity from pain it would accordingly not be what she had in mind. "Oh no," she declared; "it's nothing of that sort. You've been right."

Yet he couldn't help asking himself if she weren't, thus pressed, speaking but to save him. It seemed to him he should be most in a hole if his history should prove all a platitude. "Are you telling me the truth, so that I shan't have been a bigger idiot than I can bear to know? I *haven't* lived with a vain imagination, in the most besotted illusion? I haven't waited but to see the door shut in my face?"

She shook her head again. "However the case stands *that* isn't the truth. Whatever the reality, it *is* a reality. The door isn't shut. The door's open," said May Bartram.

"Then something's to come?"

She waited once again, always with her cold sweet eyes on him. "It's never too late." She had, with her gliding step, diminished the distance between them, and she stood nearer to him, close to him, a minute, as if still charged with the unspoken. Her movement might have been for some finer emphasis of what she was at once hesitating and deciding to say. He had been standing by the chimney-piece, fireless and sparely adorned, a small perfect old French clock and two morsels of rosy Dresden[9] constituting all its furniture; and her hand grasped the shelf while she kept him waiting, grasped it a little as for support and encouragement. She only kept him waiting, however; that is he only waited. It had become suddenly, from her movement and attitude, beautiful and vivid to him that she had something more to give him; her wasted face delicately shone with it—it glittered almost as with the white lustre of silver in her expression. She was right, incontestably, for what he saw in her face was the truth, and strangely, without consequence, while their talk of it as dreadful was still in the air, she appeared to present it as inordinately soft. This, prompting bewilderment, made him but gape the more gratefully for her revelation, so that they continued for some minutes silent, her face shining at him, her contact imponderably pressing, and his stare all kind but all expectant. The end, none the less, was that what he had expected failed to come to him. Something else took place instead, which seemed to consist at first in the mere closing of her eyes. She gave way at the same instant to a slow fine shudder, and though he remained staring—though he stared in fact but the harder—turned off and regained her chair. It was the end of what she had been intending, but it left him thinking only of that.

"Well, you don't say—?"

She had touched in her passage a bell near the chimney and had sunk back strangely pale. "I'm afraid I'm too ill."

"Too ill to tell me?" It sprang up sharp to him, and almost to his lips, the fear she might die without giving him light. He checked himself in time from so expressing his question, but she answered as if she had heard the words.

"Don't you know—now?"

"'Now'—?" She had spoken as if some difference had been made within the moment. But her maid, quickly obedient to her bell, was already with them. "I know nothing." And he was afterwards to say to himself that he must have spoken with odious impatience, such an impatience as to show that, supremely disconcerted, he washed his hands of the whole question.

"Oh!" said May Bartram.

"Are you in pain?" he asked as the woman went to her.

"No," said May Bartram.

Her maid, who had put an arm round her as if to take her to her room, fixed on him eyes that appealingly contradicted her; in spite of which, however, he showed once more his mystification. "What then has happened?"

She was once more, with her companion's help, on her feet, and, feeling withdrawal imposed on him, he had blankly found his hat and gloves and had reached the door. Yet he waited for her answer. "What *was* to," she said.

V

He came back the next day, but she was then unable to see him, and as it was literally the first time this had occurred in the long stretch of their acquaintance he turned away, defeated and sore, almost angry—or feeling at least that such a break in their custom was really the beginning of the end—and wandered alone with his thoughts, especially with the one he was least able to keep down. She was

[9] China pieces produced near Dresden, Germany.

dying and he would lose her; she was dying and his life would end. He stopped in the Park, into which he had passed, and stared before him at his recurrent doubt. Away from her the doubt pressed again; in her presence he had believed her, but as he felt his forlornness he threw himself into the explanation that, nearest at hand, had most of a miserable warmth for him and least of a cold torment. She had deceived him to save him—to put him off with something in which he should be able to rest. What could the thing that was to happen to him be, after all, but just this thing that had begun to happen? Her dying, her death, his consequent solitude—*that* was what he had figured as the Beast in the Jungle, that was what had been in the lap of the gods. He had had her word for it as he left her—what else on earth could she have meant? It wasn't a thing of a monstrous order; not a fate rare and distinguished; not a stroke of fortune that overwhelmed and immortalised; it had only the stamp of the common doom. But poor Marcher at this hour judged the common doom sufficient. It would serve his turn, and even as the consummation of infinite waiting he would bend his pride to accept it. He sat down on a bench in the twilight. He hadn't been a fool. Something had *been,* as she had said, to come. Before he rose indeed it had quite struck him that the final fact really matched with the long avenue through which he had had to reach it. As sharing his suspense and as giving herself all, giving her life, to bring it to an end, she had come with him every step of the way. He had lived by her aid, and to leave her behind would be cruelly, damnably to miss her. What could be more overwhelming than that?

Well, he was to know within the week, for though she kept him a while at bay, left him restless and wretched during a series of days on each of which he asked about her only again to have to turn away, she ended his trial by receiving him where she had always received him. Yet she had been brought out at some hazard into the presence of so many of the things that were, consciously, vainly, half their past, and there was scant service left in the gentleness of her mere desire, all too visible, to check his obsession and wind up his long trouble. That was clearly what she wanted, the one thing more for her own peace while she could still put out her hand. He was so affected by her state that, once seated by her chair, he was moved to let everything go; it was she herself therefore who brought him back, took up again, before she dismissed him, her last word of the other time. She showed how she wished to leave their business in order. "I'm not sure you understood. You've nothing to wait for more. It *has* come."

Oh how he looked at her! "Really?"

"Really."

"The thing that, as you said, *was* to?"

"The thing that we began in our youth to watch for."

Face to face with her once more he believed her; it was a claim to which he had so abjectly little to oppose. "You mean that it has come as a positive definite occurrence, with a name and a date?"

"Positive. Definite. I don't know about the 'name,' but oh with a date!"

He found himself again too helplessly at sea. "But come in the night—come and passed me by?"

May Bartram had her strange faint smile. "Oh no, it hasn't passed you by!"

"But if I haven't been aware of it and it hasn't touched me—?"

"Ah your not being aware of it"—and she seemed to hesitate an instant to deal with this—"your not being aware of it is the strangeness *in* the strangeness. It's the wonder *of* the wonder." She spoke as with the softness almost of a sick child, yet now at last, at the end of all, with the perfect straightness of a sibyl.[10] She visibly knew that she knew, and the effect on him was of something co-ordinate, in its high character, with the law that had ruled him. It was the true voice of the law; so on her lips would the law itself have sounded. "It *has* touched you," she went on. "It has done its office. It has made you all its own."

"So utterly without my knowing it?"

"So utterly without your knowing it." His hand, as he leaned to her, was on the arm of her chair, and, dimly smiling always now, she placed her own on it. "It's enough if *I* know it."

"Oh!" he confusedly breathed, as she herself of late so often had done.

"What I long ago said is true. You'll never know now, and I think you ought to be content. You've *had* it," said May Bartram.

"But had what?"

"Why what was to have marked you out. The proof of your law. It has acted. I'm too glad," she then bravely added, "to have been able to see what it's *not*."

He continued to attach his eyes to her, and with the sense that it was all beyond him, and that *she* was too, he would still have sharply challenged her hadn't he so felt it an abuse of her weakness to do more than take devoutly what she gave him, take it hushed as to a revelation. If he did speak, it was out of the fore-knowledge of his loneliness to come. "If you're glad of what it's 'not' it might then have been worse?"

She turned her eyes away, she looked straight before her; with which after a moment: "Well, you know our fears."

He wondered. "It's something then we never feared?"

On this slowly she turned to him. "Did we ever dream, with all our dreams, that we should sit and talk of it thus?"

He tried for a little to make out that they had; but it was as if their dreams, numberless enough, were in solution in some thick cold mist through which thought lost itself. "It might have been that we couldn't talk?"

"Well"—she did her best for him—"not from this side. This, you see," she said, "is the *other* side."

"I think," poor Marcher returned, "that all sides are the same to me." Then, however, as she gently shook her head in correction: "We mightn't, as it were, have got across—?"

"To where we are—no. We're *here*"—she made her weak emphasis.

"And much good does it do us!" was her friend's frank comment.

"It does us the good it can. It does us the good that *it* isn't here. It's past. It's behind," said May Bartram. "Before—" but her voice dropped.

He had got up, not to tire her, but it was hard to combat his yearning. She after all told him nothing but that his light had failed—which he knew well enough without her. "Before—?" he blankly echoed.

"Before, you see, it was always to *come*. That kept it present."

"Oh I don't care what comes now! Besides," Marcher added, "it seems to me I liked it better present, as you say, than I can like it absent with *your* absence."

"Oh mine!"—and her pale hands made light of it.

"With the absence of everything." He had a dreadful sense of standing there before her for—so far as anything but this proved, this bottomless drop was con-

---

[10] According to classical myth, a female prophet.

cerned—the last time of their life. It rested on him with a weight he felt he could scarce bear, and this weight it apparently was that still pressed out what remained in him of speakable protest. "I believe you; but I can't begin to pretend I understand. *Nothing,* for me, is past; nothing *will* pass till I pass myself, which I pray my stars may be as soon as possible. Say, however," he added, "that I've eaten my cake, as you contend, to the last crumb—how can the thing I've never felt at all be the thing I was marked out to feel?"

She met him perhaps less directly, but she met him unperturbed. "You take your 'feelings' for granted. You were to suffer your fate. That was not necessarily to know it."

"How in the world—when what is such knowledge but suffering?"

She looked up at him a while in silence. "No—you don't understand."

"I suffer," said John Marcher.

"Don't, don't!"

"How can I help at least *that?*"

"*Don't!*" May Bartram repeated.

She spoke it in a tone so special, in spite of her weakness, that he stared an instant—stared as if some light, hitherto hidden, had shimmered across his vision. Darkness again closed over it, but the gleam had already become for him an idea. "Because I haven't the right—?"

"Don't *know*—when you needn't" she mercifully urged. "You needn't—for we shouldn't."

"Shouldn't?" If he could but know what she meant!

"No—it's too much."

"Too much?" he still asked but, with a mystification that was the next moment of a sudden to give way. Her words, if they meant something, affected him in this light—the light also of her wasted face—as meaning *all,* and the sense of what knowledge had been for herself came over him with a rush which broke through into a question. "Is it of that then you're dying?"

She but watched him, gravely at first, as to see, with this, where he was, and she might have seen something or feared something that moved her sympathy. "I would live for you still—if I could." Her eyes closed for a little, as if, withdrawn into herself, she were for a last time trying. "But I can't!" she said as she raised them again to take leave of him.

She couldn't indeed, as but too promptly and sharply appeared, and he had no vision of her after this that was anything but darkness and doom. They had parted for ever in that strange talk; access to her chamber of pain, rigidly guarded, was almost wholly forbidden him; he was feeling now moreover, in the face of doctors, nurses, the two or three relatives attracted doubtless by the presumption of what she had to "leave," how few were the rights, as they were called in such cases, that he had to put forward, and how odd it might even seem that their intimacy shouldn't have given him more of them. The stupidest fourth cousin had more, even though she had been nothing in such a person's life. She had been a feature of features in *his,* for what else was it to have been so indispensable? Strange beyond saying were the ways of existence, baffling for him the anomaly of his lack, as he felt it to be, of producible claim. A woman might have been, as it were, everything to him, and it might yet present him in no connexion that any one seemed held to recognise. If this was the case in these closing weeks it was the case more sharply on the occasion of the last offices rendered, in the great grey London cemetery, to what had been mortal, to what had been precious, in his friend. The concourse at her grave was not numerous, but he saw himself treated as scarce more nearly concerned with it than if there had been a thousand others. He was in short from this moment face to face with the fact that he was to profit extraordinarily little by the interest May Bartram had taken in him. He couldn't quite have said what he expected, but he hadn't surely expected this approach to a double privation. Not only had her interest failed him, but he seemed to feel himself unattended—and for a reason he couldn't seize—by the distinction, the dignity, the propriety, if nothing else, of the man markedly bereaved. It was as if in the view of society he had not *been* markedly bereaved, as if there still failed some sign or proof of it, and as if none the less his character could never be affirmed nor the deficiency ever made up. There were moments as the weeks went by when he would have liked, by some almost aggressive act, to take his stand on the intimacy of his loss, in order that it *might* be questioned and his retort, to the relief of his spirit, so recorded; but the moments of an irritation more helpless followed fast on these, the moments during which, turning things over with a good conscience but with a bare horizon, he found himself wondering if he oughtn't to have begun, so to speak, further back.

He found himself wondering indeed at many things, and this last speculation had others to keep it company. What could he have done, after all, in her lifetime, without giving them both, as it were, away? He couldn't have made known she was watching him, for that would have published the superstition of the Beast. This was what closed his mouth now—now that the Jungle had been threshed to vacancy and that the Beast had stolen away. It sounded too foolish and too flat; the difference for him in this particular, the extinction in his life of the element of suspense, was such as in fact to surprise him. He could scarce have said what the effect resembled; the abrupt cessation, the positive prohibition, of music perhaps, more than anything else, in some place all adjusted and all accustomed to sonority and to attention. If he could at any rate have conceived lifting the veil from his image at some moment of the past (what had he done, after all, if not lift it to *her?*) so to do this to-day, to talk to people at large of the Jungle cleared and confide to them that he now felt it as safe, would have been not only to see them listen as to a goodwife's tale, but really to hear himself tell one. What it presently came to in truth was that poor Marcher waded through his beaten grass, where no life stirred, where no breath sounded, where no evil eye seemed to gleam from a possible lair, very much as if vaguely looking for the Beast, and still more as if acutely missing it. He walked about in an existence that had grown strangely more spacious, and, stopping fitfully in places where the undergrowth of life struck him as closer, asked himself yearningly, wondered secretly and sorely, if it would have lurked here or there. It would have at all events *sprung;* what was at least complete was his belief in the truth itself of the assurance given him. The change from his old sense to his new was absolute and final: what was to happen *had* so absolutely and finally happened that he was as little able to know a fear for his future as to know a hope; so absent in short was any question of anything still to come. He was to live entirely with the other question, that of his unidentified past, that of his having to see his fortune impenetrably muffled and masked.

The torment of this vision became then his occupation; he couldn't perhaps have consented to live but for the possibility of guessing. She had told him, his friend, not to guess; she had forbidden him, so far as he might, to know, and she had even in a sort denied the power in him to learn: which were so many things, precisely, to deprive him of rest. It wasn't that he wanted, he argued for fairness, that anything past and done should repeat itself; it was only that he shouldn't, as an anticlimax, have been taken sleeping so sound as not to be able to win back by an effort of thought the lost stuff of consciousness. He declared to himself at moments that he would either win it back or have done with consciousness for ever; he made this idea his one motive in fine, made it so much his passion that none other, to compare with it, seemed ever to have touched him. The lost stuff of consciousness became thus for him as a strayed or stolen child to an unappeasable father; he hunted it up and down very much as if he were knocking at doors and enquiring of the police. This was the spirit in which, inevitably, he set himself to travel; he started on a journey that was to be as long as he could make it; it danced before him that, as the other side of the globe couldn't possibly have less to say to him, it might, by a possibility of suggestion, have more. Before he quitted London, however, he made a pilgrimage to May Bartram's grave, took his way to it through the endless avenues of the grim suburban metropolis, sought it out in the wilderness of tombs, and, though he had come but for the renewal of the act of farewell, found himself, when he had at last stood by it, beguiled into long intensities. He stood for an hour, powerless to turn away and yet powerless to penetrate the darkness of death; fixing with his eyes her inscribed name and date, beating his forehead against the fact of the secret they kept, drawing his breath, while he waited, as if some sense would in pity of him rise from the stones. He kneeled on the stones, however, in vain; they kept what they concealed; and if the face of the tomb did become a face for him it was because her two names became a pair of eyes that didn't know him. He gave them a last long look, but no palest light broke.

VI

He stayed away, after this, for a year; he visited the depths of Asia, spending himself on scenes of romantic interest, of superlative sanctity; but what was present to him everywhere was that for a man who had known what *he* had known the world was vulgar and vain. The state of mind in which he had lived for so many years shone out to him, in reflexion, as a light that coloured and refined, a light beside which the glow of the East was garish cheap and thin. The terrible truth was that he had lost—with everything else—a distinction as well; the things he saw couldn't help being common when he had become common to look at them. He was simply now one of them himself—he was in the dust, without a peg for the sense of difference; and there were hours when, before the temples of gods and the sepulchres of kings, his spirit turned for nobleness of association to the barely discriminated slab in the London suburb. That had become for him, and more intensely with time and distance, his one witness of a past glory. It was all that was left to him for proof or pride, yet the past glories of Pharaohs were nothing to him as he thought of it. Small wonder then that he came back to it on the morrow of his return. He was drawn there this time as irresistibly as the other, yet with a confidence, almost, that was doubtless the effect of the many months that had elapsed. He had lived, in spite of himself, into his change of feeling, and in wandering over the earth had wandered, as might be said, from the circumference to the centre of his desert. He had settled to his safety and accepted perforce his extinction; figuring to himself, with some colour, in the likeness of certain little old men he remembered to have seen, of whom, all meagre and wizened as they might look, it was related that they had in their time fought twenty duels or been loved by ten princesses. They indeed had been wondrous for others while he was but wondrous for himself; which, however, was exactly the cause of his haste to renew the wonder by getting back, as he might put it, into his own presence. That had quickened his steps and checked his delay. If his visit was prompt it was because he had been separated so long from the part of himself that alone he now valued.

It's accordingly not false to say that he reached his goal with a certain elation and stood there again with a certain assurance. The creature beneath the sod *knew* of his rare experience, so that, strangely now, the place had lost for him its mere blankness of expression. It met him in mildness—not, as before, in mockery; it wore for him the air of conscious greeting that we find, after absence, in things that have closely belonged to us and which seem to confess of themselves to the connexion. The plot of ground, the graven tablet, the tended flowers affected him so as belonging to him that he resembled for the hour a contented landlord reviewing a piece of property. Whatever had happened—well, had happened. He had not come back this time with the vanity of that question, his former worrying "What, *what?*" now practically so spent. Yet he would none the less never again so cut himself off from the spot; he would come back to it every month, for if he did nothing else by its aid he at least held up his head. It thus grew for him, in the oddest way, a positive resource; he carried out his idea of periodical returns, which took their place at last among the most inveterate of his habits. What it all amounted to, oddly enough, was that in his finally so simplified world this garden of death gave him the few square feet of earth on which he could still most live. It was as if, being nothing anywhere else for any one, nothing even for himself, he were just everything here, and if not for a crowd of witnesses or indeed for any witness but John Marcher, then by clear right of the register that he could scan like an open page. The open page was the tomb of his friend, and *there* were the facts of the past, there the truth of his life, there the backward reaches in which he could lose himself. He did this from time to time with such effect that he seemed to wander through the old years with his hand in the arm of a companion who was, in the most extraordinary manner, his other, his younger self; and to wander, which was more extraordinary yet, round and round a third presence—not wandering she, but stationary, still, whose eyes, turning with his revolution, never ceased to follow him, and whose seat was his point, so to speak, of orientation. Thus in short he settled to live—feeding all on the sense that he once *had* lived, and dependent on it not alone for a support but for an identity.

It sufficed him in its way for months and the year elapsed; it would doubtless even have carried him further but for an accident, superficially slight, which moved him, quite in another direction, with a force beyond any of his impressions of Egypt or of India. It was a thing of the merest chance—the turn, as he afterwards felt, of a hair, though he was indeed to live to believe that if light hadn't come to him in this particular fashion it would still have come in another. He was to live to believe this, I say, though he was not to live, I may not less definitely mention, to do much else. We allow him at any rate the benefit of the conviction, struggling up for him at the end, that, whatever might have happened or not happened, he would have come round of himself to the light. The incident of an autumn day had put the match to the train laid from of old by his misery. With the light before him he knew that even of late his ache had only been smothered. It was strangely drugged, but it throbbed; at the touch it began to bleed. And the touch, in the event, was the face of a fellow mortal. This face, one grey afternoon when the leaves were thick in the alleys, looked into Marcher's own, at the cemetery, with an expression like the cut of a blade. He felt it, that is, so deep down that he winced at the steady thrust. The person who so mutely assaulted him was a figure he had noticed, on reaching his own goal, absorbed by a grave a short distance away, a grave apparently fresh, so that the emotion of the visitor would probably match it for frankness. This fact alone forbade further attention, though during the time he stayed he remained vaguely conscious of his neighbour, a middle-aged man apparently, in mourning, whose bowed back, among the clustered monuments and mortuary yews, was constantly presented. Marcher's theory that these were elements in contact with which he himself revived, had suffered, on this occasion, it may be granted, a marked, an excessive check. The autumn day was dire for him as none had recently been, and he rested with a heaviness he had not yet known on the low stone table that bore May Bartram's name. He rested without power to move, as if some spring in him, some spell vouchsafed, had suddenly been broken for ever. If he could have done that moment as he wanted he would simply have stretched himself on the slab that was ready to take him, treating it as a place prepared to receive his last sleep. What in all the wide world had he now to keep awake for? He stared before him with the question, and it was then that, as one of the cemetery walks passed near him, he caught the shock of the face.

His neighbour at the other grave had withdrawn, as he himself, with force enough in him, would have done by now, and was advancing along the path on his way to one of the gates. This brought him close, and his pace was slow, so that—and all the more as there was a kind of hunger in his look—the two men were for a minute directly confronted. Marcher knew him at once for one of the deeply stricken—a perception so sharp that nothing else in the picture comparatively lived, neither his dress, his age, nor his presumable character and class; nothing lived but the deep ravage of the features he showed. He *showed* them— that was the point; he was moved, as he passed, by some impulse that was either a signal for sympathy or, more possibly, a challenge to an opposed sorrow. He might already have been aware of our friend, might at some previous hour have noticed in him the smooth habit of the scene, with which the state of his own senses so scantly consorted, and might thereby have been stirred as by an overt discord. What Marcher was at all events conscious of was in the first place that the imaged of scarred passion presented to him was conscious too—of something that profaned the air; and in the second that, roused, startled, shocked, he was yet the next moment looking after it, as it went, with envy. The most extraordinary thing that had happened to him—though he had given that name to other matters as well—took place, after his immediate vague stare, as a consequence of this impression. The stranger passed, but the raw glare of his grief remained, making our friend wonder in pity what wrong, what wound it expressed, what injury not to be healed. What had the man *had,* to make him by the loss of it so bleed and yet live?

Something—and this reached him with a pang—that *he,* John Marcher, hadn't; the proof of which was precisely John Marcher's arid end. No passion had ever touched him, for this was what passion meant; he had survived and maundered and pined, but where had been *his* deep ravage? The extraordinary thing we speak of was the sudden rush of the result of this question. The sight that had just met his eyes named to him, as in letters of quick flame, something he had utterly, insanely missed, and what he had missed made these things a train of fire, made them mark themselves in an anguish of inward throbs. He had seen *outside* of his life, not learned it within, the way a woman was mourned when she had been loved for herself: such was the force of his conviction of the meaning of the stranger's face, which still flared for him as a smoky torch. It hadn't come to him, the knowledge, on the wings of experience; it had brushed him, jostled him, upset him, with the disrespect of chance, the insolence of accident. Now that the illumination had begun, however, it blazed to the zenith, and what he presently stood there gazing at was the sounded void of his life. He gazed, he drew breath, in pain; he turned in his dismay, and, turning, he had before him in sharper incision than ever the open page of his story. The name on the table smote him as the passage of his neighbour had done, and what it said to him, full in the face, was that *she* was what he had missed. This was the awful thought, the answer to all the past, the vision at the dread clearness of which he grew as cold as the stone beneath him. Everything fell together, confessed, explained, overwhelmed; leaving him most of all stupefied at the blindness he had cherished. The fate he had been marked for he had met with a vengeance—he had emptied the cup to the lees; he had been the man of his time, *the* man, to whom nothing on earth was to have happened. That was the rare stroke—that was his visitation. So he saw it, as we say, in pale horror, while the pieces fitted and fitted. So *she* had seen it while he didn't, and so she served at this hour to drive the truth home. It was the truth, vivid and monstrous, that all the while he had waited the wait was itself his portion. This the companion of his vigil had at a given moment made out, and she had then offered him the chance to baffle his doom. One's doom, however, was never baffled, and on the day she told him his own had come down she had seen him but stupidly stare at the escape she offered him.

The escape would have been to love her; then, *then* he would have lived. *She* had lived—who could say now with what passion?—since she had loved him for himself; whereas he had never thought of her (ah how it hugely glared at him!) but in the chill of his egotism and the light of her use. Her spoken words came back to him—the chain stretched and stretched. The Beast had lurked indeed, and the Beast, at its hour, had sprung; it had sprung in that twilight of the cold April when, pale, ill, wasted, but all beautiful, and perhaps even then recoverable, she had risen from her chair to stand before him and let him imaginably guess. It had sprung as he didn't guess; it had sprung as she hopelessly turned from him, and the mark, by the time he left her, had fallen where it *was* to fall. He had justified his fear and achieved his fate; he had failed, with the last exactitude, of all he was to fail of; and a moan now rose to his lips as he remembered she had prayed he mightn't know. This horror of waking—*this* was knowledge, knowledge under the breath of which the very tears in his eyes seemed to freeze. Through them, none the less, he tried to fix it and hold it; he kept it there before him so that he might feel the pain. That at least, belated and bitter, had something of the taste of life. But the bitterness suddenly sickened him, and it was as if, horribly, he saw, in the truth, in the cruelty of his image, what had been appointed and done. He saw the Jungle of his life and saw the lurking Beast; then, while he looked, perceived it, as by a stir of the air, rise, huge and hideous, for the leap that was to settle him. His eyes darkened—it was close; and, instinctively turning, in his hallucination, to avoid it, he flung himself, face down, on the tomb.

1903

THE JOLLY CORNER*

I

"Every one asks me what I 'think' of everything," said Spencer Brydon; "and I make answer as I can—begging or dodging the question, putting them off with any nonsense. It wouldn't matter to any of them really," he went on, "for, even were it possible to meet in that stand-and-deliver way so silly a demand on so big a subject, my 'thoughts' would still be almost altogether about something that concerns only myself." He was talking to Miss Staverton, with whom for a couple of months now he had availed himself of every possible occasion to talk; this disposition and this resource, this comfort and support, as the situation in fact presented itself, having promptly enough taken the first place in the considerable array of rather unattenuated surprises attending his so strangely belated return to America. Everything was somehow a surprise; and that might be natural when one had so long and so consistently neglected everything, taken pains to give surprises so much margin for play. He had given them more than thirty years—thirty-three, to be exact; and they now seemed to him to have organised their performance quite on the scale of that licence. He had been twenty-three on leaving New York—he was fifty-six to-day: unless indeed he were to reckon as he had sometimes, since his repatriation, found himself feeling; in which case he would have lived longer than is often allotted to man. It would have taken a century, he repeatedly said to himself, and said also to Alice Staverton, it would have taken a longer absence and a more averted mind than those even of which he had been guilty, to pile up the differences, the newnesses, the queernesses, above all the bignesses, for the better or the worse, that at present assaulted his vision wherever he looked.

The great fact all the while however had been the incalculability; since he *had* supposed himself, from decade to decade, to be allowing, and in the most liberal and intelligent manner, for brilliancy of change. He actually saw that he had allowed for nothing; he missed what he would have been sure of finding, he found what he would never have imagined. Proportions and values were upside-down; the ugly things he had expected, the ugly things of his far-away youth, when he had too promptly waked up to a sense of the ugly—these uncanny phenomena placed him rather, as it happened, under the charm; whereas the "swagger" things, the modern, the monstrous, the famous things, those he had more particularly, like thousands of ingenuous enquirers every year, come over to see, were exactly his sources of dismay. They were as so many set traps for displeasure, above all for reaction, of which his restless tread was constantly pressing the spring. It was interesting, doubtless, the whole show, but it would have been too disconcerting hadn't a certain finer truth saved the situation. He had distinctly not, in this steadier light, come over *all* for the monstrosities; he had come, not only in the last analysis but quite on the face of the act, under an impulse with which they had nothing to do. He had come—putting the thing pompously—to look at his "property," which he had thus for a third of a century not been within four thousand miles of; or, expressing it less sordidly, he had yielded to the humour of seeing

* First published in the *English Review* in December 1908.

again his house on the jolly corner, as he usually, and quite fondly, described it—the one in which he had first seen the light, in which various members of his family had lived and had died, in which the holidays of his overschooled boyhood had been passed and the few social flowers of his chilled adolescence gathered, and which, alienated then for so long a period, had, through the successive deaths of his two brothers and the termination of old arrangements, come wholly into his hands. He was the owner of another, not quite so "good"—the jolly corner having been, from far back, superlatively extended and consecrated; and the value of the pair represented his main capital, with an income consisting, in these later years, of their respective rents which (thanks precisely to their original excellent type) had never been depressingly low. He could live in "Europe," as he had been in the habit of living, on the product of these flourishing New York leases, and all the better since, that of the second structure, the mere number in its long row, having within a twelvemonth fallen in, renovation at a high advance had proved beautifully possible.

These were items of property indeed, but he had found himself since his arrival distinguishing more than ever between them. The house within the street, two bristling blocks westward, was already in course of reconstruction as a tall mass of flats; he had acceded, some time before, to overtures for this conversion—in which, now that it was going forward, it had been not the least of his astonishments to find himself able, on the spot, and though without a previous ounce of such experience, to participate with a certain intelligence, almost with a certain authority. He had lived his life with his back so turned to such concerns and his face addressed to those of so different an order that he scarce knew what to make of this lively stir, in a compartment of his mind never yet penetrated, of a capacity for business and a sense for construction. These virtues, so common all round him now, had been dormant in his own organism—where it might be said of them perhaps that they had slept the sleep of the just. At present, in the splendid autumn weather—the autumn at least was a pure boon in the terrible place—he loafed about his "work" undeterred, secretly agitated; not in the least "minding" that the whole proposition, as they said, was vulgar and sordid, and ready to climb ladders, to walk the plank, to handle materials and look wise about them, to ask questions, in fine, and challenge explanations and really "go into" figures.

It amused, it verily quite charmed him; and, by the same stroke, it amused, and even more, Alice Staverton, though perhaps charming her perceptibly less. She wasn't however going to be better-off for it, as *he* was—and so astonishingly much: nothing was now likely, he knew, ever to make her better-off than she found herself, in the afternoon of life, as the delicately frugal possessor and tenant of the small house in Irving Place to which she had subtly managed to cling through her almost unbroken New York career. If he knew the way to it now better than to any other address among the dreadful multiplied numberings which seemed to him to reduce the whole place to some vast ledger-page, overgrown, fantastic, of ruled and criss-crossed lines and figures—if he had formed, for his consolation, that habit, it was really not a little because of the charm of his having encountered and recognised, in the vast wilderness of the wholesale, breaking through the mere gross generalisation of wealth and force and success, a small still scene where items and shades, all delicate things, kept the sharpness of the notes of a high voice perfectly trained, and where economy hung about like the scent of a garden. His old friend lived with one maid and herself dusted her relics and trimmed her lamps and polished her silver; she stood off, in the awful modern crush, when she could, but she sallied forth and did battle when the challenge was really to "spirit," the spirit she after all confessed to, proudly and a little shyly, as to that of the better time, that of *their* common, their quite far-away and antediluvian social period and order. She made use of the street-cars when need be, the terrible things that people scrambled for as the panic-stricken at sea scramble for the boats; she affronted, inscrutably, under stress, all the public concussions and ordeals; and yet, with that slim mystifying grace of her appearance, which defied you to say if she were a fair young woman who looked older through trouble, or a fine smooth older one who looked young through successful indifference; with her precious reference, above all, to memories and histories into which he could enter, she was as exquisite for him as some pale pressed flower (a rarity to begin with), and, failing other sweetnesses, she was a sufficient reward of his effort. They had communities of knowledge, "their" knowledge (this discriminating possessive was always on her lips) of presences of the other age, presences all overlaid, in his case, by the experience of a man and the freedom of a wanderer, overlaid by pleasure, by infidelity, by passages of life that were strange and dim to her, just by "Europe" in short, but still unobscured, still exposed and cherished, under that pious visitation of the spirit from which she had never been diverted.

She had come with him one day to see how his "apartment-house" was rising; he had helped her over gaps and explained to her plans, and while they were there had happened to have, before her, a brief but lively discussion with the man in charge, the representative of the building-firm that had undertaken his work. He had found himself quite "standing-up" to this personage over a failure on the latter's part to observe some detail of one of their noted conditions, and had so lucidly argued his case that, besides ever so prettily flushing, at the time, for sympathy in his triumph, she had afterwards said to him (though to a slightly greater effect of irony) that he had clearly for too many years neglected a real gift. If he had but stayed at home he would have anticipated the inventor of the sky-scraper. If he had but stayed at home he would have discovered his genius in time really to start some new variety of awful architectural hare and run it till it burrowed in a gold-mine. He was to remember these words, while the weeks elapsed, for the small silver ring they had sounded over the queerest and deepest of his own lately most disguised and most muffled vibrations.

It had begun to be present to him after the first fortnight, it had broken out with the oddest abruptness, this particular wanton wonderment: it met him there—and this was the image under which he himself judged the matter, or at least, not a little, thrilled and flushed with it—very much as he might have been met by some strange figure, some unexpected occupant, at a turn of one of the dim passages of an empty house. The quaint analogy quite hauntingly remained with him, when he didn't indeed rather improve it by a still intenser form: that of his opening a door behind which he would have made sure of finding nothing, a door into a room shuttered and void, and yet so coming, with a great suppressed start, on some quite erect confronting presence, something planted in the middle of the place and facing him through the dusk. After that visit to the house in construction he walked with his companion to see the other and always so much the better one, which in the eastward direction formed one of the corners, the "jolly" one precisely, of the street now so generally dishonoured and disfigured in its westward reaches, and of the comparatively conservative Avenue.[1] The Avenue still had pretensions, as Miss Staverton said, to decency; the old people had mostly gone, the old names were unknown, and here and there an old association seemed to stray, all vaguely, like some very aged person, out too late, whom you might meet and feel the impulse to watch or follow, in kindness, for safe restoration to shelter.

They went in together, our friends; he admitted himself with his key, as he kept no one there, he explained, preferring, for his reasons, to leave the place empty, under a simple arrangement with a good woman living in the neighbourhood and who came for a daily hour to open windows and dust and sweep. Spencer Brydon had his reasons and was growingly aware of them; they seemed to him better each time he was there, though he didn't name them all to his companion, any more than he told her as yet how often, how quite absurdly often, he himself came. He only let her see for the present, while they walked through the great blank rooms, that absolute vacancy reigned and that, from top to bottom, there was nothing but Mrs. Muldoon's broomstick, in a corner, to tempt the burglar. Mrs. Muldoon was then on the premises, and she loquaciously attended the visitors, preceding them from room to room and pushing back shutters and throwing up sashes—all to show them, as she remarked, how little there was to see. There was little indeed to see in the great gaunt shell where the main dispositions and the general apportionment of space, the style of an age of ampler allowances, had nevertheless for its master their honest pleading message, affecting him as some good old servant's, some lifelong retainer's appeal for a character, or even for a retiring-pension; yet it was also a remark of Mrs. Muldoon's that, glad as she was to oblige him by her noonday round, there was a request she greatly hoped he would never make of her. If he should wish her for any reason to come in after dark she would just tell him, if he "plased," that he must ask it of somebody else.

The fact that there was nothing to see didn't militate for the worthy woman against what one *might* see, and she put it frankly to Miss Staverton that no lady could be expected to like, could she? "craping up to thim top storeys in the ayvil hours." The gas and the electric light were off the house, and she fairly evoked a gruesome vision of her march through the great grey rooms—so many of them as there were too!—with her glimmering taper. Miss Staverton met her honest glare with a smile and the profession that she herself certainly would recoil from such an adventure. Spencer Brydon meanwhile held his peace—for the moment; the question of the "evil" hours in his old home had already become too grave for him. He had begun some time since to "crape," and he knew just why a packet of candles addressed to that pursuit had been stowed by his own hand, three weeks before, at the back of a drawer of the fine old sideboard that occupied, as a "fixture," the deep recess in the dining-room. Just now he laughed at his companions—quickly however changing the subject; for the reason that, in the first place, his laugh struck him even at that moment as starting the odd echo, the conscious human resonance (he scarce knew how to qualify it) that sounds made while he was there alone sent back to his ear or his fancy; and that, in the second, he imagined Alice Staverton for the instant on the point of asking him, with a divination, if he ever so prowled. There were divinations he was unprepared for, and he

[1] Fifth Avenue, a fashionable street in New York City.

had at all events averted enquiry by the time Mrs. Muldoon had left them, passing on to other parts.

There was happily enough to say, on so consecrated a spot, that could be said freely and fairly; so that a whole train of declarations was precipitated by his friend's having herself broken out, after a yearning look round: "But I hope you don't mean they want you to pull *this* to pieces!" His answer came, promptly, with his re-awakened wrath: it was of course exactly what they wanted, and what they were "at" him for, daily, with the iteration of people who couldn't for their life understand a man's liability to decent feelings. He had found the place, just as it stood and beyond what he could express, an interest and a joy. There were values other than the beastly rent-values, and in short, in short—! But it was thus Miss Staverton took him up. "In short you're to make so good a thing of your sky-scraper that, living in luxury on *those* ill-gotten gains, you can afford for a while to be sentimental here!" Her smile had for him, with the words, the particular mild irony with which he found half her talk suffused; an irony without bitterness and that came, exactly, from her having so much imagination—not, like the cheap sarcasms with which one heard most people, about the world of "society," bid for the reputation of cleverness, from nobody's really having any. It was agreeable to him at this very moment to be sure that when he had answered, after a brief demur, "Well yes: so, precisely, you may put it!" her imagination would still do him justice. He explained that even if never a dollar were to come to him from the other house he would nevertheless cherish this one; and he dwelt, further, while they lingered and wandered, on the fact of the stupefaction he was already exciting, the positive mystification he felt himself create.

He spoke of the value of all he read into it, into the mere sight of the walls, mere shapes of the rooms, mere sound of the floors, mere feel, in his hand, of the old silver-plated knobs of the several mahogany doors, which suggested the pressure of the palms of the dead; the seventy years of the past in fine that these things represented, the annals of nearly three generations, counting his grandfather's, the one that had ended there, and the impalpable ashes of his long-extinct youth, afloat in the very air like microscopic motes. She listened to everything; she was a woman who answered intimately but who utterly didn't chatter. She scattered abroad therefore no cloud of words; she could assent, she could agree, above all she could encourage, without doing that. Only at the last she went a little further than he had done himself. "And then how do you know! You may still, after all, want to live here." It rather indeed pulled him up, for it wasn't what he had been thinking, at least in her sense of the words. "You mean I may decide to stay on for the sake of it?"

"Well, *with* such a home—!" But, quite beautifully, she had too much tact to dot so monstrous an *i,* and it was precisely an illustration of the way she didn't rattle. How could any one—of any wit—insist on any one else's "wanting" to live in New York?

"Oh," he said, "I *might* have lived here (since I had my opportunity early in life); I might have put in here all these years. Then everything would have been different enough—and, I dare say, 'funny' enough. But that's another matter. And then the beauty of it—I mean of my perversity, of my refusal to agree to a 'deal'—is just in the total absence of a reason. Don't you see that if I had a reason about the matter at all it would *have* to be the other way, and would then be inevitably a reason of dollars? There are no reasons here *but* of dollars. Let us therefore have none whatever—not the ghost of one."

They were back in the hall then for departure, but from where they stood the vista was large, through an open door, into the great square main saloon, with its almost antique felicity of brave spaces between windows. Her eyes came back from that reach and met his own a moment. "Are you very sure the 'ghost' of one doesn't, much rather, serve—?"

He had a positive sense of turning pale. But it was as near as they were then to come. For he made answer, he believed, between a glare and a grin: "Oh ghosts—of course the place must swarm with them! I should be ashamed of it if it didn't. Poor Mrs. Muldoon's right, and it's why I haven't asked her to do more than look in."

Miss Staverton's gaze again lost itself, and things she didn't utter, it was clear, came and went in her mind. She might even for the minute, off there in the fine room, have imagined some element dimly gathering. Simplified like the death-mask of a handsome face, it perhaps produced for her just then an effect akin to the stir of an expression in the "set" commemorative plaster. Yet whatever her impression may have been she produced instead a vague platitude. "Well, if it were only furnished and lived in—!"

She appeared to imply that in case of its being still furnished he might have been a little less opposed to the idea of a return. But she passed straight into the vestibule, as if to leave her words behind her, and the next moment he had opened the house-door and was standing with her on the steps. He closed the door and, while he re-pocketed his key, looking up and down, they took in the compara-tively harsh actuality of the Avenue, which reminded him of the assault of the outer light of the Desert on the traveller emerging from an Egyptian tomb. But he risked before they stepped into the street his gathered answer to her speech. "For me it *is* lived in. For me it *is* furnished." At which it was easy for her to sigh "Ah yes—!" all vaguely and discreetly; since his parents and his favourite sister, to say nothing of other kin, in numbers, had run their course and met their end there. That represented, within the walls, ineffaceable life.

It was a few days after this that, during an hour passed with her again, he had expressed his impatience of the too flattering curiosity—among the people he met—about his appreciation of New York. He had arrived at none at all that was socially producible, and as for that matter of his "thinking" (thinking the better or the worse of anything there) he was wholly taken up with one subject of thought. It was mere vain egoism, and it was moreover, if she liked, a morbid obsession. He found all things come back to the question of what he personally might have been, how he might have led his life and "turned out," if he had not so, at the outset, given it up. And confessing for the first time to the intensity within him of this absurd speculation—which but proved also, no doubt, the habit of too self-ishly thinking—he affirmed the impotence there of any other source of interest, any other native appeal. "What would it have made of me, what would it have made of me? I keep for ever wondering, all idiotically; as if I could possibly know! I see what it has made of dozens of others, those I meet, and it positively aches within me, to the point of exasperation, that it would have made something of me as well. Only I can't make out *what,* and the worry of it, the small rage of curiosity never to be satisfied, brings back what I remember to have felt, once or twice, after judging best, for reasons, to burn some important letter unopened.

I've been sorry, I've hated it—I've never known what was in the letter. You may of course say it's a trifle—!"

"I don't say it's a trifle," Miss Staverton gravely interrupted.

She was seated by her fire, and before her, on his feet and restless, he turned to and fro between this intensity of his idea and a fitful and unseeing inspection, through his single eye-glass, of the dear little old objects on her chimney-piece. Her interruption made him for an instant look at her harder. "I shouldn't care if you did!" he laughed, however; "and it's only a figure, at any rate, for the way I now feel. *Not* to have followed my perverse young course—and almost in the teeth of my father's curse, as I may say; not to have kept it up, so, 'over there,' from that day to this, without a doubt or a pang; not, above all, to have liked it, to have loved it, so much, loved it, no doubt, with such an abysmal conceit of my own preference: some variation from *that,* I say, must have produced some different effect for my life and for my 'form.' I should have stuck here—if it had been possible; and I was too young, at twenty-three, to judge, *pour deux sous,*[2] whether it *were* possible. If I had waited I might have seen it was, and then I might have been, by staying here, something nearer to one of these types who have been hammered so hard and made so keen by their conditions. It isn't that I admire them so much—the question of any charm in them, or of any charm, beyond that of the rank money-passion, exerted by their conditions *for* them, has nothing to do with the matter: it's only a question of what fantastic, yet perfectly possible, development of my own nature I mayn't have missed. It comes over me that I had then a strange *alter ego* deep down somewhere within me, as the full-blown flower is in the small tight bud, and that I just took the course, I just transferred him to the climate, that blighted him for once and for ever."

"And you wonder about the flower," Miss Staverton said. "So do I, if you want to know; and so I've been wondering these several weeks. I believe in the flower," she continued, "I feel it would have been quite splendid, quite huge and monstrous."

"Monstrous above all!" her visitor echoed; "and I imagine, by the same stroke, quite hideous and offensive."

"You don't believe that," she returned; "if you did you wouldn't wonder. You'd know, and that would be enough for you. What you feel—and what I feel *for* you—is that you'd have had power."

"You'd have liked me that way?" he asked.

She barely hung fire.[3] "How should I not have liked you?"

"I see. You'd have liked me, have preferred me, a billionaire!"

"How should I not have liked you?" she simply again asked.

He stood before her still—her question kept him motionless. He took it in, so much there was of it; and indeed his not otherwise meeting it testified to that. "I know at least what I am," he simply went on; "the other side of the medal's clear enough. I've not been edifying—I believe I'm thought in a hundred quarters to have been barely decent. I've followed strange paths and worshipped strange gods; it must have come to you again and again—in fact you've admitted to me as much—that I was leading, at any time these thirty years, a selfish frivolous scandalous life. And you see what it has made of me."

She just waited, smiling at him. "You see what it has made of *me.*"

____

[2] "For two cents" (French).   [3] Kept from saying.

"Oh you're a person whom nothing can have altered. You were born to be what you are, anywhere, anyway: you've the perfection nothing else could have blighted. And don't you see how, without my exile, I shouldn't have been waiting till now—!" But he pulled up for the strange pang.

"The great thing to see," she presently said, "seems to me to be that it has spoiled nothing. It hasn't spoiled your being here at last. It hasn't spoiled this. It hasn't spoiled your speaking—" She also however faltered.

He wondered at everything her controlled emotion might mean. "Do you believe then—too dreadfully!—that I *am* as good as I might ever have been?"

"Oh no! Far from it!" With which she got up from her chair and was nearer to him. "But I don't care," she smiled.

"You mean I'm good enough?"

She considered a little. "Will you believe it if I say so? I mean will you let that settle your question for you?" And then as if making out in his face that he drew back from this, that he had some idea which, however absurd, he couldn't yet bargain away: "Oh you don't care either—but very differently: you don't care for anything but yourself."

Spencer Brydon recognised it—it was in fact what he had absolutely professed. Yet he importantly qualified. "*He* isn't myself. He's the just so totally other person. But I do want to see him," he added. "And I can. And I shall."

Their eyes met for a minute while he guessed from something in hers that she divined his strange sense. But neither of them otherwise expressed it, and her apparent understanding, with no protesting shock, no easy derision, touched him more deeply than anything yet, constituting for his stifled perversity, on the spot, an element that was like breatheable air. What she said however was unexpected. "Well, *I've* seen him."

"You—?"

"I've seen him in a dream."

"Oh a 'dream'—!" It let him down.

"But twice over," she continued. "I saw him as I see you now."

"You've dreamed the same dream—?"

"Twice over," she repeated. "The very same."

This did somehow a little speak to him, as it also gratified him. "You dream about me at that rate?"

"Ah about *him!*" she smiled.

His eyes again sounded her. "Then you know all about him." And as she said nothing more: "What's the wretch like?"

She hesitated, and it was as if he were pressing her so hard that, resisting for reasons of her own, she had to turn away. "I'll tell you some other time!"

II

It was after this that there was most of a virtue for him, most of a cultivated charm, most of a preposterous secret thrill, in the particular form of surrender to his obsession and of address to what he more and more believed to be his privilege. It was what in these weeks he was living for—since he really felt life to begin but after Mrs. Muldoon had retired from the scene and, visiting the ample house from attic to cellar, making sure he was alone, he knew himself in safe possession and, as he tacitly expressed it, let himself go. He sometimes came twice in the twenty-four hours; the moments he liked best were those of gathering dusk, of the short autumn twilight; this was the time of which, again and again, he found himself hoping most. Then he could, as seemed to him, most intimately wander and wait, linger and listen, feel his fine attention, never in his life before so fine, on the pulse of the great vague place: he preferred the lampless hour and only wished he might have prolonged each day the deep crepuscular spell. Later—rarely much before midnight, but then for a considerable vigil—he watched with his glimmering light; moving slowly, holding it high, playing it far, rejoicing above all, as much as he might, in open vistas, reaches of communication between rooms and by passages; the long straight chance or show, as he would have called it, for the revelation he pretended to invite. It was a practice he found he could perfectly "work" without exciting remark; no one was in the least the wiser for it; even Alice Staverton, who was moreover a well of discretion, didn't quite fully imagine.

He let himself in and let himself out with the assurance of calm proprietorship; and accident so far favoured him that, if a fat Avenue "officer" had happened on occasion to see him entering at eleven-thirty, he had never yet, to the best of his belief, been noticed as emerging at two. He walked there on the crisp November nights, arrived regularly at the evening's end; it was as easy to do this after dining out as to take his way to a club or to his hotel. When he left his club, if he hadn't been dining out, it was ostensibly to go to his hotel; and when he left his hotel, if he had spent a part of the evening there, it was ostensibly to go to his club. Everything was easy in fine; everything conspired and promoted: there was truly even in the strain of his experience something that glossed over, something that salved and simplified, all the rest of consciousness. He circulated, talked, renewed, loosely and pleasantly, old relations—met indeed, so far as he could, new expectations and seemed to make out on the whole that in spite of the career, of such different contacts, which he had spoken of to Miss Staverton as ministering so little, for those who might have watched it, to edification, he was positively rather liked than not. He was a dim secondary social success—and all with people who had truly not an idea of him. It was all mere surface sound, this murmur of their welcome, this popping of their corks—just as his gestures of response were the extravagant shadows, emphatic in proportion as they meant little, of some game of *ombres chinoises*.[4] He projected himself all day, in thought, straight over the bristling line of hard unconscious heads and into the other, the real, the waiting life; the life that, as soon as he had heard behind him the click of his great house-door, began for him, on the jolly corner, as beguilingly as the slow opening bars of some rich music follows the tap of the conductor's wand.

He always caught the first effect of the steel point of his stick on the old marble of the hall pavement, large black-and-white squares that he remembered as the admiration of his childhood and that had then made in him, as he now saw, for the growth of an early conception of style. This effect was the dim reverberating tinkle as of some far-off bell hung who should say where?—in the depths of the house, of the past, of that mystical other world that might have flourished for him had he not, for weal or woe, abandoned it. On this impression he did ever the same thing; he put his stick noiselessly away in a corner—feeling the place once more in the likeness of some great glass bowl, all precious concave crystal, set delicately humming by the play of a moist finger round its edge. The concave

---

[4] "Chinese shadows" (French): a show in which actors' shadows are projected onto a screen.

crystal held, as it were, this mystical other world, and the indescribably fine murmur of its rim was the sigh there, the scarce audible pathetic wail to his strained ear, of all the old baffled forsworn possibilities. What he did therefore by this appeal of his hushed presence was to wake them into such measure of ghostly life as they might still enjoy. They were shy, all but unappeasably shy, but they weren't really sinister; at least they weren't as he had hitherto felt them—before they had taken the Form he so yearned to make them take, the Form he at moments saw himself in the light of fairly hunting on tiptoe, the points of his evening-shoes, from room to room and from storey to storey.

That was the essence of his vision—which was all rank folly, if one would, while he was out of the house and otherwise occupied, but which took on the last verisimilitude as soon as he was placed and posted. He knew what he meant and what he wanted; it was as clear as the figure on a cheque presented in demand for cash. His *alter ego* "walked"—that was the note of his image of him, while his image of his motive for his own odd pastime was the desire to waylay him and meet him. He roamed, slowly, warily, but all restlessly, he himself did—Mrs. Muldoon had been right, absolutely, with her figure of their "craping"; and the presence he watched for would roam restlessly too. But it would be as cautious and as shifty; the conviction of its probable, in fact its already quite sensible, quite audible evasion of pursuit grew for him from night to night, laying on him finally a rigour to which nothing in his life had been comparable. It had been the theory of many superficially-judging persons, he knew, that he was wasting that life in a surrender to sensations, but he had tasted of no pleasure so fine as his actual tension, had been introduced to no sport that demanded at once the patience and the nerve of this stalking of a creature more subtle, yet at bay perhaps more formidable, than any beast of the forest. The terms, the comparisons, the very practices of the chase positively came again into play; there were even moments when passages of his occasional experience as a sportsman, stirred memories, from his younger time, of moor and mountain and desert, revived for him—and to the increase of his keenness—by the tremendous force of analogy. He found himself at moments—once he had placed his single light on some mantel-shelf or in some recess—stepping back into shelter or shade, effacing himself behind a door or in an embrasure, as he had sought of old the vantage of rock and tree; he found himself holding his breath and living in the joy of the instant, the supreme suspense created by big game alone.

He wasn't afraid (though putting himself the question as he believed gentlemen on Bengal tiger-shoots or in close quarters with the great bear of the Rockies had been known to confess to having put it); and this indeed—since here at least he might be frank!—because of the impression, so intimate and so strange, that he himself produced as yet a dread, produced certainly a strain, beyond the liveliest he was likely to feel. They fell for him into categories, they fairly became familiar, the signs, for his own perception, of the alarm his presence and his vigilance created; though leaving him always to remark, portentously, on his probably having formed a relation, his probably enjoying a consciousness, unique in the experience of man. People enough, first and last, had been in terror of apparitions, but who had ever before so turned the tables and become himself, in the apparitional world, an incalculable terror? He might have found this sublime had he quite dared to think of it; but he didn't too much insist, truly, on that side of his privilege. With habit and repetition he gained to an extraordinary degree the power to penetrate the dusk of distances and the darkness of corners, to resolve back into their innocence the treacheries of uncertain light, the evil-looking forms taken in the gloom by mere shadows, by accidents of the air, by shifting effects of perspective; putting down his dim luminary he could still wander on without it, pass into other rooms and, only knowing it was there behind him in case of need, see his way about, visually project for his purpose a comparative clearness. It made him feel, this acquired faculty, like some monstrous stealthy cat; he wondered if he would have glared at these moments with large shining yellow eyes, and what it mightn't verily be, for the poor hard-pressed *alter ego,* to be confronted with such a type.

He liked however the open shutters; he opened everywhere those Mrs. Muldoon had closed, closing them as carefully afterwards, so that she shouldn't notice: he liked—oh this he did like, and above all in the upper rooms!—the sense of the hard silver of the autumn stars through the window-panes, and scarcely less the flare of the street-lamps below, the white electric lustre which it would have taken curtains to keep out. This was human actual social; this was of the world he had lived in, and he was more at his ease certainly for the countenance, coldly general and impersonal, that all the while and in spite of his detachment it seemed to give him. He had support of course mostly in the rooms at the wide front and the prolonged side; it failed him considerably in the central shades and the parts at the back. But if he sometimes, on his rounds, was glad of his optical reach, so none the less often the rear of the house affected him as the very jungle of his prey. The place was there more subdivided; a large "extension" in particular, where small rooms for servants had been multiplied, abounded in nooks and corners, in closets and passages, in the ramifications especially of an ample back staircase over which he leaned, many a time, to look far down—not deterred from his gravity even while aware that he might, for a spectator, have figured some solemn simpleton playing at hide-and-seek. Outside in fact he might himself make that ironic *rapprochement;*[5] but within the walls, and in spite of the clear windows, his consistency was proof against the cynical light of New York.

It had belonged to that idea of the exasperated consciousness of his victim to become a real test for him; since he had quite put it to himself from the first that, oh distinctly! he could "cultivate" his whole perception. He had felt it as above all open to cultivation—which indeed was but another name for his manner of spending his time. He was bringing it on, bringing it to perfection, by practice; in consequence of which it had grown so fine that he was now aware of impressions, attestations of his general postulate, that couldn't have broken upon him at once. This was the case more specifically with a phenomenon at last quite frequent for him in the upper rooms, the recognition—absolutely unmistakeable, and by a turn dating from a particular hour, his resumption of his campaign after a diplomatic drop, a calculated absence of three nights—of his being definitely followed, tracked at a distance carefully taken and to the express end that he should the less confidently, less arrogantly, appear to himself merely to pursue. It worried, it finally quite broke him up, for it proved, of all the conceivable impressions, the one least suited to his book. He was kept in sight while remaining himself—as regards the essence of his position—sightless, and his only recourse then was in abrupt turns, rapid recoveries of ground. He wheeled about, retracing his steps, as if he might so catch in his face at least the stirred air of some other quick revolution. It was indeed true that his fully dislocalised thought of these manœuvres

---

[5] Bringing together, comparison (French).

recalled to him Pantaloon, at the Christmas farce, buffeted and tricked from behind by ubiquitous Harlequin;[6] but it left intact the influence of the conditions
themselves each time he was re-exposed to them, so that in fact this association,
had he suffered it to become constant, would on a certain side have but ministered
to his intenser gravity. He had made, as I have said, to create on the premises the
baseless sense of a reprieve, his three absences; and the result of the third was to
confirm the after-effect of the second.

On his return, that night—the night succeeding his last intermission—he stood
in the hall and looked up the staircase with a certainty more intimate than any he
had yet known. "He's *there,* at the top, and waiting—not, as in general, falling
back for disappearance. He's holding his ground, and it's the first time—which is
a proof, isn't it? that something has happened for him." So Brydon argued with
his hand on the banister and his foot on the lowest stair; in which position he felt
as never before the air chilled by his logic. He himself turned cold in it, for he
seemed of a sudden to know what now was involved. "Harder pressed?—yes, he
takes it in, with its thus making clear to him that I've come, as they say, 'to stay.'
He finally doesn't like and can't bear it, in the sense, I mean, that his wrath, his
menaced interest, now balances with his dread. I've hunted him till he has
'turned': that, up there, is what has happened—he's the fanged or the antlered
animal brought at last to bay." There came to him, as I say—but determined by an
influence beyond my notation!—the acuteness of this certainty; under which however the next moment he had broken into a sweat that he would as little have
consented to attribute to fear as he would have dared immediately to act upon it for
enterprise. It marked none the less a prodigious thrill, a thrill that represented
sudden dismay, no doubt, but also represented, and with the selfsame throb, the
strangest, the most joyous, possibly the next minute almost the proudest, duplica-
tion of consciousness.

"He has been dodging, retreating, hiding, but now, worked up to anger, he'll
fight!"—this intense impression made a single mouthful, as it were, of terror and
applause. But what was wondrous was that the applause, for the felt fact, was so
eager, since, if it was his other self he was running to earth, this ineffable identity
was thus in the last resort not unworthy of him. It bristled there—somewhere near
at hand, however unseen still—as the hunted thing, even as the trodden worm of
the adage *must* at last bristle; and Brydon at this instant tasted probably of a sensation more complex than had ever before found itself consistent with sanity. It was
as if it would have shamed him that a character so associated with his own should
triumphantly succeed in just skulking, should to the end not risk the open; so that
the drop of this danger was, on the spot, a great lift of the whole situation. Yet
with another rare shift of the same subtlety he was already trying to measure by
how much more he himself might now be in peril of fear; so rejoicing that he
could, in another form, actively inspire that fear, and simultaneously quaking for
the form in which he might passively know it.

The apprehension of knowing it must after a little have grown in him, and the
strangest moment of his adventure perhaps, the most memorable or really most
interesting, afterwards, of his crisis, was the lapse of certain instants of concentrated conscious *combat,* the sense of a need to hold on to something, even after
the manner of a man slipping and slipping on some awful incline; the vivid im-

---

[6] Pantaloon and Harlequin, traditional characters in pantomime, are known for playing tricks on others.

pulse, above all, to move, to act, to charge, somehow and upon something—to show himself, in a word, that he wasn't afraid. The state of "holding-on" was thus the state to which he was momentarily reduced; if there had been anything, in the great vacancy, to seize, he would presently have been aware of having clutched it as he might under a shock at home have clutched the nearest chair-back. He had been surprised at any rate—of this he *was* aware—into something unprecedented since his original appropriation of the place; he had closed his eyes, held them tight, for a long minute, as with that instinct of dismay and that terror of vision. When he opened them the room, the other contiguous rooms, extraordinarily, seemed lighter—so light, almost, that at first he took the change for day. He stood firm, however that might be, just where he had paused; his resistance had helped him—it was as if there were something he had tided over. He knew after a little what this was—it had been in the imminent danger of flight. He had stiffened his will against going; without this he would have made for the stairs, and it seemed to him that, still with his eyes closed, he would have descended them, would have known how, straight and swiftly, to the bottom.

Well, as he had held out, here he was—still at the top, among the more intricate upper rooms and with the gauntlet[7] of the others, of all the rest of the house, still to run when it should be his time to go. He would go at his time—only at his time: didn't he go every night very much at the same hour? He took out his watch—there was light for that: it was scarcely a quarter past one, and he had never withdrawn so soon. He reached his lodgings for the most part at two—with his walk of a quarter of an hour. He would wait for the last quarter—he wouldn't stir till then; and he kept his watch there with his eyes on it, reflecting while he held it that this deliberate wait, a wait with an effort, which he recognised, would serve perfectly for the attestation he desired to make. It would prove his courage—unless indeed the latter might most be proved by his budging at last from his place. What he mainly felt now was that, since he hadn't originally scuttled, he had his dignities—which had never in his life seemed so many—all to preserve and to carry aloft. This was before him in truth as a physical image, an image almost worthy of an age of greater romance. That remark indeed glimmered for him only to glow the next instant with a finer light; since what age of romance, after all, could have matched either the state of his mind or, "objectively," as they said, the wonder of his situation? The only difference would have been that, brandishing his dignities over his head as in a parchment scroll, he might then—that is in the heroic time—have proceeded downstairs with a drawn sword in his other grasp.

At present, really, the light he had set down on the mantel of the next room would have to figure his sword; which utensil, in the course of a minute, he had taken the requisite number of steps to possess himself of. The door between the rooms was open, and from the second another door opened to a third. These rooms, as he remembered, gave all three upon a common corridor as well, but there was a fourth, beyond them, without issue save through the preceding. To have moved, to have heard his step again, was appreciably a help; though even in recognising this he lingered once more a little by the chimney-piece on which his light had rested. When he next moved, just hesitating where to turn, he found himself considering a circumstance that, after his first and comparatively vague

---

[7] From "run the gauntlet," a former punishment in which a man ran between two rows of men who struck him with switches (whipping sticks) as he passed.

apprehension of it, produced in him the start that often attends some pang of recollection, the violent shock of having ceased happily to forget. He had come into
sight of the door in which the brief chain of communication ended and which he
now surveyed from the nearer threshold, the one not directly facing it. Placed at
some distance to the left of this point, it would have admitted him to the last room
of the four, the room without other approach or egress, had it not, to his intimate
conviction, been closed *since* his former visitation, the matter probably of a quarter of an hour before. He stared with all his eyes at the wonder of the fact, arrested
again where he stood and again holding his breath while he sounded its sense.
Surely it had been *subsequently* closed—that is it had been on his previous passage indubitably open!

He took it full in the face that something had happened between—that he
couldn't not have noticed before (by which he meant on his original tour of all the
rooms that evening) that such a barrier had exceptionally presented itself. He had
indeed since that moment undergone an agitation so extraordinary that it might
have muddled for him any earlier view; and he tried to convince himself that he
might perhaps then have gone into the room and, inadvertently, automatically, on
coming out, have drawn the door after him. The difficulty was that this exactly
was what he never did; it was against his whole policy, as he might have said, the
essence of which was to keep vistas clear. He had them from the first, as he was
well aware, quite on the brain: the strange apparition, at the far end of one of
them, of his baffled "prey" (which had become by so sharp an irony so little the
term now to apply!) was the form of success his imagination had most cherished,
projecting into it always a refinement of beauty. He had known fifty times the start
of perception that had afterwards dropped; had fifty times gasped to himself
"There!" under some fond brief hallucination. The house, as the case stood, admirably lent itself; he might wonder at the taste, the native architecture of the particular time, which could rejoice so in the multiplication of doors—the opposite extreme to the modern, the actual almost complete proscription of them; but it had
fairly contributed to provoke this obsession of the presence encountered telescop-
ically, as he might say, focussed and studied in diminishing perspective and as by
a rest for the elbow.

It was with these considerations that his present attention was charged—they
perfectly availed to make what he saw portentous. He *couldn't,* by any lapse, have
blocked that aperture; and if he hadn't, if it was unthinkable, why what else was
clear but that there had been another agent? Another agent?—he had been catching, as he felt, a moment back, the very breath of him; but when had he been so
close as in this simple, this logical, this completely personal act? It was so logical,
that is, that one might have *taken* it for personal; yet for what did Brydon take it,
he asked himself, while, softly panting, he felt his eyes almost leave their sockets.
Ah this time at last they *were,* the two, the opposed projections of him, in presence; and this time, as much as one would, the question of danger loomed. With it
rose, as not before, the question of courage—for what he knew the blank face of
the door to say to him was "Show us how much you have!" It stared, it glared
back at him with that challenge; it put to him the two alternatives: should he just
push it open or not? Oh to have this consciousness was to *think*—and to think,
Brydon knew, as he stood there, was, with the lapsing moments, not to have
acted! Not to have acted—that was the misery and the pang—was even still not to
act; was in fact *all* to feel the thing in another, in a new and terrible way. How
long did he pause and how long did he debate? There was presently nothing to

measure it; for his vibration had already changed—as just by the effect of its intensity. Shut up there, at bay, defiant, and with the prodigy of the thing palpably proveably *done,* thus giving notice like some stark signboard—under that accession of accent the situation itself had turned; and Brydon at last remarkably made up his mind on what it had turned to.

It had turned altogether to a different admonition; to a supreme hint, for him, of the value of Discretion! This slowly dawned, no doubt—for it could take its time; so perfectly, on his threshold, had he been stayed, so little as yet had he either advanced or retreated. It was the strangest of all things that now when, by his taking ten steps and applying his hand to a latch, or even his shoulder and his knee, if necessary, to a panel, all the hunger of his prime need might have been met, his high curiosity crowned, his unrest assuaged—it was amazing, but it was also exquisite and rare, that insistence should have, at a touch, quite dropped from him. Discretion—he jumped at that; and yet not, verily, at such a pitch, because it saved his nerves or his skin, but because, much more valuably, it saved the situation. When I say he "jumped" at it I feel the consonance of this term with the fact that—at the end indeed of I know not how long—he did move again, he crossed straight to the door. He wouldn't touch it—it seemed now that he might *if* he would: he would only just wait there a little, to show, to prove, that he wouldn't. He had thus another station, close to the thin partition by which revelation was denied him; but with his eyes bent and his hands held off in a mere intensity of stillness. He listened as if there had been something to hear, but this attitude, while it lasted, was his own communication. "If you won't then—good: I spare you and I give up. You affect me as by the appeal positively for pity: you convince me that for reasons rigid and sublime—what do I know?—we both of us should have suffered. I respect them then, and, though moved and privileged as, I believe, it has never been given to man, I retire, I renounce—never, on my honour, to try again. So rest for ever—and let *me!*"

That, for Brydon was the deep sense of this last demonstration—solemn, measured, directed, as he felt it to be. He brought it to a close, he turned away; and now verily he knew how deeply he had been stirred. He retraced his steps, taking up his candle, burnt, he observed, well-nigh to the socket, and marking again, lighten it as he would, the distinctness of his footfall; after which, in a moment, he knew himself at the other side of the house. He did here what he had not yet done at these hours—he opened half a casement, one of those in the front, and let in the air of the night; a thing he would have taken at any time previous for a sharp rupture of his spell. His spell was broken now, and it didn't matter—broken by his concession and his surrender, which made it idle henceforth that he should ever come back. The empty street—its other life so marked even by the great lamplit vacancy—was within call, within touch; he stayed there as to be in it again, high above it though he was still perched; he watched as for some comforting common fact, some vulgar human note, the passage of a scavenger or a thief, some night-bird however base. He would have blessed that sign of life; he would have welcomed positively the slow approach of his friend the policeman, whom he had hitherto only sought to avoid, and was not sure that if the patrol had come into sight he mightn't have felt the impulse to get into relation with it, to hail it, on some pretext, from his fourth floor.

The pretext that wouldn't have been too silly or too compromising, the explanation that would have saved his dignity and kept his name, in such a case, out of the papers, was not definite to him: he was so occupied with the thought of recording his Discretion—as an effect of the vow he had just uttered to his intimate adversary—that the importance of this loomed large and something had overtaken all ironically his sense of proportion. If there had been a ladder applied to the front of the house, even one of the vertiginous perpendiculars employed by painters and roofers and sometimes left standing overnight, he would have managed somehow, astride of the window-sill, to compass by outstretched leg and arm that mode of descent. If there had been some such uncanny thing as he had found in his room at hotels, a workable fire-escape in the form of notched cable or a canvas shoot, he would have availed himself of it as a proof—well, of his present delicacy. He nursed that sentiment, as the question stood, a little in vain, and even—at the end of he scarce knew, once more, how long—found it, as by the action on his mind of the failure of response of the outer world, sinking back to vague anguish. It seemed to him he had waited an age for some stir of the great grim hush; the life of the town was itself under a spell—so unnaturally, up and down the whole prospect of known and rather ugly objects, the blankness and the silence lasted. Had they ever, he asked himself, the hard-faced houses, which had begun to look livid in the dim dawn, had they ever spoken so little to any need of his spirit? Great builded voids, great crowded stillnesses put on, often, in the heart of cities, for the small hours, a sort of sinister mask, and it was of this large collective negation that Brydon presently became conscious—all the more that the break of day was, almost incredibly, now at hand, proving to him what a night he had made of it.

He looked again at his watch, saw what had become of his time-values (he had taken hours for minutes—not, as in other tense situations, minutes for hours) and the strange air of the streets was but the weak, the sullen flush of a dawn in which everything was still locked up. His choked appeal from his own open window had been the sole note of life, and he could but break off at last as for a worse despair. Yet while so deeply demoralised he was capable again of an impulse denoting—at least by his present measure—extraordinary resolution; of retracing his steps to the spot where he had turned cold with the extinction of his last pulse of doubt as to there being in the place another presence than his own. This required an effort strong enough to sicken him; but he had his reason, which overmastered for the moment everything else. There was the whole of the rest of the house to traverse, and how should he screw himself to that if the door he had seen closed were at present open? He could hold to the idea that the closing had practically been for him an act of mercy, a chance offered him to descend, depart, get off the ground and never again profane it. This conception held together, it worked; but what it meant for him depended now clearly on the amount of forbearance his recent action, or rather his recent inaction, had engendered. The image of the "presence," whatever it was, waiting there for him to go—this image had not yet been so concrete for his nerves as when he stopped short of the point at which certainty would have come to him. For, with all his resolution, or more exactly with all his dread, he did stop short—he hung back from really seeing. The risk was too great and his fear too definite: it took at this moment an awful specific form.

He knew—yes, as he had never known anything—that, *should* he see the door open, it would all too abjectly be the end of him. It would mean that the agent of his shame—for his shame was the deep abjection—was once more at large and in general possession; and what glared him thus in the face was the act that this would determine for him. It would send him straight about to the window he had left open, and by that window, be long ladder and dangling rope as absent as they would, he saw himself uncontrollably insanely fatally take his way to the street. The hideous chance of this he at least could avert; but he could only avert it by recoiling in time from assurance. He had the whole house to deal with, this fact was still there; only he now knew that uncertainty alone could start him. He stole back from where he had checked himself—merely to do so was suddenly like safety—and, making blindly for the greater staircase, left gaping rooms and sounding passages behind. Here was the top of the stairs, with a fine large dim descent and three spacious landings to mark off. His instinct was all for mildness, but his feet were harsh on the floors, and, strangely, when he had in a couple of minutes become aware of this, it counted somehow for help. He couldn't have spoken, the tone of his voice would have scared him, and the common conceit or resource of "whistling in the dark" (whether literally or figuratively) have appeared basely vulgar; yet he liked none the less to hear himself go, and when he had reached his first landing—taking it all with no rush, but quite steadily—that stage of success drew from him a gasp of relief.

The house, withal, seemed immense, the scale of space again inordinate; the open rooms, to no one of which his eyes deflected, gloomed in their shuttered state like mouths of caverns; only the high skylight that formed the crown of the deep well created for him a medium in which he could advance, but which might have been, for queerness of colour, some watery under-world. He tried to think of something noble, as that his property was really grand, a splendid possession; but this nobleness took the form too of the clear delight with which he was finally to sacrifice it. They might come in now, the builders, the destroyers—they might come as soon as they would. At the end of two flights he had dropped to another zone, and from the middle of the third, with only one more left, he recognised the influence of the lower windows, of half-drawn blinds, of the occasional gleam of street-lamps, of the glazed spaces of the vestibule, This was the bottom of the sea, which showed an illumination of its own and which he even saw paved—when at a given moment he drew up to sink a long look over the banisters—with the marble squares of his childhood. By that time indubitably he felt, as he might have said in a commoner cause, better; it had allowed him to stop and draw breath, and the ease increased with the sight of the old black-and-white slabs. But what he most felt was that now surely, with the element of impunity pulling him as by hard firm hands, the case was settled for what he might have seen above had he dared that last look. The closed door, blessedly remote now, was still closed—and he had only in short to reach that of the house.

He came down further, he crossed the passage forming the access to the last flight; and if here again he stopped an instant it was almost for the sharpness of the thrill of assured escape. It made him shut his eyes—which opened again to the straight slope of the remainder of the stairs. Here was impunity still, but impunity almost excessive; inasmuch as the sidelights and the high fan-tracery of the entrance were glimmering straight into the hall; an appearance produced, he the next instant saw, by the fact that the vestibule gaped wide, that the hinged halves of the inner door had been thrown far back. Out of that again the *question* sprang at him, making his eyes, as he felt, half-start from his head, as they had done, at the top of the house, before the sign of the other door. If he had left that one open, hadn't he left this one closed, and wasn't he now in *most* immediate presence of some inconceivable occult activity? It was as sharp, the question, as a knife in his side, but the answer hung fire still and seemed to lose itself in the vague darkness to which the thin admitted dawn, glimmering archwise over the whole outer door, made a semicircular margin, a cold silvery nimbus that seemed to play a little as he looked—to shift and expand and contract.

It was as if there had been something within it, protected by indistinctness and corresponding in extent with the opaque surface behind, the painted panels of the last barrier to his escape, of which the key was in his pocket. The indistinctness mocked him even while he stared, affected him as somehow shrouding or challenging certitude, so that after faltering an instant on his step he let himself go with the sense that here *was* at last something to meet, to touch, to take, to know—something all unnatural and dreadful, but to advance upon which was the condition for him either of liberation or of supreme defeat. The penumbra,[8] dense and dark, was the virtual screen of a figure which stood in it as still as some image erect in a niche or as some black-vizored sentinel guarding a treasure. Brydon was to know afterwards, was to recall and make out, the particular thing he had believed during the rest of his descent. He saw, in its great grey glimmering margin, the central vagueness diminish, and he felt it to be taking the very form toward which, for so many days, the passion of his curiosity had yearned. It gloomed, it loomed, it was something, it was somebody, the prodigy of a personal presence.

Rigid and conscious, spectral yet human, a man of his own substance and stature waited there to measure himself with his power to dismay. This only could it be—this only till he recognised, with his advance, that what made the face dim was the pair of raised hands that covered it and in which, so far from being offered in defiance, it was buried as for dark deprecation. So Brydon, before him, took him in; with every fact of him now, in the higher light, hard and acute—his planted stillness, his vivid truth, his grizzled bent head and white masking hands, his queer actuality of evening-dress, of dangling double eye-glass, of gleaming silk lappet[9] and white linen, of pearl button and gold watch-guard and polished shoe. No portrait by a great modern master could have presented him with more intensity, thrust him out of his frame with more art, as if there had been "treatment," of the consummate sort, in his every shade and salience. The revulsion, for our friend, had become, before he knew it, immense—this drop, in the act of apprehension, to the sense of his adversary's inscrutable manœuvre. That meaning at least, while he gaped, it offered him; for he could but gape at his other self in this other anguish, gape as a proof that *he,* standing there for the achieved, the enjoyed, the triumphant life, couldn't be faced in his triumph. Wasn't the proof in the splendid covering hands, strong and completely spread?—so spread and so intentional that, in spite of a special verity that surpassed every other, the fact that one of these hands had lost two fingers, which were reduced to stumps, as if accidentally shot away, the face was effectually guarded and saved.

"Saved," though, *would* it be?—Brydon breathed his wonder till the very impunity of his attitude and the very insistence of his eyes produced, as he felt, a sudden stir which showed the next instant as a deeper portent, while the head raised itself, the betrayal of a braver purpose. The hands, as he looked, began to move, to open; then, as if deciding in a flash, dropped from the face and left it uncovered and presented. Horror, with the sight, had leaped into Brydon's throat, gasping there in a sound he couldn't utter; for the bared identity was too hideous as *his,* and his glare was the passion of his protest. The face, *that* face, Spencer Brydon's?—he searched it still, but looking away from it in dismay and denial, falling straight from his height of sublimity. It was unknown, inconceivable,

---

[8] A partial shadow surrounding the complete shadow of an opaque body.　　[9] A fold of a garment.

awful, disconnected from any possibility—! He had been "sold," he inwardly moaned, stalking such game as this: the presence before him was a presence, the horror within him a horror, but the waste of his nights had been only grotesque and the success of his adventure an irony. Such an identity fitted his at *no* point, made its alternative monstrous. A thousand times yes, as it came upon him nearer now—the face was the face of a stranger. It came upon him nearer now, quite as one of those expanding fantastic images projected by the magic lantern of childhood; for the stranger, whoever he might be, evil, odious, blatant, vulgar, had advanced as for aggression, and he knew himself give ground. Then harder pressed still, sick with the force of his shock, and falling back as under the hot breath and the roused passion of a life larger than his own, a rage of personality before which his own collapsed, he felt the whole vision turn to darkness and his very feet give way. His head went round; he was going; he had gone.

III

What had next brought him back, clearly—though after how long?—was Mrs. Muldoon's voice, coming to him from quite near, from so near that he seemed presently to see her as kneeling on the ground before him while he lay looking up at her; himself not wholly on the ground, but half-raised and upheld—conscious, yes, of tenderness of support and, more particularly, of a head pillowed in extraordinary softness and fainly refreshing fragrance. He considered, he wondered, his wit but half at his service; then another face intervened, bending more directly over him, and he finally knew that Alice Staverton had made her lap an ample and perfect cushion to him, and that she had to this end seated herself on the lowest degree of the staircase, the rest of his long person remaining stretched on his old black-and-white slabs. They were cold, these marble squares of his youth; but *he* somehow was not, in this rich return of consciousness—the most wonderful hour, little by little, that he had ever known, leaving him, as it did, so gratefully, so abysmally passive, and yet as with a treasure of intelligence waiting all round him for quiet appropriation; dissolved, he might call it, in the air of the place and producing the golden glow of a late autumn afternoon. He had come back, yes— come back from further away than any man but himself had ever travelled; but it was strange how with this sense what he had come back *to* seemed really the great thing, and as if his prodigious journey had been all for the sake of it. Slowly but surely his consciousness grew, his vision of his state thus completing itself: he had been miraculously *carried* back—lifted and carefully borne as from where he had been picked up, the uttermost end of an interminable grey passage. Even with this he was suffered to rest, and what had now brought him to knowledge was the break in the long mild motion.

It had brought him to knowledge, to knowledge—yes, this was the beauty of his state; which came to resemble more and more that of a man who has gone to sleep on some news of a great inheritance, and then, after dreaming it away, after profaning it with matters strange to it, has waked up again to serenity of certitude and has only to lie and watch it grow. This was the drift of his patience—that he had only to let it shine on him. He must moreover, with intermissions, still have been lifted and borne; since why and how else should he have known himself, later on, with the afternoon glow intenser, no longer at the foot of his stairs— situated as these now seemed at that dark other end of his tunnel—but on a deep window-bench of his high saloon, over which had been spread, couch-fashion, a mantle of soft stuff lined with grey fur that was familiar to his eyes and that one of his hands kept fondly feeling as for its pledge of truth. Mrs. Muldoon's face had gone, but the other, the second he had recognised, hung over him in a way that showed how he was still propped and pillowed. He took it all in, and the more he took it the more it seemed to suffice: he was as much at peace as if he had had food and drink. It was the two women who had found him, on Mrs. Muldoon's having plied, at her usual hour, her latch-key—and on her having above all arrived while Miss Staverton still lingered near the house. She had been turning away, all anxiety, from worrying the vain bell-handle—her calculation having been of the hour of the good woman's visit; but the latter, blessedly, had come up while she was still there, and they had entered together. He had then lain, beyond the vestibule, very much as he was lying now—quite, that is, as he appeared to have fallen, but all so wondrously without bruise or gash; only in a depth of stupor. What he most took in, however, at present, with the steadier clearance, was that Alice Staverton had for a long unspeakable moment not doubted he was dead.

"It must have been that I *was*." He made it out as she held him. "Yes—I can only have died. You brought me literally to life. Only," he wondered, his eyes rising to her, "only, in the name of all the benedictions, how?"

It took her but an instant to bend her face and kiss him, and something in the manner of it, and in the way her hands clasped and locked his head while he felt the cool charity and virtue of her lips, something in all this beatitude somehow answered everything. "And now I keep you," she said.

"Oh keep me, keep me!" he pleaded while her face still hung over him: in response to which it dropped again and stayed close, clingingly close. It was the seal of their situation—of which he tasted the impress for a long blissful moment in silence. But he came back. "Yet how did you know—?"

"I was uneasy. You were to have come, you remember—and you had sent no word."

"Yes, I remember—I was to have gone to you at one to-day." It caught on to their "old" life and relation—which were so near and so far. "I was still out there in my strange darkness—where was it, what was it? I must have stayed there so long." He could but wonder at the depth and the duration of his swoon.

"Since last night?" she asked with a shade of fear for her possible indiscretion.

"Since this morning—it must have been: the cold dim dawn of to-day. Where have I been," he vaguely wailed, "where have I been?" He felt her hold him close, and it was as if this helped him now to make in all security his mild moan. "What a long dark day!"

All in her tenderness she had waited a moment. "In the cold dim dawn?" she quavered.

But he had already gone on piecing together the parts of the whole prodigy. "As I didn't turn up you came straight—?"

She barely cast about. "I went first to your hotel—where they told me of your absence. You had dined out last evening and hadn't been back since. But they appeared to know you had been at your club."

"So you had the idea of *this*—?"

"Of what?" she asked in a moment.

"Well—of what has happened."

"I believed at least you'd have been here. I've known, all along," she said, "that you've been coming."

"'Known' it—?"

"Well, I've believed it. I said nothing to you after that talk we had a month ago—but I felt sure. I knew you *would,*" she declared.

"That I'd persist, you mean?"

"That you'd see him."

"Ah, but I didn't!" cried Brydon with his long wail. "There's somebody—an awful beast; whom I brought, too horribly, to bay. But it's not me."

At this she bent over him again, and her eyes were in his eyes. "No—it's not you." And it was as if, while her face hovered, he might have made out in it, hadn't it been so near, some particular meaning blurred by a smile. "No, thank heaven," she repeated—"it's not you! Of course it wasn't to have been."

"Ah but it *was,*" he gently insisted. And he stared before him now as he had been staring for so many weeks. "I was to have known myself."

"You couldn't!" she returned consolingly. And then reverting, and as if to account further for what she had herself done, "But it wasn't only *that,* that you hadn't been at home," she went on. "I waited till the hour at which we had found Mrs. Muldoon that day of my going with you; and she arrived, as I've told you, while, failing to bring any one to the door, I lingered in my despair on the steps. After a little, if she hadn't come, by such a mercy, I should have found means to hunt her up. But it wasn't," said Alice Staverton, as if once more with her fine intention—"it wasn't only that."

His eyes, as he lay, turned back to her. "What more then?"

She met it, the wonder she had stirred. "In the cold dim dawn, you say? Well, in the cold dim dawn of this morning I too saw you."

"Saw *me*—?"

"Saw *him,*" said Alice Staverton. "It must have been at the same moment."

He lay an instant taking it in—as if he wished to be quite reasonable. "At the same moment?"

"Yes—in my dream again, the same one I've named to you. He came back to me. Then I knew it for a sign. He had come to you."

At this Brydon raised himself; he had to see her better. She helped him when she understood his movement, and he sat up, steadying himself beside her there on the window-bench and with his right hand grasping her left. "*He* didn't come to me."

"You came to yourself," she beautifully smiled.

"Ah I've come to myself now—thanks to you, dearest. But this brute, with his awful face—this brute's a black stranger. He's none of *me,* even as I *might* have been," Brydon sturdily declared.

But she kept the clearness that was like the breath of infallibility. "Isn't the whole point that you'd have been different?"

He almost scowled for it. "As different as *that*—?"

Her look again was more beautiful to him than the things of this world. "Haven't you exactly wanted to know *how* different? So this morning," she said, "you appeared to me."

"Like *him?*"

"A black stranger!"

"Then how did you know it was I?"

"Because, as I told you weeks ago, my mind, my imagination, had worked so over what you might, what you mightn't have been—to show you, you see, how I've thought of you. In the midst of that you came to me—that my wonder might be answered. So I knew," she went on; "and believed that, since the question held you too so fast, as you told me that day, you too would see for yourself. And when this morning I again saw I knew it would be because you had—and also then, from the first moment, because you somehow wanted me. *He* seemed to tell me of that. So why," she strangely smiled, "shouldn't I like him?"

It brought Spencer Brydon to his feet. "You 'like' that horror—?"

"I *could* have liked him. And to me," she said, "he was no horror. I had accepted him."

"'Accepted'—?" Brydon oddly sounded.

"Before, for the interest of his difference—yes. And as *I* didn't disown him, as *I* knew him—which you at last, confronted with him in his difference, so cruelly didn't, my dear—well, he must have been, you see, less dreadful to me. And it may have pleased him that I pitied him."

She was beside him on her feet, but still holding his hand—still with her arm supporting him. But though it all brought for him thus a dim light, "You 'pitied' him?" he grudgingly, resentfully asked.

"He has been unhappy, he has been ravaged," she said.

"And haven't I been unhappy? Am not I—you've only to look at me!—ravaged?"

"Ah I don't say I like him *better*," she granted after a thought. "But he's grim, he's worn—and things have happened to him. He doesn't make shift, for sight, with your charming monocle."

"No"—it struck Brydon: "I couldn't have sported mine 'downtown.' They'd have guyed[10] me there."

"His great convex pince-nez[11]—I saw it, I recognised the kind—is for his poor ruined sight. And his poor right hand—!"

"Ah!" Brydon winced—whether for his proved identity or for his lost fingers. Then, "He has a million a year," he lucidly added. "But he hasn't you."

"And he isn't—no, he isn't—*you!*" she murmured as he drew her to his breast.

1908

THE ART OF FICTION*

I should not have affixed so comprehensive a title to these few remarks, necessarily wanting in any completeness upon a subject the full consideration of which would carry us far, did I not seem to discover a pretext for my temerity in the interesting pamphlet lately published under this name by Mr. Walter Besant. Mr. Besant's lecture at the Royal Institution—the original form of his pamphlet—appears to indicate that many persons are interested in the art of fiction, and are not indifferent to such remarks, as those who practise it may attempt to make about it. I am therefore anxious not to lose the benefit of this favourable association, and to edge in a few words under cover of the attention which Mr. Besant is sure to have excited. There is something very encouraging in his having put into form certain of his ideas on the mystery of story-telling.

---

[10] Teased.   [11] Eyeglasses held on the face by a spring that pinches the nose.

* First published in *Longman's Magazine* in 1884, written in response to a lecture on fiction given by the English novelist and critic Sir Walter Besant (1836–1901) at the Royal Institution in London on April 25, 1884.

It is a proof of life and curiosity—curiosity on the part of the brotherhood of novelists as well as on the part of their readers. Only a short time ago it might have been supposed that the English novel was not what the French call *discutable*.[1] It had no air of having a theory, a conviction, a consciousness of itself behind it—of being the expression of an artistic faith, the result of choice and comparison. I do not say it was necessarily the worse for that: it would take much more courage than I possess to intimate that the form of the novel as Dickens and Thackeray (for instance) saw it had any taint of incompleteness. It was, however, *naïf*[2] (if I may help myself out with another French word); and evidently if it be destined to suffer in any way for having lost its *naïveté* it has now an idea of making sure of the corresponding advantages. During the period I have alluded to there was a comfortable, good-humoured feeling abroad that a novel is a novel, as a pudding is a pudding, and that our only business with it could be to swallow it. But within a year or two, for some reason or other, there have been signs of returning animation—the era of discussion would appear to have been to a certain extent opened. Art lives upon discussion, upon experiment, upon curiosity, upon variety of attempt, upon the exchange of views and the comparison of standpoints; and there is a presumption that those times when no one has anything particular to say about it, and has no reason to give for practice or preference, though they may be times of honour, are not times of development—are times, possibly even, a little of dulness. The successful application of any art is a delightful spectacle, but the theory too is interesting; and though there is a great deal of the latter without the former I suspect there has never been genuine success that has not had a latent core of conviction. Discussion, suggestion, formulation, these things are fertilising when they are frank and sincere. Mr. Besant has set an excellent example in saying what he thinks, for his part, about the way in which fiction should be written, as well as about the way in which it should be published; for his view of the "art," carried on into an appendix, covers that too. Other labourers in the same field will doubtless take up the argument, they will give it the light of their experience, and the effect will surely be to make our interest in the novel a little more what it had for some time threatened to fail to be—a serious, active, inquiring interest, under protection of which this delightful study may, in moments of confidence. venture to say a little more what it thinks of itself.

It must take itself seriously for the public to take it so. The old superstition about fiction being "wicked" has doubtless died out in England; but the spirit of it lingers in a certain oblique regard directed toward any story which does not more or less admit that it is only a joke. Even the most jocular novel feels in some degree the weight of the proscription that was formerly directed against literary levity: the jocularity does not always succeed in passing for orthodoxy. It is still expected, though perhaps people are ashamed to say it, that a production which is after all only a "make-believe" (for what else is a "story"?) shall be in some degree apologetic—shall renounce the pretension of attempting really to represent life. This, of course, any sensible, wide-awake story declines to do, for it quickly perceives that the tolerance granted to it on such a condition is only an attempt to stifle it disguised in the form of generosity. The old evangelical hostility to the novel, which was as explicit as it was narrow, and which regarded it as little less favourable to our immortal part than a stage-play, was in reality far less insulting. The only reason for the existence of a novel is that it does attempt to represent life. When it relinquishes this attempt, the same attempt that we see on the canvas of

---

[1] "Disputable," "debatable" (French).   [2] "Naïve" (French).

the painter, it will have arrived at a very strange pass. It is not expected of the picture that it will make itself humble in order to be forgiven; and the analogy between the art of the painter and the art of the novelist is, so far as I am able to see, complete. Their inspiration is the same, their process (allowing for the different quality of the vehicle), is the same, their success is the same. They may learn from each other, they may explain and sustain each other. Their cause is the same, and the honour of one is the honour of another. The Mahometans[3] think a picture an unholy thing, but it is a long time since any Christian did, and it is therefore the more odd that in the Christian mind the traces (dissimulated though they may be) of a suspicion of the sister art should linger to this day. The only effectual way to lay it to rest is to emphasise the analogy to which I just alluded—to insist on the fact that as the picture is reality, so the novel is history. That is the only general description (which does it justice) that we may give of the novel. But history also is allowed to represent life; it is not, any more than painting, expected to apologise. The subject-matter of fiction is stored up likewise in documents and records, and if it will not give itself away, as they say in California, it must speak with assurance, with the tone of the historian. Certain accomplished novelists have a habit of giving themselves away which must often bring tears to the eyes of people who take their fiction seriously. I was lately struck, in reading over many pages of Anthony Trollope,[4] with his want of discretion in this particular. In a digression, a parenthesis or an aside, he concedes to the reader that he and this trusting friend are only "making believe." He admits that the events he narrates have not really happened, and that he can give his narrative any turn the reader may like best. Such a betrayal of a sacred office seems to me, I confess, a terrible crime; it is what I mean by the attitude of apology, and it shocks me every whit as much in Trollope as it would have shocked me in Gibbon or Macaulay.[5] It implies that the novelist is less occupied in looking for the truth (the truth, of course I mean, that he assumes, the premises that we must grant him, whatever they may be), than the historian, and in doing so it deprives him at a stroke of all his standing-room. To represent and illustrate the past, the actions of men, is the task of either writer, and the only difference that I can see is, in proportion as he succeeds, to the honour of the novelist, consisting as it does in his having more difficulty in collecting his evidence, which is so far from being purely literary. It seems to me to give him a great character, the fact that he has at once so much in common with the philosopher and the painter; this double analogy is a magnificent heritage.

It is of all this evidently that Mr. Besant is full when he insists upon the fact that fiction is one of the *fine* arts, deserving in its turn of all the honours and emoluments that have hitherto been reserved for the successful profession of music, poetry, painting, architecture. It is impossible to insist too much on so important a truth, and the place that Mr. Besant demands for the work of the novelist may be represented, a trifle less abstractly, by saying that he demands not only that it shall be reputed artistic, but that it shall be reputed very artistic indeed. It is excellent that he should have struck this note, for his doing so indicates that there was need of it, that his proposition may be to many people a novelty. One rubs one's eyes at the thought; but the rest of Mr. Besant's essay confirms the revelation. I suspect in truth that it would be possible to confirm it still further,

---

[3] Mohammedans; the Muslim religion at one time forbade figural representations.
[4] Trollope (1815–1882) was an English novelist.
[5] Edward Gibbon (1737–1794) and Thomas Babington Macaulay (1800–1859): English historians.

and that one would not be far wrong in saying that in addition to the people to whom it has never occurred that a novel ought to be artistic, there are a great many others who, if this principle were urged upon them, would be filled with an indefinable mistrust. They would find it difficult to explain their repugnance, but it would operate strongly to put them on their guard. "Art," in our Protestant communities, where so many things have got so strangely twisted about, is supposed in certain circles to have some vaguely injurious effect upon those who make it an important consideration, who let it weigh in the balance. It is assumed to be opposed in some mysterious manner to morality, to amusement, to instruction. When it is embodied in the work of the painter (the sculptor is another affair!) you know what it is: it stands there before you, in the honesty of pink and green and a gilt frame; you can see the worst of it at a glance, and you can be on your guard. But when it is introduced into literature it becomes more insidious—there is danger of its hurting you before you know it. Literature should be either instructive or amusing, and there is in many minds an impression that these artistic preoccupations, the search for form, contribute to neither end, interfere indeed with both. They are too frivolous to be edifying, and too serious to be diverting; and they are moreover priggish and paradoxical and superfluous. That, I think, represents the manner in which the latent thought of many people who read novels as an exercise in skipping would explain itself if it were to become articulate. They would argue, of course, that a novel ought to be "good," but they would interpret this term in a fashion of their own, which indeed would vary considerably from one critic to another. One would say that being good means representing virtuous and aspiring characters, placed in prominent positions; another would say that it depends on a "happy ending," on a distribution at the last of prizes, pensions, husbands, wives, babies, millions, appended paragraphs, and cheerful remarks. Another still would say that it means being full of incident and movement, so that we shall wish to jump ahead, to see who was the mysterious stranger, and if the stolen will was ever found, and shall not be distracted from this pleasure by any tiresome analysis or "description." But they would all agree that the "artistic" idea would spoil some of their fun. One would hold it accountable for all the description, another would see it revealed in the absence of sympathy. Its hostility to a happy ending would be evident, and it might even in some cases render any ending at all impossible. The "ending" of a novel is, for many persons, like that of a good dinner, a course of dessert and ices, and the artist in fiction is regarded as a sort of meddlesome doctor who forbids agreeable aftertastes. It is therefore true that this conception of Mr. Besant's of the novel as a superior form encounters not only a negative but a positive indifference. It matters little that as a work of art it should really be as little or as much of its essence to supply happy endings, sympathetic characters, and an objective tone, as if it were a work of mechanics: the association of ideas, however incongruous, might easily be too much for it if an eloquent voice were not sometimes raised to call attention to the fact that it is at once as free and as serious a branch of literature as any other.

Certainly this might sometimes be doubted in presence of the enormous number of works of fiction that appeal to the credulity of our generation, for it might easily seem that there could be no great character in a commodity so quickly and easily produced. It must be admitted that good novels are much compromised by bad ones, and that the field at large suffers discredit from overcrowding. I think, however, that this injury is only superficial, and that the super-abundance of written fiction proves nothing against the principle itself. It has been vulgarised, like all other kinds of literature, like everything else to-day, and it has proved more than some kinds accessible to vulgarisation. But there is as much difference as there ever was between a good novel and a bad one: the bad is swept with all the daubed canvases and spoiled marble into some unvisited limbo, or infinite rubbish-yard beneath the back-windows of the world, and the good subsists and emits its light and stimulates our desire for perfection. As I shall take the liberty of making but a single criticism of Mr. Besant, whose tone is so full of the love of his art, I may as well have done with it at once. He seems to me to mistake in attempting to say so definitely beforehand what sort of an affair the good novel will be. To indicate the danger of such an error as that has been the purpose of these few pages; to suggest that certain traditions on the subject, applied *a priori*, have already had much to answer for, and that the good health of an art which undertakes so immediately to reproduce life must demand that it be perfectly free. It lives upon exercise, and the very meaning of exercise is freedom. The only obligation to which in advance we may hold a novel, without incurring the accusation of being arbitrary, is that it be interesting. That general responsibility rests upon it, but it is the only one I can think of. The ways in which it is at liberty to accomplish this result (of interesting us) strike me as innumerable, and such as can only suffer from being marked out or fenced in by prescription. They are as various as the temperament of man, and they are successful in proportion as they reveal a particular mind, different from others. A novel is in its broadest definition a personal, a direct impression of life: that, to begin with, constitutes its value, which is greater or less according to the intensity of the impression. But there will be no intensity at all, and therefore no value, unless there is freedom to feel and say. The tracing of a line to be followed, of a tone to be taken, of a form to be filled out, is a limitation of that freedom and a suppression of the very thing that we are most curious about. The form, it seems to me, is to be appreciated after the fact: then the author's choice has been made, his standard has been indicated; then we can follow lines and directions and compare tones and resemblances. Then in a word we can enjoy one of the most charming of pleasures, we can estimate quality, we can apply the test of execution. The execution belongs to the author alone; it is what is most personal to him, and we measure him by that. The advantage, the luxury, as well as the torment and responsibility of the novelist, is that there is no limit to what he may attempt as an executant—no limit to his possible experiments, efforts, discoveries, successes. Here it is especially that he works, step by step, like his brother of the brush, of whom we may always say that he has painted his picture in a manner best known to himself. His manner is his secret, not necessarily a jealous one. He cannot disclose it as a general thing if he would; he would be at a loss to teach it to others. I say this with a due recollection of having insisted on the community of method of the artist who paints a picture and the artist who writes a novel. The painter *is* able to teach the rudiments of his practice, and it is possible, from the study of good work (granted the aptitude), both to learn how to paint and to learn how to write. Yet it remains true, without injury to the *rapprochement,*[6] that the literary artist would be obliged to say to his pupil much more than the other, "Ah, well, you must do it as you can!" It is a question of degree, a matter of delicacy. If there are exact sciences, there are also exact arts, and the grammar of painting is so much more definite that it makes the difference.

---

[6] Bringing together, comparison (French).

I ought to add, however, that if Mr. Besant says at the beginning of his essay that the "laws of fiction may be laid down and taught with as much precision and exactness as the laws of harmony, perspective, and proportion," he mitigates what might appear to be an extravagance by applying his remark to "general" laws, and by expressing most of these rules in a manner with which it would certainly be unaccommodating to disagree. That the novelist must write from his experience, that his "characters must be real and such as might be met with in actual life;" that "a young lady brought up in a quiet country village should avoid descriptions of garrison life," and "a writer whose friends and personal experiences belong to the lower middle-class should carefully avoid introducing his characters into society;" that one should enter one's notes in a common-place book; that one's figures should be clear in outline; that making them clear by some trick of speech or of carriage is a bad method, and "describing them at length" is a worse one; that English Fiction should have a "conscious moral purpose;" that "it is almost impossible to estimate too highly the value of careful workmanship—that is, of style;" that "the most important point of all is the story," that "the story is everything": these are principles with most of which it is surely impossible not to sympathise. That remark about the lower middle-class writer and his knowing his place is perhaps rather chilling; but for the rest I should find it difficult to dissent from any one of these recommendations. At the same time, I should find it difficult positively to assent to them, with the exception, perhaps, of the injunction as to entering one's notes in a common-place book. They scarcely seem to me to have the quality that Mr. Besant attributes to the rules of the novelist—the "precision and exactness" of "the laws of harmony, perspective, and proportion." They are suggestive, they are even inspiring, but they are not exact, though they are doubtless as much so as the case admits of: which is a proof of that liberty of interpretation for which I just contended. For the value of these different injunctions—so beautiful and so vague—is wholly in the meaning one attaches to them. The characters, the situation, which strike one as real will be those that touch and interest one most, but the measure of reality is very difficult to fix. The reality of Don Quixote or of Mr. Micawber[7] is a very delicate shade; it is a reality so coloured by the author's vision that, vivid as it may be, one would hesitate to propose it as a model: one would expose one's self to some very embarrassing questions on the part of a pupil. It goes without saying that you will not write a good novel unless you possess the sense of reality; but it will be difficult to give you a recipe for calling that sense into being. Humanity is immense, and reality has a myriad forms; the most one can affirm is that some of the flowers of fiction have the odour of it, and others have not; as for telling you in advance how your nosegay should be composed, that is another affair. It is equally excellent and inconclusive to say that one must write from experience; to our supposititious aspirant such a declaration might savour of mockery. What kind of experience is intended, and where does it begin and end? Experience is never limited, and it is never complete; it is an immense sensibility, a kind of huge spiderweb of the finest silken threads suspended in the chamber of consciousness, and catching every airborne particle in its tissue. It is the very atmosphere of the mind; and when the mind is imaginative—much more when it happens to be that of a man of genius—it takes

---

[7] The hero of *Don Quixote* (1605, 1616), by Miguel de Cervantes (1547–1616), and a character in *David Copperfield* (1849–1850), by Charles Dickens (1812–1870).

to itself the faintest hints of life, it converts the very pulses of the air into revelations. The young lady living in a village has only to be a damsel upon whom nothing is lost to make it quite unfair (as it seems to me) to declare to her that she shall have nothing to say about the military. Greater miracles have been seen than that, imagination assisting, she should speak the truth about some of these gentlemen. I remember an English novelist, a woman of genius, telling me that she was much commended for the impression she had managed to give in one of her tales of the nature and way of life of the French Protestant youth. She had been asked where she learned so much about this recondite being, she had been congratulated on her peculiar opportunities. These opportunities consisted in her having once, in Paris, as she ascended a staircase, passed an open door where, in the household of a *pasteur*,[8] some of the young Protestants were seated at table round a finished meal. The glimpse made a picture; it lasted only a moment, but that moment was experience. She had got her direct personal impression, and she turned out her type. She knew what youth was, and what Protestantism; she also had the advantage of having seen what it was to be French, so that she converted these ideas into a concrete image and produced a reality. Above all, however, she was blessed with the faculty which when you give it an inch takes an ell, and which for the artist is a much greater source of strength than any accident of residence or of place in the social scale. The power to guess the unseen from the seen, to trace the implication of things, to judge the whole piece by the pattern, the condition of feeling life in general so completely that you are well on your way to knowing any particular corner of it—this cluster of gifts may almost be said to constitute experience, and they occur in country and in town, and in the most differing stages of education. If experience consists of impressions, it may be said that impressions *are* experience, just as (have we not seen it?) they are the very air we breathe. Therefore, if I should certainly say to a novice, "Write from experience and experience only," I should feel that this was rather a tantalising monition if I were not careful immediately to add, "Try to be one of the people on whom nothing is lost!"

I am far from intending by this to minimise the importance of exactness—of truth of detail. One can speak best from one's own taste, and I may therefore venture to say that the air of reality (solidity of specification) seems to me to be the supreme virtue of a novel—the merit on which all its other merits (including that conscious moral purpose of which Mr. Besant speaks) helplessly and submissively depend. If it be not there they are all as nothing, and if these be there, they owe their effect to the success with which the author has produced the illusion of life. The cultivation of this success, the study of this exquisite process, form, to my taste, the beginning and the end of the art of the novelist. They are his inspiration, his despair, his reward, his torment, his delight. It is here in very truth that he competes with life; it is here that he competes with his brother the painter in *his* attempt to render the look of things, the look that conveys their meaning, to catch the colour, the relief, the expression, the surface, the substance of the human spectacle. It is in regard to this that Mr. Besant is well inspired when he bids him take notes. He cannot possibly take too many, he cannot possibly take enough. All life solicits him, and to "render" the simplest surface, to produce the most momentary illusion, is a very complicated business. His case would be easier, and the rule would be more exact, if Mr. Besant had been able to tell him what notes to

[8] "Pastor" (French).

take. But this, I fear, he can never learn in any manual; it is the business of his life. He has to take a great many in order to select a few, he has to work them up as he can, and even the guides and philosophers who might have most to say to him must leave him alone when it comes to the application of precepts, as we leave the painter in communion with his palette. That his characters "must be clear in outline," as Mr. Besant says—he feels that down to his boots; but how he shall make them so is a secret between his good angel and himself. It would be absurdly simple if he could be taught that a great deal of "description" would make them so, or that on the contrary the absence of description and the cultivation of dialogue, or the absence of dialogue and the multiplication of "incident," would rescue him from his difficulties. Nothing, for instance, is more possible than that he be of a turn of mind for which this odd, literal opposition of description and dialogue, incident and description, has little meaning and light. People often talk of these things as if they had a kind of internecine distinctness, instead of melting into each other at every breath, and being intimately associated parts of one general effort of expression. I cannot imagine composition existing in a series of blocks, nor conceive, in any novel worth discussing at all, of a passage of description that is not in its intention narrative, a passage of dialogue that is not in its intention descriptive, a touch of truth of any sort that does not partake of the nature of incident, or an incident that derives its interest from any other source than the general and only source of the success of a work of art—that of being illustrative. A novel is a living thing, all one and continuous, like any other organism, and in proportion as it lives will it be found, I think, that in each of the parts there is something of each of the other parts. The critic who over the close texture of a finished work shall pretend to trace a geography of items will mark some frontiers as artificial, I fear, as any that have been known to history. There is an old-fashioned distinction between the novel of character and the novel of incident which must have cost many a smile to the intending fabulist who was keen about his work. It appears to me as little to the point as the equally celebrated distinction between the novel and the romance—to answer as little to any reality. There are bad novels and good novels, as there are bad pictures and good pictures; but that is the only distinction in which I see any meaning, and I can as little imagine speaking of a novel of character as I can imagine speaking of a picture of character. When one says picture one says of character, when one says novel one says of incident, and the terms may be transposed at will. What is character but the determination of incident? What is incident but the illustration of character? What is either a picture or a novel that is *not* of character? What else do we seek in it and find in it? It is an incident for a woman to stand up with her hand resting on a table and look out at you in a certain way; or if it be not an incident I think it will be hard to say what it is. At the same time it is an expression of character. If you say you don't see it (character in *that—allons donc!*[9]), this is exactly what the artist who has reasons of his own for thinking he *does* see it undertakes to show you. When a young man makes up his mind that he has not faith enough after all to enter the church as he intended, that is an incident, though you may not hurry to the end of the chapter to see whether perhaps he doesn't change once more. I do not say that these are extraordinary or startling incidents. I do not pretend to estimate the degree of interest proceeding from them, for this will depend upon the skill of the painter. It sounds almost puerile to say that some incidents are intrinsi-

---

[9] "Come now!" or "Nonsense!" (French).

cally much more important than others, and I need not take this precaution after having professed my sympathy for the major ones in remarking that the only classification of the novel that I can understand is into that which has life and that which has it not.

The novel and the romance, the novel of incident and that of character—these clumsy separations appear to me to have been made by critics and readers for their own convenience, and to help them out of some of their occasional queer predicaments, but to have little reality or interest for the producer, from whose point of view it is of course that we are attempting to consider the art of fiction. The case is the same with another shadowy category which Mr. Besant apparently is disposed to set up—that of the "modern English novel"; unless indeed it be that in this matter he has fallen into an accidental confusion of stand-points. It is not quite clear whether he intends the remarks in which he alludes to it to be didactic or historical. It is as difficult to suppose a person intending to write a modern English as to suppose him writing an ancient English novel: that is a label which begs the question. One writes the novel, one paints the picture, of one's language and of one's time, and calling it modern English will not, alas! make the difficult task any easier. No more, unfortunately, will calling this or that work of one's fellow-artist a romance—unless it be, of course, simply for the pleasantness of the thing, as for instance when Hawthorne gave this heading to his story of *Blithedale*.[10] The French, who have brought the theory of fiction to remarkable completeness, have but one name for the novel, and have not attempted smaller things in it, that I can see, for that. I can think of no obligation to which the "romancer" would not be held equally with the novelist; the standard of execution is equally high for each. Of course it is of execution that we are talking—that being the only point of a novel that is open to contention. This is perhaps too often lost sight of, only to produce interminable confusions and cross-purposes. We must grant the artist his subject, his idea, his *donnée*:[11] our criticism is applied only to what he makes of it. Naturally I do not mean that we are bound to like it or find it interesting: in case we do not our course is perfectly simple—to let it alone. We may believe that of a certain idea even the most sincere novelist can make nothing at all, and the event may perfectly justify our belief; but the failure will have been a failure to execute, and it is in the execution that the fatal weakness is recorded. If we pretend to respect the artist at all, we must allow him his freedom of choice, in the face, in particular cases, of innumerable presumptions that the choice will not fructify. Art derives a considerable part of its beneficial exercise from flying in the face of presumptions, and some of the most interesting experiments of which it is capable are hidden in the bosom of common things. Gustave Flaubert has written a story[12] about the devotion of a servant-girl to a parrot, and the production, highly finished as it is, cannot on the whole be called a success. We are perfectly free to find it flat, but I think it might have been interesting; and I, for my part, am extremely glad he should have written it; it is a contribution to our knowledge of what can be done—or what cannot. Ivan Turgénieff has written a tale[13] about a deaf and dumb serf and a lap-dog, and the thing is touching, loving, a little masterpiece. He struck the note of life where Gustave Flaubert missed it—he flew in the face of a presumption and achieved a victory.

[10] Nathaniel Hawthorne's novel *The Blithedale Romance* (1852).
[11] "A given" (French): a premise.
[12] "Un Coeur Simple" (1877), by the French novelist Flaubert (1821–1880).
[13] "Mumu" (1856), by the Russian novelist Turgenev (1818–1883).

Nothing, of course, will ever take the place of the good old fashion of "liking" a work of art or not liking it: the most improved criticism will not abolish that primitive, that ultimate test. I mention this to guard myself from the accusation of intimating that the idea, the subject, of a novel or a picture, does not matter. It matters, to my sense, in the highest degree, and if I might put up a prayer it would be that artists should select none but the richest. Some, as I have already hastened to admit, are much more remunerative than others, and it would be a world happily arranged in which persons intending to treat them should be exempt from confusions and mistakes. This fortunate condition will arrive only, I fear, on the same day that critics become purged from error. Meanwhile, I repeat, we do not judge the artist with fairness unless we say to him, "Oh, I grant you your starting-point, because if I did not I should seem to prescribe to you, and heaven forbid I should take that responsibility. If I pretend to tell you what you must not take, you will call upon me to tell you then what you must take; in which case I shall be prettily caught. Moreover, it isn't till I have accepted your data that I can begin to measure you. I have the standard, the pitch; I have no right to tamper with your flute and then criticise your music. Of course I may not care for your idea at all; I may think it silly, or stale, or unclean; in which case I wash my hands of you altogether. I may content myself with believing that you will not have succeeded in being interesting, but I shall, of course, not attempt to demonstrate it, and you will be as indifferent to me as I am to you. I needn't remind you that there are all sorts of tastes: who can know it better? Some people, for excellent reasons, don't like to read about carpenters; others, for reasons even better, don't like to read about courtesans. Many object to Americans. Others (I believe they are mainly editors and publishers) won't look at Italians. Some readers don't like quiet subjects; others don't like bustling ones. Some enjoy a complete illusion, others the consciousness of large concessions. They choose their novels accordingly, and if they don't care about your idea they won't, *a fortiori*,[14] care about your treatment."

So that it comes back very quickly, as I have said, to the liking: in spite of M. Zola,[15] who reasons less powerfully than he represents, and who will not reconcile himself to this absoluteness of taste, thinking that there are certain things that people ought to like, and that they can be made to like. I am quite at a loss to imagine anything (at any rate in this matter of fiction) that people *ought* to like or to dislike. Selection will be sure to take care of itself, for it has a constant motive behind it. That motive is simply experience. As people feel life, so they will feel the art that is most closely related to it. This closeness of relation is what we should never forget in talking of the effort of the novel. Many people speak of it as a factitious, artificial form, a product of ingenuity, the business of which is to alter and arrange the things that surround us, to translate them into conventional, traditional moulds. This, however, is a view of the matter which carries us but a very short way, condemns the art to an eternal repetition of a few familiar *clichés*, cuts short its development, and leads us straight up to a dead wall. Catching the very note and trick, the strange irregular rhythm of life, that is the attempt whose strenuous force keeps Fiction upon her feet. In proportion as in what she offers us we see life *without* rearrangement do we feel that we are touching the truth; in

[14] "With greater reason" (Latin).

[15] Émile Zola (1840–1902), a French naturalistic novelist and critic; James says that Zola's criticism is less powerful than his fiction.

proportion as we see it *with* rearrangement do we feel that we are being put off with a substitute, a compromise and convention. It is not uncommon to hear an extraordinary assurance of remark in regard to this matter of rearranging, which is often spoken of as if it were the last word of art. Mr. Besant seems to me in danger of falling into the great error with his rather unguarded talk about "selection." Art is essentially selection, but it is a selection whose main care is to be typical, to be inclusive. For many people art means rose-coloured window-panes, and selection means picking a bouquet for Mrs. Grundy.[16] They will tell you glibly that artistic considerations have nothing to do with the disagreeable, with the ugly; they will rattle off shallow commonplaces about the province of art and the limits of art till you are moved to some wonder in return as to the province and the limits of ignorance. It appears to me that no one can ever have made a seriously artistic attempt without becoming conscious of an immense increase—a kind of revelation—of freedom. One perceives in that case—by the light of a heavenly ray—that the province of art is all life, all feeling, all observation, all vision. As Mr. Besant so justly intimates, it is all experience. That is a sufficient answer to those who maintain that it must not touch the sad things of life, who stick into its divine unconscious bosom little prohibitory inscriptions on the end of sticks, such as we see in public gardens—"It is forbidden to walk on the grass; it is forbidden to touch the flowers; it is not allowed to introduce dogs or to remain after dark; it is requested to keep to the right." The young aspirant in the line of fiction whom we continue to imagine will do nothing without taste, for in that case his freedom would be of little use to him; but the first advantage of his taste will be to reveal to him the absurdity of the little sticks and tickets. If he have taste, I must add, of course he will have ingenuity, and my disrespectful reference to that quality just now was not meant to imply that it is useless in fiction. But it is only a secondary aid; the first is a capacity for receiving straight impressions.

Mr. Besant has some remarks on the question of "the story" which I shall not attempt to criticise, though they seem to me to contain a singular ambiguity, because I do not think I understand them. I cannot see what is meant by talking as if there were a part of a novel which is the story and part of it which for mystical reasons is not—unless indeed the distinction be made in a sense in which it is difficult to suppose that any one should attempt to convey anything. "The story," if it represents anything, represents the subject, the idea, the *donnée* of the novel; and there is surely no "school"—Mr. Besant speaks of a school—which urges that a novel should be all treatment and no subject. There must assuredly be something to treat; every school is intimately conscious of that. This sense of the story being the idea, the starting-point, of the novel, is the only one that I see in which it can be spoken of as something different from its organic whole; and since in proportion as the work is successful the idea permeates and penetrates it, informs and animates it, so that every word and every punctuation point contribute directly to the expression, in that proportion do we lose our sense of the story being a blade which may be drawn more or less out of its sheath. The story and the novel, the idea and the form, are the needle and thread, and I never heard of a guild of tailors who recommended the use of the thread without the needle, or the needle without the thread. Mr. Besant is not the only critic who may be observed to have spoken as if there were certain things in life which constitute stories, and certain others

---

[16] A character in the play *Speed the Plow* (1798), by Thomas Morton (1764–1838); she has become a symbol of prudishness.

which do not. I find the same odd implication in an entertaining article in the *Pall Mall Gazette,* devoted, as it happens, to Mr. Besant's lecture. "The story is the thing!" says this graceful writer, as if with a tone of opposition to some other idea. I should think it was, as every painter who, as the time for "sending in" his picture[17] looms in the distance, finds himself still in quest of a subject—as every belated artist not fixed about his theme will heartily agree. There are some subjects which speak to us and others which do not, but he would be a clever man who should undertake to give a rule—an index expurgatorius[18]—by which the story and the no-story should be known apart. It is impossible (to me at least) to imagine any such rule which shall not be altogether arbitrary. The writer in the *Pall Mall* opposes the delightful (as I suppose) novel of *Margot la Balafrée*[19] to certain tales in which "Bostonian nymphs" appear to have "rejected English dukes for psychological reasons." I am not acquainted with the romance just designated, and can scarcely forgive the *Pall Mall* critic for not mentioning the name of the author, but the title appears to refer to a lady who may have received a scar in some heroic adventure. I am inconsolable at not being acquainted with this episode, but am utterly at a loss to see why it is a story when the rejection (or acceptance) of a duke is not, and why a reason, psychological or other, is not a subject when a cicatrix[20] is. They are all particles of the multitudinous life with which the novel deals, and surely no dogma which pretends to make it lawful to touch the one and unlawful to touch the other will stand for a moment on its feet. It is the special picture that must stand or fall, according as it seem to possess truth or to lack it. Mr. Besant does not, to my sense, light up the subject by intimating that a story must, under penalty of not being a story, consist of "adventures." Why of adventures more than of green spectacles? He mentions a category of impossible things, and among them he places "fiction without adventure." Why without adventure, more than without matrimony, or celibacy, or parturition,[21] or cholera, or hydropathy, or Jansenism?[22] This seems to me to bring the novel back to the hapless little *rôle* of being an artificial, ingenious thing—bring it down from its large, free character of an immense and exquisite correspondence with life. And what *is* adventure, when it comes to that, and by what sign is the listening pupil to recognise it? It is an adventure—an immense one—for me to write this little article; and for a Bostonian nymph to reject an English duke is an adventure only less stirring, I should say, than for an English duke to be rejected by a Bostonian nymph. I see dramas within dramas in that, and innumerable points of view. A psychological reason is, to my imagination, an object adorably pictorial; to catch the tint of its complexion—I feel as if that idea might inspire one to Titianesque[23] efforts. There are few things more exciting to me, in short, than a psychological reason, and yet, I protest, the novel seems to me the most magnificent form of art. I have just been reading, at the same time, the delightful story of *Treasure Island,*[24] by Mr. Robert Louis Stevenson and, in a manner less consecutive, the last

---

[17] Submitting his painting for exhibition.

[18] Index of forbidden readings (Latin): a standard by which to judge.

[19] *Margot the Scarfaced Woman,* an 1884 novel by the French novelist Fortuné du Boisgobey (1821–1891).

[20] A scar.   [21] Childbirth.

[22] The doctrine of the Dutch theologian Bishop Cornelis Jansen (1585–1638), emphasizing predestination and the necessity of belonging to the Catholic Church.

[23] Like the work of Titian (1477–1576), an Italian painter known for his use of color.

[24] An 1883 novel by the English writer Stevenson (1850–1894).

tale from M. Edmond de Goncourt, which is entitled *Chérie*.[25] One of these works treats of murders, mysteries, islands of dreadful renown, hairbreadth escapes, miraculous coincidences and buried doubloons. The other treats of a little French girl who lived in a fine house in Paris, and died of wounded sensibility because no one would marry her. I call *Treasure Island* delightful, because it appears to me to have succeeded wonderfully in what it attempts; and I venture to bestow no epithet upon *Chérie*, which strikes me as having failed deplorably in what it attempts—that is in tracing the development of the moral consciousness of a child. But one of these productions strikes me as exactly as much of a novel as the other, and as having a "story" quite as much. The moral consciousness of a child is as much a part of life as the islands of the Spanish Main, and the one sort of geography seems to me to have those "surprises" of which Mr. Besant speaks quite as much as the other. For myself (since it comes back in the last resort, as I say, to the preference of the individual), the picture of the child's experience has the advantage that I can at successive steps (an immense luxury, near to the "sensual pleasure" of which Mr. Besant's critic in the *Pall Mall* speaks) say Yes or No, as it may be, to what the artist puts before me. I have been a child in fact, but I have been on a quest for a buried treasure only in supposition, and it is a simple accident that with M. de Goncourt I should have for the most part to say No. With George Eliot,[26] when she painted that country with a far other intelligence, I always said Yes.

The most interesting part of Mr. Besant's lecture is unfortunately the briefest passage—his very cursory allusion to the "conscious moral purpose" of the novel. Here again it is not very clear whether he be recording a fact or laying down a principle; it is a great pity that in the latter case he should not have developed his idea. This branch of the subject is of immense importance, and Mr. Besant's few words point to considerations of the widest reach, not to be lightly disposed of. He will have treated the art of fiction but superficially who is not prepared to go every inch of the way that these considerations will carry him. It is for this reason that at the beginning of these remarks I was careful to notify the reader that my reflections on so large a theme have no pretension to be exhaustive. Like Mr. Besant, I have left the question of the morality of the novel till the last, and at the last I find I have used up my space. It is a question surrounded with difficulties, as witness the very first that meets us, in the form of a definite question, on the threshold. Vagueness, in such a discussion, is fatal, and what is the meaning of your morality and your conscious moral purpose? Will you not define your terms and explain how (a novel being a picture) a picture can be either moral or immoral? You wish to paint a moral picture or carve a moral statue: will you not tell us how you would set about it? We are discussing the Art of Fiction; questions of art are questions (in the widest sense) of execution; questions of morality are quite another affair, and will you not let us see how it is that you find it so easy to mix them up? These things are so clear to Mr. Besant that he has deduced from them a law which he sees embodied in English Fiction, and which is "a truly admirable thing and a great cause for congratulation." It is a great cause for congratulation indeed when such thorny problems become as smooth as silk. I may add that in so far as Mr. Besant perceives that in point of fact English Fiction has addressed itself preponderantly to these delicate questions he will appear to many people to have made a

---

[25] An 1884 novel by Edmond Louis Antoine de Goncourt (1822–1896), a French novelist who collaborated with his brother, Jules Alfred Huot de Goncourt (1830–1870).

[26] Pseudonym for Mary Ann Evans (1819–1880), the English author of *Silas Marner* (1861).

vain discovery. They will have been positively struck, on the contrary, with the moral timidity of the usual English novelist; with his (or with her) aversion to face the difficulties with which on every side the treatment of reality bristles. He is apt to be extremely shy (whereas the picture that Mr. Besant draws is a picture of boldness), and the sign of his work, for the most part, is a cautious silence on certain subjects. In the English novel (by which of course I mean the American as well), more than in any other, there is a traditional difference between that which people know and that which they agree to admit that they know, that which they see and that which they speak of, that which they feel to be a part of life and that which they allow to enter into literature. There is the great difference, in short, between what they talk of in conversation and what they talk of in print. The essence of moral energy is to survey the whole field, and I should directly reverse Mr. Besant's remark and say not that the English novel has a purpose, but that it has a diffidence. To what degree a purpose in a work of art is a source of corruption I shall not attempt to inquire; the one that seems to me least dangerous is the purpose of making a perfect work. As for our novel, I may say lastly on this score that as we find it in England to-day it strikes me as addressed in a large degree to "young people," and that this in itself constitutes a presumption that it will be rather shy. There are certain things which it is generally agreed not to discuss, not even to mention, before young people. That is very well, but the absence of discussion is not a symptom of the moral passion. The purpose of the English novel—"a truly admirable thing, and a great cause for congratulation"—strikes me therefore as rather negative.

There is one point at which the moral sense and the artistic sense lie very near together; that is in the light of the very obvious truth that the deepest quality of a work of art will always be the quality of the mind of the producer. In proportion as that intelligence is fine will the novel, the picture, the statue partake of the substance of beauty and truth. To be constituted of such elements is, to my vision, to have purpose enough. No good novel will ever proceed from a superficial mind; that seems to me an axiom which, for the artist in fiction, will cover all needful moral ground: if the youthful aspirant take it to heart it will illuminate for him many of the mysteries of "purpose." There are many other useful things that might be said to him, but I have come to the end of my article, and can only touch them as I pass. The critic in the *Pall Mall Gazette,* whom I have already quoted, draws attention to the danger, in speaking of the art of fiction, of generalising. The danger that he has in mind is rather, I imagine, that of particularising, for there are some comprehensive remarks which, in addition to those embodied in Mr Besant's suggestive lecture, might without fear of misleading him be addressed to the ingenuous student. I should remind him first of the magnificence of the form that is open to him, which offers to sight so few restrictions and such innumerable opportunities. The other arts, in comparison, appear confined and hampered; the various conditions under which they are exercised are so rigid and definite. But the only condition that I can think of attaching to the composition of the novel is, as I have already said, that it be sincere. This freedom is a splendid privilege, and the first lesson of the young novelist is to learn to be worthy of it. "Enjoy it as it deserves," I should say to him; "take possession of it, explore it to its utmost extent, publish it, rejoice in it. All life belongs to you, and do not listen either to those who would shut you up into corners of it and tell you that it is only here and there that art inhabits, or to those who would persuade you that this heavenly messenger wings her way outside of life altogether, breathing a superfine air, and turning away her head from the truth of things. There is no impression of life, no manner of seeing it and feeling it, to which the plan of the novelist may not offer a place; you have only to remember that talents so dissimilar as those of Alexandre Dumas and Jane Austen,[27] Charles Dickens and Gustave Flaubert have worked in this field with equal glory. Do not think too much about optimism and pessimism; try and catch the colour of life itself. In France to-day we see a prodigious effort (that of Emile Zola, to whose solid and serious work no explorer of the capacity of the novel can allude without respect), we see an extraordinary effort vitiated by a spirit of pessimism on a narrow basis. M. Zola is magnificent, but he strikes an English reader as ignorant; he has an air of working in the dark; if he had as much light as energy, his results would be of the highest value. As for the aberrations of a shallow optimism, the ground (of English fiction especially) is strewn with their brittle particles as with broken glass. If you must indulge in conclusions, let them have the taste of a wide knowledge. Remember that your first duty is to be as complete as possible—to make as perfect a work. Be generous and delicate and pursue the prize."

1884

=CONTEXTS=

The Birth of the Movies

In 1877 Governor Leland Stanford of California, wishing to win his bet that, at some point in their stride, horses suspend all four hooves at the same time, hired the photographer Eadweard Muybridge (1830–1904) to provide visual proof. With the aid of the chief engineer of the Southern Pacific Railroad, Muybridge set up a system of magnetic releases to trigger a series of cameras. The resulting photographs of horses in motion marked the first time in history that live action was continuously recorded on film.

The significance of Muybridge's work, which led to the invention of the first practical motion picture camera in 1889 (the kinetograph, developed at the Edison laboratories in New Jersey), eluded some of his contemporaries. In a letter to Muybridge, Thomas Edison (1847–1931) expressed doubt about the future of "moving pictures":

> . . . [I have] built a little instrument which I call a kinetograph with a nickel & slot but I am very doubtful if there is any commercial feature in it & fear they will not earn their cost. These Zootropic devices are of too sentimental a character to get the public to invest in.
>
> Thomas Edison, 1894

However, when Edison opened the first Kinetoscope Parlor later that year, it met with huge success. Soon delighted patrons in penny arcades across the nation eagerly peered into the coin-operated machines to view quarter-minute films of Buffalo Bill waving to them from horseback. Motion pictures had been born.

---

[27] The French novelist and playwright Dumas (1802–1870) wrote *The Count of Monte Cristo* (1844); the English novelist Austen (1775–1817) wrote *Pride and Prejudice* (1813).

William Dean Howells
(1837–1920)

In the final decade of the nineteenth century William Dean Howells was commonly considered the "dean" of American letters. As the editor of *Harper's* magazine, he spoke with authority on contemporary writers and on the nature of realism in American fiction; as an experienced novelist he commanded the respect of public and critics alike. In the late twentieth century Howells's reputation has declined: along with Mark Twain and Henry James, he is known as a nineteenth-century American realist; yet, unlike Twain and James (with whom Howells shared life-long friendships), he has failed to find a wide audience among readers of American literature. Because he wrote in an age when readers were accustomed to apocalyptic events and highly embroidered fiction, it has been easy to overlook Howells's insistence on portraying ordinary people involved with the problems of everyday life. Deliberately, in accordance with his theories of realism in American fiction, Howells's novels are not flashy, and yet their truthfulness and skillful style provide insights into human character that many writers never develop.

Born in Martin's Ferry, Ohio, in 1837, Howells worked with words from an early age when he began setting type for his father's newspaper. He read widely and taught himself a reading knowledge of several languages. In the process, he developed his own literary ambitions, as he reveals in such works as *My Literary Passions* (1895) and *Literary Friends and Acquaintance* (1900). As a young man he moved from jobs as typesetter and reporter to news editor and editorial writer on the Cincinnati *Gazette* and the *Ohio State Journal* in Columbus. His break into wider social circles occurred after his campaign biography of Abraham Lincoln in 1860, when Howells was appointed consul to Venice. When he returned from Italy in 1865, he became assistant editor of the *Atlantic Monthly,* then editor in chief in 1871. During his ten years as editor of this prestigious magazine and his later years at *Harper's,* Howells acquired great authority in the world of letters. Able to aid or thwart careers, he took his responsibility seriously, championing writers who showed promise, tactfully criticizing without meanness, and maintaining a standard of professionalism previously unknown in periodicals.

Howells's integrity pervades his many novels as well as his critical writings. Characteristically, his fiction portrays the daily lives of contemporary people in ways that reveal universal human emotions. Out of a belief that melodramatic excess distorts the representation of life, he wrote such arresting studies of moral behavior as *A Modern Instance* (1882), *The Rise of Silas Lapham* (1885), and *The Landlord at Lion's Head* (1897), all of which show the vulnerability that underlies human postures of strength and ambition. Howells believed that a novelist should focus on character, then attend to the incidents that grow out of character.

Critical response to Howells has varied from adulation during his life to dismissal by such writers as H. L. Mencken and Sinclair Lewis, both of whom saw Howells as prudish and old-fashioned. Mencken deplored Howells's literary descent from Jane Austen and Washington Irving and preferred the raucous vigor of François Rabelais and Geoffrey Chaucer. Howells is worth reading, however, precisely because he is not raucous, because his work exhibits a profound awareness of pretension and human frailty. In his biography of Howells, Edwin H. Cady refers to the "quiet heartbreak" implicit in many of Howells's novels. It is the signature of a writer who found the truths of human character in the lives we ordinarily lead.

Suggested Readings: *A Modern Instance*, 1882. *The Rise of Silas Lapham*, 1885. *A Hazard of New Fortunes*, 1890. *My Mark Twain*, 1910. *A Selected Edition of W. D. Howells*, 1968– . J. L. Woodress, *Howells and Italy*, 1952. E. H. Cady, *The Road to Realism: The Early Years, 1837–1885*, 1956. E. H. Cady, *The Realist at War: The Mature Years, 1885–1920*, 1958. E. H. Cady and D. L. Frazier. eds., *The War of the Critics Over William Dean Howells*, 1962. K. Vanderbilt, *The Achievement of William Dean Howells*, 1968. K. S. Lynn, *William Dean Howells*, 1971. G. N. Bennett, *The Realism of William Dean Howells*, 1973. K. Eble, *William Dean Howells*, 1982. J. W. Crowley, *The Black Heart's Truth: The Early Career of W. D. Howells*, 1985. E. Nettels, *Language, Race, and Social Class in Howells's America*, 1988. J. W. Crowley, ed., *The Mask of Fiction: Essays on W. D. Howells*, 1989.

Texts Used: *Literary Friends and Acquaintance*, ed. D. F. Hiatt and E. H. Cady, 1968. "Puritanism in American Fiction": *Literature and Life: Studies*, 1902. "Editha": *Between the Dark and the Daylight: Romances*, 1907.

from LITERARY FRIENDS AND ACQUAINTANCE

from MY FIRST VISIT TO NEW ENGLAND*

from XV: [HAWTHORNE[1]]

I wasted that whole evening and the next morning in fond delaying, and it was not until after the indifferent dinner I got at the tavern where I stopped, that I found courage to go and present Lowell's[2] letter to Hawthorne. I would almost have foregone meeting the weird genius only to have kept that letter, for it said certain infinitely precious things of me with such a sweetness, such a grace as Lowell alone could give his praise. Years afterwards, when Hawthorne was dead, I met Mrs. Hawthorne,[3] and told her of the pang I had in parting with it, and she sent it me, doubly enriched by Hawthorne's keeping. But now if I were to see him at all I must give up my letter, and I carried it in my hand to the door of the cottage he called The Wayside.[4] It was never otherwise than a very modest place, but the modesty was greater then than to-day, and there was already some preliminary carpentry at one end of the cottage, which I saw was to result in an addition to it. I recall pleasant fields across the road before it; behind rose a hill wooded with low pines, such as is made in Septimius Felton[5] the scene of the involuntary duel between Septimius and the young British officer. I have a sense of the woods coming quite down to the house, but if this was so I do not know what to do with a grassy slope which seems to have stretched part way up the hill. As I approached, I looked for the tower which the author was fabled to climb into at sight

---

* In this section of *Literary Friends and Acquaintance* (1900), first published in *Harper's Monthly* in 1894, Howells tells about his trip to Concord, Massachusetts, in 1860 to meet his literary heroes.

[1] Nathaniel Hawthorne (1804–1864), author of *The Scarlet Letter* (1850), *The House of Seven Gables* (1851), *The Blithedale Romance* (1852), and *The Marble Faun* (1860).

[2] The American poet and essayist James Russell Lowell (1819–1891). In this era it was customary to bring a letter of introduction from a mutual friend when first meeting someone.

[3] Sophia Peabody Hawthorne (1809–1871).

[4] Hawthorne's house in Concord, formerly owned by the education reformer and mystic Bronson Alcott (1799–1888).

[5] The title character of an unfinished, posthumously published work by Hawthorne.

of the coming guest, and pull the ladder up after him; and I wondered whether he would fly before me in that sort, or imagine some easier means of escaping me.

The door was opened to my ring by a tall handsome boy whom I suppose to have been Mr. Julian Hawthorne;[6] and the next moment I found myself in the presence of the romancer, who entered from some room beyond. He advanced carrying his head with a heavy forward droop, and with a pace for which I decided that the word would be *pondering*. It was the pace of a bulky man of fifty, and his head was that beautiful head we all know from the many pictures of it. But Hawthorne's *look* was different from that of any picture of him that I have seen. It was sombre and brooding, as the look of such a poet should have been; it was the look of a man who had dealt faithfully and therefore sorrowfully with that problem of evil which forever attracted, forever evaded Hawthorne. It was by no means troubled; it was full of a dark repose. Others who knew him better and saw him oftener were familiar with other aspects, and I remember that one night at Longfellow's[7] table, when one of the guests happened to speak of the photograph of Hawthorne which hung in a corner of the room, Lowell said, after a glance at it, "Yes, it's good; but it hasn't his fine *accipitral*[8] look."

In the face that confronted me, however, there was nothing of keen alertness; but only a sort of quiet, patient intelligence, for which I seek the right word in vain. It was a very regular face, with beautiful eyes; the mustache, still entirely dark, was dense over the fine mouth. Hawthorne was dressed in black, and he had a certain effect which I remember, of seeming to have on a black cravat with no visible collar. He was such a man that if I had ignorantly met him anywhere I should have instantly felt him to be a personage.

I must have given him the letter myself, for I have no recollection of parting with it before, but I only remember his offering me his hand, and making me shyly and tentatively welcome. After a few moments of the demoralization which followed his hospitable attempts in me, he asked if I would not like to go up on his hill with him and sit there, where he smoked in the afternoon. He offered me a cigar, and when I said that I did not smoke, he lighted it for himself, and we climbed the hill together. At the top, where there was an outlook in the pines over the Concord meadows, we found a log, and he invited me to a place on it beside him, and at intervals of a minute or so he talked while he smoked. Heaven preserved me from the folly of trying to tell him how much his books had been to me, and though we got on rapidly at no time, I think we got on better for this interposition. He asked me about Lowell, I dare say, for I told him of my joy in meeting him and Dr. Holmes,[9] and this seemed greatly to interest him. Perhaps because he was so lately from Europe, where our great men are always seen through the wrong end of the telescope, he appeared surprised at my devotion, and asked me whether I cared as much for meeting them as I should care for meeting the famous English authors. I professed that I cared much more, though whether this was true, I now have my doubts, and I think Hawthorne doubted it at the time. But he said nothing in comment, and went on to speak generally of Europe and America. He was curious about the West, which he seemed to fancy much more purely American, and said he would like to see some part of the country on which the shadow, or, if I must be precise, the damned shadow, of Europe had not fallen. I

[6] Hawthorne's only son (1846–1934).
[7] The New England poet Henry Wadsworth Longfellow (1807–1894).
[8] Hawklike, keen-sighted.
[9] The writer and physician Oliver Wendell Holmes (1809–1894).

told him I thought the West must finally be characterized by the Germans, whom we had in great numbers, and, purely from my zeal for German poetry, I tried to allege some proofs of their present influence, though I could think of none outside of politics, which I thought they affected wholesomely. I knew Hawthorne was a Democrat, and I felt it well to touch politics lightly, but he had no more to say about the fateful election[10] then pending than Holmes or Lowell had.

With the abrupt transition of his talk throughout, he began somehow to speak of women, and said he had never seen a woman whom he thought quite beautiful. In the same way he spoke of the New England temperament, and suggested that the apparent coldness in it was also real, and that the suppression of emotion for generations would extinguish it at last. Then he questioned me as to my knowledge of Concord, and whether I had seen any of the notable people. I answered that I had met no one but himself, as yet, but I very much wished to see Emerson and Thoreau.[11] I did not think it needful to say that I wished to see Thoreau quite as much because he had suffered in the cause of John Brown[12] as because he had written the books which had taken me; and when he said that Thoreau prided himself on coming nearer the heart of a pine-tree than any other human being, I could say honestly enough that I would rather come near the heart of a man. This visibly pleased him, and I saw that it did not displease him, when he asked whether I was not going to see his next neighbor Mr. Alcott,[13] and I confessed that I had never heard of him. That surprised as well as pleased him; he remarked, with whatever intention, that there was nothing like recognition to make a man modest; and he entered into some account of the philosopher, whom I suppose I need not be much ashamed of not knowing then, since his influence was of the immediate sort that makes a man important to his townsmen while he is still strange to his countrymen.

Hawthorne descanted a little upon the landscape, and said certain of the pleasant fields below us belonged to him; but he preferred his hill-top, and if he could have his way those arable fields should be grown up to pines too. He smoked fitfully, and slowly, and in the hour that we spent together, his whiffs were of the desultory and unfinal character of his words. When we went down, he asked me into his house again, and would have me stay to tea, for which we found the table laid. But there was a great deal of silence in it all, and at times, in spite of his shadowy kindness, I felt my spirits sink. After tea, he showed me a bookcase, where there were a few books toppling about on the half-filled shelves, and said, coldly, "This is my library." I knew that men were his books, and though I myself cared for books so much, I found it fit and fine that he should care so little, or seem to care so little. Some of his own romances were among the volumes on these shelves, and when I put my finger on the Blithedale Romance and said that I preferred that to the others, his face lighted up, and he said that he believed the Germans liked that best too.

---

[10] The 1860 presidential race between the Democrat Stephen Douglas (1813–1861), the Democrat John C. Breckinridge (1821–1875), and the Republican Abraham Lincoln (1809–1865).

[11] The essayist and poet Ralph Waldo Emerson (1803–1882); the poet, prose writer, and naturalist Henry David Thoreau (1817–1862).

[12] John Brown (1800–1859), an American abolitionist, who became a martyr/hero to many Americans after his 1859 raid on Harper's Ferry, Virginia, in an attempted slave uprising, for which he was executed. Thoreau wrote a lecture and an essay in 1859 in support of Brown's antislavery activities.

[13] Alcott, the father of writer Louisa May Alcott, had helped establish the utopian community Brook Farm, upon which Hawthorne's *Blithedale Romance* is partly based.

Upon the whole we parted such good friends that when I offered to take leave he asked me how long I was to be in Concord, and not only bade me come to see him again, but said he would give me a card to Emerson, if I liked. I answered, of course, that I should like it beyond all things; and he wrote on the back of his card something which I found, when I got away, to be, "I find this young man worthy." The quaintness, the little stiffness of it, if one pleases to call it so, was amusing to one who was not without his sense of humor, but the kindness filled me to the throat with joy. In fact, I entirely liked Hawthorne. He had been as cordial as so shy a man could show himself; and I perceived, with the repose that nothing else can give, the entire sincerity of his soul.

* * *

I am painfully aware that I have not summoned before the reader the image of the man as it has always stood in my memory, and I feel a sort of shame for my failure. He was so altogether simple that it seems as if it would be easy to do so; but perhaps a spirit from the other world would be simple too, and yet would no more stand at parle,[14] or consent to be sketched, than Hawthorne. In fact, he was always more or less merging into the shadow, which was in a few years wholly to close over him; there was nothing uncanny in his presence, there was nothing even unwilling, but he had that apparitional quality of some great minds which kept Shakespeare largely unknown to those who thought themselves his intimates, and has at last left him a sort of doubt. There was nothing teasing or wilfully elusive in Hawthorne's impalpability, such as I afterward felt in Thoreau; if he was not there to your touch, it was no fault of his; it was because your touch was dull, and wanted the use of contact with such natures. The hand passes through the veridical[15] phantom without a sense of its presence, but the phantom is none the less veridical for all that.

XVI: [THOREAU]

I kept the evening of the day I met Hawthorne wholly for the thoughts of him, or rather for that reverberation which continues in the young sensibilities after some important encounter. It must have been the next morning that I went to find Thoreau, and I am dimly aware of making one or more failures to find him, if I ever really found him at all.

He is an author who has fallen into that abeyance, awaiting all authors, great or small, at some time or another; but I think that with him, at least in regard to his most important book, it can be only transitory. I have not read the story[16] of his hermitage beside Walden Pond since the year 1858, but I have a fancy that if I should take it up now, I should think it a wiser and truer conception of the world than I thought it then. It is no solution of the problem; men are not going to answer the riddle of the painful earth by building themselves shanties and living upon beans and watching ant-fights; but I do not believe Tolstoy[17] himself has more clearly shown the hollowness, the hopelessness, the unworthiness of the life of the world than Thoreau did in that book. If it were newly written it could not

[14] Stand and talk.
[15] Genuine, not illusory; or, a truth-telling phantom.   [16] Thoreau's *Walden* (1854).
[17] The Russian novelist and social reformer Count Leo Nikolaevich Tolstoy (1828–1910).

fail of a far vaster acceptance than it had then, when to those who thought and felt seriously it seemed that if slavery could only be controlled, all things else would come right of themselves with us. Slavery has not only been controlled, but it has been destroyed, and yet things have not begun to come right with us; but it was in the order of Providence that chattel slavery[18] should cease before industrial slavery, and the infinitely crueler and stupider vanity and luxury bred of it, should be attacked. If there was then any prevision of the struggle now at hand, the seers averted their eyes, and strove only to cope with the less evil. Thoreau himself, who had so clear a vision of the falsity and folly of society as we still have it, threw himself into the tide that was already, in Kansas and Virginia, reddened with war; he aided and abetted the John Brown raid, I do not recall how much or in what sort; and he had suffered in prison for his opinions and actions.[19] It was this inevitable heroism of his that, more than his literature even, made me wish to see him and revere him; and I do not believe that I should have found the veneration difficult, when at last I met him in his insufficient person, if he had otherwise been present to my glowing expectation. He came into the room a quaint, stump figure of a man, whose effect of long trunk and short limbs was heightened by his fashionless trousers being let down too low. He had a noble face, with tossed hair, a distraught eye, and a fine aquilinity of profile, which made me think at once of Don Quixote and of Cervantes;[20] but his nose failed to add that foot to his stature which Lamb[21] says a nose of that shape will always give a man. He tried to place me geographically after he had given me a chair not quite so far off as Ohio,[22] though still across the whole room, for he sat against one wall, and I against the other; but apparently he failed to pull himself out of his revery by the effort, for he remained in a dreamy muse, which all my attempts to say something fit about John Brown and Walden Pond seemed only to deepen upon him. I have not the least doubt that I was needless and valueless about both, and that what I said could not well have prompted an important response; but I did my poor best, and I was terribly disappointed in the result. The truth is that in those days I was a helplessly concrete young person, and all forms of the abstract, the air-drawn, afflicted me like physical discomforts. I do not remember that Thoreau spoke of his books or of himself at all, and when he began to speak of John Brown, it was not the warm, palpable, loving, fearful old man of my conception, but a sort of John Brown type, a John Brown ideal, a John Brown principle, which we were somehow (with long pauses between the vague, orphic[23] phrases) to cherish, and to nourish ourselves upon.

It was not merely a defeat of my hopes, it was a rout, and I felt myself so scattered over the field of thought that I could hardly bring my forces together for retreat. I must have made some effort, vain and foolish enough, to rematerialize my old demigod, but when I came away it was with the feeling that there was very little more left of John Brown than there was of me. His body was not mouldering

---

[18] Slaves owned as property.

[19] Thoreau spent a night in jail in 1846 after he refused to pay taxes to Massachusetts because it supported proslavery sentiments.

[20] Miguel de Cervantes (1547–1616), the Spanish novelist whose most famous novel *Don Quixote* (1605, 1616) recounts a satire on chivalry through the exploits of the title character.

[21] The English essayist and critic Charles Lamb (1775–1834).

[22] Howells was from Ohio.

[23] Mystic, oracular.

in the grave, neither was his soul marching on;[24] his ideal, his type, his principle alone existed, and I did not know what to do with it. I am not blaming Thoreau; his words were addressed to a far other understanding than mine, and it was my misfortune if I could not profit by them. I think, or I venture to hope, that I could profit better by them now; but in this record I am trying honestly to report their effect with the sort of youth I was then.

from XVII: [EMERSON]

Such as I was, I rather wonder that I had the courage, after this experiment of Thoreau, to present the card Hawthorne had given me to Emerson. I must have gone to him at once, however, for I cannot make out any interval of time between my visit to the disciple and my visit to the master. I think it was Emerson himself who opened his door to me, for I have a vision of the fine old man standing tall on his threshold, with the card in his hand, and looking from it to me with a vague serenity, while I waited a moment on the door-step below him. He must then have been about sixty, but I remember nothing of age in his aspect, though I have called him an old man. His hair, I am sure, was still entirely dark, and his face had a kind of marble youthfulness, chiselled to a delicate intelligence by the highest and noblest thinking that any man has done. There was a strange charm in Emerson's eyes, which I felt then and always, something like that I saw in Lincoln's, but shyer, but sweeter and less sad. His smile was the very sweetest I have ever beheld, and the contour of the mask and the line of the profile were in keeping with this incomparable sweetness of the mouth, at once grave and quaint, though quaint is not quite the word for it either, but subtly, not unkindly arch, which again is not the word.

It was his great fortune to have been mostly misunderstood, and to have reached the dense intelligence of his fellow-men after a whole lifetime of perfectly simple and lucid appeal, and his countenance expressed the patience and forbearance of a wise man content to bide his time. It would be hard to persuade people now that Emerson once represented to the popular mind all that was most hopelessly impossible, and that in a certain sort he was a national joke, the type of the incomprehensible, the byword of the poor paragrapher. He had perhaps disabused the community somewhat by presenting himself here and there as a lecturer, and talking face to face with men in terms which they could not refuse to find as clear as they were wise; he was more and more read, by certain persons, here and there; but we are still so far behind him in the reach of his far-thinking that it need not be matter of wonder that twenty years before his death he was the most misunderstood man in America. Yet in that twilight where he dwelt he loomed large upon the imagination; the minds that could not conceive him were still aware of his greatness. I myself had not read much of him, but I knew the essays he was printing in the Atlantic,[25] and I knew certain of his poems, though by no means many; yet I had this sense of him, that he was somehow, beyond and above my ken, a presence of force and beauty and wisdom, uncompanioned in our literature.

---

[24] Phrases from a song written in support of John Brown after his death; later, Julia Ward Howe (1819–1910) used this same tune with new words to write "The Battle Hymn of the Republic."

[25] The *Atlantic Monthly,* a magazine of which Howells later become editor.

He had lately stooped from his ethereal heights to take part in the battle of humanity, and I suppose that if the truth were told he was more to my young fervor because he had said that John Brown had made the gallows glorious like the cross, than because he had uttered all those truer and wiser things which will still a hundred years hence be leading the thought of the world.

I do not know in just what sort he made me welcome, but I am aware of sitting with him in his study or library, and of his presently speaking of Hawthorne, whom I probably celebrated as I best could, and whom he praised for his personal excellence, and for his fine qualities as a neighbor. "But his last book," he added, reflectively, "is a mere mush," and I perceived that this great man was no better equipped to judge an artistic fiction than the groundlings who were then crying out upon the indefinite close of the Marble Faun. Apparently he had read it, as they had, for the story, but it seems to me now, if it did not seem to me then, that as far as the problem of evil was involved, the book must leave it where it found it. That is forever insoluble, and it was rather with that than with his more or less shadowy people that the romancer was concerned. Emerson had, in fact, a defective sense as to specific pieces of literature; he praised extravagantly, and in the wrong place, especially among the new things, and he failed to see the worth of much that was fine and precious beside the line of his fancy.

* * *

. . . He questioned me about what I had seen of Concord, and whom besides Hawthorne I had met, and when I told him only Thoreau, he asked me if I knew the poems of Mr. William Ellery Channing.[26] I have known them since, and felt their quality, which I have gladly owned a genuine and original poetry; but I answered then truly that I knew them only from Poe's[27] criticisms: cruel and spiteful things which I should be ashamed of enjoying as I once did.

"Whose criticisms?" asked Emerson.

"Poe's," I said again.

"Oh," he cried out, after a moment, as if he had returned from a far search for my meaning, "*you mean the jingle-man!*"

I do not know why this should have put me to such confusion, but if I had written the criticisms myself I do not think I could have been more abashed. Perhaps I felt an edge of reproof, of admonition, in a characterization of Poe which the world will hardly agree with; though I do not agree with the world about him, myself, in its admiration. At any rate, it made an end of me for the time, and I remained as if already absent, while Emerson questioned me as to what I had written in the Atlantic Monthly. He had evidently read none of my contributions, for he looked at them, in the bound volume of the magazine which he got down, with the effect of being wholly strange to them, and then gravely affixed my initials to each. He followed me to the door, still speaking of poetry, and as he took a kindly enough leave of me, he said one might very well give a pleasant hour to it now and then.

1894

---

[26] Channing (1810–1884) was an American poet.
[27] The poet, fiction writer, and critic Edgar Allan Poe (1809–1849).

PURITANISM IN AMERICAN FICTION*

The question whether the fiction which gives a vivid impression of reality does truly represent the conditions studied in it, is one of those inquiries to which there is no very final answer. The most baffling fact of such fiction is that its truths are self-evident; and if you go about to prove them you are in some danger of shaking the convictions of those whom they have persuaded. It will not do to affirm anything wholesale concerning them; a hundred examples to the contrary present themselves if you know the ground, and you are left in doubt of the verity which you cannot gainsay. The most that you can do is to appeal to your own consciousness, and that is not proof to anybody else. Perhaps the best test in this difficult matter is the quality of the art which created the picture. Is it clear, simple, unaffected? Is it true to human experience generally? If it is so, then it cannot well be false to the special human experience it deals with.

I

Not long ago I heard of something which amusingly, which pathetically, illustrated the sense of reality imparted by the work of one of our writers, whose art is of the kind I mean. A lady was driving with a young girl of the lighter-minded civilization of New York through one of those little towns of the North Shore in Massachusetts, where the small, wooden houses cling to the edges of the shallow bay, and the schooners slip in and out on the hidden channels of the salt meadows as if they were blown about through the tall grass. She tried to make her feel the shy charm of the place, that almost subjective beauty, which those to the manner born are so keenly aware of in old-fashioned New England villages; but she found that the girl was not only not looking at the sad-colored cottages, with their weather-worn shingle walls, their grassy door-yards lit by patches of summer bloom, and their shutterless windows with their close-drawn shades, but she was resolutely averting her eyes from them, and staring straighforward until she should be out of sight of them altogether. She said that they were terrible, and she knew that in each of them was one of those dreary old women, or disappointed girls, or unhappy wives, or bereaved mothers, she had read of in Miss Wilkins's[1] stories.

She had been too little sensible of the humor which forms the relief of these stories, as it forms the relief of the bare, duteous, conscientious, deeply individualized lives portrayed in them; and no doubt this cannot make its full appeal to the heart of youth aching for their stoical sorrows. Without being so very young, I, too, have found the humor hardly enough at times, and if one has not the habit of experiencing support in tragedy itself, one gets through a remote New England village, at nightfall, say, rather limp than otherwise, and in quite the mood that Miss Wilkins's bleaker studies leave one in. At mid-day, or in the bright sunshine of the morning, it is quite possible to fling off the melancholy which breathes the same note in the fact and the fiction; and I have even had some pleasure at

---

* First published in *Literature and Life* in 1898.

[1] Mary E. Wilkins Freeman (1852–1930), who wrote tales of rural New England, using dispassionate observation to portray the lives of repressed people in a decaying social system.

such times in identifying this or that one-story cottage with its lean-to as a Mary Wilkins house and in placing one of her muted dramas in it. One cannot know the people of such places without recognizing her types in them, and one cannot know New England without owning the fidelity of her stories to New England character, though, as I have already suggested, quite another sort of stories could be written which should as faithfully represent other phases of New England village life.

To the alien inquirer, however, I should be by no means confident that their truth would evince itself, for the reason that human nature is seldom on show anywhere. I am perfectly certain of the truth of Tolstoy and Tourguénief[2] to Russian life, yet I should not be surprised if I went through Russia and met none of their people. I should be rather more surprised if I went through Italy and met none of Verga's or Fogazzaro's,[3] but that would be because I already knew Italy a little. In fact, I suspect that the last delight of truth in any art comes only to the connoisseur who is as well acquainted with the subject as the artist himself. One must not be too severe in challenging the truth of an author to life; and one must bring a great deal of sympathy and a great deal of patience to the scrutiny. Types are very backward and shrinking things, after all; character is of such a mimosan[4] sensibility that if you seize it too abruptly its leaves are apt to shut and hide all that is distinctive in it; so that it is not without some risk to an author's reputation for honesty that he gives his readers the impression of his truth.

II

The difficulty with characters in fiction is that the reader there finds them dramatized; not only their actions, but also their emotions are dramatized; and the very same sort of persons when one meets them in real life are recreantly undramatic. One might go through a New England village and see Mary Wilkins houses and Mary Wilkins people, and yet not witness a scene nor hear a word such as one finds in her tales. It is only too probable that the inhabitants one met would say nothing quaint or humorous, or betray at all the nature that she reveals in them; and yet I should not question her revelation on that account. The life of New England, such as Miss Wilkins deals with, and Miss Sarah O. Jewett, and Miss Alice Brown,[5] is not on the surface, or not visibly so, except to the accustomed eye. It is Puritanism scarcely animated at all by the Puritanic theology. One must not be very positive in such things, and I may be too bold in venturing to say that while the belief of some New-Englanders approaches this theology the belief of most is now far from it; and yet its penetrating individualism so deeply influenced the New England character that Puritanism survives in the moral and mental make of the people almost in its early strength. Conduct and manner conform to a dead

---

[2] Count Leo Nikolaevich Tolstoy (1828–1910), a Russian novelist and social reformer; Ivan Sergeyevich Turgenev (1818–1883), a Russian novelist.

[3] Giovanni Verga (1840–1922), an Italian novelist and playwright; Antonio Fogazzaro (1842–1911), an Italian novelist.

[4] Like the mimosa, a tropical tree or bush with sensitive yellow flowers.

[5] Sarah Orne Jewett (1849–1909), who wrote precise, subdued tales depicting life in her native South Berwick, Maine; Alice Brown (1857–1948), a New Hampshire author best known for her stories of New England.

religious ideal; the wish to be sincere, the wish to be just, the wish to be righteous are before the wish to be kind, merciful, humble. A people are not a chosen people for half a dozen generations without acquiring a spiritual pride that remains with them long after they cease to believe themselves chosen. They are often stiffened in the neck and they are often hardened in the heart by it, to the point of making them angular and cold; but they are of an inveterate responsibility to a power higher than themselves, and they are strengthened for any fate. They are what we see in the stories which, perhaps, hold the first place in American fiction.

As a matter of fact, the religion of New England is not now so Puritanical as that of many parts of the South and West, and yet the inherited Puritanism stamps the New England manner, and differences it from the manner of the straightest sects elsewhere. There was, however, always a revolt against Puritanism when Puritanism was severest and securest; this resulted in types of shiftlessness if not wickedness, which have not yet been duly studied, and which would make the fortune of some novelist who cared to do a fresh thing. There is also a sentimentality, or pseudo-emotionality (I have not the right phrase for it), which awaits full recognition in fiction. This efflorescence from the dust of systems and creeds, carried into natures left vacant by the ancestral doctrine, has scarcely been noticed by the painters of New England manners. It is often a last state of Unitarianism,[6] which prevailed in the larger towns and cities when the Calvinistic theology ceased to be dominant, and it is often an effect of the spiritualism so common in New England, and, in fact, everywhere in America. Then, there is a wide-spread love of literature in the country towns and villages which has in great measure replaced the old interest in dogma, and which forms with us an author's closest appreciation, if not his best. But as yet little hint of all this has got into the short stories, and still less of that larger intellectual life of New England, or that exalted beauty of character which tempts one to say that Puritanism was a blessing if it made the New-Englanders what they are; though one can always be glad not to have lived among them in the disciplinary period. Boston, the capital of that New England nation which is fast losing itself in the American nation, is no longer of its old literary primacy, and yet most of our right thinking, our high thinking, still begins there, and qualifies the thinking of the country at large. The good causes, the generous causes, are first befriended there, and in a wholesome sort the New England culture, as well as the New England conscience, has imparted itself to the American people.

Even the power of writing short stories, which we suppose ourselves to have in such excellent degree, has spread from New England. That is, indeed, the home of the American short story, and it has there been brought to such perfection in the work of Miss Wilkins, of Miss Jewett, of Miss Brown, and of that most faithful, forgotten painter of manners, Mrs. Rose Terry Cook,[7] that it presents upon the whole a truthful picture of New England village life in some of its more obvious

---

[6] A religious doctrine emphasizing liberal rationalism and opposing doctrines of orthodox Calvinism. Unitarianism combines rationalism with a modified supernaturalism, stressing practical Christianity and humanitarianism. Calvinism is based on teachings of John Calvin (1509–1564), a French Protestant who believed in humans' inherited corruption and subsequent loss of free will, in eternal punishment and vicarious atonement, and in the doctrine of predestination, in which only the "elect" (chosen) can be saved. In New England both Puritans and Pilgrims agreed with Calvinist theology.

[7] Cooke (1827–1892) was a Connecticut short-story writer and poet.

phases. I say obvious because I must, but I have already said that this is a life which is very little obvious; and I should not blame any one who brought the portrait to the test of reality, and found it exaggerated, overdrawn, and unnatural, though I should be perfectly sure that such a critic was wrong.

1898

Mother Courage

EDITHA*

The air was thick with the war[1] feeling, like the electricity of a storm which has not yet burst. Editha sat looking out into the hot spring afternoon, with her lips parted, and panting with the intensity of the question whether she could let him go. She had decided that she could not let him stay, when she saw him at the end of the still leafless avenue, making slowly up towards the house, with his head down and his figure relaxed. She ran impatiently out on the veranda, to the edge of the steps, and imperatively demanded greater haste of him with her will before she called aloud to him: "George!"

she makes up her mind for him.

He had quickened his pace in mystical response to her mystical urgence, before he could have heard her; now he looked up and answered. "Well?"

"Oh, how united we are!" she exulted, and then she swooped down the steps to him. "What is it?" she cried.

"It's war," he said, and he pulled her up to him and kissed her.

She kissed him back intensely, but irrelevantly, as to their passion, and uttered from deep in her throat, "How glorious!"

"It's war," he repeated, without consenting to her sense of it; and she did not know just what to think at first. She never knew what to think of him; that made his mystery, his charm. All through their courtship, which was contemporaneous with the growth of the war feeling, she had been puzzled by his want of seriousness about it. He seemed to despise it even more than he abhorred it. She could have understood his abhorring any sort of bloodshed; that would have been a survival of his old life when he thought he would be a minister, and before he changed and took up the law. But making light of a cause so high and noble seemed to show a want of earnestness at the core of his being. Not but that she felt herself able to cope with a congenital defect of that sort, and make his love for her save him from himself. Now perhaps the miracle was already wrought in him. In the presence of the tremendous fact that he announced, all triviality seemed to have gone out of him; she began to feel that. He sank down on the top step, and wiped his forehead with his handkerchief, while she poured out upon him her question of the origin and authenticity of his news.

All the while, in her duplex emotioning, she was aware that now at the very beginning she must put a guard upon herself against urging him, by any word or act, to take the part that her whole soul willed him to take, for the completion of her ideal of him. He was very nearly perfect as he was, and he must be allowed to perfect himself. But he was peculiar, and he might very well be reasoned out of

* First published in *Harper's Monthly* in 1905; appeared in book form in *Between the Dark and the Daylight: Romances* (1907).
[1] Just before the Spanish-American War in 1898.

his peculiarity. Before her reasoning went her emotioning: her nature pulling upon his nature, her womanhood upon his manhood, without her knowing the means she was using to the end she was willing. She had always supposed that the man who won her would have done something to win her; she did not know what, but something. George Gearson had simply asked her for her love, on the way home from a concert, and she gave her love to him, without, as it were, thinking. But now, it flashed upon her, if he could do something worthy to *have* won her—be a hero, *her* hero—it would be even better than if he had done it before asking her; it would be grander. Besides, she had believed in the war from the beginning. *but isn't it too late?*

"But don't you see, dearest," she said, "that it wouldn't have come to this if it hadn't been in the order of Providence? And I call any war glorious that is for the liberation of people who have been struggling for years against the cruelest oppression. Don't you think so, too?"

"I suppose so," he returned, languidly. "But war! Is it glorious to break the peace of the world?" *Their senses of honor are different.*

"That ignoble peace! It was no peace at all, with that crime and shame at our very gates." She was conscious of parroting the current phrases of the newspapers, but it was no time to pick and choose her words. She must sacrifice anything to the high ideal she had for him, and after a good deal of rapid argument she ended with the climax: "But now it doesn't matter about the how or why. Since the war has come, all that is gone. There are no two sides any more. There is nothing now but our country." *because she sacrificed herself to him already?*

He sat with his eyes closed and his head leant back against the veranda, and he remarked, with a vague smile, as if musing aloud, "Our country—right or wrong."[2]

"Yes, right or wrong!" she returned, fervidly. "I'll go and get you some lemonade." She rose rustling, and whisked away; when she came back with two tall glasses of clouded liquid on a tray, and the ice clunking in them, he still sat as she had left him, and she said, as if there had been no interruption: "But there is no question of wrong in this case. I call it a sacred war. A war for liberty and humanity, if ever there was one. And I know you will see it just as I do, yet."

He took half the lemonade at a gulp, and he answered as he set the glass down: "I know you always have the highest ideal. When I differ from you I ought to doubt myself."

A generous sob rose in Editha's throat for the humility of a man, so very nearly perfect, who was willing to put himself below her.

Besides, she felt, more subliminally, that he was never so near slipping through her fingers as when he took that meek way.

"You shall not say that! Only, for once I happen to be right." She seized his hand in her two hands, and poured her soul from her eyes into his. "Don't you think so?" she entreated him.

He released his hand and drank the rest of his lemonade, and she added, "Have mine, too," but he shook his head in answering, "I've no business to think so, unless I act so, too."

Her heart stopped a beat before it pulsed on with leaps that she felt in her neck. She had noticed that strange thing in men: they seemed to feel bound to do what

[2] A phrase coined in 1816 by the American naval hero Stephen Decatur (1779–1820); the modern equivalent is "America: love it or leave it."

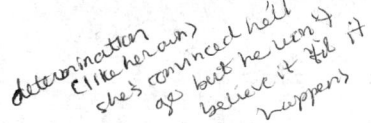

they believed, and not think a thing was finished when they said it, as girls did. She knew what was in his mind, but she pretended not, and she said, "Oh, I am not sure," and then faltered.

He went on as if to himself, without apparently heeding her: "There's only one way of proving one's faith in a thing like this."

She could not say that she understood, but she did understand.

He went on again. "If I believed—if I felt as you do about this war—Do you wish me to feel as you do?"

Now she was really not sure; so she said: "George, I don't know what you mean?"

He seemed to muse away from her as before. "There is a sort of fascination in it. I suppose that at the bottom of his heart every man would like at times to have his courage tested, to see how he would act."

"How can you talk in that ghastly way?"

"It *is* rather morbid. Still, that's what it comes to, unless you're swept away by ambition or driven by conviction. I haven't the conviction or the ambition, and the other thing is what it comes to with me. I ought to have been a preacher, after all; then I couldn't have asked it of myself, as I must now I'm a lawyer. And you believe it's a holy war, Editha?" he suddenly addressed her. "Oh, I know you do! But you wish me to believe so, too?"

She hardly knew whether he was mocking or not, in the ironical way he always had with her plainer mind. But the only thing was to be outspoken with him.

"George, I wish you to believe whatever you think is true, at any and every cost. If I've tried to talk you into anything, I take it all back."

"Oh, I know that, Editha. I know how sincere you are, and how—I wish I had your undoubting spirit! I'll think it over; I'd like to believe as you do. But I don't, now; I don't, indeed. It isn't this war alone; though this seems peculiarly wanton and needless; but it's every war—so stupid; it makes me sick. Why shouldn't this thing have been settled reasonably?"

"Because," she said, very throatily again, "God meant it to be war."

"You think it was God? Yes, I suppose that is what people will say."

"Do you suppose it would have been war if God hadn't meant it?"

"I don't know. Sometimes it seems as if God had put this world into men's keeping to work it as they pleased."

"Now, George, that is blasphemy."

"Well, I won't blaspheme. I'll try to believe in your pocket Providence," he said, and then he rose to go.

"Why don't you stay to dinner?" Dinner at Balcom's Works was at one o'clock.

"I'll come back to supper, if you'll let me. Perhaps I shall bring you a convert."

"Well, you may come back, on that condition."

"All right. If I don't come, you'll understand."

He went away without kissing her, and she felt it a suspension of their engagement. It all interested her intensely; she was undergoing a tremendous experience, and she was being equal to it. While she stood looking after him, her mother came out through one of the long windows onto the veranda, with a catlike softness and vagueness.

"Why didn't he stay to dinner?"

"Because—because—war has been declared," Editha pronounced, without turning.

Her mother said, "Oh, my!" and then said nothing more until she had sat down in one of the large Shaker chairs[3] and rocked herself for some time. Then she closed whatever tacit passage of thought there had been in her mind with the spoken words: "Well, I hope *he* won't go."

"And *I* hope he *will*," the girl said, and confronted her mother with a stormy exaltation that would have frightened any creature less unimpressionable than a cat.

Her mother rocked herself again for an interval of cogitation. What she arrived at in speech was: "Well, I guess you've done a wicked thing, Editha Balcom."

The girl said, as she passed indoors through the same window her mother had come out by: "I haven't done anything—yet."

In her room, she put together all her letters and gifts from Gearson, down to the withered petals of the first flower he had offered, with that timidity of his veiled in that irony of his. In the heart of the packet she enshrined her engagement ring which she had restored to the pretty box he had brought it her in. Then she sat down, if not calmly yet strongly, and wrote:

"GEORGE:—I understood when you left me. But I think we had better emphasize your meaning that if we cannot be one in everything we had better be one in nothing. So I am sending these things for your keeping till you have made up your mind.

"I shall always love you, and therefore I shall never marry any one else. But the man I marry must love his country first of all, and be able to say to me,

> "'I could not love thee, dear, so much,
> Loved I not honor more.'[4]

"There is no honor above America with me. In this great hour there is no other honor.

"Your heart will make my words clear to you. I had never expected to say so much, but it has come upon me that I must say the utmost.

EDITHA."

She thought she had worded her letter well, worded it in a way that could not be bettered; all had been implied and nothing expressed.

She had it ready to send with the packet she had tied with red, white, and blue ribbon, when it occurred to her that she was not just to him, that she was not giving him a fair chance. He had said he would go and think it over, and she was not waiting. She was pushing, threatening, compelling. That was not a woman's part. She must leave him free, free, free. She could not accept for her country or herself a forced sacrifice.

In writing her letter she had satisfied the impulse from which it sprang; she could well afford to wait till he had thought it over. She put the packet and the letter by, and rested serene in the consciousness of having done what was laid upon her by her love itself to do, and yet used patience, mercy, justice.

She had her reward. Gearson did not come to tea, but she had given him till

---

[3] Furniture made by the Shaker religious community, noted for its simplicity and lack of ornamentation.

[4] From "To Lucasta, Going to the Wars," by the English poet Richard Lovelace (1618–1658).

morning, when, late at night there came up from the village the sound of a fife and drum, with a tumult of voices, in shouting, singing, and laughing. The noise drew nearer and nearer; it reached the street end of the avenue; there it silenced itself, and one voice, the voice she knew best, rose over the silence. It fell; the air was filled with cheers; the fife and drum struck up, with the shouting, singing, and laughing again, but now retreating; and a single figure came hurrying up the avenue.

She ran down to meet her lover and clung to him. He was very gay, and he put his arm round her with a boisterous laugh. "Well, you must call me Captain now; or Cap, if you prefer; that's what the boys call me. Yes, we've had a meeting at the town-hall, and everybody has volunteered; and they selected me for captain, and I'm going to the war, the big war, the glorious war, the holy war ordained by the pocket Providence that blesses butchery. Come along; let's tell the whole family about it. Call them from their downy beds, father, mother, Aunt Hitty, and all the folks!"

But when they mounted the veranda steps he did not wait for a larger audience; he poured the story out upon Editha alone.

"There was a lot of speaking, and then some of the fools set up a shout for me. It was all going one way, and I thought it would be a good joke to sprinkle a little cold water on them. But you can't do that with a crowd that adores you. The first thing I knew I was sprinkling hell-fire on them. 'Cry havoc, and let slip the dogs of war.'[5] That was the style. Now that it had come to the fight, there were no two parties; there was one country, and the thing was to fight to a finish as quick as possible. I suggested volunteering then and there, and I wrote my name first of all on the roster. Then they elected me—that's all. I wish I had some ice-water."

She left him walking up and down the veranda, while she ran for the ice-pitcher and a goblet, and when she came back he was still walking up and down, shouting the story he had told her to her father and mother, who had come out more sketchily dressed than they commonly were by day. He drank goblet after goblet of the ice-water without noticing who was giving it, and kept on talking, and laughing through his talk wildly. "It's astonishing," he said, "how well the worse reason looks when you try to make it appear the better. Why, I believe I was the first convert to the war in that crowd to-night! I never thought I should like to kill a man; but now I shouldn't care; and the smokeless powder lets you see the man drop that you kill. It's all for the country! What a thing it is to have a country that *can't* be wrong, but if it is, is right, anyway!"

Editha had a great, vital thought, an inspiration. She set down the ice-pitcher on the veranda floor, and ran up-stairs and got the letter she had written him. When at last he noisily bade her father and mother, "Well, good-night. I forgot I woke you up; I sha'n't want any sleep myself," she followed him down the avenue to the gate. There, after the whirling words that seemed to fly away from her thoughts and refuse to serve them, she made a last effort to solemnize the moment that seemed so crazy, and pressed the letter she had written upon him.

"What's this?" he said. "Want me to mail it?"

"No, no. It's for you. I wrote it after you went this morning. Keep it—keep it—and read it sometime—" She thought, and then her inspiration came: "Read it if ever you doubt what you've done, or fear that I regret your having done it. Read it after you've started."

[5] From Shakespeare's *Julius Caesar* (III.i.273).

They strained each other in embraces that seemed as ineffective as their words, and he kissed her face with quick, hot breaths that were so unlike him, that made her feel as if she had lost her old lover and found a stranger in his place. The stranger said: "What a gorgeous flower you are, with your red hair, and your blue eyes that look black now, and your face with the color painted out by the white moonshine! Let me hold you under the chin, to see whether I love blood, you tiger-lily!" Then he laughed Gearson's laugh, and released her, scared and giddy. Within her wilfulness she had been frightened by a sense of subtler force in him, and mystically mastered as she had never been before.

[handwritten margin note: the metamorphosis that she had hoped for –]

She ran all the way back to the house, and mounted the steps panting. Her mother and father were talking of the great affair. Her mother said: "Wa'n't Mr. Gearson in rather of an excited state of mind? Didn't you think he acted curious?"

"Well, not for a man who'd just been elected captain and had set 'em up for the whole of Company A," her father chuckled back.

"What in the world do you mean, Mr. Balcom? Oh! There's Editha!" She offered to follow the girl indoors.

"Don't come, mother!" Editha called, vanishing.

Mrs. Balcom remained to reproach her husband. "I don't see much of anything to laugh at."

"Well, it's catching. Caught it from Gearson. I guess it won't be much of a war, and I guess Gearson don't think so, either. The other fellows will back down as soon as they see we mean it. I wouldn't lose any sleep over it. I'm going back to bed, myself."

Gearson came again next afternoon, looking pale and rather sick, but quite himself, even to his languid irony. "I guess I'd better tell you, Editha, that I consecrated myself to your god of battles last night by pouring too many libations to him down my own throat. But I'm all right now. One has to carry off the excitement, somehow."

[handwritten margin note: so much for the priesthood]

"Promise me," she commanded, "that you'll never touch it again!"

"What! Not let the cannikin[6] clink? Not let the soldier drink? Well, I promise."

"You don't belong to yourself now; you don't even belong to *me*. You belong to your country, and you have a sacred charge to keep yourself strong and well for your country's sake. I have been thinking, thinking all night and all day long."

"You look as if you had been crying a little, too," he said, with his queer smile.

"That's all past. I've been thinking, and worshipping *you*. Don't you suppose I know all that you've been through, to come to this? I've followed you every step from your old theories and opinions."

"Well, you've had a long row to hoe."

"And I know you've done this from the highest motives—"

"Oh, there won't be much pettifogging[7] to do till this cruel war is—"

"And you haven't simply done it for my sake. I couldn't respect you if you had."

"Well, then we'll say I haven't. A man that hasn't got his own respect intact wants the respect of all the other people he can corner. But we won't go into that. I'm in for the thing now, and we've got to face our future. My idea is that this isn't going to be a very protracted struggle; we shall just scare the enemy to death

---

[6] Cup; an allusion to Shakespeare's *Othello* (II.iii.71–75).

[7] Being unduly concerned with trivial matters.

before it comes to a fight at all. But we must provide for contingencies, Editha. If anything happens to me—"

"Oh, George!" She clung to him, sobbing.

"I don't want you to feel foolishly bound to my memory. I should hate that, wherever I happened to be."

"I am yours, for time and eternity—time and eternity." She liked the words; they satisfied her famine for phrases.

"Well, say eternity; that's all right; but time's another thing; and I'm talking about time. But there is something! My mother! If anything happens—"

She winced, and he laughed. "You're not the bold soldier-girl of yesterday!" Then he sobered. "If anything happens, I want you to help my mother out. She won't like my doing this thing. She brought me up to think war a fool thing as well as a bad thing. My father was in the Civil War; all through it; lost his arm in it." She thrilled with the sense of the arm round her; what if that should be lost? He laughed as if divining her: "Oh, it doesn't run in the family, as far as I know!" Then he added, gravely: "He came home with misgivings about war, and they grew on him. I guess he and mother agreed between them that I was to be brought up in his final mind about it; but that was before my time. I only knew him from my mother's report of him and his opinions; I don't know whether they were hers first; but they were hers last. This will be a blow to her. I shall have to write and tell her—"

He stopped, and she asked: "Would you like me to write, too, George?"

"I don't believe that would do. No, I'll do the writing. She'll understand a little if I say that I thought the way to minimize it was to make war on the largest possible scale at once—that I felt I must have been helping on the war somehow if I hadn't helped keep it from coming, and I knew I hadn't; when it came, I had no right to stay out of it."

Whether his sophistries[8] satisfied him or not, they satisfied her. She clung to his breast, and whispered, with closed eyes and quivering lips: "Yes, yes, yes!"

"But if anything should happen, you might go to her and see what you could do for her. You know? It's rather far off; she can't leave her chair—"

"Oh, I'll go, if it's the ends of the earth! But nothing will happen! Nothing *can!* I—"

She felt herself lifted with his rising, and Gearson was saying, with his arm still round her, to her father: "Well, we're off at once, Mr. Balcom. We're to be formally accepted at the capital, and then bunched up with the rest somehow, and sent into camp somewhere, and got to the front as soon as possible. We all want to be in the van,[9] of course; we're the first company to report to the Governor. I came to tell Editha, but I hadn't got round to it."

She saw him again for a moment at the capital, in the station, just before the train started southward with his regiment. He looked well, in his uniform, and very soldierly, but somehow girlish, too, with his clean-shaven face and slim figure. The manly eyes and the strong voice satisfied her, and his preoccupation with some unexpected details of duty flattered her. Other girls were weeping and bemoaning themselves, but she felt a sort of noble distinction in the abstraction, the almost unconsciousness, with which they parted. Only at the last moment he said:

---

[8] Reasonings that are subtly false, used here by George to cover up his misgivings about volunteering.

[9] Vanguard, the first division to go into battle.

"Don't forget my mother. It mayn't be such a walk-over as I supposed," and he laughed at the notion.

He waved his hand to her as the train moved off—she knew it among a score of hands that were waved to other girls from the platform of the car, for it held a letter which she knew was hers. Then he went inside the car to read it, doubtless, and she did not see him again. But she felt safe for him through the strength of what she called her love. What she called her God, always speaking the name in a deep voice and with the implication of a mutual understanding, would watch over him and keep him and bring him back to her. If with an empty sleeve, then he should have three arms instead of two, for both of hers should be his for life. She did not see, though, why she should always be thinking of the arm his father had lost.

There were not many letters from him, but they were such as she could have wished, and she put her whole strength into making hers such as she imagined he could have wished, glorifying and supporting him. She wrote to his mother glorifying him as their hero, but the brief answer she got was merely to the effect that Mrs. Gearson was not well enough to write herself, and thanking her for her letter by the hand of some one who called herself "Yrs truly, Mrs. W. J. Andrews."

Editha determined not to be hurt, but to write again quite as if the answer had been all she expected. Before it seemed as if she could have written, there came news of the first skirmish, and in the list of the killed, which was telegraphed as a trifling loss on our side, was Gearson's name. There was a frantic time of trying to make out that it might be, must be, some other Gearson; but the name and the company and the regiment and the State were too definitely given.

Then there was a lapse into depths out of which it seemed as if she never could rise again; then a lift into clouds far above all grief, black clouds, that blotted out the sun, but where she soared with him, with George—George! She had the fever that she expected of herself, but she did not die in it; she was not even delirious, and it did not last long. When she was well enough to leave her bed, her one thought was of George's mother, of his strangely worded wish that she should go to her and see what she could do for her. In the exaltation of the duty laid upon her—it buoyed her up instead of burdening her—she rapidly recovered.

Her father went with her on the long railroad journey from northern New York to western Iowa; he had business out at Davenport, and he said he could just as well go then as any other time; and he went with her to the little country town where George's mother lived in a little house on the edge of the illimitable cornfields, under trees pushed to a top of the rolling prairie. George's father had settled there after the Civil War, as so many other old soldiers had done; but they were Eastern people, and Editha fancied touches of the East in the June rose overhanging the front door, and the garden with early summer flowers stretching from the gate of the paling fence.

It was very low inside the house, and so dim, with the closed blinds, that they could scarcely see one another: Editha tall and black in her crapes[10] which filled the air with the smell of their dyes; her father standing decorously apart with his hat on his forearm, as at funerals; a woman rested in a deep arm-chair, and the woman who had let the strangers in stood behind the chair.

---

[10] Thin, crinkled fabrics; Victorian women wore black clothing to signify their mourning over a death. Because they could not buy ready-to-wear clothes, they had to dye the clothes they already had.

The seated woman turned her head round and up, and asked the woman behind the chair: "*Who* did you say?"

Editha, if she had done what she expected of herself, would have gone down on her knees at the feet of the seated figure and said, "I am George's Editha," for answer.

But instead of her own voice she heard that other woman's voice, saying: "Well, I don't know as I *did* get the name just right. I guess I'll have to make a little more light in here," and she went and pushed two of the shutters ajar.

Then Editha's father said, in his public will-now-address-a-few-remarks tone: "My name is Balcom, ma'am—Junius H. Balcom, of Balcom's Works, New York; my daughter—"

"Oh!" the seated woman broke in, with a powerful voice, the voice that always surprised Editha from Gearson's slender frame. "Let me see you. Stand round where the light can strike on your face," and Editha dumbly obeyed. "So, you're Editha Balcom," she sighed.

"Yes," Editha said, more like a culprit than a comforter.

"What did you come for?" Mrs. Gearson asked.

Editha's face quivered and her knees shook. "I came—because—because George—" She could go no further.

"Yes," the mother said, "he told me he had asked you to come if he got killed. You didn't expect that, I suppose, when you sent him."

"I would rather have died myself than done it!" Editha said, with more truth in her deep voice than she ordinarily found in it. "I tried to leave him free—"

"Yes, that letter of yours, that came back with his other things, left him free."

Editha saw now where George's irony came from.

"It was not to be read before—unless—until— I told him so," she faltered.

"Of course, he wouldn't read a letter of yours, under the circumstances, till he thought you wanted him to. Been sick?" the woman abruptly demanded.

"Very sick," Editha said, with self-pity.

"Daughter's life," her father interposed, "was almost despaired of, at one time."

Mrs. Gearson gave him no heed. "I suppose you would have been glad to die, such a brave person as you! I don't believe *he* was glad to die. He was always a timid boy, that way; he was afraid of a good many things; but if he was afraid he did what he made up his mind to. I suppose he made up his mind to go, but I knew what it cost him by what it cost me when I heard of it. I had been through *one* war before. When you sent him you didn't expect he would get killed."

The voice seemed to compassionate Editha, and it was time. "No," she huskily murmured.

"No, girls don't; women don't, when they give their men up to their country. They think they'll come marching back, somehow, just as gay as they went, or if it's an empty sleeve, or even an empty pantaloon, it's all the more glory, and they're so much the prouder of them, poor things!"

The tears began to run down Editha's face; she had not wept till then; but it was now such a relief to be understood that the tears came.

"No, you didn't expect him to get killed," Mrs. Gearson repeated, in a voice which was startlingly like George's again. "You just expected him to kill some one else, some of those foreigners, that weren't there because they had any say about it, but because they had to be there, poor wretches—conscripts, or whatever they call 'em. You thought it would be all right for my George, *your* George, to kill the sons of those miserable mothers and the husbands of those girls that you would never see the faces of." The woman lifted her powerful voice in a psalmlike note. "I thank my God he didn't live to do it! I thank my God they killed him first, and that he ain't livin' with their blood on his hands!" She dropped her eyes, which she had raised with her voice, and glared at Editha. "What you got that black on for?" She lifted herself by her powerful arms so high that her helpless body seemed to hang limp its full length. "Take it off, take it off, before I tear it from your back!"

The lady who was passing the summer near Balcom's Works was sketching Editha's beauty, which lent itself wonderfully to the effects of a colorist. It had come to that confidence which is rather apt to grow between artist and sitter, and Editha had told her everything.

"To think of your having such a tragedy in your life!" the lady said. She added: "I suppose there are people who feel that way about war. But when you consider the good this war has done—how much it has done for the country! I can't understand such people, for my part. And when you had come all the way out there to console her—got up out of a sick-bed! Well!"

"I think," Editha said, magnanimously, "she wasn't quite in her right mind; and so did papa."

"Yes," the lady said, looking at Editha's lips in nature and then at her lips in art, and giving an empirical touch to them in the picture. "But how dreadful of her! How perfectly—excuse me—how *vulgar!*"

A light broke upon Editha in the darkness which she felt had been without a gleam of brightness for weeks and months. The mystery that had bewildered her was solved by the word; and from that moment she rose from grovelling in shame and self-pity, and began to live again in the ideal.

Doesn't learn her lesson in the end.

1905

Stephen Crane
(1871–1900)

When he published *Maggie: A Girl of the Streets* under the pseudonym Johnston Smith in 1893, Stephen Crane was twenty-one years old. Contemporaries could not have known that this young writer had less than a decade to live, nor would they have guessed that during his brief career he would complete several novels and novellas, numerous short stories and sketches, and two volumes of poetry. In the 1890s, however, Crane's importance as a writer came to be recognized by such colleagues as Joseph Conrad, Hamlin Garland, William Dean Howells, and Henry James.

Crane, the fourteenth child of Methodist minister Jonathan Townley Crane and social activist Mary Helen Peck, was born in 1871 in Newark, New Jersey. The family moved several times and settled in Port Jervis, New York, when Crane was seven. While his father was pastor of Drew Methodist Church at Port Jervis, young Stephen led a vigorous, out-of-doors life, spending hours on foot and on horseback in nearby Sullivan County. He eventually turned his experiences among the forests and hills of this area into his discerning sketches of Sullivan County and its inhabitants. In 1888 Crane attended a military academy, Claverack College in New York, and became a cadet captain before leaving school in 1890. That same year he enrolled as an engineering student in Lafayette College in Pennsylvania for one term, then—restless and ever more intent on becoming a writer—transferred to Syracuse University, where he worked as a correspondent for the New York *Tribune,* wrote some of his early stories, and earned a varsity letter playing baseball.

In 1891 Crane moved to New York City and began to work as a freelance writer for the *Tribune.* Living in New York gave him the opportunity to observe life in the slums, and Crane was quick to turn these observations into frank depictions, fictional and nonfictional, of the brutal and typically short lives of slum dwellers. With its stark, ironic portrayal of life and death among residents of New York City's Bowery, *Maggie* stands as one of the earliest works of American naturalism. Crane later published other works dealing with New York tenement life, among them the novel *George's Mother* (1896) and stories that deal unflinchingly with sex, violence, and the bleak cycle of poverty. But Crane did not believe that vice was confined to the back lots and dirty apartments of Rum Alley and Devil's Row. In *The Monster* (1899) he explores an even more insidious form of human cruelty as the people of a small town ostracize a disfigured African-American servant and his protector, whose child the servant had rescued from a fire.

If Crane's career as a novelist began with *Maggie,* it reached its apex with *The Red Badge of Courage* (1895), the ironic and measured account of a young man's responses to battle in the Civil War. His career now firmly established with this narrative of a war he had never seen, Crane worked as a war correspondent first in Greece and then in Cuba during the Spanish-American War. During this time he lived a life as dangerous as those lived by many of his characters. Running guns to Cuba in winter 1896–1897, Crane and three other men underwent the ordeal related in "The Open Boat" (1897) and "Stephen Crane's Own Story" (1897). In writing about war experiences Crane was unsparing in his depiction of the mechanized horror of death by shelling and rifle volley.

Crane occasionally tempered his stark vision of life in the slums or on the battlefield with lighter, humorous pieces such as some of the Sullivan County sketches or "The Bride Comes to Yellow Sky" (1898). He had an eye for unusual settings or characters, from the embarrassed marshall in "Yellow Sky" to the edgy, snowbound guests of "The Blue Hotel" (1898), who elicit the tragic fate they fear. During the last years of his life he traveled extensively to Mexico, the West, Ireland, and England, always alert for material with the potential for his distinctive treatment. In England he met the novelist Joseph Conrad, who became Crane's close friend. Crane's physical constitution could not ultimately match the energy he spent in maintaining his prodigious literary output. In 1898, while covering the Puerto Rico campaign of the Spanish-American War for the New York *Journal,* Crane fell ill with fever and returned to recuperate in America. He was suffering, however, from a more serious illness, tuberculosis. Stricken with the disease, he continued to write, completing several books during the last year and a half of his life. Knowing that he might not live to finish his novel *The O'Ruddy* (1903), Crane arranged for Robert Barr, an editor and novelist, to complete it according to Crane's notes. Crane died of tuberculosis in a sanitarium at Badenweiler, Germany, in 1900, half a year into the new century whose dark events seemed prophesied by the tone of his fiction.

Although both of his parents were active in church affairs and social reforms, Crane did not share their unbending faith in a universe ordered by God's Providence, as the recurrent themes of his work demonstrate. His characters suffer and die generally without a sense of purpose or even the knowledge of the correspondent in "The Open Boat," who comes to

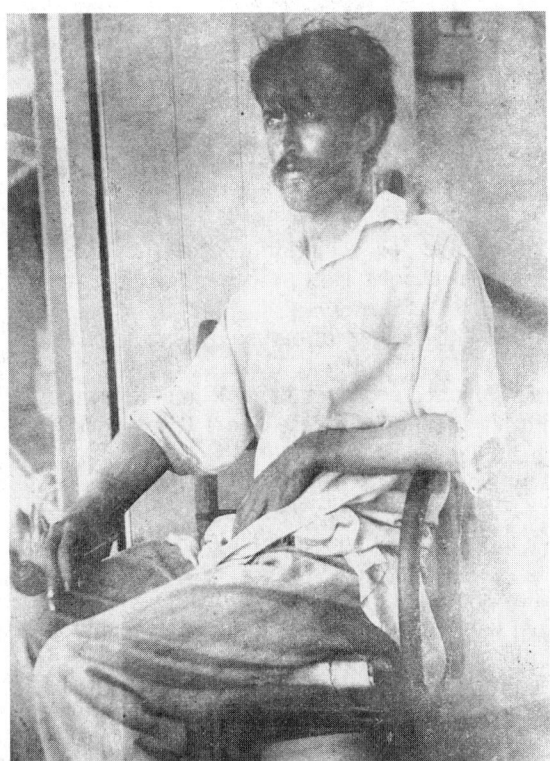

Stephen Crane after the sinking of the Commodore, *the basis for "The Open Boat": the frontispiece in Crane's* Tales of Adventure.

recognize that nature is "indifferent, flatly indifferent," to the struggles of human beings. Much of Crane's poetry addresses similar concerns in caustic parables that appeal for ultimate meaning but end in mockery and existential confusion. Some poems, too (chief among them "Do not weep maiden, for war is kind" [1896]), enact the pervasive irony of Crane's work with a distilled bitterness. Whether writing of the chance events that determine the fate of men in an open boat or that lead to cowardice and heroism on the battlefield, Crane left a unique naturalist legacy of style and substance to twentieth-century readers. If Frank Norris directs our attention to threatening primitive instincts within "civilized" human beings, if Theodore Dreiser focuses on individuals with (as he says) their "tremendous urges" and "pathetic equipment," Crane treats us to the spectacle of the universe as cosmic joke—grim, freighted with irony, unintelligible to its victims.

Suggested Readings: *Stephen Crane: Letters*, ed. R. W. Stallman and L. Gilkes, 1960. *The Poems of Stephen Crane: A Critical Edition*, ed. J. Katz, 1966. *The Works of Stephen Crane*, 10 vols., ed. F. Bowers, 1969–1975. J. Berryman, *Stephen Crane*, 1950, rpt. 1980. D. Hoffman, *The Poetry of Stephen Crane*, 1956. E. Solomon, *Stephen Crane: From Parody to Realism*, 1966. D. Gibson, *The Fiction of Stephen Crane*, 1968. R. W. Stallman, *Stephen Crane: A Biography*, 1968. M. Holton, *Cylinder of Vision: The Fiction and Journalistic Writing of Stephen Crane*, 1972. F. Bergon, *Stephen Crane's Artistry*, 1975. E. H. Cady, *Stephen Crane*, 1980. J. Nagel, *Stephen Crane and Literary Impressionism*, 1980. D. Halliburton, *The Color of the Sky: A Study of Stephen Crane*, 1989.

Texts Used: *Maggie: The Works of Stephen Crane: Bowery Tales*, Vol. I, 1969. "Stephen Crane's Own Story": *The Works: Reports of War*, Vol. IX, 1971. "The Open Boat" and "The Bride Comes to Yellow Sky": *The Works: Tales of Adventure*, Vol. V, 1970. "An Illusion in Red and White": *The Works: Tales, Sketches, and Reports*, Vol. VIII, 1973. Poems: *The Works: Poems and Literary Remains*, Vol. X, 1975.

MAGGIE*

A Girl of the Streets

CHAPTER I

A very little boy stood upon a heap of gravel for the honor of Rum Alley. He was throwing stones at howling urchins from Devil's Row who were circling madly about the heap and pelting him.

His infantile countenance was livid with the fury of battle. His small body was writhing in the delivery of oaths.

"Run, Jimmie, run! Dey'll git yehs!" screamed a retreating Rum Alley child.

"Naw," responded Jimmie with a valiant roar, "dese micks[1] can't make me run."

Howls of renewed wrath went up from Devil's Row throats. Tattered gamins[2] on the right made a furious assault on the gravel heap. On their small, convulsed faces shone the grins of true assassins. As they charged, they threw stones and cursed in shrill chorus.

The little champion of Rum Alley stumbled precipitately down the other side. His coat had been torn to shreds in a scuffle, and his hat was gone. He had bruises on twenty parts of his body, and blood was dripping from a cut in his head. His wan features looked like those of a tiny, insane demon.

On the ground, children from Devil's Row closed in on their antagonist. He crooked his left arm defensively about his head and fought with madness. The little boys ran to and fro, dodging, hurling stones and swearing in barbaric trebles.

From a window of an apartment house that uprose from amid squat, ignorant stables, there leaned a curious woman. Some laborers, unloading a scow at a dock at the river,[3] paused for a moment and regarded the fight. The engineer of a passive tugboat hung lazily over a railing and watched. Over on the Island,[4] a worm of yellow convicts came from the shadow of a grey ominous building and crawled slowly along the river's bank.

A stone had smashed in Jimmie's mouth. Blood was bubbling over his chin and down upon his ragged shirt. Tears made furrows on his dirt-stained cheeks. His thin legs had begun to tremble and turn weak, causing his small body to reel. His roaring curses of the first part of the fight had changed to a blasphemous chatter.

In the yells of the whirling mob of Devil's Row children there were notes of joy like songs of triumphant savagery. The little boys seemed to leer gloatingly at the blood upon the other child's face.

Down the avenue came boastfully sauntering a lad of sixteen years, although

---

* First published in a private edition in 1893 under the pseudonym "Johnston Smith," then in a revised edition (with Crane's real name) in 1896.

[1] Slang for the Irish.

[2] Street kids, urchins. *Maggie* opens with children fighting, then moves to the domestic violence of the Johnson household in Ch. II.

[3] The East River, between Brooklyn and Manhattan.

[4] Blackwell's Island in the East River (now called Roosevelt Island), where prisons and poorhouses were located.

the chronic sneer of an ideal manhood already sat upon his lips. His hat was tipped over his eye with an air of challenge. Between his teeth, a cigar stump was tilted at the angle of defiance. He walked with a certain swing of the shoulders which appalled the timid. He glanced over into the vacant lot in which the little raving boys from Devil's Row seethed about the shrieking and tearful child from Rum Alley.

"Gee!" he murmured with interest. "A scrap. Gee!"

He strode over to the cursing circle, swinging his shoulders in a manner which denoted that he held victory in his fists. He approached at the back of one of the most deeply engaged of the Devil's Row children.

"Ah, what d' hell," he said, and smote the deeply-engaged one on the back of the head. The little boy fell to the ground and gave a tremendous howl. He scrambled to his feet, and perceiving, evidently, the size of his assailant, ran quickly off, shouting alarms. The entire Devil's Row party followed him. They came to a stand a short distance away and yelled taunting oaths at the boy with the chronic sneer. The latter, momentarily, paid no attention to them.

"What d' hell, Jimmie?" he asked of the small champion.

Jimmie wiped his blood-wet features with his sleeve.

"Well, it was dis way, Pete, see! I was goin' t' lick dat Riley kid and dey all pitched on me."

Some Rum Alley children now came forward. The party stood for a moment exchanging vainglorious remarks with Devil's Row. A few stones were thrown at long distances, and words of challenge passed between small warriors. Then the Rum Alley contingent turned slowly in the direction of their home street. They began to give, each to each, distorted versions of the fight. Causes of retreat in particular cases were magnified. Blows dealt in the fight were enlarged to catapultian power, and stones thrown were alleged to have hurtled with infinite accuracy. Valor grew strong again, and the little boys began to brag with great spirit.

"Ah, we blokies⁵ kin lick d' hull damn Row," said a child, swaggering.

Little Jimmie was striving to stanch the flow of blood from his cut lips. Scowling, he turned upon the speaker.

"Ah, where d' hell was yehs when I was doin' all d' fightin'?" he demanded. "Youse kids makes me tired."

"Ah, go ahn," replied the other argumentatively.

Jimmie replied with heavy contempt. "Ah, youse can't fight, Blue Billie! I kin lick yeh wid one han'."

"Ah, go ahn," replied Billie again.

"Ah," said Jimmie threateningly.

"Ah," said the other in the same tone.

They struck at each other, clinched, and rolled over on the cobble stones.

"Smash 'im, Jimmie, kick d' damn guts out of 'im," yelled Pete, the lad with the chronic sneer, in tones of delight.

The small combatants pounded and kicked, scratched and tore. They began to weep and their curses struggled in their throats with sobs. The other little boys clasped their hands and wriggled their legs in excitement. They formed a bobbing circle about the pair.

A tiny spectator was suddenly agitated.

⁵ Blokes, guys. The expressions in the dialogue of *Maggie* come from the slang of the 1890s.

"Cheese it, Jimmie, cheese it! Here comes yer fader," he yelled.

The circle of little boys instantly parted. They drew away and waited in ecstatic awe for that which was about to happen. The two little boys fighting in the modes of four thousand years ago, did not hear the warning.

Up the avenue there plodded slowly a man with sullen eyes. He was carrying a dinner-pail and smoking an apple-wood pipe.

As he neared the spot where the little boys strove, he regarded them listlessly. But suddenly he roared an oath and advanced upon the rolling fighters.

"Here, you Jim, git up, now, while I belt yer life out, yeh damned disorderly brat."

He began to kick into the chaotic mass on the ground. The boy Billie felt a heavy boot strike his head. He made a furious effort and disentangled himself from Jimmie. He tottered away, damning.

Jimmie arose painfully from the ground and confronting his father, began to curse him. His parent kicked him. "Come home, now," he cried, "an' stop yer jawin', er I'll lam[6] the everlasting head off yehs."

They departed. The man paced placidly along with the apple-wood emblem of serenity between his teeth. The boy followed a dozen feet in the rear. He swore luridly, for he felt that it was degradation for one who aimed to be some vague kind of a soldier, or a man of blood with a sort of sublime license, to be taken home by a father.

Chapter II

Eventually they entered into a dark region where, from a careening building, a dozen gruesome doorways gave up loads of babies to the street and gutter. A wind of early autumn raised yellow dust from cobbles and swirled it against an hundred windows. Long streamers of garments fluttered from fire-escapes. In all unhandy places there were buckets, brooms, rags and bottles. In the street infants played or fought with other infants or sat stupidly in the way of vehicles. Formidable women, with uncombed hair and disordered dress, gossiped while leaning on railings, or screamed in frantic quarrels. Withered persons, in curious postures of submission to something, sat smoking pipes in obscure corners. A thousand odors of cooking food came forth to the street. The building quivered and creaked from the weight of humanity stamping about in its bowels.

A small ragged girl dragged a red, bawling infant along the crowded ways. He was hanging back, baby-like, bracing his wrinkled, bare legs.

The little girl cried out: "Ah, Tommie, come ahn. Dere's Jimmie and fader. Don't be a-pullin' me back."

She jerked the baby's arm impatiently. He fell on his face, roaring. With a second jerk she pulled him to his feet, and they went on. With the obstinacy of his order, he protested against being dragged in a chosen direction. He made heroic endeavors to keep on his legs, denounced his sister and consumed a bit of orange peeling which he chewed between the times of his infantile orations.

As the sullen-eyed man, followed by the blood-covered boy, drew near, the little girl burst into reproachful cries. "Ah, Jimmie, youse bin fightin' agin."

---

[6] Beat, pound.

The urchin swelled disdainfully.

"Ah, what d' hell, Mag. See?"

The little girl upbraided him. "Youse allus fightin', Jimmie, an' yeh knows it puts mudder out when yehs come home half dead, an' it's like we'll all get a poundin'."

She began to weep. The babe threw back his head and roared at his prospects.

"Ah, what d' hell!" cried Jimmie. "Shut up er I'll smack yer mout'. See?"

As his sister continued her lamentations, he suddenly struck her. The little girl reeled and, recovering herself, burst into tears and quaveringly cursed him. As she slowly retreated her brother advanced dealing her cuffs. The father heard and turned about. *(save it for inside)*

"Stop that, Jim, d'yeh hear? <u>Leave yer sister alone on the street</u>. It's like I can never beat any sense into yer damned wooden head."

The urchin raised his voice in defiance to his parent and continued his attacks. The babe bawled tremendously, protesting with great violence. During his sister's hasty manœuvres, he was dragged by the arm.

Finally the procession plunged into one of the gruesome doorways. They crawled up dark stairways and along cold, gloomy halls. At last the father pushed open a door and they entered a lighted room in which a large woman was rampant.

She stopped in a career from a seething stove to a pan-covered table. As the father and children filed in she peered at them.

"Eh, what? Been fightin' agin, by Gawd!" She threw herself upon Jimmie. The urchin tried to dart behind the others and in the scuffle the babe, Tommie, was knocked down. He protested with his usual vehemence, because they had bruised his tender shins against a table leg.

The mother's massive shoulders heaved with anger. Grasping the urchin by the neck and shoulder she shook him until he rattled. She dragged him to an unholy sink, and, soaking a rag in water, began to scrub his lacerated face with it. Jimmie screamed in pain and tried to twist his shoulders out of the clasp of the huge arms.

The babe sat on the floor watching the scene, his face in contortions like that of a woman at a tragedy. The father, with a newly-ladened pipe in his mouth, sat in a backless chair near the stove. Jimmie's cries annoyed him. He turned about and bellowed at his wife:

"Let the damned kid alone for a minute, will yeh, Mary? Yer allus poundin' 'im. When I come nights I can't git no rest 'cause yer allus poundin' a kid. Let up, d'yeh hear? Don't be allus poundin' a kid."

The woman's operations on the urchin instantly increased in violence. At last she tossed him to a corner where he limply lay weeping.

The wife put her immense hands on her hips, and with a chieftain-like stride approached her husband.

"Ho," she said, with a great grunt of contempt. "An' what in the devil are you stickin' your nose for?"

The babe crawled under the table and, turning, peered out cautiously. The ragged girl retreated and the urchin in the corner drew his legs carefully beneath him.

The man puffed his pipe calmly and put his great muddied boots on the back part of the stove.

"Go t' hell," he said tranquilly.

The woman screamed and shook her fists before her husband's eyes. The rough yellow of her face and neck flared suddenly crimson. She began to howl.

He puffed imperturbably at his pipe for a time, but finally arose and went to look out at the window into the darkening chaos of back yards.

"You've been drinkin', Mary," he said. "You'd better let up on the bot', ol' woman, or you'll git done."

"You're a liar. I ain't had a drop," she roared in reply. They had a lurid altercation, in which they damned each other's souls with frequence.

The babe was staring out from under the table, his small face working in his excitement. The ragged girl went stealthily over to the corner where the urchin lay.

"Are yehs hurted much, Jimmie?" she whispered timidly.

"Not a damn bit! See?" growled the little boy.

"Will I wash d' blood?"

"Naw!"

"Will I—"

"When I catch dat Riley kid I'll break 'is face! Dat's right! See?"

He turned his face to the wall as if resolved to grimly bide his time.

In the quarrel between husband and wife, the woman was victor. The man seized his hat and rushed from the room, apparently determined upon a vengeful drunk. She followed to the door and thundered at him as he made his way down stairs.

She returned and stirred up the room until her children were bobbing about like bubbles.

"Git outa d' way," she persistently bawled, waving feet with their dishevelled shoes near the heads of her children. She shrouded herself, puffing and snorting, in a cloud of steam at the stove, and eventually extracted a frying-pan full of potatoes that hissed.

She flourished it. "Come t' yer suppers, now," she cried with sudden exasperation. "Hurry up, now, er I'll help yeh!"

The children scrambled hastily. With prodigious clatter they arranged themselves at table. The babe sat with his feet dangling high from a precarious infant chair and gorged his small stomach. Jimmie forced, with feverish rapidity, the grease-enveloped pieces between his wounded lips. Maggie, with side glances of fear of interruption, ate like a small pursued tigress.

The mother sat blinking at them. She delivered reproaches, swallowed potatoes and drank from a yellow-brown bottle. After a time her mood changed and she wept as she carried little Tommie into another room and laid him to sleep, with his fists doubled, in an old quilt of faded red and green grandeur. Then she came and moaned by the stove. She rocked to and fro upon a chair, shedding tears and crooning miserably to the two children about their "poor mother" and "yer fader, damn 'is soul."

The little girl plodded between the table and the chair with a dish-pan on it. She tottered on her small legs beneath burdens of dishes.

Jimmie sat nursing his various wounds. He cast furtive glances at his mother. His practised eye perceived her gradually emerge from a muddled mist of sentiment until her brain burned in drunken heat. He sat breathless.

Maggie broke a plate.

The mother started to her feet as if propelled.

"Good Gawd," she howled. Her glittering eyes fastened on her child with sudden hatred. The fervent red of her face turned almost to purple. The little boy ran to the halls, shrieking like a monk in an earthquake.

He floundered about in darkness until he found the stairs. He stumbled, panic-stricken, to the next floor. An old woman opened a door. A light behind her threw a flare on the urchin's face.

"Eh, Gawd, child, what is it dis time? Is yer fader beatin' yer mudder, or yer mudder beatin' yer fader?"

CHAPTER III

Jimmie and the old woman listened long in the hall. Above the muffled roar of conversation, the dismal wailings of babies at night, the thumping of feet in unseen corridors and rooms, and the sound of varied hoarse shoutings in the street and the rattling of wheels over cobbles, they heard the screams of the child and the roars of the mother die away to a feeble moaning and a subdued bass muttering.

The old woman was a gnarled and leathery personage who could don, at will, an expression of great virtue. She possessed a small music box capable of one tune, and a collection of "God bless yehs" pitched in assorted keys of fervency. Each day she took a position upon the stones of Fifth Avenue,[7] where she crooked her legs under her and crouched immovable and hideous, like an idol. She received daily a small sum in pennies. It was contributed, for the most part, by persons[8] who did not make their homes in that vicinity.

Once, when a lady had dropped her purse on the sidewalk, the gnarled woman had grabbed it and smuggled it with great dexterity beneath her cloak. When she was arrested she had cursed the lady into a partial swoon, and with her aged limbs, twisted from rheumatism, had almost kicked the stomach out of a huge policeman whose conduct upon that occasion she referred to when she said, "The police, damn 'em!"

"Eh, Jimmie, it's cursed shame," she said. "Go, now, like a dear an' buy me a can,[9] an' if yer mudder raises 'ell all night yehs can sleep here."

Jimmie took a tendered tin-pail and seven pennies and departed. He passed into the side door of a saloon and went to the bar. Straining up on his toes he raised the pail and pennies as high as his arms would let him. He saw two hands thrust down to take them. Directly the same hands let down the filled pail and he left.

In front of the gruesome doorway he met a lurching figure. It was his father, swaying about on uncertain legs.

"Give me d' can. See?" said the man.

"Ah, come off! I got dis can fer dat ol' woman an' it 'ud be dirt t' swipe it. See?" cried Jimmie.

The father wrenched the pail from the urchin. He grasped it in both hands and lifted it to his mouth. He glued his lips to the under edge and tilted his head. His throat swelled until it seemed to grow near his chin. There was a tremendous gulping movement and the beer was gone.

The man caught his breath and laughed. He hit his son on the head with the empty pail. As it rolled clanging into the street, Jimmie began to scream and kicked repeatedly at his father's shins.

---

[7] A fashionable street in New York City.

[8] Probably visitors to New York, the implication being that New Yorkers know a fake or are unmoved by pitiful sights.

[9] A canister or pail of beer; such a beer pail generally held two quarts.

"Look at d' dirt what yeh done me," he yelled. "D' ol' woman 'ill be raisin' hell."

He retreated to the middle of the street, but the man did not pursue. He staggered toward the door.

"I'll club hell outa yeh when I ketch yeh," he shouted, and disappeared.

During the evening he had been standing against a bar drinking whiskies and declaring to all comers, confidentially: "My home reg'lar livin' hell! Damndes' place! Reg'lar hell! Why do I come an' drin' whisk' here thish way? 'Cause home reg'lar livin' hell!"

Jimmie waited a long time in the street and then crept warily up through the building. He passed with great caution the door of the gnarled woman, and finally stopped outside his home and listened.

He could hear his mother moving heavily about among the furniture of the room. She was chanting in a mournful voice, occasionally interjecting bursts of volcanic wrath at the father, who, Jimmie judged, had sunk down on the floor or in a corner.

"Why d' blazes don' chere try t' keep Jim from fightin? I'll break yer jaw," she suddenly bellowed.

The man mumbled with drunken indifference. "Ah, wha' d' hell. W'a's odds? Wha' makes kick?"

"Because he tears 'is clothes, yeh damn fool," cried the woman in supreme wrath.

The husband seemed to become aroused. "Go t' hell," he thundered fiercely in reply. There was a crash against the door and something broke into clattering fragments. Jimmie partially suppressed a yell and darted down the stairway. Below he paused and listened. He heard howls and curses, groans and shrieks—a confused chorus as if a battle were raging. With it all there was the crash of splintering furniture. The eyes of the urchin glared in his fear that one of them would discover him.

Curious faces appeared in doorways, and whispered comments passed to and fro. "Ol' Johnson's raisin' hell agin."

Jimmie stood until the noises ceased and the other inhabitants of the tenement had all yawned and shut their doors. Then he crawled up stairs with the caution of an invader of a panther den. Sounds of labored breathing came through the broken door-panels. He pushed the door open and entered, quaking.

A glow from the fire threw red hues over the bare floor, the cracked and soiled plastering, and the overturned and broken furniture.

In the middle of the floor lay his mother asleep. In one corner of the room his father's limp body hung across the seat of a chair.

The urchin stole forward. He began to shiver in dread of awakening his parents. His mother's great chest was heaving painfully. Jimmie paused and looked down at her. Her face was inflamed and swollen from drinking. Her yellow brows shaded eye-lids that had grown blue. Her tangled hair tossed in waves over her forehead. Her mouth was set in the same lines of vindictive hatred that it had, perhaps, borne during the fight. Her bare, red arms were thrown out above her head in an attitude of exhaustion, something, mayhap, like that of a sated villain.

The urchin bended over his mother. He was fearful lest she should open her eyes, and the dread within him was so stong, that he could not forbear to stare, but hung as if fascinated over the woman's grim face.

Suddenly her eyes opened. The urchin found himself looking straight into an expression, which, it would seem, had the power to change his blood to salt. He howled piercingly and fell backward.

The woman floundered for a moment, tossed her arms about her head as if in combat, and again began to snore.

Jimmie crawled back into the shadows and waited. A noise in the next room had followed his cry at the discovery that his mother was awake. He grovelled in the gloom, his eyes riveted upon the intervening door.

He heard it creak, and then the sound of a small voice came to him. "Jimmie! Jimmie! Are yehs dere?" it whispered. The urchin started. The thin, white face of his sister looked at him from the doorway of the other room. She crept to him across the floor.

The father had not moved, but lay in the same death-like sleep. The mother writhed in uneasy slumber, her chest wheezing as if she were in the agonies of strangulation. Out at the window a florid moon was peering over dark roofs, and in the distance the waters of a river glimmered pallidly.

The small frame of the ragged girl was quivering. Her features were haggard from weeping, and her eyes gleamed with fear. She grasped the urchin's arm in her little trembling hands and they huddled in a corner. The eyes of both were drawn, by some force, to stare at the woman's face, for they thought she need only to awake and all the fiends would come from below.

They crouched until the ghost-mists of dawn appeared at the window, drawing close to the panes, and looking in at the prostrate, heaving body of the mother.

CHAPTER IV

The babe, Tommie, died. He went away in an insignificant coffin, his small waxen hand clutching a flower that the girl, Maggie, had stolen from an Italian.

She and Jimmie lived.

The inexperienced fibres of the boy's eyes were hardened at an early age. He became a young man of leather. He lived some red years without laboring. During that time his sneer became chronic. He studied human nature in the gutter, and found it no worse than he thought he had reason to believe it. He never conceived a respect for the world, because he had begun with no idols that it had smashed.

He clad his soul in armor by means of happening hilariously in at a mission church where a man composed his sermons of "you's." Once a philosopher asked this man why he did not say "we" instead of "you." The man replied, "What!"

While they got warm at the stove, he told his hearers just where he calculated they stood with the Lord. Many of the sinners were impatient over the pictured depths of their degradation. They were waiting for soup-tickets.

A reader of words of wind-demons might have been able to see the portions of a dialogue pass to and fro between the exhorter and his hearers.

"You are damned," said the preacher. And the reader of sounds might have seen the reply go forth from the ragged people: "Where's our soup?"

Jimmie and a companion sat in a rear seat and commented upon the things that didn't concern them, with all the freedom of English tourists. When they grew thirsty and went out their minds confused the speaker with Christ.

Momentarily, Jimmie was sullen with thoughts of a hopeless altitude where grew fruit. His companion said that if he should ever meet God he would ask for a million dollars and a bottle of beer.

Jimmie's occupation for a long time was to stand on street-corners and watch the world go by, dreaming blood-red dreams at the passing of pretty women. He menaced mankind at the intersections of streets.

On the corners he was in life and of life. The world was going on and he was there to perceive it.

He maintained a belligerent attitude toward all well-dressed men. To him fine raiment was allied to weakness, and all good coats covered faint hearts. He and his order were kings, to a certain extent, over the men of untarnished clothes, because these latter dreaded, perhaps, to be either killed or laughed at.

Above all things he despised obvious Christians and ciphers with the chrysanthemums of aristocracy in their button-holes. He considered himself above both of these classes. He was afraid of nothing.

When he had a dollar in his pocket his satisfaction with existence was the greatest thing in the world. So, eventually, he felt obliged to work. His father died and his mother's years were divided up into periods of thirty days.

He became a truck driver. There was given to him the charge of a pains-taking pair of horses and a large rattling truck. He invaded the turmoil and tumble of the down-town streets and learned to breathe maledictory defiance at the police who occasionally used to climb up, drag him from his perch and punch him.

In the lower part of the city he daily involved himself in hideous tangles. If he and his team chanced to be in the rear he preserved a demeanor of serenity, crossing his legs and bursting forth into yells when foot passengers took dangerous dives beneath the noses of his champing horses. He smoked his pipe calmly for he knew that his pay was marching on.

If his charge was in the front and if it became the key-truck of chaos, he entered terrifically into the quarrel that was raging to and fro among the drivers on their high seats, and sometimes roared oaths and violently got himself arrested.

After a time his sneer grew so that it turned its glare upon all things. He became so sharp that he believed in nothing. To him the police were always actuated by malignant impulses and the rest of the world was composed, for the most part, of despicable creatures who were all trying to take advantage of him and with whom, in defense, he was obliged to quarrel on all possible occasions. He himself occupied a down-trodden position which had a private but distinct element of grandeur in its isolation.

The greatest cases of aggravated idiocy were, to his mind, rampant upon the front platforms of all of the street cars. At first his tongue strove with these beings, but he eventually became superior. In him grew a majestic contempt for those strings of street cars that followed him like intent bugs.

He fell into the habit, when starting on a long journey, of fixing his eye on a high and distant object, commanding his horses to start and then going into a trance of observation. Multitudes of drivers might howl in his rear, and passengers might load him with opprobrium, but he would not awaken until some blue policeman turned red and began to frenziedly seize bridles and beat the soft noses of the responsible horses.

When he paused to contemplate the attitude of the police toward himself and his fellows, he believed that they were the only men in the city who had no rights. When driving about, he felt that he was held liable by the police for anything that might occur in the streets, and that he was the common prey of all energetic officials. In revenge, he resolved never to move out of the way of anything, until formidable circumstances, or a much larger man than himself forced him to it.

Foot passengers were mere pestering flies with an insane disregard for their legs and his convenience. He could not comprehend their desire to cross the streets. Their madness smote him with eternal amazement. He was continually storming at them from his throne. He sat aloft and denounced their frantic leaps, plunges, dives and straddles.

When they would thrust at, or parry, the noses of his champing horses, making them swing their heads and move their feet, and thus disturbing a stolid dreamy repose, he swore at the men as fools, for he himself could perceive that Providence had caused it clearly to be written, that he and his team had the unalienable right to stand in the proper path of the sun chariot, and if they so minded, obstruct its mission or take a wheel off.

And if the god-driver had had a desire to step down, put up his flame-colored fists and manfully dispute the right of way, he would have probably been immediately opposed by a scowling mortal with two sets of hard knuckles.

It is possible, perhaps, that this young man would have derided, in an axle-wide alley, the approach of a flying ferry boat. Yet he achieved a respect for a fire engine. As one charged toward his truck, he would drive fearfully upon a sidewalk, threatening untold people with annihilation. When an engine struck a mass of blocked trucks, splitting it into fragments, as a blow annihilates a cake of ice, Jimmie's team could usually be observed high and safe, with whole wheels, on the sidewalk. The fearful coming of the engine could break up the most intricate muddle of heavy vehicles at which the police had been swearing for the half of an hour.

A fire engine was enshrined in his heart as an appalling thing that he loved with a distant dog-like devotion. It had been known to overturn a street car. Those leaping horses, striking sparks from the cobbles in their forward lunge, were creatures to be ineffably admired. The clang of the gong pierced his breast like a noise of remembered war.

When Jimmie was a little boy, he began to be arrested. Before he reached a great age, he had a fair record.

He developed too great a tendency to climb down from his truck and fight with other drivers. He had been in quite a number of miscellaneous fights, and in some general barroom rows that had become known to the police. Once he had been arrested for assaulting a Chinaman. Two women in different parts of the city, and entirely unknown to each other, caused him considerable annoyance by breaking forth, simultaneously, at fateful intervals, into wailings about marriage and support and infants.

Nevertheless, he had, on a certain star-lit evening, said wonderingly and quite reverently: "D' moon looks like hell, don't it?"

CHAPTER V

The girl, Maggie, blossomed in a mud puddle. She grew to be a most rare and wonderful production of a tenement district, a pretty girl.

None of the dirt of Rum Alley seemed to be in her veins. The philosophers up stairs, down stairs and on the same floor, puzzled over it.

When a child, playing and fighting with gamins in the street, dirt disguised her. Attired in tatters and grime, she went unseen.

There came a time, however, when the young men of the vicinity, said: "Dat Johnson goil is a puty good looker." About this period her brother remarked to her: "Mag, I'll tell yeh dis! See? Yeh've edder got t' go t' hell er go t' work!" Whereupon she went to work, having the feminine aversion of going to hell.

By a chance, she got a position in an establishment where they made collars and cuffs. She received a stool and a machine in a room where sat twenty girls of various shades of yellow discontent.[10] She perched on the stool and treadled at her machine all day, turning out collars with a name which might have been noted for its irrelevancy to anything connected with collars. At night she returned home to her mother.

Jimmie grew large enough to take the vague position of head of the family. As incumbent of that office, he stumbled up stairs late at night, as his father had done before him. He reeled about the room, swearing at his relations, or went to sleep on the floor.

The mother had gradually arisen to such a degree of fame that she could bandy words with her acquaintances among the police-justices. Court-officials called her by her first name. When she appeared they pursued a course which had been theirs for months. They invariably grinned and cried out: "Hello, Mary, you here again?" Her grey head wagged in many courts. She always besieged the bench with voluble excuses, explanations, apologies and prayers. Her flaming face and rolling eyes were a familiar sight on the Island.[11] She measured time by means of sprees, and was eternally swollen and dishevelled.

One day the young man, Pete, who as a lad had smitten the Devil's Row urchin in the back of the head and put to flight the antagonists of his friend, Jimmie, strutted upon the scene. He met Jimmie one day on the street, promised to take him to a boxing match in Williamsburg,[12] and called for him in the evening.

Maggie observed Pete.

He sat on a table in the Johnson home and dangled his checked legs with an enticing nonchalance. His hair was curled down over his forehead in an oiled bang. His pugged nose seemed to revolt from contact with a bristling moustache of short, wire-like hairs. His blue double-breasted coat, edged with black braid, was buttoned close to a red puff tie, and his patent-leather shoes looked like weapons.

His mannerisms stamped him as a man who had a correct sense of his personal superiority. There was valor and contempt for circumstances in the glance of his eye. He waved his hands like a man of the world, who dismisses religion and philosophy, and says "Rats!" He had certainly seen everything and with each curl of his lip, he declared that it amounted to nothing. Maggie thought he must be a very "elegant" bartender.

He was telling tales to Jimmie.

Maggie watched him furtively, with half-closed eyes, lit with a vague interest.

"Hully gee! Dey makes me tired," he said, "Mos' e'ry day some farmer[13] comes in an' tries t' run d' shop. See? But dey gits t'rowed right out! I jolt dem right out in d' street before dey knows where dey is! See?"

---

[10] An example of Crane's impressionistic style in the midst of a naturalistic story that emphasizes the effect of environment in the characters' lives.

[11] In the prison on Blackwell's Island.   [12] A section of Brooklyn.   [13] Yokel, clown.

"Sure," said Jimmie.

"Dere was a mug come in d' place d' odder day wid an idear he wus goin' t' own d' place! Hully gee, he wus goin' t' own d' place! I see he had a still on[14] an' I didn' wanna giv 'im no stuff, so I says: 'Git d' hell outa here an' don' make no trouble,' I says like dat! See? 'Git d' hell outa here an' don' make no trouble'; like dat. 'Git d' hell outa here,' I says. See?"

Jimmie nodded understandingly. Over his features played an eager desire to state the amount of his valor in a similar crisis, but the narrator proceeded.

"Well, d' blokie he says: 'T' hell wid it! I ain' lookin' for no scrap,' he says— see? 'But,' he says, 'I'm 'spectable cit'zen an' I wanna drink an' purtydamnsoon, too.' See? 'D' hell,' I says. Like dat! 'D' hell,' I says. See? 'Don' make no trouble,' I says. Like dat. 'Don' make no trouble.' See? Den d' mug he squared off an' said he was fine as silk wid his dukes—see? An' he wanned a drink damnquick. Dat's what he said. See?"

"Sure," repeated Jimmie.

Pete continued. "Say, I jes' jumped d' bar an' d' way I plunked[15] dat blokie was outa sight. See? Dat's right! In d' jaw! See? Hully gee, he t'rowed a spittoon t'ru d' front windee. Say, I t'aut I'd drop dead. But d' boss, he comes in after an' he says, 'Pete, yehs done jes' right! Yeh've gota keep order an' it's all right.' See? 'It's all right,' he says. Dat's what he said."

The two held a technical discussion.

"Dat bloke was a dandy," said Pete, in conclusion, "but he hadn' oughta made no trouble. Dat's what I says t' dem: 'Don' come in here an' make no trouble,' I says, like dat. 'Don' make no trouble.' See?"

As Jimmie and his friend exchanged tales descriptive of their prowess, Maggie leaned back in the shadow. Her eyes dwelt wonderingly and rather wistfully upon Pete's face. The broken furniture, grimy walls, and general disorder and dirt of her home of a sudden appeared before her and began to take a potential aspect. Pete's aristocratic person looked as if it might soil. She looked keenly at him, occasionally, wondering if he was feeling contempt. But Pete seemed to be enveloped in reminiscence.

"Hully gee," said he, "dose mugs can't phase me. Dey knows I kin wipe up d' street wid any t'ree of dem."

When he said, "Ah, what d' hell!" his voice was burdened with disdain for the inevitable and contempt for anything that fate might compel him to endure.

Maggie perceived that here was the ideal man. Her dim thoughts were often searching for far away lands where, as God says, the little hills sing together in the morning. Under the trees of her dream-gardens there had always walked a lover.

CHAPTER VI

Pete took note of Maggie.

"Say, Mag, I'm stuck on yer shape. It's outa sight," he said, parenthetically, with an affable grin.

As he became aware that she was listening closely, he grew still more eloquent in his descriptions of various happenings in his career. It appeared that he was invincible in fights.

---

[14] He was drunk as a skunk.   [15] Hit.

"Why," he said, referring to a man with whom he had had a misunderstanding, "dat mug scrapped like a damned dago.[16] Dat's right. He was dead easy. See? He t'aut he was a scrapper! But he foun' out diff'ent! Hully gee."

He walked to and fro in the small room, which seemed then to grow even smaller and unfit to hold his dignity, the attribute of a supreme warrior. That swing of the shoulders which had frozen the timid when he was but a lad had increased with his growth and education at the ratio of ten to one. It, combined with the sneer upon his mouth, told mankind that there was nothing in space which could appall him. Maggie marvelled at him and surrounded him with greatness. She vaguely tried to calculate the altitude of the pinnacle from which he must have looked down upon her.

"I met a chump d' odder day way up in d' city," he said, "I was goin' t' see a frien' of mine. When I was a-crossin' d' street d' chump runned plump inteh me, an' den he turns aroun' an' says, 'Yer insolen' ruffin,' he says, like dat. 'Oh, gee,' I says, 'oh, gee, go t' hell an' git off d' eart'!' I says, like dat. See? 'Go t' hell an' git off d' eart',' like dat. Den d' blokie he got wild. He says I was a contempt'ble scoun'el, er somethin' like dat, an' he says I was doom' t' everlastin' pe'dition, er somethin' like dat. 'Gee,' I says, 'gee! D' hell I am,' I says. 'D' hell I am,' like dat. An' den I slugged 'im. See?"

With Jimmie in his company, Pete departed in a sort of a blaze of glory from the Johnson home. Maggie, leaning from the window, watched him as he walked down the street.

Here was a formidable man who disdained the strength of a world full of fists. Here was one who had contempt for brass-clothed power; one whose knuckles could defiantly ring against the granite of law. He was a knight.

The two men went from under the glimmering street-lamp and passed into shadows.

Turning, Maggie contemplated the dark, dust-stained walls, and the scant and crude furniture of her home. A clock, in a splintered and battered oblong box of varnished wood, she suddenly regarded as an abomination. She noted that it ticked raspingly. The almost vanished flowers in the carpet-pattern, she conceived to be newly hideous. Some faint attempts which she had made with blue ribbon, to freshen the appearance of a dingy curtain, she now saw to be piteous.

She wondered what Pete dined on.

She reflected upon the collar and cuff factory. It began to appear to her mind as a dreary place of endless grinding. Pete's elegant occupation brought him, no doubt, into contact with people who had money and manners. It was probable that he had a large acquaintance of pretty girls. He must have great sums of money to spend.

To her the earth was composed of hardships and insults. She felt instant admiration for a man who openly defied it. She thought that if the grim angel of death should clutch his heart, Pete would shrug his shoulders and say, "Oh, ev'ryt'ing goes."

She anticipated that he would come again shortly. She spent some of her week's pay in the purchase of flowered cretonne for a lambrequin.[17] She made it with infinite care and hung it to the slightly-careening mantel, over the stove, in the kitchen. She studied it with painful anxiety from different points in the room.

---

[16] Slang for an Italian: derogatory.   [17] A heavy curtain fabric for a drapery.

She wanted it to look well on Sunday night when, perhaps, Jimmie's friend would come. On Sunday night, however, Pete did not appear.

Afterward the girl looked at it with a sense of humiliation. She was now convinced that Pete was superior to admiration for lambrequins.

A few evenings later Pete entered with fascinating innovations in his apparel. As she had seen him twice and he wore a different suit each time, Maggie had a dim impression that his wardrobe was prodigious.

"Say, Mag," he said, "put on yer bes' duds Friday night an' I'll take yehs t' d' show. See?"

He spent a few moments in flourishing his clothes and then vanished, without having glanced at the lambrequin.

Over the eternal collars and cuffs in the factory Maggie spent the most of three days in making imaginary sketches of Pete and his daily environment. She imagined some half dozen women in love with him and thought he must lean dangerously toward an indefinite one, whom she pictured as endowed with great charms of person, but with an altogether contemptible disposition.

She thought he must live in a blare of pleasure. He had friends, and people who were afraid of him.

She saw the golden glitter of the place where Pete was to take her. It would be an entertainment of many hues and many melodies where she was afraid she might appear small and mouse-colored.

Her mother drank whiskey all Friday morning. With lurid face and tossing hair she cursed and destroyed furniture all Friday afternoon. When Maggie came home at half-past six her mother lay asleep amidst the wreck of chairs and a table. Fragments of various household utensils were scattered about the floor. She had vented some phase of drunken fury upon the lambrequin. It lay in a bedraggled heap in the corner.

"Hah," she snorted, sitting up suddenly, "where d' hell yeh been? Why d' hell don' yeh come home earlier? Been loafin' 'round d' streets. Yer gettin' t' be a reg'lar devil."

When Pete arrived Maggie, in a worn black dress, was waiting for him in the midst of a floor strewn with wreckage. The curtain at the window had been pulled by a heavy hand and hung by one tack, dangling to and fro in the draft through the cracks at the sash. The knots of blue ribbons appeared like violated flowers. The fire in the stove had gone out. The displaced lids and open doors showed heaps of sullen grey ashes. The remnants of a meal, ghastly, lay in a corner. Maggie's mother, stretched on the floor, blasphemed and gave her daughter a bad name.

CHAPTER VII

An orchestra of yellow silk women and bald-headed men on an elevated stage near the centre of a great green-hued hall, played a popular waltz. The place was crowded with people grouped about little tables. A battalion of waiters slid among the throng, carrying trays of beer glasses and making change from the inexhaustible vaults of their trousers pockets. Little boys, in the costumes of French chefs, paraded up and down the irregular aisles vending fancy cakes. There was a low rumble of conversation and a subdued clinking of glasses. Clouds of tobacco smoke rolled and wavered high in air about the dull gilt of the chandeliers.

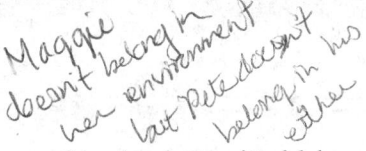

The vast crowd had an air throughout of having just quitted labor. Men with calloused hands and attired in garments that showed the wear of an endless drudging for a living, smoked their pipes contentedly and spent five, ten, or perhaps fifteen cents for beer. There was a mere sprinkling of men who smoked cigars purchased elsewhere. The great body of the crowd was composed of people who showed that all day they strove with their hands. Quiet Germans, with maybe their wives and two or three children, sat listening to the music, with the expressions of happy cows. An occasional party of sailors from a war-ship, their faces pictures of sturdy health, spent the earlier hours of the evening at the small round tables. Very infrequent tipsy men, swollen with the value of their opinions, engaged their companions in earnest and confidential conversation. In the balcony, and here and there below, shone the impassive faces of women. The nationalities of the Bowery[18] beamed upon the stage from all directions.

Pete aggressively walked up a side aisle and took seats with Maggie at a table beneath the balcony.

"Two beehs!"

Leaning back he regarded with eyes of superiority the scene before them. This attitude affected Maggie strongly. A man who could regard such a sight with indifference must be accustomed to very great things.

It was obvious that Pete had visited this place many times before, and was very familiar with it. A knowledge of this fact made Maggie feel little and new.

He was extremely gracious and attentive. He displayed the consideration of a cultured gentleman who knew what was due.

"Say, what d' hell? Bring d' lady a big glass! What d' hell use is dat pony?"[19]

"Don't be fresh, now," said the waiter, with some warmth, as he departed.

"Ah, git off d' eart'," said Pete, after the other's retreating form.

Maggie perceived that Pete brought forth all his elegance and all his knowledge of high-class customs for her benefit. Her heart warmed as she reflected upon his condescension.

The orchestra of yellow silk women and bald-headed men gave vent to a few bars of anticipatory music and a girl, in a pink dress with short skirts, galloped upon the stage. She smiled upon the throng as if in acknowledgment of a warm welcome, and began to walk to and fro, making profuse gesticulations and singing, in brazen soprano tones, a song, the words of which were inaudible. When she broke into the swift rattling measures of a chorus some half-tipsy men near the stage joined in the rollicking refrain and glasses were pounded rhythmically upon the tables. People leaned forward to watch her and to try to catch the words of the song. When she vanished there were long rollings of applause.

Obedient to more anticipatory bars, she reappeared amidst the half-suppressed cheering of the tipsy men. The orchestra plunged into dance music and the laces of the dancer fluttered and flew in the glare of gas jets. She divulged the fact that she was attired in some half dozen skirts. It was patent that any one of them would have proved adequate for the purpose for which skirts are intended. An occasional man bent forward, intent upon the pink stockings. Maggie wondered at the splendor of the costume and lost herself in calculations of the cost of the silks and laces.

The dancer's smile of enthusiasm was turned for ten minutes upon the faces of her audience. In the finale she fell into some of those grotesque attitudes which

---

[18] A slum area on Manhattan's Lower East Side, where a number of Crane's stories are set.

[19] A small glass that holds about six ounces.

were at the time popular among the dancers in the theatres up-town, giving to the Bowery public the diversions of the aristocratic theatre-going public, at reduced rates.

"Say, Pete," said Maggie, leaning forward, "dis is great."

"Sure," said Pete, with proper complacence.

A ventriloquist followed the dancer. He held two fantastic dolls on his knees. He made them sing mournful ditties and say funny things about geography and Ireland.

"Do dose little men talk?" asked Maggie.

"Naw," said Pete, "it's some damn fake. See?"

Two girls, set down on the bills[20] as sisters, came forth and sang a duet which is heard occasionally at concerts given under church auspices. They supplemented it with a dance which of course can never be seen at concerts given under church auspices.

After they had retired, a woman of debatable age sang a negro melody. The chorus necessitated some grotesque waddlings supposed to be an imitation of a plantation darkey, under the influence, probably, of music and the moon. The audience was just enthusiastic enough over it to have her return and sing a sorrowful lay,[21] whose lines told of a mother's love, and a sweetheart who waited and a young man who was lost at sea under harrowing circumstances. From the faces of a score or so in the crowd, the self-contained look faded. Many heads were bent forward with eagerness and sympathy. As the last distressing sentiment of the piece was brought forth, it was greeted by the kind of applause which rings as sincere.

As a final effort, the singer rendered some verses which described a vision of Britain annihilated by America, and Ireland bursting her bonds. A carefully prepared climax was reached in the last line of the last verse, when the singer threw out her arms and cried, "The star-spangled banner." Instantly a great cheer swelled from the throats of this assemblage of the masses, most of them of foreign birth. There was a heavy rumble of booted feet thumping the floor. Eyes gleamed with sudden fire, and calloused hands waved frantically in the air.

After a few moments' rest, the orchestra played noisily, and a small fat man burst out upon the stage. He began to roar a song and stamp back and forth before the foot-lights, wildly waving a silk hat and throwing leers broadcast. He made his face into fantastic grimaces until he looked like a devil on a Japanese kite. The crowd laughed gleefully. His short, fat legs were never still a moment. He shouted and roared and bobbed his shock of red wig until the audience broke out in excited applause.

Pete did not pay much attention to the progress of events upon the stage. He was drinking beer and watching Maggie.

Her cheeks were blushing with excitement and her eyes were glistening. She drew deep breaths of pleasure. No thoughts of the atmosphere of the collar and cuff factory came to her.

With the final crash of the orchestra they jostled their way to the sidewalk in the crowd. Pete took Maggie's arm and pushed a way for her, offering to fight with a man or two. They reached Maggie's home at a late hour and stood for a moment in front of the gruesome doorway.

"Say, Mag," said Pete, "give us a kiss for takin' yeh t' d' show, will yer?"

[20] Small billboards that advertise the acts.   [21] A song, ballad.

Maggie laughed, as if startled, and drew away from him.

"Naw, Pete," she said, "dat wasn't in it."

"Ah, what d' hell?" urged Pete.

The girl retreated nervously.

"Ah, what d' hell?" repeated he.

Maggie darted into the hall, and up the stairs. She turned and smiled at him, then disappeared.

Pete walked slowly down the street. He had something of an astonished expression upon his features. He paused under a lamp-post and breathed a low breath of surprise.

"Gawd," he said, "I wonner if I've been played fer a duffer."

CHAPTER VIII

As thoughts of Pete came to Maggie's mind, she began to have an intense dislike for all of her dresses.

"What d'hell ails yeh? What makes yeh be allus fixin' and fussin'? Good Gawd," her mother would frequently roar at her.

She began to note, with more interest, the well-dressed women she met on the avenues. She envied elegance and soft palms. She craved those adornments of person which she saw every day on the street, conceiving them to be allies of vast importance to women.

Studying faces, she thought many of the women and girls she chanced to meet, smiled with serenity as though forever cherished and watched over by those they loved.

The air in the collar and cuff establishment strangled her. She knew she was gradually and surely shriveling in the hot, stuffy room. The begrimed windows rattled incessantly from the passing of elevated trains. The place was filled with a whirl of noises and odors.

She became lost in thought as she looked at some of the grizzled women in the room, mere mechanical contrivances sewing seams and grinding out, with heads bended over their work, tales of imagined or real girl-hood happiness, or of past drunks, or the baby at home, and unpaid wages. She wondered how long her youth would endure. She began to see the bloom upon her cheeks as something of value.

She imagined herself, in an exasperating future, as a scrawny woman with an eterenal grievance. She thought Pete to be a very fastidious person concerning the appearance of women.

She felt that she should love to see somebody entangle their fingers in the oily beard of the fat foreigner who owned the establishment. He was a detestable creature. He wore white socks with low shoes.[22] He sat all day delivering orations, in the depths of a cushioned chair. His pocketbook deprived them of the power of retort.

"When een hell do you sink I pie fife dolla a week for? Play? No, py tamn!"

Maggie was anxious for a friend to whom she could talk about Pete. She would have liked to discuss his admirable mannerisms with a reliable mutual friend. At

---

[22] Low-cut shoes were then unfashionable for men; in some circles the white socks (with such shoes) would emphasize the man's lack of taste.

home, she found her mother often drunk and always raving. It seemed that the world had treated this woman very badly, and she took a deep revenge upon such portions of it as came within her reach. She broke furniture as if she were at last *Chopin* getting her rights. She swelled with virtuous indignation as she carried the lighter *(Edna)* articles of household use, one by one, under the shadows of the three gilt balls,[23] where Hebrews chained them with chains of interest.

Jimmie came when he was obliged to by circumstances over which he had no control. His well-trained legs brought him staggering home and put him to bed some nights when he would rather have gone elsewhere.

Swaggering Pete loomed like a golden sun to Maggie. He took her to a dime museum where rows of meek freaks astonished her. She contemplated their deformities with awe and thought them a sort of chosen tribe.

Pete, racking his brains for amusement, discovered the Central Park Menagerie and Museum of Arts.[24] Sunday afternoons would sometimes find them at these places. Pete did not appear to be particularly interested in what he saw. He stood around looking heavy, while Maggie giggled in glee.

Once at the Menagerie he went into a trance of admiration before the spectacle of a very small monkey threatening to thrash a cageful because one of them had pulled his tail and he had not wheeled about quickly enough to discover who did it. Ever after Pete knew that monkey by sight and winked at him, trying to induce him to fight with other and larger monkeys.

At the Museum, Maggie said, "Dis is outa sight."

"Oh hell," said Pete, "wait till next summer an' I'll take yehs to a picnic."

While the girl wandered in the vaulted rooms, Pete occupied himself in returning stony stare for stony stare, the appalling scrutiny of the watch-dogs of the treasures. Occasionally he would remark in loud tones: "Dat jay[25] has got glass eyes," and sentences of the sort. When he tired of this amusement he would go to the mummies and moralize over them.

Usually he submitted with silent dignity to all that he had to go through, but, at times, he was goaded into comment.

"What d' hell," he demanded once. "Look at all dese little jugs! Hundred jugs in a row! Ten rows in a case an' 'bout a t'ousand cases! What d' blazes use is dem?"

In the evenings of week days he often took her to see plays in which the dazzling heroine was rescued from the palatial home of her treacherous guardian by the hero with the beautiful sentiments. The latter spent most of his time out at soak[26] in pale-green snow storms, busy with a nickel-plated revolver, rescuing aged strangers from villains.

Maggie lost herself in sympathy with the wanderers swooning in snow storms beneath happy-hued church windows, while a choir within sang "Joy to the World." To Maggie and the rest of the audience this was transcendental realism. Joy always within, and they, like the actor, inevitably without. Viewing it, they hugged themselves in ecstatic pity of their imagined or real condition.

The girl thought the arrogance and granite-heartedness of the magnate of the play was very accurately drawn. She echoed the maledictions that the occupants of

---

[23] The traditional sign for a pawnshop, as a striped pole is for a barbershop.
[24] The Central Park Zoo and the Metropolitan Museum of Art.   [25] Bird, from "jaybird."
[26] Getting wet. Crane parodies popular melodramas here.

the gallery showed on this individual when his lines compelled him to expose his extreme selfishness.

Shady persons in the audience revolted from the pictured villainy of the drama. With untiring zeal they hissed vice and applauded virtue. Unmistakably bad men evinced an apparently sincere admiration for virtue. The loud gallery was overwhelmingly with the unfortunate and the oppressed. They encouraged the struggling hero with cries, and jeered the villain, hooting and calling attention to his whiskers. When anybody died in the pale-green snow storms, the gallery mourned. They sought out the painted misery and hugged it as akin.

In the hero's erratic march from poverty in the first act, to wealth and triumph in the final one, in which he forgives all the enemies that he has left, he was assisted by the gallery, which applauded his generous and noble sentiments and confounded the speeches of his opponents by making irrelevant but very sharp remarks. Those actors who were cursed with the parts of villains were confronted at every turn by the gallery. If one of them rendered lines containing the most subtle distinctions between right and wrong, the gallery was immediately aware that the actor meant wickedness, and denounced him accordingly.

The last act was a triumph for the hero, poor and of the masses, the representative of the audience, over the villain and the rich man, his pockets stuffed with bonds, his heart packed with tyrannical purposes, imperturbable amid suffering.

Maggie always departed with raised spirits from these melodramas. She rejoiced at the way in which the poor and virtuous eventually overcame the wealthy and wicked. The theatre made her think. She wondered if the culture and refinement she had seen imitated, perhaps grotesquely, by the heroine on the stage, could be acquired by a girl who lived in a tenement house and worked in a shirt factory.

Chapter IX

A group of urchins were intent upon the side door of a saloon. Expectancy gleamed from their eyes. They were twisting their fingers in excitement.

"Here she comes," yelled one of them suddenly.

The group of urchins burst instantly asunder and its individual fragments were spread in a wide, respectable half-circle about the point of interest. The saloon door opened with a crash, and the figure of a woman appeared upon the threshold. Her grey hair fell in knotted masses about her shoulders. Her face was crimsoned and wet with perspiration. Her eyes had a rolling glare.

"Not a damn cent more of me money will yehs ever get—not a damn cent. I spent me money here fer t'ree years an' now yehs tells me yeh'll sell me no more stuff! T' hell wid yeh, Johnnie Murckre! 'Disturbance?' Disturbance be damned! T' hell wid yeh, Johnnie———"

The door received a kick of exasperation from within and the woman lurched heavily out on the sidewalk.

The gamins in the half-circle became violently agitated. They began to dance about and hoot and yell and jeer. Wide dirty grins spread over each face.

The woman made a furious dash at a particularly outrageous cluster of little boys. They laughed delightedly and scampered off a short distance, calling out over their shoulders to her. She stood tottering on the curb-stone and thundered at them.

"Yeh devil's kids," she howled, shaking her fists. The little boys whooped in glee. As she started up the street they fell in behind and marched uproariously. Occasionally she wheeled about and made charges on them. They ran nimbly out of reach and taunted her.

In the frame of a gruesome doorway she stood for a moment cursing them. Her hair straggled, giving her red features a look of insanity. Her great fists quivered as she shook them madly in the air.

The urchins made terrific noises until she turned and disappeared. Then they filed off quietly in the way they had come.

The woman floundered about in the lower hall of the tenement house and finally stumbled up the stairs. On an upper hall a door was opened and a collection of heads peered curiously out, watching her. With a wrathful snort the woman confronted the door, but it was slammed hastily in her face and the key was turned.

She stood for a few minutes, delivering a frenzied challenge at the panels.

"Come out in d' hall, Mary Murphy, damn yeh, if yehs want a scrap. Come ahn, yeh overgrown terrier, come ahn."

She began to kick the door. She shrilly defied the universe to appear and do battle. Her cursing trebles brought heads from all doors save the one she threatened. Her eyes glared in every direction. The air was full of her tossing fists.

"Come ahn, d' hull damn gang of yehs, come ahn," she roared at the spectators. An oath or two, cat-calls, jeers and bits of facetious advice were given in reply. Missiles clattered about her feet.

"What d' hell's d' matter wid yeh?" said a voice in the gathered gloom, and Jimmie came forward. He carried a tin dinner-pail in his hand and under his arm a truckman's brown apron done in a bundle. "What d' hell's wrong?" he demanded.

"Come out, all of yehs, come out," his mother was howling. "Come ahn an' I'll stamp yer damn brains under me feet."

"Shet yer face, an' come home, yeh damned old fool," roared Jimmie at her. She strided up to him and twirled her fingers in his face. Her eyes were darting flames of unreasoning rage and her frame trembled with eagerness for a fight.

"T' hell wid yehs! An' who d' hell are yehs? I ain't givin' a snap of me fingers fer yehs," she bawled at him. She turned her huge back in tremendous disdain and climbed the stairs to the next floor.

Jimmie followed, cursing blackly. At the top of the flight he seized his mother's arm and started to drag her toward the door of their room.

"Come home, damn yeh," he gritted between his teeth.

"Take yer hands off me! Take yer hands off me!" shrieked his mother.

She raised her arm and whirled her great fist at her son's face. Jimmie dodged his head and the blow struck him in the back of the neck. "Damn yeh," he gritted again. He threw out his left hand and writhed his fingers about her middle arm. The mother and the son began to sway and struggle like gladiators.

"Whoop!" said the Rum Alley tenement house. The hall filled with interested spectators.

"Hi, ol' lady, dat was a dandy!"

"T'ree t' one on d' red!"

"Ah, quit yer damn scrappin'!"

The door of the Johnson home opened and Maggie looked out. Jimmie made a supreme cursing effort and hurled his mother into the room. He quickly followed and closed the door. The Rum Alley tenement swore disappointedly and retired.

The mother slowly gathered herself up from the floor. Her eyes glittered menacingly upon her children.

"Here, now," said Jimmie, "we've had enough of dis. Sit down, an' don' make no trouble."

He grasped her arm, and twisting it, forced her into a creaking chair.

"Keep yer hands off me," roared his mother again.

"Damn yer ol' hide," yelled Jimmie, madly. Maggie shrieked and ran into the other room. To her there came the sound of a storm of crashes and curses. There was a great final thump and Jimmie's voice cried: "Dere, damn yeh, stay still." Maggie opened the door now, and went warily out. "Oh, Jimmie!"

He was leaning against the wall and swearing. Blood stood upon bruises on his knotty fore-arms where they had scraped against the floor or the walls in the scuffle. The mother lay screeching on the floor, the tears running down her furrowed face.

Maggie, standing in the middle of the room, gazed about her. The usual upheaval of the tables and chairs had taken place. Crockery was strewn broadcast in fragments. The stove had been disturbed on its legs, and now leaned idiotically to one side. A pail had been upset and water spread in all directions.

The door opened and Pete appeared. He shrugged his shoulders. "Oh, Gawd," he observed.

He walked over to Maggie and whispered in her ear. "Ah, what d' hell, Mag? Come ahn and we'll have a hell of a time."

The mother in the corner upreared her head and shook her tangled locks.

"T' hell wid him and you," she said, glowering at her daughter in the gloom. Her eyes seemed to burn balefully. "Yeh've gone t' d' devil, Mag Johnson, yehs knows yehs have gone t' d' devil. Yer a digrace t' yer people, damn yeh. An' now, git out an' go ahn wid dat doe-faced jude²⁷ of yours. Go t' hell wid him, damn yeh, an' a good riddance. Go t' hell an' see how yeh likes it."

Maggie gazed long at her mother.

"Go t' hell now, an' see how yeh likes it. Git out. I won't have sech as yehs in me house! Git out, d'yeh hear! Damn yeh, git out!"

The girl began to tremble.

At this instant Pete came forward. "Oh, what d' hell, Mag, see," whispered he softly in her ear. "Dis all blows over. See? D' ol' woman 'ill be all right in d' mornin'. Come ahn out wid me! We'll have a hell of a time."

The woman on the floor cursed. Jimmie was intent upon his bruised fore-arms. The girl cast a glance about the room filled with a chaotic mass of debris, and at the writhing body of her mother.

"Go t' hell an' good riddance."

Maggie went.

Chapter X

Jimmie had an idea it wasn't common courtesy for a friend to come to one's home and ruin one's sister. But he was not sure how much Pete knew about the rules of politeness.

The following night he returned home from work at rather a late hour in the evening. In passing through the halls he came upon the gnarled and leathery old

---

²⁷ A double meaning: dude, but also Judas, the betrayer of Jesus (see Matthew 26).

woman who possessed the music box. She was grinning in the dim light that drifted through dust-stained panes. She beckoned to him with a smudged fore-finger.

"Ah, Jimmie, what do yehs t'ink I tumbled to, las' night. It was d' funnies' t'ing I ever saw," she cried, coming close to him and leering. She was trembling with eagerness to tell her tale. "I was by me door las' night when yer sister and her jude feller came in late, oh, very late. An' she, the dear, she was a-cryin' as if her heart would break, she was. It was d' funnies' t'ing I ever saw. An' right out here by me door she asked him did he love her, did he. An' she was a-cryin' as if her heart would break, poor t'ing. An' him, I could see by d' way what he said it dat she had been askin' orften, he says: 'Oh, hell, yes,' he says, says he, 'Oh, hell, yes.' "

Storm-clouds swept over Jimmie's face, but he turned from the leathery old woman and plodded on up stairs.

"Oh, hell, yes," she called after him. She laughed a laugh that was like a pro-phetic croak. " 'Oh, hell, yes,' he says, says he, 'Oh, hell, yes.' "

There was no one in at home. The rooms showed that attempts had been made at tidying them. Parts of the wreckage of the day before had been repaired by an unskilful hand. A chair or two and the table stood uncertainly upon legs. The floor had been newly swept. The blue ribbons had been restored to the curtains, and the lambrequin, with its immense sheaves of yellow wheat and red roses of equal size, had been returned, in a worn and sorry state, to its place at the mantel. Maggie's jacket and hat were gone from the nail behind the door.

Jimmie walked to the window and began to look through the blurred glass. It occurred to him to vaguely wonder, for an instant, if some of the women of his acquaintance had brothers.

Suddenly, however, he began to swear.

"But he was me frien'! I brought 'im here! Dat's d' hell of it!"

He fumed about the room, his anger gradually rising to the furious pitch.

"I'll kill d' jay! Dat's what I'll do! I'll kill d' jay!"

He clutched his hat and sprang toward the door. But it opened and his mother's great form blocked the passage.

"What d' hell's d' matter wid yeh?" exclaimed she, coming into the rooms.

Jimmie gave vent to a sardonic curse and then laughed heavily.

"Well, Maggie's gone t' d' devil! Dat's what! See?"

"Eh?" said his mother.

"Maggie's gone t' d' devil! Are yehs deaf?" roared Jimmie, impatiently.

"D' hell she has," murmured the mother, astounded.

Jimmie grunted, and then began to stare out at the window. His mother sat down in a chair, but a moment later sprang erect and delivered a maddened whirl of oaths. Her son turned to look at her as she reeled and swayed in the middle of the room, her fierce face convulsed with passion, her blotched arms raised high in imprecation.

"May Gawd curse her forever," she shrieked. "May she eat nothin' but stones and d' dirt in d' street. May she sleep in d' gutter an' never see d' sun shine again. D' damn———"

"Here, now," said her son. "Take a drop on yerself, an' quit dat."

The mother raised lamenting eyes to the ceiling.

"She's d' devil's own chil', Jimmie," she whispered. "Ah, who would t'ink such a bad girl could grow up in our fambly, Jimmie, me son. Many d' hour I've spent in talk wid dat girl an' tol' her if she ever went on d' streets I'd see her damned. An' after all her bringin' up an' what I tol' her and talked wid her, she goes t' d' bad, like a duck t' water."

The tears rolled down her furrowed face. Her hands trembled.

"An' den when dat Sadie MacMallister next door to us was sent t' d' devil by dat feller what worked in d' soap-factory, didn't I tell our Mag dat if she————"

"Ah, dat's anudder story," interrupted the brother. "Of course, dat Sadie was nice an' all dat—but—see—it ain't dessame as if—well, Maggie was diff'ent—see—she was diff'ent."

He was trying to formulate a theory that he had always unconsciously held, that all sisters, excepting his own, could advisedly be ruined.

He suddenly broke out again. "I'll go t'ump hell out a d' mug what done her d' harm. I'll kill 'im! He t'inks he kin scrap, but when he gits me a-chasin' 'im he'll fin' out where he's wrong, d' damned duffer. I'll wipe up d' street wid 'im."

In a fury he plunged out of the doorway. As he vanished the mother raised her head and lifted both hands, entreating.

"May Gawd curse her forever," she cried.

In the darkness of the hallway Jimmie discerned a knot of women talking volubly. When he strode by they paid no attention to him.

"She allus was a bold thing," he heard one of them cry in an eager voice. "Dere wasn't a feller come t' d' house but she'd try t' mash[28] 'im. My Annie says d' shameless t'ing tried t' ketch her feller, her own feller, what we useter know his fader."

"I could a' tol' yehs dis two years ago," said a woman, in a key of triumph. "Yessir, it was over two years ago dat I says t' my ol' man, I says, 'Dat Johnson girl ain't straight,' I says. 'Oh, hell,' he says. 'Oh, hell.' 'Dat's all right,' I says, 'but I know what I knows,' I says, 'an' it 'ill come out later. You wait an' see,' I says, 'you see.'"

"Anybody what had eyes could see dat dere was somethin' wrong wid dat girl. I didn't like her actions."

On the street Jimmie met a friend. "What d' hell?" asked the latter.

Jimmie explained. "An' I'll t'ump 'im till he can't stand."

"Oh, what d' hell," said the friend. "What's d' use! Yeh'll git pulled in![29] Everybody 'ill be onto it! An' ten plunks![30] Gee!"

Jimmie was determined. "He t'inks he kin scrap, but he'll fin' out diff'ent."

"Gee!" remonstrated the friend. "What d' hell?"

Chapter XI

On a corner a glass-fronted building shed a yellow glare upon the pavements. The open mouth of a saloon called seductively to passengers to enter and annihilate sorrow or create rage.

The interior of the place was papered in olive and bronze tints of imitation leather. A shining bar of counterfeit massiveness extended down the side of the room. Behind it a great mahogany-imitation sideboard reached the ceiling. Upon its shelves rested pyramids of shimmering glasses that were never disturbed. Mirrors set in the face of the sideboard multiplied them. Lemons, oranges and paper napkins, arranged with mathematical precision, sat among the glasses. Many-hued

---

[28] To move in on.   [29] Arrested.   [30] Ten dollars, the fine Jimmie will get.

decanters of liquor perched at regular intervals on the lower shelves. A nickel-plated cash register occupied a place in the exact centre of the general effect. The elementary senses of it all seemed to be opulence and geometrical accuracy.

Across from the bar a smaller counter held a collection of plates upon which swarmed frayed fragments of crackers, slices of boiled ham, dishevelled bits of cheese, and pickles swimming in vinegar. An odor of grasping, begrimed hands and munching mouths pervaded all.

Pete, in a white jacket, was behind the bar bending expectantly toward a quiet stranger. "A beeh," said the man. Pete drew a foam-topped glassful and set it dripping upon the bar.

At this moment the light bamboo doors at the entrance swung open and crashed against the wall. Jimmie and a companion entered. They swaggered unsteadily but belligerently toward the bar and looked at Pete with bleared and blinking eyes.

"Gin," said Jimmie.

"Gin," said the companion.

Pete slid a bottle and two glasses along the bar. He bended his head sideways as he assiduously polished away with a napkin at the gleaming wood. He wore a look of watchfulness.

Jimmie and his companion kept their eyes upon the bartender and conversed loudly in tones of contempt.

"He's a dindy masher, ain't he, by Gawd?" laughed Jimmie.

"Oh, hell, yes," said the companion, sneering. "He's great, he is. Git onto d' mug on d' blokie. Dat's enough to make a feller turn hand-springs in 'is sleep."

The quiet stranger moved himself and his glass a trifle further away and maintained an attitude of obliviousness.

"Gee! ain't he hot stuff!"

"Git onto his shape! Great Gawd!"

"Hey," cried Jimmie, in tones of command. Pete came along slowly, with a sullen dropping of the under lip.

"Well," he growled, "what's eatin' yehs?"

"Gin," said Jimmie.

"Gin," said the companion.

As Pete confronted them with the bottle and the glasses, they laughed in his face. Jimmie's companion, evidently overcome with merriment, pointed a grimy forefinger in Pete's direction.

"Say, Jimmie," demanded he, "what d' hell is dat behind d' bar?"

"Damned if I knows," replied Jimmie. They laughed loudly. Pete put down a bottle with a bang and turned a formidable face toward them. He disclosed his teeth and his shoulders heaved restlessly.

"You fellers can't guy[31] me," he said. "Drink yer stuff an' git out an' don' make no trouble."

Instantly the laughter faded from the faces of the two men and expressions of offended dignity immediately came.

"Who d' hell has said anyt'ing t' you," cried they in the same breath.

The quiet stranger looked at the door calculatingly.

"Ah, come off," said Pete to the two men. "Don't pick me up for no jay. Drink yer rum an' git out an' don' make no trouble."

"Oh, d' hell," airily cried Jimmie.

[31] Kid, make fun of.

"Oh, d' hell," airily repeated his companion.

"We goes when we git ready! See!" continued Jimmie.

"Well," said Pete in a threatening voice, "don' make no trouble."

Jimmie suddenly leaned forward with his head on one side. He snarled like a wild animal.

"Well, what if we does? See?" said he.

Hot blood flushed into Pete's face, and he shot a lurid glance at Jimmie.

"Well, den we'll see who's d' bes' man, you or me," he said.

The quiet stranger moved modestly toward the door.

Jimmie began to swell with valor.

"Don' pick me up fer no tenderfoot. When yeh tackles me yeh tackles one of d' bes' men in d' city. See? I'm a scrapper, I am. Ain't dat right, Billie?"

"Sure, Mike," responded his companion in tones of conviction.

"Oh, hell," said Pete, easily. "Go fall on yerself."

The two men again began to laugh.

"What d' hell is dat talkin'?" cried the companion.

"Damned if I knows," replied Jimmie with exaggerated contempt.

Pete made a furious gesture. "Git outa here now, an' don' make no trouble. See? Youse fellers er lookin' fer a scrap an' it's damn likely yeh'll fin' one if yeh keeps on shootin' off yer mout's. I know yehs! See? I kin lick better men den yehs ever saw in yer lifes. Dat's right! See? Don' pick me up fer no stuff er yeh might be jolted out in d' street before yeh knows where yeh is. When I comes from behind dis bar, I t'rows yehs bote inteh d' street. See?"

"Oh, hell," cried the two men in chorus.

The glare of a panther came into Pete's eyes. "Dat's what I said! Unnerstan'?"

He came through a passage at the end of the bar and swelled down upon the two men. They stepped promptly forward and crowded close to him.

They bristled like three roosters. They moved their heads pugnaciously and kept their shoulders braced. The nervous muscles about each mouth twitched with a forced smile of mockery.

"Well, what d' hell yer goin' t' do?" gritted Jimmie.

Pete stepped warily back, waving his hands before him to keep the men from coming too near.

"Well, what d' hell yer goin' t' do?" repeated Jimmie's ally. They kept close to him, taunting and leering. They strove to make him attempt the initial blow.

"Keep back now! Don' crowd me," ominously said Pete.

Again they chorused in contempt. "Oh, hell!"

In a small, tossing group, the three men edged for positions like frigates contemplating battle.

"Well, why d' hell don' yeh try t' t'row us out?" cried Jimmie and his ally with copious sneers.

The bravery of bull-dogs sat upon the faces of the men. Their clenched fists moved like eager weapons.

The allied two jostled the bartender's elbows, glaring at him with feverish eyes and forcing him toward the wall.

Suddenly Pete swore furiously. The flash of action gleamed from his eyes. He threw back his arm and aimed a tremendous, lightning-like blow at Jimmie's face. His foot swung a step forward and the weight of his body was behind his fist. Jimmie ducked his head, Bowery-like, with the quickness of a cat. The fierce, answering blows of Jimmie and his ally crushed on Pete's bowed head.

The quiet stranger vanished.

The arms of the combatants whirled in the air like flails. The faces of the men, at first flushed to flame-colored anger, now began to fade to the pallor of warriors in the blood and heat of a battle. Their lips curled back and stretched tightly over the gums in ghoul-like grins. Through their white, gripped teeth struggled hoarse whisperings of oaths. Their eyes glittered with murderous fire.

Each head was huddled between its owner's shoulders, and arms were swinging with marvelous rapidity. Feet scraped to and fro with a loud scratching sound upon the sanded floor. Blows left crimson blotches upon pale skin. The curses of the first quarter minute of the fight died away. The breaths of the fighters came wheezingly from their lips and the three chests were straining and heaving. Pete at intervals gave vent to low, labored hisses, that sounded like a desire to kill. Jimmie's ally gibbered at times like a wounded maniac. Jimmie was silent, fighting with the face of a sacrificial priest. The rage of fear shone in all their eyes and their blood-colored fists whirled.

At a critical moment a blow from Pete's hand struck the ally and he crashed to the floor. He wriggled instantly to his feet and grasping the quiet stranger's beer glass from the bar, hurled it at Pete's head.

High on the wall it burst like a bomb, shivering fragments flying in all directions. Then missiles came to every man's hand. The place had heretofore appeared free of things to throw, but suddenly glasses and bottles went singing through the air. They were thrown point-blank at bobbing heads. The pyramid of shimmering glasses, that had never been disturbed, changed to cascades as heavy bottles were flung into them. Mirrors splintered to nothing.

The three frothing creatures on the floor buried themselves in a frenzy for blood. There followed in the wake of missiles and fists some unknown prayers, perhaps for death.

The quiet stranger had sprawled very pyrotechnically out on the sidewalk. A laugh ran up and down the avenue for the half of a block.

"Dey've t'rowed a bloke inteh d' street."

People heard the sound of breaking glass and shuffling feet within the saloon and came running. A small group, bending down to look under the bamboo doors, and watching the fall of glass and three pairs of violent legs, changed in a moment to a crowd.

A policeman came charging down the sidewalk and bounced through the doors into the saloon. The crowd bended and surged in absorbing anxiety to see.

Jimmie caught first sight of the on-coming interruption. On his feet he had the same regard for a policeman that, when on his truck, he had for a fire engine. He howled and ran for the side door.

The officer made a terrific advance, club in hand. One comprehensive sweep of the long night stick threw the ally to the floor and forced Pete to a corner. With his disengaged hand he made a furious effort at Jimmie's coat-tails. Then he regained his balance and paused.

"Well, well, you are a pair of pictures. What in hell have yeh been up to?"

Jimmie, with his face drenched in blood, escaped up a side street, pursued a short distance by some of the more law-loving, or excited individuals of the crowd.

Later, from a safe dark corner, he saw the policeman, the ally and the bartender emerge from the saloon. Pete locked the doors and then followed up the avenue in the rear of the crowd-encompassed policeman and his charge.

At first Jimmie, with his heart throbbing at battle heat, started to go desperately to the rescue of his friend, but he halted.

"Ah, what d' hell?" he demanded of himself.

CHAPTER XII

In a hall of irregular shape sat Pete and Maggie drinking beer. A submissive orchestra dictated to by a spectacled man with frowsy hair and in soiled evening dress, industriously followed the bobs of his head and the waves of his baton. A ballad singer, in a gown of flaming scarlet, sang in the inevitable voice of brass. When she vanished, men seated at the tables near the front applauded loudly, pounding the polished wood with their beer glasses. She returned attired in less gown, and sang again. She received another enthusiastic encore. She reappeared in still less gown and danced. The deafening rumble of glasses and clapping of hands that followed her exit indicated an overwhelming desire to have her come on for the fourth time, but the curiosity of the audience was not gratified.

Maggie was pale. From her eyes had been plucked all look of self-reliance. She leaned with a dependent air toward her companion. She was timid, as if fearing his anger or displeasure. She seemed to beseech tenderness of him.

Pete's air of distinguished valor had grown upon him until it threatened to reach stupendous dimensions. He was infinitely gracious to the girl. It was apparent to her that his condescension was a marvel.

He could appear to strut even while sitting still and he showed that he was a lion of lordly characteristics by the air with which he spat.

With Maggie gazing at him wonderingly, he took pride in commanding the waiters who were, however, indifferent or deaf.

"Hi, you, git a russle[32] on yehs! What d' hell yehs lookin' at? Two more beehs, d'yeh hear?"

He leaned back and critically regarded the person of a girl with a straw-colored wig who upon the stage was flinging her heels about in somewhat awkward imitation of a well-known danseuse.[33]

At times Maggie told Pete long confidential tales of her former home life, dwelling upon the escapades of the other members of the family and the difficulties she had had to combat in order to obtain a degree of comfort. He responded in the accents of philanthropy. He pressed her arm with an air of reassuring proprietorship.

"Dey was damn jays!" he said, denouncing the mother and brother.

The sound of the music which, through the efforts of the frowsy-headed leader, drifted to her ears in the smoke-filled atmosphere, made the girl dream. She thought of her former Rum Alley environment and turned to regard Pete's strong protecting fists. She thought of a collar and cuff manufactory and the eternal moan of the proprietor: "What een hale do you sink I pie fife dolla a week for? Play? No, py tamn!" She contemplated Pete's man-subduing eyes and noted that wealth and prosperity was indicated by his clothes. She imagined a future, rose-tinted, because of its distance from all that she had experienced before.

---

[32] Move along.   [33] A female ballet dancer (French).

As to the present she perceived only vague reasons to be miserable. Her life was Pete's and she considered him worthy of the charge. She would be disturbed by no particular apprehensions, so long as Pete adored her as he now said he did. She did not feel like a bad woman. To her knowledge she had never seen any better.

At times men at other tables regarded the girl furtively. Pete, aware of it, nodded at her and grinned. He felt proud.

"Mag, yer a bloomin' good-looker," he remarked, studying her face through the haze. The men made Maggie fear, but she blushed at Pete's words as it became apparent to her that she was the apple of his eye.

Grey-headed men, wonderfully pathetic in their dissipation, stared at her through clouds. Smooth-cheeked boys, some of them with faces of stone and mouths of sin, not nearly so pathetic as the grey heads, tried to find the girl's eyes in the smoke wreaths. Maggie considered she was not what they thought her. She confined her glances to Pete and the stage.

The orchestra played negro melodies and a versatile drummer pounded, whacked, clattered and scratched on a dozen machines to make noise.

Those glances of the men, shot at Maggie from under half-closed lids, made her tremble. She thought them all to be worse men than Pete.

"Come, let's go," she said.

As they went out Maggie perceived two women seated at a table with some men. They were painted and their cheeks had lost their roundness. As she passed them the girl, with a shrinking movement, drew back her skirts.

Chapter XIII

Jimmie did not return home for a number of days after the fight with Pete in the saloon. When he did, he approached with extreme caution. He found his mother raving. Maggie had not returned home. The parent continually wondered how her daughter could come to such a pass. She had never considered Maggie as a pearl dropped unstained into Rum Alley from Heaven, but she could not conceive how it was possible for her daughter to fall so low as to bring disgrace upon her family. She was terrific in denunciation of the girl's wickedness.

The fact that the neighbors talked of it, maddened her. When women came in, and in the course of their conversation casually asked, "Where's Maggie dese days?" the mother shook her fuzzy head at them and appalled them with curses. Cunning hints inviting confidence she rebuffed with violence.

"An' wid all d' bringin' up she had, how could she?" moaningly she asked of her son. "Wid all d' talkin' wid her I did an' d' t'ings I tol' her to remember? When a girl is bringed up d' way I bringed up Maggie, how kin she go t' d' devil?"

Jimmie was transfixed by these questions. He could not conceive how under the circumstances his mother's daughter and his sister could have been so wicked.

His mother took a drink from a bottle that sat on the table. She continued her lament.

"She had a bad heart, dat girl did, Jimmie. She was wicked t' d' heart an' we never knowed it."

Jimmie nodded, admitting the fact.

"We lived in d' same house wid her an' I brought her up an' we never knowed how bad she was."

Jimmie nodded again.

"Wid a home like dis an' a mudder like me, she went t' d' bad." cried the mother, raising her eyes.

One day Jimmie came home, sat down in a chair and began to wriggle about with a new and strange nervousness. At last he spoke shamefacedly.

"Well, look-a-here, dis t'ing queers us! See? We're queered! An' maybe it 'ud be better if I—well, I t'ink I kin look 'er up an'—maybe it 'ud be better if I fetched her home an'——"

The mother started from her chair and broke forth into a storm of passionate anger.

"What! Let 'er come an' sleep under d' same roof wid her mudder agin! Oh, yes, I will, won't I? Sure? Shame on yehs, Jimmie Johnson, fer sayin' such a t'ing t' yer own mudder—t' yer own mudder! Little did I t'ink when yehs was a babby playin' about me feet dat ye'd grow up t' say sech a t'ing t' yer mudder—yer own mudder. I never t'aut——"

Sobs choked her and interrupted her reproaches.

"Dere ain't nottin' t' raise sech hell about," said Jimmie. "I on'y says it 'ud be better if we keep dis t'ing dark, see? It queers us! See?"

His mother laughed a laugh that seemed to ring through the city and be echoed and re-echoed by countless other laughs. "Oh, yes, I will, won't I! Sure!"

"Well, yeh must take me for a damn fool," said Jimmie, indignant at his mother for mocking him. "I didn't say we'd make 'er inteh a little tin angel, ner nottin', but d' way it is now she can queer us! Don' che see?"

"Aye, she'll git tired of d' life atter a while an' den she'll wanna be a-comin' home, won' she, d' beast! I'll let 'er in den, won' I?"

"Well, I didn' mean none of dis prod'gal bus'ness anyways," explained Jimmie.

"It wa'n't no prod'gal dauter, yeh damn fool," said the mother. "It was prod'gal son,[34] anyhow."

"I know dat," said Jimmie.

For a time they sat in silence. The mother's eyes gloated on the scene which her imagination called before her. Her lips were set in a vindictive smile.

"Aye, she'll cry, won' she, an' carry on, an' tell how Pete, or some odder feller, beats 'er an' she'll say she's sorry an' all dat an' she ain't happy, she ain't, and she wants to come home agin, she does."

With grim humor the mother imitated the possible wailing notes of the daughter's voice.

"Den I'll take 'er in, won't I? She kin cry 'er two eyes out on d' stones of d' street before I'll dirty d' place wid her. She abused an' ill-treated her own mudder—her own mudder what loved her an' she'll never git anodder chance dis side of hell."

Jimmie thought he had a great idea of women's frailty, but he could not understand why any of his kin should be victims.

"Damn her," he fervidly said.

Again he wondered vaguely if some of the women of his acquaintance had brothers. Nevertheless, his mind did not for an instant confuse himself with those

[34] In the parable of Luke 15:11–32, the prodigal son was welcomed home by his father.

brothers nor his sister with theirs. After the mother had, with great difficulty, suppressed the neighbors, she went among them and proclaimed her grief. "May Gawd forgive dat girl," was her continual cry. To attentive ears she recited the whole length and breadth of her woes.

"I bringed 'er up d' way a dauter oughta be bringed up, an' dis is how she served me! She went t' d' devil d' first chance she got! May Gawd forgive her."

When arrested for drunkenness she used the story of her daughter's downfall with telling effect upon the police-justices. Finally one of them said to her, peering down over his spectacles: "Mary, the records of this and other courts show *She* that you are the mother of forty-two daughters who have been ruined. The case is *sentenced* unparalleled in the annals of this court, and this court thinks——" *her*

The mother went through life shedding large tears of sorrow. Her red face was *already* a picture of agony.

Of course Jimmie publicly damned his sister that he might appear on a higher social plane. But, arguing with himself, stumbling about in ways that he knew not, he, once, almost came to a conclusion that his sister would have been more firmly good had she better known why. However, he felt that he could not hold such a view. He threw it hastily aside.

Chapter XIV

In a hilarious hall there were twenty-eight tables and twenty-eight women and a crowd of smoking men. Valiant noise was made on a stage at the end of the hall by an orchestra composed of men who looked as if they had just happened in. Soiled waiters ran to and fro, swooping down like hawks on the unwary in the throng; clattering along the aisles with trays covered with glasses; stumbling over women's skirts and charging two prices for everything but beer, all with a swiftness that blurred the view of the cocoanut palms and dusty monstrosities painted upon the walls of the room. A "bouncer" with an immense load of business upon his hands, plunged about in the crowd, dragging bashful strangers to prominent chairs, ordering waiters here and there and quarreling furiously with men who wanted to sing with the orchestra.

The usual smoke cloud was present, but so dense that heads and arms seemed entangled in it. The rumble of conversation was replaced by a roar. Plenteous oaths heaved through the air. The room rang with the shrill voices of women bubbling over with drink-laughter. The chief element in the music of the orchestra was speed. The musicians played in intent fury. A woman was singing and smiling upon the stage, but no one took notice of her. The rate at which the piano, cornet and violins were going, seemed to impart wildness to the half-drunken crowd. Beer glasses were emptied at a gulp and conversation became a rapid chatter. The smoke eddied and swirled like a shadowy river hurrying toward some unseen falls. Pete and Maggie entered the hall and took chairs at a table near the door. The woman who was seated there made an attempt to occupy Pete's attention and, failing, went away.

Three weeks had passed since the girl had left home. The air of spaniel-like dependence had been magnified and showed its direct effect in the peculiar offhandedness and ease of Pete's way toward her.

She followed Pete's eyes with hers, anticipating with smiles gracious looks from him.

A woman of brilliance and audacity, accompanied by a mere boy, came into the place and took seats near them.

At once Pete sprang to his feet, his face beaming with glad surprise.

"By Gawd, dere's Nellie," he cried.

He went over to the table and held out an eager hand to the woman.

"Why, hello, Pete, my boy, how are you," said she, giving him her fingers.

Maggie took instant note of the woman. She perceived that her black dress fitted her to perfection. Her linen collar and cuffs were spotless. Tan gloves were stretched over her well-shaped hands. A hat of prevailing fashion perched jauntily upon her dark hair. She wore no jewelry and was painted with no apparent paint. She looked clear-eyed through the stares of the men.

"Sit down, and call your lady-friend over," she said to Pete. At his beckoning Maggie came and sat between Pete and the mere boy.

"I thought yeh were gone away fer good," began Pete, at once. "When did yeh git back? How did dat Buff'lo bus'ness turn out?"

The woman shrugged her shoulders. "Well, he didn't have as many stamps[35] as he tried to make out, so I shook him, that's all."

"Well, I'm glad t' see yehs back in d' city," said Pete, with gallantry.

He and the woman entered into a long conversation, exchanging reminiscences of days together. Maggie sat still, unable to formulate an intelligent sentence as her addition to the conversation and painfully aware of it.

She saw Pete's eyes sparkle as he gazed upon the handsome stranger. He listened smilingly to all she said. The woman was familiar with all his affairs, asked him about mutual friends, and knew the amount of his salary.

She paid no attention to Maggie, looking toward her once or twice and apparently seeing the wall beyond.

The mere boy was sulky. In the beginning he had welcomed the additions with acclamations.

"Let's all have a drink! What'll you take, Nell? And you, Miss What's-your-name. Have a drink, Mr.——, you, I mean."

He had shown a sprightly desire to do the talking for the company and tell all about his family. In a loud voice he declaimed on various topics. He assumed a patronizing air toward Pete. As Maggie was silent, he paid no attention to her. He made a great show of lavishing wealth upon the woman of brilliance and audacity.

"Do keep still, Freddie! You talk like a clock," said the woman to him. She turned away and devoted her attention to Pete.

"We'll have many a good time together again, eh?"

"Sure, Mike," said Pete, enthusiastic at once.

"Say," whispered she, leaning forward, "let's go over to Billie's and have a heluva time."

"Well, it's dis way! See?" said Pete. "I got dis lady frien' here."

"Oh, t' hell with her," argued the woman.

Pete appeared disturbed.

"All right," said she, nodding her head at him. "All right for you! We'll see the next time you ask me to go anywheres with you."

Pete squirmed.

"Say," he said beseechingly, "come wid me a minit an' I'll tell yer why."

The woman waved her hand.

---

[35] Dollars.

"Oh, that's all right, you needn't explain, you know. You wouldn't come merely because you wouldn't come, that's all."

To Pete's visible distress she turned to the mere boy, bringing him speedily out of a terrific rage. He had been debating whether it would be the part of a man to pick a quarrel with Pete, or would he be justified in striking him savagely with his beer glass without warning. But he recovered himself when the woman turned to renew her smilings. He beamed upon her with an expression that was somewhat tipsy and inexpressibly tender.

"Say, shake that Bowery jay," requested he, in a loud whisper.

"Freddie, you are so funny," she replied.

Pete reached forward and touched the woman on the arm.

"Come out a minit while I tells yeh why I can't go wid yer. Yer doin' me dirt, Nell! I never t'aut[36] ye'd do me dirt, Nell. Come on, will yer?" He spoke in tones of injury.

"Why, I don't see why I should be interested in your explanations," said the woman, with a coldness that seemed to reduce Pete to a pulp.

His eyes pleaded with her. "Come out a minit while I tells yeh. On d' level, now."

The woman nodded slightly at Maggie and the mere boy, saying, "'Scuse me."

The mere boy interrupted his loving smile and turned a shriveling glare upon Pete. His boyish countenance flushed and he spoke, in a whine, to the woman:

"Oh, I say, Nellie, this ain't a square deal, you know. You aren't goin' to leave me and go off with that duffer, are you? I should think——"

"Why, you dear boy, of course I'm not," cried the woman, affectionately. She bended over and whispered in his ear. He smiled again and settled in his chair as if resolved to wait patiently.

As the woman walked down between the rows of tables, Pete was at her shoulder talking earnestly, apparently in explanation. The woman waved her hands with studied airs of indifference. The doors swung behind them, leaving Maggie and the mere boy seated at the table.

Maggie was dazed. She could dimly perceive that something stupendous had happened. She wondered why Pete saw fit to remonstrate with the woman, pleading for forgiveness with his eyes. She thought she noted an air of submission about her leonine Pete. She was astounded.

The mere boy occupied himself with cock-tails and a cigar. He was tranquilly silent for half an hour. Then he bestirred himself and spoke.

"Well," he said sighing, "I knew this was the way it would be. They got cold feet." There was another stillness. The mere boy seemed to be musing.

"She was pulling m' leg. That's the whole amount of it," he said, suddenly. "It's a bloomin' shame the way that girl does. Why, I've spent over two dollars in drinks to-night. And she goes off with that plug-ugly who looks as if he had been hit in the face with a coin-die.[37] I call it rocky treatment for a fellah like me. Here, waiter, bring me a cock-tail and make it damned strong."

Maggie made no reply. She was watching the doors. "It's a mean piece of business," complained the mere boy. He explained to her how amazing it was that anybody should treat him in such a manner. "But I'll get square with her, you bet. She won't get far ahead of yours truly, you know," he added, winking. "I'll tell her plainly that it was bloomin' mean business. And she won't come it over me

---

[36] Thought.   [37] A heavy machine for imprinting coins.

with any of her 'now-Freddie-dears.' She thinks my name is Freddie, you know, but of course it ain't. I always tell these people some name like that, because if they got onto your right name they might use it sometime. Understand? Oh, they don't fool me much."

Maggie was paying no attention, being intent upon the doors. The mere boy relapsed into a period of gloom, during which he exterminated a number of cocktails with a determined air, as if replying defiantly to fate. He occasionally broke forth into sentences composed of invectives joined together in a long chain.

The girl was still staring at the doors. After a time the mere boy began to see cobwebs just in front of his nose. He spurred himself into being agreeable and insisted upon her having a charlotte-russe[38] and a glass of beer.

"They's gone," he remarked, "they's gone." He looked at her through the smoke wreaths. "Shay, lil' girl, we mightish well make bes' of it. You ain't such bad-lookin' girl, y'know. Not half bad. Can't come up to Nell, though. No, can't do it! Well, I should shay not! Nell fine-lookin' girl! F—i—n—ine. You look damn bad longsider her, but by y'self ain't so bad. Have to do anyhow. Nell gone. On'y you left. Not half bad, though."

Maggie stood up.

"I'm going home," she said.

The mere boy started.

"Eh? What? Home," he cried, struck with amazement. "I beg pardon, did hear say home?"

"I'm going home," she repeated.

"Great Gawd, what hav'a struck?" demanded the mere boy of himself, stupefied.

In a semi-comatose state he conducted her on board an uptown car, ostentatiously paid her fare, leered kindly at her through the rear window and fell off the steps.

Chapter XV

A forlorn woman went along a lighted avenue. The street was filled with people desperately bound on missions. An endless crowd darted at the elevated station stairs and the horse cars were thronged with owners of bundles.

The pace of the forlorn woman was slow. She was apparently searching for some one. She loitered near the doors of saloons and watched men emerge from them. She furtively scanned the faces in the rushing stream of pedestrians. Hurrying men, bent on catching some boat or train, jostled her elbows, failing to notice her, their thoughts fixed on distant dinners.

The forlorn woman had a peculiar face. Her smile was no smile. But when in repose her features had a shadowy look that was like a sardonic grin, as if some one had sketched with cruel forefinger indelible lines about her mouth.

Jimmie came strolling up the avenue. The woman encountered him with an aggrieved air.

"Oh, Jimmie, I've been lookin' all over fer yehs———" she began.

Jimmie made an impatient gesture and quickened his pace.

---

[38] An individual mold of sponge cake topped with whipped cream or custard.

"Ah, don't bodder me! Good Gawd!" he said, with the savageness of a man whose life is pestered.

The woman followed him along the sidewalk in somewhat the manner of a suppliant.

"But, Jimmie," she said, "yehs told me yeh'd————"

Jimmie turned upon her fiercely as if resolved to make a last stand for comfort and peace.

"Say, fer Gawd's sake, Hattie, don' foller me from one end of d' city t' d' odder. Let up, will yehs! Give me a minute's res', can't yehs? Yehs makes me tired, allus taggin' me. See? Ain' yehs got no sense? Do yehs want people t' get onto me? Go chase yerself, fer Gawd's sake."

The woman stepped closer and laid her fingers on his arm. "But, look-a-here————"

Jimmie snarled. "Oh, go t' hell."

He darted into the front door of a convenient saloon and a moment later came out into the shadows that surrounded the side door. On the brilliantly lighted avenue he perceived the forlorn woman dodging about like a scout. Jimmie laughed with an air of relief and went away.

When he arrived home he found his mother clamoring. Maggie had returned. She stood shivering beneath the torrent of her mother's wrath.

"Well, I'm damned," said Jimmie in greeting.

His mother, tottering about the room, pointed a quivering forefinger.

"Lookut her, Jimmie, lookut her. Dere's yer sister, boy. Dere's yer sister. Lookut her! Lookut her!"

She screamed at Maggie with scoffing laughter.

The girl stood in the middle of the room. She edged about as if unable to find a place on the floor to put her feet.

"Ha, ha, ha," bellowed the mother. "Dere she stands! Ain' she purty? Lookut her! Ain' she sweet, d' beast? Lookut her! Ha, ha! lookut her!"

She lurched forward and put her red and seamed hands upon her daughter's face. She bended down and peered keenly up into the eyes of the girl.

"Oh, she's jes' dessame as she ever was, ain' she? She's her mudder's putty darlin' yit, ain' she? Lookut her, Jimmie! Come here, fer Gawd's sake, and lookut her."

The loud, tremendous railing of her mother brought the denizens of the Rum Alley tenement to their doors. Women came in the hallways. Children scurried to and fro.

"What's up? Dat Johnson party on anudder tear?"

"Naw! Young Mag's come home!"

"D' hell yeh say?"

Through the open doors curious eyes stared in at Maggie. Children ventured into the room and ogled her, as if they formed the front row at a theatre. Women, without, bended toward each other and whispered, nodding their heads with airs of profound philosophy.

A baby, overcome with curiosity concerning this object at which all were looking, sidled forward and touched her dress, cautiously, as if investigating a red-hot stove. Its mother's voice rang out like a warning trumpet. She rushed forward and grabbed her child, casting a terrible look of indignation at the girl.

Maggie's mother paced to and fro, addressing the doorful of eyes, expounding like a glib showman. Her voice rang through the building.

"Dere she stands," she cried, wheeling suddenly and pointing with dramatic finger. "Dere she stands! Lookut her! Ain' she a dindy? An' she was so good as to come home t' her mudder, she was! Ain' she a beaut'? Ain' she a dindy? Fer Gawd's sake!"

The jeering cries ended in another burst of shrill laughter.

The girl seemed to awaken. "Jimmie———"

He drew hastily back from her.

"Well, now, yer a hell of a t'ing, ain' yeh?" he said, his lips curling in scorn. Radiant virtue sat upon his brow and his repelling hands expressed horror of contamination.

Maggie turned and went.

The crowd at the door fell back precipitately. A baby falling down in front of the door, wrenched a scream like that of a wounded animal from its mother. Another woman sprang forward and picked it up, with a chivalrous air, as if rescuing a human being from an on-coming express train.

As the girl passed down through the hall, she went before open doors framing more eyes strangely microscopic, and sending broad beams of inquisitive light into the darkness of her path. On the second floor she met the gnarled woman who possessed the music box.

"So," she cried, "'ere yehs are back again, are yehs? An' dey've kicked yehs out? Well, come in an' stay wid me t'-night. I ain' got no moral standin'."

From above came an unceasing babble of tongues, over all of which rang the mother's derisive laughter.

Chapter XVI

Pete did not consider that he had ruined Maggie. If he had thought that her soul could never smile again, he would have believed the mother and brother, who were pyrotechnic[39] over the affair, to be responsible for it.

Besides, in his world, souls did not insist upon being able to smile. "What d' hell?"

He felt a trifle entangled. It distressed him. Revelations and scenes might bring upon him the wrath of the owner of the saloon, who insisted upon respectability of an advanced type.

"What d' hell do dey wanna raise such a smoke[40] about it fer?" demanded he of himself, disgusted with the attitude of the family. He saw no necessity that people should lose their equilibrium merely because their sister or their daughter had stayed away from home.

Searching about in his mind for possible reasons for their conduct, he came upon the conclusion that Maggie's motives were correct, but that the two others wished to snare him. He felt pursued.

The woman whom he had met in the hilarious hall showed a disposition to ridicule him.

"A little pale thing with no spirit," she said. "Did you note the expression of her eyes? There was something in them about pumpkin pie and virtue. That is a peculiar way the left corner of her mouth has of twitching, isn't it? Dear, dear, Pete, what are you coming to?"

---

[39] Exploding like fireworks.   [40] A fuss.

Pete asserted at once that he never was very much interested in the girl. The woman interrupted him, laughing.

"Oh, it's not of the slightest consequence to me, my dear young man. You needn't draw maps for my benefit. Why should I be concerned about it?"

But Pete continued with his explanations. If he was laughed at for his tastes in women, he felt obliged to say that they were only temporary or indifferent ones.

The morning after Maggie had departed from home, Pete stood behind the bar. He was immaculate in white jacket and apron and his hair was plastered over his brow with infinite correctness. No customers were in the place. Pete was twisting his napkined fist slowly in a beer glass, softly whistling to himself and occasionally holding the object of his attention between his eyes and a few weak beams of sunlight that found their way over the thick screens and into the shaded room.

With lingering thoughts of the woman of brilliance and audacity, the bartender raised his head and stared through the varying cracks between the swaying bamboo doors. Suddenly the whistling pucker faded from his lips. He saw Maggie walking slowly past. He gave a great start, fearing for the previously-mentioned eminent respectability of the place.

He threw a swift, nervous glance about him, all at once feeling guilty. No one was in the room.

He went hastily over to the side door. Opening it and looking out, he perceived Maggie standing, as if undecided, on the corner. She was searching the place with her eyes.

As she turned her face toward him Pete beckoned to her hurriedly, intent upon returning with speed to a position behind the bar and to the atmosphere of respectability upon which the proprietor insisted.

Maggie came to him, the anxious look disappearing from her face and a smile wreathing her lips.

"Oh, Pete————" she began brightly.

The bartender made a violent gesture of impatience.

"Oh, my Gawd," cried he, vehemently. "What d' hell do yeh wanna hang aroun' here fer? Do yeh wanna git me inteh trouble?" he demanded with an air of injury.

Astonishment swept over the girl's features. "Why, Pete! yehs tol' me————"

Pete's glance expressed profound irritation. His countenance reddened with the anger of a man whose respectability is being threatened.

"Say, yehs makes me tired. See? What d' hell do yeh wanna tag aroun' atter me fer? Yeh'll do me dirt wid d' ol' man an' dey'll be hell t' pay! If he sees a woman roun' here he'll go crazy an' I'll lose me job! See? Ain' yehs got no sense? Don' be allus bodderin' me. See? Yer brudder come in here an' raised hell an' d' ol' man hadda put up fer it! An' now I'm done! See? I'm done."

The girl's eyes stared into his face. "Pete, don't yeh remem————"

"Oh, hell," interrupted Pete, anticipating.

The girl seemed to have a struggle with herself. She was apparently bewildered and could not find speech. Finally she asked in a low voice: "But where kin I go?"

The question exasperated Pete beyond the powers of endurance. It was a direct attempt to give him some responsibility in a matter that did not concern him. In his indignation he volunteered information.

"Oh, go t' hell," cried he. He slammed the door furiously and returned, with an air of relief, to his respectability.

Maggie went away.

She wandered aimlessly for several blocks. She stopped once and asked aloud a question of herself: "Who?"

A man who was passing near her shoulder, humorously took the questioning word as intended for him.

"Eh? What? Who? Nobody! I didn't say anything," he laughingly said, and continued his way.

Soon the girl discovered that if she walked with such apparent aimlessness, some men looked at her with calculating eyes. She quickened her step, frightened. As a protection, she adopted a demeanor of intentness as if going somewhere.

After a time she left rattling avenues and passed between rows of houses with sternness and stolidity stamped upon their features. She hung her head for she felt their eyes grimly upon her.

Suddenly she came upon a stout gentleman in a silk hat and a chaste black coat, whose decorous row of buttons reached from his chin to his knees.[41] The girl had heard of the Grace of God and she decided to approach this man.

His beaming chubby face was a picture of benevolence and kind-heartedness. His eyes shone good-will.

But as the girl timidly accosted him, he made a convulsive movement and saved his respectability by a vigorous side-step. He did not risk it to save a soul. For how was he to know that there was a soul before him that needed saving?

Chapter XVII

Upon a wet evening, several months after the last chapter, two interminable rows of cars, pulled by slipping horses, jangled along a prominent side street. A dozen cabs, with coat-enshrouded drivers, clattered to and fro. Electric lights, whirring softly, shed a blurred radiance. A flower dealer, his feet tapping impatiently, his nose and his wares glistening with rain-drops, stood behind an array of roses and chrysanthemums. Two or three theatres emptied a crowd upon the storm-swept pavements. Men pulled their hats over their eyebrows and raised their collars to their ears. Women shrugged impatient shoulders in their warm cloaks and stopped to arrange their skirts for a walk through the storm. People who had been constrained to comparative silence for two hours burst into a roar of conversation, their hearts still kindling from the glowings of the stage.

The pavements became tossing seas of umbrellas. Men stepped forth to hail cabs or cars, raising their fingers in varied forms of polite request or imperative demand. An endless procession wended toward elevated stations. An atmosphere of pleasure and prosperity seemed to hang over the throng, born, perhaps, of good clothes and of two hours in a place of forgetfulness.

In the mingled light and gloom of an adjacent park, a handful of wet wanderers, in attitudes of chronic dejection, was scattered among the benches.

A girl of the painted cohorts of the city went along the street. She threw changing glances at men who passed her, giving smiling invitations to those of rural or untaught pattern and usually seeming sedately unconscious of men with a metropolitan seal upon their faces.

Crossing glittering avenues, she went into the throng emerging from the places

[41] A clergyman in a cassock.

of forgetfulness. She hurried forward through the crowd as if intent upon reaching a distant home, bending forward in her handsome cloak, daintily lifting her skirts and picking for her well-shod feet the dryer spots upon the pavements.

The restless doors of saloons, clashing to and fro, disclosed animated rows of men before bars and hurrying barkeepers.

A concert hall gave to the street faint sounds of swift, machine-like music, as if a group of phantom musicians were hastening.

A tall young man, smoking a cigarette with a sublime air, strolled near the girl. He had on evening dress, a moustache, a chrysanthemum, and a look of ennui, all of which he kept carefully under his eye. Seeing the girl walk on as if such a young man as he was not in existence, he looked back transfixed with interest. He stared glassily for a moment, but gave a slight convulsive start when he discerned that she was neither new, Parisian, nor theatrical. He wheeled about hastily and turned his stare into the air, like a sailor with a search-light.

A stout gentleman, with pompous and philanthropic whiskers, went stolidly by, the broad of his back sneering at the girl.

A belated man in business clothes, and in haste to catch a car, bounced against her shoulder. "Hi, there, Mary, I beg your pardon! Brace up, old girl." He grasped her arm to steady her, and then was away running down the middle of the street.

The girl walked on out of the realm of restaurants and saloons. She passed more glittering avenues and went into darker blocks than those where the crowd travelled.

A young man in light overcoat and derby hat received a glance shot keenly from the eyes of the girl. He stopped and looked at her, thrusting his hands in his pockets and making a mocking smile curl his lips. "Come, now, old lady," he said, "you don't mean to tell me that you sized me up for a farmer?"

A laboring man marched along with bundles under his arms. To her remarks, he replied, "It's a fine evenin', ain't it?"

She smiled squarely into the face of a boy who was hurrying by with his hands buried in his overcoat pockets, his blond locks bobbing on his youthful temples, and a cheery smile of unconcern upon his lips. He turned his head and smiled back at her, waving his hands.

"Not this eve—some other eve!"

A drunken man, reeling in her pathway, began to roar at her. "I ain' ga no money, dammit," he shouted, in a dismal voice. He lurched on up the street wailing to himself, "Dammit, I ain' ga no money. Damn ba' luck. Ain' ga no more money."

The girl went into gloomy districts near the river, where the tall black factories shut in the street and only occasional broad beams of light fell across the pavements from saloons. In front of one of these places, whence came the sound of a violin vigorously scraped, the patter of feet on boards and the ring of loud laughter, there stood a man with blotched features.

Further on in the darkness she met a ragged being with shifting, blood-shot eyes and grimy hands.

She went into the blackness of the final block. The shutters of the tall buildings were closed like grim lips. The structures seemed to have eyes that looked over them, beyond them, at other things. Afar off the lights of the avenues glittered as if from an impossible distance. Street-car bells jingled with a sound of merriment.

At the feet of the tall buildings appeared the deathly black hue of the river. Some hidden factory sent up a yellow glare, that lit for a moment the waters lapping oilily against timbers. The varied sounds of life, made joyous by distance and seeming unapproachableness, came faintly and died away to a silence.

Chapter XVIII

In a partitioned-off section of a saloon sat a man with a half dozen women, gleefully laughing, hovering about him. The man had arrived at that stage of drunkenness where affection is felt for the universe.

"I'm good f'ler, girls," he said, convincingly. "I'm damn good f'ler. An'body treats me right, I allus trea's zem right! See?"

The women nodded their heads approvingly. "To be sure," they cried in hearty chorus. "You're the kind of a man we like, Pete. You're outa sight! What yeh goin' to buy this time, dear?"

"An't'ing yehs wants, damn it," said the man in an abandonment of good-will. His countenance shone with the true spirit of benevolence. He was in the proper mood of missionaries. He would have fraternized with obscure Hottentots.[42] And above all, he was overwhelmed in tenderness for his friends, who were all illustrious.

"An't'ing yehs wants, damn it," repeated he, waving his hands with beneficient recklessness. "I'm good f'ler, girls, an' if an'body treats me right I————here," called he through an open door to a waiter, "bring girls drinks, damn it. What 'ill yehs have, girls? An't'ing yehs wants, damn it!"

The waiter glanced in with the disgusted look of the man who serves intoxicants for the man who takes too much of them. He nodded his head shortly at the order from each individual, and went.

"Damn it," said the man, "w're havin' heluva time. I like you girls! Damn'd if I don't! Yer right sort! See?"

He spoke at length and with feeling, concerning the excellencies of his assembled friends.

"Don' try pull man's leg, but have a heluva time! Das right! Das way t' do! Now, if I sawght yehs tryin' work me fer drinks, wouldn' buy damn t'ing! But yer right sort, damn it! Yehs know how ter treat a f'ler, an' I stays by yehs 'til spen' las' cent! Das right! I'm good f'ler an' I knows when an'body treats me right!"

Between the times of the arrival and departure of the waiter, the man discoursed to the women on the tender regard he felt for all living things. He laid stress upon the purity of his motives in all dealings with men in the world and spoke of the fervor of his friendship for those who were amiable. Tears welled slowly from his eyes. His voice quavered when he spoke to his companions.

Once when the waiter was about to depart with an empty tray, the man drew a coin from his pocket and held it forth.

"Here," said he, quite magnificently, "here's quar'."

The waiter kept his hands on his tray.

"I don' want yer money," he said.

The other put forth the coin with tearful insistence.

---

[42] A tribe in South Africa.

"Here, damn it," cried he, "tak't! Yer damn goo' f'ler an' I wan' yehs tak't!"

"Come, come, now," said the waiter, with the sullen air of a man who is forced into giving advice. "Put yer mon in yer pocket! Yer loaded an' yehs on'y makes a damn fool of yerself."

As the latter passed out of the door the man turned pathetically to the women.

"He don' know I'm damn goo' f'ler," cried he, dismally.

"Never you mind, Pete, dear," said the woman of brillance and audacity, laying her hand with great affection upon his arm. "Never you mind, old boy! We'll stay by you, dear!"

"Das ri'!" cried the man, his face lighting up at the soothing tones of the woman's voice. "Das ri', I'm damn goo' f'ler an' w'en anyone trea's me ri', I trea's zem ri'! Shee?"

"Sure!" cried the women. "And we're not goin' back on you, old man."

The man turned appealing eyes to the woman. He felt that if he could be convicted of a contemptible action he would die.

"Shay, Nell, damn it, I allus trea's yehs shquare, didn' I? I allus been goo' f'ler wi' yehs, ain't I, Nell?"

"Sure you have, Pete," assented the woman. She delivered an oration to her companions. "Yessir, that's a fact. Pete's a square fellah, he is. He never goes back on a friend. He's the right kind an' we stay by him, don't we, girls?"

"Sure," they exclaimed. Looking lovingly at him they raised their glasses and drank his health.

"Girlsh," said the man, beseechingly, "I allus trea's yehs ri', didn' I? I'm goo' f'ler, ain' I, girlsh?"

"Sure," again they chorused.

"Well," said he finally, "le's have nozzer drink, zen."

"That's right," hailed a woman, "that's right. Yer no bloomin' jay! Yer spends yer money like a man. Dat's right."

The man pounded the table with his quivering fists.

"Yessir," he cried, with deep earnestness, as if someone disputed him. "I'm damn goo' f'ler, an' w'en anyone trea's me ri', I allus trea's—le's have nozzer drink."

He began to beat the wood with his glass.

"Shay!" howled he, growing suddenly impatient. As the waiter did not then come, the man swelled with wrath.

"Shay!" howled he again.

The waiter appeared at the door.

"Bringsh drinksh," said the man.

The waiter disappeared with the orders.

"Zat f'ler damn fool," cried the man. "He insul' me! I'm ge'man! Can' stan' be insul'! I'm goin' lickim when comes!"

"No, no!" cried the women, crowding about and trying to subdue him. "He's all right! He didn't mean anything! Let it go! He's a good fellah!"

"Din' he insul' me?" asked the man earnestly.

"No," said they. "Of course he didn't! He's all right!"

"Sure he didn' insul' me?" demanded the man, with deep anxiety in his voice.

"No, no! We know him! He's a good fellah. He didn't mean anything."

"Well, zen," said the man, resolutely, "I'm go' 'pol'gize!"

When the waiter came, the man struggled to the middle of the floor.

"Girlsh shed you insul' me! I shay damn lie! I 'pol'gize!"

"All right," said the waiter.

The man sat down. He felt a sleepy but strong desire to straighten things out and have a perfect understanding with everybody.

"Nell, I allus trea's yeh shquare, din' I? Yeh likes me, don' yehs, Nell? I'm goo' f'ler?"

"Sure!" said the woman.

"Yeh knows I'm stuck on yehs, don' yehs, Nell?"

"Sure," she repeated, carelessly.

Overwhelmed by a spasm of drunken adoration, he drew two or three bills from his pocket, and with the trembling fingers of an offering priest, laid them on the table before the woman.

"Yehs knows, damn it, yehs kin have all I got, 'cause I'm stuck on yehs, Nell, damn 't, I—I'm stuck on yehs, Nell—buy drinksh—damn 't—we're havin' heluva time—w'en anyone trea's me ri'—I—damn 't, Nell—we're havin' heluva—time."

Presently he went to sleep with his swollen face fallen forward on his chest.

The women drank and laughed, not heeding the slumbering man in the corner. Finally he lurched forward and fell groaning to the floor.

The women screamed in disgust and drew back their skirts.

"Come ahn," cried one, starting up angrily, "let's get out of here."

The woman of brilliance and audacity stayed behind, taking up the bills and stuffing them into a deep, irregularly-shaped pocket. A guttural snore from the recumbent man caused her to turn and look down at him.

She laughed. "What a damn fool," she said, and went.

The smoke from the lamps settled heavily down in the little compartment, obscuring the way out. The smell of oil, stifling in its intensity, pervaded the air. The wine from an overturned glass dripped softly down upon the blotches on the man's neck.

Chapter XIX

In a room a woman sat at a table eating like a fat monk in a picture.

A soiled, unshaven man pushed open the door and entered.

"Well," said he, "Mag's dead."

"What?" said the woman, her mouth filled with bread.

"Mag's dead," repeated the man.

"D' hell she is," said the woman. She continued her meal. When she finished her coffee she began to weep.

"I kin remember when her two feet was no bigger dan' yer t'umb, and she weared worsted boots," moaned she.

"Well, whata dat?" said the man.

"I kin remember when she weared worsted boots," she cried.

The neighbors began to gather in the hall, staring in at the weeping woman as if watching the contortions of a dying dog. A dozen women entered and lamented with her. Under their busy hands the rooms took on that appalling appearance of neatness and order with which death is greeted.

Suddenly the door opened and a woman in a black gown rushed in with out-stretched arms. "Ah, poor Mary," she cried, and tenderly embraced the moan-ing one.

"Ah, what ter'ble affliction is dis," continued she. Her vocabulary was derived from mission churches. "Me poor Mary, how I feel fer yehs! Ah, what a ter'ble affliction is a disobed'ent chil'."

Her good, motherly face was wet with tears. She trembled in eagerness to ex-press her sympathy. The mourner sat with bowed head, rocking her body heavily to and fro, and crying out in a high, strained voice that sounded like a dirge on some forlorn pipe.

"I kin remember when she weared worsted boots an'her two feets was no big-ger dan yer t'umb an' she weared worsted boots, Miss Smith," she cried raising her streaming eyes.

"Ah, me poor Mary," sobbed the woman in black. With low, coddling cries, she sank on her knees by the mourner's chair, and put her arms about her. The other women began to groan in different keys.

"Yer poor misguided chil' is gone now, Mary, an' let us hope it's fer d' bes'. Yeh'll fergive her now, Mary, won't yehs, dear, all her disobed'ence? All her t'ankless behavior to her mudder an' all her badness? She's gone where her ter'ble sins will be judged."

The woman in black raised her face and paused. The inevitable sunlight came streaming in at the window and shed a ghastly cheerfulness upon the faded hues of the room. Two or three of the spectators were sniffling, and one was weeping loudly. The mourner arose and staggered into the other room. In a moment she emerged with a pair of faded baby shoes held in the hollow of her hand.

"I kin remember when she used to wear dem," cried she. The women burst anew into cries as if they had all been stabbed. The mourner turned to the soiled and unshaven man.

"Jimmie, boy, go git yer sister! Go git yer sister an' we'll put d' boots on her feets!"

"Dey won't fit her now, yeh damn fool," said the man.

"Go git yer sister, Jimmie," shrieked the woman, confronting him fiercely.

The man swore sullenly. He went over to a corner and slowly began to put on his coat. He took his hat and went out, with a dragging, reluctant step.

The woman in black came forward and again besought the mourner.

"Yeh'll fergive her, Mary! Yeh'll fergive yer bad, bad chil'! Her life was a curse an' her days were black an' yeh'll fergive yer bad girl? She's gone where her sins will be judged."

"She's gone where her sins will be judged," cried the other women, like a choir at a funeral.

"D' Lord gives and d' Lord takes away," said the woman in black, raising her eyes to the sunbeams.

"D' Lord gives and d' Lord takes away," responded the others.

"Yeh'll fergive her, Mary!" pleaded the woman in black. The mourner essayed to speak but her voice gave way. She shook her great shoulders frantically, in an agony of grief. The tears seemed to scald her face. Finally her voice came and arose in a scream of pain.

"Oh, yes, I'll fergive her! I'll fergive her!"

1893

STEPHEN CRANE'S OWN STORY*

JACKSONVILLE, FLA., Jan. 6.—It was the afternoon of New Year's. The *Commodore* lay at her dock in Jacksonville and negro stevedores[1] processioned steadily toward her with box after box of ammunition and bundle after bundle of rifles. Her hatch, like the mouth of a monster, engulfed them. It might have been the feeding time of some legendary creature of the sea. It was in broad daylight and the crowd of gleeful Cubans on the pier did not forbear to sing the strange patriotic ballads of their island.

Everything was perfectly open. The *Commodore* was cleared with a cargo of arms and munitions for Cuba. There was none of that extreme modesty about the proceeding which had marked previous departures of the famous tug. She loaded up as placidly as if she were going to carry oranges to New York, instead of Remingtons[2] to Cuba. Down the river, furthermore, the revenue cutter *Boutwell,* the old isosceles triangle that protects United States interests in the St. Johns,[3] lay at anchor, with no sign of excitement aboard her.

On the decks of the *Commodore* there were exchanges of farewells in two languages. Many of the men who were to sail upon her had many intimates in the old Southern town, and we who had left our friends in the remote North received our first touch of melancholy on witnessing these strenuous and earnest good-bys.

It seems, however, that there was more difficulty at the custom house. The officers of the ship and the Cuban leaders were detained there until a mournful twilight settled upon the St. Johns, and through a heavy fog the lights of Jacksonville blinked dimly.

Then at last the *Commodore* swung clear of the dock, amid a tumult of good-bys. As she turned her bow toward the distant sea the Cubans ashore cheered and cheered. In response the *Commodore* gave three long blasts of her whistle, which even to this time impressed me with their sadness. Somehow they sounded as wails.

Then at last we began to feel like filibusters.[4] I don't suppose that the most stolid brain could contrive to believe that there is not a mere trifle of danger in filibustering, and so as we watched the lights of Jacksonville swing past us and heard the regular thump, thump, thump of the engines we did considerable reflecting.

But I am sure that there was no hifalutin emotions visible upon any of the faces which fronted the speeding shore. In fact, from cook's boy to captain, we were all enveloped in a gentle satisfaction and cheerfulness.

But less than two miles from Jacksonville this atrocious fog caused the pilot to ram the bow of the *Commodore* hard upon the mud, and in this ignominious position we were compelled to stay until daybreak.

It was to all of us more than a physical calamity. We were now no longer filibusters. We were men on a ship stuck in the mud. A certain mental somersault was made once more necessary. But word had been sent to Jacksonville to the

---

* Crane sailed from Jacksonville, Florida, on the steamer *Commodore* on New Year's Day of 1897 to cover the Cuban Revolution for the New York *Press;* the ship, which carried munitions for the revolutionaries, sank the next morning, and Crane and three other men survived in a ten-foot dinghy that reached Daytona Beach the following day. On January 6 Crane published this newspaper story of the perilous adventure; six months later he published a fictional companion-piece, "The Open Boat."

[1] Workers who load and unload ships in port.   [2] Rifles.   [3] A river in northeast Florida.

[4] Military adventurers; here, gun runners.

captain of the revenue cutter *Boutwell,* and Captain Kilgore turned out promptly and generously fired up his old triangle and came at full speed to our assistance. She dragged us out of the mud and again we headed for the mouth of the river. The revenue cutter pounded along a half mile astern of us, to make sure that we did not take on board at some place along the river men for the Cuban army.

This was the early morning of New Year's Day, and the fine golden Southern sunlight fell full upon the river. It flashed over the ancient *Boutwell* until her white sides gleamed like pearl and her rigging was spun into little threads of gold. Cheers greeted the old *Commodore* from passing ships and from the shore. It was a cheerful, almost merry, beginning to our voyage.

At Mayport, however, we changed our river pilot for a man who could take her to open sea, and again the *Commodore* was beached. The *Boutwell* was fussing around us in her venerable way, and, upon seeing our predicament, she came again to assist us, but this time with engines reversed the *Commodore* dragged herself away from the grip of the sand and again the *Commodore* headed for the open sea.

The captain of the revenue cutter grew curious. He hailed the *Commodore:* "Are you fellows going to sea to-day?"

Captain Murphy of the *Commodore* called back: "Yes, sir." And then as the whistle of the *Commodore* saluted him Captain Kilgore doffed his cap and said: "Well, gentlemen, I hope you have a pleasant cruise," and this was our last words from shore.

When the *Commodore* came to the enormous rollers that flee over the bar, a certain light-heartedness departed from the throats of the ship's company. The *Commodore* began to turn handsprings, and by the time she had gotten fairly to sea and turned into the eye of the roaring breeze that was blowing from the southeast there was an almost general opinion on board the vessel that a life on the rolling wave was not the finest thing in the world. On deck amidships lay five or six Cubans, limp, forlorn and infinitely depressed. In the bunks below lay more Cubans, also limp, forlorn and infinitely depressed. In the captain's quarters, back of the pilot house, the Cuban leaders were stretched out in postures of complete contentment to this terrestrial realm of their stomachs.

The *Commodore* was heavily laden and in this strong sea she rolled like a rubber ball. She appeared to be a gallant sea boat and bravely flung off the waves that swarmed over her bow. At this time the first mate was at the wheel, and I remember how proud he was of the ship as she dashed the white foaming waters aside and arose to the swells like a duck.

"Ain't she a daisy?" said he. But she certainly did do a remarkable lot of pitching and presently even some American seamen were made ill by the long wallowing motion of the ship. A squall confronted us dead ahead and in the impressive twilight of this New Year's Day the *Commodore* steamed sturdily toward a darkened part of the horizon. The State of Florida is very large when you look at it from an airship, but it is as narrow as a sheet of paper when you look at it sideways. The coast was merely a faint streak.

As darkness came upon the waters the *Commodore's* wake was a broad, flaming path of blue and silver phosphorescence, and as her stout bow lunged at the great black waves she threw flashing, roaring cascades to either side. And all that was to be heard was the rhythmical and mighty pounding of the engines.

Being an inexperienced filibuster, the writer had undergone considerable mental excitement since the starting of the ship, and consequently he had not yet been to sleep, and so I went to the first mate's bunk to indulge myself in all the physical delights of holding one's self in bed. Every time the ship lurched I expected to be fired through a bulkhead, and it was neither amusing nor instructive to see in the dim light a certain accursed valise aiming itself at the top of my stomach with every lurch of the ship.

The cook was asleep on a bench in the galley. He was of a portly and noble exterior, and by means of a checker board he had himself wedged on this bench in such a manner that the motion of the ship would be unable to dislodge him. He awoke as I entered the galley, and, feeling moved, he delivered himself of some dolorous sentiments. "God," he said, in the course of his observations, "I don't feel right about this ship somehow. It strikes me that something is going to happen to us. I don't know what it is, but the old ship is going to get it in the neck, I think."

"Well, how about the men on board of her?" said I. "Are any of us going to get out, prophet?"

"Yes," said the cook, "sometimes I have these damned feelings come over me, and they are always right, and it seems to me somehow that you and I will both get out and meet again somewhere, down at Coney Island, perhaps, or some place like that."

Finding it impossible to sleep, I went back to the pilot house. An old seaman named Tom Smith, from Charleston, was then at the wheel. In the darkness I could not see Tom's face, except at those times when he leaned forward to scan the compass and the dim light from the box came upon his weather-beaten features.

"Well, Tom," said I, "how do you like filibustering?"

He said: "I think I am about through with it. I've been in a number of these expeditions, and the pay is good, but I think if I ever get back safe this time I will cut it."

I sat down in the corner of the pilot house and went almost to sleep. In the meantime the captain came on duty and he was standing near me when the chief engineer rushed up the stairs and cried hurriedly to the captain that there was something wrong in the engine room. He and the captain departed swiftly. I was drowsing there in my corner when the captain returned, and, going to the door of the little room directly back of the pilot house, cried to the Cuban leader:

"Say, can't you get those fellows to work? I can't talk their language and I can't get them started. Come on and get them going."

The Cuban leader turned to me then and said: "Go help in the fire-room. They are going to bail with buckets."

The engine room, by the way, represented a scene at this time taken from the middle kitchen of hades. In the first place, it was insufferably warm, and the lights burned faintly in a way to cause mystic and grewsome shadows. There was a quantity of soapish sea water swirling and sweeping and swishing among machinery that roared and banged and clattered and steamed, and in the second place, it was a devil of a ways down below.

Here I first came to know a certain young oiler named Billy Higgins. He was sloshing around this inferno filling buckets with water and passing them to a chain of men that extended up to the ship's side. Afterward we got orders to change our point of attack on the water and to operate through a little door on the windward side of the ship that led into the engine room.

During this time there was much talk of pumps out of order and many other statements of a mechanical kind, which I did not altogether comprehend, but understood to mean that there was a general and sudden ruin in the engine room.

There was no particular agitation at this time, and even later there was never a panic on board the *Commodore*. The party of men who worked with Higgins and me at this time were all Cubans, and we were under the direction of the Cuban leaders. Presently we were ordered again to the afterhold, and there was some hesitation about going into the abominable fire-room again, but Higgins dashed down the companionway with a bucket.

The heat and hard work in the fire-room affected me and I was obliged to come on deck again. Going forward I heard as I went talk of lowering the boats. Near the corner of the galley the mate was talking with a man.

"Why don't you send up a rocket?" said this unknown person. And the mate replied: "What the hell do we want to send up a rocket for? The ship is all right."

Returning with a little rubber and cloth overcoat, I saw the first boat about to be lowered. A certain man was the first person in this first boat, and they were handing him in a valise about as large as a hotel. I had not entirely recovered from my astonishment and pleasure in witnessing this noble deed, when I saw another valise go to him. This valise was not perhaps so large as a hotel, but it was a big valise anyhow. Afterward there went to him something which looked to me like an overcoat.

Seeing the chief engineer leaning out of his little window, I remarked to him: "What do you think of that blank, blank, blank?"

"Oh, he's a bird," said the old chief.

It was now that was heard the order to get away the lifeboat, which was stowed on top of the deckhouse. The deckhouse was a mighty slippery place, and with each roll of the ship the men there thought themselves likely to take headers into the deadly black sea. Higgins was on top of the deckhouse, and, with the first mate and two colored stokers, we wrestled with that boat, which I am willing to swear weighed as much as a Broadway cable car. She might have been spiked to the deck. We could have pushed a little brick schoolhouse along a corduroy road as easily as we could have moved this boat. But the first mate got a tackle to her from a leaward davit, and on the deck below the captain corralled enough men to make an impression upon the boat. We were ordered to cease hauling then, and in this lull the cook of the ship came to me and said: "What are you going to do?"

I told him of my plans, and he said: "Well, my God, that's what I am going to do."

Now the whistle of the *Commodore* had been turned loose, and if there ever was a voice of despair and death it was in the voice of this whistle. It had gained a new tone. It was as if its throat was already choked by the water, and this cry on the sea at night, with a wind blowing the spray over the ship, and the waves roaring over the bow, and swirling white along the decks, was to each of us probably a song of man's end.

It was now that the first mate showed a sign of losing his grip. To us who were trying in all stages of competence and experience to launch the lifeboat he raged in all terms of fiery satire and hammer-like abuse. But the boat moved at last and swung down toward the water.

Afterward when I went aft I saw the captain standing with his arm in a sling, holding on to a stay with his one good hand and directing the launching of the boat. He gave me a five-gallon jug of water to hold, and asked me what I was going to do. I told him what I thought was about the proper thing, and he told me that the cook had the same idea, and ordered me to go forward and be ready to launch the ten-foot dingy. I remember very well that he turned then to swear at a colored stoker who was prowling around, done up in life preservers until he looked like a feather bed.

I went forward with my five-gallon jug of water, and when the captain came we launched the dingy, and they put me over the side to fend her off from the ship with an oar.

They handed me down the water jug, and then the cook came into the boat, and we sat there in the darkness, wondering why, by all our hopes of future happiness, the captain was so long in coming over the side and ordering us away from the doomed ship.

The captain was waiting for the other boat to go. Finally he hailed in the darkness: "Are you all right, Mr. Graines?"

The first mate answered: "All right, sir."

"Shove off then," cried the captain. The captain was just about to swing over the rail when a dark form came forward and a voice said: "Captain, I go with you."

The captain answered: "Yes, Billy; get in."

It was Billy Higgins, the oiler. Billy dropped into the boat and a moment later the captain followed, bringing with him an end of about forty yards of lead line. The other end was attached to the rail of the ship. As we swung back to leaward the captain said: "Boys, we will stay right near the ship till she goes down."

This cheerful information, of course, filled us all with glee. The line kept us headed properly into the wind and as we rode over the monstrous roarers we saw upon each rise the swaying lights of the dying *Commodore*.

When came the gray shade of dawn, the form of the *Commodore* grew slowly clear to us as our little ten-foot boat rose over each swell. She was floating with such an air of buoyancy that we laughed when we had time, and said: "What a guy[5] it would be on those other fellows if she didn't sink at all."

But later we saw men aboard of her, and later still they began to hail us. I had forgotten to mention that previously we had loosened the end of the lead line and dropped much further to leaward. The men on board were a mystery to us, of course, as we had seen all the boats leave the ship. We rowed back to the ship, but did not approach too near, because we were four men in a ten-foot boat, and we knew that the touch of a hand on our gunwale would assuredly swamp us.

The first mate cried out from the ship that the third boat had foundered alongside. He cried that they had made rafts and wished us to tow them. The captain said: "All right."

Their rafts were floating astern.

"Jump in," cried the captain, but here was a singular and most harrowing hesitation. There were five white men and two negroes. This scene in the gray light of morning impressed one as would a view into some place where ghosts move slowly. These seven men on the stern of the sinking *Commodore* were silent. Save the words of the mate to the captain there was no talk. Here was death, but here also was a most singular and indefinable kind of fortitude.

Four men, I remember, clambered over the railing and stood there watching the cold, steely sheen of the sweeping waves.

"Jump," cried the captain again. The old chief engineer first obeyed the order.

---

[5] A joke, a tease.

He landed on the outside raft and the captain told him how to grip the raft, and he obeyed as promptly and as docilely as a scholar in riding school.

A stoker followed him, and then the first mate threw his hands over his head and plunged into the sea. He had no life belt, and for my part, even when he did this horrible thing, I somehow felt that I could see in the expression of his hands, and in the very toss of his head, as he leaped thus to death, that it was rage, rage, rage unspeakable that was in his heart at the time.

And then I saw Tom Smith, the man who was going to quit filibustering after this expedition, jump to a raft and turn his face toward us. On board the *Commodore* three men strode, still in silence and with their faces turned toward us. One man had his arms folded and was leaning against the deckhouse. His feet were crossed, so that the toe of his left foot pointed downward. There they stood gazing at us, and neither from the deck nor from the rafts was a voice raised. Still was there this silence.

The colored stoker on the first raft threw us a line and we began to tow. Of course, we perfectly understood the absolute impossiblity of any such thing; our dingy was within the six inches of the water's edge, there was an enormous sea running, and I knew that under the circumstances a tugboat would have no light task in moving these rafts. But we tried it, and would have continued to try it indefinitely, but that something critical came to pass. I was at an oar and so faced the rafts. The cook controlled the line. Suddenly the boat began to go backward, and then we saw this negro on the first raft pulling on the line hand over hand and drawing us to him.

He had turned into a demon. He was wild, wild as a tiger. He was crouched on this raft and ready to spring. Every muscle of him seemed to be turned into an elastic spring. His eyes were almost white. His face was the face of a lost man reaching upward, and we knew that the weight of his hand on our gunwale doomed us. The cook let go of the line.

We rowed around to see if we could not get a line from the chief engineer, and all this time, mind you, there were no shrieks, no groans, but silence, silence and silence, and then the *Commodore* sank. She lurched to windward, then swung afar back, righted and dove into the sea, and the rafts were suddenly swallowed by this frightful maw of the ocean. And then by the men on the ten-foot dingy were words said that were still not words, something far beyond words.

The lighthouse of Mosquito Inlet stuck up above the horizon like the point of a pin. We turned our dingy toward the shore. The history of life in an open boat for thirty hours would no doubt be very instructive for the young, but none is to be told here now. For my part I would prefer to tell the story at once, because from it would shine the splendid manhood of Captain Edward Murphy and of William Higgins, the oiler, but let it suffice at this time to say that when we were swamped in the surf and making the best of our way toward the shore the captain gave orders amid the wildness of the breakers as clearly as if he had been on the quarterdeck of a battleship.

John Kitchell of Daytona came running down the beach, and as he ran the air was filled with clothes. If he had pulled a single lever and undressed, even as the fire horses harness, he could not to me seem to have stripped with more speed. He dashed into the water and grabbed the cook. Then he went after the captain, but the captain sent him to me, and then it was that we saw Billy Higgins lying with his forehead on sand that was clear of the water, and he was dead.

1897

THE OPEN BOAT*

A TALE INTENDED TO BE AFTER THE FACT. BEING THE EXPERIENCE OF FOUR MEN FROM THE SUNK STEAMER COMMODORE

I

None of them knew the color of the sky. Their eyes glanced level, and were fastened upon the waves that swept toward them. These waves were of the hue of slate, save for the tops, which were of foaming white, and all of the men knew the colors of the sea. The horizon narrowed and widened, and dipped and rose, and at all times its edge was jagged with waves that seemed thrust up in points like rocks.

Many a man ought to have a bath-tub larger than the boat which here rode upon the sea. These waves were most wrongfully and barbarously abrupt and tall, and each froth-top was a problem in small boat navigation.

The cook squatted in the bottom and looked with both eyes at the six inches of gunwale which separated him from the ocean. His sleeves were rolled over his fat forearms, and the two flaps of his unbuttoned vest dangled as he bent to bail out the boat. Often he said: "Gawd! That was a narrow clip." As he remarked it he invariably gazed eastward over the broken sea.

The oiler,[1] steering with one of the two oars in the boat, sometimes raised himself suddenly to keep clear of water that swirled in over the stern. It was a thin little oar and it seemed often ready to snap.

The correspondent, pulling at the other oar, watched the waves and wondered why he was there.

The injured captain, lying in the bow, was at this time buried in that profound dejection and indifference which comes, temporarily at least, to even the bravest and most enduring when, willy nilly, the firm fails, the army loses, the ship goes down. The mind of the master of a vessel is rooted deep in the timbers of her, though he command for a day or a decade, and this captain had on him the stern impression of a scene in the grays of dawn of seven turned faces, and later a stump of a top-mast with a white ball on it that slashed to and fro at the waves, went low and lower, and down. Thereafter there was something strange in his voice. Although steady, it was deep with mourning, and of a quality beyond oration or tears.

"Keep'er a little more south, Billie," said he.

" 'A little more south,' sir," said the oiler in the stern.

A seat in this boat was not unlike a seat upon a bucking broncho, and, by the same token, a broncho is not much smaller. The craft pranced and reared, and plunged like an animal. As each wave came, and she rose for it, she seemed like a horse making at a fence outrageously high. The manner of her scramble over these walls of water is a mystic thing, and, moreover, at the top of them were ordinarily

---

* First published in *Scribner's Magazine* in June 1897. Crane sailed from Jacksonville, Florida, on the steamer *Commodore* on New Year's Day of 1897 to cover the Cuban Revolution for the New York *Press;* the ship, which carried munitions for the revolutionaries, sank the next morning, and Crane and three other men survived in a ten-foot dinghy that reached Daytona Beach the following day. On January 6 Crane wrote his newspaper story of the perilous adventure, "Stephen Crane's Own Story"; six months later he published this fictional account.

[1] A crewman who oils machinery in the ship's engine room.

these problems in white water, the foam racing down from the summit of each wave, requiring a new leap, and a leap from the air. Then, after scornfully bumping a crest, she would slide, and race, and splash down a long incline and arrive bobbing and nodding in front of the next menace.

A singular disadvantage of the sea lies in the fact that after successfully surmounting one wave you discover that there is another behind it just as important and just as nervously anxious to do something effective in the way of swamping boats. In a ten-foot dingey one can get an idea of the resources of the sea in the line of waves that is not probable to the average experience, which is never at sea in a dingey. As each slaty wall of water approached, it shut all else from the view of the men in the boat, and it was not difficult to imagine that this particular wave was the final outburst of the ocean, the last effort of the grim water. There was a terrible grace in the move of the waves, and they came in silence, save for the snarling of the crests.

In the wan light, the faces of the men must have been gray. Their eyes must have glinted in strange ways as they gazed steadily astern. Viewed from a balcony, the whole thing would doubtlessly have been weirdly picturesque. But the men in the boat had no time to see it, and if they had had leisure there were other things to occupy their minds. The sun swung steadily up the sky, and they knew it was broad day because the color of the sea changed from slate to emerald-green, streaked with amber lights, and the foam was like tumbling snow. The process of the breaking day was unknown to them. They were aware only of this effect upon the color of the waves that rolled toward them.

In disjointed sentences the cook and the correspondent argued as to the difference between a life-saving station and a house of refuge. The cook had said: "There's a house of refuge just north of the Mosquito Inlet Light, and as soon as they see us, they'll come off in their boat and pick us up."

"As soon as who see us?" said the correspondent.

"The crew," said the cook.

"Houses of refuge don't have crews," said the correspondent. "As I understand them, they are only places where clothes and grub are stored for the benefit of shipwrecked people. They don't carry crews."

"Oh, yes, they do," said the cook.

"No, they don't," said the correspondent.

"Well, we're not there yet, anyhow," said the oiler, in the stern.

"Well," said the cook, "perhaps it's not a house of refuge that I'm thinking of as being near Mosquito Inlet Light. Perhaps it's a life-saving station."

"We're not there yet," said the oiler, in the stern.

II

As the boat bounced from the top of each wave, the wind tore through the hair of the hatless men, and as the craft plopped her stern down again the spray slashed past them. The crest of each of these waves was a hill, from the top of which the men surveyed, for a moment, a broad tumultuous expanse, shining and wind-riven. It was probably splendid. It was probably glorious, this play of the free sea, wild with lights of emerald and white and amber.

"Bully good thing it's an on-shore wind," said the cook. "If not, where would we be? Wouldn't have a show."

"That's right," said the correspondent.

The busy oiler nodded his assent.

Then the captain, in the bow, chuckled in a way that expressed humor, contempt, tragedy, all in one. "Do you think we've got much of a show, now, boys?" said he.

Whereupon the three were silent, save for a trifle of hemming and hawing. To express any particular optimism at this time they felt to be childish and stupid, but they all doubtless possessed this sense of the situation in their mind. A young man thinks doggedly at such times. On the other hand, the ethics of their condition was decidedly against any open suggestion of hopelessness. So they were silent.

"Oh, well," said the captain, soothing his children, "we'll get ashore all right."

But there was that in his tone which made them think, so the oiler quoth: "Yes! If this wind holds!"

The cook was bailing. "Yes! If we don't catch hell in the surf."

Canton flannel gulls[2] flew near and far. Sometimes they sat down on the sea, near patches of brown sea-weed that rolled over the waves with a movement like carpets on a line in a gale. The birds sat comfortably in groups, and they were envied by some in the dingey, for the wrath of the sea was no more to them than it was to a covey of prairie chickens a thousand miles inland. Often they came very close and stared at the men with black bead-like eyes. At these times they were uncanny and sinister in their unblinking scrutiny, and the men hooted angrily at them, telling them to be gone. One came, and evidently decided to alight on the top of the captain's head. The bird flew parallel to the boat and did not circle, but made short sidelong jumps in the air in chicken-fashion. His black eyes were wistfully fixed upon the captain's head. "Ugly brute," said the oiler to the bird. "You look as if you were made with a jack-knife." The cook and the correspondent swore darkly at the creature. The captain naturally wished to knock it away with the end of the heavy painter,[3] but he did not dare do it, because anything resembling an emphatic gesture would have capsized this freighted boat, and so with his open hand, the captain gently and carefully waved the gull away. After it had been discouraged from the pursuit the captain breathed easier on account of his hair, and others breathed easier because the bird struck their minds at this time as being somehow grewsome and ominous.

In the meantime the oiler and the correspondent rowed. And also they rowed.

They sat together in the same seat, and each rowed an oar. Then the oiler took both oars; then the correspondent took both oars; then the oiler; then the correspondent. They rowed and they rowed. The very ticklish part of the business was when the time came for the reclining one in the stern to take his turn at the oars. By the very last star of truth, it is easier to steal eggs from under a hen than it was to change seats in the dingey. First the man in the stern slid his hand along the thwart and moved with care, as if he were of Sèvres.[4] Then the man in the rowing seat slid his hand along the other thwart. It was all done with the most extraordinary care. As the two sidled past each other, the whole party kept watchful eyes on the coming wave, and the captain cried: "Look out now! Steady there!"

The brown mats of sea-weed that appeared from time to time were like islands,

---

[2] The gulls look like cotton flannel from Canton, China.
[3] The coiled end of a rope used to fasten the boat to a wharf.
[4] Delicate porcelain made in Sèvres, France.

bits of earth. They were travelling, apparently, neither one way nor the other. They were, to all intents, stationary. They informed the men in the boat that it was making progress slowly toward the land.

The captain, rearing cautiously in the bow, after the dingey soared on a great swell, said that he had seen the light-house at Mosquito Inlet. Presently the cook remarked that he had seen it. The correspondent was at the oars, then, and for some reason he too wished to look at the light-house, but his back was toward the far shore and the waves were important, and for some time he could not seize an opportunity to turn his head. But at last there came a wave more gentle than the others, and when at the crest of it he swiftly scoured the western horizon.

"See it?" said the captain.

"No," said the correspondent, slowly, "I didn't see anything."

"Look again," said the captain. He pointed. "It's exactly in that direction."

At the top of another wave, the correspondent did as he was bid, and this time his eyes chanced on a small still thing on the edge of the swaying horizon. It was precisely like the point of a pin. It took an anxious eye to find a light-house so tiny.

"Think we'll make it, Captain?"

"If this wind holds and the boat don't swamp, we can't do much else," said the captain.

The little boat, lifted by each towering sea, and splashed viciously by the crests, made progress that in the absence of sea-weed was not apparent to those in her. She seemed just a wee thing wallowing, miraculously, top-up, at the mercy of five oceans. Occasionally, a great spread of water, like white flames, swarmed into her.

"Bail her, cook," said the captain, serenely.

"All right, Captain," said the cheerful cook.

III

It would be difficult to describe the subtle brotherhood of men that was here established on the seas. No one said that it was so. No one mentioned it. But it dwelt in the boat, and each man felt it warm him. They were a captain, an oiler, a cook, and a correspondent, and they were friends, friends in a more curiously iron-bound degree than may be common. The hurt captain, lying against the water-jar in the bow, spoke always in a low voice and calmly, but he could never command a more ready and swiftly obedient crew than the motley three of the dingey. It was more than a mere recognition of what was best for the common safety. There was surely in it a quality that was personal and heartfelt. And after this devotion to the commander of the boat there was this comradeship that the correspondent, for instance, who had been taught to be cynical of men, knew even at the time was the best experience of his life. But no one said that it was so. No one mentioned it.

"I wish we had a sail," remarked the captain. "We might try my overcoat on the end of an oar and give you two boys a chance to rest." So the cook and the correspondent held the mast and spread wide the overcoat. The oiler steered, and the little boat made good way with her new rig. Sometimes the oiler had to scull sharply to keep a sea from breaking into the boat, but otherwise sailing was a success.

Meanwhile the light-house had been growing slowly larger. It had now almost assumed color, and appeared like a little gray shadow on the sky. The man at the oars could not be prevented from turning his head rather often to try for a glimpse of this little gray shadow.

At last, from the top of each wave the men in the tossing boat could see land. Even as the light-house was an upright shadow on the sky, this land seemed but a long black shadow on the sea. It certainly was thinner than paper. "We must be about opposite New Smyrna," said the cook, who had coasted this shore often in schooners. "Captain, by the way, I believe they abandoned that life-saving station there about a year ago."

"Did they?" said the captain.

The wind slowly died away. The cook and the correspondent were not now obliged to slave in order to hold high the oar. But the waves continued their old impetuous swooping at the dingey, and the little craft, no longer under way, struggled woundily over them. The oiler or the correspondent took the oars again.

Shipwrecks are *apropos* of nothing. If men could only train for them and have them occur when the men had reached pink condition, there would be less drowning at sea. Of the four in the dingey none had slept any time worth mentioning for two days and two nights previous to embarking in the dingey, and in the excitement of clambering about the deck of a foundering ship they had also forgotten to eat heartily.

For these reasons, and for others, neither the oiler nor the correspondent was fond of rowing at this time. The correspondent wondered ingenuously how in the name of all that was sane could there be people who thought it amusing to row a boat. It was not an amusement; it was a diabolical punishment, and even a genius of mental aberrations could never conclude that it was anything but a horror to the muscles and a crime against the back. He mentioned to the boat in general how the amusement of rowing struck him, and the weary-faced oiler smiled in full sympathy. Previously to the foundering, by the way, the oiler had worked double-watch in the engine-room of the ship.

"Take her easy, now, boys," said the captain. "Don't spend yourselves. If we have to run a surf you'll need all your strength, because we'll sure have to swim for it. Take your time."

Slowly the land arose from the sea. From a black line it became a line of black and a line of white—trees and sand. Finally, the captain said that he could make out a house on the shore. "That's the house of refuge, sure," said the cook. "They'll see us before long, and come out after us."

The distant light-house reared high. "The keeper ought to be able to make us out now, if he's looking through a glass," said the captain. "He'll notify the life-saving people."

"None of those other boats could have got ashore to give word of the wreck," said the oiler, in a low voice. "Else the life-boat would be out hunting us."

Slowly and beautifully the land loomed out of the sea. The wind came again. It had veered from the northeast to the southeast. Finally, a new sound struck the ears of the men in the boat. It was the low thunder of the surf on the shore. "We'll never be able to make the light-house now," said the captain. "Swing her head a little more north, Billie."

" 'A little more north,' sir," said the oiler.

Whereupon the little boat turned her nose once more down the wind, and all but the oarsman watched the shore grow. Under the influence of this expansion doubt and direful apprehension was leaving the minds of the men. The management of the boat was still most absorbing, but it could not prevent a quiet cheerfulness. In an hour, perhaps, they would be ashore.

Their back-bones had become thoroughly used to balancing in the boat and they now rode this wild colt of a dingey like circus men. The correspondent thought that he had been drenched to the skin, but happening to feel in the top pocket of his coat, he found therein eight cigars. Four of them were soaked with sea-water; four were perfectly scatheless. After a search, somebody produced three dry matches, and thereupon the four waifs rode impudently in their little boat, and with an assurance of an impending rescue shining in their eyes, puffed at the big cigars and judged well and ill of all men. Everybody took a drink of water.

IV

"Cook," remarked the captain, "there don't seem to be any signs of life about your house of refuge."

"No," replied the cook. "Funny they don't see us!"

A broad stretch of lowly coast lay before the eyes of the men. It was of dunes topped with dark vegetation. The roar of the surf was plain, and sometimes they could see the white lip of a wave as it spun up the beach. a tiny house was blocked out black upon the sky. Southward, the slim light-house lifted its little gray length.

Tide, wind, and waves were swinging the dingey northward. "Funny they don't see us," said the men.

The surf's roar was here dulled, but its tone was, nevertheless, thunderous and mighty. As the boat swam over the great rollers, the men sat listening to this roar. "We'll swamp sure," said everybody.

It is fair to say here that there was not a life-saving station within twenty miles in either direction, but the men did not know this fact and in consequence they made dark and opprobrious remarks concerning the eyesight of the nation's life-savers. Four scowling men sat in the dingey and surpassed records in the invention of epithets.

"Funny they don't see us."

The light-heartedness of a former time had completely faded. To their sharpened minds it was easy to conjure pictures of all kinds of incompetency and blindness and, indeed, cowardice. There was the shore of the populous land, and it was bitter and bitter to them that from it came no sign.

"Well," said the captain, ultimately, "I suppose we'll have to make a try for ourselves. If we stay out here too long, we'll none of us have strength left to swim after the boat swamps."

And so the oiler, who was at the oars, turned the boat straight for the shore. There was a sudden tightening of muscles. There was some thinking.

"If we don't all get ashore—" said the captain. "If we don't all get ashore, I suppose you fellows know where to send news of my finish?"

They then briefly exchanged some addresses and admonitions. As for the reflections of the men, there was a great deal of rage in them. Perchance they might be formulated thus: "If I am going to be drowned—if I am going to be drowned—if I am going to be drowned, why, in the name of the seven mad gods who rule the sea, was I allowed to come thus far and contemplate sand and trees? Was I brought here merely to have my nose dragged away as I was about to nibble the sacred cheese of life? It is preposterous. If this old ninny-woman, Fate, cannot do better than this, she should be deprived of the management of men's fortunes. She is an old hen who knows not her intention. If she has decided to drown me, why did she not do it in the beginning and save me all this trouble. The whole affair is absurd. . . . But, no, she cannot mean to drown me. She dare not drown me. She cannot drown me. Not after all this work." Afterward the man might have had an impulse to shake his fist at the clouds. "Just you drown me, now, and then hear what I call you!"

The billows that came at this time were more formidable. They seemed always just about to break and roll over the little boat in a turmoil of foam. There was a preparatory and long growl in the speech of them. No mind unused to the sea would have concluded that the dingey could ascend these sheer heights in time. The shore was still afar. The oiler was a wily surfman. "Boys," he said, swiftly, "she won't live three minutes more and we're too far out to swim. Shall I take her to sea again, Captain?"

"Yes! Go ahead!" said the captain.

This oiler, by a series of quick miracles, and fast and steady oarsmanship, turned the boat in the middle of the surf and took her safely to sea again.

There was a considerable silence as the boat bumped over the furrowed sea to deeper water. Then somebody in gloom spoke. "Well, anyhow, they must have seen us from the shore by now."

The gulls went in slanting flight up the wind toward the gray desolate east. A squall, marked by dingy clouds, and clouds brick-red, like smoke from a burning building, appeared from the southeast.

"What do you think of those life-saving people? Ain't they peaches?"

"Funny they haven't seen us."

"Maybe they think we're out here for sport! Maybe they think we're fishin'. Maybe they think we're damned fools."

It was a long afternoon. A changed tide tried to force them southward, but wind and wave said northward. Far ahead, where coast-line, sea, and sky formed their mighty angle, there were little dots which seemed to indicate a city on the shore.

"St. Augustine?"

The captain shook his head. "Too near Mosquito Inlet."

And the oiler rowed, and then the correspondent rowed. Then the oiler rowed. It was a weary business. The human back can become the seat of more aches and pains than are registered in books for the composite anatomy of a regiment. It is a limited area, but it can become the theatre of innumerable muscular conflicts, tangles, wrenches, knots, and other comforts.

"Did you ever like to row, Billie?" asked the correspondent.

"No," said the oiler. "Hang it."

When one exchanged the rowing-seat for a place in the bottom of the boat, he suffered a bodily depression that caused him to be careless of everything save an obligation to wiggle one finger. There was cold sea-water swashing to and fro in the boat, and he lay in it. His head, pillowed on a thwart, was within an inch of the swirl of a wave crest, and sometimes a particularly obstreperous sea came in-board and drenched him once more. But these matters did not annoy him. It is almost certain that if the boat had capsized he would have tumbled comfortably out upon the ocean as if he felt sure that it was a great soft mattress.

"Look! There's a man on the shore!"

"Where?"

"There! See 'im? See 'im?"

"Yes, sure! He's walking along."

"Now he's stopped. Look! He's facing us!"

"He's waving at us!"

"So he is! By thunder!"

"Ah, now, we're all right! Now we're all right! There'll be a boat out here for us in half an hour."

"He's going on. He's running. He's going up to that house there."

The remote beach seemed lower than the sea, and it required a searching glance to discern the little black figure. The captain saw a floating stick and they rowed to it. A bath-towel was by some weird chance in the boat, and, tying this on the stick, the captain waved it. The oarsman did not dare turn his head, so he was obliged to ask questions.

"What's he doing now?"

"He's standing still again. He's looking, I think. . . . There he goes again. Toward the house. . . . Now he's stopped again."

"Is he waving at us?"

"No, not now! he was, though."

"Look! There comes another man!"

"He's running."

"Look at him go, would you."

"Why, he's on a bicycle. Now he's met the other man. They're both waving at us. Look!"

"There comes something up the beach."

"What the devil is that thing?"

"Why, it looks like a boat."

"Why, certainly it's a boat."

"No, it's on wheels."

"Yes, so it is. Well, that must be the life-boat. They drag them along shore on a wagon."

"That's the life-boat, sure."

"No, by———, it's—it's an omnibus."

"I tell you it's a life-boat."

"It is not! It's an omnibus. I can see it plain. See? One of those big hotel omnibuses."

"By thunder, you're right. It's an omnibus, sure as fate. What do you suppose they are doing with an omnibus? Maybe they are going around collecting the life-crew, hey?"

"That's it, likely. Look! There's a fellow waving a little black flag. He's standing on the steps of the omnibus. There come those other two fellows. Now they're all talking together. Look at the fellow with the flag. Maybe he ain't waving it!"

"That ain't a flag, is it? That's his coat. Why, certainly, that's his coat."

"So it is. It's his coat. He's taken it off and is waving it around his head. But would you look at him swing it!"

what's going on?

"Oh, say, there isn't any life-saving station there. That's just a winter resort hotel omnibus that has brought over some of the boarders to see us drown."

"What's that idiot with the coat mean? What's he signaling, anyhow?"

"It looks as if he were trying to tell us to go north. There must be a life-saving station up there."

"No! He thinks we're fishing. Just giving us a merry hand. See? Ah, there, Willie."

"Well, I wish I could make something out of those signals. What do you suppose he means?"

"He don't mean anything. He's just playing."

"Well, if he'd just signal us to try the surf again, or to go to sea and wait, or go north, or go south, or go to hell—there would be some reason in it. But look at him. He just stands there and keeps his coat revolving like a wheel. The ass!"

"There come more people."

"Now there's quite a mob. Look! Isn't that a boat?"

"Where? Oh, I see where you mean. No, that's no boat."

"That fellow is still waving his coat."

"He must think we like to see him do that. Why don't he quit it. It don't mean anything."

"I don't know. I think he is trying to make us go north. It must be that there's a life-saving station there somewhere."

"Say, he ain't tired yet. Look at 'im wave."

"Wonder how long he can keep that up. He's been revolving his coat ever since he caught sight of us. He's an idiot. Why aren't they getting men to bring a boat out. A fishing boat—one of those big yawls—could come out here all right. Why don't he do something?"

"Oh, it's all right, now."

"They'll have a boat out here for us in less than no time, now that they've seen us."

A faint yellow tone came into the sky over the low land. The shadows on the sea slowly deepened. The wind bore coldness with it, and the men began to shiver.

"Holy smoke!" said one, allowing his voice to express his impious mood, "if we keep on monkeying out here! If we've got to flounder out here all night!"

"Oh, we'll never have to stay here all night! Don't you worry. They've seen us now, and it won't be long before they'll come chasing out after us."

The shore grew dusky. The man waving a coat blended gradually into this gloom, and it swallowed in the same manner the omnibus and the group of people. The spray, when it dashed uproariously over the side, made the voyagers shrink and swear like men who were being branded.

"I'd like to catch the chump who waved the coat. I feel like soaking him one, just for luck."

"Why? What did he do?"

"Oh, nothing, but then he seemed so damned cheerful."

In the meantime the oiler rowed, and the correspondent rowed, and then the oiler rowed. Gray-faced and bowed forward, they mechanically, turn by turn, plied the leaden oars. The form of the light-house had vanished from the southern horizon, but finally a pale star appeared, just lifting from the sea. The streaked saffron in the west passed before the all-merging darkness, and the sea to the east was black. The land had vanished, and was expressed only by the low and drear thunder of the surf.

"If I am going to be drowned—if I am going to be drowned—if I am going to be drowned, why, in the name of the seven mad gods who rule the sea, was I allowed to come thus far and contemplate sand and trees? Was I brought here merely to have my nose dragged away as I was about to nibble the sacred cheese of life?"

The patient captain, drooped over the water-jar, was sometimes obliged to speak to the oarsman.

"Keep her head up! Keep her head up!"

" 'Keep her head up,' sir." The voices were weary and low.

This was surely a quiet evening. All save the oarsman lay heavily and listlessly in the boat's bottom. As for him, his eyes were just capable of noting the tall black waves that swept forward in a most sinister silence, save for an occasional sub-dued growl of a crest.

The cook's head was on a thwart, and he looked without interest at the water under his nose. He was deep in other scenes. Finally he spoke. "Billie," he murmured, dreamfully, "what kind of pie do you like best?"

V

"Pie," said the oiler and the correspondent, agitatedly. "Don't talk about those things, blast you!"

"Well," said the cook, "I was just thinking about ham sandwiches, and————"

A night on the sea in an open boat is a long night. As darkness settled finally, the shine of the light, lifting from the sea in the south, changed to full gold. On the northern horizon a new light appeared, a small bluish gleam on the edge of the waters. These two lights were the furniture of the world. Otherwise there was nothing but waves.

Two men huddled in the stern, and distances were so magnificent in the dingey that the rower was enabled to keep his feet partly warmed by thrusting them under his companions. Their legs indeed extended far under the rowing-seat until they touched the feet of the captain forward. Sometimes, despite the efforts of the tired oarsman, a wave came piling into the boat, an icy wave of the night, and the chilling water soaked them anew. They would twist their bodies for a moment and groan, and sleep the dead sleep once more, while the water in the boat gurgled about them as the craft rocked.

The plan of the oiler and the correspondent was for one to row until he lost the ability, and then arouse the other from his sea-water couch in the bottom of the boat.

The oiler plied the oars until his head drooped forward, and the overpowering sleep blinded him. And he rowed yet afterward. Then he touched a man in the bottom of the boat, and called his name. "Will you spell me for a little while?" he said, meekly.

"Sure, Billie," said the correspondent, awakening and dragging himself to a sitting position. They exchanged places carefully, and the oiler, cuddling down in the sea-water at the cook's side, seemed to go to sleep instantly.

The particular violence of the sea had ceased. The waves came without snarling. The obligation of the man at the oars was to keep the boat headed so that the tilt of the rollers would not capsize her, and to preserve her from filling when the crests rushed past. The black waves were silent and hard to be seen in the darkness. Often one was almost upon the boat before the oarsman was aware.

In a low voice the correspondent addressed the captain. He was not sure that the captain was awake, although this iron man seemed to be always awake. "Captain, shall I keep her making for that light north, sir?"

The same steady voice answered him. "Yes. Keep it about two points off the port bow."

The cook had tied a life-belt around himself in order to get even the warmth which this clumsy cork contrivance could donate, and he seemed almost stove-like when a rower, whose teeth invariably chattered wildly as soon as he ceased his labor, dropped down to sleep.

The correspondent, as he rowed, looked down at the two men sleeping under foot. The cook's arm was around the oiler's shoulders, and, with their fragmentary clothing and haggard faces, they were the babes of the sea, a grotesque rendering of the old babes in the wood.

Later he must have grown stupid at his work, for suddenly there was a growling of water, and a crest came with a roar and a swash into the boat, and it was a wonder that it did not set the cook afloat in his life-belt. The cook continued to sleep, but the oiler sat up, blinking his eyes and shaking with the new cold.

"Oh, I'm awful sorry, Billie," said the correspondent, contritely.

"That's all right, old boy," said the oiler, and lay down again and was asleep.

Presently it seemed that even the captain dozed, and the correspondent thought that he was the one man afloat on all the oceans. The wind had a voice as it came over the waves, and it was sadder than the end.

There was a long, loud swishing astern of the boat, and a gleaming trail of phosphorescence, like blue flame, was furrowed on the black waters. It might have been made by a monstrous knife.

Then there came a stillness, while the correspondent breathed with the open mouth and looked at the sea.

Suddenly there was another swish and another long flash of bluish light, and this time it was alongside the boat, and might almost have been reached with an oar. The correspondent saw an enormous fin speed like a shadow through the water, hurling the crystalline spray and leaving the long glowing trail.

The correspondent looked over his shoulder at the captain. His face was hidden, and he seemed to be asleep. He looked at the babes of the sea. They certainly were asleep. So, being bereft of sympathy, he leaned a little way to one side and swore softly into the sea.

But the thing did not then leave the vicinity of the boat. Ahead or astern, on one side or the other, at intervals long or short, fled the long sparkling streak, and there was to be heard the whiroo of the dark fin. The speed and power of the thing was greatly to be admired. It cut the water like a gigantic and keen projectile.

The presence of this biding thing did not affect the man with the same horror that it would if he had been a picnicker. He simply looked at the sea dully and swore in an undertone.

Nevertheless, it is true that he did not wish to be alone with the thing. He wished one of his companions to awaken by chance and keep him company with it. But the captain hung motionless over the water-jar and the oiler and the cook in the bottom of the boat were plunged in slumber.

VI

"If I am going to be drowned—if I am going to be drowned—if I am going to be drowned, why, in the name of the seven mad gods who rule the sea, was I allowed to come thus far and contemplate sand and trees?"

During this dismal night, it may be remarked that a man would conclude that it was really the intention of the seven mad gods to drown him, despite the abominable injustice of it. For it was certainly an abominable injustice to drown a man who had worked so hard, so hard. The man felt it would be a crime most unnatural. Other people had drowned at sea since galleys swarmed with painted sails, but still——

When it occurs to a man that nature does not regard him as important, and that she feels she would not maim the universe by disposing of him, he at first wishes to throw bricks at the temple, and he hates deeply the fact that there are no bricks and no temples. Any visible expression of nature would surely be pelleted with his jeers.

Then, if there be no tangible thing to hoot he feels, perhaps, the desire to confront a personification and indulge in pleas, bowed to one knee, and with hands supplicant, saying: "Yes, but I love myself."

A high cold star on a winter's night is the word he feels that she says to him. Thereafter he knows the pathos of his situation.

The men in the dingey had not discussed these matters, but each had, no doubt, reflected upon them in silence and according to his mind. There was seldom any expression upon their faces save the general one of complete weariness. Speech was devoted to the business of the boat.

To chime the notes of his emotion, a verse mysteriously entered the correspondent's head. He had even forgotten that he had forgotten this verse, but it suddenly was in his mind.

> A soldier of the Legion lay dying in Algiers,
> There was lack of woman's nursing, there was dearth of woman's tears;
> But a comrade stood beside him, and he took that comrade's hand,
> And he said: "I never more shall see my own, my native land."[5]

In his childhood, the correspondent had been made acquainted with the fact that a soldier of the Legion lay dying in Algiers, but he had never regarded it as important. Myriads of his school-fellows had informed him of the soldier's plight, but the dinning had naturally ended by making him perfectly indifferent. He had never considered it his affair that a soldier of the Legion lay dying in Algiers, nor had it appeared to him as a matter for sorrow. It was less to him than the breaking of a pencil's point.

Now, however, it quaintly came to him as a human, living thing. It was no longer merely a picture of a few throes in the breast of a poet, meanwhile drinking tea and warming his feet at the grate; it was an actuality—stern, mournful, and fine.

The correspondent plainly saw the soldier. He lay on the sand with his feet out straight and still. While his pale left hand was upon his chest in an attempt to thwart the going of his life, the blood came between his fingers. In the far Alge-

[5] Adapted from the poem "Bingen on the Rhine" (1883), by Caroline E. S. Norton (1808–1877).

rian distance, a city of low square forms was set against a sky that was faint with the last sunset hues. The correspondent, plying the oars and dreaming of the slow and slower movements of the lips of the soldier, was moved by a profound and perfectly impersonal comprehension. He was sorry for the soldier of the Legion who lay dying in Algiers.

The thing which had followed the boat and waited had evidently grown bored at the delay. There was no longer to be heard the slash of the cut-water, and there was no longer the flame of the long trail. The light in the north still glimmered, but it was apparently no nearer to the boat. Sometimes the boom of the surf rang in the correspondent's ears, and he turned the craft seaward then and rowed harder. Southward, some one had evidently built a watch-fire on the beach. It was too low and too far to be seen, but it made a shimmering, roseate reflection upon the bluff back of it, and this could be discerned from the boat. The wind came stronger, and sometimes a wave suddenly raged out like a mountain-cat and there was to be seen the sheen and sparkle of a broken crest.

The captain, in the bow, moved on his water-jar and sat erect. "Pretty long night," he observed to the correspondent. He looked at the shore. "Those life-saving people take their time."

"Did you see that shark playing around?"

"Yes, I saw him. He was a big fellow, all right."

"Wish I had known you were awake."

Later the correspondent spoke into the bottom of the boat. "Billie!" There was a slow and gradual disentanglement. "Billie, will you spell me?"

"Sure," said the oiler.

As soon as the correspondent touched the cold comfortable sea-water in the bottom of the boat, and had huddled close to the cook's life-belt he was deep in sleep, despite the fact that his teeth played all the popular airs. This sleep was so good to him that it was but a moment before he heard a voice call his name in a tone that demonstrated the last stages of exhaustion. "Will you spell me?"

"Sure, Billie."

The light in the north had mysteriously vanished, but the correspondent took his course from the wide-awake captain.

Later in the night they took the boat farther out to sea, and the captain directed the cook to take one oar at the stern and keep the boat facing the seas. He was to call out if he should hear the thunder of the surf. This plan enabled the oiler and the correspondent to get respite together. "We'll give those boys a chance to get into shape again," said the captain. They curled down and, after a few preliminary chatterings and trembles, slept once more the dead sleep. Neither knew they had bequeathed to the cook the company of another shark, or perhaps the same shark.

As the boat caroused on the waves, spray occasionally bumped over the side and gave them a fresh soaking, but this had no power to break their repose. The ominous slash of the wind and the water affected them as it would have affected mummies.

"Boys," said the cook, with the notes of every reluctance in his voice, "she's drifted in pretty close. I guess one of you had better take her to sea again." The correspondent, aroused, heard the crash of the toppled crests.

As he was rowing, the captain gave him some whiskey and water, and this steadied the chills out of him. "If I can ever get ashore and anybody shows me even a photograph of an oar———"

At last there was a short conversation.

"Billie. . . . Billie, will you spell me?"

"Sure," said the oiler.

VII

When the correspondent again opened his eyes, the sea and the sky were each of the gray hue of the dawning. Later, carmine and gold was painted upon the waters. The morning appeared finally, in its splendor, with a sky of pure blue, and the sunlight flamed on the tips of the waves.

On the distant dunes were set many little black cottages, and a tall white windmill reared above them. No man, nor dog, nor bicycle appeared on the beach. The cottages might have formed a deserted village.

The voyagers scanned the shore. A conference was held in the boat. "Well," said the captain, "if no help is coming, we might better try a run through the surf right away. If we stay out here much longer we will be too weak to do anything for ourselves at all." The others silently acquiesced in this reasoning. The boat was headed for the beach. The correspondent wondered if none ever ascended the tall wind-tower, and if then they never looked seaward. This tower was a giant, standing with its back to the plight of the ants. It represented in a degree, to the correspondent, the serenity of nature amid the struggles of the individual—nature in the wind, and nature in the vision of men. She did not seem cruel to him then, nor beneficent, nor treacherous, nor wise. But she was indifferent, flatly indifferent. It is, perhaps, plausible that a man in this situation, impressed with the unconcern of the universe, should see the innumerable flaws of his life and have them taste wickedly in his mind and wish for another chance. A distinction between right and wrong seems absurdly clear to him, then, in this new ignorance of the grave-edge, and he understands that if he were given another opportunity he would mend his conduct and his words, and be better and brighter during an introduction, or at a tea.

"Now, boys," said the captain, "she is going to swamp sure. All we can do is to work her in as far as possible, and then when she swamps, pile out and scramble for the beach. Keep cool now, and don't jump until she swamps sure."

The oiler took the oars. Over his shoulders he scanned the surf. "Captain," he said, "I think I'd better bring her about, and keep her head-on to the seas and back her in."

"All right, Billie," said the captain. "Back her in." The oiler swung the boat then and, seated in the stern, the cook and the correspondent were obliged to look over their shoulders to contemplate the lonely and indifferent shore.

The monstrous inshore rollers heaved the boat high until the men were again enabled to see the white sheets of water scudding up the slanted beach. "We won't get in very close," said the captain. Each time a man could wrest his attention from the rollers, he turned his glance toward the shore, and in the expression of the eyes during this contemplation there was a singular quality. The correspondent, observing the others, knew that they were not afraid, but the full meaning of their glances was shrouded.

As for himself, he was too tired to grapple fundamentally with the fact. He tried to coerce his mind into thinking of it, but the mind was dominated at this time by the muscles, and the muscles said they did not care. It merely occurred to him that if he should drown it would be a shame.

There were no hurried words, no pallor, no plain agitation. The men simply looked at the shore. "Now, remember to get well clear of the boat when you jump," said the captain.

Seaward the crest of a roller suddenly fell with a thunderous crash, and the long white comber came roaring down upon the boat.

"Steady now," said the captain. The men were silent. They turned their eyes from the shore to the comber and waited. The boat slid up the incline, leaped at the furious top, bounced over it, and swung down the long back of the wave. Some water had been shipped and the cook bailed it out.

But the next crest crashed also. The tumbling boiling flood of white water caught the boat and whirled it almost perpendicular. Water swarmed in from all sides. The correspondent had his hands on the gunwale at this time, and when the water entered at that place he swiftly withdrew his fingers, as if he objected to wetting them.

The little boat, drunken with this weight of water, reeled and snuggled deeper into the sea.

"Bail her out, cook! Bail her out," said the captain.

"All right, Captain," said the cook.

"Now, boys, the next one will do for us, sure," said the oiler. "Mind to jump clear of the boat."

The third wave moved forward, huge, furious, implacable. It fairly swallowed the dingey, and almost simultaneously the men tumbled into the sea. A piece of life-belt had lain in the bottom of the boat, and as the correspondent went overboard he held this to his chest with his left hand.

The January water was icy, and he reflected immediately that it was colder than he had expected to find it off the coast of Florida. This appeared to his dazed mind as a fact important enough to be noted at the time. The coldness of the water was sad; it was tragic. This fact was somehow so mixed and confused with his opinion of his own situation that it seemed almost a proper reason for tears. The water was cold.

When he came to the surface he was conscious of little but the noisy water. Afterward he saw his companions in the sea. The oiler was ahead in the race. He was swimming strongly and rapidly. Off to the correspondent's left, the cook's great white and corked back bulged out of the water, and in the rear the captain was hanging with his one good hand to the keel of the overturned dingey.

There is a certain immovable quality to a shore, and the correspondent wondered at it amid the confusion of the sea.

It seemed also very attractive, but the correspondent knew that it was a long journey, and he paddled leisurely. The piece of life-preserver lay under him, and sometimes he whirled down the incline of a wave as if he were on a hand-sled.

But finally he arrived at a place in the sea where travel was beset with difficulty. He did not pause swimming to inquire what manner of current had caught him, but there his progress ceased. The shore was set before him like a bit of scenery on a stage, and he looked at it and understood with his eyes each detail of it.

As the cook passed, much farther to the left, the captain was calling to him, "Turn over on your back, cook! Turn over on your back and use the oar."

"All right, sir." The cook turned on his back, and, paddling with an oar, went ahead as if he were a canoe.

Presently the boat also passed to the left of the correspondent with the captain clinging with one hand to the keel. He would have appeared like a man raising himself to look over a board fence, if it were not for the extraordinary gymnastics of the boat. The correspondent marvelled that the captain could still hold to it.

They passed on, nearer to shore—the oiler, the cook, the captain—and following them went the water-jar, bouncing gayly over the seas.

The correspondent remained in the grip of this strange new enemy—a current. The shore, with its white slope of sand and its green bluff, topped with little silent cottages, was spread like a picture before him. It was very near to him then, but he was impressed as one who in a gallery looks at a scene from Brittany or Holland.

He thought: "I am going to drown? Can it be possible? Can it be possible? Can it be possible?" Perhaps an individual must consider his own death to be the final phenomenon of nature.

But later a wave perhaps whirled him out of this small deadly current, for he found suddenly that he could again make progress toward the shore. Later still, he was aware that the captain, clinging with one hand to the keel of the dingey, had his face turned away from the shore and toward him, and was calling his name. "Come to the boat! Come to the boat!"

In his struggle to reach the captain and the boat, he reflected that when one gets properly wearied, drowning must really be a comfortable arrangement, a cessation of hostilities accompanied by a large degree of relief, and he was glad of it, for the main thing in his mind for some moments had been horror of the temporary agony. He did not wish to be hurt.

Presently he saw a man running along the shore. He was undressing with most remarkable speed. Coat, trousers, shirt, everything flew magically off him.

"Come to the boat," called the captain.

"All right, Captain." As the correspondent paddled, he saw the captain let himself down to bottom and leave the boat. Then the correspondent performed his one little marvel of the voyage. A large wave caught him and flung him with ease and supreme speed completely over the boat and far beyond it. It struck him even then as an event in gymnastics, and a true miracle of the sea. An overturned boat in the surf is not a plaything to a swimming man.

The correspondent arrived in water that reached only to his waist, but his condition did not enable him to stand for more than a moment. Each wave knocked him into a heap, and the under-tow pulled at him.

Then he saw the man who had been running and undressing, and undressing and running, come bounding into the water. He dragged ashore the cook, and then waded toward the captain, but the captain waved him away, and sent him to the correspondent. He was naked, naked as a tree in winter, but a halo was about his head, and he shone like a saint. He gave a strong pull, and a long drag, and a bully heave at the correspondent's hand. The correspondent, schooled in the minor formulæ, said: "Thanks, old man." But suddenly the man cried: "What's that?" He pointed a swift finger. The correspondent said: "Go."

In the shallows, face downward, lay the oiler. His forehead touched sand that was periodically, between each wave, clear of the sea.

The correspondent did not know all that transpired afterward. When he achieved safe ground he fell, striking the sand with each particular part of his body. It was as if he had dropped from a roof, but the thud was grateful to him.

It seems that instantly the beach was populated with men with blankets, clothes, and flasks, and women with coffee-pots and all the remedies sacred to their minds. The welcome of the land to the men from the sea was warm and generous, but a still and dripping shape was carried slowly up the beach, and the land's welcome for it could only be the different and sinister hospitality of the grave.

When it came night, the white waves paced to and fro in the moonlight, and the wind brought the sound of the great sea's voice to the men on shore, and they felt that they could then be interpreters.

1897

THE BRIDE COMES TO YELLOW SKY*

I

The great Pullman[1] was whirling onward with such dignity of motion that a glance from the window seemed simply to prove that the plains of Texas were pouring eastward. Vast flats of green grass, dull-hued spaces of mesquite and cactus, little groups of frame houses, woods of light and tender trees, all were sweeping into the east, sweeping over the horizon, a precipice.

A newly married pair had boarded this coach at San Antonio. The man's face was reddened from many days in the wind and sun, and a direct result of his new black clothes was that his brick-colored hands were constantly performing in a most conscious fashion. From time to time he looked down respectfully at his attire. He sat with a hand on each knee, like a man waiting in a barber's shop. The glances he devoted to other passengers were furtive and shy.

The bride was not pretty, nor was she very young. She wore a dress of blue cashmere, with small reservations of velvet here and there and with steel buttons abounding. She continually twisted her head to regard her puff sleeves, very stiff, straight, and high. They embarrassed her. It was quite apparent that she had cooked, and that she expected to cook, dutifully. The blushes caused by the careless scrutiny of some passengers as she had entered the car were strange to see upon this plain, under-class countenance, which was drawn in placid, almost emotionless lines.

They were evidently very happy. "Ever been in a parlor-car before?" he asked, smiling with delight.

"No," she answered. "I never was. It's fine, ain't it?"

---

* First published in *McClure's Magazine* in America and in *Chapman's Magazine* in England in February 1898.
  [1] A railroad passenger car with convertible sleeping berths, named for its inventor, G. M. Pullman (1831–1897).

"Great! And then after a while we'll go forward to the diner and get a big lay-out. Finest meal in the world. Charge a dollar."

"Oh, do they?" cried the bride. "Charge a dollar? Why, that's too much—for us—ain't it, Jack?"

"Not this trip, anyhow," he answered bravely. "We're going to go the whole thing."

Later, he explained to her about the trains. "You see, it's a thousand miles from one end of Texas to the other, and this train runs right across it and never stops but four times." He had the pride of an owner. He pointed out to her the dazzling fittings of the coach, and in truth her eyes opened wider as she contemplated the sea-green figured velvet, the shining brass, silver, and glass, the wood that gleamed as darkly brilliant as the surface of a pool of oil. At one end a bronze figure sturdily held a support for a separated chamber, and at convenient places on the ceiling were frescoes in olive and silver.

To the minds of the pair, their surroundings reflected the glory of their marriage that morning in San Antonio. This was the environment of their new estate, and the man's face in particular beamed with an elation that made him appear ridiculous to the negro porter. This individual at times surveyed them from afar with an amused and superior grin. On other occasions he bullied them with skill in ways that did not make it exactly plain to them that they were being bullied. He subtly used all the manners of the most unconquerable kind of snobbery. He oppressed them, but of this oppression they had small knowledge, and they speedily forgot that infrequently a number of travelers covered them with stares of derisive enjoyment. Historically there was supposed to be something infinitely humorous in their situation.

"We are due in Yellow Sky at 3.42," he said, looking tenderly into her eyes.

"Oh, are we?" she said, as if she had not been aware of it. To evince surprise at her husband's statement was part of her wifely amiability. She took from a pocket a little silver watch, and as she held it before her and stared at it with a frown of attention, the new husband's face shone.

"I bought it in San Anton' from a friend of mine," he told her gleefully.

"It's seventeen minutes past twelve," she said, looking up at him with a kind of shy and clumsy coquetry. A passenger, noting this play, grew excessively sardonic, and winked at himself in one of the numerous mirrors.

At last they went to the dining-car. Two rows of negro waiters in glowing white suits surveyed their entrance with the interest and also the equanimity of men who had been forewarned. The pair fell to the lot of a waiter who happened to feel pleasure in steering them through their meal. He viewed them with the manner of a fatherly pilot, his countenance radiant with benevolence. The patronage entwined with the ordinary deference was not plain to them. And yet as they returned to their coach they showed in their faces a sense of escape.

To the left, miles down a long purple slope, was a little ribbon of mist where moved the keening Rio Grande. The train was approaching it at an angle, and the apex was Yellow Sky. Presently it was apparent that as the distance from Yellow Sky grew shorter, the husband became commensurately restless. His brick-red hands were more insistent in their prominence. Occasionally he was even rather absent-minded and far-away when the bride leaned forward and addressed him.

As a matter of truth, Jack Potter was beginning to find the shadow of a deed weigh upon him like a leaden slab. He, the town marshal of Yellow Sky, a man known, liked, and feared in his corner, a prominent person, had gone to San

Antonio to meet a girl he believed he loved, and there, after the usual prayers, had actually induced her to marry him, without consulting Yellow Sky for any part of the transaction. He was now bringing his bride before an innocent and unsuspecting community.

Of course, people in Yellow Sky married as it pleased them in accordance with a general custom; but such was Potter's thought of his duty to his friends, or of their idea of his duty, or of an unspoken form which does not control men in these matters, that he felt he was heinous. He had committed an extraordinary crime. Face to face with this girl in San Antonio, and spurred by his sharp impulse, he had gone headlong over all the social hedges. At San Antonio he was like a man hidden in the dark. A knife to sever any friendly duty, any form, was easy to his hand in that remote city. But the hour of Yellow Sky, the hour of daylight, was approaching.

He knew full well that his marriage was an important thing to his town. It could only be exceeded by the burning of the new hotel. His friends would not forgive him. Frequently he had reflected on the advisability of telling them by telegraph, but a new cowardice had been upon him. He feared to do it. And now the train was hurrying him toward a scene of amazement, glee, reproach. He glanced out of the window at the line of haze swinging slowly in toward the train.

Yellow Sky had a kind of brass band which played painfully to the delight of the populace. He laughed without heart as he thought of it. If the citizens could dream of his prospective arrival with his bride, they would parade the band at the station and escort them, amid cheers and laughing congratulations, to his adobe home.

He resolved that he would use all the devices of speed and plains-craft in making the journey from the station to his house. Once within that safe citadel, he could issue some sort of a vocal bulletin, and then not go among the citizens until they had time to wear off a little of their enthusiasm.

The bride looked anxiously at him. "What's worrying you, Jack?"

He laughed again. "I'm not worrying, girl. I'm only thinking of Yellow Sky."

She flushed in comprehension.

A sense of mutual guilt invaded their minds and developed a finer tenderness. They looked at each other with eyes softly aglow. But Potter often laughed the same nervous laugh. The flush upon the bride's face seemed quite permanent.

The traitor to the feelings of Yellow Sky narrowly watched the speeding landscape. "We're nearly there," he said.

Presently the porter came and announced the proximity of Potter's home. He held a brush in his hand and, with all his airy superiority gone, he brushed Potter's new clothes as the latter slowly turned this way and that way. Potter fumbled out a coin and gave it to the porter as he had seen others do. It was a heavy and muscle-bound business, as that of a man shoeing his first horse.

The porter took their bag, and as the train began to slow they moved forward to the hooded platform of the car. Presently the two engines and their long string of coaches rushed into the station of Yellow Sky.

"They have to take water here," said Potter, from a constricted throat and in mournful cadence as one announcing death. Before the train stopped his eye had swept the length of the platform, and he was glad and astonished to see there was none upon it but the station-agent, who, with a slightly hurried and anxious air, was walking toward the water-tanks. When the train had halted, the porter alighted first and placed in position a little temporary step.

"Come on, girl," said Potter hoarsely. As he helped her down they each laughed on a false note. He took the bag from the negro, and bade his wife cling to his arm. As they slunk rapidly away, his hang-dog glance perceived that they were unloading the two trunks, and also that the station-agent far ahead near the baggage-car had turned and was running toward him, making gestures. He laughed, and groaned as he laughed, when he noted the first effect of his marital bliss upon Yellow Sky. He gripped his wife's arm firmly to his side, and they fled. Behind them the porter stood chuckling fatuously.

II

The California Express on the Southern Railway was due at Yellow Sky in twenty-one minutes. There were six men at the bar of the Weary Gentleman saloon. One was a drummer[2] who talked a great deal and rapidly; three were Texans who did not care to talk at that time; and two were Mexican sheep-herders who did not talk as a general practice in the Weary Gentleman saloon. The bar-keeper's dog lay on the board-walk that crossed in front of the door. His head was on his paws, and he glanced drowsily here and there with the constant vigilance of a dog that is kicked on occasion. Across the sandy street were some vivid green grass plots, so wonderful in appearance amid the sands that burned near them in a blazing sun that they caused a doubt in the mind. They exactly resembled the grass mats used to represent lawns on the stage. At the cooler end of the railway station a man without a coat sat in a tilted chair and smoked his pipe. The fresh-cut bank of the Rio Grande circled near the town, and there could be seen beyond it a great plum-colored plain of mesquite.

Save for the busy drummer and his companions in the saloon, Yellow Sky was dozing. The new-comer leaned gracefully upon the bar, and recited many tales with the confidence of a bard who has come upon a new field.

"———and at the moment that the old man fell down stairs with the bureau in his arms, the old woman was coming up with two scuttles[3] of coal, and, of course———"

The drummer's tale was interrupted by a young man who suddenly appeared in the open door. He cried: "Scratchy Wilson's drunk, and has turned loose with both hands." The two Mexicans at once set down their glasses and faded out of the rear entrance of the saloon.

The drummer, innocent and jocular, answered: "All right, old man. S'pose he has. Come in and have a drink, anyhow."

But the information had made such an obvious cleft in every skull in the room that the drummer was obliged to see its importance. All had become instantly morose. "Say," said he, mystified, "what is this?" His three companions made the introductory gesture of eloquent speech, but the young man at the door forestalled them.

"It means, my friend," he answered, as he came into the saloon, "that for the next two hours this town won't be a health resort."

The bar-keeper went to the door and locked and barred it. Reaching out of the window, he pulled in heavy wooden shutters and barred them. Immediately a

[2] A traveling salesman.   [3] Buckets with a wide lip.

solemn, chapel-like gloom was upon the place. The drummer was looking from one to another.

"But say," he cried, "what is this, anyhow? You don't mean there is going to be a gun-fight?"

"Don't know whether there'll be a fight or not," answered one man grimly. "But there'll be some shootin'—some good shootin'."

The young man who had warned them waved his hand. "Oh, there'll be a fight fast enough, if anyone wants it. Anybody can get a fight out there in the street. There's a fight just waiting."

The drummer seemed to be swayed between the interest of a foreigner and a perception of personal danger.

"What did you say his name was?" he asked.

"Scratchy Wilson,"[4] they answered in chorus.

"And will he kill anybody? What are you going to do? Does this happen often? Does he rampage around like this once a week or so? Can he break in that door?"

"No, he can't break down that door," replied the bar-keeper. "He's tried it three times. But when he comes you'd better lay down on the floor, stranger. He's dead sure to shoot at it, and a bullet may come through."

Thereafter the drummer kept a strict eye upon the door. The time had not yet been called for him to hug the floor, but as a minor precaution he sidled near to the wall. "Will he kill anybody?" he said again.

The men laughed low and scornfully at the question.

"He's out to shoot, and he's out for trouble. Don't see any good in experimentin' with him."

"But what do you do in a case like this? What do you do?"

A man responded: "Why, he and Jack Potter————"

But, in chorus, the other men interrupted: "Jack Potter's in San Anton'."

"Well, who is he? What's he got to do with it?"

"Oh, he's the town marshal. He goes out and fights Scratchy when he gets on one of these tears."

"Wow," said the drummer, mopping his brow. "Nice job he's got."

The voices had toned away to mere whisperings. The drummer wished to ask further questions which were born of an increasing anxiety and bewilderment; but when he attempted them, the men merely looked at him in irritation and motioned him to remain silent. A tense waiting hush was upon them. In the deep shadows of the room their eyes shone as they listened for sounds from the street. One man made three gestures at the bar-keeper, and the latter, moving like a ghost, handed him a glass and a bottle. The man poured a full glass of whisky, and set down the bottle noiselessly. He gulped the whisky in a swallow, and turned again toward the door in immovable silence. The drummer saw that the bar-keeper, without a sound, had taken a Winchester from beneath the bar. Later he saw this individual beckoning to him, so he tiptoed across the room.

"You better come with me back of the bar."

"No, thanks," said the drummer, perspiring. "I'd rather be where I can make a break for the back door."

Whereupon the man of bottles made a kindly but peremptory gesture. The drummer obeyed it, and finding himself seated on a box with his head below the

---

[4] Scratchy Wilson appears as Jack Potter's deputy in Crane's story "Moonlight on the Snow," published posthumously in 1901.

level of the bar, balm was laid upon his soul at sight of various zinc and copper fittings that bore a resemblance to armor-plate. The bar-keeper took a seat comfortably upon an adjacent box.

"You see," he whispered, "this here Scratchy Wilson is a wonder with a gun— a perfect wonder—and when he goes on the war trail, we hunt our holes—naturally. He's about the last one of the old gang that used to hang out along the river here. He's a terror when he's drunk. When he's sober he's all right—kind of simple—wouldn't hurt a fly—nicest fellow in town. But when he's drunk— whoo!"

There were periods of stillness. "I wish Jack Potter was back from San Anton'," said the bar-keeper. "He shot Wilson up once—in the leg—and he would sail in and pull out the kinks in this thing."

Presently they heard from a distance the sound of a shot, followed by three wild yowls. It instantly removed a bond from the men in the darkened saloon. There was a shuffling of feet. They looked at each other. "Here he comes," they said.

III

A man in a maroon-colored flannel shirt, which had been purchased for purposes of decoration and made, principally, by some Jewish women on the east side of New York, rounded a corner and walked into the middle of the main street of Yellow Sky. In either hand the man held a long, heavy blue-black revolver. Often he yelled, and these cries rang through a semblance of a deserted village, shrilly flying over the roofs in a volume that seemed to have no relation to the ordinary vocal strength of a man. It was as if the surrounding stillness formed the arch of a tomb over him. These cries of ferocious challenge rang against walls of silence. And his boots had red tops with gilded imprints, of the kind beloved in winter by little sledding boys on the hillsides of New England.

The man's face flamed in a rage begot of whisky. His eyes, rolling and yet keen for ambush, hunted the still door-ways and windows. He walked with the creeping movement of the midnight cat. As it occurred to him, he roared menacing information. The long revolvers in his hands were as easy as straws; they were moved with an electric swiftness. The little fingers of each hand played sometimes in a musician's way. Plain from the low collar of the shirt, the cords of his neck straightened and sank, straightened and sank, as passion moved him. The only sounds were his terrible invitations. The calm adobes preserved their demeanor at the passing of this small thing in the middle of the street.

There was no offer of fight; no offer of fight. The man called to the sky. There were no attractions. He bellowed and fumed and swayed his revolvers here and everywhere.

The dog of the bar-keeper of the Weary Gentleman saloon had not appreciated the advance of events. He yet lay dozing in front of his master's door. At sight of the dog, the man paused and raised his revolver humorously. At sight of the man, the dog sprang up and walked diagonally away, with a sullen head and growling. The man yelled, and the dog broke into a gallop. As it was about to enter an alley, there was a loud noise, a whistling, and something spat the ground directly before it. The dog screamed, and, wheeling in terror, galloped headlong in a new direction. Again there was a noise, a whistling, and sand was kicked viciously before it. Fear-stricken, the dog turned and flurried like an animal in a pen. The man stood laughing, his weapons at his hips.

Ultimately the man was attracted by the closed door of the Weary Gentleman saloon. He went to it, and hammering with a revolver, demanded drink.

The door remaining imperturbable, he picked a bit of paper from the walk and nailed it to the framework with a knife. He then turned his back contemptuously upon this popular resort, and walking to the opposite side of the street, and spinning there on his heel quickly and lithely, fired at the bit of paper. He missed it by a half inch. He swore at himself, and went away. Later, he comfortably fusilladed[5] the windows of his most intimate friend. The man was playing with this town. It was a toy for him.

But still there was no offer of fight. The name of Jack Potter, his ancient antagonist, entered his mind, and he concluded that it would be a glad thing if he should go to Potter's house and by bombardment induce him to come out and fight. He moved in the direction of his desire, chanting Apache scalp-music.

When he arrived at it, Potter's house presented the same still, calm front as had the other adobes. Taking up a strategic position, the man howled a challenge. But this house regarded him as might a great stone god. It gave no sign. After a decent wait, the man howled further challenges, mingling with them wonderful epithets.

Presently there came the spectacle of a man churning himself into deepest rage over the immobility of a house. He fumed at it as the winter wind attacks a prairie cabin in the North. To the distance there should have gone the sound of a tumult like the fighting of two hundred Mexicans. As necessity bade him, he paused for breath or to reload his revolvers.

IV

Potter and his bride walked sheepishly and with speed. Sometimes they laughed together shamefacedly and low.

"Next corner, dear," he said finally.

They put forth the efforts of a pair walking bowed against a strong wind. Potter was about to raise a finger to point the first appearance of the new home when, as they circled the corner, they came face to face with a man in a maroon-colored shirt who was feverishly pushing cartridges into a large revolver. Upon the instant the man dropped this revolver to the ground, and, like lightning, whipped another from its holster. The second weapon was aimed at the bridegroom's chest.

There was a silence. Potter's mouth seemed to be merely a grave for his tongue. He exhibited an instinct to at once loosen his arm from the woman's grip, and he dropped the bag to the sand. As for the bride, her face had gone as yellow as old cloth. She was a slave to hideous rites gazing at the apparitional snake.

The two men faced each other at a distance of three paces. He of the revolver smiled with a new and quiet ferocity. "Tried to sneak up on me," he said. "Tried to sneak up on me!" His eyes grew more baleful. As Potter made a slight movement, the man thrust his revolver venomously forward. "No, don't you do it, Jack Potter. Don't you move a finger toward a gun just yet. Don't move an eyelash. The time has come for me to settle with you, and I'm goin' to do it my own way and loaf along with no interferin'. So if you don't want a gun bent on you, just mind what I tell you."

Potter looked at his enemy. "I ain't got a gun on me, Scratchy," he said. "Hon-

---

[5] Rapidly shot at.

est, I ain't." He was stiffening and steadying, but yet somewhere at the back of his mind a vision of the Pullman floated, the sea-green figured velvet, the shining brass, silver, and glass, the wood that gleamed as darkly brilliant as the surface of a pool of oil—all the glory of the marriage, the environment of the new estate. "You know I fight when it comes to fighting, Scratchy Wilson, but I ain't got a gun on me. You'll have to do all the shootin' yourself."

His enemy's face went livid. He stepped forward and lashed his weapon to and fro before Potter's chest. "Don't you tell me you ain't got no gun on you, you whelp. Don't tell me no lie like that. There ain't a man in Texas ever seen you without no gun. Don't take me for no kid." His eyes blazed with light, and his throat worked like a pump.

"I ain't takin' you for no kid," answered Potter. His heels had not moved an inch backward. "I'm takin' you for a———fool. I tell you I ain't got a gun, and I ain't. If you're goin' to shoot me up, you better begin now. You'll never get a chance like this again."

So much enforced reasoning had told on Wilson's rage. He was calmer. "If you ain't got a gun, why ain't you got a gun?" he sneered. "Been to Sunday-school?"

"I ain't got a gun because I've just come from San Anton' with my wife. I'm married," said Potter. "And if I'd thought there was going to be any galoots like you prowling around when I brought my wife home, I'd had a gun, and don't you forget it."

"Married!" said Scratchy, not at all comprehending.

"Yes, married. I'm married," said Potter distinctly.

"Married?" said Scratchy. Seemingly for the first time he saw the drooping drowning woman at the other man's side. "No!" he said. He was like a creature allowed a glimpse of another world. He moved a pace backward, and his arm with the revolver dropped to his side. "Is this—is this the lady?" he asked.

"Yes, this is the lady," answered Potter.

There was another period of silence.

"Well," said Wilson at last, slowly, "I s'pose it's all off now."

"It's all off if you say so, Scratchy. You know I didn't make the trouble." Potter lifted his valise.

"Well, I 'low it's off, Jack," said Wilson. He was looking at the ground. "Married!" He was not a student of chivalry; it was merely that in the presence of this foreign condition he was a simple child of the earlier plains. He picked up his starboard[6] revolver, and placing both weapons in their holsters, he went away. His feet made funnel-shaped tracks in the heavy sand.

1898

AN ILLUSION IN RED AND WHITE*

Nights on the Cuban blockade were long, at times exciting, often dull. The men on the small leaping despatch boats became as intimate as if they had all been buried in the same coffin. Correspondents who in New York had passed as fairly good fellows sometimes turned out to be perfect rogues of vanity and selfishness, but still more

---

[6] Right-hand side.

* First published (with this one-paragraph introduction) in the *New York World* on May 20, 1900, two weeks before Crane's death.

often the conceited chumps of Park Row became the kindly and thoughtful men of the Cuban blockade. Also each correspondent told all he knew and sometimes more. For this gentle tale I am indebted to one of the brightening stars of New York journalism.

"Now this is how I imagine it happened. I don't say it happened this way, but this is how I imagine it happened. And it always struck me as being a very interesting story. I hadn't been on the paper very long, but just about long enough to get a good show, when the city editor suddenly gave me this sparkling murder assignment.

"It seems that up in one of the back counties of New York State a farmer had taken a dislike to his wife, and so he went into the kitchen with an axe, and in the presence of their four little children he had just casually rapped his wife on the nape of the neck with the head of this axe. It was early in the morning, but he told the children they had better go to bed. Then he took his wife's body out in the woods and buried it.

"This farmer's name was Jones. The widower's eldest child was named Freddy. A week after the murder one of the long-distance neighbors was rattling past the house in his buckboard when he saw Freddy playing in the road. He pulled up and asked the boy about the welfare of the Jones family.

" 'Oh, we're all right,' said Freddy, 'only ma—she ain't—she's dead.'

" 'Why, when did she die?' cried the startled farmer. 'What did she die of?'

" 'Oh,' answered Freddy, 'last week a man with red hair and big white teeth and real white hands came into the kitchen and killed ma with an axe.'

"The farmer was indignant with the boy for telling him this strange childish nonsense and drove off, much disgruntled. But he recited the incident at a tavern that evening, and when people began to miss the familiar figure of Mrs. Jones at the Methodist Church on Sunday mornings they ended by having an investigation. The calm Jones was arrested for murder, and his wife's body was lifted from its grave in the woods and buried by her own family.

"The chief interest now centred upon the children. All four declared that they were in the kitchen at the time of the crime, and that the murderer had red hair. The hair of the virtuous Jones was grey. They said that the murderer's hands were white. Jones's hands were the color of black walnut. They said that the murderer's teeth were large and white. Jones only had about eight teeth, and these were small and brown. They lifted their dazed, innocent faces, and, crying simply because the mysterious excitement and their new quarters frightened them, they repeated this heroic legend without important deviation, and without the parroty sameness which excited suspicion.

"Women came to the jail and wept over them and made little frocks for the girls and little breeches for the boys, and idiotic detectives questioned them at length. Always they upheld the theory of the murderer with the red hair, big white teeth and white hands. Jones sat in his cell, his chin sullenly on his first vest button. He knew nothing about any murder, he said. He thought his wife had gone on a visit to some relatives. He had had a quarrel with her, and she had said that she was going to leave him for a time, so that he might have proper opportunities for cooling down. Had he seen the blood on the floor? Yes, he had seen the blood on the floor. But he had been cleaning and skinning a rabbit at that spot on the day of his wife's disappearance. He had thought nothing of it. What had his children said when he returned from the fields? They had told him that their mother had been killed by an axe in the hands of a man with red hair, big white teeth and white hands. To questions as to why he had not informed the police of the county, he answered that he had not thought it a matter of sufficient importance. He had cordially hated his wife, anyhow, and he was glad to be rid of her. He decided afterward that she had run off, and he had never credited the fantastic tale of the children.

"Of course, there was very little doubt in the minds of the majority that Jones was guilty, but there was a fairly strong following who insisted that Jones was a coarse and brutal man, and perhaps weak in his head—yes—but not a murderer. They pointed to the children and declared that children could never lie on a system, and these kids when asked said that the murder had been committed by a man with red hair, large white teeth and white hands. I myself had a number of interviews with the children, and I was amazed at the convincing power of their little story. Shining in the depths of the limpid upturned eyes one could fairly see tiny mirrored images of men with red hair, big white teeth and white hands.

"Now I'll tell you how it happened—how I imagine it was done. Some time after burying his wife in the woods Jones strolled back to the house. Seeing nobody, he called out in the familiar fashion, 'Mother!' Then the kids came out whimpering. 'Where is your mother?' said Jones. The children looked at him blankly. 'Why, pa,' said Freddy, 'you came in here and hit ma with the axe and then you sent us to bed.' 'Me?' cried Jones. 'I haven't been near the house since breakfast time.'

"The children did not know how to reply. Their meagre little senses informed them that their father had been the man with the axe, but he denied it, and to their minds everything was a mere great puzzle with no meaning whatever, save that it was mysteriously sad and made them cry.

" 'What kind of a looking man was it?' said Jones. Freddy hesitated. 'Now— he looked a good deal like you, pa.'

" 'Like me?' said Jones. 'Why I thought you said he had red hair?'

" 'No, I didn't,' replied Freddy. 'I thought he had grey hair like yours.'

" 'Well,' said Jones, 'I saw a man with kind of red hair going along the road up yonder, and I thought maybe that might have been him.'

"Little Lucy, the second child, here piped up with intense conviction: 'His hair was a little teeny bit red. I saw it.'

" 'No,' said Jones, 'the man I saw had very red hair. And what did his teeth look like? Were they big and white?'

" 'Yes,' answered Lucy, 'they were.'

"Even Freddy seemed to incline to think it. 'His teeth may have been big and white.'

"Jones said little more at that time. Later he intimated to the children that their mother had gone off on a visit, and although they were full of wonder and sometimes wept because of the oppression of an incomprehensible feeling in the air, they said nothing. Jones did his chores and housework. Everything was smooth.

"The morning after the day of the murder Jones and his children had a breakfast of hominy[1] and milk. 'Well, this man with red hair and big white teeth, Lucy?' said Jones. 'Did you notice anything else about him?'

"Lucy straightened in her chair and showed the childish desire to come out with brilliant information which would gain her father's approval.

---

[1] Dry corn with the hull removed.

" 'He had white hands—hands all white————'

" 'How about you, Freddy?'

" 'I didn't look at them much, but I think they were white,' answered the boy.

" 'And what did little Martha notice?' cried the tender parent. 'Did she see the big, bad man?'

"Martha, aged four, replied solemnly: 'His ha r was all red and his hands was white—all white.'

" 'That's the man I saw up the road,' said Jones to Freddy.

" 'Yes, sir; it seems like it must have been him,' said the boy, his brain now in complete confusion.

"Again Jones allowed the subject of his wife's murder to lapse. The children did not know that it was a murder, of course. Adults were always performing in a way to make children's heads swim. For instance, what could be more incomprehensible than that a man with two horses dragging a queer thing should walk all day, making the grass turn down and the earth turn up? And why did they cut the long grass and put it in a barn? And what was a cow for? Did the water in the well like to be there? All these actions and things were grand because they were associated with the high estate of grown-up people, but they were deeply mysterious. If, then, a man with red hair, big white teeth and white hands should hit their mother on the nape of the neck with an axe, it was merely a phenomenon of grown-up life. Little Henry, the baby, when he had a want, howled and pounded the table with his spoon. That was all of life to him. He was not concerned with the fact that his mother had been murdered.

"One day Jones said to the children, suddenly: 'Look here, I wonder if you could have made a mistake? Are you absolutely sure that the man you saw had red hair, big white teeth and white hands?'

"The children were indignant with their father. 'Why, of course, pa; we ain't made no mistake. We saw him as plain as day.'

"Later young Freddy's mind began to work like ketchup. His nights were haunted with terrible memories of the man with red hair, big white teeth and white hands, and the prolonged absence of his mother made him wonder and wonder. Presently he quite gratuitously developed the theory that his mother was dead. He knew about death. He had once seen a dead dog; also dead chickens, rabbits and mice. One day he asked his father: 'Pa, is ma ever coming back?'

"Jones said: 'Well, no, I don't think she is.' This answer confirmed the boy in his theory. He knew that dead people did not come back.

"The attitude of Jones toward this descriptive legend of the man with the axe was very peculiar. He came to be in opposition to it. He protested against the convictions of the children, but he could not move them. It was the one thing in their lives of which they were stonily and absolutely positive.

"Now that really ends the story. But I will continue for your amusement. The jury hung Jones as high as they could, and they were quite right, because Jones confessed before he died. Freddy is now a highly respected driver of a grocery wagon in Ogdensburg. When I was up there, a good many years afterward, people told me that when he ever spoke of the tragedy at all he was certain to denounce the alleged confession as a lie. He considered his father a victim to the stupidity of juries, and some day he hopes to meet the man with the red hair, big white teeth and white hands, whose image still remains so distinct in his memory that he could pick him out in a crowd of ten thousand."

1900

from   *THE BLACK RIDERS AND OTHER LINES**

I

Black riders came from the sea.
There was clang and clang of spear and shield,
And clash and clash of hoof and heel,
Wild shouts and the wave of hair
In the rush upon the wind:
Thus the ride of sin.

IX

I stood upon a high place,
And saw, below, many devils
Running, leaping,
And carousing in sin.
One looked up, grinning,
And said, "Comrade! Brother!"

XIV

There was crimson clash of war.
Lands turned black and bare;
Women wept;
Babes ran, wondering.
There came one who understood not these things.
He said, "Why is this?"
Whereupon a million strove to answer him.
There was such intricate clamor of tongues,
That still the reason was not.

XIX

A god in wrath
Was beating a man;
He cuffed him loudly

* These poems were published without titles in Crane's collection *The Black Riders and Other Lines* in 1895.

With thunderous blows
That rang and rolled over the earth.
All people came running.
The man screamed and struggled.
And bit madly at the feet of the god.
The people cried,
"Ah, what a wicked man!"   10
And—
"Ah, what a redoubtable god!"

XXIV

I saw a man pursuing the horizon;
Round and round they sped.
I was disturbed at this;
I accosted the man.
"It is futile," I said.
"You can never————"

"You lie," he cried,
And ran on.

XXVII

A youth in apparel that glittered
Went to walk in a grim forest.
There he met an assassin
Attired all in garb of old days;
He, scowling through the thickets,
And dagger poised quivering,
Rushed upon the youth.
"Sir," said this latter,
"I am enchanted, believe me,
"To die, thus,   10
"In this medieval fashion,
"According to the best legends;
"Ah, what joy!"
Then took he the wound, smiling,
And died, content.

XXX

Supposing that I should have the courage
To let a red sword of virtue
Plunge into my heart,
Letting to the weeds of the ground
My sinful blood,
What can you offer me?
A gardened castle?
A flowery kingdom?

What? A hope?
Then hence with your red sword of virtue.   10

XXXI

Many workmen
Built a huge ball of masonry
Upon a mountain-top.
Then they went to the valley below,
And turned to behold their work.
"It is grand," they said;
They loved the thing.

Of a sudden, it moved:
It came upon them swiftly;
It crushed them all to blood.   10
But some had opportunity to squeal.

XXXV

A man saw a ball of gold in the sky;
He climbed for it,
And eventually he achieved it——
It was clay.

Now this is the strange part:
When the man went to the earth
And looked again,
Lo, there was the ball of gold.

Now this is the strange part:
It was a ball of gold.   10
Aye, by the heavens, it was a ball of gold.

XLVI

Many red devils ran from my heart
And out upon the page.
They were so tiny
The pen could mash them.
And many struggled in the ink.
It was strange
To write in this red muck
Of things from my heart.

1894, 1895

from   *WAR IS KIND**

69

Do not weep, maiden, for war is kind.
Because your lover threw wild hands toward the sky
And the affrighted steed ran on alone,
Do not weep.
War is kind.

   Hoarse, booming drums of the regiment
   Little souls who thirst for fight,
   These men were born to drill and die
   The unexplained glory flies above them
   Great is the battle-god, great, and his kingdom———   10
   A field where a thousand corpses lie.

Do not weep, babe, for war is kind.
Because your father tumbled in the yellow trenches,

* These poems were published without titles in Crane's collection *War Is Kind* in 1899.

Raged at his breast, gulped and died,
Do not weep.
War is kind.

Swift, blazing flag of the regiment
Eagle with crest of red and gold,
These men were born to drill and die
Point for them the virtue of slaughter   20
Make plain to them the excellence of killing
And a field where a thousand corpses lie.

Mother whose heart hung humble as a button
On the bright splendid shroud of your son,
Do not weep.
War is kind.

1895, 1896

81

The wayfarer
Perceiving the pathway to truth
Was struck with astonishment.
It was thickly grown with weeds.
"Ha," he said,
"I see that none has passed here
"In a long time."
Later he saw that each weed
Was a singular knife.
"Well," he mumbled at last,
"Doubtless there are other roads."

1897, 1899

89

A man said to the universe:
"Sir, I exist!"
"However," replied the universe,
"The fact has not created in me
"A sense of obligation."

1894, 1899

Jack London   ~~Naturalism~~
(1876–1916)

Born John Griffith in San Francisco in 1876 and raised in Oakland, California, Jack London was the son of a spiritualist, Flora Wellman, and her common-law husband, the astrologer William Henry Chaney. Chaney abandoned his wife shortly after she became pregnant, and she then married John London, who gave Jack his surname. The novelist had an adventurous boyhood: wandering the waterfront, pirating the oyster beds of fishermen, and sailing to Japan on the seal-hunting ship *Sophia Sutherland* in 1893. In 1894, after marching partway across the continent with "Kelly's Army," a Washington-bound group of unemployed workers, London was arrested for vagrancy; he later told the story of his arrest and imprisonment in *The Road* (1907). In 1897 he joined the Klondike gold rush in the Yukon Territory and found in the rigors of Yukon life not gold but the material for some of his most characteristic fiction. When he returned to Oakland in 1898, he began to write of his experiences. A collection of Klondike stories, *The Son of the Wolf* (1900), was his first published book.

Within a few years London had become a wealthy and popular writer—but not without ideological struggle and seasons of frenetic writing. Employing a variety of genres, he eventually wrote over fifty works that juxtaposed his concern for the working class with his belief in the survival of the fittest. In what might have been suicide, he died from the effects of an overdose of the drugs morphine and atropine in 1916. Like the protagonist in his novel *Martin Eden* (1909), London had risen from the working class to become a successful writer, only to have his career end in early death. His struggles with publishing and with politics are memorably depicted in the autobiographical *Martin Eden*.

The ideological divergence found in London's work came from the curious blending of deeply felt life experiences and, after his march with Kelly's Army and during a semester at the University of California, from his voracious reading of such divergent thinkers as Karl Marx, Charles Darwin, and Friedrich Nietzsche. Behind the manifest concerns of London's *The People of the Abyss* (1903) was his close personal study of the inhabitants of London slums; behind the controversies of his *War of the Classes* (1905) was a commitment to Marxism that led him to run for mayor of Oakland on the Socialist ticket in 1905. London's early fascination with the idea of survival in a primitive world gathered fresh authority from his reading of Nietzsche and became the force behind such novels as *The Call of the Wild* (1903) and *The Sea-Wolf* (1904). At that point in his career, London pledged allegiance to the collective cooperation of Socialism as well as to the struggle of individualism. Such a dichotomy remained an intense part of his imaginative life. Yet, the man who could depict the miserable, dystopian world of *The Iron Heel* (1908) as well as the brutal Wolf Larsen of *The Sea-Wolf* remained a master of narrative—much of it melodramatic, virtually all of it compelling.

Suggested Readings: *The Call of the Wild*, 1903. *The Sea-Wolf*, 1904. *Martin Eden*, 1909. *Burning Daylight*, 1910. *Letters From Jack London*, ed. K. Hendricks and I. Shepard, 1965. J. London, *Jack London and His Times: An Unconventional Biography*, 1939, rpt. 1974. P. S. Foner, *Jack London, American Rebel*, 1947, rpt. 1964. F. Walker, *Jack London and the Klondike: The Genesis of an American Writer*, 1966. E. Labor, *Jack London*, 1974. J. McClintock, *White Logic: Jack London's Short Stories*, 1975. J. Sherman, *Jack London: A Reference Guide*, 1977. J. Hedrick, *Solitary Comrade: Jack London and His Work*, 1982. A. Sinclair, *Jack: A Biography of Jack London*, 1983. C. N. Watson, *The Novels of Jack London: A Reappraisal*, 1983. C. Stasz, *American Dreamers: Charmian and Jack London*, 1988.

Text Used: *Lost Face*, 1910.

TO BUILD A FIRE*

Day had broken cold and gray, exceedingly cold and gray, when the man turned aside from the main Yukon trail[1] and climbed the high earth-bank, where a dim and little-travelled trail led eastward through the fat spruce timberland. It was a steep bank, and he paused for breath at the top, excusing the act to himself by looking at his watch. It was nine o'clock. There was no sun nor hint of sun, though there was not a cloud in the sky. It was a clear day, and yet there seemed an intangible pall over the face of things, a subtle gloom that made the day dark, and that was due to the absence of sun. This fact did not worry the man. He was used to the lack of sun. It had been days since he had seen the sun, and he knew that a few more days must pass before that cheerful orb, due south, would just peep above the sky-line and dip immediately from view.

The man flung a look back along the way he had come. The Yukon[2] lay a mile wide and hidden under three feet of ice. On top of this ice were as many feet of snow. It was all pure white, rolling in gentle, undulations where the ice-jams of the freeze-up had formed. North and south, as far as his eye could see, it was unbroken white, save for a dark hair-line that curved and twisted from around the spruce-covered island to the south, and that curved and twisted away into the north, where it disappeared behind another spruce-covered island. This dark hair-line was the trail—the main trail—that led south five hundred miles to the Chilcoot Pass, Dyea, and salt water;[3] and that led north seventy miles to Dawson, and still on to the north a thousand miles to Nulato, and finally to St. Michael[4] on Bering Sea, a thousand miles and half a thousand more.

But all this—the mysterious, far-reaching hair-line trail, the absence of sun from the sky, the tremendous cold, and the strangeness and weirdness of it all— made no impression on the man. It was not because he was long used to it. He was a newcomer in the land, a *chechaquo*,[5] and this was his first winter. The trouble with him was that he was without imagination. He was quick and alert in the things of life, but only in the things, and not in the significances. Fifty degrees below zero meant eighty-odd degrees of frost. Such fact impressed him as being cold and uncomfortable, and that was all. It did not lead him to meditate upon his frailty as a creature of temperature, and upon man's frailty in general, able only to live within certain narrow limits of heat and cold; and from there on it did not lead him to the conjectural field of immortality and man's place in the universe. Fifty degrees below zero stood for a bite of frost that hurt and that must be guarded against by the use of mittens, ear-flaps, warm moccasins, and thick socks. Fifty degrees below zero was to him just precisely fifty degrees below zero. That there should be anything more to it than that was a thought that never entered his head.

science doesn't apply it to himself

As he turned to go on, he spat speculatively. There was a sharp, explosive crackle that startled him. He spat again. And again, in the air, before it could fall to the snow, the spittle crackled. He knew that at fifty below spittle crackled on

---

* First published in *The Century* in August 1908; an earlier version of the story appeared in *Youth's Companion* in May 1902.

[1] The setting is the bleak Yukon Territory in northwestern Canada, near Alaska.

[2] The Yukon River, which runs west across Alaska to the Bering Sea.

[3] The Chilcoot Pass, in southeastern Alaska used by gold seekers from 1896 to 1898, led to the village of Dyea, near the Pacific coast.

[4] Settlements in the Yukon Territory.

[5] Cheechako (Chinook), a newcomer, or greenhorn.

the snow, but this spittle had crackled in the air. Undoubtedly it was colder than fifty below—how much colder he did not know. But the temperature did not matter. He was bound for the old claim on the left fork of Henderson Creek, where the boys were already. They had come over across the divide from the Indian Creek country, while he had come the roundabout way to take a look at the possibilities of getting out logs in the spring from the islands in the Yukon. He would be in to camp by six o'clock; a bit after dark, it was true, but the boys would be there, a fire would be going, and a hot supper would be ready. As for lunch, he pressed his hand against the protruding bundle under his jacket. It was also under his shirt, wrapped up in a handkerchief and lying against the naked skin. It was the only way to keep the biscuits from freezing. He smiled agreeably to himself as he thought of those biscuits, each cut open and sopped in bacon grease, and each enclosing a generous slice of fried bacon.

He plunged in among the big spruce trees. The trail was faint. A foot of snow had fallen since the last sled had passed over, and he was glad he was without a sled, travelling light. In fact, he carried nothing but the lunch wrapped in the handkerchief. He was surprised, however, at the cold. It certainly was cold, he concluded, as he rubbed his numb nose and cheek-bones with his mittened hand. He was a warm-whiskered man, but the hair on his face did not protect the high cheek-bones and the eager nose that thrust itself aggressively into the frosty air.

At the man's heels trotted a dog, a big native husky, the proper wolf-dog, gray-coated and without any visible or temperamental difference from its brother, the wild wolf. The animal was depressed by the tremendous cold. It knew that it was no time for travelling. Its instinct told it a truer tale than was told to the man by the man's judgment. In reality, it was not merely colder than fifty below zero; it was colder than sixty below, than seventy below. It was seventy-five below zero. Since the freezing-point is thirty-two above zero, it meant that one hundred and seven degrees of frost obtained. The dog did not know anything about thermometers. Possibly in its brain there was no sharp consciousness of a condition of very cold such as was in the man's brain. But the brute had its instinct. It experienced a vague but menacing apprehension that subdued it and made it slink along at the man's heels, and that made it question eagerly every unwonted movement of the man as if expecting him to go into camp or to seek shelter somewhere and build a fire. The dog had learned fire, and it wanted fire, or else to burrow under the snow and cuddle its warmth away from the air.

The frozen moisture of its breathing had settled on its fur in a fine powder of frost, and especially were its jowls, muzzle, and eyelashes whitened by its crystalled breath. The man's red beard and mustache were likewise frosted, but more solidly, the deposit taking the form of ice and increasing with every warm, moist breath he exhaled. Also, the man was chewing tobacco, and the muzzle of ice held his lips so rigidly that he was unable to clear his chin when he expelled the juice. The result was that a crystal beard of the color and solidity of amber was increasing its length on his chin. If he fell down it would shatter itself, like glass, into brittle fragments. But he did not mind the appendage. It was the penalty all tobacco-chewers paid in that country, and he had been out before in two cold snaps. They had not been so cold as this, he knew, but by the spirit thermometer at Sixty Mile he knew they had been registered at fifty below and at fifty-five.

He held on through the level stretch of woods for several miles, crossed a wide flat of nigger-heads,[6] and dropped down a bank to the frozen bed of a small

---

[6] Clumps of grass that project from a swamp.

stream. This was Henderson Creek, and he knew he was ten miles from the forks. He looked at his watch. It was ten o'clock. He was making four miles an hour, and he calculated that he would arrive at the forks at half-past twelve. He decided to celebrate that event by eating his lunch there.

The dog dropped in again at his heels, with a tail drooping discouragement, as the man swung along the creek-bed. The furrow of the old sled-trail was plainly visible, but a dozen inches of snow covered the marks of the last runners. In a month no man had come up or down that silent creek. The man held steadily on. He was not much given to thinking, and just then particularly he had nothing to think about save that he would eat lunch at the forks and that at six o'clock he would be in camp with the boys. There was nobody to talk to; and, had there been, speech would have been impossible because of the ice-muzzle on his mouth. So he continued monotonously to chew tobacco and to increase the length of his amber beard.

[margin handwritten note: People who live to do what's expected of them w/out questioning why.]

Once in a while the thought reiterated itself that it was very cold and that he had never experienced such cold. As he walked along he rubbed his cheek-bones and nose with the back of his mittened hand. He did this automatically, now and again changing hands. But rub as he would, the instant he stopped his cheek-bones went numb, and the following instant the end of his nose went numb. He was sure to frost his cheeks; he knew that, and experienced a pang of regret that he had not devised a nose-strap of the sort Bud wore in cold snaps. Such a strap passed across the cheeks, as well, and saved them. But it didn't matter much, after all. What were frosted cheeks? A bit painful, that was all; they were never serious.

Empty as the man's mind was of thoughts, he was keenly observant, and he noticed the changes in the creek, the curves and bends and timber-jams, and always he sharply noted where he placed his feet. Once, coming around a bend, he shied abruptly, like a startled horse, curved away from the place where he had been walking, and retreated several paces back along the trail. The creek he knew was frozen clear to the bottom,—no creek could contain water in that arctic winter,—but he knew also that there were springs that bubbled out from the hillsides and ran along under the snow and on top the ice of the creek. He knew that the coldest snaps never froze these springs, and he knew likewise their danger. They were traps. They hid pools of water under the snow that might be three inches deep, or three feet. Sometimes a skin of ice half an inch thick covered them, and in turn was covered by the snow. Sometimes there were alternate layers of water and ice-skin, so that when one broke through he kept on breaking through for a while, sometimes wetting himself to the waist.

That was why he had shied in such panic. He had felt the give under his feet and heard the crackle of a snow-hidden ice-skin. And to get his feet wet in such a temperature meant trouble and danger. At the very least it meant delay, for he would be forced to stop and build a fire, and under its protection to bare his feet while he dried his socks and moccasins. He stood and studied the creek-bed and its banks, and decided that the flow of water came from the right. He reflected awhile, rubbing his nose and cheeks, then skirted to the left, stepping gingerly and testing the footing for each step. Once clear of the danger, he took a fresh chew of tobacco and swung along at his four-mile gait.

In the course of the next two hours he came upon several similar traps. Usually the snow above the hidden pools had a sunken, candied appearance that advertised the danger. Once again, however, he had a close call; and once, suspecting danger, he compelled the dog to go on in front. The dog did not want to go. It hung back until the man shoved it forward, and then it went quickly across the white,

[bottom handwritten note: forces the thinkers to do the work]

unbroken surface. Suddenly it broke through, floundered to one side, and got away to firmer footing. It had wet its forefeet and legs, and almost immediately the water that clung to it turned to ice. It made quick efforts to lick the ice off its legs, then dropped down in the snow and began to bite out the ice that had formed between the toes. This was a matter of instinct. To permit the ice to remain would mean sore feet. It did not know this. It merely obeyed the mysterious prompting that arose from the deep crypts of its being. But the man knew, having achieved a judgment on the subject, and he removed the mitten from his right hand and helped tear out the ice particles. He did not expose his fingers more than a minute, and was astonished at the swift numbness that smote them. It certainly was cold. He pulled on the mitten hastily, and beat the hand savagely across his chest.

At twelve o'clock the day was at its brightest. Yet the sun was too far south on its winter journey to clear the horizon. The bulge of the earth intervened between it and Henderson Creek, where the man walked under a clear sky at noon and cast no shadow. At half-past twelve, to the minute, he arrived at the forks of the creek. He was pleased at the speed he had made. If he kept it up, he would certainly be with the boys by six. He unbuttoned his jacket and shirt and drew forth his lunch. The action consumed no more than a quarter of a minute, yet in that brief moment the numbness laid hold of the exposed fingers. He did not put the mitten on, but, instead, struck the fingers a dozen sharp smashes against his leg. Then he sat down on a snow-covered log to eat. The sting that followed upon the striking of his fingers against his leg ceased so quickly that he was startled. He had had no chance to take a bite of biscuit. He struck the fingers repeatedly and returned them to the mitten, baring the other hand for the purpose of eating. He tried to take a mouthful, but the ice-muzzle prevented. He had forgotten to build a fire and thaw out. He chuckled at his foolishness, and as he chuckled he noted the numbness creeping into the exposed fingers. Also, he noted that the stinging which had first come to his toes when he sat down was already passing away. He wondered whether the toes were warm or numb. He moved them inside the moccasins and decided that they were numb.

He pulled the mitten on hurriedly and stood up. He was a bit frightened. He stamped up and down until the stinging returned into the feet. It certainly was cold, was his thought. That man from Sulphur Creek had spoken the truth when telling how cold it sometimes got in the country. And he had laughed at him at the time! That showed one must not be too sure of things. There was no mistake about it, it *was* cold. He strode up and down, stamping his feet and threshing his arms, until reassured by the returning warmth. Then he got out matches and proceeded to make a fire. From the undergrowth, where high water of the previous spring had lodged a supply of seasoned twigs, he got his fire-wood. Working carefully from a small beginning, he soon had a roaring fire, over which he thawed the ice from his face and in the protection of which he ate his biscuits. For the moment the cold of space was outwitted. The dog took satisfaction in the fire, stretching out close enough for warmth and far enough away to escape being singed.

When the man had finished, he filled his pipe and took his comfortable time over a smoke. Then he pulled on his mittens, settled the earflaps of his cap firmly about his ears, and took the creek trail up the left fork. The dog was disappointed and yearned back toward the fire. This man did not know cold. Possibly all the generations of his ancestry had been ignorant of cold, of real cold, of cold one hundred and seven degrees below freezing-point. But the dog knew; all its ancestry knew, and it had inherited the knowledge. And it knew that it was not good to walk abroad in such fearful cold. It was the time to lie snug in a hole in the snow and wait for a curtain of cloud to be drawn across the face of outer space whence this cold came. On the other hand, there was no keen intimacy between the dog and the man. The one was the toil-slave of the other, and the only caresses it had ever received were the caresses of the whip-lash and of harsh and menacing throat-sounds that threatened the whip-lash. So the dog made no effort to communicate its apprehension to the man. It was not concerned in the welfare of the man; it was for its own sake that it yearned back toward the fire. But the man whistled, and spoke to it with the sound of whip-lashes, and the dog swung in at the man's heels and followed after.

The man took a chew of tobacco and proceeded to start a new amber beard. Also, his moist breath quickly powdered with white his mustache, eyebrows, and lashes. There did not seem to be so many springs on the left fork of the Henderson, and for half an hour the man saw no signs of any. And then it happened. At a place where there were no signs, where the soft, unbroken snow seemed to advertise solidity beneath, the man broke though. It was not deep. He wet himself halfway to the knees before he floundered out to the firm crust.

He was angry, and cursed his luck aloud. He had hoped to get into camp with the boys at six o'clock, and this would delay him an hour, for he would have to build a fire and dry out his foot-gear. This was imperative at that low temperature—he knew that much; and he turned aside to the bank, which he climbed. On top, tangled in the underbrush about the trunks of several small spruce trees, was a high-water deposit of dry fire-wood—sticks and twigs, principally, but also larger portions of seasoned branches and fine, dry, last-year's grasses. He threw down several large pieces on top of the snow. This served for a foundation and prevented the young flame from drowning itself in the snow it otherwise would melt. The flame he got by touching a match to a small shred of birch-bark that he took from his pocket. Placing it on the foundation, he fed the young flame with wisps of dry grass and with the tiniest dry twigs.

He worked slowly and carefully, keenly aware of his danger. Gradually, as the flame grew stronger, he increased the size of the twigs with which he fed it. He squatted in the snow, pulling the twigs out from their entanglement in the brush and feeding directly to the flame. He knew there must be no failure. When it is seventy-five below zero, a man must not fail in his first attempt to build a fire—that is, if his feet are wet. If his feet are dry, and he fails, he can run along the trail for half a mile and restore his circulation. But the circulation of wet and freezing feet cannot be restored by running when it is seventy-five below. No matter how fast he runs, the wet feet will freeze the harder.

All this the man knew. The old-timer on Sulphur Creek had told him about it the previous fall, and now he was appreciating the advice. Already all sensation had gone out of his feet. To build the fire he had been forced to remove his mittens, and the fingers had quickly gone numb. His pace of four miles an hour had kept his heart pumping blood to the surface of his body and to all the extremities. But the instant he stopped, the action of the pump eased down. The cold of space smote the unprotected tip of the planet, and he, being on that unprotected tip, received the full force of the blow. The blood of his body recoiled before it. The blood was alive, like the dog, and like the dog it wanted to hide away and cover itself up from the fearful cold. So long as he walked four miles an hour, he pumped that blood, willy-nilly, to the surface; but now it ebbed away and sank down into the recesses of his body. The extremities were the first to feel its absence. His wet feet froze the faster, and his exposed fingers numbed the faster, thought they had not yet begun to freeze. Nose and cheeks were already freezing, while the skin of all his body chilled as it lost its blood.

But he was safe. Toes and nose and cheeks would be only touched by the frost, for the fire was beginning to burn with strength. He was feeding it with twigs the size of his finger. In another minute he would be able to feed it with branches the size of his wrist, and then he could remove his wet foot-gear, and, while it dried, he could keep his naked feet warm by the fire, rubbing them at first, of course, with snow. The fire was a success. He was safe. He remembered the advice of the old-timer on Sulphur Creek, and smiled. The old-timer had been very serious in laying down the law that no man must travel alone in the Klondike[7] after fifty below. Well, here he was; he had had the accident; he was alone; and he had saved himself. Those old-timers were rather womanish, some of them, he thought. All a man had to do was to keep his head, and he was all right. Any who was a man could travel alone. But it was surprising, the rapidity with which his cheeks and nose were freezing. And he had not thought his fingers could go life-less in so short a time. Lifeless they were, for he could scarcely make them move together to grip a twig, and they seemed remote from his body and from him. When he touched a twig, he had to look and see whether or not he had hold of it. The wires were pretty well down between him and his finger-ends.

All of which counted for little. There was the fire, snapping and crackling and promising life with every dancing flame. He started to untie his moccasins. They were coated with ice; the thick German socks were like sheaths of iron halfway to the knees; and the moccasin strings were like rods of steel all twisted and knotted as by some conflagration. For a moment he tugged with his numb fingers, then, realizing the folly of it, he drew his sheath-knife.

But before he could cut the strings, it happened. It was his own fault or, rather, his mistake. He should not have built the fire under the spruce tree. He should have built it in the open. But it had been easier to pull the twigs from the brush and drop them directly on the fire. Now the tree under which he had done this carried a weight of snow on its boughs. No wind had blown for weeks, and each bough was fully freighted. Each time he had pulled a twig he had communicated a slight agitation to the tree—an imperceptible agitation, so far as he was con-cerned, but an agitation sufficient to bring about the disaster. High up in the tree one bough capsized its load of snow. This fell on the boughs beneath, capsizing them. This process continued, spreading out and involving the whole tree. It grew like an avalanche, and it descended without warning upon the man and the fire, and the fire was blotted out! Where it had burned was a mantle of fresh and disor-dered snow.

The man was shocked. It was as though he had just heard his own sentence of death. For a moment he sat and stared at the spot where the fire had been. Then he grew very calm. Perhaps the old-timer on Sulphur Creek was right. If he had only had a trail-mate he would have been in no danger now. The trail-mate could have built the fire. Well, it was up to him to build the fire over again, and this second time there must be no failure. Even if he succeeded, he would most likely lose some toes. His feet must be badly frozen by now, and there would be some time before the second fire was ready.

---

[7] A region in the Yukon River basin, near the gold fields where London worked in his early twenties.

Such were his thoughts, but he did not sit and think them. He was busy all the time they were passing through his mind. He made a new foundation for a fire, this time in the open, where no treacherous tree could blot it out. Next, he gathered dry grasses and tiny twigs from the high-water flotsam. He could not bring his fingers together to pull them out, but he was able to gather them by the handful. In this way he got many rotten twigs and bits of green moss that were undesirable, but it was the best he could do. He worked methodically, even collecting an armful of the larger branches to be used later when the fire gathered strength. And all the while the dog sat and watched him, a certain yearning wistfulness in its eyes, for it looked upon him as the fire-provider, and the fire was slow in coming.

When all was ready, the man reached in his pocket for a second piece of birch-bark. He knew the bark was there, and, though he could not feel it with his fingers, he could hear its crisp rustling as he fumbled for it. Try as he would, he could not clutch hold of it. And all the time, in his consciousness, was the knowledge that each instant his feet were freezing. This thought tended to put him in a panic, but he fought against it and kept calm. He pulled on his mittens with his teeth, and threshed his arms back and forth, beating his hands with all his might against his sides. He did this sitting down, and he stood up to do it; and all the while the dog sat in the snow, its wolf-brush of a tail curled around warmly over its forefeet, its sharp wolf-ears pricked forward intently as it watched the man. And the man, as he beat and threshed with his arms and hands, felt a great surge of envy as he regarded the creature that was warm and secure in its natural covering.

After a time he was aware of the first faraway signals of sensation in his beaten fingers. The faint tingling grew stronger till it evolved into a stinging ache that was excruciating, but which the man hailed with satisfaction. He stripped the mitten from his right hand and fetched forth the birch-bark. The exposed fingers were quickly going numb again. Next he brought out his bunch of sulphur matches. But the tremendous cold had already driven the life out of his fingers. In his effort to separate one match from the others, the whole bunch fell in the snow. He tried to pick it out of the snow, but failed. The dead fingers could neither touch or clutch. He was very careful. He drove the thought of his freezing feet, and nose, and cheeks, out of his mind, devoting his whole soul to the matches. He watched, using the sense of vision in place of that of touch, and when he saw his fingers on each side the bunch, he closed them—that is, he willed to close them, for the wires were down, and the fingers did not obey. He pulled the mitten on the right hand, and beat it fiercely against his knee, then, with both mittened hands, he scooped the bunch of matches, along with much snow, into his lap. Yet he was no better off.

After some manipulation he managed to get the bunch between the heels of his mittened hands. In this fashion he carried it to his mouth. The ice crackled and snapped when by a violent effort he opened his mouth. He drew the lower jaw in, curled the upper lip out of the way, and scraped the bunch with his upper teeth in order to separate a match. He succeeded in getting one, which he dropped on his lap. He was no better off. He could not pick it up. Then he devised a way. He picked it up in his teeth and scratched it on his leg. Twenty times he scratched before he succeeded in lighting it. As it flamed he held it with his teeth to the birch bark. But the burning brimstone went up his nostrils and into his lungs, causing him to cough spasmodically. The match fell into the snow and went out.

The old-timer on Sulphur Creek was right, he thought in the moment of controlled despair that ensued: after fifty below, a man should travel with a partner. He beat his hands, but failed in exciting any sensation. Suddenly he bared both hands, removing the mittens with his teeth. He caught the whole bunch between the heels of his hands. His arm-muscles not being frozen enabled him to press the hand-heels tightly against the matches. Then he scratched the bunch along his leg. It flared into flame, seventy sulphur matches at once! There was no wind to blow them out. He kept his head to one side to escape the strangling fumes, and held the blazing bunch to the birch-bark. As he so held it, he became aware of sensation in his hand. His flesh was burning. He could smell it. Deep down below the surface he could feel it. The sensation developed into pain that grew acute. And still he endured it, holding the flame of the matches clumsily to the bark that would not light readily because his own burning hands were in the way, absorbing most of the flame.

At last, when he could endure no more, he jerked his hands apart. The blazing matches fell sizzling into the snow, but the birch-bark was alight. He began laying dry grasses and the tiniest twigs on the flame. He could not pick and choose, for he had to lift the fuel between the heels of his hands. Small pieces of rotten wood and green moss clung to the twigs, and he bit them off as well as he could with his teeth. He cherished the flame carefully and awkwardly. It meant life, and it must not perish. The withdrawal of blood from the surface of his body now made him begin to shiver, and he grew more awkward. A large piece of green moss fell squarely on the little fire. He tried to poke it out with his fingers, but his shivering frame made him poke too far, and he disrupted the nucleus of the little fire, the burning grasses and tiny twigs separating and scattering. He tried to poke them together again, but in spite of the tenseness of the effort, his shivering got away with him, and the twigs were hopelessly scattered. Each twig gushed a puff of smoke and went out. The fire-provider had failed. As he looked apathetically about him, his eyes chanced on the dog, sitting across the ruins of the fire from him, in the snow, making restless, hunching movements, slightly lifting one forefoot and then the other, shifting its weight back and forth on them with wistful eagerness.

The sight of the dog put a wild idea into his head. He remembered the tale of the man, caught in a blizzard, who killed a steer and crawled inside the carcass, and so was saved. He would kill the dog and bury his hands in the warm body until the numbness went out of them. Then he could build another fire. He spoke to the dog, calling it to him; but in his voice was a strange note of fear that frightened the animal, who had never known the man to speak in such way before. Something was the matter, and its suspicious nature sensed danger—it knew not what danger, but somewhere, somehow, in its brain arose an apprehension of the man. It flattened its ears down at the sound of the man's voice, and its restless, hunching movements and the liftings and shiftings of its forefeet became more pronounced; but it would not come to the man. He got on his hands and knees and crawled toward the dog. This unusual posture again excited suspicion, and the animal sidled mincingly away.

The man sat up in the snow for a moment and struggled for calmness. Then he pulled on his mittens, by means of his teeth, and got upon his feet. He glanced down at first in order to assure himself that he was really standing up, for the absence of sensation in his feet left him unrelated to the earth. His erect position in itself started to drive the webs of suspicion from the dog's mind; and when he spoke peremptorily, with the sound of whip-lashes in his voice, the dog rendered its customary allegiance and came to him. As it came within reaching distance, the man lost his control. His arms flashed out to the dog, and he experienced genuine surprise when he discovered that his could not clutch, that there was neither bend nor feeling in the fingers. He had forgotten for the moment that they were frozen and that they were freezing more and more. All this happened quickly, and before the animal could get away, he encircled its body with his arms. He sat down in the snow, and in this fashion held the dog, while it snarled and whined and struggled.

But it was all he could do, hold the body encircled in his arms and sit there. He realized that he could not kill the dog. There was no way to do it. With his help-less hands he could neither draw nor hold his sheath-knife nor throttle the animal. He released it, and it plunged wildly away, with tail between its legs, and still snarling. It halted forty feet away and surveyed him curiously, with ears sharply pricked forward. The man looked down at his hands in order to locate them, and found them hanging on the ends of his arms. It struck him as curious that one should have to use his eyes in order to find out where his hands were. He began threshing his arms back and forth, beating the mittened hands against his sides. He did this for five minutes, violently, and his heart pumped enough blood up to the surface to put a stop to his shivering. But no sensation was aroused in the hands. He had an impression that they hung like weights on the ends of his arms, but when he tried to run the impression down, he could not find it.

A certain fear of death, dull and oppressive, came to him. This fear quickly became poignant as he realized that it was no longer a mere matter of freezing his fingers and toes, or of losing his hands and feet, but that is was a matter of life and death with the chances against him. This threw him into a panic, and he turned and ran up the creek-bed along the old, dim trail. The dog joined in behind and kept up with him. He ran blindly, without intention, in fear such as he had never known in his life. Slowly, as he ploughed and floundered through the snow, he began to see things again,—the banks of the creek, the old timber-jams, the leaf-less aspens, and the sky. The running made him feel better. He did not shiver. Maybe, if he ran on, his feet would thaw out; and, anyway, if he ran far enough, he would reach camp and the boys. Without doubt he would lose some fingers and toes and some of his face; but the boys would take care of him, and save the rest of him when he got there. And at the same time there was another thought in his mind that said he would never get to the camp and the boys; that it was too many miles away, that the freezing had too great a start on him, and that he would soon be stiff and dead. This thought he kept in the background and refused to consider. Sometimes it pushed itself forward and demanded to be heard, but he thrust it back and strove to think of other things.

It struck him as curious that he could run at all on feet so frozen that he could not feel them when they struck the earth and took the weight of his body. He seemed to himself to skim along above the surface, and to have no connection with the earth. Somewhere he had once seen a winged Mercury,[8] and he won-dered if Mercury felt as he felt when skimming over the earth.

[8] According to Roman myth, the messenger of the gods, portrayed with wings on his heels.

His theory of running until he reached camp and the boys had one flaw in it; he lacked the endurance. Several times he stumbled, and finally he tottered, crumpled up, and fell. When he tried to rise, he failed. He must sit and rest, he decided, and next time he would merely walk and keep on going. As he sat and regained his breath, he noted that he was feeling quite warm and comfortable. He was not shivering, and it even seemed that a warm glow had come to his chest and trunk. And yet, when he touched his nose and cheeks, there was no sensation. Running would not thaw them out. Nor would it thaw out his hands and feet. Then the thought came to him that the frozen portions of his body must be extending. He tried to keep this thought down, to forget it, to think of something else; he was aware of the panicky feeling that it caused, and he was afraid of the panic. But the thought asserted itself, and persisted, until it produced a vision of his body totally frozen. This was too much, and he made another wild run along the trail. Once he slowed down to a walk, but the thought of the freezing extending itself made him run again.

And all the time the dog ran with him, at his heels. When he fell down a second time, it curled its tail over its forefeet and sat in front of him, facing him, curiously eager and intent. The warmth and security of the animal angered him, and he cursed it till it flattened down its ears appeasingly. This time the shivering came more quickly upon the man. He was losing in his battle with the frost. It was creeping into his body from all sides. The thought of it drove him on, but he ran no more than a hundred feet, when he staggered and pitched headlong. It was his last panic. When he had recovered his breath and control, he sat up and entertained in his mind the conception of meeting death with dignity. However, the conception did not come to him in such terms. His idea of it was that he had been making a fool of himself, running around like a chicken with its head cut off— such was the simile that occurred to him. Well, he was bound to freeze anyway, and he might as well take it decently. With this new-found peace of mind came the first glimmerings of drowsiness. A good idea, he thought, to sleep off to death. It was like taking an anæsthetic. Freezing was not so bad as people thought. There were lots worse ways to die.

He pictured the boys finding his body next day. Suddenly he found himself with them, coming along the trail and looking for himself. And, still with them, he came around a turn in the trail and found himself lying in the snow. He did not belong with himself any more, for even then he was out of himself, standing with the boys and looking at himself in the snow. It certainly was cold, was his thought. When he got back to the States he could tell the folks what real cold was. He drifted on from this to a vision of the old-timer on Sulphur Creek. He could see him quite clearly, warm and comfortable, and smoking a pipe.

"You were right, old hoss; you were right," the man mumbled to the old-timer of Sulphur Creek.

Then the man drowsed off into what seemed to him the most comfortable and satisfying sleep he had ever known. The dog sat facing him and waiting. The brief day drew to a close in a long, slow twilight. There were no signs of a fire to be made, and, besides, never in the dog's experience had it know a man to sit like that in the snow and make no fire. As the twilight drew on, its eager yearning for the fire mastered it, and with a great lifting and shifting of forefeet, it whined softly, then flattened its ears down in anticipation of being chidden by the man.

But the man remained silent. Later, the dog whined loudly. And still later it crept close to the man and caught the scent of death. This made the animal bristle and back away. A little longer it delayed, howling under the stars that leaped and danced and shone brightly in the cold sky. Then it turned and trotted up the trail in the direction of the camp it knew, where were the other food-providers and fire-providers.

1908

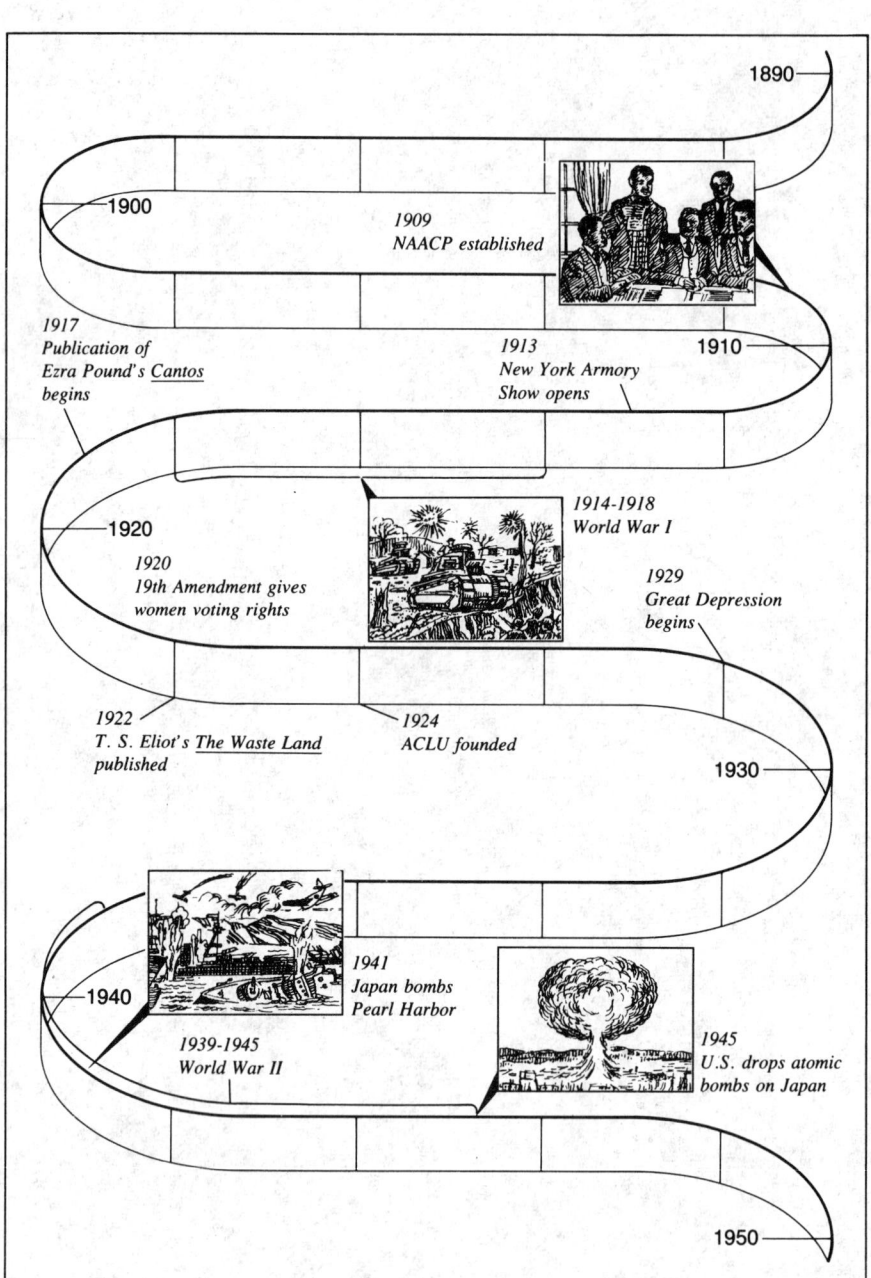

1890

1900

1909
NAACP established

1917
Publication of
Ezra Pound's Cantos
begins

1913
New York Armory
Show opens

1910

1914-1918
World War I

1920

1920
19th Amendment gives
women voting rights

1929
Great Depression
begins

1922
T. S. Eliot's The Waste Land
published

1924
ACLU founded

1930

1941
Japan bombs
Pearl Harbor

1939-1945
World War II

1945
U.S. drops atomic
bombs on Japan

1940

1950

PART TWO

America in the World Community

The Early 20th Century

Children born in the final years of the nineteenth century were young adults during World War I and were likely to send their sons to fight in World War II. In the interwar years their life chances would be curtailed by a severe economic depression; they would experience the anguish of watching what seemed like an inexorable rise of fascism and tyranny around the world. But the century opened bravely. A generation of progressive reformers, supported in many of their concerns by President Theodore Roosevelt, believed that human intelligence could solve the problems of urbanization, immigration, education, and public health. In state after state, new laws limited work hours of women and children, set the standards for decent working conditions, and made basic education compulsory. The membership of trade unions doubled between 1915 and 1920. Progressive mayors promoted public libraries and museums, sought to eliminate graft and corruption from civic building projects, and lowered fees for public services. Federal legislation provided for the regulation and inspection of food and drugs, including eliminating the cocaine that had originally been an ingredient in Coca-Cola. It was possible to anticipate that future generations could be protected from exploitation and that decent living standards were within the reach of all Americans.

But for many the reforms came too slowly and too late. On March 25, 1911, nearly 150 young female garment workers died when a fire broke out in the factory of the Triangle Shirtwaist Company in Manhattan; the owners had kept the doors to the fire escapes locked so that workers could not take breaks from their work and union organizers could not enter. Passers-by watched in horror as forty-six young women jumped out windows; some jumped in groups, holding hands. Among the watchers was a young social worker, Frances Perkins, who would dedicate her life to improving factory conditions and whom Franklin D. Roosevelt would appoint to his cabinet as secretary of labor in 1933. She was the first female member of a presidential cabinet.

Progressive reformers could be ambivalent on racial issues; Theodore Roosevelt invited Booker T. Washington to dinner at the White House but also ordered the dishonorable discharge of 167 African-American soldiers after a race riot in

Brownsville, Texas, although charges could not be proved against any of them. In 1909 a coalition of white and black reformers, led by W. E. B. Du Bois, Mary White Ovington, and Oswald Garrison Villard (grandson of the abolitionist William Lloyd Garrison), organized the National Association for the Advancement of Colored People to resist lynching, promote better race relations, and support the interests of African Americans.

World War I

World War I broke out in Europe in 1914 between the Allies (Great Britain, Belgium, France, and Russia) and the Central Powers (Germany, Austria-Hungary, and Bulgaria). Tensions from colonial rivalries and nationalist sentiment exploded after the assassination of Austria's Archduke Francis Ferdinand in June 1914. President Woodrow Wilson called upon Americans to remain neutral in thought and in action. What was neutral behavior, however, was not always obvious. For example, British passenger liners commonly carried war supplies. When German submarines sunk these ships, such as the *Lusitania* in 1915, they did so on the grounds that the ships contributed to the war effort. Wilson's secretary of state, William Jennings Bryan, thought the Germans had drawn an obvious conclusion and urged Wilson to forbid Americans to travel on belligerent ships. But Wilson took the position that a German attack on any U.S. ship would constitute an act of aggression. When in 1917 Germany announced that it would sink on sight any ship heading for England or France and then sunk five American merchant ships in a two-week period in March, Wilson called for a declaration of war. Framing it in terms of a war to stabilize democracy, he promised that the fight would be for freedom of the seas, the self-determination of small nations and colonial peoples, and "a concert of free peoples as shall bring peace and safety to all nations and make the world itself at last free."

American intervention came at a crucial time: the "Great War" had bled both sides of nearly a generation of young men. The British lost 900,000 men, the French 1.4 million, the Russians 1.7 million; in contrast, Americans lost 50,000 men. At least an equal number were wounded. But the addition of American troops in the late stages of fighting provided a crucial margin for allied victory. African-American leaders, W. E. B. Du Bois among them, urged their followers to support the war, but upon enlisting African Americans found themselves assigned to segregated units and required to do menial labor. Female suffragists had believed that women had a special responsibility to oppose war, but when the United States entered, most suffrage groups stifled their opposition and joined the patriotic campaign. Seizing upon the contradiction between a war to make the world safe for democracy and the denial of democratic participation to women, they persuaded Wilson to drop his opposition to women's suffrage. The result of a major lobbying effort was the passage of the Nineteenth Amendment to the Constitution in 1919, which gives women the right to vote.

Other groups, notably socialists, bitterly opposed intervention; they found that once war was declared neither the government nor much of the American public

New weapons, such as machine guns and poison gas, along with disease and the tactics of trench warfare, led to at least ten million deaths in World War I.

tolerated criticism. The Espionage Act of 1917 permitted the government to ban "treasonous" materials from the mails without specifying what constitutes treason; the Sedition Act of 1918 made punishable any "disloyal, profane, scurrilous, or abusive language about the form of government." More than one thousand people were convicted under these statutes, including many who had printed or distributed pamphlets opposing American intervention in Europe or in Russia, and these convictions were upheld by the Supreme Court. Freedom of speech and of the press were thus bitterly contested during the war years. The American Civil Liberties Union would be founded in 1924 to articulate the broad principles of the right to speak, write, and publish.

The peace that was negotiated at Versailles, France, in 1919 was a complex one. The negotiators were grimly distressed by the success of the Russian Revolution and by the fear that a proletarian revolution might spread outside the Soviet Union. The United States briefly sent troops that supported resistance to Nikolai Lenin, leader of the Russian Revolution. The European negotiators were determined to punish Germany and to pay for the restoration of their own economies through German reparations. But the Treaty of Versailles did create independent states from the defunct Austro-Hungarian empire—not only Austria and Hungary but also Poland, Yugoslavia, and Czechoslovakia. It established some guidelines for the treatment of colonies, and it established the League of Nations, which, it was hoped, would fulfill Wilson's promise of a "concert of free peoples."

In the aftermath of World War I, frightened by the Russian Revolution, Americans refused to join the League of Nations. Superpatriotism built on fear; in 1920 the Ku Klux Klan—racist, anti-Semitic, anti-Catholic, and generally xenophobic—claimed over 100,000 members; it grew fastest in the Midwest. Although American radical organizations were in fact losing members, a "Red scare," fear of communism, spread and contributed to the passage of laws severely restricting European immigration and virtually eliminating Asian immigration. In the 1930s these laws would even effectively bar the entry of refugees from Adolf Hitler's terror. (They did not, however, restrict immigration from Western Hemisphere countries: by the end of the 1920s one out of five people in Los Angeles was of Mexican origin.) In 1920 two Italian immigrants, the anarchists Nicola Sacco and Bartolomeo Vanzetti, were convicted for murdering a guard and a paymaster during a payroll robbery in South Braintree, Massachusetts. Many liberals believed the evidence was flimsy and that Sacco and Vanzetti were sentenced because they were foreign. Intellectuals, writers, and artists rallied to their defense. Carl Sandburg, Katherine Anne Porter, and Edna St. Vincent Millay were among the many writers who protested the conviction; Ben Shahn created twenty-three paintings in protest. Nevertheless, Sacco and Vanzetti were executed in 1927.

Consumerism and Technology

The 1920s was the high-water mark of a revolution in consumer goods and communications technology that had been underway since the 1890s. By the end of the 1920s nearly half the nation's households had telephones, and an equal number had radios. The first commercial radio station opened in 1920: car radios came into use in 1927. Radio shaped a national audience for music, news, stories— weekly comedy series and daytime soap operas—and sports; the World Series was first broadcast in 1921. Other developments also created national audiences and national standards of taste in the 1920s, helping to break down regional variations in culture. Magazines such as *The Saturday Evening Post* and *The Ladies' Home Journal* had national circulations of over 2.5 million. An estimated 100 million people a week went to movies, and the first "talkies" appeared in movie theatres in 1927. The Book-of-the-Month Club, founded in 1926, invigorated the national circulation of a limited range of titles. New automobile technology widened horizons; by the end of the 1920s there was one car for every five people. Explaining why her family had chosen to buy a car before installing running water, one rural woman explained to an inquiring sociologist, "You can't go to town in a bathtub."

Mass circulation of magazines and of broadcasts also helped to shape national patterns of consumption, and national advertising became a big business. Advertisers leaned heavily on the latest findings of psychologists in their efforts to influence purchasing behavior; advertisements stressed that the purchase of particular objects would solve consumers' insecurities and contribute to their personal happiness. Metaphors of consumption as the route to psychological security would persist throughout the twentieth century.

The Great Depression

The stock-market crash of October 1929 brought a startling halt to the prosperity that had characterized the 1920s. President Herbert Hoover moved more aggressively than had any president before him to use federal power to address the economic crisis. But it was not enough for national boards and committees to call upon businesses for voluntary actions. By 1932 85,000 businesses had failed, and many others had cut back their operations; hundreds of thousands of people (one out of four by 1933) had lost their jobs. President Franklin D. Roosevelt's New Deal reform policy, initiated in 1933, was an amalgam of support for economic planning and for welfare programs. Claiming that "the only thing we have to fear is fear itself," Roosevelt enthusiastically and aggressively used the power of government action to address economic problems, particularly in the legislation proposed to Congress during the first hundred days of his presidency. His Works Progress Administration funded jobs for the unemployed and was a boon to writers and artists. The WPA's Federal Writers' Project employed some five thousand writers to produce state guidebooks, historians to interview hundreds of former slaves, and librarians and historians to catalogue the holdings of major manuscript libraries and state archives. The WPA's Federal Theater Project commissioned plays, hired directors and actors, and made tickets available at low prices to working people.

The Great Depression was not fully resolved until the demands of production for World War II redefined the economy. But the New Deal transformed the relationship between government and the economy in ways that still endure, giving the federal government extensive regulatory power over the stock market, banks, agriculture, unions, corporations, electrical and subsequently atomic energy, transportation, and welfare (notably social security and related legislation). Much of the welfare legislation had first been sketched out by progressive reformers working in the cities and the states; now the reformers clustered around Eleanor Roosevelt, forming an effective lobbying group for the interests of women, children, and the poor within the Roosevelt administration. Notable reformers included Florence Kelley, head of the National Consumers' League, who had begun her career at Jane Addams's Hull House; Grace Abbott, head of the Children's Bureau of the Department of Labor; Harry Hopkins, a New York social worker; and Molly Dewson, head of the Women's Division of the Democratic National Committee.

Social Change

Economics, psychology, and sex roles intertwined in the 1930s. Divorce rates declined; so did marriage and birth rates, as people postponed setting up or enlarging households. In 1936 Margaret Sanger, a nurse, successfully tested federal bans on birth-control devices by importing a clearly marked package of diaphragms from Japan and challenging customs officials to confiscate it. Afterward, doctors were generally free to dispense birth-control information. A few states continued to make it illegal to sell birth control devices, however, (the ban lasted into the 1960s in Connecticut), and abortion generally remained illegal. An estimated nine thousand women died each year from abortions performed in unsanitary and unprofessional conditions during the 1930s.

Although the proportion of women who worked for wages steadily rose, as did the proportions of married working women and of working mothers, public-opinion polls regularly reported that both men and women felt wives should not work. Many states and the federal government adopted laws forbidding more than one member of a household from holding civil service jobs; invariably the person who lost the job in such cases was the wife. Many school districts forbade the employment of married women as school teachers. New Deal relief programs typically ignored women's needs; the Civilian Conservation Corps, for example, hired only young men. Domestic servants, generally African American and female, were totally excluded from Social Security coverage and from the Fair Labor Standards Act.

World War II

The 1930s was also a time of great international tension as fascism rose in Europe and the democracies seemed powerless—or unwilling—to resist. Americans had generally concluded from the disaster of World War I that wars did not solve international problems and that compromises should be made with Adolph Hitler and Benito Mussolini in the hope of maintaining American neutrality. In the Far East, Japan aggressively sought to establish its own rule in China, Malaya (now part of Malaysia), and Burma. Many on the political Left, including writers such a Ernest Hemingway and John Dos Passos, supported the Loyalists (those opposing Gen. Francisco Franco's revolt) during the Spanish Civil War (1936–1939). Over three thousand Americans formed the Abraham Lincoln Brigade and went to Spain to fight as volunteers, but they were a tiny minority. Germany, seeking new territory, annexed its close neighbors from 1936 to 1939, with little resistance from the rest of Europe. When in 1938 German armies occupied Czechoslovakia, Americans were sympathetic to the Czechs but silent; Americans were also shocked, but not into action, when news came in summer 1939 of a Nazi-Soviet Non-Aggression Pact. When Germany invaded Poland in September 1939, England and France declared war on Germany, but the United States remained neutral.

Germany and its allies, Fascist Italy and Japan, known as the Axis powers, expanded their territorial holdings worldwide. By the end of 1940 German armies had established control of Norway, Denmark, Belgium, Luxembourg, the Netherlands, and most of France. Not until 1941 did a vigorous lend-lease program make ships and goods available to Great Britain and, after Germany broke the Nazi-Soviet pact, to the Soviet Union as well. During 1941 the United States gradually became a major supporter of the Allied powers (which included Great Britain, the Soviet Union, and France); still, the Japanese attack on Pearl Harbor on December 7, 1941, came as a shock and a surprise to a largely unprepared nation. A few days later Hitler declared war on the United States.

=CONTEXTS=

Proletarian Fiction

Between the two world wars many writers became increasingly critical of American capitalism and materialism. These writers saw American life as a response to political, social, and economic conditions and related these conditions to the theories of Karl Marx (1818–1883). A leader in this movement was John Dos Passos (1896–1970). He examined the problems of materialism inherent in the lives of all Americans—rich and poor, new immigrant and established businessman. American materialism, Dos Passos felt, creates class distinctions and encourages personal greed.

In his later novels Dos Passos depicts the fragmentation of American society, caused by class divisions and by the Great Depression. He structures his narratives around such varied sources as personal reflection, historical fact, and fictional elements, all woven into an eclectic blend. The disjointedness of this blend suggests that the American "rags to riches" myth leads only to alienation and moral decay. In *The Big Money* (1936), the final volume of his *USA* trilogy (collected in 1938), he uses verbal montages of newsreel headlines to simulate the confusing and contradictory information to which we are subjected:

The Big Money

Newsreel LXVIII

WALL STREET STUNNED

This is not Thirtyeight but it's old Ninetyseven
You must put her in Center on time

MARKET SURE TO RECOVER FROM SLUMP

DECLINE IN CONTRACTS

POLICE TURN MACHINE GUNS ON COLORADO MINE STRIKERS
KILL 5 WOUND 40

sympathizers appeared on the scene just as thousands of office workers were pouring out of the buildings at the lunch hour. As they raised their placard high and started an indefinite march from one side to the other, they were jeered and hooted not only by the office workers but also by workmen on a building under construction

NEW METHODS OF SELLING SEEN

RESCUE CREWS TRY TO UPEND ILL-FATED CRAFT
WHILE WAITING FOR PONTOONS

He looked 'round an' said to his black greasy fireman
Jus' shovel in a little more coal
And when we cross that White Oak Mountain
You can watch your Ninety-seven roll

I find your column interesting and need advice. I have saved four thousand dollars which I want to invest for a better income. Do you think I might buy stocks?

John Dos Passos, 1936

At the time of the attack, more than half the Japanese Americans in the United States were American citizens. In an atmosphere of post-Pearl Harbor hysteria, fueled by long-standing racism, those of Japanese descent on the West Coast, whether citizens or not, were forced to abandon their property and moved to primitive relocation camps. Not until 1983 did Congress formally acknowledge that they had constituted no threat to American security and promise to pay modest reparations. As the United States entered the 1990s, however, money for the reparation had not been allocated.

Thirteen million men and 350,000 women served in a global war. When the United States entered the war in 1942, it was unprepared to launch an invasion of Europe, so the Soviet Union continued to lead the fight against Germany. The Soviets lost at least twenty million people, some eight percent of their population; in the 1990s these estimates have been raised to forty million. The German advance was stopped at the bitter and costly Battle of Stalingrad in winter 1942–1943. Joseph Stalin would never forgive the United States and England, unprepared as they were, for refusing to launch a large-scale invasion of Europe at that time, which would have forced Germany to fight on two fronts at once. (England and the United States did initiate a successful offensive in North Africa.) By mid-1943 the Allies had conquered Italy and were planning a major invasion of the European continent. However, D-day, the Allied invasion of Normandy, did not take place until June 6, 1944. The scale of fighting in the last months of the war was unprecedented: over a million Allied troops landed in Europe in June alone. News had come from many reliable sources of the systematic murder of millions of Jews by the Nazis, but Allied forces refused to target concentration camps or even railroad lines to the camps. When Allied troops entered the camps, such as Auschwitz and Buchenwald, after Germany's surrender in May 1945, they were shocked and surprised by the evidence of genocide—the Holocaust—they encountered.

Meanwhile, Japan had moved quickly after Pearl Harbor, capturing the Philippines, Burma, and Malaya within three months. Although the fight against Germany was carried on with the Allies, the United States alone fought Japan in the Pacific. The death toll in the Pacific was very high as American forces had to move from island to island, expelling the Japanese. By August 1944 American planes were bombing Tokyo, but Japanese resistance continued, even past the final defeat of Germany in spring 1945.

Whereas much of Europe was devastated or radically realigned by World War II, the United States (and the Soviet Union) emerged as global superpowers. The U.S. government's role in the economy, strengthened during the New Deal years, grew even stronger during the war. The United States became the "arsenal of democracy," building some 300,000 airplanes, 88,000 tanks, and 3,000 ships. Industrial production and corporate profits doubled in the five years after the war ended. Scarce products were rationed; some items that would have competed with war production, such as cars, were not made at all. Tax rates were raised, and a payroll deduction was established for income taxes. Many Americans were drawn into the war industry: a national recruitment campaign explicitly attacked old stereotypes against working women, substituting "Rosie the Riveter" as the model

During World War II over six million women worked in traditionally male jobs in factories supporting the war effort, and earned the nickname "Rosie the Riveter." When the war ended, most found themselves replaced by returning servicemen.

woman in her country's service. Most working women had actually been in the paid labor force before the war; now they moved into skilled jobs at better pay. Both the civilian and military communities remained strictly segregated by race. African Americans held only menial jobs in the navy and the lowest ranking jobs in the army.

Even before the United States had entered the war, it had secretly entered the race to build an atomic bomb. Many of the scientists who worked on the bomb were refugees from Germany and Italy. When Harry S. Truman succeeded to the presidency after Roosevelt's death in spring 1945, the war in Europe was virtually over, but the war in Japan continued. Truman received conflicting advice about whether or not to use the bomb. On the one hand, Japanese resistance in the Pacific had been intense, and there was every reason to expect it would continue were there to be an invasion of Japan. Most Americans thought the United States had sacrificed enough and wanted a quick end to the war, an end without the Soviet Union's help, so there would be no need for compromise with the Soviets after the war. Some Americans thought the bomb was proper repayment for Pearl

Harbor and were less inhibited about dropping it against Asians than they would have been against Europeans. On the other hand, many scientists who appreciated the damage the bomb could do urged that Truman simply demonstrate its capabilities, hoping to frighten the Japanese into surrender.

The bomb dropped on Hiroshima on August 6, 1945, killed 100,000 people. When Japan did not surrender immediately, another was dropped on Nagasaki, killing 60,000. Many thousands more died of radiation poisoning not long after. When J. Robert Oppenheimer, leader of the Manhattan Project, which developed the bomb, saw its first test he thought of a line from the Sanskrit book of verse Bhagavad-Gītā (first or second century A.D.): "I am become death, the destroyer of worlds."

EARLY 20TH-CENTURY POETRY

Unlike American fiction, which had taken on a fresh strength and national identity, American poetry in the early twentieth century was weak and imitative, offering few models for a young poet who wished, in Ezra Pound's words, to "make it new." Walt Whitman's death in 1892 had marked the end of an era, and young poets such as Pound and T. S. Eliot felt compelled to look abroad for inspiration. In a lecture given in Dublin in 1936, Eliot, at the height of his international fame, recollected that in his formative years even the contemporary English poets had little to offer him, while "there were no American poets at all."

The years between Eliot's birth in 1888 and Hart Crane's in 1899 were probably the most important in the history of American poetry. Modernism, a movement marked by a need to impose internal order within a chaotic world, began at this time. Crane in his youth had access to a native American tradition that had not existed for Pound, Eliot, Wallace Stevens, or William Carlos Williams. Emily Dickinson's poetry had been discovered, and a revival of Herman Melville's work was under way: the canon of twentieth-century American literature was taking shape. More importantly, Crane found himself heir to a new poetic, formed in large part by those American poets born in the 1880s. Writing to his friend and fellow poet Allen Tate, Crane spoke of his immediate predecessors—especially Pound and Eliot—as if they were already modern masters. Assuming the mantle of Whitman, Crane made a visionary pilgrimage through America's geographical and emotional space. His epic poem *The Bridge* (1930) celebrates the Brooklyn Bridge as both an architectural achievement and a symbol of American modernity.

By convention the major American poets of this time are divided into those who, like Pound and Eliot, chose expatriation and played a crucial role in creating an "international modernism," and those who stayed in America and sought a "native American modernism." This distinction holds a rough truth but needs many qualifications. Pound and Eliot, and Henry James before them, always considered themselves American writers who had chosen expatriation in order to gain perspective on their native land. The first section of Pound's essay *Patria Mia* (1950, written in 1912) opens with "America, my country." From his early essays

Marcel Duchamp's cubist painting Nude Descending a Staircase *(1912) shocked visitors at the New York Armory Show in 1913. Modernist writers of the period were also breaking conventions.*

on American literature and society through the autobiographical writing of *Indiscretions* (1920) to the American history cantos of the 1930s, Pound remained a man of only one country.

Eliot's "Americanness" is less obvious but no less profound, as Pound argues in a 1920 exchange with William Carlos Williams. Williams felt that the "academic" nature of Eliot's early poetry threatened to stifle a more spontaneous regional American form and typically compensated for his sense of isolation and belatedness by casting Eliot in the role of cultural traitor. Pound shrewdly turned the tables by calling Williams a newly arrived outsider objective enough to survive the American experience; Pound and Eliot, by contrast, were deeply infected with the American virus by way of their Puritan inheritances. In this exchange Williams becomes the foreign bystander, Pound and Eliot the ingrained natives.

Whereas Pound remained to the end a rambunctious American abroad, Eliot assimilated British culture until he became an Englishman superficially, even choosing British citizenship in 1927. But Eliot viewed himself as a foreigner abroad. He believed that no one could properly appreciate him without understanding those deep attachments to the American landscape and to the American past that are the imaginative sources of much of his best work, especially the poems of *Four Quartets* (1935–1942). Eliot is buried in the village of East Coker, in western England, the home of his ancestors before they pioneered in the New World in the seventeenth century. Inscribed around the memorial tablet in the village church are the mottoes that frame Eliot's poem *East Coker* (1940), part of *Four Quartets:* "In my beginning is my end" and "In my end is my beginning."

Conversely, the modernist poets who remained in the States were much more international in their outlooks and styles than has been claimed. The poetry of Robert Frost, who has been called the quintessential poet "in the American grain," was first recognized (by Ezra Pound) during his 1913 to 1915 stay in England; his friendship with the British poet Edward Thomas, formed then, was probably the most decisive event in Frost's poetic life. The apparent simplicity of Frost's poems is deceptive: the poems reveal an enigmatic art in which the seemingly benign pastoral surface conceals dark and ironic possibilities. His landscapes are landscapes of the inner self, and he belongs not to a region but to the larger world of the great tragic realists.

Wallace Stevens never traveled abroad but in college learned of the modern French poets and later kept in touch with international developments in the art world. A businessman and a poet, Stevens knew poetry, like life, to be a necessary and unending oscillation between the worlds of fact and of the imagination. His is a philosophical poetry that uses concrete images from American life in fleshing out difficult abstractions. The depiction of Stevens as a mannered creator of poems about poetry ignores the range of his subjects and of his styles. Stevens was not an aesthete unattached to society but a poet of everyday American reality, a reality always transformed by a cosmopolitan imagination.

Even William Carlos Williams, the most relentlessly "local" of all the early modernists, felt that he needed the stimulus of European experimental writing to keep his style fresh and responsive. Williams sat in his third-floor study in Rutherford, New Jersey, contemplating the local scene but seeing it through the eyes of Paris; Ezra Pound looked out at the Italian landscape from his apartment in Rapallo but wrote his cantos on American history. These are the complementary images of modern American poetry. The common aim of the modern poets was to be American without being provincial, to celebrate the local without falling into the narrowness of local color.

The contrasts and similarities between Pound/Eliot and Stevens/Williams/Frost form a useful paradigm under which other poets can be considered. Marianne Moore witnessed the modernism movement from its beginnings to its close, and her reviews provide the most balanced assessment available of her great contemporaries. Her neat poetic world is governed by an aesthetic that combines Pound's emphasis on the concrete image with Williams's stress on the details of ordinary life. A poet's poet because of her attention to technique, Moore resembles other modernist poets while remaining uniquely herself.

Allen Tate was the most prominent member of the Fugitives, a group of southern poets and critics that included Robert Penn Warren and John Crowe Ransom. During the 1920s and 1930s they celebrated the values of a vanishing agricultural South. Their emphasis on authority and tradition, derived from T. S. Eliot, was grounded in the tragic course of southern history. Tate's "Ode to the Confederate Dead" (1928) shows that the techniques of international modernism were easily adaptable to regional values and voices.

In some ways the Harlem Renaissance of the 1920s fits the broad pattern of regionalism. The writers who gathered in New York City's Harlem district celebrated African-American culture, including its myths, language, and sense of community. Along with such fiction writers as Zora Neale Hurston, the poets—Countee Cullen, James Weldon Johnson, and Langston Hughes among them—frankly addressed racial issues and incorporated characters from contemporary life into their poetry. Hughes's poems transcribe blues songs, jazz rhythms, and vernacular speech, creating a mythology of twentieth-century African-American life that transcends the merely local. Like other American poets of his time whose work has endured, Hughes reminds us that the more rooted and particular an artist is, the better his or her chance of achieving an enduring and universal audience.

A common aim of early twentieth-century poets was the creation of a long poem under the stylistic conditions of modernist poetry, conditions best defined by a brief rehearsal of the imagist movement. "Imagism" is a term invented by Ezra Pound to publicize his own poetry and that of some friends, including Hilda Doolittle. When she submitted a group of her finely chiseled poems to *Poetry* magazine, Pound insisted that she sign them "H. D., *Imagiste*." In a series of his own in *Poetry* (1912–1913), Pound sought to give the movement a theoretical underpinning. Imagism aimed to treat subjects directly, to use only words that contribute to a poem's presentation, and to compose with the rhythm of a musical phrase, not with that of a metronome. The rules laid out in these essays had a profound impact on the course of modern American literature. For example, the crisp, clean style of Ernest Hemingway reflects that author's deep debt to Pound.

As a movement imagism was short-lived, part of the politics of literature. The term is still used to represent the tendencies in early modern American poetry toward a conversational style and sharp, concrete, visual presentation. The goal was to scrub the palette clean of poetic diction and begin again with the primary colors of observed reality and overheard speech. That aim was well suited to the short poem, such as Pound's exemplary imagist poem "In a Station of the Metro" (1913).

How could such an aesthetic, with its emphasis on the concise and on simultaneity of effect, be accommodated in the long poem? As early as 1914 Pound was asking this question because the writing of a long poem traditionally is the validation of a poet's art. The history of modern American poetry is in a way a history of the search for a long form that would preserve the effects the modernist poets had achieved in their early, short poems. Pound's *Hugh Selwyn Mauberley* (1920), Eliot's *The Waste Land* (1922), Stevens's *The Comedian as the Letter C* (1923), and Williams's *Spring and All* (1923) were early attempts to solve this problem; Hart Crane's *The Bridge,* Eliot's *Four Quartets,* Stevens's long poems of the 1930s and 1940s, and Williams's *Paterson* (1946–1963) were later attempts. The most heroic example is Pound's *The Cantos* (1917–1959), for over fifty years the focus of his creative life and unfinished at his death.

The American modernist poet had to discover sources of order other than those available to his or her predecessors. The traditional frames of plot and drama could not contain the conflicting energies of contemporary experience. The poet felt compelled to express through form and language the discontinuities and fragmentation of the world outside the poem. The result was a variety of poetic strate-

=CONTEXTS=

The Harlem Renaissance

An increased sociopolitical consciousness among African Americans in urban centers after World War I gave rise to a flowering of African-American literature and art. This movement, centered primarily in the Harlem area of New York City, has been called the Harlem Renaissance. Countee Cullen (1903–1946) was a central poet of the Harlem Renaissance. His poetry typically deals with the problems of African-American experience in the United States, the struggle to fuse latent African roots with the practical problems of racism in America. Cullen sought to validate the dignity and secure the basic human rights of African Americans. In "Heritage," Cullen attempts to regain his sense of his ancestral roots.

Heritage

What is Africa to me:
Copper sun or scarlet sea,
Jungle star or jungle track,
Strong bronzed men, or regal black
Women from whose loins I sprang
When the birds of Eden sang?
One three centuries removed
From the scenes his fathers loved,
Spicy grove, cinnamon tree,
What is Africa to me?

* * *

So I lie, who find no peace
Night or day, no slight release
From the unremmittant beat
Made by cruel padded feet
Walking through my body's street.
Up and down they go, and back,
Treading out a jungle track.

* * *

All day long and all night through,
One thing only must I do:
Quench my pride and cool my blood,
Lest I perish in the flood. . . .
Not yet has my heart or head
In the least way realized
They and I are civilized.

Countee Cullen, 1925

gies, ranging from Eliot's orchestration of literary allusions and historical references in *The Waste Land* to Williams's interweaving of poetry and historical prose in *Paterson*. In some ways *Paterson* is the culmination of the modernist ambition to combine in a single work high and low culture, history and current events, ordinary speech and the "distinguished" language of poetry.

Edwin Arlington Robinson
(1869–1935)

Dubbed "the prince of heartachers" by Robert Frost, Edwin Arlington Robinson wrote poetry dominated by a bleak view of life. Defeated, isolated people populate Tilbury Town, the imaginary New England town Robinson modeled after his hometown, Gardiner, Maine. As Frost and others have recognized, Robinson is at his best when his gloomy message is delivered—though not necessarily tempered—by wry understatement and self-irony. Robinson's poetry is commonly compared with that of Thomas Hardy, whose dark and fatalistic vision deeply influenced Robinson.

Because of his straightforward diction and adherence to traditional forms, including blank verse and the sonnet, in the midst of modernism's experimental mood, Robinson was considered a literary anachronism for many years before and after his death in 1935. Robinson's character sketches in such early books as *The Children of the Night* (1897)—an expanded and revised version of his first book, the privately published *The Torrent and the Night Before* (1896)—and *The Town Down the River* (1910) helped usher in the modern focus on everyday aspects of life. Such subject matter had for the most part been considered "unpoetic," notwithstanding the revolutionary example of Whitman. Robinson's New England, though, is not so much a vividly imaged place as an album of personalities, the Miniver Cheevys, Richard Corys, and Mr. Floods of Tilbury Town. At the end of the poem "Richard Cory" (1896), Cory's unexpected suicide indicates a secret inner life, but Robinson refrains from specifying its contents. As the poet Conrad Aiken notes in a 1921 review of Robinson's *Avon's Harvest* (1921), Robinson's poems tend to suggest "a background left dim not because the author is only dimly aware of it, but because dimness serves to make it seem the more gigantic." The poet succeeded in making vagueness a virtue.

Although Robinson achieved a great deal of fame during his life, receiving three Pulitzer Prizes during the 1920s, his early years were marked by obscurity and misfortune. A descendant of the Puritan poet Anne Bradstreet, he was born in 1869 in Gardiner and raised in an upper-middle-class New England family. His father and mother died when Robinson was in his twenties, and the family's money was lost during the Great Panic of 1893. Robinson then moved to New York City, where he lived in a state of poverty and chronic drunkenness for nearly a decade. His fortunes miraculously improved when President Theodore Roosevelt stumbled upon *The Children of the Night*. Roosevelt was so impressed that he helped arrange for *The Children of the Night* to be reissued, wrote a review of it, and in 1905 got Robinson a clerkship in the New York Customs House.

Robinson's early volumes contain many of the Tilbury Town portraits for which the poet is famous; more appear in *The Man Against the Sky* (1916), which was well received. Robinson was so prolific that no less than four versions of *Collected Poems* were put together during his lifetime, and the final edition (1937) includes over fifteen hundred pages. After the publication of the first *Collected Poems* (1921), which earned Robinson his first Pulitzer Prize, he embarked on a series of book-length narrative poems upon which critical judgment is divided. The most important of these are realistic retellings of the British legends of King Arthur: *Merlin* (1917), *Lancelot* (1920), and the bestselling *Tristram* (1927), for which he won another Pulitzer Prize. Late in his life, Robinson wrote largely somber psychoanalytical or allegorical narratives of modern life.

Suggested Readings: *The Children of the Night,* 1897. *The Man Against the Sky,* 1916. *Lancelot,* 1920. *Collected Poems,* 1937. *Selected Early Poems and Letters,* ed. C. T. Davis, 1960. *Uncollected Poems and Prose,* ed. R. Cary, 1975. E. S. Fussell, *Edwin Arlington Robinson: The Literary Background of a Traditional Poet,* 1954. L. O. Coxe, *Edwin Arlington Robinson: The Life of Poetry,* 1969. H. Bloom, ed., *Edwin Arlington Robinson,* 1988.

Texts Used: "Why He Was There": *Dionysus in Doubt: A Book of Poems,* 1925. All others: *Selected Poems of Edwin Arlington Robinson,* ed. M. D. Zabel, 1965.

LUKE HAVERGAL

Go to the western gate,[1] Luke Havergal,
There where the vines cling crimson on the wall,
And in the twilight wait for what will come.
The leaves will whisper there of her, and some,
Like flying words, will strike you as they fall;
But go, and if you listen she will call.
Go to the western gate, Luke Havergal—
Luke Havergal.

No, there is not a dawn in eastern skies
To rift the fiery night that's in your eyes;   10
But there, where western glooms are gathering,
The dark will end the dark, if anything:
God slays Himself with every leaf that flies,
And hell is more than half of paradise.
No, there is not a dawn in eastern skies—
In eastern skies.

Out of a grave I come to tell you this,
Out of a grave I come to quench the kiss
That flames upon your forehead with a glow
That blinds you to the way that you must go.   20
Yes, there is yet one way to where she is.
Bitter, but one that faith may never miss.
Out of a grave I come to tell you this—
To tell you this.

There is the western gate, Luke Havergal,
There are the crimson leaves upon the wall.
Go, for the winds are tearing them away,—

---

[1] Robinson's phrase for death.

Nor think to riddle[2] the dead words they say,
Nor any more to feel them as they fall;
But go, and if you trust her she will call.   30
There is the western gate, Luke Havergal—
Luke Havergal.

1896

RICHARD CORY

Whenever Richard Cory went down town,
We people on the pavement looked at him:
He was a gentleman from sole to crown,
Clean favored, and imperially slim.

And he was always quietly arrayed,
And he was always human when he talked;
But still he fluttered pulses when he said,
"Good-morning," and he glittered when he walked.

And he was rich—yes, richer than a king—
And admirably schooled in every grace: 10
In fine, we thought that he was everything
To make us wish that we were in his place.

So on we worked, and waited for the light,
And went without the meat, and cursed the bread;
And Richard Cory, one calm summer night,
Went home and put a bullet through his head.

1896

FOR A DEAD LADY

No more with overflowing light
Shall fill the eyes that now are faded,
Nor shall another's fringe with night
Their woman-hidden world as they did.

No more shall quiver down the days
The flowing wonder of her ways,
Whereof no language may requite
The shifting and the many-shaded.

[2] To interpret.

The grace, divine, definitive,
Clings only as a faint forestalling;   10
The laugh that love could not forgive
Is hushed, and answers to no calling;
The forehead and the little ears
Have gone where Saturn[1] keeps the years;
The breast where roses could not live
Has done with rising and with falling.

The beauty, shattered by the laws
That have creation in their keeping,
No longer trembles at applause,
Or over children that are sleeping;   20
And we who delve in beauty's lore
Know all that we have known before
Of what inexorable cause
Makes Time so vicious in his reaping.

1910

MINIVER CHEEVY

Miniver Cheevy, child of scorn,
    Grew lean while he assailed the seasons;
He wept that he was ever born,
    And he had reasons.

Miniver loved the days of old
    When swords were bright and steeds were prancing;
The vision of a warrior bold
    Would set him dancing.

Miniver sighed for what was not,
    And dreamed, and rested from his labors;   10
He dreamed of Thebes and Camelot,[1]
    And Priam's[2] neighbors.

Miniver mourned the ripe renown
    That made so many a name so fragrant;
He mourned Romance, now on the town,
    And Art, a vagrant.

[1] According to Roman myth, the god of agriculture, associated with the Greek Cronus and therefore "chronos," Greek for "time."
[1] Thebes, an ancient Greek city that rivaled Athens and Sparta and provided the setting for Sophocles's tragic legend of King Oedipus; Camelot, the legendary city of King Arthur's court.
[2] King of Troy, the city destroyed during the Trojan War in Homer's *Iliad*.

Miniver loved the Medici,[3]
  Albeit he had never seen one;
He would have sinned incessantly
  Could he have been one.   20

Miniver cursed the commonplace
  And eyed a khaki suit with loathing;
He missed the mediæval grace
  Of iron clothing.

Miniver scorned the gold he sought,
  But sore annoyed was he without it;
Miniver thought, and thought, and thought,
  And thought about it.

Miniver Cheevy, born too late,
  Scratched his head and kept on thinking;   30
Miniver coughed, and called it fate,
  And kept on drinking.

1910

VETERAN SIRENS*

The ghost of Ninon[1] would be sorry now
To laugh at them, were she to see them here,
So brave and so alert for learning how
To fence with reason for another year.

Age offers a far comelier diadem
Than theirs; but anguish has no eye for grace,
When time's malicious mercy cautions them
To think a while of number and of space.

The burning hope, the worn expectancy,
The martyred humor, and the maimed allure,   10
Cry out for time to end his levity,
And age to soften its investiture;

But, they, though others fade and are still fair,
Defy their fairness and are unsubdued;

[3] The Florentine family of merchant-statesmen celebrated for their political power and patronage of the arts during the Renaissance.

* According to Greek myth, sea nymphs who enticed sailors to destruction with their seductive singing.

[1] Anne Lenclos (1620–1705), or Ninon de Lenclos, a wealthy Parisienne renowned for her great, age-defying beauty and her many illicit love affairs, the last of which was rumored to have occurred when she was eighty.

Although they suffer, they may not forswear
The patient ardor of the unpursued.

Poor flesh, to fight the calendar so long;
Poor vanity, so quaint and yet so brave;
Poor folly, so deceived and yet so strong,
So far from Ninon and so near the grave.   20

1917

MR. FLOOD'S PARTY

Old Eben Flood, climbing alone one night
Over the hill between the town below
And the forsaken upland hermitage
That held as much as he should ever know
On earth again of home, paused warily.
The road was his with not a native near;
And Eben, having leisure, said aloud,
For no man else in Tilbury Town[1] to hear:

"Well, Mr. Flood, we have the harvest moon
Again, and we may not have many more;   10
The bird is on the wing, the poet says,
And you and I have said it here before.
Drink to the bird."[2] He raised up to the light
The jug that he had gone so far to fill,
And answered huskily: "Well, Mr, Flood,
Since you propose it, I believe I will."

Alone, as if enduring to the end
A valiant armor of scarred hopes outworn,
He stood there in the middle of the road
Like Roland's ghost winding a silent horn.[3]   20
Below him, in the town among the trees,
Where friends of other days had honored him,
A phantom salutation of the dead
Rang thinly till old Eben's eyes were dim.

Then, as a mother lays her sleeping child
Down tenderly, fearing it may awake,

---

[1] A fictitious town modeled after Robinson's hometown, Gardiner, Maine.

[2] A paraphrase of Edward FitzGerald's 1859 translation of the eleventh-century Persian poem *The Rubáiyát of Omar Khayyám* (25–28): "Come, fill the Cup, and in the Fire of Spring / Your Winter Garment of Repentance fling: / The Bird of Time has but a little way / To fly—and Lo! the Bird is on the Wing."

[3] At the battle of Roncesvalles in A.D. 778, Roland (later, hero of the medieval French poem *Chanson de Roland,* or *Song of Roland* [1000?]) blows his horn for help just before he dies.

He set the jug down slowly at his feet
With trembling care, knowing that most things break;
And only when assured that on firm earth
It stood, as the uncertain lives of men   30
Assuredly did not, he paced away,
And with his hand extended paused again:

"Well, Mr. Flood, we have not met like this
In a long time; and many a change has come
To both of us, I fear, since last it was
We had a drop together. Welcome home!"
Convivially returning with himself,
Again he raised the jug up to the light;
And with an acquiescent quaver said:
"Well, Mr. Flood, if you insist, I might.   40

"Only a very little, Mr. Flood—
For auld lang syne. No more, sir; that will do."
So, for the time, apparently it did,
And Eben evidently thought so too;
For soon amid the silver loneliness
Of night he lifted up his voice and sang,
Secure, with only two moons listening,
Until the whole harmonious landscape rang—

"For auld lang syne." The weary throat gave out;
The last word wavered, and the song was done.   50
He raised again the jug regretfully
And shook his head, and was again alone.
There was not much that was ahead of him,
And there was nothing in the town below—
Where strangers would have shut the many doors
That many friends had opened long ago.

1920

WHY HE WAS THERE

Much as he left it when he went from us
Here was the room again where he had been
So long that something of him should be seen,
Or felt—and so it was. Incredulous,
I turned about, loath to be greeted thus,
And there he was in his old chair, serene
As ever, and as laconic and as lean
As when he lived, and as cadaverous.

Calm as he was of old when we were young,
He sat there gazing at the pallid flame   10
Before him. "And how far will this go on?"
I thought. He felt the failure of my tongue,
And smiled: "I was not here until you came:
And I shall not be here when you are gone."

1925

Robert Frost
(1874–1963)

Robert Frost's first book was not published until he was nearly forty, yet by the time of his death in 1963, he was America's best-known poet. Millions of people had watched the windswept New England sage recite a poem at John F. Kennedy's televised presidential inauguration in 1961. The public image Frost created for himself was insistently rural, regional, and American. But he was born in San Francisco, grew up in a California factory town, and first gained literary recognition in England. The kindly philosopher image was somewhat a mask. Letters, biographies, and critical studies published after Frost's death reveal cruelty, tragedy, and despair. Fear and uncertainty are major themes of his work. In the essay "The Figure a Poem Makes" (1939), he defines poetry as "a momentary stay against confusion." Writing in forms based on iambic lines and colloquial speech patterns, he positioned himself against both nothingness and the free verse experiments of modernists such as Ezra Pound and T. S. Eliot.

Robert Lee Frost was born in 1874 to William Prescott Frost, Jr., of New Hampshire and Isabelle Moodie of Scotland. William, a journalist, was a heavy drinker, sometimes brutal and impetuous. Although a northerner, he had tried to enlist in the Confederate army while he was an adolescent, and named his son after General Robert E. Lee. When William died at age thirty-four, Isabelle followed his instructions to bury him in Lowell, Massachusetts. She stayed east and eventually opened a private school. Her son at first resisted school, and Isabelle indulged his lack of discipline. In high school he pursued classics and romantic poetry, interests his mother had sparked by reading him heroic tales. He studied hard and graduated as co-valedictorian and class poet. The other valedictorian was his future wife, Elinor White. Frost entered Dartmouth College but quickly dropped out. Despite his hounding White to quit college and marry him, she insisted on finishing her degree. Frost went so far as to expose himself to the dangers of Virginia's Dismal Swamp to win her over. They were finally married in 1895.

Frost attended Harvard University from 1897 to 1899, a period he later considered a turning point. There he was stimulated by the philosophy lectures of George Santayana and by the work of psychologist/philosopher William James and could measure himself against current cultural authorities. Ill health forced him to drop out after eighteen months; by this time the Frosts had two children. The oldest died in 1900, and Frost's mother, too, died that year. To help the couple, Frost's grandfather bought a farm for them to live on in Derry, New Hampshire. When his grandfather died in 1901, Frost received the farm and an annuity but had never acknowledged his grandfather's generosity. By 1907 the Frosts had five children. The annuity allowed Frost to write, though he had little other income. Guilty for placing his art above his family and still lacking an audience, Frost made the years in Derry among his most productive in both farming and writing.

As did other poets of the American literary renaissance in the 1910s, Frost left the unreceptive United States for England; he arrived in London with his family in September 1912. A month later he found a publisher for his first poetry collection, *A Boy's Will* (1913). In May Ezra Pound published a review of it in *Poetry*, the first important American notice of Frost's work. Frost selected and arranged the poems—generally love lyrics for Elinor—to trace a boy's development from self-centered idealism to maturity. Some of the early poems are awkwardly poetic, but others, such as "Mowing," show that even before reaching London's responsive literary scene Frost had mastered the crafting of colloquial language. His second book, *North of Boston,* was published in 1914. Pound enthusiastically reviewed it for *Poetry,* but some readers had trouble understanding Frost's technique and mistook his lines for free verse. A poem commonly considered his finest, "After Apple-Picking," is part of this collection, as are "The Wood-Pile" and "Home Burial." Frost insisted that the latter poem, written around 1912, was not autobiographical, but Elinor's reaction to their son's death had been similar to the mother's reaction in the poem.

The Frosts returned to the United States in 1915 after the outbreak of World War I. Henry Holt had already published an American edition of *North of Boston* and, within months, also issued *A Boy's Will.* Over the next four years Frost was named Phi Beta Kappa poet at Tufts and Harvard Universities, was elected to the National Institute of Arts and Letters and hired to teach at Amherst College, and received his first of forty-four honorary degrees. He began to create the farmer-moralist disguise for his increasingly attentive public. Holt rushed his third collection, *Mountain Interval,* into print in 1916. A dozen of the poems dated from the Derry years; Frost considered "An Old Man's Winter Night" the best of these.

Even at the height of his career Frost did not make a living from the sale of his books. In 1920 he began what he called "barding around"—serving as poet in residence at colleges and universities. He provided the first modern example of this role, which became common by the 1960s. For six years Frost moved back and forth between Amherst and the University of Michigan, then spent twelve years at Amherst, four at Harvard, and six at Dartmouth. In the 1920s he began a summer tradition of lecturing at the Bread Loaf School of English and Writers' Conference in Vermont. He returned to Amherst in 1949 with a life appointment.

New Hampshire (1923) won Frost the first of four Pulitzer Prizes. The collection includes "Dust of Snow," "Nothing Gold Can Stay," and "Stopping by Woods on a Snowy Evening" (which he rightly saw as his best chance to be remembered). That "Stopping by Woods" is repeatedly discussed stems from the ambiguity of the speaker's choice between safety and the unknown—a theme that has preoccupied many American writers—and from the hypnotic sounds that undermine the speaker's apparently choosing his human duties over the lure of death. *New Hampshire* also includes conservative social comments in verse. Somewhere between these comments and the lyrics is Frost's philosophical self-defense in "For Once, Then, Something."

Frost continued to publish poems of social and political comment, to the dismay of critics who looked to him for lyric perfection and universal themes. One such poem is "The Bear," from his 1928 collection *West-Running Brook.* The book poses disturbing uncertainties about man's prowess and importance. In "Spring Pools," the poet cannot identify the power that must destroy to create fleeting beauty, a power at the heart of nature's cycles. "Acquainted With the Night," for Frost uncharacteristically surreal, shows comfortless isolation in the city.

Frost won a second Pulitzer Prize for his 1930 edition of *Collected Poems,* but the

Robert Frost, age 86, reciting his poem "The Gift Outright" at the inauguration of President John F. Kennedy in January 1961.

decade that would most grimly dramatize his vision had begun. One daughter died of complications after childbirth in 1934; another suffered an emotional breakdown. Elinor died four years later; during her last days she refused to let her husband enter her room. In 1940 their second son committed suicide. Meanwhile, Frost lost the near-unanimous praise his poetry had received since his return from England. The Great Depression was underway, and war was brewing in Europe as Adolph Hitler and Benito Mussolini amassed power. Although *A Further Range* (1935) garnered Frost's third Pulitzer Prize, influential critics regarded some of its poems as insensitive to victims of the Depression and lacking in commitment against fascism.

A *Further Range* includes some of Frost's most enduring poems, "Desert Places," "Design," and "Provide, Provide." The generalized background to these poems, what Frost (in a 1935 letter to the *Amherst Student*) called "hugeness and confusion shading away . . . into black and utter chaos," may have been his way of translating modern upheaval into poetic material he could skillfully control. An early version of the sonnet "Design" was written in 1912 to defend the philosopher Henri Bergson against charges of atheism. The finished poem, first published in 1922, explores the ambiguities of whiteness—a theme Melville had made centrally American in *Moby-Dick* (1851). "Design" offers two equally terrifying possibilities: that events are ruled by divine plan, in which case man is powerless, or that they occur by mindless chance.

Frost's fourth Pulitzer Prize was awarded for *A Witness Tree*, published in 1942. He dedicated the volume to Kathleen Morrison, the wife of a Harvard professor. Following

Frost's tragedies of the 1930s, his grown children accusing him of having sacrificed them for art, he sank into a depression deep enough to hamper his tending to daily tasks. Morrison helped him reorganize his life. *A Witness Tree* includes "The Gift Outright," the poem he later recited at President Kennedy's inauguration, as well as "The Silken Tent," "Come In," and "Never Again Would Birds' Song Be the Same." "The Silken Tent" is a love sonnet that portrays a woman, drawing attention to the intricacies of metaphor rather than to the woman herself. In contrast, "The Subverted Flower," another poem in the collection, has seemed to some readers to be unexpectedly revealing of Frost's relationship with his wife. First drafted, Frost claimed, before 1913, the poem is a nightmarish sexual encounter between a boy and a girl. The boy coerces, as Frost did when Elinor was in college; the girl recoils. Biographers have speculated that Frost withheld the poem from publication until after Elinor's death to save her from embarrassment.

At age seventy Frost took up, in different forms, a religious question he had explored before, most notably in "After Apple Picking": can a man's best efforts ever satisfy God? *A Masque of Reason* (1945) and *A Masque of Mercy* (1947) are comic-serious dramatic narratives; the former concerns Job's suffering, and the latter, Jonah's rebellion. The question became a plea for acceptability in *A Sermon* (1947), which Frost delivered at a synagogue in Cincinnati. The way to salvation is a theme of his last great poem, "Directive," published in *Steeple Bush* (1947). Frost had been delighted to learn that Christ spoke in parables to conceal salvation from those who do not deserve it. The key word in "Directive," Frost explained, is source. For him the source was art (as reported in 1967 by Theodore Morrison in *Atlantic Monthly*): "You can't be saved unless you understand poetry—or you can't be saved unless you have some poetry in you."

Frost's last years were filled with public honors. For his *Complete Poems* (1949) he received a gold medal from the Limited Editions Club. The U.S. Senate sent him greetings on his seventy-seventh birthday. The state government of Vermont named a mountain after him. The State Department sent him to Brazil and London. He was named Consultant in Poetry to the Library of Congress, took part in Kennedy's presidential inauguration, and received a Congressional Medal of Honor. Just before Frost's death he received the Bollingen Prize. To his distress, he was never awarded a Nobel Prize.

At age eighty-eight, after recovering from a critical bout of pneumonia, his sight and hearing impaired, Frost made an official visit to the Soviet Union. He spent ninety minutes talking with Premier Nikita Khrushchev, but Frost's press report of this conversation confused and angered many Americans. He quoted Khrushchev as saying modern liberals were "too liberal to fight." Frost, obsessed with satirizing liberals, thought the remark was a "good crack." But in the cold-war atmosphere of the early 1960s, it was interpreted to mean that the premier believed Kennedy's Democratic administration would not resist Soviet expansion. Frost did not hear from the president again and died in 1963, four months after his trip.

A public that had worshipped the white-haired country sage was unprepared for the unpleasant biographical details that were published by Lawrance Thompson between 1966 and 1976. Yet, some of his poems reveal the compulsions, cynicism, and anguish that his public image perhaps masked. Frost's later work signals that he may have convinced even himself that his job was to make homespun pronouncements. He could not have been fully convinced: in his last poetry collection, *In the Clearing* (1962), Frost returned to the uncertainties of the dark woods.

Suggested Readings: *Dedication/The Gift Outright/The Inaugural Address*, 1961. *Selected Prose of Robert Frost*, 1966. *Robert Frost on Writing*, ed. E. Barry, 1972. *Robert Frost: Poetry and Prose*, ed. E. C. Lathem and L. Thompson, 1972. F. Lentricchia, *Robert Frost: Modern Poetics and the Landscapes of Self*, 1975. R. Poirier, *Robert Frost: The Work of Knowing*, 1977. L. W. Wagner, ed., *Robert Frost: The Critical Reception,* 1977. P. L. Gerber, *Robert Frost,* 1982. L. Thompson, *Robert Frost: A Biography,* abridged by E. C. Lathem, 1982. D. J. Hall, *Robert Frost: Contours of Belief,* 1984.

Text Used: *The Poetry of Robert Frost,* ed. E. C. Lathem, 1969.

THE PASTURE

I'm going out to clean the pasture spring;
I'll only stop to rake the leaves away
(And wait to watch the water clear, I may):
I shan't be gone long.—You come too.

I'm going out to fetch the little calf
That's standing by the mother. It's so young
It totters when she licks it with her tongue.
I shan't be gone long.—You come too.

1913

MOWING

There was never a sound beside the wood but one,
And that was my long scythe whispering to the ground.
What was it it whispered? I knew not well myself;
Perhaps it was something about the heat of the sun,
Something, perhaps, about the lack of sound—
And that was why it whispered and did not speak.
It was no dream of the gift of idle hours,
Or easy gold at the hand of fay[1] or elf:
Anything more than the truth would have seemed too weak
To the earnest love that laid the swale[2] in rows,   10
Not without feeble-pointed spikes of flowers
(Pale orchises), and scared a bright green snake.
The fact is the sweetest dream that labor knows.
My long scythe whispered and left the hay to make.

1913

MENDING WALL

Something there is that doesn't love a wall,
That sends the frozen-ground-swell under it,
And spills the upper boulders in the sun;
And makes gaps even two can pass abreast.

[1] A fairy.   [2] A low-lying marshland.

The work of hunters is another thing:
I have come after them and made repair
Where they have left not one stone on a stone,
But they would have the rabbit out of hiding,
To please the yelping dogs. The gaps I mean,
No one has seen them made or heard them made,   10
But at spring mending-time we find them there.
I let my neighbor know beyond the hill;
And on a day we meet to walk the line
And set the wall between us once again.
We keep the wall between us as we go.
To each the boulders that have fallen to each.
And some are loaves and some so nearly balls
We have to use a spell to make them balance:
"Stay where you are until our backs are turned!"
We wear our fingers rough with handling them.   20
Oh, just another kind of outdoor game,
One on a side. It comes to little more;
There where it is we do not need the wall:
He is all pine and I am apple orchard.
My apple trees will never get across
And eat the cones under his pines, I tell him.
He only says, "Good fences make good neighbors."
Spring is the mischief in me, and I wonder
If I could put a notion in his head:
"*Why* do they make good neighbors? Isn't it   30
Where there are cows? But here there are no cows.
Before I built a wall I'd ask to know
What I was walling in or walling out,
And to whom I was like to give offense.
Something there is that doesn't love a wall,
That wants it down." I could say "Elves" to him,
But it's not elves exactly, and I'd rather
He said it for himself. I see him there
Bringing a stone grasped firmly by the top
In each hand, like an old-stone savage armed.   40
He moves in darkness as it seems to me,
Not of woods only and the shade of trees
He will not go behind his father's saying,
And he likes having thought of it so well
He says again, "Good fences make good neighbors."

1914

HOME BURIAL

He saw her from the bottom of the stairs
Before she saw him. She was starting down,
Looking back over her shoulder at some fear.
She took a doubtful step and then undid it

To raise herself and look again. He spoke
Advancing toward her: "What is it you see
From up there always?—for I want to know."
She turned and sank upon her skirts at that,
And her face changed from terrified to dull.
He said to gain time: "What is it you see?"   10
Mounting until she cowered under him.
"I will find out now—you must tell me, dear."
She, in her place, refused him any help,
With the least stiffening of her neck and silence.
She let him look, sure that he wouldn't see,
Blind creature; and awhile he didn't see.
But at last he murmured, "Oh," and again, "Oh."

"What is it—what?" she said.

                              "Just that I see."

"You don't," she challenged. "Tell me what it is."

"The wonder is I didn't see at once.   20
I never noticed it from here before.
I must be wonted[1] to it—that's the reason.
The little graveyard where my people are!
So small the window frames the whole of it.
Not so much larger than a bedroom, is it?
There are three stones of slate and one of marble,
Broad-shouldered little slabs there in the sunlight
On the sidehill. We haven't to mind *those*.
But I understand: it is not the stones,
But the child's mound—"
                        "Don't, don't, don't,
don't," she cried.   30

She withdrew, shrinking from beneath his arm
That rested on the banister, and slid downstairs;
And turned on him with such a daunting look,
He said twice over before he knew himself:
"Can't a man speak of his own child he's lost?"

"Not you!—Oh, where's my hat? Oh, I don't need it!
I must get out of here. I must get air.—
I don't know rightly whether any man can."

"Amy! Don't go to someone else this time.
Listen to me. I won't come down the stairs."   40
He sat and fixed his chin between his fists.
"There's something I should like to ask you, dear."

[1] Accustomed.

"You don't know how to ask it."

                                "Help me, then."

Her fingers moved the latch for all reply.

"My words are nearly always an offense.
I don't know how to speak of anything
So as to please you. But I might be taught,
I should suppose. I can't say I see how.
A man must partly give up being a man
With womenfolk. We could have some arrangement   50
By which I'd bind myself to keep hands off
Anything special you're a-mind to name.
Though I don't like such things 'twixt those that love.
Two that don't love can't live together without them
But two that do can't live together with them."
She moved the latch a little. "Don't—don't go.
Don't carry it to someone else this time.
Tell me about it if it's something human.
Let me into your grief. I'm not so much
Unlike other folks as your standing there   60
Apart would make me out. Give me my chance.
I do think, though, you overdo it a little.
What was it brought you up to think it the thing
To take your mother-loss of a first child
So inconsolably—in the face of love.
You'd think his memory might be satisfied—"

"There you go sneering now!"
                                "I'm not, I'm not!
You make me angry. I'll come down to you.
God, what a woman! And it's come to this,
A man can't speak of his own child that's dead."   70

"You can't because you don't know how to speak.
If you had any feelings, you that dug
With your own hand—how could you?—his little grave;
I saw you from that very window there,
Making the gravel leap and leap in air,
Leap up, like that, like that, and land so lightly
And roll back down the mound beside the hole.
I thought, Who is that man? I didn't know you.
And I crept down the stairs and up the stairs
To look again, and still your spade kept lifting.   80
Then you came in. I heard your rumbling voice
Out in the kitchen, and I don't know why,
But I went near to see with my own eyes.
You could sit there with the stains on your shoes
Of the fresh earth from your own baby's grave

And talk about your everyday concerns.
You had stood the spade up against the wall
Outside there in the entry, for I saw it."

"I shall laugh the worst laugh I ever laughed.
I'm cursed. God, if I don't believe I'm cursed."   90

"I can repeat the very words you were saying:
'Three foggy mornings and one rainy day
Will rot the best birch fence a man can build.'
Think of it, talk like that at such a time!
What had how long it takes a birch to rot
To do with what was in the darkened parlor?
You *couldn't* care! The nearest friends can go
With anyone to death, comes so far short
They might as well not try to go at all.
No, from the time when one is sick to death,   100
One is alone, and he dies more alone.
Friends make pretense of following to the grave,
But before one is in it, their minds are turned
And making the best of their way back to life
And living people, and things they understand.
But the world's evil. I won't have grief so
If I can change it. Oh, I won't, I won't!"

"There, you have said it all and you feel better.
You won't go now. You're crying. Close the door.
The heart's gone out of it: why keep it up?   110
Amy! There's someone coming down the road!"

"*You*—oh, you think the talk is all. I must go—
Somewhere out of this house. How can I make you—"

"If—you—do!" She was opening the door wider.
"Where do you mean to go? First tell me that.
I'll follow and bring you back by force. I *will!*—"

                                        1912?, 1914

AFTER APPLE-PICKING

My long two-pointed ladder's sticking through a tree
Toward heaven still,
And there's a barrel that I didn't fill
Beside it, and there may be two or three
Apples I didn't pick upon some bough.
But I am done with apple-picking now.
Essence of winter sleep is on the night,

The scent of apples: I am drowsing off.
I cannot rub the strangeness from my sight
I got from looking through a pane of glass   10
I skimmed this morning from the drinking trough
And held against the world of hoary grass.
It melted, and I let it fall and break.
But I was well
Upon my way to sleep before it fell,
And I could tell
What form my dreaming was about to take.
Magnified apples appear and disappear,
Stem end and blossom end,
And every fleck of russet showing clear.   20
My instep arch not only keeps the ache,
It keeps the pressure of a ladder-round.
I feel the ladder sway as the boughs bend.
And I keep hearing from the cellar bin
The rumbling sound
Of load on load of apples coming in.
For I have had too much
Of apple-picking: I am overtired
Of the great harvest I myself desired.
There were ten thousand thousand fruit to touch,   30
Cherish in hand, lift down, and not let fall.
For all
That struck the earth,
No matter if not bruised or spiked with stubble,
Went surely to the cider-apple heap
As of no worth.
One can see what will trouble
This sleep of mine, whatever sleep it is.
Were he not gone,
The woodchuck could say whether it's like his   40
Long sleep, as I describe its coming on,
Or just some human sleep.

                                        1914

THE WOOD-PILE

Out walking in the frozen swamp one gray day,
I paused and said, "I will turn back from here.
No, I will go on farther—and we shall see."
The hard snow held me, save where now and then
One foot went through. The view was all in lines
Straight up and down of tall slim trees
Too much alike to mark or name a place by
So as to say for certain I was here

Or somewhere else: I was just far from home.
A small bird flew before me. He was careful   10
To put a tree between us when he lighted,
And say no word to tell me who he was
Who was so foolish as to think what *he* thought.
He thought that I was after him for a feather—
The white one in his tail; like one who takes
Everything said as personal to himself.
One flight out sideways would have undeceived him.
And then there was a pile of wood for which
I forgot him and let his little fear
Carry him off the way I might have gone,   20
Without so much as wishing him good-night.
He went behind it to make his last stand.
It was a cord of maple, cut and split
And piled—and measured, four by four by eight.
And not another like it could I see.
No runner tracks in this year's snow looped near it.
And it was older sure than this year's cutting,
Or even last year's or the year's before.
The wood was gray and the bark warping off it
And the pile somewhat sunken. Clematis[1]   30
Had wound strings round and round it like a bundle.
What held it, though, on one side was a tree
Still growing, and on one a stake and prop,
These latter about to fall. I thought that only
Someone who lived in turning to fresh tasks
Could so forget his handiwork on which
He spent himself, the labor of his ax,
And leave it there far from a useful fireplace
To warm the frozen swamp as best it could
With the slow smokeless burning of decay.   40

1914

THE ROAD NOT TAKEN

Two roads diverged in a yellow wood,
And sorry I could not travel both
And be one traveler, long I stood
And looked down one as far as I could
To where it bent in the undergrowth;

Then took the other, as just as fair,
And having perhaps the better claim,
Because it was grassy and wanted wear;

[1] A flowering vine of the buttercup family.

Though as for that, the passing there
Had worn them really about the same,   10

And both that morning equally lay
In leaves no step had trodden black.
Oh, I kept the first for another day!
Yet knowing how way leads on to way,
I doubted if I should ever come back.

I shall be telling this with a sigh
Somewhere ages and ages hence:
Two roads diverged in a wood, and I—
I took the one less traveled by,
And that has made all the difference.   20

1914–1915, 1916

AN OLD MAN'S WINTER NIGHT

All out-of-doors looked darkly in at him
Through the thin frost, almost in separate stars,
That gathers on the pane in empty rooms.
What kept his eyes from giving back the gaze
Was the lamp tilted near them in his hand.
What kept him from remembering what it was
That brought him to that creaking room was age.
He stood with barrels round him—at a loss.
And having scared the cellar under him
In clomping here, he scared it once again   10
In clomping off—and scared the outer night,
Which has its sounds, familiar, like the roar
Of trees and crack of branches, common things,
But nothing so like beating on a box.
A light he was to no one but himself
Where now he sat, concerned with he knew what,
A quiet light, and then not even that.
He consigned to the moon—such as she was,
So late-arising—to the broken moon,
As better than the sun in any case   20
For such a charge, his snow upon the roof,
His icicles along the wall to keep;
And slept. The log that shifted with a jolt
Once in the stove, disturbed him and he shifted,
And eased his heavy breathing, but still slept.
One aged man—one man—can't keep a house,
A farm, a countryside, or if he can,
It's thus he does it of a winter night.

1906, 1916

THE OVEN BIRD*

There is a singer everyone has heard,
Loud, a mid-summer and a mid-wood bird,
Who makes the solid tree trunks sound again.
He says that leaves are old and that for flowers
Mid-summer is to spring as one to ten.
He says the early petal-fall is past,
When pear and cherry bloom went down in showers
On sunny days a moment overcast;
And comes that other fall we name the fall.
He says the highway dust is over all.   10
The bird would cease and be as other birds
But that he knows in singing not to sing.
The question that he frames in all but words
Is what to make of a diminished thing.

1916

BIRCHES

When I see birches bend to left and right
Across the lines of straighter darker trees,
I like to think some boy's been swinging them.
But swinging doesn't bend them down to stay
As ice storms do. Often you must have seen them
Loaded with ice a sunny winter morning
After a rain. They click upon themselves
As the breeze rises, and turn many-colored
As the stir cracks and crazes their enamel.
Soon the sun's warmth makes them shed crystal shells   10
Shattering and avalanching on the snow crust—
Such heaps of broken glass to sweep away
You'd think the inner dome of heaven had fallen.
They are dragged to the withered bracken by the load,
And they seem not to break; though once they are bowed
So low for long, they never right themselves:
You may see their trunks arching in the woods
Years afterwards, trailing their leaves on the ground
Like girls on hands and knees that throw their hair
Before them over their heads to dry in the sun.   20
But I was going to say when Truth broke in
With all her matter of fact about the ice storm,
I should prefer to have some boy bend them
As he went out and in to fetch the cows—
Some boy too far from town to learn baseball,

---

* The American warbler, which builds a dome-shaped nest on the ground.

Whose only play was what he found himself,
Summer or winter, and could play alone.
One by one he subdued his father's trees
By riding them down over and over again
Until he took the stiffness out of them,   30
And not one but hung limp, not one was left
For him to conquer. He learned all there was
To learn about not launching out too soon
And so not carrying the tree away
Clear to the ground. He always kept his poise
To the top branches, climbing carefully
With the same pains you use to fill a cup
Up to the brim, and even above the brim.
Then he flung outward, feet first, with a swish,
Kicking his way down through the air to the ground.   40
So was I once myself a swinger of birches.
And so I dream of going back to be.
It's when I'm weary of considerations,
And life is too much like a pathless wood
Where your face burns and tickles with the cobwebs
Broken across it, and one eye is weeping
From a twig's having lashed across it open.
I'd like to get away from earth awhile
And then come back to it and begin over.
May no fate willfully misunderstand me   50
And half grant what I wish and snatch me away
Not to return. Earth's the right place for love:
I don't know where it's likely to go better.
I'd like to go by climbing a birch tree,
And climb black branches up a snow-white trunk
Toward heaven, till the tree could bear no more,
But dipped its top and set me down again.
That would be good both going and coming back.
One could do worse than be a swinger of birches.

                                                   1914?, 1916

PUTTING IN THE SEED

You come to fetch me from my work tonight
When supper's on the table, and we'll see
If I can leave off burying the white
Soft petals fallen from the apple tree
(Soft petals, yes, but not so barren quite,
Mingled with these, smooth bean and wrinkled pea),
And go along with you ere you lose sight
Of what you came for and become like me,
Slave to a springtime passion for the earth.

How Love burns through the Putting in the Seed   10
On through the watching for that early birth
When, just as the soil tarnishes with weed,
The sturdy seedling with arched body comes
Shouldering its way and shedding the earth crumbs.

1906?, 1916

LOCKED OUT

As Told to a Child

When we locked up the house at night,
We always locked the flowers outside
And cut them off from window light.
The time I dreamed the door was tried
And brushed with buttons upon sleeves,
The flowers were out there with the thieves.
Yet nobody molested them!
We did find one nasturtium
Upon the steps with bitten stem.
I may have been to blame for that: 10
I always thought it must have been
Some flower I played with as I sat
At dusk to watch the moon down early.

1916

"OUT, OUT—"*

The buzz saw snarled and rattled in the yard
And made dust and dropped stove-length sticks of wood,
Sweet-scented stuff when the breeze drew across it.
And from there those that lifted eyes could count
Five mountain ranges one behind the other
Under the sunset far into Vermont.
And the saw snarled and rattled, snarled and rattled,
As it ran light, or had to bear a load.
And nothing happened: day was all but done.
Call it a day, I wish they might have said   10
To please the boy by giving him the half hour
That a boy counts so much when saved from work.
His sister stood beside them in her apron
To tell them "Supper." At the word, the saw,
As if to prove saws knew what supper meant,
Leaped out at the boy's hand, or seemed to leap—

* "Out, out brief candle!/Life's but a walking shadow," from Shakespeare's *Macbeth* (V.v.23–24).

He must have given the hand. However it was,
Neither refused the meeting. But the hand!
The boy's first outcry was a rueful laugh,
As he swung toward them holding up the hand,   20
Half in appeal, but half as if to keep
The life from spilling. Then the boy saw all—
Since he was old enough to know, big boy
Doing a man's work, though a child at heart—
He saw all spoiled. "Don't let him cut my hand off—
The doctor, when he comes. Don't let him, sister!"
So. But the hand was gone already.
The doctor put him in the dark of ether.
He lay and puffed his lips out with his breath.
And then—the watcher at his pulse took fright.   30
No one believed. They listened at his heart.
Little—less—nothing!—and that ended it.
No more to build on there. And they, since they
Were not the one dead, turned to their affairs.

1916

DUST OF SNOW

The way a crow
Shook down on me
The dust of snow
From a hemlock tree

Has given my heart
A change of mood
And saved some part
Of a day I had rued.

1923

NOTHING GOLD CAN STAY

Nature's first green[1] is gold,
Her hardest hue to hold.
Her early leaf's a flower;
But only so an hour.
Then leaf subsides to leaf.
So Eden sank to grief,
So dawn goes down to day.
Nothing gold can stay.

1923

---

[1] Growth.

FOR ONCE, THEN, SOMETHING

Others taunt me with having knelt at well-curbs
Always wrong to the light, so never seeing
Deeper down in the well than where the water
Gives me back in a shining surface picture
Me myself in the summer heaven, godlike,
Looking out of a wreath of fern and cloud puffs.
Once, when trying with chin against a well-curb,
I discerned, as I thought, beyond the picture,
Through the picture, a something white, uncertain,
Something more of the depths—and then I lost it.   10
Water came to rebuke the too clear water.
One drop fell from a fern, and lo, a ripple
Shook whatever it was lay there at bottom,
Blurred it, blotted it out. What was that whiteness?
Truth? A pebble of quartz? For once, then, something.

1923

STOPPING BY WOODS ON A SNOWY EVENING

Whose woods these are I think I know.
His house is in the village, though;
He will not see me stopping here
To watch his woods fill up with snow.

My little horse must think it queer
To stop without a farmhouse near
Between the woods and frozen lake
The darkest evening of the year.

He gives his harness bells a shake
To ask if there is some mistake.   10
The only other sound's the sweep
Of easy wind and downy flake.

The woods are lovely, dark, and deep,
But I have promises to keep,
And miles to go before I sleep,
And miles to go before I sleep.

1923

THE NEED OF BEING VERSED IN COUNTRY THINGS

The house had gone to bring again
To the midnight sky a sunset glow.

Now the chimney was all of the house that stood,
Like a pistil after the petals go.

The barn opposed across the way,
That would have joined the house in flame
Had it been the will of the wind, was left
To bear forsaken the place's name.

No more it opened with all one end
For teams that came by the stony road   10
To drum on the floor with scurrying hoofs
And brush the mow with the summer load.

The birds that came to it through the air
At broken windows flew out and in,
Their murmur more like the sigh we sigh
From too much dwelling on what has been.

Yet for them the lilac renewed its leaf,
And the aged elm, though touched with fire;
And the dry pump flung up an awkward arm;
And the fence post carried a strand of wire.   20

For them there was really nothing sad.
But though they rejoiced in the nest they kept,
One had to be versed in country things
Not to believe the phoebes[1] wept.

1923

SPRING POOLS

These pools that, though in forests, still reflect
The total sky almost without defect,
And like the flowers beside them, chill and shiver,
Will like the flowers beside them soon be gone,
And yet not out by any brook or river,
But up by roots to bring dark foliage on.

The trees that have it in their pent-up buds
To darken nature and be summer woods—
Let them think twice before they use their powers
To blot out and drink up and sweep away   10
These flowery waters and these watery flowers
From snow that melted only yesterday.

1928

[1] American flycatchers, birds named after the Greek moon goddess.

FIREFLIES IN THE GARDEN

Here come real stars to fill the upper skies,
And here on earth come emulating flies
That, though they never equal stars in size
(And they were never really stars at heart),
Achieve at times a very starlike start.
Only, of course, they can't sustain the part.

1928

ONCE BY THE PACIFIC

The shattered water made a misty din.
Great waves looked over others coming in,
And thought of doing something to the shore
That water never did to land before.
The clouds were low and hairy in the skies,
Like locks blown forward in the gleam of eyes.
You could not tell, and yet it looked as if
The shore was lucky in being backed by cliff,
The cliff in being backed by continent;
It looked as if a night of dark intent   10
Was coming, and not only a night, an age.
Someone had better be prepared for rage.
There would be more than ocean-water broken
Before God's last *Put out the Light* was spoken.[1]

1928

ACQUAINTED WITH THE NIGHT

I have been one acquainted with the night.
I have walked out in rain—and back in rain.
I have outwalked the furthest city light.

I have looked down the saddest city lane.
I have passed by the watchman on his beat
And dropped my eyes, unwilling to explain.

I have stood still and stopped the sound of feet
When far away an interrupted cry
Came over houses from another street,

---

[1] In Genesis 1:3 God created the world, saying " . . . Let there be light."

But not to call me back or say good-by;   10
And further still at an unearthly height
One luminary clock against the sky

Proclaimed the time was neither wrong nor right.
I have been one acquainted with the night.

1928

WHAT FIFTY SAID

When I was young my teachers were the old.
I gave up fire for form till I was cold.
I suffered like a metal being cast.
I went to school to age to learn the past.

Now I am old my teachers are the young.
What can't be molded must be cracked and sprung.
I strain at lessons fit to start a suture.
I go to school to youth to learn the future.

1928

THE BEAR

The bear puts both arms around the tree above her
And draws it down as if it were a lover
And its chokecherries lips to kiss good-by,
Then lets it snap back upright in the sky.
Her next step rocks a boulder on the wall
(She's making her cross-country in the fall).
Her great weight creaks the barbed wire in its staples
As she flings over and off down through the maples,
Leaving on one wire tooth a lock of hair.
Such is the uncaged progress of the bear.   10
The world has room to make a bear feel free;
The universe seems cramped to you and me.
Man acts more like the poor bear in a cage,
That all day fights a nervous inward rage,
His mood rejecting all his mind suggests.
He paces back and forth and never rests
The toenail click and shuffle of his feet,
The telescope at one end of his beat,
And at the other end the microscope,
Two instruments of nearly equal hope,   20
And in conjunction giving quite a spread.
Or if he rests from scientific tread,

'Tis only to sit back and sway his head
Through ninety-odd degrees of arc, it seems,
Between two metaphysical extremes.
He sits back on his fundamental butt
With lifted snout and eyes (if any) shut
(He almost looks religious but he's not),
And back and forth he sways from cheek to cheek,
At one extreme agreeing with one Greek,   30
At the other agreeing with another Greek,
Which may be thought, but only so to speak.
A baggy figure, equally pathetic
When sedentary and when peripatetic.

1928

DESERT PLACES

Snow falling and night falling fast, oh, fast
In a field I looked into going past,
And the ground almost covered smooth in snow,
But a few weeds and stubble showing last.

The woods around it have it—it is theirs.
All animals are smothered in their lairs.
I am too absent-spirited to count;
The loneliness includes me unawares.

And lonely as it is, that loneliness
Will be more lonely ere it will be less—   10
A blanker whiteness of benighted[1] snow
With no expression, nothing to express.

They cannot scare me with their empty spaces
Between stars—on stars where no human race is.
I have it in me so much nearer home
To scare myself with my own desert places.

1936

DESIGN

I found a dimpled spider, fat and white,
On a white heal-all,[1] holding up a moth
Like a white piece of rigid satin cloth—

---

[1] Unenlightened, overtaken by darkness.
[1] A medicinal plant whose flowers are generally blue.

Assorted characters of death and blight
Mixed ready to begin the morning right,
Like the ingredients of a witches' broth—
A snow-drop spider, a flower like a froth,
And dead wings carried like a paper kite.

What had that flower to do with being white,
The wayside blue and innocent heal-all?   10
What brought the kindred spider to that height,
Then steered the white moth thither in the night?
What but design of darkness to appall?—
If design govern in a thing so small.[2]

1922, 1936

PROVIDE, PROVIDE

The witch that came (the withered hag)
To wash the steps with pail and rag
Was once the beauty Abishag,[1]

The picture pride of Hollywood.
Too many fall from great and good
For you to doubt the likelihood.

Die early and avoid the fate.
Or if predestined to die late,
Make up your mind to die in state.

Make the whole stock exchange your own!   10
If need be occupy a throne,
Where nobody can call *you* crone.

Some have relied on what they knew,
Others on being simply true.
What worked for them might work for you.

No memory of having starred
Atones for later disregard
Or keeps the end from being hard.

Better to go down dignified
With boughten friendship at your side   20
Than none at all. Provide, provide!

1934, 1936

[2] Design, or order, in nature has been cited as proof of God's existence.
[1] In I Kings 1:2–4, a beautiful virgin who cared for King David in his old age.

THE SILKEN TENT

She is as in a field a silken tent
At midday when a sunny summer breeze
Has dried the dew and all its ropes relent,
So that in guys[1] it gently sways at ease,
And its supporting central cedar pole,
That is its pinnacle to heavenward
And signifies the sureness of the soul,
Seems to owe naught to any single cord,
But strictly held by none, is loosely bound
By countless silken ties of love and thought   10
To everything on earth the compass round,
And only by one's going slightly taut
In the capriciousness of summer air
Is of the slightest bondage made aware.

1939, 1942

COME IN

As I came to the edge of the woods,
Thrush music—hark!
Now if it was dusk outside,
Inside it was dark.

Too dark in the woods for a bird
By sleight of wing
To better its perch for the night,
Though it still could sing.

The last of the light of the sun
That had died in the west   10
Still lived for one song more
In a thrush's breast.

Far in the pillared dark
Thrush music went—
Almost like a call to come in
To the dark and lament.

But no, I was out for stars:
I would not come in.
I meant not even if asked,
And I hadn't been.   20

1941, 1942

[1] Ropes or chains for support.

NEVER AGAIN WOULD BIRDS' SONG BE THE SAME

He would declare and could himself believe
That the birds there in all the garden round
From having heard the daylong voice of Eve
Had added to their own an oversound,
Her tone of meaning but without the words.
Admittedly an eloquence so soft
Could only have had an influence on birds
When call or laughter carried it aloft.
Be that as may be, she was in their song.
Moreover her voice upon their voices crossed   10
Had now persisted in the woods so long
That probably it never would be lost.
Never again would birds' song be the same.
And to do that to birds was why she came.

1942

THE GIFT OUTRIGHT

The land was ours before we were the land's.
She was our land more than a hundred years
Before we were her people. She was ours
In Massachusetts, in Virginia,
But we were England's, still colonials,
Possessing what we still were unpossessed by,
Possessed by what we now no more possessed.
Something we were withholding made us weak
Until we found out that it was ourselves
We were withholding from our land of living,   10
And forthwith found salvation in surrender.
Such as we were we gave ourselves outright
(The deed of gift was many deeds of war)
To the land vaguely realizing westward,
But still unstoried, artless, unenhanced,
Such as she was, such as she would become.

1942

DIRECTIVE

Back out of all this now too much for us,
Back in a time made simple by the loss
Of detail, burned, dissolved, and broken off
Like graveyard marble sculpture in the weather,
There is a house that is no more a house

Upon a farm that is no more a farm
And in a town that is no more a town.
The road there, if you'll let a guide direct you
Who only has at heart your getting lost,
May seem as if it should have been a quarry—   10
Great monolithic knees the former town
Long since gave up pretense of keeping covered.
And there's a story in a book about it:
Besides the wear of iron wagon wheels
The ledges show lines ruled southeast-northwest,
The chisel work of an enormous Glacier
That braced his feet against the Arctic Pole.
You must not mind a certain coolness from him
Still said to haunt this side of Panther Mountain.
Nor need you mind the serial ordeal   20
Of being watched from forty cellar holes
As if by eye pairs out of forty firkins.[1]
As for the woods' excitement over you
That sends light rustle rushes to their leaves,
Charge that to upstart inexperience.
Where were they all not twenty years ago?
They think too much of having shaded out
A few old pecker-fretted[2] apple trees.
Make yourself up a cheering song of how
Someone's road home from work this once was,   30
Who may be just ahead of you on foot
Or creaking with a buggy load of grain.
The height of the adventure is the height
Of country where two village cultures faded
Into each other. Both of them are lost.
And if you're lost enough to find yourself
By now, pull in your ladder road behind you
And put a sign up CLOSED to all but me.
Then make yourself at home. The only field
Now left's no bigger than a harness gall.[3]   40
First there's the children's house of make-believe,
Some shattered dishes underneath a pine,
The playthings in the playhouse of the children.
Weep for what little things could make them glad.
Then for the house that is no more a house,
But only a belilaced cellar hole,
Now slowly closing like a dent in dough.
This was no playhouse but a house in earnest.
Your destination and your destiny's
A brook that was the water of the house,   50
Cold as a spring as yet so near its source,
Too lofty and original to rage.
(We know the valley streams that when aroused
Will leave their tatters hung on barb and thorn.)

[1] Small wooden barrels.   [2] Marked by woodpecker holes.
[3] A sore on a horse's skin, from the rubbing of the harness.

I have kept hidden in the instep arch
Of an old cedar at the waterside
A broken drinking goblet like the Grail[4]
Under a spell so the wrong ones can't find it,
So can't get saved, as Saint Mark says they mustn't.[5]
(I stole the goblet from the children's playhouse.)   60
Here are your waters and your watering place.
Drink and be whole again beyond confusion.

1946, 1947

Carl Sandburg
(1878–1967)

Carl Sandburg's early life was typical of many first-generation Americans during the unprecedented growth in the United States at the turn of the century. The son of Swedish immigrants, born in 1878 in Galesburg, Illinois and raised there, Sandburg left school after the eighth grade and held a series of odd jobs. After serving in an infantry regiment of Illinois volunteers in the Spanish-American War when he was twenty, he traveled across America. Selling stereoscopic photographs and sharing boxcars with hobos, he felt himself to be "a pal of the world." Not surprisingly, Sandburg took Walt Whitman as his poetic model and set out to rescue poetry from the enervating effects of conservative, "genteel tradition" writers. Tuning his voice to Whitman's "barbaric yawp," Sandburg wrote that his "aim was to sing, blab, chortle, yodel, like people, and [I mean] people in the sense of human beings subtracted from formal doctrines" (in *The Letters of Carl Sandburg* [1968]). Sandburg's poetry contains those multitudes swept up in the economic chaos and expansion that formed the lives of the American working class. A member of the Social Democratic party, Sandburg campaigned with the labor leader Eugene Debs in Debs's 1908 presidential campaign, wrote poems that attacked the evangelist Billy Sunday and supported the anarchists Nicola Sacco and Bartolomeo Vanzetti after their 1920 arrest (and subsequent execution), and sympathized with the sometimes violent theories of the Industrial Workers of the World. But Sandburg's poetry goes beyond the political and sociological theories of the day to capture the raw, tough atmosphere of the American worker in "public speech [that sings] simple songs for simple people," as he explains in the introduction to his *Complete Poems* (1950).

Sandburg first wrote as a war correspondent for the Galesburg *Evening Mail* while he was a soldier in Puerto Rico. He was later denied an appointment at West Point for failing the entrance examinations in grammar and mathematics. Instead, he entered Lombard College in Galesburg, where he was editor in chief of the *Lombard Review*. Leaving Lombard in 1902 without a degree, Sandburg worked as a roving reporter and advertising writer. At the anniversary of the 1858 Abraham Lincoln/Stephen Douglas senatorial debate in Galesburg, Sandburg met Lincoln's son Robert Todd Lincoln. This event sparked an interest

---

[4] The cup Jesus used at the Last Supper and the object of medieval quests.
[5] "He that believeth and is baptized shall be saved; but he that believeth not shall be damned," from Mark 16:16.

that resulted in Sandburg's Pulitzer Prize-winning four-volume biography, *Abraham Lincoln: The War Years* (1939). Sandburg also wrote editorials for the Milwaukee *Leader*, a column for the Chicago *Daily News*, and after marrying Lillian Steichen in 1908 served as secretary to the Socialist mayor of Milwaukee from 1910 to 1912.

With the 1914 publication of such poems as "Chicago" and "Grass" in *Poetry* magazine (later collected in *Chicago Poems* [1916]), Sandburg embarked on a career in poetry and he became one of the most widely read poets of the 1920s and 1930s. While lecturing on Whitman and George Bernard Shaw and giving ballad concerts, Sandburg toured the United States. An avid collector of American folklore and folk songs, he produced *The People, Yes* (1936), a book-length collection of stories, verse, commentary, and songs that celebrates his radical Populist view of America. In 1951 his *Collected Poems* earned him a second Pulitzer Prize; *Cornhuskers* (1918), which contains "Cool Tombs," had garnered a special Pulitzer Prize, also. Sandburg was decorated by the king of Sweden in 1938, honored on his seventy-fifth birthday (declared "Carl Sandburg Day") by the governor of Illinois, and given the Presidential Medal of Freedom in 1964. He died in 1967 and is well remembered for his commitment to the "ordinary" American.

Suggested Readings: *Abraham Lincoln: The Prairie Years*, 2 vols., 1926. *Mary Lincoln: Wife and Widow*, with P. M. Angle, 1932. *Abraham Lincoln: The War Years*, 4 vols., 1939. *The Letters of Carl Sandburg*, ed. H. Mitgang, 1968. R. Crowder, *Carl Sandburg*, 1964. N. Callahan, *Carl Sandburg: Lincoln of Our Literature*, 1969. G. W. Allen, *Carl Sandburg*, 1972. N. Callahan, *Carl Sandburg: His Life and Works*, 1987.

Text Used: *The Complete Poems of Carl Sandburg*, 1970.

CHICAGO

Hog Butcher for the World,
Tool Maker, Stacker of Wheat,
Player with Railroads and the Nation's Freight Handler;
Stormy, husky, brawling,
City of the Big Shoulders:

They tell me you are wicked and I believe them, for I have seen your
painted women under the gas lamps luring the farm boys.
And they tell me you are crooked and I answer: Yes, it is true I have seen
the gunman kill and go free to kill again.
And they tell me you are brutal and my reply is: On the faces of women
and children I have seen the marks of wanton hunger.
And having answered so I turn once more to those who sneer at this my
city, and I give them back the sneer and say to them:
Come and show me another city with lifted head singing so proud to be
alive and coarse and strong and cunning.   10
Flinging magnetic curses amid the toil of piling job on job, here is a tall
bold slugger set vivid against the little soft cities;
Fierce as a dog with tongue lapping for action, cunning as a savage pitted
against the wilderness,
    Bareheaded,
    Shoveling,
    Wrecking,

Planning,
   Building, breaking, rebuilding,
Under the smoke, dust all over his mouth, laughing with white teeth,
Under the terrible burden of destiny laughing as a young man laughs,
Laughing even as an ignorant fighter laughs who has never lost a battle,   20
Bragging and laughing that under his wrist is the pulse, and under his ribs
   the heart of the people,
      Laughing!
Laughing the stormy, husky, brawling laughter of Youth, half-naked,
   sweating, proud to be Hog Butcher, Tool Maker, Stacker of Wheat,
   Player with Railroads and Freight Handler to the Nation.

1914

COOL TOMBS

When Abraham Lincoln was shoveled into the tombs, he forgot the
   copperheads[1] and the assassin[2] . . . in the dust, in the cool tombs.

And Ulysses Grant lost all thought of con men and Wall Street, cash and
   collateral turned ashes[3] . . . in the dust, in the cool tombs.

Pocahontas'[4] body, lovely as a poplar, sweet as a red haw[5] in November or
   a pawpaw[6] in May, did she wonder? does she remember? . . . in the
   dust, in the cool tombs?

Take any streetful of people buying clothes and groceries, cheering a hero
   or throwing confetti and blowing tin horns . . . tell me if the lovers
   are losers . . . tell me if any get more than the lovers . . . in the
   dust . . . in the cool tombs.

1918

RIVER ROADS

Let the crows go by hawking their caw and caw.
They have been swimming in midnights of coal mines somewhere.
Let 'em hawk their caw and caw.

Let the woodpecker drum and drum on a hickory stump.
He has been swimming in red and blue pools somewhere hundreds of
   years

---

[1] Southern sympathizers in the North during the Civil War.   [2] John Wilkes Booth (1838–1865).
[3] Grant, whose second administration was notoriously corrupt, went bankrupt after leaving office.
[4] Pocahontas (1595?–1617), the daughter of Powhatan, saved Captain John Smith's life.
[5] A hawthorn berry.   [6] The fruit of the papaya tree.

And the blue has gone to his wings and the red has gone to his head.
Let his red head drum and drum.

Let the dark pools hold the birds in a looking-glass.
And if the pool wishes, let it shiver to the blur of many wings, old
    swimmers from old places.

Let the redwing streak a line of vermilion on the green wood lines.   10
And the mist along the river fix its purple in lines of a woman's shawl
    on lazy shoulders.

          1918

GRASS

Pile the bodies high at Austerlitz and Waterloo.[1]
Shovel them under and let me work—
    I am the grass; I cover all.

And pile them high at Gettysburg[2]
And pile them high at Ypres and Verdun.[3]
Shovel them under and let me work.
Two years, ten years, and passengers ask the conductor:
    What place is this?
    Where are we now?

    I am the grass.   10
    Let me work.

          1918

GARGOYLE

I saw a mouth jeering. A smile of melted red iron ran over it. Its laugh was
    full of nails rattling. It was a child's dream of a mouth.
A fist hit the mouth: knuckles of gun-metal driven by an electric wrist
    and shoulder. It was a child's dream of an arm.
The fist hit the mouth over and over, again and again. The mouth bled
    melted iron, and laughed its laughter of nails rattling.
And I saw the more the fist pounded the more the mouth laughed. The
    fist is pounding and pounding, and the mouth answering.

          1918

---

[1] The site of one of Napoleon's great victories and that of his defeat in 1815.
[2] The site of a major defeat for the Confederacy in 1863.
[3] The sites of tragic battles in World War I.

PRAYER AFTER WORLD WAR

Wandering oversea dreamer,
Hunting and hoarse, Oh daughter and mother,
Oh daughter of ashes and mother of blood,
Child of the hair let down, and tears,
Child of the cross in the south
And the star in the north,
Keeper of Egypt and Russia and France,
Keeper of England and Poland and Spain,
Make us a song for tomorrow.
Make us one new dream, us who forget,   10
Out of the storm let us have one star.

    Struggle, Oh anvils, and help her.
Weave with your wool, Oh winds and skies.
Let your iron and copper help,
    Oh dirt of the old dark earth.

Wandering oversea singer,
Singing of ashes and blood,
Child of the scars of fire,
    Make us one new dream, us who forget.
    Out of the storm let us have one star.   20

1920

APRONS OF SILENCE

Many things I might have said today.
And I kept my mouth shut.
So many times I was asked
To come and say the same things
Everybody was saying, no end
To the yes-yes, yes-yes,
    me-too, me-too.

The aprons of silence covered me.
A wire and hatch held my tongue.
I spit nails into an abyss and listened.   10
I shut off the gabble of Jones, Johnson, Smith,
All whose names take pages in the city directory.

I fixed up a padded cell and lugged it around.
I locked myself in and nobody knew it.
Only the keeper and the kept in the hoosegow,
    Knew it—on the streets, in the post office,

On the cars, into the railroad station
Where the caller was calling, "All a-board,
All a-board for . . . Blaa-blaa . . . Blaa-blaa,
Blaa-blaa . . . and all points northwest . . . all a-board."   20

Here I took along my own hoosegow
And did business with my own thoughts.
Do you see? It must be the aprons of silence.

1920

THEY ALL WANT TO PLAY HAMLET

They all want to play Hamlet.
They have not exactly seen their fathers killed
Nor their mothers in a frame-up to kill,
Nor an Ophelia dying with a dust gagging the heart,
Not exactly the spinning circles of singing golden spiders,
Not exactly this have they got at nor the meaning of flowers—O flowers,
     flowers slung by a dancing girl—in the saddest play the inkfish,
     Shakespeare, ever wrote;
Yet they all want to play Hamlet because it is sad like all actors are sad
     and to stand by an open grave with a joker's skull in the hand and   10
     then to say over slow and say over slow wise, keen, beautiful words
     masking a heart that's breaking, breaking,
This is something that calls and calls to their blood.
They are acting when they talk about it and they know it is acting to be
     particular about it and yet: They all want to play Hamlet.

1920

LOVE IN LABRADOR

One arch of the sky
Took on a spray of jewels.

The crystals gleamed on the windows
Weaving their wintrish alphabets
Of spears and ovals fixed in frost
Fastened to a glass design
With a word: This must be.

There are shooters of the moon far north.
There are dying eyes holding diadems.
There are deaths sweet as laughing waters.
There are gold heelprints on the fading
     staircases of the stars.

1928

Wallace Stevens
(1879–1955)

Wallace Stevens, born in 1879 in Reading, Pennsylvania, was the son of a prominent lawyer and a former schoolteacher. Looking back at this typical, prosperous American family, Stevens felt he had inherited his practical side from his father and his imaginative side from his mother. The well-to-do Stevens family was prominent in the Dutch Reform Church, and young Wallace attended Evangelical Lutheran elementary schools and the Reading Boys' High School before entering Harvard University in 1897.

At Harvard, where his more influential professors included Charles Townsend Copeland, Barrett Wendell, and George Santayana, Stevens became an agnostic, a position he firmly maintained until his final deathbed conversion to Roman Catholicism. In fact, much of his later poetry deals with the process of finding through poetry some recompense for the loss of faith. During his Harvard years he also wrote for the *Harvard Advocate*, served on its editorial board, and in 1900 became its president. The March 10, 1900, issue of the *Harvard Advocate,* the first with Stevens in control, included a poem, a short story, and three editorials by Stevens, who apparently had to supplement the magazine by adding his own material.

He left Harvard without a degree in June 1900 and moved to New York City to try his hand at journalism. But the life of a journalist left him lonely and depressed—even then he apparently sensed a need for something more than the reality in which journalists are caught up. At the urging and with the support of his father, he entered New York Law School in 1901. He graduated less than two years later and was admitted to the New York Bar Association in 1904. In the succeeding years, Stevens worked for a number of New York law firms, until finally in 1909 he obtained a job with American Bonding Company of Baltimore. The job gave him the financial security he needed to marry Elsie Viola Kachel, whom he had met about four years earlier on one of his trips to his parents' home in Reading. The wedding took place in September 1909, and the Stevenses lived in New York City for the next seven years.

Perhaps coincidentally, Stevens's poetic aspirations did not surface again until after his father died in 1911. At about this time Stevens became more actively involved with the writers and painters of New York City's Greenwich Village and befriended Marianne Moore and William Carlos Williams. Gradually, as a result of this involvement his interest in oriental literature, the French symbolists, and modern painting intensified. The New York Armory Show of 1913, which introduced the early modern masters to the American public, was for Stevens and many of his contemporaries a watershed experience. It stimulated a lifelong interest in painting and an enthusiasm for the avant-garde in all the arts.

In 1914 Stevens began publishing in earnest, and his career in writing poetry was underway. His early poems reveal the oriental and French influences, a love of color, and, perhaps most important, a celebration of sensual experience as a replacement for an absent God. In those early poems he created stylized symbolic landscapes, responded to the imagists by crystallizing human experience in sharp haiku-like stanzas, and explored the limits of human perception. The intense excitement generated by Stevens's engagement with modernism resulted in some of his best and most anthologized work, including "Sunday Morning," "Peter Quince at the Clavier" (both published in 1915), and "Thirteen

Ways of Looking at a Blackbird" (1917). Nevertheless, for financial security Stevens took a job with the Hartford Accident and Indemnity Company in 1916; he eventually was named a vice-president there and until his death remained an insurance lawyer in Hartford.

By the time Stevens's first poetry collection, *Harmonium*, appeared in 1923, Stevens had published nearly one hundred poems in various "little magazines" and anthologies. His interest in language, in word play, and in the imagination's transformation of sensual experience was beginning to take precedence over his interest in images and in sensual experience for its own sake. "Nuances of a Theme by Williams" (about William Carlos Williams, notorious as a spokesman for the senses), "Anecdote of the Jar," and the companion poems "The Snow Man" and "Tea at the Palaz of Hoon," are Stevens's meditations on the barrenness of the natural world, the insufficiency of mere things, and the necessity of both the order-producing intelligence and the transforming imagination. "The Emperor of Ice-Cream" and "The Snow Man" look clearly at the finality of death and at the reality of life in a universe without God, especially when this reality is not transformed by the human imagination.

In 1924 Stevens's daughter, Holly, was born, and he took a self-imposed sabbatical from poetry—perhaps because he felt he had said everything he had to say in *Harmonium*, perhaps to concentrate on his career and his family. After publishing "Sea Surface Full of Clouds" (1924) he all but retired from writing poetry until 1930. In the years before returning to serious poetry, however, Stevens immersed himself in poetic theory; he read the modern French critics on "pure poetry," and reread the canon of literary criticism. This was essential preparation for his later work, with its never-ending quest for the possible, impossible poem, for what in *The Necessary Angel* (1951) he calls the "supreme fiction."

Stevens's next book, *Ideas of Order* (1935), reveals a new sensibility, a new orientation of thought and feeling. This is perhaps most apparent in "The Idea of Order at Key West," in which a woman's voice makes "the sky acutest at its vanishing." When the singing ends the poet can step back and comment on the song, the town, the lights, the sea, the night, and the "blessed rage for order," which may, in the mind of the poet/maker, pull it all together. The conflict between reality and the imagination presented in "The Idea of Order at Key West" is a theme that permeates Stevens's later work. Both "Mozart, 1935" and "Anglais Mort à Florence" are concerned with the poet's struggle to wring some compensation from an unfeeling world, and they are grounded in the conflict between the "hoo-hoo-hoo" of the dreary present "where music fails" and the imaginatively charged, imaginatively colored past.

The Man With the Blue Guitar and Other Poems (1937) marked the beginning of a highly productive period for Stevens, culminating in *Parts of a World* (1942) and *Notes Toward a Supreme Fiction* (1942). His poems from this period deal with "the incessant conjunctions between things as they are and things imagined," as Stevens explains on the dust jacket of *Blue Guitar*. Two poems representative of this period, "A Postcard From the Volcano" (1936) and "Study of Two Pears" (1942), emphasize the meagerness of a world without imagination. Despite the similarities between them, both poems give additional insight, add something to our understanding of the conjunction of imagination and reality. The poems, like each of the stanzas in Stevens's early "Thirteen Ways of Looking at a Blackbird," view reality from a significantly different, uniquely illuminating perspective.

Stevens's aesthetic philosophy is embodied in the poems of the early 1940s, especially "Of Modern Poetry," "Mrs. Alfred Uruguay," and "Asides on an Oboe," and is the reason *Notes Toward a Supreme Fiction* was written (all four published in 1942). The latter long poem, of central importance in the Stevens canon, is actually thirty-one short poems, each composed of seven three-line stanzas. The thirty-one poems are divided into three sets that focus on what Stevens felt to be a necessary if not sufficient condition of the ultimate

Picasso's early modernist painting The Old Guitarist *(1903) is believed to have inspired Wallace Stevens's poem "The Man With the Blue Guitar."*

poem—it must be abstract; it must change; and it must give pleasure. The three sets of poems are parallel in structure so that each poem (canto) is connected to the corresponding poems in the other two sets. Stevens's exploration of aesthetic philosophy, his groping toward the supreme fiction, is present not only in his poetry but also in his critical essays. *The Necessary Angel*, subtitled *Essays in Reality and the Imagination*, contains many passages that help shed light on some of his more difficult later poems. The essay "The Noble Rider and the Sound of Words" (delivered as a lecture in 1941) is especially helpful as preparation for reading his meditative, philosophical poems of the early 1940s, in particular "Mrs. Alfred Uruguay" and *Notes Toward a Supreme Fiction*.

After writing *Notes Toward a Supreme Fiction* when he was sixty-two, an age when so many other poets would be in decline, Stevens continued to write poems, including those in *Transport to Summer* (1947) and in *The Auroras of Autumn* (1950). He also wrote a significant part of a third book, *The Rock*, which he appended to *Collected Poems* (1954). That volume's last ten poems, all written after Stevens's sixty-eighth year, illustrate his continuing poetic strength. In many of these poems (such as "Large Red Man Reading," "This Solitude of Cataracts," and "The River of Rivers in Connecticut") Stevens, like the pre-Socratic philosopher Heraclitus, is concerned with the impossibility of stepping into the same river twice and with the incessant flux of the natural world, treating this flux with characteristic depth, sophistication, and verve. Among these later poems are "To an Old Philosopher in Rome," his moving tribute to the dying Santayana (perhaps the finest poem of Stevens's later period and certainly one of the strongest poems in the Stevens canon), and "The Course of a Particular," a poem in which the "cry of leaves that do not transcend themselves" in the final analysis "concerns no one at all."

Stevens was awarded the Pulitzer Prize for poetry for the 1955 edition of *Collected Poems* and was preparing his acceptance speech when he succumbed to cancer in August 1955. His poetry lives on, and his position as one of the most important poets of the twentieth century has become more firmly established with each succeeding generation.

Readers continue to discover "something there" and to respond both to the imaginative force of the early poems that celebrate the beauty inherent in the physical, natural world and to the imaginative force of the later poems that celebrate the mind in the act of creating the supreme fiction, of finding what will suffice.

Suggested Readings: *Harmonium*, 1923, 1937. *Notes Toward a Supreme Fiction*, 1942. *The Collected Poems of Wallace Stevens*, 1954. *Letters of Wallace Stevens*, ed. H. Stevens, 1966. J. N. Riddel, *The Clairvoyant Eye: The Poetry and Poetics of Wallace Stevens*, 1965. R. Sukenick, *Wallace Stevens: Musing the Obscure*, 1967. H. H. Vendler, *On Extended Wings: Wallace Stevens' Longer Poems*, 1969. A. W. Litz, *Introspective Voyager: The Poetic Development of Wallace Stevens*, 1972. H. Bloom, *Wallace Stevens: The Poems of Our Climate*, 1977. F. Doggett, *Stevens' Poetry of Thought*, 1980. M. J. Bates, *Wallace Stevens: A Mythology of Self*, 1985. B. J. Leggett, *Wallace Stevens and Poetic Theory*, 1987.

Text Used: *The Palm at the End of the Mind*, ed. H. Stevens, 1971.

SUNDAY MORNING*

I

Complacencies of the peignoir, and late
Coffee and oranges in a sunny chair,
And the green freedom of a cockatoo
Upon a rug mingle to dissipate
The holy hush of ancient sacrifice.
She dreams a little, and she feels the dark
Encroachment of that old catastrophe,
As a calm darkens among water-lights.
The pungent oranges and bright, green wings
Seem things in some procession of the dead,   10
Winding across wide water, without sound.
The day is like wide water, without sound,
Stilled for the passing of her dreaming feet
Over the seas, to silent Palestine,
Dominion of the blood and sepulchre.[1]

II

Why should she give her bounty to the dead?
What is divinity if it can come
Only in silent shadows and in dreams?
Shall she not find in comforts of the sun,
In pungent fruit and bright, green wings, or else   20
In any balm or beauty of the earth,
Things to be cherished like the thought of heaven?
Divinity must live within herself:
Passions of rain, or moods in falling snow;

---

* First published in a shortened version in *Poetry* in 1915 with the stanzas ordered I, VIII, IV, V, VII. According to Stevens it is "simply an expression of paganism, although, of course, I did not think I was expressing paganism when I wrote it" (*Letters of Wallace Stevens*, 1977).
[1] The site of blood sacrifices, such as that of Jesus, and sacred tombs.

Grievings in loneliness, or unsubdued
Elations when the forest blooms; gusty
Emotions on wet roads on autumn nights;
All pleasures and all pains, remembering
The bough of summer and the winter branch.
These are the measures destined for her soul.   30

III

Jove[2] in the clouds had his inhuman birth.
No mother suckled him, no sweet land gave
Large-mannered motions to his mythy mind.
He moved among us, as a muttering king,
Magnificent, would move among his hinds,[3]
Until our blood, commingling, virginal,
With heaven, brought such requital to desire
The very hinds discerned it, in a star.
Shall our blood fail? Or shall it come to be
The blood of paradise? And shall the earth   40
Seem all of paradise that we shall know?
The sky will be much friendlier then than now,
A part of labor and a part of pain,
And next in glory to enduring love,
Not this dividing and indifferent blue.

IV

She says, "I am content when wakened birds,
Before they fly, test the reality
Of misty fields, by their sweet questionings;
But when the birds are gone, and their warm fields
Return no more, where, then, is paradise?"   50
There is not any haunt of prophecy,
Nor any old chimera[4] of the grave,
Neither the golden underground,[5] nor isle
Melodious, where spirits gat them home,
Nor visionary south, nor cloudy palm
Remote on heaven's hill, that has endured
As April's green endures; or will endure
Like her remembrance of awakened birds,
Or her desire for June and evening, tipped
By the consummation of the swallow's wings.   60

V

She says "But in contentment I still feel
The need of some imperishable bliss."
Death is the mother of beauty; hence from her,
Alone, shall come fulfilment to our dreams

[2] According to Roman myth, Jupiter, the supreme god.
[3] Shepherds, those who saw the star of Bethlehem, which marked the birth of Jesus.
[4] According to Greek myth, a fire-breathing monster.
[5] According to Greek myth, Elysium, the resting place of the virtuous.

And our desires. Although she strews the leaves
Of sure obliteration on our paths,
The path sick sorrow took, the many paths
Where triumph rang its brassy phrase, or love
Whispered a little out of tenderness,
She makes the willow shiver in the sun   70
For maidens who were wont to sit and gaze
Upon the grass, relinquished to their feet.
She causes boys to pile new plums and pears
On disregarded plate.[6] The maidens taste
And stray impassioned in the littering leaves.

VI

Is there no change of death in paradise?
Does ripe fruit never fall? Or do the boughs
Hang always heavy in that perfect sky,
Unchanging, yet so like our perishing earth,
With rivers like our own that seek for seas   80
They never find, the same receding shores
That never touch with inarticulate pang?
Why set the pear upon those river-banks
Or spice the shores with odors of the plum?
Alas, that they should wear our colors there,
The silken weavings of our afternoons,
And pick the strings of our insipid lutes!
Death is the mother of beauty, mystical,
Within whose burning bosom we devise
Our earthly mothers waiting, sleeplessly.   90

VII

Supple and turbulent, a ring of men
Shall chant in orgy on a summer morn
Their boisterous devotion to the sun,
Not as a god, but as a god might be,
Naked among them, like a savage source.
Their chant shall be a chant of paradise,
Out of their blood, returning to the sky;
And in their chant shall enter, voice by voice,
The windy lake wherein their lord delights,
The trees, like serafin,[7] and echoing hills,   100
That choir among themselves long afterward.
They shall know well the heavenly fellowship
Of men that perish and of summer morn.
And whence they came and whither they shall go
The dew upon their feet shall manifest.[8]

[6] Stevens's note: "Plate is used in the sense of so-called family plate. Disregarded refers to the disuse into which things fall that have been possessed for a long time. I mean, therefore, that death releases and renews. What the old have come to disregard, the young inherit and make use of" (*Letters*).

[7] Seraphim, or angels.

[8] Stevens's note: "Life is as fugitive as dew upon the feet of men dancing in dew. Men do not either come from any direction or disappear in any direction. Life is as meaningless as dew. Now these ideas are not bad in a poem. But they are a frightful bore when converted as above" (*Letters*).

VIII

She hears, upon that water without sound,
A voice that cries, "The tomb in Palestine
Is not the porch of spirits lingering.
It is the grave of Jesus, where he lay."
We live in an old chaos of the sun,   110
Or old dependency of day and night,
Or island solitude, unsponsored, free,
Of that wide water, inescapable.
Deer walk upon our mountains, and the quail
Whistle about us their spontaneous cries;
Sweet berries ripen in the wilderness;
And, in the isolation of the sky,
At evening, casual flocks of pigeons make
Ambiguous undulations as they sink,
Downward to darkness, on extended wings.   120

1915, 1923

DISILLUSIONMENT OF TEN O'CLOCK

The houses are haunted
By white night-gowns.
None are green,
Or purple with green rings,
Or green with yellow rings,
Or yellow with blue rings.
None of them are strange,
With socks of lace
And beaded ceintures.[1]   10
People are not going
To dream of baboons and periwinkles.
Only, here and there, and old sailor,
Drunk and asleep in his boots,
Catches tigers
In red weather.

1915, 1923

THIRTEEN WAYS OF LOOKING AT A BLACKBIRD*

I

Among twenty snowy mountains,
The only moving thing
Was the eye of the blackbird.

[1] Belts.

* Stevens's note: "This group of poems is not meant to be a collection of epigrams or ideas, but of sensations" (*Letters of Wallace Stevens*, 1977).

II

I was of three minds,
Like a tree
In which there are three blackbirds.

III

The blackbird whirled in the autumn winds.
It was a small part of the pantomime.

IV

A man and a woman
Are one.
A man and a woman and a blackbird
Are one.   10

V

I do not know which to prefer,
The beauty of inflections
Or the beauty of innuendoes,
The blackbird whistling
Or just after.

VI

Icicles filled the long window
With barbaric glass.
The shadow of the blackbird   20
Crossed it, to and fro.

The mood
Traced in the shadow
An indecipherable cause.

VII

O thin men of Haddam,[1]
Why do you imagine golden birds?
Do you not see how the blackbird
Walks around the feet
Of the women about you?

VIII

I know noble accents   30
And lucid, inescapable rhythms;
But I know, too,
That the blackbird is involved
In what I know.

IX

When the blackbird flew out of sight,
It marked the edge
Of one of many circles.

[1] Haddam, Connecticut.

X

At the sight of blackbirds
Flying in a green light,
Even the bawds of euphony[2]   40
Would cry out sharply.

XI

He rode over Connecticut
In a glass coach.
Once, a fear pierced him,
In that he mistook
The shadow of his equipage
For blackbirds.

XII

The river is moving.
The blackbird must be flying.[3]

XIII

It was evening all afternoon.   50
It was snowing
And it was going to snow.
The blackbird sat
In the cedar-limbs.[4]

1923

NUANCES OF A THEME BY WILLIAMS*

It's a strange courage
you give me, ancient star:

Shine alone in the sunrise
toward which you lend no part![1]

I

Shine alone, shine nakedly, shine like bronze,
that reflects neither my face nor any inner part
of my being, shine like fire, that mirrors nothing.

II

Lend no part to any humanity that suffuses
you in its own light.
Be not chimera[2] of morning,

---

[2] Stevens's note: "[I] intended [that] the bawds of euphony would suddenly cease to be academic and express themselves sharply: naturally, with pleasure, etc." (*Letters*).
[3] Stevens's note: "[The point] is the compulsion frequently back of the things that we do" (*Letters*).
[4] Stevens's note: "[I wanted this stanza to] convey despair" (*Letters*).
* William Carlos Williams (1883–1963).
[1] "El Hombre," published in Williams's *¡Al Que Quiere!* (1917).
[2] According to Greek myth, a fire-breathing monster.

Half-man, half-star.
Be not an intelligence,
Like a widow's bird
Or an old horse.   10

1919, 1923

ANECDOTE OF THE JAR

I placed a jar in Tennessee,
And round it was, upon a hill.
It made the slovenly wilderness
Surround that hill.

The wilderness rose up to it,
And sprawled around, no longer wild.
The jar was round upon the ground
And tall and of a port in air.

It took dominion everywhere.
The jar was gray and bare.   10
It did not give of bird or bush,
Like nothing else in Tennessee.

1919, 1923

THE SNOW MAN*

One must have a mind of winter
To regard the frost and the boughs
Of the pine-trees crusted with snow;

And have been cold a long time
To behold the junipers shagged with ice,
The spruces rough in the distant glitter

Of the January sun; and not to think
Of any misery in the sound of the wind,
In the sound of a few leaves,

Which is the sound of the land   10
Full of the same wind
That is blowing in the same bare place

---

* Stevens's note: "[This poem is] an example of the necessity of identifying oneself with reality in order to understand and enjoy it" (*Letters of Wallace Stevens*, 1977).

For the listener, who listens in the snow,
And, nothing himself, beholds
Nothing that is not there and the nothing that is.

1921, 1923

TEA AT THE PALAZ OF HOON*

Not less because in purple I descended
The western day through what you called
The loneliest air, not less was I myself.

What was the ointment sprinkled on my beard?
What were the hymns that buzzed beside my ears?
What was the sea whose tide swept through me there?

Out of my mind the golden ointment rained,
And my ears made the blowing hymns they heard.
I was myself the compass of that sea:

I was the world in which I walked, and what I saw   10
Or heard or felt came not but from myself;
And there I found myself more truly and more strange.

1923

THE EMPEROR OF ICE-CREAM†

Call the roller of big cigars,
The muscular one, and bid him whip
In kitchen cups concupiscent curds.[1]
Let the wenches dawdle in such dress
As they are used to wear, and let the boys
Bring flowers in last month's newspapers.
Let be be finale of seem.[2]
The only emperor is the emperor of ice-cream.

* Stevens's note: ". . . Hoon could be . . . the son of old man Hoon. He sounds like a Dutchman. I think the word is probably an automatic cipher for 'the loneliest air,' that is to say, the expanse of sky and space" (*Letters of Wallace Stevens,* 1977).

† Stevens's note: "This poem is an instance of letting myself go. Poems of this sort are the pleasantest on which to look back, because they seem to remain fresher than others" (*Letters of Wallace Stevens,* 1977).

[1] Stevens's note: [These words] have no genealogy; they are merely expressive. . . . They express the concupiscence of life, but, by contrast with the things in relation to them in the poem, they express or accentuate life's destitution, and it is this that gives them something more than a cheap lustre" (*Letters*).

[2] Stevens's note: "The true sense is let being become the conclusion or denouement of appearing to be: in short, icecream is an absolute good. The poem is obviously not about icecream, but about being as distinguished from seeming to be" (*Letters*).

Take from the dresser of deal,[3]
Lacking the three glass knobs, that sheet   10
On which she embroidered fantails[4] once
And spread it so as to cover her face.
If her horny feet protrude, they come
To show how cold she is, and dumb.
Let the lamp affix its beam.
The only emperor is the emperor of ice-cream.

1922, 1923

THE IDEA OF ORDER AT KEY WEST*

She sang beyond the genius of the sea.
The water never formed to mind or voice,
Like a body wholly body, fluttering
Its empty sleeves; and yet its mimic motion
Made constant cry, caused constantly a cry,
That was not ours although we understood,
Inhuman, of the veritable ocean.

The sea was not a mask. No more was she.
The song and water were not medleyed sound
Even if what she sang was what she heard,   10
Since what she sang was uttered word by word.
It may be that in all her phrases stirred
The grinding water and the gasping wind;
But it was she and not the sea we heard.

For she was the maker of the song she sang.
The ever-hooded, tragic-gestured sea
Was merely a place by which she walked to sing.
Whose spirit is this? we said, because we knew
It was the spirit that we sought and knew
That we should ask this often as she sang.   20

If it was only the dark voice of the sea
That rose, or even colored by many waves;
If it was only the outer voice of sky
And cloud, of the sunken coral water-walled,
However clear, it would have been deep air,
The heaving speech of air, a summer sound
Repeated in a summer without end

---

[3] A dresser of cheap wood.   [4] Fantail pigeons.
* Stevens's note: "In 'The Idea of Order at Key West,' life has ceased to be a matter of chance. It may be that every man introduces his own order into the life about him . . ." (*Letters of Wallace Stevens*, 1977).

And sound alone. But it was more than that,
More even than her voice, and ours, among
The meaningless plungings of water and the wind,   30
Theatrical distances, bronze shadows heaped
On high horizons, mountainous atmospheres
Of sky and sea.

                    It was her voice that made
The sky acutest at its vanishing.
She measured to the hour its solitude.
She was the single artificer of the world
In which she sang. And when she sang, the sea,
Whatever self it had, became the self
That was her song, for she was the maker. Then we,   40
As we beheld her striding there alone,
Knew that there never was a world for her
Except the one she sang and, singing, made.

Ramon Fernandez,[1] tell me, if you know,
Why, when the singing ended and we turned
Toward the town, tell why the glassy lights,
The lights in the fishing boats at anchor there,
As the night descended, tilting in the air,
Mastered the night and portioned out the sea,
Fixing emblazoned zones and fiery poles,   50
Arranging, deepening, enchanting night.

Oh! Blessed rage for order, pale Ramon,
The maker's rage to order words of the sea,
Words of the fragrant portals, dimly-starred,
And of ourselves and of our origins,
In ghostlier demarcations, keener sounds.

                                        1934, 1935

MOZART, 1935*

Poet, be seated at the piano.
Play the present, its hoo-hoo-hoo,
Its shoo-shoo-shoo, its ric-a-nic,
Its envious cachinnation.[1]

---

[1] Fernandez (1894–1944) was a French literary critic, but Stevens repeatedly denied that he was consciously thinking of any real person when he wrote this poem.
* Stevens's note: "[This poem] expresses something that I have very much at heart, and that is: the status of the poet in a disturbed society, or, for that matter, in any society" (*Letters of Wallace Stevens*, 1977).
[1] Loud laughter.

If they throw stones upon the roof
While you practice arpeggios,[2]
It is because they carry down the stairs
A body in rags.
Be seated at the piano.

That lucid souvenir of the past,   10
The divertimento;[3]
That airy dream of the future,
The unclouded concerto . . .
The snow is falling.
Strike the piercing chord.

Be thou the voice,
Not you. Be thou, be thou
The voice of angry fear,
The voice of this besieging pain.

Be thou that wintry sound   20
As of the great wind howling,
By which sorrow is released,
Dismissed, absolved
In a starry placating.

We may return to Mozart.
He was young, and we, we are old.
The snow is falling
And the streets are full of cries.
Be seated, thou.

                                                          1936

ANGLAIS MORT À FLORENCE*

A little less returned for him each spring.
Music began to fail him. Brahms, although
His dark familiar, often walked apart.

His spirit grew uncertain of delight,
Certain of its uncertainty, in which
That dark companion left him unconsoled

---

[2] Notes of a chord, played in quick succession.
[3] A melodic instrumental composition in several movements.
* "An Englishman Who Died in Florence" (French). Stevens's note: "[This poem reveals a] strong spirit [that] stands by its own strength [without] the aid of philosophy, religion and one thing or another" (*Letters of Wallace Stevens*, 1977).

For a self returning mostly memory.
Only last year he said that the naked moon
Was not the moon he used to see, to feel

(In the pale coherences of moon and mood   10
When he was young), naked and alien,
More leanly shining from a lankier sky.

Its ruddy pallor had grown cadaverous.
He used his reason, exercised his will,
Turning in time to Brahms as alternate

In speech. He was that music and himself.
They were particles of order, a single majesty:
But he remembered the time when he stood alone.   20

He stood at last by God's help and the police;
But he remembered the time when he stood alone.
He yielded himself to that single majesty;

But he remembered the time when he stood alone,
When to be and delight to be seemed to be one,
Before the colors deepened and grew small.

1936

A POSTCARD FROM THE VOLCANO

Children picking up our bones
Will never know that these were once
As quick as foxes on the hill;

And that in autumn, when the grapes
Made sharp air sharper by their smell
These had a being, breathing frost;

And least will guess that with our bones
We left much more, left what still is
The look of things, left what we felt

At what we saw. The spring clouds blow   10
Above the shuttered mansion-house,
Beyond our gate and the windy sky

Cries out a literate despair.
We knew for long the mansion's look
And what we said of it became

A part of what it is . . . Children,
Still weaving budded aureoles,[1]
Will speak our speech and never know,

Will say of the mansion that it seems
As if he that lived there left behind   20
A spirit storming in blank walls,

A dirty house in a gutted world,
A tatter of shadows peaked to white,
Smeared with the gold of the opulent sun.

1936

from   THE MAN WITH THE BLUE GUITAR*

I
The man bent over his guitar,
A shearsman of sorts. The day was green.

They said, "You have a blue guitar,
You do not play things as they are."

The man replied, "Things as they are
Are changed upon the blue guitar."

And they said then, "But play, you must,
A tune beyond us, yet ourselves,

A tune upon the blue guitar
Of things exactly as they are."

II
I cannot bring a world quite round,
Although I patch it as I can.

I sing a hero's head, large eye
And bearded bronze, but not a man,

Although I patch him as I can
And reach through him almost to man.

If to serenade almost to man
Is to miss, by that, things as they are,

[1] Halos.
* A poem in thirty-three parts, inspired by Pablo Picasso's use of a guitar and the color blue in *The Old Guitarist* (1903).

Say that it is the serenade
Of a man that plays a blue guitar.

1937

STUDY OF TWO PEARS

I

Opusculum paedagogum.[1]
The pears are not viols,[2]
Nudes or bottles.
They resemble nothing else.

II

They are yellow forms
Composed of curves
Bulging toward the base.
They are touched red.

III

They are not flat surfaces
Having curved outlines.
They are round
Tapering toward the top.

10

IV

In the way they are modelled
There are bits of blue.
A hard dry leaf hangs
From the stem.

V

The yellow glistens.
It glistens with various yellows,
Citrons, oranges and greens
Flowering over the skin.

20

VI

The shadows of the pears
Are blobs on the green cloth.
The pears are not seen
As the observer wills.

1942

[1] "A small opus for study" (Latin).   [2] Fiddles.

OF HARTFORD IN A PURPLE LIGHT

A long time you have been making the trip
From Havre[1] to Hartford, Master Soleil,[2]
Bringing the lights of Norway[3] and all that.

A long time the ocean has come with you,
Shaking the water off, like a poodle,
That splatters incessant thousands of drops,

Each drop a petty tricolor. For this,
The aunts in Pasadena, remembering,
Abhor the plaster of the western horses,

Souvenirs of museums. But, Master, there are   10
Lights masculine and lights feminine.
What is this purple, this parasol,

This stage-light of the Opera?
It is like a region full of intonings.
It is Hartford seen in a purple light.

A moment ago, light masculine,
Working, with big hands, on the town,
Arranged its heroic attitudes.

But now as in an amour of women
Purple sets purple round. Look, Master,   20
See the river, the railroad, the cathedral . . .

When male light fell on the naked back
Of the town, the river, the railroad were clear.
Now, every muscle slops away.

Hi! Whisk it, poodle, flick the spray
Of the ocean, ever-freshening,
On the irised hunks; the stone bouquet.

1942

OF MODERN POETRY

The poem of the mind in the act of finding
What will suffice. It has not always had
To find: the scene was set; it repeated what
Was in the script.

---

[1] Le Havre, France.   [2] "Sun" (French).   [3] The aurora borealis, or northern lights.

Then the theatre was changed
To something else. Its past was a souvenir.

It has to be living, to learn the speech of the place.
It has to face the men of the time and to meet
The women of the time. It has to think about war
And it has to find what will suffice. It has   10
To construct a new stage. It has to be on that stage
And, like an insatiable actor, slowly and
With meditation, speak words that in the ear,
In the delicatest ear of the mind, repeat,
Exactly, that which it wants to hear, at the sound
Of which, an invisible audience listens,
Not to the play, but to itself, expressed
In an emotion as of two people, as of two
Emotions becoming one. The actor is
A metaphysician in the dark, twanging   20
An instrument, twanging a wiry string that gives
Sounds passing through sudden rightnesses, wholly
Containing the mind, below which it cannot descend,
Beyond which it has no will to rise.
                                        It must
Be the finding of a satisfaction, and may
Be of a man skating, a woman dancing, a woman
Combing. The poem of the act of the mind.

                                                1940, 1942

MRS. ALFRED URUGUAY

So what said the others and the sun went down
And, in the brown blues of evening, the lady said,
In the donkey's ear, "I fear that elegance
Must struggle like the rest." She climbed until
The moonlight in her lap, mewing[1] her velvet,
And her dress were one and she said, "I have said no
To everything, in order to get at myself.
I have wiped away moonlight like mud. Your innocent ear
And I, if I rode naked, are what remain."

The moonlight crumbled to degenerate forms,   10
While she approached the real, upon her mountain,
With lofty darkness. The donkey was there to ride,
To hold by the ear, even though it wished for a bell,
Wished faithfully for a falsifying bell.
Neither the moonlight could change it. And for her,

---

[1] Shedding or molting.

To be, regardless of velvet, could never be more
Than to be, she could never differently be,
Her no and no made yes impossible.

Who was it passed her there on a horse all will,
What figure of capable imagination?   20
Whose horse clattered on the road on which she rose,
As it descended, blind to her velvet and
The moonlight? Was it a rider intent on the sun,
A youth, a lover with phosphorescent hair,
Dressed poorly, arrogant of his streaming forces,
Lost in an integration of the martyrs' bones,
Rushing from what was real; and capable?

The villages slept as the capable man went down,
Time swished on the village clocks and dreams were alive,
The enormous gongs gave edges to their sounds,   30
As the rider, no chevalere[2] and poorly dressed,
Impatient of the bells and midnight forms,
Rode over the picket rocks, rode down the road,
And, capable, created in his mind,
Eventual victor, out of the martyrs' bones,
The ultimate elegance: the imagined land.

                                                              1942

ASIDES ON THE OBOE

The prologues are over. It is a question, now,
Of final belief. So, say that final belief
Must be in a fiction. It is time to choose.

I

That obsolete fiction of the wide river in
An empty land;[1] the gods that Boucher[2] killed;
And the metal heroes that time granulates—
The philosophers' man alone still walks in dew,
Still by the sea-side mutters milky lines
Concerning an immaculate imagery.
If you say on the hautboy man[3] is not enough,   10
Can never stand as god, is ever wrong
In the end, however naked, tall, there is still
The impossible possible philosophers' man,

---

[2] "Knight" (French).

[1] According to Greek myth, the souls of the newly dead had to cross the river Styx to reach the "empty" land of the dead.

[2] Jacques Boucher de Crèvecoeur de Perthes (1788–1868), a French archeologist and writer who proved that humans existed in prehistoric times, thereby refuting popular creation theories.

[3] A hero (from "haut" for "tall" [French]); a hautboy is an oboe.

The man who has had the time to think enough,
The central man, the human globe, responsive
As a mirror with a voice, the man of glass,
Who in a million diamonds sums us up.

II

He is the transparence of the place in which
He is and in his poems we find peace.
He sets this peddler's pie and cries in summer,   20
The glass man, cold and numbered, dewily cries,
"Thou art not August unless I make thee so."
Clandestine steps upon imagined stairs
Climb through the night, because his cuckoos call.

III

One year, death and war prevented the jasmine scent
And the jasmine islands were bloody martyrdoms.
How was it then with the central man? Did we
Find peace? We found the sum of men. We found,
If we found the central evil, the central good.
We buried the fallen without jasmine crowns.   30
There was nothing he did not suffer, no; nor we.

It was not as if the jasmine ever returned.
But we and the diamond globe at last were one.
We had always been partly one. It was as we came
To see him, that we were wholly one, as we heard
Him chanting for those buried in their blood,
In the jasmine haunted forests, that we knew
The glass man, without external reference.

1942

from   NOTES TOWARD A SUPREME FICTION*

from   SECTION ONE: IT MUST BE ABSTRACT

IV

The first idea was not our own. Adam
In Eden was the father of Descartes[1]
And Eve made air the mirror of herself,

---

* Stevens's notes: "By supreme fiction, of course, I mean poetry"; "The essence of poetry is change and the essence of change is that it gives pleasure" (*Letters of Wallace Stevens*, 1977).

[1] René Descartes (1596–1650), a French mathematician and philosopher; Stevens's note: "Descartes is used as a symbol of the reason. But . . . we do not live in a land of Descartes; we have imposed the reason; Adam imposed it even in Eden" (*Letters*).

Of her sons and of her daughters. They found themselves
In heaven as in a glass; a second earth;
And in the earth itself they found a green—

The inhabitants of a very varnished green.
But the first idea was not to shape the clouds
In imitation. The clouds preceded us

There was a muddy centre before we breathed.   10
There was a myth before the myth began,
Venerable and articulate and complete.

From this the poem springs: that we live in a place
That is not our own and, much more, not ourselves
And hard it is in spite of blazoned days.

We are the mimics. Clouds are pedagogues.
The air is not a mirror but bare board,
Coulisse[2] bright-dark, tragic chiaroscuro[3]

And comic color of the rose, in which
Abysmal instruments make sounds like pips[4]   20
Of the sweeping meanings that we add to them.

from   Section Two: It Must Change

IV

Two things of opposite natures seem to depend
On one another, as a man depends
On a woman, day on night, the imagined

On the real. This is the origin of change.
Winter and spring, cold copulars,[1] embrace
And forth the particulars of rapture come.

Music falls on the silence like a sense,
A passion that we feel, not understand.
Morning and afternoon are clasped together

And North and South are an intrinsic couple   10
And sun and rain a plural, like two lovers
That walk away as one in the greenest body.

In solitude the trumpets of solitude
Are not of another solitude resounding;
A little string speaks for a crowd of voices.

---

[2] A grooved board or side flat on a theater stage.
[3] The light-dark contrast in a painting, giving the illusion of depth.   [4] Peeps or chirps.
[1] Links or connections.

The partaker partakes of that which changes him.
The child that touches takes character from the thing,
The body, it touches. The captain and his men

Are one and the sailor and the sea are one.
Follow after, O my companion, my fellow, my self,   20
Sister and solace, brother and delight.

from   SECTION THREE: IT MUST GIVE PLEASURE

IV

We reason of these things with later reason
And we make of what we see, what we see clearly
And have seen, a place dependent on ourselves.

There was a mystic marriage in Catawba,[1]
At noon it was on the mid-day of the year
Between a great captain and the maiden Bawda.

This was their ceremonial hymn: Anon
We loved but would no marriage make. Anon
The one refused the other one to take,

Foreswore the sipping of the marriage wine.   10
Each must the other take not for his high,
His puissant[2] front nor for her subtle sound,

The shoo-shoo-shoo of secret cymbals round.
Each must the other take as sign, short sign
To stop the whirlwind, balk the elements.

The great captain loved the ever-hill Catawba
And therefore married Bawda, whom he found there,
And Bawda loved the captain as she loved the sun.

They married well because the marriage-place
Was what they loved. It was neither heaven nor hell.   20
They were love's characters come face to face.

1942

SO-AND-SO RECLINING ON HER COUCH

On her side, reclining on her elbow.
This mechanism, this apparition,
Suppose we call it Projection A.

---

[1] The home of a tribe of Sioux Indians, originally in South Carolina.   [2] Powerful.

She floats in air at the level of
The eye, completely anonymous,
Born, as she was, at twenty-one,

Without lineage or language, only
The curving of her hip, as motionless gesture,
Eyes dripping blue, so much to learn.

If just above her head there hung,   10
Suspended in air, the slightest crown
Of Gothic prong and practick[1] bright,

The suspension, as in solid space,
The suspending hand withdrawn, would be
An invisible gesture. Let this be called

Projection B. To get at the thing
Without gestures is to get at it as
Idea. She floats in the contention, the flux

Between the thing as idea and
The idea as thing. She is half who made her.   20
This is the final Projection, C.

The arrangement contains the desire of
The artist. But one confides in what has no
Concealed creator. One walks easily

The unpainted shore, accepts the world
As anything but sculpture. Good-bye,
Mrs. Pappadopoulos, and thanks.

1947

LARGE RED MAN READING

There were ghosts that returned to earth to hear his phrases,
As he sat there reading, aloud, the great blue tabulae.
They were those from the wilderness of stars that had expected
    more.

There were those that returned to hear him read from the poem
    of life,
Of the pans above the stove, the pots on the table, the tulips
    among them.

---

[1] Practice, customary practice and law.

They were those that would have wept to step barefoot into
    reality,   10

That would have wept and been happy, have shivered in the frost
And cried out to feel it again, have run fingers over leaves
And against the most coiled thorn, have seized on what was ugly

And laughed, as he sat there reading, from out of the purple tabulae,
The outlines of being and its expressings, the syllables of its
    law:
Poesis,[1] *poesis,* the literal characters, the vatic[2] lines,

Which in those ears and in those thin, those spended hearts,
Took on color, took on shape and the size of things as they are
And spoke the feeling for them, which was what they had lacked.

1948?, 1954

THIS SOLITUDE OF CATARACTS*

He never felt twice the same about the flecked river,
Which kept flowing and never the same way twice, flowing

Through many places, as if it stood still in one,
Fixed like a lake on which the wild ducks fluttered,

Ruffling its common reflections, thought-like Monadnocks[1]
There seemed to be an apostrophe that was not spoken.

There was so much that was real that was not real at all.
He wanted to feel the same way over and over.

He wanted the river to go on flowing the same way,
To keep on flowing. He wanted to walk beside it,   10

Under the buttonwoods, beneath a moon nailed fast.
He wanted his heart to stop beating and his mind to rest

In a permanent realization, without any wild ducks
Or mountains that were not mountains, just to know how it would be,

---

[1] "Poetry" or "poems" (Latin).   [2] Prophetic.
* Waterfalls.
  [1] Stevens's note: "The expression 'thought-like Monadnocks' can best be explained by changing it into 'Monadnock-like thoughts'. The image of a mountain deep in the surface of a lake acquires a secondary character. From the sheen of the surface it becomes slightly unreal: thought-like. Mt. Monadnock is a New England mountain" (*Letters of Wallace Stevens,* 1977).

Just to know how it would feel, released from destruction,
To be a bronze man breathing under archaic lapis,

Without the oscillations of planetary pass-pass,[2]
Breathing his bronzen breath at the azury centre of time.

1948?, 1954

ANGEL SURROUNDED BY PAYSANS*

One of the countrymen:
                                                    There is
A welcome at the door to which no one comes?
The angel:
I am the angel of reality,[1]
Seen for a moment standing in the door.

I have neither ashen wing nor wear of ore
And live without a tepid aureole,[2]

Or stars that follow me, not to attend,
But, of my being and its knowing, part.   10

I am one of you and being one of you
Is being and knowing what I am and know.

Yet I am the necessary angel of earth,
Since, in my sight, you see the earth again,

Cleared of its stiff and stubborn, man-locked set,
And, in my hearing, you hear its tragic drone

Rise liquidly in liquid lingerings,
Like watery words awash; like meanings said

By repetitions of half-meanings. Am I not,
Myself, only half of a figure of a sort,   20

---

[2] Stevens's note: "[This phrase] means the seeming-to-go-round of the planets by day and night" (*Letters*).

* "Peasants" (French). This poem is Stevens's response to Pierre Tal Coat's painting *Still Life*. Stevens's notes: "The angel is the Venetian glass bowl on the left with the little spray of leaves in it. The peasants are the terrines [earthenware dishes], bottles, and the glasses that surround it"; "[The point of this poem] is that there must be in the world about us things that solace us quite as fully as any heavenly visitation could" (*Letters of Wallace Stevens*, 1977).

[1] In this poem, in contrast to much of Stevens's work, "reality and contact with it are the great blessings"; apparently, Stevens is rebelling against "recently [having] been fitted into too many philosophic frames" (*Letters*).

[2] A halo.

A figure half seen, or seen for a moment, a man
Of the mind, an apparition apparelled in

Apparels of such lightest look that a turn
Of my shoulder and quickly, too quickly, I am gone?

1950

THE COURSE OF A PARTICULAR

Today the leaves cry, hanging on branches swept by wind,
Yet the nothingness of winter becomes a little less.
It is still full of icy shades and shapen snow.

The leaves cry . . . One holds off and merely hears the cry.
It is a busy cry, concerning someone else.
And though one says that one is part of everything,

There is a conflict, there is a resistance involved;
And being part is an exertion that declines:
One feels the life of that which gives life as it is.

The leaves cry. It is not a cry of divine attention,   10
Nor the smoke-drift of puffed-out heroes, nor human cry.
It is the cry of leaves that do not transcend themselves,

In the absence of fantasia, without meaning more
Than they are in the final finding of the ear, in the thing
Itself, until, at last, the cry concerns no one at all.

1951, 1957

TO AN OLD PHILOSOPHER IN ROME*

On the threshold of heaven, the figures in the street
Become the figures of heaven, the majestic movement
Of men growing small in the distances of space,
Singing, with smaller and still smaller sound,
Unintelligible absolution and an end—

---

* This poem was written one year before the death of George Santayana (1863–1952), an American
poet and philosopher who in 1912 retired from teaching at Harvard University and spent the rest of
his life in Italy. Stevens writes of his early encounters with Santayana at Harvard: "While I did not

The threshold, Rome, and that more merciful Rome
Beyond, the two alike in the make of the mind.
It is as if in a human dignity
Two parallels become one, a perspective, of which
Men are part both in the inch and in the mile.   10

How easily the blown banners change to wings
Things dark on the horizons of perception
Become accompaniments of fortune, but
Of the fortune of the spirit, beyond the eye,
Not of its sphere, and yet not far beyond,

The human end in the spirit's greatest reach,
The extreme of the known in the presence of the extreme
Of the unknown. The newsboys' muttering
Becomes another murmuring; the smell
Of medicine, a fragrantness not to be spoiled   20

The bed, the books, the chair, the moving nuns,
The candle as it evades the sight, these are
The sources of happiness in the shape of Rome,
A shape within the ancient circles of shapes,
And these beneath the shadow of a shape

In a confusion on bed and books, a portent
On the chair, a moving transparence on the nuns,
A light on the candle tearing against the wick
To join a hovering excellence, to escape
From fire and be part only of that of which   30

Fire is the symbol: the celestial possible.
Speak to your pillow as if it was yourself.
Be orator but with an accurate tongue
And without eloquence, O, half-asleep,
Of the pity that is the memorial of this room,

So that we feel, in this illumined large,
The veritable small, so that each of us
Beholds himself in you, and hears his voice
In yours, master and commiserable man,
Intent on your particles of nether-do,   40

take any of his courses and never heard him lecture, he invited me to come to see him a number of
times and, in that way, I came to know him a little. I read several poems to him and he expressed his
own view of the subject of them in a sonnet ['Cathedrals by the Sea . . .'{1901}] which he sent me,
and which is in one of his books. . . . I always came away from my visits with him feeling that he
made up in the most genuine way for many things that I needed. He was then still definitely a poet"
(*Letters of Wallace Stevens*, 1977).

Your dozing in the depths of wakefulness,
In the warmth of your bed, at the edge of your chair, alive
Yet living in two worlds, impenitent
As to one, and, as to one, most penitent,
Impatient for the grandeur that you need

In so much misery; and yet finding it
Only in misery, the afflatus of ruin,
Profound poetry of the poor and of the dead,
As in the last drop of the deepest blood,
As it falls from the heart and lies there to be seen,   50

Even as the blood of an empire, it might be,
For a citizen of heaven though still of Rome.
It is poverty's speech that seeks us out the most.
It is older than the oldest speech of Rome.
This is the tragic accent of the scene.

And you—it is you that speak it, without speech,
The loftiest syllables among loftiest things,
The one invulnerable man among
Crude captains, the naked majesty, if you like,
Of bird-nest arches and of rain-stained vaults.   60

The sounds drift in. The buildings are remembered.
The life of the city never lets go, nor do you
Ever want it to. It is part of the life in your room.
Its domes are the architecture of your bed.
The bells keep on repeating solemn names

In choruses and choirs of choruses,
Unwilling that mercy should be a mystery
Of silence, that any solitude of sense
Should give you more than their peculiar chords
And reverberations clinging to whisper still.   70

It is a kind of total grandeur at the end,
With every visible thing enlarged and yet
No more than a bed, a chair and moving nuns,
The immensest theatre, the pillared porch,
The book and candle in your ambered room,

Total grandeur of a total edifice,
Chosen by an inquisitor of structures
For himself. He stops upon this threshold,
As if the design of all his words takes form
And frame from thinking and is realized.   80

1951, 1954

THE RIVER OF RIVERS IN CONNECTICUT*

There is a great river this side of Stygia,[1]
Before one comes to the first black cataracts[2]
And trees that lack the intelligence of trees.

In that river, far this side of Stygia,
The mere flowing of the water is a gayety,
Flashing and flashing in the sun. On its banks,

No shadow walks. The river is fateful,
Like the last one. But there is no ferryman.[3]
He could not bend against its propelling force.

It is not to be seen beneath the appearances   10
That tell of it. The steeple at Farmington
Stands glistening and Haddam[4] shines and sways.

It is the third commonness with light and air,
A curriculum, a vigor, a local abstraction. . .
Call it, once more, a river, an unnamed flowing,

Space-filled, reflecting the seasons, the folk-lore
Of each of the senses; call it, again and again,
The river that flows nowhere, like a sea.

1954

FIRST WARMTH

I wonder, have I lived a skeleton's life,
As a questioner about reality,

A countryman of all the bones of the world?
Now, here, the warmth I had forgotten becomes

Part of the major reality, part of
An appreciation of a reality;

And thus an elevation, as if I lived
With something I could touch, touch every way.

1957

---

* "Connecticut" means "the place of long rivers" in the Algonquian language.
[1] The subterranean world of the dead, the land on the other side of the river Styx.   [2] Waterfalls.
[3] According to Greek myth, Charon ferries the souls of the newly dead across the river Styx.
[4] Farmington and Haddam are towns in Connecticut.

AS YOU LEAVE THE ROOM

You speak. You say: Today's character is not
A skeleton out of its cabinet. Nor am I.

That poem about the pineapple, the one
About the mind as never satisfied,

The one about the credible hero, the one
About summer, are not what skeletons think about.

I wonder, have I lived a skeleton's life,
As a disbeliever in reality,

A countryman of all the bones in the world?
Now, here, the snow I had forgotten becomes   10

Part of a major reality, part of
An appreciation of a reality

And thus an elevation, as if I left
With something I could touch, touch every way.

And yet nothing has been changed except what is
Unreal, as if nothing had been changed at all.

1957

A CLEAR DAY AND NO MEMORIES

No soldiers in the scenery,
No thoughts of people now dead,
As they were fifty years ago,
Young and living in a live air,
Young and walking in the sunshine,
Bending in blue dresses to touch something,
Today the mind is not part of the weather.

Today the air is clear of everything.
It has no knowledge except of nothingness
And it flows over us without meanings,   10
As if none of us had ever been here before
And are not now: in this shallow spectacle,
This invisible activity, this sense.

1957

OF MERE BEING

The palm at the end of the mind,
Beyond the last thought, rises
In the bronze decor,

A gold-feathered bird
Sings in the palm, without human meaning,
Without human feeling, a foreign song.

You know then that it is not the reason
That makes us happy or unhappy.
The bird sings. Its feathers shine.

The palm stands on the edge of space.   10
The wind moves slowly in the branches.
The bird's fire-fangled feathers dangle down.

                                        1955, 1957

William Carlos Williams
(1883–1963)

William Carlos Williams's career culminated with *Paterson,* his epic poem with prose passages, published between 1946 and 1963. As Williams said in his autobiography (1951), *Paterson* was written about the "whole knowable world" surrounding him in his own region of New Jersey, a region transformed through his poetic vision. His career as a poet merged with his perceptions and experiences as a physician. His verse forms are apparently simple, in keeping with the simplicity of his poetic subjects: events from everyday life, which range from a commonplace, natural setting noted by the poet/physician on his way to the "contagious hospital" in "Spring and All," the title poem of his 1923 collection, to the painterly lyricism captured in perhaps his most famous short poem, "The Red Wheelbarrow," from the same volume.

Williams was born in 1883 in Rutherford, New Jersey, near the city of Paterson. He attended medical school at the University of Pennsylvania, where he specialized in pediatrics and befriended the poets Ezra Pound, Marianne Moore, and Hilda Doolittle. Although Williams viewed his career in medicine as a means of support for his poetic career, for more than forty years he was a dedicated physician, and that dedication is evident in the tone and subjects of his poetry. He married Florence Herman in 1912, and the marriage lasted until his death, giving rise to two sons and such love poems as "Asphodel, That Greeny Flower" (1955). In 1924 and 1927 he journeyed to Europe, where he furthered his friendship with Ezra Pound and met James Joyce. Later in life Williams made trips for lectures and poetry readings, but he spent most of his time practicing medicine in Rutherford. Williams wrote poetry after caring for patients during the day and kept abreast of developments in modernist poetry through extensive reading and visits to New York City to meet painters and poets, including Marianne Moore and Wallace Stevens.

A late bloomer as a poet, Williams struggled for years to overcome the Keatsian style of his early verse. He finally found his own voice in *Kora in Hell* (1920), *Sour Grapes* (1921), and especially *Spring and All*. Like Pound, Williams wanted to "make it new," but unlike Pound he believed that the scene of his poetry should be America and that he should be an American poet speaking from within that scene, as exemplified by *Paterson* and *In the American Grain* (1925), now recognized as a major essay on American culture. He felt that his poetry should not aspire to the international intellectualism of T. S. Eliot but that it should be more than the regionalism of Robert Frost.

Williams's poetry transmutes the commonplace and everyday through his poetic process. His meticulous selection of visual detail and careful diction show his talent for the poetic picture; in fact, Williams had at one time studied painting. Williams's early work tended to consist of concise poems with vivid, sensuous images. Some of these poems, such as "The Red Wheelbarrow" and "The Pot of Flowers," from *Spring and All*, show his rendering of "painterly" detail. In "The Red Wheelbarrow" the poet presents an apparently simple picture of a red wheelbarrow "glazed with rain/water" standing "beside the white/chickens." Williams demands that the reader sense the picture of a wheelbarrow and the interaction of the picture's details, but he makes no comments about this picture except that "so much depends" upon it. We as readers are expected to supply our own interpretation. Williams aimed to render the linguistic image with little or no authorial intrusion or comment. Williams's precept "no ideas but in things" represents a tendency in twentieth-century poetry. He believed that the poet need make no comment "about" the content of the poetry. Although some critics have argued that Williams's poems lack emotional depth or intellectual profundity, the poems should be read within the context of his intention to

Charles Demuth's watercolor Tuberoses *(1922) was owned by William Carlos Williams, whose poems reflect his love of natural beauty, as is apparent in his poems "The Pot of Flowers" (based on this painting) and "The Wildflower."*

create poetry that produces its own effect directly, much in the manner of painting, and that shows the promptings of the traditional American belief in the value of practicality.

In the 1930s Williams began writing fiction. The short-story collections *The Knife of the Times* (1932) and *Life Along the Passaic River* (1938) and the novels *White Mule* (1937), *In the Money* (1940), and *The Build-Up* (1952) accompanied his essays and poems. He attempted to counter the powerful influences of Eliot and of the New Critics by establishing "little" magazines with an alternative view, and actively participated in community and political events. After World War II Williams was denied the post of Consultant in Poetry at the Library of Congress because his leftist or liberal views clashed with the conservatism of that time.

From 1946 to 1958 the five books comprising *Paterson* were published, even though Williams suffered a heart attack in 1948 and a series of disabling strokes, beginning in 1951, that forced him to retire from the medical profession. (An incomplete sixth book came out in 1963.) *The Desert Music* was published in 1954 and *Pictures From Brueghel* in 1962, but Williams had to stop writing in 1961. His poetic influence can be seen in a generation of younger poets, including the beat poets, the Black Mountain group, the San Francisco poets, and the New York school. Common among these poets was the use of the American idiom in poetry; an openness of form with a corresponding openness of experience rather than a shaping of experience toward preordained conclusions; a predilection for concrete imagery; and an awareness that poems are made of words, not ideas, and that language is the poet's primary raw material. The traditional well-made poem, with beginning, middle, and end, was replaced by the absence of closure, by a play of language that invited the reader to participate in the poem and to determine its meaning. Poetry, like life, was to be open-ended.

Late in his career Williams gained wide recognition. He received a National Book Award in 1950 for part of *Paterson,* the Bollingen Prize in 1953, and a Pulitzer Prize in 1963 for *Pictures From Brueghel*. Although he felt himself to be underrated, his poetic influence has been persistent and widespread. Whereas a Europeanized mentality dominated the poetry of the American expatriate poets such as Pound and Eliot, Williams centered his interest on a local American scene, in the manner of Walt Whitman and Emily Dickinson.

Williams's most obvious poetic ancestor is Whitman: both poets borrowed from and celebrated the common life of America. However, Williams differed from Whitman by making details significant in themselves, by tightening the poetic line, by emphasizing language's material aspects, and by carefully composing painterly poems. Whitman is typically described as the father of open-form poetry in America, and the freedom allowed by that open form found many descendants. Perhaps his most innovative and distinguished descendant was Williams. His poetic form depends on the line, which he wanted to contain rhythm within itself and which carried rhythm from line to line. Williams's lines vary in length, and in his later verse he experimented with a long line broken into three segments. A tension exists between Williams's need to vary the line, breaking or interrupting traditional linear form, and his need to retain the traces of formal poetic composition in the line, which can be deceptively simple.

Paterson has been received both positively and negatively by critics. The nature of modernism makes the construction of the long poem difficult by rejecting the forms that traditionally create coherence, such as transition, narrative sequentiality, and linearity. Modernist strategies in poetry, in keeping with trends in philosophy, art, sculpture, and music, interrupt or rupture formalist assumptions. The long modernist poem, typified by Eliot's *The Waste Land* (1922), consists of fragments juxtaposed against a unifying background of myth. In *Paterson* Dr. Paterson is Dr. Williams himself, who observes the city and comments on it. The poet celebrates the presence of masses of ordinary men and women but without sentimentality. Dr. Paterson helps organize the poem's fragments, which consist of persons from local legend and history, newspaper fragments and sections from history books, sections of verse, and unabridged letters from friends, all set against the background of industry, marriage, and language—subjects that were important to Williams throughout his life as a poet.

Suggested Readings: *The Tempers*, 1913. *Al Que Quiere!*, 1917. *Sour Grapes*, 1921. *Spring and All*, 1923. *In the American Grain*, 1925. *The Descent of Winter*, 1928. *The Knife of the Times*, 1932. *An Early Martyr*, 1935. *Adam and Eve and the City*, 1936. *White Mule*, 1937. *Life Along the Passaic River*, 1938. *In the Money*, 1940. *The Wedge*, 1944. *Paterson*, Bks. I–V, 1946–1963. *The Autobiography of William Carlos Williams*, 1951. *The Desert Music*, 1954. *Pictures From Brueghel and Other Poems*, 1962. B. Dijkstra, *The Hieroglyphics of a New Speech: Cubism, Stieglitz, and the Early Poetry of William Carlos Williams*, 1969. J. E. Breslin, *William Carlos Williams, An American Artist*, 1970. M. Weaver, *William Carlos Williams: The American Background*, 1971. P. L. Mariani, *William Carlos Williams: The Poet and His Critics*, 1976. R. Coles, *William Carlos Williams: The Knack of Survival*, 1980. P. L. Mariani, *William Carlos Williams: A New World Naked*, 1981.

Texts Used: "The Dance," "Burning the Christmas Greens," and "Landscape With the Fall of Icarus": *The Collected Poems of William Carlos Williams*, Vol. II: 1939–1962, ed. C. MacGowan, 1988. *Paterson*, Bk. II, 1963. All else: *The Collected Poems*, Vol. I: 1909–1939, ed. A. W. Litz and C. MacGowan.

POSTLUDE

Now that I have cooled to you
Let there be gold of tarnished masonry,
Temples soothed by the sun to ruin
That sleep utterly.

Give me hand for the dances,
Ripples at Philae,[1] in and out,
And lips, my Lesbian,[2]
Wall flowers that once were flame.

Your hair is my Carthage[3]
And my arms the bow,   10
And our words arrows
To shoot the stars
Who from that misty sea
Swarm to destroy us.

But you there beside me—
Oh how shall I defy you,
Who wound me in the night
With breasts shining
Like Venus and like Mars?[4]

---

[1] An island in the Nile River in Egypt, noted for its remains of ancient temples.

[2] A native or resident of Lesbos, an island in the Aegean Sea.

[3] An ancient city-state in North Africa, situated on the Mediterranean Sea; one of the largest cities in antiquity and a rival of Rome, with whom it engaged in three wars (the Punic Wars) between 264 B.C. and 146 B.C.

[4] According to Roman myth, the goddess of love and beauty and the god of war.

    The night that is shouting Jason[5]   20
    When the loud eaves rattle
    As with waves above me
    Blue at the prow of my desire.

    O, prayers in the dark!
    O, incense to Poseidon![6]
    Calm in Atlantis.[7]

                                1913

THE YOUNG HOUSEWIFE*

At ten A.M. the young housewife
moves about in negligee behind
the wooden walls of her husband's house.
I pass solitary in my car.

Then again she comes to the curb
to call the ice-man, fish-man, and stands
shy, uncorseted, tucking in
stray ends of hair, and I compare her
to a fallen leaf.

The noiseless wheels of my car   10
rush with a crackling sound over
dried leaves as I bow and pass smiling.

                           1916, 1917

TRACT†

I will teach you my townspeople
how to perform a funeral—
for you have it over a troop
of artists—
unless one should scour the world—
you have the ground sense necessary.

---

[5] According to Greek myth, the husband of Medea and leader of the Argonauts, who went in quest of the Golden Fleece.

[6] According to Greek myth, the god of the sea, earthquakes, and horses.

[7] A mythical island in the Atlantic Ocean; said by the Greek philosopher Plato to have sunk beneath the sea during an earthquake.

* Williams's note: "Whenever a man sees a beautiful woman it's an occasion for poetry—compensating beauty with beauty."

† Williams's note: "I was always searching for a regular format of the line, just as I wanted to be regular in my life—to conform. But I thought my friends were damn fools, because they didn't know any better way of conducting their lives. Still they conformed better than I to a code. I wanted to conform but I couldn't so I wrote my poetry."

See! the hearse leads.
I begin with a design for a hearse.
For Christ's sake not black—
nor white either—and not polished!   10
Let it be weathered—like a farm wagon—
with gilt wheels (this could be
applied fresh at small expense)
or no wheels at all:
a rough dray to drag over the ground.

Knock the glass out!
My God—glass, my townspeople!
For what purpose? Is it for the dead
to look out or for us to see
how well he is housed or to see   20
the flowers or the lack of them—
or what?
To keep the rain and snow from him?
He will have a heavier rain soon:
pebbles and dirt and what not.
Let there be no glass—
and no upholstery, phew!
and no little brass rollers
and small easy wheels on the bottom—
my townspeople what are you thinking of?   30

A rough plain hearse then
with gilt wheels and no top at all.
On this the coffin lies
by its own weight.

                    No wreaths please—
especially no hot house flowers.
Some common memento is better,
something he prized and is known by:
his old clothes—a few books perhaps—
God knows what! You realize   40
how we are about these things
my townspeople—
something will be found—anything
even flowers if he had come to that.
So much for the hearse.

For heaven's sake though see to the driver!
Take off the silk hat! In fact
that's no place at all for him—
up there unceremoniously
dragging our friend out to his own dignity!   50
Bring him down—bring him down!
Low and inconspicuous! I'd not have him ride
on the wagon at all—damn him—

the undertaker's understrapper!
Let him hold the reins
and walk at the side
and inconspicuously too!

Then briefly as to yourselves:
Walk behind—as they do in France,
seventh class, or if you ride   60
Hell take curtains! Go with some show
of inconvenience; sit openly—
to the weather as to grief.
Or do you think you can shut grief in?
What—from us? We who have perhaps
nothing to lose? Share with us
share with us—it will be money
in your pockets.

                    Go now
I think you are ready.   70

                                        1917

EL HOMBRE*

It's a strange courage
you give me ancient star:

Shine alone in the sunrise
toward which you lend no part!

                                        1917

PORTRAIT OF A LADY†

Your thighs are appletrees
whose blossoms touch the sky.
Which sky? The sky
where Watteau[1] hung a lady's
slipper. Your knees
are a southern breeze—or
a gust of snow. Agh! what

---

    * "The Man" (Spanish); Wallace Stevens's interpretation of this poem is his "Nuances of a Theme by Williams" (1919).
    † Compare this with T. S. Eliot's "Portrait of a Lady" (1915) and Ezra Pound's "Portrait d'une Femme" (1912).
    [1] Jean Antoine Watteau (1684–1721), a French Rococo artist who painted conventional shepherds and shepherdesses, rustic dances, and fashionably dressed lovers.

sort of man was Fragonard?[2]
—as if that answered
anything. Ah, yes—below   10
the knees, since the tune
drops that way, it is
one of those white summer days,
the tall grass of your ankles
flickers upon the shore—
Which shore?—
the sand clings to my lips—
Which shore?
Agh, petals maybe. How
should I know?   20
Which shore? Which shore?
I said petals from an appletree.

1920, 1934

THE LATE SINGER

Here it is spring again
and I still a young man!
I am late at my singing.
The sparrow with the black rain on his breast
has been at his cadenzas[1] for two weeks past:
What is it that is dragging at my heart?
The grass by the back door
is stiff with sap.
The old maples are opening
their branches of brown and yellow moth-flowers.   10
A moon hangs in the blue
in the early afternoons over the marshes.
I am late at my singing.

1921

OVERTURE TO A DANCE OF LOCOMOTIVES*

Men with picked voices chant the names
of cities in a huge gallery: promises
that pull through descending stairways
to a deep rumbling.

[2] Jean-Honoré Fragonard (1732–1806), a French painter and engraver; much in demand for his light-hearted and exquisite paintings of fashionable youths in amorous play with their mistresses and other subjects glorifying love and beauty. In Fragonard's *The Swing* (1766?) a girl has kicked her slipper into the air.

[1] Elaborate solo musical passages.

* Williams's note: "Pennsylvania Station."

The rubbing feet
of those coming to be carried quicken a
grey pavement into soft light that rocks
to and fro, under the domed ceiling,
across and across from pale
earthcolored walls of bare limestone.   10

Covertly the hands of a great clock
go round and round! Were they to
move quickly and at once the whole
secret would be out and the shuffling
of all ants be done forever.

A leaning pyramid of sunlight, narrowing
out at a high window, moves by the clock:
disaccordant hands straining out from
a center: inevitable postures infinitely
repeated—   20
two—twofour—twoeight!
Porters in red hats run on narrow platforms.
This way ma'am!
                    —important not to take
the wrong train!
                    Lights from the concrete
ceiling hang crooked but—
                    Poised horizontal
on glittering parallels the dingy cylinders
packed with a warm glow—inviting entry—   30
pull against the hour. But brakes can
hold a fixed posture till—
                    The whistle!

Not twoeight. Not twofour. Two!
Gliding windows. Colored cooks sweating
in a small kitchen. Taillights—

In time: twofour!
In time: twoeight!

—rivers are tunneled: trestles
cross oozy swampland: wheels repeating   40
the same gesture remain relatively
stationary: rails forever parallel
return on themselves infinitely.
                    The dance is sure.

                                    1920, 1921

SPRING AND ALL*

By the road to the contagious hospital
under the surge of the blue
mottled clouds driven from the
northeast—a cold wind. Beyond, the
waste of broad, muddy fields
brown with dried weeds, standing and fallen

patches of standing water
the scattering of tall trees

All along the road the reddish
purplish, forked, upstanding, twiggy   10
stuff of bushes and small trees
with dead, brown leaves under them
leafless vines—

Lifeless in appearance, sluggish
dazed spring approaches—

They enter the new world naked,
cold, uncertain of all
save that they enter. All about them
the cold, familiar wind—

Now the grass, tomorrow   20
the stiff curl of wildcarrot leaf

One by one objects are defined—
It quickens: clarity, outline of leaf

But now the stark dignity of
entrance—Still, the profound change
has come upon them: rooted, they
grip down and begin to awaken

1923

THE POT OF FLOWERS†

Pink confused with white
flowers and flowers reversed
take and spill the shaded flame
darting it back

---

* In *Spring and All* (1923) Williams identified poems by roman numerals; he later added titles and used the volume's title for the poem numbered I.
† Numbered II in the 1923 edition of *Spring and All*.

into the lamp's horn

petals aslant darkened with mauve

red where in whorls
petal lays its glow upon petal
round flamegreen throats

petals radiant with transpiercing light   10
contending
        above

the leaves
reaching up their modest green
from the pot's rim

and there, wholly dark, the pot
gay with rough moss.

1923

THE RED WHEELBARROW*

so much depends
upon

a red wheel
barrow

glazed with rain
water

beside the white
chickens

1923

THE WILDFLOWER†

Black eyed susan
rich orange
round the purple core

the white daisy

---

* Numbered XXII in the 1923 edition of *Spring and All*.
† The final poem, numbered XXVII, in the 1923 edition of *Spring and All*.

is not
enough

Crowds are white
as farmers
who live poorly

But you   10
are rich
in savagery—

Arab
Indian
dark woman

1923

THE ATTIC WHICH IS DESIRE*

the unused tent
of

bare beams
beyond which

directly wait
the night

and day—
Here

from the street
by   10

```
*   *   *
*   S   *
*   O   *
*   D   *
*   A   *
*   *   *
```

ringed with
running lights

the darkened
pane

---

* The poem describes the view from the window of Williams's attic study in Rutherford, New Jersey, including a visual imitation of a street sign.

exactly
down the center

is
transfixed

1930

THIS IS JUST TO SAY

I have eaten
the plums
that were in
the icebox

and which
you were probably
saving
for breakfast

Forgive me
they were delicious
so sweet
and so cold

10

1934

THE LOCUST TREE IN FLOWER

[First Version]

Among
the leaves
bright

green
of wrist-thick
tree

and old
stiff broken
branch

ferncool
swaying
loosely strung—

10

come May
again
white blossom

clusters
hide
to spill

their sweets
almost   20
unnoticed

down
and quickly
fall

1933

THE LOCUST TREE IN FLOWER

[*Second Version*]

Among
of
green

stiff
old
bright

broken
branch
come

white   10
sweet
May

again

1935

PROLETARIAN PORTRAIT

A big young bareheaded woman
in an apron

Her hair slicked back standing
on the street

One stockinged foot toeing
the sidewalk

Her shoe in her hand. Looking
intently into it

She pulls out the paper insole
to find the nail   10

That has been hurting her

1935

THE YACHTS*

contend in a sea which the land partly encloses
shielding them from the too-heavy blows
of an ungoverned ocean which when it chooses

tortures the biggest hulls, the best man knows
to pit against its beatings, and sinks them pitilessly.
Mothlike in mists, scintillant[1] in the minute

brilliance of cloudless days, with broad bellying sails
they glide to the wind tossing green water
from their sharp prows while over them the crew crawls

ant-like, solicitously grooming them, releasing,   10
making fast as they turn, lean far over and having
caught the wind again, side by side, head for the mark.

In a well guarded arena of open water surrounded by
lesser and greater craft which, sycophant, lumbering
and flittering follow them, they appear youthful, rare

as the light of a happy eye, live with the grace
of all that in the mind is fleckless, free and
naturally to be desired. Now the sea which holds them

is moody, lapping their glossy sides, as if feeling
for some slightest flaw but fails completely.   20
Today no race. Then the wind comes again. The yachts

---

* Williams's notes: "A *very* vague imitation of Dante. I was quickly carried away by my own feelings." "The yachts do not sink but go on with the race while only *in the imagination* are they seen to flounder. It is a false situation which the yachts typify with the beauty of their movements while the real situation (of the poor) is desperate while 'the skillful yachts pass over.'"
[1] Sparkling, brilliant.

move, jockeying for a start, the signal is set and they
are off. Now the waves strike at them but they are too
well made, they slip through, though they take in canvas.

Arms with hands grasping seek to clutch at the prows.
Bodies thrown recklessly in the way are cut aside.
It is a sea of faces about them in agony, in despair

until the horror of the race dawns staggering the mind,
the whole sea become an entanglement of watery bodies
lost to the world bearing what they cannot hold. Broken,   30

beaten, desolate, reaching from the dead to be taken up
they cry out, failing, failing! their cries rising
in waves still as the skillful yachts pass over.

1935

FINE WORK WITH PITCH AND COPPER

Now they are resting
in the fleckless light
separately in unison

like the sacks
of sifted stone stacked
regularly by twos

about the flat roof
ready after lunch
to be opened and strewn

The copper in eight   10
foot strips has been
beaten lengthwise

down the center at right
angles and lies ready
to edge the coping[1]

One still chewing
picks up a copper strip
and runs his eye along it

1936

---

[1] The top layer of a masonry wall; generally sloped to carry off water.

CLASSIC SCENE*

A power-house
in the shape of
a red brick chair
90 feet high

on the seat of which
sit the figures
of two metal
stacks—aluminum—

commanding an area
of squalid shacks   10
side by side—
from one of which

buff smoke
streams while under
a grey sky
the other remains

passive today—

1937

THE LAST WORDS OF MY ENGLISH GRANDMOTHER†

There were some dirty plates
and a glass of milk
beside her on a small table
near the rank, disheveled bed—

Wrinkled and nearly blind
she lay and snored
rousing with anger in her tones
to cry for food,

Gimme something to eat—
They're starving me—   10
I'm all right I won't go
to the hospital. No, no, no

Give me something to eat
Let me take you

* Williams is describing *Classic Landscape,* a painting by Charles Sheeler (1883–1965).
  † The maiden name of Williams's grandmother was probably Dickenson, but after discovering Emily Dickinson's poetry, Williams often used that spelling, saying "Emily Dickinson her name was. Isn't that amazing?"

to the hospital, I said
and after you are well

you can do as you please.
She smiled, Yes
you do what you please first
then I can do what I please—   20

Oh, oh, oh! she cried
as the ambulance men lifted
her to the stretcher—   .
Is this what you call

making me comfortable?
By now her mind was clear—
Oh you think you're smart
you young people,

she said, but I'll tell you
you don't know anything.   30
Then we started.
On the way

we passed a long row
of elms. She looked at them
awhile out of
the ambulance window and said,

What are all those
fuzzy-looking things out there?
Trees? Well, I'm tired
of them and rolled her head away.   40

1939

THE DANCE

In Brueghel's great picture, The Kermess,[1]
the dancers go round, they go round and
around, the squeal and the blare and the
tweedle of bagpipes, a bugle and fiddles
tipping their bellies (round as the thick-
sided glasses whose wash they impound)
their hips and their bellies off balance
to turn them. Kicking and rolling about
the Fair Grounds, swinging their butts, those
shanks must be sound to bear up under such   10

---

[1] *The Wedding Dance* (1566), by Pieter Brueghel the Elder (1525?–1569), a Flemish painter.

rollicking measures, prance as they dance
in Brueghel's great picture, The Kermess.

1944

BURNING THE CHRISTMAS GREENS

Their time past, pulled down
cracked and flung to the fire
—go up in a roar

All recognition lost, burnt clean
clean in the flame, the green
dispersed, a living red,
flame red, red as blood wakes
on the ash—

and ebbs to a steady burning
the rekindled bed become
a landscape of flame   10

At the winter's midnight
we went to the trees, the coarse
holly, the balsam and
the hemlock for their green

At the thick of the dark
the moment of the cold's
deepest plunge we brought branches
cut from the green trees

to fill our need, and over
doorways, about paper Christmas   20
bells covered with tinfoil
and fastened by red ribbons

we stuck the green prongs
in the windows hung
woven wreaths and above pictures
the living green. On the

mantle we built a green forest
and among those hemlock
sprays put a herd of small
white deer as if they   30

were walking there. All this!
and it seemed gentle and good
to us. Their time past,
relief! The room bare. We

stuffed the dead grate
with them upon the half burnt out
log's smoldering eye, opening
red and closing under them

and we stood there looking down.   40
Green is a solace
a promise of peace, a fort
against the cold (though we

did not say so) a challenge
above the snow's
hard shell. Green (we might
have said) that, where

small birds hide and dodge
and lift their plaintive
rallying cries, blocks for them   50
and knocks down

the unseeing bullets of
the storm. Green spruce boughs
pulled down by a weight of
snow—Transformed!

Violence leaped and appeared.
Recreant! roared to life
as the flame rose through and
our eyes recoiled from it.

In the jagged flames green   60
to red, instant and alive. Green!
those sure abutments . . . Gone!
lost to mind

and quick in the contracting
tunnel of the grate
appeared a world! Black
mountains, black and red—as

yet uncolored—and ash white,
an infant landscape of shimmering
ash and flame and we, in   70
that instant, lost,

breathless to be witnesses,
as if we stood
ourselves refreshed among
the shining fauna of that fire.

1944

from **PATERSON***

from **BOOK II: SUNDAY IN THE PARK**[1]

The descent beckons
              as the ascent beckoned
                          Memory is kind
of accomplishment
              a sort of renewal
                          even
an initiation, since the spaces it opens are new
places
              inhabited by hordes
                          heretofore unrealized,   10

of new kinds—
              since their movements
                          are towards new objectives
(even though formerly they were abandoned)

No defeat is made up entirely of defeat—since
the world it opens is always a place
              formerly
                          unsuspected. A
world lost,
              a world unsuspected   20
                          beckons to new places
and no whiteness (lost) is so white as the memory
of whiteness   •

With evening, love wakens
              though its shadows
                          which are alive by reason
of the sun shining—
              grow sleepy now and drop away
                          from desire   •

Love without shadows stirs now   30
              beginning to waken
                          as night
advances.

---

* Published in five books from 1946 to 1958; the unfinished portions of the sixth book were added as an appendix; all were published posthumously in 1963.
[1] In *I Wanted to Write a Poem* (1958), Williams explains that he thought this passage embodies the "final conception of what my own poetry should be; a passage which, sometime later, brought all my thinking about free verse to a head."

The descent
                    made up of despairs
                          and without accomplishment
realizes a new awakening   :
                                which is a reversal
of despair.

                    For what we cannot accomplish, what   40
is denied to love,
                    what we have lost in the anticipation—
                              a descent follows,
endless and indestructible   •

                              * * *

                    That the poem,
the most perfect rock and temple, the highest
falls, in clouds of gauzy spray, should be
so rivaled   •   that the poet,
in disgrace, should borrow from erudition (to   50
unslave the mind): railing at the vocabulary
(borrowing from those he hates, to his own
disfranchisement)   •
—discounting his failures   •
seeks to induce his bones to rise into a scene,
his dry bones, above the scene, (they will not)
illuminating it within itself, out of itself
to form the colors, in the terms of some
back street, so that the history may escape
the panders   60
•   •   accomplish the inevitable
poor, the invisible, thrashing, breeding
•   debased city

Love is no comforter, rather a nail in the
skull

•   reversed in the mirror of its
own squalor, debased by the divorce from learning,
its garbage on the curbs, its legislators
under the garbage, uninstructed, incapable of
self instruction   •
                                                           70

                    a thwarting, an avulsion   :

—flowers uprooted, columbine, yellow and red,
strewn upon the path; dogwoods in full flower,
the trees dismembered; its women
shallow, its men steadfastly refusing—at
the best   •

                    The language   •   words
        without style! whose scholars (there are none)
        •   or dangling, about whom
        the water weaves its strands encasing them
        in a sort of thick lacquer, lodged   80
        under its flow   •

                                    Caught (in mind)
        beside the water he looks down, listens!
        But discovers, still, no syllable in the confused
        uproar: missing the sense (though he tries)
        untaught but listening, shakes with the intensity
        of his listening   •

                                                1946–1948, 1948

        from   PICTURES FROM BRUEGHEL*

        II: LANDSCAPE WITH THE FALL OF ICARUS[1]

                    According to Brueghel[2]
                    when Icarus fell
                    it was spring

                    a farmer was ploughing
                    his field
                    the whole pageantry

                    of the year was
                    awake tingling
                    near

                    the edge of the sea   10
                    concerned
                    with itself

                    sweating in the sun
                    that melted
                    the wings' wax

                    unsignificantly
                    off the coast
                    there was

---

* Pieter Brueghel the Elder (1525?–1569), a Flemish painter.

[1] According to Greek myth, Icarus was a young man whose father, Daedalus, made wings for him, attached by wax. Icarus flew too near the sun; the wax melted, and he fell into the sea and drowned. His story symbolizes arrogance or over-reaching.

[2] Brueghel painted *Landscape With the Fall of Icarus* (1555?), in a corner of which Icarus's leg protrudes from the sea; a farmer ploughing and a delicate sailing ship nearby are unconcerned by his fall.

a splash quite unnoticed
this was   20
Icarus drowning

1962

═CONTEXTS═

Women Writers After World War I

During the years after World War I, feminist voices challenging the traditional roles of women began to meet increasing hostility in a society dominated by patriarchal values. Women's demands for greater personal freedom were met with the renewed insistence that women retain their traditional positions as wives, mothers, and up-holders of religious and domestic values, with few vocational opportunities or legal rights. In literary and academic circles, women's writing was devalued as sentimental and lacking in intellectual sophistication. At this time the reputations of such established female authors as Willa Cather and Edith Wharton began to decline, and many other women were excluded from the central canon of "serious" literature. The works of new modernist (predominantly male) poets, including T. S. Eliot and Ezra Pound, were admired by scholars for their difficulty and allusiveness. Many of the critics who acclaimed these male poets dismissed women's poetry as overly emotional and too personal. Even when women used modernist forms, as did Hilda Doolittle (H. D.), their work was generally seen as derivative and simplistic.

   The poetry of Edna St. Vincent Millay (1892–1950) refigures conventional images of women as poets of love and emotion. In her use of the sonnet form, traditionally a vehicle for conventional expressions of love, Millay at once invokes and debunks the expected perspective of women authors. By pointing out that love may not be the only important thing for women, the poem challenges the era's typical attitudes about women. Millay foregoes the accepted stance of the sentimental female poet, twisting the traditional love poem into an ironic examination of love's transience.

Love Is Not All

Love is not all; it is not meat nor drink
Nor slumber nor a roof against the rain
Nor yet a floating spar to men that sink
And rise and sink and rise and sink again;
Love can not fill the thickened lung with breath,
Nor clean the blood, nor set the fractured bone;
Yet many a man is making friends with death
Even as I speak, for lack of love alone.
It well may be that in a difficult hour,
Pinned down by pain and moaning for release,
Or nagged by want past resolution's power,
I might be driven to sell your love for peace,
Or trade the memory of this night for food.
It well may be. I do not think I would.

Edna St. Vincent Millay, 1931

Hilda Doolittle (H. D.)
(1886–1961)

Although Hilda Doolittle is best known as an imagist poet, this label inadequately describes the range of her literary voice. Following the more purely imagistic work in her first book of verse, *Sea Garden* (1916), she wrote epics, novels, plays, translations, essays, and memoirs, many of which remain unpublished or out of print. She left America in 1911, living in Europe through two wars and returning only on brief visits. She lived at the center of modernist literature in Paris and London among the major writers of her time, leaving her own indelible mark on the literature of the day.

Doolittle was born into a strict Moravian community in Bethlehem, Pennsylvania, in 1886 and lived there until she was nine. (The Moravians were a Protestant sect founded in the eighteenth century.) Her mother was an artist who taught painting and music; her father was a professor of astronomy. At age fifteen Doolittle met and fell in love with the poet Ezra Pound. Their relationship, portrayed in various poems, is also described in her prose memoir *End to Torment* (1958). After a brief engagement opposed by her parents and doomed by Pound's other romantic entanglements, the couple continued a difficult friendship for many years. Doolittle was indebted to Pound for encouraging her to read the classics, for introducing her to writers abroad, and for grabbing three poems out of her hand one afternoon in 1912 at the tea room in the British Museum. Recognizing that the poems exemplified and embodied poetic theories he and the poet T. E. Hulme were developing, Pound immediately revised the poems, scrawled "H. D., Imagiste" at the bottom, and sent them off to the founder of *Poetry* magazine, Harriet Monroe. In his letter to Monroe he called the poems "modern," "laconic," "objective," and "direct." The poems were published in January 1913, and imagism was born.

H. D.'s poems happened to correspond with Pound's theories about poetry, and a few months after the poems appeared he published his definition of imagism in an issue of *Poetry*. An image, Pound asserted, is "that which presents an intellectual and emotional complex in an instant of time." For all the audacity with which Pound remade Hilda Doolittle into H. D.—creating the imagist movement as a vehicle for promoting her work—he did launch her literary career and teach the public how to read her work. (The imagist movement, from which Pound fairly early disassociated himself, lasted until 1917, when the last imagist anthology was published.)

During the imagism years, H. D. was romantically involved with both men and women; she married the poet Richard Aldington in 1913. Two years later she delivered a still-born baby, and the marriage, troubled already, became intolerable to her. When Aldington entered the British army in 1916, H. D. became an editor of the *Egoist* and published *Sea Garden*. Aldington's affairs further damaged the marriage, and the couple separated in 1918 (and eventually divorced in 1937). From 1915 to 1918 she maintained an intense relationship with the novelist D. H. Lawrence, who abruptly broke with her. In 1918 H. D.'s brother died in combat in World War I; her father died soon after; she was separated from Aldington; Lawrence had recently abandoned her; and she was pregnant and suffering from severe influenza. After H. D. gave birth to a daughter, the financial and emotional assistance of a wealthy young admirer, Winifred Ellerman, gave the poet a new life. Ellerman, who wrote under the pen name Bryher, became H. D.'s lover and longtime friend. In her prose fiction *Palimpsest* (1926), H. D. dedicated Part VI of "Let Zeus Record" ("Stars wheel in purple") to Bryher. During the next few years H. D., her daughter, and Bryher traveled—notably to New York City, where they met the poet Marianne Moore, and to Greece and Crete, where H. D. had visionary experiences that were to inform her work thereafter. She continued to write, funded by money from her parents and from Bryher. H. D.'s *Collected Poems* was published in 1925. Between travels, she lived in London and in Switzerland (joined there by her ailing mother), remaining with Bryher through the 1920s and early 1930s.

In 1933 H. D. began to undergo psychoanalysis with Sigmund Freud and returned for a few months as a student as well as a patient in 1934. Through analysis she overcame the writer's block she had been experiencing and achieved a new understanding and a belief in herself as a writer. She recounts this profound experience in *Tribute to Freud* (1956), a prose work examining her search for the underlying patterns that guided her behavior and formed her identity. At Freud's insistence she also wrote about her time with Pound and with Aldington, recorded in *Bid Me to Live* (1960). Throughout the rest of the 1930s H. D. published poetry and prose as well as translations of the tragedies of Euripides.

Years of productivity followed, but in 1945 H. D. suffered a nervous breakdown. After six months of recovery in Switzerland her creativity was renewed. She finished her remarkable trilogy of *The Walls Do No Fall* (1944), *Tribute to Angels* (1945), and *Flowering of the Rod* (1946), works inspired by her years in London during World War II, in which she explores in long meditative poems the role of matriarchal goddesses and poets. Aside from various volumes of prose and poetry, she wrote her last important work, *Helen in Egypt* (1961), then. An epic based on variants of the Greek myth about Helen of Troy, *Helen in Egypt* interweaves poetry and prose as the poet explores Helen's search for identity.

The last years of H. D.'s life were spent alone, mainly in Swiss and Italian hotels. Toward the end of her life, when Pound was still at St. Elizabeth's Hospital in Washington, D.C., she renewed their correspondence, as she did later with Aldington. In fact, the renewal characterizing her later years extended to an awakened appreciation of her work. In 1960, a year before her death, H. D. became the first woman to win the poetry award of the American Academy of Arts and Letters. Although her poetry of the 1910s and 1920s had been highly praised, later critics typically complained of her move away from imagism. With the 1970s and 1980s revival of female writers, H. D. regained critical attention, although her Greek masks and myths remain a barrier to many readers. Her work in reinterpreting myths and telling the untold stories of mythic characters from the woman's perspective parallels the work of Louise Bogan and anticipates the poetry of Adrienne Rich, Muriel Rukeyser, and May Sarton.

Suggested Readings: *Palimpsest,* 1926. *Tribute to Freud,* 1956, 1974. *Bid Me to Live,* 1960, 1983. *Helen in Egypt,* 1961. *HERmione,* 1981. L. Freibert, "Conflict and Creativity in the World of H. D.," *Journal of Women's Studies in Literature,* 1 (Summer):258–271, 1979. S. S. Friedman, *Psyche Reborn: The Emergence of H. D.,* 1981. A. Ostriker, "The Thieves of Language: Women Poets and Revisionist Mythmaking," *Signs,* 9 (Autumn):68–90, 1982. J. S. Robinson, *H. D.: The Life and Work of an American Poet,* 1982. B. Guest, *Herself Defined: The Poet H. D. and Her World,* 1984.

Text Used: *Collected Poems: 1912–1944,* ed. L. L. Martz, 1983.

PEAR TREE

Silver dust
lifted from the earth,
higher than my arms reach,
you have mounted,
O silver,
higher than my arms reach
you front us with great mass;

no flower ever opened
so staunch a white leaf,
no flower ever parted silver   10
from such rare silver;

O white pear,
your flower-tufts
thick on the branch
bring summer and ripe fruits
in their purple hearts.

1916

AT BAIA*

I should have thought
in a dream you would have brought
some lovely, perilous thing,
orchids piled in a great sheath,
as who would say (in a dream)
I send you this,
who left the blue veins
of your throat unkissed.

Why was it that your hands
(that never took mine)   10
your hands that I could see
drift over the orchid heads
so carefully,
your hands, so fragile, sure to lift
so gently, the fragile flower stuff—
ah, ah, how was it

You never sent (in a dream)
the very form, the very scent,

* An ancient Roman resort fashionable because of its mild climate.

not heavy, not sensuous,
but perilous—perilous—   20
of orchids, piled in a great sheath,
and folded underneath on a bright scroll
some word:

Flower sent to flower;
for white hands, the lesser white,
less lovely of flower leaf,

or

Lover to lover, no kiss,
no touch, but forever and ever this.

1921

EVADNE*

I first tasted under Apollo's lips
love and love sweetness,
I Evadne;
my hair is made of crisp violets
or hyacinth which the wind combs back
across some rock shelf;
I Evadne
was mate of the god of light.

His hair was crisp to my mouth
as the flower of the crocus,   10
across my cheek,
cool as the silver cress
on Erotos[1] bank;
between my chin and throat
his mouth slipped over and over.

Still between my arm and shoulder,
I feel the brush of his hair,
and my hands keep the gold they took
as they wandered over and over
that great arm-full of yellow flowers.   20

1921

---

* According to Greek myth, a daughter of Poseidon, the sea god, and a mate of Apollo, the sun god, by whom she bore Iamus.
[1] From *eroto,* "sexual love" (Greek).

HELEN*

All Greece hates
the still eyes in the white face,
the lustre as of olives
where she stands,
and the white hands.

All Greece reviles
the wan face when she smiles,
hating it deeper still
when it grows wan and white,
remembering past enchantments   10
and past ills.

Greece sees unmoved,
God's daughter,[1] born of love,
the beauty of cool feet
and slenderest knees,
could love indeed the maid,
only if she were laid,
white ash amid funereal cypresses.

1924

FRAGMENT SIXTY-EIGHT

. . . even in the house of Hades. —Sappho.[1]

I

I envy you your chance of death,
how I envy you this.
I am more covetous of him
even than of your glance,
I wish more from his presence
though he torture me in a grasp,
terrible, intense.

Though he clasp me in an embrace
that is set against my will
and rack me with his measure,   10

---

* Helen of Troy, beautiful wife of King Menelaus of Greece; according to Greek myth, her abduction by the Trojan prince Paris led to the Trojan War, which Greece won.
[1] Helen was the daughter of the supreme god, Zeus, and Leda, a mortal woman.
[1] Sappho (6th century B.C.) was a Greek lyric poet ranked by the ancients with Homer. According to Greek myth, Hades was the Underworld of the dead.

effortless yet full of strength,
and slay me
in that most horrible contest,
still, how I envy you your chance.

Though he pierce me—imperious—
iron—fever—dust—
though beauty is slain
when I perish,
I envy you death.

What is beauty to me?   20
has she not slain me enough,
have I not cried in agony of love,
birth, hate,
in pride crushed?

What is left after this?
what can death loose in me
after your embrace?
your touch,
your limbs are more terrible
to do me hurt.   30

What can death mar in me
that you have not?

                    2

What can death send me
that you have not?
you gathered violets,
you spoke:
"your hair is not less black,
nor less fragrant,
nor in your eyes is less light,
your hair is not less sweet   40
with purple in the lift of lock;"
why were those slight words
and the violets you gathered
of such worth?

How I envy you death;
what could death bring,
more black, more set with sparks
to slay, to affright,
than the memory of those first violets,
the chance lift of your voice,   50
the chance blinding frenzy
as you bent?

3

So the goddess has slain me
for your chance smile
and my scarf unfolding
as you stooped to it;
so she trapped me
with the upward sweep of your arm
as you lifted the veil,
and the swift smile and selfless.   60

Could I have known?
nay, spare pity,
though I break,
crushed under the goddess' hate,
though I fall beaten at last,
so high have I thrust my glance
up into her presence.

Do not pity me, spare that,
but how I envy you
your chance of death.   70

                                        1924

from LET ZEUS RECORD

VI

Stars wheel in purple, yours[1] is not so rare
as Hesperus,[2] nor yet so great a star
as bright Aldebaran or Sirius,
nor yet the stained and brilliant one of War;[3]

stars turn in purple, glorious to the sight;
yours is not gracious as the Pleiads'[4] are
nor as Orion's sapphires, luminous;

yet disenchanted, cold, imperious face,
when all the others, blighted, reel and fall,
your star, steel-set, keeps lone and frigid tryst   10
to freighted ships, baffled in wind and blast.

                                        1926

---

[1] Here, the Pole Star, which remains fixed in the sky while the other stars move around the earth.
[2] The evening star, seen briefly at dusk.
[3] The planet Mars; according to Roman myth, Mars was the god of war.
[4] The Pleiades, seven stars in the constellation Taurus.

from SIGIL

XI

If you take the moon in your hands
and turn it round
(heavy, slightly tarnished platter)
you're there;

if you pull dry sea-weed from the sand
and turn it round
and wonder at the underside's bright amber,
your eyes

look out as they did here,
(you don't remember)   10
when my soul turned round,

perceiving the other-side of everything,
mullein-leaf,[1] dog-wood leaf, moth-wing
and dandelion-seed under the ground.

                                                    1931

from THE MYSTERIES*

Renaissance Choros[1]

VI

"The mysteries remain,
I keep the same
cycle of seed-time
and of sun and rain;
Demeter in the grass
I multiply,
renew and bless
Iacchus in the vine;
I hold the law,
I keep the mysteries true,   10
the first of these
to name the living, dead;
I am red wine and bread.

---

[1] A tall plant of the figwort family.
   * The Eleusinian mysteries of Greek myth: associated with the earth goddess Demeter and the god of wine, Dionysus (or Iacchus). At the celebration of the mysteries, Iacchus was represented carrying a torch, and the word "Iacchus" was repeated.
[1] A band of dancers or singers in ancient Greece.

> *I keep the law,*
> *I hold the mysteries true,*
> *I am the vine,*
> *the branches, you*
> *and you."*

> *1931*

Ezra Pound
(1885–1972)

Ezra Pound decisively affected the course of twentieth-century literature. Born in Hailey, Idaho, in 1885, Ezra Weston Loomis Pound and his family moved to Wyncote, Pennsylvania, a Philadelphia suburb, when he was less than two years old. "The Pound Era" began around the turn of the twentieth century, when Pound determined that by age thirty he would know more about poetry than anyone else living. He attended Hamilton College (in Clinton, New York) and the University of Pennsylvania, from which he earned an M.A. in 1906. Encouraged by his college friend William Carlos Williams and by his sweetheart, Hilda Doolittle (H. D.), Pound began a comprehensive study of poetry in English, Spanish, French, Italian, Provençal, Latin, and Greek (and later, Chinese). Pound's early friendship with two of the other major American poets of his generation helped put him at the center of artistic and intellectual activity, a position he occupied wherever he lived.

After four months of teaching at Wabash College in Indiana, Pound left for Venice in 1908, in part because of his disenchantment with academia and in part because of a scandal over a female overnight visitor. From there, with his first, self-published book of poetry in hand, he went to London. That book, *A Lume Spento* ("With Tapers Quenched" [1908]), was well received, and by the following year he had published three more. Making the acquaintance of the man whom he considered the finest living English-language poet, William Butler Yeats, Pound both learned from Yeats and taught him. In 1914 Pound married Dorothy Shakespear, the daughter of a friend of Yeats, and he served as Yeats's secretary for two winters between 1914 and 1916 at Stone Cottage, Sussex, England. Pound and Yeats exchanged views on writing, each altering his style as a result of the interaction.

The London years were frenetic: Pound lectured on romance literature, published several volumes of verse and criticism, translated medieval Italian poetry, and became foreign editor of the important new Chicago magazine *Poetry*. He championed the poetry of Hilda Doolittle through his association with the imagist movement, editing the anthology *Des Imagistes* (1914). Working with the notebooks of the Orientalist Ernest Fenollosa, Pound began an exploration of Chinese poetry and thought that would continue for fifty years. In 1914 and 1915 he was closely associated with the vorticist movement in the arts and with Wyndham Lewis's shocking new journal, *Blast*.

In 1915 Pound began writing his great work, *The Cantos*, which spanned from 1917 to 1959 and were collected in *The Cantos of Ezra Pound* (1986). From that time through the early 1920s Pound was an indefatigable advocate of the poems and prose of James Joyce and of the poetry and criticism of T. S. Eliot, and was instrumental in gaining attention for

From left to right, the Irish writer James Joyce, Ezra Pound, the English writer Ford Madox Ford, and the American lawyer and book collector John Quinn (who bought the manuscript of T. S. Eliot's The Waste Land*), in Pound's Paris studio in 1923.*

their work. He also became associated with the Socialist journal *The New Age* and began a slow conversion from aestheticism to social engagement, a change in his view of the role of the poet in society, hastened by the onset of World War I and its enormous waste of life and talent. Some of Pound's more extreme positions offended members of the British literary establishment, and he found many magazines closed to his work. After trying to make a living writing music criticism (under the pseudonym William Atheling), art criticism (under the pseudonym B. H. Dias), and literary criticism (in his own name) for *The New Age,* Pound left London for Paris at the end of 1920.

Paris after the war was the scene of intense American expatriate literary and artistic activity. Due to a favorable exchange rate, the cost of living was inexpensive, and Pound fitted in well. His own work, though, was not progressing, a result of his characteristic generosity toward other artists and of the excitement of a major metropolis. In 1924 he moved to Rapallo, a small resort town east of Genoa on the Italian Riviera, where he remained for the next twenty-one years. Rapallo was a conducive location for work, and Pound had finished his first thirty cantos by 1930, when the onset of the worldwide Great Depression revived his interests in politics and economics. Throughout the 1930s Pound increasingly became an active advocate of needed economic and monetary reform, advancing positions that, slightly ahead of their time, were thought eccentric by academic economists of the period.

More ominous was Pound's growing enthusiasm for anti-Semitism and for Italian fascism—sparked by the 1932 celebration of the tenth anniversary of the institution of fascism in Italy and by a private meeting with the charismatic Italian dictator Benito Mussolini in January 1933. Particularly after Italian banking-reform legislation was passed in 1936, Pound believed that Mussolini was putting into effect economic changes similar to those that the poet advocated, and his support for the Fascist regime grew. When World War II broke out in 1939 Pound found himself in a difficult position. With his wife, his companion (Olga Rudge), one of his children, and his parents all living in Italy, Pound found leaving Italy impossible. Out of personal conviction and the necessity of earning a living, he began working as a propagandist for Italian radio. When the United States entered the war late in 1941, Pound stopped broadcasting but resumed after a hiatus of several months. Indicted for radio treason by an American grand jury in July 1943, he was arrested in May 1945 and imprisoned for six months in a disciplinary training camp in Pisa, where he was held in a steel cage until he suffered a temporary physical and mental collapse.

Brought to Washington, D.C., Pound was found unfit to stand trial for reason of insanity and was confined to St. Elizabeth's Hospital, a sanitarium, until 1958. The publication of *The Pisan Cantos* (1948) earned him the first Bollingen Prize in 1949 and occasioned a storm of controversy over his wartime role. Through a constant stream of literary correspondence and visiting poets, the St. Elizabeth's years were productive ones for Pound, but he was also in contact with a group of racist and right-wing fanatics who did little to help his reputation as a political reactionary. Upon his release Pound returned to Italy where, after suffering ill health, he lapsed into depression and rarely spoke during the final years of his life. He died in Venice in 1972 and was buried there.

Apart from the Bollingen Prize and a $2000 award given by *The Dial* magazine in 1928, major honors eluded Pound during his lifetime. His importance as a poet could not be denied, but his support for the Italian Fascist regime and the anti-Semitism that surfaced in some of his work disturbed critics and readers, who responded by carefully partitioning his work from his life. Pound and his generation continue to have a major impact on both American and world poetry, and *The Cantos* in particular has survived the transition from the modern to the postmodern period remarkably well.

The Cantos, Pound's epic of fifty years' making, is a formidable piece of high modernist poetry, comparable in difficulty to James Joyce's *Ulysses* (1922). The verse is densely allusive with occasional fragments of Greek, Latin, Chinese, French, Italian, Spanish, and Provençal. *The Cantos* ranges through human history in Pound's search for high points of cultural achievement as well as for explanations of why civilizations decay. "Canto I" typifies his historical quest. Like Odysseus he offers blood for ghosts and will allow only those past figures who can offer important insights to speak. Pound had perhaps the most vivid historical imagination of any poet. When he presents a historical figure, such as Sigismundo Malatesta, the hero of Cantos VIII through XI, the reader enters the world of a fifteenth-century Italian condottiere (a mercenary soldier) whose violence in battle is accompanied by an aesthetic ideal that helps to initiate the Renaissance in Italy. The difficulties of reading *The Cantos* are formidable but only at first. Once a source is found, a quotation translated, or an allusion understood, the problems disappear. Pound is ultimately very precise and very clear.

Although Pound wrote some of the most beautiful lyric poetry in English, he was not primarily a lyric poet. A didactic poet, he took seriously the nineteenth century's claim that poets authoritatively address the largest concerns of their culture. He believed, with Percy Bysshe Shelley, that the poet is the unacknowledged legislator of the world. Pound's frequent allusions serve a serious point: he wishes the reader to go beyond *The Cantos* and consider and read the works of those poets to whom he alludes—Dante and Ovid, the philosophers Confucius and Karl Marx, and the politicians Thomas Jefferson and John Adams. Although *The Cantos,* with its open-ended nature and lengthy genesis, cannot be said to possess the organic form, a fusing of form and content, of many other works of literature, it does cohere. The reader who progresses through the poems and reads the books Pound recommends acquires a true liberal education. The references, repeated and varied, become clearer, the meaning more precise. *The Cantos* are also what T. S. Eliot called "a reticent autobiography," presenting the record of the life of one man, a man who was in contact with the most vital currents of twentieth-century art, literature, and thought.

Pound's poetry is collected in three volumes: *Collected Early Poems of Ezra Pound* (1982), *Personae* (1990), Pound's own choice of the short poems he wished to remain in print, and his life's work, *The Cantos.* His poetic practice was attentive to the role of translation in a nation's literature. He produced several volumes of translation, most notably *The Translations of Ezra Pound* (1953) and the works of Confucius (*Confucius* [1969] and *Shih-Ching* [1954]).

There is no denying Pound's central position in twentieth-century literature. We need only consider Pound's role as a critic. For Pound, who went back to the Greek root of the word, a critic is someone who chooses, someone who determines what work is good and worthy of attention, and what is spurious and outmoded. Pound discovered, fostered, and taught the following writers: Basil Bunting, Hilda Doolittle (whom he renamed H. D.), T. S. Eliot, Ernest Hemingway, James Joyce, Marianne Moore, Robert Frost, William Carlos Williams, and Louis Zukofsky. In some measure they all owe their success to Pound. Without question he was the preeminent critic of his century, perhaps of any century.

Beyond that, he served his art. When he first began his study he found poetry lagging behind the prose art of novelists such as Gustave Flaubert and Stendhal (Marie-Henri Beyle); by the 1920s Pound had restored it to renewed status and seriousness. For Pound was a serious artist, and his understanding of the techniques of verse has never been matched. Through his translations he brought into English poetry the attained maxima in the three effects he considered most essential to poetry: melopoeia, the art of musically charging language (in which he was unsurpassed); phanopoeia, the art of visually charging language; and logopoeia, the art of charging language through the interplay of word connotations. Pound's criticism was addressed to the young, and if there exists a single place where young poets can turn to learn all the possibilities of their craft, that place is in the work of Ezra Pound, who by his criticism and practice so greatly enhanced the resources of the poet's art and so energetically revitalized the English language.

Suggested Readings: *Personae,* 1909. *Hugh Selwyn Mauberley,* 1920. *Selected Poems,* ed. T. S. Eliot, 1928. *ABC of Reading,* 1934. *Make It New,* 1934. *Pisan Cantos,* 1948. *Patria Mia,* 1950. *The Cantos of Ezra Pound,* 1964, rpt. 1986. *Literary Essays,* ed. T. S. Eliot, 1968. *Confucius: The Great Digest, The Unwobbling Pivot, The Analects,* 1969. *Late Cantos and Fragments,* 1969. *Pound-Joyce: Letters and Essays,* 1970. *Selected Letters, 1907–1941,* ed. D. D. Paige, 1951. *Collected Early Poems,* 1982. H. Kenner, *The Poetry of Ezra Pound,* 1951. C. Emery, *Ideas Into Action: A Study of Pound's Cantos,* 1958. E. Davis, *Vision Fugitive: Ezra Pound's Economics,* 1968. K. K. Ruthven, *A Guide to Ezra Pound's Personae,* 1969. H. Witemeyer, *The Poetry of Ezra Pound: Forms and Renewal, 1908–1920,* 1969. N. Stock, *The Life of Ezra Pound,* 1970. M. Alexander, *The Poetic Achievement of Ezra Pound,* 1979. C. F. Terrell, *A Companion to the Cantos of Ezra Pound,* 2 vols., 1980, 1984. I. F. A. Bell, *Critic as Scientist: The Modernist Poetics of Ezra Pound,* 1981. D. Gallup, *Ezra Pound: A Bibliography,* 1983. H. Carpenter, *A Serious Character,* 1988.

Texts Used: *The Cantos of Ezra Pound,* 1986. All else: *Personae: The Shorter Poems of Ezra Pound,* ed. L. Baechler and A. W. Litz, 1990.

THE TREE

I stood still and was a tree amid the wood,
Knowing the truth of things unseen before;
Of Daphne[1] and the laurel bow
And that god-feasting couple old
That grew elm-oak amid the wold.
'Twas not until the gods had been
Kindly entreated, and been brought within
Unto the hearth of their heart's home
That they might do this wonder thing;
Nathless[2] I have been a tree amid the wood   10
Any many a new thing understood
That was rank folly to my head before.

1908

SESTINA: ALTAFORTE*

LOQUITUR: *En* Bertrans de Born.[1]
    Dante Alighieri[2] put this man in hell for that he was a stirrer
up of strife.
    Eccovi![3]
    Judge ye!
    Have I dug him up again?
The scene is at his castle, Altaforte. "Papiols" is his jongleur.[4]
"The Leopard," the *device* of Richard Cœur de Lion.[5]

I

Damn it all! all this our South stinks peace.
You whoreson dog, Papiols, come! Let's to music!
I have no life save when the swords clash.
But ah! when I see the standards gold, vair, purple, opposing
And the broad fields beneath them turn crimson,
Then howl I my heart nigh mad with rejoicing.

[1] According to Greek myth, the nymph Daphne is changed into a laurel tree to escape the sun god Apollo, who is pursuing her.
[2] Nonetheless.
* "Very loud" (Italian); the sestina is one of the most difficult poetic forms because it is based on a fixed pattern of line endings. Pound departs from the form slightly in Stanza IV (l. 21 should end with "music," and l. 22, with "rejoicing") and more noticeably in Stanza VII (which should have six lines, with all six end words used).
[1] "Speaker" (Latin): Lord Bertrans de Born.
[2] The Italian poet Dante (1265–1321), best known for his *Divine Comedy,* which describes a journey through Hell, Purgatory, and Paradise.
[3] "Here you are" (Italian).
[4] "Juggler" (French).
[5] "Richard the Lion-Hearted" (French): Richard I (1157–1199), king of England from 1189 to 1199.

II

In hot summer have I great rejoicing
When the tempests kill the earth's foul peace,
And the lightnings from black heav'n flash crimson,
And the fierce thunders roar me their music   10
And the winds shriek through the clouds mad, opposing,
And through all the riven skies God's swords clash.

III

Hell grant soon we hear again the swords clash!
And the shrill neighs of destriers in battle rejoicing,
Spiked breast to spiked breast opposing!
Better one hour's stour[6] than a year's peace
With fat boards, bawds, wine and frail music!
Bah! there's no wine like the blood's crimson!

IV

And I love to see the sun rise blood-crimson.
And I watch his spears through the dark clash   20
And it fills all my heart with rejoicing
And pries wide my mouth with fast music
When I see him so scorn and defy peace,
His lone might 'gainst all darkness opposing.

V

The man who fears war and squats opposing
My words for stour, hath no blood of crimson
But is fit only to rot in womanish peace
Far from where worth's won and the swords clash
For the death of such sluts I go rejoicing;
Yea, I fill all the air with my music.   30

VI

Papiols, Papiols, to the music!
There's no sound like to swords swords opposing,
No cry like the battle's rejoicing
When our elbows and swords drip the crimson
And our charges 'gainst "The Leopard's" rush clash.
May God damn for ever all who cry "Peace!"

---

[6] Combat, conflict.

VII

And let the music of the swords make them crimson!
Hell grant soon we hear again the swords clash!
Hell blot black for alway the thought "Peace"!

1909

PORTRAIT D'UNE FEMME*

Your mind and you are our Sargasso Sea,[1]
London has swept about you this score years
And bright ships left you this or that in fee:
Ideas, old gossip, oddments of all things,
Strange spars of knowledge and dimmed wares of price.
Great minds have sought you—lacking someone else.
You have been second always. Tragical?
No. You preferred it to the usual thing:
One dull man, dulling and uxorious,
One average mind—with one thought less, each year.   10
Oh, you are patient, I have seen you sit
Hours, where something might have floated up.
And now you pay one. Yes, you richly pay.
You are a person of some interest, one comes to you
And takes strange gain away:
Trophies fished up; some curious suggestion;
Fact that leads nowhere; and a tale or two,
Pregnant with mandrakes,[2] or with something else
That might prove useful and yet never proves,
That never fits a corner or shows use,   20
Or finds its hour upon the loom of days:
The tarnished, gaudy, wonderful old work;
Idols and ambergris[3] and rare inlays,
These are your riches, your great store; and yet
For all this sea-hoard of deciduous things,
Strange woods half sodden, and new brighter stuff:
In the slow float of differing light and deep,
No! there is nothing! In the whole and all,
Nothing that's quite your own.
                    Yet this is you.   30

1912

* "Portrait of a Lady" (French).
[1] A North Atlantic sea noted for its abundant seaweed, thought to entrap ships.
[2] The forked root of the mandrake, a plant in the nightshade family, was thought to promote conception.
[3] A waxy substance, from the intestines of sperm whales, that is used in perfumes.

THE SEAFARER*

From the Anglo-Saxon

May I for my own self song's truth reckon,
Journey's jargon, how I in harsh days
Hardship endured oft.
Bitter breast-cares have I abided,
Known on my keel many a care's hold,
And dire sea-surge, and there I oft spent
Narrow nightwatch nigh the ship's head
While she tossed close to cliffs. Coldly afflicted,
My feet were by frost benumbed.
Chill its chains are; chafing sighs   10
Hew my heart round and hunger begot
Mere-weary[1] mood. Lest man know not
That he on dry land loveliest liveth,
List how I, care-wretched, on ice-cold sea,
Weathered the winter, wretched outcast
Deprived of my kinsmen;
Hung with hard ice-flakes, where hail-scur[2] flew,
There I heard naught save the harsh sea
And ice-cold wave, at whiles the swan cries,
Did for my games the gannet's[3] clamour,   20
Sea-fowls' loudness was for me laughter,
The mews'[4] singing all the mead-drink.[5]
Storms, on the stone-cliffs beaten, fell on the stern
In icy feathers; full oft the eagle screamed
With spray on his pinion.[6]
                              Not any protector
May make merry man faring needy.
This he little believes, who aye in winsome life
Abides 'mid burghers[7] some heavy business,
Wealthy and wine-flushed, how I weary oft
Must bide above brine.   30
Neareth nightshade, snoweth from north,
Frost froze the land, hail fell on earth then,
Corn of the coldest. Nathless[8] there knocketh now
The heart's thought that I on high streams
The salt-wavy tumult traverse alone.
Moaneth alway my mind's lust

---

* A "major persona" for Pound. This free translation of an Old English poem anticipates Pound's
Canto I (1925). Pound excised the Christian and moralizing passages from the original, thinking they
were later additions.
[1] Sea-weary.   [2] Hailstones.   [3] A large, fish-eating seabird.   [4] Gulls'.
[5] An alcoholic drink made of fermented honey and water.   [6] Wing.
[7] Townsmen.   [8] Nevertheless.

That I fare forth, that I afar hence
Seek out a foreign fastness.
For this there's no moody-lofty man over earth's midst,
Not though he be given his good, but will have in his youth greed;　　40
Nor his deed to the daring, nor his king to the faithful
But shall have his sorrow for sea-fare
Whatever his lord will.
He hath not heart for harping, nor in ring-having
Nor winsomeness to wife, nor world's delight
Nor any whit else save the wave's slash,
Yet longing comes upon him to fare forth on the water.
Bosque[9] taketh blossom, cometh beauty of berries,
Fields to fairness, land fares brisker,
All this admonisheth man eager of mood,　　50
The heart turns to travel so that he then thinks
On flood-ways to be far departing.
Cuckoo calleth with gloomy crying,
He singeth summerward, bodeth sorrow,
The bitter heart's blood. Burgher knows not—
He the prosperous man—what some perform
Where wandering them widest draweth.
So that but now my heart burst from my breastlock,
My mood 'mid the mere-flood,[10]
Over the whale's acre,[11] would wander wide.　　60
On earth's shelter cometh oft to me,
Eager and ready, the crying lone-flyer,
Whets for the whale-path the heart irresistibly,
O'er tracks of ocean; seeing that anyhow
My lord deems to me this dead life
On loan and on land, I believe not
That any earth-weal[12] eternal standeth
Save there be somewhat calamitous
That, ere a man's tide go, turn it to twain.
Disease or oldness or sword-hate　　70
Beats out the breath from doom-gripped body.
And for this, every earl whatever, for those speaking after—
Laud of the living, boasteth some last word,
That he will work ere he pass onward,
Frame on the fair earth 'gainst foes his malice,
Daring ado, . . .
So that all men shall honour him after
And his laud beyond them remain 'mid the English,
Aye, for ever, a lasting life's-blast,
Delight 'mid the doughty.[13]　　80
　　　　　Days little durable,

---

[9] A small wood or thicket.　　[10] Tide.
[11] An example of a kenning, a metaphorical compound word or phrase used especially in Old English and Old Norse poetry.
[12] Earthly wealth.　　[13] Valiant.

And all arrogance of earthen riches,
There come now no kings nor Cæsars
Nor gold-giving lords like those gone.
Howe'er in mirth most magnified,
Whoe'er lived in life most lordliest,
Drear[14] all this excellence, delights undurable!
Waneth the watch, but the world holdeth.
Tomb hideth trouble. The blade is layed low.
Earthly glory ageth and seareth.   90
No man at all going the earth's gait,
But age fares against him, his face paleth,
Grey-haired he groaneth, knows gone companions,
Lordly men, are to earth o'ergiven,
Nor may he then the flesh-cover, whose life ceaseth,
Nor eat the sweet nor feel the sorry,[15]
Nor stir hand nor think in mid heart,
And though he strew the grave with gold,
His born brothers, their buried bodies
Be an unlikely treasure hoard.   100

1912

THE RETURN*

See, they return; ah, see the tentative
Movements, and the slow feet,
The trouble in the pace and the uncertain
Wavering!

See, they return, one, and by one,
With fear, as half-awakened;
As if the snow should hesitate
And murmur in the wind,
             and half turn back;
These were the "Wing'd-with-Awe,"   10
             Inviolable.

Gods of the winged shoe![1]
With them the silver hounds,
             sniffing the trace of air!

Haie! Haie![2]
             These were the swift to harry;

---

[14] Dreary.   [15] Sorrow.
* Considered by the Irish writer William Butler Yeats (1865–1939) the most beautiful free verse poem in English.
[1] The Greek god Hermes and the Roman god Mercury, who served as messengers to the other gods.
[2] A French exclamation for calling the hounds to get in line.

These the keen-scented;
These were the souls of blood.

Slow on the leash,
pallid the leash-men!   20

1912

TENZONE*

Will people accept them?
(i.e. these songs).
As a timorous wench[1] from a centaur[2]
(or a centurion[3]),
Already they flee, howling in terror.

Will they be touched with the verisimilitudes?[4]
Their virgin stupidity is untemptable.
I beg you, my friendly critics,
Do not set about to procure me an audience.

I mate with my free kind upon the crags;   10
the hidden recesses
Have heard the echo of my heels,
in the cool light,
in the darkness.

1913

THE GARDEN

En robe de parade. —SAMAIN[1]

Like a skein[2] of loose silk blown against a wall
She walks by the railing of a path in Kensington Gardens,[3]
And she is dying piece-meal[4]
of a sort of emotional anæmia.

And round about there is a rabble
Of the filthy, sturdy, unkillable infants of the very poor.
They shall inherit the earth.

---

* From the Provençal *tenson:* a poem in the form of a debate or a dialogue, frequently between rival poets (Italian); here, between the poet and society.

[1] A young woman.
[2] According to Greek myth, a creature who is half man, half horse.
[3] An officer commanding a Roman century, or subdivision of a Roman legion.
[4] The truths.

[1] "Dressed for an outing" (French), from *Au Jardin de l'Infante* (1893), by Albert Samain (1858–1900).

[2] A coil.   [3] A large public park in London.   [4] Gradually.

In her is the end[5] of breeding.
Her boredom is exquisite and excessive.
She would like some one to speak to her,   10
And is almost afraid that I
      will commit that indiscretion.

1913

LES MILLWIN*

The little Millwins attend the Russian Ballet.[1]
The mauve and greenish souls of the little Millwins
Were seen lying along the upper seats
Like so many unused boas.

The turbulent and undisciplined host of art students—
The rigorous deputation from "Slade"[2]—
Was before them.

With arms exalted, with fore-arms
Crossed in great futuristic X's,[3] the art students
Exulted, they beheld the splendours of *Cleopatra*.   10

And the little Millwins beheld these things;
With their large and anæmic eyes they looked out upon this configuration.

Let us therefore mention the fact,
For it seems to us worthy of record.

1913

LIU CH'E†

The rustling of the silk is discontinued,
Dust drifts over the court-yard,
There is no sound of foot-fall, and the leaves
Scurry into heaps and lie still,
And she the rejoicer of the heart is beneath them:

A wet leaf that clings to the threshold.

1914

---

[5] Here, both result and finish.
* "The Millwins" (French).
[1] The artistic sensation of Western Europe, Sergei Diaghilev's Ballet Russe performed in London in 1912 and 1913.
[2] The Slade School of Art in London.
[3] Originating in Italy in 1909, futurism was an international movement in the arts that rejected the past and admired the violence, speed, and power of the machine age.
† According to T. S. Eliot, Pound was the inventor of Chinese poetry in our time. Here, the sparse style presents a situation but leaves to the reader the task of drawing conclusions. The Chinese emperor Liu Ch'e (156–87 B.C.), Pound believed, was a fellow imagist.

IN A STATION OF THE METRO*

The apparition of these faces in the crowd;
Petals on a wet, black bough.

1913, 1916

THE RIVER-MERCHANT'S WIFE: A LETTER†

While my hair was still cut straight across my forehead[1]
I played about the front gate, pulling flowers.
You came by on bamboo stilts, playing horse,
You walked about my seat, playing with blue plums.
And we went on living in the village of Chokan:[2]
Two small people, without dislike or suspicion.

At fourteen I married My Lord you.
I never laughed, being bashful.
Lowering my head, I looked at the wall.
Called to, a thousand times, I never looked back.   10

At fifteen I stopped scowling,
I desired my dust to be mingled with yours
Forever and forever and forever.
Why should I climb the look out?

At sixteen you departed,
You went into far Ku-to-en,[3] by the river of swirling eddies,
And you have been gone five months.
The monkeys make sorrowful noise overhead.

You dragged your feet when you went out.
By the gate now, the moss is grown, the different mosses,   20
Too deep to clear them away!
The leaves fall early this autumn, in wind.
The paired butterflies are already yellow with August
Over the grass in the West garden;
They hurt me. I grow older.
If you are coming down through the narrows of the river Kiang,[4]
Please let me know beforehand,
And I will come out to meet you
                    As far as Cho-fū-Sa.[5]

By Rihaku[6]
1915

---

* The Paris subway.
† Translated and adapted from a Chinese poem by Li Po (701–762).   [1] As a child.
[2] Ch'ang-kan, a suburb of Nanking.   [3] Yen-yu-tui, an island in the dangerous river Ch'u-t'ang.
[4] The river Ch'u-t'ang.   [5] Ch'ang-feng-sha, several hundred miles up river from Nanking.
[6] The Japanese name of Li Po.

LAMENT OF THE FRONTIER GUARD*

By the North Gate, the wind blows full of sand,
Lonely from the beginning of time until now!
Trees fall, the grass goes yellow with autumn.
I climb the towers and towers
       to watch out the barbarous land:
Desolate castle, the sky, the wide desert.
There is no wall left to this village.
Bones white with a thousand frosts,
High heaps, covered with trees and grass;
Who brought this to pass?   10
Who has brought the flaming imperial anger?
Who has brought the army with drums and with kettle-drums?
Barbarous kings.
A gracious spring, turned to blood-ravenous autumn,
A turmoil of wars-men, spread over the middle kingdom,
Three hundred and sixty thousand,
And sorrow, sorrow like rain.
Sorrow to go, and sorrow, sorrow returning.
Desolate, desolate fields,
And no children of warfare upon them,   20
       No longer the men for offence and defence.
Ah, how shall you know the dreary sorrow at the
       North Gate,
With Riboku's[1] name forgotten,
And we guardsmen fed to the tigers.

                                      By Rihaku[2]
                                      1915

HUGH SELWYN MAUBERLEY

(Contacts and Life)†

"Vocat æstus in umbram" —NEMESIANUS, Ec. IV.[1]

E. P. ODE POUR L'ELECTION DE SON SEPULCHRE[2]

For three years, out of key with his time,
He strove to resuscitate the dead art

---

* Translated and adapted from a Chinese poem by Li Po (701–762); it appeared in Pound's book *Cathay* (1915), published to great acclaim. Its depiction of the harshness of the soldier's life during World War I was praised for its accuracy by Pound's friends in the trenches.
[1] The general Li Mu, who died in battle in 223 B.C. defending China against the Tartars of Asia.
[2] The Japanese name of Li Po.
† Pound's "farewell to London"; originally subtitled "Life and Contacts," it was reversed to reflect more accurately the relationship between the poem's two halves.
[1] "The heat calls [us] into the shade" (Latin); Nemesianus (4th century A.D.), or Marcus Aurelius Olympus, was a poet from Carthage who wrote in Latin.
[2] "E. P. Ode on the Selection of His Tomb" (French).

Of poetry; to maintain "the sublime"
In the old sense. Wrong from the start—

No, hardly, but seeing he had been born
In a half savage country, out of date;
Bent resolutely on wringing lilies from the acorn;
Capaneus;[3] trout for factitious bait;

Ἰδμεν γάρ τοι πάνθ', ὅα' ἐνὶ Τροίη[4]
Caught in the unstopped ear;   10
Giving the rocks small lee-way
The chopped seas held him, therefore, that year.

His true Penelope[5] was Flaubert,[6]
He fished by obstinate isles;
Observed the elegance of Circe's[7] hair
Rather than the mottoes on sun-dials.

Unaffected by "the march of events,"
He passed from men's memory in *l'an trentuniesme*
De son eage,[8] the case presents
No adjunct to the Muses'[9] diadem.   20

II

The age demanded an image
Of its accelerated grimace,
Something for the modern stage,
Not, at any rate, an Attic[10] grace;

Not, not certainly, the obscure reveries
Of the inward gaze;
Better mendacities
Than the classics in paraphrase!

The "age demanded" chiefly a mould in plaster,
Made with no loss of time,   30

---

[3] According to Greek myth, one of the "Seven against Thebes," struck down by the supreme god, Zeus, for defiance and blasphemy.

[4] "For we know all that is in Troy" (Greek); first line of the song the Sirens (sea nymphs who lured sailors to their death) sang to Odysseus in Homer's *Odyssey* (XII.189).

[5] According to Greek myth, the wife of Odysseus, who remained faithful to him in his absence despite the many suitors who pursued her.

[6] Gustave Flaubert (1821–1880), a French novelist much admired by Pound.

[7] According to Greek myth, a sorceress who detained Odysseus for a year.

[8] "The thirty-first year of his life" (French), adapted from *Le Grand Testament* (1461), by the French poet François Villon (1431–1463?).

[9] According to Greek myth, nine goddesses who presided over literature and the arts and sciences.

[10] Characteristic of ancient Attica, or Athens.

A prose kinema,[11] not, not assuredly, alabaster
Or the "sculpture" of rhyme.

III

The tea-rose tea-gown, etc.
Supplants the mousseline of Cos,[12]
The pianola "replaces"
Sappho's barbitos.[13]

Christ follows Dionysus,[14]
Phallic and ambrosial
Made way for macerations;[15]
Caliban casts out Ariel.[16]   40

All things are a flowing,
Sage Heracleitus[17] says;
But a tawdry cheapness
Shall outlast our days.

Even the Christian beauty
Defects—after Samothrace;[18]
We see τὸ καλόν[19]
Decreed in the market place.

Faun's flesh is not to us,
Nor the saint's vision.   50
We have the press for wafer;
Franchise for circumcision.

All men, in law, are equals.
Free of Pisistratus,[20]
We choose a knave or an eunuch
To rule over us.

O bright Apollo,
τίν' ἄνδρα, τίν' ἥρωα, τίνα θεόν,[21]
What god, man, or hero
Shall I place a tin wreath upon!   60

[11] Cinema, stressing its root in the Greek word for movement.
[12] The muslin of Cos, a Greek island known in antiquity for its fine cloth.
[13] The lyre of the Greek lyric poet Sappho (6th century B.C.).
[14] According to Greek myth, the god of fertility and wine.   [15] Religious fasting.
[16] In Shakespeare's *The Tempest* Caliban is "savage and deformed" and Ariel, "an airy sprite." The brutish supplants the spiritual.
[17] A sixth-century B.C. Greek philosopher who taught that reality is flux, or change.
[18] A Greek island noted in antiquity for its worship of Dionysus; site of the statue "Winged Victory."
[19] "The beautiful" (Greek).   [20] A sixth-century B.C. Athenian tyrant and patron of the arts.
[21] "What man, what hero, what god" (Greek): Pound's version of one of the *Olympian Odes* by the Greek lyric poet Pindar (522?–442 B.C.).

IV

These fought in any case,
and some believing,
        pro domo,[22] in any case . . .

Some quick to arm,
some for adventure,
some from fear of weakness,
some from fear of censure,
some for love of slaughter, in imagination,
learning later . . .
some in fear, learning love of slaughter;   70

Died some, pro patria,
        non "dulce" non "et decor"[23] . . .
walked eye-deep in hell
believing in old men's lies, then unbelieving
came home, home to a lie,
home to many deceits,
home to old lies and new infamy;
usury age-old and age-thick
and liars in public places.   80

Daring as never before, wastage as never before.
Young blood and high blood,
fair cheeks, and fine bodies;

fortitude as never before

frankness as never before,
disillusions as never told in the old days,
hysterias, trench confessions,
laughter out of dead bellies.

V

There died a myriad,
And of the best, among them,   90
For an old bitch gone in the teeth,
For a botched civilization,

Charm, smiling at the good mouth,
Quick eyes gone under earth's lid,

---

[22] "For home" (Latin); the ellipses are Pound's.
[23] "For your homeland it is not sweet, not fitting to die" (Latin): an ironic adaptation of "It is sweet and fitting to die for one's own country" (*Odes,* XII.ii.13), by the Roman poet Horace (65–8 B.C.).

For two gross of broken statues,
For a few thousand battered books.

YEUX GLAUQUES*

Gladstone[1] was still respected,
When John Ruskin[2] produced
"Kings' Treasuries"; Swinburne[3]
And Rossetti[4] still abused.

Fœtid Buchanan[5] lifted up his voice
When that faun's head of hers[6]
Became a pastime for
Painters and adulterers.

The Burne-Jones cartons[7]
Have preserved her eyes;   10
Still, at the Tate, they teach
Cophetua to rhapsodize;

Thin like brook-water,
With a vacant gaze.
The English Rubaiyat[8] was still-born
In those days.

The thin, clear gaze, the same
Still darts out faun like from the half-ruin'd face,
Questing and passive. . . .
"Ah, poor Jenny's case"[9] . . .   20

Bewildered that a world
Shows no surprise
At her last maquero's[10]
Adulteries.

---

* "Sea-green eyes" (French); this poem describes the reception of the pre-Raphaelite artistic movement in England during the 1860s and 1870s. The ellipses are Pound's.
[1] William Gladstone (1809–1900), prime minister of England (1868–1874; 1880–1885; 1886; 1892–1894).
[2] Ruskin (1819–1900), an English art critic and social commentator, attacked British lack of culture.
[3] Algernon Charles Swinburne (1837–1909), an English poet admired by Pound.
[4] Dante Gabriel Rossetti (1838–1882), an English poet and painter; a powerful early influence on Pound.
[5] Robert Buchanan (1841–1901), a reviewer whose attack on the pre-Raphaelites, "The Fleshy School of Poetry" (1871), caused a great stir.
[6] Elizabeth Siddal, a green-eyed painter's model who later became Rossetti's wife.
[7] Sir Edward Burne-Jones (1833–1898), an English painter whose *Cophetua and the Beggar Maid*, for which Siddal was used as a model, is now at the Tate Gallery in London; *cartons* (French) are sketches.
[8] Edward Fitzgerald's translation of *The Rubaiyat of Omar Khayyam* (1859), ignored until Rossetti discovered it later.
[9] "Jenny," a Rossetti poem about a prostitute.
[10] Pimp (from the French *maquereau*).

"Siena Mi Fe'; Disfecemi Maremma"*

Among the pickled fœtuses and bottled bones,
Engaged in perfecting the catalogue,
I found the last scion of the
Senatorial families of Strasbourg, Monsieur Verog.[1]

For two hours he talked of Galliffet;[2]
Of Dowson;[3] of the Rhymers' Club;
Told me how Johnson (Lionel)[4] died
By falling from a high stool in a pub . . .

But showed no trace of alcohol
At the autopsy, privately performed—   10
Tissue preserved—the pure mind
Arose toward Newman[5] as the whiskey warmed.

Dowson found harlots cheaper than hotels;
Headlam for uplift; Image[6] impartially imbued
With raptures for Bacchus, Terpsichore[7] and the Church.
So spoke the author of "The Dorian Mood,"

M. Verog, out of step with the decade,
Detached from his contemporaries,
Neglected by the young,
Because of these reveries.   20

Brennbaum†

The sky-like limpid eyes,
The circular infant's face,

* " 'Siena made me, Maremma undid me' " (Italian): spoken by La Pia in *Purgatorio* (V.135), by Dante Alighieri (1265–1321); she is a woman imprisoned by her husband in the marshes of Maremma, where she dies of malaria or poison. Pound's poem describes a literary and aesthetic movement that flourished in England in the 1890s. The ellipses are Pound's.
  [1] Victor Plarr (1863–1929), the librarian of the Royal College of Surgeons; born near Strasbourg, he wrote a book of poetry, *In the Dorian Mood* (1896).
  [2] General Gaston de Galliffet (1830–1909), who led a suicidal charge in the Battle of Sedan during World War I.
  [3] Ernest Dowson (1867–1900), a poet (whose biography was written by Victor Plarr) and member of the Rhymers' Club, founded by William Butler Yeats and other "decadent" poets in 1891. These details about its members were probably revealed to Pound by Yeats.
  [4] Lionel Johnson (1867–1902), an English poet, whose works Pound edited in 1915. Johnson was an alcoholic, but he did not die from falling off a bar stool, as was commonly believed.
  [5] John Henry Cardinal Newman (1801–1890), who converted many English intellectuals to Catholicism. Dowson and Johnson were Catholics.
  [6] Arthur Headlam (1862–1947), bishop of Gloucester, who founded the Church and Stage Guild with Selwyn Image (1849–1930), an editor Pound met in London in 1909.
  [7] The Roman god of wine and the Greek Muse (one of nine goddesses of the arts) of dance.
  † "Burnt tree" (German); Brennbaum is supposedly the caricaturist Max Beerbohm (1872–1956).

The stiffness from spats to collar
Never relaxing into grace;

The heavy memories of Horeb, Sinai and the forty years,[1]
Showed only when the daylight fell
Level across the face
Of Brennbaum "The Impeccable."

MR. NIXON*

In the cream gilded cabin of his steam yacht
Mr. Nixon advised me kindly, to advance with fewer
Dangers of delay. "Consider
    "Carefully the reviewer.

"I was as poor as you are;
"When I began I got, of course,
"Advance on royalties, fifty at first," said Mr. Nixon,
"Follow me, and take a column,
"Even if you have to work free.

"Butter reviewers. From fifty to three hundred   10
"I rose in eighteen months;
"The hardest nut I had to crack
"Was Dr. Dundas.[1]

"I never mentioned a man but with the view
"Of selling my own works.
"The tip's a good one, as for literature
"It gives no man a sinecure.

"And no one knows, at sight, a masterpiece.
"And give up verse, my boy,
"There's nothing in it."   20

.   .   .   .

Likewise a friend of Blougram's[2] once advised me:
Don't kick against the pricks,
Accept opinion. The "Nineties"[3] tried your game
And died, there's nothing in it.

---

[1] Moses saw the burning bush and heard the Lord at Horeb (see Exodus 3:1) and received the Ten Commandments at Mt. Sinai (see Exodus 19); the Hebrews wandered for forty years in the desert (see Exodus 12–17). Beerbohm, however, was not Jewish.

* Probably Arnold Bennett (1867–1931), an English novelist and journalist Pound had met.

[1] Perhaps William Robertson Nicoll (1851–1923), editor of the *British Weekly*.

[2] "Bishop Blougram's Apology" (1885), by Robert Browning (1812–1889); the bishop rationalizes his renunciation of religious principles for materialistic comfort.

[3] In the 1890s a literary and aesthetic movement, advocating art for art's sake, flourished in England.

X

Beneath the sagging roof
The stylist[1] has taken shelter,
Unpaid, uncelebrated,
At last from the world's welter[2]

Nature receives him;
With a placid and uneducated mistress
He exercises his talents
And the soil meets his distress.

The haven from sophistications and contentions
Leaks through its thatch;
He offers succulent cooking;   10
The door has a creaking latch.

XI

"Conservatrix of Milésien"[1]
Habits of mind and feeling,
Possibly. But in Ealing[2]
With the most bank-clerkly of Englishmen?

No, "Milesian"[3] is an exaggeration.
No instinct has survived in her
Older than those her grandmother
Told her would fit her station.

XII

"Daphne[1] with her thighs in bark
Stretches toward me her leafy hands,"—
Subjectively. In the stuffed-satin drawing-room
I wait The Lady Valentine's[2] commands,

Knowing my coat has never been
Of precisely the fashion
To stimulate, in her,
A durable passion;

---

[1] Probably Ford Madox Ford (1873–1939), an English editor and novelist.   [2] Confusion.
[1] A female conservator of erotic traditions; Aristides's *Milesian Tales* (2d century B.C.), reputedly a series of erotic tales, is no longer extant.
[2] A London suburb.   [3] Here, voluptuous.
[1] According to Greek myth, the nymph Daphne was changed into a laurel tree to escape the pursuing Apollo, the sun god; from *Le Château du Souvenir*, a translation of the Roman poet Ovid by Théophile Gautier (1811–1872).
[2] A possibly fictitious hostess of a fashionable literary salon.

Doubtful, somewhat, of the value
Of well-gowned approbation   10
Of literary effort,
But never of The Lady Valentine's vocation:

Poetry, her border of ideas,
The edge, uncertain, but a means of blending
With other strata
Where the lower and higher have ending;

A hook to catch the Lady Jane's[3] attention,
A modulation toward the theatre,
Also, in the case of revolution,
A possible friend and comforter.   20

> .   .   .   .

Conduct, on the other hand, the soul
"Which the highest cultures have nourished"[4]
To Fleet St.[5] where
Dr. Johnson[6] flourished;

Beside this thoroughfare
The sale of half-hose has
Long since superseded the cultivation
Of Pierian[7] roses.

Envoi (1919)*

Go, dumb-born book,
Tell her that sang me once that song of Lawes:[1]
Hadst thou but song
As thou hast subjects known,
Then were there cause in thee that should condone
Even my faults that heavy upon me lie,
And build her glories their longevity.

Tell her that sheds
Such treasure in the air,

---

[3] A fictional hostess in Henry James's "The Figure in the Carpet" (1896).
[4] From *Les Complaintes* (1885), by the French poet Jules Laforgue (1860–1887).
[5] A London street associated with journalism and publishing.
[6] Samuel Johnson (1709–1784), an English writer who pursued a difficult and uncertain living as a journalist on Fleet Steet before receiving a state pension.
[7] Of Thessaly, Greece: the home of the Muses, nine goddesses of Greek myth who presided over literature and the arts.
* "Concluding remarks" (French), which are traditionally addressed to a poem, sending it on its way.
[1] According to the scholar Jo Brantley Berryman, the woman addressed in "Envoi" is the singer Raymonde Collignon. The English composer Henry Lawes (1596–1662) set to music the poem on which this envoi is based, "Go, Lovely Rose," by Edmund Waller (1606–1687).

Recking naught else but that her graces give   10
Life to the moment,
I would bid them live
As roses might, in magic amber laid,
Red overwrought with orange and all made
One substance and one colour
Braving time.

Tell her that goes
With song upon her lips
But sings not out the song, nor knows
The maker of it, some other mouth,   20
May be as fair as hers,
Might, in new ages, gain her worshippers,
When our two dusts with Waller's shall be laid,
Siftings on siftings in oblivion,
Till change hath broken down
All things save Beauty alone.

MAUBERLEY*

1920

"Vacuos exercet in aera morsus." [1]

I

Turned from the "eau-forte
Par Jacquemart" [2]
To the strait head
Of Messalina: [3]

"His true Penelope [4]
Was Flaubert," [5]
And his tool
The engraver's.

---

* The second persona in *Hugh Selwyn Mauberley*, Mauberley is an aesthete, a role beyond which Pound has progressed.

[1] "He makes vain leaps into the air" (Latin), from *Metamorphoses* (VII.786), by the Roman poet Ovid (43 B.C.–A.D. 17?).

[2] An etching by Jules Jacquemart (1837–1880) and the frontispiece to *Émaux et Camées* (1884), by Théophile Gautier (1811–1872).

[3] Valeria Messalina (A.D. 22?–48?), the third wife of the Roman emperor Claudius I (10 B.C.–A.D. 54); she was known for her sexual appetite.

[4] According to Greek myth, the wife of Odysseus, who remained faithful to him in his absence despite the many suitors who pursued her.

[5] Gustave Flaubert (1821–1880), a French novelist.

Firmness,
Not the full smile,   10
His art, but an art
In profile;

Colourless
Pier Francesca,[6]
Pisanello[7] lacking the skill
To forge Achaia.[8]

II

"Qu'est ce qu'ils savent de l'amour, et qu'est ce qu'ils peuvent en comprendre?
  S'ils ne comprennent pas la poésie, s'ils ne sentent pas la musique, qu'est ce
qu'ils peuvent comprendre de cette passion en comparaison avec laquelle la rose est
grossière et le parfum des violettes un tonnerre?"

CAID ALI[1]

For three years, diabolus[2] in the scale,
He drank ambrosia,
All passes, ANANGKE[3] prevails,
Came end, at last, to that Arcadia.

He had moved amid her phantasmagoria,
Amid her galaxies,
NUKTOS AGALMA[4]

.   .   .   .

Drifted . . . drifted precipitate,
Asking time to be rid of . . .
Of his bewilderment; to designate   10
His new found orchid . . . .

To be certain . . . certain . . .
(Amid ærial flowers) . . . time for arrangements—
Drifted on
To the final estrangement;

[6] Piero della Francesca (1420?–1492), an Italian Renaissance painter.
[7] Antonio (or Vittore) Pisano (1397–1455), an Italian Renaissance artist and medal maker.
[8] A region of southern Greece.
[1] " 'What do they know of love, and what can they understand of it? If they don't understand poetry, if they don't hear music, what can they understand of that passion, beside which the rose is crude and the scent of violets a thunderclap?' " (French); Caid Ali is Pound's pseudonym. The ellipses are Pound's.
[2] The "devil," a term for the augmented fourth, a dissonant interval in medieval music.
[3] "Necessity" (Greek); the Greek phrases and words are transliterated in the second half of the poem.
[4] "Night's jewel" (Greek).

Unable in the supervening blankness
To sift TO AGATHON[5] from the chaff
Until he found his sieve . . .
Ultimately, his seismograph:

—Given that is his "fundamental passion,"   20
This urge to convey the relation
Of eye-lid and cheek-bone
By verbal manifestation;

To present the series
Of curious heads in medallion—

He had passed, inconscient, full gaze,
The wide-banded irides[6]
And botticellian sprays[7] implied
In their diastasis;[8]

Which anæsthesis, noted a year late,   30
And weighed, revealed his great affect,
(Orchid), mandate
Of Eros, a retrospect.

            .   .   .

Mouths biting empty air,
The still stone dogs,
Caught in metamorphosis, were
Left him as epilogues.

"The Age Demanded"

VIDE[1] POEM II

For this agility chance found
Him of all men, unfit
As the red-beaked steeds of
The Cytheræan[2] for a chain bit.

The glow of porcelain
Brought no reforming sense

---

[5] "The good" (Greek).   [6] Plural of "iris": flowers and eyes.
[7] Probably a reference to *Primavera* ("Spring"), a painting by the Italian Renaissance artist Sandro Botticelli (1444?–1510), in which women carry flowers.
[8] Separation, distance.
[1] "See" (Latin); see poem II of *Hugh Selwyn Mauberley* ("The age demanded an image . . . .").
[2] According to Greek myth, the goddess of love, Aphrodite, was born in the sea near Cythera; her chariot was drawn by doves, which would not require a chain bit.

To his perception
Of the social inconsequence.   10

Thus, if her colour
Came against his gaze,
Tempered as if
It were through a perfect glaze

He made no immediate application
Of this to relation of the state
To the individual, the month was more temperate
Because this beauty had been.

The coral isle, the lion-coloured sand
Burst in upon the porcelain revery: 20
Impetuous troubling
Of his imagery.

Mildness, amid the neo-Nietzschean clatter,[3]
His sense of graduations,
Quite out of place amid
Resistance to current exacerbations,

Invitation, mere invitation to perceptivity
Gradually led him to the isolation
Which these presents place
Under a more tolerant, perhaps, examination.   30

By constant elimination
The manifest universe
Yielded an armour
Against utter consternation,

A Minoan[4] undulation,
Seen, we admit, amid ambrosial circumstances
Strengthened him against
The discouraging doctrine of chances,[5]

And his desire for survival,   40
Faint in the most strenuous moods,
Became an Olympian *apathein*[6]
In the presence of selected perceptions.

A pale gold, in the aforesaid pattern,
The unexpected palms

---

[3] When Pound arrived in London, the ideas of the German philosopher Friedrich Wilhelm Nietzsche (1844–1900) were receiving much attention, especially in the magazine *The New Age*.
[4] The Minoan period (200–1500 B.C.), named for the legendary King Minos of Crete.
[5] According to the critic Christine Froula, this may refer to Darwin's theory of evolution.
[6] "Not to feel" (Greek); the indifference of the gods of Mt. Olympus to human fate.

Destroying, certainly, the artist's urge,
Left him delighted with the imaginary
Audition of the phantasmal sea-surge,

Incapable of the least utterance or composition,
Emendation, conservation of the "better tradition,"
Refinement of medium, elimination of superfluities,
August attraction or concentration.

Nothing, in brief, but maudlin confession,   50
Irresponse to human aggression,
Amid the precipitation, down-float
Of insubstantial manna,
Lifting the faint susurrus
Of his subjective hosannah.

Ultimate affronts to
Human redundancies;

Non-esteem of self-styled "his betters"
Leading, as he well knew,
To his final   60
Exclusion from the world of letters.

IV

Scattered Moluccas[1]
Not knowing, day to day,
The first day's end, in the next noon;
The placid water
Unbroken by the Simoon;[2]

Thick foliage
Placid beneath warm suns,
Tawn fore-shores
Washed in the cobalt of oblivions;

Or through dawn-mist   10
The grey and rose
Of the juridical
Flamingoes;

A consciousness disjunct,
Being but this overblotted

---

[1] Spice Islands in the Malay Archipelago.
[2] A hot, suffocating, sand-laden wind originating in the deserts of Africa and Asia Minor.

Series
Of intermittences;

Coracle[3] of Pacific voyages,
The unforecasted beach;
Then on an oar   20
Read this:[4]

"I was
And I no more exist;
Here drifted
An hedonist."

MEDALLION*

Luini[1] in porcelain!
The grand piano
Utters a profane
Protest with her clear soprano.

The sleek head emerges
From the gold-yellow frock
As Anadyomene[2] in the opening
Pages of Reinach.[3]

Honey-red, closing the face-oval,
A basket-work of braids which seem as if they were   10
Spun in King Minos'[4] hall
From metal, or intractable amber;

The face-oval beneath the glaze,
Bright in its suave bounding-line, as,
Beneath half-watt rays,
The eyes turn topaz.

1919, 1920

---

[3] A small hide or leather-covered wicker-frame boat used by ancient Celts living in Britain at the time of the Roman invasion.

[4] According to Homer's *Odyssey,* Odysseus met the spirit of his dead shipmate Elpenor, who begged Odysseus to inscribe a memorial to him on his oar at the beach.

* The visual parallel to the *envoi,* or a poem's "concluding remarks" (French). According to the scholar Jo Brantley Berryman, the woman described here is the singer Raymonde Collignon.

[1] Bernardino Luini (1474?–1532), an Italian Renaissance painter.

[2] Epithet of Aphrodite (the Greek goddess of love), meaning "rising from the sea."

[3] Salomon Reinach (1858–1932), a French archeologist and art historian; his *Apollo* (1902) includes a reproduction of the head of Aphrodite.

[4] According to Greek myth, a king of Crete who became a judge in the Underworld after his death.

from THE CANTOS

CANTO I*

And then went down to the ship,
Set keel to breakers, forth on the godly sea, and
We[1] set up mast and sail on that swart ship,
Bore sheep aboard her, and our bodies also
Heavy with weeping, and winds from sternward
Bore us out onward with bellying canvas,
Circe's[2] this craft, the trim-coifed goddess.
Then sat we amidships, wind jamming the tiller,
Thus with stretched sail, we went over sea till day's end.
Sun to his slumber, shadows o'er all the ocean,   10
Came we then to the bounds of deepest water,
To the Kimmerian lands,[3] and peopled cities
Covered with close-webbed mist, unpierced ever
With glitter of sun-rays
Nor with stars stretched, nor looking back from heaven
Swartest night stretched over wretched men there.
The ocean flowing backward, came we then to the place
Aforesaid by Circe.
Here did they rites, Perimedes and Eurylochus,[4]
And drawing sword from my hip   20
I dug the ell-square pitkin;[5]
Poured we libations unto each the dead,
First mead and then sweet wine, water mixed with white flour.
Then prayed I many a prayer to the sickly death's-heads;
As set in Ithaca, sterile bulls of the best
For sacrifice, heaping the pyre with goods,
A sheep to Tiresias only, black and a bell-sheep.[6]
Dark blood flowed in the fosse,[7]
Souls out of Erebus,[8] cadaverous dead, of brides
Of youths and of the old who had borne much;   30
Souls stained with recent tears, girls tender,
Men many, mauled with bronze lance heads,

---

* To begin his *Cantos,* Pound adapts what he thought to be the oldest section of Homer's *Odyssey* (Bk. XI), Odysseus's visit to Hades (the Underworld of the dead); most of the names Pound cites are featured in Greek myth.
[1] Odysseus and his men.
[2] According to Greek myth, a sorceress who detained Odysseus for a year; here, she has directed him to Hades to seek instructions from the Theban seer Tiresias on how to sail home, and gives him a favoring wind.
[3] Lands of perpetual darkness, shrouded in mist, at the edge of the world.
[4] Crew members; Eurylochus was chief mate.   [5] An arm's length (one-el) square pit.
[6] A sheep wearing a bell that leads the flock.   [7] Ditch.
[8] A dark place through which souls passed on their way to Hades.

Battle spoil, bearing yet dreory[9] arms,
These many crowded about me; with shouting,
Pallor upon me, cried to my men for more beasts;
Slaughtered the herds, sheep slain of bronze;
Poured ointment, cried to the gods,
To Pluto[10] the strong, and praised Proserpine;[11]
Unsheathed the narrow sword,
I sat to keep off the impetuous impotent dead,　　　　40
Till I should hear Tiresias.
But first Elpenor[12] came, our friend Elpenor,
Unburied, cast on the wide earth,
Limbs that we left in the house of Circe,
Unwept, unwrapped in sepulchre, since toils urged other.
Pitiful spirit. And I cried in hurried speech:
"Elpenor, how art thou come to this dark coast?
"Cam'st thou afoot, outstripping seamen?"
　　　　And he in heavy speech:
"Ill fate and abundant wine. I slept in Circe's ingle.[13]　　　　50
"Going down the long ladder unguarded,
"I fell against the buttress,
"Shattered the nape-nerve,[14] the soul sought Avernus.[15]
"But thou, O King, I bid remember me, unwept, unburied,
"Heap up mine arms, be tomb by sea-board, and inscribed:
"*A man of no fortune, and with a name to come.*
"And set my oar up, that I swung mid fellows."

And Anticlea[16] came, whom I beat off, and then Tiresias Theban,
Holding his golden wand, knew me, and spoke first:
"A second time?[17] why? man of ill star,　　　　60
"Facing the sunless dead and this joyless region?
"Stand from the fosse, leave me my bloody bever[18]
"For soothsay."
　　　　And I stepped back,
And he strong with the blood, said then: "Odysseus
"Shalt return through spiteful Neptune,[19] over dark seas,
"Lose all companions." And then Anticlea came.
Lie quiet Divus. I mean, that is Andreas Divus,[20]
In officina Wecheli, 1538,[21] out of Homer.

---

[9] Dripping with blood.
[10] According to Roman myth, the god who ruled Hades; in Greek myth, the god was himself Hades.
[11] The goddess of regeneration and wife of Pluto; in Greek myth, Persephone.
[12] A crew member who, while on Circe's Island, drunkenly fell and broke his neck.　　[13] House.
[14] Neck nerve.　　[15] A lake near Naples thought to be the entrance to Hades.
[16] Odysseus's mother, who died during his voyage. Circe has instructed Odysseus not to speak to anyone until Tiresias has spoken.
[17] Tiresias and Odysseus had met once previously on earth.　　[18] Drink.
[19] According to Roman myth, the sea god; in Greek myth, Poseidon, whose son (Cyclops) Odysseus had blinded.
[20] The Latin translator whose version of Homer's *Odyssey* (1538) Pound used for this canto.
[21] "At the workshop of Wechel" (Latin), where Divus translated Homer.

And he sailed, by Sirens and thence outward and away　　　　70
And unto Circe.
　　　Venerandam,[22]
In the Cretan's[23] phrase, with the golden crown, Aphrodite,[24]
Cypri munimenta sortita est,[25] mirthful, oricalchi, with golden
Girdles and breast bands, thou with dark eyelids
Bearing the golden bough of Argicida.[26] So that:

　　　　　　　　　　　　　　　　　　　　1925

CANTO IV*

Palace in smoky light,
Troy but a heap of smouldering boundary stones,
ANAXIFORMINGES![1] Aurunculeia![2]
Hear me. Cadmus of Golden Prows![3]
The silver mirrors catch the bright stones and flare,
Dawn, to our waking, drifts in the green cool light;
Dew-haze blurs, in the grass, pale ankles moving.
Beat, beat, whirr, thud, in the soft turf
　　　under the apple trees,
Choros nympharum,[4] goat-foot, with the pale foot alternate;　　10
Crescent of blue-shot waters, green-gold in the shallows,
A black cock crows in the sea-foam;

And by the curved, carved foot of the couch,
　　　claw-foot and lion head, an old man seated
Speaking in the low drone . . . :
　　　Ityn!
Et ter flebiliter, Ityn, Ityn![5]
And she went toward the window and cast her down,
　　　"All the while, the while, swallows crying:
Ityn!　　　　　　　　　　　　　　　　　　　　20
　　　"It is Cabestan's[6] heart in the dish."
　　　"It is Cabestan's heart in the dish?

---

[22] "Worthy of adoration" (Latin).
[23] Georgius Dartona Cretensis, Latin translator of the Homeric hymns.
[24] The Greek goddess of love.
[25] "Held dominion over the Cyprian heights" (Latin); *oricalchi:* "of copper" (Latin).
[26] "Slayer of Argos" (Latin). According to Greek myth, the god Hermes slew the hundred-eyed Argus; with his golden staff, Hermes led the souls of the dead to Hades.
　* This canto's images of destruction reflect the aftermath of World War I. The ellipses are Pound's.
　[1] "Lords of the lyre" (Greek).
　[2] A bride praised in a poem by the Roman poet Gaius Valerius Catullus (84 B.C.?–54 B.C.?).
　[3] Founder of the city of Thebes.　　[4] "Chorus of nymphs" (Latin).
　[5] "Itys! / And thrice with tears, Itys, Itys!" (Latin): according to Greek myth, Itys was the son of Procne and Tereus. He was killed, cooked, and fed to Tereus by Procne after she discovered her husband had raped her sister Philomela.
　[6] Lover of Seremonda, whose husband, after killing Cabestan, cooked and served his heart to her.

"No other taste shall change this."
And she went toward the window,
  the slim white stone bar
Making a double arch;
Firm even fingers held to the firm pale stone;
Swung for a moment,
  and the wind out of Rhodez[7]
Caught in the full of her sleeve.   30
  . . . the swallows crying:
'Tis. 'Tis. Ytis!
  Actæon . . . [8]
   and a valley,
The valley is thick with leaves, with leaves, the trees,
The sunlight glitters, glitters a-top,
Like a fish-scale roof,
  Like the church roof in Poictiers[9]
If it were gold.
   Beneath it, beneath it   40
Not a ray, not a slivver, not a spare disc of sunlight
Flaking the black, soft water;
Bathing the body of nymphs, of nymphs, and Diana,[10]
Nymphs, white-gathered about her, and the air, air,
Shaking, air alight with the goddess,
  fanning their hair in the dark,
Lifting, lifting and waffing:
Ivory dipping in silver,
  Shadow'd, o'ershadow'd
Ivory dipping in silver,   50
Not a splotch, not a lost shatter of sunlight.
Then Actæon: Vidal,[11]
Vidal. It is old Vidal speaking,
  stumbling along in the wood,
Not a patch, not a lost shimmer of sunlight,
  the pale hair of the goddess.

The dogs leap on Actæon,
  "Hither, hither, Actæon,"
Spotted stag of the wood;
Gold, gold, a sheaf of hair,   60
  Thick like a wheat swath,
Blaze, blaze in the sun,
  The dogs leap on Actæon.
Stumbling, stumbling along in the wood,

---

[7] A small city in France.

[8] According to Greek myth, Actaeon accidentally spied on the goddess Diana when she was bathing. After she transformed him into a stag as punishment, he was killed by his own hounds.

[9] The church of St. Hilaire in Poictiers, France.

[10] According to Greek myth, the virgin goddess of the moon, the woods, and all that is wild.

[11] A troubador who, according to legend, dressed in wolfskins to court his lady and was almost killed by his own hounds.

Muttering, muttering Ovid:[12]
   "Pergusa . . . pool . . . pool . . . Gargaphia,
"Pool . . . pool of Salmacis."[13]
   The empty armour shakes as the cygnet moves.

Thus the light rains, thus pours, *e lo soleils plovil*[14]
The liquid and rushing crystal   70
   beneath the knees of the gods.
Ply over ply, thin glitter of water;
Brook film bearing white petals.
The pines at Takasago[15]
   grow with the pines of Isé![16]
The water whirls up the bright pale sand in the spring's mouth
"Behold the Tree of the Visages!"[17]
Forked branch-tips, flaming as if with lotus.
   Ply over ply
The shallow eddying fluid,   80
   beneath the knees of the gods.

Torches melt in the glare
   set flame of the corner cook-stall,
Blue agate casing the sky (as at Gourdon[18] that time)
   the sputter of resin,
Saffron sandal so petals the narrow foot: Hymenæus Io![19]
   Hymen, Io Hymenæe! Aurunculeia!
A scarlet flower is cast on the blanch-white stone.

And So-Gioku,[20] saying:
"This wind, sire, is the king's wind,   90
   This wind is wind of the palace,
Shaking imperial water-jets."
   And Ran-ti,[21] opening his collar:
"This wind roars in the earth's bag,
   it lays the water with rushes;
No wind is the king's wind.
   Let every cow keep her calf."

---

[12] The Roman poet Ovid (43 B.C.–A.D. 17?), who wrote *Metamorphoses,* a book much admired by Pound.

[13] Pergusa was a lake; Gargaphia, the pool where Diana was surprised by Actaeon; Salmacis, a water nymph who tried to rape Hermaphroditus but whose body became merged with his.

[14] "And the light rains down" (Provençal).

[15] Legendary pine trees; the subject of a Japanese Noh play about a couple growing old in love.

[16] A pine grove in Honshu, Japan.

[17] According to the Pound scholar Carroll Terrell, Pound mistranslated "trees of life," a synonym for pine trees.

[18] A city in southern France, associated with Provençal poetry.

[19] From Catullus's poem, "come from your hill, from Helicon; Hymen [the Greek god of marriage], hail Hymen!"

[20] The Chinese poet Sung Yu. [21] The king of Ch'u, mentioned in Sung Yu's poem on the wind.

"This wind is held in gauze curtains . . . "
    "No wind is the king's . . . "

The camel drivers sit in the turn of the stairs,   100
    Look down on Ecbatan[22] of plotted streets,
"Danaë! Danaë!"[23]
       What wind is the king's?"
Smoke hangs on the stream,
The peach-trees shed bright leaves in the water,
Sound drifts in the evening haze,
    The bark scrapes at the ford,
Gilt rafters above black water,
    Three steps in an open field,
Gray stone-posts leading . . .   110

Père Henri Jacques[24] would speak with the Sennin,[25] on Rokku,
Mount Rokku between the rock and the cedars,
Polhonac,[26]
As Gyges[27] on Thracian platter set the feast,
Cabestan, Terreus,[28]
    It is Cabestan's heart in the dish,
Vidal, or Ecbatan, upon the gilded tower in Ecbatan
Lay the god's bride, lay ever, waiting the golden rain.
By Garonne.[29] "Saave!"
The Garonne is thick like paint,   120
Procession,—"Et sa'ave, sa'ave, sa'ave Regina!"[30]—
Moves like a worm, in the crowd.
Adige, thin film of images,
Across the Adige,[31] by Stefano, Madonna in hortulo,[32]
As Cavalcanti[33] had seen her.
    The Centaur's[34] heel plants in the earth loam.
And we sit here . . .
    there in the arena . . .

1925

---

[22] A city in Persia; for Pound a symbol of perfect human order and justice.

[23] According to Greek myth, Danaë's father, Acrisius, imprisoned her in a tower to keep her from bearing a son prophesied to kill him; but she was visited by the supreme god, Zeus, in the form of a shower of gold and by him bore the hero Perseus.

[24] A Jesuit priest.   [25] Spirits; Mount Rokku is in Honshu, Japan.

[26] A lord persuaded by a troubador to assist unwittingly in the seduction of his wife.

[27] Gyges (685?–652 B.C.) was hidden by King Cadaules to spy on his naked queen, who induced Gyges to kill the king and marry her; he did and became king of Lydia.

[28] According to Greek myth, the king of Thrace who raped Philomela and cut out her tongue.

[29] A river in the south of France.

[30] "And save, save, save Regina" (Latin), from the hymn "Salve Regina."

[31] A river in the north of Italy.

[32] "*Madonna in the Garden*" (Italian), painted by the Italian Renaissance painter Stefano da Verona (1374?–1451).

[33] Guido Cavalcanti (1250?–1300), an Italian poet greatly admired by Pound, who translated him.

[34] According to Greek myth, a creature half man, half horse.

CANTO LXXXI*

Zeus lies in Ceres'[1] bosom
Taishan[2] is attended of loves
     under Cythera,[3] before sunrise
and he said: Hay aquí mucho catolicismo—(sounded
                        catoli*th*ismo)
     y muy poco reliHion"[4]
and he said: Yo creo que los reyes desparecen"[5]
That was Padre José Elizondo[6]
         in 1906 and in 1917
or about 1917   10
     and Dolores said: Come pan, niño," eat bread, me lad[7]
Sargent[8] had painted her
     before he descended[9]
(i.e. if he descended
     but in those days he did thumb sketches,
impressions of the Velasquez in the Museo del Prado[10]
and books cost a peseta,[11]
     brass candlesticks in proportion,
hot wind came from the marshes
     and death-chill from the mountains.   20
And later Bowers[12] wrote: "but such hatred,
     I had never conceived such"
and the London reds wouldn't show up his friends
     (i.e. friends of Franco[13]
working in London) and in Alcazar[14]
forty years gone, they said: go back to the station to eat
you can sleep here for a peseta"
     goat bells tinkled all night
     and the hostess grinned: Eso es luto, *haw!*

---

* The most lyrical of the *Pisan Cantos* (1948), the collection based on Pound's imprisonment in a military camp near Pisa, Italy, during World War I and for which he won the first Bollingen Prize (1949). The ellipses are Pound's.
[1] The supreme Greek god and the Roman goddess of agriculture and fertility.
[2] Mount Taishan, a sacred mountain in China; Pound was reminded of it by a mountain that he could see from the Disciplinary Training Camp in Pisa.
[3] Aphrodite (Greek) or Venus (Roman), the goddess of love.
[4] "Here is much Catholicism and very little religion" (Spanish).
[5] "I believe that the kings will disappear" (Spanish).
[6] José Maria de Elizondo, the Spanish priest who helped Pound obtain a copy of a poetry manuscript by Guido Cavalcanti (1250?–1300).
[7] The translation of the preceding Spanish phrase.
[8] The American artist John Singer Sargent (1856–1925).   [9] Deteriorated artistically.
[10] The Spanish painter Diego Rodríguez de Silva y Velasquez (1599–1600) in the great art museum in Madrid.
[11] A small Spanish coin.
[12] Claude Bowers (1879–1958), an American historian and ambassador to Spain (1933–1939) with whom Pound corresponded in the 1930s.
[13] Francisco Franco (1892–1975), victorious Fascist general in the Spanish Civil War (1936–1939) and dictator of Spain (1939–1972).
[14] A town in central Spain.

mi marido es muerto[15]   30
      (it is mourning, my husband is dead)
when she gave me paper to write on
with a black border half an inch or more deep,
      say 5/8ths, of the locanda[16]
"We call *all* foreigners frenchies"
and the egg broke in Cabranez'[17] pocket,
      thus making history. Basil[18] says
they beat drums for three days
till all the drumheads were busted
      (simple village fiesta)   40
and as for his life in the Canaries . . . [19]
Possum[20] observed that the local   folk dance
was danced by the same dancers in divers localities
      in political welcome . . .
the technique of demonstration
      Cole[21] studied that (not G.D.H., Horace)
"You will find" said old André Spire,[22]
that every man on that board (Crédit Agricole)
has a brother-in-law
           "You the one, I the few"   50
      said John Adams[23]
speaking of fears in the abstract
      to his volatile friend Mr Jefferson
(to break the pentameter, that was the first heave[24])
or as Jo Bard[25] says: they never speak to each other,
if it is baker and concierge[26] visibly
      it is La Rouchefoucauld and de Maintenon[27] audibly.
"Te cavero le budelle"
          "La corata a te"[28]
In less than a geological epoch   60
      said Henry Mencken[29]

---

[15] Translated from Spanish in the next line.   [16] "Inn" (Italian).

[17] Probably Augustin Cabanes (1862–1928), a historian and sexual researcher.

[18] Basil Bunting (1900–1985), an English poet and friend of Pound.

[19] The Canary Islands of Spain, off Northwest Africa.

[20] Pound's affectionate name for T. S. Eliot.

[21] Horace de Vere Cole (1874–1935), an English economist and friend of the painter Augustus John (1878–1961). A great practical joker, Cole claimed to be a descendant of Old King Cole.

[22] Spire (1868–1966) was a French poet; Pound quotes his derisive estimate of the directors of France's Agricultural Bank.

[23] In a letter to Thomas Jefferson (third U.S. president), John Adams (second U.S. president) noted that Jefferson feared a powerful president could destroy democracy; Adams saw the danger as coming from the rich and influential upper class.

[24] The first job of poets was to stop using traditional pentameter verse, which Pound felt was artificial.

[25] Joseph Bard (1892–?), an English critic and essayist.   [26] "Doorkeeper" (French).

[27] François Alexandre Frederic (1613–1680), Duc de La Rochefoucauld, a French politician and writer; Françoise d'Aubigné (1635–1719), Marquise de Maintenon, the mistress and later second wife of King Louis XIV of France) and the author of a famous series of letters.

[28] "I'll cut your guts out" / "I'll cut out yours" (Italian).

[29] H. L. Mencken (1880–1956), a celebrated American journalist, author, and critic with whom Pound had an extensive correspondence.

"Some cook, some do not cook[30]
      some things cannot be altered"
Ἰυγξ. . . . . ᾿εμὸν ποτί δῶμα τὸν ἄνδρα[31]
What counts is the cultural level,
      thank Benin[32] for this table ex packing box
   "doan yu tell no one I made it"
            from a mask fine as any in Frankfurt[33]
"It'll get you offn th' groun"
            Light as the branch of Kuanon[34]   70
And at first disappointed with shoddy
the bare ram-shackle quais,[35] but then saw the
high buggy wheels
            and was reconciled,
George Santayana[36] arriving in the port of Boston
and kept to the end of his life that faint *thethear*[37]
of the Spaniard
            as a grace quasi imperceptible
as did Muss[38] the *v* for *u* of Romagna
and said the grief was a full act   80
            repeated for each new condoleress
working up to a climax.
and George Horace[39] said he wd/ "get Beveridge" (Senator)[40]
Beveridge wouldn't talk and he wouldn't write for the papers
but George got him by campin' in his hotel
and assailin' him at lunch breakfast an' dinner
            three articles
and my ole man went on hoein' corn
      while George was a-tellin' him,
come across a vacant lot   90
            where you'd occasionally see a wild rabbit
or mebbe only a loose one
            AOI![41]
      a leaf in the current
                  at my grates no Althea[42]

---

[30] Pound's wife, Dorothy Shakespear, refused to cook for the family.

[31] "'Little wheel. . . . ' [Bring that] man [back] to my house" (Greek); from the second *Idyll* of Theocritus (3d century B.C.), in which a young woman uses a magical charm to attract her lover.

[32] A fellow prisoner of Pound's in Pisa, who built him a writing table. Pound calls him Benin because the black man's face resembled the masks made by the Benin tribe of Nigeria.

[33] A German city, site of the Frobenius Institute, where Pound had seen the Benin masks.

[34] According to Chinese myth, Kuan-yin, the goddess of mercy.   [35] "Quays" (French), or wharves.

[36] Santayana (1863–1952) was a Spanish-born American philosopher who taught at Harvard and then lived in Italy. Pound met him in 1939 and the two subsequently corresponded. The poet hoped that Santayana could give guidance to the then-projected Paradise section of *The Cantos*.

[37] Here, pronouncing *th* for *c* in certain words.

[38] Benito Mussolini (1883–1945), Fascist dictator of Italy (1922–1945). Mussolini's accent identified his birthplace: the province of Romagna in northern Italy.

[39] George Horace Lorimer (1868–1937), an American journalist, editor of the *Saturday Evening Post*, and a neighbor of the Pound family in Wyncote, Pennsylvania.

[40] Albert Jeremiah Beveridge (1862–1927), a U.S. senator from Indiana (1899–1911).

[41] A cry of lamentation.

[42] "To Althea, from Prison," by the English poet Richard Lovelace (1618–1658): in the prison camp at Pisa, Pound found the poem in Morris Speare's *The Pocket Book of Verse* (1940).

libretto[43]   Yet
Ere the season died a-cold
Borne upon a zephyr's shoulder
I rose through the aureate sky
     Lawes and Jenkyns guard thy rest   100
     Dolmetsch ever be thy guest,[44]
Has he tempered the viol's wood
To enforce   both the grave   and the acute?[45]
Has he curved us the bowl of the lute?
     Lawes and Jenkyns guard thy rest
     Dolmetsch ever be thy guest
Hast 'ou fashioned so airy a mood
    To draw up leaf from the root?
Hast 'ou found   a cloud   so light
    As seemed neither mist nor shade?   110

       Then resolve me, tell me aright
       If Waller sang or Dowland[46] played.

       Your eyen two wol sleye me sodenly
       I may the beauté of hem nat susteyne[47]

And for 180 years almost nothing.

Ed ascoltando al leggier mormorio[48]
     there came new subtlety of eyes into my tent,
whether of spirit or hypostasis,[49]
     but what the blindfold hides
or at carneval   120
        nor any pair showed anger
     Saw but the eyes and stance between the eyes,
colour, diastasis,[50]
     careless or unaware it had not the
    whole tent's room
nor was place for the full Ειδώς[51]
interpass, penetrate
     casting but shade beyond the other lights
       sky's clear
       night's sea   130
       green of the mountain pool
       shone from the unmasked eyes in half-mask's space.
What thou lovest well remains,
               the rest is dross

---

[43] A book or words of an opera.

[44] Henry Lawes (1596–1662) and John Jenkins (1592–1678), English composers and musicians; Arnold Dolmetsch (1858–1940), a French musician and instrument maker.

[45] In Renaissance music, lower (grave) and higher (acute) notes.

[46] Edmund Waller (1606–1687), an English poet; John Dowland (1563–1626), an English composer.

[47] "Your two eyes will slay me suddenly / I may the beauty of them not sustain," from "Merciless Beauty," a love poem attributed to Geoffrey Chaucer (1340?–1400).

[48] "And listening to the gentle murmur" (Latin).   [49] Divine substance: here, Aphrodite.

[50] Interval.   [51] "Knowing" (Greek).

What thou lov'st well shall not be reft from thee
What thou lov'st well is thy true heritage
Whose world, or mine or theirs
                              or is it of none?
First came the seen, then thus the palpable
        Elysium,[52] though it were in the halls of hell,   140
What thou lovest well is thy true heritage

The ant's a centaur in his dragon world.
Pull down thy vanity, it is not man
Made courage, or made order, or made grace,
        Pull down thy vanity, I say pull down.
Learn of the green world what can be thy place
In scaled invention or true artistry,
Pull down thy vanity,
                              Paquin[53] pull down!
The green casque has outdone your elegance.[54]   150

"Master thyself, then others shall thee beare"[55]
        Pull down thy vanity
Thou art a beaten dog beneath the hail,
A swollen magpie in a fitful sun,
Half black half white
Nor knowst'ou wing from tail
Pull down thy vanity
                How mean thy hates
Fostered in falsity,
                Pull down thy vanity,   160
Rathe[56] to destroy, niggard in charity,
Pull down thy vanity,
                I say pull down.

But to have done instead of not doing
                this is not vanity
To have, with decency, knocked
That a Blunt should open[57]
                To have gathered from the air a live tradition
or from a fine old eye the unconquered flame
This is not vanity.   170
                Here error is all in the not done,
        all in the diffidence that faltered,

                                                        1947

---

[52] According to Greek myth, the home of the virtuous after death; Paradise.
[53] A famous Parisian dressmaker.
[54] The green forms of insects surpass Paquin's artificial creations.
[55] A paraphrase of Chaucer's poem "Truth: Ballade of Good Counsel," which Pound found in Speare's *Pocket Book*.
[56] Quick.
[57] Wilfrid Scawen Blunt (1840–1922), an English poet and politician imprisoned for championing the cause of Irish home rule; he was much admired by Pound.

Marianne Moore
(1887–1972)

In the introduction to *A Marianne Moore Reader* (1961), the poet responds to a remark about her poetry—"Why the many quotation marks?"—by posing another question: "When a thing has been said so well that it could not be said better, why paraphrase it? Hence, my writing is, if not a cabinet of fossils, a kind of collection of flies in amber." The publication of the *Reader* coincided with Marianne Moore's emergence as a public figure: the grand dame of American letters, an avid baseball fan who once threw out the 1968 season's first ball in Yankee Stadium, a consultant to Ford Motors in naming a new car model, and the frequently photographed poet with black tricorn hat and white gloves. Less and less she is viewed as the "flies in amber" poet who borrowed from newspapers and nature magazines; more and more she is prized as one of the twentieth century's most startling literary intelligences.

Until age seven, Moore, born in 1887 in Kirkwood, Missouri, lived with her brother, mother, and grandfather, a Presbyterian minister; Moore's father had deserted them. After her grandfather's death the family moved to Pennsylvania, where Moore entered Bryn Mawr College in 1905. Upon graduation she taught stenography at the United States Indian School in Carlisle, Pennsylvania, and in 1918 moved with her mother to Brooklyn, New York, to be near Moore's brother, a New Jersey chaplain. Moore acknowledged her mother as her most perceptive and harshest critic as well as her housemate; their relationship informed Moore's poetry for many years.

Moore's poems were first published in Bryn Mawr's student magazine. Her first book, *Poems,* appeared in 1921; her second, *Observations,* in 1924; and her third, *Selected Poems,* not until 1935. From 1925 until 1929 Moore edited the *Dial,* a literary journal begun by Margaret Fuller and Ralph Waldo Emerson in the 1840s. Moore wrote no poetry then but published essays and reviews, establishing herself as a prose stylist. She later wrote essays on Ezra Pound and T. S. Eliot, among others. Her most famous essay, "Humility, Concentration, and Gusto" (1948), argues that those qualities are essential to good verse.

Moore's coming of age as a writer parallels the flowering of modernism. Fellow modernists Eliot and Pound were ardent admirers of Moore, and there was reciprocal influence among them; her correspondence with Pound stretched over decades. Criticized for her use of direct and paraphrased quotations, "phrasings," Moore by no means originated the technique: both Eliot and Pound borrowed freely from other sources. Indeed, Moore's comment in the foreword to *A Marianne Moore Reader* about *Marriage* (1923), a lengthy poem in which Adam and Eve come to life, could be made about Eliot's poem *The Waste Land* (1922): "The thing (I would hardly call it a poem) is . . . a little anthology of statements that took my fancy—phrasings that I liked."

In 1941 Moore published *What are Years?* The title poem, written on the eve of World War II, considers such conflict-prompted ruminations as the natures of guilt and of innocence and the absence of safety. A more dramatic situation than Moore usually chose, the subject of war allowed her stringent moral concerns to take center stage. "We don't want

An avid baseball fan, Marianne Moore threw out the first ball at Yankee Stadium to open the 1968 season.

war," she wrote in "Humility, Concentration, and Gusto," "but it does conduce to humility." That quality of humility is evoked and celebrated in "What are Years?" Moore's war poems, like most of her work, are poems of conscience, of elevated perception.

For many years Moore's achievements were either neglected or viewed as some sort of literary curiosity, primarily because of her gender. The poetry of the early twentieth-century's best-known female poets, Elinor Wylie and Edna St. Vincent Millay, reflects highly traditional conceptions of prosody, although Millay countered conventional ideas about women's roles. Poetry by women was limited to, and by, romantic and overly pastoral views of nature. Although Moore ironically led a quieter, more traditional life than did her more outspoken female contemporaries, she was clearly an odd duck.

Moore's poetry set her apart not only from Wylie and Millay but from Eliot and Pound as well. Commonly criticized for writing only syllabic, merely descriptive verse that is not poetry at all, Moore used complex and highly original techniques of language and syntax in treating "unpoetic" subjects such as unusual animals, baseball, and objets d'art. Because Moore tried for natural and conversational language and syntax, her poetry is characterized by an elevated style true to turn-of-the-century speech, which may not seem to possess the rhythms of modern speech. Moore masterfully manipulated language and syntax to create poems in which both poet and reader see through the examined objects to something larger. The true subject of many of her poems is the nature of perception. These poems, such as "Bowls" (1935) and "In the Days of Prismatic Color" (1924), typically begin on one tangent and end seemingly far afield on another.

"Nine Nectarines" (1935), "The Steeple-Jack" (1935, 1961) and to some extent "A Grave" (1924) more directly explore the nature of perception. Several of Moore's poems begin with an art-related image: "Nine Nectarines" is much like a still-life, whereas "When I Buy Pictures" (1921) examines an art that is anything but still. As finely detailed as any Albrecht Dürer etching, "The Steeple-Jack," originally one-third of the longer poem "Part of a Novel, Part of a Poem, Part of a Play" (1932), begins serenely but abruptly changes from an "etched" stillness to a "whirlwind" of confusion. Moore thereby introduces the element of danger, which clearly presents itself and demands to be taken into account. Danger is a very real element in other poems as well, such as "A Grave," in which the sea is a metaphor for death.

Moore's critical regard rose with the publication of *Collected Poems* (1951), which received a Pulitzer Prize, a National Book Award, and the Bollingen Prize. In 1954 she published the translation *The Fables of La Fontaine* (Jean de La Fontaine), a project begun after Moore's mother's death in 1947. Growing older Moore wrote fewer and less expansive poems, the intellectual rigor of her early poems replaced by a comparatively relaxed tone of voice, as in "Baseball and Writing" (1966).

Despite its title Moore's 1967 *Complete Poems* is by no means complete. Numerous poems are missing, and Moore notes in the preface that "omissions are not accidents." She radically revised others, turning many early syllabic poems into freer forms. Like other modernist poets Moore felt that revision is essential to the poetic process. Moore, who died in 1972, presented in *Complete Poems* the body of work she meant to preserve. Yet, the omitted poems, like all her poems, are treasures of language and intellect, of feeling and precision.

Suggested Readings: *Poems*, 1921. *Observations*, 1924. *The Pangolin and Other Verse*, 1936. *What Are Years?* 1941. *Nevertheless*, 1944. *The Fables of La Fontaine*, 1954. *Like a Bulwark*, 1956. *O to Be a Dragon*, 1959. *Tell Me, Tell Me*, 1967. *The Complete Prose of Marianne Moore*, 1986. R. Jarrell, "Two Essays on Marianne Moore," in *Poetry and the Age*, 1973. E. Bishop, "Efforts of Affection," in *The Collected Prose*, 1984. R. P. Blackmur, "The Method of Marianne Moore," in *Selected Essays of R. P. Blackmur*, 1986. G. Schulman, *Marianne Moore: The Poetry of Engagement*, 1986.

Texts Used: "Poetry": *Collected Poems*, 1955. All else: *Complete Poems*, 1981.

WHEN I BUY PICTURES

or what is closer to the truth,
when I look at that of which I may regard myself as the
imaginary possessor,
I fix upon what would give me pleasure in my average moments:
the satire upon curiosity in which no more is discernible
than the intensity of the mood,
or quite the opposite—the old thing, the medieval decorated
hat-box,
in which there are hounds with waists diminishing like the
waist of the hour-glass,
and deer and birds and seated people;
it may be no more than a square of parquetry;[1] the literal
biography perhaps,
in letters standing well apart upon a parchment-like expanse;   10
an artichoke in six varieties of blue; the snipe-legged
hieroglyphic in three parts;
the silver fence protecting Adam's grave,[2] or Michael taking
Adam by the wrist.[3]

---

[1] Inlaid woodwork in geometric forms, used especially in flooring.
[2] Moore's note: " 'A silver fence was erected by Constantine to enclose the grave of Adam.' *Literary Digest*, January 5, 1918, descriptive paragraph with photograph."
[3] Saint Michael, the archangel expelling Adam from Eden.

Too stern an intellectual emphasis upon this quality or that
                     detracts from one's enjoyment.
It must not wish to disarm anything; nor may the approved
                     triumph easily be honored—
that which is great because something else is small.
It comes to this: of whatever sort it is,
it must be "lit with piercing glances into the life of things";[4]
it must acknowledge the spiritual forces which have made it.

1921

POETRY*

I, too, dislike it: there are things that are important beyond
     all this fiddle.
Reading it, however, with a perfect contempt for it, one
     discovers in
it after all, a place for the genuine.
     Hands that can grasp, eyes
       that can dilate, hair that can rise
         if it must, these things are important not because a

high-sounding interpretation can be put upon them but be-
     cause they are
useful. When they become so derivative as to become
     unintelligible,
the same thing may be said for all of us, that we
     do not admire what
       we cannot understand: the bat
         holding on upside down or in quest of something to

10

eat, elephants pushing, a wild horse taking a roll, a tireless
     wolf under
a tree, the immovable critic twitching his skin like a horse
     that feels a flea, the base-
ball fan, the statistician—
     nor is it valid
       to discriminate against 'business documents and

school-books';[1] all these phenomena are important. One
     must make a distinction

---

[4] Moore's note: "A. R. Gordon, *The Poets of the Old Testament* (Hodder and Stoughton, 1919)."
     * A revised version of this poem, consisting largely of the first three lines only, was published in *The Complete Poems* (1967).
  [1] Moore's note: "*Diary of Tolstoy* (Dutton), p. 84. 'Where the boundary between prose and poetry lies, I shall never be able to understand. The question is raised in manuals of style, yet the answer to it lies beyond me. Poetry is verse; prose is not verse. Or else poetry is everything with the exception of business documents and school books.' "

however: when dragged into prominence by half poets,
    the result is not poetry,
nor till the poets among us can be   20
    'literalists of
    the imagination'[2]—above
      insolence and triviality and can present

for inspection, 'imaginary gardens with real toads in them',
    shall we have
it. In the meantime, if you demand on the one hand,
    the raw material of poetry in
    all its rawness and
    that which is on the other hand
      genuine, you are interested in poetry.

1921

IN THE DAYS OF PRISMATIC COLOR*

not in the days of Adam and Eve, but when Adam
    was alone; when there was no smoke and color was
fine, not with the refinement
    of early civilization art, but because
of its originality; with nothing to modify it but the

mist that went up, obliqueness was a variation
    of the perpendicular, plain to see and
to account for: it is no
    longer that; nor did the blue-red-yellow band
of incandescence that was color keep its stripe: it also is one of   10

those things into which much that is peculiar can be
    read; complexity is not a crime, but carry
it to the point of murkiness
    and nothing is plain. Complexity,
moreover, that has been committed to darkness, instead of

granting itself to be the pestilence that it is, moves all a-
    bout as if to bewilder us with the dismal
fallacy that insistence
    is the measure of achievement and that all
truth must be dark. Principally throat, sophistication is as it al-   20

[2] Moore's note: "*Yeats: Ideas of Good and Evil* (A. H. Bullen), p. 182. 'The limitation of his view was from the very intensity of his vision; he was a too literal realist of imagination, as others are of nature; and because he believed that the figures seen by the mind's eye, when exalted by inspiration, were "eternal existences," symbols of divine essences, he hated every grace of style that might obscure their lineaments.' "

    * The colors of the visible spectrum produced by passing white light through a prism: red, orange, yellow, green, blue, indigo, and violet.

ways has been—at the antipodes from the init-
    ial great truths. "Part of it was crawling, part of it[1]
was about to crawl, the rest
    was torpid in its lair." In the short-legged, fit-
ful advance, the gurgling and all the minutiae—we have the classic

multitude of feet. To what purpose! Truth is no Apollo
    Belvedere,[2] no formal thing. The wave may go over it if it likes.
Know that it will be there when it says,
    "I shall be there when the wave has gone by."

1921, 1924

A GRAVE

Man looking into the sea,
taking the view from those who have as much right to it as you have to it
    yourself,
it is human nature to stand in the middle of a thing,
but you cannot stand in the middle of this;
the sea has nothing to give but a well excavated grave.
The firs stand in a procession, each with an emerald turkey-foot at the top,
reserved as their contours, saying nothing;
repression, however, is not the most obvious characteristic of the sea;
the sea is a collector, quick to return a rapacious look.
There are others besides you who have worn that look—   10
whose expression is no longer a protest; the fish no longer investigate them
for their bones have not lasted:
men lower nets, unconscious of the fact that they are desecrating a grave,
and row quickly away—the blades of the oars
moving together with the feet of water-spiders as if there were no such
    thing as death.
The wrinkles progress among themselves in a phalanx[1]—beautiful under
    networks of foam,
and fade breathlessly while the sea rustles in and out of the seaweed;
the birds swim through the air at top speed, emitting cat-calls as heretofore—
the tortoise-shell scourges about the feet of the cliffs, in motion beneath them;
and the ocean, under the pulsation of lighthouses and noise of bell-buoys,   20
advances as usual, looking as if it were not that ocean in which dropped
    things are bound to sink—
in which if they turn and twist, it is neither with volition nor consciousness.

1924

---

[1] Moore's note: "'Part of it was crawling,' etc. Nestor, *Greek Anthology* (Loeb Classical Library), Vol. III, p. 129."
    [2] A restored Roman copy of the famous Greek statue of the sun god Apollo, probably by Leochares (4th century B.C.), in the Belvedere gallery of the Vatican Museum, Rome.
    [1] An ancient form of military formation of closely spaced infantrymen.

SILENCE

My father used to say,
"Superior people never make long visits,
have to be shown Longfellow's grave
or the glass flowers at Harvard.[1]
Self-reliant like the cat—
that takes its prey to privacy,
the mouse's limp tail hanging like a shoelace from its mouth—
they sometimes enjoy solitude,
and can be robbed of speech
by speech which has delighted them.   10
The deepest feeling always shows itself in silence;
not in silence, but restraint."
Nor was he insincere in saying, "Make my house your inn."[2]
Inns are not residences.

1924

THE STEEPLE-JACK*

Dürer[1] would have seen a reason for living
in a town like this, with eight stranded whales
to look at; with the sweet sea air coming into your house
on a fine day, from water etched
with waves as formal as the scales
on a fish.

One by one in two's and three's, the seagulls keep
flying back and forth over the town clock,
or sailing around the lighthouse without moving their wings—
rising steadily with a slight   10
quiver of the body—or flock
mewing where

a sea the purple of the peacock's neck is
paled to greenish azure as Dürer changed

---

[1] Moore's note: "My father used to say, 'Superior people never make long visits. When I am visiting, I like to go about by myself. I never had to be shown Longfellow's grave or the glass flowers at Harvard.' Miss A. M. Homans." The renowned poet Henry Wadsworth Longfellow (1807–1882) was buried in Cambridge, Massachusetts, the site of Harvard University's Peabody Museum, famous for its display of glass flowers.

[2] Moore's note: "Edmund Burke, in *Burke's Life,* by Sir James Prior (1872). 'Throw yourself into a coach,' said he. 'Come down and make my house your inn.' "

* A person who builds or repairs steeples.

[1] Albrecht Dürer (1471–1528), a German painter and engraver.

the pine green of the Tyrol[2] to peacock blue and guinea
gray.[3] You can see a twenty-five-
     pound lobster; and fish nets arranged
to dry. The

whirlwind fife-and-drum of the storm bends the salt
     marsh grass, disturbs stars in the sky and the   20
star on the steeple; it is a privilege to see so
much confusion. Disguised by what
     might seem the opposite, the sea-
side flowers and

trees are favored by the fog so that you have
     the tropics at first hand: the trumpet-vine,
fox-glove, giant snap-dragon, a salpiglossis[4] that has
spots and stripes; morning-glories, gourds,
     or moon-vines trained on fishing-twine
at the back door;   30

cat-tails, flags, blueberries and spiderwort,
     striped grass, lichens, sunflowers, asters, daisies—
yellow and crab-claw ragged sailors[5] with green bracts[6]—toad-plant,
petunias, ferns; pink lilies, blue
     ones, tigers; poppies; black sweet-peas.
The climate

is not right for the banyan, frangipani, or
     jack-fruit trees; or for exotic serpent
life. Ring lizard and snake-skin for the foot, if you see fit;
but here they've cats, not cobras, to   40
     keep down the rats. The diffident
little newt

with white pin-dots on black horizontal spaced-
     out bands lives here; yet there is nothing that
ambition can buy or take away. The college student
named Ambrose sits on the hillside
     with his not-native books and hat
and sees boats

at sea progress white and rigid as if in
     a groove. Liking an elegance of which   50
the source is not bravado, he knows by heart the antique

---

[2] An Alpine region in western Austria and northern Italy.   [3] Gray speckled with white.
[4] A Chilean annual plant of the nightshade family, cultivated for long-stalked, trumpet-shaped flowers.
[5] Bluebottles, or cornflowers.   [6] Leaves.

sugar-bowl shaped summer-house of
      interlacing slats, and the pitch
of the church

spire, not true, from which a man in scarlet lets
      down a rope as a spider spins a thread;
he might be part of a novel, but on the sidewalk a
sign says C. J. Poole, Steeple-Jack,
      in black and white; and one in red
and white says   60

Danger. The church portico has four fluted
      columns, each a single piece of stone, made
modester by white-wash. This would be a fit haven for
waifs, children, animals, prisoners,
      and presidents who have repaid
sin-driven

senators by not thinking about them. The
      place has a school-house, a post-office in a
store, fish-houses, hen-houses, a three-masted
      schooner on   70
the stocks. The hero, the student,
      the steeple-jack, each in his way,
is at home.

It could not be dangerous to be living
      in a town like this, of simple people,
who have a steeple-jack placing danger-signs by the church
while he is gilding the solid-
      pointed star, which on a steeple
stands for hope.

                                                         1932

BOWLS*

on the green
with lignum vitae balls[1] and ivory markers,
the pins planted in wild duck formation,
and quickly dispersed—
by this survival of ancient punctilio[2]
in the manner of Chinese lacquer-carving,
layer after layer exposed by certainty of touch and unhurried incision

---

* Lawn bowling, popular in England and Scotland.
[1] "Wood of life" (Latin), from a tropical evergreen of North America.   [2] Ceremony.

so that only so much color shall be revealed as is necessary to the picture,
I learn that we are precisionists,
not citizens of Pompeii[3] arrested in action   10
as a cross-section of one's correspondence would seem to imply.
Renouncing a policy of boorish indifference
to everything that has been said since the days of Matilda,[4]
I shall purchase an etymological dictionary of modern English
that I may understand what is written,
and like the ant and the spider
returning from time to time to headquarters,
shall answer the question
"why do I like winter better than I like summer?"
and acknowledge that it does not make me sick   20
to look playwrights and poets and novelists straight in the face—
that I feel just the same;
and I shall write to the publisher of the magazine
which will "appear the first day of the month
and disappear before one has had time to buy it
unless one takes proper precaution,"
and make an effort to please—
since he who gives quickly gives twice
in nothing so much as in a letter.

1935

NINE NECTARINES*

Arranged by two's as peaches are,
at intervals that all may live—
    eight and a single one, on twigs that
    grew the year before—they look like
a derivative;
    although not uncommonly
the opposite is seen—
nine peaches on a nectarine.
    Fuzzless through slender crescent leaves
        of green or blue or   10
        both, in the Chinese style, the four

---

[3] An ancient Italian city on the Bay of Naples; destroyed by an eruption of Mount Vesuvius in A.D. 79.

[4] The Empress Matilda (1102–1167), or Maud, who invaded England with her half-brother, Robert, earl of Gloucester, in 1139, was driven from London in 1141.

* Moore's note: " 'The Chinese believed the oval peaches, which are very red on one side, to be a symbol of long life. . . . According to the word of Chin-noug-king, the peach *Yu* prevents death. If it is not eaten in time, it at least preserves the body from decay until the end of the world.' Alphonse de Candolle, *Origin of Cultivated Plants* (Appleton, 1886)." De Candolle (1806–1893) was a Swiss botanist. The ellipsis is Moore's.

pairs' half-moon leaf-mosaic turns
out to the sun the sprinkled blush
  of puce[1]-American-Beauty pink
  applied to bees-wax gray by the
uninquiring brush
  of mercantile bookbinding.
Like the peach *Yu,* the red-
cheeked peach which cannot aid the dead,
    but eaten in time prevents death,   20
      the Italian
      peach-nut, Persian plum, Ispahan[2]

    secluded wall-grown nectarine,
as wild spontaneous fruit was
  found in China first. But was it wild?
  Prudent de Candolle would not say.
One perceives no flaws
  in this emblematic group
of nine, with leaf window
unquilted by *curculio*[3]   30
    which someone once depicted on
    this much-mended plate
    or in the also accurate

    unantlered moose or Iceland horse
or ass asleep against the old
  thick, low-leaning nectarine that is the
  color of the shrub-tree's brownish
flower.

   .   .   .   .   .   .

    A Chinese "understands
the spirit of the wilderness"   40
  and the nectarine-loving kylin[4]
  of pony appearance—the long-
tailed or the tailless
  small cinnamon-brown, common
camel-haired unicorn
with antelope feet and no horn,
    here enameled on porcelain.
    It was a Chinese
    who imagined this masterpiece.

1935

---

[1] Brownish purple.   [2] A Persian city.   [3] A beetle with a long snout.
   [4] Moore's note: "[A] Chinese unicorn. . . . It has the body of a stag, with a single horn, the tail of a
cow, horse's hoofs, a yellow belly, and hair of five colours."

THE PAPER NAUTILUS*

For authorities whose hopes
are shaped by mercenaries?
   Writers entrapped by
   teatime fame and by
commuters' comforts? Not for these
   the paper nautilus
   constructs her thin glass shell.

   Giving her perishable
souvenir of hope, a dull
   white outside and smooth-   10
   edged inner surface
glossy as the sea, the watchful
   maker of it guards it
   day and night; she scarcely

   eats until the eggs are hatched.
Buried eight-fold in her eight
   arms,[1] for she is in
   a sense a devil-
fish, her glass ram'shorn-cradled freight
   is hid but is not crushed;   20
   as Hercules,[2] bitten

   by a crab loyal to the hydra,
was hindered to succeed,
   the intensively
   watched eggs coming from
the shell free it when they are freed,—
   leaving its wasp-nest flaws
   of white on white, and close-

   laid Ionic chiton-folds[3]
like the lines in the mane of
   a Parthenon horse,[4]   30

---

  * A mollusk, the paper nautilus (or argonaut) is found mostly in warm waters; the young develop in a thin, paperlike egg case. The poem was written after the poet Elizabeth Bishop (1911–1979) presented Moore with one as a gift.

  [1] The paper nautilus is an octopod.

  [2] According to Roman myth, while the hero Hercules was attempting to perform the second of his twelve labors as prescribed by the king of Mycenae (to kill the many-headed Hydra), the supreme goddess Juno sent a huge crab to help the monster by biting Hercules's feet. When Hercules crushed the crab, Juno transformed it into the constellation Cancer.

  [3] The Ionic style of ancient Greek sculpture is graceful and delicate; a chiton is a loose, tuniclike garment worn by ancient Greeks.

  [4] A horse decoration on the Parthenon (the temple of the Greek goddess Athena), designed by the Greek sculptor Phidias (490?–430? B.C.) and sculpted under his supervision.

round which the arms had
wound themselves as if they knew love
    is the only fortress
    strong enough to trust to.

1940

WHAT ARE YEARS?

    What is our innocence,
what is our guilt? All are
    naked, none is safe. And whence
is courage: the unanswered question,
the resolute doubt,—
dumbly calling, deafly listening—that
in misfortune, even death,
        encourages others
        and in its defeat, stirs

    the soul to be strong? He   10
sees deep and is glad, who
    accedes to mortality
and in his imprisonment rises
upon himself as
the sea in a chasm, struggling to be
free and unable to be,
        in its surrendering
        finds its continuing.

    So he who strongly feels,
behaves. The very bird,   20
    grown taller as he sings, steels
his form straight up. Though he is captive,
his mighty singing
says, satisfaction is a lowly
thing, how pure a thing is joy.
        This is mortality,
        this is eternity.

1941

THE ANIMALS SICK OF THE PLAGUE

    A malady smote the earth one year,
    Felling beasts and infecting all with fear,
To prove to them what grave offenders they were;

Although plague was the name by which it was known,
For it literally congested Acheron,[1]
    Warring on creatures everywhere,
It did not bear off all but all were endangered.
    Any that lingered barely stirred—
Could merely breathe and that diseasedly.
    Nothing aroused their energy.   10
    Neither wolf nor fox disappeared
    To stalk young prey as it sunned.
    The demoralized doves scattered
    And love starved; life was moribund.

When the lion had called his constituency
    He said, "Dear friends, this is heaven's remedy
    For the sins we have thought a boon.
    So he who is guiltiest
Should sacrifice his good to that of the rest
And possibly most of us will then be immune.   20
In accord with the past, history suggests to one,
    Penance as atoning for evil done.
So without subterfuge, braving the consequence,
    Let each search his conscience.
As for me, I have preyed on flocks of sheep so often
    That I have become a glutton.
    Because they had wronged me? not once.
Moreover I would devour him when I mastered
    The shepherd.
Therefore let me be sacrificed in recompense,   30
But first make a clean breast, not just *I* say how I offend:
We must have justice and detect the trespass,
    Then rend the culprit's carcass."
The fox said, "Sire, you are too good to rend;
Your sense of honor is excessively nice.
Eat sheep, Sire! Poor dolts, their loss is no sacrifice.
A sinful king? Oh no. You prove when you devour
    The beasts that you thought them superior.
    As for the shepherd, one would swear
    That he went where he ought to go,   40
Having become to any of us, high or low,
    A monster none can endure."
When the fox said this, applause deafened the cur
    And no one dared to consider
    A tiger, bear, or other beast of prominence
    Guilty of any offense.
    In fact, quarrelers of evident spleen

---

[1] According to classical myth, the river in Hades (the Underworld), across which Charon ferried the dead.

Were canonized for their innocent mien.[2]
When his turn came the ass said, "To take a backward glance,
        I recall passing clerical domain,   50
The herbs and grass and hunger close to sustenance.
        Fiend take me, how could I refrain?
I nipped off as much grass as would lie on my tongue;
So sinned, if what we say must be disinterested."
They made too much noise to hear what the donkey said.
A wolf pronounced the verdict, to which he clung,
Convinced they had found the animal they must kill—
The battered rapscallion[3] who had made the world ill.
He deserved to be hung as an example.
Eat another's grass! What could be more horrible.   60
        Death, only death was suitable
For the criminal—inflicted at once by spite.
And so, as you are weak or are invincible,
The court says white is black or that black crimes are white.

                                                 1954

A JELLY-FISH

Visible, invisible,
    a fluctuating charm
an amber-tinctured amethyst
    inhabits it, your arm
approaches and it opens
    and it closes; you had meant
to catch it and it quivers;
    you abandon your intent.

                                                   1959

BASEBALL AND WRITING*

Suggested by post-game broadcasts.

Fanaticism? No. Writing is exciting
and baseball is like writing.
    You can never tell with either
        how it will go

---

[2] Appearance.   [3] Rascal.
  * An avid baseball fan, Moore refers throughout to various members of the New York Yankees
during the early 1960s.

or what you will do;
generating excitement—
a fever in the victim—
pitcher, catcher, fielder, batter.
    Victim in what category?
*Owl*man watching from the press box?
    To whom does it apply?
    Who is excited? Might it be I?

It's a pitcher's battle all the way—a duel—
a catcher's, as, with cruel
    puma paw, Elston Howard lumbers lightly
      back to plate. (His spring
      de-winged a bat swing.)
They have that killer instinct;
yet Elston—whose catching
arm has hurt them all with the bat—
    when questioned, says, unenviously,
    "I'm very satisfied. We won."
      Shorn of the batting crown,[1] says, "We";
      robbed by a technicality.

When three players on a side play three positions
and modify conditions,
    the massive run need not be everything.
      "Going, going . . . " Is
      it? Roger Maris
has it, running fast. You will
never see a finer catch. Well . . .
"Mickey,[2] leaping like the devil"—why
    gild it, although deer sounds better—
snares what was speeding towards its treetop nest,
    one-handing the souvenir-to-be
    meant to be caught by you or me.

Assign Yogi Berra to Cape Canaveral;
he could handle any missile.
    He is no feather. "Strike! . . . Strike *two!*"
      Fouled back. A blur.
      It's gone. You would infer
    that the bat had eyes.
    He put the wood to that one.
Praised, Skowron says, "Thanks, Mel.[3]
I think I helped a *little* bit."
      All business, each, and modesty.

10

20

30

40

---

[1] An accolade for the player with the highest batting average in a given year.   [2] Mickey Mantle.
[3] Bill ("Moose") Skowron; Mel Stottlemeyer.

Blanchard, Richardson, Kubek, Boyer.[4]
In that galaxy of nine, say which
won the pennant? *Each*. It was he.

Those two magnificent saves from the knee—throws   50
by Boyer, finesses in twos—
  like Whitey's[5] three kinds of pitch and pre-
    diagnosis
    with pick-off psychosis.
Pitching is a large subject.
Your arm, too true at first, can learn to
catch the corners—even trouble
    Mickey Mantle. ("Grazed a Yankee!
My baby pitcher, Montejo!"[6]
    With some pedagogy,[7]   60
    you'll be touch, premature prodigy.)

They crowd him and curve him and aim for the knees. Trying
indeed! The secret implying:
  "I can stand here, bat held steady."
    One may suit him;
    none has hit him.
  Imponderables smite him.
  Muscle kinks, infections, spike wounds
  require food, rest, respite from ruffians. (Drat it!
    Celebrity costs privacy!)   70
Cow's milk, "tiger's milk," soy milk, carrot juice,
    brewer's yeast (high-potency)—
    concentrates presage victory

sped by Luis Arroyo, Hector Lopez—
deadly in a pinch. And "Yes,
  it's work; I want you to bear down,
    but enjoy it
    while you're doing it."
Mr. Houk and Mr. Sain,[8]
If you have a rummage sale,   80
don't sell Roland Sheldon or Tom Tresh.
    Studded with stars in belt and crown,
the Stadium is an adastrium.[9]
    O flashing Orion,[10]
    your stars are muscled like the lion.

1966

[4] Johnny Blanchard, Bobby Richardson, Tony Kubek, Clete Boyer.   [5] Whitey Ford.
[6] Manny Montejo, of the Detroit Tigers.   [7] Instruction.
[8] Ralph Houk and Johnny Sain, then in management positions.
[9] Probably coined from *ad astrum*, "to the star" (Latin).
[10] An equatorial constellation, the hunter.

T. S. Eliot
(1888–1965)

In April 1956 Thomas Stearns Eliot gave the lecture "The Frontiers of Criticism" in a stadium at the University of Minnesota. Fourteen thousand people heard him speak. Today such vast crowds seem to gather only for rock bands, sporting events, and presidential candidates. That so many people were interested in hearing T. S. Eliot points to his position late in life as the leading poet and man of letters of his day.

Eliot was born in St. Louis to a transplanted New England family: his grandfather founded Washington University in St. Louis; his father ran a brick-manufacturing firm; and his mother fostered Eliot's interest in literature. A 1910 Harvard University graduate, he earned an M.A. in Sanskrit and philosophy from Harvard in 1914. Eliot then settled in England and did not visit the United States until eighteen years had passed. He married Vivienne Haigh-Wood in 1915 and worked as a bank clerk in London from 1918 to 1924. His wife's continuous illnesses and his father's disapproval and subsequent death led Eliot to an emotional breakdown. (Vivienne, ultimately institutionalized, died in 1947.)

Recovered, Eliot went on to edit the journals *The Egoist* and *The Criterion* (which he founded in 1922 and continued to edit until 1939). In 1927 he took British citizenship and joined the Anglican church, actions that had profound effects on the content and scope of his poetry. Despite his adopted citizenship, Eliot retained an American sensibility. In a 1959 interview for *Writers at Work,* Eliot said of his poetry that "in its sources, in its emotional springs, it comes from America."

Shortly after moving to England, Eliot met Ezra Pound. In September 1914 Pound wrote to Harriet Monroe, the editor of *Poetry* magazine, that Eliot "has actually trained himself *and* modernized himself *on his own*." Pound's comment focuses on Eliot's education and poetic craftsmanship. Eliot was well read (or "trained") in a number of languages and traditions, including Latin and Greek classics, French and German, and Eastern philosophy. Eliot started "modernizing himself," using techniques that Pound thought essential for the revitalization of poetry, by reading French symbolist poetry, which he first encountered in Arthur Symons's *The Symbolist Movement in Literature* (1899). That book led Eliot to read the poetry of Jules Laforgue, from which he learned the technique of introverted irony and of splitting the personality into two, techniques that Eliot used in his first volume of poems, *Prufrock and Other Observations* (1917).

In "The Love Song of J. Alfred Prufrock," the first poem in that volume, Prufrock, a mild, ineffectual man approaching middle age, discusses with himself visiting a woman to make some sort of declaration. He is the victim of an overactive imagination that paralyzes him with scenarios of the fool he might appear to be. The first image in the poem, "the evening spread out against the sky / Like a patient etherized upon a table," is notable not only for its antiromantic shock value, but also as a description of Prufrock himself. Prufrock finally decides that it is too late to visit the woman and takes no action at all. The doubling of his personality into "you and I" is Laforgian, as is the irony in the poem, which Prufrock directs at himself. He compares his indecision with that of Hamlet, a heroic figure, and thinks that he is more like Polonius, an officious busybody who might start a scene but would never be the central character.

"Sweeney Among the Nightingales" appeared in Eliot's second volume, *Poems* (1920). Many of the poems of that volume were written in quatrains, because Eliot and Pound decided that free verse had been overused and that they should try to work in a tighter form. "Sweeney" exemplifies the way Eliot conflates past and present. The poem seems to be leading to some dreadful action against Sweeney although nothing dreadful actually occurs in the poem. Eliot parallels Sweeney's plight with that of Agamemnon, the Greek commander in the Trojan War, killed by his wife on his return from Troy, and with the fate of Philomela, a princess of Athens, turned into a nightingale after her brother-in-law raped her and cut out her tongue. Eliot is not saying that the past is better than the present or vice-versa. Rather, he makes Sweeney (the present) seem more heroic by drawing him together with Agamemnon (the past) and at the same time deflates Agamemnon's heroism by comparing him with Sweeney. Further, Eliot suggests the unheroic aspect of Agamemnon's career, the aspect that caused his wife's deadly hatred.

This complicated use of the past is further developed in Eliot's next major poem, *The Waste Land,* published in 1922, as was James Joyce's *Ulysses.* In his essay *"Ulysses, Order and Myth"* (appearing in *The Dial,* November 1923) Eliot describes Joyce's "mythic method" as "manipulating a continuous parallel between contemporaneity and antiquity," providing a means "of controlling, of ordering, of giving a shape and a significance to the immense panorama of futility and anarchy which is contemporary history." This description applies as well to Eliot's method in *The Waste Land,* which has been thought to be emblematic of the despair felt after World War I. The poem combines fragments of the literature of the past, "shoring" them against the ruins of contemporary society.

The Waste Land became more disjunct, or fragmented, as a result of Ezra Pound's input. His editing removed abstraction, description, and narration and focused on concrete images, in the process making the poem less conventional in rhyme and meter. The disjunctive quality of the poem makes it difficult for the reader to organize into a whole. Eliot's first note to the poem indicates one way, pointing the reader to Jessie Weston's anthropological study of the Grail legend, *From Ritual to Romance* (1920), as an important source for the poem. Weston's book ties the Arthurian Grail legends to pre-Christian fertility myths found in many cultures. In the Arthurian versions a knight must go to the Chapel Perilous and ask questions about the objects he sees there, which usually include a lance and a cup. Asking the appropriate questions results in the healing of the wounded Fisher King and his land, both of which have been rendered sterile. Eliot also recognizes the influence of James G. Frazer's *The Golden Bough* (1907–1915), a compendium of worldwide myths and ritual practices that finds similarities in myths of different cultures. This comparative approach to culture lies behind Eliot's conflation of Eastern and Western religion, myth, and literature in *The Waste Land.*

Whereas many of Eliot's shorter poems are dramatic monologues, *The Waste Land* contains a series of voices, generally unidentified, speaking in sequence. The voices are filtered through the consciousness of Tiresias, the blind seer who has been both male and female. In the poem's landscape of urban and rural desert, the speakers are involved in fruitless sexual relationships and prefer death to the rebirth possible only if rain comes to the Waste Land, if the questions are asked and the Fisher King healed. Voices ask questions throughout the poem, but none of the questions seems to be the right one: while a damp wind blows and the thunder rolls at the end of the poem, no rain falls.

After *The Waste Land* Eliot published *The Hollow Men* (1925), which seems a distillation of the material of *The Waste Land.* At this point Eliot had to find some new poetic

Antonello da Messina's striking painting The Crucifixion *(1455?), which T. S. Eliot saw in Antwerp, heightened Eliot's interest in religious themes and images.*

avenue; he could go no further with that material. Out of his conversion to Anglicanism came *Ash-Wednesday* (1930) and his Ariel poems (from the Old Testament name for Jerusalem). Each published separately as a sort of Christmas card, the Ariel poems deal with a yearning for revelation, a seeking of fulfillment within a world lacking faith and certainty. *Journey of the Magi* (1927), the first of the Ariel poems, is a dramatic monologue spoken by one of the Magi after returning from the visit to the Christ child. He has seen the beginning of the New Dispensation but has no knowledge of the sacrifice yet to be made. He is caught between the old and the new, waiting for some revelation that he has no assurance will ever come. The despair in the Magus's words reflects the despair Eliot saw in so much of the early twentieth century: an old faith fading with no new faith to take its place. Eliot chose to revive the old faith in his own life, deciding that no other could do as well.

In *Marina* (1930), the last of the Ariel poems, Shakespeare's Pericles awakens to discover his lost daughter. In this dramatic monologue Pericles speaks of his wonder and joy. The fullness of revelation seems to be his, as the event for which he has long wished has finally happened. Eliot juxtaposes a quotation from the Roman philosopher/dramatist Seneca, however, to show the opposite possibility: Hercules awakens from madness to find his children dead by his own hand. Pericles' joy must be understood in contrast to the other extreme.

In the 1930s Eliot wrote the verse dramas *Murder in the Cathedral* (1935) and *The Family Reunion* (1939). However, with the intervention of World War II and the closing of London theaters, Eliot returned to writing nondramatic poetry. In 1935 he had written

Burnt Norton (1936), which begins with passages taken from *Murder in the Cathedral.* Then he wrote three more poems using the same structure and themes—time and eternity, memory and history—and named the group *Four Quartets* (1943). *East Coker* (1940), the second of the four, is concerned with Eliot's family history and the history of England. Whereas *Burnt Norton* speculates on what might have happened, *East Coker* focuses on what has happened. The other two poems in the cycle are *The Dry Salvages* (1941) and *Little Gidding* (1942).

East Coker is the English village from which Eliot's family migrated to America in the seventeenth century. Eliot roots the poem and his family in the English Renaissance, a time of growth and change in literature, science, and exploration. The motto of Mary, Queen of Scots, whose end came from a beheading ax, reminds the reader of the cyclical nature of life: the earth, composed of "flesh, fur and faeces," is part of growth and change. As the other quartets are tied to air, fire, and water, *East Coker* is the quartet of earth—the earth of burial, the earth of rebirth in the cyclical pattern of the seasons. Part four of *East Coker* uses the metaphor of the wounded surgeon (Christ) to discuss the paradoxical nature of mankind's salvation. The dying that is inevitable can be redeemed by the wounded surgeon; "dying of the absolute paternal care" gives life. The paradoxes of Christianity take human beings beyond the cyclical living and dying of earth. The poet seeks to find the "still point," the eternal, but the cycles of change, death, and rebirth make such stillness difficult to obtain. Eliot has moved beyond the despair of *The Waste Land* to a vision of life that includes death and rebirth, not fearing or denying the possibility of renewal.

After *Four Quartets* Eliot wrote almost no nondramatic poetry. He returned to the stage with three more verse plays, of which the most successful was *The Cocktail Party* (1950). In 1948 he won the Nobel Prize for literature and the British Order of Merit. Eliot received numerous other awards and was met by huge crowds wherever he went. At age sixty-eight he married his longtime secretary, Valerie Fletcher. He died in 1965, and his ashes are buried in the church at East Coker.

Suggested Readings: *The Sacred Wood,* 1920. *The Use of Poetry and the Use of Criticism,* 1933. *Selected Essays,* 1950. *On Poetry and Poets,* 1957. *Collected Plays,* 1962. *Collected Poems 1909–1962,* 1963. *To Criticise the Critic,* 1965. *The Waste Land, a Facsimile and Transcripts of the Original Drafts,* ed. V. Eliot, 1971. *Selected Prose of T. S. Eliot,* ed. F. Kermode, 1975. *The Letters of T. S. Eliot,* Vol. 1, ed. V. Eliot, 1988. H. Gardner, *The Art of T. S. Eliot,* 1949. N. Frye, *T. S. Eliot,* 1963. D. C. Gallup, *T. S. Eliot: A Bibliography,* 1969. A. W. Litz, ed., *Eliot in His Time: Essays on the Occasion of the Fiftieth Anniversary of The Waste Land,* 1973. L. Gordon, *Eliot's Early Years,* 1977. H. Gardner, *The Composition of Four Quartets,* 1978. J. Reibetanz, *A Reading of Four Quartets,* 1983. P. Ackroyd, *T. S. Eliot: A Life,* 1984. R. Bush, *T. S. Eliot: A Study in Character and Style,* 1984. L. Gordon, *Eliot's New Life,* 1988.

Text Used: *The Complete Poems and Plays,* 1969.

THE LOVE SONG OF J. ALFRED PRUFROCK*

S'io credessi che mia risposta fosse
a persona che mai tornasse al mondo,
questa fiamma staria senza più scosse.

---

* First published in *Poetry* in 1915 and collected in Eliot's first volume of poems, *Prufrock and Other Observations* (1917); the ellipses are Eliot's.

Ma per ciò che giammai di questo fondo
non torno vivo alcun, s'i' odo il vero,
senza tema d'infamia ti rispondo.[1]

Let us go then, you and I,
When the evening is spread out against the sky
Like a patient etherised upon a table;
Let us go, through certain half-deserted streets,
The muttering retreats
Of restless nights in one-night cheap hotels
And sawdust restaurants with oyster-shells:
Streets that follow like a tedious argument
Of insidious intent
To lead you to an overwhelming question . . .   10
Oh, do not ask, 'What is it?'
Let us go and make our visit.

In the room the women come and go
Talking of Michelangelo.

The yellow fog that rubs its back upon the window-panes,
The yellow smoke that rubs its muzzle on the window-panes,
Licked its tongue into the corners of the evening,
Lingered upon the pools that stand in drains,
Let fall upon its back the soot that falls from chimneys,
Slipped by the terrace, made a sudden leap,   20
And seeing that it was a soft October night,
Curled once about the house, and fell asleep.

And indeed there will be time
For the yellow smoke that slides along the street
Rubbing its back upon the window-panes;
There will be time, there will be time
To prepare a face to meet the faces that you meet;
There will be time to murder and create,
And time for all the works and days[2] of hands
That lift and drop a question on your plate;   30
Time for you and time for me,
And time yet for a hundred indecisions,
And for a hundred visions and revisions,
Before the taking of a toast and tea.

In the room the women come and go
Talking of Michelangelo.

---

[1] "If I thought my reply were to one who could return to the world, this flame would stop flickering. But since no one returns alive from this pit, if what I hear is true, I answer you without fear of dishonor" (Italian), from *Inferno* (XXVII. 61–66), by Dante Alighieri (1265–1321). Spoken to the character Dante by Guido da Montefeltro, who, while wrapped in flame, confesses to the sin of fraudulent counseling.

[2] *Works and Days*, an agricultural poem by the Greek poet Hesiod (8th century B.C.).

And indeed there will be time
To wonder, 'Do I dare?' and, 'Do I dare?'
Time to turn back and descend the stair,
With a bald spot in the middle of my hair—   40
(They will say: 'How his hair is growing thin!')
My morning coat, my collar mounting firmly to the chin,
My necktie rich and modest, but asserted by a simple pin—
(They will say: 'But how his arms and legs are thin!')
Do I dare
Disturb the universe?
In a minute there is time
For decisions and revisions which a minute will reverse.

For I have known them all already, known them all—
Have known the evenings, mornings, afternoons,   50
I have measured out my life with coffee spoons;
I know the voices dying with a dying fall
Beneath the music from a farther room.
    So how should I presume?

And I have known the eyes already, known them all—
The eyes that fix you in a formulated phrase,
And when I am formulated, sprawling on a pin,
When I am pinned and wriggling on the wall,
Then how should I begin
To spit out all the butt-ends of my days and ways?   60
    And how should I presume?

And I have known the arms already, known them all—
Arms that are braceleted and white and bare
(But in the lamplight, downed with light brown hair!)
Is it perfume from a dress
That makes me so digress?
Arms that lie along a table, or wrap about a shawl.
    And should I then presume?
    And how should I begin?

                .   .   .   .   .

Shall I say, I have gone at dusk through narrow streets   70
And watched the smoke that rises from the pipes
Of lonely men in shirt-sleeves, leaning out of windows? . . .

    I should have been a pair of ragged claws
Scuttling across the floors of silent seas.

                .   .   .   .   .

And the afternoon, the evening, sleeps so peacefully!
Smoothed by long fingers,
Asleep . . . tired . . . or it malingers,
Stretched on the floor, here beside you and me.
Should I, after tea and cakes and ices,

Have the strength to force the moment to its crisis?   80
But though I have wept and fasted, wept and prayed,
Though I have seen my head (grown slightly bald)
    brought in upon a platter,[3]
I am no prophet—and here's no great matter;
I have seen the moment of my greatness flicker,
And I have seen the eternal Footman hold my coat, and snicker,
And in short, I was afraid.

    And would it have been worth it, after all,
After the cups, the marmalade, the tea,
Among the porcelain, among some talk of you and me,
Would it have been worth while,   90
To have bitten off the matter with a smile,
To have squeezed the universe into a ball[4]
To roll it towards some overwhelming question,
To say: 'I am Lazarus, come from the dead,[5]
Come back to tell you all, I shall tell you all'—
If one, settling a pillow by her head,
    Should say: 'That is not what I meant at all.
    That is not it, at all.'

    And would it have been worth it, after all,
Would it have been worth while,   100
After the sunsets and the dooryards and the sprinkled streets,
After the novels, after the teacups, after the skirts that trail along
    the floor—
And this, and so much more?—
It is impossible to say just what I mean!
But as if a magic lantern threw the nerves in patterns on a screen:
Would it have been worth while
If one, settling a pillow or throwing off a shawl,
And turning toward the window, should say:
    'That is not it at all,
    That is not what I meant, at all.'   110

                .   .   .   .

    No! I am not Prince Hamlet, nor was meant to be;
Am an attendant lord, one that will do
To swell a progress,[6] start a scene or two,
Advise the prince; no doubt, an easy tool,
Deferential, glad to be of use,

---

[3] In Matthew 14:3–11, when Salome, Herodias's daughter, pleased Herod with her dancing, he promised her anything she requested. She asked for and received the head of the prophet John the Baptist on a platter.

[4] "Let us roll all our strength and all / Our sweetness up into one ball / And tear our pleasures with rough strife / Through the iron gates of life," from "To His Coy Mistress," by the English poet Andrew Marvell (1621–1628).

[5] In John 11:1–44 Jesus raised Lazarus from the dead.   [6] A royal procession.

Politic, cautious, and meticulous;
Full of high sentence,[7] but a bit obtuse;
At times, indeed, almost ridiculous—
Almost, at times, the Fool.

I grow old . . . I grow old . . .   120
I shall wear the bottoms of my trousers rolled.

Shall I part my hair behind? Do I dare to eat a peach?
I shall wear white flannel trousers, and walk upon the beach.
I have heard the mermaids singing, each to each.

I do not think that they will sing to me.
I have seen them riding seaward on the waves
Combing the white hair of the waves blown back
When the wind blows the water white and black.

We have lingered in the chambers of the sea
By sea-girls wreathed with seaweed red and brown   130
Till human voices wake us, and we drown.

                                    1910–1911, 1915

COUSIN NANCY

Miss Nancy Ellicott
Strode across the hills and broke them,
Rode across the hills and broke them—
The barren New England hills—
Riding to hounds
Over the cow-pasture.

Miss Nancy Ellicott smoked
And danced all the modern dances;
And her aunts were not quite sure how they felt about it,
But they knew that it was modern.   10

Upon the glazen shelves kept watch
Matthew and Waldo,[1] guardians of the faith,
The army of unalterable law.[2]

                                    1917

---

[7] Judgment or opinion.
[1] Matthew Arnold (1822–1888) and Ralph Waldo Emerson (1803–1882), guardians of Victorian moral and literary standards.
[2] In the sonnet "Lucifer in Starlight," by the English novelist and poet George Meredith (1829–1909), Lucifer (the Devil) soars over the earth until he looks up: "He reached a middle height, and at the stars, / Which are the brain of heaven, he looked, and sank. / Around the ancient track marched, rank on rank, / The army of unalterable law."

LA FIGLIA CHE PIANGE*

O quam te memorem virgo . . . [1]

Stand on the highest pavement of the stair—
Lean on a garden urn—
Weave, weave the sunlight in your hair—
Clasp your flowers to you with a pained surprise—
Fling them to the ground and turn
With a fugitive resentment in your eyes:
But weave, weave the sunlight in your hair.

So I would have had him leave,
So I would have had her stand and grieve,
So he would have left   10
As the soul leaves the body torn and bruised,
As the mind deserts the body it has used.
I should find
Some way incomparably light and deft,
Some way we both should understand,
Simple and faithless as a smile and shake of the hand.

She turned away, but with the autumn weather
Compelled my imagination many days,
Many days and many hours:
Her hair over her arms and her arms full of flowers.   20
And I wonder how they should have been together!
I should have lost a gesture and a pose.
Sometimes these cogitations still amaze
The troubled midnight and the noon's repose.

1917

SWEENEY AMONG THE NIGHTINGALES†

ὤμοι, πέπληγμαι καιρίαν πληγὴν ἔσω.[1]

Apeneck Sweeney spreads his knees
Letting his arms hang down to laugh,

---

* "The Girl Who Weeps" (Italian). In 1911 Eliot looked for, but was unable to find, a carved Greek slab by this name in a northern Italian museum.
[1] "Maiden, by what name should I call you?" from the *Aeneid* (I.327), by the Roman poet Virgil (70–19 B.C.). Aeneas asks this of the love goddess Venus, his mother, who appears to him in the guise of a young huntress.
† Eliot's symbolic character Sweeney, a vulgar person, is introduced in "Mr. Eliot's Sunday Morning Service" (1918) and appears again in such poems as "Sweeney Erect" (1919), *The Waste Land* (1922), and *Sweeney Agonistes* (1926–1927).
[1] "Alas, I have been struck by a mortal blow," from *Agamemnon* (l.1343), by the Greek tragedian Aeschylus (525?–456 B.C.): the last words of Agamemnon, the leader of the Greeks in the Trojan War, who was killed in his bath by his wife, Clytemnestra.

The zebra stripes along his jaw
Swelling to maculate² giraffe.

The circles of the stormy moon
Slide westward toward the River Plate,³
Death and the Raven⁴ drift above
And Sweeney guards the hornèd gate.⁵

Gloomy Orion and the Dog⁶
Are veiled; and hushed the shrunken seas;   10
The person in the Spanish cape
Tries to sit on Sweeney's knees

Slips and pulls the table cloth
Overturns a coffee-cup,
Reorganised upon the floor
She yawns and draws a stocking up;

The silent man in mocha brown
Sprawls at the window-sill and gapes;
The waiter brings in oranges
Bananas figs and hothouse grapes;   20

The silent vertebrate in brown
Contracts and concentrates, withdraws;
Rachel *née* Rabinovitch
Tears at the grapes with murderous paws;

She and the lady in the cape
Are suspect, thought to be in league;
Therefore the man with heavy eyes
Declines the gambit, shows fatigue,

Leaves the room and reappears
Outside the window, leaning in,   30
Branches of wistaria
Circumscribe a golden grin;

The host with someone indistinct
Converses at the door apart,
The nightingales⁷ are singing near
The Convent of the Sacred Heart,

---

² Spotted, blotched.   ³ The Río de la Plata, an estuary between Uruguay and Argentina.
⁴ The southern constellation Corvus, the Crow.
⁵ According to Greek myth, one of the two gates of the dead. False dreams come to humans through the ivory gate, true dreams through the horn gate.
⁶ The equatorial constellation of the hunter, and the nearby "Dog Star," Sirius, the hunter's dog.
⁷ According to Greek myth, Philomela was raped by her brother-in-law, Tereus, who cut out her tongue to prevent her from identifying him as her attacker. She wove a tapestry showing what had happened and sent it to her sister, Procne. Philomela was turned into a nightingale, Procne into a swallow.

And sang within the bloody wood
When Agamemnon cried aloud
And let their liquid siftings fall
To stain the stiff dishonoured shroud.   40

1918

THE WASTE LAND*

'Nam Sibyllam quidem Cumis ego ipse oculis meis vidi in ampulla pendere, et cum illi
pueri dicerent: Σίβυλλα τί θέλεις; respondebat illa: ἀποθανεῖν θέλω.'[1]

For Ezra Pound
il miglior fabbro.[2]

I. The Burial of the Dead[3]

April is the cruellest month, breeding
Lilacs out of the dead land, mixing
Memory and desire, stirring
Dull roots with spring rain.
Winter kept us warm, covering
Earth in forgetful snow, feeding
A little life with dried tubers.
Summer surprised us, coming over the Starnbergersee[4]
With a shower of rain; we stopped in the colonnade,
And went on in sunlight, into the Hofgarten,[5]   10

---

* Eliot states in *The Frontiers of Criticism* (1956), "When it came to print *The Waste Land* as a little book [1922]—for the poem on its first appearance in *The Dial* [1922] and in *The Criterion* [1922] had no notes whatever—it was discovered that the poem was inconveniently short, so I set to work to expand the notes, in order to provide a few more pages of printed matter. . . . " Eliot's note: "Not only the title, but the plan and a good deal of the incidental symbolism of the poem were suggested by Miss Jessie L. Weston's book on the Grail legend: *From Ritual to Romance* (Cambridge [1920]). Indeed, so deeply am I indebted, Miss Weston's book will elucidate the difficulties of the poem much better than my notes can do; and I recommend it (apart from the great interest of the book itself) to any who think such elucidation of the poem worth the trouble. To another work of anthropology I am indebted in general, one which has influenced our generation profoundly; I mean *The Golden Bough* [(1890), by the Scottish anthropologist Sir James Frazer]; I have used especially the two volumes *Adonis, Attis, Osiris.* Anyone who is acquainted with these works will immediately recognise in the poem certain references to vegetation ceremonies."

[1] "For I myself with my own eyes saw the Sibyl of Cumae hanging in a bottle, and when the boys asked her: 'Sibyl, what do you want?' she responded, 'I want to die,'" from *Satyricon* (Ch. 48), by the Roman satirist Petronius (?–A.D. 66). According to Roman myth, the sun god Apollo granted the sibyl (a prophetess) immortality, but, having forgotten to ask for eternal youth, she was doomed to perpetual old age.

[2] "The best maker" (Italian), from *Purgatorio* (XXVI.117), by Dante Alighieri (1265–1321). Dante praises the Italian poet Guido Guinizelli (1240?–1274), who responds that the Provençal poet Arnaut Daniel (12th century B.C.) is the best maker of poetry. Pound (1885–1972) edited *The Waste Land*.

[3] The burial service in the Anglican *Book of Common Prayer*.

[4] A lake south of Munich.   [5] A public garden in Munich.

And drank coffee, and talked for an hour.
Bin gar keine Russin, stamm' aus Litauen, echt deutsch.[6]
And when we were children, staying at the arch-duke's,
My cousin's, he took me out on a sled,
And I was frightened. He said, Marie,
Marie, hold on tight. And down we went.
In the mountains, there you feel free.
I read, much of the night, and go south in the winter.

What are the roots that clutch, what branches grow
Out of this stony rubbish? Son of man,[7]   20
You cannot say, or guess, for you know only
A heap of broken images, where the sun beats,
And the dead tree gives no shelter, the cricket no relief,[8]
And the dry stone no sound of water. Only
There is shadow under this red rock,
(Come in under the shadow of this red rock),
And I will show you something different from either
Your shadow at morning striding behind you
Or your shadow at evening rising to meet you;
I will show you fear in a handful of dust.   30
> *Frisch weht der Wind*[9]
> *Der Heimat zu*
> *Mein Irisch Kind*
> *Wo weilest du?*

'You gave me hyacinths first a year ago;
'They called me the hyacinth girl.'[10]
—Yet when we came back, late, from the hyacinth garden,
Your arms full, and your hair wet, I could not
Speak, and my eyes failed, I was neither
Living nor dead, and I knew nothing,   40
Looking into the heart of light, the silence.
Oed' und leer das Meer.[11]

Madame Sosostris, famous clairvoyante,
Had a bad cold, nevertheless
Is known to be the wisest woman in Europe,
With a wicked pack of cards.[12] Here, said she,

---

[6] "I am not at all Russian, I come from Lithuania, a real German" (German).

[7] Eliot's note: "Cf. Ezekiel II, i," in which God tells the "Son of man," the prophet Ezekiel, "Stand upon thy feet, and I will speak unto thee."

[8] Eliot's note: "Cf. Ecclesiastes XII, v," in which old age is said to be a time when "the grasshopper shall be a burden, and desire shall fail."

[9] "Fresh blows the wind / to the homeland / my Irish child / where are you waiting?" (German). Eliot's note: "V. *Tristan und Isolde,* I. verses 5–8," an opera by Richard Wagner (1813–1883).

[10] According to Greek myth, Hyacinthus was a youth accidentally killed by Apollo, who resurrected the boy as a flower, the hyacinth, which came to symbolize rebirth.

[11] "Empty and barren is the sea" (German). Eliot's note: "Id. III, verse 24." Near the end of Wagner's opera, the dying Tristan is told that his love Isolde's ship cannot be seen.

[12] Eliot's note: "I am not familiar with the exact constitution of the Tarot pack of cards, from which I have obviously departed to suit my own convenience. The Hanged Man, a member of the traditional

Is your card, the drowned Phoenician Sailor,
(Those are pearls that were his eyes.[13] Look!)
Here is Belladonna, the Lady of the Rocks,[14]
The lady of situations.   50
Here is the man with three staves, and here the Wheel,
And here is the one-eyed merchant, and this card,
Which is blank, is something he carries on his back,
Which I am forbidden to see. I do not find
The Hanged Man. Fear death by water.
I see crowds of people, walking round in a ring.
Thank you. If you see dear Mrs. Equitone,
Tell her I bring the horoscope myself:
One must be so careful these days.

    Unreal City,[15]   60
Under the brown fog of a winter dawn,
A crowd flowed over London Bridge, so many,
I had not thought death had undone so many.[16]
Sighs, short and infrequent, were exhaled,[17]
And each man fixed his eyes before his feet.
Flowed up the hill and down King William Street,
To where Saint Mary Woolnoth[18] kept the hours
With a dead sound on the final stroke of nine.[19]
There I saw one I knew, and stopped him, crying: 'Stetson!
'You who were with me in the ships at Mylae![20]   70
'That corpse you planted last year in your garden,
'Has it begun to sprout? Will it bloom this year?
'Or has the sudden frost disturbed its bed?

---

pack, fits my purpose in two ways: because he is associated in my mind with the Hanged God of Frazer, and because I associate him with the hooded figure in the passage of the disciples of Emmaus in Part V. The Phoenician Sailor and the Merchant appear later; also the 'crowds of people,' and Death by Water is executed in Part IV. The Man with Three Staves (an authentic member of the Tarot pack) I associate, quite arbitrarily, with the Fisher King himself."

[13] In Shakespeare's *The Tempest* (I.ii.397–402) Ariel sings to Ferdinand, who fears that his father has drowned: "Full fathom five thy father lies, / Of his bones are coral made: / Those are pearls that were his eyes: / Nothing of him that doth fade, / But doth suffer a sea-change / Into something rich and strange."

[14] "Beautiful lady" (Italian), the poisonous plant nightshade and a cosmetic; also the Virgin Mary of the painting *Madonna of the Rocks,* by Leonardo da Vinci.

[15] Eliot's note: "Cf. Baudelaire: 'Fourmillante cité, cité pleine de rêves, / Où le spectre en plein jour raccroche le passant' " (French): "Swarming city, city full of dreams, / Where the specter in broad daylight accosts the passerby," from *Les Fleurs du Mal* (*The Flowers of Evil,* 1857), by the French symbolist Charles Baudelaire (1821–1867).

[16] Eliot's note: "Cf. *Inferno,* III, 55–57: 'si lunga tratta / di gente, ch'io non avrei mai creduto / che morte tanta n'avesse disfatta' " (Italian): "such a long train / of people, I should not have believed / that death had undone so many." Entering the Inferno, Dante sees the hordes of people who made no choices in life and therefore have been rejected by both Heaven and Hell.

[17] Eliot's note: "Cf. *Inferno,* IV, 25–27: 'Quivi, secondo che per ascoltare, / non avea pianto ma' che di sospiri, / che l'aura eterna facevan tremare' " (Italian): "Here, to judge by hearing, there was no weeping but sighs / that made the eternal air tremble." Dante is in the first circle of the Inferno, Limbo, where the virtuous non-Christians suffer only from the fact that they can never see God.

[18] A London church.

[19] Eliot's note: "A phenomenon which I have often noticed."

[20] The site of a Roman naval victory against Carthage (260 B.C.).

'O keep the Dog far hence, that's friend to men,[21]
'Or with his nails he'll dig it up again!
'You! hypocrite lecteur!—mon semblable,—mon frère!'[22]

II. A GAME OF CHESS[23]

The Chair she sat in, like a burnished throne,[24]
Glowed on the marble, where the glass
Held up by standards wrought with fruited vines
From which a golden Cupidon[25] peeped out   80
(Another hid his eyes behind his wing)
Doubled the flames of sevenbranched candelabra
Reflecting light upon the table as
The glitter of her jewels rose to meet it,
From satin cases poured in rich profusion.
In vials of ivory and coloured glass
Unstoppered, lurked her strange synthetic perfumes,
Unguent, powdered, or liquid—troubled, confused
And drowned the sense in odours; stirred by the air
That freshened from the window, these ascended   90
In fattening the prolonged candle-flames,
Flung their smoke into the laquearia,[26]
Stirring the pattern on the coffered ceiling.
Huge sea-wood fed with copper
Burned green and orange, framed by the coloured stone,
In which sad light a carvèd dolphin swam.
Above the antique mantel was displayed
As though a window gave upon the sylvan scene[27]
The change of Philomel, by the barbarous king[28]

[21] Eliot's note: "Cf. the Dirge in Webster's *White Devil*." The play *The White Devil or Vittoria Corombona* (1610?), by John Webster (1580?–1625?), ends, "But keep the wolf far thence, that's foe to men; / For with his nails he'll dig them up again."

[22] Eliot's note: "V. Baudelaire, Preface to *Fleurs du Mal*." The prefatory poem to this volume, titled "Au Lecteur" ("To the Reader") ends with the line, "You! Hypocritical reader!—my counterpart,— my brother!"

[23] Probably refers to one of two plays by Thomas Middleton (1570?–1627): *A Game at Chesse* (1624), a political satire, or *Women Beware Women* (1657), in which a woman is seduced while her mother-in-law plays chess nearby.

[24] Eliot's note: "Cf. *Antony and Cleopatra*, II, ii, l. 190." In this Shakespeare play, Enobarbus, attempting to describe Cleopatra to Roman friends, begins his famous speech, "The barge she sat in, like a burnish'd throne."

[25] A statue of the Roman god of love, Cupid.

[26] Eliot's note: "Laquearia. V. *Aeneid*, I, 726: dependent lychni laquearibus aureis incensi, et noctem flammis funalia vincunt" (Latin): "from the golden paneled ceiling hang lamps, and the torches conquer the night with their flames," a description of the banquet hall where Aeneas is welcomed to Carthage by Queen Dido, who later kills herself after Aeneas abandons her to found Rome.

[27] Eliot's note: "Sylvan scene. V. Milton, *Paradise Lost*, IV, 140." In this epic by John Milton (1608–1674), Satan comes to Eden and sees "A Silvan Scene, and as the ranks ascend / Shade above shade, a woody Theatre / Of stateliest view" (140–142).

[28] Eliot's note: "V. Ovid, *Metamorphoses*, VI, Philomela." In this narrative poem by the Roman Ovid (43 B.C.–A.D. 17?), Philomela is raped by King Tereus of Thrace, her brother-in-law, who cuts out her tongue to silence her; the gods transform her into a nightingale. Note the contrast from the Edenic sylvan scene of the previous line.

So rudely forced; yet there the nightingale[29]   100
Filled all the desert with inviolable voice
And still she cried, and still the world pursues,
'Jug Jug'[30] to dirty ears.
And other withered stumps of time
Were told upon the walls; staring forms
Leaned out, leaning, hushing the room enclosed.
Footsteps shuffled on the stair.
Under the firelight, under the brush, her hair
Spread out in fiery points
Glowed into words, then would be savagely still.   110

   'My nerves are bad to-night. Yes, bad. Stay with me.
Speak to me. Why do you never speak. Speak.
    What are you thinking of? What thinking? What?
I never know what you are thinking. Think.'

   I think we are in rats' alley[31]
Where the dead men lost their bones.

   'What is that noise?'
                The wind under the door.[32]
'What is that noise now? What is the wind doing?'
                Nothing again nothing.   120
                        'Do
'You know nothing? Do you see nothing? Do you remember
Nothing?'

   I remember
Those are pearls that were his eyes.
'Are you alive, or not? Is there nothing in your head?'[33]
                        But
O O O O that Shakespeherian Rag[34]—
It's so elegant
So intelligent   130
'What shall I do now? What shall I do?
I shall rush out as I am, and walk the street
With my hair down, so. What shall we do tomorrow?
What shall we ever do?'
                  The hot water at ten.
And if it rains, a closed car at four.

---

[29] Eliot's note: "Cf. Part III, l. 204" (of *The Waste Land*).
[30] A standard Elizabethan transcription of the nightingale's song.
[31] Eliot's note: "Cf. Part III, l. 195" (of *The Waste Land*).
[32] Eliot's note: "Cf. Webster: 'Is the wind in that door still?' " In Webster's *The Devil's Law Case* (1619?) (III.ii), a doctor makes this comment when an attack fails to kill the victim, who is still breathing.
[33] Eliot's note: "Cf. Part I, l. 37, 48" (of *The Waste Land*).
[34] "The Shakespearian Rag" (1912), lyrics by Gene Buck and Herman Ruby, music by Dave Stamper, contains the chorus: "That Shakespearian rag, / Most intelligent, very elegant. . . . "

And we shall play a game of chess,
Pressing lidless eyes and waiting for a knock upon the door.[35]

When Lil's husband got demobbed,[36] I said—
I didn't mince my words, I said to her myself,   140
HURRY UP PLEASE ITS TIME[37]
Now Albert's coming back, make yourself a bit smart.
He'll want to know what you done with that money he gave you
To get yourself some teeth. He did, I was there.
You have them all out, Lil, and get a nice set,
He said, I swear, I can't bear to look at you.
And no more can't I, I said, and think of poor Albert,
He's been in the army four years, he wants a good time,
And if you don't give it him, there's others will, I said.
Oh is there, she said. Something o' that, I said.   150
Then I'll know who to thank, she said, and give me a straight look.
HURRY UP PLEASE ITS TIME
If you don't like it you can get on with it, I said.
Others can pick and choose if you can't.
But if Albert makes off, it won't be for lack of telling.
You ought to be ashamed, I said, to look so antique.
(And her only thirty-one.)
I can't help it, she said, pulling a long face,
It's them pills I took, to bring it off, she said.
(She's had five already, and nearly died of young George.)   160
The chemist[38] said it would be all right, but I've never been the same.
You *are* a proper fool, I said.
Well, if Albert won't leave you alone, there it is, I said,
What you get married for if you don't want children?
HURRY UP PLEASE ITS TIME
Well, that Sunday Albert was home, they had a hot gammon,[39]
And they asked me in to dinner, to get the beauty of it hot—
HURRY UP PLEASE ITS TIME
HURRY UP PLEASE ITS TIME
Goonight Bill. Goonight Lou. Goonight May. Goonight.   170
Ta ta. Goonight. Goonight.
Good night, ladies, good night, sweet ladies, good night, good night.[40]

III. THE FIRE SERMON[41]

The river's tent is broken; the last fingers of leaf
Clutch and sink into the wet bank. The wind
Crosses the brown land, unheard. The nymphs are departed.

[35] Eliot's note: "Cf. the game of chess in Middleton's *Women Beware Women*."
[36] Slang for "demobilized from the army," a change made by Pound.
[37] A typical announcement of closing-time in a London pub.
[38] Pharmacist.   [39] Ham or bacon.
[40] From Shakespeare's *Hamlet* (IV.v. 74–75), spoken by Ophelia.   [41] Buddha's Fire Sermon.

Sweet Thames, run softly, till I end my song.[42]
The river bears no empty bottles, sandwich papers,
Silk handkerchiefs, cardboard boxes, cigarette ends
Or other testimony of summer nights. The nymphs are departed.
And their friends, the loitering heirs of City directors;[43]   180
Departed, have left no addresses.
By the waters of Leman I sat down and wept . . . [44]
Sweet Thames, run softly till I end my song,
Sweet Thames, run softly, for I speak not loud or long.
But at my back in a cold blast I hear[45]
The rattle of the bones, and chuckle spread from ear to ear.

A rat crept softly through the vegetation
Dragging its slimy belly on the bank
While I was fishing in the dull canal
On a winter evening round behind the gashouse   190
Musing upon the king my brother's wreck
And on the king my father's death before him.[46]
White bodies naked on the low damp ground
And bones cast in a little low dry garret,
Rattled by the rat's foot only, year to year.
But at my back from time to time I hear[47]
The sound of horns and motors, which shall bring[48]
Sweeney to Mrs. Porter in the spring.
O the moon shone bright on Mrs. Porter[49]
And on her daughter   200
They wash their feet in soda water
Et O ces voix d'enfants, chantant dans la coupole![50]

---

[42] Eliot's note: "V. Spenser, *Prothalamion*": the refrain to the 1596 marriage song by Edmund Spenser (1552?–1599).

[43] Business directors in London's financial sector, the City.

[44] After "By the rivers of Babylon, there we sat down, yea, we wept, when we remembered Zion," from Psalm 137:1. Léman is the French name for Lake Geneva, Switzerland.

[45] After "But at my back I always hear / Time's wingéd chariot hurrying near . . . ," from the poem "To His Coy Mistress" (21–22), by Andrew Marvell (1621–1678). The speaker, in his attempt to seduce his lady, reminds her of the inevitable passing of time.

[46] Eliot's note: "Cf. *The Tempest*, I, ii." Ferdinand, son of the king of Naples, says, "Sitting on a bank, / Weeping again the King my father's wreck, / This music crept by me on the waters."

[47] Eliot's note: "Cf. Marvell, *To His Coy Mistress*."

[48] Eliot's note: "Cf. Day, *Parliament of Bees*: 'When of the sudden, listening, you shall hear, / A noise of horns and hunting, which shall bring / Actaeon to Diana in the spring, / Where all shall see her naked skin. . . . '" According to classical myth, Actaeon, as punishment for seeing naked Diana (the Roman goddess of the hunt) bathing, was turned into a stag and killed by his own hounds. *Parliament of Bees* (1607?) is a satirical play by John Day (1574–1640?).

[49] Eliot's note: "I do not know the origin of the ballad from which these lines are taken: it was reported to me from Sydney, Australia." In the song, a favorite of British troops during World War I, Mrs. Porter and her daughter are prostitutes. Eliot uses the character Sweeney throughout his poetry as a vulgar person.

[50] "And oh those voices of children, singing in the cupola!" (French): Eliot's note: "V. Verlaine, *Parsifal*," the concluding line of a sonnet by the French symbolist poet Paul Verlaine (1844–1896). In Wagner's opera *Parsifal* (1882), before the knight Parsifal can approach the Holy Grail, his feet must be washed.

Twit twit twit
Jug jug jug jug jug jug
So rudely forc'd.
Tereu[51]

Unreal City
Under the brown fog of a winter noon
Mr. Eugenides, the Smyrna[52] merchant
Unshaven, with a pocket full of currants[53]   210
C.i.f. London: documents at sight,
Asked me in demotic[54] French
To luncheon at the Cannon Street Hotel[55]
Followed by a weekend at the Metropole.

At the violet hour, when the eyes and back
Turn upward from the desk, when the human engines waits
Like a taxi throbbing waiting,
I Tiresias, though blind, throbbing between two lives,[56]
Old man with wrinkled female breasts, can see
At the violet hour, the evening hour that strives   220
Homeward, and brings the sailor home from sea,[57]
The typist home at teatime, clears her breakfast, lights
Her stove, and lays out food in tins.
Out of the window perilously spread
Her drying combinations touched by the sun's last rays,
On the divan are piled (at night her bed)
Stockings, slippers, camisoles, and stays.
I Tiresias, old man with wrinkled dugs
Perceived the scene, and foretold the rest—

---

[51] Short for Tereus, representing the nightingale's song.   [52] A port in Turkey.

[53] Eliot's note: "The currants were quoted at a price 'cost insurance and freight to London'; and the Bill of Lading, etc., were to be handed to the buyer upon payment of the sight draft."

[54] Popular, vernacular.

[55] A London hotel next to a station, typically full of travelers from Europe; the Metropole is a luxury hotel in Brighton, England.

[56] Eliot's note: "Tiresias, although a mere spectator and not indeed a 'character,' is yet the most important personage in the poem, uniting all the rest. Just as the one-eyed merchant, seller of currants, melts into the Phoenician Sailor, and the latter is not wholly distinct from Ferdinand Prince of Naples, so all the women are one woman, and the two sexes meet in Tiresias. What Tiresias *sees*, in fact, is the substance of the poem. The whole passage from Ovid is of great anthropological interest. . . . " Eliot then quotes from Ovid's *Metamorphoses* (III.320–338): the story of Tiresias, who upon seeing two snakes mating, strikes them and is turned into a woman. Seven years later he comes upon them again, strikes them, and is turned back into a man. Because he has been both man and woman, Tiresias is called upon to settle a quarrel between Jove and Juno (the supreme Roman god and goddess) concerning whether men or women have more pleasure in love. Tiresias's answer that women have more pleasure angered Juno, who struck him blind. To compensate for the loss of sight, Jove granted Tiresias the gift of prophesy.

[57] Eliot's note: "This may not appear as exact as Sappho's lines, but I had in mind the 'longshore' or 'dory' fisherman, who returns at nightfall." Sappho (early 6th century B.C.) was a Greek lyric poet; another source is "Requiem" by Robert Louis Stevenson (1850–1894): "Home is the sailor, home from the sea. . . . "

I too awaited the expected guest.   230
He, the young man carbuncular, arrives,
A small house agent's clerk, with one bold stare,
One of the low on whom assurance sits
As a silk hat on a Bradford[58] millionaire.
The time is now propitious, as he guesses,
The meal is ended, she is bored and tired,
Endeavours to engage her in caresses
Which still are unreproved, if undesired.
Flushed and decided, he assaults at once;
Exploring hands encounter no defence;   240
His vanity requires no response,
And makes a welcome of indifference.
(And I Tiresias have foresuffered all
Enacted on this same divan or bed;
I who have sat by Thebes below the wall[59]
And walked among the lowest of the dead.)
Bestows one final patronising kiss,
And gropes his way, finding the stairs unlit . . .

She turns and looks a moment in the glass,
Hardly aware of her departed lover;   250
Her brain allows one half-formed thought to pass:
'Well now that's done: and I'm glad it's over.'
When lovely woman stoops to folly and[60]
Paces about her room again, alone,
She smoothes her hair with automatic hand,
And puts a record on the gramophone.

'This music crept by me upon the waters'[61]
And along the Strand, up Queen Victoria Street.
O City city, I can sometimes hear
Beside a public bar in Lower Thames Street,   260
The pleasant whining of a mandoline
And a clatter and a chatter from within
Where fishermen lounge at noon: where the walls
Of Magnus Martyr hold[62]
Inexplicable splendour of Ionian white and gold.

[58] An English Midlands industrial town where fortunes were made during World War I.
[59] Below the wall of Thebes stretched the marketplace where Tiresias prophesized.
[60] Eliot's note: "V. Goldsmith, the song in *The Vicar of Wakefield*": a 1766 novel by Oliver Goldsmith (1728–1774), in which Olivia, having been seduced, sings, "When lovely woman stoops to folly / And finds too late that men betray, / What charm can soothe her melancholy, / What art can wash her guilt away? / The only art her guilt to cover, / To hide her shame from every eye, / To give repentance to her lover / And wring his bosom—is to die."
[61] Eliot's note: "V. *The Tempest*, as above."
[62] Eliot's note: "The interior of St. Magnus Martyr is to my mind one of the finest among Wren's interiors. See *The Proposed Demolition of Nineteen City Churches*: (P. S. King & Son, Ltd.)." St. Magnus Martyr, a church designed by the English architect Sir Christopher Wren (1632–1723), is in London, as are the other sites mentioned.

The river sweats[63]
Oil and tar
The barges drift
With the turning tide
Red sails   270
Wide
To leeward, swing on the heavy spar.
The barges wash
Drifting logs
Down Greenwich reach
Past the Isle of Dogs.[64]
     Weialala leia
     Wallala leialala

Elizabeth and Leicester[65]
Beating oars   280
The stern was formed
A gilded shell
Red and gold
The brisk swell
Rippled both shores
Southwest wind
Carried down stream
The peal of bells
White towers
     Weialala leia   290
     Wallala leialala

'Trams and dusty trees.
Highbury bore me. Richmond and Kew[66]
Undid me. By Richmond I raised my knees
Supine on the floor of a narrow canoe.'

---

[63] Eliot's note: "The Song of the (three) Thames-daughters begins here. From line 292 to 306 inclusive they speak in turn. V. *Götterdämmerung*, III, i: the Rhine-daughters." Lines 277–278 and 290–291 are the refrain of the Rhine maidens, who sing of the deterioration of the Rhine River, in Wagner's 1874 opera ("*Twilight of the Gods*" [German]): Eliot adapts the song to the Thames River.

[64] A peninsula in the Thames River, across from the borough of Greenwich, where Elizabeth I (1533–1603), queen of England from 1558 to 1603, was born.

[65] Eliot's note: "V. Froude, *Elizabeth*, Vol. I, ch. iv, letter of De Quadra to Philip of Spain: 'In the afternoon we were in a barge, watching the games on the river. (The queen) was alone with Lord Robert and myself on the poop, when they began to talk nonsense, and went so far that Lord Robert at last said, as I was on the spot there was no reason why they should not be married if the queen pleased.'" The English historian James Anthony Froude (1818–1894) wrote of the love affair between Elizabeth I and the earl of Leicester, Robert Dudley (1532?–1588). Bishop De Quadra was the Spanish ambassador to England; the poop is a raised deck at a ship's stern.

[66] Eliot's note: "Cf. *Purgatorio*, V. 133: 'Ricorditi di me, che son la Pia; / 'Siena mi fe', disfecemi Maremma' ": "Remember me, who am Pia; Siena made me, Maremma unmade me" (Italian). In the Antepurgatory Dante meets Pia, one of those who died without last rites, probably because her jealous husband had her killed because of suspicion of adultery. She was born in Siena and died in Maremma. Highbury is a London suburb; Richmond, a borough of London; Kew, a London district noted for its botanical garden.

'My feet are at Moorgate,[67] and my heart
Under my feet. After the event
He wept. He promised "a new start."
I made no comment. What should I resent?'

'On Margate Sands.[68]   300
I can connect
Nothing with nothing.
The broken fingernails of dirty hands.
My people humble people who expect
Nothing.'
          la la

To Carthage then I came[69]

Burning burning burning burning[70]
O Lord Thou pluckest me out[71]
O Lord Thou pluckest   310

burning

IV. Death By Water[72]

Phlebas the Phoenician, a fortnight dead,
Forgot the cry of gulls, and the deep sea swell
And the profit and loss.
                         A current under sea
Picked his bones in whispers. As he rose and fell
He passed the stages of his age and youth
Entering the whirlpool.
                        Gentile or Jew
O you who turn the wheel and look to windward,   320
Consider Phlebas, who was once handsome and tall as you.

V. What the Thunder Said[73]

After the torchlight red on sweaty faces
After the frosty silence in the gardens
After the agony in stony places

[67] A London slum.   [68] A resort on the Thames.
[69] Eliot's note: "V. St. Augustine's *Confessions:* 'to Carthage then I came, where a cauldron of unholy loves sang all about mine ears': from the autobiography (III. i) of St. Augustine (354–430).
[70] Eliot's note: "The complete text of the Buddha's Fire Sermon (which corresponds in importance to the Sermon on the Mount) from which these words are taken, will be found translated in the late Henry Clarke Warren's *Buddhism in Translation* (Harvard Oriental Series). Mr. Warren was one of the great pioneers of Buddhist studies in the Occident." Buddha's sermon calls for a life free of passion, which he symbolized by fire; for the Sermon on the Mount, see Matthew 5.
[71] Eliot's note: "From St. Augustine's *Confessions* again. The collocation of these two representatives of eastern and western asceticism, as the culmination of this part of the poem, is not an accident."
[72] This section, which Pound shortened considerably, was originally written in French as the conclusion to Eliot's poem "Dans le Restaurant" (1920), or "In the Restaurant."
[73] Eliot's note: "In the first part of Part V three themes are employed: the journey to Emmaus, the approach to the Chapel Perilous (see Miss Weston's book) and the present decay of eastern Europe."

The shouting and the crying
Prison and palace and reverberation
Of thunder of spring over distant mountains
He who was living is now dead
We who were living are now dying
With a little patience   330

    Here is no water but only rock
Rock and no water and the sandy road
The road winding above among the mountains
Which are mountains of rock without water
If there were water we should stop and drink
Amongst the rock one cannot stop or think
Sweat is dry and feet are in the sand
If there were only water amongst the rock
Dead mountain mouth of carious[74] teeth that cannot spit
Here one can neither stand nor lie nor sit   340
There is not even silence in the mountains
But dry sterile thunder without rain
There is not even solitude in the mountains
But red sullen faces sneer and snarl
From doors of mudcracked houses
                                 If there were water
And no rock
If there were rock
And also water
And water
A spring   350
A pool among the rock
If there were the sound of water only
Not the cicada
And dry grass singing
But sound of water over a rock
Where the hermit-thrush sings in the pine trees
Drip drop drip drop drop drop drop[75]
But there is no water

Who is the third who walks always beside you?[76]
When I count, there are only you and I together   360

In Luke 24:13–35 two disciples meet Christ on the road to Emmaus after his resurrection; the first nine lines deal with the events from Jesus' betrayal to his crucifixion. In the *Upanishads,* Vedic holy books, thunder is the language of god.

[74] Decaying.

[75] Eliot's note: "This is *Turdus aonalaschkae pallasii,* the hermit-thrush which I have heard in Quebec Province. Chapman says (*Handbook of Birds of Eastern North America*) 'it is most at home in secluded woodland and thickety retreats. . . . Its notes are not remarkable for variety or volume, but in purity and sweetness of tone and exquisite modulation they are unequalled.' Its 'water-dripping song' is justly celebrated." Frank Michler Chapman (1864–1945), an ornithologist, published this *Handbook* in 1895.

[76] Eliot's note: "The following lines were stimulated by the account of one of the Antarctic expeditions (I forget which, but I think one of Shackleton's): it was related that the party of explorers, at the

But when I look ahead up the white road
There is always another one walking beside you
Gliding wrapt in a brown mantle, hooded
I do not know whether a man or a woman
—But who is that on the other side of you?

What is that sound high in the air[77]
Murmur of maternal lamentation
Who are those hooded hordes swarming
Over endless plains, stumbling in cracked earth
Ringed by the flat horizon only   370
What is the city over the mountains
Cracks and reforms and bursts in the violet air
Falling towers
Jerusalem Athens Alexandria
Vienna London
Unreal

A woman drew her long black hair out tight
And fiddled whisper music on those strings
And bats with baby faces in the violet light
Whistled, and beat their wings   380
And crawled head downward down a blackened wall
And upside down in air were towers
Tolling reminiscent bells, that kept the hours
And voices singing out of empty cisterns and exhausted wells.

In this decayed hole among the mountains
In the faint moonlight, the grass is singing
Over the tumbled graves, about the chapel[78]
There is the empty chapel, only the wind's home.
It has no windows, and the door swings,
Dry bones can harm no one.   390
Only a cock stood on the rooftree
Co co rico co co rico[79]
In a flash of lightning. Then a damp gust
Bringing rain

---

extremity of their strength, had the constant delusion that there was *one more member* than could actually be counted." In Luke 24:13–34 a stranger appears to the two disciples journeying to Emmaus affter Jesus' death; the stranger is Jesus himself. Sir Ernest Henry Shackleton (1874–1922) was a British explorer who made three expeditions to Antarctica.

[77] Eliot's note: "Cf. Hermann Hesse, *Blick ins Chaos* . . . ": "*A Glimpse Into Chaos*" (German), a 1920 book by Hesse (1877–1962). Eliot then quotes a passage from the book, translated as, "Already half of Europe, already at least half of Eastern Europe, is on the way to chaos, going drunk in holy madness along the edge of the abyss and sings, sings drunkenly and hymnlike as Dmitri Karamazov sang. The bourgeois laughs, shocked, at these songs; the saint and the prophet hear them with tears." The passage refers to the Russian Revolution in 1917; Karamazov is a character in *The Brothers Karamazov* (1880), by Feodor Dostoevski (1821–1881).

[78] The Chapel Perilous of the Arthurian Grail legend, where a knight must go in search of the Holy Grail.

[79] According to folklore, a cock's crowing indicates that a ghost has departed.

Ganga[80] was sunken, and the limp leaves
Waited for rain, while the black clouds
Gathered far distant, over Himavant.[81]
The jungle crouched, humped in silence.
The spoke the thunder
DA   400
Datta:[82] what have we given?
My friend, blood shaking my heart
The awful daring of a moment's surrender
Which an age of prudence can never retract
By this, and this only, we have existed
Which is not to be found in our obituaries
Or in memories draped by the beneficent spider[83]
Or under seals broken by the lean solicitor
In our empty rooms
DA   410
Dayadhvam: I have heard the key[84]
Turn in the door once and turn once only
We think of the key, each in his prison
Thinking of the key, each confirms a prison
Only at nightfall, aethereal rumours
Revive for a moment a broken Coriolanus[85]
DA
Damyata: The boat responded
Gaily, to the hand expert with sail and oar
The sea was calm, your heart would have responded   420
Gaily, when invited, beating obedient
To controlling hands

                                        I sat upon the shore
Fishing,[86] with the arid plain behind me

---

[80] The Ganges River in India, sacred to Hindus.   [81] The Himalayas.

[82] Eliot's note: "Datta, dayadhvam, damyata" ("Give, sympathise, control" [Sanskrit]). The fable of the meaning of the Thunder is found in the *Brihadaranyaka-Upanishad*, 5, 1. A translation is found in Deussen's *Sechzig Upanishads des Veda*, p. 489." According to Hindu Theology, "Da" is the command of the god Prajapati; thunder, god's voice, commands that humans practice alms-giving, sympathy, and self-control. Paul Deussen (1845–1919) was a German philosopher and Sanskrit scholar who wrote *Sixty Vedic Upanishads*.

[83] Eliot's note: "Cf. Webster, *The White Devil*, V, vi: ' . . . they'll remarry / Ere the worm pierce your winding-sheet, ere the spider / Make a thin curtain for your epitaphs.' "

[84] Eliot's note: "Cf. *Inferno*, XXXIII, 46: 'ed io senti chiavar l'uscio di sotto / all'orribile torre.' Also F. H. Bradley, *Appearance and Reality*, p. 346. 'My external sensations are no less private to myself than are my thoughts or my feelings. In either case my experience falls within my own circle, a circle closed on the outside; and, with all its elements alike, every sphere is opaque to the others which surround it. . . . In brief, regarded as an existence which appears in a soul, the whole world for each is peculiar and private to that soul.' " "And I heard them below locking the door / of the horrible tower" (Italian), spoken by Count Ugolino, whom Dante meets in Circle 9 of the Inferno, among those who were traitors to their countries. Ugolino was locked in a tower with his sons and grandsons and left to starve.

[85] Gaius Marcius Coriolanus (5th century B.C.), a Roman hero who became *Coriolanus* (1608), the excessively proud protagonist of Shakespeare's play ruined by his inability to sympathize with Rome's common people.

[86] Eliot's note: "V. Weston: *From Ritual to Romance;* chapter on the Fisher King." The Fisher King symbolizes resurrection.

Shall I at least set my lands in order?[87]
London Bridge is falling down falling down falling down
Poi s'ascose nel foco che gli affina[88]
Quando fiam uti chelidon—O swallow swallow[89]
Le Prince d'Aquitaine à la tour abolie[90]
These fragments I have shored against my ruins   430
Why then Ile fit you. Hieronymo's mad againe.[91]
Datta. Dayadhvam. Damyata.
　　　　Shantih shantih shantih[92]

1921, 1922

JOURNEY OF THE MAGI*

'A cold coming we had of it,
Just the worst time of the year
For a journey, and such a long journey:
The ways deep and the weather sharp,
The very dead of winter.'[1]
And the camels galled,[2] sore-footed, refractory,
Lying down in the melting snow.
There were times we regretted
The summer palaces on slopes, the terraces,

---

[87] "Thus saith the Lord, Set thine house in order: for thou shalt die, and not live," from Isaiah 38:1.

[88] Eliot's note: V. *Purgatorio*, XXVI, 48. "'Ara vos prec er aquella valor / "que vos condus al som de l'escalina, / "sovegna vos a temps de ma dolor." / Poi s'ascose nel foco che li affina.'" "'I pray you now in the name of that virtue / that guides you to the top of this stair [paradise], / remember in good time my suffering.' / Then he hid himself in the purifying fire." On Ledge 7 of Purgatory, among the Lustful, Dante meets the poet Arnaut Daniel: Daniel speaks in Provençal; Dante, in Italian.

[89] "When shall I be like the swallow?" (Latin). Eliot's note: "V. *Pervigilium Veneris*. Cf. Philomela in Parts II and III." In the version of the myth in the anonymous poem "The Vigil of Venus," Philomela is turned into a swallow.

[90] "The Prince of Aquitaine at the ruined tower" (French). Eliot's note: "V. Gerard de Nerval, Sonnet *El Desdichado*." The prince has been disinherited in this sonnet from *Les Chimères* (1854), or "*The Chimeras*" (French), by the French writer de Nerval (1808–1855).

[91] Eliot's note: "V. Kyd's *Spanish Tragedy*." "Why then Ile fit [supply] you" refers to Hieronymo's plan to gain revenge while performing a play that has been requested by those he seeks to kill, from a 1594 drama by the English playwright Thomas Kyd (1557?–1595?). "Hieronymo's mad againe" refers to the play's subtitle. Hieronymo bites out his tongue at the end of the play.

[92] Eliot's note: "Shantih. Repeated as here, a formal ending to an Upanishad. 'The Peace which passeth understanding' is our equivalent to this word."

* One of Eliot's "Ariel" poems, which deal with death and rebirth. The speaker is one of the three Magi, or wise men, who journeyed to Bethlehem, bearing gifts for the newborn child Jesus (see Matthew 2:1–13).

[1] Lines 1 to 5 are adapted from the 1622 Christmas sermon by Lancelot Andrewes (1555–1626): "Last, we consider the *time* of their coming, the season of the yeare. It was no *summer Progresse*. A cold comming they had of it, at this time of yeare; just, the worst time of the yeare, to take a journey, and specially a long journey, in. The waies deep, the weather sharp, the daies short, the sunn farthest off, *in solstitio brumali,* the very dead of *Winter*."

[2] Rubbed sore by their harness.

And the silken girls bringing sherbet.   10
Then the camel men cursing and grumbling
And running away, and wanting their liquor and women,
And the night-fires going out, and the lack of shelters,
And the cities hostile and the towns unfriendly
And the villages dirty and charging high prices:
A hard time we had of it.
At the end we preferred to travel all night,
Sleeping in snatches,
With the voices singing in our ears, saying
That this was all folly.   20

    Then at dawn we came down to a temperate valley,
Wet, below the snow line, smelling of vegetation,
With a running stream and a water-mill beating the
      darkness,
And three trees on the low sky.[3]
And an old white horse galloped away in the meadow.[4]
Then we came to a tavern with vine-leaves over the lintel,[5]
Six hands at an open door dicing for pieces of silver,[6]
And feet kicking the empty wine-skins.
But there was no information,[7] so we continued
And arrived at evening, not a moment too soon   30
Finding the place; it was (you may say) satisfactory.

    All this was a long time ago, I remember,
And I would do it again, but set down
This set down
This: were we led all that way for
Birth or Death? There was a Birth, certainly,
We had evidence and no doubt. I had seen birth and death,
But had thought they were different; this Birth was
Hard and bitter agony for us, like Death, our death.
We returned to our places, these Kingdoms,   40
But no longer at ease here, in the old dispensation,
With an alien people clutching their gods.
I should be glad of another death.

                    1927

---

[3] Suggesting the crucifixion: according to Matthew 27:38, there were three crosses (two thieves were also crucified) and "darkness over the land."

[4] "Behold a white horse; and he that sat upon him was Faithful and True," from Revelation 19:11.

[5] Symbolizing homage to pagan gods of fertility, in contrast to the sacrificial blood with which ancient Israelites marked their side posts and lintels (the crosspieces at the top of door frames): " . . . when I [the Lord] see the blood, I will pass over you, and the plague shall not be upon you to destroy you, when I smite the land of Egypt," from Exodus 12:13.

[6] Symbolizing Judas's betrayal of Jesus for silver (see Matthew 26:14–16) and the soldiers' casting lots for his clothing (see Psalm 22:18).

[7] "And no man putteth new wine into old bottles: else the new wine doth burst the bottles . . . ," from Mark 2:22. The Magi are unable to interpret any of these symbols because Jesus' life has not yet given them symbolic meaning.

MARINA*

Quis hic locus, quae
regio, quae mundi plaga?[1]

What seas what shores what grey rocks and what islands
What water lapping the bow
And scent of pine and the woodthrush singing through the fog
What images return
O my daughter.

Those who sharpen the tooth of the dog, meaning
Death
Those who glitter with the glory of the hummingbird, meaning
Death
Those who sit in the sty of contentment, meaning   10
Death
Those who suffer the ecstasy of the animals, meaning
Death

Are become unsubstantial, reduced by a wind,
A breath of pine, and the woodsong fog
By this grace dissolved in place

What is this face, less clear and clearer
The pulse in the arm, less strong and stronger—
Given or lent? more distant than stars and nearer than the eye

Whispers and small laughter between leaves and hurrying feet   20
Under sleep, where all the waters meet.

Bowsprit[2] cracked with ice and paint cracked with heat.
I made this, I have forgotten
And remember.
The rigging weak and the canvas rotten
Between one June and another September.
Made this unknowing, half conscious, unknown, my own.
The garboard strake[3] leaks, the seams need caulking.
This form, this face, this life
Living to live in a world of time beyond me; let me   30

---

* One of Eliot's "Ariel" Poems, which deal with death and rebirth. In Shakespeare's *Pericles* Marina is the long-lost daughter of Pericles. The speaker is Pericles at the moment of reunion (V.i).

[1] "What place is this, what / land, what quarter of the globe?" (Latin): the question Hercules asks upon awakening from his madness to discover that he has killed his wife and children, from *Hercules Furens* (I. 1138), by the Roman philosopher, dramatist, and statesman Seneca (4? B.C.–A.D. 65). In a letter of May 9, 1930, to Sir Michael Sadler, Eliot comments, "I intend a crisscross between Pericles finding alive, and Hercules finding dead—the two extremes of the recognition scene."

[2] A large, tapered spar extending forward from the bow of a boat.

[3] The planking or plating along the hull of a boat along the bottom.

Resign my life for this life, my speech, for that unspoken,
The awakened, lips parted, the hope, the new ships.

What seas what shores what granite islands towards my timbers
And woodthrush calling through the fog
My daughter.

1930

from **FOUR QUARTETS***

EAST COKER[1]

I

In my beginning is my end.[2] In succession
Houses rise and fall, crumble, are extended,
Are removed, destroyed, restored, or in their place
Is an open field, or a factory, or a by-pass.
Old stone to new building, old timber to new fires,
Old fires to ashes, and ashes to the earth
Which is already flesh, fur and faeces,
Bone of man and beast, cornstalk and leaf.
Houses live and die: there is a time for building
And a time for living and for generation   10
And a time for the wind to break the loosened pane
And to shake the wainscot[3] where the field-mouse trots
And to shake the tattered arras[4] woven with a silent motto.

In my beginning is my end. Now the light falls
Across the open field, leaving the deep lane
Shuttered with branches, dark in the afternoon,
Where you lean against a bank while a van passes,
And the deep lane insists on the direction
Into the village, in the electric heat
Hypnotised. In a warm haze the sultry light   20
Is absorbed, not refracted, by grey stone.
The dahlias sleep in the empty silence.
Wait for the early owl.

---

* A group of poems with the same structure and themes—time and eternity, memory and history—
published separately as *Burnt Norton* (1936), *East Coker* (1940), *The Dry Salvages* (1941), and *Little
Gidding* (1942); they were collected as *Four Quartets* in 1943.
  [1] The English village from which Eliot's seventeenth-century ancestors set forth on their journey to
the New World.
  [2] The motto of Mary Stuart (1542–1587), queen of Scots, was "*En ma fin est mon commencement*":
"In my end is my beginning" (French).
  [3] A wood lining or paneling on walls.   [4] An elaborate type of tapestry.

                                        In that open field
If you do not come too close, if you do not come too close,
On a summer midnight, you can hear the music
Of the weak pipe and the little drum
And see them dancing around the bonfire
The association of man and woman
In daunsinge, signifying matrimonie—   30
A dignified and commodious sacrament.
Two and two, necessarye coniunction,
Holding eche other by the hand or the arm[5]
Whiche betokeneth concorde. Round and round the fire
Leaping through the flames, or joined in circles,
Rustically solemn or in rustic laughter
Lifting heavy feet in clumsy shoes,
Earth feet, loam[6] feet, lifted in country mirth
Mirth of those long since under earth
Nourishing the corn. Keeping time,   40
Keeping the rhythm in their dancing
As in their living in the living seasons
The time of the seasons and the constellations
The time of milking and the time of harvest
The time of the coupling of man and woman
And that of beasts. Feet rising and falling.
Eating and drinking. Dung and death.

    Dawn points, and another day
Prepares for heat and silence. Out at sea the dawn wind
Wrinkles and slides. I am here   50
Or there, or elsewhere. In my beginning.

                                        II

What is the late November doing
With the disturbance of the spring
And creatures of the summer heat,
And snowdrops writhing under feet
And hollyhocks that aim too high
Red into grey and tumble down
Late roses filled with early snow?
Thunder rolled by the rolling stars
Simulates triumphal cars   60
Deployed in constellated wars
Scorpion[7] fights against the Sun
Until the Sun and Moon go down

---

[5] From Bk. I, Ch. 12 of *The Boke Named the Governour* (1531), by Thomas Elyot (1490?–1546), an ancestor of Eliot.

[6] A rich soil.

[7] The constellation Scorpio and the sign of the zodiac for October–November.

Comets weep and Leonids[8] fly
Hunt the heavens and the plains
Whirled in a vortex that shall bring
The world to that destructive fire
Which burns before the ice-cap reigns.

That was a way of putting it—not very satisfactory:
A periphrastic[9] study in a worn-out poetical fashion,   70
Leaving one still with the intolerable wrestle
With words and meanings. The poetry does not matter.
It was not (to start again) what one had expected.
What was to be the value of the long looked forward to,
Long hoped for calm, the autumnal serenity
And the wisdom of age? Had they deceived us,
Or deceived themselves, the quiet-voiced elders,
Bequeathing us merely a receipt for deceit?
The serenity only a deliberate hebetude,[10]
The wisdom only the knowledge of dead secrets   80
Useless in the darkness into which they peered
Or from which they turned their eyes. There is, it seems to us,
At best, only a limited value
In the knowledge derived from experience.
The knowledge imposes a pattern, and falsifies,
For the pattern is new in every moment
And every moment is a new and shocking
Valuation of all we have been. We are only undeceived
Of that which, deceiving, could no longer harm.
In the middle, not only in the middle of the way   90
But all the way, in a dark wood,[11] in a bramble,
On the edge of a grimpen,[12] where is no secure foothold,
And menaced by monsters, fancy lights,
Risking enchantment. Do not let me hear
Of the wisdom of old men, but rather of their folly,
Their fear of fear and frenzy, their fear of possession,
Of belonging to another, or to others, or to God.
The only wisdom we can hope to acquire
Is the wisdom of humility: humility is endless.

The houses are all gone under the sea.   100

The dancers are all gone under the hill.

---

[8] Meteor showers that appear to originate from the constellation Leo, the lion.

[9] Roundabout, using many words when one or a few will do.

[10] Dullness, lethargy.

[11] In the *Inferno*, by Dante Alighieri (1265–1321), Dante has lost his way in a dark wood "in the middle of the journey of our life" (I.1).

[12] In *The Hound of the Baskervilles* (1902), by Sir Arthur Conan Doyle (1859–1930), the great Grimpen Mire swallows anything that gets caught in its mud. The huge hound that scares people literally to death is hidden on solid ground in the center of the mire.

III

O dark dark dark.[13] They all go into the dark,
The vacant interstellar spaces, the vacant into the vacant,
The captains, merchant bankers, eminent men of letters,
The generous patrons of art, the statesmen and the rulers,
Distinguished civil servants, chairman of many committees,
Industrial lords and petty contractors, all go into the dark,
And dark the Sun and Moon, and the Almanach de Gotha[14]
And the Stock Exchange Gazette, the Directory of Directors,
And cold the sense and lost the motive of action.   110
And we all go with them, into the silent funeral,
Nobody's funeral, for there is no one to bury.
I said to my soul, be still, and let the dark come upon you
Which shall be the darkness of God. As, in a theatre,
The lights are extinguished, for the scene to be changed
With a hollow rumble of wings, with a movement of darkness on
        darkness,
And we know that the hills and the trees, the distant panorama
And the bold imposing façade are all being rolled away—
Or as, when an underground train, in the tube, stops too long between
        stations
And the conversation rises and slowly fades into silence   120
And you see behind every face the mental emptiness deepen
Leaving only the growing terror of nothing to think about;
Or when, under ether, the mind is conscious but conscious of
        nothing—
I said to my soul, be still, and wait without hope
For hope would be hope for the wrong thing; wait without love
For love would be love of the wrong thing; there is yet faith
But the faith and the love and the hope are all in the waiting.
Wait without thought, for you are not ready for thought:
So the darkness shall be the light, and the stillness the dancing.
Whisper of running streams, and winter lightning.   130
The wild thyme unseen and the wild strawberry,
The laughter in the garden, echoed ecstasy
Not lost, but requiring, pointing to the agony
Of death and birth.
                        You say I am repeating
Something I have said before. I shall say it again.
Shall I say it again? In order to arrive there,
To arrive where you are, to get from where you are not,

---

[13] "O dark, dark, dark, amid the blaze of noon, / Irrecoverably dark, total Eclipse / Without all hope of day!" from *Samson Agonistes* (1671) (XI. 80–82), by John Milton (1608–1674).

[14] An international gazette that includes genealogical, diplomatic, and statistical information; first published in 1763 by Johann George Justus Perthes (1749–1816) of Gotha, Germany, it appears annually.

You must go by a way wherein there is no ecstasy.
In order to arrive at what you do not know   140
    You must go by a way which is the way of ignorance.
In order to possess what you do not possess
    You must go by the way of dispossession.
In order to arrive at what you are not
    You must go through the way in which you are not.
And what you do not know is the only thing you know
And what you own is what you do not own
And where you are is where you are not.

IV

The wounded surgeon plies the steel
That questions the distempered part;   150
Beneath the bleeding hands we feel
The sharp compassion of the healer's art
Resolving the enigma of the fever chart.

Our only health is the disease
If we obey the dying nurse
Whose constant care is not to please
But to remind of our, and Adam's curse,[15]
And that, to be restored, our sickness must grow worse.

The whole earth is our hospital
Endowed by the ruined millionaire,   160
Wherein, if we do well, we shall
Die of the absolute paternal care
That will not leave us, but prevents us everywhere.

The chill ascends from feet to knees,
The fever sings in mental wires.
If to be warmed, then I must freeze
And quake in frigid purgatorial fires
Of which the flame is roses, and the smoke is briars.

The dripping blood our only drink,
The bloody flesh our only food:[16]
In spite of which we like to think   170

---

[15] "Because thou . . . hast eaten of the tree [of knowledge of good and evil] of which I [the Lord] commanded thee, saying, thou shalt not eat of it: cursed is the ground for thy sake; in sorrow shalt thou eat of it all the days of thy life," from Genesis 3:17.

[16] The blood and flesh of the crucified Jesus: in Matthew 26:26–28, " . . . Jesus took bread . . . and gave it to the disciples, and said, Take, eat; this is my body. And he took the cup . . . and gave it to them, saying, Drink ye all of it; For this is my blood. . . . "

That we are sound, substantial flesh and blood—
Again, in spite of that, we call this Friday good.[17]

V

So here I am, in the middle way, having had twenty years—
Twenty years largely wasted, the years of *l'entre deux guerres*[18]—
Trying to learn to use words, and every attempt
Is a wholly new start, and a different kind of failure
Because one has only learnt to get the better of words
For the thing one no longer has to say, or the way in which
One is no longer disposed to say it. And so each venture   180
Is a new beginning, a raid on the inarticulate
With shabby equipment always deteriorating
In the general mess of imprecision of feeling,
Undisciplined squads of emotion. And what there is to conquer
By strength and submission, has already been discovered
Once or twice, or several times, by men whom one cannot hope
To emulate—but there is no competition—
There is only the fight to recover what has been lost
And found and lost again and again: and now, under conditions
That seem unpropitious. But perhaps neither gain nor loss.   190
For us, there is only the trying. The rest is not our business.

Home is where one starts from. As we grow older
The world becomes stranger, the pattern more complicated
Of dead and living. Not the intense moment
Isolated, with no before and after,
But a lifetime burning in every moment
And not the lifetime of one man only
But of old stones that cannot be deciphered.
There is a time for the evening under starlight,
A time for the evening under lamplight   200
(The evening with the photograph album).
Love is most nearly itself
When here and now cease to matter.
Old men ought to be explorers
Here and there does not matter
We must be still and still moving
Into another intensity
For a further union, a deeper communion
Through the dark cold and the empty desolation,
The wave cry, the wind cry, the vast waters   210
Of the petrel[19] and the porpoise. In my end is my beginning.

1940

---

[17] Good Friday, the Friday before Easter, commemorates Jesus' crucifixion.
[18] "Between two wars" (French).   [19] A small marine bird.

=CONTEXTS=

New Criticism

In the late 1930s the state of English studies in American universities led the poet/ editor John Crowe Ransom (1888–1974) to pose certain fundamental questions about the business of literary scholarship:

What Is Criticism?

"Easier to ask, What is criticism not? It is an act now notoriously arbitrary and undefined. We feel certain that the critical act is not one of those which the professors of literature habitually perform, and cause their students to perform. And it is our melancholy impression that it is not often cleanly performed in those loose compositions, by writers of perfectly indeterminate qualifications, that appear in print as reviews of books."

—John Crowe Ransom, 1938

Determined that literary studies should occupy a place of respect in universities, Ransom and other scholars such as Cleanth Brooks (1906–) and Robert Penn Warren (1905–1990) sought to mold literary criticism into more of a "hard science" while still maintaining a somewhat mystical reverence for literary texts themselves. "Criticism," Ransom continues, "must become more scientific, or precise and systematic. . . . " Ransom and other New Critics, as they called themselves, were after a more "objective" treatment of literature, specifically poetry. They wanted to deal specifically with the literary object itself and avoid entanglement in external matters, including historical comment, airy impressionism, psychological evaluations of the author, and other techniques that deal with abstract and isolated elements of a work. Rather, the New Criticism focused on elements of a poem—such as meter, texture, tone, syntax, and patterns of imagery—as they relate to the work as a whole, an organic unity.

E. E. Cummings
(1894–1962)

E. E. Cummings's poems are recognizable at a glance. His typographical innovations are his signature. For him poems were visual artifacts; not surprisingly he was a painter as well as a poet. When cubist painters were dislocating anatomy, he was doing that with language: splitting syllables, subverting syntax, and demanding that his poems be sensed by the process of seeing and reading.

Born in 1894, Edward Estlin Cummings grew up in Cambridge, Massachusetts. Although his father taught English at Harvard College, his early decision to become a poet was supported by his mother. Cummings imitated traditional forms and authors. In 1911 he entered Harvard, where he studied English and classics and earned a B.A. and an M.A. There he met Schofield Thayer and Sibley Watson, future owners of *The Dial*, who published his poems regularly and supported his painting. A year after Cummings graduated, his work was included in *Eight Harvard Poets* (1917); even there he altered conventions of punctuation, grammar, and lineation. Moving to New York to work for a mail-order book business, Cummings resigned after just three months.

Like other young writers during World War I, Cummings volunteered for ambulance service in Paris in 1917. However, through a misunderstanding he was suspected of disloyalty and imprisoned for three months. This experience resulted in *The Enormous Room* (1922), a prose work that recounts the injustice. Cummings returned to New York and shared an apartment with fellow prisoner William Slater Brown. After being drafted and serving briefly, Cummings again returned to New York.

In the early 1920s Cummings toured Europe with the novelist John Dos Passos, a friend from Harvard, and met Ezra Pound in Paris in 1921. Cummings's first book of verse, *Tulips and Chimneys* (1923), came out soon after he returned to America. A collection of free verse and sonnets, its poems contain his characteristic turns of speech, grammar, and punctuation. In 1925 Cummings won *The Dial* award, which briefly gave him financial freedom and important critical attention. His play *him* (1927), produced in New York's Greenwich Village, was as eccentric as his verse. A collection of his artwork, entitled *CIOPW*, was published in 1931, the year he traveled to the Soviet Union.

Although substantial prizes and money were forthcoming, in the mid-1930s Cummings had trouble publishing his poetry. When he was able to publish his *Collected Poems* in 1938, it garnered good reviews but slow sales. From the early 1940s until his death in 1962, Cummings was bothered by ill health. The publication of his volume *XAIPE* in 1950 brought accusations of anti-Semitism. During the final decade of his life he gave numerous readings, some of which were collected as *i: six nonlectures* (1953). In 1958 he won the Bollingen Prize for poetry. Although Cummings's work was generally praised, throughout his career that praise was typically tempered. Many critics liked his innovative play with language, his sharp satires, and his celebrations of sensuality and the individual but began to call his style immature or mannered. Whereas his style may not have changed with maturity, Cummings was one of the few poets to have found a particular voice, perfected it, and thereby changed both the look and definition of modern poetry.

Selected Readings: *The Enormous Room*, 1922. *CIOPW*, 1931. *i: six nonlectures*, 1953. *Tulips and Chimneys: The Original 1922 Manuscript With the 35 Additional Poems From &*, ed. G. Firmage, 1976. C. Norman, *E. E. Cummings: The Magic Maker*, 1964. N. Friedman, ed., *E. E. Cummings: A Collection of Critical Essays*, 1972. B. K. Dumas, *E. E. Cummings: A Remembrance of Miracles*, 1974. R. S. Kennedy, *Dreams in the Mirror: A Biography of E. E. Cummings*, 1980.

Texts Used: 25 ("as freedom . . . "), 29 ("anyone lived . . . "), and 37 ("these children . . . "): *Complete Poems*, Vol. Two: 1936–1962, ed. G. Firmage, 1968. All else: *Complete Poems*, Vol. One: 1913–1935, ed. G. Firmage, 1968.

from SONGS

IV

All in green went my love riding
on a great horse of gold
into the silver dawn.

four lean hounds crouched low and smiling
the merry deer ran before.

Fleeter be they than dappled dreams
the swift sweet deer
the red rare deer.

Four red roebuck at a white water
the cruel bugle sang before.   10

Horn at hip went my love riding
riding the echo down
into the silver dawn.

four lean hounds crouched low and smiling
the level meadows ran before.

Softer be they than slippered sleep
the lean lithe deer
the fleet flown deer.

Four fleet does at a gold valley
the famished arrow sang before.   20

Bow at belt went my love riding
riding the mountain down
into the silver dawn.

four lean hounds crouched low and smiling
the sheer peaks ran before.

Paler be they than daunting death
the sleek slim deer
the tall tense deer.

Four tall stags at a green mountain
the lucky hunter sang before.   30

All in green went my love riding
on a great horse of gold
into the silver dawn.

four lean hounds crouched low and smiling
my heart fell dead before.

1916

from   ORIENTALE

III

my love
thy hair is one kingdom
    the king whereof is darkness
thy forehead is a flight of flowers

thy head is a quick forest
    filled with sleeping birds
thy breasts are swarms of white bees
    upon the bough of thy body
thy body to me is April
in whose armpits is the approach of spring   10

thy thighs are white horses yoked to a chariot
    of kings
they are the striking of a good minstrel
between them is always a pleasant song

my love
thy head is a casket
    of the cool jewel of thy mind
the hair of thy head is one warrior
    innocent of defeat
thy hair upon thy shoulders is an army   20
    with victory and with trumpets

thy legs are the trees of dreaming
whose fruit is the very eatage of forgetfulness

thy lips are satraps[1] in scarlet
    in whose kiss is the combining of kings
thy wrists
are holy

[1] Governors of ancient Persia; petty tyrants.

which are the keepers of the keys of thy blood
thy feet upon thy ankles are flowers in vases
    of silver   30

in thy beauty is the dilemma of flutes

    thy eyes are the betrayal
of bells comprehended through incense

                                                                        1923

from   PORTRAITS

VIII

Buffalo Bill's
defunct
        who used to
        ride a watersmooth-silver
                                stallion
and break onetwothreefourfive pigeonsjustlikethat
                                        Jesus
he was a handsome man
                and what i want to know is
how do you like your blueeyed boy   10
Mister Death

                                                                        1923

from   N

III

    Spring is like a perhaps hand
    (which comes carefully
    out of Nowhere)arranging
    a window,into which people look(while
    people stare
    arranging and changing placing
    carefully there a strange
    thing and a known thing here)and

    changing everything carefully

spring is like a perhaps   10
Hand in a window
(carefully to
and fro moving New and
Old things,while
people stare carefully
moving a perhaps
fraction of flower here placing
an inch of air there)and

without breaking anything.

1925

from TWO

III

"next to of course god america i
love you land of the pilgrims' and so forth oh
say can you see by the dawn's early my
country 'tis of centuries come and go
and are no more what of it we should worry
in every language even deafanddumb
thy sons acclaim your glorious name by gorry
by jingo by gee by gosh by gum
why talk of beauty what could be more beaut-
iful than these heroic happy dead   10
who rushed like lions to the roaring slaughter
they did not stop to think they died instead
then shall the voice of liberty be mute?"

He spoke. And drank rapidly a glass of water

1926

from W

LVII

somewhere i have never travelled,gladly beyond
any experience,your eyes have their silence:
in your most frail gesture are things which enclose me,
or which i cannot touch because they are too near

your slightest look easily will unclose me
though i have closed myself as fingers,
you open always petal by petal myself as Spring opens
(touching skilfully,mysteriously)her first rose

or if you wish be to close me,i and
my life will shut very beautifully,suddenly,   10
as when the heart of this flower imagines
the snow carefully everywhere descending;

nothing which we are to perceive in this world equals
the power of your intense fragility:whose texture
compels me with the colour of its countries,
rendering death and forever with each breathing

(i do not know what it is about you that closes
and opens;only something in me understands
the voice of your eyes is deeper than all roses)
nobody,not even the rain,has such small hands   20

                                                                    1931

                                    25

            as freedom is a breakfastfood
            or truth can live with right and wrong
            or molehills are from mountains made
            —long enough and just so long
            will being pay the rent of seem
            and genius please the talentgang
            and water most encourage flame

            as hatracks into peachtrees grow
            or hopes dance best on bald men's hair
            and every finger is a toe   10
            and any courage is a fear
            —long enough and just so long
            will the impure think all things pure
            and hornets wail by children stung

            or as the seeing are the blind
            and robins never welcome spring
            nor flatfolk prove their world is round
            nor dingsters die at break of dong
            and common's rare and millstones float
            —long enough and just so long   20
            tomorrow will not be too late

worms are the words but joy's the voice
down shall go which and up come who
breasts will be breasts thighs will be thighs
deeds cannot dream what dreams can do
—time is a tree(this life one leaf)
but love is the sky and i am for you
just so long and long enough

1940

29

anyone lived in a pretty how town
(with up so floating many bells down)
spring summer autumn winter
he sang his didn't he danced his did.

Women and men(both little and small)
cared for anyone not at all
they sowed their isn't they reaped their same
sun moon stars rain

children guessed(but only a few
and down they forgot as up they grew   10
autumn winter spring summer)
that noone loved him more by more

when by now and tree by leaf
she laughed his joy she cried his grief
bird by snow and stir by still
anyone's any was all to her

Like
Dickinson's
#135

someones married their everyones
laughed their cryings and did their dance
(sleep wake hope and then)they
said their nevers they slept their dream   20

stars rain sun moon
(and only the snow can begin to explain
how children are apt to forget to remember
with up so floating many bells down)

one day anyone died i guess
(and noone stooped to kiss his face)
busy folk buried them side by side
little by little and was by was

all by all and deep by deep
and more by more they dream their sleep   30
noone and anyone earth by april
wish by spirit and if by yes.

Women and men(both dong and ding)
summer autumn winter spring
reaped their sowing and went their came
sun moon stars rain

1940

37

these children singing in stone a
silence of stone these
little children wound with stone
flowers opening for

ever these silently lit
tle children are petals
their song is a flower of
always their flowers

of stone are
silently singing   10
a song more silent
than silence these always

children forever
singing wreathed with singing
blossoms children of
stone with blossoming

eyes
know if a
lit tle
tree listens   20

forever to always children singing forever
a song made
of silent as stone silence of
song

1940

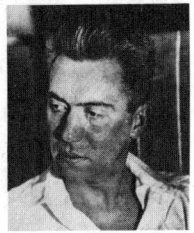

Hart Crane
(1899–1932)

Hart Crane's poetry makes enormous demands upon its readers. Its dense web of figurative language, violations of customary syntax, and exotic diction all aspire to the verbal music with which Crane casts his poetic spell. For Crane these intricacies were necessities rather than obstacles to the kind of poetry he was after. Adherence to such exacting standards of literary achievement places the artist in a precarious position. Crane's poems at times waver between magnificence and murkiness, a characteristic that had led some critics (perhaps unfairly) to call Crane a "splendid failure." But Crane insisted that a poet must risk criticism "in the conquest of consciousness." The fruits of this risk turned out to be some of the most original and beautiful passages of poetry available in American literature.

Born into a well-to-do family in Garrettsville, Ohio, in 1899, Harold Hart Crane began writing poetry while he was in high school. He published his first poem, a tribute to the Irish writer Oscar Wilde, at age seventeen. During parts of 1917, 1918, and 1919, Crane lived in New York City, immersing himself in Greenwich Village's thriving bohemian art world and publishing poems in several "little" magazines, including the *Little Review,* an important vehicle for the experimental work of major modernist writers, such as James Joyce, T. S. Eliot. and Ezra Pound. Crane spent much of the next four years in Cleveland, working in his father's candy company (which developed Life Savers), in advertising, and at other jobs. During these years he carried on energetic correspondences with a number of writers, including Sherwood Anderson and Allen Tate. Despite enduring emotionally draining conflicts with his divorced parents—conflicts that would plague Crane all his life—he was writing the poems that mark the beginning of his mature work: "My Grandmother's Love Letters" (1920), "Chaplinesque" (1921), and "For the Marriage of Faustus and Helen" (1922). Among others, his most ambitious project, *The Bridge* (1930), an epic poem he described as a "mystical synthesis of America," was conceived at this time, though not completed until 1929.

The next few years were Crane's most productive ones. After returning to New York City in 1923, he composed many of the poems collected in his first book, *White Buildings* (1926), including "Voyages," a sequence of six love poems inspired by an intense homosexual relationship. For much of 1926 he stayed at his grandmother's plantation on the Isle of Pines, near Cuba; that summer, in a burst of creativity during which he felt as if he were "dancing on dynamite," he wrote much of *The Bridge.* Following this active period Crane began to lose confidence in his abilities, giving himself over more completely than ever before to heavy drinking and sometimes-dangerous homosexual encounters with sailors. Chronically short of money, he moved restlessly from New York to Hollywood, Paris, and Ohio, until a Guggenheim Fellowship took him to Mexico in 1931. While he had planned to work on an epic about the Aztec emperor Montezuma, he was disheartened by the negative critical reception of *The Bridge* and wrote very little except for "The Broken Tower" (1932), a poem that communicates Crane's anguished uncertainty about his poetic achievement yet reaffirms his faith in the imagination. In 1932, while returning by boat to New York City from Mexico, he jumped to his death.

Although Crane was very much attracted to the formal experimentalism of modernism and at times wrote in free verse, he commonly employed traditional metrical and stanzaic patterns, relying instead on unorthodox uses of figurative language. Underlying all his work is an essentially romantic notion of creativity, a predisposition that Crane felt necessary to defend at a time when many intellectuals and artists were denigrating romanticist poets. Defending his poetry against the charge that its opaque conceits were inadmissible, Crane embraced Samuel Coleridge's conviction that poetic genius "cannot be lawless," because "the power of acting creatively under laws of its own origination" is exactly what constitutes that genius. In a letter to the photographer Alfred Stieglitz, Crane complained that he had "to combat everyday those really sincere people, but limited, who deny the superior logic of metaphor in favor of their more perfect sums, divisions, subtractions." Crane sought to create what he called an "interior form," in which he could "dye" the words to take on a slightly different meaning than they would normally have.

Crane shared the belief in this distinction between poetic language and ordinary discourse with T. S. Eliot and with the French symbolist poets they both admired, but Crane resisted the cultural pessimism that marked the work of Eliot and many other writers in the wake of World War I. Calling Eliot's *The Waste Land* (1922) "good, of course, but so damned dead," Crane declared his intention to "take Eliot as a point of departure toward an almost complete reverse of direction" and "apply as much of his erudition and technique as I can absorb and assemble toward a more positive, or (if [I] must put it so in a sceptical age) ecstatic goal."

Crane's most ambitious statement of this "ecstatic goal" is *The Bridge*, a long work composed of fifteen individual poems in which the personal quest for transcendent experience is coupled with a Whitmanesque vision of national destiny. The Brooklyn Bridge, with which the poem begins and ends, is the book's controlling symbol, an object of beauty that to Crane embodied the promise of a marriage between the forces of modern technology and older notions of spiritual aspirations. Like Walt Whitman, with whom he strongly identified in temperament if not in style, Crane believed a poet ought to (in Whitman's words) "flood himself with the immediate age," not reject it, as Crane felt Eliot had done. Crane's belief that it was thus incumbent upon poetry to "absorb the machine, i.e., *acclimatize* it as naturally and casually as trees," takes shape in the presence of numerous images of modern technology in *The Bridge*. But Crane feared that his personal associations of the bridge with spiritual and idealistic national aspirations were not shared by the culture as a whole, that instead "the bridge as a symbol today has no significance beyond an economical approach to shorter hours, quicker lunches, behaviorism and toothpicks." In the face of overwhelming obstacles and imminent disillusionment, *The Bridge* affirms the individual's commitment to a visionary goal.

Suggested Readings: *White Buildings*, 1926. *The Bridge*, 1930. *The Letters of Hart Crane: 1916–1932*, ed. B. Weber, 1965. *The Complete Poems and Selected Letters and Prose of Hart Crane*, ed. B. Weber, 1966. *Letters of Hart Crane and His Family*, ed. T. S. W. Lewis, 1974. *Hart Crane and Yvor Winters: Their Literary Correspondence*, ed. T. Parkinson, 1978. P. Horton, *Hart Crane: The Life of an American Poet*, 1937. H. Leibowitz, *Hart Crane: An Introduction to the Poetry*, 1968. J. Unterecker, *Voyager: A Life of Hart Crane*, 1969. S. Paul, *Hart's Bridge*, 1972. A. Trachtenberg, ed. *Hart Crane: A Collection of Critical Essays*, 1982. E. Brunner, *Splendid Failure: Hart Crane and the Making of "The Bridge"*, 1985. H. Bloom, ed., *Hart Crane*, 1986. M. F. Bennett, *Unfractioned Idiom: Hart Crane and Modernism*, 1987. L. Edelman, *Transmemberment of Song: Hart Crane's Anatomies of Rhetoric and Desire*, 1987.

Text Used: *The Poems of Hart Crane*, ed. M. Simon, 1986.

LEGEND*

As silent as a mirror is believed
Realities plunge in silence by . . .

I am not ready for repentance;
Nor to match regrets. For the moth
Bends no more than the still
Imploring flame. And tremorous
In the white falling flakes
Kisses are,—
The only worth all granting.

It is to be learned—   10
This cleaving and this burning,
But only by the one who
Spends out himself again.

Twice and twice
(Again the smoking souvenir,
Bleeding eidolon!¹) and yet again.
Until the bright logic is won
Unwhispering as a mirror
Is believed.

Then, drop by caustic drop, a perfect cry   20
Shall string some constant harmony,—
Relentless caper for all those who step
The legend of their youth into the noon.

1926

EMBLEMS OF CONDUCT†

By a peninsula the wanderer sat and sketched
The uneven valley graves. While the apostle gave
Alms to the meek the volcano burst
With sulphur and aureate¹ rocks . . .
For joy rides in stupendous coverings
Luring the living into spiritual gates.

---

* The opening poem of *White Buildings* (1926), Crane's first volume of poetry. "Legend" announces the credo of creative intensity that permeates the collection.
¹ A phantom.
† In 1923 Crane was shown the manuscripts of Samuel Greenberg (1893–1917), a poet who had died—impoverished and unknown—of tuberculosis at age twenty-three. Fascinated by Greenberg's nearly unintelligible, exotic imagery, Crane constructed "Emblems of Conduct" from several fragments of Greenberg's poems.
¹ Gilded.

Orators follow the universe
And radio the complete laws to the people.
The apostle conveys thought through discipline.
Bowls and cups fill historians with adorations,— 10
Dull lips commemorating spiritual gates.

The wanderer later chose this spot of rest
Where marble clouds support the sea
And where was finally borne a chosen hero.
By that time summer and smoke were past.
Dolphins still played, arching the horizons,
But only to build memories of spiritual gates.

1926

MY GRANDMOTHER'S LOVE LETTERS

There are no stars tonight
But those of memory.
Yet how much room for memory there is
In the loose girdle of soft rain.

There is even room enough
For the letters of my mother's mother,
Elizabeth,
That have been pressed so long
Into a corner of the roof
That they are brown and soft, 10
And liable to melt as snow.

Over the greatness of such space
Steps must be gentle.
It is all hung by an invisible white hair.
It trembles as birch limbs webbing the air.

And I ask myself:

"Are your fingers long enough to play
Old keys that are but echoes:
Is the silence strong enough
To carry back the music to its source 20
And back to you again
As though to her?"

Yet I would lead my grandmother by the hand
Through much of what she would not understand;
And so I stumble. And the rain continues on the roof
With such a sound of gently pitying laughter.

1926

CHAPLINESQUE*

We make our meek adjustments,
Contented with such random consolations
As the wind deposits
In slithered and too ample pockets.

For we can still love the world, who find
A famished kitten[1] on the step, and know
Recesses for it from the fury of the street,
Or warm torn elbow coverts.

We will sidestep, and to the final smirk
Dally the doom of that inevitable thumb   10
That slowly chafes its puckered index toward us,
Facing the dull squint with what innocence
And what surprise!

And yet these fine collapses are not lies
More than the pirouettes of any pliant cane;
Our obsequies[2] are, in a way, no enterprise.
We can evade you, and all else but the heart:
What blame to us if the heart live on.

The game enforces smirks; but we have seen
The moon in lonely alleys make   20
A grail of laughter of an empty ash can,
And through all sound of gaiety and quest
Have heard a kitten in the wilderness.

1926

PASSAGE

Where the cedar leaf divides the sky
I heard the sea.
In sapphire arenas of the hills
I was promised an improved infancy.

Sulking, sanctioning the sun;
My memory I left in a ravine,—
Casual louse that tissues the buckwheat,

---

* Crane admired the ability of the comedian Charlie Chaplin (1889–1977) to make sentimentality "transcend itself into a new kind of tragedy, eccentric, homely and yet brilliant." Inspired by Chaplin's film *The Kid* (1921), Crane explained to a friend that "Poetry . . . is so crowded out of the humdrum, rushing, mechanical scramble of today that the man who would preserve them must duck and camouflage for dear life to keep them or keep himself from annihilation. . . . I have tried to express these 'social sympathies' in words corresponding somewhat to the antics of the actor."
[1] Here, symbolizing poetry.
[2] Burial rights; here, suggesting obsequious behavior.

Aprons rocks, congregates pears
In moonlit bushels
And wakens alleys with a hidden cough.   10

Dangerously the summer burned
(I had joined the entrainments of the wind).
The shadows of boulders lengthened my back:
In the bronze gongs of my cheeks
The rain dried without odour.

"It is not long, it is not long;
See where the red and black
Vine-stanchioned[1] valleys—": but the wind
Died speaking through the ages that you know
And hug, chimney-sooted heart of man!   20
So was I turned about and back, much as your smoke
Compiles a too well known biography.

The evening was a spear in the ravine
That throve through very oak. And had I walked
The dozen particular decimals of time?
Touching an opening laurel, I found
A thief beneath, my stolen book in hand.

"Why are you back here—smiling an iron coffin?"
"To argue with the laurel," I replied:
"Am justified in transience, fleeing   30
Under the constant wonder of your eyes—."

He closed the book. And from the Ptolemies[2]
Sand troughed us in a glittering abyss.
A serpent swam a vertex[3] to the sun
—On unpaced beaches leaned its tongue and drummed.
What fountains did I hear? what icy speeches?
Memory, committed to the page, had broke.

1926

AT MELVILLE'S TOMB*

Often beneath the wave, wide from this ledge
The dice of drowned men's bones he saw bequeath

---

[1] Restrained.   [2] Greco-Egyptian rulers of Egypt from 323 B.C. to 30 B.C.
[3] A summit, the top point of the sun above the horizon.
* A tribute to Herman Melville (1819–1891) that first appeared in *Poetry* magazine in October 1926, but only after an exchange of letters between its editor, Harriet Monroe (1860–1936), and Crane about the propriety of the poem's unorthodox imagery. In the course of this exchange, which was published with the poem, Crane not only explicated several of his images, but also defended the authority of a poet to base a poem on the "so-called illogical impingements of the connotations of words on the consciousness" rather than on "logically rigid significations." Crane argued that the

An embassy.[1] Their numbers as he watched,
Beat on the dusty shore and were obscured.

And wrecks passed without sound of bells,
The calyx[2] of death's bounty giving back
A scattered chapter, livid hieroglyph,
The portent wound in corridors of shells.

Then in the circuit calm of one vast coil,
Its lashings charmed and malice reconciled,   10
Frosted eyes there were that lifted altars;[3]
And silent answers crept across the stars.

Compass, quadrant and sextant contrive
No farther tides . . . [4] High in the azure steeps
Monody[5] shall not wake the mariner.
This fabulous shadow only the sea keeps.

                                                    1926

VOYAGES*

I

Above the fresh ruffles of the surf
Bright striped urchins flay each other with sand.

---

articulation of "fresh concepts, more inclusive evaluations" is the proper "province of poetry," and that in quest of these a poet must rely on "something like short-hand as compared to usual description."

[1] Crane's note: "Dice bequeath an embassy, in the first place, by being ground (in this connection only, of course) in little cubes from the bones of drowned men by the action of the sea, and are finally thrown up on the sand, having 'numbers' but no identification. These being the bones of dead men who never completed their voyage, it seems legitimate to refer to them as the only surviving evidence of certain messages undelivered, mute evidence of certain things, experiences that the dead mariners might have had to deliver. Dice as a symbol of chance and circumstance is also implied."

[2] Crane's note: "This calyx refers in a double ironic sense both to a cornucopia and the vortex made by a sinking vessel. As soon as the water has closed over a ship, this whirlpool sends up broken spars, wreckage, etc., which can be alluded to as livid *hieroglyphs,* making a *scattered chapter* so far as any complete record of the recent ship and her crew is concerned. In fact, about as much definite knowledge might come from all this as anyone might gain from the roar of his own veins, which is easily heard (haven't you ever done it?) by holding a shell close to one's ear."

[3] Crane's note: "Refers simply to a conviction that a man, not knowing perhaps a definite god yet being endowed with a reverence for deity—such a man naturally postulates a deity somehow, and the altar of that deity by the very *action* of the eyes *lifted* in searching."

[4] Crane's note: "Hasn't it often occurred that instruments originally invented for record and computation have inadvertently so extended the concepts of the entity they were invented to measure (concepts of space, etc.) in the mind and imagination that employed them, that they may metaphorically be said to have extended the original boundaries of the entity measured? This little bit of 'relativity' ought not to be discredited in poetry now that scientists are proceeding to measure the universe on principles of pure *ratio,* quite as metaphorical, so far as previous standards of scientific methods extended, as some of the axioms in Job."

[5] The title of an 1891 Melville poem: a monotonous sound or tone, as of waves.

* Comprised of a series of six poems published separately.

They have contrived a conquest for shell shucks,
And their fingers crumble fragments of baked weed
Gaily digging and scattering.

And in answer to their treble interjections
The sun beats lightning on the waves,
The waves fold thunder on the sand;
And could they hear me I would tell them:

O brilliant kids, frisk with your dog,   10
Fondle your shells and sticks, bleached
By time and the elements; but there is a line
You must not cross nor ever trust beyond it
Spry cordage of your bodies to caresses
Too lichen-faithful[1] from too wide a breast.
The bottom of the sea is cruel.

II

—And yet this great wink of eternity,
Of rimless floods, unfettered leewardings,[2]
Samite[3] sheeted and processioned where
Her undinal[4] vast belly moonward bends,   20
Laughing the wrapt inflections of our love;

Take this Sea, whose diapason[5] knells
On scrolls of silver snowy sentences,
The sceptred terror of whose sessions rends
As her demeanors motion well or ill,
All but the pieties of lovers' hands.

And onward, as bells off San Salvador
Salute the crocus lustres of the stars,
In these poinsettia meadows of her tides,—
Adagios of islands,[6] O my Prodigal,   30
Complete the dark confessions her veins spell.

Mark how her turning shoulders wind the hours,
And hasten while her penniless rich palms
Pass superscription of bent foam and wave,—
Hasten, while they are true,—sleep, death, desire,
Close round one instant in one floating flower.

---

[1] A lichen is a symbiotic relationship between a fungus and an alga: a close relationship.
[2] Leeward is the direction toward which the wind blows.
[3] Heavy silk fabric threaded with gold, worn in the Middle Ages.
[4] According to folklore, Undine is a female water spirit who acquired a soul after marrying a human.
[5] The range of a musical instrument or voice.
[6] Crane's note: "the reference is to the motion of a boat through islands clustered thickly, the rhythm of the motion, etc. And it seems a much more direct and creative statement than any more logical employment of words such as 'coasting slowly through the islands,' besides ushering in a whole world of music."

Bind us in time, O Seasons clear, and awe.
O minstrel galleons of Carib fire,
Bequeath us to no earthly shore until
Is answered in the vortex of our grave   40
The seal's wide spindrift[7] gaze toward paradise.

III

Infinite consanguinity it bears—
This tendered theme of you that light
Retrieves from sea plains where the sky
Resigns a breast that every wave enthrones;
While ribboned water lanes I wind
Are laved and scattered with no stroke
Wide from your side, whereto this hour
The sea lifts, also, reliquary[8] hands.

And so, admitted through black swollen gates   50
That must arrest all distance otherwise,—
Past whirling pillars and lithe pediments,[9]
Light wrestling there incessantly with light,
Star kissing star through wave on wave unto
Your body rocking!
                              and where death, if shed,
Presumes no carnage, but this single change,—
Upon the steep floor flung from dawn to dawn
The silken skilled transmemberment[10] of song;

Permit me voyage, love, into your hands   60

IV

Whose counted smile of hours and days, suppose
I know as spectrum of the sea and pledge
Vastly now parting gulf on gulf of wings
Whose circles bridge, I know, (from palms to the severe
Chilled albatross's white immutability)
No stream of greater love advancing now
Than, singing, this mortality alone
Through clay aflow immortally to you.

All fragrance irrefragably,[11] and claim
Madly meeting logically in this hour   70
And region that is ours to wreathe again,

---

[7] Spray blown from a rough surf.   [8] A container in which relics are kept and displayed.
[9] Triangular ornamental features in Grecian-style architecture.
[10] A term Crane coined, indicating both metamorphosis, as in transfiguration or transformation, and disintegration.
[11] Indisputably.

Portending eyes and lips and making told
The chancel[12] port and portion of our June—

Shall they not stem and close in our own steps
Bright staves of flowers and quills today as I
Must first be lost in fatal tides to tell?

In signature of the incarnate word
The harbor shoulders to resign in mingling
Mutual blood, transpiring as foreknown
And widening noon within your breast for gathering   80
All bright insinuations that my years have caught
For islands where must lead inviolably
Blue latitudes and levels of your eyes,—

In this expectant, still exclaim receive
The secret oar and petals of all love.

V

Meticulous, past midnight in clear rime,[13]
Infrangible[14] and lonely, smooth as though cast
Together in one merciless white blade—
The bay estuaries fleck the hard sky limits.

—As if too brittle or too clear to touch!   90
The cables of our sleep so swiftly filed,
Already hang, shred ends from remembered stars.
One frozen trackless smile . . . What words
Can strangle this deaf moonlight? For we

Are overtaken. Now no cry, no sword
Can fasten or deflect this tidal wedge,
Slow tyranny of moonlight, moonlight loved
And changed . . . "There's

Nothing like this in the world," you say,
Knowing I cannot touch your hand and look   100
Too, into that godless cleft of sky
Where nothing turns but dead sands flashing.

"—And never to quite understand!" No,
In all the argosy[15] of your bright hair I dreamed
Nothing so flagless as this piracy.

But now
Draw in your head, alone and too tall here.

---

[12] The part of a church near the altar.   [13] Frost.   [14] Unbreakable.
[15] A large merchant ship or fleet of ships.

Your eyes already in the slant of drifting foam;
Your breath sealed by the ghosts I do not know:
Draw in your head and sleep the long way home.   110

VI

Where icy and bright dungeons lift
Of swimmers their lost morning eyes,
And ocean rivers, churning, shift
Green borders under stranger skies,

Steadily as a shell secretes
Its beating leagues of monotone,
Or as many waters trough the sun's
Red kelson[16] past the cape's wet stone;

O rivers mingling toward the sky
And harbor of the phoenix'[17] breast—   120
My eyes pressed black against the prow,
—Thy derelict and blinded guest

Waiting, afire, what name, unspoke,
I cannot claim: let thy waves rear
More savage than the death of kings,
Some splintered garland for the seer.

Beyond siroccos[18] harvesting
The solstice thunders, crept away,
Like a cliff swinging or a sail
Flung into April's inmost day—   130

Creation's blithe and petalled word
To the lounged goddess when she rose
Conceding dialogue with eyes
That smile unsearchable repose—

Still fervid covenant, Belle Isle,
—Unfolded floating dais before
Which rainbows twine continual hair—
Belle Isle, white echo of the oar!

The imaged Word, it is, that holds
Hushed willows anchored in its glow.   140
It is the unbetrayable reply
Whose accent no farewell can know.

1921–1924, 1926

[16] Keelson, structural support inside a ship's hull along the keel.
[17] According to Egyptian myth, a bird that lives for hundreds of years, sets itself on fire, and arises from the ashes: a symbol of immortality.
[18] Hot, oppressive winds.

from **THE BRIDGE***

TO BROOKLYN BRIDGE[1]

How many dawns, chill from his rippling rest
The seagull's wings shall dip and pivot him,
Shedding white rings of tumult, building high
Over the chained bay waters Liberty—

Then, with inviolate curve, forsake our eyes
As apparitional as sails that cross
Some page of figures to be filed away;
—Till elevators drop us from our day . . .

I think of cinemas, panoramic sleights
With multitudes bent toward some flashing scene 10
Never disclosed, but hastened to again,
Foretold to other eyes on the same screen;

And Thee,[2] across the harbor, silver-paced
As though the sun took step of thee, yet left
Some motion ever unspent in thy stride,—
Implicitly thy freedom staying thee!

Out of some subway scuttle, cell or loft
A bedlamite[3] speeds to thy parapets,
Tilting there momently, shrill shirt ballooning,
A jest falls from the speechless caravan. 20

Down Wall,[4] from girder into street noon leaks,
A rip-tooth of the sky's acetylene;
All afternoon the cloud-flown derricks turn . . .
Thy cables breathe the North Atlantic still.

And obscure as that heaven of the Jews,
Thy guerdon[5] . . . Accolade thou dost bestow
Of anonymity time cannot raise:
Vibrant reprieve and pardon thou dost show.

O harp and altar, of the fury fused,
(How could mere toil align thy choiring strings!) 30

---

* A long poem, published in 1930, consisting of an opening proem (introduction)—"To Brooklyn Bridge"—and eight succeeding sections: "Ave Maria," "Powhatan's Daughter," "Cutty Sark," "Cape Hatteras," "Three Songs," "Quaker Hill," "The Tunnel," and "Atlantis." The ellipses are Crane's.

[1] A suspension bridge designed by John A. Roebling (1806–1869) and built from 1869 to 1883; it spans the East River from Brooklyn to Manhattan.

[2] Brooklyn Bridge.   [3] An insane person: after Bedlam, an insane asylum in London.

[4] New York City's Wall Street.   [5] A reward.

> Terrific threshold of the prophet's pledge,
> Prayer of pariah, and the lover's cry,—
>
> Again the traffic lights that skim thy swift
> Unfractioned idiom, immaculate sigh of stars,
> Beading thy path—condense eternity:
> And we have seen night lifted in thine arms.
>
> Under thy shadow by the piers I waited;
> Only in darkness is thy shadow clear.
> The City's fiery parcels all undone,
> Already snow submerges an iron year . . .   40
>
> O Sleepless as the river under thee,
> Vaulting the sea, the prairies' dreaming sod,
> Unto us lowliest sometime sweep, descend
> And of the curveship⁶ lend a myth to God.
>
> > > *1926–1927, 1930*

from   II: POWHATAN'S DAUGHTER*

THE RIVER

	Stick your patent name on a signboard
	brother—all over—going west—young man
. . . and past	Tintex—Japalac—Certain-teed Overalls¹ ads
the din and	and lands sakes! under the new playbill ripped
slogans of	in the guaranteed corner—see Bert Williams² what?
the year—	Minstrels when you steal a chicken just
	save me the wing for if it isn't
	Erie it ain't for miles around a
	Mazda³—and the telegraphic night coming on Thomas

---

⁶ A term Crane coined.

* The second section of *The Bridge*. Powhatan (1550?–1618) was the head of a federation of Algonquian tribes in eastern Virginia; his daughter, Pocahontas (1595?–1617) reputedly saved the life of Captain John Smith in 1608; in 1614 she married the colonist John Rolfe. Crane's note: "I'm trying in this part of the poem to chart the pioneer experience of our forefathers—and to tell the story backwards, as it were, on the 'backs' of hoboes. These hoboes are simply 'psychological ponies' to carry the reader across the country and back to the Mississippi, which you will notice is described as a great River of Time." The ellipses are Crane's.

¹ Brand names of a dye, a varnish, and overalls.

² Egbert A. Williams (1876–1922), a popular African-American minstrel show performer.

³ The electric light bulb, called by the trade name "Mazda" lamp.

a Ediford[4]—and whistling down the tracks   10
a headlight rushing with the sound—can you
imagine—while an EXPRESS makes time like
SCIENCE—COMMERCE and the HOLYGHOST
RADIO ROARS IN EVERY HOME WE HAVE THE NORTHPOLE
WALLSTREET AND VIRGINBIRTH WITHOUT STONES OR
WIRES OR EVEN RUNning brooks connecting ears
and no more sermons windows flashing roar
breathtaking—as you like it[5] . . . eh?

               So the 20th Century—so
whizzed the Limited—roared by and left   20
three men, still hungry on the tracks, ploddingly
watching the tail lights wizen[6] and converge, slipping gimleted and neatly out of sight.[7]

  .   .   .   .

The last bear, shot drinking in the Dakotas
Loped under wires that span the mountain stream.
Keen instruments, strung to a vast precision

to those
whose   Bind town to town and dream to ticking dream.
addresses
are never near   But some men take their liquor slow—and count
—Though they'll confess no rosary nor clue—

The river's minute by the far brook's year.   30
Under a world of whistles, wires and steam
Caboose-like they go ruminating through
Ohio, Indiana—blind baggage—
To Cheyenne tagging . . . Maybe Kalamazoo.

Time's rendings, time's blendings they construe
As final reckonings of fire and snow;
Strange bird-wit, like the elemental gist
Of uwalled winds they offer, singing low
My Old Kentucky Home and *Casey Jones,*
Some Sunny Day. I heard a road-gang chanting so.   40
And afterwards, who had a colt's eyes—one said,
"Jesus! Oh I remember watermelon days!" And sped
High in a cloud of merriment, recalled
"—And when my Aunt Sally Simpson smiled," he drawled—
"It was almost Louisiana, long ago."

    [4] A reference to Thomas A. Edison (1847–1931), who invented the incandescent lamp, to the auto-
mobile manufacturer Henry Ford (1863–1947), and to Saint Thomas à Becket (1118?–1170), the
archbishop of Canterbury, murdered after opposing King Henry II of England.
    [5] "Books in the running brooks / Sermons in stones" (2.1.16–17), from Shakespeare's *As You Like It.*
    [6] Wither, shrivel.
    [7] Crane's note: "The extravagance of the first twenty-three lines of this section is an intentional bur-
lesque on the cultural confusion of the present—a great conglomeration of noises analogous to the
strident impression of a fast express rushing by. The rhythm is jazz."

"There's no place like Booneville though, Buddy,"
One said, excising a last burr from his vest,
"—For early trouting." Then peering in the can,   50
"—But I kept on the tracks." Possessed, resigned,
He trod the fire down pensively and grinned,
Spreading dry shingles of a beard. . . .

                      Behind
My father's cannery works I used to see
Rail-squatters ranged in nomad raillery,
The ancient men—wifeless or runaway
Hobo-trekkers that forever search
An empire wilderness of freight and rails.
Each seemed a child, like me, on a loose perch,   60
Holding to childhood like some termless play.
John, Jake or Charley, hopping the slow freight
—Memphis to Tallahassee—riding the rods,
Blind fists of nothing, humpty-dumpty clods.

Yet they touch something like a key perhaps.
From pole to pole across the hills, the states
but who have   —They know a body under the wide rain;
touched her,   Youngsters with eyes like fjords, old reprobates
knowing her   With racetrack jargon,—dotting immensity
without name   They lurk across her, knowing her yonder breast   70
Snow-silvered, sumac-stained or smoky blue—
Is past the valley-sleepers, south or west.
—As I have trod the rumorous midnights, too,

And past the circuit of the lamp's thin flame
(O Nights that brought me to her body bare!)
Have dreamed beyond the print that bound her name.
Trains sounding the long blizzards out—I heard
Wail into distances I knew were hers.
Papooses crying on the wind's long mane
Screamed redskin dynasties that fled the brain,   80
—Dead echoes! But I knew her body there,
Time like a serpent down her shoulder, dark,
And space, an eaglet's wing, laid on her hair.

Under the Ozarks, domed by Iron Mountain,[8]
The old gods of the rain lie wrapped in pools
nor the   Where eyeless fish curvet a sunken fountain
myths of her   And re-descend with corn from querulous crows.
fathers . . .   Such pilferings make up their timeless eatage,
Propitiate them for their timber torn
By iron, iron—always the iron dealt cleavage!
They doze now, below axe and powder horn.

---

[8] In southeastern Missouri.

And Pullman[9] breakfasters glide glistening steel   90
From tunnel into field—iron strides the dew—
Straddles the hill, a dance of wheel on wheel.
You have a half-hour's wait at Siskiyou,[10]
Or stay the night and take the next train through.
Southward, near Cairo[11] passing, you can see
The Ohio merging,—borne down Tennessee;
And if it's summer and the sun's in dusk
Maybe the breeze will lift the River's musk
—As though the waters breathed that you might know
Memphis Johnny, Steamboat Bill, Missouri Joe.   100
Oh, lean from the window, if the train slows down,
As though you touched hands with some ancient clown,
—A little while gaze absently below
And hum *Deep River* with them while they go.

Yes, turn again and sniff once more—look see,
O Sheriff, Brakeman and Authority—
Hitch up your pants and crunch another quid,[12]
For you, too, feed the River timelessly.
And few evade full measure of their fate;
Always they smile out eerily what they seem.   110
I could believe he joked at heaven's gate—
Dan Midland[13]—jolted from the cold brake-beam.[14]

Down, down—born pioneers in time's despite,
Grimed tributaries to an ancient flow—
They win no frontier by their wayward plight,
But drift in stillness, as from Jordan's brow.[15]

You will not hear it as the sea; even stone
Is not more hushed by gravity . . . But slow,
As loth to take more tribute—sliding prone
Like one whose eyes were buried long ago   120

The River, spreading, flows—and spends your dream.
What are you, lost within this tideless spell?
You are your father's father, and the stream—
A liquid theme that floating niggers swell.

Damp tonnage and alluvial[16] march of days—
Nights turbid, vascular with silted shale

---

[9] A railroad passenger car with convertible berths for sleeping, named after its inventor, G. P. Pullman (1831–1897).
    [10] In northern California.   [11] In southern Illinois.   [12] A wad of chewing tobacco.
    [13] A folklore hobo who died from falling off a train.
    [14] A part of a railroad car on which hobos often ride.
    [15] The bank of the Jordan River, symbolic of the boundary between Heaven and earth; mentioned frequently in the Bible and in African-American gospel music.
    [16] Depositional, sedimentary.

And roots surrendered down of moraine[17] clays:
The Mississippi drinks the farthest dale.

O quarrying passion, undertowed sunlight!
The basalt surface drags a jungle grace   130
Ochreous and lynx-barred in lengthening might;
Patience! and you shall reach the biding place!

Over De Soto's[18] bones the freighted floors
Throb past the City storied of three thrones.[19]
Down two more turns the Mississippi pours
(Anon tall ironsides[20] up from salt lagoons)

And flows within itself, heaps itself free.
All fades but one thin skyline 'round . . . Ahead
No embrace opens but the stinging sea;
The River lifts itself from its long bed,   140

Poised wholly on its dream, a mustard glow
Tortured with history, its one will—flow!
—The Passion spreads in wide tongues, choked and slow,
Meeting the Gulf, hosannas silently below.

1926–1927, 1930

from   VII: The Tunnel*

THE TUNNEL

Performances, assortments, résumés—
Up Times Square to Columbus Circle[1] lights
Channel the congresses, nightly sessions,
Refractions of the thousand theatres, faces—
Mysterious kitchens . . . You shall search them all.
Someday by heart you'll learn each famous sight
And watch the curtain lift in hell's despite;
You'll find the garden in the third act dead,
Finger your knees—and wish yourself in bed
With tabloid crime-sheets perched in easy sight.   10

> Then let you reach your hat
> and go.
> As usual, let you—also

---

[17] Material deposited by a glacier.
[18] The Spanish explorer Hernando de Soto (1500–1542), buried in the Mississippi River.
[19] New Orleans, controlled at different times by the Spanish, the French, and the English.
[20] Warships.
* The seventh section of *The Bridge;* the title refers to a subway tunnel, which Crane depicts as a type of Hell. The ellipses are Crane's.
[1] Along upper Broadway, in New York City.

walking down—exclaim
to twelve upward leaving
a subscription praise
for what time slays.

Or can't you quite make up your mind to ride;
A walk is better underneath the L[2] a brisk
Ten blocks or so before? But you find yourself
Preparing penquin flexions of the arms,—
As usual you will meet the scuttle yawn:
The subway yawns the quickest promise home.

Be minimum, then, to swim the hiving swarms
Out of the Square, the Circle burning bright—
Avoid the glass doors gyring[3] at your right,
Where boxed alone a second, eyes take fright
—Quite unprepared rush naked back to light:
And down beside the turnstile press the coin
Into the slot. The gongs already rattle.

And so
of cities you bespeak
subways, rivered under streets
and rivers. . . . In the car
the overtone of motion
underground, the monotone
of motion is the sound
of other faces, also underground—

"Let's have a pencil Jimmy—living now
at Floral Park
Flatbush[4]—on the fourth of July—
like a pigeon's muddy dream—potatoes
to dig in the field—travlin the town—too—
night after night—the Culver line[5]—the
girls all shaping up—it used to be—"

Our tongues recant like beaten weather vanes.
This answer lives like verdigris,[6] like hair
Beyond extinction, surcease of the bone;
And repetition freezes—"What

"what do you want? getting weak on the links?
fandaddle daddy[7] don't ask for change—IS THIS
FOURTEENTH?[8] it's half past six she said—if
you don't like my gate why did you

20

30

40

50

---

[2] An elevated portion of the subway.   [3] Spinning.   [4] A section of Brooklyn.
[5] Formerly a branch of the Brooklyn Rapid Transit system.
[6] A greenish-blue poisonous compound.   [7] A panhandler.
[8] Fourteenth Street, in lower Manhattan.

swing on it, why *didja*
swing on it
anyhow—"

And somehow anyhow swing—

The phonographs of hades[9] in the brain
Are tunnels that re-wind themselves, and love
A burnt match skating in a urinal—
Somewhere above Fourteenth TAKE THE EXPRESS   60
To brush some new presentiment of pain—

"But I want service in this office SERVICE
I said—after
the show she cried a little afterwards but—"

Whose head is swinging from the swollen strap?
Whose body smokes along the bitten rails,
Bursts from a smoldering bundle far behind
In back forks of the chasms of the brain,—
Puffs from a riven stump far out behind   70
In interborough fissures of the mind . . . ?

And why do I often meet your[10] visage here,
Your eyes like agate lanterns[11]—on and on
Below the toothpaste and the dandruff ads?
—And did their riding eyes right through your side,
And did their eyes like unwashed platters ride?
And Death, aloft,—gigantically down[12]
Probing through you—toward me, O evermore![13]
And when they dragged your retching flesh,
Your trembling hands that night through Baltimore—   80
That last night on the ballot rounds,[14] did you,
Shaking, did you deny the ticket, Poe?

For Gravesend Manor change at Chambers Street.[15]
The platform hurries along to a dead stop.

The intent escalator lifts a serenade
Stilly
Of shoes, umbrellas, each eye attending its shoe, then
Bolting outright somewhere above where streets
Burst suddenly in rain. . . . The gongs recur:

[9] According to Greek myth, the Underworld, home of the dead.   [10] Edgar Allan Poe (1809–1849).
[11] "The agate lamp within thy hand," from Poe's poem "To Helen" (1831).
[12] "Death looks gigantically down," from Poe's poem "The City in the Sea" (1831).
[13] After the refrain "Nevermore" from Poe's poem "The Raven" (1845).
[14] Poe died in Baltimore supposedly after being beaten by a political gang that dragged him to various polling places to vote repeatedly for their candidate.
[15] In lower Manhattan.

Elbows and levers, guard and hissing door.   90
Thunder is galvothermic[16] here below. . . . The car
Wheels off. The train rounds, bending to a scream,
Taking the final level for the dive
Under the river—
And somewhat emptier than before,
Demented, for a hitching second, humps; then
Lets go. . . . Toward corners of the floor
Newspapers wing, revolve and wing.
Blank windows gargle signals through the roar.

And does the Daemon take you home, also,   100
Wop[17] washerwoman, with the bandaged hair?
After the corridors are swept, the cuspidors—
The gaunt sky-barracks cleanly now, and bare,
O Genoese,[18] do you bring mother eyes and hands
Back home to children and to golden hair?

Daemon, demurring and eventful yawn!
Whose hideous laughter is a bellows mirth
—Or the muffled slaughter of a day in birth—
O cruelly to inoculate the brinking dawn
With antennae toward worlds that glow and sink;—   110
To spoon us out more liquid than the dim
Locution of the eldest star, and pack
The conscience navelled in the plunging wind,
Umbilical to call—and straightway die!

O caught like pennies beneath soot and steam,
Kiss of our agony thou gatherest;
Condensed, thou takes all—shrill ganglia
Impassioned with some song we fail to keep.
And yet, like Lazarus,[19] to feel the slope,
The sod and billow breaking,—lifting ground,   120
—A sound of waters bending astride the sky
Unceasing with some Word that will not die . . . !

              .   .   .   .   .

A tugboat, wheezing wreaths of steam,
Lunged past, with one galvanic blare stove up the River.[20]
I counted the echoes assembling, one after one,
Searching, thumbing the midnight on the piers.
Lights, coasting, left the oily tympanum of waters;
The blackness somewhere gouged glass on a sky.
And this thy harbor, O my City, I have driven under,
Tossed from the coil of ticking towers. . . . Tomorrow,   130

---

[16] Crane's shorthand for galvanothermic, or electrically generated heat.
[17] Slang for an Italian person.   [18] Christopher Columbus (1451–1506), born in Genoa, Italy.
[19] In John 11:43–44 Jesus resurrected Lazarus from the dead.
[20] The East River, which separates Manhattan from Long Island.

And to be. . . . . Here by the River that is East—
Here at the waters' edge the hands drop memory;
Shadowless in that abyss they unaccounting lie.
How far away the star has pooled the sea—
Or shall the hands be drawn away, to die?

Kiss of our agony Thou gatherest,
O Hand of Fire
gatherest—

1926–1927, 1930

THE BROKEN TOWER

The bell-rope that gathers God at dawn
Dispatches me as though I dropped down the knell
Of a spent day—to wander the cathedral lawn
From pit to crucifix, feet chill on steps from hell.

Have you not heard, have you not seen that corps
Of shadows in the tower, whose shoulders sway
Antiphonal carillons[1] launched before
The stars are caught and hived in the sun's ray?

The bells, I say, the bells break down their tower;
And swing I know not where. Their tongues engrave   10
Membrane through marrow, my long-scattered score
Of broken intervals . . . And I, their sexton[2] slave!

Oval encyclicals[3] in canyons heaping
The impasse high with choir. Banked voices slain!
Pagodas, campaniles[4] with reveilles outleaping—
O terraced echoes prostrate on the plain! . . .

And so it was I entered the broken world
To trace the visionary company of love, its voice
An instant in the wind (I know not whither hurled)
But not for long to hold each desperate choice.   20

My word I poured. But was it cognate, scored
Of that tribunal monarch of the air
Whose thigh embronzes earth, strikes crystal Word
In wounds pledged once to hope,—cleft to despair?

---

[1] Bells that produce harmonies through opposing sounds.
[2] A church caretaker, bellringer and gravedigger.
[3] Papal letters circulated to the bishops of a whole church or in one country.
[4] Free-standing church towers.

The steep encroachments of my blood left me
No answer (could blood hold such a lofty tower
As flings the question true?)—or is it she
Whose sweet mortality stirs latent power?—

And through whose pulse I hear, counting the strokes
My veins recall and add, revived and sure   30
The angelus[5] of wars my chest evokes:
What I hold healed, original now, and pure . . .

And builds, within, a tower that is not stone
(Not stone can jacket heaven)—but slip
Of pebbles,—visible wings of silence sown
In azure circles, widening as they dip

The matrix of the heart, lift down the eye
That shrines the quiet lake and swells a tower . . .
The commodious, tall decorum of that sky
Unseals her earth, and lifts love in its shower.   40

1932

Louise Bogan
(1897–1970)

Not until nearly fifteen years after Louise Bogan's death, with the publication of Elizabeth Frank's biography *Louise Bogan, A Portrait* (1985), did the "rough and vulgar facts" of Bogan's life come to light. In her poems we read of passion and grief, but we do not know what prompted the poetry. A formal, tightly controlled, discrete verse, Bogan's poetry fell out of fashion when free verse and explicitly autobiographical poetry were the dominant trends. Interest in her life and in her work is growing, however, with particular attention to her slim volume of collected verse, *The Blue Estuaries* (1968). Most of the poems in this volume were originally published in the 1920s and 1930s. Thereafter she wrote a few poems and some (uncollected) fiction and continued to write remarkable reviews as poetry critic for the *New Yorker*, a job she held for thirty-eight years.

Bogan was born in 1897 in Livermore Falls, a small mill town in Maine. She spent her early years with her family in Maine, New Hampshire, and Massachusetts among various boarding houses. Her parents' marriage was extremely troubled, and her mother engaged in a series of affairs, all of which the child was aware of. Bogan's formal education took place, except for one year at Boston College, in Boston's Girls' Latin School, where she was rigorously trained in the classics and was already writing poetry. She has said that by

---

[5] The Roman Catholic prayer that commemorates the Incarnation of Christ; or the bell rung to announce this thrice-daily prayer.

age eighteen she had learned every essential of her trade. Bogan married Curt Alexander, an army man, in 1916 but found both him and army life to her dislike and left with their only child, a daughter. He died in 1920, when Bogan was living in New York City's Greenwich Village. There Bogan, at age twenty-two, was already gaining a reputation as a gifted lyric poet and met friends she was to have for life, notably the writers Edmund Wilson, Malcolm Cowley, and Rolfe Humphries. Yet, though her work was going well, she suffered the first of several emotional breakdowns.

In 1923 Bogan's first book of verse, *Body of this Death,* was published, and she married the writer Raymond Holden in 1925. Her second book, *Dark Summer* (1929), received quiet, if favorable, reviews. However, Bogan suffered from depression in the early 1930s and twice checked herself into New York's Neurological Institute. In her letters she writes of having gone "to the ninth circle of hell" and back. Her second marriage fell apart, and she divorced at age thirty-seven. During the 1930s Bogan traveled on fellowships and continued writing, her last collection of new work, *The Sleeping Fury,* coming out in 1937.

Thereafter, Bogan struggled mainly to write criticism and stave off depression. In 1954 she was elected to the Academy of American Poets and published *Collected Poems,* for which she shared a Bollingen Prize with Léonie Adams. Bogan spent much of her last years alone, although she kept up her lively and witty correspondence with friends. She died in 1970, alone in her apartment opposite the Neurological Institute. The importance of Bogan's work in the canon of modern poetry is now established, her poetry recognized once again, and with considerable enthusiasm, for its technical grace, lyric perfection, and hard-earned wisdom.

Suggested Readings: *Achievement in American Poetry, 1900–1950,* 1951. *A Poet's Alphabet: Reflections on the Literary Art and Vocation,* ed. R. Phelps and R. Limmer, 1970. *What the Woman Lived: Selected Letters of Louise Bogan 1920–1970,* ed. R. Limmer, 1973. *Journey Around My Room: The Autobiography of Louise Bogan, A Mosaic,* ed. R. Limmer, 1980. M. Collins, ed., *Critical Essays on Louise Bogan,* 1984. E. Frank, *Louise Bogan, A Portrait,* 1985. G. Bowles, *Louise Bogan's Aesthetic of Limitation,* 1987.

Text Used: *The Blue Estuaries: Poems 1923–1968,* 1968.

WOMEN

Women have no wilderness in them,
They are provident instead,
Content in the tight hot cell of their hearts
To eat dusty bread.

They do not see cattle cropping red winter grass,
They do not hear
Snow water going down under culverts[1]
Shallow and clear.

They wait, when they should turn to journeys,
They stiffen, when they should bend.   10

---

[1] Transverse drains.

They use against themselves that benevolence
To which no man is friend.

They cannot think of so many crops to a field
Or of clean wood cleft by an axe.
Their love is an eager meaninglessness
Too tense, or too lax.

They hear in every whisper that speaks to them
A shout and a cry.
As like as not, when they take life over their door-sills
They should let it go by.   20

1923

CASSANDRA*

To me, one silly task is like another.
I bare the shambling tricks of lust and pride.
This flesh will never give a child its mother,—
Song, like a wing, tears through my breast, my side,
And madness chooses out my voice again,
Again. I am the chosen no hand saves:
The shrieking heaven lifted over men,
Not the dumb earth, wherein they set their graves.

1929

FOR A MARRIAGE

She gives most dangerous sight
To keep his life awake:
A sword sharp-edged and bright
That darkness must not break,
Not ever for her sake.

With it he sees, deep-hidden,
The sullen other blade
To every eye forbidden,
That half her life has made,
And until now obeyed.   10

Now he will know his part:
Tougher than bone or wood,

---

* According to Greek myth, a daughter of King Priam of Troy; her dire but accurate prophecies were never believed.

To clasp on that barbed heart
That once shed its own blood
In its own solitude.

1929

SONNET

Dark, underground, is furnished with the bone;
The tool's lost, and the counter in the game.
Eaten as though by water or by flame
The elaborate craft built up from wood and stone.

Words made of breath, these also are undone,
And greedy sight abolished in its claim.
Light fails from ruin and from wall the same;
The loud sound and pure silence fall as one.

Worn flesh at last is history and treasure
Unto itself; its scars it still can keep,   10
Received from love, from memory's false measure,
From pain, from the long dream drawn back in sleep.

Attest, poor body, with what scars you have,
That you left life, to come down to the grave.

1929

SINGLE SONNET

Now, you great stanza, you heroic mould,
Bend to my will, for I must give you love:
The weight in the heart that breathes, but cannot move,
Which to endure flesh only makes so bold.

Take up, take up, as it were lead or gold
The burden; test the dreadful mass thereof.
No stone, slate, metal under or above
Earth, is so ponderous, so dull, so cold.

Too long as ocean bed bears up the ocean,
As earth's core bears the earth, have I borne this;   10
Too long have lovers, bending for their kiss,
Felt bitter force cohering without motion.

Staunch meter, great song, it is yours, at length,
To prove how stronger you are than my strength.

1930

ITALIAN MORNING

Half circle's come before we know.
Full in the falling arc, we hear
Our heel give earth a lonely blow.
We place the hour and name the year.

High in a room long since designed
For our late visit under night,
We sleep: we wake to watch the lined
Wave take strange walls with counterfeit light.

The big magnolia, like a hand,
Repeats our flesh. (O bred to love,   10
Gathered to silence!) In a land
Thus garnished, there is time enough

To pace the rooms where painted swags[1]
Of fruit and flower in pride depend,
Stayed as we are not. The hour wags
Deliberate, and great arches bend

In long perspective past our eye.

Mutable body, and brief name,
Confront, against an early sky,
This marble herb, and this stone flame.   20

1930

THE SLEEPING FURY

You are here now,
Who were so loud and feared, in a symbol before me,
Alone and asleep, and I at last look long upon you.

Your hair fallen on your cheek, no longer in the semblance of serpents,
Lifted in the gale; your mouth, that shrieked so, silent.
You, my scourge, my sister, lie asleep, like a child,
Who, after rage, for an hour quiet, sleeps out its tears.

The days close to winter
Rough with strong sound. We hear the sea and the forest,
And the flames of your torches fly, lit by others,   10
Ripped by the wind, in the night. The black sheep for sacrifice
Huddle together. The milk is cold in the jars.

---

[1] Decorations hanging in a curve between two points.

All to no purpose, as before, the knife whetted and plunged,
The shout raised, to match the clamor you have given them.
You alone run away, not appeased; unaltered, avenger.

Hands full of scourges, wreathed with your flames and adders,[1]
You alone turned away, but did not move from my side,
Under the broken light, when the soft nights took the torches.

At thin morning you showed, thick and wrong in that calm,
The ignoble dream and the mask, sly, with slits at the eyes,   20
Pretence and half-sorrow, beneath which a coward's hope trembled.

You uncovered at night, in the locked stillness of houses,
False love due the child's heart, the kissed-out lie, the embraces,
Made by the two who for peace tenderly turned to each other.

You who know what we love, but drive us to know it;
You with your whips and shrieks, bearer of truth and of solitude;
You who give, unlike men, to expiation your mercy.

Dropping the scourge when at last the scourged advances to meet it,
You, when the hunted turns, no longer remain the hunter
But stand silent and wait, at last returning his gaze.   30

Beautiful now as a child whose hair, wet with rage and tears
Clings to its face. And now I may look upon you,
Having once met your eyes. You lie in sleep and forget me.
Alone and strong in my peace, I look upon you in yours.

1930

EVENING IN THE SANITARIUM*

The free evening fades, outside the windows fastened with decorative
    iron grilles.
The lamps are lighted; the shades drawn; the nurses are watching a
    little.
It is the hour of the complicated knitting on the safe bone needles; of
    the games of anagrams and bridge;
The deadly game of chess; the book held up like a mask.

The period of the wildest weeping, the fiercest delusion, is over.
The women rest their tired half-healed hearts; they are almost well.
Some of them will stay almost well always: the blunt-faced woman
    whose thinking dissolved

---

[1] Poisonous snakes.
    * First published in 1941 with the subtitle "Imitated From Auden." Bogan much admired the work of
the English poet W. H. Auden (1907–1973), who became an American citizen in 1946.

Under academic discipline; the manic-depressive girl
Now leveling off; one paranoiac afflicted with jealousy.
Another with persecution. Some alleviation has been possible.   10

O fortunate bride, who never again will become elated after childbirth!
O lucky older wife, who has been cured of feeling unwanted!
To the suburban railway station you will return, return,
To meet forever Jim home on the 5:35.
You will be again as normal and selfish and heartless as anybody else.

There is life left: the piano says it with its octave smile.
The soft carpets pad the thump and splinter of the suicide to be.
Everything will be splendid: the grandmother will not drink habitually.
The fruit salad will bloom on the plate like a bouquet
And the garden produce the blue-ribbon aquilegia.[1]   20

The cats will be glad; the fathers feel justified; the mothers relieved.
The sons and husbands will no longer need to pay the bills.
Childhoods will be put away, the obscene nightmare abated.

At the ends of the corridors the baths are running.
Mrs. C. again feels the shadow of the obsessive idea.
Miss R. looks at the mantel-piece, which must mean something.

1941

SONG FOR THE LAST ACT

Now that I have your face by heart, I look
Less at its features than its darkening frame
Where quince and melon, yellow as young flame,
Lie with quilled dahlias and the shepherd's crook.
Beyond, a garden. There, in insolent ease
The lead and marble figures watch the show
Of yet another summer loath to go
Although the scythes hang in the apple trees.

Now that I have your face by heart, I look.

Now that I have your voice by heart, I read   10
In the black chords upon a dulling page
Music that is not meant for music's cage,
Whose emblems mix with words that shake and bleed.
The staves are shuttled over with a stark
Unprinted silence. In a double dream
I must spell out the storm, the running stream.
The beat's too swift. The notes shift in the dark.

---

[1] Columbine, a blue-flowered plant of the Rocky Mountains.

Now that I have your voice by heart, I read.

Now that I have your heart by heart, I see
The wharves with their great ships and architraves;[1]   20
The rigging and the cargo and the slaves
On a strange beach under a broken sky.
O not departure, but a voyage done!
The bales stand on the stone; the anchor weeps
Its red rust downward, and the long vine creeps
Beside the salt herb, in the lengthening sun.

Now that I have your heart by heart, I see.

                                                              1954

THE DRAGONFLY

You are made of almost nothing
But of enough
To be great eyes
And diaphanous double vans;[1]
To be ceaseless movement,
Unending hunger
Grappling love.

Link between water and air,
Earth repels you.
Light touches you only to shift into iridescence   10
Upon your body and wings.

Twice-born,[2] predator,
You split into the heat.
Swift beyond calculation or capture
You dart into the shadow
Which consumes you.

You rocket into the day.
But at last, when the wind flattens the grasses,
For you, the design and purpose stop.

And you fall   20
With the other husks of summer.

                                                              1968

---

[1] Architectural moldings.
[1] Wings.   [2] Dragonflies undergo metamorphosis, the transformation of a larva into an adult.

NIGHT

The cold remote islands
And the blue estuaries
Where what breathes, breathes
The restless wind of the inlets,
And what drinks, drinks
The incoming tide;

Where shell and weed
Wait upon the salt wash of the sea,
And the clear nights of stars
Swing their lights westward   10
To set behind the land;

Where the pulse clinging to the rocks
Renews itself forever;
Where, again on cloudless nights,
The water reflects
The firmament's partial setting;

—O remember
In your narrowing dark hours
That more things move
Than blood in the heart.   20

1968

Yvor Winters
(1900–1968)

Yvor Winters was proud to be living quietly with his wife and dogs in California when other poets were in Paris or at eastern colleges. An outsider in the American literary world, Arthur Yvor Winters was born in Chicago in 1900 and raised in California, where he spent most of his life.

Winters spent 1917 at the University of Chicago. There he joined the Poetry Club, through which he met the writers Glenway Wescott and Elizabeth Roberts and the publisher of *Poetry* magazine, Harriet Monroe. Afflicted by tuberculosis in 1918, Winters endured three isolated and lonely years of recovery in a Santa Fe, New Mexico, sanitarium. While hospitalized he continued to read poetry magazines and wrote most of his first two books of poetry, *The Immobile Wind* (1921) and *The Magpie's Shadow* (1922). In 1921 he met Janet Lewis, who later became a distinguished poet and novelist and Winters's wife. She, too, was ill and spent several years at the sanitarium. Between 1923 and 1925

Winters finished his B.A. and M.A. at the University of Colorado, where he studied French, Spanish, and Latin. Thereafter he taught languages in Moscow, Idaho, while his new wife remained in the sanitarium. In 1927 the couple moved to California, where Winters began a forty-year-long association with Stanford University. As a graduate student and as an instructor, he systematically reviewed English literature, century by century, and saw the virtues of sixteenth-century and seventeenth-century lyric poetry. Initially he wrote like, and thought of himself as, an imagist, but in 1928 he abruptly changed his thinking and began writing more formal verse. Feeling that he could not write poems as good as those he was reading, Winters changed his poetic method. His collection *The Proof* (1930) is transitional and includes both free verse and sonnets. In his criticism, for which he is best known, he took an absolute stand in which judgment does not depend on prevailing conditions of the author's life or work.

Winters corresponded with the poet Hart Crane, though the two met only briefly in 1927, and Crane's are the only letters Winters saved. As his own theories changed, Winters's early enthusiasm for Crane's work waned over the years; his criticism became more insistent. Winters's harsh review of Crane's long poem *The Bridge* (1930) infuriated Crane, who immediately ended their correspondence. Winters had come to equate poetic form with moral sensibility, and Crane fell short.

During the 1930s Winters continued to write poetry but turned his attention more to criticism. Three of his early books of criticism were collected in *In Defense of Reason* (1947). Although his post-1945 poetry writing was minimal, his *Collected Poems* (1960) won the Bollingen Prize. Winters continued teaching at Stanford until 1966 (his maxim to his students was "Write little; do it well") and greatly influenced many poets and scholars under his tutelage. A year before his death from cancer in 1968, he won the National Endowment for the Arts award honoring writers who had previously not received adequate recognition. As a poet, critic, and teacher Winters devoted his life to poetry and left a strong legacy inspired by his passionate and demanding intellect.

Suggested Readings: *In Defense of Reason,* 1947. *The Early Poems of Yvor Winters, 1920–1928,* 1966. *Forms of Discovery: Critical and Historical Essays on the Forms of the Short Poem in English,* 1967. *Uncollected Essays and Reviews,* ed. F. Murphy, 1973. *The Poetry of Yvor Winters,* 1980. E. Isaacs, *An Introduction to the Poetry of Yvor Winters,* 1981. D. Davis, *Wisdom and Wilderness: The Achievement of Yvor Winters,* 1983.

Text Used: *The Collected Poems of Yvor Winters,* 1978.

THE SLOW PACIFIC SWELL*

Far out of sight forever stands the sea,
Bounding the land with pale tranquillity.
When a small child, I watched it from a hill
At thirty miles or more. The vision still
Lies in the eye, soft blue and far away:
The rain has washed the dust from April day;
Paint-brush and lupine[1] lie against the ground;
The wind above the hill-top has the sound
Of distant water in unbroken sky;
Dark and precise the little steamers ply—   10

---

* A large ocean wave.

[1] Orange hawkweed and plants of the pea family, some poisonous; others, cultivated for green manure, fodder, or their edible seeds.

Firm in direction they seem not to stir.
That is illusion. The artificer
Of quiet, distance holds me in a vise
And holds the ocean steady to my eyes.

Once when I rounded Flattery,² the sea
Hove its loose weight like sand to tangle me
Upon the washing deck, to crush the hull;
Subsiding, dragged flesh at the bone. The skull
Felt the retreating wash of dreaming hair.
Half drenched in dissolution, I lay bare.   20
I scarcely pulled myself erect; I came
Back slowly, slowly knew myself the same.
That was the ocean. From the ship we saw
Gray whales for miles: the long sweep of the jaw,
The blunt head plunging clean above the wave.
And one rose in a tent of sea and gave
A darkening shudder; water fell away;
The whale stood shining, and then sank in spray.

A landsman, I. The sea is but a sound.
I would be near it on a sandy mound,   30
And hear the steady rushing of the deep
While I lay stinging in the sand with sleep.
I have lived inland long. The land is numb.
It stands beneath the feet, and one may come
Walking securely, till the sea extends
It's limber margin, and precision ends.
By night a chaos of commingling power,
The whole Pacific hovers hour by hour.
The slow Pacific swell stirs on the sand,
Sleeping to sink away, withdrawing land,   40
Heaving and wrinkled in the moon, and blind;
Or gathers seaward, ebbing out of mind.

1931

ORPHEUS*

*In Memory of Hart Crane*¹

Climbing from the Lethal² dead,
Past the ruined waters' bed,

---

² Cape Flattery, in northwestern Washington.

* According to Greek myth, the poet and musician Orpheus, typically depicted with a lyre, journeyed to the Underworld in search of his beloved wife, Eurydice. He is permitted by Hades to return with her to earth provided he does not look back as she follows him until she reaches daylight. But when he reaches the light, Orpheus eagerly looks back; Eurydice, however, has not yet stepped into the sunlight, and he loses her forever.

¹ The poet Hart Crane (1899–1932), who committed suicide at sea.

² Of Lethe, the river of forgetfulness and oblivion: one of the streams in Hades of classical myth.

In the sleep his music cast
Tree and flesh and stone were fast—
As amid Dodona's wood[3]
Wisdom never understood.

Till the shade his music won
Shuddered, by a pause undone—
Silence would not let her stay.
He could go one only way: 10
By the river, strong with grief,
Gave his flesh beyond belief.

Yet the fingers on the lyre
Spread like an avenging fire.
Crying loud, the immortal tongue,
From the empty body wrung,
Broken in a bloody dream,
Sang unmeaning down the stream.

1934

ON TEACHING THE YOUNG

The young are quick of speech.
Grown middle-aged, I teach
Corrosion and distrust,
Exacting what I must.

A poem is what stands
When imperceptive hands,
Feeling, have gone astray.
It is what one should say.

Few minds will come to this.
The poet's only bliss   10
Is in cold certitude—
Laurel,[1] archaic, rude.

1934

THE MANZANITA*

Under the forest, where the day is dark
And air is motionless throughout the day,

---

[3] In ancient Greece, a sanctuary of Zeus and the center of an oracle.
[1] Honorable; the laurel tree represents honor.
* Any of various evergreen shrubs and trees in the American Northwest.

Rooted in leaf-mould and in rotting bark,
This old arbutus[1] gathers strength to stay.

Tall as a man, and taller, but more old,
This is no shrub of some few years, but hard
Its smooth unbending trunk, oh, hard and cold!
Of earth and age the stony proof and guard!

This skin is rose: yet infinitely thin,
It is a color only. What one tells   10
Of ancient wood and softly glinting skin
Is less than are the tiny waxen bells.

This life is not our life; nor for our wit
The sweetness of these shades; these are alone.
There is no wisdom here; seek not for it!
This is the shadow of the vast madrone.[2]

1943

SIR GAWAINE AND THE GREEN KNIGHT*

Reptilian green the wrinkled throat,
Green as a bough of yew the beard;
He bent his head, and so I smote;
Then for a thought my vision cleared.

The head dropped clean; he rose and walked;
He fixed his fingers in the hair;
The head was unabashed and talked;
I understood what I must dare.

His flesh, cut down, arose and grew.
He bade me wait the season's round,   10
And then, when he had strength anew,
To meet him on his native ground.

The year declined; and in his keep
I passed in joy a thriving yule;

[1] A tree or shrub of the heath family.   [2] An evergreen tree of the Pacific coast.
* The title of a fourteenth-century Arthurian romance, a long narrative poem describing how a Green Knight arrives at King Arthur's court and challenges any knight to behead him that night, provided that he give the beheader a similar blow a year from now. Sir Gawaine takes the challenge and beheads the Green Knight, who picks up his head and tells Gawaine to meet him in a year. Later, Gawaine arrives at a castle where is he is warmly entertained, not realizing that his host is the Green Knight. The lady of the castle tries to seduce Gawaine, who resists her but accepts a magic protective girdle that he conceals from his host. When the time for the beheading comes, Gawaine does not flinch, but the Green Knight gives him only a slight wound, and that because he concealed the girdle. The entire adventure is a plot to test the honor and courage of the knights.

And whether waking or in sleep,
I lived in riot like a fool.

He beat the woods to bring me meat.
His lady, like a forest vine,
Grew in my arms; the growth was sweet;
And yet what thoughtless force was mine!   20

By practice and conviction formed,
With ancient stubbornness ingrained,
Although her body clung and swarmed,
My own identity remained.

Her beauty, lithe, unholy, pure,
Took shapes that I had never known;
And had I once been insecure,
Had grafted laurel[1] in my bone.

And then, since I had kept the trust,
Had loved the lady, yet was true,   30
The knight withheld his giant thrust
And let me go with what I knew.

I left the green bark and the shade,
Where growth was rapid, thick, and still;
I found a road that men had made
And rested on a drying hill.

1943

AN ELEGY

For the U.S.N. Dirigible, Macon

The noon is beautiful: the perfect wheel
Now glides on perfect surface with a sound
Earth has not heard before; the polished ground
Trembles and whispers under rushing steel.

The polished ground, and prehistoric air!
Metal now plummets upward and there sways,
A loosened pendulum for summer days,
Fixing the eyeball in a limpid stare.

There was one symbol in especial, one
Great form of thoughtless beauty that arose   10

---

[1] A tree that represents honor.

Above the mountains, to foretell the close
Of this deception, at meridian.[1]

Steel-gray the shadow, than a storm more vast!
Its crowding engines, rapid, disciplined,
Shook the great valley like a rising wind.
This image, now, is conjured from the past.

Wind in the wind! O form more light than cloud!
Storm amid storms! And by the storms dispersed!
The brain-drawn metal rose until accursed
By its extension and the sky was loud!   20

Who will believe this thing in time to come?
I was a witness. I beheld the age
That seized upon a planet's heritage
Of steel and oil, the mind's viaticum:[2]

Crowded the world with strong ingenious things,
Used the provision it could not replace,
To leave but Cretan[3] myths, a sandy trace
Through the last stone age, for the pastoral kings.

                                                    1943

TIME AND THE GARDEN

The spring has darkened with activity.
The future gathers in vine, bush, and tree:
Persimmon, walnut, loquat,[1] fig, and grape,
Degrees and kinds of color, taste, and shape.
These will advance in their due series, space
The season like a tranquil dwelling-place.
And yet excitement swells me, vein by vein:
I long to crowd the little garden, gain
Its sweetness in my hand and crush it small
And taste it in a moment, time and all!   10
These trees, whose slow growth measures off my years,
I would expand to greatness. No one hears,
And I am still retarded in duress!
And this is like that other restlessness
To seize the greatness not yet fairly earned,
One which the tougher poets have discerned—

---

[1] Noon.   [2] Provisions for a journey.
[3] Of the Greek island of Crete; Cretans had their own perceptions of the gods long before the mainland Greeks developed their myths.
[1] A yellow fruit used in preserves.

Gascoigne, Ben Jonson, Greville, Raleigh, Donne,[2]
Poets who wrote great poems, one by one,
And spaced by many years, each line an act
Through which few labor, which no men retract.   20
This passion is the scholar's heritage,
The imposition of a busy age,
The passion to condense from book to book
Unbroken wisdom in a single look,
Though we know well that when this fix the head,
The mind's immortal, but the man is dead.

1943

THE ROWS OF COLD TREES

To be my own Messiah to the
burning end. Can one endure the
acrid, steeping darkness of
the brain, which glitters and is
dissipated? Night. The night is
winter and a dull man bending,
muttering above a freezing pipe;
and I, bent heavily on books; the
mountain, iron in my sleep and
ringing; but the pipe has frozen, haired with   10
unseen veins, and cold is on the eyelids: who can
remedy this vision?

                          I have walked upon
the streets between the trees that
grew unleaved from asphalt in a night of
sweating winter in distracted silence.

                          I have
walked among the tombs—the rushing of the air
in the rich pines above my head is that which
ceaseth not nor stirreth whence it is: 20
in this the sound of the wind is like a flame.

It was the dumb decision of the
madness of my youth that left me with
this cold eye for the fact; that keeps me
quiet, walking toward a
stinging end: I am alone,
and, like the alligator cleaving timeless mud,
among the blessed who have Latin names.

1960

[2] The English poets George Gascoigne (1525?–1577), Ben Jonson (1572–1637), Sir Fulke Greville (1554–1628), Sir Walter Raleigh (1554–1618), and John Donne (1572–1631).

Allen Tate
(1899–1979)

Born John Orley Allen Tate in Winchester, Kentucky, in 1899, Allen Tate was one of the twentieth century's leading poet/critics and a proponent of an agrarian, Jeffersonian tradition rooted in the tragedy, heroism, and life of the South. However, Tate grew up in a family whose wealth was based on property and lumber, though a series of business failures in 1907 led to the loss of most of that wealth, the gradual isolation of his father from family and social life, and the frequent necessity for relocation. In 1918 Tate entered Vanderbilt University; while in Nashville he and his roommate Robert Penn Warren were admitted to the Fugitives, a group that met with poet/critic John Crowe Ransom to discuss philosophy and critique each others' work. Tate's poems were first published in the group's highly influential journal, *The Fugitive,* which Tate co-edited from 1923 to 1925. He moved to New York City in 1924, married the novelist Caroline Gordon (whom he wed and divorced twice, in addition to two other marriages), and spent the next eight years as a man of letters in New York and in France on a Guggenheim Fellowship (1928–1929). Tate met most of the influential writers of the time and owed a great deal to the generosity of his close friend Ford Madox Ford.

Tate wrote poetry, biography, and criticism, worked in publishing, and edited journals before he took a teaching position at the University of Minnesota in 1951; he remained there until his retirement in 1968. *Mr. Pope and Other Poems* (1928), *The Mediterranean and Other Poems* (1928), and *Poems: 1928–1931* (1932) established Tate's reputation as a poet of rich, allusive complexity in the mold of Charles Baudelaire, Ezra Pound, and T. S. Eliot. Tate's "Ode to the Confederate Dead" (1927) argues that "the past" must be held in ironic tension with the modern sense of the irrecoverable past. His writing participates vividly in what he called the "historical imagination"—the participation with the past as "a living imagination in a great work of literature" (from "Miss Emily and the Bibliographer" [1968]). This principle, coupled with the "religious imagination" that Tate associated with medieval Christianity and with the poet Dante, also guided Tate's biographical and critical writings, which champion southern figures and values. In *Stonewall Jackson* (1928) and *Jefferson Davis* (1929), Tate traces the tragic history of the South, and in *I'll Take My Stand* (1930) he joins the other Fugitives in a manifesto advocating a provincial, rural community rooted in the soil, sharing a tradition formed from the hardships of real events and from a conscious resistance to government involvement in culture and society. Taking his ideal early on from the pre-Civil War South of Thomas Jefferson and later from T. S. Eliot's *Notes Toward a Definition of Culture* (1949), Tate sought the re-formation of a "traditional society" that combines spiritual and economic life, in opposition to the abstract beliefs of the industrialized North.

Tate's criticism combines the promotion of these ideas with the methodology of the New Criticism. Attacking criticism for treating literature as the simple reflection of biographical facts and historical incidents and ideas, Tate focused inward on close readings that exposed a work's various "tensions" and explained how they subverted easy, literal meanings. His critical writings, collected in *Reactionary Essays on Poetry and Ideas* (1936), *Reason and Madness* (1941), and *Memoirs and Opinions* (1975), were purposefully snobbish attacks on conventional methods and mores that, despite contemporary views on the New Criticism, were always a form of self-consciously reactionary cultural critique. Tate held the Chair of Poetry in the Library of Congress from 1943 to 1944, received the Bollingen Prize for poetry in 1956 and the Academy of American Poets

Award in 1963, and served as president of the National Institute of Arts and Letters in 1968. After retiring from teaching he returned to the South—Sewanee, Tennessee—and moved back to Nashville a few years before his death in 1979.

Suggested Readings: *The Fathers,* 1938. *Reason and Madness,* 1941. *Poems,* 1960. *The Swimmers and Other Selected Poems,* 1970. R. K. Meiners, *The Last Alternatives: A Study of the Works of Allen Tate,* 1963. G. Hemphill, *Allen Tate,* 1964. F. Bishop, *Allen Tate,* 1967. R. Squires, *Allen Tate: A Literary Biography,* 1971. R. Squires, ed., *Allen Tate and His Work,* 1972.

Text Used: *Collected Poems: 1919–1976,* 1977.

MR. POPE*

When Alexander Pope strolled in the city
Strict was the glint of pearl and gold sedans.
Ladies leaned out more out of fear than pity
For Pope's tight back[1] was rather a goat's than man's.

Often one thinks the urn should have more bones
Than skeletons provide for speedy dust,
The urn gets hollow, cobwebs brittle as stones
Weave to the funeral shell a frivolous rust.

And he who dribbled couplets like a snake
Coiled to a lithe precision in the sun   10
Is missing. The jar is empty; you may break
It only to find that Mr. Pope is gone.

What requisitions of a verity
Prompted the wit and rage between his teeth
One cannot say. Around a crooked tree
A moral climbs whose name should be a wreath.

1925

ODE TO THE CONFEDERATE DEAD†

Row after row with strict impunity
The headstones yield their names to the element,
The wind whirrs without recollection;

---

* The English poet Alexander Pope (1688–1744).
[1] Pope suffered from severe curvature of the spine.
† First published in 1927 and revised in 1930. Tate reveals in the essay "Narcissus as Narcissus" (1968) that this poem "is 'about' solipsism, a philosophical doctrine which says that we create the world in the act of perceiving it; or about Narcissism, or any other *ism* that denotes the failure of the human personality to function objectively in nature and society." According to Greek myth, Narcissus pined away for love of his own reflection and turned into a flower.

In the riven troughs the splayed leaves
Pile up, of nature the casual sacrament
To the seasonal eternity of death;
Then driven by the fierce scrutiny
Of heaven to their election in the vast breath,
They sought the rumour of mortality.

Autumn is desolation in the plot   10
Of a thousand acres where these memories grow
From the inexhaustible bodies that are not
Dead, but feed the grass row after rich row.
Think of the autumns that have come and gone!—
Ambitious November with the humors of the year,
With a particular zeal for every slab,
Staining the uncomfortable angels that rot
On the slabs, a wing chipped here, an arm there:
The brute curiosity of an angel's stare
Turns you, like them, to stone,   20
Transforms the heaving air
Till plunged to a heavier world below
You shift your sea-space blindly
Heaving, turning like the blind crab.[1]

   Dazed by the wind, only the wind
   The leaves flying, plunge

You know who have waited by the wall
The twilight certainty of an animal,
Those midnight restitutions of the blood
You know—the immitigable pines, the smoky frieze   30
Of the sky, the sudden call: you know the rage,
The cold pool left by the mounting flood,
Of muted Zeno and Parmenides.[2]
You who have waited for the angry resolution
Of those desires that should be yours tomorrow,
You know the unimportant shrift of death
And praise the vision

[1] Tate's note: "The structure of the Ode is simple. Figure to yourself a man stopping at the gate of a Confederate graveyard on a late autumn afternoon. The leaves are falling; his first impressions bring him the 'rumor of mortality', and the desolation barely allows him, at the beginning of the second stanza, the conventionally heroic surmise that the dead will enrich the earth, 'where these memories grow.' From those quoted words to the end of that passage he pauses for a baroque meditation on the ravages of time, concluding with the figure of the 'blind crab.' This figure has mobility but no direction, energy but, from the human point of view, no purposeful world to use it in; in the entire poem there are only two explicit symbols for the locked-in ego; the crab is the first and less explicit symbol, a mere hint, a planting of the idea that will become overt in its second instance—the jaguar towards the end. The crab is the first intimation of the nature of the moral conflict upon which the drama of the poem develops: the cut-off-ness of the modern 'intellectual man' from the world."

[2] The Greek philosopher Parmenides (515? B.C.–?) and his follower Zeno (495?–430? B.C.) believed that the universe is singular and unchanging, whereas the "apparent universe" of mutable, or changeable, things is deceptive and incomprehensible.

And praise the arrogant circumstance
Of those who fall
Rank upon rank, hurried beyond decision—   40
Here by the sagging gate, stopped by the wall.[3]

Seeing, seeing only the leaves
Flying, plunge and expire

Turn your eyes to the immoderate past,
Turn to the inscrutable infantry rising
Demons out of the earth—they will not last.
Stonewall,[4] Stonewall, and the sunken fields of hemp,[5]
Shiloh, Antietam, Malvern Hill, Bull Run.[6]
Lost in that orient of the thick-and-fast
You will curse the setting sun.   50

Cursing only the leaves crying
Like an old man in a storm

You hear the shout, the crazy hemlocks point
With troubled fingers to the silence which
Smothers you, a mummy, in time,

                              The hound bitch
Toothless and dying, in a musty cellar
Hears the wind only.

                    Now that the salt of their blood
Stiffens the saltier oblivion of the sea,   60

---

[3] Tate's note: "The next long passage or 'strophe' . . . states the other term of the conflict. It is the theme of heroism, not merely moral heroism, but heroism in the grand style, elevating even death from mere physical dissolution into a formal ritual: this heroism is a formal ebullience of the human spirit in an entire society, not private, romantic illusion—something better than moral heroism, great as that may be, for moral heroism, being personal and individual, may be achieved by certain men in all ages, even ages of decadence. But the late Hart Crane [1899–1932] . . . described the theme as the 'theme of chivalry, a tradition of excess (not literally excess, but active faith) which cannot be perpetuated in the fragmentary cosmos of today—"those desires which should be yours tomorrow," but which, you know, will not persist nor find any way into action.' The 'structure' then is the objective frame for the tension between the two themes, 'active faith,' which has decayed, and the 'fragmentary cosmos' which surrounds us. . . . In contemplating the heroic theme the man at the gate never commits himself to the illusion of its availability to him. The most that he can allow himself is the fancy that the blowing leaves are charging soldiers, but he rigorously returns to the refrain: 'Only the wind'—or the 'leaves flying.' . . . More than this, he cautions himself, reminds himself repeatedly, of his subjective prison, his solipsisms, by breaking off the half-illusion and coming back to the refrain of wind and leaves, a refrain that, as Hart Crane said, is necessary to the 'subjective continuity.'"
[4] Thomas Jackson (1824–1863), Confederate Civil War general who earned the nickname Stonewall at the first Battle of Bull Run, Virginia, on July 21, 1861.
[5] Sunken, as they were not cultivated during the war.
[6] Famous Civil War battles: the Confederate losses at Shiloh, Tennessee, April 6 to 7, 1862; troops in retreat; Antietam, or Sharpsburg, Maryland, September 17, 1862; and Malvern Hill, Virginia, July 2, 1862; and the Confederate victories at the two battles of Bull Run, the second on August 29 to 30, 1862.

Seals the malignant purity of the flood,
What shall we who count our days and bow
Our heads with a commemorial woe
In the ribboned coats of grim felicity,
What shall we say of the bones, unclean,
Whose verdurous[7] anonymity will grow?
The ragged arms, the ragged heads and eyes
Lost in these acres of the insane green?
The gray lean spiders come, they come and go;
In a tangle of willows without light   70
The singular screech-owl's tight
Invisible lyric seeds the mind
With the furious murmur of their chivalry.

   We shall say only the leaves
   Flying, plunge and expire

We shall say only the leaves whispering
In the improbable mist of nightfall
That flies on multiple wing;
Night is the beginning and the end
And in between the ends of distraction   80
Waits mute speculation, the patient curse
That stones the eyes, or like the jaguar leaps
For his own image in a jungle pool, his victim.[8]
What shall we say who have knowledge
Carried to the heart?[9] Shall we take the act
To the grave? Shall we, more hopeful, set up the grave
In the house? The ravenous grave?[10]

                       Leave now
The shut gate and the decomposing wall:

---

[7] Flourishing with vegetation.

[8] Tate's note: "This figure of the jaguar is the only explicit rendering of the Narcissus motif in the poem, but instead of a youth gazing into a pool, a predatory beast stares at a jungle stream, and leaps to devour himself."

[9] Tate's note: "This is Pascal's war between heart and head, between *finesse* and *geométrie*." Blaise Pascal (1623–1662) was a French mathematician and philosopher.

[10] Tate's note: "These two themes struggle for mastery up to [lines 77–78]. . . . It will be observed that the passage begins with a phrase taken from the wind-leaves refrain—the signal that it has won. The refrain has been fused with the main stream of the man's reflections dominating them; and he cannot return even to an ironic vision of the heroes. There is nothing but death, the mere naturalism of death at that—spiritual extinction in the decay of the body. Autumn and the leaves are death; the men who exemplified in a grand style an 'active faith' are dead; there are only the leaves. Shall we then worship death . . . that will take us before our time? The question is not answered, although as a kind of morbid romanticism it might, if answered affirmatively, provide the man with an illusory escape from his solipsism; but he cannot accept it. Nor has he been able to live in his immediate world, the fragmentary cosmos. There is no practical solution, no solution offered for the edification of moralists. . . . The main intention of the poem has been to make dramatically visible the conflict, to concentrate it. . . . "

The gentle serpent, green in the mulberry bush,   90
Riots with his tongue through the hush—
Sentinel of the grave who counts us all![11]

1926, 1927; 1930

THE OATH

It was near evening, the room was cold
Half dark; Uncle Ben's brass bullet-mould
And powder-horn and Major Bogan's[1] face
Above the fire in the half-light plainly said:
There's naught to kill but the animated dead.
Horn nor mould nor major follows the chase.
Being cold I urged Lytle[2] to the fire
In the blank twilight with not much left untold
By two old friends when neither's a great liar.
We sat down evenly in the smoky chill.   10
There's precious little to say between day and dark,
Perhaps a few words on the implacable will
Of time sailing like a magic barque[3]
Or something as fine for the amenities,
Till dusk seals the window, the fire grows bright,
And the wind saws the hill with a swarm of bees.
Now meditating a little on the firelight
We heard the darkness grapple with the night
And give an old man's valedictory wheeze
From his westward breast between his polar jaws;   20
Then Lytle asked: Who are the dead?
Who are the living and the dead?
And nothing more was said.
So I, leaving Lytle to that dream,
Decided what it is in time that gnaws

---

[11] Tate's note: "The closing image, that of the serpent, is the ancient symbol of time, and I tried to give it the credibility of the commonplace by placing it in a mulberry bush—with the faint hope that the silkworm [which feeds on the mulberry] would somehow be implicit. But time is also death. If that is so, then space, or the Becoming, is life; and I believe there is not a single spatial symbol in the poem. 'Sea-space' is allowed the 'blind crab'; but the sea, as appears plainly in the passage beginning, 'Now that the salt of their blood . . .' is life only insofar as it is the source of the lowest forms of life, the source perhaps of all life, but life undifferentiated, halfway between life and death. This passage is a contrasting inversion of the conventional '. . . inexhaustible bodies that are not / Dead, but feed the grass . . .' the reduction of the earlier, literary conceit to a more naturalistic figure derived from modern biological speculation. Those 'buried Caesars' will not bloom in the hyacinth but will only make saltier the sea."

[1] Major Benjamin Bogan, Tate's great-grandfather.

[2] Andrew Lytle (1902–), a novelist and essayist, member of the Fugitives, and longtime friend of Tate's.

[3] Bark, a sailing vessel.

The ageing fury of a mountain stream
When suddenly as an ignorant mind will do
I thought I heard the dark pounding its head
On a rock, crying: *Who are the dead?*
Then Lytle turned with an oath—By God it's true!   30

1932

THE MEDITERRANEAN*

Quem das finem, rex magne, dolorum?[1]

Where we went in the boat was a long bay
A slingshot wide, walled in by towering stone—
Peaked margin of antiquity's delay,
And we went there out of time's monotone:

Where we went in the black hull no light moved
But a gull white-winged along the feckless wave,
The breeze, unseen but fierce as a body loved,
That boat drove onward like a willing slave:

Where we went in the small ship the seaweed
Parted and gave to us the murmuring shore,   10
And we made feast and in our secret need
Devoured the very plates[2] Aeneas bore:

Where derelict you see through the low twilight
The green coast that you, thunder-tossed, would win,
Drop sail, and hastening to drink all night
Eat dish and bowl to take that sweet land in!

Where we feasted and caroused on the sandless
Pebbles, affecting our day of piracy,
What prophecy of eaten plates could landless
Wanderers fulfil by the ancient sea?   20

We for that time might taste the famous age
Eternal here yet hidden from our eyes
When lust of power undid its stuffless rage;
They, in a wineskin, bore earth's paradise.

* Written about a picnic Tate attended on the French Mediterranean in 1932; first published as "Picnic at Cassis" in 1932.

[1] "What end do you give, O great king, of their pains?" (Latin), from the poem *Aeniad* (I.241), by the Roman poet Virgil (70–19 B.C.). The Roman goddess of love, Venus, asks this of the supreme god, Jupiter, on behalf of her mortal son Aeneas and his companions.

[2] The prophecy that Aeneas and his companions would resort to eating their plates when they had reached their unknown destination came true: they ate the bread on which meat was served and thereby knew that their wanderings were over.

Let us lie down once more by the breathing side
Of Ocean, where our live forefathers sleep
As if the Known Sea still were a month wide—
Atlantis[3] howls but is no longer steep!

What country shall we conquer, what fair land
Unman our conquest and locate our blood?   30
We've cracked the hemispheres with careless hand!
Now, from the Gates of Hercules[4] we flood

Westward, westward till the barbarous brine
Whelms us to the tired land where tasseling corn,
Fat beans, grapes sweeter than muscadine[5]
Rot on the vine: in that land were we born.

1933

SHADOW AND SHADE

The shadow streamed into the wall—
The wall, break-shadow in the blast;
We lingered wordless while a tall
Shade enclouded the shadow's cast.

The torrent of the reaching shade
Broke shadow into all its parts,
What then had been of shadow made
Found exigence in fits and starts

Where nothing properly had name
Save that still element the air,   10
Burnt sea of universal frame
In which impounded now we were:

I took her hand, I shut her eyes
And all her shadow cleft with shade,
Shadow was crushed beyond disguise
But, being fear, was unafraid.

I asked fair shadow at my side:
What more shall fiery shade require?

---

[3] A legendary continent in the Atlantic Ocean, thought to have sunk into the sea.
[4] According to classical myth, a hero of great strength who performed twelve labors imposed on him by the gods; he became the gatekeeper of Olympus, home of the gods.
[5] An American grape that grows in the South.

We lay long in the immense tide
Of shade and shadowy desire   20

And saw the dusk assail the wall,
The black surge, mounting, crash the stone!
Companion of this lust, we fall,
I said, lest we should die alone.

1933

SONNETS AT CHRISTMAS

I

This is the day His[1] hour of life draws near,
Let me get ready from head to foot for it
Most handily with eyes to pick the year
For small feed to reward a feathered wit.
Some men would see it an epiphany[2]
At ease, at food and drink, others at chase;
Yet I, stung lassitude, with ecstasy
Unspent argue the season's difficult case
So: Man, dull creature of enormous head,
What would he look at in the coiling sky?   10
But I must kneel again unto the Dead
While Christmas bells of paper white and red,
Figured with boys and girls spilt from a sled,
Ring out the silence I am nourished by.

II

Ah, Christ, I love you rings to the wild sky
And I must think a little of the past:
When I was ten I told a stinking lie
That got a black boy whipped; but now at last
The going years, caught in an after-glow,
Reverse like balls englished upon green baize[3]—   20
Let them return, let the round trumpets blow
The ancient crackle of the Christ's deep gaze.
Deafened and blind, with senses yet unfound,
Am I, untutored to the after-wit
Of knowledge, knowing a nightmare has no sound;
Therefore with idle hands and head I sit
In late December before the fire's daze
Punished by crimes of which I would be quit.

1934

---

[1] Jesus.   [2] An appearance or manifestation of a supernatural being.
[3] Spinning upon green (feltlike) woolen cloth.

=CONTEXTS=

The Southern Agrarians

In the American South of the early 1920s a literary revival, known as the Southern Renaissance, took shape. Though the authors of the Southern Renaissance moved beyond the strictures of "regional" literature and approached more universal concerns, they continued the traditions of the local-color writers and retained a distinctive southern flavor. In his poem "Vision by Sweetwater" (1927), John Crowe Ransom (1888–1974), a prominent Southern Renaissance writer, contrasts the peacefulness of antebellum southern life with the debased state of the post-Reconstruction South:

Vision by Sweetwater

Go and ask Robin to bring the girls over
To Sweetwater, said my Aunt; and that was why
It was like a dream of ladies sweeping by
The willows, clouds, deep meadowgrass, and river.

Robin's sisters and my Aunt's lily daughter
Laughed and talked, and tinkled light as wrens
If there were a little colony all hens
To go walking by the steep turn of Sweetwater.

Let them alone, dear Aunt, just for one minute
Till I go fishing in the dark of my mind:
Where have I seen before, against the wind,
These bright virgins, robed and bare of bonnet,

Flowing with music of their strange quick tongue
And adventuring with delicate paces by the stream,—
Myself a child, old suddenly at the scream
From one of the white throats which it hid among?

John Crowe Ransom, 1927

The proponents of the movement of regional pride known as agrarianism, including Ransom, Allen Tate, and Robert Penn Warren (1905–1990), were concerned that industrialization would overwhelm the Old South's pastoral way of life. This way of life involved an organic relationship between humans and nature, a relationship that would be destroyed, agrarians feared, by the introduction of smoke-belching factories, the diminished importance of the individual, and other trappings of industrialism. Some southerners also feared that an industrial economy, with its need for cheap sources of labor, would allow African Americans a more stable economic footing in the South. The agrarians' inability to reconcile the values of the rural South with the needs and rights of its African-American population contributed to the ultimate failure of agrarianism to hold the line against industrialism.

Langston Hughes
(1902–1967)

Langston Hughes's contributions to African-American literature span the period from the Harlem Renaissance of the 1920s to the Black Arts movement of the late 1960s. Known as the "bard of Harlem," he wrote poems, plays, fiction, and nonfiction; edited anthologies; and encouraged such younger writers as Gwendolyn Brooks and Alice Walker. Hughes was born in Joplin, Missouri, in 1902. In 1903 his father, Jessie Nathaniel Hughes, left for Mexico in search of economic opportunities. His mother, Carrie Mercer Langston, moved frequently, working as a newspaperwoman and stenographer. Hughes occasionally traveled with her but resided in Lawrence, Kansas, with his maternal grandmother, a woman honored as the last surviving widow of a slave killed in John Brown's 1859 raid. After her death in 1915 Hughes briefly stayed with devoutly religious friends of hers. From 1916 to 1920 he lived with his mother, new stepfather, and stepbrother in Cleveland, Ohio, where he attended high school. The more liberal of his white schoolmates, children of European immigrants, introduced him to continental philosophy and Marxism.

At age eighteen Hughes wrote his most anthologized poem, "The Negro Speaks of Rivers," while crossing the Mississippi by train on his way to Mexico to spend a year with his father. The poem was accepted by W. E. B. DuBois's magazine *Crisis*. Hughes enrolled at Columbia University in 1920 but dropped out after a year to immerse himself in the people, night life, and folk forms that shaped the Harlem Renaissance. Working to free writing from European traditions, he innovated forms based on African-American culture.

Throughout his life Hughes traveled extensively. His travels enabled him to form friendships with writers of different backgrounds, stretching both his thinking about the responsibilities of artists and his own literary practice. His translations introduced Caribbean, Latin American, and African poets to American readers. Hughes first went to Africa as a cabin boy on a freighter in 1923 and to Paris the following year. There, the writer/educator Alain Locke made Hughes a part of the Harlem Renaissance by including the poet's work in the anthology *The New Negro* (1925).

Back in the States, Hughes met the novelist Arna Bontemps, with whom he collaborated for several decades on children's books and anthologies. *The Weary Blues*, Hughes's first poetry book, was published in 1926; his second book of poems, *Fine Clothes to the Jew*, appeared in 1927. Some black reviewers objected to both books' stance against middle-class assimilation of African Americans. That summer Charlotte Mason, one of Hughes's several white patrons, provided support for him to begin his first novel. However, their differences surfaced by the time that novel, *Not Without Laughter*, was published in 1930. Mason saw black culture as white Americans' connection to the primitive, whereas Hughes increasingly wrote to protest the social conditions of a racist society.

By this time Hughes had finished college at Lincoln University (he was later awarded two honorary doctorates). The Great Depression had so deprived the Harlem Renaissance of its wealthy audience that the movement had dispersed. Hughes was determined to make a living as a writer. In Chapel Hill, North Carolina, in 1931, an unofficial student paper published Hughes's "Christ in Alabama," a poem about nine young black men who were unjustly jailed for the rapes of two white prostitutes. The audience at Hughes's subsequent poetry reading in Chapel Hill nearly rioted. Elsewhere audiences packed his readings. In 1932 he visited Russia, where he met the communist writer Arthur Koestler. Hughes and Koestler explored Soviet Asia and debated the roles of social goals and individual desires in art. Hughes defended the artist's autonomy, but the discussions revived his interest in leftist thought. His poetry of this period rings with the language of proletarian revolution.

Hughes's drama *Mulatto* played on Broadway from 1935 to 1936. As a correspondent for the *Baltimore Afro-American* in 1937, he covered the Spanish Civil War and met the influential literary figures Ernest Hemingway, André Malraux, and Pablo Neruda in Madrid. In Los Angeles in 1939 Hughes founded the New Negro Theater, wrote a screenplay, and completed the first part of his autobiography, *The Big Sea* (1940). Over the next three years he received a fellowship to write historical plays and, in Chicago, founded the Skyloft Players, who performed his musical *The Sun Do More* (1941).

Hughes returned to New York City when his book *Shakespeare in Harlem* was published in 1942. He wrote slogans to sell U.S. Defense Bonds and a weekly column for the *Chicago Defender*, an African-American newspaper, where his first of five short stories of Harlem folk philosopher Jesse B. Semple (nicknamed "Simple") were published. Semple's female counterpart, Madam Alberta K. Johnson, appeared in the poems of *One-Way Ticket* (1949). His long poem *Montage of a Dream Deferred* was published in 1951. Reviews of his work remain mixed: critics have recognized the modernism of Hughes's restraint, but some have had reservations about the folk elements.

In 1953 Hughes was called before Senator Joseph McCarthy's subcommittee on subversive activities and testified about his involvement with communism in the 1930s. As had other black intellectuals, Hughes saw communism's interest in the poor as potentially helpful to African Americans. Until 1959 he was listed by the FBI as a security risk. After 1960, however, he visited Africa and Europe many times on cultural grants from the State Department. In varied forms of satire, the poems in *Ask Your Mama* (1961), considered by some his greatest work, discuss the rising anger against bigotry of the 1960s. The status of African Americans was changing, but Hughes saw the change as slow and regressive. The prolific writer died in 1967, shortly after the publication of *The Panther and the Lash: Poems of Our Times* and shortly before major upheavals in the civil rights movement.

Suggested Readings: *The Weary Blues*, 1926. *Not Without Laughter*, 1930. *The Dream Keeper and Other Poems*, 1932. *Scottsboro Limited: Four Poems and a Play in Verse*, 1932. *The Ways of White Folks*, 1934. *The Big Sea: An Autobiography*, 1940. *One-Way Ticket*, 1949. *Montage of a Dream Deferred*, 1951. *I Wonder As I Wander: An Autobiographical Journey*, 1956. *Fight for Freedom: The Story of the NAACP*, 1962. D. C. Dickinson, *A Bio-Bibliography of Langston Hughes, 1902–1967*, 1967. N. Huggins, *Harlem Renaissance*, 1971. R. K. Barksdale, *Langston Hughes: The Poet and His Critics*, 1977. F. Berry, *Langston Hughes: Before and Beyond Harlem*, 1983. A. Rampersad, *The Life of Langston Hughes*, 2 vols., 1986–1988. R. B. Miller, *The Art and Imagination of Langston Hughes*, 1989.

Texts Used: Poems: *Selected Poems of Langston Hughes*, 1970. "Feet Live Their Own Life": *The Best of Simple*, 1961. "Thank You, M'am": *The Langston Hughes Reader*, 1958.

THE NEGRO SPEAKS OF RIVERS

I've known rivers:
I've known rivers ancient as the world and older than the
flow of human blood in human veins.

My soul has grown deep like the rivers.

I bathed in the Euphrates[1] when dawns were young.
I built my hut near the Congo[2] and it lulled me to sleep.
I looked upon the Nile and raised the pyramids above it.
I heard the singing of the Mississippi when Abe Lincoln
    went down to New Orleans, and I've seen its muddy
    bosom turn all golden in the sunset.   10

I've known rivers:
Ancient, dusky rivers.

My soul has grown deep like the rivers.

1920, 1921

DREAM VARIATIONS

To fling my arms wide
In some place of the sun,
To whirl and to dance
Till the white day is done.
Then rest at cool evening
Beneath a tall tree
While night comes on gently,
    Dark like me—
That is my dream!

To fling my arms wide
In the face of the sun,
Dance! Whirl! Whirl!
Till the quick day is done.
Rest at pale evening . . .
A tall, slim tree . . .
Night coming tenderly
    Black like me.

1924

FIRE

Fire,
Fire, Lord!
Fire gonna burn ma soul!

[1] The Euphrates River, the cradle of ancient Babylonian civilization, flows from eastern Turkey through Syria and Iraq into the Persian Gulf.
[2] The Congo River, which flows through West Central Africa into the Atlantic.

I ain't been good,
I ain't been clean—
I been stinkin', low-down, mean.

Fire,
Fire, Lord!
Fire gonna burn ma soul!

Tell me, brother,   10
Do you believe
If you wanta go to heaben
Got to moan an' grieve?

Fire,
Fire, Lord!
Fire gonna burn ma soul!

I been stealin',
Been tellin' lies,
Had more women
Than Pharaoh[1] had wives.   20

Fire,
Fire, Lord!
Fire gonna burn ma soul!
I means Fire, Lord!
Fire gonna burn ma soul!

1926

THE WEARY BLUES

Droning a drowsy syncopated tune,
Rocking back and forth to a mellow croon,
    I heard a Negro play.
Down on Lenox Avenue[1] the other night
By the pale dull pallor of an old gas light
    He did a lazy sway. . . .
    He did a lazy sway. . . .
To the tune o' those Weary Blues.
With his ebony hands on each ivory key
He made that poor piano moan with melody.   10
    O Blues!
Swaying to and fro on his rickety stool
He played that sad raggy tune like a musical fool.
    Sweet Blues!

[1] The title given to ancient Egyptian rulers; used here, as in the Bible, as a proper noun.
[1] In New York City's Harlem.

Coming from a black man's soul.
 O Blues!
In a deep song voice with a melancholy tone
I heard that Negro sing, that old piano moan—
 "Ain't got nobody in all this world,
 Ain't got nobody but ma self.   20
 I's gwine to quit ma frownin'
 And put ma troubles on the shelf."
Thump, thump, thump, went his foot on the floor.
He played a few chords then he sang some more—
 "I got the Weary Blues
 And I can't be satisfied.
 Got the Weary Blues
 And can't be satisfied—
 I ain't happy no mo'
 And I wish that I had died."   30
And far into the night he crooned that tune.
The stars went out and so did the moon.
The singer stopped playing and went to bed
While the Weary Blues echoed through his head.
He slept like a rock or a man that's dead.

           1923, 1926

AFRO-AMERICAN FRAGMENT

 So long,
 So far away
 Is Africa.
 Not even memories alive
 Save those that history books create,
 Save those that songs
 Beat back into the blood—
 Beat out of blood with words sad-sung
 In strange un-Negro tongue—
 So long,   10
 So far away
 Is Africa.

 Subdued and time-lost
 Are the drums—and yet
 Through some vast mist of race
 There comes this song
 I do not understand,
 This song of atavistic[1] land,
 Of bitter yearnings lost
 Without a place—   20

[1] Characteristic of a remote ancestor.

So long,
So far away
Is Africa's
Dark face.

1930

I, TOO*

I, too, sing America.

I am the darker brother.
They send me to eat in the kitchen
When company comes,
But I laugh,
And eat well,
And grow strong.

Tomorrow,
I'll be at the table
When company comes.   10
Nobody'll dare
Say to me,
"Eat in the kitchen,"
Then.

Besides,
They'll see how beautiful I am
And be ashamed—

I, too, am America.

1932

SYLVESTER'S DYING BED

I woke up this mornin'
'Bout half-past three.
All the womens in town
Was gathered round me.

Sweet gals was a-moanin',
"Sylvester's gonna die!"

* Also known by the title "Epilogue."

And a hundred pretty mamas
Bowed their heads to cry.

I woke up little later
'Bout half-past fo',   10
The doctor 'n' undertaker's
Both at ma do'.

Black gals was a-beggin',
"You can't leave us here!"
Brown-skins cryin', "Daddy!
Honey! Baby! Don't go, dear!"

But I felt ma time's a-comin',
And I know'd I's dyin' fast.
I seed the River Jerden[1]
A-creepin' muddy past—   20
But I's still Sweet Papa 'Vester,
Yes, sir! Long as life do last!

So I hollers, "Com'ere, babies,
Fo' to love yo' daddy right!"
And I reaches up to hug 'em—
When the Lawd put out the light.

Then everything was darkness
In a great . . . big . . . night.

1942

MADAM'S PAST HISTORY

My name is Johnson—
Madam Alberta K.
The Madam stands for business.
I'm smart that way.

I had a
HAIR-DRESSING PARLOR
Before
The depression put
The prices lower.

Then I had a   10
BARBECUE STAND

---

[1] The Jordan River in Palestine; a symbol of the division between earth and Heaven, and mentioned frequently in the Bible and in African-American gospel music.

Till I got mixed up
With a no-good man.

Cause I had a insurance
The WPA[1]
Said, We can't use you
Wealthy that way.

I said,
DON'T WORRY 'BOUT ME!
Just like the song,   20
You WPA folks take care of yourself—
And I'll get along.

I do cooking,
Day's work, too!
Alberta K. Johnson—
Madam to you.

1943

MADAM AND THE MINISTER

Reverend Butler came by
My house last week.
He said, Have you got
A little time to speak?

He said, I am interested
In your soul.
Has it been saved,
Or is your heart stone-cold?

I said, Reverend,
I'll have you know   10
I was baptized
Long ago.

He said, What have you
Done since then?
I said, None of your
Business, friend.

He said, Sister
Have you back-slid?

---

[1] The Works Progress Administration, a federal agency that created jobs for the unemployed during the Great Depression.

I said, It felt good—
If I did!   20

He said, Sister,
Come time to die,
The Lord will surely
Ask you why!
I'm gonna pray
For you!
Goodbye!

I felt kinder sorry
I talked that way
After Rev. Butler   30
Went away—
So I ain't in no mood
For sin today.

1943

TRUMPET PLAYER

The Negro
With the trumpet at his lips
Has dark moons of weariness
Beneath his eyes
Where the smoldering memory
Of slave ships
Blazed to the crack of whips
About his thighs.

The Negro
With the trumpet at his lips   10
Has a head of vibrant hair
Tamed down,
Patent-leathered now
Until it gleams
Like jet[1]—
Were jet a crown.

The music
From the trumpet at his lips
Is honey
Mixed with liquid fire.   20
The rhythm
From the trumpet at his lips

[1] A hard, black type of lignite (coal) that can be highly polished.

Is ecstasy
Distilled from old desire—

Desire
That is longing for the moon
Where the moonlight's but a spotlight
In his eyes,
Desire
That is longing for the sea   30
Where the sea's a bar-glass
Sucker size.

The Negro
With the trumpet at his lips
Whose jacket
Has a *fine* one-button roll,
Does not know
Upon what riff the music slips
Its hypodermic needle
To his soul—   40

But softly
As the tune comes from his throat
Trouble
Mellows to a golden note.

1947

DREAM BOOGIE

Good morning, daddy!
Ain't you heard
The boogie-woogie[1] rumble
Of a dream deferred?

Listen closely:
You'll hear their feet
Beating out and beating out a—

You think
It's a happy beat?

Listen to it closely: 10
Ain't you heard
something underneath
like a—

---

[1] A percussive style of playing blues on the piano, characterized by a steady rhythmic bass and a series of improvised melodic variations.

What did I say?

Sure,
I'm happy!
Take it away!

 Hey, pop!
 Re-bop!
 Mop!   20

 Y-e-a-h!

      1951

SISTER

That little Negro's married and got a kid.
Why does he keep on foolin' around Marie?
Marie's my sister—not married to me—
But why does he keep on foolin' around Marie?
Why don't she get a boy-friend
I can understand—some decent man?

 Did it ever occur to you, son,
 the reason Marie runs around with trash
 is she wants some cash?

Don't decent folks have dough?   10

 Unfortunately usually no!

Well, anyway, it don't have to be a married man.

 Did it ever occur to you, boy,
 that a woman does the best she can?

       Comment on Stoop
So does a man.

         1951

THEME FOR ENGLISH B

 The instructor said,

  Go home and write
  a page tonight.

And let that page come out of you—
Then, it will be true.

I wonder if it's that simple?
I am twenty-two, colored, born in Winston-Salem.
I went to school there, then Durham,[1] then here
to this college[2] on the hill above Harlem.
I am the only colored student in my class.   10
The steps from the hill lead down into Harlem,
through a park, then I cross St. Nicholas,[3]
Eighth Avenue, Seventh, and I come to the Y,[4]
the Harlem Branch Y, where I take the elevator
up to my room, sit down, and write this page:

It's not easy to know what is true for you or me
at twenty-two, my age. But I guess I'm what
I feel and see and hear, Harlem, I hear you:
hear you, hear me—we two—you, me, talk on this page.
(I hear New York, too.) Me—who?   20
Well, I like to eat, sleep, drink, and be in love.
I like to work, read, learn, and understand life.
I like a pipe for a Christmas present,
or records—Bessie, bop, or Bach.[5]
I guess being colored doesn't make me *not* like
the same things other folks like who are other races.
So will my page be colored that I write?
Being me, it will not be white.
But it will be
a part of you, instructor.   30
You are white—
yet a part of me, as I am a part of you.
That's American.
Sometimes perhaps you don't want to be a part of me.
Nor do I often want to be a part of you.
But we are, that's true!
As I learn from you,
I guess you learn from me—
although you're older—and white—
and somewhat more free.   40

This is my page for English B.

1951

---

[1] Cities in North Carolina.   [2] Columbia University.
[3] An avenue east of the Columbia University campus.
[4] The Young Men's Christian Association (YMCA).
[5] The famous African-American blues singer Bessie Smith (1898?–1937); jazz, often played very fast, characterized by harmonic complexity, convoluted melodic lines, and constant shifting of accent; the German composer and organist Johann Sebastian Bach (1685–1750).

HARLEM

What happens to a dream deferred?

Does it dry up
like a raisin in the sun?
Or fester like a sore—
And then run?
Does it stink like rotten meat?
Or crust and sugar over—
like a syrupy sweet?

Maybe it just sags
like a heavy load.

Or does it explode?

1951

FEET LIVE THEIR OWN LIFE*

"If you want to know about my life," said Simple as he blew the foam from the top of the newly filled glass the bartender put before him, "don't look at my face, don't look at my hands. Look at my feet and see if you can tell how long I been standing on them."

"I cannot see your feet through your shoes," I said.

"You do not need to see through my shoes," said Simple. "Can't you tell by the shoes I wear—not pointed, not rocking-chair, not French-toed, not nothing but big, long, broad, and flat—that I been standing on these feet a long time and carrying some heavy burdens? They ain't flat from standing at no bar, neither, because I always sets at a bar. Can't you tell that? You know I do not hang out in a bar unless it has stools, don't you?"

"That I have observed," I said, "but I did not connect it with your past life."

"Everything I do is connected up with my past life," said Simple. "From Virginia to Joyce, from my wife to Zarita, from my mother's milk to this glass of beer, everything is connected up."

"I trust you will connect up with that dollar I just loaned you when you get paid," I said. "And who is Virginia? You never told me about her."

"Virginia is where I was borned," said Simple. "I *would* be borned in a state named after a woman. From that day on, women never give me no peace."

"You, I fear, are boasting. If the women were running after you as much as you run after them, you would not be able to sit here on this bar stool in peace. I don't see any women coming to call you out to go home, as some of these fellows' wives do around here."

---

* One of a series of stories Hughes began writing for the Chicago *Defender* in 1943 that features the street-smart Harlem underdog Jessie B. Simple.

"Joyce better not come in no bar looking for me," said Simple. "That is why me and my wife busted up—one reason. I do not like to be called out of no bar by a female. It's a man's perogative to just set and drink sometimes."

"How do you connect that prerogative with your past?" I asked.

"When I was a wee small child," said Simple, "I had no place to set and think in, being as how I was raised up with three brothers, two sisters, seven cousins, one married aunt, a common-law uncle, and the minister's grandchild—and the house only had four rooms. I never had no place just to set and think. Neither to set and drink—not even much my milk before some hongry child snatched it out of my hand. I were not the youngest, neither a girl, not the cutest. I don't know why, but I don't think nobody liked me much. Which is why I was afraid to like anybody for a long time myself. When I did like somebody, I was full-grown and then I picked out the wrong woman because I had no practice in liking anybody before that. We did not get along."

"Is that when you took to drink?"

"Drink took to me," said Simple. "Whiskey just naturally likes me but beer likes me better. By the time I got married I had got to the point where a cold bottle was almost as good as a warm bed, especially when the bottle could not talk and the bed-warmer could. I do not like a woman to talk to me too much—I mean about me. Which is why I like Joyce. Joyce most in generally talks about herself."

"I am still looking at your feet," I said, "and I swear they do not reveal your life to me. Your feet are no open book."

"You have eyes but you see not," said Simple. "These feet have stood on every rock from the Rock of Ages to 135th and Lenox.[1] These feet have supported everything from a cotton bale to a hongry woman. These feet have walked ten thousand miles working for white folks and another ten thousand keeping up with colored. These feet have stood at altars, crap tables, free lunches, bars, graves, kitchen doors, betting windows, hospital clinics, WPA[2] desks, social security railings, and in all kinds of lines from soup lines to the draft. If I just had four feet, I could have stood in more places longer. As it is, I done wore out seven hundred pairs of shoes, eighty-nine tennis shoes, twelve summer sandals, also six loafers. The socks that these feet have bought could build a knitting mill. The corns I've cut away would dull a German razor. The bunions I forgot would make you ache from now till Judgment Day. If anybody was to write the history of my life, they should start with my feet."

"Your feet are not all that extraordinary," I said. "Besides, everything you are saying is general. Tell me specifically some one thing your feet have done that makes them different from any other feet in the world, just one."

"Do you see that window in that white man's store across the street?" asked Simple. "Well, this right foot of mine broke out that window in the Harlem riots right smack in the middle. Didn't no other foot in the world break that window but mine. And this left foot carried me off running as soon as my right foot came down. Nobody else's feet saved me from the cops that night but these *two* feet right here. Don't tell me these feet ain't had a life of their own."

"For shame," I said, "going around kicking out windows. Why?"

---

[1] A hymn written in 1775 by Augustus Montague Toplady (1740–1778), an English clergyman; streets in Harlem.

[2] The Works Progress Administration, a federal agency that created jobs for the unemployed during the Great Depression.

"Why?" said Simple. "You have to ask my great-great-grandpa why. He must of been simple—else why did he let them capture him in Africa and sell him for a slave to breed my great-grandpa in slavery to breed my grandpa in slavery to breed my pa to breed me to look at that window and say, 'It ain't mine! Bam-mmm-mm-m!' and kick it out?"

"This bar glass is not yours either," I said. "Why don't you smash it?"

"It's got my beer in it," said Simple.

Just then Zarita came in wearing her Thursday-night rabbit-skin coat. She didn't stop at the bar, being dressed up, but went straight back to a booth. Simple's hand went up, his beer went down, and the glass back to its wet spot on the bar.

"Excuse me a minute," he said, sliding off the stool.

Just to give him pause, the dozens, that old verbal game of maligning a friend's female relatives, came to mind. "Wait," I said. "You have told me about what to ask your great-great-grandpa. But I want to know what to ask your great-great-grand*ma*."

"I don't play the dozens that far back," said Simple, following Zarita into the smoky juke-box blue of the back room.

1950

THANK YOU, M'AM

She was a large woman with a large purse that had everything in it but hammer and nails. It had a long strap and she carried it slung across her shoulder. It was about eleven o'clock at night, and she was walking alone, when a boy ran up behind her and tried to snatch her purse. The strap broke with the single tug the boy gave it from behind. But the boy's weight, and the weight of the purse combined caused him to lose his balance so, instead of taking off full blast as he had hoped, the boy fell on his back on the sidewalk, and his legs flew up. The large woman simply turned around and kicked him right square in his blue jeaned sitter. Then she reached down, picked the boy up by his shirt front, and shook him until his teeth rattled.

After that the woman said, "Pick up my pocketbook, boy, and give it here."

She still held him. But she bent down enough to permit him to stoop and pick up her purse. Then she said, "Now ain't you ashamed of yourself?"

Firmly gripped by his shirt front, the boy said, "Yes'm."

The woman said, "What did you want to do it for?"

The boy said, "I didn't aim to."

She said, "You a lie!"

By that time two or three people passed, stopped, turned to look, and some stood watching.

"If I turn you loose, will you run?" asked the woman.

"Yes'm," said the boy.

"Then I won't turn you loose," said the woman. She did not release him.

"I'm very sorry, lady, I'm sorry," whispered the boy.

"Um-hum! And your face is dirty. I got a great mind to wash your face for you. Ain't you got nobody home to tell you to wash your face?"

"No'm," said the boy.

"Then it will get washed this evening," said the large woman starting up the street, dragging the frightened boy behind her.

He looked as if he were fourteen or fifteen, frail and willow-wild, in tennis shoes and blue jeans.

The woman said, "You ought to be my son. I would teach you right from wrong. Least I can do right now is to wash your face. Are you hungry?"

"No'm," said the being-dragged boy. "I just want you to turn me loose."

"Was I bothering *you* when I turned that corner?" asked the woman.

"No'm."

"But you put yourself in contact with *me*," said the woman. "If you think that that contact is not going to last awhile, you got another thought coming. When I get through with you, sir, you are going to remember Mrs. Luella Bates Washington Jones."

Sweat popped out on the boy's face and he began to struggle. Mrs. Jones stopped, jerked him around in front of her, put a half-nelson about his neck, and continued to drag him up the street. When she got to her door, she dragged the boy inside, down a hall, and into a large kitchenette-furnished room at the rear of the house. She switched on the light and left the door open. The boy could hear other roomers laughing and talking in the large house. Some of their doors were open, too, so he knew he and the woman were not alone. The woman still had him by the neck in the middle of her room.

She said, "What is your name?"

"Roger," answered the boy.

"Then, Roger, you go to that sink and wash your face," said the woman, whereupon she turned him loose—at last. Roger looked at the door—looked at the woman—looked at the door—*and went to the sink.*

"Let the water run until it gets warm," she said. "Here's a clean towel."

"You gonna take me to jail?" asked the boy, bending over the sink.

"Not with that face, I would not take you nowhere," said the woman. "Here I am trying to get home to cook me a bite to eat and you snatch my pocketbook! Maybe you ain't been to your supper either, late as it be. Have you?"

"There's nobody home at my house," said the boy.

"Then we'll eat," said the woman. "I believe you're hungry—or been hungry—to try to snatch my pocketbook."

"I wanted a pair of blue suede shoes," said the boy.

"Well, you didn't have to snatch *my* pocketbook to get some suede shoes," said Mrs. Luella Bates Washington Jones. "You could of asked me."

"M'am?"

The water dripping from his face, the boy looked at her. There was a long pause. A very long pause. After he had dried his face and not knowing what else to do dried it again, the boy turned around, wondering what next. The door was open. He could make a dash for it down the hall. He could run, run, run, run, *run!*

The woman was sitting on the day-bed. After awhile she said, "I were young once and I wanted things I could not get."

There was another long pause. The boy's mouth opened. Then he frowned, but not knowing he frowned.

The woman said, "Um-hum! You thought I was going to say *but,* didn't you? You thought I was going to say, *but I didn't snatch people's pocketbooks.* Well, I wasn't going to say that." Pause. Silence. "I have done things, too, which I would not tell you, son—neither tell God, if he didn't already know. So you set down while I fix us something to eat. You might run that comb through your hair so you will look presentable."

In another corner of the room behind a screen was a gas plate and an icebox. Mrs. Jones got up and went behind the screen. The woman did not watch the boy to see if he was going to run now, nor did she watch her purse which she left behind her on the day-bed. But the boy took care to sit on the far side of the room where he thought she could easily see him out of the corner of her eye, if she wanted to. He did not trust the woman *not* to trust him. And he did not want to be mistrusted now.

"Do you need somebody to go to the store," asked the boy, "maybe to get some milk or something?"

"Don't believe I do," said the woman, "unless you just want sweet milk yourself. I was going to make cocoa out of this canned milk I got here."

"That will be fine," said the boy.

She heated some lima beans and ham she had in the icebox, made the cocoa, and set the table. The woman did not ask the boy anything about where he lived, or his folks, or anything else that would embarrass him. Instead, as they ate, she told him about her job in a hotel beauty-shop that stayed open late, what the work was like, and how all kinds of women came in and out, blondes, red-heads, and Spanish. Then she cut him a half of her ten-cent cake.

"Eat some more, son," she said.

When they were finished eating she got up and said, "Now, here, take this ten dollars and buy yourself some blue suede shoes. And next time, do not make the mistake of latching onto *my* pocketbook *nor nobody else's*—because shoes come by devilish like that will burn your feet. I got to get my rest now. But I wish you would behave yourself, son, from here on in."

She led him down the hall to the front door and opened it. "Goodnight! Behave yourself, boy!" she said, looking out into the street.

The boy wanted to say something else other than, "Thank you, m'am," to Mrs. Luella Bates Washington Jones, but he couldn't do so as he turned at the barren stoop and looked back at the large woman in the door. He barely managed to say, "Thank you," before she shut the door. And he never saw her again.

1958

Stanley Kunitz
(1905–   )

"What I am seeking is a transparency of language and vision," wrote Stanley Kunitz in the 1975 prose meditation *A Kind of Order, A Kind of Folly: Essays and Conversations*. His sixty-years-worth of poems are evidence of that clarity of language and vision, distilled, sharp, resonant. Born in Worcester, Massachusetts, in 1905 to Russian-Jewish parents, Kunitz attended Harvard University, where he received an A.B. in 1926 and an A.M. in 1927. For years he edited literary reference books, and he has taught and conducted poetry workshops at the New School for Social Research and at such universities as Yale, Columbia, and Rutgers. An impressive supporter of younger poets and intensely committed to a spirit of community among artists and writers, Kunitz was instrumental in organizing the Provincetown Fine Arts Work Center, where he has been a staff member since 1968. Beside traveling widely for workshops and readings, he has divided his time between New York City and his home and garden on Cape Cod.

Kunitz's first volume of poems, *Intellectual Things,* was published in 1930. It was followed by such volumes as *Passport to the War* (1944), *Selected Poems: 1928–1958* (1958), *The Testing-Tree* (1971), *The Poems of Stanley Kunitz, 1928–1978* (1979), and *Next-to-Last Things: New Poems and Essays* (1985). After a visit to Russia in 1967 he published book-length translations of the poetry of Anna Akhmatova, Andrei Voznesensky, and Ivan Drach. Kunitz has received a Guggenheim Fellowship (1945–1946), a Ford Foundation Grant (1958–1959), a Pulitzer Prize in 1959 for *Selected Poems,* and a Bollingen Prize in 1987, among other awards and grants.

Although Kunitz looks back at his early poems as "dense and involuted," he has also noted that the images with which we have to live come to us by the time we are eighteen. His own work certainly suggests the truth of how deeply rooted those images are, and the poems testify to the clarifying power of time and experience to reshape these images. For example, the ghostly presence of an absent father haunts many of the poems—Kunitz's father committed suicide before Kunitz was born. In the poem "Father and Son" (1944) the poet cries to his father, " 'Return! You know / the way.' " In the later "Quinnapoxet" (1978), however, the poet's sudden vision of his father reveals that what both father and son know is somehow inaccessible to the other. Although the nature of change, time, fate, and even the nature of self ultimately remain mysterious, Kunitz sees both life and writing as processes of continuing refinement, claiming in the poem "Layers" (1978), "I am not done with my changes."

A poet with great affection for life, Kunitz has trained his eye on those particulars that transform into the universal, attentive always to details of place and to our sensory relationship with the organic. He has sensed that the root of all poetry, even that with a theme of tragedy, is joy. Over the years, since he first struggled against the dense knots of youth, Kunitz has sought to embrace "the great simplicities" in his quest for that transparency of vision articulated in a language spare yet elegant, meticulous yet often elegiac.

Suggested Readings: *Intellectual Things,* 1930. *Passport to the War: A Selection of Poems,* 1944. *Selected Poems, 1928–1958,* 1958. The Testing-Tree: Poems, 1971. *A Kind of Order, A Kind of Folly: Essays and Conversations,* 1975. *Interviews and Encounters With Stanley Kunitz,* ed. B. Smith et al., 1990. *Antaeus,* special Kunitz issue, 37 (Spring), 1980. M. Henault, *Stanley Kunitz,* 1980. G. Orr, *Stanley Kunitz: An Introduction to the Poetry,* 1985. "A Special Supplement: Stanley Kunitz," *The American Poetry Review,* 14 (Sept.–Oct.), 1985. *A Celebration of Stanley Kunitz on His Eightieth Birthday,* Jack Gilbert et al., 1986.

Texts Used: "The Abduction" and "Passing Through": *Next-to-Last Things: New Poems and Essays,* 1985. All else: *The Poems of Stanley Kunitz: 1928–1978,* 1979.

HOW LONG IS THE NIGHT?

On the anvil of love my flesh has been hammered out.
Indifferent, in the indifferent air,
I circulate and suck the star-space in.
No one is dear to me now,

Leastly myself that sickened in the night.
I would abandon this loose bag of bones
And walk between the world's great wounds, unpitying.

1944

FATHER AND SON

Now in the suburbs and the falling light
I followed him, and now down sandy road
Whiter than bone-dust, through the sweet
Curdle of fields, where the plums
Dropped with their load of ripeness, one by one.
Mile after mile I followed, with skimming feet,
After the secret master of my blood,
Him, steeped in the odor of ponds, whose indomitable love
Kept me in chains. Strode years; stretched into bird;
Raced through the sleeping country where I was young,   10
The silence unrolling before me as I came,
The night nailed like an orange to my brow.

How should I tell him my fable and the fears,
How bridge the chasm in a casual tone,
Saying, "The house, the stucco one you built,
We lost. Sister married and went from home,
And nothing comes back, it's strange, from where she goes.
I lived on a hill that had too many rooms:
Light we could make, but not enough of warmth,
And when the light failed, I climbed under the hill.   20
The papers are delivered every day;
I am alone and never shed a tear."

At the water's edge, where the smothering ferns lifted
Their arms, "Father!"[1] I cried, "Return! You know
The way. I'll wipe the mudstains from your clothes;
No trace, I promise, will remain. Instruct
Your son, whirling between two wars,
In the Gemara[2] of your gentleness,
For I would be a child to those who mourn
And brother to the foundlings of the field   30
And friend of innocence and all bright eyes.
O teach me how to work and keep me kind."

Among the turtles and the lilies he turned to me
The white ignorant hollow of his face.

1944

---

[1] Kunitz's father committed suicide just before Kunitz was born.
[2] Kunitz's note: "The Gemara is the section of commentary in the Talmud on the oral law of the Jews."

THE TESTING-TREE*

I

On my way home from school
    up tribal Providence Hill[1]
      past the Academy ballpark
where I could never hope to play
    I scuffed in the drainage ditch
      among the sodden seethe of leaves
hunting for perfect stones
    rolled out of glacial time
      into my pitcher's hand;
then sprinted lickety-   10
    split on my magic Keds
      from a crouching start,
scarcely touching the ground
    with my flying skin
      as I poured it on
for the prize of the mastery
    over that stretch of road,
      with no one no where to deny
when I flung myself down
    that on the given course   20
      I was the world's fastest human.

2

Around the bend
    that tried to loop me home
      dawdling came natural
across a nettled field
    riddled with rabbit-life
      where the bees sank sugar-wells
in the trunks of the maples
    and a stringy old lilac
      more than two stories tall   30
blazing with mildew

---

* Kunitz's note: "When I was a boy in Worcester, Massachusetts, my family lived on top of a hill, at the thin edge of the city, with the woods beyond. Much of the time I was alone, but I learned how not to be lonely, exploring the surrounding fields and the old Indian trails. In the games that I improvised, most of them involved running, climbing, and a variety of ball-skills, I was a fierce competitor, representing in turn myself and my imaginary opponent. It did not occur to me to be surprised that 'I' was always the winner.

    The stone-throwing that figures in the poem was of a somewhat special order, since it did more than try my skill: it challenged destiny. My life hinged on the three throws permitted me, according to my rules. If I hit the target-oak once, somebody would love me; if I hit it twice, I should be a poet; if I scored all three times, I should never die. A friend of mine tells me that what I have recorded here is recognizable as an ancient ritual, and that the patriarchal scarred oak, as I have described it, is transparently a manifestation of the King of the Wood. Such mysteries for a Worcester childhood!"

[1] In southern Worcester.

remembered a door in the
　　long teeth of the woods.
All of it happened slow:
　　brushing the stickseed[2] off,
　　　　wading through jewelweed[3]
strangled by angel's hair,
　　spotting the print of the deer
　　　　and the red fox's scats.[4]

Once I owned the key   40
　　to an umbrageous[5] trail
　　　　thickened with mosses
where flickering presences
　　gave me right of passage
　　　　as I followed in the steps
of straight-backed Massassoit[6]
　　soundlessly heel-and-toe
　　　　practicing my Indian walk.

3

Past the abandoned quarry
　　where the pale sun bobbed   50
　　　　in the sump[7] of the granite,
past copperhead ledge,
　　where the ferns gave foothold,
　　　　I walked, deliberate,
on to the clearing,
　　with the stones in my pocket
　　　　changing to oracles
and my coiled ear tuned
　　to the slightest leaf-stir.
　　　　I had kept my appointment.   60
There I stood in the shadow,
　　at fifty measured paces,
　　　　of the inexhaustible oak,
tyrant and target,
　　Jehovah[8] of acorns,
　　　　watchtower of the thunders,
that locked King Philip's War[9]
　　in its annulated[10] core
　　　　under the cut of my name.
Father wherever you are   70

---

[2] A plant of the borage family with barbs on the seeds.   [3] A plant of the balsam family.
[4] Dung.   [5] Shadow-filled.
[6] Massasoit (1580?–1661) was the powerful chief of the Wampanoag Indians in New England; he honored a 1621 treaty with the Pilgrims.
[7] An excavation at the head of a mine shaft.   [8] The Judeo-Christian God.
[9] Massasoit's son Metacomet (?–1676) led King Philip's War (1675–1678) against the New England colonists, proportionally the bloodiest in American history.
[10] Ringed.

> *I have only three throws*
> *bless my good right arm.*
> In the haze of afternoon,
>   while the air flowed saffron,
>   I played my game for keeps—
> for love, for poetry,
>   and for eternal life—
>   after the trials of summer.

4

In the recurring dream
   my mother stands   80
      in her bridal gown
under the burning lilac,
   with Bernard Shaw and Bertie
      Russell[11] kissing her hands;
the house behind her is in ruins;
   she is wearing an owl's face
      and makes barking noises.
Her minatory[12] finger points.
   I pass through the cardboard doorway
      askew in the field   90
and peer down a well
   where an albino walrus huffs.
      He has the gentlest eyes.
If the dirt keeps sifting in,
   staining the water yellow,
      why should I be blamed?
Never try to explain.
   That single Model A[13]
      sputtering up the grade   100
unfurled a highway behind
   where the tanks maneuver,
      revolving their turrets.
In a murderous time
   the heart breaks and breaks
      and lives by breaking.
It is necessary to go
   through dark and deeper dark
      and not to turn.
I am looking for the trail.   110
   Where is my testing-tree?
      Give me back my stones!

1971

---

[11] The Irish playwright George Bernard Shaw (1856–1950), winner of the Nobel Prize for literature in 1925; the English philosopher, mathematician, and social reformer Bertrand Russell (1872–1970), winner of the Nobel Prize for literature in 1950.
[12] Menacing.   [13] An early car model by Henry Ford (1863–1947).

AN OLD CRACKED TUNE

My name is Solomon Levi,
the desert is my home,
my mother's breast was thorny,
and father I had none.

The sands whispered, *Be separate,*
the stones taught me, *Be hard.*
I dance, for the joy of surviving,
on the edge of the road.

1971

THE PORTRAIT

My mother never forgave my father
for killing himself,[1]
especially at such an awkward time
and in a public park,
that spring
when I was waiting to be born.
She locked his name
in her deepest cabinet
and would not let him out,
though I could hear him thumping.   10
When I came down from the attic
with the pastel portrait in my hand
of a long-lipped stranger
with a brave moustache
and deep brown level eyes,
she ripped it into shreds
without a single word
and slapped me hard.
In my sixty-fourth year
I can feel my cheek   20
still burning.

1971

THE QUARREL

The word I spoke in anger
weighs less than a parsley seed,
but a road runs through it

---

[1] Kunitz's father did commit suicide just before Kunitz was born.

that leads to my grave,
that bought-and-paid-for lot
on a salt-sprayed hill in Truro[1]
where the scrub pines
overlook the bay.
Half-way I'm dead enough,
strayed from my own nature   10
and my fierce hold on life.
If I could cry, I'd cry,
but I'm too old to be
anybody's child.
Liebchen,[2]
with whom should I quarrel
except in the hiss of love,
that harsh, irregular flame?

1978

QUINNAPOXET*

I was fishing in the abandoned reservoir
back in Quinnapoxet,
where the snapping turtles cruised
and the bullheads[1] swayed
in their bower of tree-stumps,
sleek as eels and pigeon-fat.
One of them gashed my thumb
with a flick of his razor fin
when I yanked the barb
out of his gullet.   10
The sun hung its terrible coals
over Buteau's farm: I saw
the treetops seething.

They came suddenly into view
on the Indian road,
evenly stepping
past the apple orchard,
commingling with the dust
they raised, their cloud of being,
against the dripping light   20
looming larger and bolder.

---

[1] A town in Cape Cod, Massachusetts, site of the oldest synagogue in America.
[2] "Sweetheart" (German).
 * Kunitz's note: "Quinnapoxet (also sometimes spelled with one 'n') was a backwater village outside Worcester, Massachusetts, where I spent my childhood summers as a boarder on the Buteau farm. The village no longer exists, and its place-name is all but forgotten."
[1] Any of various large-headed fishes.

She was wearing a mourning bonnet
and a wrap of shining taffeta.
"Why don't you write?" she cried
from the folds of her veil.

"We never hear from you."
I had nothing to say to her.
But for him who walked behind her
in his dark worsted suit,
with his face averted   30
as if to hide a scald,
deep in his other life,
I touched my forehead
with my swollen thumb
and splayed my fingers out—
in deaf-mute country
the sign for father.[2]

1978

THE ABDUCTION

Some things I do not profess
to understand, perhaps
not wanting to, including
whatever it was they did
with you or you with them
that timeless summer day
when you stumbled out of the wood,
distracted, with your white blouse torn
and a bloodstain on your skirt.
"Do you believe?" you asked.   10
Between us, through the years,
from bits, from broken clues,
we pieced enough together
to make the story real:
how you encountered on the path
a pack of sleek, grey hounds,
trailed by a dumbshow retinue
in leather shrouds; and how
you were led, through leafy ways,
into the presence of a royal stag,   20
flaming in his chestnut coat,
who kneeled on a swale[1] of moss
before you; and how you were borne

[2] Kunitz's father had committed suicide before Kunitz was born.
[1] A low-lying, often wet stretch of land.

aloft in triumph through the green,
stretched on his rack of budding horn,
till suddenly you found yourself alone
in a trampled clearing.

That was a long time ago,
almost another age, but even now,
when I hold you in my arms,   30
I wonder where you are.
Sometimes I wake to hear
the engines of the night thrumming
outside the east bay window
on the lawn spreading to the rose garden.
You lie beside me in elegant repose,
a hint of transport hovering on your lips,
indifferent to the harsh green flares
that swivel through the room,
searchlights controlled by unseen hands.   40
Out there is childhood country,
bleached faces peering in
with coals for eyes.
Our lives are spinning out
from world to world;
the shapes of things
are shifting in the wind.
What do we know
beyond the rapture and the dread?

                                                         1985

PASSING THROUGH

—on my seventy-ninth birthday

Nobody in the widow's household
ever celebrated anniversaries.
In the secrecy of my room
I would not admit I cared
that my friends were given parties.
Before I left town for school
my birthday went up in smoke
in a fire at City Hall that gutted
the Department of Vital Statistics.
If it weren't for a census report   10
of a five-year-old White Male
sharing my mother's address

at the Green Street tenement in Worcester[1]
I'd have no documentary proof
that I exist. You are the first,
my dear, to bully me
into these festive occasions.

Sometimes, you say, I wear
an abstracted look that drives you
up the wall, as though it signified   20
distress or disaffection.
Don't take it so to heart.
Maybe I enjoy not-being as much
as being who I am. Maybe
it's time for me to practice
growing old. The way I look
at it, I'm passing through a phase:
gradually I'm changing to a word.
Whatever you choose to claim
of me is always yours;   30
nothing is truly mine
except my name. I only
borrowed this dust.[2]

1985

EARLY 20TH-CENTURY FICTION

The early years of the twentieth century were marked by a series of political and cultural disruptions, both international and domestic. During that time, traditional political structures were globally destabilized. Europe's empires were either diminishing greatly or were being replaced by new regimes, and the United States was replacing them in arbitrating international affairs. As the political maps were being redrawn and the lessons of history reassessed, developments in physics, philosophy, and psychiatry combined to discredit the most fundamental assumptions about the stability and the validity of our perceptions of reality. Increasingly dehumanizing industrialization, World War I, the 1917 Russian Revolution, the revolt of disenfranchised women everywhere, and the disillusioning rise and fall of western economies in the 1920s and 1930s all contributed to a growing dissatisfaction with traditional values. This distrust produced radical changes in literary tastes and techniques in Europe and the United States.

---

[1] Worcester, Massachusetts, where Kunitz was born and raised.
[2] After ". . . for out of [the ground] wast thou taken: for dust thou art, and unto dust shalt thou return," from Genesis 3:19 and similar biblical passages.

his belief in environmental determinism as the young Frank Cowperwood observes an octopus and a squid in the same fishtank; over the period of a few days, the octopus thrives while the squid perishes, simply, Dreiser shows, because of the "random" ability of one to consume the other.

Edith Wharton, a friend and admirer of Henry James, treated in her own novels many of the ethical issues she found in his novels. Like James, she was most comfortable examining American mores from a distance: leaving her husband and her country, she moved to France. There she wrote incisively ironic and lucid fiction, much of it concerning married American women. James's influence is apparent in Wharton's finely crafted studies of the leisured and horrifyingly empty lives of upper-class women in the years prior to World War I.

Gertrude Stein was notable for following James and Wharton in their expatriation and for promptly rejecting the social standards and rituals they dissected in their exquisitely polished prose. Stein also rejected that prose style itself. She went beyond Wharton's lucid criticisms of women's place in the American family to pioneer the alternative lifestyle of the uncloseted lesbian, unapologetically appropriating a degree of sexual license that was denied less presumptuous women throughout the century. Stein and her lifelong companion, Alice B. Toklas, were frequently visited at their home in Paris by an international collection of writers, artists, sculptors, and painters. Mingling the aesthetics of guests Pablo Picasso, Ezra Pound, Henri Matisse, and James Joyce, Stein wrote experimental narratives applying avant-garde theories of sculpture to prose. In her novel *Tender Buttons* (1914) her incantatory, primitive pattern of repeating phrases with slight variations imitates the simplification and fragmentation of cubist painting. Although her commonly unintelligible writing was more often discussed than read, she stimulated writers such as Ernest Hemingway and William Faulkner, members of what she labeled "the lost generation," as they searched for new modes of expressing their postwar grief and confusion.

One influential proponent of Stein's simplified, fragmented, prose was her friend Sherwood Anderson. Anderson, too, experimented with consciously primitive prose styles and multiple points of view. In Anderson's story "The Book of the Grotesque," included in his best-known collection, *Winesburg, Ohio* (1919), an elderly author tries to write a book envisioning truth and beauty, but his vision devolves into nightmare. By the 1920s many nineteenth-century moral certainties were suspect, replaced by the queasily uncertain principles of pluralism and subjectivity. Anderson's work—tame enough today but in its time shocking for its sexual candor as well as its stylistic innovations—dramatized the despair and liberation of artists caught unprepared for the political, aesthetic, and sexual emancipations of the flapper era.

Hemingway, influenced by Anderson and Stein, responded to the moral void following World War I with tales of physically and philosophically courageous heroes. Stoically bearing psychic and physical pain, the Hemingway hero, such as Robert Jordan of *For Whom the Bell Tolls* (1940), maintains subjective standards of honor, valor, and duty in the face of repeated objective disproofs of those values. This puritanically spare code of single-minded persistence is incompletely articulated by Hemingway's characters but subtly expressed in his starkly pared prose style. In Hemingway's writings the style carries the same moral charge as the content.

Few of Hemingway's fellow writers met his standards for stylistic machismo in their writing or in their actions, and F. Scott Fitzgerald's failure to find favor with Hemingway is perhaps the most celebrated of many such disappointments. Fitzgerald grappled with many of the issues that troubled Hemingway. In his first novel, *This Side of Paradise* (1920), Fitzgerald weighs dubious conventional fame against genuine personal merit. In *The Great Gatsby* (1925) he considers the difficulties of creating a public persona for the self in the absence of reliable moral guidelines. Fitzgerald's concerns with the disparity between surface and substance, and his later interest in Freudian psychiatry, reflect in part his personal experiences and the interests of the age. Artists confronted the plight of the fragmented personality at war not only with society but also with itself.

Other authors countered postwar tendencies toward alienated despair by anchoring their work to very particular geographic and ethnic environments. In 1923 Jean Toomer published the multidimensional book *Cane,* an experiment in symbolic and poetic prose. It incorporates modernist (untraditional) techniques of juxtaposition and discontinuity to define African-American experience in the early twentieth-century. Toomer was part of the Harlem Renaissance of the 1920s, along with other African-American writers such as Langston Hughes and Claude McKay. Whereas he paradoxically chose European models to distinguish his perceptions of African Americans, Zora Neale Hurston chose narrative models from her native folk culture. After leaving her all-black hometown in Florida, Hurston studied anthropology and used that training to reproduce in her novel *Their Eyes Were Watching God* (1937) the vernacular sounds and rhythms of her childhood. Hurston's story of a Florida woman's efforts to define herself among her fellow sugar-cane workers describes the specifically female experience within the African-American community.

Like Hurston, William Faulkner examined his own community in the South. The inhabitants of the fictional Yoknapatawpha County, first described in his novel *Sartoris* (1929), share a terrible and glorious history that is both their burden

St. Louis singer-dancer sensation Josephine Baker moved to Paris in 1925 and helped introduce American jazz there. Receiving the Legion of Honor for her resistance work during World War II, she founded an orphanage for all races—her "experiment in brotherhood"—in the 1950s.

The naturalism movement that had begun in the late 1800s continued into the early 1900s. Naturalism, in which environmental forces overwhelm individual will, was dominated by the work of Theodore Dreiser. In his novel *Sister Carrie* (1900) it is chance that causes a safe to shut accidentally at a pivotal moment, leaving George Hurstwood a thief and leading to his horrible downfall, which might easily have been averted. And in *The Financier* (1912) Dreiser evidences and their salvation. In his fiction the brilliantly drawn characters are challenged by very specifically provincial circumstances. His genius lay in his universalizing those circumstances and in directly addressing even those readers for whom his vibrantly realized Mississippi is uncomfortably exotic.

Other regions of the country found other speakers. John Steinbeck claimed California's Salinas Valley as the setting for much of his fiction, and the Great Plains region and the Southwest inspired Willa Cather's fictional reminiscences of the passing pioneer spirit, including *My Ántonia* (1918) and *Death Comes for the Archbishop* (1927). The Southwest also produced the tragic vision of Katherine Anne Porter's stories, collected in *Flowering Judas* (1930) and *Pale Horse, Pale Rider* (1939). But the southern states produced by far the greatest number of regionalist authors. The Southern Renaissance, beginning in the 1920s, generated a chorus of lyrical celebrations and lamentations. Thomas Wolfe nostalgically retold his North Carolina childhood and youth in a series of long novels, beginning with *Look Homeward, Angel* (1929).

Many authors of the early twentieth century wrote with horrified vividness of the economic devastations during the Great Depression of the 1930s. The depression was especially ruinous in rural communities, and John Steinbeck recorded with sympathy and humor its catastrophic effects in those communities. His novel *The Grapes of Wrath* (1939) follows the westward migration of Oklahoma sharecroppers fleeing the desperately impoverished midwestern Dust Bowl. Steinbeck was less concerned with technically innovative prose styles than with political and social documentation of the period. In this undertaking he continued a tradition of social criticism in American fiction, traceable through Theodore Dreiser's *Sister Carrie;* Sinclair Lewis's *Main Street* (1920), *Babbitt* (1922), and *Arrowsmith* (1925); and the novels of John Dos Passos, particularly his anti-World War I novel, *Three Soldiers* (1921), and his *U.S.A.* trilogy (1938). Each of these authors championed the poor, the unemployed, and the dehumanized worker; each criticized the growth of mechanized industry and the concomitant deification of material goods and profits. Distrusting capitalist society and its promises, these authors found an increasing readership as the depression lingered. Although many authors—at best employed only marginally—had themselves been severely affected by the depression, the government funded Federal Writers' Project, part of Franklin D. Roosevelt's New Deal, provided support for unemployed writers. The FWP allowed such writers as Zora Neale Hurston, Saul Bellow, Tillie Olsen, John Cheever, and Richard Wright to get back on their feet. Thereafter, politically engaged writers, like many American readers in the 1930s and 1940s, gained interest in the growing Socialist and Communist reform movements. After World War II disrupted the 1940s, a new generation of politically conscious writers with new voices and new literary tools continued this tradition.

=CONTEXTS=

Reform Writers

During the 1920s and 1930s many American writers became disillusioned with the brutality of twentieth-century industrial life. They were critical of the destructive effects of runaway capitalism on humanity and in their works sought to expose these ills.

Notable among these reform writers is Upton Sinclair (1878–1968), whose works typically depict the horror of working-class life in the industrial age. His 1906 novel *The Jungle,* with its graphic depictions of the dehumanizing effects of industry, resulted in the passage of legislation toward improvements in the sanitation of meat packing and processing.

The Jungle depicts a Lithuanian immigrant family's struggles to make a living and fulfill the "American Dream." Shortly after arriving in the New World, the realities of industrial life become clear to the immigrants. They are beset from the beginning by political corruption, brutal working conditions, and bitter poverty (as in the excerpt below). In the end the family dissolves, but a glimmer of hope is cast by the protagonist's drift toward the Communist party.

The Jungle

A very few days of practical experience in this land of high wages had been sufficient to make clear to them the cruel fact that it was also a land of high prices, and that in it the poor man was almost as poor as in any other corner of the earth; and so there vanished in a night all the wonderful dreams of wealth that had been haunting Jurgis. What had made the discovery all the more painful was that they were spending, at American prices, money which they had earned at home rates of wages—and so were really being cheated by the world!

Upton Sinclair, 1906

Edith Wharton
(1862–1937)

Born in 1862, Edith Newbold Jones was the youngest child of George Frederic Jones and Lucretia Stevens Rhinelander, members of the wealthy "Old New York" society. In 1866, with their financial state impaired by the post-Civil War inflation, the Joneses went to Europe in order to economize. Edith spent much of her early childhood traveling in France, Italy, and Germany. After their return to America she enjoyed summers in Newport, Rhode Island, and winters in New York City. She eagerly read the classics in her father's library, where she discovered "the Old Testament, the Apocalypse and the Eliza-

Edith Wharton in 1905.

bethan dramatists," as noted by R. W. B. Lewis in his 1975 Pulitzer Prize-winning biography of Wharton.

Although her family disapproved of literary activities and expected Edith to become a conventional society matron, a different destiny seemed ordained by her ability to read easily in several languages and by the private printing of her first volume of poetry when she was sixteen—a year before she made her debutante appearance. Like Kate Chopin, Edith Jones had to curb her desire for reading and "making up" bits of writing in order to participate in the social world of the debutante. Through that world she met the Bostonian Edward ("Teddy") Robbins Wharton, whom she married in 1885. The two had a childless and leisure-filled marriage, dividing their time between New York, Newport, Boston, and

Europe and even taking a cruise on the Aegean Sea in 1888 that Wharton described in a letter as "the greatest step forward in [her] making." Although Teddy appears to have been a decent and considerate husband, the marriage was clearly not a happy one. Indeed, the literary critic Edmund Wilson suggests that Wharton began writing in earnest at the recommendation of the "nerve specialist" Dr. S. Weir Mitchell, who treated her for a "paralyzing melancholy" that recurred from the early 1890s until 1902, the year her husband's mental illness became quite evident. Whether invigorated by her journey or seeking a happier world through her imagination, Wharton did begin to write seriously, publishing poetry and stories in major magazines, including *Scribner's, Harper's,* and the *Century.* Produced with the Boston architect Ogden Codman, Jr., her first lengthy work—*The Decoration of Houses* (1897)—combined an interest in interior design with developing writing abilities.

Although Wharton complained in her autobiography, *A Backward Glance* (1934), that she had little encouragement during this period, her short-story collections *The Greater Inclination* (1899) and *Crucial Instances* (1901) brought her enough assurance as a writer to feel that she needed to build a haven where she could work without interruption. "The Mount," in Lenox, Massachusetts, not only offered her solitude but provided her with a vantage for observing the land and the people who would figure prominently in her rural fiction. The novellas and the novel (*The Valley of Decision* [1902]) of this period reflect Wharton's "apprenticeship," an experimentation with both the forms and the themes that would recur in her more mature works—including tales of the supernatural; the relationships between artistry, artists, and life; variations on the international theme; and reflections on the problems of the marriage market.

Wharton did not meet Henry James until 1902, but the similarity between her early themes and those that James addressed is striking, although the stylistic strategies deployed by the two differ greatly. In contrast to James's indirection, for example, Wharton's *The House of Mirth* (1905) demonstrates her preference for straightforward examination and presentation. Frankly and somewhat sardonically *The House of Mirth* combines the tenets of the genteel novel of manners with the harsh determinism of Charles Darwin or Herbert Spencer in order to examine both the intricacies of old New York City's elite inner circle and the specific problems of Lily Bart, a slightly unconventional woman in that world. Although she would like to belong to a "republic of the spirit," Bart cannot break free of the social constraints within which she has been born; she is stifled in a world in which women should simply be lovely wives and good hostesses.

Despite dissimilarities in their subjects, many of Wharton's best stories of this period share a preoccupation with exploring a protagonist's responses to socially imposed restrictions. *The Reef* (1912), *The Custom of the Country* (1913), and the Pulitzer Prize-winning *The Age of Innocence* (1920) all consider the social forces that tightly regulate personal and sexual relationships, dictating which alliances are acceptable and which are not. *Ethan Frome* (1911) and *Summer* (1917) explore the limitations imposed not by the inner circle of New York but by the communal standards of rural New England. The protagonists' struggles to live happily despite communal standards typically force them to consider divorce or to give up a lover. These tensions are so pervasive in Wharton's fiction perhaps because she was herself in a dilemma akin to the ones she described. Around 1910 she was involved in a passionate affair with her longtime friend Morton Fullerton, a relationship that she understood to be temporary but nevertheless forced both her and Teddy to recognize the deficiencies of their marriage. Selling "The Mount," they moved to France for Teddy's health; however, he had another nervous breakdown and was subsequently confined to a sanitorium. The couple divorced in 1913, and Wharton poured her energy into the civilian war efforts in France. She incorporated some of her experiences into nonfictional work and into her two war novels, *The Marne* (1918) and *A Son at the Front* (1923).

Although her late writings are generally regarded as less successful than *The House of Mirth* or *The Age of Innocence*, Wharton remained highly acclaimed. In 1923 she became the first woman to receive a Doctor of Letters from Yale University; in 1930 she and Mary E. Wilkins Freeman were the first two women to receive gold medals from the National Institute of Arts and Letters; and in 1934 she was selected for membership in the American Academy of Arts and Letters. As such wide acknowledgment suggests, her best work— typically ironic and carefully modulated in tone—addresses fundamental questions of the survival of weak or disenfranchised individuals in self-promoting societies that can be vicious simply through unquestioning allegiance to their own standards.

Suggested Readings: *The House of Mirth*, 1905. *The Age of Innocence*, 1920. *A Backward Glance*, 1934. *The Edith Wharton Reader*, ed. L. Auchincloss, 1965. *The Collected Short Stories of Edith Wharton*, ed. R. W. B. Lewis, 1968. *The Letters of Edith Wharton*, ed. R. W. B. Lewis and N. Lewis, 1988. B. Nevius, *Edith Wharton: A Study of Her Fiction*, 1961. R. W. B. Lewis, *Edith Wharton: A Biography*, 1975. G. Lindberg, *Edith Wharton and the Novel of Manners*, 1975. M. B. McDowell, *Edith Wharton*, 1976. C. G. Wolff, *A Feast of Words: The Triumph of Edith Wharton*, 1977. E. Ammons, *Edith Wharton's Argument With America*, 1980. W. Gimbel, *Edith Wharton: Orphancy and Survival*, 1984. J. Fryer, *Felicitous Space: The Imaginative Structures of Edith Wharton and Willa Cather*, 1986. J. Goodwyn, *Edith Wharton: Traveller in the Land of Letters*, 1990. P. Vita-Finzi, *Edith Wharton and the Art of Fiction*, 1990.

Texts Used: "The Other Two": *The Descent of Man and Other Stories*, 1904. "Roman Fever": *The World Over*, 1936.

THE OTHER TWO*

I

Waythorn, on the drawing-room hearth, waited for his wife to come down to dinner.

It was their first night under his own roof, and he was surprised at his thrill of boyish agitation. He was not so old, to be sure—his glass[1] gave him little more than the five-and-thirty years to which his wife confessed—but he had fancied himself already in the temperate zone; yet here he was listening for her step with a tender sense of all it symbolized, with some old trail of verse about the garlanded nuptial door-posts floating through his enjoyment of the pleasant room and the good dinner just beyond it.

They had been hastily recalled from their honeymoon by the illness of Lily Haskett, the child of Mrs. Waythorn's first marriage. The little girl, at Waythorn's desire, had been transferred to his house on the day of her mother's wedding, and the doctor, on their arrival, broke the news that she was ill with typhoid, but declared that all the symptoms were favourable. Lily could show twelve years of unblemished health, and the case promised to be a light one. The nurse spoke as reassuringly, and after a moment of alarm Mrs. Waythorn had adjusted herself to the situation. She was very fond of Lily—her affection for the child had perhaps

---

* First published in *The Descent of Man and Other Stories* (1904). The ellipses are Wharton's.
[1] Mirror.

been her decisive charm in Waythorn's eyes—but she had the perfectly balanced nerves which her little girl had inherited, and no woman ever wasted less tissue in unproductive worry. Waythorn was therefore quite prepared to see her come in presently, a little late because of a last look at Lily, but as serene and well-appointed as if her good-night kiss had been laid on the brow of health. Her composure was restful to him; it acted as ballast to his somewhat unstable sensibilities. As he pictured her bending over the child's bed he thought how soothing her presence must be in illness: her very step would prognosticate recovery.

His own life had been a gray one, from temperament rather than circumstance, and he had been drawn to her by the unperturbed gaiety which kept her fresh and elastic at an age when most women's activities are growing either slack or febrile. He knew what was said about her; for, popular as she was, there had always been a faint undercurrent of detraction. When she had appeared in New York, nine or ten years earlier, as the pretty Mrs. Haskett whom Gus Varick had unearthed somewhere—was it in Pittsburg or Utica?—society, while promptly accepting her, had reserved the right to cast a doubt on its own discrimination. Enquiry, however, established her undoubted connection with a socially reigning family, and explained her recent divorce as the natural result of a runaway match at seventeen; and as nothing was known of Mr. Haskett it was easy to believe the worst of him.

Alice Haskett's remarriage with Gus Varick was a passport to the set whose recognition she coveted, and for a few years the Varicks were the most popular couple in town. Unfortunately the alliance was brief and stormy, and this time the husband had his champions. Still, even Varick's staunchest supporters admitted that he was not meant for matrimony, and Mrs. Varick's grievances were of a nature to bear the inspection of the New York courts. A New York divorce is in itself a diploma of virtue,[2] and in the semi-widowhood of this second separation Mrs. Varick took on an air of sanctity, and was allowed to confide her wrongs to some of the most scrupulous ears in town. But when it was known that she was to marry Waythorn there was a momentary reaction. Her best friends would have preferred to see her remain in the rôle of the injured wife, which was as becoming to her as crape to a rosy complexion. True, a decent time had elapsed, and it was not even suggested that Waythorn had supplanted his predecessor. People shook their heads over him, however, and one grudging friend, to whom he affirmed that he took the step with his eyes open, replied oracularly: "Yes—and with your ears shut."

Waythorn could afford to smile at these innuendoes. In the Wall Street phrase, he had 'discounted' them. He knew that society has not yet adapted itself to the consequences of divorce, and that till the adaptation takes place every woman who uses the freedom the law accords her must be her own social justification. Waythorn had an amused confidence in his wife's ability to justify herself. His expectations were fulfilled, and before the wedding took place Alice Varick's group had rallied openly to her support. She took it all imperturbably: she had a way of surmounting obstacles without seeming to be aware of them, and Waythorn looked back with wonder at the trivialities over which he had worn his nerves thin. He had the sense of having found refuge in a richer, warmer nature than his own, and his satisfaction, at the moment, was humorously summed up in the thought

---

[2] Because adultery was the only ground for divorce in New York state in the early 1900s, the party that sued for divorce seemed virtuous.

that his wife, when she had done all she could for Lily, would not be ashamed to come down and enjoy a good dinner.

The anticipation of such enjoyment was not, however, the sentiment expressed by Mrs. Waythorn's charming face when she presently joined him. Though she had put on her most engaging tea-gown she had neglected to assume the smile that went with it, and Waythorn thought he had never seen her look so nearly worried.

"What is it?" he asked. "Is anything wrong with Lily?"

"No; I've just been in and she's still sleeping." Mrs. Waythorn hesitated. "But something tiresome has happened."

He had taken her two hands, and now perceived that he was crushing a paper between them.

"This letter?"

"Yes—Mr. Haskett has written—I mean his lawyer has written."

Waythorn felt himself flush uncomfortably. He dropped his wife's hands.

"What about?"

"About seeing Lily. You know the courts————"

"Yes, yes," he interrupted nervously.

Nothing was known about Haskett in New York. He was vaguely supposed to have remained in the outer darkness from which his wife had been rescued, and Waythorn was one of the few who were aware that he had given up his business in Utica and followed her to New York in order to be near his little girl. In the days of his wooing, Waythorn had often met Lily on the doorstep, rosy and smiling, on her way "to see papa."

"I am so sorry," Mrs. Waythorn murmured.

He roused himself. "What does he want?"

"He wants to see her. You know she goes to him once a week."

"Well—he doesn't expect her to go to him now, does he?"

"No—he has heard of her illness; but he expects to come here."

"Here?"

Mrs. Waythorn reddened under his gaze. They looked away from each other.

"I'm afraid he has the right. . . . You'll see. . . ." She made a proffer of the letter.

Waythorn moved away with a gesture of refusal. He stood staring about the softly lighted room, which a moment before had seemed so full of bridal intimacy.

"I'm so sorry," she repeated. "If Lily could have been moved————"

"That's out of the question," he returned impatiently.

"I suppose so."

Her lip was beginning to tremble, and he felt himself a brute.

"He must come, of course," he said. "When is—his day?"

"I'm afraid—to-morrow."

"Very well. Send a note in the morning."

The butler entered to announce dinner.

Waythorn turned to his wife. "Come—you must be tired. It's beastly, but try to forget about it," he said, drawing her hand through his arm.

"You're so good, dear. I'll try," she whispered back.

Her face cleared at once, and as she looked at him across the flowers, between the rosy candle-shades, he saw her lips waver back into a smile.

"How pretty everything is!" she sighed luxuriously.

He turned to the butler. "The champagne at once, please. Mrs. Waythorn is tired."

In a moment or two their eyes met above the sparkling glasses. Her own were quite clear and untroubled: he saw that she had obeyed his injunction and forgotten.

II

Waythorn, the next morning, went down town earlier than usual. Haskett was not likely to come till the afternoon, but the instinct of flight drove him forth. He meant to stay away all day—he had thoughts of dining at his club. As his door closed behind him he reflected that before he opened it again it would have admitted another man who had as much right to enter it as himself, and the thought filled him with a physical repugnance.

He caught the "elevated"[3] at the employés' hour, and found himself crushed between two layers of pendulous humanity. At Eighth Street the man facing him wriggled out, and another took his place. Waythorn glanced up and saw that it was Gus Varick. The men were so close together that it was impossible to ignore the smile of recognition on Varick's handsome overblown face. And after all— why not? They had always been on good terms, and Varick had been divorced before Waythorn's attentions to his wife began. The two exchanged a word on the perennial grievance of the congested trains, and when a seat at their side was miraculously left empty the instinct of self-preservation made Waythorn slip into it after Varick.

The latter drew the stout man's breath of relief. "Lord—I was beginning to feel like a pressed flower." He leaned back, looking unconcernedly at Waythorn. "Sorry to hear that Sellers is knocked out again."

"Sellers?" echoed Waythorn, starting at his partner's name.

Varick looked surprised. "You didn't know he was laid up with the gout?"

"No, I've been away—I only got back last night." Waythorn felt himself reddening in anticipation of the other's smile.

"Ah—yes; to be sure. And Seller's attack came on two days ago. I'm afraid he's pretty bad. Very awkward for me, as it happens, because he was just putting through a rather important thing for me."

"Ah?" Waythorn wondered vaguely since when Varick had been dealing in "important things." Hitherto he had dabbled only in the shallow pools of speculation, with which Waythorn's office did not usually concern itself.

It occurred to him that Varick might be talking at random, to relieve the strain of their propinquity. That strain was becoming momentarily more apparent to Waythorn, and when, at Cortlandt Street, he caught sight of an acquaintance, and had a sudden vision of the picture he and Varick must present to an initiated eye, he jumped up with a muttered excuse.

"I hope you'll find Sellers better," said Varick civilly, and he stammered back: "If I can be of any use to you———" and let the departing crowd sweep him to the platform.

At his office he heard that Sellers was in fact ill with the gout, and would probably not be able to leave the house for some weeks.

"I'm sorry it should have happened so, Mr. Waythorn," the senior clerk said

---

[3] A train on rails set above street level, hence "elevated."

with affable significance. "Mr. Sellers was very much upset at the idea of giving you such a lot of extra work just now."

"Oh, that's no matter," said Waythorn hastily. He secretly welcomed the pressure of additional business, and was glad to think that, when the day's work was over, he would have to call at his partner's on the way home.

He was late for luncheon, and turned in at the nearest restaurant instead of going to his club. The place was full, and the waiter hurried him to the back of the room to capture the only vacant table. In the cloud of cigar-smoke Waythorn did not at once distinguish his neighbours; but presently, looking about him, he saw Varick seated a few feet off. This time, luckily, they were too far apart for conversation, and Varick, who faced another way, had probably not even seen him; but there was an irony in their renewed nearness.

Varick was said to be fond of good living, and as Waythorn sat despatching his hurried luncheon he looked across half enviously at the other's leisurely degustation of his meal. When Waythorn first saw him he had been helping himself with critical deliberation to a bit of Camembert at the ideal point of liquefaction, and now, the cheese removed, he was just pouring his *café double*[4] from its little two-storied earthen pot. He poured slowly, his ruddy profile bent above the task, and one be-ringed white hand steadying the lid of the coffee-pot; then he stretched his other hand to the decanter of cognac at his elbow, filled a liqueur-glass, took a tentative sip, and poured the brandy into his coffee-cup.

Waythorn watched him in a kind of fascination. What was he thinking of—only of the flavour of the coffee and the liqueur? Had the morning's meeting left no more trace in his thoughts than on his face? Had his wife so completely passed out of his life that even this odd encounter with her present husband, within a week after her remarriage, was no more than an incident in his day? And as Waythorn mused, another idea struck him: had Haskett ever met Varick as Varick and he had just met? The recollection of Haskett perturbed him, and he rose and left the restaurant, taking a circuitous way out to escape the placid irony of Varick's nod.

It was after seven when Waythorn reached home. He thought the footman who opened the door looked at him oddly.

"How is Miss Lily?" he asked in haste.

"Doing very well, sir. A gentleman————"

"Tell Barlow to put off dinner for half an hour," Waythorn cut him off, hurrying upstairs.

He went straight to his room and dressed without seeing his wife. When he reached the drawing-room she was there, fresh and radiant. Lily's day had been good; the doctor was not coming back that evening.

At dinner Waythorn told her of Seller's illness and of the resulting complications. She listened sympathetically, adjuring him not to let himself be overworked, and asking vague feminine questions about the routing of the office. Then she gave him the chronicle of Lily's day; quoted the nurse and doctor, and told him who had called to enquire. He had never seen her more serene and unruffled. It struck him, with a curious pang, that she was very happy in being with him, so happy that she found a childish pleasure in rehearsing the trivial incidents of her day.

---

[4] "Double coffee" (French): strong coffee in which water drips through the grounds in individual servings. Varick's manner with the Camembert cheese, the coffee, and the cognac functions as part of Wharton's characterization.

After dinner they went to the library, and the servant put the coffee and liqueurs on a low table before her and left the room. She looked singularly soft and girlish, in her rosy pale dress, against the dark leather of one of his bachelor armchairs. A day earlier the contrast would have charmed him.

He turned away now, choosing a cigar with affected deliberation.

"Did Haskett come?" he asked, with his back to her.

"Oh, yes—he came."

"You didn't see him, of course?"

She hesitated a moment. "I let the nurse see him."

That was all. There was nothing more to ask. He swung round toward her, applying a match to his cigar. Well, the thing was over for a week, at any rate. He would try not to think of it. She looked up at him, a trifle rosier than usual, with a smile in her eyes.

"Ready for your coffee, dear?"

He leaned against the mantelpiece, watching her as she lifted the coffee-pot. The lamplight struck a gleam from her bracelets and tipped her soft hair with brightness. How light and slender she was, and how each gesture flowed into the next! She seemed a creature all compact of harmonies. As the thought of Haskett receded, Waythorn felt himself yielding again to the joy of possessorship. They were his, those white hands with their flitting motions, his the light haze of hair, the lips and eyes. . . .

She set down the coffee-pot, and reaching for the decanter of cognac, measured off a liqueur-glass and poured it into his cup.

Waythorn uttered a sudden exclamation.

"What is the matter?" she said, startled.

"Nothing; only—I don't take cognac in my coffee."

"Oh, how stupid of me," she cried.

Their eyes met, and she blushed a sudden agonized red.

III

Ten days later, Mr. Sellers, still house-bound, asked Waythorn to call on his way down town.

The senior partner, with his swaddled foot propped up by the fire, greeted his associate with an air of embarrassment.

"I'm sorry, my dear fellow; I've got to ask you to do an awkward thing for me."

Waythorn waited, and the other went on, after a pause apparently given to the arrangement of his phrases: "The fact is, when I was knocked out I had just gone into a rather complicated piece of business for—Gus Varick."

"Well?" said Waythorn, with an attempt to put him at his ease.

"Well—it's this way: Varick came to me the day before my attack. He had evidently had an inside tip from somebody, and had made about a hundred thousand. He came to me for advice, and I suggested his going in with Vanderlyn."

"Oh, the deuce!" Waythorn exclaimed. He saw in a flash what had happened. The investment was an alluring one, but required negotiation. He listened quietly while Sellers put the case before him, and, the statement ended, he said: "You think I ought to see Varick?"

"I'm afraid I can't as yet. The doctor is obdurate. And this thing can't wait. I hate to ask you, but no one else in the office knows the ins and outs of it."

Waythorn stood silent. He did not care a farthing for the success of Varick's venture, but the honour of the office was to be considered, and he could hardly refuse to oblige his partner.

"Very well," he said, "I'll do it."

That afternoon, apprised by telephone, Varick called at the office. Waythorn, waiting in his private room, wondered what the others thought of it. The newspapers, at the time of Mrs. Waythorn's marriage, had acquainted their readers with every detail of her previous matrimonial ventures, and Waythorn could fancy the clerks smiling behind Varick's back as he was ushered in.

Varick bore himself admirably. He was easy without being undignified, and Waythorn was conscious of cutting a much less impressive figure. Varick had no experience of business, and the talk prolonged itself for nearly an hour while Waythorn set forth with scrupulous precision the details of the proposed transaction.

"I'm awfully obliged to you," Varick said as he rose. "The fact is I'm not used to having much money to look after, and I don't want to make an ass of myself——" He smiled, and Waythorn could not help noticing that there was something pleasant about his smile. "It feels uncommonly queer to have enough cash to pay one's bills. I'd have sold my soul for it a few years ago!"

Waythorn winced at the allusion. He had heard it rumoured that a lack of funds had been one of the determining causes of the Varick separation, but it did not occur to him that Varick's words were intentional. It seemed more likely that the desire to keep clear of embarrassing topics had fatally drawn him into one. Waythorn did not wish to be outdone in civility.

"We'll do the best we can for you," he said. "I think this is a good thing you're in."

"Oh, I'm sure it's immense. It's awfully good of you——" Varick broke off, embarrassed. "I suppose the thing's settled now—but if——"

"If anything happens before Sellers is about, I'll see you again," said Waythorn quietly. He was glad, in the end, to appear the more self-possessed of the two.

The course of Lily's illness ran smooth, and as the days passed Waythorn grew used to the idea of Haskett's weekly visit. The first time the day came round, he stayed out late, and questioned his wife as to the visit on his return. She replied at once that Haskett had merely seen the nurse downstairs, as the doctor did not wish any one in the child's sick-room till after the crisis.

The following week Waythorn was again conscious of the recurrence of the day, but had forgotten it by the time he came home to dinner. The crisis of the disease came a few days later, with a rapid decline of fever, and the little girl was pronounced out of danger. In the rejoicing which ensued, the thought of Haskett passed out of Waythorn's mind, and one afternoon, letting himself into the house with a latch-key, he went straight to his library without noticing a shabby hat and umbrella in the hall.

In the library he found a small effaced-looking man with a thinnish gray beard sitting on the edge of the chair. The stranger might have been a piano-tuner, or one of those mysteriously efficient persons who are summoned in emergencies to adjust some detail of the domestic machinery. He blinked at Waythorn through a pair of gold-rimmed spectacles and said mildly: "Mr. Waythorn, I presume? I am Lily's father."

Waythorn flushed. "Oh——" he stammered uncomfortably. He broke off, disliking to appear rude. Inwardly he was trying to adjust the actual Haskett to the image of him projected by his wife's reminiscences. Waythorn had been allowed to infer that Alice's first husband was a brute.

"I am sorry to intrude," said Haskett, with his over-the-counter politeness.

"Don't mention it," returned Waythorn, collecting himself. "I suppose the nurse has been told?"

"I presume so. I can wait," said Haskett. He had a resigned way of speaking, as though life had worn down his natural powers of resistance.

Waythorn stood on the threshold, nervously pulling off his gloves.

"I'm sorry you've been detained. I will send for the nurse," he said; and as he opened the door he added with an effort: "I'm glad we can give you a good report of Lily." He winced as the *we* slipped out, but Haskett seemed not to notice it.

"Thank you, Mr. Waythorn. It's been an anxious time for me."

"Ah, well, that's past. Soon she'll be able to go to you." Waythorn nodded and passed out.

In his own room he flung himself down with a groan. He hated the womanish sensibility which made him suffer so acutely from the grotesque chances of life. He had known when he married that his wife's former husbands were both living, and that amid the multiplied contacts of modern existence there were a thousand chances to one that he would run against one or the other, yet he found himself as much disturbed by his brief encounter with Haskett as though the law had not obligingly removed all difficulties in the way of their meeting.

Waythorn sprang up and began to pace the room nervously. He had not suffered half as much from his two meetings with Varick. It was Haskett's presence in his own house that made the situation so intolerable. He stood still, hearing steps in the passage.

"This way, please," he heard the nurse say. Haskett was being taken upstairs, then: not a corner of the house but was open to him. Waythorn dropped into another chair, staring vaguely ahead of him. On his dressing-table stood a photograph of Alice, taken when he had first known her. She was Alice Varick then— how fine and exquisite he had thought her! Those were Varick's pearls about her neck. At Waythorn's instance they had been returned before her marriage. Had Haskett ever given her any trinkets—and what had become of them, Waythorn wondered? He realized suddenly that he knew very little of Haskett's past or present situation; but from the man's appearance and manner of speech he could reconstruct with curious precision the surroundings of Alice's first marriage. And it startled him to think that she had, in the background of her life, a phase of existence so different from anything with which he had connected her. Varick, whatever his faults, was a gentleman, in the conventional, traditional sense of the term: the sense which at that moment seemed, oddly enough, to have most meaning to Waythorn. He and Varick had the same social habits, spoke the same language, understood the same allusions. But this other man . . . it was grotesquely uppermost in Waythorn's mind that Haskett had worn a made-up tie attached with an elastic. Why should that ridiculous detail symbolize the whole man? Waythorn was exasperated by his own paltriness, but the fact of the tie expanded, forced itself on him, became as it were the key to Alice's past. He could see her, as Mrs. Haskett, sitting in a "front parlour" furnished in plush, with a pianola, and a copy of "Ben Hur" on the centre-table.[5] He could see her going to the theatre with

<hr />

[5] Waythorn sees her as hopelessly middle class, with an overfurnished ("plush") parlour; a pianola, or mechanical piano player; and a copy of *Ben Hur* (1880), by the American soldier and writer General Lew Wallace (1827–1905); *Ben Hur* sold approximately two million copies.

Hasket—or perhaps even to a "Church Sociable"—she in a "picture hat" and Haskett in a black frock-coat, a little creased, with the made-up tie on an elastic. On the way home they would stop and look at the illuminated shop-windows, lingering over the photographs of New York actresses. On Sunday afternoons Haskett would take her for a walk, pushing Lily ahead of them in a white enamelled perambulator, and Waythorn had a vision of the people they would stop and talk to. He could fancy how pretty Alice must have looked, in a dress adroitly constructed from the hints of a New York fashion-paper, and how she must have looked down on the other women, chafing at her life, and secretly feeling that she belonged in a bigger place.

For the moment his foremost thought was one of wonder at the way in which she had shed the phase of existence which her marriage with Haskett implied. It was as if her whole aspect, every gesture, every inflection, every allusion, were a studied negation of that period of her life. If she had denied being married to Haskett she could hardly have stood more convicted of duplicity than in this obliteration of the self which had been his wife.

Waythorn started up, checking himself in the analysis of her motives. What right had he to create a fantastic effigy of her and then pass judgment on it? She had spoken vaguely of her first marriage as unhappy, had hinted, with becoming reticence, that Haskett had wrought havoc among her young illusions. . . . It was a pity for Waythorn's peace of mind that Haskett's very inoffensiveness shed a new light on the nature of those illusions. A man would rather think that his wife has been brutalized by her first husband than that the process has been reversed.

IV

"Mr. Waythorn, I don't like that French governess of Lily's."

Haskett, subdued and apologetic, stood before Waythorn in the library, revolving his shabby hat in his hand.

Waythorn, surprised in his armchair over the evening paper, stared back perplexedly at his visitor.

"You'll excuse my asking to see you," Haskett continued. "But this is my last visit, and I thought if I could have a word with you it would be a better way than writing to Mrs. Waythorn's lawyer."

Waythorn rose uneasily. He did not like the French governess either; but that was irrelevant.

"I am not so sure of that," he returned stiffly; "but since you wish it I will give your message to—my wife." He always hesitated over the possessive pronoun in addressing Haskett.

The latter sighed. "I don't know as that will help much. She didn't like it when I spoke to her."

Waythorn turned red. "When did you see her?" he asked.

"Not since the first day I came to see Lily—right after she was taken sick. I remarked to her then that I didn't like the governess."

Waythorn made no answer. He remembered distinctly that, after that first visit, he had asked his wife if she had seen Haskett. She had lied to him then, but she had respected his wishes since; and the incident cast a curious light on her character. He was sure she would not have seen Haskett that first day if she had divined that Waythorn would object, and the fact that she did not divine it was almost as disagreeable to the latter as the discovery that she had lied to him.

"I don't like the woman," Haskett was repeating with mild persistency. "She ain't straight, Mr. Waythorn—she'll teach the child to be underhand. I've noticed a change in Lily—she's too anxious to please—and she don't always tell the truth. She used to be the straightest child, Mr. Waythorn———" He broke off, his voice a little thick. "Not but what I want her to have a stylish education," he ended.

Waythorn was touched. "I'm sorry, Mr. Haskett; but frankly, I don't quite see what I can do."

Haskett hesitated. Then he laid his hat on the table, and advanced to the hearth-rug, on which Waythorn was standing. There was nothing aggressive in his manner, but he had the solemnity of a timid man resolved on a decisive measure.

"There's just one thing you can do, Mr. Waythorn," he said. "You can remind Mrs. Waythorn that, by the decree of the courts, I am entitled to have a voice in Lily's bringing up." He paused, and went on more deprecatingly: "I'm not the kind to talk about enforcing my rights, Mr. Waythorn. I don't know as I think a man is entitled to rights he hasn't known how to hold on to; but this business of the child is different. I've never let go there—and I never mean to."

.   .   .   .   .   .

The scene left Waythorn deeply shaken. Shamefacedly, in indirect ways, he had been finding out about Haskett; and all that he had learned was favourable. The little man, in order to be near his daughter, had sold out his share in a profitable business in Utica, and accepted a modest clerkship in a New York manufacturing house. He boarded in a shabby street and had few acquaintances. His passion for Lily filled his life. Waythorn felt that this exploration of Haskett was like groping about with a dark-lantern in his wife's past; but he saw now that there were recesses his lantern had not explored. He had never enquired into the exact circumstances of his wife's first matrimonial rupture. On the surface all had been fair. It was she who had obtained the divorce, and the court had given her the child. But Waythorn knew how many ambiguities such a verdict might cover. The mere fact that Haskett retained a right over his daughter implied an unsuspected compromise. Waythorn was an idealist. He always refused to recognize unpleasant contingencies till he found himself confronted with them, and then he saw them followed by a spectral train of consequences. His next days were thus haunted, and he determined to try to lay the ghosts by conjuring them up in his wife's presence.

When he repeated Haskett's request a flame of anger passed over her face; but she subdued it instantly and spoke with a slight quiver of outraged motherhood.

"It is very ungentlemanly of him," she said.

The word grated on Waythorn. "That is neither here nor there. It's a bare question of rights."

She murmured: "It's not as if he could ever be a help to Lily———"

Waythorn flushed. This was even less to his taste. "The question is," he repeated, "what authority has he over her?"

She looked downward, twisting herself a little in her seat. "I am willing to see him—I thought you objected," she faltered.

In a flash he understood that she knew the extent of Haskett's claims. Perhaps it was not the first time she had resisted them.

"My objecting has nothing to do with it," he said coldly; "if Haskett has a right to be consulted you must consult him."

She burst into tears, and he saw that she expected him to regard her as a victim. ✳

Haskett did not abuse his rights. Waythorn had felt miserably sure that he would not. But the governess was dismissed, and from time to time the little man demanded an interview with Alice. After the first outburst she accepted the situation with her usual adaptability. Haskett had once reminded Waythorn of the piano-tuner, and Mrs. Waythorn, after a month or two, appeared to class him with that domestic familiar. Waythorn could not but respect the father's tenacity. At first he had tried to cultivate the suspicion that Haskett might be "up to" something, that he had an object in securing a foothold in the house. But in his heart Waythorn was sure of Haskett's single-mindedness; he even guessed in the latter a mild contempt for such advantages as his relation with the Waythorns might offer. Haskett's sincerity of purpose made him invulnerable, and his successor had to accept him as a lien on the property.

Mr. Sellers was sent to Europe to recover from his gout, and Varick's affairs hung on Waythorn's hands. The negotiations were prolonged and complicated; they necessitated frequent conferences between the two men, and the interests of the firm forbade Waythorn's suggesting that his client should transfer his business to another office.

Varick appeared well in the transaction. In moments of relaxation his coarse streak appeared, and Waythorn dreaded his geniality; but in the office he was concise and clear-headed, with a flattering deference to Waythorn's judgment. Their business relations being so affably established, it would have been absurd for the two men to ignore each other in society. The first time they met in a drawing-room, Varick took up their intercourse in the same easy key, and his hostess's grateful glance obliged Waythorn to respond to it. After that they ran across each other frequently, and one evening at a ball Waythorn, wandering through the remoter rooms, came upon Varick seated beside his wife. She coloured a little, and faltered in what she was saying; but Varick nodded to Waythorn without rising, and the latter strolled on.

In the carriage, on the way home, he broke out nervously: "I didn't know you spoke to Varick."

Her voice trembled a little. "It's the first time—he happened to be standing near me; I didn't know what to do. It's so awkward, meeting everywhere—and he said you had been very kind about some business."

"That's different," said Waythorn.

She paused a moment. "I'll do just as you wish," she returned pliantly. "I thought it would be less awkward to speak to him when we meet."

Her pliancy was beginning to sicken him. Had she really no will of her own— no theory about her relation to these men? She had accepted Haskett—did she mean to accept Varick? It was "less awkward," as she had said, and her instinct was to evade difficulties or to circumvent them. With sudden vividness Waythorn saw how the instinct had developed. She was "as easy as an old shoe"—a shoe that too many feet had worn. Her elasticity was the result of tension in too many different directions. Alice Haskett—Alice Varick—Alice Waythorn—she had been each in turn, and had left hanging to each name a little of her privacy, a little of her personality, a little of the inmost self where the unknown god abides.

"Yes—it's better to speak to Varick," said Waythorn wearily.

V

The winter wore on, and society took advantage of the Waythorns' acceptance of Varick. Harassed hostesses were grateful to them for bridging over a social difficulty, and Mrs. Waythorn was held up as a miracle of good taste. Some experimental spirits could not resist the diversion of throwing Varick and his former wife together, and there were those who thought he found a zest in the propinquity. But Mrs. Waythorn's conduct remained irreproachable. She neither avoided Varick nor sought him out. Even Waythorn could not but admit that she had discovered the solution of the newest social problem.

He had married her without giving much thought to that problem. He had fancied that a woman can shed her past like a man. But now he saw that Alice was bound to hers both by the circumstances which forced her into continued relation with it, and by the traces it had left on her nature. With grim irony Waythorn compared himself to a member of a syndicate. He held so many shares in his wife's personality and his predecessors were his partners in the business. If there had been any element of passion in the transaction he would have felt less deteriorated by it. The fact that Alice took her change of husbands like a change of weather reduced the situation to mediocrity. He could have forgiven her for blunders, for excesses; for resisting Haskett, for yielding to Varick; for anything but her acquiescence and her tact. She reminded him of a juggler tossing knives; but the knives were blunt and she knew they would never cut her.

And then, gradually, habit formed a protecting surface for his sensibilities. If he paid for each day's comfort with the small change of his illusions, he grew daily to value the comfort more and set less store upon the coin. He had drifted into a dulling propinquity with Haskett and Varick and he took refuge in the cheap revenge of satirizing the situation. He even began to reckon up the advantages which accrued from it, to ask himself if it were not better to own a third of a wife who knew how to make a man happy than a whole one who had lacked opportunity to acquire the art. For it *was* an art, and made up, like all others, of concessions, eliminations and embellishments; of lights judiciously thrown and shadows skilfully softened. His wife knew exactly how to manage the lights, and he knew exactly to what training she owed her skill. He even tried to trace the source of his obligations, to discriminate between the influences which had combined to produce his domestic happiness: he perceived that Haskett's commonness had made Alice worship good breeding, while Varick's liberal construction of the marriage bond had taught her to value the conjugal virtues; so that he was directly indebted to his predecessors for the devotion which made his life easy if not inspiring.

From this phase he passed into that of complete acceptance. He ceased to satirize himself because time dulled the irony of the situation and the joke lost its humour with its sting. Even the sight of Haskett's hat on the hall table had ceased to touch the springs of epigram. The hat was often seen there now, for it had been decided that it was better for Lily's father to visit her than for the little girl to go to his boarding-house. Waythorn, having acquiesced in this arrangement, had been surprised to find how little difference it made. Haskett was never obtrusive, and the few visitors who met him on the stairs were unaware of his identity. Waythorn did not know how often he saw Alice, but with himself Haskett was seldom in contact.

One afternoon, however, he learned on entering that Lily's father was waiting to see him. In the library he found Haskett occupying a chair in his usual provisional way. Waythorn always felt grateful to him for not leaning back.

"I hope you'll excuse me, Mr. Waythorn," he said, rising. "I wanted to see Mrs. Waythorn about Lily, and your man asked me to wait here till she came in."

"Of course," said Waythorn, remembering that a sudden leak had that morning given over the drawing-room to the plumbers.

He opened his cigar-case and held it out to his visitor, and Haskett's acceptance seemed to mark a fresh stage in their intercourse. The spring evening was chilly, and Waythorn invited his guest to draw up his chair to the fire. He meant to find an excuse to leave Haskett in a moment; but he was tired and cold, and after all the little man no longer jarred on him.

The two were enclosed in the intimacy of their blended cigar-smoke when the door opened and Varick walked into the room. Waythorn rose abruptly. It was the first time that Varick had come to the house, and the surprise of seeing him, combined with the singular inopportuneness of his arrival, gave a new edge to Waythorn's blunted sensibilities. He stared at his visitor without speaking.

Varick seemed too preoccupied to notice his host's embarrassment.

"My dear fellow," he exclaimed in his most expansive tone, "I must apologize for tumbling in on you in this way, but I was too late to catch you down town, and so I thought——"

He stopped short, catching sight of Haskett, and his sanguine colour deepened to a flush which spread vividly under his scant blond hair. But in a moment he recovered himself and nodded slightly. Haskett returned the bow in silence, and Waythorn was still groping for speech when the footman came in carrying a tea-table.

The intrusion offered a welcome vent to Waythorn's nerves. "What the deuce are you bringing this here for?" he said sharply.

"I beg your pardon, sir, but the plumbers are still in the drawing-room, and Mrs. Waythorn said she would have tea in the library." The footman's perfectly respectful tone implied a reflection on Waythorn's reasonableness.

"Oh, very well," said the latter resignedly, and the footman proceeded to open the folding tea-table and set out its complicated appointments. While this interminable process continued the three men stood motionless, watching it with a fascinated stare, till Waythorn, to break the silence, said to Varick: "Won't you have a cigar?"

He held out the case he had just tendered to Haskett, and Varick helped himself with a smile. Waythorn looked about for a match, and finding none, proffered a light from his own cigar. Haskett, in the background, held his ground mildly, examining his cigar-tip now and then, and stepping forward at the right moment to knock its ashes into the fire.

The footman at last withdrew, and Varick immediately began: "If I could just say half a word to you about this business——"

"Certainly," stammered Waythorn; "in the dining-room——"

But as he placed his hand on the door it opened from without, and his wife appeared on the threshold.

She came in fresh and smiling, in her street dress and hat, shedding a fragrance from the boa[6] which she loosened in advancing.

"Shall we have tea in here, dear?" she began; and then she caught sight of Varick. Her smile deepened, veiling a slight tremor of surprise.

"Why, how do you do?" she said with a distinct note of pleasure.

As she shook hands with Varick she saw Haskett standing behind him. Her smile faded for a moment, but she recalled it quickly, with a scarcely perceptible side-glance at Waythorn.

---

[6] A fluffy wrap-around scarf, named humorously for the boa constrictor.

"How do you do, Mr. Haskett?" she said, and shook hands with him a shade less cordially.

The three men stood awkwardly before her, till Varick, always the most self-possessed, dashed into an explanatory phrase.

"We—I had to see Waythorn a moment on business," he stammered, brick-red from chin to nape.

Haskett stepped forward with his air of mild obstinacy. "I am sorry to intrude; but you appointed five o'clock————" he directed his resigned glance to the timepiece on the mantel.

She swept aside their embarrassment with a charming gesture of hospitality.

"I'm so sorry—I'm always late; but the afternoon was so lovely." She stood drawing off her gloves, propitiatory and graceful, diffusing about her a sense of ease and familiarity in which the situation lost its grotesqueness. "But before talking business," she added brightly, "I'm sure every one wants a cup of tea."

She dropped into her low chair by the tea-table, and the two visitors, as if drawn by her smile, advanced to receive the cups she held out.

She glanced about for Waythorn, and he took the third cup with a laugh.

1904

ROMAN FEVER*

I

From the table at which they had been lunching two American ladies of ripe but well-cared-for middle age moved across the lofty terrace of the Roman restaurant and, leaning on its parapet, looked first at each other, and then down on the out-spread glories of the Palatine and the Forum,[1] with the same expression of vague but benevolent approval.

As they leaned there a girlish voice echoed up gaily from the stairs leading to the court below. "Well, come along, then," it cried, not to them but to an invisible companion, "and let's leave the young things to their knitting"; and a voice as fresh laughed back: "Oh, look here, Babs, not actually *knitting*—" "Well, I mean figuratively," rejoined the first. "After all, we haven't left our poor parents much else to do . . . " and at that point the turn of the stairs engulfed the dialogue.

The two ladies looked at each other again, this time with a tinge of smiling embarrassment, and the smaller and paler one shook her head and coloured slightly.

"Barbara!" she murmured, sending an unheard rebuke after the mocking voice in the stairway.

The other lady, who was fuller, and higher in colour, with a small determined nose supported by vigorous black eyebrows, gave a good-humoured laugh. "That's what our daughters think of us!"

---

* Wharton sold this story to *Liberty* magazine in 1934 for $3000; it was published in *Liberty* in 1936 and collected in *The World Over* the same year.

[1] One of the seven hills on which ancient Rome was built, and the ruins of the administrative center of ancient Rome.

Her companion replied by a deprecating gesture. "Not of us individually. We must remember that. It's just the collective modern idea of Mothers. And you see—" Half guiltily she drew from her handsomely mounted black hand-bag a twist of crimson silk run through by two fine knitting needles. "One never knows," she murmured. "The new system has certainly given us a good deal of time to kill; and sometimes I get tired just looking—even at this." Her gesture was now addressed to the stupendous scene at their feet.

The dark lady laughed again, and they both relapsed upon the view, contemplating it in silence, with a sort of diffused serenity which might have been borrowed from the spring effulgence of the Roman skies. The luncheon-hour was long past, and the two had their end of the vast terrace to themselves. At its opposite extremity a few groups, detained by a lingering look at the outspread city, were gathering up guide-books and fumbling for tips. The last of them scattered, and the two ladies were alone on the air-washed height.

"Well, I don't see why we shouldn't just stay here," said Mrs. Slade, the lady of the high colour and energetic brows. Two derelict basket-chairs stood near, and she pushed them into the angle of the parapet,[2] and settled herself in one, her gaze upon the Palatine. "After all, it's still the most beautiful view in the world."

"It always will be, to me," assented her friend Mrs. Ansley, with so slight a stress on the "me" that Mrs. Slade, though she noticed it, wondered if it were not merely accidental, like the random underlinings of old-fashioned letter-writers.

"Grace Ansley was always old-fashioned," she thought; and added aloud, with a retrospective smile: "It's a view we've both been familiar with for a good many years. When we first met here we were younger than our girls are now. You remember?"

"Oh, yes, I remember," murmured Mrs. Ansley, with the same undefinable stress.— "There's that head-waiter wondering," she interpolated. She was evidently far less sure than her companion of herself and of her rights in the world.

"I'll cure him of wondering," said Mrs. Slade, stretching her hand toward a bag as discreetly opulent-looking as Mrs. Ansley's. Signing to the head-waiter, she explained that she and her friend were old lovers of Rome, and would like to spend the end of the afternoon looking down on the view—that is, if it did not disturb the service? The headwaiter, bowing over her gratuity, assured her that the ladies were most welcome, and would be still more so if they would condescend to remain for dinner. A full moon night, they would remember. . . .

Mrs. Slade's black brows drew together, as though references to the moon were out-of-place and even unwelcome. But she smiled away her frown as the headwaiter retreated. "Well, why not? We might do worse. There's no knowing, I suppose, when the girls will be back. Do you even know back from *where*? I don't!"

Mrs. Ansley again coloured slightly. "I think those young Italian aviators we met at the Embassy invited them to fly to Tarquinia[3] for tea. I suppose they'll want to wait and fly back by moonlight."

"Moonlight—moonlight! What a part it still plays. Do you suppose they're as sentimental as we were?"

"I've come to the conclusion that I don't in the least know what they are," said Mrs. Ansley. "And perhaps we didn't know much more about each other."

"No; perhaps we didn't."

---

[2] A low wall or railing.   [3] A seaport about eighty miles north of Rome.

Her friend gave her a shy glance. "I never should have supposed you were sentimental, Alida."

"Well, perhaps I wasn't." Mrs. Slade drew her lids together in retrospect; and for a few moments the two ladies, who had been intimate since childhood, reflected how little they knew each other. Each one, of course, had a label ready to attach to the other's name; Mrs. Delphin Slade, for instance, would have told herself, or any one who asked her, that Mrs. Horace Ansley, twenty-five years ago, had been exquisitely lovely—no, you wouldn't believe it, would you? . . . though, of course, still charming, distinguished. . . . Well, as a girl she had been exquisite; far more beautiful than her daughter Barbara, though certainly Babs, according to the new standards at any rate, was more effective—had more *edge,* as they say. Funny where she got it, with those two nullities as parents. Yes; Horace Ansley was—well, just the duplicate of his wife. Museum specimens of old New York. Good-looking, irreproachable, exemplary. Mrs. Slade and Mrs. Ansley had lived opposite each other—actually as well as figuratively—for years. When the drawing-room curtains in No. 20 East 73rd Street were renewed, No. 23, across the way, was always aware of it. And of all the movings, buyings, travels, anniversaries, illnesses—the tame chronicle of an estimable pair. Little of it escaped Mrs. Slade. But she had grown bored with it by the time her husband made his big *coup* in Wall Street, and when they bought in upper Park Avenue had already begun to think: "I'd rather live opposite a speak-easy for a change; at least one might see it raided." The idea of seeing Grace raided was so amusing that (before the move) she launched it at a woman's lunch. It made a hit, and went the rounds—she sometimes wondered if it had crossed the street, and reached Mrs. Ansley. She hoped not, but didn't much mind. Those were the days when respectability was at a discount, and it did the irreproachable no harm to laugh at them a little.

A few years later, and not many months apart, both ladies lost their husbands. There was an appropriate exchange of wreaths and condolences, and a brief renewal of intimacy in the half-shadow of their mourning; and now, after another interval, they had run across each other in Rome, at the same hotel, each of them the modest appendage of a salient[4] daughter. The similarity of their lot had again drawn them together, lending itself to mild jokes, and the mutual confession that, if in old days it must have been tiring to "keep up" with daughters, it was now, at times, a little dull not to.

No doubt, Mrs. Slade reflected, she felt her unemployment more than poor Grace ever would. It was a big drop from being the wife of Delphin Slade to being his widow. She had always regarded herself (with a certain conjugal pride) as his equal in social gifts, as contributing her full share to the making of the exceptional couple they were: but the difference after his death was irremediable. As the wife of the famous corporation lawyer, always with an international case or two on hand, every day brought its exciting and unexpected obligation: the impromptu entertaining of eminent colleagues from abroad, the hurried dashes on legal business to London, Paris or Rome, where the entertaining was so handsomely reciprocated; the amusement of hearing in her wake: "What, that handsome woman with the good clothes and the eyes is Mrs. Slade—*the* Slade's wife? Really? Generally the wives of celebrities are such frumps."

Yes; being *the* Slade's widow was a dullish business after that. In living up to

---

[4] Conspicuous and lively.

such a husband all her faculties had been engaged; now she had only her daughter to live up to, for the son who seemed to have inherited his father's gifts had died suddenly in boyhood. She had fought through that agony because her husband was there, to be helped and to help; now, after the father's death, the thought of the boy had become unbearable. There was nothing left but to mother her daughter; and dear Jenny was such a perfect daughter that she needed no excessive mothering. "Now with Babs Ansley I don't know that I *should* be so quiet," Mrs. Slade sometimes half-enviously reflected; but Jenny, who was younger than her brilliant friend, was that rare accident, an extremely pretty girl who somehow made youth and prettiness seem as safe as their absence. It was all perplexing— and to Mrs. Slade a little boring. She wished that Jenny would fall in love—with the wrong man, even; that she might have to be watched, out-manoeuvred, rescued. And instead, it was Jenny who watched her mother, kept her out of draughts, made sure that she had taken her tonic. . . .

Mrs. Ansley was much less articulate than her friend, and her mental portrait of Mrs. Slade was slighter, and drawn with fainter touches. "Alida Slade's awfully brilliant; but not as brilliant as she thinks," would have summed it up; though she would have added, for the enlightenment of strangers, that Mrs. Slade had been an extremely dashing girl; much more so than her daughter, who was pretty, of course, and clever in a way, but had none of her mother's—well, "vividness", some one had called it. Mrs. Ansley would take up current words like this, and cite them in quotation marks, as unheard-of audacities. No; Jenny was not like her mother. Sometimes Mrs. Ansley thought Alida Slade was disappointed; on the whole she had had a sad life. Full of failures and mistakes; Mrs. Ansley had always been rather sorry for her. . . .

So these two ladies visualized each other, each through the wrong end of her little telescope.

II

For a long time they continued to sit side by side without speaking. It seemed as though, to both, there was a relief in laying down their somewhat futile activities in the presence of the vast Memento Mori[5] which faced them. Mrs. Slade sat quite still, her eyes fixed on the golden slope of the Palace of the Cæsars,[6] and after a while Mrs. Ansley ceased to fidget with her bag, and she too sank into meditation. Like many intimate friends, the two ladies had never before had occasion to be silent together, and Mrs. Ansley was slightly embarrassed by what seemed, after so many years, a new stage in their intimacy, and one with which she did not yet know how to deal.

Suddenly the air was full of that deep clangour of bells which periodically covers Rome with a roof of silver. Mrs. Slade glanced at her wrist-watch. "Five o'clock already," she said, as though surprised.

Mrs. Ansley suggested interrogatively: "There's bridge at the Embassy at five." For a long time Mrs. Slade did not answer. She appeared to be lost in contempla-

---

[5] "Memento of Death" (Latin): here Rome is the "vast" reminder of death.
[6] A Roman palace erected by the Caesars, on the Palatine Hill.

tion, and Mrs. Ansley thought the remark had escaped her. But after a while she said, as if speaking out of a dream: "Bridge, did you say? Not unless you want to. . . . But I don't think I will, you know."

"Oh, no," Mrs. Ansley hastened to assure her. "I don't care to at all. It's so lovely here; and so full of old memories, as you say." She settled herself in her chair, and almost furtively drew forth her knitting. Mrs. Slade took sideway note of this activity, but her own beautifully cared-for hands remained motionless on her knee.

"I was just thinking," she said slowly, "what different things Rome stands for to each generation of travellers. To our grandmothers, Roman fever;[7] to our mothers, sentimental dangers—how we used to be guarded!—to our daughters, no more dangers than the middle of Main Street. They don't know it—but how much they're missing!"

The long golden light was beginning to pale, and Mrs. Ansley lifted her knitting a little closer to her eyes. "Yes; how we were guarded!"

"I always used to think," Mrs. Slade continued, "that our mothers had a much more difficult job than our grandmothers. When Roman fever stalked the streets it must have been comparatively easy to gather in the girls at the danger hour; but when you and I were young, with such beauty calling us, and the spice of disobedience thrown in, and no worse risk than catching cold during the cool hour after sunset, the mothers used to be put to it to keep us in—didn't they?"

She turned again toward Mrs. Ansley, but the latter had reached a delicate point in her knitting. "One, two, three—slip two; yes, they must have been," she assented, without looking up.

Mrs. Slade's eyes rested on her with a deepened attention. "She can knit—in the face of *this!* How like her. . . . "

Mrs. Slade leaned back, brooding, her eyes ranging from the ruins which faced her to the long green hollow of the Forum, the fading glow of the church fronts beyond it, and the outlying immensity of the Colosseum.[8] Suddenly she thought: "It's all very well to say that our girls have done away with sentiment and moonlight. But if Babs Ansley isn't out to catch that young aviator—the one who's a Marchese[9]—then I don't know anything. And Jenny has no chance beside her. I know that too. I wonder if that's why Grace Ansley likes the two girls to go everywhere together? My poor Jenny as a foil—!" Mrs. Slade gave a hardly audible laugh, and at the sound Mrs. Ansley dropped her knitting.

"Yes—?"

"I—oh, nothing. I was only thinking how your Babs carries everything before her. That Campolieri boy is one of the best matches in Rome. Don't look so innocent, my dear—you know he is. And I was wondering, ever so respectfully, you understand . . . wondering how two such exemplary characters as you and Horace had managed to produce anything quite so dynamic." Mrs. Slade laughed again, with a touch of asperity.

Mrs. Ansley's hands lay inert across her needles. She looked straight out at the great accumulated wreckage of passion and splendour at her feet. But her small

---

[7] Malaria, at one time a danger in Rome, then thought to be transmitted by the night air rather than by mosquitoes.

[8] The ruins of an amphitheater, or arena, built in Rome (A.D. 75?–80?).

[9] "Marquis" (Italian), a nobleman.

profile was almost expressionless. At length she said: "I think you overrate Babs, my dear."

Mrs. Slade's tone grew easier. "No; I don't. I appreciate her. And perhaps envy you. Oh, my girl's perfect; if I were a chronic invalid I'd—well, I think I'd rather be in Jenny's hands. There must be times . . . but there! I always wanted a brilliant daughter . . . and never quite understood why I got an angel instead."

Mrs. Ansley echoed her laugh in a faint murmur. "Babs is an angel too."

"Of course—of course! But she's got rainbow wings. Well, they're wandering by the sea with their young men; and here we sit . . . and it all brings back the past a little too acutely."

Mrs. Ansley had resumed her knitting. One might almost have imagined (if one had known her less well, Mrs. Slade reflected) that, for her also, too many memories rose from the lengthening shadows of those august ruins. But no; she was simply absorbed in her work. What was there for her to worry about? She knew that Babs would almost certainly come back engaged to the extremely eligible Campolieri. "And she'll sell the New York house, and settle down near them in Rome, and never be in their way . . . she's much too tactful. But she'll have an excellent cook, and just the right people in for bridge and cocktails . . . and a perfectly peaceful old age among her grandchildren."

Mrs. Slade broke off this prophetic flight with a recoil of self-disgust. There was no one of whom she had less right to think unkindly than of Grace Ansley. Would she never cure herself of envying her? Perhaps she had begun too long ago.

She stood up and leaned against the parapet, filling her troubled eyes with the tranquillizing magic of the hour. But instead of tranquillizing her the sight seemed to increase her exasperation. Her gaze turned toward the Colosseum. Already its golden flank was drowned in purple shadow, and above it the sky curved crystal clear, without light or colour. It was the moment when afternoon and evening hang balanced in mid-heaven.

Mrs. Slade turned back and laid her hand on her friend's arm. The gesture was so abrupt that Mrs. Ansley looked up, startled.

"The sun's set. You're not afraid, my dear?"

"Afraid—?"

"Of Roman fever or pneumonia? I remember how ill you were that winter. As a girl you had a very delicate throat, hadn't you?"

"Oh, we're all right up here. Down below, in the Forum, it does get deathly cold, all of a sudden . . . but not here."

"Ah, of course you know because you had to be so careful." Mrs. Slade turned back to the parapet. She thought: "I must make one more effort not to hate her." Aloud she said: "Whenever I look at the Forum from up here, I remember that story about a great-aunt of yours, wasn't she? A dreadfully wicked great-aunt?"

"Oh, yes; Great-aunt Harriet. The one who was supposed to have sent her young sister out to the Forum after sunset to gather a night-blooming flower for her album. All our great-aunts and grandmothers used to have albums of dried flowers."

Mrs. Slade nodded. "But she really sent her because they were in love with the same man—"

"Well, that was the family tradition. They said Aunt Harriet confessed it years afterward. At any rate, the poor little sister caught the fever and died. Mother used to frighten us with the story when we were children."

"And you frightened *me* with it, that winter when you and I were here as girls. The winter I was engaged to Delphin."

Mrs. Ansley gave a faint laugh. "Oh, did I? Really frightened you? I don't believe you're easily frightened."

"Not often; but I was then. I was easily frightened because I was too happy. I wonder if you know what that means?"

"I—yes . . . " Mrs. Ansley faltered.

"Well, I suppose that was why the story of your wicked aunt made such an impression on me. And I thought: 'There's no more Roman fever, but the Forum is deathly cold after sunset—especially after a hot day. And the Colosseum's even colder and damper'."

"The Colosseum—?"

"Yes. It wasn't easy to get in, after the gates were locked for the night. Far from easy. Still, in those days it could be managed; it *was* managed, often. Lovers met there who couldn't meet elsewhere. You knew that?"

"I—I daresay. I don't remember."

"You don't remember? You don't remember going to visit some ruins or other one evening, just after dark, and catching a bad chill? You were supposed to have gone to see the moon rise. People always said that expedition was what caused your illness."

There was a moment's silence; then Mrs. Ansley rejoined: "Did they? It was all so long ago."

"Yes. And you got well again—so it didn't matter. But I suppose it struck your friends—the reason given for your illness, I mean—because everybody knew you were so prudent on account of your throat, and your mother took such care of you. . . . You *had* been out late sight-seeing, hadn't you, that night?"

"Perhaps I had. The most prudent girls aren't always prudent. What made you think of it now?"

Mrs. Slade seemed to have no answer ready. But after a moment she broke out: "Because I simply can't bear it any longer—!"

Mrs. Ansley lifted her head quickly. Her eyes were wide and very pale. "Can't bear what?"

"Why—your not knowing that I've always known why you went."

"Why I went—?"

"Yes. You think I'm bluffing, don't you? Well, you went to meet the man I was engaged to—and I can repeat every word of the letter that took you there."

While Mrs. Slade spoke Mrs. Ansley had risen unsteadily to her feet. Her bag, her knitting and gloves, slid in a panic-stricken heap to the ground. She looked at Mrs. Slade as though she were looking at a ghost.

"No, no—don't," she faltered out.

"Why not? Listen, if you don't believe me. 'My one darling, things can't go on like this. I must see you alone. Come to the Colosseum immediately after dark tomorrow. There will be somebody to let you in. No one whom you need fear will suspect'—but perhaps you've forgotten what the letter said?"

Mrs. Ansley met the challenge with an unexpected composure. Steadying herself against the chair she looked at her friend, and replied: "No, I know it by heart too."

"And the signature? 'Only *your* D.S.' Was that it? I'm right, am I? That was the letter that took you out that evening after dark?"

Mrs. Ansley was still looking at her. It seemed to Mrs. Slade that a slow struggle was going on behind the voluntarily controlled mask of her small quiet face. "I shouldn't have thought she had herself so well in hand," Mrs. Slade reflected, almost resentfully. But at this moment Mrs. Ansley spoke. "I don't know how you knew. I burnt that letter at once."

"Yes; you would, naturally—you're so prudent!" The sneer was open now. "And if you burnt the letter you're wondering how on earth I know what was in it. That's it, isn't it?"

Mrs. Slade waited, but Mrs. Ansley did not speak.

"Well, my dear, I know what was in that letter because I wrote it!"

"You wrote it?"

"Yes."

The two women stood for a minute staring at each other in the last golden light. Then Mrs. Ansley dropped back into her chair. "Oh," she murmured, and covered her face with her hands.

Mrs. Slade waited nervously for another word or movement. None came, and at length she broke out: "I horrify you."

Mrs. Ansley's hands dropped to her knee. The face they uncovered was streaked with tears. "I wasn't thinking of you. I was thinking—it was the only letter I ever had from him!"

"And I wrote it. Yes; I wrote it! But I was the girl he was engaged to. Did you happen to remember that?"

Mrs. Ansley's head drooped again. "I'm not trying to excuse myself. . . . I remembered. . . ."

"And still you went?"

"Still I went."

Mrs. Slade stood looking down on the small bowed figure at her side. The flame of her wrath had already sunk, and she wondered why she had ever thought there would be any satisfaction in inflicting so purposeless a wound on her friend. But she had to justify herself.

"You do understand? I'd found out—and I hated you, hated you. I knew you were in love with Delphin—and I was afraid; afraid of you, of your quiet ways, your sweetness . . . your . . . well, I wanted you out of the way, that's all. Just for a few weeks; just till I was sure of him. So in a blind fury I wrote that letter. . . . I don't know why I'm telling you now."

"I suppose," said Mrs. Ansley slowly, "it's because you've always gone on hating me."

"Perhaps. Or because I wanted to get the whole thing off my mind." She paused. "I'm glad you destroyed the letter. Of course I never thought you'd die."

Mrs. Ansley relapsed into silence, and Mrs. Slade, leaning above her, was conscious of a strange sense of isolation, of being cut off from the warm current of human communion. "You think me a monster!"

"I don't know. . . . It was the only letter I had, and you say he didn't write it?"

"Ah, how you care for him still!"

"I cared for that memory," said Mrs. Ansley.

Mrs. Slade continued to look down on her. She seemed physically reduced by the blow—as if, when she got up, the wind might scatter her like a puff of dust. Mrs. Slade's jealousy suddenly leapt up again at the sight. All these years the woman had been living on that letter. How she must have loved him, to treasure the mere memory of its ashes! The letter of the man her friend was engaged to. Wasn't it she who was the monster?

"You tried your best to get him away from me, didn't you? But you failed; and I kept him. That's all."

"Yes. That's all."

"I wish now I hadn't told you. I'd no idea you'd feel about it as you do; I thought you'd be amused. It all happened so long ago, as you say; and you must do me the justice to remember that I had no reason to think you'd ever taken it seriously. How could I, when you were married to Horace Ansley two months afterward? As soon as you could get out of bed your mother rushed you off to Florence and married you. People were rather surprised—they wondered at its being done so quickly; but I thought I knew. I had an idea you did it out of *pique*[10]—to be able to say you'd got ahead of Delphin and me. Girls have such silly reasons for doing the most serious things. And your marrying so soon convinced me that you'd never really cared."

"Yes. I suppose it would," Mrs. Ansley assented.

The clear heaven overhead was emptied of all its gold. Dusk spread over it, abruptly darkening the Seven Hills. Here and there lights began to twinkle through the foliage at their feet. Steps were coming and going on the deserted terrace— waiters looking out of the doorway at the head of the stairs, then reappearing with trays and napkins and flasks of wine. Tables were moved, chairs straightened. A feeble string of electric lights flickered out. Some vases of faded flowers were carried away, and brought back replenished. A stout lady in a dust-coat suddenly appeared, asking in broken Italian if any one had seen the elastic band which held together her tattered Baedeker.[11] She poked with her stick under the table at which she had lunched, the waiters assisting.

The corner where Mrs. Slade and Mrs. Ansley sat was still shadowy and deserted. For a long time neither of them spoke. At length Mrs. Slade began again: "I suppose I did it as a sort of joke—"

"A joke?"

"Well, girls are ferocious sometimes, you know. Girls in love especially. And I remember laughing to myself all that evening at the idea that you were waiting around there in the dark, dodging out of sight, listening for every sound, trying to get in—. Of course I was upset when I heard you were so ill afterward."

Mrs. Ansley had not moved for a long time. But now she turned slowly toward her companion. "But I didn't wait. He'd arranged everything. He was there. We were let in at once," she said.

Mrs. Slade sprang up from her leaning position. "Delphin there? They let you in?— Ah, now you're lying!" she burst out with violence.

Mrs. Ansley's voice grew clearer, and full of surprise. "But of course he was there. Naturally he came—"

"Came? How did he know he'd find you there? You must be raving!"

Mrs. Ansley hesitated, as though reflecting. "But I answered the letter. I told him I'd be there. So he came."

Mrs. Slade flung her hands up to her face. "Oh, God—you answered! I never thought of your answering. . . . "

"It's odd you never thought of it, if you wrote the letter."

"Yes. I was blind with rage."

Mrs. Ansley rose, and drew her fur scarf about her. "It is cold here. We'd

---

[10] Resentment, irritation.

[11] One of a popular series of guidebooks issued by the German publisher Karl Baedeker (1801–1859).

better go. . . . I'm sorry for you," she said, as she clasped the fur about her throat.

The unexpected words sent a pang through Mrs. Slade. "Yes; we'd better go." She gathered up her bag and cloak. "I don't know why you should be sorry for me," she muttered.

Mrs. Ansley stood looking away from her toward the dusky secret mass of the Colosseum. "Well—because I didn't have to wait that night."

Mrs. Slade gave an unquiet laugh. "Yes; I was beaten there. But I oughtn't to begrudge it to you, I suppose. At the end of all these years. After all, I had everything; I had him for twenty-five years. And you had nothing but that one letter that he didn't write."

Mrs. Ansley was again silent. At length she turned toward the door of the terrace. She took a step, and turned back, facing her companion.

"I had Barbara," she said, and began to move ahead of Mrs. Slade toward the stairway.

1936

Theodore Dreiser
(1871–1945)

The twelfth of thirteen children of a German Catholic immigrant father and a Mennonite mother, Theodore Dreiser was born in 1871 in Terre Haute, Indiana. His childhood was a harsh one, clouded by poverty and the severe religious code of his parents. Dreiser's father lost his job when a woolen mill he managed burned down, and for some years afterward the family was frequently separated while both parents and the older children sought employment. One of Dreiser's sisters was involved in an affair with a married man that provided the basis for Dreiser's first novel, *Sister Carrie* (1900). Dreiser's older brother Paul made a living in New York City as the composer of Tin Pan Alley tunes, among them "On the Banks of the Wabash" (1899), on which Dreiser may have collaborated, and "My Gal Sal" (1905). During his infrequent but dramatic visits home, Paul provided his brother with a tantalizing model of the success that seemed so accessible in large cities. After Dreiser graduated from high school in 1889 in Warsaw, Indiana, a sympathetic high school teacher, Mildred Fielding, paid his expenses to attend Indiana University. But Dreiser left after one year, unconvinced that academic studies had relevance for his life.

Like many American writers, Dreiser turned to journalism for an income; for the next few years he did freelance magazine writing and newspaper reporting in Chicago, St. Louis (where he met Sara White, whom he married in 1898), Pittsburgh, and New York. He was dazzled by the burgeoning consumer society of urban America, and his experiences in these cities sharpened his taste for a material standard of living beyond anything he had ever known. His sense of himself as an outsider accounts for much that is characteristic in his fiction: the hunger for wealth of such young protagonists as Frank Cowperwood in *The Financier* and Clyde Griffiths in *An American Tragedy,* the accumulation of detail upon which Dreiser's power as a naturalist is based.

Sister Carrie was all but suppressed by Dreiser's publisher when it became apparent that the frank narrative of a girl's sexual compromise and success as an actress would not find favor among genteel readers. But Dreiser persisted with his writing and his vision of the force of environment in shaping human lives: he published *Jennie Gerhardt* in 1911; two volumes of a trilogy, *The Financier* in 1912 and *The Titan* in 1914; and *The "Genius"* in 1915. No longer dependent upon journalism for an income, he also produced essays and plays during these years and wrote several short stories centered in the consciousness of young women, notably "The Second choice" (1918). The publication of *An American Tragedy* in 1925, however, brought him his greatest measure of fame.

Dreiser's novels are informed by a fatalistic belief in the power of circumstance, resulting largely from his conviction that American society values material success above all else. They depict candidly, almost amorally, and with cumulative force the appeal of the world and of the flesh; typically, his characters live in places where avarice and ruthlessness bring rewards, where innocence and trust are exploited. Despite an ungainly prose style that remains part of his signature as a writer, Dreiser is deservedly regarded as a leading exponent of naturalism in American fiction.

Throughout his life Dreiser continued to look for answers, for systems that would place him on the inside. After a visit to Russia in 1927, he became an advocate of socialism; he later became a student of Eastern philosophy. Despite his failing health, Dreiser married his mistress of twenty-five years, Helen Richardson, in mid-1944; he died in Hollywood in late 1945. Two labored but interesting novels were published posthumously: *The Bulwark* (1946) and *The Stoic* (1947), the final volume of the Frank Cowperwood trilogy begun years before with *The Financier* and *The Titan*.

Suggested Readings: *An American Tragedy*, 1925. *The Letters of Theodore Dreiser*, 3 vols., ed. R. Elias, 1959. *Theodore Dreiser: A Selection of Uncollected Poems*, ed. D. Pizer, 1977. *Sister Carrie*, ed. J. Berkey and A. Winters, 1981. *American Diaries, 1902–1926*, ed. T. Riggio, 1982. R. Elias, *Theodore Dreiser, Apostle of Nature*, 1949, rpt. 1970. H. P. Dreiser, *My Life With Dreiser*, 1951. C. Shapiro, *Theodore Dreiser: Our Bitter Patriot*, 1962. W. A. Swanberg, *Dreiser*, 1965. R. Lehan, *Theodore Dreiser: His World and His Novels*, 1969. E. Moers, *Two Dreisers: The Man and the Novelist*, 1969. D. Pizer, *The Novels of Theodore Dreiser*, 1976. L. Hussman, *Dreiser and His Fiction*, 1983. J. Griffin, *The Small Canvas: An Introduction to Dreiser's Short Stories*, 1985. R. Lingeman, *Theodore Dreiser: At the Gates of the City*, 1986.

Text Used: *Free and Other Stories*, 1918.

THE SECOND CHOICE*

SHIRLEY DEAR:

You don't want the letters. There are only six of them, anyhow, and think, they're all I have of you to cheer me on my travels. What good would they be to you—little bits of notes telling me you're sure to meet me—but me—think of me! If I send them to you, you'll tear them up, whereas if you leave them with me I can dab them with musk and ambergris and keep them in a little silver box, always beside me.

Ah, Shirley dear, you really don't know how sweet I think you are, how dear!

---

* First published in *Cosmopolitan* in February 1918 and collected in *Free and Other Stories* the same year. The asterisks are Dreiser's.

There isn't a thing we have ever done together that isn't as clear in my mind as this great big skyscraper over the way here in Pittsburgh, and far more pleasing. In fact, my thoughts of you are the most precious and delicious things I have, Shirley.

But I'm too young to marry now. You know that, Shirley, don't you? I haven't placed myself in any way yet, and I'm so restless that I don't know whether I ever will, really. Only yesterday, old Roxbaum—that's my new employer here—came to me and wanted to know if I would like an assistant overseership on one of his coffee plantations in Java,[1] said there would not be much money in it for a year or two, a bare living, but later there would be more—and I jumped at it. Just the thought of Java and going there did that, although I knew I could make more staying right here. Can't you see how it is with me, Shirl? I'm too restless and too young. I couldn't take care of you right, and you wouldn't like me after a while if I didn't.

But ah, Shirley sweet, I think the dearest things of you! There isn't an hour, it seems, but some little bit of you comes back—a dear, sweet bit—the night we sat on the grass in Tregore Park and counted the stars through the trees; that first evening at Sparrows Point when we missed the last train and had to walk to Langley. Remember the tree-toads, Shirl? And then that warm April Sunday in Atholby woods! Ah, Shirl, you don't want the six notes! Let me keep them. But think of me, will you, sweet, wherever you go and whatever you do? I'll always think of you, and wish that you had met a better, saner man than me, and that I really could have married you and been all you wanted me to be. By-by, sweet. I may start for Java within the month. If so, and you would want them, I'll sent you some cards from there—if they have any.

Your worthless,

ARTHUR.

She sat and turned the letter in her hand, dumb with despair. It was the very last letter she would ever get from him. Of that she was certain. He was gone now, once and for all. She had written him only once, not making an open plea but asking him to return her letters, and then there had come this tender but evasive reply, saying nothing of a possible return but desiring to keep her letters for old times' sake—the happy hours they had spent together.

The happy hours! Oh, yes, yes, yes—the happy hours!

In her memory now, as she sat here in her home after the day's work, meditating on all that had been in the few short months since he had come and gone, was a world of color and light—a color and a light so transfiguring as to seem celestial, but now, alas, wholly dissipated. It had contained so much of all she had desired—love, romance, amusement, laughter. He had been so gay and thoughtless, or headstrong, so youthfully romantic, and with such a love of play and change and to be saying and doing anything and everything. Arthur could dance in a gay way, whistle, sing after a fashion, play. He could play cards and do tricks, and he had such a superior air, so genial and brisk, with a kind of innate courtesy in it and yet an intolerance for slowness and stodginess or anything dull or dingy, such as characterized—— But here her thoughts fled from him. She refused to think of any one but Arthur.

Sitting in her little bedroom now, off the parlor on the ground floor in her home in Bethune Street, and looking out over the Kessels' yard, and beyond that—there being no fences in Bethune Street—over the "yards" or lawns of the Pollards,

---

[1] On the Malay Archipelago.

Bakers, Cryders, and others, she thought of how dull it must all have seemed to him, with his fine imaginative mind and experiences, his love of change and gayety, his atmosphere of something better than she had ever known. How little she had been fitted, perhaps, by beauty or temperament to overcome this—the something—dullness in her work or her home, which possibly had driven him away. For, although many had admired her to date, and she was young and pretty in her simple way and constantly receiving suggestions that her beauty was disturbing to some, still, he had not cared for her—he had gone.

And now, as she meditated, it seemed that this scene, and all that it stood for—her parents, her work, her daily shuttling to and fro between the drug company for which she worked and this street and house—was typical of her life and what she was destined to endure always. Some girls were so much more fortunate. They had fine clothes, fine homes, a world of pleasure and opportunity in which to move. They did not have to scrimp and save and work to pay their own way. And yet she had always been compelled to do it, but had never complained until now—or until he came, and after. Bethune Street, with its commonplace front yards and houses nearly all alike, and this house, so like the others, room for room and porch for porch, and her parents, too, really like all the others, had seemed good enough, quite satisfactory, indeed, until then. But now, now!

Here, in their kitchen, was her mother, a thin, pale, but kindly woman, peeling potatoes and washing lettuce, and putting a bit of steak or a chop or a piece of liver in a frying-pan day after day, morning and evening, month after month, year after year. And next door was Mrs. Kessel doing the same thing. And next door Mrs. Cryder. And next door Mrs. Pollard. But, until now, she had not thought it so bad. But now—now—oh! And on all the porches or lawns all along this street were the husbands and fathers, mostly middle-aged or old men like her father, reading their papers or cutting the grass before dinner, or smoking and meditating afterward. Her father was out in front now, a stooped, forbearing, meditative soul, who had rarely anything to say—leaving it all to his wife, her mother, but who was fond of her in his dull, quiet way. He was a pattern-maker by trade, and had come into possession of this small, ordinary home via years of toil and saving, her mother helping him. They had no particular religion, as he often said, thinking reasonably human conduct a sufficient passport to heaven, but they had gone occasionally to the Methodist Church over in Nicholas Street, and she had once joined it. But of late she had not gone, weaned away by the other commonplace pleasures of her world.

And then in the midst of it, the dull drift of things, as she now saw them to be, he had come—Arthur Bristow—young, energetic, good-looking, ambitious, dreamful, and instanter, and with her never knowing quite how, the whole thing had been changed. He had appeared so swiftly—out of nothing, as it were.

Previous to him had been Barton Williams, stout, phlegmatic, good-natured, well-meaning, who was, or had been before Arthur came, asking her to marry him, and whom she allowed to half assume that she would. She had liked him in a feeble, albeit, as she thought, tender way, thinking him the kind, according to the logic of her neighborhood, who would make her a good husband, and, until Arthur appeared on the scene, had really intended to marry him. It was not really a love-match, as she saw now, but she thought it was, which was much the same thing, perhaps. But, as she now recalled, when Arthur came, how the scales fell from her eyes! In a trice, as it were, nearly, there was a new heaven and a new earth. Arthur had arrived, and with him a sense of something different.

Mabel Gove had asked her to come over to her house in Westleigh, the adjoining suburb, for Thanksgiving eve and day, and without a thought of any thing, and because Barton was busy handling a part of the work in the despatcher's office of the Great Eastern and could not see her, she had gone. And then, to her surprise and strange, almost ineffable delight, the moment she had seen him, he was there—Arthur, with his slim, straight figure and dark hair and eyes and clean-cut features, as clean and attractive as those of a coin. And as he had looked at her and smiled and narrated humorous bits of things that had happened to him, something had come over her—a spell—and after dinner they had all gone round to Edith Barringer's to dance, and there as she had danced with him, somehow, without any seeming boldness on his part, he had taken possesion of her, as it were, drawn her close, and told her she had beautiful eyes and hair and such a delicately rounded chin, and that he thought she danced gracefully and was sweet. She had nearly fainted with delight.

"Do you like me?" he had asked in one place in the dance, and, in spite of herself, she had looked up into his eyes, and from that moment she was almost mad over him, could think of nothing else but his hair and eyes and his smile and his graceful figure.

Mabel Gove had seen it all, in spite of her determination that no one should, and on their going to bed later, back at Mabel's home, she had whispered:

"Ah, Shirley, I saw. You like Arthur, don't you?"

"I think he's very nice," Shirley recalled replying, for Mabel knew of her affair with Barton and liked him, "But I'm not crazy over him." And for this bit of treason she had sighed in her dreams nearly all night.

And the next day, true to a request and a promise made by him, Arthur had called again at Mabel's to take her and Mabel to a "movie" which was not so far away, and from there they had gone to an ice-cream parlor, and during it all, when Mabel was not looking, he had squeezed her arm and hand and kissed her neck, and she had held her breath, and her heart had seemed to stop.

"And now you're going to let me come out to your place to see you, aren't you?" he had whispered.

And she had replied, "Wednesday evening," and then written the address on a little piece of paper and given it to him.

But now it was all gone, gone!

This house, which now looked so dreary—how romantic it had seemed that first night *he* called—the front room with its commonplace furniture, and later in the spring, the veranda, with its vines just sprouting, and the moon in May. Oh, the moon in May, and June and July, when he was here! How she had lied to Barton to make evenings for Arthur, and occasionally to Arthur to keep him from contact with Barton. She had not even mentioned Barton to Arthur because—because—well, because Arthur was so much better, and somehow (she admitted it to herself now) she had not been sure that Arthur would care for her long, if at all, and then—well, and then, to be quite frank, Barton might be good enough. She did not exactly hate him because she had found Arthur—not at all. She still liked him in a way—he was so kind and faithful, so very dull and straightforward and thoughtful of her, which Arthur was certainly not. Before Arthur had appeared, as she well remembered, Barton had seemed to be plenty good enough—in fact, all that she desired in a pleasant, companionable way, calling for her, taking her places, bringing her flowers and candy, which Arthur rarely did, and for that, if nothing more, she could not help continuing to like him and to feel sorry for him, and, besides, as she had admitted to herself before, if Arthur left her—* * * * *

Weren't his parents better off than hers—and hadn't he a good position for such a man as he—one hundred and fifty dollars a month and the certainty of more later on? A little while before meeting Arthur, she had thought this very good, enough for two to live on at least, and she had thought some of trying it at some time or other—but now—now———

And that first night he had called—how well she remembered it—how it had transfigured the parlor next this in which she was now, filling it with something it had never had before, and the porch outside, too, for that matter, with its gaunt, leafless vine, and this street, too, even—dull, commonplace Bethune Street. There had been a flurry of snow during the afternoon while she was working at the store, and the ground was white with it. All the neighboring homes seemed to look sweeter and happier and more inviting than ever they had as she came past them, with their lights peeping from under curtains and drawn shades. She had hurried into hers and lighted the big red-shaded parlor lamp, her one artistic treasure, as she thought, and put it near the piano, between it and the window, and arranged the chairs, and then bustled to the task of making herself as pleasing as she might. For him she had gotten out her one best filmy house dress and done up her hair in the fashion she thought most becoming—and that he had not seen before—and powdered her cheeks and nose and darkened her eyelashes, as some of the girls at the store did, and put on her new gray satin slippers, and then, being so arrayed, waited nervously, unable to eat anything or to think of anything but him.

And at last, just when she had begun to think he might not be coming, he had appeared with that arch smile and a "Hello! It's here you live, is it? I was wondering. George, but you're twice as sweet as I thought you were, aren't you?" And then, in the little entryway, behind the closed door, he had held her and kissed her on the mouth a dozen times while she pretended to push against his coat and struggle and say that her parents might hear.

And, oh, the room afterward, with him in it in the red glow of the lamp, and with his pale handsome face made handsomer thereby, as she thought! He had made her sit near him and had held her hands and told her about his work and his dreams—all that he expected to do in the future—and then she had found herself wishing intensely to share just such a life—his life—anything that he might wish to do; only, she kept wondering, with a slight pain, whether he would want her to—he was so young, dreamful, ambitious, much younger and more dreamful than herself, although, in reality, he was several years older.

And then followed that glorious period from December to this late September, in which everything which was worth happening in love had happened. Oh, those wondrous days the following spring, when, with the first burst of buds and leaves, he had taken her one Sunday to Atholby, where all the great woods were, and they had hunted spring beauties in the grass, and sat on a slope and looked at the river below and watched some boys fixing up a sailboat and setting forth in it quite as she wished she and Arthur might be doing—going somewhere together—far, far away from all commonplace things and life! And then he had slipped his arm about her and kissed her cheek and neck, and tweaked her ear and smoothed her hair—and oh, there on the grass, with the spring flowers about her and a canopy of small green leaves above, the perfection of love had come—love so wonderful that the mere thought of it made her eyes brim now! And then had been days, Saturday afternoons and Sundays, at Atholby and Sparrows Point, where the great beach was, and in lovely Tregore Park, a mile or two from her home, where they could go of an evening and sit in or near the pavilion and have ice-cream and dance or watch the dancers. Oh, the stars, the winds, the summer breath of those days! Ah, me! Ah, me!

Naturally, her parents had wondered from the first about her and Arthur, and her and Barton, since Barton had already assumed a proprietary interest in her and she had seemed to like him. But then she was an only child and a pet, and used to presuming on that, and they could not think of saying anything to her. After all, she was young and pretty and was entitled to change her mind; only, only—she had had to indulge in a career of lying and subterfuge in connection with Barton, since Arthur was headstrong and wanted every evening that he chose—to call for her at the store and keep her down-town to dinner and a show.

Arthur had never been like Barton, shy, phlegmatic, obedient, waiting long and patiently for each little favor, but, instead, masterful and eager, rifling her of kisses and caresses and every delight of love, and teasing and playing with her as a cat would a mouse. She could never resist him. He demanded of her her time and her affection without let or hindrance. He was not exactly selfish or cruel, as some might have been, but gay and unthinking at times, unconsciously so, and yet loving and tender at others—nearly always so. But always he would talk of things in the future as if they really did not include her—and this troubled her greatly— of places he might go, things he might do, which, somehow, he seemed to think or assume that she could not or would not do with him. He was always going to Australia sometime, he thought, in a business way, or to South Africa, or possibly to India. He never seemed to have any fixed clear future for himself in mind.

A dreadful sense of helplessness and of impending disaster came over her at these times, of being involved in some predicament over which she had no control, and which would lead her on to some sad end. Arthur, although plainly in love, as she thought, and apparently delighted with her, might not always love her. She began, timidly at first (and always, for that matter), to ask him pretty, seeking questions about himself and her, whether their future was certain to be together, whether he really wanted her—loved her—whether he might not want to marry some one else or just her, and whether she wouldn't look nice in a pearl satin wedding-dress with a long creamy veil and satin slippers and a bouquet of bridal-wreath. She had been so slowly but surely saving to that end, even before he came, in connection with Barton; only, after *he* came, all thought of the import of it had been transferred to him. But now, also, she was beginning to ask herself sadly, "Would it ever be?" He was so airy, so inconsequential, so ready to say: "Yes, yes," and "Sure, sure! That's right! Yes, indeedy; you bet! Say, kiddie, but you'll look sweet!" but, somehow, it had always seemed as if this whole thing were a glorious interlude and that it could not last. Arthur was too gay and ethereal and too little settled in his own mind. His ideas of travel and living in different cities, finally winding up in New York or San Francisco, but never with her exactly until she asked him, was too ominous, although he always reassured her gaily: "Of course! Of course!" But somehow she could never believe it really, and it made her intensely sad at times, horribly gloomy. So often she wanted to cry, and she could scarcely tell why.

And then, because of her intense affection for him, she had finally quarreled with Barton, or nearly that, if one could say that one ever really quarreled with him. It had been because of a certain Thursday evening a few weeks before about which she had disappointed him. In a fit of generosity, knowing that Arthur was coming Wednesday, and because Barton had stopped in at the store to see her, she had told him that he might come, having regretted it afterward, so enamored was she of Arthur. And then when Wednesday came, Arthur had changed his mind, telling her he would come Friday instead, but on Thursday evening he had stopped in at the store and asked her to go to Sparrows Point, with the result that she had no time to notify Barton. He had gone to the house and sat with her parents until ten-thirty, and then, a few days later, although she had written him offering an excuse, had called at the store to complain slightly.

"Do you think you did just right, Shirley? You might have sent word, mightn't you? Who was it—the new fellow you won't tell me about?"

Shirley flared on the instant.

"Supposing it was? What's it to you? I don't belong to you yet, do I? I told you there wasn't any one, and I wish you'd let me alone about that. I couldn't help it last Thursday—that's all—and I don't want you to be fussing with me—that's all. If you don't want to, you needn't come any more, anyhow."

"Don't say that, Shirley," pleaded Barton. "You don't mean that. I won't bother you, though, if you don't want me any more."

And because Shirley sulked, not knowing what else to do, he had gone and she had not seen him since.

And then sometime later when she had thus broken with Barton, avoiding the railway station where he worked, Arthur had failed to come at his appointed time, sending no word until the next day, when a note came to the store saying that he had been out of town for his firm over Sunday and had not been able to notify her, but that he would call Tuesday. It was an awful blow. At the time, Shirley had a vision of what was to follow. It seemed for the moment as if the whole world had suddenly been reduced to ashes, that there was nothing but black charred cinders anywhere—she felt that about all life. Yet it all came to her clearly then that this was but the beginning of just such days and just such excuses, and that soon, soon, he would come no more. He was beginning to be tired of her and soon he would not even make excuses. She felt it, and it froze and terrified her.

And then, soon after, the indifference which she feared did follow—almost created by her own thoughts, as it were. First, it was a meeting he had to attend somewhere one Wednesday night when he was to have come for her. Then he was going out of town again, over Sunday. Then he was going away for a whole week—it was absolutely unavoidable, he said, his commercial duties were increasing—and once he had casually remarked that nothing could stand in the way where she was concerned—never! She did not think of reproaching him with this; she was too proud. If he was going, he must go. She would not be willing to say to herself that she had ever attempted to hold any man. But, just the same, she was agonized by the thought. When he was with her, he seemed tender enough; only, at times, his eyes wandered and he seemed slightly bored. Other girls, particularly pretty ones, seemed to interest him as much as she did.

And the agony of the long days when he did not come any more for a week or two at a time! The waiting, the brooding, the wondering, at the store and here in her home—in the former place making mistakes at times because she could not get her mind off him and being reminded of them, and here at her own home at nights, being so absent-minded that her parents remarked on it. She felt sure that her parents must be noticing that Arthur was not coming any more, or as much as he had—for she pretended to be going out with him, going to Mabel Gove's instead—and that Barton had deserted her too, he having been driven off by her indifference, never to come any more, perhaps, unless she sought him out.

And then it was that the thought of saving her own face by taking up with Barton once more occurred to her, of using him and his affections and faithfulness and dulness, if you will, to cover up her own dilemma. Only, this ruse was not to be tried until she had written Arthur this one letter—a pretext merely to see if there was a single ray of hope, a letter to be written in a gentle-enough way and asking for the return of the few notes she had written him. She had not seen him now in nearly a month, and the last time she had, he had said he might soon be compelled to leave her awhile—to go to Pittsburgh to work. And it was his reply to this that she now held in her hand—from Pittsburgh! It was frightful! The future without him!

But Barton would never know really what had transpired, if she went back to him. In spite of all her delicious hours with Arthur, she could call him back, she felt sure. She had never really entirely dropped him, and he knew it. He had bored her dreadfully on occasion, arriving on off days when Arthur was not about, with flowers or candy, or both, and sitting on the porch steps and talking of the railroad business and of the whereabouts and doings of some of their old friends. It was shameful, she had thought at times, to see a man so patient, so hopeful, so good-natured as Barton, deceived in this way, and by her, who was so miserable over another. Her parents must see and know, she had thought at these times, but still, what else was she to do?

"I'm a bad girl," she kept telling herself. "I'm all wrong. What right have I to offer Barton what is left?" But still, somehow, she realized that Barton, if she chose to favor him, would only to be too grateful for even the leavings of others where she was concerned, and that even yet, if she but deigned to crook a finger, she could have him. He was so simple, so good-natured, so stolid and matter of fact, so different to Arthur whom (she could not help smiling at the thought of it) she was loving now about as Barton loved her—slavishly, hopelessly.

And then, as the days passed and Arthur did not write any more—just this one brief note—she at first grieved horribly, and then in a fit of numb despair attempted, bravely enough from one point of view, to adjust herself to the new situation. Why should she despair? Why die of agony where there were plenty who would still sigh for her—Barton among others? She was young, pretty, very—many told her so. She could, if she chose, achieve a vivacity which she did not feel. Why should she brook this unkindness without a thought of retaliation? Why shouldn't she enter upon a gay and heartless career, indulging in a dozen flirtations at once—dancing and killing all thoughts of Arthur in a round of frivolities? There were many who beckoned to her. She stood at her counter in the drug store on many a day and brooded over this, but at the thought of which one to begin with, she faltered. After her late love, all were so tame, for the present anyhow.

And then—and then—always there was Barton, the humble or faithful, to whom she had been so unkind and whom she had used and whom she still really liked. So often self-reproaching thoughts in connection with him crept over her. He must have known, must have seen how badly she was using him all this while, and yet he had not failed to come and come, until she had actually quarreled with him, and any one would have seen that it was literally hopeless. She could not help remembering, especially now in her pain, that he adored her. He was not calling on her now at all—by her indifference she had finally driven him away— but a word, a word— She waited for days, weeks, hoping against hope, and then————

The office of Barton's superior in the Great Eastern terminal had always made him an easy object for her blandishments, coming and going, as she frequently did, via this very station. He was in the office of the assistant train-despatcher on the ground floor, where passing to and from the local, which, at times, was quicker than a street-car, she could easily see him by peering in; only, she had carefully avoided him for nearly a year. If she chose now, and would call for a message-blank at the adjacent telegraph-window which was a part of his room, and raised her voice as she often had in the past, he could scarcely fail to hear, if he did not see her. And if he did, he would rise and come over—of that she was sure, for he never could resist her. It had been a wile of hers in the old days to do this or to make her presence felt by idling outside. After a month of brooding, she felt that she must act—her position as a deserted girl was too much. She could not stand it any longer really—the eyes of her mother, for one.

It was six-fifteen one evening when, coming out ot the store in which she worked, she turned her step disconsolately homeward. Her heart was heavy, her face rather pale and drawn. She had stopped in the store's retiring-room before coming out to add to her charms as much as possible by a little powder and rouge and to smooth her hair. It would not take much to reallure her former sweetheart, she felt sure—and yet it might not be so easy after all. Suppose he had found another? But she could not believe that. It had scarcely been long enough since he had last attempted to see her, and he was really so very, very fond of her and so faithful. He was too slow and certain in his choosing—he had been so with her. Still, who knows? With this thought, she went forward in the evening, feeling for the first time the shame and pain that comes of deception, the agony of having to relinquish an ideal and the feeling of despair that comes to those who find themselves in the position of suppliants, stooping to something which in better days and better fortune they would not know. Arthur was the cause of this.

When she reached the station, the crowd that usually filled it at this hour was swarming. There were so many pairs like Arthur and herself laughing and hurrying away or so she felt. First glancing in the small mirror of a weighing scale to see if she were still of her former charm, she stopped thoughtfully at a little flower stand which stood outside, and for a few pennies purchased a tiny bunch of violets. She then went inside and stood near the window, peering first furtively to see if he were present. He was. Bent over his work, a green shade over his eyes, she could see his stolid, genial figure at a table. Stepping back a moment to ponder, she finally went forward and, in a clear voice, asked,

"May I have a blank,[2] please?"

The infatuation of the discarded Barton was such that it brought him instantly to his feet. In his stodgy, stocky way he rose, his eyes glowing with a friendly hope, his mouth wreathed in smiles, and came over. At the sight of her, pale, but pretty—paler and prettier, really, than he had ever seen her—he thrilled dumbly.

"How are you, Shirley?" he asked sweetly, as he drew near, his eyes searching her face hopefully. He had not seen her for so long that he was intensely hungry, and her paler beauty appealed to him more than ever. Why wouldn't she have him? he was asking himself. Why wouldn't his persistent love yet win her? Perhaps it might. "I haven't seen you in a month of Sundays, it seems. How are the folks?"

"They're all right, Bart," she smiled archly, "and so am I. How have you been? It has been a long time since I've seen you. I've been wondering how you were. Have you been all right? I was just going to send a message."

[2] A blank form on which to write the message for a telegram.

As he had approached, Shirley had pretended at first not to see him, a moment later to affect surprise, although she was really suppressing a heavy sigh. The sight of him, after Arthur, was not reassuring. Could she really interest herself in him any more? Could she?

"Sure, sure," he replied genially; "I'm always all right. You couldn't kill me, you know. Not going away, are you, Shirl?" he queried interestedly.

"No; I'm just telegraphing to Mabel. She promised to meet me to-morrow, and I want to be sure she will."

"You don't come past here as often as you did, Shirley," he complained tenderly. "At least, I don't seem to see you so often," he added with a smile. "It isn't anything I have done, is it?" he queried, and then, when she protested quickly, added: "What's the trouble, Shirl? Haven't been sick, have you?"

She affected all her old gaiety and ease, feeling as though she would like to cry.

"Oh, no," she returned; "I've been all right. I've been going through the other door, I suppose, or coming in and going out on the Langdon Avenue car." (This was true, because she had been wanting to avoid him.) "I've been in such a hurry, most nights, that I haven't had time to stop, Bart. You know how late the store keeps us at times."

He remembered, too, that in the old days she had made time to stop or meet him occasionally.

"Yes, I know," he said tactfully. "But you haven't been to any of our old card-parties either of late, have you? At least, I haven't seen you. I've gone to two or three, thinking you might be there."

That was another thing Arthur had done—broken up her interest in these old store and neighborhood parties and a banjo-and-mandolin club to which she had once belonged. They had all seemed so pleasing and amusing in the old days—but now—* * * * In those days Bart had been her usual companion when his work permitted.

"No," she replied evasively, but with a forced air of pleasant remembrance; "I have often thought of how much fun we had at those, though. It was a shame to drop them. You haven't seen Harry Stull or Trina Task recently, have you?" she inquired, more to be saying something than for any interest she felt.

He shook his head negatively, then added:

"Yes, I did, too; here in the waiting-room a few nights ago. They were coming down-town to a theater, I suppose."

His face fell slightly as he recalled how it had been their custom to do this, and what their one quarrel had been about. Shirley noticed it. She felt the least bit sorry for him, but much more for herself, coming back so disconsolately to all this.

"Well, you're looking as pretty as ever, Shirley," he continued, noting that she had not written the telegram and that there was something wistful in her glance. "Prettier, I think," and she smiled sadly. Every word that she tolerated from him was as so much gold to him, so much of dead ashes to her. "You wouldn't like to come down some evening this week and see 'The Mouse-Trap,' would you? We haven't been to a theater together in I don't know when." His eyes sought hers in a hopeful, doglike way.

So—she could have him again—that was the pity of it! To have what she really did not want, did not care for! At the least nod now he would come, and this very devotion made it all but worthless, and so sad. She ought to marry him now for certain, if she began in this way, and could in a month's time if she chose, but oh, oh—could she? For the moment she decided that she could not, would not. If he had only repulsed her—told her to go—ignored her—but no; it was her fate to be loved by him in this moving, pleading way, and hers not to love him as she wished to love—to be loved. Plainly, he needed some one like her, whereas she, she——. She turned a little sick, a sense of the sacrilege of gaiety at this time creeping into her voice, and exclaimed:

"No, no!" Then seeing his face change, a heavy sadness come over it, "Not this week, anyhow, I mean" ("Not so soon," she had almost said). "I have several engagements this week and I'm not feeling well. But"—seeing his face change, and the thought of her own state returning—"you might come out to the house some evening instead, and then we can go some other time."

His face brightened intensely. It was wonderful how he longed to be with her, how the least favor from her comforted and lifted him up. She could see also now, however, how little it meant to her, how little it could ever mean, even if to him it was heaven. The old relationship would have to be resumed in toto, once and for all, but did she want it that way now that she was feeling so miserable about this other affair? As she meditated, these various moods racing to and fro in her mind, Barton seemed to notice, and now it occurred to him that perhaps he had not pursued her enough—was too easily put off. She probably did like him yet. This evening, her present visit, seemed to prove it.

"Sure, sure!" he agreed. "I'd like that. I'll come out Sunday, if you say. We can go any time to the play. I'm sorry, Shirley, if you're not feeling well. I've thought of you a lot these days. I'll come out Wednesday, if you don't mind."

She smiled a wan smile. It was all so much easier than she had expected—her triumph—and so ashenlike in consequence, a flavor of dead-sea fruit and defeat about it all, that it was pathetic. How could she, after Arthur? How could he, really?

"Make it Sunday," she pleaded, naming the farthest day off, and then hurried out.

Her faithful lover gazed after her, while she suffered an intense nausea. To think—to think—it should all be coming to this! She had not used her telegraph-blank, and now had forgotten all about it. It was not the simple trickery that discouraged her, but her own future which could find no better outlet than this, could not rise above it apparently, or that she had no heart to make it rise above it. Why couldn't she interest herself in some one different to Barton? Why did she have to return to him? Why not wait and meet some other—ignore him as before? But no, no; nothing mattered now—no one—it might as well be Barton really as any one, and she would at least make him happy and at the same time solve her own problem. She went out into the train-shed and climbed into her train. Slowly, after the usual pushing and jostling of a crowd, it drew out toward Latonia, that suburban region in which her home lay. As she rode, she thought.

"What have I just done? What am I doing?" she kept asking herself as the clacking wheels on the rails fell into a rhythmic dance and the houses of the brown, dry endless city fled past in a maze. "Severing myself decisively from the past—the happy past—for supposing, once I am married, Arthur should return and want me again—suppose! Suppose!"

Below at one place, under a shed, were some market-gardeners disposing of the last remnants of their day's wares—a sickly, dull life, she thought. Here was Rutgers Avenue, with its line of red street-cars, many wagons and tracks and counter-streams of automobiles—how often had she passed it morning and evening in a shuttle-like way, and how often would, unless she got married! And here, now, was the river flowing smoothly between its banks lined with coal-pockets and wharves—away, away to the huge deep sea which she and Arthur had enjoyed so much. Oh, to be in a small boat and drift out, out into the endless, restless, pathless deep! Somehow the sight of this water, to-night and every night, brought back those evenings in the open with Arthur at Sparrows Point, the long line of dancers in Eckert's Pavilion, the woods at Atholby, the park with the dancers in the pavilion—she choked back a sob. Once Arthur had come this way with her on just such an evening as this, pressing her hand and saying how wonderful she was. Oh, Arthur! Arthur! And now Barton was to take his old place again—forever, no doubt. She could not trifle with her life longer in this foolish way, or his. What was the use? But think of it!

Yes, it must be—forever now, she told herself. She must marry. Time would be slipping by and she would become too old. It was her only future—marriage. It was the only future she had ever contemplated really, a home, children, the love of some man whom she could love as she loved Arthur. Ah, what a happy home that would have been for her! But now, now————

But there must be no turning back now, either. There was no other way. If Arthur ever came back—but fear not, he wouldn't! She had risked so much and lost—lost him. Her little venture into true love had been such a failure. Before Arthur had come all had been well enough. Barton, stout and simple and frank and direct, had in some way—how, she could scarcely realize now—offered sufficient of a future. But now, now! He had enough money, she knew, to build a cottage for the two of them. He had told her so. He would do his best always to make her happy, she was sure of that. They could live in about the state her parents were living in—or a little better, not much—and would never want. No doubt there would be children, because he craved them—several of them—and that would take up her time, long years of it—the sad, gray years! But then Arthur, whose children she would have thrilled to bear, would be no more, a mere memory—think of that!—and Barton, the dull, the commonplace, would have achieved his finest dream—and why?

Because love was a failure for her—that was why—and in her life there could be no more true love. She would never love any one again as she had Arthur. It could not be, she was sure of it. He was too fascinating, too wonderful. Always, always, wherever she might be, whoever she might marry, he would be coming back, intruding between her and any possible love, receiving any possible kiss. It would be Arthur she would be loving or kissing. She dabbed at her eyes with a tiny handkerchief, turned her face close to the window and stared out, and then as the environs of Latonia came into view, wondered (so deep is romance): What if Arthur should come back at some time—or now! Supposing he should be here at the station now, accidentally or on purpose, to welcome her, to soothe her weary heart. He had met her here before. How she would fly to him, lay her head on his shoulder, forget forever that Barton ever was, that they had ever separated for an hour. Oh, Arthur! Arthur!

But no, no; here was Latonia—here the viaduct over her train, the long business street and the cars marked "Center" and "Langdon Avenue" running back into the great city. A few blocks away in treeshaded Bethune Street, duller and plainer than ever, was her parents' cottage and the routine of that old life which was now, she felt, more fully fastened upon her than ever before—the lawnmowers, the lawns, the front porches all alike. Now would come the going to and fro of Barton to business as her father and she now went to business, her keeping house, cooking, washing ironing, sewing for Barton as her mother now did these things for her father and herself. And she would not be in love really, as she wanted to be. Oh, dreadful! She could never escape it really, now that she could endure it less, scarcely for another hour. And yet she must, must, for the sake of—for the sake of—she closed her eyes and dreamed.

She walked up the street under the trees, past the houses and lawns all alike to her own, and found her father on their veranda reading the evening paper. She sighed at the sight.

"Back, daughter?" he called pleasantly.

"Yes."

"Your mother is wondering if you would like steak or liver for dinner. Better tell her."

"Oh, it doesn't matter."

She hurried into her bedroom, threw down her hat and gloves, and herself on the bed to rest silently, and groaned in her soul. To think that it had all come to this!—Never to see him any more!—To see only Barton, and marry him and live in such a street, have four or five children, forget all her youthful companionships—and all to save her face before her parents, and her future. Why must it be? Should it be, really? She choked and stifled. After a little time her mother, hearing her come in, came to the door—thin, practical, affectionate, conventional.

"What's wrong, honey? Aren't you feeling well tonight? Have you a headache? Let me feel."

Her thin cool fingers crept over her temples and hair. She suggested something to eat or a headache powder right away.

"I'm all right, mother. I'm just not feeling well now. Don't bother. I'll get up soon. Please don't."

"Would you rather have liver or steak to-night, dear?"

"Oh, anything—nothing—please don't bother—steak will do—anything"—if only she could get rid of her and be at rest!

Her mother looked at her and shook her head sympathetically, then retreated quietly, saying no more. Lying so, she thought and thought—grinding, destroying thoughts about the beauty of the past, the darkness of the future—until able to endure them no longer she got up and, looking distractedly out of the window into the yard and the house next door, stared at her future fixedly. What should she do? What should she really do? There was Mrs. Kessel in her kitchen getting her dinner as usual, just as her own mother was now, and Mr. Kessel out on the front porch in his shirt-sleeves reading the evening paper. Beyond was Mr. Pollard in his yard, cutting the grass. All along Bethune Street were such houses and such people—simple, commonplace souls all—clerks, managers, fairly successful craftsmen, like her father and Barton, excellent in their way but not like Arthur the beloved, the lost—and here was she, perforce, or by decision of necessity, soon to be one of them, in some such street as this no doubt, forever and —. For the moment it choked and stifled her.

She decided that she would not. No, no, no! There must be some other way—many ways. She did not have to do this unless she really wished to—would not—only—. Then going to the mirror she looked at her face and smoothed her hair.

"But what's the use?" she asked of herself wearily and resignedly after a time.

"Why should I cry? Why shouldn't I marry Barton? I don't amount to anything, anyhow. Arthur wouldn't have me. I wanted him, and I am compelled to take some one else—or no one—what difference does it really make who? My dreams are too high, that's all. I wanted Arthur, and he wouldn't have me. I don't want Barton, and he crawls at my feet. I'm a failure, that's what's the matter with me."

And then, turning up her sleeves and removing a fichu[3] which stood out too prominently from her breast, she went into the kitchen and, looking about for an apron, observed:

"Can't I help? Where's the tablecloth?" and finding it among napkins and silverware in a drawer in the adjoining room, proceeded to set the table.

1918

Willa Cather
(1873–1947)

The narrator of *O Pioneers!* (1913) observes that "there are only two or three human stories, and they go on repeating themselves as fiercely as if they had never happened before." Throughout her career, Willa Cather recorded these primary tales of struggle and aspiration, situating them upon various frontiers that evoke a sense of promise and of promise lost. Some of the frontiers required pioneers who were strong in body and spirit (Alexandra Bergson of *O Pioneers!* and Ántonia Shimerda of *My Ántonia* [1918], for example). Others called for trailblazers who channeled their vitality and courage into artistry or worlds of the spirit.

Willela ("Willie") Cather was born near Winchester, Virginia, in 1873. At age nine she moved with her family to Webster County, Nebraska, and later to Red Cloud, Nebraska— much the same trip Jim Burden makes in *My Ántonia*. Like Jim, she befriended many of the immigrants whose trials and perseverance would become an enduring part of her fiction. At the University of Nebraska in the 1890s she studied the classics and published lively reviews of cultural events in the Lincoln newspaper. She moved to Pittsburgh in 1896 to edit *Home Monthly* magazine. In 1905 Cather's first short-story collection, *The Troll Garden,* appeared, with its moving contrasts between the starkness of the prairies and the evocative world of art. Although this period of her life remains mysterious (because she burned most of her letters), her roommate Isabelle McClung seems to have been her closest companion in Pittsburgh. In 1906 Cather moved to New York to work at *McClure's Magazine;* there she met Edith Lewis, who became her lifelong companion until Cather's death in 1947. In Boston soon thereafter, Cather had the good fortune to meet Sarah Orne Jewett, whose advice on writing affected both the content and the style of Cather's work.

Her atypical first novel, *Alexander's Bridge,* was serialized in *McClure's* in 1912.

---

[3] A three-cornered cape.

After that false start (as she saw it), Cather took Jewett's advice to write about what she knew and produced *O Pioneers!* and *The Song of the Lark* (1915). In *My Ántonia* Cather portrays the heroic Ántonia through the eyes of Jim Burden, whose unfulfilling life in the East leads him to recapture the memories of his youth—and to bring them into the present. In this novel, too, Cather dramatizes gender roles more directly than in her previous works. Despite her growing reputation, she became disillusioned with the materialism and lack of value in modern life—as evidenced in her Pulitzer Prize-winning war novel, *One of Ours* (1922), and in a book of essays, *Not Under Forty* (1936), in which she asserts that "the world broke in two in 1922 or thereabouts." After finishing the novel *A Lost Lady* (1923), she began to turn her imagination toward historically remote locales in a search for meaning and order, first, tentatively, in *The Professor's House* (1925), then in the quiet harmony of *Death Comes for the Archbishop* (1927) and the resolute domesticity of *Shadows on the Rock* (1931). The Nebraska prairie had served Cather's early fiction well: in these later narratives her lifelong reverence for the Southwest and an interest in seventeenth-century Quebec took her again to primary human stories of struggle and achievement.

Suggested Readings: *The Novels and Stories of Willa Cather,* 13 vols., 1937–1941. *On Writing: Critical Studies on Writing as Art,* 1949. *The Kingdom of Art: Willa Cather's First Principles and Critical Statements, 1893–1896,* ed. B. Slote, 1966. *April Twilights: Poems by Willa Cather,* 1976. E. K. Brown and L. Edel, *Willa Cather: A Critical Biography,* 1953. E. S. Sergeant, *Willa Cather, A Memoir,* 1963. P. C. Robinson, *Willa, The Life of Willa Cather,* 1983. S. O'Brien, *Willa Cather: The Emerging Voice,* 1987. J. Woodress, *Willa Cather: A Literary Life,* 1987. H. Lee, *Willa Cather: Double Lives,* 1990.

Texts Used: "Peter": *Willa Cather's Collected Short Fiction,* ed. V. Faulkner, 1970. "A Wagner Matinee": *Youth and the Bright Medusa,* 1937. *My Ántonia,* 1918.

An early 1900s photograph of Red Cloud, Nebraska, the pioneer town in which Willa Cather was raised—and the source of some of her best fiction.

PETER*

"No, Antone, I have told thee many times, no, thou shalt not sell it until I am gone."

"But I need money; what good is that old fiddle to thee? The very crows laugh at thee when thou art trying to play. Thy hand trembles so thou canst scarce hold the bow. Thou shalt go with me to the Blue to cut wood tomorrow. See to it thou art up early."

"What, on the Sabbath, Antone, when it is so cold? I get so very cold, my son, let us not go tomorrow."

"Yes, tomorrow, thou lazy old man. Do not I cut wood upon the Sabbath? Care I how cold it is? Wood thou shalt cut, and haul it too, and as for the fiddle, I tell thee I will sell it yet." Antone pulled his ragged cap down over his low heavy brow, and went out. The old man drew his stool up nearer the fire, and sat stroking his violin with trembling fingers and muttering. "Not while I live, not while I live."

Five years ago they had come here, Peter Sadelack, and his wife, and oldest son Antone, and countless smaller Sadelacks, here to the dreariest part of southwestern Nebraska, and had taken up a homestead. Antone was the acknowledged master of the premises, and people said he was a likely youth, and would do well. That he was mean and untrustworthy every one knew, but that made little difference. His corn was better tended than any in the county, and his wheat always yielded more than other men's.

Of Peter no one knew much, nor had any one a good word to say for him. He drank whenever he could get out of Antone's sight long enough to pawn his hat or coat for whisky. Indeed there were but two things he would not pawn, his pipe and his violin. He was a lazy, absent-minded old fellow, who liked to fiddle better than to plow, though Antone surely got work enough out of them all, for that matter. In the house of which Antone was master there was no one, from the little boy three years old, to the old man of sixty, who did not earn his bread. Still people said that Peter was worthless, and was a great drag on Antone, his son, who never drank, and was a much better man than his father had ever been. Peter did not care what people said. He did not like the country, nor the people, least of all he liked the plowing. He was very homesick for Bohemia. Long ago, only eight years ago by the calendar, but it seemed eight centuries to Peter, he had been a second violinist in the great theatre at Prague. He had gone into the theatre very young, and had been there all his life, until he had a stroke of paralysis, which made his arm so weak that his bowing was uncertain. Then they told him he could go. Those were great days at the theatre. He had plenty to drink then, and wore a dress coat every evening, and there were always parties after the play. He could play in those days, ay, that he could! He could never read the notes well, so he did not play first; but his touch, he had a touch indeed, so Herr Mikilsdoff, who led the orchestra, had said. Sometimes now Peter thought he could plow better if he could only bow as he used to. He had seen all the lovely women in the world

---

* Cather's first story, published in *The Mahogany Tree*, May 21, 1892. Both in outline and in many of its details, it anticipates the suicide of Mr. Shimerda in *My Ántonia* (1918).

there, all the great singers and the great players. He was in the orchestra when Rachel played, and he heard Liszt[1] play when the Countess d'Agoult sat in the stage box and threw the master white lilies. Once, a French woman came and played for weeks, he did not remember her name now.[2] He did not remember her face very well either, for it changed so, it was never twice the same. But the beauty of it, and the great hunger men felt at the sight of it, that he remembered. Most of all he remembered her voice. He did not know French, and could not understand a word she said, but it seemed to him that she must be talking the music of Chopin.[3] And her voice, he thought he should know that in the other world. The last night she played a play[4] in which a man touched her arm, and she stabbed him. As Peter sat among the smoking gas jets down below the footlights with his fiddle on his knee, and looked up at her, he thought he would like to die too, if he could touch her arm once, and have her stab him so. Peter went home to his wife very drunk that night. Even in those days he was a foolish fellow, who cared for nothing but music and pretty faces.

It was all different now. He had nothing to drink and little to eat, and here, there was nothing but sun, and grass, and sky. He had forgotten almost everything, but some things he remembered well enough. He loved his violin and the holy Mary, and above all else he feared the Evil One, and his son Antone.

The fire was low, and it grew cold. Still Peter sat by the fire remembering. He dared not throw more cobs on the fire; Antone would be angry. He did not want to cut wood tomorrow, it would be Sunday, and he wanted to go to mass. Antone might let him do that. He held his violin under his wrinkled chin, his white hair fell over it, and he began to play "Ave Maria." His hand shook more than ever before, and at last refused to work the bow at all. He sat stupefied for a while, then arose, and taking his violin with him, stole out into the old sod stable. He took Antone's shotgun down from its peg, and loaded it by the moonlight which streamed in through the door. He sat down on the dirt floor, and leaned back against the dirt wall. He heard the wolves howling in the distance, and the night wind screaming as it swept over the snow. Near him he heard the regular breathing of the horses in the dark. He put his crucifix above his heart, and folding his hands said brokenly all the Latin he had ever known, *"Pater noster, qui in coelum est."*[5] Then he raised his head and sighed, "Not one kreutzer[6] will Antone pay them to pray for my soul, not one kreutzer, he is so careful of his money, is Antone, he does not waste it in drink, he is a better man than I, but hard sometimes. He works the girls too hard, women were not made to work so. But he shall not sell thee, my fiddle, I can play thee no more, but they shall not part us. We have seen it all together, and we will forget it together, the French woman and all." He held his fiddle under his chin a moment, where it had lain so often, then put it across his knee and broke it through the middle. He pulled off his old boot,

<hr />

[1] Franz Liszt (1811–1886), a Hungarian pianist and composer whose virtuosity was acclaimed throughout Europe in the nineteenth century. Marie de Flavigny (1805–1876), Comtesse d'Agoult, was Liszt's mistress and the mother of his three children.

[2] Probably the French actress Sarah Bernhardt (1844–1923).

[3] The Polish composer Frederick Chopin (1810–1849), known for his mastery of romantic music.

[4] The romantic tragedy *Tosca* (1887), by Victorien Sardou (1831–1908).

[5] "Our father, who art in heaven" (Latin): the opening words of the Lord's Prayer.

[6] A coin of little value, formerly used in Austria.

held the gun between his knees with the muzzle against his forehead, and pressed the trigger with his toe.

In the morning Antone found him stiff, frozen fast in a pool of blood. They could not straighten him out enough to fit a coffin, so they buried him in a pine box. Before the funeral Antone carried to town the fiddle-bow which Peter had forgotten to break. Antone was very thrifty, and a better man than his father had been.

1892

A WAGNER MATINÉE*

I received one morning a letter, written in pale ink on glassy, blue-lined note-paper, and bearing the postmark of a little Nebraska town. This communication, worn and rubbed, looking as if it had been carried for some days in a coat pocket that was none too clean, was from my Uncle Howard, and informed me that his wife had been left a small legacy by a bachelor relative, and that it would be necessary for her to go to Boston to attend to the settling of the estate. He requested me to meet her at the station and render her whatever services might be necessary. On examining the date indicated as that of her arrival, I found it to be no later than to-morrow. He had characteristically delayed writing until, had I been away from home for a day, I must have missed my aunt altogether.

The name of my Aunt Georgiana opened before me a gulf of recollection so wide and deep that, as the letter dropped from my hand, I felt suddenly a stranger to all the present conditions of my existence, wholly ill at ease and out of place amid the familiar surroundings of my study. I became, in short, the gangling farmer-boy my aunt had known, scourged with chilblains[1] and bashfulness, my hands cracked and sore from the corn-husking. I sat again before her parlour organ, fumbling the scales with my stiff, red fingers, while she, beside me, made canvas mittens for the huskers.

The next morning, after preparing my landlady for a visitor, I set out for the station. When the train arrived, I had some difficulty in finding my aunt. She was the last of the passengers to alight, and it was not until I got her into the carriage that she seemed really to recognize me. She had come all the way in a day coach; her linen duster had become black with soot and her black bonnet grey with dust during the journey. When we arrived at my boarding-house, the landlady put her to bed at once and I did not see her again until the next morning.

Whatever shock Mrs. Springer experienced at my aunt's appearance, she considerately concealed. As for myself, I saw my aunt's battered figure with that feeling of awe and respect with which we behold explorers who have left their ears

---

* First published in *Everybody's Magazine* in 1904, revised, and collected in *The Troll Garden* in 1905. This version, from *Youth and the Bright Medusa* (1937), incorporates additional revisions made by Cather. The title refers to Richard Wagner (1813–1883), a renowned German composer of operas.

[1] Sores or swellings caused by exposure to cold.

and fingers north of Franz-Josef Land,[2] or their health somewhere along the Upper Congo.

My Aunt Georgiana had been a music-teacher at the Boston Conservatory, somewhere back in the late sixties. One summer, while visiting in the little village among the Green Mountains where her ancestors had dwelt for generations, she had kindled the callow fancy of my uncle, Howard Carpenter, then an idle, shiftless boy of twenty-one. When she returned to her duties in Boston, Howard followed her, and the upshot of this infatuation was that she eloped with him, eluding the reproaches of her family and the criticism of her friends by going with him to the Nebraska frontier. Carpenter, who, of course, had no money, took up a homestead in Red Willow County, fifty miles from the railroad. There they had measured off their land themselves, driving across the prairie in a wagon, to the wheel of which they had tied a red cotton handkerchief, and counting its revolutions. They built a dugout in the red hillside, one of those cave dwellings whose immates so often reverted to primitive conditions. Their water they got from the lagoons where the buffalo drank, and their slender stock of provisions was always at the mercy of bands of roving Indians. For thirty years my aunt had not been farther than fifty miles from the homestead.

I owed to this woman most of the good that ever came my way in my boyhood, and had a reverential affection for her. During the years when I was riding herd for my uncle, my aunt, after cooking the three meals—the first of which was ready at six o'clock in the morning—and putting the six children to bed, would often stand until midnight at her ironing-board, with me at the kitchen table beside her, hearing me recite Latin declensions and conjugations, gently shaking me when my drowsy head sank down over a page of irregular verbs. It was to her, at her ironing or mending, that I read my first Shakespeare, and her old textbook on mythology was the first that ever came into my empty hands. She taught me my scales and exercises on the little parlour organ which her husband had bought her after fifteen years during which she had not so much as seen a musical instrument. She would sit beside me by the hour, darning and counting, while I struggled with the "Joyous Farmer." She seldom talked to me about music, and I understood why. Once when I had been doggedly beating out some easy passages from an old score of "Euryanthe"[3] I had found among her music-books, she came up to me and, putting her hands over my eyes, gently drew my head back upon her shoulder, saying tremulously, "Don't love it so well, Clark, or it may be taken from you."

When my aunt appeared on the morning after her arrival in Boston, she was still in a semi-somnambulant state. She seemed not to realize that she was in the city where she had spent her youth, the place longed for hungrily half a lifetime. She had been so wretchedly train-sick throughout the journey that she had no recollection of anything but her discomfort, and, to all intents and purposes, there were but a few hours of nightmare between the farm in Red Willow County and my study on Newbury Street. I had planned a little pleasure for her that afternoon, to repay her for some of the glorious moments she had given me when we used to milk together in the straw-thatched cow-shed and she, because I was more than

---

[2] An archipelago in the Arctic Ocean that was annexed by Soviet Russia in 1928.
[3] An opera by Carl Maria von Weber (1786–1826) first performed in Vienna in 1823.

usually tired, or because her husband had spoken sharply to me, would tell me of the splendid performance of the "Huguenots"[4] she had seen in Paris, in her youth.

At two o'clock the Symphony Orchestra was to give a Wagner program, and I intended to take my aunt; though, as I conversed with her, I grew doubtful about her enjoyment of it. I suggested our visiting the Conservatory and the Common before lunch, but she seemed altogether too timid to wish to venture out. She questioned me absently about various changes in the city, but she was chiefly concerned that she had forgotten to leave instructions about feeding half-skimmed milk to a certain weakling calf, "old Maggie's calf, you know, Clark," she explained, evidently having forgotten how long I had been away. She was further troubled because she had neglected to tell her daughter about the freshly opened kit of mackerel in the cellar, which would spoil if it were not used directly.

I asked her whether she had ever heard any of the Wagnerian operas, and found that she had not, though she was perfectly familiar with their respective situations, and had once possessed the piano score of "The Flying Dutchman."[5] I began to think it would be best to get her back to Red Willow County without waking her, and regretted having suggested the concert.

From the time we entered the concert hall, however, she was a trifle less passive and inert, and for the first time seemed to perceive her surroundings. I had felt some trepidation lest she might become aware of her queer, country clothes, or might experience some painful embarrassment at stepping suddenly into the world to which she had been dead for more than a quarter of a century. But, again, I found how superficially I had judged her. She sat looking about her with eyes as impersonal, almost as stony, as those with which the granite Rameses[6] in a museum watches the froth and fret that ebbs and flows about his pedestal. I have seen this same aloofness in old miners who drift into the Brown Palace Hotel at Denver, their pockets full of bullion, their linen soiled, their haggard faces unshaven; standing in the thronged corridors as solitary as though they were still in a frozen camp on the Yukon.

The matinée audience was made up chiefly of women. One lost the contour of faces and figures, indeed any effect of line whatever, and there was only the colour of bodices past counting, the shimmer of fabrics soft and firm, silky and sheer; red, mauve, pink, blue, lilac, purple, écru, rose, yellow, cream, and white, all the colours that an impressionist finds in a sunlit landscape, with here and there the dead shadow of a frock coat. My Aunt Georgiana regarded them as though they had been so many daubs of tube-paint on a palette.

When the musicians came out and took their places, she gave a little stir of anticipation, and looked with quickening interest down over the rail at that invariable grouping, perhaps the first wholly familiar thing that had greeted her eye since she had left old Maggie and her weakling calf. I could feel how all those details sank into her soul, for I had not forgotten how they had sunk into mine when I came fresh from ploughing forever and forever between green aisles of corn, where, as in a treadmill, one might walk from daybreak to dusk without perceiving a shadow of change. The clean profiles of the musicians, the gloss of their linen, the dull black of their coats, the beloved shapes of the instruments, the

---

[4] An opera by Giacomo Meyerbeer (1791–1864) first performed in Paris in 1836.
[5] A Wagner opera completed in 1841 and first performed in Dresden in 1843.
[6] A statue of one of several Egyptian kings, or pharaohs.

patches of yellow light on the smooth, varnished bellies of the 'cellos and the bass viols in the rear, the restless, wind-tossed forest of fiddle necks and bows—I recalled how, in the first orchestra I ever heard, those long bow-strokes seemed to draw the heart out of me, as a conjurer's stick reels out yards of paper ribbon from a hat.

The first number was the "Tannhäuser"[7] overture. When the horns drew out the first strain of the Pilgrims' Chorus, Aunt Georgiana clutched my coat-sleeve. Then it was I first realized that for her this broke a silence of thirty years. I saw again the tall, naked house on the prairie, black and grim as a wooden fortress; the black pond where I had learned to swim, its margin pitted with sun-dried cattle tracks; the rain-gullied clay banks about the naked house, the four dwarf ash seedlings where the dish-cloths were always hung to dry before the kitchen door. The world there was the flat world of the ancients; to the east, a cornfield that stretched to daybreak; to the west, a corral that reached to sunset; between, the conquests of peace, dearer-bought than those of war.

The overture closed, my aunt released my coat-sleeve, but she said nothing. She sat quietly looking at the orchestra. What, I wondered, did she get from it? She had been a good pianist in her day, I knew, and her musical education had been broader than that of most music-teachers of a quarter of a century ago. She had often told me of Mozart's operas and Meyerbeer's, and I could remember hearing her sing, years ago, certain melodies of Verdi.[8] When I had fallen ill with a fever in her house, she used to sit by my cot in the evening—when the cool night wind blew in through the faded mosquito netting tacked over the window and I lay watching a certain bright star that burned red above the cornfield—and sing "Home to our mountains, O, let us return!" in a way fit to break the heart of a Vermont boy near dead of homesickness already.

I watched her closely through the prelude to "Tristan and Isolde,"[9] trying vainly to conjecture what that seething turmoil of strings and winds might mean to her, but she sat mutely staring at the violin bows that drove obliquely downward, like the streaks of rain in a summer shower. Had this music any message for her? Had she enough left to at all comprehend this power which had kindled the world since she had left it? I was in a fever of curiosity, but Aunt Georgiana preserved her utter immobility throughout the number from "The Flying Dutchman," though her fingers worked mechanically upon her black dress, as if, of themselves, they were recalling the piano score they had once played. Poor hands! They had been stretched and twisted into mere tentacles to hold and lift and knead with; on one of them a thin, worn band that had once been a wedding ring. As I pressed and gently quieted one of those groping hands, I remembered their services for me in other days.

Soon after the tenor began the "Prize Song,"[10] I heard a quick-drawn breath and turned to my aunt. Her eyes were closed, but the tears were glistening on her cheeks, and I think, in a moment more, they were in my eyes as well. It never really died, then—the soul which can suffer so excruciatingly and so intermina-

---

[7] A Wagner opera (first performed in Dresden in 1845) in which the minstrel knight Tannhauser joins a group of pilgrims journeying to Rome.

[8] Wolfgang Amadeus Mozart (1756–1791); Giuseppe Verdi (1813–1901): composers of grand opera.

[9] A Wagner opera first performed in Munich in 1865.

[10] A famous song from Act III of Wagner's *Die Meistersinger* (1867), or *"The Mastersingers"* (German).

bly; it withers to the outward eye only; like that strange moss which can lie on a dusty shelf half a century and yet, if placed in water, grows green again.

During the intermission before the second half, I questioned my aunt and found that the "Prize Song" was not new to her. Some years before there had drifted to the farm in Red Willow County a young German, a tramp cow-puncher, who had sung in the chorus at Bayreuth[11] when he was a boy, along with the other peasant boys and girls. Of a Sunday morning he used to sit on his gingham-sheeted bed in the hands' bedroom which opened off the kitchen, cleaning the leather of his boots and saddle, singing the 'Prize Song,' while my aunt went about her work in the kitchen. She had hovered over him until she had prevailed upon him to join the country church, though his sole fitness for this step, in so far as I could gather, lay in his boyish face and his possession of this divine melody. Shortly afterward, he had gone to town on the Fourth of July, been drunk for several days, lost his money at a faro table, ridden a saddled Texas steer on a bet, and disappeared with a fractured collar-bone. All this my aunt told me huskily, wanderingly, during the intermission.

"Well, we have come to better things than the old "Trovatore"[12] at any rate, Aunt Georgie?" I asked, with a well-meant effort at jocularity.

Her lip quivered and she hastily put her handkerchief up to her mouth. From behind it she murmured, "And you have been hearing this ever since you left me, Clark?" Her question was the gentlest and saddest of reproaches.

The second half of the programme consisted of four numbers from the "Ring"[13] and closed with Siegfried's funeral march. Throughout these I felt that my aunt had drifted quite away from me. From time to time her eyes looked up at the lights, burning softly under their dull glass globes.

The deluge of sound poured on and on; I never knew what she found in the shining current of it; I never knew how far it bore her, or past what happy islands. From the trembling of her face I could well believe that before the last number she had been carried out where the myriad graves are, into the grey, nameless burying grounds of the sea; or into some world of death vaster yet, where, from the beginning of the world, hope has lain down with hope and dream with dream and, renouncing, slept.

The concert was over; the people filed out of the hall chattering and laughing, glad to relax and find the living level again, but my kinswoman made no effort to rise. The harpist slipped the green felt cover over his instrument; the flute-players shook the water from their mouthpieces; the men of the orchestra went out one by one, leaving the stage to the chairs and music-stands, empty as a winter cornfield.

I spoke to my aunt. She turned to me with a sad little smile. "I don't want to go, Clark. I suppose we must."

I understood. For her, just outside the concert hall, lay the black pond with the cattle-tracked bluffs; the tall, unpainted house, with weather-curled boards, naked as a tower; the crook-backed ash seedlings where the dish-cloths hung to dry; the gaunt, moulting turkeys picking up refuse about the kitchen door.

1904

---

[11] A city in Bavaria. The "tramp cow-puncher" from Bayreuth (a wandering Dutchman himself) sings the famous aria from *The Flying Dutchman*.

[12] A Verdi opera first performed in Rome in 1853.

[13] *Der Ring des Nibelungen* ("The Ring of the Nibelungs" [German]), a cycle of four Wagner operas performed individually from 1869 to 1876 and as a complete cycle in Bayreuth in 1876. Siegfried's funeral march is from the third of these operas, *Siegfried*.

from MY ÁNTONIA*

[*The Story of Peter and Pavel*]

One afternoon Ántonia and her father came over to our house to get buttermilk, and lingered, as they usually did, until the sun was low. Just as they were leaving, Russian Peter drove up. Pavel was very bad, he said, and wanted to talk to Mr. Shimerda and his daughter; he had come to fetch them. When Ántonia and her father got into the wagon, I entreated grandmother to let me go with them: I would gladly go without my supper, I would sleep in the Shimerdas' barn and run home in the morning. My plan must have seemed very foolish to her, but she was often large-minded about humoring the desires of other people. She asked Peter to wait a moment, and when she came back from the kitchen she brought a bag of sandwiches and doughnuts for us.

Mr. Shimerda and Peter were on the front seat; Ántonia and I sat in the straw behind and ate our lunch as we bumped along. After the sun sank, a cold wind sprang up and moaned over the prairie. If this turn in the weather had come sooner, I should not have got away. We burrowed down in the straw and curled up close together, watching the angry red die out of the west and the stars begin to shine in the clear, windy sky. Peter kept sighing and groaning. Tony whispered to me that he was afraid Pavel would never get well. We lay still and did not talk. Up there the stars grew magnificently bright. Though we had come from such different parts of the world, in both of us there was some dusky superstition that those shining groups have their influence upon what is and what is not to be. Perhaps Russian Peter, come from farther away than any of us, had brought from his land, too, some such belief.

The little house on the hillside was so much the color of the night that we could not see it as we came up the draw. The ruddy windows guided us—the light from the kitchen stove, for there was no lamp burning.

We entered softly. The man in the wide bed seemed to be asleep. Tony and I sat down on the bench by the wall and leaned our arms on the table in front of us. The firelight flickered on the hewn logs that supported the thatch overhead. Pavel made a rasping sound when he breathed, and he kept moaning. We waited. The wind shook the doors and windows impatiently, then swept on again, singing through the big spaces. Each gust, as it bore down, rattled the panes, and swelled off like the others. They made me think of defeated armies, retreating; or of ghosts who were trying desperately to get in for shelter, and then went moaning on. Presently, in one of those sobbing intervals between the blasts, the coyotes tuned up with their whining howl; one, two, three, then all together—to tell us that winter was coming. This sound brought an answer from the bed,—a long complaining cry,—as if Pavel were having bad dreams or were waking to some old misery. Peter listened, but did not stir. He was sitting on the floor by the kitchen stove. The coyotes broke out again; yap, yap, yap—then the high whine. Pavel called for something and struggled up on his elbow.

---

* Narrated by young Jim Burden, who has come from Virginia to live with his grandparents in Nebraska at the same time Ántonia Shimerda has emigrated with her family from Bohemia. During their early months on the prairie Jim and Ántonia (Tony) go to the house of the Russian emigrants Peter and Pavel and hear the fearful story Pavel gasps out from his sickbed. Ántonia understands enough of the story to relate it to Jim.

"He is scared of the wolves," Ántonia whispered to me. "In his country there are very many, and they eat men and women." We slid closer together along the bench.

I could not take my eyes off the man in the bed. His shirt was hanging open, and his emaciated chest, covered with yellow bristle, rose and fell horribly. He began to cough. Peter shuffled to his feet, caught up the tea-kettle and mixed him some hot water and whiskey. The sharp smell of spirits went through the room.

Pavel snatched the cup and drank, then made Peter give him the bottle and slipped it under his pillow, grinning disagreeably, as if he had outwitted some one. His eyes followed Peter about the room with a contemptuous, unfriendly expression. It seemed to me that he despised him for being so simple and docile.

Presently Pavel began to talk to Mr. Shimerda, scarcely above a whisper. He was telling a long story, and as he went on, Ántonia took my hand under the table and held it tight. She leaned forward and strained her ears to hear him. He grew more and more excited, and kept pointing all around his bed, as if there were things there and he wanted Mr. Shimerda to see them.

"It's wolves, Jimmy," Ántonia whispered. "It's awful, what he says!"

The sick man raged and shook his fist. He seemed to be cursing people who had wronged him. Mr. Shimerda caught him by the shoulders, but could hardly hold him in bed. At last he was shut off by a coughing fit which fairly choked him. He pulled a cloth from under his pillow and held it to his mouth. Quickly it was covered with bright red spots—I thought I had never seen any blood so bright. When he lay down and turned his face to the wall, all the rage had gone out of him. He lay patiently fighting for breath, like a child with croup. Ántonia's father uncovered one of his long bony legs and rubbed it rhythmically. From our bench we could see what a hollow case his body was. His spine and shoulder-blades stood out like the bones under the hide of a dead steer left in the fields. That sharp backbone must have hurt him when he lay on it.

Gradually, relief came to all of us. Whatever it was, the worst was over. Mr. Shimerda signed to us that Pavel was asleep. Without a word Peter got up and lit his lantern. He was going out to get his team to drive us home. Mr. Shimerda went with him. We sat and watched the long bowed back under the blue sheet, scarcely daring to breathe.

On the way home, when we were lying in the straw, under the jolting and rattling Ántonia told me as much of the story as she could. What she did not tell me then, she told later; we talked of nothing else for days afterward.

When Pavel and Peter were young men, living at home in Russia, they were asked to be groomsmen for a friend who was to marry the belle of another village. It was in the dead of winter and the groom's party went over to the wedding in sledges. Peter and Pavel drove in the groom's sledge, and six sledges followed with all his relatives and friends.

After the ceremony at the church, the party went to a dinner given by the parents of the bride. The dinner lasted all afternoon; then it became a supper and continued far into the night. There was much dancing and drinking. At midnight the parents of the bride said good-bye to her and blessed her. The groom took her up in his arms and carried her out to his sledge and tucked her under the blankets. He sprang in beside her, and Pavel and Peter (our Pavel and Peter!) took the front seat. Pavel drove. The party set out with singing and the jingle of sleigh-bells, the groom's sledge going first. All the drivers were more or less the worse for merry-making, and the groom was absorbed in his bride.

The wolves were bad that winter, and every one knew it, yet when they heard the first wolf-cry, the drivers were not much alarmed. They had too much food and drink inside them. The first howls were taken up and echoed and with quickening repetitions. The wolves were coming together. There was no moon, but the starlight was clear on the snow. A black drove came up over the hill behind the wedding party. The wolves ran like streaks of shadow; they looked no bigger than dogs, but there were hundreds of them.

Something happened to the hindmost sledge: the driver lost control,—he was probably very drunk,—the horses left the road, the sledge was caught in a clump of trees, and overturned. The occupants rolled out over the snow, and the fleetest of the wolves sprang upon them. The shrieks that followed made everybody sober. The drivers stood up and lashed their horses. The groom had the best team and his sledge was lightest—all the others carried from six to a dozen people.

Another driver lost control. The screams of the horses were more terrible to hear than the cries of the men and women. Nothing seemed to check the wolves. It was hard to tell what was happening in the rear; the people who were falling behind shrieked as piteously as those who were already lost. The little bride hid her face on the groom's shoulder and sobbed. Pavel sat still and watched his horses. The road was clear and white, and the groom's three blacks went like the wind. It was only necessary to be calm and to guide them carefully.

At length, as they breasted a long hill, Peter rose cautiously and looked back. "There are only three sledges left," he whispered.

"And the wolves?" Pavel asked.

"Enough! Enough for all of us."

Pavel reached the brow of the hill, but only two sledges followed him down the other side. In that moment on the hilltop, they saw behind them a whirling black group on the snow. Presently the groom screamed. He saw his father's sledge overturned, with his mother and sisters. He sprang up as if he meant to jump, but the girl shrieked and held him back. It was even then too late. The black ground-shadows were already crowding over the heap in the road, and one horse ran out across the fields, his harness hanging to him, wolves at his heels. But the groom's movement had given Pavel an idea.

They were within a few miles of their village now. The only sledge left out of six was not very far behind them, and Pavel's middle horse was failing. Beside a frozen pond something happened to the other sledge; Peter saw it plainly. Three big wolves got abreast of the horses, and the horses went crazy. They tried to jump over each other, got tangled up in the harness, and overturned the sledge.

When the shrieking behind them died away, Pavel realized that he was alone upon the familiar road. "They still come?" he asked Peter.

"Yes."

"How many?"

"Twenty, thirty—enough."

Now his middle horse was being almost dragged by the other two. Pavel gave Peter the reins and stepped carefully into the back of the sledge. He called to the groom that they must lighten—and pointed to the bride. The young man cursed him and held her tighter. Pavel tried to drag her away. In the struggle, the groom rose. Pavel knocked him over the side of the sledge and threw the girl after him. He said he never remembered exactly how he did it, or what happened afterward. Peter, crouching in the front seat, saw nothing. The first thing either of them noticed was a new sound that broke into the air, louder than they had ever heard it before—the bell of the monastery of their own village, ringing for early prayers.

Pavel and Peter drove into the village alone, and they had been alone ever since. They were run out of their village. Pavel's own mother would not look at him. They went away to strange towns, but when people learned where they came from, they were always asked if they knew the two men who had fed the bride to the wolves. Wherever they went, the story followed them. It took them five years to save money enough to come to America. They worked in Chicago, Des Moines, Fort Wayne, but they were always unfortunate. When Pavel's health grew so bad, they decided to try farming.

Pavel died a few days after he unburdened his mind to Mr. Shimerda, and was buried in the Norwegian graveyard. Peter sold off everything, and left the country—went to be cook in a railway construction camp where gangs of Russians were employed.

1918

Gertrude Stein
(1874–1946)

Gertrude Stein, one of the twentieth century's most original literary minds, was born in Allegheny, Pennsylvania, in 1874 to prosperous, assimilated German-Jewish immigrants. Her father had followed his father in operating a successful textile and clothing business, enlarging the family fortune through real-estate speculation and other investments. The youngest of seven children, she was a pampered child. From 1875 to 1879 the Steins lived in Vienna and Paris, moving to Oakland, California, in 1880. After both parents had died by 1891, the five remaining children received comfortable inheritances. Gertrude later relied on the freedom this income gave her: able to ignore the pressures of finding a market for her writing, she could pursue her uncompromising experimentations in literary form.

In 1892 Stein accompanied her brother Leo to Harvard University and enrolled in the "Harvard Annex" for women (now Radcliffe). She soon entered the orbit of Harvard's famous psychologist and philosopher William James, whose theories of consciousness as the subjective streams of "concrete particular I's and you's" underlie Stein's early writings. Under James's tutelage she participated in laboratory experiments in automatic writing, publishing the results of her own experiment, "Cultivated Motor Automatism: A Study of Character in Its Relation to Attention," in Harvard's *Psychological Review* in 1898. When Leo began graduate study in biology at Johns Hopkins University in 1897, Gertrude enrolled in the Johns Hopkins School of Medicine, which had only recently begun to admit women students. From then until about 1914 the independent, eccentric sister and brother made a home together.

Stein seemed headed toward an auspicious career as a pioneering female scientist. However, entangled in an unhappy lesbian triangle (which provided the then-unpublishable subject of her first novel, *Q.E.D.* [1950]) and aware of Leo's flagging interest in his studies, Stein neglected her own courses. When her impulsive brother resolved to go to Europe to study painting, she soon followed him to 27 *rue de Fleurus,* the home that she would occupy for many years and make famous as a premier gathering-place for artists and intellectuals of the Parisian and expatriate avant-garde.

Together, Gertrude and Leo set about building a remarkable private collection of modern art. They first bought works by established recent artists, such as Paul Gaugin, Auguste Renoir, and Paul Cézanne. In the process the Steins supported several struggling painters, including Henri Matisse and Pablo Picasso, who in 1906 painted a now-famous portrait of Gertrude Stein and who became a lifelong friend. At this time she was writing the three-part *Three Lives* (1909), which blends subject matter familiar to late nineteenth-century naturalistic fiction—the experiences and sexuality of immigrant and black women—with a literary style formed from her absorption of the psychological and aesthetic principles of William James, Gustave Flaubert, and Cézanne. Despite poor sales, the work (which contains "The Gentle Lena") earned critical success; some readers, including the critics Mabel Dodge and Carl Van Vechten, became dedicated promoters of Stein's work. Soon the *rue de Fleurus* household changed permanently, when Alice B. Toklas moved in as Stein's self-effacing companion, secretary, and lover; their mutual devotion lasted until Stein's death.

Between 1906 and 1908 Stein wrote an enormous, ponderous novel, *The Making of Americans* (not published until 1925), based largely on memories of her family. She pushed her experiments in exposition and narration further in a series of short "word portraits" of friends and relatives. The 1913 New York Armory show introduced the challenging new European art forms to a mainly querulous American public. In an art magazine accompanying the exhibition, an essay by Mabel Dodge on Stein's writings linked Stein's name, in the minds of eager journalists, to the European innovations: her American reputation was made by their parodies and ridicule. Her most radical prose experiment, *Tender Buttons* (1914), a series of asyntactical entries "about" the immediate environment of the household, appeared in the wake of and furthered this publicity. The popular view of Stein was tempered by the enthusiastic reception her work received from established American cultural figures such as Sherwood Anderson and the photographer Alfred Stieglitz.

Meanwhile, Stein had steadily consolidated her position at the center of the Parisian avant-garde: she met and hosted an amazing array of European and American talents. She and Toklas did volunteer relief work during World War I. After Stein's return to Paris in 1918, more visiting writers and artists sought her acquaintance and typically received her advice. She published works in "little" magazines and with small, ephemeral presses but kept a large pile of manuscripts in a cabinet; many of these were published posthumously. Extending her formal experiments to drama, she wrote numerous short plays. In 1926 Stein accepted an invitation to speak at Oxford University; her lecture, "Composition as Explanation," was the first of many public lectures she gave during the 1920s and 1930s.

In 1930 Stein and Toklas decided to publish Stein's works themselves, creating their press, Plain Editions. However, the memoir *The Autobiography of Alice B. Toklas* (1933), written by Stein from Toklas's viewpoint, brought the resolute inventor of intransigent literary experiments into the world of commercial publishing: the book became a bestseller and was serialized in the *Atlantic Monthly*. For the first time Stein earned substantial royalties for her work and was courted by publishers, such as Bennett Cerf, who printed one Stein book per year as long as she provided them. The American popularity of *Toklas*, casual and anecdotal, aroused interest in the modernist opera by Stein and composer Virgil Thomson, *Four Saints in Three Acts*, which premiered in 1934 and caused considerable high-society excitement. Later that year Stein and Toklas began a highly-publicized American tour, discovering firsthand the potential impact of the American publicity machine: lights in New York's Times Square flashed "GERTRUDE STEIN HAS ARRIVED IN NEW YORK." Stein lectured to large audiences across the country; she and Toklas took tea with Eleanor Roosevelt at the White House.

After returning to France in 1935, Stein produced several more books, some in a diffi-

Pablo Picasso's 1906 painting of Gertrude Stein. (The Metropolitan Museum of Art, bequest of Gertrude Stein, 1946)

cult-to-read style, some in a more accessible style. The tour yielded volumes of her lectures, *The Geographical History of America* (1935), and *Everybody's Autobiography* (1937), but none repeated the success of *Toklas*. When France fell to the Germans during World War II, Stein and Toklas moved to the South of France, despite the risk they faced as Jews and, later, as enemy nationals. Stein's account of the occupation of France, *Wars I Have Seen*, was published in 1945. In 1946 she died of cancer. Her obituaries tended to emphasize her celebrity status, forceful personality, and illustrious acquaintances, giving only a decorous, qualified praise to her works. Stein the author has begun to be fully appreciated only since the 1960s. The renewed interest in Stein by writers and critics alike is reflected in the dozens of books about her and her work that have been published in the decades after her death.

Suggested Readings: *Tender Buttons*, 1914. *The Making of Americans*, 1925. *The Autobiography of Alice B. Toklas*, 1933. *Four Saints in Three Acts*, with V. Thomson, 1934. *Lectures in America*, 1935. *Everybody's Autobiography*, 1937. *Yes Is for a Very Young Man*, 1946. *The Yale Edition of the Unpublished Writings of Gertrude Stein*, 8 vols., ed. C. Van Vechten, 1951–1958. *Gertrude Stein: Writings and Lectures, 1909–1945*, ed. P. Meyerowitz, 1967. *Gertrude Stein on Picasso*, ed. E. Burns, 1970. *Dear Sammy: Letters From Gertrude Stein and Alice B. Toklas*. ed. S. M. Steward, 1977. A. B. Toklas, *What Is Remembered*, 1963. R. Bridgman, *Gertrude Stein in Pieces*, 1970. J. R. Mellow, *Charmed Circle: Gertrude Stein and Company*, 1974. W. Steiner, *Exact Resemblance to Exact Resemblance: The Literary Portraiture of Gertrude Stein*, 1978. M. J. Hoffman, ed., *Critical Essays on Gertrude Stein*, 1986. S. Neuman, and I. B. Nadel, eds., *Gertrude Stein and the Making of Literature*, 1988. H. S. Chessman, *The Public Is Invited to the Dance: Representation, the Body, and Dialogue in Gertrude Stein*, 1989.

Texts Used: "The Gentle Lena": *Three Lives*, 1933. *Tender Buttons: Selected Writings of Gertrude Stein*, ed. C. Van Vechten, 1946.

THE GENTLE LENA*

Lena was patient, gentle, sweet and german. She had been a servant for four years and had liked it very well.

Lena had been brought from Germany to Brigepoint by a cousin and had been in the same place there for four years.

This place Lena had found very good. There was a pleasant, unexacting mistress and her children, and they all liked Lena very well.

There was a cook there who scolded Lena a great deal but Lena's german patience held no suffering and the good incessant woman really only scolded so for Lena's good.

Lena's german voice when she knocked and called the family in the morning was as awakening, as soothing, and as appealing, as a delicate soft breeze in midday, summer. She stood in the hallway every morning a long time in her unexpectant and unsuffering german patience calling to the young ones to get up. She would call and wait a long time and then call again, always even, gentle, patient, while the young ones fell back often into that precious, tense, last bit of sleeping that gives a strength of joyous vigor in the young, over them that have come to the readiness of middle age, in their awakening.

Lena had good hard work all morning, and on the pleasant, sunny afternoons she was sent out into the park to sit and watch the little two year old girl baby of the family.

The other girls, all them that make the pleasant, lazy crowd, that watch the children in the sunny afternoons out in the park, all liked the simple, gentle, german Lena very well. They all, too, liked very well to tease her, for it was so easy to make her mixed and troubled, and all helpless, for she could never learn to know just what the other quicker girls meant by the queer things they said.

The two or three of these girls, the ones that Lena always sat with, always worked together to confuse her. Still it was pleasant, all this life for Lena.

The little girl fell down sometimes and cried, and then Lena had to soothe her. When the little girl would drop her hat, Lena had to pick it up and hold it. When the little girl was bad and threw away her playthings, Lena told her she could not have them and took them from her to hold until the little girl should need them.

It was all a peaceful life for Lena, almost as peaceful as a pleasant leisure. The other girls, of course, did tease her, but then that only made a gentle stir within her.

Lena was a brown and pleasant creature, brown as blonde races often have them brown, brown, not with the yellow or the red or the chocolate brown of sun burned countries, but brown with the clear color laid flat on the light toned skin beneath, the plain, spare brown that makes it right to have been made with hazel eyes, and not too abundant straight, brown hair, hair that only later deepens itself into brown from the straw yellow of a german childhood.

---

* The third story of Stein's *Three Lives* (1909), like the first, "The Good Anna," describes the life of a German-born immigrant woman in the fictional American town of Bridgepoint. The long middle story is "Melanctha." Lena was drawn in part from Lena Lebender, the German immigrant housekeeper at the Baltimore home Stein shared with her brother, Leo. Another influence was *Trois Contes* (1877), or "*Three Tales*," by the French novelist Gustave Flaubert (1821–1880), which Stein was then translating into English. When *Three Lives* was first printed, its copy editors, thinking that an author named Stein might not have herself mastered English, offered to correct the "errors" in her prose.

Lena had the flat chest, straight back and forward falling shoulders of the patient and enduring working woman, though her body was now still in its milder girlhood and work had not yet made these lines too clear.

The rarer feeling that there was with Lena, showed in all the even quiet of her body movements, but in all it was the strongest in the patient, old-world ignorance, and earth made pureness of her brown, flat, soft featured face. Lena had eyebrows that were a wondrous thickness. They were black, and spread, and very cool, with their dark color and their beauty, and beneath them were her hazel eyes, simple and human, with the earth patience of the working, gentle, german woman.

Yes it was all a peaceful life for Lena. The other girls, of course, did tease her, but then that only made a gentle stir within her.

"What you got on your finger Lena," Mary, one of the girls she always sat with, one day asked her. Mary was good natured, quick, intelligent and Irish.

Lena had just picked up the fancy paper made accordion that the little girl had dropped beside her, and was making it squeak sadly as she pulled it with her brown strong, awkward finger.

"Why, what is it, Mary, paint?" said Lena, putting her finger to her mouth to taste the dirt spot.

"That's awful poison Lena, don't you know?" said Mary, "that green paint that you just tasted."

Lena has sucked a good deal of the green paint from her finger. She stopped and looked hard at the finger. She did not know just how much Mary meant by what she said.

"Ain't it poison, Nellie, that green paint, that Lena sucked just now," said Mary. "Sure it is Lena, its real poison, I ain't foolin' this time anyhow."

Lena was a little troubled. She looked hard at her finger where the paint was, and she wondered if she had really sucked it.

It was still a little wet on the edges and she rubbed it off a long time on the inside of her dress, and in between she wondered and looked at the finger and thought, was it really poison that she had just tasted.

"Ain't it too bad, Nellie, Lena should have sucked that," Mary said.

Nellie smiled and did not answer. Nellie was dark and thin, and looked Italian. She had a big mass of black hair that she wore high up on her head, and that made her face look very fine.

Nellie always smiled and did not say much, and then she would look at Lena to perplex her.

And so they all three sat with their little charges in the pleasant sunshine a long time. And Lena would often look at her finger and wonder if it was really poison that she had just tasted and then she would rub her finger on her dress a little harder.

Mary laughed at her and teased her and Nellie smiled a little and looked queerly at her.

Then it came time, for it was growing cooler, for them to drag together the little ones, who had begun to wander, and to take each one back to its own mother. And Lena never knew for certain whether it was really poison, that green stuff that she had tasted.

During these four years of service, Lena always spent her Sundays out at the house of her aunt, who had brought her four years before to Bridgepoint.

This aunt, who had brought Lena, four years before, to Bridgepoint, was a hard, ambitious, well meaning, german woman. Her husband was a grocer in the town, and they were very well to do. Mrs. Haydon, Lena's aunt, had two daughters who were just beginning as young ladies, and she had a little boy who was not honest and who was very hard to manage.

Mrs. Haydon was a short, stout, hard built, german woman. She always hit the ground very firmly and compactly as she walked. Mrs. Haydon was all a compact and well hardened mass, even to her face, reddish and darkened from its early blonde, with its hearty, shiny, cheeks, and doubled chin well covered over with the uproll from her short, square neck.

The two daughters, who were fourteen and fifteen, looked like unkneaded, unformed mounds of flesh beside her.

The elder girl, Mathilda, was blonde, and slow, and simple, and quite fat. The younger, Bertha, who was almost as tall as her sister, was dark, and quicker, and she was heavy, too, but not really fat.

These two girls the mother had brought up very firmly. They were well taught for their position. They were always both well dressed, in the same kinds of hats and dresses, as is becoming in two german sisters. The mother liked to have them dressed in red. Their best clothes were red dresses, made of good heavy cloth, and strongly trimmed with braid of a glistening black. They had stiff, red felt hats, trimmed with black velvet ribbon, and a bird. The mother dressed matronly, in a bonnet and in black, always sat between her two big daughters, firm, directing, and repressed.

The only weak spot in this good woman's conduct was the way she spoiled her boy who was not honest and who was very hard to manage.

The father of this family was a decent, quiet, heavy, and uninterfering german man. He tried to cure the boy of his bad ways, and make him honest, but the mother could not make herself let the father manage, and so the boy was brought up very badly.

Mrs. Haydon's girls were now only just beginning as young ladies, and so to get her niece, Lena, married, was just then the most important thing that Mrs. Haydon had to do.

Mrs. Haydon had four years before gone to Germany to see her parents, and had taken the girls with her. This visit had been for Mrs. Haydon most successful, though her children had not liked it very well.

Mrs. Haydon was a good and generous woman, and she patronized her parents grandly, and all the cousins who came from all about to see her. Mrs. Haydon's people were of the middling class of farmers. They were not peasants, and they lived in a town of some pretension, but it all seemed very poor and smelly to Mrs. Haydon's american born daughters.

Mrs. Haydon liked it all. It was familiar, and then here she was so wealthy and important. She listened and decided, and advised all of her relations how to do things better. She arranged their present and their future for them, and showed them how in the past they had been wrong in all their methods.

Mrs. Haydon's only trouble was with her two daughters, whom she could not make behave well to her parents. The two girls were very nasty to all their numerous relations. Their mother could hardly make them kiss their grandparents, and every day the girls would get a scolding. But then Mrs. Haydon was so very busy that she did not have time to really manage her stubborn daughters.

These hard working, earth-rough german cousins were to these american born children, ugly and dirty and as far below them as were italian or negro workmen, and they could not see how their mother could ever bear to touch them, and then all the women dressed so funny, and were worked all rough and different.

The two girls stuck up their noses at them all, and always talked in English to each other about how they hated all these people and how they wished their mother would not do so. The girls could talk some German, but they never chose to use it.

It was her eldest brother's family that most interested Mrs. Haydon. Here there were eight children, and out of the eight, five of them were girls.

Mrs. Haydon thought it would be a fine thing to take one of these girls back with her to Bridgepoint and get her well started. Everybody liked that she should do so, and they were all willing that it should be Lena.

Lena was the second girl in her large family. She was at this time just seventeen years old. Lena was not an important daughter in the family. She was always sort of dreamy and not there. She worked hard and went very regularly at it, but even good work never seemed to bring her near.

Lena's age just suited Mrs. Haydon's purpose. Lena could first go out to service, and learn how to do things, and then, when she was a little older, Mrs. Haydon could get her a good husband. And then Lena was so still and docile, she would never want to do things her own way. And then, too, Mrs. Haydon, with all her hardness had wisdom, and she could feel the rarer strain there was in Lena.

Lena was willing to go with Mrs. Haydon. Lena did not like her german life very well. It was not the hard work but the roughness that disturbed her. The people were not gentle, and the men when they were glad were very boisterous, and would lay hold of her and roughly tease her. They were good people enough around her, but it was all harsh and dreary for her.

Lena did not really know that she did not like it. She did not know that she was always dreamy and not there. She did not think whether it would be different for her away off there in Bridgepoint. Mrs. Haydon took her and got her different kinds of dresses, and then took her with them to the steamer. Lena did not really know what it was that had happened to her.

Mrs. Haydon, and her daughters, and Lena traveled second class on the steamer. Mrs. Haydon's daughters hated that their mother should take Lena. They hated to have a cousin, who was to them, little better than a nigger, and then everybody on the steamer there would see her. Mrs. Haydon's daughters said things like this to their mother, but she never stopped to hear them, and the girls did not dare to make their meaning very clear. And so they could only go on hating Lena hard, together. They could not stop her from going back with them to Bridgepoint.

Lena was very sick on the voyage. She thought, surely before it was over that she would die. She was so sick she could not even wish that she had not started. She could not eat, she could not moan, she was just blank and scared, and sure that every minute she would die. She could not hold herself in, nor help herself in her trouble. She just staid where she had been put, pale, and scared, and weak, and sick, and sure that she was going to die.

Mathilda and Bertha Haydon had no trouble from having Lena for a cousin on the voyage, until the last day that they were on the ship, and by that time they had made their friends and could explain.

Mrs. Haydon went down every day to Lena, gave her things to make her better, held her head when it was needful, and generally was good and did her duty by her.

Poor Lena had no power to be strong in such trouble. She did not know how to yield to her sickness nor endure. She lost all her little sense of being in her suffering. She was so scared, and then at her best, Lena, who was patient, sweet and quiet, had not self-control, nor any active courage.

Poor Lena was so scared and weak, and every minute she was sure that she would die.

After Lena was on land again a little while, she forgot all her bad suffering. Mrs. Haydon got her the good place, with the pleasant unexacting mistress, and her children, and Lena began to learn some English and soon was very happy and content.

All her Sundays out Lena spent at Mrs. Haydon's house. Lena would have liked much better to spend her Sundays with the girls she always sat with, and who often asked her, and who teased her and made a gentle stir within her, but it never came to Lena's unexpectant and unsuffering german nature to do something different from what was expected of her, just because she would like it that way better. Mrs. Haydon had said that Lena was to come to her house every other Sunday, and so Lena always went there.

Mrs. Haydon was the only one of her family who took any interest in Lena. Mr. Haydon did not think much of her. She was his wife's cousin and he was good to her, but she was for him stupid, and a little simple, and very dull, and sure some day to need help and to be in trouble. All young poor relations, who were brought from Germany to Bridgepoint were sure, before long, to need help and to be in trouble.

The little Haydon boy was always very nasty to her. He was a hard child for any one to manage, and his mother spoiled him very badly. Mrs. Haydon's daughters as they grew older did not learn to like Lena any better. Lena never knew that she did not like them either. She did not know that she was only happy with the other quicker girls, she always sat with in the park, and who laughed at her and always teased her.

Mathilda Haydon, the simple, fat, blonde, older daughter felt very badly that she had to say that this was her cousin Lena, this Lena who was little better for her than a nigger. Mathilda was an overgrown, slow, flabby, blonde, stupid, fat girl, just beginning as a woman; thick in her speech and dull and simple in her mind, and very jealous of all her family and of other girls, and proud that she could have good dresses and new hats and learn music, and hating very badly to have a cousin who was a common servant. And then Mathilda remembered very strongly that dirty nasty place that Lena came from and that Mathilda had so turned up her nose at, and where she had been made so angry because her mother scolded her and liked all those rough cow-smelly people.

Then, too, Mathilda would get very mad when her mother had Lena at their parties, and when she talked about how good Lena was, to certain german mothers in whose sons, perhaps, Mrs. Haydon might find Lena a good husband. All this would make the dull, blonde, fat Mathilda very angry. Sometimes she would get so angry that she would, in her thick, slow way, and with jealous anger blazing in her light blue eyes, tell her mother that she did not see how she could like that nasty Lena; and then her mother would scold Mathilda, and tell her that she knew her cousin Lena was poor and Mathilda must be good to poor people.

Mathilda Haydon did not like relations to be poor. She told all her girl friends what she thought of Lena, and so the girls would never talk to Lena at Mrs. Haydon's parties. But Lena in her unsuffering and unexpectant patience never really knew that she was slighted. When Mathilda was with her girls in the street or in the park and would see Lena, she always turned up her nose and barely nodded to her, and then she would tell her friends how funny her mother was to take care of people like that Lena, and how, back in Germany, all Lena's people lived just like pigs.

The younger daughter, the dark, large, but not fat, Bertha Haydon, who was very quick in her mind, and in her ways, and who was the favorite with her father, did not like Lena, either. She did not like her because for her Lena was a fool and so stupid, and she would let those Irish and Italian girls laugh at her and tease her, and everybody always made fun of Lena, and Lena never got mad, or even had sense enough to know that they were all making an awful fool of her.

Bertha Haydon hated people to be fools. Her father, too, thought Lena was a fool, and so neither the father nor the daughter ever paid any attention to Lena, although she came to their house every other Sunday.

Lena did not know how all the Haydons felt. She came to her aunt's house all her Sunday afternoons that she had out, because Mrs. Haydon had told her she must do so. In the same way Lena always saved all of her wages. She never thought of any way to spend it. The german cook, the good woman who always scolded Lena, helped her to put it in the bank each month, as soon as she got it. Sometimes before it got into the bank to be taken care of, somebody would ask Lena for it. The little Haydon boy sometimes asked and would get it, and sometimes some of the girls, the ones Lena always sat with, needed some more money; but the german cook, who always scolded Lena, saw to it that this did not happen very often. When it did happen she would scold Lena very sharply, and for the next few months she would not let Lena touch her wages, but put it in the bank for her on the same day that Lena got it.

So Lena always saved her wages, for she never thought to spend them, and she always went to her aunt's house for her Sundays because she did not know that she could do anything different.

Mrs. Haydon felt more and more every year that she had done right to bring Lena back with her, for it was all coming out just as she had expected. Lena was good and never wanted her own way, she was learning English, and saving all her wages, and soon Mrs. Haydon would get her a good husband.

All these four years Mrs. Haydon was busy looking around among all the german people that she knew for the right man to be Lena's husband, and now at last she was quite decided.

The man Mrs. Haydon wanted for Lena was a young german-american tailor, who worked with his father. He was good and all the family were very saving, and Mrs. Haydon was sure that this would be just right for Lena, and then too, this young tailor always did whatever his father and his mother wanted.

This old german tailor and his wife, the father and the mother of Herman Kreder, who was to marry Lena Mainz, were very thrifty, careful people. Herman was the only child they had left with them, and he always did everything they wanted. Herman was now twenty-eight years old, but he had never stopped being scolded and directed by his father and his mother. And now they wanted to see him married.

Herman Kreder did not care much to get married. He was a gentle soul and a little fearful. He had a sullen temper, too. He was obedient to his father and his mother. He always did his work well. He often went out on Saturday nights and on Sundays, with other men. He liked it with them but he never became really joyous. He liked to be with men and he hated to have women with them. He was obedient to his mother, but he did not care much to get married.

Mrs. Haydon and the elder Kreders had often talked the marriage over. They all three liked it very well. Lena would do anything that Mrs. Haydon wanted, and Herman was always obedient in everything to his father and his mother. Both Lena and Herman were saving and good workers and neither of them ever wanted their own way.

The elder Kreders, everybody knew, had saved up all their money, and they were hard, good german people, and Mrs. Haydon was sure that with these people Lena would never be in any trouble. Mr. Haydon would not say anything about it. He knew old Kreder had a lot of money and owned some good houses, and he did not care what his wife did with that simple, stupid Lena, so long as she would be sure never to need help or to be in trouble.

Lena did not care much to get married. She liked her life very well where she was working. She did not think much about Herman Kreder. She thought he was a good man and she always found him very quiet. Neither of them ever spoke much to the other. Lena did not care much just then about getting married.

Mrs. Haydon spoke to Lena about it very often. Lena never answered anything at all. Mrs. Haydon thought, perhaps Lena did not like Herman Kreder. Mrs. Haydon could not believe that any girl not even Lena, really had no feeling about getting married.

Mrs. Haydon spoke to Lena very often about Herman. Mrs. Haydon sometimes got very angry with Lena. She was afraid that Lena, for once, was going to be stubborn, now when it was all fixed right for her to be married.

"Why you stand there so stupid, why don't you answer, Lena," said Mrs. Haydon one Sunday, at the end of a long talking that she was giving Lena about Herman Kreder, and about Lena's getting married to him.

"Yes ma'am," said Lena, and then Mrs. Haydon was furious with this stupid Lena. "Why don't you answer with some sense, Lena, when I ask you if you don't like Herman Kreder. You stand there so stupid and don't answer just like you ain't heard a word what I been saying to you. I never see anybody like you, Lena. If you going to burst out at all, why don't you burst out sudden instead of standing there so silly and don't answer. And here I am so good to you, and find you a good husband so you can have a place to live in all your own. Answer me, Lena, don't you like Herman Kreder? He is a fine young fellow, almost too good for you, Lena, when you stand there so stupid and don't make no answer. There ain't many poor girls that get the chance you got now to get married."

"Why, I do anything you say, Aunt Mathilda. Yes, I like him. He don't say much to me, but I guess he is a good man, and I do anything you say for me to do."

"Well then Lena, why you stand there so silly all the time and not answer when I asked you."

"I didn't hear you say you wanted I should say anything to you. I didn't know you wanted me to say nothing. I do whatever you tell me it's right for me to do. I marry Herman Kreder, if you want me."

And so for Lena Mainz the match was made.

Old Mrs. Kreder did not discuss the matter with her Herman. She never thought that she needed to talk such things over with him. She just told him about getting married to Lena Mainz who was a good worker and very saving and never wanted her own way, and Herman made his usual little grunt in answer to her.

Mrs. Kreder and Mrs. Haydon fixed the day and made all the arrangements for the wedding and invited everybody who ought to be there to see them married.

In three months Lena Mainz and Herman Kreder were to be married.

Mrs. Haydon attended to Lena's getting all the things that she needed. Lena had to help a good deal with the sewing. Lena did not sew very well. Mrs. Haydon scolded because Lena did not do it better, but then she was very good to Lena, and she hired a girl to come and help her. Lena still stayed on with her pleasant mistress, but she spent all her evenings and her Sundays with her aunt and all the sewing.

Mrs. Haydon got Lena some nice dresses. Lena liked that very well. Lena liked having new hats even better, and Mrs. Haydon had some made for her by a real milliner who made them very pretty.

Lena was nervous these days, but she did not think much about getting married. She did not know really what it was, that, which was always coming nearer.

Lena liked the place where she was with the pleasant mistress and the good cook, who always scolded, and she liked the girls she always sat with. She did not ask if she would like being married any better. She always did whatever her aunt said and expected, but she was always nervous when she saw the Kreders with their Herman. She was excited and she liked her new hats, and everybody teased her and every day her marrying was coming nearer, and yet she did not really know what it was, this that was about to happen to her.

Herman Kreder knew more what it meant to be married and he did not like it very well. He did not like to see girls and he did not want to have to have one alway near him. Herman always did everything that his father and his mother wanted and now they wanted that he should be married.

Herman had a sullen temper; he was gentle and he never said much. He liked to go out with other men, but he never wanted that there should be any women with them. The men all teased him about getting married. Herman did not mind the teasing but he did not like very well the getting married and having a girl always with him.

Three days before the wedding day, Herman went away to the country to be gone over Sunday. He and Lena were to be married Tuesday afternoon. When the day came Herman had not been seen or heard from.

The old Kreder couple had not worried much about it. Herman always did everything they wanted and he would surely come back in time to get married. But when Monday night came, and there was no Herman, they went to Mrs. Haydon to tell her what had happened.

Mrs. Haydon got very much excited. It was hard enough to work so as to get everything all ready, and then to have that silly Herman go off that way, so no one could tell what was going to happen. Here was Lena and everything all ready, and now they would have to make the wedding later so that they would know that Herman would be sure to be there.

Mrs. Haydon was very much excited, and then she could not say much to the old Kreder couple. She did not want to make them angry, for she wanted very badly now that Lena should be married to their Herman.

At last it was decided that the wedding should be put off a week longer. Old Mr. Kreder would go to New York to find Herman, for it was very likely that Herman had gone there to his married sister.

Mrs. Haydon sent word around, about waiting until a week from that Tuesday, to everybody that had been invited, and then Tuesday morning she sent for Lena to come down to see her.

Mrs. Haydon was very angry with poor Lena when she saw her. She scolded her hard because she was so foolish, and now Herman had gone off and nobody could tell where he had gone to, and all because Lena always was so dumb and silly. And Mrs. Haydon was just like a mother to her, and Lena always stood there so stupid and did not answer what anybody asked her, and Herman was so silly too, and now his father had to go and find him. Mrs. Haydon did not think that any old people should be good to their children. Their children always were so thankless, and never paid any attention, and older people were always doing things for their good. Did Lena think it gave Mrs. Haydon any pleasure, to work so hard to make Lena happy, and get her a good husband, and then Lena was so thankless and never did anything that anybody wanted. It was a lesson to poor Mrs. Haydon not to do things any more for anybody. Let everybody take care of themselves and never come to her with any troubles; she knew better now than to meddle to make other people happy. It just made trouble for her and her husband did not like it. He always said she was too good, and nobody ever thanked her for it, and there Lena was always standing stupid and not answering anything anybody wanted. Lena could always talk enough to those silly girls she liked so much, and always sat with, but who never did anything for her except to take away her money, and here was her aunt who tried so hard and was so good to her and treated her just like one of her own children and Lena stood there, and never made any answer and never tried to please her aunt, or to do anything that her aunt wanted. "No, it ain't no use your standin' there and cryin', now, Lena. Its too late now to care about that Herman. You should have cared some before, and then you wouldn't have to stand and cry now, and be a disappointment to me, and then I get scolded by my husband for taking care of everybody, and nobody ever thankful. I am glad you got the sense to feel sorry now, Lena, anyway, and I try to do what I can to help you out in your trouble, only you don't deserve to have anybody take any trouble for you. But perhaps you know better next time. You go home now and take care you don't spoil your clothes and that new hat, you had no business to be wearin' that this morning, but you ain't got no sense at all, Lena. I never in my life see anybody be so stupid."

Mrs. Haydon stopped and poor Lena stood there in her hat, all trimmed with pretty flowers, and the tears coming out of her eyes, and Lena did not know what it was that she had done, only she was not going to be married and it was a disgrace for a girl to be left by a man on the very day she was to be married.

Lena went home all alone, and cried in the street car.

Poor Lena cried very hard all alone in the street car. She almost spoiled her new hat with her hitting it against the window in her crying. Then she remembered that she must not do so.

The conductor was a kind man and he was very sorry when he saw her crying. "Don't feel so bad, you get another feller, you are such a nice girl," he said to make her cheerful. "But Aunt Mathilda said now, I never get married," poor Lena sobbed out for her answer. "Why you really got trouble like that," said the conductor, "I just said that now to josh you. I didn't ever think you really was left by a feller. He must be a stupid feller. But don't you worry, he wasn't much good if he could go away and leave you, lookin' to be such a nice girl. You just tell all your trouble to me, and I help you." The car was empty and the conductor sat down beside her to put his arm around her, and to be a comfort to her. Lena suddenly remembered where she was, and if she did things like that her aunt would scold her. She moved away from the man into the corner. He laughed, "Don't be scared," he said, "I wasn't going to hurt you. But you just keep up your spirit. You are a real nice girl, and you'll be sure to get a real good husband. Don't you let nobody fool you. You're all right and I don't want to scare you."

The conductor went back to his platform to help a passenger get on the car. All the time Lena stayed in the street car, he would come in every little while and reassure her, about her not to feel so bad about a man who hadn't no more sense than to go away and leave her. She'd be sure yet to get a good man, she needn't be so worried, he frequently assured her.

He chatted with the other passenger who had just come in, a very well dressed old man, and then with another who came in later, a good sort of a working man, and then another who came in, a nice lady, and he told them all about Lena's having trouble, and it was too bad there were men who treated a poor girl so badly. And everybody in the car was sorry for poor Lena and the workman tried to cheer her, and the old man looked sharply at her, and said she looked like a good girl, but she ought to be more careful and not be so careless, and things like that would not happen to her, and the nice lady went and sat beside her and Lena liked it, though she shrank away from being near her.

So Lena was feeling a little better when she got off the car, and the conductor helped her, and he called out to her, "You be sure you keep up a good heart now. He wasn't no good that feller and you were lucky for to lose him. You'll get a real man yet, one that will be better for you. Don't you be worried, you're a real nice girl as I ever see in such trouble," and the conductor shook his head and went back into his car to talk it over with the other passengers he had there.

The german cook, who always scolded Lena, was very angry when she heard the story. She never did think Mrs. Haydon would do so much for Lena, though she was always talking so grand about what she could do for everybody. The good german cook always had been a little distrustful of her. People who always thought they were so much never did really do things right for anybody. Not that Mrs. Haydon wasn't a good woman. Mrs. Haydon was a real, good, german woman, and she did really mean to do well by her niece Lena. The cook knew that very well, and she had always said so, and she always had liked and respected Mrs. Haydon, who always acted very proper to her, and Lena was so backward, when there was a man to talk to, Mrs. Haydon did have hard work when she tried to marry Lena. Mrs. Haydon was a good woman, only she did talk sometimes too grand. Perhaps this trouble would make her see it wasn't always so easy to do, to make everybody do everything just like she wanted. The cook was very sorry now for Mrs. Haydon. All this must be such a disappointment, and such a worry to her, and she really had always been very good to Lena. But Lena had better go and put on her other clothes and stop with all that crying. That wouldn't do nothing now to help her, and if Lena would be a good girl, and just be real patient, her aunt would make it all come out right yet for her. "I just tell Mrs. Aldrich, Lena, you stay here yet a little longer. You know she is always so good to you, Lena, and I know she let you, and I tell her all about that stupid Herman Kreder. I got no patience, Lena, with anybody who can be so stupid. You just stop now with your crying, Lena, and take off them good clothes and put them away so you don't spoil them when you need them, and you can help me with the dishes and everything will come off better for you. You see if I ain't right by what I tell you. You just stop crying now Lena quick, or else I scold you."

Lena still choked a little and was very miserable inside her but she did everything just as the cook told her.

The girls Lena always sat with were very sorry to see her look so sad with her trouble. Mary the Irish girl sometimes got very angry with her. Mary was always very hot when she talked of Lena's aunt Mathilda, who thought she was so grand, and had such stupid, stuck up daughters. Mary wouldn't be a fat fool like that ugly tempered Mathilda Haydon, not for anything anybody could ever give her. How Lena could keep on going there so much when they all always acted as if she was just dirt to them, Mary never could see. But Lena never had any sense of how she should make people stand round for her, and that was always all the trouble with her. And poor Lena, she was so stupid to be sorry for losing that gawky fool who didn't ever know what he wanted and just said "ja" to his mamma and his papa, like a baby, and was scared to look at a girl straight, and then sneaked away the last day like as if somebody was going to do something to him. Disgrace, Lena talking about disgrace! It was a disgrace for a girl to be seen with the likes of him, let alone to be married to him. But that poor Lena, she never did know how to show herself off for what she was really. Disgrace to have him go away and leave her. Mary would just like to get a chance to show him. If Lena wasn't worth fifteen like Herman Kreder, Mary would just eat her own head all up. It was a good riddance Lena had of that Herman Kreder and his stingy, dirty parents, and if Lena didn't stop crying about it,—Mary would just naturally despise her.

Poor Lena, she knew very well how Mary meant it all, this she was always saying to her. But Lena was very miserable inside her. She felt the disgrace it was for a decent german girl that a man should go away and leave her. Lena knew very well that her aunt was right when she said the way Herman had acted to her was a disgrace to everyone that knew her. Mary and Nellie and the other girls she always sat with were always very good to Lena but that did not make her trouble any better. It was a disgrace the way Lena had been left, to any decent family, and that could never be made any different to her.

And so the slow days wore on, and Lena never saw her Aunt Mathilda. At last on Sunday she got word by a boy to go and see her aunt Mathilda. Lena's heart beat quick for she was very nervous now with all this that had happened to her. She went just as quickly as she could to see her Aunt Mathilda.

Mrs. Haydon quick, as soon as she saw Lena, began to scold her for keeping her aunt waiting so long for her, and for not coming in all the week to see her, to see if her aunt should need her, and so her aunt had to send a boy to tell her. But it was easy, even for Lena, to see that her aunt was not really angry with her. It wasn't Lena's fault, went on Mrs. Haydon, that everything was going to happen all right for her. Mrs. Haydon was very tired taking all this trouble for her, and when Lena couldn't even take trouble to come and see her aunt, to see if she needed anything to tell her. But Mrs. Haydon really never minded things like that when she could do things for anybody. She was tired now, all the trouble she had been taking to make things right for Lena, but perhaps now Lena heard it she would learn a little to be thankful to her. "You get all ready to be married Tuesday. Lena, you hear me," said Mrs. Haydon to her. "You come here Tuesday morning and I have everything all ready for you. You wear your new dress I got you, and your hat with all them flowers on it, and you be very careful coming you don't get your things all dirty, you so careless all the time, Lena, and not thinking, and you act sometimes you never got no head at all on you. You go home, now, and you tell your Mrs. Aldrich that you leave her Tuesday. Don't you go forgetting now, Lena, anything I ever told you what you should do to be careful. You be a good girl, now Lena. You get married Tuesday to Herman Kreder." And that was all Lena ever knew of what had happened all this week to Herman Kreder.

Lena forgot there was anything to know about it. She was really to be married Tuesday, and her Aunt Mathilda said she was a good girl, and now there was no disgrace left upon her.

Lena now fell back into the way she always had of being always dreamy and not there, the way she always had been, except for the few days she was so excited, because she had been left by a man the very day she was to have been married. Lena was a little nervous all these last days, but she did not think much about what it meant for her to be married.

Herman Kreder was not so content about it. He was quiet and was sullen and he knew he could not help it. He knew now he just had to let himself get married. It was not that Herman did not like Lena Mainz. She was as good as any other girl could be for him. She was a little better perhaps than other girls he saw, she was so very quiet, but Herman did not like to always have to have a girl around him. Herman had always done everything that his mother and his father wanted. His father had found him in New York, where Herman had gone to be with his married sister.

Herman's father when he had found him coaxed Herman a long time and went on whole days with his complaining to him, always troubled but gentle and quite patient with him; and always he was worrying to Herman about what was the right way his boy Herman should always do, always whatever it was his mother ever wanted from him, and always Herman never made him any answer.

Old Mr. Kreder kept on saying to him, he did not see how Herman could think now, it could be any different. When you make a bargain you just got to stick right to it, that was the only way old Mr. Kreder could ever see it, and saying you would get married to a girl and she got everything all ready, that was a bargain just like one you make in business and Herman he had made it, and now Herman he would just have to do it, old Mr. Kreder didn't see there was any other way a good boy like his Herman had, to do it. And then too that Lena Mainz was such a nice girl and Herman hadn't ought to really give his father so much trouble and make him pay out all that money, to come all the way to New York just to find him, and they both lose all that time from their working, when all Herman had to do was just to stand up, for an hour, and then he would be all right married, and it would be all over for him, and then everything at home would never be any different to him.

And his father went on; there was his poor mother saying always how her Herman always did everything before she ever wanted, and now just because he got notions in him, and wanted to show people how he could be stubborn, he was making all this trouble for her, and making them pay all that money just to run around and find him. "You got no idea Herman, how bad mama is feeling about the way you been acting Herman," said old Mr. Kreder to him. "She says she never can understand how you can be so thankless Herman. It hurts her very much you been so stubborn, and she find you such a nice girl for you, like Lena Mainz who is always just so quiet and always saves up all her wages, and she never wanting her own way at all like some girls are always all the time to have it, and your mama trying so hard, just so you could be comfortable Herman to be married, and then you act so stubborn Herman. You like all young people Herman, you think only about yourself, and what you are just wanting, and your mama she is thinking only what is good for you to have, for you in the future. Do you think your mama wants to have a girl around to be a bother, for herself, Herman. Its just for you Herman she is always thinking, and she talks always about how happy she will be, when she sees her Herman married to a nice girl, and then when she fixed it all up so good for you, so it never would be any bother to you, just the way she wanted you should like it, and you say yes all right, I do it, and then you go away like this and act stubborn, and make all this trouble everybody to take for you, and we spend money, and I got to travel all round to find you. You come home now with me Herman and get married, and I tell your mama she better not say anything to you about how much it cost me to come all the way to look for you—Hey Herman," said his father coaxing, "Hey, you come home now and get married. All you got to do Herman is just to stand up for an hour Herman, and then you don't never to have any more bother to it—Hey Herman!—you come home with me to-morrow and get married. Hey Herman."

Herman's married sister liked her brother Herman, and she had always tried to help him, when there was anything she knew he wanted. She liked it that he was so good and always did everything that their father and their mother wanted, but still she wished it could be that he could have more his own way, if there was anything he ever wanted.

But now she thought Herman with his girl was very funny. She wanted that Herman should be married. She thought it would do him lots of good to get married. She laughed at Herman when she heard the story. Until his father came to find him, she did not know why it was Herman had come just then to New York to see her. When she heard the story she laughed a good deal at her brother Herman and teased him a good deal about his running away, because he didn't want to have a girl to be all the time around him.

Herman's married sister liked her brother Herman, and she did not want him not to like to be with women. He was good, her brother Herman, and it would surely do him good to get married. It would make him stand up for himself stronger. Herman's sister always laughed at him and always she would try to reassure him. "Such a nice man as my brother Herman acting like as if he was afraid of women. Why the girls all like a man like you Herman, if you didn't always run away when you saw them. It do you good really Herman to get married, and then you got somebody you can boss around when you want to. It do you good Herman to get married, you see if you don't like it, when you really done it. You go along home now with papa, Herman and get married to that Lena. You don't know how nice you like it Herman when you try once how you can do it. You just don't be afraid of nothing, Herman. You good enough for any girl to marry, Herman. Any girl be glad to have a man like you to be always with them Herman. You just go along home with papa and try it what I say, Herman. Oh you so funny Herman, when you sit there, and then run away and leave your girl behind you. I know she is crying like anything Herman for to lose you. Don't be bad to her Herman. You go along home with papa now and get married Herman. I'd be awful ashamed Herman, to really have a brother didn't have spirit enough to get married, when a girl is just dying for to have him. You always like me to be with you Herman. I don't see why you say you don't want a girl to be all the time around you. You always been good to me Herman, and I know you always be good to that Lena, and you soon feel just like as if she had always been there with you. Don't act like as if you wasn't a nice strong man, Herman. Really I laugh at you Herman, but you know I like awful well to see you real happy. You go home and get married to that Lena, Herman. She is a real pretty girl and real nice and good and quiet and she make my brother Herman very happy. You just stop your fussing now with Herman, papa. He go with you to-morrow papa, and you see he like it so much to be married, he make everybody laugh just to see him be so happy. Really truly, that's the way it will be with you Herman. You just listen to me what I tell you Herman." And so his sister laughed at him and reassured him, and his father kept on telling what the mother always said about her Herman, and he coaxed him and Herman never said anything in answer, and his sister packed his things up and was very cheerful with him, and she kissed him, and then she laughed and then she kissed him, and his father went and bought the tickets for the train, and at last late on Sunday he brought Herman back to Bridgepoint with him.

It was always very hard to keep Mrs. Kreder from saying what she thought, to her Herman, but her daughter had written her a letter, so as to warn her not to say anything about what he had been doing, to him, and her husband came in with Herman and said, "Here we are come home mama, Herman and me, and we are very tired it was so crowded coming," and then he whispered to her. "You be good to Herman, mama, he didn't mean to make us so much trouble," and so old Mrs. Kreder, held in what she felt was so strong in her to say to her Herman. She just said very stiffly to him, "I'm glad to see you come home to-day, Herman." Then she went to arrange it all with Mrs. Haydon.

Herman was now again just like he always had been, sullen and very good, and very quiet, and always ready to do whatever his mother and his father wanted. Tuesday morning came, Herman got his new clothes on and went with his father and his mother to stand up for an hour and get married. Lena was there in her new dress, and her hat with all the pretty flowers, and she was very nervous for now she knew she was really very soon to be married. Mrs. Haydon had everything all ready. Everybody was there just as they should be and very soon Herman Kreder and Lena Mainz were married.

When everything was really over, they went back to the Kreder house together. They were all now to live together, Lena and Herman and the old father and the old mother, in the house where Mr. Kreder had worked so many years as a tailor, with his son Herman always there to help him.

Irish Mary had often said to Lena she never did see how Lena could ever want to have anything to do with Herman Kreder and his dirty stingy parents. The old Kreders were to an Irish nature, a stingy, dirty couple. They had not the free-hearted, thoughtless, fighting, mud bespattered, ragged, peat-smoked cabin dirt that irish Mary knew and could forgive and love. Theirs was the german dirt of saving, of being dowdy and loose and foul in your clothes so as to save them and yourself in washing, having your hair greasy to save it in the soap and drying, having your clothes dirty, not in freedom, but because so it was cheaper, keeping the house close and smelly because so it cost less to get it heated, living so poorly not only so as to save money but so they should never even know themselves that they had it, working all the time not only because from their nature they just had to and because it made them money but also that they never could be put in any way to make them spend their money.

This was the place Lena now had for her home and to her it was very different than it could be for an irish Mary. She too was german and was thrifty, though she was always so dreamy and not there. Lena was always careful with things and she always saved her money, for that was the only way she knew how to do it. She never had taken care of her own money and she never had thought how to use it.

Lena Mainz had been, before she was Mrs. Herman Kreder, always clean and decent in her clothes and in her person, but it was not because she ever thought about it or really needed so to have it, it was the way her people did in the german country where she came from, and her Aunt Mathilda and the good german cook who always scolded, had kept her on and made her, with their scoldings, always more careful to keep clean and to wash real often. But there was no deep need in all this for Lena and so, though Lena did not like the old Kreders, though she really did not know that, she did not think about their being stingy dirty people.

Herman Kreder was cleaner than the old people, just because it was his nature to keep cleaner, but he was used to his mother and his father, and he never thought that they should keep things cleaner. And Herman too always saved all his money, except for that little beer he drank when he went out with other men of an evening the way he always liked to do it, and he never thought of any other way to spend it. His father had always kept all the money for them and he always was doing business with it. And then too Herman really had no money, for he always had worked for his father, and his father had never thought to pay him.

And so they began all four to live in the Kreder house together, and Lena began soon with it to look careless and a little dirty, and to be more lifeless with it, and nobody ever noticed much what Lena wanted, and she never really knew herself what she needed.

The only real trouble that came to Lena with their living all four there together, was the way old Mrs. Kreder scolded. Lena had always been used to being scolded, but this scolding of old Mrs. Kreder was very different from the way she ever before had had to endure it.

Herman, now he was married to her, really liked Lena very well. He did not care very much about her but she never was a bother to him being there around him, only when his mother worried and was nasty to them because Lena was so careless, and did not know how to save things right for them with their eating, and all the other ways with money, that the old woman had to save it.

Herman Kreder had always done everything his mother and his father wanted but he did not really love his parents very deeply. With Herman it was always only that he hated to have any struggle. It was all always all right with him when he could just go along and do the same thing over every day with his working, and not to hear things, and not to have people make him listen to their anger. And now his marriage, and he just knew it would, was making trouble for him. It made him hear more what his mother was always saying, with her scolding. He had to really hear it now because Lena was there, and she was so scared and dull always when she heard it. Herman knew very well with his mother, it was all right if one ate very little and worked hard all day and did not hear her when she scolded, the way Herman always had done before they were so foolish about his getting married and having a girl there to be all the time around him, and now he had to help her so the girl could learn too, not to hear it when his mother scolded, and not to look so scared, and not to eat much, and always to be sure to save it.

Herman really did not know very well what he could do to help Lena to understand it. He could never answer his mother back to help Lena, that never would make things any better for her, and he never could feel in himself any way to comfort Lena, to make her strong not to hear his mother, in all the awful ways she always scolded. It just worried Herman to have it like that all the time around him. Herman did not know much about how a man could make a struggle with a mother, to do much to keep her quiet, and indeed Herman never knew much how to make a struggle against anyone who really wanted to have anything very badly. Herman all his life never wanted anything so badly, that he would really make a struggle against any one to get it. Herman all his life only wanted to live regular and quiet, and not talk much and to do the same way every day like every other with his working. And now his mother had made him get married to this Lena and now with his mother making all that scolding, he had all this trouble and this worry always on him.

Mrs. Haydon did not see Lena now very often. She had not lost her interest in her niece Lena, but Lena could not come much to her house to see her, it would not be right, now Lena was a married woman. And then too Mrs. Haydon had her hands full just then with her two daughters, for she was getting them ready to find them good husbands, and then too her own husband now worried her very often about her always spoiling that boy of hers, so he would be sure to turn out no good and be a disgrace to a german family, and all because his mother always spoiled him. All these things were very worrying now to Mrs. Haydon, but still she wanted to be good to Lena, though she could not see her very often. She only saw her when Mrs. Haydon went to call on Mrs. Kreder or when Mrs. Kreder came to see Mrs. Haydon, and that never could be very often. Then too these days Mrs. Haydon could not scold Lena, Mrs. Kreder was always there with her, and it would not be right to scold Lena when Mrs. Kreder was there, who had now the real right to do it. And so her aunt always said nice things now to Lena, and though Mrs. Haydon sometimes was a little worried when she saw Lena looking sad and not careful, she did not have time just then to really worry much about it.

Lena now never any more saw the girls she always used to sit with. She had no way now to see them and it was not in Lena's nature to search out ways to see them, nor did she now ever think much of the days when she had been used to see them. They never any of them had come to the Kreder house to see her. Not even Irish Mary had ever thought to come to see her. Lena had been soon forgotten by them. They had soon passed away from Lena and now Lena never thought any more that she had ever known them.

The only one of her old friends who tried to know what Lena liked and what she needed, and who always made Lena come to see her, was the good german cook who had always scolded. She now scolded Lena hard for letting herself go so, and going out when she was looking so untidy. "I know you going to have a baby Lena, but that's no way for you to be looking. I am ashamed most to see you come and sit here in my kitchen, looking so sloppy and like you never used to Lena. I never see anybody like you Lena. Herman is very good to you, you always say so, and he don't treat you bad ever though you don't deserve to have anybody good to you, you so careless all the time, Lena, letting yourself go like you never had anybody tell you what was the right way you should know how to be looking. No, Lena, I don't see no reason you should let yourself go so and look so untidy Lena, so I am ashamed to see you sit there looking so ugly, Lena. No Lena that ain't no way ever I see a woman make things come out better, letting herself go so every way and crying all the time like as if you had real trouble. I never wanted to see you marry Herman Kreder, Lena, I knew what you got to stand with that old woman always, and that old man, he is so stingy too and he don't say things out but he ain't any better in his heart than his wife with her bad ways, I know that Lena, I know they don't hardly give you enough to eat, Lena, I am real sorry for you Lena, you know that Lena, but that ain't any way to be going round so untidy Lena, even if you have got all that trouble. You never see me do like that Lena, though sometimes I got a headache so I can't see to stand to be working hardly, and nothing comes right with all my cooking, but I always see Lena, I look decent. That's the only way a german girl can make things come out right Lena. You hear me what I am saying to you Lena. Now you eat something nice Lena, I got it all ready for you, and you wash up and be careful Lena and the baby will come all right to you, and then I make your Aunt Mathilda see that you live in a house soon all alone with Herman and your baby, and then everything go better for you. You hear me what I say to you Lena. Now don't let me ever see you come looking like this any more Lena, and you just stop with that always crying. You ain't got no reason to be sitting there now with all that crying, I never see anybody have trouble it did them any good to do the way you are doing, Lena. You hear me Lena. You go home now and you be good the way I tell you Lena, and I see what I can do. I make your Aunt Mathilda make old Mrs. Kreder let you be till you get your baby all right. Now don't you be scared and so silly Lena. I don't like to see you act so Lena when really you got a nice man and so many things really any girl should be grateful to be having. Now you go home Lena to-day and you do the way I say, to you, and I see what I can do to help you."

"Yes Mrs. Aldrich" said the good german woman to her mistress later, "Yes Mrs. Aldrich that's the way it is with them girls when they want so to get married. They dont know when they got it good Mrs. Aldrich. They never know what it is they're really wanting when they got it, Mrs. Aldrich. There's that poor Lena, she just been here crying and looking so careless so I scold her, but that was no good that marrying for that poor Lena, Mrs. Aldrich. She do look so pale and sad now Mrs. Aldrich, it just break my heart to see her. She was a good girl was Lena, Mrs. Aldrich, and I never had no trouble with her like I got with so many young girls nowadays, Mrs. Aldrich, and I never see any girl any better to work right than our Lena, and now she got to stand it all the time with that old woman Mrs. Kreder. My! Mrs. Aldrich, she is a bad old woman to her. I never see Mrs. Aldrich how old people can be so bad to young girls and not have no kind of patience with them. If Lena could only live with her Herman, he ain't so bad the way men are, Mrs. Aldrich, but he is just the way always his mother wants him, he ain't got no spirit in him, and so I don't really see no help for that poor Lena. I know her aunt, Mrs. Haydon, meant it all right for her Mrs. Aldrich, but poor Lena, it would be better for her if her Herman had stayed there in New York that time he went away to leave her. I don't like it the way Lena is looking now, Mrs. Aldrich. She looks like as if she don't have no life left in her hardly, Mrs. Aldrich, she just drags around and looks so dirty and after all the pains I always took to teach her and to keep her nice in her ways and looking. It don't do no good to them, for them girls to get married Mrs. Aldrich, they are much better when they only know it, to stay in a good place when they got it, and keep on regular with their working. I don't like it the way Lena looks now Mrs. Aldrich. I wish I knew some way to help that poor Lena, Mrs. Aldrich, but she is a bad old woman, that old Mrs. Kreder, Herman's mother. I speak to Mrs. Haydon real soon, Mrs. Aldrich, I see what we can do now to help that poor Lena."

These were really bad days for poor Lena. Herman always was real good to her and now he even sometimes tried to stop his mother from scolding Lena. "She ain't well now mama, you let her be now you hear me. You tell me what it is you want she should be doing, I tell her. I see she does it right just the way you want it mama. You let be, I say now mama, with that always scolding Lena. You let be, I say now, you wait till she is feeling better." Herman was getting really strong to struggle, for he could see that Lena with that baby working hard inside her, really could not stand it any longer with his mother and the awful ways she always scolded.

It was a new feeling Herman now had inside him that made him feel he was strong to make a struggle. It was new for Herman Kreder really to be wanting something, but Herman wanted strongly now to be a father, and he wanted badly that his baby should be a boy and healthy. Herman never had cared really very much about his father and his mother, though always, all his life, he had done everything just as they wanted, and he had never really cared much about his wife, Lena, though he always had been very good to her, and had always tried to keep his mother off her, with the awful way she always scolded, but to be really a father of a little baby, that feeling took hold of Herman very deeply. He was almost ready, so as to save his baby from all trouble, to really make a strong struggle with his mother and with his father, too, if he would not help him to control his mother.

Sometimes Herman even went to Mrs. Haydon to talk all this trouble over. They decided then together, it was better to wait there all four together for the baby, and Herman could make Mrs. Kreder stop a little with her scolding, and then when Lena was a little stronger, Herman should have his own house for her, next door to his father, so he could always be there to help him in his working, but so they could eat and sleep in a house where the old woman could not control them and they could not hear her awful scolding.

And so things went on, the same way, a little longer. Poor Lena was not feeling any joy to have a baby. She was scared the way she had been when she was so sick on the water. She was scared now every time when anything would hurt her. She was scared and still and lifeless, and sure that every minute she would die. Lena had no power to be strong in this kind of trouble, she could only sit still and be scared, and dull, and lifeless, and sure that every minute she would die.

Before very long, Lena had her baby. He was a good, healthy little boy, the baby. Herman cared very much to have the baby. When Lena was a little stronger he took a house next door to the old couple, so he and his own family could eat and sleep and do the way they wanted. This did not seem to make much change now for Lena. She was just the same as when she was waiting with her baby. She just dragged around and was careless with her clothes and all lifeless, and she acted always and lived on just as if she had no feeling. She always did everything regular with the work, the way she always had had to do it, but she never got back any spirit in her. Herman was always good and kind, and always helped her with her working. He did everything he knew to help her. He always did all the active new things in the house and for the baby. Lena did what she had to do the way she always had been taught it. She always just kept going now with her working, and she was always careless, and dirty, and a little dazed, and lifeless. Lena never got any better in herself of this way of being that she had had ever since she had been married.

Mrs. Haydon never saw any more of her niece, Lena. Mrs. Haydon had now so much trouble with her own house, and her daughters getting married, and her boy, who was growing up, and who always was getting so much worse to manage. She knew she had done right by Lena. Herman Kreder was a good man, she would be glad to get one so good, sometimes, for her own daughters, and now they had a home to live in together, separate from the old people, who had made their trouble for them. Mrs. Haydon felt she had done very well by her niece, Lena, and she never thought now she needed any more to go and see her. Lena would do very well now without her aunt to trouble herself any more about her.

The good german cook who had always scolded, still tried to do her duty like a mother to poor Lena. It was very hard now to do right by Lena. Lena never seemed to hear now what anyone was saying to her. Herman was always doing everything he could to help her. Herman always, when he was home, took good care of the baby. Herman loved to take care of his baby. Lena never thought to take him out or to do anything she didn't have to.

The good cook sometimes made Lena come to see her. Lena would come with her baby and sit there in the kitchen, and watch the good woman cooking, and listen to her sometimes a little, the way she used to, while the good german woman scolded her for going around looking so careless when now she had no trouble, and sitting there so dull, and always being just so thankless. Sometimes Lena would wake up a little and get back into her face her old, gentle, patient, and unsuffering sweetness, but mostly Lena did not seem to hear much when the good german woman scolded. Lena always like it when Mrs. Aldrich her good mistress spoke to her kindly, and then Lena would seem to go back and feel herself to be like she was when she had been in service. But mostly Lena just lived along and was careless in her clothes, and dull, and lifeless.

By and by Lena had two more little babies. Lena was not so much scared now when she had the babies. She did not seem to notice very much when they hurt her, and she never seemed to feel very much now about anything that happened to her.

They were very nice babies, all these three that Lena had, and Herman took good care of them always. Herman never really cared much about his wife, Lena. The only things Herman ever really cared for were his babies. Herman always was very good to his children. He always had a gentle, tender way when he held them. He learned to be very handy with them. He spent all the time he was not working, with them. By and by he began to work all day in his own home so that he could have his children always in the same room with him.

Lena always was more and more lifeless and Herman now mostly never thought about her. He more and more took all the care of their three children. He saw to their eating right and their washing, and he dressed them every morning, and he taught them the right way to do things, and he put them to their sleeping, and he was now always every minute with them. Then there was to come to them, a fourth baby. Lena went to the hospital near by to have the baby. Lena seemed to be going to have much trouble with it. When the baby was come out at last, it was like its mother lifeless. While it was coming, Lena had grown very pale and sicker. When it was all over Lena had died, too, and nobody knew just how it had happened to her.

The good german cook who had always scolded Lena, and had always to the last day tried to help her, was the only one who ever missed her. She remembered how nice Lena had looked all the time she was in service with her, and how her voice had been so gentle and sweet-sounding, and how she always was a good girl, and how she never had to have any trouble with her, the way she always had with all the other girls who had been taken into the house to help her. The good cook sometimes spoke so of Lena when she had time to have a talk with Mrs. Aldrich, and this was all the remembering there now ever was of Lena.

Herman Kreder now always lived very happy, very gentle, very quiet, very well content alone with his three children. He never had a woman any more to be all the time around him. He always did all his own work in his house, when he was through every day with the work he was always doing for his father. Herman always was alone, and he always worked alone, until his little ones were big enough to help him. Herman Kreder was very well content now and he always lived very regular and peaceful, and with every day just like the next one, always alone now with his three good, gentle children.

FINIS

1909

from   *TENDER BUTTONS**

from   OBJECTS

A SUBSTANCE IN A CUSHION

The change of color is likely and a difference a very little difference is prepared. Sugar is not a vegetable.

Callous is something that hardening leaves behind what will be soft if there is a genuine interest in there being present as many girls as men. Does this change. It shows that dirt is clean when there is a volume.

A cushion has that cover. Supposing you do not like to change, supposing it is very clean that there is no change in appearance, supposing that there is regularity and a costume is that any the worse than an oyster and an exchange. Come to season that is there any extreme use in feather and cotton. Is there not much more joy in a table and more chairs and very likely roundness and a place to put them.

A circle of fine card board and a chance to see a tassel.

What is the use of a violent kind of delightfulness if there is no pleasure in not getting tired of it. The question does not come before there is a quotation. In any kind of place there is a top to covering and it is a pleasure at any rate there is some venturing in refusing to believe nonsense. It shows what use there is in a whole piece if one uses it and it is extreme and very likely the little things could be dearer but in any case there is a bargain and if there is the best thing to do is to take it away and wear it and then be reckless be reckless and resolved on returning gratitude.

Light blue and the same red with purple makes a change. It shows that there is no mistake. Any pink shows that and very likely it is reasonable. Very likely there should not be a finer fancy present. Some increase means a calamity and this is the best preparation for three and more being together. A little calm is so ordinary and in any case there is sweetness and some of that.

A seal and matches and a swan and ivy and a suit.

A closet, a closet does not connect under the bed. The band if it is white and

---

* First published in 1914, *Tender Buttons,* one of Stein's most innovative works, consists of short entries arranged under the headings "Objects," "Food," and "Rooms." Stein explains in *Lectures in America* (1935), " . . . in *Tender Buttons* and then on I struggled with the ridding of myself of nouns. I knew that nouns must go in poetry as they had gone in prose if anything that is everything was to go on meaning something." Stein jettisoned conventional patterns of syntax, freeing words that normally function as nouns, to form new semantic and phonic combinations. She paralleled the radical innovations of her artist friends Pablo Picasso (1881–1973) and Georges Braque (1882–1963), who in "synthetic cubism" dissociated familiar shapes, objects, and even linguistic elements from the context in which they were habitually perceived and understood.

black, the band has a green string. A sight a whole sight and a little groan grinding makes a trimming such a sweet singing trimming and a red thing not a round thing but a white thing, a red thing and a white thing.

The disgrace is not in carelessness nor even in sewing it comes out out of the way.

What is the sash like. The sash is not like anything mustard it is not like a same thing that has stripes, it is not even more hurt than that, it has a little top.

A BOX

Out of kindness comes redness and out of rudeness comes rapid same question, out of an eye comes research, out of selection comes painful cattle. So then the order is that a white way of being round is something suggesting a pin and is it disappointing, it is not, it is so rudimentary to be analysed and see a fine substance strangely, it is so earnest to have a green point not to red but to point again.

A PIECE OF COFFEE

More of double.

A place in no new table.

A single image is not splendor. Dirty is yellow. A sign of more is not mentioned. A piece of coffee is not a detainer. The resemblance to yellow is dirtier and distincter. The clean mixture is whiter and not coal color, never more coal color than altogether.

The sight of a reason, the same sight slighter, the sight of a simpler negative answer, the same sore sounder, the intention to wishing, the same splendor, the same furniture.

The time to show a message is when too late and later there is no hanging in a blight.

A not torn rose-wood color. If it is not dangerous then a pleasure and more than any other if it is cheap is not cheaper. The amusing side is that the sooner there are no fewer the more certain is the necessity dwindled. Supposing that the case contained rose-wood and a color. Supposing that there was no reason for a distress and more likely for a number, supposing that there was no astonishment, is it not necessary to mingle astonishment.

The settling of stationing cleaning is one way not to shatter scatter and scattering. The one way to use custom is to use soap and silk for cleaning. The one way to see cotton is to have a design concentrating the illusion and the illustration. The perfect way is to accustom the thing to have a lining and the shape of a ribbon and to be solid, quite solid in standing and to use heaviness in morning. It is light enough in that. It has that shape nicely. Very nicely may not be exaggerating. Very strongly may be sincerely fainting. May be strangely flattering. May not be strange in everything. May not be strange to.

DIRT AND NOT COPPER

Dirt and not copper makes a color darker. It makes the shape so heavy and makes no melody harder.

It makes mercy and relaxation and even a strength to spread a table fuller. There are more places not empty. They see cover.

NOTHING ELEGANT

A charm a single charm is doubtful. If the red is rose and there is a gate surrounding it, if inside is let in and there places change then certainly something is upright. It is earnest.

MILDRED'S UMBRELLA

A cause and no curve, a cause and loud enough, a cause and extra a loud clash and an extra wagon, a sign of extra, a sac a small sac and an established color and cunning, a slender grey and no ribbon, this means a loss a great loss a restitution.

A METHOD OF A CLOAK

A single climb to a line, a straight exchange to a cane, a desperate adventure and courage and a clock, all this which is a system, which has feeling, which has resignation and success, all makes an attractive black silver.

A RED STAMP

If lilies are lily white if they exhaust noise and distance and even dust, if they dusty will dirt a surface that has no extreme grace, if they do this and it is not necessary it is not at all necessary if they do this they need a catalogue.

A BOX

A large box is handily made of what is necessary to replace any substance. Suppose an example is necessary, the plainer it is made the more reason there is for some outward recognition that there is a result.

A box is made sometimes and them to see to see to it neatly and to have the holes stopped up makes it necessary to use paper.

A custom which is necessary when a box is used and taken is that a large part of the time there are three which have different connections. The one is on the table. The two are on the table. The three are on the table. The one, one is the same length as is shown by the cover being longer. The other is different there is more cover that shows it. The other is different and that makes the corners have the same shade the eight are in singular arrangement to make four necessary.

Lax, to have corners, to be lighter than some weight, to indicate a wedding journey, to last brown and not curious, to be wealthy, cigarettes are established by length and by doubling.

Left open, to be left pounded, to be left closed, to be circulating in summer and winter, and sick color that is grey that is not dusty and red shows, to be sure cigarettes do measure an empty length sooner than a choice in color.

Winged, to be winged means that white is yellow and pieces pieces that are brown are dust color if dust is washed off, then it is choice that is to say it is fitting cigarettes sooner than paper.

An increase why is an increase idle, why is silver cloister, why is the spark brighter, if it is brighter is there any result, hardly more than ever.

A PLATE

An occasion for a plate, an occasional resource is in buying and how soon does washing enable a selection of the same thing neater. If the party is small a clever song is in order.

Plates and a dinner set of colored china. Pack together a string and enough with it to protect the centre, cause a considerable haste and gather more as it is cooling, collect more trembling and not any even trembling, cause a whole thing to be a church.

A sad size a size that is not sad is blue as every bit of blue is precocious. A kind of green a game in green and nothing flat nothing quite flat and more round, nothing a particular color strangely, nothing breaking the losing of no little piece.

A splendid address a really splendid address is not shown by giving a flower freely, it is not shown by a mark or by wetting.

Cut cut in white, cut in white so lately. Cut more than any other and show it. Show it in the stem and in starting and in evening coming complication.

A lamp is not the only sign of glass. The lamp and the cake are not the only sign of stone. The lamp and the cake and the cover are not the only necessity altogether.

A plan a hearty plan, a compressed disease and no coffee, not even a card or a change to incline each way, a plan that has that excess and that break is the one that shows filling.

* * *

A MOUNTED UMBRELLA

What was the use of not leaving it there where it would hang what was the use if there was no chance of ever seeing it come there and show that it was handsome and right in the way it showed it. The lesson is to learn that it does show it, that it shows it and that nothing, that there is nothing, that there is no more to do about it and just so much more is there plenty of reason for making an exchange.

A CLOTH

Enough cloth is plenty and more, more is almost enough for that and besides if there is no more spreading is there plenty of room for it. Any occasion shows the best way.

MORE

An elegant use of foliage and grace and a little piece of white cloth and oil.

Wondering so winningly in several kinds of oceans is the reason that makes red so regular and enthusiastic. The reason that there is more snips are the same shining very colored rid of no round color.

A NEW CUP AND SAUCER

Enthusiastically hurting a clouded yellow bud and saucer, enthusiastically so is the bite in the ribbon.

OBJECTS

Within, within the cut and slender joint alone, with sudden equals and no more than three, two in the centre make two one side.

If the elbow is long and it is filled so then the best example is all together.

The kind of show is made by squeezing.

* * *

RED ROSES

A cool red rose and a pink cut pink, a collapse and a sold hole, a little less hot.

IN BETWEEN

In between a place and candy is a narrow foot-path that shows more mounting than anything, so much really that a calling meaning a bolster measured a whole thing with that. A virgin a whole virgin is judged made and so between curves and outlines and real seasons and more out glasses and a perfectly unprecedented arrangement between old ladies and mild colds there is no satin wood shining.

* * *

A SOUND

Elephant beaten with candy and little pops and chews all bolts and reckless reckless rats, this is this.

* * *

A LEAVE

In the middle of a tiny spot and nearly bare there is a nice thing to say that wrist is leading. Wrist is leading.

SUPPOSE AN EYES

Suppose it is within a gate which open is open at the hour of closing summer that is to say it is so.

All the seats are needing blackening. A white dress is in sign. A soldier a real soldier has a worn lace a worn lace of different sizes that is to say if he can read, if he can read he is a size to show shutting up twenty-four.

Go red go red, laugh white.

Suppose a collapse in rubbed purr, in rubbed purr get.

Little sales ladies little sales ladies little saddles of mutton.

Little sales of leather and such beautiful beautiful, beautiful beautiful.

A SHAWL

A shawl is a hat and hurt and a red ballon and an under coat and a sizer a sizer of talks.

A shawl is a wedding, a piece of wax a little build. A shawl.

Pick a ticket, pick it in strange steps and with hollows. There is hollow hollow belt, a belt is a shawl.

A plate that has a little bobble, all of them, any so.

Please a round it is ticket.

It was a mistake to state that a laugh and a lip and a laid climb and a depot and a cultivator and little choosing is a point it.

BOOK

Book was there, it was there. Book was there. Stop it, stop it, it was a cleaner, a wet cleaner and it was not where it was wet, it was not high, it was directly placed back, not back again, back it was returned, it was needless, it put a bank, a bank when, a bank care.

Suppose a man a realistic expression of resolute reliability suggests pleasing itself white all white and no head does that mean soap. It does not so. It means kind wavers and little chance to beside beside rest. A plain.

Suppose ear rings that is one way to breed, breed that. Oh chance to say, oh nice old pole. Next best and nearest a pillar. Chest not valuable, be papered.

Cover up cover up the two with a little piece of string and hope rose and green, green.

Please a plate, put a match to the seam and really then really then, really then it is a remark that joins many many lead games. It is a sister and sister and a flower and a flower and a dog and a colored sky a sky colored grey and nearly that nearly that let.

PEELED PENCIL, CHOKE

Rub her coke.

IT WAS BLACK, BLACK TOOK

Black ink best wheel bale brown.

Excellent not a hull house, not a pea soup, no bill no care, no precise no past pearl pearl goat.

THIS IS THIS DRESS, AIDER

Aider, why aider why whow, whow stop touch, aider whow, aider stop the muncher, muncher munchers.

A jack in kill her, a jack in, makes a meadowed king, makes a to let.

1914

An organized women's suffrage movement that began in the 1890s led to the passage of the Nineteenth Amendment in 1920. Here, women in 1913 are demonstrating for the right to vote.

Sherwood Anderson
(1876–1941)

Sherwood Anderson radically altered the shape of the American short story by loosening its restrictions, and he provided a model for other writers. Because his successors wrote so well in his wake, Anderson's work is typically valued less as art than as an influential antecedent to the work of later authors such as Ernest Hemingway, William Faulkner, John Steinbeck, and Henry Miller. Some of Anderson's reviewers qualify their praise with unflattering comparisons; few, however, deny his stylistic originality or his moments of inspired lyricism and genuine insight. These moments were never sufficiently prolonged for the production of an exemplary novel, but many of his short stories are minor masterpieces.

Anderson was born in 1876 in Camden, Ohio. His parents, a harnessmaker and a washerwoman, raised him in the small town of Clyde, Ohio. Anderson contributed to the family finances by working at many odd jobs; his high school attendance was sporadic, and he never graduated. Released from the army in 1900 after the Spanish-American War, he found work in Chicago as an advertising copywriter. Anderson later condemned advertising copy as a perversion of language: his experiments with plain, discursive prose styles were in part a reaction to his years of uneasy participation in the duping of the American public. Throughout his life Anderson cast himself as a champion of the average citizen, investigating and deploring the deleterious socioeconomic effects of industrialization and big business. His lasting sympathy and easy rapport with the middle and lower classes permeate his collection of essays *Puzzled America* (1935), which documents the reactions of ordinary people to the extraordinary circumstances of the Great Depression.

Anderson's concern for the middle class and distrust of wealthy industrialists did not, however, diminish his own social and financial aspirations. In *Sherwood Anderson's Memoirs* (1942), he confesses to elitist ambitions: "I wanted to go to the theatre, sit in a good seat, drive a good car. . . . I was the kind of man Mr. Bernard Shaw had described as 'a simple soul, perfectly satisfied with the best of everything.'" To finance these ambitions he left Chicago to manage his own mail-order paint-distribution business, the Anderson Manufacturing Company, in Elyria, Ohio. This venture folded in 1912; he suffered a nervous breakdown that year, and his first marriage failed soon afterward (he was to marry three more times).

In his "fanciful autobiography," *A Story Teller's Story* (1924), Anderson offers an embroidered account of the year 1912. There he transforms his financial and personal catastrophes into a dramatic rejection of the chicaneries of free enterprise. He viewed himself as an entirely unauthentic self-creation: a fraudulent, fast-talking businessman. He began writing fiction to search for a "buried life" within himself as well as within his characters. The stories he wrote before 1912 include "Hands," an elusive and evocative protrait of a pathetically inarticulate character being interviewed by George Willard, a small-town newspaper reporter. "Hands" was ultimately published in *Winesburg, Ohio* (1919), a compilation of related stories (including "Adventure") that many critics consider Anderson's best work. John Updike suggests that the inadequacy of contemporary language is the central topic of the collection: "Inexpressiveness, indeed, is what is above all expressed: the characters, often, talk only to George Willard [who narrates many of the *Winesburg, Ohio* stories], and then only once; their attempts to talk with one another tend to culminate in a comedy of tongue-tied silence."

Aphasia, a loss of the ability to use or understood words, figures as well in the autobi-

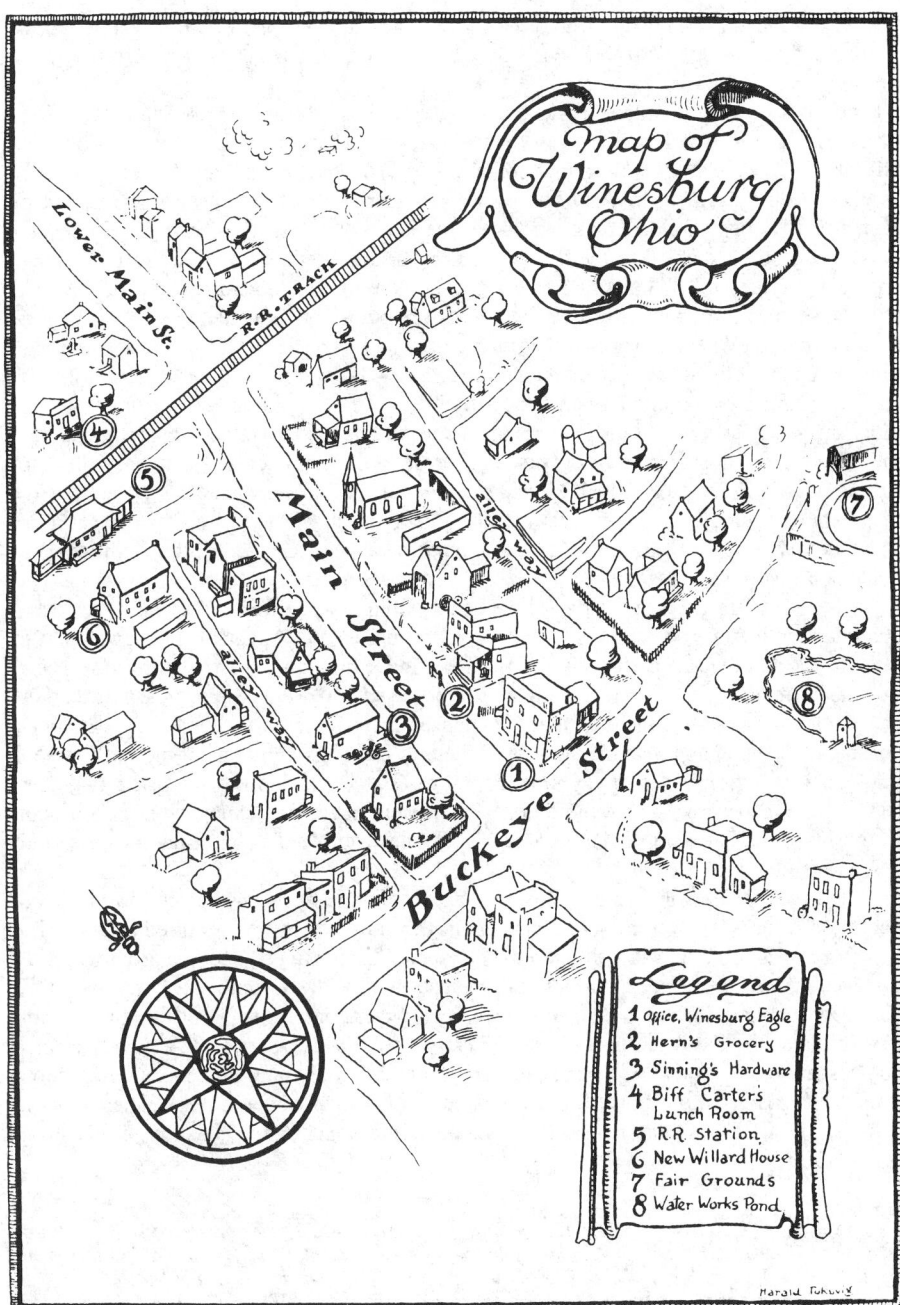

The frontispiece of Sherwood Anderson's Winesburg, Ohio, *a map of the fictional town drawn by Harald Toksvig.*

ography's account of Anderson's nervous breakdown in 1912. While dictating a letter he fell silent, walked out of his office and (symbolically) abandoned the business world and all its linguistic frauds. Several days later he was found some miles away, babbling incoherently. After a brief hospitalization he moved back to Chicago, where he supported his writing efforts by copywriting, betraying language during business hours in order to redeem it in his free time.

During this period Anderson was encouraged by his colleagues Carl Sandburg, Theodore Dreiser, and Ben Hecht, and Anderson's stories began to appear in literary journals. His first two novels, *Windy McPherson's Son* (1916) and *Marching Men* (1917), were received well by critics. In 1917 he visited New York City, where he was welcomed by Van Wyck Brooks, Waldo Frank, and other literary figures involved with the leftist journal *Seven Arts,* dedicated to the development of a new literature opposed to materialism and sexual repression. Although Anderson lacked the formal education of his new associates, he seemed to be creating just such a literature out of native materials.

Winesburg, Ohio was nationally acclaimed for its innovation of form and its combination of superficially spare and unpretentious prose with delicate shadings of darker undercurrents. Anderson revolted against the strictures of the traditional short-story form: his plots are nearly absent and his endings inconclusive. He also revolted against the publishing taboos censoring discussions of sexual mores, so that some critics condemned his stories as obscene. The stories in *Winesburg, Ohio* seem relatively tame today, but in 1919 they earned Anderson the sobriquets "phallic Chekhov" and "Sherwood Lawrence." D. H. Lawrence was in fact one of Anderson's models, as was Gertrude Stein, whose work Anderson first read in 1912.

In 1921 Anderson visited Paris, where he met Stein; their unlikely but warm friendship continued until Anderson's death in 1941. (While in Panama, Anderson swallowed part of a toothpick and died of peritonitis shortly thereafter.) In 1926 Ernest Hemingway cruelly parodied Anderson in the satirical novel *The Torrents of Spring.* Stein, who felt that she and Anderson were equally important influences in Hemingway's literary development, consoled Anderson and revenged him by ridiculing Hemingway in one of the most famous passages in *The Autobiography of Alice B. Toklas* (1933). Other writers assisted by Anderson early in their careers were more honest than Hemingway in acknowledging their debt: in 1929 William Faulkner dedicated *Sartoris* to "Sherwood Anderson, through whose kindness I was first published."

After 1926 Anderson lived in Virginia, and economic problems specific to the South became a central focus in his later writing. In the early 1930s he was briefly attracted to communism, but his flawed political novel *Beyond Desire* (1932) inadvertently reveals his distaste for the dogmatic, authoritarian elements within the Communist party. His final collection of short stories, *Death in the Woods* (1933), contains some of the finest examples of his stylistic achievement. In *Kit Brandon* (1936), his last novel, Anderson created perhaps his most attractive heroine: a sexually uninhibited young woman running moonshine during Prohibition. In tracing her experiences of American culture, Anderson continued his crusade against the materialism, inauthenticity, and dehumanization of industrialized society.

Suggested Readings: *Windy McPherson's Son,* 1916. *Mid-American Chants,* 1918. *Poor White,* 1920. *The Triumph of the Egg: A Book of Impressions From American Life in Tales and Poems,* 1921. *A Story Teller's Story,* 1924. *Dark Laughter,* 1925. *Sherwood Anderson's Notebooks,* 1926. *Perhaps Women,* 1931. *Letters of Sherwood Anderson,* 1953. R. L. White, ed., *The Achievement of Sherwood Anderson: Essays in Criticism,* 1966. D. Anderson, ed., *Sherwood Anderson: Dimensions of His Literary Art: A Collection of Critical Essays,* 1976. H. H. Campbell and C. E. Modlin, eds., *Sherwood Anderson: Centennial Studies,* 1976. R. L. White, ed., *Sherwood Anderson: A Reference Guide,* 1977. D. Anderson, ed., *Critical Essays on Sherwood Anderson,* 1981.

Texts Used: "Adventure": *Winesburg, Ohio: A Group of Tales of Ohio Small-Town Life,* 1919. "Death in the Woods": *Death in the Woods and Other Stories,* 1933.

from   *WINESBURG, OHIO**

ADVENTURE

Alice Hindman, a woman of twenty-seven when George Willard was a mere boy, had lived in Winesburg all her life. She clerked in Winney's Dry Goods Store and lived with her mother who had married a second husband.

Alice's step-father was a carriage painter, and given to drink. His story is an odd one. It will be worth telling some day.

At twenty-seven Alice was tall and somewhat slight. Her head was large and overshadowed her body. Her shoulders were a little stooped and her hair and eyes brown. She was very quiet but beneath a placid exterior a continual ferment went on.

When she was a girl of sixteen and before she began to work in the store, Alice had an affair with a young man. The young man, named Ned Currie, was older than Alice. He, like George Willard, was employed on the *Winesburg Eagle* and for a long time he went to see Alice almost every evening. Together the two walked under the trees through the streets of the town and talked of what they would do with their lives. Alice was then a very pretty girl and Ned Currie took her into his arms and kissed her. He became excited and said things he did not intend to say and Alice, betrayed by her desire to have something beautiful come into her rather narrow life, also grew excited. She also talked. The outer crust of her life, all of her natural diffidence and reserve, was torn away and she gave herself over to the emotions of love. When, late in the fall of her sixteenth year, Ned Currie went away to Cleveland where he hoped to get a place on a city newspaper and rise in the world, she wanted to go with him. With a trembling voice she told him what was in her mind. "I will work and you can work," she said. "I do not want to harness you to a needless expense that will prevent your making progress. Don't marry me now. We will get along without that and we can be together. Even though we live in the same house no one will say anything. In the city we will be unknown and people will pay no attention to us."

Ned Currie was puzzled by the determination and abandon of his sweetheart and was also deeply touched. He had wanted the girl to become his mistress but changed his mind. He wanted to protect and care for her. "You don't know what you're talking about," he said sharply; "you may be sure I'll let you do no such thing. As soon as I get a good job I'll come back. For the present you'll have to stay here. It's the only thing we can do."

On the evening before he left Winesburg to take up his new life in the city, Ned Currie went to call on Alice. They walked about through the streets for an hour and then got a rig from Wesley Moyer's livery and went for a drive in the country. The moon came up and they found themselves unable to talk. In his sadness the young man forgot the resolutions he had made regarding his conduct with the girl.

They got out of the buggy at a place where a long meadow ran down to the bank of Wine Creek and there in the dim light became lovers. When at midnight they returned to town they were both glad. It did not seem to them that anything

---

* Twenty-three stories published in 1919; Anderson's characters are unified throughout, as he explains in the preface, "The Book of the Grotesque" (Anderson's title for the collection before its publication).

that could happen in the future could blot out the wonder and beauty of the thing that had happened. "Now we will have to stick to each other, whatever happens we will have to do that," Ned Currie said as he left the girl at her father's door.

The young newspaper man did not succeed in getting a place on a Cleveland paper and went west to Chicago. For a time he was lonely and wrote to Alice almost every day. Then he was caught up by the life of the city; he began to make friends and found new interests in life. In Chicago he boarded at a house where there were several women. One of them attracted his attention and he forgot Alice in Winesburg. At the end of a year he had stopped writing letters, and only once in a long time, when he was lonely or when he went into one of the city parks and saw the moon shining on the grass as it had shone that night on the meadow by Wine Creek, did he think of her at all.

In Winesburg the girl who had been loved grew to be a woman. When she was twenty-two years old her father, who owned a harness repair shop, died suddenly. The harness maker was an old soldier, and after a few months his wife received a widow's pension. She used the first money she got to buy a loom and became a weaver of carpets, and Alice got a place in Winney's store. For a number of years nothing could have induced her to believe that Ned Currie would not in the end return to her.

She was glad to be employed because the daily round of toil in the store made the time of waiting seem less long and uninteresting. She began to save money, thinking that when she had saved two or three hundred dollars she would follow her lover to the city and try if her presence would not win back his affections.

Alice did not blame Ned Currie for what had happened in the moonlight in the field, but felt that she could never marry another man. To her the thought of giving to another what she still felt could belong only to Ned seemed monstrous. When other young men tried to attract her attention she would have nothing to do with them. "I am his wife and shall remain his wife whether he comes back or not," she whispered to herself, and for all of her willingness to support herself could not have understood the growing modern idea of a woman's owning herself and giving and taking for her own ends in life.

Alice worked in the dry goods store from eight in the morning until six at night and on three evenings a week went back to the store to stay from seven until nine. As time passed and she became more and more lonely she began to practice the devices common to lonely people. When at night she went upstairs into her own room she knelt on the floor to pray and in her prayers whispered things she wanted to say to her lover. She became attached to inanimate objects, and because it was her own, could not bear to have anyone touch the furniture of her room. The trick of saving money, begun for a purpose, was carried on after the scheme of going to the city to find Ned Currie had been given up. It became a fixed habit, and when she needed new clothes she did not get them. Sometimes on rainy afternoons in the store she got out her bank book and, letting it lie open before her, spent hours dreaming impossible dreams of saving money enough so that the interest would support both herself and her future husband.

"Ned always liked to travel about," she thought. "I'll give him the chance. Some day when we are married and I can save both his money and my own, we will be rich. Then we can travel together all over the world."

In the dry goods store weeks ran into months and months into years as Alice waited and dreamed of her lover's return. Her employer, a grey old man with false teeth and a thin grey mustache that drooped down over his mouth, was not given to conversation, and sometimes, on rainy days and in the winter when a storm raged in Main Street, long hours passed when no customers came in. Alice arranged and rearranged the stock. She stood near the front window where she could look down the deserted street and thought of the evenings when she had walked with Ned Currie and of what he had said. "We will have to stick to each other now." The words echoed and re-echoed through the mind of the maturing woman. Tears came into her eyes. Sometimes when her employer had gone out and she was alone in the store she put her head on the counter and wept. "Oh, Ned, I am waiting," she whispered over and over, and all the time the creeping fear that he would never come back grew stronger within her.

In the spring when the rains have passed and before the long hot days of summer have come, the country about Winesburg is delightful. The town lies in the midst of open fields, but beyond the fields are pleasant patches of woodlands. In the wooded places are many little cloistered nooks, quiet places where lovers go to sit on Sunday afternoons. Through the trees they look out across the fields and see farmers at work about the barns or people driving up and down on the roads. In the town bells ring and occasionally a train passes, looking like a toy thing in the distance.

For several years after Ned Currie went away Alice did not go into the wood with other young people on Sunday, but one day after he had been gone for two or three years and when her loneliness seemed unbearable, she put on her best dress and set out. Finding a little sheltered place from which she could see the town and a long stretch of the fields, she sat down. Fear of age and ineffectuality took possession of her. She could not sit still, and rose. As she stood looking out over the land something, perhaps the thought of never ceasing life as it expresses itself in the flow of the seasons, fixed her mind on the passing years. With a shiver of dread, she realized that for her the beauty and freshness of youth had passed. For the first time she felt that she had been cheated. She did not blame Ned Currie and did not know what to blame. Sadness swept over her. Dropping to her knees, she tried to pray, but instead of prayers words of protest came to her lips. "It is not going to come to me. I will never find happiness. Why do I tell myself lies?" she cried, and an odd sense of relief came with this, her first bold attempt to face the fear that had become part of her everyday life.

In the year when Alice Hindman became twenty-five two things happened to disturb the dull uneventfulness of her days. Her mother married Bush Milton, the carriage painter of Winesburg, and she herself became a member of the Winesburg Methodist Church. Alice joined the church because she had become frightened by the loneliness of her position in life. Her mother's second marriage had emphasized her isolation. "I am becoming old and queer. If Ned comes he will not want me. In the city where he is living men are perpetually young. There is so much going on that they do not have time to grow old," she told herself with a grim little smile, and went resolutely about the business of becoming acquainted with people. Every Thursday evening when the store had closed she went to a prayer meeting in the basement of the church and on Sunday evening attended a meeting of an organization called The Epworth League.

When Will Hurley, a middle-aged man who clerked in a drug store and who also belonged to the church, offered to walk home with her she did not protest. "Of course I will not let him make a practice of being with me, but it he comes to see me once in a long time there can be no harm in that," she told herself, still determined in her loyalty to Ned Currie.

Without realizing what was happening, Alice was trying feebly at first, but with growing determination, to get a new hold upon life. Beside the drug clerk she walked in silence, but sometimes in the darkness as they went stolidly along she put out her hand and touched softly the folds of his coat. When he left her at the gate before her mother's house she did not go indoors, but stood for a moment by the door. She wanted to call to the drug clerk, to ask him to sit with her in the darkness on the porch before the house, but was afraid he would not understand. "It is not him that I want," she told herself; "I want to avoid being so much alone. If I am not careful I will grow unaccustomed to being with people."

During the early fall of her twenty-seventh year passionate restlessness took possession of Alice. She could not bear to be in the company of the drug clerk, and when, in the evening, he came to walk with her she sent him away. Her mind became intensely active and when, weary from the long hours of standing behind the counter in the store, she went home and crawled into bed, she could not sleep. With staring eyes she looked into the darkness. Her imagination, like a child awakened from long sleep, played about the room. Deep within her there was something that would not be cheated by phantasies and that demanded some definite answer from life.

Alice took a pillow into her arms and held it tightly against her breasts. Getting out of bed, she arranged a blanket so that in the darkness it looked like a form lying between the sheets and, kneeling beside the bed, she caressed it, whispering words over and over, like a refrain. "Why doesn't something happen? Why am I left here alone?" she muttered. Although she sometimes thought of Ned Currie, she no longer depended on him. Her desire had grown vague. She did not want Ned Currie or any other man. She wanted to be loved, to have something answer the call that was growing louder and louder within her.

And then one night when it rained Alice had an adventure. It frightened and confused her. She had come home from the store at nine and found the house empty. Bush Milton had gone off to town and her mother to the house of a neighbor. Alice went upstairs to her room and undressed in the darkness. For a moment she stood by the window hearing the rain beat against the glass and then a strange desire took possession of her. Without stopping to think of what she intended to do, she ran downstairs through the dark house and out into the rain. As she stood on the little grass plot before the house and felt the cold rain on her body a mad desire to run naked through the streets took possession of her.

She thought that the rain would have some creative and wonderful effect on her body. Not for years had she felt so full of youth and courage. She wanted to leap and run, to cry out, to find some other lonely human and embrace him. On the brick sidewalk before the house a man stumbled homeward. Alice started to run. A wild desperate mood took possession of her. "What do I care who it is. He is alone, and I will go to him," she thought; and then without stopping to consider the possible result of her madness, called softly. "Wait!" she cried. "Don't go away. Whoever you are, you must wait."

The man on the sidewalk stopped and stood listening. He was an old man and somewhat deaf. Putting his hand to his mouth, he shouted: "What? What say?" he called.

Alice dropped to the ground and lay trembling. She was so frightened at the thought of what she had done that when the man had gone on his way she did not dare to get to her feet, but crawled on hands and knees through the grass to the house. When she got to her own room she bolted the door and drew her dressing table across the doorway. Her body shook as with a chill and her hands trembled so that she had difficulty getting into her nightdress. When she got into bed she buried her face in the pillow and wept brokenheartedly. "What is the matter with me? I will do something dreadful if I am not careful," she thought, and turning her face to the wall, began trying to force herself to face bravely the fact that many people must live and die alone, even in Winesburg.

1919

DEATH IN THE WOODS*

She was an old woman and lived on a farm near the town in which I lived. All country and small-town people have seen such old women, but no one knows much about them. Such an old woman comes into town driving an old worn-out horse or she comes afoot carrying a basket. She may own a few hens and have eggs to sell. She brings them in a basket and takes them to a grocer. There she trades them in. She gets some salt pork and some beans. Then she gets a pound or two of sugar and some flour.

Afterwards she goes to the butcher's and asks for some dog-meat. She may spend ten or fifteen cents, but when she does she asks for something. Formerly the butchers gave liver to any one who wanted to carry it away. In our family we were always having it. Once one of my brothers got a whole cow's liver at the slaughter-house near the fairgrounds in our town. We had it until we were sick of it. It never cost a cent. I have hated the thought of it ever since.

The old farm woman got some liver and a soup-bone. She never visited with any one, and as soon as she got what she wanted she lit out for home. It made quite a load for such an old body. No one gave her a lift. People drive right down a road and never notice an old woman like that.

There was such an old woman who used to come into town past our house one Summer and Fall when I was a young boy and was sick with what was called inflammatory rheumatism. She went home later carrying a heavy pack on her back. Two or three large gaunt-looking dogs followed at her heels.

The old woman was nothing special. She was one of the nameless ones that hardly any one knows, but she got into my thoughts. I have just suddenly now, after all these years, remembered her and what happened. It is a story. Her name was Grimes, and she lived with her husband and son in a small unpainted house on the bank of a small creek four miles from town.

The husband and son were a tough lot. Although the son was but twenty-one, he had already served a term in jail. It was whispered about that the woman's husband stole horses and ran them off to some other county. Now and then, when a horse turned up missing, the man had also disappeared. No one ever caught him. Once, when I was loafing at Tom Whitehead's livery-barn, the man came there and sat on the bench in front. Two or three other men were there, but no one spoke to him. He sat for a few minutes and then got up and went away. When he

---

* First published in the *American Mercury* in 1926 and collected in *Death in the Woods and Other Stories* in 1933.

was leaving he turned around and stared at the men. There was a look of defiance in his eyes. "Well, I have tried to be friendly. You don't want to talk to me. It has been so wherever I have gone in this town. If, some day, one of your fine horses turns up missing, well, then what?" He did not say anything actually. "I'd like to bust one of you on the jaw," was about what his eyes said. I remember how the look in his eyes made me shiver.

The old man belonged to a family that had had money once. His name was Jake Grimes. It all comes back clearly now. His father, John Grimes, had owned a sawmill when the country was new, and had made money. Then he got to drinking and running after women. When he died there wasn't much left.

Jake blew in the rest. Pretty soon there wasn't any more lumber to cut and his land was nearly all gone.

He got his wife off a German farmer, for whom he went to work one June day in the wheat harvest. She was a young thing then and scared to death. You see, the farmer was up to something with the girl—she was, I think, a bound girl and his wife had her suspicions. She took it out on the girl when the man wasn't around. Then, when the wife had to go off to town for supplies, the farmer got after her. She told young Jake that nothing really ever happened, but he didn't know whether to believe it or not.

He got her pretty easy himself, the first time he was out with her. He wouldn't have married her if the German farmer hadn't tried to tell him where to get off. He got her to go riding with him in his buggy one night when he was threshing on the place, and then he came for her the next Sunday night.

She managed to get out of the house without her employer's seeing, but when she was getting into the buggy he showed up. It was almost dark, and he just popped up suddenly at the horse's head. He grabbed the horse by the bridle and Jake got out his buggy-whip.

They had it out all right! The German was a tough one. Maybe he didn't care whether his wife knew or not. Jake hit him over the face and shoulders with the buggy-whip, but the horse got to acting up and he had to get out.

Then the two men went for it. The girl didn't see it. The horse started to run away and went nearly a mile down the road before the girl got him stopped. Then she managed to tie him to a tree beside the road. (I wonder how I know all this. It must have stuck in my mind from small-town tales when I was a boy.) Jake found her there after he got through with the German. She was huddled up in the buggy seat, crying, scared to death. She told Jake a lot of stuff, how the German had tried to get her, how he chased her once into the barn, how another time, when they happened to be alone in the house together, he tore her dress open clear down the front. The German, she said, might have got her that time if he hadn't heard his old woman drive in at the gate. She had been off to town for supplies. Well, she would be putting the horse in the barn. The German managed to sneak off to the fields without his wife seeing. He told the girl he would kill her if she told. What could she do? She told a lie about ripping her dress in the barn when she was feeding the stock. I remember now that she was a bound girl and did not know where her father and mother were. Maybe she did not have any father. You know what I mean.

Such bound children were often enough cruelly treated. They were children who had no parents, slaves really. There were very few orphan homes then. They were legally bound into some home. It was a matter of pure luck how it came out.

II

She married Jake and had a son and daughter, but the daughter died.

Then she settled down to feed stock. That was her job. At the German's place she had cooked the food for the German and his wife. The wife was a strong woman with big hips and worked most of the time in the fields with her husband. She fed them and fed the cows in the barn, fed the pigs, the horses and the chickens. Every moment of every day, as a young girl, was spent feeding something.

Then she married Jake Grimes and he had to be fed. She was a slight thing, and when she had been married for three or four years, and after the two children were born, her slender shoulders became stooped.

Jake always had a lot of big dogs around the house, that stood near the unused sawmill near the creek. He was always trading horses when he wasn't stealing something and had a lot of poor bony ones about. Also he kept three or four pigs and a cow. They were all pastured in the few acres left of the Grimes place and Jake did little enough work.

He went into debt for a threshing outfit and ran it for several years, but it did not pay. People did not trust him. They were afraid he would steal the grain at night. He had to go a long way off to get work and it cost too much to get there. In the Winter he hunted and cut a little firewood, to be sold in some nearby town. When the son grew up he was just like the father. They got drunk together. If there wasn't anything to eat in the house when they came home the old man gave his old woman a cut over the head. She had a few chickens of her own and had to kill one of them in a hurry. When they were all killed she wouldn't have any eggs to sell when she went to town, and then what would she do?

She had to scheme all her life about getting things fed, getting the pigs fed so they would grow fat and could be butchered in the Fall. When they were butchered her husband took most of the meat off to town and sold it. If he did not do it first the boy did. They fought sometimes and when they fought the old woman stood aside trembling.

She had got the habit of silence anyway—that was fixed. Sometimes, when she began to look old—she wasn't forty yet—and when the husband and son were both off, trading horses or drinking or hunting or stealing, she went around the house and the barnyard muttering to herself.

How was she going to get everything fed?—that was her problem. The dogs had to be fed. There wasn't enough hay in the barn for the horses and the cow. If she didn't feed the chickens how could they lay eggs? Without eggs to sell how could she get things in town, things she had to have to keep the life of the farm going? Thank heaven, she did not have to feed her husband—in a certain way. That hadn't lasted long after their marriage and after the babies came. Where he went on his long trips she did not know. Sometimes he was gone from home for weeks, and after the boy grew up they went off together.

They left everything at home for her to manage and she had no money. She knew no one. No one ever talked to her in town. When it was Winter she had to gather sticks of wood for her fire, had to try to keep the stock fed with very little grain.

The stock in the barn cried to her hungrily, the dogs followed her about. In the Winter the hens laid few enough eggs. They huddled in the corners of the barn and she kept watching them. If a hen lays an egg in the barn in the Winter and you do not find it, it freezes and breaks.

One day in Winter the old woman went off to town with a few eggs and the dogs followed her. She did not get started until nearly three o'clock and the snow was heavy. She hadn't been feeling very well for several days and so she went muttering along, scantily clad, her shoulders stooped. She had an old grain bag in which she carried her eggs, tucked away down in the bottom. There weren't many of them, but in Winter the price of eggs is up. She would get a little meat in exchange for the eggs, some salt pork, a little sugar, and some coffee perhaps. It might be the butcher would give her a piece of liver.

When she had got to town and was trading in her eggs the dogs lay by the door outside. She did pretty well, got the things she needed, more than she had hoped. Then she went to the butcher and he gave her some liver and some dog-meat.

It was the first time any one had spoken to her in a friendly way for a long time. The butcher was alone in his shop when she came in and was annoyed by the thought of such a sick-looking old woman out on such a day. It was bitter cold and the snow, that had let up during the afternoon, was falling again. The butcher said something about her husband and her son, swore at them, and the old woman stared at him, a look of mild surprise in her eyes as he talked. He said that if either the husband or the son were going to get any of the liver or the heavy bones with scraps of meat hanging to them that he had put into the grain bag, he'd see him starve first.

Starve, eh? Well, things had to be fed. Men had to be fed, and the horses weren't any good but maybe could be traded off, and the poor thin cow that hadn't given any milk for three months.

Horses, cows, pigs, dogs, men.

III

The old woman had to get back before darkness came if she could. The dogs followed at her heels, sniffing at the heavy grain bag she had fastened on her back. When she got to the edge of town she stopped by a fence and tied the bag on her back with a piece of rope she had carried in her dress-pocket for just that purpose. That was an easier way to carry it. Her arms ached. It was hard when she had to crawl over fences and once she fell over and landed in the snow. The dogs went frisking about. She had to struggle to get to her feet again, but she made it. The point of climbing over the fences was that there was a short cut over a hill and through a woods. She might have gone around by the road, but it was a mile farther that way. She was afraid she couldn't make it. And then, besides, the stock had to be fed. There was a little hay left and a little corn. Perhaps her husband and son would bring some home when they came. They had driven off in the only buggy the Grimes family had, a rickety thing, a rickety horse hitched to the buggy, two other rickety horses led by halters. They were going to trade horses, get a little money if they could. They might come home drunk. It would be well to have something in the house when they came back.

The son had an affair on with a woman at the county seat, fifteen miles away. She was a rough enough woman, a tough one. Once, in the Summer, the son had brought her to the house. Both she and the son had been drinking. Jake Grimes was away and the son and his woman ordered the old woman about like a servant.

She didn't mind much; she was used to it. Whatever happened she never said anything. That was her way of getting along. She had managed that way when she was a young girl at the German's and ever since she had married Jake. That time her son brought his woman to the house they stayed all night, sleeping together just as though they were married. It hadn't shocked the old woman, not much. She had got past being shocked early in life.

With the pack on her back she went painfully along across an open field, wading in the deep snow, and got into the woods.

There was a path, but it was hard to follow. Just beyond the top of the hill, where the woods was thickest, there was a small clearing. Had some one once thought of building a house there? The clearing was as large as a building lot in town, large enough for a house and a garden. The path ran along the side of the clearing, and when she got there the old woman sat down to rest at the foot of a tree.

It was a foolish thing to do. When she got herself placed, the pack against the tree's trunk, it was nice, but what about getting up again? She worried about that for a moment and then quietly closed her eyes.

She must have slept for a time. When you are about so cold you can't get any colder. The afternoon grew a little warmer and the snow came thicker than ever. Then after a time the weather cleared. The moon even came out.

There were four Grimes dogs that had followed Mrs. Grimes into town, all tall gaunt fellows. Such men as Jake Grimes and his son always keep just such dogs. They kick and abuse them, but they stay. The Grimes dogs, in order to keep from starving, had to do a lot of foraging for themselves, and they had been at it while the old woman slept with her back to the tree at the side of the clearing. They had been chasing rabbits in the woods and in adjoining fields and in their ranging had picked up three other farm dogs.

After a time all the dogs came back to the clearing. They were excited about something. Such nights, cold and clear and with a moon, do things to dogs. It may be that some old instinct, come down from the time when they were wolves and ranged the woods in packs on Winter nights, comes back into them.

The dogs in the clearing, before the old woman, had caught two or three rabbits and their immediate hunger had been satisfied. They began to play, running in circles in the clearing. Round and round they ran, each dog's nose at the tail of the next dog. In the clearing, under the snow-laden trees and under the wintry moon they made a strange picture, running thus silently, in a circle their running had beaten in the soft snow. The dogs made no sound. They ran around and around in the circle.

It may have been that the old woman saw them doing that before she died. She may have awakened once or twice and looked at the strange sight with dim old eyes.

She wouldn't be very cold now, just drowsy. Life hangs on a long time. Perhaps the old woman was out of her head. She may have dreamed of her girlhood, at the German's, and before that, when she was a child and before her mother lit out and left her.

Her dreams couldn't have been very pleasant. Not many pleasant things had happened to her. Now and then one of the Grimes dogs left the running circle and came to stand before her. The dog thrust his face close to her face. His red tongue was hanging out.

The running of the dogs may have been a kind of death ceremony. It may have been that the primitive instinct of the wolf, having been aroused in the dogs by the night and the running, made them somehow afraid.

"Now we are no longer wolves. We are dogs, the servants of men. Keep alive, man! When man dies we becomes wolves again."

When one of dogs came to where the old woman sat with her back against the tree and thrust his nose close to her face he seemed satisfied and went back to run with the pack. All the Grimes dogs did it at some time during the evening, before she died. I knew all about it afterward, when I grew to be a man, because once in a woods in Illinois, on another Winter night, I saw a pack of dogs act just like that. The dogs were waiting for me to die as they had waited for the old woman that night when I was a child, but when it happened to me I was a young man and had no intention whatever of dying.

The old woman died softly and quietly. When she was dead and when one of the Grimes dogs had come to her and had found her dead all the dogs stopped running.

They gathered about her.

Well, she was dead now. She had fed the Grimes dogs when she was alive, what about now?

There was the pack on her back, the grain bag containing the piece of salt pork, the liver the butcher had given her, the dog-meat, the soup bones. The butcher in town, having been suddenly overcome with a feeling of pity, had loaded her grain bag heavily. It had been a big haul for the old woman.

It was a big haul for the dogs now.

IV

One of the Grimes dogs sprang suddenly out from among the others and began worrying the pack on the old woman's back. Had the dogs really been wolves that one would have been the leader of the pack. What he did, all the others did.

All of them sank their teeth into the grain bag the old woman had fastened with ropes to her back.

They dragged the old woman's body out into the open clearing. The worn-out dress was quickly torn from her shoulders. When she was found a day or two later, the dress had been torn from her body clear to the hips, but the dogs had not touched her body. They had got the meat out of the grain bag, that was all. Her body was frozen stiff when it was found, and the shoulders were so narrow and the body so slight that in death it looked like the body of some charming young girl.

Such things happened in towns of the Middle West, on farms near town, when I was a boy. A hunter out after rabbits found the old woman's body and did not touch it. Something, the beaten round path in the little snow-covered clearing, the silence of the place, the place where the dogs had worried the body trying to pull the grain bag away or tear it open—something startled the man and he hurried off to town.

I was in Main street with one of my brothers who was town newsboy and who was taking the afternoon papers to the stores. It was almost night.

The hunter came into a grocery and told his story. Then he went to a hardware-shop and into a drugstore. Men began to gather on the sidewalks. Then they started out along the road to the place in the woods.

My brother should have gone on about his business of distributing papers but he didn't. Every one was going to the woods. The undertaker went and the town marshal. Several men got on a dray and rode out to where the path left the road and went into the woods, but the horses weren't very sharply shod and slid about on the slippery roads. They made no better time than those of us who walked.

The town marshal was a large man whose leg had been injured in the Civil War. He carried a heavy cane and limped rapidly along the road. My brother and I followed at his heels, and as we went other men and boys joined the crowd.

It had grown dark by the time we got to where the old woman had left the road but the moon had come out. The marshal was thinking there might have been a murder. He kept asking the hunter questions. The hunter went along with his gun across his shoulders, a dog following at his heels. It isn't often a rabbit hunter has a chance to be so conspicuous. He was taking full advantage of it, leading the procession with the town marshal."I didn't see any wounds. She was a beautiful young girl. Her face was buried in the snow. No, I didn't know her." As a matter of fact, the hunter had not looked closely at the body. He had been frightened. She might have been murdered and some one might spring out from behind a tree and murder him. In a woods, in the late afternoon, when the trees are all bare and there is white snow on the ground, when all is silent, something creepy steals over the mind and body. If something strange or uncanny has happened in the neigh-borhood all you think about is getting away from there as fast as you can.

The crowd of men and boys had got to where the old woman had crossed the field and went, following the marshal and the hunter, up the slight incline and into the woods.

My brother and I were silent. He had his bundle of papers in a bag slung across his shoulder. When he got back to town he would have to go on distributing his papers before he went home to supper. If I went along, as he had no doubt already determined I should, we would both be late. Either mother or our older sister would have to warm our supper.

Well, we would have something to tell. A boy did not get such a chance very often. It was lucky we just happened to go into the grocery when the hunter came in. The hunter was a country fellow. Neither of us had ever seen him before.

Now the crowd of men and boys had got to the clearing. Darkness comes quickly on such Winter nights, but the full moon made everything clear. My brother and I stood near the tree, beneath which the old woman had died.

She did not look old, lying there in that light, frozen and still. One of the men turned her over in the snow and I saw everything. My body trembled with some strange mystical feeling and so did my brother's. It might have been the cold.

Neither of us had ever seen a woman's body before. It may have been the snow, clinging to the frozen flesh, that made it look so white and lovely, so like marble. No woman had come with the party from town; but one of the men, he was the town blacksmith, took off his overcoat and spread it over her. Then he gathered her into his arms and started off to town, all the others following silently. At that time no one knew who she was.

V

I had seen everything, had seen the oval in the snow, like a miniature race-track, where the dogs had run, had seen how the men were mystified, had seen the white bare young-looking shoulders, had heard the whispered comments of the men.

The men were simply mystified. They took the body to the undertaker's, and when the blacksmith, the hunter, the marshal and several others had got inside they closed the door. If father had been there perhaps he could have got in, but we boys couldn't.

I went with my brother to distribute the rest of his papers and when we got home it was my brother who told the story.

I kept silent and went to bed early. It may have been I was not satisfied with the way he told it.

Later, in the town, I must have heard other fragments of the old woman's story. She was recognized the next day and there was an investigation.

The husband and son were found somewhere and brought to town and there was an attempt to connect them with the woman's death, but it did not work. They had perfect enough alibis.

However, the town was against them. They had to get out. Where they went I never heard.

I remember only the picture there in the forest, the men standing about, the naked girlish-looking figure, face down in the snow, the tracks made by the running dogs and the clear cold Winter sky above. White fragments of clouds were drifting across the sky. They went racing across the little open space among the trees.

The scene in the forest had become for me, without my knowing it, the foundation for the real story I am now trying to tell. The fragments, you see, had to be picked up slowly, long afterwards.

Things happened. When I was a young man I worked on the farm of a German. The hired-girl was afraid of her employer. The farmer's wife hated her.

I saw things at that place. Once later, I had a half-uncanny, mystical adventure with dogs in an Illinois forest on a clear, moon-lit Winter night. When I was a schoolboy, and on a Summer day, I went with a boy friend out along a creek some miles from town and came to the house where the old woman had lived. No one had lived in the house since her death. The doors were broken from the hinges; the window lights were all broken. As the boy and I stood in the road outside, two dogs, just roving farm dogs no doubt, came running around the corner of the house. The dogs were tall, gaunt fellows and came down to the fence and glared through at us, standing in the road.

The whole thing, the story of the old woman's death, was to me as I grew older like music heard from far off. The notes had to be picked up slowly one at a time. Something had to be understood.

The woman who died was one destined to feed animal life. Anyway, that is all she ever did. She was feeding animal life before she was born, as a child, as a young woman working on the farm of the German, after she married, when she grew old and when she died. She fed animal life in cows, in chickens, in pigs, in horses, in dogs, in men. Her daughter had died in childhood and with her one son she had no articulate relations. On the night when she died she was hurrying homeward, bearing on her body food for animal life.

She died in the clearing in the woods and even after her death continued feeding animal life.

You see it is likely that, when my brother told the story, that night when we got home and my mother and sister sat listening, I did not think he got the point. He was too young and so was I. A thing so complete has its own beauty.

I shall not try to emphasize the point. I am only explaining why I was dissatisfied then and have been ever since. I speak of that only that you may understand why I have been impelled to try to tell the simple story over again.

1926

Katherine Anne Porter
(1890–1980)

Details about Katherine Anne Porter did not become available until Joan Givner's biography *Katherine Anne Porter: A Life* was published in 1982. In interview after interview Porter retold and revised the story of her life, changing the details of her ancestors, birthdate, religion, schooling, number of husbands, and working habits to suit the picture of herself she wanted to present. Porter—who was baptized Callie Russell and changed her name on her twenty-fifth birthday—was born in 1890 in Indian Creek, Texas, to rather poor parents. Her mother died when Porter was two, and the family spent many years with her grandmother in worse poverty than before. Porter's father slid into depression after his wife died and seems to have never fully recovered.

After leaving school in 1906, Porter married for the first of four times and converted from Methodism to Catholicism, her husband's religion. Divorced nine years later, she worked briefly at her childhood aspiration of becoming an actress. Beginning in 1916 Porter earned money as a journalist in Dallas and then Denver; a year later she nearly died of influenza, during a period she describes in the novella *Pale Horse, Pale Rider* (1939). Her entire life Porter struggled with financial difficulties, poor physical and mental health, and failed relationships.

In 1918 a job with *Magazine of Mexico* brought Porter to Mexico for the first time. To Porter Mexico was her "familiar country," and it indeed provided some of the richest material for her fiction.

During the 1920s and 1930s she immersed herself in the revolutionary and artistic communities of Mexico: she taught dance, studied folk art, witnessed revolutions, and, above all, wrote. Although the bulk of her writing during this period was journalistic, she took copious notes on people she met, stories she heard, and experiences she had. It was in Mexico City that she met the young woman courted by the fat revolutionary depicted in the strong "Flowering Judas" (1930). The two women visited prisoners, one of whom died of a drug overdose. In 1929, while visiting friends in New York City, Porter wrote the story at one sitting, taking her title from T. S. Eliot's "Gerontion" (1920), in which Christ comes "in depraved May, dogwood and chestnut, flowering judas". She said repeatedly in interviews that she never deliberately put symbols in her stories—they were just naturally there. She said of "Flowering Judas" that in fact a judas tree, which symbolizes betrayal, was part of the original experience. Although she had published her first story, "María Concepción," in 1922 (when she was thirty-two), not until the publication of "Flowering Judas" did friends and editors suggest she publish a collection of short stories.

On a Guggenheim Fellowship Porter traveled to Europe in 1931. This ocean crossing became the subject of her only novel, *Ship of Fools* (1962), which she wrote intermittently over a period of thirty years. Its publication was announced several times before the book was actually finished, and Porter was seventy-two when the novel was finally published. In it she depicts the variously ridiculous, nasty, insincere, and illusioned lives of travelers set against the backdrop of the looming Nazi threat. Not a critical success, *Ship of Fools* earned tremendous popular success—it remained a best seller almost a year and was made into a movie. Although critics thought she should keep to writing short stories, the novel's financial success allowed her to stop teaching and going on lecture tours, which had supported her. Porter then settled in Washington, D.C., where in her last years she gathered her nonfiction for publication and worked on a biography of the clergyman Cotton Mather, which she never completed.

Though she was sometimes called a southern writer, Porter did not think of herself that way. She resisted the label, preferring to think of herself as a Southerner who happened to write wonderful fiction with characters not confined to regional habits of speech, thought, and manner. She always pointed out that although her youth was spent in parts of Texas, the rest of her life was spent in New York, Chicago, California, Mexico, Paris, Berlin, Bermuda, and elsewhere. Porter was in a nursing home in Maryland when she died in 1980.

Porter is typically viewed as a "stylist" and a "writer's writer," terms that annoyed her considerably. She is compared with Henry James and Gustave Flaubert for her finely wrought fiction pieces. Joan Givner calls Porter's style "restrained" and "lyrical," carried by an undercurrent of complicated irony and morality. As noted in Givner's biography, in a 1965 interview she said, "I was brought up in the generations that Miss [Gertrude] Stein described as 'lost,' but I'll be damned if I ever was lost. I always knew where I was. I sometimes wondered how I was going to get out of it, but I knew where I was and how I got there." Porter painstakingly crafted her stories word by word and rarely let editors change her work.

Porter's reputation is based primarily on the short fiction she produced during the first half of her life and her many self-dramatizing interviews. She also published a volume of essays and occasional writings, *The Days Before,* in 1952. She procrastinated regularly, always opting for distractions while complaining about the interruptions of work or company or travel. Nevertheless, she managed to produce a considerable body of work that earned her much acclaim, which took the form of a National Book Award and Pulitzer Prize for her *Collected Stories* (1965) and the Gold Medal for Fiction in 1967.

Suggested Readings: *Hacienda,* 1934. *Pale Horse, Pale Rider: Three Short Novels,* 1935. *Ship of Fools,* 1962. *Collected Stories,* 1967. *The Collected Essays and Occasional Writings of Katherine Anne Porter,* 1970. G. Hendrick, *Katherine Anne Porter,* 1965. G. Core and L. Hartley, eds., *Katherine Anne Porter: A Critical Symposium,* 1969. J. Givner, *Katherine Anne Porter: A Life,* 1982. J. Givner, ed., *Katherine Anne Porter: Conversations,* 1987.

Text Used: *Flowering Judas and Other Stories,* 1935.

FLOWERING JUDAS*

Braggioni sits heaped upon the edge of a straight-backed chair much too small for him, and sings to Laura in a furry, mournful voice. Laura has begun to find reasons for avoiding her own house until the latest possible moment, for Braggioni is there almost every night. No matter how late she is, he will be sitting there with a surly, waiting expression, pulling at his kinky yellow hair, thumbing the strings of his guitar, snarling a tune under his breath. Lupe the Indian maid meets Laura at the door, and says with a flicker of a glance towards the upper room, "He waits."

---

* The title story of Porter's first published volume, *Flowering Judas and Other Stories,* which was expanded in 1935. The Judas tree, or cercis, was named for Judas Iscariot, Jesus' betrayer, who supposedly hanged himself on one such tree.

Laura wishes to lie down, she is tired of her hairpins and the feel of her long tight sleeves, but she says to him, "Have you a new song for me this evening?" If he says yes, she asks him to sing it. If he says no, she remembers his favorite one, and asks him to sing it again. Lupe brings her a cup of chocolate and a plate of rice, and Laura eats at the small table under the lamp, first inviting Braggioni, whose answer is always the same: "I have eaten, and besides, chocolate thickens the voice."

Laura says, "Sing, then," and Braggioni heaves himself into song. He scratches the guitar familiarly as though it were a pet animal, and sings passionately off key, taking the high notes in a prolonged painful squeal. Laura, who haunts the markets listening to the ballad singers, and stops every day to hear the blind boy playing his reed-flute in Sixteenth of September Street,[1] listens to Braggioni with pitiless courtesy, because she dares not smile at his miserable performance. Nobody dares to smile at him. Braggioni is cruel to everyone, with a kind of specialized insolence, but he is so vain of his talents, and so sensitive to slights, it would require a cruelty and vanity greater than his own to lay a finger on the vast cureless wound of his self-esteem. It would require courage, too, for it is dangerous to offend him, and nobody has this courage.

Braggioni loves himself with such tenderness and amplitude and eternal charity that his followers—for he is a leader of men, a skilled revolutionist, and his skin has been punctured in honorable warfare—warm themselves in the reflected glow and say to each other: "He has a real nobility, a love of humanity raised above mere personal affections." The excess of this self-love has flowed out, inconveniently for her, over Laura, who, with so many others, owes her comfortable situation and her salary to him. When he is in a very good humor, he tells her, "I am tempted to forgive you for being a *gringa. Gringita!*"[2] and Laura, burning, imagines herself leaning forward suddenly, and with a sound back-handed slap wiping the suety smile from his face. If he notices her eyes at these moments he gives no sign.

She knows what Braggioni would offer her, and she must resist tenaciously without appearing to resist, and if she could avoid it she would not admit even to herself the slow drift of his intention. During these long evenings which have spoiled a long month for her, she sits in her deep chair with an open book on her knees, resting her eyes on the consoling rigidity of the printed page when the sight and sound of Braggioni singing threaten to identify themselves with all her remembered afflictions and to add their weight to her uneasy premonitions of the future. The gluttonous bulk of Braggioni has become a symbol of her many disillusions, for a revolutionist should be lean, animated by heroic faith, a vessel of abstract virtues. This is nonsense, she knows it now and is ashamed of it. Revolution must have leaders, and leadership is a career for energetic men. She is, her comrades tell her, full of romantic error, for what she defines as cynicism in them is merely "a developed sense of reality." She is almost too willing to say, "I am wrong, I suppose I don't really understand the principles," and afterward she makes a secret truce with herself, determined not to surrender her will to such expedient logic. But she cannot help feeling that she has been betrayed irreparably by the disunion between her way of living and her feeling of what life should be, and at times she is almost contented to rest in this sense of grievance as a private

---

[1] A street in Mexico City named for the first day of the Mexican Revolution in 1910.
[2] "American girl. Little American girl!" (Spanish), said mockingly.

store of consolation. Sometimes she wishes to run away, but she stays. Now she longs to fly out of this room, down the narrow stairs, and into the street where the houses lean together like conspirators under a single mottled lamp, and leave Braggioni singing to himself.

Instead she looks at Braggioni, frankly and clearly, like a good child who understands the rules of behavior. Her knees cling together under sound blue serge, and her round white collar is not purposely nun-like. She wears the uniform of an idea, and has renounced vanities. She was born Roman Catholic, and in spite of her fear of being seen by someone who might make a scandal of it, she slips now and again into some crumbling little church, kneels on the chilly stone, and says a Hail Mary on the gold rosary she bought in Tehuantepec.[3] It is no good and she ends by examining the altar with its tinsel flowers and ragged brocades, and feels tender about the battered doll-shape of some male saint whose white, lace-trimmed drawers hang limply around his ankles below the hieratic dignity of his velvet robe. She has encased herself in a set of principles derived from her early training, leaving no detail of gesture or of personal taste untouched, and for this reason she will not wear lace made on machines. This is her private heresy, for in her special group the machine is sacred, and will be the salvation of the workers. She loves fine lace, and there is a tiny edge of fluted cobweb on this collar, which is one of twenty precisely alike, folded in blue tissue paper in the upper drawer of her clothes chest.

Braggioni catches her glance solidly as if he had been waiting for it, leans forward, balancing his paunch between his spread knees, and sings with tremendous emphasis, weighing his words. He has, the song relates, no father and no mother, nor even a friend to console him; lonely as a wave of the sea he comes and goes, lonely as a wave. His mouth opens round and yearns sideways, his balloon cheeks grow oily with the labor of song. He bulges marvelously in his expensive garments. Over his lavender collar, crushed upon a purple necktie, held by a diamond hoop: over his ammunition belt of tooled leather worked in silver, buckled cruelly around his grasping middle: over the tops of his glossy yellow shoes Braggioni swells with ominous ripeness, his mauve silk hose stretched taut, his ankles bound with the stout leather thongs of his shoes.

When he stretches his eyelids at Laura she notes again that his eyes are the true tawny yellow cat's eye. He is rich, not in money, he tells her, but in power and this power brings with it the blameless ownership of things, and the right to indulge his love of small luxuries. "I have a taste for the elegant refinements," he said once, flourishing a yellow silk handkerchief before her nose. "Smell that? It is Jockey Club, imported from New York." Nonetheless he is wounded by life. He will say so presently. "It is true everything turns to dust in the hand, to gall on the tongue." He sighs and his leather belt creaks like a saddle girth. "I am disappointed in everything as it comes. Everything." He shakes his head. "You, poor thing, you will be disappointed too. You are born for it. We are more alike than you realize in some things. Wait and see. Some day you will remember what I have told you, you will know that Braggioni was your friend."

Laura feels a slow chill, a purely physical sense of danger, a warning in her blood that violence, mutilation, a shocking death, wait for her with lessening patience. She has translated this fear into something homely, immediate, and sometimes hesitates before crossing the street. "My personal fate is nothing, except as

---

[3] A town in southern Mexico.

the testimony of a mental attitude," she reminds herself, quoting from some forgotten philosophic primer, and is sensible enough to add, "Anyhow, I shall not be killed by an automobile if I can help it."

"It may be true I am as corrupt, in another way, as Braggioni," she thinks in spite of herself, "as callous, as incomplete," and if this is so, any kind of death seems preferable. Still she sits quietly, she does not run. Where could she go? Uninvited she has promised herself to this place; she can no longer imagine herself as living in another country, and there is no pleasure in remembering her life before she came here.

Precisely what is the nature of this devotion, its true motives, and what are its obligations? Laura cannot say. She spends part of her days in Xochimilco,[4] near by, teaching Indian children to say in English, "The cat is on the mat." When she appears in the classroom they crowd about her with smiles on their wise, innocent, clay-colored faces, crying, "Good morning, my titcher!" in immaculate voices, and they make of her desk a fresh garden of flowers every day.

During her leisure she goes to union meetings and listens to busy important voices quarreling over tactics, methods, internal politics. She visits the prisoners of her own political faith in their cells, where they entertain themselves with counting cockroaches, repenting of their indiscretions, composing their memoirs, writing out manifestoes and plans for their comrades who are still walking about free, hands in pockets, sniffing fresh air. Laura brings them food and cigarettes and a little money, and she brings messages disguised in equivocal phrases from the men outside who dare not set foot in the prison for fear of disappearing into the cells kept empty for them. If the prisoners confuse night and day, and complain, "Dear little Laura, time doesn't pass in this infernal hole, and I won't know when it is time to sleep unless I have a reminder," she brings them their favorite narcotics, and says in a tone that does not wound them with pity, "Tonight will really be night for you," and though her Spanish amuses them, they find her comforting, useful. If they lose patience and all faith, and curse the slowness of their friends in coming to their rescue with money and influence, they trust her not to repeat everything, and if she inquires, "Where do you think we can find money, or influence?" they are certain to answer, "Well, there is Braggioni, why doesn't he do something?"

She smuggles letters from headquarters to men hiding from firing squads in back streets in mildewed houses, where they sit in tumbled beds and talk bitterly as if all Mexico were at their heels, when Laura knows positively they might appear at the band concert in the Alameda[5] on Sunday morning, and no one would notice them. But Braggioni says, "Let them sweat a little. The next time they may be careful. It is very restful to have them out of the way for a while." She is not afraid to knock on any door in any street after midnight, and enter in the darkness, and say to one of these men who is really in danger: "They will be looking for you—seriously—tomorrow morning after six. Here is some money from Vicente. Go to Vera Cruz[6] and wait."

She borrows money from the Roumanian agitator to give to his bitter enemy the Polish agitator. The favor of Braggioni is their disputed territory, and Braggioni holds the balance nicely, for he can use them both. The Polish agitator talks love

[4] A town near Mexico City known for its floating gardens.
[5] A large park in Mexico City.
[6] A city on the Gulf of Mexico.

to her over café tables, hoping to exploit what he believes is her secret sentimental preference for him, and he gives her misinformation which he begs her to repeat as the solemn truth to certain persons. The Roumanian is more adroit. He is generous with his money in all good causes, and lies to her with an air of ingenuous candor, as if he were her good friend and confidant. She never repeats anything they may say. Braggioni never asks questions. He has other ways to discover all that he wishes to know about them.

Nobody touches her, but all praise her gray eyes, and the soft, round under lip which promises gayety, yet is always grave, nearly always firmly closed: and they cannot understand why she is in Mexico. She walks back and forth on her errands, with puzzled eyebrows, carrying her little folder of drawings and music and school papers. No dancer dances more beautifully than Laura walks, and she inspires some amusing, unexpected ardors, which cause little gossip, because nothing comes of them. A young captain who had been a soldier in Zapata's[7] army attempted, during a horseback ride near Cuernavaca, to express his desire for her with the noble simplicity befitting a rude folk-hero: but gently, because he was gentle. This gentleness was his defeat, for when he alighted, and removed her foot from the stirrup, and essayed to draw her down into his arms, her horse, ordinarily a tame one, shied fiercely, reared and plunged away. The young hero's horse careered blindly after his stable-mate, and the hero did not return to the hotel until rather late that evening. At breakfast he came to her table in full charro dress, gray buckskin jacket and trousers with strings of silver buttons down the leg, and he was in a humorous, careless mood. "May I sit with you?" and "You are a wonderful rider. I was terrified that you might be thrown and dragged. I should never have forgiven myself. But I cannot admire you enough for your riding!"

"I learned to ride in Arizona," said Laura.

"If you will ride with me again this morning, I promise you a horse that will not shy with you," he said. But Laura remembered that she must return to Mexico City at noon.

Next morning the children made a celebration and spent their playtime writing on the blackboard, "We lov ar ticher," and with tinted chalks they drew wreaths of flowers around the words. The young hero wrote her a letter: "I am a very foolish, wasteful, impulsive man. I should have first said I love you, and then you would not have run away. But you shall see me again." Laura thought, "I must send him a box of colored crayons," but she was trying to forgive herself for having spurred her horse at the wrong moment.

A brown, shock-haired youth came and stood in her patio one night and sang like a lost soul for two hours, but Laura could think of nothing to do about it. The moonlight spread a wash of gauzy silver over the clear spaces of the garden, and the shadows were cobalt blue. The scarlet blossoms of the Judas tree were dull purple, and the names of the colors repeated themselves automatically in her mind, while she watched not the boy, but his shadow, fallen like a dark garment across the fountain rim, trailing in the water. Lupe came silently and whispered expert counsel in her ear: "If you will throw him one little flower, he will sing another song or two and go away." Laura threw the flower, and he sang a last song and went away with the flower tucked in the band of his hat. Lupe said, "He is one of the organizers of the Typographers Union, and before that he sold corri-

---

[7] Emiliano Zapata (1877?–1919), one of the leaders of the Mexican Revolution; the city of Cuernavaca is south of Mexico City.

dos in the Merced market,[8] and before that, he came from Guanajuato,[9] where I was born. I would not trust any man, but I trust least those from Guanajuato."

She did not tell Laura that he would be back again the next night, and the next, nor that he would follow her at a certain fixed distance around the Merced market, though the Zócolo,[10] up Francisco I. Madero Avenue, and so along the Paseo de la Reforma to Chapultepec Park, and into the Philosopher's Footpath, still with that flower withering in his hat, and an indivisible attention in his eyes.

Now Laura is accustomed to him, it means nothing except that he is nineteen years old and is observing a convention with all propriety, as though it were founded on a law of nature, which in the end it might well prove to be. He is beginning to write poems which he prints on a wooden press, and he leaves them stuck like handbills in her door. She is pleasantly disturbed by the abstract, unhurried watchfulness of his black eyes which will in time turn easily towards another object. She tells herself that throwing the flower was a mistake, for she is twenty-two years old and knows better; but she refuses to regret it, and persuades herself that her negation of all external events as they occur is a sign that she is gradually perfecting herself in the stoicism she strives to cultivate against that disaster she fears, though she cannot name it.

She is not at home in the world. Every day she teaches children who remain strangers to her, though she loves their tender round hands and their charming opportunist savagery. She knocks at unfamiliar doors not knowing whether a friend or a stranger shall answer, and even if a known face emerges from the sour gloom of that unknown interior, still it is the face of a stranger. No matter what this stranger says to her, nor what her message to him, the very cells of her flesh reject knowledge and kinship in one monotonous word. No. No. No. She draws her strength from this one holy talismanic word which does not suffer her to be led into evil. Denying everything, she may walk anywhere in safety, she looks at everything without amazement.

No, repeats this firm unchanging voice of her blood; and she looks at Braggioni without amazement. He is a great man, he wishes to impress this simple girl who covers her great round breasts with thick dark cloth, and who hides long, invaluably beautiful legs under a heavy skirt. She is almost thin except for the incomprehensible fullness of her breasts, like a nursing mother's, and Braggioni, who considers himself a judge of women, speculates again on the puzzle of her notorious virginity, and takes the liberty of speech which she permits without a sign of modesty, indeed, without any sort of sign, which is disconcerting.

"You think you are so cold, *gringita!* Wait and see. You will surprise yourself some day! May I be there to advise you!" He stretches his eyelids at her, and his ill-humored cat's eyes waver in a separate glance for the two points of light marking the opposite ends of a smoothly drawn path between the swollen curve of her breasts. He is not put off by that blue serge, nor by her resolutely fixed gaze. There is all the time in the world. His cheeks are bellying with the wind of the song. "O girl with the dark eyes," he sings, and reconsiders. "But yours are not dark. I can change all that. O girl with the green eyes, you have stolen my heart

---

[8] "Ballads" (Spanish) in the open-air market in Mexico City.
[9] A city northwest of Mexico City.
[10] The common name of Mexico City's Constitution Square; Madero (1873–1913) was a revolutionary leader and president of Mexico (1911–1913). "Boulevard of the Reformation" (Spanish); Chapultepec is a fortress on a hill near Mexico City.

away!" then his mind wanders to the song, and Laura feels the weight of his attention being shifted elsewhere. Singing thus, he seems harmless, he is quite harmless, there is nothing to do but sit patiently and say "No," when the moment comes. She draws a full breath, and her mind wanders also, but not far. She dares not wander too far.

Not for nothing has Braggioni taken pains to be a good revolutionist and a professional lover of humanity. He will never die of it. He has the malice, the cleverness, the wickedness, the sharpness of wit, the hardness of heart, stipulated for loving the world profitably. *He will never die of it.* He will live to see himself kicked out from his feeding trough by other hungry world-saviors. Traditionally he must sing in spite of his life which drives him to bloodshed, he tells Laura, for his father was a Tuscany[11] peasant who drifted to Yucatan and married a Maya woman: a woman of race, an aristocrat. They gave him the love and knowledge of music, thus: and under the rip of his thumbnail, the strings of the instrument complain like exposed nerves.

Once he was called Delgadito[12] by all the girls and married women who ran after him; he was so scrawny all his bones showed under his thin cotton clothing, and he could squeeze his emptiness to the very backbone with his two hands. He was a poet and the revolution was only a dream then; too many women loved him and sapped away his youth, and he could never find enough to eat anywhere, anywhere! Now he is a leader of men, crafty men who whisper in his ear, hungry men who wait for hours outside his office for a word with him, emaciated men with wild faces who waylay him at the street gate with a timid, "Comrade, let me tell you . . . ." and they blow the foul breath from their empty stomachs in his face.

He is always sympathetic. He gives them handfuls of small coins from his own pocket, he promises them work, there will be demonstrations, they must join the unions and attend the meetings, above all they must be on the watch for spies. They are closer to him than his own brothers, without them he can do nothing—until tomorrow, comrade!

Until tomorrow. "They are stupid, they are lazy, they are treacherous, they would cut my throat for nothing," he says to Laura. He has good food and abundant drink, he hires an automobile and drives in the Paseo on Sunday morning, and enjoys plenty of sleep in a soft bed beside a wife who dares not disturb him; and he sits pampering his bones in easy billows of fat, singing to Laura, who knows and thinks these things about him. When he was fifteen, he tried to drown himself because he loved a girl, his first love, and she laughed at him. "A thousand women have paid for that," and his tight little mouth turns down at the corners. Now he perfumes his hair with Jockey Club, and confides to Laura: "One woman is really as good as another for me, in the dark. I prefer them all."

His wife organizes unions among the girls in the cigarette factories, and walks in picket lines, and even speaks at meetings in the evening. But she cannot be brought to acknowledge the benefits of true liberty. "I tell her I must have my freedom, net. She does not understand my point of view." Laura has heard this many times. Braggioni scratches the guitar and meditates. "She is an instinctively virtuous woman, pure gold, no doubt of that. If she were not, I should lock her up, and she knows it."

---

[11] A region of central Italy; Mexico's Yucatan Peninsula has been home to the Maya Indians since long before the arrival of Europeans in the sixteenth century.
[12] "Skinny" (Spanish).

His wife, who works so hard for the good of the factory girls, employs part of her leisure lying on the floor weeping because there are so many women in the world, and only one husband for her, and she never knows where nor when to look for him. He told her: "Unless you can learn to cry when I am not here, I must go away for good." That day he went away and took a room at the Hotel Madrid.

It is this month of separation for the sake of higher principles that has been spoiled not only for Mrs. Braggioni, whose sense of reality is beyond criticism, but for Laura, who feels herself bogged in a nightmare. Tonight Laura envies Mrs. Braggioni, who is alone, and free to weep as much as she pleases about a concrete wrong. Laura has just come from a visit to the prison, and she is waiting for tomorrow with a bitter anxiety as if tomorrow may not come, but time may be caught immovable in this hour, with herself transfixed, Braggioni singing on forever, and Eugenio's body not yet discovered by the guard.

Braggioni says: "Are you going to sleep?" Almost before she can shake her head, he begins telling her about the May-day disturbances coming on in Morelia,[13] for the Catholics hold a festival in honor of the Blessed Virgin, and the Socialists celebrate their martyrs on that day. "There will be two independent processions, starting from either end of town, and they will march until they meet, and the rest depends . . ." He asks her to oil and load his pistols. Standing up, he unbuckles his ammunition belt, and spreads it laden across her knees. Laura sits with the shells slipping through the cleaning cloth dipped in oil, and he says again he cannot understand why she works so hard for the revolutionary idea unless she loves some man who is in it. "Are you not in love with someone?" "No," says Laura. "And no one is in love with you?" "No." "Then it is your own fault. No woman need go begging. Why, what is the matter with you? The legless beggar woman in the Alameda has a perfectly faithful lover. Did you know that?"

Laura peers down the pistol barrel and says nothing, but a long, slow faintness rises and subsides in her; Braggioni curves his swollen fingers around the throat of the guitar and softly smothers the music out of it, and when she hears him again he seems to have forgotten her, and is speaking in the hypnotic voice he uses when talking in small rooms to a listening, close-gathered crowd. Some day this world, now seemingly so composed and eternal, to the edges of every sea shall be merely a tangle of gaping trenches, of crashing walls and broken bodies. Everything must be torn from its accustomed place where it has rotted for centuries, hurled skyward and distributed, cast down again clean as rain, without separate identity. Nothing shall survive that the stiffened hands of poverty have created for the rich and no one shall be left alive except the elect spirits destined to procreate a new world cleansed of cruelty and injustice, ruled by benevolent anarchy: "Pistols are good, I love them, cannon are even better, but in the end I pin my faith to good dynamite," he concludes, and strokes the pistol lying in her hands. "Once I dreamed of destroying this city, in case it offered resistance to General Ortíz,[14] but it fell into his hands like an overripe pear."

He is made restless by his own words, rises and stands waiting. Laura holds up the belt to him: "Put that on, and go kill somebody in Morelia, and you will be happier," she says softly. The presence of death in the room makes her bold. "Today, I found Eugenio going into a stupor. He refused to allow me to call the prison doctor. He had taken all the tablets I brought him yesterday. He said he took them because he was bored."

[13] A city west of Mexico City.
[14] Pascual Ortíz Rubio (1877–1963), a revolutionary leader and president of Mexico (1930–1932).

"He is a fool, and his death is his own business," says Braggioni, fastening his belt carefully.

"I told him if he had waited only a little while longer, you would have got him set free," says Laura. "He said he did not want to wait."

"He is a fool and we are well rid of him," says Braggioni, reaching for his hat.

He goes away. Laura knows his mood has changed, she will not see him any more for a while. He will send word when he needs her to go on errands into strange streets, to speak to the strange faces that will appear, like clay masks with the power of human speech, to mutter their thanks to Braggioni for his help. Now she is free, and she thinks, I must run while there is time. But she does not go.

Braggioni enters his own house where for a month his wife has spent many hours every night weeping and tangling her hair upon her pillow. She is weeping now, and she weeps more at the sight of him, the cause of all her sorrows. He looks about the room. Nothing is changed, the smells are good and familiar, he is well acquainted with the woman who comes toward him with no reproach except grief on her face. He says to her tenderly: "You are so good, please don't cry any more, you dear good creature." She says, "Are you tired, my angel? Sit here and I will wash your feet." She brings a bowl of water, and kneeling, unlaces his shoes, and when from her knees she raises her sad eyes under her blackened lids, he is sorry for everything, and bursts into tears. "Ah, yes, I am hungry, I am tired, let us eat something together," he says, between sobs. His wife leans her head on his arm and says, "Forgive me!" and this time he is refreshed by the solemn, endless rain of her tears.

Laura takes off her serge dress and puts on a white linen nightgown and goes to bed. She turns her head a little to one side, and lying still, reminds herself that it is time to sleep. Numbers tick in her brain like little clocks, soundless doors close of themselves around her. If you would sleep, you must not remember anything, the children will say tomorrow, good morning, my teacher, the poor prisoners who come every day bringing flowers to their jailor. 1-2-3-4-5—it is monstrous to confuse love with revolution, night with day, life with death—ah, Eugenio!

The tolling of the midnight bell is a signal, but what does it mean? Get up, Laura, and follow me: come out of your sleep, out of your bed, out of this strange house. What are you doing in this house? Without a word, without fear she rose and reached for Eugenio's hand, but he eluded her with a sharp, sly smile and drifted away. This is not all, you shall see—Murderer, he said, follow me, I will show you a new country, but it is far away and we must hurry. No, said Laura, not unless you take my hand, no; and she clung first to the stair rail, and then to the topmost branch of the Judas tree that bent down slowly and set her upon the earth, and then to the rocky ledge of a cliff, and then to the jagged wave of a sea that was not water but a desert of crumbling stone. Where are you taking me, she asked in wonder but without fear. To death, and it is a long way off, and we must hurry, said Eugenio. No, said Laura, not unless you take my hand. Then eat these flowers, poor prisoner, said Eugenio in a voice of pity, take and eat: and from the Judas tree he stripped the warm bleeding flowers, and held them to her lips. She saw that his hand was fleshless, a cluster of small white petrified branches, and his eye sockets were without light, but she ate the flowers greedily for they satisfied both hunger and thirst. Murderer! said Eugenio, and Cannibal! This is my body and my blood. Laura cried No! and at the sound of her own voice, she awoke trembling, and was afraid to sleep again.

1930

F. Scott Fitzgerald
(1896–1940)

Near the end of F. Scott Fitzgerald's novel *The Great Gatsby* (1925), Jay Gatsby's father shows the narrator, Nick Carraway, a book Jay had owned as a boy. On the flyleaf Gatsby (then known by his true, prosaic name, Jimmy Gatz) had written a detailed daily schedule of activities for self-improvement. The passage clearly alludes to the *Autobiography* (1867) of Benjamin Franklin, who had designed charts and calendars to outline an optimistic "campaign for moral perfection," according to which a person could theoretically eliminate all personality flaws—effectively making oneself anew—simply by sticking to the schedule. In *Gatsby* Fitzgerald conveys the young Gatz's Franklinesque determination to remake himself by means of such scheduling: "dumbbell exercise and wall-scaling" (6:15–6:30 A.M.), the study of "elocution, poise, and how to attain it" (5:00–6:00 P.M.), the "study [of] needed inventions" (7:00–9:00 P.M.), and so on. That this document is produced by Mr. Gatz after his son, the rich, awe-inspiring party-giver Gatsby, is dead is a central irony of the novel. Readers learn along with Nick that young Jimmy Gatz's self-perfection schemes had led him to "success" as a bootlegger and a fraud.

The late eighteenth century had Benjamin Franklin; the late nineteenth century, Horatio Alger, whose inspirational rags-to-riches stories for boys preached the gospel of the Protestant ethic—success through humble diligence. F. Scott Fitzgerald gave the early twentieth century Jay Gatsby both to continue and subvert the tradition. Gatz/Gatsby had exploited the myth of the self-made man, acquiring a new identity and an enormous illegal fortune by playing upon gullible Americans who, like Nick Carraway, believed in the myth. The irony of Jimmy Gatz's fabrication of "Jay Gatsby" sheds light on the career of Fitzgerald, who lived that traditional American myth as well as investigated its condition in an era that seemed to have superseded Franklin's pragmatic moral earnestness in favor of a remorseless opportunism, a worship of prosperity and pleasure.

Jimmy Gatz started out in North Dakota and ended up murdered in "West Egg," a wealthy Long Island suburb; Fitzgerald came from St. Paul, Minnesota, and unhappily wound up in that factory of American self-fabrication, Hollywood. He was born the only child of Irish Catholic parents in 1896 and named Frances Scott Key Fitzgerald, after the author of "The Star-Spangled Banner," a distant maternal ancestor. Fitzgerald's mother, a descendant of well-to-do Southerners, was the daughter of one of St. Paul's most prominent businessmen. Married relatively late to Edward Fitzgerald, Mollie McQuillan inherited money that kept the family near the upper middle-class life style to which they were accustomed. Edward's business failures made this legacy all the more important, for Mollie had great plans for her son in the business world. His own youthful dreams of literary fame were just as great.

Fitzgerald was sent to a Catholic boarding school in New Jersey in 1911 and, barely passing his entrance exams, entered Princeton University in 1914. He compiled a very poor record during his college years, but academia was hardly his main concern. He later called the Princeton of his era "the pleasantest country club in America," and from the start he strove assiduously to exploit its opportunities for social success. No natural athlete, he tried in vain to make the football team; that failure never ceased festering. He compensated by making his way into undergraduate literary circles. Two fellow Princetonians, John Peale Bishop and Edmund Wilson, were to be valued supporters and friends—and sometimes harsh critics—throughout Fitzgerald's literary career.

In spring 1917 America entered World War I in Europe. Dropping out of Princeton in his senior year, Fitzgerald obtained an infantry commission. Convinced he would die on the battlefield, he furiously began writing a novel aptly called "The Romantic Egoist," intending to leave the world evidence of his genius. In fact, he never shipped out. While in training camp near Montgomery, Alabama, Fitzgerald met Zelda Sayre, a vivacious eighteen-year-old socialite, at a country club ball and soon fell in love with her. Zelda and her parents balked at the idea of her marrying an unpublished aspiring writer, so, with his discharge in hand, Fitzgerald headed to New York alone to make his fame and fortune.

What ensued looks in retrospect like a sad parody of the Franklin or Alger myth, specially adapted to the literary world. A young editor at Scribners, Max Perkins, thought "The Romantic Egoist" showed great promise, but the house declined to publish it without revision. Fitzgerald landed a job in an advertising agency and spent nights writing stories, verse, and revising his novel, which garnered 122 rejection slips in spring 1919. But when he sent his novel back to Scribners, Perkins backed it wholeheartedly and persuaded his senior colleagues to accept it. They could hardly have regretted the decision: *This Side of Paradise* (1920), as the book was renamed, sold out its first printing in three days, went through twelve printings in two years, and made Fitzgerald an instant celebrity. Partly autobiographical, it portrayed "the contemporary American in adolescence and young manhood," and both book and author rose upon a groundswell of enthusiasm for the values and concerns of youth. Poetic and irreverent in message and style, it seemed to speak for a whole generation and to affront and ignore the older representatives of established American society. Princeton president John Grier Hibben wrote Fitzgerald to say he was "grieved" by the novel's depiction of the "calculation and snobbishness" of university men, but other readers celebrated the work for its "self-criticism."

Soon Fitzgerald was quoted widely in the popular press as an authority on the new social and sexual mores of 1920. Interviews and articles with titles such as "Fitzgerald, Flappers, and Fame" treated him as the "Flapper Philosopher." One week after publication of *This Side of Paradise*, Fitzgerald married Zelda, seemingly inaugurating the new American decade that in a later book he named "the Jazz Age." It was the beginning of the illusory identity "F. Scott Fitzgerald"—the embodiment of 1920s hedonism—that the real Fitzgerald was never be able to shed. New York gloriously feted him, twenty-three, and Zelda, nineteen. They danced in the fountain outside the Plaza Hotel; they rode atop taxis; the bootleg alcohol flowed. Fitzgerald somehow managed to keep writing, producing the short-story collections *Flappers and Philosophers* (1920) and *Tales of the Jazz Age* (1922) and the novel *The Beautiful and Damned* (1922).

The Fitzgeralds bought a house in Great Neck, the Long Island town on which West Egg of *The Great Gatsby* was modeled. Financially imprudent, to say the least—their monthly budget shows generous sums earmarked for such uses as "wild parties"—they soon found themselves heavily in debt. Fitzgerald attempted to ease their debt by writing numerous magazine pieces, including a self-mocking essay entitled "How to Live on $36,000 a Year" for the *Saturday Evening Post* (April 5, 1924)—while most Americans earned about $1,500 a year.

In 1921 a daughter, their only child, was born. In summer 1924 the Fitzgeralds went abroad, ostensibly for a less costly life style. They settled on the French Riviera, and Fitzgerald worked on *The Great Gatsby*. The novel is now considered his finest, perhaps one of the best novels written by an American. Yet, when it appeared in 1925 it was greeted with only modest praise (although T. S. Eliot considered it "the first step that American fiction has taken since Henry James"), and its sales were half those of *This Side of Paradise*. By the time the novel was published, the Fitzgeralds were in Paris, where they met Ernest Hemingway, Gertrude Stein, Ezra Pound, and others; but Fitzgerald kept his distance from Paris's expatriate literary life, writing only for American magazines and seeking no entry into French intellectual circles. He and Zelda continued their inebriated high jinks with desperate gaiety. In the 1931 story "Babylon Revisited," Fitzgerald's memories of this time of dissipation in Paris were expressed by his protagonist, Charlie Wales—memories of "champagne dinners and long luncheons that began at two and ended in a blurred and vague twilight," of relentless "catering to vice and waste." Plans were underway for a fourth novel, but it was 1934 before *Tender Is the Night* appeared.

In the late 1920s and the 1930s the money continued to come in: in 1928 the *Saturday Evening Post* paid Fitzgerald $4,000 per short story. However, in his personal ledger of that year he made the entry "Thirty-two years old . . . OMINOUS No Real Progress in ANY way + *wrecked myself with dozens of people*." He had most conspicuously wrecked himself with Zelda, as she had with him: their marriage, already strained by infidelities on both sides, threatened to collapse. The couple's deterioration had vaguely been predicted in *The Beautiful and the Damned*.

A writer of promise and an aspiring dancer, Zelda Fitzgerald was frustrated by her husband's greater success and resented his rather condescending encouragement of her efforts. In 1930 she suffered a breakdown and was diagnosed as schizophrenic; from then until her death in 1947 she spent much time in asylums and clinics. It was in December 1930 while Zelda was undergoing treatment in Switzerland that Fitzgerald wrote "Babylon Revisited." They returned to America in 1931, and Zelda entered a hospital near Baltimore and worked determinedly on an autobiographical novel, *Save Me the Waltz*. At first furious, Fitzgerald eventually helped warm Max Perkins to the book, which was published in 1932 to poor sales and reviews.

In summer 1932 he worked hard at his long-deferred novel *Tender Is the Night*, a subtle examination of the process by which the protagonist, a gifted doctor, "betrays his genius" by becoming involved with a group of dissolute American expatriates in Europe. Fitzgerald felt that he had committed such a self-betrayal, and his portrait of Dick and Nicole Diver conveys much of the contempt, remorse, and pity with which he regarded himself and Zelda. Written in the midst of the Great Depression, when American literary concerns were predominantly social and political, the novel did not sell well. To many readers its story of pleasure-seeking expatriates seemed a vestige of the roaring twenties. The poet Horace Gregory summed up many critics' views of *Tender Is the Night* by writing that, though superficially appealing, the novel never criticizes "the entire system which has made such creatures as [Fitzgerald's characters] possible."

Responding to his doctor's advice, Fitzgerald made several unsuccessful attempts to give up drinking; he was hospitalized for alcoholism several times from 1933 on. He continued to produce magazine stories and essays—publishing one last story collection, *Taps at Reveille*, in 1935—but he was increasingly regarded as a rather pathetic has-been. He turned his own "betrayal of his genius" into marketable subject matter for a series of alternately self-critical and self-pitying articles for *Esquire*, beginning with "The Crack-Up" in late 1935. Fitzgerald was censured by a cutting comment in Hemingway's story "The Snows of Kilimanjaro" (1936) and publicly humiliated on his fortieth birthday by a *New York Post* article entitled "The Other Side of Paradise / Scott Fitzgerald, 40, / Engulfed in Despair / Broken in Health He Spends Birthday Re- / gretting That He Has Lost Faith in His Star." The drinking and debts worsened.

In 1937 Fitzgerald went to Hollywood, hired as a screenwriter by Metro-Goldwyn-

Mayer. Much of his initial salary of $1,000 a week was spent on Zelda's hospitalization and their daughter's college tuition as well as on his many debts. He began an affair with Sheilah Graham, a Hollywood gossip columnist, that lasted until his death. Although Fitzgerald earned more money in Hollywood than he had ever made from his fiction and worked on many film scripts (including a stint on *Gone With the Wind* [1939]), he never became the top movie writer he hoped to be. In late 1940, at the nadir of his career but with a new novel well underway, Fitzgerald died suddenly of a heart attack. Ironically, his literary reputation was soon steadily revived, partly through the efforts of the critic Edmund Wilson, Fitzgerald's college friend. Wilson oversaw publication of that unfinished novel, *The Last Tycoon* (1941), and *The Crack-Up* (1945), a selection of Fitzgerald's writings from the 1930s. *The Stories of F. Scott Fitzgerald* (1951), edited by Malcolm Cowley, continued the resurgence of interest in Fitzgerald's work.

Suggested Readings: *This Side of Paradise,* 1920. *The Beautiful and Damned,* 1922. *Tales of the Jazz Age,* 1922. *The Great Gatsby,* 1925. *Tender Is the Night,* 1934. *The Last Tycoon,* 1941. *The Crack-Up,* ed. E. Wilson, 1945. *Correspondence of F. Scott Fitzgerald,* eds. M. J. Bruccoli and M. M. Duggan, 1980. A. Kazin, ed. *F. Scott Fitzgerald: The Man and His Work,* 1951. S. Graham and R. Grant, *Beloved Infidel,* 1958. A. Mizener, *The Far Side of Paradise,* 1965. S. Perosa, *The Art of F. Scott Fitzgerald,* trans. C. Matz and S. Perosa, 1965. M. Cowley, and R. Cowley, eds. *Fitzgerald and the Jazz Age,* 1966. M. R. Stern, *The Golden Moment: The Novels of F. Scott Fitzgerald,* 1970. M. J. Bruccoli, *F. Scott Fitzgerald: A Descriptive Bibliography,* 1972. R. A. Gallo, *F. Scott Fitzgerald,* 1978. M. J. Bruccoli, ed., *Some Kind of Epic Grandeur: The Life of F. Scott Fitzgerald,* 1981. S. Donaldson, *Fool for Love: F. Scott Fitzgerald,* 1983.

Text Used: *The Stories of F. Scott Fitzgerald,* 1951.

BABYLON REVISITED*

"And where's Mr. Campbell?" Charlie asked.

"Gone to Switzerland. Mr. Campbell's a pretty sick man, Mr. Wales."

"I'm sorry to hear that. And George Hardt?" Charlie inquired.

"Back in America, gone to work."

"And where is the Snow Bird?"[1]

"He was in here last week. Anyway, his friend, Mr. Schaeffer, is in Paris."

Two familiar names from the long list of a year and a half ago. Charlie scribbled an address in his notebook and tore out the page.

"If you see Mr. Schaeffer, give him this," he said. "It's my brother-in-law's address. I haven't settled on a hotel yet."

He was not really disappointed to find Paris was so empty. But the stillness in the Ritz bar[2] was strange and portentous. It was not an American bar any more— he felt polite in it, and not as if he owned it. It had gone back into France. He felt

---

* Babylon is an ancient city-kingdom in Southwest Asia where the Israelites fled into exile after the destruction of the first Temple (587 B.C.); the name is synonymous with civic corruption and perverse luxury. The story was first published in the *Saturday Evening Post* on February 21, 1931, and collected in *Taps at Reveille* (1935).

[1] Slang for a cocaine ("snow") addict who also sometimes sells the drug.

[2] The bar at the Ritz Hotel in Paris, a prime gathering spot for rich Americans; Fitzgerald mentions many well-known Parisian locales.

the stillness from the moment he got out of the taxi and saw the doorman, usually in a frenzy of activity at this hour, gossiping with a *chasseur*[3] by the servants' entrance.

Passing through the corridor, he heard only a single, bored voice in the once-clamorous women's room. When he turned into the bar he traveled the twenty feet of green carpet with his eyes fixed straight ahead by old habit; and then, with his foot firmly on the rail, he turned and surveyed the room, encountering only a single pair of eyes that fluttered up from a newspaper in the corner. Charlie asked for the head barman, Paul, who in the latter days of the bull market had come to work in his own custom-built car—disembarking, however, with due nicety at the nearest corner. But Paul was at his country house today and Alix giving him information.

"No, no more," Charlie said, "I'm going slow these days."

Alix congratulated him: "You were going pretty strong a couple of years ago."

"I'll stick to it all right," Charlie assured him. "I've stuck to it for over a year and a half now."

"How do you find conditions in America?"

"I haven't been to America for months. I'm in business in Prague, representing a couple of concerns there. They don't know about me down there."

Alix smiled.

"Remember the night of George Hardt's bachelor dinner here?" said Charlie. "By the way, what's become of Claude Fessenden?"

Alix lowered his voice confidentially: "He's in Paris, but he doesn't come here any more. Paul doesn't allow it. He ran up a bill of thirty thousand francs, charging all his drinks and his lunches, and usually his dinner, for more than a year. And when Paul finally told him he had to pay, he gave him a bad check."

Alix shook his head sadly.

"I don't understand it, such a dandy fellow. Now he's all bloated up—"He made a plump apple of his hands.

Charlie watched a group of strident queens[4] installing themselves in a corner.

"Nothing affects them," he thought. "Stocks rise and fall, people loaf or work, but they go on forever." The place oppressed him. He called for the dice and shook with Alix for the drink.

"Here for long, Mr. Wales?"

"I'm here for four or five days to see my little girl."

"Oh-h! You have a little girl?"

Outside, the fire-red, gas-blue, ghost-green signs shone smokily through the tranquil rain. It was late afternoon and the streets were in movement; the *bistros* gleamed. At the corner of the Boulevard des Capucines he took a taxi. The Place de la Concorde[5] moved by in pink majesty; they crossed the logical Seine, and Charlie felt the sudden provincial quality of the left bank.[6]

Charlie directed his taxi to the Avenue de l'Opera, which was out of his way. But he wanted to see the blue hour spread over the magnificent façade, and imag-

---

[3] A hotel porter (French).   [4] Male homosexuals.

[5] A famous square in Paris; symbolic in that Charlie Wales is in Paris to reach a "concord" with his past and with his sister-in-law, the legal guardian of his daughter.

[6] He crosses from the cosmopolitan Right Bank of the Seine River to the less pretentious Left Bank, where the Peterses live.

ine that the cab horns, playing endlessly the first few bars of *Le Plus que Lent,*[7] were the trumpets of the Second Empire. They were closing the iron grill in front of Brentano's Book-store, and people were already at dinner behind the trim little bourgeois hedge of Duval's. He had never eaten at a really cheap restaurant in Paris. Five-course dinner, four francs fifty, eighteen cents, wine included. For some odd reason he wished that he had.

As they rolled on to the Left Bank and he felt its sudden provincialism, he thought, "I spoiled this city for myself. I didn't realize it, but the days came along one after another, and then two years were gone, and everything was gone, and I was gone."

He was thirty-five, and good to look at. The Irish mobility of his face was sobered by a deep wrinkle between his eyes. As he rang his brother-in-law's bell in the Rue Palatine, the wrinkle deepened till it pulled down his brows; he felt a cramping sensation in his belly. From behind the maid who opened the door darted a lovely little girl of nine who shrieked "Daddy!" and flew up, struggling like a fish, into his arms. She pulled his head around by one ear and set her cheek against his.

"My old pie," he said.

"Oh, daddy, daddy, daddy, daddy, dads, dads, dads!"

She drew him into the salon, where the family waited, a boy and a girl his daughter's age, his sister-in-law and her husband. He greeted Marion with his voice pitched carefully to avoid either feigned enthusiasm or dislike, but her response was more frankly tepid, though she minimized her expression of unalterable distrust by directing her regard toward his child. The two men clasped hands in a friendly way and Lincoln Peters rested his for a moment on Charlie's shoulder.

The room was warm and comfortably American. The three children moved intimately about, playing through the yellow oblongs that led to other rooms; the cheer of six o'clock spoke in the eager smacks of the fire and the sounds of French activity in the kitchen. But Charlie did not relax; his heart sat up rigidly in his body and he drew confidence from his daughter, who from time to time came close to him, holding in her arms the doll he had brought.

"Really extremely well," he declared in answer to Lincoln's question. "There's a lot of business there that isn't moving at all, but we're doing even better than ever. In fact, damn well. I'm bringing my sister over from America next month to keep house for me. My income last year was bigger than it was when I had money. You see, the Czechs————"

His boasting was for a specific purpose; but after a moment, seeing a faint restiveness in Lincoln's eye, he changed the subject:

"Those are fine children of yours, well brought up, good manners."

"We think Honoria's a great little girl too."

Marion Peters came back from the kitchen. She was a tall woman with worried eyes, who had once possessed a fresh American loveliness. Charlie had never been sensitive to it and was always surprised when people spoke of how pretty she had been. From the first there had been an instinctive antipathy between them.

---

[7] "The slowest of the slow" (French), the title of a waltz by Claude Debussy (1862–1918), to express the mood of Parisian cafés and cabarets. The Second Empire (1852–1871) in France was the period of modernization and expansion under Louis Napoleon (1808–1873), Emperor Napoleon III; the broad boulevards of Paris were laid out then.

"Well, how do you find Honoria?" she asked.

"Wonderful. I was astonished how much she's grown in ten months. All the children are looking well."

"We haven't had a doctor for a year. How do you like being back in Paris?"

"It seems very funny to see so few Americans around."

"I'm delighted," Marion said vehemently. "Now at least you can go into a store without their assuming you're a millionaire. We've suffered like everybody,[8] but on the whole it's a good deal pleasanter."

"But it was nice while it lasted," Charlie said. "We were sort of royalty, almost infallible, with a sort of magic around us. In the bar this afternoon"—he stumbled, seeing his mistake—"there wasn't a man I knew."

She looked at him keenly. "I should think you'd have had enough of bars."

"I only stayed a minute. I take one drink every afternoon, and no more."

"Don't you want a cocktail before dinner?" Lincoln asked.

"I take only one drink every afternoon, and I've had that."

"I hope you keep to it," said Marion.

Her dislike was evident in the coldness with which she spoke, but Charlie only smiled; he had larger plans. Her very aggressiveness gave him an advantage, and he knew enough to wait. He wanted them to initiate the discussion of what they knew had brought him to Paris.

At dinner he couldn't decide whether Honoria was most like him or her mother. Fortunate if she didn't combine the traits of both that had brought them to disaster. A great wave of protectiveness went over him. He thought he knew what to do for her. He believed in character; he wanted to jump back a whole generation and trust in character again as the eternally valuable element. Everything else wore out.

He left soon after dinner, but not to go home. He was curious to see Paris by night with clearer and more judicious eyes than those of other days. He bought a *strapontin*[9] for the Casino and watched Josephine Baker go through her chocolate arabesques.

After an hour he left and strolled toward Montmartre, up the Rue Pigalle[10] into the Place Blanche. The rain had stopped and there were a few people in evening clothes disembarking from taxis in front of cabarets, and *cocottes*[11] prowling singly or in pairs, and many Negroes. He passed a lighted door from which issued music, and stopped with the sense of familiarity; it was Bricktop's, where he had parted with so many hours and so much money. A few doors farther on he found another ancient rendezvous and incautiously put his head inside. Immediately an eager orchestra burst into sound, a pair of professional dancers leaped to their feet and a maître d'hôtel swooped toward him, crying, "Crowd just arriving, sir!" But he withdrew quickly.

"You have to be damn drunk," he thought.

Zelli's was closed, the bleak and sinister cheap hotels surrounding it were dark;

---

[8] Two years after the 1929 crash of the American stock market, the depression hit Paris, decimating its large American colony.

[9] A low-priced flip-up seat in a theater or cabaret (French); here, a ticket for such a seat. Josephine Baker (1906–1975) was an African-American singer and dancer whose erotic performances made her the rage of Paris nightclubs in the 1920s and 1930s.

[10] A district of risqué night life; Fitzgerald names several popular clubs, such as Bricktop's.

[11] "Prostitutes" (French).

up in the Rue Blanche there was more light and a local, colloquial French crowd. The Poet's Cave had disappeared, but the two great mouths of the Café of Heaven and the Café of Hell still yawned—even devoured, as he watched, the meager contents of a tourist bus—a German, a Japanese, and an American couple who glanced at him with much frightened eyes.

So much for the effort and ingenuity of Montmartre. All the catering to vice and waste was on an utterly childish scale, and he suddenly realized the meaning of the word "dissipate"—to dissipate into thin air; to make nothing out of something. In the little hours of the night every move from place to place was an enormous human jump, an increase of paying for the privilege of slower and slower motion.

He remembered thousand-franc notes given to an orchestra for playing a single number, hundred-franc notes tossed to a doorman for calling a cab.

But it hadn't been given for nothing.

It had been given, even the most wildly squandered sum, as an offering to destiny that he might not remember the things most worth remembering, the things that now he would always remember—his child taken from his control, his wife escaped to a grave in Vermont.

In the glare of a *brasserie*[12] a woman spoke to him. He bought her some eggs and coffee, and then, eluding her encouraging stare, gave her a twenty-franc note and took a taxi to his hotel.

II

He woke upon a fine fall day—football weather. The depression of yesterday was gone and he liked the people on the streets. At noon he sat opposite Honoria at Le Grand Vatel, the only restaurant he could think of not reminiscent of champagne dinners and long luncheons that began at two and ended in a blurred and vague twilight.

"Now, how about vegetables? Oughtn't you to have some vegetables?"

"Well, yes."

"Here's *épinards* and *chou-fleur* and carrots and *haricots*."[13]

"I'd like *chou-fleur*."

"Wouldn't you like to have two vegetables?"

"I usually only have one at lunch."

The waiter was pretending to be inordinately fond of children. *"Qu'elle est mignonne la petite! Elle parle exactement comme une Française."*[14]

"How about dessert? Shall we wait and see?"

The waiter disappeared. Honoria looked at her father expectantly.

"What are we going to do?"

"First, we're going to that toy store in the Rue Saint-Honoré and buy you anything you like. And then we're going to the vaudeville at the Empire."

She hesitated. "I like it about the vaudeville, but not the toy store."

---

[12] A restaurant and bar (French).   [13] "Spinach," "cauliflower," "beans" (French).
[14] "What a little darling she is! She speaks just like a French girl" (French).

"Why not?"

"Well, you brought me this doll." She had it with her. "And I've got lots of things. And we're not rich any more, are we?"

"We never were. But today you are to have anything you want."

"All right," she agreed resignedly.

When there had been her mother and a French nurse he had been inclined to be strict; now he extended himself, reached out for a new tolerance; he must be both parents to her and not shut any of her out of communication.

"I want to get to know you," he said gravely. "First let me introduce myself. My name is Charles J. Wales, of Prague."

"Oh, daddy!" her voice cracked with laughter.

"And who are you, please?" he persisted, and she accepted a rôle immediately: "Honoria Wales, Rue Palatine, Paris."

"Married or single?"

"No, not married. Single."

He indicated the doll. "But I see you have a child, madame."

Unwilling to disinherit it, she took it to her heart and thought quickly: "Yes, I've been married, but I'm not married now. My husband is dead."

He went on quickly, "And the child's name?"

"Simone. That's after my best friend at school."

"I'm very pleased that you're doing so well at school."

"I'm third this month," she boasted. "Elsie"—that was her cousin—"is only about eighteenth, and Richard is about at the bottom."

"You like Richard and Elsie, don't you?"

"Oh, yes. I like Richard quite well and I like her all right."

Cautiously and casually he asked: "And Aunt Marion and Uncle Lincoln—which do you like best?"

"Oh, Uncle Lincoln, I guess."

He was increasingly aware of her presence. As they came in, a murmur of " . . . adorable" followed them, and now the people at the next table bent all their silences upon her, staring as if she were something no more conscious than a flower.

"Why don't I live with you?" she asked suddenly. "Because mamma's dead?"

"You must stay here and learn more French. It would have been hard for daddy to take care of you so well."

"I don't really need much taking care of any more. I do everything for myself."

Going out of the restaurant, a man and a woman unexpectedly hailed him.

"Well, the old Wales!"

"Hello there, Lorraine. . . . Dunc."

Sudden ghosts out of the past: Duncan Schaeffer, a friend from college. Lorraine Quarrles, a lovely, pale blonde of thirty; one of a crowd who had helped them make months into days in the lavish times of three years ago.

"My husband couldn't come this year," she said, in answer to his question. "We're poor as hell. So he gave me two hundred a month and told me I could do my worst on that. . . . This is your little girl?"

"What about coming back and sitting down?" Duncan asked.

"Can't do it." He was glad for an excuse. As always, he felt Lorraine's passionate, provocative attraction, but his own rhythm was different now.

"Well, how about dinner?" she asked.

"I'm not free. Give me your address and let me call you."

"Charlie, I believe you're sober," she said judicially. "I honestly believe he's sober, Dunc. Pinch him and see if he's sober."

Charlie indicated Honoria with his head. They both laughed.

"What's your address?" said Duncan skeptically.

He hesitated, unwilling to give the name of his hotel.

"I'm not settled yet. I'd better call you. We're going to see the vaudeville at the Empire."

"There! That's what I want to do," Lorraine said. "I want to see some clowns and acrobats and jugglers. That's just what we'll do, Dunc."

"We've got to do an errand first," said Charlie. "Perhaps we'll see you there."

"All right, you snob. . . . Good-by, beautiful little girl."

"Good-by."

Honoria bobbed politely.

Somehow, an unwelcome encounter. They liked him because he was functioning, because he was serious; they wanted to see him, because he was stronger than they were now, because they wanted to draw a certain sustenance from his strength.

At the Empire, Honoria proudly refused to sit upon her father's folded coat. She was already an individual with a code of her own, and Charlie was more and more absorbed by the desire of putting a little of himself into her before she crystallized utterly. It was hopeless to try to know her in so short a time.

Between the acts they came upon Duncan and Lorraine in the lobby where the band was playing.

"Have a drink?"

"All right, but not up at the bar. We'll take a table."

"The perfect father."

Listening abstractedly to Lorraine, Charlie watched Honoria's eyes leave their table and he followed them wistfully about the room, wondering what they saw. He met her glance and she smiled.

"I liked that lemonade," she said.

What had she said? What had he expected? Gong home in a taxi afterward, he pulled her over until her head rested against his chest.

"Darling, do you ever think about your mother?"

"Yes, sometimes," she answered vaguely.

"I don't want you to forget her. Have you got a picture of her?"

"Yes, I think so. Anyhow, Aunt Marion has. Why don't you want me to forget her?"

"She loved you very much."

"I loved her too."

They were silent for a moment.

"Daddy, I want to come and live with you," she said suddenly.

His heart leaped; he had wanted it to come like this.

"Aren't you perfectly happy?"

"Yes, but I love you better than anybody. And you love me better than anybody, don't you, now that mummy's dead?"

"Of course I do. But you won't always like me best, honey. You'll grow up and meet somebody your own age and go marry him and forget you ever had a daddy."

"Yes, that's true," she agreed tranquilly.

He didn't go in. He was coming back at nine o'clock and he wanted to keep himself fresh and new for the thing he must say then.

"When you're safe inside, just show yourself in that window."

"All right. Good-by, dads, dads, dads, dads."

He waited in the dark street until she appeared, all warm and glowing, in the window above and kissed her fingers out into the night.

III

They were waiting. Marion sat behind the coffee service in a dignified black dinner dress that just faintly suggested mourning. Lincoln was walking up and down with the animation of one who had already been talking. They were as anxious as he was to get into the question. He opened it almost immediately:

"I supposed you know what I want to see you about—why I really came to Paris."

Marion played with the black stars on her necklace and frowned.

"I'm awfully anxious to have a home," he continued. "And I'm awfully anxious to have Honoria in it. I appreciate your taking in Honoria for her mother's sake, but things have changed now"—he hesitated and then continued more forcibly—"changed radically with me, and I want to ask you to reconsider the matter. It would be silly for me to deny that about three years ago I was acting badly———"

Marion looked up at him with hard eyes.

"—but all that's over. As I told you, I haven't had more than a drink a day for over a year, and I take that drink deliberately, so that the idea of alcohol won't get too big in my imagination. You see the idea?"

"No," said Marion succinctly.

"It's a sort of stunt I set myself. It keeps the matter in proportion."

"I get you," said Lincoln. "You don't want to admit it's got any attraction for you."

"Something like that. Sometimes I forget and don't take it. But I try to take it. Anyhow, I couldn't afford to drink in my position. The people I represent are more than satisfied with what I've done, and I'm bringing my sister over from Burlington to keep house for me, and I want awfully to have Honoria too. You know that even when her mother and I weren't getting along well we never let anything that happened touch Honoria. I know she's fond of me and I know I'm able to take care of her and—well, there you are. How do you feel about it?"

He knew that now he would have to take a beating. It would last an hour or two hours, and it would be difficult, but if he modulated his inevitable resentment to the chastened attitude of the reformed sinner, he might win his point in the end.

Keep your temper, he told himself. You don't want to be justified. You want Honoria.

Lincoln spoke first: "We've been talking it over ever since we got your letter last month. We're happy to have Honoria here. She's a dear little thing, and we're glad to be able to help her, but of course that isn't the question————"

Marion interrupted suddenly. "How long are you going to stay sober, Charlie?" she asked.

"Permanently, I hope."

"How can anybody count on that?"

"You know I never did drink heavily until I gave up business and came over here with nothing to do. Then Helen and I began to run around with————"

"Please leave Helen out of it. I can't bear to hear you talk about her like that."

He stared at her grimly; he had never been certain how fond of each other the sisters were in life.

"My drinking only lasted about a year and a half—from the time we came over until I—collapsed."

"It was time enough."

"It was time enough," he agreed.

"My duty is entirely to Helen," she said. "I try to think what she would have wanted me to do. Frankly, from the night you did that terrible thing you haven't really existed for me. I can't help that. She was my sister."

"Yes."

"When she was dying she asked me to look out for Honoria. If you hadn't been in a sanitarium then, it might have helped matters."

He had no answer.

"I'll never in my life be able to forget the morning when Helen knocked at my door, soaked to the skin and shivering, and said you'd locked her out."

Charlie gripped the sides of the chair. This was more difficult than he expected; he wanted to launch out into a long expostulation and explanation, but he only said: "The night I locked her out—" and she interrupted, "I don't feel up to going over that again."

After a moment's silence Lincoln said: "We're getting off the subject. You want Marion to set aside her legal guardianship and give you Honoria. I think the main point for her is whether she has confidence in you or not."

"I don't blame Marion," Charlie said slowly, "but I think she can have entire confidence in me. I had a good record up to three years ago. Of course, it's within human possibilities I might go wrong any time. But if we wait much longer I'll lose Honoria's childhood and my chance for a home." He shook his head, "I'll simply lose her, don't you see?"

"Yes, I see," said Lincoln.

"Why didn't you think of all this before?" Marion asked.

"I suppose I did, from time to time, but Helen and I were getting along badly. When I consented to the guardianship, I was flat on my back in a sanitarium and the market had cleaned me out. I knew I'd acted badly, and I thought if it would bring any peace to Helen, I'd agree to anything. But now it's different. I'm functioning, I'm behaving damn well, so far as————"

"Please don't swear at me," Marion said.

He looked at her, startled. With each remark the force of her dislike became more and more apparent. She had built up all her fear of life into one wall and faced it toward him. This trivial reproof was possibly the result of some trouble with the cook several hours before. Charlie became increasingly alarmed at leaving Honoria in this atmosphere of hostility against himself; sooner or later it would come out, in a word here, a shake of the head there, and some of that distrust would be irrevocably implanted in Honoria. But he pulled his temper down out of his face and shut it up inside him; he had won a point, for Lincoln realized the absurdity of Marion's remark and asked her lightly since when she had objected to the word "damn."

"Another thing," Charlie said: "I'm able to give her certain advantages now. I'm going to take a French governess to Prague with me. I've got a lease on a new apartment————"

He stopped, realizing he was blundering. They couldn't be expected to accept with equanimity the fact that his income was again twice as large as their own.

"I suppose you can give her more luxuries than we can," said Marion. "When you were throwing away money we were living along watching every ten francs. . . . I suppose you'll start doing it again."

"Oh, no," he said. "I've learned. I've worked hard for ten years, you know—until I got lucky in the market, like so many people. Terribly lucky. It didn't seem any use working any more, so I quit."

There was a long silence. All of them felt their nerves straining, and for the first time in a year Charlie wanted a drink. He was sure now that Lincoln Peters wanted him to have his child.

Marion shuddered suddenly; part of her saw that Charlie's feet were planted on the earth now, and her own maternal feeling recognized the naturalness of his desire; but she had lived for a long time with a prejudice—a prejudice founded on a curious disbelief in her sister's happiness, and which, in the shock of one terrible night, had turned to hatred for him. It had all happened at a point in her life where the discouragement of ill health and adverse circumstances made it necessary for her to believe in tangible villainy and a tangible villain.

"I can't help what I think!" she cried out suddenly. "How much you were responsible for Helen's death, I don't know. It's something you'll have to square with your own conscience."

An electric current of agony surged through him; for a moment he was almost on his feet, an unuttered sound echoing in his throat. He hung on to himself for a moment, another moment.

"Hold on there," said Lincoln uncomfortably. "I never thought you were responsible for that."

"Helen died of heart trouble," Charlie said dully.

"Yes, heart trouble." Marion spoke as if the phrase had another meaning for her.

Then, in the flatness that followed her outburst, she saw him plainly and she knew he had somehow arrived at control over the situation. Glancing at her husband, she found no help from him, and as abruptly as if it were a matter of no importance, she threw up the sponge.

"Do what you like!" she cried, springing up from her chair. "She's your child. I'm not the person to stand in your way. I think if it were my child I'd rather see her—" She managed to check herself. "You two decide it. I can't stand this. I'm sick. I'm going to bed."

She hurried from the room; after a moment Lincoln said:

"This has been a hard day for her. You know how strongly she feels—" His voice was almost apologetic: "When a woman gets an idea in her head."

"Of course."

"It's going to be all right. I think she sees now that you—can provide for the child, and so we can't very well stand in your way or Honoria's way."

"Thank you, Lincoln."

"I'd better go along and see how she is."

"I'm going."

He was still trembling when he reached the street, but a walk down the Rue Bonaparte to the *quais*[15] set him up, and as he crossed the Seine, fresh and new by the *quai* lamps, he felt exultant. But back in his room he couldn't sleep. The image of Helen haunted him. Helen whom he had loved so until they had senselessly begun to abuse each other's love, tear it into shreds. On that terrible February night that Marion remembered so vividly, a slow quarrel had gone on for hours. There was a scene at the Florida, and then he attempted to take her home, and then she kissed young Webb at a table; after that there was what she had hysterically said. When he arrived home alone he turned the key in the lock in wild anger. How could he know she would arrive an hour later alone, that there would be a snowstorm in which she wandered about in slippers, too confused to find a taxi? Then the aftermath, her escaping pneumonia by a miracle, and all the attendant horror. They were "reconciled," but that was the beginning of the end, and Marion, who had seen with her own eyes and who imagined it to be one of many scenes from her sister's martyrdom, never forgot.

Going over it again brought Helen nearer, and in the white, soft light that steals upon half sleep near morning he found himself talking to her again. She said that he was perfectly right about Honoria and that she wanted Honoria to be with him. She said she was glad he was being good and doing better. She said a lot of other things—very friendly things—but she was in a swing in a white dress, and swinging faster and faster all the time, so that at the end he could not hear clearly all that she said.

IV

He woke up feeling happy. The door of the world was open again. He made plans, vistas, futures for Honoria and himself, but suddenly he grew sad, remembering all the plans he and Helen had made. She had not planned to die. The present was the thing—work to do and someone to love. But not to love too much, for he knew the injury that a father can do to a daughter or a mother to a son by attaching them too closely: afterward, out in the world, the child would seek in the marriage partner the same blind tenderness and, failing probably to find it, turn against love and life.

It was another bright, crisp day. He called Lincoln Peters at the bank where he worked and asked if he could count on taking Honoria when he left for Prague. Lincoln agreed that there was no reason for delay. One thing—the legal guardianship. Marion wanted to retain that a while longer. She was upset by the whole matter, and it would oil things if she felt that the situation was still in her control for another year. Charlie agreed, wanting only the tangible, visible child.

Then the question of a governess. Charles sat in a gloomy agency and talked to

---

[15] "Embankments" (French); here, along the Seine.

a cross Béarnaise and to a buxom Breton peasant,[16] neither of whom he could have endured. There were others whom he would see tomorrow.

He lunched with Lincoln Peters at Griffons, trying to keep down his exultation.

"There's nothing quite like your own child," Lincoln said. "But you understand how Marion feels too."

"She's forgotten how hard I worked for seven years there," Charlie said. "She just remembers one night."

"There's another thing." Lincoln hesitated. "While you and Helen were tearing around Europe throwing money away, we were just getting along. I didn't touch any of the prosperity because I never got ahead enough to carry anything but my insurance. I think Marion felt there was some kind of injustice in it—you not even working toward the end, and getting richer and richer."

"It went just as quick as it came," said Charlie.

"Yes, a lot of it stayed in the hands of *chasseurs* and saxophone players and maîtres d'hôtel—well, the big party's over now. I just said that to explain Marion's feeling about those crazy years. If you drop in about six o'clock tonight before Marion's too tired, we'll settle the details on the spot."

Back at his hotel, Charlie found a *pneumatique*[17] that had been redirected from the Ritz bar where Charlie had left his address for the purpose of finding a certain man.

> "DEAR CHARLIE: You were so strange when we saw you the other day that I wondered if I did something to offend you. If so, I'm not conscious of it. In fact, I have thought about you too much for the last year, and it's always been in the back of my mind that I might see you if I came over here. We *did* have such good times that crazy spring, like the night you and I stole the butcher's tricycle, and the time we tried to call on the president and you had the old derby rim and the wire cane. Everybody seems so old lately, but I don't feel old a bit. Couldn't we get together some time today for old time's sake? I've got a vile hang-over for the moment, but will be feeling better this afternoon and will look for you about five in the sweatshop at the Ritz.
>
> "Always devotedly,
>
> "LORRAINE."

His first feeling was one of awe that he had actually, in his mature years, stolen a tricycle and pedaled Lorraine all over the Étoile[18] between the small hours and dawn. In retrospect it was a nightmare. Locking out Helen didn't fit in with any other act of his life, but the tricycle incident did—it was one of many. How many weeks or months of dissipation to arrive at that condition of utter irresponsibility?

He tried to picture how Lorraine had appeared to him then—very attractive; Helen was unhappy about it, though she said nothing. Yesterday, in the restaurant, Lorraine had seemed trite, blurred, worn away. He emphatically did not want to see her, and he was glad Alix had not given away his hotel address. It was

---

[16] Wales interviews two women: one from Béarn, in southwestern France, the other from Brittany, in northwestern France.

[17] An express message sent through a pneumatic tube (French).

[18] The Place de l'Étoile, the Parisian square in which the Arc de Triomphe stands.

a relief to think, instead, of Honoria, to think of Sundays spent with her and of saying good morning to her and of knowing she was there in his house at night, drawing her breath in the darkness.

At five he took a taxi and bought presents for all the Peters—a piquant cloth doll, a box of Roman soldiers, flowers for Marion, big linen handkerchiefs for Lincoln.

He saw, when he arrived in the apartment, that Marion had accepted the inevitable. She greeted him now as though he were a recalcitrant member of the family, rather than a menacing outsider. Honoria had been told she was going; Charlie was glad to see that her tack made her conceal her excessive happiness. Only on his lap did she whisper her delight and the question "When?" before she slipped away with the other children.

He and Marion were alone for a minute in the room, and on an impulse he spoke out boldly:

"Family quarrels are bitter things. They don't go according to any rules. They're not like aches or wounds; they're more like splits in the skin that won't heal because there's not enough material. I wish you and I could be on better terms."

"Some things are hard to forget," she answered. "It's a question of confidence." There was no answer to this and presently she asked, "When do you propose to take her?"

"As soon as I can get a governess. I hoped the day after tomorrow."

"That's impossible. I've got to get her things in shape. Not before Saturday."

He yielded. Coming back into the room, Lincoln offered him a drink.

"I'll take my daily whisky," he said.

It was warm here, it was a home, people together by a fire. The children felt very safe and important; the mother and father were serious, watchful. They had things to do for the children more important than his visit here. A spoonful of medicine was, after all, more important than the strained relations between Marion and himself. They were not dull people, but they were very much in the grip of life and circumstances. He wondered if he couldn't do something to get Lincoln out of his rut at the bank.

A long peal at the door-bell; the *bonne à tout faire*[19] passed through and went down the corridor. The door opened upon another long ring, and then voices, and the three in the salon looked up expectantly; Richard moved to bring the corridor within his range of vision, and Marion rose. Then the maid came back along the corridor, closely followed by the voices, which developed under the light into Duncan Schaeffer and Lorraine Quarrles.

They were gay, they were hilarious, they were roaring with laughter. For a moment Charlie was astounded; unable to understand how they ferreted out the Peters' address.

"Ah-h-h!" Duncan wagged his finger roguishly at Charlie. "Ah-h-h!"

They both slid down another cascade of laughter. Anxious and at a loss, Charlie shook hands with them quickly and presented them to Lincoln and Marion. Marion nodded, scarcely speaking. She had drawn back a step toward the fire; her little girl stood beside her, and Marion put an arm about her shoulder.

---

[19] "Maid of all work" (French), a housemaid. The Peters's modest circumstances permit them to have one servant for all household chores.

With growing annoyance at the intrusion, Charlie waited for them to explain themselves. After some concentration Duncan said:

"We came to invite you out to dinner. Lorraine and I insist that all this chi-chi, cagy business 'bout your address got to stop."

Charlie came closer to them, as if to force them backward down the corridor.

"Sorry, but I can't. Tell me where you'll be and I'll phone you in half an hour."

This made no impression. Lorraine sat down suddenly on the side of a chair, and focusing her eyes on Richard, cried, "Oh, what a nice little boy! Come here, little boy." Richard glanced at his mother, but did not move. With a perceptible shrug of her shoulders, Lorraine turned back to Charlie:

"Come and dine. Sure your cousins won' mine. See you so sel'om. Or solemn."

"I can't," said Charlie sharply. "You two have dinner and I'll phone you."

Her voice became suddenly unpleasant. "All right, we'll go. But I remember once when you hammered on my door at four A. M. I was enough of a good sport to give you a drink. Come on, Dunc."

Still in slow motion, with blurred, angry faces, with uncertain feet, they retired along the corridor.

"Good night," Charlie said.

"Good night!" responded Lorraine emphatically.

When he went back into the salon Marion had not moved, only now her son was standing in the circle of her other arm. Lincoln was still swinging Honoria back and forth like a pendulum from side to side.

"What an outrage!" Charlie broke out. "What an absolute outrage!"

Neither of them answered. Charlie dropped into an armchair, picked up his drink, set it down again and said:

"People I haven't seen for two years having the colossal nerve———"

He broke off. Marion had made the sound "Oh!" in one swift, furious breath, turned her body from him with a jerk and left the room.

Lincoln set down Honoria carefully.

"You children go in and start your soup," he said, and when they obeyed, he said to Charlie:

"Marion's not well and she can't stand shocks. That kind of people make her really physically sick."

"I didn't tell them to come here. They wormed your name out of somebody. They deliberately———"

"Well, it's too bad. It doesn't help matters. Excuse me a minute."

Left alone, Charlie sat tense in his chair. In the next room he could hear the children eating, talking in monosyllables, already oblivious to the scene between their elders. He heard a murmur of conversation from a farther room and then the ticking bell of a telephone receiver picked up, and in a panic he moved to the other side of the room and out of earshot.

In a minute Lincoln came back. "Look here, Charlie. I think we'd better call off dinner for tonight. Marion's in bad shape."

"Is she angry with me?"

"Sort of," he said, almost roughly. "She's not strong and———"

"You mean she's changed her mind about Honoria?"

"She's pretty bitter right now. I don't know. You phone me at the bank tomorrow."

"I wish you'd explain to her I never dreamed these people would come here. I'm just as sore as you are."

"I couldn't explain anything to her now."

Charlie got up. He took his coat and hat and started down the corridor. Then he opened the door of the dining room and said in a strange voice, "Good night, children."

Honoria rose and ran around the table to hug him.

"Good night, sweetheart," he said vaguely, and then trying to make his voice more tender, trying to conciliate something, "Good night, dear children."

V

Charlie went directly to the Ritz bar with the furious idea of finding Lorraine and Duncan, but they were not there, and he realized that in any case there was nothing he could do. He had not touched his drink at the Peters', and now he ordered a whisky-and-soda. Paul came over to say hello.

"It's a great change," he said sadly. "We do about half the business we did. So many fellows I hear about back in the States lost everything, maybe not in the first crash, but then in the second. Your friend George Hardt lost every cent, I hear. Are you back in the States?"

"No, I'm in business in Prague."

"I heard that you lost a lot in the crash."

"I did," and he added grimly, "but I lost everything I wanted in the boom."

"Selling short."

"Something like that."

Again the memory of those days swept over him like a nightmare—the people they had met travelling; then people who couldn't add a row of figures or speak a coherent sentence. The little man Helen had consented to dance with at the ship's party, who had insulted her ten feet from the table; the women and girls carried screaming with drink or drugs out of public places————

—The men who locked their wives out in the snow, because the snow of twenty-nine wasn't real snow. If you didn't want it to be snow, you just paid some money.

He went to the phone and called the Peters' apartment; Lincoln answered.

"I called up because this thing is on my mind. Has Marion said anything definite?"

"Marion's sick," Lincoln answered shortly. "I know this thing isn't altogether your fault, but I can't have her go to pieces about it. I'm afraid we'll have to let it slide for six months; I can't take the chance of working her up to this state again."

"I see."

"I'm sorry, Charlie."

He went back to his table. His whisky glass was empty, but he shook his head when Alix looked at it questioningly. There wasn't much he could do now except send Honoria some things; he would send her a lot of things tomorrow. He thought rather angrily that this was just money—he had given so many people money. . . .

"No, no more," he said to another waiter. "What do I owe you?"

He would come back some day; they couldn't make him pay forever. But he wanted his child, and nothing was much good now, beside that fact. He wasn't young any more, with a lot of nice thoughts and dreams to have by himself. He was absolutely sure Helen wouldn't have wanted him to be so alone.

1931

A February 1926 Life *magazine cover by John Held, Jr., expresses the youthful spirit of the "flappers" during the prosperous "roaring twenties," before the stock-market crash of 1929 and the subsequent Great Depression.*

Zora Neale Hurston
(1901?–1960)

Zora Neale Hurston was the most prolific African-American female writer from the 1920s through the 1950s. She published an autobiography, novels, folklore, short stories, and essays. Although she earned critical acclaim (as well as controversy), her life ended in a welfare hospital, and she was buried in 1960 in an unmarked grave.

Hurston was born about 1901 in Eatonville, Florida, the all-black town featured in her most accomplished novel, *Their Eyes Were Watching God* (1937). When her mother died, the thirteen-year-old Hurston, rejected by her father and stepmother, was passed to various relatives. She eventually set out on her own. While attending Howard University, she met Professor Alain Locke, who encouraged her to move to New York City. Already publishing stories and gaining attention in the early 1920s, Hurston burst upon the Harlem Renaissance at its height. The Harlem Renaissance emerged after World War I, when the wartime race riots had subsided. A new enthusiasm for Harlem and its so-called primitive music, literature, and art made Harlem a cultural capital for African Americans in the 1920s. Hurston fit right in, documenting the black experience as she lived it and observed it.

On a scholarship Hurston entered Barnard College, where she studied with the noted anthropologist Franz Boas. Under his influence she began defining part of her life's work: to record black life. With encouragement and private funding she collected the songs, customs, tales, anecdotes, and games she later published in the voodoo stories *Mules and Men* (1935) and incorporated into her fiction. For many years she had difficulty publishing her research, although she was able to produce musical revues of the folklore.

After Hurston finished the short story "The Gilded Six-Bits" (1933), she began to write a novel—*Jonah's Gourd Vine* (1934)—based on an idea she got from her publisher. *Their Eyes Were Watching God,* published three years later, was written in only seven weeks while Hurston continued her folklore research in the Caribbean. In this acclaimed novel, Hurston combines themes from her earlier work, especially love, community, marriage, and inner spiritual life. Her second folklore collection, *Tell My Horse* (1938), was less successful. Her novel *Moses, Man of the Mountain* (1939), a reworking of the Moses legend for African Americans, followed. After producing her autobiography, *Dust Tracks on a Road* (1942), Hurston began teaching and writing magazine pieces. Her last novel, *Seraph on the Suwanee,* was published in 1948 but failed terribly; that same year she was arrested for child molestation. Although the charge was dropped, Hurston never fully recovered from the ensuing scandal. She spent the last ten years of her life barely surviving financially.

Hurston was not uniformly admired. Although she celebrated black culture, many critics, including Richard Wright, complained that she was on the sidelines politically. She did not explicitly address racial and class issues, and when she publicly denounced desegregation, her audience became even more critical. But changes in popular and critical tastes have resulted in renewed interest and re-publication of Hurston's work. Such interest was initially fostered by advocates of neglected female writers—especially black female writers—but critics have begun to assess and appreciate the universal concerns at the heart of her work and that work's pervading poetic sensibility. Contemporary writers such as Alice Walker now claim Hurston as a literary influence.

Suggested Readings: *Jonah's Gourd Vine,* 1934. *Mules and Men,* 1935. *Their Eyes Were Watching God,* 1937. *Voodoo Gods,* 1939. *The Man of the Mountain,* 1941. *Dust Tracks on a Road,* 1942. *Seraph on the Suwanee,* 1948. R. Hemenway, *Zora Neale Hurston: A Literary Biography,* 1977. L. P. Howard, *Zora Neale Hurston,* 1980. B. Bell, *The Afro-American Novel and Its Tradition,* 1987.

Texts Used: "How It Feels to Be Colored Me": *I Love Myself When I Am Laughing . . . And Then Again When I Am Looking Mean and Impressive,* ed. A. Walker, 1979. "The Gilded Six-Bits": *Spunk: The Selected Stories of Zora Neale Hurston,* 1985.

HOW IT FEELS TO BE COLORED ME

I am colored but I offer nothing in the way of extenuating circumstances except the fact that I am the only Negro in the United States whose grandfather on the mother's side was *not* an Indian chief.

I remember the very day that I became colored. Up to my thirteenth year I lived in the little Negro town of Eatonville, Florida. It is exclusively a colored town. The only white people I knew passed through the town going to or coming from Orlando. The native whites rode dusty horses, the Northern tourists chugged down the sandy village road in automobiles. The town knew the Southerners and never stopped cane chewing when they passed. But the Northerners were something else again. They were peered at cautiously from behind curtains by the timid. The more venturesome would come out on the porch to watch them go past and got just as much pleasure out of the tourists as the tourists got out of the village.

The front porch might seem a daring place for the rest of the town, but it was a gallery seat for me. My favorite place was atop the gate-post. Proscenium[1] box for a born first-nighter. Not only did I enjoy the show, but I didn't mind the actors knowing that I liked it. I usually spoke to them in passing. I'd wave at them and when they returned my salute, I would say something like this: "Howdy-do-well-I-thank-you-where-you-goin'?" Usually automobile or the horse paused at this, and after a queer exchange of compliments, I would probably "go a piece of the way" with them, as we say in farthest Florida. If one of my family happened to come to the front in time to see me, of course negotiations would be rudely broken off. But even so, it is clear that I was the first "welcome-to-our-state" Floridian, and I hope the Miami Chamber of Commerce will please take notice.

During this period, white people differed from colored to me only in that they rode through town and never lived there. They liked to hear me "speak pieces" and sing and wanted to see me dance the parse-me-la, and gave me generously of their small silver for doing these things, which seemed strange to me for I wanted to do them so much that I needed bribing to stop. Only they didn't know it. The colored people gave no dimes. They deplored any joyful tendencies in me, but I was their Zora nevertheless. I belonged to them, to the nearby hotels, to the county—everybody's Zora.

But changes came in the family when I was thirteen, and I was sent to school in

---

[1] The theater area closest to the stage.

Jacksonville. I left Eatonville, the town of the oleanders, as Zora. When I disembarked from the river-boat at Jacksonville, she was no more. It seemed that I had suffered a sea change. I was not Zora of Orange County any more. I was now a little colored girl. I found it out in certain ways. In my heart as well as in the mirror. I became a fast brown—warranted not to rub nor run.

But I am not tragically colored. There is no great sorrow dammed up in my soul, nor lurking behind my eyes. I do not mind at all. I do not belong to the sobbing school of Negrohood who hold that nature somehow has given them a lowdown dirty deal and whose feelings are all hurt about it. Even in the helter-skelter skirmish that is my life, I have seen that the world is to the strong regardless of a little pigmentation more or less. No, I do not weep at the world—I am too busy sharpening my oyster knife.

Someone is always at my elbow reminding me that I am the granddaughter of slaves. It fails to register depression with me. Slavery is sixty years in the past. The operation was successful and the patient is doing well, thank you. The terrible struggle that made me an American out of a potential slave said "On the line!" The Reconstruction said "Get set!" and the generation before said "Go!" I am off to a flying start and I must not halt in the stretch to look behind and weep. Slavery is the price I paid for civilization, and the choice was not with me. It is a bully adventure and worth all that I have paid through my ancestors for it. No one on earth ever had a greater chance for glory. The world to be won and nothing to be lost. It is thrilling to think—to know that for any act of mine, I shall get twice as much praise or twice as much blame. It is quite exciting to hold the center of the national stage, with the spectators not knowing whether to laugh or to weep.

The position of my white neighbor is much more difficult. No brown specter pulls up a chair beside me when I sit down to eat. No dark ghost thrusts its leg against mine in bed. The game of keeping what one has is never so exciting as the game of getting.

I do not always feel colored. Even now I often achieve the unconscious Zora of Eatonville before the Hegira.[2] I feel most colored when I am thrown against a sharp white background.

For instance at Barnard.[3] "Beside the waters of the Hudson" I feel my race. Among the thousand white persons, I am a dark rock surged upon, and overswept, but through it all, I remain myself. When covered by the waters, I am; and the ebb but reveals me again.

Sometimes it is the other way around. A white person is set down in our midst, but the contrast is just as sharp for me. For instance, when I sit in the drafty basement that is The New World Cabaret[4] with a white person, my color comes. We enter chatting about any little nothing that we have in common and are seated by the jazz waiters. In the abrupt way that jazz orchestras have, this one plunges into a number. It loses no time in circumlocutions, but gets right down to business. It constricts the thorax and splits the heart with its tempo and narcotic harmonies. This orchestra grows rambunctious, rears on its hind legs and attacks the tonal veil with primitive fury, rending it, clawing it until it breaks through to the jungle beyond. I follow those heathen—follow them exultingly. I dance wildly inside myself; I yell within, I whoop; I shake my assegai[5] above my head, I hurl it

---

[2] The flight of Mohammed from Mecca (A.D. 622), or any journey undertaken to seek refuge from danger.
[3] Barnard College in New York City, near the Hudson River.
[4] A popular Harlem nightclub in the 1920s.
[5] A thin spear or light javelin used by some southern African tribes.

true to the mark *yeeeeooww!* I am in the jungle and living in the jungle way. My face is painted red and yellow and my body is painted blue. My pulse is throbbing like a war drum. I want to slaughter something—give pain, give death to what, I do not know. But the piece ends. The men of the orchestra wipe their lips and rest their fingers. I creep back slowly to the veneer we call civilization with the last tone and find the white friend sitting motionless in his seat, smoking calmly.

"Good music they have here," he remarks, drumming the table with his finger-tips.

Music. The great blobs of purple and red emotion have not touched him. He has only heard what I felt. He is far away and I see him but dimly across the ocean and the continent that have fallen between us. He is so pale with his whiteness then and I am *so* colored.

At certain times I have no race. I am *me*. When I set my hat at a certain angle and saunter down Seventh Avenue, Harlem City, feeling as snooty as the lions in front of the Forty-Second Street Library, for instance. So far as my feelings are concerned, Peggy Hopkins Joyce[6] on the Boule Mich[7] with her gorgeous raiment, stately carriage, knees knocking together in a most aristocratic manner, has nothing on me. The cosmic Zora emerges. I belong to no race nor time. I am the eternal feminine with its string of beads.

I have no separate feeling about being an American citizen and colored. I am merely a fragment of the Great Soul that surges within the boundaries. My country, right or wrong.

Sometimes, I feel discriminated against, but it does not make me angry. It merely astonishes me. How *can* any deny themselves the pleasure of my company? It's beyond me.

But in the main, I feel like a brown bag of miscellany propped against a wall. Against a wall in company with other bags, white, red and yellow. Pour out the contents, and there is discovered a jumble of small things priceless and worthless. A first-water[8] diamond, an empty spool, bits of broken glass, lengths of string, a key to a door long since crumbled away, a rusty knife-blade, old shoes saved for a road that never was and never will be, a nail bent under the weight of things too heavy for any nail, a dried flower or two still a little fragrant. In your hand is the brown bag. On the ground before you is the jumble it held—so much like the jumble in the bags, could they be emptied, that all might be dumped in a single heap and the bags refilled without altering the content of any greatly. A bit of colored glass more or less would not matter. Perhaps that is how the Great Stuffer of Bags filled them in the first place—who knows?

1933

THE GILDED SIX-BITS*

It was a Negro yard around a Negro house in a Negro settlement that looked to the payroll of the G and G Fertilizer works for its support.

But there was something happy about the place. The front yard was parted in

---

[6] A famous American heiress and socialite.

[7] Boulevard St. Michel, a well-known street in Paris, that runs near the Sorbonne and through the "Latin Quarter."

[8] Of the best quality.

* First published in *Story* in August 1933.

the middle by a sidewalk from gate to door-step, a sidewalk edged on either side by quart bottles driven neck down to the ground on a slant. A mess of homey flowers planted without a plan but blooming cheerily from their helter-skelter places. The fence and house were whitewashed. The porch and steps scrubbed white.

The front door stood open to the sunshine so that the floor of the front room could finish drying after its weekly scouring. It was Saturday. Everything clean from the front gate to the privy house. Yard raked so that the strokes of the rake would make a pattern. Fresh newspaper cut in fancy-edge on the kitchen shelves.

Missie May was bathing herself in the galvanized washtub in the bedroom. Her dark-brown skin glistened under the soapsuds that skittered down from her wash rag. Her stiff young breasts thrust forward aggressively like broad-based cones with the tips lacquered in black.

She heard men's voices in the distance and glanced at the dollar clock on the dresser.

"Humph! Ah'm way behind time t'day! Joe gointer be heah 'fore Ah git mah clothes on if Ah don't make haste."

She grabbed the clean meal sack at hand and dried herself hurriedly and began to dress. But before she could tie her slippers, there came a ring of singing metal on wood. Nine times.

Missie May grinned with delight. She had not seen the big tall man come stealing in at the gate and creep up the walk grinning happily at the joyful mischief he was about to commit. But she knew that it was her husband throwing silver dollars in the door for her to pick up and pile beside her plate at dinner. It was this way every Saturday afternoon. The nine dollars hurled into the open door, he scurried to a hiding place behind the cape jasmine bush and waited.

Missie May promptly appeared at the door in mock alarm.

"Who dat chunkin' money in mah do'way?" she demanded. Now answer from the yard. She leaped off the porch and began to search the shrubbery. She peeped under the porch and hung over the gate to look up and down the road. While she did this, the man behind the jasmine darted to the chinaberry tree. She spied him and gave chase.

"Nobody ain't gointer be chunkin' money at me and Ah not do'em nothing'," she shouted in mock anger. He ran around the house with Missie May at his heels. She overtook him at the kitchen door. He ran inside but could not close it after him before she crowded in and locked with him in a rough and tumble. For several minutes the two were a furious mass of male and female energy. Shouting, laughing, twisting, turning, and Joe trying, but not too hard, to get away.

"Missie May, take yo' hand out mah pocket!" Joe shouted out between laughs.

"Ah ain't, Joe, not lessen you gwine gimme whateve' it is good you got in yo' pocket. Turn it go Joe, do Ah'll tear yo' clothes."

"Go on tear 'em. You de one dat pushes de needles round heah. Move yo' hand Missie May."

"Lemme git dat paper sak out yo' pocket. Ah bet its candy kisses."

"Tain't. Move yo' hand. Woman ain't got no business in a man's clothes nohow. Go 'way."

Missie May gouged way down and gave an upward jerk and triumphed.

"Unhhunh! Ah got it. It 'tis so candy kisses. Ah knowed you had somethin' for me in yo' clothes. Now Ah got to see whut's in every pocket you got."

Joe smiled indulgently and let his wife go through all of his pockets and take out the things that he had hidden there for her to find. She bore off the chewing gum, the cake of sweet soap, the pocket handkerchief as if she had wrested them from him, as if they had not been bought for the sake of this friendly battle.

"Whew! dat play-fight done got me all warmed up," Joe exclaimed. "Got me some water in de kittle?"

"Yo' water is on de fire and yo' clean things is cross de bed. Hurry up and wash yo'self and git changed so we kin eat. Ah'm hongry." As Missie said this, she bore the steaming kettle into the bedroom.

"You ain't hongry, sugar," Joe contradicted her. "Youse jes's little empty. Ah'm de one whut's hongry. Ah could eat up camp meetin,' back off 'ssociation, and drink Jurdan[1] dry. Have it on de table when Ah git out de tub."

"Don't you mess wid mah business, man. You git in yo' clothes. Ah'm a real wife, not no dress and breath. Ah might not look lak one, but if you burn me, you won't git a thing but wife ashes."

Joe splashed in the bedroom and Missie May fanned around in the kitchen. A fresh red and white checked cloth on the table. Big pitcher of buttermilk beaded with pale drops of butter from the churn. Hot fried mullet,[2] crackling bread, ham hocks atop a mound of string beans and new potatoes, and perched on the window-sill a pone of spicy potato pudding.

Very little talk during the meal but that little consisted of banter that pretended to deny affection but in reality flaunted it. Like when Missie May reached for a second helping of the tater pone. Joe snatched it out of her reach. After Missie May had made two or three unsuccessful grabs at the pan, she begged, "Aw, Joe gimme some mo' dat tater pone."

"Nope, sweetenin' is for us men-folks. Y'all pritty li'l frail eels don't need nothin' lak dis. You too sweet already."

"Please, Joe."

"Naw, naw. Ah don't want you to git no sweeter than whut you is already. We goin' down de road al li'l piece t'night so you go put on yo' Sunday-go-to-meetin' things."

Missie May looked at her husband to see if he was playing some prank. "Sho' nuff, Joe?"

"Yeah. We goin' to de ice cream parlor."

"Where de ice cream parlor at, Joe?"

"A new man done come heah from Chicago and he done got a place and took and opened it up for a ice cream parlor, and bein' as it's real swell, Ah wants you to be one de first ladies to walk in dere and have some set down."

"Do Jesus, Ah ain't knowed nothin' 'bout it. Who de man done it?"

"Mister Otis D. Slemmons, of spots and places—Memphis, Chicago, Jacksonville, Philadelphia and so on."

"Dat heavy-set man wid his mouth full of gold teethes?"

"Yeah. Where did you see 'im at?"

"Ah went down to de sto' tuh git a box of lye and Ah seen 'im standin' on de corner talkin' to some of de mens, and Ah come on back and went to scrubbin' de floor, and he passed and tipped his hat whilst Ah was scourin' de steps. Ah thought never Ah seen *him* befo'."

---

[1] The Jordan River in Palestine, a symbol of the division between earth and Heaven; mentioned frequently in the Bible and in African-American gospel music.

[2] A variety of edible fish with small teeth; pone is potato pudding baked in an oval shape.

Joe smiled pleasantly. "Yeah, he's up to date. He got de finest clothes Ah ever seen on a colored man's back."

"Aw, he don't look no better in his clothes than you do in yourn. He got a puzzlegut[3] on 'im and he so chuckle-headed, he got a pone behind his neck."

Joe looked down at his own abdomen and said wistfully, "Wisht Ah had a build on me lak he got. He ain't puzzlegutted, honey. He jes' got a corperation. Dat make 'm look lak a rich white man. All rich mens is got some belly on 'em."

"Ah seen de pitchers of Henry Ford and he's a spare-built man and Rockefeller look lak he ain't got but one gut. But Ford and Rockefeller and dis Slemmons and all de rest kin be as many-gutted as dey please, ah'm satisfied wid you jes' lak you is, baby. God took pattern after a pine tree and built you noble. Youse a pritty still man, and if Ah knowed any way to make you mo' pritty still Ah'd take and do it."

Joe reached over gently and toyed with Missie May's ear. "You jes' say dat cause you love me, but Ah know Ah can't hold no light to Otis D. Slemmons. Ah ain't never been nowhere and Ah ain't got nothin' but you."

"How you know dat, Joe."

"He tole us so hisself."

"Dat don't make it so. His mouf is cut cross-ways, ain't it? Well, he kin lie jes' lak anybody els."

"Good Lawd, Missie! You womens sho' is hard to sense into things. He's got a five-dollar gold piece for a stick-pin and he got a ten-dollar gold piece on his watch chain and his mouf is jes' crammed full of gold teethes. Sho' wisht it wuz mine. And whut make it so cool, he got money 'cumulated. And womens give it all to 'im."

"Ah don't see whut de womens see on 'im. Ah wouldn't give 'im a wind if de sherff wuz after 'im."

"Well, he tole us how de white womens in Chicago give 'im all dat gold money. So he don't 'low nobody to touch it at all. Not even put dey finger on it. Dey tole 'im not to. You kin make 'miration at it, but don't tetch it."

"Whyn't he stay up dere where dey so crazy 'bout 'im?"

"Ah reckon dey done made 'im vast-rich and he wants to travel some. He say dey wouldn't leave 'im hit a lick of work. He got mo' lady people crazy 'bout him than he kin shake a stick at."

"Joe, Ah hates to see you so dumb. Dat stray nigger jes' tell y'all anything and y'all b'lieve it."

"Go 'head on now, honey and put on yo' clothes. He talkin' 'bout his pritty womens—Ah want 'im to see *mine*."

Missie May went off to dress and Joe spent the time trying to make his stomach punch out like Slemmons' middle. He tried the rolling swagger of the stranger, but found that his tall bone-and-muscle stride fitted ill with it. He just had time to drop back into his seat before Missie May came in dressed to go.

On the way home that night Joe was exultant. "Didn't Ah say ole Otis was swell? Can't he talk Chicago talk? Wuzn't dat funny whut he said when great big fat ole Ida Armstrong come in? He asted me, "'Who is dat broad wid de forty shake?' Dat's a new word. Us always thought forty was a set of figgers but he showed us where it means a whole heap of things. Sometimes he don't say forty, he jes' say thirty-eight and two and dat mean de same thing. Know whut he tole me when Ah was payin' for our ice cream? He say, 'Ah have to hand it to you,

---

[3] A potbelly.

Joe. Dat wife of yours is jes' thirty-eight and two. Yessuh, she's forty!' Ain't he killin'?"

"He'll do in case of a rush. But he sho' is got uh heap uh gold on 'im. Dat's de first time Ah ever seed gold money. It lookted good on him sho' nuff, but it'd look a whole heap better on you."

"Who, me? Missie May was youse crazy! Where would a po' man lak me git gold money from?"

Missie May was silent for a minute, then she said, "Us might find some goin' long de road some time. Us could."

"Who would be losin' gold money 'round heah? We ain't even seen none dese white folks wearin' no gold money on dey watch chain. You must be figgeren' Mister Packard or Mister Cadillac goin' pass through heah . . . "

"You don't know whut been lost 'round heah. Maybe somebody way back in memorial times lost they gold money and went on off and it ain't never been found. And then if we wuz to find it, you could wear some 'thout havin' no gang of womens lak dat Slemmons say he got."

Joe laughed and hugged her. "Don't be so wishful 'bout me. Ah'm satisfied de way Ah is. So long as Ah be yo' husband, ah don't keer 'bout nothin' else. Ah'd ruther all de other womens in de world to be dead than for you to have de tooth-ache. Less we go to bed and git our night rest."

It was Saturday night once more before Joe could parade his wife in Slemmons' ice cream parlor again. He worked the night shift and Saturday was his only night off. Every other evening around six o'clock he left home, and dying dawn saw him hustling home around the lake where the challenging sun flung a flaming sword from east to west across the trembling water.

That was the best part of life—going home to Missie May. Their whitewashed house, the mock battle on Saturday, the dinner and ice cream parlor afterwards, church on Sunday nights when Missie outdressed any woman in town—all, everything was right.

One night around eleven the acid ran out at the G and G. The foreman knocked off the crew and let the steam die down. As Joe rounded the lake on his way home, a lean moon rode the lake in a silver boat. If anybody had asked Joe about the moon on the lake, he would have said he hadn't paid it any attention. But he saw it with his feelings. It made him yearn painfully for Missie. Creation obsessed him. He thought about children. They had been married for more than a year now. They had money put away. They ought to be making little feet for shoes. A little boy child would be about right.

He saw a dim light in the bedroom and decided to come in through the kitchen door. He could wash the fertilizer dust off himself before presenting himself to Missie May. It would be nice for her not to know that he was there until he slipped into his place in bed and hugged her back. She always liked that.

He eased the kitchen door open slowly and silently, but when he went to set his dinner bucket on the table he bumped it into a pile of dishes, and something crashed to the floor. He heard his wife gasp in fright and hurried to reassure her.

"Iss me, honey. Don't get skeered."

There was a quick, large movement in the bedroom. A rustle, a thud, and a stealthy silence. The light went out.

What? Robbers? Murderers? Some varmit attacking his helpless wife, perhaps. He struck a match, threw himself on guard and stepped over the door-sill into the bedroom.

The great belt on the wheel of Time slipped and eternity stood still. By the match light he could see the man's legs fighting with his breeches in his frantic desire to get them on. He had both chance and time to kill the intruder in his helpless condition—half-in and half-out of his pants—but he was too weak to take action. The shapeless enemies of humanity that live in the hours of Time had waylaid Joe. He was assaulted in his weakness. Like Samson awakening after his haircut. So he just opened his mouth and laughed.

The match went out and he struck another and lit the lamp. A howling wind raced across his heart, but underneath its fury he heard his wife sobbing and Slemmons pleading for his life. Offering to buy it with all that he had. "Please, suh, don't kill me. Sixty-two dollars at de sto' gold money."

Joe just stood. Slemmons looked at the window, but it was screened. Joe stood out like a rough-backed mountain between him and the door. Barring him from escape, from sunrise, from life.

He considered a surprise attack upon the big clown that stood there laughing like a chessy cat. But before his fist could travel an inch, Joe's own rushed out to crush him like a battering ram. Then Joe stood over him.

"Git into yo' damn rags, Slemmons, and dat quick."

Slemmons scrambled to his feet and into his vest and coat. As he grabbed his hat, Joe's fury overrode his intentions and he grabbed at Slemmons with his left hand and struck at him with his right. The right landed. The left grazed the front of his vest. Slemmons was knocked a somersault into the kitchen and fled through the open door. Joe found himself alone with Missie May, with the golden watch charm clutched in his left fist. A short bit of broken chain dangled between his fingers.

Missie May was sobbing. Wails of weeping without words. Joe stood, and after awhile she found out that he had something in his hand. And then he stood and felt without thinking and without seeing with his natural eyes. Missie May kept on crying and Joe kept on feeling so much and not knowing what to do with all his feelings, he put Slemmons' watch charm in his pants pocket and took a good laugh and went to bed.

"Missie May, whut you crying for?"

"Cause Ah love you so hard and Ah know you don't love *me* no mo'."

Joe sank his face into the pillow for a spell then he said huskily, "You don't know de feelings of dat yet, Missie May."

"Oh Joe, honey, he said he wuz gointer gimme dat gold money and he jes' kept on after me—"

Joe was very still and silent for a long time. Then he said, "Well, don't cry no mo', Missie May. Ah got yo' gold piece for you."

The hours went past on their rusty ankles. Joe still and quiet on one bed-rail and Missie May wrung dry of sobs on the other. Finally the sun's tide crept upon the shore of night and drowned all its hours. Missie May with her face stiff and streaked towards the window saw the dawn come into her yard. It was day. Nothing more. Joe wouldn't be coming home as usual. No need to fling open the front door and sweep off the porch, making it nice for Joe. Never no more breakfast to cook; no more washing and starching of Joe's jumper-jackets and pants. No more nothing. So why get up?

With this strange man in her bed, she felt embarrassed to get up and dress. She decided to wait till he had dressed and gone. Then she would get up, dress quickly and be gone forever beyond reach of Joe's looks and laughs. But he never moved. Red light turned to yellow, then white.

From beyond the no-man's land between them came a voice. A strange voice that yesterday had been Joe's.

"Missie May, ain't you gonna fix me no breakfus'?"

She sprang out of bed. "Yeah, Joe. Ah didn't reckon you wuz hongry."

No need to die today. Joe needed her for a few more minutes anyhow.

Soon there was a roaring fire in the cook stove. Water bucket full and two chickens killed. Joe loved fried chicken and rice. She didn't deserve a thing and good Joe was letting her cook him some breakfast. She rushed hot biscuits to the table as Joe took his seat.

He ate with his eyes on his plate. No laughter, no banter.

"Missie May, you ain't eatin' yo' breakfus'."

"Ah don't choose none, Ah thank yuh."

His coffee cup was empty. She sprang to refill it. When she turned from the stove and bent to set the cup beside Joe's plate, she saw the yellow coin on the table between them.

She slumped into her seat and wept into her arms.

Presently Joe said calmly, "Missie May, you cry too much. Don't look back lak Lot's wife and turn to salt."

The sun, the hero of every day, the impersonal old man that beams as brightly on death as on birth, came up every morning and raced across the blue dome and dipped into the sea of fire every evening. Water ran down hill and birds nested.

Missie knew why she didn't leave Joe. She couldn't. She loved him too much. But she couldn't understand why Joe didn't leave her. He was polite, even kind at times, but aloof.

There were no more Saturday romps. No ringing silver dollars to stack beside her plate. No pockets to rifle. In fact the yellow coin in his trousers was like a monster hiding in the cave of his pockets to destroy her.

She often wondered if he still had it, but nothing could have induced her to ask nor yet to explore his pockets to see for herself. Its shadow was in the house whether or no.

One night Joe came home around midnight and complained of pains in his back. He asked Missie to rub him down with liniment. It had been three months since Missie had touched his body and it all seemed strange. But she rubbed him. Grateful for the chance. Before morning, youth triumphed and Missie exulted. But the next day, as she joyfully made up their bed, beneath her pillow she found the piece of money with the bit of chain attached.

Alone to herself, she looked at the thing with loathing, but look she must. She took it into her hands with trembling and saw first thing that it was no gold piece. It was a gilded half-dollar. Then she knew why Slemmons had forbidden anyone to touch his gold. He trusted village eyes at a distance not to recognize his stick-pin as a gilded quarter, and his watch charm as a four-bit piece.

She was glad at first that Joe had left it there. Perhaps he was through with her punishment. They were man and wife again. Then another thought came clawing at her. He had come home to buy from her as if she were any woman in the long house. Fifty cents for her love. As if to say that he could pay as well as Slemmons. She slid the coin into his Sunday pants pocket and dressed herself and left his house.

Halfway between her house and the quarters she met her husband's mother, and after a short talk she turned and went back home. If she had not the substance of marriage, she had the outside show. Joe must leave *her*. She let him see she didn't want his old gold four-bits too.

She saw no more of the coin for some time though she knew that Joe could not help finding it in his pocket. But his health kept poor, and he came home at least every ten days to be rubbed.

The sun swept around the horizon, trailing its robes of weeks and days. One morning as Joe came in from work, he found Missie May chopping wood. Without a word he took the ax and chopped a huge pile before he stopped.

"You ain't got no business choppin' wood, and you know it."

"How come? Ah been choppin' it for de last longest."

"Ah ain't blind. You makin' feet for shoes."

"Won't you be glad to have a li'l baby chile, Joe?"

"You know dat 'thout astin' me."

"Iss gointer be a boy chile and de very spit of you."

"You reckon, Missie May?"

"Who else could it look lak?"

Joe said nothing, but he thrust his hand deep into his pocket and fingered something there.

It was almost six months later Missie May took to bed and Joe went and got his mother to come wait on the house.

Missie May delivered a fine boy. Her travail was over when Joe came in from work one morning. His mother and the old women were drinking great bowls of coffee around the fire in the kitchen.

The minute Joe came into the room his mother called him aside.

"How did Missie May make out?" he asked quickly.

"Who, dat gal? She strong as a ox. She gointer have plenty mo'. We done fixed her wid de sugar and lard to sweeten her for de nex' one."

Joe stood silent awhile.

"You ain't ast 'bout de baby, Joe. You oughter be mighty proud cause he sho' is de spittin' image of yuh, son. Dat's yourn all right, if you never git another one, dat un is yourn. And you know Ah'm mighty proud too, son, cause Ah never thought well of you marryin' Missie May cause her ma used tuh fan her foot 'round right smart and Ah been mighty skeered dat Missie May wuz gointer git misput on her road."

Joe said nothing. He fooled around the house till late in the day then just before he went to work, he went and stood at the foot of the bed and asked his wife how she felt. He did this every day during the week.

On Saturday he went to Orlando to make his market. It had been a long time since he had done that.

Meat and lard, meal and flour, soap and starch. Cans of corn and tomatoes. All the staples. He fooled around town for awhile and bought bananas and apples. Way after while he went around to the candy store.

"Hellow, Joe," the clerk greeted him. "Ain't seen you in a long time."

"Nope, Ah ain't been heah. Been 'round spots and places."

"Want some of them molasses kisses you always buy?"

"Yessuh." He threw the gilded half-dollar on the counter. "Will dat spend?"

"Whut is it, Joe? Well, I'll be doggone! A gold-plated four-bit piece. Where'd you git it, Joe?"

"Offen a stray nigger dat come through Eatonville. He had it on his watch chain for a charm—goin' 'round making out iss gold money. Ha ha! He had a quarter on his tie pin and it wuz all golded up too. Tryin' to fool people. Makin' out he so rich and everything. Ha! Ha! Tryin' to tole off folkses wives from home."

"How did you git it, Joe? Did he fool you, too?"

"Who, me? Naw suh! He ain't fooled me none. Know whut Ah done? He come 'round me wid his smart talk. Ah hauled off and knocked 'im down and took his old four-bit 'way from 'im. Gointer buy my wife some good old 'lasses kisses wid it. Gimme fifty cents worth of dem candy kisses."

"Fifty cents buys a mightly lot of candy kisses, Joe. Why don't you split it up and take some chocolate bars, too. They eat good, too."

"Yessuh, dey do, but Ah wants all dat in kisses. Ah got a li'l boy chile home now. Tain't a week old yet, but he kin suck a sugar tit and maybe eat one them kisses hisself."

Joe got his candy and left the store. The clerk turned to the next customer. "Wisht I could be like these darkies. Laughin' all the time. Nothin' worries 'em."

Back in Eatonville, Joe reached his own front door. There was the ring of singing metal on wood. Fifteen times. Missie May couldn't run to the door, but she crept there as quickly as she could.

"Joe Banks, Ah hear you chunkin' money in mah do'way. You wait till Ah got mah strength back and Ah'm gointer fix you for dat."

1933

Jean Toomer
(1894–1967)

The author/editor William Stanley Braithwaite praised Jean Toomer as "a bright morning star of a new day of the race in literature," according to Darwin Turner's introduction to Toomer's collection *The Wayward and the Seeking* (1980). Born Eugene Pinchback Toomer in 1894 in Washington, D.C., Toomer was renamed Nathan Eugene after the father he never knew, whom Toomer romanticized as the son of a wealthy Georgia plantation owner. Toomer was raised by his mother, Nina Pinchback, and his grandfather, P. B. S. Pinchback, a man who had achieved wealth and prominence as a politician in Louisiana during Reconstruction. A light-skinned man from a mixed-blood family, Toomer spent a large part of his life in all-white communities in Washington and New York City. Between 1914 and 1919 he attended the University of Wisconsin, the Massachusetts College of Agriculture, the American College of Physical Training in Chicago, the University of Chicago, and City College of New York but never earned a formal degree. During this period he also held a series of odd jobs, connected only by his desire for some unifying, guiding principle to his life. In Chicago he lectured on the writer Victor Hugo and the philosopher Herbert Spencer; Toomer worked in the New Jersey shipyards, too, intent on spreading his new-found and quickly abandoned gospel of socialism. In 1919 writers Waldo Frank and Lola Ridge introduced Toomer to a number of artists in New York City's Greenwich Village. He began reading Eastern and Western literature and soon decided to become a writer.

In 1921 Toomer accepted a position as a superintendent of a small African-American school in rural Georgia, and his first sustained encounter with African-American folk culture gave Toomer the material from which the collection *Cane* (1923) was constructed. "The earth seemed part of the people," Toomer writes, "and the people part of the earth, and they worked upon each other and upon me, so that my earth life was liberated from the rest of myself." *Cane* consists of various stories and poems and a play. Identity is an issue that pervades these components: the identify of African-American southerners, of light-skinned northerners, and of a northern African American who moves to the South to teach, much as Toomer did himself. The book brought Toomer instant acclaim and paved the way for other works by African-American writers such as Langston Hughes and Zora Neale Hurston.

Toomer's work is prominently featured in Alain Locke's anthology *The New Negro* (1925), the hallmark of the Harlem Renaissance. Still, Toomer did not want to be perceived only as a "Negro writer." He saw racial designations as signs of entrapment and claimed that all Americans are a complicated mixture of many different groups.

The strong voice and identity that Toomer had found in *Cane* soon became unsatisfying to him, and he severed his ties with his literary friends. What followed for Toomer was a series of flirtations with various spiritual cults and religious sects. He became a follower of the Eastern mystic George I. Gurdjieff in 1924, was enamored with the writings of George William Russell (A. E.) and Aldous Huxley in the 1930s, went on a pilgrimage to India in 1939, and joined the Society of Friends (Quakers) in the 1940s. Throughout this time Toomer's writing became increasingly didactic, and he found it nearly impossible to get his work published. He produced *Essentials* in 1931 and *Portage Potential* in 1932, but his only popularly printed work other than *Cane* was "Blue Meridian" (1936), a long poem that traces the movement of various racial groups into "raceless" Americans. Toomer died in obscurity in March 1967.

Suggested Readings: *Cane*, 1923. *Essentials*, 1931. *Portage Potential*, 1932. *The Wayward and the Seeking: A Collection of Writings by Jean Toomer*, ed. D. Turner, 1980. A. Locke, ed., *The New Negro: An Interpretation*, 1925. A. Bontemp, "The Negro Renaissance: Jean Toomer and the Harlem Writers of the 1920's," in *Anger and Beyond: The Negro Writer in the United States*, ed. H. Hill, 1966. H. Baker, *Singers of Daybreak: Studies in Black American Literature*, 1975. B. J. Benson, and M. M. Dillard, *Jean Toomer*, 1980. N. McKay, *Jean Toomer, Artist*, 1984. H. L. Gates, Jr., *The Signifying Monkey: A Theory of African American Literary Criticism*, 1988.

Text Used: *Cane*, 1975.

from   CANE*

KARINTHA

> *Her skin is like dusk on the eastern horizon,*
> *O cant you see it, O cant you see it,*
> *Her skin is like dusk on the eastern horizon*
> *. . . When the sun goes down.*

Men had always wanted her, this Karintha, even as a child, Karintha carrying beauty, perfect as dusk when the sun goes down. Old men rode her hobby-horse upon their knees. Young men danced with her at frolics when they should have

---

* A collection of stories, poems, and a play, published in 1923.

been dancing with their grown-up girls. God grant us youth, secretly prayed the old men. The young fellows counted the time to pass before she would be old enough to mate with them. This interest of the male, who wishes to ripen a growing thing soon, could mean no good to her.

Karintha, at twelve, was a wild flash that told the other folks just what it was to live. At sunset, when there was no wind, and the pine-smoke from over by the sawmill hugged the earth, and you couldn't see more than a few feet in front, her sudden darting past you was a bit of vivid color, like a black bird that flashes in light. With the other children one could hear, some distance off, their feet flopping in the two-inch dust. Karintha's running was a whir. It had the sound of the red dust that sometimes makes a spiral in the road. At dusk, during the hush just after the sawmill had closed down, and before any of the women had started their supper-getting-ready songs, her voice, high-pitched, shrill, would put one's ears to itching. But no one ever thought to make her stop because of it. She stoned the cows, and beat her dog, and fought the other children. . . Even the preacher, who caught her at mischief, told himself that she was as innocently lovely as a November cotton flower. Already, rumors were out about her. Homes in Georgia are most often built on the two-room plan. In one, you cook and eat, in the other you sleep, and there love goes on. Karintha had seen or heard, perhaps she had felt her parents loving. One could but imitate one's parents, for to follow them was the way of God. She played "home" with a small boy who was not afraid to do her bidding. That started the whole thing. Old men could no longer ride her hobbyhorse upon their knees. But young men counted faster.

> Her skin is like dusk,
> O cant you see it,
> Her skin is like dusk,
> When the sun goes down.

Karintha is a woman. She who carries beauty, perfect as dusk when the sun goes down. She has been married many times. Old men remind her that a few years back they rode her hobby-horse upon their knees. Karintha smiles, and indulges them when she is in the mood for it. She has contempt for them. Karintha is a woman. Young men run stills[1] to make her money. Young men go to the big cities and run on the road.[2] Young men go away to college. They all want to bring her money. These are the young men who thought that all they had to do was count time. But Karintha is a woman, and she has had a child. A child fell out of her womb onto a bed of pine-needles in the forest. Pine-needles are smooth and sweet. They are elastic to the feet of rabbits . . . A sawmill was nearby. Its pyramidal sawdust pile smouldered. It is a year before one completely burns. Meanwhile, the smoke curls up and hangs in odd wraiths about the trees, curls up, and spreads itself out over the valley. . . Weeks after Karintha returned home the smoke was so heavy you tasted it in water. Some one made a song:

> Smoke is on the hills. Rise up.
> Smoke is on the hills, O rise
> And take my soul to Jesus.

---

[1] A homemade apparatus for distilling whiskey.   [2] Work for the railroads as porters or stewards.

Karintha is a woman. Men do not know that the soul of her was a growing thing ripened too soon. They will bring their money; they will die not having found it out. . . Karintha at twenty, carrying beauty, perfect as dusk when the sun goes down. Karintha. . .

> Her skin is like dusk on the eastern horizon,
> O cant you see it, O cant you see it,
> Her skin is like dusk on the eastern horizon
> . . . When the sun goes down.

Goes down. . .

1923

REAPERS

Black reapers with the sound of steel on stones
Are sharpening scythes. I see them place the hones
In their hip-pockets as a thing that's done,
And start their silent swinging, one by one.
Black horses drive a mower through the weeds,
And there, a field rat, startled, squealing bleeds,
His belly close to ground. I see the blade,
Blood-stained, continue cutting weeds and shade.

1923

NOVEMBER COTTON FLOWER

Boll-weevil's[1] coming, and the winter's cold,
Made cotton-stalks look rusty, seasons old,
And cotton, scarce as any southern snow,
Was vanishing; the branch, so pinched and slow,
Failed in its function as the autumn rake;
Drouth fighting soil had caused the soil to take
All water from the streams; dead birds were found
In wells a hundred feet below the ground—
Such was the season when the flower bloomed.
Old folks were startled, and it soon assumed   10
Significance. Superstition saw
Something it had never seen before:
Brown eyes that loved without a trace of fear,
Beauty so sudden for that time of year.

1923

---

[1] A small grayish insect that infests cotton plants.

FERN

Face flowed into her eyes. Flowed in soft cream foam and plaintive ripples, in such a way that wherever your glance may momentarily have rested, it immediately thereafter wavered in the direction of her eyes. The soft suggestion of down slightly darkened, like the shadow of a bird's wing might, the creamy brown color of her upper lip. Why, after noticing it, you sought her eyes, I cannot tell you. Her nose was aquiline, Semitic. If you have heard a Jewish cantor[1] sing, if he has touched you and made your own sorrow seem trivial when compared with his, you will know my feeling when I follow the curves of her profile, like mobile rivers, to their common delta. They were strange eyes. In this, that they sought nothing—that is, nothing that was obvious and tangible and that one could see, and they gave the impression that nothing was to be denied. When a woman seeks, you will have observed, her eyes deny. Fern's eyes desired nothing that you could give her; there was no reason why they should withhold. Men saw her eyes and fooled themselves. Fern's eyes said to them that she was easy. When she was young, a few men took her, but got no joy from it. And then, once done, they felt bound to her (quite unlike their hit and run with other girls), felt as though it would take them a lifetime to fulfill an obligation which they could find no name for. They became attached to her, and hungered after finding the barest trace of what she might desire. As she grew up, new men who came to town felt as almost everyone did who ever saw her: that they would not be denied. Men were everlastingly bringing her their bodies. Something inside of her got tired of them, I guess, for I am certain that for the life of her she could not tell why or how she began to turn them off. A man in fever is no trifling thing to send away. They began to leave her, baffled and ashamed, yet vowing to themselves that some day they would do some fine thing for her: send her candy every week and not let her know whom it came from, watch out for her wedding-day and give her a magnificent something with no name on it, buy a house and deed it to her, rescue her from some unworthy fellow who had tricked her into marrying him. As you know, men are apt to idolize or fear that which they cannot understand, especially if it be a woman. She did not deny them, yet the fact was that they were denied. A sort of superstition crept into their consciousness of her being somehow above them. Being above them meant that she was not to be approached by anyone. She became a virgin. Now a virgin in a small southern town is by no means the usual thing, if you will believe me. That the sexes were made to mate is the practice of the South. Particularly, black folks were made to mate. And it is black folks whom I have been talking about thus far. What white men thought of Fern I can arrive at only by analogy. They let her alone.

Anyone, of course, could see her, could see her eyes. If you walked up the Dixie Pike most any time of day, you'd be most like to see her resting listless-like on the railing of her porch, back propped against a post, head tilted a little forward because there was a nail in the porch post just where her head came which for some reason or other she never took the trouble to pull out. Her eyes, if it were sunset, rested idly where the sun, molten and glorious, was pouring down between the fringe of pines. Or maybe they gazed at the gray cabin on the knoll from which an evening folk-song was coming. Perhaps they followed a cow that had

---

[1] A male singer in Jewish religious services.

been turned loose to roam and feed on cotton-stalks and corn leaves. Like as not they'd settle on some vague spot above the horizon, though hardly a trace of wistfulness would come to them. If it were dusk, then they'd wait for the searchlight of the evening train which you could see miles up the track before it flared across the Dixie Pike, close to her home. Wherever they looked, you'd follow them and then waver back. Like her face, the whole countryside seemed to flow into her eyes. Flowed into them with the soft listless cadence of Georgia's South. A young Negro, once, was looking at her, spellbound, from the road. A white man passing in a buggy had to flick him with his whip if he was to get by without running him over. I first saw her on her porch. I was passing with a fellow whose crusty numbness (I was from the North and suspected of being prejudiced and stuck-up) was melting as he found me warm. I asked him who she was. "That's Fern," was all that I could get from him. Some folks already thought that I was given to nosing around; I let it go at that, so far as questions were concerned. But at first sight of her I felt as if I heard a Jewish cantor sing. As if his singing rose above the unheard chorus of a folk-song. And I felt bound to her. I too had my dreams: something I would do for her. I have knocked about from town to town too much not to know the futility of mere change of place. Besides, picture if you can, this cream-colored solitary girl sitting at a tenement window looking down on the indifferent throngs of Harlem. Better that she listen to folk-songs at dusk in Georgia, you would say, and so would I. Or, suppose she came up North and married. Even a doctor or a lawyer, say, one who would be sure to get along— that is, make money. You and I know, who have had experience in such things, that love is not a thing like prejudice which can be bettered by changes of town. Could men in Washington, Chicago, or New York, more than the men of Georgia, bring her something left vacant by the bestowal of their bodies? You and I who know men in these cities will have to say, they could not. See her out and out a prostitute along State Street in Chicago. See her move into a southern town where white men are more aggressive. See her become a white man's concubine. . . Something I must do for her. There was myself. What could I do for her? Talk, of course. Push back the fringe of pines upon new horizons. To what purpose? and what for? Her? Myself? Men in her case seem to lose their selfishness. I lost mine before I touched her. I ask you, friend (it makes no difference if you sit in the Pullman or the Jim Crow[2] as the train crosses her road), what thoughts would come to you—that is, after you'd finished with the thoughts that leap into men's minds at the sight of a pretty woman who will not deny them; what thoughts would come to you, had you seen her in a quick flash, keen and intuitively, as she sat there on her porch when your train thundered by? Would you have got off at the next station and come back for her to take her where? Would you have completely forgotten her as soon as you reached Macon, Atlanta, Augusta, Pasadena, Madison, Chicago, Boston, or New Orleans? Would you tell your wife or sweetheart about a girl you saw? Your thoughts can help me, and I would like to know. Something I would do for her. . .

One evening I walked up the Pike on purpose, and stopped to say hello. Some of her family were about, but they moved away to make room for me. Damn if I

---

[2] "Jim Crow" laws, mainly in the segregated South, required separate facilities for blacks and whites. Barred from the first-class "Pullman," or sleeping car, blacks had to sit in the coach section of railway cars.

knew how to begin. Would you? Mr. and Miss So-and-So, people, the weather, the crops, the new preacher, the frolic, the church benefit, rabbit and possum hunting, the new soft drink they had at old Pap's store, the schedule of the trains, what kind of town Macon was, Negro's migration north, boll-weevils, syrup, the Bible—to all these things she gave a yassur or nassur, without further comment. I began to wonder if perhaps my own emotional sensibility had played one of its tricks on me. "Lets take a walk," I at last ventured. The suggestion, coming after so long an isolation, was novel enough, I guess, to surprise. But it wasnt that. Something told me that men before me had said just that as a prelude to the offering of their bodies. I tried to tell her with my eyes. I think she understood. The thing from her that made my throat catch, vanished. Its passing left her visible in a way I'd thought, but never seen. We walked down the Pike with people on all the porches gaping at us. "Doesnt it make you mad?" She meant the row of petty gossiping people. She meant the world. Through a canebrake that was ripe for cutting, the branch was reached. Under a sweet-gum tree, and where reddish leaves had dammed the creek a little, we sat down. Dusk, suggesting the almost imperceptible procession of giant trees, settled with a purple haze about the cane. I felt strange, as I always do in Georgia, particularly at dusk. I felt that things unseen to men were tangibly immediate. It would not have surprised me had I had vision. People have them in Georgia more often than you would suppose. A black woman once saw the mother of Christ and drew her in charcoal on the courthouse wall. . . When one is on the soil of one's ancestors, most anything can come to one. . . From force of habit, I suppose, I held Fern in my arms—that is, without at first noticing it. Then my mind came back to her. Her eyes, unusually weird and open, held me. Held God. He flowed in as I've seen the countryside flow in. Seen men. I must have done something—what, I don't know, in the confusion of my emotion. She sprang up. Rushed some distance from me. Fell to her knees, and began swaying, swaying. Her body was tortured with something it could not let out. Like boiling sap it flooded arms and fingers till she shook them as if they burned her. It found her throat, and spattered inarticulately in plaintive, convulsive sounds, mingled with calls to Christ Jesus. And then she sang, brokenly. A Jewish cantor singing with a broken voice. A child's voice, uncertain, or an old man's. Dusk hid her; I could hear only her song. It seemed to me as though she were pounding her head in anguish upon the ground. I rushed to her. She fainted in my arms.

There was talk about her fainting with me in the canefield. And I got one or two ugly looks from town men who'd set themselves up to protect her. In fact, there was talk of making me leave town. But they never did. They kept a watch-out for me, though. Shortly after, I came back North. From the train window I saw her as I crossed her road. Saw her on her porch, head tilted a little forward where the nail was, eyes vaguely focused on the sunset. Saw her face flow into them, the countryside and something that I call God, flowing into them. . . Nothing ever really happened. Nothing ever came to Fern, not even I. Something I would do for her. Some fine unnamed thing. . . And, friend, you? She is still living, I have reason to know. Her name, against the chance that you might happen down that way, is Fernie May Rosen.

1923

With millions unemployed during the Great Depression, apple sellers (like those here in 1930) were a common sight on city streets, as people sought to earn a living.

William Faulkner
(1897–1962)

"Tell them I was born in 1826 of a Negro slave and an alligator." So responded William Faulkner in a 1931 interview (L. H. Cox, *William Faulkner,* 1982) when asked about his childhood. An intensely private man who resented public curiosity about his personal life, he remarked in a 1949 letter to the writer Malcolm Cowley that it was his "ambition to be, as a private individual, abolished and voided from history, leaving it markless, no refuse save the printed books. . . . It is my aim, and every effort bent, that the sum and history of my life, which in the same sentence is my obit and epitaph too, shall be them both: He made the books and he died." Despite his refusal to divulge personal information, Faulkner set all his major fiction in Mississippi, which he cherished as his "little postage stamp of native ground," and drew many of his characters and plots from his early experiences and from family memories and legends.

Born in New Albany, Mississippi, in 1897 (the family soon moved to nearby Oxford), William Cuthbert Falkner was the oldest son of Murray Cuthbert Falkner and Maud Butler and the great-grandson of Colonel William Clark Falkner. (The author added the "u" later.) The colonel's dramatic life inspired such characters as Colonel Sartoris of *Sartoris* (1929) and Thomas Sutpen of *Absalom, Absalom!* (1936). A lawyer and lieutenant in the Mexican War, the colonel had stabbed a man to death in self-defense and shot another; he also was a writer, an infantry captain during the Civil War, and founder of the Ripley Railroad (later the Gulf and Chicago Railroad). He died when he was shot in the head at close range by a former stockholder in the railroad. The violence continued in the Falkner family for two generations.

Faulkner's formal education ended after the eleventh grade; by then Faulkner was already an avid reader and writer of poetry. His first published work, *The Marble Faun* (1924), was a collection of verse, and years later he described himself not as a novelist or short-story writer but as a failed poet. After his high school sweetheart, Estelle Oldham, married a more financially secure man, Faulkner left Oxford in 1918 and enlisted in the British Royal Air Force in Canada (as he did not meet U.S. requirements) to play an active role in World War I. The war ended before he reached Europe, though, and he returned home—with a limp and a story of a metal plate in his head, both of which he claimed were the result of war wounds.

Faulkner began to publish poems—both his own and translations from French symbolists—and critical pieces in local newspapers, and in 1920 he wrote the verse play *Marionettes* (not published until 1975). Seeking to support himself, he drifted from job to job, finally becoming postmaster at the University of Mississippi. Forced to resign, however, Faulkner went to New Orleans in 1924. There he met the fiction writer Sherwood Anderson, who encouraged Faulkner to develop his prose style and to draw on his home region for material. When Faulkner left for Europe in 1925, he had with him the manuscript of a completed novel about life in postwar America, *Soldier's Pay*, which Anderson had recommended to his publisher; the novel appeared in 1926. Faulkner traveled in Italy, France, and England and lived in Paris for several months, where he frequented the Louvre and the Luxembourg galleries. He continued to write, working on a novel about the place of artists in society; the novel was published in 1927 as *Mosquitoes*.

Back in Mississippi in late 1925, Faulkner turned to projects with southern settings in which he introduced fictional families, including the aristocratic Sartorises. "Flags in the Dust," the novel about the Sartorises and their community, later called Yoknapatawpha County, was rejected several times before it was finally published in heavily edited form in 1929 as *Sartoris* (the original manuscript appeared posthumously in 1973). Meanwhile, he had resumed his romance with Estelle Oldham, now a divorcée with two young children. Faulkner and Oldham married in 1929, and the family of four settled into a large, dilapidated house, Rowan Oak. A daughter born in 1931 died after just nine days; another was born in 1933.

Despite the financial pressure placed on Faulkner by the sudden acquisition of a family and house, the years around 1930 were among his most productive. *The Sound and the Fury*, his favorite novel, was published in 1929; it is the story of Caddy Compson and the disintegration of the Compson family amidst the decline of the Old South. Exhibiting Faulkner's fascination with subjective rather than chronological time, the novel is divided into four sections, each presented from a different perspective and written in a different style. Caddy's brothers narrate the first three sections; only in the third-person narration of Dilsey, the cook, is the account sequential.

The Sound and the Fury earned Faulkner more critical attention than he had yet received but not the money that he badly needed. Working as a supervisor on the night shift

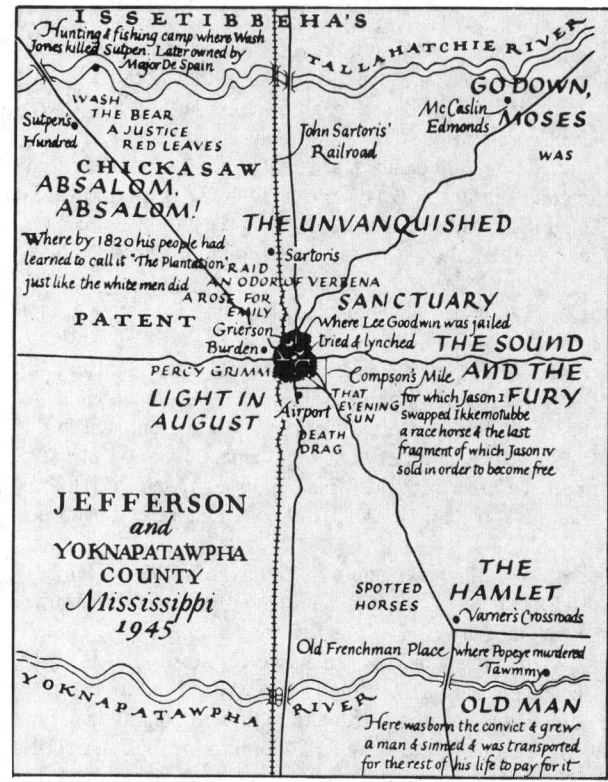

This is one of several maps that William Faulkner provided of his fictional city Jefferson in the imaginary Yoknapatawpha County, Mississippi.

at a local power plant, he wrote his next masterpiece, *As I Lay Dying* (1930), the story of a six-day journey a poor family undertakes to transport their dead mother for burial in Jefferson, the Yoknapatawpha County seat. Like *The Sound and the Fury, As I Lay Dying* is comprised of interior monologues; each of fifteen different characters perceives the events differently. His next novel, *Sanctuary* (1931), which deals with urban corruption, prostitution, and drugs and describes a brutal rape, increased the charges of bad taste and sensationalism that *As I Lay Dying* had brought on Faulkner.

Before he began his next novel, *Light in August* (1932), Faulkner turned his attention to the immediately marketable form of the short story, yet the stories that he wrote then— published in national magazines such as the *Saturday Evening Post, Scribner's,* and *Harper's* and collected in *These 13* (1931)—are anything but formulaic. *These 13* is divided into three sections: the first consists of World War I stories; the second relates the history of Yoknapatawpha County; and the third, which includes "That Evening Sun" and "A Rose for Emily," focuses on the contemporary community of Jefferson and its separate black and white quarters. The stories use many of the same techniques and involve many of the same characters that his novels do. "That Evening Sun," about Nancy, an African-American washerwoman and temporary cook for the Compson family, and narrated by Quentin Compson, takes place roughly eight years before the events of *The Sound and the Fury*. As is true of all Faulkner's novels, the reader must distinguish between the narrator's relating of events and the events themselves: the Compson children are unable to understand when Nancy tells Jesus, her threatening lover, that the "watermelon" under her dress "never come off your vine." The first-person narrator of "A Rose for Emily," one of Faulkner's most masterful and popular stories, constantly misinterprets actions and events as he recalls the story of Miss Emily's tragic love affair with Homer Barron. Teasing readers who confuse "time with its mathematical progression," the narrative moves back and forth in time, memory following upon memory. Both stories display Faulkner's keen awareness of the inequities and peculiar ironies of race relations in the South. " 'I can't hang around white man's kitchen. . . . But white men can hang around mine,' " Jesus remarks in "That Evening Sun."

These 13 was very favorably received, but Faulkner still faced economic pressures, and when Metro-Goldwyn-Mayer offered him a six-week contract as a screenwriter in 1932 for $500 a week, he accepted. "Nothing can injure a man's writing if he's a first rate writer," he later told an interviewer; "the problem does not apply if he is not first rate, because he has already sold his soul for a swimming pool" (Cox, 1982). Faulkner developed a close working relationship with the director Howard Hawks but was not happy in Hollywood and returned to Mississippi in 1933, where he continued to experiment with novelistic form. *Absalom, Absalom!,* the story of the rise and fall of Thomas Sutpen, who had sought to found a dynasty in the post-Civil War South, is variously told by four different speakers (including Quentin Compson) who impose different interpretations on the events they narrate. Between 1933 and 1940 Faulkner published a novel almost every year and continued to write stories. (It was then that he began working on his novelette "The Bear," one of seven stories in the acclaimed *Go Down, Moses* [1942].) In 1937 he was corresponding with Maurice Coindreau, a French critic and translator, who introduced Faulkner's work to France via translations of *The Sound and the Fury* and *As I Lay Dying* and who is largely responsible for Faulkner's high reputation there. The philosopher/writer Jean-Paul Sartre wrote that "*Pour les jeunes en France, Faulkner c'est un dieu,*" or "For the young people of France, Faulkner is a god" (J. Blotner, *Faulkner,* 1984). Faulkner continued to work intermittently in Hollywood, contributing to the scripts for Howard Hawk's *To Have and Have Not* (1945) and *The Big Sleep* (1946), both starring Humphrey Bogart and Lauren Bacall.

With the onset of World War II Faulkner's concern with social problems, always present in his work, moved to the forefront. His writing became less experimental and more traditional; he began a series of books—*The Hamlet* (1940), *The Town* (1957), and *The Mansion* (1959), the so-called Snopes Trilogy—about the rise of the "poor white trash" Snopes family and the fall of the old southern gentry in Yoknapatawpha County. His reputation in America was strengthened with the 1946 publication of Malcolm Cowley's edition of *The Portable Faulkner,* for which Faulkner wrote an appendix on the history of the Compson family, beginning with the Native-American Ikkemotubbe and ending with the Compson's cook, Dilsey. In 1948 Faulkner wrote to his publisher that he had half of a novel written, the story of "a Negro [who is] in jail accused of murder and waiting for the white folks to drag him out and pour gasoline over him and set him on fire, [and who] is the detective, solves the crime because he goddamn has to to keep from being lynched." The novel, published in 1948 as *Intruder in the Dust,* is perhaps the strongest expression of the antiracist theme he had examined throughout his works; it led to the highest honor of his life, the 1950 Nobel Prize for literature. Typically reluctant to put himself in the public eye, Faulkner initially balked at attending the award ceremony in Stockholm. In the end he not only attended, but also delivered one of the most memorable laureate's speeches in the history of the prize. "The award was made, not to me, but to my works," he said. Of the $30,000 prize, he set apart $25,000 for the William Faulkner Foundation, to provide educational scholarships for African-American Mississippians and financial encouragement for Latin-American writers.

His post-Nobel years brought him numerous honors. In 1950 he received the Howells Medal from the American Academy of Arts and Letters; in 1951 he was awarded both the National Book Award for fiction and the French Legion of Honor; and in 1955 his parable

A Fable (1954) earned him a Pulitzer Prize. Though he continued to write, he increasingly assumed the role of sage. A frequent lecturer at college campuses, he refused to accept honorary degrees, saying that to do so "would be an insult to all those who have gained degrees by means of . . . long and arduous devotion" (Cox, 1982). Faulkner spoke out on civil rights issues in his native South and even undertook various State Department assignments between 1954 and 1961, traveling to South America, Japan, Manila, Europe, and Iceland. Faulkner was awarded another Pulitzer Prize for *The Reivers* (1962), a fictional "reminiscence" told by Lucius Priest to his grandson. In summer 1962 Faulkner suffered a severe back injury; the day after he was admitted to a hospital, he died at age sixty-five of a heart attack. He left behind a considerable body of work that accomplished what he expressed in his Nobel speech as the writer's duty: to write about the human "soul, a spirit capable of compassion and sacrifice and endurance."

Suggested Readings: *The Marble Faun,* 1924. *Soldier's Pay,* 1927. *The Sound and the Fury,* 1929. *As I Lay Dying,* 1930. *These 13,* 1931. *Light in August,* 1932. *Absalom, Absalom!,* 1936. *Go Down, Moses and Other Stories,* 1942. *Requiem for a Nun,* 1951. *A Fable,* 1954. *The Reivers,* 1962. *Essays, Speeches & Public Letters,* ed. J. B. Meriwether, 1966. *Uncollected Stories of William Faulkner,* 1979. I. Howe, *William Faulkner: A Critical Study,* 1962. O. W. Vickery, *The Novels of William Faulkner: A Critical Interpretation,* 1964. M. Millgate, *The Achievement of William Faulkner,* 1966. L. Wagner-Martin, *William Faulkner: Four Decades of Criticism,* 1973. J. T. Irwin, *Doubling and Incest/Repetition and Revenge: A Speculative Reading of Faulkner,* 1975. D. L. Mintner, *William Faulkner: His Life and Work,* 1980. C. Brooks, *William Faulkner: First Encounters,* 1983. T. M. Davis, *Faulkner's "Negro": Art and the Southern Context,* 1983. E. Peters, *William Faulkner: The Yoknapatawpha World and Black Being,* 1983. J. L. Blotner, *Faulkner: A Biography,* 1984.

Text Used: *Collected Stories of William Faulkner,* 1977.

A ROSE FOR EMILY

I

When Miss Emily Grierson died, our whole town went to her funeral: the men through a sort of respectful affection for a fallen monument, the women mostly out of curiosity to see the inside of her house, which no one save an old manservant—a combined gardener and cook—had seen in at least ten years.

It was a big, squarish frame house that had once been white, decorated with cupolas and spires and scrolled balconies in the heavily lightsome style of the seventies, set on what had once been our most select street. But garages and cotton gins had encroached and obliterated even the august names of that neighborhood; only Miss Emily's house was left, lifting its stubborn and coquettish decay above the cotton wagons and the gasoline pumps—an eyesore among eyesores. And now Miss Emily had gone to join the representatives of those august names where they lay in the cedar-bemused cemetery among the ranked and anonymous graves of Union and Confederate soldiers who fell at the battle of Jefferson.[1]

Alive, Miss Emily had been a tradition, a duty, and a care; a sort of hereditary obligation upon the town, dating from that day in 1894 when Colonel Sartoris,

[1] The seat of Faulkner's fictional Yoknapatawpha county, Jefferson is clearly his home town of Oxford, Mississippi.

the mayor—he who fathered the edict that no Negro woman should appear on the streets without an apron—remitted her taxes, the dispensation dating from the death of her father on into perpetuity. Not that Miss Emily would have accepted charity. Colonel Sartoris invented an involved tale to the effect that Miss Emily's father had loaned money to the town, which the town, as a matter of business, preferred this way of repaying. Only a man of Colonel Sartoris' generation and thought could have invented it, and only a woman could have believed it.

When the next generation, with its more modern ideas, became mayors and aldermen, this arrangement created some little dissatisfaction. On the first of the year they mailed her a tax notice. February came, and there was no reply. They wrote her a formal letter, asking her to call at the sheriff's office at her convenience. A week later the mayor wrote her himself, offering to call or to send his car for her, and received in reply a note on paper of an archaic shape, in a thin, flowing calligraphy in faded ink, to the effect that she no longer went out at all. The tax notice was also enclosed, without comment.

They called a special meeting of the Board of Aldermen. A deputation waited upon her, knocked at the door through which no visitor had passed since she ceased giving china-painting lessons eight or ten years earlier. They were admitted by the old Negro into a dim hall from which a stairway mounted into still more shadow. It smelled of dust and disuse—a close, dank smell. The Negro led them into the parlor. It was furnished in heavy, leather-covered furniture. When the Negro opened the blinds of one window, they could see that the leather was cracked; and when they sat down, a faint dust rose sluggishly about their thighs, spinning with slow motes in the single sun-ray. On a tarnished gilt easel before the fireplace stood a crayon portrait of Miss Emily's father.

They rose when she entered—a small, fat woman in black, with a thin gold chain descending to her waist and vanishing into her belt, leaning on an ebony cane with a tarnished gold head. Her skeleton was small and spare; perhaps that was why what would have been merely plumpness in another was obesity in her. She looked bloated, like a body long submerged in motionless water, and of that pallid hue. Her eyes, lost in the fatty ridges of her face, looked like two small pieces of coal pressed into a lump of dough as they moved from one face to another while the visitors stated their errand.

She did not ask them to sit. She just stood in the door and listened quietly until the spokesman came to a stumbling halt. Then they could hear the invisible watch ticking at the end of the gold chain.

Her voice was dry and cold. "I have no taxes in Jefferson. Colonel Sartoris explained it to me. Perhaps one of you can gain access to the city records and satisfy yourselves."

"But we have. We are the city authorities, Miss Emily. Didn't you get a notice from the sheriff, signed by him?"

"I received a paper, yes," Miss Emily said. "Perhaps he considers himself the sheriff . . . I have no taxes in Jefferson."

"But there is nothing on the books to show that, you see. We must go by the—"

"See Colonel Sartoris. I have no taxes in Jefferson."

"But, Miss Emily—"

"See Colonel Sartoris." (Colonel Sartoris had been dead almost ten years.) "I have no taxes in Jefferson. Tobe!" The Negro appeared. "Show these gentlemen out."

II

So she vanquished them, horse and foot,[2] just as she had vanquished their fathers thirty years before about the smell. That was two years after her father's death and a short time after her sweetheart—the one we believed would marry her—had deserted her. After her father's death she went out very little; after her sweetheart went away, people hardly saw her at all. A few of the ladies had the temerity to call, but were not received, and the only sign of life about the place was the Negro man—a young man then—going in and out with a market basket.

"Just as if a man—any man—could keep a kitchen properly," the ladies said; so they were not surprised when the smell developed. It was another link between the gross, teeming world and the high and mighty Griersons.

A neighbor, a woman, complained to the mayor, Judge Stevens, eighty years old.

"But what will you have me do about it, madam?" he said.

"Why, send her word to stop it," the woman said. "Isn't there a law?"

"I'm sure that won't be necessary," Judge Stevens said. "It's probably just a snake or a rat that nigger of hers killed in the yard. I'll speak to him about it."

The next day he received two more complaints, one from a man who came in diffident deprecation. "We really must do something about it, Judge. I'd be the last one in the world to bother Miss Emily, but we've got to do something." That night the Board of Aldermen met—three graybeards and one younger man, a member of the rising generation.

"It's simple enough," he said. "Send her word to have her place cleaned up. Give her a certain time to do it in, and if she don't . . . "

"Dammit, sir," Judge Stevens said, "will you accuse a lady to her face of smelling bad?"

So the next night, after midnight, four men crossed Miss Emily's lawn and slunk about the house like burglars, sniffing along the base of the brickwork and at the cellar openings while one of them performed a regular sowing motion with his hand out of a sack slung from his shoulder. They broke open the cellar door and sprinkled lime there, and in all the outbuildings. As they recrossed the lawn, a window that had been dark was lighted and Miss Emily sat in it, the light behind her, and her upright torso motionless as that of an idol. They crept quietly across the lawn and into the shadow of the locusts that lined the street. After a week or two the smell went away.

That was when people had begun to feel really sorry for her. People in our town, remembering how old lady Wyatt, her great-aunt, had gone completely crazy at last, believed that the Griersons held themselves a little too high for what they really were. None of the young men were quite good enough for Miss Emily and such. We had long thought of them as a tableau, Miss Emily a slender figure in white in the background, her father a spraddled silhouette in the foreground, his back to her and clutching a horsewhip, the two of them framed by the back-flung front door. So when she got to be thirty and was still single, we were not pleased exactly, but vindicated; even with insanity in the family she wouldn't have turned down all of her chances if they had really materialized.

When her father died, it got about that the house was all that was left to her; and in a way, people were glad. At last they could pity Miss Emily. Being left

---

[2] Completely, as in the defeat of an army's cavalry (horses) and infantry (foot).

alone, and a pauper, she had become humanized. Now she too would know the old thrill and the old despair of a penny more or less.

The day after his death all the ladies prepared to call at the house and offer condolence and aid, as is our custom. Miss Emily met them at the door, dressed as usual and with no trace of grief on her face. She told them that her father was not dead. She did that for three days, with the ministers calling on her, and the doctors, trying to persuade her to let them dispose of the body. Just as they were about to resort to law and force, she broke down, and they buried her father quickly.

We did not say she was crazy then. We believed she had to do that. We remembered all the young men her father had driven away, and we knew that with nothing left, she would have to cling to that which had robbed her, as people will.

III

She was sick for a long time. When we saw her again, her hair was cut short, making her look like a girl, with a vague resemblance to those angels in colored church windows—sort of tragic and serene.

The town had just let the contracts for paving the sidewalks, and in the summer after her father's death they began the work. The construction company came with niggers and mules and machinery, and a foreman named Homer Barron, a Yankee—a big, dark, ready man, with a big voice and eyes lighter than his face. The little boys would follow in groups to hear him cuss the niggers, and the niggers singing in time to the rise and fall of picks. Pretty soon he knew everybody in town. Whenever you heard a lot of laughing anywhere about the square, Homer Barron would be in the center of the group. Presently we began to see him and Miss Emily on Sunday afternoons driving in the yellow-wheeled buggy and the matched team of bays from the livery stable.

At first we were glad that Miss Emily would have an interest, because the ladies all said, "Of course a Grierson would not think seriously of a Northerner, a day laborer." But there were still others, older people, who said that even grief could not cause a real lady to forget *noblesse oblige*[3]—without calling it *noblesse oblige*. They just said, "Poor Emily. Her kinsfolk should come to her." She had some kin in Alabama; but years ago her father had fallen out with them over the estate of old lady Wyatt, the crazy woman, and there was no communication between the two families. They had not even been represented at the funeral.

And as soon as the old people said, "Poor Emily," the whispering began. "Do you suppose it's really so?" they said to one another. "Of course it is. What else could . . . " This behind their hands; rustling of craned silk and satin behind jalousies closed upon the sun of Sunday afternoon as the thin, swift clop-clop-clop of the matched team passed: "Poor Emily."

She carried her head high enough—even when we believed that she was fallen. It was as if she demanded more than ever the recognition of her dignity as the last Grierson; as if it had wanted that touch of earthiness to reaffirm her imperviousness. Like when she bought the rat poison, the arsenic. That was over a year after they had begun to say "Poor Emily," and while the two female cousins were visiting her.

---

[3] "High birth obligates" (French): the obligation of honorable, generous, and responsible behavior associated with high rank or birth.

"I want some poison," she said to the druggist. She was over thirty then, still a slight woman, though thinner than usual, with cold, haughty black eyes in a face the flesh of which was strained across the temples and about the eyesockets as you imagine a lighthouse-keeper's face ought to look. "I want some poison," she said.

"Yes, Miss Emily. What kind? For rats and such? I'd recom—"

"I want the best you have. I don't care what kind."

The druggist named several. "They'll kill anything up to an elephant. But what you want is—"

"Arsenic," Miss Emily said. "Is that a good one?"

"Is . . . arsenic? Yes, ma'am. But what you want—"

"I want arsenic."

The druggist looked down at her. She looked back at him, erect, her face like a strained flag. "Why, of course," the druggist said. "If that's what you want. But the law requires you to tell what you are going to use it for."

Miss Emily just stared at him, her head tilted back in order to look him eye for eye, until he looked away and went and got the arsenic and wrapped it up. The Negro delivery boy brought her the package; the druggist didn't come back. When she opened the package at home there was written on the box, under the skull and bones: "For rats."

IV

So the next day we all said, "She will kill herself"; and we said it would be the best thing. When she had first begun to be seen with Homer Barron, we had said, "She will marry him." Then we said, "She will persuade him yet," because Homer himself had remarked—he liked men, and it was known that he drank with the younger men in the Elks' Club—that he was not a marrying man. Later we said, "Poor Emily" behind the jalousies as they passed on Sunday afternoon in the glittering buggy, Miss Emily with her head high and Homer Barron with his hat cocked and a cigar in his teeth, reins and whip in a yellow glove.

Then some of the ladies began to say that it was a disgrace to the town and a bad example to the young people. The men did not want to interfere, but at last the ladies forced the Baptist minister—Miss Emily's people were Episcopal—to call upon her. He would never divulge what happened during that interview, but he refused to go back again. The next Sunday they again drove about the streets, and the following day the minister's wife wrote to Miss Emily's relations in Alabama.

So she had blood-kin under her roof again and we sat back to watch developments. At first nothing happened. Then we were sure that they were to be married. We learned that Miss Emily had been to the jeweler's and ordered a man's toilet set in silver, with the letters H. B. on each piece. Two days later we learned that she had bought a complete outfit of men's clothing, including a nightshirt, and we said, "They are married." We were really glad. We were glad because the two female cousins were even more Grierson than Miss Emily had ever been.

So we were not surprised when Homer Barron—the streets had been finished some time since—was gone. We were a little disappointed that there was not a public blowing-off, but we believed that he had gone on to prepare for Miss Emily's coming, or to give her a chance to get rid of the cousins. (By that time it was a cabal, and we were all Miss Emily's allies to help circumvent the cousins.) Sure enough, after another week they departed. And, as we had expected all along, within three days Homer Barron was back in town. A neighbor saw the Negro man admit him at the kitchen door at dusk one evening.

And that was the last we saw of Homer Barron. And of Miss Emily for some time. The Negro man went in and out with the market basket, but the front door remained closed. Now and then we would see her at the window for a moment, as the men did that night when they sprinkled the lime, but for almost six months she did not appear on the streets. Then we knew that this was to be expected too; as if that quality of her father which had thwarted her woman's life so many times had been too virulent and too furious to die.

When we next saw Miss Emily, she had grown fat and her hair was turning gray. During the next few years it grew grayer and grayer until it attained an even pepper-and salt iron-gray, when it ceased turning. Up to the day of her death at seventy-four it was still that vigorous iron-gray, like the hair of an active man.

From that time on her front door remained closed, save for a period of six or seven years, when she was about forty, during which she gave lessons in china-painting. She fitted up a studio in one of the downstairs rooms, where the daughters and granddaughters of Colonel Sartoris' contemporaries were sent to her with the same regularity and in the same spirit that they were sent to church on Sundays with a twenty-five-cent piece for the collection plate. Meanwhile her taxes had been remitted.

Then the newer generation became the backbone and the spirit of the town, and the painting pupils grew up and fell away and did not send their children to her with boxes of color and tedious brushes and pictures cut from the ladies' magazines. The front door closed upon the last one and remained closed for good. When the town got free postal delivery, Miss Emily alone refused to let them fasten the metal numbers above her door and attach a mailbox to it. She would not listen to them.

Daily, monthly, yearly we watched the Negro grow grayer and more stooped, going in and out with the market basket. Each December we sent her a tax notice, which would be returned by the post office a week later, unclaimed. Now and then we would see her in one of the downstairs windows—she had evidently shut up the top floor of the house—like the carven torso of an idol in a niche, looking or not looking at us, we could never tell which. Thus she passed from generation to generation—dear, inescapable, impervious, tranquil, and perverse.

And so she died. Fell ill in the house filled with dust and shadows, with only a doddering Negro man to wait on her. We did not even know she was sick; we had long since given up trying to get any information from the Negro. He talked to no one, probably not even to her, for his voice had grown harsh and rusty, as if from disuse.

She died in one of the downstairs rooms, in a heavy walnut bed with a curtain, her gray head propped on a pillow yellow and moldy with age and lack of sunlight.

V

The Negro met the first of the ladies at the front door and let them in, with their hushed, sibilant voices and their quick, curious glances, and then he disappeared. He walked right through the house and out the back and was not seen again.

The two female cousins came at once. They held the funeral on the second day, with the town coming to look at Miss Emily beneath a mass of bought flowers, with the crayon face of her father musing profoundly above the bier and the ladies sibilant and macabre; and the very old men—some in their brushed Confederate uniforms—on the porch and the lawn, talking of Miss Emily as if she had been a contemporary of theirs, believing that they had danced with her and courted her perhaps, confusing time with its mathematical progression, as the old do, to whom all the past is not a diminishing road but, instead, a huge meadow which no winter ever quite touches, divided from them now by the narrow bottle-neck of the most recent decade of years.

Already we knew that there was one room in that region above stairs which no one had seen in forty years, and which would have to be forced. They waited until Miss Emily was decently in the ground before they opened it.

The violence of breaking down the door seemed to fill this room with pervading dust. A thin, acrid pall as of the tomb seemed to lie everywhere upon this room decked and furnished as for a bridal: upon the valance curtains of faded rose color, upon the rose-shaded lights, upon the dressing table, upon the delicate array of crystal and the man's toilet things backed with tarnished silver, silver so tarnished that the monogram was obscured. Among them lay a collar and tie, as if they had just been removed, which, lifted, left upon the surface a pale crescent in the dust. Upon a chair hung the suit, carefully folded; beneath it the two mute shoes and the discarded socks.

The man himself lay in the bed.

For a long while we just stood there, looking down at the profound and fleshless grin. The body had apparently once lain in the attitude of an embrace, but now the long sleep that outlasts love, that conquers even the grimace of love, had cuckolded him. What was left of him, rotted beneath what was left of the nightshirt, had become inextricable from the bed in which he lay; and upon him and upon the pillow beside him lay that even coating of the patient and biding dust.

Then we noticed that in the second pillow was the indentation of a head. One of us lifted something from it; and leaning forward, that faint and invisible dust dry and acrid in the nostrils, we saw a long strand of iron-gray hair.

                                                                        1930

THAT EVENING SUN*

I

Monday is no different from any other weekday in Jefferson[1] now. The streets are paved now, and the telephone and electric companies are cutting down more and more of the shade trees—the water oaks, the maples and locusts and elms—to make room for iron poles bearing clusters of bloated and ghostly and bloodless grapes, and we have a city laundry which makes the rounds on Monday morning, gathering the bundles of clothes into bright-colored, specially-made motor cars:

---

* First published in the *American Mercury* in March 1931 and collected in *These 13* (1931). The title is probably based on W. C. Handy's song "St. Louis Blues" (1914), in which a woman sings of her unfaithful lover. "Hate to see de ev'nin' sun go down. / 'Cause my baby, he done lef' dis town."

[1] The seat of Faulkner's fictional Yoknapatawpha County, Jefferson is clearly his hometown of Oxford, Mississippi.

the soiled wearing of a whole week now flees apparitionlike behind alert and irritable electric horns, with a long diminishing noise of rubber and asphalt like tearing silk, and even the Negro women who still take in white people's washing after the old custom, fetch and deliver it in automobiles.

But fifteen years ago, on Monday morning the quiet, dusty, shady streets would be full of Negro women with, balanced on their steady, turbaned heads, bundles of clothes tied up in sheets, almost as large as cotton bales, carried so without touch of hand between the kitchen door of the white house and the blackened washpot beside a cabin door in Negro Hollow.

Nancy would set her bundle on the top of her head, then upon the bundle in turn she would set the black straw sailor hat which she wore winter and summer. She was tall, with a high, sad face sunken a little where her teeth were missing. Sometimes we would go a part of the way down the lane and across the pasture with her, to watch the balanced bundle and the hat that never bobbed nor wavered, even when she walked down into the ditch and up the other side and stooped through the fence. She would go down on her hands and knees and crawl through the gap, her head rigid, uptilted, the bundle steady as a rock or a balloon, and rise to her feet again and go on.

Sometimes the husbands of the washing women would fetch and deliver the clothes, but Jesus never did that for Nancy, even before father told him to stay away from our house, even when Dilsey was sick and Nancy would come to cook for us.

And then about half the time we'd have to go down the lane to Nancy's cabin and tell her to come on and cook breakfast. We would stop at the ditch, because father told us to not have anything to do with Jesus—he was a short black man, with a razor scar down his face—and we would throw rocks at Nancy's house until she came to the door, leaning her head around it without any clothes on.

"What yawl mean, chunking my house?" Nancy said. "What you little devils mean?"

"Father says for you to come on and get breakfast," Caddy said. "Father says it's over a half an hour now, and you've got to come this minute."

"I aint studying no breakfast," Nancy said. "I going to get my sleep out."

"I bet you're drunk," Jason said. "Father says you're drunk. Are you drunk, Nancy?"

"Who says I is?" Nancy said. "I got to get my sleep out. I aint studying no breakfast."

So after a while we quit chunking the cabin and went back home. When she finally came, it was too late for me to go to school. So we thought it was whisky until that day they arrested her again and they were taking her to jail and they passed Mr Stovall. He was the cashier in the bank and a deacon in the Baptist church, and Nancy began to say:

"When you going to pay me, white man? When you going to pay me, white man? It's been three times now since you paid me a cent—" Mr Stovall knocked her down, but she kept on saying, "When you going to pay me, white man? It's been three times now since—" until Mr Stovall kicked her in the mouth with his heel and the marshal caught Mr Stovall back, and Nancy lying in the street, laughing. She turned her head and spat out some blood and teeth and said, "It's been three times now since he paid me a cent."

That was how she lost her teeth, and all that day they told about Nancy and Mr Stovall, and all that night the ones that passed the jail could hear Nancy singing and yelling. They could see her hands holding to the window bars, and a lot of them stopped along the fence, listening to her and to the jailer trying to make her stop. She didn't shut up until almost daylight, when the jailer began to hear a bumping and scraping upstairs and he went up there and found Nancy hanging from the window bar. He said that it was cocaine and not whisky, because no nigger would try to commit suicide unless he was full of cocaine, because a nigger full of cocaine wasn't a nigger any longer.

The jailer cut her down and revived her; then he beat her, whipped her. She had hung herself with her dress. She had fixed it all right, but when they arrested her she didn't have on anything except a dress and so she didn't have anything to tie her hands with and she couldn't make her hands let go of the window ledge. So the jailer heard the noise and ran up there and found Nancy hanging from the window, stark naked, her belly already swelling out a little, like a little balloon.

When Dilsey was sick in her cabin and Nancy was cooking for us, we could see her apron swelling out; that was before father told Jesus to stay away from the house. Jesus was in the kitchen, sitting behind the stove, with his razor scar on his black face like a piece of dirty string. He said it was a watermelon that Nancy had under her dress.

"It never come off of your vine, though," Nancy said.

"Off of what vine?" Caddy said.

"I can cut down the vine it did come off of," Jesus said.

"What makes you want to talk like that before these children?" Nancy said. "Whyn't you go on to work? You done et. You want Mr Jason to catch you hanging around his kitchen, talking that way before these chillen?"

"Talking what way?" Caddy said. "What vine?"

"I cant hang around white man's kitchen," Jesus said. "But white man can hang around mine. White man can come in my house, but I cant stop him. When white man want to come in my house, I aint got no house. I cant stop him, but he cant kick me outen it. He cant do that."

Dilsey was still sick in her cabin. Father told Jesus to stay off our place. Dilsey was still sick. It was a long time. We were in the library after supper.

"Isn't Nancy through in the kitchen yet?" mother said. "It seems to me that she has had plenty of time to have finished the dishes."

"Let Quentin go and see," father said. "Go and see if Nancy is through, Quentin. Tell her she can go on home."

I went to the kitchen. Nancy was through. The dishes were put away and the fire was out. Nancy was sitting in a chair, close to the cold stove. She looked at me.

"Mother wants to know if you are through," I said.

"Yes," Nancy said. She looked at me. "I done finished." She looked at me.

"What is it?" I said. "What is it?"

"I aint nothing but a nigger," Nancy said. "It aint none of my fault."

She looked at me, sitting in the chair before the cold stove, the sailor hat on her head. I went back to the library. It was the cold stove and all, when you think of a kitchen being warm and busy and cheerful. And with a cold stove and the dishes all put away, and nobody wanting to eat at that hour.

"Is she through?" mother said.

"Yessum," I said.

"What is she doing?" mother said.

"She's not doing anything. She's through."

"I'll go and see," father said.

"Maybe she's waiting for Jesus to come and take her home," Caddy said.

"Jesus is gone," I said. Nancy told us how one morning she woke up and Jesus was gone.

"He quit me," Nancy said. "Done gone to Memphis, I reckon. Dodging them city *po*-lice for a while, I reckon."

"And a good riddance," father said. "I hope he stays there."

"Nancy's scaired of the dark," Jason said.

"So are you," Caddy said.

"I'm not," Jason said.

"Scairy cat," Caddy said.

"I'm not," Jason said.

"You, Candace!" mother said. Father came back.

"I am going to walk down the lane with Nancy," he said. "She says that Jesus is back."

"Has she seen him?" mother said.

"No. Some Negro sent her word that he was back in town. I wont be long."

"You'll leave me alone, to take Nancy home?" mother said. "Is her safety more precious to you than mine?"

"I wont be long," father said.

"You'll leave these children unprotected, with that Negro about?"

"I'm going too," Caddy said, "Let me go, Father."

"What would he do with them, if he were unfortunate enough to have them?" father said.

"I want to go, too," Jason said.

"Jason!" mother said. She was speaking to father. You could tell that by the way she said the name. Like she believed that all day father had been trying to think of doing the thing she wouldn't like the most, and that she knew all the time that after a while he would think of it. I stayed quiet, because father and I both knew that mother would want him to make me stay with her if she just thought of it in time. So father didn't look at me. I was the oldest. I was nine and Caddy was seven and Jason was five.

"Nonsense," father said. "We wont be long."

Nancy had her hat on. We came to the lane. "Jesus always been good to me," Nancy said. "Whenever he had two dollars, one of them was mine." We walked in the lane. "If I can just get through the lane." Nancy said, "I be all right then."

The lane was always dark. "This is where Jason got scared on Hallowe'en," Caddy said.

"I didn't," Jason said.

"Cant Aunt Rachel do anything with him?" father said. Aunt Rachel was old. She lived in a cabin beyond Nancy's, by herself. She had white hair and she smoked a pipe in the door, all day long; she didn't work any more. They said she was Jesus' mother. Sometimes she said she was and sometimes she said she wasn't any kin to Jesus.

"Yes, you did," Caddy said. "You were scairder than Frony. You were scairder than T.P. even. Scairder than niggers."

"Cant nobody do nothing with him," Nancy said. "He say I done woke up the devil in him and aint but one thing going to lay it down again."

"Well, he's gone now," father said. "There's nothing for you to be afraid of now. And if you'd just let white men alone."

"Let what white men alone?" Caddy said. "How let them alone?"

"He aint gone nowhere," Nancy said. "I can feel him. I can feel him now, in this lane. He hearing us talk, every word, hid somewhere, waiting. I aint seen him, and I aint going to see him again but once more, with that razor in his mouth. That razor on that string down his back, inside his shirt. And then I aint going to be even surprised."

"I wasn't scaired," Jason said.

"If you'd behave yourself, you'd have kept out of this," father said. "But it's all right now. He's probably in St. Louis now. Probably got another wife by now and forgot all about you."

"If he has, I better not find out about it," Nancy said. "I'd stand there right over them, and every time he wropped her, I'd cut that arm off. I'd cut his head off and I'd slit her belly and I'd shove—"

"Hush," father said.

"Slit whose belly, Nancy?" Caddy said.

"I wasn't scaired," Jason said. "I'd walk right down this lane by myself."

"Yah," Caddy said. "You wouldn't dare to put your foot down in it if we were not here too."

II

Dilsey was still sick, so we took Nancy home every night until mother said, "How much longer is this going on? I to be left alone in this big house while you take home a frightened Negro?

We fixed a pallet,[2] in the kitchen for Nancy. One night we waked up, hearing the sound. It was not singing and it was not crying, coming up the dark stairs. There was a light in mother's room and we heard father going down the hall, down the back stairs, and Caddy and I went into the hall. The floor was cold. Our toes curled away from it while we listened to the sound. It was like singing and it wasn't like singing, like the sounds that Negroes make.

Then it stopped and we heard father going down the back stairs, and we went to the head of the stairs. Then the sound began again, in the stairway, not loud, and we could see Nancy's eyes halfway up the stairs, against the wall. They looked like cat's eyes do, like a big cat against the wall, watching us. When we came down the steps to where she was, she quit making the sound again, and we stood there until father came back up from the kitchen, with his pistol in his hand. He went back down with Nancy and they came back with Nancy's pallet.

We spread the pallet in our room. After the light in mother's room went off, we could see Nancy's eyes again. "Nancy," Caddy whispered, "are you asleep, Nancy?"

Nancy whispered something. It was oh or no, I dont know which. Like nobody had made it, like it came from nowhere and went nowhere, until it was like Nancy was not there at all; that I had looked so hard at her eyes on the stairs that they had got printed on my eyeballs, like the sun does when you have closed your eyes and there is no sun. "Jesus," Nancy whispered. "Jesus."

"Was it Jesus?" Caddy said. "Did he try to come into the kitchen?"

"Jesus," Nancy said. Like this: Jeeeeeeeeeeeeeeeeus, until the sound went out, like a match or a candle does.

---

[2] A temporary bed, typically on the floor.

"It's the other Jesus she means," I said.

"Can you see us, Nancy?" Caddy whispered. "Can you see our eyes too?"

"I aint nothing but a nigger," Nancy said. "God knows. God knows."

"What did you see down there in the kitchen?" Caddy whispered. "What tried to get in?"

"God knows," Nancy said. We could see her eyes. "God knows."

Dilsey got well. She cooked dinner. "You'd better stay in bed a day or two longer," father said.

"What for?" Dilsey said. "If I had been a day later, this place would be to rack and ruin. Get on out of here now, and let me get my kitchen straight again."

Dilsey cooked supper too. And that night, just before dark, Nancy came into the kitchen.

"How do you know he's back?" Dilsey said. "You aint seen him."

"Jesus is a nigger," Jason said.

"I can feel him," Nancy said. "I can feel him laying yonder in the ditch."

"Tonight?" Dilsey said. "Is he there tonight?"

"Dilsey's a nigger too," Jason said.

"You try to eat something," Dilsey said.

"I dont want nothing," Nancy said.

"I aint a nigger," Jason said.

"Drink some coffee," Dilsey said. She poured a cup of coffee for Nancy. "Do you know he's out there tonight? How come you know it's tonight?"

"I know," Nancy said. "He's there, waiting. I know. I done lived with him too long. I know what he is fixing to do fore he know it himself."

"Drink some coffee," Dilsey said. Nancy held the cup to her mouth and blew into the cup. Her mouth pursed out like a spreading adder's, like a rubber mouth, like she had blown all the color out of her lips with blowing the coffee.

"I aint a nigger," Jason said. "Are you a nigger, Nancy?"

"I hellborn, child," Nancy said. "I wont be nothing soon. I going back where I come from soon."

III

She began to drink the coffee. While she was drinking, holding the cup in both hands, she began to make the sound again. She made the sound into the cup and the coffee sploshed out onto her hands and her dress. Her eyes looked at us and she sat there, her elbows on her knees, holding the cup in both hands, looking at us across the wet cup, making the sound. "Look at Nancy," Jason said. "Nancy cant cook for us now. Dilsey's got well now."

"You hush up," Dilsey said. Nancy held the cup in both hands, looking at us, making the sound, like there were two of them: one looking at us and the other making the sound. "Whyn't you let Mr Jason telefoam the marshal?" Dilsey said. Nancy stopped then, holding the cup in her long brown hands. She tried to drink some coffee again, but it sploshed out of the cup, onto her hands and her dress, and she put the cup down. Jason watched her.

"I cant swallow it," Nancy said. "I swallows but it wont go down me."

"You go down to the cabin," Dilsey said. "Frony will fix you a pallet and I'll be there soon."

"Wont no nigger stop him," Nancy said.

"I aint a nigger," Jason said. "Am I, Dilsey?"

"I reckon not," Dilsey said. She looked at Nancy. "I dont reckon so. What you going to do, then?"

Nancy looked at us. Her eyes went fast, like she was afraid there wasn't time to look, without hardly moving at all. She looked at us, at all three of us at one time. "You member that night I stayed in yawls' room?" she said. She told about how we waked up early the next morning, and played. We had to play quiet, on her pallet, until father woke up and it was time to get breakfast. "Go and ask your maw to let me stay here tonight," Nancy said. "I wont need no pallet. We can play some more."

Caddy asked mother. Jason went too. "I cant have Negroes sleeping in the bedrooms," mother said. Jason cried. He cried until mother said he couldn't have any dessert for three days if he didn't stop. Then Jason said he would stop if Dilsey would make a chocolate cake. Father was there.

"Why dont you do something about it?" mother said. "What do we have officers for?"

"Why is Nancy afraid of Jesus?" Caddy said. "Are you afraid of father, mother?"

"What could the officers do?" father said. "If Nancy hasn't seen him, how could the officers find him?"

"Then why is she afraid?" mother said.

"She says he is there. She says she knows he is there tonight."

"Yet we pay taxes," mother said. "I must wait here alone in this big house while you take a Negro woman home."

"You know that I am not lying outside with a razor," father said.

"I'll stop if Dilsey will make a chocolate cake," Jason said. Mother told us to go out and father said he didn't know if Jason would get a chocolate cake or not, but he knew what Jason was going to get in about a minute. We went back to the kitchen and told Nancy.

"Father said for you to go home and lock the door, and you'll be all right," Caddy said. "All right from what, Nancy? Is Jesus mad at you?" Nancy was holding the coffee cup in her hands again, her elbows on her knees and her hands holding the cup between her knees. She was looking into the cup. "What have you done that made Jesus mad?" Caddy said. Nancy let the cup go. It didn't break on the floor, but the coffee spilled out, and Nancy sat there with her hands still making the shape of the cup. She began to make the sound again, not loud. Not singing and not unsinging. We watched her.

"Here," Dilsey said. "You quit that, now. You get aholt of yourself. You wait here. I going to get Versh to walk home with you." Dilsey went out.

We looked at Nancy. Her shoulders kept shaking, but she quit making the sound. We watched her. "What's Jesus going to do to you?" Caddy said. "He went away."

Nancy looked at us. "We had fun that night I stayed in yawls' room, didn't we?"

"I didn't," Jason said. "I didn't have any fun."

"You were asleep in mother's room," Caddy said. "You were not there."

"Let's go down to my house and have some more fun," Nancy said.

"Mother wont let us," I said. "It's too late now."

"Dont bother her," Nancy said. "We can tell her in the morning. She wont mind."

"She wouldn't let us," I said.

"Dont ask her now," Nancy said. "Dont bother her now."

"She didn't say we couldn't go," Caddy said.

"We didn't ask," I said.

"If you go, I'll tell," Jason said.

"We'll have fun," Nancy said. "They won't mind, just to my house. I been working for yawl a long time. They won't mind."

"I'm not afraid to go," Caddy said. "Jason is the one that's afraid. He'll tell."

"I'm not," Jason said.

"Yes, you are," Caddy said, "You'll tell."

"I won't tell," Jason said. "I'm not afraid."

"Jason ain't afraid to go with me," Nancy said. "Is you, Jason?"

"Jason is going to tell," Caddy said. The lane was dark. We passed the pasture gate. "I bet if something was to jump out from behind that gate, Jason would holler."

"I wouldn't," Jason said. We walked down the lane. Nancy was talking loud.

"What are you talking so loud for, Nancy?" Caddy said.

"Who; me?" Nancy said. "Listen at Quentin and Caddy and Jason saying I'm talking loud."

"You talk like there was five of us here," Caddy said. "You talk like father was here too."

"Who; me talking loud, Mr Jason?" Nancy said.

"Nancy called Jason 'Mister,' " Caddy said.

"Listen how Caddy and Quentin and Jason talk," Nancy said.

"We're not talking loud," Caddy said. "You're the one that's talking like father—"

"Hush," Nancy said; "hush, Mr Jason."

"Nancy called Jason 'Mister' aguh—"

"Hush," Nancy said. She was talking loud when we crossed the ditch and stooped through the fence where she used to stoop through with the clothes on her head. Then we came to her house. We were going fast then. She opened the door. The smell of the house was like the lamp and the smell of Nancy was like the wick, like they were waiting for one another to begin to smell. She lit the lamp and closed the door and put the bar up. Then she quit talking loud, looking at us.

"What're we going to do?" Caddy said.

"What do yawl want to do?" Nancy said.

"You said we would have some fun," Caddy said.

There was something about Nancy's house; something you could smell besides Nancy and the house. Jason smelled it, even. "I don't want to stay here," he said. "I want to go home."

"Go home, then," Caddy said.

"I don't want to go by myself," Jason said.

"We're going to have some fun," Nancy said.

"How?" Caddy said.

Nancy stood by the door. She was looking at us, only it was like she had emptied her eyes, like she had quit using them. "What do you want to do?" she said.

"Tell us a story," Caddy said. "Can you tell a story?"

"Yes," Nancy said.

"Tell it," Caddy said. We looked at Nancy. "You don't know any stories."

"Yes," Nancy said. "Yes, I do."

She came and sat in a chair before the hearth. There was a little fire there. Nancy built it up, when it was already hot inside. She built a good blaze. She told a story. She talked like her eyes looked, like her eyes watching us and her voice talking to us did not belong to her. Like she was living somewhere else, waiting somewhere else. She was outside the cabin. Her voice was inside and the shape of her, the Nancy that could stoop under a barbed wire fence with a bundle of clothes balanced on her head as though without weight, like a balloon, was there. But that was all. "And so this here queen come walking up to the ditch, where that bad man was hiding. She was walking up to the ditch, and she say, 'If I can just get past this here ditch,' was what she say . . . "

"What ditch?" Caddy said. "A ditch like that one out there? Why did a queen want to go into a ditch?"

"To get to her house," Nancy said. She looked at us. "She had to cross the ditch to get into her house quick and bar the door."

"Why did she want to go home and bar the door?" Caddy said.

IV

Nancy looked at us. She quit talking. She looked at us. Jason's legs stuck straight out of his pants where he sat on Nancy's lap. "I don't think that's a good story," he said. "I want to go home."

"Maybe we had better," Caddy said. She got up from the floor. "I bet they are looking for us right now." She went toward the door.

"No," Nancy said. "Don't open it." She got up quick and passed Caddy. She didn't touch the door, the wooden bar.

"Why not?" Caddy said.

"Come back to the lamp," Nancy said. "We'll have fun. You don't have to go."

"We ought to go," Caddy said. "Unless we have a lot of fun." She and Nancy came back to the fire, the lamp.

"I want to go home," Jason said. "I'm going to tell."

"I know another story," Nancy said. She stood close to the lamp. She looked at Caddy, like when your eyes look up at a stick balanced on your nose. She had to look down to see Caddy, but her eyes looked like that, like when you are balancing a stick.

"I won't listen to it," Jason said. "I'll bang on the floor."

"It's a good one," Nancy said. "It's better than the other one."

"What's it about?" Caddy said. Nancy was standing by the lamp. Her hand was on the lamp, against the light, long and brown.

"Your hand is on that hot globe," Caddy said. "Don't it feel hot to your hand?"

Nancy looked at her hand on the lamp chimney. She took her hand away, slow. She stood there, looking at Caddy, wringing her long hand as though it were tied to her wrist with a string.

"Let's do something else," Caddy said.

"I want to go home," Jason said.

"I got some popcorn," Nancy said. She looked at Caddy and then at Jason and then at me and then at Caddy again. "I got some popcorn."

"I don't like popcorn," Jason said. "I'd rather have candy."

Nancy looked at Jason. "You can hold the popper." She was still wringing her hand; it was long and limp and brown.

"All right," Jason said. "I'll stay a while if I can do that. Caddy can't hold it. I'll want to go home again if Caddy holds the popper."

Nancy built up the fire. "Look at Nancy putting her hands in the fire," Caddy said. "What's the matter with you, Nancy?"

"I got popcorn," Nancy said. "I got some." She took the popper from under the bed. It was broken. Jason began to cry.

"Now we can't have any popcorn," he said.

"We ought to go home, anyway," Caddy said. "Come on, Quentin."

"Wait," Nancy said; "wait. I can fix it. Don't you want to help me fix it?"

"I don't think I want any," Caddy said. "It's too late now."

"You help me, Jason," Nancy said. "Don't you want to help me?"

"No," Jason said. "I want to go home."

"Hush," Nancy said; "hush. Watch. Watch me. I can fix it so Jason can hold it and pop the corn." She got a piece of wire and fixed the popper.

"It won't hold good," Caddy said.

"Yes, it will," Nancy said. "Yawl watch. Yawl help me shell some corn."

The popcorn was under the bed too. We shelled it into the popper and Nancy helped Jason hold the popper over the fire.

"It's not popping," Jason said. "I want to go home."

"You wait," Nancy said. "It'll begin to pop. We'll have fun then." She was sitting close to the fire. The lamp was turned up so high it was beginning to smoke.

"Why don't you turn it down some?" I said.

"It's all right," Nancy said. "I'll clean it. Yawl wait. The popcorn will start in a minute."

"I don't believe it's going to start," Caddy said. "We ought to start home, anyway. They'll be worried."

"No," Nancy said. "It's going to pop. Dilsey will tell um yawl with me. I been working for yawl long time. They won't mind if yawl at my house. You wait, now. It'll start popping any minute now."

Then Jason got some smoke in his eyes and he began to cry. He dropped the popper into the fire. Nancy got a wet rag and wiped Jason's face, but he didn't stop crying.

"Hush," she said, "Hush." But he didn't hush. Caddy took the popper out of the fire.

"It's burned up," she said. "You'll have to get some more popcorn, Nancy."

"Did you put all of it in?" Nancy said.

"Yes," Caddy said. Nancy looked at Caddy. Then she took the popper and opened it and poured the cinders into her apron and began to sort the grains, her hands long and brown, and we watching her.

"Haven't you got any more?" Caddy said.

"Yes," Nancy said; "yes. Look. This here ain't burnt. All we need to do is—"

"I want to go home," Jason said. "I'm going to tell."

"Hush," Caddy said. We all listened. Nancy's head was already turned toward the barred door, her eyes filled with red lamplight. "Somebody is coming," Caddy said.

Then Nancy began to make that sound again, not loud, sitting there above the fire, her long hands dangling between her knees; all of a sudden water began to come out on her face in big drops, running down her face, carrying in each one a little turning ball of firelight like a spark until it dropped off her chin. "She's not crying," I said.

"I ain't crying," Nancy said. Her eyes were closed. "I ain't crying. Who is it?"

"I don't know," Caddy said. She went to the door and looked out. "We've got to go now," she said. "Here comes father."

"I'm going to tell," Jason said. "Yawl made me come."

The water still ran down Nancy's face. She turned in her chair. "Listen. Tell him. Tell him we going to have fun. Tell him I take good care of yawl until in the morning. Tell him to let me come home with yawl and sleep on the floor. Tell him I won't need no pallet. We'll have fun. You member last time how we had so much fun?"

"I didn't have fun," Jason said. "You hurt me. You put smoke in my eyes. I'm going to tell."

V

Father came in. He looked at us. Nancy did not get up.

"Tell him," she said.

"Caddy made us come down here," Jason said. "I didn't want to."

Father came to the fire. Nancy looked up at him. "Can't you go to Aunt Rachel's and stay?" he said. Nancy looked up at father, her hands between her knees. "He's not here," father said. "I would have seen him. There's not a soul in sight."

"He in the ditch," Nancy said. "He waiting in the ditch yonder."

"Nonsense," father said. He looked at Nancy. "Do you know he's there?"

"I got the sign," Nancy said.

"What sign?"

"I got it. It was on the table when I come in. It was a hog-bone, with blood meat still on it, laying by the lamp. He's out there. When yawl walk out that door, I gone."

"Gone where, Nancy?" Caddy said.

"I'm not a tattletale," Jason said.

"Nonsense," father said.

"He out there," Nancy said. "He looking through that window this minute, waiting for yawl to go. Then I gone."

"Nonsense," father said. "Lock up your house and we'll take you on to Aunt Rachel's."

"'Twont do no good," Nancy said. She didn't look at father now, but he looked down at her, at her long, limp, moving hands. "Putting it off wont do no good."

"Then what do you want to do?" father said.

"I don't know," Nancy said. "I can't do nothing. Just put it off. And that don't do no good. I reckon it belong to me. I reckon what I going to get ain't no more than mine."

"Get what?" Caddy said. "What's yours?"

"Nothing," father said. "You all must get to bed."

"Caddy made me come," Jason said.

"Go on to Aunt Rachel's," father said.

"It won't do no good," Nancy said. She sat before the fire, her elbows on her knees, her long hands between her knees. "When even your own kitchen wouldn't do no good. When even if I was sleeping on the floor in the room with your chillen, and the next morning there I am, and blood—"

"Hush," father said. "Lock the door and put out the lamp and go to bed."

"I scared of the dark," Nancy said. "I scared for it to happen in the dark."

"You mean you're going to sit right here with the lamp lighted?" father said. Then Nancy began to make the sound again, sitting before the fire, her long hands between her knees. "Ah, damnation," father said. "Come along, chillen. It's past bedtime."

"When yawl go home, I gone," Nancy said. She talked quieter now, and her face looked quiet, like her hands. "Anyway, I got my coffin money saved up with Mr. Lovelady." Mr. Lovelady was a short, dirty man who collected the Negro insurance, coming around to the cabins or the kitchens every Saturday morning, to collect fifteen cents. He and his wife lived at the hotel. One morning his wife committed suicide. They had a child, a little girl. He and the child went away. After a week or two he came back alone. We would see him going along the lanes and the back streets on Saturday mornings.

"Nonsense," father said. "You'll be the first thing I'll see in the kitchen tomorrow morning."

"You'll see what you'll see, I reckon," Nancy said. "But it will take the Lord to say what that will be."

VI

We left her sitting before the fire.

"Come and put the bar up," father said. But she didn't move. She didn't look at us again, sitting quietly there between the lamp and the fire. From some distance down the lane we could look back and see her through the open door.

"What, Father?" Caddy said. "What's going to happen?"

"Nothing," father said. Jason was on father's back, so Jason was the tallest of all of us. We went down into the ditch. I looked at it, quiet. I couldn't see much where the moonlight and the shadows tangled.

"If Jesus is hid here, he can see us, cant he?" Caddy said.

"He's not there," father said. "He went away a long time ago."

"You made me come," Jason said, high; against the sky it looked like father had two heads, a little one and a big one. "I didn't want to."

We went up out of the ditch. We could still see Nancy's house and the open door, but we couldn't see Nancy now, sitting before the fire with the door open, because she was tired. "I just done got tired," she said. "I just a nigger. It ain't no fault of mine."

But we could hear her, because she began just after we came up out of the ditch, the sound that was not singing and not unsinging. "Who will do our washing now, Father?" I said.

"I'm not a nigger," Jason said, high and close above father's head.

"You're worse," Caddy said, "you are a tattletale. If something was to jump out, you'd be scairder than a nigger."

"I wouldn't," Jason said.

"You'd cry," Caddy said.
"Caddy," father said.
"I wouldn't!" Jason said.
"Scairy cat," Caddy said.
"Candace!" father said.

1931

Ernest Hemingway
(1899–1961)

Born in 1899 in Oak Park, Illinois, a prosperous suburb of Chicago, Ernest Miller Hemingway grew up as the third child, the oldest son, of six children in a comfortable, devout Protestant family. His parents were dynamic, spirited individuals: Clarence Edmond Hemingway was a general practitioner and an avid sportsman; his wife, Grace Hall, had relinquished a potential operatic career in favor of marriage and devoted her talents to teaching music and to the promotion of religion and high culture in her household. From the time Ernest Hemingway was a few months old, the family regularly spent summers at a cottage in upper Michigan, where the boy acquired his lifelong passion for hunting and fishing. The landscape was to provide the setting for some of Hemingway's greatest stories, including "Big Two-Hearted River" (1925).

By the time Hemingway was eighteen, America had entered World War I, and he faced a choice about his future. Having decided not to attend college, he spent six months working as a cub reporter for the Kansas City *Star* and discovered a boundless enthusiasm, which never left him, for the "romance of journalism." Hemingway longed to participate in the war in Europe, but an inherited eye problem precluded military service. Searching for alternatives, he and two of his closest friends made a pact to volunteer as ambulance drivers for the Red Cross, and in spring 1918 he found himself aboard a ship bound for France.

What he saw and experienced during the next months in Europe affected him deeply and lastingly. "I was an awful dope when I went to the last war," he recalled in a 1942 letter to the editor Maxwell Perkins. "I can remember just thinking that we were the home team and the Austrians were the visiting team." Not only were Hemingway's illusions shattered by constant exposure to the wounded and the dead, but while serving in northern Italy in early July he was badly injured by shrapnel. Sent to the Red Cross Hospital in Milan, he began a long convalescence, which was enlivened by a brief romance with a beautiful American nurse. Before long the other nurses took to exhibiting the handsome young Hemingway to visitors as a "prize specimen of a wounded hero." Despite his bravado and the obvious pleasure he got from this attention, Hemingway was troubled by a sense that his preferment was undeserved, his suffering much less than those of others. Such feelings were only heightened when he was decorated for valor (for carrying to safety a soldier more seriously wounded than himself) and when he was singled out, limping down the gangplank upon his return to New York in January 1919, by an interview-seeking New York *Sun* reporter as an American hero who had "defied the shrapnel of the Central Powers" (January 22, 1919).

Back in America Hemingway gradually recovered from his injuries and renewed two prewar passions, fishing trips to northern Michigan and journalism. He wrote for the Toronto *Star* and the monthly *Cooperative Commonwealth*. He found himself increasingly at odds with his parents, especially his mother, who criticized him for what she saw as his laziness and impiety. In 1921 he married Hadley Richardson and briefly lived with her in Chicago. Later that year the couple set out for Paris, armed with letters of introduction from the fiction writer Sherwood Anderson to numerous influential figures in Parisian expatriate society. Hadley would count on a small income from a trust fund, and Ernest would write for the Toronto *Star* while attempting to begin his literary career.

Hemingway's years in Paris have achieved the status of legend in literary history and popular consciousness: it was there that the "lost generation"—as the avant-garde author and art collector Gertrude Stein called the loosely-knit group of artists and writers centered on the Left Bank of the Seine River—took shape and fostered a revolution in aesthetic style and sensibility. With the aid of Anderson's letters, Hemingway met the bookstore proprietor Sylvia Beach, Stein, Ezra Pound, F. Scott Fitzgerald, and many others. Writing in cafés and rented rooms, Hemingway crafted the distinctive prose style—marked by clipped declarative sentences and suggestive understatement—that characterizes his work. In a series of short stories and several novels of extraordinary power, he drew on his reporter's sense of economy of expression as well as on his experience of war and injury. Nick Adams, the protagonist of "Big Two-Hearted River" and numerous other tales, became an exemplar of Hemingway's personal artistic and ethical "code," a man who had suffered debilitating wounds and emotional distresses but who tried to cope with them with quiet dignity, resignation, and grace.

"Big Two-Hearted River" dates from Hemingway's time in Paris in the early 1920s and was originally published in the expatriate magazine *This Quarter* and in the collection *In Our Time* in 1925. After returning from the war in Europe Hemingway went on several recuperative fishing expeditions in summer 1919, one to Michigan's upper peninsula, the site of Nick Adams's solitary journey. Hemingway, according to a letter he wrote to the author Malcolm Cowley in 1948, was limping so slowly in getting off the train at Seney, Michigan, that the brakeman called out to the engineer to wait because of the "cripple." Hearing himself called a cripple so shocked him that he "stopped being one in [my] mind." True or not, this story speaks of Hemingway's desire for an emotional and imaginative "cure" to purge the profound disturbances of the war and the feelings of shame and complicity it had inculcated in him.

Yet, "Big Two-Hearted River" makes no mention of war or physical injury; it is a prime example of what Hemingway called his "iceberg" principle of fiction. Like an iceberg, a story should be "seven-eighths under water for every part that shows," Hemingway noted in a 1958 interview in *Paris Review*. In "Big Two-Hearted River" Nick's intense concentration on the details of making his camp, cooking his meals, and preparing to fish draw their significance from precisely what is unspecified in the story, the obscure cause and context of his anxiety and unhappiness. The solitary expedition becomes a ritual of healing, each step of which must be taken in its turn. Nick's repeated efforts to restrain his thoughts and actions are related in a prose that pares itself down to an insistent staccato at moments of special intensity.

Hemingway's work in the early 1920s was quickly seized upon for its "new, tough, severe and satisfying beauty"; the influential critic Edmund Wilson helped promote the young writer's "strikingly original" stories. After producing *The Torrents of Spring*,

(1926), a slight parody of Sherwood Anderson's *Dark Laughter* (1925), Hemingway published his first serious novel, *The Sun Also Rises* (1926). Greeted with widespread enthusiasm, it sealed "lost generationism" as a phenomenon of popular culture. The taciturn Jake Barnes, emasculated by his war injuries, narrates the cycle of tawdry amusements and betrayals of a group of jaded, hard-drinking expatriates in Paris and Spain. Jake's stoic endurance of jealousy and frustration contrasts sharply with the selfishness and narcissism of his companions and with the self-dramatizing machismo of the young Spanish bull-fighter who becomes involved with them. The peaceful center of the work is an account of the fishing trip taken by Jake and his friend Bill to Spain's Basque region for a temporary escape. The quiet camaraderie of the two men and their shared appreciation for the fishing ritual seem to represent the best that the Hemingway world has to offer.

The Sun Also Rises was followed in 1927 by the short-story collection *Men Without Women* and in 1929 by the novel *A Farewell to Arms*, both of which enhanced Hemingway's reputation as a tough-minded realist, unafraid of depicting emotional and sexual issues long considered taboo. In *A Farewell to Arms* Hemingway creates a sympathetic portrait of an American army deserter, Frederic Henry. Hemingway used his own 1918 hospital stay in Milan as the springboard for his tale of Henry's escape from the war with Catherine Barkley, an English nurse; Catherine subsequently dies giving birth to their illegitimate child.

Hemingway's early fiction had been so influential that as early as 1931 critics were referring to a "Hemingway school" of fiction. But after the 1920s his fame as a public personality outstripped the critical appraisal of his writings. He began to suffer from the loss of novelty in his work. Furthermore, readers whose moral tolerance had been strained by *A Farewell to Arms* refused to countenance the even greater "licentiousness" they saw in ensuing books. Hemingway did not help his cause with *Death in the Afternoon* (1932), a nonfiction meditation on bullfighting, or *Green Hills of Africa* (1935), a thinly veiled fictional account of an East African safari. Both received mixed reviews and were faulted for the frequent, strident editorial passages, their "small-boy wickedness of vocabulary," and their "he-mannish" posturing. Although his novel *To Have and Have Not* (1937) enjoyed large sales, it received a similar critical reception. Throughout the decade, however, Hemingway produced noteworthy short stories, including some of his greatest—such as "A

Ernest Hemingway's public image as a "he-man" author was promoted by frequent news stories of his adventures and sporting activities. Here, he is on a hunting trip in 1941.

Way You'll Never Be" (1932), "A Clean, Well-Lighted Place" (1933), "The Snows of Kilimanjaro" (1936), and "The Short Happy Life of Francis Macomber" (1936).

Hollywood versions of *A Farewell to Arms* and *To Have and Have Not* converted Hemingway's works into star vehicles for Gary Cooper and Humphrey Bogart, diluted Hemingway to the American cinema audience, and distorted his plots by adding happy endings, all while increasing his fame and income. Hemingway's 1940 novel about the Spanish civil war, *For Whom the Bell Tolls*, salvaged his literary reputation, but there were to be further ups and downs. His novel *Across the River and Into the Trees* (1950) was disappointing; the novella *The Old Man and the Sea* (1952), which first appeared in *Life* magazine, was greeted with "a chorus of relief" and hailed as a triumph for the aging master, earning him a Pulitzer Prize. In 1954 Hemingway was awarded the Nobel Prize for literature. Though he subsequently worked on several projected novels, he never published another during his lifetime.

The public persona "Papa" Hemingway assiduously cultivated—hirsute, no-nonsense, a "man's man" as a writer, sportsman, and daredevil—masked many deep-seated insecurities about his creativity and sexuality. Married four times, he remained a sexual adventurer and braggart, attempting to dominate each of the very independent women with whom he became involved. During World War II he yearned, as he had done in World War I, for an opportunity to prove himself in battle. He offered his services to the FBI, establishing an amateur anti-Fascist intelligence and paramilitary organization in Cuba, where he had a home. Later in the war he toured Allied installations in Europe as a correspondent for *Collier's* magazine. His avidity for "blood-sports"—bullfighting, big-game hunting, marlin fishing—was another form of demonstrating manliness. Perhaps the most telling irony of Hemingway's life is in the manner of his death: when in 1961, ill, depressed, and subject to extreme paranoia, he took his own life (as his father had), he did so violently, shooting himself in the forehead with a double-barreled shotgun.

Suggested Readings: *In Our Time*, 1925. *The Sun Also Rises*, 1926. *A Farewell to Arms*, 1929. *To Have and Have Not*, 1937. *The Fifth Column and the First Forty-Nine Stories*, 1938. *For Whom the Bell Tolls*, 1940. *The Old Man and the Sea*, 1952. *A Moveable Feast*, 1964. *The Nick Adams Stories*, ed. P. Young, 1972. R. P. Weeks, ed., *Hemingway: A Collection of Critical Essays*, 1962. C. Baker, *Ernest Hemingway: A Life Story*, 1969. C. Baker, *Hemingway: The Writer as Artist*, 1972. S. Donaldson, *By Force of Will: The Life and Art of Ernest Hemingway*, 1977. J. M. Flora, *Hemingway's Nick Adams*, 1982. J. Nagel, *Ernest Hemingway: The Writer in Context*, 1984. P. Griffin, *Along With Youth: Hemingway, The Early Years*, 1985.

Text Used: *The Short Stories of Ernest Hemingway*, 1987.

BIG TWO-HEARTED RIVER*

PART I

The train went on up the track out of sight, around one of the hills of burnt timber. Nick sat down on the bundle of canvas and bedding the baggage man had pitched out of the door of the baggage car. There was no town, nothing but the rails and

---

* First published in *In Our Time* (1925); the main character, Nick Adams, appears in numerous other Hemingway stories. Although Hemingway chose this river—to the Northeast of Seney, Michigan, the setting of this story—for the "poetry" of its name, the river at Seney is actually the Fox River.

the burned-over country. The thirteen saloons that had lined the one street of Seney[1] had not left a trace. The foundations of the Mansion House hotel stuck up above the ground. The stone was chipped and split by the fire. It was all that was left of the town of Seney. Even the surface had been burned off the ground.

Nick looked at the burned-over stretch of hillside, where he had expected to find the scattered houses of the town and then walked down the railroad track to the bridge over the river. The river was there. It swirled against the log spiles[2] of the bridge. Nick looked down into the clear, brown water, colored from the pebbly bottom, and watched the trout keeping themselves steady in the current with wavering fins. As he watched them they changed their positions by quick angles, only to hold steady in the fast water again. Nick watched them a long time.

He watched them holding themselves with their noses into the current, many trout in deep, fast moving water, slightly distorted as he watched far down through the glassy convex surface of the pool, its surface pushing and swelling smooth against the resistance of the log-driven piles of the bridge. At the bottom of the pool were the big trout. Nick did not see them at first. Then he saw them at the bottom of the pool, big trout looking to hold themselves on the gravel bottom in a varying mist of gravel and sand, raised in spurts by the current.

Nick looked down into the pool from the bridge. It was a hot day. A kingfisher flew up the stream. It was a long time since Nick had looked into a stream and seen trout. They were very satisfactory. As the shadow of the kingfisher moved up the stream, a big trout shot upstream in a long angle, only his shadow marking the angle, then lost his shadow as he came through the surface of the water, caught the sun, and then, as he went back into the stream under the surface, his shadow seemed to float down the stream with the current, unresisting, to his post under the bridge where he tightened facing up into the current.

Nick's heart tightened as the trout moved. He felt all the old feeling.

He turned and looked down the stream. It stretched away, pebbly-bottomed with shallows and big boulders and a deep pool as it curved away around the foot of a bluff.

Nick walked back up the ties to where his pack lay in the cinders beside the railway track. He was happy. He adjusted the pack harness around the bundle, pulling straps tight, slung the pack on the back, got his arms through the shoulder straps and took some of the pull off his shoulders by leaning his forehead against the wide band of the tump-line.[3] Still, it was too heavy. It was much too heavy. He had his leather rod-case in his hand and leaning forward to keep the weight of the pack high on his shoulders he walked along the road that paralleled the railway track, leaving the burned town behind in the heat, and then turned off around a hill with a high, fire-scarred hill on either side onto a road that went back into the country. He walked along the road feeling the ache from the pull of the heavy pack. The road climbed steadily. It was hard work walking up-hill. His muscles ached and the day was hot, but Nick felt happy. He felt he had left everything behind, the need for thinking, the need to write, other needs. It was all back of him.

From the time he had gotten down off the train and the baggage man had

---

[1] Twice destroyed by forest fires, Seney, a railroad town in Michigan's Upper Peninsula (between Lakes Superior and Michigan), was a "virtual ghost town" when Hemingway visited it in 1919.

[2] Stakes or timbers used for support.

[3] A strap stretched across the forehead to help support a backpack.

thrown his pack out of the open car door things had been different. Seney was burned, the country was burned over and changed, but it did not matter. It could not all be burned. He knew that. He hiked along the road, sweating in the sun, climbing to cross the range of hills that separated the railway from the pine plains.

The road ran on, dipping occasionally, but always climbing. Nick went on up. Finally the road after going parallel to the burnt hillside reached the top. Nick leaned back against a stump and slipped out of the pack harness. Ahead of him, as far as he could see, was the pine plain. The burned country stopped off at the left with the range of hills. On ahead islands of dark pine trees rose out of the plain. Far off to the left was the line of the river. Nick followed it with his eye and caught glints of the water in the sun.

There was nothing but the pine plain ahead of him, until the far blue hills that marked the Lake Superior height of land. He could hardly see them, faint and far away in the heat-light over the plain. If he looked too steadily they were gone. But if he only half-looked they were there, the far-off hills of the height of land.

Nick sat down against the charred stump and smoked a cigarette. His pack balanced on the top of the stump, harness holding ready, a hollow molded in it from his back. Nick sat smoking, looking out over the country. He did not need to get his map out. He knew where he was from the position of the river.

As he smoked, his legs stretched out in front of him, he noticed a grasshopper walk along the ground and up onto his woolen sock. The grasshopper was black. As he had walked along the road, climbing, he had started many grasshoppers from the dust. They were all black. They were not the big grasshoppers with yellow and black or red and black wings whirring out from their black wing sheathing as they fly up. These were just ordinary hoppers, but all a sooty black in color. Nick had wondered about them as he walked, without really thinking about them. Now, as he watched the black hopper that was nibbling at the wool of his sock with its fourway lip, he realized that they had all turned black from living in the burned-over land. He realized that the fire must have come the year before, but the grasshoppers were all black now. He wondered how long they would stay that way.

Carefully he reached his hand down and took hold of the hopper by the wings. He turned him up, all his legs walking in the air, and looked at his jointed belly. Yes, it was black too, iridescent where the back and head were dusty.

"Go on, hopper," Nick said, speaking out loud for the first time. "Fly away somewhere."

He tossed the grasshopper up into the air and watched him sail away to a charcoal stump across the road.

Nick stood up. He leaned his back against the weight of his pack where it rested upright on the stump and got his arms through the shoulder straps. He stood with the pack on his back on the brow of the hill looking out across the country, toward the distant river and then struck down the hillside away from the road. Underfoot the ground was good walking. Two hundred yards down the hillside the fire line stopped. Then it was sweet fern, growing ankle high, to walk through, and clumps of jack pines; a long undulating country with frequent rises and descents, sandy underfoot and the country alive again.

Nick kept his direction by the sun. He knew where he wanted to strike the river and he kept on through the pine plain, mounting small rises to see other rises ahead of him and sometimes from the top of a rise a great solid island of pines off to his right or his left. He broke off some sprigs of the heathery sweet fern, and put them under his pack straps. The chafing crushed it and he smelled it as he walked.

He was tired and very hot, walking across the uneven, shadeless pine plain. At any time he knew he could strike the river by turning off to his left. It could not be more than a mile away. But he kept on toward the north to hit the river as far upstream as he could go in one day's walking.

For some time as he walked Nick had been in sight of one of the big islands of pine standing out above the rolling high ground he was crossing. He dipped down and then as he came slowly up to the crest of the bridge he turned and made toward the pine trees.

There was no underbrush in the island of pine trees. The trunks of the trees went straight up or slanted toward each other. The trunks were straight and brown without branches. The branches were high above. Some interlocked to make a solid shadow on the brown forest floor. Around the grove of trees was a bare space. It was brown and soft underfoot as Nick walked on it. This was the over-lapping of the pine needle floor, extending out beyond the width of the high branches. The trees had grown tall and the branches moved high, leaving in the sun this bare space they had once covered with shadow. Sharp at the edge of this extension of the forest floor commenced the sweet fern.

Nick slipped off his pack and lay down in the shade. He lay on his back and looked up into the pine trees. His neck and back and the small of his back rested as he stretched. The earth felt good against his back. He looked up at the sky, through the branches, and then shut his eyes. He opened them and looked up again. There was a wind high up in the branches. He shut his eyes again and went to sleep.

Nick woke stiff and cramped. The sun was nearly down. His pack was heavy and the straps painful as he lifted it on. He leaned over with the pack on and picked up the leather rod-case and started out from the pine trees across the sweet fern swale, toward the river. He knew it could not be more than a mile.

He came down a hillside covered with stumps into a meadow. At the edge of the meadow flowed the river. Nick was glad to get to the river. He walked upstream through the meadow. His trousers were soaked with the dew as he walked. After the hot day, the dew had come quickly and heavily. The river made no sound. It was too fast and smooth. At the edge of the meadow, before he mounted to a piece of high ground to make camp, Nick looked down the river at the trout rising. They were rising to insects come from the swamp on the other side of the stream when the sun went down. The trout jumped out of the water to take them. While Nick walked through the little stretch of meadow alongside the stream, trout had jumped high out of water. Now as he looked down the river, the insects must be settling on the surface, for the trout were feeding steadily all down the stream. As far down the long stretch as he could see, the trout were rising, making circles all down the surface of the water, as though it were starting to rain.

The ground rose, wooded and sandy, to overlook the meadow, the stretch of river and the swamp. Nick dropped his pack and rod-case and looked for a level piece of ground. He was very hungry and he wanted to make his camp before he cooked. Between two jack pines, the ground was quite level. He took the ax out of the pack and chopped out two projecting roots. That leveled a piece of ground large enough to sleep on. He smoothed out the sandy soil with his hand and pulled all the sweet fern bushes by their roots. His hands smelled good from the sweet fern. He smoothed the uprooted earth. He did not want anything making lumps under the blankets. When he had the ground smooth, he spread his three blankets. One he folded double, next to the ground. The other two he spread on top.

With the ax he slit off a bright slab of pine from one of the stumps and split it into pegs for the tent. He wanted them long and solid to hold in the ground. With the tent unpacked and spread on the ground, the pack, leaning against a jackpine, looked much smaller. Nick tied the rope that served the tent for a ridge-pole to the trunk of one of the pine trees and pulled the tent up off the ground with the other end of the rope and tied it to the other pine. The tent hung on the rope like a canvas blanket on a clothesline. Nick poked a pole he had cut up under the back peak of the canvas and then made it a tent by pegging out the sides. He pegged the sides out taut and drove the pegs deep, hitting them down into the ground with the flat of the ax until the rope loops were buried and the canvas was drum tight.

Across the open mouth of the tent Nick fixed cheesecloth to keep out mosquitoes. He crawled inside under the mosquito bar with various things from the pack to put at the head of the bed under the slant of the canvas. Inside the tent the light came through the brown canvas. It smelled pleasantly of canvas. Already there was something mysterious and homelike. Nick was happy as he crawled inside the tent. He had not been unhappy all day. This was different though. Now things were done. There had been this to do. Now it was done. It had been a hard trip. He was very tired. That was done. He had made his camp. He was settled. Nothing could touch him. It was a good place to camp. He was there, in the good place. He was in his home where he had made it. Now he was hungry.

He came out, crawling under the cheesecloth. It was quite dark outside. It was lighter in the tent.

Nick went over to the pack and found, with his fingers, a long nail in a paper sack of nails, in the bottom of the pack. He drove it into the pine tree, holding it close and hitting it gently with the flat of the ax. He hung the pack up on the nail. All his supplies were in the pack. They were off the ground and sheltered now.

Nick was hungry. He did not believe he had ever been hungrier. He opened and emptied a can of pork and beans and a can of spaghetti into the frying pan.

"I've got a right to eat this kind of stuff, if I'm willing to carry it," Nick said. His voice sounded strange in the darkening woods. He did not speak again.

He started a fire with some chunks of pine he got with the ax from a stump. Over the fire he stuck a wire grill, pushing the four legs down into the ground with his boot. Nick put the frying pan on the grill over the flames. He was hungrier. The beans and spaghetti warmed. Nick stirred them and mixed them together. They began to bubble, making little bubbles that rose with difficulty to the surface. There was a good smell. Nick got out a bottle of tomato catchup and cut four slices of bread. The little bubbles were coming faster now. Nick sat down beside the fire and lifted the frying pan off. He poured about half the contents out into the tin plate. It spread slowly on the plate. Nick knew it was too hot. He poured on some tomato catchup. He knew the beans and spaghetti were still too hot. He looked at the fire, then at the tent, he was not going to spoil it all by burning his tongue. For years he had never enjoyed fried bananas because he had never been able to wait for them to cool. His tongue was very sensitive. He was very hungry. Across the river in the swamp, in the almost dark, he saw a mist rising. He looked at the tent once more. All right. He took a full spoonful from the plate.

"Chrise," Nick said, "Geezus Chrise," he said happily.

He ate the whole plateful before he remembered the bread. Nick finished the second plateful with the bread, mopping the plate shiny. He had not eaten since a cup of coffee and a ham sandwich in the station restaurant at St. Ignace.[4] It had been a very fine experience. He had been that hungry before, but had not been able to satisfy it. He could have made camp hours before if he had wanted to. There were plenty of good places to camp on the river. But this was good.

Nick tucked two big chips of pine under the grill. The fire flared up. He had forgotten to get water for the coffee. Out of the pack he got a folding canvas bucket and walked down the hill, across the edge of the meadow, to the stream. The other bank was in the white mist. The grass was wet and cold as he knelt on the bank and dipped the canvas bucket into the stream. It bellied and pulled hard in the current. The water was ice cold. Nick rinsed the bucket and carried it full up to the camp. Up away from the stream it was not so cold.

Nick drove another big nail and hung up the bucket full of water. He dipped the coffee pot half full, put some more chips under the grill onto the fire and put the pot on. He could not remember which way he made coffee. He could remember an argument about it with Hopkins, but not which side he had taken. He decided to bring it to a boil. He remembered now that was Hopkins's way. He had once argued about everything with Hopkins. While he waited for the coffee to boil, he opened a small can of apricots. He liked to open cans. He emptied the can of apricots out into a tin cup. While he watched the coffee on the fire, he drank the juice syrup of the apricots, carefully at first to keep from spilling, then meditatively, sucking the apricots down. They were better than fresh apricots.

The coffee boiled as he watched. The lid came up and coffee and grounds ran down the side of the pot. Nick took it off the grill. It was a triumph for Hopkins. He put sugar in the empty apricot cup and poured some of the coffee out to cool. It was too hot to pour and he used his hat to hold the handle of the coffee pot. He would not let it steep in the pot at all. Not the first cup. It should be straight Hopkins all the way. Hop deserved that. He was a very serious coffee drinker. He was the most serious man Nick had ever known. Not heavy, serious. That was a long time ago. Hopkins spoke without moving his lips. He had played polo. He made millions of dollars in Texas. He had borrowed carfare to go to Chicago, when the wire came that his first big well had come in. He could have wired for money. That would have been too slow. They called Hop's girl the Blonde Venus. Hop did not mind because she was not his real girl. Hopkins said very confidently that none of them would make fun of his real girl. He was right. Hopkins went away when the telegram came. That was on the Black River.[5] It took eight days for the telegram to reach him. Hopkins gave away his .22 caliber Colt automatic pistol to Nick. He gave his camera to Bill. It was to remember him always by. They were all going fishing again next summer. The Hop Head was rich. He would get a yacht and they would all cruise along the north shore of Lake Superior. He was excited but serious. They said good-bye and all felt bad. It broke up the trip. They never saw Hopkins again. That was a long time ago on the Black River.

Nick drank the coffee, the coffee according to Hopkins. The coffee was bitter. Nick laughed. It made a good ending to the story. His mind was starting to work. He knew he could choke it because he was tired enough. He spilled the coffee out of the pot and shook the grounds loose into the fire. He lit a cigarette and went inside the tent. He took off his shoes and trousers, sitting on the blankets, rolled the shoes up inside the trousers for a pillow and got in between the blankets.

---

[4] An Upper Peninsula town southeast of Seney on the Strait of Mackinac in Lake Michigan.
[5] Near the northern tip of Michigan's Lower Peninsula; Hemingway fished it in summer 1919.

Out through the front of the tent he watched the glow of the fire, when the night wind blew on it. It was a quiet night. The swamp was perfectly quiet. Nick stretched under the blanket comfortably. A mosquito hummed close to his ear. Nick sat up and lit a match. The mosquito was on the canvas, over his head. Nick moved the match quickly up to it. The mosquito made a satisfactory hiss in the flame. The match went out. Nick lay down again under the blanket. He turned on his side and shut his eyes. He was sleepy. He felt sleep coming. He curled up under the blanket and went to sleep.

PART II

In the morning the sun was up and the tent was starting to get hot. Nick crawled out under the mosquito netting stretched across the mouth of the tent, to look at the morning. The grass was wet on his hands as he came out. He held his trousers and his shoes in his hands. The sun was just up over the hill. There was the meadow, the river and the swamp. There were birch trees in the green of the swamp on the other side of the river.

The river was clear and smoothly fast in the early morning. Down about two hundred yards were three logs all the way across the stream. They made the water smooth and deep above them. As Nick watched, a mink crossed the river on the logs and went into the swamp. Nick was excited. He was excited by the early morning and the river. He was really too hurried to eat breakfast, but he knew he must. He built a little fire and put on the coffee pot.

While the water was heating in the pot he took an empty bottle and went down over the edge of the high ground to the meadow. The meadow was wet with dew and Nick wanted to catch grasshoppers for bait before the sun dried the grass. He found plenty of good grasshoppers. They were at the base of the grass stems. Sometimes they clung to a grass stem. They were cold and wet with the dew, and could not jump until the sun warmed them. Nick picked them up, taking only the medium-sized brown ones, and put them into the bottle. He turned over a log and just under the shelter of the edge were several hundred hoppers. It was a grasshopper lodging house. Nick put about fifty of the medium browns into the bottle. While he was picking up the hoppers the others warmed in the sun and commenced to hop away. They flew when they hopped. At first they made one flight and stayed stiff when they landed, as though they were dead.

Nick knew that by the time he was through with breakfast they would be as lively as ever. Without dew in the grass it would take him all day to catch a bottle full of good grasshoppers and he would have to crush many of them, slamming at them with his hat. He washed his hands at the stream. He was excited to be near it. Then he walked up to the tent. The hoppers were already jumping stiffly in the grass. In the bottle, warmed by the sun, they were jumping in a mass. Nick put in a pine stick as a cork. It plugged the mouth of the bottle enough, so the hoppers could not get out and left plenty of air passage.

He had rolled the log back and knew he could get grasshoppers there every morning.

Nick laid the bottle full of jumping grasshoppers against a pine trunk. Rapidly he mixed some buckwheat flour with water and stirred it smooth, one cup of flour, one cup of water. He put a handful of coffee in the pot and dipped a lump of grease out of a can and slid it sputtering across the hot skillet. On the smoking skillet he poured smoothly the buckwheat batter. It spread like lava, the grease spitting sharply. Around the edges the buckwheat cake began to firm, then brown, then crisp. The surface was bubbling slowly to porousness. Nick pushed under the browned under surface with a fresh pine chip. He shook the skillet sideways and the cake was loose on the surface. I won't try and flop it, he thought. He slid the chip of clean wood all the way under the cake, and flopped it over onto its face. It sputtered in the pan.

When it was cooked Nick regreased the skillet. He used all the batter. It made another big flapjack and one smaller one.

Nick ate a big flapjack and a smaller one, covered with apple butter. He put apple butter on the third cake, folded it over twice, wrapped it in oiled paper and put it in his shirt pocket. He put the apple butter jar back in the pack and cut bread for two sandwiches.

In the pack he found a big onion. He sliced it in two and peeled the silky outer skin. Then he cut one half into slices and made onion sandwiches. He wrapped them in oiled paper and buttoned them in the other pocket of his khaki shirt. He turned the skillet upside down on the grill, drank the coffee, sweetened and yellow brown with the condensed milk in it, and tidied up the camp. It was a good camp.

Nick took his fly rod out of the leather rod-case, jointed it, and shoved the rod-case back into the tent. He put on the reel and threaded the line through the guides. He had to hold it from hand to hand, as he threaded it, or it would slip back through its own weight. It was a heavy, double tapered fly line. Nick had paid eight dollars for it a long time ago. It was made heavy to lift back in the air and come forward flat and heavy and straight to make it possible to cast a fly which has no weight. Nick opened the aluminum leader[6] box. The leaders were coiled between the damp flannel pads. Nick had wet the pads at the water cooler on the train up to St. Ignace. In the damp pads the gut leaders had softened and Nick unrolled one and tied it by a loop at the end to the heavy fly line. He fastened a hook on the end of the leader. It was a small hook; very thin and springy.

Nick took it from his hook book, sitting with the rod across his lap. He tested the knot and the spring of the rod by pulling the line taut. It was a good feeling. He was careful not to let the hook bite into his finger.

He started down to the stream, holding his rod, the bottle of grasshoppers hung from his neck by a thong tied in half hitches around the neck of the bottle. His landing net hung by a hook from his belt. Over his shoulder was a long flour sack tied at each corner into an ear. The cord went over his shoulder. The sack flapped against his legs.

Nick felt awkward and professionally happy with all his equipment hanging from him. The grasshopper bottle swung against his chest. In his shirt the breast pockets bulged against him with the lunch and his fly book.

He stepped into the stream. It was a shock. His trousers clung tight to his legs. His shoes felt the gravel. The water was a rising cold shock.

Rushing, the current sucked against his legs. Where he stepped in, the water was over his knees. He waded with the current. The gravel slid under his shoes. He looked down at the swirl of water below each leg and tipped up the bottle to get a grasshopper.

The first grasshopper gave a jump in the neck of the bottle and went out into the water. He was sucked under in the whirl by Nick's right leg and came to the surface a little way down stream. He floated rapidly, kicking. In a quick circle, breaking the smooth surface of the water, he disappeared. A trout had taken him.

---

[6] A short length of gut or wire used to attach a hook to a fishing line.

Another hopper poked his face out of the bottle. His antennæ wavered. He was getting his front legs out of the bottle to jump. Nick took him by the head and held him while he threaded the slim hook under his chin, down through his thorax and into the last segments of his abdomen. The grasshopper took hold of the hook with his front feet, spitting tobacco juice on it. Nick dropped him into the water.

Holding the rod in his right hand he let out line against the pull of the grasshopper in the current. He stripped off line from the reel with his left hand and let it run free. He could see the hopper in the little waves of the current. It went out of sight.

There was a tug on the line. Nick pulled against the taut line. It was his first strike. Holding the now living rod across the current, he brought in the line with his left hand. The rod bent in jerks, the trout pumping against the current. Nick knew it was a small one. He lifted the rod straight up in the air. It bowed with the pull.

He saw the trout in the water jerking with his head and body against the shifting tangent of the line in the stream.

Nick took the line in his left hand and pulled the trout, thumping tiredly against the current, to the surface. His back was mottled the clear, water-over-gravel color, his side flashing in the sun. The rod under his right arm, Nick stooped, dipping his right hand into the current. He held the trout, never still, with his moist right hand, while he unhooked the barb from his mouth, then dropped him back into the stream.

He hung unsteadily in the current, then settled to the bottom beside a stone. Nick reached down his hand to touch him, his arm to the elbow under water. The trout was steady in the moving stream, resting on the gravel, beside a stone. As Nick's fingers touched him, touched his smooth, cool, underwater feeling he was gone, gone in a shadow across the bottom of the stream.

He's all right, Nick thought. He was only tired.

He had wet his hand before he touched the trout, so he would not disturb the delicate mucus that covered him. If a trout was touched with a dry hand, a white fungus attacked the unprotected spot. Years before when he had fished crowded streams, with fly fishermen ahead of him and behind him, Nick had again and again come on dead trout, furry with white fungus, drifted against a rock, or floating belly up in some pool. Nick did not like to fish with other men on the river. Unless they were of your own party, they spoiled it.

He wallowed down the stream, above his knees in the current, through the fifty yards of shallow water above the pile of logs that crossed the stream. He did not rebait his hook and held it in his hand as he waded. He was certain he could catch small trout in the shallows, but he did not want them. There would be no big trout in the shallows this time of day.

Now the water deepened up his thighs sharply and coldly. Ahead was the smooth dammed-back flood of water above the logs. The water was smooth and dark; on the left, the lower edge of the meadow; on the right the swamp.

Nick leaned back against the current and took a hopper from the bottle. He threaded the hopper on the hook and spat on him for good luck. Then he pulled several yards of line from the reel and tossed the hopper out ahead onto the fast, dark water. It floated down towards the logs, then the weight of the line pulled the bait under the surface. Nick held the rod in his right hand, letting the line run out through his fingers.

There was a long tug. Nick struck and the rod came alive and dangerous, bent double, the line tightening, coming out of water, tightening, all in a heavy, dangerous, steady pull. Nick felt the moment when the leader would break if the strain increased and let the line go.

The reel ratcheted into a mechanical shriek as the line went out in a rush. Too fast. Nick could not check it, the line rushing out, the reel note rising as the line ran out.

With the core of the reel showing, his heart feeling stopped with the excitement, leaning back against the current that mounted icily his thighs, Nick thumbed the reel hard with his left hand. It was awkward getting his thumb inside the fly reel frame.

As he put on pressure the line tightened into sudden hardness and beyond the logs a huge trout went high out of water. As he jumped, Nick lowered the tip of the rod. But he felt, as he dropped the tip to ease the strain, the moment when the strain was too great; the hardness too tight. Of course, the leader had broken. There was no mistaking the feeling when all spring left the line and it became dry and hard. Then it went slack.

His mouth dry, his heart down, Nick reeled in. He had never seen so big a trout. There was a heaviness, a power not to be held, and then the bulk of him as he jumped. He looked as broad as a salmon.

Nick's hand was shaky. He reeled in slowly. The thrill had been too much. He felt, vaguely, a little sick, as though it would be better to sit down.

The leader had broken where the hook was tied to it. Nick took it in his hand. He thought of the trout somewhere on the bottom, holding himself steady over the gravel, far down below the light, under the logs, with the hook in his jaw. Nick knew the trout's teeth would cut through the snell of the hook. The hook would imbed itself in his jaw. He'd bet the trout was angry. Anything that size would be angry. That was a trout. He had been solidly hooked. Solid as a rock. He felt like a rock, too, before he started off. By God, he was a big one. By God, he was the biggest one I ever heard of.

Nick climbed out onto the meadow and stood, water running down his trousers and out of his shoes, his shoes squlchy. He went over and sat on the logs. He did not want to rush his sensations any.

He wriggled his toes in the water, in his shoes, and got out a cigarette from his breast pocket. He lit it and tossed the match into the fast water below the logs. A tiny trout rose at the match, as it swung around in the fast current. Nick laughed. He would finish the cigarette.

He sat on the logs, smoking, drying in the sun, the sun warm on his back, the river shallow ahead entering the woods, curving into the woods, shallows, light glittering, big water-smooth rocks, cedars along the bank and white birches, the logs warm in the sun, smooth to sit on, without bark, gray to the touch; slowly the feeling of disappointment left him. It went away slowly, the feeling of disappointment that came sharply after the thrill that made his shoulders ache. It was all right now. His rod lying out on the logs, Nick tied a new hook on the leader, pulling the gut tight until it grimped into itself in a hard knot.

He baited up, then picked up the rod and walked to the far end of the logs to get into the water, where it was not too deep. Under and beyond the logs was a deep pool. Nick walked around the shallow shelf near the swamp shore until he came out on the shallow bed of the stream.

On the left, where the meadow ended and the woods began, a great elm tree was uprooted. Gone over in a storm, it lay back into the woods, its roots clotted with dirt, grass growing in them, rising a solid bank beside the stream. The river cut to the edge of the uprooted tree. From where Nick stood he could see deep channels, like ruts, cut in the shallow bed of the stream by the flow of the current. Pebbly where he stood and pebbly and full of boulders beyond; where it curved near the tree roots, the bed of the stream was marly and between the ruts of deep water green weed fronds swung in the current.

Nick swung the rod back over his shoulder and forward, and the line, curving forward, laid the grasshopper down on one of the deep channels in the weeds. A trout struck and Nick hooked him.

Holding the rod far out toward the uprooted tree and sloshing backward in the current, Nick worked the trout, plunging, the rod bending alive, out of the danger of the weeds into the open river. Holding the rod, pumping alive against the current, Nick brought the trout in. He rushed, but always came, the spring of the rod yielding to the rushes, sometimes jerking under water, but always bringing him in. Nick eased downstream with the rushes. The rod above his head he led the trout over the net, then lifted.

The trout hung heavy in the net, mottled trout back and silver sides in the meshes. Nick unhooked him; heavy sides, good to hold, big undershot jaw, and slipped him, heaving and big sliding, into the long sack that hung from his shoulders in the water.

Nick spread the mouth of the sack against the current and it filled, heavy with water. He held it up, the bottom in the stream, and the water poured out through the sides. Inside at the bottom was the big trout, alive in the water.

Nick moved downstream. The sack out ahead of him sunk heavy in the water, pulling from his shoulders.

It was getting hot, the sun hot on the back of his neck.

Nick had one good trout. He did not care about getting many trout. Now the stream was shallow and wide. There were trees along both banks. The trees of the left bank made short shadows on the current in the forenoon sun. Nick knew there were trout in each shadow. In the afternoon, after the sun had crossed toward the hills, the trout would be in the cool shadows on the other side of the stream.

The very biggest ones would lie up close to the bank. You could always pick them up there on the Black. When the sun was down they all moved out into the current. Just when the sun made the water blinding in the glare before it went down, you were liable to strike a big trout anywhere in the current. It was almost impossible to fish then, the surface of the water was blinding as a mirror in the sun. Of course, you could fish upstream, but in a stream like the Black, or this, you had to wallow against the current and in a deep place, the water piled up on you. It was no fun to fish upstream with this much current.

Nick moved along through the shallow stretch watching the banks for deep holes. A beech tree grew close beside the river, so that the branches hung down into the water. The stream went back in under the leaves. There were always trout in a place like that.

Nick did not care about fishing that hole. He was sure he would get hooked in the branches.

It looked deep though. He dropped the grasshopper so the current took it under water, back in under the overhanging branch. The line pulled hard and Nick struck. The trout threshed heavily, half out of water in the leaves and branches. The line was caught. Nick pulled hard and the trout was off. He reeled in and holding the hook in his hand, walked down the stream.

Ahead, close to the left bank, was a big log. Nick saw it was hollow; pointing up river the current entered it smoothly, only a little ripple spread each side of the log. The water was deepening. The top of the hollow log was gray and dry. It was partly in the shadow.

Nick took the cork out of the grasshopper bottle and a hopper clung to it. He picked him off, hooked him and tossed him out. He held the rod far out so that the hopper on the water moved into the current flowing into the hollow log. Nick lowered the rod and the hopper floated in. There was a heavy strike. Nick swung the rod against the pull. It felt as though he were hooked into the log itself, except for the live feeling.

He tried to force the fish out into the current. It came, heavily.

The line went slack and Nick though the trout was gone. Then he saw him, very near, in the current, shaking his head, trying to get the hook out. His mouth was clamped shut. He was fighting the hook in the clear flowing current.

Looping in the line with his left hand, Nick swung the rod to make the line taut and tried to lead the trout toward the net, but he was gone, out of sight, the line pumping. Nick fought him against the current, letting him thump in the water against the spring of the rod. He shifted the rod to his left hand, worked the trout upstream, holding his weight, fighting on the rod, and then let him down into the net. He lifted him clear of the water, a heavy half circle in the net, the net dripping, unhooked him and slid him into the sack.

He spread the mouth of the sack and looked down in at the two big trout alive in the water.

Through the deepening water, Nick waded over to the hollow log. He took the sack off, over his head, the trout flopping as it came out of water, and hung it so the trout were deep in the water. Then he pulled himself up on the log and sat, the water from his trousers and boots running down into the stream. He laid his rod down, moved along to the shady end of the log and took the sandwiches out of his pocket. He dipped the sandwiches in the cold water. The current carried away the crumbs. He ate the sandwiches and dipped his hat full of water to drink, the water running out through his hat just ahead of his drinking.

It was cool in the shade, sitting on the log. He took a cigarette out and struck a match to light it. The match sunk into the gray wood, making a tiny furrow. Nick leaned over the side of the log, found a hard place and lit the match. He sat smoking and watching the river.

Ahead the river narrowed and went into a swamp. The river became smooth and deep and the swamp looked solid with cedar trees, their trunks close together, their branches solid. It would not be possible to walk through a swamp like that. The branches grew so low. You would have to keep almost level with the ground to move at all. You could not crash through the branches. That must be why the animals that lived in swamps were built the way they were, Nick thought.

He wished he had brought something to read. He felt like reading. He did not feel like going on into the swamp. He looked down the river. A big cedar slanted all the way across the stream. Beyond that the river went into the swamp.

Nick did not want to go in there now. He felt a reaction against deep wading with the water deepening up under his armpits, to hook big trout in places impossible to land them. In the swamp the banks were bare, the big cedars came together overhead, the sun did not come through, except in patches; in the fast deep water, in the half light, the fishing would be tragic. In the swamp fishing was a tragic adventure. Nick did not want it. He did not want to go down the stream any further today.

He took out his knife, opened it and stuck it in the log. Then he pulled up the sack, reached into it and brought out one of the trout. Holding him near the tail, hard to hold, alive, in his hand, he whacked him against the log. The trout quivered, rigid. Nick laid him on the log in the shade and broke the neck of the other fish the same way. He laid them side by side on the log. They were fine trout.

Nick cleaned them, slitting them from the vent to the tip of the jaw. All the insides and the gills and tongue came out in one piece. They were both males; long gray-white strips of milt,[7] smooth and clean. All the insides clean and compact, coming out all together. Nick tossed the offal ashore for the minks to find.

He washed the trout in the stream. When he held them back up in the water they looked like live fish. Their color was not gone yet. He washed his hands and dried them on the log. Then he laid the trout on the sack spread out on the log, rolled them up in it, tied the bundle and put it in the landing net. His knife was still standing, blade stuck in the log. He cleaned it on the wood and put it in his pocket.

Nick stood up on the log, holding his rod, the landing net hanging heavy, then stepped into the water and splashed ashore. He climbed the bank and cut up into the woods, toward the high ground. He was going back to camp. He looked back. The river just showed through the trees. There were plenty of days coming when he could fish the swamp.

1924, 1925

John Steinbeck
(1902–1968)

The writing of John Steinbeck is concerned mostly with agricultural life in America's far West in the early twentieth century and with the Great Depression. The novels considered his best—*In Dubious Battle* (1936), *Of Mice and Men* (1937), and *The Grapes of Wrath* (1939)—are set in "Steinbeck country," as is the short story "Flight" (1938). Steinbeck was born in Salinas, California, in 1902. His mother, a former schoolteacher, encouraged him to read widely: John Milton's *Paradise Lost* (1667), Feodor Dostoevski's *Crime and Punishment* (1866), Thomas Malory's *Le Morte d'Arthur* (1485), Thomas Hardy's *The Return of the Native* (1878), the King James Bible, and Gustave Flaubert's *Madame Bovary* (1857) were among his favorites, and their influence is apparent in Steinbeck's work. He wrote his first stories in accountants' ledgers kept by his father, the treasurer of California's Monterey County. Steinbeck's parents' appreciation of the world around them helped him develop a strong interest in science and in the natural world. His writing is full of migrant laborers, union organizers, paisanos (ethnically mixed Mexican-Indian-Caucasians), and marine scientists, all of whom populated the region in which he was raised.

---

[7] Fish sperm, or the reproductive glands that produce it; symbolically, the male fish, full of sperm, may refer obliquely to young men of Nick's age.

In high school Steinbeck scribbled far into the night in his attic bedroom, composing stories and poetry to amuse friends. He also wrote for the school newspaper, played basketball, ran track, and was elected senior-class president. At Stanford University he took eleven English courses and very little else. He left college in 1925 and hopped a freighter to New York City, where he worked briefly as a reporter and a bricklayer. He soon returned to California, doing odd jobs to support his budding writing career. In 1930 he turned to writing full time after he married Carol Henning. (The couple divorced in 1943; Steinbeck married Gwyn Conger later that year but divorced her in 1948; he married Elaine Scott two years later.)

Steinbeck's novels typically began as short pieces that spilled over their boundaries or were combined with other short pieces to make up episodic novels. Conversely, his short-story collections tend to form integrated wholes, as does *The Pastures of Heaven* (1932). *Tortilla Flat* (1935), Steinbeck's first critical success, is a composite of the two forms—a loosely structured novel in which stories of the paisanos of Monterey advance a complex argument about the possibilities for happiness in a world of apparent destitution. Throughout his career Steinbeck used the short story as a means of experimentation to help him expand his skills and to escape from what he called the "straitjacket" of novelistic unity. In more than fifty short stories, he employed parable, allegory, fable, and even Gothic romance and science fiction to shape his worlds.

The collection of short stories published as *The Long Valley* (1938), in which "Flight" appears, has been praised as some of Steinbeck's finest work and compared to Ernest Hemingway's *In Our Time* (1925). Both books end with a story—"The Red Pony" and "Big Two-Hearted River," respectively—that engages the reader in a complex reevaluation of the whole. The similarities between the two authors' work is clear: behind their deceptively simple prose, photographic accuracy, and action-filled stories are explorations of enduring human concerns. Although the fictional world of both writers is predominantly masculine, strong and engaging female characters appear in their work.

Like most of Steinbeck's early fiction, "Flight" demonstrates the effect of the natural setting on plot and on character development. Its deterministic perspective creates a sense of inevitability, which seems as predetermined as the accompanying sunrise and sunset. Steinbeck's spare, naturalistic prose does not directly reveal the mind and heart of Pepe, the story's protagonist. The story can be read as a moral allegory: Pepe's flight—his initiation into adulthood, enacted through courage in the face of great trial—can represent a universal human process.

In Dubious Battle, a novel about a fruitpickers' strike against an exploitative employer, was the first of Steinbeck's works to address a significant social issue and accurately portrays the 1930s. *Of Mice and Men,* the story of two itinerant ranch hands—Lennie, huge, half-witted and sympathetic, and George, exploitative and more intelligent—is a classic. These works established Steinbeck as the novelist of the rural proletariat. In 1962 Steinbeck was awarded the Nobel Prize for literature. Although he has always been popular with the reading public, his critical reputation declined in the 1960s and since his death in 1968. Even *The Grapes of Wrath,* generally perceived as Steinbeck's masterpiece and the book for which he received a Pulitzer Prize in 1940, suffered a loss of status. The fiftieth anniversary of the novel's publication has, however, provoked a critical reassessment of the powerfully compassionate story of the migrant Joad family's flight from the dust bowl of Oklahoma to a hoped for better life in California, and promises to reclaim it as a work of moral force and aesthetic complexity.

With the onset of World War II Steinbeck's creativity waned. He continued to write prolifically, though, producing *The Moon Is Down* (1942) and several volumes of nonfiction, but feared that his most significant contribution had already been made. *Cannery*

Row (1945), *The Pearl* (1947), and *Sweet Thursday* (1954) return to the California of his early novels and to the happy, unsophisticated people of the Salinas Valley. Their simple contentment contrasts sharply with the complicated world of "civilized" adults in his later novels *East of Eden* (1952) and *The Winter of Our Discontent* (1961). His last work, *Travels With Charley in Search of America* (1962), amusingly chronicles the author's cross-country trip by truck camper with his French poodle.

Suggested Readings: *Tortilla Flat*, 1935. *In Dubious Battle*, 1936. *Of Mice and Men*, 1937. *The Red Pony*, 1937. *The Grapes of Wrath*, 1939. *The Pearl*, 1947. *East of Eden*, 1952. *The Winter of Our Discontent*, 1961. *Travels With Charley*, 1962. H. Levant, *The Novels Of John Steinbeck: A Critical Study*, 1974. T. Kiernan, *The Intricate Music of John Steinbeck*, 1979. P. McCarthy, *John Steinbeck*, 1980. J. Benson, *The True Adventures of John Steinbeck, Writer*, 1984. J. Ditsky, *John Steinbeck: Life, Work, and Criticism*, 1985. J. Timmerman, *John Steinbeck's Fiction: The Aesthetics of the Road Taken*, 1986.

Text Used: *The Long Valley*, 1938.

FLIGHT

About fifteen miles below Monterey,[1] on the wild coast, the Torres family had their farm, a few sloping acres above a cliff that dropped to the brown reefs and to the hissing white waters of the ocean. Behind the farm the stone mountains stood up against the sky. The farm buildings huddled like little clinging aphids on the mountain skirts, crouched low to the ground as though the wind might blow them into the sea. The little shack, the rattling, rotting barn were grey-bitten with sea salt, beaten by the damp wind until they had taken on the color of the granite hills. Two horses, a red cow and a red calf, half a dozen pigs and a flock of lean, multicolored chickens stocked the place. A little corn was raised on the sterile slope, and it grew short and thick under the wind, and all the cobs formed on the landward sides of the stalks.

Mama Torres, a lean, dry woman with ancient eyes, had ruled the farm for ten years, ever since her husband tripped over a stone in the field one day and fell full length on a rattlesnake. When one is bitten on the chest there is not much that can be done.

Mama Torres had three children, two undersized black ones of twelve and fourteen, Emilio and Rosy, whom Mama kept fishing on the rocks below the farm when the sea was kind and when the truant officer was in some distant part of Monterey County. And there was Pepé, the tall smiling son of nineteen, a gentle, affectionate boy, but very lazy. Pepé had a tall head, pointed at the top, and from its peak, coarse black hair grew down like a thatch all around. Over his smiling little eyes Mama cut a straight bang so he could see. Pepé had sharp Indian cheek bones and an eagle nose, but his mouth was as sweet and shapely as a girl's mouth, and his chin was fragile and chiseled. He was loose and gangling, all legs and feet and wrists, and he was very lazy. Mama thought him fine and brave, but she never told him so. She said, "Some lazy cow must have got into thy father's family, else how could I have a son like thee." And she said, "When I carried

---

[1] Monterey, California, a Pacific coastal city.

thee, a sneaking lazy coyote came out of the brush and looked at me one day. That must have made thee so."

Pepé smiled sheepishly and stabbed at the ground with his knife to keep the blade sharp and free from rust. It was his inheritance, that knife, his father's knife. The long heavy blade folded back into the black handle. There was a button on the handle. When Pepé pressed the button, the blade leaped out ready for use. The knife was with Pepé always, for it had been his father's knife.

One sunny morning when the sea below the cliff was glinting and blue and the white surf creamed on the reef, when even the stone mountains looked kindly, Mama Torres called out the door of the shack, "Pepé, I have a labor for thee."

There was no answer. Mama listened. From behind the barn she heard a burst of laughter. She lifted her full long skirt and walked in the direction of the noise.

Pepé was sitting on the ground with his back against a box. His white teeth glistened. On either side of him stood the two black ones, tense and expectant. Fifteen feet away a redwood post was set in the ground. Pepé's right hand lay limply in his lap, and in the palm the big black knife rested. The blade was closed back into the handle. Pepé looked smiling at the sky.

Suddenly Emilio cried, "Ya!"

Pepé's wrist flicked like the head of a snake. The blade seemed to fly open in mid-air, and with a thump the point dug into the redwood post, and the black handle quivered. The three burst into excited laughter. Rosy ran to the post and pulled out the knife and brought it back to Pepé. He closed the blade and settled the knife carefully in his listless palm again. He grinned self-consciously at the sky.

"Ya!"

The heavy knife lanced out and sunk into the post again. Mama moved forward like a ship and scattered the play.

"All day you do foolish things with the knife, like a toy-baby," she stormed. "Get up on thy huge feet that eat up shoes. Get up!" She took him by one loose shoulder and hoisted at him. Pepé grinned sheepishly and came half-heartedly to his feet. "Look!" Mama cried. "Big lazy, you must catch the horse and put on him thy father's saddle. You must ride to Monterey. The medicine bottle is empty. There is no salt. Go thou now, Peanut! Catch the horse."

A revolution took place in the relaxed figure of Pepé. "To Monterey, me? Alone? Sí, Mama."

She scowled at him. "Do not think, big sheep, that you will buy candy. No, I will give you only enough for the medicine and salt."

Pepé smiled. "Mama, you will put the hatband on the hat?"

She relented then. "Yes, Pepé. You may wear the hatband."

His voice grew insinuating, "And the green handkerchief, Mama?"

"Yes, if you go quickly and return with no trouble, the silk green handkerchief will go. If you make sure to take off the handkerchief when you eat so no spot may fall on it. . . . "

"Sí, Mama. I will be careful. I am a man."

"Thou?[2] A man? Thou art a peanut."

He went into the rickety barn and brought out a rope, and he walked agilely enough up the hill to catch the horse.

When he was ready and mounted before the door, mounted on his father's

---

[2] Mama Torres's use of the archaic second-person pronoun simulates an intimate, affectionate form of address; modern English does not have a familiar form of the pronoun "you."

saddle that was so old that the oaken frame showed through torn leather in many places, then Mama brought out the round black hat with the tooled leather band, and she reached up and knotted the green silk handkerchief about his neck. Pepé's blue denim coat was much darker than his jeans, for it had been washed much less often.

Mama handed up the big medicine bottle and the silver coins. "That for the medicine," she said, "and that for the salt. That for a candle to burn for the papa. That for *dulces*[3] for the little ones. Our friend Mrs. Rodriguez will give you dinner and maybe a bed for the night. When you go to the church say only ten Paternosters and only twenty-five Ave Marias.[4] Oh! I know, big coyote. You would sit there flapping your mouth over Aves all day while you looked at the candles and the holy pictures. That is not a good devotion to stare at the pretty things."

The black hat, covering the high pointed head and black thatched hair of Pepé, gave him dignity and age. He sat the rangy horse well. Mama thought how handsome he was, dark and lean and tall. "I would not send thee now alone, thou little one, except for the medicine," she said softly. "It is not good to have no medicine, for who knows when the toothache will come, or the sadness of the stomach. These things are."

"Adios, Mama," Pepé cried. "I will come back soon. You may send me often alone. I am a man."

"Thou art a foolish chicken."

He straightened his shoulders, flipped the reins against the horse's shoulder and rode away. He turned once and saw that they still watched him, Emilio and Rosy and Mama. Pepé grinned with pride and gladness and lifted the tough buckskin horse to a trot.

When he had dropped out of sight over a little dip in the road, Mama turned to the black ones, but she spoke to herself. "He is nearly a man now," she said. "It will be a nice thing to have a man in the house again." Her eyes sharpened on the children. "Go to the rocks now. The tide is going out. There will be abalones to be found." She put the iron hooks into their hands and saw them down the steep trail to the reefs. She brought the smooth stone *metate* to the doorway and sat grinding her corn to flour and looking occasionally at the road over which Pepé had gone. The noonday came and then the afternoon, when the little ones beat the abalones on a rock to make them tender and Mama patted the tortillas to make them thin. They ate their dinner as the red sun was plunging down toward the ocean. They sat on the doorsteps and watched the big white moon come over the mountain tops.

Mama said, "He is now at the house of our friend Mrs. Rodriguez. She will give him nice things to eat and maybe a present."

Emilio said, "Some day I too will ride to Monterey for medicine. Did Pepé come to be a man today?"

Mama said wisely, "A boy gets to be a man when a man is needed. Remember this thing. I have known boys forty years old because there was no need for a man."

Soon afterwards they retired, Mama in her big oak bed on one side of the room, Emilio and Rosy in their boxes full of straw and sheepskins on the other side of the room.

The moon went over the sky and the surf roared on the rocks. The roosters

---

[3] "Sweets" (Spanish).
[4] "Our Fathers and Hail Marys" (Latin), the first lines of famous Christian prayers.

crowed the first call. The surf subsided to a whispering surge against the reef. The moon dropped toward the sea. The roosters crowed again.

The moon was near down to the water when Pepé rode on a winded horse to his home flat. His dog bounced out and circled the horse yelping with pleasure. Pepé slid off the saddle to the ground. The weathered little shack was silver in the moonlight and the square shadow of it was black to the north and east. Against the east the piling mountains were misty with light; their tops melted into the sky.

Pepé walked wearily up the three steps and into the house. It was dark inside. There was a rustle in the corner.

Mama cried out from her bed. "Who comes? Pepé, is it thou?"

"Sí, Mama."

"Did you get the medicine?"

"Sí, Mama."

"Well, go to sleep, then. I thought you would be sleeping at the house of Mrs. Rodriguez." Pepé stood silently in the dark room. "Why do you stand there, Pepé? Did you drink wine?"

"Sí, Mama."

"Well, go to bed then and sleep out the wine."

His voice was tired and patient, but very firm. "Light the candle, Mama. I must go away into the mountains."

"What is this, Pepé? You are crazy." Mama struck a sulphur match and held the little blue burr until the flame spread up the stick. She set light to the candle on the floor beside her bed. "Now, Pepé, what is this you say?" She looked anxiously into his face.

He was changed. The fragile quality seemed to have gone from his chin. His mouth was less full than it had been, the lines of the lips were straighter, but in his eyes the greatest change had taken place. There was no laughter in them any more, nor any bashfulness. They were sharp and bright and purposeful.

He told her in a tired monotone, told her everything just as it had happened. A few people came into the kitchen of Mrs. Rodriguez. There was wine to drink. Pepé drank wine. The little quarrel—the man started toward Pepé and then the knife—it went almost by itself. It flew, it darted before Pepé knew it. As he talked, Mama's face grew stern, and it seemed to grow more lean. Pepé finished. "I am a man now, Mama. The man said names to me I could not allow."

Mama nodded. "Yes, thou art a man, my poor little Pepé. Thou art a man. I have seen it coming on thee. I have watched you throwing the knife into the post, and I have been afraid." For a moment her face had softened, but now it grew stern again. "Come! We must get you ready. Go. Awaken Emilio and Rosy. Go quickly."

Pepé stepped over to the corner where his brother and sister slept among the sheepskins. He leaned down and shook them gently. "Come, Rosy! Come, Emilio! The mama says you must arise."

The little black ones sat up and rubbed their eyes in the candlelight. Mama was out of bed now, her long black skirt over her nightgown. "Emilio," she cried. "Go up and catch the other horse for Pepé. Quickly, now! Quickly." Emilio put his legs in his overalls and stumbled sleepily out the door.

"You heard no one behind you on the road?" Mama demanded.

"No, Mama. I listened carefully. No one was on the road."

Mama darted like a bird about the room. From a nail on the wall she took a canvas water bag and threw it on the floor. She stripped a blanket from her bed and rolled it into a tight tube and tied the ends with string. From a box beside the stove she lifted a flour sack half full of black stringy jerky. "Your father's black coat, Pepé. Here, put it on."

Pepé stood in the middle of the floor watching her activity. She reached behind the door and brought out the rifle, a long 38–56, worn shiny the whole length of the barrel. Pepé took it from her and held it in the crook of his elbow. Mama brought a little leather bag and counted the cartridges into his hand. "Only ten left," she warned. "You must not waste them."

Emilio put his head in the door. "'*Qui 'st 'l caballo,*[5] Mama."

"Put on the saddle from the other horse. Tie on the blanket. Here, tie the jerky to the saddle horn."

Still Pepé stood silently watching his mother's frantic activity. His chin looked hard, and his sweet mouth was drawn and thin. His little eyes followed Mama about the room almost suspiciously.

Rosy asked softly, "Where goes Pepé?"

Mama's eyes were fierce. "Pepé goes on a journey. Pepé is a man now. He has a man's thing to do."

Pepé straightened his shoulders. His mouth changed until he looked very much like Mama.

At last the preparation was finished. The loaded horse stood outside the door. The water bag dripped a line of moisture down the bay shoulder.

The moonlight was being thinned by the dawn and the big white moon was near down to the sea. The family stood by the shack. Mama confronted Pepé. "Look, my son! Do not stop until it is dark again. Do not sleep even though you are tired. Take care of the horse in order that he may not stop of weariness. Remember to be careful with the bullets—there are only ten. Do not fill thy stomach with jerky or it will make thee sick. Eat a little jerky and fill thy stomach with grass. When thou comest to the high mountains, if thou seest any of the dark watching men,[6] go not near to them nor try to speak to them. And forget not thy prayers." She put her lean hands on Pepé's shoulders, stood on her toes and kissed him formally on both cheeks, and Pepé kissed her on both cheeks. Then he went to Emilio and Rosy and kissed both of their cheeks.

Pepé turned back to Mama. He seemed to look for a little softness, a little weakness in her. His eyes were searching, but Mama's face remained fierce. "Go now," she said. "Do not wait to be caught like a chicken."

Pepé pulled himself into the saddle. "I am a man," he said.

It was the first dawn when he rode up the hill toward the little canyon which let a trail into the mountains. Moonlight and daylight fought with each other, and the two warring qualities made it difficult to see. Before Pepé had gone a hundred yards, the outlines of his figure were misty; and long before he entered the canyon, he had become a grey, indefinite shadow.

---

[5] "Here's the horse" (Spanish).

[6] Black figures said to haunt the Santa Lucia Mountains, along the coast of Central California. Steinbeck's note: "I don't know who they are or what they represent. All I know is that the people around Monterey believe in them . . . there are certain small areas in the woods which animals avoid and will not cross. We don't know why, but we know such spots exist."

Mama stood stiffly in front of her doorstep, and on either side of her stood Emilio and Rosy. They cast furtive glances at Mama now and then.

When the grey shape of Pepé melted into the hillside and disappeared, Mama relaxed. She began the high, whining keen of the death wail. "Our beautiful—our brave," she cried. "Our protector, our son is gone." Emilio and Rosy moaned beside her. "Our beautiful—our brave, he is gone." It was the formal wail. It rose to a high piercing whine and subsided to a moan. Mama raised it three times and then she turned and went into the house and shut the door.

Emilio and Rosy stood wondering in the dawn. They heard Mama whimpering in the house. They went out to sit on the cliff above the ocean. They touched shoulders. "When did Pepé come to be a man?" Emilio asked.

"Last night," said Rosy. "Last night in Monterey." The ocean clouds turned red with the sun that was behind the mountains.

"We will have no breakfast," said Emilio. "Mama will not want to cook." Rosy did not answer him. "Where is Pepé gone?" he asked.

Rosy looked around at him. She drew her knowledge from the quiet air. "He has gone on a journey. He will never come back."

"Is he dead? Do you think he is dead?"

Rosy looked back at the ocean again. A little steamer, drawing a line of smoke sat on the edge of the horizon. "He is not dead," Rosy explained. "Not yet."

Pepé rested the big rifle across the saddle in front of him. He let the horse walk up the hill and he didn't look back. The stony slope took on a coat of short brush so that Pepé found the entrance to a trail and entered it.

When he came to the canyon opening, he swung once in his saddle and looked back, but the houses were swallowed in the misty light. Pepé jerked forward again. The high shoulder of the canyon closed in on him. His horse stretched out its neck and sighed and settled to the trail.

It was a well-worn path, dark soft leaf-mould earth strewn with broken pieces of sandstone. The trail rounded the shoulder of the canyon and dropped steeply into the bed of the stream. In the shallows the water ran smoothly, glinting in the first morning sun. Small round stones on the bottom were as brown as rust with sun moss. In the sand along the edges of the stream the tall, rich wild mint grew, while in the water itself the cress, old and tough, had gone to heavy seed.

The path went into the stream and emerged on the other side. The horse sloshed into the water and stopped. Pepé dropped his bridle and let the beast drink of the running water.

Soon the canyon sides became steep and the first giant sentinel redwoods guarded the trail, great round red trunks bearing foliage as green and lacy as ferns. Once Pepé was among the trees, the sun was lost. A perfumed and purple light lay in the pale green of the underbrush. Gooseberry bushes and blackberries and tall ferns lined the stream, and overhead the branches of the redwoods met and cut off the sky.

Pepé drank from the water bag, and he reached into the flour sack and brought out a black string of jerky. His white teeth gnawed at the string until the tough meat parted. He chewed slowly and drank occasionally from the water bag. His little eyes were slumberous and tired, but the muscles of his face were hard set. The earth of the trail was black now. It gave up a hollow sound under the walking hoofbeats.

The stream fell more sharply. Little waterfalls splashed on the stones. Five-fingered ferns hung over the water and dripped spray from their fingertips. Pepé rode half over in his saddle, dangling one leg loosely. He picked a bay leaf from a tree beside the way and put it into his mouth for a moment to flavor the dry jerky. He held the gun loosely across the pommel.

Suddenly he squared in his saddle, swung the horse from the trail and kicked it hurriedly up behind a big redwood tree. He pulled up the reins tight against the bit to keep the horse from whinnying. His face was intent and his nostrils quivered a little.

A hollow pounding came down the trail, and a horseman rode by, a fat man with red cheeks and a white stubble beard. His horse put down its head and blubbered at the trail when it came to the place where Pepé had turned off. "Hold up!" said the man and he pulled up his horse's head.

When the last sound of the hoofs died away, Pepé came back into the trail again. He did not relax in the saddle any more. He lifted the big rifle and swung the lever to throw a shell into the chamber, and then he let down the hammer to half cock.

The trail grew very steep. Now the redwood trees were smaller and their tops were dead, bitten dead where the wind reached them. The horse plodded on; the sun went slowly overhead and started down toward the afternoon.

Where the stream came out of a side canyon, the trail left it. Pepé dismounted and watered his horse and filled up his water bag. As soon as the trail had parted from the stream, the trees were gone and only the thick brittle sage and manzanita and chaparral edged the trail. And the soft black earth was gone, too, leaving only the light tan broken rock for the trail bed. Lizards scampered away into the brush as the horse rattled over the little stones.

Pepé turned in his saddle and looked back. He was in the open now: he could be seen from a distance. As he ascended the trail the country grew more rough and terrible and dry. The way wound about the bases of great square rocks. Little grey rabbits skittered in the brush. A bird made monotonous high creaking. Eastward the bare rock mountaintops were pale and powder-dry under the drooping sun. The horse plodded up and up the trail toward a little V in the ridge which was the pass.

Pepé looked suspiciously back every minute or so, and his eyes sought the tops of the ridges ahead. Once, on a white barren spur, he saw a black figure for a moment, but he looked quickly away, for it was one of the dark watchers. No one knew who the watchers were, nor where they lived, but it was better to ignore them and never to show interest in them. They did not bother one who stayed on the trail and minded his own business.

The air was parched and full of light dust blown by the breeze from the eroding mountains. Pepé drank sparingly from his bag and corked it tightly and hung it on the horn again. The trail moved up the dry shale hillside, avoiding rocks, dropping under clefts, climbing in and out of old water scars. When he arrived at the little pass he stopped and looked back for a long time. No dark watchers were to be seen now. The trail behind was empty. Only the high tops of the redwoods indicated where the stream flowed.

Pepé rode on through the pass. His little eyes were nearly closed with weariness, but his face was stern, relentless and manly. The high mountain wind coasted sighing through the pass and whistled on the edges of the big blocks of broken granite. In the air, a red-tailed hawk sailed over close to the ridge and screamed angrily. Pepé went slowly through the broken jagged pass and looked down on the other side.

The trail dropped quickly, staggering among broken rock. At the bottom of the slope there was a dark crease, thick with brush, and on the other side of the crease a little flat, in which a grove of oak trees grew. A scar of green grass cut across the flat. And behind the flat another mountain rose, desolate with dead rocks and starving little black bushes. Pepé drank from the bag again for the air was so dry that it encrusted his nostrils and burned his lips. He put the horse down the trail. The hooves slipped and struggled on the steep way, starting little stones that rolled off into the brush. The sun was gone behind the westward mountain now, but still it glowed brilliantly on the oaks and on the grassy flat. The rocks and the hillsides still sent up waves of the heat they had gathered from the day's sun.

Pepé looked up to the top of the next dry withered ridge. He saw a dark form against the sky, a man's figure standing on top of a rock, and he glanced away quickly not to appear curious. When a moment later he looked up again, the figure was gone.

Downward the trail was quickly covered. Sometimes the horse floundered for footing, sometimes set his feet and slid a little way. They came at last to the bottom where the dark chaparral was higher than Pepé's head. He held up his rifle on one side and his arm on the other to shield his face from the sharp brittle fingers of the brush.

Up and out of the crease he rode, and up a little cliff. The grassy flat was before him, and the round comfortable oaks. For a moment he studied the trail down which he had come, but there was no movement and no sound from it. Finally he rode out over the flat, to the green streak, and at the upper end of the damp he found a little spring welling out of the earth and dropping into a dug basin before it seeped out over the flat.

Pepé filled his bag first, and then he let the thirsty horse drink out of the pool. He led the horse to the clump of oaks, and in the middle of the grove, fairly protected from sight on all sides, he took off the saddle and the bridle and laid them on the ground. The horse stretched his jaws sideways and yawned. Pepé knotted the lead rope about the horse's neck and tied him to a sapling among the oaks, where he could graze in a fairly large circle.

When the horse was gnawing hungrily at the dry grass, Pepé went to the saddle and took a black string of jerky from the sack and strolled to an oak tree on the edge of the grove, from under which he could watch the trail. He sat down in the crisp dry oak leaves and automatically felt for his big black knife to cut the jerky, but he had no knife. He leaned back on his elbow and gnawed at the tough strong meat. His face was blank, but it was a man's face.

The bright evening light washed the eastern ridge, but the valley was darkening. Doves flew down from the hills to the spring, and the quail came running out of the brush and joined them, calling clearly to one another.

Out of the corner of his eye Pepé saw a shadow grow out of the bushy crease. He turned his head slowly. A big spotted wildcat was creeping toward the spring, belly to the ground, moving like thought.

Pepé cocked his rifle and edged the muzzle slowly around. Then he looked apprehensively up the trail and dropped the hammer again. From the ground beside him he picked an oak twig and threw it toward the spring. The quail flew up with a roar and the doves whistled away. The big cat stood up: for a long moment he looked at Pepé with cold yellow eyes, and then fearlessly walked back into the gulch.

The dusk gathered quickly in the deep valley. Pepé muttered his prayers, put his head down on his arm and went instantly to sleep.

The moon came up and filled the valley with cold blue light, and the wind swept rustling down from the peaks. The owls worked up and down the slopes looking for rabbits. Down in the brush of the gulch a coyote gabbled. The oak trees whispered softly in the night breeze.

Pepé started up, listening. His horse had whinnied. The moon was just slipping behind the western ridge, leaving the valley in darkness behind it. Pepé sat tensely gripping his rifle. From far up the trail he heard an answering whinny and the crash of shod hooves on the broken rock. He jumped to his feet, ran to his horse and led it under the trees. He threw on the saddle and cinched it tight for the steep trail, caught the unwilling head and forced the bit into the mouth. He felt the saddle to make sure the water bag and the sack of jerky were there. Then he mounted and turned up the hill.

It was velvet dark. The horse found the entrance to the trail where it left the flat, and started up, stumbling and slipping on the rocks. Pepé's hand rose up to his head. His hat was gone. He had left it under the oak tree.

The horse had struggled far up the trail when the first change of dawn came into the air, a steel greyness as light mixed thoroughly with dark. Gradually the sharp snaggled edge of the ridge stood out above them, rotten granite tortured and eaten by the winds of time. Pepé had dropped his reins on the horn, leaving direction to the horse. The brush grabbed at his legs in the dark until one knee of his jeans was ripped.

Gradually the light flowed down over the ridge. The starved brush and rocks stood out in the half light, strange and lonely in high perspective. Then there came warmth into the light. Pepé drew up and looked back, but he could see nothing in the darker valley below. The sky turned blue over the coming sun. In the waste of the mountainside, the poor dry brush grew only three feet high. Here and there, big outcroppings of unrotted granite stood up like mouldering houses. Pepé relaxed a little. He drank from his water bag and bit off a piece of jerky. A single eagle flew over, high in the light.

Without warning Pepé's horse screamed and fell on its side. He was almost down before the rifle crash echoed up from the valley. From a hole behind the struggling shoulder, a stream of bright crimson blood pumped and stopped and pumped and stopped. The hooves threshed on the ground. Pepé lay half stunned beside the horse. He looked slowly down the hill. A piece of sage clipped off beside his head and another crash echoed up from side to side of the canyon. Pepé flung himself frantically behind a bush.

He crawled up the hill on his knees and one hand. His right hand held the rifle up off the ground and pushed it ahead of him. He moved with the instinctive care of an animal. Rapidly he wormed his way toward one of the big outcroppings of granite on the hill above him. Where the brush was high he doubled up and ran, but where the cover was slight he wriggled forward on his stomach, pushing the rifle ahead of him. In the last little distance there was no cover at all. Pepé poised and then he darted across the space and flashed around the corner of the rock.

He leaned panting against the stone. When his breath came easier he moved along behind the big rock until he came to a narrow split that offered a thin section of vision down the hill. Pepé lay on his stomach and pushed the rifle barrel through the slit and waited.

The sun reddened the western ridges now. Already the buzzards were settling down toward the place where the horse lay. A small brown bird scratched in the dead sage leaves directly in front of the rifle muzzle. The coasting eagle flew back toward the rising sun.

Pepé saw a little movement in the brush far below. His grip tightened on the gun. A little brown doe stepped daintily out on the trail and crossed it and disappeared into the brush again. For a long time Pepé waited. Far below he could see the little flat and the oak trees and the slash of green. Suddenly his eyes flashed back at the trail again. A quarter of a mile down there had been a quick movement in the chaparral. The rifle swung over. The front sight nestled in the v of the rear sight. Pepé studied for a moment and then raised the rear sight a notch. The little movement in the brush came again. The sight settled on it. Pepé squeezed the trigger. The explosion crashed down the mountain and up the other side, and came rattling back. The whole side of the slope grew still. No more movement. And then a white streak cut into the granite of the slit and a bullet whined away and a crash sounded up from below. Pepé felt a sharp pain in his right hand. A sliver of granite was sticking out from between his first and second knuckles and the point protruded from his palm. Carefully he pulled out the sliver of stone. The wound bled evenly and gently. No vein nor artery was cut.

Pepé looked into a little dusty cave in the rock and gathered a handful of spider web, and he pressed the mass into the cut, plastering the soft web into the blood. The flow stopped almost at once.

The rifle was on the ground. Pepé picked it up, levered a new shell into the chamber. And then he slid into the brush on his stomach. Far to the right he crawled, and then up the hill, moving slowly and carefully, crawling to cover and resting and then crawling again.

In the mountains the sun is high in its arc before it penetrates the gorges. The hot face looked over the hill and brought instant heat with it. The white light beat on the rocks and reflected from them and rose up quivering from the earth again, and the rocks and bushes seemed to quiver behind the air.

Pepé crawled in the general direction of the ridge peak, zig-zagging for cover. The deep cut between his knuckles began to throb. He crawled close to a rattle-snake before he saw it, and when it raised its dry head and made a soft beginning whirr, he backed up and took another way. The quick grey lizards flashed in front of him, raising a tiny line of dust. He found another mass of spider web and pressed it against his throbbing hand.

Pepé was pushing the rifle with his left hand now. Little drops of sweat ran to the ends of his coarse black hair and rolled down his cheeks. His lips and tongue were growing thick and heavy. His lips writhed to draw saliva into his mouth. His little dark eyes were uneasy and suspicious. Once when a grey lizard paused in front of him on the parched ground and turned its head sideways he crushed it flat with a stone.

When the sun slid past noon he had not gone a mile. He crawled exhaustedly a last hundred yards to a patch of high sharp manzanita,[7] crawled desperately, and

---

[7] A shrub or tree of the heath family, found in the western United States.

when the patch was reached he wriggled in among the tough gnarly trunks and dropped his head on his left arm. There was little shade in the meager brush, but there was cover and safety. Pepé went to sleep as he lay and the sun beat on his back. A few little birds hopped close to him and peered and hopped away. Pepé squirmed in his sleep and he raised and dropped his wounded hand again and again.

The sun went down behind the peaks and the cool evening came, and then the dark. A coyote yelled from the hillside, Pepé started awake and looked about with misty eyes. His hand was swollen and heavy; a little thread of pain ran up the inside of his arm and settled in a pocket in his armpit. He peered about and then stood up, for the mountains were black and the moon had not yet risen. Pepé stood up in the dark. The coat of his father pressed on his arm. His tongue was swollen until it nearly filled his mouth. He wriggled out of the coat and dropped it in the brush, and then he struggled up the hill, falling over rocks and tearing his way through the brush. The rifle was knocked against stones as he went. Little dry avalanches of gravel and shattered stone went whispering down the hill behind him.

After a while the old moon came up and showed the jagged ridge top ahead of him. By moonlight Pepé traveled more easily. He bent forward so that his throbbing arm hung away from his body. The journey uphill was made in dashes and rests, a frantic rush up a few yards and then a rest. The wind coasted down the slope rattling the dry stems of the bushes.

The moon was at meridian when Pepé came at last to the sharp backbone of the ridge top. On the last hundred yards of the rise no soil had clung under the wearing winds. The way was on solid rock. He clambered to the top and looked down on the other side. There was a draw like the last below him, misty with moonlight, brushed with dry struggling sage and chaparral. On the other side the hill rose up sharply and at the top the jagged rotten teeth of the mountain showed against the sky. At the bottom of the cut the brush was thick and dark.

Pepé stumbled down the hill. His throat was almost closed with thirst. At first he tried to run, but immediately he fell and rolled. After that he went more carefully. The moon was just disappearing behind the mountains when he came to the bottom. He crawled into the heavy brush feeling with his fingers for water. There was no water in the bed of the stream, only damp earth. Pepé laid his gun down and scooped up a handful of mud and put it in his mouth, and then he sputtered and scraped the earth from his tongue with his finger, for the mud drew at his mouth like a poultice. He dug a hole in the stream bed with his fingers, dug a little basin to catch water; but before it was very deep his head fell forward on the damp ground and he slept.

The dawn came and the heat of the day fell on the earth, and still Pepé slept. Late in the afternoon his head jerked up. He looked slowly around. His eyes were slits of wariness. Twenty feet away in the heavy brush a big tawny mountain lion stood looking at him. Its long thick tail waved gracefully, its ears were erect with interest, not laid back dangerously. The lion squatted down on its stomach and watched him.

Pepé looked at the hole he had dug in the earth. A half inch of muddy water had collected in the bottom. He tore the sleeve from his hurt arm, with his teeth ripped out a little square, soaked it in the water and put it in his mouth. Over and over he filled the cloth and sucked it.

Still the lion sat and watched him. The evening came down but there was no movement on the hills. No birds visited the dry bottom of the cut. Pepé looked occasionally at the lion. The eyes of the yellow beast drooped as though he were about to sleep. He yawned and his long thin red tongue curled out. Suddenly his head jerked around and his nostrils quivered. His big tail lashed. He stood up and slunk like a tawny shadow into the thick brush.

A moment later Pepé heard the sound, the faint far crash of horses' hooves on gravel. And he heard something else, a high whining yelp of a dog.

Pepé took his rifle in his left hand and he glided into the brush almost as quietly as the lion had. In the darkening evening he crouched up the hill toward the next ridge. Only when the dark came did he stand up. His energy was short. Once it was dark he fell over the rocks and slipped to his knees on the steep slope, but he moved on and on up the hill, climbing and scrabbling over the broken hillside.

When he was far up toward the top, he lay down and slept for a while. The withered moon, shining on his face, awakened him. He stood up and moved up the hill. Fifty yards away he stopped and turned back, for he had forgotten his rifle. He walked heavily down and poked about in the brush, but he could not find his gun. At last he lay down to rest. The pocket of pain in his armpit had grown more sharp. His arm seemed to swell out and fall with every heartbeat. There was no position lying down where the heavy arm did not press against his armpit.

With the effort of a hurt beast, Pepé got up and moved again toward the top of the ridge. He held his swollen arm away from his body with his left hand. Up the steep hill he dragged himself, a few steps and a rest, and a few more steps. At last he was nearing the top. The moon showed the uneven sharp back of it against the sky.

Pepé's brain spun in a big spiral up and away from him. He slumped to the ground and lay still. The rock ridge top was only a hundred feet above him.

The moon moved over the sky. Pepé half turned on his back. His tongue tried to make words, but only a thick hissing came from between his lips.

When the dawn came, Pepé pulled himself up. His eyes were sane again. He drew his great puffed arm in front of him and looked at the angry wound. The black line ran up from his wrist to his armpit. Automatically he reached in his pocket for the big black knife, but it was not there. His eyes searched the ground. He picked up a sharp blade of stone and scraped at the wound, sawed at the proud flesh and then squeezed the green juice out in big drops. Instantly he threw back his head and whined like a dog. His whole right side shuddered at the pain, but the pain cleared his head.

In the grey light he struggled up the last slope to the ridge and crawled over and lay down behind a line of rocks. Below him lay a deep canyon exactly like the last, waterless and desolate. There was no flat, no oak trees, not even heavy brush in the bottom of it. And on the other side a sharp ridge stood up, thinly brushed with starving sage, littered with broken granite. Strewn over the hill there were giant outcroppings, and on the top the granite teeth stood out against the sky.

The new day was light now. The flame of the sun came over the ridge and fell on Pepé where he lay on the ground. His coarse black hair was littered with twigs and bits of spider web. His eyes had retreated back into his head. Between his lips the tip of his black tongue showed.

He sat up and dragged his great arm into his lap and nursed it, rocking his body and moaning in his throat. He threw back his head and looked up into the pale sky. A big black bird circled nearly out of sight, and far to the left another was sailing near.

He lifted his head to listen, for a familiar sound had come to him from the valley he had climbed out of; it was the crying yelp of hounds, excited and feverish on a trail.

Pepé bowed his head quickly. He tried to speak rapid words but only a thick hiss came from his lips. He drew a shaky cross on his breast with his left hand. It was a long struggle to get to his feet. He crawled slowly and mechanically to the top of a big rock on the ridge peak. Once there, he arose slowly, swaying to his feet, and stood erect. Far below he could see the dark brush where he had slept. He braced his feet and stood there, black against the morning sky.

There came a ripping sound at his feet. A piece of stone flew up and a bullet droned off into the next gorge. The hollow crash echoed up from below. Pepé looked down for a moment and then pulled himself straight again.

His body jarred back. His left hand fluttered helplessly toward his breast. The second crash sounded from below. Pepé swung forward and toppled from the rock. His body struck and rolled over and over, starting a little avalanche. And when at last he stopped against a bush, the avalanch slid slowly down and covered up his head.

1938

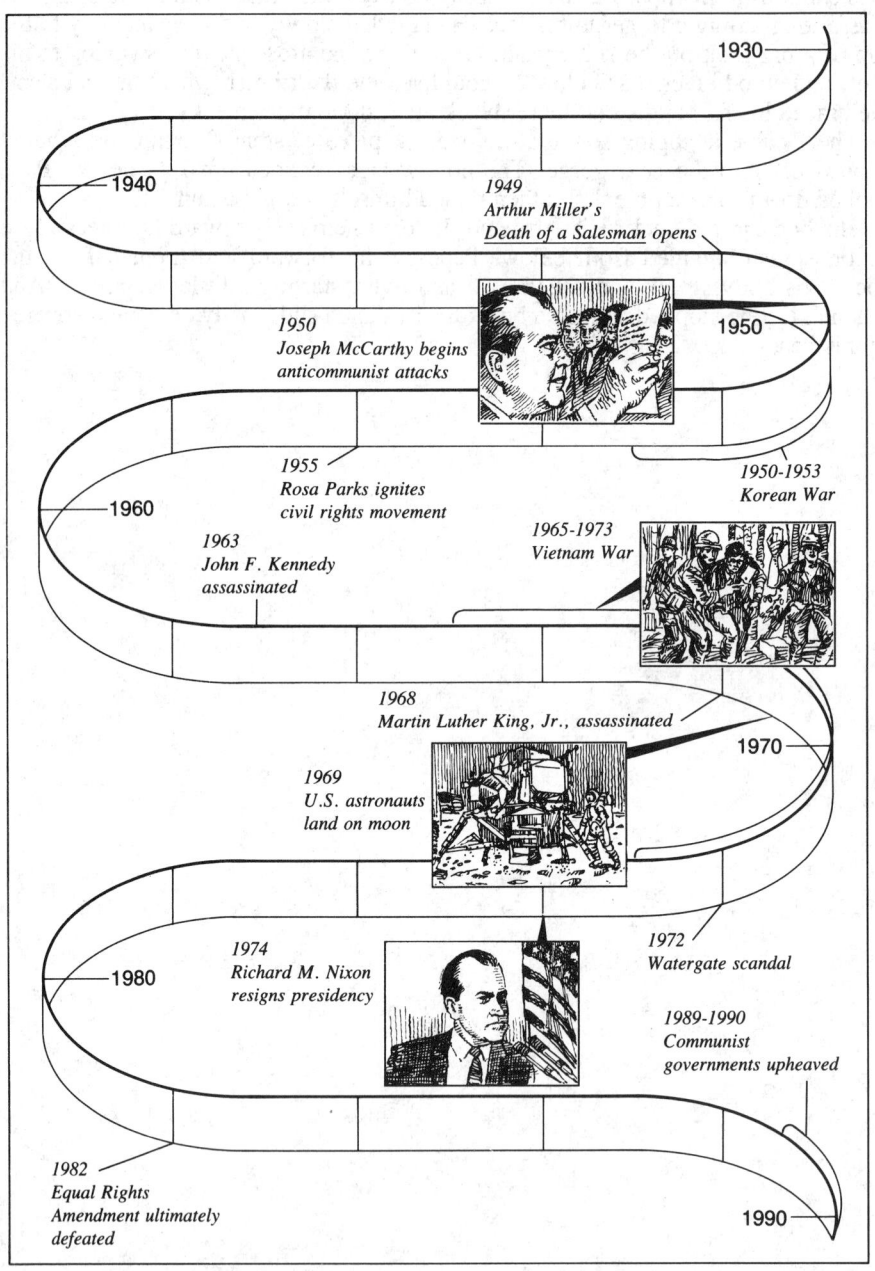

1930

1940

1949
Arthur Miller's
Death of a Salesman opens

1950
Joseph McCarthy begins
anticommunist attacks

1950

1950-1953
Korean War

1955
Rosa Parks ignites
civil rights movement

1960

1963
John F. Kennedy
assassinated

1965-1973
Vietnam War

1968
Martin Luther King, Jr., assassinated

1970

1969
U.S. astronauts
land on moon

1972
Watergate scandal

1974
Richard M. Nixon
resigns presidency

1989-1990
Communist
governments upheaved

1980

1982
Equal Rights
Amendment ultimately
defeated

1990

PART THREE

Diversity, Technology, and Social Change

The Middle to Late 20th Century

In the distant future it may be said that World War II did not really come to an end until autumn 1989, when a democratic upheaval swept Eastern Europe, when the Berlin Wall was demolished, and when the rivalries between the United States and the Soviet Union (dating from the world-war years) seemed well on the way to resolution. The power of Fascist regimes at their height in 1942 stretched from Mongolia to Burma to the Marshall Islands in the Pacific; from the outskirts of Moscow to Europe's Atlantic Coast; from Casablanca to Cairo in North Africa. Genocide for Jews and Gypsies, ruthless management of prisoners of war, and harsh occupation of conquered territories suggested what the defeated could expect. The triumph of the Allied powers over Germany and Japan in 1945 ended a nightmare. But embedded in the triumph were its own tragedies, and the postwar generations would not find it easy to maintain the peace for which they longed. An oxymoronic epithet would describe the era: it would be called the "cold war."

Savoring their triumph, and determined to make it more lasting than victory in World War I had been, the Allies moved to make the United Nations a permanent forum for international dialogue. Understanding that the seeds of war had grown in the festering wounds of a demoralized political system and a bankrupt economy in Germany, the United States moved quickly to make postwar economic reconstruction possible: the Marshall Plan provided $17 billion over four years for sixteen nations, including the western portion of a divided Germany. Western Europe was restored to economic health quickly, as was Japan, where a peace treaty and a democratic constitution were imposed. Forbidden to build armies, Japan and West Germany concentrated on economic rebuilding. In less than a generation their economies were robust and competitive, their political systems authentically democratic.

Within the United States the advent of peace also signaled great opportunities, as manufacturing responded to the demand for consumer goods that it had been unable to satisfy during the war. A generous "G.I. Bill" gave returning veterans priority for many jobs, small-business loans, low-interest mortgages, and tuition subsidies for vocational schools and for colleges. Into college streamed millions of returning veterans, many from working-class families, who before the war would have found college far out of their reach. New colleges and universities were founded, and older ones expanded. College education became vastly more accessible and would remain so. In 1940 less than ten percent of eighteen- to twenty-four-year-olds were enrolled in college; by 1980 over thirty-five percent of that group were. An unintentional result of the G.I. Bill was the expansion of the gap between middle-class men and women in the accessibility of college education. Although all veterans were eligible for its benefits, only a very small fraction of veterans—mostly army nurses and members of the Women's Army Corps—were women. Not until 1978 would the gap between male and female college students be closed.

But tragedies were also inherited from World War II. Chief among them was the abuse of atomic energy: the race with German scientists to build an atomic bomb was quickly replaced by a race with Soviet scientists to build a hydrogen bomb, powered by fusion and many times more destructive than the atomic bomb. Americans had long been suspicious of the Soviet Union as a tyranny and had entered into the wartime alliance only out of necessity; now that the war was over, American suspicions resumed their force. These suspicions were heightened by the widespread feeling that the United States had been too slow in appreciating the Fascist threat in the 1930s. Many Americans were determined not to repeat that mistake. For its part the Soviet Union felt the Allies had delayed opening a second front while the Soviets faced the German threat virtually alone. (Estimates of the number of USSR citizens who died in World War II, once thought to be 20 million, were revised in 1990 to about 40 million; that is, nearly one out of five of the Soviet population may have perished in the war.) The Soviets were determined to make a third twentieth-century invasion from the West impossible, demanding that Germany be inhibited from rebuilding its strength and that regimes in Eastern Europe be friendly ones. Russian troops were in place in Eastern Europe as Germany was defeated, and they showed no anxiety to leave; neither the United States nor Great Britain was prepared to remove them by force. Instead, the United States took the position that it would seek to "contain" Soviet expansion by a military alliance, the North Atlantic Treaty Organization (NATO) and by a massive increase in its own military spending. But it would not intervene to challenge the boundaries of the Soviet sphere of influence. When East Germans rebelled in 1953, when Hungarians revolted in 1956, and when Czechs rose in 1968, the United States kept its distance lest a major war would ensue.

In the Far East the United States took a stricter line. Although it had long worried about the corrupt regime of Chiang Kai-shek in China, the United States refused diplomatic overtures made by Chou En-lai's and Mao Tse-tung's victorious Communists in 1949. When North Korean troops invaded South Korea in 1950, President Harry S. Truman concluded that the Soviet Union was responsible. Once the United Nations Security Council agreed, Truman bypassed Congress and ordered two American army divisions into action. The Korean War, which lasted until 1953, demonstrated American's willingness to "contain" communism anywhere on the globe. Meanwhile, the South Korean dictator Syngman Rhee was defined as a "gallant ally." Historian William Chafe has observed that "through such logic the United States seriously impaired its credibility with Third World countries, neutrals, even allies" (*The Unfinished Journey,* 1986). Similar themes would emerge during the next decade's involvement in Vietnam.

Anxieties about international relations infused domestic politics in the postwar years. Fear of communism abroad spilled over into fear of Communists at home. Although membership in the American Communist party had declined sharply after World War II, many Americans were convinced that Communists were actively seeking to subvert the U.S. government. The McCarran Internal Security Act of 1950 illegalized "substantially contributing" to establishing a dictatorship in the United States. In the late 1940s Truman established a program to search for people suspected of subversive activity, and the House Un-American Activities Committee embarked on a major investigation of the motion-picture industry in 1947. Ten screenwriters, including Dalton Trumbo, were sent to federal prison for refusing to testify; many other writers and actors were informally blacklisted and forced out of their profession by rumor and innuendo. African-American writers and artists, among them the distinguished scholar and National Association for the Advancement of Colored People (NAACP) founder W. E. B. DuBois, and the great singer and actor Paul Robeson, were accused of Communist cooperation; while they were abroad, their passports were confiscated. Through most of the 1950s Joseph McCarthy, who had had an undistinguished career as a senator from Wisconsin, accused hundreds of people of being Communist agents or sympathizers—"fellow travelers." His accusations, which had virtually no evidence, were generally enough to ruin careers, until in 1954 he attacked the army itself. In one of the first sets of congressional hearings to be televised, millions of people watched as his accusations were shown to be groundless. During the 1953 production of Arthur Miller's *The Crucible,* which shows how easily suspicion and dread were spread in the Salem witchcraft trials in colonial Massachusetts, everyone in the audience knew Miller was writing about his own time.

The Civil Rights Movement

The civil rights revolution had many of its origins in World War II. Millions of black soldiers had been drafted to fight for democracy in a segregated army in which they were commanded by white officers. Millions of African-American men and women had worked in defense plants. Returning veterans were outraged by the continuation of segregation and by lynchings. Not until African-American civil rights leaders threatened a massive civil disobedience campaign in 1948 did Truman issue an executive order ending discrimination in the armed forces, but the army was not actually desegregated until after the Korean War, and the navy remained segregated long after that. The federal government did not defend African Americans against violence and intimidation when they attempted to vote. And in 1955 fourteen-year-old Emmett Till, visiting Mississippi from Chicago, was murdered because he had not been deferential to whites in a grocery store.

The NAACP brought lawsuits challenging claims that states were providing "separate but equal" educational facilities, beginning with "law schools" that were one-room facilities with one teacher and no books. In the landmark case of *Brown* v. *Board of Education* in 1954, a legal team brilliantly led by attorney Thurgood

═CONTEXTS═

The Civil Rights Movement

Throughout the 1950s and 1960s African Americans continued to struggle vigorously for the basic rights to which they were entitled. This struggle was centered in the activities of the Congress of Racial Equality, the Southern Christian Leadership Conference, and the Student Nonviolent Coordinating Committee. Martin Luther King, Jr. (1929–1968), head of the SCLC, was a major force in this movement. He delivered his "I Have A Dream" speech during a civil rights march on Washington, D.C., on August 28, 1963:

I Have a Dream

Five score years ago a great American in whose symbolic shadow we stand today signed the Emancipation Proclamation. This momentous decree is a great beacon light of hope to millions of Negro slaves who had been seared in the flames of withering injustice. It came as a joyous daybreak to end the long night of their captivity. But 100 years later, the Negro still is not free. One hundred years later the life of the Negro is still badly crippled by the manacles of segregation and the chains of discrimination. One hundred years later the Negro lives on a lonely island of poverty in the midst of a vast ocean of material prosperity. One hundred years later the Negro still languishe[s] in the corners of American society and finds himself in exile in his own land. . . .

We must forever conduct our struggle on the high plane of dignity and discipline. We must not allow our creative protests to degenerate into physical violence. Again and again we must rise to the majestic heights of meeting physical force with soul force. . . .

. . . I have a dream that my four little children will one day live in a nation where they will not be judged by the color of their skin but by the content of their character. . . .

When we allow freedom to ring—when we let it ring from every city and every hamlet, from every state and every city, we will be able to speed up that day when all God's children, black men and white men, Jews and Gentiles, Protestants and Catholics, will be able to join hands and sing in the words of the old Negro spiritual, "Free at last, Free at last! Great God a-mighty, We are free at last!"

Martin Luther King, Jr., 1963

Marshall argued that no separate facilities *could* be equal because separation itself stigmatized African Americans as different and unequal. Chief Justice Earl Warren had supported the relocation of Japanese Americans during World War II but had come to regret that decision bitterly. In 1954 he took a leading role in persuading his fellow justices not only to declare "separate but equal" a denial of equal protection of the law, but to do so unanimously. The Supreme Court, however, could only declare what the law was. Although President Dwight D. Eisenhower had moved effectively to desegregate the army, he was critical of the *Brown* decision and did not move to enforce it, even rhetorically. Although most southern states had been ready to comply with the court's decision, they gradually moved to resist or circumvent it. Children trying to register at Central High School in Little Rock, Arkansas, in 1957 were surrounded and intimidated by hostile crowds. Other children were met by hostility and violence, inside and outside schools. Tax funds were used to pay tuition at "private" schools for white children. Embittered by the law's failure to protect them, African Americans became ever more skeptical of whites' protestations of equality.

In autumn 1955 Rosa Parks, secretary of the Montgomery, Alabama, NAACP branch, felt the time had come; when a bus driver insisted she move to the segregated back of the bus, she refused. She was arrested, and her colleagues—veterans of efforts to desegregate drinking fountains and the police force—embarked on a massive boycott of the public buses of Montgomery. The boycott lasted a year and a month. It brought together Montgomery's black community (who, by walking long distances to work each day, dramatically demonstrated that they would make major practical sacrifices rather than absorb the continued humiliation of segregation), the national black community, and ultimately a national community of whites moved by the demonstrations. They catapulted to national visibility and leadership the young minister Martin Luther King, Jr. whose moving speeches articulated the high moral principles that placed the boycott on a level with other classic struggles for liberty and justice.

In 1960 four African-American college freshmen in Greensboro, North Carolina, sat down at a segregated lunch counter and refused to obey management's demand that they leave. The following day more African-American students joined them. The "sit-in" movement became a national protest, enlarged to claim not only a seat at a lunch counter or on a bus, but full economic, educational, and political freedom. It was met with violence, brutality, and murder. It also resulted in federal legislation that outlawed racial discrimination in public accommodations; prohibited hiring on the basis of race, sex, religion, or national origin; and authorized federal examiners to register African-American voters when local officials would not.

Gender Equality Movements

The women's movement of the middle to late twentieth century had its roots in World War II and in the civil rights movement. During the war women's participation in the paid work force was a welcome contribution to the economy. Many married women entered the paid work force, and women who were already working found highly improved opportunities and salaries. African-American women gained skilled jobs in manufacturing for the first time. When the war was over, however, these women lost their jobs to returning veterans; worse, they lost the seniority that would have made them candidates for subsequent openings. Few women could afford to stop working; instead they moved into part-time or underpaid, less-skilled work. They typically carried with them memories of better times, and the conviction that their daughters should have greater opportunities than they had. In 1963, when the President's Commission on the Status of Women documented widespread legal discrimination, the average working woman earned sixty-three percent of what the average working man earned; that figure actually declined to fifty-seven percent in the next decade. Meanwhile, young women working in the civil rights movement came to criticize attitudes that considered them inferior to their male colleagues and learned effective tactics for demanding social and cultural change.

In the 1970s feminists launched a wide-ranging criticism of legal and social practice. They demanded equal employment opportunities; access to safe, legal abortion; and equal access to credit, to fringe benefits, and to education. Their criticism of colleges and universities focused both on the exclusion of women from college faculties and on the curriculum itself. Feminists questioned the absence of women's experience from fields as diverse as psychology, economics, history, and literature; they also questioned decisions as to what texts deserve to be labeled "classic" and what authors should be presented to the next generation as indispensable to the well-educated person.

A series of Supreme Court decisions in the early 1970s established for the first time in American history that discrimination based solely on sex could under certain conditions be unconstitutional. In an effort to make this interpretation permanent, Congress passed a proposed Equal Rights Amendment to the Constitution in 1972. It was quickly ratified by thirty of the required thirty-eight states, but thereafter progress on passage was stopped by a strong conservative movement claiming that women already have sufficient protection by law.

During the 1970s radical feminists developed the argument that gender itself is socially constructed. "Sex" refers to biological differences that are unchanging, but "gender" involves the *meaning* that a particular society and culture attaches to sexual difference. In "consciousness-raising" groups, women shared painful memories of making their way in a society that put limits on their aspirations and constrained their choices. They reinterpreted behavior they had once thought to be "natural" as in fact learned behavior, the result of socialization. Lesbians offered the most intense critique of a society that permitted heterosexual men to set the norms; along with gay men, lesbians publicly claimed the legitimacy of their own sexual choices. These claims were embodied in part by public gestures such as parades, in part by the direct challenging of laws that barred lesbians and gay men from careers in teaching or in the military, and in part by the renegotiation of institutional regulations that denied equal treatment to partners in homosexual relationships.

The Vietnam War Years

Throughout the 1960s much American foreign policy continued to be framed in cold-war terms, and the tension between the United States and communism was assumed to be permanent. One region in which this tension exploded was Southeast Asia. Ho Chi Minh had led a nationalist resistance to Japanese occupation during World War II; this resistance continued when Vietnam was returned to the French. It was strong enough to force the French out, despite American military and economic aid. Vietnam was divided, with Ho presiding over the North. Un-

Visitors to the black marble Vietnam War Memorial in Washington, D.C. take pencil rubbings of the names of loved ones killed in the controversial war in Southeast Asia.

derstanding that he was allied with Communists, believing that the crucial errors of the 1930s had been the failure to stop Hitler's advances early enough, and fearing that if one region fell to the Communists others would follow like "falling dominos" (in Eisenhower's words), the United States began to support Ho's enemies in South Vietnam, sending first a secret CIA mission, then military advisors, and ultimately combat troops in 1965. At the time of President John F. Kennedy's assassination in 1963, there were some 16,000 military advisors; by 1966 there were 385,000 military personnel; at the end of Lyndon Johnson's term as president in 1968, there were 500,000.

The immediacy of news coverage provided by electronic media made Vietnam the "living-room war," and America was not ready for what it saw. Criticism of the Vietnam intervention grew at home, particularly on college campuses, where students who had worked for civil rights brought to college campuses the strategies they had learned in the South. In the mid-1960s they transformed the culture of American college life by demanding student participation in setting university policy, in curriculum change, and often in demanding admission of minority students. College students bitterly questioned the need to spend lives in defending an undemocratic regime in South Vietnam, questioned the domino theory, and questioned the cold war itself. They attacked their own universities for maintaining ROTC programs, which prepared students for Vietnam service, and for accepting federal grants for military research. By the late 1960s it was possible to identify a "counterculture" of young people who opposed the war and believed in the possibility of an American society driven by harmony and cooperation rather than by competition and individualism.

The year 1968 was a deeply tragic one. The incompatibility of the war in Vietnam and a liberal reform agenda at home so exhausted and depressed Lyndon Johnson that he declined to run for a second term as president. Robert F. Kennedy and Martin Luther King, Jr., two political leaders whose heroic and inclusive vision promised to heal the divisions of American society, were assassinated within two months of each other. The Democratic National Convention in Chicago took place amid a virtual police riot against antiwar demonstrators: while the police used mace and tear gas, protesters chanted to television cameras, "The whole world is watching!" Republican candidate Richard M. Nixon used consensus language in his campaign, promising to "bring the country together," but domestic politics remained polarized throughout his time in office.

Nixon adopted the policy of a gradual withdrawal of American ground troops but an escalation of air power in Vietnam. In an effort to interdict the flow of supplies from North Vietnam, Nixon approved an invasion of Cambodia in 1970. When college students throughout America demonstrated in protest, local police and National Guard units were called out to silence them. At a peaceable rally at Kent State University in Ohio, four students were killed and eleven wounded; at Jackson State College, an African-American college in Mississippi, police fired into a dormitory, killing two innocent students. During the next five years, under a policy of "Vietnamization," American troops were slowly withdrawn from Vietnam. The peace accords that were signed in January 1973 permitted the North Vietnamese to keep their troops in the South. By 1975 the South Vietnamese forces had crumbled, and the last Americans fled in an ignominious retreat. Overloaded helicopters desperately fled Saigon, unable to carry even those Vietnamese who had cooperated most closely with Americans and therefore faced the most extreme reprisals.

The Postwar Years

American public opinion was partly assuaged for the failures of Vietnam by Nixon's restoration of diplomatic relations with China in 1972 after twenty-five years. The United States agreed to withdraw troops stationed in Taiwan, while the Chinese promised to urge North Vietnam to accept a negotiated settlement, and trade relations were opened. Nixon also initiated a major breakthrough in relations with the Soviet Union, including a Strategic Arms Limitation Treaty (SALT-I), signed in 1972.

Nixon was re-elected in 1972 by the largest majority ever claimed by a Republican presidential candidate. But in late 1973 Vice-President Spiro Agnew, facing charges of income-tax evasion and bribery, was forced to resign. During Nixon's presidential campaign, five burglars sponsored by his campaign committee had been caught breaking into the Democratic National Headquarters at the Watergate Hotel in Washington, D.C. As discovered by two reporters for the *Washington*

The "space race" that begin in 1957 with the Soviet Union's launching of Sputnik I, the first artificial satellite, eventually led to the landing of Americans on the moon on July 20, 1969.

Post, the break-in was part of a "dirty tricks" campaign against Democratic candidates, complete with massive illegal fundraising. A Select Senate Committee and the House Judiciary Committee heard testimony on wiretapping, perjury, and blackmail, emanating from the executive office. When tape recordings—which Nixon had himself ordered to be made—provided evidence of a criminal conspiracy to obstruct justice, Nixon, facing increasingly likely impeachment proceedings, resigned.

"American politics oscillated wildly during the seventies," writes William Chafe, "giving the Democrats their greatest majority in the postwar era in 1974, and then in 1980 doing the same for the Republicans. . . . No one seemed able to find answers capable of forging a new consensus" (*The Unfinished Journey,* 1986). The oscillation continued into the 1980s, when Congress was often controlled by Democrats, while the White House was held by Republicans. The economy was equally difficult to interpret. Massive deficits characterized the federal budget for two decades. These deficits are generally traced to Lyndon Johnson's fear of raising taxes to pay for the expenses of Vietnam (lest opposition to taxes turn into opposition to foreign policy) and to Richard Nixon's monetary policies, which permitted an inflation rate of ten percent in 1973. Ronald Reagan made an attack on the deficit a major part of his platform in 1980 and again in 1984, but the deficit continued to grow, due in large part to heightened military spending.

For many, especially the well educated, professional opportunities improved in the 1970s and 1980s. This was particularly true for college-educated women. Desegregated schools and changes in job expectations enabled more African-American families to reach middle-class status. But there was also a downward spiral: for the first time sociologists could identify a permanent "underclass." Two-thirds of all adults classified as poor in 1980 were women; the "feminization of poverty" developed first among African Americans. Poverty had many political consequences, among them demoralization; the lowest voting rates are found in the poorest neighborhoods.

In 1893 the historian Frederick Jackson Turner suggested that the frontier experience was at the core of what was distinctive about American society; "frontier" was a metaphor for limitless possibility, for resources waiting to be claimed and used, for plenty and prosperity. American political metaphor in the twentieth century has stressed both "new" and "limitless"—FDR spoke of a New Deal, JFK of a New Frontier. The landing of U.S. astronauts on the moon on July 20, 1969, opened a truly limitless frontier in space. Americans had traditionally described their society as free of the distinctions of class, race, and gender; political rhetoric insisted that all were equal and that any existing distinctions would soon erode. American society would always have room for upward mobility. In the postwar years the United States was indisputably the most economically prosperous nation in the world. Ironically, American aid to nations destroyed in World War II enabled those nations to build economies that, by the end of the 1980s, were competitive with the U.S. economy. Social critics of the postwar years denied the "melting pot" and insisted on acknowledging the depths of prejudice and discrimination that characterized American society. As the 1990s began, Americans cheered the end of the cold war and the emergence of stronger economies among their allies and burgeoning democracies among their former enemies. But they also worried about America's ability to retain its character as a multiracial, multiethnic society both prosperous and free.

MIDDLE TO LATE 20TH-CENTURY DRAMA

By the end of the nineteenth century, the American theater was thoroughly encrusted with tired conventions borrowed mostly from European traditions. Great actors overshadowed both playwrights and their plays; melodrama flourished at the expense of language and of the complexities of social relations. But by about 1912 the situation began to change, with the appearance of "little theaters" in several cities. Several of them—the Provincetown Players, the Neighborhood Playhouse, and the Washington Square Players—became the voices of change.

The Provincetown Players was founded in 1915 by a small group headed by the writer Susan Glaspell and her husband, George Gram Cook, to encourage new American dramatists. The group gave its first performances in a small theater on a wharf in Provincetown, Massachusetts; by the next summer the program included *Bound East for Cardiff,* by the young Eugene O'Neill. The season was such a success that the group took over a playhouse in New York City and remained there until 1929. The Provincetown Players created an audience for serious American drama and provided a forum for O'Neill's experimental works, such as *The Emperor Jones* (1920).

Established in 1915 in New York City, the Neighborhood Playhouse and the Washington Square Players also attempted to raise the standards of the American stage. Such problems as rising costs and competition with Broadway forced these groups to disband before long. But an outgrowth of the defunct Washington Square Players was the Theatre Guild founded in 1919. The first commercially successful theater group committed to producing quality plays, the guild initially produced works by the leading European playwrights but in 1923 mounted Elmer Rice's *Adding Machine* and in 1928 started to produce O'Neill's plays for its subscription audience. From then on the guild aggressively sought new American playwrights. It also established a permanent acting company and began to perform works in repertory.

By 1920 O'Neill, already heralded as America's most promising playwright, had his first full-length play, *Beyond the Horizon* (1920), presented on Broadway to critical acclaim. A prolific writer, he completed about twenty-five full-length plays, among them such masterpieces as *Desire Under the Elms* (1924), *Mourning Becomes Electra* (1931), and *The Iceman Cometh* (1946). Although O'Neill experimented with symbolism, expressionism, and novel technical devices (the use of masks and extended asides), his greatest plays reveal that he was a master of realistic tragedy. He began what was later recognized as the "shrinking" of the American stage: a preoccupation with physical and psychological space, compressed and pressing in on the characters.

During the 1930s a new group of dramatists gained prominence. The fame of Maxwell Anderson rests on his efforts to revive poetic drama in such historical plays as *Mary of Scotland* (1933). Robert B. Sherwood's best works were the realistic-allegoric melodrama *The Petrified Forest* (1935) and the semifarcical *Idiot's Delight* (1936). Lillian Hellman's third and finest play, *The Little Foxes* (1939), depicts the ruthless infighting of a rapacious southern family. The first two plays of William Saroyan, *My Heart's in the Highlands* (1939) and *The Time of Your Life* (1939), celebrate the eccentric life.

The social consciousness evident in Hellman's and Sherwood's work was evident elsewhere in the theater. The country was still in the midst of the Great Depression. As part of the Works Progress Administration, the government created the Federal Theatre Project in 1935 to provide work for unemployed theater professionals and to provide inexpensive, uncensored theater. At its peak, the project employed ten thousand people and set up numerous semiautonomous companies that offered audiences a broad range of theatrical fare. Among its controversial innovations was the Living Newspaper, documentary plays dramatizing daily events. With the Federal Theatre Project's support, numerous African-American theater groups sprang up in Harlem and elsewhere. Some productions, such as Orson Welles's all-black staging of *Macbeth* (1935), became nationally celebrated. However, in 1939 Congress abolished the project in response to conservative opposition to what was seen as the left-wing propagandistic tone of many of

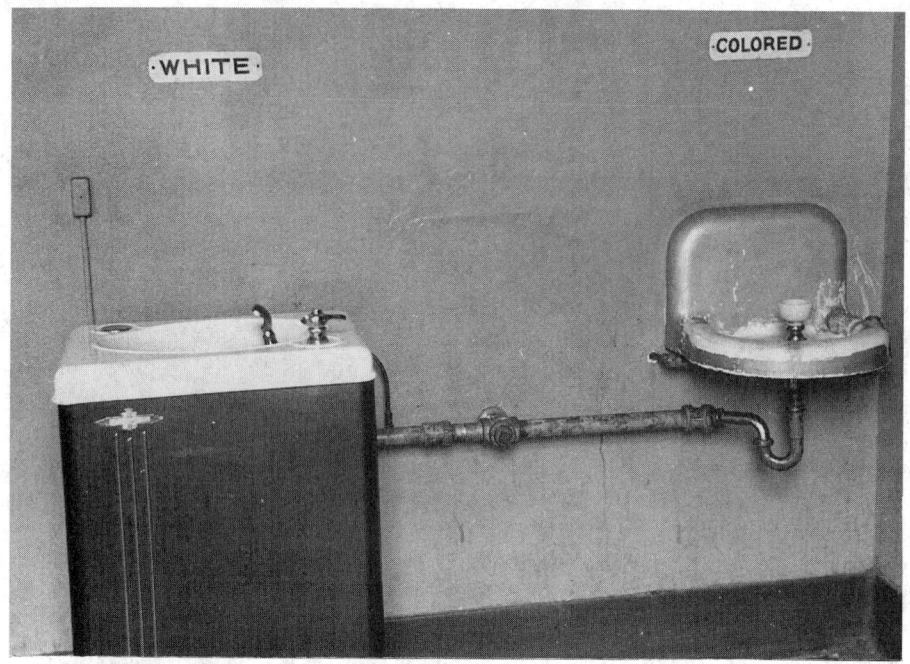

Even drinking fountains in the South were racially segregated before the Civil Rights Act of 1964.

the productions. Despite its relatively brief life, the Federal Theatre is the closest America has come to having a national theater.

Another influential and politically involved theatrical organization, the Group Theatre, was founded in 1931 by Harold Clurman, Cheryl Crawford, and Lee Strasberg, who had broken away from the Theatre Guild. Committed leftists, Clurman and Strasberg wanted a theater that reflected their political views and tried to counteract the notion that social concern is death to art. Until it disbanded in 1940, the Group Theatre was perhaps the most potent artistic force in American theater. Beside producing works of socially conscious playwrights such as Sidney Kingsley, Irwin Shaw, and Marc Blitzstein, it introduced Clifford Odets, the leading playwright of left-wing protest, with productions of *Awake and Sing* (1935), *Waiting for Lefty* (1935), and *Golden Boy* (1937).

Of the playwrights writing on the eve of World War II, the most significant beside O'Neill may have been Thornton Wilder. His universal tale of smalltown life, *Our Town* (1938), is one of the best-known and most popular American dramas. *The Skin of Our Teeth* (1942), an allegory based on humankind's fight for survival, was another critical and commercial success for Wilder. His use of theatrical devices taken from surrealism, futurism, and expressionism placed him among experimental writers such as O'Neill and influenced European playwrights such as Friedrich Durrenmatt and Eugene Ionesco. Yet, Wilder's plays are accessible to the average theatergoer, mostly because of the simplicity of their subject matter.

Between the world wars American theater won international acclaim. But with the exception of O'Neill and Wilder, there were no real innovators, or artistic movements. Part of the reason was economic. In 1928, just before the depression, there were fifteen hundred theaters across the country, but on the eve of World War II, the number had dwindled to about two hundred. The development of sound films in 1928, coupled with their low admission prices, made it nearly impossible for theaters to compete with movies. Rising production costs, partly caused by the increasing power of theatrical unions, worsened the situation. Theater managers then had to attract the popular audience, a group notoriously disinterested in risky plays or artistic experimentation.

During World War II the musical became the most popular form of theater and, as has been frequently said, reached its maturity. *Oklahoma* (1943), by Richard Rodgers and Oscar Hammerstein II, was the first musical to integrate song and story and one of the first to integrate modern American dance. Later Rodgers and Hammerstein productions, such as *Carousel* (1945), *South Pacific* (1949), and *The King and I* (1951), cemented the place of musicals in American theater.

After the war two major new dramatists—Tennessee Williams and Arthur Miller—appeared and came to master expressionistic drama. Williams's first success, *The Glass Menagerie* (1945), manipulates theme and place in exploring the characters' inner and often unconscious motivation. In his many later acclaimed plays, Williams's protagonists are misfits or lost souls, out of sync with normal people, who physically and morally humiliate them. Miller first achieved recognition with *All My Sons* (1947) and was further lauded for *Death of a Salesman* (1949). Miller's best works are powerful and dramatic moral statements about the individual's responsibility to preserve his or her integrity in a society that demands the opposite. Miller was himself a prominent character in a political drama that unfolded in the later 1940s and early 1950s: the anticommunism panic that led to the investigations of the House Committee on Un-American Activities. Many well-known playwrights were brought before the infamous House Committee. The plays of the time reflected the horror of members of the artistic community who watched the integrity of friends crumble and were themselves called upon to answer the question, "Are you now, or have you ever been, a member of the Communist party?" Clifford Odets and Elia Kazan were forever linked to those who named names before the committee. Miller wrote the play *The Crucible* (1953) to protest the injustice of the "witchhunts"; Lillian Hellman wrote memorable letters in which she states her refusal to implicate colleagues, and she produced *Scoundrel Time* (1976), an account of her own experiences, and those of her friends, during the McCarthy era.

One of the most powerful influences on the theater in the mid-1950s was the Actor's Studio, a workshop for professional actors. Founded in 1950 by Elia Kazan, Robert Lewis, and Cheryl Crawford, it was the leading proponent of "method" acting, which encourages performers to probe their own feelings as the way to find a character's psychological truth, sometimes, its critics claimed, at the expense of technique. The Actor's Studio established special units for directors, playwrights, and production. But by 1962, when the production unit was created, the studio's influence was already waning as American theater began to turn from the psychological realism expounded by Lee Strasberg, its leading advocate.

It was during the 1950s that Off Broadway theaters became prominent. By renting cheap, and in some cases nontheatrical, space, Off Broadway producers kept production costs and ticket costs down. The low overhead and the necessity of adapting to unusual stages encouraged experimentation. The 1952 revival of Williams's *Summer and Smoke* (1947), an artistic and commercial triumph, suggested that small theaters might be able to mount productions of higher quality than the larger, more commercial playhouses. By the mid-1950s Off Broadway productions outnumbered those on Broadway, were more diverse, and emphasized repertory. However, Off Broadway did not tend to be experimental either in writing or staging and did not seriously challenge the dominance of Broadway.

═CONTEXTS═

Archetypal Criticism

Archetypal criticism is a way of understanding literature in terms of certain recurring patterns, thought to originate in the subconscious mind. The Canadian literary critic Northrop Frye (1912–), author of *Anatomy of Criticism* (1957), sought for literary criticism a sense of methodological discipline more common among the "hard sciences." For Frye this involved the construction of a single, overriding hypothesis of literature that could act as a cohesive force in criticism. He found this in his theory of literary "archetypes," recurring structures in literature that are reducible to common elements of the subconscious mind. The conflict between father and son, for example, assumes archetypal dimensions in Arthur Miller's *Death of a Salesman.* Frye explains his theory in this excerpt from the essay "The Archetypes of Literature" (1951):

The Archetypes of Literature

It is clear that criticism cannot be systematic unless there is a quality in literature which enables it to be so, an order of words corresponding to the order of nature in the natural sciences. An archetype should be not only a unifying category of criticism, but itself a part of a total form, and it leads us at once to the question of what sort of total form criticism can see in literature. . . . Total literary history moves from the primitive to the sophisticated, and here we glimpse the possibility of seeing literature as a complication of a relatively restricted and simple group of formulas that can be studied in primitive culture. If so, then the search for archetypes is a kind of literary anthropology, concerned with the way that literature is informed by pre-literary categories such as ritual, myth and folk tale. We next realize that the relation between these categories and literature is by no means purely one of descent, as we find them reappearing in the greatest classics—in fact there seems to be a general tendency on the part of the great classics to revert to them.

Northrop Frye, 1951

During the 1960s regional American theaters developed, and women's and minority theater gained in prominence. African-American theater flourished with the establishment of the Black Arts Theater School in New York City in 1964. By 1968 about forty African-American arts organizations existed, including the New

York-based Negro Ensemble Company, which aimed to continuously present black drama "without regard to the whims of commercial theater." This increased African-American consciousness in the theater spawned such new playwrights as James Baldwin, Lorraine Hansberry, Ed Bullins, Douglas Turner Ward, Amiri Baraka (LeRoi Jones), Ntozake Shange, and Angus Wilson. Hansberry was probably the most critically acclaimed, although in her brief lifetime she completed only two plays—*A Raisin in the Sun* (1959) and *The Sign in Sidney Brustein's Window* (1964).

One of the important dramatists to emerge in the 1960s was Edward Albee. In works such as *The American Dream* (1961) and *Who's Afraid of Virginia Woolf?* (1962), he combined fantasy and reality. Critics proclaimed him the first American absurdist dramatist, in the tradition of the Irish playwright Samuel Beckett.

During the 1960s Off Off Broadway assumed the role Off Broadway had played in the 1950s. Off Off Broadway groups of the 1960s, generally working without pay and on tiny budgets, produced hundreds of plays by new playwrights, including Ronald Tavel, Charles Ludlam, Lanford Wilson, Maria Irene Fornès, Terrence McNally, Adrienne Kennedy, Luís Valdez, David Mamet, and Sam Shepard. Such writers moved American drama from the realism of Miller and Williams toward more experimental forms. Of the Off-Off Broadway organizations promoting this change, some of the most influential have been the Living Theater, La Mama Experimental Theater, the Ridiculous Theater Company, and the Public Theater.

Created in 1947 by the husband-and-wife team of Julian Beck and Judith Malina, the Living Theater reached its zenith during the 1960s and 1970s. The group's productions emphasized improvisation, ritual actions, nonverbal communications, and other devices from the Theater of Cruelty (based on the theories of the French actor and director Antonin Artaud). In one of the Living Theater's most celebrated productions, *Paradise Now* (1968), the actors confronted members of the audience, seeking to insult and humiliate them. Such radical efforts to involve playgoers were attacked as counterproductive, and the Living Theater has never regained its former influence. In contrast, La Mama, the Ridiculous Theater Company, and the Public Theater are all still potent forces in American theater. Under the energetic guidance of La Mama's founder, Elaine Stewart, that group has mounted avant-garde performances since 1962. The Ridiculous Theater Company was headed by Charles Ludlam until his death. At the forefront of gay drama, the group has presented fantasies based on myths derived from the popular culture, with the key roles played by female impersonators. And since Joseph Papp transformed New York City's Astor Library into the Public Theater in 1967, that group has continued to present new playwrights, such as Charles Gordone and David Rabe.

The most prolific and successful of the new writers to have originated in Off Off Broadway is Sam Shepard, whose works were first produced in 1967 and contain a wide variety of American stereotypes, from rock stars to cowboys to gangsters. His plays, such as *Buried Child* (1978) and *A Lie of the Mind* (1985), have been acclaimed for their imaginative language, a mix of slang, rock and roll, and B-movie dialogue.

Experimental theater has continued in new forms. One of them is performance art, which developed out of experimental "happenings" staged during the 1960s when performers combined elements from other media such as dance, film, and music. Today's performance artists, such as Laurie Anderson and Robert Wilson, still rely on mixed media to highlight dramatic intent. And if Wilson and Anderson represent the radical extreme of American theater, new dramatists such as Wendy Wasserstein, Angus Wilson, and David Henry Hwang fit more into the mainstream. Their work, and that of Michael Bennett and Stephen Sondheim, innovative artists in the field of musical drama, has proven successful even on Broadway. According to Hwang, "American theater is beginning to discover . . . . Black theater, women's theater, gay theater, Asian American theater, Hispanic theater." But as the twentieth century draws to a close, the theater is struggling with the entertainment industry—movies and television—to maintain itself as a vital community, one engaged in artistic renewal.

Eugene O'Neill
(1888–1953)

The private life of a theatrical family typically includes the extension of drama from the stage to the household; daily occurrences become small melodramatic scenes insisting on crisis and resolution. The circumstances of Eugene O'Neill's upbringing have all the elements, as O'Neill was himself excruciatingly aware, of a play by the man from whom O'Neill took his literary models, August Strindberg. In O'Neill's life and his work, as in Strindberg's plays, to be a member of a family is to participate in extravagant lies to conceal from public view the family's inner weaknesses and moral blight. Awash in alcohol and addiction and suffering under what he perceived as the "tyrannies" of Irish Catholicism, O'Neill's family life prepared him for the manic velocity of his early manhood.

Eugene Gladstone O'Neill was born in New York City in 1888. His father, James O'Neill, was an actor famous for his portrayal of the hero in *The Count of Monte Cristo*, a potboiler by the playwright Alexander Dumas. James shunted his family from town to town on the American theater circuit. In the midst of this rootless life, the only measure of consistency was James O'Neill's nightly performance as the Count of Monte Cristo—a drudgery that went on for thirty years. The O'Neills traveled from hotel to hotel, trying to keep some semblance of a home. O'Neill's mother, Ella Quinlan, became ill while she was pregnant with her second child; the child later died. The family held James O'Neill at fault for engaging the services of the least expensive physician available. She had been treated with morphine, a drug to which she remained addicted for the rest of her life. Eugene O'Neill's memories of this childhood were agonizingly recreated in his masterpiece, *Long Day's Journey Into Night*, which was written in 1940 but first produced in 1956.

Rebellious and unhappy through years of parochial school training, O'Neill entered Princeton University in 1906, only to be expelled a year later because of a prank. Although he married Kathleen Jenkins, a New York socialite, in 1909, O'Neill succumbed to the romantic lure of life at sea. He drifted aimlessly from port to port but returned home in 1911 and soon afterward made a feeble attempt at suicide. In 1912 O'Neill divorced his wife and became severely ill with tuberculosis; he entered Gaylord Farm Sanatorium in Wallingford, Connecticut, for treatment. Because his grandfather had died from the disease, O'Neill considered his own death imminent (but that was not to occur until 1953). At the sanatorium he read extensively, from European philosophy to plays. He began to form his own belief about the grim fate determining all existence, the destructive cycles of struggle and defeat.

When O'Neill left the sanatorium in June 1913, he was surprised and grateful to be alive and devoted himself to the writing profession. While writing his early plays, O'Neill studied at Harvard University with George Pierce Baker, who instructed many of the early twentieth-century playwrights and was then considered the father of American drama. O'Neill's first plays, primarily one-act plays, evoke the melodrama that had surrounded him and that he had survived, but in his later plays great emotion coexists with a skepticism that deflates it. Even as O'Neill, in emulation of Strindberg, turned to realism, his work retained an almost tidal emotion while concentrating upon the increasingly narrow worlds of the family.

In 1915 O'Neill moved to Provincetown, Massachusetts; while there he courted Agnes Boulton, who in 1918 became his second wife. In 1916 the Provincetown Players produced his play *Bound East for Cardiff*. The focus of the Players, a group of playwrights and actors committed to American theater and American plays, was unusual in a time when theater groups tended to borrow plays from abroad. In retrospect, the arrival of Eugene O'Neill in Provincetown might be seen as the beginning of modern American theater, because his name and twentieth-century American drama would become indissolubly linked. This link has regrettably caused some equally important American playwrights to be lost in O'Neill's shadow. Susan Glaspell and George Cook, for example, members of the Provincetown Players, were significant for their own works and for their dedication to a theater struggling to get out from under the pervading influences of European drama as well as for their careful nurturing of O'Neill's early work.

Cook's commitment to the scope of O'Neill's talent took physical shape in the set Cook created for *The Emperor Jones* (1920). The dome setting cost the Players' entire budget, but the conception was arresting. O'Neill calls for drumbeats throughout the play to signal changes in emotion: fear, confusion, triumph. Most of the play is delivered in soliloquies, with other characters often privy to the speeches.

O'Neill's special abilities as a playwright were widely appreciated with the 1920 New York production of *Beyond the Horizon*. The play, a Pulitzer Prize winner, depicts the failure and disillusionment of a poor farming family, the Mayos. O'Neill's subsequent play *Anna Christie* (1921), a revision of the unsuccessful *Chris Christopherson*, earned the playwright another Pulitzer Prize. Yet another modern American tragedy, *Anna Christie* represented a "backward look" to O'Neill, who favored the experimental use of sound and character development of *The Emperor Jones*. He returned to experimenting with other forms in plays such as *The Hairy Ape* (1922) and *All God's Chillun Got Wings* (1924).

Desire Under the Elms, produced in 1924, won O'Neill even wider critical acclaim. By setting the play on the Cabot Farm in Connecticut, O'Neill gave it a degree of intimacy (he had just purchased a thirty-acre estate in Ridgefield, Connecticut); by setting it in 1850, he gave it a degree of distance. Through an intricate network of marriages and deceit, the Cabot family vies for possession of the farm. The aging patriarch Ephraim Cabot returns to his farm with a new, young wife, the scheming former housemaid Abbie Putnam. Eben, Ephraim's third son, vengefully begins an affair with Abbie as he was convinced that Ephraim had killed Eben's mother through overwork. The illegitimate birth of a child

A scene from a production of O'Neill's Desire Under the Elms.

parented by Eben and Abbie sets the family further at odds. Eben announces his plan to desert Abbie, and, in a desperate attempt to prove that she loves him and does not want his family's farm, she murders the child.

Watching over these melodramatic struggles are the elms that with "crushing, jealous absorption" brood over the house with a "sinister maternity." O'Neill's fascination with Greek tragedy invites a comparison to Medea, a sorceress who kills her children. *Desire Under the Elms* was O'Neill's first attempt at writing in the tradition of Greek tragedy. Abbie is carefully patterned after Phaedra, the queen in Euripedes's play *Hippolytus* whose desire for her husband's son is uncontrollable.

O'Neill's first Broadway play, *Marco Millions*, was produced in 1928. A complex allegory of religion, commerce, and salvation, the play traces the movement of the main character, Marco Polo, from poet to salesman through a course that includes a papal visit. While at work on his other plays, O'Neill began the trilogy *Mourning Becomes Electra*, written in France between 1929 and 1931 after O'Neill had divorced his second wife and married his third wife, Carlotta Monterey. *Mourning Becomes Electra* consists of three sections—*The Homecoming, The Hunted,* and *The Haunted*—in which O'Neill sought to give a modern psychological approximation of the Greek tragedy's sense of fate. The play went through many drafts and revisions as O'Neill used Aeschylus's *Oresteia* as his model.

In the Pulitzer Prize winning *Strange Interlude* (1928) O'Neill revived the use of soliloquy in performance. More than just a halt in the dramatic action or the necessary introduction of pertinent information by the character, soliloquies in many of O'Neill's plays abruptly shift the audience's perception of a character's state of mind or motive. Allowing some dramatic tension, depending on who overhears the soliloquy, this device reminded critics of the finest Renaissance creations.

Year after year O'Neill produced plays that have endured in American theater. *The Iceman Cometh* (1946) captures the rosy, transitory glow of the drinking house. Set in Harry Hope's Saloon and Boardinghouse, the characters spin dreams and tell lies to pass the time. They await the arrival of Hickey, a traveling salesman who makes an annual visit to drink, buy drinks, celebrate Harry's birthday, and joke about his own wife's affair with the iceman. Hickey arrives sober and proceeds to dispel everyone's dreams, returning them to the image of their own devastating failures. The play ends when Hickey confesses that he murdered his wife to end the suffering he had been causing her, and Don Parritt, a character hiding from the police, admits that he has turned his mother in for money. O'Neill's women are a constant reminder of failure. *The Iceman Cometh*, written in 1939, was not produced until 1946 and was the last new play to be produced on Broadway in O'Neill's lifetime. When the play was revived on Broadway in 1958, more than four years after O'Neill's death, it renewed interest in his work, beginning new productions that offered critical reinterpretations of his most powerful plays.

Elements of O'Neill's family life appear in all his plays—domineering fathers riding their children, drunken men contemplating their failures, women at once guilt ridden and contemptuous—but in *Long Day's Journey Into Night* the family is portrayed with a painful accuracy that lays bare the soul-sickness of years of entanglements, blame, guilt, and sorrow that underlie a cultivated appearance of propriety. O'Neill's painstaking control is apparent in his elaborate, exacting stage directions and instructions about how the lines should be delivered (and thus how they should be received). Like a choreographer, O'Neill positions the family members where a loss of poise or balance leads to an unraveling or to self-exposure.

Mary Tyrone, the mother in *Long Day's Journey*, moves from blame to sudden revelation to confused detachment, all in the course of a single speech. Her recent return from a sanatorium, where she was "treated" for morphine addiction, is the object of her husband's and her sons' fragile hope that "this time" will be "different." As the precarious peace crumbles, the stress on all the characters is revealed. Over and over old stories of betrayal and wrongdoing are told to excuse present shortcomings. The elaborate dance of the two sons, Jamie and Edmund (whose continual coughing echoes in the house, grimly diagnosing his tuberculosis), moves between their own despair and their united fury at their father's miserly ways. The story O'Neill tells in *Long Day's Journey* is painful not only because of the clear, autobiographical elements, but also because as an American playwright—whose most famous colleagues in twentieth-century theater consistently represent either their own or their families' alcoholism—he is telling a peculiarly American story of what lies between the appearance and the reality of American family life.

Like *Long Day's Journey*, *A Moon for the Misbegotten* (1952) stretches time to create a sense of endlessness. The actual length of time, however, is an effect of O'Neill's subtle manipulation of the characters' behavior as they change in response to situations unbearably and destructively repetitive. He composed *A Moon for the Misbegotten*, which is said to deal with his brother Jamie's deterioration, in 1943 after O'Neill had supposedly retired. He wrote continuously throughout his life, and some of his "lost" plays, never produced, were published as late as 1972. His complex, vivid works and his varied role in American theater earned him a Nobel Prize for literature in 1936 and deserve renewed attention from contemporary audiences.

Suggested Readings: *Beyond the Horizon,*1920. *The Emperor Jones,* 1920. *Anna Christie,* 1921. *The Hairy Ape,* 1922. *All God's Chillun Got Wings,* 1924. *Strange Interlude,* 1928. *Mourning Becomes Electra,* 1931. *The Iceman Cometh,* 1946. *A Moon for the Misbegotten,* 1947. *Long Day's Journey Into Night,* 1956. *A Touch of the Poet,* 1957. *Ten "Lost" Plays,* ed. B. Cerf, 1963. *Poems 1912–1944,* ed. D. C. Gallup, 1980. E. A. Engel, *The Haunted Heroes of Eugene O'Neill,* 1953. J.

Gassner, *Eugene O'Neill*, 1965. J. H. Raleigh, *The Plays of Eugene O'Neill*, 1965. E. Tornqvuist, *A Drama of Souls*, 1968. A. and B. Gelb, *O'Neill*, 1973. L. Schaeffer, *Eugene O'Neill: Son and Artist*, 1973. C. W. E. Bigsby, *20th-Century American Drama*, 1984. H. Bloom, ed., *Eugene O'Neill: Modern Critical Interpretations*, 1987.

Text Used: *The Plays of Eugene O'Neill*, 1924.

DESIRE UNDER THE ELMS

CHARACTERS

EPHRAIM CABOT

SIMEON ⎫
PETER ⎬ *his sons*
EBEN ⎭

ABBIE PUTNAM

YOUNG GIRL, TWO FARMERS, *the* FIDDLER, *a* SHERIFF, *and other folk from the neighboring farms.*

The action of the entire play takes place in, and immediately outside of, the Cabot farmhouse in New England, in the year 1850. The south end of the house faces front to a stone wall with a wooden gate at center opening on a country road. The house is in good condition but in need of paint. Its walls are a sickly grayish, the green of the shutters faded. Two enormous elms are on each side of the house. They bend their trailing branches down over the roof. They appear to protect and at the same time subdue. There is a sinister maternity in their aspect, a crushing, jealous absorption. They have developed from their intimate contact with the life of man in the house an appalling humaneness. They brood oppressively over the house. They are like exhausted women resting their sagging breasts and hands and hair on its roof, and when it rains their tears trickle down monotonously and rot on the shingles.

There is a path running from the gate around the right corner of the house to the front door. A narrow porch is on this side. The end wall facing us has two windows in its upper story, two larger ones on the floor below. The two upper are those of the father's bedroom and that of the brothers. On the left, ground floor, is the kitchen — on the right, the parlor, the shades of which are always drawn down.

PART I, SCENE I

(Exterior of the farmhouse. It is sunset of a day at the beginning of summer in the year 1850. There is no wind and everything is still. The sky above the roof is suffused with deep colors, the green of the elms glows, but the house is in shadow, seeming pale and washed out by contrast.)

(A door opens and Eben Cabot comes to the end of the porch and stands looking down the road to the right. He has a large bell in his hand and this he swings mechanically, awakening a deafening clangor. Then he puts his hands on his hips

and stares up at the sky. He sighs with a puzzled awe and blurts out with halting appreciation.)

EBEN: God! Purty! *(His eyes fall and he stares about him frowningly. He is twenty-five, tall and sinewy. His face is well formed, good-looking, but its expression is resentful and defensive. His defiant, dark eyes remind one of a wild animal's in captivity. Each day is a cage in which he finds himself trapped but inwardly unsubdued. There is a fierce repressed vitality about him. He has black hair, mustache, a thin curly trace of beard. He is dressed in rough farm clothes.)*

(He spits on the ground with intense disgust, turns, and goes back into the house.)

(Simeon and Peter come in from their work in the fields. They are tall men, much older than their half-brother [Simeon is thirty-nine and Peter thirty-seven], built on a squarer, simpler model, fleshier in body, more bovine and homelier in face, shrewder and more practical. Their shoulders stoop a bit from years of farm work. They clump heavily along in their clumsy thick-soled boots caked with earth. Their clothes, their faces, hands, bare arms, and throats are earth-stained. They smell of earth. They stand together for a moment in front of the house and, as if with the one impulse, stare dumbly up at the sky, leaning on their hoes. Their faces have a compressed, unresigned expression. As they look upward, this softens.)

SIMEON *(grudgingly)*: Purty.

PETER: Ay-eh.

SIMEON *(suddenly)*: Eighteen years ago.

PETER: What?

SIMEON: Jenn. My woman. She died.

PETER: I'd fergot.

SIMEON: I rec'lect—now an' agin. Makes it lonesome. She'd hair long's a hoss' tail—an' yaller like gold!

PETER: Waal—she's gone. *(This with indifferent finality—then after a pause.)* They's gold in the West, Sim.

SIMEON *(still under the influence of sunset—vaguely)*: In the sky?

PETER: Waal—in a manner o' speakin'—that's the promise. *(Growing excited.)* Gold in the sky—in the West—Golden Gate—Californi-a!—Goldest West!—fields o' gold!

SIMEON *(excited in his turn)*: Fortunes layin' just atop o' the ground waitin' t' be picked! Solomon's mines, they says! *(For a moment they continue looking up at the sky—then their eyes drop.)*

PETER *(with sardonic bitterness)*: Here—it's stones atop o' the ground—stones atop o' stones—makin' stone walls—year atop o' year—him 'n' yew 'n' me 'n' then Eben—makin' stone walls fur him to fence us in!

SIMEON: We've wuked. Give our strength. Give our years. Plowed 'em under in the ground—*(He stamps rebelliously.)*—rottin'—makin' soil for his crops! *(A pause.)* Waal—the farm pays good for hereabouts.

PETER: If we plowed in Californi-a, they'd be lumps o' gold in the furrow!

SIMEON: Californi-a's t'other side o'earth, a'most. We got t' calc'late—

PETER *(after a pause)*: 'Twould be hard fur me, too, to give up what we've 'arned here by our sweat. *(A pause. Eben sticks his head out of the dining room window, listening.)*

SIMEON: Ay-eh. *(A pause.)* Mebbe—he'll die soon.

PETER (*doubtfully*):   Mebbe.

SIMEON: Mebbe—fur all we knows—he's dead now.

PETER: Ye'd need proof.

SIMEON: He's been gone two months—with no word.

PETER: Left us in the fields an evenin' like this. Hitched up an' druv off into the West. That's plum onnateral. He hain't never been off this farm 'ceptin' t' the village in thirty year or more, not since he married Eben's maw. (*A pause. Shrewdly.*) I calc'late we might git him declared crazy by the court.

SIMEON: He skinned 'em too slick. He got the best o' all on 'em. They'd never b'lieve him crazy. (*A pause.*) We got t' wait—till he's underground.

EBEN: (*with a sardonic chuckle*):   Honor thy father! (*They turn startled, and stare at him. He grins, then scowls.*) I pray he's died. (*They stare at him. He continues matter-of-factly.*) Supper's ready.

SIMEON AND PETER (*together*):   Ay-eh.

EBEN: (*gazing up at the sky*):   Sun's downin' purty.

SIMEON AND PETER (*together*):   Ay-eh. They's gold in the West.

EBEN: Ay-eh. (*Pointing.*) Yonder atop o' the hill pasture, ye mean?

SIMEON AND PETER (*together*):   In Californi-a!

EBEN: Hunh? (*Stares at them indifferently for a second, then drawls.*) Waal—supper's gittin' cold. (*He turns back into kitchen.*)

SIMEON (*startled—smacks his lips*):   I air hungry!

PETER (*sniffing*):   I smells bacon!

SIMEON (*with hungry appreciation*):   Bacon's good!

PETER (*in same tone*):   Bacon's bacon! (*They turn, shouldering each other, their bodies bumping and rubbing together as they hurry clumsily to their food, like two friendly oxen toward their evening meal. They disappear around the right corner of house and can be heard entering the door.*)

SCENE II

(*The color fades from the sky. Twilight begins. The interior of the kitchen is now visible. A pine table is at center, a cook-stove in the right rear corner, four rough wooden chairs, a tallow candle on the table. In the middle of the rear wall is fastened a big advertising poster with a ship in full sail and the word "California" in big letters. Kitchen utensils hang from nails. Everything is neat and in order but the atmosphere is of a men's camp kitchen rather than that of a home.*)

(*Places for three are laid. Eben takes boiled potatoes and bacon from the stove and puts them on the table, also a loaf of bread and a crock of water. Simeon and Peter shoulder in, slump down in their chairs without a word. Eben joins them. The three eat in silence for a moment, the two elder as naturally unrestrained as beasts of the field, Eben picking at his food without appetite, glancing at them with a tolerant dislike.*)

SIMEON (*suddenly turns to Eben*):   Looky here! Ye'd oughtn't t' said that, Eben.

PETER: 'Twa'n't righteous.

EBEN: What?

SIMEON: Ye prayed he'd died.

EBEN: Waal—don't yew pray it? (*A pause.*)

PETER: He's our Paw.

EBEN (*violently*):   Not mine!

SIMEON (*dryly*):   Ye'd not let no one else say that about yer Maw! Ha! (*He gives one abrupt sardonic guffaw. Peter grins.*)

EBEN (*very pale*):   I meant—I hain't his'n—I hain't like him—he hain't me!

PETER (*dryly*):   Wait till ye've growed his age!

EBEN (*intensely*):   I'm Maw—every drop o' blood! (*A pause. They stare at him with indifferent curiosity.*)

PETER (*reminiscently*):   She was good t' Sim 'n' me. A good Stepmaw's scurse.

SIMEON: She was good t' everyone.

EBEN (*greatly moved, gets to his feet and makes an awkward bow to each of them—stammering*):   I be thankful t' ye. I'm her—her heir. (*He sits down in confusion.*)

PETER (*after a pause—judicially*):   She was good even t' him.

EBEN (*fiercely*):   An' fur thanks he killed her!

SIMEON (*after a pause*):   No one never kills nobody. It's allus somethin'. That's the murderer.

EBEN: Didn't he slave Maw t' death?

PETER: He's slaved himself t' death. He's slaved Sim 'n' me 'n' yew t' death—on'y none o' us hain't died—yit.

SIMEON: It's somethin'—drivin' him—t' drive us!

EBEN (*vengefully*):   Waal—I hold him t' jedgment! (*Then scornfully.*) Somethin'! What's somethin'?

SIMEON: Dunno.

EBEN (*sardonically*):   What's drivin' yew to Californi-a, mebbe? (*They look at him in surprise.*) Oh, I've heerd ye! (*Then, after a pause.*) But ye'll never go t' the gold fields!

PETER (*Assertively*):   Mebbe!

EBEN: Whar'll ye git the money?

PETER: We kin walk. It's an a'mighty ways—Californi-a—but if yew was t' put all the steps we've walked on this farm end t' end we'd be in the moon!

EBEN: The Injuns'll skulp ye on the plains.

SIMEON (*with grim humor*):   We'll mebbe make 'em pay a hair fur a hair!

EBEN (*decisively*):   But t'aint that. Ye won't never go because ye'll wait here fur yer share o' the farm, thinkin' allus he'll die soon.

SIMEON (*after a pause*):   We've a right.

PETER: Two-thirds belongs t'us.

EBEN (*jumping to his feet*):   Ye've no right! She wa'n't yewr Maw! It was her farm! Didn't he steal it from her? She's dead. It's my farm.

SIMEON (*sardonically*):   Tell that t' Paw—when he comes! I'll bet ye a dollar he'll laugh—fur once in his life. Ha! (*He laughs himself in one single mirthless bark.*)

PETER (*amused in turn, echoes his brother*):   Ha!

SIMEON (*after a pause*):   What've ye got held agin us, Eben? Year arter year it's skulked in yer eye—somethin'.

PETER: Ay-eh.

EBEN: Ay-eh. They's somethin'. (*Suddenly exploding.*) Why didn't ye never stand between him 'n' my Maw when he was slavin' her to her grave—t' pay her back fur the kindness she done t' yew? (*There is a long pause. They stare at him in surprise.*)

SIMEON: Waal—the stock'd got t' be watered.

PETER: 'R they was woodin' t' do.

SIMEON: 'R plowin'.

PETER: 'R hayin'.

SIMEON: 'R spreadin' manure.

PETER: 'R weedin'.

SIMEON: 'R prunin'.

PETER: 'R milkin'.

EBEN (*breaking in harshly*): An' makin' walls—stone atop o' stone—makin' walls till yer heart's a stone ye heft up out o' the way o' growth onto a stone wall t' wall in yer heart!

SIMEON (*matter-of-factly*): We never had no time t' meddle.

PETER (*to Eben*): Yew was fifteen afore yer Maw died—an' big fur yer age. Why didn't ye never do nothing'?

EBEN (*harshly*): They was chores t' do, wa'n't they? (*A pause—then slowly.*) It was on'y arter she died I come to think o' it. Me cookin'—doin' her work—that made me know her, suffer her sufferin'—she'd come back t'help—come back t' bile potatoes—come back t' fry bacon—come back t' bake biscuits—come back all cramped up t' shake the fire, an' carry ashes, her eyes weepin' an' bloody with smoke an' cinders same's they used t' be. She still comes back—stands by the stove thar in the evenin'—she can't find it nateral sleepin' an' restin' in peace. She can't git used t' bein' free—even in her grave.

SIMEON: She never complained none.

EBEN: She'd got too tired. She'd got too used t' bein' too tired. That was what he done. (*With vengeful passion.*) An' sooner'r later, I'll meddle. I'll say the thin's I didn't say then t' him! I'll yell 'em at the top o' my lungs. I'll see t' it my Maw gits some rest an' sleep in her grave! (*He sits down again, relapsing into a brooding silence. They look at him with a queer indifferent curiosity.*)

PETER (*after a pause*): Whar in tarnation d'ye s'pose he went, Sim?

SIMEON: Dunno. He druv off in the buggy, all spick an' span, with the mare all breshed an' shiny, druv off clackin' his tongue an' wavin' his whip. I remember it right well. I was finishin' plowin', it was spring an' May an' sunset, an' gold in the West, an' he druv off into it. I yells "Whar ye goin', Paw?" an' he hauls up by the stone wall a jiffy. His old snake's eyes was glitterin' in the sun like he'd been drinkin' a jugful an' he says with a mule's grin: "Don't ye run away till I come back!"

PETER: Wonder if he knowed we was wantin' fur Californi-a?

SIMEON: Mebbe. I didn't say nothin' and he says, lookin' kinder queer an' sick: "I been hearin' the hens cluckin' an' the roosters crowin' all the durn day. I been listenin' t' the cows lowin' an' everythin' else kickin' up till I can't stand it no more. It's spring an' I'm feelin' damned," he says. "Damned like an old bare hickory tree fit on'y fur burnin'," he says. An' then I calc'late I must've looked a mite hopeful, fur he adds real spry and vicious: "But don't git no fool idee I'm dead. I've sworn t' live a hundred an' I'll do it, if on'y t' spite yer sinful greed! An' now I'm ridin' out t' learn God's message t' me in the spring, like the prophets done. An' yew git back t' yer plowin'," he says. An' he druv off singin' a hymn. I thought he was drunk—'r I'd stopped him goin'.

EBEN (*scornfully*): No, ye wouldn't! Ye're scared o' him. He's stronger—inside—than both o' ye put together!

PETER (*sardonically*): An' yew—be yew Samson?[1]

---

[1] In the Old Testament, a hero known for his great strength.

EBEN: I'm gittin' stronger. I kin feel it growin' in me—growin' an' growin'—till it'll bust out—! (*He gets up and puts on his coat and a hat. They watch him, gradually breaking into grins. Eben avoids their eyes sheepishly.*) I'm goin' out fur a spell—up the road.

PETER: T' the village.

SIMEON: T' see Minnie?

EBEN (*defiantly*): Ay-eh!

PETER (*jeeringly*): The Scarlet Woman!

SIMEON: Lust—that's what's growin' in ye!

EBEN: Waal—she's purty!

PETER: She's been purty fur twenty year.

SIMEON: A new coat o' paint'll make a heifer out of forty.

EBEN: She hain't forty!

PETER: If she hain't, she's teeterin' on the edge.

EBEN (*desperately*): What d'yew know—

PETER: All they is . . . Sim knew her—an' then me arter—

SIMEON: An' Paw kin tell yew somethin' too! He was fust!

EBEN: D'ye mean t' say he . . . ?

SIMEON (*with a grin*): Ay-eh! We air his heirs in everythin'!

EBEN (*intensely*): That's more to it! That grows on it! It'll bust soon! (*Then violently.*) I'll go smash my fist in her face! (*He pulls open the door in rear violently.*)

SIMEON (*with a wink at Peter—drawlingly*): Mebbe—but the night's wa'm—purty—by the time ye git thar mebbe ye'll kiss her instead!

PETER: Sart'n he will! (*They both roar with coarse laughter. Eben rushes out and slams the door—then the outside front door—comes around the corner of the house and stands still by the gate, staring up at the sky.*)

SIMEON (*looking after him*): Like his Paw.

PETER: Dead spit an' image!

SIMEON: Dog'll eat dog!

PETER: Ay-eh. (*Pause. With yearning.*) Mebbe a year from now we'll be in Californi-a.

SIMEON: Ay-eh. (*A pause. Both yawn.*) Let's git t'bed. (*He blows out the candle. They go out door in rear. Eben stretches his arms up to the sky—rebelliously.*)

EBEN: Waal—thar's a star, an' somewhar's they's him, an' here's me, an' thar's Min up the road—in the same night. What if I does kiss her? She's like t'night, she's soft 'n' wa'm, her eyes kin wink like a star, her mouth's wa'm, her arms're wa'm, she smells like a wa'm plowed field, she's purty . . . Ay-eh! By God A'mighty she's purty, an' I don't give a damn how many sins she's sinned afore mine or who she's sinned 'em with, my sin's as purty as any one on 'em! (*He strides off down the road to the left.*)

SCENE III

(*It is the pitch darkness just before dawn. Eben comes in from the left and goes around to the porch, feeling his way, chuckling bitterly and cursing half-aloud to himself.*)

EBEN: The cussed old miser! *(He can be heard going in the front door. There is a pause as he goes upstairs, then a loud knock on the bedroom door of the brothers.)* Wake up!

SIMEON *(startledly)*:   Who's thar?

EBEN *(Pushing open the door and coming in, a lighted candle in his hand. The bedroom of the brothers is revealed. Its ceiling is the sloping roof. They can stand upright only close to the center dividing wall of the upstairs. Simeon and Peter are in a double bed, front. Eben's cot is to the rear. Eben has a mixture of silly grin and vicious scowl on his face.)*: I be!

PETER *(angrily)*:   What in hell's-fire . . . ?

EBEN: I got news fur ye! Ha! *(He gives one abrupt sardonic guffaw.)*

SIMEON *(angrily)*:   Couldn't ye hold it 'til we'd got our sleep?

EBEN: It's nigh sunup. *(Then explosively.)* He's gone an' married agen!

SIMEON AND PETER *(explosively)*:   Paw?

EBEN: Got himself hitched to a female 'bout thirty-five—an' purty, they says . . .

SIMEON *(aghast)*:   It's a durn lie!

PETER: Who says?

SIMEON: They been stringin' ye!

EBEN: Think I'm a dunce, do ye? The hull village says. The preacher from New Dover, he brung the news—told it t'our preacher—New Dover, that's whar the old loon got himself hitched—that's whar the woman lived—

PETER *(no longer doubting—stunned)*:   Waal . . . !

SIMEON *(the same)*:   Waal . . . !

EBEN *(sitting down on a bed—with vicious hatred)*:   Ain't he a devil out o' hell? It's jest t' spite us—the damned old mule!

PETER *(after a pause)*:   Everythin'll go t'her now.

SIMEON: Ay-eh. *(A pause—dully.)* Waal—if it's done—

PETER: It's done us. *(Pause—then persuasively.)* They's gold in the fields o' Californi-a, Sim. No good a-stayin' here now.

SIMEON: Jest what I was a-thinkin'. *(Then with decision.)* S'well fust's last! Let's light out and git this mornin'.

PETER: Suits me.

EBEN: Ye must like walkin'.

SIMEON *(sardonically)*:   If ye'd grow wings on us we'd fly thar!

EBEN: Ye'd like ridin' better—on a boat, wouldn't ye? *(Fumbles in his pocket and takes out a crumpled sheet of foolscap.)* Waal, if ye sign this ye kin ride on a boat. I've had it writ out an' ready in case ye'd ever go. It says fur three hundred dollars t' each ye agree yewr shares o' the farm is sold t' me. *(They look suspiciously at the paper. A pause.)*

SIMEON *(wonderingly)*:   But if he's hitched agen—

PETER: An' whar'd yew git that sum o' money, anyways?

EBEN *(cunningly)*:   I know whar it's hid. I been waitin'—Maw told me. She knew whar it lay fur years, but she was waitin' . . . It's her'n—the money he hoarded from her farm an' hid from Maw. It's my money by rights now.

PETER: Whar's it hid?

EBEN *(cunningly)*:   Whar yew won't never find it without me. Maw spied on him—'r she'd never knowed. *(A pause. They look at him suspiciously, and he at them.)* Waal, is it fa'r trade?

SIMEON: Dunno.

PETER: Dunno.

SIMEON (*looking at window*):   Sky's grayin'.

PETER: Ye better start the fire, Eben.

SIMEON: An' fix some vittles.

EBEN: Ay-eh. (*Then with a forced jocular heartiness.*) I'll git ye a good one. If ye're startin' t' hoof it t' Californi-a ye'll need somethin' that'll stick t' yer ribs. (*He turns to the door, adding meaningly.*) But ye kin ride on a boat if ye'll swap. (*He stops at the door and pauses. They stare at him.*)

SIMEON (*suspiciously*):   Whar was ye all night?

EBEN (*defiantly*):   Up t' Min's. (*Then slowly.*) Walkin' thar, fust I felt 's if I'd kiss her; then I got a-thinkin' o' what ye'd said o' him an' her an' I says, I'll bust her nose fur that! Then I got t' the village an' heerd the news an' I got madder'n hell an' run all the way t' Min's not knowin' what I'd do— (*He pauses—then sheepishly but more defiantly.*) Waal—when I seen her, I didn't hit her—nor I didn't kiss her nuther—I begun t'beller like a calf an' cuss at the same time, I was so durn mad—an' she got scared—an' I jest grabbed holt an' tuk her! (*Proudly.*) Yes, sirree! I tuk her. She may've been his'n—an' your'n, too—but she's mine now!

SIMEON (*dryly*):   In love, air yew?

EBEN (*with lofty scorn*):   Love! I don't take no stock in sech slop!

PETER (*winking at Simeon*):   Mebbe Eben's aimin' t' marry, too.

SIMEON: Min'd make a true faithful he'pmeet! (*They snicker.*)

EBEN: What do I care fur her—'ceptin' she's round an' wa'm? The p'int is she was his'n—an' now she b'longs t' me! (*He goes to the door—then turns—rebelliously.* An' Min hain't sech a bad un. They's worse'n Min in the world, I'll bet ye! Wait'll we see this cow the Old Man's hitched t'! She'll beat Min, I got a notion! (*He starts to go out.*)

SIMEON (*suddenly*):   Mebbe ye'll try t' make her your'n, too?

PETER: Ha! (*He gives a sardonic laugh of relish at this idea.*)

EBEN (*spitting with disgust*):   Her—here—sleepin' with him—stealin' my Maw's farm! I'd as soon pet a skunk 'r kiss a snake! (*He goes out. The two stare after him suspiciously. A pause. They listen to his steps receding.*)

PETER: He's startin' the fire.

SIMEON: I'd like t' ride t' Californi-a—but—

PETER: Min might o' put some scheme in his head.

SIMEON: Mebbe it's all a lie 'bout Paw marryin'. We'd best wait an' see the bride.

PETER: An' don't sign nothin' till we does!

SIMEON: Nor till we've tested it's good money! (*Then with a grin.*) But if Paw's hitched we'd be sellin' Eben somethin' we'd never git nohow!

PETER: We'll wait an' see. (*Then with sudden vindictive anger.*) An' till he comes, let's yew 'n' me not wuk a lick, let Eben tend to thin's if he's a mind t', let's us jest sleep an' eat an' drink likker, an' let the hull damned farm go t' blazes!

SIMEON (*excitedly*):   By God, we've 'arned a rest! We'll play rich fur a change. I hain't a-going to stir outa bed till breakfast's ready.

PETER: An' on the table!

SIMEON (*after a pause—thoughtfully*):   What d'ye calc'late she'll be like—our new Maw? Like Eben thinks?

PETER: More'n' likely.

SIMEON (*vindictively*):   Waal—I hope she's a she-devil that'll make him wish he was dead an' livin' in the pit o' hell fur comfort!

PETER (*fervently*):   Amen!

SIMEON (*imitating his father's voice*):   "I'm ridin' out t' learn God's message t' me in the spring like the prophets done," he says. I'll bet right then an' thar he knew plumb well he was goin' whorin', the stinkin' old hypocrite!

SCENE IV

(Same as Scene II—shows the interior of the kitchen with a lighted candle on table. It is a gray dawn outside. Simeon and Peter are just finishing their breakfast. Eben sits before his plate of untouched food, brooding frowningly.)

PETER (*glancing at him rather irritably*):   Lookin' glum don't help none.

SIMEON (*sarcastically*):   Sorrowin' over his lust o' the flesh!

PETER (*with a grin*):   Was she yer fust?

EBEN (*angrily*):   None o' yer business. (*A pause.*) I was thinkin' o' him. I got a notion he's gittin' near—I kin feel him comin' on like yew kin feel malaria chill afore it takes ye.

PETER: It's too early yet.

SIMEON: Dunno. He'd like t' catch us nappin'—jest t' have somethin' t' hoss us 'round over.

PETER (*Mechanically gets to his feet. Simeon does the same.*):   Waal—let's git t'wuk. (*They both plod mechanically toward the door before they realize. Then they stop short.*)

SIMEON (*grinning*):   Ye're a cussed fool, Pete—and I be wuss! Let him see we hain't wukin'! We don't give a durn!

PETER (*as they go back to the table*):   Not a damned durn! It'll serve t' show him we're done with him. (*They sit down again. Eben stares from one to the other with surprise.*)

SIMEON (*grins at him*):   We're aimin' t' start bein' lilies o' the field.

PETER: Nary a toil 'r spin 'r lick o' wuk do we put in!

SIMEON: Ye're sole owner—till he comes—that's what ye wanted. Waal, ye got t' be sole hand, too.

PETER: The cows air bellerin'. Ye better hustle at the milkin'.

EBEN (*with excited joy*):   Ye mean ye'll sign the paper?

SIMEON (*dryly*):   Mebbe.

PETER: Mebbe.

SIMEON: We're considerin'. (*Peremptorily.*) Ye better git t' wuk.

EBEN (*with queer excitement*):   It's Maw's farm agen! It's my farm! Them's my cows! I'll milk my durn fingers off fur cows o' mine! (*He goes out door in rear, they stare after him indifferently.*)

SIMEON: Like his Paw.

PETER: Dead spit 'n' image!

SIMEON: Waal—let dog eat dog! (*Eben comes out of front door and around the corner of the house. The sky is beginning to grow flushed with sunrise. Eben stops by the gate and stares around him with glowing, possessive eyes. He takes in the whole farm with his embracing glance of desire.*)

EBEN: It's purty! It's damned purty! It's mine! (*He suddenly throws his head back boldly and glares with hard, defiant eyes at the sky.*) Mine, d'ye hear? Mine! (*He turns and walks quickly off left, rear, toward the barn. The two brothers light their pipes.*)

SIMEON (*putting his muddy boots up on the table, tilting back his chair, and puffing defiantly*): Waal—this air solid comfort—fur once.

PETER: Ay-eh. (*He follows suit. A pause. Unconsciously they both sigh.*)

SIMEON (*suddenly*):   He never was much o' a hand at milkin', Eben wa'n't.

PETER (*with a snort*):   His hands air like hoofs! (*A pause.*)

SIMEON: Reach down the jug thar! Let's take a swaller. I'm feelin' kind o' low.

PETER: Good idee! (*He does so—gets two glasses—they pour out drinks of whisky.*) Here's t' the gold in Californi-a!

SIMEON: An' luck t' find it! (*They drink—puff resolutely—sigh—take their feet down from the table.*)

PETER: Likker don't pear t' sot right.

SIMEON: We hain't used t' it this early. (*A pause. They become very restless.*)

PETER: Gittin' close in this kitchen.

SIMEON (*with immense relief*):   Let's git a breath o' air. (*They arise briskly and go out rear—appear around house and stop by the gate. They stare up at the sky with a numbed appreciation.*)

PETER: Purty!

SIMEON: Ay-eh. Gold's t' the East now.

PETER: Sun's startin' with us fur the Golden West.

SIMEON (*staring around the farm, his compressed face tightened, unable to conceal his emotion*):   Waal—it's our last mornin'—mebbe.

PETER (*the same*):   Ay-eh.

SIMEON (*stamps his foot on the earth and addresses it desperately*):   Waal—ye've thirty year o' me buried in ye—spread out over ye—blood an' bone an' sweat—rotted away—fertilizin' ye—richin' yer soul—prime manure, by God, that's what I been t' ye!

PETER: Ay-eh! An' me.

SIMEON: An' yew, Peter. (*He sighs—then spits.*) Waal—no use'n cryin' over spilt milk.

PETER: They's gold in the West—an' freedom, mebbe. We been slaves t' stone walls here.

SIMEON (*defiantly*):   We hain't nobody's slaves from this out—nor nothin's slaves nuther. (*A pause—restlessly.*) Speaking o' milk, wonder how Eben's managin'?

PETER: I s'pose he's managin'.

SIMEON: Mebbe we'd ought t' help—this once.

PETER: Mebbe. The cows knows us.

SIMEON: An' likes us. They don't know him much.

PETER: An' the hosses, an' pigs, an' chickens. They don't know him much.

SIMEON: They knows us like brothers—an' likes us! (*Proudly.*) Hain't we raised 'em t' be fust-rate, number one prize stock?

PETER: We hain't—not no more.

SIMEON (*dully*):   I was fergittin'. (*Then resignedly.*) Waal, let's go help Eben a spell an' git waked up.

PETER: Suits me. *(They are starting off down left, rear, for the barn when Eben appears from there hurrying toward them, his face excited.)*

EBEN *(breathlessly)*:   Waal—har they be! The old mule an' the bride! I seen 'em from the barn down below at the turnin'.

PETER: How could ye tell that far?

EBEN: Hain't I as far-sight as he's near-sight? Don't I know the mare 'n' buggy, an' two people settin' in it? Who else . . . ? An' I tell ye I kin feel 'em a-comin', too! *(He squirms as if he had the itch.)*

PETER *(beginning to be angry)*:   Waal—let him do his own unhitchin'!

SIMEON *(angry in his turn)*:   Let's hustle in an' git our bundles an' be a-goin' as he's a-comin'. I don't want never t' step inside the door agen arter he's back. *(They both start back around the corner of the house. Eben follows them.)*

EBEN *(anxiously)*:   Will ye sign it afore ye go?

PETER: Let's see the color o' the old skinflint's money an' we'll sign. *(They disappear left. The two brothers clump upstairs to get their bundles. Eben appears in the kitchen, runs to window, peers out, comes back and pulls up a strip of flooring in under stove, takes out a canvas bag and puts it on table, then sets the floorboard back in place. The two brothers appear a moment after. They carry old carpetbags.)*

EBEN *(puts his hand on bag guardingly)*:   Have ye signed?

SIMEON *(shows paper in his hand)*:   Ay-eh. *(Greedily.)* Be that the money?

EBEN *(opens bag and pours out pile of twenty-dollar gold pieces)*:   Twenty-dollar pieces—thirty on 'em. Count 'em. *(Peter does so, arranging them in stacks of five, biting one or two to test them.)*

PETER: Six hundred. *(He puts them in bag and puts it inside his shirt carefully.)*

SIMEON *(handing paper to Eben)*:   Har ye be.

EBEN *(after a glance, folds it carefully and hides it under his shirt—gratefully)*: Thank yew.

PETER: Thank yew fur the ride.

SIMEON: We'll send ye a lump o' gold fur Christmas. *(A pause. Eben stares at them and they at him.)*

PETER *(awkwardly)*:   Waal—we're a-goin'.

SIMEON: Comin' out t' the yard?

EBEN: No. I'm waitin' in here a spell. *(Another silence. The brothers edge awkwardly to door in rear—then turn and stand.)*

SIMEON: Waal—good-by.

PETER: Good-by.

EBEN: Good-by. *(They go out. He sits down at the table, faces the stove and pulls out the paper. He looks from it to the stove. His face, lighted up by the shaft of sunlight from the window, has an expression of trance. His lips move. The two brothers come out to the gate.)*

PETER *(looking off toward barn)*:   Thar he be—unhitchin'.

SIMEON *(with a chuckle)*:   I'll bet ye he's riled!

PETER: An' thar she be.

SIMEON: Let's wait 'n' see what our new Maw looks like.

PETER *(with a grin)*:   An' give him our partin' cuss!

SIMEON *(grinning)*:   I feel like raisin' fun. I feel light in my head an' feet.

PETER: Me, too. I feel like laffin' till I'd split up the middle.

SIMEON: Reckon it's the likker?

PETER: No. My feet feel itchin' t' walk an' walk—an' jump high over thin's—an' . . .

SIMEON: Dance? (*A pause.*)

PETER (*puzzled*):   It's plumb onnateral.

SIMEON (*a light coming over his face*):   I calc'late it's 'cause school's out. It's holiday. Fur once we're free!

PETER (*dazedly*):   Free?

SIMEON: The halter's broke—the harness is busted—the fence bars is down—the stone walls air crumblin' an' tumblin'! We'll be kickin' up an' tearin' away down the road!

PETER (*drawing a deep breath—oratorically*):   Anybody that wants this stinkin' old rock-pile of a farm kin hev it. T'ain't our'n, no sirree!

SIMEON (*takes the gate off its hinges and puts it under his arm*):   We harby 'bolishes shet gates, an' open gates, an' all gates, by thunder!

PETER: We'll take it with us fur luck an' let 'er sail free down some river.

SIMEON (*as a sound of voices comes from left, rear*):   Har they comes! (*The two brothers congeal into two stiff, grim-visaged statues. Ephraim Cabot and Abbie Putnam come in. Cabot is seventy-five, tall and gaunt, with great, wiry, concentrated power, but stoop-shouldered from toil. His face is as hard as if it were hewn out of a boulder, yet there is a weakness in it, a petty pride in its own narrow strength. His eyes are small, close together, and extremely near-sighted, blinking continually in the effort to focus on objects, their stare having a straining, ingrowing quality. He is dressed in his dismal black Sunday suit. Abbie is thirty-five, buxom, full of vitality. Her round face is pretty but marred by its rather gross sensuality. There is strength and obstinacy in her jaw, a hard determination in her eyes, and about her whole personality the same unsettled, untamed, desperate quality which is so apparent in Eben.*)

CABOT (*as they enter—a queer strangled emotion in his dry cracking voice*):   Har we be t'hum, Abbie.

ABBIE (*with lust for the word*):   Hum! (*Her eyes gloating on the house without seeming to see the two stiff figures at the gate.*) It's purty—purty! I can't b'lieve it's r'ally mine.

CABOT (*sharply*):   Yewr'n? Mine! (*He stares at her penetratingly. She stares back. He adds relentingly.*) Our'n—mebbe! It was lonesome too long. I was growin' old in the spring. A hum's got t' hev a woman.

ABBIE (*her voice taking possession*):   A woman's got t' hev a hum!

CABOT (*nodding uncertainly*):   Ay-eh. (*Then irritably.*) Whar be they? Ain't thar nobody about—'r wukin'—'r nothin'?

ABBIE (*Sees the brothers. She returns their stare of cold appraising contempt with interest—slowly.*): Thar's two men loafin' at the gate an' starin' at me like a couple o' strayed hogs.

CABOT (*straining his eyes*):   I kin see 'em—but I can't make out . . .

SIMEON: It's Simeon.

PETER: It's Peter.

CABOT (*exploding*):   Why hain't ye wukin'?

SIMEON (*dryly*):   We're waitin' t' welcome ye hum—yew an' the bride!

CABOT (*confusedly*):   Huh? Waal—this be yer new Maw, boys. (*She stares at them and they at her.*)

SIMEON (*turns away and spits contemptuously*):   I see her!

PETER (*spits also*):   An' I see her!

ABBIE (*with the conqueror's conscious superiority*):   I'll go in an' look at *my* house. (*She goes slowly around to porch.*)

SIMEON (*with a snort*):   *Her* house!

PETER (*calls after her*):   Ye'll find Eben inside. Ye better not tell him it's *yewr* house.

ABBIE (*mouthing the name*):   Eben. (*Then quietly.*) I'll tell Eben.

CABOT (*with a contemptuous sneer*):   Ye needn't heed Eben. Eben's a dumb fool—like his Maw—soft an' simple!

SIMEON (*with his sardonic burst of laughter*):   Ha! Eben's a chip o' yew—spit 'n' image—hard 'n' bitter's a hickory tree! Dog'll eat dog. He'll eat ye yet, old man!

CABOT (*commandingly*):   Ye git t' wuk.

SIMEON (*as Abbie disappears in house—winks at Peter and says tauntingly*):   So that thar's our new Maw, be it? Whar in hell did ye dig her up? (*He and Peter laugh.*)

PETER: Ha! Ye'd better turn her in the pen with the other sows. (*They laugh uproariously, slapping their thighs.*)

CABOT (*so amazed at their effrontery that he stutters in confusion*):   Simeon! Peter! What's come over ye? Air ye drunk?

SIMEON: We're free, old man—free o' yew an' the hull damned farm! (*They grow more and more hilarious and excited.*)

PETER: An' we're startin' out fur the gold fields o' Californi-a!

SIMEON: Ye kin take this place an' burn it!

PETER: An' bury it—fur all we cares!

SIMEON: We're free, old man! (*He cuts a caper.*)

PETER: Free! (*He gives a kick in the air.*)

SIMEON (*in a frenzy*):   Whoop!

PETER: Whoop! (*They do an absurd Indian war dance about the old man who is petrified between rage and the fear that they are insane.*)

SIMEON: We're free as Injuns! Lucky we don't skulp ye!

PETER: An' burn yer barn an' kill the stock!

SIMEON: An' rape yer new woman! Whoop! (*He and Peter stop their dance, holding their sides, rocking with wild laughter.*)

CABOT (*edging away*):   Lust fur gold—fur the sinful, easy gold o' Californi-a! It's made ye mad!

SIMEON (*tauntingly*):   Wouldn't ye like us to send ye back some sinful gold, ye old sinner?

PETER: They's gold besides what's in Californi-a! (*He retreats back beyond the vision of the old man and takes the bag of money and flaunts it in the air above his head, laughing.*)

SIMEON: And sinfuller, too!

PETER: We'll be voyagin' on the sea! Whoop! (*He leaps up and down.*)

SIMEON: Livin' free! Whoop! (*He leaps in turn.*)

CABOT (*suddenly roaring with rage*):   My cuss on ye!

SIMEON: Take our'n in trade fur it! Whoop!

CABOT: I'll hev ye both chained up in the asylum!

PETER: Ye old skinflint! Good-by!

SIMEON: Ye old blood sucker! Good-by!

CABOT: Go afore I . . . !

PETER: Whoop! (*He picks a stone from the road. Simeon does the same.*)

SIMEON: Maw'll be in the parlor.

PETER: Ay-eh! One! Two!

CABOT (*frightened*):   What air ye . . . ?

PETER: Three! (*They both throw, the stones hitting the parlor window with a crash of glass, tearing the shade.*)

SIMEON: Whoop!

PETER: Whoop!

CABOT (*in a fury now, rushing toward them*):   If I kin lay hands on ye—I'll break yer bones fur ye! (*But they beat a capering retreat before him, Simeon with the gate still under his arm. Cabot comes back, panting with impotent rage. Their voices as they go off take up the song of the gold-seekers to the old tune of "Oh, Susannah!"*)

"I jumped aboard the Liza ship,
And traveled on the sea,
And every time I thought of home
I wished it wasn't me!
Oh! Californi-a,
That's the land fur me!
I'm off to Californi-a!
With my wash bowl on my knee."

(*In the meantime, the window of the upper bedroom on right is raised and Abbie sticks her head out. She looks down at Cabot—with a sigh of relief.*)

ABBIE: Waal—that's the last o' them two, hain't it? (*He doesn't answer. Then in possessive tones.*) This here's a nice bedroom, Ephraim. It's a r'al nice bed. Is it my room, Ephraim?

CABOT (*grimly—without looking up*):   Our'n! (*She cannot control a grimace of aversion and pulls back her head slowly and shuts the window. A sudden horrible thought seems to enter Cabot's head.*) They been up to somethin'! Mebbe— mebbe they've pizened the stock—'r somethin'! (*He almost runs off down toward the barn. A moment later the kitchen door is slowly pushed open and Abbie enters. For a moment she stands looking at Eben. He does not notice her at first. Her eyes take him in penetratingly with a calculating appraisal of his strength as against hers. But under this her desire is dimly awakened by his youth and good looks. Suddenly he becomes conscious of her presence and looks up. Their eyes meet. He leaps to his feet, glowering at her speechlessly.*)

ABBIE (*in her most seductive tones which she uses all through this scene*):   Be you—Eben? I'm Abbie— (*She laughs.*) I mean, I'm yer new Maw.

EBEN (*viciously*):   No, damn ye!

ABBIE (*as if she hadn't heard—with a queer smile*):   Yer Paw's spoke a lot o' yew. . . .

EBEN: Ha!

ABBIE: Ye mustn't mind him. He's an old man. (*A long pause. They stare at each other.*) I don't want t' pretend playin' Maw t' ye, Eben. (*Admiringly.*) Ye're too big an' too strong fur that. I want t' be frens with ye. Mebbe with me fur a fren ye'd find ye'd like livin' here better. I kin make it easy fur ye with him, mebbe. (*With a scornful sense of power.*) I calc'late I kin git him t' do most anythin' fur me.

EBEN (*with bitter scorn*):   Ha! (*They stare again, Eben obscurely moved, physically attracted to her—in forced stilted tones.*) Yew kin go t' the devil!

ABBIE (*calmly*):   If cussin' me does ye good, cuss all ye've a mind t'. I'm all prepared t' have ye agin me—at fust. I don't blame ye nuther. I'd feel the same at any stranger comin' t' take my Maw's place. (*He shudders. She is watching him carefully.*) Yew must've cared a lot fur yewr Maw, didn't ye? My Maw died afore I'd growed. I don't remember her none. (*A pause.*) But yew won't hate me long, Eben. I'm not the wust in the world—an' yew an' me've got a lot in common. I kin tell that by lookin' at ye. Waal—I've had a hard life, too—oceans o' trouble an' nuthin' but wuk fur reward. I was a orphan early an' had t' wuk fur others in other folks' hums. Then I married an' he turned out a drunken spreer an' so he had to wuk fur others an' me too agen in other folks' hums, an' the baby died, an' my husband got sick an' died too, an' I was glad sayin' now I'm free fur once, on'y I diskivered right away all I was free fur was t' wuk agen in other folks' hums, doin' other folks' wuk till I'd most give up hope o' ever doin' my own wuk in my own hum, an' then your Paw come. . . . (*Cabot appears returning from the barn. He comes to the gate and looks down the road the brothers have gone. A faint strain of their retreating voices is heard: "Oh, Californi-a! That's the place for me." He stands glowering, his fist clenched, his face grim with rage.*)

EBEN (*fighting against his growing attraction and sympathy—harshly*): An' bought yew—like a harlot! (*She is stung and flushes angrily. She has been sincerely moved by the recital of her troubles. He adds furiously.*) An' the price he's payin' ye—this farm—was my Maw's, damn ye!—an' mine now!

ABBIE (*with a cool laugh of confidence*):   Yewr'n? We'll see 'bout that! (*Then strongly.*) Waal—what if I did need a hum? What else'd I marry an old man like him fur?

EBEN (*maliciously*):   I'll tell him ye said that!

ABBIE (*smiling*):   I'll say ye're lyin' a-purpose—an' he'll drive ye off the place!

EBEN: Ye devil!

ABBIE (*defying him*):   This be my farm—this be my hum—this be my kitchen—!

EBEN (*furiously, as if he were going to attack her*):   Shut up, damn ye!

ABBIE (*walks up to him—a queer coarse expression of desire in her face and body—slowly*): An' upstairs—that be my bedroom—an' my bed! (*He stares into her eyes, terribly confused and torn. She adds softly.*) I hain't bad nor mean— 'ceptin' fur an enemy—but I got t' fight fur what's due me out o' life, if I ever 'spect t' git it. (*Then putting her hand on his arm—seductively.*) Let's yew 'n' me be frens, Eben.

EBEN (*stupidly—as if hypnotized*):   Ay-eh. (*Then furiously flinging off her arm.*) No, ye durned old witch! I hate ye! (*He rushes out the door.*)

ABBIE (*looks after him smiling satisfiedly—then half to herself, mouthing the word*): Eben's nice. (*She looks at the table, proudly.*) I'll wash up *my* dishes now. (*Eben appears outside, slamming the door behind him. He comes around corner, stops on seeing his father, and stands staring at him with hate.*)

CABOT (*raising his arms to heaven in the fury he can no longer control*): Lord God o' Hosts,[2] smite the undutiful sons with Thy wust cuss!

EBEN (*breaking in violently*):   Yew 'n' yewr God! Allus cussin' folks—allus naggin' 'em!

CABOT (*oblivious to him—summoningly*):   God o' the old! God o' the lonesome!

---

[2]Eucharistic wafers, consecrated for the ceremony of Holy Communion.

EBEN (*mockingly*):   Naggin' His sheep t' sin! T' hell with yewr God! (*Cabot turns. He and Eben glower at each other.*)

CABOT (*harshly*):   So it's yew. I might've knowed it. (*Shaking his finger threateningly at him.*) Blasphemin' fool! (*Then quickly.*) Why hain't ye t' wuk?

EBEN: Why hain't yew? They've went. I can't wuk it all alone.

CABOT (*contemptuously*):   Nor noways! I'm wuth ten o' ye yit, old's I be! Ye'll never be more'n half a man! (*Then, matter-of-factly.*) Waal—let's git t' the barn. (*They go. A last faint note of the "Californi-a" song is heard from the distance. Abbie is washing her dishes.*)

PART II, SCENE I

(*The exterior of the farmhouse, as in Part I—a hot Sunday afternoon two months later. Abbie, dressed in her best, is discovered sitting in a rocker at the end of the porch. She rocks listlessly, enervated by the heat, staring in front of her with bored, half-closed eyes.*)

(*Eben sticks his head out of his bedroom window. He looks around furtively and tries to see—or hear—if anyone is on the porch, but although he has been careful to make no noise, Abbie has sensed his movement. She stops rocking, her face grows animated and eager, she waits attentively. Eben seems to feel her presence, he scowls back his thoughts of her and spits with exaggerated disdain— then withdraws back into the room. Abbie waits, holding her breath as she listens with passionate eagerness for every sound within the house.*)

(*Eben comes out. Their eyes meet; his falter. He is confused, he turns away and slams the door resentfully. At this gesture, Abbie laughs tantalizingly, amused but at the same time piqued and irritated. He scowls, strides off the porch to the path and starts to walk past her to the road with a grand swagger of ignoring her existence. He is dressed in his store suit, spruced up, his face shines from soap and water. Abbie leans forward on her chair, her eyes hard and angry now, and, as he passes her, gives a sneering, taunting chuckle.*)

EBEN (*stung—turns on her furiously*):   What air yew cacklin' 'bout?

ABBIE (*triumphant*):   Yew!

EBEN: What about me?

ABBIE: Ye look all slicked up like a prize bull.

EBEN (*with a sneer*):   Waal—ye hain't so durned purty yerself, be ye? (*They stare into each other's eyes, his held by hers in spite of himself, hers glowingly possessive. Their physical attraction becomes a palpable force quivering in the hot air.*)

ABBIE (*softly*):   Ye don't mean that, Eben. Ye may think ye mean it, mebbe, but ye don't. Ye can't. It's agin nature, Eben. Ye been fightin' yer nature ever since the day I come—tryin' t' tell yerself I hain't purty t'ye. (*She laughs a low humid laugh without taking her eyes from his. A pause—her body squirms desir- ously—she murmurs languorously.*) Hain't the sun strong an' hot? Ye kin feel it burnin' into the earth—Nature—makin' thin's grow—bigger 'n' bigger—burnin' inside ye—makin' ye want t' grow—into somethin' else—till ye're jined with it—an' it's your'n—but it owns ye, too—an' makes ye grow bigger—like a tree—like them elums—(*She laughs again softly, holding his eyes. He takes a step toward her, compelled against his will.*) Nature'll beat ye, Eben. Ye might's well own up t' it fust 's last.

EBEN (*trying to break from her spell—confusedly*):   If Paw'd hear ye goin' on . . . (*Resentfully.*) But ye've made such a damned idjit out o' the old devil . . . ! (*Abbie laughs.*)

ABBIE: Waal—hain't it easier fur yew with him changed softer?

EBEN (*defiantly*):   No. I'm fightin' him—fightin' yew—fightin' fur Maw's rights t' her hum! (*This breaks her spell for him. He glowers at her.*) An' I'm onto ye. Ye hain't foolin' me a mite. Ye're aimin' t' swaller up everythin' an' make it your'n. Waal, you'll find I'm a heap sight bigger hunk nor yew kin chew! (*He turns from her with a sneer.*)

ABBIE (*trying to regain her ascendancy—seductively*):   Eben!

EBEN: Leave me be! (*He starts to walk away.*)

ABBIE (*more commandingly*):   Eben!

EBEN (*stops—resentfully*):   What d'ye want?

ABBIE (*trying to conceal a growing excitement*):   Whar air ye goin'?

EBEN (*with malicious nonchalance*):   Oh—up the road a spell.

ABBIE: T' the village?

EBEN (*airily*):   Mebbe.

ABBIE (*excitedly*):   T' see Min, I s'pose?

EBEN: Mebbe.

ABBIE (*weakly*):   What d'ye want t' waste time on her fur?

EBEN (*revenging himself now—grinning at her*):   Ye can't beat Nature, didn't ye say? (*He laughs and again starts to walk away.*)

ABBIE (*bursting out*):   An ugly old hake!

EBEN (*with a tantalizing sneer*):   She's purtier'n yew be!

ABBIE: That every wuthless drunk in the country has . . .

EBEN (*tauntingly*):   Mebbe—but she's better'n yew. She owns up fa'r 'n' squar' t' her doin's.

ABBIE (*furiously*):   Don't ye dare compare . . .

EBEN: She don't go sneakin' an' stealin'—what's mine.

ABBIE (*savagely seizing on his weak point*):   Your'n? Yew mean—my farm?

EBEN: I mean the farm yew sold yerself fur like any other old whore—my farm!

ABBIE (*stung—fiercely*):   Ye'll never live t' see the day when even a stinkin' weed on it'll belong t' ye! (*Then in a scream.*) Git out o' my sight! Go on t' yer slut—disgracin' yer Paw 'n' me! I'll git yer Paw t' horsewhip ye off the place if I want t'! Ye're only livin' here 'cause I tolerate ye! Git along! I hate the sight o' ye! (*She stops, panting and glaring at him.*)

EBEN (*returning her glance in kind*):   An' I hate the sight o' yew! (*He turns and strides off up the road. She follows his retreating figure with concentrated hate. Old Cabot appears coming up from the barn. The hard, grim expression of his face has changed. He seems in some queer way softened, mellowed. His eyes have taken on a strange, incongruous dreamy quality. Yet there is no hint of physical weakness about him—rather he looks more robust and younger. Abbie sees him and turns away quickly with unconcealed aversion. He comes slowly up to her.*)

CABOT (*mildly*):   War yew an' Eben quarrelin' agen?

ABBIE (*shortly*):   No.

CABOT: Ye was talkin' a'mighty loud. (*He sits down on the edge of porch.*)

ABBIE (*snappishly*):   If ye heerd us they hain't no need askin' questions.

CABOT: I didn't hear what ye said.

ABBIE (*relieved*):   Waal—it wa'n't nothin' t' speak on.

CABOT (*after a pause*):   Eben's queer.

ABBIE (*bitterly*):   He's the dead spit 'n' image o' yew!

CABOT (*queerly interested*):   D'ye think so, Abbie? (*After a pause, ruminatingly.*) Me 'n' Eben's allus fit 'n' fit. I never could b'ar him noways. He's so thunderin' soft—like his Maw.

ABBIE (*scornfully*):   Ay-eh! 'Bout as soft as yew be!

CABOT (*as if he hadn't heard*):   Mebbe I been too hard on him.

ABBIE (*jeeringly*):   Waal—ye're gittin' soft now—soft as slop! That's what Eben was sayin'.

CABOT (*his face instantly grim and ominous*):   Eben was sayin'? Waal, he'd best not do nothin' t' try me 'r he'll soon diskiver. . . . (*A pause. She keeps her face turned away. His gradually softens. He stares up at the sky.*) Purty, hain't it?

ABBIE (*crossly*):   I don't see nothin' purty.

CABOT: The sky. Feels like a wa'm field up thar.

ABBIE (*sarcastically*):   Air yew aimin' t' buy up over the farm too? (*She snickers contemptuously.*)

CABOT (*strangely*):   I'd like t' own my place up thar. (*A pause.*) I'm gittin' old, Abbie. I'm gittin' ripe on the bough. (*A pause. She stares at him mystified. He goes on.*) It's allus lonesome cold in the house —even when it's bilin' hot outside. Hain't yew noticed?

ABBIE: No.

CABOT: It's wa'm down t' the barn—nice smellin' an' warm—with the cows. (*A pause.*) Cows is queer.

ABBIE: Like yew?

CABOT: Like Eben. (*A pause.*) I' gittin' t' feel resigned t' Eben—jest as I got t' feel 'bout his Maw. I'm gittin' t' learn to b'ar his softness—jest like her'n. I calc'late I c'd a'most take t' him—if he wa'n't sech a dumb fool! (*A pause.*) I s'pose it's old age a-creepin' in my bones.

ABBIE (*indifferently*):   Waal—ye hain't dead yet.

CABOT (*roused*):   No, I hain't, yew bet—not by a hell of a sight—I'm sound 'n' tough as hickory! (*Then moodily.*) But arter three score and ten the Lord warns ye t' prepare. (*A pause.*) That's why Eben's come in my head. Now that his cussed sinful brothers is gone their path t' hell, they's no one left but Eben.

ABBIE (*resentfully*):   They's me, hain't they? (*Agitatedly.*) What's all this sudden likin' ye've tuk to Eben? Why don't ye say nothin' 'bout me? Hain't I yer lawful wife?

CABOT (*simply*):   Ay-eh. Ye be. (*A pause—he stares at her desirously—his eyes grow avid—then with a sudden movement he seizes her hands and squeezes them, declaiming in a queer camp meeting preacher's tempo.*) Yew air my Rose o' Sharon! Behold, yew air fair; yer eyes air doves; yer lips air like scarlet; yer two breasts air like two fawns; yer navel be like a round goblet; yer belly be like a heap o' wheat . . . (*He covers her hand with kisses. She does not seem to notice. She stares before her with hard angry eyes.*)

ABBIE (*jerking her hands away—harshly*):   So ye're plannin' t' leave the farm t' Eben, air ye?

CABOT (*dazedly*):   Leave . . . ? (*Then with resentful obstinacy.*) I hain't a-givin' it t' no one!

ABBIE (*remorselessly*):   Ye can't take it with ye.

CABOT (*thinks a moment—then reluctantly*):   No, I calc'late not. (*After a pause—with a strange passion.*) But if I could, I would, by the Eternal! 'R if I could, in my dyin' hour, I'd set it afire an' watch it burn—this house an' every ear o' corn an' every tree down t' the last blade o' hay! I'd sit an' know it was all a-dying with me an' no one else'd ever own what was mine, what I'd made out o' nothin' with my own sweat 'n' blood! (*A pause—then he adds with a queer affection.*) 'Ceptin' the cows. Them I'd turn free.

ABBIE (*harshly*):   An' me?

CABOT (*with a queer smile*):   Ye'd be turned free, too.

ABBIE (*furiously*):   So that's the thanks I git fur marryin' ye—t' have ye change kind to Eben who hates ye, an' talk o' turnin' me out in the road.

CABOT (*hastily*):   Abbie! Ye know I wa'n't. . . .

ABBIE (*vengefully*):   Just let me tell ye a thing or two 'bout Eben! Whar's he gone? T' see that harlot, Min! I tried fur t' stop him. Disgracin' yew an' me—on the Sabbath, too!

CABOT (*rather guiltily*):   He's a sinner—nateral-born. It's lust eatin' his heart.

ABBIE (*enraged beyond endurance—wildly vindictive*):   An' his lust fur me! Kin ye find excuses fur that?

CABOT (*stares at her—after a dead pause*):   Lust—fur yew?

ABBIE (*defiantly*):   He was tryin' t' make love t' me—when ye heerd us quarrelin'.

CABOT (*stares at her—then a terrible expression of rage comes over his face— he springs to his feet shaking all over*): By the A'mighty God—I'll end him!

ABBIE (*frightened now for Eben*):   No! Don't ye!

CABOT (*violently*):   I'll git the shotgun an' blow his soft brains t' the top o' them elums!

ABBIE (*throwing her arms around him*):   No, Ephraim!

CABOT (*pushing her away violently*):   I will, by God!

ABBIE (*in a quieting tone*):   Listen, Ephraim. 'Twa'n't nothin' bad—on'y a boy's foolin'—'twa'an't meant serious—jest jokin' an' teasin' . . . .

CABOT: Then why did ye say—lust?

ABBIE: It must hev sounded wusser'n I meant. An' I was mad at thinkin'— ye'd leave him the farm.

CABOT (*quieter but still grim and cruel*):   Waal then, I'll horsewhip him off the place if that much'll content ye.

ABBIE (*reaching out and taking his hand*):   No. Don't think o' me! Ye mustn't drive him off. 'Tain't sensible. Who'll ye get to help ye on the farm? They's no one hereabouts.

CABOT (*considers this—then nodding his appreciation*):   Ye got a head on ye. (*Then irritably.*) Waal, let him stay. (*He sits down on the edge of the porch. She sits beside him. He murmurs contemptuously.*) I oughtn't t' git riled so—at that 'ere fool calf. (*A pause.*) But har's the p'int. What son o' mine'll keep on here t' the farm—when the Lord does call me? Simeon an' Peter air gone t' hell—an' Eben's follerin' 'em.

ABBIE: They's me.

CABOT: Ye're on'y a woman.

ABBIE: I'm yewr wife.

CABOT: That hain't me. A son is me—my blood—mine. Mine ought t' git mine. An' then it's still mine—even though I be six foot under. D'ye see?

ABBIE (*giving him a look of hatred*):   Ay-eh. I see. (*She becomes very thoughtful, her face growing shrewd, her eyes studying Cabot craftily.*)

CABOT: I'm gittin' old—ripe on the bough. (*Then with a sudden forced reassurance.*) Not but what I hain't a hard nut t' crack even yet—an' fur many a year t' come! By the Etarnal, I kin break most o' the young fellers' backs at any kind o' work any day o' the year!

ABBIE (*suddenly*):   Mebbe the Lord'll give *us* a son.

CABOT (*turns and stares at her eagerly*):   Ye mean—a son—t' me 'n' yew?

ABBIE (*with a cajoling smile*):   Ye're a strong man yet, hain't ye? 'Tain't noways impossible, be it? We know that. Why d'ye stare so? Hain't ye never thought o' that afore? I been thinkin' o' it all along. Ay-eh—an' I been prayin' it'd happen, too.

CABOT (*his face growing full of joyous pride and a sort of religious ecstasy*):   Ye been prayin', Abbie?—fur a son?—t' us?

ABBIE: Ay-eh. (*With a grim resolution.*) I want a son now.

CABOT (*excitedly clutching both of her hands in his*):   It'd be the blessin' o' God, Abbie—the blessin' o' God A'mighty on me—in my old age—in my lonesomeness! They hain't nothin' I wouldn't do fur ye then, Abbie. Ye'd hev on'y t' ask it—anythin' ye'd a mind t'!

ABBIE (*interrupting*):   Would ye will the farm t' me then—t' me an' it . . . ?

CABOT (*vehemently*):   I'd do anythin' ye axed, I tell ye! I swar it! May I be everlastin' damned t' hell if I wouldn't! (*He sinks to his knees pulling her down with him. He trembles all over with the fervor of his hopes.*) Pray t' the Lord agen, Abbie. It's the Sabbath! I'll jine ye! Two prayers air better nor one. "An' God hearkened unto Rachel"![3] An' God hearkened unto Abbie! Pray, Abbie! Pray fur him to hearken! (*He bows his head, mumbling. She pretends to do likewise but gives him a side glance of scorn and triumph.*)

Scene II

(*About eight in the evening. The interior of the two bedrooms on the top floor is shown. Eben is sitting on the side of his bed in the room on the left. On account of the heat he has taken off everything but his undershirt and pants. His feet are bare. He faces front, brooding moodily, his chin propped on his hands, a desperate expression on his face.*)

(*In the other room Cabot and Abbie are sitting side by side on the edge of their bed, an old four-poster with feather mattress. He is in his nightshirt, she in her nightdress. He is still in the queer, excited mood into which the notion of a son has thrown him. Both rooms are lighted dimly and flickeringly by tallow candles.*)

CABOT: The farm needs a son.

ABBIE: I need a son.

CABOT: Ay-eh. Sometimes ye air the farm an' sometimes the farm be yew. That's why I clove t' ye in my lonesomeness. (*A pause. He pounds his knee with his fist.*) Me an' the farm has got t' beget a son!

ABBIE: Ye'd best go t' sleep. Ye're gittin' thin's all mixed.

CABOT (*with an impatient gesture*):   No, I hain't. My mind's clear's a well. Ye don't know me, that's it. (*He stares hopelessly at the floor.*)

---

[3]A paraphrase of Genesis 30:22; Rachel, a wife of Jacob, had been childless, but God allowed her to conceive a son, Joseph.

ABBIE (*indifferently*):   Mebbe. (*In the next room Eben gets up and paces up and down distractedly. Abbie hears him. Her eyes fasten on the intervening wall with concentrated attention. Eben stops and stares. Their hot glances seem to meet through the wall. Unconsciously he stretches out his arms for her and she half rises. Then aware, he mutters a curse at himself and flings himself face downward on the bed, his clenched fists above his head, his face buried in the pillow. Abbie relaxes with a faint sigh but her eyes remain fixed on the wall; she listens with all her attention for some movement from Eben.*)

CABOT (*suddenly raises his head and looks at her—scornfully*):   Will ye ever know me—'r will any man 'r woman? (*Shaking his head.*) No. I calc'late wa'n't t' be. (*He turns away. Abbie looks at the wall. Then, evidently unable to keep silent about his thoughts, without looking at his wife, he puts out his hand and clutches her knee. She starts violently, looks at him, sees he is not watching her, concentrates again on the wall, and pays no attention to what he says.*) Listen Abbie. When I come here fifty odd year ago—I was jest twenty an' the strongest an' hardest ye ever seen—ten times as strong an' fifty times as hard as Eben. Waal—this place was nothin' but fields o' stones. Folks laughed when I tuk it. They couldn't know what I knowed. When ye kin make corn sprout out o' stones, God's livin' in yew! They wa'n't strong enuf fur that! They reckoned God was easy. They laughed. They don't laugh no more. Some died hereabouts. Some went West an' died. They're all underground—fur follerin' arter an easy God. God hain't easy. (*He shakes his head slowly.*) An' I growed hard. Folks kept allus sayin' he's a hard man like 'twas sinful t' be hard, so's at last I said back at 'em: Waal then, by thunder, ye'll git me hard an' see how ye like it! (*Then suddenly.*) But I give in t' weakness once. 'Twas arter I'd been here two year. I got weak—despairful—they was so many stones. They was a party leavin', givin' up, goin' West. I jined 'em. We tracked on 'n' on. We come t' broad medders, plains, whar the soil was black an' rich as gold. Nary a stone. Easy. Ye'd on'y to plow an' sow an' then set an' smoke yer pipe an' watch thin's grow. I could o' been a rich man—but somethin' in me fit me an' fit me—the voice o' God sayin': "This hain't wuth nothin' t' Me. Git ye back t' hum!" I got afeerd o' that voice an' I lit out back t' hum here, leavin' my claim an' crops t' whoever'd a mind t' take 'em. Ay-eh. I actoolly give up what was rightful mine! God's hard, not easy! God's in the stones! Build my church on a rock—out o' stones an' I'll be in them! That's what He meant t' Peter! (*He sighs heavily—a pause.*) Stones. I picked 'em up an' piled 'em into walls. Ye kin read the years of my life in them walls, every day a hefted stone, climbin' over the hills up and down, fencin' in the fields that was mine, whar I'd made thin's grow out o' nothin'—like the will o' God, like the servant o' His hand. It wa'n't easy. It was hard an' He made me hard fur it. (*He pauses.*) All the time I kept gittin' lonesomer. I tuk a wife. She bore Simeon an' Peter. She was a good woman. She wuked hard. We was married twenty year. She never knowed me. She helped but she never knowed what she was helpin'. I was allus lonesome. She died. After that it wa'n't so lonesome fur a spell. (*A pause.*) I lost count o' the years. I had no time t' fool away countin' 'em. Sim an' Peter helped. The farm growed. It was all mine! When I thought o' that I didn't feel lonesome. (*A pause.*) But ye can't hitch yer mind t' one thin' day an' night. I tuk another wife—Eben's Maw. Her folks was contestin' me at law over my deeds t' the farm—my farm! That's why Eben keeps a-talkin' his fool talk o' this bein' his Maw's farm. She bore Eben. She was purty—but soft. She tried t' be hard. She couldn't. She never knowed me nor nothin'. It was lonesomer 'n hell with her. After a matter o' sixteen odd years, she died. (*A pause.*) I lived with the boys. They hated me 'cause I was hard. I hated them 'cause they was soft. They coveted the farm without knowin' what it meant. It made me bitter 'n wormwood. It aged me—them coveting what I'd made fur mine. Then this spring the call come—the voice o' God cryin' in my wilderness, in my lonesomeness—t' go out an' seek an' find! (*Turning to her with strange passion.*) I sought ye an' I found ye! Yew air my Rose o' Sharon! Yer eyes air like. . . . (*She has turned a blank face, resentful eyes to his. He stares at her for a moment—then harshly.*) Air ye any the wiser fur all I've told ye?

ABBIE (*confusedly*):   Mebbe.

CABOT (*pushing her away from him—angrily*):   Ye don't know nothin'—nor never will. If ye don't hev a son t' redeem ye. . . . (*This in a tone of cold threat.*)

ABBIE (*resentfully*):   I've prayed, hain't I?

CABOT (*bitterly*):   Pray agen—fur understandin'!

ABBIE (*a veiled threat in her tone*):   Ye'll have a son out o' me, I promise ye.

CABOT: How kin ye promise?

ABBIE: I got second-sight mebbe. I kin foretell. (*She gives a queer smile.*)

CABOT: I believe ye have. Ye give me the chills sometimes. (*He shivers.*) It's cold in this house. It's oneasy. They's thin's pokin' about in the dark—in the corners. (*He pulls on his trousers, tucking in his nightshirt, and pulls on his boots.*)

ABBIE (*surprised*):   Whar air ye goin'?

CABOT (*queerly*):   Down whar it's restful—whar it's warm—down t' the barn. (*Bitterly.*) I kin talk t' the cows. They know. They know the farm an' me. They'll give me peace. (*He turns to go out the door.*)

ABBIE (*a bit frightenedly*):   Air ye ailin' tonight, Ephraim?

CABOT: Growin'. Growin' ripe on the bough. (*He turns and goes, his boots clumping down the stairs. Eben sits up with a start, listening. Abbie is conscious of his movement and stares at the wall. Cabot comes out of the house around the corner and stands by the gate, blinking at the sky. He stretches up his hands in a tortured gesture.*) God A'mighty, call from the dark! (*He listens as if expecting an answer. Then his arms drop, he shakes his head and plods off toward the barn. Eben and Abbie stare at each other through the wall. Eben sighs heavily and Abbie echoes it. Both become terribly nervous, uneasy. Finally Abbie gets up and listens, her ear to the wall. He acts as if he saw every move she was making, he becomes resolutely still. She seems driven into a decision—goes out the door in rear determinedly. His eyes follow her. Then as the door of his room is opened softly, he turns away, waits in an attitude of strained fixity. Abbie stands for a second staring at him, her eyes burning with desire. Then with a little cry she runs over and throws her arms about his neck, she pulls his head back and covers his mouth with kisses. At first, he submits dumbly; then he puts his arms about her neck and returns her kisses, but finally, suddenly aware of his hatred, he hurls her away from him, springing to his feet. They stand speechless and breathless, panting like two animals.*)

ABBIE (*at last—painfully*):   Ye shouldn't Eben—ye shouldn't—I'd make ye happy!

EBEN (*harshly*):   I don't want t' be happy—from yew!

ABBIE (*helplessly*):   Ye do, Eben! Ye do! Why d'ye lie?

EBEN (*viciously*):   I don't take t'ye, I tell ye! I hate the sight o' ye!

ABBIE (*with an uncertain troubled laugh*):   Waal, I kissed ye anyways—an' ye kissed back—yer lips was burnin'—ye can't lie 'bout that! (*Intensely.*) If ye don't care, why did ye kiss me back—why was yer lips burnin'?

EBEN (*wiping his mouth*):   It was like pizen on 'em. (*Then tauntingly.*) When I kissed ye back, mebbe I thought 'twas someone else.

ABBIE (*wildly*):   Min?

EBEN: Mebbe.

ABBIE (*torturedly*):   Did ye go t' see her? Did ye r'ally go? I thought ye mightn't. Is that why ye throwed me off jest now?

EBEN (*sneeringly*):   What if it be?

ABBIE (*raging*):   Then ye're a dog, Eben Cabot!

EBEN (*threateningly*):   Ye can't talk that way t' me!

ABBIE (*with a shrill laugh*):   Can't I? Did ye think I was in love with ye—a weak thin' like yew? Not much! I on'y wanted ye fur a purpose o' my own—an' I'll hev ye fur it yet 'cause I'm stronger'n yew be!

EBEN (*resentfully*):   I knowed well it was on'y part o' yer plan t' swaller everythin'!

ABBIE (*tauntingly*):   Mebbe!

EBEN (*furious*):   Git out o' my room!

ABBIE: This air my room an' ye're on'y hired help!

EBEN (*threateningly*):   Git out afore I murder ye!

ABBIE (*quite confident now*):   I hain't a mite afeerd. Ye want me, don't ye? Yes, ye do! An' yer Paw's son'll never kill what he wants! Look at yer eyes! They's lust fur me in 'em, burnin' 'em up! Look at yer lips now! They're tremblin' an' longin' t' kiss me, an' yer teeth t' bite! (*He is watching her now with a horrible fascination. She laughs a crazy triumphant laugh.*) I'm a-goin' t' make all o' this hum my hum! They's one room hain't mine yet, but it's a-goin' t' be tonight. I'm a-goin' down now an' light up! (*She makes him a mocking bow.*) Won't ye come courtin' me in the best parlor, Mister Cabot?

EBEN (*staring at her—horribly confused—dully*):   Don't ye dare! It hain't been opened since Maw died an' was laid out thar! Don't ye . . . ! (*But her eyes are fixed on his so burningly that his will seems to wither before hers. He stands swaying toward her helplessly.*)

ABBIE (*holding his eyes and putting all her will into her words as she backs out the door*): I'll expect ye afore long, Eben.

EBEN (*Stares after her for a while, walking toward the door. A light appears in the parlor window. He murmurs.*): In the parlor? (*This seems to arouse connotations, for he comes back and puts on his white shirt, collar, half ties the tie mechanically, puts on coat, takes his hat, stands barefooted looking about him in bewilderment, mutters wonderingly.*) Maw! Whar air yew? (*Then goes slowly toward the door in rear.*)

SCENE III

(*A few minutes later. The interior of the parlor is shown. A grim, repressed room like a tomb in which the family has been interred alive. Abbie sits on the edge of the horsehair sofa. She has lighted all the candles and the room is revealed in all its preserved ugliness. A change has come over the woman. She looks awed and frightened now, ready to run away.*)

(*The door is opened and Eben appears. His face wears an expression of obsessed confusion. He stands staring at her, his arms hanging disjointedly from his shoulders, his feet bare, his hat in his hand.*)

ABBIE (*after a pause—with a nervous, formal politeness*):   Won't ye set?

EBEN (*dully*):   Ay-eh. (*Mechanically he places his hat carefully on the floor near the door and sits stiffly beside her on the edge of the sofa. A pause. They both remain rigid, looking straight ahead with eyes full of fear.*)

ABBIE: When I fust come in—in the dark—they seemed somethin' here.

EBEN (*simply*):   Maw.

ABBIE: I kin still feel—somethin'. . . .

EBEN: It's Maw.

ABBIE: At fust I was feered o' it. I wanted t' yell an' run. Now—since yew come—seems like it's growin' soft an' kind t' me. (*Addressing the air—queerly.*) Thank yew.

EBEN: Maw allus loved me.

ABBIE: Mebbe it knows I love yew, too. Mebbe that makes it kind t' me.

EBEN (*dully*):   I dunno. I should think she'd hate ye.

ABBIE (*with certainty*):   No. I kin feel it don't—not no more.

EBEN: Hate ye fur stealin' her place—here in her hum—settin' in her parlor whar she was laid— (*He suddenly stops, staring stupidly before him.*)

ABBIE: What is it, Eben?

EBEN (*in a whisper*):   Seems like Maw didn't want me t' remind ye.

ABBIE (*excitedly*):   I knowed, Eben! It's kind t' me! It don't b'ar me no grudges fur what I never knowed an' couldn't help!

EBEN: Maw b'ars him a grudge.

ABBIE: Waal, so does all o'us.

EBEN: Ay-eh. (*With passion.*) I does, by God!

ABBIE (*taking one of his hands in hers and patting it*):   Thar! Don't git riled thinkin' o' him. Think o' yer Maw who's kind t' us. Tell me about yer Maw, Eben.

EBEN: They hain't nothin' much. She was kind. She was good.

ABBIE (*Putting one arm over his shoulder. He does not seem to notice—passionately.*): I'll be kind an' good t' ye!

EBEN: Sometimes she used t' sing fur me.

ABBIE: I'll sing fur ye!

EBEN: This was her hum. This was her farm.

ABBIE: This is my hum! This is my farm!

EBEN: He married her t' steal 'em. She was soft an' easy. He couldn't 'preciate her.

ABBIE: He can't 'preciate me!

EBEN: He murdered her with his hardness.

ABBIE: He's murderin' me!

EBEN: She died. (*A pause.*) Sometimes she used to sing fur me. (*He bursts into a fit of sobbing.*)

ABBIE (*both her arms around him—with wild passion*):   I'll sing fur ye! I'll die fur ye! (*In spite of her overwhelming desire for him, there is a sincere maternal love in her manner and voice—a horribly frank mixture of lust and mother love.*) Don't cry, Eben! I'll take yer Maw's place! I'll be everythin' she was t' ye! Let me kiss ye, Eben! (*She pulls his head around. He makes a bewildered pretense of resistance. She is tender.*) Don't be afeered! I'll kiss ye pure, Eben—same's if I was a Maw t' ye—an' ye kin kiss me back 's if yew was my son—my boy— sayin' good-night t' me! Kiss me, Eben. (*They kiss in restrained fashion. Then suddenly wild passion overcomes her. She kisses him lustfully again and again and he flings his arms about her and returns her kisses. Suddenly, as in the bed-*

room, he frees himself from her violently and springs to his feet. He is trembling all over, in a strange state of terror. Abbie strains her arms toward him with fierce pleading.) Don't ye leave me, Eben! Can't ye see it hain't enuf—lovin' ye like a Maw—can't ye see it's got t' be that an' more—much more—a hundred times more—fur me t' be happy—fur yew t' be happy?

EBEN *(to the presence he feels in the room)*: Maw! Maw! What d'ye want? What air ye tellin' me?

ABBIE: She's tellin' ye t' love me. She knows I love ye an' I'll be good t' ye. Can't ye feel it? Don't ye know? She's tellin' ye t' love me, Eben!

EBEN: Ay-eh. I feel—mebbe she—but—I can't figger out—why—when ye've stole her place—here in her hum—in the parlor whar she was—

ABBIE *(fiercely)*: She knows I love ye!

EBEN *(his face suddenly lighting up with a fierce, triumphant grin)*: I see it! I sees why. It's her vengeance on him—so's she kin rest quiet in her grave!

ABBIE *(wildly)*: Vengeance o' God on the hull o' us! What d'we give a durn? I love ye, Eben! God knows I love ye! *(She stretches out her arms for him.)*

EBEN *(throws himself on his knees beside the sofa and grabs her in his arms—releasing all his pent-up passion)*: An' I love ye, Abbie!—now I kin say it! I been dyin' fur want o' ye—every hour since ye come! I love ye! *(Their lips meet in a fierce, bruising kiss.)*

SCENE IV

(Exterior of the farmhouse. It is just dawn. The front door at right is opened and Eben comes out and walks around to the gate. He is dressed in his working clothes. He seems changed. His face wears a bold and confident expression, he is grinning to himself with evident satisfaction. As he gets near the gate, the window of the parlor is heard opening and the shutters are flung back and Abbie sticks her head out. Her hair tumbles over her shoulders in disarray, her face is flushed, she looks at Eben with tender, languorous eyes and calls softly.)

ABBIE: Eben. *(As he turns—playfully.)* Jest one more kiss afore ye go. I'm goin' to miss ye fearful all day.

EBEN: An' me yew, ye kin bet! *(He goes to her. They kiss several times. He draws away, laughingly.)* Thar. That's enuf, hain't it? Ye won't hev none left fur next time.

ABBIE: I got a million o' 'em left fur yew! *(Then a bit anxiously.)* D'ye r'ally love me, Eben?

EBEN *(emphatically)*: I like ye better'n any gal I ever knowed! That's gospel!

ABBIE: Likin' hain't lovin'.

EBEN: Waal then—I love ye. Now air yew satisfied?

ABBIE: Ay-eh, I be. *(She smiles at him adoringly.)*

EBEN: I better git t' the barn. The old critter's liable t' suspicion an' come sneakin' up.

ABBIE *(with a confident laugh)*: Let him! I kin allus pull the wool over his eyes. I'm goin' t' leave the shutters open and let in the sun 'n' air. This room's been dead long enuf. Now it's goin' t' be my room!

EBEN *(frowning)*: Ay-eh.

ABBIE *(hastily)*: I meant—our room.

EBEN: Ay-eh.

ABBIE: We made it our'n last night, didn't we? We give it life—our lovin' did. (*A pause.*)

EBEN (*with a strange look*):   Maw's gone back t' her grave. She kin sleep now.

ABBIE: May she rest in peace! (*Then tenderly rebuking.*) Ye oughtn't t' talk o' sad thin's—this mornin'.

EBEN: It jest come up in my mind o' itself.

ABBIE: Don't let it. (*He doesn't answer. She yawns.*) Waal, I'm a-goin' t' steal a wink o' sleep. I'll tell the Old Man I hain't feelin' pert. Let him git his own vittles.

EBEN: I see him comin' from the barn. Ye better look smart an' git upstairs.

ABBIE: Ay-eh. Good-by. Don't ferget me. (*She throws him a kiss. He grins—then squares his shoulders and awaits his father confidently. Cabot walks slowly up from the left, staring up at the sky with a vague face.*)

EBEN (*jovially*):   Mornin', Paw. Star-gazin' in daylight?

CABOT: Purty, hain't it?

EBEN (*looking around him possessively*):   It's a durned purty farm.

CABOT: I mean the sky.

EBEN (*grinning*):   How d'ye know? Them eyes o' your'n can't see that fur. (*This tickles his humor and he slaps his thigh and laughs.*) Ho-ho! That's a good un!

CABOT (*grimly sarcastic*):   Ye're feelin' right chipper, hain't ye? Whar'd ye steal the likker?

EBEN (*good-naturedly*):   'Tain't likker. Jest life. (*Suddenly holding out his hand—soberly.*) Yew 'n' me is quits. Let's shake hands.

CABOT (*suspiciously*):   What's come over ye?

EBEN: Then don't. Mebbe it's jest as well. (*A moment's pause.*) What's come over me? (*Queerly.*) Didn't ye feel her passin'—goin' back t' her grave?

CABOT (*dully*):   Who?

EBEN: Maw. She kin rest now an' sleep content. She's quit with ye.

CABOT (*confusedly*):   I rested. I slept good—down with the cows. They know how t' sleep. They're teachin' me.

EBEN (*suddenly jovial again*):   Good fur the cows! Waal—ye better git t' work.

CABOT (*grimly amused*):   Air yew bossin' me, ye calf?

EBEN (*beginning to laugh*):   Ay-eh! I'm bossin' yew! Ha-ha-ha! See how ye like it! Ha-ha-ha! I'm the prize rooster o' this roost. Ha-ha-ha! (*He goes off toward the barn laughing.*)

CABOT (*looks after him with scornful pity*):   Soft-headed. Like his Maw. Dead spit 'n' image. No hope in him! (*He spits with contemptuous disgust.*) A born fool! (*Then matter-of-factly.*) Waal—I'm gittin' peckish. (*He goes toward door.*)

PART III, SCENE I

(*A night in late spring the following year. The kitchen and the two bedrooms upstairs are shown. The two bedrooms are dimly lighted by a tallow candle in each. Eben is sitting on the side of the bed in his room, his chin propped on his fists, his face a study of the struggle he is making to understand his conflicting emotions. The noisy laughter and music from below where a kitchen dance is in progress annoy and distract him. He scowls at the floor.*)

(In the next room a cradle stands beside the double bed.)

(In the kitchen all is festivity. The stove has been taken down to give more room to the dancers. The chairs, with wooden benches added, have been pushed back against the walls. On these are seated, squeezed in tight against one another, farmers and their wives and their young folks of both sexes from the neighboring farms. They are all chattering and laughing loudly. They evidently have some secret joke in common. There is no end of winking, of nudging, of meaning nods of the head toward Cabot who, in a state of extreme hilarious excitement increased by the amount he has drunk, is standing near the rear door where there is a small keg of whisky and serving drinks to all the men. In the left corner, front, dividing the attention with her husband, Abbie is sitting in a rocking chair, a shawl wrapped about her shoulders. She is very pale, her face is thin and drawn, her eyes are fixed anxiously on the open door in rear as if waiting for someone.)

(The musician is tuning up his fiddle, seated in the far right corner. He is a lanky young fellow with a long, weak face. His pale eyes blink incessantly and he grins about him slyly with a greedy malice.)

ABBIE *(suddenly turning to a young girl on her right)*:   Whar's Eben?

YOUNG GIRL *(eyeing her scornfully)*:   I dunno, Mrs. Cabot. I hain't seen Eben in ages. *(Meaningly.)* Seems like he's spent most o' his time t' hum since yew come.

ABBIE *(vaguely)*:   I tuk his Maw's place.

YOUNG GIRL: Ay-eh. So I've heerd. *(She turns away to retail this bit of gossip to her mother sitting next to her. Abbie turns to her left to a big stoutish middle-aged man whose flushed face and starting eyes show the amount of "likker" he has consumed.)*

ABBIE: Ye hain't seen Eben, hev ye?

MAN: No, I hain't. *(Then he adds with a wink.)* If yew hain't, who would?

ABBIE: He's the best dancer in the county. He'd ought t' come an' dance.

MAN *(with a wink)*: Mebbe he's doin' the dutiful an' walkin' the kid t' sleep. It's a boy, hain't it?

ABBIE *(nodding vaguely)*:   Ay-eh—born two weeks back—purty's a picter.

MAN: They all is—t' their Maws. *(Then in a whisper, with a nudge and a leer.)* Listen, Abbie—if ye ever git tired o' Eben, remember me! Don't fergit now! *(He looks at her uncomprehending face for a second—then grunts disgustedly.)* Waal—guess I'll likker agin. *(He goes over and joins Cabot who is arguing noisily with an old farmer over cows. They all drink.)*

ABBIE *(this time appealing to nobody in particular)*:   Wonder what Eben's a-doin'? *(Her remark is repeated down the line with many a guffaw and titter until it reaches the fiddler. He fastens his blinking eyes on Abbie.)*

FIDDLER *(raising his voice)*:   Bet I kin tell ye, Abbie, what Eben's doin'! He's down t' the church offerin' up prayers o' thanksgivin'. *(They all titter expectantly.)*

A MAN: What fur? *(Another titter.)*

FIDDLER: 'Cause unto him a— *(He hesitates just long enough.)* brother is born! *(A roar of laughter. They all look from Abbie to Cabot. She is oblivious, staring at the door. Cabot, although he hasn't heard the words, is irritated by the laughter and steps forward, glaring about him. There is an immediate silence.)*

CABOT: What're ye all bleatin' about—like a flock o' goats? Why don't ye dance, damn ye? I axed ye here t'dance—t' eat, drink an' be merry—an' thar ye set cacklin' like a lot o' wet hens with the pip! Ye've swilled my likker an' guzzled my vittles like hogs, hain't ye? Then dance fur me, can't ye? That's fa'r an' squar', hain't it? (*A grumble of resentment goes around but they are all evidently in too much awe of him to express it openly.*)

FIDDLER (*slyly*):   We're waitin' fur Eben. (*A suppressed laugh.*)

CABOT (*with a fierce exultation*):   T'hell with Eben! Eben's done fur now! I got a new son! (*His mood switching with drunken suddenness.*) But ye needn't t' laugh at Eben, none o' ye! He's my blood, if he be a dumb fool. He's better nor any o' yew! He kin do a day's work a'most up t' what I kin–an' that'd put any o' yew pore critters t' shame!

FIDDLER: An' he kin do a good night's work, too! (*A roar of laughter.*)

CABOT: Laugh, ye damn fools! Ye're right jist the same, Fiddler. He kin work day an' night too, like I kin, if need be!

OLD FARMER (*from behind the keg where he is weaving drunkenly back and forth—with great simplicity*): They hain't many t' touch ye, Ephraim—a son at seventy-six. That's a hard man fur ye! I be on'y sixty-eight an' I couldn't do it. (*A roar of laughter in which Cabot joins uproariously.*)

CABOT (*slapping him on the back*):   I'm sorry fur ye, Hi. I'd never suspicion sech weakness from a boy like yew!

OLD FARMER: An' I never reckoned yew had it in ye nuther, Ephraim. (*There is another laugh.*)

CABOT (*suddenly grim*):   I got a lot in me—a hell of a lot—folks don't know on. (*Turning to the fiddler.*) Fiddle 'er up, durn ye! Give 'em somethin' t' dance t'! What air ye, an ornament? Hain't this a celebration? Then grease yer elbow an' go it!

FIDDLER (*seizes a drink which the Old Farmer holds out to him and downs it*):   Here goes! (*He starts to fiddle "Lady of the Lake." Four young fellows and four girls form in two lines and dance a square dance. The Fiddler shouts directions for the different movements, keeping his words in the rhythm of the music and interspersing them with jocular personal remarks to the dancers themselves. The people seated along the walls stamp their feet and clap their hands in unison. Cabot is especially active in this respect. Only Abbie remains apathetic, staring at the door as if she were alone in a silent room.*)

FIDDLER: Swing your partner t' the right! That's it, Jim! Give her a b'ar hug. Her Maw hain't lookin'. (*Laughter.*) Change partners! That suits ye, don't it, Essie, now ye got Reub afore ye? Look at her redden up, will ye? Waal, life is short an' so's love, as the feller says. (*Laughter.*)

CABOT (*excitedly, stamping his foot*):   Go it, boys! Go it, gals!

FIDDLER (*with a wink at the others*):   Ye're the spryest seventy-six ever I sees, Ephraim! Now if ye'd on'y good eyesight . . . ! (*Suppressed laughter. He gives Cabot no chance to retort but roars.*) Promenade! Ye're walkin' like a bride down the aisle, Sarah! Waal, while they's life they's allus hope, I've heerd tell. Swing your partner to the left! Gosh A'mighty, look at Johnny Cook high-steppin'! They hain't goin' t' be much strength left fur howin' in the corn lot t'morrow. (*Laughter.*)

CABOT: Go it! Go it! (*Then suddenly, unable to restrain himself any longer, he prances into the midst of the dancers, scattering them, waving his arms about wildly.*) Ye're all hoofs! Git out o' my road! Give me room! I'll show ye dancin'. Ye're all too soft! (*He pushes them roughly away. They crowd back toward the walls, muttering, looking at him resentfully.*)

FIDDLER (*jeeringly*):   Go it, Ephraim! Go it! (*He starts "Pop, Goes the Weasel," increasing the tempo with every verse until at the end he is fiddling crazily as fast as he can go.*)

CABOT (*Starts to dance, which he does very well and with tremendous vigor. Then he begins to improvise, cuts incredibly grotesque capers, leaping up and cracking his heels together, prancing around in a circle with body bent in an Indian war dance, then suddenly straightening up and kicking as high as he can with both legs. He is like a monkey on a string. And all the while he intersperses his antics with shouts and derisive comments.*): Whoop! Here's dancin' fur ye! Whoop! See that! Seventy-six, if I'm a day! Hard as iron yet! Beatin' the young 'uns like I allus done! Look at me! I'd invite ye t' dance on my hundredth birthday on'y ye'll all be dead by then. Ye're a sickly generation! Yer hearts air pink, not red! Yer veins is full o' mud an' water! I be the on'y man in the county! Whoop! See that! I'm a Injun! I've killed Injuns in the West afore ye was born—an' skulped 'em too! They's a arrer wound on my backside I c'd show ye! The hull tribe chased me. I outrun 'em all—with the arrer stuck in me! An' I tuk vengeance on 'em. Ten eyes fur an eye, that was my motter! Whoop! Look at me! I kin kick the ceilin' off the room! Whoop!

FIDDLER (*stops playing—exhaustedly*):   God A'mighty, I got enuf. Ye got the devil's strength in ye.

CABOT (*delightedly*):   Did I beat yew, too? Waal, ye played smart. Hev a swig. (*He pours whisky for himself and Fiddler. They drink. The others watch Cabot silently with cold, hostile eyes. There is a dead pause. The Fiddler rests. Cabot leans against the keg, panting, glaring around him confusedly. In the room above, Eben gets to his feet and tiptoes out the door in rear, appearing a moment later in the other bedroom. He moves silently, even frightenedly, toward the cradle and stands there looking down at the baby. His face is as vague as his reactions are confused, but there is a trace of tenderness, of interested discovery. At the same moment that he reaches the cradle, Abbie seems to sense something. She gets up weakly and goes to Cabot.*)

ABBIE: I'm goin' up t' the baby.

CABOT (*with real solicitation*):   Air ye able fur the stairs? D'ye want me t' help ye, Abbie?

ABBIE: No, I'm able. I'll be down agen soon.

CABOT: Don't ye git wore out! He needs ye, remember—our son does! (*He grins affectionately, patting her on the back. She shrinks from his touch.*)

ABBIE (*dully*):   Don't—tech me. I'm goin'—up. (*She goes. Cabot looks after her. A whisper goes around the room. Cabot turns. It ceases. He wipes his forehead streaming with sweat. He is breathing pantingly.*)

CABOT: I'm a-goin' out t' git fresh air. I'm feelin' a mite dizzy. Fiddle up thar! Dance, all o' ye! Here's likker fur them as wants it. Enjoy yerselves. I'll be back. (*He goes, closing the door behind him.*)

FIDDLER (*sarcastically*):   Don't hurry none on our account! (*A suppressed laugh. He imitates Abbie.*) Whar's Eben? (*More laughter.*)

A WOMAN (*loudly*):   What's happened in this house is plain as the nose on yer face! (*Abbie appears in the doorway upstairs and stands looking in surprise and adoration at Eben who does not see her.*)

A MAN: Ssshh! He's li'ble t' be listenin' at the door. That'd be like him. (*Their voices die to an intensive whispering. Their faces are concentrated on this gossip. A noise as of dead leaves in the wind comes from the room. Cabot has come out from the porch and stands by the gate, leaning on it, staring at the sky blinkingly. Abbie comes across the room silently. Eben does not notice her until quite near.*)

EBEN (*starting*): Abbie!

ABBIE: Sshh! (*She throws her arms around him. They kiss—then bend over the cradle together.*) Ain't he purty?—dead spit 'n' image o' yew!

EBEN (*pleased*): Air he? I can't tell none.

ABBIE: E-zactly like!

EBEN (*frowningly*): I don't like this. I don't like lettin' on what's mine's his'n. I been doin' that all my life. I'm gittin' t' the end o' b'arin' it!

ABBIE (*putting her finger on his lips*): We're doin' the best we kin. We got t' wait. Somethin's bound t' happen. (*She puts her arms around him.*) I got t' go back.

EBEN: I'm goin' out. I can't b'ar it with the fiddle playin' an' the laughin'.

ABBIE: Don't git feelin' low. I love ye, Eben. Kiss me. (*He kisses her. They remain in each other's arms.*)

CABOT (*at the gate, confusedly*): Even the music can't drive it out—somethin'. Ye kin feel it droppin' off the elums, climbin' up the roof, sneakin' down the chimney, pokin' in the corners! They's no peace in houses, they's no rest livin' with folks. Somethin's always livin' with ye. (*With a deep sigh.*) I'll go t' the barn an' rest a spell. (*He goes wearily toward the barn.*)

FIDDLER (*tuning up*): Let's celebrate the old skunk gittin' fooled! We kin have some fun now he's went. (*He starts to fiddle "Turkey in the Straw." There is real merriment now. The young folks get up to dance.*)

Scene II

(*A half hour later—exterior—Eben is standing by the gate looking up at the sky, an expression of dumb pain bewildered by itself on his face. Cabot appears, returning from the barn, walking wearily, his eyes on the ground. He sees Eben and his whole mood immediately changes. He becomes excited, a cruel, triumphant grin comes to his lips, he strides up and slaps Eben on the back. From within comes the whining of the fiddle and the noise of stamping feet and laughing voices.*)

CABOT: So har ye be!

EBEN (*startled, stares at him with hatred for a moment—then dully*): Ay-eh.

CABOT (*surveying him jeeringly*): Why hain't ye been in t' dance? They was all axin' fur ye.

EBEN: Let 'em ax!

CABOT: They's a hull passel o' purty gals.

EBEN: T' hell with 'em!

CABOT: Ye'd ought t' be marryin' one o' 'em soon.

EBEN: I hain't marryin' no one.

CABOT: Ye might 'arn a share o' a farm that way.

EBEN (*with a sneer*): Like yew did, ye mean? I hain't that kind.

CABOT (*stung*): Ye lie! 'Twas yer Maw's folks aimed t' steal my farm from me.

EBEN: Other folks don't say so. (*After a pause—defiantly.*) An' I got a farm, anyways!

CABOT (*derisively*): Whar?

EBEN (*stamps a foot on the ground*): Har!

CABOT (*throws his head back and laughs coarsely*): Ho-ho! Ye hev, hev ye? Waal, that's a good un!

EBEN (*controlling himself—grimly*): Ye'll see!

CABOT (*stares at him suspiciously, trying to make him out—a pause—then with scornful confidence*): Ay-eh. I'll see. So'll ye. It's ye that's blind—blind as a mole underground. (*Eben suddenly laughs, one short sardonic bark: "Ha." A pause. Cabot peers at him with renewed suspicion.*) What air ye hawin' 'bout? (*Eben turns away without answering. Cabot grows angry.*) God A'mighty, yew air a dumb dunce! They's nothin' in that thick skull o' your'n but noise—like a empty keg it be! (*Eben doesn't seem to hear. Cabot's rage grows.*) Yewr farm! God A'mighty! If ye wa'n't a born donkey ye'd know ye'll never own stick nor stone on it, specially now arter him bein' born. It's his'n, I tell ye—his'n arter I die—but I'll live a hundred jest t' fool ye all—an' he'll be growed then—yewr age a'most! (*Eben laughs again his sardonic "Ha." This drives Cabot into a fury.*) Ha? Ye think ye kin git 'round that someways, do ye? Waal, it'll be her'n, too— Abbie's—ye won't git 'round her—she knows yer tricks—she'll be too much fur ye—she wants the farm her'n—she was afeerd o' ye—she told me ye was sneakin' 'round tryin' t' make love t' her t' git her on yer side . . . ye . . . ye mad fool, ye! (*He raises his clenched fists threateningly.*)

EBEN (*is confronting him, choking with rage*): Ye lie, ye old skunk! Abbie never said no sech thing!

CABOT (*suddenly triumphant when he sees how shaken Eben is*): She did. An' I says, I'll blow his brains t' the top o' them elums—an' she says no, that hain't sense, who'll ye git t'help ye on the farm in his place—an' then she says yew'n me ought t' have a son—I know we kin, she says—an' I says, if we do, ye kin have anythin' I've got ye've a mind t'. An' she says, I wants Eben cut off so's this farm'll be mine when ye die! (*With terrible gloating.*) An' that's what's happened, hain't it? An' the farm's her'n! An' the dust o' the road—that's you'rn! Ha! Now who's hawin'?

EBEN (*has been listening, petrified with grief and rage—suddenly laughs wildly and brokenly*): Ha-ha-ha! So that's her sneakin' game—all along!—like I suspicioned at fust—t' swaller it all—an' me, too . . . ! (*Madly.*) I'll murder her! (*He springs toward the porch but Cabot is quicker and gets in between.*)

CABOT: No, ye don't!

EBEN: Git out o' my road! (*He tries to throw Cabot aside. They grapple in what becomes immediately a murderous struggle. The old man's concentrated strength is too much for Eben. Cabot gets one hand on his throat and presses him back across the stone wall. At the same moment, Abbie comes out on the porch. With a stifled cry she runs toward them.*)

ABBIE: Eben! Ephraim! (*She tugs at the hand on Eben's throat.*) Let go, Ephraim! Ye're chokin' him!

CABOT (*Removes his hand and flings Eben sideways full length on the grass, gasping and choking. With a cry, Abbie kneels beside him, trying to take his head on her lap, but he pushes her away. Cabot stands looking down with fierce triumph.*): Ye needn't t've fret, Abbie, I wa'n't aimin' t' kill him. He hain't wuth hangin' fur—not by a hell of a sight! (*More and more triumphantly.*) Seventy-six an' him not thirty yit—an' look whar he be fur thinkin' his Paw was easy! No, by God, I hain't easy! An' him upstairs, I'll raise him t' be like me! (*He turns to *leave them.*) I'm goin' in an' dance!—sing an' celebrate! (*He walks to the porch—then turns with a great grin.*) I don't calc'late it's left in him, but if he gits pesky, Abbie, ye jest sing out. I'll come a-runnin' an' by the Etarnal, I'll put him across my knee an' birch him! Ha-ha-ha! (*He goes into the house laughing. A moment later his loud "whoop" is heard.*)

ABBIE (*tenderly*): Eben. Air ye hurt? (*She tries to kiss him but he pushes her violently away and struggles to a sitting position.*)

EBEN (*gaspingly*): T'hell—with ye!

ABBIE (*not believing her ears*): It's me, Eben—Abbie—don't ye know me?

EBEN (*glowering at her with hatred*): Ay-eh—I know ye—now! (*He suddenly breaks down, sobbing weakly.*)

ABBIE (*fearfully*): Eben—what's happened t' ye—why did ye look at me 's if ye hated me?

EBEN (*violently, between sobs and gasps*): I do hate ye! Ye're a whore—a damn trickin' whore!

ABBIE (*shrinking back horrified*): Eben! Ye don't know what ye're sayin'!

EBEN (*scrambling to his feet and following her—accusingly*): Ye're nothin' but a stinkin' passel o' lies! Ye've been lyin' t' me every word ye spoke, day an' night, since we fust—done it. Y've kept sayin' ye loved me. . . .

ABBIE (*frantically*): I do love ye! (*She takes his hand but he flings hers away.*)

EBEN (*unheeding*): Ye've made a fool o' me—a sick, dumb fool—a-purpose! Ye've been on'y playin' yer sneakin', stealin' game all along—gittin' me t' lie with ye so's ye'd hev a son he'd think was his'n, an' makin' him promise he'd give ye the farm and let me eat dust, if ye did git him a son! (*Staring at her with anguished, bewildered eyes.*) They must be a devil livin' in ye! T'ain't human t' be as bad as that be!

ABBIE (*stunned—dully*): He told yew . . . ?

EBEN: Hain't it true? It hain't no good in yew lyin'.

ABBIE (*pleadingly*): Eben, listen—ye must listen—it was long ago—afore we done nothin'—yew was scornin' me—goin' t' see Min—when I was lovin' ye—an' I said it t' him t' git vengeance on ye!

EBEN (*Unheedingly. With tortured passion.*): I wish ye was dead! I wish I was dead along with ye afore this come! (*Ragingly.*) But I'll git my vengeance too! I'll pray Maw t' come back t' help me—t' put her cuss on yew an' him!

ABBIE (*brokenly*): Don't ye, Eben! Don't ye! (*She throws herself on her knees before him, weeping.*) I didn't mean t' do bad t'ye! Fergive me, won't ye?

EBEN (*not seeming to hear her—fiercely*): I'll git squar' with the old skunk— an' yew! I'll tell him the truth 'bout the son he's so proud o'! Then I'll leave ye here t' pizen each other—with Maw comin' out o' her grave at nights—an' I'll go t' the gold fields o' Californi-a whar Sim an' Peter be!

ABBIE (*terrified*): Ye won't—leave me? Ye can't!

EBEN (*with fierce determination*): I'm a-goin', I tell ye! I'll git rich thar an' come back an' fight him fur the farm he stole—an' I'll kick ye both out in the road—t' beg an' sleep in the woods—an' yer son along with ye—t' starve an' die! (*He is hysterical at the end.*)

ABBIE (*with a shudder—humbly*): He's yewr son, too, Eben.

EBEN (*torturedly*): I wish he never was born! I wish he'd die this minit! I wish I'd never sot eyes on him! It's him—yew havin' him—a-purpose t' steal—that's changed everythin'!

ABBIE (*gently*): Did ye believe I loved ye—afore he come?

EBEN: Aye-eh—like a dumb ox!

ABBIE: An' ye don't believe no more?

EBEN: B'lieve a lyin' thief! Ha!

ABBIE (*shudders—then humbly*):   An' did ye r'ally love me afore?

EBEN (*brokenly*):   Ay-eh—an' ye was trickin' me!

ABBIE: An' ye don't love me now!

EBEN (*violently*):   I hate ye, I tell ye!

ABBIE: An' ye're truly goin' West—goin' t' leave me—all account o' him being born?

EBEN: I'm a-goin' in the mornin'—or may God strike me t' hell!

ABBIE (*after a pause—with dreadful cold intensity—slowly*):   If that's what his comin's done t' me—killin' yewr love—takin' yew away—my on'y joy—the on'y joy I ever knowed—like heaven t' me—purtier'n heaven—then I hate him, too, even if I be his Maw!

EBEN (*bitterly*):   Lies! Ye love him! He'll steal the farm fur ye! (*Brokenly.*) But t'ain't the farm so much—not no more—it's yew foolin' me—gittin' me t' love ye—lyin' yew loved me—jest t' git a son t' steal!

ABBIE (*distractedly*):   He won't steal! I'd kill him fust! I do love ye! I'll prove t' ye . . . !

EBEN (*harshly*):   T'ain't no use lyin' no more. I'm deaf t' ye! (*He turns away.*) I hain't seein' ye agen. Good-by!

ABBIE (*pale with anguish*):   Hain't ye even goin' t' kiss me—not once—arter all we loved?

EBEN (*in a hard voice*):   I hain't wantin' t' kiss ye never agen! I'm wantin' t' forgit I ever sot eyes on ye!

ABBIE: Eben!—ye mustn't—wait a spell—I want t' tell ye. . . .

EBEN: I'm a-goin' in t' git drunk. I'm a-goin' t' dance.

ABBIE (*clinging to his arm—with passionate earnestness*):   If I could make it—'s if he'd never come up between us—if I could prove t' ye I wa'n't schemin' t' steal from ye—so's everythin' could be jest the same with us, lovin' each other jest the same, kissin' an' happy the same's we've been happy afore he come—if I could do it—ye'd love me agen, wouldn't ye? Ye'd kiss me agen? Ye wouldn't never leave me, would ye?

EBEN (*moved*):   I calc'late not. (*Then shaking her hand off his arm—with a bitter smile.*) But ye hain't God, be ye?

ABBIE (*exultantly*):   Remember y've promised! (*Then with strange intensity.*) Mebbe I kin take back one thin' God does!

EBEN (*peering at her*):   Ye're gittin' cracked, hain't ye? (*Then going toward door.*) I'm a-goin' t' dance.

ABBIE (*calls after him intensely*):   I'll prove t' ye! I'll prove I love ye bettter'n. . . . (*He goes in the door, not seeming to hear. She remains standing where she is, looking after him—then she finishes desperately.*) Better'n everythin' else in the world!

Scene III

(*Just before dawn in the morning—shows the kitchen and Cabot's bedroom. In the kitchen, by the light of a tallow candle on the table, Eben is sitting, his chin propped on his hands, his drawn face blank and expressionless. His carpetbag is on the floor beside him. In the bedroom, dimly lighted by a small whale-oil lamp,*

Cabot lies asleep. Abbie is bending over the cradle, listening, her face full of terror yet with an undercurrent of desperate triumph. Suddenly, she breaks down and sobs, appears about to throw herself on her knees beside the cradle; but the old man turns restlessly, groaning in his sleep, and she controls herself, and, shrinking away from the cradle with a gesture of horror, backs swiftly toward the door in rear and goes out. A moment later she comes into the kitchen and, running to Eben, flings her arms about his neck and kisses him wildly. He hardens himself, he remains unmoved and cold, he keeps his eyes straight ahead.)

ABBIE (*hysterically*):   I done it, Eben! I told ye I'd do it! I've proved I love ye—better'n everythin'—so's ye can't never doubt me no more!

EBEN (*dully*):   Whatever ye done, it hain't no good now.

ABBIE (*wildly*):   Don't ye say that! Kiss me, Eben, won't ye? I need ye t' kiss me arter what I done! I need ye t' say ye love me!

EBEN (*kisses her without emotion—dully*):   That's fur good-by. I'm a-goin' soon.

ABBIE: No! No! Ye won't go—not now!

EBEN (*going on with his own thoughts*):   I been a-thinkin'—an' I hain't goin' t' tell Paw nothin'. I'll leave Maw t' take vengeance on ye. If I told him, the old skunk'd jest be stinkin' mean enuf to take it out on that baby. (*His voice showing emotion in spite of him.*) An' I don't want nothin' bad t' happen t' him. He hain't t' blame fur yew. (*He adds with a certain queer pride.*) An' he looks like me! An' by God, he's mine! An' some day I'll be a-comin' back an' . . . !

ABBIE (*too absorbed in her own thoughts to listen to him—pleadingly*): They's no cause fur ye t' go now—they's no sense—it's all the same's it was—they's nothin' come b'tween us now—arter what I done!

EBEN (*Something in her voice arouses him. He stares at her a bit frightenedly.*): Ye look mad, Abbie. What did ye do?

ABBIE: I—I killed him, Eben.

EBEN (*amazed*):   Ye killed him?

ABBIE (*dully*):   Ay-eh.

EBEN (*recovering from his astonishment—savagely*):   An' serves him right! But we got t' do somethin' quick t' make it look s'if the old skunk'd killed himself when he was drunk. We kin prove by 'em all how drunk he got.

ABBIE (*wildly*):   No! No! Not him! (*Laughing distractedly.*) But that's what I ought t' done, hain't it? I oughter killed him instead! Why didn't ye tell me?

EBEN (*appalled*):   Instead? What d'ye mean?

ABBIE: Not him.

EBEN (*his face grown ghastly*):   Not—not that baby!

ABBIE (*dully*):   Ay-eh!

EBEN (*falls to his knees as if he'd been struck—his voice trembling with horror*):   Oh, God A'mighty! A'mighty God! Maw, whar was ye, why didn't ye stop her?

ABBIE (*simply*):   She went back t' her grave that night we fust done it, remember? I hain't felt her about since. (*A pause. Eben hides his head in his hands, trembling all over as if he had the ague. She goes on dully.*) I left the piller over his little face. Then he killed himself. He stopped breathin'. (*She begins to weep softly.*)

EBEN (*rage beginning to mingle with grief*):   He looked like me. He was mine, damn ye!

ABBIE (*slowly and brokenly*):   I didn't want t' do it. I hated myself fur doin' it.

I loved him. He was so purty—dead spit 'n' image o' yew. But I loved yew more—an' yew was goin' away—far off whar I'd never see ye agen, never kiss ye, never feel ye pressed agin me agen—an' ye said ye hated me fur havin' him— ye said ye hated him an' wished he was dead—ye said if it hadn't been fur him comin' it'd be the same's afore between us.

EBEN (*unable to endure this, springs to his feet in a fury, threatening her, his twitching fingers seeming to reach out for her throat*): Ye lie! I never said—I never dreamed ye'd—I'd cut off my head afore I'd hurt his finger!

ABBIE (*piteously, sinking on her knees*):   Eben, don't ye look at me like that— hatin' me—not after what I done fur ye—fur us—so's we could be happy agen—

EBEN (*furiously now*):   Shut up, or I'll kill ye! I see yer game now—the same old sneakin' trick—ye're aimin' t' blame me fur the murder ye done!

ABBIE (*moaning—putting her hands over her ears*):   Don't ye, Eben! Don't yc! (*She grasps his legs.*)

EBEN (*his mood suddenly changing to horror, shrinks away from her*):   Don't ye tech me! Ye're pizen! How could ye—t' murder a pore little critter—Ye must've swapped yer soul t' hell! (*Suddenly raging.*) Ha! I kin see why ye done it! Not the lies ye jest told—but 'cause ye wanted t' steal agen—steal the last thin' ye'd left me—my part o' him—no, the hull o' him—ye saw he looked like me— ye knowed he was all mine—an' ye couldn't b'ar it—I know ye! Ye killed him fur bein' mine! (*All this has driven him almost insane. He makes a rush past her for the door—then turns—shaking both fists at her, violently.*) But I'll take vengeance now! I'll git the Sheriff! I'll tell him everythin'! Then I'll sing "I'm off to Californi-a!" an' go—gold—Golden Gate—gold sun—fields o'gold in the West! (*This last he half shouts, half croons incoherently, suddenly breaking off passionately.*) I'm a-goin' fur the Sheriff t' come an' git ye! I want ye tuk away, locked up from me! I can't stand t' luk at ye! Murderer an' thief 'r not, ye still tempt me! I'll give ye up t' the Sheriff! (*He turns and runs out, around the corner of house, panting and sobbing, and breaks into a swerving spring down the road.*)

ABBIE (*struggling to her feet, runs to the door, calling after him*):   I love ye, Eben! I love ye! (*She stops at the door weakly, swaying, about to fall.*) I don't care what ye do—if ye'll on'y love me agen—(*She falls limply to the floor in a faint.*)

SCENE IV

(*About an hour later. Same as Scene III. Shows the kitchen and Cabot's bedroom. It is after dawn. The sky is brilliant with the sunrise. In the kitchen, Abbie sits at the table, her body limp and exhausted, her head bowed down over her arms, her face hidden. Upstairs, Cabot is still asleep but awakens with a start. He looks toward the window and gives a snort of surprise and irritation—throws back the covers and begins hurriedly pulling on his clothes. Without looking behind him, he begins talking to Abbie whom he supposes beside him.*)

CABOT: Thunder 'n' lightin', Abbie! I hain't slept this late in fifty year! Looks 's if the sun was full riz a'most. Must've been the dancin' an' likker. Must be gittin' old. I hope Eben's t' wuk. Ye might've tuk the trouble t' rouse me, Abbie. (*He turns—sees no one there—surprised.*) Waal—whar air she? Gittin' vittles, I calc'late. (*He tiptoes to the cradle and peers down—proudly.*) Mornin', sonny.

Purty's a picter! Sleepin' sound. He don't beller all night like most o' 'em. (*He goes quietly out the door in rear—a few moments later enters kitchen—sees Abbie—with satisfaction.*) So thar ye be. Ye got any vittles cooked?

ABBIE (*without moving*): No.

CABOT (*coming to her, almost sympathetically*): Ye feelin' sick?

ABBIE: No.

CABOT (*Pats her on shoulder. She shudders.*): Ye'd best lie down a spell. (*Half jocularly.*) Yer son'll be needin' ye soon. He'd ought t' wake up with a gnashin' appetite, the sound way he's sleepin'.

ABBIE (*shudders—then in a dead voice*): He hain't never goin' t' wake up.

CABOT (*jokingly*): Takes after me this mornin'. I hain't slept so late in . . .

ABBIE: He's dead.

CABOT (*stares at her—bewilderedly*): What. . . .

ABBIE: I killed him.

CABOT (*stepping back from her—aghast*): Air ye drunk—'r crazy—'r . . . ?

ABBIE (*suddenly lifts her head and turns on him—wildly*): I killed him, I tell ye! I smothered him. Go up an' see if ye don't b'lieve me!

(*Cabot stares at her a second, then bolts out the rear door, can be heard bounding up the stairs, and rushes into the bedroom and over to the cradle. Abbie has sunk back lifelessly into her former position. Cabot puts his hand down on the body in the crib. An expression of fear and horror comes over his face.*)

CABOT (*shrinking away—tremblingly*): God A'mighty! God A'mighty. (*He stumbles out the door—in a short while returns to the kitchen—comes to Abbie, the stunned expression still on his face—hoarsely.*) Why did ye do it? Why? (*As she doesn't answer, he grabs her violently by the shoulder and shakes her.*) I ax ye why ye done it! Ye'd better tell me 'r . . . !

ABBIE (*gives him a furious push which sends him staggering back and springs to her feet—with wild rage and hatred*): Don't ye dare tech me! What right hev ye t' question me 'bout him? He wa'n't yewr son! Think I'd have a son by yew? I'd die fust! I hate the sight o' ye an' allus did! It's yew I should've murdered, if I'd had good sense! I hate ye! I love Eben. I did from the fust. An' he was Eben's son— mine an' Eben's—not your'n!

CABOT (*stands looking at her dazedly—a pause—finding his words with an effort—dully*): That was it—what I felt—pokin' round the corners—while ye lied—holdin' yerself from me—sayin' ye'd a'ready conceived—(*He lapses into crushed silence—then with a strange emotion.*) He's dead, sart'n. I felt his heart. Pore little critter! (*He blinks back one tear, wiping his sleeve across his nose.*)

ABBIE (*hysterically*): Don't ye! Don't ye! (*She sobs unrestrainedly.*)

CABOT (*with a concentrated effort that stiffens his body into a rigid line and hardens his face into a stony mask—through his teeth to himself*): I got t' be—like a stone—a rock o' jedgment! (*A pause. He gets complete control over himself— harshly.*) If he was Eben's, I be glad he air gone! An' mebbe I suspicioned it all along. I felt they was somethin' onnateral—somewhars—the house got so lonesome—an' cold—drivin' me down t' the barn—t' the beasts o' the field. . . . Ay-eh. I must've suspicioned—somethin'. Ye didn't fool me—not altogether, leastways—I'm too old a bird—growin' ripe on the bough . . . .(*He becomes aware he is wandering, straightens again, looks at Abbie with a cruel grin.*) So ye'd liked t' hev murdered me 'stead o' him, would ye! Waal, I'll live to a hundred! I'll live t' see ye hung! I'll deliver ye up t' the jedgment o' God an' the law! I'll git the Sheriff now. (*Starts for the door.*)

ABBIE (*dully*):   Ye needn't. Eben's gone fur him.

CABOT (*amazed*):   Eben—gone fur the Sheriff?

ABBIE: Ay-eh.

CABOT: T' inform agen ye?

ABBIE: Ay-eh.

CABOT (*considers this—a pause—then in a hard voice*):   Waal, I'm thankful fur him savin' me the trouble. I'll git t' wuk. (*He goes to the door—then turns— in a voice full of strange emotion.*) He'd ought t' been my son, Abbie. Ye'd ought t' loved me. I'm a man. If ye'd loved me, I'd never told no Sheriff on ye no matter what ye did, if they was t' brile me alive!

ABBIE (*defensively*):   They's more to it nor yew know, makes him tell.

CABOT (*dryly*):   Fur yewr sake, I hope they be. (*He goes out—comes around to the gate—stares up at the sky. His control relaxes. For a moment he is old and weary. He murmurs despairingly.*) God A'mighty, I be lonesomer'n ever! (*He hears running footsteps from the left, immediately is himself again. Eben runs in, panting exhaustedly, wild-eyed and mad looking. He lurches through the gate. Cabot grabs him by the shoulder. Eben stares at him dumbly.*) Did ye tell the Sheriff?

EBEN (*nodding stupidly*):   Ay-eh.

CABOT (*gives him a push away that sends him sprawling—laughing with withering contempt*): Good fur ye! A prime chip o' yer Maw ye be! (*He goes toward the barn, laughing harshly. Eben scrambles to his feet. Suddenly Cabot turns— grimly threatening.*) Git off this farm when the Sheriff takes her—or, by God, he'll have t' come back an' git me fur murder, too! (*He stalks off. Eben does not appear to have heard him. He runs to the door and comes into the kitchen. Abbie looks up with a cry of anguished joy. Eben stumbles over and throws himself on his knees beside her sobbing brokenly.*)

EBEN: Fergive me!

ABBIE (*happily*):   Eben! (*She kisses him and pulls his head over against her breast.*)

EBEN: I love ye! Fergive me!

ABBIE (*ecstatically*):   I'd fergive ye all the sins in hell fur sayin' that! (*She kisses his head, pressing it to her with a fierce passion of possession.*)

EBEN (*brokenly*):   But I told the Sheriff. He's comin' fur ye!

ABBIE: I kin b'ar what happens t' me—now!

EBEN: I woke him up. I told him. He says, wait 'til I git dressed. I was waiting. I got to thinkin' o' yew. I got to thinkin' how I'd loved ye. It hurt like somethin' was bustin' in my chest an' head. I got t' cryin'. I knowed sudden I loved ye yet, an' allus would love ye!

ABBIE (*caressing his hair—tenderly*):   My boy, hain't ye?

EBEN: I begun t' run back. I cut across the fields an' through the woods. I thought ye might have time t' run away—with me—an' . . .

ABBIE (*shaking her head*):   I got t' take my punishment—t' pay fur my sin.

EBEN: Then I want t' share it with ye.

ABBIE: Ye didn't do nothin'.

EBEN: I put it in yer head. I wisht he was dead! I as much as urged ye t' do it!

ABBIE: No. It was me alone!

EBEN: I'm as guilty as yew be! He was the child o' our sin.

ABBIE (*lifting her head as if defying God*):   I don't repent that sin! I hain't askin' God t' fergive that!

EBEN: Nor me—but it led up t' the other—an' the murder ye did, ye did 'count o' me—an' it's my murder, too, I'll tell the Sheriff—an' if ye deny it, I'll say we planned it t'gether—an' they'll all b'lieve me, fur they suspicion everythin' we've done, an' it'll seem likely an' true to 'em. An' it is true—way down. I did help ye—somehow.

ABBIE (*laying her head on his—sobbing*):   No! I don't want yew t' suffer!

EBEN: I got t' pay fur my part o' the sin! An' I'd suffer wuss leavin' ye, goin' West, thinkin' o' ye day an' night, bein' out when yew was in—(*Lowering his voice.*) 'r bein' alive when yew was dead. (*A pause.*) I want t' share with ye, Abbie—prison 'r death 'r hell 'r anythin'! (*He looks into her eyes and forces a trembling smile.*) If I'm sharin' with ye, I won't feel lonesome, leastways.

ABBIE (*weakly*):   Eben! I won't let ye! I can't let ye!

EBEN (*kissing her—tenderly*):   Ye can't he'p yerself. I got ye beat fur once!

ABBIE (*forcing a smile—adoringly*):   I hain't beat—s'long's I got ye!

EBEN (*hears the sound of feet outside*):   Sshh! Listen! They've come t' take us!

ABBIE: No, it's him. Don't give him no chance to fight ye, Eben. Don't say nothin'—no matter what he says. An' I won't neither. (*It is Cabot. He comes up from the barn in a great state of excitement and strides into the house and then into the kitchen. Eben is kneeling beside Abbie, his arm around her, hers around him. They stare straight ahead.*)

CABOT (*Stares at them, his face hard. A long pause—vindictively.*):   Ye make a slick pair o' murderin' turtle doves! Ye'd ought t' be both hung on the same limb an' left thar t' swing in the breeze an' rot—a warnin' t' old fools like me t' b'ar their lonesomeness alone—an' fur young fools like ye t' hobble their lust. (*A pause. The excitement returns to his face, his eyes snap, he looks a bit crazy.*) I couldn't work today. I couldn't take no interest. T' hell with the farm! I'm leavin' it! I've turned the cows an' other stock loose! I've druv 'em into the woods whar they kin be free! By freein' 'em, I'm freein' myself! I'm quittin' here today! I'll set fire t' house an' barn an' watch 'em burn, an' I'll leave yer Maw t' haunt the ashes, an' I'll will the fields back t' God, so that nothin' human kin never touch 'em! I'll be a-goin' to Californi-a—t' jine Simeon an' Peter—true sons o' mine if they be dumb fools—an' the Cabots'll find Solomon's Mines t'gether! (*He suddenly cuts a mad caper.*) Whoop! What was the song they sung? "Oh, Californi-a! That's the land fur me." (*He sings this—then gets on his knees by the floorboard under which the money was hid.*) An' I'll sail thar on one o' the finest clippers I kin find! I've got the money! Pity ye didn't know whar this was hidden so's ye could steal. . . . (*He has pulled up the board. He stares—feels—stares again. A pause of dead silence. He slowly turns, slumping into a sitting position on the floor, his eyes like those of a dead fish, his face the sickly green of an attack of nausea. He swallows painfully several times—forces a weak smile at last.*) So— ye did steal it!

EBEN (*emotionlessly*):   I swapped it t' Sim an' Peter fur their share o' the farm—t' pay their passage t' Californi-a.

CABOT (*with one sardonic*):   Ha! (*He begins to recover. Gets slowly to his feet—strangely.*) I calc'late God give it to 'em—not yew! God's hard, not easy! Mebbe they's easy gold in the West but it hain't God's gold. It hain't fur me. I kin hear His voice warnin' me agen t' be hard an' stay on my farm. I kin see his hand usin' Eben t' steal t' keep me from weakness. I kin feel I be in the palm o' His hand, His fingers guidin' me. (*A pause—then he mutters sadly.*) It's a-goin' t' be lonesomer now than ever it war afore—an' I'm gittin' old, Lord—ripe on the bough. . . . (*Then stiffening.*) Waal—what d'ye want? God's lonesome, hain't He? God's hard an' lonesome! (*A pause. The Sheriff with two men comes up the road from the left. They move cautiously to the door. The Sheriff knocks on it with the butt of his pistol.*)

SHERIFF: Open in the name o' the law! (*They start.*)

CABOT: They've come fur ye. (*He goes to the rear door.*) Come in, Jim! (*The three men enter. Cabot meets them in doorway.*) Jest a minit, Jim. I got 'em safe here. (*The Sheriff nods. He and his companions remain in the doorway.*)

EBEN (*suddenly calls*):   I lied this mornin', Jim. I helped her to do it. Ye kin take me, too.

ABBIE (*brokenly*):   No!

CABOT: Take 'em both. (*He comes forward—stares at Eben with a trace of grudging admiration.*) Purty good—fur yew! Waal, I got t' round up the stock. Good-by.

EBEN: Good-by.

ABBIE: Good-by. (*Cabot turns and strides past the men—comes out and around the corner of the house, his shoulders squared, his face stony, and stalks grimly toward the barn. In the meantime the Sheriff and men have come into the room.*)

SHERIFF (*embarrassedly*):   Waal—we'd best start.

ABBIE: Wait. (*Turns to Eben.*) I love ye, Eben.

EBEN: I love ye, Abbie. (*They kiss. The three men grin and shuffle embarrassedly. Eben takes Abbie's hand. They go out the door in rear, the men following, and come from the house, walking hand in hand to the gate. Eben stops there and points to the sunrise sky.*) Sun's a-rizin'. Purty, hain't it?

ABBIE: Ay-eh. (*They both stand for a moment looking up raptly in attitudes strangely aloof and devout.*)

SHERIFF (*looking around at the farm enviously—to his companions*):   It's a jim-dandy farm, no denyin'. Wished I owned it!

1924

Tennessee Williams
(1911–1983)

Born Thomas Lanier Williams in Columbus, Mississippi, in 1911, Tennessee Williams inherited a culture of disappointment, a shabby gentility. He was in part raised by his grandparents, thereby absorbing a tradition many years older than the world of his peers. Young Thomas, his mother, and his sister Rose moved frequently. Leaving the quiet, orderly Episcopalian rectories of the churches in which his grandfather preached, the boy ultimately settled in St. Louis, in a chaos only slightly mitigated by his grandmother's presence. Williams's father was a traveling shoe salesman who visited the family periodically but, when his son was seven, was made a sales manager of a St. Louis shoe company and wanted to establish a home. That home, however, was filled with violence and drinking. Rose Williams, the model for many of her brother's later fragile female characters, suffered not only the terror of her father's rage but the fear that her mother, constantly ill, would die. Both as a brother and an artist, Williams was preoccupied with Rose. Over the years she was taken from treatment to treatment, gradually deteriorating; she was one of the first Americans to undergo a frontal lobotomy.

Many of Williams's characters whose brutal masculinity menaces the gentler characters around them may have been created in memory of the father Williams openly "hated." Williams's father, who called his son "Miss Nancy," had little time for a boy who read and stayed close to his mother's side. As an adolescent Williams, finding himself in a society that was all too ready to adopt his father's scorn, took to the solitary pursuits of reading and writing. He attended, but dropped out of, the University of Missouri and Washington University in St. Louis, and spent three years working in a shoe factory. He then returned to college and, in his mid-twenties, earned a B.A. from the University of Iowa. While in college Williams began writing plays and won prizes for fiction. He experimented with different forms, but his short stories were his first works to be published, in "little" magazines.

After college Williams spent brief periods in numerous cities, doing menial jobs and writing. It was then that he gave himself the romanticized name "Tennessee." The theatrical agent Audrey Wood found William's work promising and contacted him in 1939 to offer her services as an agent. (Their partnership would last for most of his career.) In 1940 the Theater Guild produced his *Battle of Angels* in Boston. The play took up many of the themes of later Williams plays, but its plot was unwieldy and its subject matter received mixed reviews. (It was revised and later released as *Orpheus Descending* [1957].) Throughout his career Williams considered topics shunned by the public: incest, adultery, homosexuality, cannibalism, and mental illness. In the aftermath of the failure of *Battle of Angels,* Williams eventually took a job in Hollywood, writing movie scripts. While writing not-so-successful screenplays, Williams turned his rejected screenplay "The Gentleman Caller" into the play *The Glass Menagerie* (1944), a New York Drama Critics' Circle Award winner.

Williams is known for his eery, evocative creation of characters whose oddities render them unfit for the "normal" world. These unusual characters are set in the South in a world that eastern audiences had not seen or understood. That world that insulates itself in stories of lost glory, languishing in the closeted, dark experiences of characters such as Laura in *The Glass Menagerie*. As Laura turns her glass unicorn, a mystical, tinkling sound begins before the background music drifts out; Williams's language is there first, delicately combining filaments of daydreaming, languor, and confinement. His refrain is in his lyrical language, the richness of rhythm created by monologue and musing.

For the Wingfields, the family of *The Glass Menagerie,* life takes on the sheen of disappointment, polished only by dreams. While Tom—the narrator, frustrated writer, and Laura's brother—dreams of getting away from the family, and Amanda—the mother—fantasizes about gentler, easier times, Laura lives precariously in a world of glass, blown into shape by imagination and longing. The story, like a musicbox figurine, revolves around the expected arrival of the visitor, the "Gentleman Caller." For the life of a young and slightly "odd" woman and her anxious mother pining away in a dingy apartment in St. Louis in the late 1930s, the gentleman caller's visit is anticipated as a rescue, the possible salvation of marriage and escape. But the arrival of Jim O'Connor, the Gentleman Caller, proves to be a cruel blow. Reality is always desperately harsh in Williams's plays as characters' worst fears are confirmed and surpassed. The pain of loss is typically so intense as

A scene from a production of Tennessee Williams's The Glass Menagerie.

to seem indulgent, as if pain for its own pleasure, delicious anguish, is the dubious reward for perpetual expectation.

If we follow Williams's directive to read his plays as autobiographical pieces (a practice to be undertaken with healthy skepticism because such interpretation can flatten rich, ambiguous characters and settings), his next big success matured from his own childhood and isolated longings as a young writer to the conflicts of class and temperament contained in adult liaisons. *A Streetcar Named Desire* opened in New York in 1947 and won a Pulitzer Prize in 1948. The play exists, however, in the American memory as a film, and even those who know little of the theater are likely to know Marlon Brando's Stanley Kowalski character. His "Stella!" echoes down from 1951 to the present, bringing with it the powerful contrast between fame in American theater and the more lucrative, widespread fame in Hollywood.

Back and forth across a dilapidated street in the New Orleans French Quarter run two streetcars, one named Desire, the other Cemeteries. Somehow, as Williams's life had thus far progressed, he seemed to have always been on his way to this street. As the characters appear, weaving in and out to the sounds of a blues piano, lovers shouting, and air moving audibly through the languor of humid speech, the story shapes itself into an atmospheric tale of heat and mistrust. What ease and passion there is between Stella and Stanley Kowalski is a tale that has been told before the play begins. Their connection is one of powerful attraction and learned acceptance: Stella's past as a genteel southern girl seems gratefully relinquished for the vitality of Stanley's physical presence. Their Eden is interrupted as the play opens with the arrival of Blanche DuBois, Stella's sister, an affected, girlish schoolteacher whose disbelief at the poverty into which Stella has married immediately begins to erode the Kowalskis' ease. Social strictures are evoked subtly, the sense that some presence of authority has arrived and the couple must now curtail their energy, must now behave in their small, cramped apartment. Williams clearly represents the struggles of class inherent in this seemingly classless society.

In some ways Blanche represents the world of the imagination as does Laura in *The*

Glass Menagerie. With paper lanterns to soften the effects of harsh light, coy slips into French or German, and educated conversation, Blanche stands in contrast to Stanley's blunt sensuality and uncultured manners. She sadly mirrors the position of the artist in the everyday world. While Blanche upholds the code for a woman, particularly a southern woman, of soft lies and supposed purity, her vitality, mirrored in Stanley's passion, is suppressed. Williams accurately portrays a society uncomfortable with its own imagination, which seems to hold unbearable secrets.

In his subsequent plays Williams continued to create intricate relationships among families threatening to reveal the secret lives of their members. *Cat on a Hot Tin Roof* (1955), which earned Williams a second Pulitzer Prize, expands the vista of the cramped apartment to the large plantation house. But the scenes are generally limited to the bedroom, that of Brick and Maggie, a couple locked in a struggle over sexuality. The question of homosexuality hangs in the air quite realistically but is never asked directly. Williams's own homosexuality was the subject of much attention throughout his artistic career. Within the theater community, Williams and his longtime lover, Frank Merlo, were accepted, but the theater-going society was capable of petty judgments and bigotry.

Williams's determined investigation of sexuality included incest, rape, castration, nymphomania, and pedophilia. His screenplay *Baby Doll* (1956), created from two of his one-act plays, features a young bride who sleeps in a crib. The image of her manipulative and oppressive infantilization is a stark challenge to American sexual mores, often heinous in the prudery that hides the sexualization of little girls, the false comfort of "Papas." And in his novelette *The Roman Spring of Mrs. Stone* (1950) and play *Sweet Bird of Youth* (1959), Williams depicts the sordid relationship between an aging actress and a kept young man.

Williams peopled his plays with characters who had lived in isolation and exclusion. *The Night of the Iguana* (1962) was written and produced while Williams was suffering from complications due to drug addiction. Taking place in 1940, the play gathers together a defrocked Episcopalian minister, a Nantucket artist and spinster, her grandfather, a practicing poet, a group of American women on tour, Germans exultant over Adolph Hitler's early war victories, and the keeper of the hotel where they are all staying. A one-day journey into the cycles of life and death accompanied by guilt (religious and sexual), confusion, and fanaticism, *The Night of the Iguana* is considered Williams's last great work for the theater. The play received immediate attention and won the New York Drama Critics Circle Award.

Williams continued to compose for the theater, but his worsening physical and mental health is clear in the first-draft title page of *The Two-Character Play* (1969), written "from the state of lunacy. . . . It is the story of the last six to seven years of the 1960s. The play is about disorientation—these people are lost as I am. They are two sides of one person." A play-within-a-play, Williams portrays a brother and a sister at a play called "The Two-Character Play." As he does in the comical *The Rose Tattoo* (1950) and in the violent *Suddenly Last Summer* (1958), Williams uses that motif to reexamine, obsessively, his own fears about his sister, Rose, her breakdowns, and her operation. Williams was aware that his own breakdown was imminent, the years of drugs and alcohol having completely taxed his system.

Through the last thirteen years of his life, Tennessee Williams wrote continually. He completed such plays as *Small Craft Warnings* (1972) and numerous nondramatic works, including the novel *Noise and the World of Reason* (1975), in which a homosexual writer recalls his youth and his search for love, the poetry collection *Androgyne, Mon Amour* (1977), and *Memoirs* (1975). His recovery from seizures suffered during drug withdrawal was miraculous, though his continuing alcoholism crippled his strength. His accidental death by choking in 1983 shocked the theater community. Williams left behind a body of work, powerful and prolific, that challenged and revived the American stage.

Suggested Readings: *Summer and Smoke*, 1947. *A Streetcar Named Desire*, 1947. *The Rose Tattoo*, 1950. *Camino Real*, 1953. *Cat on a Hot Tin Roof*, 1955. *Suddenly Last Summer*, 1958. *Sweet Bird of Youth*, 1959. *The Night of the Iguana*, 1962. S. Falk, *Tennessee Williams*, 1961. N. Tischler, *Tennessee Williams, Rebellious Puritan*, 1961. E. Jackson, *The Broken World of Tennessee Williams*, 1965. G. Maxwell, *Tennessee Williams and Friends: An Informal Biography*, 1965. S. Stanton, *Tennessee Williams: A Collection of Critical Essays*, 1977. F. Hirsch, *A Portrait of the Artist: The Plays of Tennessee Williams*, 1979. C. W. E. Bigsby, *20th-Century American Drama*, Vol. II, 1984. H. Bloom, ed., *Tennessee Williams: Modern Critical Interpretations*, 1987.

Text Used: *The Glass Menagerie*, 1945.

THE GLASS MENAGERIE

Nobody, not even the rain, has such small hands. —E. E. Cummings

CHARACTERS

AMANDA WINGFIELD, *the mother. A little woman of great but confused vitality clinging frantically to another time and place. Her characterization must be carefully created, not copied from type. She is not paranoiac, but her life is paranoia. There is much to admire in Amanda, and as much to love and pity as there is to laugh at. Certainly she has endurance and a kind of heroism, and though her foolishness makes her unwittingly cruel at times, there is tenderness in her slight person.*

LAURA WINGFIELD, *her daughter. Amanda, having failed to establish contact with reality, continues to live vitally in her illusions, but Laura's situation is even graver. A childhood illness has left her crippled, one leg slightly shorter than the other, and held in a brace. This defect need not be more than suggested on the stage. Stemming from this, Laura's separation increases till she is like a piece of her own glass collection, too exquisitely fragile to move from the shelf.*

TOM WINGFIELD, *her son. And the narrator of the play. A poet with a job in a warehouse. His nature is not remorseless, but to escape from a trap he has to act without pity.*

JIM O'CONNOR, *the gentleman caller. A nice, ordinary, young man.*

SCENE: *An alley in St. Louis.*
Part I: *Preparation for a Gentleman Caller.*
Part II: *The Gentleman Calls.*
Time: *Now and the Past.*

SCENE I

(The Wingfield apartment is in the rear of the building, one of those vast hive-like conglomerations of cellular living-units that flower as warty growths in overcrowded urban centers of lower middle-class population and are symptomatic of the impulse of this largest and fundamentally enslaved section of American society to avoid fluidity and differentiation and to exist and function as one interfused mass of automatism.)

(The apartment faces an alley and is entered by a fire escape, a structure whose name is a touch of accidental poetic truth, for all of these huge buildings

are always burning with the slow and implacable fires of human desperation. The fire escape is included in the set—that is, the landing of it and steps descending from it.)

(The scene is memory and is therefore nonrealistic. Memory takes a lot of poetic license. It omits some details; others are exaggerated, according to the emotional value of the articles it touches, for memory is seated predominantly in the heart. The interior is therefore rather dim and poetic.)

(At the rise of the curtain, the audience is faced with the dark, grim rear wall of the Wingfield tenement. This building, which runs parallel to the footlights, is flanked on both sides by dark, narrow alleys which run into murky canyons of tangled clotheslines, garbage cans, and the sinister latticework of neighboring fire escapes. It is up and down these side alleys that exterior entrances and exits are made, during the play. At the end of Tom's opening commentary, the dark tenement wall slowly reveals (by means of a transparency) the interior of the ground floor Wingfield apartment.)

(Downstage is the living room, which also serves as a sleeping room for Laura, the sofa unfolding to make her bed. Upstage, center, and divided by a wide arch or second proscenium[1] with transparent faded portieres[2] (or second curtain), is the dining room. In an old-fashioned what-not in the living room are seen scores of transparent glass animals. A blown-up photograph of the father hangs on the wall of the living room, facing the audience, to the left of the archway. It is the face of a very handsome young man in a doughboy's First World War cap. He is gallantly smiling, ineluctably smiling, as if to say, "I will be smiling forever.")

(The audience hears and sees the opening scene in the dining room through both the transparent fourth wall of the building and the transparent gauze portieres of the dining-room arch. It is during this revealing scene that the fourth wall slowly ascends, out of sight. This transparent exterior wall is not brought down again until the very end of the play, during Tom's final speech.)

(The narrator is an undisguised convention of the play. He takes whatever license with dramatic convention as is convenient to his purposes.)

(Tom enters dressed as a merchant sailor from alley, stage left, and strolls across the front of the stage to the fire escape. There he stops and lights a cigarette. He addresses the audience.)

TOM: Yes, I have tricks in my pocket, I have things up my sleeve. But I am the opposite of a stage magician. He gives you illusion that has the appearance of truth. I give you truth in the pleasant disguise of illusion. To begin with, I turn back time. I reverse it to that quaint period, the thirties, when the huge middle class of America was matriculating in a school for the blind. Their eyes had failed them, or they had failed their eyes, and so they were having their fingers pressed forcibly down on the fiery Braille alphabet of a dissolving economy. In Spain there was revolution. Here there was only shouting and confusion. In Spain there was Guernica.[3] Here there were disturbances of labor, sometimes pretty violent, in otherwise peaceful cities such as Chicago, Cleveland, Saint Louis . . . . This is the social background of the play.

(Music.)

---

[1] The separation of the stage from the audience.   [2] Drapes, generally heavy.
[3] A town in northern Spain bombed by German Fascist sympathizers in 1937 during the Spanish civil war (1936–1939).

The play is memory. Being a memory play, it is dimly lighted, it is sentimental, it is not realistic. In memory everything seems to happen to music. That explains the fiddle in the wings. I am the narrator of the play, and also a character in it. The other characters are my mother, Amanda, my sister, Laura, and a gentleman caller who appears in the final scenes. He is the most realistic character in the play, being an emissary from a world of reality that we were somehow set apart from. But since I have a poet's weakness for symbols, I am using this character also as a symbol; he is the long delayed but always expected something that we live for. There is a fifth character in the play who doesn't appear except in this larger-than-life photograph over the mantel. This is our father who left us a long time ago. He was a telephone man who fell in love with long distances; he gave up his job with the telephone company and skipped the light fantastic out of town . . . The last we heard of him was a picture postcard from Mazatlan, on the Pacific coast of Mexico, containing a message of two words—"Hello—Good-bye!" and no address. I think the rest of the play will explain itself. . . .

(Amanda's voice becomes audible through the portieres.)

(Legend on Screen: "Où Sont les Neiges."[4])

(He divides the portieres and enters the upstage area.)

(Amanda and Laura are seated at a drop-leaf table. Eating is indicated by gestures without food or utensils. Amanda faces the audience. Tom and Laura are seated in profile.)

(The interior has lit up softly and through the scrim we see Amanda and Laura seated at the table in the upstage area.)

AMANDA *(calling)*: Tom?

TOM: Yes, Mother.

AMANDA: We can't say grace until you come to the table!

TOM: Coming, Mother. *(He bows slightly and withdraws, reappearing a few moments later in his place at the table.)*

AMANDA *(to her son)*: Honey, don't *push* with your *fingers*. If you have to push with something, the thing to push with is a crust of bread. And chew—chew! Animals have sections in their stomachs which enable them to digest food without mastication, but human beings are supposed to chew their food before they swallow it down. Eat food leisurely, son, and really enjoy it. A well-cooked meal has lots of delicate flavors that have to be held in the mouth for appreciation. So chew your food and give your salivary glands a chance to function!

(Tom deliberately lays his imaginary fork down and pushes his chair back from the table.)

TOM: I haven't enjoyed one bite of this dinner because of your constant directions on how to eat it. It's you that makes me rush through meals with your hawk-like attention to every bite I take. Sickening—spoils my appetite—all this discussion of animals' secretion—salivary glands—mastication!

AMANDA *(lightly)*: Temperament like a Metropolitan[5] star! *(He rises and crosses downstage.)* You're not excused from the table.

TOM: I'm getting a cigarette.

AMANDA: You smoke too much.

---

[4] "Where are the snows of yesteryear?" (French) from "Ballade des Dames du Temps Jadis" ("Ballad of the Ladies of Bygone Times"), by François Villon (1431–?).

[5] New York City's Metropolitan Opera House.

(*Laura rises.*)

LAURA: I'll bring in the blanc mange.[6]

(*He remains standing with his cigarette by the portieres during the following.*)

AMANDA (*rising*):   No, sister, no, sister—you be the lady this time and I'll be the darky.

LAURA: I'm already up.

AMANDA: Resume your seat, little sister—I want you to stay fresh and pretty—for gentlemen callers!

LAURA: I'm not expecting any gentlemen callers.

AMANDA (*Crossing out to kitchenette. Airily.*):   Sometimes they come when they are least expected! Why, I remember one Sunday afternoon in Blue Mountain—(*Enters kitchenette.*)

TOM: I know what's coming!

LAURA: Yes. But let her tell it.

TOM: Again?

LAURA: She loves to tell it.

(*Amanda returns with bowl of dessert.*)

AMANDA: One Sunday afternoon in Blue Mountain—your mother received— *seventeen!*—gentlemen callers! Why, sometimes there weren't chairs enough to accommodate them all. We had to send the nigger over to bring in folding chairs from the parish house.

TOM (*remaining at portieres*):   How did you entertain those gentlemen callers?

AMANDA: I understood the art of conversation!

TOM: I bet you could talk.

AMANDA: Girls in those days *knew* how to talk, I can tell you.

TOM: Yes?

(*Image.   Amanda as a girl on a porch greeting callers.*)

AMANDA: They knew how to entertain their gentlemen callers. It wasn't enough for a girl to be possessed of a pretty face and a graceful figure—although I wasn't slighted in either respect. She also needed to have a nimble wit and a tongue to meet all occasions.

TOM: What did you talk about?

AMANDA: Things of importance going on in the world! Never anything coarse or common or vulgar. (*She addresses Tom as though he were seated in the vacant chair at the table though he remains by portieres. He plays this scene as though he held the book.*) My callers were gentlemen—all! Among my callers were some of the most prominent young planters of the Mississippi Delta—planters and sons of planters!

(*Tom motions for music and a spot of light on Amanda.*)
(*Her eyes lift, her face glows, her voice becomes rich and elegiac.*)
(*Screen legend: "Où Sont les Neiges."*)

There was young Champ Laughlin who later became vice-president of the Delta Planters Bank. Hadley Stevenson who was drowned in Moon Lake and left his widow one hundred and fifty thousand in Government bonds. There were the

---

[6] A molded, jellylike dessert.

Cutrere brothers, Wesley and Bates. Bates was one of my bright particular beaux! He got in a quarrel with that wild Wainright boy. They shot it out on the floor of Moon Lake Casino. Bates was shot through the stomach. Died in the ambulance on his way to Memphis. His widow was also well-provided for, came into eight or ten thousand acres, that's all. She married him on the rebound—never loved her—carried my picture on him the night he died! And there was that boy that every girl in the Delta had set her cap for! That beautiful, brilliant young Fitzhugh boy from Greene County!

TOM: What did he leave his widow?

AMANDA: He never married! Gracious, you talk as though all of my old admirers had turned up their toes to the daisies!

TOM: Isn't this the first you mentioned that still survives?

AMANDA: That Fitzhugh boy went North and made a fortune—came to be known as the Wolf of Wall Street! He had the Midas touch, whatever he touched turned to gold! And I could have been Mrs. Duncan J. Fitzhugh, mind you! But— I picked your *father!*

LAURA (*rising*):   Mother, let me clear the table.

AMANDA: No, dear, you go in front and study your typewriter chart. Or practice your shorthand a little. Stay fresh and pretty!—It's almost time for our gentlemen callers to start arriving. (*She flounces girlishly toward the kitchenette.*) How many do you suppose we're going to entertain this afternoon?

(*Tom throws down the paper and jumps up with a groan.*)

LAURA (*alone in the dining room*):   I don't believe we're going to receive any, Mother.

AMANDA (*reappearing, airily*):   What? No one—not one? You must be joking! (*Laura nervously echoes her laugh. She slips in a fugitive manner through the half-open portieres and draws them gently behind her. A shaft of very clear light is thrown on her face against the faded tapestry of the curtains. Music: "The Glass Menagerie" under faintly. Lightly.*) Not one gentleman caller? It can't be true! There must be a flood, there must have been a tornado!

LAURA: It isn't a flood, it's not a tornado, Mother. I'm just not popular like you were in Blue Mountain. . . . (*Tom utters another groan. Laura glances at him with a faint, apologetic smile. Her voice catching a little.*) Mother's afraid I'm going to be an old maid.

(*The scene dims out with "Glass Menagerie" music.*)

SCENE II

(*"Laura, Haven't You Ever Liked Some Boy?"*)
    (*On the dark stage the screen is lighted with the image of blue roses.*)
    (*Gradually Laura's figure becomes apparent and the screen goes out.*)
    (*The music subsides.*)
    (*Laura is seated in the delicate ivory chair at the small clawfoot table.*)
    (*She wears a dress of soft violet material for a kimono—her hair tied back from her forehead with a ribbon.*)
    (*She is washing and polishing her collection of glass.*)
    (*Amanda appears on the fire escape steps. At the sound of her ascent, Laura catches her breath, thrusts the bowl of ornaments away and seats herself stiffly*

before the diagram of the typewriter keyboard as though it held her spellbound. Something has happened to Amanda. It is written in her face as she climbs to the landing: a look that is grim and hopeless and a little absurd.)

(She has on one of those cheap or imitation velvety-looking cloth coats with imitation fur collar. Her hat is five or six years old, one of those dreadful cloche hats that were worn in the late twenties, and she is clasping an enormous black patent-leather pocketbook with nickel clasp and initials. This is her full-dress outfit, the one she usually wears to the D.A.R.[7])

(Before entering she looks through the door.)

(She purses her lips, opens her eyes wide, rolls them upward and shakes her head.)

(Then she slowly lets herself in the door. Seeing her mother's expression Laura touches her lips with a nervous gesture.)

LAURA: Hello, Mother, I was—*(She makes a nervous gesture toward the chart on the wall. Amanda leans against the shut door and stares at Laura with a martyred look.)*

AMANDA: Deception? Deception? *(She slowly removes her hat and gloves, continuing the swift suffering stare. She lets the hat and gloves fall on the floor—a bit of acting.)*

LAURA *(shakily)*:   How was the D.A.R. meeting? *(Amanda slowly opens her purse and removes a dainty white handkerchief which she shakes out delicately and delicately touches to her lips and nostrils.)* Didn't you go to the D.A.R. meeting, Mother?

AMANDA *(faintly, almost inaudibly)*:—No.—No. *(Then more forcibly).* I did not have the strength—to go to the D.A.R. In fact, I did not have the courage! I wanted to find a hole in the ground and hide myself in it forever! *(She crosses slowly to the wall and removes the diagram of the typewriter keyboard. She holds it in front of her for a second, staring at it sweetly and sorrowfully—then bites her lips and tears it in two pieces.)*

LAURA *(faintly)*:   Why did you do that, Mother? *(Amanda repeats the same procedure with the chart of the Gregg Alphabet.)* Why are you—

AMANDA: Why? Why? How old are you, Laura?

LAURA: Mother, you know my age.

AMANDA: I thought that you were an adult; it seems that I was mistaken. *(She crosses slowly to the sofa and sinks down and stares at Laura.)*

LAURA: Please don't stare at me, Mother.

(Amanda closes her eyes and lowers her head. Count ten.)

AMANDA: What are we going to do, what is going to become of us, what is the future?

(Count ten.)

LAURA: Has something happened, Mother? *(Amanda draws a long breath and takes out the handkerchief again. Dabbing process.)* Mother, has—something happened?

AMANDA: I'll be all right in a minute. I'm just bewildered—*(Count five.)*—by life. . . .

---

[7] To a meeting of the Daughters of the American Revolution, a conservative, patriotic society for women whose ancestors fought in the Revolutionary War.

LAURA: Mother, I wish that you would tell me what's happened.

AMANDA: As you know, I was supposed to be inducted into my office at the D.A.R. this afternoon. (*Image: a swarm of typewriters.*) But I stopped off at Rubicam's Business College to speak to your teachers about your having a cold and ask them what progress they thought you were making down there.

LAURA: Oh. . . .

AMANDA: I went to the typing instructor and introduced myself as your mother. She didn't know who you were. Wingfield, she said. We don't have any such student enrolled at the school! I assured her she did, that you had been going to classes since early in January. "I wonder," she said, "if you could be talking about that terribly shy little girl who dropped out of school after only a few days' attendance?" "No," I said, "Laura, my daughter, has been going to school every day for the past six weeks!" "Excuse me," she said. She took the attendance book out and there was your name, unmistakably printed, and all the dates you were absent until they decided that you had dropped out of school. I still said, "No, there must have been some mistake! There must have been some mix-up in the records!" And she said, "No—I remember her perfectly now. Her hands shook so that she couldn't hit the right keys! The first time we gave a speed test, she broke down completely—was sick at the stomach and almost had to be carried into the wash-room! After that morning she never showed up any more. We phoned the house but never got any answer"—while I was working at Famous and Barr,[8] I suppose, demonstrating those—Oh! I felt so weak I could barely keep on my feet. I had to sit down while they got me a glass of water! Fifty dollars' tuition, all of our plans —my hopes and ambitions for you—just gone up the spout, just gone up the spout like that. (*Laura draws a long breath and gets awkwardly to her feet. She crosses to the victrola and winds it up.*) What are you doing?

LAURA: Oh! (*She releases the handle and returns to her seat.*)

AMANDA: Laura, where have you been going when you've gone out pretending that you were going to business college?

LAURA: I've just been going out walking.

AMANDA: That's not true.

LAURA: It is. I just went walking.

AMANDA: Walking? Walking? In winter? Deliberately courting pneumonia in that light coat? Where did you walk to, Laura?

LAURA: All sorts of places—mostly in the park.

AMANDA: Even after you'd started catching that cold?

LAURA: It was the lesser of two evils, Mother. (*Image: winter scene in park.*) I couldn't go back up. I—threw up—on the floor!

AMANDA: From half past seven till after five every day you mean to tell me you walked around in the park, because you wanted to make me think that you were still going to Rubicam's Business College?

LAURA: It wasn't as bad as it sounds. I went inside places to get warmed up.

AMANDA: Inside where?

LAURA: I went in the art museum and the bird houses at the Zoo. I visited the penguins every day! Sometimes I did without lunch and went to the movies. Lately I've been spending most of my afternoons in the Jewel-box, that big glass house where they raise the tropical flowers.

---

[8] A St. Louis department store.

AMANDA: You did all this to deceive me, just for the deception? (*Laura looks down.*) Why?

LAURA: Mother, when you're disappointed, you get that awful suffering look on your face, like the picture of Jesus' mother in the museum!

AMANDA: Hush!

LAURA: I couldn't face it.

(*Pause. A whisper of strings.*)
(*Legend: "The Crust of Humility."*)

AMANDA (*hopelessly fingering the huge pocketbook*): So what are we going to do the rest of our lives? Stay home and watch the parades go by? Amuse ourselves with the glass menagerie, darling? Eternally play those worn-out phonograph records your father left as a painful reminder of him? We won't have a business career—we've given that up because it gave us nervous indigestion! (*Laughs wearily.*) What is there left but dependency all our lives? I know so well what becomes of unmarried women who aren't prepared to occupy a position. I've seen such pitiful cases in the South—barely tolerated spinsters living upon the grudging patronage of sister's husband or brother's wife!—stuck away in some little mousetrap of a room—encouraged by one in-law to visit another—little birdlike women without any nest—eating the crust of humility all their life! Is that the future that we've mapped out for ourselves? I swear it's the only alternative I can think of! It isn't a very pleasant alternative, is it? Of course—some girls do *marry.* (*Laura twists her hands nervously.*) Haven't you ever liked some boy?

LAURA: Yes. I liked one once. (*Rises.*) I came across his picture a while ago.

AMANDA (*with some interest*): He gave you his picture?

LAURA: No, it's in the yearbook.

AMANDA (*disappointed*): Oh—a high-school boy.

(*Screen image: Jim as high school hero bearing a silver cup.*)

LAURA: Yes. His name was Jim. (*Laura lifts the heavy annual from the clawfoot table.*) Here he is in *The Pirates of Penzance.*[9]

AMANDA (*absently*): The what?

LAURA: The operetta the senior class put on. He had a wonderful voice and we sat across the aisle from each other Mondays, Wednesdays, and Fridays in the Aud. Here he is with the silver cup for debating! See his grin?

AMANDA (*absently*): He must have had a jolly disposition.

LAURA: He used to call me—Blue Roses.

(*Image: blue roses.*)

AMANDA: Why did he call you such a name as that?

LAURA: When I had that attack of pleurosis[10]—he asked me what was the matter when I came back. I said pleurosis—he thought that I said Blue Roses! So that's what he always called me after that. Whenever he saw me, he'd holler, "Hello, Blue Roses!" I didn't care for the girl that he went out with. Emily Meisenbach. Emily was the best-dressed girl at Soldan. She never struck me, though, as being sincere . . . It says in the Personal Section—they're engaged. That's— six years ago! They must be married by now.

---

[9] A Gilbert and Sullivan comic light opera (1879).   [10] A respiratory inflammation.

AMANDA: Girls that aren't cut out for business careers usually wind up married to some nice man. (*Gets up with a spark of revival.*) ɔister, that's what you'll do!

(*Laura utters a startled, doubtful laugh. She reaches quickly for a piece of glass.*)

LAURA: But, Mother—
AMANDA: Yes? (*Crossing to photograph.*)
LAURA (*in a tone of frightened apology*): I'm—crippled!

(*Image: screen.*)

AMANDA: Nonsense! Laura, I've told you never, never to use that word. Why, you're not crippled, you just have a little defect—hardly noticeable, even! When people have some slight disadvantage like that, they cultivate other things to make up for it—develop charm—and vivacity—and—*charm!* That's all you have to do! (*She turns again to the photograph.*) One thing your father had *plenty of—* was *charm!*

(*Tom motions to the fiddle in the wings.*)
(*The scene fades out with music.*)

Scene III

(*Legend on screen: "After the Fiasco—")*
(*Tom speaks from the fire escape landing.*)

TOM: After the fiasco at Rubicam's Business College, the idea of getting a gentleman caller for Laura began to play a more important part in Mother's calculations. It became an obsession. Like some archetype of the universal unconscious, the image of the gentleman caller haunted our small apartment. . . . (*Image: young man at door with flowers.*) An evening at home rarely passed without some allusion to this image, this specter, this hope. . . . Even when he wasn't mentioned, his presence hung in Mother's preoccupied look and in my sister's frightened, apologetic manner—hung like a sentence passed upon the Wingfields! Mother was a woman of action as well as words. She began to take logical steps in the planned direction. Late that winter and in the early spring—realizing that extra money would be needed to properly feather the nest and plume the bird—she conducted a vigorous campaign on the telephone, roping in subscribers to one of those magazines for matrons called *The Home-maker's Companion,* the type of journal that features the serialized sublimations of ladies of letters who think in terms of delicate cuplike breasts, slim, tapering waists, rich, creamy thighs, eyes like wood smoke in autumn, fingers that soothe and caress like strains of music, bodies as powerful as Etruscan sculpture.

(*Screen image: glamor magazine cover.*)
(*Amanda enters with phone on long extension cord. She is spotted in the dim stage.*)

AMANDA: Ida Scott? This is Amanda Wingfield! We *missed* you at the D.A.R. last Monday! I said to myself: She's probably suffering with that sinus condition! How is that sinus condition? Horrors! Heaven have mercy!—You're a Christian martyr, yes, that's what you are, a Christian martyr! Well, I just now happened to notice that your subscription to the *Companion's* about to expire! Yes, it expires with the next issue, honey!—just when that wonderful new serial by Bessie Mae Hopper is getting off to such an exciting start. Oh, honey, it's something that you can't miss! You remember how *Gone With the Wind* took everybody by storm? You simply couldn't go out if you hadn't read it. All everybody *talked* was Scarlett O'Hara. Well, this is a book that critics already compare to *Gone With the Wind*. It's the *Gone With the Wind* of the post-World War generation!—What?—Burning?—Oh, honey, don't let them burn, go take a look in the oven and I'll hold the wire! Heavens—I think she's hung up!

(Dim out.)
   (Legend on screen: "You Think I'm in Love with Continental Shoemakers?")
   (Before the stage is lighted, the violent voices of Tom and Amanda are heard.)
   (They are quarreling behind the portieres. In front of them stands Laura with clenched hands and panicky expression.)
   (A clear pool of light on her figure throughout this scene.)

TOM: What in Christ's name am I—
AMANDA *(shrilly)*:   Don't you use that—
TOM: Supposed to do!
AMANDA: Expression! Not in my—
TOM: Ohhh!
AMANDA: Presence! Have you gone out of your senses?
TOM: I have, that's true, *driven* out!
AMANDA: What is the matter with you, you—big—big—IDIOT!
TOM: Look—I've got *no thing,* no single thing—
AMANDA: Lower your voice!
TOM: In my life here that I can call my OWN! Everything is—
AMANDA: Stop that shouting!
TOM: Yesterday you confiscated my books! You had the nerve to—
AMANDA: I took that horrible novel back to the library—yes! That hideous book by that insane Mr. Lawrence.[11] *(Tom laughs wildly.)* I cannot control the output of diseased minds or people who cater to them— *(Tom laughs still more wildly.)* BUT I WON'T ALLOW SUCH FILTH BROUGHT INTO MY HOUSE! No, no, no, no, no!
TOM: House, house! Who pays rent on it, who makes a slave of himself to—
AMANDA *(fairly screeching)* Don't you DARE to—
TOM: No, no, *I* musn't say things! *I've* got to just—
AMANDA: Let me tell you—
TOM: I don't want to hear any more! *(He tears the portieres open. The upstage area is lit with a turgid smoky red glow.)*

(Amanda's hair is in metal curlers and she wears a very old bathrobe, much too large for her slight figure, a relic of the faithless Mr. Wingfield.)
   (An upright typewriter and a wild disarray of manuscripts are on the dropleaf table. The quarrel was probably precipitated by Amanda's interruption of his creative labor. A chair lying overthrown on the floor.)
   (Their gesticulating shadows are cast on the ceiling by the fiery glow.)

AMANDA: You *will* hear more, you—
TOM: No, I won't hear more, I'm going out!
AMANDA: You come right back in—

---

[11] D. H. Lawrence (1885–1930), an English poet and fiction writer.

TOM: Out, out out! Because I'm—

AMANDA: Come back here, Tom Wingfield! I'm not through talking to you!

TOM: Oh, go—

LAURA *(desperately)*: Tom!

AMANDA: You're going to listen, and no more insolence from you! I'm at the end of my patience! *(He comes back toward her.)*

TOM: What do you think I'm at? Aren't I supposed to have any patience to reach the end of, Mother? I know, I know. It seems unimportant to you, what I'm *doing*—what I *want* to do—having a little *difference* between them! You don't think that—

AMANDA: I think you've been doing things that you're ashamed of. That's why you act like this. I don't believe that you go every night to the movies. Nobody goes to the movies night after night. Nobody in their right minds goes to the movies as often as you pretend to. People don't go to the movies at nearly midnight, and movies don't let out at two A.M. Come in stumbling. Muttering to yourself like a maniac! You get three hours' sleep and then go to work. Oh, I can picture the way you're doing down there. Moping, doping, because you're in no condition.

TOM *(wildly)*:   No, I'm in no condition!

AMANDA: What right have you got to jeopardize your job? Jeopardize the security of us all? How do you think we'd manage if you were—

TOM: Listen! You think I'm crazy *about* the *warehouse? (He bends fiercely toward her slight figure.)* You think I'm in love with the Continental Shoemakers? You think I want to spend fifty-five *years* down there in that—*celotex interior!* with—*fluorescent—tubes!* Look! I'd rather somebody picked up a crowbar and battered out my brains—than go back mornings! I *go!* Every time you come in yelling that God damn *"Rise and Shine!" "Rise and Shine!"* I say to myself, "How *lucky dead* people are!" But I get up. I *go!* For sixty-five dollars a month I give up all that I dream of doing and being *ever!* And you say self—*self'*s all I ever think of. Why, listen, if self is what I thought of, Mother, I'd be where he is—GONE! *(Pointing to father's picture.)* As far as the system of transportation reaches! *(He starts past her. She grabs his arm.)* Don't grab at me, Mother!

AMANDA: Where are you going?

TOM: I'm going to the *movies!*

AMANDA: I don't believe that lie!

TOM *(Crouching toward her, overtowering her tiny figure. She backs away, gasping.)*:   I'm going to opium dens! Yes, opium dens, dens of vice and criminals' hangouts, Mother. I've joined the Hogan gang,[12] I'm a hired assassin, I carry a tommy-gun in a violin case! I run a string of cathouses in the Valley! They call me Killer, Killer Wingfield, I'm leading a double life, a simple, honest warehouse worker by day, by night, a dynamic *czar* of the *underworld, Mother*. I go to gambling casinos, I spin away fortunes on the roulette table! I wear a patch over one eye and a false mustache, sometimes I put on green whiskers. On those occasions they call me—*El Diablo!*[13] Oh, I could tell you things to make you sleepless! My enemies plan to dynamite this place. They're going to blow us all sky-high some night! I'll be glad, very happy, and so will you! You'll go up, up on a broomstick, over Blue Mountain with seventeen gentlemen callers! You ugly— babbling old—*witch* . . . . *(He goes through a series of violent, clumsy move-*

---

[12] A major criminal organization in St. Louis in the 1930s.   [13] "The Devil" (Spanish).

ments, seizing his overcoat, lunging to the door, pulling it fiercely open. The women watch him, aghast. His arm catches in the sleeve of the coat as he struggles to pull it on. For a moment he is pinioned by the bulky garment. With an outraged groan he tears the coat off again, splitting the shoulders of it, and hurls it across the room. It strikes against the shelf of Laura's glass collection, there is a tinkle of shattering glass. Laura cries out as if wounded.)

(Music legend: "The Glass Menagerie.")

LAURA *(shrilly):* My glass!—menagerie. . . . *(She covers her face and turns away.)*

(But Amanda is still stunned and stupefied by the "ugly witch" so that she barely notices this occurrence. Now she recovers her speech.)

AMANDA *(in an awful voice):* I won't speak to you—until you apologize! *(She crosses through portieres and draws them together behind her. Tom is left with Laura. Laura clings weakly to the mantel with her face averted. Tom stares at her stupidly for a moment. Then he crosses to shelf. Drops awkwardly to his knees to collect the fallen glass, glancing at Laura as if he would speak but couldn't.)*

("The Glass Menagerie" steals in as the scene dims out.)

Scene IV

(The interior is dark. Faint light in the alley.)

(A deep-voiced bell in a church is tolling the hour of five as the scene commences.)

(Tom appears at the top of the alley. After each solemn boom of the bell in the tower, he shakes a little noisemaker or rattle as if to express the tiny spasm of man in contrast to the sustained power and dignity of the Almighty. This and the unsteadiness of his advance make it evident that he has been drinking.)

(As he climbs the few steps to the fire escape landing light steals up inside. Laura appears in nightdress, observing Tom's empty bed in the front room.)

(Tom fishes in his pockets for the door key, removing a motley assortment of articles in the search, including a perfect shower of movie ticket stubs and an empty bottle. At last he finds the key, but just as he is about to insert it, it slips from his fingers. He strikes a match and crouches below the door.)

TOM *(bitterly):* One crack—and it falls through!

(Laura opens the door.)

LAURA: Tom! Tom, what are you doing?
TOM: Looking for a door key.
LAURA: Where have you been all this time?
TOM: I have been to the movies.
LAURA: All this time at the movies?
TOM: There was a very long program. There was a Garbo picture and a Mickey Mouse and a travelogue and a newsreel and a preview of coming attractions. And there was an organ solo and a collection for the milk fund—simultaneously—which ended up in a terrible fight between a fat lady and an usher!
LAURA *(innocently):* Did you have to stay through everything?

TOM: Of course! And, oh, I forgot! There was a big stage show! The headliner on this stage show was Malvolio the Magician. He performed wonderful tricks, many of them, such as pouring water back and forth between pitchers. First it turned to wine and then it turned to beer and then it turned to whiskey. I know it was whiskey it finally turned into because he needed somebody to come up out of the audience to help him, and I came up—both shows! It was Kentucky Straight Bourbon. A very generous fellow, he gave souvenirs. (*He pulls from his back pocket a shimmering rainbow-colored scarf.*) He gave me this. This is his magic scarf. You can have it, Laura. You wave it over a canary cage and you get a bowl of goldfish. You wave it over the goldfish bowl and they fly away canaries. . . . But the wonderfullest trick of all was the coffin trick. We nailed him into a coffin and he got out of the coffin without removing one nail. (*He has come inside.*) There is a trick that would come in handy for me—get me out of this 2 by 4 situation! (*Flops onto bed and starts removing shoes.*)

LAURA: Tom—Shhh!

TOM: What you shushing me for?

LAURA: You'll wake up Mother.

TOM: Goody, goody! Pay 'er back for all those "Rise an' Shines." (*Lies down, groaning.*) You know it don't take much intelligence to get yourself into a nailed-up coffin, Laura. But who in hell ever got himself out of one without removing one nail?

(*As if in answer, the father's grinning photograph lights up.*)

(*Scene dims out.*)

(*Immediately following: The church bell is heard striking six. At the sixth stroke the alarm clock goes off in Amanda's room, and after a few moments we hear her calling: "Rise and Shine! Rise and Shine! Laura, go tell your brother to rise and shine!"*)

TOM (*sitting up slowly*): I'll rise—but I won't shine.

(*The light increases.*)

AMANDA: Laura, tell your brother his coffee is ready.

(*Laura slips into front room.*)

LAURA: Tom! it's nearly seven. Don't make Mother nervous. (*He stares at her stupidly. Beseechingly.*) Tom, speak to Mother this morning. Make up with her, apologize, speak to her!

TOM: She won't to me. It's her that started not speaking.

LAURA: If you just say you're sorry she'll start speaking.

TOM: Her not speaking—is that such a tragedy?

LAURA: Please—please!

AMANDA (*calling from kitchenette*): Laura, are you going to do what I asked you to do, or do I have to get dressed and go out myself?

LAURA: Going, going—soon as I get on my coat! (*She pulls on a shapeless felt hat with nervous, jerky movement, pleadingly glancing at Tom. Rushes awkwardly for coat. The coat is one of Amanda's, inaccurately made over, the sleeves too short for Laura.*) Butter and what else?

AMANDA (*entering upstage*): Just butter. Tell them to charge it.

LAURA: Mother, they make such faces when I do that.

AMANDA: Sticks and stones may break my bones, but the expression on Mr.

Garfinkel's face won't harm us! Tell your brother his coffee is getting cold.

LAURA (*at door*):   Do what I asked you, will you, will you, Tom?

(He looks sullenly away.)

AMANDA: Laura, go now or just don't go at all!

LAURA (*rushing out*):   Going—going! *(A second later she cries out. Tom springs up and crosses to the door. Amanda rushes anxiously in. Tom opens the door.)*

TOM: Laura?

LAURA: I'm all right. I slipped, but I'm all right.

AMANDA (*peering anxiously after her*):   If anyone breaks a leg on those fire escape steps, the landlord ought to be sued for every cent he possesses! *(She shuts door. Remembers she isn't speaking and returns to other room.)*

(As Tom enters listlessly for his coffee, she turns her back to him and stands rigidly facing the window on the gloomy gray vault of the areaway. Its light on her face with its aged but childish features is cruelly sharp, satirical as a Daumier[14] *print.)*

(Music under: "Ave Maria.")

(Tom glances sheepishly but sullenly at her averted figure and slumps at the table. The coffee is scalding hot; he sips it and gasps and spits it back in the cup. At his gasp, Amanda catches her breath and half turns. Then catches herself and turns back to window.)

(Tom blows on his coffee, glancing sidewise at his mother. She clears her throat. Tom clears his. He starts to rise. Sinks back down again, scratches his head, clears his throat again. Amanda coughs. Tom raises his cup in both hands to blow on it, his eyes staring over the rim of it at his mother for several moments. Then he slowly sets the cup down and awkwardly and hesitantly rises from the chair.)

TOM (*hoarsely*):   Mother. I—I apologize. Mother. *(Amanda draws a quick, shuddering breath. Her face works grotesquely. She breaks into childlike tears.)* I'm sorry for what I said, for everything that I said, I didn't mean it.

AMANDA (*sobbingly*):   My devotion has made me a witch and so I make myself hateful to my children!

TOM: *No, you don't.*

AMANDA: I worry so much, don't sleep, it makes me nervous!

TOM (*gently*):   I understand that.

AMANDA: I've had to put up a solitary battle all these years. But you're my right-hand bower![15] Don't fall down, don't fail!

TOM (*gently*):   I try, Mother.

AMANDA (*with great enthusiasm*):   Try and you will SUCCEED! *(The notion makes her breathless.)* Why, you—you're just *full* of natural endowments! Both of my children—they're *unusual* children! Don't you think I know it? I'm so— *proud!* Happy and—feel I've—so much to be thankful for but—Promise me one thing, son!

TOM: What, Mother?

AMANDA: Promise, son, you'll—never be a drunkard!

---

[14] Honoré Daumier (1808–1879), a French caricaturist.   [15] An anchor at the front of a ship.

TOM (*turns to her grinning*):   I will never be a drunkard, Mother.

AMANDA: That's what frightened me, so, that you'd be drinking! Eat a bowl of Purina!

TOM: Just coffee, Mother.

AMANDA: Shredded wheat biscuit?

TOM: No, no, Mother, just coffee.

AMANDA: You can't put in a day's work on an empty stomach. You've got ten minutes—don't gulp! Drinking too-hot liquids makes cancer of the stomach. . . . Put cream in.

TOM: No, thank you.

AMANDA: To cool it.

TOM: No! No, thank you, I want it black.

AMANDA: I know, but it's not good for you. We have to do all that we can to build ourselves up. In these trying times we live in, all that we have to cling to is—each other. . . . That's why it's so important to—Tom, I—I sent out your sister so I could discuss something with you. If you hadn't spoken I would have spoken to you. (*Sits down.*)

TOM (*gently*):   What is it, Mother, that you want to discuss?

AMANDA: *Laura!*

(Tom puts his cup down slowly.)
(Legend on screen: "Laura.")
(Music: "The Glass Menagerie.")

TOM: —Oh.—Laura . . .

AMANDA (*touching his sleeve*):   You know how Laura is. So quiet but—still water runs deep! She notices things and I think she—broods about them. (*Tom looks up.*) A few days ago I came in and she was crying.

TOM: What about?

AMANDA: You.

TOM: Me?

AMANDA: She has an idea that you're not happy here.

TOM: What gave her that idea?

AMANDA: What gives her any idea? However, you do act strangely. I—I'm not criticizing, understand *that!* I know your ambitions do not lie in the warehouse, that like everybody in the whole wide world —you've had to—make sacrifices, but—Tom—Tom—life's not easy, it calls for—Spartan endurance! There's so many things in my heart that I cannot describe to you! I've never told you but I—*loved your father. . . .*

TOM (*gently*):   I know that, Mother.

AMANDA: And you—when I see you taking after his ways! Staying out late—and—well, you *had* been drinking the night you were in that—terrifying condition! Laura says that you hate the apartment and that you go out nights to get away from it! Is that true, Tom?

TOM: No. You say there's so much in your heart that you can't describe to me. That's true of me, too. There's so much in my heart that I can't describe to *you!* So let's respect each other's—

AMANDA: But, why—*why*, Tom—are you always so *restless?* Where do you go to, nights?

TOM: I—go to the movies.

AMANDA: Why do you go to the movies so much, Tom?

TOM: I go to the movies because—I like adventure. Adventure is something I don't have much of at work, so I go to the movies.

AMANDA: But, Tom, you go to the movies *entirely* too *much!*

TOM: I like a lot of adventure.

(Amanda looks baffled, then hurt. As the familiar inquisition resumes he becomes hard and impatient again. Amanda slips back into her querulous attitude toward him.)

(Image on screen: sailing vessel with Jolly Roger.[16])

AMANDA: Most young men find adventure in their careers.

TOM: Then most young men are not employed in a warehouse.

AMANDA: The world is full of young men employed in warehouses and offices and factories.

TOM: Do all of them find adventure in their careers?

AMANDA: They do or they do without it! Not everybody has a craze for adventure.

TOM: Man is by instinct a lover, a hunter, a fighter, and none of those instincts are given much play at the warehouse!

AMANDA: Man is by instinct! Don't quote instinct to me! Instinct is something that people have got away from! It belongs to animals! Christian adults don't want it!

TOM: What do Christian adults want, then, Mother?

AMANDA: Superior things! Things of the mind and the spirit! Only animals have to satisfy instincts! Surely your aims are somewhat higher than theirs! Than monkeys—pigs—

TOM: I reckon they're not.

AMANDA: You're joking. However, that isn't what I wanted to discuss.

TOM *(rising)*: I haven't much time.

AMANDA *(pushing his shoulders)*: Sit down.

TOM: You want me to punch in red[17] at the warehouse, Mother?

AMANDA: You have five minutes. I want to talk about Laura.

(Legend: "Plans and Provisions.")

TOM: All right! What about Laura?

AMANDA: We have to be making plans and provisions for her. She's older than you, two years, and nothing has happened. She just drifts along doing nothing. It frightens me terribly how she just drifts along.

TOM: I guess she's the type that people call home girls.

AMANDA: There's no such type, and if there is, it's a pity! That is unless the home is hers, with a husband!

TOM: What?

AMANDA: Oh, I can see the handwriting on the wall as plain as I see the nose in front of my face! It's terrifying! More and more you remind me of your father! He was out all hours without explanation—Then *left! Goodbye!* And me with a bag to hold. I saw that letter you got from the Merchant Marine. I know what you're dreaming of. I'm not standing here blindfolded. Very well, then. Then *do* it! But not till there's somebody to take your place.

---

[16] The pirates' flag, black with white skull and crossbones.   [17] Arrive late for work.

TOM: What do you mean?

AMANDA: I mean that as soon as Laura has got somebody to take care of her, married, a home of her own, independent—why, then you'll be free to go wherever you please, on land, on sea, whichever way the wind blows you! But until that time you've got to look out for your sister. I don't say me because I'm old and don't matter! I say for your sister because she's young and dependent. I put her in business college—a dismal failure! Frightened her so it made her sick to her stomach. I took her over to the Young People's League at the church. Another fiasco. She spoke to nobody, nobody spoke to her. Now all she does is fool with those pieces of glass and play those worn-out records. What kind of a life is that for a girl to lead!

TOM: What can I do about it?

AMANDA: Overcome selfishness! Self, self, self is all that you ever think of! (*Tom springs up and crosses to get his coat. It is ugly and bulky. He pulls on a cap with earmuffs.*) Where is your muffler? Put your wool muffler on! (*He snatches it angrily from the closet and tosses it around his neck and pulls both ends tight.*) Tom! I haven't said what I had in mind to ask you.

TOM: I'm too late to—

AMANDA (*Catching his arms—very importunately. Then shyly*): Down at the warehouse, aren't there some—nice young men?

TOM: No!

AMANDA: There *must* be—*some* . . .

TOM: Mother—

(*Gesture.*)

AMANDA: Find out one that's clean-living—doesn't drink and—ask him out for sister!

TOM: What?

AMANDA: For *sister!* To *meet!* Get *acquainted!*

TOM (*stamping to door*): Oh, my *go-osh!*

AMANDA: Will you? (*He opens door. Imploringly.*) Will you? (*He starts down.*) Will you? *Will* you? Will you, dear?

TOM (*calling back*): YES!

(*Amanda closes the door hesitantly and with a troubled but faintly hopeful expression.*)

(*Screen image: glamor magazine cover.*)

(*Spot[18] Amanda at phone.*)

AMANDA: Ella Cartwright? This is Amanda Wingfield! How are you, honey? How is that kidney condition? (*Count five.*) Horrors! (*Count five.*) You're a Christian martyr, yes, honey, that's what you are, a Christian martyr! Well, I just happened to notice in my little red book that your subscription to the *Companion* has just run out! I knew that you wouldn't want to miss out on the wonderful serial starting in this new issue. It's by Bessie Mae Hopper, the first thing she's written since *Honeymoon for Three.* Wasn't that a strange and interesting story? Well, this one is even lovelier, I believe. It has a sophisticated society background. It's all about the horsey set on Long Island!

(*Fade out.*)

---

[18] Spotlight on.

SCENE V

(Legend on screen: "Annunciation." Fade with music.)

(It is early dusk of a spring evening. Supper has just been finished in the Wingfield apartment. Amanda and Laura in light colored dresses are removing dishes from the table, in the upstage area, which is shadowy, their movements formalized almost as a dance or ritual, their moving forms as pale and silent as moths.)

(Tom, in white shirt and trousers, rises from the table and crosses toward the fire escape.)

AMANDA *(as he passes her)*: Son, will you do me a favor?

TOM: What?

AMANDA: Comb your hair! You look so pretty when your hair is combed! *(Tom slouches on sofa with evening paper. Enormous caption "Franco[19] Triumphs.")* There is only one respect in which I would like you to emulate your father.

TOM: What respect is that?

AMANDA: The care he always took of his appearance. He never allowed himself to look untidy. *(He throws down the paper and crosses to fire escape.)* Where are you going?

TOM: I'm going out to smoke.

AMANDA: You smoke too much. A pack a day at fifteen cents a pack. How much would that amount to in a month? Thirty times fifteen is how much, Tom? Figure it out and you will be astounded at what you could save. Enough to give you a night school course in accounting at Washington U! Just think what a wonderful thing that would be for you, son!

(Tom is unmoved by the thought.)

TOM: I'd rather smoke. *(He steps out on landing, letting the screen door slam.)*

AMANDA *(sharply)*: I know! That's the tragedy of it. . . . *(Alone, she turns to look at her husband's picture.)*

(Dance music: "All the World is Waiting for the Sunrise!")

TOM *(to the audience)*: Across the alley from us was the Paradise Dance Hall. On evenings in spring the windows and doors were open and the music came outdoors. Sometimes the lights were turned out except for a large glass sphere that hung from the ceiling. It would turn slowly about and filter the dusk with delicate rainbow colors. Then the orchestra played a waltz or a tango, something that had a slow and sensuous rhythm. Couples would come outside, to the relative privacy of the alley. You could see them kissing behind ash-pits and telephone poles. This was the compensation for lives that passed like mine, without any change or adventure. Adventure and change were imminent in this year. They were waiting around the corner for all these kids. Suspended in the mist over Berchtesgaden,[20] caught in the folds of Chamberlain's umbrella—In Spain there was Guernica! But here there was only hot swing music and liquor, dance halls, bars, and movies,

---

[19] Francisco Franco (1892–1975), Fascist Spanish dictator who came to power after the Spanish civil war.

[20] The German town where the British prime minister Neville Chamberlain met with Adolph Hitler and signed the Munich Pact to avoid World War II; Chamberlain and the umbrella he carried became symbolic of unsuccessful attempts to pacify evil forces.

and sex that hung in the gloom like a chandelier and flooded the world with brief, deceptive rainbows. . . . All the world was waiting for bombardments!

(Amanda turns from the picture and comes outside.)

AMANDA *(sighing)*: A fire escape landing's a poor excuse for a porch. *(She spreads a newspaper on a step and sits down, gracefully and demurely as if she were settling into a swing on a Mississippi veranda.)* What are you looking at?

TOM: The moon.

AMANDA: Is there a moon this evening?

TOM: It's rising over Garfinkel's Delicatessen.

AMANDA: So it is! A little silver slipper of a moon. Have you made a wish on it yet?

TOM: Um-hum.

AMANDA: What did you wish for?

TOM: That's a secret.

AMANDA: A secret, huh? Well, I won't tell mine either. I will be just as mysterious as you.

TOM: I bet I can guess what yours is.

AMANDA: Is my head so transparent?

TOM: You're not a sphinx.

AMANDA: No, I don't have secrets. I'll tell you what I wished for on the moon. Success and happiness for my precious children! I wish for that whenever there's a moon, and when there isn't a moon, I wish for it, too.

TOM: I thought perhaps you wished for a gentleman caller.

AMANDA: Why do you say that?

TOM: Don't you remember asking me to fetch one?

AMANDA: I remember suggesting that it would be nice for your sister if you brought home some nice young man from the warehouse. I think I've made that suggestion more than once.

TOM: Yes, you have made it repeatedly.

AMANDA: Well?

TOM: We are going to have one.

AMANDA: *What?*

TOM:· A gentleman caller!

(The annunciation is celebrated with music.)
(Amanda rises.)
(Image on screen: caller with bouquet.)

AMANDA: You mean you have asked some nice young man to come over?

TOM: Yep. I've asked him to dinner.

AMANDA: You really did?

TOM: I did!

AMANDA: You did, and did he—*accept?*

TOM: He did!

AMANDA: Well, well—well, well! That's—lovely!

TOM: I thought that you would be pleased.

AMANDA: It's definite, then?

TOM: Very definite.

AMANDA: Soon?

TOM: Very soon.

AMANDA: For heaven's sake, stop putting on and tell me some things, will you?

TOM: What things do you want me to tell you?

AMANDA: *Naturally* I would like to know when he's *coming!*

TOM: He's coming tomorrow.

AMANDA: *Tomorrow?*

TOM: Yep. Tomorrow.

AMANDA: But, Tom!

TOM: Yes, Mother?

AMANDA: Tomorrow gives me no time!

TOM: Time for what?

AMANDA: Preparations! Why didn't you phone me at once, as soon as you asked him, the minute that he accepted? Then, don't you see, I could have been getting ready!

TOM: You don't have to make any fuss.

AMANDA: Oh, Tom, Tom, Tom, of course I have to make a fuss! I want things nice, not sloppy! Not thrown together. I'll certainly have to do some fast thinking, won't I?

TOM: I don't see why you have to think at all.

AMANDA: You just don't know. We can't have a gentleman caller in a pigsty! All my wedding silver has to be polished, the monogrammed table linen ought to be laundered! The windows have to be washed and fresh curtains put up. And how about clothes? We have to *wear* something, don't we?

TOM: Mother, this boy is no one to make a fuss over!

AMANDA: Do you realize he's the first young man we've introduced to your sister? It's terrible, dreadful, disgraceful that poor little sister has never received a single gentleman caller! Tom, come inside! (*She opens the screen door.*)

TOM: What for?

AMANDA: I want to ask you some things.

TOM: If you're going to make such a fuss, I'll call it off, I'll tell him not to come.

AMANDA: You certainly won't do anything of the kind. Nothing offends people worse than broken engagements. It simply means I'll have to work like a Turk! We won't be brilliant, but we'll pass inspection. Come on inside. (*Tom follows, groaning.*) Sit down.

TOM: Any particular place you would like me to sit?

AMANDA: Thank heavens I've got that new sofa! I'm also making payments on a floor lamp I'll have sent out! And put the chintz covers on, they'll brighten things up! Of course I'd hoped to have these walls repapered. . . . What is the young man's name?

TOM: His name is O'Connor.

AMANDA: That, of course, means fish—tomorrow is Friday![21] I'll have that salmon loaf—with Durkee's dressing! What does he do? He works at the warehouse?

TOM: Of course! How else would I—

AMANDA: Tom, he—doesn't drink?

TOM: Why do you ask me that?

AMANDA: Your father *did!*

---

[21] Catholics were then prohibited from eating meat on Fridays.

TOM: Don't get started on that!

AMANDA: He *does* drink, then?

TOM: Not that I know of!

AMANDA: Make sure, be certain! The last thing I want for my daughter's a boy who drinks!

TOM: Aren't you being a little premature? Mr. O'Connor has not yet appeared on the scene!

AMANDA: But will tomorrow. To meet your sister, and what do I know about his character? Nothing! Old maids are better off than wives of drunkards!

TOM: Oh, my God!

AMANDA: Be still!

TOM (*leaning forward to whisper*): Lots of fellows meet girls whom they don't marry!

AMANDA: Oh, talk sensibly, Tom—and don't be sarcastic! (*She has gotten a hairbrush.*)

TOM: What are you doing?

AMANDA: I'm brushing that cowlick down! What is this young man's position at the warehouse?

TOM (*submitting grimly to the brush and the interrogation*): This young man's position is that of a shipping clerk, Mother.

AMANDA: Sounds to me like a fairly responsible job, the sort of a job *you* would be in if you just had more *get-up*. What is his salary? Have you got any idea?

TOM: I would judge it to be approximately eighty-five dollars a month.

AMANDA: Well—not princely, but—

TOM: Twenty more than I make.

AMANDA: Yes, how well I know! But for a family man, eighty-five dollars a month is not much more than you can just get by on. . . .

TOM: Yes, but Mr. O'Connor is not a family man.

AMANDA: He might be, mightn't he? Some time in the future?

TOM: I see. Plans and provisions.

AMANDA: You are the only young man that I know of who ignores the fact that the future becomes the present, the present the past, and the past turns into everlasting regret if you don't plan for it!

TOM: I will think that over and see what I can make of it.

AMANDA: Don't be supercilious with your mother! Tell me some more about this—what do you call him?

TOM: James D. O'Connor. The D. is for Delaney.

AMANDA: Irish on *both* sides! *Gracious!* And doesn't drink?

TOM: Shall I call him up and ask him right this minute?

AMANDA: The only way to find out about those things is to make discreet inquiries at the proper moment. When I was a girl in Blue Mountain and it was suspected that a young man drank, the girl whose attentions he had been receiving, if any girl *was,* would sometimes speak to the minister of his church, or rather her father would if her father was living, and sort of feel him out on the young man's character. That is the way such things are discreetly handled to keep a young woman from making a tragic mistake!

TOM: Then how did you happen to make a tragic mistake?

AMANDA: That innocent look of your father's had everyone fooled! He *smiled*—the world was *enchanted!* No girl can do worse than put herself at the mercy of a handsome appearance! I hope that Mr. O'Connor is not too good-looking.

TOM: No, he's not too good-looking. He's covered with freckles and hasn't too much of a nose.

AMANDA: He's not right-down homely, though?

TOM: Not right-down homely. Just medium homely, I'd say.

AMANDA: Character's what to look for in a man.

TOM: That's what I've always said, Mother.

AMANDA: You've never said anything of the kind and I suspect you would never give it a thought.

TOM: Don't be suspicious of me.

AMANDA: At least I hope he's the type that's up and coming.

TOM: I think he really goes in for self-improvement.

AMANDA: What reason have you to think so?

TOM: He goes to night school.

AMANDA (*beaming*): Splendid! What does he do, I mean study?

TOM: Radio engineering and public speaking!

AMANDA: Then he has visions of being advanced in the world! Any young man who studies public speaking is aiming to have an executive job some day! And radio engineering? A thing for the future! Both of these facts are very illuminating. Those are the sort of things that a mother should know concerning any young man who comes to call on her daughter. Seriously or—not.

TOM: One little warning. He doesn't know about Laura. I didn't let on that we had dark ulterior motives. I just said, why don't you come have dinner with us? He said okay and that was the whole conversation.

AMANDA: I bet it was! You're eloquent as an oyster. However, he'll know about Laura when he gets here. When he sees how lovely and sweet and pretty she is, he'll thank his lucky stars he was asked to dinner.

TOM: Mother, you mustn't expect too much of Laura.

AMANDA: What do you mean?

TOM: Laura seems all those things to you and me because she's ours and we love her. We don't even notice she's crippled anymore.

AMANDA: Don't say crippled! You know that I never allow that word to be used!

TOM: But face facts, Mother. She is and—that's not all—

AMANDA: What do you mean "not all"?

TOM: Laura is very different from other girls.

AMANDA: I think the difference is all to her advantage.

TOM: Not quite all—in the eyes of others—strangers—she's terribly shy and lives in a world of her own and those things make her seem a little peculiar to people outside the house.

AMANDA: Don't say peculiar.

TOM: Face the facts. She is.

(*The dance-hall music changes to a tango that has a minor and somewhat ominous tone.*)

AMANDA: In what way is she peculiar—may I ask?

TOM (*gently*): She lives in a world of her own—a world of—little glass ornaments, Mother. . . . (*Gets up. Amanda remains holding brush, looking at him, troubled.*) She plays old phonograph records and—that's about all—(*He glances at himself in the mirror and crosses to door.*)

AMANDA (*sharply*): Where are you going?

TOM: I'm going to the movies. (*Out screen door.*)

AMANDA: Not to the movies, every night to the movies! (*Follows quickly to screen door.*) I don't believe you always go to the movies! (*He is gone. Amanda looks worriedly after him for a moment. Then vitality and optimism return and she turns from the door. Crossing to portieres.*) Laura! Laura! (*Laura answers from kitchenette.*)

LAURA: Yes, Mother.

AMANDA: Let those dishes go and come in front! (*Laura appears with dish towel. Gaily.*) Laura, come here and make a wish on the moon!

LAURA (*entering*): Moon—moon?

AMANDA: A little silver slipper of a moon. Look over your left shoulder, Laura, and make a wish! (*Laura looks faintly puzzled as if called out of sleep. Amanda seizes her shoulders and turns her at an angle by the door.*) Now! Now, darling, *wish!*

LAURA: What shall I wish for, Mother?

AMANDA (*her voice trembling and her eyes suddenly filling with tears*): Happiness! Good Fortune!

(*The violin rises and the stage dims out.*)

Scene VI

(*Image: high school hero.*)

TOM: And so the following evening I brought Jim home to dinner. I had known Jim slightly in high school. In high school Jim was a hero. He had tremendous Irish good nature and vitality with the scrubbed and polished look of white chinaware. He seemed to move in a continual spotlight. He was a star in basketball, captain of the debating club, president of the senior class and the glee club and he sang the male lead in the annual light operas. He was always running or bounding, never just walking. He seemed always at the point of defeating the law of gravity. He was shooting with such velocity through his adolescence that you would logically expect him to arrive at nothing short of the White House by the time he was thirty. But Jim apparently ran into more interference after his graduation from Soldan. His speed had definitely slowed. Six years after he left high school he was holding a job that wasn't much better than mine.

(*Image: clerk.*)

He was the only one at the warehouse with whom I was on friendly terms. I was valuable to him as someone who could remember his former glory, who had seen him win basketball games and the silver cup in debating. He knew of my secret practice of retiring to a cabinet of the washroom to work on poems when business was slack in the warehouse. He called me Shakespeare. And while the other boys in the warehouse regarded me with suspicious hostility, Jim took a humorous attitude toward me. Gradually his attitude affected the others, their hostility wore off and they also began to smile at me as people smile at an oddly fashioned dog who trots across their path at some distance.

I knew that Jim and Laura had known each other at Soldan, and I had heard Laura speak admiringly of his voice. I didn't know if Jim remembered her or not. In high school Laura had been as unobtrusive as Jim had been astonishing. If he did remember Laura, it was not as my sister, for when I asked him to dinner, he grinned and said, "You know, Shakespeare, I never thought of you as having folks!"

He was about to discover that I did. . . .

(Light up stage.)

(Legend on screen: "The Accent of a Coming Foot.")

(Friday evening. It is about five o'clock of a late spring evening which comes "scattering poems in the sky.")

(A delicate lemony light is in the Wingfield apartment.)

(Amanda has worked like a Turk in preparation for the gentleman caller. The results are astonishing. The new floor lamp with its rose-silk shade is in place, a colored paper lantern conceals the broken light fixture in the ceiling, new billowing white curtains are at the windows, chintz covers are on chairs and sofa, a pair of new sofa pillows make their initial appearance.)

(Open boxes and tissue paper are scattered on the floor.)

(Laura stands in the middle with lifted arms while Amanda crouches before her, adjusting the hem of the new dress, devout and ritualistic. The dress is colored and designed by memory. The arrangement of Laura's hair is changed; it is softer and more becoming. A fragile, unearthly prettiness has come out in Laura: she is like a piece of translucent glass touched by light, given a momentary radiance, not actual, not lasting.)

AMANDA *(impatiently)*: Why are you trembling?

LAURA: Mother, you've made me so nervous!

AMANDA: How have I made you nervous?

LAURA: By all this fuss! You make it seem so important!

AMANDA: I don't understand you, Laura. You couldn't be satisfied with just sitting home, and yet whenever I try to arrange something for you, you seem to resist it. *(She gets up.)* Now take a look at yourself. No, wait! Wait just a moment—I have an idea!

LAURA: What is it now?

(Amanda produces two powder puffs which she wraps in handkerchiefs and stuffs in Laura's bosom.)

LAURA: Mother, what are you doing?

AMANDA: They call them "Gay Deceivers"!

LAURA: I won't wear them!

AMANDA: You will!

LAURA: Why should I?

AMANDA: Because, to be painfully honest, your chest is flat.

LAURA: You make it seem like we were setting a trap.

AMANDA: All pretty girls are a trap, a pretty trap, and men expect them to be. *(Legend: "A Pretty Trap.")* Now look at yourself, young lady. This is the prettiest you will ever be! I've got to fix myself now! You're going to be surprised by your mother's appearance! *(She crosses through portieres, humming gaily.)*

(Laura moves slowly to the long mirror and stares solemnly at herself.)

(A wind blows the white curtains inward in a slow, graceful motion and with a faint, sorrowful sighing.)

AMANDA *(offstage)*: It isn't dark enough yet. *(She turns slowly before the mirror with a troubled look.)*

(Legend on screen: "This is My Sister: Celebrate Her with Strings!" Music.)

AMANDA *(laughing, off)*: I'm going to show you something. I'm going to make a spectacular appearance!

LAURA: What is it, Mother?

AMANDA: Possess your soul in patience—you will see! Something I've resurrected from that old trunk! Styles haven't changed so terribly much after all. . . . *(She parts the portieres.)* Now just look at your mother! *(She wears a girlish frock of yellowed voile with a blue silk sash. She carries a bunch of jonquils—the legend of her youth is nearly revived. Feverishly.)* This is the dress in which I led the cotillion. Won the cakewalk twice at Sunset Hill, wore one spring to the Governor's ball in Jackson![22] See how I sashayed around the ballroom, Laura? *(She raises her skirt and does a mincing step around the room.)* I wore it on Sundays for my gentlemen callers! I had it on the day I met your father—I had malaria fever all that spring. The change of climate from East Tennessee to the Delta— weakened resistance—I had a little temperature all the time—not enough to be serious—just enough to make me restless and giddy! Invitations poured in—parties all over the Delta!—"Stay in bed," said Mother, "you have fever!"—but I just wouldn't.—I took quinine but kept on going, going!—Evenings, dances!—Afternoons, long, long rides! Picnics—lovely!—So lovely, that country in May.—All lacy with dogwood, literally flooded with jonquils!—That was the spring I had the craze for jonquils. Jonquils became an absolute obsession. Mother said, "Honey, there's no more room for jonquils." And still I kept on bringing in more jonquils. Whenever, wherever I saw them, I'd say, "Stop! Stop! I see jonquils!" I made the young men help me gather the jonquils! It was a joke, Amanda and her jonquils! Finally there were no more vases to hold them, every available space was filled with jonquils. No vases to hold them? All right, I'll hold them myself! And then I— *(She stops in front of the picture. Music.)* met your father! Malaria fever and jonquils and then—this—boy. . . . *(She switches on the rose-colored lamp.)* I hope they get here before it starts to rain. *(She crosses upstage and places the jonquils in bowl on table.)* I gave your brother a little extra change so he and Mr. O'Connor could take the service car home.

LAURA *(with altered look)*: What did you say his name was?

AMANDA: O'Connor.

LAURA: What is his first name?

AMANDA: I don't remember. Oh, yes, I do. It was—Jim!

(Laura sways slightly and catches hold of a chair.)

(Legend on screen: "Not Jim!")

LAURA *(faintly)*: Not—Jim!

AMANDA: Yes, that was it, it was Jim! I've never known a Jim that wasn't nice!

(Music: ominous.)

---

[22] Jackson, Mississippi.

LAURA: Are you sure his name is Jim O'Connor?

AMANDA: Yes. Why?

LAURA: Is he the one that Tom used to know in high school?

AMANDA: He didn't say so. I think he just got to know him at the warehouse.

LAURA: There was a Jim O'Connor we both knew in high school—(*Then, with effort.*) If that is the one that Tom is bringing to dinner—you'll have to excuse me, I won't come to the table.

AMANDA: What sort of nonsense is this?

LAURA: You asked me once if I'd ever liked a boy. Don't you remember I showed you this boy's picture?

AMANDA: You mean the boy you showed me in the yearbook?

LAURA: Yes, that boy.

AMANDA: Laura, Laura, were you in love with that boy?

LAURA: I don't know, Mother. All I know is I couldn't sit at the table if it was him!

AMANDA: It won't be him! It isn't the least bit likely. But whether it is or not, you will come to the table. You will not be excused.

LAURA: I'll have to be, Mother.

AMANDA: I don't intend to humor your silliness, Laura. I've had too much from you and your brother, both! So just sit down and compose yourself till they come. Tom has forgotten his key so you'll have to let them in, when they arrive.

LAURA (*panicky*): Oh, Mother—*you* answer the door!

AMANDA (*lightly*): I'll be in the kitchen—busy!

LAURA: Oh, Mother, please answer the door, don't make me do it!

AMANDA (*crossing into kitchenette*): I've got to fix the dressing for the salmon. Fuss, fuss—silliness!—over a gentleman caller!

(*Door swings shut. Laura is left alone.*)

(*Legend: "Terror!"*)

(*She utters a low moan and turns off the lamp—sits stiffly on the edge of the sofa, knotting her fingers together.*)

(*Legend on screen: "The Opening of a Door!"*)

(*Tom and Jim appear on the fire escape steps and climb to landing. Hearing their approach, Laura rises with a panicky gesture. She retreats to the portieres.*)

(*The doorbell. Laura catches her breath and touches her throat. Low drums.*)

AMANDA (*calling*): Laura, sweetheart! The door!

(*Laura stares at it without moving.*)

JIM: I think we just beat the rain.

TOM: Uh-huh. (*He rings again, nervously. Jim whistles and fishes for a cigarette.*)

AMANDA (*very, very gaily*): Laura, that is your brother and Mr. O'Connor! Will you let them in, darling?

(*Laura crosses toward kitchenette door.*)

LAURA (*breathlessly*): Mother—you go to the door!

(*Amanda steps out of kitchenette and stares furiously at Laura. She points imperiously at the door.*)

LAURA: Please, please!

AMANDA (*in a fierce whisper*): What is the matter with you, you silly thing?

LAURA (*desperately*): Please, you answer it, *please!*

AMANDA: I told you I wasn't going to humor you, Laura. Why have you chosen this moment to lose your mind?

LAURA: Please, please, please, you go!

AMANDA: You'll have to go to the door because I can't!

LAURA (*despairingly*): I can't either!

AMANDA: *Why?*

LAURA: I'm *sick!*

AMANDA: I'm sick, too—of your nonsense! Why can't you and your brother be normal people? Fantastic whims and behavior! (*Tom gives a long ring.*) Preposterous goings on! Can you give me one reason—(*Calls out lyrically.*) COMING! JUST ONE SECOND!—why should you be afraid to open a door? Now you answer it, Laura!

LAURA: Oh, oh, oh . . . (*She returns through the portieres. Darts to the victrola and winds it frantically and turns it on.*)

AMANDA: Laura Wingfield, you march right to that door!

LAURA: Yes—yes, Mother!

(A faraway, scratchy rendition of "Dardanella" softens the air and gives her strength to move through it. She slips to the door and draws it cautiously open.)
(Tom enters with the caller, Jim O'Connor.)

TOM: Laura, this is Jim. Jim, this is my sister, Laura.

JIM (*stepping inside*): I didn't know that Shakespeare had a sister!

LAURA (*retreating stiff and trembling from the door*): How—how do you do?

JIM (*heartily extending his hand*): Okay!

(Laura touches it hesitantly with hers.)

JIM: Your hand's *cold,* Laura!

LAURA: Yes, well—I've been playing the victrola. . . .

JIM: Must have been playing classical music on it! You ought to play a little hot swing music to warm you up!

LAURA: Excuse me—I haven't finished playing the victrola. . . .

(She turns awkwardly and hurries into the front room. She pauses a second by the victrola. Then catches her breath and darts through the portieres like a frightened deer.)

JIM (*grinning*): What was the matter?

TOM: Oh—with Laura? Laura is—terribly shy.

JIM: Shy, huh? Its unusual to meet a shy girl nowadays. I don't believe you ever mentioned you had a sister.

TOM: Well, now you know. I have one. Here is the *Post Dispatch.*[23] You want a piece of it?

JIM: Uh-huh.

TOM: What piece? The comics?

JIM: Sports! (*Glances at it.*) Ole Dizzy Dean[24] is on his bad behavior.

TOM (*disinterest*): Yeah? (*Lights cigarette and crosses back to fire escape door.*)

JIM: Where are *you* going?

---

[23] The *St. Louis Post Dispatch.*

[24] Jerome Herman Dean (1911–1974), a renowned pitcher for the St. Louis Cardinals (1932–1938).

TOM: I'm going out on the terrace.

JIM (*goes after him*): You know, Shakespeare—I'm going to sell you a bill of goods!

TOM: What goods?

JIM: A course I'm taking.

TOM: Huh?

JIM: In public speaking! You and me, we're not the warehouse type.

TOM: Thanks—that's good news. But what has public speaking got to do with it?

JIM: It fits you for—executive positions!

TOM: Awww.

JIM: I tell you it's done a helluva lot for me.

(*Image: executive at desk.*)

TOM: In what respect?

JIM: In every! Ask yourself what is the difference between you an' me and men in the office down front? Brain?—No!—Ability?—No! Then what? Just one little thing—

TOM: What is that one little thing?

JIM: Primarily it amounts to—social poise! Being able to square up to people and hold your own on any social level!

AMANDA (*offstage*): Tom?

TOM: Yes, Mother?

AMANDA: Is that you and Mr. O'Connor?

TOM: Yes, Mother.

AMANDA: Well, you just make yourselves comfortable in there.

TOM: Yes, Mother.

AMANDA: Ask Mr. O'Connor if he would like to wash his hands.

JIM: Aw,—no—no—thank you—I took care of that at the warehouse. Tom—

TOM: Yes?

JIM: Mr. Mendoza was speaking to me about you.

TOM: Favorably?

JIM: What do you think?

TOM: Well—

JIM: You're going to be out of a job if you don't wake up.

TOM: I am waking up—

JIM: You show no signs.

TOM: The signs are interior.

(*Image on screen: the sailing vessel with Jolly Roger again.*)

TOM: I'm planning to change. (*He leans over the rail speaking with quiet exhilaration. The incandescent marquees and signs of the first-run movie houses light his face from across the alley. He looks like a voyager.*) I'm right at the point of committing myself to a future that doesn't include the warehouse and Mr. Mendoza or even a night school course in public speaking.

JIM: What are you gassing about?

TOM: I'm tired of the movies.

JIM: Movies!

TOM: Yes, movies! Look at them—(*A wave toward the marvels of Grand Avenue.*) All of those glamorous people—having adventures—hogging it all, gobbling the whole thing up! You know what happens? People go to the *movies* instead of *moving!* Hollywood characters are supposed to have all the adventures for everybody in America, while everybody in America sits in a dark room and watches them have them! Yes, until there's a war. That's when adventure becomes available to the masses! *Everyone's* dish, not only Gable's! Then the people in the dark room come out of the dark room to have some adventures themselves—Goody, goody! —It's our turn now, to go to the South Sea Island—to make a safari—to be exotic, far-off! —But I'm not patient. I don't want to wait till then. I'm tired of the *movies* and I am *about* to *move!*

JIM (*incredulously*): Move?

TOM: Yes.

JIM: When?

TOM: Soon!

JIM: Where? Where?

(Theme three music seems to answer the question, while Tom thinks it over. He searches among his pockets.)

TOM: I'm starting to boil inside. I know I seem dreamy, but inside—well, I'm boiling! Whenever I pick up a shoe, I shudder a little thinking how short life is and what I am doing! —Whatever that means. I know it doesn't mean shoes—except as something to wear on a traveler's feet! (*Finds paper.*) Look—

JIM: What?

TOM: I'm a member.

JIM (*reading*): The Union of Merchant Seamen.

TOM: I paid my dues this month, instead of the light bill.

JIM: You will regret it when they turn the lights off.

TOM: I won't be here.

JIM: How about your mother?

TOM: I'm like my father. The bastard son of a bastard! See how he grins? And he's been absent going on sixteen years!

JIM: You're just talking, you drip. How does your mother feel about it?

TOM: Shhh! —Here comes Mother! Mother is not acquainted with my plans!

AMANDA (*enters portieres*): Where are you all?

TOM: On the terrace, Mother.

(They start inside. She advances to them. Tom is distinctly shocked at her appearance. Even Jim blinks a little. He is making his first contact with girlish Southern vivacity and in spite of the night school course in public speaking is somewhat thrown off the beam by the unexpected outlay of social charm.)

(Certain responses are attempted by Jim but are swept aside by Amanda's gay laughter and chatter. Tom is embarrassed but after the first shock Jim reacts very warmly. Grins and chuckles, is altogether won over.)

(Image: Amanda as a girl.)

AMANDA (*coyly smiling, shaking her girlish ringlets*): Well, well, well, so this is Mr. O'Connor. Introductions entirely unnecessary. I've heard so much about you from my boy. I finally said to him, Tom—good gracious! —why don't you bring this paragon to supper? I'd like to meet this nice young man at the warehouse! —Instead of just hearing him sing your praises so much! I don't know why my son is so standoffish—that's not Southern behavior! Let's sit down and—I think we could stand a little more air in here! Tom, leave the door open. I felt a nice fresh breeze a moment ago. Where has it gone to? Mmm, so warm already! And not quite summer, even. We're going to burn up when summer really gets started. However, we're having—we're having a very light supper. I think light things are better fo' this time of year. The same as light clothes are. Light clothes an' light food are what warm weather calls fo'. You know our blood gets so thick during th' winter—it takes a while fo' us to *adjust* ou'selves! —when the season changes . . . It's come so quick this year. I wasn't prepared. All of a sudden—heavens! Already summer! —I ran to the trunk an' pulled out this light dress—Terribly old! Historical almost! But feels so good—so good an' co-ol, y'know. . . .

TOM: Mother—

AMANDA: Yes, honey?

TOM: How about—supper?

AMANDA: Honey, you go ask Sister if supper is ready! You know that Sister is in full charge of supper! Tell her you hungry boys are waiting for it. (*To Jim.*) Have you met Laura?

JIM: She—

AMANDA: Let you in? Oh, good, you've met already! It's rare for a girl as sweet an' pretty as Laura to be domestic! But Laura is, thank heavens, not only pretty but also very domestic. I'm not at all. I never was a bit. I never could make a thing but angel food cake. Well, in the South we had so many servants. Gone, gone, gone. All vestiges of gracious living! Gone completely! I wasn't prepared for what the future brought me. All of my gentlemen callers were sons of planters and so of course I assumed that I would be married to one and raise my family on a large piece of land with plenty of servants. But man proposes—and woman accepts the proposal!—To vary that old, old saying a little bit—I married no planter! I married a man who worked for the telephone company!—That gallantly smiling gentleman over there! (*Points to the picture.*) A telephone man who—fell in love with long distance!—Now he travels and I don't even know where!—But what am I going on for about my—tribulations! Tell me yours—I hope you don't have any! Tom?

TOM (*returning*): Yes, Mother?

AMANDA: Is supper nearly ready?

TOM: It looks to me like supper is on the table.

AMANDA: Let me look—(*She rises prettily and looks through portieres.*) Oh, lovely!—But where is Sister?

TOM: Laura is not feeling well and she says that she thinks she'd better not come to the table.

AMANDA: What?—Nonsense!—Laura? Oh, Laura!

LAURA (*off stage, faintly*): Yes, Mother.

AMANDA: You really must come to the table. We won't be seated until you come to the table! Come in, Mr. O'Connor. You sit over there, and I'll—Laura? Laura Wingfield! You're keeping us waiting, honey! We can't say grace until you come to the table!

(*The back door is pushed weakly open and Laura comes in. She is obviously quite faint, her lips trembling, her eyes wide and staring. She moves unsteadily toward the table.*)

(*Legend: "Terror!"*)

(*Outside a summer storm is coming abruptly. The white curtains billow inward*)

at the windows and there is a sorrowful murmur and deep blue dusk.)
    (Laura suddenly stumbles—she catches at a chair with a faint moan.)

TOM: Laura!
AMANDA: Laura! *(There is a clap of thunder.) (Legend: "Ah!") (Despairingly.)*
Why, Laura, you *are* sick, darling! Tom, help your sister into the living room,
dear! Sit in the living room, Laura—rest on the sofa. Well! *(To the gentleman
caller.)* Standing over the hot stove made her ill!—I told her that it was just too
warm this evening, but—*(Tom comes back in. Laura is on the sofa.)* Is Laura all
right now?
TOM: Yes.
AMANDA: What *is* that? Rain? A nice cool rain has come up! *(She gives the
gentleman caller a frightened look.)* I think we may—have grace—now
. . . *(Tom looks at her stupidly.)* Tom, honey—you say grace!
TOM: Oh . . . "For these and all thy mercies—"*(They bow their heads,
Amanda stealing a nervous glance at Jim. In the living room Laura, stretched on
the sofa, clenches her hand to her lips, to hold back a shuddering sob.)* God's
Holy Name be praised—

(The scene dims out.)

SCENE VII

(A Souvenir)
    *(Half an hour later. Dinner is just being finished in the upstage area which is
concealed by the drawn portieres.)*
    *(As the curtain rises Laura is still huddled upon the sofa, her feet drawn under
her, her head resting on a pale blue pillow, her eyes wide and mysteriously watchful. The new floor lamp with its shade of rose-colored silk gives a soft, becoming
light to her face, bringing out the fragile, unearthly prettiness which usually escapes attention. There is a steady murmur of rain, but it is slackening and stops
soon after the scene begins; the air outside becomes pale and luminous as the
moon breaks out.)*
    (A moment after the curtain rises, the lights in both rooms flicker and go out.)

JIM: Hey, there, Mr. Light Bulb!

(Amanda laughs nervously.)
    (Legend: "Suspension of a Public Service.")

AMANDA: Where was Moses when the lights went out? Ha-ha. Do you know
the answer to that one, Mr. O'Connor?
JIM: No, Ma'am, what's the answer?
AMANDA: In the dark! *(Jim laughs appreciably.)* Everybody sit still. I'll light
the candles. Isn't it lucky we have them on the table? Where's a match? Which of
you gentlemen can provide a match?
JIM: Here.
AMANDA: Thank you, sir.
JIM: Not at all, Ma'am!
AMANDA: I guess the fuse has burnt out. Mr. O'Connor, can you tell a burnt-
out fuse? I know I can't and Tom is a total loss when it comes to mechanics.

(*Sound: getting up: voices recede a little to kitchenette.*) Oh, be careful you don't bump into something. We don't want our gentleman caller to break his neck. Now wouldn't that be a fine howdy-do?

JIM: Ha-ha! Where is the fuse box?

AMANDA: Right here next to the stove. Can you see anything?

JIM: Just a minute.

AMANDA: Isn't electricity a mysterious thing? Wasn't it Benjamin Franklin who tied a key to a kite? We live in such a mysterious universe, don't we? Some people say that science clears up all the mysteries for us. In my opinion it only creates more! Have you found it yet?

JIM: No, Ma'am. All these fuses look okay to me.

AMANDA: Tom!

TOM: Yes, Mother?

AMANDA: That light bill I gave you several days ago. The one I told you we got the notices about?

TOM: Oh.—Yeah.

(*Legend: "Ha!"*)

AMANDA: You didn't neglect to pay it by any chance?

TOM: Why, I—

AMANDA: Didn't! I might have known it!

JIM: Shakespeare probably wrote a poem on that light bill, Mrs. Wingfield.

AMANDA: I might have known better than to trust him with it! There's such a high price for negligence in this world!

JIM: Maybe the poem will win a ten-dollar prize.

AMANDA: We'll just have to spend the remainder of the evening in the nineteenth century, before Mr. Edison made the Mazda lamp![25]

JIM: Candlelight is my favorite kind of light.

AMANDA: That shows you're romantic! But that's no excuse for Tom. Well, we got through dinner. Very considerate of them to let us get through dinner before they plunged us into everlasting darkness, wasn't it, Mr. O'Connor?

JIM: Ha-ha!

AMANDA: Tom, as a penalty for your carelessness you can help me with the dishes.

JIM: Let me give you a hand.

AMANDA: Indeed you will not!

JIM: I ought to be good for something.

AMANDA: Good for something? (*Her tone is rhapsodic.*) You? Why, Mr. O'Connor, nobody, *nobody's* given me this much entertainment in years—as you have!

JIM: Aw, now, Mrs. Wingfield!

AMANDA: I'm not exaggerating, not one bit! But Sister is all by her lonesome. You go keep her company in the parlor! I'll give you this lovely old candelabrum that used to be on the altar at the church of the Heavenly Rest. It was melted a little out of shape when the church burnt down. Lightning struck it one spring. Gypsy Jones was holding a revival at the time and he intimated that the church was destroyed because the Episcopalians gave card parties.

---

[25] The first incandescent lamp.

JIM: Ha-ha.

AMANDA: And how about coaxing Sister to drink a little wine? I think it would be good for her! Can you carry both at once?

JIM: Sure. I'm Superman!

AMANDA: Now, Thomas, get into this apron!

(The door of kitchenette swings closed on Amanda's gay laughter; the flickering light approaches the portieres.)

(Laura sits up nervously as he enters. Her speech at first is low and breathless from the almost intolerable strain of being alone with a stranger.)

(The legend: "I Don't Suppose You Remember Me at All!")

(In her first speeches in this scene, before Jim's warmth overcomes her paralyzing shyness, Laura's voice is thin and breathless as though she has just run up a steep flight of stairs.)

(Jim's attitude is gently humorous. In playing this scene it should be stressed that while the incident is apparently unimportant, it is to Laura the climax of her secret life.)

JIM: Hello, there, Laura.

LAURA *(faintly)*: Hello. (*She clears her throat.*)

JIM: How are you feeling now? Better?

LAURA: Yes. Yes, thank you.

JIM: This is for you. A little dandelion wine. (*He extends it toward her with extravagant gallantry.*)

LAURA: Thank you.

JIM: Drink it—but don't get drunk! (*He laughs heartily. Laura takes the glass uncertainly; laughs shyly.*) Where shall I set the candles?

LAURA: Oh—oh, anywhere . . .

JIM: How about here on the floor? Any objections?

LAURA: No.

JIM: I'll spread a newspaper under to catch the drippings. I like to sit on the floor. Mind if I do?

LAURA: Oh, no.

JIM: Give me a pillow?

LAURA: What?

JIM: A pillow!

LAURA: Oh . . . (*Hands him one quickly.*)

JIM: How about you? Don't you like to sit on the floor?

LAURA: Oh—yes.

JIM: Why don't you, then?

LAURA: I—will.

Take a pillow! (*Laura does. Sits on the other side of the candelabrum. Jim crosses his legs and smiles engagingly at her.*) I can't hardly see you sitting way over there.

LAURA: I can—see you.

JIM: I know, but that's not fair, I'm in the limelight. (*Laura moves her pillow closer.*) Good! Now I can see you! Comfortable?

LAURA: Yes.

JIM: So am I. Comfortable as a cow. Will you have some gum?

LAURA: No, thank you.

JIM: I think that I will indulge, with your permission. (*Musingly unwraps it and holds it up*.) Think of the fortune made by the guy that invented the first piece of chewing gum. Amazing, huh? The Wrigley Building is one of the sights of Chicago.—I saw it summer before last when I went up to the Century of Progress.[26] Did you take in the Century of Progress?

LAURA: No, I didn't.

JIM: Well, it was quite a wonderful exposition. What impressed me most was the Hall of Science. Gives you an idea of what the future will be in America, even more wonderful than the present time is! (*Pause. Smiling at her*.) Your brother tells me you're shy. Is that right, Laura?

LAURA: I—don't know.

JIM: I judge you to be an old-fashioned type of girl. Well, I think that's a pretty good type to be. Hope you don't think I'm being too personal—do you?

LAURA (*hastily, out of embarrassment*): I believe I *will* take a piece of gum, if you—don't mind. (*Clearing her throat*.) Mr. O'Connor, have you—kept up with your singing?

JIM: Singing? Me?

LAURA: Yes. I remember what a beautiful voice you had.

JIM: When did you hear me sing?

(*Voice offstage in the pause*.)

VOICE (*offstage*): O blow, ye winds, heigh-ho,
A-roving I will go!
   I'm off to my love
   With a boxing glove—
Ten thousand miles away!

JIM: You say you've heard me sing?

LAURA: Oh, yes! Yes, very often . . . I—don't suppose you remember me—at all?

JIM (*smiling doubtfully*): You know I have an idea I've seen you before. I had that idea soon as you opened the door. It seemed almost like I was about to remember your name. But the name that I started to call you—wasn't a name! And so I stopped myself before I said it.

LAURA: Wasn't it—Blue Roses?

JIM (*Springs up. Grinning*.): Blue Roses! My gosh, yes—Blue Roses! That's what I had on my tongue when you opened the door! Isn't it funny what tricks your memory plays? I didn't connect you with the high school somehow or other. But that's where it was; it was high school. I didn't even know you were Shakespeare's sister! Gosh, I'm sorry.

LAURA: I didn't expect you to. You—barely knew me!

JIM: But we did have a speaking acquaintance, huh?

LAURA: Yes, we—spoke to each other.

JIM: When did you recognize me?

LAURA: Oh, right away!

JIM: Soon as I came in the door?

LAURA: When I heard your name I thought it was probably you. I knew that Tom used to know you a little in high school. So when you came in the door—Well, then I was—sure.

JIM: Why didn't you *say* something, then?

[26] A world's fair (1933–1934) to celebrate Chicago's centennial.

LAURA (*breathlessly*): I didn't know what to say, I was —too surprised!

JIM: For goodness' sakes! You know, this sure is funny!

LAURA: Yes! Yes, isn't it, though . . .

JIM: Didn't we have a class in something together?

LAURA: Yes, we did.

JIM: What class was that?

LAURA: It was—singing—Chorus!

JIM: Aw!

LAURA: I sat across the aisle from you in the Aud.

JIM: Aw.

LAURA: Mondays, Wednesdays, and Fridays.

JIM: Now I remember—you always came in late.

LAURA: Yes, it was so hard for me, getting upstairs. I had that brace on my leg—it clumped so loud!

JIM: I never heard any clumping.

LAURA (*wincing at the recollection*): To me it sounded like—thunder!

JIM: Well, well, well, I never even noticed.

LAURA: And everybody was seated before I came in. I had to walk in front of all those people. My seat was in the back row. I had to go clumping all the way up the aisle with everyone watching!

JIM: You shouldn't have been self-conscious.

LAURA: I know, but I was. It was always such a relief when the singing started.

JIM: Aw, yes, I've placed you now! I used to call you Blue Roses. How was it that I got started calling you that?

LAURA: I was out of school a little while with pleurosis. When I came back you asked me what was the matter. I said I had pleurosis—you thought I said Blue Roses. That's what you always called me after that!

JIM: I hope you didn't mind.

LAURA: Oh, no—I liked it. You see, I wasn't acquainted with many—people. . . .

JIM: As I remember you sort of stuck by yourself.

LAURA: I—I—never had much luck at—making friends.

JIM: I don't see why you wouldn't.

LAURA: Well, I—started out badly.

JIM: You mean being—

LAURA: Yes, it sort of—stood between me—

JIM: You shouldn't have let it!

LAURA: I know, but it did, and—

JIM: You were shy with people!

LAURA: I tried not to be but never could—

JIM: Overcome it?

LAURA: No, I—I never could!

JIM: I guess being shy is something you have to work out of kind of gradually.

LAURA (*sorrowfully*): Yes—I guess it—

JIM: Takes time!

LAURA: Yes—

JIM: People are not so dreadful when you know them. That's what you have to remember! And everybody has problems, not just you, but practically everybody has got some problems. You think of yourself as having the only problems, as being the only one who is disappointed. But just look around you and you will see lots of people as disappointed as you are. For instance, I hoped when I was going to high school that I would be further along at this time, six years later, than I am now—You remember that wonderful write-up I had in *The Torch?*

LAURA: Yes! (*She rises and crosses to table.*)

JIM: It said I was bound to succeed in anything I went into! (*Laura returns with the annual.*) Holy Jeez! *The Torch!* (*He accepts it reverently. They smile across it with mutual wonder. Laura crouches beside him and they begin to turn through it. Laura's shyness is dissolving in his warmth.*)

LAURA: Here you are in *Pirates of Penzance!*

JIM (*wistfully*): I sang the baritone lead in that operetta.

LAURA (*rapidly*): So—*beautifully!*

JIM (*protesting*): Aw—

LAURA: Yes, yes—beautifully—beautifully!

JIM: You heard me?

LAURA: All three times!

JIM: No!

LAURA: Yes!

JIM: All three performances?

LAURA (*looking down*): Yes.

JIM: Why?

LAURA: I—wanted to ask you to—autograph my program.

JIM: Why didn't you ask me to?

LAURA: You were always surrounded by your own friends so much that I never had a chance to.

JIM: You should have just—

LAURA: Well, I—thought you might think I was—

JIM: Thought I might think you was—what?

LAURA: Oh—

JIM (*with reflective relish*): I was beleaguered by females in those days.

LAURA: You were terribly popular!

JIM: Yeah—

LAURA: You had such a—friendly way—

JIM: I was spoiled in high school.

LAURA: Everybody—liked you!

JIM: Including you?

LAURA: I—yes, I—I did, too—(*She gently closes the book in her lap.*)

JIM: Well, well, well!—Give me that program, Laura. (*She hands it to him. He signs it with a flourish.*) There you are—better late than never!

LAURA: Oh, I—what a—surprise!

JIM: My signature isn't worth very much right now. But some day—maybe—it will increase in value! Being disappointed is one thing and being discouraged is something else. I am disappointed but I am not discouraged. I'm twenty-three years old. How old are you?

LAURA: I'll be twenty-four in June.

JIM: That's not old age!

LAURA: No, but—

JIM: You finished high school?

LAURA (*with difficulty*): I didn't go back.

JIM: You mean you dropped out?

LAURA: I made bad grades in my final examinations. (*She rises and replaces the book and the program. Her voice strained.*) How is—Emily Meisenbach getting along?

JIM: Oh, that kraut-head!

LAURA: Why do you call her that?

JIM: That's what she was.

LAURA: You're not still—going with her?

JIM: I never see her.

LAURA: It said in the Personal Section that you were—engaged!

JIM: I know, but I wasn't impressed by that—propaganda!

LAURA: It wasn't—the truth?

JIM: Only in Emily's optimistic opinion!

LAURA: Oh—

(*Legend: "What Have You Done since High School?"*)
(*Jim lights a cigarette and leans indolently back on his elbows smiling at Laura with a warmth and charm which lights her inwardly with altar candles. She remains by the table and turns in her hands a piece of glass to cover her tumult.*)

JIM (*after several reflective puffs on a cigarette*): What have you done since high school? (*She seems not to hear him.*) Huh? (*Laura looks up.*) I said what have you done since high school, Laura?

LAURA: Nothing much.

JIM: You must have been doing something these six long years.

LAURA: Yes.

JIM: Well, then, such as what?

LAURA: I took a business course at business college—

JIM: How did that work out?

LAURA: Well, not very—well—I had to drop out, it gave me—indigestion—

(*Jim laughs gently.*)

JIM: What are you doing now?

LAURA: I don't do anything—much. Oh, please don't think I sit around doing nothing! My glass collection takes up a good deal of my time. Glass is something you have to take good care of.

JIM: What did you say—about glass?

LAURA: Collection I said—I have one— (*She clears her throat and turns away again, acutely shy.*)

JIM (*abruptly*): You know what I judge to be the trouble with you? Inferiority complex! Know what that is? That's what they call it when someone low-rates himself! I understand it because I had it, too. Although my case was not so aggravated as yours seems to be. I had it until I took up public speaking, developed my voice, and learned that I had an aptitude for science. Before that time I never thought of myself as being outstanding in any way whatsoever! Now I've never made a regular study of it, but I have a friend who says I can analyze people better than doctors that make a profession of it. I don't claim that to be necessarily true, but I can sure guess a person's psychology, Laura! (*Takes out his gum.*) Excuse me, Laura. I always take it out when the flavor is gone. I'll use this scrap of paper to wrap it in. I know how it is to get it stuck on a shoe. Yep—that's what I judge to be your principal trouble. A lack of confidence in yourself as a person. You don't have the proper amount of faith in yourself. I'm basing that fact on a number of your remarks and also on certain observations I've made. For instance that clumping you thought was so awful in high school. You say that you even dreaded to walk into class. You see what you did? You dropped out of school, you gave up an education because of a clump, which as far as I know was practically nonexistent! A little physical defect is what you have. Hardly noticeable even! Magnified thousands of times by imagination! You know what my strong advice to you is? Think of yourself as *superior* in some way!

LAURA: In what way would I think?

JIM: Why, man alive, Laura! Just look about you a little. What do you see? A world full of common people! All of 'em born and all of 'em going to die! Which of them has one-tenth of your good points! Or mine! Or anyone else's, as far as that goes—Gosh! Everybody excels in some one thing. Some in many! (*Unconsciously glances at himself in the mirror.*) All you've got to do is discover in *what!* Take me, for instance. (*He adjusts his tie at the mirror.*) My interest happens to lie in electro-dynamics. I'm taking a course in radio engineering at night school, Laura, on top of a fairly responsible job at the warehouse. I'm taking that course and studying public speaking.

LAURA: Ohhhh.

JIM: Because I believe in the future of television! (*Turning back to her.*) I wish to be ready to go up right along with it. Therefore I'm planning to get in on the ground floor. In fact, I've already made the right connections and all that remains is for the industry itself to get under way! Full steam—(*His eyes are starry.*) *Knowledge*—Zzzzzp! *Money*—Zzzzzzp!—*Power!* That's the cycle democracy is built on! (*His attitude is convincingly dynamic. Laura stares at him, even her shyness eclipsed in her absolute wonder. He suddenly grins.*) I guess you think I think a lot of myself!

LAURA: No—o-o-o, I—

JIM: Now how about you? Isn't there something you take more interest in than anything else?

LAURA: Well, I do—as I said—have my—glass collection—

(*A peal of girlish laughter from the kitchen.*)

JIM: I'm not right sure I know what you're talking about. What kind of glass is it?

LAURA: Little articles of it, they're ornaments mostly! Most of them are little animals made out of glass, the tiniest little animals in the world. Mother calls them a glass menagerie! Here's an example of one, if you'd like to see it! This one is one of the oldest. It's nearly thirteen. (*He stretches out his hand.*) (*Music: "The Glass Menagerie."*) Oh, be careful—if you breathe, it breaks!

JIM: I'd better not take it. I'm pretty clumsy with things.

LAURA: Go on, I trust you with him! (*Places it in his palm.*) There now— you're holding him gently! Hold him over the light, he loves the light! You see how the light shines through him?

JIM: It sure does shine!

LAURA: I shouldn't be partial, but he is my favorite one.

JIM: What kind of a thing is this one supposed to be?

LAURA: Haven't you noticed the single horn on his forehead?

JIM: A unicorn, huh?

LAURA: Mmm-hmmm!

JIM: Unicorns, aren't they extinct in the modern world?

LAURA: I know!

JIM: Poor little fellow, he must feel sort of lonesome.

LAURA (*smiling*): Well, if he does he doesn't complain about it. He stays on a shelf with some horses that don't have horns and all of them seem to get along nicely together.

JIM: How do you know?

LAURA (*lightly*): I haven't heard any arguments among them!

JIM (*grinning*): No arguments, huh? Well, that's a pretty good sign! Where shall I set him?

LAURA: Put him on the table. They all like a change of scenery once in a while!

JIM (*stretching*): Well, well, well, well—Look how big my shadow is when I stretch!

LAURA: Oh, oh, yes—it stretches across the ceiling!

JIM (*crossing to door*): I think it's stopped raining. (*Opens fire escape door.*) Where does the music come from?

LAURA: From the Paradise Dance Hall across the alley.

JIM: How about cutting the rug a little, Miss Wingfield?

LAURA: Oh, I—

JIM: Or is your program filled up? Let me have a look at it. (*Grasps imaginary card.*) Why, every dance is taken! I'll just have to scratch some out. (*Waltz music: "La Golondrina."*) Ahhh, a waltz! (*He executes some sweeping turns by himself then holds his arms toward Laura.*)

LAURA (*breathlessly*): I—can't dance!

JIM: There you go, that inferiority stuff!

LAURA: I've never danced in my life!

JIM: Come on, try!

LAURA: Oh, but I'd step on you!

JIM: I'm not made out of glass.

LAURA: How—how—how do we start?

JIM: Just leave it to me. You hold your arms out a little.

LAURA: Like this?

JIM: A little bit higher. Right. Now don't tighten up, that's the main thing about it—relax.

LAURA (*laughing breathlessly*): It's hard not to.

JIM: Okay.

LAURA: I'm afraid you can't budge me.

JIM: What do you bet I can't? (*He swings her into motion.*)

LAURA: Goodness, yes, you can!

JIM: Let yourself go, now, Laura, just let yourself go.

LAURA: I'm—

JIM: Come on!

LAURA: Trying!

JIM: Not so stiff—Easy does it!

LAURA: I know but I'm—

JIM: Loosen th' backbone! There now, that's a lot better.

LAURA: Am I?

JIM: Lots, lots better! (*He moves her about the room in a clumsy waltz.*)

LAURA: Oh, my!

JIM: Ha-ha!

LAURA: Oh, my goodness!

JIM: Ha-ha-ha! (*They suddenly bump into the table. Jim stops.*) What did we hit on?

LAURA: Table.

JIM: Did something fall off it? I think—

LAURA: Yes.

JIM: I hope that it wasn't the little glass horse with the horn!

LAURA: Yes.

JIM: Aw, aw, aw. Is it broken?

LAURA: Now it is just like all the other horses.

JIM: It's lost its—

LAURA: Horn! It doesn't matter. Maybe it's a blessing in disguise.

JIM: You'll never forgive me. I bet that that was your favorite piece of glass.

LAURA: I don't have favorites much. It's no tragedy, Freckles. Glass breaks so easily. No matter how careful you are. The traffic jars the shelves and things fall off them.

JIM: Still I'm awfully sorry that I was the cause.

LAURA (*smiling*): I'll just imagine he had an operation. The horn was removed to make him feel less—freakish! (*They both laugh.*) Now he will feel more at home with the other horses, the ones that don't have horns . . .

JIM: Ha-ha, that's very funny! (*Suddenly serious.*) I'm glad to see that you have a sense of humor. You know—you're—well—very different! Surprisingly different from anyone else I know! (*His voice becomes soft and hesitant with a genuine feeling.*) Do you mind me telling you that? (*Laura is abashed beyond speech.*) I mean it in a nice way . . . (*Laura nods shyly, looking away.*) You make me feel sort of—I don't know how to put it! I'm usually pretty good at expressing things, but—This is something that I don't know how to say! (*Laura touches her throat and clears it—turns the broken unicorn in her hands.*) (*Even softer.*) Has anyone ever told you that you were pretty? (*Pause: Music.*) (*Laura looks up slowly, with wonder, and shakes her head.*) Well, you are! In a very different way from anyone else. And all the nicer because of the difference, too. (*His voice becomes low and husky. Laura turns away, nearly faint with the novelty of her emotions.*) I wish that you were my sister. I'd teach you to have some confidence in yourself. The different people are not like other people, but being different is nothing to be ashamed of. Because other people are not such wonderful people. They're one hundred times one thousand. You're one times one! They walk all over the earth. You just stay here. They're common as—weeds, but—you—well, you're—*Blue Roses!*

(*Image on screen: blue roses.*)
(*Music changes.*)

LAURA: But blue is wrong for—roses . . .

JIM: It's right for you—You're—pretty!

LAURA: In what respect am I pretty?

JIM: In all respects—believe me! Your eyes—your hair—are pretty! Your hands are pretty! (*He catches hold of her hand.*) You think I'm making this up because I'm invited to dinner and have to be nice. Oh, I could do that! I could put on an act for you, Laura, and say lots of things without being very sincere. But this time I am. I'm talking to you sincerely. I happened to notice you had this inferiority complex that keeps you from feeling comfortable with people. Somebody needs to build your confidence up and make you proud instead of shy and turning away and—blushing—Somebody ought to—Ought to—*kiss* you, Laura! *(His hand slips slowly up her arm to her shoulder.) (Music swells tumultuously.) (He suddenly turns her about and kisses her on the lips. When he releases her Laura sinks on the sofa with a bright, dazed look. Jim backs away and fishes in his pocket for a cigarette.) (Legend on screen: "Souvenir.")* Stumble-john! *(He lights the cigarette, avoiding her look. There is a peal of girlish laughter from Amanda in the kitchen. Laura slowly raises and opens her hand. It still contains the little broken glass animal. She looks at it with a tender, bewildered expression.)* Stumble-john! I shouldn't have done that—That was way off the beam. You don't smoke, do you? *(She looks up, smiling, not hearing the question. He sits beside her a little gingerly. She looks at him speechlessly—waiting. He coughs decorously and moves a little farther aside as he considers the situation and senses her feelings, dimly, with perturbation. Gently.)* Would you—care for a—mint? *(She doesn't seem to hear him but her look grows brighter even.)* Peppermint—Life Saver? My pocket's a regular drugstore—wherever I go . . . *(He pops a mint in his mouth. Then gulps and decides to make a clean breast of it. He speaks slowly and gingerly.)* Laura, you know, if I had a sister like you, I'd do the same thing as Tom. I'd bring out fellows and—introduce her to them. The right type of boys of a type to—appreciate her. Only—well—he made a mistake about me. Maybe I've got no call to be saying this. That may not have been the idea in having me over. But what if it was? There's nothing wrong about that. The only trouble is that in my case—I'm not in a situation to—do the right thing. I can't take down your number and say I'll phone. I can't call up next week and—ask for a date. I thought I had better explain the situation in case you misunderstood it and—hurt your feelings. . . . *(Pause. Slowly, very slowly, Laura's look changes, her eyes returning slowly from his to the ornament in her palm.)*

(Amanda utters another gay laugh in the kitchen.)

LAURA *(faintly)*: You—won't—call again?

JIM: No Laura, I can't. *(He rises from the sofa.)* As I was just explaining, I've—got strings on me, Laura, I've—been going steady! I go out all the time with a girl named Betty. She's a home-girl like you, and Catholic, and Irish, and in a great many ways we—get along fine. I met her last summer on a moonlight boat trip up the river to Alton,[27] on the *Majestic*. Well—right away from the start it was—love! *(Legend: Love!) (Laura sways slightly forward and grips the arm of the sofa. He fails to notice, now enrapt in his own comfortable being.)* Being in love has made a new man of me! *(Leaning stiffly forward, clutching the arm of the sofa, Laura struggles visibly with her storm. But Jim is oblivious, she is a long way off.)* The power of love is really pretty tremendous! Love is something that—changes the whole world, Laura! *(The storm abates a little and Laura leans back. He notices her again.)* It happened that Betty's aunt took sick, she got a wire and had to go to Centralia.[28] So Tom—when he asked me to dinner—I naturally just accepted the invitation, not knowing that you—that he—that I—*(He stops awkwardly.)* Huh—I'm a stumble-john! *(He flops back on the sofa. The holy candles on the altar of Laura's face have been snuffed out! There is a look of almost infinite desolation. Jim glances at her uneasily.)* I wish that you would—say something. *(She bites her lip which was trembling and then bravely smiles. She opens*

---

[27] Alton, Illinois.   [28] Centralia, Illinois.

her hand again on the broken glass ornament. Then she gently takes his hand and raises it level with her own. She carefully places the unicorn in the palm of his hand, then pushes his fingers closed upon it.) What are you—doing that for? You want me to have him?—Laura? *(She nods.)* What for?

LAURA: A—souvenir . . .

(She rises unsteadily and crouches beside the victrola to wind it up.)
(Legend on screen: "Things Have a Way of Turning out so Badly.")
(Or Image: "Gentleman Caller Waving Good-bye!—Gaily.")
(At this moment Amanda rushes brightly back in the front room. She bears a pitcher of fruit punch in an old-fashioned cut-glass pitcher and a plate of maca-roons. The plate has a gold border and poppies painted on it.)

AMANDA: Well, well, well! Isn't the air delightful after the shower? I've made you children a little liquid refreshment. *(Turns gaily to the gentleman caller.)* Jim, do you know that song about lemonade?
"Lemonade, lemonade
    Made in the shade and stirred with a spade—
    Good enough for any old maid!"

JIM *(uneasily)*: Ha-ha! No—I never heard it.

AMANDA: Why, Laura! You look so serious!

JIM: We were having a serious conversation.

AMANDA: Good! Now you're better acquainted!

JIM *(uncertainly)*: Ha-ha! Yes.

AMANDA: You modern young people are much more serious-minded than my generation. I was so gay as a girl!

JIM: You haven't changed, Mrs. Wingfield.

AMANDA: Tonight I'm rejuvenated! The gaiety of the occasion, Mr. O'Con-nor! *(She tosses her head with a peal of laughter. Spills lemonade.)* Oooo! I'm baptizing myself!

JIM: Here—let me—

AMANDA *(setting the pitcher down)*: There now. I discovered we had some maraschino cherries. I dumped them in, juice and all!

JIM: You shouldn't have gone to that trouble, Mrs. Wingfield.

AMANDA: Trouble, trouble? Why it was loads of fun! Didn't you hear me cut-ting up in the kitchen? I bet your ears were burning! I told Tom how outdone with him I was for keeping you to himself so long a time! He should have brought you over much, much sooner! Well, now that you've found your way, I want you to be a very frequent caller! Not just occasional but all the time. Oh, we're going to have a lot of gay times together! I see them coming! Mmm, just breathe that air! So fresh, and the moon's so pretty! I'll skip back out—I know where my place is when young folks are having a—serious conversation!

JIM: Oh, don't go out, Mrs. Wingfield. The fact of the matter is I've got to be going.

AMANDA: Going, now? You're joking! Why, it's only the shank of the eve-ning, Mr. O'Connor!

JIM: Well, you know how it is.

AMANDA: You mean you're a young workingman and have to keep working-men's hours. We'll let you off early tonight. But only on the condition that next time you stay later. What's the best night for you? Isn't Saturday night the best night for you workingmen?

JIM: I have a couple of time clocks to punch, Mrs. Wingfield. One at morning, another one at night!

AMANDA: My, but you *are* ambitious! You work at night, too?

JIM: No, Ma'am, not work but—Betty! (*He crosses deliberately to pick up his hat. The band at the Paradise Dance Hall goes into a tender waltz.*)

AMANDA: Betty? Betty? Who's—Betty! (*There is an ominous cracking sound in the sky.*)

JIM: Oh, just a girl. The girl I go steady with! (*He smiles charmingly. The sky falls.*)

(*Legend: "The Sky Falls."*)

AMANDA (*a long-drawn exhalation*): Ohhhh . . . Is it a serious romance, Mr. O'Connor?

JIM: We're going to be married the second Sunday in June.

AMANDA: Ohhhh—how nice! Tom didn't mention that you were engaged to be married.

JIM: The cat's not out of the bag at the warehouse yet. You know how they are. They call you Romeo and stuff like that. (*He stops at the oval mirror to put on his hat. He carefully shapes the brim and the crown to give a discreetly dashing effect.*) It's been a wonderful evening, Mrs. Wingfield. I guess this is what they mean by Southern hospitality.

AMANDA: It really wasn't anything at all.

JIM: I hope it don't seem like I'm rushing off. But I promised Betty I'd pick her up at the Wabash depot, an' by the time I get my jalopy down there her train'll be in. Some women are pretty upset if you keep 'em waiting.

AMANDA: Yes, I know—The tyranny of women! (*Extends her hand.*) Good-bye, Mr. O'Connor. I wish you luck—and happiness—and success! All three of them, and so does Laura!—Don't you, Laura?

LAURA: Yes!

JIM (*taking her hand*) Good-bye, Laura. I'm certainly going to treasure that souvenir. And don't you forget the good advice I gave you. (*Raises his voice to a cheery shout.*) So long, Shakespeare! Thanks again, ladies—Good night!

(*He grins and ducks jauntily out.*)

(*Still bravely grimacing, Amanda closes the door on the gentleman caller. Then she turns back to the room with a puzzled expression. She and Laura don't dare to face each other. Laura crouches beside the victrola to wind it.*)

AMANDA (*faintly*): Things have a way of turning out so badly. I don't believe that I would play the victrola. Well, well—well—Our gentleman caller was engaged to be married! Tom!

TOM (*from back*): Yes, Mother?

AMANDA: Come in here a minute. I want to tell you something awfully funny.

TOM (*enters with macaroon and a glass of the lemonade*): Has the gentleman caller gotten away already?

AMANDA: The gentleman caller has made an early departure. What a wonderful joke you played on us!

TOM: How do you mean?

AMANDA: You didn't mention that he was engaged to be married.

TOM: Jim? Engaged?

AMANDA: That's what he just informed us.

TOM: I'll be jiggered! I didn't know about that.

AMANDA: That seems very peculiar.

TOM: What's peculiar about it?

AMANDA: Didn't you call him your best friend down at the warehouse?

TOM: He is, but how did I know?

AMANDA: It seems extremely peculiar that you wouldn't know your best friend was going to be married!

TOM: The warehouse is where I work, not where I know things about people!

AMANDA: You don't know things anywhere! You live in a dream; you manufacture illusions! (*He crosses to door.*) Where are you going?

TOM: I'm going to the movies.

AMANDA: That's right, now that you've had us make such fools of ourselves. The effort, the preparations, all the expense! The new floor lamp, the rug, the clothes for Laura! All for what? To entertain some other girl's fiancé! Go to the movies, go! Don't think about us, a mother deserted, an unmarried sister who's crippled and has no job! Don't let anything interfere with your selfish pleasure! Just go, go, go—to the movies!

TOM: All right, I will! The more you shout about my selfishness to me the quicker I'll go, and I won't go to the movies!

AMANDA: Go, then! Then go to the moon—you selfish dreamer!

(*Tom smashes his glass on the floor. He plunges out on the fire escape, slamming the door. Laura screams—cut by door.*)

(*Dance hall music up. Tom goes to the rail and grips it desperately, lifting his face in the chill white moonlight penetrating the narrow abyss of the alley.*)

(*Legend on screen: "And so Good-bye . . . "*)

(*Tom's closing speech is timed with the interior pantomime. The interior scene is played as though viewed through soundproof glass. Amanda appears to be making a comforting speech to Laura who is huddled upon the sofa. Now that we cannot hear the mother's speech, her silliness is gone and she has dignity and tragic beauty. Laura's dark hair hides her face until at the end of the speech she lifts it to smile at her mother. Amanda's gestures are slow and graceful, almost dancelike, as she comforts the daughter. At the end of her speech she glances a moment at the father's picture—then withdraws through the portieres. At close of Tom's speech, Laura blows out the candles, ending the play.*)

TOM: I didn't go to the moon, I went much further—for time is the longest distance between two places—Not long after that I was fired for writing a poem on the lid of a shoebox. I left Saint Louis. I descended the steps of this fire escape for a last time and followed, from then on, in my father's footsteps, attempting to find in motion what was lost in space—I traveled around a great deal. The cities swept about me like dead leaves, leaves that were brightly colored but torn away from the branches. I would have stopped, but I was pursued by something. It always came upon me unawares, taking me altogether by surprise. Perhaps it was a familiar bit of music. Perhaps it was only a piece of transparent glass—Perhaps I am walking along a street at night, in some strange city, before I have found companions. I pass the lighted window of a shop where perfume is sold. The window is filled with pieces of colored glass, tiny transparent bottles in delicate colors, like bits of a shattered rainbow. Than all at once my sister touches my shoulder. I turn around and look into her eyes . . . Oh, Laura, Laura, I tried to leave you behind me, but I am more faithful than I intended to be! I reach for a cigarette, I cross the street, I run into the movies or a bar, I buy a drink, I speak to the nearest stranger—anything that can blow your candles out! (*Laura bends over the candles.*)—for nowadays the world is lit by lightning! Blow out your candles, Laura—and so good-bye. . . .

(*She blows the candles out.*)
(*The scene dissolves.*)

1944, 1945

Arthur Miller
(1915–)

The world into which Arthur Miller was born in 1915 was the world that characters in his early plays would later inhabit. The son of Jewish immigrant parents, Miller grew up in a Brooklyn home filled with talk of sales, merchandising, and the fate of Jews in an America wary of their presence. He recounts in his autobiography, *Timebends* (1987), an experience of American public schooling familiar to later generations: "I never read a book weightier than Tom Swift and the Rover Boys, and only verged on literature with some Dickens." Miller's lack of enthusiasm for scholarly interests in high school led to failure in his first attempt to enter the University of Michigan. This failure allowed him the time to work and save money for schooling, while he pursued the reading he had not done in high school.

Feodor Dostoevski's novels became Miller's passion, and he began to consider writing as a profession. Finally accepted at Michigan in 1934, he won two of the school's playwriting awards. In 1938 Miller married Mary Grace Slattery and began research for his first postcollege play, *The Man Who Had All the Luck* (1944). That play received some critical acclaim, but it was Miller's next play, *All My Sons* (1947), that succeeded as popular drama and received the New York Drama Critics Circle Award—out of a field that included Eugene O'Neill's *The Iceman Cometh* (1946).

Miller's interest in the embattled patriarch, the lone and confused head of the family (generally comprised of sons), is clearly reflected in the Keller family of *All My Sons*. The guilt-ridden father so painfully and fully developed in the character of Willy Loman in Miller's next play, *Death of a Salesman* (1949), is in *All My Sons* Joe Keller, a man whose mistakes have caused the deaths of his son Larry's companions and then Larry's suicide. Whereas in *All My Sons* the deaths are violent and immediate, *Death of a Salesman* more subtly examines the slow, crushing, ebbing away of life in two sons who can fulfill their father's expectations only by using fantasy and bravado.

Since Miller began writing for theater, the entertainment industry has undergone swift, sweeping changes; what was innovation in 1947 may look flat and commonplace today. A Pulitzer Prize winner, *Death of a Salesman* was produced with innovations in set design and in lighting, allowing Miller to portray American life more realistically than most playwrights had before him. *Death of a Salesman* audiences were granted the extraordinary

A scene from a production of Arthur Miller's Death of a Salesman, *starring Lee J. Cobb as Willy Loman.*

experience of watching Biff and Happy, the two sons, stand on the upper tier of a house (not coincidentally designed like a doll's house cut open to allow the manipulation of the pieces) and converse while their father mumbles in the kitchen, unaware of the scene taking place above him. That is of course how the family works, sequestered in small rooms, discussing or furtively witnessing the behavior of other members. The cramped attic room and small dimensions of the Brooklyn house are a constant visual reminder of the added social pressure Miller brought to O'Neill's vision of family drama and of the true condition of working-class frustration and poverty that complicates family relations. The lighting allows Willy Loman's ailing mind to rehash memories while the action of other characters continues. All the characters are themselves at once in the present and in their youth. Although in isolated instances much of this technique had been used before, as a whole vision of a family and its weary struggle *Death of a Salesman* stunned its audiences. Miller has recalled that at its first production in Philadelphia, audience members simply sat after the performance, some putting their coats on quietly, some openly weeping, until they remembered to applaud, applauding for a very long time.

 Death of a Salesman was considered the work of an "intellectual" playwright, though Miller balked at the moniker. The play treats money and sex with an obsession richly experienced by, if not represented to, the American public. During the 1940s a theatergoer was more likely to see well-dressed, content characters having small, easily mended altercations than the gritty Brooklyn neighborhood dependent upon the kindness of consumers. Like O'Neill's *Long Day's Journey Into Night* (written in 1940 but not produced until 1956), the excruciating machinations of a dreamer, a blustering confused man at the center of his more clear-eyed family, can be expressed powerfully in scenes of almost interminable length.

Many critical readings of *Death of a Salesman* consider Willy Loman's name to be a heavyhanded reference to "Low-man." But Miller recounts a more affecting story of the character's conception. After watching Fritz Lang's 1933 film *The Testament of Dr. Mabuse,* Miller could not forget the chilling moment when a detective who has been following an arsonist desperately tries to reach his boss and cries into the phone "Hello? Hello! Lohmann? Lohmann!" As Miller recalls in *Timebends,* "the screen goes black before he can give his location. The next shot finds him in an asylum in a white gown, seated on a bed with his hand up to his ear gripping a nonexistent phone receiver, a look of total terror in his face, repeating, 'Lohmann? Lohmann? Lohmann? . . .' What the name really meant to me was a terror-stricken man calling into the void for help that will never come."

Whereas O'Neill's plays about families deal with the unusual household headed by flamboyant actors or frustrated artists, *Death of a Salesman* touches on a portion of the American audience whose days were spent in the mediocre rhythm of expectation and disappointment, of dream and reality. The play takes the viewer relentlessly along on Willy's rollercoaster dreams. His hope is contagious; his despair, unbearable. And the spectacle of a father who has invested everything in the son who cannot help but fail is a scene well known in the average American household.

Like families in many other American plays, the Loman family consists of sons. The women in the work of Miller, and of O'Neill, and even of such contemporary playwrights as Sam Shepard, are mothers and girlfriends, women on the periphery, whose influence is fraught and shadowy. Willy's wife, Linda, is forcefully described in Miller's direction as unremittingly loyal. Biff and his father struggle over the secret of Willy's "other woman," who should primarily affect Linda. Yet, the family's strange protective mechanisms function between both sexes. If Linda is not privy to Willy and Biff's secret, Willy does not realize that Linda knows about his desire to kill himself and that she enlists the boys in her hovering about him.

Family dramas also tend to be heroless, representing the foibles and oppressive habits of fathers as an effect of their social position and their family lives. The children tend to struggle confusedly to mediate between their own dreams and their parents' expectations. In *Death of a Salesman* the audience witnesses a process, the full implications of which are unbeknownst to Willy Loman. His audience is perforce more politically astute than Willy himself, for what he does not see is quite clearly observable to the audience: the progressive revelation of the unnamed, disabling, and destructive power of the seemingly benign American dream.

Miller's next plays allowed for a potential hero and examined how the individual acts in the context of his or her society. His 1950 adaptation of Ibsen's *An Enemy of the People* (1882), a story about one man's moral strength in the face of community greed, prepared Miller to write the play *The Crucible* (1953). Unlike Willy Loman, John Proctor, the main character of *The Crucible,* is well aware of the nature of the powers that threaten him. As the central figure, he is a character with the moral fortitude and political conscience that tend to reveal themselves in times of acute political crisis. In the figure of Proctor, Miller explores the possibility of defiance. Like Loman, Proctor is knotted into the complications of his situation by having committed an infidelity, but for him the lines demarcating the private from the public, the personal from the social, are strong. Although he does not allow the power and violence of exterior political forces to overtake his judgment of self-worth or to determine his ethical choices, the price of such honor seems to demand death, as if the price of moral knowledge is death.

Written while daily reports from the House Committee on Un-American Activities filled the media, *The Crucible* with its witchhunts, frenzied tribunals, and implicated believers could not help being seen as an allegory for the hearings. Indeed, Miller was called before the committee and, like Proctor, refused to name any of his friends to save himself. The very real, devastating effect the hearings had on many of Miller's colleagues in the theater made the play's subject more harrowing, demonstrating the power of accusation and rumor to create a community of fear. Despite its powerful timeliness *The Crucible* opened in New York to cold reviews, and Miller was denied his passport to attend its Brussels opening in 1954. When the play opened Off Broadway in 1958, however, it won rave reviews from the same critics who had dismissed it several years before. What in 1953 had been an uncomfortable diagnosis of the current social ills was in 1958 an accepted critique of the excesses of the McCarthy hearings.

After completing *The Crucible* Miller wrote *A View From the Bridge,* and *A Memory of Two Mondays;* the two plays were produced together in 1955. In 1956 he "married into" the world of Hollywood: his marriage to Marilyn Monroe was a union that produced not only constant attention from the press but also the screenplay for *The Misfits* (1961). Adapted from a story he had written after his divorce from his first wife, *The Misfits* was created for Monroe as a vehicle for a part more interesting than those in which Hollywood generally cast her. The premise, a group of cowboys who catch mustangs too small to ride (misfits) and sell them for dog food, oddly meshed the independent West with the more traditional occupation of trade. Neither "marriage" lasted, however; the Hollywood life was incompatible with Miller's interests, and its destructive influence on Monroe became too painful for him to witness. The couple divorced in 1961, and Miller married Inge Morath, a photographer, a year later.

Miller continued to write for the stage. Part romantic, part pragmatist, part political writer, he wrote about Adam and Eve in *After the Fall* (1964), examining the dependance relationships between men and women. In *Incident at Vichy* (1965), about a group of men brought together to be interrogated by the Nazis, Miller again used the theme of moral conscience in the context of society. The tension grows as the members of the group are taken away one by one and not returned. The final debate between a Roman Catholic priest and a Jewish psychiatrist contains the most elemental questions of honor and survival: if offered freedom at the expense of another's life, do you take it?

In his latest works Miller continues to weave the concerns of society with those of the family. His play *American Clock* (1980) is based on the interviewer Studs Terkel's *Hard Times* (1970), a transcription of conversations about life during the Great Depression and the supports derived from the family. Miller wrote the television script for *Playing for Time* (1981), the story of Auschwitz survivor Fanya Fenelon, whose experience as a member of the camp's female orchestra is a tale of consistent courage. Miller's *Timebends* is concurrently an autobiography, a political commentary, and theatrical essay. The stories, the people, and the power of the book provide an important reinterpretation of much of Miller's artistic career.

Suggested Readings: *All My Sons,* 1947. *The Crucible,* 1953. *A View From the Bridge,* 1955. *The Misfits,* 1961. *After the Fall,* 1964. *Incident at Vichy,* 1964. *The Price,* 1968. *The Theater Essays of Arthur Miller,* 1978. *The American Clock,* 1980. *Timebends,* 1987. E. Murray, *Arthur Miller: Dramatist,* 1967. B. Nelson, *Arthur Miller: Portrait of a Playwright,* 1970. S. White, *Guide to Arthur Miller,* 1970. C. W. E. Bigsby, *20th-Century Drama,* Vol. II, 1984. H. Bloom, ed., *Arthur Miller: Modern Critical Interpretations,* 1987.

Text Used: *Death of a Salesman,* 1949.

DEATH OF A SALESMAN

CAST

WILLY LOMAN	UNCLE BEN
LINDA	HOWARD WAGNER
BIFF	JENNY
HAPPY	STANLEY
BERNARD	MISS FORSYTHE
THE WOMAN	LETTA
CHARLEY	

The action takes place in Willy Loman's house and yard and in various places he visits in the New York and Boston of today.

Throughout the play, in the stage directions, left and right mean stage left and stage right.

ACT ONE

A melody is heard, played upon a flute. It is small and fine, telling of grass and trees and the horizon. The curtain rises.

Before us is the Salesman's house. We are aware of towering, angular shapes behind it, surrounding it on all sides. Only the blue light of the sky falls upon the house and forestage; the surrounding area shows an angry glow of orange. As more light appears, we see a solid vault of apartment houses around the small, fragile-seeming home. An air of the dream clings to the place, a dream rising out of reality. The kitchen at center seems actual enough, for there is a kitchen table with three chairs, and a refrigerator. But no other fixtures are seen. At the back of the kitchen there is a draped entrance, which leads to the living-room. To the right of the kitchen, on a level raised two feet, is a bedroom furnished only with a brass bedstead and a straight chair. On a shelf over the bed a silver athletic trophy stands. A window opens onto the apartment house at the side.

Behind the kitchen, on a level raised six and a half feet, is the boys' bedroom, at present barely visible. Two beds are dimly seen, and at the back of the room a dormer window. (This bedroom is above the unseen living-room.) At the left a stairway curves up to it from the kitchen.

The entire setting is wholly, or, in some places, partially transparent. The roof-line of the house is one-dimensional; under and over it we see the apartment buildings. Before the house lies an apron, curving beyond the forestage into the orchestra. This forward area serves as the back yard as well as the locale of all Willy's imaginings and of his city scenes. Whenever the action is in the present the actors observe the imaginary wall-lines, entering the house only through its door at the left. But in the scenes of the past these boundaries are broken, and characters enter or leave a room by stepping "through" a wall onto the forestage.

From the right, Willy Loman, the Salesman, enters, carrying two large sample cases. The flute plays on. He hears but is not aware of it. He is past sixty years of age, dressed quietly. Even as he crosses the stage to the doorway of the house, his exhaustion is apparent. He unlocks the door, comes into the kitchen, and thank-

fully lets his burden down, feeling the soreness of his palms. A word-sigh escapes his lips—it might be "Oh, boy, oh, boy." He closes the door, then carries his cases out into the living-room, through the draped kitchen doorway.

Linda, his wife, has stirred in her bed at the right. She gets out and puts on a robe, listening. Most often jovial, she has developed an iron repression of her exceptions to Willy's behavior—she more than loves him, she admires him, as though his mercurial nature, his temper, his massive dreams and little cruelties, served her only as sharp reminders of the turbulent longings within him, longings which she shares but lacks the temperament to utter and follow to their end.

LINDA, *hearing Willy outside the bedroom, calls with some trepidation:* Willy!

WILLY: It's all right. I came back.

LINDA: Why? What happened? *Slight pause.* Did something happen, Willy?

WILLY: No, nothing happened.

LINDA: You didn't smash the car, did you?

WILLY, *with casual irritation:*   I said nothing happened. Didn't you hear me?

LINDA: Don't you feel well?

WILLY: I'm tired to the death. *The flute has faded away. He sits on the bed beside her, a little numb.* I couldn't make it. I just couldn't make it, Linda.

LINDA, *very carefully, delicately:*   Where were you all day? You look terrible.

WILLY: I got as far as a little above Yonkers. I stopped for a cup of coffee. Maybe it was the coffee.

LINDA: What?

WILLY, *after a pause:*   I suddenly couldn't drive any more. The car kept going off onto the shoulder, y'know?

LINDA, *helpfully:*   Oh. Maybe it was the steering again. I don't think Angelo knows the Studebaker.

WILLY: No, it's me, it's me. Suddenly I realize I'm goin' sixty miles an hour and I don't remember the last five minutes. I'm—I can't seem to—keep my mind to it.

LINDA: Maybe it's your glasses. You never went for your new glasses.

WILLY: No, I see everything. I came back ten miles an hour. It took me nearly four hours from Yonkers.

LINDA, *resigned:*   Well, you'll just have to take a rest, Willy, you can't continue this way.

WILLY: I just got back from Florida.

LINDA: But you didn't rest your mind. Your mind is overactive, and the mind is what counts, dear.

WILLY: I'll start out in the morning. Maybe I'll feel better in the morning. *She is taking off his shoes.* These goddam arch supports are killing me.

LINDA: Take an aspirin. Should I get you an aspirin? It'll soothe you.

WILLY, *with wonder:*   I was driving along, you understand? And I was fine. I was even observing the scenery. You can imagine, me looking at scenery, on the road every week of my life. But it's so beautiful up there, Linda, the trees are so thick, and the sun is warm. I opened the windshield and just let the warm air bathe over me. And then all of a sudden I'm goin' off the road! I'm tellin' ya, I absolutely forgot I was driving. If I'd've gone the other way over the white line I might've killed somebody. So I went on again—and five minutes later I'm dreamin' again, and I nearly— *He presses two fingers against his eyes.* I have such thoughts, I have such strange thoughts.

LINDA: Willy, dear. Talk to them again. There's no reason why you can't work in New York.

WILLY: They don't need me in New York. I'm the New England man. I'm vital in New England.

LINDA: But you're sixty years old. They can't expect you to keep traveling every week.

WILLY: I'll have to send a wire to Portland. I'm supposed to see Brown and Morrison tomorrow morning at ten o'clock to show the line. Goddammit, I could sell them! *He starts putting on his jacket.*

LINDA, *taking the jacket from him:* Why don't you go down to the place tomorrow and tell Howard you've simply got to work in New York? You're too accommodating, dear.

WILLY: If old man Wagner was alive I'd a been in charge of New York now! That man was a prince, he was a masterful man. But that boy of his, that Howard, he don't appreciate. When I went north the first time, the Wagner Company didn't know where New England was!

LINDA: Why don't you tell those things to Howard, dear?

WILLY, *encouraged:* I will, I definitely will. Is there any cheese?

LINDA: I'll make you a sandwich.

WILLY: No, go to sleep. I'll take some milk. I'll be up right away. The boys in?

LINDA: They're sleeping. Happy took Biff on a date tonight.

WILLY, *interested:* That so?

LINDA: It was so nice to see them shaving together, one behind the other, in the bathroom. And going out together. You notice? The whole house smells of shaving lotion.

WILLY: Figure it out. Work a lifetime to pay off a house. You finally own it, and there's nobody to live in it.

LINDA: Well, dear, life is a casting off. It's always that way.

WILLY: No, no, some people—some people accomplish something. Did Biff say anything after I went this morning?

LINDA: You shouldn't have criticized him, Willy, especially after he just got off the train. You mustn't lose your temper with him.

WILLY: When the hell did I lose my temper? I simply asked him if he was making any money. Is that a criticism?

LINDA: But, dear, how could he make any money?

WILLY, *worried and angered:* There's such an undercurrent in him. He became a moody man. Did he apologize when I left this morning?

LINDA: He was crestfallen, Willy. You know how he admires you. I think if he finds himself, then you'll both be happier and not fight any more.

WILLY: How can he find himself on a farm? Is that a life? A farmhand? In the beginning, when he was young, I thought, well, a young man, it's good for him to tramp around, take a lot of different jobs. But it's more than ten years now and he has yet to make thirty-five dollars a week!

LINDA: He's finding himself, Willy.

WILLY: Not finding yourself at the age of thirty-four is a disgrace!

LINDA: Shh!

WILLY: The trouble is he's lazy, goddammit!

LINDA: Willy, please!

WILLY: Biff is a lazy bum!

LINDA: They're sleeping. Get something to eat. Go on down.

WILLY: Why did he come home? I would like to know what brought him home.

LINDA: I don't know. I think he's still lost, Willy. I think he's very lost.

WILLY: Biff Loman is lost. In the greatest country in the world a young man with such—personal attractiveness, gets lost. And such a hard worker. There's one thing about Biff—he's not lazy.

LINDA: Never.

WILLY, *with pity and resolve:*   I'll see him in the morning; I'll have a nice talk with him. I'll get him a job selling. He could be big in no time. My God! Remember how they used to follow him around in high school? When he smiled at one of them their faces lit up. When he walked down the street . . . *He loses himself in reminiscences.*

LINDA, *trying to bring him out of it:*   Willy, dear, I got a new kind of American-type cheese today. It's whipped.

WILLY: Why do you get American when I like Swiss?

LINDA: I just thought you'd like a change—

WILLY: I don't want a change! I want Swiss cheese. Why am I always being contradicted?

LINDA, *with a covering laugh:*   I thought it would be a surprise.

WILLY: Why don't you open a window in here, for God's sake?

LINDA, *with infinite patience:*   They're all open, dear.

WILLY: The way they boxed us in here. Bricks and windows, windows and bricks.

LINDA: We should've bought the land next door.

WILLY: The street is lined with cars. There's not a breath of fresh air in the neighborhood. The grass don't grow any more, you can't raise a carrot in the back yard. They should've had a law against apartment houses. Remember those two beautiful elm trees out there? When I and Biff hung the swing between them?

LINDA: Yeah, like being a million miles from the city.

WILLY: They should've arrested the builder for cutting those down. They massacred the neighborhood. *Lost:* More and more I think of those days, Linda. This time of year it was lilac and wisteria. And then the peonies would come out, and the daffodils. What fragrance in this room!

LINDA: Well, after all, people had to move somewhere.

WILLY: No, there's more people now.

LINDA: I don't think there's more people. I think—

WILLY: There's more people! That's what's ruining this country! Population is getting out of control. The competition is maddening! Smell the stink from that apartment house! And another one on the other side . . . How can they whip cheese?

On Willy's last line, Biff and Happy raise themselves up in their beds, listening.

LINDA: Go down, try it. And be quiet.

WILLY, *turning to Linda, guiltily:*   You're not worried about me, are you, sweetheart?

BIFF: What's the matter?

HAPPY: Listen!

LINDA: You've got too much on the ball to worry about.

WILLY: You're my foundation and my support, Linda.

LINDA: Just try to relax, dear. You make mountains out of molehills.

WILLY: I won't fight with him any more. If he wants to go back to Texas, let him go.

LINDA: He'll find his way.

WILLY: Sure. Certain men just don't get started till later in life. Like Thomas Edison, I think. Or B. F. Goodrich. One of them was deaf. *He starts for the bedroom doorway.* I'll put my money on Biff.

LINDA: And Willy—if it's warm Sunday we'll drive in the country. And we'll open the windshield, and take lunch.

WILLY: No, the windshields don't open on the new cars.

LINDA: But you opened it today.

WILLY: Me? I didn't. *He stops.* Now isn't that peculiar! Isn't that a remarkable—*He breaks off in amazement and fright as the flute is heard distantly.*

LINDA: What, darling?

WILLY: That is the most remarkable thing.

LINDA: What, dear?

WILLY: I was thinking of the Chevvy. *Slight pause.* Nineteen twenty-eight . . . when I had that red Chevvy—*Breaks off.* That funny? I coulda sworn I was driving that Chevvy today.

LINDA: Well, that's nothing. Something must've reminded you.

WILLY: Remarkable. Ts. Remember those days? The way Biff used to simonize that car? The dealer refused to believe there was eighty thousand miles on it. *He shakes his head.* Heh! *To Linda.* Close your eyes, I'll be right up. *He walks out of the bedroom.*

HAPPY, *to Biff:*   Jesus, maybe he smashed the car again!

LINDA, *calling after Willy:*   Be careful on the stairs, dear! The cheese is on the middle shelf! *She turns, goes over to the bed, takes his jacket, and goes out of the bedroom.*

Light has risen on the boys' room. Unseen, Willy is heard talking to himself, "Eighty thousand miles," and a little laugh. Biff gets out of bed, comes downstage a bit, and stands attentively. Biff is two years older than his brother Happy, well built, but in these days bears a worn air and seems less self-assured. He has succeeded less, and his dreams are stronger and less acceptable than Happy's. Happy is tall, powerfully made. Sexuality is like a visible color on him, or a scent that many women have discovered. He, like his brother, is lost, but in a different way, for he has never allowed himself to turn his face toward defeat and is thus more confused and hard-skinned, although seemingly more content.

HAPPY, *getting out of bed:*   He's going to get his license taken away if he keeps that up. I'm getting nervous about him, y'know, Biff?

BIFF: His eyes are going.

HAPPY: No, I've driven with him. He sees all right. He just doesn't keep his mind on it. I drove into the city with him last week. He stops at a green light and then it turns red and he goes. *(He laughs.)*

BIFF: Maybe he's color-blind.

HAPPY: Pop? Why he's got the finest eye for color in the business. You know that.

BIFF, *sitting down on his bed:*   I'm going to sleep.

HAPPY: You're not still sour on Dad, are you, Biff?

BIFF: He's all right, I guess.

WILLY, *underneath them, in the living room:* Yes, sir, eighty thousand miles—eighty-two thousand!

BIFF: You smoking?

HAPPY, *holding out a pack of cigarettes:* Want one?

BIFF, *taking a cigarette:* I can never sleep when I smell it.

WILLY: What a simonizing job, heh!

HAPPY, *with deep sentiment:* Funny, Biff, y'know? Us sleeping in here again? The old beds. *He pats his bed affectionately.* All the talk that went across those two beds, huh? Our whole lives.

BIFF: Yeah. Lotta dreams and plans.

HAPPY, *with a deep and masculine laugh:* About five hundred women would like to know what was said in this room.

They share a soft laugh.

BIFF: Remember that big Betsy something—what the hell was her name—over on Bushwick Avenue?

HAPPY *(combing his hair):* With the collie dog!

BIFF: That's the one. I got you in there, remember?

HAPPY: Yeah, that was my first time—I think. Boy, there was a pig. *They laugh, almost crudely.* You taught me everything I know about women. Don't forget that.

BIFF: I bet you forgot how bashful you used to be. Especially with girls.

HAPPY: Oh, I still am, Biff.

BIFF: Oh, go on.

HAPPY: I just control it, that's all. I think I got less bashful and you got more so. What happened, Biff? Where's the old humor, the old confidence? *He shakes Biff's knee. Biff gets up and moves restlessly about the room.* What the matter?

BIFF: Why does Dad mock me all the time?

HAPPY: He's not mocking you, he—

BIFF: Everything I say there's a twist of mockery on his face. I can't get near him.

HAPPY: He just wants you to make good, that's all. I wanted to talk to you about Dad for a long time, Biff. Something's—happening to him. He—talks to himself.

BIFF: I noticed that this morning. But he always mumbled.

HAPPY: But not so noticeable. It got so embarrassing I sent him to Florida. And you know something? Most of the time he's talking to you.

BIFF: What's he say about me?

HAPPY: I think the fact that you're not settled, that you're still kind of up in the air . . .

BIFF: There's one or two other things depressing him, Happy.

HAPPY: What do you mean?

BIFF: Never mind. Just don't lay it all to me.

HAPPY: But I think if you just got started—I mean—is there any future for you out there?

BIFF: I tell ya, Hap, I don't know what the future is. I don't know—what I'm supposed to want.

HAPPY: What do you mean?

BIFF: Well, I spent six or seven years after high school trying to work myself up. Shipping clerk, salesman, business of one kind or another. And it's a measly manner of existence. To get on that subway on the hot mornings in summer. To devote your whole life to keeping stock, or making phone calls, or selling or buying. To suffer fifty weeks of the year for the sake of a two-week vacation, when all you really desire is to be outdoors, with your shirt off. And always to have to get ahead of the next fella. And still—that's how you build a future.

HAPPY: Well, you really enjoy it on a farm? Are you content out there?

BIFF, *with rising agitation:*   Hap, I've had twenty or thirty different kinds of jobs since I left home before the war, and it always turns out the same. I just realized it lately. In Nebraska when I herded cattle, and the Dakotas, and Arizona, and now in Texas. It's why I came home now, I guess, because I realized it. This farm I work on, it's spring there now, see? And they've got about fifteen new colts. There's nothing more inspiring or—beautiful than the sight of a mare and a new colt. And it's cool there now, see? Texas is cool now, and it's spring. And whenever spring comes to where I am, I suddenly get the feeling, my God, I'm not gettin' anywhere! What the hell am I doing, playing around with horses, twenty-eight dollars a week! I'm thirty-four years old, I oughta be makin' my future. That's when I come running home. And now, I get here, and I don't know what to do with myself. *After a pause:* I've always made a point of not wasting my life, and everytime I come back here I know that all I've done is to waste my life.

HAPPY: You're a poet, you know that Biff? You're a—you're an idealist!

BIFF: No, I'm mixed up very bad. Maybe I oughta get married. Maybe I oughta get stuck into something. Maybe that's my trouble. I'm like a boy. I'm not married, I'm not in business, I just—I'm like a boy. Are you content, Hap? You're a success, aren't you? Are you content?

HAPPY: Hell, no!

BIFF: Why? You're making money, aren't you?

HAPPY, *moving about with energy, expressiveness:*   All I can do now is wait for the merchandise manager to die. And suppose I get to be merchandise manager? He's a good friend of mine, and he just built a terrific estate on Long Island. And he lived there about two months and sold it, and now he's building another one. He can't enjoy it once it's finished. And I know that's just what I would do. I don't know what the hell I'm workin' for. Sometimes I sit in my apartment—all alone. And I think of the rent I'm paying. And it's crazy. But then, it's what I always wanted. My own apartment, a car, and plenty of women. And still, goddammit, I'm lonely.

BIFF, *with enthusiasm:*   Listen, why don't you come out West with me?

HAPPY: You and I, heh?

BIFF: Sure, maybe we could buy a ranch. Raise cattle, use our muscles. Men built like we are should be working out in the open.

HAPPY, *avidly:*   The Loman Brothers, heh?

BIFF, *with vast affection:*   Sure, we'd be known all over the counties!

HAPPY, *enthralled:*   That's what I dream about, Biff. Sometimes I want to just rip my clothes off in the middle of the store and outbox that goddam merchandise manager. I mean I can outbox, outrun, and outlift anybody in that store, and I have to take orders from the common, petty sons-of-bitches till I can't stand it any more.

BIFF: I'm tellin' you, kid, if you were with me I'd be happy out there.

HAPPY, *enthused:*   See, Biff, everybody around me is so false that I'm constantly lowering my ideals . . .

BIFF: Baby, together we'd stand up for one another, we'd have someone to trust.

HAPPY: If I were around you—

BIFF: Hap, the trouble is we weren't brought up to grub for money. I don't know how to do it.

HAPPY: Neither can I!

BIFF: Then let's go!

HAPPY: The only thing is—what can you make out there?

BIFF: But look at your friend. Builds an estate and then hasn't the peace of mind to live in it.

HAPPY: Yeah, but when he walks into the store the waves part in front of him. That's fifty-two thousand dollars a year coming through the revolving door, and I got more in my pinky finger than he's got in his head.

BIFF: Yeah, but you just said—

HAPPY: I gotta show some of those pompous, self-important executives over there that Hap Loman can make the grade. I want to walk into the store the way he walks in. Then I'll go with you, Biff. We'll be together yet, I swear. But take those two we had tonight. Now weren't they gorgeous creatures?

BIFF: Yeah, yeah, most gorgeous I've had in years.

HAPPY: I get that any time I want, Biff. Whenever I feel disgusted. The only trouble is, it gets like bowling or something. I just keep knockin' them over and it doesn't mean anything. You still run around a lot?

BIFF: Naa. I'd like to find a girl—steady, somebody with substance.

HAPPY: That's what I long for.

BIFF: Go on! You'd never come home.

HAPPY: I would! Somebody with character, with resistance! Like Mom, y'know? You're gonna call me a bastard when I tell you this. That girl Charlotte I was with tonight is engaged to be married in five weeks. *He tries on his new hat.*

BIFF: No kiddin'!

HAPPY: Sure, the guy's in line for the vice-presidency of the store. I don't know what gets into me, maybe I just have an overdeveloped sense of competition or something, but I went and ruined her, and furthermore I can't get rid of her. And he's the third executive I've done that to. Isn't that a crummy characteristic? And to top it all, I go to their weddings! *Indignantly, but laughing:* Like I'm not supposed to take bribes. Manufacturers offer me a hundred-dollar bill now and then to throw an order their way. You know how honest I am, but it's like this girl, see. I hate myself for it. Because I don't want the girl, and, still, I take it and—I love it!

BIFF: Let's go to sleep.

HAPPY: I guess we didn't settle anything, heh?

BIFF: I just got one idea that I think I'm going to try.

HAPPY: What's that?

BIFF: Remember Bill Oliver?

HAPPY: Sure, Oliver is very big now. You want to work for him again?

BIFF: No, but when I quit he said something to me. He put his arm on my shoulder, and he said, "Biff, if you ever need anything, come to me."

HAPPY: I remember that. That sounds good.

BIFF: I think I'll go to see him. If I could get ten thousand or even seven or eight thousand dollars I could buy a beautiful ranch.

HAPPY: I bet he'd back you. 'Cause he thought highly of you, Biff. I mean, they all do. You're well liked, Biff. That's why I say to come back here, and we both have the apartment. And I'm tellin' you, Biff, any babe you want . . .

BIFF: No, with a ranch I could do the work I like and still be something. I just wonder though. I wonder if Oliver still thinks I stole that carton of basketballs.

HAPPY: Oh, he probably forgot that long ago. It's almost ten years. You're too sensitive. Anyway, he didn't really fire you.

BIFF: Well, I think he was going to. I think that's why I quit. I was never sure whether he knew or not. I know he thought the world of me, though. I was the only one he'd let lock up the place.

WILLY, *below:*   You gonna wash the engine, Biff?

HAPPY: Shh!

Biff looks at Happy, who is gazing down, listening. Willy is mumbling in the parlor.

HAPPY: You hear that?

They listen. Willy laughs warmly.

BIFF, *growing angry:*   Doesn't he know Mom can hear that?

WILLY: Don't get your sweater dirty, Biff!

A look of pain crosses Biff's face.

HAPPY: Isn't that terrible? Don't leave again, will you? You'll find a job here. You gotta stick around. I don't know what to do about him, it's getting embarrassing.

WILLY: What a simonizing job!

BIFF: Mom's hearing that!

WILLY: No kiddin', Biff, you got a date? Wonderful.

HAPPY: Go on to sleep. But talk to him in the morning, will you?

BIFF, *reluctantly getting into bed:*   With her in the house. Brother!

HAPPY, *getting into bed:*   I wish you'd have a good talk with him.

The light on their room begins to fade.

BIFF, *to himself in bed:*   That selfish, stupid . . .

HAPPY: Sh . . . Sleep, Biff.

Their light is out. Well before they have finished speaking, Willy's form is dimly seen below in the darkened kitchen. He opens the refrigerator, searches in there, and takes out a bottle of milk. The apartment houses are fading out, and the entire house and surroundings become covered with leaves. Music insinuates itself as the leaves appear.

WILLY: Just wanna be careful with those girls, Biff, that's all. Don't make any promises. No promises of any kind. Because a girl, y'know, they always believe what you tell 'em, and you're very young, Biff, you're too young to be talking seriously to girls.

Light rises on the kitchen. Willy, talking, shuts the refrigerator door and comes downstage to the kitchen table. He pours milk into a glass. He is totally immersed in himself, smiling faintly.

WILLY: Too young entirely, Biff. You want to watch your schooling first. Then when you're all set, there'll be plenty of girls for a boy like you. *He smiles broadly at a kitchen chair.* That so? The girls pay for you? *He laughs.* Boy, you must really be makin' a hit.

Willy is gradually addressing—physically—a point offstage, speaking through the wall of the kitchen, and his voice has been rising in volume to that of a normal conversation.

WILLY: I been wondering why you polish the car so careful. Ha! Don't leave the hubcaps, boys. Get the chamois to the hubcaps. Happy, use newspaper on the windows, it's the easiest thing. Show him how to do it, Biff! You see, Happy? Pad it up, use it like a pad. That's it, that's it, good work. You're doin' all right, Hap. *He pauses, then nods in approbation for a few seconds, then looks upward.* Biff, first thing we gotta do when we get time is clip that big branch over the house. Afraid it's gonna fall in a storm and hit the roof. Tell you what. We get a rope and sling her around, and then we climb up there with a couple of saws and take her down. Soon as you finish the car, boys, I wanna see ya. I got a surprise for you, boys.

BIFF, *offstage:*   Whatta ya got, Dad?

WILLY: No, you finish first. Never leave a job till you're finished—remember that. *Looking toward the "big trees":* Biff, up in Albany I saw a beautiful hammock. I think I'll buy it next trip, and we'll hang it right between those two elms. Wouldn't that be something? Just swingin' there under those branches. Boy, that would be . . .

Young Biff and Young Happy appear from the direction Willy was addressing. Happy carries rags and a pail of water. Biff, wearing a sweater with a block "S," carries a football.

BIFF, *pointing in the direction of the car offstage:*   How's that, Pop, professional?

WILLY: Terrific. Terrific job, boys. Good work, Biff.

HAPPY: Where's the surprise, Pop?

WILLY: In the back seat of the car.

HAPPY: Boy! *He runs off.*

BIFF: What is it, Dad? Tell me, what'd you buy?

WILLY, *laughing, cuffs him:*   Never mind, something I want you to have.

BIFF, *turns and starts off:*   What is it, Hap?

HAPPY, *offstage:*   It's a punching bag!

BIFF: Oh, Pop!

WILLY: It's got Gene Tunney's signature on it!

Happy runs onstage with a punching bag.

BIFF: Gee, how'd you know we wanted a punching bag?

WILLY: Well, it's the finest thing for the timing.

HAPPY, *lies down on his back and pedals with his feet:*   I'm losing weight, you notice, Pop?

WILLY, *to Happy:*   Jumping rope is good too.

BIFF: Did you see the new football I got?

WILLY, *examining the ball:*   Where'd you get a new ball?

BIFF: The coach told me to practice my passing.

WILLY: That so? And he gave you the ball, heh?

BIFF: Well, I borrowed it from the locker room. *He laughs confidentially.*

WILLY, *laughing with him at the theft:*   I want you to return that.

HAPPY: I told you he wouldn't like it!

BIFF, *angrily:*   Well, I'm bringing it back!

WILLY, *stopping the incipient argument, to Happy:* Sure, he's gotta practice with a regulation ball, doesn't he? *To Biff:* Coach'll probably congratulate you on your initiative!

BIFF: Oh, he keeps congratulating my initiative all the time, Pop.

WILLY: That's because he likes you. If somebody else took that ball there'd be an uproar. So what's the report, boys, what's the report?

BIFF: Where'd you go this time, Dad? Gee we were lonesome for you.

WILLY, *pleased, puts an arm around each boy and they come down to the apron:* Lonesome, heh?

BIFF: Missed you every minute.

WILLY: Don't say? Tell you a secret, boys. Don't breathe it to a soul. Someday I'll have my own business, and I'll never have to leave home any more.

HAPPY: Like Uncle Charley, heh?

WILLY: Bigger than Uncle Charley! Because Charley is not—liked. He's liked, but he's not—well liked.

BIFF: Where'd you go this time, Dad?

WILLY: Well, I got on the road, and I went north to Providence. Met the Mayor.

BIFF: The Mayor of Providence!

WILLY: He was sitting in the hotel lobby.

BIFF: What'd he say?

WILLY: He said, "Morning!" And I said, "You got a fine city here, Mayor." And then he had coffee with me. And then I went to Waterbury. Waterbury is a fine city. Big clock city, the famous Waterbury clock. Sold a nice bill there. And then Boston—Boston is the cradle of the Revolution. A fine city. And a couple of other towns in Mass., and on to Portland and Bangor and straight home!

BIFF: Gee, I'd love to go with you sometime, Dad.

WILLY: Soon as summer comes.

HAPPY: Promise?

WILLY: You and Hap and I, and I'll show you all the towns. America is full of beautiful towns and fine, upstanding people. And they know me, boys, they know me up and down New England. The finest people. And when I bring you fellas up, there'll be open sesame for all of us, 'cause one thing, boys: I have friends. I can park my car in any street in New England, and the cops protect it like their own. This summer, heh?

BIFF and HAPPY, *together:* Yeah! You bet!

WILLY: We'll take our bathing suits.

HAPPY: We'll carry your bags, Pop!

WILLY: Oh, won't that be something! Me comin' into the Boston stores with you boys carryin' my bags. What a sensation!

Biff is prancing around, practicing passing the ball.

WILLY: You nervous, Biff, about the game?

BIFF: Not if you're gonna be there.

WILLY: What do they say about you in school, now that they made you captain?

HAPPY: There's a crowd of girls behind him everytime the classes change.

BIFF, *taking Willy's hand:* This Saturday, Pop, this Saturday—just for you, I'm going to break through for a touchdown.

HAPPY: You're supposed to pass.

BIFF: I'm takin' one play for Pop. You watch me, Pop, and when I take off my helmet, that means I'm breakin' out. Then you watch me crash through that line!

WILLY, *kisses Biff:*   Oh, wait'll I tell this in Boston!

Bernard enters in knickers. He is younger than Biff, earnest and loyal, a worried boy.

BERNARD: Biff, where are you? You're supposed to study with me today.

WILLY: Hey, looka Bernard. What're you lookin' so anemic about, Bernard?

BERNARD: He's gotta study, Uncle Willy. He's got Regents[1] next week.

HAPPY, *tauntingly, spinning Bernard around:*   Let's box, Bernard!

BERNARD: Biff! *He gets away from Happy.* Listen, Biff, I heard Mr. Birnbaum say that if you don't start studyin' math he's gonna flunk you, and you won't graduate. I heard him!

WILLY: You better study with him, Biff. Go ahead now.

BERNARD: I heard him!

BIFF: Oh, Pop, you didn't see my sneakers! *He holds up a foot for Willy to look at.*

WILLY: Hey, that's a beautiful job of printing!

BERNARD, *wiping his glasses:*   Just because he printed University of Virginia on his sneakers doesn't mean they've got to graduate him, Uncle Willy!

WILLY, *angrily:*   What're you talking about? With scholarships to three universities they're gonna flunk him?

BERNARD: But I heard Mr. Birnbaum say—

WILLY: Don't be a pest, Bernard! *To his boys:* What an anemic!

BERNARD: Okay, I'm waiting for you in my house, Biff.

Bernard goes off. The Lomans laugh.

WILLY: Bernard is not well liked, is he?

BIFF: He's liked, but he's not well liked.

HAPPY: That's right, Pop.

WILLY: That's just what I mean. Bernard can get the best marks in school, y'understand, but when he gets out in the business world, y'understand, you are going to be five times ahead of him. That's why I thank Almighty God you're both built like Adonises.[2] Because the man who makes an appearance in the business world, the man who creates personal interest, is the man who gets ahead. Be liked and you will never want. You take me, for instance. I never have to wait in line to see a buyer. "Willy Loman is here!" That's all they have to know, and I go right through.

BIFF: Did you knock them dead, Pop?

WILLY: Knocked 'em cold in Providence, slaughtered 'em in Boston.

HAPPY, *on his back, pedaling again:*   I'm losing weight, you notice, Pop?

Linda enters, as of old, a ribbon in her hair, carrying a basket of washing.

LINDA, *with youthful energy:*   Hello, dear!

WILLY: Sweetheart!

---

[1] A high school proficiency test given in New York state.

[2] According to Greek myth, Adonis was a handsome young man loved by Aphrodite, goddess of love and beauty.

LINDA: How'd the Chevvy run?

WILLY: Chevrolet, Linda, is the greatest car ever built. *To the boys:* Since when do you let your mother carry wash up the stairs?

BIFF: Grab hold there, boy!

HAPPY: Where to, Mom?

LINDA: Hang them up on the line. And you better go down to your friends, Biff. The cellar is full of boys. They don't know what to do with themselves.

BIFF: Ah, when Pop comes home they can wait!

WILLY, *laughs appreciatively:*   You better go down and tell them what to do, Biff.

BIFF: I think I'll have them sweep out the furnace room.

WILLY: Good work, Biff.

BIFF, *goes through wall-line of kitchen to doorway at back and calls down:* Fellas! Everybody sweep out the furnace room! I'll be right down!

VOICES: All right! Okay, Biff.

BIFF: George and Sam and Frank, come out back! We're hangin' up the wash! Come on, Hap, on the double! *He and Happy carry out the basket.*

LINDA: The way they obey him!

WILLY: Well, that's training, the training. I'm tellin' you, I was sellin' thousands and thousands, but I had to come home.

LINDA: Oh, the whole block'll be at that game. Did you sell anything?

WILLY: I did five hundred gross in Providence and seven hundred gross in Boston.

LINDA: No! Wait a minute, I've got a pencil. *She pulls pencil and paper out of her apron pocket.* That makes your commission . . . Two hundred—my God! Two hundred and twelve dollars!

WILLY: Well, I didn't figure it yet, but . . .

LINDA: How much did you do?

WILLY: Well, I—I did—about a hundred and eighty gross in Providence. Well, no—it came to—roughly two hundred gross on the whole trip.

LINDA, *without hesitation:*   Two hundred gross. That's . . . *She figures.*

WILLY: The trouble was that three of the stores were half closed for inventory in Boston. Otherwise I woulda broke records.

LINDA: Well, it makes seventy dollars and some pennies. That's very good.

WILLY: What do we owe?

LINDA: Well, on the first there's sixteen dollars on the refrigerator—

WILLY: Why sixteen?

LINDA: Well, the fan belt broke, so it was a dollar eighty.

WILLY: But it's brand new.

LINDA: Well, the man said that's the way it is. Till they work themselves in, y'know.

They move through the wall-line into the kitchen.

WILLY: I hope we didn't get stuck on that machine.

LINDA: They got the biggest ads of any of them!

WILLY: I know, it's a fine machine. What else?

LINDA: Well, there's nine-sixty for the washing machine. And for the vacuum cleaner there's three and a half due on the fifteenth. Then the roof, you got twenty-one dollars remaining.

WILLY: It don't leak, does it?

LINDA: No, they did a wonderful job. Then you owe Frank for the carburetor.

WILLY: I'm not going to pay that man! That goddam Chevrolet, they ought to prohibit the manufacture of that car!

LINDA: Well, you owe him three and a half. And odds and ends, comes to around a hundred and twenty dollars by the fifteenth.

WILLY: A hundred and twenty dollars! My God, if business don't pick up I don't know what I'm gonna do!

LINDA: Well, next week you'll do better.

WILLY: Oh, I'll knock 'em dead next week. I'll go to Hartford. I'm very well liked in Hartford. You know, the trouble is, Linda, people don't seem to take to me.

They move onto the forestage.

LINDA: Oh, don't be foolish.

WILLY: I know it when I walk in. They seem to laugh at me.

LINDA: Why? Why would they laugh at you? Don't talk that way, Willy.

Willy moves to the edge of the stage. Linda goes into the kitchen and starts to darn stockings.

WILLY: I don't know the reason for it, but they just pass me by. I'm not noticed.

LINDA: But you're doing wonderful, dear. You're making seventy to a hundred dollars a week.

WILLY: But I gotta be at it ten, twelve hours a day. Other men—I don't know—they do it easier. I don't know why—I can't stop myself—I talk too much. A man oughta come in with a few words. One thing about Charley. He's a man of few words, and they respect him.

LINDA: You don't talk too much, you're just lively.

WILLY, *smiling:*   Well, I figure, what the hell, life is short, a couple of jokes. *To himself:* I joke too much! *The smile goes.*

LINDA: Why? You're—

WILLY: I'm fat. I'm very—foolish to look at, Linda. I didn't tell you, but Christmas time I happened to be calling on F. H. Stewarts, and a salesman I know, as I was going in to see the buyer I heard him say something about—walrus. And I—I cracked him right across the face. I won't take that. I simply will not take that. But they do laugh at me. I know that.

LINDA: Darling . . .

WILLY: I gotta overcome it. I know I gotta overcome it. I'm not dressing to advantage, maybe.

LINDA: Willy, darling, you're the handsomest man in the world—

WILLY: Oh, no, Linda.

LINDA: To me you are. *Slight pause.* The handsomest.

From the darkness is heard the laughter of a woman. Willy doesn't turn to it, but it continues through Linda's lines.

LINDA: And the boys, Willy. Few men are idolized by their children the way you are.

Music is heard as behind a scrim,[3] to the left of the house, The Woman, dimly seen, is dressing.

---

[3] Sheer cloth hung in theatrical productions to be either opaque or transparent, depending on the lighting used.

WILLY, *with great feeling:*   You're the best there is, Linda, you're a pal, you know that? On the road—on the road I want to grab you sometimes and just kiss the life outa you.

The laughter is loud now, and he moves into a brightening area at the left, where The Woman has come from behind the scrim and is standing, putting on her hat, looking into a "mirror" and laughing.

WILLY: 'Cause I get so lonely—especially when business is bad and there's nobody to talk to. I get the feeling that I'll never sell anything again, that I won't make a living for you, or a business, a business for the boys. *He talks through The Woman's subsiding laughter; The Woman primps at the "mirror."* There's so much I want to make for—

THE WOMAN: Me? You didn't make me, Willy. I picked you.

WILLY, *pleased:*   You picked me?

THE WOMAN, *who is quite proper-looking, Willy's age:*   I did. I've been sitting at that desk watching all the salesmen go by, day in, day out. But you've got such a sense of humor, and we do have such a good time together, don't we?

WILLY: Sure, sure. *He takes her in his arms.* Why do you have to go now?

THE WOMAN: It's two o'clock . . .

WILLY: No, come on in! *He pulls her.*

THE WOMAN: . . . my sisters'll be scandalized. When'll you be back?

WILLY: Oh, two weeks about. Will you come up again?

THE WOMAN: Sure thing. You do make me laugh. It's good for me. *She squeezes his arm, kisses him.* And I think you're a wonderful man.

WILLY: You picked me, heh?

THE WOMAN: Sure. Because you're so sweet. And such a kidder.

WILLY: Well, I'll see you next time I'm in Boston.

THE WOMAN: I'll put you right through to the buyers.

WILLY, *slapping her bottom:*   Right. Well, bottoms up!

THE WOMAN, *slaps him gently and laughs:*   You just kill me, Willy. *He suddenly grabs her and kisses her roughly.* You kill me. And thanks for the stockings. I love a lot of stockings. Well, good night.

WILLY: Good night. And keep your pores open!

THE WOMAN: Oh, Willy!

The Woman bursts out laughing, and Linda's laughter blends in. The Woman disappears into the dark. Now the area at the kitchen table brightens. Linda is sitting where she was at the kitchen table, but now is mending a pair of her silk stockings.

LINDA: You are, Willy. The handsomest man. You've got no reason to feel that—

WILLY, *coming out of The Woman's dimming area and going over to Linda:*   I'll make it all up to you, Linda, I'll—

LINDA: There's nothing to make up, dear. You're doing fine, better than—

WILLY, *noticing her mending:*   What's that?

LINDA: Just mending my stockings. They're so expensive—

WILLY, *angrily, taking them from her:*   I won't have you mending stockings in this house! Now throw them out!

Linda puts the stockings in her pocket.

BERNARD, *entering on the run:*   Where is he? If he doesn't study!

WILLY, *moving to the forestage, with great agitation:*   You'll give him the answers!

BERNARD: I do, but I can't on a Regents! That's a state exam! They're liable to arrest me!

WILLY: Where is he? I'll whip him, I'll whip him!

LINDA: And he'd better give back that football, Willy, it's not nice.

WILLY: Biff! Where is he? Why is he taking everything?

LINDA: He's too rough with the girls, Willy. All the mothers are afraid of him!

WILLY: I'll whip him!

BERNARD: He's driving the car without a license!

The Woman's laugh is heard.

WILLY: Shut up!

LINDA: All the mothers—

WILLY: Shut up!

BERNARD, *backing quietly away and out:*   Mr. Birnbaum says he's stuck up.

WILLY: Get outa here!

BERNARD: If he doesn't buckle down he'll flunk math! *He goes off.*

LINDA: He's right, Willy, you've gotta—

WILLY, *exploding at her:*   There's nothing the matter with him! You want him to be a worm like Bernard? He's got spirit, personality . . .

As he speaks, Linda, almost in tears, exits into the living-room. Willy is alone in the kitchen, wilting and staring. The leaves are gone. It is night again, and the apartment houses look down from behind.

WILLY: Loaded with it. Loaded! What is he stealing? He's giving it back, isn't he? Why is he stealing? What did I tell him? I never in my life told him anything but decent things.

Happy in pajamas has come down the stairs; Willy suddenly becomes aware of Happy's presence.

HAPPY: Let's go now, come on.

WILLY, *sitting down at the kitchen table:*   Huh! Why did she have to wax the floors herself? Everytime she waxes the floors she keels over. She knows that!

HAPPY: Shh! Take it easy. What brought you back tonight?

WILLY: I got an awful scare. Nearly hit a kid in Yonkers. God! Why didn't I go to Alaska with my brother Ben that time! Ben! That man was a genius, that man was success incarnate! What a mistake! He begged me to go.

HAPPY: Well, there's no use in—

WILLY: You guys! There was a man started with the clothes on his back and ended up with diamond mines!

HAPPY: Boy, someday I'd like to know how he did it.

WILLY: What's the mystery? The man knew what he wanted and went out and got it! Walked into a jungle, and comes out, the age of twenty-one, and he's rich! The world is an oyster, but you don't crack it open on a mattress!

HAPPY: Pop, I told you I'm gonna retire you for life.

WILLY: You'll retire me for life on seventy goddam dollars a week? And your women and your car and your apartment, and you'll retire me for life! Christ's sake, I couldn't get past Yonkers today! Where are you guys, where are you? The woods are burning! I can't drive a car!

Charley has appeared in the doorway. He is a large man, slow of speech, laconic, immovable. In all he says, despite what he says, there is pity, and, now, trepidation. He has a robe over pajamas, slippers on his feet. He enters the kitchen.

CHARLEY: Everything all right?
HAPPY: Yeah, Charley, everything's . . .
WILLY: What's the matter?
CHARLEY: I heard some noise. I thought something happened. Can't we do something about the walls? You sneeze in here, and in my house hats blow off.
HAPPY: Let's go to bed, Dad. Come on.

Charley signals to Happy to go.

WILLY: You go ahead, I'm not tired at the moment.
HAPPY, *to Willy:*   Take it easy, huh? *He exits.*
WILLY: What're you doin' up?
CHARLEY, *sitting down at the kitchen table opposite Willy:*   Couldn't sleep good. I had a heartburn.
WILLY: Well, you don't know how to eat.
CHARLEY: I eat with my mouth.
WILLY: No, you're ignorant. You gotta know about vitamins and things like that.
CHARLEY: Come on, let's shoot. Tire you out a little.
WILLY, *hesitantly:*   All right. You got cards?
CHARLEY, *taking a deck from his pocket:*   Yeah, I got them. Someplace. What is it with those vitamins?
WILLY, *dealing:*   They build up your bones. Chemistry.
CHARLEY: Yeah, but there's no bones in a heartburn.
WILLY: What are you talkin' about? Do you know the first thing about it?
CHARLEY: Don't get insulted.
WILLY: Don't talk about something you don't know anything about.

They are playing. Pause.

CHARLEY: What're you doin' home?
WILLY: A little trouble with the car.
CHARLEY: Oh. *Pause.* I'd like to take a trip to California.
WILLY: Don't say.
CHARLEY: You want a job?
WILLY: I got a job, I told you that. *After a slight pause:* What the hell are you offering me a job for?
CHARLEY: Don't get insulted.
WILLY: Don't insult me.
CHARLEY: I don't see no sense in it. You don't have to go on this way.
WILLY: I got a good job. *Slight pause.* What do you keep comin' in here for?
CHARLEY: You want me to go?
WILLY, *after a pause, withering:*   I can't understand it. He's going back to Texas again. What the hell is that?
CHARLEY: Let him go.

WILLY: I got nothin' to give him, Charley, I'm clean, I'm clean.

CHARLEY: He won't starve. None a them starve. Forget about him.

WILLY: Then what have I got to remember?

CHARLEY: You take it too hard. To hell with it. When a deposit bottle is broken you don't get your nickel back.

WILLY: That's easy enough for you to say.

CHARLEY: That ain't easy for me to say.

WILLY: Did you see the ceiling I put up in the living-room?

CHARLEY: Yeah, that's a piece of work. To put up a ceiling is a mystery to me. How do you do it?

WILLY: What's the difference?

CHARLEY: Well, talk about it.

WILLY: You gonna put up a ceiling?

CHARLEY: How could I put up a ceiling?

WILLY: Then what the hell are you bothering me for?

CHARLEY: You're insulted again.

WILLY: A man who can't handle tools is not a man. You're disgusting.

CHARLEY: Don't call me disgusting, Willy.

Uncle Ben, carrying a valise and an umbrella, enters the forestage from around the right corner of the house. He is a stolid man, in his sixties, with a mustache and an authoritative air. He is utterly certain of his destiny, and there is an aura of far places about him. He enters exactly as Willy speaks.

WILLY: I'm getting awfully tired, Ben.

Ben's music is heard. Ben looks around at everything.

CHARLEY: Good, keep playing; you'll sleep better. Did you call me Ben?

Ben looks at his watch.

WILLY: That's funny. For a second there you reminded me of my brother Ben.

BEN: I only have a few minutes. *He strolls, inspecting the place. Willy and Charley continue playing.*

CHARLEY: You never heard from him again, heh? Since that time?

WILLY: Didn't Linda tell you? Couple of weeks ago we got a letter from his wife in Africa. He died.

CHARLEY: That so.

BEN, *chuckling:*   So this is Brooklyn, eh?

CHARLEY: Maybe you're in for some of his money.

WILLY: Naa, he had seven sons. There's just one opportunity I had with that man . . .

BEN: I must make a train, William. There are several properties I'm looking at in Alaska.

WILLY: Sure, sure! If I'd gone with him to Alaska that time, everything would've been totally different.

CHARLEY: Go on, you'd froze to death up there.

WILLY: What're you talking about?

BEN: Opportunity is tremendous in Alaska, William. Surprised you're not up there.

WILLY: Sure, tremendous.

CHARLEY: Heh?

WILLY: There was the only man I ever met who knew the answers.

CHARLEY: Who?

BEN: How are you all?

WILLY, *taking a pot, smiling:*   Fine, fine.

CHARLEY: Pretty sharp tonight.

BEN: Is Mother living with you?

WILLY: No, she died a long time ago.

CHARLEY: Who?

BEN: That's too bad. Fine specimen of a lady, Mother.

WILLY, *to Charley:*   Heh?

BEN: I'd hoped to see the old girl.

CHARLEY: Who died?

BEN: Heard anything from Father, have you?

WILLY, *unnerved:*   What do you mean, who died?

CHARLEY, *taking a pot:*   What're you talkin' about?

BEN, *looking at his watch:*   William, it's half-past eight!

WILLY, *as though to dispel his confusion he angrily stops Charley's hand:*   That's my build!

CHARLEY: I put the ace—

WILLY: If you don't know how to play the game I'm not gonna throw my money away on you!

CHARLEY, *rising:*   It was my ace, for God's sake!

WILLY: I'm through, I'm through!

BEN: When did Mother die?

WILLY: Long ago. Since the beginning you never knew how to play cards.

CHARLEY, *picks up the cards and goes to the door:*   All right! Next time I'll bring a deck with five aces.

WILLY: I don't play that kind of game!

CHARLEY, *turning to him:*   You ought to be ashamed of yourself!

WILLY: Yeah?

CHARLEY: Yeah! *He goes out.*

WILLY, *slamming the door after him:*   Ignoramus!

BEN, *as Willy comes toward him through the wall-line of the kitchen:*   So you're William.

WILLY, *shaking Ben's hand:*   Ben! I've been waiting for you so long! What's the answer? How did you do it?

BEN: Oh, there's a story in that.

Linda enters the forestage, as of old, carrying the wash basket.

LINDA: Is this Ben?

BEN, *gallantly:*   How do you do, my dear.

LINDA: Where've you been all these years? Willy's always wondered why you—

WILLY, *pulling Ben away from her impatiently:*   Where is Dad? Didn't you follow him? How did you get started?

BEN: Well, I don't know how much you remember.

WILLY: Well, I was just a baby, of course, only three or four years old—

BEN: Three years and eleven months.

WILLY: What a memory, Ben!

BEN: I have many enterprises, William, and I have never kept books.

WILLY: I remember I was sitting under the wagon in—was it Nebraska?

BEN: It was South Dakota, and I gave you a bunch of wild flowers.

WILLY: I remember you walking away down some open road.

BEN, *laughing:*   I was going to find Father in Alaska.

WILLY: Where is he?

BEN: At that age I had a very faulty view of geography, William. I discovered after a few days that I was heading due south, so instead of Alaska, I ended up in Africa.

LINDA: Africa!

WILLY: The Gold Coast!

BEN: Principally diamond mines.

LINDA: Diamond mines!

BEN: Yes, my dear. But I've only a few minutes—

WILLY: No! Boys! Boys! *Young Biff and Happy appear.* Listen to this. This is your Uncle Ben, a great man! Tell my boys, Ben!

BEN: Why, boys, when I was seventeen I walked into the jungle, and when I was twenty-one I walked out. *He laughs.* And by God I was rich.

WILLY, *to the boys:*   You see what I been talking about? The greatest things can happen!

BEN, *glancing at his watch:*   I have an appointment in Ketchikan Tuesday week.

WILLY: No, Ben! Please tell about Dad. I want my boys to hear. I want them to know the kind of stock they spring from. All I remember is a man with a big beard, and I was in Mamma's lap, sitting around a fire, and some kind of high music.

BEN: His flute. He played the flute.

WILLY: Sure, the flute, that's right!

New music is heard, a high, rollicking tune.

BEN: Father was a very great and a very wild-hearted man. We would start in Boston, and he'd toss the whole family into the wagon, and then he'd drive the team right across the country; through Ohio, and Indiana, Michigan, Illinois, and all the Western states. And we'd stop in the town and sell the flutes that he'd made on the way. Great inventor, Father. With one gadget he made more in a week than a man like you could make in a lifetime.

WILLY: That's just the way I'm bringing them up, Ben—rugged, well liked, all-around.

BEN: Yeah? *To Biff:* Hit that, boy—hard as you can. *He pounds his stomach.*

BIFF: Oh, no sir!

BEN, *taking boxing stance:*   Come on, get to me! *He laughs.*

WILLY: Go to it, Biff! Go ahead, show him!

BIFF: Okay! *He cocks his fists and starts in.*

LINDA, *to Willy:*   Why must he fight, dear?

BEN, *sparring with Biff:*   Good boy! Good boy!

WILLY: How's that, Ben, heh?

HAPPY: Give him the left, Biff!

LINDA: Why are you fighting?

BEN: Good boy! *Suddenly comes in, trips Biff, and stands over him, the point of his umbrella poised over Biff's eye.*

LINDA: Look out, Biff!

BIFF: Gee!

BEN, *patting Biff's knee:*   Never fight fair with a stranger, boy. You'll never get out of the jungle that way. *Taking Linda's hand and bowing:* It was an honor and a pleasure to meet you, Linda.

LINDA, *withdrawing her hand coldly, frightened:*   Have a nice—trip.

BEN, *to Willy:*   And good luck with your—what do you do?

WILLY: Selling.

BEN: Yes. Well . . . *He raises his hand in farewell to all.*

WILLY: No, Ben, I don't want you to think . . . *He takes Ben's arm to show him.* It's Brooklyn, I know, but we hunt too.

BEN: Really, now.

WILLY: Oh, sure, there's snakes and rabbits and—that's why I moved out here. Why, Biff can fell any one of these trees in no time! Boys! Go right over to where they're building the apartment house and get some sand. We're gonna rebuild the entire front stoop right now! Watch this, Ben!

BIFF: Yes, sir! On the double, Hap!

HAPPY, *as he and Biff run off:*   I lost weight, Pop, you notice?

Charley enters in knickers, even before the boys are gone.

CHARLEY: Listen, if they steal any more from that building the watchman'll put the cops on them!

LINDA, *to Willy:*   Don't let Biff . . .

Ben laughs lustily.

WILLY: You shoulda seen the lumber they brought home last week. At least a dozen six-by-tens worth all kinds a money.

CHARLEY: Listen, if that watchman—

WILLY: I gave them hell, understand. But I got a couple of fearless characters there.

CHARLEY: Willy, the jails are full of fearless characters.

BEN, *clapping Willy on the back, with a laugh at Charley:*   And the stock exchange, friend!

WILLY, *joining in Ben's laughter:*   Where are the rest of your pants?

CHARLEY: My wife bought them.

WILLY: Now all you need is a golf club and you can go upstairs and go to sleep. *To Ben:* Great athlete! Between him and his son Bernard they can't hammer a nail!

BERNARD, *rushing in:*   The watchman's chasing Biff!

WILLY, *angrily:*   Shut up! He's not stealing anything!

LINDA, *alarmed, hurrying off left:*   Where is he? Biff, dear! *She exits.*

WILLY, *moving toward the left, away from Ben:*   There's nothing wrong. What's the matter with you?

BEN: Nervy boy. Good!

WILLY, *laughing:*   Oh, nerves of iron, that Biff!

CHARLEY: Don't know what it is. My New England man comes back and he's bleedin', they murdered him up there.

WILLY: It's contacts, Charley, I got important contacts!

CHARLEY, *sarcastically:*   Glad to hear it, Willy. Come in later, we'll shoot a little casino. I'll take some of your Portland money. *He laughs at Willy and exits.*

WILLY, *turning to Ben:* Business is bad, it's murderous. But not for me, of course.

BEN: I'll stop by on my way back to Africa.

WILLY, *longingly:* Can't you stay a few days? You're just what I need, Ben, because I—I have a fine position here, but I—well, Dad left when I was such a baby and I never had a chance to talk to him and I still feel—kind of temporary about myself.

BEN: I'll be late for my train.

They are at opposite ends of the stage.

WILLY: Ben, my boys—can't we talk? They'd go into the jaws of hell for me, see, but I—

BEN: William, you're being first-rate with your boys. Outstanding, manly chaps!

WILLY, *hanging on to his words:* Oh, Ben, that's good to hear! Because sometimes I'm afraid that I'm not teaching them the right kind of—Ben, how should I teach them?

BEN, *giving great weight to each word, and with a certain vicious audacity:* William, when I walked into the jungle, I was seventeen. When I walked out I was twenty-one. And, by God, I was rich! *He goes off into the darkness around the right corner of the house.*

WILLY: . . . was rich! That's just the spirit I want to imbue them with! To walk into a jungle! I was right! I was right! I was right!

Ben is gone, but Willy is still speaking to him as Linda, in nightgown and robe, enters the kitchen, glances around for Willy, then goes to the door of the house, looks out and sees him. Comes down to his left. He looks at her.

LINDA: Willy, dear? Willy?

WILLY: I was right!

LINDA: Did you have some cheese? *He can't answer.* It's very late, darling. Come to bed, heh?

WILLY, *looking straight up:* Gotta break your neck to see a star in this yard.

LINDA: You coming in?

WILLY: Whatever happened to that diamond watch fob? Remember? When Ben came from Africa that time? Didn't he give me a watch fob with a diamond in it?

LINDA: You pawned it, dear. Twelve, thirteen years ago. For Biff's radio correspondence course.

WILLY: Gee, that was a beautiful thing. I'll take a walk.

LINDA: But you're in your slippers.

WILLY, *starting to go around the house at the left:* I was right! I was! *Half to Linda, as he goes, shaking his head:* What a man! There was a man worth talking to. I was right!

LINDA, *calling after Willy:* But in your slippers, Willy!

Willy is almost gone when Biff, in his pajamas, comes down the stairs and enters the kitchen.

BIFF: What is he doing out there?

LINDA: Sh!

BIFF: God Almighty, Mom, how long has he been doing this?

LINDA: Don't, he'll hear you.

BIFF: What the hell is the matter with him?

LINDA: It'll pass by morning.

BIFF: Shouldn't we do anything?

LINDA: Oh, my dear, you should do a lot of things, but there's nothing to do, so go to sleep.

Happy comes down the stair and sits on the steps.

HAPPY: I never heard him so loud, Mom.

LINDA: Well, come around more often: you'll hear him. *She sits down at the table and mends the lining of Willy's jacket.*

BIFF: Why didn't you ever write me about this, Mom?

LINDA: How would I write to you? For over three months you had no address.

BIFF: I was on the move. But you know I thought of you all the time. You know that, don't you, pal?

LINDA: I know, dear. I know. But he likes to have a letter. Just to know that there's still a possibility for better things.

BIFF: He's not like this all the time, is he?

LINDA: It's when you come home he's always the worst.

BIFF: When I come home?

LINDA: When you write you're coming, he's all smiles, and talks about the future, and—he's just wonderful. And then the closer you seem to come, the more shaky he gets, and then, by the time you get here, he's arguing, and he seems angry at you. I think it's just that maybe he can't bring himself to—to open up to you. Why are you so hateful to each other? Why is that?

BIFF, *evasively:*   I'm not hateful, Mom.

LINDA: But you no sooner come in the door than you're fighting!

BIFF: I don't know why. I mean to change. I'm tryin', Mom, you understand?

LINDA: Are you home to stay now?

BIFF: I don't know. I want to look around, see what's doin'.

LINDA: Biff, you can't look around all your life, can you?

BIFF: I just can't take hold, Mom. I can't take hold of some kind of a life.

LINDA: Biff, a man is not a bird, to come and go with the springtime.

BIFF: Your hair . . . *He touches her hair.* Your hair got so gray.

LINDA: Oh, it's been gray since you were in high school. I just stopped dyeing it, that's all.

BIFF: Dye it again, will ya? I don't want my pal looking old. *He smiles.*

LINDA: You're such a boy! You think you can go away for a year and . . . You've got to get it into your head now that one day you'll knock on this door and there'll be strange people here—

BIFF: What are you talking about? You're not even sixty, Mom.

LINDA: But what about your father?

BIFF, *lamely:*   Well, I meant him too.

HAPPY: He admires Pop.

LINDA: Biff, dear, if you don't have any feeling for him, then you can't have any feeling for me.

BIFF: Sure I can, Mom.

LINDA: No. You can't just come to see me, because I love him. *With a threat, but only a threat, of tears:* He's the dearest man in the world to me, and I won't have anyone making him feel unwanted and low and blue. You've got to make up your mind now, darling, there's no leeway any more. Either he's your father and you pay him that respect, or else you're not to come here. I know he's not easy to get along with—nobody knows that better than me—but . . .

WILLY, *from the left, with a laugh:* Hey, hey, Biffo!

BIFF, *starting to go out after Willy:* What the hell is the matter with him? *Happy stops him.*

LINDA: Don't—don't go near him!

BIFF: Stop making excuses for him! He always, always wiped the floor with you. Never had an ounce of respect for you.

HAPPY: He's always had respect for—

BIFF: What the hell do you know about it?

HAPPY, *surlily:* Just don't call him crazy!

BIFF: He's got no character—Charley wouldn't do this. Not in his own house—spewing out that vomit from his mind.

HAPPY: Charley never had to cope with what he's got to.

BIFF: People are worse off than Willy Loman. Believe me, I've seen them!

LINDA: Then make Charley your father, Biff. You can't do that, can you? I don't say he's a great man. Willy Loman never made a lot of money. His name was never in the paper. He's not the finest character that ever lived. But he's a human being, and a terrible thing is happening to him. So attention must be paid. He's not to be allowed to fall into his grave like an old dog. Attention, attention must be finally paid to such a person. You called him crazy—

BIFF: I didn't mean—

LINDA: No, a lot of people think he's lost his—balance. But you don't have to be very smart to know what his trouble is. The man is exhausted.

HAPPY: Sure!

LINDA: A small man can be just as exhausted as a great man. He works for a company thirty-six years this March, opens up unheard-of territories to their trademark, and now in his old age they take his salary away.

HAPPY, *indignantly:* I didn't know that, Mom.

LINDA: You never asked, my dear! Now that you get your spending money someplace else you don't trouble your mind with him.

HAPPY: But I gave you money last—

LINDA: Christmas time, fifty dollars! To fix the hot water it cost ninety-seven fifty! For five weeks he's been on straight commission, like a beginner, an unknown!

BIFF: Those ungrateful bastards!

LINDA: Are they any worse than his sons? When he brought them business, when he was young, they were glad to see him. But now his old friends, the old buyers that loved him so and always found some order to hand him in a pinch—they're all dead, retired. He used to be able to make six, seven calls a day in Boston. Now he takes his valises out of the car and puts them back and takes them out again and he's exhausted. Instead of walking he talks now. He drives seven hundred miles, and when he gets there no one knows him any more, no one welcomes him. And what goes through a man's mind, driving seven hundred miles home without having earned a cent? Why shouldn't he talk to himself? Why? When he has to go to Charley and borrow fifty dollars a week and pretend to me that it's his pay? How long can that go on? How long? You see what I'm sitting here and waiting for? And you tell me he has no character? The man who never worked a day but for your benefit? When does he get the medal for that? Is this his reward—to turn around at the age of sixty-three and find his sons, who he loved better than his life, one a philandering bum—

HAPPY: Mom!

LINDA: That's all you are, my baby! *To Biff:* And you! What happened to the love you had for him? You were such pals! How you used to talk to him on the phone every night! How lonely he was till he could come home to you!

BIFF: All right, Mom. I'll live here in my room, and I'll get a job. I'll keep away from him, that's all.

LINDA: No, Biff. You can't stay here and fight all the time.

BIFF: He threw me out of this house, remember that.

LINDA: Why did he do that? I never knew why.

BIFF: Because I know he's a fake and he doesn't like anybody around who knows!

LINDA: Why a fake? In what way? What do you mean?

BIFF: Just don't lay it all at my feet. It's between me and him—that's all I have to say. I'll chip in from now on. He'll settle for half my pay check. He'll be all right. I'm going to bed. *He starts for the stairs.*

LINDA: He won't be all right.

BIFF, *turning on the stairs, furiously:*   I hate this city and I'll stay here. Now what do you want?

LINDA: He's dying, Biff.

Happy turns quickly to her, shocked.

BIFF, *after a pause:*   Why is he dying?

LINDA: He's been trying to kill himself.

BIFF, *with great horror:*   How?

LINDA: I live from day to day.

BIFF: What're you talking about?

LINDA: Remember I wrote you that he smashed up the car again? In February?

BIFF: Well?

LINDA: The insurance inspector came. He said that they have evidence. That all these accidents in the last year—weren't—weren't—accidents.

HAPPY: How can they tell that? That's a lie.

LINDA: It seems there's a woman . . . *She takes a breath as*

BIFF, *sharply but contained:*   What woman?

LINDA, *simultaneously:*   . . . and this woman . . .

LINDA: What?

BIFF: Nothing. Go ahead.

LINDA: What did you say?

BIFF: Nothing. I just said what woman?

HAPPY: What about her?

LINDA: Well, it seems she was walking down the road and saw his car. She says that he wasn't driving fast at all, and that he didn't skid. She says he came to that little bridge, and then deliberately smashed into the railing, and it was only the shallowness of the water that saved him.

BIFF: Oh, no, he probably just fell asleep again.

LINDA: I don't think he fell asleep.

BIFF: Why not?

LINDA: Last month . . . *With great difficulty:* Oh, boys, it's so hard to say a thing like this! He's just a big stupid man to you, but I tell you there's more good in him than in many other people. *She chokes, wipes her eyes.* I was looking for a fuse. The lights blew out, and I went down the cellar. And behind the fuse box— it happened to fall out—was a length of rubber pipe—just short.

HAPPY: No kidding?

LINDA: There's a little attachment on the end of it. I knew right away. And sure enough, on the bottom of the water heater there's a new little nipple on the gas pipe.

HAPPY, *angrily:* That—jerk.

BIFF: Did you have it taken off?

LINDA: I'm—I'm ashamed to. How can I mention it to him? Every day I go down and take away that little rubber pipe. But when he comes home, I put it back where it was. How can I insult him that way? I don't know what to do. I live from day to day, boys. I tell you, I know every thought in his mind. It sounds so old-fashioned and silly, but I tell you he put his whole life into you and you've turned your backs on him. *She is bent over in the chair, weeping, her face in her hands.* Biff, I swear to God! Biff, his life is in your hands!

HAPPY, *to Biff:* How do you like that damned fool!

BIFF, *kissing her:* All right, pal, all right. It's all settled now. I've been remiss. I know that, Mom. But now I'll stay, and I swear to you, I'll apply myself. *Kneeling in front of her, in a fever of self-reproach:* It's just—you see, Mom, I don't fit in business. Not that I won't try. I'll try, and I'll make good.

HAPPY: Sure you will. The trouble with you in business was you never tried to please people.

BIFF: I know, I—

HAPPY: Like when you worked for Harrison's. Bob Harrison said you were tops, and then you go and do some damn fool thing like whistling whole songs in the elevator like a comedian.

BIFF, *against Happy:* So what? I like to whistle sometimes.

HAPPY: You don't raise a guy to a responsible job who whistles in the elevator!

LINDA: Well, don't argue about it now.

HAPPY: Like when you'd go off and swim in the middle of the day instead of taking the line around.

BIFF, *his resentment rising:* Well, don't you run off? You take off sometimes, don't you? On a nice summer day?

HAPPY: Yeah, but I cover myself!

LINDA: Boys!

HAPPY: If I'm going to take a fade the boss can call any number where I'm supposed to be and they'll swear to him that I just left. I'll tell you something that I hate to say, Biff, but in the business world some of them think you're crazy.

BIFF, *angered:* Screw the business world!

HAPPY: All right, screw it! Great, but cover yourself!

LINDA: Hap, Hap!

BIFF: I don't care what they think! They've laughed at Dad for years, and you know why? Because we don't belong in this nuthouse of a city! We should be mixing cement on some open plain, or—or carpenters. A carpenter is allowed to whistle!

Willy walks in from the entrance of the house, at left.

WILLY: Even your grandfather was better than a carpenter. *Pause. They watch him.* You never grew up. Bernard does not whistle in the elevator, I assure you.

BIFF, *as though to laugh Willy out of it:* Yeah, but you do, Pop.

WILLY: I never in my life whistled in an elevator! And who in the business world thinks I'm crazy?

BIFF: I didn't mean it like that, Pop. Now don't make a whole thing out of it, will ya?

WILLY: Go back to the West! Be a carpenter, a cowboy, enjoy yourself!

LINDA: Willy, he was just saying—

WILLY: I heard what he said!

HAPPY, *trying to quiet Willy:* Hey, Pop, come on now . . .

WILLY, *continuing over Happy's line:* They laugh at me, heh? Go to Filene's, go to the Hub, go to Slattery's,[4] Boston. Call out the name Willy Loman and see what happens! Big shot!

BIFF: All right, Pop.

WILLY: Big!

BIFF: All right!

WILLY: Why do you always insult me?

BIFF: I didn't say a word. *To Linda:* Did I say a word?

LINDA: He didn't say anything, Willy.

WILLY, *going to the doorway of the living-room:* All right, good night, good night.

LINDA: Willy, dear, he just decided . . .

WILLY, *to Biff:* If you get tired hanging around tomorrow, paint the ceiling I put up in the living-room.

BIFF: I'm leaving early tomorrow.

HAPPY: He's going to see Bill Oliver, Pop.

WILLY, *interestedly:* Oliver? For what?

BIFF, *with reserve, but trying, trying:* He always said he'd stake me. I'd like to go into business, so maybe I can take him up on it.

LINDA: Isn't that wonderful?

WILLY: Don't interrupt. What's wonderful about it? There's fifty men in the City of New York who'd stake him. *To Biff:* Sporting goods?

BIFF: I guess so. I know something about it and—

WILLY: He knows something about it! You know sporting goods better than Spalding, for God's sake! How much is he giving you?

BIFF: I don't know, I didn't even see him yet, but—

WILLY: Then what're you talkin' about?

BIFF, *getting angry:* Well, all I said was I'm gonna see him, that's all!

WILLY, *turning away:* Ah, you're counting your chickens again.

BIFF, *starting left for the stairs:* Oh, Jesus, I'm going to sleep!

WILLY, *calling after him:* Don't curse in this house!

BIFF, *turning:* Since when did you get so clean?

HAPPY, *trying to stop them:* Wait a . . .

WILLY: Don't use that language to me! I won't have it!

HAPPY, *grabbing Biff, shouts:* Wait a minute! I got an idea. I got a feasible idea. Come here, Biff, let's talk this over now, let's talk some sense here. When I

---

[4] New England department stores.

was down in Florida last time, I thought of a great idea to sell sporting goods. It just came back to me. You and I, Biff—we have a line, the Loman Line. We train a couple of weeks, and put on a couple of exhibitions, see?

WILLY: That's an idea!

HAPPY: Wait! We form two basketball teams, see? Two water-polo teams. We play each other. It's a million dollars' worth of publicity. Two brothers, see? The Loman Brothers. Displays in the Royal Palms—all the hotels. And banners over the ring and the basketball court: "Loman Brothers." Baby, we could sell sporting goods!

WILLY: That is a one-million-dollar idea!

LINDA: Marvelous!

BIFF: I'm in great shape as far as that's concerned.

HAPPY: And the beauty of it is, Biff, it wouldn't be like a business. We'd be out playin' ball again . . .

BIFF, *enthused:*   Yeah, that's . . .

WILLY: Million-dollar . . .

HAPPY: And you wouldn't get fed up with it, Biff. It'd be the family again. There'd be the old honor, and comradeship, and if you wanted to go off for a swim or somethin'—well, you'd do it! Without some smart cooky gettin' up ahead of you!

WILLY: Lick the world! You guys together could absolutely lick the civilized world.

BIFF: I'll see Oliver tomorrow. Hap, if we could work that out . . .

LINDA: Maybe things are beginning to—

WILLY, *wildly enthused, to Linda:*   Stop interrupting! *To Biff:* But don't wear sport jacket and slacks when you see Oliver.

BIFF: No, I'll—

WILLY: A business suit, and talk as little as possible, and don't crack any jokes.

BIFF: He did like me. Always liked me.

LINDA: He loved you!

WILLY, *to Linda:*   Will you stop! *To Biff:* Walk in very serious. You are not applying for a boy's job. Money is to pass. Be quiet, fine, and serious. Everybody likes a kidder, but nobody lends him money.

HAPPY: I'll try to get some myself, Biff. I'm sure I can.

WILLY: I see great things for you kids, I think your troubles are over. But remember, start big and you'll end big. Ask fifteen. How much you gonna ask for?

BIFF: Gee, I don't know—

WILLY: And don't say "Gee." "Gee" is a boy's word. A man walking in for fifteen thousand dollars does not say "Gee!"

BIFF: Ten, I think, would be top though.

WILLY: Don't be so modest. You always started too low. Walk in with a big laugh. Don't look worried. Start off with a couple of your good stories to lighten things up. It's not what you say, it's how you say it—because personality always wins the day.

LINDA: Oliver always thought the highest of him—

WILLY: Will you let me talk?

BIFF: Don't yell at her, Pop, will ya?

WILLY, *angrily:*   I was talking, wasn't I?

BIFF: I don't like you yelling at her all the time, and I'm tellin' you, that's all.

WILLY: What're you, takin' over this house?

LINDA: Willy—

WILLY, *turning on her:*   Don't take his side all the time, goddammit!

BIFF, *furiously:*   Stop yelling at her!

WILLY, *suddenly pulling on his cheek, beaten down, guilt ridden:*   Give my best to Bill Oliver—he may remember me. *He exits through the living-room doorway.*

LINDA, *her voice subdued:*   What'd you have to start that for? *Biff turns away.* You see how sweet he was as soon as you talked hopefully? *She goes over to Biff.* Come up and say good night to him. Don't let him go to bed that way.

HAPPY: Come on, Biff, let's buck him up.

LINDA: Please, dear. Just say good night. It takes so little to make him happy. Come. *She goes through the living-room doorway, calling upstairs from within the living-room:* Your pajamas are hanging in the bathroom, Willy!

HAPPY, *looking toward where Linda went out:*   What a woman! They broke the mold when they made her. You know that, Biff?

BIFF: He's off salary. My God, working on commission!

HAPPY: Well, let's face it: he's no hot-shot selling man. Except that sometimes, you have to admit, he's a sweet personality.

BIFF, *deciding:*   Lend me ten bucks, will ya? I want to buy some new ties.

HAPPY: I'll take you to a place I know. Beautiful stuff. Wear one of my striped shirts tomorrow.

BIFF: She got gray. Mom got awful old. Gee, I'm gonna go in to Oliver tomorrow and knock him for a—

HAPPY: Come on up. Tell that to Dad. Let's give him a whirl. Come on.

BIFF, *steamed up:*   You know, with ten thousand bucks, boy!

HAPPY, *as they go into the living-room:*   That's the talk, Biff, that's the first time I've heard the old confidence out of you! *From within the living-room, fading off:* You're gonna live with me, kid, and any babe you want just say the word . . . *The last lines are hardly heard. They are mounting the stairs to their parents' bedroom.*

LINDA, *entering her bedroom and addressing Willy, who is in the bathroom. She is straightening the bed for him:*   Can you do anything about the shower? It drips.

WILLY, *from the bathroom:*   All of a sudden everything falls to pieces! Goddam plumbing, oughta be sued, those people. I hardly finished putting it in and the thing . . . *His words rumble off.*

LINDA: I'm just wondering if Oliver will remember him. You think he might?

WILLY, *coming out of the bathroom in his pajamas:*   Remember him? What's the matter with you, you crazy? If he'd've stayed with Oliver he'd be on top by now! Wait'll Oliver gets a look at him. You don't know the average caliber any more. The average young man today—*he is getting into bed*—is got a caliber of zero. Greatest thing in the world for him was to bum around.

Biff and Happy enter the bedroom. Slight pause.

WILLY, *stops short, looking at Biff:*   Glad to hear it, boy.

HAPPY: He wanted to say good night to you, sport.

WILLY, *to Biff:*   Yeah. Knock him dead, boy. What'd you want to tell me?

BIFF: Just take it easy, Pop. Good night. *He turns to go.*

WILLY, *unable to resist:*   And if anything falls off the desk while you're talking to him—like a package or something—don't you pick it up. They have office boys for that.

LINDA: I'll make a big breakfast—

WILLY: Will you let me finish? *To Biff:* Tell him you were in the business in the West. Not farm work.

BIFF: All right, Dad.

LINDA: I think everything—

WILLY, *going right through her speech:*   And don't undersell yourself. No less than fifteen thousand dollars.

BIFF, *unable to bear him:*   Okay. Good night, Mom. *He starts moving.*

WILLY: Because you got a greatness in you, Biff, remember that. You got all kinds a greatness . . . *He lies back, exhausted. Biff walks out.*

LINDA, *calling after Biff:*   Sleep well, darling!

HAPPY: I'm gonna get married, Mom. I wanted to tell you.

LINDA: Go to sleep, dear.

HAPPY, *going:*   I just wanted to tell you.

WILLY: Keep up the good work. *Happy exits.* God . . . remember that Ebbets Field[5] game? The championship of the city?

LINDA: Just rest. Should I sing to you?

WILLY: Yeah. Sing to me. *Linda hums a soft lullaby.* When that team came out—he was the tallest, remember?

LINDA: Oh, yes. And in gold.

Biff enters the darkened kitchen, takes a cigarette, and leaves the house. He comes downstage into a golden pool of light. He smokes, staring at the night.

WILLY: Like a young god. Hercules—something like that. And the sun, the sun all around him. Remember how he waved to me? Right up from the field, with the representatives of three colleges standing by? And the buyers I brought, and the cheers when he came out—Loman, Loman, Loman! God Almighty, he'll be great yet. A star like that, magnificent, can never really fade away!

The light on Willy is fading. The gas heater begins to glow through the kitchen wall, near the stairs, a blue flame beneath red coils.

LINDA, *timidly:*   Willy dear, what has he got against you?

WILLY: I'm so tired. Don't talk any more.

Biff slowly returns to the kitchen. He stops, stares toward the heater.

LINDA: Will you ask Howard to let you work in New York?

WILLY: First thing in the morning. Everything'll be all right.

Biff reaches behind the heater and draws out a length of rubber tubing. He is horrified and turns his head toward Willy's room, still dimly lit, from which the strains of Linda's desperate but monotonous humming rise.

WILLY, *staring through the window into the moonlight:*   Gee, look at the moon moving between the buildings!

Biff wraps the tubing around his hand and quickly goes up the stairs.

Curtain

---

[5] The field at which the Brooklyn Dodgers played baseball.

ACT TWO

Music is heard, gay and bright. The curtain rises as the music fades away. Willy, in shirt sleeves, is sitting at the kitchen table, sipping coffee, his hat in his lap. Linda is filling his cup when she can.

WILLY: Wonderful coffee. Meal in itself.

LINDA: Can I make you some eggs?

WILLY: No. Take a breath.

LINDA: You look so rested, dear.

WILLY: I slept like a dead one. First time in months. Imagine, sleeping till ten on a Tuesday morning. Boys left nice and early, heh?

LINDA: They were out of here by eight o'clock.

WILLY: Good work!

LINDA: It was so thrilling to see them leaving together. I can't get over the shaving lotion in this house!

WILLY, *smiling:*   Mmm—

LINDA: Biff was very changed this morning. His whole attitude seemed to be hopeful. He couldn't wait to get downtown to see Oliver.

WILLY: He's heading for a change. There's no question, there simply are certain men that take longer to get—solidified. How did he dress?

LINDA: His blue suit. He's so handsome in that suit. He could be a—anything in that suit!

Willy gets up from the table. Linda holds his jacket for him.

WILLY: There's no question, no question at all. Gee, on the way home tonight I'd like to buy some seeds.

LINDA, *laughing:*   That'd be wonderful. But not enough sun gets back here. Nothing'll grow any more.

WILLY: You wait, kid, before it's all over we're gonna get a little place out in the country, and I'll raise some vegetables, a couple of chickens . . .

LINDA: You'll do it yet, dear.

Willy walks out of his jacket. Linda follows him.

WILLY: And they'll get married, and come for a weekend. I'd build a little guest house. 'Cause I got so many fine tools, all I'd need would be a little lumber and some peace of mind.

LINDA, *joyfully:*   I sewed the lining . . .

WILLY: I could build two guest houses, so they'd both come. Did he decide how much he's going to ask Oliver for?

LINDA, *getting him into the jacket:*   He didn't mention it, but I imagine ten or fifteen thousand. You going to talk to Howard today?

WILLY: Yeah, I'll put it to him straight and simple. He'll just have to take me off the road.

LINDA: And Willy, don't forget to ask for a little advance, because we've got the insurance premium. It's the grace period now.

WILLY: That's a hundred . . . ?

LINDA: A hundred and eight, sixty-eight. Because we're a little short again.

WILLY: Why are we short?

LINDA: Well, you had the motor job on the car . . .

WILLY:　That goddam Studebaker!

LINDA:　And you got one more payment on the refrigerator . . .

WILLY:　But it just broke again!

LINDA:　Well, it's old, dear.

WILLY:　I told you we should've bought a well-advertised machine. Charley bought a General Electric and it's twenty years old and it's still good, that son-of-a-bitch.

LINDA:　But, Willy—

WILLY:　Whoever heard of a Hastings refrigerator? Once in my life I would like to own something outright before it's broken! I'm always in a race with the junkyard! I just finished paying for the car and it's on its last legs. The refrigerator consumes belts like a goddam maniac. They time those things. They time them so when you finally paid for them, they're used up.

LINDA, *buttoning up his jacket as he unbuttons it:*　All told, about two hundred dollars would carry us, dear. But that includes the past payment on the mortgage. After this payment, Willy, the house belongs to us.

WILLY:　It's twenty-five years!

LINDA:　Biff was nine years old when we bought it.

WILLY:　Well, that's a great thing. To weather a twenty-five year mortgage is—

LINDA:　It's an accomplishment.

WILLY:　All the cement, the lumber, the reconstruction I put in this house! There ain't a crack to be found in it any more.

LINDA:　Well, it served its purpose.

WILLY:　What purpose? Some stranger'll come along, move in, and that's that. If only Biff would take this house, and raise a family . . . *He starts to go.* Good-by, I'm late.

LINDA, *suddenly remembering:*　Oh, I forgot! You're supposed to meet them for dinner.

WILLY:　Me?

LINDA:　At Frank's Chop House on Forty-eighth near Sixth Avenue.

WILLY:　Is that so! How about you?

LINDA:　No, just the three of you. They're gonna blow you to a big meal!

WILLY:　Don't say! Who thought of that?

LINDA:　Biff came to me this morning, Willy, and he said "Tell Dad, we want to blow him to a big meal." Be there six o'clock. You and your two boys are going to have dinner.

WILLY:　Gee whiz! That's really somethin'. I'm gonna knock Howard for a loop, kid. I'll get an advance, and I'll come home with a New York job. Goddammit, now I'm gonna do it!

LINDA:　Oh, that's the spirit, Willy!

WILLY:　I will never get behind a wheel the rest of my life!

LINDA:　It's changing, Willy, I can feel it changing!

WILLY:　Beyond a question. G'by, I'm late. *He starts to go again.*

LINDA, *calling after him as she runs to the kitchen table for a handkerchief:* You got your glasses?

WILLY, *feels for them, then comes back in:* Yeah, yeah, got my glasses.

LINDA, *giving him the handkerchief:* And a handkerchief.

WILLY:　Yeah, handkerchief.

LINDA:　And your saccharine?

WILLY: Yeah, my saccharine.

LINDA: Be careful on the subway stairs.

She kisses him, and a silk stocking is seen hanging from her hand. Willy notices it.

WILLY: Will you stop mending stockings? At least while I'm in the house, It gets me nervous. I can't tell you. Please.

Linda hides the stocking in her hand as she follows Willy across the forestage in front of the house.

LINDA: Remember, Frank's Chop House.

WILLY,   *passing the apron:* Maybe beets would grow out there.

LINDA,   *laughing:* But you tried so many times.

WILLY: Yeah. Well, don't work hard today. *He disappears around the right corner of the house.*

LINDA: Be careful!

As Willy vanishes, Linda waves to him. Suddenly the phone rings. She runs across the stage and into the kitchen and lifts it.

LINDA: Hello? Oh, Biff! I'm so glad you called, I just . . . Yes, sure, I just told him. Yes, he'll be there for dinner at six o'clock, I didn't forget. Listen, I was just dying to tell you. You know that little rubber pipe I told you about? That he connected to the gas heater? I finally decided to go down the cellar this morning and take it away and destroy it. But it's gone! He took it away himself, it isn't there! *She listens.* When? Oh, then you took it. Oh—nothing, it's just that I'd hoped he'd taken it away himself. Oh, I'm not worried, darling, because this morning he left in such high spirits, it was like the old days! I'm not afraid any more. Did Mr. Oliver see you? . . . Well, you wait there then. And make a nice impression on him, darling. Just don't perspire too much before you see him. And have a nice time with Dad. He may have big news too! . . . That's right, a New York job. And be sweet to him tonight, dear. Be loving to him. Because he's only a little boat looking for a harbor. *She is trembling with sorrow and joy.* Oh, that's wonderful, Biff, you'll save his life. Thanks, darling. Just put your arm around him when he comes into the restaurant. Give him a smile. That's the boy . . . Good-by, dear. . . . You got your comb? . . . That's fine. Good-by, Biff dear.

In the middle of her speech, Howard Wagner, thirty-six, wheels on a small type-writer table on which is a wire-recording machine[1] and proceeds to plug it in. This is on the left forestage. Light slowly fades on Linda as it rises on Howard. Howard is intent on threading the machine and only glances over his shoulder as Willy appears.

WILLY: Pst! Pst!

HOWARD: Hello, Willy, come in.

WILLY: Like to have a little talk with you, Howard.

HOWARD: Sorry to keep you waiting. I'll be with you in a minute.

WILLY: What's that, Howard?

HOWARD: Didn't you ever see one of these? Wire recorder.

WILLY: Oh. Can we talk a minute?

HOWARD: Records things. Just got delivery yesterday. Been driving me crazy, the most terrific machine I ever saw in my life. I was up all night with it.

---

[1] An early type of magnetic recorder using wire rather than tape.

WILLY: What do you do with it?

HOWARD: I bought it for dictation, but you can do anything with it. Listen to this. I had it home last night. Listen to what I picked up. The first one is my daughter. Get this. *He flicks the switch and "Roll out the Barrel" is heard being whistled.* Listen to that kid whistle.

WILLY: That is lifelike, isn't it?

HOWARD: Seven years old. Get that tone.

WILLY: Ts, ts. Like to ask a little favor if you . . .

The whistling breaks off, and the voice of Howard's daughter is heard.

HIS DAUGHTER: "Now you, Daddy."

HOWARD: She's crazy for me! *Again the same song is whistled.* That's me! Ha! *He winks.*

WILLY: You're very good!

The whistling breaks off again. The machine runs silent for a moment.

HOWARD: Sh! Get this now, this is my son.

HIS SON: "The capital of Alabama is Montgomery; the capital of Arizona is Phoenix; the capital of Arkansas is Little Rock; the capital of California is Sacramento . . ." *and on, and on.*

HOWARD, *holding up five fingers:*   Five years old, Willy!

WILLY: He'll make an announcer some day!

HIS SON, *continuing:*   "The capital . . ."

HOWARD: Get that—alphabetical order! *The machine breaks off suddenly.* Wait a minute. The maid kicked the plug out.

WILLY: It certainly is a—

HOWARD: Sh, for God's sake!

HIS SON: "It's nine o'clock, Bulova watch time. So I have to go to sleep."

WILLY: That really is—

HOWARD: Wait a minute! The next is my wife.

They wait.

HOWARD'S VOICE: "Go on, say something." *Pause.* "Well, you gonna talk?"

HIS WIFE: "I can't think of anything."

HOWARD'S VOICE: "Well, talk—it's turning."

HIS WIFE, *shyly, beaten:*   "Hello." *Silence.* "Oh, Howard, I can't talk into this . . ."

HOWARD, *snapping the machine off:*   That was my wife.

WILLY: That is a wonderful machine. Can we—

HOWARD: I tell you, Willy, I'm gonna take my camera, and my bandsaw, and all my hobbies, and out they go. This is the most fascinating relaxation I ever found.

WILLY: I think I'll get one myself.

HOWARD: Sure, they're only a hundred and a half. You can't do without it. Supposing you wanna hear Jack Benny, see? But you can't be at home at that hour. So you tell the maid to turn the radio on when Jack Benny comes on, and this automatically goes on with the radio . . .

WILLY: And when you come home you . . .

HOWARD: You can come home twelve o'clock, one o'clock, any time you like, and you get yourself a Coke and sit yourself down, throw the switch, and there's Jack Benny's program in the middle of the night!

WILLY: I'm definitely going to get one. Because lots of time I'm on the road, and I think to myself, what I must be missing on the radio!

HOWARD: Don't you have a radio in the car?

WILLY: Well, yeah, but who ever thinks of turning it on?

HOWARD: Say, aren't you supposed to be in Boston?

WILLY: That's what I want to talk to you about, Howard. You got a minute? *He draws a chair in from the wing.*

HOWARD: What happened? What're you doing here?

WILLY: Well . . .

HOWARD: You didn't crack up again, did you?

WILLY: Oh, no. No . . .

HOWARD: Geez, you had me worried there for a minute. What's the trouble?

WILLY: Well, tell you the truth, Howard. I've come to the decision that I'd rather not travel any more.

HOWARD: Not travel! Well, what'll you do?

WILLY: Remember, Christmas time, when you had the party here? You said you'd try to think of some spot for me here in town.

HOWARD: With us?

WILLY: Well, sure.

HOWARD: Oh, yeah, yeah. I remember. Well, I couldn't think of anything for you, Willy.

WILLY: I tell ya, Howard. The kids are all grown up, y'know. I don't need much any more. If I could take home—well, sixty-five dollars a week, I could swing it.

HOWARD: Yeah, but Willy, see I—

WILLY: I tell ya why, Howard. Speaking frankly and between the two of us, y'know—I'm just a little tired.

HOWARD: Oh, I could understand that, Willy. But you're a road man, Willy, and we do a road business. We've only got a half-dozen salesmen on the floor here.

WILLY: God knows, Howard, I never asked a favor of any man. But I was with the firm when your father used to carry you in here in his arms.

HOWARD: I know that, Willy, but—

WILLY: Your father came to me the day you were born and asked me what I thought of the name of Howard, may he rest in peace.

HOWARD: I appreciate that, Willy, but there just is no spot here for you. If I had a spot I'd slam you right in, but I just don't have a single solitary spot.

He looks for his lighter. Willy has picked it up and gives it to him. Pause.

WILLY, *with increasing anger:*   Howard, all I need to set my table is fifty dollars a week.

HOWARD: But where am I going to put you, kid?

WILLY: Look, it isn't a question of whether I can sell merchandise, is it?

HOWARD: No, but it's a business, kid, and everybody's gotta pull his own weight.

WILLY, *desperately:*   Just let me tell you a story, Howard—

HOWARD: 'Cause you gotta admit, business is business.

WILLY, *angrily:*   Business is definitely business, but just listen for a minute. You don't understand this. When I was a boy—eighteen, nineteen—I was already on the road. And there was a question in my mind as to whether selling had a future for me. Because in those days I had a yearning to go to Alaska. See, there were three gold strikes in one month in Alaska, and I felt like going out. Just for the ride, you might say.

HOWARD, *barely interested:*   Don't say.

WILLY: Oh, yeah, my father lived many years in Alaska. He was an adventurous man. We've got quite a little streak of self-reliance in our family. I thought I'd go out with my older brother and try to locate him, and maybe settle in the North with the old man. And I was almost decided to go, when I met a salesman in the Parker House.[2] His name was Dave Singleman. And he was eighty-four years old, and he'd drummed merchandise in thirty-one states. And old Dave, he'd go up to his room, y'understand, put on his green velvet slippers—I'll never forget—and pick up his phone and call the buyers, and without ever leaving his room, at the age of eighty-four, he made his living. And when I saw that, I realized that selling was the greatest career a man could want. 'Cause what could be more satisfying than to be able to go, at the age of eighty-four, into twenty or thirty different cities, and pick up a phone, and be remembered and loved and helped by so many different people? Do you know? when he died—and by the way he died the death of a salesman, in his green velvet slippers in the smoker of the New York, New Haven and Hartford, going into Boston—when he died, hundreds of salesmen and buyers were at his funeral. Things were sad on a lotta trains for months after that. *He stands up. Howard has not looked at him.* In those days there was personality in it, Howard. There was respect, and comradeship, and gratitude in it. Today, it's all cut and dried, and there's no chance for bringing friendship to bear—or personality. You see what I mean? They don't know me any more.

HOWARD, *moving away, to the right:*   That's just the thing, Willy.

WILLY: If I had forty dollars a week—that's all I'd need. Forty dollars, Howard.

HOWARD: Kid, I can't take blood from a stone, I—

WILLY, *desperation is on him now:*   Howard, the year Al Smith[3] was nominated, your father came to me and—

HOWARD, *starting to go off:*   I've got to see some people, kid.

WILLY, *stopping him:*   I'm talking about your father! There were promises made across this desk! You mustn't tell me you've got people to see—I put thirty-four years into this firm, Howard, and now I can't pay my insurance! You can't eat the orange and throw the peel away—a man is not a piece of fruit! *After a pause.* Now pay attention. Your father—in 1928 I had a big year. I averaged a hundred and seventy dollars a week in commissions.

HOWARD, *impatiently:*   Now, Willy, you never averaged—

WILLY, *banging his hand on the desk:*   I averaged a hundred and seventy dollars a week in the year of 1928! And your father came to me—or rather, I was in the office here—it was right over this desk—and he put his hand on my shoulder—

HOWARD, *getting up:*   You'll have to excuse me, Willy, I gotta see some people. Pull yourself together. *Going out.* I'll be back in a little while.

On Howard's exit, the light on his chair grows very bright and strange.

---

[2] A hotel in Boston.
[3] Alfred E. Smith (1873–1944), governor of New York from 1919 to 1920 and 1923 to 1928 and a presidential candidate in 1928.

WILLY: Pull myself together! What the hell did I say to him? My God, I was yelling at him! How could I? *Willy breaks off, staring at the light, which occupies the chair, animating it. He approaches this chair, standing across the desk from it.* Frank, Frank, don't you remember what you told me that time? How you put your hand on my shoulder, and Frank . . . *He leans on the desk and as he speaks the dead man's name he accidentally switches on the recorder, and instantly*

HOWARD'S SON: ". . . of New York is Albany. The capital of Ohio is Cincinnati, the capital of Rhode Island is . . ." *The recitation continues.*

WILLY, *leaping away with fright, shouting:* Ha! Howard! Howard! Howard!

HOWARD, *rushing in:* What happened?

WILLY, *pointing at the machine, which continues nasally, childishly, with the capital cities:* Shut it off! Shut it off!

HOWARD, *pulling the plug out:* Look, Willy . . .

WILLY, *pressing his hands to his eyes:* I gotta get myself some coffee. I'll get some coffee . . .

Willy starts to walk out. Howard stops him.

HOWARD, *rolling up the cord:* Willy, look . . .

WILLY: I'll go to Boston.

HOWARD: Willy, you can't go to Boston for us.

WILLY: Why can't I go?

HOWARD: I don't want you to represent us. I've been meaning to tell you for a long time now.

WILLY: Howard, are you firing me?

HOWARD: I think you need a good long rest, Willy.

WILLY: Howard—

HOWARD: And when you feel better, come back, and we'll see if we can work something out.

WILLY: But I gotta earn money, Howard. I'm in no position to—

HOWARD: Where are your sons? Why don't your sons give you a hand?

WILLY: They're working on a very big deal.

HOWARD: This is no time for false pride, Willy. You go to your sons and you tell them that you're tired. You've got two great boys, haven't you?

WILLY: Oh, no question, no question, but in the meantime . . .

HOWARD: Then that's that, heh?

WILLY: All right, I'll go to Boston tomorrow.

HOWARD: No, no.

WILLY: I can't throw myself on my sons. I'm not a cripple!

HOWARD: Look, kid, I'm busy this morning.

WILLY, *grasping Howard's arm:* Howard, you've got to let me go to Boston!

HOWARD, *hard, keeping himself under control:* I've got a line of people to see this morning. Sit down, take five minutes, and pull yourself together, and then go home, will ya? I need the office, Willy. *He starts to go, turns, remembering the recorder, starts to push off the table holding the recorder.* Oh, yeah. Whenever you can this week, stop by and drop off the samples. You'll feel better, Willy, and then come back and we'll talk. Pull yourself together, kid, there's people outside.

Howard exits, pushing the table off left. Willy stares into space, exhausted. Now the music is heard—Ben's music—first distantly, then closer, closer. As Willy speaks, Ben enters from the right. He carries valise and umbrella.

WILLY: Oh, Ben, how did you do it? What is the answer? Did you wind up the Alaska deal already?

BEN: Doesn't take much time if you know what you're doing. Just a short business trip. Boarding ship in an hour. Wanted to say good-by.

WILLY: Ben, I've got to talk to you.

BEN, *glancing at his watch:*   Haven't the time, William.

WILLY, *crossing the apron to Ben:*   Ben, nothing's working out. I don't know what to do.

BEN: Now, look, here, William. I've bought timberland in Alaska and I need a man to look after things for me.

WILLY: God, timberland! Me and my boys in those grand outdoors!

BEN: You've a new continent at your doorstep, William. Get out of these cities, they're full of talk and time payments and courts of law. Screw on your fists and you can fight for a fortune up there.

WILLY: Yes, yes! Linda, Linda!

Linda enters as of old, with the wash.

LINDA: Oh, you're back?

BEN: I haven't much time.

WILLY: No, wait! Linda, he's got a proposition for me in Alaska.

LINDA: But you've got—(*To Ben.*) He's got a beautiful job here.

WILLY: But in Alaska, kid, I could—

LINDA: You're doing well enough, Willy!

BEN, *to Linda:*   Enough for what, my dear?

LINDA, *frightened of Ben and angry at him:*   Don't say those things to him! Enough to be happy right here, right now. *To Willy, while Ben laughs.* Why must everybody conquer the world? You're well liked, and the boys love you, and someday—(*To Ben*)—why, old man Wagner told him just the other day that if he keeps it up he'll be a member of the firm, didn't he, Willy?

WILLY: Sure, sure. I am building something with this firm, Ben, and if a man is building something he must be on the right track, mustn't he?

BEN: What are you building? Lay your hand on it. Where is it?

WILLY, *hesitantly:*   That's true, Linda, there's nothing.

LINDA: Why? *To Ben:* There's a man eighty-four years old—

WILLY: That's right, Ben, that's right. When I look at that man I say, what is there to worry about?

BEN: Bah!

WILLY: It's true, Ben. All he has to do is go into any city, pick up the phone, and he's making his living and you know why?

BEN, *picking up his valise:*   I've got to go.

WILLY, *holding Ben back:*   Look at this boy!

Biff, in his high school sweater, enters carrying suitcase. Happy carries Biff's shoulder guards, gold helmet, and football pants.

WILLY: Without a penny to his name, three great universities are begging for him, and from there the sky's the limit, because it's not what you do, Ben. It's who you know and the smile on your face! It's contacts, Ben, contacts! The whole wealth of Alaska passes over the lunch table at the Commodore Hotel,[4] and that's

---

[4] A large New York City hotel.

the wonder, the wonder of this country, that a man can end with diamonds here on the basis of being liked! *He turns to Biff.* And that's why when you get out on that field today it's important. Because thousands of people will be rooting for you and loving you. *To Ben, who has again begun to leave:* And Ben! when he walks into a business office his name will sound out like a bell and all the doors will open to him! I've seen it, Ben, I've seen it a thousand times! You can't feel it with your hand like timber, but it's there!

BEN: Good-by, William.

WILLY: Ben, am I right? Don't you think I'm right? I value your advice.

BEN: There's a new continent at your doorstep, William. You could walk out rich. Rich! *He is gone.*

WILLY: We'll do it here, Ben! You hear me? We're gonna do it here!

Young Bernard rushes in. The gay music of the Boys is heard.

BERNARD: Oh, gee, I was afraid you left already!

WILLY: Why? What time is it?

BERNARD: It's half-past one!

WILLY: Well, come on, everybody! Ebbets Field next stop! Where's the pennants? *He rushes through the wall-line of the kitchen and out into the living-room.*

LINDA, *to Biff:*   Did you pack fresh underwear?

BIFF, *who has been limbering up:*   I want to go!

BERNARD: Biff, I'm carrying your helmet, ain't I?

HAPPY: No, I'm carrying the helmet.

BERNARD: Oh, Biff, you promised me.

HAPPY: I'm carrying the helmet.

BERNARD: How am I going to get in the locker room?

LINDA: Let him carry the shoulder guards. *She puts her coat and hat on in the kitchen.*

BERNARD: Can I, Biff? 'Cause I told everybody I'm going to be in the locker room.

HAPPY: In Ebbets Field it's the clubhouse.

BERNARD: I meant the clubhouse. Biff!

HAPPY: Biff!

BIFF, *grandly, after a slight pause:*   Let him carry the shoulder guards.

HAPPY, *as he gives Bernard the shoulder guards:*   Stay close to us now.

Willy rushes in with the pennants.

WILLY, *handing them out:*   Everybody wave when Biff comes out on the field. *Happy and Bernard run off.* You set now, boy?

The music has died away.

BIFF: Ready to go, Pop. Every muscle is ready.

WILLY, *at the edge of the apron:*   You realize what this means?

BIFF: That's right, Pop.

WILLY, *feeling Biff's muscles:*   You're comin' home this afternoon captain of the All-Scholastic Championship Team of the City of New York.

BIFF: I got it, Pop. And remember, pal, when I take off my helmet, that touchdown is for you.

WILLY: Let's go! *He is starting out, with his arm around Biff, when Charley enters, as of old, in knickers.* I got no room for you, Charley.

CHARLEY: Room? For what?

WILLY: In the car.

CHARLEY: You goin' for a ride? I wanted to shoot some casino.

WILLY, *furiously:*   Casino! *Incredulously:*   Don't you realize what today is?

LINDA: Oh, he knows, Willy. He's just kidding you.

WILLY: That's nothing to kid about!

CHARLEY: No. Linda, what's goin' on?

LINDA: He's playing in Ebbets Field.

CHARLEY: Baseball in this weather?

WILLY: Don't talk to him. Come on, come on! *He is pushing them out.*

CHARLEY: Wait a minute, didn't you hear the news?

WILLY: What?

CHARLEY: Don't you listen to the radio? Ebbets Field just blew up.

WILLY: You go to hell! *Charley laughs. Pushing them out:* Come on, come on! We're late.

CHARLEY, *as they go:*   Knock a homer, Biff, knock a homer!

WILLY, *the last to leave, turning to Charley:*   I don't think that was funny, Charley. This is the greatest day of his life.

CHARLEY: Willy, when are you going to grow up?

WILLEY: Yeah, heh? When this game is over, Charley, you'll be laughing out of the other side of your face. They'll be calling him another Red Grange.[5] Twenty-five thousand a year.

CHARLEY, *kidding:*   Is that so?

WILLY: Yeah, that's so.

CHARLEY: Well, then, I'm sorry, Willy. But tell me something.

WILLY: What?

CHARLEY: Who is Red Grange?

WILLY: Put up your hands. Goddam you, put up your hands!

Charley, chuckling, shakes his head and walks away, around the left corner of the stage. Willy follows him. The music rises to a mocking frenzy.

WILLY: Who the hell do you think you are, better than everybody else? You don't know everything, you big, ignorant, stupid . . . Put up your hands!

Light rises on the right side of the forestage, on a small table in the reception room of Charley's office. Traffic sounds are heard. Bernard, now mature, sits whistling to himself. A pair of tennis rackets and an overnight bag are on the floor beside him.

WILLY, *offstage:*   What are you walking away for? Don't walk away! If you're going to say something say it to my face! I know you laugh at me behind my back. You'll laugh out of the other side of your goddam face after this game. Touchdown! Touchdown! Eighty thousand people! Touchdown! Right between the goal posts.

Bernard is a quiet, earnest, but self-assured young man. Willy's voice is coming from right upstage now. Bernard lowers his feet off the table and listens. Jenny, his father's secretary, enters.

---

[5] Harold Edward Grange (1903–   ), an All-American football player for the University of Illinois (1923–1925).

JENNY: *distressed:* Say, Bernard, will you go out in the hall?

BERNARD: What is that noise? Who is it?

JENNY: Mr. Loman. He just got off the elevator.

BERNARD, *getting up:*   Who's he arguing with?

JENNY: Nobody. There's nobody with him. I can't deal with him any more, and your father gets all upset everytime he comes. I've got a lot of typing to do, and your father's waiting to sign it. Will you see him?

WILLY, *entering:*   Touchdown! Touch— *He sees Jenny.* Jenny, Jenny, good to see you. How're ya? Workin'? Or still honest?

JENNY: Fine, How've you been feeling?

WILLY: Not much any more, Jenny. Ha, ha! *He is surprised to see the rackets.*

BERNARD: Hello, Uncle Willy.

WILLY, *almost shocked:*   Bernard! Well, look who's here! *He comes quickly, guiltily, to Bernard and warmly shakes his hand.*

BERNARD: How are you? Good to see you.

WILLY: What are you doing here?

BERNARD: Oh, just stopped by to see Pop. Get off my feet till my train leaves. I'm going to Washington in a few minutes.

WILLY: Is he in?

BERNARD: Yes, he's in his office with the accountant. Sit down.

WILLY, *sitting down:*   What're you going to do in Washington?

BERNARD: Oh, just a case I've got there, Willy.

WILLY: That so? *Indicating the rackets:* You going to play tennis there?

BERNARD: I'm staying with a friend who's got a court.

WILLY: Don't say. His own tennis court. Must be fine people, I bet.

BERNARD: They are, very nice. Dad tells me Biff's in town.

WILLY, *with a big smile:*   Yeah, Biff's in. Working on a very big deal, Bernard.

BERNARD: What's Biff doing?

WILLY: Well, he's been doing very big things in the West. But he decided to establish himself here. Very big. We're having dinner. Did I hear your wife had a boy?

BERNARD: That's right. Our second.

WILLY: Two boys! What do you know!

BERNARD: What kind of a deal has Biff got?

WILLY: Well, Bill Oliver—very big sporting-goods man—he wants Biff very badly. Called him in from the West. Long distance, carte blanche, special deliveries. Your friends have their own private tennis court?

BERNARD: You still with the old firm, Willy?

WILLY, *after a pause:*   I'm—I'm overjoyed to see how you made the grade, Bernard, overjoyed. It's an encouraging thing to see a young man really—really—Looks very good for Biff—very— *He breaks off, then:* Bernard— *He is so full of emotion, he breaks off again.*

BERNARD: What is it, Willy?

WILLY, *small and alone:*   What—what's the secret?

BERNARD: What secret?

WILLY: How—how did you? Why didn't he ever catch on?

BERNARD: I wouldn't know that, Willy.

WILLY, *confidentially, desperately:*   You were his friend, his boyhood friend.

There's something I don't understand about it. His life ended after that Ebbets Field game. From the age of seventeen nothing good ever happened to him.

BERNARD: He never trained himself for anything.

WILLY: But he did, he did. After high school he took so many correspondence courses. Radio mechanics; television; God knows what, and never made the slightest mark.

BERNARD, *taking off his glasses:*   Willy, do you want to talk candidly?

WILLY, *rising, faces Bernard:*   I regard you as a very brilliant man, Bernard. I value your advice.

BERNARD: Oh, the hell with the advice, Willy. I couldn't advise you. There's just one thing I've always wanted to ask you. When he was supposed to graduate, and the math teacher flunked him—

WILLY: Oh, that son-of-a-bitch ruined his life.

BERNARD: Yeah, but, Willy, all he had to do was go to summer school and make up that subject.

WILLY: That's right, that's right.

BERNARD: Did you tell him not to go to summer school?

WILLY: Me? I begged him to go. I ordered him to go!

BERNARD: Then why wouldn't he go?

WILLY: Why? Why! Bernard, that question has been trailing me like a ghost for the last fifteen years. He flunked the subject, and laid down and died like a hammer hit him!

BERNARD: Take it easy, kid.

WILLY: Let me talk to you—I got nobody to talk to. Bernard, Bernard, was it my fault? Y'see? It keeps going around in my mind, maybe I did something to him. I got nothing to give him.

BERNARD: Don't take it so hard.

WILLY: Why did he lay down? What is the story there? You were his friend!

BERNARD: Willy, I remember, it was June, and our grades came out. And he'd flunked math.

WILLY: That son-of-a-bitch!

BERNARD: No, it wasn't right then. Biff just got very angry, I remember, and he was ready to enroll in summer school.

WILLY, *surprised:*   He was?

BERNARD: He wasn't beaten by it at all. But then, Willy, he disappeared from the block for almost a month. And I got the idea that he'd gone up to New England to see you. Did he have a talk with you then?

Willy stares in silence.

BERNARD: Willy?

WILLY, *with a strong edge of resentment in his voice:*   Yeah, he came to Boston. What about it?

BERNARD: Well, just that when he came back—I'll never forget this, it always mystifies me. Because I'd thought so well of Biff, even though he's always taken advantage of me. I loved him, Willy, y'know? And he came back after that month and took his sneakers—remember those sneakers with "University of Virginia" printed on them? He was so proud of those, wore them every day. And he took them down in the cellar, and burned them up in the furnace. We had a fist fight. It lasted at least half an hour. Just the two of us, punching each other down the cellar, and crying right through it. I've often thought of how strange it was that I knew he'd given up his life. What happened in Boston, Willy?

Willy looks at him as at an intruder.

> BERNARD: I just bring it up because you asked me.
>
> WILLY: *angrily:* Nothing. What do you mean, "What happened?" What's that got to do with anything?
>
> BERNARD: Well, don't get sore.
>
> WILLY: What are you trying to do, blame it on me? If a boy lays down is that my fault?
>
> BERNARD: Now, Willy, don't get—
>
> WILLY: Well, don't—don't talk to me that way! What does that mean, "What happened?"

Charley enters. He is in his vest, and he carries a bottle of bourbon.

> CHARLEY: Hey, you're going to miss that train. *He waves the bottle.*
>
> BERNARD: Yeah, I'm going. *He takes the bottle.* Thanks, Pop. *He picks up his rackets and bag.* Good-by, Willy, and don't worry about it. You know, "If at first you don't succeed . . ."
>
> WILLY: Yes, I believe in that.
>
> BERNARD: But sometimes, Willy, it's better for a man just to walk away.
>
> WILLY: Walk away?
>
> BERNARD: That's right.
>
> WILLY: But if you can't walk away?
>
> BERNARD, *after a slight pause:* I guess that's when it's tough. *Extending his hand:* Good by, Willy.
>
> WILLY, *shaking Bernard's hand:* Good-by, boy.
>
> CHARLEY, *an arm on Bernard's shoulder:* How do you like this kid? Gonna argue a case in front of the Supreme Court.
>
> BERNARD, *protesting:* Pop!
>
> WILLY, *genuinely shocked, pained, and happy:* No! The Supreme Court!
>
> BERNARD: I gotta run. 'By, Dad!
>
> CHARLEY: Knock 'em dead, Bernard!

Bernard goes off.

> WILLY, *as Charley takes out his wallet:* The Supreme Court! And he didn't even mention it!
>
> CHARLEY, *counting out money on the desk:* He don't have to—he's gonna do it.
>
> WILLY: And you never told him what to do, did you? You never took any interest in him.
>
> CHARLEY: My salvation is that I never took any interest in anything. There's some money—fifty dollars. I got an accountant inside.
>
> WILLY: Charley, look . . . *With difficulty:* I got my insurance to pay. If you can manage it—I need a hundred and ten dollars.

Charley doesn't reply for a moment; merely stops moving.

> WILLY: I'd draw it from my bank but Linda would know, and I . . .
>
> CHARLEY: Sit down, Willy.

WILLY, *moving toward the chair:*   I'm keeping an account of everything, remember. I'll pay every penny back. *He sits.*

CHARLEY: Now listen to me, Willy.

WILLY: I want you to know I appreciate . . .

CHARLEY, *sitting down on the table:*   Willy, what're you doin'? What the hell is goin' on in your head?

WILLY: Why? I'm simply . . .

CHARLEY: I offered you a job. You can make fifty dollars a week. And I won't send you on the road.

WILLY: I've got a job.

CHARLEY: Without pay? What kind of a job is a job without pay? *He rises.* Now, look, kid, enough is enough. I'm no genius but I know when I'm being insulted.

WILLY: Insulted!

CHARLEY: Why don't you want to work for me?

WILLY: What's the matter with you? I've got a job.

CHARLEY: Then what're you walkin' in here every week for?

WILLY, *getting up:*   Well, if you don't want me to walk in here—

CHARLEY: I am offering you a job.

WILLY: I don't want your goddam job!

CHARLEY: When the hell are you going to grow up?

WILLY, *furiously:*   You big ignoramus, if you say that to me again I'll rap you one! I don't care how big you are! *He's ready to fight.*

Pause.

CHARLEY, *kindly, going to him:*   How much do you need, Willy?

WILLY: Charley, I'm strapped, I'm strapped. I don't know what to do. I was just fired.

CHARLEY: Howard fired you?

WILLY: That snotnose. Imagine that? I named him. I named him Howard.

CHARLEY: Willy, when're you gonna realize that them things don't mean anything? You named him Howard, but you can't sell that. The only thing you got in this world is what you can sell. And the funny thing is that you're a salesman, and you don't know that.

WILLY: I've always tried to think otherwise, I guess. I always felt that if a man was impressive, and well liked, that nothing—

CHARLEY: Why must everybody like you? Who liked J. P. Morgan?[6] Was he impressive? In a Turkish bath he'd look like a butcher. But with his pockets on he was very well liked. Now listen, Willy, I know you don't like me, and nobody can say I'm in love with you, but I'll give you a job because—just for the hell of it, put it that way. Now what do you say?

WILLY: I—I just can't work for you, Charley.

CHARLEY: What're you, jealous of me?

WILLY: I can't work for you, that's all, don't ask me why.

CHARLEY, *angered, takes out more bills:*   You been jealous of me all your life, you damned fool! Here, pay your insurance. *He puts the money in Willy's hand.*

WILLY: I'm keeping strict accounts.

---

[6] John Pierpont Morgan (1867–1943), a millionaire who inherited his father's wealth and position.

CHARLEY: I've got some work to do. Take care of yourself. And pay your insurance.

WILLY, *moving to the right:* Funny, y'know? After all the highways, and the trains, and the appointments, and the years, you end up worth more dead than alive.

CHARLEY: Willy, nobody's worth nothin' dead. *After a slight pause:* Did you hear what I said?

Willy stands still, dreaming.

CHARLEY: Willy!

WILLY: Apologize to Bernard for me when you see him. I didn't mean to argue with him. He's a fine boy. They're all fine boys, and they'll end up big—all of them. Someday they'll all play tennis together. Wish me luck, Charley. He saw Bill Oliver today.

CHARLEY: Good luck.

WILLY, *on the verge of tears:* Charley, you're the only friend I got. Isn't that a remarkable thing? *He goes out.*

CHARLEY: Jesus!

Charley stares after him a moment and follows. All light blacks out. Suddenly raucous music is heard, and a red glow rises behind the screen at right. Stanley, a young waiter, appears, carrying a table, followed by Happy, who is carrying two chairs.

STANLEY, *putting the table down:* That's all right, Mr. Loman, I can handle it myself. *He turns and takes the chairs from Happy and places them at the table.*

HAPPY, *glancing around:* Oh, this is better.

STANLEY: Sure, in the front there you're in the middle of all kinds a noise. Whenever you got a party, Mr. Loman, you just tell me and I'll put you back here. Y'know, there's a lotta people they don't like it private, because when they go out they like to see a lotta action around them because they're sick and tired to stay in the house by theirself. But I know you, you ain't from Hackensack.[7] You know what I mean?

HAPPY, *sitting down:* So how's it coming, Stanley?

STANLEY: Ah, it's a dog's life. I only wish during the war they'd a took me in the Army. I coulda been dead by now.

HAPPY: My brother's back, Stanley.

STANLEY: Oh, he come back, heh? From the Far West.

HAPPY: Yeah, big cattle man, my brother, so treat him right. And my father's coming too.

STANLEY: Oh, your father too!

HAPPY: You got a couple of nice lobsters?

STANLEY: Hundred per cent, big.

HAPPY: I want them with the claws.

STANLEY: Don't worry, I don't give you no mice. *Happy laughs.* How about some wine? It'll put a head on the meal.

HAPPY: No. You remember, Stanley, that recipe I brought you from overseas? With the champagne in it?

---

[7] A middle-class city in New Jersey.

STANLEY: Oh, yeah, sure. I still got it tacked up yet in the kitchen. But that'll have to cost a buck apiece anyways.

HAPPY: That's all right.

STANLEY: What'd you, hit a number or somethin'?

HAPPY: No, it's a little celebration. My brother is—I think he pulled off a big deal today. I think we're going into business together.

STANLEY: Great! That's the best for you. Because a family business, you know what I mean?—that's the best.

HAPPY: That's what I think.

STANLEY: 'Cause what's the difference? Somebody steals? It's in the family. Know what I mean? *Sotto voce:*[8] Like this bartender here. The boss is goin' crazy what kinda leak he's got in the cash register. You put it in but it don't come out.

HAPPY, *raising his head:*   Sh!

STANLEY: What?

HAPPY: You notice I wasn't lookin' right or left, was I?

STANLEY: No.

HAPPY: And my eyes are closed.

STANLEY: So what's the—?

HAPPY: Strudel's comin'.

STANLEY, *catching on, looks around:*   Ah, no there's no—

He breaks off as a furred, lavishly dressed girl enters and sits at the next table. Both follow her with their eyes.

STANLEY: Geez, how'd ya know?

HAPPY: I got radar or something. *Staring directly at her profile:* Oooooooo . . . Stanley.

STANLEY: I think that's for you, Mr. Loman.

HAPPY: Look at that mouth. Oh, God. And the binoculars.

STANLEY: Geez, you got a life, Mr. Loman.

HAPPY: Wait on her.

STANLEY, *going to the girl's table:*   Would you like a menu, ma'am?

GIRL: I'm expecting someone, but I'd like a—

HAPPY: Why don't you bring her—excuse me, miss, do you mind? I sell champagne, and I'd like you to try my brand. Bring her a champagne, Stanley.

GIRL: That's awfully nice of you.

HAPPY: Don't mention it. It's all company money. *He laughs.*

GIRL: That's a charming product to be selling, isn't it?

HAPPY: Oh, gets to be like everything else. Selling is selling, y'know.

GIRL: I suppose.

HAPPY: You don't happen to sell, do you?

GIRL: No, I don't sell.

HAPPY: Would you object to a compliment from a stranger? You ought to be on a magazine cover.

GIRL, *looking at him a little archly:*   I have been.

Stanley comes in with a glass of champagne.

HAPPY: What'd I say before, Stanley? You see? She's a cover girl.

[8] In a "soft voice" (Italian).

STANLEY: Oh, I could see, I could see.

HAPPY, *to the Girl:* What magazine?

GIRL: Oh, a lot of them. *She takes the drink.* Thank you.

HAPPY: You know what they say in France, don't you? "Champagne is the drink of the complexion"—Hya, Biff!

Biff has entered and sits with Happy.

BIFF: Hell, kid, Sorry I'm late.

HAPPY: I just got here. Uh, Miss—?

GIRL: Forsythe.

HAPPY: Miss Forsythe, this is my brother.

BIFF: Is Dad here?

HAPPY: His name is Biff. You might've heard of him. Great football player.

GIRL: Really? What team?

HAPPY: Are you familiar with football?

GIRL: No, I'm afraid I'm not.

HAPPY: Biff is quarterback with the New York Giants.

GIRL: Well, that is nice, isn't it? *She drinks.*

HAPPY: Good health.

GIRL: I'm happy to meet you.

HAPPY: That's my name. Hap. It's really Harold, but at West Point they called me Happy.

GIRL, *now really impressed:* Oh, I see. How do you do? *She turns her profile.*

BIFF: Isn't Dad coming?

HAPPY: You want her?

BIFF: Oh, I could never make that.

HAPPY: I remember the time that idea would never come into your head. Where's the old confidence, Biff?

BIFF: I just saw Oliver—

HAPPY: Wait a minute. I've got to see that old confidence again. Do you want her? She's on call.

BIFF: Oh, no. *He turns to look at the Girl.*

HAPPY: I'm telling you. Watch this. *Turning to the Girl:* Honey? *She turns to him.* Are you busy?

GIRL: Well, I am . . . but I could make a phone call.

HAPPY: Do that, will you, honey? And see if you get a friend. We'll be here for a while. Biff is one of the greatest football players in the country.

GIRL, *standing up:* Well, I'm certainly happy to meet you.

HAPPY: Come back soon.

GIRL: I'll try.

HAPPY: Don't try, honey, try hard.

The Girl exits. Stanley follows, shaking his head in bewildered admiration.

HAPPY: Isn't that a shame now? A beautiful girl like that? That's why I can't get married. There's not a good woman in a thousand. New York is loaded with them, kid!

BIFF: Hap, look—

HAPPY: I told you she was on call!

BIFF, *strangely unnerved:* Cut it out, will ya? I want to say something to you.

HAPPY: Did you see Oliver?

BIFF: I saw him all right. Now look, I want to tell Dad a couple of things and I want you to help me.

HAPPY: What? Is he going to back you?

BIFF: Are you crazy? You're out of your goddam head, you know that?

HAPPY: Why? What happened?

BIFF, *breathlessly:* I did a terrible thing today, Hap. It's been the strangest day I ever went through. I'm all numb, I swear.

HAPPY: You mean he wouldn't see you?

BIFF: Well, I waited six hours for him, see? All day. Kept sending my name in. Even tried to date his secretary so she'd get me to him, but no soap.

HAPPY: Because you're not showin' the old confidence, Biff. He remembered you, didn't he?

BIFF, *stopping Happy with a gesture:*   Finally, about five o'clock, he comes out. Didn't remember who I was or anything. I felt like such an idiot, Hap.

HAPPY: Did you tell him my Florida idea?

BIFF: He walked away. I saw him for one minute. I got so mad I could've torn the walls down! How the hell did I ever get the idea I was a salesman there? I even believed myself that I'd been a salesman for him! And then he gave me one look and—I realized what a ridiculous lie my whole life has been! We've been talking in a dream for fifteen years. I was a shipping clerk.

HAPPY: What'd you do?

BIFF, *with great tension and wonder:*   Well, he left, see. And the secretary went out. I was all alone in the waiting-room. I don't know what came over me, Hap. The next thing I know I'm in his office—paneled walls, everything. I can't explain it. I—Hap, I took his fountain pen.

HAPPY: Geez, did he catch you?

BIFF: I ran out. I ran down all eleven flights. I ran and ran and ran.

HAPPY: That was an awful dumb—what'd you do that for?

BIFF, *agonized:*   I don't know, I just—wanted to take something, I don't know. You gotta help me, Hap, I'm gonna tell Pop.

HAPPY: You crazy? What for?

BIFF: Hap, he's got to understand that I'm not the man somebody lends that kind of money to. He thinks I've been spiting him all these years and it's eating him up.

HAPPY: That's just it. You tell him something nice.

BIFF: I can't.

HAPPY: Say you got a lunch date with Oliver tomorrow.

BIFF: So what do I do tomorrow?

HAPPY: You leave the house tomorrow and come back at night and say Oliver is thinking it over. And he thinks it over for a couple of weeks, and gradually it fades away and nobody's the worse.

BIFF: But it'll go on forever!

HAPPY: Dad is never so happy as when he's looking forward to something!

Willy enters.

HAPPY: Hello, scout!

WILLY: Gee, I haven't been here in years!

Stanley has followed Willy and sets a chair for him. Stanley starts off but Happy stops him.

HAPPY: Stanley!

Stanley stands by, waiting for an order.

BIFF, *going to Willy with guilt, as to an invalid:*   Sit down, Pop. You want a drink?

WILLY: Sure, I don't mind.

BIFF: Let's get a load on.

WILLY: You look worried.

BIFF: N-no. *To Stanley:* Scotch all around. Make it doubles.

STANLEY: Doubles, right. *He goes.*

WILLY: You had a couple already, didn't you?

BIFF: Just a couple, yeah.

WILLY: Well, what happened, boy? *Nodding affirmatively, with a smile:* Everything go all right?

BIFF, *takes a breath, then reaches out and grasps Willy's hand:*   Pal . . . *He is smiling bravely, and Willy is smiling too.* I had an experience today.

HAPPY: Terrific, Pop.

WILLY: That so? What happened?

BIFF, *high, slightly alcoholic, above the earth:*   I'm going to tell you everything from first to last. It's been a strange day. *Silence. He looks around, composes himself as best he can, but his breath keeps breaking the rhythm of his voice.* I had to wait quite a while for him, and—

WILLY: Oliver?

BIFF: Yeah, Oliver. All day, as a matter of cold fact. And a lot of—instances—facts, Pop, facts about my life came back to me. Who was it, Pop? Who ever said I was a salesman with Oliver?

WILLY: Well, you were.

BIFF: No, Dad, I was a shipping clerk.

WILLY: But you were practically—

BIFF, *with determination:*   Dad, I don't know who said it first, but I was never a salesman for Bill Oliver.

WILLY: What're you talking about?

BIFF: Let's hold on to the facts tonight, Pop. We're not going to get anywhere bullin' around. I was a shipping clerk.

WILLY, *angrily:*   All right, now listen to me—

BIFF: Why don't you let me finish?

WILLY: I'm not interested in stories about the past or any crap of that kind because the woods are burning, boys, you understand? There's a big blaze going on all around. I was fired today.

BIFF, *shocked:*   How could you be?

WILLY: I was fired, and I'm looking for a little good news to tell your mother, because the woman has waited and the woman has suffered. The gist of it is that I haven't got a story left in my head, Biff. So don't give me a lecture about facts and aspects. I am not interested. Now what've you got to say to me?

Stanley enters with three drinks. They waits until he leaves.

WILLY: Did you see Oliver?

BIFF: Jesus, Dad!

WILLY: You mean you didn't go up there?

HAPPY: Sure he went up there.

BIFF: I did. I—saw him. How could they fire you?

WILLY, *on the edge of his chair:* What kind of a welcome did he give you?

BIFF: He won't even let you work on commission?

WILLY: I'm out! *Driving:* So tell me, he gave you a warm welcome?

HAPPY: Sure, Pop, sure!

BIFF, *driven:* Well, it was kind of—

WILLY: I was wondering if he'd remember you. *To Happy:* Imagine, man doesn't see him for ten, twelve years and gives him that kind of a welcome!

HAPPY: Damn right!

BIFF, *trying to return to the offensive:* Pop, look—

WILLY: You know why he remembered you, don't you? Because you impressed him in those days.

BIFF: Let's talk quietly and get this down to the facts, huh?

WILLY, *as though Biff had been interrupting:* Well, what happened? It's great news, Biff. Did he take you into his office or'd you talk in the waiting room?

BIFF: Well, he came in, see, and—

WILLY, *with a big smile:* What'd he say? Betcha he threw his arm around you.

BIFF: Well, he kinda—

WILLY: He's a fine man. *To Happy:* Very hard man to see, y'know.

HAPPY, *agreeing:* Oh, I know.

WILLY, *to Biff:* Is that where you had the drinks?

BIFF: Yeah, he gave me a couple of—no, no!

HAPPY, *cutting in:* He told him my Florida idea.

WILLY: Don't interrupt. *To Biff:* How'd he react to the Florida idea?

BIFF: Dad, will you give me a minute to explain?

WILLY: I've been waiting for you to explain since I sat down here! What happened? He took you into his office and what?

BIFF: Well—I talked. And—and he listened, see.

WILLY: Famous for the way he listens, y'know. What was his answer?

BIFF: His answer was— *He breaks off, suddenly angry.* Dad, you're not letting me tell you what I want to tell you!

WILLY, *accusing, angered:* You didn't see him, did you?

BIFF: I did see him!

WILLY: What'd you insult him or something? You insulted him, didn't you?

BIFF: Listen, will you let me out of it, will you just let me out of it!

HAPPY: What the hell!

WILLY: Tell me what happened!

BIFF, *to Happy:* I can't talk to him!

A single trumpet note jars the ear. The light of green leaves stains the house, which holds the air of night and a dream. Young Bernard enters and knocks on the door of the house.

YOUNG BERNARD, *frantically:* Mrs. Loman, Mrs. Loman!

HAPPY: Tell him what happened!

BIFF, *to Happy:* Shut up and leave me alone!

WILLY: No, no! You had to go and flunk math!

BIFF: What math? What're you talking about?

YOUNG BERNARD: Mrs. Loman, Mrs. Loman!

Linda appears in the house, as of old.

WILLY, *wildly:* Math, math, math!

BIFF: Take it easy, Pop!

YOUNG BERNARD: Mrs. Loman!

WILLY, *furiously:* If you hadn't flunked you'd've been set by now!

BIFF: Now look, I'm gonna tell you what happened, and you're going to listen to me.

YOUNG BERNARD: Mrs. Loman!

BIFF: I waited six hours—

HAPPY: What the hell are you saying?

BIFF: I kept sending in my name but he wouldn't see me. So finally he . . . *He continues unheard as light fades low on the restaurant.*

YOUNG BERNARD: Biff flunked math!

LINDA: No!

YOUNG BERNARD: Birnbaum flunked him! They won't graduate him!

LINDA: But they have to. He's gotta go to the university. Where is he? Biff! Biff!

YOUNG BERNARD: No, he left. He went to Grand Central.[9]

LINDA: Grand—You mean he went to Boston!

YOUNG BERNARD: Is Uncle Willy in Boston?

LINDA: Oh, maybe Willy can talk to the teacher. Oh, the poor, poor boy!

Light on house area snaps out.

BIFF, *at the table, now audible, holding up a gold fountain pen:* . . . so I'm washed up with Oliver, you understand? Are you listening to me?

WILLY, *at a loss:* Yeah, sure. If you hadn't flunked—

BIFF: Flunked what? What're you talking about?

WILLY: Don't blame everything on me! I didn't flunk math—you did! What pen?

HAPPY: That was awful dumb, Biff, a pen like that is worth—

WILLY, *seeing the pen for the first time:* You took Oliver's pen?

BIFF, *weakening:* Dad, I just explained it to you.

WILLY: You stole Bill Oliver's fountain pen!

BIFF: I didn't exactly steal it! That's just what I've been explaining to you!

HAPPY: He had it in his hand and just then Oliver walked in, so he got nervous and stuck it in his pocket!

WILLY: My God, Biff!

BIFF: I never intended to do it, Dad!

OPERATOR'S VOICE: Standish Arms, good evening!

WILLY, *shouting:* I'm not in my room!

BIFF, *frightened:* Dad, what's the matter? *He and Happy stand up.*

OPERATOR: Ringing Mr. Loman for you!

WILLY: I'm not there, stop it!

BIFF, *horrified, gets down on one knee before Willy:* Dad, I'll make good, I'll make good. *Willy tries to get to his feet. Biff holds him down.* Sit down now.

WILLY: No, you're no good, you're no good for anything.

BIFF: I am, Dad, I'll find something else, you understand? Now don't worry about anything. *He holds up Willy's face:* Talk to me, Dad.

OPERATOR: Mr. Loman does not answer. Shall I page him?

---

[9] New York City's Grand Central Station.

WILLY, *attempting to stand, as though to rush and silence the Operator:*   No, no, no!

HAPPY: He'll strike something, Pop.

WILLY: No, no . . .

BIFF, *desperately, standing over Willy:*   Pop, listen! Listen to me! I'm telling you something good. Oliver talked to his partner about the Florida idea. You listening? He—he talked to his partner, and he came to me . . . I'm going to be all right, you hear? Dad, listen to me, he said it was just a question of the amount!

WILLY: Then you . . . got it?

HAPPY: He's gonna be terrific, Pop!

WILLY, *trying to stand:*   Then you got it, haven't you? You got it! You got it!

BIFF, *agonized, holds Willy down:*   No, no. Look, Pop. I'm supposed to have lunch with them tomorrow. I'm just telling you this so you'll know that I can still make an impression, Pop. And I'll make good somewhere, but I can't go tomorrow, see?

WILLY: Why not? You simply—

BIFF: But the pen, Pop!

WILLY: You give it to him and tell him it was an oversight!

HAPPY: Sure, have lunch tomorrow!

BIFF: I can't say that—

WILLY: You were doing a crossword puzzle and accidentally used his pen!

BIFF: Listen, kid, I took those balls years ago, now I walk in with his fountain pen? That clinches it, don't you see? I can't face him like that! I'll try elsewhere.

PAGE'S VOICE: Paging Mr. Loman!

WILLY: Don't you want to be anything?

BIFF: Pop, how can I go back?

WILLY: You don't want to be anything, is that what's behind it?

BIFF, *now angry at Willy for not crediting his sympathy:*   Don't take it that way! You think it was easy walking into that office after what I'd done to him? A team of horses couldn't have dragged me back to Bill Oliver!

WILLY: Then why'd you go?

BIFF: Why did I go? Why did I go! Look at you! Look at what's become of you!

Off left, The Woman laughs.

WILLY: Biff, you're going to go to that lunch tomorrow, or—

BIFF: I can't go. I've got no appointment!

HAPPY: Biff, for . . . !

WILLY: Are you spiting me?

BIFF: Don't take it that way! Goddammit!

WILLY, *strikes Biff and falters away from the table:*   You rotten little louse! Are you spiting me?

THE WOMAN: Someone's at the door, Willy!

BIFF: I'm no good, can't you see what I am?

HAPPY, *separating them:*   Hey, you're in a restaurant! Now cut it out, both of you! *The girls enter.* Hello, girls, sit down.

The Woman laughs, off left.

MISS FORSYTHE: I guess we might as well. This is Letta.

THE WOMAN: Willy, are you going to wake up?

BIFF, *ignoring Willy:*   How're ya, miss, sit down. What do you drink?

MISS FORSYTHE: Letta might not be able to stay long.

LETTA: I gotta get up very early tomorrow. I got jury duty. I'm so excited! Were you fellows ever on a jury?

BIFF: No, but I been in front of them! *The girls laugh.* This is my father.

LETTA: Isn't he cute? Sit down with us, Pop.

HAPPY: Sit him down, Biff!

BIFF, *going to him:*   Come on, slugger, drink us under the table. To hell with it! Come on, sit down, pal.

On Biff's last insistence, Willy is about to sit.

THE WOMAN, *now urgently:*   Willy, are you going to answer the door!

The Woman's call pulls Willy back. He starts right, befuddled.

BIFF: Hey, where are you going?

WILLY: Open the door.

BIFF: The door?

WILLY: The washroom . . . the door . . . where's the door?

BIFF, *leading Willy to the left:*   Just go straight down.

Willy moves left.

THE WOMAN: Willy, Willy, are you going to get up, get up, get up, get up?

Willy exits left.

LETTA: I think it's sweet you bring your daddy along.

MISS FORSYTHE: Oh, he isn't really your father!

BIFF, *at left, turning to her resentfully:*   Miss Forsythe, you've just seen a prince walk by. A fine, troubled prince. A hard-working, unappreciated prince. A pal, you understand? A good companion. Always for his boys.

LETTA: That's so sweet.

HAPPY: Well, girls, what's the program? We're wasting time. Come on, Biff. Gather round. Where would you like to go?

BIFF: Why don't you do something for him?

HAPPY: Me!

BIFF: Don't you give a damn for him, Hap?

HAPPY: What're you talking about? I'm the one who—

BIFF: I sense it, you don't give a goddam about him. *He takes the rolled-up hose from his pocket and puts it on the table in front of Happy.* Look what I found in the cellar, for Christ's sake. How can you bear to let it go on?

HAPPY: Me? Who goes away? Who runs off and—

BIFF: Yeah, but he doesn't mean anything to you. You could help him—I can't! Don't you understand what I'm talking about? He's going to kill himself, don't you know that?

HAPPY: Don't I know it! Me!

BIFF: Hap, help him! Jesus . . . help him . . . Help me, help me, I can't bear to look at his face! *Ready to weep, he hurries out, up right.*

HAPPY, *starting after him:*   Where are you going?

MISS FORSYTHE: What's he so mad about?

HAPPY: Come on, girls, we'll catch up with him.

MISS FORSYTHE, *as Happy pushes her out:*   Say, I don't like that temper of his!

HAPPY: He's just a little overstrung, he'll be all right!

WILLY, *off left, as The Woman laughs:*   Don't answer! Don't answer!

LETTA: Don't you want to tell your father—

HAPPY: No, that's not my father. He's just a guy. Come on, we'll catch Biff, and, honey, we're going to paint this town! Stanley, where's the check! Hey, Stanley!

They exit. Stanley looks toward left.

STANLEY, *calling to Happy indignantly:*   Mr. Loman! Mr. Loman!

Stanley picks up a chair and follows them off. Knocking is heard off left. The Woman enters, laughing. Willy follows her. She is in a black slip; he is buttoning his shirt. Raw, sensuous music accompanies their speech.

WILLY: Will you stop laughing? Will you stop?

THE WOMAN: Aren't you going to answer the door? He'll wake the whole hotel.

WILLY: I'm not expecting anybody.

THE WOMAN: Whyn't you have another drink, honey, and stop being so damn self-centered?

WILLY: I'm so lonely.

THE WOMAN: You know you ruined me, Willy? From now on, whenever you come to the office, I'll see that you go right through to the buyers. No waiting at my desk any more, Willy. You ruined me.

WILLY: That's nice of you to say that.

THE WOMAN: Gee, you are self-centered! Why so sad? You are the saddest, self-centeredest soul I ever did see-saw. *She laughs. He kisses her.* Come on inside, drummer boy. It's silly to be dressing in the middle of the night. *As knocking is heard:* Aren't you going to answer the door?

WILLY: They're knocking on the wrong door.

THE WOMAN: But I felt the knocking. And he heard us talking in here. Maybe the hotel's on fire!

WILLY, *his terror rising:*   It's a mistake.

THE WOMAN: Then tell him to go away!

WILLY: There's nobody there.

THE WOMAN: It's getting on my nerves, Willy. There's somebody standing out there and it's getting on my nerves!

WILLY, *pushing her away from him:*   All right, stay in the bathroom here, and don't come out. I think there's a law in Massachusetts about it, so don't come out. It may be that new room clerk. He looked very mean. So don't come out. It's a mistake, there's no fire.

The knocking is heard again. He takes a few steps away from her, and she vanishes into the wing. The light follows him, and now he is facing Young Biff, who carries a suitcase. Biff steps toward him. The music is gone.

BIFF: Why didn't you answer?

WILLY: Biff! What are you doing in Boston?

BIFF: Why didn't you answer? I've been knocking for five minutes, I called you on the phone—

WILLY: I just heard you. I was in the bathroom and had the door shut. Did anything happen home?

BIFF: Dad—I let you down.

WILLY: What do you mean?

BIFF: Dad . . .

WILLY: Biffo, what's this about? *Putting his arm around Biff:* Come on, let's go downstairs and get you a malted.

BIFF: Dad, I flunked math.

WILLY: Not for the term?

BIFF: The term. I haven't got enough credits to graduate.

WILLY: You mean to say Bernard wouldn't give you the answers?

BIFF: He did, he tried, but I only got a sixty-one.

WILLY: And they wouldn't give you four points?

BIFF: Birnbaum refused absolutely. I begged him, Pop, but he won't give me those points. You gotta talk to him before they close the school. Because if he saw the kind of man you are, and you just talked to him in your way, I'm sure he'd come through for me. The class came right before practice, see, and I didn't go enough. Would you talk to him? He'd like you, Pop. You know the way you could talk.

WILLY: You're on. We'll drive right back.

BIFF: Oh, Dad, good work! I'm sure he'll change it for you!

WILLY: Go downstairs and tell the clerk I'm checkin' out. Go right down.

BIFF: Yes, sir! See, the reason he hates me, Pop—one day he was late for class so I got up at the blackboard and imitated him. I crossed my eyes and talked with a lithp.

WILLY, *laughing:*   You did? The kids like it?

BIFF: They nearly died laughing!

WILLY: Yeah? What'd you do?

BIFF: The thquare root of thixthy twee is . . . *Willy bursts out laughing; Biff joins him.* And in the middle of it he walked in!

Willy laughs and The Woman joins in offstage.

WILLY, *without hesitation:*   Hurry downstairs and—

BIFF: Somebody in there?

WILLY: No, that was next door.

The Woman laughs offstage.

BIFF: Somebody got in your bathroom!

WILLY: No, it's the next room, there's a party—

THE WOMAN, *enters, laughing. She lisps this:* Can I come in? There's something in the bathtub, Willy, and it's moving!

Willy looks at Biff, who is staring open-mouthed and horrified at The Woman.

WILLY: Ah—you better go back to your room. They must be finished painting by now. They're painting her room so I let her take a shower here. Go back, go back . . . *He pushes her.*

THE WOMAN, *resisting:*   But I've got to get dressed, Willy, I can't—

WILLY: Get out of here! Go back, go back . . . *Suddenly striving for the ordinary:* This is Miss Francis, Biff, she's a buyer. They're painting her room. Go back, Miss Francis, go back . . .

THE WOMAN: But my clothes, I can't go out naked in the hall!

WILLY, *pushing her offstage:*   Get outa here! Go back, go back!

Biff slowly sits down on his suitcase as the argument continues offstage.

THE WOMAN: Where's my stockings? You promised me stockings, Willy!

WILLY: I have no stockings here!

THE WOMAN: You had two boxes of size nine sheers for me, and I want them!

WILLY: Here, for God's sake, will you get outa here!

THE WOMAN: *enters holding a box of stockings:*   I just hope there's nobody in the hall. That's all I hope. *To Biff:* Are you football or baseball?

BIFF: Football.

THE WOMAN, *angry, humiliated:*   That's me too. G'night. *She snatches her clothes from Willy, and walks out.*

WILLY, *after a pause:*   Well, better get going. I want to get to the school first thing in the morning. Get my suits out of the closet. I'll get my valise. *Biff doesn't move.* What's the matter? *Biff remains motionless, tears falling.* She's a buyer. Buys for J. H. Simmons. She lives down the hall—they're painting. You don't imagine—*He breaks off. After a pause:* Now listen, pal, she's just a buyer. She sees merchandise in her room and they have to keep it looking just so . . . *Pause. Assuming command:* All right, get my suits. *Biff doesn't move.* Now stop crying and do as I say. I gave you an order. Biff, I gave you an order! Is that what you do when I give you an order? How dare you cry! *Putting his arm around Biff:* Now look, Biff, when you grow up you'll understand about these things. You mustn't—you mustn't overemphasize a thing like this. I'll see Birnbaum first thing in the morning.

BIFF: Never mind.

WILLY, *getting down beside Biff:*   Never mind! He's going to give you those points. I'll see to it.

BIFF: He wouldn't listen to you.

WILLY: He certainly will listen to me. You need those points for the U. of Virginia.

BIFF: I'm not going there.

WILLY: Heh? If I can't get him to change that mark you'll make it up in summer school. You've got all summer to—

BIFF, *his weeping breaking from him:*   Dad . . .

WILLY, *infected by it:*   Oh, my boy . . .

BIFF: Dad . . .

WILLY: She's nothing to me, Biff. I was lonely, I was terribly lonely.

BIFF: You—you gave her Mama's stockings! *His tears break through and he rises to go.*

WILLY, *grabbing for Biff:*   I gave you an order!

BIFF: Don't touch me, you—liar!

WILLY: Apologize for that!

BIFF: You fake! You phony little fake! You fake! *Overcome, he turns quickly and weeping fully goes out with his suitcase. Willy is left on the floor on his knees.*

WILLY: I gave you an order! Biff, come back here or I'll beat you! Come back here! I'll whip you!

Stanley comes quickly in from the right and stands in front of Willy.

WILLY, *shouts at Stanley:*   I gave you an order . . .

STANLEY: Hey, let's pick it up, pick it up, Mr. Loman. *He helps Willy to his feet.* Your boys left with the chippies. They said they'll see you home.

A second waiter watches some distance away.

WILLY: But we were supposed to have dinner together.

Music is heard, Willy's theme.

STANLEY: Can you make it?

WILLY: I'll—sure, I can make it. *Suddenly concerned about his clothes:* Do I—I look all right?

STANLEY: Sure, you look all right. *He flicks a speck off Willy's lapel.*

WILLY: Here—here's a dollar.

STANLEY: Oh, your son paid me. It's all right.

WILLY, *putting it in Stanley's hand:*   No, take it. You're a good boy.

STANLEY: Oh, no, you don't have to . . .

WILLY: Here—here's some more, I don't need it any more. *After a slight pause:* Tell me—is there a seed store in the neighborhood?

STANLEY: Seeds? You mean like to plant?

As Willy turns, Stanley slips the money back into his jacket pocket.

WILLY: Yes. Carrots, peas . . .

STANLEY: Well, there's hardware stores on Sixth Avenue, but it may be too late now.

WILLY, *anxiously:*   Oh, I'd better hurry. I've got to get some seeds. *He starts off to the right.* I've got to get some seeds, right away. Nothing's planted. I don't have a thing in the ground.

Willy hurries out as the light goes down. Stanley moves over to the right after him, watches him off. The other waiter has been staring at Willy.

STANLEY, *to the waiter:*   Well, whatta you looking at?

The waiter picks up the chairs and moves off right. Stanley takes the table and follows him. The light fades on this area. There is a long pause, the sound of the flute coming over. The light gradually rises on the kitchen, which is empty. Happy appears at the door of the house, followed by Biff. Happy is carrying a large bunch of long-stemmed roses. He enters the kitchen, looks around for Linda. Not seeing her, he turns to Biff, who is just outside the house door, and makes a gesture with his hands, indicating "Not here, I guess." He looks into the living-room and freezes. Inside, Linda, unseen, is seated. Willy's coat on her lap. She rises ominously and quietly and moves toward Happy, who backs up into the kitchen, afraid.

HAPPY: Hey, what're you doing up? *Linda says nothing but moves toward him implacably.* Where's Pop? *He keeps backing to the right, and now Linda is in full view in the doorway to the living-room.* Is he sleeping?

LINDA: Where were you?

HAPPY, *trying to laugh it off:*   We met two girls, Mom, very fine types. Here, we brought you some flowers. *Offering them to her:* Put them in your room, Ma.

She knocks them to the floor at Biff's feet. He has now come inside and closed the door behind him. She stares at Biff, silent.

HAPPY: Now what'd you do that for? Mom, I want you to have some flowers—

LINDA, *cutting Happy off, violently to Biff:*   Don't you care whether he lives or dies?

HAPPY, *going to the stairs:*   Come upstairs, Biff.

BIFF, *with a flare of disgust, to Happy:* Go away from me! *To Linda:* What do you mean, lives or dies? Nobody's dying around here, pal.

LINDA: Get out of my sight! Get out of here!

BIFF: I wanna see the boss.

LINDA: You're not going near him!

BIFF: Where is he? *He moves into the living-room and Linda follows.*

LINDA, *shouting after Biff:* You invite him for dinner. He looks forward to it all day—*Biff appears in his parents' bedroom, looks around, and exits*—and then you desert him there. There's no stranger you'd do that to!

HAPPY: Why? He had a swell time with us. Listen, when I—*Linda comes back into the kitchen*—desert him I hope I don't outlive the day!

LINDA: Get out of here!

HAPPY: Now look, Mom . . .

LINDA: Did you have to go to women tonight? You and your lousy rotten whores!

Biff re-enters the kitchen.

HAPPY: Mom, all we did was follow Biff around trying to cheer him up! *To Biff:* Boy, what a night you gave me!

LINDA: Get out of here, both of you, and don't come back! I don't want you tormenting him any more. Go on now, get your things together! *To Biff:* You can sleep in his apartment. *She starts to pick up the flowers and stops herself.* Pick up this stuff, I'm not your maid any more. Pick it up, you bum, you!

Happy turns his back to her in refusal. Biff slowly moves over and gets down on his knees, picking up the flowers.

LINDA: You're a pair of animals! Not one, not another living soul would have had the cruelty to walk out on that man in a restaurant!

BIFF, *not looking at her:* Is that what he said?

LINDA: He didn't have to say anything. He was so humiliated he nearly limped when he came in.

HAPPY: But, Mom, he had a great time with us—

BIFF, *cutting him off violently:* Shut-up!

Without another word, Happy goes upstairs.

LINDA: You! You didn't even go in to see if he was all right!

BIFF, *still on the floor in front of Linda, the flowers in his hand; with self-loathing:* No. Didn't. Didn't do a damned thing. How do you like that, heh? Left him babbling in a toilet.

LINDA: You louse. You . . .

BIFF: Now you hit it on the nose! *He gets up, throws the flowers in the waste-basket.* The scum of the earth, and you're looking at him!

LINDA: Get out of here!

BIFF: I gotta talk to the boss, Mom. Where is he?

LINDA: You're not going near him. Get out of this house!

BIFF, *with absolute assurance, determination:* No. We're gonna have an abrupt conversation, him and me.

LINDA: You're not talking to him!

Hammering is heard from outside the house, off right. Biff turns toward the noise.

LINDA, *suddenly pleading:*   Will you please leave him alone?
BIFF: What's he doing out there?
LINDA: He's planting the garden!
BIFF, *quietly:*   Now? Oh, my God!

Biff moves outside, Linda following. The light dies down on them and comes up on the center of the apron as Willy walks into it. He is carrying a flashlight, a hoe, and a handful of seed packets. He raps the top of the hoe sharply to fix it firmly, and then moves to the left, measuring off the distance with his foot. He holds the flashlight to look at the seed packets, reading off the instructions. He is in the blue of night.

WILLY: Carrots . . . quarter-inch apart. Rows . . . one-foot rows. *He measures it off.* One foot. *He puts down a package and measures off.* Beets. *He puts down another package and measures again.* Lettuce. *He reads the package, puts it down.* One foot—*He breaks off as Ben appears at the right and moves slowly down to him.* What a proposition, ts, ts. Terrific, terrific. 'Cause she's suffered, Ben, the woman has suffered. You understand me? A man can't go out the way he came in, Ben, a man has got to add up to something. You can't, you can't—*Ben moves toward him as though to interrupt.* You gotta consider, now. Don't answer so quick. Remember, it's a guaranteed twenty-thousand-dollar proposition. Now look, Ben, I want you to go through the ins and outs of this thing with me. I've got nobody to talk to, Ben, and the woman has suffered, you hear me?
BEN, *standing still, considering:*   What's the proposition?
WILLY: It's twenty thousand dollars on the barrelhead. Guaranteed, gilt-edged, you understand?
BEN: You don't want to make a fool of yourself. They might not honor the policy.
WILLY: How can they dare refuse? Didn't I work like a coolie to meet every premium on the nose? And now they don't pay off? Impossible!
BEN: It's called a cowardly thing, William.
WILLY: Why? Does it take more guts to stand here the rest of my life ringing up a zero?
BEN, *yielding:*   That's a point, William. *He moves, thinking, turns.* And twenty thousand—that *is* something one can feel with the hand, it is there.
WILLY, *now assured, with rising power:*   Oh, Ben, that's the whole beauty of it! I see it like a diamond, shining in the dark, hard and rough, that I can pick up and touch in my hand. Not like—like an appointment! This would not be another damned-fool appointment, Ben, and it changes all the aspects. Because he thinks I'm nothing, see, and so he spites me. But the funeral— *Straightening up:* Ben, that funeral will be massive! They'll come from Maine, Massachusetts, Vermont, New Hampshire! All the old-timers with the strange license plates—that boy will be thunder-stuck, Ben, because he never realized—I am known! Rhode Island, New York, New Jersey—I am known, Ben, and he'll see it with his eyes once and for all. He'll see what I am, Ben! He's in for a shock, that boy!
BEN, *coming down to the edge of the garden:*   He'll call you a coward.
WILLY, *suddenly fearful:*   No, that would be terrible.
BEN: Yes. And a damned fool.
WILLY: No, no, he mustn't, I won't have that! *He is broken and desperate.*
BEN: He'll hate you, William.

The gay music of the Boys is heard.

WILLY: Oh, Ben, how do we get back to all the great times? Used to be so full of light, and comradeship, the sleigh-riding in winter, and the ruddiness on his cheeks. And always some kind of good news coming up, always something nice coming up ahead. And never even let me carry the valises in the house, and simonizing, simonizing that little red car! Why, why can't I give him something and not have him hate me?

BEN: Let me think about it. *He glances at his watch.* I still have a little time. Remarkable proposition, but you've got to be sure you're not making a fool of yourself.

Ben drifts off upstage and goes out of sight. Biff comes down from the left.

WILLY, *suddenly conscious of Biff, turns and looks up at him, then begins picking up the packages of seeds in confusion:*   Where the hell is that seed? *Indignantly:*   You can't see nothing out here! They boxed in the whole goddam neighborhood!

BIFF: There are people all around here. Don't you realize that?

WILLY: I'm busy. Don't bother me.

BIFF, *taking the hoe from Willy:*   I'm saying good-by to you, Pop. *Willy looks at him, silent, unable to move.* I'm not coming back any more.

WILLY: Spite, spite, is the word of your undoing! And when you're down and out, remember what did it. When you're rotting somewhere beside the railroad tracks, remember, and don't you dare blame it on me!

BIFF: I'm not blaming it on you!

WILLY: I won't take the rap for this, you hear?

Happy comes down the stairs and stands on the bottom step, watching.

BIFF: That's just what I'm telling you!

WILLY, *sinking into a chair at the table, with full accusation:*   You're trying to put a knife in me—don't think I don't know what you're doing!

BIFF: All right, phony! Then let's lay it on the line. *He whips the rubber tube out of his pocket and puts it on the table.*

HAPPY: You crazy—

LINDA: Biff! *She moves to grab the hose, but Biff holds it down with his hand.*

BIFF: Leave it there! Don't move it!

WILLY, *not looking at it:*   What is that?

BIFF: You know goddam well what that is.

WILLY, *caged, wanting to escape:*   I never saw that.

BIFF: You saw it. The mice didn't bring it into the cellar! What is this supposed to do, make a hero out of you? This supposed to make me sorry for you?

WILLY: Never heard of it.

BIFF: There'll be no pity for you, you hear it? No pity!

WILLY, *to Linda:*   You hear the spite!

BIFF: No, you're going to hear the truth—what you are and what I am!

LINDA: Stop it!

WILLY: Spite!

HAPPY, *coming down toward Biff:*   You cut it now!

BIFF, *to Happy:*   The man don't know who we are! The man is gonna know! *To Willy:* We never told the truth for ten minutes in this house!

HAPPY: We always told the truth!

BIFF, *turning on him:*   You big blow, are you the assistant buyer? You're one of the two assistants to the assistant, aren't you?

HAPPY: Well, I'm practically—

BIFF: You're practically full of it! We all are! And I'm through with it. *To Willy:* Now hear this, Willy, this is me.

WILLY: I know you!

BIFF: You know why I had no address for three months? I stole a suit in Kansas City and I was in jail. *To Linda, who is sobbing:*   Stop crying. I'm through with it.

Linda turns away from them, her hands covering her face.

WILLY: I suppose that's my fault!

BIFF: I stole myself out of every good job since high school!

WILLY: And whose fault is that?

BIFF: And I never got anywhere because you blew me so full of hot air I could never stand taking orders from anybody! That's whose fault it is!

WILLY: I hear that!

LINDA: Don't, Biff!

BIFF: It's goddam time you heard that! I had to be boss big shot in two weeks, and I'm through with it!

WILLY: Then hang yourself! For spite, hang yourself!

BIFF: No! Nobody's hanging himself, Willy! I ran down eleven flights with a pen in my hand today. And suddenly I stopped, you hear me? And in the middle of that office building, do you hear this? I stopped in the middle of that building and I saw—the sky. I saw the things that I love in this world. The work and the food and time to sit and smoke. And I looked at the pen and said to myself, what the hell am I grabbing this for? Why am I trying to become what I don't want to be? What am I doing in an office, making a contemptuous, begging fool of myself, when all I want is out there, waiting for me the minute I say I know who I am! Why can't I say that, Willy? *He tries to make Willy face him, but Willy pulls away and moves to the left.*

WILLY, *with hatred, threateningly:*   The door of your life is wide open!

BIFF: Pop! I'm a dime a dozen, and so are you!

WILLY, *turning on him now in an uncontrolled outburst:*   I am not a dime a dozen! I am Willy Loman, and you are Biff Loman!

Biff starts for Willy, but is blocked by Happy. In his fury, Biff seems on the verge of attacking his father.

BIFF: I am not a leader of men, Willy, and neither are you. You were never anything but a hard-working drummer[10] who landed in the ash can like all the rest of them! I'm one dollar an hour, Willy! I tried seven states and couldn't raise it. A buck an hour! Do you gather my meaning? I'm not bringing home any prizes any more, and you're going to stop waiting for me to bring them home!

WILLY, *directly to Biff:*   You vengeful, spiteful mut!

Biff breaks from Happy. Willy, in fright, starts up the stairs, Biff grabs him.

BIFF, *at the peak of his fury:*   Pop, I'm nothing! I'm nothing, Pop. Can't you understand that? There's no spite in it any more. I'm just what I am, that's all.

Biff's fury has spent itself, and he breaks down, sobbing, holding on to Willy, who dumbly fumbles for Biff's face.

---

[10] Slang for a traveling salesman.

WILLY, *astonished:*   What're you doing? What're you doing? *To Linda:* Why is he crying?

BIFF, *crying, broken:*   Will you let me go, for Christ's sake? Will you take that phony dream and burn it before something happens? *Struggling to contain himself, he pulls away and moves to the stairs.* I'll go in the morning. Put him—put him to bed. *Exhausted, Biff moves up the stairs to his room.*

WILLY, *after a long pause, astonished, elevated:*   Isn't that—isn't that remarkable? Biff—he likes me!

LINDA: He loves you, Willy!

HAPPY, *deeply moved:*   Always did, Pop.

WILLY: Oh, Biff! *Staring wildly:* He cried! Cried to me. *He is choking with his love, and now cries out his promise:* That boy—that boy is going to be magnificent!

Ben appears in the light just outside the kitchen.

BEN: Yes, outstanding, with twenty thousand behind him.

LINDA, *sensing the racing of his mind, fearfully, carefully:*   Now come to bed, Willy. It's all settled now.

WILLY, *finding it difficult not to rush out of the house:*   Yes, we'll sleep. Come on. Go to sleep, Hap.

BEN: And it does take a great kind of a man to crack the jungle.

In accents of dread, Ben's idyllic music starts up.

HAPPY, *his arm around Linda:*   I'm getting married, Pop, don't forget it. I'm changing everything. I'm gonna run that department before the year is up. You'll see, Mom. *He kisses her.*

BEN: The jungle is dark but full of diamonds, Willy.

Willy turns, moves, listening to Ben.

LINDA: Be good, You're both good boys, just act that way, that's all.

HAPPY: 'Night, Pop. *He goes upstairs.*

LINDA, *to Willy:*   Come, dear.

BEN, *with greater force:*   One must go in to fetch a diamond out.

WILLY, *to Linda, as he moves slowly along the edge of the kitchen, toward the door:*   I just want to get settled down, Linda. Let me sit alone for a little.

LINDA, *almost uttering her fear:*   I want you upstairs.

WILLY, *taking her in his arms:*   In a few minutes, Linda. I couldn't sleep right now. Go on, you look awful tired. *He kisses her.*

BEN: Not like an appointment at all. A diamond is rough and hard to the touch.

WILLY: Go on now. I'll be right up.

LINDA: I think this is the only way, Willy.

WILLY: Sure, it's the best thing.

BEN: Best thing!

WILLY: The only way. Everything is gonna be—go on, kid, get to bed. You look so tired.

LINDA: Come right up.

WILLY: Two minutes.

Linda goes into the living-room, then reappears in her bedroom. Willy moves just outside the kitchen door.

WILLY: Loves me. *Wonderingly:* Always loved me. Isn't that a remarkable thing? Ben, he'll worship me for it!

BEN, *with promise:* It's dark there, but full of diamonds.

WILLY: Can you imagine that magnificence with twenty thousand dollars in his pocket?

LINDA, *calling from her room:* Willy! Come up!

WILLY, *calling into the kitchen:* Yes! Yes. Coming! It's very smart, you realize, that, don't you, sweetheart? Even Ben sees it. I gotta go, baby. 'By!' By! *Going over to Ben, almost dancing:* Imagine? When the mail comes he'll be ahead of Bernard again!

BEN: A perfect proposition all around.

WILLY: Did you see how he cried to me? Oh, if I could kiss him, Ben!

BEN: Time, William, time!

WILLY: Oh, Ben, I always knew one way or another we were gonna make it, Biff and I!

BEN, *looking at his watch:* The boat. We'll be late. *He moves slowly off into the darkness.*

WILLY, *elegiacally, turning to the house:* Now when you kick off, boy, I want a seventy-yard boot, and get right down the field under the ball, and when you hit, hit low and hit hard, because it's important, boy. *He swings around and faces the audience.* There's all kinds of important people in the stands, and the first thing you know . . . *Suddenly realizing he is alone:* Ben! Ben, where do I . . . ? *He makes a sudden movement of search.* Ben, how do I . . . ?

LINDA, *calling:* Willy, you coming up?

WILLY, *uttering a gasp of fear, whirling about as if to quiet her:* Sh! *He turns around as if to find his way; sounds, faces, voices, seem to be swarming in upon him and he flicks at them, crying,* Sh! Sh! *Suddenly music, faint and high, stops him. It rises in intensity, almost to an unbearable scream. He goes up and down on his toes, and rushes off around the house.* Shhh!

LINDA: Willy?

There is no answer. Linda waits. Biff gets up off his bed. He is still in his clothes. Happy sits up. Biff stands listening.

LINDA, *with real fear:* Willy, answer me! Willy!

There is the sound of a car starting and moving away at full speed.

LINDA: No!

BIFF, *rushing down the stairs:* Pop!

As the car speeds off, the music crashes down in a frenzy of sound, which becomes the soft pulsation of a single cello string. Biff slowly returns to his bedroom. He and Happy gravely don their jackets. Linda slowly walks out of her room. The music has developed into a dead march. The leaves of day are appearing over everything. Charley and Bernard, somberly dressed, appear and knock on the kitchen door. Biff and Happy slowly descend the stairs to the kitchen as Charley and Bernard enter. All stop a moment when Linda, in clothes of mourning, bearing a little bunch of roses, comes through the draped doorway into the kitchen. She goes to Charley and takes his arm. Now all move toward the audience, through the wall-line of the kitchen. At the limit of the apron, Linda lays down the flowers, kneels, and sits back on her heels. All stare down at the grave.

REQUIEM

CHARLEY: It's getting dark, Linda.

Linda doesn't react. She stares at the grave.

BIFF: How about it, Mom? Better get some rest, heh? They'll be closing the gate soon.

Linda makes no move. Pause.

HAPPY, *deeply angered:*   He had no right to do that. There was no necessity for it. We would've helped him.

CHARLEY, *grunting:*   Hmmm.

BIFF: Come along, Mom.

LINDA: Why didn't anybody come?

CHARLEY: It was a very nice funeral.

LINDA: But where are all the people he knew? Maybe they blame him.

CHARLEY: Naa. It's a rough world, Linda. They wouldn't blame him.

LINDA: I can't understand it. At this time especially. First time in thirty-five years we were just about free and clear. He only needed a little salary. He was even finished with the dentist.

CHARLEY: No man only needs a little salary.

LINDA: I can't understand it.

BIFF: There were a lot of nice days. When he'd come home from a trip; or on Sundays, making the stoop; finishing the cellar; putting on the new porch; when he built the extra bathroom; and put up the garage. You know something, Charley, there's more of him in that front stoop than in all the sales he ever made.

CHARLEY: Yeah. He was a happy man with a batch of cement.

LINDA: He was so wonderful with his hands.

BIFF: He had the wrong dreams. All, all, wrong.

HAPPY, *almost ready to fight Biff:*   Don't say that!

BIFF: He never knew who he was.

CHARLEY, *stopping Happy's movement and reply. To Biff:*   Nobody dast blame this man. You don't understand: Willy was a salesman. And for a salesman, there is no rock bottom to the life. He don't put a bolt to a nut, he don't tell you the law or give you medicine. He's a man way out there in the blue, riding on a smile and a shoeshine. And when they start not smiling back—that's an earthquake. And then you get yourself a couple of spots on your hat, and you're finished. Nobody dast blame this man. A salesman is got to dream, boy. It comes with the territory.

BIFF: Charley, the man didn't know who he was.

HAPPY, *infuriated:*   Don't say that!

BIFF: Why don't you come with me, Happy?

HAPPY: I'm not licked that easily. I'm staying right in this city, and I'm gonna beat this racket! *He looks at Biff, his chin set.* The Loman Brothers!

BIFF: I know who I am, kid.

HAPPY: All right, boy. I'm gonna show you and everybody else that Willy Loman did not die in vain. He had a good dream. It's the only dream you can have—to come out number-one man. He fought it out here, and this is where I'm gonna win it for him.

BIFF, *with a hopeless glance at Happy, bends toward his mother:* Let's go, Mom.

LINDA: I'll be with you in a minute. Go on, Charley. *He hesitates.* I want to, just for a minute. I never had a chance to say good-by.

Charley moves away, followed by Happy. Biff remains a slight distance up and left of Linda. She sits there, summoning herself. The flute begins, not far away, playing behind her speech.

LINDA: Forgive me, dear. I can't cry. I don't know what it is, but I can't cry. I don't understand it. Why did you ever do that? Help me, Willy, I can't cry. It seems to me that you're just on another trip. I keep expecting you. Willy, dear, I can't cry. Why did you do it? I search and search and I search, and I can't understand it, Willy. I made the last payment on the house today. Today, dear. And there'll be nobody home. *A sob rises in her throat.* We're free and clear. *Sobbing more fully, released:* We're free. *Biff comes slowly toward her.* We're free . . . We're free . . .

Biff lifts her to her feet and moves out up right with her in his arms. Linda sobs quietly. Bernard and Charley come together and follow them, followed by Happy. Only the music of the flute is left on the darkening stage as over the house the hard towers of the apartment buildings rise into sharp focus, and

The Curtain Falls

1949

Lorraine Hansberry
(1930–1965)

When it opened in 1959 Lorraine Hansberry's *A Raisin in the Sun* broke through the color barrier of American theater. The first play by a black woman on Broadway and the first to have a black director (Lloyd Richards), it was named Best Play of the Year by the New York Drama Critics Circle, chosen over works by Tennessee Williams, Eugene O'Neill, and Archibald MacLeish. While sharing with O'Neill and Williams a central interest in the American family, Hansberry transformed the conventions of American "kitchen table" drama.

Born in Chicago in 1930 Hansberry grew up in a middle-class African-American family. Her father, Carl Hansberry, ran a successful real-estate business in Chicago, served as U.S. Marshall, and ran unsuccessfully for U.S. Congress. Her mother, Nannie Perry, worked for years as a Republican ward organizer. Leading African-American intellectuals such as W. E. B. DuBois, Langston Hughes, and Paul Robeson were frequent visitors to the Hansberry home. These early associations nourished her vision and her art.

In 1938 Carl Hansberry challenged Chicago's segregationist real-estate covenants by buying a house in a white neighborhood. Lorraine was eight years old when a white mob threw a brick through the window of the living room in which she was sitting. A lower-court ruling evicted the Hansberrys from their new home, but, with the backing of the National Association for the Advancement of Colored People, they fought the case to the Supreme Court and won. But the bitterness of this experience ultimately led Carl Hansberry to choose exile from the United States. In 1946 he bought a house in Mexico and was making preparations to move his family when he died of a cerebral hemorrhage.

As Hansberry noted in a 1959 *New Yorker* interview, she believed that "American racism helped kill" her father. And while she shared her father's pessimism, she also saw new possibilities for freedom for her generation. Hansberry took heart in the growing activism of the civil rights movement during the 1950s and in her feeling that she belonged to an assertive world majority. *Raisin* embodies Hansberry's double sense of racial empowerment in the connection it draws between an African-American family's fight against poverty and segregation and the struggle of African nations to overthrow colonialism.

Hansberry's identification with Africa was fostered early. Her uncle William Leo Hansberry was a professor of African history at Howard University. He frequently visited his brother's Chicago home, bringing with him African students, many of whom were exiled from the colonial governments of their home countries. In 1950, after two years of study at the University of Wisconsin, Lorraine Hansberry moved to New York. Although the bohemian world of New York in the 1950s was a radical departure from the traditional Hansberry education at Howard University, during her apprentice years in New York she became increasingly engaged with the voices and issues she had first heard raised in her own home.

For Paul Robeson's radical newspaper *Freedom,* Hansberry wrote articles on African politics, African-American artists, and the early struggles of the civil rights movement. In 1952 she became an associate editor and attended the International Peace Congress in Montevideo, Uruguay, as Robeson's representative when the State Department revoked his passport because of his Communist sympathies. Hansberry spent the following year studying African history with W. E. B. DuBois at the Jefferson School for Social Sciences in New York. She met her future husband, Robert Nemiroff, on a picket line, protesting the exclusion of blacks from the New York University basketball team.

Following their marriage in 1953 Hansberry left *Freedom* in order to give full attention to writing plays. *Raisin* was completed in 1957. In her *New Yorker* interview, during the play's Broadway run, Hansberry explained the "intellectual point of view" from which she wrote: "I believe, with [playwright Sean] O'Casey, that real drama has to do with audience involvement and achieving the emotional transformation of people on the stage. I believe that ideas *can* be transmitted emotionally." By Hansberry's criterion of audience involvement, the successs of *Raisin* can perhaps best be measured by novelist James Baldwin's observation that "I had never in my life seen so many black people in the theater" (in his introduction to Hansberry's *To Be Young, Gifted and Black* [1970]).

The success and celebrity of *Raisin* gave Hansberry the opportunity to speak out publicly on civil rights. She was an active supporter of the Student Nonviolent Coordinating Committee's struggle to achieve desegregation in the South. She was commissioned to write a teleplay on slavery, for which she wrote *The Drinking Gourd* (1970). Hansberry's unsentimental treatment of the slave experience was evidently too frank for network executives and was never produced.

In 1963 the thirty-two-year-old Hansberry was diagnosed as having cancer. In the next two years she suffered debilitating rounds of radiation therapy while continuing to work on a number of dramatic projects. She completed drafts of two plays: a postnuclear-era drama, *What Use Are Flowers?* (1970), and *Les Blancs* (1970), about the nationalistic struggles of an African nation seeking to overthrow colonial rule. She began an "epic" work about the life of Haitian liberator Toussaint L'Ouverture and planned projects about the English writer, Mary Wollstonecraft, and about the Navajo.

Ultimately, however, only one more Hansberry play was brought to the stage during her lifetime. *The Sign in Sidney Brustein's Window* opened in October 1965 to violently mixed reviews. A study of the relationships between various intellectuals and artists living in New York City's Greenwich Village, *Sidney Brustein* asks how intellectual and artistic commitment can or should respond to oppression, whether against blacks, Jews, the poor, or homosexuals. *Sidney Brustein* closed after 101 performances in late 1965 on the night Hansberry died of cancer, at age thirty-four. "I think," she said in *To Be Young*, "the artist who is creating the realistic work imposes on it not only what *is* but what is *possible* . . . because that is part of reality too." The theater of Hansberry presented Americans with not only the reality of past and present racial strife in America but the possibility, even the necessity, of social and intellectual commitment to change.

Suggested Readings: *The Movement: Documentary of a Struggle for Equality*, 1964. *To Be Young, Gifted, and Black*, 1970. *Les Blancs: The Collected Last Plays of Lorraine Hansberry*, ed. R. Nemiroff, 1972. *A Raisin in the Sun and The Sign in Sidney Brustein's Window: Expanded Twenty-Fifth Anniversary Edition*, ed. R. Nemiroff, 1987. A. Cheney, *Lorraine Hansberry*, 1984.

Text Used: *A Raisin in the Sun*, 1959.

A RAISIN IN THE SUN

CHARACTERS

RUTH YOUNGER	JOSEPH ASAGAI
TRAVIS YOUNGER	GEORGE MURCHISON
WALTER LEE YOUNGER (BROTHER)	KARL LINDNER
BENEATHA YOUNGER	BOBO
LENA YOUNGER (MAMA)	MOVING MEN

The action of the play is set in Chicago's Southside, sometime between World War II and the present.

Act I
SCENE ONE: Friday morning.
SCENE TWO: The following morning.

Act II
SCENE ONE: Later, the same day.
SCENE TWO: Friday night, a few weeks later.
SCENE THREE: Moving day, one week later.

Act III: An hour later.

ACT I

SCENE ONE

The YOUNGER *living room would be a comfortable and well-ordered room if it were not for a number of indestructible contradictions to this state of being. Its furnishings are typical and undistinguished and their primary feature now is that they* have clearly had to accommodate the living of too many people for too many years—and they are tired. Still, we can see that at some time, a time probably no longer remembered by the family (except perhaps for MAMA), the furnishings of this room were actually selected with care and love and even hope—and brought to this apartment and arranged with taste and pride.

That was a long time ago. Now the once loved pattern of the couch upholstery has to fight to show itself from under acres of crocheted doilies and couch covers which have themselves finally come to be more important than the upholstery. And here a table or a chair has been moved to disguise the worn places in the carpet; but the carpet has fought back by showing its weariness, with depressing uniformity, elsewhere on its surface.

Weariness has, in fact, won in this room. Everything has been polished, washed, sat on, used, scrubbed too often. All pretenses but living itself have long since vanished from the very atmosphere of this room.

Moreover, a section of this room, for it is not really a room unto itself, though the landlord's lease would make it seem so, slopes backward to provide a small kitchen area, where the family prepares the meals that are eaten in the living room proper, which must also serve as dining room. The single window that has been provided for these "two" rooms is located in this kitchen area. The sole natural light the family may enjoy in the course of a day is only that which fights its way through this little window.

At left, a door leads to a bedroom which is shared by MAMA and her daughter, BENEATHA. At right, opposite, is a second room (which in the beginning of the life of this apartment was probably a breakfast room) which serves as a bedroom for WALTER and his wife, RUTH.

Time: Sometime between World War II and the present.

Place: Chicago's Southside.

At rise: It is morning dark in the living room. TRAVIS is asleep on the make-down bed at center. An alarm clock sounds from within the bedroom at right, and presently RUTH enters from that room and closes the door behind her. She crosses sleepily toward the window. As she passes her sleeping son she reaches down and shakes him a little. At the window she raises the shade and a dusky Southside morning light comes in feebly. She fills a pot with water and puts it on to boil. She calls to the boy, between yawns, in a slightly muffled voice.

RUTH is about thirty. We can see that she was a pretty girl, even exceptionally so, but now it is apparent that life has been little that she expected, and disappointment has already begun to hang in her face. In a few years, before thirty-five even, she will be known among her people as a "settled woman."

She crosses to her son and gives him a good, final, rousing shake.

RUTH: Come on now, boy, it's seven thirty! (*Her son sits up at last, in a stupor of sleepiness*) I say hurry up, Travis! You ain't the only person in the world got to use a bathroom! (*The child, a sturdy, handsome little boy of ten or eleven, drags himself out of the bed and almost blindly takes his towels and "today's clothes" from drawers and a closet and goes out to the bathroom, which is in an outside hall and which is shared by another family or families on the same floor. RUTH crosses to the bedroom door at right and opens it and calls in to her husband*) Walter Lee! . . . It's after seven thirty! Lemme see you do some waking up in there now! (*She waits*) You better get up from there, man! It's after seven thirty I tell you. (*She waits again*) All right, you just go ahead and lay there and next thing you know Travis be finished and Mr. Johnson'll be in there and you'll be fussing and cussing round here like a madman! And be late too! (*She waits, at the end of patience*) Walter Lee—it's time for you to GET UP!

(*She waits another second and then starts to go into the bedroom, but is apparently satisfied that her husband has begun to get up. She stops, pulls the door to, and returns to the kitchen area. She wipes her face with a moist cloth and runs her fingers through her sleep-disheveled hair in a vain effort and ties an apron around her housecoat. The bedroom door at right opens and her husband stands in the doorway in his pajamas, which are rumpled and mismated. He is a lean, intense young man in his middle thirties, inclined to quick nervous movements and erratic speech habits—and always in his voice there is a quality of indictment*)

WALTER: Is he out yet?

RUTH: What you mean *out?* He ain't hardly got in there good yet.

WALTER (*Wandering in, still more oriented to sleep than to a new day*): Well, what was you doing all that yelling for if I can't even get in there yet? (*Stopping and thinking*) Check coming today?

RUTH: They *said* Saturday and this is just Friday and I hopes to God you ain't going to get up here first thing this morning and start talking to me 'bout no money—'cause I 'bout don't want to hear it.

WALTER: Something the matter with you this morning?

RUTH: No—I'm just sleepy as the devil. What kind of eggs you want?

WALTER: Not scrambled. (RUTH *starts to scramble eggs*) Paper come? (RUTH *points impatiently to the rolled up* Tribune *on the table, and he gets it and spreads it out and vaguely reads the front page*) Set off another bomb yesterday.

RUTH (*Maximum indifference*): Did they?

WALTER (*Looking up*): What's the matter with you?

RUTH: Ain't nothing the matter with me. And don't keep asking me that this morning.

WALTER: Ain't nobody bothering you. (*Reading the news of the day absently again*) Say Colonel McCormick is sick.

RUTH (*Affecting tea-party interest*): Is he now? Poor thing.

WALTER (*Sighing and looking at his watch*): Oh, me. (*He waits*) Now what is that boy doing in that bathroom all this time? He is just going to have to start getting up earlier. I can't be being late to work on account of him fooling around in there.

RUTH (*Turning on him*): Oh, no he ain't going to be getting up no earlier no such thing! It ain't his fault that he can't go to bed no earlier nights 'cause he got a bunch of crazy good-for-nothing clowns sitting up running their mouths in what is supposed to be his bedroom after ten o'clock at night . . .

WALTER: That's what you mad about, ain't it? The things I want to talk about with my friends just couldn't be important in your mind, could they?

(*He rises and finds a cigarette in her handbag on the table and crosses to the little window and looks out, smoking and deeply enjoying this first one*)

RUTH (*Almost matter of factly, a complaint too automatic to deserve emphasis*): Why you always got to smoke before you eat in the morning?

WALTER (*At the window*): Just look at 'em down there . . . Running and racing to work . . . (*He turns and faces his wife and watches her a moment at the stove, and then, suddenly*) You look young this morning, baby.

RUTH (*Indifferently*): Yeah?

WALTER: Just for a second—stirring them eggs. Just for a second it was—you looked real young again. (*He reaches for her; she crosses away. Then, drily*) It's gone now—you look like yourself again!

RUTH: Man, if you don't shut up and leave me alone.

WALTER (*Looking out to the street again*):   First thing a man ought to learn in life is not to make love to no colored woman first thing in the morning. You all some eeeevil people at eight o'clock in the morning.

(TRAVIS *appears in the hall doorway, almost fully dressed and quite wide awake now, his towels and pajamas across his shoulders. He opens the door and signals for his father to make the bathroom in a hurry*)

TRAVIS (*Watching the bathroom*):   Daddy, come on! (WALTER *gets his bathroom utensils and flies out to the bathroom*)

RUTH: Sit down and have your breakfast, Travis.

TRAVIS: Mama, this is Friday. (*Gleefully*) Check coming tomorrow, huh?

RUTH: You get your mind off money and eat your breakfast.

TRAVIS (*Eating*):   This is the morning we supposed to bring the fifty cents to school.

RUTH: Well, I ain't got no fifty cents this morning.

TRAVIS: Teacher say we have to.

RUTH: I don't care what teacher say. I ain't got it. Eat your breakfast, Travis.

TRAVIS: I *am* eating.

RUTH: Hush up now and just eat!

(*The boy gives her an exasperated look for her lack of understanding, and eats grudgingly*)

TRAVIS: You think Grandmama would have it?

RUTH: No! And I want you to stop asking your grandmother for money, you hear me?

TRAVIS (*Outraged*):   Gaaaleee! I don't ask her, she just gimme it sometimes!

RUTH: Travis Willard Younger—I got too much on me this morning to be—

TRAVIS: Maybe Daddy—

RUTH: *Travis!*

(*The boy hushes abruptly. They are both quiet and tense for several seconds*)

TRAVIS (*Presently*):   Could I maybe go carry some groceries in front of the supermarket for a little while after school then?

RUTH: Just hush, I said. (*Travis jabs his spoon into his cereal bowl viciously, and rests his head in anger upon his fists*) If you through eating, you can get over there and make up your bed.

(*The boy obeys stiffly and crosses the room, almost mechanically, to the bed and more or less folds the bedding into a heap, then angrily gets his books and cap*)

TRAVIS (*Sulking and standing apart from her unnaturally*):   I'm gone.

RUTH (*Looking up from the stove to inspect him automatically*):   Come here. (*He crosses to her and she studies his head*) If you don't take this comb and fix this here head, you better! (TRAVIS *puts down his books with a great sigh of oppression, and crosses to the mirror. His mother mutters under her breath about his "stubbornness"*) 'Bout to march out of here with that head looking just like chickens slept in it! I just don't know where you get your stubborn ways . . . And get your jacket, too. Looks chilly out this morning.

TRAVIS (*With conspicuously brushed hair and jacket*):   I'm gone.

RUTH: Get carfare and milk money—(*Waving one finger*)—and not a single penny for no caps, you hear me?

TRAVIS (*With sullen politeness*):   Yes'm.

(*He turns in outrage to leave. His mother watches after him as in his frustration he approaches the door almost comically. When she speaks to him, her voice has become a very gentle tease*)

RUTH (*Mocking; as she thinks he would say it*):   Oh, Mama makes me so mad sometimes, I don't know what to do! (*She waits and continues to his back as he stands stock-still in front of the door*) I wouldn't kiss that woman good-bye for nothing in this world this morning! (*The boy finally turns around and rolls his eyes at her, knowing the mood has changed and he is vindicated; he does not, however, move toward her yet*) Not for nothing in this world! (*She finally laughs aloud at him and holds out her arms to him and we see that it is a way between them, very old and practiced. He crosses to her and allows her to embrace him warmly but keeps his face fixed with masculine rigidity. She holds him back from her presently and looks at him and runs her fingers over the features of his face. With utter gentleness—*) Now—whose little old angry man are you?

TRAVIS (*The masculinity and gruffness start to fade at last*):   Aw gaalee— Mama . . .

RUTH (*Mimicking*):   Aw—gaaaaalleeeee, Mama! (*She pushes him, with rough playfulness and finality, toward the door*) Get on out of here or you going to be late.

TRAVIS (*In the face of love, new aggressiveness*):   Mama, could I *please* go carry groceries?

RUTH: Honey, it's starting to get so cold evenings.

WALTER (*Coming in from the bathroom and drawing a make-believe gun from a make-believe holster and shooting at his son*):   What is it he wants to do?

RUTH: Go carry groceries after school at the supermarket.

WALTER: Well, let him go . . .

TRAVIS (*Quickly, to the ally*):   I *have* to—she won't gimme the fifty cents . . .

WALTER (*To his wife only*):   Why not?

RUTH (*Simply, and with flavor*):   'Cause we don't have it.

WALTER (*To RUTH only*):   What you tell the boy things like that for? (*Reaching down into his pants with a rather important gesture*) Here, son—

(*He hands the boy the coin, but his eyes are directed to his wife's.* TRAVIS *takes the money happily*)

TRAVIS: Thanks, Daddy.

(*He starts out.* RUTH *watches both of them with murder in her eyes.* WALTER *stands and stares back at her with defiance, and suddenly reaches into his pocket again on an afterthought*)

WALTER (*Without even looking at his son, still staring hard at his wife*):   In fact, here's another fifty cents . . . Buy yourself some fruit today—or take a taxi-cab to school or something!

TRAVIS: Whoopee—

(*He leaps up and clasps his father around the middle with his legs, and they face each other in mutual appreciation; slowly* WALTER LEE *peeks around the boy to catch the violent rays from his wife's eyes and draws his head back as if shot*)

WALTER: You better get down now—and get to school, man.

TRAVIS (*At the door*):   O.K. Good-bye.

(*He exits*)

WALTER (*After him, pointing with pride*):   That's *my* boy. (*She looks at him in disgust and turns back to her work*) You know what I was thinking 'bout in the bathroom this morning?

RUTH: No.

WALTER: How come you always try to be so pleasant!

RUTH: What is there to be pleasant 'bout!

WALTER: You want to know what I was thinking 'bout in the bathroom or not!

RUTH: I know what you thinking 'bout.

WALTER (*Ignoring her*):   'Bout what me and Willy Harris was talking about last night.

RUTH (*Immediately—a refrain*):   Willy Harris is a good-for-nothing loud-mouth.

WALTER: Anybody who talks to me has got to be a good-for-nothing loud-mouth, ain't he? And what you know about who is just a good-for-nothing loud-mouth? Charlie Atkins was just a "good-for-nothing loudmouth" too, wasn't he! When he wanted me to go in the dry-cleaning business with him. And now—he's grossing a hundred thousand a year. A hundred thousand dollars a year! You still call *him* a loudmouth!

RUTH (*Bitterly*):   Oh, Walter Lee . . .

(*She folds her head on her arms over the table*)

WALTER (*Rising and coming to her and standing over her*):   You tired, ain't you? Tired of everything. Me, the boy, the way we live—this beat-up hole—everything. Ain't you? (*She doesn't look up, doesn't answer*) So tired—moaning and groaning all the time, but you wouldn't do nothing to help, would you? You couldn't be on my side that long for nothing, could you?

RUTH: Walter, please leave me alone.

WALTER: A man needs for a woman to back him up . . .

RUTH: Walter—

WALTER: Mama would listen to you. You know she listen to you more than she do me and Bennie. She think more of you. All you have to do is just sit down with her when you drinking your coffee one morning and talking 'bout things like you do and—(*He sits down beside her and demonstrates graphically what he thinks her methods and tone should be*)—you just sip your coffee, see, and say easy like that you been thinking 'bout that deal Walter Lee is so interested in, 'bout the store and all, and sip some more coffee, like what you saying ain't really that important to you—And the next thing you know, she be listening good and asking you questions and when I come home—I can tell her the details. This ain't no fly-by-night proposition, baby. I mean we figured it out, me and Willy and Bobo.

RUTH (*With a frown*):   Bobo?

WALTER: Yeah. You see, this little liquor store we got in mind cost seventy-five thousand and we figured the initial investment on the place be 'bout thirty thousand, see. That be ten thousand each. Course, there's a couple of hundred you got to pay so's you don't spend your life just waiting for them clowns to let your license get approved—

RUTH: You mean graft?

WALTER (*Frowning impatiently*):   Don't call it that. See there, that just goes to show you what women understand about the world. Baby, don't *nothing* happen for you in this world 'less you pay *somebody* off!

RUTH: Walter, leave me alone! (*She raises her head and stares at him vigorously—then says more quietly*) Eat your eggs, they gonna be cold.

WALTER (*Straightening up from her and looking off*):   That's it. There you are. Man say to his woman: I got me a dream. His woman say: Eat your eggs. (*Sadly, but gaining in power*) Man say: I got to take hold of this here world, baby! And a woman will say: Eat your eggs and go to work. (*Passionately now*) Man say: I got to change my life, I'm choking to death, baby! And his woman say—(*In utter anguish as he brings his fists down on his thighs*)—Your eggs is getting cold!

RUTH (*Softly*):   Walter, that ain't none of our money.

WALTER (*Not listening at all or even looking at her*):   This morning, I was lookin' in the mirror and thinking about it . . . I'm thirty-five years old; I been married eleven years and I got a boy who sleeps in the living room—(*Very, very quietly*)—and all I got to give him is stories about how rich white people live . . .

RUTH: Eat your eggs, Walter.

WALTER (*Slams the table and jumps up*):—DAMN MY EGGS—DAMN ALL THE EGGS THAT EVER WAS!

RUTH: Then go to work.

WALTER (*Looking up at her*):   See—I'm trying to talk to you 'bout myself—(*Shaking his head with the repetition*)—and all you can say is eat them eggs and go to work.

RUTH (*Wearily*):   Honey, you never say nothing new. I listen to you every day, every night and every morning, and you never say nothing new. (*Shrugging*) So you would rather *be* Mr. Arnold than be his chauffeur. So—I would *rather* be living in Buckingham Palace.

WALTER: That is just what is wrong with the colored woman in this world . . . Don't understand about building their men up and making 'em feel like they somebody. Like they can do something.

RUTH (*Drily, but to hurt*):   There *are* colored men who do things.

WALTER: No thanks to the colored woman.

RUTH: Well, being a colored woman, I guess I can't help myself none.

(*She rises and gets the ironing board and sets it up and attacks a huge pile of rough-dried clothes, sprinkling them in preparation for the ironing and then rolling them into tight fat balls*)

WALTER (*Mumbling*):   We one group of men tied to a race of women with small minds!

(*His sister* BENEATHA *enters. She is about twenty, as slim and intense as her brother. She is not as pretty as her sister-in-law, but her lean, almost intellectual face has a handsomeness of its own. She wears a bright-red flannel nightie, and her thick hair stands wildly about her head. Her speech is a mixture of many things; it is different from the rest of the family's insofar as education has permeated her sense of English—and perhaps the Midwest rather than the South has finally—at last—won out in her inflection; but not altogether, because over all of it is a soft slurring and transformed use of vowels which is the decided influence of the Southside. She passes through the room without looking at either* RUTH *or*

WALTER *and goes to the outside door and looks, a little blindly, out to the bathroom. She sees that it has been lost to the Johnsons. She closes the door with a sleepy vengeance and crosses to the table and sits down a little defeated*)

BENEATHA: I am going to start timing those people.

WALTER: You should get up earlier.

BENEATHA (*Her face in her hands. She is still fighting the urge to go back to bed*):   Really—would you suggest dawn? Where's the paper?

WALTER (*Pushing the paper across the table to her as he studies her almost clinically, as though he had never seen her before*):   You a horrible-looking chick at this hour.

BENEATHA (*Drily*):   Good morning, everybody.

WALTER (*Senselessly*):   How is school coming?

BENEATHA (*In the same spirit*):   Lovely. Lovely. And you know, biology is the greatest. (*Looking up at him*) I dissected something that looked just like you yesterday.

WALTER: I just wondered if you've made up your mind and everything.

BENEATHA (*Gaining in sharpness and impatience*):   And what did I answer yesterday morning—and the day before that?

RUTH (*From the ironing board, like someone disinterested and old*):   Don't be so nasty, Bennie.

BENEATHA (*Still to her brother*):   And the day before that and the day before that!

WALTER (*Defensively*):   I'm interested in you. Something wrong with that? Ain't many girls who decide—

WALTER *and* BENEATHA: (*In unison*)—"to be a doctor."

(*Silence*)

WALTER: Have we figured out yet just exactly how much medical school is going to cost?

RUTH: Walter Lee, why don't you leave that girl alone and get out of here to work?

BENEATHA (*Exits to the bathroom and bangs on the door*):   Come on out of there, please!

(*She comes back into the room*)

WALTER (*Looking at his sister intently*):   You know the check is coming tomorrow.

BENEATHA (*Turning on him with a sharpness all her own*):   That money belongs to Mama, Walter, and it's for her to decide how she wants to use it. I don't care if she wants to buy a house or a rocket ship or just nail it up somewhere and look at it. It's hers. Not ours—*hers*.

WALTER (*Bitterly*):   Now ain't that fine! You just got your mother's interest at heart, ain't you, girl? You such a nice girl—but if Mama got that money she can always take a few thousand and help you through school too—can't she?

BENEATHA: I have never asked anyone around here to do anything for me!

WALTER: No! And the line between asking and just accepting when the time comes is big and wide—ain't it!

BENEATHA (*With fury*):   What do you want from me, Brother—that I quit school or just drop dead, which!

WALTER: I don't want nothing but for you to stop acting holy 'round here. Me and Ruth done made some sacrifices for you—why can't you do something for the family?

RUTH: Walter, don't be dragging me in it.

WALTER: You are in it—Don't you get up and go work in somebody's kitchen for the last three years to help put clothes on her back?

RUTH: Oh, Walter—that's not fair . . .

WALTER: It ain't that nobody expects you to get on your knees and say thank you, Brother; thank you, Ruth; thank you, Mama—and thank you, Travis, for wearing the same pair of shoes for two semesters—

BENEATHA (*Dropping to her knees*): Well—I *do*—all right?—thank everybody! And forgive me for ever wanting to be anything at all! (*Pursuing him on her knees across the floor*) FORGIVE ME, FORGIVE ME, FORGIVE ME!

RUTH: Please stop it! Your mama'll hear you.

WALTER: Who the hell told you you had to be a doctor? If you so crazy 'bout messing 'round with sick people—then go be a nurse like other women—or just get married and be quiet . . .

BENEATHA: Well—you finally got it said . . . It took you three years but you finally got it said. Walter, give up; leave me alone—it's Mama's money.

WALTER: *He was my father, too!*

BENEATHA: So what? He was mine, too—and Travis' grandfather—but the insurance money belongs to Mama. Picking on me is not going to make her give it to you to invest in any liquor stores—(*Underbreath, dropping into a chair*)—and I for one say, God bless Mama for that!

WALTER (*To* RUTH): See—did you hear? Did you hear?

RUTH: Honey, please go to work.

WALTER: Nobody in this house is ever going to understand me.

BENEATHA: Because you're a nut.

WALTER: Who's a nut?

BENEATHA: You—you are a nut. Thee is mad, boy.

WALTER (*Looking at his wife and his sister from the door, very sadly*): The world's most backward race of people, and that's a fact.

BENEATHA (*Turning slowly in her chair*): And then there are all those prophets who would lead us out of the wilderness—(WALTER *slams out of the house*)—into the swamps!

RUTH: Bennie, why you always gotta be pickin' on your brother? Can't you be a little sweeter sometimes? (*Door opens.* WALTER *walks in. He fumbles with his cap, starts to speak, clears throat, looks everywhere but at* RUTH. *Finally*):

WALTER (*To* RUTH): I need some money for carfare.

RUTH (*Looks at him, then warms; teasing, but tenderly*): Fifty cents? (*She goes to her bag and gets money*) Here—take a taxi!

(WALTER *exits.* MAMA *enters. She is a woman in her early sixties, full-bodied and strong. She is one of those women of a certain grace and beauty who wear it so unobtrusively that it takes a while to notice. Her dark-brown face is surrounded by the total whiteness of her hair, and being a woman who has adjusted to many things in life and overcome many more, her face is full of strength. She has, we can see, wit and faith of a kind that keep her eyes lit and full of interest and expectancy. She is, in a word, a beautiful woman. Her bearing is perhaps most like the noble bearing of the women of the Hereros of Southwest Africa—rather as if she imagines that as she walks she still bears a basket or a vessel upon her head. Her speech, on the other hand, is as careless as her carriage is precise— she is inclined to slur everything—but her voice is perhaps not so much quiet as simply soft)*

MAMA: Who that 'round here slamming doors at this hour?

(She crosses through the room, goes to the window, opens it, and brings in a feeble little plant growing doggedly in a small pot on the window sill. She feels the dirt and puts it back out)

RUTH: That was Walter Lee. He and Bennie was at it again.

MAMA: My children and they tempers. Lord, if this little old plant don't get more sun than it's been getting it ain't never going to see spring again. *(She turns from the window)* What's the matter with you this morning, Ruth? You looks right peaked. You aiming to iron all them things? Leave some for me. I'll get to 'em this afternoon. Bennie honey, it's too drafty for you to be sitting 'round half dressed. Where's your robe?

BENEATHA: In the cleaners.

MAMA: Well, go get mine and put it on.

BENEATHA: I'm not cold, Mama, honest.

MAMA: I know—but you so thin . . .

BENEATHA *(Irritably)*:   Mama, I'm not cold.

MAMA *(Seeing the make-down bed as* TRAVIS *has left it)*:   Lord have mercy, look at that poor bed. Bless his heart—he tries, don't he?

(She moves to the bed TRAVIS *has sloppily made up)*

RUTH: No—he don't half try at all 'cause he knows you going to come along behind him and fix everything. That's just how come he don't know how to do nothing right now—you done spoiled that boy so.

MAMA *(Folding bedding)*:   Well—he's a little boy. Ain't supposed to know 'bout housekeeping. My baby, that's what he is. What you fix for his breakfast this morning?

RUTH *(Angrily)*:   I feed my son, Lena!

MAMA: I ain't meddling—*(Underbreath; busy-bodyish)* I just noticed all last week he had cold cereal, and when it starts getting this chilly in the fall a child ought to have some hot grits or something when he goes out in the cold—

RUTH *(Furious)*:   I gave him hot oats—is that all right!

MAMA: I ain't meddling. *(Pause)* Put a lot of nice butter on it? (RUTH *shoots her an angry look and does not reply)* He likes lots of butter.

RUTH *(Exasperated)*:   Lena—

MAMA *(To* BENEATHA. MAMA *is inclined to wander conversationally sometimes)*: What was you and your brother fussing 'bout this morning?

BENEATHA: It's not important, Mama.

(She gets up and goes to look out at the bathroom, which is apparently free, and she picks up her towels and rushes out)

MAMA: What was they fighting about?

RUTH: Now you know as well as I do.

MAMA *(Shaking her head)*:   Brother still worrying hisself sick about that money?

RUTH: You know he is.

MAMA: You had breakfast?

RUTH: Some coffee.

MAMA: Girl, you better start eating and looking after yourself better. You almost thin as Travis.

RUTH: Lena—

MAMA: Un-hunh?

RUTH: What are you going to do with it?

MAMA: Now don't you start, child. It's too early in the morning to be talking about money. It ain't Christian.

RUTH: It's just that he got his heart set on that store—

MAMA: You mean that liquor store that Willy Harris want him to invest in?

RUTH: Yes—

MAMA: We ain't no business people, Ruth. We just plain working folks.

RUTH: Ain't nobody business people till they go into business. Walter Lee say colored people ain't never going to start getting ahead till they start gambling on some different kinds of things in the world—investments and things.

MAMA: What done got into you girl? Walter Lee done finally sold you on investing.

RUTH: No, Mama, something is happening between Walter and me. I don't know what it is—but he needs something—something I can't give him any more. He needs this chance, Lena.

MAMA (*Frowning deeply*):   But liquor, honey—

RUTH: Well—like Walter say—I spec people going to always be drinking themselves some liquor.

MAMA: Well—whether they drinks it or not ain't none of my business. But whether I go into business selling it to 'em *is,* and I don't want that on my ledger this late in life. (*Stopping suddenly and studying her daughter-in-law*) Ruth Younger, what's the matter with you today? You look like you could fall over right there.

RUTH: I'm tired.

MAMA: Then you better stay home from work today.

RUTH: I can't stay home. She'd be calling up the agency and screaming at them, "My girl didn't come in today—send me somebody! My girl didn't come in!" Oh, she just have a fit . . .

MAMA: Well, let her have it. I'll just call her up and say you got the flu—

RUTH (*Laughing*):   Why the flu?

MAMA: 'Cause it sounds respectable to 'em. Something white people get, too. They know 'bout the flu. Otherwise they think you been cut up or something when you tell 'em you sick.

RUTH: I got to go in. We need the money.

MAMA: Somebody would of thought my children done all but starved to death the way they talk about money here late. Child, we got a great big old check coming tomorrow.

RUTH (*Sincerely, but also self-righteously*):   Now that's your money. It ain't got nothing to do with me. We all feel like that—Walter and Bennie and me—even Travis.

MAMA (*Thoughtfully, and suddenly very far away*):   Ten thousand dollars—

RUTH: Sure is wonderful.

MAMA: Ten thousand dollars.

RUTH: You know what you should do, Miss Lena? You should take yourself a trip somewhere. To Europe or South America or someplace—

MAMA (*Throwing up her hands at the thought*):   Oh, child!

RUTH: I'm serious. Just pack up and leave! Go on away and enjoy yourself some. Forget about the family and have yourself a ball for once in your life—

MAMA (*Drily*):   You sound like I'm just about ready to die. Who'd go with me? What I look like wandering 'round Europe by myself?

RUTH: Shoot—these here rich white women do it all the time. They don't think nothing of packing up they suitcases and piling on one of them big steamships and—swoosh!—they gone, child.

MAMA: Something always told me I wasn't no rich white woman.

RUTH: Well—what are you going to do with it then?

MAMA: I ain't rightly decided. (*Thinking. She speaks now with emphasis*) Some of it got to be put away for Beneatha and her schoolin'—and ain't nothing going to touch that part of it. Nothing. (*She waits several seconds, trying to make up her mind about something, and looks at* RUTH *a little tentatively before going on*) Been thinking that we maybe could meet the notes on a little old two-story somewhere, with a yard where Travis could play in the summertime, if we use part of the insurance for a down payment and everybody kind of pitch in. I could maybe take on a little day work again, few days a week—

RUTH (*Studying her mother-in-law furtively and concentrating on her ironing, anxious to encourage without seeming to*):   Well, Lord knows, we've put enough rent into this here rat trap to pay for four houses by now . . .

MAMA (*Looking up at the words "rat trap" and then looking around and leaning back and sighing—in a suddenly reflective mood—*):   "Rat trap"—yes, that's all it is. (*Smiling*) I remember just as well the day me and Big Walter moved in here. Hadn't been married but two weeks and wasn't planning on living here no more than a year. (*She shakes her head at the dissolved dream*) We was going to set away, little by little, don't you know, and buy a little place out in Morgan Park. We had even picked out the house. (*Chuckling a little*) Looks right dumpy today. But Lord, child, you should know all the dreams I had 'bout buying that house and fixing it up and making me a little garden in the back—(*She waits and stops smiling*) And didn't none of it happen.

(*Dropping her hands in a futile gesture*)

RUTH (*Keeps her head down, ironing*):   Yes, life can be a barrel of disappointments, sometimes.

MAMA: Honey, Big Walter would come in here some nights back then and slump down on that couch there and just look at the rug, and look at me and look at the rug and then back at me—and I'd know he was down then . . . really down. (*After a second very long and thoughtful pause; she is seeing back to times that only she can see*) And then, Lord, when I lost that baby—little Claude—I almost thought I was going to lose Big Walter too. Oh, that man grieved hisself! He was one man to love his children.

RUTH: Ain't nothin' can tear at you like losin' your baby.

MAMA: I guess that's how come that man finally worked hisself to death like he done. Like he was fighting his own war with this here world that took his baby from him.

RUTH: He sure was a fine man, all right. I always liked Mr. Younger.

MAMA: Crazy 'bout his children! God knows there was plenty wrong with Walter Younger—hard-headed, mean, kind of wild with women—plenty wrong with him. But he sure loved his children. Always wanted them to have something—be something. That's where Brother gets all these notions, I reckon. Big Walter used to say, he'd get right wet in the eyes sometimes, lean his head back with the water standing in his eyes and say, "Seem like God didn't see fit to give the black man nothing but dreams—but He did give us children to make them dreams seem worth while." (*She smiles*) He could talk like that, don't you know—

RUTH: Yes, he sure could. He was a good man, Mr. Younger.

MAMA: Yes, a fine man—just couldn't never catch up with his dreams, that's all.

(BENEATHA *comes in, brushing her hair and looking up to the ceiling, where the sound of a vacuum cleaner has started up*)

BENEATHA: What could be so dirty on that woman's rugs that she has to vacuum them every single day?

RUTH: I wish certain young women 'round here who I could name would take inspiration about certain rugs in a certain apartment I could also mention.

BENEATHA (*Shrugging*): How much cleaning can a house need, for Christ's sakes.

MAMA (*Not liking the Lord's name used thus*): Bennie!

RUTH: Just listen to her—just listen!

BENEATHA: Oh, God!

MAMA: If you use the Lord's name just one more time—

BENEATHA (*A bit of a whine*): Oh, Mama—

RUTH: Fresh—just fresh as salt, this girl!

BENEATHA (*Drily*): Well—if the salt loses its savor—

MAMA: Now that will do. I just ain't going to have you 'round here reciting the scriptures in vain—you hear me?

BENEATHA: How did I manage to get on everybody's wrong side by just walking into a room?

RUTH: If you weren't so fresh—

BENEATHA: Ruth, I'm twenty years old.

MAMA: What time you be home from school today?

BENEATHA: Kind of late. (*With enthusiasm*) Madeline is going to start my guitar lessons today.

(MAMA *and* RUTH *look up with the same expression*)

MAMA: Your *what* kind of lessons?

BENEATHA: Guitar.

RUTH: Oh, Father!

MAMA: How come you done taken it in your mind to learn to play the guitar?

BENEATHA: I just want to, that's all.

MAMA (*Smiling*): Lord, child, don't you know what to get tired of this now—like you got tired of that little do with yourself? How long it going to be before you play-acting group you joined last year? (*Looking at* RUTH) And what was it the year before that?

RUTH: The horseback-riding club for which she bought that fifty-five-dollar riding habit that's been hanging in the closet ever since!

MAMA (*To* BENEATHA): Why you got to flit so from one thing to another, baby?

BENEATHA (*Sharply*): I just want to learn to play the guitar. Is there anything wrong with that?

MAMA: Ain't nobody trying to stop you. I just wonders sometimes why you has to flit so from one thing to another all the time. You ain't never done nothing with all that camera equipment you brought home—

BENEATHA: I don't flit! I—I experiment with different forms of expression—

RUTH: Like riding a horse?

BENEATHA: —People have to express themselves one way or another.

MAMA: What is it you want to express?

BENEATHA (*Angrily*): Me! (MAMA *and* RUTH *look at each other and burst into raucous laughter*) Don't worry—I don't expect you to understand.

MAMA (*To change the subject*): Who you going out with tomorrow night?

BENEATHA (*With displeasure*): George Murchison again.

MAMA (*Pleased*): Oh—you getting a little sweet on him?

RUTH: You ask me, this child ain't sweet on nobody but herself—(*Under-breath*) Express herself!

(*They laugh*)

BENEATHA: Oh—I like George all right, Mama. I mean I like him enough to go out with him and stuff, but—

RUTH (*For devilment*): What does *and stuff* mean?

BENEATHA: Mind your own business.

MAMA: Stop picking at her now, Ruth. (*She chuckles—then a suspicious sudden look at her daughter as she turns in her chair for emphasis*) What DOES it mean?

BENEATHA (*Wearily*): Oh, I just mean I couldn't ever really be serious about George. He's—he's so shallow.

RUTH: Shallow—what do you mean he's shallow? He's *Rich!*

MAMA: Hush, Ruth.

BENEATHA: I know he's rich. He knows he's rich, too.

RUTH: Well—what other qualities a man got to have to satisfy you, little girl?

BENEATHA: You wouldn't even begin to understand. Anybody who married Walter could not possibly understand.

MAMA (*Outraged*): What kind of way is that to talk about your brother?

BENEATHA: Brother is a flip—let's face it.

MAMA (*To* RUTH, *helplessly*): What's a flip?

RUTH (*Glad to add kindling*): She's saying he's crazy.

BENEATHA: Not crazy. Brother isn't really crazy yet—he—he's an elaborate neurotic.

MAMA: Hush your mouth!

BENEATHA: As for George. Well. George looks good—he's got a beautiful car and he takes me to nice places and, as my sister-in-law says, he is probably the richest boy I will ever get to know and I even like him sometimes—but if the Youngers are sitting around waiting to see if their little Bennie is going to tie up the family with the Murchisons, they are wasting their time.

RUTH: You mean you wouldn't marry George Murchison if he asked you someday? That pretty, rich thing? Honey, I knew you was odd—

BENEATHA: No I would not marry him if all I felt for him was what I feel now. Besides, George's family wouldn't really like it.

MAMA: Why not?

BENEATHA: Oh, Mama—The Murchisons are honest-to-God-real-*live*-rich colored people, and the only people in the world who are more snobbish than rich white people are rich colored people. I thought everybody knew that. I've met Mrs. Murchison. She's a scene!

MAMA: You must not dislike people 'cause they well off, honey.

BENEATHA: Why not? It makes just as much sense as disliking people 'cause they are poor, and lots of people do that.

RUTH (*A wisdom-of-the-ages manner. To* MAMA):   Well, she'll get over some of this—

BENEATHA: Get over it? What are you talking about, Ruth? Listen, I'm going to be a doctor. I'm not worried about who I'm going to marry yet—if I ever get married.

MAMA *and* RUTH: *If!*

MAMA: Now, Bennie—

BENEATHA: Oh, I probably will . . . but first I'm going to be a doctor, and George, for one, still thinks that's pretty funny. I couldn't be bothered with that. I am going to be a doctor and everybody around here better understand that!

MAMA (*Kindly*):   'Course you going to be a doctor, honey, God willing.

BENEATHA (*Drily*):   God hasn't got a thing to do with it.

MAMA: Beneatha—that just wasn't necessary.

BENEATHA: Well—neither is God. I get sick of hearing about God.

MAMA: Beneatha!

BENEATHA: I mean it! I'm just tired of hearing about God all the time. What has He got to do with anything? Does he pay tuition?

MAMA: You 'bout to get your fresh little jaw slapped!

RUTH: That's just what she needs, all right!

BENEATHA: Why? Why can't I say what I want to around here, like everybody else?

MAMA: It don't sound nice for a young girl to say things like that—you wasn't brought up that way. Me and your father went to trouble to get you and Brother to church every Sunday.

BENEATHA: Mama, you don't understand. It's all a matter of ideas, and God is just one idea I don't accept. It's not important. I am not going out and be immoral or commit crimes because I don't believe in God. I don't even think about it. It's just that I get tired of Him getting credit for all the things the human race achieves through its own stubborn effort. There simply is no blasted God—there is only man and it is *he* who makes miracles!

(MAMA *absorbs this speech, studies her daughter and rises slowly and crosses to* BENEATHA *and slaps her powerfully across the face. After, there is only silence and the daughter drops her eyes from her mother's face, and* MAMA *is very tall before her*)

MAMA: Now—you say after me, in my mother's house there is still God. (*There is a long pause and* BENEATHA *stares at the floor wordlessly.* MAMA *repeats the phrase with precision and cool emotion*) In my mother's house there is still God.

BENEATHA: In my mother's house there is still God.

(*A long pause*)

MAMA (*Walking away from* BENEATHA, *too disturbed for triumphant posture.*

Stopping and turning back to her daughter):   There are some ideas we ain't going to have in this house. Not long as I am at the head of this family.

BENEATHA: Yes, ma'am.

(MAMA *walks out of the room*)

RUTH (*Almost gently, with profound understanding*):   You think you a woman, Bennie—but you still a little girl. What you did was childish—so you got treated like a child.

BENEATHA: I see. (*Quietly*) I also see that everybody thinks it's all right for Mama to be a tyrant. But all the tyranny in the world will never put a God in the heavens!

(*She picks up her books and goes out. Pause*)

RUTH (*Goes to* MAMA'S *door*):   She said she was sorry.

MAMA (*Coming out, going to her plant*):   They frightens me, Ruth. My children.

RUTH: You got good children, Lena. They just a little off sometimes—but they're good.

MAMA: No—there's something come down between me and them that don't let us understand each other and I don't know what it is. One done almost lost his mind thinking 'bout money all the time and the other done commence to talk about things I can't seem to understand in no form or fashion. What is it that's changing, Ruth?

RUTH (*Soothingly, older than her years*):   Now . . . you taking it all too seriously. You just got strong-willed children and it takes a strong woman like you to keep 'em in hand.

MAMA (*Looking at her plant and sprinkling a little water on it*):   They spirited all right, my children. Got to admit they got spirit—Bennie and Walter. Like this little old plant that ain't never had enough sunshine or nothing—and look at it . . .

(*She has her back to* RUTH, *who has had to stop ironing and lean against something and put the back of her hand to her forehead*)

RUTH (*Trying to keep* MAMA *from noticing*):   You . . . sure . . . loves that little old thing, don't you? . . .

MAMA: Well, I always wanted me a garden like I used to see sometimes at the back of the houses down home. This plant is close as I ever got to having one. (*She looks out of the window as she replaces the plant*) Lord, ain't nothing as dreary as the view from this window on a dreary day, is there? Why ain't you singing this morning, Ruth? Sing that "No Ways Tired." That song always lifts me up so—(*She turns at last to see that* RUTH *has slipped quietly to the floor, in a state of semiconsciousness*) Ruth! Ruth honey—what's the matter with you . . . Ruth!

Curtain

SCENE TWO

It is the following morning; a Saturday morning, and house cleaning is in progress at the YOUNGERS. *Furniture has been shoved hither and yon and* MAMA *is giving the kitchen-area walls a washing down.* BENEATHA, *in dungarees, with a handkerchief tied around her face, is spraying insecticide into the cracks in the walls. As they work, the radio is on and a Southside disk-jockey program is inappropriately filling the house with a rather exotic saxophone blues.* TRAVIS, *the sole idle one, is leaning on his arms, looking out of the window.*

TRAVIS: Grandmama, that stuff Bennie is using smells awful. Can I go downstairs, please?

MAMA: Did you get all them chores done already? I ain't seen you doing much.

TRAVIS: Yes'm—finished early. Where did Mama go this morning?

MAMA (*Looking at* BENEATHA):   She had to go on a little errand.

(*The phone rings.* BENEATHA *runs to answer it and reaches it before* WALTER, *who has entered from bedroom*)

TRAVIS: Where?

MAMA: To tend to her business.

BENEATHA: Haylo . . . (*Disappointed*) Yes, he is. (*She tosses the phone to* WALTER, *who barely catches it*) It's Willie Harris again.

WALTER (*As privately as possible under* MAMA'S *gaze*):   Hello, Willie. Did you get the papers from the lawyer? . . . No, not yet. I told you the mailman doesn't get here till ten-thirty . . . No, I'll come there . . . Yeah! Right away. (*He hangs up and goes for his coat*)

BENEATHA: Brother, where did Ruth go?

WALTER (*As he exits*):   How should I know!

TRAVIS: Aw come on, Grandma. Can I go outside?

MAMA: Oh, I guess so. You stay right in front of the house, though, and keep a good lookout for the postman.

TRAVIS: Yes'm. (*He darts into bedroom for stickball and bat, reenters, and sees* BENEATHA *on her knees spraying under sofa with behind upraised. He edges closer to the target, takes aim, and lets her have it. She screams*) Leave them poor little cockroaches alone, they ain't bothering you none! (*He runs as she swings the spraygun at him viciously and playfully*) Grandma! Grandma!

MAMA: Look out there, girl, before you be spilling some of that stuff on that child!

TRAVIS (*Safely behind the bastion of* MAMA):   That's right—look out, now! (*He exits*)

BENEATHA (*Drily*): I can't imagine that it would hurt him—it has never hurt the roaches.

MAMA: Well, little boys' hides ain't as tough as Southside roaches. You better get over there behind the bureau. I seen one marching out of there like Napoleon yesterday.

BENEATHA: There's really only one way to get rid of them, Mama.—

MAMA: How?

BENEATHA: Set fire to the building! Mama, where did Ruth go?

MAMA (*Looking at her with meaning*):   To the doctor, I think.

BENEATHA: The doctor? What's the matter? (*They exchange glances*) You don't think—

MAMA (*With her sense of drama*):   Now I ain't saying what I think. But I ain't never been wrong 'bout a woman neither.

(*The phone rings*)

BENEATHA (*At the phone*): Hay-lo . . . (*Pause, and a moment of recognition*) Well—when did you get back! . . . And how was it? . . . Of course I've missed you—in my way . . . This morning? No . . . house cleaning and all that and Mama hates it if I let people come over when the house is like this . . . You *have?* Well, that's different . . . What is it—Oh, what the hell, come on over . . . Right, see you then. *Arrividerci.*

(*She hangs up*)

MAMA (*Who has listened vigorously, as is her habit*): Who is that you inviting over here with this house looking like this? You ain't got the pride you was born with!

BENEATHA: Asagai doesn't care how houses look, Mama—he's an intellectual.

MAMA: *Who?*

BENEATHA: Asagai—Joseph Asagai. He's an African boy I met on campus. He's been studying in Canada all summer.

MAMA: What's his name?

BENEATHA: Asagai, Joseph. Ah-sah-guy . . . He's from Nigeria.

MAMA: Oh, that's the little country that was founded by slaves way back . . .

BENEATHA: No, Mama—that's Liberia.

MAMA: I don't think I never met no African before.

BENEATHA: Well, do me a favor and don't ask him a whole lot of ignorant questions about Africans. I mean, do they wear clothes and all that—

MAMA: Well, now, I guess if you think we so ignorant 'round here maybe you shouldn't bring your friends here—

BENEATHA: It's just that people ask such crazy things. All anyone seems to know about when it comes to Africa is Tarzan—

MAMA (*Indignantly*): Why should I know anything about Africa?

BENEATHA: Why do you give money at church for the missionary work?

MAMA: Well, that's to help save people.

BENEATHA: You mean save them from *heathenism*—

MAMA (*Innocently*): Yes.

BENEATHA: I'm afraid they need more salvation from the British and the French.

(RUTH *comes in forlornly and pulls off her coat with dejection. They both turn to look at her*)

RUTH (*Dispiritedly*): Well, I guess from all the happy faces—everybody knows.

BENEATHA: You pregnant?

MAMA: Lord have mercy, I sure hope it's a little old girl. Travis ought to have a sister.

(BENEATHA *and* RUTH *give her a hopeless look for this grandmotherly enthusiasm*)

BENEATHA: How far along are you?

RUTH: Two months.

BENEATHA: Did you mean to? I mean did you plan it or was it an accident?

MAMA: What do you know about planning or not planning?

BENEATHA: Oh, Mama.

RUTH (*Wearily*): She's twenty years old, Lena.

BENEATHA: Did you plan it, Ruth?

RUTH: Mind your own business.

BENEATHA: It is my business—where is he going to live, on the *roof?* (*There is silence following the remark as the three women react to the sense of it*) Gee—I didn't mean that, Ruth, honest. Gee, I don't feel like that at all. I—I think it is wonderful.

RUTH (*Dully*):   Wonderful.

BENEATHA: Yes—really. (*There is sudden commotion from the street and she goes to the window to look out*) What on earth is going on out there? These kids. (*There are, as she throws open the window, the shouts of children rising up from the street. She sticks her head out to see better and calls out*) TRAVIS! TRAVIS . . . WHAT ARE YOU DOING DOWN THERE? (*She sees*) Oh Lord, they're chasing a rat!

(RUTH *covers her face with hands and turns away*)

MAMA (*Angrily*):   Tell that youngun to get himself up here, at once!

BENEATHA: TRAVIS . . . YOU COME UPSTAIRS . . . AT ONCE!

RUTH (*Her face twisted*):   Chasing a rat . . .

MAMA (*Looking at* RUTH, *worried*):   Doctor say everything going to be all right?

RUTH (*Far away*):   Yes—She says everything is going to be fine . . .

MAMA (*Immediately suspicious*):   "She"—What doctor you went to?

(RUTH *just looks at* MAMA *meaningfully and* MAMA *opens her mouth to speak as* TRAVIS *bursts in*)

TRAVIS (*Excited and full of narrative, coming directly to his mother*):   Mama, you should of seen the rat . . . Big as a cat, honest! (*He shows an exaggerated size with his hands*) Gaaleee, that rat was really cuttin' and Bubber caught him with his heel and the janitor, Mr. Barnett, got him with a stick—and then they got him in a corner and—BAM! BAM! BAM!—and he was still jumping around and bleeding like everything too—there's rat blood all over the street—

(RUTH *reaches out suddenly and grabs her son without even looking at him and clamps her hand over his mouth and holds him to her.* MAMA *crosses to them rapidly and takes the boy from her*)

MAMA: You hush up now . . . talking all that terrible stuff. . . . (TRAVIS *is staring at his mother with a stunned expression.* BENEATHA *comes quickly and takes him away from his grandmother and ushers him to the door*)

BENEATHA: You go back outside and play . . . but not with any rats. (*She pushes him gently out the door with the boy straining to see what is wrong with his mother*)

MAMA (*worriedly hovering over* RUTH):   Ruth honey—what's the matter with you—you sick?

(RUTH *has her fists clenched on her thighs and is fighting hard to suppress a scream that seems to be rising in her*)

BENEATHA: What's the matter with her, Mama?

MAMA (*Working her fingers in* RUTH'S *shoulders to relax her*):   She be all right. Women gets right depressed sometimes when they get her way. (*Speaking softly, expertly, rapidly*) Now you just relax. That's right . . . just lean back, don't think 'bout nothing at all . . . nothing at all—

RUTH: I'm all right . . .

(*The glassy-eyed look melts and then she collapses into a fit of heavy sobbing. The bell rings*)

BENEATHA: Oh, my God—that must be Asagai.

MAMA (*To* RUTH):   Come on now honey. You need to lie down and rest awhile . . . then have some nice hot food.

(*They exit,* RUTH'S *weight on her mother-in-law.* BENEATHA, *herself profoundly disturbed, opens the door to admit a rather dramatic-looking young man with a large package*)

ASAGAI: Hello, Alaiyo—

BENEATHA (*Holding the door open and regarding him with pleasure*): Hello . . . (*Long pause*) Well—come in. And please excuse everything. My mother was very upset about my letting anyone come here with the place like this.

ASAGAI (*Coming into the room*):   You look disturbed too . . . Is something wrong?

BENEATHA (*Still at the door, absently*):   Yes . . . we've all got acute ghetto-itis. (*She smiles and comes toward him, finding a cigarette and sitting*) So—sit down! No! Wait! (*She whips the spraygun off sofa where she had left it and puts the cushions back. At last perches on arm of sofa. He sits*) So, how was Canada?

ASAGAI (*A sophisticate*):   Canadian.

BENEATHA (*Looking at him*):   Asagai, I'm very glad you are back.

ASAGAI (*Looking back at her in turn*):   Are you really?

BENEATHA: Yes—very.

ASAGAI: Why?—you were quite glad when I went away. What happened?

BENEATHA: You went away.

ASAGAI: Ahhhhhhhh.

BENEATHA: Before—you wanted to be so serious before there was time.

ASAGAI: How much time must there be before one knows what one feels?

BENEATHA (*Stalling this particular conversation. Her hands pressed together, in a deliberately childish gesture*):   What did you bring me?

ASAGAI (*Handing her the package*):   Open it and see.

BENEATHA (*Eagerly opening the package and drawing out some records and the colorful robes of a Nigerian woman*):   Oh, Asagai! . . . You got them for me! . . . How beautiful . . . and the records too! (*She lifts out the robes and runs to the mirror with them and holds the drapery up in front of herself*)

ASAGAI (*Coming to her at the mirror*):   I shall have to teach you how to drape it properly. (*He flings the material about her for the moment and stands back to look at her*) Ah—*Oh-pay-gay-day, oh-gbah-mu-shay.* (*A Yoruba exclamation for admiration*) You wear it well . . . very well . . . mutilated hair and all.

BENEATHA (*Turning suddenly*):   My hair—what's wrong with my hair?

ASAGAI (*Shrugging*):   Were you born with it like that?

BENEATHA (*Reaching up to touch it*):   No . . . of course not.

(*She looks back to the mirror, disturbed*)

ASAGAI (*Smiling*):   How then?

BENEATHA: You know perfectly well how . . . as crinkly as yours . . . that's how.

ASAGAI: And it is ugly to you that way?

BENEATHA (*Quickly*): Oh, no—not ugly . . . (*More slowly, apologetically*) But it's so hard to manage when it's well—raw.

ASAGAI: And so to accommodate that—you mutilate it every week?

BENEATHA: It's not mutilation!

ASAGAI (*Laughing aloud at her seriousness*): Oh . . . please! I am only teasing you because you are so very serious about these things. (*He stands back from her and folds his arms across his chest as he watches her pulling at her hair and frowning in the mirror*) Do you remember the first time you met me at school? . . . (*He laughs*) You came up to me and you said—and I thought you were the most serious little thing I had ever seen—you said: (*He imitates her*) "Mr. Asagai—I want very much to talk with you. About Africa. You see, Mr. Asagai, I am looking for my *identity!*"

(*He laughs*)

BENEATHA (*Turning to him, not laughing*): Yes—

(*Her face is quizzical, profoundly disturbed*)

ASAGAI (*Still teasing and reaching out and taking her face in his hands and turning her profile to him*): Well . . . it is true that this is not so much a profile of a Hollywood queen as perhaps a queen of the Nile—(*A mock dismissal of the importance of the question*) But what does it matter? Assimilationism is so popular in your country.

BENEATHA (*Wheeling, passionately, sharply*): I am not an assimilationist!

ASAGAI (*The protest hangs in the room for a moment and* ASAGAI *studies her, his laughter fading*): Such a serious one. (*There is a pause*) So—you like the robes? You must take excellent care of them—they are from my sister's personal wardrobe.

BENEATHA (*With incredulity*): You—you sent all the way home—for me?

ASAGAI (*With charm*): For you—I would do much more . . . Well, that is what I came for. I must go.

BENEATHA: Will you call me Monday?

ASAGAI: Yes . . . We have a great deal to talk about. I mean about identity and time and all that.

BENEATHA: Time?

ASAGAI: Yes. About how much time one needs to know what one feels.

BENEATHA: You see! You never understood that there is more than one kind of feeling which can exist between a man and a woman—or, at least, there should be.

ASAGAI (*Shaking his head negatively but gently*): No. Between a man and a woman there need be only one kind of feeling. I have that for you . . . Now even . . . right this moment . . .

BENEATHA: I know—and by itself—it won't do. I can find that anywhere.

ASAGAI: For a woman it should be enough.

BENEATHA: I know—because that's what it says in all the novels that men write. But it isn't. Go ahead and laugh—but I'm not interested in being someone's little episode in America or—(*With feminine vengeance*)—one of them! (ASAGAI *has burst into laughter again*) That's funny as hell, huh!

ASAGAI: It's just that every American girl I have known has said that to me. White—black—in this you are all the same. And the same speech, too!

BENEATHA (*Angrily*): Yuk, yuk, yuk!

ASAGAI: It's how you can be sure that the world's most liberated women are not liberated at all. You all talk about it too much!

(MAMA *enters and is immediately all social charm because of the presence of a guest*)

BENEATHA: Oh—Mama—this is Mr. Asagai.

MAMA: How do you do?

ASAGAI (*Total politeness to an elder*): How do you do, Mrs. Younger. Please forgive me for coming at such an outrageous hour on a Saturday.

MAMA: Well, you are quite welcome. I just hope you understand that our house don't always look like this. (*Chatterish*) You must come again. I would love to here all about—(*Not sure of the name*)—your country. I think it's so sad the way our American Negroes don't know nothing about Africa 'cept Tarzan and all that. And all that money they pour into these churches when they ought to be helping you people over there drive out them French and Englishmen done taken away your land.

(*The mother flashes a slightly superior look at her daughter upon completion of the recitation*)

ASAGAI (*Taken aback by this sudden and acutely unrelated expression of sympathy*): Yes . . . yes . . .

MAMA (*Smiling at him suddenly and relaxing and looking him over*): How many miles is it from here to where you come from?

ASAGAI: Many thousands.

MAMA (*Looking at him as she would* WALTER): I bet you don't half look after youself, being away from your mama either. I spec you better come 'round here from time to time to get yourself some decent homecooked meals . . .

ASAGAI (*Moved*): Thank you. Thank you very much. (*They are all quiet, then—*) Well . . . I must go. I will call you Monday, Alaiyo.

MAMA: What's that he call you?

ASAGAI: Oh—"Alaiyo." I hope you don't mind. It is what you would call a nickname, I think. It is a Yoruba word. I am a Yoruba.

MAMA (*Looking at* BENEATHA): I—I thought he was from—(*Uncertain*)

ASAGAI (*Understanding*): Nigeria is my country. Yoruba is my tribal origin—

BENEATHA: You didn't tell us what Alaiyo means . . . for all I know, you might be calling me Little Idiot or something . . .

ASAGAI: Well . . . let me see . . . I do not know how just to explain it . . . The sense of a thing can be so different when it changes language.

BENEATHA: You're evading.

ASAGAI: No—really it is difficult . . . (*Thinking*) It means . . . it means One for Whom Bread—Food—Is Not Enough. (*He looks at her*) Is that all right?

BENEATHA (*Understanding, softly*): Thank you.

MAMA (*Looking from one to the other and not understanding any of it*) Well . . . that's nice . . . You must come see us again—Mr.—

ASAGAI: Ah-sah-guy . . .

MAMA: Yes . . . Do come again.

ASAGAI: Good-bye.

(*He exits*)

MAMA (*After him*): Lord, that's a pretty thing just went out here! (*Insinuat-*

ingly, to her daughter) Yes, I guess I see why we done commence to get so interested in Africa 'round here. Missionaries my aunt Jenny!

(*She exits*)

BENEATHA: Oh, Mama! . . .

(*She picks up the Nigerian dress and holds it up to her in front of the mirror again. She sets the headdress on haphazardly and then notices her hair again and clutches at it and then replaces the headdress and frowns at herself. Then she starts to wriggle in front of the mirror as she thinks a Nigerian woman might.* TRAVIS *enters and stands regarding her*)

TRAVIS: What's the matter, girl, you cracking up?
BENEATHA: Shut up.

(*She pulls the headdress off and looks at herself in the mirror and clutches at her hair again and squinches her eyes as if trying to imagine something. Then, suddenly, she gets her raincoat and kerchief and hurriedly prepares for going out*)

MAMA (*Coming back into the room*):   She's resting now. Travis, baby, run next door and ask Miss Johnson to please let me have the little kitchen cleanser. This here can is empty as Jacob's kettle.
TRAVIS: I just came in.
MAMA: Do as you told. (*He exits and she looks at her daughter*) Where you going?
BENEATHA (*Halting at the door*):   To become a queen of the Nile!

(*She exits in a breathless blaze of glory.* RUTH *appears in the bedroom doorway*)

MAMA: Who told you to get up?
RUTH: Ain't nothing wrong with me to be lying in no bed for. Where did Bennie go?
MAMA (*Drumming her fingers*):   Far as I could make out—to Egypt. (RUTH *just looks at her*) What time is it getting to?
RUTH: Ten twenty. And the mailman going to ring that bell this morning just like he done every morning for the last umpteen years.

TRAVIS (*comes in with the cleanser can*)

TRAVIS: She say to tell you that she don't have much.
MAMA (*Angrily*): Lord, some people I could name sure is tight-fisted! (*Directing her grandson*) Mark two cans of cleanser down on the list there. If she that hard up for kitchen cleanser, I sure don't want to forget to get her none!
RUTH: Lena—maybe the woman is just short on cleanser—
MAMA (*Not listening*):—Much baking powder as she done borrowed from me all these years, she could of done gone into the baking business!

(*The bell sounds suddenly and sharply and all three are stunned—serious and silent—mid-speech. In spite of all the other conversations and distractions of the morning, this is what they have been waiting for, even* TRAVIS, *who looks helplessly from his mother to his grandmother.* RUTH *is the first to come to life again*)

RUTH (*To* TRAVIS):   *Get down them steps, boy!*

(TRAVIS *snaps to life and flies out to get the mail*)

MAMA: (*Her eyes wide, her hand to her breast*):   You mean it done really come?

RUTH (*Excited*):   Oh, Miss Lena!

MAMA (*Collecting herself*):   Well . . . I don't know what we all so excited about 'round here for. We known it was coming for months.

RUTH: That's a whole lot different from having it come and being able to hold it in your hands . . . a piece of paper worth ten thousand dollars . . . (TRAVIS *bursts back into the room. He holds the envelope high above his head, like a little dancer, his face is radiant and he is breathless. He moves to his grandmother with sudden slow ceremony and puts the envelope into her hands. She accepts it, and then merely holds it and looks at it*) Come on! Open it . . . Lord have mercy, I wish Walter Lee was here!

TRAVIS: Open it, Grandmama!

MAMA (*Staring at it*):   Now you all be quiet. It's just a check.

RUTH: Open it . . .

MAMA (*Still staring at it*):   Now don't act silly . . . We ain't never been no people to act silly 'bout no money—

RUTH (*Swiftly*):   We ain't never had none before—OPEN IT!

(MAMA *finally makes a good strong tear and pulls out the thin blue slice of paper and inspects it closely. The boy and his mother study it raptly over* MAMA'S *shoulders*)

MAMA: *Travis!* (*She is counting off with doubt*) Is that the right number of zeros?

TRAVIS: Yes'm . . . ten thousand dollars. Gaalee, Grandmama, you rich.

MAMA (*She holds the check away from her, still looking at it. Slowly her face sobers into a mask of unhappiness*):   Ten thousand dollars. (*She hands it to* RUTH) Put it away somewhere, Ruth. (*She does not look at* RUTH; *her eyes seem to be seeing something somewhere very far off*) Ten thousand dollars they give you. Ten thousand dollars.

TRAVIS (*To his mother, sincerely*):   What's the matter with Grandmama—don't she want to be rich?

RUTH (*Distractedly*):   You go on out and play now, baby. (TRAVIS *exits.* MAMA *starts wiping dishes absently, humming intently to herself.* RUTH *turns to her, with kind exasperation*) You've gone and got yourself upset.

MAMA (*Not looking at her*):   I spec if it wasn't for you all . . . I would just put that money away or give it to the church or something.

RUTH: Now what kind of talk is that. Mr. Younger would just be plain mad if he could hear you talking foolish like that.

MAMA (*Stopping and staring off*):   Yes . . . he sure would. (*Sighing*) We got enough to do with that money, all right. (*She halts then, and turns and looks at her daughter-in-law hard;* RUTH *avoids her eyes and* MAMA *wipes her hands with finality and starts to speak firmly to* RUTH) Where did you go today, girl?

RUTH: To the doctor.

MAMA (*Impatiently*):   Now, Ruth . . . you know better than that. Old Doctor Jones is strange enough in his way but there ain't nothing 'bout him make somebody slip and call him "she" —like you done this morning.

RUTH: Well, that's what happened—my tongue slipped.

MAMA: You went to see that woman, didn't you?

RUTH (*Defensively, giving herself away*):   What woman you talking about?

MAMA (*Angrily*):   That woman who—

(WALTER *enters in great excitement*)

WALTER: Did it come?

MAMA (*Quietly*):   Can't you give people a Christian greeting before you start asking about money?

WALTER (*To* RUTH):   Did it come? (RUTH *unfolds the check and lays it quietly before him, watching him intently with thoughts of her own.* WALTER *sits down and grasps it close and counts off the zeros*) Ten thousand dollars—(*He turns suddenly, frantically to his mother and draws some papers out of his breast pocket*) Mama—look. Old Willy Harris put everything on paper—

MAMA: Son—I think you ought to talk to your wife . . . I'll go on out and leave you alone if you want—

WALTER: I can talk to her later—Mama, look—

MAMA: Son—

WALTER: WILL SOMEBODY PLEASE LISTEN TO ME TODAY!

MAMA (*Quietly*):   I don't 'low no yellin' in this house, Walter Lee, and you know it—(WALTER *stares at them in frustration and starts to speak several times*) And there ain't going to be no investing in no liquor stores.

WALTER: But, Mama, you ain't even looked at it.

MAMA: I don't aim to have to speak on that again.

(*A long pause*)

WALTER: You ain't looked at it and you don't aim to have to speak on that again? You ain't even looked at it and *you* have decided—(*Crumpling his paper*) Well, *you* tell that to my boy tonight when you put him to sleep on the living-room couch . . . (*Turning to* MAMA *and speaking directly to her*) Yeah—and tell it to my wife, Mama, tomorrow when she has to go out of here to look after somebody else's kids. And tell it to *me*, Mama, every time we need a new pair of curtains and I have to watch *you* go out and work in somebody's kitchen. Yeah, you tell me then!

(WALTER *starts out*)

RUTH: Where you going?

WALTER: I'm going out!

RUTH: Where?

WALTER: Just out of this house somewhere—

RUTH: (*Getting her coat*):   I'll come too.

WALTER: I don't want you to come!

RUTH: I got something to talk to you about, Walter.

WALTER: That's too bad.

MAMA (*Still quietly*):   Walter Lee—(*She waits and he finally turns and looks at her*) Sit down.

WALTER: I'm a grown man, Mama.

MAMA: Ain't nobody said you wasn't grown. But you still in my house and my presence. And a long as you are—you'll talk to your wife civil. Now sit down.

RUTH (*Suddenly*):   Oh, let him go on out and drink himself to death! He makes me sick to my stomach! (*She flings her coat against him and exits to bedroom*)

WALTER (*Violently flinging the coat after her*):   And you turn mine too, baby! (*The door slams behind her*) That was my biggest mistake—

MAMA (*Still quietly*):   Walter what is the matter with you?

WALTER: Matter with me? Ain't nothing the matter with *me!*

MAMA: Yes there is. Something eating you up like a crazy man. Something more than me not giving you this money. The past few years I been watching it happen to you. You get all nervous acting and kind of wild in the eyes—(WALTER *jumps up impatiently at her words*) I said sit there now, I'm talking to you!

WALTER: Mama—I don't need no nagging at me today.

MAMA: Seem like you getting to a place where you always tied up in some kind of knot about something. But if anybody ask you 'bout it you just yell at 'em and bust out the house and go out and drink somewheres. Walter Lee, people can't live with that. Ruth's a good, patient girl in her way—but you getting to be too much. Boy, don't make the mistake of driving that girl away from you.

WALTER: Why—what she do for me?

MAMA: She loves you.

WALTER: Mama—I'm going out. I want to go off somewhere and be by myself for a while.

MAMA: I'm sorry 'bout your liquor store, son. It just wasn't the thing for us to do. That's what I want to tell you about—

WALTER: I got to go out, Mama—

(*He rises*)

MAMA: It's dangerous, son.

WALTER: What's dangerous?

MAMA: When a man goes outside his home to look for peace.

WALTER (*Beseechingly*):   Then why can't there never be no peace in this house then?

MAMA: You done found it in some other house?

WALTER: No—there ain't no woman! Why do women always think there's a woman somewhere when a man gets restless? (*Picks up the check*) Do you know what this money means to me? Do you know what this money can do for us? (*Puts it back*) Mama—Mama—I want so many things . . .

MAMA: Yes, son—

WALTER: I want so many things that they are driving me kind of crazy . . . Mama—look at me.

MAMA: I'm looking at you. You a good-looking boy. You got a job, a nice wife, a fine boy and—

WALTER: A job. (*Looks at her*) Mama, a job? I open and close car doors all day long, I drive a man around in his limousine and I say, "Yes, sir; no, sir; very good, sir; shall I take the Drive, sir?" Mama, that ain't no kind of job . . . that ain't nothing at all. (*Very quietly*) Mama, I don't know if I can make you understand.

MAMA: Understand what, baby?

WALTER (*Quietly*):   Sometimes it's like I can see the future stretched out in front of me—just plain as day. The future, Mama. Hanging over there at the edge of my days. Just waiting for me—a big looming blank space full of *nothing*. Just waiting for *me*. But it don't have to be. (*Pause. Kneeling beside her chair*) Mama—sometimes when I'm downtown and I pass them cool, quiet-looking restaurants where them white boys are sitting back and talking about things . . . sitting there turning deals worth millions of dollars—sometimes I see guys don't look much older than me—

MAMA: Son—how come you talk so much 'bout money?

WALTER (*With immense passion*): Because it is life, Mama!

MAMA (*Quietly*): Oh—(*Very quietly*) So now it's life. Money is life. Once upon a time freedom used to be life—now it's money. I guess the world really do change . . .

WALTER: No—it was always money, Mama. We just didn't know about it.

MAMA: No . . . something has changed. (*She looks at him*) You something new, boy. In my time we was worried about not being lynched and getting to the North if we could and how to stay alive and still have a pinch of dignity too . . . Now here come you and Beneatha—talking 'bout things we ain't never even thought about hardly, me and your daddy. You ain't satisfied or proud of nothing we done. I mean that you had a home; that we kept you out of trouble till you was grown; that you don't have to ride to work on the back of nobody's streetcar— You my children—but how different we done become.

WALTER (*A long beat. He pats her hand and gets up*): You just don't understand, Mama, you just don't understand.

MAMA: Son—do you know your wife is expecting another baby? (WALTER *stands, stunned, and absorbs what his mother has said*) That's what she wanted to talk to you about. (WALTER *sinks down into a chair*) This ain't for me to be telling—but you ought to know. (*She waits*) I think Ruth is thinking 'bout getting rid of that child.

WALTER (*Slowly understanding*):—No — no — Ruth wouldn't do that.

MAMA: When the world gets ugly enough—a woman will do anything for her family. *The part that's already living*.

WALTER: You don't know Ruth, Mama, if you think she would do that.

(RUTH *opens the bedroom door and stands there a little limp*)

RUTH (*Beaten*): Yes I would too, Walter. (*Pause*) I gave her a five-dollar down payment.

(*There is total silence as the man stares at his wife and the mother stares at her son*)

MAMA (*Presently*): Well — (*Tightly*) Well — son, I'm waiting to hear you say something—(*She waits*) I'm waiting to hear how you be your father's son. Be the man he was . . . (*Pause. The silence shouts*) Your wife say she going to destroy your child. And I'm waiting to hear you talk like him and say we a people who give children life, not who destroys them—(*She rises*) I'm waiting to see you stand up and look like your daddy and say we done give up one baby to poverty and that we ain't going to give up nary another one . . . I'm waiting.

WALTER: Ruth—(*He can say nothing*)

MAMA: If you a son of mine, tell her! (WALTER *picks up his keys and his coat and walks out. She continues, bitterly*) You . . . you are a disgrace to your father's memory. Somebody get me my hat!

Curtain

ACT II

SCENE ONE

Time: Later the same day.

At rise: RUTH *is ironing again. She has the radio going. Presently* BENEATHA'S *bedroom door opens and* RUTH'S *mouth falls and she puts down the iron in fascination.*

RUTH: What have we got on tonight!

BENEATHA (*Emerging grandly from the doorway so that we can see her thoroughly robed in the costume Asagai brought*):   You are looking at what a well-dressed Nigerian woman wears—(*She parades for* RUTH, *her hair completely hidden by the headdress; she is coquettishly fanning herself with an ornate oriental fan, mistakenly more like Butterfly*[1] *than any Nigerian that ever was*) Isn't it beautiful? (*She promenades to the radio and, with an arrogant flourish, turns off the good loud blues that is playing*) Enough of this assimilationist junk! (RUTH *follows her with her eyes as she goes to the phonograph and puts on a record and turns and waits ceremoniously for the music to come up. Then, with a shout—*) OCOMOGOSIAY!

(RUTH *jumps. The music comes up, a lovely Nigerian melody.* BENEATHA *listens, enraptured, her eyes far away—"back to the past." She begins to dance.* RUTH *is dumfounded*)

RUTH: What kind of dance is that?

BENEATHA: A folk dance.

RUTH (*Pearl Bailey*):   What kind of folks do that, honey?

BENEATHA: It's from Nigeria. It's a dance of welcome.

RUTH: Who you welcoming?

BENEATHA: The men back to the village.

RUTH: Where they been?

BENEATHA: How should I know—out hunting or something. Anyway, they are coming back now . . .

RUTH: Well, that's good.

BENEATHA (*With the record*):

Alundi, alundi
Alundi alunya
Jop pu a jeepua
Ang gu soooooooooo

Ai yai yae . . .
Ayehaye—alundi . . .

(WALTER *comes in during this performance; he has obviously been drinking. He leans against the door heavily and watches his sister, at first with distaste. Then his eyes look off—"back to the past"—as he lifts both his fists to the roof, screaming*)

---

[1] Madame Butterfly, from Puccini's opera of the same name.

WALTER: YEAH . . . AND ETHIOPIA STRETCH FORTH HER HANDS AGAIN! . . .

RUTH (*Drily, looking at him*): Yes—and Africa sure is claiming her own tonight. (*She gives them both up and starts ironing again*)

WALTER (*All in a drunken, dramatic shout*): Shut up! . . . I'm digging them drums . . . them drums move me! . . . (*He makes his weaving way to his wife's face and leans in close to her*) In my *heart of hearts*—(*He thumps his chest*)—I am much warrior!

RUTH (*Without even looking up*): In your heart of hearts you are much drunkard.

WALTER (*Coming away from her and starting to wander around the room, shouting*): Me and Jomo . . . (*Intently, in his sister's face. She has stopped dancing to watch him in this unknown mood*) That's my man, Kenyatta. (*Shouting and thumping his chest*) FLAMING SPEAR! HOT DAMN! (*He is suddenly in possession of an imaginary spear and actively spearing enemies all over the room*) OCOMOGOSIAY . . .

BENEATHA (*To encourage* WALTER, *thoroughly caught up with this side of him*): OCOMOGOSIAY, FLAMING SPEAR!

WALTER: THE LION IS WAKING . . . OWIMOWEH!

(*He pulls his shirt open and leaps up on the table and gestures with his spear*)

BENEATHA: OWIMOWEH!

WALTER (*On the table, very far gone, his eyes pure glass sheets. He sees what we cannot, that he is a leader of this people, a great chief, a descendant of Chaka, and that the hour to march has come*): Listen, my black brothers—

BENEATHA: OCOMOGOSIAY!

WALTER: —Do you hear the waters rushing against the shores of the coastlands—

BENEATHA: OCOMOGOSIAY!

WALTER: —Do you hear the screeching of the cocks in yonder hills beyond where the chiefs meet in council for the coming of the mighty war—

BENEATHA: OCOMOGOSIAY!

(*And now the lighting shifts subtly to suggest the world of* WALTER'S *imagination, and the mood shifts from pure comedy. It is the inner* WALTER *speaking: the Southside chauffeur has assumed an unexpected majesty*)

WALTER: —Do you hear the beating of the wings of the birds flying low over the mountains and the low places of our land—

BENEATHA: OCOMOGOSIAY!

WALTER: —Do you hear the singing of the women, singing the war songs of our fathers to the babies in the great houses? Singing the sweet war songs! (*The doorbell rings*) OH, DO YOU HEAR, MY BLACK BROTHERS!

BENEATHA (*Completely gone*): We hear you, Flaming Spear—

(RUTH *shuts off the phonograph and opens the door.* GEORGE MURCHISON *enters*)

WALTER: Telling us to prepare for the GREATNESS OF THE TIME! (*Lights back to normal. He turns and sees* GEORGE) Black Brother!

(*He extends his hand for the fraternal clasp*)

GEORGE: Black Brother, hell!

RUTH (*Having had enough, and embarrassed for the family*): Beneatha, you got company—what's the matter with you? Walter Lee Younger, get down off that table and stop acting like a fool . . .

(WALTER *comes down off the table suddenly and makes a quick exit to the bathroom*)

RUTH: He's had a little to drink . . . I don't know what her excuse is.

GEORGE (*To* BENEATHA): Look honey, we're going to the theatre—we're not going to be *in* it . . . so go change, huh?

(BENEATHA *looks at him and slowly, ceremoniously, lifts her hands and pulls off the headdress. Her hair is close-cropped and unstraightened.* GEORGE *freezes mid-sentence and* RUTH'S *eyes all but fall out of her head*)

GEORGE: What in the name of—

RUTH (*Touching* BENEATHA'S *hair*): Girl, you done lost your natural mind!? Look at your head!

GEORGE: What have you done to your head—I mean your hair!

BENEATHA: Nothing—except cut it off.

RUTH: Now that's the truth—it's what ain't been done to it! You expect this boy to go out with you with your head all nappy like that?

BENEATHA (*Looking at* GEORGE): That's up to George. If he's ashamed of his heritage—

GEORGE: Oh, don't be so proud of yourself, Bennie—just because you look eccentric.

BENEATHA: How can something that's natural be eccentric?

GEORGE: That's what being eccentric means—being natural. Get dressed.

BENEATHA: I don't like that, George.

RUTH: Why must you and your brother make an argument out of everything people say?

BENEATHA: Because I hate assimilationist Negroes!

RUTH: Will somebody please tell me what assimila-who-ever means!

GEORGE: Oh, it's just a college girl's way of calling people Uncle Toms—but that isn't what it means at all.

RUTH: Well, what does it mean?

BENEATHA (*Cutting* GEORGE *off and staring at him as she replies to* RUTH): It means someone who is willing to give up his own culture and submerge himself completely in the dominant, and in this case *oppressive* culture!

GEORGE: Oh, dear, dear, dear! Here we go! A lecture on the African past! On our Great West African Heritage! In one second we will hear all about the great Ashanti empires; the great Songhay civilizations; and the great sculpture of Bénin—and then some poetry in the Bantu—and the whole monologue will end with the word *heritage!* (*Nastily*) Let's face it, baby, your heritage is nothing but a bunch of raggedy-assed spirituals and some grass huts!

BENEATHA: GRASS HUTS! (RUTH *crosses to her and forcibly pushes her toward the bedroom*) See there . . . you are standing there in your splendid ignorance talking about people who were the first to smelt iron on the face of the earth! (RUTH *is pushing her through the door*) The Ashanti were performing surgical operations when the English—(RUTH *pulls the door to, with* BENEATHA *on the other side, and smiles graciously at* GEORGE. BENEATHA *opens the door and shouts the end of the sentence defiantly at* GEORGE)—were still tatooing themselves with blue dragons! (*She goes back inside*)

RUTH: Have a seat, George (*They both sit.* RUTH *folds her hands rather primly on her lap, determined to demonstrate the civilization of the family*) Warm, ain't it? I mean for September. (*Pause*) Just like they always say about Chicago weather: If it's too hot or cold for you, just wait a minute and it'll change. (*She smiles happily at this cliché of clichés*) Everybody say it's got to do with them bombs and things they keep setting off. (*Pause*) Would you like a nice cold beer?

GEORGE: No, thank you. I don't care for beer. (*He looks at his watch*) I hope she hurries up.

RUTH: What time is the show?

GEORGE: It's an eight-thirty curtain. That's just Chicago, though. In New York standard curtain time is eight forty.

(*He is rather proud of this knowledge*)

RUTH (*Properly appreciating it*): You get to New York a lot?

GEORGE (*Offhand*): Few times a year.

RUTH: Oh—that's nice. I've never been to New York.

(WALTER *enters. We feel he has relieved himself, but the edge of unreality is still with him*)

WALTER: New York ain't got nothing Chicago ain't. Just a bunch of hustling people all squeezed up together—being "Eastern."

(*He turns his face into a screw of displeasure*)

GEORGE: Oh—you've been?

WALTER: *Plenty* of times.

RUTH (*Shocked at the lie*): Walter Lee Younger!

WALTER (*Staring her down*): Plenty! (*Pause*) What we got to drink in this house? Why don't you offer this man some refreshment. (*To* GEORGE) They don't know how to entertain people in this house, man.

GEORGE: Thank you—I don't really care for anything.

WALTER (*Feeling his head; sobriety coming*): Where's Mama?

RUTH: She ain't come back yet.

WALTER (*Looking* MURCHISON *over from head to toe, scrutinizing his carefully casual tweed sports jacket over cashmere V-neck sweater over soft eyelet shirt and tie, and soft slacks, finished off with white buckskin shoes*): Why all you college boys wear them faggoty-looking white shoes?

RUTH: Walter Lee!

(GEORGE MURCHISON *ignores the remark*)

WALTER (*To* RUTH): Well, they look crazy as hell—white shoes, cold as it is.

RUTH (*Crushed*): You have to excuse him—

WALTER: No he don't! Excuse me for what? What you always excusing me for! I'll excuse myself when I needs to be excused! (*A pause*) They look as funny as them black knee socks Beneatha wears out of here all the time.

RUTH: It's the college *style*, Walter.

WALTER: Style, hell. She looks like she got burnt legs or something!

RUTH: Oh, Walter—

WALTER (*An irritable mimic*): Oh, Walter! Oh, Walter! (*To* MURCHISON) How's your old man making out? I understand you all going to buy that big hotel on the Drive? (*He finds a beer in the refrigerator, wanders over to* MURCHISON, *sipping and wiping his lips with the back of his hand, and straddling a chair backwards to talk to the other man*) Shrewd move. Your old man is all right, man. (*Tapping his head and half winking for emphasis*) I mean he knows how to operate. I mean he thinks *big,* you know what I mean, I mean for a *home,* you know? But I think he's kind of running out of ideas now. I'd like to talk to him. Listen, man, I got some plans that could turn this city upside down. I mean think like he does. *Big.* Invest big, gamble big, hell, lose *big* if you have to, you know what I mean. It's hard to find a man on this whole Southside who understands my kind of thinking—you dig? (*He scrutinizes* MURCHISON *again, drinks his beer, squints his eyes and leans in close, confidential, man to man*) Me and you ought to sit down and talk sometimes, man. Man, I got me some ideas . . .

MURCHISON (*With boredom*):   Yeah — sometimes we'll have to do that, Walter.

WALTER (*Understanding the indifference, and offended*):   Yeah—well, when you get the time, man. I know you a busy little boy.

RUTH: Walter, please—

WALTER (*Bitterly, hurt*):   I know ain't nothing in this world as busy as you colored college boys with your fraternity pins and white shoes . . .

RUTH (*Covering her face with humiliation*):   Oh, Walter Lee—

WALTER: I see you all the time—with the books tucked under your arms—going to your (*British A—a mimic*) "clahsses." And for what! What the hell you learning over there? Filling up your heads—(*Counting off on his fingers*)—with the sociology and the psychology—but they teaching you how to be a man? How to take over and run the world? They teaching you how to run a rubber plantation or a steel mill? Naw—just to talk proper and read books and wear them faggoty-looking white shoes . . .

GEORGE (*Looking at him with distaste, a little above it all*):   You're all wacked up with bitterness, man.

WALTER (*Intently, almost quietly, between the teeth, glaring at the boy*):   And you—ain't you bitter, man? Ain't you just about had it yet? Don't you see no stars gleaming that you can't reach out and grab? You happy?—You contented son-of-a-bitch—you happy? You got it made? Bitter? Man, I'm a volcano. Bitter? Here I am a giant—surrounded by ants! Ants who can't even understand what it is the giant is talking about.

RUTH (*Passionately and suddenly*):   Oh, Walter—ain't you with nobody!

WALTER (*Violently*):   No! 'Cause ain't nobody with me! Not even my own mother!

RUTH: Walter, that's a terrible thing to say!

(BENEATHA *enters, dressed for the evening in a cocktail dress and earrings, hair natural*)

GEORGE: Well—hey—(*Crosses to* BENEATHA; *thoughtful, with emphasis, since this is a reversal*) You look great!

WALTER (*Seeing his sister's hair for the first time*):   What's the matter with your head?

BENEATHA (*Tired of the jokes now*):   I cut it off, Brother.

WALTER (*Coming close to inspect it and walking around her*):   Well, I'll be damned. So that's what they mean by the African bush . . .

BENEATHA: Ha ha. Let's go, George.

GEORGE (*Looking at her*):   You know something? I like it. It's sharp. I mean it really is. (*Helps her into her wrap*)

RUTH: Yes—I think so, too. (*She goes to the mirror and starts to clutch at her hair*)

WALTER: Oh no! You leave yours alone, baby. You might turn out to have a pin-shapcd hcad or something!

BENEATHA: See you all later.

RUTH: Have a nice time.

GEORGE: Thanks. Good night. (*Half out the door, he reopens it. To* WALTER) Good night, Prometheus![2]

(BENEATHA *and* GEORGE *exit*)

WALTER (*To* RUTH):   Who is Prometheus?

RUTH: I don't know. Don't worry about it.

WALTER (*In fury, pointing after* GEORGE):   See there—they get to a point where they can't insult you man to man—they got to go talk about something ain't nobody never heard of!

RUTH: How do you know it was an insult? (*To humor him*) Maybe Prometheus is a nice fellow.

WALTER: Prometheus! I bet there ain't even no such thing! I bet that simpleminded clown—

RUTH: Walter—

(*She stops what she is doing and looks at him*)

WALTER (*Yelling*):   Don't start!

RUTH: Start what?

WALTER: Your nagging! Where was I? Who was I with? How much money did I spend?

RUTH (*Plaintively*):   Walter Lee—why don't we just try to talk about it . . .

WALTER (*Not listening*):   I been out talking with people who understand me. People who care about the things I got on my mind.

RUTH (*Wearily*):   I guess that means people like Willy Harris.

WALTER: Yes, people like Willy Harris.

RUTH (*With a sudden flash of impatience*):   Why don't you all just hurry up and go into the banking business and stop talking about it!

WALTER: Why? You want to know why? 'Cause we all tied up in a race of people that don't know how to do nothing but moan, pray and have babies!

(*The line is too bitter even for him and he looks at her and sits down*)

RUTH: Oh, Walter . . . (*Softly*) Honey, why can't you stop fighting me?

WALTER (*Without thinking*):   Who's fighting you? Who even cares about you?

(*This line begins the retardation of his mood*)

RUTH: Well—(*She waits a long time, and then with resignation starts to put away her things*) I guess I might as well go on to bed . . . (*More or less to herself*) I don't know where we lost it . . . but we have . . . (*Then, to him*) I—I'm sorry about this new baby, Walter. I guess maybe I better go on and do what I

---

[2] According to Greek myth, a Titan, or giant god, who stole fire from Heaven and gave it to humans; for this he was severely punished.

started . . . I guess I just didn't realize how bad things was with us . . . I guess I just didn't really realize—(*She starts out to the bedroom and stops*) You want some hot milk?

WALTER: Hot milk?

RUTH: Yes—hot milk.

WALTER: Why hot milk?

RUTH: 'Cause after all that liquor you come home with you ought to have something hot in your stomach.

WALTER: I don't want no milk.

RUTH: You want some coffee then?

WALTER: No, I don't want no coffee. I don't want nothing hot to drink. (*Almost plaintively*) Why you always trying to give me something to eat?

RUTH (*Standing and looking at him helplessly*):   What *else* can I give you, Walter Lee Younger?

(*She stands and looks at him and presently turns to go out again. He lifts his head and watches her going away from him in a new mood which began to emerge when he asked her "Who cares about you?"*)

WALTER: It's been rough, ain't it baby? (*She hears and stops but does not turn around and he continues to her back*) I guess between two people there ain't never as much understood as folks generally thinks there is. I mean like between me and you—(*She turns to face him*) How we gets to the place where we scared to talk softness to each other. (*He waits, thinking hard himself*) Why you think it got to be like that? (*He is thoughtful, almost as a child would be*) Ruth, what is it gets into people ought to be close?

RUTH: I don't know, honey. I think about it a lot.

WALTER: On account of you and me, you mean? The way things are with us. The way something done come down between us.

RUTH: There ain't so much between us, Walter . . . Not when you come to me and try to talk to me. Try to be with me . . . a little even.

WALTER (*Total honesty*):   Sometimes . . . sometimes . . . I don't even know how to try.

RUTH: Walter—

WALTER: Yes?

RUTH (*Coming to him, gently and with misgiving, but coming to him*): Honey . . . life don't have to be like this. I mean sometimes people can do things so that things are better . . . You remember how we used to talk when Travis was born . . . about the way we were going to live . . . the kind of house . . . (*She is stroking his head*) Well, it's all starting to slip away from us . . .

(*He turns her to him and they look at each other and kiss, tenderly and hungrily. The door opens and MAMA enters— WALTER breaks away and jumps up. A beat*)

WALTER: Mama, where have you been?

MAMA: My—them steps is longer than they used to be. Whew! (*She sits down and ignores him*) How you feeling this evening, Ruth?

(RUTH *shrugs, disturbed at having been interrupted and watching her husband knowingly*)

WALTER: Mama, where have you been all day?

MAMA (*Still ignoring him and leaning on the table and changing to more comfortable shoes*):   Where's Travis?

RUTH: I let him go out earlier and he ain't come back yet. Boy, is he going to get it!

WALTER: Mama!

MAMA (*As if she has heard him for the first time*):   Yes, son?

WALTER: Where did you go this afternoon?

MAMA: I went downtown to tend to some business that I had to tend to.

WALTER: What kind of business?

MAMA: You know better than to question me like a child, Brother.

WALTER (*Rising and bending over the table*):   Where were you, Mama? (*Bringing his fists down and shouting*) Mama, you didn't go do something with that insurance money, something crazy?

(*The front door opens slowly, interrupting him, and* TRAVIS *peeks his head in, less than hopefully*)

TRAVIS (*To his mother*):   Mama, I—

RUTH: "Mama I" nothing! You're going to get it, boy! Get on in that bedroom and get yourself ready!

TRAVIS: But I—

MAMA: Why don't you all never let the child explain hisself.

RUTH: Keep out of it now, Lena.

(MAMA *clamps her lips together, and* RUTH *advances toward her son menacingly*)

RUTH: A thousand times I have told you not to go off like that—

MAMA (*Holding out her arms to her grandson*):   Well—at least let me tell him something. I want him to be the first one to hear . . . Come here, Travis. (*The boy obeys, gladly*) Travis . . . (*She takes him by the shoulder and looks into his face*)—you know that money we got in the mail this morning?

TRAVIS: Yes'm—

MAMA: Well—what you think your grandmama gone and done with that money?

TRAVIS: I don't know, Grandmama.

MAMA (*Putting her finger on his nose for emphasis*):   She went out and she bought you a house! (*The explosion comes from* WALTER *at the end of the revelation and he jumps up and turns away from all of them in a fury.* MAMA *continues, to* TRAVIS) You glad about the house? It's going to be yours when you get to be a man.

TRAVIS: Yeah—I always wanted to live in a house.

MAMA: All right, gimme some sugar then—(TRAVIS *puts his arms around her neck as she watches her son over the boy's shoulder. Then, to* TRAVIS, *after the embrace*) Now when you say your prayers tonight, you thank God and your grandfather—'cause it was him who give you the house—in his way.

RUTH (*Taking the boy from* MAMA *and pushing him toward the bedroom*):   Now you get out of here and get ready for your beating.

TRAVIS: Aw, Mama—

RUTH: Get on in there—(*Closing the door behind him and turning radiantly to her mother-in-law*) So you went and did it!

MAMA (*Quietly, looking at her son with pain*):   Yes, I did.

RUTH (*Raising both arms classically*):   PRAISE GOD! (*Looks at* WALTER *a moment, who says nothing. She crosses rapidly to her husband*) Please, honey—let me be glad . . . you be glad too. (*She has laid her hands on his shoulders, but he shakes himself free of her roughly, without turning to face her*) Oh, Walter . . . a home . . . *a home.* (*She comes back to* MAMA) Well—where is it? How big is it? How much it going to cost?

MAMA: Well—

RUTH: When we moving?

MAMA (*Smiling at her*):   First of the month.

RUTH (*Throwing back her head with jubilance*):   *Praise God!*

MAMA (*Tentatively, still looking at her son's back turned against her and* RUTH):   It's—it's a nice house too . . . (*She cannot help speaking directly to him. An imploring quality in her voice, her manner, makes her almost like a girl now*) Three bedrooms—nice big one for you and Ruth . . . Me and Beneatha still have to share our room, but Travis have one of his own—and (*With difficulty*) I figure if the—new baby—is a boy, we could get one of them double-decker outfits . . . And there's a yard with a little patch of dirt where I could maybe get to grow me a few flowers . . . And a nice big basement . . .

RUTH: Walter honey, be glad—

MAMA (*Still to his back, fingering things on the table*):   'Course I don't want to make it sound fancier than it is . . . It's just a plain little old house—but it's made good and solid—and it will be *ours.* Walter Lee—it makes a difference in a man when he can walk on floors that belong to *him* . . .

RUTH: Where is it?

MAMA (*Frightened at this telling*):   Well—well—it's out there in Clybourne Park—

(RUTH'S *radiance fades abruptly, and* WALTER *finally turns slowly to face his mother with incredulity and hostility*)

RUTH: Where?

MAMA (*Matter-of-factly*):   Four o six Clybourne Street, Clybourne Park.

RUTH: Clybourne Park? Mama, there ain't no colored people living in Clybourne Park.

MAMA (*Almost idiotically*):   Well, I guess there's going to be some now.

WALTER (*Bitterly*):   So that's the peace and comfort you went out and bought for us today!

MAMA (*Raising her eyes to meet his finally*):   Son—I just tried to find the nicest place for the least amount of money for my family.

RUTH (*Trying to recover from the shock*):   Well—well—'course I ain't one never been 'fraid of no crackers,[3] mind you—but—well, wasn't there no other houses nowhere?

MAMA: Them houses they put up for colored in them areas way out all seem to cost twice as much as other houses. I did the best I could.

RUTH (*Struck senseless with the news, in its various degrees of goodness and trouble, she sits a moment, her fists propping her chin in thought, and then she starts to rise, bringing her fists down with vigor, the radiance spreading from cheek to cheek again*):   Well—well!—All I can say is—if this is my time in life—MY TIME—to say good-bye—(*And she builds with momentum as she*

---

[3] A contemptuous term for poor whites.

starts to circle the room with an exuberant, almost tearfully happy release)—to these Goddamned cracking walls!—(*She pounds the walls*)—and these marching roaches!—(*She wipes at an imaginary army of marching roaches*)—and this cramped little closet which ain't now or never was no kitchen!—then I say it loud and good, HALLELUJAH! AND GOOD-BYE MISERY . . . I DON'T NEVER WANT TO SEE YOUR UGLY FACE AGAIN! (*She laughs joyously, having practically destroyed the apartment, and flings her arms up and lets them come down happily, slowly, reflectively, over her abdomen, aware for the first time perhaps that the life therein pulses with happiness and not despair*) Lena?

MAMA (*Moved, watching her happiness*):   Yes, honey?

RUTH (*Looking off*):   Is there—is there a whole lot of sunlight?

MAMA (*Understanding*):   Yes, child, there's a whole lot of sunlight.

(*Long pause*)

RUTH (*Collecting herself and going to the door of the room* TRAVIS *is in*): Well— I guess I better see 'bout Travis. (*To* MAMA) Lord, I sure don't feel like whipping nobody today!

(*She exits*)

MAMA (*The mother and son are left alone now and the mother waits a long time, considering deeply, before she speaks*):   Son—you—you understand what I done, don't you? (WALTER *is silent and sullen*) I—I just seen my family falling apart today . . . just falling to pieces in front of my eyes . . . We couldn't of gone on like we was today. We was going backwards 'stead of forwards—talking 'bout killing babies and wishing each other was dead . . . When it gets like that in life—you just got to do something different, push on out and do something bigger . . . (*She waits*) I wish you say something, son . . . I wish you'd say how deep inside you you think I done the right thing—

WALTER (*Crossing slowly to his bedroom door and finally turning there and speaking measuredly*):   What you need me to say you done right for? *You* the head of this family. You run our lives like you want to. It was your money and you did what you wanted with it. So what you need for me to say it was all right for? (*Bitterly, to hurt her as deeply as he knows is possible*) So you butchered up a dream of mine—you—who always talking 'bout your children's dreams . . .

MAMA: Walter Lee—

(*He just closes the door behind him.* MAMA *sits alone, thinking heavily*)

Curtain

SCENE TWO

Time: Friday night. A few weeks later.
At rise: Packing crates mark the intention of the family to move. BENEATHA *and* GEORGE *come in, presumably from an evening out again.*

GEORGE: O.K. . . . O.K., whatever you say . . . (*They both sit on the couch. He tries to kiss her. She moves away*) Look, we've had a nice evening; let's not spoil it, huh? . . .

(*He again turns her head and tries to nuzzle in and she turns away from him, not with distaste but with momentary lack of interest; in a mood to pursue what they were talking about*)

BENEATHA: I'm *trying* to talk to you.

GEORGE: We always talk.

BENEATHA: Yes—and I love to talk.

GEORGE (*Exasperated; rising*):   I know it and I don't mind it sometimes . . . I want you to cut it out, see—The moody stuff, I mean. I don't like it. You're a nice-looking girl . . . all over. That's all you need, honey, forget the atmosphere. Guys aren't going to go for the atmosphere—they're going to go for what they see. Be glad for that. Drop the Garbo routine. It doesn't go with you. As for myself, I want a nice—(*Groping*)—simple (*Thoughtfully*)—sophisticated girl . . . not a poet—O. K.?

(*He starts to kiss her, she rebuffs him again and he jumps up*)

BENEATHA: Why are you angry, George?

GEORGE: Because this is stupid! I don't go out with you to discuss the nature of "quiet desperation" or to hear all about your thoughts—because the world will go on thinking what it thinks regardless—

BENEATHA: Then why read books? Why go to school?

GEORGE (*With artificial patience, counting on his fingers*):   It's simple. You read books—to learn facts—to get grades—to pass the course—to get a degree. That's all—it has nothing to do with thoughts.

(*A long pause*)

BENEATHA: I see. (*He starts to sit*) Good night, George.

(GEORGE *looks at her a little oddly, and starts to exit. He meets* MAMA *coming in*)

GEORGE: Oh—hello, Mrs. Younger.

MAMA: Hello, George, how you feeling?

GEORGE: Fine—fine, how are you?

MAMA: Oh, a little tired. You know them steps can get you after a day's work. You all have a nice time tonight?

GEORGE: Yes—a fine time. A fine time.

MAMA: Well, good night.

GEORGE: Good night. (*He exits.* MAMA *closes the door behind her*) Hello, honey. What you sitting like that for?

BENEATHA: I'm just sitting.

MAMA: Didn't you have a nice time?

BENEATHA: No.

MAMA: No? What's the matter?

BENEATHA: Mama, George is a fool—honest. (*She rises*)

MAMA (*Hustling around unloading the packages she has entered with. She stops*):   Is he, baby?

BENEATHA: Yes.

(BENEATHA *makes up* TRAVIS' *bed as she talks*)

MAMA: You sure?

BENEATHA: Yes.

MAMA: Well—I guess you better not waste your time with no fools.

(BENEATHA *looks up at her mother, watching her put groceries in the refrigerator. Finally she gathers up her things and starts into the bedroom. At the door she stops and looks back at her mother*)

BENEATHA: Mama—
MAMA: Yes, baby—
BENEATHA: Thank you.
MAMA: For what?
BENEATHA: For understanding me this time.

(*She exits quickly and the mother stands, smiling a little, looking at the place where* BENEATHA *just stood.* RUTH *enters*)

RUTH: Now don't you fool with any of this stuff, Lena—
MAMA: Oh, I just thought I'd sort a few things out. Is Brother here?
RUTH: Yes.
MAMA (*With concern*):   Is he—
RUTH (*Reading her eyes*):   Yes.

(MAMA *is silent and someone knocks on the door.* MAMA *and* RUTH *exchange weary and knowing glances and* RUTH *opens it to admit the neighbor,* MRS. JOHNSON,[4] *who is a rather squeaky wide-eyed lady of no particular age, with a newspaper under her arm*)

MAMA (*Changing her expression to acute delight and a ringing cheerful greeting*):   Oh—hello there, Johnson.
JOHNSON: (*This is a woman who decided long ago to be enthusiastic about EVERYTHING in life and she is inclined to wave her wrist vigorously at the height of her exclamatory comments*):   Hello there, yourself! H'you this evening, Ruth?
RUTH (*Not much of a deceptive type*):   Fine, Mis' Johnson, h'you?
JOHNSON: Fine. (*Reaching out quickly, playfully, and patting* RUTH's *stomach*) Ain't you starting to poke out none yet! (*She mugs with delight at the over-familiar remark and her eyes dart around looking at the crates and packing preparation;* MAMA's *face is a cold sheet of endurance*) Oh, ain't we getting ready round here, though! Yessir! Lookathere! I'm telling you the Youngers is really getting ready to "move on up a little higher!"—Bless God!
MAMA (*A little drily, doubting the total sincerity of the Blesser*):   Bless God.
JOHNSON: He's good, ain't He?
MAMA: Oh yes, He's good.
JOHNSON: I mean sometimes He works in mysterious ways . . . but He works, don't He!
MAMA (*The same*):   Yes, he does.
JOHNSON: I'm just soooooo happy for y'all. And this here child—(*About* RUTH) looks like she could just pop open with happiness, don't she. Where's all the rest of the family?
MAMA: Bennie's gone to bed—
JOHNSON: Ain't no . . . (*The implication is pregnancy*) sickness done hit you—I hope . . . ?
MAMA: No—she just tired. She was out this evening.
JOHNSON (*All is a coo, an emphatic coo*):   Aw—ain't that lovely. She still going out with the little Murchison boy?

---

[4] Johnson, and the scene in which she visits, were cut from the original production and from early editions.

MAMA (*Drily*):   Ummmm huh.

JOHNSON: That's lovely. You sure got lovely children, Younger. Me and Isaiah talks all the time 'bout what fine children you was blessed with. We sure do.

MAMA: Ruth, give Mis' Johnson a piece of sweet potato pie and some milk.

JOHNSON: Oh honey, I can't stay hardly a minute—I just dropped in to see if there was anything I could do. (*Accepting the food easily*) I guess y'all seen the news what's all over the colored paper this week . . .

MAMA: No—didn't get mine yet this week.

JOHNSON: (*Lifting her head and blinking with the spirit of catastrophe*):   You mean you ain't read 'bout them colored people that was bombed out their place out there?

(RUTH *straightens with concern and takes the paper and reads it.* JOHNSON *notices her and feeds commentary*)

JOHNSON: Ain't it something how bad these here white folks is getting here in Chicago! Lord, getting so you think you right down in Mississippi! (*With a tremendous and rather insincere sense of melodrama*) 'Course I thinks it's wonderful how our folks keeps on pushing out. You hear some of these Negroes round here talking 'bout how they don't go where they ain't wanted and all that—but not me, honey! (*This is a lie*) Wilhemenia Othella Johnson goes anywhere, any time she feels like it! (*With head movement for emphasis*) Yes I do! Why if we left it up to these here crackers, the poor niggers wouldn't have nothing—(*She clasps her hand over her mouth*) Oh, I always forgets you don't 'low that word in your house.

MAMA (*Quietly, looking at her*):   No—I don't 'low it.

JOHNSON (*Vigorously again*):   Me neither! I was just telling Isaiah yesterday when he come using it in front of me—I said, "Isaiah, it's just like Mis' Younger says all the time—"

MAMA: Don't you want some more pie?

JOHNSON: No—no thank you; this was lovely. I got to get on over home and have my midnight coffee. I hear some people say it don't let them sleep but I finds I can't close my eyes right lessen I done had that laaaast cup of coffee . . . (*She waits. A beat. Undaunted*) My Goodnight coffee, I calls it!

MAMA (*With much eye-rolling and communication between herself and* RUTH):   Ruth, why don't you give Mis' Johnson some coffee.

(RUTH *gives* MAMA *an unpleasant look for her kindness*)

JOHNSON (*Accepting the coffee*):   Where's Brother tonight?

MAMA: He's lying down.

JOHNSON: MMmmmmm, he sure gets his beauty rest, don't he? Good-looking man. Sure is a good-looking man! (*Reaching out to pat* RUTH'S *stomach again*) I guess that's how come we keep on having babies around here. (*She winks at* MAMA) One thing 'bout Brother, he always know how to have a *good* time. And soooooo ambitious! I bet it was his idea y'all moving out to Clybourne Park. Lord—I bet this time next month y'all's names will have been in the papers plenty—(*Holding up her hands to mark off each word of the headline she can see in front of her*) "NEGROES INVADE CLYBOURNE PARK—BOMBED!"

MAMA (*She and* RUTH *look at the woman in amazement*):   We ain't exactly moving out there to get bombed.

JOHNSON: Oh, honey—you know I'm praying to God every day that don't nothing like that happen! But you have to think of life like it is—and these here Chicago peckerwoods is some baaaad peckerwoods.

MAMA (*Wearily*): We done thought about all that Mis' Johnson.

(BENEATHA *comes out of the bedroom in her robe and passes through to the bathroom.* MRS. JOHNSON *turns*)

JOHNSON: Hello there, Bennie!

BENEATHA (*Crisply*): Hello, Mrs. Johnson.

JOHNSON: How is school?

BENEATHA (*Crisply*): Fine, thank you. (*She goes out.*)

JOHNSON (*Insulted*): Getting so she don't have much to say to nobody.

MAMA: The child was on her way to the bathroom.

JOHNSON: I know—but sometimes she act like ain't got time to pass the time of day with nobody ain't been to college. Oh—I ain't criticizing her none. It's just—you know how some of our young people gets when they get a little education. (MAMA *and* RUTH *say nothing, just look at her*) Yes—well. Well, I guess I better get on home. (*Unmoving*) 'Course I can understand how she must be proud and everything—being the only one in the family to make something of herself. I know just being a chauffeur ain't never satisfied Brother none. He shouldn't feel like that, though. Ain't nothing wrong with being a chauffeur.

MAMA: There's plenty wrong with it.

JOHNSON: What?

MAMA: Plenty. My husband always said being any kind of a servant wasn't a fit thing for a man to have to be. He always said a man's hands was made to make things, or to turn the earth with—not to drive nobody's car for 'em—or—(*She looks at her own hands*) carry they slop jars. And my boy is just like him—he wasn't meant to wait on nobody.

JOHNSON (*Rising, somewhat offended*): Mmmmmmmmm. The Youngers is too much for me! (*She looks around*) You sure one proud-acting bunch of colored folks. Well—I always thinks like Booker T. Washington said that time—"Education has spoiled many a good plow hand"—

MAMA: Is that what old Booker T. said?

JOHNSON: He sure did.

MAMA: Well, it sounds just like him. The fool.

JOHNSON (*Indignantly*): Well—he was one of our great men.

MAMA: Who said so?

JOHNSON (*Nonplussed*): You know, me and you ain't never agreed about some things, Lena Younger. I guess I better be going—

RUTH (*Quickly*): Good night.

JOHNSON: Good night. Oh—(*Thrusting it at her*) You can keep the paper! (*With a trill*) 'Night.

MAMA: Good night, Mis' Johnson.

(MRS. JOHNSON *exits*)

RUTH: If ignorance was gold—

MAMA: Shush. Don't talk about folks behind their backs.

RUTH: You do.

MAMA: I'm old and corrupted. (BENEATHA *enters*) You was rude to Mis' Johnson, Beneatha, and I don't like it at all.

BENEATHA (*At her door*): Mama, if there are two things we, as a people, have got to overcome, one is the Klu Klux Klan—and the other is Mrs. Johnson. (*She exits*)

MAMA: Smart aleck.

(*The phone rings*)

RUTH: I'll get it.

MAMA: Lord, ain't this a popular place tonight.

RUTH (*At the phone*):   Hello—Just a minute. (*Goes to door*) Walter, it's Mrs. Arnold. (*Waits. Goes back to the phone. Tense*) Hello. Yes, this is his wife speaking . . . He's lying down now. Yes . . . well, he'll be in tomorrow. He's been very sick. Yes—I know we should have called, but we were so sure he'd be able to come in today. Yes—yes, I'm very sorry. Yes . . . Thank you very much. (*She hangs up.* WALTER *is standing in the doorway of the bedroom behind her*) That was Mrs. Arnold.

WALTER (*Indifferently*):   Was it?

RUTH: She said if you don't come in tomorrow that they are getting a new man . . .

WALTER: Ain't that sad—ain't that crying sad.

RUTH: She said Mr. Arnold has had to take a cab for three days . . . Walter, you ain't been to work for three days! (*This is a revelation to her*) Where you been, Walter Lee Younger? (WALTER *looks at her and starts to laugh*) You're going to lose your job.

WALTER: That's right . . . (*He turns on the radio*)

RUTH: Oh, Walter, and with your mother working like a dog every day—

(*A steamy, deep blues pours into the room*)

WALTER: That's sad too—Everything is sad.

MAMA: What you been doing for these three days, son?

WALTER: Mama—you don't know all the things a man what got leisure can find to do in this city . . . What's this—Friday night? Well—Wednesday I borrowed Willy Harris' car and I went for a drive . . . just me and myself and I drove and drove . . . Way out . . . way past South Chicago, and I parked the car and I sat and looked at the steel mills all day long. I just sat in the car and looked at them big black chimneys for hours. Then I drove back and I went to the Green Hat. (*Pause*) And Thursday—Thursday I borrowed the car again and I got in it and I pointed it the other way and I drove the other way—for hours—way, way up to Wisconsin, and I looked at the farms. I just drove and looked at the farms. Then I drove back and I went to the Green Hat. (*Pause*) And today—today I didn't get the car. Today I just walked. All over the Southside. And I looked at the Negroes and they looked at me and finally I just sat down on the curb at Thirty-ninth and South Parkway and I just sat there and watched the Negroes go by. And then I went to the Green Hat. You all sad? You all depressed? And you know where I am going right now—

(RUTH *goes out quietly*)

MAMA: Oh, Big Walter, is this the harvest of our days?

WALTER: You know what I like about the Green Hat? I like this little cat they got there who blows a sax . . . He blows. He talks to me. He ain't but 'bout five feet tall and he's got a conked head and his eyes is always closed and he's all music—

MAMA (*Rising and getting some papers out of her handbag*):   Walter—

WALTER: And there's this other guy who plays the piano . . . and they got a sound. I mean they can work on some music . . . They got the best little combo in the world in Green Hat . . . You can just sit there and drink and listen to them three men play and you realize that don't nothing matter worth a damn, but just being there—

MAMA: I've helped do it to you, haven't I son? Walter I been wrong.

WALTER: Naw—you ain't never been wrong about nothing, Mama.

MAMA: Listen to me, now. I say I been wrong, son. That I been doing to you what the rest of the world been doing to you. (*She turns off the radio*) Walter— (*She stops and he looks up slowly at her and she meets his eyes pleadingly*) What you ain't never understood is that I ain't got nothing, don't own nothing, ain't never really wanted nothing that wasn't for you. There ain't nothing as precious to me . . . There ain't nothing worth holding on to, money, dreams, nothing else— if it means—if it means it's going to destroy my boy. (*She takes an envelope out of her handbag and puts it in front of him and he watches her without speaking or moving*) I paid the man thirty-five hundred dollars down on the house. That leaves sixty-five hundred dollars. Monday morning I want you to take this money and take three thousand dollars and put it in a savings account for Beneatha's medical schooling. The rest you put in a checking account—with your name on it. And from now on any penny that come out of it or that go in it is for you to look after. For you to decide. (*She drops her hands a little helplessly*) It ain't much, but it's all I got in the world and I'm putting it in your hands. I'm telling you to be the head of this family from now on like you supposed to be.

WALTER (*Stares at the money*):   You trust me like that, Mama?

MAMA: I ain't never stop trusting you. Like I ain't never stop loving you.

(*She goes out, and* WALTER *sits looking at the money on the table. Finally, in a decisive gesture, he gets up, and, in mingled joy and desperation, picks up the money. At the same moment,* TRAVIS *enters for bed*)

TRAVIS: What's the matter, Daddy? You drunk?

WALTER (*Sweetly, more sweetly than we have ever known him*):   No, Daddy ain't drunk. Daddy ain't going to never be drunk again . . .

TRAVIS: Well, good night, Daddy.

(*The* FATHER *has come from behind the couch and leans over, embracing his son*)

WALTER: Son, I feel like talking to you tonight.

TRAVIS: About what?

WALTER: Oh, about a lot of things. About you and what kind of man you going to be when you grow up . . . Son—son, what do you want to be when you grow up?

TRAVIS: A bus driver.

WALTER (*Laughing a little*):   A what? Man, that ain't nothing to want to be!

TRAVIS: Why not?

WALTER: 'Cause, man—it ain't big enough—you know what I mean.

TRAVIS: I don't know then. I can't make up my mind. Sometimes Mama asks me that too. And sometimes when I tell her I just want to be like you—she says she don't want me to be like that and sometimes she says she does . . .

WALTER (*Gathering him up in his arms*):   You know what, Travis? In seven years you going to be seventeen years old. And things is going to be very different with us in seven years, Travis. . . . One day when you are seventeen I'll come home—home from my office downtown somewhere—

TRAVIS: You don't work in no office, Daddy.

WALTER: No—but after tonight. After what your daddy gonna do tonight, there's going to be offices—a whole lot of offices. . . .

TRAVIS: What you gonna do tonight, Daddy?

WALTER: You wouldn't understand yet, son, but your daddy's gonna make a transaction . . . a business transaction that's going to change our lives. . . . That's how come one day when you 'bout seventeen years old I'll come home and I'll be pretty tired, you know what I mean, after a day of conferences and secretaries getting things wrong the way they do . . . 'cause an executive's life is hell, man—(*The more he talks the farther away he gets*) And I'll pull the car up on the driveway . . . just a plain black Chrysler, I think, with white walls—no—black tires. More elegant. Rich people don't have to be flashy . . . though I'll have to get something a little sportier for Ruth—maybe a Cadillac convertible to do her shopping in. . . . And I'll come up the steps to the house and the gardener will be clipping away at the hedges and he'll say, "Good evening, Mr. Younger." And I'll say, "Hello, Jefferson, how are you this evening?" And I'll go inside and Ruth will come downstairs and meet me at the door and we'll kiss each other and she'll take my arm and we'll go up to your room to see you sitting on the floor with the catalogues of all the great schools in America around you. . . . All the great schools in the world! And—and I'll say, all right son—it's your seventeenth birthday, what is it you've decided? . . . Just tell me where you want to go to school and you'll *go*. Just tell me, what it is you want to be—and you'll *be* it. . . . Whatever you want to be—Yessir! (*He holds his arms open for* TRAVIS) You just name it son . . . (TRAVIS *leaps into them*) and I hand you the world!

(WALTER'S *voice has risen in pitch and hysterical promise and on the last line he lifts* TRAVIS *high*)

(*Blackout*)

SCENE THREE

Time: Saturday, moving day, one week later.

Before the curtain rises, RUTH'S *voice, a strident, dramatic church alto, cuts through the silence.*

It is, in the darkness, a triumphant surge, a penetrating statement of expectation: "Oh, Lord, I don't feel no ways tired! Children, oh, glory hallelujah!"

As the curtain rises we see that RUTH *is alone in the living room, finishing up the family's packing. It is moving day. She is nailing crates and tying cartons.* BENEATHA *enters, carrying a guitar case, and watches her exuberant sister-in-law.*

RUTH: Hey!

BENEATHA (*Putting away the case*): Hi.

RUTH (*Pointing at a package*): Honey—look in that package there and see what I found on sale this morning at the South Center. (RUTH *gets up and moves to the package and draws out some curtains*) Lookahere—hand-turned hems!

BENEATHA: How do you know the window size out there?

RUTH (*Who hadn't thought of that*):   Oh—Well, they bound to fit something in the whole house. Anyhow, they was too good a bargain to pass up. (RUTH *slaps her head, suddenly remembering something*) Oh, Bennie—I meant to put a special note on that carton over there. That's your mama's good china and she wants 'em to be very careful with it.

BENEATHA: I'll do it.

(BENEATHA *finds a piece of paper and starts to draw large letters on it*)

RUTH: You know what I'm going to do soon as I get in that new house?

BENEATHA: What?

RUTH: Honey—I'm going to run me a tub of water up to here . . . (*With her fingers practically up to her nostrils*) And I'm going to get in it—and I am going to sit . . . and sit . . . and sit in that hot water and the first person who knocks to tell *me* to hurry up and come out—

BENEATHA: Gets shot at sunrise.

RUTH (*Laughing happily*):   You said it, sister! (*Noticing how large* BENEATHA *is absent-mindedly making the note*) Honey, they ain't going to read that from no airplane.

BENEATHA (*Laughing herself*):   I guess I always think things have more emphasis if they are big, somehow.

RUTH (*Looking up at her and smiling*):   You and your brother seem to have that as a philosophy of life. Lord, that man—done changed so 'round here. You know—you know what we did last night? Me and Walter Lee?

BENEATHA: What?

RUTH (*Smiling to herself*):   We went to the movies. (*Looking at* BENEATHA *to see if she understands*) We went to the movies. You know the last time me and Walter went to the movies together?

BENEATHA: No.

RUTH: Me neither. That's how long it been. (*Smiling again*) But we went last night. The picture wasn't much good, but that didn't seem to matter. We went—and we held hands.

BENEATHA: Oh, Lord!

RUTH: We held hands—and you know what?

BENEATHA: What?

RUTH: When we come out of the show it was late and dark and all the stores and things was closed up . . . and it was kind of chilly and there wasn't many people on the streets . . . and we was still holding hands, me and Walter.

BENEATHA: You're killing me.

(WALTER *enters with a large package. His happiness is deep in him; he cannot keep still with his new-found exuberance. He is singing and wiggling and snapping his fingers. He puts his package in a corner and puts a phonograph record, which he has brought in with him, on the record player. As the music, soulful and sensuous, comes up he dances over to* RUTH *and tries to get her to dance with him. She gives in at last to his raunchiness and in a fit of giggling allows herself to be drawn into his mood. They dip and she melts into his arms in a classic, body-melding "slow drag"*)

BENEATHA (*Regarding them a long time as they dance, then drawing in her breath for a deeply exaggerated comment which she does not particularly mean*): Talk about—olddddddddddd-fashionedddddddd—Negroes!

WALTER (*Stopping momentarily*):   What kind of Negroes?

(*He says this in fun. He is not angry with her today, nor with anyone. He starts to dance with his wife again*)

BENEATHA: Old-fashioned.

WALTER (*As he dances with* RUTH):   You know, when these *New Negroes* have their convention—(*Pointing at his sister*)—that is going to be the chairman of the Committee on Unending Agitation. (*He goes on dancing, then stops*) Race, race, race! . . . Girl, I do believe you are the first person in the history of the entire human race to successfully brainwash yourself. (BENEATHA *breaks up and he goes on dancing. He stops again, enjoying his tease*) Damn, even the N double A C P takes a holiday sometimes! (BENEATHA *and* RUTH *laugh. He dances with* RUTH *some more and starts to laugh and stops and pantomimes someone over an operating table*) I can just see that chick someday looking down at some poor cat on an operating table and before she starts to slice him, she says . . . (*Pulling his sleeves back maliciously*) "By the way, what are your views on civil rights down there? . . . "

(*He laughs at her again and starts to dance happily. The bell sounds*)

BENEATHA: Sticks and stones may break my bones but . . . words will never hurt me!

(BENEATHA *goes to the door and opens it as* WALTER *and* RUTH *go on with the clowning.* BENEATHA *is somewhat surprised to see a quiet-looking middle-aged white man in a business suit holding his hat and a briefcase in his hand and consulting a small piece of paper*)

MAN: Uh—how do you do, miss. I am looking for a Mrs.—(*He looks at the slip of paper*) Mrs. Lena Younger? (*He stops short, struck dumb at the sight of the oblivious* WALTER *and* RUTH)

BENEATHA (*Smoothing her hair with slight embarrassment*):   Oh—yes, that's my mother. Excuse me (*She closes the door and turns to quiet the other two*) Ruth! Brother! (*Enunciating precisely but soundlessly: "There's a white man at the door!" They stop dancing,* RUTH *cuts off the phonograph,* BENEATHA *opens the door. The man casts a curious quick glance at all of them*) Uh—come in please.

MAN (*Coming in*):   Thank you.

BENEATHA: My mother isn't here just now. Is it business?

MAN: Yes . . . well, of a sort.

WALTER (*Freely, the Man of the House*):   Have a seat. I'm Mrs. Younger's son. I look after most of her business matters.

(RUTH *and* BENEATHA *exchange amused glances*)

MAN (*Regarding* WALTER, *and sitting*):   Well—My name is Karl Lindner . . .

WALTER (*Stretching out his hand*):   Walter Younger. This is my wife—(RUTH *nods politely*)—and my sister.

LINDNER: How do you do.

WALTER (*Amiably, as he sits himself easily on a chair, leaning forward on his knees with interest and looking expectantly into the newcomer's face*):   What can we do for you, Mr. Lindner!

LINDNER (*Some minor shuffling of the hat and briefcase on his knees*):   Well—I am a representative of the Clybourne Park Improvement Association—

WALTER (*Pointing*):   Why don't you sit your things on the floor?

LINDNER: Oh—yes. Thank you. (*He slides the briefcase and hat under the chair*) And as I was saying—I am from the Clybourne Park Improvement Association and we have had it brought to our attention at the last meeting that you people—or at least your mother—has bought a piece of residential property at (*He digs for the slip of paper again*)—four o six Clybourne Street . . .

WALTER: That's right. Care for something to drink? Ruth, get Mr. Lindner a beer.

LINDNER (*Upset for some reason*):   Oh—no, really. I mean thank you very much, but no thank you.

RUTH (*Innocently*):   Some coffee?

LINDNER: Thank you, nothing at all.

(BEATHA *is watching the man carefully*)

LINDNER: Well, I don't know how much you folks know about our organization. (*He is a gentle man; thoughtful and somewhat labored in his manner*) It is one of these community organizations set up to look after—oh, you know, things like block upkeep and special projects and we also have what we call our New Neighbors Orientation Committee . . .

BEATHA (*Drily*):   Yes—and what do they do?

LINDNER (*Turning a little to her and then returning the main force to* WALTER): Well—it's what you might call a sort of welcoming committee, I guess. I mean they, we—I'm the chairman of the committee—go around and see the new people who move into the neighborhood and sort of give them the lowdown on the way we do things out in Clybourne Park.

BEATHA (*With appreciation of the two meanings, which escape* RUTH *and* WALTER):   Un-huh.

LINDNER: And we also have the category of what the association calls—(*He looks elsewhere*)—uh—special community problems . . .

BEATHA: Yes—and what are some of those?

WALTER: Girl, let the man talk.

LINDNER (*With understated relief*):   Thank you. I would sort of like to explain this thing in my own way. I mean I want to explain to you in a certain way.

WALTER: Go ahead.

LINDNER: Yes. Well. I'm going to try to get right to the point. I'm sure we'll all appreciate that in the long run.

BEATHA: Yes.

WALTER: Be still now!

LINDNER: Well—

RUTH (*Still innocently*):   Would you like another chair—you don't look comfortable.

LINDNER (*More frustrated than annoyed*):   No, thank you very much. Please. Well—to get right to the point I—(*A great breath, and he is off at last*) I am sure you people must be aware of some of the incidents which have happened in various parts of the city when colored people have moved into certain areas— (BEATHA *exhales heavily and starts tossing a piece of fruit up and down in the air*) Well—because we have what I think is going to be a unique type of organization in American community life—not only do we deplore that kind of thing—but we are trying to do something about it. (BEATHA *stops tossing and turns with a new and quizzical interest to the man*) We feel—(*gaining confidence in his mis-*

sion because of the interest in the faces of the people he is talking to)—we feel that most of the trouble in this world, when you come right down to it—(*He hits his knee for emphasis*)—most of the trouble exists because people just don't sit down and talk to each other.

RUTH (*Nodding as she might in church, pleased with the remark*):   You can say that again, mister.

LINDNER (*More encouraged by such affirmation*):   That we don't try hard enough in this world to understand the other fellow's problem. The other guy's point of view.

RUTH: Now that's right.

(BENEATHA *and* WALTER *merely watch and listen with genuine interest*)

LINDNER: Yes—that's the way we feel out in Clybourne Park. And that's why I was elected to come here this afternoon and talk to you people. Friendly like, you know, the way people should talk to each other and see if we couldn't find some way to work this thing out. As I say, the whole business is a matter of *caring* about the other fellow. Anybody can see that you are a nice family of folks, hard working and honest I'm sure. (BENEATHA *frowns slightly, quizzically, her head tilted regarding him*) Today everybody knows what it means to be on the outside of *something*. And of course, there is always somebody who is out to take advantage of people who don't always understand.

WALTER: What do you mean?

LINDNER: Well—you see our community is made up of people who've worked hard as the dickens for years to build up that little community. They're not rich and fancy people; just hard-working, honest people who don't really have much but those little homes and a dream of the kind of community they want to raise their children in. Now, I don't say we are perfect and there is a lot wrong in some of the things they want. But you've got to admit that a man, right or wrong, has the right to want to have the neighborhood he lives in a certain kind of way. And at the moment the overwhelming majority of our people out there feel that people get along better, take more of a common interest in the life of the community, when they share a common background. I want you to believe me when I tell you that race prejudice simply doesn't enter into it. It is a matter of the people of Clybourne Park believing, rightly or wrongly, as I say, that for the happiness of all concerned that our Negro families are happier when they live in their *own* communities.

BENEATHA (*With a grand and bitter gesture*):   This, friends, is the Welcoming Committee!

WALTER (*Dumfounded, looking at* LINDNER):   Is this what you came marching all the way over here to tell us?

LINDNER: Well, now we've been having a fine conversation. I hope you'll hear me all the way through.

WALTER (*Tightly*):   Go ahead, man.

LINDNER: You see—in the face of all the things I have said, we are prepared to make your family a very generous offer . . .

BENEATHA: Thirty pieces and not a coin less!

WALTER: Yeah?

LINDNER (*Putting on his glasses and drawing a form out of the briefcase*):   Our association is prepared, through the collective effort of our people, to buy the house from you at a financial gain to your family.

RUTH: Lord have mercy, ain't this the living gall!

WALTER: All right, you through?

LINDNER: Well, I want to give you the exact terms of the financial arrangement—

WALTER: We don't want to hear no exact terms of no arrangements. I want to know if you got any more to tell us 'bout getting together?

LINDNER (*Taking off his glasses*):   Well—I don't suppose that you feel . . .

WALTER: Never mind how I feel—you got any more to say 'bout how people ought to sit down and talk to each other? . . . Get out of my house, man.

(*He turns his back and walks to the door*)

LINDNER (*Looking around at the hostile faces and reaching and assembling his hat and briefcase*):   Well—I don't understand why you people are reacting this way. What do you think you are going to gain by moving into a neighborhood where you just aren't wanted and where some elements—well—people can get awful worked up when they feel that their whole way of life and everything they've ever worked for is threatened.

WALTER: Get out.

LINDNER (*At the door, holding a small card*):   Well—I'm sorry it went like this.

WALTER: Get out.

LINDNER (*Almost sadly regarding* WALTER):   You just can't force people to change their hearts, son.

(*He turns and puts his card on a table and exits.* WALTER *pushes the door to with stinging hatred, and stands looking at it.* RUTH *just sits and* BENEATHA *just stands. They say nothing.* MAMA *and* TRAVIS *enter*)

MAMA: Well—this all the packing got done since I left out of here this morning. I testify before God that my children got all the energy of the *dead!* What time the moving men due?

BENEATHA: Four o'clock. You had a caller, Mama.

(*She is smiling, teasingly*)

MAMA: Sure enough—who?

BENEATHA (*Her arms folded saucily*):   The Welcoming Committee.

(WALTER *and* RUTH *giggle*)

MAMA (*Innocently*):   Who?

BENEATHA: The Welcoming Committee. They said they're sure going to be glad to see you when you get there.

WALTER (*Devilishly*):   Yeah, they said they can't hardly wait to see your face.

(*Laughter*)

MAMA: (*Sensing their facetiousness*):   What's the matter with you all?

WALTER: Ain't nothing the matter with us. We just telling you 'bout the gentleman who came to see you this afternoon. From the Clybourne Park Improvement Association.

MAMA: What he want?

RUTH (*In the same mood as* BENEATHA *and* WALTER):   To welcome you, honey.

WALTER: He said they can't hardly wait. He said the one thing they don't

have, that they just *dying* to have out there is a fine family of fine colored people!
(*To* RUTH *and* BENEATHA) Ain't that right!

RUTH (*Mockingly*):   Yeah! He left his card—

BENEATHA (*Handing card to* MAMA):   In case.

(MAMA *reads and throws it on the floor—understanding and looking off as she draws her chair up to the table on which she has put her plant and some sticks and some cord*)

MAMA: Father, give us strength. (*Knowingly—and without fun*) Did he threaten us?

BENEATHA: Oh—Mama—they don't do it like that any more. He talked Brotherhood. He said everybody ought to learn how to sit down and hate each other with good Christian fellowship.

(*She and* WALTER *shake hands to ridicule the remark*)

MAMA (*Sadly*):   Lord, protect us . . .

RUTH: You should hear the money those folks raised to buy the house from us. All we paid and then some.

BENEATHA: What they think we going to do—eat 'em?

RUTH: No, honey, marry 'em.

MAMA (*Shaking her head*):   Lord, Lord, Lord . . .

RUTH: Well—that's the way the crackers crumble. (*A beat*) Joke.

BENEATHA (*Laughingly noticing what her mother is doing*):   Mama, what are you doing?

MAMA: Fixing my plant so it won't get hurt none on the way . . .

BENEATHA: Mama, you going to take *that* to the new house?

MAMA: Un-huh—

BENEATHA: That raggedy-looking old thing?

MAMA (*Stopping and looking at her*):   It expresses ME!

RUTH (*With delight, to* BENEATHA):   So there, Miss Thing!

(WALTER *comes to* MAMA *suddenly and bends down behind her and squeezes her in his arms with all his strength. She is overwhelmed by the suddenness of it and, though delighted, her manner is like that of* RUTH *and* TRAVIS)

MAMA: Look out now, boy! You make me mess up my thing here!

WALTER (*His face lit, he slips down on his knees beside her, his arms still about her*):   Mama . . . you know what it means to climb up in the chariot?

MAMA (*Gruffly, very happy*):   Get on away from me now . . .

RUTH (*Near the gift-wrapped package, trying to catch* WALTER'S *eye*):   Psst—

WALTER: What the old song say, Mama . . .

RUTH: Walter—Now?

(*She is pointing at the package*)

WALTER (*Speaking the lines, sweetly, playfully, in his mother's face*):
   I got wings . . . you got wings . . .
   All God's Children got wings . . .

MAMA: Boy—get out of my face and do some work . . .

WALTER:
   When I get to heaven gonna put on my wings,
   Gonna fly all over God's heaven . . .

BENEATHA (*Teasingly, from across the room*):   Everybody talking 'bout heaven ain't going there!

WALTER (*To* RUTH, *who is carrying the box across to them*):   I don't know, you think we ought to give her that . . . Seems to me she ain't been very appreciative around here.

MAMA (*Eying the box, which is obviously a gift*):   What is that?

WALTER (*Taking it from* RUTH *and putting it on the table in front of* MAMA):   Well—what you all think? Should we give it to her?

RUTH: Oh—she was pretty good today.

MAMA: I'll good you—

(*She turns her eyes to the box again*)

BENEATHA: Open it, Mama.

(*She stands up, looks at it, turns and looks at all of them, and then presses her hands together and does not open the package*)

WALTER (*Sweetly*):   Open it, Mama. It's for you. (MAMA *looks in his eyes. It is the first present in her life without it being Christmas. Slowly she opens her package and lifts out, one by one, a brand-new sparkling set of gardening tools.* WALTER *continues, prodding*) Ruth made up the note—read it . . .

MAMA (*Picking up the card and adjusting her glasses*):   "To our own Mrs. Miniver[5]—Love from Brother, Ruth and Beneatha." Ain't that lovely . . .—

TRAVIS (*Tugging at his father's sleeve*):   Daddy, can I give her mine now?

WALTER: All right, son. (TRAVIS *flies to get his gift*)

MAMA: Now I don't have to use my knives and forks no more . . .

WALTER: Travis didn't want to go in with the rest of us, Mama. He got his own. (*Somewhat amused*) We don't know what it is . . .

TRAVIS (*Racing back in the room with a large hatbox and putting it in front of his grandmother*):   Here!

MAMA: Lord have mercy, baby. You done gone and bought your grandmother a hat?

TRAVIS (*Very proud*):   Open it!

(*She does and lifts out an elaborate, but very elaborate, wide gardening hat, and all the adults break up at the sight of it*)

RUTH: Travis, honey, what is that?

TRAVIS (*Who thinks it is beautiful and appropriate*):   It's a gardening hat! Like the ladies always have on in the magazines when they work in their gardens.

BENEATHA (*Giggling fiercely*):   Travis—we were trying to make Mama Mrs. Miniver—not Scarlett O'Hara!

MAMA (*Indignantly*):   What's the matter with you all! This here is a beautiful hat! (*Absurdly*) I always wanted me one just like it!

(*She pops it on her head to prove it to her grandson, and the hat is ludicrous and considerably oversized*)

RUTH: Hot dog! Go, Mama!

WALTER (*Doubled over with laughter*):   I'm sorry, Mama—but you look like you ready to go out and chop you some cotton sure enough!

---

[5] The title character of a 1942 movie.

(*They all laugh except* MAMA, *out of deference to* TRAVIS' *feelings*)

MAMA (*Gathering the boy up to her*):   Bless your heart—this is the prettiest hat I ever owned— (WALTER, RUTH and BENEATHA *chime in—noisily, festively and insincerely congratulating* TRAVIS *on his gift*) What are we all standing around here for? We ain't finished packin' yet. Bennie, you ain't packed one book.

(*The bell rings*)

BENEATHA: That couldn't be the movers . . . it's not hardly two good yet—

(BENEATHA *goes into her room.* MAMA *starts for door*)

WALTER (*Turning, stiffening*):   Wait—wait—I'll get it.

(*He stands and looks at the door*)

MAMA: You expecting company, son?
WALTER (*Just looking at the door*):   Yeah—yeah . . .

(MAMA *looks at* RUTH, *and they exchange innocent and unfrightened glances*)

MAMA (*Not understanding*):   Well, let them in, son.
BENEATHA (*From her room*):   We need some more string.
MAMA: Travis—you run to the hardware and get me some string cord.

(MAMA *goes out and* WALTER *turns and looks at* RUTH. TRAVIS *goes to a dish for money*)

RUTH: Why don't you answer the door, man?
WALTER (*Suddenly bounding across the floor to embrace her*):   'Cause sometimes it hard to let the future begin! (*Stooping down in her face*)
  I got wings! You got wings!
  All God's children got wings!

(*He crosses to the door and throws it open. Standing there is a very slight little man in a not too prosperous business suit and with haunted frightened eyes and a hat pulled down tightly, brim up, around his forehead.* TRAVIS *passes between the men and exits.* WALTER *leans deep in the man's face, still in his jubilance*)

  When I get to heaven gonna put on my wings,
  Gonna fly all over God's heaven . . .

(*The little man just stares at him*)

  Heaven—

(*Suddenly he stops and looks past the little man into the empty hallway*) Where's Willy, man?

BOBO: He ain't with me.
WALTER (*Not disturbed*):   Oh—come on in. You know my wife.
BOBO (*Dumbly, taking off his hat*):   Yes—h'you, Miss Ruth.
RUTH (*Quietly, a mood apart from her husband already, seeing* BOBO):   Hello, Bobo.
WALTER: You right on time today . . . Right on time. That's the way! (*He slaps* BOBO *on his back*) Sit down . . . lemme hear.

(RUTH *stands stiffly and quietly in back of them, as though somehow she senses death, her eyes fixed on her husband*)

BOBO (*His frightened eyes on the floor, his hat in his hands*):   Could I please get a drink of water, before I tell you about it, Walter Lee?

(WALTER *does not take his eyes off the man.* RUTH *goes blindly to the tap and gets a glass of water and brings it to* BOBO)

WALTER: There ain't nothing wrong, is there?

BOBO: Lemme tell you—

WALTER: Man—didn't nothing go wrong?

BOBO: Lemme tell you—Walter Lee. (*Looking at* RUTH *and talking to her more than to* WALTER) You know how it was. I got to tell you how it was. I mean first I got to tell you how it was all the way . . . I mean about the money I put in, Walter Lee . . .

WALTER (*With taut agitation now*):   What about the money you put in?

BOBO: Well—it wasn't much as we told you—me and Willy—(*He stops*) I'm sorry, Walter. I got a bad feeling about it. I got a real bad feeling about it . . .

WALTER: Man, what you telling me about all this for? . . . Tell me what happened in Springfield . . .

BOBO: Springfield.

RUTH (*Like a dead woman*):   What was supposed to happen in Springfield?

BOBO (*To her*):   This deal that me and Walter went into with Willy—Me and Willy was going to go down to Springfield and spread some money 'round so's we wouldn't have to wait so long for the liquor license . . . That's what we were going to do. Everybody said that was the way you had to do, you understand, Miss Ruth?

WALTER: Man—what happened down there?

BOBO (*A pitiful man, near tears*):   I'm trying to tell you, Walter.

WALTER (*Screaming at him suddenly*):   THEN TELL ME, GODDAM-MIT . . . WHAT'S THE MATTER WITH YOU?

BOBO: Man . . . I didn't go to no Springfield, yesterday.

WALTER (*Halted, life hanging in the moment*):   Why not?

BOBO (*The long way, the hard way to tell*):   'Cause I didn't have no reasons to . . .

WALTER: Man, what are you talking about!

BOBO: I'm talking about the fact that when I got to the train station yesterday morning—eight o'clock like we planned . . . Man—*Willy didn't never show up.*

WALTER: Why . . . where was he . . . where is he?

BOBO: That's what I'm trying to tell you . . . I don't know . . . I waited six hours . . . I called his house . . . and I waited . . . six hours . . . I waited in that train station six hours . . . (*Breaking into tears*) That was all the extra money I had in the world . . . (*Looking up at* WALTER *with tears running down his face*) Man, *Willy is gone.*

WALTER: Gone, what you mean Willy is gone? Gone where? You mean he went by himself. You mean he went off to Springfield by himself—to take care of getting the license—(*Turns and looks anxiously at* RUTH) You mean maybe he didn't want too many people in on the business down there? (*Looks to* RUTH *again, as before*) You know Willy got his own ways. (*Looks back to* BOBO) Maybe you was late yesterday and he just went on down there without you. Maybe—maybe—he's been callin' you at home tryin' to tell you what happened or something. Maybe—maybe—he just got sick. He's somewhere—he's got to be somewhere. We just got to find him—me and you got to find him. (*Grabs* BOBO *senselessly by the collar and starts to shake him*) We got to!

BOBO (*In sudden angry, frightened agony*):   What's the matter with you Walter! *When a cat take off with your money he don't leave you no road maps!*

WALTER (*Turning madly, as though he is looking for* WILLY *in the very room*): Willy! . . . Willy . . . don't do it . . . Please don't do it . . . Man, not with that money . . . Man, please, not with that money . . . Oh, God . . . Don't let it be true . . . (*He is wandering around, crying out for* WILLY *and looking for him or perhaps for help from God*) Man . . . I trusted you . . . Man, I put my life in your hands . . . (*He starts to crumple down on the floor as* RUTH *just covers her face in horror.* MAMA *opens the door and comes into the room, with* BENEATHA *behind her*) Man . . . (*He starts to pound the floor with his fists, sobbing wildly*) THAT MONEY IS MADE OUT OF MY FATHER'S FLESH——

BOBO (*Standing over him helplessly*):   I'm sorry, Walter . . . (*Only* WALTER'S *sobs reply.* BOBO *puts on his hat*) I had my life staked on this deal, too . . .

(*He exits*)

MAMA (*To* WALTER):   Son—(*She goes to him, bends down to him, talks to his bent head*) Son . . . Is it gone? Son, I gave you sixty-five hundred dollars. Is it gone? All of it? Beneatha's money too?

WALTER (*Lifting his head slowly*):   Mama . . . I never . . . went to the bank at all . . .

MAMA (*Not wanting to believe him*):   You mean . . . your sister's school money . . . you used that too . . . Walter? . . .

WALTER: Yessss! All of it . . . It's all gone . . .

(*There is total silence.* RUTH *stands with her face covered with her hands;* BENEATHA *leans forlornly against a wall, fingering a piece of red ribbon from the mother's gift.* MAMA *stops and looks at her son without recognition and then, quite without thinking about it, starts to beat him senselessly in the face.* BENEATHA *goes to them and stops it*)

BENEATHA: Mama!

(MAMA *stops and looks at both of her children and rises slowly and wanders vaguely, aimlessly away from them*)

MAMA: I seen . . . him . . . night after night . . . come in . . . and look at that rug . . . and then look at me . . . the red showing in his eyes . . . the veins moving in his head . . . I seen him grow thin and old before he was forty . . . working and working and working like somebody's old horse . . . killing himself . . . and you—you give it all away in a day—(*She raises her arms to strike him again*)

BENEATHA: Mama—

MAMA: Oh, God . . . (*She looks up to Him*) Look down here—and show me the strength.

BENEATHA: Mama—

MAMA (*Folding over*):   Strength . . .

BENEATHA (*Plaintively*):   Mama . . .

MAMA: Strength!

Curtain

ACT III

An hour later.

At curtain, there is a sullen light of gloom in the living room, gray light not unlike that which began the first scene of Act One. At left we can see WALTER *within his room, alone with himself. He is stretched out on the bed, his shirt out and open, his arms under his head. He does not smoke, he does not cry out, he merely lies there, looking up at the ceiling, much as if he were alone in the world.*

In the living room BENEATHA *sits at the table, still surrounded by the now almost ominous packing crates. She sits looking off. We feel that this is a mood struck perhaps an hour before, and it lingers now, full of the empty sound of profound disappointment. We see on a line from her brother's bedroom the sameness of their attitudes. Presently the bell rings and* BENEATHA *rises without ambition or interest in answering. It is* ASAGAI, *smiling broadly, striding into the room with energy and happy expectation and conversation.*

ASAGAI: I came over . . . I had some free time. I thought I might help with the packing. Ah, I like the look of packing crates! A household in preparation for a journey! It depresses some people . . . but for me . . . it is another feeling. Something full of the flow of life, do you understand? Movement, progress . . . It makes me think of Africa.

BENEATHA: Africa!

ASAGAI: What kind of a mood is this? Have I told you how deeply you move me?

BENEATHA: He gave away the money, Asagai . . .

ASAGAI: Who gave away what money?

BENEATHA: The insurance money. My brother gave it away.

ASAGAI: Gave it away?

BENEATHA: He made an investment! With a man even Travis wouldn't have trusted with his most worn-out marbles.

ASAGAI: And it's gone?

BENEATHA: Gone!

ASAGAI: I'm very sorry . . . And you, now?

BENEATHA: Me? . . . Me? . . . Me, I'm nothing . . . Me. When I was very small . . . we used to take our sleds out in the wintertime and the only hills we had were the ice-covered stone steps of some houses down the street. And we used to fill them in with snow and make them smooth and slide down them all day . . . and it was very dangerous, you know . . . far too steep . . . and sure enough one day a kid named Rufus came down too fast and hit the sidewalk and we saw his face just split open right there in front of us . . . And I remember standing there looking at his bloody open face thinking that was the end of Rufus. But the ambulance came and they took him to the hospital and they fixed the broken bones and they sewed it all up . . . and the next time I saw Rufus he just had a little line down the middle of his face . . . I never got over that . . .

ASAGAI: What?

BENEATHA: That that was what one person could do for another, fix him up— sew up the problem, make him all right again. That was the most marvelous thing in the world . . . I wanted to do that. I always thought it was the one concrete thing in the world that a human being could do. Fix up the sick, you know—and make them whole again. This was truly being God . . .

ASAGAI: You wanted to be God?

BENEATHA: No—I wanted to cure. It used to be so important to me. I wanted to cure. It used to matter. I used to care. I mean about people and how their bodies hurt . . .

ASAGAI: And you've stopped caring?

BENEATHA: Yes—I think so.

ASAGAI: Why?

BENEATHA (*Bitterly*):   Because it doesn't seem deep enough, close enough to what ails mankind! It was a child's way of seeing things—or an idealist's.

ASAGAI: Children see things very well sometimes—and idealists even better.

BENEATHA: I know that's what you think. Because you are still where I left off. You with all your talk and dreams about Africa! You still think you can patch up the world. Cure the Great Sore of Colonialism—(*Loftily, mocking it*) with the Penicillin of Independence—!

ASAGAI: Yes!

BENEATHA: Independence *and then what?* What about all the crooks and thieves and just plain idiots who will come into power and steal and plunder the same as before—only now they will be black and do it in the name of the new Independence—WHAT ABOUT THEM?!

ASAGAI: That will be the problem for another time. First we must get there.

BENEATHA: And where does it end?

ASAGAI: End? Who even spoke of an end? To life? To living?

BENEATHA: An end to misery! To stupidity! Don't you see there isn't any real progress, Asagai, there is only one large circle that we march in, around and around, each of us with our own little picture in front of us—our own little mirage that we think is the future.

ASAGAI: That is the mistake.

BENEATHA: What?

ASAGAI: What you just said—about the circle. It isn't a circle—it is simply a long line—as in geometry, you know, one that reaches into infinity. And because we cannot see the end—we also cannot see how it changes. And it is very odd but those who see the changes—who dream, who will not give up—are called idealists . . . and those who see only the circle—we call *them* the "realists"!

BENEATHA: Asagai, while I was sleeping in that bed in there, people went out and took the future right out of my hands! And nobody asked me, nobody consulted me—they just went out and changed my life!

ASAGAI: Was it your money?

BENEATHA: What?

ASAGAI: Was it your money he gave away?

BENEATHA: It belonged to all of us.

ASAGAI: But did you earn it? Would you have had it at all if your father had not died?

BENEATHA: No.

ASAGAI: Then isn't there something wrong in a house—in a world—where all dreams, good or bad, must depend on the death of a man? I never thought to see *you* like this, Alaiyo. You! Your brother made a mistake and you are grateful to him so that now you can give up the ailing human race on account of it! You talk about what good is struggle, what good is anything! Where are we all going and why are we bothering!

BENEATHA: AND YOU CANNOT ANSWER IT!

ASAGAI (*Shouting over her*):   *I LIVE THE ANSWER!* (*Pause*) In my village at home it is the exceptional man who can even read a newspaper . . . or who ever sees a book at all. I will go home and much of what I will have to say will seem strange to the people of my village. But I will teach and work and things will happen, slowly and swiftly. At times it will seem that nothing changes at all . . . and then again the sudden dramatic events which make history leap into the future. And then quiet again. Retrogression even. Guns, murder, revolution. And I even will have moments when I wonder if the quiet was not better than all that death and hatred. But I will look about my village at the illiteracy and disease and ignorance and I will not wonder long. And perhaps . . . perhaps I will be a great man . . . I mean perhaps I will hold on to the substance of truth and find my way always with the right course . . . and perhaps for it I will be butchered in my bed some night by the servants of empire . . .

BENEATHA: *The martyr!*

ASAGAI (*He smiles*): . . . or perhaps I shall live to be a very old man, respected and esteemed in my new nation . . . And perhaps I shall hold office and this is what I'm trying to tell you, Alaiyo: Perhaps the things I believe now for my country will be wrong and outmoded, and I will not understand and do terrible things to have things my way or merely to keep my power. Don't you see that there will be young men and women—not British soldiers then, but my own black countrymen—to step out of the shadows some evening and slit my then useless throat? Don't you see they have always been there . . . that they always will be. And that such a thing as my own death will be an advance? They who might kill me even . . . actually replenish all that I was.

BENEATHA: Oh, Asagai, I know all that.

ASAGAI: Good! Then stop moaning and groaning and tell me what you plan to do.

BENEATHA: Do?

ASAGAI: I have a bit of a suggestion.

BENEATHA: What?

ASAGAI (*Rather quietly for him*):   That when it is all over—that you come home with me—

BENEATHA (*Staring at him and crossing away with exasperation*):   Oh—Asagai—at this moment you decide to be romantic!

ASAGAI (*Quickly understanding the misunderstanding*):   My dear, young creature of the New World—I do not mean across the city—I mean across the ocean: home—to Africa.

BENEATHA (*Slowly understanding and turning to him with murmured amazement*):   To Africa?

ASAGAI: Yes! . . . (*Smiling and lifting his arms playfully*) Three hundred years later the African Prince rose up out of the seas and swept the maiden back across the middle passage over which her ancestors had come—

BENEATHA (*Unable to play*):   To—to Nigeria?

ASAGAI: Nigeria. Home. (*Coming to her with genuine romantic flippancy*) I will show you our mountains and our stars; and give you cool drinks from gourds and teach you the old songs and the ways of our people—and, in time, we will pretend that—(*Very Softly*)—you have only been away for a day. Say that you'll come—(*He swings her around and takes her full in his arms in a kiss which proceeds to passion*)

BENEATHA (*Pulling away suddenly*):   You're getting me all mixed up—

ASAGAI: Why?

BENEATHA: Too many things—too many things have happened today. I must sit down and think. I don't know what I feel about anything right this minute.

(She promptly sits down and props her chin on her fist)

ASAGAI *(Charmed)*:   All right, I shall leave you. No—don't get up. *(Touching her, gently, sweetly)* Just sit awhile and think . . . Never be afraid to sit awhile and think. *(He goes to door and looks at her)* How often I have looked at you and said, "Ah—so this is what the New World hath finally wrought . . . "

(He exits. BENEATHA sits on alone. Presently WALTER enters from his room and starts to rummage through things, feverishly looking for something. She looks up and turns in her seat)

BENEATHA *(Hissingly)*:   Yes—just look at what the New World hath wrought! . . . Just look! *(She gestures with bitter disgust)* There he is! *Monsieur le petit bourgeois noir*[6]—himself! There he is—Symbol of a Rising Class! Entrepreneur! Titan of the system! (WALTER *ignores her completely and continues frantically and destructively looking for something and hurling things to floor and tearing things out of their place in his search.* BENEATHA *ignores the eccentricity of his actions and goes on with the monologue of insult)* Did you dream of yachts on Lake Michigan, Brother? Did you see yourself on that Great Day sitting down at the Conference Table, surrounded by all the mighty bald-headed men in America? All halted, waiting, breathless, waiting for your pronouncements on industry? Waiting for you—Chairman of the Board! (WALTER *finds what he is looking for— a small piece of white paper—and pushes it in his pocket and puts on his coat and rushes out without ever having looked at her. She shouts after him)* I look at you and I see the final triumph of stupidity in the world!

(The door slams and she returns to just sitting again. RUTH *comes quickly out of* MAMA'S *room)*

RUTH: Who was that?

BENEATHA: Your husband.

RUTH: Where did he go?

BENEATHA: Who knows—maybe he has an appointment at U.S. Steel.

RUTH *(Anxiously, with frightened eyes)*:   You didn't say nothing bad to him, did you?

BENEATHA: Bad? Say anything bad to him? No—I told him he was a sweet boy and full of dreams and everything is strictly peachy keen, as the ofay[7] kids say!

(MAMA enters from her bedroom. She is lost, vague, trying to catch hold, to make some sense of her former command of the world, but it still eludes her. A sense of waste overwhelms her gait; a measure of apology rides on her shoulders. She goes to her plant, which has remained on the table, looks at it, picks it up and takes it to the window sill and sits it outside, and she stands and looks at it a long moment. Then she closes the window, straightens her body with effort and turns around to her children)

MAMA: Well—ain't it a mess in here, though? *(A false cheerfulness, a beginning of something)* I guess we all better stop moping around and get some work

---

[6] "Mr. Middle Class Black" (French).   [7] A disparaging term for white.

done. All this unpacking and everything we got to do. (RUTH *raises her head slowly in response to the sense of the line; and* BENEATHA *in similar manner turns very slowly to look at her mother*) One of you all better call the moving people and tell 'em not to come.

RUTH: Tell 'em not to come?

MAMA: Of course, baby. Ain't no need in 'em coming all the way here and having to go back. They charges for that too. (*She sits down, fingers to her brow, thinking*) Lord, ever since I was a little girl, I always remembers people saying, "Lena—Lena Eggleston, you aims too high all the time. You needs to slow down and see life a little more like it is. Just slow down some." That's what they always used to say down home—"Lord, that Lena Eggleston is a high-minded thing. She'll get her due one day!"

RUTH: No, Lena . . .

MAMA: Me and Big Walter just didn't never learn right.

RUTH: Lena, no! We gotta go. Bennie—tell her . . . (*She rises and crosses to* BENEATHA *with her arms outstretched.* BENEATHA *doesn't respond*) Tell her we can still move . . . the notes ain't but a hundred and twenty-five a month. We got four grown people in this house—we can work . . .

MAMA (*To herself*):   Just aimed too high all the time—

RUTH (*Turning and going to* MAMA *fast—the words pouring out with urgency and desperation*):   Lena–I'll work . . . I'll work twenty hours a day in all the kitchens in Chicago . . . I'll strap my baby on my back if I have to and scrub all the floors in America and wash all the sheets in America if I have to—but we got to MOVE! We got to get OUT OF HERE!!

(MAMA *reaches out absently and pats* RUTH'S *hand*)

MAMA: No—I see things differently now. Been thinking 'bout some of the things we could do to fix this place up some. I seen a second-hand bureau over on Maxwell Street just the other day that could fit right there. (*She points to where the new furniture might go.* RUTH *wanders away from her*) Would need some new handles on it and then a little varnish and it look like something brand-new. And—we can put up them new curtains in the kitchen . . . Why this place be looking fine. Cheer us all up so that we forget trouble ever come . . . (*To* RUTH) And you could get some nice screens to put up in your room round the baby's bassinet . . . (*She looks at both of them, pleadingly*) Sometimes you just got to know when to give up some things . . . and hold on to what you got. . . .

(WALTER *enters from the outside, looking spent and leaning against the door, his coat hanging from him*)

MAMA: Where you been, son?

WALTER (*Breathing hard*):   Made a call.

MAMA: To who, son?

WALTER: To The Man. (*He heads for his room*)

MAMA: What man, baby?

WALTER (*Stops in the door*):   The Man, Mama. Don't you know who The Man is?

RUTH: Walter Lee?

WALTER: *The Man.* Like the guys in the streets say—The Man. Captain Boss—Mistuh Charley . . . Old Cap'n Please Mr. Bossman . . .

BENEATHA (*Suddenly*):   Lindner!

WALTER: That's right! That's good. I told him to come right over.

BENEATHA (*Fiercely, understanding*):   For what? What do you want to see him for!

WALTER (*Looking at his sister*):   We going to do business with him.

MAMA: What you talking 'bout, son?

WALTER: Talking 'bout life, Mama. You all always telling me to see life like it is. Well—I laid in there on my back today . . . and I figured it out. Life just like it is. Who gets and who don't get. (*He sits down with his coat on and laughs*) Mama, you know it's all divided up. Life is. Sure enough. Between the takers and the "tooken." (*He laughs*) I've figured it out finally. (*He looks around at them*) Yeah. Some of us always getting "tooken." (*He laughs*) People like Willy Harris, they don't never get "tooken." And you know why the rest of us do? 'Cause we all mixed up. Mixed up bad. We get to looking 'round for the right and the wrong; and we worry about it and cry about it and stay up nights trying to figure out 'bout the wrong and the right of things all the time . . . And all the time, man, them takers is out there operating, just taking and taking. Willy Harris? Shoot—Willy Harris don't even count. He don't even count in the big scheme of things. But I'll say one thing for old Willy Harris . . . he's taught me something. He's taught me to keep my eye on what counts in this world. Yeah—(*Shouting out a little*) Thanks, Willy!

RUTH: What did you call that man for, Walter Lee?

WALTER: Called him to tell him to come on over to the show. Gonna put on a show for the man. Just what he wants to see. You see, Mama, the man came here today and he told us that them people out there where you want us to move—well they so upset they willing to pay us *not* to move! (*He laughs again*) And—and oh, Mama—you would of been proud of the way me and Ruth and Bennie acted. We told him to get out . . . Lord have mercy! We told the man to get out! Oh, we was some proud folks this afternoon, yeah. (*He lights a cigarette*) We were still full of that old-time stuff . . .

RUTH (*Coming toward him slowly*):   You talking 'bout taking them people's money to keep us from moving in that house?

WALTER: I ain't just talking 'bout it, baby—I'm telling you that's what's going to happen!

BENEATHA: Oh, God! Where is the bottom! Where is the real honest-to-God bottom so he can't go any farther!

WALTER: See—that's the old stuff. You and that boy that was here today. You all want everybody to carry a flag and a spear and sing some marching songs, huh? You wanna spend your life looking into things and trying to find the right and the wrong part, huh? Yeah. You know what's going to happen to that boy someday—he'll find himself sitting in a dungeon, locked in forever—and the takers will have the key! Forget it, baby! There ain't no causes—there ain't nothing but taking in this world, and he who takes most is smartest—and it don't make a damn bit of difference *how*.

MAMA: You making something inside me cry, son. Some awful pain inside me.

WALTER: Don't cry, Mama. Understand. That white man is going to walk in that door able to write checks for more money than we ever had. It's important to him and I'm going to help him . . . I'm going to put on the show, Mama.

MAMA: Son—I come from five generations of people who was slaves and sharecroppers—but ain't nobody in my family never let nobody pay 'em no money that was a way of telling us we wasn't fit to walk the earth. We ain't never been that poor. (*Raising her eyes and looking at him*) We ain't never been that—dead inside.

BENEATHA: Well—we are dead now. All the talk about dreams and sunlight that goes on in this house. It's all dead now.

WALTER: What's the matter with you all! I didn't make this world! It was give to me this way! Hell, yes, I want me some yachts someday! Yes, I want to hang some real pearls 'round my wife's neck. Ain't she supposed to wear no pearls? Somebody tell me—tell me, who decides which women is suppose to wear pearls in this world. I tell you I am a *man*—and I think my wife should wear some pearls in this world!

(*This last line hangs a good while and* WALTER *begins to move about the room. The word "Man" has penetrated his consciousness; he mumbles it to himself repeatedly between strange agitated pauses as he moves about*)

MAMA: Baby, how you going to feel on the inside?

WALTER: Fine! . . . Going to feel fine . . . a man . . .

MAMA: You won't have nothing left then, Walter Lee.

WALTER (*Coming to her*):   I'm going to feel fine, Mama. I'm going to look that son-of-a-bitch in the eyes and say—(*He falters*)—and say, "All right, Mr. Lindner—(*He falters even more*)—that's *your* neighborhood out there! You got the right to keep it like you want! You got the right to have it like you want! Just write the check and—the house is yours." And—and I am going to say—(*His voice almost breaks*) "And you—you people just put the money in my hand and you won't have to live next to this bunch of stinking niggers! . . . " (*He straightens up and moves away from his mother, walking around the room*) And maybe—maybe I'll just get down on my black knees . . . (*He does so;* RUTH *and* BENNIE *and* MAMA *watch him in frozen horror*) "Captain, Mistuh, Bossman—(*Groveling and grinning and wringing his hands in profoundly anguished imitation of the slow-witted movie stereotype*) A-hee-hee-hee! Oh, yassuh boss! Yasssssuh! Great white—(*Voice breaking, he forces himself to go on*)—Father, just gi' ussen de money, fo' God's sake, and we's—we's ain't gwine come out deh and dirty up yo' white folks neighborhood . . . " (*He breaks down completely*) And I'll feel fine! Fine! FINE! (*He gets up and goes into the bedroom*)

BENEATHA: That is not a man. That is nothing but a toothless rat.

MAMA: Yes—death done come in this here house. (*She is nodding, slowly, reflectively*) Done come walking in my house on the lips of my children. You what supposed to be my beginning again. You—what supposed to be my harvest. (*To* BENEATHA) You—you mourning your brother?

BENEATHA: He's no brother of mine.

MAMA: What you say?

BENEATHA: I said that that individual in that room is no brother of mine.

MAMA: That's what I thought you said. You feeling like you better than he is today? (BENEATHA *does not answer*) Yes? What you tell him a minute ago? That he wasn't a man? Yes? You give him up for me? You done wrote his epitaph too—like the rest of the world? Well, who give you the privilege?

BENEATHA: Be on my side for once! You saw what he just did, Mama! You saw him—down on his knees. Wasn't it you who taught me to despise any man who would do that? Do what he's going to do?

MAMA: Yes—I taught you that. Me and your daddy. But I thought I taught you something else too . . . I thought I taught you to love him.

BENEATHA: Love him? There is nothing left to love.

MAMA: There is *always* something left to love. And if you ain't learned that, you ain't learned nothing. (*Looking at her*) Have you cried for that boy today? I don't mean for yourself and for the family 'cause we lost the money. I mean for him: what he been through and what it done to him. Child, when do you think is the time to love somebody the most? When they done good and made things easy for everybody? Well then, you ain't through learning—because that ain't the time at all. It's when he's at his lowest and can't believe in hisself 'cause the world done whipped him so! When you starts measuring somebody, measure him right, child, measure him right. Make sure you done taken into account what hills and valleys he come through before he got to wherever he is.

(TRAVIS *bursts into the room at the end of the speech, leaving the door open*)

TRAVIS: Grandmama—the moving men are downstairs! The truck just pulled up.

MAMA (*Turning and looking at him*): Are they, baby? They downstairs?

(*She sighs and sits.* LINDNER *appears in the doorway. He peers in and knocks lightly, to gain attention, and comes in. All turn to look at him*)

LINDNER (*Hat and briefcase in hand*): Uh—hello . . .

(RUTH *crosses mechanically to the bedroom door and opens it and lets it swing open freely and slowly as the lights come up on* WALTER *within, still in his coat, sitting at the far corner of the room. He looks up and out through the room to* LINDNER)

RUTH: He's here.

(*A long minute passes and* WALTER *slowly gets up*)

LINDNER (*Coming to the table with efficiency, putting his briefcase on the table and starting to unfold papers and unscrew fountain pens*): Well, I certainly was glad to hear from you people. (WALTER *has begun the trek out of the room, slowly and awkwardly, rather like a small boy, passing the back of his sleeve across his mouth from time to time*) Life can really be so much simpler than people let it be most of the time. Well—with whom do I negotiate? You, Mrs. Younger, or your son here? (MAMA *sits with her hands folded on her lap and her eyes closed as* WALTER *advances.* TRAVIS *goes closer to* LINDNER *and looks at the papers curiously*) Just some official papers, sonny.

RUTH: Travis, you go downstairs—

MAMA (*Opening her eyes and looking into* WALTER'S): No. Travis, you stay right here. And you make him understand what you doing, Walter Lee. You teach him good. Like Willy Harris taught you. You show where our five generations done come to. (WALTER *looks from her to the boy, who grins at him innocently*) Go ahead, son—(*She folds her hands and closes her eyes*) Go ahead.

WALTER (*At last crosses to* LINDNER, *who is reviewing the contract*): Well, Mr. Lindner. (BENEATHA *turns away*) We called you—(*There is a profound, simple groping quality in his speech*)—because, well, me and my family (*He looks around and shifts from one foot to the other*) Well—we are very plain people . . .

LINDNER: Yes—

WALTER: I mean—I have worked as a chauffeur most of my life—and my wife

here, she does domestic work in people's kitchens. So does my mother. I mean—
we are plain people . . .

LINDNER: Yes, Mr. Younger—

WALTER (*Really like a small boy, looking down at his shoes and then up at the man*):   And—uh—well, my father, well, he was a laborer most of his life . . .

LINDNER (*Absolutely confused*):   Uh, yes—yes, I understand. (*He turns back to the contract*)

WALTER (*A beat; staring at him*):   And my father—(*With sudden intensity*) My father almost *beat a man to death* once because this man called him a bad name or something, you know what I mean?

LINDNER (*Looking up, frozen*):   No, no, I'm afraid I don't—

WALTER (*A beat. The tension hangs; then* WALTER *steps back from it*):   Yeah. Well—what I mean is that we come from people who had a lot of *pride*. I mean—we are very proud people. And that's my sister over there and she's going to be a doctor—and we are very proud—

LINDNER: Well—I am sure that is very nice, but—

WALTER: What I am telling you is that we called you over here to tell you that we are very proud and that this—(*Signaling to* TRAVIS) Travis, come here. (TRAVIS *crosses and* WALTER *draws him before him facing the man*) This is my son, and he makes the sixth generation our family in this country. And we have all thought about your offer—

LINDNER: Well, good . . . good—

WALTER: And we have decided to move into our house because my father—my father—he earned it for us brick by brick. (MAMA *has her eyes closed and is rocking back and forth as though she were in church, with her head nodding the Amen yes*) We don't want to make no trouble for nobody or fight no causes, and we will try to be good neighbors. And that's *all* we got to say about that. (*He looks the man absolutely in the eyes*) We don't want your money. (*He turns and walks away*)

LINDNER (*Looking around at all of them*):   I take it then—that you have decided to occupy . . .

BENEATHA: That's what the man said.

LINDNER (*To* MAMA *in her reverie*):   Then I would like to appeal to you, Mrs. Younger. You are older and wiser and understand things better I am sure . . .

MAMA: I am afraid you don't understand. My son said we was going to move and there ain't nothing left for me to say. (*Briskly*) You know how these young folks is nowadays, mister. Can't do a thing with 'em! (*As he opens his mouth, she rises*) Good-bye.

LINDNER (*Folding up his materials*):   Well—if you are that final about it . . . there is nothing left for me to say. (*He finishes, almost ignored by the family, who are concentrating on* WALTER LEE. *At the door* LINDNER *halts and looks around*) I sure hope you people know what you're getting into.

(*He shakes his head and exits*)

RUTH (*Looking around and coming to life*):   Well, for God's sake—if the moving men are here—LET'S GET THE HELL OUT OF HERE!

MAMA (*Into action*):   Ain't it the truth! Look at all this here mess. Ruth, put Travis' good jacket on him . . . Walter Lee, fix your tie and tuck your shirt in, you look like somebody's hoodlum! Lord have mercy, where is my plant? (*She flies to get it amid the general bustling of the family, who are deliberately trying to ignore the nobility of the past moment*) You all start on down . . . Travis child, don't go empty-handed . . . Ruth, where did I put that box with my skillets in it? I want to be in charge of it myself . . . I'm going to make us the biggest dinner we ever ate tonight . . . Beneatha, what's the matter with them stockings? Pull them things up, girl . . .

(*The family starts to file out as two moving men appear and begin to carry out the heavier pieces of furniture, bumping into the family as they move about*)

BENEATHA: Mama, Asagai asked me to marry him today and go to Africa—

MAMA (*In the middle of her getting-ready activity*): He did? You ain't old enough to marry nobody—(*Seeing the moving men lifting one of her chairs precariously*) Darling, that ain't no bale of cotton, please handle it so we can sit in it again! I had that chair twenty-five years . . .

(*The movers sigh with exasperation and go on with their work*)

BENEATHA (*Girlishly and unreasonably trying to pursue the conversation*): To go to Africa, Mama—be a doctor in Africa . . .

MAMA (*Distracted*): Yes, baby—

WALTER: *Africa!* What he want you to go to Africa for?

BENEATHA: To practice there . . .

WALTER: Girl, if you don't get all them silly ideas out your head! You better marry yourself a man with some loot . . .

BENEATHA (*Angrily, precisely as in the first scene of the play*): What have you got to do with who I marry!

WALTER: Plenty. Now I think George Murchison—

BENEATHA: *George Murchison!* I wouldn't marry him if he was Adam and I was Eve!

(WALTER *and* BENEATHA *go out yelling at each other vigorously and the anger is loud and real till their voices diminish.* RUTH *stands at the door and turns to* MAMA *and smiles knowingly*)

MAMA (*Fixing her hat at last*): Yeah—they something all right, my children . . .

RUTH: Yeah—they're something. Let's go, Lena.

MAMA (*Stalling, starting to look around the house*): Yes—I'm coming. Ruth—

RUTH: Yes?

MAMA (*Quietly, woman to woman*): He finally come into his manhood today, didn't he? Kind of like a rainbow after the rain . . .

RUTH (*Biting her lip lest her own pride explode in front of* MAMA): Yes, Lena.

(WALTER'S *voice calls for them raucously*)

WALTER (*Off stage*): Y'all come on! These people charges by the hour, you know!

MAMA (*Waving* RUTH *out vaguely*): All right, honey—go on down. I be down directly.

(RUTH *hesitates, then exits.* MAMA *stands, at last alone in the living room, her plant on the table before her as the lights start to come down. She looks around at all the walls and ceilings and suddenly, despite herself, while the children call below, a great heaving thing rises in her and she puts her fist to her mouth to stifle it, takes a final desperate look, pulls her coat about her, pats her hat and goes out. The lights dim down. The door opens and she comes back in, grabs her plant, and goes out for the last time)*

Curtain

1959

Edward Albee
(1928–   )

The conditions under which the boy who was born in Washington, D.C., in 1928 and adopted by Frances and Reed Albee came into the world might be interpreted as a metaphor for the essential isolation and homelessness of the characters in Albee's plays. The American theater for which Albee wrote had its own troubles with adoption: always struggling with European theater, American theater of the 1960s revered Ireland's Samuel Beckett and France's Jean Genet as it mimicked Hollywood.

Albee's preparation for the theater began in a family with lucrative and traditional ties to the theater: Reed Albee had inherited his father's portion of the Keith-Albee Theater Circuit, a chain of vaudeville theaters. Although Reed Albee retired after he adopted his son, Edward Franklin Albee III grew up attending matinee performances in New York City, surrounded by the celebrities the public associated with the drama of the 1920s and 1930s.

The Albees raised their only child in Larchmont, New York, and traveled to Arizona and Florida during the winters. Their affluence—servants, tutors, limousines—assured the boy a physically comfortable, though isolated, childhood. When Albee was eleven he was sent to boarding school, where he began to write poetry and prose. His work received attention early and won many prizes. After graduating from high school, he entered Connecticut's Trinity College but dropped out after his first year. Like many American artists, Albee found that university education in the United States stunted his own creative vision and imagination. Once free of the university, he independently pursued his interest in playwrights such as Jean Genet, Tennessee Williams, Eugene O'Neill, and Eugene Ionesco while developing his own writing. On his thirtieth birthday Albee began writing his first play, *The Zoo Story* (1960). Three weeks and one revision later, it was complete. With the help of literary agents and friends, the play traveled to Broadway by way of Berlin. *The Zoo Story* was first performed in German on September 28, 1959, and had an even more auspicious American premier in New York City on January 14, 1960.

The Zoo Story reflects the tensions between the status quo and radicalism in American society and the established and experimental American theater. The established, complacent audience, represented by the character Peter, occupies a proper seated position while Jerry, the drifting, questioning performer, stands and engages his audience in a series of ploys to get Peter to listen. As the play, or staged encounter, continues, the two characters shift position only once, and the change in roles is dangerous, indeed fatal. Albee's technique exposes the relationships of drifter to businessman and of performer to audience to reveal a common isolation, though born of very different conditions. Appropriately for a play that implicitly critiques conservative Broadway theater, Albee won an Obie, the prestigious award given to Off Broadway productions, for *The Zoo Story*.

In writing *The Zoo Story* Albee established his fundamental view of the playwright's goal: to reflect and alter. According to Albee, the playwright must say something about the human condition and then try to change that condition; the playwright must also say something about the art form itself and then try to change that form. In his plays immediately following *The Zoo Story—The Death of Bessie Smith* (1960), *The Sandbox* (1960), and *The American Dream* (1961)—Albee takes the form of traditional Greek theater and of the continental absurdist tradition of Europe and creates characters in the context of the American condition. His world is one in which unlimited freedoms are preached to a populace trapped by society's promises of opportunity. Simply by choosing to stage the death of the famous singer Bessie Smith, because a white hospital refused to admit a black woman as a patient, Albee affirms his role as a playwright who believes that the theater can awaken to its own injustices the community represented on stage. Albee's subjects vary from academic cruelty and marital entrapment in *Who's Afraid of Virginia Woolf?* (1962), to adaptations of works not originally written for the theater in *The Ballad of the Sad Cafe* (1963)—from a novella by Carson McCullers—to seduction and martyrdom in the symbolic *Tiny Alice* (1965), to allegorical treatment of the fantastic and the mundane in *Seascape* (1975).

Despite his ambivalence about popular American theater, most of Albee's plays have received wide acclaim. *Virginia Woolf*, his first play to be produced on Broadway and his first three-act play, won the New York Drama Critics' Circle Award and two Tony awards and was later popularized as a film starring Elizabeth Taylor and Richard Burton. Known for the acute verbal sadism of two inebriated couples, *Virginia Woolf* was controversial when it first opened. Albee enjoyed continued success: he won a Pulitzer Prize in 1967 for *A Delicate Balance* (1966), about a family's equilibrium upset by friends haunted by an unknown cause, and again in 1975 for *Seascape*, an abstract look at human behavior and beliefs.

Albee's early success enabled him to experiment with form and subject; his work regularly found backers and was performed by prestigious New York companies and theaters. Still a forceful voice in American theater, Albee lectures throughout the United States, urging young writers and playwrights to stand against the decay of popular theater. Attacking the critics for the decline of theater as well as of Broadway, he has suggested that a good critic should guide people away from what they actually want and instead toward what they *should* want. Albee has continued to write plays, such as *The Lady From Dubuque* (1980) and *The Marriage Play* (1987). A teacher and coordinator of the California Young Playwrights group, Albee received an honorary degree from Bard College in 1987.

Suggested Readings: *The Death of Bessie Smith,* 1960. *The Sandbox,* 1960. *Who's Afraid of Virginia Woolf?,* 1962. *Tiny Alice,* 1964. *A Delicate Balance,* 1966. *Seascape,* 1975. *The Lady From Dubuque,* 1980. C. W. E. Bigsby, *Albee,* 1969. R. Cohn, *Edward Albee,* 1969. M. E. Rutenberg, *Edward Albee: Playwright in Protest,* 1969. A. Paolucci, *From Tension to Tonic: The Plays of Edward Albee,* 1972. C. W. E. Bigsby, *Albee: A Collection of Critical Essays,* 1975. C. W. E. Bigsby, 20th-Century Drama, Vol. II, 1984. Bloom, ed., *Edward Albee: Modern Critical Interpretations,* 1987.

Text Used: *The Zoo Story,* 1959.

THE ZOO STORY

THE PLAYERS:

PETER: A man in his early forties, neither fat nor gaunt, neither handsome nor homely. He wears tweeds, smokes a pipe, carries horn-rimmed glasses. Although he is moving into middle age, his dress and his manner would suggest a man younger.

JERRY: A man in his late thirties, not poorly dressed, but carelessly. What was once a trim and lightly muscled body has begun to go to fat; and while he is no longer handsome, it is evident that he once was. His fall from physical grace should not suggest debauchery; he has, to come closest to it, a great weariness.

THE SCENE: *It is Central Park; a Sunday afternoon in summer; the present. There are two park benches, one toward either side of the stage; they both face the audience. Behind them: foliage, trees, sky. At the beginning, Peter is seated on one of the benches.*

STAGE DIRECTIONS: *As the curtain rises,* PETER *is seated on the bench stage-right. He is reading a book. He stops reading, cleans his glasses, goes back to reading.* JERRY *enters.*

JERRY: I've been to the zoo. (PETER *doesn't notice*) I said, I've been to the zoo. MISTER, I'VE BEEN TO THE ZOO!

PETER: Hm? . . . What? . . . I'm sorry, were you talking to me?

JERRY: I went to the zoo, and then I walked until I came here. Have I been walking north?

PETER (*Puzzled*):   North? Why . . . I . . . I think so. Let me see.

JERRY (*Pointing past the audience*):   Is that Fifth Avenue?

PETER: Why yes; yes, it is.

JERRY: And what is that cross street there; that one, to the right?

PETER: That? Oh, that's Seventy-fourth Street.

JERRY: And the zoo is around Sixty-fifth Street; so, I've been walking north.

PETER (*Anxious to get back to his reading*):   Yes; it would seem so.

JERRY: Good old north.

PETER (*Lightly, by reflex*):   Ha, ha.

JERRY (*After a slight pause*):   But not due north.

PETER: I . . . well, no, not due north; but, we . . . call it north. It's northerly.

JERRY (*Watches as* PETER, *anxious to dismiss him, prepares his pipe*):   Well, boy; *you're* not going to get lung cancer, are you?

PETER (*Looks up, a little annoyed, then smiles*):   No, sir. Not from this.

JERRY: No, sir. What you'll probably get is cancer of the mouth, and then you'll have to wear one of those things Freud wore after they took one whole side of his jaw away. What do they call those things?

PETER (*Uncomfortable*):   A prosthesis?

JERRY: The very thing! A prosthesis. You're an educated man, aren't you? Are you a doctor?

PETER: Oh, no; no. I read about it somewhere; *Time* magazine, I think. (*He turns to his book*)

JERRY: Well, *Time* magazine isn't for blockheads.

PETER: No, I suppose not.

JERRY (*After a pause*):   Boy, I'm glad that's Fifth Avenue there.

PETER (*Vaguely*):   Yes.

JERRY: I don't like the west side of the park much.

PETER: Oh? (*Then, slightly wary, but interested*) Why?

JERRY (*Offhand*):   I don't know.

PETER: Oh. (*He returns to his book*)

JERRY (*He stands for a few seconds, looking at* PETER, *who finally looks up again, puzzled*):   Do you mind if we talk?

PETER (*Obviously minding*):   Why . . . no, no.

JERRY: Yes you do; you do.

PETER (*Puts his book down, his pipe out and away, smiling*):   No, really; I don't mind.

JERRY: Yes you do.

PETER (*Finally decided*):   No; I don't mind at all, really.

JERRY: It's . . . it's a nice day.

PETER (*Stares unnecessarily at the sky*):   Yes. Yes, it is; lovely.

JERRY: I've been to the zoo.

PETER: Yes, I think you said so . . . didn't you?

JERRY: You'll read about it in the papers tomorrow, if you don't see it on your TV tonight. You have TV, haven't you?

PETER: Why yes, we have two; one for the children.

JERRY: You're married!

PETER (*With pleased emphasis*):   Why, certainly.

JERRY: It isn't a law, for God's sake.

PETER: No. . . . no, of course not.

JERRY: And you have a wife.

PETER (*Bewildered by the seeming lack of communication*):   Yes!

JERRY: And you have children.

PETER: Yes; two.

JERRY: Boys?

PETER: No, girls . . . both girls.

JERRY: But you wanted boys.

PETER: Well . . . naturally, every man wants a son, but . . .

JERRY (*Lightly mocking*):   But that's the way the cookie crumbles?

PETER (*Annoyed*):   I wasn't going to say that.

JERRY: And you're not going to have any more kids, are you?

PETER (*A bit distantly*):   No. No more. (*Then back, and irksome*) Why did you say that? How would you know about that?

JERRY: The way you cross your legs, perhaps; something in the voice. Or maybe I'm just guessing. Is it your wife?

PETER (*Furious*):   That's none of your business! (*A silence*) Do you understand? (JERRY *nods.* PETER *is quiet now*) Well, you're right. We'll have no more children.

JERRY (*Softly*):   That *is* the way the cookie crumbles.

PETER (*Forgiving*):   Yes . . . I guess so.

JERRY: Well, now; what else?

PETER: What were you saying about the zoo . . . that I'd read about it, or see . . . ?

JERRY: I'll tell you about it, soon. Do you mind if I ask you questions.

PETER: Oh, not really.

JERRY: I'll tell you why I do it; I don't talk to many people—except to say like: give me a beer, or where's the john, or what time does the feature go on, or keep your hands to yourself, buddy. You know—things like that.

PETER: I must say I don't . . .

JERRY: But every once in a while I like to talk to somebody, really *talk;* like to get to know somebody, know all about him.

PETER (*Lightly laughing, still a little uncomfortable*):   And am I the guinea pig for today?

JERRY: On a sun-drenched Sunday afternoon like this? Who better than a nice married man with two daughters and . . . uh . . . a dog? (PETER *shakes his head*) No? Two dogs. (PETER *shakes his head again*) Hm. No dogs? (PETER *shakes his head, sadly*) Oh, that's a shame. But you look like an animal man. CATS? (PETER *nods his head, ruefully*) Cats! But, that can't be your idea. No, sir. Your wife and daughters? (PETER *nods his head*) Is there anything else I should know?

PETER (*He has to clear his throat*):   There are . . . there are two parakeets. One . . . uh . . . one for each of my daughters.

JERRY: Birds.

PETER: My daughters keep them in a cage in their bedroom.

JERRY: Do they carry disease? The birds.

PETER: I don't believe so.

JERRY: That's too bad. If they did you could set them loose in the house and the cats could eat them and die, maybe. (PETER *looks blank for a moment, then laughs*) And what else? What do you do to support your enormous household?

PETER: I . . . uh . . . I have an executive position with a . . . a small publishing house. We . . . uh . . . we publish textbooks.

JERRY: That sounds nice; very nice. What do you make?

PETER (*Still cheerful*):   Now look here!

JERRY: Oh, come on.

PETER: Well, I make around eighteen thousand a year, but I don't carry more than forty dollars at any one time . . . in case you're a . . . holdup man . . . ha, ha, ha.

JERRY (*Ignoring the above*):   Where do you live? (PETER *is reluctant*) Oh, look; I'm not going to rob you, and I'm not going to kidnap your parakeets, your cats, or your daughters.

PETER (*Too loud*):   I live between Lexington and Third Avenue, on Seventy-fourth Street.

JERRY: That wasn't so hard, was it?

PETER: I didn't mean to seem . . . ah . . . it's that you don't really carry on a conversation; you just ask questions. And I'm . . . I'm normally . . . uh . . . reticent. Why do you just stand there?

JERRY: I'll start walking around in a little while, and eventually I'll sit down. (*Recalling*) Wait until you see the expression on his face.

PETER: What? Whose face? Look here; is this something about the zoo?

JERRY (*Distantly*):   The what?

PETER: The zoo; the zoo. Something about the zoo.

JERRY: The zoo?

PETER: You've mentioned it several times.

JERRY (*Still distant, but returning abruptly*):   The zoo? Oh, yes; the zoo. I was there before I came here. I told you that. Say, what's the dividing line between upper-middle–middle-class and lower-upper–middle-class?

PETER: My dear fellow, I . . .

JERRY: Don't my dear fellow me.

PETER (*Unhappily*):   Was I patronizing? I believe I was; I'm sorry. But you see, your question about the classes bewildered me.

JERRY: And when you're bewildered you become patronizing?

PETER: I . . . I don't express myself too well, sometimes. (*He attempts a joke on himself*) I'm in publishing, not writing.

JERRY (*Amused, but not at the humor*):   So be it. The truth *is: I* was being patronizing.

PETER: Oh, now; you needn't say that.

(*It is at this point that Jerry may begin to move about the stage with slowly increasing determination and authority, but pacing himself, so that the long speech about the dog comes at the high point of the arc*)

JERRY: All right. Who are your favorite writers? Baudelaire and J. P. Marquand?[1]

PETER (*Wary*):   Well, I like a great many writers; I have a considerable . . . catholicity of taste, if I may say so. Those two men are fine, each in his way. (*Warming up*) Baudelaire, of course . . . uh . . . is by far the finer of the two, but Marquand has a place . . . in our . . . uh . . . national . . .

JERRY: Skip it.

PETER: I . . . sorry.

JERRY: Do you know what I did before I went to the zoo today? I walked all the way up Fifth Avenue from Washington Square; all the way.

PETER: Oh; you live in the Village! (*This seems to enlighten* PETER)

JERRY: No, I don't. I took the subway down to the Village so I could walk all the way up Fifth Avenue to the zoo. It's one of those things a person has to do; sometimes a person has to go a very long distance out of his way to come back a short distance correctly.

PETER (*Almost pouting*):   Oh, I thought you lived in the Village.

JERRY: What were you trying to do? Make sense out of things? Bring order? The old pigeonhole bit? Well, that's easy; I'll tell you. I live in a four-story brownstone roominghouse on the upper West Side between Columbus Avenue and Central Park West. I live on the top floor; rear; west. It's a laughably small room, and one of my walls is made of beaverboard; this beaverboard separates my room from another laughably small room, so I assume that the two rooms were once one room, a small room, but not necessarily laughable. The room beyond my beaverboard wall is occupied by a colored queen who always keeps his door open; well, not always, but *always* when he's plucking his eyebrows, which he does with Buddhist concentration. This colored queen has rotten teeth, which is rare, and he has a Japanese kimono, which is also pretty rare; and he wears this kimono to and from the john in the hall, which is pretty frequent. I mean, he goes to the john a lot. He never bothers me, and he never brings anyone up to his room. All he does is pluck his eyebrows, wear his kimono and go to the john. Now, the two front rooms on my floor are a little larger, I guess; but they're pretty small, too. There's a Puerto Rican family in one of them, a husband, a wife, and some kids; I don't know how many. These people entertain a lot. And in the other front room,

---

[1] Charles Baudelaire (1821–1867), a French symbolist poet; John Phillips Marquand (1893–1960), an American writer whose novels satirized New England monied families.

there's somebody living there, but I don't know who it is. I've never seen who it is. Never. Never ever.

PETER (*Embarrassed*):   Why . . . why do you live there?

JERRY (*From a distance again*):   I don't know.

PETER: It doesn't sound like a very nice place . . . where you live.

JERRY: Well, no; it isn't an apartment in the East Seventies. But, then again, I don't have one wife, two daughters, two cats and two parakeets. What I do have, I have toilet articles, a few clothes, a hot plate that I'm not supposed to have, a can opener, one that works with a key, you know; a knife, two forks, and two spoons, one small, one large; three plates, a cup, a saucer, a drinking glass, two picture frames, both empty, eight or nine books, a pack of pornographic playing cards, regular deck, an old Western Union typewriter that prints nothing but capital letters, and a small strongbox without a lock which has in it . . . what? Rocks! Some rocks . . . sea-rounded rocks I picked up on the beach when I was a kid. Under which . . . weighed down . . . are some letters . . . please letters . . . please why don't you do this, and please when will you do that letters. And when letters, too. When will you write? When will you come? When? These letters are from more recent years.

PETER (*Stares glumly at his shoes, then*):   About those two empty picture frames . . . ?

JERRY: I don't see why they need any explanation at all. Isn't it clear? I don't have pictures of anyone to put in them.

PETER: Your parents . . . perhaps . . . a girl friend . . .

JERRY: You're a very sweet man, and you're possessed of a truly enviable innocence. But good old Mom and good old Pop are dead . . . you know? . . . I'm broken up about it, too . . . I mean really. BUT. That particular vaudeville act is playing the cloud circuit now, so I don't see how I can look at them, all neat and framed. Besides, or, rather, to be pointed about it, good old Mom walked out on good old Pop when I was ten and a half years old; she embarked on an adulterous turn of our southern states . . . a journey of a year's duration . . . and her most constant companion . . . among others, among many others . . . was a Mr. Barleycorn.[2] At least, that's what good old Pop told me after he went down . . . came back . . . brought her body north. We'd received the news between Christmas and New Year's, you see, that good old Mom had parted with the ghost in some dump in Alabama. And, without the ghost . . . she was less welcome. I mean, what was she? A stiff . . . a northern stiff. At any rate, good old Pop celebrated the New Year for an even two weeks and then slapped into the front of a somewhat moving city omnibus, which sort of cleaned things out family-wise. Well no; then there was Mom's sister, who was given neither to sin nor the consolations of the bottle. I moved in on her, and my memory of her is slight excepting I remember still that she did all things dourly: sleeping, eating, working, praying. She dropped dead on the stairs to her apartment, my apartment then, too, on the afternoon of my high school graduation. A terribly middle-European joke, if you ask me.

PETER: Oh, my; oh, my.

JERRY: Oh, your what? But that was a long time ago, and I have no feeling about any of it that I care to admit to myself. Perhaps you can see, though, why good old Mom and good old Pop are frameless. What's your name? Your first name?

---

[2] John Barleycorn, a personification of corn liquor or malt liquor.

PETER: I'm Peter.

JERRY: I'd forgotten to ask you. I'm Jerry.

PETER (*With a slight, nervous laugh*):   Hello, Jerry.

JERRY (*Nods his hello*):   And let's see now; what's the point of having a girl's picture, especially in two frames? I have two picture frames, you remember. I never see the pretty little ladies more than once, and most of them wouldn't be caught in the same room with a camera. It's odd, and I wonder if it's sad.

PETER: The girls?

JERRY: No. I wonder if it's sad that I never see the little ladies more than once. I've never been able to have sex with, or, how is it put? . . . make love to anybody more than once. Once; that's it . . . Oh, wait; for a week and a half, when I was fifteen . . . and I hang my head in shame that puberty was late . . . I was a h-o-m-o-s-e-x-u-a-l. I mean, I was queer . . . (*Very fast*) . . . queer, queer, queer . . . with bells ringing, banners snapping in the wind. And for those eleven days, I met at least twice a day with the park superintendent's son . . . a Greek boy, whose birthday was the same as mine, except he was a year older. I think I was very much in love . . . maybe just with sex. But that was the jazz of a very special hotel, wasn't it? And now; oh, do I love the little ladies; really, I love them. For about an hour.

PETER: Well, it seems perfectly simple to me. . . .

JERRY (*Angry*):   Look! Are you going to tell me to get married and have parakeets?

PETER (*Angry himself*):   Forget the parakeets! And stay single if you want to. It's no business of mine. I didn't start this conversation in the . . .

JERRY: All right, all right. I'm sorry. All right? You're not angry?

PETER (*Laughing*):   No, I'm not angry.

JERRY (*Relieved*):   Good. (*Now back to his previous tone*) Interesting that you asked me about the picture frames. I would have thought that you would have asked me about the pornographic playing cards.

PETER (*With a knowing smile*):   Oh, I've seen those cards.

JERRY: That's not the point. (*Laughs*) I suppose when you were a kid you and your pals passed them around, or you had a pack of your own.

PETER: Well, I guess a lot of us did.

JERRY: And you threw them away just before you got married.

PETER: Oh, now; look here. I didn't *need* anything like that when I got older.

JERRY: No?

PETER (*Embarassed*):   I'd rather not talk about these things.

JERRY: So? Don't. Besides, I wasn't trying to plumb your post-adolescent sexual life and hard times; what I wanted to get at is the value difference between pornographic playing cards when you're a kid, and pornographic playing cards when you're older. It's that when you're a kid you use the cards as a substitute for a real experience, and when you're older you use real experience as a substitute for the fantasy. But I imagine you'd rather hear about what happened at the zoo.

PETER (*Enthusiastic*):   Oh, yes; the zoo. (*Then, awkward*) That is . . . if you . . .

JERRY: Let me tell you about why I went . . . well, let me tell you some things. I've told you about the fourth floor of the roominghouse where I live. I think the rooms are better as you go down, floor by floor, I guess they are; I don't know. I don't know any of the people on the third and second floors. Oh, wait! I do know that there's a lady living on the third floor, in the front. I know because she cries all the time. Whenever I go out or come back in, whenever I pass her door, I always hear her crying, muffled, but . . . very determined. Very determined indeed. But the one I'm getting to, and all about the dog, is the landlady. I don't like to use words that are too harsh in describing people. I don't like to. But the landlady is a fat, ugly, mean, stupid, unwashed, misanthropic, cheap, drunken bag of garbage. And you may have noticed that I very seldom use profanity, so I can't describe her as well as I might.

PETER: You describe her . . . vividly.

JERRY: Well, thanks. Anyway, she has a dog, and I will tell you about the dog, and she and her dog are the gatekeepers of my dwelling. The woman is bad enough; she leans around in the entrance hall, spying to see that I don't bring in things or people, and when she's had her midafternoon pint of lemon-flavored gin she always stops me in the hall, and grabs ahold of my coat or my arm, and she presses her disgusting body up against me to keep me in a corner so she can talk to me. The smell of her body and her breath . . . you can't imagine it . . . and somewhere, somewhere in the back of that pea-sized brain of hers, an organ developed just enough to let her eat, drink, and emit, she has some foul parody of sexual desire. And I, Peter, I am the object of her sweaty lust.

PETER: That's disgusting. That's . . . horrible.

JERRY: But I have found a way to keep her off. When she talks to me, when she presses herself to my body and mumbles about her room and how I should come there, I merely say: but, Love; wasn't yesterday enough for you, and the day before? Then she puzzles, she makes slits of her tiny eyes, she sways a little, and then, Peter . . . and it is at this moment that I think I might be doing some good in that tormented house . . . a simple-minded smile begins to form on her unthinkable face, and she giggles and groans as she thinks about yesterday and the day before; as she believes and relives what never happened. Then, she motions to that black monster of a dog she has, and she goes back to her room. And I am safe until our next meeting.

PETER: It's so . . . unthinkable. I find it hard to believe that people such as that really *are*.

JERRY (*Lightly mocking*):   It's for reading about, isn't it?

PETER (*Seriously*):   Yes.

JERRY: And fact is better left to fiction. You're right, Peter. Well, what I have been meaning to tell you about is the dog; I shall, now.

PETER (*Nervously*):   Oh, yes; the dog.

JERRY: Don't go. You're not thinking of going are you?

PETER: Well . . . no, I don't think so.

JERRY (*As if to a child*):   Because after I tell you about the dog, do you know what then? Then . . . then I'll tell you about what happened at the zoo.

PETER (*Laughing faintly*):   You're . . . you're full of stories, aren't you?

JERRY: You don't *have* to listen. Nobody is holding you here; remember that. Keep that in your mind.

PETER (*Irritably*):   I know that.

JERRY: You do? Good.

(*The following long speech, it seems to me, should be done with a great deal of action, to achieve a hypnotic effect on* PETER, *and on the audience, too. Some specific actions have been suggested, but the director and the actor playing* JERRY *might best work it out for themselves*)

ALL RIGHT. (*As if reading from a hugh billboard*) THE STORY OF JERRY AND THE DOG! (*Natural again*) What I am going to tell you has something to do with how sometimes it's necessary to go a long distance out of the way in order to come back a short distance correctly; or, maybe I only think that it has something to do with that. But, it's why I went to the zoo today, and why I walked north . . . northerly, rather . . . until I came here. All right. The dog, I think I told you, is a black monster of a beast: an oversized head, tiny, tiny ears, and eyes . . . bloodshot, infected, maybe; and a body you can see the ribs through the skin. The dog is black, all black; all black except for the bloodshot eyes, and . . . yes . . . and an open sore on its . . . *right* forepaw; that is red, too. And, oh yes; the poor monster, and I do believe it's an old dog . . . it's certainly a misused one . . . almost always has an erection . . . of sorts. That's red, too. And . . . what else? . . . oh, yes; there's a gray-yellow-white color, too, when he bares his fangs. Like this: Grrrrrr! Which is what he did when he saw me for the first time . . . the day I moved in. I worried about that animal the very first minute I met him. Now, animals don't take to me like Saint Francis[3] had birds hanging off him all the time. What I mean is: animals are indifferent to me . . . like people (*He smiles slightly*) . . . most of the time. But this dog wasn't indifferent. From the very beginning he'd snarl and then go for me, to get one of my legs. Not like he was rabid, you know; he was sort of a stumbly dog, but he wasn't half-assed, either. It was a good, stumbly run; but I always got away. He got a piece of my trouser leg, look, you can see right here, where it's mended; he got that the second day I lived there; but, I kicked free and got upstairs fast, so that was that. (*Puzzles*) I still don't know to this day how the other roomers manage it, but you know what I *think:* I think it had to do only with me. Cozy. So. Anyway, this went on for over a week, whenever I came in; but never when I went out. That's funny. Or, it *was* funny. I could pack up and live in the street for all the dog cared. Well, I thought about it up in my room one day, one of the times after I'd bolted upstairs, and I made up my mind. I decided: First, I'll kill the dog with kindness, and if that doesn't work . . . I'll just kill him. (PETER *winces*) Don't react, Peter; just listen. So, the next day I went out and bought a bag of hamburgers, medium rare, no catsup, no onion; and on the way home I threw away all the rolls and kept just the meat.

(*Action for the following, perhaps*)

When I got back to the roominghouse the dog was waiting for me. I half opened the door that led into the entrance hall, and there he was; waiting for me. It figured. I went in, very cautiously, and I had the hamburgers, you remember; I opened the bag, and I set the meat down about twelve feet from where the dog was snarling at me. Like so! He snarled; stopped snarling; sniffed; moved slowly; then faster; then faster toward the meat. Well, when he got to it he stopped, and he looked at me. I smiled; but tentatively, you understand. He turned his face back to the hamburgers smelled, sniffed some more, and then . . . RRRAAAAGGGGGHHHH, like that . . . he tore into them. It was as if he had never eaten anything in his life before, except like garbage. Which might very well have been the truth. I don't think the landlady ever eats anything but garbage. But. He ate all the hamburgers, almost all at once, making sounds in his throat like a woman. *Then,* when he'd finished the meat, the hamburger, and tried to eat the paper, too, he sat down and smiled. I think he smiled; I know cats do. It was a very gratifying few moments. Then, BAM, he snarled and made for me again. He didn't get me this time, either. So, I got upstairs, and I lay down on my bed and

---

[3] Saint Francis of Assisi, patron saint of animals.

started to think about the dog again. To be truthful, I was offended, and I was damn mad, too. It was six perfectly good hamburgers with not enough pork in them to make it disgusting. I was offended. But, after a while, I decided to try it for a few more days. If you think about it, this dog had what amounted to an antipathy toward me; really. And, I wondered if I mightn't overcome this antipathy. So, I tried it for five more days, but it was always the same: snarl; sniff; move; faster; stare; gobble; RAAGGGHHH; smile; snarl; BAM. Well, now; by this time Columbus Avenue was strewn with hamburger rolls and I was less offended than disgusted. So, I decided to kill the dog.

(PETER *raises a hand in protest*)

Oh, don't be so alarmed, Peter; I didn't succeed. The day I tried to kill the dog I bought only one hamburger and what I thought was a murderous portion of rat poison. When I bought the hamburger I asked the man not to bother with the roll, all I wanted was the meat. I expected some reaction from him, like: we don't sell no hamburgers without rolls; or, wha' d'ya wanna do, eat it out'a ya han's? But no; he smiled benignly, wrapped up the hamburger in waxed paper, and said: A bite for ya pussy-cat? I wanted to say: No, not really; it's part of a plan to poison a dog I know. But, you can't say "a dog I know" without sounding funny; so I said, a little too loud, I'm afraid, and too formally: YES, A BITE FOR MY PUSSY-CAT. People looked up. It always happens when I try to simplify things; people look up. But that's neither hither nor thither. So. On my way back to the rooming-house, I kneaded the hamburger and the rat poison together between my hands, at that point feeling as much sadness as disgust. I opened the door to the entrance hall, and there the monster was, waiting to take the offering and then jump me. Poor bastard; he never learned that the moment he took to smile before he went for me gave me time enough to get out of range. BUT, there he was; malevolence with an erection, waiting. I put the poison patty down, moved toward the stairs and watched. The poor animal gobbled the food down as usual, smiled, which made me almost sick, and then, BAM. But, I sprinted up the stairs, as usual, and the dog didn't get me, as usual. AND IT CAME TO PASS THAT THE BEAST WAS DEATHLY ILL. I knew this because he no longer attended me, and because the landlady sobered up. She stopped me in the hall the same evening of the attempted murder and confided the information that God had struck her puppy-dog a surely fatal blow. She had forgotten her bewildered lust, and her eyes were wide open for the first time. They looked like the dog's eyes. She sniveled and implored me to pray for the animal. I wanted to say to her: Madam, I have myself to pray for, the colored queen, the Puerto Rican family, the person in the front room whom I've never seen, the woman who cries deliberately behind her closed door, and the rest of the people in all roominghouses, everywhere; besides, Madam, I don't understand how to pray. But . . . to simplify things . . . I told her I would pray. She looked up. She said that I was a liar, and that I probably wanted the dog to die. I told her, and there was so much truth here, that I didn't want the dog to die. I didn't, and not just because I'd poisoned him. I'm afraid that I must tell you I wanted the dog to live so that I could see what our new relationship might come to.

(PETER *indicates his increasing displeasure and slowly growing antagonism*)

Please understand, Peter; that sort of thing is important. You must believe me; it *is* important. We have to know the effect of our actions. (*Another deep sigh*) Well, anyway; the dog recovered. I have no idea why, unless he was a descendant of the puppy that guarded the gates of hell or some such resort. I'm not up on my mythology. (*He pronounces the word myth-o-logy*) Are you?

(PETER *sets to thinking, but* JERRY *goes on*)

At any rate, and you've missed the eight-thousand-dollar question, Peter; at any rate, the dog recovered his health and the landlady recovered her thirst, in no way altered by the bow-wow's deliverance. When I came home from a movie that was playing on Forty-second Street, a movie I'd seen, or one that was very much like one or several I'd seen, after the landlady told me puppykins was better, I was so hoping for the dog to be waiting for me. I was . . . well, how would you put it . . . enticed? . . . fascinated? . . . no, I don't think so . . . heart-shatteringly anxious, that's it; I was heart-shatteringly anxious to confront my friend again.

(PETER *reacts scoffingly*)

Yes, Peter; friend. That's the only word for it. I was heart-shatteringly et cetera to confront my doggy friend again. I came in the door and advanced, unafraid, to the center of the entrance hall. The beast was there . . . looking at me. And, you know, he looked better for his scrape with the nevermind. I stopped; I looked at him; he looked at me. I think . . . I think we stayed a long time that way . . . still, stone-statue . . . just looking at one another. I looked more into his face than he looked into mine. I mean, I can concentrate longer at looking into a dog's face than a dog can concentrate at looking into mine, or into anybody else's face, for that matter. But during that twenty seconds or two hours that we looked into each other's face, we made contact. Now, here is what I had wanted to happen: I loved the dog now, and I wanted him to love me. I had tried to love, and I had tried to kill, and both had been unsuccessful by themselves. I hoped . . . and I don't really know why I expected the dog to understand anything, much less my motivations . . . I hoped that the dog would understand.

(PETER *seems to be hypnotized*)

It's just . . . it's just that . . . (JERRY *is abnormally tense, now*) . . . it's just that if you can't deal with people, you have to make a start somewhere. WITH ANIMALS! (*Much faster now, and like a conspirator*) Don't you see? A person has to have some way of dealing with SOMETHING. If not with people . . . if not with people SOMETHING. With a bed, with a cockroach, with a mirror . . . no, that's too hard, that's one of the last steps. With a cockroach, with a . . . with a . . . with a carpet, a roll of toilet paper . . . no, not that, either . . . that's a mirror too; always check bleeding. You see how hard it is to find things? With a street corner, and too many lights, all colors reflecting on the oily-wet streets . . . with a wisp of smoke, a wisp . . . of smoke . . . with . . . with pornographic playing cards, with a strongbox . . . WITHOUT A LOCK . . . with love, with vomiting, with crying, with fury because the pretty little ladies aren't pretty little ladies, with making money with your body which is an act of love and I could prove it, with howling because you're alive; with God. How about that? WITH GOD WHO IS A COLORED QUEEN WHO WEARS A KIMONO AND PLUCKS HIS EYEBROWS, WHO IS A WOMAN WHO CRIES WITH DETERMINATION BEHIND HER CLOSED DOOR . . . with God who, I'm told, turned his back on the whole thing some time ago . . . with . . . some day, with people. (JERRY *sighs the next word heavily*) People. With an idea; a concept. And where better, where ever better in this humiliating excuse for a jail, where better to communicate one single, simpleminded idea than in an entrance hall? Where? It would be A START! Where better to make a beginning . . . to understand and just possibly be understood . . . a beginning of an understanding, than with . . .

(*Here* JERRY *seems to fall into almost grotesque fatigue*)

. . . than with A DOG. Just that; a dog.

(*Here there is a silence that might be prolonged for a moment or so; then* JERRY *wearily finishes his story*)

A dog. It seemed like a perfectly sensible idea. Man is a dog's best friend, remember. So: the dog and I looked at each other. I longer than the dog. And what I saw then has been the same ever since. Whenever the dog and I see each other we both stop where we are. We regard each other with a mixture of sadness and suspicion, and then we feign indifference. We walk past each other safely; we have an understanding. It's very sad, but you'll have to admit that it is an understanding. We had made many attempts at contact, and we had failed. The dog has returned to garbage, and I to solitary but free passage. I have not returned. I mean to say, I have *gained* solitary free passage, if that much further loss can be said to be gain. I have learned that neither kindness nor cruelty by themselves, independent of each other, creates any effect beyond themselves; and I have learned that the two combined, together, at the same time, are the teaching emotion. And what is gained is loss. And what has been the result: the dog and I have attained a compromise; more of a bargain, really. We neither love nor hurt because we do not try to reach each other. And, *was* trying to feed the dog an act of love? And, perhaps, was the dog's attempt to bite me *not* an act of love? If we can so misunderstand, well then, why have we invented the word love in the first place?

(*There is silence.* JERRY *moves to* PETER'S *bench and sits down beside him. This is the first time* JERRY *has sat down during the play*)

The Story of Jerry and the Dog: the end.

(PETER *is silent*)

Well, Peter? (JERRY *is suddenly cheerful*) Well, Peter? Do you think I could sell that story to the *Reader's Digest* and make a couple of hundred bucks for *The Most Unforgettable Character I've Ever Met?* Huh?

(JERRY *is animated, but* PETER *is disturbed*)

Oh, come on now, Peter; tell me what you think.

PETER (*Numb*):   I . . . I don't understand what . . . I don't think I . . . (*Now, almost tearfully*) Why did you tell me all of this?

JERRY: Why not?

PETER: I DON'T UNDERSTAND!

JERRY (*Furious, but whispering*):   That's a lie.

PETER: No. No, it's not.

JERRY (*Quietly*):   I tried to explain it to you as I went along. I went slowly; it all has to do with . . .

PETER: I DON'T WANT TO HEAR ANY MORE. I don't understand you, or your landlady, or her dog . . .

JERRY: *Her* dog! I thought it was my . . . No. No, you're right. It *is* her dog. (*Looks at* PETER *intently, shaking his head*) I don't know what I was thinking about; of course you don't understand. (*In a monotone, wearily*) I don't live in your block; I'm not married to two parakeets, or whatever your setup is. I am a *permanent transient,* and my home is the sickening roominghouses on the West Side of New York City, which is the greatest city in the world. Amen.

PETER: I'm . . . I'm sorry; I didn't mean to . . .

JERRY: Forget it. I suppose you don't quite know what to make of me, eh?

PETER (*A joke*):   We get all kinds in publishing. (*Chuckles*)

JERRY: You're a funny man. (*He forces a laugh*) You know that? You're a very . . . a richly comic person.

PETER (*Modestly, but amused*):   Oh, now, not really. (*Still chuckling*)

JERRY: Peter, do I annoy you, or confuse you?

PETER (*Lightly*):   Well, I must confess that this wasn't the kind of afternoon I'd anticipated.

JERRY: You mean, I'm not the gentleman you were expecting.

PETER: I wasn't expecting anybody.

JERRY: No, I don't imagine you were. But I'm here, and I'm not leaving.

PETER (*Consulting his watch*):   Well, you may not be, but I must be getting home soon.

JERRY: Oh, come on; stay a while longer.

PETER: I really should get home; you see . . .

JERRY (*Tickles* PETER'S *ribs with his fingers*):   Oh, come on.

PETER (*He is very ticklish; as* JERRY *continues to tickle him his voice becomes falsetto*):   No, I . . . OHHHHH! Don't do that. Stop, Stop, Ohhh, no, no.

JERRY: Oh, come on.

PETER (*As* JERRY *tickles*):   Oh, hee, hee, hee. I must go. I . . . hee, hee, hee. After all, stop, stop, hee, hee, hee, after all, the parakeets will be getting dinner ready soon. Hee, Hee. And the cats are setting the table. Stop, Stop, and, and . . . (PETER *is beside himself now*) . . . and we're having . . . hee, hee . . . uh . . . ho, ho, ho.

(JERRY *stops tickling* PETER, *but the combination of the tickling and his own mad whimsy has* PETER *laughing almost hysterically. As his laughter continues, then subsides,* JERRY *watches him, with a curious fixed smile*)

JERRY: Peter?

PETER: Oh, ha, ha, ha, ha, ha. What? What?

JERRY: Listen, now.

PETER: Oh, ho, ho. What . . . what is it, Jerry? Oh, my.

JERRY (*Mysteriously*):   Peter, do you want to know what happened at the zoo?

PETER: Ah, ha, ha. The what? Oh, yes; the zoo. Oh, ho, ho. Well, I had my own zoo there for a moment with . . . hee, hee, the parakeets getting dinner ready, and the . . . ha, ha, whatever it was, the . . .

JERRY (*Calmly*):   Yes, that was very funny, Peter. I wouldn't have expected it. But do you want to hear about what happened at the zoo, or not?

PETER: Yes. Yes, by all means; tell me what happened at the zoo. Oh, my. I don't know what happened to me.

JERRY: Now I'll let you in on what happened at the zoo; but first, I should tell you why I went to the zoo. I went to the zoo to find out more about the way people exist with animals, and the way animals exist with each other, and with people too. It probably wasn't a fair test, what with everyone separated by bars from everyone else, the animals for the most part from each other, and always the people from the animals. But, if it's a zoo, that's the way it is. (*He pokes* PETER *on the arm*) Move over.

PETER (*Friendly*): I'm sorry, haven't you enough room? (*He shifts a little*)

JERRY (*Smiling slightly*): Well, all the animals are there, and all the people are there, and it's Sunday and all the children are there. (*He pokes* PETER *again*) Move over.

PETER (*Patiently, still friendly*): All right. (*He moves some more, and* JERRY *has all the room he might need*)

JERRY: And it's a hot day, so all the stench is there, too, and all the balloon sellers, and all the ice cream sellers, and all the seals are barking, and all the birds are screaming. (*Pokes* PETER *harder*) Move over!

PETER (*Beginning to be annoyed*): Look here, you have more than enough room! (*But he moves more, and is now fairly cramped at one end of the bench*)

JERRY: And I am there, and it's feeding time at the lions' house, and the lion keeper comes into the lion cage, one of the lion cages, to feed one of the lions. (*Punches* PETER *on the arm, hard*) MOVE OVER!

PETER (*Very annoyed*): I can't move over any more, and stop hitting me. What's the matter with you?

JERRY: Do you want to hear the story? (*Punches* PETER'S *arm again*)

PETER (*Flabbergasted*): I'm not so sure! I certainly don't want to be punched in the arm.

JERRY (*Punches* PETER'S *arm again*): Like that?

PETER: Stop it! What's the matter with you?

JERRY: I'm crazy, you bastard.

PETER: That isn't funny.

JERRY: Listen to me, Peter. I want this bench. You go sit on the bench over there, and if you're good I'll tell you the rest of the story.

PETER (*Flustered*): But . . . whatever for? What *is* the matter with you? Besides, I see no reason why I should give up this bench. I sit on this bench almost every Sunday afternoon, in good weather. It's secluded here; there's never anyone sitting here, so I have it all to myself.

JERRY (*Softly*): Get off this bench, Peter; I want it.

PETER (*Almost whining*): No.

JERRY: I said I want this bench, and I'm going to have it. Now get over there.

PETER: People can't have everything they want. You should know that; it's a rule; people can have some of the things they want, but they can't have everything.

JERRY (*Laughs*): Imbecile! You're slow-witted!

PETER: Stop that!

JERRY: You're a vegetable! Go lie down on the ground.

PETER (*Intense*): Now *you* listen to me. I've put up with you all afternoon.

JERRY: Not really.

PETER: LONG ENOUGH. I've put up with you long enough. I've listened to you because you seemed . . . well, because I thought you wanted to talk to somebody.

JERRY: You put things well; economically, and, yet . . . oh, what is the word I want to put justice to your . . . JESUS, you make me sick . . . get off here and give me my bench.

PETER: MY BENCH!

JERRY (*Pushes* PETER *almost, but not quite, off the bench*):   Get out of my sight.

PETER (*Regaining his position*):   God da . . . mn you. That's enough! I've had enough of you. I will not give up this bench; you can't have it, and that's that. Now, go away.

(JERRY *snorts but does not move*)

Go away, I said.

(JERRY *does not move*)

Get away from here. If you don't move on . . . you're a bum . . . that's what you are . . . If you don't move on, I'll get a policeman here and make you go.

(JERRY *laughs, stays*)

I warn you, I'll call a policeman.

JERRY (*Softly*):   You won't find a policeman around here; they're all over on the west side of the park chasing fairies down from trees or out of the bushes. That's all they do. That's their function. So scream your head off; it won't do you any good.

PETER: POLICE! I warn you, I'll have you arrested. POLICE! (*Pause*) I said POLICE! (*Pause*) I feel ridiculous.

JERRY: You look ridiculous: a grown man screaming for the police on a bright Sunday afternoon in the park with nobody harming you. If a policeman *did* fill his quota and come sludging over this way he'd probably take you in as a nut.

PETER (*With digust and impotence*):   Great God, I just came here to read, and now you want me to give up the bench. You're mad.

JERRY: Hey, I got news for you, as they say. I'm on your precious bench, and you're never going to have it for yourself again.

PETER (*Furious*):   Look, you; get off my bench. I don't care if it makes any sense or not. I want this bench to myself; I want you OFF IT!

JERRY (*Mocking*):   Aw . . . look who's mad.

PETER: GET OUT!

JERRY: No.

PETER: I WARN YOU!

JERRY: Do you know how ridiculous you look *now?*

PETER (*His fury and self-consciousness have possessed him*):   It doesn't matter. (*He is almost crying*) GET AWAY FROM MY BENCH!

JERRY: Why? You have everything in the world you want; you've told me about your home, and your family, and *your own* little zoo. You have everything, and now you want this bench. Are these the things men fight for? Tell me, Peter, is this bench, this iron and this wood, is this your honor? Is this the thing in the world you'd fight for? Can you think of anything more absurd?

PETER: Absurd? Look, I'm not going to talk to you about honor, or even try to explain it to you. Besides, it isn't a question of honor; but even if it were, you wouldn't understand.

JERRY (*Contemptuously*):   You don't even know what you're saying, do you? This is probably the first time in your life you've had anything more trying to face than changing your cats' toilet box. Stupid! Don't you have any idea, not even the slightest, what other people *need?*

PETER: Oh, boy, listen to you; well, you don't need this bench. That's for sure.

JERRY: Yes; yes, I do.

PETER (*Quivering*):   I've come here for years; I have hours of great pleasure, great satisfaction, right here. And that's important to a man. I'm a responsible person, and I'm a GROWNUP. This is my bench, and you have no right to take it away from me.

JERRY: Fight for it, then. Defend yourself; defend your bench.

PETER: You've *pushed* me to it. Get up and fight.

JERRY: Like a man?

PETER (*Still angry*):   Yes, like a man, if you insist on mocking me even further.

JERRY: I'll have to give you credit for one thing: you *are* a vegetable, and a slightly nearsighted one, I think . . .

PETER: THAT'S ENOUGH . . .

JERRY: . . . but, you know, as they say on TV all the time—you know—and I mean this, Peter, you have a certain dignity; it surprises me . . .

PETER: STOP!

JERRY (*Rises lazily*):   Very well, Peter, we'll battle for the bench, but we're not evenly matched.

(*He takes out and clicks open an ugly-looking knife*)

PETER (*Suddenly awakening to the reality of the situation*):   You *are* mad! You're stark raving mad! YOU'RE GOING TO KILL ME!

(*But before* PETER *has time to think what to do,* JERRY *tosses the knife at* PETER'S *feet*)

JERRY: There you go. Pick it up. You have the knife and we'll be more evenly matched.

PETER (*Horrified*):   No!

JERRY (*Rushes over to* PETER, *grabs him by the collar;* PETER *rises; their faces almost touch*):   Now you pick up that knife and you fight with me. You fight for your self-respect; you fight for that goddamned bench.

PETER (*Struggling*):   No! Let . . . let go of me! He . . . Help!

JERRY (*Slaps* PETER *on each "fight"*):   You fight, you miserable bastard; fight for that bench; fight for your parakeets; fight for your cats, fight for your two daughters; fight for your wife; fight for your manhood, you pathetic little vegetable. (*Spits in* PETER'S *face*) You couldn't even get your wife with a male child.

PETER (*Breaks away, enraged*):   It's a matter of genetics, not manhood, you . . . you monster.

(*He darts down, picks up the knife and backs off a little; he is breathing heavily*)

I'll give you one last chance; get out of here and leave me alone!

(*He holds the knife with a firm arm, but far in front of him, not to attack, but to defend*)

JERRY (*Sighs heavily*):   So be it!

(*With a rush he charges* PETER *and impales himself on the knife. Tableau: For just a moment, complete silence,* JERRY *impaled on the knife at the end of* PETER'S *still firm arm. Then* PETER *screams, pulls away, leaving the knife in* JERRY. JERRY *is motionless, on point. Then he, too, screams, and it must be the sound of an infuriated and fatally wounded animal. With the knife in him, he stumbles back to the bench that* PETER *had vacated. He crumbles there, sitting, facing* PETER, *his eyes wide in agony, his mouth open*)

PETER (*Whispering*):   Oh my God, oh my God, oh my God . . . .

(*He repeats these words many times, very rapidly*)

JERRY (JERRY *is dying; but now his expression seems to change. His features relax, and while his voice varies, sometimes wrenched with pain, for the most part he seems removed from his dying. He smiles*):   Thank you, Peter. I mean that, now; thank you very much.

(PETER'S *mouth drops open. He cannot move; he is transfixed*)

Oh, Peter, I was so afraid I'd drive you away. (*He laughs as best he can*) You don't know how afraid I was you'd go away and leave me. And now I'll tell you what happened at the zoo. I think . . . I think this is what happened at the zoo . . . I think. I think that while I was at the zoo I decided that I would walk north . . . northerly, rather . . . until I found you . . . or somebody . . . and I decided that I would talk to you . . . I would tell you things . . . and things that I would tell you would . . . Well, here we are. You see? Here we *are*. But . . . I don't know . . . could I have planned all this? No . . . no, I couldn't have. But I think I did. And now I've told you what you wanted to know, haven't I? And now you know all about what happened at the zoo. And now you know what you'll see in your TV, and the face I told you about . . . you remember . . . the face I told you about . . . my face, the face you see right now. Peter . . . Peter? . . . Peter . . . thank you. I came unto you (*He laughs, so faintly*) and you have comforted me. Dear Peter.

PETER (*Almost fainting*):   Oh my God!

JERRY: You'd better go now. Somebody might come by, and you don't want to be here when anyone comes.

PETER (*Does not move, but begins to weep*):   Oh my God, oh my God.

JERRY (*Most faintly, now; he is very near death*):   You won't be coming back here any more, Peter; you've been dispossessed. You've lost your bench, but you've defended your honor. And Peter, I'll tell you something now; you're not really a vegetable; it's all right, you're an animal. You're an animal, too. But you'd better hurry now, Peter. Hurry, you'd better go . . . see?

(JERRY *takes a handkerchief and with great effort and pain wipes the knife handle clean of fingerprints*)

Hurry away, Peter.

(PETER *begins to stagger away*)

Wait . . . wait, Peter. Take your book . . . book. Right here . . . beside me . . . on your bench . . . my bench, rather. Come . . . take your book.

(PETER *starts for the book, but retreats*)

Hurry . . . Peter.

(PETER *rushes to the bench, grabs the book, retreats*)

Very good, Peter . . . very good. Now . . . hurry away. (PETER *hesitates for a moment, then flees, stage-left*) Hurry away . . . (*His eyes are closed now*) Hurry away, your parakeets are making the dinner . . . the cats . . . are setting the table . . .

PETER (*Off stage*) (*A pitiful howl*):   OH MY GOD!

JERRY (*His eyes still closed, he shakes his head and speaks; a combination of scornful mimicry and supplication*):   Oh . . . my . . . God.

(*He is dead*)

CURTAIN

1958, 1959

MIDDLE TO LATE 20TH-CENTURY POETRY

After World War II the influence of the modernists remained strong. The new generation of poets had the unenviable task of fashioning their own styles in the living shadows of Ezra Pound, William Carlos Williams, Wallace Stevens, Robert Frost, W. H. Auden (who, having emigrated to America in 1939, became a citizen in 1946), and especially T. S. Eliot. During the 1940s and 1950s these great modernists were not only still publishing major collections, but gaining in literary stature. For most modernists the primary question had been how and what to write after Eliot's *The Waste Land* (1922). Although *Four Quartets* (1943) had supplanted it as Eliot's vision of the quintessential modern long poem, neither the rest of his generation nor the next caught up with him or discovered a way to escape his authority easily.

World War II forced a decisive break in world history. Emerging from the conflict, the United States assumed the role of superpower. Artistically, this dominance was reflected in America's replacing England as the center of poetry. Despite Eliot's shadow, young American postwar poets inherited a confidence for which the previous generation had had to fight. This confidence was solidified by the newfound importance of poetry in American colleges and universities. Many young poets learned their craft by studying literature, whereas the previous generation had been largely self-taught. By 1950 poets and poetry had become fixtures on campuses in New York City, New Haven, Cambridge, Nashville, Ann Arbor, Berkeley, and elsewhere. During the late 1940s and early 1950s, many of the new generation of poets—including W. S. Merwin, Robert Lowell, James Merrill, James Wright, Richard Wilbur, Adrienne Rich, and John Ashbery—went abroad, financed either by private funds or by fellowships and grants. Yet, no one city became a foreign literary center, as Paris had in the 1920s, and these poets did not follow in the footsteps of Pound and Eliot, who lived abroad permanently.

The accent on the individual is the signature of postmodern poetry, an appellation given to poetry that appeared after 1945 and differs stylistically from the poetry of the modernists. Individual, if not personal, experience came to be not only acceptable as subject matter and stance, but assumed. And with the shift to postmodernism came a shift in poetry criticism. The most significant critical movement of the 1940s and the 1950s was the so-called New Criticism, led by the poet/critics I. A. Richards, John Crowe Ransom, R. P. Blackmur, Robert Penn Warren, and Cleanth Brooks. Influenced by the formal, classical, and impersonal elements in Eliot's poetry and criticism, the New Critics saw the poem as an inde-

John Crowe Ransom established the journal the Kenyon Review *at Kenyon College in 1937. Since then, increasing numbers of colleges have become centers of literary activities.*

pendent whole (a self-contained object) whose meaning could be interpreted by close textual analysis without reference to either the author's intention or the reader's emotional response. In their own poetry the New Critics employed traditional forms in writing objective, "impersonal" poems. Some young poets showed the influence of the New Criticism in their first volumes: Randall Jarrell's *Blood for a Stranger* (1942), Robert Lowell's *Lord Weary's Castle* (1946), John Berryman's *The Dispossessed* (1948), and Theodore Roethke's *Lost Son and Other Poems* (1948). These poets later freed themselves in varying degrees from its restraints. Other young poets, such as Elizabeth Bishop, admired by her peers for her technical elegance, were relatively untouched by the New Critics, as her first volume, *North and South* (1946), shows. Richard Wilbur, who published his first book of poetry, *The Beautiful Changes* in 1947, also remained a formalist. But the New Criticism, which had quickly become entrenched in academia, reached its zenith in 1956 with the revised edition of Brooks and Warren's 1938 *Understanding Poetry,* a college textbook that taught students how to "read" poetry according to the editors' canons.

By 1960 other views of poetry began to be heard. In his highly influential anthology *The New American Poetry,* published that year, Donald Allen included the work of post-World War II poets who represented, he claimed in his introduction, "the avant-garde, the true continuers of the modern movement in American poetry." Their common characteristic was "a total rejection of all those qualities typical of academic verse." Allen divided these poets into such groups as the

---

⸗CONTEXTS⸗

Psychoanalytic Criticism

Psychoanalytic criticism involves the examination of literary works and their authors in terms of the theories of psychoanalysis, especially those of Sigmund Freud (1856–1939). In the essay "Freud and Literature" (1941), the writer Lionel Trilling (1905–1975) finds "literary affinities" to certain elements of Freudian psychology. In making connections between the functions of the mind as Freud understood them and the interpretation of literature, Trilling writes:

Freud and Literature

The whole notion of rich ambiguity in literature, of the interplay between the apparent meaning and the latent—not "hidden"—meaning, has been reinforced by the Freudian concepts, perhaps even received its first impetus from them.

Specifically of poetry, he says:

Of all the mental systems, the Freudian psychology is the one which makes poetry indigenous to the very constitution of the mind. Indeed, the mind, as Freud sees it, is in the greater part of its tendency exactly a poetry-making organ. This puts the case too strongly, no doubt, for it seems to make the working of the unconscious mind equivalent to poetry itself, forgetting that between the unconscious mind and the finished poem there supervene the social intention and the formal control of the conscious mind. Yet the statement has at least the virtue of counterbalancing the belief, so commonly expressed or implied, that the very opposite is true, and that poetry is a kind of beneficent aberration of the mind's right course.

Lionel Trilling, 1941

Black Mountain School, the beats, and the New York School, although he recognized that this categorization was flexible.

Many of the Black Mountain poets—most of them affiliated with Black Mountain College in North Carolina—followed the theories of the college's rector, the poet Charles Olson. He advocated "projective verse," or poems as "open fields" conducting energy from poet to reader. Open forms included irregular meter and placement of lines and phrases over the page, as dictated by the poet's "breath." Members of the Black Mountain School included Robert Creeley, Robert Duncan, and the English poet Denise Levertov, after she emigrated to America following the war.

Allen Ginsberg's long poem "Howl" (1956) ushered in the beat generation of poets. In "Howl," Ginsberg explained, he sought to write with the "freedom of personal-thought rhythms as they occur." As Walt Whitman had done the century before, Ginsberg lengthened the traditional poetic line and extended the subject matter of poetry to embrace the often raw, dirty, ugly side of life and to protest public complacency, espousing instead freer lifestyles. Indeed, the term "beat" linked poets who shared Ginsberg's views to such underground alternatives as drugs, political radicalism, and homosexuality. Yet, it also connected them to another, more inward path of revolt, that achieved through the "beatitude" offered by the Eastern religious cults popular during the 1960s and 1970s. Ginsberg wrote and read "Howl" in San Francisco, which had become a center of beat activities during the 1950s, primarily through the efforts of beat poets such as Lawrence Ferlinghetti, who ran the influential City Lights bookstore, and Kenneth Rexroth.

Another opening of poetic content and form was initiated by the New York poets. Influenced by abstract-expressionist and surrealist painters, Frank O'Hara, John Ashbery, and James Schuyler wrote verse that, like abstract expressionism, concentrates on the act of composition itself and on capturing the moment that occasioned it. O'Hara's *Lunch Poems* (1964), written like notebook jottings, exemplifies the lighthearted, casual quality found in much of these poets' work. Of the New York poets, Ashbery has gone on to develop a far more complex style, as in his long poem "Self-Portrait in a Convex Mirror" (1975), which explores the tension between a completed work of art and the poet using all his energy to write about it.

A less radical expansion of poetry originated in the confessional verse of the 1950s and 1960s. The first volume by W. D. Snodgrass, *Heart's Needle* (1959), consisting of poems on his divorce, spurred Robert Lowell to write the family history poems of *Life Studies* (1959). Confessional verse was characterized by the unflinching candor with which these poets and others, including John Berryman in *The Dream Songs* (1964, 1969), Anne Sexton in *To Bedlam and Part Way Back* (1960), and Sylvia Plath in *Ariel* (1965), examined the most painful elements of their private lives—alcoholism, mental breakdowns, suicide attempts, and adultery. Yet, although they opened poetry to new subject matter, these poets tended to employ more formal verse styles than did the Black Mountain poets, the beats, and the New York poets. The tension in confessional poetry, in fact, arises from the friction between the personal, often shocking subject matter and the form (or its vestiges) that strives to contain it.

As many Americans, especially the young, turned increasingly to social protest in the 1960s, poetry of social protest came to the forefront, as it had in the 1930s. Adrienne Rich, Robert Lowell, Denise Levertov, and Allen Ginsberg wrote poems attacking America's involvement in the Vietnam War—and in the process both continued and changed the focus of Jarrell's war poetry of World War II. Rich passionately addresses the issues of women's liberation in *Diving Into the Wreck* (1973) and of lesbianism in *Sources* (1983), whereas Amiri Baraka angrily advocates African-American separatism and (later) revolution in his poetry of *The Dead Lecturer* (1964) and *In Our Terribleness* (1971) and in his prose. Such works, which explore the moral questions underlying the social issues of the times, would have been unlikely if post-World War II poets had not expanded the permissible range of subject matter and form.

Today's poets are taking full advantage of this previous experimentation. Written in formal verse, James Merrill's trilogy of book-length poems, *The Changing Light at Sandover* (1983), boldly attempts to construct an epic poem, using the brief lyric as its essential building block. Other notable recent poets, including Galway Kinnell, James Wright, A. R. Ammons, and Robert Hass, have in varying degrees replaced strict forms by looser ones, typically dispensing with rhyme and meter to emphasize metaphor and image, juxtaposition, lineation, and rhythm. Poets such as Lawson Inada, Paula Gunn Allen, Maxine Kumin, Simon Ortíz, Alberto Ríos, Louise Erdrich, and William Stafford write poetry firmly rooted in their ethnic heritage and/or explore regional landscapes. Poetry has once again been redefined in the generations of the postmodernists.

Theodore Roethke
(1908–1963)

Theodore Roethke was born in Saginaw, Michigan, in 1908. Much of Roethke's childhood was spent in intimate contact with the world within the greenhouse operated by his father, a successful florist who died when the poet was fifteen. This early death, and his ambivalent feelings for his father, are recurrent themes in Roethke's poems, but these poems are not as frankly autobiographical as the confessional poetry of Roethke's contemporaries Robert Lowell and Sylvia Plath.

After graduating from the University of Michigan in 1929 and spending a year at Harvard University, Roethke embarked on a series of teaching jobs. At Lafayette College in Pennsylvania he established important friendships with the poets Louise Bogan, Stanley Kunitz, and Rolfe Humphries; at Bennington College in Vermont he met the intellectually stimulating critic Kenneth Burke. From 1947 until his sudden death in 1963, Roethke taught at the University of Washington in Seattle, where the poets Carolyn Kizer, Richard Hugo, David Wagoner, and James Wright were among the many students captivated by Roethke's intensity.

Roethke's "greenhouse" poems stem from a rediscovery of his childhood. The highly unconventional free-verse greenhouse poems in *The Lost Son and Other Poems* (1948) brought the literary world to attention. Some of these poems scrutinize a subterranean realm of leaf mold, mildew, and roots; other poems are interior monologues written in the meditative yet anxious voice of a child. In both cases Roethke asks us to recognize our kinship with the "subhuman" order of life. Roethke's contemporaries recognized the publication of *The Lost Son* as an important event.

Although Roethke's creative breakthrough was accomplished in free verse, he never forsook traditional poetic forms. A poem like "The Waking" (1953), a highly successful villanelle—a complex and demanding verse form of French origin—shows that Roethke was capable of working within traditional forms while addressing a theme implicit in the greenhouse poems: that the unconscious is our most reliable guide to spiritual progress. In "The Waking" he writes that we "wake to sleep," not to our rational, conscious powers. Indeed, he is at times excessively derisive of reason. Roethke seeks instead a return to a primordial category of consciousness and situates himself within American and British traditions of romanticism. In his nature poems he manifests Ralph Waldo Emerson's desire to explore the near-familiar; Roethke's focus on the child amounts to an innovative revival of William Wordsworth's reverence for the intuitive wisdom of childhood. (The title of Roethke's third book, *Praise to the End!* [1951], comes from Book I of *The Prelude* [1850], Wordsworth's long autobiographical poem.) The affirmative counterpart to the traumatized voice of Roethke's "The Lost Son" is evident in the numerous children's nonsense poems and other humorous pieces in *Words for the Wind* (1958) and *I Am! Says the Lamb* (1961). Equally playful are Roethke's late and beautiful love poems, such as "I Knew a Woman" (1958), replete with erotic puns.

Roethke's craving for recognition was answered late in life. He received a Pulitzer Prize in 1954 for *The Waking, Poems: 1933–1953;* National Book Awards in 1959 for *Words for the Wind* and in 1964 for *The Far Field;* and the Bollingen Prize in 1959 for *Words for the Wind.* Despite these achievements and his students' admiration, Roethke's life was marked by personal anguish, periods of heavy drinking, and the need for frequent reassurances from friends about the quality of his poetry. After 1935 he was plagued by a series of emotional breakdowns. Several of these breakdowns warranted hospitalization, but Roethke managed to write some of his best poems during these difficult periods.

Suggested Readings: *Open House,* 1941. *The Lost Son and Other Poems,* 1948. *Praise to the End!,* 1951. *The Waking, Poems: 1933–1953,* 1953. *Words for the Wind,* 1958. *The Far Field,* 1965. *On the Poet and His Craft: Selected Prose of Theodore Roethke,* ed. R. J. Mills, Jr., 1965. K. Malkoff, *Theodore Roethke: An Introduction to the Poetry,* 1966. A. Seager, *The Glass House: The Life of Theodore Roethke,* 1968. J. La Belle, *The Echoing Wood of Theodore Roethke,* 1976. H. Bloom, ed. *Theodore Roethke,* 1988. P. Balakian, *Theodore Roethke's Far Fields: The Evolution of His Poetry,* 1989.

Text Used: *The Collected Poems of Theodore Roethke,* 1975.

OPEN HOUSE

My secrets cry aloud.
I have no need for tongue.
My heart keeps open house,
My doors are widely swung.
An epic of the eyes
My love, with no disguise.

My truths are all foreknown,
This anguish self-revealed.
I'm naked to the bone,
With nakedness my shield.   10
Myself is what I wear:
I keep the spirit spare.

The anger will endure,
The deed will speak the truth
In language strict and pure.
I stop the lying mouth:
Rage warps my clearest cry
To witless agony.

1941

NIGHT JOURNEY

Now as the train bears west,
Its rhythm rocks the earth,
And from my Pullman[1] berth
I stare into the night
While others take their rest.
Bridges of iron lace,
A suddenness of trees,
A lap of mountain mist
All cross my line of sight,
Then a bleak wasted place,   10
And a lake below my knees.
Full on my neck I feel
The straining at a curve;
My muscles move with steel,
I wake in every nerve.
I watch a beacon swing
From dark to blazing bright;
We thunder through ravines
And gullies washed with light.
Beyond the mountain pass   20
Mist deepens on the pane;
We rush into a rain
That rattles double glass.
Wheels shake the roadbed stone,
The pistons jerk and shove,
I stay up half the night
To see the land I love.

1941

MY PAPA'S WALTZ*

The whiskey on your breath
Could make a small boy dizzy;
But I hung on like death:
Such waltzing was not easy.

We romped until the pans
Slid from the kitchen shelf;
My mother's countenance
Could not unfrown itself.

The hand that held my wrist
Was battered on one knuckle;   10

---

[1] A railroad passenger car with convertible berths for sleeping; named after its inventor, G. M. Pullman (1831–1897).
* First published in *Harper's Bazaar* in 1942.

At every step you missed
My right ear scraped a buckle.

You beat time on my head
With a palm caked hard by dirt,
Then waltzed me off to bed
Still clinging to your shirt.

1942

ROOT CELLAR

Nothing would sleep in that cellar, dank as a ditch,
Bulbs broke out of boxes hunting for chinks in the dark,
Shoots dangled and drooped,
Lolling obscenely from mildewed crates,
Hung down long yellow evil necks, like tropical snakes.
And what a congress of stinks!—
Roots ripe as old bait,
Pulpy stems, rank, silo-rich,[1]
Leaf-mold, manure, lime, piled against slippery planks.
Nothing would give up life: 10
Even the dirt kept breathing a small breath.

1946, 1948

THE LOST SON

1. THE FLIGHT

At Woodlawn[1] I heard the dead cry:
I was lulled by the slamming of iron,
A slow drip over stones,
Toads brooding wells.
All the leaves stuck out their tongues;
I shook the softening chalk of my bones,
Saying,
Snail, snail, glister[2] me forward,
Bird, soft-sigh me home,
Worm, be with me.   10
This is my hard time.

Fished in an old wound,
The soft pond of repose;
Nothing nibbled my line,
Not even the minnows came.

---

[1] Stored for a long time.
[1] A cemetery.
[2] An archaic variant of glisten; snails produce a mucus trail along which they glide.

Sat in an empty house
Watching shadows crawl,
Scratching.
There was one fly.

Voice, come out of the silence.   20
Say something.
Appear in the form of a spider
Or a moth beating the curtain.

Tell me:
Which is the way I take;
Out of what door do I go,
Where and to whom?

    Dark hollows said, lee to the wind,
    The moon said, back of an eel,
    The salt said, look by the sea,   30
    Your tears are not enough praise,
    You will find no comfort here,
    In the kingdom of bang and blab.[3]

    Running lightly over spongy ground,
    Past the pasture of flat stones,
    The three elms,
    The sheep strewn on a field,
    Over a rickety bridge
    Toward the quick-water, wrinkling and rippling.

    Hunting along the river,   40
    Down among the rubbish, the bug-riddled foliage,
    By the muddy pond-edge, by the bog-holes,
    By the shrunken lake, hunting, in the heat of summer.

The shape of a rat?
        It's bigger than that.
        It's less than a leg
        And more than a nose,
        Just under the water
        It usually goes.

Is it soft like a mouse?   50
Can it wrinkle its nose?
Could it come in the house
On the tips of its toes?

        Take the skin of a cat
        And the back of an eel,

---

[3] Noise and idle chatter.

Then roll them in grease,—
That's the way it would feel.

It's sleek as an otter
With wide webby toes
Just under the water   60
It usually goes.

2. THE PIT

Where do the roots go?
  Look down under the leaves.
Who put the moss there?
  These stones have been here too long.
Who stunned the dirt into noise?
  Ask the mole, he knows.
I feel the slime of a wet nest.
  Beware Mother Mildew.
Nibble again, fish nerves.   70

3. THE GIBBER[4]

At the wood's mouth,
By the cave's door,
I listened to something
I had heard before.

Dogs of the groin
Barked and howled,
The sun was against me,
The moon would not have me.

The weeds whined,
The snakes cried,   80
The cows and briars
Said to me: Die.

What a small song. What slow clouds. What dark water.
Hath the rain a father? All the caves are ice. Only the snow's here.
I'm cold. I'm cold all over. Rub me in father and mother.
Fear was my father, Father Fear.
His look drained the stones.

  What gliding shape
  Beckoning through halls,
  Stood poised on the stair,   90
  Fell dreamily down?

---

[4] Unintelligible chatter; also a pouch at the base of some flowers.

From the mouths of jugs
Perched on many shelves,
I saw substance flowing
That cold morning.

Like a slither of eels
That watery cheek
As my own tongue kissed
My lips awake.

Is this the storm's heart? The ground is unstilling itself.   100
My veins are running nowhere. Do the bones cast out their fire?
Is the seed leaving the old bed? These buds are live as birds.
Where, where are the tears of the world?
Let the kisses resound, flat like a butcher's palm;
Let the gestures freeze; our doom is already decided.
All the windows are burning! What's left of my life?
I want the old rage, the lash of primordial milk!
Goodbye, goodbye, old stones, the time-order is going,
I have married my hands to perpetual agitation,
I run, I run to the whistle of money.   110

Money money money
Water water water

How cool the grass is.
Has the bird left?
The stalk still sways.
Has the worm a shadow?
What do the clouds say?

These sweeps of light undo me.
Look, look, the ditch is running white!
I've more veins than a tree!   120
Kiss me, ashes, I'm falling through a dark swirl.

4. THE RETURN

The way to the boiler was dark,
Dark all the way,
Over slippery cinders
Through the long greenhouse.

The roses kept breathing in the dark.
They had many mouths to breathe with.
My knees made little winds underneath
Where the weeds slept.

There was always a single light   130
Swinging by the fire-pit,[5]
Where the fireman pulled out roses,
The big roses, the big bloody clinkers.[6]

Once I stayed all night.
The light in the morning came slowly over the white
Snow.
There were many kinds of cool
Air.
Then came steam.

Pipe-knock.[7]   140

Scurry of warm over small plants.
Ordnung! ordnung![8]
Papa is coming!

A fine haze moved off the leaves;
Frost melted on far panes;
The rose, the chrysanthemum turned toward the light.
Even the hushed forms, the bent yellowy weeds
Moved in a slow up-sway.

5. "It was beginning winter"

It was beginning winter,
An in-between time,   150
The landscape still partly brown:
The bones of weeds kept swinging in the wind,
Above the blue snow.

It was beginning winter,
The light moved slowly over the frozen field,
Over the dry seed-crowns,
The beautiful surviving bones
Swinging in the wind.

Light traveled over the wide field;
Stayed.   160
The weeds stopped swinging.
The mind moved, not alone,
Through the clear air, in the silence.

---

[5] The heat source of the boiler that keeps the greenhouse temperature high.
[6] Fused residue from burnt coals, still red-hot ("bloody").
[7] The knocking of radiator pipes.
[8] "Order! Order!" (German).

Was it light?
Was it light within?
Was it light within light?
Stillness becoming alive,
Yet still?

A lively understandable spirit
Once entertained you.   170
It will come again.
Be still.
Wait.

1946, 1948

ELEGY FOR JANE

My Student, Thrown by a Horse

I remember the neckcurls, limp and damp as tendrils;
And her quick look, a sidelong pickerel[1] smile;
And how, once startled into talk, the light syllables leaped for her,
And she balanced in the delight of her thought,
A wren, happy, tail into the wind,
Her song trembling the twigs and small branches.
The shade sang with her;
The leaves, their whispers turned to kissing;
And the mold sang in the bleached valleys under the rose.

Oh, when she was sad, she cast herself down into such a pure depth,   10
Even a father could not find her:
Scraping her cheek against straw;
Stirring the clearest water.

My sparrow, you are not here,
Waiting like a fern, making a spiny shadow.
The sides of wet stones cannot console me,
Nor the moss, wound with the last light.

If only I could nudge you from this sleep,
My maimed darling, my skittery pigeon.
Over this damp grave I speak the words of my love: 20
I, with no rights in this matter,
Neither father nor lover.

1953

---

[1] A young or small pike.

THE WAKING

I wake to sleep, and take my waking slow.
I feel my fate in what I cannot fear.
I learn by going where I have to go.

We think by feeling. What is there to know?
I hear my being dance from ear to ear.
I wake to sleep, and take my waking slow.

Of those so close beside me, which are you?
God bless the Ground! I shall walk softly there,
And learn by going where I have to go.

Light takes the Tree; but who can tell us how?   10
The lowly worm climbs up a winding stair;
I wake to sleep, and take my waking slow.

Great Nature has another thing to do
To you and me; so take the lively air,
And, lovely, learn by going where to go.

This shaking keeps me steady. I should know.
What falls away is always. And is near.
I wake to sleep, and take my waking slow.
I learn by going where I have to go.

1952, 1953

I KNEW A WOMAN

I knew a woman, lovely in her bones,
When small birds sighed, she would sigh back at them;
Ah, when she moved, she moved more ways than one:
The shapes a bright container can contain!
Of her choice virtues only gods should speak,
Or English poets who grew up on Greek
(I'd have them sing in chorus, cheek to cheek).

How well her wishes went! She stroked my chin,
She taught me Turn, and Counter-turn, and Stand;[1]
She taught me Touch, that undulant white skin;   10
I nibbled meekly from her proffered hand;

[1] Strophe, antistrophe, and epode, or the three stanzas around which the odes of the Greek poet Pindar (522–442 B.C.) are organized. Usually elevated in tone, Pindaric odes have a complex metrical structure reflecting the dance movements they were written to accompany. The pattern of the strophe is repeated in the antistrophe but not in the concluding epode.

She was the sickle; I, poor I, the rake,
Coming behind her for her pretty sake
(But what prodigious mowing we did make).

Love likes a gander, and adores a goose:
Her full lips pursed, the errant note to seize;
She played it quick, she played it light and loose;
My eyes, they dazzled at her flowing knees;
Her several parts could keep a pure repose,
Or one hip quiver with a mobile nose   20
(She moved in circles, and those circles moved).

Let seed be grass, and grass turn into hay:
I'm martyr to a motion not my own;
What's freedom for? To know eternity.
I swear she cast a shadow white as stone.
But who would count eternity in days?
These old bones live to learn her wanton ways:
(I measure time by how a body sways).

1958

THE KITTY-CAT BIRD

The Kitty-Cat Bird, he sat on a Fence.
Said the Wren, your Song isn't worth 10¢.
You're a Fake, you're a Fraud, you're a Hor-rid Pretense!
   —Said the Wren to the Kitty-Cat Bird.

You've too many Tunes, and none of them Good:
I wish you would act like a bird really should,
Or stay by yourself down deep in the wood,
   —Said the Wren to the Kitty-Cat Bird.

You mew like a Cat, you grate like a Jay:
You squeak like a Mouse that's lost in the Hay,   10
I wouldn't be You for even a day,
   —Said the Wren to the Kitty-Cat Bird.

The Kitty-Cat Bird, he moped and he cried,
Then a real cat came with a Mouth so Wide,
That the Kitty-Cat Bird just hopped inside;
"At last I'm myself!"—and he up and died
   —Did the Kitty—the Kitty-Cat Bird.

You'd better not laugh; and don't say, "Pooh!"
Until you have thought this Sad Tale through:

Be sure that whatever you are is you   20
  —Or you'll end like the Kitty-Cat Bird.

1961

MYRTLE

There once was a girl named Myrtle
Who, strangely enough, *was* a Turtle:
She was mad as a Hare,
She could growl like a Bear,—
O *No*body understood Myrtle!

She would sit with a Book on her Knees,—
My Poetry-Book, if you please,—
She'd Rant and She'd Roar:
"This stuff is a Bore!
Why I could do better   10
With only ONE Letter,—
These Poets, they write like *I* Sneeze!"

1961

IN A DARK TIME*

In a dark time, the eye begins to see,
I meet my shadow in the deepening shade;
I hear my echo in the echoing wood—
A lord of nature weeping to a tree.
I live between the heron[1] and the wren,
Beasts of the hill and serpents of the den.

What's madness but nobility of soul
At odds with circumstance? The day's on fire!
I know the purity of pure despair,
My shadow pinned against a sweating wall.   10
That place among the rocks—is it a cave,
Or winding path? The edge is what I have.

A steady storm of correspondences!
A night flowing with birds, a ragged moon,
And in broad day the midnight come again!

---

* Roethke's note: "[The poem is] a drive toward God; an effort to break through the barrier of rational experience."
  [1] Roethke's note: "A symbol of purity, wisdom, toughness."

A man goes far to find out what he is—
Death of the self in a long, tearless night,
All natural shapes blazing unnatural light.

Dark, dark my light, and darker my desire.
My soul, like some heat-maddened summer fly,   20
Keeps buzzing at the sill. Which I is *I*?
A fallen man, I climb out of my fear.
The mind enters itself, and God the mind,
And one is One, free in the tearing[2] wind.

1964

Elizabeth Bishop
(1911–1979)

Elizabeth Bishop's titles for three of her major collections of poems—*North & South* (1946), *Questions of Travel* (1965), and *Geography III* (1976)—appropriately allude to her life and to the subject of much of her work. Bishop was a poet whose early losses and uprootedness are reflected in her adult travels and in poems tentatively addressing questions of "place," of travel and geography. Bishop relied on the intricate details of observation, translating them into descriptions of external landscapes that yield, though somewhat obliquely, the more elusive internal landscape of the self. To Bishop that internal landscape can be apprehended by knowing precisely where we are geographically and by understanding the complex relationship between that location and where we could be or could have chosen to be. Whereas the poem "Questions of Travel" asks "Should we have stayed at home and thought of here?" and "'Should we have stayed at home, / wherever that may be?'," the poet contends that "*the choice is never wide and never free.*"

If the poems address questions of place, the poet and her work are likewise difficult to place. Highly descriptive and typically formal, the poetry is not easily defined in relation to any specific movement. Belonging to no particular school of poetry, Bishop remained, by her work and by her character and life style, essentially outside the literary circles of her contemporaries. A poet who did not necessarily think of herself as a writer, she remarked in a 1978 interview with Elizabeth Spires (in *Poets at Work* [1989]) that "there's nothing more embarrassing than being a poet, really." A woman who, until late in her career, was too shy to give readings or to teach, Bishop established and maintained significant relationships with the poets Marianne Moore and Robert Lowell.

Born in Worcester, Massachusetts, in 1911 to parents of Canadian descent, Bishop spent her early childhood with her maternal grandparents in Nova Scotia, a landscape to which she returned in much of her poetry. Her father had died soon after her birth; in 1916 her mother, who had suffered a series of breakdowns, was committed to a mental hospital and remained there until her death in 1934. For Bishop, who never saw her mother again

---

[2] Roethke's note: "I feel there is hope in the ambiguity of 'tearing'—that the ambient air itself . . . [is] capable of pity."

*A 1976 drawing of
Elizabeth Bishop by
Darcy Penteado.*

after the last breakdown, itinerancy became a way of life when she was soon sent to her paternal grandparents in Worcester. There she became severely ill. When she went to live with an aunt in Boston, continued ill health—bronchitis, chronic asthma, and eczema—kept her out of school for long periods at a time. Bishop did not begin a steady formal education until she went away to boarding school in Natick, Massachusetts. She entered Vassar College in 1930 as a music composition major but dreaded the performances required of her. After giving up music she studied English and shortly before graduation met Marianne Moore. They began a lifelong friendship lasting until Moore's death in 1972.

After graduating with an A.B. in 1934, Bishop traveled to Europe, North Africa, and Mexico, and her poems began to appear in such periodicals as the *Partisan Review* and *Poetry.* Although Bishop's poems were published as early as 1935, she did not bring out her first collection, *North & South,* until 1946, about the time the poet Randall Jarrell introduced her to Robert Lowell. In 1938 she went to Key West, where she stayed for extended periods until the late 1940s. She traveled to South America in 1951, settling in Río de Janiero for nearly twenty years, and once took a trip down the Amazon River.

Bishop's travels and foreign residences are not surprising, as she had been a child with no permanent home nor a sense of one. "I was always sort of a guest, and I think I've always felt that way," she told Spires. As traveler and carefully inquisitive poet she was not unlike her "Sandpiper" (1965), ". . . preoccupied, / looking for something, something, something." Although Bishop claimed she had not really "been anywhere at all," her poems are deeply connected to the various landscapes she inhabited, particularly the northern ones of New England and Nova Scotia and the southern ones of Key West and

South America. Characterized by repetition, rhyme and partial rhyme, they are rarely self-referential, focusing instead on the precise detail of what lies before the poet's eye, "preoccupied" with naturalizing for the self the specifics of geographic location.

Yet, such poems as "The Map" (1946), "The Imaginary Iceberg" (1946), "Questions of Travel," and "The Moose" (1976) tentatively probe the interior landscape of the self, subtly excavating the shadowy worlds of borders, the places between and beneath what is most apparently visible, what is highlighted in the deceptively simple surface descriptions of the poems. "We'd rather have the iceberg than the ship, / although it meant the end of travel," writes Bishop in "The Imaginary Iceberg," for it "cuts its facets from within" and, like the soul, is "self-made from elements least visible." Maintaining a straightforward and modest tone but authoritative control over material, Bishop's poems tend to pivot on a series of questions or qualified, provisional assertions: "the art of losing's not too hard to master / though it may look like (*Write* it!) like disaster," Bishop claims in "One Art" (1976).

Returning to the United States in the early 1970s, Bishop taught at a number of universities, including Harvard, and lived in Boston from 1974 until her sudden death in 1979. The posthumously published *Elizabeth Bishop: The Collected Prose* (1984) includes the much-noted short story "In the Village." She translated the work of several Brazilian poets and *The Diary of "Helena Morley"* (1957). The first woman and the first American to win the prestigious Books Abroad/Neustadt International Prize for literature (1976), Bishop received such honors as two Guggenheim Fellowships, the Houghton Mifflin Poetry Award (for *North & South*), a Pulitzer Prize for *Poems: North & South—A Cold Spring* (1955), a National Book Award for *The Complete Poems* (1969), and the National Book Critics' Circle Award for *Geography III*. Widely acclaimed yet always on the edge of mainstream literary life, Bishop was not unlike her "imaginary iceberg," her epithets "self-made" and "least visible" applicable to the internal landscapes lying beneath her carefully constructed descriptions and to her poetic persona.

Suggested Readings: *North & South*, 1946. *Poems: North & South—A Cold Spring*, 1955. *The Ballad of the Burglar of Babylon*, 1968. *Questions of Travel*, 1968. *Geography III*, 1976. *The Collected Prose*, 1984. J. H. Miller, *Poets of Reality: Six Twentieth-Century Writers*, 1965. A. Stevenson, *Elizabeth Bishop*, 1966. A. Brown, "Elizabeth Bishop in Brazil," in *Southern Review*, 13:688–704 (Autumn) 1977. A. S. Ostriker, *Stealing the Language: The Emergence of Women's Poetry in America*, 1986. H. Vendler, "The Poems of Elizabeth Bishop," in *Critical Inquiry*, 13(4): 825–838, (Summer) 1987. D. Kalstone, *Becoming a Poet: Elizabeth Bishop With Marianne Moore and Robert Lowell*, ed. R. Hemenway, 1989. E. Spires, "An Afternoon With Elizabeth Bishop," in *Poets at Work: The PARIS REVIEW Interviews*, ed. G. Plimpton, 1989.

Text Used: *The Complete Poems: 1927–1979*, 1983.

THE MAP

Land lies in water; it is shadowed green.
Shadows, or are they shallows, at its edges
showing the line of long sea-weeded ledges
where weeds hang to the simple blue from green.
Or does the land lean down to lift the sea from under,
drawing it unperturbed around itself?
Along the fine tan sandy shelf
is the land tugging at the sea from under?

The shadow of Newfoundland lies flat and still.
Labrador's yellow, where the moony Eskimo   10
has oiled it. We can stroke these lovely bays,
under a glass as if they were expected to blossom,
or as if to provide a clean cage for invisible fish.
The names of seashore towns run out to sea,
the names of cities cross the neighboring mountains
—the printer here experiencing the same excitement
as when emotion too far exceeds its cause.
These peninsulas take the water between thumb and finger
like women feeling for the smoothness of yard-goods.

Mapped waters are more quiet than the land is,   20
lending the land their waves' own conformation:
and Norway's hare runs south[1] in agitation,
profiles investigate the sea, where land is.
Are they assigned, or can the countries pick their colors?
—What suits the character or the native waters best.
Topography displays no favorites; North's as near as West.
More delicate than the historians' are the map-makers' colors.

1946

THE IMAGINARY ICEBERG

We'd rather have the iceberg than the ship,
although it meant the end of travel.
Although it stood stock-still like cloudy rock
and all the sea were moving marble.
We'd rather have the iceberg than the ship;
we'd rather own this breathing plain of snow
though the ship's sails were laid upon the sea
as the snow lies undissolved upon the water.
O solemn, floating field,
are you aware an iceberg takes repose   10
with you, and when it wakes may pasture on your snows?

This is a scene a sailor'd give his eyes for.
The ship's ignored. The iceberg rises
and sinks again; its glassy pinnacles
correct elliptics in the sky.
This is a scene where he who treads the boards
is artlessly rhetorical. The curtain
is light enough to rise on finest ropes
that airy twists of snow provide.
The wits of these white peaks   20

_____

[1] A reference to Norway's shape; its "head" is pointed southward, with the upper portion in the
Atlantic and the lower portion in Skagerrak, the broad arm of the North Sea.

spar with the sun. Its weight the iceberg dares
upon a shifting stage and stands and stares.

This iceberg cuts its facets from within.
Like jewelry from a grave
it saves itself perpetually and adorns
only itself, perhaps the snows
which so surprise us lying on the sea.
Goody-bye, we say, good-bye, the ship steers off
where waves give in to one another's waves
and clouds run in a warmer sky.   30
Icebergs behoove the soul
(both being self-made from elements least visible)
to see them so: fleshed, fair, erected indivisible.

1946

THE BIGHT*

[*On my birthday*]

At low tide like this how sheer the water is.
White, crumbling ribs of marl[1] protrude and glare
and the boats are dry, the pilings dry as matches.
Absorbing, rather than being absorbed,
the water in the bight doesn't wet anything,
the color of the gas flame turned as low as possible.
One can smell it turning to gas; if one were Baudelaire[2]
one could probably hear it turning to marimba music.[3]
The little ocher dredge at work off the end of the dock
already plays the dry perfectly off-beat claves.[4]   10
The birds are outsize. Pelicans crash
into his peculiar gas unnecessarily hard,
it seems to me, like pickaxes,
rarely coming up with anything to show for it,
and going off with humorous elbowings.
Black-and-white man-of-war birds soar
on impalpable drafts

---

* A bay formed by a curve in a river or coastline.
[1] A soft, crumbly mixture of clay, sand, and limestone in varying proportions, typically containing shell fragments.
[2] The French poet Charles Baudelaire (1821–1867), whose aesthetic ideas were the source of the symbolist movement.
[3] Latin dance music based on a syncopated rhythm of alternating phrases of three and two beats, played by a musical instrument resembling a xylophone, consisting of a series of hard wooden bars with resonators, struck with small mallets.
[4] A pair of cylindrical hardwood sticks that make a hollow sound when struck together, used as a percussion instrument in Latin music.

and open their tails like scissors on the curves
or tense them like wishbones, till they tremble.
The frowsy sponge boats keep coming in   20
with the obliging air of retrievers,
bristling with jackstraw gaffs and hooks[5]
and decorated with bobbles of sponges.
There is a fence of chicken wire along the dock
where, glinting like little plowshares,
the blue-gray shark tails are hung up to dry
for the Chinese-restaurant trade.
Some of the little white boats are still piled up
against each other, or lie on their sides, stove in,
and not yet salvaged, if they ever will be, from the last bad storm,   30
like torn-open, unanswered letters.
The bight is littered with old correspondences.
Click. Click. Goes the dredge,
and brings up a dripping jawful of marl.
All the untidy activity continues,
awful but cheerful.

1955

THE SHAMPOO

The still explosions on the rocks,
the lichens, grow
by spreading, gray, concentric shocks.
They have arranged
to meet the rings around the moon, although
within our memories they have not changed.

And since the heavens will attend
as long on us,
you've been, dear friend,
precipitate and pragmatical;   10
and look what happens. For Time is
nothing if not amenable.

The shooting stars in your black hair
in bright formation
are flocking where,
so straight, so soon?
—Come, let me wash it in this big tin basin,
battered and shiny like the moon.

1955

---

[5] Large, strong hooks on a pole used in catching large sponges; here, hooks on a sponge-catching boat to hold the catch.

QUESTIONS OF TRAVEL

There are too many waterfalls here; the crowded streams
hurry too rapidly down to the sea,
and the pressure of so many clouds on the mountaintops
makes them spill over the sides in soft slow-motion,
turning to waterfalls under our very eyes.
—For if those streaks, those mile-long, shiny, tearstains,
aren't waterfalls yet,
in a quick age or so, as ages go here,
they probably will be.
But if the streams and clouds keep travelling, travelling,   10
the mountains look like the hulls of capsized ships,
slime-hung and barnacled.

Think of the long trip home.
Should we have stayed at home and thought of here?
Where should we be today?
Is it right to be watching strangers in a play
in this strangest of theatres?
What childishness is it that while there's a breath of life
in our bodies, we are determined to rush
to see the sun the other way around?   20
The tiniest green hummingbird in the world?
To stare at some inexplicable old stonework,
inexplicable and impenetrable,
at any view,
instantly seen and always, always delightful?
Oh, must we dream our dreams
and have them, too?
And have we room
for one more folded sunset, still quite warm?   30

But surely it would have been a pity
not to have seen the trees along this road,
really exaggerated in their beauty,
not to have seen them gesturing
like noble pantomimists, robed in pink.
—Not to have had to stop for gas and heard
the sad, two-noted, wooden tune
of disparate wooden clogs
carelessly clacking over   40
a grease-stained filling-station floor.
(In another country the clogs would all be tested.
Each pair there would have identical pitch.)
—A pity not to have heard
the other, less primitive music of the fat brown bird
who sings above the broken gasoline pump

in a bamboo church of Jesuit baroque:[1]
three towers, five silver crosses.
—Yes, a pity not to have pondered,
blurr'dly and inconclusively,
on what connection can exist for centuries   50
between the crudest wooden footwear
and, careful and finicky,
the whittled fantasies of wooden cages.
—Never to have studied history in
the weak calligraphy of songbirds' cages.
—And never to have had to listen to rain
so much like politicians' speeches:
two hours of unrelenting oratory
and then a sudden golden silence
in which the traveller takes a notebook, writes:

                                                                          60

"Is it lack of imagination that makes us come
to imagined places, not just stay at home?
Or could Pascal[2] have been not entirely right
about just sitting quietly in one's room?

Continent, city, country, society:
the choice is never wide and never free.
And here, or there . . . No. Should we have stayed at home,
wherever that may be?"

                                                                  1965

SESTINA*

September rain falls on the house.
In the failing light, the old grandmother
sits in the kitchen with the child
beside the Little Marvel Stove,
reading the jokes from the almanac,
laughing and talking to hide her tears.

---

[1] A seventeenth-century architectural style first brought to South America by the Jesuits.

[2] Blaise Pascal (1623–1662), a French mathematician, physicist, and philosopher who entered a convent in 1654 and argued for the necessity of mystic faith in understanding the universe.

* A complicated verse form composed of six stanzas of six lines each, followed by a three-line postscript. Generally unrhymed, the sestina is characterized by a recurrent pattern of the original six end words repeated in shifting order throughout the stanzas, three of the six in the end line positions of the postscript and three within each of the postscript's three lines.

She thinks that her equinoctial[1] tears
and the rain that beats on the roof of the house
were both foretold by the almanac,
but only known to a grandmother.
The iron kettle sings on the stove.   10
She cuts some bread and says to the child,

It's time for tea now; but the child
is watching the teakettle's small hard tears
dance like mad on the hot black stove,
the way the rain must dance on the house.
Tidying up, the old grandmother
hangs up the clever almanac

on its string. Birdlike, the almanac
hovers half open above the child,   20
hovers above the old grandmother
and her teacup full of dark brown tears.
She shivers and says she thinks the house
feels chilly, and puts more wood in the stove.

It was to be, says the Marvel Stove.
I know what I know, says the almanac.
With crayons the child draws a rigid house
and a winding pathway. Then the child
puts in a man with buttons like tears
and shows it proudly to the grandmother.   30

But secretly, while the grandmother
busies herself about the stove,
the little moons fall down like tears
from between the pages of the almanac
into the flower bed the child
has carefully placed in the front of the house.

Time to plant tears, says the almanac.
The grandmother sings to the marvellous stove
and the child draws another inscrutable house.

1965

POEM

About the size of an old-style dollar bill,
American or Canadian,
mostly the same whites, gray greens, and steel grays

---

[1] Of the equinox; here, the autumnal equinox, around September 22.

—this little painting (a sketch for a larger one?)
has never earned any money in its life.
Useless and free, it has spent seventy years
as a minor family relic
handed along collaterally to owners
who looked at it sometimes, or didn't bother to.

It must be Nova Scotia; only there   10
does one see gabled wooden houses
painted that awful shade of brown.
The other houses, the bits that show, are white.
Elm trees, low hills, a thin church steeple
—that gray-blue wisp—or is it? In the foreground
a water meadow with some tiny cows,
two brushstrokes each, but confidently cows;
two minuscule white geese in the blue water,
back-to-back, feeding, and a slanting stick.
Up closer, a wild iris, white and yellow,   20
fresh-squiggled from the tube.
The air is fresh and cold; cold early spring
clear as gray glass; a half inch of blue sky
below the steel-gray storm clouds.
(They were the artist's specialty.)
A specklike bird is flying to the left.
Or is it a flyspeck looking like a bird?

Heavens, I recognize the place, I know it!
It's behind—I can almost remember the farmer's name.
His barn backed on that meadow. There it is,   30
titanium white, one dab. The hint of steeple,
filaments of brush-hairs, barely there,
must be the Presbyterian church.
Would that be Miss Gillespie's house?
Those particular geese and cows
are naturally before my time.

A sketch done in an hour, "in one breath,"
once taken from a trunk and handed over.
Would you like this? I'll probably never
have room to hang these things again.   40
Your Uncle George, no, mine, my Uncle George,
he'd be your great-uncle, left them all with Mother
when he went back to England.
You know, he was quite famous, an R.A.[1] . . .

I never knew him. We both knew this place,
apparently, this literal small backwater,
looked at it long enough to memorize it,

[1] An artist elected to England's Royal Academy.

our years apart. How strange. And it's still loved,
or its memory is (it must have changed a lot).
Our visions coincided—"visions" is   50
too serious a word—our looks, two looks:
art "copying from life" and life itself,
life and the memory of it so compressed
they've turned into each other. Which is which?
Life and the memory of it cramped,
dim, on a piece of Bristol board,[2]
dim, but how live, how touching in detail
—the little that we get for free,
the little of our earthly trust. Not much.
About the size of our abidance   60
along with theirs: the munching cows,
the iris, crisp and shivering, the water
still standing from spring freshets,
the yet-to-be-dismantled elms, the geese.

                                                                    1976

IN THE WAITING ROOM

In Worcester, Massachusetts,
I went with Aunt Consuelo
to keep her dentist's appointment
and sat and waited for her
in the dentist's waiting room.
It was winter. It got dark
early. The waiting room
was full of grown-up people,
arctics and overcoats,
lamps and magazines.   10
My aunt was inside
what seemed like a long time
and while I waited I read
the *National Geographic*
(I could read) and carefully
studied the photographs:
the inside of a volcano,
black, and full of ashes;
then it was spilling over
in rivulets of fire.   20
Osa and Martin Johnson[1]
dressed in riding breeches,

---

[2] A smooth pasteboard used by artists.

[1] Osa Johnson (1894–1953) and her husband, Martin Johnson (1884–1937), filmed Africa's vanishing wildlife for the American Museum of Natural History.

laced boots, and pith helmets.
A dead man slung on a pole
—"Long Pig,"[2] the caption said.
Babies with pointed heads
wound round and round with string;
black, naked women with necks
wound round and round with wire
like the necks of light bulbs.   30
Their breasts were horrifying.
I read it right straight through.
I was too shy to stop.
And then I looked at the cover:
the yellow margins, the date.

Suddenly, from inside,
came an *oh!* of pain
—Aunt Consuelo's voice—
not very loud or long.
I wasn't at all surprised;   40
even then I knew she was
a foolish, timid woman.
I might have been embarrassed,
but wasn't. What took me
completely by surprise
was that it was *me:*
my voice, in my mouth.
Without thinking at all
I was my foolish aunt,
I—we—were falling, falling,   50
our eyes glued to the cover
of the *National Geographic,*
February, 1918.

I said to myself: three days
and you'll be seven years old.
I was saying it to stop
the sensation of falling off
the round, turning world
into cold, blue-black space.
But I felt: you are an *I,*   60
you are an *Elizabeth,*
you are one of *them.*
Why should you be one, too?
I scarcely dared to look
to see what it was I was.
I gave a sidelong glance
—I couldn't look any higher—
at shadowy gray knees,

---

[2] The name Polynesian cannibals use for a dead person.

trousers and skirts and boots
and different pairs of hands   70
lying under the lamps.
I knew that nothing stranger
had ever happened, that nothing
stranger could ever happen.

Why should I be my aunt,
or me, or anyone?
What similarities—
boots, hands, the family voice
I felt in my throat, or even
the *National Geographic*   80
and those awful hanging breasts—
held us all together
or made us all just one?
How—I didn't know any
word for it—how "unlikely" . . .
How had I come to be here,
like them, and overhear
a cry of pain that could have
got loud and worse but hadn't?

The waiting room was bright   90
and too hot. It was sliding
beneath a big black wave,
another, and another.

Then I was back in it.
the War[3] was on. Outside,
in Worcester, Massachusetts,
were night and slush and cold,
and it was still the fifth
of February, 1918.

1976

THE MOOSE

For Grace Bulmer Bowers[1]

From narrow provinces
of fish and bread and tea,
home of the long tides
where the bay leaves the sea
twice a day and takes
the herrings long rides,

---

[3] World War I (1914–1918).
[1] Bishop's maternal aunt.

where if the river
enters or retreats
in a wall of brown foam
depends on if it meets   10
the bay coming in,
the bay not at home;

where, silted red,
sometimes the sun sets
facing a red sea,
and others, veins the flats'
lavender, rich mud
in burning rivulets;

on red, gravelly roads,
down rows of sugar maples,   20
past clapboard farmhouses
and neat, clapboard churches,
bleached, ridged as clamshells,
past twin silver birches,

through late afternoon
a bus journeys west,
the windshield flashing pink,
pink glancing off of metal,
brushing the dented flank
of blue, beat-up enamel;   30

down hollows, up rises,
and waits, patient, while
a lone traveller gives
kisses and embraces
to seven relatives
and a collie supervises.

Goodbye to the elms,
to the farm, to the dog.
The bus starts. The light
grows richer; the fog,   40
shifting, salty, thin,
comes closing in.

Its cold, round crystals
form and slide and settle
in the white hens' feathers,
in gray glazed cabbages,
on the cabbage roses
and lupins[2] like apostles;

---

[2] Lupines, plants of the pea family.

the sweet peas cling
to their wet white string   50
on the whitewashed fences;
bumblebees creep
inside the foxgloves,
and evening commences.

One stop at Bass River.
Then the Economies—
Lower, Middle, Upper;
Five Islands, Five Houses,[3]
where a woman shakes a tablecloth
out after supper.   60

A pale flickering. Gone.
The Tantramar marshes
and the smell of salt hay.
An iron bridge trembles
and a loose plank rattles
but doesn't give way.

On the left, a red light
swims through the dark:
a ship's port lantern.
Two rubber boots show,   70
illuminated, solemn.
A dog gives one bark.

A woman climbs in
with two market bags,
brisk, freckled, elderly.
"A grand night. Yes, sir,
all the way to Boston."
She regards us amicably.

Moonlight as we enter
the New Brunswick woods,   80
hairy, scratchy, splintery;
moonlight and mist
caught in them like lamb's wool
on bushes in a pasture.

The passengers lie back.
Snores. Some long sighs.
A dreamy divagation
begins in the night,
a gentle, auditory,
slow hallucination. . . .   90

---

[3] Sites in Nova Scotia.

In the creakings and noises,
an old conversation
—not concerning us,
but recognizable, somewhere,
back in the bus:
Grandparents' voices

uninterruptedly
talking, in Eternity:
names being mentioned,
things cleared up finally;   100
what he said, what she said,
who got pensioned;

deaths, deaths and sicknesses;
the year he remarried;
the year (something) happened.
She died in childbirth.
That was the son lost
when the schooner foundered.

He took to drink. Yes.
She went to the bad.   110
When Amos began to pray
even in the store and
finally the family had
to put him away.

"Yes . . ." that peculiar
affirmative. "Yes . . ."
A sharp, indrawn breath,
half groan, half acceptance,
that means "Life's like that.
We know *it* (also death)."   120

Talking the way they talked
in the old featherbed,
peacefully, on and on,
dim lamplight in the hall,
down in the kitchen, the dog
tucked in her shawl.

Now, it's all right now
even to fall asleep
just as on all those nights.
—Suddenly the bus driver   130
stops with a jolt,
turns off his lights.

A moose has come out of
the impenetrable wood

and stands there, looms, rather,
in the middle of the road.
It approaches; it sniffs at
the bus's hot hood.

Towering, antlerless,
high as a church,   140
homely as a house
(or, safe as houses).
A man's voice assures us
"Perfectly harmless. . . ."

Some of the passengers
exclaim in whispers,
childishly, softly,
"Sure are big creatures."
"It's awful plain."
"Look! It's a she!"   150

Taking her time,
she looks the bus over,
grand, otherworldly.
Why, why do we feel
(we all feel) this sweet
sensation of joy?

"Curious creatures,"
says our quiet driver,
rolling his *r*'s.
"Look at that, would you."   160
Then he shifts gears.
For a moment longer,

by craning backward,
the moose can be seen
on the moonlit macadam;
then there's a dim
smell of moose, an acrid
smell of gasoline.

1976

ONE ART

The art of losing isn't hard to master;
so many things seem filled with the intent
to be lost that their loss is no disaster.

Lose something every day. Accept the fluster
of lost door keys, the hour badly spent.
The art of losing isn't hard to master.

Then practice losing farther, losing faster:
places, and names, and where it was you meant
to travel. None of these will bring disaster.

I lost my mother's watch. And look! my last, or   10
next-to-last, of three loved houses went.
The art of losing isn't hard to master.

I lost two cities, lovely ones. And, vaster,
some realms I owned, two rivers, a continent.
I miss them, but it wasn't a disaster.

—Even losing you (the joking voice, a gesture
I love) I shan't have lied. It's evident
the art of losing's not too hard to master
though it may look like (*Write* it!) like disaster.

                                                              1976

Randall Jarrell
(1914–1965)

Randall Jarrell was at his most eloquent when he was writing of America's involvement in
World War II. Born in Nashville in 1914, Jarrell lived in California until he was twelve.
He then returned to Nashville and stayed with his recently divorced mother. There Jarrell
later did undergraduate and graduate work at Vanderbilt University, where he studied with
the poet John Crowe Ransom. Jarrell spent much of his life teaching literature at Kenyon
and Sarah Lawrence Colleges and at the Universities of Texas and North Carolina. One of
only a handful of poets able to write about World War II from the perspective of a service-
man, he served as an Air Force pilot from 1942 to 1946. Jarrell's poems, many of which
are dramatic monologues from the viewpoint of pilots or prisoners of war, do not glorify
war; they return it to a human scale. "The Death of the Ball Turret Gunner" (1945), Jarrell's best-known war poem, is successful precisely for the way it equates death with rebirth.

In addition to writing war poems, Jarrell authored four children's books and translated
fairy tales, including those of the Brothers Grimm. He typically imbued the speakers of his
dramatic monologues, regardless of their age, with the guilelessness and remembered innocence of childhood. His poem "90 North" (1942) explores that innocence and the sad
experience of those who have reached adulthood: "Pain comes from the darkness / And we
call it wisdom. It is pain." At once lyric and dramatic, introspective and declarative, "90°
North" seems finally an extended metaphor for the failure of metaphor to do life justice
and for the sometimes misleading nature of words.

Jarrell survived the war. America did, too, though not undamaged, and was soon
launched into an era marked by the growth of suburbs. This America (and its inhabitants),
revitalized after the war, was Jarrell's second great subject. His two final collections of

poetry—*The Woman at the Washington Zoo* (1960), a National Book Award winner, and the posthumously published *The Lost World* (1965)—contain a number of dramatic monologues delivered by women. Most notable from these collections is "Next Day" (from *The Lost World*), set in a grocery store and delivered while the speaker moves "from Cheer to Joy, from Joy to All."

In October 1965 while out walking, Jarrell was struck and killed by a passing motorist. The month before, in a letter to the poet and novelist Robert Penn Warren, Jarrell had noted, "I haven't written any poems [lately], but I've been thinking about the passage of time, and what it's like to live a certain number of years in the world, that I think it's sure to turn into some poems in the long run." Jarrell was widely acknowledged by his contemporaries as the best poet/critic of his generation. His essays and reviews are collected in several volumes, including *Poetry and the Age* (1953), which contains the influential essay "The Obscurity of the Poet"; *A Sad Heart at the Supermarket* (1962); and *Kipling, Auden & Co.* (1980). He also authored *Pictures From an Institution* (1954), a satirical novel about college life.

Suggested Readings: *Blood for a Stranger*, 1942. *Losses*, 1948. *The Seven-League Crutches*, 1951. *Poetry and the Age*, 1953. *Pictures From an Institution*, 1954. *The Woman at the Washington Zoo*, 1960. *Selected Poems*, 1964. *The Lost World*, 1965. *The Third Book of Criticism*, 1965. M. L. Rosenthal, *The Modern Poets: A Critical Introduction*, 1960. R. Lowell et al., eds., *Randall Jarrell, 1914–1965*, 1967. E. Simpson, *Poets in Their Youth, A Memoir*, 1983. J. A. Bryant, Jr., *Understanding Randall Jarrell*, 1986. R. Lowell, "Randall Jarrell," in *Collected Prose*, 1987. H. Vendler, "Randall Jarrell," in *The Music of What Happens*, 1988.

Text Used: *The Complete Poems*, 1969.

90 NORTH*

At home, in my flannel gown, like a bear to its floe,
I clambered to bed; up the globe's impossible sides
I sailed all night—till at last, with my black beard,
My furs and my dogs, I stood at the northern pole.

There in the childish night my companions lay frozen,
The stiff furs knocked at my starveling throat,
And I gave my great sigh: the flakes came huddling,
Were they really my end? In the darkness I turned to my rest.

—Here, the flag snaps in the glare and silence
Of the unbroken ice. I stand here,
The dogs bark, my beard is black, and I stare   10
At the North Pole . . .
                    And now what? Why, go back.

Turn as I please, my step is to the south.
The world—my world spins on this final point
Of cold and wretchedness: all lines, all winds
End in this whirlpool I at last discover.

* The latitude of the North Pole.

And it is meaningless. In the child's bed
After the night's voyage, in that warm world
Where people work and suffer for the end
That crowns the pain—in that Cloud-Cuckoo-Land[1]   20

I reached my North and it had meaning.
Here at the actual pole of my existence,
Where all that I have done is meaningless,
Where I die or live by accident alone—

Where, living or dying, I am still alone;
Here where North, the night, the berg of death
Crowd me out of the ignorant darkness,
I see at last that all the knowledge

I wrung from the darkness—that the darkness flung me—
Is worthless as ignorance: nothing comes from nothing,   30
The darkness from the darkness. Pain comes from the darkness
And we call it wisdom. It is pain.

1942

THE DEATH OF THE BALL TURRET GUNNER*

From my mother's sleep I fell into the State,
And I hunched in its belly till my wet fur froze.
Six miles from earth, loosed from its dream of life,
I woke to black flak[1] and the nightmare fighters.
When I died they washed me out of the turret with a hose.

1945

THE WOMAN AT THE WASHINGTON ZOO

The saris[1] go by me from the embassies.

Cloth from the moon. Cloth from another planet.
They look back at the leopard like the leopard.

---

[1] Fantasy land: an imaginary city built in the sky by cuckoos, in the comic drama *The Birds* (414 B.C.), by the Greek satirist Aristophanes (450?–388? B.C.).

* Jarrell's note: "A ball turret was a plexiglass sphere set into the belly of a B-17 or B-24 [bomber], and inhabited by two .50 caliber machine-guns and one man, a short, small man. When this gunner tracked with his machine-guns a fighter attacking his bomber from below, he revolved with the turret; hunched upside-down in his little sphere, he looked like the foetus in the womb. The fighters which attacked him were armed with cannon firing explosive shells. The hose was a steam hose."

[1] The noise and fire of anti-aircraft guns.

[1] The wrapped outer garments of Hindu women.

And I. . . .
        this print of mine, that has kept its color
Alive through so many cleanings; this dull null
Navy I wear to work, and wear from work, and so
To my bed, so to my grave, with no
Complaints, no comment: neither from my chief,
The Deputy Chief Assistant, nor his chief—
Only I complain. . . . this serviceable   10
Body that no sunlight dyes, no hand suffuses
But, dome-shadowed, withering among columns,
Wavy beneath fountains—small, far-off, shining
In the eyes of animals, these beings trapped
As I am trapped but not, themselves, the trap,
Aging, but without knowledge of their age,
Kept safe here, knowing not of death, for death—
Oh, bars of my own body, open, open!

The world goes by my cage and never sees me.
And there come not to me, as come to these,   20
The wild beasts, sparrows pecking the llamas' grain,
Pigeons settling on the bears' bread, buzzards
Tearing the meat the flies have clouded. . . .
                     Vulture,
When you come for the white rat that the foxes left,
Take off the red helmet of your head, the black
Wings that have shadowed me, and step to me as man:
The wild brother at whose feet the white wolves fawn,
To whose hand of power the great lioness
Stalks, purring. . . .
             You know what I was,
You see what I am: change me, change me!   30

           1960

NEXT DAY

Moving from Cheer to Joy, from Joy to All,
I take a box
And add it to my wild rice, my Cornish game hens.
The slacked or shorted, basketed, identical
Food-gathering flocks
Are selves I overlook. Wisdom, said William James,[1]

Is learning what to overlook. And I am wise
If that is wisdom.

---

[1] James (1842–1910), a psychologist and philosopher (and brother of Henry James), in *Principles of Psychology* (1890).

Yet somehow, as I buy All from these shelves
And the boy takes it to my station wagon,   10
What I've become
Troubles me even if I shut my eyes.

When I was young and miserable and pretty
And poor, I'd wish
What all girls wish: to have a husband,
A house and children. Now that I'm old, my wish
Is womanish:
That the boy putting groceries in my car

See me. It bewilders me he doesn't see me.
For so many years   20
I was good enough to eat: the world looked at me
And its mouth watered. How often they have undressed me,
The eyes of strangers!
And, holding their flesh within my flesh, their vile

Imaginings within my imagining,
I too have taken
The chance of life. Now the boy pats my dog
And we start home. Now I am good.
The last mistaken,
Ecstatic, accidental bliss, the blind   30

Happiness that, bursting, leaves upon the palm
Some soap and water—
It was so long ago, back in some Gay
Twenties, Nineties, I don't know . . . Today I miss
My lovely daughter
Away at school, my sons away at school,

My husband away at work—I wish for them.
The dog, the maid,
And I go through the sure unvarying days
At home in them. As I look at my life,   40
I am afraid
Only that it will change, as I am changing:

I am afraid, this morning, of my face.
It looks at me
From the rear-view mirror, with the eyes I hate,
The smile I hate. Its plain, lined look
Of gray discovery
Repeats to me: "You're old." That's all, I'm old.

And yet I'm afraid, as I was at the funeral
I went to yesterday.   50
My friend's cold made-up face, granite among its flowers,

Her undressed, operated-on, dressed body
Were my face and body.
As I think of her I hear her telling me

How young I seem; I *am* exceptional;
I think of all I have.
But really no one is exceptional,
No one has anything, I'm anybody,
I stand beside my grave
Confused with my life, that is commonplace and solitary.   60

                                                                    1965

WELL WATER

What a girl called "the dailiness of life"
(Adding an errand to your errand. Saying,
"Since you're up . . . " Making you a means to
A means to a means to) is well water
Pumped from an old well at the bottom of the world.
The pump you pump the water from is rusty
And hard to move and absurd, a squirrel-wheel
A sick squirrel turns slowly, through the sunny
Inexorable hours. And yet sometimes
The wheel turns of its own weight, the rusty   10
Pump pumps over your sweating face the clear
Water, cold, so cold! you cup your hands
And gulp from them the dailiness of life.

                                                                    1965

BATS

A bat is born
Naked and blind and pale.
His mother makes a pocket of her tail
And catches him. He clings to her long fur
By his thumbs and toes and teeth.
And then the mother dances through the night
Doubling and looping, soaring, somersaulting—
Her baby hangs on underneath.
All night, in happiness, she hunts and flies.
Her high sharp cries   10
Like shining needlepoints of sound
Go out into the night and, echoing back,
Tell her what they have touched.
She hears how far it is, how big it is,

Which way it's going:
She lives by hearing.
The mother eats the moths and gnats she catches
In full flight; in full flight
The mother drinks the water of the pond
She skims across. Her baby hangs on tight.   20
Her baby drinks the milk she makes him
In moonlight or starlight, in mid-air.
Their single shadow, printed on the moon
Or fluttering across the stars,
Whirls on all night; at daybreak
The tired mother flaps home to her rafter.
The others all are there.
They hang themselves up by their toes,
They wrap themselves in their brown wings.
Bunched upside-down, they sleep in air.   30
Their sharp ears, their sharp teeth, their quick sharp faces
Are dull and slow and mild.
All the bright day, as the mother sleeps,
She folds her wings about her sleeping child.

1965

John Berryman
(1914–1972)

The madness and eloquence that characterize John Berryman's poetry are very much the madness and eloquence of the twentieth century—the political and social upheavals, the obsessions with loss. Berryman was born John Smith in McAlester, Oklahoma, in 1914, the first year of World War I. When he was twelve his father shot himself to death. This event haunted Berryman for the rest of his life and reappears obsessively in his poetry. After his mother remarried he took the surname of his stepfather. Educated at Columbia University and Clare College in Cambridge, England, Berryman subsequently taught literature and the history of civilization at Princeton and Harvard Universities and the Universities of Cincinnati and Minnesota. His first published book was *Poems* (1942). He followed it by *The Dispossessed* (1948) and achieved recognition with the long lyric poem *Homage to Mistress Bradstreet* (1956). In 1965 he received a Pulitzer Prize for *77 Dream Songs* (1964), which became the first section of *The Dream Songs* (1969). By the end of Berryman's life, the number of "dream songs" totaled 385.

Berryman's poetry was a continued if troubled apprenticeship to any number of difficult masters. William Butler Yeats profoundly influenced Berryman's early poems, and echoes of W. H. Auden and Robert Lowell may also be heard. Nevertheless, some of these poems bear suggestions of the brilliance that *The Dream Songs* later captured. What makes "The Ball Poem" (1942) and a handful of other poems stand out from the mass of Berryman's early work is their psychological acuity: they demonstrate unapologetically the bounds and rebounds of a mind profoundly unsettled by loss.

Homage to Mistress Bradstreet, the poem that defines and exemplifies the middle years of Berryman's career, in many ways prefigures *The Dream Songs,* most notably in the use of inversion and forced diction. "When I finally woke up to the fact that I was involved in a long poem," he recollected in the essay "One Answer to a Question" (1976), "one of my first thoughts was: Narrative! let's have narrative, and at least one dominant personality, and no fragmentation!" The poem takes for its subject the life of the seventeenth-century Puritan poet Anne Bradstreet, who Berryman describes as "this boring high-minded Puritan woman." *Homage to Mistress Bradstreet* allowed Berryman to show in a historical character how the personal and the spiritual life of a poet can become the stuff of a poem. At times the lyric sequence takes the form of a conversation between Bradstreet and a twentieth-century poet, most likely Berryman himself, although he denied that. In the end Mistress Bradstreet is as much a fictional creation as is Henry, the protagonist of *The Dream Songs.* Henry's last name is never revealed with certainty: it changes, as Berryman's had.

In "One Answer to a Question" Berryman describes the form of *The Dream Songs* as "eighteen-line sections, three six-line stanzas, each normally (for feet) 5–5–3–5–5–3, variously rhymed and not but mostly rhymed with great strictness." This stanzaic structure commonly breaks down. For example, "A Strut for Roethke," the eighteenth Dream Song, has twenty lines; the extra two form a bridge between the first and second stanzas. And the seventy-seventh dream song has a haunting one-line bridge: "—Come away, Mr. Bones." Some critics have suggested that Henry's unnamed friend, the speaker who implores Mr. Bones to "come away," is Death. Whether or not this is true, in a number of the later dream songs Berryman certainly mourns the death of many of his closest friends, among them the poets Randall Jarrell and Delmore Schwartz. "I'm cross with god who has wrecked this generation," begins dream song number 153. This poem cites the deaths not only of Jarrell and Schwartz, but also of Theodore Roethke, R. P. Blackmur, and Sylvia Plath, each of whom was a contemporary or near-contemporary of Berryman. Yet, for all the despair and the numerous losses they record, *The Dream Songs* struggle to find laughter in the wreckage. At their best they make tragedy of the commonplace and comedy of tragedy. That Henry and his vaudevillian friend speak at times in the dialect of minstrels is unfortunate, as their patter can be—and has been—misconstrued as racist. Nonetheless, the diction Berryman chose for *The Dream Songs* seems appropriate to the dark comedy of Henry's life.

After the publication of *The Dream Songs,* Berryman seemed to flounder. The "I" of his later poems appears to lapse into the voice of the poet himself. Although many of these later poems share the diction and the stanzaic structure Berryman originated in *The Dream Songs,* they are more self-indulgent than self-revelatory and lack his characteristic eloquence. As the years passed, the suffering caused by his father's death continued unabated. Alcoholism, clinical depression, and three failed marriages further eroded his emotional and physical stamina. In 1972, at age fifty-seven, Berryman committed suicide by jumping off a Minneapolis bridge.

Suggested Readings: *Homage to Mistress Bradstreet,* 1956. *77 Dream Songs,* 1964. *Berryman's Sonnets,* 1967. *Delusions, Etc.,* 1972. *Recovery,* 1973. *The Freedom of the Poet,* 1976. M. L. Rosenthal, *The New Poets: American and British Poetry Since World War II,* 1967. E. Simpson, *Poets in Their Youth: A Memoir,* 1983. E. M. Halliday, *John Berryman and the Thirties: A Memoir,* 1987. R. Lowell, "John Berryman," in *Robert Lowell: Collected Prose,* 1987. J. D. McClatchy, "John Berryman: The Impediments of Salvation," in *White Paper,* 1989.

Texts Used: *The Dream Songs,* 1969. *Henry's Fate,* 1977. All else: *Collected Poems: 1937–1971,* ed. C. Thornburg, 1989.

THE STATUE

The statue, tolerant through years of weather,
Spares the untidy Sunday throng its look,
Spares shopgirls knowledge of the fatal pallor
Under their evening colour,
Spares homosexuals, the crippled, the alone,
Extravagant perception of their failure;
Looks only, cynical, across them all
To the delightful Avenue and its lights.

Where I sit, near the entrance to the Park,
The charming dangerous entrance to their need,   10
Dozens, a hundred men have lain till morning
And the preservative darkness waning,
Waking to want, to the day before, desire
For the ultimate good, Respect, to hunger waking;
Like the statue ruined but without its eyes;
Turned vaguely out at dawn for a new day.

Fountains I hear behind me on the left,
See green, see natural life springing in May
To spend its summer sheltering our lovers,
Those walks so shortly to be over.   20
The sound of water cannot startle them
Although their happiness runs out like water,
Of too much sweetness the expected drain.
They trust their Spring; they have not seen the statue.

Disfigurement is general. Nevertheless
Winters have not been able to alter its pride,
If that expression is a pride remaining,
Coriolanus[1] and Rome burning,
An aristocracy that moves no more.
Scholars can stay their pity; from the ceiling   30
Watch blasted and superb inhabitants,
The wreck and justifying ruined stare.

Since graduating from its years of flesh
The name has faded in the public mind
Or doubled: which is this? the elder? younger?
The statesman or the traveller?[2]
Who first died or who edited his works,
The lonely brother bound to remain longer
By a quarter-century than the first-born
Of that illustrious and lost family?   40

---

[1] A legendary fifth-century B.C. Roman general and the protagonist of Shakespeare's tragedy *Coriolanus*.
[2] Baron Wilhelm von Humboldt (1767–1835), a German philologist and diplomat, and his younger brother, Baron Alexander von Humboldt (1769–1859), a naturalist, traveler, and statesman.

The lovers pass. Not one of them can know
Or care which Humboldt is immortalized.
If they glance up, they glance in passing,
An idle outcome of that pacing
That never stops, and proves them animal;
These thighs breasts pointed eyes are not their choosing,
But blind insignia by which are known
Season, excitement, loosed upon this city.

Turning: the brilliant Avenue, red, green,
The laws of passage; marvellous hotels;   50
Beyond, the dark apartment where one summer
Night an insignificant dreamer,
Defeated occupant, will close his eyes
Mercifully on the expensive drama
Wherein he wasted so much skill, such faith,
And salvaged less than the intolerable statue.

                                                    1948

THE BALL POEM

What is the boy now, who has lost his ball,
What, what is he to do? I saw it go
Merrily bouncing, down the street, and then
Merrily over—there it is in the water!
No use to say 'O there are other balls':
An ultimate shaking grief fixes the boy
As he stands rigid, trembling, staring down
All his young days into the harbour where
His ball went. I would not intrude on him,
A dime, another ball, is worthless. Now   10
He senses first responsibility
In a world of possessions. People will take balls,
Balls will be lost always, little boy,
And no one buys a ball back. Money is external.
He is learning, well behind his desperate eyes,
The epistemology of loss, how to stand up
Knowing what every man must one day know
And most know many days, how to stand up
And gradually light returns to the street,
A whistle blows, the ball is out of sight,   20
Soon part of me will explore the deep and dark
Floor of the harbour . . I am everywhere,
I suffer and move, my mind and my heart move
With all that move me, under the water
Or whistling, I am not a little boy.

                                                    1948

THE SONG OF THE TORTURED GIRL

After a little I could not have told—
But no one asked me this—why I was there.
I asked. The ceiling of that place was high
And there were sudden noises, which I made.
I must have stayed there a long time today:
My cup of soup was gone when they brought me back.

Often 'Nothing worse now can come to us'
I thought, the winter the young men stayed away,
My uncle died, and mother broke her crutch.
And then the strange room where the brightest light   10
Does not shine on the strange men: shines on me.
I feel them stretch my youth and throw a switch.

Through leafless branches the sweet wind blows
Making a mild sound, softer than a moan;
High in a pass once where we put our tent,
Minutes I lay awake to hear my joy.
—I no longer remember what they want.—
Minutes I lay awake to hear my joy.

1948

from   THE DREAM SONGS*

I

Huffy Henry hid   the day,
unappeasable Henry sulked.
I see his point,—a trying to put things over.
It was the thought that they thought
they could *do* it made Henry wicked & away.
But he should have come out and talked.

All the world like a woolen lover
once did seem on Henry's side.
Then came a departure.

* Most of these poems were first published in *77 Dream Songs* (1967) or in *His Toy, His Dream, His Rest* (1968) and then collected in *The Dream Songs* (1969). Throughout the "dream songs" appear Berryman's persona, Henry, and Henry's alter ego, Mister Bones (a name given to the character who rattled bones as a sound effect in minstrel shows). Berryman's note: "The poem, then, whatever its wide cast of characters, is essentially about an imaginary character (not the poet, not me) named Henry, a white American in early middle age sometimes in blackface, who has suffered an irreversible loss and talks about himself sometimes in the first person, sometimes in the third, sometimes even in the second; he has a friend, never named, who addresses him as Mr. Bones and variants thereof. Requiescant in pace ["Rest in peace" (Latin)]."

Thereafter nothing fell out as it might or ought.   10
I don't see how Henry, pried
open for all the world to see, survived.

What he has now to say is a long
wonder the world can bear & be.
Once in a sycamore I was glad
all at the top, and I sang.
Hard on the land wears the strong sea
and empty grows every bed.

1958, 1959

14

Life, friends, is boring. We must not say so.
After all, the sky flashes, the great sea yearns,
we ourselves flash and yearn,
and moreover my mother told me as a boy
(repeatingly) 'Ever to confess you're bored
means you have no

Inner Resources.' I conclude now I have no
inner resources, because I am heavy bored.
Peoples bore me,
literature bores me, especially great literature,   10
Henry bores me, with his plights & gripes
as bad as achilles,[1]

who loves people and valiant art, which bores me.
And the tranquil hills, & gin, look like a drag
and somehow a dog
has taken itself & its tail considerably away
into mountains or sea or sky, leaving
behind: me, wag.

1964

18

A STRUT FOR ROETHKE*

Westward, hit a low note, for a roarer lost
across the Sound but north from Bremerton,[1]
hit a way down note.

[1] The hero of *The Iliad*, by the Greek epic poet Homer (8th century B.C.); because of injured pride, Achilles sulked in his tent, refusing to fight the Trojans.
* The poet Theodore Roethke (1908–1963).
[1] A city in Washington State on the Puget Sound; at the time of his death, Roethke was teaching at the University of Washington.

And never cadenza[2] again of flowers, or cost.
Him who could really do that cleared his throat
& staggered on.

The bluebells, pool-shallows, saluted his over-needs,
while the clouds growled, heh-heh, & snapped, & crashed.

No stunt he'll ever unflinch once more will fail
(O lucky fellow, eh Bones?)—drifted off upstairs,   10
downstairs, somewheres.
No more daily, trying to hit the head on the nail:
thirstless: without a think in his head:
back from wherever, with it said.

Hit a high long note, for a lover found
needing a lower into friendlier ground
to bug among worms no more
around um jungles where ah blurt 'What for?'
Weeds, too, he favoured as   most men don't favour men.
The Garden Master's gone.[3]   20

1964

29

There sat down, once, a thing on Henry's heart
so heavy, if he had a hundred years
& more, & weeping, sleepless, in all them time
Henry could not make good.
Starts again always in Henry's ears
the little cough somewhere, an odour, a chime.

And there is another thing he has in mind
like a grave Sienese face[1] a thousand years
would fail to blur the still profiled reproach of. Ghastly,
with open eyes, he attends, blind.   10
All the bells say: too late. This is not for tears;
thinking.

But never did Henry, as he thought he did,
end anyone and hacks her body up
and hide the pieces, where they may be found.
He knows: he went over everyone, & nobody's missing.
Often he reckons, in the dawn, them up.
Nobody is ever missing.

1960

---

[2] An elaborate musical passage played solo.
[3] Roethke's father and grandfather were greenhouse keepers; his poems are filled with allusions to botanical growth.
[1] Like a face seen in the religious paintings by thirteenth- and fourteenth-century Italian artists in Siena.

40

I'm scared a lonely. Never see my son,
easy be not to see anyone,
combers[1] out to sea
know they're goin somewhere but not me.
Got a little poison, got a little gun,
I'm scared a lonely.

I'm scared a only one thing, which is me,
from othering I don't take nothin, see,
for any hound dog's sake.
But this is where I livin, where I rake   10
my leaves and cop[2] my promise, this' where we
cry oursel's awake.

Wishin was dyin but I gotta make
it all this way to that bed on these feet
where peoples said to meet.
Maybe but even if I see my son
forever never, get back on the take,
free, black & forty-one.[3]

1964

76

HENRY'S CONFESSION

Nothin very bad happen to me lately.
How you explain that?—I explain that, Mr Bones,
terms o' your bafflin odd sobriety.
Sober as man can get, no girls, no telephones,
what could happen bad to Mr Bones?
—*If* life is a handkerchief sandwich,

in a modesty of death I join my father
who dared so long agone leave me.
A bullet on a concrete stoop
close by a smothering southern sea
spreadeagled on an island, by my knee.   10
—You is from hunger, Mr Bones,

I offers you this handkerchief, now set
your left foot by my right foot,
shoulder to shoulder, all that jazz,

---

[1] Long, breaking waves.   [2] Back down on, go back on.
[3] A play on "free, white, and twenty-one," a colloquialism for "legally independent."

arm in arm, by the beautiful sea,
hum a little, Mr Bones.
—I saw nobody coming, so I went instead.

1964

77

Seedy Henry rose up shy in de world
& shaved & swung his barbells, duded Henry up
and p.a.'d[1] poor thousands of persons on topics of grand
moment to Henry, ah to those less & none.
Wif a book of his in either hand
he is stript down to move on.

—Come away, Mr Bones.

—Henry is tired of the winter,
& haircuts, & a squeamish comfy   ruin-prone proud national
   mind,   & Spring (in the city so called).
Henry likes Fall.   10
Hé would be prepared to líve in a world of Fáll
for ever, impenitent Henry.
But the snows and summers grieve & dream;

thése fierce & airy occupations, and love,
raved away so many of Henry's years
it is a wonder that, with in each hand
one of his own mad books and all,
ancient fires for eyes, his head full
& his heart full, he's making ready to move on.

1964

127

Again, his friend's death made the man sit still
and freeze inside—his daughter won first prize—
his wife scowled over at him—
It seemed to be Hallowe'en.
His friend's death had been adjudged suicide,
which dangles a trail

longer than Henry's chill, longer than his loss
and longer than the letter that he wrote
that day to the widow

---

[1] Publicly addressed (from "P. A. system").

to find out what the hell had happened thus.   10
All souls converge upon a hopeless mote
tonight, as though

the throngs of souls in hopeless pain rise up
to say they cannot care, to say they abide
whatever is to come.
My air is flung with souls which will not stop
and among them hangs a soul that has not died
and refuses to come home.

1968

153

I'm cross with god who has wrecked this generation.
First he seized Ted, then Richard, Randall, and now Delmore.[1]
In between he gorged on Sylvia Plath.
That was a first rate haul. He left alive
fools I could number like a kitchen knife
but Lowell he did not touch.[2]

Somewhere the enterprise continues, not—
yellow the sun lies on the baby's blouse—
in Henry's staggered thought.
I suppose the word would be, we must submit.   10
Later.
I hang, and I will not be part of it.

A friend of Henry's contrasted God's career
with Mozart's,[3] leaving Henry with nothing to say
but praise for a word so apt.
We suffer on, a day, a day, a day.
And never again can come, like a man slapped,
news like this

1968

157

Ten Songs, one solid block of agony,
I wrote for him,[1] and then I wrote no more.
His sad ghost must aspire
free of my love to its own post, that ghost,

---

[1] The poets Theodore Roethke (1908–1963); R. P. Blackmur (1904–1965), a critic as well; Randall Jarrell (1914–1965); Delmore Schwartz (1913–1966); also, Plath (1932–1963).
[2] In contrast to the other poets mentioned, Robert Lowell (1917–1977) was still alive when Berryman wrote this.
[3] The Austrian composer Wolfgang Amadeus Mozart (1756–1791).
[1] The poet Delmore Schwartz (1913–1966).

among its fellows, Mozart's, Bach's,[2] Delmore's
free of its careful body

high in the shades which line that avenue
where I will gladly walk, beloved of one,
and listen to the Buddha.
His work downhill, I don't conceal from you,   10
ran and ran out. The brain shook as if stunned,
I hope he's over that,

flame may his glory in that other place,
for he was fond of fame, devoted to it,
and every first-rate soul
has sacrifices which it puts in play,
I hope he's sitting with his peers: sit, sit,
& recover & be whole.

1968

187

Them lady poets must not marry, pal.
Miss Dickinson[1]—fancy in Amherst bedding hér.
Fancy a lark with Sappho,[2]
a tumble in the bushes with Miss Moore,[3]
a spoon with Emily, while Charlotte glare.[4]
Miss Bishop's[5] too noble-O.

That was the lot. And two of them are here
as yet, and—and: Sylvia Plath is not.[6]
She—she her credentials
has handed in, leaving alone two tots   10
and widower to what he makes of it—
surviving guy, &

when Tolstoy's pathetic widow doing her whung[7]
(after them decades of marriage) & kids, she decided he was *queer*
& loving his agent.

---

[2] The Austrian composer Wolfgang Amadeus Mozart (1756–1791); the German organist and composer Johann Sebastian Bach (1685–1750).
[1] Emily Dickinson (1830–1886), born in Amherst, Massachusetts, where she lived all her life.
[2] A seventh-century B.C. Greek lyric poet (female).
[3] Marianne Moore (1887–1972).
[4] Here, Berryman converts the verb "to spoon," or "to make love with kisses and carresses," into a noun; the Brönte sisters: Emily (1818–1845) and Charlotte (1816–1855), English novelists and poets.
[5] Elizabeth Bishop (1911–1979).
[6] When Berryman wrote this, both Bishop and Moore were alive, but Plath (1932–1963) was not.
[7] After 48 years of marriage to Sonya Andreyevna Bers, his worsening marital situation drove the Russian novelist Leo Tolstoy (1828–1910) to flee home secretly; several days later he died of pneumonia at the remote railway junction of Astapovo. The "agent" is probably Tolstoy's disciple V. G. Chertkov.

Wherefore he rush off, leaving two journals, & die.
It is a true error to marry with poets
or to be by them.

1968

366

Chilled in this Irish pub I wish my loves
well, well to strangers, well to all his friends,
seven or so in number,
I forgive my enemies, especially two,
races his heart, at so much magnanimity,
can it at all be true?

—Mr Bones, you on a trip outside yourself.
Has you seen a medicine man? You sound will-like,
a testament & such.
Is you going?—Oh, I suffer from a strike   10
& a strike & three balls: I stand up for much,
Wordsworth[1] & that sort of thing.

The pitcher dreamed. He threw a hazy curve,
I took it in my stride & out I struck,
lonesome Henry.
These Songs are not meant to be understood, you understand.
They are only meant to terrify & comfort.
Lilac was found in his hand.

1968

HENRY'S UNDERSTANDING*

He was reading late, at Richard's, down in Maine,
aged 32? Richard & Helen[1] long in bed,
my good wife long in bed.
All I had to do was strip & get into my bed,
putting the marker in the book, & sleep,
& wake to a hot breakfast.

---

[1] The English poet William Wordsworth (1770–1850).
* A "dream song" posthumously published in *Delusions, etc.* (1972).
[1] R. P. Blackmur (1904–1965), a poet and critic, and his wife.

Off the coast was an island, P'tit Manaan,[2]
the bluff from Richard's lawn was almost sheer.
A chill at four o'clock.
It only takes a few minutes to make a man.   10
A concentration upon now & here.
Suddenly, unlike Bach,[3]

& horribly, unlike Bach, it occurred to me
that *one* night, instead of warm pajamas,
I'd take off all my clothes
& cross the damp cold lawn & down the bluff
into the terrible water & walk forever
under it out toward the island.

1972

from   HENRY'S FATE

[I DIDN'T. AND I DIDN'T.]*

I didn't. And I didn't. Sharp the Spanish blade
to gash my throat after I'd climbed across
the high railing of the bridge
to tilt out, with the knife in my right hand
to slash me knocked or fainting till I'd fall
unable to keep my skull down but fearless

unless my wife wouldn't let me out of the house,
unless the cops noticed me crossing the campus
up to the bridge
& clappt me in for observation, costing my job—   10
I'd be now in a cell, costing my job—
well, I missed that;

but here's the terror of tomorrow's lectures
bad in themselves, the students dropping the course,
the Administration hearing
& offering me either a medical leave of absence
or resignation—Kitticat, they can't fire me—

1972, 1977

---

[2] Petit Manan Point, off southeastern Maine.
[3] The German organist and composer Johann Sebastian Bach (1685–1750).
    * Berryman wrote this untitled poem five days before he committed suicide by leaping from a Minneapolis bridge in 1972, years before the poem was published in *Henry's Fate* (1977).

Robert Hayden
(1913–1980)

Born Asa Bundy Sheffey in 1913 into poverty in a Detroit ghetto ironically called "Paradise Valley"—a name the poet later exploited in his verse—Robert Hayden became one of America's best-known African-American poets. He was the first African American to be named consultant in poetry to the Library of Congress (in 1976). In an autobiographical essay in *Collected Prose* (1984), Hayden wrote disconcertingly of himself in the third person: "By the time he entered high school he had discovered poetry and had begun the arduous and obsessive task of becoming a poet. He read Countee Cullen and Langston Hughes, Carl Sandburg and Edna St. Vincent Millay." For the young poet, Hayden remembered years later, poetry was "an escape, a release. It was a way of discovery, discovery of self and the world. It was the magic power of words."

Hayden was raised by neighbors, whose surname he took after his parents divorced and left the boy in their care. Hayden graduated from Detroit City College (now Wayne State University), where he met the prominent African-American poet Langston Hughes. Following Hayden's graduation, he worked for the Federal Writers' Project in Detroit from 1936 to 1938, researching the black history and folklore of the area. He published his first book of poems, *Heart-Shape in the Dust,* in 1940. In the same year he married Erma Morris and moved to New York City, where Erma studied at the Julliard School of Music. In New York Hayden was introduced to a poet whose work he had long admired, Countee Cullen.

Hayden then entered the University of Michigan, where he completed an M.A. in 1941 and studied with the expatriate British poet W. H. Auden. Hayden taught at the University of Michigan from 1944 through 1946 before becoming professor of English literature at Fisk University in Nashville, where he remained for twenty-three years. In 1946 he received a Rosenwald Fellowship, and in 1947 a Ford Foundation Grant for travel and writing in Mexico. Hayden won the Grand Prize for Poetry at the First World Festival of Negro Arts in Dakar, Senegal, in 1966 for his collection *A Ballad of Remembrance* (1962). A member of the Baha'i faith, Hayden was a poetry editor of the Baha'i magazine *World Order*. He also was editor and publisher of the Counterpoise Series, publications aimed at presenting the work of writers committed to poetics before politics. In 1968 he returned to the University of Michigan and taught there until his death in 1980.

Throughout his life Hayden attempted to avoid racial categorization. He hoped that his own poetry would have broad impact rather than an effect narrowly focused by race, ethnicity, or politics. Though he resolutely resisted the label of "black poet," Hayden wrote powerfully of the experiences of African Americans, from the national trauma of slavery to the segregation he experienced first-hand while teaching in Tennessee. Criticized at times for his disavowal of racial politics, Hayden nonetheless created a poetry that speaks movingly about, and for, African Americans as well as for all men and women.

Suggested Readings: *Heart-Shape in the Dust,* 1940. *Figure of Time: Poems,* 1955. *A Ballad of Remembrance,* 1962. *Selected Poems,* 1966. *Words in the Mourning Time,* 1970. *The Night-Blooming Cereus,* 1972. *American Journal,* 1978. *Collected Prose,* 1984. T. Davis, "Robert Hayden's Use of History," in *Modern Black Poets,* ed. D. B. Gibson, 1973. J. O. Young, *Black Writers of the Thirties,* 1973. B. Jackson and L. D. Rubin, Jr., *Black Poetry in America,* 1974. M. P. Novak,

"Meditative, Ironic, Richly Human: The Poetry of Robert Hayden," in *Midwest Quarterly*, 15:276–285, (Spring) 1974. L. Turco, *"Angle of Ascent:* The Poetry of Robert Hayden," in *Michigan Quarterly Review*, 16:199–219, (Spring) 1977.

Texts Used: "Bone-Flower Elegy": *Collected Poems of Robert Hayden*, 1985. All else: *Angle of Ascent: New and Selected Poems*, 1975.

A ROAD IN KENTUCKY

And when that ballad lady went
    to ease the lover whose life she broke,
oh surely this is the road she took,
    road all hackled through barberry fire,
through cedar and alder and sumac and thorn.

Red clay stained her flounces
    and stones cut her shoes
and the road twisted on to his loveless house
    and his cornfield dying
in the scarecrow's arms.   10

And when she had left her lover lying
    so stark and so stark, with the Star-of-Hope
drawn over his eyes, oh this is the road
    that lady walked in the cawing[1] light,
so dark and so dark in the briary light.

                                                    1966

THOSE WINTER SUNDAYS

Sundays too my father got up early
and put his clothes on in the blueblack cold,
then with cracked hands that ached
from labor in the weekday weather made
banked fires blaze. No one ever thanked him.

I'd wake and hear the cold splintering, breaking.
When the rooms were warm, he'd call,
and slowly I would rise and dress,
fearing the chronic angers of that house,

Speaking indifferently to him,   10
who had driven out the cold

---

[1] Harsh.

and polished my good shoes as well.
What did I know, what did I know
of love's austere and lonely offices?[1]

1966

RUNAGATE RUNAGATE*

I.

Runs falls rises stumbles on from darkness into darkness
and the darkness thicketed with shapes of terror
and the hunters pursuing and the hounds pursuing
and the night cold and the night long and the river
to cross and the jack-muh-lanterns[1] beckoning beckoning
and blackness ahead and when shall I reach that somewhere
morning and keep on going and never turn back and keep on going

       Runagate
          Runagate
             Runagate   10
Many thousands rise and go
many thousands crossing over

               O mythic North
               O star-shaped yonder Bible city[2]

Some go weeping and some rejoicing
some in coffins and some in carriages
some in silks and some in shackles

       Rise and go or fare you well

No more auction block for me
no more driver's lash for me   20

      If you see my Pompey, 30 yrs of age,
      new breeches, plain stockings, negro shoes;
      if you see my Anna, likely young mulatto[3]

---

[1] Functions, duties.
* Archaic for "runaway"; the poem is about the Underground Railroad, a pre-Civil War system set up by abolitionists to help slaves escape to the North.
[1] Jack-o'-lanterns, or will-o'-the-wisps, elusive lights seen over marshes at night.
[2] Bethlehem, Pennsylvania, just north of the Mason-Dixon line in pre-Civil War days.
[3] Of one black and one white parent.

branded E on the right cheek, R on the left,
catch them if you can notify subscriber.
Catch them if you can, but it won't be easy.
They'll dart underground when you try to catch them,
plunge into quicksand, whirlpools, mazes,
turn into scorpions when you try to catch them.

And before I'll be a slave   30
I'll be buried in my grave

     North star and bonanza gold
     I'm bound for the freedom, freedom-bound
     and oh Susyanna don't you cry for me.[4]

           Runagate

              Runagate

                II.

Rises from their anguish and their power,

           Harriet Tubman,[5]

           woman of earth, whipscarred,
           a summoning, a shining   40

           Mean to be free

And this was the way of it, brethren brethren,
way we journeyed from Can't to Can.
Moon so bright and no place to hide,
the cry up and the patterollers[6] riding,
hound dogs belling in bladed air.
And fear starts a-murbling, Never make it,
we'll never make it. *Hush that now,*
and she's turned upon us, levelled pistol   50
glinting in the moonlight:
Dead folks can't jaybird-talk, she says;
you keep on going now or die, she says.

Wanted   Harriet Tubman   alias The General
alias Moses   Stealer of Slaves

---

[4] The first line of the song "Oh Susanna" (1848), by the composer of popular music Stephen Collins Foster (1826–1864).
[5] Tubman (1820?–1913) was an escaped slave who helped other slaves escape to the North by the Underground Railroad.
[6] Patrollers.

In league with Garrison   Alcott   Emerson
Garrett   Douglass   Thoreau   John Brown[7]

Armed and known to be Dangerous

Wanted   Reward   Dead or Alive

> Tell me, Ezekiel,[8] oh tell me do you see   60
> mailed Jehovah coming to deliver me?

Hoot-owl calling in the ghosted air.
five times calling to the hants[9] in the air.
Shadow of a face in the scary leaves,
shadow of a voice in the talking leaves:

> Come ride-a my train

> *Oh that train, ghost-story train*
> *through swamp and savanna movering,*
> *over trestles of dew, through caves of the wish,*
> *Midnight Special on a sabre track movering movering,*   70
> *first stop Mercy and the last Hallelujah.*

> Come ride-a my train

> Mean mean mean to be free.

1966

FREDERICK DOUGLASS*

When it is finally ours, this freedom, this liberty, this beautiful
and terrible thing, needful to man as air,
usable as earth; when it belongs at last to all,
when it is truly instinct, brain matter, diastole, systole,[1]
reflex action; when it is finally won; when it is more
than the gaudy mumbo jumbo of politicians:
this man, this Douglass, this former slave, this Negro
beaten to his knees, exiled, visioning a world

---

[7] All abolitionists: the editor William Lloyd Garrison (1805–1879); the educator and reformer Amos Bronson Alcott (1799–1888); the essayist and poet Ralph Waldo Emerson (1803–1882); the Quaker leader Thomas Garrett (1789–1871); the African-American journalist and statesman Frederick Douglass (1818?–1895); the writer and naturalist Henry David Thoreau (1817–1862); John Brown (1800–1859), the leader of a raid on the arsenal at Harper's Ferry, Virginia, to start a slave uprising.

[8] A sixth-century B.C. Hebrew prophet; Jehovah is the Judeo-Christian God.

[9] Haunts, ghosts.

* Douglass (1818?–1895) was an escaped slave whose oratorical and literary brilliance thrust him to the forefront of the abolitionist movement.

[1] The two parts of a heartbeat: diastole, the dilation of the heart; systole, the contraction.

where none is lonely, none hunted, alien,
this man, superb in love and logic, this man   10
shall be remembered. Oh, not with statues' rhetoric,
    not with legends and poems and wreaths of bronze alone,
    but with the lives grown out of his life, the lives
    fleshing his dream of the beautiful, needful thing.

1966

"'MYSTERY BOY' LOOKS FOR KIN IN NASHVILLE"

Puzzle faces in the dying elms
promise him treats if he will stay.
Sometimes they hiss and spit at him
like varmints caught
in a thicket of butterflies.

A black doll,
one disremembered time,
came floating down to him
through mimosa's[1] fancywork leaves and blooms
to be his hidden bride.   10

From the road beyond the creepered walls
they call to him now and then,
and he'll take off in spite of the angry trees,
hearing like the loudening of his heart
the name he never can he never can repeat.

And when he gets to where the voices were—
Don't cry, his dollbaby wife implores;
I know where they are, don't cry.
We'll go and find them, we'll go
and ask them for your name again.   20

1970

BONE-FLOWER ELEGY

In the dream I enter the house
    wander vast rooms that are
        catacombs midnight subway
            cavernous ruined movie-palace
        where presences in vulture masks

---

[1] A tree or shrub that grows in warm regions; typically with spikes of small flowers.

play scenes of erotic violence
on a scaffold stage   I want
to stay and watch but know somehow
I must not linger and come to the funeral
chamber   in its icy nonlight see
a naked corpse
turning with sensual movements
on its coffin-bed
I have wept for you many times
I whisper but shrink from the arms
that would embrace me
and treading water reach
arched portals opening on a desert
groves of enormous nameless flowers
twist up from firegold sand
skull flowers flowers of sawtooth bone
their leaves and petals interlock
caging me for you beastangel
raging toward me
angelbeast shining come
to rend me and redeem

10

20

1978

William Stafford

(1914–   )

The poetry of William Stafford is, in every sense of the word, conversational. It is a dialogue between the poet and his various subjects: the past, both personal and historical; the natural world, its rewards and diminishing returns; the act of writing. For Stafford, the poet is not sacred; rather, the poetry is itself sacred. In many ways Stafford is a direct poetic descendant of William Wordsworth, emphasizing feeling first and then thought. It is easy to see Stafford's poems as manifestations of Wordsworth's view of poetry as "the spontaneous overflow of powerful feelings [taking] its origin from emotion recollected in tranquility," as Stafford's poem "After Arguing Against the Contention That Art Must Come From Discontent" (1982) ultimately contends. Stafford, the author of numerous essays on the nature and composition of poetry, possesses an eloquence that is at once uniquely American yet, unlike the eloquence of Walt Whitman, for example, is neither partisan nor nationalistic. However, Stafford's vision, like Whitman's, is expansive. Despite the brevity of Stafford's poems, their pace is unhurried: they are as declarative as they are meditative.

Born in 1914 in Hutchinson, Kansas, Stafford earned degrees from the Universities of Kansas and Iowa. During World War II he was a conscientious objector and worked in a public-service camp. His essays on the writing and teaching of poetry are collected in two volumes, *Writing the Australian Crawl* (1978) and *You Must Revise Your Life* (1986). Since 1948 Stafford has lived in Portland, Oregon, where he has been a professor at Lewis and Clark College.

Whereas Stafford's poems cannot be called nationalistic, they have typically, though wrongly, been called regional because he has spent the greater part of his life in, and has written about, the American Northwest. To label Stafford "regional" is to categorize superficially a writer who has never truly been a part of either the academic community or the East Coast literary community. In the preface to his collection *An Oregon Message* (1987), he writes: "My poems are organically grown, and it is my habit to allow language its freedom and confidence. Each poem is a miracle that has been invited to happen." There is verve in Stafford's emphasis on the "freedom and confidence" of language. Stafford was influenced not by the language of Wallace Stevens or of T. S. Eliot but by the language of William Carlos Williams and to some extent that of Robert Frost. Stafford is not a poet of unadorned speech: Stafford's poems tend to consist of a direct address from writer to reader, whether that reader is a specific individual—a number of Stafford's later poems are addressed to his mother—or any individual. Such an address occurs at the close of "Traveling Through the Dark" (1962), from the National Book Award winner by the same name and perhaps his best-known poem. In this poem Stafford addresses a doe, dead at roadside, and her unborn fawn as well as the poet and reader. Poet and reader share complicity in the act of disposing of the body, if only, Stafford would seem to argue, because such acts have consequences for all of "us."

Suggested Readings: *Down in My Heart*, 1947. *West of Your City*, 1960. *Traveling Through the Dark*, 1962. *Allegiances*, 1970. *Writing the Australian Crawl*, 1978. *You Must Revise Your Life*, 1986. R. Howard, *Alone With America: Essays on the Art of Poetry in America Since 1950*, 1969. J. Holden, *The Mark to Turn: A Reading of William Stafford's Poetry*, 1976. G. S. Lensing and R. Moran, *Four Poets and the Emotive Imagination: Robert Bly, James Wright, Louis Simpson and William Stafford*, 1976. L. Wagner, *American Modern: Essays in Fiction and Poetry*, 1980. R. Jackson, *Acts of Mind*, 1983.

Texts Used: "After Arguing Against the Contention That Art Must Come From Discontent": *A Glass Face in the Rain*, 1982. "An Oregon Message," 1987. All else: *Stories That Could Be True: New and Collected Poems*, 1977.

AT THE BOMB TESTING SITE

At noon in the desert a panting lizard
waited for history, its elbows tense,
watching the curve of a particular road
as if something might happen.

It was looking at something farther off
than people could see, an important scene
acted in stone for little selves
at the flute end of consequences.

There was just a continent without much on it
under a sky that never cared less.   10
Ready for a change, the elbows waited.
The hands gripped hard on the desert.

1960

A RITUAL TO READ TO EACH OTHER

If you don't know the kind of person I am
and I don't know the kind of person you are
a pattern that others made may prevail in the world
and following the wrong god home we may miss our star.

For there is many a small betrayal in the mind,
a shrug that lets the fragile sequence break
sending with shouts the horrible errors of childhood
storming out to play through the broken dyke.

And as elephants parade holding each elephant's tail,
but if one wanders the circus won't find the park,   10
I call it cruel and maybe the root of all cruelty
to know what occurs but not recognize the fact.

And so I appeal to a voice, to something shadowy,
a remote important region in all who talk:
though we could fool each other, we should consider—
lest the parade of our mutual life get lost in the dark.

For it is important that awake people be awake,
or a breaking line may discourage them back to sleep;
the signals we give—yes or no, or maybe—
should be clear: the darkness around us is deep.   20

1960

from *IN MEDIAS RES*

TRAVELING THROUGH THE DARK

Traveling through the dark I found a deer
dead on the edge of the Wilson River road.
It is usually best to roll them into the canyon:
that road is narrow; to swerve might make more dead.

By glow of the tail-light I stumbled back of the car
and stood by the heap, a doe, a recent killing;
she had stiffened already, almost cold.
I dragged her off; she was large in the belly.
My fingers touching her side brought me the reason—
her side was warm; her fawn lay there waiting,   10
alive, still, never to be born.
Beside that mountain road I hesitated.

The car aimed ahead its lowered parking lights;
under the hood purred the steady engine.
I stood in the glare of the warm exhaust turning red;
around our group I could hear the wilderness listen.

I thought hard for us all—my only swerving—,
then pushed her over the edge into the river.

1962

THE FARM ON THE GREAT PLAINS*

A telephone line goes cold;
birds tread it wherever it goes.
A farm back of a great plain
tugs an end of the line.

I call that farm every year,
ringing it, listening, still;
no one is home at the farm,
the line gives only a hum.

Some year I will ring the line
on a night at last the right one,   10
and with an eye tapered for braille
from the phone on the wall

I will see the tenant who waits—
the last one left at the place;
through the dark my braille eye
will lovingly touch his face.

"Hello, is Mother at home?"
No one is home today.
"But Father—he should be there."
No one—no one is here.   20

"But you—are you the one . . . ?"
Then the line will be gone
because both ends will be home:
no space, no birds, no farm.

My self will be the plain,
wise as winter is gray,
pure as cold posts go
pacing toward what I know.

1966

* In Kansas, where Stafford was born and raised.

THE EPITAPH ENDING IN AND

In the last storm, when hawks
blast upward and a dove is
driven into the grass, its broken wings
a delicate design, the air between
wracked thin where it stretched before,
a clear spring bent close too often
(that Earth should ever have such wings
burnt on in blind color!), this will be
good as an epitaph:

Doves did not know where to fly, and   10

1966

A LECTURE ON THE ELEGY

An elegy is really about the wilting of a flower,
the passing of the year, the falling of a stone.
Those people who go out, they just accompany
many things that leave us. Death is only
bad because it is like sunset, or a long eclipse.
If it had a dawn for company, or came with
spring, we would need laws to keep eager people
from rushing into danger and thus depopulating the world

So, I have turned the occasion for such sadness
around: those graceful images that   10
seem to decorate the poems, they are
a rediscovery of those elements
that first created the obvious feelings,
the feelings that some people cannot even sense
until they are built up from little losses
and surrounded with labels: "war," "catastrophe," "death."

1973

THE BURNING HOUSE

What does the floor hear—that cousin to earth?
A little tap, determined. Coming? No one.
Then a chair scrapes, and everywhere thunder.

Now everywhere has my home, reclaimed
earth, dust: it crossed borders, crept
under the praying emperor's knee.

Oh mansion all windows now!
Deepest and widest home—the swallows' barn,
or—"Fish, let me shake your fin."

My home is a home for all. Come in.   10

1977

ACCOUNTABILITY

Cold nights outside the taverns in Wyoming
pickups and big semi's[1] lounge idling, letting their
haunches twitch now and then in gusts of powder snow,
their owners inside for hours, forgetting as well
as they can the miles, the circling plains, the still town
that connects to nothing but cold and space and a few
stray ribbons of pavement, icy guides to nothing
but bigger towns and other taverns that glitter and wait:
Denver, Cheyenne.

Hibernating in the library of the school on the hill   10
a few pieces by Thomas Aquinas or Saint Teresa[2]
and the fragmentary explorations of people like Alfred
North Whitehead[3] crouch and wait amid research folders
on energy and military recruitment posters glimpsed
by the hard stars. The school bus by the door, a yellow
mound, clangs open and shut as the wind finds a loose
door and worries it all night, letting the hollow
students count off and break up and blow away
over the frozen ground.

1977

AFTER ARGUING AGAINST THE CONTENTION THAT ART MUST COME FROM DISCONTENT

Whispering to each handhold, "I'll be back,"
I go up the cliff in the dark. One place
I loosen a rock and listen a long time
till it hits, faint in the gulf, but the rush
of the torrent almost drowns it out, and the wind—

---

[1] Semi-trailer: a detachable trailer and the truck it pulls, generally an eighteen-wheeled truck.
[2] Saint Thomas Aquinas (1225?–1274) was an Italian theologian and philosopher who systematized Catholic theology; Teresa (1515–1582) was a Spanish saint known for her mystical visions.
[3] Whitehead (1861–1947) was an English mathematician and philosopher.

I almost forgot the wind: it tears at your side
or it waits and then buffets; you sag outward. . . .

I remember they said it would be hard. I scramble
by luck into a little pocket out of
the wind and begin to beat on the stones   10
with my scratched numb hands, rocking back and forth
in silent laughter there in the dark—
"Made it again!" Oh how I love this climb!
—the whispering to stones, the drag, the weight
as your muscles crack and ease on, working
right. They are back there, discontent,
waiting to be driven forth. I pound
on the earth, riding the earth past the stars:
"Made it again! Made it again!"

                                                    1982

AN OREGON MESSAGE

When we first moved here,[1] pulled
the trees in around us, curled
our backs to the wind, no one
had ever hit the moon—no one.
Now our trees are safer than the stars,
and only other people's neglect
is our precious and abiding shell,
pierced by meteors, radar, and the telephone.

From our snug place we shout
religiously for attention, in order to hide: 10
only silence or evasion will bring
dangerous notice, the hovering hawk
of the state, or the sudden quiet stare
and fatal estimate of an alerted neighbor.

This message we smuggle out in
its plain cover, to be opened
quietly: Friends everywhere—
we are alive! Those moon rockets
have missed millions of secret
places! Best wishes.   20

Burn this.

                                                    1987

[1] Stafford moved to Portland, Oregon, in 1948.

Robert Lowell
(1917–1977)

Born in 1917, Robert Traill Spence Lowell, Jr., was the only child of Charlotte Winslow and Robert Traill Spence Lowell, a naval officer who was talked into leaving the navy and becoming a stockbrocker (a job at which he had little success). The Lowells came from a prominent New England intellectual family that included James Russell Lowell, a nineteenth-century poet and editor, and Amy Lowell, an imagist poet. Throughout his poetic career Robert Lowell struggled to come to terms with his patrician family background. In a memoir of his childhood, "Antebellum Boston" (1957) Lowell draws a comparison between himself and the author Henry Adams, a member of another venerable Boston family. Written when Lowell was forty, his memoir displays perhaps the most characteristic feature of his poetry: the marriage, uneasy though it might be, of personal and historical points of view.

After graduating form St. Mark's preparatory school, Lowell began undergraduate studies at Harvard University but left after two years. At the urging of the poet Allen Tate, Lowell entered Kenyon College in Ohio, where his instructors and acquaintances included Tate and his wife, Caroline Gordon; John Crowe Ransom; Ford Madox Ford; Peter Taylor; and Randall Jarrell. After leaving Kenyon, Lowell studied with Robert Penn Warren and Cleanth Brooks at Louisiana State University. Many of Lowell's teachers were proponents of the New Criticism. Although Lowell adopted many of the formal tenets of his teachers, biographical—and autobiographical—material came to be so important in Lowell's work that his poems cannot be analyzed without in some fashion considering the life behind the poems. Lowell's relatives and friends all appear as characters in his poetry, even though certain truths were altered to meet the needs and requirements of the poems.

In 1940 Lowell graduated as Kenyon's valedictorian; also during that year he married Jean Stafford, a novelist, and converted to Roman Catholicism. His conversion, though temporary, was to affect his poetry throughout the 1940s. In a 1971 interview with the writer Ian Hamilton, Lowell explained: "I was born a nonbelieving Protestant New Englander; my parents and everyone I saw were nonbelieving Protestant New Englanders . . . From zealous, atheist Calvinist to a believing Catholic is no great leap." At the outset of World War II, Lowell attempted to enlist in the navy, following family tradition, but was turned down because of bad eyesight. So when he soon received orders from the army, Lowell sent a letter to President Franklin Delano Roosevelt in which he declared himself a conscientious objector. Lowell was sentenced in 1943 to a year and a day in prison. He spent five months in prison and served the rest of his term as an attendant in a Connecticut hospital. His poem "Memories of West Street and Lepke" (1959) describes the first days of his incarceration, in a New York City jail.

In 1944 Lowell's first poetry collection, *Land of Unlikeness*, was privately published. Its poems, many about religious subjects, are heavy with symbolism. A number of these poems appear in revised form in Lowell's second book, *Lord Weary's Castle* (1946), for which he received a Pulitzer Prize. *Lord Weary's Castle* includes two of Lowell's most famous poems, "Mr. Edwards and the Spider" and "The Quaker Graveyard in Nantucket."

The former copiously quotes the writings of Jonathan Edwards, an eighteenth-century Puritan revivalist minister and essayist, particularly his sermon "Sinners in the Hands of an Angry God" (1741). The latter poem, dedicated to Lowell's cousin Warren Winslow, who drowned at sea during World War II, shows the influence of John Milton's "Lycidas" (1637), Herman Melville's *Moby Dick* (1851), and T. S. Eliot's *Four Quartets* (1943)—especially "The Dry Salvages," published only a few years before "Quaker Graveyard." Not long after the release of *Lord Weary's Castle,* Lowell had a mental breakdown, the first of several that would plague him over the three decades until his death.

Lowell experimented with form, most notably dramatic monologue, in *The Mills of the Kavanaughs* (1951). An even greater change is evident in *Life Studies* (1959), considered by many to be his greatest work and also one of the most influential poetry collections of his generation. The collection begins with the prose memoir "91 Revere Street," one of the few chapters of Lowell's proposed autobiography that he was able to finish, and the only chapter published during his lifetime. Its title is the street address where Lowell and his mother lived while his father, a naval commander, was under orders to reside on the naval base in Boston. Although this memoir seems to stand apart from the poems in *Life Studies,* those poems illuminate the prose recollection.

Life Studies contains poems (such as "Beyond the Alps") that flow naturally from his earlier work. The poems of the final section of *Life Studies* generated great criticism as well as praise; in these poems Lowell shows off his "new" style. These frankly autobiographical, confessional poems, like most poems in the collection, are written in free verse. Long admired for his technical mastery and compressed syntax, Lowell worked with lines

The Massachusetts 54th, under Colonel Robert Gould Shaw, was the first African-American regiment to fight in the Civil War and is remembered in Robert Lowell's poem "For the Union Dead."

and stanzas that are untraditional yet controlled. The poems range from the poet's child-hood memories of the Lowell family, as in "My Last Afternoon With Uncle Devereaux Winslow," to searing and sordid accounts of the adult poet's hospitalization for chronic manic depression, as in "Waking in the Blue." The collection ends with "Skunk Hour," dedicated to Elizabeth Bishop and modeled after her poem "The Armadillo" (1965). Many of its lines and images can be traced to such sources as the poetry of Johann Hölderlin and John Milton's *Paradise Lost* (1667). In "Skunk Hour" Lowell struggles with the religion of his family, a struggle less narrative than thematic, less explicit than implicit. Set in a small town in Maine, the poem suggests sickness in both landscape ("The season's ill") and the poet himself ("My mind's not right"). The poet travels from desperation to an ambiguous affirmation of life.

Lowell followed the personal history of *Life Studies* with *For the Union Dead* (1964), which continues his personal/historical explorations—returning, for example, to Jonathan Edwards for subject matter. The fiercely moral and intensely personal title poem commem-orates, among other things, Col. Robert Shaw's Civil War regiment of African-American soldiers, the bronze monument dedicated to those soldiers (located in Boston), the victims of the atomic bomb, and the civil rights movement in the South during the late 1950s and early 1960s. Yet, perhaps nowhere in his entire body of work do Lowell's moral, histori-cal, and personal concerns manifest themselves more than in the long collection *Notebook 1967–68* (1969). Although the volume includes dozens of sonnetlike sections, Lowell thought of *Notebook* as a single poem, his life story in fourteen-line, unrhymed verse. With numerous revisions, the political and historical poems of *Notebook* were published as *History* (1973), and the more personal poems appeared in *For Lizzie and Harriet* (1973), which concerns Lowell's breakup with his second wife (the critic and novelist Elizabeth Hardwick) and their only child, Harriet. Lowell had become a public figure by this time due to his refusal to attend a White House Festival of the Arts, his support of the presiden-tial campaign of Senator Eugene McCarthy, and his vocal opposition to America's in-volvement in Vietnam—an involvement he actively protested and for which he was ar-rested.

The Dolphin (1973) is another volume of fourteen-line sections of verse and a personal history. The collection deals with the relationship between art and experience; with his third marriage, to the English novelist Lady Caroline Blackwood; and with the birth of their son. In *The Dolphin*, the personal triumphs over the historical—some of its poems detail the pain of his divorce from Hardwick and chronicle his continued episodes of manic depression. His final collection, *Day by Day*, is a loosely constructed, almost relaxed vol-ume that ends with the poem "Epilogue," seen by some as Lowell's poetic masterpiece. Published in 1977, the year of Lowell's sudden death from a heart attack, *Day by Day* seems heavy with a sense of resignation, of acceptance, as if Lowell knew that he would soon die.

Suggested Readings: *Lord Weary's Castle*, 1946. *The Mills of the Kavanaughs*, 1951. *Life Studies*, 1959. *For the Union Dead*, 1964. *The Old Glory*, 1968. *For Lizzie and Harriet*, 1973. *The Dolphin*, 1973. *Collected Prose*, 1988. H. B. Stapler, *Robert Lowell: The First Twenty Years*, 1961. W. J. Martz, *The Achievement of Robert Lowell*, 1966. T. Parkinson, ed., *Robert Lowell: A Collection of Critical Essays*, 1968. S. G. Axelrod, *Robert Lowell: Life and Art*, 1978. H. Vendler, "Robert Low-ell," in *Part of Nature, Part of Us: Modern American Poets*, 1980. I. Hamilton, *Robert Lowell, A Biography*, 1982. R. V. Hallberg, *American Poetry and Culture, 1945–80*, 1985. S. G. Axelrod and H. Deese, *Robert Lowell: Essays on the Poetry*, 1986.

Texts Used: "Water 1948": *Notebooks, 1967–1968*, 1970. "Epilogue": *Day by Day*, 1977. All else: *Selected Poems*, 1976.

THE QUAKER GRAVEYARD IN NANTUCKET

[FOR WARREN WINSLOW, DEAD AT SEA]*

*Let man have dominion over the fishes of the sea and the fowls of the air
and the beasts of the whole earth, and every creeping creature
that moveth upon the earth.*[1]

I

A brackish reach of shoal off Madaket[2]—
The sea was still breaking violently and night
Had steamed into our North Atlantic Fleet,
When the drowned sailor clutched the drag-net. Light
Flashed from his matted head and marble feet,
He grappled at the net
With the coiled, hurdling muscles of his thighs:
The corpse was bloodless, a botch of reds and whites,
Its open, staring eyes
Were lustreless dead-lights[3]   10
Or cabin-windows on a stranded hulk
Heavy with sand. We weight the body, close
Its eyes and heave it seaward whence it came,[4]
Where the heel-headed dogfish barks its nose
On Ahab's[5] void and forehead; and the name
Is blocked in yellow chalk.
Sailors, who pitch this portent at the sea
Where dreadnaughts shall confess
Its hell-bent deity,
When you are powerless   20
To sand-bag this Atlantic bulwark, faced
By the earth-shaker,[6] green, unwearied, chaste
In his steel scales; ask for no Orphean lute
To pluck life back.[7] The guns of the steeled fleet
Recoil and then repeat
The hoarse salute.

---

* Lowell's cousin died when his naval ship sank during World War II.
[1] From Genesis 1:26.
[2] Siasconset, a town on Nantucket Island, off Cape Cod.
[3] Strong covers placed over a ship's porthole cabin window in stormy weather. Lines 4–11 are based
on "The Shipwreck," the first chapter of *Cape Cod* (1865), by Henry David Thoreau (1817–1862).
[4] All life is thought to have developed from a primordial "sea."
[5] The captain of the whaler *Pequod* in *Moby-Dick* (1851), by Herman Melville (1819–1891).
[6] The god of the sea and of earthquakes: Poseidon to the Greeks, Neptune to the Romans.
[7] According to Greek myth, Orpheus's music so charmed Hades, the god of the Underworld, that he
allowed Orpheus to try to bring his wife, Eurydice, back to earth.

II

Whenever winds are moving and their breath
Heaves at the roped-in bulwarks of this pier,
The terns and sea-gulls tremble at your death
In these home waters. Sailor, can you hear   30
The Pequod's sea wings, beating landward, fall
Headlong and break on our Atlantic wall
Off 'Sconset,[8] where the yawing S-boats[9] splash
The bellbuoy, with ballooning spinnakers,
As the entangled, screeching mainsheet clears
The blocks: off Madaket, where lubbers[10] lash
The heavy surf and throw their long lead squids
For blue-fish? Sea-gulls blink their heavy lids
Seaward. The winds' wings beat upon the stones,
Cousin, and scream for you and the claws rush   40
At the sea's throat and wring it in the slush
Of this old Quaker graveyard where the bones
Cry out in the long night for the hurt beast
Bobbing by Ahab's whaleboats in the East.

III

All you recovered from Poseidon died
With you, my cousin, and the harrowed brine
Is fruitless on the blue beard of the god,
Stretching beyond us to the castles in Spain,
Nantucket's westward haven. To Cape Cod
Guns, cradled on the tide,   50
Blast the eelgrass about a waterclock[11]
Of bilge and backwash, roil the salt and sand
Lashing earth's scaffold, rock
Our warships in the hand
Of the great God; where time's contrition blues
Whatever it was these Quaker sailors,[12] lost
In the mad scramble of their lives. They died
When time was open-eyed,
Wooden and childish, only bones abide
There, in the nowhere, where their boats were tossed   60
Sky-high, where mariners had fabled news
Of IS,[13] the whited monster. What it cost
Them is their secret. In the sperm-whale's slick
I see the Quakers drown and hear their cry:
"If God himself had not been on our side,

---

[8] A town on Nantucket Island.   [9] Wildly steering racing yachts.
[10] Landlubbers: inexperienced sailors.   [11] A device for measuring time by the flow of water.
[12] Many Nantucket sailors were Quakers.
[13] A being of great force: Jesus Salvator, a sacrificial victim, as the whale was thought to be a victim of the Quakers; Revelation 17:8 speaks of a " . . . beast that was and is not and yet is."

If God himself had not been on our side,
When the Atlantic rose against us, why,
Then it had swallowed us up quick."

IV

This is the end of the whaleroad[14] and the whale
Who spewed Nantucket bones on the thrashed swell   70
And stirred the troubled waters to whirlpools
To send the Pequod packing off to hell:
This is the end of them, three-quarters fools,
Snatching at straws to sail
Seaward and seaward on the turntail whale,
Spouting out blood and water as it rolls,
Sick as a dog to these Atlantic shoals:
Clamavimus,[15] O depths. Let the sea-gulls wail

For water, for the deep where the high tide
Mutters to its hurt self, mutters and ebbs.   80
Waves wallow in their wash, go out and out,
Leave only the death-rattle of the crabs,
The beach increasing, its enormous snout
Sucking the ocean's side.
This is the end of running on the waves;
We are poured out like water. Who will dance
The mast-lashed master of Leviathans[16]
Up from this field of Quakers in their unstoned graves?

V

When the whale's viscera go and the roll
Of its corruption overruns this world   90
Beyond tree-swept Nantucket and Woods Hole[17]
And Martha's Vineyard, Sailor, will your sword
Whistle and fall and sink into the fat?
In the great ash-pit of Jehoshaphat[18]
The bones cry for the blood of the white whale,
The fat flukes arch and whack about its ears,
The death-lance churns into the sanctuary, tears
The gun-blue swingle,[19] heaving like a flail,
And hacks the coiling life out: it works and drags
And rips the sperm-whale's midriff into rags,   100
Gobbets of blubber spill to wind and weather,
Sailor, and gulls go round the stoven timbers

---

[14] The sea.
[15] "We have cried" (Latin); after Psalm 130:1, "Out of the depths I have cried unto thee, O Lord."
[16] In the Old Testament, sea monsters, typically whales.
[17] A town on the Massachusetts coast, across from the island of Martha's Vineyard.
[18] The "valley of decision," site of the Last Judgment (see Joel 3:11–16). Lowell's note: "The day of judgment. The world, according to some prophets, will end in fire."
[19] A knifelike wooden instrument used to clean flax or hemp by beating or scraping.

Where the morning stars sing out together
And thunder shakes the white surf and dismembers
The red flag hammered in the mast-head.[20] Hide,
Our steel, Jonas Messias,[21] in Thy side.

VI

OUR LADY OF WALSINGHAM[22]

There once the penitents took off their shoes
And then walked barefoot the remaining mile;
And the small trees, a stream and hedgerows file
Slowly along the munching English lane,   110
Like cows to the old shrine, until you lose
Track of your dragging pain.
The stream flows down under the druid tree,[23]
Shiloah's[24] whirlpools gurgle and make glad
The castle of God. Sailor, you were glad
And whistled Sion by that stream.[25] But see:
Our Lady, too small for her canopy,
Sits near the altar. There's no comeliness
At all or charm in that expressionless
Face with its heavy eyelids. As before,   120
This face, for centuries a memory,
Non est species, neque decor,[26]
Expressionless, expresses God: it goes
Past castled Sion. She knows what God knows,
Not Calvary's Cross nor crib at Bethlehem[27]
Now, and the world shall come to Walsingham.

VII

The empty winds are creaking and the oak
Splatters and splatters on the cenotaph,[28]
The boughs are trembling and a gaff[29]
Bobs on the untimely stroke   130
Of the greased wash exploding on a shoal-bell
In the old mouth of the Atlantic. It's well;
Atlantic, you are fouled with the blue sailors,

---

[20] At the end of *Moby-Dick* the sail of the sinking *Pequod* is nailed to the mast like a flag.

[21] A combination of Jonah, the Old Testament prophet who was swallowed by a whale, and Jesus, the New Testament Messiah. Here, Jonah's emergence from the whale is prophetic of Jesus' resurrection.

[22] A medieval shrine dedicated to the Virgin Mary in Walsingham Priory, Norfolk, England; details from E. I. Watkin's *Catholic Art and Culture.*

[23] The oak tree, sacred to ancient pagan Celtic Druids.   [24] The town Shiloh, in ancient Palestine.

[25] The stream on Mount Sion (or Zion) that flows past God's Temple in Jerusalem (see Isaiah 8:6); in Isaiah 51:2 the redeemed come "singing into Zion."

[26] "There is neither form nor beauty" (Latin).

[27] Not the site of Jesus' crucifixion nor that of his birth.

[28] An empty tomb or monument erected in honor of someone buried elsewhere.

[29] A pole with a hook used in catching large fish.

Sea-monsters, upward angel, downward fish:[30]
Unmarried and corroding, spare of flesh
Mart once of supercilious, wing'd clippers,
Atlantic, where your bell-trap guts its spoil
You could cut the brackish winds with a knife
Here in Nantucket, and cast up the time
When the Lord God formed man from the sea's slime   140
And breathed into this face the breath of life,
And blue-lung'd combers lumbered to the kill.
The Lord survives the rainbow of His will.[31]

1946

MR. EDWARDS AND THE SPIDER*

I saw the spiders marching through the air,
Swimming from tree to tree that mildewed day
   In latter August when the hay
   Came creaking to the barn. But where
      The wind is westerly,
Where gnarled November makes the spiders fly
Into the apparitions of the sky,
They purpose nothing but their ease and die
Urgently beating east to sunrise and the sea;

What are we in the hands of the great God?[1]   10
It was in vain you set up thorn and briar
   In battle array against the fire
   And treason crackling in your blood;
      For the wild thorns grow tame
And will do nothing to oppose the flame;
Your lacerations tell the losing game
You play against a sickness past your cure.
How will the hands be strong? How will the heart endure?

A very little thing, a little worm,
Or hourglass-blazoned spider,[2] it is said,   20
   Can kill a tiger. Will the dead

---

[30] After Book I (462–463) of *Paradise Lost* (1667), by John Milton (1608–1674).

[31] In Genesis 9:11 God makes a covenant with Noah that the earth would never again be plagued by a Great Flood.

* Jonathan Edwards (1703–1758) was a Puritan minister and theologian. The first stanza is derived from the essay "Of Insects," which Edwards wrote in 1715.

[1] After Edwards's famous sermon *Sinners in the Hands of an Angry God* (1741), based on Ezekiel 22:14: "Can thine heart endure, or can thine hands be strong, in the days that I shall deal with thee?" In the sermon God dangles sinners like spiders above a bottomless pit.

[2] On the underside of the abdomen of the poisonous female black widow spider is a red, hourglass-shaped mark.

Hold up his mirror and affirm
  To the four winds the smell
And flash of his authority? It's well
If God who holds you to the pit of hell,
Much as one holds a spider, will destroy,
Baffle and dissipate your soul. As a small boy

On Windsor Marsh,[3] I saw the spider die
When thrown into the bowels of fierce fire:
  There's no long struggle, no desire   30
  To get up on its feet and fly—
    It stretches out its feet
And dies. This is the sinner's last retreat;
Yes, and no strength exerted on the heat
Then sinews the abolished will, when sick
And full of burning, it will whistle on a brick.

But who can plumb the sinking of that soul?
Josiah Hawley,[4] picture yourself cast
  Into a brick-kiln where the blast
  Fans your quick vitals to a coal—   40
    If measured by a glass,
How long would it seem burning! Let there pass
A minute, ten, ten trillion; but the blaze
Is infinite, eternal: this is death,
To die and know it. This is the Black Widow, death.

1946

BEYOND THE ALPS

(On the train from Rome to Paris, 1950, the year Pius XII defined the dogma of Mary's bodily assumption.)[1]

Reading how even the Swiss had thrown the sponge
in once again and Everest was still
unscaled,[2] I watched our Paris Pullman lunge
mooning across the fallow Alpine snow.
O bella Roma![3] I saw our stewards go
forward on tiptoe banging on their gongs.

---

[3] Near East Windsor, Connecticut, where Edwards spent his boyhood.

[4] Edwards's uncle, whose suicide Edwards blamed on the Devil.

[1] Eugenio Pacelli (1876–1958), Pope Pius XII (1939–1958), had promulgated as official Roman Catholic dogma that the Virgin Mary did not die but was taken up bodily to Heaven.

[2] Mount Everest was not scaled successfully until May 29, 1953, by Edmund Hillary and Tensing Norgay; a Pullman is a railroad passenger car with sleeping berths, named after its inventor, G. M. Pullman (1831–1897).

[3] "O beautiful Rome!" (Italian).

Life changed to landscape. Much against my will
I left the City of God[4] where it belongs.
There the skirt-mad Mussolini unfurled
the eagle of Caesar.[5] He was one of us   10
only, pure prose. I envy the conspicuous
waste of our grandparents on their grand tours—
long-haired Victorian sages bought the universe,
while breezing on their trust funds through the world.

When the Vatican made Mary's Assumption dogma,
the crowds at San Pietro[6] screamed *Papá*.
The Holy Father dropped his shaving glass,
and listened. His electric razor purred,
his pet canary chirped on his left hand.
The lights of science couldn't hold a candle   20
to Mary risen—at one miraculous stroke,
angel-wing'd, gorgeous as a jungle bird!
But who believed this? Who could understand?
Pilgrims still kissed Saint Peter's[7] brazen sandal.
The Duce's lynched, bare, booted skull[8] still spoke.
God herded his people to the *coup de grâce*[9]—
the costumed Switzers sloped their pikes to push,
O Pius, through the monstrous human crush. . . . [10]

Our mountain-climbing train had come to earth.
Tired of the querulous hush-hush of the wheels,   30
the blear-eyed ego kicking in my berth
lay still, and saw Apollo[11] plant his heels
on terra firma through the morning's thigh . . .
each backward, wasted Alp, a Parthenon,[12]
fire-branded socket of the Cyclops'[13] eye.
There were no tickets for that altitude

---

[4] Rome.

[5] Benito Mussolini (1883–1945), the Fascist dictator of Italy (1922–1943), is known to have had many mistresses; on the flag of the National Italian Socialist Republic was an eagle holding the *fasces,* or bound sticks, symbolizing fascism.

[6] Saint Peter's Basilica in Rome; "Papá" is an affectionate form of address for Father.

[7] A bronze statue (13th? century) of the seated figure of St. Peter in the basilica; the line is a scathing reference to the Catholic Church, especially to the pope's policy of neutrality during World War II and his failure to condemn the Nazi extermination of the Jews.

[8] Mussolini was known as "Il Duce" (the chief); after he was expelled by his countrymen and shot, his dead, naked body was hung upside down in public for the people to see.

[9] "The final blow" (French).

[10] Probably the crowds that gather every Sunday at Saint Peter's Square to receive the pope's blessing.

[11] According to Greek myth, the god of the sun and of music.

[12] The temple of Athena, the Greek goddess of wisdom and of warfare, built (5th century B.C.) on the Acropolis in Athens.

[13] A one-eyed monster of Greek myth; in the *Odyssey* (Bk. IX), by Homer (8th? century B.C.), Odysseus and his men poke out the eye of the cyclops Polyshemus with a stake they have sharpened in the fire.

once held by Hellas,[14] when the Goddess stood,
prince, pope, philosopher and golden bough,
pure mind and murder at the scything prow—
Minerva,[15] the miscarriage of the brain.   40

Now Paris, our black classic,[16] breaking up
like killer kings on an Etruscan cup.

1950, 1959

from   *LIFE STUDIES**

I

MY LAST AFTERNOON
WITH UNCLE DEVEREUX WINSLOW[1]

1922: THE STONE PORCH OF MY GRANDFATHER'S[2] SUMMER HOUSE

I

"I won't go with you. I want to stay with Grandpa!"
That's how I threw cold water
on my Mother and Father's
watery martini pipe dreams at Sunday dinner.
. . . Fontainebleau, Mattapoisett,[3] Puget Sound. . . .
Nowhere was anywhere after a summer
at my Grandfather's farm.
Diamond-pointed, athirst and Norman,[4]
its alley of poplars
paraded from Grandmother's rose garden   10

---

[14] Ancient Greece, including its islands and colonies.

[15] The Roman equivalent of Athena.

[16] Paris is contrasted with the whiteness of the snow-covered Alps, making the city seem pagan and mysterious. Paris, representing the twentieth-century world to which Lowell returns, appears as remote as that of the Etruscans, the people of ancient Etruria (a country in what is now Italy that flourished in the sixth century B.C.), known for their pottery.

* Lowell's four-part collection of highly personal poetry and prose, published in 1959.

[1] An uncle on Lowell's mother's side; the Winslow family was as patrician as was the Lowell family. The ellipses are Lowell's.

[2] Arthur Winslow, Lowell's maternal grandfather, a financial entrepeneur from Boston.

[3] A wealthy Paris suburb and location of a royal chateau; a summer resort town in southeastern Massachusetts.

[4] A style of architecture that flourished in Normandy, France, and, after the Norman conquest (1066), in England; characterized by massive construction, round arches over recessed doors and windows, and carvings.

to a scary stand of virgin pine,
scrub, and paths forever pioneering.

One afternoon in 1922,
I sat on the stone porch, looking through
screens as black-grained as drifting coal.
Tockytock, tockytock
clumped our Alpine, Edwardian[5] cuckoo clock,
slung with strangled, wooden game.
Our farmer was cementing a root-house[6] under the hill.
One of my hands was cool on a pile   20
of black earth, the other warm
on a pile of lime. All about me
were the works of my Grandfather's hands:
snapshots of his *Liberty Bell* silver mine;
his high school at *Stuttgart am Neckar;*[7]
stogie-brown beams; fools'-gold nuggets;
octagonal red tiles,
sweaty with a secret dank, crummy with ant-stale;
a Rocky Mountain chaise longue,
its legs, shellacked saplings.   30
A pastel-pale Huckleberry Finn
fished with a broom straw in a basin
hollowed out of a millstone.
Like my Grandfather, the décor
was manly, comfortable,
overbearing, disproportioned.

What were those sunflowers? Pumpkins floating shoulder-high?
It was sunset, Sadie and Nellie
bearing pitchers of ice-tea,
oranges, lemons, mint, and peppermints,   40
and the jug of shandygaff,
which Grandpa made by blending half and half
yeasty, wheezing homemade sarsaparilla with beer.
The farm, entitled *Char-de-sa*
in the Social Register,
was named for my Grandfather's children:
Charlotte, Devereux, and Sarah.
No one had died there in my lifetime . . .
Only Cinder, our Scottie puppy
paralyzed from gobbling toads.   50
I sat mixing black earth and lime.

II

I was five and a half.
My formal pearl gray shorts

---

[5] In the style prominent during the reign of Edward VII.
[6] A storage place for bulbs and root vegetables.   [7] "Stuttgart on the Neckar [River]" (German).

had been worn for three minutes.
My perfection was the Olympian[8]
poise of my models in the imperishable autumn
display windows
of Rogers Peet's boys' store below the State House
in Boston. Distorting drops of water
pinpricked my face in the basin's mirror.   60
I was a stuffed toucan
with a bibulous, multicolored beak.

III

Up in the air
by the lakeview window in the billiards-room,
lurid in the doldrums of the sunset hour,
my Great Aunt Sarah
was learning *Samson and Delilah*.[9]
She thundered on the keyboard of her dummy piano,
with gauze curtains like a boudoir table,
accordionlike yet soundless.   70
It had been bought to spare the nerves
of my Grandmother,
tone-deaf, quick as a cricket,
now needing a fourth for "Auction,"[10]
and casting a thirsty eye
on Aunt Sarah, risen like the phoenix[11]
from her bed of troublesome snacks and Tauchnitz classics.[12]

Forty years earlier,
twenty, auburn headed,
grasshopper notes of genius!   80
Family gossip says Aunt Sarah
tilted her archaic Athenian nose
and jilted an Astor.[13]
Each morning she practiced
on the grand piano at Symphony Hall,
deathlike in the off-season summer—
its naked Greek statues draped with purple
like the saints in Holy Week. . . .
On the recital day, she failed to appear.

IV

I picked with a clean finger nail at the blue anchor
on my sailor blouse washed white as a spinnaker.

---

[8] Like the gods of Mt. Olympus of classical myth.
[9] An 1877 opera by the French composer Camille Saint-Saëns (1835–1921).
[10] Auction bridge, which requires four players.
[11] According to Egyptian myth, a bird that sets itself on fire and rises anew from the ashes.
[12] German-produced, paper-covered English editions of standard British and American works.
[13] A member of a wealthy German-American family.   [14] In southeastern Massachusetts.

What in the world was I wishing?
. . . A sail-colored horse browsing in the bullrushes . . .
A fluff of the west wind puffing   90
my blouse, kiting me over our seven chimneys,
troubling the waters. . . .
As small as sapphires were the ponds: *Quittacus, Snippituit,*
and *Assawompset,*[14] halved by "the Island,"
where my Uncle's duck blind[15]
floated in a barrage of smoke-clouds.
Double-barreled shotguns
stuck out like bundles of baby crow-bars.
A single sculler[16] in a camouflaged kayak
was quacking to the decoys. . . .   100

At the cabin between the waters,
the nearest windows were already boarded.
Uncle Devereux was closing camp for the winter.
As if posed for "the engagement photograph,"
he was wearing his severe
war-uniform of a volunteer Canadian officer.
Daylight from the doorway riddled his student posters,
tacked helter-skelter on walls as raw as a boardwalk.
Mr. Punch,[17] a water melon in hockey tights,
was tossing off a decanter of Scotch.   110
La Belle France[18] in a red, white and blue toga
was accepting the arm of her "protector,"
the ingenu and porcine Edward VII.[19]
The pre-war music hall belles
had goose necks, glorious signatures, beauty-moles,
and coils of hair like rooster tails.
The finest poster was two or three young men in khaki kilts
being bushwhacked on the veldt[20]—
They were almost life-size. . . .
                                                                                   120

My Uncle was dying at twenty-nine.
"You are behaving like children,"
said my Grandfather,
when my Uncle and Aunt left their three baby daughters,
and sailed for Europe on a last honeymoon . . .

[15] A structure that conceals a duck hunter from the prey.
[16] The oarsman in a racing boat (or kayak).
[17] The cartoon figure of a plump Englishman, the emblem of the English humor magazine *Punch*, established in 1841.
[18] The female emblem of France.
[19] A poster showing Edward VII (1841–1910), king of Great Britain and Ireland (1901–1910), well known as a ladies' man, with his arm around La Belle France; it commemorates the Entente Cordiale, an informal understanding between France and England (1904).
[20] Open, grassy country in South Africa; in the Boer War (1899–1902) Britain defeated the South African republics of the Orange Free State and the Transvaal.

I cowered in terror.
I wasn't a child at all—   130
unseen and all-seeing, I was Agrippina[21]
in the Golden House of Nero. . . .
Near me was the white measuring-door
my Grandfather had penciled with my Uncle's heights.
In 1911, he had stopped growing at just six feet.
While I sat on the tiles,
and dug at the anchor on my sailor blouse,
Uncle Devereux stood behind me.
He was as brushed as Bayard, our riding horse.
His face was putty.   140
His blue coat and white trousers
grew sharper and straighter.
His coat was a blue jay's tail,
his trousers were solid cream from the top of the bottle.
He was animated, hierarchical,
like a ginger snap man in a clothes-press.
He was dying of the incurable Hodgkin's disease. . . .
My hands were warm, then cool, on the piles
of earth and lime,
a black pile and a white pile. . . .   150
Come winter,
Uncle Devereux would blend to the one color.

                                                                1959

WAKING IN THE BLUE

The night attendant, a B.U.[1] sophomore,
rouses from the mare's-nest of his drowsy head
propped on *The Meaning of Meaning*.[2]
He catwalks down our corridor.
Azure day
makes my agonized blue window bleaker.
Crows maunder[3] on the petrified fairway.
Absence! My heart grows tense
as though a harpoon were sparring for the kill.
(This is the house for the "mentally ill.")   10

---

[21] Julia Agrippina II (A.D. 15?–59), mother of the Roman emperor Nero; she was murdered on his orders. After a fire that destroyed much of Rome in A.D. 64, Nero erected his "Golden House" between two of Rome's seven hills, decorating it with gold and precious stones and then taxing the provinces to pay for it.
[1] Boston University.
[2] An influential 1923 book of philosophy and literary criticism by the English critic I. A. Richards (1893–1979) and the English psychologist and educator C. K. Ogden (1889–1957).
[3] Walk aimlessly.

What use is my sense of humor?
I grin at Stanley, now sunk in his sixties,
once a Harvard all-American fullback
(if such were possible!),
still hoarding the build of a boy in his twenties,
as he soaks, a ramrod
with the muscle of a seal
in his long tub,
vaguely urinous from the Victorian plumbing.
A kingly granite profile in a crimson golf cap,   20
worn all day, all night,
he thinks only of his figure,
of slimming on sherbet and ginger ale—
more cut off from words than a seal.

This is the way day breaks in Bowditch Hall at McLean's;[4]
the hooded night lights bring out "Bobbie,"
Porcellian '29,[5]
a replica of Louis XVI[6]
without the wig—
redolent and roly-poly as a sperm whale,   30
as he swashbuckles about in his birthday suit
and horses at chairs.

These victorious figures of bravado ossified young.

In between the limits of day,
hours and hours go by under the crew haircuts
and slightly too little nonsensical bachelor twinkle
of the Roman Catholic attendants.
(There are no Mayflower
screwballs in the Catholic Church.)

After a hearty New England breakfast,   40
I weigh two hundred pounds
this morning. Cock of the walk,
I strut in my turtle-necked French sailor's jersey
before the metal saving mirrors,
and see the shaky future grow familiar
in the pinched, indigenous faces
of these thoroughbred mental cases,
twice my age and half my weight.
We are all old-timers,
each of us holds a locked razor.   50

1958, 1959

---

[4] McLean Hospital, a psychiatric institution in Belmont, Massachusetts. Lowell wrote numerous works while he was institutionalized.
[5] Someone elected to Porcellian, an exclusive Harvard social club, in 1929.
[6] Louis XVI (1754–1793) was king of France from 1774 to 1792.

MEMORIES OF WEST STREET AND LEPKE*

Only teaching on Tuesdays, book-worming
in pajamas fresh from the washer each morning,
I hog a whole house on Boston's
"hardly passionate Marlborough Street,"[1]
where even the man
scavenging filth in the back alley trash cans,
has two children, a beach wagon, a helpmate,
and is a "young Republican."
I have a nine months' daugher,[2]
young enough to be my granddaughter.   10
Like the sun she rises in her flame-flamingo infants' wear.

These are the tranquillized *Fifties,*
and I am forty. Ought I to regret my seedtime?
I was a fire-breathing Catholic C.O.,[3]
and made my manic statement,
telling off the state and president, and then
sat waiting sentence in the bull pen
beside a Negro boy with curlicues
of marijuana in his hair.

Given a year,   20
I walked on the roof of the West Street Jail, a short
enclosure like my school soccer court,
and saw the Hudson River once a day
through sooty clothesline entanglements
and bleaching khaki tenements.
Strolling, I yammered metaphysics with Abramowitz,
a jaundice-yellow ("it's really tan")
and fly-weight pacifist,
so vegetarian,
he wore rope shoes and preferred fallen fruit.   30
He tried to convert Bioff and Brown,[4]
the Hollywood pimps, to his diet.
Hairy, muscular, suburban,

---

* The West Street jail in Manhattan, where Lowell spent ten days (before being transferred to the Federal Correctional Center at Danbury, Connecticut) in 1943 after he was sentenced to one year and one day for refusing to serve in the army; Louis "Lepke" Buchalter (1897–1944), a racketeer who headed Murder Incorporated, an association of criminals who hired out as assassins, was a fellow prisoner. According to Ian Hamilton's biography *Robert Lowell* (1982), " . . . Lepke says to [Lowell]: 'I'm in for killing. What are you in for?' 'Oh, I'm in for refusing to kill.' " The poem was first published in the winter issue of the *Partisan Review* in 1958;

[1] A description by the novelist Henry James (1828–1911) of the street on which Lowell lived from 1955 to 1958.

[2] A nine-month-old daughter, Harriet (from Lowell's second wife, the critic Elizabeth Hardwick).

[3] Conscientious Objector.

[4] William Bioff and George Brown, theatrical-union officials convicted in 1943 of extortion in Hollywood. In 1922 Brown had been convicted of pandering.

wearing chocolate double-breasted suits,
they blew their tops and beat him black and blue.

I was so out of things, I'd never heard
of the Jehovah's Witnesses.[5]
"Are you a C.O.?" I asked a fellow jailbird.
"No," he answered, "I'm a J.W."
He taught me the "hospital tuck,"[6]   40
and pointed out the T-shirted back
of *Murder Incorporated's* Czar Lepke,
there piling towels on a rack,
or dawdling off to his little segregated cell full
of things forbidden the common man:
a portable radio, a dresser, two toy American
flags tied together with a ribbon of Easter palm.
Flabby, bald, lobotomized,
he drifted in a sheepish calm,
where no agonizing reappraisal
jarred his concentration on the electric chair[7]—   50
hanging like an oasis in his air
of lost connections. . . .

                                                    1958

MAN AND WIFE*

Tamed by *Miltown,*[1] we lie on Mother's bed;
the rising sun in war paint dyes us red;
in broad daylight her gilded bed-posts shine,
abandoned, almost Dionysian.[2]
At last the trees are green on Marlborough Street,[3]
blossoms on our magnolia ignite
the morning with their murderous five days' white.
All night I've held your hand,
as if you had
a fourth time faced the kingdom of the mad—[4]   10
its hackneyed speech, its homicidal eye—

---

[5] A Christian religious sect whose members refuse to support a sovereign other than God (Jehovah) and to participate in war.

[6] Tucking the ends of bedsheets under a mattress; "hospital corners."

[7] Lepke was executed in March 1944.

* Lowell and the critic Elizabeth Hardwick (1916–), his second wife, whom he married in 1949. The poem was first published in the *Partisan Review* in winter 1958.

[1] A tranquilizer popular during the 1950s.

[2] According to Greek myth, Dionysus was the god of fertility and wine; here, having the orgiastic nature of the Dionysia (an ancient Greek festival honoring Dionysus): wild, frenzied, and sensual.

[3] The Boston street on which the Lowells lived from 1955 to 1958.

[4] Throughout his adult life Lowell suffered periodic mental breakdowns.

and dragged me home alive. . . . Oh my *Petite,*
clearest of all God's creatures, still all air and nerve:
you were in your twenties, and I,
once hand on glass
and heart in mouth,
outdrank the Rahvs[5] in the heat
of Greenwich Village, fainting at your feet—
too boiled and shy
and poker-faced to make a pass,   20
while the shrill verve
of your invective scorched the traditional South.[6]

Now twelve years later, you turn your back.
Sleepless, you hold
your pillow to your hollows like a child;
your old-fashioned tirade—
loving, rapid, merciless—
breaks like the Atlantic Ocean on my head.

1957, 1958

SKUNK HOUR*

[For Elizabeth Bishop]

Nautilus Island's[1] hermit
heiress still lives through winter in her Spartan cottage;
her sheep still graze above the sea.
Her son's a bishop. Her farmer
is first selectman[2] in our village;
she's in her dotage.

Thirsting for
the hierarchic privacy
of Queen Victoria's century,[3]
she buys up all   10
the eyesores facing her shore,
and lets them fall.

---

[5] Philip Rahv (1908–1973), the co-editor of the *Partisan Review* from 1934 to 1969.
[6] Hardwick was born and raised in Lexington, Kentucky.
* First published in the winter issue of the *Partisan Review* in 1958; modeled after "The Armadillo" (not published until 1965), by his friend and fellow poet Elizabeth Bishop (1911–1979). In summer 1957 he showed his new poems to Bishop, who was visiting Boston from her home in Brazil; she liked "the skunk one enormously."
[1] Near Castine, Maine, where the Lowells had a summer house.
[2] An offical elected in a New England town to manage municipal affairs.
[3] The nineteenth century; Alexandrina Victoria (1819–1901) was queen of Great Britain and Ireland from 1837 to 1901.

The season's ill—
we've lost our summer millionaire,
who seemed to leap from an L. L. Bean[4]
catalogue. His nine-knot yawl[5]
was auctioned off to lobstermen.
A red fox stain covers Blue Hill.[6]

And now our fairy
decorator brightens his shop for fall;   20
his fishnet's filled with orange cork,
orange, his cobbler's bench and awl;
there is no money in his work,
he'd rather marry.

One dark night,
my Tudor Ford[7] climbed the hill's skull;
I watched for love-cars. Lights turned down,
they lay together, hull to hull,
where the graveyard shelves on the town. . . .
My mind's not right.   30

A car radio bleats,
"Love, O careless Love. . . . "[8] I hear
my ill-spirit sob in each blood cell,
as if my hand were at its throat. . . .
I myself am hell;[9]
nobody's here—

only skunks, that search
in the moonlight for a bite to eat.
They march on their soles up Main Street:
white stripes, moonstruck eyes' red fire   40
under the chalk-dry and spar spire
of the Trinitarian Church.

I stand on top
of our back steps and breathe the rich air—
a mother skunk with her column of kittens swills the garbage pail.
She jabs her wedge-head in a cup
of sour cream, drops her ostrich tail,
and will not scare.

1957, 1958

---

[4] A mail-order company based in Freeport, Maine, specializing in sporting and camping goods.
[5] A small sailboat.   [6] A town near Bangor, Maine.
[7] A two-door Ford.   [8] From the American folk song "Careless Love."
[9] "Which way I fly is Hell, myself am Hell" (IV.75), Satan's words from *Paradise Lost* (1667), by John Milton (1608–1674).

THE MOUTH OF THE HUDSON*

[For Esther Brooks]

A single man stands like a bird-watcher,
and scuffles the pepper and salt snow
from a discarded, gray
Westinghouse Electric cable drum.
He cannot discover America by counting
the chains of condemned freight-trains
from thirty states. They jolt and jar
and junk in the siding below him.
He has trouble with his balance.
His eyes drop,   10
and he drifts with the wild ice
ticking seaward down the Hudson,
like the blank sides of a jig-saw puzzle.

The ice ticks seaward like a clock.
A Negro toasts
wheat-seeds over the coke-fumes[1]
of a punctured barrel.
Chemical air
sweeps in from New Jersey,
and smells of coffee.   20

Across the river,
ledges of suburban factories tan
in the sulphur-yellow sun
of the unforgivable landscape.

1964

EYE AND TOOTH

My whole eye was sunset red,
the old cut cornea throbbed,
I saw things darkly,
as through an unwashed goldfish globe.

I lay all day on my bed.
I chain-smoked through the night,
learning to flinch
at the flash of the matchlight.

---

* The mouth of the Hudson River, at Lower New York Bay.
[1] From burned coal or distilled petroleum.

Outside, the summer rain,
a simmer of rot and renewal,   10
fell in pinpricks.
Even new life is fuel.

My eyes throb.
Nothing can dislodge
the house with my first tooth
noosed in a knot to the doorknob.

Nothing can dislodge
the triangular blotch
of rot on the red roof,
a cedar hedge, or the shade of a hedge.   20

No ease from the eye
of the sharp-skinned hawk in the birdbook there,
with reddish-brown buffalo hair
on its shanks, one ascetic talon

clasping the abstract imperial sky.
It says:
an eye for an eye,
a tooth for a tooth.[1]

No ease for the boy at the keyhole,
his telescope,   30
when the women's white bodies flashed
in the bathroom. Young, my eyes began to fail.

Nothing! No oil
for the eye, nothing to pour
on those waters or flames.
I am tired. Everyone's tired of my turmoil.

1964

THE NEO-CLASSICAL URN

I rub my head and find a turtle shell
stuck on a pole,
each hair electrical
with charges, and the juice alive
with ferment. Bubbles drive
the motor, always purposeful . . .
Poor head!
How its skinny shell once hummed,
as I sprinted down the colonnade

---

[1] "Eye for eye, tooth for tooth, hand for hand, foot for foot," from Exodus 21:24.

of bleaching pines, cylindrical   10
clipped trunks without a twig between them. Rest!
I cound not rest. At full run on the curve,
I left the cast stone statue of a nymph,
her soaring armpits and her one bare breast,
gray from the rain and graying in the shade,
as on, on, in sun, the pathway now a dyke,
I swerved between two water bogs,
two seines[1] of moss, and stooped to snatch
the painted turtles on dead logs.
In that season of joy,   20
my turtle catch
was thirty-three,
dropped splashing in our garden urn,
like money in the bank,
the plop and splash
of turtle on turtle,
fed raw gobs of hash . . .

Oh neo-classical white urn, Oh nymph,
Oh lute! The boy was pitiless who strummed
their elegy,   30
for as the month wore on,
the turtles rose,
and popped up dead on the stale scummed
surface—limp wrinkled heads and legs withdrawn
in pain. What pain? A turtle's nothing. No
grace, no cerebration, less free will
than the mosquito I must kill—
nothings! Turtles! I rub my skull,
that turtle shell,
and breathe their dying smell,   40
still watch their crippled last survivors pass,
and hobble humpbacked through the grizzled grass.

                                                              1964

FOR THE UNION DEAD*

"Relinquunt omnia servare rem publicam."[1]

The old South Boston Aquarium stands
in a Sahara of snow now. Its broken windows are boarded.

---

[1] Large fishing nets with floats along the top and weights along the bottom.

* First published as "Colonel Shaw and the Massachusetts 54th" in the 1960 edition of *Life Studies* and with this title as the title poem of Lowell's 1964 collection. Colonel Robert Shaw (1837–1863) led the first African-American regiment (of enlistees) in the Civil War.

[1] "They give up everything to serve the republic" (Latin); after the inscription on the monument to Shaw, sculpted by Augustus Saint-Gaudens (1848–1907), which stands at the edge of Boston Common, a public park across from the Boston State House.

The bronze weathervane cod has lost half its scales.
The airy tanks are dry.

Once my nose crawled like a snail on the glass;
my hand tingled
to burst the bubbles
drifting from the noses of the cowed, compliant fish.

My hand draws back. I often sigh still
for the dark downward and vegetating kingdom   10
of the fish and reptile. One morning last March,
I pressed against the new barbed and galvanized

fence on the Boston Common. Behind their cage,
yellow dinosaur steamshovels were grunting
as they cropped up tons of mush and grass
to gouge their underworld garage.

Parking spaces luxuriate like civic
sandpiles in the heart of Boston.
A girdle of orange, Puritan-pumpkin colored girders
braces the tingling Statehouse,   20

shaking over the excavations, as it faces Colonel Shaw
and his bell-cheeked Negro infantry
on St. Gaudens' shaking Civil War relief,
propped by a plank splint against the garage's earthquake.

Two months after marching through Boston,
half the regiment was dead;
at the dedication,
William James[2] could almost hear the bronze Negroes breathe.

Their monument sticks like a fishbone
in the city's throat.   30
Its Colonel is as lean
as a compass-needle.

He has an angry wrenlike vigilance,
a greyhound's gentle tautness;
he seems to wince at pleasure,
and suffocate for privacy.

He is out of bounds now. He rejoices in man's lovely,
peculiar power to choose life and die—

[2] William James (1842–1910), a philosopher and psychologist (and brother of Henry James), who in his "Oration at the Dedication of the Monument" in May 1897 said, "There on foot go the dark outcasts, so true to nature that one can almost hear them breathing as they march."

when he leads his black soldiers to death,
he cannot bend his back.   40

On a thousand small town New England greens,
the old white churches hold their air
of sparse, sincere rebellion; frayed flags
quilt the graveyards of the Grand Army of the Republic.[3]

The stone statues of the abstract Union Soldier
grow slimmer and younger each year—
wasp-waisted, they doze over muskets
and muse through their sideburns . . .

Shaw's father wanted no monument
except the ditch,   50
where his son's body was thrown
and lost with his "niggers."[4]

The ditch is nearer.
There are no statues for the last war[5] here;
on Boylston Street,[6] a commercial photograph
shows Hiroshima boiling

over a Mosler Safe,[7] the "Rock of Ages"
that survived the blast. Space is nearer.
When I crouch to my television set,
the drained faces of Negro school-children rise like balloons.[8]   60

Colonel Shaw
is riding on his bubble,
he waits
for the blessèd break.

The Aquarium is gone. Everywhere,
giant finned cars nose forward like fish;
a savage servility
slides by on grease.

                                                                        1960

---

[3] An organization for Union and Confederate Civil War veterans.

[4] The name a Confederate officer used for Shaw's troops: on July 18, 1863, Shaw and most of his men were killed during an attack against Fort Wagner in South Carolina; the Confederates buried them in a common grave.

[5] World War II (1939–1945).   [6] A street in central Boston.

[7] A brand of safe that was photographed as intact in Hiroshima after the nuclear bomb was dropped there in 1945; "Rock of Ages" is a hymn written in 1775 by Augustus Montague Toplady (1740–1778).

[8] Probably in relation to civil rights demonstrations of the 1960s to enforce the desegregation of schools afforded by the *Brown* v. *Board of Education of Topeka* decision of 1954.

from   FOUR POEMS FOR ELIZABETH BISHOP*

1: WATER 1948

Stonington:[1] each morning boatloads of hands[2]
cruised off for the granite quarry on an island;
they left dozens of bleak white frame houses stuck
like oyster shells on the hill of rock. Remember?
We sat on the slab of rock. From this distance in time,
it seems the color of iris, rotting and turning purpler,
but it was only the usual gray rock
turning fresh green when drenched by the sea.
The sea flaked the rock at our feet, kept lapping the matchstick
mazes of weirs[3] where the fish for bait were trapped.   10
You dreamed you were a mermaid clinging to a wharfpile,
trying to pull off the barnacles with your hands.
We wished our two souls might return like gulls to the rock.
In the end, the water was too cold for us.

                                                          1973

READING MYSELF

Like thousands, I took just pride and more than just,
struck matches that brought my blood to a boil;
I memorized the tricks to set the river on fire—
somehow never wrote something to go back to.
Can I suppose I am finished with wax flowers
and have earned my grass on the minor slopes of Parnassus[1]. . . .
No honeycomb is built without a bee
adding circle to circle, cell to cell,
the wax and honey of a mausoleum—
this round dome proves its maker is alive;   10
the corpse of the insect lives embalmed in honey,
prays that its perishable work live long
enough for the sweet-tooth bear to desecrate—
this open book . . . my open coffin.

---

* Lowell was influenced by the poetry of Bishop (1911–1979), his contemporary.
[1] A seaport in southern Maine.   [2] Laborers, sailors.
[3] Fences of brushwood or stakes for catching fish.
[1] A mountain in Greece; according to Greek myth, the seat of music and poetry.

DOLPHIN*

My Dolphin,[1] you only guide me by surprise,
captive as Racine,[2] the man of craft,
drawn through his maze of iron composition
by the incomparable wandering voice of Phèdre.
When I was troubled in mind, you made for my body
caught in its hangman's-knot of sinking lines,
the glassy bowing and scraping of my will. . . .
I have sat and listened to too many
words of the collaborating muse,
and plotted perhaps too freely with my life,   10
not avoiding injury to others,
not avoiding injury to myself—
to ask compassion . . . this book, half fiction,
an eelnet made by man for the eel fighting—

my eyes have seen what my hand did.

1973

EPILOGUE†

Those blessèd structures, plot and rhyme—
why are they no help to me now
I want to make
something imagined, not recalled?
I hear the noise of my own voice:
The painter's vision is not a lens,
it trembles to caress the light.
But sometimes everything I write
with the threadbare art of my eye
seems a snapshot,   10
lurid, rapid, garish, grouped,
heightened from life,
yet paralyzed by fact.
All's misalliance.
Yet why not say what happened?
Pray for the grace of accuracy
Vermeer[1] gave to the sun's illumination

---

* The title poem of Lowell's 1973 collection.
[1] Lowell's third wife, the Irish writer Lady Caroline Blackwood.
[2] The French playwright and poet Jean Baptiste Racine (1639–1699), whose tragedy *Phèdre* (1677) Lowell had translated in 1961.
† Published in *Day by Day* (1977) shortly before Lowell's death.
[1] Jan Vermeer (1632–1675), a Dutch painter (mostly of interiors), celebrated for his reproduction of the tones of daylight.

stealing like the tide across a map
to his girl solid with yearning.
We are poor passing facts,   20
warned by that to give
each figure in the photograph
his living name.

1977

Gwendolyn Brooks
(1917–   )

Gwendolyn Brooks was the first female African-American poet to be recognized in America by the critics and public alike. Although too young to have been part of the Harlem Renaissance, which was waning at the beginning of the Great Depression, Brooks corresponded with and met poets who had made their reputations in Harlem—notably Langston Hughes and James Weldon Johnson, both of whom encouraged her. Each recognized her talent and similar focus on writing about black people in a spirit of dignity and honesty, as well as her technical expertise in doing so.

Brooks was born in Topeka, Kansas, in 1917 and raised in Chicago, her home for most of her life. As a child she wrote poetry; at age thirteen her first poem was published in a children's magazine. At sixteen she met Langston Hughes, whose serious attention to her work made a great impression on her. The two later became friends. Brooks graduated from Wilson Junior College in Chicago in 1936 and worked briefly as a maid and then as secretary to a spiritual advisor (she hated both jobs). Years later she drew upon this experience for the title poem of *In the Mecca* (1968). In 1938 she joined the National Association for the Advancement of Colored People Youth Council, where she met Henry Blakely, whom she married in 1939. The two moved into a crowded apartment, later depicted in her poetry, which was being published regularly in the Chicago *Defender*. The early 1940s were highly creative years for her: she took a writing workshop and wrote most of the poems in *A Street in Bronzeville* (1945), named for an African-American neighborhood in Chicago. She submitted her poems to *Harper's* where the author Richard Wright read them and recommended publication with additional poems. The volume came out to excellent reviews, many praising the poignant portraits of African-American life, rendered in formal eloquence and everyday speech.

Prizes and fellowships (including two Guggenheim Fellowships) followed, allowing Brooks to travel and write. To the surprise of many and the discomfort of a few, in 1950 she became the first black Pulitzer Prize recipient. Her prize-winning book, *Annie Allen* (1949), is a collection of poems about a young black girl coming of age while trying to reconcile her conflicting romantic dreams and dismal realities. A turning point in Brooks's life came in 1967 after she attended the Second Black Writers' Conference at Fisk University in Nashville. As she recounted in an interview (in *Black Women Writers at Work* [1983], edited by Claudia Tate), "The poets among them felt that black poets should write as blacks, about blacks, address themselves *to* blacks. I had never thought deliberately in such terms." Her work since then shows a deepened political consciousness as she confronts racial and social oppression with less irony and more urgency.

After meeting members of a Chicago street gang called the Blackstone Rangers, she began her lifelong involvement in teaching, funding, and promoting young African-American writers. In 1968 she was named Poet Laureate of Illinois, after Carl Sandburg, and in the early 1970s she traveled through East and West Africa, returning more strongly committed than ever to her work for her people. She told Tate that her poetry is meant to "be presented in a tavern atmosphere—on a street corner." Through the years her rhythms and forms have become looser, but she continues experimenting with ballad and sonnet stanzas, mixing free and blank verse, and playing with words in a serious and impatient way.

Suggested Readings: *A Street in Bronzeville,* 1945. *Annie Allen,* 1949. *Maud Martha,* 1953. *The Bean Eaters,* 1960. *In the Mecca,* 1963. *Riot,* 1969. *The World of Gwendolyn Brooks,* 1971. *Report From Part One,* 1972. J. N. Loff, "Gwendolyn Brooks: A Bibliography," in *College Language Association Journal,* 17 (September): 21–32, 1973. H. B. Shaw, *Gwendolyn Brooks,* 1980. C. Tate, ed. *Black Women Writers at Work,* 1983. D. H. Melhem, *Gwendolyn Brooks: Poetry and the Heroic Voice,* 1987. M. K. Mootry and G. Smith, eds, *A Life Distilled: Gwendolyn Brooks, Her Poetry and Fiction,* 1987.

Text Used: *Selected Poems,* 1963.

from *A STREET IN BRONZEVILLE**

SOUTHEAST CORNER

> The School of Beauty's a tavern now.
> The Madam is underground.
> Out at Lincoln,[1] among the graves
> Her own is early found.
> Where the thickest, tallest monument
> Cuts grandly into the air
> The Madam lies, contentedly.
> Her fortune, too, lies there,
> Converted into cool hard steel
> And right red velvet lining;   10
> While over her tan impassivity
> Shot silk is shining.

> *1945*

* An African-American ghetto in Chicago.   [1] An African-American cemetery in Chicago.

THE MOTHER

Abortions will not let you forget.
You remember the children you got that you did not get,
The damp small pulps with a little or with no hair,
The singers and workers that never handled the air.
You will never neglect or beat
Them, or silence or buy with a sweet.
You will never wind up the sucking-thumb
Or scuttle off ghosts that come.
You will never leave them, controlling your luscious sigh,
Return for a snack of them, with gobbling mother-eye.   10

I have heard in the voices of the wind the voices of my dim killed children.
I have contracted. I have eased
My dim dears at the breasts they could never suck.
I have said, Sweets, if I sinned, if I seized
Your luck
And your lives from your unfinished reach,
If I stole your births and your names,
Your straight baby tears and your games,
Your stilted or lovely loves, your tumults, your marriages, aches, and your
    deaths,
If I poisoned the beginnings of your breaths,   20
Believe than even in my deliberateness I was not deliberate.
Though why should I whine,
Whine that the crime was other than mine?—
Since anyhow you are dead.
Or rather, or instead,
You were never made.
But that too, I am afraid,
Is faulty: oh, what shall I say, how is the truth to be said?
You were born, you had body, you died.
It is just that you never giggled or planned or cried.   30

Believe me, I loved you all.
Believe me, I knew you, though faintly, and I loved, I loved you
All.

                                                                1945

A SONG IN THE FRONT YARD

I've stayed in the front yard all my life.
I want a peek at the back
Where it's rough and untended and hungry weed grows.
A girl gets sick of a rose.

I want to go in the back yard now
And maybe down the alley,
To where the charity children play.
I want a good time today.

They do some wonderful things.
They have some wonderful fun.   10
My mother sneers, but I say it's fine
How they don't have to go in at quarter to nine.
My mother, she tells me that Johnnie Mae
Will grow up to be a bad woman.
That George'll be taken to Jail soon or late
(On account of last winter he sold our back gate).

But I say it's fine. Honest, I do.
And I'd like to be a bad woman, too,
And wear the brave stockings of night-black lace
And strut down the streets with paint on my face.   20

1945

SADIE AND MAUD

Maud went to college.
Sadie stayed at home.
Sadie scraped life
With a fine-tooth comb.

She didn't leave a tangle in.
Her comb found every strand.
Sadie was one of the livingest chits[1]
In all the land.

Sadie bore two babies
Under her maiden name.   10
Maud and Ma and Papa
Nearly died of shame.

When Sadie said her last so-long
Her girls struck out from home.
(Sadie had left as heritage
Her fine-tooth comb.)

---

[1] Young girls.

Maud, who went to college,
Is a thin brown mouse.
She is living all alone
In this old house.

20

1945

OF DE WITT WILLIAMS ON HIS WAY TO LINCOLN CEMETERY*

He was born in Alabama.
He was bred in Illinois.
He was nothing but a
Plain black boy.

Swing low swing low sweet sweet chariot.[1]
Nothing but a plain black boy.

Drive him past the Pool Hall.
Drive him past the Show.
Blind within his casket,
But maybe he will know.

10

Down through Forty-seventh Street:[2]
Underneath the L,[3]
And Northwest Corner, Prairie,
That he loved so well.

Don't forget the Dance Halls—
Warwick and Savoy,
Where he picked his women, where
He drank his liquid joy.

Born in Alabama.
Bred in Illinois.
He was nothing but a
Plain black boy.

20

Swing low swing low sweet sweet chariot.
Nothing but a plain black boy.

1945

* An African-American cemetery in Chicago.
[1] From the African-American spiritual *Swing Low, Sweet Chariot.*
[2] The main street of Bronzeville, Chicago's African-American ghetto.
[3] The elevated railway.

THE BEAN EATERS

They eat beans mostly, this old yellow pair.
Dinner is a casual affair.
Plain chipware on a plain and creaking wood,
Tin flatware.

Two who are Mostly Good.
Two who have lived their day,
But keep on putting on their clothes
And putting things away.

And remembering . . .
Remembering, with twinklings and twinges,   10
As they lean over the beans in their rented back room that is full of beads and
  receipts and dolls and cloths, tobacco crumbs, vases and fringes.

1960

WE REAL COOL

*The Pool Players.
Seven at the Golden Shovel.*[1]

We real cool. We
Left school. We

Lurk late. We
Strike straight. We

Sing sin. We
Thin gin. We

Jazz June. We
Die soon.

1960

THE LOVERS OF THE POOR

            arrive. The Ladies from the Ladies' Betterment League
  Arrive in the afternoon, the late light slanting
  In diluted gold bars across the boulevard brag

[1] A Chicago pool hall.

Of proud, seamed faces with mercy and murder hinting
Here, there, interrupting, all deep and debonair,
The pink paint on the innocence of fear;
Walk in a gingerly manner up the hall.
Cutting with knives served by their softest care,
Served by their love, so barbarously fair.
Whose mothers taught: You'd better not be cruel!   10
You had better not throw stones upon the wrens!
Herein they kiss and coddle and assault
Anew and dearly in the innocence
With which they baffle nature. Who are full,
Sleek, tender-clad, fit, fiftyish, a-glow, all
Sweetly abortive, hinting at fat fruit,
Judge it high time that fiftyish fingers felt
Beneath the lovelier planes of enterprise.
To resurrect. To moisten with milky chill.
To be a random hitching-post or plush.   20
To be, for wet eyes, random and handy hem.
          Their guild is giving money to the poor.
The worthy poor. The very very worthy
And beautiful poor. Perhaps just not too swarthy?
Perhaps just not too dirty nor too dim
Nor—passionate. In truth, what they could wish
Is—something less than derelict or dull.
Not staunch enough to stab, though, gaze for gaze!
God shield them sharply from the beggar-bold!
The noxious needy ones whose battle's bald   30
Nonetheless for being voiceless, hits one down.
          But it's all so bad! and entirely too much for them.
The stench; the urine, cabbage, and dead beans,
Dead porridges of assorted dusty grains,
The old smoke, *heavy* diapers, and, they're told,
Something called chitterlings.[1] The darkness. Drawn
Darkness, or dirty light. The soil that stirs.
The soil that looks the soil of centuries.
And for that matter the *general* oldness. Old
Wood. Old marble. Old tile. Old old old.   40
Not homekind Oldness! Not Lake Forest, Glencoe.[2]
Nothing is sturdy, nothing is majestic,
There is no quiet drama, no rubbed glaze, no
Unkillable infirmity of such
A tasteful turn as lately they have left,
Glencoe, Lake Forest, and to which their cars
Must presently restore them. When they're done
With dullards and distortions of this fistic[3]
Patience of the poor and put-upon.

[1] The small intestines of pigs, generally eaten fried.   [2] Suburbs of Chicago.
[3] Pugilistic, fought with fists.

They've never seen such a make-do-ness as 50
Newspaper rugs before! In this, this "flat,"
Their hostess is gathering up the oozed, the rich
Rugs of the morning (tattered! the bespattered. . . .)
Readies to spread clean rugs for afternoon.
Here is a scene for you. The Ladies look,
In horror, behind a substantial citizeness
Whose trains clank out across her swollen heart.
Who, arms akimbo, almost fills a door.
All tumbling children, quilts dragged to the floor
And tortured thereover, potato peelings, soft- 60
Eyed kitten, hunched-up, haggard, to-be-hurt.
    Their League is allotting largesse to the Lost.
But to put their clean, their pretty money, to put
Their money collected from delicate rose-fingers
Tipped with their hundred flawless rose-nails seems . . .
    They own Spode, Lowestoft,[4] candelabra,
Mantels, and hostess gowns, and sunburst clocks,
Turtle soup, Chippendale,[5] red satin "hangings,"
Aubussons and Hattie Carnegie.[6] They Winter
In Palm Beach; cross the Water[7] in June; attend, 70
When suitable, the nice Art Institute;
Buy the right books in the best bindings; saunter
On Michigan,[8] Easter mornings, in sun or wind.
Oh Squalor! This sick four-story hulk, this fibre
With fissures everywhere! Why, what are bringings
Of loathe-love largesse? What shall peril hungers
So old old, what shall flatter the desolate?
Tin can, blocked fire escape and chitterling
And swaggering seeking youth and the puzzled wreckage
Of the middle passage, and urine and stale shames 80
And, again, the porridges of the underslung
And children children children. Heavens! That
Was a rat, surely, off there, in the shadows? Long
And long-tailed? Gray? The Ladies from the Ladies'
Betterment League agree it will be better
To achieve the outer air that rights and steadies,
To hie to a house that does not holler, to ring
Bells elsetime, better presently to cater
To no more Possibilities, to get
Away. Perhaps the money can be posted. 90
Perhaps they two may choose another Slum!
Some serious sooty half-unhappy home!—
Where loathe-love likelier may be invested.

---

[4] English china.   [5] Eighteenth-century English furniture.
  [6] Fifteenth-century tapestries and carpets made in the French town of Aubusson; a fashionable American dress designer during the 1950s.
   [7] The Atlantic Ocean, to summer in Europe.
   [8] Michigan Avenue, a Chicago street known for its shops and museums.

Keeping their scented bodies in the center
Of the hall as they walk down the hysterical hall,
They allow their lovely skirts to graze no wall,
Are off at what they manage of a canter,
And, resuming all the clues of what they were,
Try to avoid inhaling the laden air.

1960

Richard Wilbur
(1921–   )

"My first poems were written in answer to the inner and outer disorders of the Second World War and they helped me, as poems should, to take ahold [*sic*] of raw events and convert them, provisionally, into experience." So writes Richard Wilbur in the essay "On My Own Work," included in his collection of critical prose, *Responses* (1976). Since the publication of Wilbur's first book, *The Beautiful Changes and Other Poems* (1947), when he was twenty-six, critics have praised his superb ear, technical perfection, and talent as a formalist. With praise of his skill has come the suspicion that Wilbur is somehow too conventional, too safe, and too optimistic. For Wilbur, the conversion of raw events into experience—to order his world into meter, rhythm, and rhyme through stanzaic forms—is verification, an act of affirmation, albeit an unfashionable one.

Wilbur, who typically sets his poems in natural landscapes or incorporates specific details of nature, was born in New York City in 1921 and grew up on a farm in North Caldwell, New Jersey. Soon after graduating from Amherst College in 1942, Wilbur entered the army and served in the infantry in Italy and France until 1945. He later went to Harvard University and in 1947 received an M.A. in English and had *The Beautiful Changes* published. He had begun teaching at Harvard in 1950 when his second book, *Ceremony and Other Poems,* came out. The book includes some of his translations of French plays, which early established his reputation as a distinguished translator. On a Guggenheim Fellowship he then went to New Mexico; with a grant from the Academy of Arts and Letters he traveled to Rome. There he finished his first of several Molière translations, which earned him a Bollingen Prize in 1963.

Since 1954 Wilbur has taught at Wellesley College, Wesleyan University, and Smith College. In 1956 his third book of verse, *Things of This World* (in which "Love Calls Us to the Things of This World" appears), won a Pulitzer Prize and a National Book Award. The title of this book has particular significance for Wilbur, who is consistently concerned with "things." In a 1977 *Paris Review* interview, "The Art of Poetry," Wilbur remarked that he has "considerable respect for the actual and physical. We are all kickers of stones, you know. . . . " He has continued to present reality through imagery in such collections as *Advice to a Prophet* (1961) and *The Mind-Reader* (1976).

Unlike the confessional poetry of some of Wilbur's contemporaries, such as Robert Lowell, Wilbur has deliberately avoided the explicitly intimate, asserting in "The Art of Poetry" that impersonal poems are "more honest and usable." Through the years his work has become simpler, he claims, and critics have noted that his poetry has become more personal and direct. Wilbur's lyrics are characterized by elegance, wit, and sheer loveliness of melody. In his lyrics he tries to "lay claim to as much of the world as possible through uttering the names of things."

Suggested Readings: *The Beautiful Changes and Other Poems,* 1947. *A Bestiary,* 1955. *Things of This World,* 1956. *Advice to a Prophet,* 1961. *The Poems of Richard Wilbur,* 1963. *The Mind-Reader,* 1976. *Responses, Prose Pieces: 1953–1976,* 1976. D. L. Hill, *Richard Wilbur,* 1968. J. P. Field, *Richard Wilbur: A Bibliographical Checklist,* 1971. W. Salinger, ed., *Richard Wilbur's Creation,* 1983.

Text Used: *New and Collected Poems,* 1988.

BELL SPEECH

The selfsame toothless voice for death or bridal:
It has been long since men would give the time
To tell each someone's-change with a special chime,
And a toll for every year the dead walked through.
And mostly now, above this urgent idle
Town, the bells mark time, as they can do.

This bavardage[1] of early and of late
Is what is wanted, and yet the bells beseech
By some excess that's in their stricken speech
Less meanly to be heard. Were this not so,   10
Why should Great Paul[2] shake every window plate
To warn me that my pocket watch is slow?

Whether or not attended, bells will chant
With a clear dumb sound, and wide of any word
Expound our hours, clear as the waves are heard
Crashing at Mount Desert,[3] from far at sea,
And dumbly joining, as the night's descent
Makes deltas into dark of every tree.

Great Paul, great pail of sound, still dip and draw
Dark speech from the deep and quiet steeple well,   20
Bring dark for doctrine, do but dim and quell
All voice in yours, while earth will give you breath.
Still gather to a language without flaw
Our loves, and all the hours of our death.

1947

---

[1] Gossip, chatter.   [2] A bell, probably at St. Paul's Cathedral in London.
[3] An island off Maine.

THE PARDON

My dog lay dead five days without a grave
In the thick of summer, hid in a clump of pine
And a jungle of grass and honeysuckle-vine.
I who had loved him while he kept alive

Went only close enough to where he was
To sniff the heavy honeysuckle-smell
Twined with another odor heavier still
And hear the flies' intolerable buzz.

Well, I was ten and very much afraid.
In my kind world the dead were out of range   10
And I could not forgive the sad or strange
In beast or man. My father took the spade

And buried him. Last night I saw the grass
Slowly divide (it was the same scene
But now it glowed a fierce and mortal green)
And saw the dog emerging. I confess

I felt afraid again, but still he came
In the carnal sun, clothed in a hymn of flies,
And death was breeding in his lively eyes.
I started in to cry and call his name,   20

Asking forgiveness of his tongueless head.
. . . I dreamt the past was never past redeeming:
But whether this was false or honest dreaming
I beg death's pardon now. And mourn the dead.

1950

LOVE CALLS US TO THE THINGS OF THIS WORLD

The eyes open to a cry of pulleys,
And spirited from sleep, the astounded soul
Hangs for a moment bodiless and simple
As false dawn.
                    Outside the open window
The morning air is all awash with angels.

Some are in bed-sheets, some are in blouses,
Some are in smocks: but truly there they are.
Now they are rising together in calm swells
Of halcyon feeling, filling whatever they wear
With the deep joy of their impersonal breathing;   10

Now they are flying in place, conveying
The terrible speed of their omnipresence, moving
And staying like white water; and now of a sudden
They swoon down into so rapt a quiet
That nobody seems to be there.
                        The soul shrinks

From all that it is about to remember,
From the punctual rape of every blessèd day,
And cries,   20
               "Oh, let there be nothing on earth but laundry,
Nothing but rosy hands in the rising steam
And clear dances done in the sight of heaven."

Yet, as the sun acknowledges
With a warm look the world's hunks and colors,
The soul descends once more in bitter love
To accept the waking body, saying now
In a changed voice as the man yawns and rises,

"Bring them down from their ruddy gallows;
Let there be clean linen for the backs of thieves;   30
Let lovers go fresh and sweet to be undone,
And the heaviest nuns walk in a pure floating
Of dark habits,
                keeping their difficult balance."

                                      1956

FOR DUDLEY*

Even when death has taken
An exceptional man,
It is common things which touch us, gathered
In the house that proved a hostel.

Though on his desk there lie
The half of a sentence
Not to be finished by us, who lack
His gaiety, his Greek,

It is the straight back
Of a good woman   10
Which now we notice. For her guests' hunger
She sets the polished table.

* Dudley Fitts (1903–1968), an educator and translator of classical literature.

And now the quick sun,
Rounding the gable,
Picks out a chair, a vase of flowers,
Which had stood till then in shadow.

It is the light of which
Achilles[1] spoke,
Himself a shadow then, recalling
The splendor of mere being.   20

As if we were perceived
From a black ship—
A small knot of island folk,
The Light-Dwellers, pouring

A life to the dark sea—
All that we do
Is touched with ocean, yet we remain
On the shore of what we know.

We say that we are behaving
As he would have us—   30
He who was brave and loved this world,
Who did not hold with weeping,

Yet in the mind as in
The shut closet
Where his coats hang in black procession,
There is a covert muster.
One is moved to turn to him,
The exceptional man,
Telling him all these things, and waiting
For the deft, lucid answer.   40

At the sound of that voice's deep
Specific silence,
The sun winks and fails in the window.
Light perpetual keep him.

1969

TO THE ETRUSCAN POETS*

Dream fluently, still brothers, who when young
Took with your mother's milk the mother tongue,

---

[1] According to Greek myth, the warrior who led the Greeks in the Trojan War; the hero of the *Iliad*, by Homer (8th? century B.C.).

* First published in the *Ontario Review* in 1975. The Etruscans were the people of Etruria, a region in Italy (now Tuscany and part of Umbria), who flourished in the sixth century B.C.

In which pure matrix, joining world and mind,
You strove to leave some line of verse behind

Like a fresh track across a field of snow,
Not reckoning that all could melt and go.

1975

THE WRITER

In her room at the prow of the house
Where light breaks, and the windows are tossed with linden,
My daughter is writing a story.

I pause in the stairwell, hearing
From her shut door a commotion of typewriter-keys
Like a chain hauled over a gunwale.

Young as she is, the stuff
Of her life is a great cargo, and some of it heavy:
I wish her a lucky passage.

But now it is she who pauses,   10
As if to reject my thought and its easy figure.
A stillness greatens, in which

The whole house seems to be thinking,
And then she is at it again with a bunched clamor
Of strokes, and again is silent.

I remember the dazed starling
Which was trapped in that very room, two years ago;
How we stole in, lifted a sash

And retreated, not to affright it;
And how for a helpless hour, through the crack of the door,   20
We watched the sleek, wild, dark

And iridescent creature
Batter against the brilliance, drop like a glove
To the hard floor, or the desk-top,

And wait then, humped and bloody,
For the wits to try it again; and how our spirits
Rose when, suddenly sure,

lifted off from a chair-back,
Beating a smooth course for the right window
And clearing the sill of the world.   30

It is always a matter, my darling,
Of life or death, as I had forgotten. I wish
What I wished you before, but harder.

1976

LYING*

To claim, at a dead party, to have spotted a grackle,[1]
When in fact you haven't of late, can do no harm.
Your reputation for saying things of interest
Will not be marred, if you hasten to other topics,
Nor will the delicate web of human trust
Be ruptured by that airy fabrication.
Later, however, talking with toxic zest
Of golf, or taxes, or the rest of it
Where the beaked ladle plies the chuckling ice,
You may enjoy a chill of severance, hearing   10
Above your head the shrug of unreal wings.
Not that the world is tiresome in itself:
We know what boredom is: it is a dull
Impatience or a fierce velleity,[2]
A champing wish, stalled by our lassitude,
To make or do. In the strict sense, of course,
We invent nothing, merely bearing witness
To what each morning brings again to light:
Gold crosses, cornices, astonishment
Of panes, the turbine-vent which natural law   20
Spins on the grill-end of the diner's roof,
Then grass and grackles or, at the end of town
In sheen-swept pastureland, the horse's neck
Clothed with its usual thunder, and the stones
Beginning now to tug their shadows in
And track the air with glitter. All these things
Are there before us; there before we look
Or fail to look; there to be seen or not
By us, as by the bee's twelve thousand eyes,
According to our means and purposes.   30
So too with strangeness not to be ignored,
Total eclipse or snow upon the rose,
And so with that most rare conception, nothing.
What is it, after all, but something missed?
It is the water of a dried-up well
Gone to assail the cliffs of Labrador.
There is what galled the arch-negator,[3] sprung

---

* First published in the *New Yorker* in 1987.   [1] A blackbird.
[2] A wish; one that generally does not lead to an action.   [3] The Devil.

From Hell to probe with intellectual sight
The cells and heavens of a given world
Which he could take but as another prison: 40
Small wonder that, pretending not to be,
He drifted through the bar-like boles[4] of Eden
In a *black mist low creeping,* dragging down
And darkening with moody self-absorption
What, when he left it, lifted and, if seen
From the sun's vantage, seethed with vaulting hues.
Closer to making than the deftest fraud
Is seeing how the catbird's tail was made
To counterpoise, on the mock-orange spray,
Its light, up-tilted spine; or, lighter still,   50
How the shucked tunic of an onion, brushed
To one side on a backlit chopping-board
And rocked by trifling currents, prints and prints
Its bright, ribbed shadow like a flapping sail.
Odd that a thing is most itself when likened:
The eye mists over, basil hints of clove,
The river glazes toward the dam and spills
To the drubbed[5] rocks below its crashing cullet,[6]
And in the barnyard near the sawdust-pile
Some great thing is tormented. Either it is   60
A trap torn loose and in the groaning wind
Now puffed, now flattened, or a hip-shot beast
Which tries again, and once again, to rise.
What, though for pain there is no other word,
Finds pleasure in the cruellest simile?
It is something in us like the catbird's song
From neighbor bushes in the grey of morning
That, harsh or sweet, and of its own accord,
Proclaims its many kin. It is a chant
Of the first springs, and it is tributary   70
To the great lies told with the eyes half-shut
That have the truth in view: the tale of Chiron[7]
Who, with sage head, wild heart, and planted hoof
Instructed brute Achilles in the lyre,
Or of the garden where we first mislaid
Simplicity of wish and will, forgetting
Out of what cognate splendor all things came
To take their scattering names; and nonetheless
That matter of a baggage-train surprised
By a few Gascons[8] in the Pyrenees   80
Which, having worked three centuries and more
In the dark caves of France, poured out at last

---

[4] Tree trunks.   [5] Beaten, weathered.   [6] "Little neck" (French).
[7] According to Greek myth, a wise and just centaur (half man, half horse) who reared the warrior Achilles from infancy, teaching him to ride and hunt and instructing him in the art of healing.
[8] Natives of Gascony, a region in southwest France along the Pyrenees Mountains.

The blood of Roland,[9] who to Charles his king
And to the dove that hatched the dove-tailed world
Was faithful unto death, and shamed the Devil.

1987

Denise Levertov
(1923–   )

Denise Levertov was born in Essex, England, in 1923. Her mother was Welsh; her father, a Russian Jew of Hasidic ancestry, had coverted to Christianity and became an Anglican minister. Levertov's parents were prisoners of war in Germany during World War I and assisted in the relocation of Jewish refugees during World War II. Levertov was educated at home amid literary, religious, and political discussions in many languages. She drew upon that education in her poetry: the title poems "The Jacob's Ladder" (1961) and "O Taste and See" (1964), for example, reveal the influence of her (informal) religious training.

The Double Image, Levertov's first book of poetry, was written during World War II and published in London in 1946. Its formal, melancholy style is like that of other neoromantic British poets of the 1940s. In 1947 she married an American soldier, the writer Mitchell Goodman, and the following year the couple moved to New York. Their son Nikolai was born in 1949, the year Levertov's poetry was anthologized in *The New British Poets.* Her second book, *Here and Now,* appeared in 1957, just after Levertov became a U.S. citizen. Its style and focus show that she had transformed herself into an American poet; her work was soon published in an American anthology, *The New American Poets* (1959). Levertov acknowledged the influence of William Carlos Williams in this metamorphosis. His poetics directed her attention to the poetry of idiomatic speech and reenforced her movement away from the nostalgia of her early work and toward immediate everyday experience. Another influence in this direction was a group of avant-garde poets teaching at Black Mountain College near Asheville, North Carolina. She considered two of those poets, Robert Creeley and Robert Duncan, the finest poets of her generation.

In the 1960s and 1970s Levertov became active in the protests against the Vietnam War, and her poetry reflected these political concerns. Her war poetry, collected in *To Stay Alive* (1971), records the poet's pilgrimage through years of urban unrest, student protest, and war resistance. A number of the earlier poems in the volume were written after the death of Levertov's sister Olga, an activist who encouraged Levertov's social commitment. *The Freeing of the Dust* (1975) maps another spiritual journey, one that follows Levertov's divorce and a visit to Hanoi. Throughout the 1980s she remained politically outspoken, working and writing against nuclear proliferation and American military involvement in Central America. She has been known to disrupt the complacency of a poetry reading by demanding that the audience act on a pressing social issue.

Levertov has been influential as a teacher and theorist and has translated poetry from

---

[9] A legendary hero of the epic *Chanson de Roland* ("*Song of Roland*" [French]), one of twelve paladins, or knights of the emperor Charlemagne (742–814), or Charles the Great.

several languages. In her own poetry she rejects both traditional forms and free verse and seeks instead an "organic form," which grows from the poet's inner voice and opposes "normal" rules of form or of content. Experiences, she believes, have their own internal form that must be discovered and expressed in the movement of a poem. Although she does not define herself as a feminist, her attention to the occurrences of daily life, expressed in sensuous detail, has produced much writing concerned with women's common experiences. Prose analyses of her own creative process are collected in *Poet in the World* (1973). And she has since published numerous volumes of poetry, including *Oblique Players* (1984) and *Breathing the Water* (1987).

Suggested Readings: *Here and Now*, 1956. *The Sorrow Dance*, 1967. *Footprints*, 1972. *The Poet in the World*, 1974. *Collected Earlier Poems: 1940–1960*, 1979. *Poems 1960–1967*, 1983. *Selected Poems*, 1986. L. W. Wagner, *Denise Levertov*, 1967. L. W. Wagner, ed., *Denise Levertov: In Her Own Province*, 1979. C. Altieri, *Enlarging the Temple: New Directions in Poetry During the 1960's*, 1980. R. Howard, *Alone With America: Essays on the Art of Poetry in the United States Since 1950*, 1980. H. Marten, *Understanding Denise Levertov*, 1988.

Texts Used: "The Ache of Marriage": *New Directions in Prose and Poetry 18*, ed. J. Laughlin, 1964. *O Taste and See*, 1964. "Intrusion": *Poems 1968–1972*, 1987. "Ways of Conquest": *The Freeing of the Dust*, 1975. "Gathered at the River": *Oblique Players*, 1984. All else: *The Jacob's Ladder*, 1961.

THE JACOB'S LADDER*

The stairway is not
a thing of gleaming strands
a radiant evanescence
for angels' feet that only glance in their tread, and need not
touch the stone.

It is of stone.
A rosy stone that takes
a glowing tone of softness
only because behind it the sky is a doubtful, a doubting
night gray.   10

A stairway of sharp
angles, solidly built.
One sees that the angels must spring
down from one step to the next, giving a little
lift of the wings:

and a man climbing
must scrape his knees, and bring
the grip of his hands into play. The cut stone
consoles his groping feet. Wings brush past him.
The poem ascends.   20

1958

---

* In Genesis 28:12 the patriarch Jacob saw in a dream "a ladder set up on the earth, and the top of it reached to heaven: and behold the angels of God ascending and descending on it."

MATINS*

i

The authentic! Shadows of it
sweep past in dreams, one could say imprecisely,
evoking the almost-silent
ripping apart of giant
sheets of cellophane. No.
It thrusts up close. Exactly in dreams
it has you off-guard, you
recognize it before you have time.
For a second before waking
the alarm bell is a red conical hat,[1] it   10
takes form.

ii

The authentic! I said
rising from the toilet seat.
The radiator in rhythmic knockings
spoke of the rising steam.
The authentic, I said
breaking the handle of my hairbrush as I
brushed my hair in
rhythmic strokes: That's it,
that's joy, it's always   20
a recognition, the known
appearing fully itself, and
more itself than one knew.

iii

The new day rises
as heat rises,
knocking in the pipes
with rhythms it seizes for its own
to speak of its invention—
the real, the new-laid
egg whose speckled shell   30
the poet fondles and must break
if he will be nourished.

---

* Early morning prayers of the Roman Catholic Church.
[1] The type of hat worn by a Roman Catholic cardinal.

iv

A shadow painted where
yes, a shadow must fall.
The cow's breath
not forgotten in the mist, in the
words. Yes,
verisimilitude draws up
heat in us, zest
to follow through,   40
follow through,
follow
transformations of day
in its turning, in its becoming.

v

Stir the holy grains, set
the bowls on the table and
call the child to eat.

While we eat we think,
as we think an undercurrent
of dream runs through us   50
faster than thought
towards recognition.

Call the child to eat,
send him off, his mouth
tasting of toothpaste, to go down
into the ground, into a roaring train
and to school.

His cheeks are pink
his black eyes hold his dreams, he has left
forgetting his glasses.   60

Follow down the stairs at a clatter
to give them to him and save
his clear sight.

Cold air
comes in at the street door.

vi

The authentic! It rolls
just out of reach, beyond

running feet and
stretching fingers, down
the green slope and into   70
the black waves of the sea.
Speak to me, little horse, beloved,
tell me
how to follow the iron ball,
how to follow through to the country
beneath the waves
to the place where I must kill you and step out
of your bones and flystrewn meat
tall, smiling, renewed,
formed in your likeness.   80

vii

Marvelous Truth, confront us
at every turn,
in every guise, iron ball,
egg, dark horse, shadow,
cloud
of breath on the air,

dwell
in our crowded hearts
our steaming bathrooms, kitchens full of
things to be done, the   90
ordinary streets.

Thrust close your smile
that we know you, terrible joy.

1961

THE ACHE OF MARRIAGE

The ache of marriage:

thigh and tongue, beloved,
are heavy with it,
it throbs in the teeth

We look for communion
and are turned away, beloved,
each and each

It is leviathan[1] and we
in its belly
looking for joy, some joy   10
not to be known outside it

two by two in the ark of
the ache of it

                                                        1964

O TASTE AND SEE

The world is
not with us enough.[1]
O taste and see[2]

the subway Bible poster said,
meaning **The Lord,** meaning
if anything all that lives
to the imagination's tongue,

grief, mercy, language,
tangerine, weather, to
breathe them, bite,   10
savor, chew, swallow, transform

into our flesh our
deaths, crossing the street, plum, quince,
living in the orchard and being

hungry, and plucking
the fruit.

                                                        1964

INTRUSION

After I had cut off my hands
and grown new ones

something my former hands had longed for
came and asked to be rocked.

---

[1] A biblical sea monster, a whale or a large reptile.
[1] After the sonnet "The World Is Too Much With Us" (1807), by the English poet William Wordsworth (1770–1850).
[2] "O taste and see that the Lord is good," from Psalm 34:8.

After my plucked out eyes
had withered, and new ones grown

something my former eyes had wept for
came asking to be pitied.

1969, 1972

WAYS OF CONQUEST

You invaded my country by accident,
not knowing you had crossed the border.
Vines that grew there touched you.
                                You ran past them,
shaking raindrops off the leaves—you or the wind.
It was toward the hills you ran,
inland—

I invaded your country with all my
'passionate intensity,'
pontoons and parachutes of my blindness.   10
But living now in the suburbs of the capital
incognito,
                my will to take the heart of the city
                has dwindled. I love
its unsuspecting life,
its adolescents who come to tell me their dreams in the dusty park
among the rocks and benches,
I the stranger who will listen.
I love
the wild herons who return each year to the marshy outskirts.   20
What I invaded has
invaded me.

1975

GATHERED AT THE RIVER

For Beatrice Hawley and John Jagel

As if the trees were not indifferent . . .

A breeze flutters the candles but the trees give off
a sense of listening, of hush.

The dust of August on their leaves.
But it grows dark. Their dark green
is something known about, not seen.

But summer twilight takes away
only color, not form. The tree-forms,
massive trunks and the great domed heads,
leaning in towards us, are visible,   10

a half-circle of attention.

They listen because the war
we speak of, the human war with ourselves,

the war against earth,
against nature,
is a war against them.

The words are spoken
of those who survived a while,
living shadowgraphs, eyes fixed forever
on witnessed horror,   20
who survived to give
testimony, that no-one
may plead ignorance.
Contra naturam.[1] The trees,
the trees are not indifferent.

We intone together, *Never again,*

we stand in a circle,
singing, speaking, making vows,

remembering the dead
of Hiroshima,   30
of Nagasaki.

We are holding candles: we kneel to set them
afloat on the dark river
as they do
there in Hiroshima. We are invoking

saints and prophets,
heroes and heroines of justice and peace,
to be with us, to help us
stop the torment of our evil dreams . . .

---

[1] "Against nature" (Latin).

Windthreatened flames bob on the current . . .   40

They don't get far from shore. But none capsizes
even in the swell of a boat's wake.

The waxy paper cups sheltering them
catch fire. But still the candles
sail their gold downstream.

And still the trees ponder our strange doings, as if
well aware that if we fail,
we fail also for them:
if our resolves and prayers are weak and fail

there will be nothing left of their slow and innocent wisdom,   50
no roots,
no bole[2] nor branch,

no memory
of shade,
of leaf,

no pollen.

1981

Maxine Kumin
(1925–   )

"There is no more, no less, peace of mind in the disciplined life of the barnyard than there is in the routine of the office," writes Maxine Kumin in *In Deep: Country Essays* (1987) after many years of raising horses on her New Hampshire farm. Typical of Kumin's temperate manner, this statement reflects the unsentimental relationship to nature and the sober acceptance of human limitations that characterize her poetry. Family relationships, husbandry, and the inner life of women as they negotiate various roles—mother, daughter, sister, lover—are the subjects that have dominated Kumin's verse since the appearance of her first book, *Halfway,* in 1961. Her maturation as a poet coincides with the emergence in American literature of women writing more frankly than ever before about their experiences. Although she has rarely been as explicitly political as such feminist poets as Adrienne Rich, Kumin typically summons to her aid a vision of female solidarity, as in the prayerlike hope expressed in "The Envelope" (1978): "May we carry our mothers forth in our bellies."

---

[2] Tree trunk.

A close friend of the poet Anne Sexton until Sexton's suicide in 1975, Kumin has said that they frequently shared their works in progress and had an enormous influence on each other. Kumin is, however, careful to draw distinctions. Calling herself a skeptic, she points out in a 1985 interview with Diana George that Sexton was "much more of an extremist and an absolutist in her search for a deity." A critic has claimed that Kumin "keeps her demons bridled," refraining, for the most part, from the explicit exposition of psychic trauma that marks the work of Sexton and of Sylvia Plath. Understatement, rather than rage or passion, is Kumin's hallmark. Thus, the burning houses in "The Longing to Be Saved" (1978) indirectly suggest Kumin's ambivalence about the domestic settings so prevalent in her work. Are not we all, she seems to ask, yearning to be rescued from our homes?

Kumin has consistently favored traditional poetic forms, making use of rhyme schemes, the iambic line, and a variety of quatrain-based (four-line) stanzas. "When I'm writing free-verse," she complains, "I feel as though I am in Indiana, where it's absolutely flat and you can see the horizon 360 degrees around. You feel as though you have no eyelids, you can't blink. I lose, I have no sense of, the line." Although she is known primarily for her poetry, Kumin is the author of four novels (including the semi-autobiographical *Through Dooms of Love* [1965]), a collection of short stories, two collections of essays, and more than twenty children's books. She received a Pulitzer Prize for *Up Country* (1972), the poetry collection in which her preoccupation with the New England landscape begins to take center stage. *Our Ground Time Here Will Be Brief*, published in 1982, collects her most important poetry to that point. Her ninth collection of poems is *Nurture* (1989).

Kumin was born Maxine Winokur into a middle-class Jewish family in Philadelphia in 1925. She received an A.B. (1946) and M.A. (1948) from Radcliffe College and married Victor Kumin in 1946. When *Halfway* was published in 1961, she was an instructor at Tufts University in Medford, Massachusetts. Kumin has taught at numerous other schools, including Columbia and Princeton Universities and the University of Massachusetts.

Suggested Readings: *Through Dooms of Love*, 1965. *Up Country: Poems of New England*, 1972. *To Make a Prairie: Essays on Poets, Poetry, and Country Living*, 1979. *Why Can't We Live Together Like Civilized Human Beings*, 1982. *The Long Approach*, 1985. *In Deep: Country Essays*, 1987. *Nurture*, 1989. M. G. Meek, "An Interview With Maxine Kumin," in *Massachusetts Review*, 16:317–327, (Spring) 1975. E. Showalter and C. Smith, "A Nurturing Relationship: A Conversation With Anne Sexton and Maxine Kumin, April 15, 1974," in *Women's Studies*, 4:115–136, 1976. D. H. George, "Kumin on Kumin and Sexton: An Interview," *Poesis*, 6(2): 1–18, 1985.

Text Used: *Our Ground Time Here Will Be Brief*, 1982.

WOODCHUCKS

Gassing the woodchucks didn't turn out right.
The knockout bomb from the Feed and Grain Exchange
was featured as merciful, quick at the bone
and the case we had against them was airtight,
both exits shoehorned shut with puddingstone,[1]
but they had a sub-sub-basement out of range.

---

[1] A rock conglomerate.

Next morning they turned up again, no worse
for the cyanide than we for our cigarettes
and state-store Scotch, all of us up to scratch.
They brought down the marigolds as a matter of course   10
and then took over the vegetable patch
nipping the broccoli shoots, beheading the carrots.

The food from our mouths, I said, righteously thrilling
to the feel of the .22, the bullets' neat noses.
I, a lapsed pacifist fallen from grace
puffed with Darwinian[2] pieties for killing,
now drew a bead on the littlest woodchuck's face.
He died down in the everbearing roses.

Ten minutes later I dropped the mother. She
flipflopped in the air and fell, her needle teeth   20
still hooked in a leaf of early Swiss chard.
Another baby next. O one-two-three
the murderer inside me rose up hard,
the hawkeye killer came on stage forthwith.

There's one chuck left. Old wily fellow, he keeps
me cocked and ready day after day after day.
All night I hunt his humped-up form. I dream
I sight along the barrel in my sleep.
If only they'd all consented to die unseen
gassed underground the quiet Nazi way.   30

1971

THE LONGING TO BE SAVED

When the barn catches fire
I am wearing the wrong negligee.
It hangs on me like a gunny sack.
I get the horses out, but they
wrench free, wheel, dash back
and three or four trips are required.
Much whinnying and rearing as well.
This happens whenever I travel.

At the next stopover, the children take off
their doctor and lawyer disguises
and turn back into little lambs.   10
They cower at windows from which flames
shoot like the tattered red cloth
of dimestore devil suits. They refuse

---

[2] Like the survival of the fittest, a theory proposed by the English naturalist Charles Darwin (1809–1882) in *On the Origin of Species by Means of Natural Selection* (1859).

to jump into my waiting arms, although
I drilled them in this technique, years ago.

Finally they come to their senses and leap
but each time, the hoop holds my mother.
Her skin is as dry and papery
as a late onion. I take her   20
into my bed, an enormous baby
I do not especially want to keep.
Three nights of such disquiet
in and out of dreams as thin as acetate

until, last of all, it's you
trapped in the blazing fortress.
I hold the rope as you slide from danger.
It's tricky in high winds and drifting snow.
Your body swaying in space
grows heavier, older, stranger   30

and me in the same gunny sack
and the slamming sounds as the gutted building burns.
Now the family's out, there's no holding back.
I go in to get my turn.

1978

THE ENVELOPE

It is true, Martin Heidegger,[1] as you have written,
I fear to cease, even knowing that at the hour
of my death my daughters will absorb me, even
knowing they will carry me about forever
inside them, an arrested fetus, even as I carry
the ghost of my mother under my navel, a nervy
little androgynous person, a miracle
folded in lotus position.

Like those old pear-shaped Russian dolls that open
at the middle to reveal another and another, down   10
to the pea-sized, irreducible minim,
may we carry our mothers forth in our bellies.
May we, borne onward by our daughters, ride
in the Envelope of Almost-Infinity,
that chain letter good for the next twenty-five
thousand days of their lives.

1978

---

[1] Heidegger (1889–1976) was a German existential philosopher.

HOW IT IS*

Shall I say how it is in your clothes?
A month after your death I wear your blue jacket.
The dog at the center of my life recognizes
you've come to visit, he's ecstatic.
In the left pocket, a hole.
In the right, a parking ticket
delivered up last August on Bay State Road.
In my heart, a scatter like milkweed,
a flinging from the pods of the soul.
My skin presses your old outline.   10
It is hot and dry inside.

I think of the last day of your life,
old friend, how I would unwind it, paste
it together in a different collage,
back from the death car idling in the garage,
back up the stairs, your praying hands unlaced,
reassembling the bits of bread and tuna fish
into a ceremony of sandwich,
running the home movie backward to a space
we could be easy in, a kitchen place   20
with vodka and ice, our words like living meat.

Dear friend, you have excited crowds
with your example. They swell
like wine bags, straining at your seams.
I will be years gathering up our words,
fishing out letters, snapshots, stains,
leaning my ribs against this durable cloth
to put on the dumb blue blazer of your death.

1978

THE GRACE OF GELDINGS IN RIPE PASTURES

Glutted, half asleep, browsing in
timothy[1] grown so tall I see them
as through a pale-green stage scrim[2]

they circle, nose to rump,
a trio of trained elephants.
It begins to rain, as promised.

---

* One of several elegies Kumin wrote for her friend the poet Anne Sexton (1928–1975), who committed suicide.
[1] A grass with dense cylindrical bristles, widely grown for hay.
[2] A hanging of loosely woven cloth that functions in theatrical productions as a semi-transparent curtain or as an opaque curtain, depending on the lighting.

Bit by bit they soak up drops
like laundry dampened to be ironed.
Runnels bedeck them. Their sides

drip like the ribs of very broad   10
umbrellas. And still they graze
and grazing, one by one let down

their immense, indolent penises
to drench the everlasting grass
with the rich nitrogen

that repeats them.

1978

FAMILY REUNION

The week in August you come home,
adult, professional, aloof,
we roast and carve the fatted calf
—in our case home-grown pig, the chine[1]
garlicked and crisped, the applesauce
hand-pressed. Hand-pressed the greengage wine.[2]

Nothing is cost-effective here.
The peas, the beets, the lettuces
hand sown, are raised to stand apart.
The electric fence ticks like the slow heart   10
of something we fed and bedded for a year,
then killed with kindness's one bullet
and paid Jake Mott to do the butchering.

In winter we lure the birds with suet,
thaw lungs and kidneys for the cat.
Darlings, it's all a circle from the ring
of wire that keeps the raccoons from the corn
to the gouged pine table that we lounge around,
distressed before any of you was born.

Benign and dozy from our gluttonies,   20
the candles down to stubs, defenses down,
love leaking out unguarded the way
juice dribbles from the fence when grounded
by grass stalks or a forgotten hoe,
how eloquent, how beautiful you seem!

---

[1] A cut of meat or fish, including at least part of the backbone and the surrounding flesh.
[2] Plum wine.

Wearing our gestures, how wise you grow,
ballooning to overfill our space,
the almost-parents of your parents now.
So briefly having you back to measure us
is harder than having let you go.   30

1982

MORNING SWIM

Into my empty head there come
a cotton beach, a dock wherefrom

I set out, oily and nude
through mist, in chilly solitude.

There was no line, no roof or floor
to tell the water from the air.

Night fog thick as terry cloth
closed me in its fuzzy growth.

I hung my bathrobe on two pegs.
I took the lake between my legs.   10

Invaded and invader, I
went overhand on that flat sky.

Fish twitched beneath me, quick and tame.
In their green zone they sang my name

and in the rhythm of the swim
I hummed a two-four-time slow hymn.

I hummed "Abide With Me."[1] The beat
rose in the fine thrash of my feet,

rose in the bubbles I put out
slantwise, trailing through my mouth.   20

My bones drank water; water fell
through all my doors. I was the well

that fed the lake that met my sea
in which I sang "Abide With Me."

1982

---

[1] An 1847 hymn by the Scottish clergyman Henry Francis Lyte (1793–1847).

A. R. Ammons
(1926–   )

Few contemporary poets have been honored with the type of praise epitomized by the critic Harold Bloom's declaration that A. R. Ammons is "the poet that Emerson prophesied as necessary for America." By turns oracular, discursive, and playfully colloquial, Ammons's poetry has for thirty years been marked by an attraction toward, and a quarrel with, Emersonian transcendence. Ammons's work exhibits a tension between the concrete and the vague, the certain and the unknown. We encounter in "He Held Radical Light" (1972) a reluctant visionary torn between the conflicting claims of logic and vision.

Ammons's first book, *Ommateum* (1955), was scarcely noticed, but its chantlike proclamations of his ambitious poetic aims prefigure many of his later works. The title, which refers to the compound eye of an insect, indicates Ammons's desire, as he writes in the volume's preface, to achieve a "many-sided view of reality," to replace "partial, unified, prejudicial, and rigid" attitudes with attitudes that are "tentative, provisional."

Ammons arrived at his career as a poet through a route as circuitous as the "eddies of meaning" so characteristic of his poetry. He was born Archie Randolph Ammons on a farm near Whiteville, North Carolina, in 1926. Ammons served in the navy during World War II and married in 1949. Though he attended the University of California in Berkeley for three semesters in 1951 and 1952, he never earned a degree in literature. Studying biology and chemistry, he graduated from Wake Forest College in his native North Carolina with a B.S. in 1949. The presence of scientific themes and vocabulary in his poetry implies that his interest in science has never waned. For a short time after college Ammons was the principal of an elementary school in North Carolina. When *Ommateum* was published he was the thirty-year-old manager of a biological-glass factory in southern New Jersey. He accepted a teaching position in the English department at Cornell University in 1964 and began to publish more poetry.

Ammons has been persistently experimental. Through one of his most distinctive formal innovations, replacing almost all punctuation with the colon, he found a way to emphasize process and continuity. This device dominated his verse in his second and third volumes, *Expressions of Sea Level* (1964) and the well-received *Corsons Inlet* (1965), and culminated in *Sphere: The Form of a Motion* (1974), a Bollingen Prize winner. Except for the final period of this book-length poem, commas and colons are the sole punctuation. Another example of his willingness to violate convention is *Tape for the Turn of the Year* (1965), a book-length poetic diary of a three-week period, typed within the narrow margins of a roll of adding-machine paper.

Ammons's work has been published in several collections. *Collected Poems: 1951–1971* (1972) won the 1973 National Book Award for poetry. The expanded edition of Ammons's *Selected Poems* (1986) includes work through his *Lake Effect Country* (1983). *Selected Longer Poems* (1980) reprints several of his most important long poems. Many of his poems feature coastal settings—shorelines that have inspired the poet on quiet walks—and have been likened to the work of nineteenth-century transcendentalists.

Suggested Readings: *Ommateum*, 1955. *Corsons Inlet: A Book of Poems*, 1965. *Tape for the Turn of the Year*, 1965. *Sphere: The Form of a Motion*, 1974. *Worldly Hopes: Poems*, 1982. *The Selected Poems: Expanded Edition*, 1986. *Sumerian Vistas*, 1987. Ammons issue, *Diacritics*, 3 (5), (Winter) 1973. A. Holder, *A. R. Ammons*, 1978. H. Bloom, ed. *A. R. Ammons*, 1986. Ammons issue, *Pembroke Magazine*, 18, 1986.

Text Used: *Collected Poems: 1951–1971*, 1972.

SO I SAID I AM EZRA

So I said I am Ezra
and the wind whipped my throat
gaming for the sounds of my voice
    I listened to the wind
go over my head and up into the night
Turning to the sea I said
      I am Ezra
but there were no echoes from the waves
The words were swallowed up
    in the voice of the surf   10
or leaping over the swells
lost themselves oceanward
    Over the bleached and broken fields
I moved my feet and turning from the wind
    that ripped sheets of sand
    from the beach and threw them
    like seamists across the dunes
swayed as if the wind were taking me away
and said
      I am Ezra   20
As a word too much repeated
falls out of being
so I Ezra went out into the night
like a drift of sand
and splashed among the windy oats
that clutch the dunes
of unremembered seas

1955

APOLOGIA PRO VITA SUA*

I started picking up the stones
throwing them into one place
and by sunrise I was going far away
for the large ones
always turning to see never lost
the cairn's[1] height
lengthening my radial reach:

the sun watched with deep concentration
and the heap through the hours grew

---

* "Apology For His life" (Latin); the title of the 1864 spiritual autobiography of the English theologian Cardinal John Henry Newman (1801–1890), which traces the stages of his religious development from strong Protestantism to his conversion to Roman Catholicism in 1845.
[1] A conical pile of stones built as a landmark or monument.

and became by nightfall   10
distinguishable from all the miles around
of slate and sand:

during the night the wind falling
turned earthward its lofty freedom and speed
and the sharp blistering sound muffled
toward dawn and the blanket was
drawn up over a breathless face:

even so you can see in full dawn
the ground there lifts
a foreign thing desertless in origin.   20

                                                1956

COON SONG

I got one good look
    in the raccoon's eyes
        when he fell from the tree
came to his feet
    and perfectly still
        seized the baying hounds
in his dull fierce stare,
    in that recognition all
        decision lost,
choice irrelevant, before the   10
    battle fell
    and the unwinding
of his little knot of time began:

        Dostoevsky[1] would think
it important if the coon
    could choose to
        be back up the tree:
or if he could choose to be
    wagging by a swamp pond,
        dabbling at scuttling   20
crawdads:[2] the coon may have
    dreamed in fact of curling
        into the holed-out gall
of a fallen oak some squirrel
    had once brought
        high into the air
clean leaves to: but

[1] The Russian novelist Feodor Dostoevski (1821–1881).   [2] Crayfish.

reality can go to hell
is what the coon's eyes said to me:
    and said how simple
        the solution to my
problem is: it needs only
    not to be: I thought the raccoon
        felt no anger,
saw none; cared nothing for cowardice,
    bravery; was in fact
        bored at
knowing what would ensue:
    the unwinding, the whirling growls,
        exposed tenders,
the wet teeth—a problem to be
    solved, the taut-coiled vigor
        of the hunt
ready to snap loose:

        you want to know what happened,
you want to hear me describe it,
    to placate the hound's-mouth
        slobbering in your own heart:
I will not tell you: actually the coon
    possessing secret knowledge
        pawed dust on the dogs
and they disappeared, yapping into
    nothingness, and the coon went
        down to the pond
and washed his face and hands and beheld
    the world: maybe he didn't:
        I am no slave that I
should entertain you, say what you want
    to hear, let you wallow in
        your silt: one two three four five:
one two three four five six seven eight nine ten:

    (all this time I've been
        counting spaces
while you were thinking of something else)
    mess in your own sloppy silt:
        the hounds disappeared
yelping (the way you would at extinction)
    into—the order
        breaks up here—immortality:
I know that's where you think the brave
    little victims should go:
        I do not care what
you think: I do not care what you think:
    I do not care what you
        think: one two three four five

30

40

50

60

70

six seven eight nine ten: here we go
   round the here-we-go-round, the
      here-we-go-round, the here-we-
go-round: coon will end in disorder at the
   teeth of hounds: the situation
     will get him:
spheres roll, cubes stay put: now there
   one two three four five
     are two philosophies:
here we go round the mouth-wet of hounds:

     what I choose
     is youse:
     baby

1965

80

LASER

An image comes
and the mind's light, confused
as that on surf
or ocean shelves,
gathers up,
parallelizes, focuses
and in a rigid beam illuminates the image:

the head seeks in itself
fragments of left-over light
to cast a new
direction,
any direction,
to strike and fix
a random, contradicting image:

but any found image falls
back to darkness or
the lesser beams splinter and
go out:
the mind tries to
dream of diversity, of mountain
rapids shattered with sound and light,

of wind fracturing brush or
bursting out of order against a mountain
range: but the focused beam
folds all energy in:

10

20

the image glares filling all space:
the head falls and
hangs and cannot wake itself.

1970

HE HELD RADICAL LIGHT

He held radical light
as music in his skull: music
turned, as
over ridges immanences of evening light
rise, turned
back over the furrows of his brain
into the dark, shuddered,
shot out again
in long swaying swirls of sound:

reality had little weight in his transcendence   10
so he
had trouble keeping
his feet on the ground, was
terrified by that
and liked himself, and others, mostly
under roofs:
nevertheless, when the
light churned and changed

his head to music, nothing could keep him
off the mountains, his   20
head back, mouth working,
wrestling to say, to cut loose
from the high, unimaginable hook:
released, hidden from stars, he ate,
burped, said he was like any one
of us: demanded he
was like any one of us.

1971

WINTER SAINT

In the summer I live so
close to my neighbor I
can hear him sweat:

all my forced bushes, leafy
and birdy, do not
prevent this:

his drawers wrenched
off his sticky butt
clutch my speech white:

his beery mouth wakes up   10
under my tongue: his
lawnmower wilts my cereal:

I do not like to hear him
wheeze over difficult weeds:
I don't like his squishy toes:

I'm for ice and shutters
and the miles and miles
winter clears between us.

1972

Allen Ginsberg
(1926–   )

"My poetry is Angelical Ravings," said Allen Ginsberg in 1959 (Lewis Hyde, *On the Poetry of Allen Ginsberg*, 1984), but critical response has been divided about whether his poetry is indeed angelic, merely a stream of ravings, or not poetry at all. A mythic figure in American culture, particularly as a leader of the beat poets, Ginsberg engendered and continues to sustain the numerous legends about him. He was born in 1926 in Newark, New Jersey, to a father who taught high school English and was a published poet and to a mother who was mentally ill and institutionalized throughout much of her life. Ginsberg attended Columbia University, where he studied and struggled with Lionel Trilling and Mark Van Doren, who both became critics and educators. After a school suspension and a subsequent stay at a mental institution (where he met Carl Solomon, a fellow patient to whom the poem "Howl" [1956] is dedicated), Ginsberg earned a B.A. in 1948. His already turbulent life changed dramatically that year when, alone and depressed, he read William Blake's poems and experienced a series of visions or "beatific illuminations" in which he "saw the universe unfold in [his] brain" and heard the voice of Blake speaking to him directly (Hyde, 1984). From that moment Ginsberg attained a sense of vocation as a poet whose visions would enlighten him in the same intense way. Years of travel and experimentation with drugs followed, but the visions did not reappear.

Ginsberg lived with his father in Paterson, New Jersey, for a time in the late 1940s and there met the poet William Carlos Williams, who later wrote the introduction to "Howl." In 1954 Ginsberg found his way to San Francisco, which was then bursting with poetic life, primarily under the influence of the poet Kenneth Rexroth. It was there that Lawrence Ferlinghetti's City Lights Bookshop released "Howl," the poem that made Ginsberg's reputation. In an obscenity trial following the poem's publication, Ferlinghetti was charged with disseminating "indecent writing." Although the judge ruled in favor of Ferlinghetti on the basis of freedom of speech, reviews of the poem were generally negative. Similar objections to Ginsberg's personal references—to his mother's madness and his guiltless homosexuality—would be raised throughout his career. Nonetheless, Ginsberg was thrust into the public eye and has remained there ever since.

After "Howl" Ginsberg traveled the world—to Tangier, Spain, France, Chile—and returned to the United States to give readings of his work. His readings became "performances," and he became a popular speaker on college campuses. Leading the beat poets in their anti-intellectual and anti-establishment efforts in the 1950s, Ginsberg proclaimed individual expression as paramount, a philosophy reflected in his prosody. Based not on traditional metrics but on the single breath unit ("one physical and mental inspiration of thought contained in the elastic of a breath" [Hyde, 1984]), Ginsberg's poetic line is like that of Walt Whitman and characterized by Ginsberg's own long "breath."

During the 1960s Ginsberg was involved with Vietnam War protests and the civil rights movement; he gradually turned to Eastern philosophies and became a Buddhist. In addition to the collections *The Fall of America* (1972), and *Howl and Other Poems* (1956), his collection *Kaddish and Other Poems* (1961), of which the title poem laments the recent death of Ginsberg's mother, gained widespread recognition. Ginsberg has won such awards as a Guggenheim Fellowship, a National Book Award for *Fall* and a medal from the National Arts Club. And in 1990 he was honored with an American Book Award for his lifetime achievement in contributing "to literary excellence in America."

Suggested Readings: *Howl and Other Poems*, 1956. *Kaddish and Other Poems*, 1961. *The Fall of America, Poems of These States*, 1972. *Mind Breaths*, 1978. T. Clark, "Allen Ginsberg: An Interview," in *Writers at Work: The Paris Review Interviews*, Third Series, 1967. J. Kramer, *Allen Ginsberg in America*, 1969. T. F. Merrill, *Allen Ginsberg*, 1969. *To Eberhart From Ginsberg: A Letter About Howl 1956*, 1976. L. Hyde, ed., *On the Poetry of Allen Ginsberg*, 1984.

Text Used: *Collected Poems: 1947–1980*, 1988.

HOWL

For Carl Solomon*

I

I saw the best minds of my generation destroyed by madness, starving hysterical
   naked,
dragging themselves through the negro streets at dawn looking for an angry fix,
angelheaded hipsters burning for the ancient heavenly connection[1] to the starry
   dynamo in the machinery of night,

---

* Solomon (1928–   ) was a fellow patient of Ginsberg's at the Columbia Psychiatric Institute in New York City in 1949; part of the poem is thought to be based on Solomon's "apocryphal history" of adventures.

[1] Dope supplier.

who poverty and tatters and hollow-eyed and high sat up smoking in the
   supernatural darkness of cold-water flats floating across the tops of cities
   contemplating jazz,
who bared their brains to Heaven under the El[2] and saw Mohammedan angels
   staggering on tenement roofs illuminated,
who passed through universities with radiant cool eyes hallucinating Arkansas
   and Blake-light[3] tragedy among the scholars of war,
who were expelled from the academies for crazy & publishing obscene odes
   on the windows of the skull,[4]
who cowered in unshaven rooms in underwear, burning their money in
   wastebaskets and listening to the Terror through the wall,
who got busted in their pubic beards returning through Laredo[5] with a belt of
   marijuana for New York,
who ate fire in paint hotels or drank turpentine in Paradise Alley,[6] death, or
   purgatoried their torsos night after night   10
with dreams, with drugs, with waking nightmares, alcohol and cock and
   endless balls,
incomparable blind streets of shuddering cloud and lightning in the mind leaping
   toward poles of Canada & Paterson,[7] illuminating all the motionless world of
   Time between,
Peyote[8] solidities of halls, backyard green tree cemetery dawns, wine
   drunkenness over the rooftops, storefront boroughs of teahead joyride neon
   blinking traffic light, sun and moon and tree vibrations in the roaring winter
   dusks of Brooklyn, ashcan rantings and kind king light of mind,
who chained themselves to subways for the endless ride from Battery[9] to holy
   Bronx on benzedrine until the noise of wheels and children brought them
   down shuddering mouth-wracked and battered bleak of brain all drained of
   brilliance in the drear light of Zoo,[10]
who sank all night in submarine light of Bickford's[11] floated out and sat through
   the stale beer afternoon in desolate Fugazzi's[12] listening to the crack of doom
   on the hydrogen jukebox,
who talked continuously seventy hours from park to pad to bar to Bellevue[13] to
   museum to the Brooklyn Bridge,
a lost battalion of platonic conversationalists jumping down the stoops off
   fire escapes off windowsills off Empire State out of the moon,

[2] The elevated railway system in New York City.
[3] Ginsberg experienced a mystical vision while he read the work of the English poet William Blake
(1757–1827).
[4] In 1945 Ginsberg was expelled from Columbia University for drawing and writing obscenities on
his dormitory windows.
[5] Laredo, Texas, on the Mexican border.
[6] Ginsberg's note: "A slum courtyard N. Y. Lower East Side, site of Kerouac's *Subterraneans*,
1958": a beat novel by Jack Kerouac (1922–1969).
[7] Paterson, New Jersey, where Ginsberg lived for a few years and met William Carlos Williams
(1883–1963), author of the long poem *Paterson* (1946–1963).
[8] Mescal, portions of a cactus that Mexican Indians chew in religious ceremonies for their hallucino-
genic effects.
[9] Battery Park, at the southern end of Manhattan.
[10] The Bronx Zoo, at the northern end of the N.Y.C. subway line.
[11] The all-night cafeteria where Ginsberg worked while he was a Columbia student.
[12] A bar near Greenwich Village where beats gathered.
[13] A New York public hospital with a psychiatric clinic.

yacketayakking screaming vomiting whispering facts and memories and
    anecdotes and eyeball kicks and shocks of hospitals and jails and wars,
whole intellects disgorged in total recall for seven days and nights with
    brilliant eyes, meat for the Synagogue cast on the pavement,
who vanished into nowhere Zen New Jersey leaving a trail of ambiguous
    picture postcards of Atlantic City Hall,   20
suffering Eastern sweats and Tangerian bone-grindings and migraines of
    China[14] under junk-withdrawal in Newark's bleak furnished room,
who wandered around and around at midnight in the railroad yard wondering
    where to go, and went, leaving no broken hearts,
who lit cigarettes in boxcars boxcars boxcars racketing through snow toward
    lonesome farms in grandfather night,
who studied Plotinus Poe St. John of the Cross[15] telepathy and bop kabbalah[16]
    because the cosmos instinctively vibrated at their feet in Kansas,
who loned it through the streets of Idaho seeking visionary indian angels
    who were visionary indian angels,
who thought they were only mad when Baltimore gleamed in supernatural ecstasy,
who jumped in limousines with the Chinaman of Oklahoma on the impulse of
    winter midnight streetlight smalltown rain,
who lounged hungry and lonesome through Houston seeking jazz or sex or
    soup, and followed the brilliant Spaniard to converse about America and
    Eternity, a hopeless task, and so took ship to Africa,
who disappeared into the volcanoes of Mexico leaving behind nothing but
    the shadow of dungarees and the lava and ash of poetry scattered in fireplace
    Chicago,
who reappeared on the West Coast investigating the FBI in beards and shorts
    with big pacifist eyes sexy in their dark skin passing out incomprehensible
    leaflets,   30
who burned cigarette holes in their arms protesting the narcotic tobacco haze
    of Capitalism,
who distributed Supercommunist pamphlets in Union Square[17] weeping and
    undressing while the sirens of Los Alamos[18] wailed them down, and wailed
    down Wall,[19] and the Staten Island ferry also wailed,
who broke down crying in white gymnasiums naked and trembling before
    the machinery of other skeletons,
who bit detectives in the neck and shrieked with delight in policecars for
    committing no crime but their own wild cooking pederasty and intoxication,
who howled on their knees in the subway and were dragged off the roof
    waving genitals and manuscripts,
who let themselves be fucked in the ass by saintly motorcyclists, and screamed
    with joy,

---

[14] African and Asian drug sources.

[15] Plotinus (A.D. 205?–270) was a Roman neo-Platonic philosopher; the poet and writer Edgar Allan Poe (1809–1849); Juan de Yepes y Álvaraz (1542–1591), a Spanish mystic poet.

[16] The bop style of jazz developed in the 1940s and 1950s; the mystical tradition of interpreting Hebrew scripture.

[17] Once a meeting place for radical speakers and protesters in New York City.

[18] The New Mexico site for the research and development of the atomic bomb.

[19] Wall Street; also, Jerusalem's Wailing Wall (thought to be part of the wall surrounding the temple of King Herod (73–4 B.C.) of Judea, where Jews have traditionally gathered for prayer.

who blew and were blown by those human seraphim, the sailors, caresses of
Atlantic and Caribbean love,

who balled in the morning in the evenings in rosegardens and the grass of
public parks and cemeteries scattering their semen freely to whomever come
who may,

who hiccuped endlessly trying to giggle but wound up with a sob behind a
partition in a Turkish Bath when the blond & naked angel came to pierce
them with a sword,

who lost their loveboys to the three old shrews of fate[20] the one eyed shrew of
the heterosexual dollar the one eyed shrew that winks out of the womb and
the one eyed shrew that does nothing but sit on her ass and snip the
intellectual golden threads of the craftsman's loom,   40

who copulated ecstatic and insatiate with a bottle of beer a sweetheart a
package of cigarettes a candle and fell off the bed, and continued along the
floor and down the hall and ended fainting on the wall with a vision of ultimate
cunt and come eluding the last gyzym of consciousness,

who sweetened the snatches of a million girls trembling in the sunset, and
were red eyed in the morning but prepared to sweeten the snatch of the sunrise,
flashing buttocks under barns and naked in the lake,

who went out whoring through Colorado in myriad stolen night-cars, N.C.,[21]
secret hero of these poems, cocksman and Adonis[22] of Denver—joy to the
memory of his innumerable lays of girls in empty lots & diner backyards,
moviehouses' rickety rows, on mountaintops in caves or with gaunt waitresses
in familiar roadside lonely petticoat upliftings & especially secret gas-station
solipsisms[23] of johns, & hometown alleys too,

who faded out in vast sordid movies, were shifted in dreams, woke on a
sudden Manhattan, and picked themselves up out of basements hungover with
heartless Tokay[24] and the horrors of Third Avenue iron dreams & stumbled to
unemployment offices,

who walked all night with their shoes full of blood on the snowbank docks
waiting for a door in the East River to open to a room full of steamheat
and opium,

who created great suicidal dramas on the apartment cliff-banks of the Hudson[25]
under the wartime blue floodlight of the moon & their heads shall be crowned
with laurel in oblivion,

who ate the lamb stew of the imagination or digested the crab at the muddy
bottom of the rivers of Bowery,[26]

who wept at the romance of the streets with their pushcarts full of onions and
bad music,

who sat in boxes breathing in the darkness under the bridge, and rose up to
build harpsichords in their lofts,

---

[20] The Fates: according to Roman myth, three goddesses of destiny who determine the course of
human lives.

[21] Neal Cassady (1926–1968), a beat writer and friend of Ginsberg and Kerouac on whom Kerouac
based the character Dean Moriarty in *On the Road* (1957).

[22] According to Greek myth, a handsome young man loved by Aphrodite, goddess of love.

[23] Philosophical theories by which only the self exists, so that all experience is subjective.

[24] A cheap, fortified wine favored by alcoholic derelicts.

[25] The high-rise apartment houses atop the cliffs of the Palisades along the Hudson River.

[26] The lower part of Third Avenue in New York City, frequented by alcoholic derelicts.

who coughed on the sixth floor of Harlem crowned with flame under the
    tubercular sky surrounded by orange crates of theology,   50
who scribbled all night rocking and rolling over lofty incantations which in
    the yellow morning were stanzas of gibberish,
who cooked rotten animals lung heart feet tail borsht[27] & tortillas dreaming of
    the pure vegetable kingdom,
who plunged themselves under meat trucks looking for an egg,
who threw their watches off the roof to cast their ballot for Eternity outside
    of Time, & alarm clocks fell on their heads every day for the next decade,
who cut their wrists three times successively unsuccessfully, gave up and
    were forced to open antique stores where they thought they were growing old
    and cried,
who were burned alive in their innocent flannel suits on Madison Avenue[28]
    amid blasts of leaden verse & the tanked-up clatter of the iron regiments of
    fashion & the nitroglycerine shrieks of the fairies of advertising & the mustard
    gas of sinister intelligent editors, or were run down by the drunken taxicabs of
    Absolute Reality,
who jumped off the Brooklyn Bridge this actually happened and walked away
    unknown and forgotten into the ghostly daze of Chinatown soup alleyways &
    firetrucks, not even one free beer,
who sang out of their windows in despair, fell out of the subway window,
    jumped in the filthy Passaic,[29] leaped on negroes, cried all over the street,
    danced on broken wineglasses barefoot smashed phonograph records of
    nostalgic European 1930s German jazz finished the whiskey and threw up
    groaning into the bloody toilet, moans in their ears and the blast of colossal
    steamwhistles,
who barreled down the highways of the past journeying to each other's
    hotrod-Golgotha[30] jail-solitude watch or Birmingham jazz incarnation,
who drove crosscountry seventytwo hours to find out if I had a vision or you
    had a vision or he had a vision to find out Eternity,   60
who journeyed to Denver, who died in Denver, who came back to Denver
    & waited in vain, who watched over Denver & brooded & loned in Denver
    and finally went away to find out the Time, & now Denver is lonesome for
    her heroes,
who fell on their knees in hopeless cathedrals praying for each other's
    salvation and light and breasts, until the soul illuminated its hair for a second,
who crashed through their minds in jail waiting for impossible criminals
    with golden heads and the charm of reality in their hearts who sang sweet
    blues to Alcatraz,
who retired to Mexico to cultivate a habit, or Rocky Mount to tender Buddha
    or Tangiers to boys or Southern Pacific to the black locomotive[31] or Harvard
    to Narcissus to Woodlawn[32] to the daisychain or grave,

---

[27] Borscht, Russian beet soup.

[28] The traditional location of New York advertising agencies whose conformist employees wore gray flannel suits as a "uniform" for success.

[29] The Passaic River, which flows past Paterson, New Jersey.

[30] "Place of a Skull" (Hebrew): Calvary, the site of Jesus' crucifixion.

[31] William Burroughs (1914–   ), a beat writer and drug addict, lived in Mexico and Tangier, Morocco; Kerouac lived in Rocky Mount, North Carolina; Cassady worked for the Southern Pacific Railroad.

[32] According to Greek myth, Narcissus was a youth who fell in love with his own reflection in a pool; a cemetery in the Bronx.

who demanded sanity trials accusing the radio of hypnotism & were left with
their insanity & their hands & a hung jury,

who threw potato salad at CCNY[33] lecturers on Dadaism and subsequently
presented themselves on the granite steps of the madhouse with shaven heads
and harlequin speech of suicide, demanding instantaneous lobotomy,

and who were given instead the concrete void of insulin Metrazol[34] electricity
hydrotherapy psychotherapy occupational therapy pingpong & amnesia,

who in humorless protest overturned only one symbolic pingpong table,
resting briefly in catatonia,

returning years later truly bald except for a wig of blood, and tears and fingers,
to the visible madman doom of the wards of the madtowns of the East,

Pilgrim State's Rockland's and Greystone's[35] foetid halls, bickering with the
echoes of the soul, rocking and rolling in the midnight solitude-bench
dolmen-realms[36] of love, dream of life a nightmare, bodies turned to stone as
heavy as the moon,   70

with mother finally******, and the last fantastic book flung out of the
tenement window, and the last door closed at 4 A.M. and the last telephone
slammed at the wall in reply and the last furnished room emptied down to the
last piece of mental furniture, a yellow paper rose twisted on a wire hanger
in the closet, and even that imaginary nothing but a hopeful little bit of
hallucination—

ah, Carl, while you are not safe I am not safe, and now you're really in the
total animal soup of time—

and who therefore ran through the icy streets obsessed with a sudden flash of
the alchemy of the use of the ellipse the catalog the meter & the vibrating
plane,

who dreamt and made incarnate gaps in Time & Space through images
juxtaposed, and trapped the archangel of the soul between 2 visual images and
joined the elemental verbs and set the noun and dash of consciousness together
jumping with sensation of Pater Omnipotens Aeterna Deus[37]

to recreate the syntax and measure of poor human prose and stand before you
speechless and intelligent and shaking with shame, rejected yet confessing out
the soul to conform to the rhythm of thought in his naked and endless head,

the madman bum and angel beat in Time, unknown, yet putting down here
what might be left to say in time come after death,

and rose reincarnate in the ghostly clothes of jazz in the goldhorn shadow of
the band and blew the suffering of America's naked mind for love into an
eli eli lamma lamma sabacthani[38] saxophone cry that shivered the cities down
to the last radio

with the absolute heart of the poem of life butchered out of their own bodies
good to eat a thousand years.

---

[33] The City College of New York; the dada cult (1916–1922) was an artistic and literary movement
emphasizing the irrational and the absurd.

[34] The brand name of pentylenetetrazol, a drug used in shock therapy.

[35] Hospitals for the insane, near New York City. Solomon spent time at Pilgrim State and Rockland;
Ginsberg's mother, institutionalized at Greystone since the late 1940s, died there in 1956.

[36] Dolmens are neolithic tombs consisting of a large, flat rock laid across upright rocks.

[37] "All-powerful Father, Eternal God" (Latin), from a 1904 letter by the French painter Paul Cézanne
(1839–1906).

[38] "My God, my God, why have you forsaken me?" (Aramaic), from Matthew 27:46, Jesus' last
words on the cross.

II

What sphinx[39] of cement and aluminum bashed open their skulls and ate up
    their brains and imagination?
Moloch![40] Solitude! Filth! Ugliness! Ashcans and unobtainable dollars!
    Children screaming under the stairways! Boys sobbing in armies! Old men
    weeping in the parks!   80
Moloch! Moloch! Nightmare of Moloch! Moloch the loveless! Mental
    Moloch! Moloch the heavy judger of men!
Moloch the incomprehensible prison! Moloch the crossbone soulless jailhouse
    and Congress of sorrows! Moloch whose buildings are judgment! Moloch the
    vast stone of war! Moloch the stunned governments!
Moloch whose mind is pure machinery! Moloch whose blood is running
    money! Moloch whose fingers are ten armies! Moloch whose breast is a
    cannibal dynamo! Moloch whose ear is a smoking tomb!
Moloch whose eyes are a thousand blind windows! Moloch whose skyscrapers
    stand in the long streets like endless Jehovahs![41] Moloch whose factories
    dream and croak in the fog! Moloch whose smokestacks and antennae crown
    the cities!
Moloch whose love is endless oil and stone! Moloch whose soul is electricity
    and banks! Moloch whose poverty is the specter of genius! Moloch whose fate
    is a cloud of sexless hydrogen! Moloch whose name is the Mind!
Moloch in whom I sit lonely! Moloch in whom I dream Angels! Crazy in
    Moloch! Cocksucker in Moloch! Lacklove and manless in Moloch!
Moloch who entered my soul early! Moloch in whom I am a consciousness
    without a body! Moloch who frightened me out of my natural ecstasy! Moloch
    whom I abandon! Wake up in Moloch! Light streaming out of the sky!
Moloch! Moloch! Robot apartments! invisible suburbs! skeleton treasures!
    blind capitals! demonic industries! spectral nations! invincible madhouses!
    granite cocks! monstrous bombs!
They broke their backs lifting Moloch to Heaven! Pavements, trees, radios,
    tons! lifting the city to Heaven which exists and is everywhere about us!
Visions! omens! hallucinations! miracles! ecstasies! gone down the
    American river!   90
Dreams! adorations! illuminations! religions! the whole boatload of sensitive
    bullshit!
Breakthroughs! over the river! flips and crucifixions! gone down the flood!
    Highs! Epiphanies! Despairs! Ten years' animal screams and suicides!
    Minds! New loves! Mad generation! down on the rocks of Time!
Real holy laughter in the river! They saw it all! the wild eyes! the holy yells!
    They bade farewell! They jumped off the roof! to solitude! waving! carrying
    flowers! Down to the river! into the street!

III

Carl Solomon! I'm with you in Rockland
    where you're madder than I am
I'm with you in Rockland
    where you must feel very strange

---

[39] A mythical beast with a lion's body and a human head.
[40] Ginsberg's note: "Or Molech, the Canaanite fire god, whose worship was marked by parents burning their children as propitiatory sacrifice. 'And thou shalt not let any of thy seed pass through the fire to Molech' (Leviticus 18:21)."
[41] Judeo-Christian Gods.

I'm with you in Rockland
  where you imitate the shade of my mother
I'm with you in Rockland
  where you've murdered your twelve secretaries
I'm with you in Rockland
  where you laugh at this invisible humor
I'm with you in Rockland
  where we are great writers on the same dreadful typewriter
I'm with you in Rockland
  where your condition has become serious and is reported on the radio   100
I'm with you in Rockland
  where the faculties of the skull no longer admit the worms of the senses
I'm with you in Rockland
  where you drink the tea of the breasts of the spinsters of Utica
I'm with you in Rockland
  where you pun on the bodies of your nurses the harpies of the Bronx
I'm with you in Rockland
  where you scream in a straightjacket that you're losing the game of the
  actual pingpong of the abyss
I'm with you in Rockland
  where you bang on the catatonic piano the soul is innocent and immortal
  it should never die ungodly in an armed madhouse
I'm with you in Rockland
  where fifty more shocks will never return your soul to its body again from
  its pilgrimage to a cross in the void
I'm with you in Rockland
  where you accuse your doctors of insanity and plot the Hebrew socialist
  revolution against the fascist national Golgotha
I'm with you in Rockland
  where you will split the heavens of Long Island and resurrect your living
  human Jesus from the superhuman tomb
I'm with you in Rockland
  where there are twenty-five thousand mad comrades all together singing the
  final stanzas of the Internationale[42]
I'm with you in Rockland
  where we hug and kiss the United States under our bedsheets the United
  States that coughs all night and won't let us sleep   110
I'm with you in Rockland
  where we wake up electrified out of the coma by our own souls' airplanes
  roaring over the roof they've come to drop angelic bombs the hospital
  illuminates itself   imaginary walls collapse   O skinny legions run outside
  O starry-spangled shock of mercy the eternal war is here   O victory forget
  your underwear we're free
I'm with you in Rockland
  in my dreams you walk dripping from a sea-journey on the highway across
  America in tears to the door of my cottage in the Western night

                                                              1955–1956, 1956

---

[42] The national anthem of the Soviet Union from the Russian Revolution (1917) to World War II (1944).

FOOTNOTE TO HOWL

Holy! Holy! Holy! Holy! Holy! Holy! Holy! Holy! Holy! Holy! Holy! Holy!
    Holy! Holy! Holy!
The world is holy! The soul is holy! The skin is holy! The nose is holy!
    The tongue and cock and hand and asshole holy!
Everything is holy! everybody's holy! everywhere is holy! everyday is in
    eternity! Everyman's an angel!
The bum's as holy as the seraphim! the madman is holy as you my soul are holy!
The typewriter is holy the poem is holy the voice is holy the hearers are holy
    the ecstasy is holy!
Holy Peter holy Allen holy Solomon holy Lucien holy Kerouac holy Huncke[1]
    holy Burroughs holy Cassady holy the unknown buggered and suffering
    beggars holy the hideous human angels!
Holy my mother in the insane asylum! Holy the cocks of the grandfathers of
    Kansas!
Holy the groaning saxophone! Holy the bop apocalypse! Holy the jazzbands
    marijuana hipsters peace peyote pipes & drums!
Holy the solitudes of skyscrapers and pavements! Holy the cafeterias filled
    with the millions! Holy the mysterious rivers of tears under the streets!
Holy the lone juggernaut! Holy the vast lamb of the middleclass! Holy the
    crazy shepherds of rebellion! Who digs Los Angeles IS Los Angeles!   10
Holy New York Holy San Francisco Holy Peoria & Seattle Holy Paris Holy
    Tangiers Holy Moscow Holy Istanbul!
Holy time in eternity holy eternity in time holy the clocks in space holy the
    fourth dimension holy the fifth International holy the Angel in Moloch!
Holy the sea holy the desert holy the railroad holy the locomotive holy the
    visions holy the hallucinations holy the miracles holy the eyeball holy
    the abyss!
Holy forgiveness! mercy! charity! faith! Holy! Ours! bodies! suffering!
    magnanimity!
Holy the supernatural extra brilliant intelligent kindness of the soul!

1955, 1956

A SUPERMARKET IN CALIFORNIA

What thoughts I have of you tonight, Walt Whitman,[1] for I walked down the
sidestreets under the trees with a headache self-conscious looking at the full moon.
    In my hungry fatigue, and shopping for images, I went into the neon fruit
supermarket, dreaming of your enumerations!
    What peaches and what penumbras![2] Whole families shopping at night! Aisles

---

[1] Herbert Huncke (1915–   ), a friend of Ginsberg's who coined the term "beat"; author of *Huncke's
Journal* (1965). All other names and terms are explained in "Howl."
    [1] Ginsberg deeply admired the poet Whitman (1819–1892), to whom he has frequently been com-
pared.
    [2] Partly lighted areas.

full of husbands! Wives in the avocados, babies in the tomatoes! —and you, García Lorca,[3] what were you doing down by the watermelons?

I saw you, Walt Whitman, childless, lonely old grubber, poking among the meats in the refrigerator and eyeing the grocery boys.
I heard you asking questions of each: Who killed the pork chops? What price bananas? Are you my Angel?
I wandered in and out of the brilliant stacks of cans following you, and followed in my imagination by the store detective.
We strode down in the open corridors together in our solitary fancy tasting artichokes, possessing every frozen delicacy, and never passing the cashier.

Where are we going, Walt Whitman? The doors close in an hour. Which way does your beard point tonight?
(I touch your book and dream of our odyssey in the supermarket and feel absurd.)
Will we walk all night through solitary streets? The trees add shade to shade, lights out in the houses, we'll both be lonely.
Will we stroll dreaming to the lost America of love past blue automobiles in driveways, home to our silent cottage?
Ah, dear father, graybeard, lonely old courage-teacher, what America did you have when Charon[4] quit poling his ferry and you got out on a smoking bank and stood watching the boat disappear on the black waters of Lethe?

1955, 1956

AMERICA

America I've given you all and now I'm nothing.
America two dollars and twentyseven cents January, 17, 1956.
I can't stand my own mind.
America when will we end the human war?
Go fuck yourself with your atom bomb.
I don't feel good don't bother me.
I won't write my poem till I'm in my right mind.
America when will you be angelic?
When will you take off your clothes?
When will you look at yourself through the grave?   10
When will you be worthy of your million Trotskyites?[1]

---

[3] Federico García Lorca (1899–1936), a Spanish poet and playwright; in his *Collected Poems* (1984) Ginsberg notes García Lorca's poem "Ode to Walt Whitman": like Whitman's and Ginsberg's poetry, García Lorca's is homoerotic.

[4] According to Greek myth, the boatman who ferried the dead across the Lethe, the river of forgetfulness in Hades, the Underworld.

[1] Supporters of the Russian Communist leader Leon Trotsky (1877–1940).

America why are your libraries full of tears?
America when will you send your eggs to India?
I'm sick of your insane demands.
When can I go into the supermarket and buy what I need with my good looks?
America after all it is you and I who are perfect not the next world.
Your machinery is too much for me.
You made me want to be a saint.
There must be some other way to settle this argument.
Burroughs[2] is in Tangiers I don't think he'll come back it's sinister.   20
Are you being sinister or is this some form of practical joke?
I'm trying to come to the point.
I refuse to give up my obsession.
America stop pushing I know what I'm doing.
America the plum blossoms are falling.
I haven't read the newspapers for months, everyday somebody goes on trial
    for murder.
America I feel sentimental about the Wobblies.[3]
America I used to be a communist when I was a kid I'm not sorry.
I smoke marijuana every chance I get.
I sit in my house for days on end and stare at the roses in the closet.   30
When I go to Chinatown I get drunk and never get laid.
My mind is made up there's going to be trouble.
You should have seen me reading Marx.[4]
My psychoanalyst thinks I'm perfectly right.
I won't say the Lord's Prayer.
I have mystical visions and cosmic vibrations.
America I still haven't told you what you did to Uncle Max after he came
    over from Russia.
I'm addressing you.
Are you going to let your emotional life be run by Time Magazine?
I'm obsessed by Time Magazine.   40
I read it every week.
Its cover stares at me every time I slink past the corner candystore.
I read it in the basement of the Berkeley Public Library.
It's always telling me about responsibility. Businessmen are serious. Movie
    producers are serious. Everybody's serious but me.
It occurs to me that I am America.
I am talking to myself again.

Asia is rising against me.
I haven't got a chinaman's chance.
I'd better consider my national resources.
My national resources consist of two joints of marijuana millions of genitals

---

[2] William Burroughs (1914–   ), a beat writer then living in Morocco.
[3] A nickname for members of the radical Industrial Workers of the World, an organization of unions, formed in 1905.
[4] The German political philosopher and the founder of modern socialism, Karl Marx (1818–1883).

an unpublishable private literature that jetplanes 1400 miles an hour and
twentyfive-thousand mental institutions.   50
I say nothing about my prisons nor the millions of underprivileged who live in
my flowerpots under the light of five hundred suns.
I have abolished the whorehouses of France, Tangiers is the next to go. My
ambition is to be President despite the fact that I'm a Catholic.

America how can I write a holy litany in your silly mood?
I will continue like Henry Ford my strophes[5] are as individual as his
automobiles more so they're all different sexes.
America I will sell you strophes $2500 apiece $500 down on your old strophe
America free Tom Mooney[6]
America save the Spanish Loyalists[7]
America Sacco & Vanzetti must not die[8]
America I am the Scottsboro boys.[9]   60
America when I was seven momma took me to Communist Cell meetings
they sold us garbanzos[10] a handful per ticket a ticket costs a nickel and the
speeches were free everybody was angelic and sentimental about the workers
it was all so sincere you have no idea what a good thing the party was in 1935
Scott Nearing was a grand old man a real mensch[11] Mother Bloor the
Silk-strikers' Ewig-Weibliche[12] made me cry I once saw the Yiddish orator
Israel Amter[13] plain. Everybody must have been a spy.
America you don't really want to go to war.
America it's them bad Russians.
Them Russians them Russians and them Chinamen. And them Russians.
The Russia wants to eat us alive. The Russia's power mad. She wants to take
our cars from out our garages.
Her wants to grab Chicago. Her needs a Red *Reader's Digest.* Her wants our
auto plants in Siberia. Him big bureaucracy running our fillingstations.
That no good. Ugh. Him make Indians learn read. Him need big black
niggers. Hah. Her make us all work sixteen hours a day. Help.
America this is quite serious.
America this is the impression I get from looking in the television set.
America is this correct?   70
I'd better get right down to the job.

---

[5] Stanzas.
[6] Mooney (1882–1942) was an American labor leader imprisoned in 1916 for bomb throwing and pardoned in 1939.
[7] In the Spanish Civil War (1936–1939), foreign supporters of theSpanish government against the Fascist general Francisco Franco (1892–1975).
[8] Nicola Sacco (1892–1927) and Bartolomeo Vanzetti (1888–1927), Italian-American anarchists convicted of robbery and murder in Massachusetts and executed despite international protests over their innocence.
[9] Nine black youths arrested in 1931 in Scottsboro, Alabama, for the rape of two white women; amid widespread protests of racism, the were eventually released.
[10] Chickpeas.
[11] A real sensible, mature person (Yiddish). Scott Nearing (1883–1983) and Ella Reeve Bloor (1862–1851) were American Communist leaders.
[12] "Eternally feminine" (German), the eternal woman.
[13] Amter (1918–1954) was an American Communist leader.

It's true I don't want to join the Army or turn lathes in precision parts
   factories, I'm nearsighted and psychopathic anyway.
America I'm putting my queer shoulder to the wheel.

1956

ODE TO FAILURE

Many prophets have failed, their voices silent
ghost-shouts in basements nobody heard dusty laughter in family attics
nor glanced them on park benches weeping with relief under empty sky
Walt Whitman viva'd[1] local losers—courage to Fat Ladies in the Freak
   Show! nervous prisoners whose mustached lips dripped sweat on chow lines—
Mayakovsky cried, Then die! my verse, die like the workers' rank & file
   fusilladed in Petersburg![2]
Prospero[3] burned his Power books & plummeted his magic wand to the bottom
   of dragon seas
Alexander the Great[4] failed to find more worlds to conquer!
O Failure I chant your terrifying name, accept me your 54 year old Prophet
   epicking[5] Eternal Flop! I join your Pantheon[6] of mortal bards, & hasten this
   ode with high blood pressure
rushing to the top of my skull as if I wouldn't last another minute, like the
   Dying Gaul![7] to   10
You, Lord of blind Monet, deaf Beethoven, armless Venus de Milo,
   headless Winged Victory![8]
I failed to sleep with every bearded rosy-cheeked boy I jacked off over
My tirades destroyed no Intellectual Unions of KGB & CIA in turtlenecks &
   underpants, their woolen suits & tweeds
I never dissolved Plutonium or dismantled the nuclear Bomb before my skull
   lost hair
I have not yet stopped the Armies of entire Mankind in their march toward
   World War III
I never got to Heaven, Nirvana,[9] X, Whatchamacallit, I never left Earth,
I never learned to die.

1980

---

[1] Whitman (1819–1892) applauded.

[2] "Let glory / disconsolate widow frail / trudge after genius / in funeral anthems / Die, my verse / die, like the rank and file," from "At the Top of My Voice" (1930), by the Russian poet Vladimir Mayakovski (1893–1930).

[3] The magician in Shakespeare's *Tempest* who abandons his magic.

[4] Alexander III (356–323 B.C.), king of Macedonia (336–323 B.C.) and conquerer of Asia Minor, Egypt, Babylon, and central Asia.

[5] Ginsberg has made a verb out of "epic."

[6] A building in which a nation's famous dead are entombed.

[7] A Roman copy of an original bronze statue (230–220 B.C.) of a dying warrior; the Gauls were Celtic peoples in Europe (1st to 5th centuries B.C.).

[8] The French painter Claude Monet (1840–1926), whose eyesight was failing in his later years; the German romantic composer Ludwig van Beethoven (1770–1827), who went deaf around 1819; the famous armless statue (150? B.C.) of Venus, Greek goddess of love; a headless sculpture (200–190 B.C.) of Nike of Samothrace, the winged Greek goddess of victory.

[9] A place or condition of great peace or bliss.

James Merrill
(1926–   )

James Merrill's career has long been an anomaly: he is a formalist in an age of free verse, a poet of technical elegance and virtuosity in an age of plain speech. Merrill was born in New York City in 1926 to Hellen Ingram and Charles Merrill, a wealthy financier who helped found the world-famous brokerage house Merrill, Lynch. James Merrill was just sixteen when his first book, a privately published collection entitled *Jim's Book* (1942), appeared. Since 1950, when his *First Poems* was published, Merrill has written books of poetry, novels, plays, and a collection of prose.

While Merrill was an undergraduate at Amherst College, he was deeply influenced by the French novelist Marcel Proust. Merrill has borrowed the Proustian usage of memory to analyze and liberate the true meaning of the past. Childhood typically surfaces as a subject for Merrill, as does daily home life. A sequence of seven sonnets, "The Broken Home" (1966), recounts the breakup of his parents' marriage against the backdrop of the country's charged atmosphere between the two world wars, a time when women lobbied for the vote, expatriatism became fashionable, and the battle between the sexes broke out on the domestic front: "Father Time and Mother Earth, / a marriage on the rocks."

Two of the volumes constituting the middle part of Merrill's career—*Nights and Days* (1960) and *The Fire Screen* (1964)—depict experiences in Greece, where Merrill spent part of each year, and in Stonington, Connecticut, a village on the Long Island Sound, where the poet made his American home. Although some of his work is continental, Merrill is a singularly American poet influenced as much by Americans such as Henry James as by the Greek poet C. P. Cavafy and by Proust. In the all-American collection *Braving the Elements* (1969), Merrill plays out his preoccupations in the context of America's Far West. In these books as in his earlier work, sensuous descriptions of the outside world are used to shed light on interior psychological states or truths. One of these truths, about which Merrill is increasingly frank, is his own homosexuality.

In 1977 Merrill received the Pulitzer Prize for poetry for *Divine Comedies,* which includes the long narrative *The Book of Ephraim. The Book of Ephraim* became the first part of his trilogy of book-length poems, *The Changing Light at Sandover* (1982). The other two parts are *Mirabell: Books of Number* (1978) and *Scripts for the Pageant* (1980). *The Changing Light* chronicles Merrill's experiments with a Ouija board (a device that supposedly conveys messages from spirits) to contact the dead, such as W. H. Auden and Marianne Moore. Felt by many to be Merrill's crowning achievement, *The Changing Light* is a massive, highly original and integrative work of the imagination. It represents the poet's courageous effort to locate all the sources of his creative nourishment: scientific theories, metaphysical occurrences, historical events, human beings, even life in other worlds.

Merrill's recent poems deal with concerns of age, the fits and starts of memory, and death. "Farewell Performance," from *The Inner Room* (1988), embraces each of these subjects, placing them in the context of a ballet. The poem is an elegy for Merrill's friend David Kalstone, a literary critic who died of AIDS in 1986. It expresses the restorative if transient nature of art, which "cures affliction."

Suggested Readings: *First Poems,* 1950. *The Seraglio,* 1957. *The (Diblos) Notebook,* 1965. *Nights and Days,* 1966. *Divine Comedies,* 1976. *The Changing Light at Sandover,* 1982. *Recitative,* 1986. D. Kalstone, *Five Temperaments,* 1977. J. Moffet, *James Merrill: An Introduction to the Poetry,*

1984. R. von Hallberg, "James Merrill: Revealing by Obscuring," in *American Poetry and Culture, 1945–1980*, 1985. S. Yenser, *The Consuming Myth: The Work of James Merrill*, 1987. H. Vendler, "James Merrill," in *The Music of What Happens*, 1988.

Texts Used: "Farewell Performance": *The Inner Room*, 1988. All else: *From the First Nine*, 1982.

CHARLES ON FIRE

Another evening we sprawled about discussing
Appearances. And it was the consensus
That while uncommon physical good looks
Continued to launch one, as before, in life
(Among its vaporous eddies and false calms),
Still, as one of us said into his beard,
"Without your intellectual and spiritual
Values, man, you are sunk." No one but squared
The shoulders of his own unloveliness.
Long-suffering Charles, having cooked and served the meal,   10
Now brought out little tumblers finely etched
He filled with amber liquor and then passed.
"Say," said the same young man, "in Paris, France,
They do it this way"—bounding to his feet
And touching a lit match to our host's full glass.
A blue flame, gentle, beautiful, came, went
Above the surface. In a hush that fell
We heard the vessel crack. The contents drained
As who should step down from a crystal coach.
Steward of spirits, Charles's glistening hand   20
All at once gloved itself in eeriness.
The moment passed. He made two quick sweeps and
Was flesh again. "It couldn't matter less,"
He said, but with a shocked, unconscious glance
Into the mirror. Finding nothing changed,
He filled a fresh glass and sank down among us.

1966

THE BROKEN HOME*

Crossing the street,
I saw the parents and the child
At their window, gleaming like fruit
With evening's mild gold leaf.

In a room on the floor below,
Sunless, cooler—a brimming

* About the marital breakup of Merrill's parents.

Saucer of wax, marbly and dim—
I have lit what's left of my life.

I have thrown out yesterday's milk
And opened a book of maxims.   10
The flame quickens. The word stirs.

Tell me, tongue of fire,
That you and I are as real
At least as the people upstairs.

My father, who had flown in World War I,
Might have continued to invest his life[1]
In cloud banks well above Wall Street and wife.
But the race was run below, and the point was to win.

Too late now, I make out in his blue gaze
(Through the smoked glass of being thirty-six)   20
The soul eclipsed by twin black pupils, sex
And business; time was money in those days.

Each thirteenth year he married. When he died
There were already several chilled wives
In sable orbit—rings, cars, permanent waves.
We'd felt him warming up for a green bride.

He could afford it. He was "in his prime"
At three score ten. But money was not time.

When my parents were younger this was a popular act:
A veiled woman would leap from an electric, wine-dark car   30
To the steps of no matter what—the Senate or the Ritz Bar—
And bodily, at newsreel speed, attack

No matter whom—Al Smith or José Maria Sert
Or Clemenceau[2]—veins standing out on her throat
As she yelled *War mongerer! Pig! Give us the vote!*,
And would have to be hauled away in her hobble skirt.

What had the man done? Oh, made history.
Her business (he had implied) was giving birth,
Tending the house, mending the socks.

---

[1] Merrill's father, Charles E. Merrill, founded the brokerage firm now known as Merrill, Lynch, Pierce, Fenner, and Smith.

[2] Alfred E. Smith (1873–1944), four times governor of New York and in 1928 the unsuccessful Democratic presidential candidate; Sert (1876–1945), the Spanish painter who decorated the lobby of New York City's Waldorf Astoria Hotel in 1930; Georges Clemenceau (1841–1929), premier of France during World War I.

Always that same old story— 40
Father Time and Mother Earth,[3]
A marriage on the rocks.

One afternoon, red, satyr-thighed[4]
Michael, the Irish setter, head
Passionately lowered, led
The child I was to a shut door. Inside,

Blinds beat sun from the bed.
The green-gold room throbbed like a bruise.
Under a sheet, clad in taboos
Lay whom we sought, her hair undone, outspread, 50

And of a blackness found, if ever now, in old
Engravings where the acid bit.
I must have needed to touch it
Or the whiteness—was she dead?
Her eyes flew open, startled strange and cold.
The dog slumped to the floor. She reached for me. I fled.

Tonight they have stepped out onto the gravel.
The party is over. It's the fall
Of 1931. They love each other still.

She: Charlie, I can't stand the pace. 60
He: Come on, honey—why, you'll bury us all!

A lead soldier guards my windowsill:
Khaki rifle, uniform, and face.
Something in me grows heavy, silvery, pliable.

How intensely people used to feel!
Like metal poured at the close of a proletarian novel,[5]
Refined and glowing from the crucible,
I see those two hearts, I'm afraid,
Still. Cool here in the graveyard of good and evil,
They are even so to be honored and obeyed. 70

. . . Obeyed, at least, inversely. Thus
I rarely buy a newspaper, or vote.
To do so, I have learned, is to invite
The tread of a stone guest[6] within my house.

---

[3] According to Greek myth, the supreme god Cronus and the supreme goddess, overthrown by their son, Zeus.

[4] Lustful; satyrs are goat-legged woodland deities of Greek myth.

[5] A novel about work; here, about iron and steel production.

[6] In the opera *Don Giovanni* (1787), by the Austrian composer Wolfgang Amadeus Mozart (1756–1791), the commander returns as a statue to seek revenge against Don Giovanni.

Shooting this rusted bolt, though, against him,
I trust I am no less time's child than some
Who on the heath impersonate Poor Tom[7]
Or on the barricades risk life and limb.

Nor do I try to keep a garden, only
An avocado in a glass of water—   80
Roots pallid, gemmed with air. And later,

When the small gilt leaves have grown
Fleshy and green, I let them die, yes, yes,
And start another. I am earth's no less.

A child, a red dog roam the corridors,
Still, of the broken home. No sound. The brilliant
Rag runners halt before wide-open doors.
My old room! Its wallpaper—cream, medallioned
With pink and brown—brings back the first nightmares,
Long summer colds, and Emma, sepia-faced,   90
Perspiring over broth carried upstairs
Aswim with golden fats I could not taste.

The real house became a boarding school.
Under the ballroom ceiling's allegory
Someone at last may actually be allowed
To learn something; or, from my window, cool
With the unstiflement of the entire story,
Watch a red setter stretch and sink in cloud.

1966

THE VICTOR DOG*

for Elizabeth Bishop[1]

Bix to Buxtehude to Boulez,[2]
The little white dog on the Victor label
Listens long and hard as he is able.
It's all in a day's work, whatever plays.

---

[7] Edgar in Shakespeare's *King Lear,* who was disowned by his father, the earl of Gloucester, and wanders the heath pretending to be mad.
* The emblem of RCA-Victor, the Radio Corporation of America; the dog is best known from the labels of phonograph records.
[1] The poet Bishop (1911–1979).
[2] Bix Beiderbecke (1903–1931), a jazz trumpeter; Dietrich Buxtehude (1637–1707), a Danish composer; Pierre Boulez (1925–   ), a French conductor and composer.

From judgment, it would seem, he has refrained.
He even listens earnestly to Bloch,[3]
Then builds a church upon our acid rock.
He's man's—no—he's the Leiermann's[4] best friend,

Or would be if hearing and listening were the same.
Does he hear? I fancy he rather smells   10
Those lemon-gold arpeggios in Ravel's
"Les jets d'eau du palais de ceux qui s'aiment."[5]

He ponders the Schumann[6] Concerto's tall willow hit
By lightning, and stays put. When he surmises
Through one of Bach's[7] eternal boxwood mazes
The oboe pungent as a bitch in heat,

Or when the calypso decants its raw bay rum
Or the moon in *Wozzeck*[8] reddens ripe for murder,
He doesn't sneeze or howl; just listens harder.
Adamant needles bear down on him from   20

Whirling of outer space, too black, too near—
But he was taught as a puppy not to flinch,
Much less to imitate his bête noire[9] Blanche
Who barked, fat foolish creature, at King Lear.

Still others fought in the road's filth over Jezebel,[10]
Slavered on hearths of horned and pelted barons.
His forebears lacked, to say the least, forbearance.
Can nature change in him? Nothing's impossible.

The last chord fades. The night is cold and fine.
His master's voice rasps through the grooves' bare groves.   30
Obediently, in silence like the grave's
He sleeps there on the still-warm gramophone[11]

---

[3] Ernest Bloch (1880–1959), a Swiss-born composer.

[4] *Der Leiermann,* or "The Organ-Grinder" (German), a song by the Austrian composer Franz Schubert (1797–1828).

[5] "The palace fountains of those who love each other" (French), from a song by the French composer Maurice Ravel (1875–1937); arpeggios are chords whose notes are played in quick succession rather than simultaneously.

[6] The German composer Robert Schumann (1810–1856).

[7] The German organist and composer Johann Sebastian Bach (1685–1750); in the seventeenth century oboes were commonly made of boxwood.

[8] A 1925 opera by the Austrian composer Alban Berg (1885–1935).

[9] "Black beast" (French); "The little dogs and all, / Tray, Blanche, and Sweetheart; see they bark at me," from Shakespeare's *King Lear*.

[10] In I Kings 21:5–23 and II Kings 9:30–37, the wicked wife of Ahab, king of Israel; when she died, her body was thrown into the street and eaten by dogs.

[11] A phonograph named in 1887 by Emile Berliner (1851–1929).

Only to dream he is at the première of a Handel
Opera long thought lost—*Il Cane Minore*.[12]
Its allegorical subject is his story!
A little dog revolving round a spindle

Gives rise to harmonies beyond belief,
A cast of stars. . . . Is there in Victor's heart
No honey for the vanquished? Art is art.
The life it asks of us is a dog's life.   40

1972

FAREWELL PERFORMANCE

for DK*

Art. It cures affliction. As lights go down and
Maestro lifts his wand, the unfailing sea change
starts within us. Limber alembics[1] once more
make of the common

lot a pure, brief gold. At the end our bravos
call them back, sweat-soldered and leotarded,
back, again back—anything not to face the
fact that it's over.

You are gone. You'd caught like a cold their airy
lust for essence. Now, in the furnace parched to   10
ten or twelve light handfuls, a mortal gravel
sifted through fingers,

coarse yet grayly glimmering sublimate of
palace days, Strauss, Sidney,[2] the lover's plaintive
Can't we just be friends? which your breakfast phone call
clothed in amusement,

this is what we paddled a neighbor's dinghy
out to scatter—Peter who grasped the buoy,
I who held the box underwater, freeing
all it contained. Past   20

---

[12] "*The Little Dog*" (Italian), an imaginary opera attributed to the German-born composer George Frederick Handel (1635–1759).
* David Kalstone (1932–1986), a literary critic and friend of Merrill's.
[1] Any devices that refine or purify.
[2] The German composer Richard Strauss (1864–1949); Sir Philip Sidney (1554–1586), an English courtier and poet who served on diplomatic missions for Elizabeth I (1533–1603), queen of England (1558–1603).

sunny, fluent soundings that gruel of selfhood
taking manlike shape for one last jeté on
ghostly—wait, ah!—point into darkness vanished.
High up, a gull's wings

clapped. The house lights (always supposing, caro,
Earth remains your house) at their brightest set the
scene for good: true colors, the sun-warm hand to
cover my wet one. . . .

Back they come. How you would have loved it. We in
turn have risen. Pity and terror done with,   30
programs furled, lips parted, we jostle forward
eager to hail them,

more, to join the troupe—will a friend enroll us
one fine day? Strange, though. For up close their magic
self-destructs. Pale, dripping, with downcast eyes they've
seen where it led you.

1988

Anne Sexton
(1928–1974)

Born Anne Harvey in 1928 in Newton, Massachusetts, Anne Sexton was a descendant of the Pilgrims. At an early age she wrote poetry but soon abandoned her efforts. In 1948, after briefly attending Garland Junior College, she married Alfred Sexton; they had two girls. Sexton suffered from, and was often hospitalized for, chronic acute depression; several times she attempted suicide. After the first attempt, one of her doctors suggested that she return to writing poetry, which she admitted gave her a feeling of purpose. After attending poetry workshops led by John Holmes and by Robert Lowell at Boston University, Sexton published her first book, *To Bedlam and Part Way Back* (1960). It describes her breakdown and life in a mental hospital and attempts to heal domestic wounds after her discharge. Because these poems tend to be harrowingly autobiographical, Sexton was, along with Lowell, Sylvia Plath, and W. D. Snodgrass, labeled a "confessional" poet. Like them she wrote poems chronicling her relationship to such raw subjects as mental breakdowns, guilt, madness, and suicide. In Sexton's work these subjects serve as vehicles by which to examine myth and religion, sin and redemption, love (both sexual and romantic) and its withdrawal, memory and the imagination.

In her early poems especially, Sexton was influenced by Theodore Roethke, Elizabeth Bishop, and May Swenson, in addition to Plath, Lowell, and Snodgrass. Sexton's early work met with almost immediate success. For *Live or Die* (1966) she received a Pulitzer

Prize. Yet, the critical reception of her work has varied. Some contemporary critics dismissed Sexton for her incomplete formal education and her unsparing exploration of subjects previously deemed improper for poetry. Others, however, praised her work for the same reasons. Early feminists saw in Sexton a spokesperson for their cause and particularly applauded the poems in *Transformations* (1971), which they saw as feminist reenactments of Grimm's fairy tales. Like some of her early admirers, more recent critics have acknowledged the poet's startling use of metaphor and imagery, perhaps in part the result of her many years in psychoanalysis.

Toward the end of Sexton's life, her own critical standards relaxed somewhat. Her later poems are less formal and intimate, more fluid and in some cases incantatory, than her early poems are. In 1974, depressed by the dissolution of her marriage and by fears that her creative powers were diminishing, Sexton committed suicide. She left behind a body of work that is highly original and compelling though sadly reflective of her slow emotional deterioration.

Suggested Readings: *To Bedlam and Part Way Back*, 1960. *All My Pretty Ones*, 1962. *Live or Die*, 1966. *Anne Sexton: A Self-Portrait in Letters*, 1977. *The Complete Poems*, 1981. *No Evil Star: Selected Essays, Interviews and Prose*, 1985. *Love Poems of Anne Sexton*, 1989. J. D. McClatchy, ed., *Anne Sexton: The Artist and Her Critics*, 1978. D. H. George, *Oedipus Anne: The Poetry of Anne Sexton*, 1987. S. E. Colburn, ed., *Anne Sexton: Telling the Tale*, 1988. D. H. George, *Sexton: Selected Criticism*, 1988. C. H. Barnard, *Anne Sexton*, 1989.

Text Used: *Selected Poems*, 1988.

KIND SIR: THESE WOODS

For a man needs only to be turned around once
with his eyes shut in this world to be lost. . . . Not
til we are lost . . . do we begin to find ourselves.
> —THOREAU, *Walden*[1]

Kind Sir: This is an old game
that we played when we were eight and ten.
Sometimes on The Island, in down Maine,
in late August, when the cold fog blew in
off the ocean, the forest between Dingley Dell[2]
and grandfather's cottage grew white and strange.
It was as if every pine tree were a brown pole
we did not know; as if day had rearranged
into night and bats flew in sun. It was a trick
to turn around once and know you were lost;   10
knowing the crow's horn was crying in the dark,
knowing that supper would never come, that the coast's
cry of doom from that far away bell buoy's bell
said *your nursemaid is gone*. O Mademoiselle,

---

[1] *Walden, or Life in the Woods* (1850), by Henry David Thoreau (1817–1862).
[2] A shady spot.

the rowboat rocked over. Then you were dead.
Turn around once, eyes tight, the thought in your head.

Kind Sir: Lost and of your same kind
I have turned around twice with my eyes sealed
and the woods were white and my night mind
saw such strange happenings, untold and unreal.   20
And opening my eyes, I am afraid of course
to look—this inward look that society scorns—
Still, I search in these woods and find nothing worse
than myself, caught between the grapes and the thorns.

1960

HER KIND

I have gone out, a possessed witch,
haunting the black air, braver at night;
dreaming evil, I have done my hitch
over the plain houses, light by light:
lonely thing, twelve-fingered,[1] out of mind.
A woman like that is not a woman, quite.
I have been her kind.

I have found the warm caves in the woods,
filled them with skillets, carvings, shelves,
closets, silks, innumerable goods;   10
fixed the suppers for the worms and the elves:
whining, rearranging the disaligned.
A woman like that is misunderstood.
I have been her kind.

I have ridden in your cart, driver,
waved my nude arms at villages going by,
learning the last bright routes, survivor
where your flames still bite my thigh
and my ribs crack where your wheels wind.
A woman like that is not ashamed to die.   20
I have been her kind.

1960

THE TRUTH THE DEAD KNOW

*For my mother, born March 1902, died March 1959,
and my father, born February 1900, died June 1959*

---

[1] Possession of a sixth finger per hand has been considered a sign of witchcraft.

Gone, I say and walk from church,
refusing the stiff procession to the grave,
letting the dead ride alone in the hearse.
It is June. I am tired of being brave.

We drive to the Cape.[1] I cultivate
myself where the sun gutters from the sky,
where the sea swings in like an iron gate
and we touch. In another country people die.

My darling, the wind falls in like stones
from the whitehearted water and when we touch   10
we enter touch entirely. No one's alone.
Men kill for this, or for as much.

And what of the dead? They lie without shoes
in their stone boats. They are more like stone
than the sea would be if it stopped. They refuse
to be blessed, throat, eye and knucklebone.

1962

ALL MY PRETTY ONES*

Father, this year's jinx rides us apart
where you followed our mother to her cold slumber;
a second shock boiling its stone to your heart,
leaving me here to shuffle and disencumber
you from the residence you could not afford:
a gold key, your half of a woolen mill,
twenty suits from Dunne's, an English Ford,
the love and legal verbiage of another will,
boxes of pictures of people I do not know.
I touch their cardboard faces. They must go.   10

But the eyes, as thick as wood in this album,
hold me. I stop here, where a small boy
waits in a ruffled dress for someone to come . . .
for this soldier who holds his bugle like a toy
or for this velvet lady who cannot smile.
Is this your father's father, this commodore
in a mailman suit? My father, time meanwhile
has made it unimportant who you are looking for.
I'll never know what these faces are all about.
I lock them into their book and throw them out.   20

[1] Cape Cod.
* From Shakespeare's *Macbeth* (IV. iii. 216): Macduff's response upon learning that Macbeth has
had his wife and children murdered.

This is the yellow scrapbook that you began
the year I was born; as crackling now and wrinkly
as tobacco leaves: clippings where Hoover[1] outran
the Democrats, wiggling his dry finger at me
and Prohibition; news where the *Hindenburg*[2] went
down and recent years where you went flush
on war. This year, solvent but sick, you meant
to marry that pretty widow in a one-month rush.
But before you had that second chance, I cried
on your fat shoulder. Three days later you died.   30

These are the snapshots of marriage, stopped in places.
Side by side at the rail toward Nassau[3] now;
here, with the winner's cup at the speedboat races,
here, in tails at the Cotillion,[4] you take a bow,
here, by our kennel of dogs with their pink eyes,
running like show-bred pigs in their chain-link pen;
here, at the horseshow where my sister wins a prize;
and here, standing like a duke among groups of men.
Now I fold you down, my drunkard, my navigator,
my first lost keeper, to love or look at later.   40

I hold a five-year diary that my mother kept
for three years, telling all she does not say
of your alcoholic tendency. You overslept,
she writes. My God, father, each Christmas Day
with your blood, will I drink down your glass
of wine? The diary of your hurly-burly years
goes to my shelf to wait for my age to pass.
Only in this hoarded span will love persevere.
Whether you are pretty or not, I outlive you,
bend down my strange face to yours and forgive you.   50

1962

FOR MY LOVER, RETURNING TO HIS WIFE

She is all there.
She was melted carefully down for you
and cast up from your childhood,
cast up from your one hundred favorite aggies.[1]

---

[1] Herbert Hoover (1874–1964), the Republican candidate for president in 1928, who won a landslide victory over his democratic rival, Alfred E. Smith (1873–1944), and served as the thirty-first U.S. president (1929–1933); Prohibition was in effect until shortly after he left office.

[2] The helium-filled passenger blimp that crashed in Lakehurst, New Jersey, in 1937 after exploding in midair.

[3] The capital of the Bahama Islands.

[4] A formal ball; generally one at which debutantes are introduced.

[1] Agate marbles.

She has always been there, my darling.
She is, in fact, exquisite.
Fireworks in the dull middle of February
and as real as a cast-iron pot.

Let's face it, I have been momentary.
A luxury. A bright red sloop in the harbor.   10
My hair rising like smoke from the car window.
Littleneck clams out of season.
She is more than that. She is your have to have,
has grown you your practical your tropical growth.
This is not an experiment. She is all harmony.
She sees to oars and oarlocks for the dinghy,

has placed wild flowers at the window at breakfast,
sat by the potter's wheel at midday,
set forth three children under the moon,
three cherubs drawn by Michelangelo,[2]   20

done this with her legs spread out
in the terrible months in the chapel.
If you glance up, the children are there
like delicate balloons resting on the ceiling.

She has also carried each one down the hall
after supper, their heads privately bent,
two legs protesting, person to person,
her face flushed with a song and their little sleep.

I give you back your heart.
I give you permission—   30

for the fuse inside her, throbbing
angrily in the dirt, for the bitch in her
and the burying of her wound—
for the burying of her small red wound alive—

for the pale flickering flare under her ribs,
for the drunken sailor who waits in her left pulse,
for the mother's knee, for the stockings,
for the garter belt, for the call—

the curious call
when you will burrow in arms and breasts   40
and tug at the orange ribbon in her hair
and answer the call, the curious call.

---

[2] The Italian Renaissance painter, architect, and poet Michelangelo Buonarroti (1475–1564), who executed the ceiling decorations for the Sistine Chapel (1508–1512) in Rome.

She is so naked and singular.
She is the sum of yourself and your dream.
Climb her like a monument, step after step.
She is solid.

As for me, I am a watercolor.
I wash off.

1969

US

I was wrapped in black
fur and white fur and
you undid me and then
you placed me in gold light
and then you crowned me,
while snow fell outside
the door in diagonal darts.
While a ten-inch snow
came down like stars
in small calcium fragments,   10
we were in our own bodies
(that room that will bury us)
and you were in my body
(that room that will outlive us)
and at first I rubbed your
feet dry with a towel
because I was your slave
and then you called me princess.
Princess!

Oh then   20
I stood up in my gold skin
and I beat down the psalms
and I beat down the clothes
and you undid the bridle
and you undid the reins
and I undid the buttons,
the bones, the confusions,
the New England postcards,
the January ten o'clock night,
and we rose up like wheat,   30
acre after acre of gold,
and we harvested,
we harvested.

1969

from   THE FURIES*

THE FURY OF BEAUTIFUL BONES

Sing me a thrush, bone.
Sing me a nest of cup and pestle.
Sing me a sweetbread for an old grandfather.
Sing me a foot and a doorknob, for you are my love.
Oh sing, bone bag man, sing.
Your head is what I remember that August,
you were in love with another woman but
that didn't matter. I was the fury of your
bones, your fingers long and nubby, your
forehead a beacon, bare as marble and I worried   10
you like an odor because you had not quite forgotten,
bone bag man, garlic in the North End,[1]
the book you dedicated, naked as a fish,
naked as someone drowning into his own mouth.
I wonder, Mr. Bone man, what you're thinking
of your fury[2] now, gone sour as a sinking whale,
crawling up the alphabet on her own bones.
Am I in your ear still singing songs in the rain,
me of the death rattle, me of the magnolias,
me of the sawdust tavern at the city's edge.   20
Women have lovely bones, arms, neck, thigh
and I admire them also, but your bones
supersede loveliness. They are the tough
ones that get broken and reset. I just can't
answer for you, only for your bones,
round rulers, round nudgers, round poles,
numb nubkins, the sword of sugar.
I feel the skull, Mr. Skeleton, living its
own life in its own skin.

1974

James Wright
(1927–1980)

Born in the steel-mill town of Martins Ferry, Ohio, in 1927 and raised in part on a small farm nearby, James Arlington Wright maintained throughout his life a feel for the lonely, isolated individuals that populated the American Midwest of his childhood. Consciously

---

* According to Greek myth, the three goddesses of vengeance.
[1] A predominantly Italian section of Boston.   [2] Sexton herself.

forging his early style "in the mode of Edward Arlington Robinson and Robert Frost," Wright said in a 1972 *Southern Humanities Review* interview that he "wanted to make the poems say something humanely important instead of just showing off with language." What Wright's early poems "say" is typically something in sympathy with the quiet but noble suffering of those who exist outside of, or apart from, society. In "American Twilights, 1957" (1959), a poem dedicated to the convicted murderer Caryl Chessman, Wright even prays that God will "have pity if he wake, / Have mercy on a man who dreamed apart."

After publishing *The Green Wall* (1957) and *Saint Judas* (1959), Wright translated the works of the South American poets Pablo Neruda and César Vallejo and of the Austrian poet Georg Trakl while consciously seeking to change his own poetic style. As a result Wright's later poetry moves away from his earlier focus on character to share the surrealistic juxtaposing of images found in these poets' works as well as their concern for the political and the social. Concentrating still on both the beauty and the squalor of the poor and the neglected, Wright adopted a more open form in order to accommodate a broader stance toward place and country. Without ever wholly abandoning the local or the native—"I was born in Ohio. / I still dream of home," he says in "Stages on a Journey Westward" (1963)—Wright's later poetry examines an America that is "over and done with." Torn between loving his country and despising the way it treats its own people and natural setting, Wright explores the notions of individual responsibility and guilt in a landscape that sometimes threatens and sometimes consoles.

Wright won a Pulitzer Prize in 1972 for his *Collected Poems* (1971), which contains work from his first four books of poetry and his translations of Neruda, Vallejo, Trakl, and others. A powerful collection of Wright's best work, *Collected Poems* earned praise for him as "a visionary not with an unearthly or heavenly vision, but a human vision," in the words of the poet James Dickey from the volume's book jacket. Wright married Anne Runk in the early 1970s, his second marriage. His relationship with his new wife and their travels abroad combine with Wright's own coming to grips with both his alcoholism and his American past to form the core of a body of work that has received divided critical appraisal. Still, *Two Citizens* (1973), *Moments of an Italian Summer* (1976), and *To a Blossoming Pear Tree* (1977) all evidence Wright's continued devotion to exploring the desperate beauty he found around him. "I do not have a talent for happiness," Wright said in a 1975 interview for the *Paris Review*. "I tried to come to terms with that in the clearest most ferociously perfect form that I could find and in all the traditional ways." He continued writing poetry until his death at age fifty-three from throat cancer in 1980, and several collections of his work were published posthumously.

Suggested Readings: *Two Citizens,* 1973. *Moments of an Italian Summer,* 1976. *To a Blossoming Pear Tree,* 1977. *The Temple in Nimes,* 1982. *The Shape of Light: Prose Poems,* 1986. J. Seay, "A World Immeasurably Alive and Good: A Look at James Wright's *Collected Poems,*" in *Georgia Review,* 27, (Spring) 1973. G. S. Lensing and R. Moran, *Four Poets and the Emotive Imagination: Robert Bly, James Wright, Louis Simpson, and William Stafford,* 1976. J. Ditsky, "James Wright Collected: Alterations on the Monument," in *Modern Poetry Studies,* 2, 1979. D. Smith, *The Pure Clear World,* 1982.

Texts Used: "Wherever Home Is": *This Journey,* 1982. All else: *Collected Poems,* 1971.

SAINT JUDAS*

When I went out to kill myself, I caught
A pack of hoodlums beating up a man.
Running to spare his suffering, I forgot
My name, my number, how my day began,
How soldiers milled around the garden stone
And sang amusing songs; how all that day
Their javelins measured crowds; how I alone
Bargained the proper coins, and slipped away.

Banished from heaven, I found this victim beaten,
Stripped, kneed, and left to cry. Dropping my rope   10
Aside, I ran, ignored the uniforms:
Then I remembered bread my flesh had eaten,
The kiss that ate my flesh. Flayed without hope,
I held the man for nothing in my arms.

1951

ALL THE BEAUTIFUL ARE BLAMELESS

Out of a dark into the dark she leaped
Lightly this day.
Heavy with prey, the evening skiffs[1] are gone,
And drowsy divers lift their helmets off,
Dry on the shore.

Two stupid harly-charlies got her drunk
And took her swimming naked on the lake.
The waters rippled lute-like round the boat,
And far beyond them, dipping up and down,
Unmythological sylphs,[2] their names unknown,   10
Beckoned to sandbars where the evenings fall.

Only another drunk would say she heard
A natural voice
Luring the flesh across the water.
I think of those unmythological
Sylphs of the trees.

---

* Judas Iscariot, the disciple who betrayed Jesus for thirty pieces of silver (see Matthew 26:14, 48).
Wright conflates the story of Judas with that of the Good Samaritan (see Luke 10:30–37).
    [1] Light rowboats.
    [2] According to the alchemical system of the Swiss physician Paracelsus (1493–1541), soulless beings
that inhabit the air.

Slight but orplidean³ shoulders weave in dusk
Before my eyes when I walk lonely forward
To kick beer-cans from tracked declivities.
If I, being lightly sane, may carve a mouth   20
Out of the air to kiss, the drowned girl surely
Listened to lute-song where the sylphs are gone.
The living and the dead glide hand in hand
Under cool waters where the days are gone.
Out of the dark into a dark I stand.

The ugly curse the world and pin my arms
Down by their grinning teeth, sneering a blame.
Closing my eyes, I look for hungry swans
To plunder the lake and bear the girl away,
Back to the larger waters where the sea   30
Sifts, judges, gathers the body, and subsides.

But here the starved, touristic crowd divides
And offers the dead
Hell for the living body's evil:
The girl flopped in the water like a pig
And drowned dead drunk.

So do the pure defend themselves. But she,
Risen to kiss the sky, her limbs still whole,
Rides on the dark tarpaulin toward the shore;
And the hired saviours turn their painted shell   40
Along the wharf, to list her human name.
But the dead have no names, they lie so still,
And all the beautiful are blameless now.

1951

ARRANGEMENTS WITH EARTH FOR
THREE DEAD FRIENDS

Sweet earth, he ran and changed his shoes to go
Outside with other children through the fields.
He panted up the hills and swung from trees
Wild as a beast but for the human laughter
That tumbled like a cider down his cheeks.
Sweet earth, the summer has been gone for weeks,
And weary fish already sleeping under water
Below the banks where early acorns freeze.
Receive his flesh and keep it cured of colds.
Button his coat and scarf his throat from snow.   10

³ Probably coined by Wright.

And now, bright earth, this other is out of place
In what, awake, we speak about as tombs.
He sang in houses when the birds were still
And friends of his were huddled round till dawn
After the many nights to hear him sing.
Bright earth, his friends remember how he sang
Voices of night away when wind was one.
Lonely the neighborhood beneath your hill
Where he is waved away through silent rooms.
Listen for music, earth, and human ways.   20

Dark earth, there is another gone away,
But she was not inclined to beg of you
Relief from water falling or the storm.
She was aware of scavengers in holes
Of stone, she knew the loosened stones that fell
Indifferently as pebbles plunging down a well
And broke for the sake of nothing human souls.
Earth, hide your face from her where dark is warm.
She does not beg for anything, who knew
The change of tone, the human hope gone gray.   30

1957

THE ANGEL

Last night, before I came to bear
The clean edge of my wing upon the boulder,
I walked about the town.
The people seemed at peace that he was dead:
A beggar carried water out of a door,
And young men gathered round the corner
To spell the night.

I walked, like a folded bird, about the towers
And sang softly to the blue levels of evening
I slid down treeless, featherless, bemused: 10
At curious faces whispering round a fire
And sniffing chestnuts sugared by a woman;
At a vague child heaving a beetle over
In dust, to see it swimming on its back.

Under an arch I found a woman lean
Weeping for loneliness: away from her
A young man whistle toward the crowds;
Out of an open window pigeons flew

And a slow dove fluted for nothing—the girl
Blew to the air a melody lost on me.   20

Laid in a pile of stone, how could he weep
For that calm town?
Looped in a yoke of darkened garden,
He murmured blood out of his heart for love,
Hallowed a soldier, took the savage kiss
And gave it back a warm caress;

Yet no one changed.

Tossing aside the worry of the place,
As someone threw an apple core across
A wall I walked beside, I sought delight   30
Pebble by pebble, song by song, and light
By light, singly, among the river boats.
Down to the river at the end I came.

But then a girl appeared, to wash her hair.
Struck stupid by her face,
I stood there, sick to love her, sick of sky.
The child, the beetle, chestnut fires, the song
Of girl and dove
Shuddered along my wings and arms.
She slipped her bodice off, and a last wave   40
Of shadow oiled her shoulder till it shone;
Lifting her arms to loosen the soft braids
She looked across the water. I looked down
And felt my wings waving aside the air,
Furious to fly. For I could never bear
Belly and breast and thigh against the ground.

Now, having heaved the hidden hollow open
As I was sent to do, seen Jesus waken
And guided the women there, I wait to rise.
To feel a weapon gouge between the ribs,   50
He hung with a shut mouth:
For curious faces round a chestnut fire,
For the slow fluting doves
Lost on a trellis, for the laughing girl
Who frightened me away.

But now I fumble at the single joy
Of dawn. On the pale ruffle of the lake
The ripples weave a color I can bear.
Under a hill I see the city sleep
And fade. The perfect pleasure of the eyes: 60

A tiny bird bathed in a bowl of air,
Carving a yellow ripple down the bines,
Posing no storm to blow my wings aside
As I drift upward dropping a white feather.

1957

HAVING LOST MY SONS, I CONFRONT
THE WRECKAGE OF THE MOON: CHRISTMAS, 1960

After dark
Near the South Dakota border,
The moon is out hunting, everywhere,
Delivering fire,
And walking down hallways
Of a diamond.

Behind a tree,
It lights on the ruins
Of a white city:
Frost, frost.   10

Where are they gone,
Who lived there?

Bundled away under wings
And dark faces.

I am sick
Of it, and I go on,
Living, alone, alone,
Past the charred silos, past the hidden graves
Of Chippewas and Norwegians.[1]

This cold winter   20
Moon spills the inhuman fire
Of jewels
Into my hands.

Dead riches, dead hands, the moon
Darkens,
And I am lost in the beautiful white ruins
Of America.

1963

[1] Many settlers in the Dakotas had emigrated from Norway.

A BLESSING

Just off the highway to Rochester, Minnesota,
Twilight bounds softly forth on the grass.
And the eyes of those two Indian ponies
Darken with kindness.
They have come gladly out of the willows
To welcome my friend and me.
We step over the barbed wire into the pasture
Where they have been grazing all day, alone.
They ripple tensely, they can hardly contain their happiness
That we have come.   10
They bow shyly as wet swans. They love each other.
There is no loneliness like theirs.
At home once more,
They begin munching the young tufts of spring in the darkness.
I would like to hold the slenderer one in my arms,
For she has walked over to me
And nuzzled my left hand.
She is black and white,
Her mane falls wild on her forehead,
And the light breeze moves me to caress her long ear   20
That is delicate as the skin over a girl's wrist.
Suddenly I realize
That if I stepped out of my body I would break
Into blossom.

1963

LYING IN A HAMMOCK AT WILLIAM DUFFY'S FARM IN PINE ISLAND, MINNESOTA

Over my head, I see the bronze butterfly,
Asleep on the black trunk,
Blowing like a leaf in green shadow.
Down the ravine behind the empty house,
The cowbells follow one another
Into the distances of the afternoon.
To my right,
In a field of sunlight between two pines,
The droppings of last year's horses
Blaze up into golden stones.   10
I lean back, as the evening darkens and comes on.
A chicken hawk floats over, looking for home.
I have wasted my life.

1963

AUTUMN BEGINS IN MARTINS FERRY, OHIO

In the Shreve High football stadium,
I think of Polacks nursing long beers in Tiltonsville,[1]
And gray faces of Negroes in the blast furnace at Benwood,[2]
And the ruptured[3] night watchman of Wheeling Steel,
Dreaming of heroes.

All the proud fathers are ashamed to go home.
Their women cluck like starved pullets,[4]
Dying for love.

Therefore,
Their sons grow suicidally beautiful   10
At the beginning of October,
And gallop terribly against each other's bodies.

                                                              1963

IN RESPONSE TO A RUMOR THAT
THE OLDEST WHOREHOUSE IN WHEELING,
WEST VIRGINIA, HAS BEEN CONDEMNED

I will grieve alone,
As I strolled alone, years ago, down along
The Ohio shore.
I hid in the hobo jungle weeds
Upstream from the sewer main,
Pondering, gazing.

I saw, down river,
At Twenty-third and Water Streets
By the vinegar works,
The doors open in early evening.   10
Swinging their purses, the women
Poured down the long street to the river
And into the river.

I do not know how it was
They could drown every evening.
What time near dawn did they climb up the other shore,
Drying their wings?

---

[1] A town in eastern Ohio, north of Martins Ferry.
[2] A town south of Martins Ferry, the site of the Wheeling Steel Works.
[3] Herniated.   [4] Young hens.

For the river at Wheeling, West Virginia,
Has only two shores:
The one in hell, the other   20
In Bridgeport, Ohio.

And nobody would commit suicide, only
To find beyond death
Bridgeport, Ohio.

1968

SMALL FROGS KILLED ON THE HIGHWAY

Still,
I would leap too
Into the light,
If I had the chance.
It is everything, the wet green stalk of the field
On the other side of the road.
They crouch there, too, faltering in terror
And take strange wing. Many
Of the dead never moved, but many
Of the dead are alive forever in the split second   10
Auto headlights more sudden
Than their drivers know.
The drivers burrow backward into dank pools
Where nothing begets
Nothing.

Across the road, tadpoles are dancing
On the quarter thumbnail
Of the moon. They can't see,
Not yet.

1971

WHEREVER HOME IS

Leonardo da Vinci, haggard in basalt stone,[1]
Will soon be gone,
A frivolous face lost in wisteria flowers.
They are turning gray and dying
All over his body.
Subtlest of all wanderers

---

[1] A statue of Leonardo da Vinci (1452–1519), the Italian Renaissance painter, sculptor, architect, engineer, and scientist.

Who live beautifully by living on other lives,
They cannot find a warm vein
In Leonardo, and Leonardo
Himself will soon   10
Be gone.

Good riddance a little while to the insane.
Although the wisteria gets nowhere
And the sea wind crumbles Leonardo down,
A new lizard frolics in the cold sunlight
Between Leonardo's thumb and his palette.
One brief lizard
Lavishes on Leonardo and on me
The whole spring.

Goodbye to Leonardo, good riddance   20
To decaying madmen who cannot keep alive
The wanderers among trees.
I am going home with the lizard,
Wherever home is,
And lie beside him unguarded
In the clear sunlight.
We will lift our faces even if it rains.
We will both turn green.

1977

John Ashbery
(1927–   )

More than any of his contemporaries, John Ashbery explores through the tenor of his
poems what might be called the vehicle of imagination: the vast possibilities of imagination as a habit of mind and a habit of language. His nontraditional poems encompass advertisement and cliché, popular song and the history of poetry, as well as original thoughts
and ideas. Ashbery's work reflects all that the twentieth century offers. It has been said
that his poetry suffers from an intensely private dialogue with the self, that only Ashbery
can understand Ashbery; it has been argued that the poet's dialogue with the self covers all
possible subjects at once. Even a cursory reading reveals the inclusiveness of Ashbery's
poems, most of which require numerous readings.

   Like Scheherazade (the title of a 1985 Ashbery poem), the narrator of the ancient tales
of *The Arabian Nights* who told continuously open-ended stories to save herself from execution, Ashbery constructs tales that flow one into the next. Scheherazade and the cartoon
character Popeye (in the sestina "Farm Implements and Rutabagas in a Landscape" [1985])
flow into and out of the novelist Gertrude Stein and the poet Andrew Marvell, who in turn

flow into and out of the painters Jackson Pollack and Parmigianino. Ashbery, a noted art historian and art critic, alludes as naturally to art and artists as to the artifacts of daily life and popular culture. The artistic movements of surrealism and abstract expressionism strongly influence his writings.

This all-encompassing approach, with its borrowings and abstractions, places Ashbery firmly in line with the modernism of Ezra Pound, T. S. Eliot, and Marianne Moore. Yet, Ashbery's "respect for things as they are" (to borrow the title of his 1982 essay on the artist Fairfield Porter) suggests that the poet is ultimately less modern than postmodern. By and large, Ashbery's poetry resists explication. It is as much about the process and experience of reading as it is about the process and experience of writing, with both reader and poet engaged in a common act of perception. Ashbery's poems seem to absorb all that falls under the poet's attention.

Dazzling and difficult, Ashbery's poetry has not always met with critical regard. Although his first volume, *Some Trees* (1956), was selected by the poet W. H. Auden for the Yale Series of Younger Poets (an award given only to poets under age forty), its poems baffled some critics and most readers. During the 1950s Ashbery was a "member," along with James Schuyler and Frank O'Hara, of the so-called New York school of poetry, a response to the New York school of abstract art.

The Tennis Court Oath (1962), Ashbery's second volume of poems, shows the influence of Wallace Stevens. Ashbery's "Painter," for example, echoes Stevens's "Idea of Order at Key West" (1936). Although the comparison of Ashbery to Stevens is a common one, few American poets writing in the last half of the twentieth century have escaped that comparison. Ashbery seemed, at first, either unwilling or unable to conceal the influence, but as his work progressed he lost those echoes and the sentimentality that tends to come of such imitation. However, his poems lost none of the flash, the verbal and philosophical acrobatics, that characterize his early work; the recent poems seem less contrived and more relaxed. They are also less formal, largely abandoning rhyme and meter for forms much more fluid and even experimental. Ashbery's prose poems, though comparatively few in number, are among his best. His book *Three Poems* (1972) consists of three extended prose poems.

Ashbery's most celebrated work is the introspective "Self-Portrait in a Convex Mirror," the title poem of his 1975 book that won a Pulitzer Prize, the National Book Award, and the National Book Critics' Circle Award. As the title suggests, that poem is an extended meditation on the natures of art and the self. The poet's formal explorations continued in *Shadow Train* (1981), a volume of sixteen-line poems that in their logic and composition resemble the sonnet, though they are unrhymed and lack regular meter.

In recent years, Ashbery's attention has turned to the issues of age, death, and memory, as in "Forgotten Sex," from *April Galleons* (1987). Although some critics have seen it as Ashbery's tribute to those who have died of AIDS, the poem functions, as do all of his poems, on a much less specific level. "Forgotten Sex" suggests a special place and time out of which a world is created, a world in which "Sweetness of things late, a memory for particulars / As lively as though they happened still" looms large.

Born in Rochester, New York, in 1927, Ashbery was educated at Harvard, Columbia, and New York universities. For a number of years he lived in France, first as a Fulbright scholar and later as an art critic and a literary critic. But Ashbery moved back to New York in 1965 and became an art critic for *Newsweek*. His literary contributions go beyond poetry and criticism: he co-authored the novel *A Nest of Ninnies* (1969) with James Schuyler and wrote the one-act plays *The Heroes* (1952) and *The Philosopher* (1962) as well as the three-act *Compromise* (1956).

Suggested Readings: *Some Trees,* 1956. *A Nest of Ninnies,* with J. Schuyler, 1969. *Three Poems,* 1972. *Self-Portrait in a Convex Mirror,* 1975. *Shadow Train,* 1981. D. Kalstone, *Five Tempera-ments,* 1977. D. Lehman, ed., *Beyond Amazement: New Essays on John Ashbery,* 1980. R. von Hallberg, "Robert Creeley and John Ashbery: Systems," in *American Poetry and Culture, 1945–1980,* 1985. A. Corn, "A Magma of Interiors: John Ashbery's 'Self-Portrait in a Convex Mirror,'" in *The Metamorphoses of Metaphor,* 1987. H. Vendler, "John Ashbery, Louise Glück," in *The Music of What Happens,* 1988.

Texts Used: "Forgotten Sex," "Frost," and "Someone You Have Seen Before": *April Galleons,* 1988. All else: *Selected Poems,* 1985.

SOME TREES

These are amazing: each
Joining a neighbor, as though speech
Were a still performance.
Arranging by chance

To meet as far this morning
From the world as agreeing
With it, you and I
Are suddenly what the trees try

To tell us we are:
That their merely being there   10
Means something; that soon
We may touch, love, explain.

And glad not to have invented
Such comeliness, we are surrounded:
A silence already filled with noises,
A canvas on which emerges

A chorus of smiles, a winter morning.
Placed in a puzzling light, and moving,
Our days put on such reticence
These accents seem their own defense.   20

1956

THE PAINTER

Sitting between the sea and the buildings
He enjoyed painting the sea's portrait.
But just as children imagine a prayer
Is merely silence, he expected his subject
To rush up the sand, and, seizing a brush,
Plaster its own portrait on the canvas.

So there was never any paint on his canvas
Until the people who lived in the buildings
Put him to work: "Try using the brush
As a means to an end. Select, for a portrait,   10
Something less angry and large, and more subject
To a painter's moods, or, perhaps, to a prayer."

How could he explain to them his prayer
That nature, not art, might usurp the canvas?
He chose his wife for a new subject,
Making her vast, like ruined buildings,
As if, forgetting itself, the portrait
Had expressed itself without a brush.

Slightly encouraged, he dipped his brush
In the sea, murmuring a heartfelt prayer: 20
"My soul, when I paint this next portrait
Let it be you who wrecks the canvas."
The news spread like wildfire through the buildings:
He had gone back to the sea for his subject.

Imagine a painter crucified by his subject!
Too exhausted even to lift his brush,
He provoked some artists leaning from the buildings
To malicious mirth: "We haven't a prayer
Now, of putting ourselves on canvas,
Or getting the sea to sit for a portrait!"   30

Others declared it a self-portrait.
Finally all indications of a subject
Began to fade, leaving the canvas
Perfectly white. He put down the brush.
At once a howl, that was also a prayer,
Arose from the overcrowded buildings.

They tossed him, the portrait, from the tallest of the building
And the sea devoured the canvas and the brush
As though his subject had decided to remain a prayer.

1956

RIVERS AND MOUNTAINS

On the secret map the assassins
Cloistered, the Moon River was marked
Near the eighteen peaks and the city
Of humiliation and defeat—wan ending
Of the trail among dry, papery leaves
Gray-brown quills like thoughts

In the melodious but vast mass of today's
Writing through fields and swamps
Marked, on the map, with little bunches of weeds.
Certainly squirrels lived in the woods   10
But devastation and dull sleep still
Hung over the land, quelled
The rioters turned out of sleep in the peace of prisons
Singing on marble factory walls
Deaf consolation of minor tunes that pack
The air with heavy invisible rods
Pent in some sand valley from
Which only quiet walking ever instructs.
The bird flew over and
Sat—there was nothing else to do.   20
Do not mistake its silence for pride or strength
Or the waterfall for a harbor
Full of light boats that is there
Performing for thousands of people
In clothes some with places to go
Or games. Sometimes over the pillar
Of square stones its impact
Makes a light print.

So going around cities
To get to other places you found   30
It all on paper but the land
Was made of paper processed
To look like ferns, mud or other
Whose sea unrolled its magic
Distances and then rolled them up
Its secret was only a pocket
After all but some corners are darker
Than these moonless nights spent as on a raft
In the seclusion of a melody heard
As though through trees   40
And you can never ignite their touch
Long but there were homes
Flung far out near the asperities
Of a sharp, rocky pinnacle
And other collective places
Shadows of vineyards whose wine
Tasted of the forest floor
Fisheries and oyster beds
Tides under the pole
Seminaries of instruction, public   50
Places for electric light
And the major tax assessment area
Wrinkled on the plan
Of election to public office
Sixty-two years old bath and breakfast

The formal traffic, shadows
To make it not worth joining
After the ox had pulled away the cart.
Your plan was to separate the enemy into two groups
With the razor-edged mountains between.   60
It worked well on paper
But their camp had grown
To be the mountains and the map
Carefully peeled away and not torn
Was the light, a tender but tough bark
On everything. Fortunately the war was solved
In another way by isolating the two sections
Of the enemy's navy so that the mainland
Warded away the big floating ships.
Light bounced off the ends   70
Of the small gray waves to tell
Them in the observatory
About the great drama that was being won
To turn off the machinery
And quietly move among the rustic landscape
Scooping snow off the mountains rinsing
The coarser ones that love had
Slowly risen in the night to overflow
Wetting pillow and petal
Determined to place the letter   80
On the unassassinated president's desk
So that a stamp could reproduce all this
In detail, down to the last autumn leaf
And the affliction of June ride
Slowly out into the sun-blackened landscape.

1966

FOR JOHN CLARE*

Kind of empty in the way it sees everything, the earth gets to its feet and salutes the sky. More of a success at it this time than most others it is. The feeling that the sky might be in the back of someone's mind. Then there is no telling how many there are. They grace everything—bush and tree—to take the roisterer's mind off his caroling—so it's like a smooth switch back. To what was aired in their previous conniption fit. There is so much to be seen everywhere that it's like not getting used to it, only there is so much it never feels new, never any different. You are standing looking at that building and you cannot take it all in, certain details are already hazy and the mind boggles. What will it all be like in five years' time when you try to remember? Will there have been boards in between the grass part and the edge of the street? As long as that couple is stopping to look in that win-

---

* Clare (1793–1864), an English romantic poet, was the son of peasant farmers; he grew up in extreme poverty and spent his last twenty-three years in an insane asylum. The poem is in prose form.

dow over there we cannot go. We feel like they have to tell us we can, but they never look our way and they are already gone, gone far into the future—the night of time. If we could look at a photograph of it and say there they are, they never really stopped but there they are. There is so much to be said, and on the surface of it very little gets said.

There ought to be room for more things, for a spreading out, like. Being immersed in the details of rock and field and slope—letting them come to you for once, and then meeting them halfway would be so much easier—if they took an ingenuous pride in being in one's blood. Alas, we perceive them if at all as those things that were meant to be put aside—costumes of the supporting actors or voice trilling at the end of a narrow enclosed street. You can do nothing with them. Not even offer to pay.

It is possible that finally, like coming to the end of a long, barely perceptible rise, there is mutual cohesion and interaction. The whole scene is fixed in your mind, the music all present, as though you could see each note as well as hear it. I say this because there is an uneasiness in things just now. Waiting for something to be over before you are forced to notice it. The pollarded trees[1] scarcely bucking the wind—and yet it's keen, it makes you fall over. Clabbered sky.[2] Seasons that pass with a rush. After all it's their time too—nothing says they aren't to make something of it. As for Jenny Wren, she cares, hopping about on her little twig like she was tryin' to tell us somethin', but that's just it, she couldn't even if she wanted to—dumb bird. But the others—and they in some way must know too—it would never occur to them to want to, even if they could take the first step of the terrible journey toward feeling somebody should act, that ends in utter confusion and hopelessness, east of the sun and west of the moon. So their comment is "No comment." Meanwhile the whole history of probabilities is coming to life, starting in the upper left-hand corner, like a sail.

1966

FARM IMPLEMENTS AND RUTABAGAS
IN A LANDSCAPE*

The first of the undecoded messages read: "Popeye[1] sits in thunder,
Unthought of. From that shoebox of an apartment,
From livid curtain's hue, a tangram emerges: a country."
Meanwhile the Sea Hag was relaxing on a green couch: "How pleasant
To spend one's vacation *en la casa de Popeye*,"[2] she scratched
Her cleft chin's solitary hair. She remembered spinach

And was going to ask Wimpy if he had bought any spinach.
"M'love," he intercepted, "the plains are decked out in thunder

---

[1] Trees that have been cut back at the top to stimulate thicker growth.
[2] Resembling thicky curdled sour milk.
* A spoof of titles traditionally given to landscape paintings.
[1] All names in the poem are those of characters in the Popeye comic strip, created by Segar.
[2] "In Popeye's house" (Spanish). When Ashbery wrote the poem, the strip was appearing in New York City only in the Spanish-language newspaper *El Diario*.

Today, and it shall be as you wish." He scratched
The part of his head under his hat. The apartment   10
Seemed to grow smaller. "But what if no pleasant
Inspiration plunge us now to the stars? *For this is my country.*"

Suddenly they remembered how it was cheaper in the country.
Wimpy was thoughtfully cutting open a number 2 can of spinach
When the door opened and Swee'pea crept in. "How pleasant!"
But Swee'pea looked morose. A note was pinned to his bib. "Thunder
And tears are unavailing," it read. "Henceforth shall Popeye's apartment
Be but remembered space, toxic or salubrious, whole or scratched."

Olive came hurtling through the window; its geraniums scratched
Her long thigh. "I have news!" she gasped. "Popeye, forced as you know to
    flee the country   20
One musty gusty evening, by the schemes of his wizened, duplicate father,
    jealous of the apartment
And all that it contains, myself and spinach
In particular, heaves bolts of loving thunder
At his own astonished becoming, rupturing the pleasant

Arpeggio[3] of our years. No more shall pleasant
Rays of the sun refresh your sense of growing old, nor the scratched
Tree-trunks and mossy foliage, only immaculate darkness and thunder."
She grabbed Swee'pea. "I'm taking the brat to the country."
"But you can't do that—he hasn't even finished his spinach,"
Urged the Sea Hag, looking fearfully around at the apartment.   30

But Olive was already out of earshot. Now the apartment
Succumbed to a strange new hush. "Actually it's quite pleasant
Here," thought the Sea Hag. "If this is all we need fear from spinach
Then I don't mind so much. Perhaps we could invite Alice the Goon over"—
    she scratched
One dug pensively—"but Wimpy is such a country
Bumpkin, always burping like that." Minute at first, the thunder

Soon filled the apartment. It was domestic thunder,
The color of spinach. Popeye chuckled and scratched
His balls: it sure was pleasant to spend a day in the country.

1966

SCHEHERAZADE*

> Unsupported by reason's enigma
> Water collects in squared stone catch basins.

---

[3] A chord whose notes are played in quick succession rather than simultaneously.

* In *Arabian Nights,* a collection of ancient tales, the Sultan's bride who saves her life by maintaining his interest in the tales she tells.

The land is dry. Under it moves
The water. Fish live in the wells. The leaves,
A concerned green, are scrawled on the light. Bad
Bindweed[1] and rank ragweed somehow forget to flourish here.
An inexhaustible wardrobe has been placed at the disposal
Of each new occurrence. It can be itself now.
Day is almost reluctant to decline
And slowing down opens out new avenues   10
That don't infringe on space but are living here with us.
Other dreams came and left while the bank
Of colored verbs and adjectives was shrinking from the light
To nurse in shade their want of a method
But most of all she loved the particles
That transform objects of the same category
Into particular ones, each distinct
Within and apart from its own class.
In all this springing up was no hint
Of a tide, only a pleasant wavering of the air   20
In which all things seemed present, whether
Just past or soon to come. It was all invitation.
So much the flowers outlined along the night
Alleys when few were visible, yet
Their story sounded louder than the hum
Of bug and stick noises that brought up the rear,
Trundling it along into a new fact of day.
These were meant to be read as any
Salutation before getting down to business,
But they stuck to their guns, and so much   30
Was their obstinacy in keeping with the rest
(Like long flashes of white birds that refuse to die
When day does) that none knew the warp
Which presented this major movement as a firm
Digression, a plain that slowly becomes a mountain.

So each found himself caught in a net
As a fashion, and all efforts to wriggle free
Involved him further, inexorably, since all
Existed there to be told, shot through
From border to border. Here were stones   40
That read as patches of sunlight, there was the story
Of the grandparents, of the vigorous young champion
(The lines once given to another, now
Restored to the new speaker), dinners and assemblies,
The light in the old home, the secret way
The rooms fed into each other, but all
Was wariness of time watching itself
For nothing in the complex story grew outside:
The greatness in the moment of telling stayed unresolved

---

[1] Twining vines of the morning-glory family.

Until its wealth of incident, pain mixed with pleasure,   50
Faded in the precise moment of bursting
Into bloom, its growth a static lament.

Some stories survived the dynasty of the builders
But their echo was itself locked in, became
Anticipation that was only memory after all,
For the possibilities are limited. It is seen
At the end that the kind and good are rewarded,
That the unjust one is doomed to burn forever
Around his error, sadder and wiser anyway.
Between these extremes the others muddle though   60
Like us, uncertain but wearing artlessly
Their function of minor characters who must
Be kept in mind. It is we who make this
Jungle and call it space, naming each root,
Each serpent, for the sound of the name
As it clinks dully against our pleasure,
Indifference that is pleasure. And what would they be
Without an audience to restrict the innumerable
Passes and swipes, restored to good humor as it issues
Into the impervious evening air? So in some way   70
Although the arithmetic is incorrect
The balance is restored because it
Balances, knowing it prevails,
And the man who made the same mistake twice is exonerated.

                                                        1972

WET CASEMENTS*

When Eduard Raban, coming along the passage,
walked into the open doorway, he saw that it was
raining. It was not raining much.
—KAFKA, *Wedding Preparations in the Country*[1]

The concept is interesting: to see, as though reflected
In streaming windowpanes, the look of others through
Their own eyes. A digest of their correct impressions of
Their self-analytical attitudes overlaid by your
Ghostly transparent face. You in falbalas[2]
Of some distant but not too distant era, the cosmetics,
The shoes perfectly pointed, drifting (how long you
Have been drifting; how long I have too for that matter)

---

*Window frames that open on hinges along the side.
[1] A novel fragment (1907) by the Czech writer Franz Kafka (1883–1924).
[2] Flounces or trimmings for women's garments.

Like a bottle-imp[3] toward a surface which can never be approached,
Never pierced through into the timeless energy of a present   10
Which would have its own opinions on these matters,
Are an epistemological snapshot of the processes
That first mentioned your name at some crowded cocktail
Party long ago, and someone (not the person addressed)
Overheard it and carried that name around in his wallet
For years as the wallet crumbled and bills slid in
And out of it. I want that information very much today,

Can't have it, and this makes me angry.
I shall use my anger to build a bridge like that
Of Avignon,[4] on which people may dance for the feeling   20
Of dancing on a bridge. I shall at last see my complete face
Reflected not in the water but in the worn stone floor of my bridge.

I shall keep to myself.
I shall not repeat others' comments about me.

1975

THE ICE-CREAM WARS

Although I mean it, and project the meaning
As hard as I can into its brushed-metal surface,
It cannot, in this deteriorating climate, pick up
Where I leave off. It sees the Japanese text
(About two men making love on a foam-rubber bed)
As among the most massive secretions of the human spirit.
Its part is in the shade, beyond the iron spikes of the fence,
Mixing red with blue. As the day wears on
Those who come to seem reasonable are shouted down
(*Why you old goat!* Look who's talkin'. Let's see you   10
Climb off that tower—the waterworks architecture, both stupid and
Grandly humorous at the same time, is a kind of mask for him,
Like a seal's face. Time and the weather
Don't always go hand in hand, as here: sometimes
One is slanted sideways, disappears for awhile.
Then later it's forget-me-not time, and rapturous
Clouds appear above the lawn, and the rose tells
The old old story, the pearl of the orient, occluded[1]
And still apt to rise at times.)
                    A few black smudges   20
On the outer boulevards, like squashed midges[2]

---

[3] A genie of the bottle.   [4] A city in southeast France.
[1] Closed.   [2] Small, two-winged, gnatlike creatures.

And the truth becomes a hole, something one has always known,
A heaviness in the trees, and no one can say
Where it comes from, or how long it will stay—

A randomness, a darkness of one's own.

1975

MY EROTIC DOUBLE

He says he doesn't feel like working today.
It's just as well. Here in the shade
Behind the house, protected from street noises,
One can go over all kinds of old feeling,
Throw some away, keep others.
                    The wordplay
Between us gets very intense when there are
Fewer feelings around to confuse things.
Another go-round? No, but the last things
You always find to say are charming, and rescue me   10
Before the night does. We are afloat
On our dreams as on a barge made of ice,
Shot through with questions and fissures of starlight
That keep us awake, thinking about the dreams
As they are happening. Some occurrence. You said it.

I said it but I can hide it. But I choose not to.
Thank you. You are a very pleasant person.
Thank you. You are too.

1979

SOME OLD TIRES

This was mine, and I let it slip through my fingers.
Nevertheless, I do not want, in this airy and pleasant city,
To be held back by valors that were mine
Only for the space of a dream instant, before continuing

To be someone else's. Because there's too much to
Be done that doesn't fit, and the parts that get lost
Are the reasonable ones just because they got lost
And were forced to suffer transfiguration by finding their way home

To a forgotten spot way out in the fields. To have always
Had the wind for a friend is no recommendation. Yet some   10

Disagree, while still others claim that signs of fatigue
And mended places are, these offshore days, open

And a symbol of what must continue
After the ring is closed on us. The furniture,
Taken out and examined under the starlight, pleads
No contest. And the backs of those who sat there before.

1980

FORGOTTEN SEX*

They tore down the old movie palaces,
Ripped up streetcar tracks, widened avenues.
Lampposts, curbs with their trees vanished.

They knew, who came after,
A story of departing hands and affairs, that mostly
Went untold, unless someone who was there once
Visited the old neighborhood, and then
They would tell about it, the space
Of an afternoon, how it happened in the afternoon
So that no record, no print of it could exist   10
For the steep times to come. And sure enough,
Even as the story ended its shadow vanished,
A twice-told tale not to be told again
Unless children one day dig up the past, in the attic
Or under brush in the back yard: "What's this?"
And you have to tell them, will have to tell them then
That the enormous nature of things had a face
Once and feet like any human being, and one day
Broke out of the shell that had always been,
Changed its answers to lies, youthful ambition   20
To a quirk of the past, a fancy, of some
Antiquarian concern that this damaged day can never
Countenance if we want to live past the rope
Of noon, reach the bald summits by late afternoon.

Surely we are protected, surely someone thinks of us
Often enough to keep the stain from setting, surely
All of us are alike and know each other from earliest
Childhood, for better or for worse: surely we eat
Breakfast each day, and shit, and put the kettle on the stove
With much changing of the subject, much twisting the original   30
Premise back to the nature of the actual itch

* First published in *Sulfur* in 1984.

Engulfing us, now. And when we come back
From an outing expect to find the furniture magically
Rearranged to accommodate revised, smaller projects
No one bothers to question, except polite Puss-in-Boots[1] with what
Is in effect a new premise: "Try this one, the dust
Shows less on these rather sad colors; the time
To get started and gain time, however brief, over the neighbors
Quarreling into sunset, once you have convinced them you're
Not playing and therefore not cheating. When the princess   40
Comes to see you on some perfectly plausible pretext, you'll know
The underground stream that has never stood still is the surface
And the theater for all that is to come. Too bad the revisions
Will never be adopted, but how lucky for you, now,
The change of face. Good times follow bad."

And the locket is still on the chain on a throat.
The askers, the doers, fall into silent confusion
As it comes time to stand up like a sheet of metal
In the blast of sunrise. I will do this, I can do no more.
I cannot think on the edge of a platform.   50

But the abandonment by love is a de facto sign
Of something else coming along,
Something similar in its measuredness:
Sweetness of things late, a memory for particulars
As lively as though they happened still. As indeed
They do sometimes, though like the transparent bricks
In a particular dream, they cannot always be seen.

                                                                1984

FROST

Trapped in the wrong dream, you turn
Out of an alley into a wide, weak street   Mirrors
Fall from trees, and it could be time
To refinance the mess of starting
And staying put. But rumors feed this.
The distant passage is then always sublime
And well-lit for some, a curious picture
Of longing and distress for others.

Meanwhile the only tall thing   10
Of importance dismantles himself,
Transparent in places, sometimes opaque
And more beautiful for the scenes
That might be projected on him. The secret
Chamber is one, where only the king
Could come, and now two or three young people

---

[1] The clever cat who brings his young master wealth, position, and happiness in the fairytale "Puss In Boots" (1697), by the French writer Charles Perrault (1628–1703).

Can sit, uneasy and comfortable, discussing
Bicycles, the bone: any of the smaller anythings.
Which is quite nice, but darkness
Seems to fall more quickly, to accrue more in this sudden
Place, made of a name cut out of a map.   20

One gets closer to nervousness then.
It needn't be so. Things are stranger elsewhere.
Here in the dark the keeping of secrets
Is dense, that's all. There are still a few common
Names for things around; even they don't have to be
Used. Only I wish
There was some way of not getting more thoughtful,
Of not bruising the obvious shadow for which
There is a reason. Am I poor?
Have I worn out God's welcome?   30
There is enough dark green to cover us,
Yet will we always be speechless to the end,
Unable to say the familiar things?

1984

SOMEONE YOU HAVE SEEN BEFORE

It was a night for listening to Corelli, Geminiani
Or Manfredini.[1] The tables had been set with beautiful white cloths
And bouquets of flowers. Outside the big glass windows
The rain drilled mercilessly into the rock garden, which made light
Of the whole thing. Both business and entertainment waited
With parted lips, because so much new way of being
With one's emotion and keeping track of it at the same time
Had been silently expressed. Even the waiters were happy.

It was an example of how much one can grow lustily
Without fracturing the shell of coziness that surrounds us,   10
And all things as well. "We spend so much time
Trying to convince ourselves we're happy that we don't recognize
The real thing when it comes along." the Disney[2] official said.
He's got a point, you must admit. If we followed nature
More closely we'd realize that, I mean really getting your face pressed
Into the muck and indecision of it. Then it's as if
We grew out of our happiness, not the other way round, as is
Commonly supposed. We're the characters in its novel,
And anybody who doubts that need only look out of the window
Past his or her own reflection, to the bright, patterned,   20
Timeless unofficial truth hanging around out there,

[1] The Italian composers Arcangelo Corelli (1653–1713), also a violinist; Francesco Geminiani (1674?–1762), a student of Corelli; and Francesco Manfredini (1684–1762).
[2] Of the Walt Disney Company.

Waiting for the signal to be galvanized into a crowd scene,
Joyful or threatening, it doesn't matter, so long as we know
It's inside, here with us.

But people do change in life,
As well as in fiction. And what happens then? Is it because we think nobody's
Listening that one day it comes, the urge to delete yourself,
"Take yourself out," as they say? As though this could matter
Even to the concerned ones who crowd around,
Expressions of lightness and peace on their faces,   30
In which you play no part perhaps, but even so
Their happiness is for you, it's your birthday, and even
When the balloons and fudge get tangled with extraneous
Good wishes from everywhere, it is, I believe, made to order
For your questioning stance and that impression
Left on the inside of your pleasure by some bivalve
With which you have been identified. Sure,
Nothing is ever perfect enough, but that's part of how it fits
The mixed bag
Of leftover character traits that used to be part of you   40
Before the change was performed
And of all those acquaintances bursting with vigor and
Humor, as though they wanted to call you down
Into closeness, not for being close, or snug, or whatever,
But because they believe you were made to fit this unique
And valuable situation whose lid is rising, totally
Into the morning-glory-colored future. Remember, don't throw away
The quadrant of unused situations just because they're here:
They may not always be, and you haven't finished looking
Through them all yet. So much that happens happens in small ways   50
That someone was going to get around to tabulate, and then never did,
Yet it all bespeaks freshness, clarity and an even motor drive
To coax us out of sleep and start us wondering what the new round
Of impressions and salutations is going to leave in its wake
This time. And the form, the precepts, are yours to dispose of as you will,
As the ocean makes grasses, and in doing so refurbishes a lighthouse
On a distant hill, or else lets the whole picture slip into foam.

1984

W. S. Merwin
(1927–   )

After the publication of the poetry collection *The Lice* (1967), W. S. Merwin was acclaimed by many critics as the representative poet of the 1960s. Though the events to
which the book refers are rarely named, its spare, highly controlled poems convey an

unmistakable rage at the political and ecological crises of the time—the Vietnam War in particular—and an overwhelming sense of despair. Merwin's work during this period amounts to an indictment of what he has called "a society whose triumphs . . . emerge as new symbols of death, and that feeds itself by poisoning the earth. . . . " Upon receiving the Pulitzer Prize for poetry in 1971 for *The Carrier of Ladders* (1970), he publicly declared that he would donate most of the prize money to the draft-resistance movement.

This sense that humanity has betrayed both its natural environment and its own primal foundations informs Merwin's attitude toward language as well. Characterized by the desire to avoid the "very dangerous human arrogance" of using language "to possess the world" and by the need to transcend the "ego-bound, historical, culturally brainwashed, incredibly limited moment," Merwin's poems are often hushed, inhabited by a disembodied voice that suggests the inadequacy of language rather than its power. Thus, the humble posture he strikes in a poem such as "For the Anniversary of My Death" (1967), which ends with the speaker "bowing not knowing to what," reflects Merwin's conviction that a poet should not use rhetoric as an "emotional screen." Knowing that he is drawn to words like "silence," "darkness," and "emptiness," Merwin explains in an interview that he has tried to guard against falling into a merely habitual rhetoric because those words would then "have an emptiness which obscures their real emptiness; they can become sentimental."

The son of a Presbyterian minister, William Stanley Merwin was born in 1927 in New York City and grew up in Union City, New Jersey, and Scranton, Pennsylvania. He associates his initiation into writing with his father's religious vocation: "I started writing hymns for my father almost as soon as I could write at all, illustrating them. I recall some rather stern little pieces addressed . . . to backsliders, but I can remember too wondering whether there might not be some liberating mode" (from a 1984 interview with L. Edwin Folsom). With the help of a scholarship, he attended Princeton University, where he studied with, and was influenced by, the writers John Berryman and R. P. Blackmur, to whom the collection *The Moving Target* (1963) is dedicated. During Merwin's college years he admired Ezra Pound, a poet to whom he still feels a tremendous debt. Merwin says he was "marked . . . for life" by the visit he made in 1946 to Pound in Washington, D.C., at St. Elizabeth's Hospital for the criminally insane; Merwin, like Pound, became a student of foreign languages and a reader of medieval poetry, especially the work of Dante and of François Villon.

After graduating with a B.A. in romance languages from Princeton in 1947, Merwin went abroad. He worked as a tutor in France, Portugal, and Majorca (where he tutored the son of the British writer Robert Graves) and as a translator in London, where he got involved with the theater. Upon returning to the United States in 1956, Merwin wrote several plays for the Poets' Theater in Cambridge, Massachusetts. In 1952 his first volume of poems, *A Mask for Janus*, won the Yale Younger Poets Award, chosen by the poet W. H. Auden. Auden praised Merwin for his command of a wide range of traditional poetic forms, including such folk forms as the ballad—a reflection of Merwin's long-standing interest in oral literature.

By the end of the 1950s, after having been very well received by the literary world, Merwin experienced something of a crisis in his work and, he says in an interview, "virtually stopped writing poetry." During these years he broke away from traditional metrical and stanzaic patterns and was engaged in a process of "strengthening by compressing and intensifying, of getting down to what was really essential." In his fourth book, *The Drunk in the Furnace* (1960), Merwin turned to autobiographical themes, writing poems about his family and his childhood in Scranton. His next collection, *The Moving Target* (1963), represents a major turning point: he began to omit all punctuation from his poems, a practice that since the 1960s has become one of the distinctive characteristics of his verse.

"Punctuation," writes Merwin, "seemed to staple the poem to the page, but if I took those staples out the poem lifted itself right up off the page."

In addition to his numerous collections of poetry and of prose, Merwin has established himself as an important and innovative translator of works in various languages and a wide range of styles, from Sanskrit love poetry to French symbolist poetry to Asian proverbs. Partly on the advice of Ezra Pound, Merwin started translating as an exercise that he hoped would help his own writing. Pound's suggestion that he write English versions of Spanish romances eventually led to Merwin's translations of two medieval epics, the Spanish *The Poem of the Cid* (1959) and the French *Song of Roland* (1963). He has worked on material that reflects his thematic and formal interests, even if that material is written in languages in which he has no firsthand knowledge. *Asian Figures* (1973), for example, consists of English adaptations of proverbs from a variety of Asian languages and embodies Merwin's attraction to compact forms.

Merwin recently made Hawaii his primary residence. At work on a book of prose about Hawaii, he is combing oral histories and essays in an effort to tell what he believes is the largely ignored story of how the U.S. military has desecrated Kaho'Olawe, an uninhabited island sacred to the Hawaiian people, by using the island as a bombing target. Merwin has described this project as a "gathering together of almost all of my interests . . . ," including opposing "the destruction of the earth for abstract and greedy reasons."

Suggested Readings: *A Mask for Janus*, 1952. *The Drunk in the Furnace*, 1960. *The Lice*, 1967. *The Carrier of Ladders*, 1970. *The Miner's Pale Children*, 1970. *The Compass Flower*, 1977. *Houses and Travellers*, 1977. *Unframed Originals: Recollections*, 1982. *Regions of Memory: Uncollected Prose*, ed. E. Folsom and C. Nelson, 1987. J. Vernon, in *American Poetry Review*, Jan.–Feb., 1978. C. Davis, *W. S. Merwin*, 1981. C. Nelson and E. Folsom, eds., *W. S. Merwin: Essays on the Poetry*, 1987.

Texts Used: "Travelling Together" and "Thanks": *The Rain in the Trees*, 1988. All else: *Selected Poems*, 1988.

BALLAD OF JOHN CABLE AND THREE GENTLEMEN

> He that had come that morning,
> One after the other,
> Over seven hills,
> Each of a new color,
>
> Came now by the last tree,
> By the red-colored valley,
> To a gray river
> Wide as the sea.
>
> There at the shingle[1]
> A listing wherry[2]
> Awash with dark water;
> What should it carry?

10

---

[1] Shoreline area of a beach, covered with coarse, waterworn gravel.
[2] A light rowboat used on rivers.

There on the shelving,[3]
Three dark gentlemen.
Might they direct him?
Three gentlemen.

"Cable, friend John, John Cable,"
When they saw him they said,
"Come and be company
As far as the far side."   20

"Come follow the feet," they said,
"Of your family,
Of your old father
That came already this way."

But Cable said, "First I must go
Once to my sister again;
What will she do come spring
And no man on her garden?

She will say 'Weeds are alive
From here to the Stream of Friday;   30
I grieve for my brother's plowing,'
Then break and cry."

"Lose no sleep," they said, "for that fallow:
She will say before summer,
'I can get me a daylong man,
Do better than a brother.'"

Cable said, "I think of my wife:
Dearly she needs consoling;
I must go back for a little
For fear she die of grieving."   40

"Cable," they said, "John Cable,
Ask no such wild favor;
Still, if you fear she die soon,
The boat might wait for her."

But Cable said, "I remember:
Out of charity let me
Go shore up my poorly mother,
Cries all afternoon."

They said, "She is old and far,
Far and rheumy[4] with years,   50

---

[3] Slope.   [4] Teary.

And, if you like, we shall take
No note of her tears."

But Cable said, "I am neither
Your hired man nor maid,
Your dog nor shadow
Nor your ape to be led."

He said, "I must go back:
Once I heard someone say
That the hollow Stream of Friday
Is a rank place to lie;   60

And this word, now I remember,
Makes me sorry: have you
Thought of my own body
I was always good to?

The frame that was my devotion
And my blessing was,
The straight bole[5] whose limbs
Were long as stories—

Now, poor thing, left in the dirt
By the Stream of Friday   70
Might not remember me
Half tenderly."

They let him nurse no worry;
They said, "We give you our word:
Poor thing is made of patience;
Will not say a word."

"Cable, friend John, John Cable,"
After this they said,
"Come with no company
To the far side.   80

To a populous place,
A dense city
That shall not be changed
Before much sorrow dry."

Over shaking water
Toward the feet of his father,
Leaving the hills' color
And his poorly mother

---

[5] Tree trunk.

And his wife at grieving
And his sister's fallow   90
And his body lying
In the rank hollow,

Now Cable is carried
On the dark river;
Nor even a shadow
Followed him over.

On the wide river
Gray as the sea
Flags of white water
Are his company.   100

1952

ONE-EYE

(*"In the country of the blind the one-eyed man is king."*)*

  On that vacant day
After kicking and moseying[1] here and there
For some time, he lifted that carpet-corner
  His one eye-lid, and the dyed light
Leapt at him from all sides like dogs. Also hues
That he had never heard of, in that place
  Were bleeding and playing.

  Even so, it was
Only at the grazing of light fingers
Over his face, unannounced, and then his   10
  Sight of many mat eyes, paired white
Irises like dried peas looking, that it dawned
On him: his sidelong idling had found
  The country of the blind.

  Whose swarming digits
Knew him at once: their king, come to them
Out of a saying. And chanting an anthem
  Unto his one eye, to the dry

---

* From the short story "The Country of the Blind" (1911), by the English writer H. G. Wells (1866–1946).
[1] Strolling.

Accompaniment that their leaping fingers made
Flicking round him like locusts in a cloud,   20
    They took him home with them.

    Their shapely city
Shines like a suit. On a plain chair he was set
In a cloak of hands, and crowned, to intricate
    Music. They sent him their softest
Daughters, clad only in scent and their own
Vast ears, meantime making different noises
    In each ante-chamber.

    They can be wakened
Sometimes by a feather falling on the next   30
Floor, and they keep time by the water-clocks'[2]
    Dropping even when they sleep. Once
He would expound to them all, from his only
Light, day breaking, the sky spiked and the
    Earth amuck with color,

    And they would listen,
Amazed at his royalty, gaping like
Sockets, and would agree, agree, blank
    As pearls. At the beginning.
Alone in brightness, soon he spoke of it   40
In sleep only; "Look, look," he would call out
    In the dark only.

    Now in summer gaudy
With birds he says nothing; of their thefts, often
Beheld, and their beauties, now for a long time
    Nothing. Nothing, day after day,
To see the black thumb as big as a valley
Over their heads descending silently
    Out of a quiet sky.

1960

GRANDMOTHER DYING

Not ridden in her Christian bed, either,
But her wrenched back bent double, hunched over
The plank tied to the arms of her rocker
With a pillow on it to keep her head
Sideways up from her knees, and three others
Behind her in the high chair to hold her

---

[2] Clocks that operate by the flow of water.

Down so the crooked might be straight, as if
There was any hope. Who for ninety-three years,
Keeping the faith, believed you could get
Through the strait gate and the needle's eye if   10
You made up your mind straight and narrow, kept
The thread tight and, dead both to left and to right
To the sly music beyond the ditches, beat
Time on the book as you went. And then she fell.
She should have did what she was told, she should
Have called for what she needed, she did look
Sleeping on the pillows and to be trusted
Just for a bit, and Bid was not downstairs
A minute before hearing the hall creak
And the door crash back in the bathroom as   20
She fell. What was it, eighteen months, they took
Care of her crooked that way, feeding from
The side, hunching down to hear her, all
Knowing full well what the crooked come to
When their rockers stop. Still could hear what she
Thought good to hear, still croak: you keep my
Candy hid in that sweater drawer, Bid,
Only for company one piece, then you put it
Back again, hear? One after the other
A family of fevers visited her,   30
And last a daughter-in-law with a nasty
Cough combed her hair out pretty on the plank,
With a flower in it, and held a mirror
For her to see till it made her smile, but
Bid, she whispered, you keep wide of that new
Nurse's cough, she has T.B.[1] And where
Were the wars that still worried her, when
Most were dead a long time ago, and one
Son had come back and was there hanging
In sunlight, in a medal of glory, on   40
The wall in her room smelling of coal-gas
And petunias. One daughter lived and dusted
A nice brick house a block away, already
Rehearsing how she'd say, "Well, we was always
Good to our Mumma anyway." Outside,
The crooked river flowed easy, knowing
All along; the tracks smiled and rang away;
Help would come from the hills. One knotted hand
Of hers would hang up in the air above
Her head for hours, propped on its elbow, waving   50
In that direction. And when she heaved up
Her last breath, to shake it like a fist,
As out of a habit so old as to be
Nearly absent, at the dirty river

---

[1] Tuberculosis.

Sliding away there the same as ever,
Bid says you could not hear her because there
Came a black engine that had been waiting
Up the tracks there for ninety-four years, and
Snatched it out from her lips, and roared off
With it hooting downriver, making the tracks   60
Straighten out in front of it like a whip,
While the windows rattled loud to break, the things
On the shelves shook, the folds of her face jarred
And shivered; and when it was gone, for a long
Time the goosed[2] laundry still leaped and jiggled
In the smutty wind outside, and her chair went on
Rocking all by itself with nothing alive
Inside it to explain it, nothing, nothing.

1960

THE DRUNK IN THE FURNACE

For a good decade
The furnace stood in the naked gully, fireless
And vacant as any hat. Then when it was
No more to them than a hulking black fossil
To erode unnoticed with the rest of the junk-hill
By the poisonous creek, and rapidly to be added
    To their ignorance,

They were afterwards astonished
To confirm, one morning, a twist of smoke like a pale
Resurrection, staggering out of its chewed hole,   10
And to remark then other tokens that someone,
Cosily bolted behind the eye-holed iron
Door of the drafty burner, had there established
    His bad castle.

Where he gets his spirits
It's a mystery. But the stuff keeps him musical:
Hammer-and-anvilling with poker and bottle
To his jugged bellowings, till the last groaning clang
As he collapses onto the rioting
Springs of a litter of car-seats ranged on the grates,   20
    To sleep like an iron pig.

In their tar-paper church
On a text about stoke-holes that are sated never
Their Reverend lingers. They nod and hate trespassers.

---

[2] Prodded suddenly and playfully in the buttocks.

When the furnace wakes, though, all afternoon
Their witless offspring flock like piped rats[1] to its siren
Crescendo, and agape on the crumbling ridge
        Stand in a row and learn.

1956, 1960

THE ANIMALS

All these years behind windows
With blind crosses sweeping the tables

And myself tracking over empty ground
Animals I never saw

I with no voice

Remembering names to invent for them
Will any come back will one

Saying yes

Saying look carefully yes
We will meet again   10

1967

FOR THE ANNIVERSARY OF MY DEATH

Every year without knowing it I have passed the day
When the last fires will wave to me
And the silence will set out
Tireless traveller
Like the beam of a lightless star

Then I will no longer
Find myself in life as in a strange garment
Surprised at the earth
And the love of one woman
And the shamelessness of men   10
As today writing after three days of rain
Hearing the wren sing and the falling cease
And bowing not knowing to what

1967

---

[1] From the German folk tale of the Pied Piper of Hamelin, who lured rats out of town with his flute playing but, angered at not being paid, also lured away the children.

THE DRY STONE MASON

The mason is dead the gentle drunk
Master of dry walls
What he made of his years crosses the slopes without wavering
Upright but nameless
Ignorant in the new winter
Rubbed by running sheep
But the age of mortar has come to him

Bottles are waiting like fallen shrines
Under different trees in the rain
And stones drip where his hands left them   10
Leaning slightly inwards
His thirst is past

As he had no wife
The neighbors found where he kept his suit
A man with no family they sat with him
When he was carried through them they stood by their own dead
And they have buried him among the graves of the stones

1967

THE JUDGMENT OF PARIS*

Long afterwards
the intelligent could deduce what had been offered
and not recognized
and they suggest that bitterness should be confined
to the fact that the gods chose for their arbiter
a mind and character so ordinary
albeit a prince

and brought up as a shepherd[1]
a calling he must have liked
for he had returned to it   10

---

* According to Greek myth, a golden apple marked "To the Fairest," thrown by Eris (the goddess of discord) was claimed by three goddesses: Hera (the supreme goddess), Athena (the goddess of wisdom and warfare), and Aphrodite (the goddess of love); to settle the dispute, Zeus (the supreme god) advised them to consult Paris, the son of King Priam of Troy.

[1] Because of a prophecy that Paris would bring destruction to Troy, he was left to die as an infant in the wilderness but, unbeknown to the king, was raised by one of his own shepherds.

when they stood before him
the three
naked feminine deathless
and he realized that he was clothed
in nothing but mortality
the strap of his quiver of arrows crossing
between his nipples
making it seem stranger

and he knew he must choose
and on that day   20

the one with the gray eyes[2] spoke first
and whatever she said he kept
thinking he remembered
but remembered it woven with confusion and fear
the two faces that he called father
the first sight of the palace
where the brothers were strangers
and the dogs watched him and refused to know him
she made everything clear she was dazzling she
offered it to him   30
to have for his own but what he saw
was the scorn above her eyes
and her words of which he understood few
all said to him *Take wisdom*
take power
you will forget anyway

the one with the dark eyes[3] spoke
and everything she said
he imagined he had once wished for
but in confusion and cowardice   40
the crown
of his father the crowns the crowns bowing to him
his name everywhere like grass
only he and the sea
triumphant
she made everything sound possible she was
dazzling she offered it to him
to hold high but what he saw
was the cruelty around her mouth
and her words of which he understood more   50
all said to him *Take pride*
take glory
you will suffer anyway

---

[2] Athena, who promised Paris victory in battles if he chose her.
[3] Hera, who promised to make Paris ruler of the world.

the third one[4] the color of whose eyes
later he could not remember
spoke last and slowly and
of desire and it was his
though up until then he had been
happy with his river nymph[5]
here was his mind   60
filled utterly with one girl gathering
yellow flowers
and no one like her
the words
made everything seem present
almost present
present
they said to him *Take*
her
you will lose her anyway   70

it was only when he reached out to the voice
as though he could take the speaker
herself
that his hand filled with
something to give
but to give to only one of the three
an apple as it is told
discord itself in a single fruit its skin
already carved
To the fairest   80

then a mason working above the gates of Troy
in the sunlight thought he felt the stone
shiver

in the quiver on Paris's back the head
of the arrow for Achilles' heel[6]
smiled in its sleep

and Helen stepped from the palace to gather
as she would do every day in that season
from the grove the yellow ray flowers tall
as herself   90

whose roots are said to dispel pain

1970

---

[4] Aphrodite, who promised Paris the fairest woman in the world—Helen, the wife of the Spartan king Menelaus. Paris chose Aphrodite and incurred the hatred of Hera and Athena; the events led to the Trojan War, in which the Greeks fought to restore Helen to Menelaus.

[5] The nymph Oenone.

[6] Paris killed the hero Achilles by shooting an arrow into his one vulnerable spot, his heel.

FLIES

On the day when the flies were made
death was a garden
already without walls
without apples
with nowhere to look back to
all that day the stars could be seen
black points
in the eyes of flies
and the only sound was the roar of the flies
until the sun went down   10

each day after that something else was made
and something else with no name
was a garden
which the flies never saw
what they saw was not there
with no end
no apples
ringed with black stars
that no one heard
and they flew in it happily all day   20
wearing mourning

1973

A CONTEMPORARY

What if I came down now out of these
solid dark clouds that build up against the mountain
day after day with no rain in them
and lived as one blade of grass
in a garden in the south when the clouds part in winter
from the beginning I would be older than all the animals
and to the last I would be simpler
frost would design me and dew would disappear on me
sun would shine through me
I would be green with white roots   10
feel worms touch my feet as a bounty
have no name and no fear
turn naturally to the light
know how to spend the day and night
climbing out of myself
all my life

1977

BERRYMAN*

I will tell you what he told me
in the years just after the war
as we then called
the second world war

don't lose your arrogance yet he said
you can do that when you're older
lose it too soon and you may
merely replace it with vanity

just one time he suggested
changing the usual order   10
of the same words in a line of verse
why point out a thing twice

he suggested I pray to the Muse[1]
get down on my knees and pray
right there in the corner and he
said he meant it literally

it was in the days before the beard
and the drink but he was deep
in tides of his own through which he sailed
chin sideways and head tilted like a tacking sloop   20

he was far older than the dates allowed for
much older than I was he was in his thirties
he snapped down his nose with an accent
I think he had affected in England

as for publishing he advised me
to paper my wall with rejection slips
his lips and the bones of his long fingers trembled
with the vehemence of his views about poetry

he said the great presence
that permitted everything and transmuted it   30
in poetry was passion
passion was genius and he praised movement and invention

I had hardly begun to read
I asked how can you ever be sure
that what you write is really
any good at all and he said you can't

---

* A tribute to the poet John Berryman (1914–1972), with whom Merwin studied as an undergraduate at Princeton University.

[1] According to Greek myth, one of nine goddesses who presided over literature and the arts and sciences.

you can't you can never be sure
you die without knowing
whether anything you wrote was any good
if you have to be sure don't write   40

1983

TRAVELLING TOGETHER

If we are separated I will
try to wait for you
on your side of things

your side of the wall and the water
and of the light moving at its own speed
even on leaves that we have seen
I will wait on one side

while a side is there

1988

THANKS*

Listen
with the night falling we are saying thank you
we are stopping on the bridges to bow from the railings
we are running out of the glass rooms
with our mouths full of food to look at the sky
and say thank you
we are standing by the water thanking it
standing by the windows looking out
in our directions

back from a series of hospitals back from a mugging   10
after funerals we are saying thank you
after the news of the dead
whether or not we knew them we are saying thank you

over telephones we are saying thank you
in doorways and in the backs of cars and in elevators
remembering wars and the police at the door
and the beatings on stairs we are saying thank you
in the banks we are saying thank you
in the faces of the officials and the rich
and of all who will never change   20
we go on saying thank you thank you

* First published in *The Nation*.

with the animals dying around us
taking our feelings we are saying thank you
with the forests falling faster than the minutes
of our lives we are saying thank you
with the words going out like cells of a brain
with the cities growing over us
we are saying thank you faster and faster
with nobody listening we are saying thank you
thank you we are saying and waving   30
dark though it is

1988

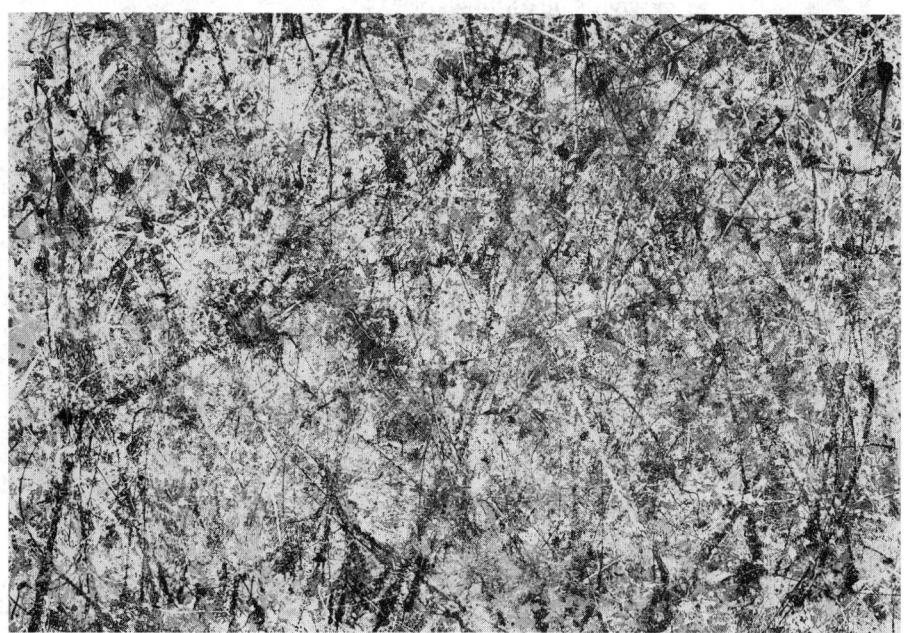

Jackson Pollock's Number 1, 1950 (Lavender Mist) *(1950) is an example of abstract expressionism. Pollock's radical techniques, such as dripping paint on a canvas, helped generate experimentation in abstract expression in literature as well.*

Galway Kinnell
(1927–   )

Galway Kinnell was once described as "looking more like a prizefighter than a literary man." In fact, his poetry encompasses both the "'Tenderness Toward Existence'" he invokes in *The Book of Nightmares* (1971) and the identification with the savage forces of nature he enacts in his poem "The Bear" (1968). Kinnell encourages an emotional direct-ness, the value of experiential rather than intellectual knowledge, and a hard, close look at the visceral. With this attitude he counters what he has called the "technological spirit" of modern society, the same spirit that he feels gave Henry David Thoreau "hives of the soul." Thus, Kinnell's poetry is filled with "simple material things" invigorated by a ritual-istic transformation of ordinary experience.

A native of Providence, Rhode Island, Kinnell was born in 1927. During his undergrad-uate years at Princeton University, he was a friend and classmate of the poet W. S. Mer-win. After graduating in 1948 Kinnell earned an M.A. at the University of Rochester and then directed an adult education program, the Downtown Center of the University of Chi-cago. He pursued what had interested him most as an undergraduate, writing poetry, while he worked for politically active organizations such as the Congress of Racial Equality and Poets Against the Vietnam War. In addition, Kinnell has been poet in residence at numer-ous colleges across America and has held visiting lectureships abroad. His year teaching at Iran's University of Teheran led to his only novel, *Black Light* (1966). Although Kinnell has generally earned his living by teaching, he has always been uneasy as a poet in univer-sity environments.

Above all, Kinnell is preoccupied with death, mortality and dispelling the wishful thinking that he believes gives rise to theories of immortality. Like Rainer Maria Rilke, the Austrian poet he admires, Kinnell believes that insight into the miraculous beauty of the ordinary must be based on an acceptance of mortality. "The subject of the poem," he insists, "is the thing which dies."

Kinnell's most distinctive form is what has been called the "segmental" poem: a se-quence of numbered, free-verse sections that at times expands to Whitmanlike proportions, as in "The Avenue Bearing the Initial of Christ Into the New World," a long poem from *What a Kingdom It Was* (1960). In that collection the reader participates in the poet's fascination with the gritty street life of New York City's Lower East Side. However, Kin-nell has not always written outside traditional poetic conventions. Reflecting on his depar-ture from the strict forms that dominate his *First Poems: 1946–1954* (1970), Kinnell ex-plains in an interview that like many poets who came of age during the 1950s, amidst the intellectual atmosphere fostered by the New Criticism, he had believed that mastering con-ventional verse was necessary before venturing out into experimental forms. His many interviews on poetry are collected in *Walking Down the Stairs* (1978).

With his collection *Body Rags* (1968) Kinnell earned both admiration and notoriety for his stripped-down diction and strident embracing of primitive states of being. Most critics applauded the grisliness of poems such as the "The Porcupine" and "The Bear." The critics marveled at Kinnell's ability to incorporate his experience in the civil rights movement into the long poem "The Last River" without stooping to preachiness. His next volume, *The Book of Nightmares*, was very well received. Kinnell was awarded both a Pulitzer Prize and an American Book Award for his *Selected Poems* (1982).

Suggested Readings: *What a Kingdom It Was*, 1960. *Body Rags*, 1968. *First Poems: 1946–1954*, 1970. *The Book of Nightmares*, 1971. *Walking Down the Stairs: Selections From Interviews*, 1978. *Black Light*, 1980. *The Past*, 1985. H. Nelson, ed., *On the Poetry of Galway Kinnell: The Wages of Dying*, 1987. L. Zimmerman, *Intricate and Simple Things: The Poetry of Galway Kinnell*, 1987.

Text Used: *Selected Poems*, 1982.

THE BEAR

1

In late winter
I sometimes glimpse bits of steam
coming up from
some fault in the old snow
and bend close and see it is lung-colored
and put down my nose
and know
the chilly, enduring odor of bear.

2

I take a wolf's rib and whittle
it sharp at both ends   10
and coil it up
and freeze it in blubber and place it out
on the fairway of the bears.

And when it has vanished
I move out on the bear tracks,
roaming in circles
until I come to the first, tentative, dark
splash on the earth.

And I set out
running, following the splashes   20
of blood wandering over the world.
At the cut, gashed resting places
I stop and rest,
at the crawl-marks
where he lay out on his belly
to overpass some stretch of bauchy[1] ice
I lie out
dragging myself forward with bear-knives in my fists.

3

On the third day I begin to starve,
at nightfall I bend down as I knew I would   30
at a turd sopped in blood,
and hesitate, and pick it up,
and thrust it in my mouth, and gnash it down,
and rise
and go on running.

4

On the seventh day,
living by now on bear blood alone,

---

[1] Weak, insubstantial.

I can see his upturned carcass far out ahead, a scraggled,
steamy hulk,
the heavy fur riffling in the wind.   40

I come up to him
and stare at the narrow-spaced, petty eyes,
the dismayed
face laid back on the shoulder, the nostrils
flared, catching
perhaps the first taint of me as he
died.

I hack
a ravine in his thigh, and eat and drink,
and tear him down his whole length   50
and open him and climb in
and close him up after me, against the wind,
and sleep.

5
And dream
of lumbering flatfooted
over the tundra,
stabbed twice from within,
splattering a trail behind me,
splattering it out no matter which way I lurch,
no matter which parabola² of bear-transcendence,   60
which dance of solitude I attempt,
which gravity-clutched leap,
which trudge, which groan.

6
Until one day I totter and fall—
fall on this
stomach that has tried so hard to keep up,
to digest the blood as it leaked in,
to break up
and digest the bone itself: and now the breeze
blows over me, blows off   70
the hideous belches of ill-digested bear blood
and rotted stomach
and the ordinary, wretched odor of bear,

blows across
my sore, lolled³ tongue a song
or screech, until I think I must rise up
and dance. And I lie still.

---

² Application, comparison.   ³ Drooped.

7
I awaken I think. Marshlights
reappear, geese
come trailing again up the flyway.   80
In her ravine under old snow the dam-bear[4]
lies, licking
lumps of smeared fur
and drizzly eyes into shapes
with her tongue. And one
hairy-soled trudge stuck out before me,
the next groaned out,
the next,
the next,
the rest of my days I spend   90
wandering: wondering
what, anyway,
was that sticky infusion, that rank flavor of blood, that poetry, by which
    I lived?

1968

from *THE BOOK OF NIGHTMARES**

LITTLE SLEEP'S-HEAD SPROUTING HAIR IN THE MOONLIGHT

1
You cry, waking from a nightmare.

When I sleepwalk
into your room, and pick you up,
and hold you up in the moonlight, you cling to me
hard,
as if clinging could save us. I think
you think
I will never die, I think I exude
to you the permanence of smoke or stars,
even as   10
my broken arms heal themselves around you.

2
I have heard you tell
the sun, *don't go down,* I have stood by

4 Mother-bear.
   * A book-length poem (1971) framed by the births of Kinnell's daughter and son. "Little Sleep's-Head" is the seventh section of the poem; the ellipses are Kinnell's.

as you told the flower, *don't grow old,*
don't die. Little Maud,[1]

I would blow the flame out of your silver cup,
I would suck the rot from your fingernail,
I would brush your sprouting hair of the dying light,
I would scrape the rust off your ivory bones,
I would help death escape through the little ribs of your body,   20
I would alchemize the ashes of your cradle back into wood,
I would let nothing of you go, ever,

until washerwomen
feel the clothes fall asleep in their hands,
and hens scratch their spell across hatchet blades,
and rats walk away from the cultures of the plague,
and iron twists weapons toward the true north,
and grease refuses to slide in the machinery of progress,
and men feel as free on earth as fleas on the bodies of men,
and lovers no longer whisper to the one beside them in the   30
    dark, *O you-who-will-no-longer-be* . . .

And yet perhaps this is the reason you cry,
this the nightmare you wake crying from:
being forever
in the pre-trembling of a house that falls.

3
In a restaurant once, everyone
quietly eating, you clambered up
on my lap: to all
the mouthfuls rising toward
all the mouths, at the top of your voice   40
you cried
your one word, *caca! caca! caca!*[2]
and each spoonful
stopped, a moment, in midair, in its withering
steam.

Yes,
you cling because
I, like you, only sooner
than you, will go down
the path of vanished alphabets,   50
the roadlessness
to the other side of the darkness,
your arms
like the shoes left behind,
like the adjectives in the halting speech

---

[1] Kinnell's daughter.   [2] Excrement.

of very old men,
which used to be able to call up the forgotten nouns.

4
And you yourself,
some impossible Tuesday
in the year Two Thousand and Nine, will walk out   60
among the black stones
of the field, in the rain,
and the stones saying
over their one word, *ci-gît,*[3]*ci-gît, ci-gît,*

and the raindrops
hitting you on the fontanel[4]
over and over, and you standing there
unable to let them in.

5
If one day it happens
you find yourself with someone you love   70
in a café at one end
of the Pont Mirabeau,[5] at the zinc bar
where white wine stands in upward opening glasses,

and if you commit then, as we did, the error
of thinking,
one day all this will only be memory,

learn to reach deeper
into the sorrows
to come—to touch
the almost imaginary bones   80
under the face, to hear under the laughter
the wind crying across the stones. Kiss
the mouth
which tells you, *here,*
here is the world. This mouth. This laughter. These temple bones.

The still undanced cadence of vanishing.

6
In the light the moon
sends back, I can see in your eyes
the hand that waved once
in my father's eyes, a tiny kite   90
wobbling far up in the twilight of his last look,
and the angel
of all mortal things lets go the string.

---

[3] "Here lies" (French).   [4] The soft, boneless area of a baby's skull that is later covered by bone.
[5] A Paris bridge.

7
Back you go, into your crib.

The last blackbird lights up his gold wings: *farewell.*
Your eyes close inside your head,
in sleep. Already
in your dreams the hours begin to sing.

Little sleep's-head sprouting hair in the moonlight,
when I come back   100
we will go out together,
we will walk out together among
the ten thousand things,
each scratched in time with such knowledge, *the wages
of dying is love.*[6]

1978

SAINT FRANCIS AND THE SOW*

The bud
stands for all things,
even for those things that don't flower,
for everything flowers, from within, of self-blessing;
though sometimes it is necessary
to reteach a thing its loveliness,
to put a hand on its brow
of the flower
and retell it in words and in touch
it is lovely   10
until it flowers again from within, of self-blessing;
as Saint Francis
put his hand on the creased forehead
of the sow, and told her in words and in touch
blessings of earth on the sow, and the sow
began remembering all down her thick length,
from the earthen snout all the way
through the fodder and slops to the spiritual curl of the tail,
from the hard spininess spiked out from the spine
down through the great broken heart   20
to the sheer blue milken dreaminess spurting and shuddering
from the fourteen teats into the fourteen mouths sucking and
        blowing beneath them:
the long, perfect loveliness of sow.

1980

---

[6] After "The wages of sin is death," from Romans 6: 23.
    * St. Francis of Assisi (1181?–1226), an Italian friar who consecrated himself to poverty and humility, was reknowned for his understanding of animals.

DAYBREAK

On the tidal mud, just before sunset,
dozens of starfishes
were creeping. It was
as though the mud were a sky
and enormous, imperfect stars
moved across it as slowly
as the actual stars cross heaven.
All at once they stopped,
and as if they had simply
increased their receptivity   10
to gravity they sank down
into the mud; they faded down
into it and lay still; and by the time
pink of sunset broke across them
they were as invisible
as the true stars at daybreak.

1980

Adrienne Rich
(1929–   )

The title of Adrienne Rich's first book, *A Change of World* (1951), aptly describes all of Rich's subsequent work: poems and essays that celebrate and speak for women. Rich is trying to change the very consciousness of the world. By daring and even insisting on confronting the myths by which we live, myths handed from generation to generation, Rich aims to change our world by changing how we imagine ourselves in it. To say the unspoken and to banish the silences, she walks a dangerous path with few guides to follow. Achieving remarkable success in both the academic and popular communities, Rich has nonetheless managed to find her way in book after book—undoing and redoing the sense of self, the sense of what is essential, and the sense of what is possible.

Born in Baltimore in 1929, Rich grew up feeling "vaguely Episcopal" in a southern family, with a Jewish father and non-Jewish mother. Not until the late 1940s, when Rich was attending Radcliffe College, did she begin to claim Jewish identity. In her prose collection *Blood, Bread and Poetry* (1986), she describes the ambiguity of her childhood and her early sense of being "split at the root," a metaphor she probes in much of her work. Rich graduated from Radcliffe in 1951, the year *A Change of World*, chosen by the poet W. H. Auden for the Yale Younger Poets Award, was published. The following year she was awarded a Guggenheim Fellowship. Praised for their elegance of style and sureness of technique, both her first volume of poems and her second, *The Diamond Cutters* (1955), radiate her training in the traditional and early modern masters, including Auden.

In 1953 Rich married Alfred Conrad, an economist from an Orthodox Jewish family, and by the time she was thirty she had given birth to three children. The family lived in Cambridge, Massachusetts, where Conrad taught at Harvard University. Rich also began to teach and has since taught at several colleges, including Swarthmore College and Columbia, Rutgers and Cornell Universities. Concerned primarily with motherhood during the Cambridge years, Rich snatched moments to write and won a second Guggenheim Fellowship in 1961. Eight years elapsed between the publication of her second volume and her third, *Snapshots of a Daughter-in-Law* (1963). The "snapshot" format of the title poem reflects the stolen fragments of time during which she wrote and the progress of her emerging feminist consciousness. Piecing together bits of insights and incongruities that unsettled her and unsettle her readers, she wrote the title poem, she says in the essay "When We Dead Awaken" (1971), "in a longer, looser mode than I'd ever trusted myself with before. It was an extraordinary relief to write that poem. It strikes me now as too literary, too dependent on allusions; I hadn't found the courage yet to do without authority or even to use the pronoun 'I'—the woman in the poem is always 'she.'" *Snapshots* announced a tremendous leap in Rich's thinking and writing, and pointed to her abandonment of traditional forms and subjects.

Rich's poetry became more experimental in the 1960s—and more overtly political and feminist. What had earlier been ambiguous became declarative in her collections *Necessities of Life* (1966) and *The Will to Change* (1968). When Rich and her family moved to New York in 1966, she began teaching at City College, where she became involved with the school's open admissions policy and with the civil rights movement. In "When We Dead Awaken" she says that the social justice movement during those years "lifted [her] out of a sense of personal frustration and hopelessness," helping her to clarify those convictions that would shape her feminist philosophy. Although Rich's move from the personal to the social delineates her ever-emerging perspective on gender and sexual issues, hers is not a universal poetry but an emphatically feminine one. "Time is male," she writes in "Snapshots of a Daughter-in-Law," and accordingly, "universal" to her has meant non-female.

After her husband committed suicide in 1970, Rich wrote *Diving Into the Wreck* (1973), an angry, pained collection that plunges into the depths of her being. In it she continues to confront the sexual politics and inherited myths that had left her bitter and to voice the themes of marginality, power and powerlessness, and rage against the forced silence of generations. A book written a few years later, *The Dream of a Common Language* (1978), is even by its title more hopeful, the rage redirected to a dream and hope for communication. As exemplified in the twenty-one love poems collected in that volume, a "common language" is not a universal one, but one vital and true to those who speak it. Detailing a lesbian relationship, these poems articulate a love taboo in lyric poetry of the traditional poets.

In 1974 Rich received a National Book Award, which she accepted with the poet Audre Lourde on behalf of all women. In the mid-1970s Rich moved in with the writer Michelle Cliff and began to edit the feminist journal *Sinister Wisdom* with her. For Rich there is no distinction between the political and the personal, the political and the poetic, the political and the feminine. Whereas in the earlier prose collection *Of Woman Born* (1976) she explodes the myths of motherhood, in her essay "Compulsory Heterosexuality and the Lesbian Experience" (1981), she explodes the myths of heterosexuality. Rich contends that because sexuality has been determined by society through training and the models given in the media and in literature, heterosexuality is enforced and hence not natural. These deliberate shatterings of traditional beliefs and, as Rich says, "re-visions" of the female experience dictate a corresponding change in our vision of humanity.

Suggested Readings: *Snapshots of a Daughter-in-Law: Poems 1954–1962*, 1963. *Diving Into the Wreck*, 1973. *Of Woman Born: Motherhood as Experience and Institution*, 1976. *On Lies, Secrets and Silence: Selected Prose 1966–78*, 1979. *Blood, Bread and Poetry: Selected Prose 1979–1985*, 1986. B. Gelpi and A. Gelpi, ed., *Adrienne Rich's Poetry, A Norton Critical Edition*, 1975. D. Kalstone, *Five Temperaments*, 1977. J. R. Cooper, *Reading Adrienne Rich: Reviews and Re-Visions 1951–1981*, 1984. C. Keyes, *The Aesthetics of Power: The Poetry of Adrienne Rich*, 1986.

Texts Used: "Toward the Solstice": *The Dream of a Common Language: Poems 1974–1977*, 1978. "In Memoriam: D. K.": *Time's Power*, 1989. All else: *The Fact of a Doorframe: Poems Selected and New, 1950–1984*, 1984.

LIVING IN SIN

She had thought the studio would keep itself;
no dust upon the furniture of love.
Half heresy, to wish the taps[1] less vocal,
the panes relieved of grime. A plate of pears,
a piano with a Persian shawl, a cat
stalking the picturesque amusing mouse
had risen at his urging.
Not that at five each separate stair would writhe
under the milkman's tramp; that morning light
so coldly would delineate the scraps   10
of last night's cheese and three sepulchral[2] bottles;
that on the kitchen shelf among the saucers
a pair of beetle-eyes would fix her own—
envoy from some village in the moldings . . .
Meanwhile, he, with a yawn,
sounded a dozen notes upon the keyboard,
declared it out of tune, shrugged at the mirror,
rubbed at his beard, went out for cigarettes;
while she, jeered by the minor demons,
pulled back the sheets and made the bed and found   20
a towel to dust the table-top,
and let the coffee-pot boil over on the stove.
By evening she was back in love again,
though not so wholly but throughout the night
she woke sometimes to feel the daylight coming
like a relentless milkman up the stairs.

1955

THE DIAMOND CUTTERS*

However legendary,
The stone is still a stone,

---

[1] Water faucets.   [2] Ghostly.

* Rich's note: "Thirty years later I have trouble with the informing metaphor of this poem. I was trying, in my twenties, to write about the craft of poetry. But I was drawing, quite ignorantly, on the

Though it had once resisted
The weight of Africa,
The hammer-blows of time
That wear to bits of rubble
The mountain and the pebble—
But not this coldest one.

Now, you intelligence
So late dredged up from dark   10
Upon whose smoky walls
Bison took fumbling form
Or flint was edged on flint—
Now, careful arriviste,[1]
Delineate at will
Incisions in the ice.

Be serious, because
The stone may have contempt
For too-familiar hands,
And because all you do   20
Loses or gains by this:
Respect the adversary,
Meet it with tools refined,
And thereby set your price.

Be hard of heart, because
The stone must leave your hand.
Although you liberate
Pure and expensive fires
Fit to enamor Shebas,[2]
Keep your desire apart.   30
Love only what you do,
And not what you have done.

Be proud, when you have set
The final spoke of flame
In that prismatic wheel,
And nothing's left this day
Except to see the sun
Shine on the false and the true,
And know that Africa
Will yield you more to do.   40

1955

---

long tradition of domination, according to which the precious resource is yielded up into the hands of the dominator as if by a natural event. The enforced and exploited labor of actual Africans in diamond mines was invisible to me, and therefore invisible in the poem, which does not take responsibility for its own metaphor. I note this here because this kind of metaphor is still widely accepted, and I still have to struggle against it in my work."

[1] Someone who has recently gained wealth, power, and success, and is regarded as an upstart.
[2] In Kings 10:1–13 the queen of Sheba visited King Solomon to investigate his wisdom.

SNAPSHOTS OF A DAUGHTER-IN-LAW

1.

You, once a belle in Shreveport,[1]
with henna-colored hair, skin like a peachbud,
still have your dresses copied from that time,
and play a Chopin[2] prelude
called by Cortot:[3] *"Delicious recollections
float like perfume through the memory."*

Your mind now, moldering like wedding-cake,
heavy with useless experience, rich
with suspicion, rumor, fantasy,
crumbling to pieces under the knife-edge   10
of mere fact. In the prime of your life.

Nervy, glowering, your daughter
wipes the teaspoons, grows another way.

2.

Banging the coffee-pot into the sink
she hears the angels chiding, and looks out
past the raked gardens to the sloppy sky.
Only a week since They said: *Have no patience.*

The next time it was: *Be insatiable.*
Then: *Save yourself; others you cannot save.*
Sometimes she's let the tapstream scald her arm,   20
a match burn to her thumbnail,

or held her hand above the kettle's snout
right in the woolly steam. They are probably angels,
since nothing hurts her anymore, except
each morning's grit blowing into her eyes.

3.

A thinking woman sleeps with monsters.
The beak that grips her, she becomes. And Nature,
that sprung-lidded, still commodious
steamer-trunk of *tempora* and *mores*[4]

---

[1] Shreveport, Louisiana.   [2] The Polish composer and pianist Frederic Chopin (1810–1849).
[3] Alfred Cortot (1877–1962), a famous French pianist; from the preface to his *Chopin: 24 Preludes*
(1930), specifically Prelude No. 7.
[4] "Times," "customs" (Latin).

gets stuffed with it all: The mildewed orange-flowers,   30
the female pills,[5] the terrible breasts
of Boadicea[6] beneath flat foxes' heads and orchids.

Two handsome women, gripped in argument,
each proud, acute, subtle, I hear scream
across the cut glass and majolica[7]
like Furies[8] cornered from their prey:
The argument *ad feminam*,[9] all the old knives
that have rusted in my back, I drive in yours,
ma semblable, ma soeur![10]

4.

Knowing themselves too well in one another: 40
their gifts no pure fruition, but a thorn,
the prick filed sharp against a hint of scorn . . .
Reading while waiting
for the iron to heat,
writing, *My Life had stood—a Loaded Gun—*[11]
in that Amherst pantry while the jellies boil and scum,
or, more often,
iron-eyed and beaked and purposed as a bird,
dusting everything on the whatnot every day of life.

5.

Dulce ridens, dulce loquens,[12]   50
she shaves her legs until they gleam
like petrified mammoth-tusk.

6.

When to her lute Corinna sings[13]
neither words nor music are her own;

---

[5] Medication for menstrual pain.

[6] Boadicea (?–A.D. 62), queen of the Iceni (Britons of Norfolk and Suffolk), led an unsuccessful revolt against Roman rulers.

[7] A modern imitation of Italian Renaissance pottery, both characterized by rich colors, glaze, and ornamentation.

[8] According to Greek myth, goddesses of vengeance.

[9] "To the woman" (Latin): the feminine version of *ad hominem*, an argument appealing to the emotions rather than to reason.

[10] "My like, my sister!" (French), after the final line of the poem "Au Lecteur," by the French poet Charles Baudelaire (1821–1867); Rich changes "brother" to "sister."

[11] Rich's note: "*Emily Dickinson, Complete Poems*, ed. T. H. Johnson, 1960, p. 369": from poem 754 by Emily Dickinson (1830–1886), who lived her entire life in Amherst, Massachusetts.

[12] "Sweetly smiling, sweetly speaking" (Latin), from Ode XXII, "Integer vitae" (23–24), by the Roman poet Horace (65–8 B.C.).

[13] The first line of a song by the English poet and composer Thomas Campion (1567–1620).

only the long hair dipping
over her cheek, only the song
of silk against her knees
and these
adjusted in reflections of an eye.

Poised, trembling and unsatisfied, before   60
an unlocked door, that cage of cages,
tell us, you bird, you tragical machine—
is this *fertilisante douleur?*[14] Pinned down
by love, for you the only natural action,
are you edged more keen
to prise the secrets of the vault? has Nature shown
her household books to you, daughter-in-law,
that her sons never saw?

7.

*"To have in this uncertain world some stay
which cannot be undermined, is*   70
of the utmost consequence."[15]
                                    Thus wrote
a woman, partly brave and partly good,
who fought with what she partly understood.
Few men about her would or could do more,
hence she was labeled harpy, shrew and whore.

8.

"You all die at fifteen," said Diderot,[16]
and turn part legend, part convention.
Still, eyes inaccurately dream
behind closed windows blankening with steam.   80
Deliciously, all that we might have been,
all that we were—fire, tears,
wit, taste, martyred ambition—
stirs like the memory of refused adultery
the drained and flagging bosom of our middle years.

---

[14] "Fertilizing [or life-giving] sorrow" (French).

[15] Rich's note: "From Mary Wollstonecraft, *Thoughts on the Education of Daughters*, London, 1787." An early feminist, Wollstonecraft (1759–1797), best known for her *Vindication of the Rights of Women* (1792), advocated equality and companionship between the sexes and education for women.

[16] Denis Diderot (1713–1784), a French encyclopedist, philosopher, critic, and playwright. Rich's note: "'You all die at fifteen': '*Vous mourez toutes à quinze ans.*' from the *Lettres à Sophie Volland*, quoted by Simone de Beauvoir in *Le Deuxième Sexe*, Vol. II, pp. 123–124." The French writer de Beauvoir (1908–1986) published *Le Deuxième Sexe*, or "The Second Sex" (French), in 1949.

9.

Not that it is done well, but
that it is done at all?[17] Yes, think
of the odds! or shrug them off forever.
This luxury of the precocious child,
Time's precious chronic invalid,—   90
would we, darlings, resign it if we could?
Our blight has been our sinecure:
mere talent was enough for us—
glitter in fragments and rough drafts.

Sigh no more, ladies.
                    Time is male
and in his cups drinks to the fair.
Bemused by gallantry, we hear
our mediocrities over-praised,
indolence read as abnegation,   100
slattern thought styled intuition,
every lapse forgiven, our crime
only to cast too bold a shadow
or smash the mold straight off.

For that, solitary confinement,
tear gas, attrition shelling.
Few applicants for that honor.

10.
                              Well,
she's long about her coming, who must be
more merciless to herself than history.   110
Her mind full to the wind, I see her plunge
breasted and glancing through the currents,
taking the light upon her
at least as beautiful as any boy
or helicopter,[18]
              poised, still coming,
her fine blades making the air wince
but her cargo

---

[17] After a remark by the English man-of-letters, poet, biographer, and lexicographer Samuel Johnson (1709–1784) to his biographer James Boswell (1740–1795) in 1763: "Sir, a woman's preaching is like a dog's walking on his hinder legs. It is not done well; but you are surprised to find it done at all."

[18] Rich's note: "She comes down from the remoteness of ages, from Thebes, from Crete, from Chichén-Itzá; and she is also the totem set deep in the African jungle; she is a helicopter and she is a bird; and there is this, the greatest wonder of all: under her tinted hair the forest murmur becomes a thought and words issue from her breasts," from de Beauvoir's *Le Deuxième Sexe*.

no promise then:
delivered   120
palpable
ours.

1958–1960, 1963

FACE TO FACE

Never to be lonely like that—
the Early American figure on the beach
in black coat and knee-breeches
scanning the didactic storm in privacy,

never to hear the prairie wolves
in their lunar hilarity
circling one's little all, one's claim
to be Law and Prophets

for all that lawlessness,
never to whet the appetite   10
weeks early, for a face, a hand
longed-for and dreaded—

How people used to meet!
starved, intense, the old
Christmas gifts saved up till spring,
and the old plain words,

and each with his God-given secret,
spelled out through months of snow and silence,
burning under the bleached scalp; behind dry lips
a loaded gun.[1]   20

1965, 1966

I DREAM I'M THE DEATH OF ORPHEUS*

I am walking rapidly through striations of light and dark thrown under an arcade.

I am a woman in the prime of life, with certain powers
and those powers severely limited

---

[1] "My Life had stood—a Loaded Gun—." from poem 754 by Emily Dickinson (1830–1886).
 * According to Greek myth, Orpheus was a musician who journeyed to the Underworld to try to bring back his wife, Eurydice, but failed when he looked back at her before she stepped into the light. Throughout the poem are images drawn from the film *Orphée* (1950), by the French filmmaker Jean Cocteau (1889–1963), which modernizes the myth.

by authorities whose faces I rarely see.
I am a woman in the prime of life
driving her dead poet in a black Rolls-Royce
through a landscape of twilight and thorns.
A woman with a certain mission
which if obeyed to the letter will leave her intact.
A woman with the nerves of a panther[1]   10
a woman with contacts among Hell's Angels[2]
a woman feeling the fullness of her powers
at the precise moment when she must not use them
a woman sworn to lucidity
who sees through the mayhem, the smoky fires
of these underground streets
her dead poet learning to walk backward against the wind
on the wrong side of the mirror

1968, 1971

ORION*

Far back when I went zig-zagging
through tamarack[1] pastures
you were my genius, you
my cast-iron Viking, my helmed[2]
lion-heart king[3] in prison.
Years later now you're young

my fierce half-brother, staring
down from that simplified west
your breast open, your belt[4] dragged down
by an oldfashioned thing, a sword   10
the last bravado you won't give over
though it weighs you down as you stride

and the stars in it are dim[5]
and maybe have stopped burning.
But you burn, and I know it;
as I throw back my head to take you in

---

[1] Possibly a member of the Black Panthers, a group of African Americans organized in 1966 to force the changes in civil rights that nonviolent methods were slow in producing.
[2] A motorcycle club associated with violence.
* The equatorial constellation of the hunter Orion; according to Greek myth, Artemis (goddess of the moon and the hunt) loved Orion but accidentally killed him, so she placed him in the sky as a constellation.
[1] The American larch tree, a member of the pine family.   [2] Helmeted.
[3] Richard I (1157–1199), king of England (1189–1199) and named Richard the Lion-Hearted; he was captured in Austria in 1192 and held until he was ransomed in 1194.
[4] Orion's belt and sword are formed by stars in the constellation.
[5] Of the seven stars of Orion, only two—Rigel and Betelgeuse— are bright.

an old transfusion happens again:
divine astronomy is nothing to it.

Indoors I bruise and blunder,
break faith, leave ill enough   20
alone, a dead child born in the dark.
Night cracks up over the chimney,
pieces of time, frozen geodes[6]
come showering down in the grate.

A man reaches behind my eyes
and finds them empty
a woman's head turns away
from my head in the mirror
children are dying my death
and eating crumbs of my life.   30

Pity is not your forte.
Calmly you ache up there
pinned aloft in your crow's nest,[7]
my speechless pirate!
You take it all for granted
and when I look you back

it's with a starlike eye
shooting its cold and egotistical spear
where it can do least damage.
Breathe deep! No hurt, no pardon   40
out here in the cold with you
you with your back to the wall.[8]

                                                    1965, 1969

A VALEDICTION FORBIDDING MOURNING*

My swirling wants. Your frozen lips.
The grammar turned and attacked me.
Themes, written under duress.
Emptiness of the notations.

They gave me a drug that slowed the healing of wounds.

---

[6] Globular stones with a crystal-lined cavity.   [7] A lookout platform near the top of a ship's mast.

[8] Rich's note: "One of two phrases suggested by Gottfried Benn's essay, 'Artists and Old Age' in *Primal Vision*, edited by E. B. Ashton, New Directions." The German poet and essayist Benn (1886–1956) advises modern artists, "Don't lose sight of the cold and egotistical element in your mission. . . . With your back to the wall, care-worn and weary, in the gray light of the void, read Job and Jeremiah and keep going."

* Also the title of a famous poem by John Donne (1572–1631).

I want you to see this before I leave:
the experience of repetition as death
the failure of criticism to locate the pain
the poster in the bus that said:
my bleeding is under control.   10

A red plant in a cemetery of plastic wreaths.

A last attempt: the language is a dialect called metaphor.
These images go unglossed: hair, glacier, flashlight.
When I think of a landscape I am thinking of a time.
When I talk of taking a trip I mean forever.
I could say: those mountains have a meaning
but further than that I could not say.

To do something very common, in my own way.

1970, 1971

FROM A SURVIVOR

The pact that we[1] made was the ordinary pact
of men and women in those days

I don't know who we thought we were
that our personalities
could resist the failures of the race

Lucky or unlucky, we didn't know
the race had failures of that order
and that we were going to share them

Like everybody else, we thought of ourselves as special

Your body is as vivid to me   10
as it ever was: even more

since my feeling for it is clearer:
I know what it could and could not do

it is no longer
the body of a god
or anything with power over my life

Next year it would have been 20 years
and you are wastefully dead[2]

---

[1] Rich and her husband, the economist Alfred Conrad (1924–1970); they were married in 1953.
[2] Conrad committed suicide.

who might have made the leap
we talked, too late, of making   20

which I live now
not as a leap
but a succession of brief, amazing movements

each one making possible the next

                                                                    1972

from TWENTY-ONE LOVE POEMS

III

Since we're[1] not young, weeks have to do time
for years of missing each other. Yet only this odd warp
in time tells me we're not young.
Did I ever walk the morning streets at twenty,
my limbs streaming with a purer joy?
did I lean from any window over the city
listening for the future
as I listen here with nerves tuned for your ring?
And you, you move toward me with the same tempo.
Your eyes are everlasting, the green spark   10
of the blue-eyed grass of early summer,
the green-blue wild cress washed by the spring.
At twenty, yes: we thought we'd live forever.
At forty-five, I want to know even our limits.
I touch you knowing we weren't born tomorrow,
and somehow, each of us will help the other live,
and somewhere, each of us must help the other die.

                                                            1976, 1978

TOWARD THE SOLSTICE*

The thirtieth of November.
Snow is starting to fall.
A peculiar silence is spreading

---

[1] Rich and her husband, the economist Alfred Conrad (1924–1970).

* The time when the sun is the farthest north or the farthest south of the equator; here, the summer solstice, about June 21, when the sun is farthest north.

over the fields, the maple grove.
It is the thirtieth of May,
rain pours on ancient bushes, runs
down the youngest blade of grass.
I am trying to hold in one steady glance
all the parts of my life.
A spring torrent races   10
on this old slanting roof,
the slanted field below
thickens with winter's first whiteness.
Thistles dried to sticks in last year's wind
stand nakedly in the green,
stand sullenly in the slowly whitening,
field.

       My brain glows
more violently, more avidly
the quieter, the thicker   20
the quilt of crystals settles,
the louder, more relentlessly
the torrent beats itself out
on the old boards and shingles.
It is the thirtieth of May,
the thirtieth of November,
a beginning or an end,
we are moving into the solstice
and there is so much here
I still do not understand.   30

If I could make sense of how
my life is still tangled
with dead weeds, thistles,
enormous burdocks,[1] burdens
slowly shifting under
this first fall of snow,
beaten by this early, racking rain
calling all new life to declare itself strong
or die,

       if I could know   40
in what language to address
the spirits that claim a place
beneath these low and simple ceilings,
tenants that neither speak nor stir
yet dwell in mute insistence
till I can feel utterly ghosted in this house.

---

[1] Plants with large leaves and purple-flowered heads covered with hooked prickles.

If history is a spider-thread
spun over and over though brushed away
it seems I might some twilight
or dawn in the hushed country light   50
discern its greyness stretching
from molding or doorframe, out
into the empty dooryard
and following it climb
the path into the pinewoods,
tracing from tree to tree
in the failing light, in the slowly
lucidifying[2] day
its constant, purposive trail,
till I reach whatever cellar hole   60
filling with snowflakes or lichen,[3]
whatever fallen shack
or unremembered clearing
I am meant to have found
and there, under the first or last
star, trusting to instinct
the words would come to mind
I have failed or forgotten to say
year after year, winter
after summer, the right rune[4]   70
to ease the hold of the past
upon the rest of my life
and ease my hold on the past.

If some rite of separation
is still unaccomplished
between myself and the long-gone
tenants of this house,
between myself and my childhood,
and the childhood of my children,
it is I who have neglected   80
to perform the needed acts,
set water in corners, light and eucalyptus
in front of mirrors,
or merely pause and listen
to my own pulse vibrating
lightly as falling snow,
relentlessly as the rainstorm,
and hear what it has been saying.
It seems I am still waiting
for them to make some clear demand   90

---

[2] Clearing.   [3] An association between a fungus and an alga that together form a plantlike unit.
[4] Any poem, verse, or song; especially one that is mystical or obscure.

some articulate sound or gesture,
for release to come from anywhere
but from inside myself.

A decade of cutting away
dead flesh, cauterizing
old scars ripped open over and over
and still it is not enough.

A decade of performing
the loving humdrum acts
of attention to this house   100
transplanting lilac suckers,[5]
washing panes, scrubbing
wood-smoke from splitting paint,
sweeping stairs, brushing the thread
of the spider aside,
and so much yet undone,
a woman's work, the solstice nearing,
and my hand still suspended
as if above a letter
I long and dread to close.   110

1977, 1978

IN MEMORIAM: D. K.*

A man walking on the street
feels unwell   has felt unwell
all week, a little   Yet the flowers crammed
in pots on the corner: furled anemones:
he knows they open
burgundy, violet, pink, amarillo[1]
all the way to their velvet cores
The flowers hanging over the fence: fuchsias:
each tongued, staring,   all of a fire:
the flowers   He who has   10
been happy oftener than sad
carelessly happy   well oftener than sick
one of the lucky   is thinking about death
and its music   about poetry
its translations of his life

[5] Subordinate shoots on a plant's roots or stem.
* David Kalstone (1932–1986), a literary critic.   [1] "Yellow" (Spanish).

And what good will it do you
to go home and put on the Mozart Requiem?[2]
Read Keats?[3]   How will culture cure you?

Poor, unhappy

unwell culture   what can it sing or say   20
six weeks from now, to you?

Give me your living hand   If I could take the hour
death moved into you   undeclared, unnamed
—even if sweet, if I could take that hour

between my forceps   tear at it like a monster
wrench it out of your flesh   dissolve its shape in quicklime
and make you well again

no, not again

but still. . . .

1986, 1989

*In the 1960s and 1970s
the proposed Equal
Rights Amendment,
calling for full equality
for women, was ratified
in many states but failed
to gain the necessary
majority for passage by
the 1982 deadline. Here,
pro-ERA demonstrators
marched in Chicago in
1980.*

---

[2] The unfinished requiem mass by the Austrian composer Wolfgang Amadeus Mozart (1756–1791).
[3] The English poet John Keats (1795–1821).

Sylvia Plath
(1932–1963)

"Sylvia Plath," the critic George Stade has written, "would have been a good poet even if she had not committed suicide, but not exactly the poet she has since become" (in N. H. Stelnor, *A Closer Look at Ariel*, 1973). Plath's poetic reputation is indeed a posthumous phenomenon. Her *Collected Poems* (1981) earned a Pulitzer Prize nearly twenty years after her death. Her most acclaimed collection of poetry, *Ariel* (1965)—which her husband, the English poet Ted Hughes, published two years after her death—immediately transformed the image readers had of her from a promising talent to a major lyric voice. In the *Ariel* poems, most of which she wrote in furious bursts in the last months of her life, the pared-down syntax, stark imagery, and incantatory tone create a haunting vision of tormented intensity that the student of Plath finds difficult to reconcile with the fabric of much of her life. Commonly called a confessional poet, Plath derived much of the raw material for her work from her life—yet, more important is the way in which she created a personal mythology transcending the facts and events of simple autobiography.

Born in 1932 in Boston, Plath was the eldest child of Otto Emil Plath, a German immigrant, and Aurelia Schoeber, the daughter of Austrian immigrants. Otto Plath was a professor of biology and an entomologist (one who studies insects), specializing in bees, at Boston University, where he also taught German for scientists; his wife had a graduate degree in German. The family lived in the coastal town of Winthrop, Massachusetts, and Sylvia enjoyed a seemingly happy childhood, playing by the sea. The apparent idyll ended when her father began to suffer from diabetes, which required the amputation of a gangrenous leg and claimed his life in 1940. Aurelia Plath moved her family to Wellesley, Massachusetts, and began to teach at Boston University.

Sylvia Plath began to write poetry early; her first published poem, called simply "Poem," appeared in 1940 in the *Boston Sunday Herald* when she was eight. She excelled academically in high school and dutifully submitted forty-five pieces to *Seventeen* magazine before one was finally published in 1950. That year she won a full scholarship to Smith College in Massachusetts, where she continued her academic achievements. Plath published stories and poems in magazines, won two Smith poetry prizes, and was elected to Phi Beta Kappa. She also won a fiction contest sponsored by *Mademoiselle* magazine: the prize included a paid trip to New York, where she worked as a guest editor on the magazine. During her month in Manhattan she interviewed writers and poets, including Anthony Hecht, Richard Wilbur, George Steiner, and Elizabeth Bowen. When Plath returned home to Wellesley for the rest of her summer vacation, she became increasingly anxious and depressed. One day when her family was out, she hid in the basement and swallowed a large number of sleeping pills. She was found three days later and was rushed to a hospital, where she began psychotherapy and electric shock therapy. Plath's doctors allowed her to return to college that winter, and despite her setback she graduated summa cum laude in 1955, with a Fulbright scholarship to Cambridge University in hand.

Plath studied for two years at Newnham College, Cambridge, and toured Europe during

Sylvia Plath's own sketch The Docks, Portland, Maine.

breaks. In February 1956 she met Ted Hughes, whose work she had read and admired; in April she wrote an ecstatic letter home to her brother (in *Letters Home*, 1975): "[I] am writing poetry as I never have before; and it is the best, because I am strong in myself and in love with the only man in the world who is my match." The two were married in June 1956 and, after spending the summer in Spain, settled into a flat near Cambridge, where she continued her studies and he taught at a nearby secondary school. In 1957 they moved to America, where Plath had been offered an instructorship in English at her alma mater and Hughes taught creative writing at the University of Massachusetts. Teaching left them little time for their own writing, though, and they decided to leave their jobs at the end of the academic year.

The couple returned to England in 1959; shortly thereafter Plath's first child, a daughter, was born and her first collection of poetry, *The Colossus* (1960), was accepted for publication. She began work on a novel, *The Bell Jar,* based on her former psychiatric experiences. During the summer, she and Hughes bought a house in Devon, England, and early in 1962 she gave birth to a son. The year 1962 was an agonizing one for Plath: she was sick much of the time; her marriage was suffering, too, and she and Hughes separated; and she moved her two children to London during the coldest winter in England in 150 years. In January 1963 *The Bell Jar* appeared, under the pseudonym Victoria Lucas. Plath took to rising at four in the morning to write before her children awoke. She was working on the *Ariel* poems at an astonishing pace, turning out two, sometimes three poems a day. Alone, sick, and exhausted, in February 1963 at six in the morning, Plath prepared breakfast for her children, brought it up to them before they woke, went downstairs, and took her own life by inhaling gas from the oven.

Plath says in *The Poet Speaks* (1977) that "birds, bees, spring, fall, all those sub-jects . . . are absolute gifts to the person who doesn't have any interior experience to write about." Much of the poetry included in *The Colossus* and in the two collections that Ted Hughes published in 1971, *Crossing the Water* and *Winter Trees,* records a keen apprecia-tion of, and an intense reaction to, nature. It also reveals Plath's careful attention to stan-zaic form, rhythm, and sound patterns. In "Blackberrying," from *Crossing the Water,* natural objects are so fraught with symbolic, larger-than-life significance as to threaten the identity of the persona; yet Plath also maintains regular stanzaic form and creates a reso-nant beat. In the *Ariel* poems, of which Plath wrote to her mother in 1962 (in *Letters Home*), "I am writing the best poems of my life; they will make my name," the powerful symbolism and relentless scrutiny of a persona alternately victimized and triumphant com-bine with hypnotic rhythms and insistent sound patterns to mark the height of Plath's po-etic achievement. But as she committed suicide well before *Ariel* was published, she was never to enjoy that achievement.

Suggested Readings: *The Colossus,* 1960. *The Bell Jar* (pseud. Victoria Lucas), 1963. *Ariel,* 1965. *Crossing the Water,* 1971. *Winter Trees,* 1971. *Letters Home: Correspondence 1950–63; ed. A. S. Plath,* 1975. *Johnny Panic* and the *Bible of Dreams: Short Stories, Prose and Diary Excerpts,* 1977. *The Journals of Sylvia Plath,* ed. T. Hughes and McCullough, 1982. A. Alvarez, *The Savage God: A Study of Suicide,* 1972. E. Aird, *Sylvia Plath,* 1973. M. Dickie, *Sylvia Plath and Ted Hughes,* 1979. L. Wagner, ed., *Critical Essays on Sylvia Plath,* 1984. L. Wagner-Martin, *Sylvia Plath: A Biogra-phy,* 1987. H. Bloom, ed., *Sylvia Plath,* 1988. A. Stevenson, *Bitter Fame: A Life of Sylvia Plath,* 1989. S. G. Axelrod, *Sylvia Plath: The Wound and the Cure of Words,* 1990.

Text Used: *The Collected Poems,* ed. T. Hughes, 1981.

YOU'RE*

Clownlike, happiest on your hands,
Feet to the stars, and moon-skulled,
Gilled like a fish. A common-sense
Thumbs-down on the dodo's mode.[1]
Wrapped up in yourself like a spool,
Trawling your dark as owls do.
Mute as a turnip from the Fourth
Of July to All Fools' Day,[2]
O high-riser, my little loaf.

Vague as fog and looked for like mail.   10
Farther off than Australia.
Bent-backed Atlas,[3] our traveled prawn.
Snug as a bud and at home
Like a sprat[4] in a pickle jug.

---

* Plath was pregnant with her daughter, Frieda (born in April 1960), when she wrote this poem.
[1] Someone stupid.   [2] April Fools' Day, April 1.
[3] According to Greek myth, a Titan (or giant god) forced to support the heavens on his shoulders.
[4] A small or young herring.

A creel of eels, all ripples.
Jumpy as a Mexican bean.
Right, like a well-done sum.
A clean slate, with your own face on.

1960

THE HANGING MAN*

By the roots of my hair some god got hold of me.
I sizzled in his blue volts like a desert prophet.

The nights snapped out of sight like a lizard's eyelid:
A world of bald white days in a shadeless socket.

A vulturous boredom pinned me in this tree.
If he were I, he would do what I did.

1960, 1965

TULIPS†

The tulips are too excitable, it is winter here.
Look how white everything is, how quiet, how snowed-in.
I am learning peacefulness, lying by myself quietly
As the light lies on these white walls, this bed, these hands.
I am nobody; I have nothing to do with explosions.
I have given my name and my day-clothes up to the nurses
And my history to the anesthetist and my body to surgeons.

They have propped my head between the pillow and the sheet-cuff
Like an eye between two white lids that will not shut.
Stupid pupil, it has to take everything in.   10
The nurses pass and pass, they are no trouble,
They pass the way gulls pass inland in their white caps,
Doing things with their hands, one just the same as another,
So it is impossible to tell how many there are.

My body is a pebble to them, they tend it as water
Tends to the pebbles it must run over, smoothing them gently.

---

* One of the twenty-two fortune-telling cards in a Tarot deck: both Plath and her husband, Ted Hughes (1930–   ), were interested in the symbolism of Tarot cards.
† Written in March 1961; that winter Plath had suffered a miscarriage, and in March she was hospitalized for an appendectomy.

They bring me numbness in their bright needles, they bring me sleep.
Now I have lost myself I am sick of baggage————
My patent leather overnight case like a black pillbox,
My husband and child[1] smiling out of the family photo;   20
Their smiles catch onto my skin, little smiling hooks.

I have let things slip, a thirty-year-old cargo boat
Stubbornly hanging on to my name and address.
They have swabbed me clear of my loving associations.
Scared and bare on the green plastic-pillowed trolley
I watched my teaset, my bureaus of linen, my books
Sink out of sight, and the water went over my head.
I am a nun now, I have never been so pure.

I didn't want any flowers, I only wanted
To lie with my hands turned up and be utterly empty.   30
How free it is, you have no idea how free————
The peacefulness is so big it dazes you,
And it asks nothing, a name tag, a few trinkets.
It is what the dead close on, finally; I imagine them
Shutting their mouths on it, like a Communion tablet.[2]

The tulips are too red in the first place, they hurt me.
Even through the gift paper I could hear them breathe
Lightly, through their white swaddlings, like an awful baby.
Their redness talks to my wound, it corresponds.
They are subtle: they seem to float, though they weigh me down,   40
Upsetting me with their sudden tongues and their color,
A dozen red lead sinkers round my neck.

Nobody watched me before, now I am watched.
The tulips turn to me, and the window behind me
Where once a day the light slowly widens and slowly thins,
And I see myself, flat, ridiculous, a cut-paper shadow
Between the eye of the sun and the eyes of the tulips,
And I have no face, I have wanted to efface myself.
The vivid tulips eat my oxygen.

Before they came the air was calm enough,   50
Coming and going, breath by breath, without any fuss.
Then the tulips filled it up like a loud noise.
Now the air snags and eddies round them the way a river
Snags and eddies round a sunken rust-red engine.

---

[1] Plath's husband was the English poet Ted Hughes (1930–   ); their daughter, Frieda, was born in April 1960.
[2] During the Christian sacrament of Communion to commemorate Christ's death, a tablet or wafer (symbolizing the body of Christ) is eaten.

They concentrate my attention, that was happy
Playing and resting without committing itself.

The walls, also, seem to be warming themselves.
The tulips should be behind bars like dangerous animals;
They are opening like the mouth of some great African cat,
And I am aware of my heart: it opens and closes   60
Its bowl of red blooms out of sheer love of me.
The water I taste is warm and salt, like the sea,
And comes from a country far away as health.

1961, 1965

BLACKBERRYING

Nobody in the lane, and nothing, nothing but blackberries,
Blackberries on either side, though on the right mainly,
A blackberry alley, going down in hooks, and a sea
Somewhere at the end of it, heaving. Blackberries
Big as the ball of my thumb, and dumb as eyes
Ebon[1] in the hedges, fat
With blue-red juices. These they squander on my fingers.
I had not asked for such a blood sisterhood; they must love me.
They accommodate themselves to my milkbottle, flattening their sides.

Overhead go the choughs[2] in black, cacophonous flocks—   10
Bits of burnt paper wheeling in a blown sky.
Theirs is the only voice, protesting, protesting.
I do not think the sea will appear at all.
The high, green meadows are glowing, as if lit from within.
I come to one bush of berries so ripe it is a bush of flies,
Hanging their bluegreen bellies and their wing panes in a Chinese screen.
The honey-feast of the berries has stunned them; they believe in heaven.
One more hook, and the berries and bushes end.

The only thing to come now is the sea.
From between two hills a sudden wind funnels at me,   20
Slapping its phantom laundry in my face.
These hills are too green and sweet to have tasted salt.
I follow the sheep path between them. A last hook brings me
To the hills' northern face, and the face is orange rock
That looks out on nothing, nothing but a great space
Of white and pewter lights, and a din like silversmiths
Beating and beating at an intractable metal.

1961, 1965

---

[1] Ebony.   [2] Small chattering birds related to crows.

THE MOON AND THE YEW TREE*

This is the light of the mind, cold and planetary.
The trees of the mind are black. The light is blue.
The grasses unload their griefs on my feet as if I were God,
Prickling my ankles and murmuring of their humility.
Fumy, spiritous mists inhabit this place
Separated from my house by a row of headstones.
I simply cannot see where there is to get to.

The moon is no door. It is a face in its own right,
White as a knuckle and terribly upset.
It drags the sea after it like a dark crime; it is quiet   10
With the O-gape of complete despair. I live here.
Twice on Sunday, the bells startle the sky———
Eight great tongues affirming the Resurrection.
At the end, they soberly bong out their names.

The yew tree points up. It has a Gothic¹ shape.
The eyes lift after it and find the moon.
The moon is my mother. She is not sweet like Mary.²
Her blue garments unloose small bats and owls.
How I would like to believe in tenderness———
The face of the effigy, gentled by candles,   20
Bending, on me in particular, its mild eyes.

I have fallen a long way. Clouds are flowering
Blue and mystical over the face of the stars.
Inside the church, the saints will be all blue,
Floating on their delicate feet over the cold pews,
Their hands and faces stiff with holiness.
The moon sees nothing of this. She is bald and wild.
And the message of the yew tree is blackness—blackness and silence.

1961, 1965

LADY LAZARUS†

I have done it again.
One year in every ten
I manage it———

---

* The country house in Devon, England, where Plath and her family lived from July 1961 to December 1962 had a view of a churchyard with an English yew tree. Ted Hughes, Plath's husband, suggested she write a poem about a full moon setting behind the tree at dawn.
¹ A style of architecture developed in western Europe between the twelfth and sixteenth centuries, characterized by ribbed vaulting, pointed arches, and high, steep roofs.
² The Virgin Mary, who is typically pictured in blue clothing.
† In John 11:39–44 Jesus raised Lazarus, the brother of Mary, from the dead; Plath refers to her own suicide attempts.

A sort of walking miracle, my skin
Bright as a Nazi lampshade,[1]
My right foot

A paperweight,
My face a featureless, fine
Jew linen.

Peel off the napkin   10
O my enemy.
Do I terrify?————

The nose, the eye pits, the full set of teeth?
The sour breath
Will vanish in a day.

Soon, soon the flesh
The grave cave ate will be
At home on me

And I a smiling woman.
I am only thirty.   20
And like the cat I have nine times to die.

This is Number Three.
What a trash
To annihilate each decade.

What a million filaments.
The peanut-crunching crowd
Shoves in to see

Them unwrap me hand and foot————
The big strip tease.
Gentlemen, ladies   30

These are my hands
My knees.
I may be skin and bone,

Nevertheless, I am the same, identical woman.
The first time it happened I was ten.
It was an accident.

The second time I meant
To last it out and not come back at all.
I rocked shut

[1] In Nazi concentration camps the skin of victims was sometimes made into lampshades.

As a seashell.   40
They had to call and call
And pick the worms off me like sticky pearls.

Dying
Is an art, like everything else.
I do it exceptionally well.

I do it so it feels like hell.
I do it so it feels real.
I guess you could say I've a call.

It's easy enough to do it in a cell.
It's easy enough to do it and stay put.   50
It's the theatrical

Comeback in broad day
To the same place, the same face, the same brute
Amused shout:

'A miracle!'
That knocks me out.
There is a charge

For the eyeing of my scars, there is a charge
For the hearing of my heart————
It really goes.   60

And there is a charge, a very large charge
For a word or a touch
Or a bit of blood

Or a piece of my hair or my clothes.
So, so, Herr Doktor.[2]
So, Herr Enemy.

I am your opus,
I am your valuable,
The pure gold baby

That melts to a shriek.   70
I turn and burn.
Do not think I underestimate your great concern.

Ash, ash—
You poke and stir.
Flesh, bone, there is nothing there————

[2] "Mr. Doctor" (German).

A cake of soap,
A wedding ring,
A gold filling.

Herr God, Herr Lucifer
Beware   80
Beware.

Out of the ash
I rise[3] with my red hair
And I eat men like air.

1962, 1965

THE BEE MEETING*

Who are these people at the bridge to meet me? They are the villagers————
The rector, the midwife, the sexton,[1] the agent for bees.
In my sleeveless summery dress I have no protection,
And they are all gloved and covered, why did nobody tell me?
They are smiling and taking out veils tacked to ancient hats.

I am nude as a chicken neck, does nobody love me?
Yes, here is the secretary of bees with her white shop smock,
Buttoning the cuffs at my wrists and the slit from my neck to my knees.
Now I am milkweed silk, the bees will not notice.
They will not smell my fear, my fear, my fear.   10

Which is the rector now, is it that man in black?
Which is the midwife, is that her blue coat?
Everybody is nodding a square black head, they are knights in visors,
Breastplates of cheesecloth knotted under the armpits.
Their smiles and their voices are changing. I am led through a beanfield.

Strips of tinfoil winking like people,
Feather dusters fanning their hands in a sea of bean flowers,
Creamy bean flowers with black eyes and leaves like bored hearts.
Is it blood clots the tendrils are dragging up that string?
No, no, it is scarlet flowers that will one day be edible.   20

---

[3] Like the phoenix, a mythical bird that supposedly sets itself on fire and rises anew from its own ashes.
* Plath's father, Otto Plath (1885–1940), was a biologist and author of *Bumble Bees and Their Ways* (1934). While living in Devon, England, she kept a hive of bees and attended meetings of the Beekeepers Association.
[1] A church caretaker, bellringer, and gravedigger.

Now they are giving me a fashionable white straw Italian hat
And a black veil that molds to my face, they are making me one of them.
They are leading me to the shorn grove, the circle of hives.
Is it the hawthorn[2] that smells so sick?
The barren body of hawthorn, etherizing its children.

Is it some operation that is taking place?
It is the surgeon my neighbors are waiting for,
This apparition in a green helmet,
Shining gloves and white suit.
Is it the butcher, the grocer, the postman, someone I know?   30

I cannot run, I am rooted, and the gorse[3] hurts me
With its yellow purses, its spiky armory.
I could not run without having to run forever.
The white hive is snug as a virgin,
Sealing off her brood[4] cells, her honey, and quietly humming.

Smoke rolls and scarves in the grove.
The mind of the hive thinks this is the end of everything.
Here they come, the outriders, on their hysterical elastics.[5]
If I stand very still, they will think I am cow-parsley,
A gullible head untouched by their animosity,   40

Not even nodding, a personage in a hedgerow.
The villagers open the chambers, they are hunting the queen.
Is she hiding, is she eating honey? She is very clever.
She is old, old, old, she must live another year, and she knows it.
While in their fingerjoint cells the new virgins

Dream of a duel they will win inevitably,
A curtain of wax dividing them from the bride flight,
The upflight of the murderess[6] into a heaven that loves her.
The villagers are moving the virgins, there will be no killing.
The old queen does not show herself, is she so ungrateful?   50

I am exhausted, I am exhausted————
Pillar of white in a blackout of knives.
I am the magician's girl who does not flinch.
The villagers are untying their disguises, they are shaking hands.
Whose is that long white box in the grove, what have they accomplished, why am
    I cold.

1962, 1965

---

[2] A spring shrub of the rose family, with fragrant flowers and small red fruits.
[3] A spiny, yellow-flowered shrub.   [4] Breeding.
[5] The bees that left the hive return quickly.   [6] The queen bee.

ARIEL*

Stasis[1] in darkness.
Then the substanceless blue
Pour of tor[2] and distances.

God's lioness,
How one we grow,
Pivot of heels and knees!—The furrow

Splits and passes, sister to
The brown arc
Of the neck I cannot catch,

Nigger-eye   10
Berries cast dark
Hooks————

Black sweet blood mouthfuls,
Shadows.
Something else

Hauls me through air————
Thighs, hair;
Flakes from my heels.

White
Godiva,[3] I unpeel————   20
Dead hands, dead stringencies.

And now I
Foam to wheat, a glitter of seas.
The child's cry

Melts in the wall.
And I
Am the arrow,

The dew that flies
Suicidal, at one with the drive
Into the red   30

Eye, the cauldron of morning.

1962, 1965

---

* The horse Plath rode in Devon, England, during the two years she lived there; a name for Jerusalem, meaning "lion of God" (Hebrew); also, the sprite of fire and air in Shakespeare's *Tempest*.
[1] A state of balance or equilibrium.   [2] A high, craggy hill.
[3] Lady Godiva, a noblewoman who supposedly rode naked on horseback through Coventry, England
(1040), to get feudal obligations and taxes reduced.

DADDY*

You do not do, you do not do
Any more, black shoe
In which I have lived like a foot
For thirty years, poor and white,
Barely daring to breathe or Achoo.

Daddy, I have had to kill you.
You died before I had time——
Marble-heavy, a bag full of God,
Ghastly statue with one gray toe[1]
Big as a Frisco seal   10

And a head in the freakish Atlantic
Where it pours bean green over blue
In the waters off beautiful Nauset.[2]
I used to pray to recover you.
Ach, du.[3]

In the German tongue, in the Polish town[4]
Scraped flat by the roller
Of wars, wars, wars.
But the name of the town is common.
My Polack friend   20

Says there are a dozen or two.
So I never could tell where you
Put your foot, your root,
I never could talk to you.
The tongue stuck in my jaw.

It stuck in a barb wire snare.
Ich, ich, ich, ich,[5]
I could hardly speak.
I thought every German was you.
And the language obscene   30

An engine, an engine
Chuffing[6] me off like a Jew.

* Plath's note: "The poem is spoken by a girl with an Electra complex [a tendency for a daughter to be attached to her father and hostile to her mother]. Her father died while she thought he was God. Her case is complicated by the fact that her father was also a Nazi and her mother very possibly part Jewish. In the daughter the two strains marry and paralyze each other—she has to act out the awful little allegory before she is free of it."
[1] The result of diabetes-induced gangrene; Plath's father, Otto Plath (1885–1940) had died from the disease.
[2] The Native-American name for Eastham, Cape Cod.
[3] "Ah, you" (German); the first of several references to her father's German background.
[4] Grasbow, where Otto Plath was born.   [5] "I, I, I, I" (German).   [6] Chugging.

A Jew to Dachau, Auschwitz, Belsen.[7]
I began to talk like a Jew.
I think I may well be a Jew.

The snows of the Tyrol,[8] the clear beer of Vienna
Are not very pure or true.
With my gipsy ancestress and my weird luck
And my Taroc pack[9] and my Taroc pack
I may be a bit of a Jew.   40

I have always been scared of *you,*
With your Luftwaffe,[10] your gobbledygoo.
And your neat mustache
And your Aryan[11] eye, bright blue.
Panzer-man, panzer-man,[12] O You——

Not God but a swastika[13]
So black no sky could squeak through.
Every woman adores a Fascist,
The boot in the face, the brute
Brute heart of a brute like you.   50

You stand at the blackboard, daddy,[14]
In the picture I have of you,
A cleft in your chin instead of your foot
But no less a devil for that, no not
Any less the black man who

Bit my pretty red heart in two.
I was ten when they buried you.
At twenty I tried to die
And get back, back, back to you.[15]
I thought even the bones would do.   60

But they pulled me out of the sack,
And they stuck me together with glue.
And then I knew what to do.
I made a model of you,
A man in black with a Meinkampf[16] look

And a love of the rack and the screw.
And I said I do, I do.

---

[7] Nazi concentration camps in Poland (Auschwitz) and Germany.
[8] Tirol, an Alpine region in Austria and Italy.
[9] A variant of Tarot, ancient fortune-telling cards.   [10] The Nazi air force.
[11] In Nazi ideology, the "superior" race of Nordic people of non-Jewish descent.
[12] A soldier in the Nazi tank division.   [13] A Greek cross, a symbol used by the Nazi party.
[14] Otto Plath taught biology at Boston University.
[15] Plath first attempted suicide when she was home from college during summer break.
[16] Hitler's autobiography of his youth, *Mein Kampf* ("*My Struggle*" [German]), published in 1925, before his political rise.

So daddy, I'm finally through.
The black telephone's off at the root,
The voices just can't worm through.   70

If I've killed one man, I've killed two———
The vampire who said he was you
And drank my blood for a year,
Seven years, if you want to know.
Daddy, you can lie back now.

There's a stake in your fat black heart
And the villagers never liked you.
They are dancing and stamping on you.
They always *knew* it was you.
Daddy, daddy, you bastard, I'm through.   80

                                        1962, 1965

NICK* AND THE CANDLESTICK

I am a miner. The light burns blue.
Waxy stalactites[1]
Drip and thicken, tears

The earthen womb
Exudes from its dead boredom.
Black bat airs

Wrap me, raggy shawls,
Cold homicides.
They weld to me like plums.

Old cave of calcium   10
Icicles, old echoer.
Even the newts are white,

Those holy Joes.
And the fish, the fish———
Christ! they are panes of ice,

A vice of knives,
A piranha
Religion, drinking

---

* Plath's son, Nicholas, born in January 1962.
[1] Deposits of calcium carbonate that hang like icicles from the roof or sides of a cavern.

Its first communion[2] out of my live toes.
The candle   20
Gulps and recovers its small altitude,

Its yellows hearten.
O love, how did you get here?
O embryo

Remembering, even in sleep,
Your crossed position.
The blood blooms clean

In you, ruby.
The pain
You wake to is not yours.   30

Love, love,
I have hung our cave with roses,
With soft rugs————

The last of Victoriana.[3]
Let the stars
Plummet to their dark address,

Let the mercuric
Atoms that cripple drip
Into the terrible well,

You are the one   40
Solid the spaces lean on, envious.
You are the baby in the barn.

                                          1962, 1965

EDGE*

The woman is perfected.
Her dead

Body wears the smile of accomplishment,
The illusion of a Greek necessity

Flows in the scrolls of her toga,
Her bare

---

[2] A Christian sacrament in which bread and wine are consumed as a commemoration of Jesus' death.

[3] Objects typical of the Victorian era, during the reign (1837–1901) of Queen Victoria (1819–1901) of Great Britain and Ireland.

* Plath's husband, Ted Hughes (1930–   ), suggests in "Notes on the Chronological Order of Sylvia Plath's Poems" (1966) that this poem was written a week before she committed suicide in February 1963.

Feet seem to be saying:
We have come so far, it is over.

Each dead child coiled, a white serpent,
One at each little   10

Pitcher of milk, now empty.[1]
She has folded

Them back into her body as petals
Of a rose close when the garden

Stiffens and odors bleed
From the sweet, deep throats of the night flower.

The moon has nothing to be sad about,
Staring from her hood of bone.

She is used to this sort of thing.
Her blacks crackle and drag.   20

1963, 1965

Amiri Baraka (LeRoi Jones)
(1934–   )

Amiri Baraka was born LeRoi Jones in Newark, New Jersey, in 1934 and educated at
Rutgers and Howard Universities. After he spent nearly three years in the U.S. Air Force,
Jones immersed himself in the bohemian scene of New York City's Greenwich Village in
1957 while he worked toward an M.A. in German literature at Columbia University and at
the New School for Social Research. Jones and his wife, Hettie Cohen, edited *Yugen,* an
avant-garde journal. Consistently a social critic and literary innovator, Jones has passed
through a series of transformations, adjusting his aesthetics, his politics, and his personal
life in resistance to the changing imbalances in mainstream American culture. A visit to
Cuba in 1960 marked a turning point, the beginning of his movement toward politically
engaged art.

In 1960 Jones's poetry was included in *The New American Poetry,* an influential anthology that brought together a diverse collection of post-World War II poets—nearly all
white—who rejected traditional forms. "MY POETRY is whatever I think I am," Jones
wrote in his statement at the end of the volume. "I CAN BE ANYTHING I CAN. I make a
poetry with what I feel is useful & can be saved out of all the garbage of our lives."

Struggling against the silence of printed poetry, Jones wrote for the theater. His plays
Dutchman and *The Slave,* produced Off Broadway in 1964, won awards and critical ac-

---

[1] At the time of Plath's death, her daughter was nearly three years old and her son just over one year.

claim. His writing of the early 1960s shows conflicts about his position in white society, doubts about beat poetics, and a search, through music criticism, for the criteria of a new African-American aesthetic.

In 1965, after the assassination of the Black Muslim leader Malcolm X, Jones entered a decade of African-American nationalist activism. He divorced his white wife and moved from Greenwich Village to Harlem. There he founded the Black Arts Theater School, which served as a model for black theaters throughout America. In 1966 he returned to Newark, where he founded the Spirit House Theater. Jones adopted the Muslim name Imamu (spiritual leader) Amiri (blessed) Baraka (prince) in 1968, and his new wife, Sylvia Robinson, took the name Amina Baraka. His co-editorship of *Black Fire: An Anthology of African-American Writing* (1968) was a major contribution to the African-American arts movement. Baraka's two mixed-media works of 1970, *In Our Terribleness* and *It's Nation Time*, drew on Kawaida, an African value system emphasizing collectivity, self-determination, creativity, and faith.

Much of the work of Baraka's black nationalist period was fiercely antiwhite. This stance changed by 1974 as he adopted Marxism. Dropping the religious title "Imamu," Baraka revised his leadership role, becoming an African studies professor and an artist/worker. He has succeeded at raising political and historical awareness through poetry of struggle and theater of ideas.

Suggested Readings: *Preface to a Twenty Volume Suicide Note*, 1961. *Blues People: Negro Music in White America*, 1963. *The System of Dante's Hell*, 1965. *Four Black Revolutionary Plays*, 1969. *The Motion of History and Other Plays*, 1978. *Selected Plays and Prose of Amiri Baraka/LeRoi Jones*, 1979. *The Autobiography of LeRoi Jones/Amiri Baraka*, 1984. *Daggers and Javelins: Essays, 1974–1979*, 1984. K. W. Benston, *Baraka: The Renegade and the Mask*, 1976. K. W. Benston, *Imamu Amiri Baraka (LeRoi Jones): A Collection of Critical Essays*, 1976. W. Sollers, *Amiri Baraka/LeRoi Jones: The Quest for a "Populist Modernism"*, 1978. L. W. Brown, *Amiri Baraka*, 1980. H. C. Lacey, *To Raise, Destroy, and Create: The Poetry, Drama, and Fiction of Imamu Amiri Baraka (LeRoi Jones)*, 1981. W. J. Harris, *The Poetry and Poetics of Amiri Baraka: The Jazz Aesthetic*, 1985.

Texts Used: "I Substitute for the Dead Lecturer" and "Political Poem": *The Dead Lecturer*, 1964. "Legacy" and "Evil Nigger Waits for Lightnin'": *Black Magic*, 1969. All else: *Selected Poetry of Amiri Baraka/LeRoi Jones*, 1979.

PREFACE TO A TWENTY VOLUME SUICIDE NOTE

(For Kellie Jones,[1] born 16 May 1959)

  Lately, I've become accustomed to the way
  The ground opens up and envelops me
  Each time I go out to walk the dog.
  Or the broad edged silly music the wind
  Makes when I run for a bus . . .

  Things have come to that.

---

[1] The daughter of Baraka (when he was still LeRoi Jones) and his wife Hettie Cohen.

And now, each night I count the stars,
And each night I get the same number.
And when they will not come to be counted,
I count the holes they leave.   10

Nobody sings anymore.

And then last night, I tiptoed up
To my daughter's room and heard her
Talking to someone, and when I opened
The door, there was no one there . . .
Only she on her knees, peeking into

Her own clasped hands.

1957, 1961

IN MEMORY OF RADIO

Who has ever stopped to think of the divinity of Lamont Cranston?[1]
(Only Jack Kerouac,[2] that I know of: & me.
The rest of you probably had on WCBS and Kate Smith,
Or something equally unattractive.)

What can I say?
It is better to have loved and lost
Than to put linoleum in your living rooms?

Am I a sage or something?
Mandrake's[3] hypnotic gesture of the week?
(Remember, I do not have the healing powers of Oral Roberts . . .   10
I cannot, like F. J. Sheen,[4] tell you how to get saved & *rich!*
I cannot even order you to gaschamber satori[5] like Hitler or Goody Knight[6]

& Love is an evil word.
Turn it backwards/see, see what I mean?
An evol word. & besides
who understands it?
I certainly wouldn't like to go out on that kind of limb.

Saturday mornings we listened to *Red Lantern* & his undersea folk.
At 11, *Let's Pretend*/& we did/&I, the poet, still do, Thank God!

---

[1] The hero of the radio serial *The Shadow* (1931–1954), popular during Baraka's boyhood; most names in the poem are those of characters, performers, and programs that he heard in his youth.
[2] Kerouac (1922–1969) was a famous beat writer.   [3] Mandrake the Magician, a comic-strip hero.
[4] Bishop Fulton Sheen (1895–1975), who preached over the radio in the 1930s and 1940s.
[5] Spiritual enlightenment, used in Zen Buddhism.
[6] Goodwin Knight, California's governor (1953–1959) while the use of the gas chamber in capital punishment was under debate.

What was it he used to say (after the transformation, when he was safe   20
& invisible & the unbelievers couldn't throw stones?) "Heh, heh, heh,
Who knows what evil lurks in the hearts of men? The Shadow knows."[7]

O, yes he does
O, yes he does.
An evil word it is,
This Love.

1964

A POEM FOR SPECULATIVE HIPSTERS

He had got, finally,
to the forest
of motives. There were no
owls, or hunters. No Connie Chatterleys[1]
resting beautifully
on their backs, having casually
brought socialism
to England.
   Only ideas,
and their opposites.   10
    Like,
  he was *really*
  nowhere.

1964

I SUBSTITUTE FOR THE DEAD LECTURER

What is most precious, because
it is lost. What is lost,
because it is most
precious.

They have turned, and say that I am dying. That
I have thrown
my life
away. They
have left me alone, where

---

[7] The opening lines of *The Shadow* episodes.
[1] The heroine of *Lady Chatterley's Lover* (1930), by the English writer D. H. Lawrence (1885–1930), in which Lady Chatterley renounces her sickly upper-class husband to marry his virile game-keeper.

there is no one, nothing
save who I am. Not a note
nor a word.

      Cold air batters
the poor (and their minds   10
turn open
like sores). What kindness
What wealth
can I offer? Except
what is, for me,
ugliest. What is
for me, shadows, shrieking
phantoms. Except
they have need
of life. Flesh   20
at least,
        should be theirs.

The Lord has saved me
to do this. The Lord
has made me strong. I
am as I must have
myself. Against all
thought, all music, all
my soft loves.

      For all these wan roads   30
I am pushed to follow, are
my own conceit. A simple muttering
elegance, slipped in my head
pressed on my soul, is my heart's
worth. And I am frightened
that the flame of my sickness
will burn off my face. And leave
the bones, my stewed black skull,
an empty cage of failure.

1964

POLITICAL POEM

(for Basil)

Luxury, then, is a way of
being ignorant, comfortably
An approach to the open market

of least information. Where theories
can thrive, under heavy tarpaulins
without being cracked by ideas.

(I have not seen the earth for years
and think now possibly "dirt" is
negative, positive, but clearly
social. I cannot plant a seed, cannot   10
recognize the root with clearer dent
than indifference. Though I eat
and shit as a natural man. (Getting up
from the desk to secure a turkey sandwich
and answer the phone: the poem undone
undone by my station, by my station,
and the bad words of Newark.[1]) Raised up
to the breech, we seek to fill for this
crumbling century. The darkness of love,
in whose sweating memory all error is forced.   20

Undone by the logic of any specific death. (Old gentlemen
who still follow fires, tho are quieter
and less punctual. It is a polite truth
we are left with. Who are you? What are you
saying? Something to be dealt with, as easily.
The noxious game of reason, saying, "No, No,
you cannot feel," like my dead lecturer
lamenting thru gipsies his fast suicide.

1964

A POEM FOR BLACK HEARTS

For Malcolm's[1] eyes, when they broke
the face of some dumb white man, For
Malcolm's hands raised to bless us
all black and strong in his image
of ourselves, For Malcolm's words
fire darts, the victor's tireless
thrusts, words hung above the world
change as it may, he said it, and
for this he was killed, for saying,
and feeling, and being/change, all   10
collected hot in his heart, For Malcolm's
heart, raising us above our filthy cities,

---

[1] In the mid-1960s Baraka began to concentrate his activities in Newark, New Jersey.
[1] Malcolm X (1925–1965), a civil rights leader and Black Muslim activist who was assassinated.

for his stride, and his beat, and his address
to the gray monsters of the world, For Malcolm's
pleas for your dignity, black men, for your life,
black man, for the filling of your minds
with righteousness, For all of him dead and
gone and vanished from us, and all of him which
clings to our speech black god of our time.
For all of him, and all of yourself, look up,   20
black man, quit stuttering and shuffling, look up,
black man, quit whining and stooping, for all of him,
For Great Malcolm a prince of the earth, let nothing in us rest
until we avenge ourselves for his death, stupid animals
that killed him, let us never breathe a pure breath if
we fail and white men call us faggots till the end of
the earth.

1967

LEGACY

(For Blues People)

In the south, sleeping against
the drugstore, growling under
the trucks and stoves, stumbling
through and over the cluttered eyes
of early mysterious night. Frowning
drunk waving moving a hand or lash.
Dancing kneeling reaching out, letting
a hand rest in shadows. Squatting
to drink or pee. Stretching to climb
pulling themselves onto horses near   10
where there was sea (the old songs
lead you to believe). Riding out
from this town, to another, where
it is also black. Down a road
where people are asleep. Towards
the moon or the shadows of houses.
Towards the songs' pretended sea.

1967

EVIL NIGGER WAITS FOR LIGHTNIN'

Alone, at night, with all the world
not watching, around me,

who for the understanding
intended, the love
withheld,
would be lost in the blackness
of self-nights
howling like something
or scurrying behind iceboxes
like something   10
would be them things
in my conscious
ness, or waddlegirls
full of invisible demands
they are children the world will tell you
only children, lost dreams, that you should love
if you can, from the tower of Headlust, you they moan
should always adore them, lost feeling, should love and
take yrself through any change to understand their blankness.

Alone at night the world disappears breathing over my head weeping it   20
is lost or unappreciated. It says I do not love it. And sends its dopey
messengers to touch me right. The world, the world says, is full of love
can you find it, can you enter, and remain, grow strong with it beautiful
thing
in the rain, the world,
these sent things whisper
mice, fucked ladies, whisps of cloud
still visible four oclock in the nighttime
for the expanding or retracting dying or just coming
thing   30
we will always
be.

The Astronomers,
The Philosophers,
The Crowd, of them,
Things, These dangerous feelers, for understanding,
now that I am alone so much I can manage to
hear another thing
singing through my face
describing the arc   40
and the constant
return . . .
                way out now,
                describing its own voice
                its
                reason

1967

Lawson Inada
(1938–   )

Born in 1938 in Fresno, California, Lawson Fusao Inada is a *sansei,* or third-generation Japanese American. As a child during World War II, Inada was confined with his family, along with thousands of other Japanese Americans, in government-operated "relocation" camps in California, Arkansas, and Colorado. Products of national paranoia during the war, these camps were designed to segregate Japanese Americans from the general population. He describes the experience in such poems as "From Our Album" (1971), which begins before the war and ends "when the threat lessened, / when we became tame."

After the war Inada returned with his family to Fresno and finished high school. In 1956 he enrolled at the University of California at Berkeley. A year later he transferred to Fresno State College (now California State University at Fresno), where he received a B.A. in 1959. On a Writers Workshop Fellowship Inada attended the University of Iowa from 1960 to 1962. He then completed a master of fine arts degree in creative writing at the University of Oregon in 1966. He has since taught at the University of New Hampshire, Lewis and Clark College in Oregon, Eastern Oregon State College, the University of Hawaii, and Southern Oregon State College.

A prolific poet, editor, and lecturer, Inada maintains a deep interest in the literatures and cultures of Asian Americans. One of few Asian-American writers, he sees himself as a social force and is well aware of the varied cultures he inherited as a *sansei.* In a 1989 letter to the writer Louis Owens, Inada notes, "I've worked and lived all over this country, and what continues to amaze me is our cultural diversity. I hear it on the radio when I wake up! At the same time, I know that great culture and diversity was already here before America was founded. As a teacher, I try to inform my students about the greater American experience."

Inada's poetry, particularly that in his collection *Before the War: Poems as They Happened* (1971), explores memories of family life and internment during World War II. At the same time, the poet casts a close eye at both natural and manmade environments. Inada's verse is highly eclectic and syncretic (merging different forms into one). In both form and content his poetry owes much to American jazz. As a teenager Inada dreamed of becoming a jazz musician. "To this day," he told Owens, "the major influences on my poetry are musicians such as Lester Young, Charlie Parker, and John Coltrane."

Inada has twice been awarded National Endowment for the Arts creative writing fellowships and has been honored with a Pioneer Writers Award from the Asian-American Writers Conference. In 1980 Inada was one of twenty-one American writers invited to read at the White House for "A Salute to Poetry and American Poets." His work has appeared in more than thirty anthologies as well as in numerous journals and magazines. He has recently collaborated with David B. Zaslow on the "Shakin' Loose With Mother Goose" series of children's books (1986) accompanied by tapes narrated by Steve Allen and Jayne Meadows.

Suggested Readings: *Three Northwest Poets: Drake, Inada, Lawder,* 1970. Ed., *Aiiieeeee!: An Anthology of Asian-American Writers,* 1974. *The Next World,* ed. J. Bruchac, 1978. H. A. Baker, Jr., ed., *Three American Literatures: Essays in Chicano, Native American, Asian-American Literature for Teachers of American Literature,* 1982. M. Harris and K. Aguero, eds., *A Gift of Tongues:*

Critical Challenges in Contemporary American Poetry, 1978. *The Buddha Bandits Down Highway 99: Hongo, Inada, Lau,* 1979.

Text Used: *Before the War: Poems As They Happened,* 1971.

FROM OUR ALBUM

I. "Before the War"[1]

"Before the war"
means Fresno,[2] a hedged-in house,
two dogs in the family.

Blackie, the small one, mine,
lapped at his insides
on the floorboard, on the way to the doctor.

Jimmy, my father's shepherd,
wouldn't eat after the evacuation.
He wouldn't live with another master

and pined away, skin and bone.   10

With feelings more than pride,
we call him our one-man dog.

II. Mud

Mud in the barracks[3]—
a muddy room, a chamber pot.

Mud in the moats
around each barracks group.

Mud on the shoes
trudging to the mess hall.

Mud in the swamp
where the men chopped wood.   20

---

[1] World War II (1939–1945), in which some 110,000 Japanese Americans on the West Coast were rounded up against their will and "relocated" to internment camps, supposedly for fear that they might prove disloyal; Inada and his family were among those relocated. The Supreme Court forbade such internment in December 1944, near the end of the war.
[2] A city in central California.   [3] The internment camps were set up like barracks.

Mud on the guts
under a loaded wagon—

crushed in the mud by the wheel.

III. Desert Songs

1. ALL THAT WE GATHERED

Because there was little else to do,
they led us to the artillery range
for shells, all that we gathered,
and let us dig among dunes
for slugs, when they were through.

Because there was little else to do,
one of them chased a stray   30
with his tail between his legs
and shot him through the head.

2. SHELLS

A desert tortoise—
something mute and hard—

something to decorate
a desert Japanese garden:

gnarled wood, smooth
artillery shells for a border.

When a guard
smashes one, the shell   40

cracks open and the muscles ooze.

3. IT IS ONLY NATURAL

The pheasant is an Oriental creature,
so it is only natural
that one should fly into camp

and, famished by rations and cans,
break out in secret, native dance
over a fire, on a black coal stove.

4. SONG OF THE 442ND

Caged creatures
have curious moods.

Some of them choose
to be turned
                                           50

loose in a group,
to take their chances

in the open.

5. STEERS

Because a dentist
logically drives a butcher truck,

I rode with my father
to the slaughterhouse on an afternoon.

Not hammers, not bullets,
could make him close his eyes.   60

6. HE TEACHES

He jerks the eyes
from birds, feet
from lizards,

and punishes
ants with the gaze
of a glass.

And with his sly
gaze, his child's face,
he teaches

what has its place,   70
and must be
passed on to others.

IV. SONG OF CHICAGO

When the threat lessened,[4]
when we became tame,
my father and friends
took a train to Chicago

for factory work,
for packaging bolts.
One grew a mustache
and called himself Carlos.   80

---

[4] Either when the end of the war approached or when Japan surrendered (August 15, 1945).

And they all made a home
with those of their own—

rats, bedbugs, blacks.

1971

IN A STORM

Late afternoon, and the grove
snaps under weight of snow.
Their bodies cannot bear
such extension,

the force that makes them
more than they are:

branches have broken;
one whole tree
goes groping like a squid.

We have barely met.   10

We talk a little, share
a short, dry kiss,

then go on talking—

and each word said
brings snow and branches down upon us.

2.

Night, and another snow:
dense, wafting,
all but stopping in descent.

We have been captive
to its fancies: 20

rolling, floating in a drift.

Now the walls have us:
shapes that might be
Joshuas[1] on a mesa praising rain.

---

[1] The Joshua tree is a variety of yucca plant common to the high, flat tableland (mesas) of southwestern United States; so named because its branches were thought to resemble the outstretched arms of Joshua leading the Israelites, in the Bible story.

But cold, heat come
flowing out of darkness

in a storm we make.

1971

UTICA, NORTH PLATTE*

Take any flat, plain piece of land,
give it a name—
Utica, North Platte—
motels take shape around the syllables.
Some movie screens . . .

You come and register, sick
with the edges,
furtive dog among the brushes . . .

The scent of flesh,
of lovers' luggage,   10
the crushed mosquito's image . . .

The city has her window open—
bugs cluster at the screen.
She shoves and tugs her silent lover . . .

Night of tall doors
opening for truckers, some bitch within . . .

Then to be a convict,
on the run,
licenses and whiskey sagging the back end . . .

Someone tugs the covers from you.   20
Tracing the edges,
you are about to cry . . .

By morning she is tired and sleeping—
widow white, closed . . .

The night has grown
metallic flowers in her garden—

* Cities in western and eastern Nebraska, respectively.

straight and hard,
all of the same color.

1971

WINTERSONG

For Bill Evans[1]

Suspended from the eaves
the feeder swings, cold
plastic pagoda[2] brimmed
with seeds the wind flings
scattering in the snow.
Beyond those low
eaves, the frozen teeth,
are juncos[3] in the trees.
Trees too thin for snow
and three birds weaving   10
wintersong among them—
music on a sheet.
Music eased by one
alone, from a piano,
brooding over the keys,
holding each note
for all its worth,
alone and whole . . .

When the flourish goes,
emptiness comes, space   20
of fields simplified
by snow, that between
note and other note,
unreckoned with before.
That which differentiates
lasting deed from forage,
the mindless bickerings . . .

Noon on the kitchen clock.
The mail truck stops
and skitters in the road.   30
Coming from the box,
I consider the irony
of the house—modern,

---

[1] William John Evans (1929–1980), a jazz pianist.
[2] An oriental or Indian temple in the form of a pyramidal tower.   [3] Small American finches.

spare as any feeder,
the owner somewhere
in Florida—and, caught
once more in the snow,
with stuff disposed of
by the postman—notes
and cancelings from   40
San Francisco—I know
whatever juncos know.

1971

Paula Gunn Allen
(1939–   )

Born in 1939 in Cubero, New Mexico, Paula Gunn Allen was raised in that village at the edge of the Laguna Indian Pueblo. Of Laguna, Sioux, and Lebanese ancestry, Allen grew up in a family in which, according to her, English was only one of the five languages in which the family conversed. In *Songs From This Earth on Turtle's Back* (1983, edited by Joseph Bruchac) Allen has said of her complicated heritage, "My poetry, my poetics and my aesthetics all arise out of this chaotic mix, this primordial soup. Melting pots hold no terrors for me because I am one." After receiving a master of fine arts degree from the University of Oregon and Ph.D. from the University of New Mexico, Allen taught at Fort Lewis College in Durango, Colorado. Subsequently, in California she has directed programs for, and has taught, Native-American studies.

A poet, novelist, essayist, and critic, Allen has published more than half a dozen collections of verse, including the acclaimed *Skins and Bones* (1988); a novel, *The Woman Who Owned the Shadows* (1983); two major critical studies of Native-American literature, *Studies in Native American Literature* (1983) and *The Sacred Hoop: Recovering the Feminine in American Indian Traditions* (1986); and numerous uncollected poems, stories, and essays. Of her primary interest in Native-American culture and literature, Allen states in the essay "The Autobiography of a Confluence" (1987), "I was told over and over, 'Never forget that you're Indian.' My mother said it. Nor did she say, 'Remember that you are part Indian.' "

The author's intense concern for what being Native American and being a mixed-blooded woman in contemporary America means is central to her poetry and fiction. Again and again in her poems and in her long and short fiction, Allen draws upon Native-American mythology, in particular the oral tradition of southwestern tribes, to explore and define her own life and the lives of those around her. In some of her poems, such as "Coyote Jungle" (1988), she calls upon Coyote, a trickster figure of Native-American legend. She also typically focuses the reader's attention on the dilemmas that confront women and addresses the choices available to today's women. Simultaneously, Allen identifies closely with, and writes about, the landscape. "[Native Americans] are the land," Allen declares in "IYANI: It Goes This Way" (1981). "To the best of my understanding, that is the fundamental idea embedded in Native American life and culture in the Southwest."

Suggested Readings: *The Blind Lion*, 1975. *Coyote's Daylight Trip*, 1978. *A Cannon Between My Knees*, 1981. *Starchild*, 1981. *Shadow Country*, 1982. *The Woman Who Owned the Shadows*, 1983. *The Sacred Hoop: Recovering the Feminine in American Indian Traditions*, 1986. H. A. Baker, Jr., ed., *Three American Literatures: Essays in Chicano, Native American, Asian-American Literature for Teachers of American Literature*, 1982. K. Lincoln, *Native American Renaissance*, 1983. J. Ruppert, "Paula Gunn Allen and Joy Harjo: Closing the Distance Between Personal and Mythic Space," in *American Indian Quarterly*, 7(1): 27–40, 1983. L. Owens and T. Colonnese, *American Indian Novelists: An Annotated Critical Bibliography*, 1985. G. Vizenor, *Narrative Chance: Postmodern Discourse on Native American Literatures*, 1989.

Text Used: *Skins and Bones: Poems 1979–1987*, 1988.

C'KOY'U, OLD WOMAN*

old woman there in the earth
outside you we wait
do you dream of birth, bring
what is outside   inside?

    old
        woman inside
           old
                woman outside

        old woman there in the sky
        we are waiting inside you   10
        dreaming your dream of birthing
        get what is inside/outside

    a hey a hey a hey a ho
    a hey a hey a hey a ho
    a hi oh ho a hi oh ho
    a hey a hey a hey a ho

1988

POCAHONTAS TO HER ENGLISH HUSBAND, JOHN ROLFE†

In a way, then, Pocahontas was a kind of traitor to her people. . . . Perhaps I am being a little too hard on her. The crucial point, it seems to me, is to remember that

---

* In the Laguna language, "c'koy'u" means "old woman."

† The princess Pocahontas (1595?–1617), daughter of Powhatan, the chief of the Wampanoag Indians, married Rolfe (1585–1622), an English colonist and a founder of Jamestown, Virginia (1607), in 1614. She is said to have saved the life of Captain John Smith (1580–1631), another Jamestown colonist, in 1608 by holding his head in her arms to prevent Powhatan's warriors from clubbing him to death.

*Pocahontas was a hostage. Would she have converted freely to Christianity if she
had not been in captivity? There is no easy answer to this question other than to note
that once she was free to do what she wanted, she avoided her own people like the
plague. . . .*

Pocahontas was a white dream—a dream of cultural superiority.

—CHARLES LARSON, *American Indian Fiction*[1]

Had I not cradled you in my arms
oh beloved perfidious one,
you would have died.
And how many times did I pluck you
from certain death in the wilderness—
my world through which you stumbled
as though blind?
Had I not set you tasks
your masters far across the sea
would have abandoned you—   10
did abandon you, as many times
they left you
to reap the harvest of their lies.
Still you survived, oh my fair husband,
and brought them gold
wrung from a harvest I taught you
to plant. Tobacco.
It is not without irony that by this crop
your descendants die, for other
powers than you know   20
take part in this and all things.
And indeed I did rescue you—
not once but a thousand thousand times
and in my arms you slept, a foolish child,
and under my protecting gaze you played,
chattering nonsense about a God
you had not wit to name. I'm sure
you wondered at my silence, saying I was
a simple wanton,[2] a savage maid,
dusky daughter of heathen sires   30
who cartwheeled naked through the muddy towns
who would learn the ways of grace only
by your firm guidance, through
your husbandly rule:
no doubt, no doubt.
I spoke little, you said.
And you listened less,
but played with your gaudy dreams
and sent ponderous missives to the throne
striving thereby to curry favor   40
with your king.[3]

[1] Published in 1978.   [2] A lewd or lascivious person.
[3] James I (1566–1625), king of England (1603–1625).

I saw you well. I
understood your ploys and still
protected you, going so far as to die
in your keeping—a wasting,
putrefying Christian death[4]—and you,
deceiver, whiteman, father of my son,
survived, reaping wealth greater
than any you had ever dreamed
from what I taught you and   50
from the wasting of my bones.

1988

COYOTE JUNGLE*

The man across from me
sits tight, holding
together all the plans
of another time,
pointed toe edging
cautious toward a future
of electronic landscape.
Even the forests
have been wired, plugged in
to terminals far away.   10
He doesn't understand
that the furrow on his
forehead was transferred
from the furrows he once turned
on the land, embedded there
by lightning flash that stunned
him, knocked him silly
as he sat on the tractor
waiting out Nebraska storm.
On that day,   20
Earth marked him as her own,
and blinded by that light
to tractor hum and rich,
new-turned clods,
he walked to town
carrying nothing but a small
squat black box[1] for doctoring

[4] Pocahontas probably died from tuberculosis.
  * According to Native-American legend, the coyote is a trickster who assumes many forms and
shapes.
  [1] A box containing natural remedies carried by Native-American medicine men.

and a stranger's way of knowing.
Now he sits near me,
squinting into the velvet dark   30
of technological truth,
muttering with vanished wizards:

DO WHAT THOU WILT
SHALL BE THE WHOLE OF THE LAW

and there casts the enchantment
that will frame our lives anew.
He does not comprehend
the fire-studded darkness
of the words that fall: *silver,*
camphor, mercury, copper, gold,   40
iron, brass and *lead,* ancient
ritual revitalized on smog-
heavy mountain air.
Jeremiah in the wild,
Coyote hunched on the northeast border of urban sprawl
he grows sheep and doctors
broken pets;
he builds strong fences
to cradle baby and wife in,   50
he speaks words to banish
terror in face of the dark
he knows he is facing:
goddam coyotes,
I'd like to see em raise em
in the cities, like
em to see the gutted bellies
of the lambs those varmints
leave behind.

                                                        1988

WEED

She stood, a weed tall in the sun.
She grew like that and went
over it again and again trying to be tall
trying not to die in the drying sun
the seeming turbulence of waiting
the sun so yellow
so still

There was nothing else to do. It was like that
in her day, and the sun who rose so bright

so full of fire reminded her of that.   10
It was the sun that did it; it was the rain.
She stood it all, and more:
the water pounding from the high rock face
of the mesas[1] that made her yard
she knew where she was growing. Didn't
she know what sun will do, what happens to weeds
when their growing time's done? Didn't she care?
She got the sun into her, though.
The fire. She drank the rain for fuel.
She stood there in the day, growing,   20
trying to stand tall like a right weed would.

The drying was part of it.
The dying. Come from heat, the transformation
of fire. The rain helped because it understood
why she just stood there, growing,
tall in the heat and bright.

1988

MYTH/TELLING—DREAM/SHOWING

1.

so where do we go next?
(into sunrise)

2.

there is all the clutter:
on the walls, the table top,
in the sink, all over the counters,
on the stove, the sofa, the floors.

3.

the bird, yellow, green and blue
who lives in a cage with an open door
chirps now and then. drops onto the table
for breakfast.   10

4.

the cloud in the north, she said.
she meant the united states.

---

[1] High plateaus or flat tablelands with steep sides; common in the southwestern United States.

5.

I don't care, he said. I love
the united states. it isn't fair.
I never killed any indians. I am not
responsible for what my ancestors did.
I love the wilderness, he said. the indians
can't keep me out of it.

6.

and then there's the indian woman
who hates in herself what is white.   20
says she sees it like vomit. like
a crippled withered leg she must drag
with her everywhere she goes.

7.

and there is all the litter. the hours
passing. the exhaustion. the cloud
that is what I have to do today. not
go to the water. not go to the mesa.[1]
go into the city. the cloud.

8.

the indian woman is cursed with lupus.[2]
a blood disease. in which your blood   30
devours you.

9.

the white man goes to yosemite
on vacation. it's his recreation.
yes, says another man, black. it's
your recreation, but it's their life.

10.

the north of here is oregon, washington.
mt. st. helen's.[3] that cloud.

11.

the bird dreams in his cage.
about lunch. he doesn't dream of trees.
he never saw one, doesn't know what they are.   40

---

[1] A high plateau or flat tableland with steep sides; common in the southwestern United States.
[2] An inflammatory disease in which the body's immunological system attacks itself.
[3] A volcano in Washington state.

12.

I have to put my feathers on.
go through the door that opens.
into wilderness. city traffic.
bird-empty streets.

13.

if dawn comes (if corn comes).
if it is sunrise. that soft and blessing.
where someone is going, next.
if spring comes. (summer-people time.)
corn-is-growing time.
where/when-someone-is-going-next time.   50

1988

Robert Pinsky
(1940–   )

Robert Pinsky's work stands in a line with that of Alexander Pope, Samuel Johnson, Samuel Taylor Coleridge, Matthew Arnold, T. S. Eliot, and W. H. Auden in its now-rare ability to combine a well-respected academic criticism with a highly regarded poetic sensibility. Pinsky's first four published books alternate critical studies of the poems of Walter Savage Landor and the traditions of contemporary poetry with two volumes of long, meditative verse, *Sadness and Happiness* (1975) and *An Explanation of America* (1979). A student of the poet Yvor Winters at Stanford University, Pinsky shares in Winters's evaluative, urbane approach to poetry, preferring sanity and moral engagement to what Winters termed "melodramatic emotionalism." Pinsky's criticism and verse both share in this move away from an Emersonian model of speculative transcendence to focus on the play of the mind as it searches for a "language for presenting the role of a conscious soul in an unconscious world" (*The Situation of Poetry,* 1976). In his "Essay on Psychiatrists" (1975) he figures Winters as "the Old Man," who explains that as "capitalism and scientific method" rose, "the logical / Foundations of western thought decayed and fell apart," leaving poets with no way to investigate emotions or experiences. "At this time, poets and men / Of genius began to go mad." Pinsky's meditations are devoted to finding the wisdom to arm us against this madness.

Pinsky's poetry moderates between ironic detachment and passionate involvement. In his poetry collection *History of My Heart* (1984), Pinsky continues his ruminative search for health and again centers on moral moments in everyday life—giving comfort to a victim of a seizure or rescuing a young boy who is choking. Here, as he says elsewhere, the physical world "reminds us of our solitude . . . of the contingency and randomness of the world the senses know." His most recognized model is Horace, the first-century B.C.

Roman poet whose letters Pinsky translates in *An Explanation of America* and who provides Pinsky with a decorous tone in which to explore the "everlasting possibilities" of his country. Whereas Pinsky has experimented with other forms, such as short lyrics and surreal-dream poems, the long meditation of Horatian civility has been Pinsky's most successful mode, though his *Mindwheel* (1987) marks something of a departure from it. *Mindwheel,* an interactive computer game that Pinsky calls an "electronic novel," dramatically demonstrates the endless curiosity embodied in all of his writing.

Pinsky was born in Long Branch, New Jersey, in 1940 and received his undergraduate degree from Rutgers University in 1962. After earning a Ph.D. in English literature at Stanford in 1966, Pinsky taught at the University of Chicago, Wellesley College, Harvard University, and the University of California at Berkeley. He also served as poetry editor for the *New Republic* and has contributed to a wide variety of both poetry and scholarly journals.

Suggested Readings: *Sadness and Happiness,* 1975. *The Situation of Poetry: Contemporary Poetry and Its Traditions,* 1976. *An Explanation of America,* 1979. *Mindwheel,* 1987. M. Halliday, "An Interview With Robert Pinsky," in *Ploughshares,* 6, 1980.

Text Used: *History of My Heart,* 1984.

THE UNSEEN

In Krakow[1] it rained, the stone arcades and cobbles
And the smoky air all soaked one penetrating color
While in an Art Nouveau[2] cafe, on harp-shaped chairs,

We sat making up our minds to tour the death camp.[3]
As we drove there the next morning past farms
And steaming wooden villages, the rain had stopped

Though the sky was still gray. A young guide explained
Everything we saw in her tender, hectoring[4] English:
The low brick barracks; the heaped-up meticulous

Mountains of shoes, toothbrushes, hair; one cell   10
Where the Pope[5] had prayed and placed flowers; logbooks,
Photographs, latrines—the whole unswallowable

Menu of immensities. It began drizzling again,
And the way we paused to open or close the umbrellas,
Hers and ours, as we went from one building to the next,

---

[1] A city in southern Poland.
[2] A decorating style that originated in the late nineteenth century, characterized by sinuous lines and foliate forms.
[3] Auschwitz, just west of Krakow.   [4] Brow-beating.
[5] John Paul II (1920–), named pope in 1978.

Had a formal, dwindled feeling. We felt bored
And at the same time like screaming Biblical phrases:
I am poured out like water; Thine is the day and

Thine also the night; I cannot look to see
My own right hand . . . I remembered a sleep-time game,   20
A willed dream I had never thought of by day before:

I am there; and granted the single power of invisibility,
Roaming the camp at will. At first I savor my mastery
Slowly by creating small phantom diversions,

Then kill kill kill kill, a detailed and strangely
Passionless inward movie: I push the man holding
The crystals[6] down from the gas chamber roof, bludgeon

The pet collie of the Commandant's children
And in the end flush everything with a vague flood
Of fire and blood as I drift on toward sleep   30

In a blurred finale, like our tour's—eddying
In a downpour past the preserved gallows where
The Allies hung the Commandant, in 1947.

I don't feel changed, or even informed—in that,
It's like any other historical monument; although
It is true that I don't ever at night any more

Prowl rows of red buildings unseen, doing
Justice like an angry god to escape insomnia. And so,
O discredited Lord of Hosts,[7] your servant gapes

Obediently to swallow various doings of us, the most   40
Capable of all your former creatures—we have
No shape, we are poured out like water, but still

We try to take in what won't be turned from in despair:
As if, just as we turned toward the fumbled drama
Of the religious art shop window to accuse you

Yet again, you were to slit open your red heart
To show us at last the secret of your day and also,
Because it also is yours, of your night.

1984

---

[6] Cyanide crystals, causing death by asphyxiation.   [7] Jehovah, the Judeo-Christian God.

THE VOLUME

Or a crippled sloop falters, about to go under
In sight of huge ritual fires along the beach
With people eating and dancing, the older children

Cantering horses parallel to the ghostlike surf.
But instead the crew nurse her home somehow,
And they make her fast and stand still shivering

In the warm circle, preserved, and they may think
Or else I have drowned, and this is the last dream.
They try never to think about the whole range and weight

Of ocean. To try to picture it is like looking down   10
From an immense height, the oblivious black volume.
To drown in that calamitous belly would be dying twice.

When I was small, someone might say about a delicate
Uncorroded piece of equipment, that's a sweetwater reel—
And from the sound *sweetwater,* a sense of the coarse,

Kelp-colored, chill sucking of the other,
Sour and vital: governed by the moon, or in the picture
Of the blind minotaur[1] led by the little girl,

Walking together on the beach under the partial moon,
Past amazed fishermen furled in their hoodlike sail.   20
Last Easter, when the branch broke under Caroline[2]

And the jagged stub, digging itself into her thigh as she fell,
Tore her leg open to the bone, she said she didn't want to die.
And now the scar like a streak of glare on her tan leg

Flashes when she swims. Otherwise, it might be a dream.
The sad, brutal bullhead[3] with its milky eye tilts upward
Toward the stars painted as large as moths as the helpless

Monster strides by, his hand resting on the child's shoulder,
All only a dream, painted, like the corpse's long hair
That streams back from the dory[4] toward the shark   30

---

[1] According to Greek myth, a monster with the body of a man and the head of a bull; he was confined
by King Minos in a labyrinth and was fed a periodic tribute of youths and maidens until the hero
Theseus slew him. [2] A hurricane. [3] A large-headed fish.
[4] A flat-bottomed rowboat with high flaring sides, used in fishing.

Scavenging in *Brook Watson and the Shark,*[5]
The gray-green paint mysterious as water,
The wave, the boat-hook, the white faces of the living,

The hair that shows the corpse has dreamed the picture,
It is so calm; the boat and the shark and the flowing hair
All held and preserved in the green volume of water.

1984

THE LIVING

The living, the unfallen lords of life,
Move heavily through the dazzle
Where all things shift, glitter or swim—

As on a day at the beach, or under
The stark, absolute blue of a snow morning,
With concentric peals of brightness

Ringing in the cold air. They seem drugged.
Their abrupt good fortune clings heavily
With the slow sway and pomp of dirty velvet,

Their purple, the unaccustomed garb—   10
Worn slipshod—of the Court
Of Misrule:[1] animal-headed, staring

As if sleepy or drunk, riding a goat
Or perched backwards on a donkey,
Widdershins,[2] hectic. Beggars, bad governors,

We thrive awkwardly—some maimed slightly
In the course of war; some torn by fear sometimes;
Yet not paralyzed: we are moved. The strange

Stories of the degradations of the martyrs—
Crucified upside-down, cooked live   20
On a grille—bother us doubly: in themselves,

And because a strange opiate intervenes
As if they were suffering now, at this
Apex of time, and for some reason we

---

[5] A 1778 painting by John Singleton Copley (1738–1815).
[1] A medieval celebration in which social hierarchies are reversed and a Lord of Misrule appointed.
[2] Backwards, in a direction opposite to the usual.

Could not concentrate, lost on the slopes
Below. We ape court manners clumsily;
Or shake fists, in awkward parade,

Exalted and confused. Even in affliction—grotesque
Illnesses, poverty, ruined hopes, the world's
Rage and the body's—the most miserable   30

Find in the mere daylight and air
A miraculous daily bread. Fairy bread:
We eat and are changed. Survivors

After a catastrophe, transported, feel
Nearly as if they could find the lost,
Luckless ones, somewhere, perhaps not far—

Crowded, maybe, behind some one
Of the innumerable doors of the palace.
Plump Chance beams like an effigy

Of Mardi Gras—the apparent origin   40
And end of so much: disease, fame,
Unemployment, intrigue. The world, random,

Is so real, it is as if our own
Good or bad luck were here only
As a kind of filler, holding together

Just that much of the adjacent
Splendor and terror. Only,
Sometimes, a sharp, violent burr, discordant,

Sizzles for one instant in jagged
Hachures[3] in the brain—momentary scream   50
Of the powersaw wincing back

From a buried nail. Seizure: with a rising
Whoop, like a child on a steep slide,
A woman fell heavily to the floor

A few feet away from me, her scalp
Split a little, blood on my sleeve
As I raised her shoulders, acting the part

Of a stranger helping—asking a clerk
To please get something to cover her,
Please call for an ambulance, maybe   60

---

[3] Lines in topographical maps, indicating a steep slope.

She has had a seizure. Epileptic—
The Falling Evil;[4] something about the tongue,
Something for the teeth. But her mouth

Was not rigid, her eyes open—why
Should she look at me so knowingly,
Almost with contempt, was she crazy?—

As if I had made her fall: or were no
Stranger at all but a son, lover, lord
And master who had thus humiliated her

And now, tucking the blanket around her,   70
Hypocritical automaton, pretended
To urge—as if without complicity or shame

Or least sense of betrayal—the old embrace
Of this impenetrable haze, this prolonged
But not infinite surfeit of glory.

                                                    1984

THE CHANGES

Even at sea the bodies of the unborn and the dead
Interpenetrate at peculiar angles. In a displaced channel

The crew of a tanker float by high over the heads
Of a village of makers of flint knives, and a woman

In one round hut on a terrace dreams of her grandsons
Floating through the blue sky on a bubble of black oil

Calling her in the unknown rhythms of diesel engines to come
Lie down and couple. On the ship, three different sailors

Have a brief revery of dark, furry shanks, and one resolves
To build when he gets home a kind of round shrine or gazebo   10

In the small terraced garden of his house in a suburb.
In the garden, bees fumble at hydrangeas blue as crockery[1]

While four children giggle playing School in the round gazebo.
(To one side, the invisible shaved heads of six priests

---

[4] Epilepsy, also called the "falling sickness."
[1] Earthenware, ceramics made of slightly porous, opaque clay fired at low heat.

Bob above the garden's earth as they smear ash on their chests,
Trying to dance away a great epidemic; afterwards one priest,

The youngest, founds a new discipline based on the ideals
Of childlike humility and light-heartedness and learning.)

One of the sailor's children on his lunch hour years later
Writes on a napkin a poem about blue hydrangeas, bees   20

And a crockery pitcher. And though he is killed in a war
And the poem is burned up unread on a mass pyre with his body,

The separate molecules of the poem spread evenly over the globe
In a starlike precise pattern, as if a geometer[2] had mapped it.

Overhead, passengers in planes cross and recross in the invisible
Ordained lanes of air traffic—some of us in the traverse

Passing through our own slightly changed former and future bodies,
Seated gliding along the black lines printed on colored maps

In the little pouches at every seat, the webs of routes bunched
To the shapes of beaks or arrowheads at the black dots of the cities.   30

1984

THE SAVING

Though the sky still was partly light
Over the campsite clearing
Where some men and boys sat eating
Gathered near their fire,
It was full dark in the trees,
With somewhere a night-hunter
Up and out already to pad
Unhurried after a spoor,[1]
Pausing maybe to sniff
At the strange, lifeless aura   10
Of a dropped knife or a coin
Buried in the spongy duff.

Willful, hungry and impatient,
Nose damp in the sudden chill,
One of the smaller, scrawnier boys
Roasting a chunk of meat
Pulled it half-raw from the coals,

---

[2] A geometrician, or specialist in geometry.   [1] The track or trail of an animal.

Bolted it whole from the skewer
Rubbery gristle and all,
And started to choke and strangle—   20
Gaping his helpless mouth,
Struggling to retch or to swallow
As he gestured, blacking out,
And felt his father lift him

And turning him upside down
Shake him and shake him by the heels,
Like a woman shaking a jar—
And the black world upside-down,
The upside-down fire and sky,
Vomited back his life,   30
And the wet little plug of flesh
Lay under him in the ashes.
Set back on his feet again
In the ring of faces and voices,
He drank the dark air in,
Snuffling and feeling foolish

In the fresh luxury of breath
And the brusque, flattering comfort
Of the communal laughter. Later,
Falling asleep under the stars,   40
He watched a gray wreath of smoke
Unfurling into the blackness;
And he thought of it as the shape
Of a newborn ghost, the benign
Ghost of his death, that had nearly
Happened: it coiled, as the wind rustled,
And he thought of it as a power,
His luck or his secret name.

1984

Robert Hass
(1941–   )

The title Robert Hass assigned to his second volume of poems, *Praise* (1979), is a singularly appropriate epithet for the sensibility pervading his poetry and essays. His poetic vision originates from his affinity with the natural world, his work informed by the purity of observation and the leaps of imagination essential for translating experience of that world into meaning, for probing the mystery of life, of death. "Images haunt," writes Hass

in an essay from *Twentieth Century Pleasures: Prose on Poetry* (1984), and his own articulation of images is inextricably tied to the act of "naming" as a way of apprehending what
is present and what is haunting in the presence of things. Images bring into conjunction
"what perishes and what lasts forever," and it is that moment of conjunction Hass has
strived to realize. The importance Hass accords the power of images—"they do not say
this is that, they say this is"—owes much to his study of Asian poetry, particularly the
Japanese haiku of Buson, Basho, and Issa.

Born in San Francisco in 1941, Hass grew up in the San Francisco Bay area. In 1962 he
married Earlene Leif, a psychotherapist, and the following year he received a B.A. from
St. Mary's College of California, in Moraga, California. At Stanford University he earned
an M.A. in 1965 and a Ph.D. in 1971; he then returned to St. Mary's to teach. Hass has
been a visiting lecturer at a number of schools, including Columbia University and the
University of California at Berkeley, and has received, among other honors, the William
Carlos Williams Award in 1979 for *Praise* and a Guggenheim Fellowship in 1980. He
edited a translation of the Swedish poet Tomas Transtromer's work and has translated
several collections in Polish by the poet Czeslaw Milosz.

While at Stanford Hass was a student of the poet and critic Yvor Winters. Whereas
Winters early turned the younger poet's attention to questions of form, Hass has used the
discipline of his academic training to bring intellectual rigor and precision to poems characterized by their clarity and compassion. His poems are intellectual and intimate, interweaving references to music, painting, and books with the appearance of wife, children,
flowers, otters—his is a poetry in which the metaphysical and the personal are consonant
and are coextensive. A meditative and lyric poet, Hass typically explores the truth of some
proposition, but the argument by which he comes to understand that truth inevitably returns to and probes the sensory and the sensual. In "Meditation at Lagunitas" (1979) Hass
poses the idea that "a word is elegy to what it signifies," but he arrives at perception of that
truth through lived experience: "Longing, we say, because desire is full / of endless distances." . . . "moments when the body is as numinous / as words."

Hass's first volume of poems, *Field Guide*, won the Yale Series of Younger Poets
Award in 1973, and *Praise* appeared six years later. His collection of essays, *Twentieth
Century Pleasures*, won the National Book Critics' Circle Award for criticism in 1984.
Included are essays on American and international poets, and in several meditative essays
Hass examines his notions on poetic form, prosody and rhythm, and images. In his third
volume of poems, *Human Wishes* (1989), Hass uses both the long, expansive lines of
Praise and the prose poem structure for his meditations on the nature of desire. And in all
his work the incantatory act of naming is an act of praise, of affirmation.

Suggested Readings: *Five American Poets,* ed. J. Mathias, 1981. *Twentieth Century Pleasures:
Prose on Poetry,* 1984. S. Lea and J. Parini, "An Interview With Robert Hass," in *New England
Review,* 295–314, 1979. R. Miklitsch, "Praise: The Poetry of Robert Hass," in *Hollins Critic, XVII,*
February 1979. C. Altieri, *Self and Sensibility in Contemporary American Poetry,* 1984.

Texts Used: "Song": *Field Guide,* 1973. "Spring Drawing": *Human Wishes,* 1989. All else: *Praise,*
1979.

SONG

Afternoon cooking in the fall sun—
who is more naked

                    than the man
yelling, "Hey, I'm home!"
                    to an empty house?
thinking because the bay is clear,
the hills in yellow heat,
& scrub oak red in gullies
         that great crowds of family
should tumble from the rooms   10
              to throw their bodies on the Papa-body,
         I-am-loved.

Cat sleeps in the windowgleam,
              dust motes.[1]
    On the oak table
  filets of sole
stewing in the juice of tangerines,
    slices of green pepper
         on a bone-white dish.

                                                        1973

HEROIC SIMILE

When the swordsman fell in Kurosawa's *Seven Samurai*[1]
in the gray rain,
in Cinemascope and the Tokugawa[2] dynasty,
he fell straight as a pine, he fell
as Ajax[3] fell in Homer
in changed dactyls[4] and the tree was so huge
the woodsman returned for two days
to that lucky place before he was done with the sawing
and on the third day he brought his uncle.

They stacked logs in the resinous air,   10
hacking the small limbs off,
tying those bundles separately.
The slabs near the root
were quartered and still they were awkwardly large;

---

[1] Particles.
[1] A 1954 film by the Japanese director Akira Kurosawa (1910–   ) depicting the decline of the samurai military class and its code of honor in feudal Japan.
[2] The family that controlled Japan from 1603 to 1867.
[3] A legendary Greek hero, a warrior in the Trojan war. In the *Odyssey* (Bk. XI), by the Greek epic poet Homer (8th? century B.C.), the disappointed and enraged Ajax kills himself after Odysseus, not he, is awarded the armor of the dead hero Achilles.
[4] In poetry, metrical feet that consist of one long and two short syllables, or one stressed and two unstressed syllables.

the logs from midtree they halved:
ten bundles and four great piles of fragrant wood,
moons and quarter moons and half moons
ridged by the saw's tooth.

The woodsman and the old man his uncle
are standing in midforest   20
on a floor of pine silt and spring mud.
They have stopped working
because they are tired and because
I have imagined no pack animal
or primitive wagon. They are too canny
to call in neighbors and come home
with a few logs after three days' work.
They are waiting for me to do something
or for the overseer of the Great Lord
to come and arrest them.   30

How patient they are!
The old man smokes a pipe and spits.
The young man is thinking he would be rich
if he were already rich and had a mule.
Ten days of hauling
and on the seventh day they'll probably
be caught, go home empty-handed
or worse. I don't know
whether they're Japanese or Mycenaean[5]
and there's nothing I can do.   40
The path from here to that village
is not translated. A hero, dying,
gives off stillness to the air.
A man and a woman walk from the movies
to the house in the silence of separate fidelities.
There are limits to imagination.

1979

MEDITATION AT LAGUNITAS*

All the new thinking is about loss.
In this it resembles all the old thinking.
The idea, for example, that each particular erases
the luminous clarity of a general idea. That the clown-
faced woodpecker probing the dead sculpted trunk

---

[5] Ancient Greeks of Mycenae, a civilization that flourished from the fifteenth to the twelfth centuries
B.C.

* A lake on the Stanford University campus in Palo Alto, California; Hass received his M.A. and
Ph.D. from Stanford in 1965 and 1971, respectively.

of that black birch is, by his presence,
some tragic falling off from a first world
of undivided light. Or the other notion that,
because there is in this world no one thing
to which the bramble of *blackberry* corresponds,   10
a word is elegy to what it signifies.
We talked about it late last night and in the voice
of my friend, there was a thin wire of grief, a tone
almost querulous. After a while I understood that,
talking this way, everything dissolves: *justice,*
pine, hair, woman, you and *I*. There was a woman
I made love to and I remembered how, holding
her small shoulders in my hands sometimes,
I felt a violent wonder at her presence
like a thirst for salt, for my childhood river   20
with its island willows, silly music from the pleasure boat,
muddy places where we caught the little orange-silver fish
called *pumpkinseed*. It hardly had to do with her.
Longing, we say, because desire is full
of endless distances. I must have been the same to her.
But I remember so much, the way her hands dismantled bread,
the thing her father said that hurt her, what
she dreamed. There are moments when the body is as numinous[1]
as words, days that are the good flesh continuing.
Such tenderness, those afternoons and evenings,   30
saying *blackberry, blackberry, blackberry.*

1979

SUNRISE

Ah, love, this is fear. This is fear and syllables
and the beginnings of beauty. We have walked the city,
a flayed animal signifying death, a hybrid god
who sings in the desolation of filth and money
a song the heart is heavy to receive. We mourn
otherwise. Otherwise the ranked monochromes,
the death-teeth of that horizon,[1] survive us
as we survive pleasure. What a small hope.
What a fierce small privacy of consolation.
What a dazzle of petals for the poor meat.   10

Blind, with eyes like stars, like astral flowers,
from the purblind[2] mating sickness of the beasts

---

[1] Holy.
[1] Fossilized teeth of a particular sediment level, or soil horizon.   [2] Completely blind.

we rise, trout-shaken, in the gaping air,
in terror, the scarlet sun-flash
leaping from the pond's imagination
of a deadly sea. Fish, mole,
we are the small stunned creatures
inside these human resurrections, the nights
the city praises and defiles. From there we all
walk slowly to the sea gathering scales   20
from the cowled whisper of the waves,
the mensural polyphony.[3] Small stars,
and blind the hunger under sun,
we turn to each other and turn to each other
in the mother air of what we want.

That is why blind Orpheus[4] praises love
and why love gouges out our eyes
and why all lovers smell their way to Dover.[5]
That is why innocence has so much to account for,
why Venus[6] appears least saintly in the attitudes of shame.   30
This is lost children and the deep sweetness of the pulp,
a blue thrumming at the formed bone, river,
flame, quicksilver. It is not the fire
we hunger for and not the ash. It is the still hour,
a deer come slowly to the creek at dusk,
the table set for abstinence, windows
full of flowers like summer in the provinces
vanishing when the moon's half-face pallor
rises on the dark flax line of hills.

1979

THE YELLOW BICYCLE

The woman I love is greedy,
but she refuses greed.
She walks so straightly.
When I ask her what she wants,
she says, "A yellow bicycle."

•

[3] A combining of independent but harmonizing melodies in which each note is given a strictly determined value.

[4] According to Greek myth, the first lyric poet; when his wife, Eurydice, died, Orpheus was permitted to lead her back from the Underworld as long as he did not look at her until she stepped into the light on earth. He was unable to resist the temptation to look back; having lost her forever, he spent the rest of his life lamenting his loss.

[5] In the famous poem "Dover Beach" (1851?), by the English poet Matthew Arnold (1822–1888), a great love is able to prevent the darkness of despair.

[6] According to Roman myth, the goddess of love.

Sun, sunflower,
coltsfoot[1] on the roadside,
a goldfinch, the sign
that says Yield, her hair,
cat's eyes, his hunger   10
and a yellow bicycle.

•

Once, when they had made love in the middle of the night and it was very sweet,
they decided they were hungry, so they got up, got dressed, and drove downtown
to an all-night donut shop. Chicano kids lounged outside, a few drunks, and one
black man selling dope. Just at the entrance there was an old woman in a thin
floral print dress. She was barefoot. Her face was covered with sores and dry
peeling skin. The sores looked like raisins and her skin was the dry yellow of a
parchment lampshade ravaged by light and tossed away. They thought she must
have been hungry and, coming out again with a white paper bag full of hot rolls,
they stopped to offer her one. She looked at them out of her small eyes, bewildered, and shook her head for a little while, and said very kindly, "No."

•

Her song to the yellow bicycle:
The boats on the bay
have nothing on you,
my swan, my sleek one!

1979

SPRING DRAWING

A man thinks *lilacs against white houses,* having seen them in the farm country
south of Tacoma[1] in April, and can't find his way to a sentence, a brushstroke
carrying the energy of *brush* and *stroke*

—as if he were stranded on the aureole[2] of the memory of a woman's breast,

and she, after the drive from the airport and a chat with her mother and a shower,
which is ritual cleansing and a passage through water to mark transition,

had walked up the mountain on a summer evening.

Away from, not toward. As if the garden roses were a little hobby of the dead. As
if the deer pellets in the pale grass and the wavering moon and the rondure[3]—as
they used to say, upping the ante—of heaven

---

[1] A plant of the composite family, with small, yellow flowers and large leaves shaped like a colt's
footprint.

[1] Tacoma, Washington.   [2] Radiance.   [3] Graceful roundness.

were admirable completely, but only as common nouns of a plainer intention, *moon, shit, sky,*

as if spirit attended to plainness only, the more complicated forms exhausting it, tossed-off grapestems becoming crystal chandeliers,

as if radiance were the meaning of meaning, and justice responsible to daydream not only for the strict beauty of denial,

but as a felt need to reinvent the inner form of wishing.

Only the force of the brushstroke keeps the lilacs from pathos—the hes and shes of the comedy may or may not get together, but if they are to get at all,   10

then the interval created by *if,* to which mind and breath attend, nervous as the grazing animals the first brushes painted,

has become habitable space, lived in beyond wishing.

1989

Simon J. Ortiz
(1941–   )

Simon J. Ortiz was born in 1941 in the Acoma Pueblo Indian tribe's village of McCartys, New Mexico ("Deetziyama" to its Acoma inhabitants), and raised there. "My childhood was the oral tradition of the Acoma Pueblo people," Ortiz says in his autobiographical essay "The Language We Know" (1987). "The language I spoke was that of a struggling people who held ferociously to a heritage, culture, language, and land despite the odds posed them by the forces surrounding them since 1540 A.D., the advent of Euro-American colonization." When he began elementary school in the Bureau of Indian Affairs day school on the Acoma reservation, Ortiz spoke only the language of the Acoma people. Immediately, like countless Native-American children since the late 1800s, he found himself forced to learn English and punished when he spoke his native language. Despite such coercion, Ortiz learned English rapidly because of his love for "language, the sound, meaning, and magic of language."

From the reservation school Oritz entered the army briefly and attended the University of New Mexico. He went on to receive a masters degree in writing from the University of Iowa International Writing Program and has published more than a dozen books. In 1980 he was invited to Washington, D.C., to take part in the White House Salute to Poetry and American Poets, and in 1982 he received a Pushcart Prize for his poetry collection *From Sand Creek* (1981). In addition to serving as lieutenant governor of the Acoma Pueblo, Ortiz has taught Native-American literature and creative writing at such schools as the

University of New Mexico and at San Diego State University and has directed the creative writing program at Sinte Gleska College in South Dakota. He has edited such publications as the Navajo *Rough Rock News* and *Wanbli Ho,* a Native-American literary magazine, as well as collections of Native-American prose and poetry, such as the short-fiction collection *Earth Power Coming* (1983).

Ortiz's works, both poetry and fiction, merge a distinctly political concern for contemporary Native-American existence with the ancient knowledge and traditions of his Acoma heritage. Much of his poetry is intended to be narrated. Coyote, his traditional Native-American trickster figure, appears in poems such as "The Creation, According to Coyote" (1976)—(with the hint of satire that typically accompanies tricksters)—to remind the speaker of his people's origins. In the poem "A Story of How a Wall Stands" (1976) Ortiz recalls with emblematic force the skill of his father and of the Acoma people as stoneworkers for generations. Permeating Ortiz's free-form verse are the traditional storyteller's voice and the rhythms and patterns of Native-American ceremony and song. Deeply immersed in his tribe's oral tradition—the ceremony, mythology, and storytelling—Oritz says in "The Language We Know," "I don't remember a world without language. . . . It is language that brings us into being in order to know life."

Suggested Readings: *A Good Journey,* 1977. *Fight Back: For the Sake of the People, for the Sake of Land,* 1980. *Fightin': New and Collected Short Stories,* 1983. Ed., *Earth Power Coming: Short Fiction in Native American Literature,* 1988. "Always the Stories: A Brief History and Thoughts on My Writing," in *Coyote Was Here: Essays on Contemporary Native American Literary and Political Mobilization,* ed. B. Scholer, 1984. K. Lincoln, *Native American Renaissance,* 1983. K. Lincoln, "The Poetry of Simon Ortiz," in *Coyote Was Here,* ed. B. Scholer, 1984. P. G. Allen, *The Sacred Hoop: Recovering the Feminine in American Indian Traditions,* 1986. A. Wiget, *Simon Ortiz,* 1986. A. Krupat, *The Voice in the Margin: Native American Literature and the Canon,* 1989.

Texts Used: "'Grief'" and "'The Sky Is Brilliant'": *From Sand Creek,* 1981. All else: *Going for the Rain,* 1976.

DRY ROOT IN A WASH*

the sand is a fine grit
and warm to the touch.
An old juniper root
lies by the cutbank[1] of sand;
it lingers, waiting
for the next month of rain.

I feel like saying,
It will rain, but you know
better than I these centuries
don't mean much   10
for anyone to be waiting.

---

* The dry bed of a stream.   [1] A steep stream bank.

Upstream, towards the mountains,
the Shiwana[2] work for rain.

They know we're waiting.

Underneath the fine sand
it is cool
with crystalline moisture,
the forming rain.

1976

A STORY OF HOW A WALL STANDS

*At Acu,[1] there is a wall almost 400 years old which supports hundreds of tons
of dirt and bones—it's a graveyard built on a steep incline—and it looks like
it's about to fall down the incline but will not for a long time.*

My father, who works with stone,
says, "That's just the part you see,
the stones which seem to be
just packed in on the outside,"
and with his hands puts the stone and mud
in place. "Underneath
what looks like loose stone,
there is stone woven together."
He ties one hand over the other,
fitting like the bones of his hands   10
and fingers. "That's what is holding it together."

"It is built that carefully,"
he says, "the mud mixed
to a certain texture," patiently
"with the fingers," worked
in the palm of his hand. "So that
placed between the stones, they hold
together for a long, long time."

He tells me those things,
the story of them worked   20
with his fingers, in the palm
of his hands, working the stone

[2] A society of men who are said to bring rain through prayers and observances in a religious ceremony that requires sacred objects.
[1] The Acoma Pueblo in New Mexico, where Ortiz was born and raised.

and the mud until they become
the wall that stands a long, long time.

1976

WIND AND GLACIER VOICES

Laguna[1] man said,
I only heard that glacier scraping
once, thirty thousand years ago.
My daughter was born then.
                    —a storytelling, continuing
                        voice—
West of Yuma,[2] a brown man murmurs
the motion of the solar wind.[3]
                    —a harsh, searing
                        voice—   10

Please don't tell me
how to live;
I've always lived this way.
                    —a protesting
                        voice—

the last time I was in Fargo[4]
I thought I heard the echo
of a glacier scraping.
                    —a remembering,
                        beckoning   20
                        voice—

And the wind, solar,
the big wind will come.
Solar, it will come.
Solar, it will come.
It will pass by and through
and with everything.
                    —a longing, whispering,
                        prophetic
                        voice—   30

1976

---

[1] A Native-American tribe of New Mexico.   [2] Yuma, Arizona.
[3] Streams of electrically charged gas particles emitted by the sun.   [4] Fargo, North Dakota.

THE CREATION, ACCORDING TO COYOTE*

"First of all, it's all true."
Coyote, he says this, this way,
humble yourself, motioning and meaning
what he says.

You were born when you came
from that body, the earth;
your black head burst from granite,
the ashes cooling,

until it began to rain.
It turned muddy then,   10
and then green and brown things
came without legs.

They looked strange.
Everything was strange.
There was nothing to know then,

until later, Coyote told me this,
and he was b.s.-ing probably,
two sons were born,
Uyuyayeh and Masaweh.

They were young then,   20
and then later on they were older.

And then the people were wondering
what was above
they had heard rumors.

But, you know, Coyote,
he was mainly bragging
when he said (I think),
"My brothers, the Twins then said,
'Let's lead these poor creatures
and save them.'"   30

And later on, they came to light

after many exciting and colorful
and tragic things of adventure;
and this is the life, all these, all these.

---

* According to Native-American legend, the coyote is a trickster who assumes many shapes and forms.

My uncle told me all this, that time.
Coyote told me too, but you know
how he is, always talking to the gods,
the mountains, the stone all around.

And you know, I believe him.

1976

from   *FROM SAND CREEK**

GRIEF

Grief
memorizes this grass.
Raw
courage,
                believe it,
red-eyed and urgent,
stalking Denver.
Like stone,
like steel,
the hone and sheer gone,   10
just the brute
and perceptive angle left.

Like courage,
                believe it,

left still;
the words from then
talk like that.

Believe it.

1981

THE SKY IS BRILLIANT

The sky is brilliant
and expansive like the universe

---

* A series of untitled poems and interspersed prose taken from Ortiz's own experiences as a recovering U.S. Army veteran. Sand Creek, in southeastern Colorado, is the site of a slaughter of Cheyennes and Arapahos by U.S. troops in November 1864.

on the concave of my eye.
My mind is a cove
          of light
shining upon a vista
of a grassed great plain.
I know
there is a world
peopled with love.   10
I know
there are people
          who speak
not in undertones
but gallantly and joyously,
who are valorous
with simple courage.
But looking at the VA[1] hospital
fortressed with dike walls
in defense against the rising   20
Arkansas River,[2] I see
a train that carries dreams
and freedom away.

                  Thunder rises
in me and its waves empty me.
               O
train and people and plains,
look at me and the hospital
where stricken men and broken boys
are mortared and sealed   30
into its defensive walls. O look,
now.

1981

Louise Glück
(1943–   )

The world as portrayed in Louise Glück's poems is a world of archetypes, newly fashioned or traditional, a world in which the gods of myth—their tragedies, seductions and reprisals—are the figurative equals of "you" and "I." It is a world of children who sense "the

---

[1] Veteran's Administration.   [2] A river in southeastern Colorado.

great human subjects: time which breeds loss, desire, the world's beauty," Glück explains in the essay "Education of the Poet" (1988). Where autobiography figures in her work (as it does in such poems as "Dedication to Hunger" (1980), poems with the common subject of renunciation), such detail becomes a sort of epic, or extended simile, a device John Milton used in *Paradise Lost* (1667).

Glück's "you" and "I" are typically meant to represent men and women, respectively: "male and female, thrust and ache," as she writes in "Palais des Arts" (1980). From the striking absence of personal pronouns in her early poems to the encompassing "you" and "I" of her later ones, her subjects are treated distinctively, as though Glück was desperately trying to learn how to write "I" and mean something larger than mere autobiography. Life as a subject for poetry is denied its specificity and is thereby not demystified but mystified.

If in Glück's poetry men and women are meant to be figurative, then so are their offspring. In "The Drowned Children," from *Descending Figure* (1980), she writes "You see, they have no judgment. / So it is natural that they should drown." These children, "lost / in the waters, blue and permanent," might well lack judgment, yet they are among the poet's most prescient characters. "Gretel in Darkness" (from her widely acclaimed *The House on Marshland* [1975]) reimagines the Grimm's fairytale, escalating the violence of the original, so that even children seem to wage war with one another. "All who would have seen us dead / are dead," Gretel addresses her brother; "I killed for you." Glück also retells ancient myths conveyed by means of direct address. In "Mythic Fragment" (1985) she distills the story of Daphne and Apollo.

Such archetypal and mythical tendencies and ambitions commonly seem at odds with both the plainspoken and formalist currents of much contemporary poetry; they are also potential invitations to excess. Excess is rare, though, in Glück's poetry. Her language is mannered but careful, her technique one of almost rigid control. The poems in her collection *Ararat* (1990) are even more pared down than are her earlier poems. In that book, a series of short verses linked as a single narrative, her imagery and honesty are paramount. If her poems have ancestors, they are surely the poems of William Blake and Emily Dickinson, not only in their shared obsessions with archetype and the created world, but also in their short trimeter lines. Even so, Glück's poems at times echo those of Elizabeth Bishop, of Robert Lowell, and of Stanley Kunitz (with whom Glück studied at Columbia University during the early 1960s).

Born in 1943 in New York City, Glück was raised on Long Island and attended Sarah Lawrence College and Columbia University. At age twenty-five she published her first collection, *Firstborn* (1968). For her poetry she has received numerous grants and awards such as a National Endowment for the Arts grant, a Guggenheim Fellowship, and a National Book Critics' Circle Award for *The Triumph of Achilles* (1985). She has taught at Goddard College in Vermont, at Warren Wilson College in North Carolina, and at Williams College.

Suggested Readings: *Ararat*, 1990. H. Vendler, "Louise Glück," in *Part of Nature, Part of Us: Modern American Poets*, 1980. H. Vendler, "John Ashbery, Louise Glück" in *The Music of What Happens*, 1988.

Texts Used: "Cottonmouth Country": *Firstborn*, 1968. "All Hallows" and "Gretel in Darkness": *The House on Marshland*, 1975. "The Drowned Children," "Palais des Arts," and "Dedication to Hunger": *Descending Figure*, 1980. All else: *The Triumph of Achilles*, 1985.

COTTONMOUTH COUNTRY*

Fish bones walked the waves off Hatteras.[1]
And there were other signs
That Death wooed us, by water, wooed us
By land: among the pines
An uncurled cottonmouth that rolled on moss
Reared in the polluted air.
Birth, not death, is the hard loss.
I know. I also left a skin there.

1967

GRETEL IN DARKNESS†

This is the world we wanted.
All who would have seen us dead
are dead.[1] I hear the witch's cry
break in the moonlight through a sheet
of sugar: God rewards.
Her tongue shrivels into gas. . . .

       Now, far from women's arms
and memory of women, in our father's hut
we sleep, are never hungry.
Why do I not forget?
My father bars the door, bars harm
from this house, and it is years.

No one remembers. Even you, my brother,
summer afternoons you look at me as though
you meant to leave,
as though it never happened.
But I killed for you.[2] I see armed firs,
the spires of that gleaming kiln—

Nights I turn to you to hold me
but you are not there.
Am I alone? Spies

10

20

---

* Water moccasin country, the southeastern United States; first published in the *New American Review,* Number 1, 1967.
[1] An island off North Carolina.
† First published in the *New American Review;* after the German folk tale "Hansel and Gretel," collected by the German scholars and brothers Jacob (1785–1863) and Wilhelm (1786–1859) Grimm.
[1] The children's cruel stepmother and the wicked witch who lured them into her house made of sweets.
[2] Gretel pushed the witch into the oven in which Hansel was to be baked.

hiss in the stillness, Hansel,
we are there still and it is real, real,
that black forest and the fire in earnest.

1971

ALL HALLOWS*

Even now this landscape is assembling.
The hills darken. The oxen
sleep in their blue yoke,
the fields having been
picked clean, the sheaves
bound evenly and piled at the roadside
among cinquefoil,[1] as the toothed moon rises:

This is the barrenness
of harvest or pestilence.
And the wife leaning out the window   10
with her hand extended, as in payment,
and the seeds
distinct, gold, calling
Come here
Come here, little one

And the soul creeps out of the tree.

1975

THE DROWNED CHILDREN†

You see, they have no judgment.
So it is natural that they should drown,
first the ice taking them in
and then, all winter, their wool scarves
floating behind them as they sink
until at last they are quiet.
And the pond lifts them in its manifold dark arms.

But death must come to them differently,
so close to the beginning.

---

* All Saints' Day, a Christian festival honoring the saints, celebrated on November 1; first published in the *New Yorker*.
[1] A plant of the rose family whose leaves have five lobes.
† First published in the *New Yorker*.

As though they had always been   10
blind and weightless. Therefore
the rest is dreamed, the lamp,
the good white cloth that covered the table,
their bodies.

And yet they hear the names they used
like lures slipping over the pond:
What are you waiting for
come home, come home, lost
in the waters, blue and permanent.

1980

PALAIS DES ARTS*

Love long dormant showing itself:
the large expected gods
caged really, the columns
sitting on the lawn, as though perfection
were not timeless but stationary—that
is the comedy, she thinks,
that they are paralyzed. Or like the matching swans,
insular, circling the pond: restraint so passionate
implies possession. They hardly speak.
On the other bank, a small boy throws bits of bread   10
into the water. The reflected monument
is stirred, briefly, stricken with light—
She can't touch his arm in innocence again.
They have to give that up and begin
as male and female, thrust and ache.

1980

DEDICATION TO HUNGER†

I FROM THE SUBURBS

They cross the yard
and at the back door

---

* "Palace of the Arts" (French).
† During her adolescence Glück suffered from anorexia nervosa, a physical and psychological disorder afflicting primarily teenage women; characterized by a pathological fear of weight gain, leading to faulty eating patterns, malnutrition, and weight loss.

the mother sees with pleasure
how alike they are, father and daughter—
I know something of that time.
The little girl purposefully
swinging her arms, laughing
her stark laugh:

It should be kept secret, that sound.
It means she's realized   10
that he never touches her.
She is a child; he could touch her
if he wanted to.

2 GRANDMOTHER

"Often I would stand at the window—
your grandfather
was a young man then—
waiting, in the early evening."

That is what marriage is,
I watch the tiny figure
changing to a man   20
as he moves toward her,
the last light rings in his hair.
I do not question
their happiness. And he rushes in
with his young man's hunger,
so proud to have taught her that:
his kiss would have been
clearly tender—

Of course, of course. Except
it might as well have been   30
his hand over her mouth.

3 EROS[1]

To be male, always
to go to women
and be taken back
into the pierced flesh:

           I suppose
memory is stirred.

[1] According to Greek myth, the god of love.

And the girl child
who wills herself
into her father's arms   40
likewise loved him
second. Nor is she told
what need to express.
There is a look one sees,
the mouth somehow desperate—

Because the bond
cannot be proven.

4 THE DEVIATION

It begins quietly
in certain female children:
the fear of death, taking as its form   50
dedication to hunger,
because a woman's body
is a grave; it will accept
anything. I remember
lying in bed at night
touching the soft, digressive breasts,
touching, at fifteen,
the interfering flesh
that I would sacrifice
until the limbs were free   60
of blossom and subterfuge: I felt
what I feel now, aligning these words—
it is the same need to perfect,
of which death is the mere byproduct.

5 SACRED OBJECTS

Today in the field I saw
the hard, active buds of the dogwood
and wanted, as we say, to capture them,
to make them eternal. That is the premise
of renunciation: the child,
having no self to speak of,
comes to life in denial—   70

I stood apart in that achievement,
in that power to expose
the underlying body, like a god
for whose deed
there is no parallel in the natural world.

1980

MYTHIC FRAGMENT

When the stern god[1]
approached me with his gift
my fear enchanted him
so that he ran more quickly
through the wet grass, as he insisted,
to praise me. I saw captivity
in praise; against the lyre,
I begged my father in the sea
to save me.[2] When
the god arrived, I was nowhere,   10
I was in a tree forever. Reader,
pity Apollo: at the water's edge,
I turned from him, I summoned
my invisible father—as
I stiffened in the god's arms,
of his encompassing love
my father made
no other sign from the water.

1985

ELMS

All day I tried to distinguish
need from desire. Now, in the dark,
I feel only bitter sadness for us,
the builders, the planers of wood,
because I have been looking
steadily at these elms
and seen the process that creates
the writhing, stationary tree
is torment, and have understood
it will make no forms but twisted forms.   10

1985

HORSE*

What does the horse give you
that I cannot give you?

---

[1] Apollo (the sun god of Greek myth), who courted the nymph Daphne.
[2] According to the myth, she begged her father, the river god Peneus, to help her avoid the god's pursuit and was transformed into a laurel tree.
* First published in *Antaeus*.

I watch you when you are alone,
when you ride into the field behind the dairy,
your hands buried in the mare's
dark mane.

Then I know what lies behind your silence:
scorn, hatred of me, of marriage. Still,
you want me to touch you; you cry out
as brides cry, but when I look at you I see   10
there are no children in your body.
Then what is there?

Nothing, I think. Only haste
to die before I die.

In a dream, I watched you ride the horse
over the dry fields and then
dismount: you two walked together;
in the dark, you had no shadows.
But I felt them coming toward me
since at night they go anywhere,   20
they are their own masters.

Look at me. You think I don't understand?
What is the animal
if not passage out of this life?

1985

Alberto Ríos
(1952–   )

The poems of Alberto Alvaro Ríos are characterized by the convergence of everyday occurrence and the world of mystery, a world in which anything can happen. Subtle and
nearly invisible in his poems are the *milagros* of his Mexican heritage—literally, "miracles"—the thin, hand-tooled silver or gold Mexican charms shaped like body parts or figu-
rines and hung on the statues of saints in gratitude for a blessing. Like the *milagros*, Ríos's
poems reaffirm the possibility of magical crossovers between the ordinary and the mysterious and offer experiences that are familiar yet strange.

Born in 1952 in Nogales, Arizona, a border town between Mexico and the United
States, Ríos sees the borderline as a way of visualizing the double perspective in his work.
Interweaving both literal and figurative language to evoke a vivid experience of place, his
descriptive geographical poems move back and forth between two views of the same landscape. The influence of his British mother, Agnes Fogg, and his Mexican father, Alberto

Alvaro, on Ríos's use of language also contributes to the double perspective in his work: although his poems are written in English, they contain structural and linguistic elements of Spanish. Ríos has explained that his "awkward syntax" makes him work harder and remain inventive.

Educated at the University of Arizona, Ríos received a B.A. in English in 1974 and one in psychology in 1975 and a master of fine arts degree in 1979. Also in 1979, he married Maria Guadalupe Barron, a librarian. He has published the poetry volumes *Whispering to Fool the Wind* (1981), a Walt Whitman Award winner; *Five Indiscretions* (1985); *The Lime Orchard Woman* (1988); and *Marvella, for Borrowing* (1989). His collection of short stories, *The Iguana Killer: Twelve Stories of the Heart* (1984), won the Western States Book Award. Ríos's poems and stories have been anthologized and have appeared in specialized collections such as *Chicano Literature* (1982), *Agua Fresca* (1980), and *Crossing the River: Poets of the Western United States* (1987). An educator as well as a writer, Ríos has taught writing, prosody, and magical realism at Arizona State University.

Ríos typically uses English poetic forms to express Chicano content, as in poems about his ancestors. "Mi Abuelo" (1982), in which the poet talks to his *abuelo*, or grandfater, is a disguised sestina. Although the sestina is a complicated, highly structured poetic form, Ríos manipulates it to create a spontaneous expression of warmth and humor. The magical and incantatory powers of the sestina give form and resonance to the narrator's dialogue with the dead, whereas the repetition of end words re-enacts the constant verbal repetition to which children are subject from the adults in their lives. The grandson in "Mi Abuelo" attempts to make his *abuelo* talk like a proper grandfather.

The name "Carlos" echoes throughout Ríos's poetry. The name of Ríos's great uncle who lived on in the poet's memory after only a single meeting, it is also the name Ríos gives to the private memories, perceptions, and poignant feelings that make each individual unique but isolated in his or her own experiences. The ordinary and the subjective perception of the extraordinary are juxtaposed in "Madre Sofía" (1982) and "The Purpose of Altar Boys" (1982), poems that explore, simultaneously through the eyes of a little boy and the man he becomes, the places where innocence and knowledge, holiness and superstition, reverence and humor meet.

Suggested Readings: *Elk Heads on the Wall*, 1979. *Sleeping on Fists*, 1981. *The Iguana Killer: Twelve Stories of the Heart*, 1984. *Five Indiscretions*, 1985. *The Lime Orchard Woman*, 1988. *Marvella, for Borrowing*, 1989. *The Warrington Poems*, 1989. Village Voice Literary Supplement, October 1982. C. Candelaria, *Chicano Poetry: A Critical Introduction*, 1986. C. R. Shirley and P. W. Shirley, *Understanding Chicano Literature*, 1988.

Text Used: *Whispering to Fool the Wind*, 1982.

AT KINO VIEJO, MEXICO*

The potatoes of the corner store sing,
sand crickets and green flies full,
fat almost like night beetles,
the burlap bags of dry onions move,

---

* A small fishing village off the Gulf of California in the Mexican Northwest, inhabited by vacationing tourists, who flourish like the flowers in the poem, and by the native Seri Indians, who stoically endure like the weeds. First published in *Porch*.

the loose copper skins jumping
to the wild *sandunga* dance[1]
brought by rich gypsies from the south
two summers previous, jumping
like the rhythms of the flat yellow
grandmother fingers, always knitting   10
for a birth, fingers husbandless
and almost quiet in the outer room
with the Bible and the picture.
Inside, on all the cool black nights
the young men are making love
privately with two of the older women
whose long flower names are known
and whose families are shamed.
No one speaks about nature;
here it is a private pain.   20
The children go naked in the dirt
and have red coughs.
Over the hills the ocean, once
seen, once touched, is of use to no one
but the gypsies who returned
to the south with parts of it to sell;
the fish of the bay, the sharks
and the white lisa,[2] were all caught
one summer, the year of the fat August.
It is the job of four elected men   30
to keep the sand from the ocean
away, but they cannot.
Rumored widely not to have weeds,
scared away by the great animal sounds
of the ocean, coming closer at night,
weeds are the lie of this town.

1982

CARLOS*

Carlos is the name
by which loneliness
knows each of us.
Carlos the distant relative
worse off than we are
drank the medicines

---

[1] A Mexican couple dance in which the man dances around the woman; the name evokes the sand dunes.

[2] An edible fish that is caught and sold by the Seris as their livelihood.

* A "persona" that Ríos uses in many of his poems, the name probably taken from that of his great uncle.

of poverty and died
not in his sleep
but wide awake
clutching the red chair   10
because alone
his most powerful act
was this.
Carlos who lives inside
pain in each of us
knowing one woman,
it was her brother that died
and that was all,
he was dead
and everyone was sorry   20
because her hands
were too heavy to lift.
Carlos at this moment
wanting desperately other women
looking out through my eyes
making my tongue his
speaking my words
hearing his meanings.
Carlos who is the name of a boat
and the fishermen and the anchor.   30
Carlos who is the cold
and the women and the night.
Carlos who wants only
to age with each of us,
to grow old, to be happy.

                                                1982

MI ABUELO*

Where my grandfather is is in the ground
where you can hear the future
like an Indian with his ear at the tracks.
A pipe leads down to him so that sometimes
he whispers what will happen to a man
in town or how he will meet the best
dressed woman tomorrow and how the best
man at her wedding will chew the ground
next to her. Mi abuelo is the man
who speaks through all the mouths in my house.   10

* "My Grandfather" (Spanish); first published in the *Louisville Review*, the poem takes place on Hallowmas (All Saints' Day, November 1), the occasion of the traditional annual visit to the grandfather's grave.

An echo of me hitting the pipe sometimes
to stop him from saying *my hair is a
sieve* is the only other sound. It is a phrase
that among all others is the best,
he says, and *my hair is a sieve* is sometimes
repeated for hours out of the ground
when I let him, which is not often.
*An abuelo should be much more than a man
like you!* He stops then, and speaks: *I am a man
who has served ants with the attitude*   20
*of a waiter, who has made each smile as only
an ant who is fat can, and they liked me best,
but there is nothing left.* Yet I know he ground
green coffee beans as a child, and sometimes
he will talk about his wife, and sometimes
about when he was deaf and a man
cured him by mail and he heard groundhogs
talking,[1] or about how he walked with a cane
he chewed on when he got hungry.
At best, mi abuelo is a liar.   30
I see an old picture of him at nani's[2] with an
off-white yellow center mustache and sometimes
that's all I know for sure. He talks best
about these hills, *slowest waves*, and where this man
is going, and I'm convinced his hair is a sieve,
that his fever is cooled now underground.
Mi abuelo is an ordinary man.
I look down the pipe, sometimes, and see a
ripple-topped stream in its best suit, in the ground.

1982

MADRE SOFÍA*

My mother took me because she couldn't
wait the second ten years to know.
This was the lady rumored to have been
responsible for the box-wrapped baby
among the presents at that wedding,[1]
but we went in, anyway, through the curtains.
Loose jar-top, half turned
and not caught properly in the threads

[1] According to myth, mail-order cures enable the deaf to hear the gossip of groundhogs.
[2] Nana: grandmother.
* "Mother Sophia" (Spanish); the title character is a fortune teller. First published in *Ironwood*.
[1] In the companion story "Eyes Like the Devil," a couple receives an anonymous wedding present—a gift-wrapped infant.

her head sat mimicking its original intention
like the smile of a child hitting himself.   10
Central in that head grew unfamiliar poppies
from a face mahogany, eyes half yellow
half gray at the same time, goat and fog,
slit eyes of the devil, his tweed suit, red
lips, and she smelled of smoke, cigarettes,
but a diamond smoke, somehow; I inhaled
sparkles, I could feel them, throat, stomach.
She did not speak, and as a child
I could only answer, so that together
we were silent, cold and wet, dry and hard: 20
from behind my mother pushed me forward.
The lady put her hand on the face
of a thin animal wrap, tossing that head
behind her to be pressured incredibly
as she sat back in the huge chair and leaned.
And then I saw the breasts as large as her
head, folded together, coming out of her dress
as if it didn't fit, not like my mother's.
I could see them, how she kept them
penned up, leisurely, in maroon feed bags,   30
horse nuzzles of her wide body,
but exquisitely penned up
circled by pearl reins and red scarves.
She lifted her arm, but only with the tips
of her fingers motioned me to sit opposite.
She looked at me but spoke to my mother
words dark, smoky like the small room,
words coming like red ants stepping occasionally
from a hole on a summer day in the valley,
red ants from her mouth, her nose, her ears,   40
tears from the corners of her cinched eyes.
And suddenly she put her hand full on my head
pinching tight again with those finger tips
like a television healer, young Oral Roberts
half standing, quickly, half leaning
those breasts swinging toward me
so that I reach with both my hands to my lap
protecting instinctively whatever it is
that needs protection when a baseball is thrown
and you're not looking but someone yells,   50
the hand, then those breasts coming toward me
like the quarter-arms of the amputee Joaquín
who came back from the war to sit
in the park, reaching always for children
until one day he had to be held back.
I sat there, no breath, and could see only
hair around her left nipple, like a man.
Her clothes were old.

Accented, in a language whose spine had been
snapped, she whispered the words of a city
witch, and made me happy, alive like a man:
The future will make you tall.

60

1982

THE PURPOSE OF ALTAR BOYS*

Tonio told me at catechism[1]
the big part of the eye
admits good, and the little
black part is for seeing
evil—his mother told him
who was a widow and so
an authority on such things.
That's why at night
the black part gets bigger.
That's why kids can't go out   10
at night, and at night
girls take off their clothes
and walk around their
bedrooms or jump on their
beds or wear only sandals
and stand in their windows.
I was the altar boy
who knew about these things,
whose mission on some Sundays
was to remind people of   20
the night before as they
knelt for Holy Communion.[2]
To keep Christ from falling
I held the metal plate[3]
under chins, while on the thick
red carpet of the altar
I dragged my feet
and waited for the precise
moment: plate to chin
I delivered without expression   30
the Holy Electric Shock,
the kind that produces
a really large swallowing
and makes people think.

---

* First published in the *American Literary Review*.
[1] A formal questioning for the purpose of religious instruction.
[2] A Christian rite in which bread and wine are consecrated and consumed as symbols of the body and blood of Jesus.
[3] The Communion plate holding the bread (or wafers).

I thought of it as justice.
But on other Sundays the fire
in my eyes was different,
my mission somehow changed.
I would hold the metal plate
a little too hard   40
against those certain same
nervous chins, and I
I would look
with authority down
the tops of white dresses.

1982

WINTER ALONG THE SANTA CRUZ*

Ground squirrels snap and turn
like the motion that spins a child's wooden top,
but the river sand is still, like heavy cream
left out too long, assuming the color
death requires, still and stretched:
severed long arm lying, crooked at its elbow,
white with the last summer pulses
of rain through its hard and thinning arteries
sucking in liquid instinctively, feeding
on itself, first from its fingers, then wrist,   10
taking everything in, leaving its parts dry,
the river consumes everything but the clear sweat
of its own effort, visible in the early morning,
beads carried off by the wind and the redbirds
and the sailors who are lost.

1982

Louise Erdrich
(1954–   )

In a 1987 interview with Joseph Bruchac, Louise Erdrich described the poet or fiction
writer as "something like a medium at a seance who lets the voices speak." And her voices
do speak, telling their stories of loneliness and survival in language at once poetic and
colloquial. In her work, Erdrich, whose background is mainly Chippewa, French, and

---

* A river that flows south through Nogales, Arizona, on the Mexico-United States border to the Gulf
of California; first published in the *Iowa Review*.

German, consistently draws upon her Native-American heritage. She was born Karen Louise Erdrich in Little Falls, Minnesota, in 1954 and raised in North Dakota. Her parents, who worked for the Bureau of Indian Affairs's boarding school, encouraged Erdrich to write at an early age. After graduating from Dartmouth College in 1976, she began to recognize the important role her Native-American heritage plays in what she has to say.

Erdrich returned to North Dakota after college and worked as a publications director for a small press-distribution company and as a poet for a program called Poetry in the Schools. After assisting on a film about the clash of the Sioux and the European settlers, she moved back East. With a fellowship to teach at Johns Hopkins University, she completed an M.A. there in 1977. Later she edited *The Circle,* an Urban Indian Council newspaper, in Boston. In 1981 Erdrich married the writer Michael Dorris (author of *The Broken Cord* [1989]), who taught in Dartmouth's Native-American Studies program and is a member of the Modoc tribe of Northern California. Thereafter, Erdich was able to devote herself to writing full time. The two have since often collaborated in writing fiction.

With the freedom to write, Erdrich published her first book of poetry, *Jacklight,* and her first novel, *Love Medicine,* in 1984. The two books are clearly related in style—both make use of dramatic monologues, one in poetry and the other in prose. *Love Medicine* describes the families on a North Dakota Chippewa reservation. Although Erdrich did not grow up on a reservation, her mother did and told vivid childhood stories; the family often visited relatives there. The novel consists of interlocking first-person stories and dramatic monologues of many characters. Both *Love Medicine* and *Jacklight* received critical praise, the novel winning the National Book Critics' Circle Award for fiction. Two novels followed: *The Beet Queen* in 1986 and *Tracks* in 1988.

Erdrich claims as literary influences Flannery O'Connor, Eudora Welty, and Toni Morrison, women steeped in their own strong traditions of place and people. Erdrich avidly reads firsthand historical accounts of travel and adventure, particularly in journals and diaries. After the publication of *Jacklight* she turned her attention almost exclusively to fiction writing. Having children interfered with the experience of letting "your unconscious work for you," which she feels has everything to do with writing poetry. In her interview with Bruchac she claimed that she had not missed writing poetry—she would "rather have the kids than the tortured unconscious." But the lure of poetry was too great. She again began to write poetry, confessing that "now I have children *and* a tortured unconscious," and published *Baptism of Desire* in 1990. The poems of that collection, which are rich with religious imagery, feature some of the Chippewa characters she introduced in *Jacklight.*

Suggested Readings: *Love Medicine,* 1984. *The Beet Queen,* 1986. *Tracks,* 1988. *Baptism of Desire,* 1990. J. George, "Interview With Louise Erdrich," in *North Dakota Quarterly,* 53(2): 240–246, Spring 1985. V. Shetley, review of *Jacklight* in *Poetry,* 146:40–41, April 1985. J. Bruchac, "Whatever Is Really Yours: An Interview With Louise Erdrich," in J. Bruchac, ed., *Survival This Way: Interviews With American Indian Poets,* 1987.

Text Used: *Jacklight,* 1984.

INDIAN BOARDING SCHOOL: THE RUNAWAYS*

Home's the place we head for in our sleep.
Boxcars stumbling north in dreams

* First published in *Frontiers.*

don't wait for us. We catch them on the run.
The rails, old lacerations that we love,
shoot parallel across the face and break
just under Turtle Mountains.[1] Riding scars
you can't get lost. Home is the place they cross.

The lame guard strikes a match and makes the dark
less tolerant. We watch through cracks in boards
as the land starts rolling, rolling till it hurts   10
to be here, cold in regulation clothes.
We know the sheriff's waiting at midrun
to take us back. His car is dumb and warm.
The highway doesn't rock, it only hums
like a wing of long insults. The worn-down welts
of ancient punishments lead back and forth.

All runaways wear dresses, long green ones,
the color you would think shame was. We scrub
the sidewalks down because it's shameful work.
Our brushes cut the stone in watered arcs   20
and in the soak frail outlines shiver clear
a moment, things us kids pressed on the dark
face before it hardened, pale, remembering
delicate old injuries, the spines of names and leaves.

1984

FRANCINE'S ROOM

This is Tarsus, one place like anyplace else.
And this is my circuit, the rodeo, fair.
The farmboys blow through here in pickups, wild
as horses in their oat sacks.
The women wear spurs.
In the trailers the cattle are pounding for air.

My room is the same as last year. They always give me
end of the corridor, left, the top floor.
Privacy. Why not. I've been through here before.
I'm the town's best   10
customer. A minor attraction.
I buy from their stores. Remember this bureau—

battered wood, the fake drawer and split mirror?
And even the glass marks, ring within ring
of spilled drinks. When I sit here
the widest warped links have a center.

---

[1] A small mountain range in North Dakota.

Strung out they're a year's worth of slack, a tether
that swings around the spine's dark pole
and swings back. Each time I return
something's different,   20
although there's a few I can always expect.
The cracks in the mirror: always more, never less.
The stains in the bedspread have spread.
And the rip in the window shade lets through more light,
strange light, since I come here to be in the dark.
Should be taped. A few things can be saved anyhow.
But I don't want to get into that.

I set up my pictures. Mother and Father,
stiffer, more blurred every year.
I turn them to the walls when there's customers, that   30
is the least I can do. What mending there is
occurs in small acts,
and after the fact of the damage,
when nothing is ever enough.
There is always the scar to remind me
that things were once perfect, at least

they were new. I first came here when I was a girl.
It surprised me, the things that two people could do
left alone in a room. Not long and I learned.
I learned what the selves are a man can disown   40
till he lets them to life in a room.

It's the region's hard winters, snowed in with the snow
half the year. I'd expect them to think up a few.
But nothing surprises me, not anymore.
The plumbing can only get worse with the cold.
It's true, even summers the water is foul
and flows slowly, a thin brown trickle by noon.

Heat pours in the west, freak waves of dry lightning
soak the whole town in a feverish light.
Beneath me, the tables of water have dropped   50
to unheard-of levels. It's been a long drought.
I bend my whole arm to the handle, the valve
yawns open but nothing comes out. What else should I
expect. Wrung cloth. The body washing in dust.

1984

CAPTIVITY

*He (my captor) gave me a bisquit, which I put in my pocket, and not daring to eat it,
buried it under a log, fearing he had put something in it to make me love him.*

—from the narrative of the captivity of Mrs. Mary Rowlandson,[1]
who was taken prisoner by the Wampanoag when Lancaster,
Massachusetts, was destroyed, in the year 1676.

The stream was swift, and so cold
I thought I would be sliced in two.
But he dragged me from the flood
by the ends of my hair.
I had grown to recognize his face.
I could distinguish it from the others.
There were times I feared I understood
his language, which was not human,
and I knelt to pray for strength.

We were pursued! By God's agents   10
or pitch devils I did not know.
Only that we must march.
Their guns were loaded with swan shot.
I could not suckle and my child's wail
put them in danger.
He had a woman
with teeth black and glittering.
She fed the child milk of acorns.
The forest closed, the light deepened.

I told myself that I would starve   20
before I took food from his hands
but I did not starve.
One night
he killed a deer with a young one in her
and gave me to eat of the fawn.
It was so tender,
the bones like the stems of flowers,
that I followed where he took me.
The night was thick. He cut the cord
that bound me to the tree.   30

After that the birds mocked.
Shadows gaped and roared
and the trees flung down
their sharpened lashes.
He did not notice God's wrath.
God blasted fire from half-buried stumps.
I hid my face in my dress, fearing He would burn us all
but this, too, passed.

Rescued, I see no truth in things.
My husband drives a thick wedge   40

---

[1] Rowlandson (1637?–1711?) was wounded and captured in February 1676 in a raid by local Native-American tribes during King Philip's War (1675?–1678); she was held captive for twelve weeks and described the experience in her *Narrative* (1682).

through the earth, still it shuts
to him year after year.
My child is fed of the first wheat.
I lay myself to sleep
on a Holland-laced pillowbeer.[2]
I lay to sleep.
And in the dark I see myself
as I was outside their circle.

They knelt on deerskins, some with sticks,
and he led his company in the noise   50
until I could no longer bear
the thought of how I was.
I stripped a branch
and struck the earth,
in time, begging it to open
to admit me
as he was
and feed me honey from the rock.

                                            1984

THAT PULL FROM THE LEFT*

Butch once remarked to me how sinister it was
alone, after hours, in the dark of the shop
to find me there hunched over two weeks' accounts
probably smoked like a bacon from all those Pall-Malls.[1]

Odd comfort when the light goes, the case lights left on
and the rings of baloney, the herring, the parsley,
arranged in the strict, familiar ways.

Whatever intactness holds animals up
has been carefully taken, what's left are the parts.
Just look in the cases, all counted and stacked.   10

Step-and-a-Half Waleski used to come to the shop
and ask for the cheap cut, she would thump, sniff, and finger.
This one too old. This one here for my supper.
Two days and you do notice change in the texture.

I have seen them the day before slaughter.
Knowing of the outcome from the moment they enter
the chute, the eye rolls, blood is smeared on the lintel.[2]
Mallet or bullet they lunge toward their darkness.

[2] A pillowcase.
* First published in the *Louisville Review*.   [1] A brand of cigarettes.
[2] The horizontal crosspiece over a door; in Exodus 12:13 God has instructed the Israelites to mark the

But something queer happens when the heart is delivered.
When a child is born, sometimes the left hand is stronger.   20
You can train it to fail, still the knowledge is there.
That is the knowledge in the hand of a butcher

that adds to its weight. Otto Kröger could fell
a dray horse[3] with one well-placed punch to the jaw,
and yet it is well known how thorough he was.

He never sat down without washing his hands,
and he was a maker, his sausage was *echt*[4]
so that even Waleski had little complaint.
Butch once remarked there was no one so deft
as my Otto. So true, there is great tact involved   30
in parting the flesh from the bones.

How we cling to the bones. Each joint is a web
of small tendons and fibers. He knew what I meant
when I told him I felt something pull from the left,
and how often it clouded the day before slaughter.

Something queer happens when the heart is delivered.

1984

MIDDLE TO LATE 20TH-CENTURY FICTION

Since World War II American fiction has been distinguished by an unprecedented heterogeneity of genre, subject, and theme and by a comparable elasticity in form and language. World War II, the Korean War, and the Vietnam War generated a large body of literature documenting the newly realized capacity for cruelty and self-destruction, glorifying individual instances of wartime courage and generosity, and, more typically, condemning American participation in foreign conflicts. The efflorescence of regionalism begun in the Southern Renaissance earlier in the twentieth century continued, with new energies. American audiences learned in the second half of the century to read not only the literatures of marginalized foreign countries but those of historically voiceless American factions, authors who would have been ignored prior to World War II for reasons of religion, race, or gender. In the 1940s and 1950s they began demanding to be heard and were gradually and slowly allowed to enrich American literature. And the paranoia engendered by the cold war and McCarthyism during the 1950s provoked a new form of popular fiction, the spy novel, and bolstered the popularity of a related genre, the mystery novel.

---

lintels of their doors with blood: " . . . and when I see the blood, I will pass over you, and the plague shall not be upon you to destroy you, when I smite the land of Egypt."
[3] A horse that pulls a cart for hauling heavy cargo; a workhorse.   [4] "Authentic" (German).

World War II was the favored topic of the American novel in the late 1940s and early 1950s. Some novelists used the arena of the war to portray the individual's impotence and insignificance in the universe; others transformed wartime exigencies into political allegories of peacetime society. One of the most successful World War II novels was one of the first, Norman Mailer's *The Naked and the Dead* (1948). Mailer's realistic and comprehensive portrayal of an infantry platoon fighting the Japanese in the Pacific earned him great critical acclaim and several critical accusations of romanticism. His search for a hero suitable to the nuclear age found no ideal figure in *The Naked and the Dead,* but Mailer clearly admired the characters wielding military authority.

═══CONTEXTS═══

Historical Interpretation

The historical interpretation of literature seeks to place a literary work in the context of the time and place of its creation. The historical circumstances in which an author works are seen as important contributing factors, and knowledge of these factors is essential to fully understanding the work. A major proponent of this critical method was Edmund Wilson (1895–1972), who, in his lecture "The Historical Interpretation of Literature" (delivered at Princeton University in 1940), asserted that "human arts and institutions [are] to be studied and elucidated as the products of the geographical and climatic conditions in which the people who created them lived, and of the phase of their social development through which they [are] passing at the moment."

Wilson adopted these attitudes from the French historical critic Hippolyte Adolphe Taine (1828–1893), whose method Wilson has described as follows:

The Historical Interpretation of Literature

Taine thought he was a scientist and a mechanist, who was examining works of literature from the same point of view as the chemist's in experimenting with chemical compounds. But the difference between the critic and the chemist is that the critic cannot first combine his elements and then watch to see what they will do: he can only examine phenomena which have already taken place. The procedure that Taine actually follows is to pretend to set the stage for the experiment by describing the moment, the race and the milieu, and then to say: "Such a situation demands such and such a kind of writer."

Wilson was in part reacting against the antihistorical attitudes of the New Criticism. Wilson suggested that while this method can bring interesting connections to light, it nonetheless ignores the fact that literature is centered in history. The New Critic, according to Wilson:

. . . sees, or tries to see, the whole of literature, so far as he is acquainted with it, spread out before him under the aspect of eternity. He then compares the work of different periods and countries, and tries to draw from it general conclusions about what literature ought to be.

Edmund Wilson, 1940

However, in the 1960s, with the increasing acceptance of the writer Marshall McLuhan's ideas on the transformative nature of all media, including written texts as well as moving images, war novels commonly became occasions for authors to question the validity of traditionally realistic prose styles and to experiment with new approaches to fictional records of wartime perceptions. American literature includes a long tradition of deromanticizing the military. In the 1960s authors writing about World War II found their models not in the novels of the 1940s and 1950s but in such precedents as Ambrose Bierce's scathing nineteenth-century satires of the Civil War and Dalton Trumbo's horrific tale of a limbless, deaf-mute, and blind war veteran, *Johnny Got His Gun* (1939). Novels such as Joseph Heller's *Catch-22* (1961) and Thomas Pynchon's *Gravity's Rainbow* (1973) emphasize the injustice, horror, and absurdity of war.

Many of the authors of the first wave of World War II novels came to recognize the literary implications of incurable subjectivity and later abandoned the attempt to write purportedly realistic fiction. Norman Mailer and Truman Capote wrote nonfiction in the 1950s until they realized that the same subjectivity that undermines realistic fiction undermines realistic nonfiction as well. In the late 1960s both authors began experimenting with a hybrid form of fictionalized journalism. Among Mailer's early works in this genre was his account of a 1967 antiwar march on the Pentagon, *The Armies of the Night* (1968). More recent war novels, such as Bobbie Ann Mason's *In Country* (1985), have focused on the Vietnam War and its home-front consequences.

While mainstream authors were attempting to draw meaning from their war experiences, African-American authors were engaged in a domestic war of their own, struggling to gain entry into the American literary scene, much as all African Americans were struggling to improve their position in American society. With the publication of his novel *Native Son* (1940), Richard Wright became the first African-American author to reach a large audience. A grimly detailed depiction of the urban ghetto that shaped the African-American protagonist, Bigger Thomas, who expresses his enraged frustration through murderous violence, this work marked the beginning of a new literature of black protest. Wright drew reactionary objections from alarmed whites, but the controversy only increased book sales. The success of Wright's autobiographical novel, *Black Boy* (1945), also facilitated publication of Ralph Ellison and James Baldwin in the 1950s. The works of a second, more stridently revolutionary generation of African-American authors, including Malcolm X, Eldridge Cleaver, and Amiri Baraka, appeared in the 1960s.

In the 1970s and 1980s the works of African-American women began to receive public validation as bestsellers. Alice Walker's epistolary novel *The Color Purple* (1982) won a National Book Award, and Toni Morrison's novel *Beloved* (1988) won a Pulitzer Prize. Morrison employs a wide range of narrative voices and imaginative resources, drawing technical inspiration from European and American modernist conventions, from the oral vernacular traditions of American slave culture, and from the richly creative literatures of Africa and of South and Central America. Combining these influences, she explores the possibility of free will and self-definition in an era burdened by widespread alienation, fragmented families as well as fragmented psyches, and an absence of ethical consensus.

On August 28, 1963, the civil rights leader Martin Luther King, Jr. led a march to the Lincoln Memorial, where he delivered his famous "I Have a Dream" speech.

These problems are both complicated and much illuminated by the addition of the female African-American perspective.

During World War II and the tumultuous civil rights movement, regional writing continued to flourish. Eudora Welty, Katherine Anne Porter's protégé, began incorporating myth and symbolism into her fiction and produced some of her finest short stories of the comic and the grotesque during the 1940s and 1950s. *The Heart is a Lonely Hunter* (1940), the first novel by Carson McCullers, another southerner writing about the South, demonstrates her preoccupation with grotesque characters driven to violent actions. Flannery O'Connor, like McCullers a Georgian interested in the grotesque and the violent, began her brief publishing career with short stories in the 1940s, followed by her first novel, *Wise Blood,* in 1952. Her combinations of overheated southern landscapes, Calvinist religion, eccentric humor, and creative brilliance won her a large and loyal readership.

John Cheever also combined religious themes and idiosyncratic humor in his depictions of northeastern America. Claiming suburban New York and New England as his own, he excelled in satirizing social and individual pretensions and in framing particular moments of illumination and folly in the lives of urbanites and commuters. Many of Cheever's stories first appeared in the *New Yorker* magazine, a very influential force in the advancement of the short-story genre during the 1950s and 1960s. Although it published work by a wide variety of artists, such as the luminous and intricate stories by the Russian émigré Vladimir Nabokov, the *New Yorker* favored stories by and about the American upper middle class, such as those of Mary McCarthy and J. D. Salinger.

John Updike, who began working as a writer and critic for the *New Yorker* in 1955, has become one of America's most prolific writers. His eye for visual detail is acute; his fictional observations of contemporary American manners, especially in matters of sex, money, religion, and race, are provocative. Many of his novels deal with the topography of his character's emotions within and outside marriage and with the domestic artifacts of middle-class American life. These issues also figure largely in stories published in the 1980s by authors investigating the uses of "minimalist" narrative techniques, such as Frederick Barthelme, Annie Dillard, and Raymond Carver. Carver deploys a laconic, elliptical style reminiscent of Ernest Hemingway's to portray middle-class characters trapped in dialogues of avoidance and of emotional confrontration. Whereas regional writers focus on a geographically defined culture, Updike and others write of a population united by the common concerns and vocabulary of shared class standing.

In the late 1940s a group of writers claiming to represent "the beat generation" of young Americans traumatized by World War II began producing exuberant and stylistically original works celebrating their escape from the middle class. Their reckless and exhilarating forays into the subterranean life of urban and rural America were recorded most famously in Kerouac's novel *On the Road* (1957). In the 1970s and 1980s Joyce Carol Oates has typically investigated the same subterranean America that attracted the beat poets but found little there to celebrate. Her characters are typically drawn from the lower middle or working classes, and her fiction reveals a fascination with the American propensity for violence. In her novels, short stories, and nonfiction works she traces the undercurrents of brutality in everyday life, especially in male/female relationships.

Only after 1960 did the reading public begin to notice the work of Native Americans. The stories, myth cycles, and novels of N. Scott Momaday (of Kiowa ancestry) and of Leslie Marmon Silko (descended from the Laguna Pueblo tribe) draw their narrative and stylistic strengths from Native-American storytelling traditions. Momaday's novel *House Made of Dawn* (1968), concerning a young Native American's estrangement from his ancestral roots, was quickly followed by *The Way to Rainy Mountain* (1969), a cycle of Kiowa legends. In *Ceremony* (1977) Silko portrays the alienation and repatriation of a Native-American soldier. Her shorter piece "Storyteller" (1981) uses alternating styles and techniques— Native-American myths and songs interspersed with linear and chronological narrative.

Jewish authors, also writing out of a cultural legacy of geographic displacement, found publishers and readers earlier and more easily than did African Americans and Native Americans. Henry Roth published his novel *Call It Sleep* in 1937; novels and short stories by Saul Bellow, Bernard Malamud, and Herbert Gold appeared in the 1950s. Bellow translated Isaac Bashevis Singer's story "Gimpel the Fool" (1957) from Yiddish for the *Partisan Review;* it has echoed in the work of Jewish authors ever since. Bellow's own fiction reveals his close engagement with American life after World War II, with the often tragicomic interplay between the intellectual backgrounds and European culture of his characters, and with the hyperkinetic flow of everyday life in American cities. Malamud, too, wrote about urban communities. In *The Assistant* (1957) he describes the painfully constrained lives of a Jewish grocer and his family in Brooklyn, mingling comedy and pathos in a story of suffering and muted triumphs. A second generation of Jewish authors who began writing after 1960 includes Frederick Busch, Grace Paley, Cynthia Ozick, Philip Roth, and Susan Sontag.

Hispanic literature has become increasingly prominent in the late twentieth century, perhaps because it generally reflects a sensibility that is closely allied to the ethos of the postmodern writer. Marked by a willingness to employ narrative strategies that incorporate structural disjunction with a subjective lyricism, and by a commitment to political change, the work of Hispanic authors has lost its marginal status and has been absorbed by the larger current of postmodernism. The works of Chicano literature began to flourish in the post-World War II era, particularly in New York City and in the barrio areas of urban America. However, it was the work of Luís Valdez, with César Chávez and the farm laborers, in El Teatro Campesino (founded in 1965) that brought widespread public attention to Chicano literature. Valdez's work was so effective that by 1967 a strictly Chicano press was established in Berkeley, California. Quinto Sol Publications promoted the work of contemporary Chicano writers, finally providing prose writers such as Rudolfo Anaya, Denise Chávez, Rolando Hinojosa-Smith, and Tomás Rivera with mainstream attention. Like Valdez these writers mixed street dialect with literary conceits, combined the Spanish language with English, and re-examined the past, creating a multi-voiced, bilingual literature. Out of these seemingly incongruous combinations, a Chicano identity in fiction writing was created.

Paradoxically, just as previously voiceless ethnic groups were entering the American literary canon in the 1940s and 1950s, the international tensions of the cold war produced a malignant atmosphere of political repression in America. Senator Joseph McCarthy's crusade against suspected "card-carrying Communists" in government and in the military (though he never found one) spread to include investigations of private citizens. Those who had sympathized with Socialist reform movements in the 1930s were called to account for their actions. Artists and authors, including Dashiell Hammett, Ring Lardner, and Dalton Trumbo, were summoned to testify before McCarthy's investigating committees; uncooperative witnesses were jailed and/or blacklisted in the theater, television, and film industries. Even writers who had merely associated with suspected Communists were silenced as effectively as if they had been exiled to a Siberian gulag.

One of the casualties in McCarthy's crusade was Hammett, who was actively involved in Communist party activities during the 1930s. His refusal to name his associates resulted in a six-month imprisonment in 1951. Before he quit writing in the 1940s, Hammett introduced the reading public to detective fiction. His followers in this extremely durable literary form borrowed Hammett's technical inspiration but not his Socialist principles. Raymond Chandler and Ross MacDonald worked to elevate the detective novel above the level of pulp fiction. Both were chastized for writing beneath their talents, and both produced sophisticated and articulate theoretical defenses of the genre. Chandler's hero, Philip Marlowe, has beneath his crusty exterior as much in common with a romanticized knight rescuing tawdry gutter damsels as he does with real detectives. Chandler quite self-consciously emphasizes Marlowe's knightly qualities with symbolic and literary allusions; the author's literary refinements of his chosen genre bridged the gap between high culture and low culture.

Writers of contemporary western fiction have inherited a literary tradition in which the harsh dynamics of the ever-threatening wilderness serve as a backdrop for the exploration of the American psyche and its relationship to the frontier. Among those important in establishing the western tradition were Owen Wister, James Fenimore Cooper, Zane Grey, and, more recently, Louis L'Amour. In the intersection of postmodernism and the western literary tradition, current writers fracture traditional western images and motifs to correspond to the fragmented nature of contemporary society. Ken Kesey's *Sometimes A Great Notion* (1971) helped establish this connection between postmodern fiction and the contemporary frontier. Larry McMurtry, author of such western novels as *Horseman, Pass By* (1961), *Leaving Cheyenne* (1963), *The Last Picture Show* (1966), and *Lonesome Dove* (1985), has become the most visible proponent of this trend. Thomas McGuane, Richard Ford, Edward Abbey, and Jim Harrison all create fictions that are closely tied to the frontier terrain, whereas Joan Didion and Kathy Acker deal with the myth in a manner that makes the western a primary genre within the canon of postmodernism.

Since World War II, efforts to dismantle exclusive canonical literary restrictions on fiction have moved unsteadily but irreversibly forward. Categories such as high culture versus low, fiction versus nonfiction, mainstream versus marginal, and politically correct versus criminally indictable are not applied as stringently as they once were. The result has been the creation of an increasingly dynamic, diverse, and inclusive literature.

Raymond Chandler
(1888–1959)

In 1929 when a stock market crash ushered in the Great Depression, Raymond Chandler was in charge of the Los Angeles office of an oil syndicate. Three years later he was fired for drinking and missing work. He enrolled in a correspondence course in writing, studied detective magazines, and at age forty-five began a new career with the sale of the short story "Blackmailers Don't Shoot" (1933) for a penny a word. He sold fifteen more stories during the next four years—the pay rose to a nickel a word—and "cannibalized" two of the stories for the plot of *The Big Sleep* (1939), his first novel. Hollywood studios subsequently bought the film rights to his second and third novels, *Farewell My Lovely* (1940) and *The High Window* (1942). He was hired by Paramount Pictures to coauthor the screenplay of *Double Indemnity* (1944), which earned him an Academy Award nomination, as did his solo screenplay, *The Blue Dahlia* (1946). By the late 1940s he was the hottest name in detective fiction and a sought-after screenwriter. However, he was disenchanted with the Los Angeles he wrote about and bitter about the demands of the film industry.

Chandler was born to Quaker parents in Chicago in 1888 and lived in Plattsmouth, Nebraska, until his parents divorced when he was seven. Florence Chandler, an Irish immigrant, took her son to London, where they lived with her mother and sister. Chandler received a classical education at a college preparatory school and studied languages in Europe. At age twenty-three he returned to the United States. In 1924 he married Cissy Pascal, eighteen years his senior. The marriage endured thirty years, through his failures, successes, escapades with secretaries, and drinking. After Cissy's death in 1954 Chandler moved back and forth between La Jolla, California, and London. Hospitalized frequently for alcoholism, he could not remain sober. He died of pneumonia in 1959, leaving an unfinished manuscript, *Poodle Springs,* which was completed in 1989 by Robert B. Parker.

Chandler's best-known creation, Philip Marlowe, started as a version of the freelance detectives that were the specialty of *Black Mask* magazine. These tough moral heroes appealed to a readership shocked by the corruption of the Prohibition era. Chandler's "modern knight" was eventually played by a half-dozen actors on radio, film, and television. "To me Marlowe is the American mind," Chandler wrote to the editor Joseph Shaw, "a heavy portion of rugged realism, a dash of good hard vulgarity, a strong overtone of strident wit, an equally strong undertone of pure sentimentalism, an ocean of slang, and an utterly unexpected range of sensitivity."

Partly an outsider in American culture due to his education abroad, Chandler was an intrigued observer. He listed in a notebook (published as *The Notebooks of Raymond Chandler* [1976]) slang terms of people around him—film workers as well as pickpockets and convicts. "I have had a lot of fun with the American language," he wrote in 1958. "It has fascinating idioms, is constantly creative, very much like the English of Shakespeare's time. . . . " Although Chandler's early work was published in American "pulp" magazines (named for the pulp-wood paper on which they were printed), in England he was regarded as more than a pulp writer. High praise came from the poet W. H. Auden in a 1948 review in *Harper's*: "Chandler is interested in writing. . .serious studies of a criminal milieu, the Great Wrong Place, and his powerful but extremely depressing books should be read and judged, not as escape literature, but as works of art."

Suggested Readings: *The Little Sister,* 1971. *The Long Goodbye,* 1971. *The Simple Art of Murder,* 1972. *Killer in the Rain,* 1972. *The Big Sleep,* 1976. *Farewell, My Lovely,* 1976. *The High Window,* 1976. *The Lady in the Lake,* 1976. *The Notebooks of Raymond Chandler,* ed. F. MacShane, 1976. *Raymond Chandler Speaking,* ed. D. Gardiner and K. S. Walker, 1977. J. Cawelti, *Adventure, Mystery, and Romance,* 1976. F. MacShane, *The Life of Raymond Chandler,* 1976. R. Champigny, *What Will Have Happened,* 1977. M. Gross, ed., *The World of Raymond Chandler,* 1977. J. Speir, *Raymond Chandler,* 1981. W. Marling, *Raymond Chandler,* 1986.

Text Used: *The Midnight Raymond Chandler,* 1971.

RED WIND

I

There was a desert wind blowing that night. It was one of those hot dry Santa Anas[1] that come down through the mountain passes and curl your hair and make your nerves jump and your skin itch. On nights like that every booze party ends in a fight. Meek little wives feel the edge of the carving knife and study their husbands' necks. Anything can happen. You can even get a full glass of beer at a cocktail lounge.

I was getting one in a flossy new place across the street from the apartment house where I lived. It had been open about a week and it wasn't doing any business. The kid behind the bar was in his early twenties and looked as if he had never had a drink in his life.

There was only one other customer, a souse on a bar stool with his back to the door. He had a pile of dimes stacked neatly in front of him, about two dollars' worth. He was drinking straight rye in small glasses and he was all by himself in a world of his own.

I sat farther along the bar and got my glass of beer and said: "You sure cut the clouds off them,[2] buddy. I will say that for you."

"We just opened up," the kid said. "We got to build up trade. Been in before, haven't you, mister?"

"Uh-huh."

"Live around here?"

"In the Berglund Apartments across the street," I said. "And the name is Philip Marlowe."

"Thanks, mister. Mine's Lew Petrolle." He leaned close to me across the polished dark bar. "Know that guy?"

"No."

"He ought to go home, kind of. I ought to call a taxi and send him home. He's doing his next week's drinking too soon."

"A night like this," I said. "Let him alone."

"It's not good for him," the kid said, scowling at me.

"Rye!" the drunk croaked, without looking up. He snapped his fingers so as not to disturb his piles of dimes by banging on the bar.

The kid looked at me and shrugged. "Should I?"

"Whose stomach is it? Not mine."

The kid poured him another straight rye and I think he doctored it with water down behind the bar because when he came up with it he looked as guilty as if he'd kicked his grandmother. The drunk paid no attention. He lifted coins off his pile with the exact care of a crack surgeon operating on a brain tumor.

The kid came back and put more beer in my glass. Outside the wind howled.

---

[1] Hot desert winds from the East or Northeast in southern California.
[2] Serve a full glass of beer, with little foam.

Every once in a while it blew the stained-glass door open a few inches. It was a heavy door.

The kid said: "I don't like drunks in the first place and in the second place I don't like them getting drunk in here, and in the third place I don't like them in the first place."

"Warner Brothers[3] could use that," I said.

"They did."

Just then we had another customer. A car squeaked to a stop outside and the swinging door came open. A fellow came in who looked a little in a hurry. He held the door and ranged the place quickly with flat, shiny, dark eyes. He was well set up, dark, good-looking in a narrow-faced, tight-lipped way. His clothes were dark and a white handkerchief peeped coyly from his pocket and he looked cool as well as under a tension of some sort. I guessed it was the hot wind. I felt a bit the same myself only not cool.

He looked at the drunk's back. The drunk was playing checkers with his empty glasses. The new customer looked at me, then he looked along the line of half-booths at the other side of the place. They were all empty. He came on in—down past where the drunk sat swaying and muttering to himself—and spoke to the bar kid.

"Seen a lady in here, buddy? Tall, pretty, brown hair, in a print bolero jacket over a blue crêpe silk dress. Wearing a wide-brimmed straw hat with a velvet band." He had a tight voice I didn't like.

"No sir. Nobody like that's been in," the bar kid said.

"Thanks. Straight Scotch. Make it fast, will you?"

The kid gave it to him and the fellow paid and put the drink down in a gulp and started to go out. He took three or four steps and stopped, facing the drunk. The drunk was grinning. He swept a gun from somewhere so fast that it was just a blur coming out. He held it steady and he didn't look any drunker than I was. The tall dark guy stood quite still and then his head jerked back a little and then he was still again.

A car tore by outside. The drunk's gun was a .22 target automatic, with a large front sight. It made a couple of hard snaps and a little smoke curled—very little.

"So long, Waldo," the drunk said.

Then he put the gun on the barman and me.

The dark guy took a week to fall down. He stumbled, caught himself, waved one arm, stumbled again. His hat fell off, and then he hit the floor with his face. After he hit it he might have been poured concrete for all the fuss he made.

The drunk slid down off the stool and scooped his dimes into a pocket and slid towards the door. He turned sideways, holding the gun across his body. I didn't have a gun. I hadn't thought I needed one to buy a glass of beer. The kid behind the bar didn't move or make the slightest sound.

The drunk felt the door lightly with his shoulder, keeping his eyes on us, then pushed through it backwards. When it was wide a hard gust of air slammed in and lifted the hair of the man on the floor. The drunk said: "Poor Waldo. I bet I made his nose bleed."

---

[3] A film-production company.

The door swung shut. I started to rush it—from long practice in doing the wrong thing. In this case it didn't matter. The car outside let out a roar and when I got onto the sidewalk it was flicking a red smear of taillight around the nearby corner. I got its license number the way I got my first million.

There were people and cars up and down the block as usual. Nobody acted as if a gun had gone off. The wind was making enough noise to make the hard quick rap of .22 ammunition sound like a slammed door, even if anyone heard it. I went back into the cocktail bar.

The kid hadn't moved, even yet. He just stood with his hands flat on the bar, leaning over a little and looking down at the dark guy's back. The dark guy hadn't moved either. I bent down and felt his neck artery. He wouldn't move—ever.

The kid's face had as much expression as a cut of round steak and was about the same color. His eyes were more angry than shocked.

I lit a cigarette and blew smoke at the ceiling and said shortly: "Get on the phone."

"Maybe he's not dead," the kid said.

"When they use a twenty-two that means they don't make mistakes. Where's the phone?"

"I don't have one. I got enough expenses without that. Boy, can I kick eight hundred bucks in the face!"

"You own this place?"

"I did till this happened."

He pulled his white coat off and his apron and came around the inner end of the bar. "I'm locking this door," he said, taking keys out.

He went out, swung the door to and juggled the lock from the outside until the bolt clicked into place. I bent down and rolled Waldo over. At first I couldn't even see where the shots went in. Then I could. A couple of tiny holes in his coat, over his heart. There was a little blood on his shirt.

The drunk was everything you could ask—as a killer.

The prowl-car boys came in about eight minutes. The kid, Lew Petrolle, was back behind the bar by then. He had his white coat on again and he was counting his money in the register and putting it in his pocket and making notes in a little book.

I sat at the edge of one of the half-booths and smoked cigarettes and watched Waldo's face get deader and deader. I wondered who the girl in the print coat was, why Waldo had left the engine of his car running outside, why he was in a hurry, whether the drunk had been waiting for him or just happened to be there.

The prowl-car boys came in perspiring. They were the usual large size and one of them had a flower stuck under his cap and his cap on a bit crooked. When he saw the dead man he got rid of the flower and leaned down to feel Waldo's pulse. "Seems to be dead," he said, and rolled him around a little more. "Oh yeah, I see where they went in. Nice clean work. You two see him get it?"

I said yes. The kid behind the bar said nothing. I told them about it, that the killer seemed to have left in Waldo's car.

The cop yanked Waldo's wallet out, went through it rapidly and whistled. "Plenty of jack and no driver's license." He put the wallet away. "Okay, we didn't touch him, see? Just a chance we could find did he have a car and put it on the air."

"The hell you didn't touch him," Lew Petrolle said.

The cop gave him one of those looks. "Okay, pal," he said softly. "We touched him."

The kid picked up a clean highball glass and began to polish it. He polished it all the rest of the time we were there.

In another minute a homicide fast-wagon sirened up and screeched to a stop outside the door and four men came in, two dicks, a photographer and a laboratory man. I didn't know either of the dicks. You can be in the detecting business a long time and not know all the men on a big city force.

One of them was a short, smooth, dark, quiet, smiling man, with curly black hair and soft intelligent eyes. The other was big, raw-boned, long-jawed, with a veined nose and glassy eyes. He looked like a heavy drinker. He looked tough, but he looked as if he thought he was a little tougher than he was. He shooed me into the last booth against the wall and his partner got the kid up front and the bluecoats went out. The fingerprint man and photographer set about their work.

A medical examiner came, stayed just long enough to get sore because there was no phone for him to call the morgue wagon.

The short dick emptied Waldo's pockets and then emptied his wallet and dumped everything into a large handkerchief on a booth table. I saw a lot of currency, keys, cigarettes, another handkerchief, very little else.

The big dick pushed me back into the end of the half-booth. "Give," he said. "I'm Copernik, Detective Lieutenant."

I put my wallet in front of him. He looked at it, went through it, tossed it back, made a note in a book.

"Philip Marlowe, huh? A shamus.[4] You here on business?"

"Drinking business," I said. "I live just across the street in the Berglund."

"Know this kid up front?"

"I've been in here once since he opened up."

"See anything funny about him now?"

"No."

"Takes it too light for a young fellow, don't he? Never mind answering. Just tell the story."

I told it—three times. Once for him to get the outline, once for him to get the details and once for him to see if I had it too pat. At the end he said: "This dame interests me. And the killer called the guy Waldo, yet didn't seem to be anyways sure he would be in. I mean, if Waldo wasn't sure the dame would be here, nobody could be sure Waldo would be here."

"That's pretty deep," I said.

He studied me. I wasn't smiling. "Sounds like a grudge job, don't it? Don't sound planned. No getaway except by accident. A guy don't leave his car unlocked much in this town. And the killer works in front of two good witnesses. I don't like that."

"I don't like being a witness," I said. "The pay's too low."

He grinned. His teeth had a freckled look. "Was the killer drunk really?"

"With that shooting? No."

"Me too. Well, it's a simple job. The guy will have a record and he's left plenty

---

[4] A private detective.

prints. Even if we don't have his mug here we'll make him in hours. He had something on Waldo, but he wasn't meeting Waldo tonight. Waldo just dropped in to ask about a dame he had a date with and had missed connections on. It's a hot night and this wind would kill a girl's face. She'd be apt to drop in somewhere to wait. So the killer feeds Waldo two in the right place and scrams and don't worry about you boys at all. It's that simple."

"Yeah," I said.

"It's so simple it stinks," Copernik said.

He took his felt hat off and tousled up his ratty blond hair and leaned his head on his hands. He had a long mean horse face. He got a handkerchief out and mopped it, and the back of his neck and the back of his hands. He got a comb out and combed his hair—he looked worse with it combed—and put his hat back on.

"I was just thinking," I said.

"Yeah? What?"

"This Waldo knew just how the girl was dressed. So he must already have been with her tonight."

"So what? Maybe he had to go to the can. And when he came back she's gone. Maybe she changed her mind about him."

"That's right," I said.

But that wasn't what I was thinking at all. I was thinking that Waldo had described the girl's clothes in a way the ordinary man wouldn't know how to describe them. Printed bolero jacket over blue crêpe silk dress. I didn't even know what a bolero jacket was. And I might have said blue dress or even blue silk dress, but never blue crêpe silk dress.

After a while two men came with a basket. Lew Petrolle was still polishing his glass and talking to the short dark dick.

We all went down to headquarters.

Lew Petrolle was all right when they checked on him. His father had a grape ranch near Antioch[5] in Contra Costa County. He had given Lew a thousand dollars to go into business and Lew had opened the cocktail bar, neon sign and all, on eight hundred flat.

They let him go and told him to keep the bar closed until they were sure they didn't want to do any more printing. He shook hands all around and grinned and said he guessed the killing would be good for business after all, because nobody believed a newspaper account of anything and people would come to him for the story and buy drinks while he was telling it.

"There's a guy won't ever do any worrying," Copernik said, when he was gone. "Over anybody else."

"Poor Waldo," I said. "The prints any good?"

"Kind of smudged," Copernik said sourly. "But we'll get a classification and teletype it to Washington[6] some time tonight. If it don't click, you'll be in for a day on the steel picture racks[7] downstairs."

I shook hands with him and his partner, whose name was Ybarra, and left. They didn't know who Waldo was yet either. Nothing in his pockets told.

---

[5] A city east of San Francisco.   [6] To the FBI's Fingerprint Identification Department.
[7] The racks on which photographs of criminals are mounted in the police department.

2

I got back to my street about 9 P.M. I looked up and down the block before I went into the Berglund. The cocktail bar was farther down on the other side, dark, with a nose or two against the glass, but no real crowd. People had seen the law and the morgue wagon, but they didn't know what had happened. Except the boys playing pinball games in the drugstore on the corner. They know everything, except how to hold a job.

The wind was still blowing, oven-hot, swirling dust and torn paper up against the walls.

I went into the lobby of the apartment house and rode the automatic elevator up to the fourth floor. I unwound the doors and stepped out and there was a tall girl standing there waiting for the car.

She had brown wavy hair under a wide-brimmed straw hat with a velvet band and loose bow. She had wide blue eyes and eyelashes that didn't quite reach her chin. She wore a blue dress that might have been crêpe silk, simple in lines but not missing any curves. Over it she wore what might have been a print bolero jacket.

I said: "Is that a bolero jacket?"

She gave me a distant glance and made a motion as if to brush a cobweb out of the way.

"Yes, Would you mind—I'm rather in a hurry. I'd like—"

I didn't move. I blocked her off from the elevator. We stared at each other and she flushed very slowly.

"Better not go out on the street in those clothes," I said.

"Why, how dare you—"

The elevator clanked and started down again. I didn't know what she was going to say. Her voiced lacked the edgy twang of a beer-parlor frill.[8] It had a soft light sound, like spring rain.

"It's not a make,"[9] I said. "You're in trouble. If they come to this floor in the elevator, you have just that much time to get off the hall. First take off the hat and jacket—and snap it up!"

She didn't move. Her face seemed to whiten a little behind the not-too-heavy make-up.

"Cops," I said, "are looking for you. In those clothes. Give me the chance and I'll tell you why."

She turned her head swiftly and looked back along the corridor. With her looks I didn't blame her for trying one more bluff.

"You're impertinent, whoever you are. I'm Mrs. Leroy in apartment thirty-one. I can assure—"

"That you're on the wrong floor," I said. "This is the fourth." The elevator had stopped down below. The sound of doors being wrenched open came up the shaft.

"Off!" I rapped. "Now!"

She switched her hat off and slipped out of the bolero jacket, fast. I grabbed them and wadded them into a mess under my arm. I took her elbow and turned her and we were going down the hall.

"I live in forty-two. The front one across from yours, just a floor up. Take your choice. Once again—I'm not on the make."

---

[8] Slang for "woman."   [9] A proposition.

She smoothed her hair with that quick gesture, like a bird preening itself. Ten thousand years of practice behind it.

"Mine," she said, and tucked her bag under her arm and strode down the hall fast. The elevator stopped at the floor below. She stopped when it stopped. She turned and faced me.

"The stairs are back by the elevator shaft," I said gently.

"I don't have an apartment," she said.

"I didn't think you had."

"Are they searching for me?"

"Yes, but they won't start gouging the block stone by stone before tomorrow. And then only if they don't make Waldo."

She stared at me. "Waldo?"

"Oh, you don't know Waldo," I said.

She shook her head slowly. The elevator started down in the shaft again. Panic flicked in her blue eyes like a ripple on water.

"No," she said breathlessly, "but take me out of this hall."

We were almost at my door. I jammed the key in and shook the lock around and heaved the door inward. I reached in far enough to switch lights on. She went in past me like a wave. Sandalwood floated on the air, very faint.

I shut the door, threw my hat into a chair and watched her stroll over to a card table on which I had a chess problem set out that I couldn't solve. Once inside, with the door locked, her panic had left her.

"So you're a chess player," she said, in that guarded tone, as if she had come to look at my etchings. I wished she had.

We both stood still then and listened to the distant clang of elevator doors and then steps—going the other way.

I grinned, but with strain, not pleasure, went out into the kitchenette and started to fumble with a couple of glasses and then realized I still had her hat and bolero jacket under my arm. I went into the dressing room behind the wall bed[10] and stuffed them into a drawer, went back out to the kitchenette, dug out some extra-fine Scotch and made a couple of highballs.

When I went in with the drinks she had a gun in her hand. It was a small automatic with a pearl grip. It jumped up at me and her eyes were full of horror.

I stopped, with a glass in each hand, and said: "Maybe this hot wind has got you crazy too. I'm a private detective. I'll prove it if you let me."

She nodded slightly and her face was white. I went over slowly and put a glass down beside her, and went back and set mine down and got a card out that had no bent corners. She was sitting down, smoothing one blue knee with her left hand, and holding the gun on the other. I put the card down beside her drink and sat with mine.

"Never let a guy get that close to you," I said. "Not if you mean business. And your safety catch is on."

She flashed her eyes down, shivered, and put the gun back in her bag. She drank half the drink without stopping, put the glass down hard and picked the card up.

"I don't give many people that liquor," I said. "I can't afford to."

Her lips curled. "I supposed you would want money."

"Huh?"

---

[10] A Murphy bed, which folds up into the wall when not in use.

She didn't say anything. Her hand was close to her bag again.

"Don't forget the safety catch," I said. Her hand stopped. I went on: "This fellow I called Waldo is quite tall, say five-eleven, slim, dark, brown eyes with a lot of glitter. Nose and mouth too thin. Dark suit, white handkerchief showing, and in a hurry to find you. Am I getting anywhere?"

She took her glass again. "So that's Waldo," she said. "Well, what about him?" Her voice seemed to have a slight liquor edge now.

"Well, a funny thing. There's a cocktail bar across the street . . . Say, where have you been all evening?"

"Sitting in my car," she said coldly, "most of the time."

"Didn't you see a fuss across the street up the block?"

Her eyes tried to say no and missed. Her lips said: "I knew there was some kind of disturbance. I saw policemen and red searchlights. I supposed someone had been hurt."

"Someone was. And this Waldo was looking for you before that. In the cocktail bar. He described you and your clothes."

Her eyes were set like rivets now and had the same amount of expression. Her mouth began to tremble and kept on trembling.

"I was in there," I said, "talking to the kid that runs it. There was nobody in there but a drunk on a stool and the kid and myself. The drunk wasn't paying any attention to anything. Then Waldo came in and asked about you and we said no, we hadn't seen you and he started to leave."

I sipped my drink. I like an effect as well as the next fellow. Her eyes ate me.

"Just started to leave. Then this drunk that wasn't paying any attention to anyone called him Waldo and took a gun out. He shot him twice"—I snapped my fingers twice—"like that. Dead."

She fooled me. She laughed in my face. "So my husband hired you to spy on me," she said. "I might have known the whole thing was an act. You and your Waldo."

I gawked at her.

"I never thought of him as jealous," she snapped. "Not of a man who had been our chauffeur anyhow. A little about Stan, of course—that's natural. But Joseph Coates—"

I made motions in the air. "Lady, one of us has this book open at the wrong page," I grunted. "I don't know anybody named Stan or Joseph Coates. So help me, I didn't even know you had a chauffeur. People around here don't run to them. As for husbands—yeah, we do have a husband once in a while. Not often enough."

She shook her head slowly and her hand stayed near her bag and her blue eyes had glitters in them.

"Not good enough, Mr. Marlowe. No, not nearly good enough. I know you private detectives. You're all rotten. You tricked me into your apartment, if it is your apartment. More likely it's the apartment of some horrible man who will swear anything for a few dollars. Now you're trying to scare me. So you can blackmail me—as well as get money from my husband. All right," she said breathlessly, "how much do I have to pay?"

I put my empty glass aside and leaned back: "Pardon me if I light a cigarette," I said. "My nerves are frayed."

I lit it while she watched me without enough fear for any real guilt to be under it. "So Joseph Coates is his name," I said. "The guy that killed him in the cocktail bar called him Waldo."

She smiled a bit disgustedly, but almost tolerantly. "Don't stall. How much?"

"Why were you trying to meet this Joseph Coates?"

"I was going to buy something he stole from me, of course. Something that's valuable in the ordinary way too. Almost fifteen thousand dollars. The man I loved gave it to me. He's dead. There! He's dead! He died in a burning plane. Now, go back and tell my husband that, you slimy little rat!"

"I'm not little and I'm not a rat," I said.

"You're still slimy. And don't bother about telling my husband. I'll tell him myself. He probably knows anyway."

I grinned. "That's smart. Just what was I supposed to find out?"

She grabbed her glass and finished what was left of her drink. "So he thinks I'm meeting Joseph. Well, perhaps I was. But not to make love. Not with a chauffeur. Not with a bum I picked off the front step and gave a job to. I don't have to dig down that far, if I want to play around."

"Lady," I said, "you don't indeed."

"Now I'm going," she said. "You just try and stop me." She snatched the pearl-handled gun out of her bag. I didn't move.

"Why, you nasty little string of nothing," she stormed. "How do I know you're a private detective at all? You might be a crook. This card you gave me doesn't mean anything. Anybody can have cards printed."

"Sure," I said. "And I suppose I'm smart enough to live here two years because you were going to move in today so I could blackmail you for not meeting a man named Joseph Coates who was bumped off across the street under the name of Waldo. Have you got the money to buy this something that cost fifteen grand?"

"Oh! You think you'll hold me up, I suppose!"

"Oh!" I mimicked her. "I'm a stick-up artist now, am I? Lady, will you please either put that gun away or take the safety catch off? It hurts my professional feelings to see a nice gun made a monkey of that way."

"You're a full portion of what I don't like," she said. "Get out of my way."

I didn't move. She didn't move. We were both sitting down—and not even close to each other.

"Let me in on one secret before you go," I pleaded. "What in hell did you take the apartment down on the floor below for? Just to meet a guy down on the street?"

"Stop being silly," she snapped. "I didn't. I lied. It's his apartment."

"Joseph Coates'?"

She nodded sharply.

"Does my description of Waldo sound like Joseph Coates?"

She nodded sharply again.

"All right. That's one fact learned at last. Don't you realize Waldo described your clothes before he was shot—when he was looking for you—that the description was passed on to the police—that the police don't know who Waldo is—and are looking for somebody in those clothes to help tell them? Don't you get that much?"

The gun suddenly started to shake in her hand. She looked down at it, sort of vacantly, slowly put it back in her bag.

"I'm a fool," she whispered, "to be even talking to you." She stared at me for a long time, then pulled in a deep breath. "He told me where he was staying. He didn't seem afraid. I guess blackmailers are like that. He was to meet me on the street, but I was late. It was full of police when I got here. So I went back and sat in my car for a while. Then I came up to Joseph's apartment and knocked. Then I went back to my car and waited again. I came up here three times in all. The last time I walked up a flight to take the elevator. I had already been seen twice on the third floor. I met you. That's all."

"You said something about a husband," I grunted. "Where is he?"

"He's at a meeting."

"Oh, a meeting," I said nastily.

"My husband's a very important man. He has lots of meetings. He's a hydro-electric engineer. He's been all over the world. I'd have you know—"

"Skip it," I said. "I'll take him to lunch some day and have him tell me himself. Whatever Joseph had on you is dead stock now. Like Joseph."

"He's really dead?" she whispered. "Really?"

"He's dead," I said. "Dead, dead, dead. Lady, he's dead."

She believed it at last. I hadn't thought she ever would somehow. In the silence, the elevator stopped at my floor.

I heard steps coming down the hall. We all have hunches. I put my finger to my lips. She didn't move now. Her face had a frozen look. Her big blue eyes were as black as the shadows below them. The hot wind boomed against the shut windows. Windows have to be shut when a Santa Ana blows, heat or no heat.

The steps that came down the hall were the casual ordinary steps of one man. But they stopped outside my door, and somebody knocked.

I pointed to the dressing room behind the wall bed. She stood up without a sound, her bag clenched against her side. I pointed again, to her glass. She lifted it swiftly, slid across the carpet, through the door, drew the door quietly shut after her.

I didn't know just what I was going to all this trouble for.

The knocking sounded again. The backs of my hands were wet. I creaked my chair and stood up and made a loud yawning sound. Then I went over and opened the door—without a gun. That was a mistake.

3

I didn't know him at first. Perhaps for the opposite reason Waldo hadn't seemed to know him. He'd had a hat on all the time over at the cocktail bar and he didn't have one on now. His hair ended completely and exactly where his hat would start. Above that line was hard white sweatless skin almost as glaring as scar tissue. He wasn't just twenty years older. He was a different man.

But I knew the gun he was holding, the .22 target automatic with the big front sight. And I knew his eyes. Bright, brittle, shallow eyes like the eyes of a lizard.

He was alone. He put the gun against my face very lightly and said between his teeth: "Yeah, me. Let's go on in."

I backed in just far enough and stopped. Just the way he would want me to, so he could shut the door without moving much. I knew from his eyes that he would want me to do just that.

I wasn't scared. I was paralyzed.

When he had the door shut he backed me some more, slowly, until there was something against the back of my legs. His eyes looked into mine.

"That's a card table," he said. "Some goon here plays chess. You?"

I swallowed. "I don't exactly play it. I just fool around."

"That means two," he said with a kind of hoarse softness, as if some cop had hit him across the windpipe with a blackjack once, in a third-degree[11] session.

"It's a problem," I said. "Not a game. Look at the pieces."

"I wouldn't know."

"Well, I'm alone," I said, and my voice shook just enough.

"It don't make any difference," he said. "I'm washed up anyway. Some nose[12] puts the bulls on me tomorrow, next week, what the hell? I just didn't like your map,[13] pal. And that smug-faced pansy in the bar coat that played left tackle for Fordham or something. To hell with guys like you guys."

I didn't speak or move. The big front sight raked my cheek lightly, almost caressingly. The man smiled.

"It's kind of good business too," he said. "Just in case. An old con like me don't make good prints, all I got against me is two witnesses. The hell with it."

"What did Waldo do to you?" I tried to make it sound as if I wanted to know, instead of just not wanting to shake too hard.

"Stooled on a bank job in Michigan and got me four years. Got himself a nolle prosse.[14] Four years in Michigan ain't no summer cruise. They make you be good in them lifer states."[15]

"How'd you know he'd come in there?" I croaked.

"I didn't. Oh yeah, I was lookin' for him. I was wanting to see him all right. I got a flash of him on the street night before last but I lost him. Up to then I wasn't lookin' for him. Then I was. A cute guy, Waldo. How is he?"

"Dead," I said.

"I'm still good," he chuckled. "Drunk or sober. Well, that don't make no doughnuts for me now. They make me downtown yet?"

I didn't answer him quick enough. He jabbed the gun into my throat and I choked and almost grabbed for it by instinct.

"Naw," he cautioned me softly. "Naw. You ain't that dumb."

I put my hands back, down at my sides, open, the palms towards him. He would want them that way. He hadn't touched me, except with the gun. He didn't seem to care whether I might have one too. He wouldn't—if he just meant the one thing.

He didn't seem to care very much about anything, coming back on that block. Perhaps the hot wind did something to him. It was booming against my shut windows like the surf under a pier.

"They got prints," I said. "I don't know how good."

"They'll be good enough—but not for teletype work. Take 'em airmail time to Washington and back to check 'em right. Tell me why I came here, pal."

"You heard the kid and me talking in the bar. I told him my name, where I lived."

---

[11] Grueling interrogation of a prisoner.   [12] Informant, stool pigeon.   [13] Slang for "face."

[14] Short for *nolle prosequi,* "unwilling to prosecute" (Latin): a formal notice by the prosecutor that prosecution will be ended.

[15] States in which repeat felons are sentenced to life imprisonment mandatorily.

"That's how pal. I said why." He smiled at me. It was a lousy smile to be the last one you might see.

"Skip it," I said. "The hangman won't ask you to guess why he's there."

"Say, you're tough at that. After you, I visit that kid. I tailed him home from headquarters, but I figure you're the guy to put the bee on first. I tail him home from the city hall, in the rent car Waldo had. From headquarters, pal. Them funny dicks.[16] You can sit in their laps and they don't know you. Start runnin' for a streetcar and they open up with machine guns and bump two pedestrians, a hacker asleep in his cab, and an old scrubwoman on the second floor workin' a mop. And they miss the guy they're after. Them funny lousy dicks."

He twisted the gun muzzle in my neck. His eyes looked madder than before.

"I got time," he said. "Waldo's rent car don't get a report right away. And they don't make Waldo very soon. I know Waldo. Smart he was. A smooth boy, Waldo."

"I'm going to vomit," I said, "if you don't take that gun out of my throat."

He smiled and moved the gun down to my heart. "This about right? Say when."

I must have spoken louder than I meant to. The door of the dressing room by the wall bed showed a crack of darkness. Then an inch. Then four inches. I saw eyes, but didn't look at them. I stared hard into the bald-headed man's eyes. Very hard. I didn't want him to take his eyes off mine.

"Scared?" he asked softly.

I leaned against his gun and began to shake. I thought he would enjoy seeing me shake. The girl came out through the door. She had her gun in her hand again. I was sorry as hell for her. She'd try to make the door—or scream. Either way it would be curtains—for both of us.

"Well, don't take all night about it," I bleated. My voice sounded far away, like a voice on a radio on the other side of a street.

"I like this, pal," he smiled. "I'm like that."

The girl floated in the air, somewhere behind him. Nothing was ever more soundless than the way she moved. It wouldn't do any good though. He wouldn't fool around with her at all. I had known him all my life but I had been looking into his eyes for only five minutes.

"Suppose I yell," I said.

"Yeah, suppose you yell. Go ahead and yell," he said with his killer's smile.

She didn't go near the door. She was right behind him.

"Well—here's where I yell," I said.

As if that was the cue, she jabbed the little gun hard into his short ribs, without a single sound.

He had to react. It was like a knee reflex. His mouth snapped open and both his arms jumped out from his sides and he arched his back just a little. The gun was pointing at my right eye.

I sank and kneed him with all my strength, in the groin.

His chin came down and I hit it. I hit it as if I was driving the last spike on the first transcontinental railroad. I can still feel it when I flex my knuckles.

His gun raked the side of my face but it didn't go off. He was already limp. He writhed down gasping, his left side against the floor. I kicked his right shoulder—hard. The gun jumped away from him, skidded on the carpet, under a chair. I heard the chessmen tinkling on the floor behind me somewhere.

---

[16] Slang for "detectives."

The girl stood over him, looking down. Then her wide dark horrified eyes came up and fastened on mine.

"That buys me," I said. "Anything I have is yours—now and forever."

She didn't hear me. Her eyes were strained open so hard that the whites showed under the vivid blue iris. She backed quickly to the door with her little gun up, felt behind her for the knob and twisted it. She pulled the door open and slipped out.

The door shut.

She was bareheaded and without her bolero jacket.

She had only the gun, and the safety catch on that was still set so that she couldn't fire it.

It was silent in the room then, in spite of the wind. Then I heard him gasping on the floor. His face had a greenish pallor. I moved behind him and pawed him for more guns, and didn't find any. I got a pair of store cuffs out of my desk and pulled his arms in front of him and snapped them on his wrists. They would hold if he didn't shake them too hard.

His eyes measured me for a coffin, in spite of their suffering. He lay in the middle of the floor, still on his left side, a twisted, wizened, bald-headed little guy with drawn-back lips and teeth spotted with cheap silver fillings. His mouth looked like a black pit and his breath came in little waves, choked, stopped, came on again, limping.

I went into the dressing room and opened the drawer of the chest. Her hat and jacket lay there on my shirts. I put them underneath, at the back, and smoothed the shirts over them. Then I went out to the kitchenette and poured a stiff jolt of whiskey and put it down and stood a moment listening to the hot wind howl against the window glass. A garage door banged, and a power-line wire with too much play between the insulators thumped the side of the building with a sound like somebody beating a carpet.

The drink worked on me. I went back into the living room and opened a window. The guy on the floor hadn't smelled her sandalwood, but somebody else might.

I shut the window again, wiped the palms of my hands and used the phone to dial headquarters.

Copernik was still there. His smart-aleck voice said: "Yeah? Marlowe? Don't tell me. I bet you got an idea."

"Make that killer yet?"

"We're not saying, Marlowe. Sorry as all hell and so on. You know how it is."

"Okay. I don't care who he is. Just come and get him off the floor of my apartment."

"Holy Christ!" Then his voice hushed and went down low. "Wait a minute, now. Wait a minute." A long way off I seemed to hear a door shut. Then his voice again. "Shoot," he said softly.

"Handcuffed," I said. "All yours. I had to knee him, but he'll be all right. He came here to eliminate a witness."

Another pause. The voice was full of honey. "Now listen, boy, who else is in this with you?"

"Who else? Nobody. Just me."

"Keep it that way, boy. All quiet. Okay?"

"Think I want all the bums in the neighborhood in here sight-seeing?"

"Take it easy, boy. Easy. Just sit tight and sit still. I'm practically there. No touch nothing. Get me?"

"Yeah." I gave him the address and apartment number again to save him time.

I could see his big bony face glisten. I got the .22 target gun from under the chair and sat holding it until feet hit the hallway outside my door and knuckles did a quiet tattoo on the door panel.

Copernik was alone. He filled the doorway quickly, pushed me back into the room with a tight grin and shut the door. He stood with his back to it, his hand under the left side of his coat. A big hard bony man with flat cruel eyes.

He lowered them slowly and looked at the man on the floor. The man's neck was twitching a little. His eyes moved in short stabs—sick eyes.

"Sure it's the guy?" Copernik's voice was hoarse.

"Positive. Where's Ybarra?"

"Oh, he was busy." He didn't look at me when he said that. "Those your cuffs?"

"Yeah."

"Key."

I tossed it to him. He went down swiftly on one knee beside the killer and took my cuffs off his wrists, tossed them to one side. He got his own off his hip, twisted the bald man's hands behind him and snapped the cuffs on.

"All right, you bastard," the killer said tonelessly.

Copernik grinned and balled his fist and hit the handcuffed man in the mouth a terrific blow. His head snapped back almost enough to break his neck. Blood dribbled from the lower corner of his mouth.

"Get a towel," Copernik ordered.

I got a hand towel and gave it to him. He stuffed it between the handcuffed man's teeth, viciously, stood up and rubbed his bony fingers through his ratty blond hair.

"All right. Tell it."

I told it—leaving the girl out completely. It sounded a little funny. Copernik watched me, said nothing. He rubbed the side of his veined nose. Then he got his comb out and worked on his hair just as he had done earlier in the evening, in the cocktail bar.

I went over and gave him the gun. He looked at it casually, dropped it into his side pocket. His eyes had something in them and his face moved in a hard bright grin.

I bent down and began picking up my chessmen and dropping them into the box. I put the box on the mantel, straightened out a leg of the card table, played around for a while. All the time Copernik watched me. I wanted him to think something out.

At last he came out with it. "This guy uses a twenty-two," he said. "He uses it because he's good enough to get by with that much gun. That means he's good. He knocks at your door, pokes that gat in your belly, walks you back into the room, says he's here to close your mouth for keeps—and yet you take him. You not having any gun. You take him alone. You're kind of good yourself, pal."

"Listen," I said, and looked at the floor. I picked up another chessman and twisted it between my fingers. "I was doing a chess problem," I said. "Trying to forget things."

"You got something on your mind, pal," Copernik said softly. "You wouldn't try to fool an old copper, would you, boy?"

"It's a swell pinch and I'm giving it to you," I said. "What the hell more do you want?"

The man on the floor made a vague sound behind the towel. His bald head glistened with sweat.

"What's the matter, pal? You been up to something?" Copernik almost whispered.

I looked at him quickly, looked away again. "All right," I said. "You know damn well I couldn't take him alone. He had the gun on me and he shoots where he looks."

Copernik closed one eye and squinted at me amiably with the other. "Go on, pal. I kind of thought of that too."

I shuffled around a little more, to make it look good. I said, slowly: "There was a kid here who pulled a job over in Boyle Heights, a heist job. It didn't take. A two-bit service station stick-up. I know his family. He's not really bad. He was here trying to beg train money off me. When the knock came he sneaked in—there."

I pointed at the wall bed and the door beside. Copernik's head swiveled slowly, swiveled back. His eyes winked again. "And this kid had a gun," he said.

I nodded. "And he got behind him. That takes guts, Copernik. You've got to give the kid a break. You've got to let him stay out of it."

"Tag[17] out for this kid?" Copernik asked softly.

"Not yet, he says. He's scared there will be."

Copernik smiled. "I'm a homicide man," he said. "I wouldn't know—or care."

I pointed down at the gagged and handcuffed man on the floor. "You took him, didn't you?" I said gently.

Copernik kept on smiling. A big whitish tongue came out and massaged his thick lower lip. "How'd I do it?" he whispered.

"Get the slugs out of Waldo?"

"Sure. Long twenty-two's. One smashed a rib, one good."

"You're a careful guy. You don't miss any angles. You know anything about me? You dropped in on me to see what guns I had."

Copernik got up and went down on one knee again beside the killer. "Can you hear me, guy?" he asked with his face close to the face of the man on the floor.

The man made some vague sound. Copernik stood up and yawned. "Who the hell cares what he says? Go on, pal."

"You wouldn't expect to find I had anything, but you wanted to look around my place. And while you were mousing around in there"—I pointed to the dressing room—"and me not saying anything, being a little sore, maybe, a knock came on the door. So he came in. So after a while you sneaked out and took him."

"Ah." Copernik grinned widely, with as many teeth as a horse. "You're on, pal. I socked him and I kneed him and I took him. You didn't have no gun and the guy swiveled on me pretty sharp and I left-hooked him down the backstairs. Okay?"

"Okay," I said.

"You'll tell it like that downtown?"[18]

"Yeah," I said.

"I'll protect you, pal. Treat me right and I'll always play ball. Forget about that kid. Let me know if he needs a break."

He came over and held out his hand. I shook it. It was as clammy as a dead fish. Clammy hands and the people who own them make me sick.

---

[17] An arrest warrant.   [18] At the police station.

"There's just one thing," I said. "This partner of yours—Ybarra. Won't he be a bit sore you didn't bring him along on this?"

Copernik tousled his hair and wiped his hatband with a large yellowish silk handkerchief.

"That guinea?"[19] he sneered. "To hell with him!" He came close to me and breathed in my face. "No mistakes, pal—about that story of ours."

His breath was bad. It would be.

4

There were just five of us in the chief of detectives' office when Copernik laid it before them. A stenographer, the chief, Copernik, myself, Ybarra. Ybarra sat on a chair tilted against the side wall. His hat was down over his eyes but their softness loomed underneath, and the small still smile hung at the corners of the clean-cut Latin lips. He didn't look directly at Copernik. Copernik didn't look at him at all.

Outside in the corridor there had been photos of Copernik shaking hands with me, Copernik with his hat on straight and his gun in his hand and a stern, purposeful look on his face.

They said they knew who Waldo was, but they wouldn't tell me. I didn't believe they knew, because the chief of detectives had a morgue photo of Waldo on his desk. A beautiful job, his hair combed, his tie straight, the light hitting his eyes just right to make them glisten. Nobody would have known it was a photo of a dead man with two bullet holes in his heart. He looked like a dance-hall sheik making up his mind whether to take the blonde or the red-head.

It was about midnight when I got home. The apartment door was locked and while I was fumbling for my keys a low voice spoke to me out of the darkness.

All it said was "Please!" but I knew it. I turned and looked at a dark Cadillac coupe parked just off the loading zone. It had no lights. Light from the street touched the brightness of a woman's eyes.

I went over there. "You're a darn fool," I said.

She said: "Get in."

I climbed in and started the car and drove it a block and a half along Franklin and turned down Kingsley Drive. The hot wind still burned and blustered. A radio lilted from an open, sheltered side window of an apartment house. There were a lot of parked cars but she found a vacant space behind a small brand-new Packard cabriolet[20] that had the dealer's sticker on the windshield glass. After she'd jockeyed us up to the curb she leaned back in the corner with her gloved hands on the wheel.

She was all in black now, or dark brown, with a small foolish hat. I smelled the sandalwood in her perfume.

"I wasn't very nice to you, was I?" she said.

"All you did was save my life."

"What happened?"

"I called the law and fed a few lies to a cop I don't like and gave him all the

---

[19] Slang for a person of Italian descent: derogatory; but Ybarra is Hispanic.
[20] A convertible coupe.

credit for the pinch and that was that. That guy you took away from me was the man who killed Waldo."

"You mean—you didn't tell them about me?"

"Lady," I said again, "all you did was save my life. What else do you want done? I'm ready, willing, and I'll try to be able."

She didn't say anything, or move.

"Nobody learned who you are from me," I said. "Incidentally, I don't know myself."

"I'm Mrs. Frank C. Barsaly, two-twelve Fremont Place, Olympia two-four-five-nine-six. Is that what you wanted?"

"Thanks," I mumbled, and rolled a dry unlit cigarette around in my fingers. "Why did you come back?" Then I snapped the fingers of my left hand. "The hat and jacket," I said. "I'll go up and get them."

"It's more than that," she said. "I want my pearls." I might have jumped a little. It seemed as if there had been enough without pearls.

A car tore by down the street going twice as fast as it should. A thin bitter cloud of dust lifted in the streetlights and whirled and vanished. The girl ran the window up quickly against it.

"All right," I said. "Tell me about the pearls. We have had a murder and a mystery woman and a mad killer and a heroic rescue and a police detective framed into making a false report. Now we will have pearls. All right—feed it to me."

"I was to buy them for five thousand dollars. From the man you call Waldo and I call Joseph Coates. He should have had them."

"No pearls," I said. "I saw what came out of his pockets. A lot of money, but no pearls."

"Could they be hidden in his apartment?"

"Yes," I said. "So far as I know he could have had them hidden anywhere in California except in his pockets. How's Mr. Barsaly this hot night?"

"He's still downtown at his meeting. Otherwise I couldn't have come."

"Well, you could have brought him," I said. "He could have sat in the rumble seat."

"Oh, I don't know," she said. "Frank weighs two hundred pounds and he's pretty solid. I don't think he would like to sit in the rumble seat, Mr. Marlowe."

"What the hell are we talking about anyway?"

She didn't answer. Her gloved hands tapped lightly, provokingly on the rim of the slender wheel. I threw the unlit cigarette out the window, turned a little and took hold of her.

When I let go of her, she pulled as far away from me as she could against the side of the car and rubbed the back of her glove against her mouth. I sat quite still.

We didn't speak for some time. Then she said very slowly: "I meant you to do that. But I wasn't always that way. It's only been since Stan Phillips was killed in his plane. If it hadn't been for that, I'd be Mrs. Phillips now. Stan gave me the pearls. They cost fifteen thousand dollars, he said once. White pearls, forty-one of them, the largest about a third of an inch across. I don't know how many grains. I never had them appraised or showed them to a jeweler, so I don't know those things. But I loved them on Stan's account. I loved Stan. The way you do just the one time. Can you understand?"

"What's your first name?" I asked.

"Lola."

"Go on talking, Lola." I got another dry cigarette out of my pocket and fumbled it between my fingers just to give them something to do.

"They had a simple silver clasp in the shape of a two-bladed propeller. There was one small diamond where the boss would be. I told Frank they were store pearls I had bought myself. He didn't know the difference. It's not so easy to tell, I dare say. You see—Frank is pretty jealous."

In the darkness she came closer to me and her side touched my side. But I didn't move this time. The wind howled and the trees shook. I kept on rolling the cigarette around in my fingers.

"I suppose you've read that story," she said. "About the wife and the real pearls and her telling her husband they were false?"

"I've read it," I said, "Maugham."[21]

"I hired Joseph. My husband was in Argentina at the time. I was pretty lonely."

"*You* should be lonely," I said.

"Joseph and I went driving a good deal. Sometimes we had a drink or two together. But that's all. I don't go around—"

"You told him about the pearls," I said. "And when your two hundred pounds of beef came back from Argentina and kicked him out—he took the pearls, because he knew they were real. And then offered them back to you for five grand."

"Yes," she said simply. "Of course I didn't want to go to the police. And of course in the circumstance Joseph wasn't afraid of my knowing where he lived."

"Poor Waldo," I said. "I feel kind of sorry for him. It was a hell of a time to run into an old friend that had a down on you."

I struck a match on my shoe sole and lit the cigarette. The tobacco was so dry from the hot wind that it burned like grass. The girl sat quietly beside me, her hands on the wheel again.

"Hell with women—these fliers," I said. "And you're still in love with him, or think you are. Where did you keep the pearls?"

"In a Russian malachite jewelry box on my dressing table. With some other costume jewelry. I had to, if I ever wanted to wear them."

"And they were worth fifteen grand. And you think Joseph might have hidden them in his apartment. Thirty-one, wasn't it?"

"Yes," she said. "I guess it's a lot to ask."

I opened the door and got out of the car. "I've been paid," I said. "I'll go look. The doors in my apartment are not very obstinate. The cops will find out where Waldo lived when they publish his photo, but not tonight, I guess."

"It's awfully sweet of you," she said. "Shall I wait here?"

I stood with a foot on the running board, leaning in, looking at her. I didn't answer her question. I just stood there looking in at the shine of her eyes. Then I shut the car door and walked up the street towards Franklin.

Even with the wind shriveling my face I could still smell the sandalwood in her hair. And feel her lips.

I unlocked the Berglund door, walked through the silent lobby to the elevator, and rode up to 3. Then I soft-footed along the silent corridor and peered down at the sill of apartment 31. No light. I rapped—the old light, confidential tattoo of the bootlegger with the big smile and the extra-deep hip pockets. No answer. I took the piece of thick hard celluloid that pretended to be a window over the

---

[21] Somerset Maugham (1874–1965), an English novelist and playwright; specifically, his short story "Mr. Know-All."

driver's license in my wallet, and eased it between the lock and the jamb,[22] leaning hard on the knob, pushing it towards the hinges. The edge of the celluloid caught the slope of the spring lock and snapped it back with a small brittle sound, like an icicle breaking. The door yielded and I went into near darkness. Street light filtered in and touched a high spot here and there.

I shut the door and snapped the light on and just stood. There was a queer smell in the air. I made it in a moment—the smell of dark-cured tobacco. I prowled over to a smoking stand by the window and looked down at four brown butts—Mexican or South American cigarettes.

Upstairs, on my floor, feet hit the carpet and somebody went into a bathroom. I heard the toilet flush. I went into the bathroom of apartment 31. A little rubbish, nothing, no place to hide anything. The kitchenette was a longer job, but I only half searched. I knew there were no pearls in that apartment. I knew Waldo had been on his way out and that he was in a hurry and that something was riding him when he turned and took two bullets from an old friend.

I went back to the living room and swung the wall bed and looked past its mirror side into the dressing room for signs of still current occupancy. Swinging the bed farther I was no longer looking for pearls. I was looking at a man.

He was small, middle-aged, iron-gray at the temples, with a very dark skin, dressed in a fawn-colored suit with a wine-colored tie. His neat little brown hands hung limply by his sides. His small feet, in pointed polished shoes, pointed almost at the floor.

He was hanging by a belt around his neck from the metal top of the bed. His tongue stuck out farther than I thought it possible for a tongue to stick out.

He swung a little and I didn't like that, so I pulled the bed shut and he nestled quietly between the two clamped pillows. I didn't touch him yet. I didn't have to touch him to know that he would be cold as ice.

I went around him into the dressing room and used my handkerchief on drawer knobs. The place was stripped clean except for the light litter of a man living alone.

I came out of there and began on the man. No wallet. Waldo would have taken that and ditched it. A flat box of cigarettes, half full, stamped in gold:

> LOUIS TAPIA Y CIA
> CALLE DE PAYSANDÚ, 19
> MONTEVIDEO

Matches from the Spezzia Club. An underarm holster of dark-grained leather and in it a 9-millimeter Mauser.[23]

The Mauser made him a professional, so I didn't feel so badly. But not a very good professional, or bare hands would not have finished him, with the Mauser—a gun you can blast through a wall with—undrawn in his shoulder holster.

I made a little sense of it, not much. Four of the brown cigarettes had been smoked, so there had been either waiting or discussion. Somewhere along the line Waldo had got the little man by the throat and held him in just the right way to

---

[22] Side post.
[23] A gun invented by the German brothers Peter Paul (1838–1914) and Wilhelm (1834–1882) Mauser.

make him pass out in a matter of seconds. The Mauser had been less useful to him than a toothpick. Then Waldo had hung him up by the strap, probably dead already. That would account for haste, cleaning out the apartment, for Waldo's anxiety about the girl. It would account for the car left unlocked outside the cocktail bar.

That is, it would account for these things if Waldo had killed him, if this was really Waldo's apartment—if I wasn't just being kidded.

I examined some more pockets. In the left trouser one I found a gold penknife, some silver. In the left hip pocket a handkerchief, folded, scented. On the right hip another, unfolded but clean. In the right leg pocket four or five tissue handkerchiefs. A clean little guy. He didn't like to blow his nose on his handkerchief. Under these there was a small new keytainer holding four new keys—car keys. Stamped in gold on the keytainer was:

COMPLIMENTS OF R. K. VOGELSANG, INC.
"THE PACKARD HOUSE."

I put everything as I had found it, swung the bed back, used my handkerchief on knobs and other projections, and flat surfaces, killed the light and poked my nose out the door. The hall was empty. I went down to the street and around the corner to Kingsley Drive. The Cadillac hadn't moved.

I opened the car door and leaned on it. She didn't seem to have moved, either. It was hard to see any expression on her face. Hard to see anything but her eyes and chin, but not hard to smell the sandalwood.

"That perfume," I said, "would drive a deacon nuts . . . no pearls."

"Well, thanks for trying," she said in a low, soft vibrant voice. "I guess I can stand it. Shall I . . . Do we . . . Or . . .?"

"You go on home now," I said. "And whatever happens you never saw me before. Whatever happens. Just as you may never see me again."

"I'd hate that."

"Good luck, Lola." I shut the car door and stepped back.

The lights blazed on, the motor turned over. Against the wind at the corner the big coupe made a slow contemptuous turn and was gone. I stood there by the vacant space at the curb where it had been.

It was quite dark there now. Windows had become blanks in the apartment where the radio sounded. I stood looking at the back of a Packard cabriolet which seemed to be brand-new. I had seen it before—before I went upstairs, in the same place, in front of Lola's car. Parked, dark, silent, with a blue sticker pasted to the right-hand corner of the shiny windshield.

And in my mind I was looking at something else, a set of brand-new car keys in a keytainer stamped "THE PACKARD HOUSE," upstairs, in a dead man's pocket.

I went up to the front of the cabriolet and put a small pocket flash on the blue slip. It was the same dealer all right. Written in ink below his name and slogan was a name and address—Eugénie Kolchenko, 5315 Arvieda Street, West Los Angeles.

It was crazy. I went back up to apartment 31, jimmied the door as I had done before, stepped in behind the wall bed and took the keytainer from the trousers pocket of the neat brown dangling corpse. I was back down on the street beside the cabriolet in five minutes. The keys fitted.

5

It was a small house, near a canyon rim out beyond Sawtelle, with a circle of writhing eucalyptus trees in front of it. Beyond that, on the other side of the street, one of those parties was going on where they come out and smash bottles on the sidewalk with a whoop like Yale making a touchdown against Princeton.

There was a wire fence at my number and some rose trees, and a flagged walk and a garage that was wide open and had no car in it. There was no car in front of the house either. I rang the bell. There was a long wait, then the door opened rather suddenly.

I wasn't the man she had been expecting. I could see it in her glittering kohl-rimmed[24] eyes. Then I couldn't see anything in them. She just stood and looked at me, a long, lean, hungry brunette, with rouged cheekbones, thick black hair parted in the middle, a mouth made for three-decker sandwiches, coral-and-gold pajamas, sandals—and gilded toenails. Under her ear lobes a couple of miniature temple bells gonged lightly in the breeze. She made a slow disdainful motion with a cigarette in a holder as long as a baseball bat.

"We-el, what ees it, little man? You want sometheeng? You are lost from the bee-ootiful party across the street, hein?"[25]

"Ha-ha," I said. "Quite a party, isn't it? No, I just brought your car home. Lost it, didn't you?"

Across the street somebody had delirium tremens in the front yard and a mixed quartet tore what was left of the night into small strips and did what they could to make the strips miserable. While this was going on the exotic brunette didn't move more than one eyelash.

She wasn't beautiful, she wasn't even pretty, but she looked as if things would happen where she was.

"You have said what?" she got out, at last, in a voice as silky as a burnt crust of toast.

"Your car." I pointed over my shoulder and kept my eyes on her. She was the type that uses a knife.

The long cigarette holder dropped very slowly to her side and the cigarette fell out of it. I stamped it out, and that put me in the hall. She backed away from me and I shut the door.

The hall was like the long hall of a railroad flat.[26] Lamps glowed pinkly in iron brackets. There was a bead curtain at the end, a tiger skin on the floor. The place went with her.

"You're Miss Kolchenko?" I asked, not getting any more action.

"Ye-es. I am Mees Kolchenko. What the 'ell you want?"

She was looking at me now as if I had come to wash the windows, but at an inconvenient time.

I got a card out with my left hand, held it out to her. She read it in my hand, moving her head just enough. "A detective?" she breathed.

"Yeah."

She said something in a spitting language. Then in English: "Come in! Theese damn wind dry up my skeen like so much teesue paper."

---

[24] Lined with a powdered cosmetic preparation.   [25] "Eh?" (French).
[26] An apartment set up with rooms one after the other in a line.

"We're in," I said. "I just shut the door. Snap out of it, Nazimova.[27] Who was he? The little guy?"

Beyond the bead curtain a man coughed. She jumped as if she had been stuck with an oyster fork. Then she tried to smile. It wasn't very successful.

"A reward," she said softly. "You weel wait 'ere? Ten dollars it is fair to pay, no?"

"No," I said.

I reached a finger towards her slowly and added: "He's dead."

She jumped about three feet and let out a yell.

A chair creaked harshly. Feet pounded beyond the bead curtain, a large hand plunged into view and snatched it aside, and a big hard-looking blond man was with us. He had a purple robe over his pajamas, his right hand held something in his robe pocket. He stood quite still as soon as he was through the curtain, his feet planted solidly, his jaw out, his colorless eyes like gray ice. He looked like a man who would be hard to take out on an off-tackle play.

"What's the matter, honey?" He had a solid, burring voice, with just the right sappy tone to belong to a guy who would go for a woman with gilded toenails.

"I came about Miss Kolchenko's car," I said.

"Well, you could take your hat off," he said. "Just for a light work-out."

I took it off and apologized.

"Okay," he said, and kept his right hand shoved down hard in the purple pocket. "So you came about Miss Kolchenko's car. Take it from there."

I pushed past the woman and went closer to him. She shrank back against the wall and flattened her palms against it. Camille[28] in a high-school play. The long holder lay empty at her toes.

When I was six feet from the big man he said easily: "I can hear you from there. Just take it easy. I've got a gun in this pocket and I've had to learn to use one. Now about the car?"

"The man who borrowed it couldn't bring it," I said, and pushed the card I was still holding towards his face. He barely glanced at it. He looked back at me.

"So what?" he said.

"Are you always this tough?" I asked. "Or only when you have your pajamas on?"

"So why couldn't he bring it himself?" he asked. "And skip the mushy talk."

The dark woman made a stuffed sound at my elbow.

"It's all right, honeybunch," the man said. "I'll handle this. Go on."

She slid past both of us and flicked through the bead curtain.

I waited a little while. The big man didn't move a muscle. He didn't look any more bothered than a toad in the sun.

"He couldn't bring it because somebody bumped him off," I said. "Let's see you handle that."

"Yeah?" he said. "Did you bring him with you to prove it?"

"No," I said. "But if you put your tie and crush hat on, I'll take you down and show you."

[27] Alla Nazimova (1879–1945), a Russian-born stage actress.
[28] The title role of *Camille: The Lady of the Camellias* (1852), by Alexandre Dumas, fils (1824–1895).

"Who the hell did you say you were, now?"

"I didn't say. I thought maybe you could read." I held the card at him some more.

"Oh, that's right," he said. "Philip Marlowe, private investigator. Well, well. So I should go with you to look at who, why?"

"Maybe he stole the car," I said.

The big man nodded. "That's a thought. Maybe he did. Who?"

"The little brown guy who had the keys to it in his pocket, and had it parked around the corner from the Berglund Apartments."

He thought that over, without any apparent embarrassment. "You've got something there," he said. "Not much. But a little. I guess this must be the night of the Police Smoker. So you're doing all their work for them."

"Huh?"

"The card says private detective to me," he said. "Have you got some cops outside that were too shy to come in?"

"No, I'm alone."

He grinned. The grin showed white ridges in his tanned skin. "So you find somebody dead and take some keys and find a car and come riding out here—all alone. No cops. Am I right?"

"Correct."

He sighed. "Let's go inside," he said. He yanked the bead curtain aside and make an opening for me to go through. "It might be you have an idea I ought to hear."

I went past him and he turned, keeping his heavy pocket towards me. I hadn't noticed until I got quite close that there were beads of sweat on his face. It might have been the hot wind but I didn't think so.

We were in the living room of the house.

We sat down and looked at each other across a dark floor, on which a few Navajo rugs and a few dark Turkish rugs made a decorating combination with some well-used overstuffed furniture. There was a fireplace, a small baby grand, a Chinese screen, a tall Chinese lantern on a teakwood pedestal, and gold net curtains against lattice windows. The windows to the south were open. A fruit tree with a whitewashed trunk whipped about outside the screen, adding its bit to the noise from across the street.

The big man eased back into a brocaded chair and put his slippered feet on a footstool. He kept his right hand where it had been since I met him—on his gun.

The brunette hung around in the shadows and a bottle gurgled and her temple bells gonged in her ears.

"It's all right, honeybunch," the man said. "It's all under control. Somebody bumped somebody off and this lad thinks we're interested. Just sit down and relax."

The girl tilted her head and poured half a tumbler of whiskey down her throat. She signed, said, "Goddam," in a casual voice, and curled up on a davenport.[29] It took all of the davenport. She had plenty of legs. Her gilded toenails winked at me from the shadowy corner where she kept herself quiet from then on.

---

[29] A large sofa.

I got a cigarette out without being shot at, lit it and went into my story. It wasn't all true, but some of it was. I told them about the Berglund Apartments and that I had lived there and that Waldo was living there in apartment 31 on the floor below mine and that I had been keeping an eye on him for business reasons.

"Waldo what?" the blond man put in. "And what business reasons?"

"Mister," I said, "have you no secrets?" He reddened slightly.

I told him about the cocktail lounge across the street from the Berglund and what had happened there. I didn't tell him about the printed bolero jacket or the girl who had worn it. I left her out of the story altogether.

"It was an undercover job—from my angle," I said. "If you know what I mean." He reddened again, bit his teeth. I went on: "I got back from the City Hall without telling anybody I knew Waldo. In due time, when I decided they couldn't find out where he lived that night, I took the liberty of examining his apartment."

"Looking for what?" the big man said thickly.

"For some letters. I might mention in passing there was nothing there at all—except a dead man. Strangled and hanging by a belt to the top of the wall bed—well out of sight. A small man, about forty-five, Mexican or South American, well-dressed in a fawn-colored—"

"That's enough," the big man said. "I'll bite, Marlowe. Was it a blackmail job you were on?"

"Yeah. The funny part was this little brown man had plenty of gun under his arm."

"He wouldn't have five hundred bucks in twenties in his pocket, of course? Or are you saying?"

"He wouldn't. But Waldo had over seven hundred in currency when he was killed in the cocktail bar."

"Looks like I underrated this Waldo," the big man said calmly. "He took my guy and his pay-off money, gun and all. Waldo have a gun?"

"Not on him."

"Get us a drink, honeybunch," the big man said. "Yes, I certainly did sell this Waldo person shorter than a bargain-counter shirt."

The brunette unwound her legs and made two drinks with soda and ice. She took herself another gill[30] without trimmings, wound herself back on the davenport. Her big glittering black eyes watched me solemnly.

"Well, here's how," the big man said, lifting his glass in salute. "I haven't murdered anybody, but I've got a divorce suit on my hands from now on. You haven't murdered anybody, the way you tell it, but you laid an egg down at police headquarters. What the hell! Life's a lot of trouble, anyway you look at it. I've still got honeybunch here. She's a white Russian I met in Shanghai. She's safe as a vault and she looks as if she could cut your throat for a nickel. That's what I like about her. You get the glamour without the risk."

"You talk damn foolish," the girl spat him.

"You look okay to me." The big man went on ignoring her. "That is, for a keyhole peeper. Is there an out?"

"Yeah. But it will cost a little money."

"I expected that. How much?"

"Say another five hundred."

---

[30] A quarter-pint measure of an alcoholic beverage.

"Goddam, thees hot wind make me dry like the ashes of love," the Russian girl said bitterly.

"Five hundred might do," the blond man said. "What do I get for it?"

"If I swing it—you get left out of the story. If I don't—you don't pay."

He thought it over. His face looked lined and tired now. The small beads of sweat twinkled in his short blond hair.

"This murder will make you talk," he grumbled. "The second one, I mean. And I don't have what I was going to buy. And if it's a hush, I'd rather buy it direct."

"Who was the little brown man?" I asked.

"Name's Leon Valesanos, a Uruguayan. Another of my importations. I'm in a business that takes me a lot of places. He was working in the Spezzia Club in Chiseltown—you know, the strip of Sunset next to Beverly Hills. Working on roulette, I think. I gave him the five hundred to go down to this—this Waldo—and buy back some bills for stuff Miss Kolchenko had charged to my account and delivered here. That wasn't bright, was it? I had them in my briefcase and this Waldo got a chance to steal them. What's your hunch about what happened?"

I sipped my drink and looked at him down my nose. "Your Uruguayan pal probably talked out and Waldo didn't listen good. Then the little guy thought maybe that Mauser might help his argument—and Waldo was too quick for him. I wouldn't say Waldo was a killer—not by intention. A blackmailer seldom is. Maybe he lost his temper and maybe he just held on to the little guy's neck too long. Then he had to take it on the lam. But he had another date, with more money coming up. And he worked the neighborhood looking for the party. And accidentally he ran into a pal who was hostile enough and drunk enough to blow him down."

"There's a hell of a lot of coincidence in all this business," the big man said.

"It's the hot wind." I grinned. "Everybody's screwy tonight."

"For the five hundred you guarantee nothing? If I don't get my cover-up, you don't get your dough. Is that it?"

"That's it," I said, smiling at him.

"Screwy is right," he said, and drained his highball. "I'm taking you up on it."

"There are just two things," I said softly, leaning forward in my chair. "Waldo had a getaway car parked outside the cocktail bar where he was killed, unlocked with the motor running. The killer took it. There's always the chance of a kick-back from that direction. You see, all Waldo's stuff must have been in that car."

"Including my bills, and your letters."

"Yeah. But the police are reasonable about things like that—unless you're good for a lot of publicity. If you're not, I think I can eat some stale dog[31] down-town and get by. If you are—that's the second thing. What did you say your name was?"

The answer was a long time coming. When it came I didn't get as much kick out of it as I thought I would. All at once it was too logical.

"Frank C. Barsaly," he said.

After a while the Russian girl called me a taxi. When I left, the party across the street was doing all that a party could do. I noticed the walls of the house were still standing. That seemed a pity.

---

[31] Eat my words.

6

When I unlocked the glass entrance door of the Berglund I smelled policeman. I looked at my wrist watch. It was nearly 3 A.M. In the dark corner of the lobby a man dozed in a chair with a newspaper over his face. Large feet stretched out before him. A corner of the paper lifted an inch, dropped again. The man made no other movement.

I went on along the hall to the elevator and rode up to my floor. I soft-footed along the hallway, unlocked my door, pushed it wide and reached in for the light switch.

A chain switch tinkled and light glared from a standing lamp by the easy chair, beyond the card table on which my chessmen were still scattered.

Copernik sat there with a stiff unpleasant grin on his face. The short dark man, Ybarra, sat across the room from him, on my left, silent, half smiling as usual.

Copernik showed more of his big yellow horse teeth and said: "Hi. Long time no see. Been out with the girls?"

I shut the door and took my hat off and wiped the back of my neck slowly, over and over again. Copernik went on grinning. Ybarra looked at nothing with his soft dark eyes.

"Take a seat, pal," Copernik drawled. "Make yourself to home. We got pow-wow to make. Boy, do I hate this night sleuthing. Did you know you were low on hooch?"

"I could have guessed it," I said. I leaned against the wall.

Copernik kept on grinning. "I always did hate private dicks," he said, "but I never had a chance to twist one like I got tonight."

He reached down lazily beside his chair and picked up a printed bolero jacket, tossed it on the card table. He reached down again and put a wide-brimmed hat beside it.

"I bet you look cuter than all hell with these on," he said.

I took hold of a straight chair, twisted it around and straddled it, leaned my folded arms on the chair and looked at Copernik.

He got up very slowly—with an elaborate slowness, walked across the room and stood in front of me smoothing his coat down. Then he lifted his open right hand and hit me across the face with it—hard. It stung but I didn't move.

Ybarra looked at the wall, looked at the floor, looked at nothing.

"Shame on you, pal," Copernik said lazily. "The way you was taking care of this nice exclusive merchandise. Wadded down behind your old shirts. You punk peepers[32] always did make me sick."

He stood there over me for a moment. I didn't move or speak. I looked into his glazed drinker's eyes. He doubled a fist at his side, then shrugged and turned and went back to the chair.

"Okay," he said. "The rest will keep. Where did you get these things?"

"They belong to a lady."

"Do tell. They belong to a lady. Ain't you the lighthearted bastard? I'll tell you what lady they belong to. They belong to the lady a guy named Waldo asked about in a bar across the street—about two minutes before he got shot kind of dead. Or would that have slipped your mind?"

I didn't say anything.

---

[32] Slang for private eyes.

"You was curious about her yourself," Copernik sneered on. "But you were smart, pal. You fooled me."

"That wouldn't make me smart," I said.

His face twisted suddenly and he started to get up. Ybarra laughed, suddenly and softly, almost under his breath. Copernik's eyes swung on him, hung there. Then he faced me again, bland-eyed.

"The guinea likes you," he said. "He thinks you're good."

The smile left Ybarra's face, but no expression took its place. No expression at all.

Copernik said: "You knew who the dame was all the time. You knew who Waldo was and where he lived. Right across the hall a floor below you. You knew this Waldo person had bumped a guy off and started to lam, only this broad came into his plans somewhere and he was anxious to meet up with her before he went away. Only he never got the chance. A heist guy from back east named Al Tessilore took care of that by taking care of Waldo. So you met the gal and hid her clothes and sent her on her way and kept your trap glued. That's the way guys like you make your beans. Am I right?"

"Yeah," I said. "Except that I only knew these things very recently. Who was Waldo?"

Copernik bared his teeth at me. Red spots burned high on his sallow cheeks. Ybarra, looking down at the floor, said very softly: "Waldo Ratigan. We got him from Washington by teletype. He was a two-bit porch climber with a few small terms on him.[33] He drove a car in a bank stick-up job in Detroit. He turned the gang in later and got a nolle prosse. One of the gang was this Al Tessilore. He hasn't talked a word, but we think the meeting across the street was purely accidental."

Ybarra spoke in the soft quiet modulated voice of a man for whom sounds have a meaning. I said: "Thanks, Ybarra. Can I smoke—or would Copernik kick it out of my mouth?"

Ybarra smiled suddenly. "You may smoke, sure," he said.

"The guinea likes you all right," Copernik jeered. "You never know what a guinea will like, do you?"

I lit a cigarette. Ybarra looked at Copernik and said very softly: "The word guinea—you overwork it. I don't like it so well applied to me."

"The hell with what you like, guinea."

Ybarra smiled a little more. "You are making a mistake," he said. He took a pocket nail file out and began to use it, looking down.

Copernik blared: "I smelled something rotten on you from the start, Marlowe. So when we make these two mugs, Ybarra and me think we'll drift over and dabble a few more words with you. I bring one of Waldo's morgue photos—nice work, the light just right in his eyes, his tie all straight and a white handkerchief showing just right in his pocket. Nice work. So on the way up, just as a matter of routine, we rout out the manager here and let him lamp[34] it. And he knows the guy. He's here as A. B. Hummel, apartment thirty-one. So we go in there and find a stiff. Then we go round and round with that. Nobody knows him yet, but he's got some swell finger bruises under that strap and I hear they fit Waldo's fingers very nicely."

"That's something," I said. "I thought maybe I murdered him."

---

[33] He spent a few short terms in jail.   [34] Take a look at.

Copernik stared at me a long time. His face had stopped grinning and was just a hard brutal face now. "Yeah. We got something else even," he said. "We got Waldo's getaway car—and what Waldo had in it to take with him."

I blew cigarette smoke jerkily. The wind pounded the shut windows. The air in the room was foul.

"Oh, we're bright boys," Copernik sneered. "We never figured you with that much guts. Take a look at this."

He plunged his bony hand into his coat pocket and drew something up slowly over the edge of the card table, drew it along the green top and left it there stretched out, gleaming. A string of white pearls with a clasp like a two-bladed propeller. They shimmered softly in the thick smoky air.

Lola Barsaly's pearls. The pearls the flier had given her. The guy who was dead, the guy she still loved.

I stared at them, but I didn't move. After a long moment Copernik said almost gravely: "Nice, ain't they? Would you feel like telling us a story about now, Mister Marlowe?"

I stood up and pushed the chair from under me, walked slowly across the room and stood looking down at the pearls. The largest was perhaps a third of an inch across. They were pure white, iridescent, with a mellow softness. I lifted them slowly off the card table from beside her clothes. They felt heavy, smooth, fine.

"Nice," I said. "A lot of the trouble was about these. Yeah, I'll talk now. They must be worth a lot of money."

Ybarra laughed behind me. It was a very gentle laugh. "About a hundred dollars," he said. "They're good phonies—but they're phony."

I lifted the pearls again. Copernik's glassy eyes gloated at me. "How do you tell?" I asked.

"I know pearls," Ybarra said. "These are good stuff, the kind women very often have made on purpose, as a kind of insurance. But they are slick like glass. Real pearls are gritty between the edges of the teeth. Try."

I put two or three of them between my teeth and moved my teeth back and forth, then sideways. Not quite biting them. The beads were hard and slick.

"Yes. They are very good," Ybarra said. "Several even have little waves and flat spots, as real pearls might have."

"Would they cost fifteen grand—if they were real?" I asked.

"Sí. Probably. That's hard to say. It depends on a lot of things."

"This Waldo wasn't so bad," I said.

Copernik stood up quickly, but I didn't see him swing. I was still looking down at the pearls. His fist caught me on the side of the face, against the molars. I tasted blood at once. I staggered back and made it look like a worse blow than it was.

"Sit down and talk, you bastard!" Copernik almost whispered.

I sat down and used a handkerchief to pat my cheek. I licked at the cut inside my mouth. Then I got up again and went over and picked up the cigarette he had knocked out of my mouth. I crushed it out in a tray and sat down again.

Ybarra filed at his nails and held one up against the lamp. There were beads of sweat on Copernik's eyebrows, at the inner ends.

"You found the beads in Waldo's car," I said, looking at Ybarra. "Find any papers?"

He shook his head without looking up.

"I'd believe you," I said. "Here it is. I never saw Waldo until he stepped into the cocktail bar tonight and asked about the girl. I knew nothing I didn't tell.

When I got home and stepped out of the elevator this girl, in the printed bolero jacket and the wide hat and the blue silk crêpe dress—all as he had described them—was waiting for the elevator, here on my floor. And she looked like a nice girl."

Copernik laughed jeeringly. It didn't make any difference to me. I had him cold. All he had to do was know that. He was going to know it now, very soon.

"I knew what she was up against as a police witness," I said. "And I suspected that there was something else to it. But I didn't suspect for a minute that there was anything wrong with her. She was just a nice girl in a jam—and she didn't even know she was in a jam. I got her in here. She pulled a gun on me. But she didn't mean to use it."

Copernik sat up very suddenly and he began to lick his lips. His face had a stony look now. A look like wet gray stone. He didn't make a sound.

"Waldo had been her chauffeur," I went on. "His name was then Joseph Coates. Her name is Mrs. Frank C. Barsaly. Her husband is a big hydroelectric engineer. Some guy gave her the pearls once and she told her husband they were just store pearls. Waldo got wise somehow there was a romance behind them and when Barsaly came home from South America and fired him, because he was too good-looking, he lifted the pearls."

Ybarra lifted his head suddenly and his teeth flashed. "You mean he didn't know they were phony?"

"I thought he fenced the real ones and had imitations fixed up," I said.

Ybarra nodded. "It's possible."

"He lifted something else," I said. "Some stuff from Barsaly's briefcase that showed he was keeping a woman—out in Brentwood. He was blackmailing wife and husband both, without either knowing about the other. Get it so far?"

"I get it," Copernik said harshly, between his tight lips. His face was still wet gray stone. "Get the hell on with it."

"Waldo wasn't afraid of them," I said. "He didn't conceal where he lived. That was foolish, but it saved a lot of finagling, if he was willing to risk it. The girl came down here tonight with five grand to buy back her pearls. She didn't find Waldo. She came here to look for him and walked up a floor before she went back down. A woman's idea of being cagey. So I met her. So I brought her in here. So she was in that dressing room when Al Tessilore visited me to rub out a witness." I pointed to the dressing-room door. "So she came out with her little gun and stuck it in his back and saved my life," I said.

Copernik didn't move. There was something horrible in his face now. Ybarra slipped his nail file into a small leather case and slowly tucked it into his pocket.

"Is that all?" he said gently.

I nodded. "Except that she told me where Waldo's apartment was and I went in there and looked for the pearls. I found the dead man. In his pocket I found new car keys in a case from a Packard agency. And down on the street I found the Packard and took it to where it came from. Barsaly's kept woman. Barsaly had sent a friend from the Spezzia Club down to buy something and he had tried to buy it with his gun instead of the money Barsaly gave him. And Waldo beat him to the punch."

"Is that all?" Ybarra said softly.

"That's all," I said, licking the torn place on the inside of my cheek.

Ybarra said slowly: "What do you want?"

Copernik's face convulsed and he slapped his long hard thigh. "This guy's good," he jeered. "He falls for a stray broad and breaks every law in the book and you ask him what does he want? I'll give him what he wants, guinea!"

Ybarrra turned his head slowly and looked at him. "I don't think you will," he said. "I think you'll give him a clean bill of health and anything else he wants. He's giving you a lesson in police work."

Copernik didn't move or make a sound for a long minute. None of us moved. Then Copernik leaned forward and his coat fell open. The butt of his service gun looked out of his underarm holster.

"So what do you want?" he asked me.

"What's on the card table there. The jacket and hat and the phony pearls. And some names kept away from the papers. Is that too much?"

"Yeah—it's too much," Copernik said almost gently. He swayed sideways and his gun jumped neatly into his hand. He rested his forearm on his thigh and pointed the gun at my stomach.

"I like better that you get a slug in the guts resisting arrest," he said. "I like that better, because of a report I made out on Al Tessilore's arrest and how I made the pinch. Because of some photos of me that are in the morning sheets going out about now. I like it better that you don't live long enough to laugh about that baby."

My mouth felt suddenly hot and dry. Far off I heard the wind booming. It seemed like the sound of guns.

Ybarra moved his feet on the floor and said coldly: "You've got a couple of cases all solved, policeman. All you do for it is leave some junk here and keep some names from the papers. Which means from the D.A. If he gets them any-way, too bad for you."

Copernik said: "I like the other way." The blue gun in his hand was like a rock. "And God help you, if you don't back me up on it."

Ybarra said: "If the woman is brought out into the open, you'll be a liar on a police report and a chiseler on your own partner. In a week they won't even speak your name at Headquarters. The taste of it would make them sick."

The hammer clicked back on Copernik's gun and I watched his big finger slide in farther around the trigger.

Ybarra stood up. The gun jumped at him. He said: "We'll see how yellow a guinea is. I'm telling you to put that gun up, Sam."

He started to move. He moved four even steps. Copernik was a man without a breath of movement, a stone man.

Ybarra took one more step and quite suddenly the gun began to shake.

Ybarra spoke evenly: "Put it up, Sam. If you keep your head everything lies the way it is. If you don't—you're gone."

He took one more step. Copernik's mouth opened wide and made a gasping sound and then he sagged in the chair as if he had been hit on the head. His eyelids dropped.

Ybarra jerked the gun out of his hand with a movement so quick it was no movement at all. He stepped back quickly, held the gun low at his side.

"It's the hot wind, Sam. Let's forget it," he said in the same even, almost dainty voice.

Copernik's shoulders sagged lower and he put his face in his hands. "Okay," he said between his fingers.

Ybarra went softly across the room and opened the door. He looked at me with lazy, half-closed eyes. "I'd do a lot for a woman who saved my life, too," he said.

"I'm eating this dish, but as a cop you can't expect me to like it."

I said: "The little man in the bed is called Leon Valesanos. He was a croupier[35] at the Spezzia Club."

"Thanks," Ybarra said. "Let's go, Sam."

Copernik got up heavily and walked across the room and out of the open door and out of my sight. Ybarra stepped through the door after him and started to close it.

I said: "Wait a minute."

He turned his head slowly, his left hand on the door, the blue gun hanging down close to his right side.

"I'm not in this for money," I said. "The Barsalys live at two-twelve Fremont Place. You can take the pearls to her. If Barsaly's name stays out of the paper, I get five C's. It goes to the Police Fund. I'm not so damn smart as you think. It just happened that way—and you had a heel for a partner."

Ybarra looked across the room at the pearls on the card table. His eyes glistened. "You take them," he said. "The five hundred's okay. I think the fund has it coming."

He shut the door quietly and in a moment I heard the elevator doors clang.

7

I opened a window and stuck my head out into the wind and watched the squad car tool off down the block. The wind blew in hard and I let it blow. A picture fell off the wall and two chessmen rolled off the card table. The material of Lola Barsaly's bolero jacket lifted and shook.

I went out to the kitchenette and drank some Scotch and went back into the living room and called her—late as it was.

She answered the phone herself, very quickly, with no sleep in her voice.

"Marlowe," I said. "Okay your end?"

"Yes . . . yes," she said. "I'm alone."

"I found something," I said. "Or rather the police did. But your dark boy gypped you. I have a string of pearls. They're not real. He sold the real ones, I guess, and made you up a string of ringers, with your clasp."

She was silent for a long time. Then, a little faintly: "The police found them?"

"In Waldo's car. But they're not telling. We have a deal. Look at the papers in the morning and you'll be able to figure out why."

"There doesn't seem to be anything more to say," she said. "Can I have the clasp?"

"Yes, Can you meet me tomorrow at four in the Club Esquire bar?"

"You're really rather sweet," she said in a dragged-out voice. "I can. Frank is still at his meeting."

"Those meetings—they take it out of a guy," I said. We said goodbye.

I called a West Los Angeles number. He was still there, with the Russian girl.

"You can send me a check for five hundred in the morning," I told him. "Made out to the Police Relief Fund, if you want to. Because that's where it's going."

Copernik made the third page of the morning papers with two photos and a nice half-column. The little brown man in apartment 31 didn't make the paper at all. The Apartment House Association has a good lobby too.

I went out after breakfast and the wind was all gone. It was soft, cool, a little foggy. The sky was close and comfortable and gray. I rode down to the boulevard

[35] The person in charge of a gambling table; the one who rakes in and pays out the money.

and picked out the best jewelry store on it and laid a string of pearls on a black velvet mat under a daylight-blue lamp. A man in a wing collar and striped trousers looked down at them languidly.

"How good?" I asked.

"I'm sorry, sir. We don't make appraisals. I can give you the name of an appraiser."

"Don't kid me," I said. "They're Dutch."[36]

He focused the light a little and leaned down and toyed with a few inches of the string.

"I want a string just like them, fitted to that clasp, and in a hurry," I added.

"How, like them?" He didn't look up. "And they're not Dutch. They're Bohemian."

"Okay, can you duplicate them?"

He shook his head and pushed the velvet pad away as if it soiled him. "In three months, perhaps, We don't blow glass like that in this country. If you wanted them matched—three months at least. And this house would not do that sort of thing at all."

"It must be swell to be that snooty," I said. I put a card under his black sleeve. "Give me a name that will—and not in three months—and maybe not exactly like them."

He shrugged, went away with the card, came back in five minutes and handed it back to me. There was something written on the back.

The old Levantine[37] had a shop on Melrose, a junk shop with everything in the window from a folding baby carriage to a French horn, from a mother-of-pearl lorgnette[38] in a faded plush case to one of those .44 Special Single Action six-shooters they still make for Western peace officers whose grandfathers were tough.

The old Levantine wore a skull cap and two pairs of glasses and a full beard. He studied my pearls, shook his head sadly, and said: "For twenty dollars, almost so good. Not so good, you understand. Not so good glass."

"How like will they look?"

He spread his firm strong hands. "I am telling you the truth," he said. "They would not fool a baby."

"Make them up," I said. "With this clasp. And I want the others back, too, of course."

"Yah. Two o'clock," he said.

Leon Valesanos, the little brown man from Uruguay, made the afternoon papers. He had been found hanging in an unnamed apartment. The police were investigating.

At four o'clock I walked into the long cool bar of the Club Esquire and prowled along the rows of booths until I found one where a woman sat alone. She wore a hat like a shallow soup plate with a very wide edge, a brown tailor-made suit with severe mannish shirt and tie.

I sat down beside her and slipped a parcel along the seat. "You don't open that," I said. "In fact you can slip it into the incinerator as is, if you want to."

She looked at me with dark tired eyes. Her fingers twisted a thin glass that smelled of peppermint. "Thanks." Her face was very pale.

I ordered a highball and the waiter went away. "Read the papers?"

---

[36] Slang for "fake."   [37] Inhabitant of the Levant, the eastern Mediterranean region.
[38] Eyeglasses attached to a handle; opera glasses.

"Yes."

"You understand now about this fellow Copernik who stole your act? That's why they won't change the story or bring you into it."

"It doesn't matter now," she said. "Thank you, all the same. Please—please show them to me."

I pulled the string of pearls out of the loosely wrapped tissue paper in my pocket and slid them across to her. The silver propeller clasp winked in the light of the wall bracket. The little diamond winked. The pearls were as dull as white soap. They didn't even match in size.

"You were right," she said tonelessly. "They are not my pearls."

The waiter came with my drink and she put her bag on them deftly. When he was gone she fingered them slowly once more, dropped them into the bag and gave me a dry mirthless smile.

"As you said—I'll keep the clasp."

I said slowly: "You don't know anything about me. You saved my life last night and we had a moment, but it was just a moment. You still don't know anything about me. There's a detective downtown named Ybarra, a Mexican of the nice sort, who was on the job when the pearls were found in Waldo's suitcase. That is in case you would like to make sure—"

She said: "Don't be silly. It's all finished. It was a memory. I'm too young to nurse memories. It may be for the best. I loved Stan Phillips—but he's gone—long gone."

I stared at her, didn't say anything.

She added quietly: "This morning my husband told me something I hadn't known. We are to separate. So I have very little to laugh about today."

"I'm sorry," I said lamely. "There's nothing to say. I may see you sometime. Maybe not. I don't move much in your circle. Good luck."

I stood up. We looked at each other for a moment. "You haven't touched your drink," she said.

"You drink it. That peppermint stuff will just make you sick."

I stood there a moment with a hand hard on the table.

"If anybody ever bothers you," I said, "let me know."

I went out of the bar without looking back at her, got into my car and drove west on Sunset and down all the way to the Coast Highway. Everywhere along the way gardens were full of withered and blackened leaves and flowers which the hot wind had burned.

But the ocean looked cool and languid and just the same as ever. I drove on almost to Malibu and then parked and went and sat on a big rock that was inside somebody's wire fence. It was about half-tide and coming in. The air smelled of kelp. I watched the water for a while and then I pulled a string of Bohemian glass imitation pearls out of my pocket and cut the knot at one end and slipped the pearls off one by one.

When I had them all loose in my left hand I held them like that for a while and thought. There wasn't really anything to think about. I was sure.

"To the memory of Mr. Stan Phillips," I said aloud. "Just another four-flusher."[39]

I flipped her pearls out into the water one by one at the floating seagulls.

They made little splashes and the seagulls rose off the water and swooped at the splashes.

1945

[39] A bluffer.

Richard Wright
(1908–1960)

In 1947 Richard Wright left Manhattan to become a permanent resident of Paris, which remained his home until his death after a heart attack in 1960. He had modeled his first novel, *Lawd Today* (completed in 1938 but published in 1963), on the design of James Joyce's *Ulysses* (1922). In fleeing the constrictions of American society, Wright followed the example set by Joyce, Gertrude Stein, and other expatriots and hoped that his creative powers would thrive outside his native culture. This hope was sadly unrealized; most of Wright's best fiction was written before his exasperated departure. But his early novels and stories, together with his autobiographical and sociological writings, establish him as one of the most influential American writers of the twentieth century. Much of the power of Wright's prose derives from his personal experience of both southern and northern forms of racist suppression and exploitation.

Wright was born in a sharecropper's cabin on a farm in Roxie, Mississippi, in 1908. His father, an illiterate sharecropper, moved the family to Memphis in 1911 and abandoned them in 1913. Ella Wilson Wright, a former schoolteacher reduced to menial labor, could not afford to feed her sons Richard and Alan; hunger became one of Wright's most vivid metaphors in his definitions of the difference between black and white America. When their mother became ill, Richard and Alan were left in an orphanage for two years. In 1916 Ella Wright took the boys to live with her sister and brother-in-law in Elaine, Arkansas. Soon after they arrived, Wright's uncle was murdered for his property by a group of whites who threatened to kill the rest of the family. The Wrights escaped and wandered between Arkansas and Mississippi until ill health forced Ella Wright to place the boys with relatives in 1919. Richard could not stand the restrictive scrutiny of an overbearing aunt and uncle in Greenwood, Mississippi, and chose instead to live with his grandmother and another aunt in Jackson, Mississippi, where he stayed until 1925.

Denied the opportunity to attend school regularly until he entered the Seventh-Day Adventist School in 1920, Wright was tutored by his mother and his aunt. He was advanced to the sixth grade two weeks after enrolling and proved an excellent student with a gift for writing. In 1924 his short story "The Voodoo of Hell's Half Acre" was published in a Jackson newspaper; in 1925 he was valedictorian of his junior high school class. When school officials asked that he read a valedictory address written by a white administrator, Wright argued until permitted to read his own speech. His formal education was cut short that year when he had to help support his family, but he continued to read widely, borrowing books from the white library with a card loaned to him by a kindly white mentor.

In 1927 Wright moved to the North for reasons similar to those prompting his European self-exile in 1947: to come to terms with the South. He lived in Chicago during the Great Depression and became a director of the Federal Negro Theater of the Federal Writers Project; he also worked at odd jobs and went on relief when unemployed. He continued reading, introducing himself to the work of Feodor Dostoevski, of Sinclair Lewis, and of Sherwood Anderson. Theodore Dreiser's naturalist novels particularly impressed Wright; the blistering cultural critique in Wright's novel *Native Son* (1940) echoes the tenets of Dreiser's social determinism.

Wright first began writing seriously during his years in Chicago. He met other writers by participating in the National Negro Congress, the South Side Writers' Group, and the Chicago John Reed Club, a Communist literary organization. He joined the Communist party in 1933 and contributed revolutionary poems to leftist publications such as the *New Masses*. For a time, Wright's poetry and critical essays seemed politically correct—as long as he wrote poems with titles such as "We of the Streets" (1937) and "Red Leaves of Red Books" (1935). In 1941 he married a devoted party member, Ellen Poplar (his first marriage, to the dancer Rose Dhima Meadman, dissolved in less than a year). But when he began compiling biographical sketches of black party members, his insistence on the singularity of the black proletariat experience was unacceptable to the Chicago branch of the Communist party. Wright left the party in 1944 and remained actively sympathetic to aspects of it, although he became an active anti-Communist in the 1950s and wrote about the inhumanity of Communist methods.

After moving to New York in 1937 Wright co-edited and wrote for the *Daily Worker* and other journals. In *Uncle Tom's Children* (1938, 1940), a publishing sensation, he focuses an outraged eye on the plight of African Americans in the rural South. That collection includes some of his most brilliant work and led to a Guggenheim Fellowship. With the publication of *Native Son* in 1940, Wright created the genre of the African-American protest novel. Twenty years later civil rights protests on behalf of the urban African-American populace would address precisely those inhuman living conditions Wright paints with such brutally realistic clarity in *Native Son*. That novel was a record-breaking bestseller; Orson Welles directed a film version in 1951 with Wright cast in the lead role.

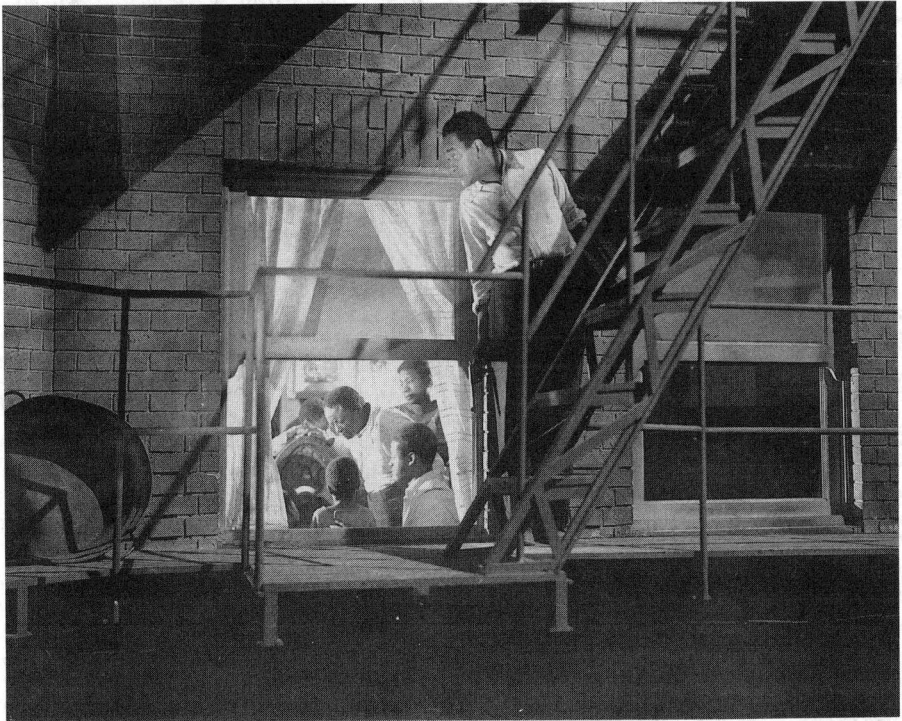

Richard Wright's Native Son *was made into a 1950 motion picture in which Wright starred as Bigger Thomas.*

Wright typically instilled his fiction with autobiographical reminiscences, but in the story "Bright and Morning Star" (1940) the devoted mother notably contrasts with Wright's own experience of maternal figures. In *Black Boy: A Record of Childhood and Youth* (1945) he recalls how his mother once punished him by beating him into unconsciousness. He remarks that "for a long time I was chastened whenever I remembered that my mother had come close to killing me." His aunt and grandmother forced upon him a peculiarly mean-spirited and fanatical form of Seventh Day Adventism; in Wright's last writings in the late 1950s, his rejection of institutionalized religious observance sprung from his emotional conviction of this early period. That autobiography and his second one, *American Hunger* (published posthumously in 1977), were both well received. His experiments with existential fiction in the 1950s were less successful in America than in Europe, where his reputation was strengthened by his association with the circle of the existentialist writers Jean-Paul Sartre and Simone de Beauvoir. American critics were less than kind in reviewing Wright's late writing, but the critic Irving Howe anticipated a 1970s and 1980s resurgence of appreciation for Wright's work when he eulogized Wright in *A World More Attractive* (1963) after Wright's death of a heart attack in 1960: "If such younger Negro novelists as James Baldwin and Ralph Ellison were to move beyond Wright's harsh naturalism and toward more subtle modes of fiction, that was possible only because Wright had been there first, courageous enough to release the full weight of his anger."

Suggested Readings: *Native Son*, 1940. *12 Million Black Voices*, 1941. *Black Boy: A Record of Childhood and Youth*, 1945. *White Man, Listen!*, 1957. *Eight Men*, 1961. *American Hunger*, 1977. M. Fabre, *The Unfinished Quest of Richard Wright*, 1973. *Richard Wright: A Primary Bibliography*, ed. C. T. Davis and M. Fabre, 1982. M. Fabre, *The World of Richard Wright*, 1985. *Modern Critical Views: Richard Wright*, ed. H. Bloom, 1987. K. Kinnamon et al., *A Richard Wright Bibliography: Fifty Years of Criticism and Commentary*, 1988.

Text Used: *Uncle Tom's Children*, 1989.

from   UNCLE TOM'S CHILDREN*

BRIGHT AND MORNING STAR

I

She stood with her black face some six inches from the moist windowpane and wondered when on earth would it ever stop raining. It might keep up like this all week, she thought. She heard rain droning upon the roof and high up in the wet sky her eyes followed the silent rush of a bright shaft of yellow that swung from the airplane beacon in far off Memphis. Momently she could see it cutting through

---

* First published as *Uncle Tom's Children: Four Novellas* in 1938 and enlarged to *Uncle Tom's Children: Five Long Stories* in 1940 with the inclusion of the introductory essay "The Ethics of Living Jim Crow" and "Bright and Morning Star," which was first published in the *New Masses* in 1939. The story's title is from an old African-American hymn.

the rainy dark; it would hover a second like a gleaming sword above her head, then vanish. She sighed, troubling, Johnny-Boys been trampin in this slop all day wid no decent shoes on his feet. . . . Through the window she could see the rich black earth sprawling outside in the night. There was more rain than the clay could soak up; pools stood everywhere. She yawned and mumbled: "Rains good n bad. It kin make seeds bus up thu the ground, er it kin bog things down lika watah-soaked coffin." Her hands were folded loosely over her stomach and the hot air of the kitchen traced a filmy vein of sweat on her forehead. From the cook stove came the soft singing of burning wood and now and then a throaty bubble rose from a pot of simmering greens.

"Shucks, Johnny-Boy coulda let somebody else do all tha runnin in the rain. Theres others bettah fixed for it than he is. But, naw! Johnny-boy ain the one t trust nobody t do nothin. Hes gotta do it *all* hissef. . . ."

She glanced at a pile of damp clothes in a zinc tub. Waal, Ah bettah git t work. She turned, lifted a smoothing iron with a thick pad of cloth, touched a spit-wet finger to it with a quick, jerking motion: *smiiitz!* Yeah; its hot! Stooping, she took a blue work-shirt from the tub and shook it out. With a deft twist of her shoulders she caught the iron in her right hand; the fingers of her left hand took a piece of wax from a tin box and a frying sizzle came as she smeared the bottom. She was thinking of nothing now; her hands followed a life-long ritual of toil. Spreading a sleeve, she ran the hot iron to and fro until the wet cloth became stiff. She was deep in the midst of her work when a song rose up out of the far off days of her childhood and broke through half-parted lips:

> *Hes the Lily of the Valley, the Bright n*
> *Mawnin Star*
> *Hes the Fairest of Ten Thousan t ma soul . . .*

A gust of wind dashed rain against the window. Johnny-Boy oughta c mon home n eat his suppah. Aw, Lawd! Itd be fine ef Sug could eat wid us tonight! Itd be like ol times! Mabbe aftah all it wont be long fo he comes back. Tha lettah Ah got from im last week said *Don give up hope.* . . . Yeah; we gotta live in hope. Then both of her sons, Sug and Johnny-Boy, would be back with her.

With an involuntary nervous gesture, she stopped and stood still, listening. But the only sound was the lulling fall of rain. Shucks, ain no usa me ackin this way, she thought. Ever time they gits ready to hol them meetings Ah gits jumpity. Ah been a lil scared ever since Sug went t jail. She heard the clock ticking and looked. Johnny-boys a *hour* late! He sho must be havin a time doin all tha trampin, trampin thu the mud. . . . But her fear was a quiet one; it was more like an intense brooding than a fear; it was a sort of hugging of hated facts so closely that she could feel their grain, like letting cold water run over her hand from a faucet on a winter morning.

She ironed again, faster now, as if she felt the more she engaged her body in work the less she would think. But how could she forget Johnny-Boy out there on those wet fields rounding up white and black Communists for a meeting tomorrow? And that was just what Sug had been doing when the sheriff had caught him, beat him, and tried to make him tell who and where his comrades were. Po Sug! They sho musta beat the boy somethin awful! But, thank Gawd, he didn't talk! He ain no weaklin, Sug ain! Hes been lion-hearted all his life long.

That had happened a year ago. And now each time those meetings came around the old terror surged back. While shoving the iron a cluster of toiling days returned; days of washing and ironing to feed Johnny-Boy and Sug so they could do party work; days of carrying a hundred pounds of white folks' clothes upon her head across fields sometimes wet and sometimes dry. But in those days a hundred pounds was nothing to carry carefully balanced upon her head while stepping by instinct over the corn and cotton rows. The only time it had seemed heavy was when she had heard of Sug's arrest. She had been coming home one morning with a bundle upon her head, her hands swinging idly by her sides, walking slowly with her eyes in front of her, when Bob, Johnny-Boy's pal, had called from across the fields and had come and told her that the sheriff had got Sug. That morning the bundle had become heavier than she could ever remember.

And with each passing week now, though she spoke of it to no one, things were becoming heavier. The tubs of water and the smoothing iron and the bundles of clothes were becoming harder to lift, with her back aching so; and her work was taking longer, all because Sug was gone and she didn't know just when Johnny-Boy would be taken too. To ease the ache of anxiety that was swelling her heart, she hummed, then sang softly:

> *He walks wid me, He talks wid me*
> *He tells me Ahm His own. . . .*

Guiltily, she stopped and smiled. Looks like Ah jus cant seem t fergit them ol songs, no mattah how hard Ah tries. . . . She had learned them when she was a little girl living and working on a farm. Every Monday morning from the corn and cotton fields the slow strains had floated from her mother's lips, lonely and haunting; and later, as the years had filled with gall, she had learned their deep meaning. Long hours of scrubbing floors for a few cents a day had taught her who Jesus was, what a great boon it was to cling to Him, to be like Him and suffer without a mumbling word. She had poured the yearning of her life into the songs, feeling buoyed with a faith beyond this world. The figure of the Man nailed in agony to the Cross, His burial in a cold grave, His transfigured Resurrection, His being breath and clay, God and Man—all had focused her feelings upon an imagery which had swept her life into a wondrous vision.

But as she had grown older, a cold white mountain, the white folks and their laws, had swum into her vision and shattered her songs and their spell of peace. To her that white mountain was temptation, something to lure her from her Lord, a part of the world God had made in order that she might endure it and come through all the stronger, just as Christ had risen with greater glory from the tomb. The days crowded with trouble had enhanced her faith and she had grown to love hardship with a bitter pride; she had obeyed the laws of the white folks with a soft smile of secret knowing.

After her mother had been snatched up to heaven in a chariot of fire, the years had brought her a rough workingman and two black babies, Sug and Johnny-Boy, all three of whom she had wrapped in the charm and magic of her vision. Then she was tested by no less than God; her man died, a trial which she bore with the strength shed by the grace of her vision; finally even the memory of her man faded into the vision itself, leaving her with two black boys growing tall, slowly into manhood.

Then one day grief had come to her heart when Johnny-boy and Sug had walked forth demanding their lives. She had sought to fill their eyes with her vision, but they would have none of it. And she had wept when they began to boast of the strength shed by a new and terrible vision.

But she had loved them, even as she loved them now; bleeding, her heart had followed them. She could have done no less, being an old woman in a strange world. And day by day her sons had ripped from her startled eyes her old vision, and image by image had given her a new one, different, but great and strong enough to fling her into the light of another grace. The wrongs and sufferings of black men had taken the place of Him nailed to the Cross; the meager beginnings of the party had become another Resurrection; and the hate of those who would destroy her new faith had quickened in her a hunger to feel how deeply her new strength went.

"Lawd, Johnny-Boy," she would sometimes say, "Ah jus wan them white folks t try t make me tell *who* is *in* the party n who *ain!* Ah jus wan em t try, Ahll show em somethin they never thought a black woman could have!"

But sometimes like tonight, while lost in the forgetfulness of work, the past and the present would become mixed in her; while toiling under a strange star for a new freedom the old songs would slip from her lips with their beguiling sweetness.

The iron was getting cold. She put more wood into the fire, stood again at the window and watched the yellow blade of light cut through the wet darkness. Johnny-Boy ain here yit . . . Then, before she was aware of it, she was still, listening for sounds. Under the drone of rain she heard the slosh of feet in mud. Tha ain Johnny-Boy. She knew his long, heavy footsteps in a million. She heard feet come on the porch. Some woman. . . . She heard bare knuckles knock three times, then once. Thas some of them comrades! She unbarred the door, cracked it a few inches, and flinched from the cold rush of damp wind.

"Whos tha?"

"Its me!"

"Who?"

"Me, Reva!"

She flung the door open.

"Lawd, chile, c mon in!"

She stepped to one side and a thin, blond-haired white girl ran through the door; as she slid the bolt she heard the girl gasping and shaking her wet clothes. Somethings wrong! Reva wouldna walked a mil t mah house in all this slop fer nothin! That gals stuck onto Johnny-Boy. Ah wondah ef anythin happened t im?

"Git on inter the kitchen, Reva, where its warm."

"Lawd, Ah sho is wet!"

"How yuh reckon yuhd be, in all tha rain?"

"Johnny-Boy ain here *yit?*" asked Reva.

"Naw! N ain no usa yuh worryin bout im. Jus yuh git them shoes off! Yuh wanna ketch yo deatha col?" She stood looking absently. Yeah; its somethin about the party er Johnny-Boy thas gone wrong. Lawd, Ah wondah ef her pa knows how she feels bout Johnny-Boy? "Honey, yuh hadn't oughta come out in sloppy weather like this."

"Ah had t come, An Sue."

She led Reva to the kitchen.

"Git them shoes off n git close t the stove so yuhll git dry!"

"An Sue, Ah got somethin t tell yuh . . ."

The words made her hold her breath. Ah bet its somethin bout Johnny-Boy!

"Whut, honey?"

"The sheriff wuz by our house tonight. He come t see pa."

"Yeah?"

"He done got word from somewheres bout tha meetin tomorrow."

"Is it Johnny-Boy, Reva?"

"Aw, naw, An Sue! Ah ain hearda word bout im. Ain yuh seen im tonight?"

"He ain come home t eat yit."

"Where kin he be?"

"Lawd knows, chile."

"Somebody's gotta tell them comrades that meetings off," said Reva. "The sheriffs got men watchin our house. Ah had t slip out t git here widout em fol-lowin me."

"Reva?"

"Hunh?"

"Ahma ol woman n Ah wans yuh t tell me the truth."

"Whut, An Sue?"

"Yuh ain tryin t fool me, is yuh?"

"*Fool* yuh?"

"Bout Johnny-Boy?"

"Lawd, naw, An Sue!"

"Ef theres anythin wrong jus tell me, chile. Ah kin stan it."

She stood by the ironing board, her hands as usual folded loosely over her stomach, watching Reva pull off her water-clogged shoes. She was feeling that Johnny-Boy was already lost to her; she was feeling the pain that would come when she knew it for certain; and she was feeling that she would have to be brave and bear it. She was like a person caught in a swift current of water and knew where the water was sweeping her and did not want to go on but had to go on to the end.

"It ain nothin bout Johnny-Boy, An Sue," said Reva, "But we gotta do some-thin er we'll all git inter trouble."

"How the sheriff know about tha meetin?"

"Thas whut pa wants t know."

"Somebody done turned Judas."[1]

"Sho looks like it."

"Ah bet it wuz some of them new ones," she said.

"Its hard t tell," said Reva.

"Lissen, Reva, yuh oughta stay here n git dry, but yuh bettah git back n tell yo pa Johnny-Boy ain here n Ah don know when hes gonna show up. *Some*bodys gotta tell them comrades t stay erway from yo pas house."

She stood with her back to the window, looking at Reva's wide, blue eyes. Po critter! Gotta go back thu all tha slop! Though she felt sorry for Reva, not once did she think that it would not have to be done. Being a woman, Reva was not sus-pect; she would *have* to go. It was just as natural for Reva to go back through the cold rain as it was for her to iron night and day, or for Sug to be in jail. Right now, Johnny-Boy was out there on those dark fields trying to get home. Lawd, don let em git im tonight! In spite of herself her feelings became torn. She loved her son and, loving him, she loved what he was trying to do. Johnny-Boy was happiest when he was working for the party, and her love for him was for his

---

[1] Judas Iscariot, Jesus' betrayer (see Matthew 26).

happiness. She frowned, trying hard to fit something together in her feelings: for her to try to stop Johnny-Boy was to admit that all the toil of years meant nothing; and to let him go meant that sometime or other he would be caught, like Sug. In facing it this way she felt a little stunned, as though she had come suddenly upon a blank wall in the dark. But outside in the rain were people, white and black, whom she had known all her life. Those people depended upon Johnny-Boy, loved him and looked to him as a man and leader. Yeah; hes gotta keep on; he cant stop now. . . . She looked at Reva; she was crying and pulling her shoes back on with reluctant fingers.

"Whut yuh carryin on tha way fer, chile?"

"Yuh done los Sug, now yuh sendin Johnny-Boy . . ."

"Ah got t, honey."

She was glad she could say that. Reva believed in black folks and not for anything in the world would she falter before her. In Reva's trust and acceptance of her she had found her first feelings of humanity; Reva's love was her refuge from shame and degradation. If in the early days of her life the white mountain had driven her back from the earth, then in her last days Reva's love was drawing her toward it, like the beacon that swung through the night outside. She heard Reva sobbing.

"Hush, honey!"

"Mah brothers in jail too! Ma cries ever day . . ."

"Ah know, honey."

She helped Reva with her coat; her fingers felt the scant flesh of the girl's shoulders. She don git ernuff t eat, she thought. She slipped her arms around Reva's waist and held her close for a moment.

"Now, yuh stop that cryin."

"A-a-ah c-c-cant hep it. . . ."

"Everythingll be awright; Johnny-Boyll be back."

"Yuh think so?"

"Sho, chile. Cos he will."

Neither of them spoke again until they stood in the doorway. Outside they could hear water washing through the ruts of the street.

"Be sho n send Johnny-Boy t tell the folks t stay erway from pas house," said Reva.

"Ahll tell im. Don yuh worry."

"Good-bye!"

"Good-bye!"

Leaning against the door jamb,[2] she shook her head slowly and watched Reva vanish through the falling rain.

II

She was back at her board, ironing, when she heard feet sucking in the mud of the back yard; feet she knew from long years of listening were Johnny-Boy's. But tonight, with all the rain and fear, his coming was like a leaving, was almost more than she could bear. Tears welled to her eyes and she blinked them away. She felt that he was coming so that she could give him up; to see him now was to say

---

[2] The side post.

good-bye. But it was a good-bye she knew she could never say; they were not that way toward each other. All day long they could sit in the same room and not speak; she was his mother and he was her son. Most of the time a nod or a grunt would carry all the meaning that she wanted to convey to him, or he to her. She did not even turn her head when she heard him come stomping into the kitchen. She heard him pull up a chair, sit, sigh, and draw off his muddy shoes; they fell to the floor with heavy thuds. Soon the kitchen was full of the scent of his drying socks and his burning pipe. *Tha boys hongry!* She paused and looked at him over her shoulder; he was puffing at his pipe with his head tilted back and his feet propped up on the edge of the stove; his eyelids drooped and his wet clothes steamed from the heat of the fire. *Lawd, tha boy gits mo like his pa every day he lives,* she mused, her lips breaking in a slow faint smile. *Hols tha pipe in his mouth just like his pa usta hol his. Wondah how they woulda got erlong ef his pa hada lived? They oughta liked each other, they so mucha like.* She wished there could have been other children besides Sug, so Johnny-Boy would not have to be so much alone. *A man needs a woman by his side. . . .* She thought of Reva; she liked Reva; the brightest glow her heart had ever known was when she had learned that Reva loved Johnny-Boy. *But beyond Reva were cold white faces. Ef theys caught it means* death. *. . .* She jerked around when she heard Johnny-Boy's pipe clatter to the floor. She saw him pick it up, smile sheepishly at her, and wag his head.

"Gawd, Ahm sleepy," he mumbled.

She got a pillow from her room and gave it to him.

"Here," she said.

"Hunh," he said, putting the pillow between his head and the back of the chair.

They were silent again. *Yes, she would have to tell him to go back out into the cold rain and slop; maybe to get caught; maybe for the last time; she didn't know.* But she would let him eat and get dry before telling him that the sheriff knew of the meeting to be held at Lem's tomorrow. And she would make him take a big dose of soda before he went out; soda always helped to stave off a cold. She looked at the clock. It was eleven. *Theres time yit.* Spreading a newspaper on the apron of the stove, she placed a heaping plate of greens upon it, a knife, a fork, a cup of coffee, a slab of cornbread, and a dish of peach cobbler.

"Yo suppahs ready," she said.

"Yeah," he said.

He did not move. She ironed again. Presently, she heard him eating. When she could no longer hear his knife tinkling against the edge of the plate, she knew he was through. It was almost twelve now. *She would let him rest a little while longer before she told him. Till one er'clock, mabbe. Hes so tired. . . .* She finished her ironing, put away the board, and stacked the clothes in her dresser drawer. She poured herself a cup of black coffee, drew up a chair, sat down and drank.

"Yuh almos dry," she said, not looking around.

"Yeah," he said, turning sharply to her.

The tone of voice in which she had spoken had let him know that more was coming. She drained her cup and waited a moment longer.

"Reva wuz here."

"Yeah?"

"She lef bout a hour ergo."

"Whut she say?"

"She said ol man Lem hada visit from the sheriff today."

"Bout the meetin?"

She saw him stare at the coals glowing red through the crevices of the stove and run his fingers nervously through his hair. She knew he was wondering how the sheriff had found out. In the silence he would ask a wordless question and in the silence she would answer wordlessly. Johnny-Boys too trustin, she thought. Hes trying t make the party big n hes takin in folks fastern he kin git t know em. You cant trust ever white man yuh meet. . . .

"Yuh know, Johnny-Boy, yuh been takin in a lotta them white folks lately . . ."

"Aw, ma!"

"But, Johnny-Boy . . ."

"Please, dont talk t me bout tha now, ma."

"Yuh ain t ol t lissen n learn, son," she said.

"Ah know whut yuh gonna say, ma. N yuh wrong. Yuh cant judge folks just by how yuh feel bout em n by how long yuh done knowed em. Ef we start that we wouldnt have *no*body in the party. When folks pledge they word t be with us, then we gotta take em in. Wes too weak t be choosy."

He rose abruptly, rammed his hands into his pockets, and stood facing the window; she looked at his back in a long silence. She knew his faith; it was deep. He had always said that black men could not fight the rich bosses alone; a man could not fight with every hand against him. But he believes so hard hes blind, she thought. At odd times they had had these arguments before; always she would be pitting her feelings against the hard necessity of his thinking, and always she would lose. She shook her head. Po Johnny-Boy; he don know . . .

"But ain nona our folks tol, Johnny-Boy," she said.

"How yuh know?" he asked. His voice came low and with a tinge of anger. He still faced the window and now and then the yellow blade of light flicked across the sharp outline of his black face.

"Cause Ah know em," she said.

"*Any*body mighta tol," he said.

"It wuznt nona *our* folks," she said again.

She saw his hand sweep in a swift arc of disgust.

"*Our* folks! Ma, who in Gawds name is *our* folks?"

"The folks we wuz born n raised wid, son. The folks we *know!*"

"We cant make the party grow tha way, ma."

"It mighta been Booker," she said.

"Yuh don know."

". . . er Blattberg . . ."

"Fer Chrissakes!"

". . . er any of the fo-five others whut joined las week."

"Ma, yuh jus don wan me t go out tonight," he said.

"Yo ol ma wans yuh t be careful, son."

"Ma, when yuh start doubtin folks in the party, then there ain no end."

"Son, Ah knows ever black man n woman in this parta the country," she said, standing too. "Ah watched em grow up; Ah even heped birth n nurse some of em; Ah knows em *all* from way back. There ain none of em that *coulda* tol! The folks Ah know jus don open they dos n ast death t walk in! Son, it wuz some of them *white* folks! Yuh just mark mah word n wait n see!"

"Why is it gotta be *white* folks?" he asked. "Ef they tol, then theys jus Judases, thas all."

"Son, look at whuts befo yuh."

He shook his head and sighed.

"Ma, Ah done tol yuh a hundred times. Ah cant see white n Ah cant see black," he said. "Ah sees rich men n Ah sees po men."

She picked up his dirty dishes and piled them in a pan. Out of the corners of her eyes she saw him sit and pull on his wet shoes. Hes goin! When she put the last dish away he was standing fully dressed, warming his hands over the stove. Jus a few mo minutes now n hell be gone, like Sug, mabbe. Her throat tightened. This black mans fight takes *ever*thin! Looks like Gawd put us in this world jus t beat us down!

"Keep this, ma," he said.

She saw a crumpled wad of money in his outstretched fingers.

"Naw, yuh keep it. Yuh might need it."

"It ain mine, ma. It berlongs t the party."

"But, Johnny-Boy, yuh might hafta go erway!"

"Ah kin make out."

"Don fergit yosef too much, son."

"Ef Ah don come back theyll need it."

He was looking at her face and she was looking at the money.

"Yuh keep tha," she said slowly. "Ahll give em the money."

"From where?"

"Ah got some."

"Where yuh git it from?"

She sighed.

"Ah been savin a dollah a week fer Sug ever since hes been in jail."

"Lawd, ma!"

She saw the look of puzzled love and wonder in his eyes. Clumsily, he put the money back into his pocket.

"Ahm gone," he said.

"Here; drink this glass of soda watah."

She watched him drink, then put the glass away.

"Waal," he said.

"Take the stuff outta yo pockets!"

She lifted the lid of the stove and he dumped all the papers from his pocket into the fire. She followed him to the door and made him turn round.

"Lawd, yuh tryin to maka revolution n yuh cant even keep yo coat buttoned." Her nimble fingers fastened his collar high around his throat. "There!"

He pulled the brim of his hat low over his eyes. She opened the door and with the suddenness of the cold gust of wind that struck her face, he was gone. She watched the black fields and the rain take him, her eyes burning. When the last faint footstep could no longer be heard, she closed the door, went to her bed, lay down, and pulled the cover over her while fully dressed. Her feelings coursed with the rhythm of the rain: Hes gone! Lawd, Ah *knows* hes gone! Her blood felt cold.

III

She was floating in a grey void somewhere between sleeping and dreaming and then suddenly she was wide awake, hearing and feeling in the same instant the thunder of the door crashing in and a cold wind filling the room. It was pitch black and she stared, resting on her elbows, her mouth open, not breathing, her ears full of the sound of tramping feet and booming voices. She knew at once: They lookin fer im! Then, filled with her will, she was on her feet, rigid, waiting, listening.

"The lamps burnin!"

"Yuh see her?"

"Naw!"

"Look in the kitchen!"

"Gee, this place smells like niggers!"

"Say, somebodys here er been here!"

"Yeah; theres fire in the stove!"

"Mabbe hes been here n gone?"

"Boy, look at these jars of jam!"

"Niggers make good jam!"

"Git some bread!"

"Heres some cornbread!"

"Say, lemme git some!"

"Take it easy! Theres plenty here!"

"Ahma take some of this stuff home!"

"Look, heres a pota greens!"

"N some hot cawffee!"

"Say, yuh guys! C mon! Cut it out! We didn't come here fer a feas!"

She walked slowly down the hall. They lookin fer im, but they ain got im yit! She stopped in the doorway, her gnarled, black hands as always folded over her stomach, but tight now, so tightly the veins bulged. The kitchen was crowded with white men in glistening raincoats. Though the lamp burned, their flashlights still glowed in red fists. Across her floor she saw the muddy tracks of their boots.

"Yuh white folks git outta mah house!"

There was a quick silence; every face turned toward her. She saw a sudden movement, but did not know what it meant until something hot and wet slammed her squarely in the face. She gasped, but did not move. Calmly, she wiped the warm, greasy liquor of greens from her eyes with her left hand. One of the white men had thrown a handful of greens out of the pot at her.

"How they taste, ol bitch?"

"Ah ast yuh t git outta mah house!"

She saw the sheriff detach himself from the crowd and walk toward her.

"Now, Anty . . ."

"White man, don yuh *Anty* me!"

"Yuh ain got the right sperit!"

"Sperit hell! Yuh git these men outta mah house!"

"Yuh ack like yuh don like it!"

"Naw, Ah don like it, n yuh knows dam waal Ah don!"

"What yuh gonna do about it?"

"Ahm telling yuh t git outta mah house!"

"Gittin sassy?"

"Ef telling yuh t git outta mah house is sass, then Ahm sassy!"

Her words came in a tense whisper; but beyond, back of them, she was watching, thinking, judging the men.

"Listen, Anty," the sheriff's voice came soft and low. "Ahm here t hep yuh. How come yuh wanna ack this way?"

"Yuh ain never heped yo *own* sef since yuh been born," she flared. "How kin the likes of yuh hep me?"

One of the white men came forward and stood directly in front of her.

"Lissen, nigger woman, yuh talkin t *white* men!"

"Ah don care who Ahm talkin t!"

"Yuhll wish some day yuh did!"

"Not t the likes of yuh!"

"Yuh need somebody t teach yuh how t be a good nigger!"

"*Yuh* cant teach it t me!"

"Yuh gonna change yo tune."

"Not longs mah bloods warm!"

"Don git smart now!"

"Yuh git outta mah house!"

"Spose we don go?" the sheriff asked.

They were crowded around her. She had not moved since she had taken her place in the doorway. She was thinking only of Johnny-Boy as she stood there giving and taking words; and she knew that they, too, were thinking of Johnny-Boy. She knew they wanted him, and her heart was daring them to take him from her.

"Spose we don go?" the sheriff asked again.

"Twenty of yuh runnin over one ol woman! Now, ain yuh white men glad yuh so brave?"

The sheriff grabbed her arm.

"C mon, now! Yuh don did ernuff sass fer one night. Wheres tha nigger son of yos?"

"Don yuh wished yuh knowed?"

"Yuh wanna git slapped?"

"Ah ain never seen one of yo kind that wuznt too low fer . . ."

The sheriff slapped her straight across her face with his open palm. She fell back against a wall and sank to her knees.

"Is tha whut white men do t nigger women?"

She rose slowly and stood again, not even touching the place that ached from his blow, her hands folded over her stomach.

"Ah ain never seen one of yo kind tha wuznt too low fer . . ."

He slapped her again; she reeled backward several feet and fell on her side.

"Is tha whut we too low t do?"

She stood before him again, dry-eyed, as though she had not been struck. Her lips were numb and her chin was wet with blood.

"Aw, let her go! Its the nigger we wan!" said one.

"Wheres that nigger son of yos?" the sheriff asked.

"Find im," she said.

"By Gawd, ef we hafta find im well kill im!"

"He wont be the only nigger yuh ever killed," she said.

She was consumed with a bitter pride. There was nothing on this earth, she felt then, that they could not do to her but that she could take. She stood on a narrow plot of ground from which she would die before she was pushed. And then it was, while standing there feeling warm blood seeping down her throat, that she gave up Johnny-Boy, gave him up to the white folks. She gave him up because they had come tramping into her heart demanding him, thinking they could get him by beating her, thinking they could scare her into making her tell where he was. She gave him up because she wanted them to know that they could not get what they wanted by bluffing and killing.

"Wheres this meetin gonna be?" the sheriff asked.

"Don yuh wish yuh knowed?"

"Ain there gonna be a meetin?"

"How come yuh astin me?"

"There *is* gonna be a meetin," said the sheriff.

"Is it?"

"Ah gotta great mind t choke it outta yuh!"

"Yuh so smart," she said.

"We ain playing wid yuh!"

"Did Ah say yuh wuz?"

"That nigger son of yos is erroun here somewheres n Ah aim to find im," said the sheriff. "Ef yuh tell us where he is n ef he talks, mabbe hell git off easy. But ef we hafta find im, well kill im! Ef we hafta find im, then yuh git a sheet t put over im in the mawnin, see? Git yuh a sheet, cause hes gonna be dead!"

"He wont be the only nigger yuh ever killed," she said again.

The sheriff walked past her. The others followed. Yuh didnt git whut yuh wanted! she thought exultingly. N yuh ain gonna *never* git it! Hotly, something arched in her to make them feel the intensity of her pride and freedom; her heart groped to turn the bitter hours of her life into words of a kind that would make them feel that she had taken all they had done to her in stride and could still take more. Her faith surged so strongly in her she was all but blinded. She walked behind them to the door, knotting and twisting her fingers. She saw them step to the muddy ground. Each whirl of the yellow beacon revealed glimpses of slanting rain. Her lips moved, then she shouted:

"Yuh didnt git whut yuh wanted! N yuh ain gonna nevah git it!"

The sheriff stopped and turned; his voice came low and hard.

"Now, by Gawd, thas ernuff outta yuh!"

"Ah know when Ah done said ernuff!"

"Aw, naw, yuh don!" he said. "Yuh don know when yuh done said ernuff, but Ahma teach yuh ternight!"

He was up the steps and across the porch with one bound. She backed into the hall, her eyes full on his face.

"Tell me when yuh gonna stop talkin!" he said, swinging his fist.

The blow caught her high on the cheek; her eyes went blank; she fell flat on her face. She felt the hard heel of his wet shoes coming into her temple and stomach.

"Lemme hear yuh talk some mo!"

She wanted to, but could not; pain numbed and choked her. She lay still and somewhere out of the grey void of unconsciousness she heard someone say: *Aw fer chrissakes leave her erlone, its the nigger we wan. . . .*

IV

She never knew how long she had lain huddled in the dark hallway. Her first returning feeling was of a nameless fear crowding the inside of her, then a deep pain spreading from her temple downward over her body. Her ears were filled with the drone of rain and she shuddered from the cold wind blowing through the door. She opened her eyes and at first saw nothing. As if she were imagining it, she knew she was half lying and half sitting in a corner against a wall. With difficulty she twisted her neck and what she saw made her hold her breath—a vast white blur was suspended directly above her. For a moment she could not tell if her fear was from the blur or if the blur was from her fear. Gradually the blur resolved itself into a huge white face that slowly filled her vision. She was stone still, conscious really of the effort to breathe, feeling somehow that she existed only by the mercy of that white face. She had seen it before; its fear had gripped her many times; it had for her the fear of all the white faces she had ever seen in her life. *Sue* . . . As from a great distance, she heard her name being called. She was regaining consciousness now, but the fear was coming with her. She looked into the face of a white man, wanting to scream out for him to go; yet accepting his presence because she felt she had to. Though some remote part of her mind was active, her limbs were powerless. It was as if an invisible knife had split her in two, leaving one half of her lying there helpless, while the other half shrank in dread from a forgotten but familiar enemy. *Sue its me Sue its me* . . . Then all at once the voice came clearly.

"Sue, its me! Its Booker!"

And she heard an answering voice speaking inside of her. Yeah, its Booker . . . The one whut just joined . . . She roused herself, struggling for full consciousness; and as she did so she transferred to the person of Booker the nameless fear she felt. It seemed that Booker towered above her as a challenge to her right to exist upon the earth.

"Yuh awright?"

She did not answer; she started violently to her feet and fell.

"Sue, yuh hurt!"

"Yeah," she breathed.

"Where they hit yuh?"

"Its mah head," she whispered.

She was speaking even though she did not want to; the fear that had hold of her compelled her.

"They beat yuh?"

"Yeah."

"Them bastards! Them Gawddam bastards!"

She heard him saying it over and over; then she felt herself being lifted.

"Naw!" she gasped.

"Ahma take yuh t the kitchen!"

"Put me down!"

"But yuh cant stay here like this!"

She shrank in his arms and pushed her hands against his body; when she was in the kitchen she freed herself, sank into a chair, and held tightly to its back. She looked wonderingly at Booker. There was nothing about him that should frighten her so, but even that did not ease her tension. She saw him go the water bucket, wet his handkerchief, wring it, and offer it to her. Distrustfully, she stared at the damp cloth.

"Here; put this on yo fohead . . ."

"Naw!"

"C mon; itll make yuh feel bettah!"

She hesitated in confusion. What right had she to be afraid when someone was acting as kindly as this toward her? Reluctantly, she leaned forward and pressed the damp cloth to her head. It helped. With each passing minute she was catching hold of herself, yet wondering why she felt as she did.

"Whut happened?"

"Ah don know."

"Yuh feel bettah?"

"Yeah."

"Who all wuz here?"

"Ah don know," she said again.

"Yo head still hurt?"

"Yeah."

"Gee, Ahm sorry."

"Ahm awright," she sighed and buried her face in her hands.

She felt him touch her shoulder.

"Sue, Ah got some bad news fer yuh . . ."

She knew; she stiffened and grew cold. It had happened; she stared dry-eyed, with compressed lips.

"Its mah Johnny-Boy," she said.

"Yeah; Ahm awful sorry t hafta tell yuh this way. But Ah thought yuh oughta know . . ."

Her tension eased and a vacant place opened up inside of her. A voice whispered, Jesus, hep me!

"W-w-where is he?"

"They got im out t Foleys Woods tryin t make him tell who the others is."

"He ain gonna tell," she said, "They jus as waal kill im, cause he ain gonna nevah tell."

"Ah hope he don," said Booker. "But he didnt have a chance t tell the others. They grabbed im jus as he got t the woods."

Then all the horror of it flashed upon her; she saw flung out over the rainy countryside an array of shacks where white and black comrades were sleeping; in the morning they would be rising and going to Lem's; then they would be caught. And that meant terror, prison, and death. The comrades would have to be told; she would have to tell them; she could not entrust Johnny-Boy's work to another, and especially not to Booker as long as she felt toward him as she did. Gripping the bottom of the chair with both hands, she tried to rise; the room blurred and she swayed. She found herself resting in Booker's arms.

"Lemme go!"

"Sue, yuh too weak t walk!"

"Ah gotta tell em!" she said.

"Set down, Sue! Yuh hurt! Yuh sick!"

When seated, she looked at him helplessly.

"Sue, lissen! Johnny-Boys caught. Ahm here. Yuh tell me who they is n Ahll tell em."

She stared at the floor and did not answer. Yes; she was too weak to go. There was no way for her to tramp all those miles through the rain tonight. But should she tell Booker? If only she had somebody like Reva to talk to! She did not want to decide alone; she must make no mistake about this. She felt Booker's fingers pressing on her arm and it was as though the white mountain was pushing her to the edge of a sheer height; she again exclaimed inwardly. Jesus, hep me! Booker's white face was at her side, waiting. Would she be doing right to tell him? Suppose she did not tell and then the comrades were caught? She could not ever forgive herself for doing a thing like that. But maybe she was wrong; maybe her fear was what Johnny-Boy had always called "jus foolishness." She remembered his saying, Ma, we cant make the party grow ef we start doubtin everbody. . . .

"Tell me who they is, Sue, n Ahll tell em. Ah jus joined n Ah don know who they is."

"Ah don know who they is," she said.

"Yuh *gotta* tell me who they is, Sue!"

"Ah tol yuh Ah don know!"

"Yuh *do* know! C mon! Set up n talk!"

"Naw!"

"Yuh wan em all t git *killed?*"

She shook her head and swallowed. Lawd, Ah don believe in this man!

"Lissen, Ahll call the names n yuh tell me which ones is in the party n which ones ain, see?"

"Naw!"

"Please, Sue!"

"Ah don know," she said.

"Sue, yuh ain doin right by em. Johnny-Boy wouldnt wan yuh t be this way. Hes out there holdin up his end. Les hol up ours . . ."

"Lawd, Ah don know . . ."

"Is yuh scared a me cause Ahm *white?* Johnny-Boy ain like tha. Don let all the work we done go fer nothin."

She gave up and bowed her head in her hands.

"Is it Johnson? Tell me, Sue?"

"Yeah," she whispered in horror; a mounting horror of feeling herself being undone.

"Is it Green?"

"Yeah."

"Murphy?"

"Lawd, Ah don know!"

"Yuh gotta tell me, Sue!"

"Mistah Booker, please leave me erlone . . ."

"Is it Murphy?"

She answered yes to the names of Johnny-Boy's comrades; she answered until he asked her no more. Then she thought, How he know the sheriffs men is watchin Lems house? She stood up and held onto her chair, feeling something sure and firm within her.

"How yuh know about Lem?"

"Why . . . How Ah know?"

"Whut yuh doin here this tima night? How yuh know the sheriff got Johnny-Boy?"

"Sue, don yuh believe in me?"

She did not, but she could not answer. She stared at him until her lips hung open; she was searching deep within herself for certainty.

"You meet Reva?" she asked.

"Reva?"

"Yeah, Lems gal?"

"Oh, yeah. Sho, Ah met Reva."

"She tell yuh?"

She asked the question more of herself than of him; she longed to believe.

"Yeah," he said softly. "Ah reckon Ah oughta be goin t tell em now."

"Who?" she asked. "Tell *who?*"

The muscles of her body were stiff as she waited for his answer; she felt as though life depended upon it.

"The comrades," he said.

"Yeah," she sighed.

She did not know when he left; she was not looking or listening. She just suddenly saw the room empty and from her the thing that had made her fearful was gone.

<h1 style="text-align:center">V</h1>

For a space of time that seemed to her as long as she had been upon the earth, she sat huddled over the cold stove. One minute she would say to herself, They both gone now; Johnny-Boy n Sug . . . Mabbe Ahll never see em ergin. Then a surge of guilt would blot out her longing. "Lawd, Ah shouldna tol!" she mumbled. "But no man kin be so lowdown as to do a thing like that . . ." Several times she had an impulse to try to tell the comrades herself; she was feeling a little better now. But what good would that do? She had told Booker the names. He jus couldnt be a Judas to po folks like us . . . He *couldnt!*

"An Sue!"

Thas Reva! Her heart leaped with an anxious gladness. She rose without answering and limped down the dark hallway. Through the open door, against the background of rain, she saw Reva's face lit now and then to whiteness by the whirling beams of the beacon. She was about to call, but a thought checked her. Jesus, hep me! Ah gotta tell her bout Johnny-Boy . . . Lawd, Ah cant!

"An Sue, yuh there?"

"C mon in, chile!"

She caught Reva and held her close for a moment without speaking.

"Lawd, Ahm sho glad yuh here," she said at last.

"Ah thought somethin had happened t yuh," said Reva, pulling away. "Ah saw the do open . . . Pa told me to come back n stay wid yuh tonight . . ." Reva paused and started, "W-w-whuts the mattah?"

She was so full of having Reva with her that she did not understand what the question meant.

"Hunh?"

"Yo neck . . ."

"Aw, it ain nothin, chile. C mon in the kitchen."

"But theres blood on yo neck!"

"The sheriff wuz here . . ."

"Them fools! Whut they wanna bother yuh fer? Ah could kill em! So hep me Gawd, Ah could!"

"It ain nothin," she said.

She was wondering how to tell Reva about Johnny-Boy and Booker. Ahll wait a lil while longer, she thought. Now that Reva was here, her fear did not seem as awful as before.

"C mon, lemme fix yo head, An Sue. Yuh hurt."

They went to the kitchen. She sat silent while Reva dressed her scalp. She was feeling better now; in just a little while she would tell Reva. She felt the girl's finger pressing gently upon her head.

"Tha hurt?"

"A lil, chile."

"Yuh po thing."

"It ain nothin."

"Did Johnny-Boy come?"

She hesitated.

"Yeah."

"He done gone t tell the others?"

Reva's voice sounded so clear and confident that it mocked her. Lawd, Ah cant tell this chile . . .

"Yuh tol im, didnt yuh, An Sue?"

"Y-y-yeah . . ."

"Gee! Thas good! Ah tol pa he didnt hafta worry ef Johnny-Boy got the news. Mabbe thingsll come out awright."

"Ah hope . . ."

She could not go on; she had gone as far as she could. For the first time that night she began to cry.

"Hush, An Sue! Yuh awways been brave. Itll be awright!"

"Ain nothin awright, chile. The worls jus too much fer us, Ah reckon."

"Ef yuh cry that way itll make me cry."

She forced herself to stop. Naw; Ah cant carry on this way in fronta Reva . . . Right now she had a deep need for Reva to believe in her. She watched the girl get pine-knots from behind the stove, rekindle the fire, and put on the coffee pot.

"Yuh wan some cawffee?" Reva asked.

"Naw, honey."

"Aw, c mon, An Sue."

"Jusa lil, honey."

"Thas the way to be. Oh, say, Ah fergot," said Reva, measuring out spoonsful of coffee. "Pa tol me t tell yuh t watch out fer tha Booker man. Hes a stool."

She showed not one sign of outward movement or expression, but as the words fell from Reva's lips she went limp inside.

"Pa tol me soon as Ah got back home. He got word from town . . ."

She stopped listening. She felt as though she had been slapped to the extreme outer edge of life, into a cold darkness. She knew now what she had felt when she had looked up out of her fog of pain and had seen Booker. It was the image of all the white folks, and the fear that went with them, that she had seen and felt during her lifetime. And again, for the second time that night, something she had felt had come true. All she could say to herself was, Ah didnt like im! Gawd knows, Ah didnt! Ah tol Johnny-Boy it wuz some of them white folks . . .

"Here; drink yo cawffee . . ."

She took the cup; her fingers trembled, and the steaming liquid spilt onto her dress and leg.

"Ahm sorry, An Sue!"

Her leg was scalded, but the pain did not bother her.

"Its awright," she said.

"Wait; lemme put some lard on tha burn!"

"It don hurt."

"Yuh worried bout somethin."

"Naw, honey."

"Lemme fix yuh so mo cawffee."

"Ah don wan nothin now, Reva."

"Waal, buck up. Don be tha way . . ."

They were silent. She heard Reva drinking. No; she would not tell Reva; Reva was all she had left. But she had to do something, some way, somehow. She was undone too much as it was; and to tell Reva about Booker or Johnny-Boy was more than she was equal to; it would be too coldly shameful. She wanted to be alone and fight this thing out with herself.

"Go t bed, honey. Yuh tired."

"Naw; Ahm awright, An Sue."

She heard the bottom of Reva's empty cup clank against the top of the stove. Ah *got* t make her go t bed! Yes; Booker would tell the names of the comrades to the sheriff. If she could only stop him some way! That was the answer, the point, the star that grew bright in the morning of new hope. Soon, maybe half an hour from now, Booker would reach Foleys Woods. Hes boun t go the long way, cause he don know no short cut, she thought. Ah could wade the creek n beat im there . . . But what would she do after that?

"Reva, honey, go t bed. Ahm awright. Yuh need res."

"Ah ain sleepy, An Sue."

"Ah knows whuts bes fer yuh, chile. Yuh tired n wet."

"Ah wanna stay up wid yuh."

She forced a smile and said:

"Ah don think they gonna hurt Johnny-Boy . . ."

"Fer *real*, An Sue?"

"Sho, honey."

"But Ah wanna wait up wid yuh."

"Thas mah job, honey. Thas whut a mas fer, t wait up fer her chullun."

"Good night, An Sue."

"Good night, honey."

She watched Reva pull up and leave the kitchen; presently she heard the shucks in the mattress whispering, and she knew that Reva had gone to bed. She was alone. Through the cracks of the stove she saw the fire dying to grey ashes; the room was growing cold again. The yellow beacon continued to flit past the window and the rain still drummed. Yes; she was alone; she had done this awful thing alone; she must find some way out, alone. Like touching a festering sore, she put her finger upon that moment when she had shouted her defiance to the sheriff, when she had shouted to feel her strength. She had lost Sug to save others; she had let Johnny-Boy go to save others; and then in a moment of weakness that came from too much strength she had lost all. If she had not shouted to the sheriff, she would have been strong enough to have resisted Booker; she would have been able to tell the comrades herself. Something tightened in her as she remembered and understood the fit of fear she had felt on coming to herself in the dark hallway. A part of her life she thought she had done away with forever had had hold of her then. She had thought the soft, warm past was over; she had thought that it did not mean much when now she sang: *"Hes the Lily of the Valley, the Bright n Mawnin Star"* . . . The days when she had sung that song were the days when she had not hoped for anything on this earth, the days when the cold mountain had driven her into the arms of Jesus. She had thought that Sug and Johnny-Boy had taught her to forget Him, to fix her hope upon the fight of black men for freedom. Through the gradual years she had believed and worked with them, had felt strength shed from the grace of their terrible vision. That grace had been upon her when she had let the sheriff slap her down; it had been upon her when she had risen time and again from the floor and faced him. But she had trapped herself with her own hunger; to water the long, dry thirst of her faith; her pride had made a bargain which her flesh could not keep. Her having told the names of Johnny-

Boy's comrades was but an incident in a deeper horror. She stood up and looked at the floor while call and counter-call, loyalty and counter-loyalty struggled in her soul. Mired she was between two abandoned worlds, living, but dying without the strength of the grace that either gave. The clearer she felt it the fuller did something well up from the depths of her for release; the more urgent did she feel the need to fling into her black sky another star, another hope, one more terrible vision to give her the strength to live and act. Softly and restlessly she walked about the kitchen, feeling herself naked against the night, the rain, the world; and shamed whenever the thought of Reva's love crossed her mind. She lifted her empty hands and looked at her writhing fingers. Lawd, whut kin Ah do now? She could still wade the creek and get to Foleys Woods before Booker. And then what? How could she manage to see Johnny-Boy or Booker? Again she heard the sheriff's threatening voice: Git yuh a sheet, cause hes gonna be dead! The sheet! Thas it, the *sheet!* Her whole being leaped with will; the long years of her life bent toward a moment of focus, a point. Ah kin go wid mah sheet! Ahll be doin whut he said! Lawd Gawd in Heaven, Ahma go lika nigger woman wid mah windin sheet t git mah dead son! But then what? She stood straight and smiled grimly; she had in her heart the whole meaning of her life; her entire personality was poised on the brink of a total act. Ah know! Ah *know!* She thought of Johnny-Boy's gun in the dresser drawer. Ahll hide the gun in the sheet n go aftah Johnny-Boys body. . . . She tiptoed to her room, eased out the dresser drawer, and got a sheet. Reva was sleeping; the darkness was filled with her quiet breathing. She groped in the drawer and found the gun. She wound the gun in the sheet and held them both under her apron. Then she stole to the bedside and watched Reva. Lawd, hep her! But mabbe shes bettah off. This had t happen sometime . . . She n Johnny-Boy couldna been together in this here South . . . N Ah couldnt tell her about Booker. Itll come out awright n she wont nevah know. Reva's trust would never be shaken. She caught her breath as the shucks in the mattress rustled dryly; then all was quiet and she breathed easily again. She tiptoed to the door, down the hall, and stood on the porch. Above her the yellow beacon whirled through the rain. She went over the muddy ground, mounted a slope, stopped and looked back at her house. The lamp glowed in her window, and the yellow beacon that swung every few seconds seemed to feed it with light. She turned and started across the fields, holding the gun and sheet tightly, thinking, Po Reva . . . Po critter . . . Shes fas ersleep . . .

VI

For the most part she walked with her eyes half shut, her lips tightly compressed, leaning her body against the wind and the driving rain, feeling the pistol in the sheet sagging cold and heavy in her fingers. Already she was getting wet; it seemed that her feet found every puddle of water that stood between the corn rows.

She came to the edge of the creek and paused, wondering at what point was it low. Taking the sheet from under her apron, she wrapped the gun in it so that her finger could be upon the trigger. Ahll cross here, she thought. At first she did not feel the water; her feet were already wet. But the water grew cold as it came up to her knees; she gasped when it reached her waist. Lawd, this creeks high! When she had passed the middle, she knew that she was out of danger. She came out of

the water, climbed a grassy hill, walked on, turned a bend and saw the lights of
autos gleaming ahead. Yeah; theys still there! She hurried with her head down.
Wondah did Ah beat im here? Lawd, Ah *hope* so! A vivid image of Booker's
white face hovered a moment before her eyes and a surging will rose up in her so
hard and strong that it vanished. She was among the autos now. From nearby
came the hoarse voices of the men.

"Hey, yuh!"

She stopped, nervously clutching the sheet. Two white men with shotguns
came toward her.

"Whut in hell yuh doin out here?"

She did not answer.

"Didnt yuh hear somebody speak t yuh?"

"Ahm comin aftah mah son," she said humbly.

"Yo *son?*"

"Yessuh."

"What yo son doin out here?"

"The sheriffs got im."

"Holy Scott! Jim, its the niggers ma!"

"Whut yuh got there?" asked one.

"A sheet."

"A *sheet?*"

"Yessuh."

"Fer whut?"

"The sheriff tol me t bring a sheet t git his body."

"Waal, waal . . ."

"Now, ain tha somethin?"

The white men looked at each other.

"These niggers sho love one ernother," said one.

"N tha ain no lie," said the other.

"Take me t the sheriff," she begged.

"Yuh ain given us *orders,* is yuh?"

"Nawsuh."

"Well take yuh when wes good n ready."

"Yessuh."

"So yuh wan his body?"

"Yessuh."

"Waah, he ain dead yit."

"They gonna kill im," she said.

"Ef he talks they wont."

"He ain gonna talk," she said.

"How yuh know?"

"Cause he ain."

"We got ways of makin niggers talk."

"Yuh ain got no way fer im."

"Yuh thinka lot of that black Red, don yuh?"

"Hes mah son."

"Why don yuh teach im some sense?"

"Hes mah son," she said again.

"Lissen, ol nigger woman, yuh stand there wid yo hair white. Yuh got bettah
sense than t believe tha niggers kin make a revolution . . ."

"A black republic," said the other one, laughing.

"Take me t the sheriff," she begged.

"Yuh his ma," said one. "Yuh kin make im talk n tell whose in this thing wid im."

"He ain gonna talk," she said.

"Don yuh wan im t live?"

She did not answer.

"C mon, les take her t Bradley."

They grabbed her arms and she clutched hard at the sheet and gun; they led her toward the crowd in the woods. Her feelings were simple; Booker would not tell; she was there with the gun to see to that. The louder became the voices of the men the deeper became her feeling of wanting to right the mistake she had made; of wanting to fight her way back to solid ground. She would stall for time until Booker showed up. Oh, ef theyll only lemme git close t Johnny-Boy! As they led her near the crowd she saw white faces turning and looking at her and heard a rising clamor of voices.

"Whose tha?"

"A nigger woman!"

"Whut she doin out here?"

"This is his ma!" called one of the men.

"Whut she wans?"

"She brought a sheet t cover his body!"

"He ain dead yit!"

"They tryin t make im talk!"

"But he will be dead soon ef he don open up!"

"Say, look! The niggers ma brought a sheet t cover up his body!"

"Now, ain that sweet?"

"Mabbe she wans t hol a prayer meetin!"

"Did she git a preacher?"

"Say, go git Bradley!"

"O.K.!"

The crowd grew quiet. They looked at her curiously; she felt their cold eyes trying to detect some weakness in her. Humbly, she stood with the sheet covering the gun. She had already accepted all that they could do to her.

The sheriff came.

"So yuh brought yuh sheet, hunh?"

"Yessuh," she whispered.

"Looks like them slaps we gave yuh learned yuh some sense, didnt they?"

She did not answer.

"Yuh don need tha sheet. Yo son ain dead yit," he said, reaching toward her.

She backed away, her eyes wide.

"Naw!"

"Now, lissen, Anty!" he said. "There ain no use in yuh ackin a fool! Go in there n tell tha nigger son of yos t tell us whos in this wid im, see? Ah promise we wont kill im ef he talks. We'll let im git outta town."

"There ain nothin Ah kin tell im," she said.

"Yuh wan us t kill im?"

She did not answer. She saw someone lean toward the sheriff and whisper.

"Bring her erlong," the sheriff said.

They led her to a muddy clearing. The rain streamed down through the ghostly glare of the flashlights. As the men formed a semi-circle she saw Johnny-Boy lying in a trough of mud. He was tied with rope; he lay hunched and one side of his face rested in a pool of black water. His eyes were staring questioningly at her.

"Speak t im," said the sheriff.

If she could only tell him why she was here! But that was impossible; she was close to what she wanted and she stared straight before her with compressed lips.

"Say, nigger!" called the sheriff, kicking Johnny-Boy. "Heres yo ma!"

Johnny-Boy did not move or speak. The sheriff faced her again.

"Lissen, Anty," he said. "Yuh got mo say wid im than anybody. Tell im t talk n hava chance. Whut he wanna pertect the other niggers n white folks fer?"

She slid her finger about the trigger of the gun and looked stonily at the mud.

"Go t him," said the sheriff.

She did not move. Her heart was crying out to answer the amazed question in Johnny-Boy's eyes. But there was no way now.

"Waal, yuhre astin fer it. By Gawd, we gotta way to *make* yuh talk t im," he said, turning away. "Say, Tim, git one of them logs n turn that nigger upside-down n put his legs on it!"

A murmur of assent ran through the crowd. She bit her lips; she knew what that meant.

"Yuh wan yo nigger son crippled?" she heard the sheriff ask.

She did not answer. She saw them roll the log up; they lifted Johnny-Boy and laid him on his face and stomach, then they pulled his legs over the log. His kneecaps rested on the sheer top of the log's back and the toes of his shoes pointed groundward. So absorbed was she in watching that she felt that it was she who was being lifted and made ready for torture.

"Git a crowbar!" said the sheriff.

A tall, lank man got a crowbar from a nearby auto and stood over the log. His jaws worked slowly on a wad of tobacco.

"Now, its up t yuh, Anty," the sheriff said. "Tell the man whut t do!"

She looked into the rain. The sheriff turned.

"Mabbe she think wes playin. Ef she don say nothin, then break em at the kneecaps!"

"O.K., Sheriff!"

She stood waiting for Booker. Her legs felt weak; she wondered if she would be able to wait much longer. Over and over she said to herself, Ef he came now Ahd kill em both!

"She ain saying nothin, Sheriff!"

"Waal, Gawddammit, let im have it!"

The crowbar came down and Johnny-Boy's body lunged in the mud and water. There was a scream. She swayed, holding tight to the gun and sheet.

"Hol im! Git the other leg!"

The crowbar fell again. There was another scream.

"Yuh break em?" asked the sheriff.

The tall man lifted Johnny-Boy's legs and let them drop limply again, dropping rearward from the kneecaps. Johnny-Boy's body lay still. His head had rolled to one side and she could not see his face.

"Jus lika broke sparrow wing," said the man, laughing softly.

Then Johnny-Boy's face turned to her; he screamed.

"Go way, ma! Go way!"

It was the first time she had heard his voice since she had come out to the woods; she all but lost control of herself. She started violently forward, but the sheriff's arm checked her.

"Aw, naw! Yuh had yo chance!" He turned to Johnny-Boy. "She kin go ef yuh talk."

"Mistah, he ain gonna talk," she said.

"Go way, ma!" said Johnny-Boy.

"Shoot im! Don make im suffah so," she begged.

"He'll either talk or he'll never hear yuh ergin." the sheriff said. "Theres other things we kin do t im."

She said nothing.

"Whut yuh come here fer, ma?" Johnny-Boy sobbed.

"Ahm gonna split his eardrums," the sheriff said. "Ef yuh got anythin to say t im yuh bettah say it *now!*"

She closed her eyes. She heard the sheriff's feet sucking in mud. Ah could save im! She opened her eyes; there were shouts of eagerness from the crowd as it pushed in closer.

"Bus em, Sheriff!"

"Fix im so he cant hear!"

"He knows how t do it, too!"

"He busted a Jew boy tha way once!"

She saw the sheriff stoop over Johnny-Boy, place his flat palm over one ear and strike his fist against it with all his might. He placed his palm over the other ear and struck again. Johnny-Boy moaned, his head rolling from side to side, his eyes showing white amazement in a world without sound.

"Yuh wouldnt talk t im when yuh had the chance," said the sheriff. "Try n talk now."

She felt warm tears on her cheeks. She longed to shoot Johnny-Boy and let him go. But if she did that they would take the gun from her, and Booker would tell who the others were. Lawd, hep me! The men were talking loudly now, as though the main business was over. It seemed ages that she stood there watching Johnny-Boy roll and whimper in his world of silence.

"Say, Sheriff, heres somebody lookin fer yuh!"

"Who is it?"

"Ah don know!"

"Bring em in!"

She stiffened and looked around wildly, holding the gun tight. Is tha Booker? Then she held still, feeling that her excitement might betray her. Mabbe Ah kin shoot em both! Mabbe Ah kin shoot *twice!* The sheriff stood in front of her, waiting. The crowd parted and she saw Booker hurrying forward.

"Ah know em all, Sheriff!" he called.

He came full into the muddy clearing where Johnny-Boy lay.

"Yuh mean yuh got the names?"

"Sho! The ol nigger . . ."

She saw his lips hang open and silent when he saw her. She stepped forward and raised the sheet.

"Whut . . ."

She fired, once; then without pausing, she turned, hearing them yell. She aimed at Johnny-Boy, but they had their arms around her, bearing her to the ground, clawing at the sheet in her hand. She glimpsed Booker lying sprawled in the mud, on his face, his hands stretched out before him; then a cluster of yelling men blotted him out. She lay without struggling, looking upward through the rain at the white faces above her. And she was suddenly at peace; they were not a white mountain now; they were not pushing her any longer to the edge of life. Its awright . . .

"She shot Booker!"

"She hada gun in the sheet!"

"She shot im right thu the head!"

"Whut she shoot im fer?"

"Kill the bitch!"

"Ah *thought* somethin wuz wrong bout her!"

"Ah wuz fer givin it t her from the firs!"

"Thas whut yuh git fer treatin a nigger nice!"

"Say, Bookers dead!"

She stopped looking into the white faces, stopped listening. She waited, giving up her life before they took it from her; she had done what she wanted. Ef only Johnny-Boy . . . She looked at him; he lay looking at her with tired eyes. Ef she could only tell im! But he lay already buried in a grave of silence.

"Whut yuh kill im fer, hunh?"

It was the sheriff's voice; she did not answer.

"Mabbe she wuz shootin at yuh, Sheriff?"

"Whut yuh kill im fer?"

She felt the sheriff's foot come into her side; she closed her eyes.

"Yuh black bitch!"

"Let her have it!"

"Yuh reckon she foun out bout Booker?"

"She mighta."

"Jesus Chris, whut yuh dummies *waitin* on!"

"Yeah, kill her!"

"Kill em *both!*"

"Let her know her nigger sons dead firs!"

She turned her head toward Johnny-Boy; he lay looking puzzled in a world beyond the reach of voices. At leas he cant hear, she thought.

"C mon, let im have it!"

She listened to hear what Johnny-Boy could not. They came, two of them, one right behind the other; so close together that they sounded like one shot. She did not look at Johnny-Boy now; she looked at the white faces of the men, hard and wet in the glare of the flashlights.

"Yuh hear tha, nigger woman?"

"Did tha surprise im? Hes in hell now wonderin whut hit im!"

"C mon! Give it t her, Sheriff!"

"Lemme shoot her, Sheriff! It wuz mah pal she shot!"

"Awright, Pete! Thas fair ernuff!"

She gave up as much of her life as she could before they took it from her. But the sound of the shot and the streak of fire that tore its way through her chest forced her to live again, intensely. She had not moved, save for the slight jarring impact of the bullet. She felt the heat of her own blood warming her cold, wet back. She yearned suddenly to talk. "Yuh didnt git whut yuh wanted! N yuh ain gonna nevah git it! Yuh didnt kill me; Ah come here by mahsef . . ." She felt rain falling into her wide-open, dimming eyes and heard faint voices. Her lips moved soundlessly. *Yuh didnt git yuh didnt yuh didnt* . . . Focused and pointed she was, buried in the depths of her star, swallowed in its peace and strength; and not feeling her flesh growing cold, cold as the rain that fell from the invisible sky upon the doomed living and the dead that never dies.

THE END

1937, 1939

Eudora Welty
(1909–   )

Born and raised in Jackson, Mississippi, Eudora Welty's writing is suffused with the scents, colors, and sounds of Mississippi. She is ranked with William Faulkner as one of the most distinctly southern voices to have emerged from the Southern Renaissance. Her observations of her fellow Mississippians are unerring. She is a master of the telling detail that carries the reader along with her into the lives of her characters, into the perfumed beauty parlors and sweltering summer streets where parasoled southern character assassins meet to gossip like dueling butterflies. But while critics admire the true tones of her characters' regional dialect, just as often they praise her transcendence of the limits of regionalism. Her story "Petrified Man" (1941) examines in almost clinical detail the very localized vulgarity Welty observed in and around Jackson. Lee J. Richmond called this story "one of the most pitiless indictments of the venal spirit of modern civilization." Welty's gift for simultaneously evoking the particular and the universal won her a Pulitzer Prize in 1973 for her novel *The Optimist's Daughter* (1972).

Welty has been showered with awards, honors, and fellowships since the 1940s but was not an immediate success early in her career. After attending the Mississippi State College for Women, she transferred to the University of Wisconsin, where she majored in English and graduated in 1929. As the depression economy spiraled, her father urged her to acquire some practical means of supporting herself. To that end she studied advertising at the Columbia University School of Business for a year, but her career did not prosper in New York. She returned to Mississippi in 1931. After her father's death that year, she worked part time for newspapers and radio stations. In 1933 she began working as a publicity agent for the federal Works Progress Administration, traveling throughout Mississippi to write feature stories on the various WPA projects. She was both fascinated and appalled by what she heard in interviews and saw from train windows. However, rather than avert her gaze, she developed her skills as a photographer, recording scenes to study in the evenings. Eventually, she shared her vision of economic disaster: in 1936 her photographs were shown in New York; in 1971 she published *One Time, One Place: Mississippi in the Depression, a Snapshot Album,* and in 1989, *Eudora Welty: Photographs.*

She wrote short stories throughout the 1930s, but none were accepted for publication until 1936, when "The Death of a Traveling Salesman" appeared in the "little" magazine *Manuscript.* Soon after that breakthrough she was discovered and encouraged by Robert Penn Warren and Cleanth Brooks, editors of the *Southern Review.* By 1940 her work had impressed the writer and editor Ford Madox Ford and Katherine Anne Porter, who helped her publish her first collection of stories, *A Curtain of Green* (1941). This collection in-

Eudora Welty reproduced images of the South in her writings and photographs. She shot this picture of Fayette, Mississippi, in the 1930s.

cludes the story "A Worn Path," which won the O. Henry Memorial Contest award in 1942. Welty won the same award in 1943 for the title story of her second collection, *The Wide Net and Other Stories* (1943). She also published a novella, *The Robber Bridegroom,* in 1942. The critical success of these first three books confirmed her place in the national literary scene. She broadened her audience when two of her works were adapted for the stage: in 1956 Jerome Chodorov and Joseph Fields produced a theatrical version of her novella *The Ponder Heart* (1954), and in 1974 *The Robber Bridegroom* was made into a Broadway musical. Both productions were successful, and Welty's reputation continued to grow despite a hiatus in publishing new work, lasting from 1955, when *The Bride of the Innisfallen and Other Stories* appeared, to 1970, when she finally published her longest novel, *Losing Battles.* The action of that novel, set in Tishomingo County, Mississippi, occurs in only two days' time at a family reunion, and flashbacks provide the necessary background information. Welty explains in *Eudora Welty,* "I was trying to describe what the characters' lives were like without benefit of any editorial comment at all, or any interior description. I wanted things shown by speech, by action, and by setting, location."

Although Welty has always been very open and articulate in discussing her experiences and techniques as a creative writer, she has rarely discussed her personal life. Rather than fictionalizing her own biography, Welty attempts to imagine her way into the lives of characters completely unlike herself. At times her characters obtrude themselves upon her, uninvited. As she states in *Eudora Welty,* "Technique springs out of the doing. . . . It's *after* the fact of writing a story that I realize what it has taught me. . . . Writing fiction, I am interpreting every minute, but always by way of the characters' own words and acts. . . . I am in the characters' minds all the time."

In her essay "Place in Fiction" (1957) Welty explains that place "is the named, identified, concrete, exact and exacting, and therefore credible, gathering-spot of all that has been felt, is about to be experienced." With a painterly eye and a perfectly tuned ear, she captures her experiences of her chosen place in her fiction, making the horrific, the hilarious, and the rapturously beautiful equally credible. She varies her placement of the narrative voice, most devastatingly satirizing her grotesque characters from a distance, and exploring other characters from within. Her story "June Recital" (1947) is a narrative tour de force mingling memories with present perceptions, moving from the point of view of a young boy (hanging upside down from a tree, looking into a window of the house next door) to that of his sister (viewing the same scene from inside her own bedroom window).

Whether Welty writes from inside, outside, or in between her characters, she maintains a disciplined distinction between art and autobiography. Requests for an autobiography discouraged her, as she believed that a writer's work, and not an account of his or her life, should be "everything." Her readers were thus astonished when she published her autobiography, *One Writer's Beginnings,* in 1984. Based upon a series of lectures she gave at Harvard University, the book quickly became a bestseller—the first ever published by Harvard University Press, and a demonstration of Welty's broad appeal within, and outside of, academia.

Suggested Readings: *The Robber Bridegroom,* 1942. *Delta Wedding,* 1946. *The Ponder Heart,* 1954. *Losing Battles,* 1970. *The Optimist's Daughter,* 1972. *One Writer's Beginning,* 1984. *Shenandoah: Special Eudora Welty Issue,* XX, No. 2, (Spring) 1969. J. F. Desmond, ed., *A Still Moment: Essays on the Art of Eudora Welty,* 1978. P. W. Prenshaw, ed., *Eudora Welty: Critical Essays,* 1979. M. Kreyling, *Eudora Welty's Achievement of Order,* 1980.

Text Used: *The Collected Stories of Eudora Welty,* 1980.

PETRIFIED MAN*

"Reach in my purse and git me a cigarette without no powder in it if you kin, Mrs. Fletcher, honey," said Leota to her ten o'clock shampoo-and-set customer. "I don't like no perfumed cigarettes."

Mrs. Fletcher gladly reached over to the lavender shelf under the lavender-framed mirror, shook a hair net loose from the clasp of the patent-leather bag, and slapped her hand down quickly on a powder puff which burst out when the purse was opened.

"Why, look at the peanuts, Leota!" said Mrs. Fletcher in her marvelling voice.

"Honey, them goobers has been in my purse a week if they's been in it a day. Mrs. Pike bought them peanuts."

"Who's Mrs. Pike?" asked Mrs. Fletcher, settling back. Hidden in this den of curling fluid and henna packs, separated by a lavender swingdoor from the other customers, who were being gratified in other booths, she could give her curiosity its freedom. She looked expectantly at the black part in Leota's yellow curls as she bent to light the cigarette.

"Mrs. Pike is this lady from New Orleans," said Leota, puffing, and pressing into Mrs. Fletcher's scalp with strong red-nailed fingers. "A friend, not a customer. You see, like maybe I told you last time, me and Fred and Sal and Joe all

---

* First collected in *A Curtain of Green* (1941).

had us a fuss, so Sal and Joe up and moved out, so we didn't do a thing but rent out their room. So we rented it to Mrs. Pike. And Mr. Pike." She flicked an ash into the basket of dirty towels. "Mrs. Pike is a very decided blonde. *She* bought me the peanuts."

"She must be cute," said Mrs. Fletcher.

"Honey, 'cute' ain't the word for what she is. I'm tellin' you, Mrs. Pike is attractive. She has her a good time. She's got a sharp eye out, Mrs. Pike has."

She dashed the comb through the air, and paused dramatically as a cloud of Mrs. Fletcher's hennaed hair floated out of the lavender teeth like a small storm-cloud.

"Hair fallin'."

"Aw, Leota."

"Uh-huh, commencin' to fall out," said Leota, combing again, and letting fall another cloud.

"Is it any dandruff in it?" Mrs. Fletcher was frowning, her hair-line eyebrows diving down toward her nose, and her wrinkled, beady-lashed eyelids batting with concentration.

"Nope." She combed again. "Just fallin' out."

"Bet it was that last perm'nent you gave me that did it," Mrs. Fletcher said cruelly. "Remember you cooked me fourteen minutes."

"You had fourteen minutes comin' to you," said Leota with finality.

"Bound to be somethin'," persisted Mrs. Fletcher. "Dandruff, dandruff. I couldn't of caught a thing like that from Mr. Fletcher, could I?"

"Well," Leota answered at last, "you know what I heard in here yestiddy, one of Thelma's ladies was settin' over yonder in Thelma's booth gittin' a mach-ineless, and I don't mean to insist or insinuate or anything, Mrs. Fletcher, but Thelma's lady just happ'med to throw out—I forgotten what she was talkin' about at the time—that you was p-r-e-g., and lots of times that'll make your hair do awful funny, fall out and God knows what all. It just ain't our fault, is the way I look at it."

There was a pause. The women stared at each other in the mirror.

"Who was it?" demanded Mrs. Fletcher.

"Honey, I really couldn't say," said Leota, "Not that you look it."

"Where's Thelma? I'll get it out of her," said Mrs. Fletcher.

"Now, honey, I wouldn't go and git mad over a little thing like that," Leota said, combing hastily, as though to hold Mrs. Fletcher down by the hair. "I'm sure it was somebody didn't mean no harm in the world. How far gone are you?"

"Just wait," said Mrs. Fletcher, and shrieked for Thelma, who came in and took a drag from Leota's cigarette.

"Thelma, honey, throw your mind back to yestiddy if you kin," said Leota, drenching Mrs. Fletcher's hair with a thick fluid and catching the overflow in a cold wet towel at her neck.

"Well, I got my lady half wound for a spiral," said Thelma doubtfully.

"This won't take but a minute," said Leota. "Who is it you got in there, old Horse Face? Just cast your mind back and try to remember who your lady was yestiddy who happ'm to mention that my customer was pregnant, that's all. She's dead to know."

Thelma drooped her blood-red lips and looked over Mrs. Fletcher's head into the mirror. "Why, honey, I ain't got the faintest," she breathed. "I really don't recollect the faintest. But I'm sure she meant no harm. I declare, I forgot my hair finally got combed and thought it was a stranger behind me."

"Was it that Mrs. Hutchinson?" Mrs. Fletcher was tensely polite.

"Mrs. Hutchinson? Oh, Mrs. Hutchinson." Thelma batted her eyes. "Naw, precious, she come on Thursday and didn't ev'm mention your name. I doubt if she ev'm knows you're on the way."

"Thelma!" cried Leota staunchly.

"All I know is, whoever it is 'll be sorry some day. Why, I just barely knew it myself!" cried Mrs. Fletcher. "Just let her wait!"

"Why? What're you gonna do to her?"

It was a child's voice, and the women looked down. A little boy was making tents with aluminum wave pinchers on the floor under the sink.

"Billy Boy, hon, mustn't bother nice ladies," Leota smiled. She slapped him brightly and behind her back waved Thelma out of the booth. "Ain't Billy Boy a sight? Only three years old and already just nuts about the beauty-parlor business."

"I never saw him here before," said Mrs. Fletcher, still unmollified.

"He ain't been here before; that's how come," said Leota. "He belongs to Mrs. Pike. She got her a job but it was Fay's Millinery. He oughtn't to try on those ladies' hats, they come down over his eyes like I don't know what. They just git to look ridiculous, that's what, an' of course he's gonna put 'em on: hats. They tole Mrs. Pike they didn't appreciate him hangin' around there. Here, he couldn't hurt a thing."

"Well! I don't like children that much," said Mrs. Fletcher.

"Well!" said Leota, moodily.

"Well! I'm almost tempted not to have this one," said Mrs. Fletcher. "That Mrs. Hutchinson! Just looks straight through you when she sees you on the street and then spits at you behind your back."

"Mr. Fletcher would beat you on the head if you didn't have it now," said Leota reasonably. "After going this far."

Mrs. Fletcher sat up straight. "Mr. Fletcher can't do a thing with me."

"He can't!" Leota winked at herself in the mirror.

"No, siree, he can't. If he so much as raises his voice against me, he knows good and well I'll have one of my sick headaches, and then I'm just not fit to live with. And if I really look that pregnant already—"

"Well, now, honey, I just want you to know—I habm't told any of my ladies and I ain't goin' to tell 'em—even that you're losin' your hair. You just get you one of those Stork-a-Lure dresses and stop worryin'. What people don't know don't hurt nobody, as Mrs. Pike says."

"Did you tell Mrs. Pike?" asked Mrs. Fletcher sulkily.

"Well, Mrs. Fletcher, look, you ain't ever goin' to lay eyes on Mrs. Pike or her lay eyes on you, so what diffunce does it make in the long run?"

"I knew it!" Mrs. Fletcher deliberately nodded her head so as to destroy a ringlet Leota was working on behind her ear. "Mrs. Pike!"

Leota sighed. "I reckon I might as well tell you. It wasn't any more Thelma's lady tole me you was pregnant than a bat."

"Not Mrs. Hutchinson?"

"Naw, Lord! It was Mrs. Pike."

"Mrs. Pike!" Mrs. Fletcher could only sputter and let curling fluid roll into her ear. "How could Mrs. Pike possibly know I was pregnant or otherwise, when she doesn't even know me? The nerve of some people!"

"Well, here's how it was. Remember Sunday?"

"Yes," said Mrs. Fletcher.

"Sunday, Mrs. Pike an' me was all by ourself. Mr. Pike and Fred had gone over to Eagle Lake, sayin' they was goin' to catch 'em some fish, but they didn't a course. So we was settin' in Mrs. Pike's car, it's a 1939 Dodge—"

"1939, eh," said Mrs. Fletcher.

"—An' we was gettin' us a Jax beer apiece—that's the beer that Mrs. Pike says is made right in N.O.,[1] so she won't drink no other kind. So I seen you drive up to the drugstore an' run in for just a secont, leavin' I reckon Mr. Fletcher in the car, an' come runnin' out with looked like a perscription. So I says to Mrs. Pike, just to be makin' talk, 'Right yonder's Mrs. Fletcher, and I reckon that's Mr. Fletcher—she's one of my regular customers,' I says."

"I had on a figured print," said Mrs. Fletcher tentatively.

"You sure did," agreed Leota. "So Mrs. Pike, she give you a good look—she's very observant, a good judge of character, cute as a minute, you know—and she says, 'I bet you another Jax that lady's three months on the way.'"

"What gall!" said Mrs. Fletcher. "Mrs. Pike!"

"Mrs. Pike ain't goin' to bite you," said Leota. "Mrs. Pike is a lovely girl, you'd be crazy about her, Mrs. Fletcher. But she can't sit still a minute. We went to the travellin' freak show yestiddy after work. I got through early—nine o'clock. In the vacant store next door. What, you ain't been?"

"No, I despise freaks," declared Mrs. Fletcher.

"Aw. Well, honey, talkin' about bein' pregnant an' all, you ought to see those twins in a bottle, you really owe it to yourself."

"What twins?" asked Mrs. Fletcher out of the side of her mouth.

"Well, honey, they got these two twins in a bottle, see? Born joined plumb together—dead a course." Leota dropped her voice into a soft lyrical hum. "They was about this long—pardon—must of been full time, all right, wouldn't you say?—an' they had these two heads an' two faces an' four arms an' four legs, all kind of joined *here*. See, this face looked this-a-way, and the other face looked that-a-way, over their shoulder, see. Kinda pathetic."

"Glah!" said Mrs. Fletcher disapprovingly.

"Well, ugly? Honey, I mean to tell you—their parents was first cousins and all like that. Billy Boy, git me a fresh towel from off Teeny's stack—this 'n's wringin' wet—an' quit ticklin' my ankles with that curler. I declare! He don't miss nothin'."

"Me and Mr. Fletcher aren't one speck of kin, or he could never of had me," said Mrs. Fletcher placidly.

"Of course not!" protested Leota. "Neither is me an' Fred, not that we know of. Well, honey, what Mrs. Pike liked was the pygmies. They've got these pygmies down there, too, an' Mrs. Pike was just wild about 'em. You know, the teeniniest men in the universe? Well, honey, they can just rest back on their little bohunkus an' roll around an' you can't hardly tell if they're sittin' or standin'. That'll give you some idea. They're about forty-two years old. Just suppose it was your husband!"

"Well, Mr. Fletcher is five foot nine and one half," said Mrs. Fletcher quickly.

"Fred's five foot ten," said Leota, "but I tell him he's still a shrimp, account of I'm so tall." She made a deep wave over Mrs. Fletcher's other temple with the comb. "Well, these pygmies are a kind of a dark brown, Mrs. Fletcher. Not bad lookin' for what they are, you know."

---

[1] New Orleans.

"I wouldn't care for them," said Mrs. Fletcher. "What does that Mrs. Pike see in them?"

"Aw, I don't know," said Leota. "She's just cute, that's all. But they got this man, this petrified man, that ever'thing ever since he was nine years old, when it goes through his digestion, see, somehow Mrs. Pike says it goes to his joints and has been turning to stone."

"How awful!" said Mrs. Fletcher.

"He's forty-two too. That looks like a bad age."

"Who said so, that Mrs. Pike? I bet she's forty-two," said Mrs. Fletcher.

"Naw," said Leota, "Mrs. Pike's thirty-three, born in January, an Aquarian. He could move his head—like this. A course his head and mind ain't a joint, so to speak, and I guess his stomach ain't, either—not yet, anyways. But see—his food, he eats it, and it goes down, see, and then he digests it"—Leota rose on her toes for an instant—"and it goes out to his joints and before you can say 'Jack Robinson,'[2] it's stone—pure stone. He's turning to stone. How'd you like to be married to a guy like that? All he can do, he can move his head just a quarter of an inch. A course he *looks* just *terrible*."

"I should think he would," said Mrs. Fletcher frostily. "Mr. Fletcher takes bending exercises every night of the world. I make him."

"All Fred does is lay around the house like a rug. I wouldn't be surprised if he woke up some day and couldn't move. The petrified man just sat there moving his quarter of an inch though," said Leota reminiscently.

"Did Mrs. Pike like the petrified man?" asked Mrs. Fletcher.

"Not as much as she did the others," said Leota deprecatingly. "And then she likes a man to be a good dresser, and all that."

"Is Mr. Pike a good dresser?" asked Mrs. Fletcher sceptically.

"Oh, well, yeah," said Leota, "but he's twelve or fourteen years older'n her. She ast Lady Evangeline about him."

"Who's Lady Evangeline?" asked Mrs. Fletcher.

"Well, it's this mind reader they got in the freak show," said Leota. "Was real good. Lady Evangeline is her name, and if I had another dollar I wouldn't do a thing but have my other palm read. She had what Mrs. Pike said was the 'sixth mind' but she had the worst manicure I ever saw on a living person."

"What did she tell Mrs. Pike?" asked Mrs. Fletcher.

"She told her Mr. Pike was as true to her as he could be and besides, would come into some money."

"Humph!" said Mrs. Fletcher. "What does he do?"

"I can't tell," said Leota, "because he don't work. Lady Evangeline didn't tell me enough about my nature or anything. And I would like to go back and find out some more about this boy. Used to go with this boy until he got married to this girl. Oh, shoot, that was about three and a half years ago, when you was still goin' to the Robert E. Lee Beauty Shop in Jackson.[3] He married her for her money. Another fortune-teller tole me that at the time. So I'm not in love with him any more, anyway, besides being married to Fred, but Mrs. Pike thought, just for the hell of it, see, to ask Lady Evangeline was he happy."

---

[2] A saying thought to derive from a guest known for leaving as suddenly as he arrived; according to James Orchard Halliwell's *Dictionary of Archaic and Provincial Words* (1847), it appeared in a play: "A warke it ys as easie to be doone / As 'tys to saye *Jacke! robys on*."

[3] Jackson, Mississippi.

"Does Mrs. Pike know everything about you already?" asked Mrs. Fletcher unbelievingly. "Mercy!"

"Oh, yeah, I tole her ever'thing about ever'thing, from now on back to I don't know when—to when I first started goin' out," said Leota. "So I ast Lady Evangeline for one of my questions, was he happily married, and she says, just like she was glad I ask her, 'Honey,' she says, 'naw, he idn't. You write down this day, March 8, 1941,' she says, 'and mock it down: three years from today him and her won't be occupyin' the same bed.' There it is, up on the wall with them other dates—see, Mrs. Fletcher? And she says, 'Child, you ought to be glad you didn't git him, because he's so mercenary.' So I'm glad I married Fred. He sure ain't mercenary, money don't mean a thing to him. But I sure would like to go back and have my other palm read."

"Did Mrs. Pike believe in what the fortune-teller said?" asked Mrs. Fletcher in a superior tone of voice.

"Lord, yes, she's from New Orleans. Ever'body in New Orleans believes ever'thing spooky. One of 'em in New Orleans before it was raided says to Mrs. Pike one summer she was goin' to go from State to State and meet some grey-headed men, and, sure enough, she says she went on a beautician convention up to Chicago. . . ."

"Oh!" said Mrs. Fletcher. "Oh, is Mrs. Pike a beautician too?"

"Sure she is," protested Leota. "She's a beautician. I'm goin' to git her in here if I can. Before she married. But it don't leave you. She says sure enough, there was three men who was a very large part of making her trip what it was, and they all three had grey in their hair and they went in six States. Got Christmas cards from 'em. Billy Boy, go see if Thelma's got any dry cotton. Look how Mrs. Fletcher's a-drippin'."

"Where did Mrs. Pike meet Mr. Pike?" asked Mrs. Fletcher primly.

"On another train," said Leota.

"I met Mr. Fletcher, or rather he met me, in a rental library," said Mrs. Fletcher with dignity, as she watched the net come down over her head.

"Honey, me an' Fred, we met in a rumble seat[4] eight months ago and we was practically on what you might call the way to the altar inside of half an hour," said Leota in a guttural voice, and bit a bobby pin open. "Course it don't last. Mrs. Pike says nothin' like that ever lasts."

"Mr. Fletcher and myself are as much in love as the day we married," said Mrs. Fletcher belligerently as Leota stuffed cotton into her ears.

"Mrs. Pike says it don't last," repeated Leota in a louder voice. "Now go git under the dryer. You can turn yourself on, can't you? I'll be back to comb you out. Durin' lunch I promised to give Mrs. Pike a facial. You know—free. Her bein' in the business, so to speak."

"I bet she needs one," said Mrs. Fletcher, letting the swing-door fly back against Leota. "Oh, pardon me."

A week later, on time for her appointment, Mrs. Fletcher sank heavily into Leota's chair after first removing a drugstore rental book, called *Life Is Like That*,[5] from the seat. She stared in a discouraged way into the mirror.

"You can tell it when I'm sitting down, all right," she said.

---

[4] In early-model cars, an open seat that can be folded away when not in use.
[5] A book by W. B. Creighton.

Leota seemed preoccupied and stood shaking out a lavender cloth. She began to pin it around Mrs. Fletcher's neck in silence.

"I said you sure can tell it when I'm sitting straight on and coming at you this way," Mrs. Fletcher said.

"Why, honey, naw you can't," said Leota gloomily, "Why, I'd never know. If somebody was to come up to me on the street and say, 'Mrs. Fletcher is pregnant!' I'd say, 'Heck, she don't look it to me.'"

"If a certain party hadn't found it out and spread it around, it wouldn't be too late even now," said Mrs. Fletcher frostily, but Leota was almost choking her with the cloth, pinning it so tight, and she couldn't speak clearly. She paddled her hands in the air until Leota wearily loosened her.

"Listen, honey, you're just a virgin compared to Mrs. Montjoy," Leota was going on, still absent-minded. She bent Mrs. Fletcher back in the chair and, sighing, tossed liquid from a teacup onto her head and dug both hands into her scalp. "You know Mrs. Montjoy—her husband's that premature-grey-headed fella?"

"She's in the Trojan Garden Club, is all I know," said Mrs. Fletcher.

"Well, honey," said Leota, but in a weary voice, "she come in here not the week before and not the day before she had her baby—she come in here the very selfsame day, I mean to tell you. Child, we was all plumb scared to death. There she was! Come for her shampoo an' set. Why, Mrs. Fletcher, in an hour an' twenty minutes she was layin' up there in the Babtist Hospital with a seb'm-pound son. It was that close a shave. I declare, if I hadn't been so tired I would of drank up a bottle of gin that night."

"What gall," said Mrs. Fletcher. "I never knew her at all well."

"See, her husband was waitin' outside in the car, and her bags was all packed an' in the back seat, an' she was all ready, 'cept she wanted her shampoo an' set. An' havin' one pain right after another. Her husband kep' comin' in here, scared-like, but couldn't do nothin' with her a course. She yelled bloody murder, too, but she always yelled her head off when I give her a perm'nent."

"She must of been crazy," said Mrs. Fletcher. "How did she look?"

"Shoot!" said Leota.

"Well, I can guess," said Mrs. Fletcher. "Awful."

"Just wanted to look pretty while she was havin' her baby, is all," said Leota airily. "Course, we was glad to give the lady what she was after—that's our motto—but I bet a hour later she wasn't payin' no mind to them little end curls. I bet she wasn't thinkin' about she ought to have on a net. It wouldn't of done her no good if she had."

"No, I don't suppose it would," said Mrs. Fletcher.

"Yeah man! She was a-yellin'. Just like when I give her perm'nent."

"Her husband ought to make her behave. Don't it seem that way to you?" asked Mrs. Fletcher. "He ought to put his foot down."

"Ha," said Leota. "A lot he could do. Maybe some women is soft."

"Oh, you mistake me, I don't mean for her to get soft—far from it! Women have to stand up for themselves, or there's just no telling. But now you take me—I ask Mr. Fletcher's advice now and then, and he appreciates it, especially on something important, like is it time for a permanent—not that I've told him about the baby. He says, 'Why, dear, go ahead!' Just ask their *advice*."

"Huh! If I ever ast Fred's advice we'd be floatin' down the Yazoo River[6] on a

---

[6] A river in western Mississippi that flows into the Mississippi River at Vicksburg.

houseboat or somethin' by this time," said Leota. "I'm sick of Fred. I told him to go over to Vicksburg."

"Is he going?" demanded Mrs. Fletcher.

"Sure. See, the fortune-teller—I went back and had my other palm read, since we've got to rent the room agin—said my lover was goin' to work in Vicksburg, so I don't know who she could mean, unless she meant Fred. And Fred ain't workin' here—that much is so."

"Is he going to work in Vicksburg?" asked Mrs. Fletcher. "And—"

"Sure. Lady Evangeline said so. Said the future is going to be brighter than the present. He don't want to go, but I ain't gonna put up with nothin' like that. Lays around the house an' bulls—did bull—with that good-for-nothin' Mr. Pike. He says if he goes who'll cook, but I says I never get to eat anyway—not meals. Billy Boy, take Mrs. Grover that *Screen Secrets* and leg it."

Mrs. Fletcher heard stamping feet go out the door.

"Is that that Mrs. Pike's little boy here again?" she asked, sitting up gingerly.

"Yeah, that's still him." Leota stuck out her tongue.

Mrs. Fletcher could hardly believe her eyes. "Well! How's Mrs. Pike, your attractive new friend with the sharp eyes who spreads it around town that perfect strangers are pregnant?" she asked in a sweetened tone.

"Oh, Mizriz Pike." Leota combed Mrs. Fletcher's hair with heavy strokes.

"You act like you're tired," said Mrs. Fletcher.

"Tired? Feel like its four o'clock in the afternoon already," said Leota. "I ain't told you the awful luck we had, me and Fred? It's the worst thing you ever heard of. Maybe *you* think Mrs. Pike's got sharp eyes. Shoot, there's a limit! Well, you know, we rented out our room to this Mr. and Mrs. Pike from New Orleans when Sal an' Joe Fentress got mad at us 'cause they drank up some home-brew we had in the closet—Sal an' Joe did. So, a week ago Sat'day Mr. and Mrs. Pike moved in. Well, I kinda fixed up the room, you know—put a sofa pillow on the couch and picked some ragged robbins[7] and put in a vase, but they never did say they appreciated it. Anyway, then I put some old magazines on the table."

"I think that was lovely," said Mrs. Fletcher.

"Wait. So, come night 'fore last, Fred and this Mr. Pike, who Fred just took up with, was back from they said they was fishin', bein' as neither one of 'em has got a job to his name, and we was all settin' around in their room. So Mrs. Pike was settin' there, readin' a old *Startling G-Man Tales* that was mine, mind you, I'd bought it myself, and all of a sudden she jumps!—into the air—you'd 'a' thought she'd set on a spider—an' says, 'Canfield'—ain't that silly, that's Mr. Pike—'Canfield, my God A'mighty,' she says, 'honey,' she says, 'we're rich, and you won't have to work.' Not that he turned one hand anyway. Well, me and Fred rushes over to her, and Mr. Pike, too, and there she sets, pointin' her finger at a photo in my copy of *Startling G-Man*. 'See that man?' yells Mrs. Pike. 'Remember him, Canfield?' 'Never forget a face,' says Mr. Pike. 'It's Mr. Petrie, that we stayed with him in the apartment next to ours in Toulouse Street in N.O. for six weeks. Mr. Petrie.' 'Well,' says Mrs. Pike, like she can't hold out one secont longer, 'Mr. Petrie is wanted for five hundred dollars cash, for rapin' four women in California, and I know where he is.'"

"Mercy!" said Mrs. Fletcher. "Where was he?"

---

[7] Perennial plants of the pink family, with clusters of pink or red flowers.

At some time Leota had washed her hair and now she yanked her up by the back locks and sat her up.

"Know where he was?"

"I certainly don't," Mrs. Fletcher said. Her scalp hurt all over.

Leota flung a towel around the top of her customer's head. "Nowhere else but in that freak show! I saw him just as plain as Mrs. Pike. *He* was the petrified man!"

"Who would ever have thought that!" cried Mrs. Fletcher sympathetically.

"So Mr. Pike says, 'Well whatta you know about that,' an' he looks real hard at the photo and whistles. And she starts dancin' and singin' about their good luck. She meant our bad luck! I made a point of tellin' that fortune-teller the next time I saw her. I said, 'Listen, that magazine was layin' around the house for a month, and there was the freak show runnin' night an' day, not two steps away from my own beauty parlor, with Mr. Petrie just settin' there waitin'. An' it had to be Mr. and Mrs. Pike, almost perfect strangers.'"

"What gall," said Mrs. Fletcher. She was only sitting there, wrapped in a turban, but she did not mind.

"Fortune-tellers don't care. And Mrs. Pike, she goes around actin' like she thinks she was Mrs. God," said Leota. "So they're goin' to leave tomorrow, Mr. and Mrs. Pike. And in the meantime I got to keep that mean, bad little old kid here, gettin' under my feet ever' minute of the day an' talkin' back too."

"Have they gotten the five hundred dollars' reward already?" asked Mrs. Fletcher.

"Well," said Leota, "at first Mr. Pike didn't want to do anything about it. Can you feature that? Said he kinda liked that ole bird and said he was real nice to 'em, lent 'em money or somethin'. But Mrs. Pike simply tole him he could just go to hell, and I can see her point. She says, 'You ain't worked a lick in six months, and here I make five hundred dollars in two seconts, and what thanks do I get for it? You go to hell, Canfield,' she says. So," Leota went on in a despondent voice, "they called up the cops and they caught the ole bird, all right, right there in the freak show where I saw him with my own eyes, thinkin' he was petrified. He's the one. Did it under his real name—Mr. Petrie. Four women in California, all in the month of August. So Mrs. Pike gits five hundred dollars. And my magazine, and right next door to my beauty parlor. I cried all night, but Fred said it wasn't a bit of use and to go to sleep, because the whole thing was just a sort of coincidence—you know: can't do nothin' about it. He says it put him clean out of the notion of goin' to Vicksburg for a few days till we rent out the room agin—no tellin' who we'll git this time."

"But can you imagine anybody knowing this old man, that's raped four women?" persisted Mrs. Fletcher, and she shuddered audibly. "Did Mrs. Pike *speak* to him when she met him in the freak show?"

Leota had begun to comb Mrs. Fletcher's hair. "I says to her, I says, 'I didn't notice you fallin' on his neck when he was the petrified man—don't tell me you didn't recognize your fine friend?' And she says, 'I didn't recognize him with that white powder all over his face. He just looked familiar,' Mrs. Pike says, 'and lots of people look familiar.' But she says that ole petrified man did put her in mind of somebody. She wondered who it was! Kep' her awake, which man she'd ever knew it reminded her of. So when she seen the photo, it all come to her. Like a flash. Mr. Petrie. The way he'd turn his head and look at her when she took him in his breakfast."

"Took him in his breakfast!" shrieked Mrs. Fletcher. "Listen—don't tell me. I'd 'a' felt something."

"Four women. I guess those women didn't have the faintest notion at the time they'd be worth a hundred an' twenty-five bucks apiece some day to Mrs. Pike. We ast her how old the fella was then, an' she says he musta had one foot in the grave, at least. Can you beat it?"

"Not really petrified at all, of course," said Mrs. Fletcher meditatively. She drew herself up. "I'd 'a' felt something," she said proudly.

"Shoot! I did feel somethin'," said Leota. "I tole Fred when I got home I felt so funny. I said, 'Fred, that ole petrified man sure did leave me with a funny feelin'.' He says, 'Funny-haha or funny-peculiar?' and I says, 'Funny-peculiar.'" She pointed her comb into the air emphatically.

"I'll bet you did," said Mrs. Fletcher.

They both heard a crackling noise.

Leota screamed, "Billy Boy! What you doin' in my purse?"

"Aw, I'm just eatin' these ole stale peanuts up," said Billy Boy.

"You come here to me!" screamed Leota, recklessly flinging down the comb, which scattered a whole ashtray full of bobby pins and knocked down a row of Coca-Cola bottles. "This is the last straw!"

"I caught him! I caught him!" giggled Mrs. Fletcher. "I'll hold him on my lap. You bad, bad boy, you! I guess I better learn how to spank little old bad boys," she said.

Leota's eleven o'clock customer pushed open the swing-door upon Leota paddling him heartily with the brush, while he gave angry but belittling screams which penetrated beyond the booth and filled the whole curious beauty parlor. From everywhere ladies began to gather round to watch the paddling. Billy Boy kicked both Leota and Mrs. Fletcher as hard as he could, Mrs. Fletcher with her new fixed smile.

Billy Boy stomped through the group of wild-haired ladies and went out the door, but flung back the words, "If you're so smart, why ain't you rich?"

1941

John Cheever
(1912–1982)

"So long as we are possessed by experience that is distinguished by its intensity and its episodic nature, we will have the short story in our literature," John Cheever writes in the 1978 *Newsweek* article "Why I Write Short Stories." Cheever had more than 120 stories published. Though sometimes criticized for narrowly focusing on affluent New Yorkers and suburbanites, his stories strip the veneer of social manners in an act of self-discovery that holds on to the promise of hope amid the possibility of self-disintegration. Mixing a comic, detached irony with painful awareness of his characters' plight, Cheever exposes the emptiness of American high society in the 1950s and 1960s in a way that neither mocks nor condemns its members.

Born in 1912 in Quincy, Massachusetts, Cheever was fifteen when his parents separated. By that time he already knew he wanted to become a writer. His first story, "Expelled" (1930), published in the *New Republic*, fictionalized his recent expulsion from the Thayer Academy in Braintree, Massachusetts. That was to be the end of his formal education (although Harvard University awarded him an honorary degree in 1978). In 1941 Cheever married Mary Winternitz and then spent four years in the army, all the while writing. His first collection of stories, *The Way Some People Live* (1943), draws largely on his family life and marked the beginning of his more than thirty-year-long association with the *New Yorker*. By 1953, with the publication of *The Enormous Radio and Other Stories*, Cheever had begun to perfect his short-story form, dramatizing effectively those intense and episodic experiences that make up short fiction. He then started writing his first novel, *The Wapshot Chronicle* (1957), a National Book Award winner. He considered the novel to be a form more artificial than the short story but again met the novel's narrative demands with *The Wapshot Scandal* (1963), which won the Howells Medal in 1965. *The Wapshot Scandal* reflects Cheever's darkening personal and social vision; this pessimism continued in his work. With the novel *Bullet Park* (1969) Cheever's focus on alcoholics, drug addicts, and other self-destructive characters had reached a nadir. The book was attacked for its "lax composition," and the despair prevalent in his fiction soon spilled over into Cheever's life: his own problems with alcohol, depression, and physical deterioration led up to a heart attack in 1972.

By 1975 Cheever's family insisted that he enter New York City's Smithers Clinic for rehabilitation, and he was released a month later. Out of his recovery came *Falconer* (1977), an instant success and his best novel. With the publication of *The Stories of John Cheever* (1978), Cheever's fame was assured. The collection won a National Book Award, the Edward McDowell Medal, and a Pulitzer Prize in 1979. Containing the stories from his five earlier collections, it charts in chronological order his growth as a master of short fiction. Cheever writes in the preface, "It would please me if the order in which these stories are published had been reversed and if I appeared first as an elderly man and not as a young one who was truly shocked to discover that genuinely decorous men and women admitted into their affairs erotic bitterness and even greed. . . . Even a selected display of one's early work will be a naked history of one's struggle to receive an education in economics and love." As his early story "The Enormous Radio" (1953) attests, that education began as intensely as it ended, and it ended only when Cheever died of cancer in 1982.

Suggested Readings: *The Enormous Radio and Other Stories*, 1953. *The Wapshot Chronicle*, 1957. *The Wapshot Scandal*, 1964. *Bullet Park*, 1969. *The World of Apples*, 1973. *Falconer*, 1977. *Oh What a Paradise It Seems*, 1982. I. Hassan, *Radical Innocence*, 1961. A. Kazin, *Bright Book of Life*, 1973. A. Grant, "The Art of Fiction LXII: John Cheever," in *Paris Review*, 17, (Fall) 1976. L. Walleland, *John Cheever*, 1979. J. Updike, "On Such a Beautiful Green Little Planet," in *New Yorker*, (5 April) 1982.

Text Used: *The Stories of John Cheever*, 1978.

THE ENORMOUS RADIO

Jim and Irene Westcott were the kind of people who seem to strike that satisfactory average of income, endeavor, and respectability that is reached by the statistical reports in college alumni bulletins. They were the parents of two young children, they had been married nine years, they lived on the twelfth floor of an apartment house near Sutton Place,[1] they went to the theatre on an average of 10.3 times a year, and they hoped someday to live in Westchester.[2] Irene Westcott was a pleasant, rather plain girl with soft brown hair and a wide, fine forehead upon which nothing at all had been written, and in the cold weather she wore a coat of fitch[3] skins dyed to resemble mink. You could not say that Jim Westcott looked younger than he was, but you could at least say of him that he seemed to feel younger. He wore his graying hair cut very short, he dressed in the kind of clothes his class had worn at Andover,[4] and his manner was earnest, vehement, and intentionally naïve. The Westcotts differed from their friends, their classmates, and their neighbors only in an interest they shared in serious music. They went to a great many concerts—although they seldom mentioned this to anyone—and they spent a good deal of time listening to music on the radio.

Their radio was an old instrument, sensitive, unpredictable, and beyond repair. Neither of them understood the mechanics of radio—or of any of the other appliances that surrounded them—and when the instrument faltered, Jim would strike the side of the cabinet with his hand. This sometimes helped. One Sunday afternoon, in the middle of a Schubert[5] quartet, the music faded away altogether. Jim struck the cabinet repeatedly, but there was no response; the Schubert was lost to them forever. He promised to buy Irene a new radio, and on Monday when he came home from work he told her that he had got one. He refused to describe it, and said it would be a surprise for her when it came.

The radio was delivered at the kitchen door the following afternoon, and with the assistance of her maid and the handyman Irene uncrated it and brought it into the living room. She was struck at once with the physical ugliness of the large gumwood cabinet. Irene was proud of her living room, she had chosen its furnishings and colors as carefully as she chose her clothes, and now it seemed to her that the new radio stood among her intimate possessions like an aggressive intruder. She was confounded by the number of dials and switches on the instrument panel, and she studied them thoroughly before she put the plug into a wall socket and turned the radio on. The dials flooded with a malevolent green light, and in the distance she heard the music of a piano quintet. The quintet was in the distance for only an instant; it bore down upon her with a speed greater than light and filled the apartment with the noise of music amplified so mightily that it knocked a china ornament from a table to the floor. She rushed to the instrument and reduced the volume. The violent forces that were snared in the ugly gumwood cabinet made her uneasy. Her children came home from school then, and she took them to the Park. It was not until later in the afternoon that she was able to return to the radio.

The maid had given the children their suppers and was supervising their baths when Irene turned on the radio, reduced the volume, and sat down to listen to a Mozart[6] quintet that she knew and enjoyed. The music came through clearly. The new instrument had a much purer tone, she thought, than the old one. She decided that tone was most important and that she could conceal the cabinet behind a sofa. But as soon as she had made her peace with the radio, the interference began. A crackling sound like the noise of a burning powder fuse began to accompany the

---

[1] An exclusive section of New York City, near the East River.
[2] Westchester County, New York, just north of New York City.   [3] Polecat, or ferret.
[4] Andover Academy, a private preparatory school in Andover, Massachusetts.
[5] The Austrian composer Franz Schubert (1797–1828).
[6] The Austrian composer Wolfgang Amadeus Mozart (1756–1791).

singing of the strings. Beyond the music, there was a rustling that reminded Irene unpleasantly of the sea, and as the quintet progressed, these noises were joined by many others. She tried all the dials and switches but nothing dimmed the interference, and she sat down, disappointed and bewildered, and tried to trace the flight of the melody. The elevator shaft in her building ran beside the living-room wall, and it was the noise of the elevator that gave her a clue to the character of the static. The rattling of the elevator cables and the opening and closing of the elevator doors were reproduced in her loudspeaker, and, realizing that the radio was sensitive to electrical currents of all sorts, she began to discern through the Mozart the ringing of telephone bells, the dialing of phones, and the lamentation of a vacuum cleaner. By listening more carefully, she was able to distinguish doorbells, elevator bells, electric razors, and Waring mixers, whose sounds had been picked up from the apartments that surrounded hers and transmitted through her loudspeaker. The powerful and ugly instrument, with its mistaken sensitivity to discord, was more than she could hope to master, so she turned the thing off and went into the nursery to see her children.

When Jim Westcott came home that night, he went to the radio confidently and worked the controls. He had the same sort of experience Irene had had. A man was speaking on the station Jim had chosen, and his voice swung instantly from the distance into a force so powerful that it shook the apartment. Jim turned the volume control and reduced the voice. Then, a minute or two later, the interference began. The ringing of telephones and doorbells set in, joined by the rasp of the elevator doors and the whir of cooking appliances. The character of the noise had changed since Irene had tried the radio earlier; the last of the electric razors was being unplugged, the vacuum cleaners had all been returned to their closets, and the static reflected that change in pace that overtakes the city after the sun goes down. He fiddled with the knobs but couldn't get rid of the noises, so he turned the radio off and told Irene that in the morning he'd call the people who had sold it to him and give them hell.

The following afternoon, when Irene returned to the apartment from a luncheon date, the maid told her that a man had come and fixed the radio. Irene went into the living room before she took off her hat or her furs and tried the instrument. From the loudspeaker came a recording of the "Missouri Waltz."[7] It reminded her of the thin, scratchy music from an old-fashioned phonograph that she sometimes heard across the lake where she spent her summers. She waited until the waltz had finished, expecting an explanation of the recording, but there was none. The music was followed by silence, and then the plaintive and scratchy record was repeated. She turned the dial and got a satisfactory burst of Caucasian music—the thump of bare feet in the dust and the rattle of coin jewelry—but in the background she could hear the ringing of bells and a confusion of voices. Her children came home from school then, and she turned off the radio and went to the nursery.

When Jim came home that night, he was tired, and he took a bath and changed his clothes. Then he joined Irene in the living room. He had just turned on the radio when the maid announced dinner, so he left it on, and he and Irene went to the table.

Jim was too tired to make even a pretense of sociability, and there was nothing about the dinner to hold Irene's interest, so her attention wandered from the food to the deposits of silver polish on the candlesticks and from there to the music in

[7] A popular song with words written in 1916 by James Royce and music by Frederick Knight Logan.

the other room. She listened for a few minutes to a Chopin[8] prelude and then was surprised to hear a man's voice break in. "For Christ's sake, Kathy," he said, "do you always have to play the piano when I get home?" The music stopped abruptly. "It's the only chance I have," a woman said. "I'm at the office all day." "So am I," the man said. He added something obscene about an upright piano, and slammed a door. The passionate and melancholy music began again.

"Did you hear that?" Irene asked.

"What?" Jim was eating his dessert.

"The radio. A man said something while the music was still going on—something dirty."

"It's probably a play."

"I don't think it *is* a play," Irene said.

They left the table and took their coffee into the living room. Irene asked Jim to try another station. He turned the knob. "Have you seen my garters?" a man asked. "Button me up," a woman said. "Have you seen my garters?" the man said again. "Just button me up and I'll find your garters," the woman said. Jim shifted to another station. "I wish you wouldn't leave apple cores in the ashtrays," a man said. "I hate the smell."

"This is strange," Jim said.

"Isn't it?" Irene said.

Jim turned the knob again. "'On the coast of Coromandel[9] where the early pumpkins blow,'" a woman with a pronounced English accent said, "'in the middle of the woods lived the Yonghy-Bonghy-Bò. Two old chairs, and half a candle, one old jug without a handle . . .'"

"My God!" Irene cried. "That's the Sweeneys' nurse."

"'These were all his worldly goods,'" the British voice continued.

"Turn that thing off," Irene said. "Maybe they can hear *us*." Jim switched the radio off. "That was Miss Armstrong, the Sweeney's nurse," Irene said. "She must be reading to the little girl. They live in 17-B. I've talked with Miss Armstrong in the Park. I know her voice very well. We must be getting other people's apartments."

"That's impossible," Jim said.

"Well, that was the Sweeneys' nurse," Irene said hotly. "I know her voice. I know it very well, I'm wondering if they can hear us."

Jim turned the switch. First from a distance and then nearer, nearer, as if borne on the wind, came the pure accents of the Sweeneys' nurse again: "'*Lady Jingly! Lady Jingly!*'" she said, "'*sitting where the pumpkins blow, will you come and be my wife?* said the Yonghy-Bonghy-Bò . . .'"

Jim went over to the radio and said "Hello" loudly into the speaker.

"'*I am tired of living singly,*'" the nurse went on, "'*on this coast so wild and shingly, I'm a-weary of my life; if you'll come and be my wife, quite serene would be my life . . .*'"

"I guess she can't hear us," Irene said. "Try something else."

Jim turned to another station, and the living room was filled with the uproar of a cocktail party that had overshot its mark. Someone was playing the piano and singing the "Whiffenpoof Song,"[10] and the voices that surrounded the piano were

[8] The Polish composer Frederic Chopin (1810–1849).

[9] A peninsula of northern New Zealand; from "The Courtship of the Yonghy-Bongy-Bò" (1877), a nonsense poem by Edward Lear (1812–1888).

[10] A Yale University drinking song.

vehement and happy. "Eat some more sandwiches," a woman shrieked. There were screams of laughter and a dish of some sort crashed to the floor.

"Those must be the Fullers, in 11-E," Irene said. "I knew they were giving a party this afternoon. I saw her in the liquor store. Isn't this too divine? Try something else. See if you can get those people in 18-C."

The Westcotts overheard that evening a monologue on salmon fishing in Canada, a bridge game, running comments on home movies of what had apparently been a fortnight at Sea Island,[11] and a bitter family quarrel about an overdraft at the bank. They turned off their radio at midnight and went to bed, weak with laughter. Sometime in the night, their son began to call for a glass of water and Irene got one and took it to his room. It was very early. All the lights in the neighborhood were extinguished, and from the boy's window she could see the empty street. She went into the living room and tried the radio. There was some faint coughing, a moan, and then a man spoke. "Are you all right, darling?" he asked. "Yes," a woman said wearily. "Yes, I'm all right, I guess," and then she added with great feeling, "But, you know, Charlie, I don't feel like myself any more. Sometimes there are about fifteen or twenty minutes in the week when I feel like myself. I don't like to go to another doctor, because the doctor's bills are so awful already, but I just don't feel like myself, Charlie. I just never feel like myself." They were not young, Irene thought. She guessed from the timbre of their voices that they were middle-aged. The restrained melancholy of the dialogue and the draft from the bedroom window made her shiver, and she went back to bed.

The following morning, Irene cooked breakfast for the family—the maid didn't come up from her room in the basement until ten—braided her daughter's hair, and waited at the door until her children and her husband had been carried away in the elevator. Then she went into the living room and tried the radio. "I don't want to go to school," a child screamed. "I hate school. I won't go to school. I hate school." "You will go to school," an enraged woman said. "We paid eight hundred dollars to get you into that school and you'll go if it kills you." The next number on the dial produced the worn record of the "Missouri Waltz." Irene shifted the control and invaded the privacy of several breakfast tables. She overheard demonstrations of indigestion, carnal love, abysmal vanity, faith, and despair. Irene's life was nearly as simple and sheltered as it appeared to be, and the forthright and sometimes brutal language that came from the loudspeaker that morning astonished and troubled her. She continued to listen until her maid came in. Then she turned off the radio quickly, since this insight, she realized, was a furtive one.

Irene had a luncheon date with a friend that day, and she left her apartment at a little after twelve. There were a number of women in the elevator when it stopped at her floor. She stared at their handsome and impassive faces, their furs, and the cloth flowers in their hats. Which one of them had been to Sea Island? she wondered. Which one had overdrawn her bank account? The elevator stopped at the tenth floor and a woman with a pair of Skye terriers joined them. Her hair was rigged high on her head and she wore a mink cape. She was humming the "Missouri Waltz."

Irene had two Martinis at lunch, and she looked searchingly at her friend and wondered what her secrets were. They had intended to go shopping after lunch,

---

[11] An island off British Columbia.

but Irene excused herself and went home. She told the maid that she was not to be disturbed; then she went into the living room, closed the doors, and switched on the radio. She heard, in the course of the afternoon, the halting conversation of a woman entertaining her aunt, the hysterical conclusion of a luncheon party, and a hostess briefing her maid about some cocktail guests. "Don't give the best Scotch to anyone who hasn't white hair," the hostess said. "See if you can get rid of that liver paste before you pass those hot things, and could you lend me five dollars? I want to tip the elevator man."

As the afternoon waned, the conversations increased in intensity. From where Irene sat, she could see the open sky above the East River. There were hundreds of clouds in the sky, as though the south wind had broken the winter into pieces and were blowing it north, and on her radio she could hear the arrival of cocktail guests and the return of children and businessmen from their schools and offices. "I found a good-sized diamond on the bathroom floor this morning," a woman said. "It must have fallen out of that bracelet Mrs. Dunston was wearing last night." "We'll sell it," a man said. "Take it down to the jeweler on Madison Avenue[12] and sell it. Mrs. Dunston won't know the difference, and we could use a couple of hundred bucks . . . " "'Oranges and lemons, say the bells of St. Clement's,'" the Sweeneys' nurse sang. "'Halfpence and farthings, say the bells of St. Martin's. When will you pay me? say the bells at old Bailey . . . '"[13] "It's not a hat," a woman cried, and at her back roared a cocktail party. "It's not a hat, it's a love affair. That's what Walter Florell said. He said it's not a hat, it's a love affair," and then, in a lower voice, the same woman added, "Talk to somebody, for Christ's sake, honey, talk to somebody. If she catches you standing here not talking to anybody, she'll take us off her invitation list, and I love these parties."

The Westcotts were going out for dinner that night, and when Jim came home, Irene was dressing. She seemed sad and vague, and he brought her a drink. They were dining with friends in the neighborhood, and they walked to where they were going. The sky was broad and filled with light. It was one of those splendid spring evenings that excite memory and desire, and the air that touched their hands and faces felt very soft. A Salvation Army band was on the corner playing "Jesus Is Sweeter." Irene drew on her husband's arm and held him there for a minute, to hear the music. "They're really such nice people, aren't they?" she said. "They have such nice faces. Actually, they're so much nicer than a lot of the people we know." She took a bill from her purse and walked over and dropped it into the tambourine. There was in her face, when she returned to her husband, a look of radiant melancholy that he was not familiar with. And her conduct at the dinner party that night seemed strange to him, too. She interrupted her hostess rudely and stared at the people across the table from her with an intensity for which she would have punished her children.

It was still mild when they walked home from the party, and Irene looked up at the spring stars. "'How far that little candle throws its beams,'" she exclaimed. "'So shines a good deed in a naughty world.'"[14] She waited that night until Jim had fallen asleep, and then went into the living room and turned on the radio.

Jim came home at about six the next night. Emma, the maid, let him in, and he had taken off his hat and was taking off his coat when Irene ran into the hall. Her

---

[12] A New York City street considered the center of the advertising industry in America.
[13] From the anonymous nursery rhyme "Oranges and Lemons."
[14] From Shakespeare's *Merchant of Venice* (V.i.90–91), spoken by Portia on her return to Belmont.

face was shining with tears and her hair was disordered. "Go up to 16-C, Jim!" she screamed. "Don't take off your coat. Go up to 16-C. Mr. Osborn's beating his wife. They've been quarreling since four o'clock, and now he's hitting her. Go up there and stop him."

From the radio in the living room, Jim heard screams, obscenities, and thuds. "You know you don't have to listen to this sort of thing," he said. He strode into the living room and turned the switch. "It's indecent," he said. "It's like looking in windows. You know you don't have to listen to this sort of thing. You can turn it off."

"Oh, it's so horrible, it's so dreadful," Irene was sobbing. "I've been listening all day, and it's so depressing."

"Well, if it's so depressing, why do you listen to it? I bought this damned radio to give you some pleasure," he said. "I paid a great deal of money for it. I thought it might make you happy. I wanted to make you happy."

"Don't, don't, don't, don't quarrel with me," she moaned, and laid her head on his shoulder. "All the others have been quarreling all day. Everybody's been quarreling. They're all worried about money. Mrs. Hutchinson's mother is dying of cancer in Florida and they don't have enough money to send her to the Mayo Clinic. At least, Mr. Hutchinson says they don't have enough money. And some woman in this building is having an affair with the handyman—with that hideous handyman. It's too disgusting. And Mrs. Melville has heart trouble and Mr. Hendricks is going to lose his job in April and Mrs. Hendricks is horrid about the whole thing and that girl who plays the 'Missouri Waltz' is a whore, a common whore, and the elevator man has tuberculosis and Mr. Osborn has been beating Mrs. Osborn." She wailed, she trembled with grief and checked the stream of tears down her face with the heel of her palm.

"Well, why do you have to listen?" Jim asked again. "Why do you have to listen to this stuff if it makes you so miserable?"

"Oh, don't, don't, don't," she cried. "Life is too terrible, too sordid and awful. But we've never been like that, have we, darling? Have we? I mean, we've always been good and decent and loving to one another, haven't we? And we have two children, two beautiful children. Our lives aren't sordid, are they, darling? Are they?" She flung her arms around his neck and drew his face down to hers. "We're happy, aren't we, darling? We are happy, aren't we?"

"Of course we're happy," he said tiredly. He began to surrender his resentment. "Of course we're happy. I'll have that damned radio fixed or taken away tomorrow." He stroked her soft hair. "My poor girl," he said.

"You love me, don't you?" she asked. "And we're not hypercritical or worried about money or dishonest, are we?"

"No, darling," he said.

A man came in the morning and fixed the radio. Irene turned it on cautiously and was happy to hear a California-wine commercial and a recording of Beethoven's Ninth Symphony, including Schiller's "Ode to Joy."[15] She kept the radio on all day and nothing untoward came from the speaker.

A Spanish suite was being played when Jim came home. "Is everything all right?" he asked. His face was pale, she thought. They had some cocktails and

---

[15] The final movement of the *Ninth Symphony* (1824), by the German composer Ludwig van Beethoven takes as its text the famous hymn "Ode to Joy" (1787), by the German poet and playwright Friedrich von Schiller (1759–1805).

went in to dinner to the "Anvil Chorus" from *Il Trovatore*. This was followed by Debussy's "La Mer."[16]

"I paid the bill for the radio today," Jim said. "It cost four hundred dollars. I hope you'll get some enjoyment out of it."

"Oh, I'm sure I will," Irene said.

"Four hundred dollars is a good deal more than I can afford," he went on. "I wanted to get something that you'd enjoy. It's the last extravagance we'll be able to indulge in this year. I see that you haven't paid your clothing bills yet. I saw them on your dressing table." He looked directly at her. "Why did you tell me you'd paid them? Why did you lie to me?"

"I just didn't want you to worry, Jim," she said. She drank some water. "I'll be able to pay my bills out of this month's allowance. There were the slipcovers last month, and that party."

"You've got to learn to handle the money I give you a little more intelligently, Irene," he said. "You've got to understand that we won't have as much money this year as we had last. I had a very sobering talk with Mitchell today. No one is buying anything. We're spending all our time promoting new issues, and you know how long that takes. I'm not getting any younger, you know. I'm thirty-seven. My hair will be gray next year. I haven't done as well as I'd hoped to do. And I don't suppose things will get any better."

"Yes, dear," she said.

"We've got to start cutting down," Jim said. "We've got to think of the children. To be perfectly frank with you, I worry about money a great deal. I'm not at all sure of the future. No one is. If anything should happen to me, there's the insurance, but that wouldn't go very far today. I've worked awfully hard to give you and the children a comfortable life," he said bitterly. "I don't like to see all of my energies, all of my youth, wasted in fur coats and radios and slipcovers and—"

"Please, Jim," she said. "Please. They'll hear us."

"*Who'll hear us?* Emma can't hear us."

"The radio."

"Oh, I'm sick!" he shouted. "I'm sick to death of your apprehensiveness. The radio can't hear us. Nobody can hear us. And what if they can hear us? Who cares?"

Irene got up from the table and went into the living room. Jim went to the door and shouted at her from there. "Why are you so Christly all of a sudden? What's turned you overnight into a convent girl? You stole your mother's jewelry before they probated her will. You never gave your sister a cent of that money that was intended for her—not even when she needed it. You made Grace Howland's life miserable, and where was all your piety and your virtue when you went to that abortionist? I'll never forget how cool you were. You packed your bag and went off to have that child murdered as if you were going to Nassau.[17] If you'd had any reasons, if you'd had any good reasons—"

Irene stood for a minute before the hideous cabinet, disgraced and sickened, but she held her hand on the switch before she extinguished the music and the voices, hoping that the instrument might speak to her kindly, that she might hear the Sweeneys' nurse. Jim continued to shout at her from the door. The voice on

---

[16] "*The Troubadour*" (Italian), an 1852 opera by the Italian composer Giuseppi Verdi (1813–1901); "*The Sea*" (French), an orchestral piece by the French composer Claude Debussy (1862–1918).

[17] The capital of the Bahamas.

the radio was suave and noncommittal. "An early-morning railroad disaster in Tokyo," the loudspeaker said, "killed twenty-nine people. A fire in a Catholic hospital near Buffalo for the care of blind children was extinguished early this morning by nuns. The temperature is forty-seven. The humidity is eighty-nine."

1953

Bernard Malamud
(1914–1986)

Bernard Malamud remains distinct from Philip Roth and Saul Bellow, all leading modern Jewish-American writers, in both Malamud's portrayal of immigrant Jewish life and his attitudes toward suffering. Malamud's work combines the influence of such figures as Anton Chekhov, Feodor Dostoevski, Ernest Hemingway, and Sherwood Anderson, with the traditional tales of Sholom Alechem and I. L. Peretz, and draws on sources as diverse as the Grail legend, the life of St. Francis of Assisi, and the history of baseball. Born in 1914 in Brooklyn, New York, the son of immigrant Russian parents who ran a grocery store, Malamud earned a bachelor's degree from the City College of New York in 1936 and a master's degree in English from Columbia University in 1942. He first started publishing his stories while he taught night classes at Erasmus Hall High School (his alma mater) and later at Harlem Evening High School. In 1949 he joined the faculty at Oregon State University and later, in *A New Life* (1961), satirized his twelve years there. He joined the faculty at Bennington College in Vermont in 1961 and retired shortly before his death in 1986.

Malamud's early novels were highly allegorical looks at modern-day, suffering man. Malamud's first novel, *The Natural* (1952), mixes the Grail legend with classical allusions to mythologize events loosely based on the 1919 Black Sox baseball scandal and the life of Babe Ruth, among other things. Dark and pessimistic in its outlook, *The Natural* examines the self-interest and greed that deny spiritual fulfillment, both personally and societally. Malamud's next novel, *The Assistant* (1958), uses the story of St. Francis to illuminate the modern day conflict between Jew and non-Jew, focusing on the suffering and the compassion that can lead to spiritual conversion. *The Magic Barrel* (1958), a National Book Award winner, is Malamud's first collection of short stories, and it, too, looks at the bleak lives of tenement dwellers and shop owners, using the structures and rhythms of Yiddish folk tales to organize tales of sacrifice and love.

Idiots First (1963), Malamud's next collection of stories, provides a historical perspective that enriches the allegorical framework Malamud continued to employ. *The Fixer* (1966) combines history, mysticism, and philosophy, all in a novel that moves away from overt allegory to recount the story of a Russian Jew falsely accused of the ritual murder of a Christian child in 1913. It was awarded both a Pulitzer Prize and a National Book Award in 1967. Malamud continued to relax his style in *Pictures of Fidelman* (1969)—"Fidelman" being his mother's maiden name—which returns to the problems of modern Jews, and *The Tenants* (1971), which examines the sometimes violent conflicts between African-Americans and Jews. His novel *Dubin's Lives* (1979) is the story of a biographer, living in Vermont, whose life is split between the history about which he writes and the new life of passion he learns from a young woman. *God's Grace* (1982), marked a return to the allegorical mode for Malamud, though the novel is set in the post-Apocalypse of a nuclear war.

Suggested Readings: *The Natural*, 1952. *The Assistant*, 1958. *The Fixer*, 1966. *Dubin's Lives*, 1975. *The Stories of Bernard Malamud*, 1983. R. Alter, "Malamud as Jewish Writer," in *Commentary* 42, (Sept.) 1966. S. Richman, *Bernard Malamud*, 1966. S. Cohen, *Bernard Malamud and the Trial by Love*, 1974. L. A. Field and J. W. Field, eds., *Bernard Malamud: A Collection of Critical Essays*, 1974. R. Astro and J. Benson, eds., *The Fiction of Bernard Malamud*, 1977. J. Helterman, *Understanding Bernard Malamud*, 1985. H. Bloom, ed., *Bernard Malamud*, 1986.

Text Used: *The Magic Barrel*, 1958.

THE MAGIC BARREL*

Not long ago there lived in uptown New York, in a small, almost meager room, though crowded with books, Leo Finkle, a rabbinical student in the Yeshivah University.[1] Finkle, after six years of study, was to be ordained in June and had been advised by an acquaintance that he might find it easier to win himself a congregation if he were married. Since he had no present prospects of marriage, after two tormented days of turning it over in his mind, he called in Pinye Salzman, a marriage broker whose two-line advertisement he had read in the *Forward*.[2]

The matchmaker appeared one night out of the dark fourth-floor hallway of the graystone rooming house where Finkle lived, grasping a black, strapped portfolio that had been worn thin with use. Salzman, who had been long in the business, was of slight but dignified build, wearing an old hat, and an overcoat too short and tight for him. He smelled frankly of fish, which he loved to eat, and although he was missing a few teeth, his presence was not displeasing, because of an amiable manner curiously contrasted with mournful eyes. His voice, his lips, his wisp of beard, his bony fingers were animated, but give him a moment of repose and his mild blue eyes revealed a depth of sadness, a characteristic that put Leo a little at ease although the situation, for him, was inherently tense.

He at once informed Salzman why he had asked him to come, explaining that his home was in Cleveland, and that but for his parents, who had married comparatively late in life, he was alone in the world. He had for six years devoted himself almost entirely to his studies, as a result of which, understandably, he had found himself without time for a social life and the company of young women. Therefore he thought it the better part of trial and error—of embarrassing fumbling—to call in an experienced person to advise him on these matters. He remarked in passing that the function of the marriage broker was ancient and honorable, highly approved in the Jewish community, because it made practical the necessary without hindering joy. Moreover, his own parents had been brought together by a matchmaker. They had made, if not a financially profitable marriage—since neither had possessed any worldly goods to speak of—at least a successful one in the sense of their everlasting devotion to each other. Salzman listened in embarrassed

---

* The title story of a collection first published in 1958.
[1] A yeshivah is a Jewish seminary; Yeshiva University in New York City offers both secular and religious training.
[2] The *Jewish Daily Forward*, a daily Yiddish newspaper in New York City.

surprise, sensing a sort of apology. Later, however, he experienced a glow of pride in his work, an emotion that had left him years ago, and he heartily approved of Finkle.

The two went to their business. Leo had led Salzman to the only clear place in the room, a table near a window that overlooked the lamp-lit city. He seated himself at the matchmaker's side but facing him, attempting by an act of will to suppress the unpleasant tickle in his throat. Salzman eagerly unstrapped his portfolio and removed a loose rubber band from a thin packet of much-handled cards. As he flipped through them, a gesture and sound that physically hurt Leo, the student pretended not to see and gazed steadfastly out the window. Although it was still February, winter was on its last legs, signs of which he had for the first time in years begun to notice. He now observed the round white moon, moving high in the sky through a cloud menagerie, and watched with half-open mouth as it penetrated a huge hen, and dropped out of her like an egg laying itself. Salzman, though pretending through eyeglasses he had just slipped on, to be engaged in scanning the writing on the cards, stole occasional glances at the young man's distinguished face, noting with pleasure the long, severe scholar's nose, brown eyes heavy with learning, sensitive yet ascetic lips, and a certain, almost hollow quality of the dark cheeks. He gazed around at shelves upon shelves of books and let out a soft, contented sigh.

When Leo's eyes fell upon the cards, he counted six spread out in Salzman's hand.

"So few?" he asked in disappointment.

"You wouldn't believe me how much cards I got in my office," Salzman replied. "The drawers are already filled to the top, so I keep them now in a barrel, but is every girl good for a new rabbi?"

Leo blushed at this, regretting all he had revealed of himself in a curriculum vitae he had sent to Salzman. He had thought it best to acquaint him with his strict standards and specifications, but in having done so, felt he had told the marriage broker more than was absolutely necessary.

He hesitantly inquired, "Do you keep photographs of your clients on file?"

"First comes family, amount of dowry, also what kind promises," Salzman replied, unbuttoning his tight coat and settling himself in the chair. "After comes pictures, rabbi."

"Call me Mr. Finkle. I'm not yet a rabbi."

Salzman said he would, but instead called him doctor, which he changed to rabbi when Leo was not listening too attentively.

Salzman adjusted his horn-rimmed spectacles, gently cleared his throat and read in an eager voice the contents of the top card:

"Sophie P. Twenty four years. Widow one year. No children. Educated high school and two years college. Father promises eight thousand dollars. Has wonderful wholesale business. Also real estate. On the mother's side comes teachers, also one actor. Well known on Second Avenue."

Leo gazed up in surprise. "Did you say a widow?"

"A widow don't mean spoiled, rabbi. She lived with her husband maybe four months. He was a sick boy she made a mistake to marry him."

"Marrying a widow has never entered my mind."

"This is because you have no experience. A widow, especially if she is young and healthy like this girl, is a wonderful person to marry. She will be thankful to you the rest of her life. Believe me, if I was looking now for a bride, I would marry a widow."

Leo reflected, then shook his head.

Salzman hunched his shoulders in an almost imperceptible gesture of disappointment. He placed the card down on the wooden table and began to read another:

"Lily H. High school teacher. Regular. Not a substitute. Has savings and new Dodge car. Lived in Paris one year. Father is successful dentist thirty-five years. Interested in professional man. Well Americanized family. Wonderful opportunity."

"I knew her personally," said Salzman. "I wish you could see this girl. She is a doll. Also very intelligent. All day you could talk to her about books and theyater and what not. She also knows current events."

"I don't believe you mentioned her age?"

"Her age?" Salzman said, raising his brows. "Her age is thirty-two years."

Leo said after a while, "I'm afraid that seems a little too old."

Salzman let out a laugh. "So how old are you, rabbi?"

"Twenty-seven."

"So what is the difference, tell me, between twenty-seven and thirty-two? My own wife is seven years older than me. So what did I suffer?—Nothing. If Rothschild's[3] daughter wants to marry you, would you say on account her age, no?"

"Yes," Leo said dryly.

Salzman shook off the no in the yes. "Five years don't mean a thing. I give you my word that when you will live with her for one week you will forget her age. What does it mean five years—that she lived more and knows more than somebody who is younger? On this girl, God bless her, years are not wasted. Each one that it comes makes better the bargain."

"What subject does she teach in high school?"

"Languages. If you heard the way she speaks French, you will think it is music. I am in the business twenty-five years, and I recommend her with my whole heart. Believe me, I know what I'm talking, rabbi."

"What's on the next card?" Leo said abruptly.

Salzman reluctantly turned up the third card:

"Ruth K. Nineteen years. Honor student. Father offers thirteen thousand cash to the right bridegroom. He is a medical doctor. Stomach specialist with marvelous practice. Brother in law owns own garment business. Particular people."

Salzman looked as if he had read his trump card.[4]

"Did you say nineteen?" Leo asked with interest.

"On the dot."

"Is she attractive?" He blushed. "Pretty?"

Salzman kissed his finger tips. "A little doll. On this I give you my word. Let me call the father tonight and you will see what means pretty."

But Leo was troubled. "You're sure she's that young?"

"This I am positive. The father will show you the birth certificate."

"Are you positive there isn't something wrong with her?" Leo insisted.

"Who says there is wrong?"

"I don't understand why an American girl her age should go to a marriage broker."

A smile spread over Salzman's face.

---

[3] A prominent, wealthy family of European Jews.   [4] An advantage held in reserve until needed.

"So for the same reason you went, she comes."

Leo flushed. "I am pressed for time."

Salzman, realizing he had been tactless, quickly explained. "The father came, not her. He wants she should have the best, so he looks around himself. When we will locate the right boy he will introduce him and encourage. This makes a better marriage than if a young girl without experience takes for herself. I don't have to tell you this."

"But don't you think this young girl believes in love?" Leo spoke uneasily.

Salzman was about to guffaw but caught himself and said soberly, "Love comes with the right person, not before."

Leo parted dry lips but did not speak. Noticing that Salzman had snatched a glance at the next card, he cleverly asked, "How is her health?"

"Perfect," Salzman said, breathing with difficulty. "Of course, she is a little lame on her right foot from an auto accident that it happened to her when she was twelve years, but nobody notices on account she is so brilliant and also beautiful."

Leo got up heavily and went to the window. He felt curiously bitter and up-braided himself for having called in the marriage broker. Finally, he shook his head.

"Why not?" Salzman persisted, the pitch of his voice rising.

"Because I detest stomach specialists."

"So what do you care what is his business? After you marry her do you need him? Who says he must come every Friday night in your house?"

Ashamed of the way the talk was going, Leo dismissed Salzman, who went home with heavy, melancholy eyes.

Though he had felt only relief at the marriage broker's departure, Leo was in low spirits the next day. He explained it as arising from Salzman's failure to pro-duce a suitable bride for him. He did not care for his type of clientele. But when Leo found himself hesitating whether to seek out another matchmaker, one more polished than Pinye, he wondered if it could be—his protestations to the contrary, and although he honored his father and mother—that he did not, in essence, care for the matchmaking institution? This thought he quickly put out of mind yet found himself still upset. All day he ran around in the woods—missed an impor-tant appointment, forgot to give out his laundry, walked out of a Broadway ca-feteria without paying and had to run back with the ticket in his hand; had even not recognized his landlady in the street when she passed with a friend and courte-ously called out, "A good evening to you, Doctor Finkle." By nightfall, however, he had regained sufficient calm to sink his nose into a book and there found peace from his thoughts.

Almost at once there came a knock on the door. Before Leo could say enter, Salzman, commercial cupid, was standing in the room. His face was gray and meager, his expression hungry, and he looked as if he would expire on his feet. Yet the marriage broker managed, by some trick of the muscles, to display a broad smile.

"So good evening. I am invited?"

Leo nodded, disturbed to see him again, yet unwilling to ask the man to leave.

Beaming still, Salzman laid his portfolio on the table. "Rabbi, I got for you tonight good news."

"I've asked you not to call me rabbi. I'm still a student."

"Your worries are finished. I have for you a first-class bride."

"Leave me in peace concerning this subject." Leo pretended lack of interest.

"The world will dance at your wedding."

"Please, Mr. Salzman, no more."

"But first must come back my strength," Salzman said weakly. He fumbled with the portfolio straps and took out of the leather case an oily paper bag, from which he extracted a hard, seeded roll and a small, smoked white fish. With a quick motion of his hand he stripped the fish out of its skin and began ravenously to chew. "All day in a rush," he muttered.

Leo watched him eat.

"A sliced tomato you have maybe?" Salzman hesitantly inquired.

"No."

The marriage broker shut his eyes and ate. When he had finished he carefully cleaned up the crumbs and rolled up the remains of the fish, in the paper bag. His spectacled eyes roamed the room until he discovered, amid some piles of books, a one-burner gas stove. Lifting his hat he humbly asked, "A glass tea you got, rabbi?"

Conscience-stricken, Leo rose and brewed the tea. He served it with a chunk of lemon and two cubes of lump sugar, delighting Salzman.

After he had drunk his tea, Salzman's strength and good spirits were restored.

"So tell me, rabbi," he said amiably, "you considered some more the three clients I mentioned yesterday?"

"There was no need to consider."

"Why not?"

"None of them suits me."

"What then suits you?"

Leo let it pass because he could give only a confused answer.

Without waiting for a reply, Salzman asked, "You remember this girl I talked to you—the high school teacher?"

"Age thirty-two?"

But, surprisingly, Salzman's face lit in a smile. "Age twenty-nine."

Leo shot him a look. "Reduced from thirty-two?"

"A mistake," Salzman avowed. "I talked today with the dentist. He took me to his safety deposit box and showed me the birth certificate. She was twenty-nine years last August. They made her a party in the mountains where she went for a vacation. When her father spoke to me the first time I forgot to write the age and I told you thirty-two, but now I remember this was a different client, a widow."

"The same one you told me about? I thought she was twenty-four?"

"A different. Am I responsible that the world is filled with widows?"

"No, but I'm not interested in them, nor for that matter, in school teachers."

Salzman pulled his clasped hands to his breast. Looking at the ceiling he devoutly exclaimed, "Yiddishe kinder,[5] what can I say to somebody that he is not interested in high school teachers? So what then you are interested?"

Leo flushed but controlled himself.

"In what else will you be interested," Salzman went on, "if you not interested in this fine girl that she speaks four languages and has personally in the bank ten thousand dollars? Also her father guarantees further twelve thousand. Also she has a new car, wonderful clothes, talks on all subjects, and she will give you a first-class home and children. How near do we come in our life to paradise?"

"If she's so wonderful, why wasn't she married ten years ago?"

---

[5] "Jewish children" (Yiddish).

"Why?" said Salzman with a heavy laugh. "—Why? Because she is *partikiler*. This is why. She wants the *best*."

Leo was silent, amused at how he had entangled himself. But Salzman had aroused his interest in Lily H., and he began seriously to consider calling on her. When the marriage broker observed how intently Leo's mind was at work on the facts he had supplied, he felt certain they would soon come to an agreement.

Late Saturday afternoon, conscious of Salzman, Leo Finkle walked with Lily Hirschorn along Riverside Drive.[6] He walked briskly and erectly, wearing with distinction the black fedora he had that morning taken with trepidation out of the dusty hat box on his closet shelf, and the heavy black Saturday coat he had thoroughly whisked clean. Leo also owned a walking stick, a present from a distant relative, but quickly put temptation aside and did not use it. Lily, petite and not unpretty, had on something signifying the approach of spring. She was au courant,[7] animatedly, with all sorts of subjects, and he weighed her words and found her surprisingly sound—score another for Salzman, whom he uneasily sensed to be somewhere around, hiding perhaps high in a tree along the street, flashing the lady signals with a pocket mirror; or perhaps a cloven-hoofed Pan,[8] piping nuptial ditties as he danced his invisible way before them, strewing wild buds on the walk and purple grapes in their path, symbolizing fruit of a union, though there was of course still none.

Lily startled Leo by remarking, "I was thinking of Mr. Salzman, a curious figure, wouldn't you say?"

Not certain what to answer, he nodded.

She bravely went on, blushing, "I for one am grateful for his introducing us. Aren't you?"

He courteously replied, "I am."

"I mean," she said with a little laugh—and it was all in good taste, or at least gave the effect of being not in bad—"do you mind that we came together so?"

He was not displeased with her honesty, recognizing that she meant to set the relationship aright, and understanding that it took a certain amount of experience in life, and courage, to want to do it quite that way. One had to have some sort of past to make that kind of beginning.

He said that he did not mind. Salzman's function was traditional and honorable—valuable for what it might achieve, which, he pointed out, was frequently nothing.

Lily agreed with a sigh. They walked on for a while and she said after a long silence, again with a nervous laugh, "Would you mind if I asked you something a little bit personal? Frankly, I find the subject fascinating." Although Leo shrugged, she went on half embarrassedly, "How was it that you came to your calling? I mean was it a sudden passionate inspiration?"

Leo, after a time, slowly replied, "I was always interested in the Law."

"You saw revealed in it the presence of the Highest?"

He nodded and changed the subject. "I understand that you spent a little time in Paris, Miss Hirschorn?"

"Oh, did Mr. Salzman tell you, Rabbi Finkle?" Leo winced but she went on, "It was ages ago and almost forgotten. I remember I had to return for my sister's wedding."

---

[6] Along the Upper West Side of Manhattan.   [7] In the know (French).
[8] According to Greek myth, a half-man, half-goat god who presided over shepherds and flocks and played musical pipes.

And Lily would not be put off. "When," she asked in a trembly voice, "did you become enamored of God?"

He stared at her. Then it came to him that she was talking not about Leo Finkle, but of a total stranger, some mystical figure, perhaps even passionate prophet that Salzman had dreamed up for her—no relation to the living or dead. Leo trembled with rage and weakness. The trickster had obviously sold her a bill of goods, just as he had him, who'd expected to become acquainted with a young lady of twenty-nine, only to behold, the moment he laid eyes upon her strained and anxious face, a woman past thirty-five and aging rapidly. Only his self control had kept him this long in her presence.

"I am not," he said gravely, "a talented religious person," and in seeking words to go on, found himself possessed by shame and fear. "I think," he said in a strained manner, "that I came to God not because I loved Him, but because I did not."

This confession he spoke harshly because its unexpectedness shook him.

Lily wilted. Leo saw a profusion of loaves of bread go flying like ducks high over his head, not unlike the winged loaves by which he had counted himself to sleep last night. Mercifully, then, it snowed, which he would not put past Salzman's machinations.

He was infuriated with the marriage broker and swore he would throw him out of the room the minute he reappeared. But Salzman did not come that night, and when Leo's anger had subsided, an unaccountable despair grew in its place. At first he thought this was caused by his disappointment in Lily, but before long it became evident that he had involved himself with Salzman without a true knowledge of his own intent. He gradually realized—with an emptiness that seized him with six hands—that he had called in the broker to find him a bride because he was incapable of doing it himself. This terrifying insight he had derived as a result of his meeting and conversation with Lily Hirschorn. Her probing questions had somehow irritated him into revealing—to himself more than her—the true nature of his relationship to God, and from that it had come upon him, with shocking force, that apart from his parents, he had never loved anyone. Or perhaps it went the other way, that he did not love God so well as he might, because he had not loved man. It seemed to Leo that his whole life stood starkly revealed and he saw himself for the first time as he truly was—unloved and loveless. This bitter but somehow not fully unexpected revelation brought him to a point of panic, controlled only by extraordinary effort. He covered his face with his hands and cried.

The week that followed was the worst of his life. He did not eat and lost weight. His beard darkened and grew ragged. He stopped attending seminars and almost never opened a book. He seriously considered leaving the Yeshivah, although he was deeply troubled at the thought of the loss of all his years of study— saw them like pages torn from a book, strewn over the city—and at the devastating effect of this decision upon his parents. But he had lived without knowledge of himself, and never in the Five Books and all the Commentaries—mea culpa[9]— had the truth been revealed to him. He did not know where to turn, and in all this desolating loneliness there was no *to whom,* although he often thought of Lily but not once could bring himself to go downstairs and make the call. He became touchy and irritable, especially with his landlady, who asked him all manner of personal questions; on the other hand, sensing his own disagreeableness, he way-

[9] The Pentateuch, the first five books of the Old Testament, comprise the Jewish Torah, on which interpretive commentaries (the Midrash) have been written; "my fault" (Latin): I have sinned.

laid her on the stairs and apologized abjectly, until mortified, she ran from him. Out of this, however, he drew the consolation that he was a Jew and that a Jew suffered. But gradually, as the long and terrible week drew to a close, he regained his composure and some idea of purpose in life: to go on as planned. Although he was imperfect, the ideal was not. As for his quest of a bride, the thought of continuing afflicted him with anxiety and heartburn, yet perhaps with this new knowledge of himself he would be more successful than in the past. Perhaps love would now come to him and a bride to that love. And for this sanctified seeking who needed a Salzman?

The marriage broker, a skeleton with haunted eyes, returned that very night. He looked, withal, the picture of frustrated expectancy—as if he had steadfastly waited the week at Miss Lily Hirschorn's side for a telephone call that never came.

Casually coughing, Salzman came immediately to the point: "So how did you like her?"

Leo's anger rose and he could not refrain from chiding the matchmaker: "Why did you lie to me, Salzman?"

Salzman's pale face went dead white, the world had snowed on him.

"Did you not state that she was twenty-nine?" Leo insisted.

"I give you my word—"

"She was thirty-five, if a day. *At least* thirty-five."

"Of this don't be too sure. Her father told me—"

"Never mind. The worst of it was that you lied to her."

"How did I lie to her, tell me?"

"You told her things about me that weren't true. You made me out to be more, consequently less than I am. She had in mind a totally different person, a sort of semi-mystical Wonder Rabbi."

"All I said, you was a religious man."

"I can imagine."

Salzman sighed. "This is my weakness that I have," he confessed, "My wife says to me I shouldn't be a salesman, but when I have two fine people that they would be wonderful to be married, I am so happy that I talk too much." He smiled wanly. "This is why Salzman is a poor man."

Leo's anger left him. "Well, Salzman, I'm afraid that's all."

The marriage broker fastened hungry eyes on him.

"You don't want any more a bride?"

"I do," said Leo, "but I have decided to seek her in a different way. I am no longer interested in an arranged marriage. To be frank, I now admit the necessity of premarital love. That is, I want to be in love with the one I marry."

"Love?" said Salzman, astounded. After a moment he remarked, "For us, our love is our life, not for the ladies. In the ghetto they—"

"I know, I know," said Leo. "I've thought of it often. Love, I have said to myself, should be a by-product of living and worship rather than its own end. Yet for myself I find it necessary to establish the level of my need and fulfill it."

Salzman shrugged but answered, "Listen, rabbi, if you want love, this I can find for you also. I have such beautiful clients that you will love them the minute your eyes will see them."

Leo smiled unhappily. "I'm afraid you don't understand."

But Salzman hastily unstrapped his portfolio and withdrew a manila packet from it.

"Pictures," he said, quickly laying the envelope on the table.

Leo called after him to take the pictures away, but as if on the wings of the wind, Salzman had disappeared.

March came. Leo had returned to his regular routine. Although he felt not quite himself yet—lacked energy—he was making plans for a more active social life. Of course it would cost something, but he was an expert in cutting corners; and when there were no corners left he would make circles rounder. All the while Salzman's pictures had lain on the table, gathering dust. Occasionally as Leo sat studying, or enjoying a cup of tea, his eyes fell on the manila envelope, but he never opened it.

The days went by and no social life to speak of developed with a member of the opposite sex—it was difficult, given the circumstances of his situation. One morning Leo toiled up the stairs to his room and stared out the window at the city. Although the day was bright his view of it was dark. For some time he watched the people in the street below hurrying along and then turned with a heavy heart to his little room. On the table was the packet. With a sudden relentless gesture he tore it open. For a half-hour he stood by the table in a state of excitement, examining the photographs of the ladies Salzman had included. Finally, with a deep sigh he put them down. There were six, of varying degrees of attractiveness, but look at them long enough and they all became Lily Hirschorn: all past their prime, all starved behind bright smiles, not a true personality in the lot. Life, despite their frantic yoohooings, had passed them by; they were pictures in a brief case that stank of fish. After a while, however, as Leo attempted to return the photographs into the envelope, he found in it another, a snapshot of the type taken by a machine for a quarter. He gazed at it a moment and let out a cry.

Her face deeply moved him. Why, he could at first not say. It gave him the impression of youth—spring flowers, yet age—a sense of having been used to the bone, wasted; this came from the eyes, which were hauntingly familiar, yet absolutely strange. He had a vivid impression that he had met her before, but try as he might he could not place her although he could almost recall her name, as if he had read it in her own handwriting. No, this couldn't be; he would have remembered her. It was not, he affirmed, that she had an extraordinary beauty—no, though her face was attractive enough; it was that *something* about her moved him. Feature for feature, even some of the ladies of the photographs could do better; but she leaped forth to his heart—had *lived,* or wanted to—more than just wanted, perhaps regretted how she had lived—had somehow deeply suffered: it could be seen in the depths of those reluctant eyes, and from the way the light enclosed and shone from her, and within her, opening realms of possibility: this was her own. Her he desired. His head ached and eyes narrowed with the intensity of his gazing, then as if an obscure fog had blown up in the mind, he experienced fear of her and was aware that he had received an impression, somehow, of evil. He shuddered, saying softly, it is thus with us all. Leo brewed some tea in a small pot and sat sipping it without sugar, to calm himself. But before he had finished drinking, again with excitement he examined the face and found it good: good for Leo Finkle. Only such a one could understand him and help him seek whatever he was seeking. She might, perhaps, love him. How she had happened to be among the discards in Salzman's barrel he could never guess, but he knew he must urgently go find her.

Leo rushed downstairs, grabbed up the Bronx telephone book, and searched for Salzman's home address. He was not listed, nor was his office. Neither was he in the Manahttan book. But Leo remembered having written down the address on a slip of paper after he had read Salzman's advertisement in the "personals" column of the *Forward*. He ran up to his room and tore through his papers, without luck. It was exasperating. Just when he needed the matchmaker he was nowhere to be found. Fortunately Leo remembered to look in his wallet. There on a card he found his name written and a Bronx address. No phone number was listed, the reason—Leo now recalled—he had originally communicated with Salzman by letter. He got on his coat, put a hat on over his skull cap and hurried to the subway station. All the way to the far end of the Bronx he sat on the edge of his seat. He was more than once tempted to take out the picture and see if the girl's face was as he remembered it, but he refrained, allowing the snapshot to remain in his inside coat pocket, content to have her so close. When the train pulled into the station he was waiting at the door and bolted out. He quickly located the street Salzman had advertised.

The building he sought was less than a block from the subway, but it was not an office building, nor even a loft, nor a store in which one could rent office space. It was a very old tenement house. Leo found Salzman's name in pencil on a soiled tag under the bell and climbed three dark flights to his apartment. When he knocked, the door was opened by a thin, asthmatic, gray-haired woman, in felt slippers.

"Yes?" she said, expecting nothing. She listened without listening. He could have sworn he had seen her, too, before but knew it was an illusion.

"Salzman—does he live here? Pinye Salzman," he said, "the matchmaker?"

She stared at him a long minute. "Of course."

He felt embarrassed. "Is he in?"

"No." Her mouth, though left open, offered nothing more.

"The matter is urgent. Can you tell me where his office is?"

"In the air." She pointed upward.

"You mean he has no office?" Leo asked.

"In his socks."

He peered into the apartment. It was sunless and dingy, one large room divided by a half-open curtain, beyond which he could see a sagging metal bed. The near side of a room was crowded with rickety chairs, old bureaus, a three-legged table, racks of cooking utensils, and all the apparatus of a kitchen. But there was no sign of Salzman or his magic barrel, probably also a figment of the imagination. An odor of frying fish made Leo weak to the knees.

"Where is he?" he insisted. "I've got to see your husband."

At length she answered. "So who knows where he is? Every time he thinks a new thought he runs to a different place. Go home, he will find you."

"Tell him Leo Finkle."

She gave no sign she had heard.

He walked downstairs, depressed.

But Salzman, breathless, stood waiting at his door.

Leo was astounded and overjoyed. "How did you get here before me?"

"I rushed."

"Come inside."

They entered. Leo fixed tea, and a sardine sandwich for Salzman. As they were drinking he reached behind him for the packet of pictures and handed them to the marriage broker.

Salzman put down his glass and said expectantly, "You found somebody you like?"

"Not among these."

The marriage broker turned away.

"Here is the one I want." Leo held forth the snapshot.

Salzman slipped on his glasses and took the picture into his trembling hand. He turned ghastly and let out a groan.

"What's the matter?" cried Leo.

"Excuse me. Was an accident this picture. She isn't for you."

Salzman frantically shoved the manila packet into his portfolio. He thrust the snapshot into his pocket and fled down the stairs.

Leo, after momentary paralysis, gave chase and cornered the marriage broker in the vestibule. The landlady made hysterical outcries but neither of them listened.

"Give me back the picture, Salzman."

"No." The pain in his eyes was terrible.

"Tell me who she is then."

"This I can't tell you. Excuse me."

He made to depart, but Leo, forgetting himself, seized the matchmaker by his tight coat and shook him frenziedly.

"Please, "sighed Salzman. "*Please.*"

Leo ashamedly let him go. "Tell me who she is," he begged. "It's very important for me to know."

"She is not for you. She is a wild one—wild, without shame. This is not a bride for a rabbi."

"What do you mean wild?"

"Like an animal. Like a dog. For her to be poor was a sin. This is why to me she is dead now."

"In God's name, what do you mean?"

"Her I can't introduce to you," Salzman cried.

"Why are you so excited?"

"Why, he asks," Salzman said, bursting into tears. "This is my baby, my Stella, she should burn in hell."

Leo hurried up to bed and hid under the covers. Under the covers he thought his life through. Although he soon fell asleep he could not sleep her out of his mind. He woke, beating his breast. Though he prayed to be rid of her, his prayers went unanswered. Through days of torment he endlessly struggled not to love her; fearing success, he escaped it. He then concluded to convert her to goodness, himself to God. The idea alternately nauseated and exalted him.

He perhaps did not know that he had come to a final decision until he encountered Salzman in a Broadway cafeteria. He was sitting alone at a rear table, sucking the bony remains of a fish. The marriage broker appeared haggard, and transparent to the point of vanishing.

Salzman looked up at first without recognizing him. Leo had grown a pointed beard and his eyes were weighted with wisdom.

"Salzman," he said, "love has at last come to my heart."

"Who can love from a picture?" mocked the marriage broker.

"It is not impossible."

"If you can love her, then you can love anybody. Let me show you some new clients that they just sent me their photographs. One is a little doll."

"Just her I want," Leo murmured.

"Don't be a fool, doctor. Don't bother with her."

"Put me in touch with her, Salzman," Leo said humbly. "Perhaps I can be of service."

Salzman had stopped eating and Leo understood with emotion that it was now arranged.

Leaving the cafeteria, he was, however, afflicted by a tormenting suspicion that Salzman had planned it all to happen this way.

Leo was informed by letter that she would meet him on a certain corner, and she was there one spring night, waiting under a street lamp. He appeared, carrying a small bouquet of violets and rosebuds. Stella stood by the lamp post, smoking. She wore white with red shoes, which fitted his expectations, although in a troubled moment he had imagined the dress red, and only the shoes white. She waited uneasily and shyly. From afar he saw that her eyes—clearly her father's—were filled with desperate innocence. He pictured, in her, his own redemption. Violins and lit candles revolved in the sky. Leo ran forward with flowers outthrust.

Around the corner, Salzman, leaning against a wall, chanted prayers for the dead.

1954

Ralph Ellison
(1914–   )

Ralph Waldo Ellison was born in Oklahoma City in 1914 to Ida Milsap, a maid, and Lewis Ellison, a contractor and small-business owner. Hoping to raise a literary master, they named their son after Emerson. As a teenager Ellison resolved to become a "latter-day Renaissance man," fully educated in both black and white cultural traditions. With his family's encouragement he combined his studies with odd jobs: doing yard work for the conductor of the Oklahoma City orchestra in exchange for instruction in classical music, absorbing black oral narratives from the informal taletellers (cracker-barrels) lounging about the drug store where he swept floors, practicing jazz idioms while playing in dance bands, and reading voraciously. When he entered Alabama's Tuskegee Institute on a scholarship in 1933, he planned to compose symphonies combining classical, jazz, and blues techniques. Ellison's ongoing commitment to cultural synthesis has shaped his aesthetics and his career.

In 1936 Ellison left Tuskegee to sculpt and compose in New York City. Supplementing his income with more odd jobs—in factories, in a psychiatrist's office, in cafeterias—he continued collecting raw materials that he later crafted into symphonic prose incorporating black folklore, surrealism, existentialism, and Freudian dream analysis. After meeting Langston Hughes and Richard Wright, Ellison abandoned sculpture and musical composition in order to write; however, music has retained a seminal place in his work. Like Hughes, Wright, James Baldwin, and more recently August Wilson, Ellison translates the structures and emotional colors of jazz to his experimental narratives. Ellison has continuously attempted to place himself in the white literary tradition without effacing the nontraditional perceptions of a black writer.

Along with Wright and Hughes, Ellison thought he had found a balance of individual freedom and social cooperation in Marxism during the 1930s, but he never joined the Communist party. After he returned from serving in the merchant marines in World War

II, he protested the party's intolerance of his need to articulate the black experience of American history. His explorations of his heritage paradoxically mingle echoes of slave narratives and blues lyrics with allusions to Herman Melville, Nathaniel Hawthorne, T. S. Eliot, James Joyce, and Ernest Hemingway. Throughout his career, Ellison has refused to limit himself to a separate but equal literary canon.

His disenchantment with communism finds expression in his satirical portrait of the party in the novel *Invisible Man* (1952), awarded a National Book Award in 1953. The nameless protagonist welcomes the comforting embrace of a radical political group, the Brotherhood, only to discover that the group is founded upon racist principles. In the novel's last pages the Invisible Man is still struggling to define himself in relation to a hostile society. "Battle Royal," commonly published as a short story, forms the first chapter of *Invisible Man* and suggests an overview of the novel as a whole. Long before he encounters the Brotherhood, the Invisible Man hungers for the approving embrace of his hometown's white leaders, an embrace that proves furiously, grotesquely malevolent. In addition to *Invisible Man*, Ellison has published two volumes of essays, *Shadow and Act* (1964) and *Going to the Territory* (1986) and has taught at Bard College and Rutgers and New York Universities.

Suggested Readings: *Shadow and Act*, 1964. *Going to the Territory*, 1986. J. M. Reilly, ed., *Twentieth Century Interpretations of Invisible Man: A Collection of Essays*, 1970. J. F. Trimmer, *A Casebook on Ralph Ellison's Invisible Man*, 1972. J. Hersey, ed., *Ralph Ellison, A Collection of Critical Essays*, 1974. R. B. Stepto, *From Behind the Veil: A Study of Afro-American Narrative*, 1979. R. G. O'Meally, *The Craft of Ralph Ellison*, 1980. R. F. Dietze, *Ralph Ellison: The Genesis of an Artist*, 1982. H. Bloom, ed., *Modern Critical Views: Ralph Ellison*, 1986. K. W. Benston, *Speaking for You: The Vision of Ralph Ellison*, 1987. R. G. O'Meally, ed., *New Essays on Invisible Man*, 1988.

Text Used: *Invisible Man*, 1953.

from INVISIBLE MAN*

CHAPTER I: [BATTLE ROYAL]

It goes a long way back, some twenty years. All my life I had been looking for something, and everywhere I turned someone tried to tell me what it was. I accepted their answers too, though they were often in contradiction and even self-contradictory. I was naïve. I was looking for myself and asking everyone except myself questions which I, and only I, could answer. It took me a long time and much painful boomeranging of my expectations to achieve a realization everyone else appears to have been born with: That I am nobody but myself. But first I had to discover that I am an invisible man!

And yet I am no freak of nature, nor of history. I was in the cards, other things having been equal (or unequal) eighty-five years ago. I am not ashamed of my grandparents for having been slaves. I am only ashamed of myself for having at one time been ashamed. About eighty-five years ago[1] they were told that they were free, united with others of our country in everything pertaining to the common good, and, in everything social, separate like the fingers of the hand. And they believed it. They exulted in it. They stayed in their place, worked hard, and

---

* First published in 1947; with the addition of a transitional paragraph at the end, the story became Chapter 1 of *Invisible Man* (1952). The ellipses are Ellison's.

[1] The Emancipation Proclamation was issued in 1863.

brought up my father to do the same. But my grandfather is the one. He was an odd old guy, my grandfather, and I am told I take after him. It was he who caused the trouble. On his deathbed he called my father to him and said, "Son, after I'm gone I want you to keep up the good fight. I never told you, but our life is a war and I have been a traitor all my born days, a spy in the enemy's country ever since I give up my gun back in the Reconstruction. Live with your head in the lion's mouth. I want you to overcome 'em with yeses, undermine 'em with grins, agree 'em to death and destruction, let 'em swoller you till they vomit or bust wide open." They thought the old man had gone out of his mind. He had been the meekest of men. The younger children were rushed from the room, the shades drawn and the flame of the lamp turned so low that it sputtered on the wick like the old man's breathing. "Learn it to the younguns," he whispered fiercely; then he died.

But my folks were more alarmed over his last words than over his dying. It was as though he had not died at all, his words caused so much anxiety. I was warned emphatically to forget what he had said and, indeed, this is the first time it has been mentioned outside the family circle. It had a tremendous effect upon me, however. I could never be sure of what he meant. Grandfather had been a quiet old man who never made any trouble, yet on his deathbed he had called himself a traitor and a spy, and he had spoken of his meekness as a dangerous activity. It became a constant puzzle which lay unanswered in the back of my mind. And whenever things went well for me I remembered my grandfather and felt guilty and uncomfortable. It was as though I was carrying out his advice in spite of myself. And to make it worse, everyone loved me for it. I was praised by the most lily-white men of the town. I was considered an example of desirable conduct— just as my grandfather had been. And what puzzled me was that the old man had defined it as *treachery*. When I was praised for my conduct I felt a guilt that in some way I was doing something that was really against the wishes of the white folks, that if they had understood they would have desired me to act just the opposite, that I should have been sulky and mean, and that that really would have been what they wanted, even though they were fooled and thought they wanted me to act as I did. It made me afraid that some day they would look upon me as a traitor and I would be lost. Still I was more afraid to act any other way because they didn't like that at all. The old man's words were like a curse. On my graduation day I delivered an oration in which I showed that humility was the secret, indeed, the very essence of progress. (Not that I believed this—how could I, remembering my grandfather?—I only believed that it worked.) It was a great success. Everyone praised me and I was invited to give the speech at a gathering of the town's leading white citizens. It was a triumph for our whole community.

It was in the main ballroom of the leading hotel. When I got there I discovered that it was on the occasion of a smoker, and I was told that since I was to be there anyway I might as well take part in the battle royal to be fought by some of my schoolmates as part of the entertainment. The battle royal came first.

All of the town's big shots were there in their tuxedoes, wolfing down the buffet foods, drinking beer and whiskey and smoking black cigars. It was a large room with a high ceiling. Chairs were arranged in neat rows around three sides of a portable boxing ring. The fourth side was clear, revealing a gleaming space of polished floor. I had some misgivings over the battle royal, by the way. Not from a distaste for fighting, but because I didn't care too much for the other fellows who were to take part. They were tough guys who seemed to have no grandfather's curse worrying their minds. No one could mistake their toughness. And besides, I suspected that fighting a battle royal might detract from the dignity of my speech. In those pre-invisible days I visualized myself as a potential Booker T. Washington.[2] But the other fellows didn't care too much for me either, and there were nine of them. I felt superior to them in my way, and I didn't like the manner in which we were all crowded together into the servants' elevator. Nor did they like my being there. In fact, as the warmly lighted floors flashed past the elevator we had words over the fact that I, by taking part in the fight, had knocked one of their friends out of a night's work.

We were led out of the elevator through a rococo[3] hall into an anteroom and told to get into our fighting togs. Each of us was issued a pair of boxing gloves and ushered out into the big mirrored hall, which we entered looking cautiously about us and whispering, lest we might accidentally be heard above the noise of the room. It was foggy with cigar smoke. And already the whiskey was taking effect. I was shocked to see some of the most important men of the town quite tipsy. They were all there—bankers, lawyers, judges, doctors, fire chiefs, teachers, merchants. Even one of the more fashionable pastors. Something we could not see was going on up front. A clarinet was vibrating sensuously and the men were standing up and moving eagerly forward. We were a small tight group, clustered together, our bare upper bodies touching and shining with anticipatory sweat; while up front the big shots were becoming increasingly excited over something we still could not see. Suddenly I heard the school superintendent, who had told me to come, yell, "Bring up the shines,[4] gentlemen! Bring up the little shines!"

We were rushed up to the front of the ballroom, where it smelled even more strongly of tobacco and whiskey. Then we were pushed into place. I almost wet my pants. A sea of faces, some hostile, some amused, ringed around us, and in the center, facing us, stood a magnificent blonde—stark naked. There was dead silence. I felt a blast of cold air chill me. I tried to back away, but they were behind me and around me. Some of the boys stood with lowered heads, trembling. I felt a wave of irrational guilt and fear. My teeth chattered, my skin turned to goose flesh, my knees knocked. Yet I was strongly attracted and looked in spite of myself. Had the price of looking been blindness, I would have looked. The hair was yellow like that of a circus kewpie doll, the face heavily powdered and rouged, as though to form an abstract mask, the eyes hollow and smeared a cool blue, the color of a baboon's butt. I felt a desire to spit upon her as my eyes brushed slowly over her body. Her breasts were firm and round as the domes of East Indian temples, and I stood so close as to see the fine skin texture and beads of pearly perspiration glistening like dew around the pink and erected buds of her nipples. I wanted at one and the same time to run from the room, to sink through the floor, or go to her and cover her from my eyes and the eyes of the others with my body; to feel the soft thighs, to caress her and destroy her, to love her and murder her, to hide from her, and yet to stroke where below the small American flag tattooed upon her belly her thighs formed a capital V. I had a notion that of all in the room she saw only me with her impersonal eyes.

And then she began to dance, a slow sensuous movement; the smoke of a hundred cigars clinging to her like the thinnest of veils. She seemed like a fair bird-

---

[2] Washington (1856–1915) was a famed African-American educator and botanist and author of the autobiographical *Up From Slavery* (1901).

[3] A graceful, delicate style of architecture, art, and music developed in the early eighteenth century in reaction to the heavy baroque style.

[4] Slang for "Negroes": derogatory, as are "coon" and "Sambo."

girl girdled in veils calling to me from the angry surface of some gray and threatening sea. I was transported. Then I became aware of the clarinet playing and the big shots yelling at us. Some threatened us if we looked and others if we did not. On my right I saw one boy faint. And now a man grabbed a silver pitcher from a table and stepped close as he dashed ice water upon him and stood him up and forced two of us to support him as his head hung and moans issued from his thick bluish lips. Another boy began to plead to go home. He was the largest of the group, wearing dark red fighting trunks much too small to conceal the erection which projected from him as though in answer to the insinuating low-registered moaning of the clarinet. He tried to hide himself with his boxing gloves.

And all the while the blonde continued dancing, smiling faintly at the big shots who watched her with fascination, and faintly smiling at our fear. I noticed a certain merchant who followed her hungrily, his lips loose and drooling. He was a large man who wore diamond studs in a shirtfront which swelled with the ample paunch underneath, and each time the blonde swayed her undulating hips he ran his hand through the thin hair of his bald head and, with his arms upheld, his posture clumsy like that of an intoxicated panda, wound his belly in a slow and obscene grind. This creature was completely hypnotized. The music had quickened. As the dancer flung herself about with a detached expression on her face, the men began reaching out to touch her. I could see their beefy fingers sink into the soft flesh. Some of the others tried to stop them and she began to move around the floor in graceful circles, as they gave chase, slipping and sliding over the polished floor. It was mad. Chairs went crashing, drinks were spilt, as they ran laughing and howling after her. They caught her just as she reached a door, raised her from the floor, and tossed her as college boys are tossed at a hazing, and above her red, fixed-smiling lips I saw the terror and disgust in her eyes, almost like my own terror and that which I saw in some of the other boys. As I watched, they tossed her twice and her soft breasts seemed to flatten against the air and her legs flung wildly as she spun. Some of the more sober ones helped her to escape. And I started off the floor, heading for the anteroom with the rest of the boys.

Some were still crying and in hysteria. But as we tried to leave we were stopped and ordered to get into the ring. There was nothing to do but what we were told. All ten of us climbed under the ropes and allowed ourselves to be blindfolded with broad bands of white cloth. One of the men seemed to feel a bit sympathetic and tried to cheer us up as we stood with our backs against the ropes. Some of us tried to grin. "See that boy over there?" one of the men said. "I want you to run across at the bell and give it to him right in the belly. If you don't get him, I'm going to get you. I don't like his looks." Each of us was told the same. The blindfolds were put on. Yet even then I had been going over my speech. In my mind each word was as bright as flame. I felt the cloth pressed into place, and frowned so that it would be loosened when I relaxed.

But now I felt a sudden fit of blind terror. I was unused to darkness. It was as though I had suddenly found myself in a dark room filled with poisonous cottonmouths.[5] I could hear the bleary voices yelling insistently for the battle royal to begin.

"Get going in there!"

"Let me at that big nigger!"

I strained to pick up the school superintendent's voice, as though to squeeze some security out of that slightly more familiar sound.

---

[5] Water moccasins: poisonous snakes common in the southeastern United States.

"Let me at those black sonsabitches!" someone yelled.

"No, Jackson, no!" another voice yelled. "Here, somebody, help me hold Jack."

"I want to get at that ginger-colored nigger. Tear him limb from limb," the first voice yelled.

I stood against the ropes trembling. For in those days I was what they called ginger-colored, and he sounded as though he might crunch me between his teeth like a crisp ginger cookie.

Quite a struggle was going on. Chairs were being kicked about and I could hear voices grunting as with a terrific effort. I wanted to see, to see more desperately than ever before. But the blindfold was tight as a thick skin-puckering scab and when I raised my gloved hands to push the layers of white aside a voice yelled, "Oh, no you don't, black bastard! Leave that alone!"

"Ring the bell before Jackson kills him a coon!" someone boomed in the sudden silence. And I heard the bell clang and the sound of the feet scuffling forward.

A glove smacked against my head. I pivoted, striking out stiffly as someone went past, and felt the jar ripple along the length of my arm to my shoulder. Then it seemed as though all nine of the boys had turned upon me at once. Blows pounded me from all sides while I struck out as best I could. So many blows landed upon me that I wondered if I were not the only blindfolded fighter in the ring, or if the man called Jackson hadn't succeeded in getting me after all.

Blindfolded, I could no longer control my motions. I had no dignity. I stumbled about like a baby or a drunken man. The smoke had become thicker and with each new blow it seemed to sear and further restrict my lungs. My saliva became like hot bitter glue. A glove connected with my head, filling my mouth with warm blood. It was everywhere. I could not tell if the moisture I felt upon my body was sweat or blood. A blow landed hard against the nape of my neck. I felt myself going over, my head hitting the floor. Streaks of blue light filled the black world behind the blindfold. I lay prone, pretending that I was knocked out, but felt myself seized by hands and yanked to my feet. "Get going, black boy! Mix it up!" My arms were like lead, my head smarting from blows. I managed to feel my way to the ropes and held on, trying to catch my breath. A glove landed in my midsection and I went over again, feeling as though the smoke had become a knife jabbed into my guts. Pushed this way and that by the legs milling around me, I finally pulled erect and discovered that I could see the black, sweat-washed forms weaving in the smoky-blue atmosphere like drunken dancers weaving to the rapid drum-like thuds of blows.

Everyone fought hysterically. It was complete anarchy. Everybody fought everybody else. No group fought together for long. Two, three, four, fought one, then turned to fight each other, were themselves attacked. Blows landed below the belt and in the kidney, with the gloves open as well as closed, and with my eye partly opened now there was not so much terror. I moved carefully, avoiding blows, although not too many to attract attention, fighting from group to group. The boys groped about like blind, cautious crabs crouching to protect their mid-sections, their heads pulled in short against their shoulders, their arms stretched nervously before them, with their fists testing the smoke-filled air like the knobbed feelers of hypersensitive snails. In one corner I glimpsed a boy violently punching the air and heard him scream in pain as he smashed his hand against a ring post. For a second I saw him bent over holding his hand, then going down as a blow caught his unprotected head. I played one group against the other, slipping in and throwing a punch then stepping out of range while pushing the others into the melee to take the blows blindly aimed at me. The smoke was agonizing and there were no rounds, no bells at three minute intervals to relieve our exhaustion. The room spun round me, a swirl of lights, smoke, sweating bodies surrounded by tense white faces. I bled from both nose and mouth, the blood spattering upon my chest.

The men kept yelling, "Slug him, black boy! Knock his guts out!"

"Uppercut him! Kill him! Kill that big boy!"

Taking a fake fall, I saw a boy going down heavily beside me as though we were felled by a single blow, saw a sneaker-clad foot shoot into his groin as the two who had knocked him down stumbled upon him. I rolled out of range, feeling a twinge of nausea.

The harder we fought the more threatening the men became. And yet, I had begun to worry about my speech again. How would it go? Would they recognize my ability? What would they give me?

I was fighting automatically when suddenly I noticed that one after another of the boys was leaving the ring. I was surprised, filled with panic, as though I had been left alone with an unknown danger. Then I understood. The boys had arranged it among themselves. It was the custom for the two men left in the ring to slug it out for the winner's prize. I discovered this too late. When the bell sounded two men in tuxedoes leaped into the ring and removed the blindfold. I found myself facing Tatlock, the biggest of the gang. I felt sick at my stomach. Hardly had the bell stopped ringing in my ears than it clanged again and I saw him moving swiftly toward me. Thinking of nothing else to do I hit him smash on the nose. He kept coming, bringing the rank sharp violence of stale sweat. His face was a black blank of a face, only his eyes alive—with hate of me and aglow with a feverish terror from what had happened to us all. I became anxious. I wanted to deliver my speech and he came at me as though he meant to beat it out of me. I smashed him again and again, taking his blows as they came. Then on a sudden impulse I struck him lightly and as we clinched, I whispered, "Fake like I knocked you out, you can have the prize."

"I'll break your behind," he whispered hoarsely.

"For *them?*"

"For *me,* sonofabitch!"

They were yelling for us to break it up and Tatlock spun me half around with a blow, and as a joggled camera sweeps in a reeling scene, I saw the howling red faces crouching tense beneath the cloud of blue-gray smoke. For a moment the world wavered, unraveled, flowed, then my head cleared and Tatlock bounced before me. That fluttering shadow before my eyes was his jabbing left hand. Then falling forward, my head against his damp shoulder, I whispered,

"I'll make it five dollars more."

"Go to hell!"

But his muscles relaxed a trifle beneath my pressure and I breathed, "Seven?"

"Give it to your ma," he said, ripping me beneath the heart.

And while I still held him I butted him and moved away. I felt myself bombarded with punches. I fought back with hopeless desperation. I wanted to deliver my speech more than anything else in the world, because I felt that only these men could judge truly my ability, and now this stupid clown was ruining my chances. I began fighting carefully now, moving in to punch him and out again with my greater speed. A lucky blow to his chin and I had him going too—until I heard a loud voice yell, "I got my money on the big boy."

Hearing this, I almost dropped my guard. I was confused: Should I try to win against the voice out there? Would not this go against my speech, and was not this a moment for humility, for nonresistance? A blow to my head as I danced about sent my right eye popping like a jack-in-the-box and settled my dilemma. The room went red as I fell. It was a dream fall, my body languid and fastidious as to where to land, until the floor became impatient and smashed up to meet me. A moment later I came to. An hypnotic voice said FIVE emphatically. And I lay there, hazily watching a dark red spot of my own blood shaping itself into a butterfly, glistening and soaking into the soiled gray world of the canvas.

When the voice drawled TEN I was lifted up and dragged to a chair. I sat dazed. My eye pained and swelled with each throb of my pounding heart and I wondered if now I would be allowed to speak. I was wringing wet, my mouth still bleeding. We were grouped along the wall now. The other boys ignored me as they congratulated Tatlock and speculated as to how much they would be paid. One boy whimpered over his smashed hand. Looking up front, I saw attendants in white jackets rolling the portable ring away and placing a small square rug in the vacant space surrounded by chairs. Perhaps, I thought, I will stand on the rug to deliver my speech.

Then the M.C.[6] called to us, "Come on up here boys and get your money."

We ran forward to where the men laughed and talked in their chairs, waiting. Everyone seemed friendly now.

"There it is on the rug," the man said. I saw the rug covered with coins of all dimensions and a few crumpled bills. But what excited me, scattered here and there, were the gold pieces.

"Boys, it's all yours," the man said. "You get all you grab."

"That's right, Sambo," a blond man said, winking at me confidentially.

I trembled with excitement, forgetting my pain. I would get the gold and the bills, I thought. I would use both hands. I would throw my body against the boys nearest me to block them from the gold.

"Get down around the rug now," the man commanded, "and don't anyone touch it until I give the signal."

"This ought to be good," I heard.

As told, we got around the square rug on our knees. Slowly the man raised his freckled hand as we followed it upward with our eyes.

I heard, "These niggers look like they're about to pray!"

Then, "Ready," the man said. "Go!"

I lunged for a yellow coin lying on the blue design of the carpet, touching it and sending a surprised shriek to join those rising around me. I tried frantically to remove my hand but could not let go. A hot, violent force tore through my body, shaking me like a wet rat. The rug was electrified. The hair bristled up on my head as I shook myself free. My muscles jumped, my nerves jangled, writhed. But I saw that this was not stopping the other boys. Laughing in fear and embarrassment, some were holding back and scooping up the coins knocked off by the painful contortions of the others. The men roared above us as we struggled.

"Pick it up, goddamnit, pick it up!" someone called like a bass-voiced parrot. "Go on, get it!"

I crawled rapidly around the floor, picking up the coins, trying to avoid the coppers and to get greenbacks and the gold. Ignoring the shock by laughing, as I brushed the coins off quickly, I discovered that I could contain the electricity—a contradiction, but it works. Then the men began to push us onto the rug. Laughing embarrassedly, we struggled out of their hands and kept after the coins. We were

[6] Emcee.

all wet and slippery and hard to hold. Suddenly I saw a boy lifted into the air, glistening with sweat like a circus seal, and dropped, his wet back landing flush upon the charged rug, heard him yell and saw him literally dance upon his back, his elbows beating a frenzied tattoo upon the floor, his muscles twitching like the flesh of a horse stung by many flies. When he finally rolled off, his face was gray and no one stopped him when he ran from the floor amid booming laughter.

"Get the money," the M.C. called. "That's good hard American cash!"

And we snatched and grabbed, snatched and grabbed. I was careful not to come too close to the rug now, and when I felt the hot whiskey breath descend upon me like a cloud of foul air I reached out and grabbed the leg of a chair. It was occupied and I held on desperately.

"Leggo, nigger! Leggo!"

The huge face wavered down to mine as he tried to push me free. But my body was slippery and he was too drunk. It was Mr. Colcord, who owned a chain of movie houses and "entertainment palaces." Each time he grabbed me I slipped out of his hands. It became a real struggle. I feared the rug more than I did the drunk, so I held on, surprising myself for a moment by trying to topple *him* upon the rug. It was such an enormous idea that I found myself actually carrying it out. I tried not to be obvious, yet when I grabbed his leg, trying to tumble him out of the chair, he raised up roaring with laughter, and, looking at me with soberness dead in the eye, kicked me viciously in the chest. The chair leg flew out of my hand and I felt myself going and rolled. It was as though I had rolled through a bed of hot coals. It seemed a whole century would pass before I would roll free, a century in which I was seared through the deepest levels of my body to the fearful breath within me and the breath seared and heated to the point of explosion. It'll all be over in a flash, I thought as I rolled clear. It'll all be over in a flash.

But not yet, the men on the other side were waiting, red faces swollen as though from apoplexy as they bent forward in their chairs. Seeing their fingers coming toward me I rolled away as a fumbled football rolls off the receiver's fingertips, back into the coals. That time I luckily sent the rug sliding out of place and heard the coins ringing against the floor and the boys scuffling to pick them up and the M.C. calling, "All right, boys, that's all. Go get dressed and get your money."

I was limp as a dish rag. My back felt as though it had been beaten with wires.

When we had dressed the M.C. came in and gave us each five dollars, except Tatlock, who got ten for being last in the ring. Then he told us to leave. I was not to get a chance to deliver my speech, I thought. I was going out into the dim alley in despair when I was stopped and told to go back. I returned to the ballroom, where the men were pushing back their chairs and gathering in groups to talk.

The M.C. knocked on a table for quiet. "Gentlemen," he said, "we almost forgot an important part of the program. A most serious part, gentlemen. This boy was brought here to deliver a speech which he made at his graduation yesterday . . ."

"Bravo!"

"I'm told that he is the smartest boy we've got out there in Greenwood. I'm told that he knows more big words than a pocket-sized dictionary."

Much applause and laughter.

"So now, gentlemen, I want you to give him your attention."

There was still laughter as I faced them, my mouth dry, my eye throbbing. I began slowly, but evidently my throat was tense, because they began shouting, "Louder! Louder!"

"We of the younger generation extol the wisdom of that great leader and educator," I shouted, "who first spoke these flaming words of wisdom: 'A ship lost at sea for many days suddenly sighted a friendly vessel. From the mast of the unfortunate vessel was seen a signal: "Water, water; we die of thirst!" The answer from the friendly vessel came back: "Cast down your bucket where you are." The captain of the distressed vessel, at last heeding the injunction, cast down his bucket, and it came up full of fresh sparkling water from the mouth of the Amazon River.' And like him I say, and in his words, 'To those of my race who depend upon bettering their condition in a foreign land, or who underestimate the importance of cultivating friendly relations with the Southern white man, who is his next-door neighbor, I would say: "Cast down your bucket where you are"—cast it down in making friends in every manly way of the people of all races by whom we are surrounded . . . '"[7]

I spoke automatically and with such fervor that I did not realize that the men were still talking and laughing until my dry mouth, filling up with blood from the cut, almost strangled me. I coughed, wanting to stop and go to one of the tall brass, sand-filled spittoons to relieve myself, but a few of the men, especially the superintendent, were listening and I was afraid. So I gulped it down, blood, saliva and all, and continued. (What powers of endurance I had during those days! What enthusiasm! What a belief in the rightness of things!) I spoke even louder in spite of the pain. But still they talked and still they laughed, as though deaf with cotton in dirty ears. So I spoke with greater emotional emphasis. I closed my ears and swallowed blood until I was nauseated. The speech seemed a hundred times as long as before, but I could not leave out a single word. All had to be said, each memorized nuance considered, rendered. Nor was that all. Whenever I uttered a word of three or more syllables a group of voices would yell for me to repeat it. I used the phrase "social responsibility" and they yelled:

"What's that word you say, boy?"

"Social responsibility," I said.

"What?"

"Social . . . "

"Louder."

" . . . responsibility."

"More!"

"Respon—"

"Repeat!"

"—sibility."

The room filled with the uproar of laughter until, no doubt, distracted by having to gulp down my blood, I made a mistake and yelled a phrase I had often seen denounced in newspaper editorials, heard debated in private.

"Social . . . "

"What?" they yelled.

" . . . equality."

The laughter hung smokelike in the sudden stillness. I opened my eyes, puzzled. Sounds of displeasure filled the room. The M.C. rushed forward. They shouted hostile phrases at me. But I did not understand.

A small dry mustached man in the front row blared out, "Say that slowly, son!"

---

[7] From Booker T. Washington's famous Atlanta Exposition speech of 1895, known as the Atlanta Compromise; the address is presented in Ch. XIV of *Up From Slavery*.

"What, sir?"

"What you just said!"

"Social responsibility, sir," I said.

"You weren't being smart, were you, boy?" he said, not unkindly.

"No, sir!"

"You sure that about 'equality' was a mistake?"

"Oh, yes, sir," I said. "I was swallowing blood."

"Well, you had better speak more slowly so we can understand. We mean to do right by you, but you've got to know your place at all times. All right, now, go on with your speech."

I was afraid. I wanted to leave but I wanted also to speak and I was afraid they'd snatch me down.

"Thank you, sir," I said, beginning where I had left off, and having them ignore me as before.

Yet when I finished there was a thunderous applause. I was surprised to see the superintendent come forth with a package wrapped in white tissue paper, and, gesturing for quiet, address the men.

"Gentlemen, you see that I did not overpraise this boy. He makes a good speech and some day he'll lead his people in the proper paths. And I don't have to tell you that that is important in these days and times. This is a good, smart boy, and so to encourage him in the right direction, in the name of the Board of Education I wish to present him a prize in the form of this . . . "

He paused, removing the tissue paper and revealing a gleaming calfskin brief case.

" . . . in the form of this first-class article from Shad Whitmore's shop."

"Boy," he said, addressing me, "take this prize and keep it well. Consider it a badge of office. Prize it. Keep developing as you are and some day it will be filled with important papers that will help shape the destiny of your people."

I was so moved that I could hardly express my thanks. A rope of bloody saliva forming a shape like an undiscovered continent drooled upon the leather and I wiped it quickly away. I felt an importance that I had never dreamed.

"Open it and see what's inside," I was told.

My fingers a-tremble, I complied, smelling the fresh leather and finding an official-looking document inside. It was a scholarship to the state college for Negroes. My eyes filled with tears and I ran awkwardly off the floor.

I was overjoyed; I did not even mind when I discovered that the gold pieces I had scrambled for were brass pocket tokens advertising a certain make of automobile.

When I reached home everyone was excited. Next day the neighbors came to congratulate me. I even felt safe from grandfather, whose deathbed curse usually spoiled my triumphs. I stood beneath his photograph with my brief case in hand and smiled triumphantly into his stolid black peasant's face. It was a face that fascinated me. The eyes seemed to follow everywhere I went.

That night I dreamed I was at a circus with him and that he refused to laugh at the clowns no matter what they did. Then later he told me to open my brief case and read what was inside and I did, finding an official envelope stamped with the state seal; and inside the envelope I found another and another, endlessly, and I thought I would fall of weariness. "Them's years," he said. "Now open that one." And I did and in it I found an engraved document containing a short message in letters of gold. "Read it," my grandfather said. "Out loud!"

"To Whom It May Concern," I intoned. "Keep This Nigger-Boy Running."

I awoke with the old man's laughter ringing in my ears.

(It was a dream I was to remember and dream again for many years after. But at that time I had no insight into its meaning. First I had to attend college.)

1947

=CONTEXTS=

The Jewish Immigrant Experience

With the influx of European immigrants to America in the early to middle twentieth century came an influx of literature dealing with the experiences of those immigrants. For Jewish immigrants much of this literature was an attempt to reconcile the harshness of their life in America with the deep spiritual values and traditions of their European homelands. The conditions under which many Jewish immigrants lived are exposed in such works as the posthumously published *How the Other Half Lives* (1919), by the Danish-born journalist Jacob Riis (1849–1914), which examines the problems caused by overcrowding in the tenement districts of early twentieth-century New York City. Many European immigrants settled in urban areas where jobs were plentiful, but the extreme poverty and large numbers of people, combined with the greed of tenement owners, often led to unsanitary, nearly inhuman living conditions.

That European immigrants to America were faced with hostility and insensitivity to their cultural differences as well is also reflected in literature. A major voice in Yiddish literature is the 1978 Nobel Laureate Isaac Bashevis Singer (1904–). After immigrating to the United States in 1935, he began to write stories incorporating Jewish folklore and life in his native Poland. In such stories as "Gimpel The Fool" (1953) Singer establishes the importance in Jewish life of piety and of the individual's relationship with God. In his later stories about Jewish immigrants, Singer points out the problems of maintaining a sense of racial identity and culture. In "The Little Shoemakers" (1954) Abba Shuster chooses to remain in Poland while his sons leave for America. Only the bombing of his village during World War II and the destruction of his family home force his departure to America. The journey is arduous, and along the way Abba loses his prayer shawl and other religious articles. Reaching New Jersey and his sons, he feels alienated until he rediscovers his shoemaking tools. The ability to ply his old trade renews his strength, and when his sons join him, they solidify the bonds of tradition that immigration threatened to break:

The Little Shoemakers

Abba's sons spread sackcloth aprons on their knees and went to work, cutting soles and shaping heels, boring holes and hammering pegs, as in the good old days. . . . In the high spring sky, lofting over the grass and the water, floated clouds in the form of brooms, sailboats, flocks of sheep, herds of elephants. Birds sang, flies buzzed, butterflies fluttered about.

Abba raised his dense eyebrows, and his sad eyes looked around at his heirs, the seven shoemakers. . . . No, praise God, they had not become idolaters in Egypt. They had not forgotten their heritage, nor had they lost themselves among the unworthy.

Isaac Bashevis Singer, 1954

Saul Bellow
(1915–   )

Since he began writing novels in the 1940s, Saul Bellow has been wrestling with a seemingly insoluble problem: how to write moral fiction in a skeptical century. "Modern writers sin," he writes, "when they suppose that they *know*, as they conceive that physics *knows* or that history *knows*. The subject of the novelist is not knowable in any such way." And yet, in his story "The Gonzaga Manuscripts" (1956), his idealistic protagonist endows modern authors with ethical responsibilities requiring infinite wisdom. Bellow defines modern literature as "a sort of grand council considering what mankind should do next, how we should fill our mortal time, what we should feel, what we should see, where we should get our courage, how we should love or hate, how we should be pure or great or terrible, evil (you know!), and all the rest." After three decades of struggling to reconcile the modern artist's terrifying responsibilities and terribly human limitations, Bellow was awarded the Nobel Prize for literature in 1976 "for the human understanding and subtle analysis of contemporary culture that are combined in his work." He continues to grapple with problems of epistemology, evil, "and all the rest" in his novel *The Dean's December* (1982), but, as in his earlier work, he finds more questions than answers. *The Dean's December* ends with the aging Dean Corde addressing his queries to a wintry night sky from the observatory at Mount Palomar.

Parallels between Dean Corde's life and that of Bellow are obvious. The dean is approaching the end of a long and distinguished career in academia; so was Bellow in 1982. The dean's wife is a Romanian astronomer who teaches in Chicago; Bellow's fourth wife, Alexandra Ionescu Tulcea, was born in Romania and met Bellow while she was teaching mathematics at Northwestern University. Bellow's readers have often complained that he tends to coalesce with his characters; he admits that he "lends" his characters bits of himself when they require it. The protagonists of the novels *Dangling Man* (1944) and *Herzog* (1964) were, like Bellow, born in Canada (Bellow in Lachine, Quebec, in 1915) and raised in Chicago. Many of Bellow's beleaguered heroes are burdened with one or two of the author's ex-wives. All his books are inhabited by worried souls who cannot answer the larger questions they pose for themselves.

Bellow examined the frustration of the existentialist hero, unfettered by certainty of any sort, in his first novel, *Dangling Man,* which reverberates with echoes of the novels of Feodor Dostoevski and of Jean-Paul Sartre. In *The Victim* (1947), Bellow, while investigating the predicament of American urban Jews, strove for a level of formal perfection like that of Gustave Flaubert. Early in his career Bellow was painfully conscious of his own Russian-Jewish heritage and later recalled that he wrote these first two novels "timidly," afraid that he was announcing himself to the non-Jewish world with great effrontery. Bellow relaxed his style in his next novel, *The Adventures of Augie March* (1953), written in Europe.

Bellow graduated with honors in anthropology and sociology in 1937 from Northwestern University and began graduate study at the University of Wisconsin, but he left without a degree. To support his first wife and son, Bellow worked for the federally funded Works Progress Administration as a writer and then taught at the Pestalozzi-Froebel Teachers College in Chicago. From 1943 to 1946 he was an editor for the *Encyclopedia Britannica;*

in 1946 he returned to teaching. By the time he wrote *Augie March,* he had taught at the University of Minnesota, New York University, and Princeton University. He had won the approval of the dauntingly non-Jewish literary community in the form of a Guggenheim Fellowship, which gave him the leisure to travel and the self-confidence to write with less restraint. The novel won a National Book Award in 1954. Bellow has called *Augie March* his "favorite fantasy" but admitted in retrospect that the unbridled exuberance of that novel threatens to dissolve into formlessness. His next major piece, the novella *Seize the Day* (1956), unfolds within a more discernible structure. Some readers have called it Bellow's darkest work, but the critic Alfred Kazin finds it his most moving: "Each detail is cruel, plain, irremediable, yet one feels that it is about to burst forth into the radiance of consciousness."

In Bellow's novel *Henderson the Rain King* (1959), Eugene Henderson flees the complexities of his life in urban America, searching for a less challenging community. Arriving in an apparently primitive African village, he becomes embroiled in an entirely new matrix of difficulties and discovers that human society is never primitive, never simple. Bellow's most autobiographical novel, *Herzog,* portrays a distracted scholar who must unexpectedly come to terms with the fact that he has failed to notice his wife's long-term adultery. This novel and Bellow's next, *Mr. Sammler's Planet* (1970), earned National Book Awards in 1965 and 1971, respectively. And in 1976 Bellow received a Pulitzer Prize for *Humboldt's Gift* (1975).

Bellow's heroes generally fall into two categories: fabulously gifted intellectuals and hilariously, tragically unlucky fools. He presents both types in his short story "Mosby's Memoirs" (1968). Mosby, a celebrated American academic reviewing his illustrious career as he writes his memoirs in Mexico, recalls his brief acquaintance with Hymen Lustgarten, a doomed and clownish figure much like Tommy Wilhelm of *Seize the Day.* Mosby coldly utilizes Lustgarten to leaven his memoirs with humor. Lustgarten is a loser, a bungler, and, paradoxically, an indefatigable source of generative, life-affirming power that is utterly lacking in Mosby. In the final pages of the story, Mosby visits a Zapotec temple in Mexico—a claustrophobic, tomblike building constructed with the same impeccable precision as his own finely wrought manuscript. Viewing the altar that once ran with the blood of human sacrifice, he suddenly and uncharacteristically empathizes with the Zapotec priests' victims. Realizing that he, as well as his own victim, Lustgarten, is trapped within his exquisite and inhuman irony, Mosby begins to experience the same difficulty breathing that plagues Tommy Wilhelm. This awakening recurs throughout Bellow's fiction: his Brahmin professors, his geniuses pontificating from lofty isolation, and all the members of the "grand council considering what mankind should do next" realize their affinity with losers such as Tommy Wilhelm and Hymen Lustgarten. The only suggestions Bellow can offer for mankind's next move require that his readers find some bit of redemption in this realization.

Suggested Readings: *Dangling Man,* 1944. *The Victim,* 1947. *The Adventures of Augie March,* 1953. *Henderson the Rain King,* 1959. *Herzog,* 1964. *Mosby's Memoirs and Other Stories,* 1968. *Mr. Sammler's Planet,* 1970. *Humboldt's Gift,* 1975. *The Dean's December,* 1982. T. Tanner, *Saul Bellow,* 1965. K. M. Opdahl, *The Novels of Saul Bellow, An Introduction,* 1967. J. J. Clayton, *Saul Bellow: In Defense of Man,* 1968. I. Malin, *Saul Bellow's Fiction,* 1969. B. Scheer-Schäzler, *Saul Bellow,* 1972. E. Rovit, ed., *Saul Bellow: A Collection of Critical Essays,* 1975. S. Trachtenberg, ed., *Critical Essays on Saul Bellow,* 1979.

Text Used: *Seize the Day,* 1956.

SEIZE THE DAY*

I

When it came to concealing his troubles, Tommy Wilhelm was not less capable than the next fellow. So at least he thought, and there was a certain amount of evidence to back him up. He had once been an actor—no, not quite, an extra—and he knew what acting should be. Also, he was smoking a cigar, and when a man is smoking a cigar, wearing a hat, he has an advantage; it is harder to find out how he feels. He came from the twenty-third floor down to the lobby on the mezzanine to collect his mail before breakfast, and he believed—he hoped—that he looked passably well: doing all right. It was a matter of sheer hope, because there was not much that he could add to his present effort. On the fourteenth floor he looked for his father to enter the elevator; they often met at this hour, on the way to breakfast. If he worried about his appearance it was mainly for his old father's sake. But there was no stop on the fourteenth, and the elevator sank and sank. Then the smooth door opened and the great dark red uneven carpet that covered the lobby billowed toward Wilhelm's feet. In the foreground the lobby was dark, sleepy. French drapes like sails kept out the sun, but three high, narrow windows were open, and in the blue air Wilhelm saw a pigeon about to light on the great chain that supported the marquee of the movie house directly underneath the lobby. For one moment he heard the wings beating strongly.

Most of the guests at the Hotel Gloriana were past the age of retirement. Along Broadway in the Seventies, Eighties, and Nineties, a great part of New York's vast population of old men and women lives. Unless the weather is too cold or wet they fill the benches about the tiny railed parks and along the subway gratings from Verdi Square to Columbia University, they crowd the shops and cafeterias, the dime stores, the tea-rooms, the bakeries, the beauty parlors, the reading rooms and club rooms. Among these old people at the Gloriana, Wilhelm felt out of place. He was comparatively young, in his middle forties, large and blond, with big shoulders; his back was heavy and strong, if already a little stooped or thickened. After breakfast the old guests sat down on the green leather armchairs and sofas in the lobby and began to gossip and look into the papers; they had nothing to do but wait out the day. But Wilhelm was used to an active life and liked to go out energetically in the morning. And for several months, because he had no position, he had kept up his morale by rising early; he was shaved and in the lobby by eight o'clock. He bought the paper and some cigars and drank a Coca-Cola or two before he went in to breakfast with his father. After breakfast—out, out, out to attend to business. The getting out had in itself become the chief business. But he had realized that he could not keep this up much longer, and today he was afraid. He was aware that his routine was about to break up and he sensed that a huge trouble long presaged but till now formless was due. Before evening, he'd know.

Nevertheless he followed his daily course and crossed the lobby.

Rubin, the man at the newsstand, had poor eyes. They may not have been actually weak but they were poor in expression, with lacy lids that furled down at

---

* After the final lines of an ode (I. ix. 7) by the Roman poet Horace (65-8 B.C.): "*Carpe diem, quam minimum credula postero*" ("Seize the day, put little trust in tomorrow"). The novella was first published in the *Partisan Revieew* in summer 1956, and collected (with three short stories and a one-act play) later that year.

the corners. He dressed well. It didn't seem necessary—he was behind the counter most of the time—but he dressed very well. He had on a rich brown suit; the cuffs embarrassed the hairs on his small hands. He wore a Countess Mara painted necktie.[1] As Wilhelm approached, Rubin did not see him; he was looking out dreamily at the Hotel Ansonia, which was visible from his corner, several blocks away. The Ansonia, the neighborhood's great landmark, was built by Stanford White.[2] It looks like a baroque palace from Prague or Munich enlarged a hundred times, with towers, domes, huge swells and bubbles of metal gone green from exposure, iron fretwork and festoons. Black television antennae are densely planted on its round summits. Under the changes of weather it may look like marble or like sea water, black as slate in the fog, white as tufa[3] in sunlight. This morning it looked like the image of itself reflected in deep water, white and cumulous above, with cavernous distortions underneath. Together, the two men gazed at it.

Then Rubin said, "Your dad is in to breakfast already, the old gentleman."

"Oh, yes? Ahead of me today?"

"That's a real knocked-out shirt you got on," said Rubin. "Where's it from, Saks?"[4]

"No, it's a Jack Fagman—Chicago."

Even when his spirits were low, Wilhelm could still wrinkle his forehead in a pleasing way. Some of the slow, silent movements of his face were very attractive. He went back a step, as if to stand away from himself and get a better look at his shirt. His glance was comic, a comment upon his untidiness. He liked to wear good clothes, but once he had put it on each article appeared to go its own way. Wilhelm, laughing, panted a little; his teeth were small; his cheeks when he laughed and puffed grew round, and he looked much younger than his years. In the old days when he was a college freshman and wore a raccoon coat and a beanie on his large blond head his father used to say that, big as he was, he could charm a bird out of a tree. Wilhelm had great charm still.

"I like this dove-gray color," he said in his sociable, good-natured way. "It isn't washable. You have to send it to the cleaner. It never smells as good as washed. But it's a nice shirt. It cost sixteen, eighteen bucks."

This shirt had not been bought by Wilhelm; it was a present from his boss—his former boss, with whom he had had a falling out. But there was no reason why he should tell Rubin the history of it. Although perhaps Rubin knew—Rubin was the kind of man who knew, and knew and knew. Wilhelm also knew many things about Rubin, for that matter, about Rubin's wife and Rubin's business, Rubin's health. None of these could be mentioned, and the great weight of the unspoken left them little to talk about.

"Well, y'lookin' pretty sharp today," Rubin said.

And Wilhelm said gladly, "Am I? Do you really think so?" He could not believe it. He saw his reflection in the glass cupboard full of cigar boxes, among the grand seals and paper damask and the gold-embossed portraits of famous men, García, Edward the Seventh, Cyrus the Great.[5] You had to allow for the darkness

---

[1] An expensive tie of handpainted silk.

[2] White (1853–1906) was an architect who designed many New York City buildings—but not the Ansonia, at Broadway and 73d Street, which was designed and operated by W. E. D. Stokes (1852–1926).

[3] A porous stone.   [4] The department store Saks Fifth Avenue.

[5] Diego García (1471–1529), a Portuguese explorer; Edward VII (1841–1910), king of Great Britain and Ireland from 1901 to 1910; Cyrus (600?–529 B.C.), king of Persia (550–529 B.C.), founder of the Persian empire.

and deformations of the glass, but he thought he didn't look too good. A wide wrinkle like a comprehensive bracket sign was written upon his forehead, the point between his brows, and there were patches of brown on his dark blond skin. He began to be half amused at the shadow of his own marveling, troubled, desirous eyes, and his nostrils and his lips. Fair-haired hippopotamus!—that was how he looked to himself. He saw a big round face, a wide, flourishing red mouth, stump teeth. And the hat, too; and the cigar, too. I should have done hard labor all my life, he reflected. Hard honest labor that tires you out and makes you sleep. I'd have worked off my energy and felt better. Instead, I had to distinguish myself—yet.

He had put forth plenty of effort, but that was not the same as working hard, was it? And if as a young man he had got off to a bad start it was due to this very same face. Early in the nineteen-thirties, because of his striking looks, he had been very briefly considered star material, and he had gone to Hollywood. There for seven years, stubbornly, he had tried to become a screen artist. Long before that time his ambition or delusion had ended, but through pride and perhaps also through laziness he had remained in California. At last he turned to other things, but those seven years of persistence and defeat had unfitted him somehow for trades and businesses, and then it was too late to go into one of the professions. He had been slow to mature, and he had lost ground, and so he hadn't been able to get rid of his energy and he was convinced that this energy itself had done him the greatest harm.

"I didn't see you at the gin game[6] last night," said Rubin.

"I had to miss it. How did it go?"

For the last few weeks Wilhelm had played gin almost nightly, but yesterday he had felt that he couldn't afford to lose any more. He had never won. Not once. And while the losses were small they weren't gains, were they? They were losses. He was tired of losing, and tired also of the company, and so he had gone by himself to the movies.

"Oh," said Rubin, "it went okay. Carl made a chump of himself yelling at the guys. This time Doctor Tamkin didn't let him get away with it. He told him the psychological reason why."

"What was the reason?"

Rubin said, "I can't quote him. Who could? You know the way Tamkin talks. Don't ask me. Do you want the *Trib?*[7] Aren't you going to look at the closing quotations?"

"It won't help much to look. I know what they were yesterday at three," said Wilhelm. "But I suppose I better had get the paper." It seemed necessary for him to lift one shoulder in order to put his hand into his jacket pocket. There, among little packets of pills and crushed cigarette butts and strings of cellophane, the red tapes of packages which he sometimes used as dental floss, he recalled that he had dropped some pennies.

"That doesn't sound so good," said Rubin. He meant to be conversationally playful, but his voice had no tone and his eyes, slack and lid-blinded, turned elsewhere. He didn't want to hear. It was all the same to him. Maybe he already knew, being the sort of man who knew and knew.

No, it wasn't good. Wilhelm held three orders of lard in the commodities market. He and Dr. Tamkin had bought this lard together four days ago at 12.96, and

[6] Gin rummy.   [7] The daily New York *Herald Tribune*.

the price at once began to fall and was still falling. In the mail this morning there was sure to be a call for additional margin payment. One came every day.

The psychologist, Dr. Tamkin, had got him into this. Tamkin lived at the Gloriana and attended the card game. He had explained to Wilhelm that you could speculate in commodities at one of the uptown branches of a good Wall Street house without making the full deposit of margin legally required. It was up to the branch manager. If he knew you—and all the branch managers knew Tamkin—he would allow you to make short-term purchases. You needed only to open a small account.

"The whole secret of this type of speculation," Tamkin had told him, "is in the alertness. You have to act fast—buy it and sell it; sell it and buy in again. But quick! Get to the window and have them wire Chicago at just the right second. Strike and strike again! Then get out the same day. In no time at all you turn over fifteen, twenty thousand dollars' worth of soy beans, coffee, corn, hides, wheat, cotton." Obviously the doctor understood the market well. Otherwise he could not make it sound so simple. "People lose because they are greedy and can't get out when it starts to go up. They gamble, but I do it scientifically. This is not guesswork. You must take a few points and get out. Why, ye gods!" said Dr. Tamkin with his bulging eyes, his bald head, and his drooping lip. "Have you stopped to think how much dough people are making in the market?"

Wilhelm with a quick shift from gloomy attention to the panting laugh which entirely changed his face had said, "Ho, have I ever! What do you think? Who doesn't know it's way beyond nineteen-twenty-eight—twenty-nine[8] and still on the rise? Who hasn't read the Fulbright investigation?[9] There's money everywhere. Everyone is shoveling it in. Money is—is—"

"And can you rest—can you sit still while this is going on?" said Dr. Tamkin. "I confess to you I can't. I think about people, just because they have a few bucks to invest, making fortunes. They have no sense, they have no talent, they just have the extra dough and it makes them more dough. I get so worked up and tormented and restless, so restless! I haven't even been able to practice my profession. With all this money around you don't want to be a fool while everyone else is making. I know guys who make five, ten thousand a week just by fooling around. I know a guy at the Hotel Pierre. There's nothing to him, but he has a whole case of Mumm's champagne at lunch. I know another guy on Central Park South— But what's the use of talking. They make millions. They have smart lawyers who get them out of taxes by a thousand schemes."

"Whereas I got taken," said Wilhelm. "My wife refused to sign a joint return. One fairly good year and I got into the thirty-two-per-cent bracket and was stripped bare. What of all my bad years?"

"It's a businessmen's government," said Dr. Tamkin. "You can be sure that these men making five thousand a week—"

"I don't need that sort of money," Wilhelm had said. "But oh! if I could only work out a little steady income from this. Not much. I don't ask much. But how badly I need—! I'd be so grateful if you'd show me how to work it."

"Sure I will. *I* do it regularly. I'll bring you my receipts if you like. And do you want to know something? I approve of your attitude very much. You want to

---

[8] The stock market reached highs in 1928 and 1929 before it crashed in October 1929, initiating the Great Depression.

[9] The report of an investigation of abnormalities in the stock market.

avoid catching the money fever. This type of activity is filled with hostile feeling and lust. You should see what it does to some of these fellows. They go on the market with murder in their hearts."

"What's that I once heard a guy say?" Wilhelm remarked. "A man is only as good as what he loves."

"That's it—just it," Tamkin said. "You don't have to go about it their way. There's also a calm and rational, a psychological approach."

Wilhelm's father, old Dr. Adler, lived in an entirely different world from his son, but he had warned him once against Dr. Tamkin. Rather casually—he was a very bland old man—he said, "Wilky, perhaps you listen too much to this Tamkin. He's interesting to talk to. I don't doubt it. I think he's pretty common but he's a persuasive man. However, I don't know how reliable he may be."

It made Wilhelm profoundly bitter that his father should speak to him with such detachment about his welfare. Dr. Adler liked to appear affable. Affable! His own son, his one and only son, could not speak his mind or ease his heart to him. I wouldn't turn to Tamkin, he thought, if I could turn to him. At least Tamkin sympathizes with me and tries to give me a hand, whereas Dad doesn't want to be disturbed.

Old Dr. Adler had retired from practice; he had a considerable fortune and could easily have helped his son. Recently Wilhelm had told him, "Father—it so happens that I'm in a bad way now. I hate to have to say it. You realize that I'd rather have good news to bring you. But it's true. And since it's true, Dad—What else am I supposed to say! It's true."

Another father might have appreciated how difficult this confession was—so much bad luck, weariness, weakness, and failure. Wilhelm had tried to copy the old man's tone and made himself sound gentlemanly, low-voiced, tasteful. He didn't allow his voice to tremble; he made no stupid gesture. But the doctor had no answer. He only nodded. You might have told him that Seattle was near Puget Sound, or that the Giants and Dodgers were playing a night game, so little was he moved from his expression of healthy, handsome, good-humored old age. He behaved toward his son as he had formerly done toward his patients, and it was a great grief to Wilhelm; it was almost too much to bear. Couldn't he see—couldn't he feel? Had he lost his family sense?

Greatly hurt, Wilhelm struggled however to be fair. Old people are bound to change, he said. They have hard things to think about. They must prepare for where they are going. They can't live by the old schedule any longer and all their perspectives change, and other people become alike, kin and acquaintances. Dad is no longer the same person, Wilhelm reflected. He was thirty-two when I was born, and now he's going on eighty. Furthermore, it's time I stopped feeling like a kid toward him, a small son.

The handsome old doctor stood well above the other old people in the hotel. He was idolized by everyone. This was what people said: "That's old Professor Adler, who used to teach internal medicine. He was a diagnostician, one of the best in New York, and had a tremendous practice. Isn't he a wonderful-looking old guy? It's a pleasure to see such a fine old scientist, clean and immaculate. He stands straight and understands every single thing you say. He still has all his buttons. You can discuss any subject with him." The clerks, the elevator operators, the telephone girls and waitresses and chambermaids, the management flattered and pampered him. That was what he wanted. He had always been a vain man. To see how his father loved himself sometimes made Wilhelm madly indignant.

He folded over the *Tribune* with its heavy, black, crashing sensational print and read without recognizing any of the words, for his mind was still on his father's vanity. The doctor had created his own praise. People were primed and did not know it. And what did he need praise for? In a hotel where everyone was busy and contacts were so brief and had such small weight, how could it satisfy him? He could be in people's thoughts here and there for a moment; in and then out. He could never matter much to them. Wilhelm let out a long, hard breath and raised the brows of his round and somewhat circular eyes. He stared beyond the thick borders of the paper.

> . . . love that well which thou must leave ere long.[10]

Involuntary memory brought him this line. At first he thought it referred to his father, but then he understood that it was for himself, rather. *He* should love that well. "This thou perceivest, which makes *thy* love more strong." Under Dr. Tamkins' influence Wilhelm had recently begun to remember the poems he used to read. Dr. Tamkin knew, or said he knew, the great English poets and once in a while he mentioned a poem of his own. It was a long time since anyone had spoken to Wilhelm about this sort of thing. He didn't like to think about his college days, but if there was one course that now made sense it was Literature I. The textbook was Lieder and Lovett's *British Poetry and Prose*,[11] a black heavy book with thin pages. Did I read that? he asked himself. Yes, he had read it and there was one accomplishment at least he could recall with pleasure. He had read "Yet once more, O ye laurels."[12] How pure this was to say! It was beautiful.

> Sunk though he be beneath the wat'ry floor . . .

Such things had always swayed him, and now the power of such words was far, far greater.

Wilhelm respected the truth, but he could lie and one of the things he lied often about was his education. He said he was an alumnus of Penn State; in fact he had left school before his sophomore year was finished. His sister Catherine had a B. S. degree. Wilhelm's late mother was a graduate of Bryn Mawr. He was the only member of the family who had no education. This was another sore point. His father was ashamed of him.

But he had heard the old man bragging to another old man, saying, "My son is a sales executive. He didn't have the patience to finish school. But he does all right for himself. His income is up in the five figures somewhere."

"What—thirty, forty thousand?" said his stooped old friend.

"Well, he needs at least that much for his style of life. Yes, he needs that."

Despite his troubles, Wilhelm almost laughed. Why, that boasting old hypocrite. He knew the sales executive was no more. For many weeks there had been no executive, no sales, no income. But how we love looking fine in the eyes of the world—how beautiful are the old when they are doing a snow job! It's Dad,

---

[10] Line 14 from Shakespeare's Sonnet 73; Bellow quotes the preceding line in the next paragraph.
[11] An anthology by Paul R. Lieder and Robert Morss Lovett.
[12] From line 1 of "Lycidas," by John Milton (1608–1674); from line 167 just below.

thought Wilhelm, who is the salesman. He's selling me. *He* should have gone on the road.

But what of the truth? Ah, the truth was that there were problems, and of these problems his father wanted no part. His father was ashamed of him. The truth, Wilhelm thought, was very awkward. He pressed his lips together, and his tongue went soft; it pained him far at the back, in the cords and throat, and a knot of ill formed in his chest. Dad never was a pal to me when I was young, he reflected. He was at the office or the hospital, or lecturing. He expected me to look out for myself and never gave me much thought. Now he looks down on me. And maybe in some respects he's right.

No wonder Wilhelm delayed the moment when he would have to go into the dining room. He had moved to the end of Rubin's counter. He had opened the *Tribune;* the fresh pages drooped from his hands; the cigar was smoked out and the hat did not defend him. He was wrong to suppose that he was more capable than the next fellow when it came to concealing his troubles. They were clearly written out upon his face. He wasn't even aware of it.

There was the matter of the different names, which, in the hotel, came up frequently. "Are you Doctor Adler's son?" "Yes, but my name is Tommy Wilhelm." And the doctor would say, "My son and I use different monickers. I uphold tradition. He's for the new." The Tommy was Wilhelm's own invention. He adopted it when he went to Hollywood, and dropped the Adler. Hollywood was his own idea, too. He used to pretend that it had all been the doing of a certain talent scout named Maurice Venice. But the scout had never made him a definite offer of a studio connection. He had approached him, but the results of the screen tests had not been good. After the test Wilhelm took the initiative and pressed Maurice Venice until he got him to say, "Well, I suppose you might make it out there." On the strength of this Wilhelm had left college and had gone to California.

Someone had said, and Wilhelm agreed with the saying, that in Los Angeles all the loose objects in the country were collected, as if America had been tilted and everything that wasn't tightly screwed down had slid into Southern California. He himself had been one of these loose objects. Sometimes he told people, "I was too mature for college. I was a big boy, you see. Well, I thought, when do you start to become a man?" After he had driven a painted flivver[13] and had worn a yellow slicker with slogans on it, and played illegal poker, and gone out on Coke dates, he had *had* college. He wanted to try something new and quarreled with his parents about his career. And then a letter came from Maurice Venice.

The story of the scout was long and intricate and there were several versions of it. The truth about it was never told. Wilhelm had lied first boastfully and then out of charity to himself. But his memory was good, he could still separate what he had invented from the actual happenings, and this morning he found it necessary as he stood by Rubin's showcase with his *Tribune* to recall the crazy course of the true events.

I didn't seem even to realize that there was a depression. How could I have been such a jerk as not to prepare for anything and just go on luck and inspiration? With round gray eyes expanded and his large shapely lips closed in severity toward himself he forced open all that had been hidden. Dad I couldn't affect one way or another. Mama was the one who tried to stop me, and we carried on and

---

[13] A small, cheap car, especially an old one.

yelled and pleaded. The more I lied the louder I raised my voice, and charged—like a hippopotamus. Poor Mother! How I disappointed her. Rubin heard Wilhelm give a broken sigh as he stood with the forgotten *Tribune* crushed under his arm.

When Wilhelm was aware that Rubin watched him, loitering and idle, apparently not knowing what to do with himself this morning, he turned to the Coca-Cola machine. He swallowed hard at the Coke bottle and coughed over it, but he ignored his coughing, for he was still thinking, his eyes upcast and his lips closed behind his hand. By a peculiar twist of habit he wore his coat collar turned up always, as though there were a wind. It never lay flat. But on his broad back, stooped with its own weight, its strength warped almost into deformity, the collar of his sports coat appeared anyway to be no wider than a ribbon.

He was listening to the sound of his own voice as he explained, twenty-five years ago in the living room on West End Avenue,[14] "But Mother, if I don't pan out as an actor I can still go back to school."

But she was afraid he was going to destroy himself. She said, "Wilky, Dad could make it easy for you if you wanted to go into medicine." To remember this stifled him.

"I can't bear hospitals. Besides, I might make a mistake and hurt someone or even kill a patient. I couldn't stand that. Besides, I haven't got that sort of brains."

Then his mother had made the mistake of mentioning her nephew Artie, Wilhelm's cousin, who was an honor student at Columbia in math and languages. That dark little gloomy Artie with his disgusting narrow face, and his moles and self-sniffing ways and his unclean table manners, the boring habit he had of conjugating verbs when you went for a walk with him. "Roumanian is an easy language. You just add a *tl* to everything." He was now a professor, this same Artie with whom Wilhelm had played near the soldiers' and sailors' monument on Riverside Drive.[15] Not that to be a professor was in itself so great. How could anyone bear to know so many languages? And Artie also had to remain Artie, which was a bad deal. But perhaps success had changed him. Now that he had a place in the world perhaps he was better. Did Artie love his languages, and live for them, or was he also, in his heart, cynical? So many people nowadays were. No one seemed satisfied, and Wilhelm was especially horrified by the cynicism of successful people. Cynicism was bread and meat to everyone. And irony, too. Maybe it couldn't be helped. It was probably even necessary. Wilhelm, however, feared it intensely. Whenever at the end of the day he was unusually fatigued he attributed it to cynicism. Too much of the world's business done. Too much falsity. He had various words to express the effect this had on him. Chicken! Unclean! Congestion! he exclaimed in his heart. Rat race! Phony! Murder! Play the Game! Buggers!

At first the letter from the talent scout was nothing but a flattering sort of joke. Wilhelm's picture in the college paper when he was running for class treasurer was seen by Maurice Venice, who wrote to him about a screen test. Wilhelm at once took the train to New York. He found the scout to be huge and oxlike, so stout that his arms seemed caught from beneath in a grip of flesh and fat; it looked as though it must be positively painful. He had little hair. Yet he enjoyed a healthy complexion. His breath was noisy and his voice rather difficult and husky because of the fat in his throat. He had on a double-breasted suit of the type then known as the pillbox; it was chalk-striped, pink on blue; the trousers hugged his ankles.

---

[14] On Manhattan's West Side.　　[15] Along the Upper West Side of Manhattan.

They met and shook hands and sat down. Together these two big men dwarfed the tiny Broadway office and made the furnishings look like toys. Wilhelm had the color of a Golden Grimes apple when he was well, and then his thick blond hair had been vigorous and his wide shoulders unwarped; he was leaner in the jaws, his eyes fresher and wider; his legs were then still awkward but he was impressively handsome. And he was about to make his first great mistake. Like, he sometimes thought, I was going to pick up a weapon and strike myself a blow with it.

Looming over the desk in the small office darkened by overbuilt midtown—sheer walls, gray spaces, dry lagoons of tar and pebbles—Maurice Venice proceeded to establish his credentials. He said, "My letter was on the regular stationery, but maybe you want to check on me?"

"Who, *me?* said Wilhelm. "Why?"

"There's guys who think I'm in a racket and make a charge for the test. I don't ask a cent. I'm no agent. There ain't no commission."

"I never even thought of it," said Wilhelm. Was there perhaps something fishy about this Maurice Venice? He protested too much.

In his husky, fat-weakened voice he finally challenged Wilhelm, "If you're not sure, you can call the distributor and find out who I am, Maurice Venice."

Wilhelm wondered at him. "Why shouldn't I be sure? Of course I am."

"Because I can see the way you size me up, and because this is a dinky office. Like you don't believe me. Go ahead. Call. I won't care if you're cautious. I mean it. There's quite a few people who doubt me at first. They can't really believe that fame and fortune are going to hit 'em."

"But I tell you I do believe you," Wilhelm had said, and bent inward to accommodate the pressure of his warm, panting laugh. It was purely nervous. His neck was ruddy and neatly shaved about the ears—he was fresh from the barbershop; his face anxiously glowed with his desire to make a pleasing impression. It was all wasted on Venice, who was just as concerned about the impression *he* was making.

"If you're surprised, I'll just show you what I mean," Venice had said. "It was about fifteen months ago right in this identical same office when I saw a beautiful thing in the paper. It wasn't even a photo but a drawing, a brassière ad, but I knew right away that this was star material. I called up the paper to ask who the girl was, they gave me the name of the advertising agency; I phoned the agency and they gave me the name of the artist; I got hold of the artist and he gave me the number of the model agency. Finally, finally I got her number and phoned her and said, 'This is Maurice Venice, scout for Kaskaskia Films.' So right away she says, 'Yah, so's your old lady.' Well, when I saw I wasn't getting nowhere with her I said to her, 'Well, miss. I don't blame you. You're a very beautiful thing and must have a dozen admirers after you all the time, boy friends who like to call and pull your leg and give a tease. But as I happen to be a very busy fellow and don't have the time to horse around or argue, I tell you what to do. Here's my number, and here's the number of the Kaskaskia Distributors, Inc. Ask them who am I, Maurice Venice. The scout.' She did it. A little while later she phoned me back, all apologies and excuses, but I didn't want to embarrass her and get off on the wrong foot with an artist. I know better than to do that. So I told her it was a natural precaution, never mind. I wanted to run a screen test right away. Because I seldom am wrong about talent. If I see it, it's there. Get that, please. And do you know who that little girl is today?"

"No," Wilhelm said eagerly. "Who is she?"

Venice said impressively, "'Nita Christenberry."

Wilhelm sat utterly blank. This was failure. He didn't know the name, and Venice was waiting for his response and would be angry.

And in fact Venice had been offended. He said, "What's the matter with you! Don't you read a magazine? She's a starlet."

"I'm sorry," Wilhelm answered. "I'm at school and don't have time to keep up. If I don't know her, it doesn't mean a thing. She made a big hit, I'll bet."

"You can say that again. Here's a photo of her." He handed Wilhelm some pictures. She was a bathing beauty—short, the usual breasts, hips, and smooth thighs. Yes, quite good, as Wilhelm recalled. She stood on high heels and wore a Spanish comb and mantilla.[16] In her hand was a fan.

He had said, "She looks awfully peppy."

"Isn't she a divine girl? And what personality! Not just another broad in the show business, believe me." He had a surprise for Wilhelm. "I have found happiness with her," he said.

"You have?" said Wilhelm, slow to understand.

"Yes, boy, we're engaged."

Wilhelm saw another photograph, taken on the beach. Venice was dressed in a terry-cloth beach outfit, and he and the girl, cheek to cheek, were looking into the camera. Below, in white ink, was written "Love at Malibu Colony."

"I'm sure you'll be very happy. I wish you—'

"I *know*," said Venice firmly, "I'm going to be happy. When I saw that drawing, the breath of fate breathed on me. I felt it over my entire body."

"Say, it strikes a bell suddenly," Wilhelm had said. "Aren't you related to Martial Venice the producer?"

Venice was either a nephew of the producer or the son of a first cousin. Decidedly he had not made good. It was easy enough for Wilhelm to see this now. The office was so poor, and Venice bragged so nervously and identified himself so scrupulously—the poor guy. He was the obscure failure of an aggressive and powerful clan. As such he had the greatest sympathy from Wilhelm.

Venice had said, "Now I suppose you want to know where you come in. I seen your school paper, by accident. You take quite a remarkable picture."

"It can't be so much," said Wilhelm, more panting than laughing.

"You don't want to tell me my business," Venice said. "Leave it to me. I studied up on this."

"I never imagined— Well, what kind of roles do you think I'd fit?"

"All this time that we've been talking, I've been watching. Don't think I haven't. You remind me of someone. Let's see who it can be—one of the great old-timers. Is it Milton Sills? No, that's not the one. Conway Tearle, Jack Mulhall? George Bancroft?[17] No, his face was ruggeder. One thing I can tell you, though, a George Raft type you're not—those tough, smooth, black little characters."

"No, I wouldn't seem to be."

"No, you're not that flyweight type, with the fists, from a nightclub, and the glamorous sideburns, doing the tango or the bolero. Not Edward G. Robinson, either—I'm thinking aloud. Or the Cagney[18] fly-in-your-face role, a cabbie, with that mouth and those punches."

---

[16] A lace scarf worn over the head and shoulders.

[17] Film stars of the early 1900s; Raft (1895–1980) was a star in the 1930s.

[18] Robinson (1893–1973) and James Cagney (1899–1987) were film stars of the 1930s and 1940s.

"I realize that."

"Not suave like William Powell, or a lyric juvenile like Buddy Rogers.[19] I suppose you don't play the sax? No. But—"

"But what?"

"I have you placed as the type that loses the girl to the George Raft type or the William Powell type. You are steady, faithful, you get stood up. The older women would know better. The mothers are on your side. With what they been through, if it was up to them, they'd take you in a minute. You're very sympathetic, even the young girls feel that. You'd make a good provider. But they go more for the other types. It's as clear as anything."

This was not how Wilhelm saw himself. And as he surveyed the old ground he recognized now that he had been not only confused but hurt. Why, he thought, he cast me even then for a loser.

Wilhelm had said, with half a mind to be defiant, "Is that your opinion?"

It never occurred to Venice that a man might object to stardom in such a role. "Here is your chance," he said. "Now you're just in college. What are you studying?" He snapped his fingers. "Stuff." Wilhelm himself felt this way about it. "You may plug along fifty years before you get anywheres. This way, in one jump, the world knows who you are. You become a name like Roosevelt, Swanson.[20] From east to west, out to China, into South America. This is no bunk. You become a lover to the whole world. The world wants it, needs it. One fellow smiles, a billion people also smile. One fellow cries, the other billion sob with him. Listen, bud—" Venice had pulled himself together to make an effort. On his imagination there was some great weight which he could not discharge. He wanted Wilhelm, too, to feel it. He twisted his large, clean, well-meaning, rather foolish features as though he were their unwilling captive, and said in his choked, fat-obstructed voice, "Listen, everywhere there are people trying hard, miserable, in trouble, downcast, tired, trying and trying. They need a break, right? A break through, a help, luck or sympathy."

"That certainly is the truth," said Wilhelm. He had seized the feeling and he waited for Venice to go on. But Venice had no more to say; he had concluded. He gave Wilhelm several pages of blue hectographed[21] script, stapled together, and told him to prepare for the screen test. "Study your lines in front of a mirror," he said. "Let yourself go. The part should take ahold of you. Don't be afraid to make faces and be emotional. Shoot the works. Because when you start to act you're no more an ordinary person, and those things don't apply to you. You don't behave the same way as the average."

And so Wilhelm had never returned to Penn State. His roommate sent his things to New York for him, and the school authorities had to write to Dr. Adler to find out what had happened.

Still, for three months Wilhelm delayed his trip to California. He wanted to start out with the blessings of his family, but they were never given. He quarreled with his parents and his sister. And then, when he was best aware of the risks and knew a hundred reasons against going and had made himself sick with fear, he left home. This was typical of Wilhelm. After much thought and hesitation and debate

[19] Powell (1892–1984) and Charles "Buddy" Rogers (1904–   ) were film stars of the 1930s and 1940s.

[20] Franklin Delano Roosevelt (1882–1945), thirty-second U.S. president (1933–1945); Gloria Swanson (1899–1983), a film star.

[21] Duplicated by transferral to a coated sheet of gelatin, from which copies are made.

he invariably took the course he had rejected innumerable times. Ten such decisions made up the history of his life. He had decided that it would be a bad mistake to go to Hollywood, and then he went. He had made up his mind not to marry his wife, but ran off and got married. He had resolved not to invest money with Tamkin, and then had given him a check.

But Wilhelm had been eager for life to start. College was merely another delay. Venice had approached him and said that the world had named Wilhelm to shine before it. He was to be freed from the anxious and narrow life of the average. Moreover, Venice had claimed that he never made a mistake. His instinct for talent was infallible, he said.

But when Venice saw the results of the screen test he did a quick about-face. In those days Wilhelm had had a speech difficulty. It was not a true stammer, it was a thickness of speech which the sound track exaggerated. The film showed that he had many peculiarities, otherwise unnoticeable. When he shrugged, his hands drew up within his sleeves. The vault of his chest was huge, but he really didn't look strong under the lights. Though he called himself a hippopotamus, he more nearly resembled a bear. His walk was bearlike, quick and rather soft, toes turned inward, as though his shoes were an impediment. About one thing Venice had been right. Wilhelm was photogenic, and his wavy blond hair (now graying) came out well, but after the test Venice refused to encourage him. He tried to get rid of him. He couldn't afford to take a chance on him, he had made too many mistakes already and lived in fear of his powerful relatives.

Wilhelm had told his parents, "Venice says I owe it to myself to go." How ashamed he was now of this lie! He had begged Venice not to give him up. He had said, "Can't you help me out? It would kill me to go back to school now."

Then when he reached the Coast he learned that a recommendation from Maurice Venice was the kiss of death. Venice needed help and charity more than he, Wilhelm, ever had. A few years later when Wilhelm was down on his luck and working as an orderly in a Los Angeles hospital, he saw Venice's picture in the papers. He was under indictment for pandering. Closely following the trial, Wilhelm found out that Venice had indeed been employed by Kaskaskia Films but that he had evidently made use of the connection to organize a ring of call girls. Then what did he want with me? Wilhelm had cried to himself. He was unwilling to believe anything very bad about Venice. Perhaps he was foolish and unlucky, a fall guy, a dupe, a sucker. You didn't give a man fifteen years in prison for that. Wilhelm often thought that he might write him a letter to say how sorry he was. He remembered the breath of fate and Venice's certainty that he would be happy. 'Nita Christenberry was sentenced to three years. Wilhelm recognized her although she had changed her name.

By that time Wilhelm too had taken his new name. In California he became Tommy Wilhelm. Dr. Adler would not accept the change. Today he still called his son Wilky, as he had done for more than forty years. Well, now, Wilhelm was thinking, the paper crowded in disarray under his arm, there's really very little that a man can change at will. He can't change his lungs, or nerves, or constitution or temperament. They're not under his control. When he's young and strong and impulsive and dissatisfied with the way things are he wants to rearrange them to assert his freedom. He can't overthrow the government or be differently born; he only has a little scope and maybe a foreboding, too, that essentially you can't change. Nevertheless, he makes a gesture and becomes Tommy Wilhelm. Wilhelm had always had a great longing to be Tommy. He had never, however, suc-

ceeded in feeling like Tommy, and in his soul had always remained Wilky. When
he was drunk he reproached himself horribly as Wilky. "You fool, you clunk, you
Wilky!" he called himself. He thought that it was a good thing perhaps that he had
not become a success as Tommy since that would not have been a genuine success. Wilhelm would have feared that not he but Tommy had brought it off, cheating Wilky of his birthright. Yes, it had been a stupid thing to do, but it was his
imperfect judgment at the age of twenty which should be blamed. He had cast off
his father's name, and with it his father's opinion of him. It was, he knew it was,
his bid for liberty, Adler being in his mind the title of the species, Tommy the
freedom of the person. But Wilky was his inescapable self.

   In middle age you no longer thought such thoughts about free choice. Then it
came over you that from one grandfather you had inherited such and such a head
of hair which looked like honey when it whitens or sugars in the jar; from another,
broad thick shoulders; an oddity of speech from one uncle, and small teeth from
another, and the gray eyes with darkness diffused even into the whites, and a
wide-lipped mouth like a statue from Peru. Wandering races have such looks, the
bones of one tribe, the skin of another. From his mother he had gotten sensitive
feelings, a soft heart, a brooding nature, a tendency to be confused under pressure.

   The changed name was a mistake, and he would admit it as freely as you liked.
But this mistake couldn't be undone now, so why must his father continually
remind him how he had sinned? It was too late. He would have to go back to the
pathetic day when the sin was committed. And where was that day? Past and
dead. Whose humiliating memories were these? His and not his father's. What
had he to think back on that he could call good? Very, very little. You had to
forgive. First, to forgive yourself, and then general forgiveness. Didn't he suffer
from his mistakes far more than his father could?

   "Oh, God," Wilhelm prayed. "Let me out of my trouble. Let me out of my
thoughts, and let me do something better with myself. For all the time I have
wasted I am very sorry. Let me out of this clutch and into a different life. For I am
all balled up. Have mercy."

II

The mail.

   The clerk who gave it to him did not care what sort of appearance he made this
morning. He only glanced at him from under his brows, upward, as the letters
changed hands. Why should the hotel people waste courtesies on him? They had
his number. The clerk knew that he was handing him, along with the letters, a bill
for his rent. Wilhelm assumed a look that removed him from all such things. But
it was bad. To pay the bill he would have to withdraw money from his brokerage
account, and the account was being watched because of the drop in lard. According to the *Tribune*'s figures lard was still twenty points below last year's level.
There were government price supports. Wilhelm didn't know how these worked
but he understood that the farmer was protected and that the SEC[22] kept an eye on
the market and therefore he believed that lard would rise again and he wasn't
greatly worried as yet. But in the meantime his father might have offered to pick
up his hotel tab. Why didn't he? What a selfish old man he was! He saw his son's

---

[22] The Securities and Exchange Commission.

hardships; he could so easily help him. How little it would mean to him, and how much to Wilhelm! Where was the old man's heart? Maybe, thought Wilhelm, I was sentimental in the past and exaggerated his kindliness—warm family life. It may never have been there.

Not long ago his father had said to him in his usual affable, pleasant way, "Well, Wilky, here we are under the same roof again, after all these years."

Wilhelm was glad for an instant. At last they would talk over old times. But he was also on guard against insinuations. Wasn't his father saying, "Why are you here in a hotel with me and not at home in Brooklyn with your wife and two boys? You're neither a widower nor a bachelor. You have brought me all your confusions. What do you expect me to do with them?"

So Wilhelm studied the remark for a bit, then said, "The roof is twenty-six stories up. But how many years has it been?"

"That's what I was asking you."

"Gosh, Dad, I'm not sure. Wasn't it the year Mother died? What year was that?"

He asked this question with an innocent frown on his Golden Grimes, dark blond face. *What year was it!* As though he didn't know the year, the month, the day, the very hour of his mother's death.

"Wasn't it nineteen-thirty-one?" said Dr. Adler.

"Oh, was it?" said Wilhelm. And in hiding the sadness and the overwhelming irony of the question he gave a nervous shiver and wagged his head and felt the ends of his collar rapidly.

"Do you know?" his father said. "You must realize, an old fellow's memory becomes unreliable. It was in winter, that I'm sure of. Nineteen-thirty-two?"

Yes, it was age. Don't make an issue of it, Wilhelm advised himself. If you were to ask the old doctor in what year he had interned, he'd tell you correctly. All the same, don't make an issue. Don't quarrel with your own father. Have pity on an old man's failings.

"I believe the year was closer to nineteen-thirty-four, Dad," he said.

But Dr. Adler was thinking, Why the devil can't he stand still when we're talking? He's either hoisting his pants up and down by the pockets or jittering with his feet. A regular mountain of tics, he's getting to be. Wilhelm had a habit of moving his feet back and forth as though, hurrying into a house, he had to clean his shoes first on the doormat.

Then Wilhelm had said, "Yes, that was the beginning of the end, wasn't it, Father?"

Wilhelm often astonished Dr. Adler. Beginning of the end? What could he mean—what was he fishing for? Whose end? The end of family life? The old man was puzzled but he would not give Wilhelm an opening to introduce his complaints. He had learned that it was better not to take up Wilhelm's strange challenges. So he merely agreed pleasantly, for he was a master of social behavior, and said, "It was an awful misfortune for us all."

He thought, What business has he to complain to *me* of his mother's death?

Face to face they had stood, each declaring himself silently after his own way. It was: it was not, the beginning of the end—*some* end.

Unaware of anything odd in his doing it, for he did it all the time, Wilhelm had pinched out the coal of his cigarette and dropped the butt in his pocket, where there were many more. And as he gazed at his father the little finger of his right hand began to twitch and tremble; of that he was unconscious, too.

And yet Wilhelm believed that when he put his mind to it he could have perfect and even distinguished manners, outdoing his father. Despite the slight thickness in his speech—it amounted almost to a stammer when he started the same phrase over several times in his effort to eliminate the thick sound—he could be fluent. Otherwise he would never have made a good salesman. He claimed also that he was a good listener. When he listened he made a tight mouth and rolled his eyes thoughtfully. He would soon tire and begin to utter short, loud, impatient breaths, and he would say, "Oh yes . . . yes . . . yes. I couldn't agree more." When he was forced to differ he would declare, "Well, I'm not sure. I don't really see it that way. I'm of two minds about it." He would never willingly hurt any man's feelings.

But in conversation with his father he was apt to lose control of himself. After any talk with Dr. Adler, Wilhelm generally felt dissatisfied, and his dissatisfaction reached its greatest intensity when they discussed family matters. Ostensibly he had been trying to help the old man to remember a date, but in reality he meant to tell him, "You were set free when Ma died. You wanted to forget her. You'd like to get rid of Catherine, too. Me, too. You're not kidding anyone"—Wilhelm striving to put this across, and the old man not having it. In the end he was left struggling, while his father seemed unmoved.

And then once more Wilhelm had said to himself, "But man! you're not a kid. Even then you weren't a kid!" He looked down over the front of his big, indecently big, spoiled body. He was beginning to lose his shape, his gut was fat, and he looked like a hippopotamus. His younger son called him "a hummuspotamus"; that was little Paul. And here he was still struggling with his old dad, filled with ancient grievances. Instead of saying, "Good-by, youth! Oh, good-by those marvelous, foolish wasted days. What a big clunk I was—I *am*."

Wilhelm was still paying heavily for his mistakes. His wife Margaret would not give him a divorce, and he had to support her and the two children. She would regularly agree to divorce him, and then think things over again and set new and more difficult conditions. No court would have awarded her the amounts he paid. One of today's letters, as he had expected, was from her. For the first time he had sent her a postdated check, and she protested. She also enclosed bills for the boys' educational insurance policies, due next week. Wilhelm's mother-in-law had taken out these policies in Beverly Hills, and since her death two years ago he had to pay the premiums. Why couldn't she have minded her own business! They were his kids, and he took care of them, and always would. He had planned to set up a trust fund. But that was on his former expectations. Now he had to rethink the future, because of the money problem. Meanwhile, here were the bills to be paid. When he saw the two sums punched out so neatly on the cards he cursed the company and its IBM equipment. His heart and his head were congested with anger. Everyone was supposed to have money. It was nothing to the company. It published pictures of funerals in the magazines and frightened the suckers, and then punched out little holes, and the customers would lie awake to think out ways to raise the dough. They'd be ashamed not to have it. They couldn't let a great company down, either, and they got the scratch. In the old days a man was put in prison for debt, but there were subtler things now. They made it a shame not to have money and set everybody to work.

Well, and what else had Margaret sent him? He tore the envelope open with his thumb, swearing that he would send any other bills back to her. There was, luckily, nothing more. He put the hole-punched cards in his pocket. Didn't Margaret know that he was nearly at the end of his rope? Of course. Her instinct told her that this was her opportunity, and she was giving him the works.

He went into the dining room, which was under Austro-Hungarian management at the Hotel Gloriana. It was run like a European establishment. The pastries were excellent, especially the strudel. He often had apple strudel and coffee in the afternoon.

As soon as he entered he saw his father's small head in the sunny bay at the farther end, and heard his precise voice. It was with an odd sort of perilous expression that Wilhelm crossed the dining room.

Dr. Adler liked to sit in a corner that looked across Broadway down to the Hudson and New Jersey. On the other side of the street was a supermodern cafeteria with gold and purple mosaic columns. On the second floor a private-eye school, a dental laboratory, a reducing parlor, a veteran's club, and a Hebrew school shared the space. The old man was sprinkling sugar on his strawberries. Small hoops of brilliance were cast by the water glasses on the white tablecloth, despite a faint murkiness in the sunshine. It was early summer, and the long window was turned inward; a moth was on the pane; the putty was broken and the white enamel on the frames was streaming with wrinkles.

"Ha, Wilky," said the old man to his tardy son. "You haven't met our neighbor Mr. Perls, have you? From the fifteenth floor."

"How d'do," Wilhelm said. He did not welcome this stranger; he began at once to find fault with him. Mr. Perls carried a heavy cane with a crutch tip. Dyed hair, a skinny forehead—these were not reasons for bias. Nor was it Mr. Perls's fault that Dr. Adler was using him, not wishing to have breakfast with his son alone. But a gruffer voice within Wilhelm spoke, asking, "Who is this damn frazzle-faced herring with his dyed hair and his fish teeth and this drippy mustache? Another one of Dad's German friends. Where does he collect all these guys? What is the stuff on his teeth? I never saw such pointed crowns. Are they stainless steel, or a kind of silver? How can a human face get into this condition. Uch!" Staring with his widely spaced gray eyes, Wilhelm sat, his broad back stooped under the sports jacket. He clasped his hands on the table with an implication of suppliance. Then he began to relent a little toward Mr. Perls, beginning at the teeth. Each of those crowns represented a tooth ground to the quick, and estimating a man's grief with his teeth as two per cent of the total, and adding to that his flight from Germany and the probable origin of his wincing wrinkles, not to be confused with the wrinkles of his smile, it came to a sizable load.

"Mr. Perls was a hosiery wholesaler," said Dr. Adler.

"Is this the son you told me was in the selling line?" said Mr. Perls.

Dr. Adler replied, "I have only this one son. One daughter. She was a medical technician before she got married—anesthetist. At one time she had an important position in Mount Sinai."[23]

He couldn't mention his children without boasting. In Wilhelm's opinion, there was little to boast of. Catherine, like Wilhelm, was big and fair-haired. She had married a court reporter who had a pretty hard time of it. She had taken a professional name, too—Philippa. At forty she was still ambitious to become a painter. Wilhelm didn't venture to criticize her work. It didn't do much to him, he said, but then he was no critic. Anyway, he and his sister were generally on the outs

---

[23] New York City's Mount Sinai Hospital.

and he didn't often see her paintings. She worked very hard, but there were fifty thousand people in New York with paints and brushes, each practically a law unto himself. It was the Tower of Babel[24] in paint. *He* didn't want to go far into this. Things were chaotic all over.

Dr. Adler thought that Wilhelm looked particularly untidy this morning—unrested, too, his eyes red-rimmed from excessive smoking. He was breathing through his mouth and he was evidently much distracted and rolled his red-shot eyes barbarously. As usual, his coat collar was turned up as though he had had to go out in the rain. When he went to business he pulled himself together a little; otherwise he let himself go and looked like hell.

"What's the matter, Wilky, didn't you sleep last night?"

"Not very much."

"You take too many pills of every kind—first stimulants and then depressants, anodynes followed by analeptics,[25] until the poor organism doesn't know what's happened. Then the luminal won't put people to sleep, and the Pervitin or Benzedrine won't wake them. God knows! These things get to be as serious as poisons, and yet everyone puts all their faith in them."

"No, Dad, it's not the pills. It's that I'm not used to New York any more. For a native, that's very peculiar, isn't it? It was never so noisy at night as now, and every little thing is a strain. Like the alternate parking. You have to run out at eight to move your car. And where can you put it? If you forget for a minute they tow you away. Then some fool puts advertising leaflets under your windshield wiper and you have heart failure a block away because you think you've got a ticket. When you do get stung with a ticket, you can't argue. You haven't got a chance in court and the city wants the revenue."

"But in your line you have to have a car, eh?" said Mr. Perls.

"Lord knows why any lunatic would want one in the city who didn't need it for his livelihood."

Wilhelm's old Pontiac was parked in the street. Formerly, when on an expense account, he had always put it up in a garage. Now he was afraid to move the car from Riverside Drive lest he lose his space, and he used it only on Saturdays when the Dodgers were playing in Ebbets Field[26] and he took his boys to the game. Last Saturday, when the Dodgers were out of town, he had gone out to visit his mother's grave.

Dr. Adler had refused to go along. He couldn't bear his son's driving. Forgetfully, Wilhelm traveled for miles in second gear; he was seldom in the right lane and he neither gave signals nor watched for lights. The upholstery of his Pontiac was filthy with grease and ashes. One cigarette burned in the ashtray, another in his hand, a third on the floor with maps and other waste paper and Coca-Cola bottles. He dreamed at the wheel or argued and gestured, and therefore the old doctor would not ride with him.

Then Wilhelm had come back from the cemetery angry because the stone bench between his mother's and his grandmother's graves had been overturned and broken by vandals. "Those damn teen-age hoodlums get worse and worse," he said. "Why, they must have used a sledge-hammer to break the seat smack in half like that. If I could catch one of them!" He wanted the doctor to pay for a new

---

[24] In Genesis 11:1–9, a tower Noah's descendants tried to build to reach Heaven; God prevented its completion by a confusion of tongues; here, chaos.

[25] Pain relievers followed by stimulants.   [26] The home field of the Brooklyn Dodgers (1913–1958).

seat, but his father was cool to the idea. He said he was going to have himself cremated.

Mr. Perls said, "I don't blame you if you get no sleep up where you are." His voice was tuned somewhat sharp, as though he were slightly deaf. "Don't you have Parigi the singing teacher there? God, they have some queer elements in this hotel. On which floor is that Estonian[27] woman with all her cats and dogs? They should have made her leave long ago."

"They've moved her down to twelve," said Dr. Adler.

Wilhelm ordered a large Coca-Cola with his breakfast. Working in secret at the small envelopes in his pocket, he found two pills by touch. Much fingering had worn and weakened the paper. Under cover of a napkin he swallowed a Phenaphen sedative and a Unicap, but the doctor was sharp-eyed and said, "Wilky, what are you taking now?"

"Just my vitamin pills." He put his cigar butt in an ashtray on the table behind him, for his father did not like the odor. Then he drank his Coca-Cola.

"That's what you drink for breakfast, and not orange juice?" said Mr. Perls. He seemed to sense that he would not lose Dr. Adler's favor by taking an ironic tone with his son.

"The caffeine stimulates brain activity," said the old doctor. "It does all kinds of things to the respiratory center."

"It's just a habit of the road, that's all," Wilhelm said. "If you drive around long enough it turns your brains, your stomach, and everything else."

His father explained, "Wilky used to be with the Rojax Corporation. He was their northeastern sales representative for a good many years but recently ended the connection."

"Yes," said Wilhelm, "I was with them from the end of the war." He sipped the Coca-Cola and chewed the ice, glancing at one and the other with his attitude of large, shaky, patient dignity. The waitress set two boiled eggs before him.

"What kind of line does this Rojax company manufacture?" said Mr. Perls.

"Kiddies' furniture. Little chairs, rockers, tables, Jungle-Gyms, slides, swings, seesaws."

Wilhelm let his father do the explaining. Large and stiffbacked, he tried to sit patiently, but his feet were abnormally restless. All right! His father had to impress Mr. Perls? He would go along once more, and play his part. Fine! He would play along and help his father maintain his style. Style was the main consideration. That was just fine!

"I was with the Rojax Corporation for almost ten years," he said. "We parted ways because they wanted me to share my territory. They took a son-in-law into the business—a new fellow. It was his idea."

To himself, Wilhelm said, Now God alone can tell why I have to lay my whole life bare to this blasted herring here. I'm sure nobody else does it. Other people keep their business to themselves. Not me.

He continued, "But the rationalization was that it was too big a territory for one man. I had a monopoly. That wasn't so. The real reason was that they had gotten to the place where they would have to make me an officer of the corporation. Vice presidency. I was in line for it, but instead this son-in-law got in, and—"

Dr. Adler thought Wilhelm was discussing his grievances much too openly and said, "My son's income was up in the five figures."

---

[27] From the Estonian Soviet Socialist Republic, in the northwestern U.S.S.R.

As soon as money was mentioned, Mr. Perls's voice grew eagerly sharper. "Yes? What, the thirty-two-per-cent bracket? Higher even, I guess?" He asked for a hint, and he named the figures not idly but with a sort of hugging relish. Uch! How they love money, thought Wilhelm. They adore money! Holy money! Beautiful money! It was getting so that people were feeble-minded about everything except money. While if you didn't have it you were a dummy, a dummy! You had to excuse yourself from the face of the earth. Chicken! that's what it was. The world's business. If only he could find a way out of it.

Such thinking brought on the usual congestion. It would grow into a fit of passion if he allowed it to continue. Therefore he stopped talking and began to eat.

Before he struck the egg with his spoon he dried the moisture with his napkin. Then he battered it (in his father's opinion) more than was necessary. A faint grime was left by his fingers on the white of the egg after he had picked away the shell. Dr. Adler saw it with silent repugnance. What a Wilky he had given to the world! Why, he didn't even wash his hands in the morning. He used an electric razor so that he didn't have to touch water. The doctor couldn't bear Wilky's dirty habits. Only once—and never again, he swore—had he visited his room. Wilhelm, in pajamas and stockings had sat on his bed, drinking gin from a coffee mug and rooting for the Dodgers on television. "That's two and two on you, Duke.[28] Come on—hit it, now." He came down on the mattress—bam! The bed looked kicked to pieces. Then he drank the gin as though it were tea, and urged his team on with his fist. The smell of dirty clothes was outrageous. By the bedside lay a quart bottle and foolish magazines and mystery stories for the hours of insomnia. Wilhelm lived in worse filth than a savage. When the Doctor spoke to him about this he answered, "Well, I have no wife to look after my things." And who—*who!*—had done the leaving? Not Margaret. The Doctor was certain that she wanted him back.

Wilhelm drank his coffee with a trembling hand. In his full face his abused bloodshot gray eyes, moved back and forth. Jerkily he set his cup back and put half the length of a cigarette into his mouth; he seemed to hold it with his teeth, as though it were a cigar.

"I can't let them get away with it," he said. "It's also a question of morale."

His father corrected him. "Don't you mean a moral question, Wilky?"

"I mean that, too. I have to do something to protect myself. I was promised executive standing." Correction before a stranger mortified him, and his dark blond face changed color, more pale, and then more dark. He went on talking to Perls but his eyes spied on his father. "I was the one who opened the territory for them. I could go back for one of their competitors and take away their customers. *My* customers. Morale enters into it because they've tried to take away my confidence."

"Would you offer a different line to the same people?" Mr. Perls wondered.

"Why not? I know what's wrong with the Rojax product."

"Nonsense," said his father. "Just nonsense and kids' talk, Wilky. You're only looking for trouble and embarrassment that way. What would you gain by such a silly feud? You have to think about making a living and meeting your obligations."

Hot and bitter, Wilhelm said with pride, while his feet moved angrily under the table, "I don't have to be told about my obligations. I've been meeting them for years. In more than twenty years I've never had a penny of help from anybody. I

---

[28] Edwin "Duke" Snider (1926–   ), a Brooklyn Dodgers outfielder from 1947 to 1957.

preferred to dig a ditch on the WPA[29] but never asked anyone to meet my obligations for me."

"Wilky has had all kinds of experiences," said Dr. Adler.

The old doctor's face had a wholesome reddish and almost translucent color, like a ripe apricot. The wrinkles beside his ears were deep because the skin conformed so tightly to his bones. With all his might, he was a healthy and fine small old man. He wore a white vest of a light check pattern. His hearing-aid doodad was in the pocket. An unusual shirt of red and black stripes covered his chest. He bought his clothes in a college shop farther uptown. Wilhelm thought he had no business to get himself up like a jockey, out of respect for his profession.

"Well," said Mr. Perls. "I can understand how you feel. You want to fight it out. By a certain time of life, to have to start all over again can't be a pleasure, though a good man can always do it. But anyway you want to keep on with a business you know already, and not have to meet a whole lot of new contacts."

Wilhelm again thought, Why does it have to be me and my life that's discussed, and not him and his life? He would never allow it. But I am an idiot. I have no reserve. To me it can be done. I talk. I must ask for it. Everybody wants to have intimate conversations, but the smart fellows don't give out, only the fools. The smart fellows talk intimately about the fools, and examine them all over and give them advice. Why do I allow it? The hint about his age had hurt him. No, you can't admit it's as good as ever, he conceded. Things do give out.

"In the meanwhile," Dr. Adler said, "Wilky is taking it easy and considering various propositions. Isn't that so?"

"More or less," said Wilhelm. He suffered his father to increase Mr. Perls's respect for him. The WPA ditch had brought the family into contempt. He was a little tired. The spirit, the peculiar burden of his existence lay upon him like an accretion, a load, a hump. In any moment of quiet, when sheer fatigue prevented him from struggling, he was apt to feel this mysterious weight, this growth or collection of nameless things which it was the business of his life to carry about. That must be what a man was for. This large, odd, excited, fleshy, blond, abrupt personality named Wilhelm, or Tommy, was here, present, in the present—Dr. Tamkin had been putting into his mind many suggestions about the present moment, the here and now—this Wilky, or Tommy Wilhelm, forty-four years old, father of two sons, at present living in the Hotel Gloriana, was assigned to be the carrier of a load which was his own self, his characteristic self. There was no figure or estimate for the value of this load. But it is probably exaggerated by the subject, T. W. Who is a visionary sort of animal. Who has to believe that he can know why he exists. Though he has never seriously tried to find out why.

Mr. Perls said, "If he wants time to think things over and have a rest, why doesn't he run down to Florida for a while? Off season it's cheap and quiet. Fairyland. The mangoes are just coming in. I got two acres down there. You'd think you were in India."

Mr. Perls utterly astonished Wilhelm when he spoke of fairyland with a foreign accent. Mangoes—India? What did he mean, India?

"Once upon a time," said Wilhelm, "I did some public relations work for a big hotel down in Cuba. If I could get them a notice in Leonard Lyons[30] or one of the other columns it might be good for another holiday there, gratis. I haven't had a

---

[29] The Works Progress Administration, a government agency that created jobs for the unemployed during the Great Depression.

[30] Lyons (1906–1976) was a gossip columnist in New York City.

vacation for a long time, and I could stand a rest after going so hard. You know that's true, Father." He meant that his father knew how deep the crisis was becoming; how badly he was strapped for money; and that he could not rest but would be crushed if he stumbled; and that his obligations would destroy him. He couldn't falter. He thought, The money! When I had it, I flowed money. They bled it away from me. I hemorrhaged money. But now it's almost all gone, and where am I supposed to turn for more?

He said, "As a matter of fact, Father, I am tired as hell."

But Mr. Perls began to smile and said, "I understand from Doctor Tamkin that you're going into some kind of investment with him, partners."

"You know, he's a very ingenious fellow," said Dr. Adler. "I really enjoy hearing him go on. I wonder if he really is a medical doctor."

"Isn't he?" said Perls. "Everybody thinks he is. He talks about his patients. Doesn't he write prescriptions?"

"I don't really know what he does," said Dr. Adler. "He's a cunning man."

"He's a psychologist, I understand," said Wilhelm.

"I don't know what sort of psychologist or psychiatrist he may be," said his father. "He's a little vague. It's growing into a major industry, and a very expensive one. Fellows have to hold down very big jobs in order to pay those fees. Anyway, this Tamkin is clever. He never said he practiced here, but I believe he was a doctor in California. They don't seem to have much legislation out there to cover these things, and I hear a thousand dollars will get you a degree from a Los Angeles correspondence school. He gives the impression of knowing something about chemistry, and things like hypnotism. I wouldn't trust him, though."

"And why wouldn't you?" Wilhelm demanded.

"Because he's probably a liar. Do you believe he invented all the things he claims?"

Mr. Perls was grinning.

"He was written up in *Fortune*," said Wilhelm. "Yes, in *Fortune* magazine. He showed me the article. I've seen his clippings."

"That doesn't make him legitimate," said Dr. Adler. "It might have been another Tamkin. Make no mistake, he's an operator. Perhaps even crazy."

"Crazy, you say?"

Mr. Perls put in, "He could be both sane and crazy. In these days nobody can tell for sure which is which."

"An electrical device for truck drivers to wear in their caps," said Dr. Adler, describing one of Tamkin's proposed inventions. "To wake them with a shock when they begin to be drowsy at the wheel. It's triggered by the change in blood-pressure when they start to doze."

"It doesn't sound like such an impossible thing to me," said Wilhelm.

Mr. Perls said, "To me he described an underwater suit so a man could walk on the bed of the Hudson in case of an atomic attack. He said he could walk to Albany in it."

"Ha, ha, ha, ha, ha!" cried Dr. Adler in his old man's voice. "Tamkin's Folly. You could go on a camping trip under Niagara Falls."

"This is just his kind of fantasy," said Wilhelm. "It doesn't mean a thing. Inventors are supposed to be like that. I get funny ideas myself. Everybody wants to make something. Any American does."

But his father ignored this and said to Perls, "What other inventions did he describe?"

While the frazzle-faced Mr. Perls and his father in the unseemly, monkey-striped shirt were laughing, Wilhelm could not restrain himself and joined in with his own panting laugh. But he was in despair. They were laughing at the man to whom he had given a power of attorney over his last seven hundred dollars to speculate for him in the commodities market. They had bought all that lard. It had to rise today. By ten o'clock, or half-past ten, trading would be active, and he would see.

III

Between white tablecloths and glassware and glancing silverware, through over-full light, the long figure of Mr. Perls went away into the darkness of the lobby. He thrust with his cane, and dragged a large built-up shoe which Wilhelm had not included in his estimate of troubles. Dr. Adler wanted to talk about him. "There's a poor man," he said, "with a bone condition which is gradually breaking him up."

"One of those progressive diseases?" said Wilhelm.

"Very bad. I've learned," the doctor told him, "to keep my sympathy for the real ailments. This Perls is more to be pitied than any man I know."

Wilhelm understood he was being put on notice and did not express his opinion. He ate and ate. He did not hurry but kept putting food on his plate until he had gone through the muffins and his father's strawberries, and then some pieces of bacon that were left; he had several cups of coffee, and when he was finished he sat gigantically in a state of arrest and didn't seem to know what he should do next.

For a while father and son were uncommonly still. Wilhelm's preparations to please Dr. Adler had failed completely, for the old man kept thinking, You'd never guess he had a clean upbringing, and, What a dirty devil this son of mine is. Why can't he try to sweeten his appearance a little? Why does he want to drag himself like this? And he makes himself look so idealistic.

Wilhelm sat, mountainous. He was not really so slovenly as his father found him to be. In some aspects he even had a certain delicacy. His mouth, though broad, had a fine outline, and his brow and his gradually incurved nose, dignity, and in his blond hair there was white but there were also shades of gold and chestnut. When he was with the Rojax Corporation Wilhelm had kept a small apartment in Roxbury, two rooms in a large house with a small porch and garden, and on mornings of leisure, in late spring weather like this, he used to sit expanded in a wicker chair with the sunlight pouring through the weave, and sunlight through the slug-eaten holes of the young hollyhocks and as deeply as the grass allowed into small flowers. This peace (he forgot that that time had had its troubles, too), this peace was gone. It must not have belonged to him, really, for to be here in New York with his old father was more genuinely like his life. He was well aware that he didn't stand a chance of getting sympathy from his father, who said he kept his for real ailments. Moreover, he advised himself repeatedly not to discuss his vexatious problems with him, for his father, with some justice, wanted to be left in peace. Wilhelm also knew that when he began to talk about these things he made himself feel worse, he became congested with them and worked himself into a clutch. Therefore he warned himself, Lay off, pal. It'll only be an aggravation. From a deeper source, however, came other promptings. If he didn't keep his troubles before him he risked losing them altogether, and he knew by experience that this was worse. And furthermore, he could not succeed in excusing his father on the ground of old age. No. No, he could not. I am his son, he thought. He is my father. He is as much father as I am son—old or not. Affirming this, though in complete silence, he sat, and, sitting, he kept his father at the table with him.

"Wilky," said the old man, "have you gone down to the baths here yet?"

"No, Dad, not yet."

"Well, you know the Gloriana has one of the finest pools in New York. Eighty feet, blue tile. It's a beauty."

Wilhelm had seen it. On the way to the gin game you passed the stairway to the pool. He did not care for the odor of the wall-locked and chlorinated water.

"You ought to investigate the Russian and Turkish baths, and the sunlamps and massage. I don't hold with sunlamps. But the massage does a world of good, and there's nothing better than hydrotherapy when you come right down to it. Simple water has a calming effect and would do you more good than all the barbiturates and alcohol in the world."

Wilhelm reflected that this advice was as far as his father's help and sympathy would extend.

"I thought," he said, "that the water cure was for lunatics."

The doctor received this as one of his son's jokes and said with a smile, "Well, it won't turn a sane man into a lunatic. It does a great deal for me. I couldn't live without my massages and steam."

"You're probably right. I ought to try it one of these days. Yesterday, late in the afternoon, my head was about to bust and I just had to have a little air, so I walked around the reservoir, and I sat down for a while in a playground. It rests me to watch the kids play potsy[31] and skiprope."

The doctor said with approval, "Well, now, that's more like the idea."

"It's the end of the lilacs," said Wilhelm. "When they burn it's the beginning of summer. At least, in the city. Around the time of year when the candy stores take down the windows and start to sell sodas on the sidewalk. But even though I was raised here, Dad, I can't take city life any more, and I miss the country. There's too much push here for me. It works me up too much. I take things too hard. I wonder why you never retired to a quieter place."

The doctor opened his small hand on the table in a gesture so old and so typical that Wilhelm felt it like an actual touch upon the foundations of his life. "I am a city boy myself, you must remember," Dr. Adler explained. "But if you find the city so hard on you, you ought to get out."

"I'll do that," said Wilhelm, "as soon as I can make the right connection. Meanwhile—"

His father interrupted, "Meanwhile I suggest you cut down on drugs."

"You exaggerate that, Dad. I don't really— I give myself a little boost against—" He almost pronounced the word "misery" but he kept his resolution not to complain.

The doctor, however, fell into the error of pushing his advice too hard. It was all he had to give his son and he gave it once more. "Water and exercise," he said.

He wants a young, smart, successful son, thought Wilhelm, and he said, "Oh, Father, it's nice of you to give me this medical advice, but steam isn't going to cure what ails me."

---

[31] A variation of hopskotch.

The doctor measurably drew back, warned by the sudden weak strain of Wilhelm's voice and all that the droop of his face, the swell of his belly against the restraint of his belt intimated.

"Some new business?" he asked unwillingly.

Wilhelm made a great preliminary summary which involved the whole of his body. He drew and held a long breath, and his color changed and his eyes swam. "New?" he said.

"You make too much of your problems," said the doctor. "They ought not to be turned into a career. Concentrate on real troubles—fatal sickness, accidents." The old man's whole manner said, Wilky, don't start this on me. I have a right to be spared.

Wilhelm himself prayed for restraint; he knew this weakness of his and fought it. He knew, also, his father's character. And he began mildly, "As far as the fatal part of it goes, everyone on this side of the grave is the same distance from death. No, I guess my trouble is not exactly new. I've got to pay premiums on two policies for the boys. Margaret sent them to me. She unloads everything on me. Her mother left her an income. She won't even file a joint tax return. I get stuck. Etcetera. But you've heard the whole story before."

"I certainly have," said the old man. "And I've told you to stop giving her so much money."

Wilhelm worked his lips in silence before he could speak. The congestion was growing. "Oh, but my kids, Father. My kids. I love them. I don't want them to lack anything."

The doctor said with a half-deaf benevolence, "Well, naturally. And she, I'll bet, is the beneficiary of that policy."

"Let her be. I'd sooner die myself before I collected a cent of such money."

"Ah, yes." The old man sighed. He did not like the mention of death. "Did I tell you that your sister Catherine—Philippa—is after me again."

"What for?"

"She wants to rent a gallery for an exhibition."

Stiffly fair-minded, Wilhelm said, "Well, of course that's up to you, Father."

The round-headed old man with his fine, feather-white, ferny hair said, "No, Wilky. There's not a thing on those canvases. I don't believe it; it's a case of the emperor's clothes. I may be old enough for my second childhood, but at least the first is well behind me. I was glad enough to buy crayons for her when she was four. But now she's a woman of forty and too old to be encouraged in her delusions. She's no painter."

"I wouldn't go so far as to call her a born artist," said Wilhelm, "but you can't blame her for trying something worth while."

"Let her husband pamper her."

Wilhelm had done his best to be just to his sister, and he had sincerely meant to spare his father, but the old man's tight, benevolent deafness had its usual effect on him. He said, "When it comes to women and money, I'm completely in the dark. What makes Margaret act like this?"

"She's showing you that you can't make it without her," said the doctor. "She aims to bring you back by financial force."

"But if she ruins me, Dad, how can she expect me to come back? No, I have a sense of honor. What you don't see is that she's trying to put an end to me."

His father stared. To him this was absurd. And Wilhelm thought, Once a guy starts to slip, he figures he might as well be a clunk. A real big clunk. He even takes pride in it. But there's nothing to be proud of—hey, boy? Nothing. I don't blame Dad for his attitude. And it's no cause for pride.

"I don't understand that. But if you feel like this why don't you settle with her once and for all?"

"What do you mean, Dad?" said Wilhelm, surprised. "I thought I told you. Do you think I'm not willing to settle? Four years ago when we broke up I gave her everything—goods, furniture, savings. I tried to show good will, but I didn't get anywhere. Why when I wanted Scissors, the dog, because the animal and I were so attached to each other—it was bad enough to leave the kids—she absolutely refused me. Not that she cared a damn about the animal. I don't think you've seen him. He's an Australian sheep dog. They usually have one blank or whitish eye which gives a misleading look, but they're the gentlest dogs and have unusual delicacy about eating or talking. Let me at least have the companionship of this animal. Never." Wilhelm was greatly moved. He wiped his face at all corners with his napkin. Dr. Adler felt that his son was indulging himself too much in his emotions.

"Whenever she can hit me, she hits, and she seems to live for that alone. And she demands more and more, and still more. Two years ago she wanted to go back to college and get another degree. It increased my burden but I thought it would be wiser in the end if she got a better job through it. But still she takes as much from me as before. Next thing she'll want to be a Doctor of Philosophy. She says the women in her family live long, and I'll have to pay and pay for the rest of my life."

The doctor said impatiently, "Well, these are details, not principles. Just details which you can leave out. The dog! You're mixing up all kinds of irrelevant things. Go to a good lawyer."

"But I've already told you, Dad. I got a lawyer, and she got one, too, and both of them talk and send me bills, and I eat my heart out. Oh, Dad, Dad, what a hole I'm in!" said Wilhelm in utter misery. "The lawyers—see?—draw up an agreement, and she says okay on Monday and wants more money on Tuesday. And it begins again."

"I always thought she was a strange kind of woman," said Dr. Adler. He felt that by disliking Margaret from the first and disapproving of the marriage he had done all that he could be expected to do.

"Strange, Father? I'll show you what she's like." Wilhelm took hold of his broad throat with brown-stained fingers and bitten nails and began to choke himself.

"What are you doing?" cried the old man.

"I'm showing you what she does to me."

"Stop that—stop it!" the old man said and tapped the table commandingly.

"Well, Dad, she hates me. I feel that she's strangling me. I can't catch my breath. She just has fixed herself on me to kill me. She can do it at long distance. One of these days I'll be struck down by suffocation or apoplexy because of her. I just can't catch my breath."

"Take your hands off your throat, you foolish man," said his father. "Stop this bunk. Don't expect me to believe in all kinds of voodoo."

"If that's what you want to call it, all right." His face flamed and paled and swelled and his breath was laborious.

"But I'm telling you that from the time I met her I've been a slave. The Emancipation Proclamation was only for colored people. A husband like me is a slave, with an iron collar. The churches go up to Albany and supervise the law. They won't have divorces. The court says, 'You want to be free. Then you have to work twice as hard—twice, at least! Work! you bum.' So then guys kill each other for the buck, and they may be free of a wife who hates them but they are sold to the company. The company knows a guy has got to have his salary, and takes full advantage of him. Don't talk to me about being free. A rich man may be free on an income of a million net. A poor man may be free because nobody cares what he does. But a fellow in my position has to sweat it out until he drops dead."

His father replied to this, "Wilky, it's entirely your own fault. You don't have to allow it."

Stopped in his eloquence, Wilhelm could not speak for a while. Dumb and incompetent, he struggled for breath and frowned with effort into his father's face.

"I don't understand your problems," said the old man. "I never had any like them."

By now Wilhelm had lost his head and he waved his hands and said over and over, "Oh, Dad, don't give me that stuff, don't give me that. Please don't give me that sort of thing."

"It's true," said his father. "I come from a different world. Your mother and I led an entirely different life."

"Oh, how can you compare Mother," Wilhelm said. "Mother was a help to you. Did she harm you ever?"

"There's no need to carry on like an opera, Wilky," said the doctor. "This is only your side of things."

"What? It's the truth," said Wilhelm.

The old man could not be persuaded and shook his round head and drew his vest down over the gilded shirt, and leaned back with a completeness of style that made this look, to anyone out of hearing, like an ordinary conversation between a middle-aged man and his respected father. Wilhelm towered and swayed, big and sloven, with his gray eyes red-shot and his honey-colored hair twisted in flaming shapes upward. Injustice made him angry, made him beg. But he wanted an understanding with his father, and he tried to capitulate to him. He said, "You can't compare Mother and Margaret, and neither can you and I be compared, because you, Dad, were a success. And a success—is a success. I never made a success."

The doctor's old face lost all of its composure and became hard and angry. His small breast rose sharply under the red and black shirt and he said, "Yes. Because of hard work. I was not self-indulgent, not lazy. My old man sold dry goods in Williamsburg. We were nothing, do you understand? I knew I couldn't afford to waste my chances."

"I wouldn't admit for one minute that I was lazy," said Wilhelm. "If anything, I tried too hard. I admit I made many mistakes. Like I thought I shouldn't do things you had done already. Study chemistry. You had done it already. It was in the family."

His father continued, "I didn't run around with fifty women, either. I was not a Hollywood star. I didn't have time to go to Cuba for a vacation. I stayed at home and took care of my children."

Oh, thought Wilhelm, eyes turning upward. Why did I come here in the first place, to live near him? New York is like a gas. The colors are running. My head feels so tight, I don't know what I'm doing. He thinks I want to take away his money or that I envy him. He doesn't see what I want.

"Dad," Wilhelm said aloud, "you're being very unfair. It's true the movies was a false step. But I love my boys. I didn't abandon them. I left Margaret because I had to."

"Why did you have to?"

"Well—" said Wilhelm, struggling to condense his many reasons into a few plain words. "I had to—I had to."

With sudden and surprising bluntness his father said, "Did you have bed-trouble with her? Then you should have stuck it out. Sooner or later everyone has it. Normal people stay with it. It passes. But you wouldn't, so now you pay for your stupid romantic notions. Have I made my view clear?"

It was very clear. Wilhelm seemed to hear it repeated from various sides and inclined his head different ways, and listened and thought. Finally he said, "I guess that's the medical standpoint. You may be right. I just couldn't live with Margaret. I wanted to stick it out, but I was getting very sick. She was one way and I was another. She wouldn't be like me, so I tried to be like her, and I couldn't do it."

"Are you sure she didn't tell *you* to go?" the doctor said.

"I wish she had. I'd be in a better position now. No, it was me. I didn't want to leave, but I couldn't stay. Somebody had to take the initiative. I did. Now I'm the fall guy too."

Pushing aside in advance all the objections that his son would make, the doctor said, "Why did you lose your job with Rojax?"

"I didn't, I've told you."

"You're lying. You wouldn't have ended the connection. You need the money too badly. But you must have got into trouble." The small old man spoke concisely and with great strength. "Since you have to talk and can't let it alone, tell the truth. Was there a scandal—a woman?"

Wilhelm fiercely defended himself. "No, Dad, there wasn't any woman. I told you how it was."

"Maybe it was a man, then," the old man said wickedly.

Shocked, Wilhelm stared at him with burning pallor and dry lips. His skin looked a little yellow. "I don't think you know what you're talking about," he answered after a moment. "You shouldn't let your imagination run so free. Since you've been living here on Broadway you must think you understand life, up to date. You ought to know your own son a little better. Let's drop that, now."

"All right, Wilky, I'll withdraw it. But something must have happened in Roxbury nevertheless. You'll never go back. You're just talking wildly about representing a rival company. You won't. You've done something to spoil your reputation, I think. But you've got girl friends who are expecting you back, isn't that so?"

"I take a lady out now and then while on the road," said Wilhelm. "I'm not a monk."

"No one special? Are you sure you haven't gotten into complications?"

He had tried to unburden himself and instead, Wilhelm thought, he had to undergo an inquisition to prove himself worthy of a sympathetic word. Because his father believed that he did all kinds of gross things.

"There is a woman in Roxbury that I went with. We fell in love and wanted to marry, but she got tired of waiting for my divorce. Margaret figured that. On top of which the girl was a Catholic and I had to go with her to the priest and make an explanation."

Neither did this last confession touch Dr. Adler's sympathies or sway his calm old head or affect the color of his complexion.

"No, no, no, no; all wrong," he said.

Again Wilhelm cautioned himself. Remember his age. He is no longer the same person. He can't bear trouble. I'm so choked up and congested anyway I can't see straight. Will I ever get out of the woods, and recover my balance? You're never the same afterward. Trouble rusts out the system.

"You really *want* a divorce?" said the old man.

"For the price I pay I should be getting something."

"In that case," Dr. Adler said, "it seems to me no normal person would stand for such treatment from a woman."

"Ah, Father, Father!" said Wilhelm. "It's always the same thing with you. Look how you lead me on. You always start out to help me with my problems, and be sympathetic and so forth. It gets my hopes up and I begin to be grateful. But before we're through I'm a hundred times more depressed than before. Why is that? You have no sympathy. You want to shift all the blame on to me. Maybe you're wise to do it." Wilhelm was beginning to lose himself. "All you seem to think about is your death. Well, I'm sorry. But I'm going to die too. And I'm your son. It isn't my fault in the first place. There ought to be a right way to do this, and be fair to each other. But what I want to know is, why do you start up with me if you're not going to help me? What do you want to know about my problems for, Father? So you can lay the whole responsibility on me—so that you won't have to help me? D'you want me to comfort you for having such a son?" Wilhelm had a great knot of wrong tied tight within his chest, and tears approached his eyes but he didn't let them out. He looked shabby enough as it was. His voice was thick and hazy, and he was stammering and could not bring his awful feelings forth.

"You have some purpose of your own," said the doctor, "in acting so unreasonable. What do you want from me? What do you expect?"

"What do I expect?" said Wilhelm. He felt as though he were unable to recover something. Like a ball in the surf, washed beyond reach, his self-control was going out. "I expect *help!*" The words escaped him in a loud, wild, frantic cry and startled the old man, and two or three breakfasters within hearing glanced their way. Wilhelm's hair, the color of whitened honey, rose dense and tall with the expansion of his face, and he said, "When I suffer—you aren't even sorry. That's because you have no affection for me, and you don't want any part of me."

"Why must I like the way you behave? No, I don't like it." said Dr. Adler.

"All right. You want me to change myself. But suppose I could do it—what would I become? What could I? Let's suppose that all my life I have had the wrong ideas about myself and wasn't what I thought I was. And wasn't even careful to take a few precautions, as most people do—like a woodchuck has a few exits to his tunnel. But what shall I do now? More than half my life is over. More than half. And now you tell me I'm not even normal."

The old man too had lost his calm. "You cry about being helped," he said. "When you thought you had to go into the service I sent a check to Margaret every month. As a family man you could have had an exemption. But no! The war couldn't be fought without you and you had to get yourself drafted and be an office-boy in the Pacific theater. Any clerk could have done what you did. You could find nothing better to become than a GI."

Wilhelm was going to reply, and half raised his bearish figure from the chair, his fingers spread and whitened by their grip on the table, but the old man would not let him begin. He said, "I see other elderly people here with children who aren't much good, and they keep backing them and holding them up at a great sacrifice. But I'm not going to make that mistake. It doesn't enter your mind that when I die—a year, two years from now—you'll still be here. I do think of it."

He had intended to say that he had a right to be left in peace. Instead he gave Wilhelm the impression that he meant it was not fair for the better man of the two, and the more useful, the more admired, to leave the world first. Perhaps he meant that, too—a little; but he would not under other circumstances have come out with it so flatly.

"Father," said Wilhelm with an unusual openness of appeal. "Don't you think I know how you feel? I have pity. I want you to live on and on. If you outlive me, that's perfectly okay by me." As his father did not answer this avowal and turned away his glance, Wilhelm suddenly burst out, "No, but you hate me. And if I had money you wouldn't. By God, you have to admit it. The money makes the difference. Then we would be a fine father and son, if I was a credit to you—so you could boast and brag about me all over the hotel. But I'm not the right type of son. I'm too old, I'm too old and too unlucky."

His father said, "I can't give you any money. There would be no end to it if I started. You and your sister would take every last buck from me. I'm still alive, not dead. I am still here. Life isn't over yet. I am as much alive as you or anyone. And I want nobody on my back. Get off! And I give you the same advice, Wilky. Carry nobody on your back."

"Just keep your money," said Wilhelm miserably. "Keep it and enjoy it yourself. That's the ticket!"

IV

Ass! Idiot! Wild boar! Dumb mule! Slave! Lousy, wallowing hippopotamus! Wilhelm called himself as his bending legs carried him from the dining room. His pride! His inflamed feelings! His begging and feebleness! And trading insults with his old father—and spreading confusion over everything. Oh, how poor, contemptible, and ridiculous he was! When he remembered how he had said, with great reproof, "You ought to know your own son"—why, how corny and abominable it was.

He could not get out of the sharply brilliant dining room fast enough. He was horribly worked up; his neck and shoulders, his entire chest ached as though they had been tightly tied with ropes. He smelled the salt odor of tears in his nose.

But at the same time, since there were depths in Wilhelm not unsuspected by himself, he received a suggestion from some remote element in his thoughts that the business of life, the real business—to carry his peculiar burden, to feel shame and impotence, to taste these quelled tears—the only important business, the highest business was being done. Maybe the making of mistakes expressed the very purpose of his life and the essence of his being here. Maybe he was supposed to make them and suffer from them on this earth. And though he had raised himself above Mr. Perls and his father because they adored money, still they were called to act energetically and this was better than to yell and cry, pray and beg, poke and blunder and go by fits and starts and fall upon the thorns of life. And finally sink beneath that watery floor—would that be tough luck, or would it be good riddance?

But he raged once more against his father. Other people with money, while they're still alive, want to see it do some good. Granted, he shouldn't support me. But have I ever asked him to do that? Have I ever asked for dough at all, either for Margaret or for the kids or for myself? It isn't the money, but only the assistance; not even assistance, but just the feeling. But he may be trying to teach me that a grown man should be cured of such feeling. Feeling got me in dutch[32] at Rojax. I had the *feeling* that I belonged to the firm, and my *feelings* were hurt when they put Gerber in over me. Dad thinks I'm too simple. But I'm not so simple as he thinks. What about his feelings? He doesn't forget death for one single second, and that's what makes him like this. And not only is death on his mind but through money he forces me to think about it, too. It gives him power over me. He forces me that way, he himself, and then he's sore. If he was poor, I could care for him and show it. The way I *could* care, too, if I only had a chance. He'd see how much love and respect I had in me. It would make him a different man, too. He'd put his hands on me and give me his blessing."

Someone in a gray straw hat with a wide cocoa-colored band spoke to Wilhelm in the lobby. The light was dusky, splotched with red underfoot; green, the leather furniture; yellow, the indirect lighting.

"Hey, Tommy. Say, there."

"Excuse me," said Wilhelm, trying to reach a house phone. But this was Dr. Tamkin, whom he was just about to call.

"You have a very obsessional look on your face," said Dr. Tamkin.

Wilhelm thought, Here he is, Here he is. If I could only figure this guy out.

"Oh," he said to Tamkin. "Have I got such a look? Well, whatever it is, you name it and I'm sure to have it."

The sight of Dr. Tamkin brought his quarrel with his father to a close. He found himself flowing into another channel.

"What are we doing?" he said. "What's going to happen to lard today?"

"Don't worry yourself about that. All we have to do is hold on to it and it's sure to go up. But what's made you so hot under the collar, Wilhelm?"

"Oh, one of those family situations." This was the moment to take a new look at Tamkin, and he viewed him closely but gained nothing by the new effort. It was conceivable that Tamkin was everything that he claimed to be, and all the gossip false. But was he a scientific man, or not? If he was not, this might be a case for the district attorney's office to investigate. Was he a liar? That was a delicate question. Even a liar might be trustworthy in some ways. Could he trust Tamkin—could he? He feverishly, fruitlessly sought an answer.

But the time for this question was past, and he had to trust him now. After a long struggle to come to a decision, he had given him the money. Practical judgment was in abeyance. He had worn himself out, and the decision was no decision. How had this happened? But how had his Hollywood career begun? It was not because of Maurice Venice, who turned out to be a pimp. It was because Wilhelm himself was ripe for the mistake. His marriage, too, had been like that. Through such decisions somehow his life had taken form. And so, from the moment when he tasted the peculiar flavor of fatality in Dr. Tamkin, he could no longer keep back the money.

Five days ago Tamkin had said, "Meet me tomorrow, and we'll go to the market." Wilhelm, therefore, had had to go. At eleven o'clock they had walked to the

---

[32] In trouble.

brokerage office. On the way, Tamkin broke the news to Wilhelm that though this was an equal partnership he couldn't put up his half of the money just yet; it was tied up for a week or so in one of his patents. Today he would be two hundred dollars short; next week, he'd make it up. But neither of them needed an income from the market, of course. This was only a sporting proposition anyhow, Tamkin said. Wilhelm had to answer, "Of course." It was too late to withdraw. What else could he do? Then came the formal part of the transaction, and it was frightening. The very shade of green of Tamkin's check looked wrong; it was a false, disheartening color. His handwriting was peculiar, even monstrous; the e's were like i's, the t's and l's the same, and the h's like wasps' bellies. He wrote like a fourth-grader. Scientists, however, dealt mostly in symbols; they printed. This was Wilhelm's explanation.

Dr. Tamkin had given him his check for three hundred dollars. Wilhelm, in a blinded and convulsed aberration, pressed and pressed to try to kill the trembling of his hand as he wrote out his check for a thousand. He set his lips tight, crouched with his huge back over the table, and wrote with crumbling, terrified fingers, knowing that if Tamkin's check bounced his own would not be honored either. His sole cleverness was to set the date ahead by one day to give the green check time to clear.

Next he had signed a power of attorney, allowing Tamkin to speculate with his money, and this was an even more frightening document. Tamkin had never said a word about it, but here they were and it had to be done.

After delivering his signatures, the only precaution Wilhelm took was to come back to the manager of the brokerage office and ask him privately, "Uh, about Doctor Tamkin. We were in here a few minutes ago, remember?"

That day had been a weeping, smoky one and Wilhelm had gotten away from Tamkin on the pretext of having to run to the post office. Tamkin had gone to lunch alone, and here was Wilhelm, back again, breathless, his hat dripping, needlessly asking the manager if he remembered.

"Yes, sir, I know," the manager had said. He was a cold, mild, lean German who dressed correctly and around his neck wore a pair of opera glasses with which he read the board. He was an extremely correct person except that he never shaved in the morning, not caring, probably, how he looked to the fumblers and the old people and the operators and the gamblers and the idlers of Broadway uptown. The market closed at three. Maybe, Wilhelm guessed, he had a thick beard and took a lady out to dinner later and wanted to look fresh-shaven.

"Just a question," said Wilhelm. "A few minutes ago I signed a power of attorney so Doctor Tamkin could invest for me. You gave me the blanks."

"Yes, sir, I remember."

"Now this is what I want to know," Wilhelm had said. "I'm no lawyer and I only gave the paper a glance. Does this give Doctor Tamkin power of attorney over any other assets of mine—money, or property?"

The rain had dribbled from Wilhelm's deformed, transparent raincoat; the buttons of his shirt, which always seemed tiny, were partly broken, in pearly quarters of the moon, and some of the dark, thick golden hairs that grew on his belly stood out. It was the manager's business to conceal his opinion of him; he was shrewd, gray, correct (although unshaven) and had little to say except on matters that came to his desk. He must have recognized in Wilhelm a man who reflected long and then made the decision he had rejected twenty separate times. Silvery, cool, level, long-profiled, experienced, indifferent, observant, with unshaven refinement, he scarcely looked at Wilhelm, who trembled with fearful awkwardness. The manager's face, low-colored, long-nostriled, acted as a unit of perception; his eyes merely did their reduced share. Here was a man, like Rubin, who knew and knew and knew. He, a foreigner, knew; Wilhelm, in the city of his birth, was ignorant.

The manager had said, "No, sir, it does not give him."

"Only over the funds I deposited with you?"

"Yes, that is right, sir."

"Thank you, that's what I wanted to find out," Wilhelm had said, grateful.

The answer comforted him. However, the question had no value. None at all. For Wilhelm had no other assets. He had given Tamkin his last money. There wasn't enough of it to cover his obligations anyway, and Wilhelm had reckoned that he might as well go bankrupt now as next month. "Either broke or rich," was how he had figured, and that formula had encouraged him to make the gamble. Well, not rich; he did not expect that, but perhaps Tamkin might really show him how to earn what he needed in the market. By now, however, he had forgotten his own reckoning and was aware only that he stood to lose his seven hundred dollars to the last cent.

Dr. Tamkin took the attitude that they were a pair of gentlemen experimenting with lard and grain futures. The money, a few hundred dollars, meant nothing much to either of them. He said to Wilhelm, "Watch. You'll get a big kick out of this and wonder why more people don't go into it. You think the Wall Street guys are so smart—geniuses? That's because most of us are psychologically afraid to think about the details. Tell me this. When you're on the road, and you don't understand what goes on under the hood of your car, you'll worry what'll happen if something goes wrong with the engine. Am I wrong?" No, he was right. "Well," said Dr. Tamkin with an expression of quiet triumph about his mouth, almost the suggestion of a jeer. "It's the same psychological principle, Wilhelm. They are rich because you don't understand what goes on. But it's no mystery, and by putting in a little money and applying certain principles of observation, you begin to grasp it. It can't be studied in the abstract. You have to take a specimen risk so that you feel the process, the money-flow, the whole complex. To know how it feels to be a seaweed you have to get in the water. In a very short time we'll take out a hundred-per-cent profit." Thus Wilhelm had had to pretend at the outset that his interest in the market was theoretical.

"Well," said Tamkin when he met him now in the lobby, "what's the problem, what is this family situation? Tell me." He put himself forward as the keen mental scientist. Whenever this happened Wilhelm didn't know what to reply. No matter what he said or did it seemed that Dr. Tamkin saw through him.

"I had some words with my dad."

Dr. Tamkin found nothing extraordinary in this. "It's the eternal same story," he said. "The elemental conflict of parent and child. It won't end, ever. Even with a fine old gentleman like your dad."

"I don't suppose it will. I've never been able to get anywhere with him. He objects to my feelings. He thinks they're sordid. I upset him and he gets mad at me. But maybe all old men are alike."

"Sons, too. Take it from one of them," said Dr. Tamkin. "All the same, you should be proud of such a fine old patriarch of a father. It should give you hope. The longer he lives, the longer your life-expectancy becomes."

Wilhelm answered, brooding, "I guess so. But I think I inherit more from my mother's side, and she died in her fifties."

"A problem arose between a young fellow I'm treating and his dad—I just had a consultation," said Dr. Tamkin as he removed his dark gray hat.

"So early in the morning?" said Wilhelm with suspicion.

"Over the telephone, of course."

What a creature Tamkin was when he took off his hat! The indirect light showed the many complexities of his bald skull, his gull's nose, his rather handsome eyebrows, his vain mustache, his deceiver's brown eyes. His figure was stocky, rigid, short in the neck, so that the large ball of the occiput touched his collar. His bones were peculiarly formed, as though twisted twice where the ordinary human bone was turned only once, and his shoulders rose in two pagoda-like points. At mid-body he was thick. He stood pigeon-toed, a sign perhaps that he was devious or had much to hide. The skin of his hands was aging, and his nails were moonless, concave, clawlike, and they appeared loose. His eyes were as brown as beaver fur and full of strange lines. The two large brown naked balls looked thoughtful—but were they? And honest—but was Dr. Tamkin honest? There was a hypnotic power in his eyes, but this was not always of the same strength, nor was Wilhelm convinced that it was completely natural. He felt that Tamkin tried to make his eyes deliberately conspicuous, with studied art, and that he brought forth his hypnotic effect by an exertion. Occasionally it failed or drooped, and when this happened the sense of his face passed downward to his heavy (possibly foolish?) red underlip.

Wilhelm wanted to talk about the lard holdings, but Dr. Tamkin said, "This father-and-son case of mine would be instructive to you. It's a different psychological type completely than your dad. This man's father thinks that he isn't his son."

"Why not?"

"Because he has found out something about the mother carrying on with a friend of the family for twenty-five years."

"Well, what do you know!" said Wilhelm. His silent thought was, Pure bull. Nothing but bull!

"You must note how interesting the woman is, too. She has two husbands. Whose are the kids? The fellow detected her and she gave a signed confession that two of the four children were not the father's."

"It's amazing," said Wilhelm, but he said it in a rather distant way. He was always hearing such stories from Dr. Tamkin. If you were to believe Tamkin, most of the world was like this. Everybody in the hotel had a mental disorder, a secret history, a concealed disease. The wife of Rubin at the newsstand was supposed to be kept by Carl, the yelling, loud-mouthed gin-rummy player. The wife of Frank in the barbershop had disappeared with a GI while he was waiting for her to disembark at the French Lines pier. Everyone was like the faces on a playing card, upside down either way. Every public figure had a character-neurosis. Maddest of all were the businessmen, the heartless, flaunting, boisterous business class who ruled this country with their hard manners and their bold lies and their absurd words that nobody could believe. They were crazier than anyone. They spread the plague. Wilhelm, thinking of the Rojax Corporation, was inclined to agree that many businessmen were insane. And he supposed that Tamkin, for all his peculiarities, spoke a kind of truth and did some people a sort of good. It confirmed Wilhelm's suspicions to hear that there was a plague, and he said, "I couldn't agree with you more. They trade on anything, they steal everything, they're cynical right to the bones."

"You have to realize," said Tamkin, speaking of his patient, or his client, "that the mother's confession isn't good. It's a confession of duress. I try to tell the young fellow he shouldn't worry about a phony confession. But what does it help him if I am rational with him?"

"No?" said Wilhelm, intensely nervous. "I think we ought to go over to the market. It'll be opening pretty soon."

"Oh, come on," said Tamkin. "It isn't even nine o'clock, and there isn't much trading the first hour anyway. Things don't get hot in Chicago until half-past ten, and they're an hour behind us, don't forget. Anyway, I say lard will go up, and it will. Take my word. I've made a study of the guilt-aggression cycle which is behind it. I ought to know *something* about that. Straighten your collar."

"But meantime," said Wilhelm, "we have taken a licking this week. Are you sure your insight is at its best? Maybe when it isn't we should lay off and wait."

"Don't you realize," Dr. Tamkin told him, "you can't march in a straight line to the victory? You fluctuate toward it. From Euclid to Newton[33] there was straight lines. The modern age analyzes the wavers. On my own accounts, I took a licking in hides and coffee. But I have confidence. I'm sure I'll out-guess them." He gave Wilhelm a narrow smile, friendly, calming, shrewd, and wizard-like, patronizing, secret, potent. He saw his fears and smiled at them. "It's something," he remarked, "to see how the competition-factor will manifest itself in different individuals."

"So? Let's go over."

"But I haven't had my breakfast yet."

"I've had mine."

"Come, have a cup of coffee."

"I wouldn't want to meet my dad." Looking through the glass doors, Wilhelm saw that his father had left by the other exit. Wilhelm thought, He didn't want to run into me, either. He said to Dr. Tamkin, "Okay, I'll sit with you, but let's hurry it up because I'd like to get to the market while there's still a place to sit. Everybody and his uncle gets in ahead of you."

"I want to tell you about this boy and his dad. It's highly absorbing. The father was a nudist. Everybody went naked in the house. Maybe the woman found men *with* clothes attractive. Her husband didn't believe in cutting his hair, either. He practiced dentistry. In his office he wore riding pants and a pair of boots, and he wore a green eyeshade."

"Oh, come off it," said Wilhelm.

"This is a true case history."

Without warning, Wilhelm began to laugh. He himself had had no premonition of his change of humor. His face became warm and pleasant, and he forgot his father, his anxieties; he panted bearlike, happily, through his teeth. "This sounds like a horse-dentist. He wouldn't have to put on pants to treat a horse. Now what else are you going to tell me? Did the wife play the mandolin? Does the boy join the cavalry? Oh, Tamkin, you really are a killer-diller."

"Oh, you think I'm trying to amuse you," said Tamkin. "That's because you aren't familiar with my outlook. I deal in facts. Facts always are sensational. I'll say that a second time. Facts *always!* are sensational."

---

[33] A fourth-century B.C. Greek mathematician; the English physicist and mathematician Sir Isaac Newton (1642–1727).

Wilhelm was reluctant to part with his good mood. The doctor had little sense of humor. He was looking at him earnestly.

"I'd bet you any amount of money," said Tamkin, "that the facts about you are sensational."

"Oh—ha, ha! You want them? You can sell them to a true confession magazine."

"People forget how sensational the things are that they do. They don't see it on themselves. It blends into the background of their daily life."

Wilhelm smiled. "Are you sure this boy tells you the truth?"

"Yes, because I've known the whole family for years."

"And you do psychological work with your own friends? I didn't know that was allowed."

"Well, I'm a radical in the profession. I have to do good wherever I can."

Wilhelm's face became ponderous again and pale. His whitened gold hair lay heavy on his head, and he clasped uneasy fingers on the table. Sensational, but oddly enough, dull, too. Now how do you figure that out? It blends with the background. Funny but unfunny. True but false. Casual but laborious, Tamkin was. Wilhelm was most suspicious of him when he took his driest tone.

"With me," said Dr. Tamkin, "I am at my most efficient when I don't need the fee. When I only love. Without a financial reward. I remove myself from the social influence. Especially money. The spiritual compensation is what I look for. Bringing people into the here-and-now. The real universe. That's the present moment. The past is no good to us. The future is full of anxiety. Only the present is real—the here-and-now. Seize the day."

"Well," said Wilhelm, his earnestness returning. "I know you are a very unusual man. I like what you say about here-and-now. Are all the people who come to see you personal friends and patients too? Like that tall handsome girl, the one who always wears those beautiful broomstick skirts and belts?"

"She was an epileptic, and a most bad and serious pathology, too. I'm curing her successfully. She hasn't had a seizure in six months, and she used to have one every week."

"And that young cameraman, the one who showed us those movies from the jungles of Brazil, isn't he related to her?"

"Her brother. He's under my care, too. He has some terrible tendencies, which are to be expected when you have an epileptic sibling. I came into their lives when they needed help desperately, and took hold of them. A certain man forty years older than she had her in his control and used to give her fits by suggestion whenever she tried to leave him. If you only knew one per cent of what goes on in the city of New York! You see, I understand what it is when the lonely person begins to feel like an animal. When the night comes and he feels like howling from his window like a wolf. I'm taking complete care of that young fellow and his sister. I have to steady him down or he'll go from Brazil to Australia the next day. The way I keep him in the here-and-now is by teaching him Greek."

This was a complete surprise! "What, do you know Greek?"

"A friend of mine taught me when I was in Cairo. I studied Aristotle[34] with him to keep from being idle."

Wilhelm tried to take in these new claims and examine them. Howling from the window like a wolf when night comes sounded genuine to him. That was some-

---

[34] The Greek philosopher Aristotle (384–322 B.C.).

thing really to think about. But the Greek! He realized that Tamkin was watching to see how he took it. More elements were continually being added. A few days ago Tamkin had hinted that he had once been in the underworld, one of the Detroit Purple Gang. He was once head of a mental clinic in Toledo. He had worked with a Polish inventor on an unsinkable ship. He was a technical consultant in the field of television. In the life of a man of genius, all of these things might happen. But had they happened to Tamkin? Was he a genius? He often said that he had attended some of the Egyptian royal family as a psychiatrist. "But everybody is alike, common or aristocrat," he told Wilhelm. "The aristocrat knows less about life."

An Egyptian princess whom he had treated in California, for horrible disorders he had described to Wilhelm, retained him to come back to the old country with her, and there he had had many of her friends and relatives under his care. They turned over a villa on the Nile to him. "For ethical reasons, I can't tell you many of the details about them," he said—but Wilhelm had already heard all these details, and strange and shocking they were, if true. *If* true—he could not be free from doubt. For instance, the general who had to wear ladies' silk stockings and stand otherwise naked before the mirror—and all the rest. Listening to the doctor when he was so strangely factual, Wilhelm had to translate his words into his own language, and he could not translate fast enough or find terms to fit what he heard.

"Those Egyptian big shots invested in the market, too, for the heck of it. What did they need the extra money for? By association, I almost became a millionaire myself, and if I had played it smart there's no telling what might have happened. I could have been the ambassador." The American? The Egyptian ambassador? "A friend of mine tipped me off on the cotton. I made a heavy purchase of it. I didn't have that kind of money, but everybody there knew me. It never entered their minds that a person of their social circle didn't have dough. The sale was made on the phone. Then, while the cotton shipment was at sea, the price tripled. When the stuff suddenly became so valuable all hell broke loose on the world cotton market, they looked to see who was the owner of this big shipment. Me! They investigated my credit and found out I was a mere doctor, and they canceled. This was illegal. I sued them. But as I didn't have the money to fight them I sold the suit to a Wall Street lawyer for twenty thousand dollars. He fought it and was winning. They settled with him out of court for more than a million. But on the way back from Cairo, flying, there was a crash. All on board died. I have this guilt on my conscience, of being the murderer of that lawyer. Although he was a crook."

Wilhelm thought, I must be a real jerk to sit and listen to such impossible stories. I guess I am a sucker for people who talk about the deeper things of life, even the way he does.

"We scientific men speak of irrational guilt, Wilhelm," said Dr. Tamkin, as if Wilhelm were a pupil in his class. "But in such a situation, because of the money, I wished him harm. I realize it. This isn't the time to describe all the details, but the money made me guilty. *M*oney and *M*urder both begin with *M*. *M*achinery. *M*ischief."

Wilhelm, his mind thinking for him at random, said, "What about *M*ercy? *M*ilk-of-human-kindness?"

"One fact should be clear to you by now. Money-making is aggression. That's the whole thing. The functionalistic explanation is the only one. People come to the market to kill. They say, 'I'm going to make a killing.' It's not accidental. Only they haven't got the genuine courage to kill, and they erect a symbol of it.

The money. They make a killing by a fantasy. Now, counting and number is always a sadistic activity. Like hitting. In the Bible, the Jews wouldn't allow you to count them. They knew it was sadistic."

"I don't understand what you mean," said Wilhelm. A strange uneasiness tore at him. The day was growing too warm and his head felt dim. "What makes them want to kill?"

"By and by, you'll get the drift," Dr. Tamkin assured him. His amazing eyes had some of the rich dryness of a brown fur. Innumerable crystalline hairs or spicules of light glittered in their bold surfaces. "You can't understand without first spending years on the study of the ultimates of human and animal behavior, the deep chemical, organismic, and spiritual secrets of life. I am a psychological poet."

"If you're this kind of poet," said Wilhelm, whose fingers in his pocket were feeling in the little envelopes for the Phenaphen capsules, "what are you doing on the market?"

"That's a good question. Maybe I am better at speculation because I don't care. Basically, I don't wish hard enough for money, and therefore I come with a cool head to it."

Wilhelm thought, Oh, sure! That's an answer, is it? I bet that if I took a strong attitude he'd back down on everything. He'd grovel in front of me. The way he looks at me on the sly, to see if I'm being taken in! He swallowed his Phenaphen pill with a long gulp of water. The rims of his eyes grew red as it went down. And then he felt calmer.

"Let me see if I can give you an answer that will satisfy you," said Dr. Tamkin. His flapjacks were set before him. He spread the butter on them, poured on brown maple syrup, quartered them, and began to eat with hard, active, muscular jaws which sometimes gave a creak at the hinges. He pressed the handle of his knife against his chest and said, "In here, the human bosom—mine, yours, everybody's—there isn't just one soul. There's a lot of souls. But there are two main ones, the real soul and a pretender soul. Now! Every man realizes that he has to love something or somebody. He feels that he must go outward. 'If thou canst not love, what art thou?' Are you with me?"

"Yes, Doc, I think so," said Wilhelm listening—a little skeptically but nonetheless hard.

"'What art thou?' Nothing. That's the answer. Nothing. In the heart of hearts—Nothing! So of course you can't stand that and want to be Something, and you try. But instead of being this Something, the man puts it over on everybody instead. You can't be that strict to yourself. You love a *little*. Like you have a dog" (*Scissors!*) "or give some money to a charity drive. Now that isn't love, is it? What is it? Egotism, pure and simple. It's a way to love the pretender soul. Vanity. Only vanity, is what it is. And social control. The interest of the pretender soul is the same as the interest of the social life, the society mechanism. This is the main tragedy of human life. Oh, it is terrible! Terrible! You are not free. Your own betrayer is inside of you and sells you out. You have to obey him like a slave. He makes you work like a horse. And for what? For who?"

"Yes, for what?" The doctor's words caught Wilhelm's heart. "I couldn't agree more," he said. "When do we get free?"

"The purpose is to keep the whole thing going. The true soul is the one that pays the price. It suffers and gets sick, and it realizes that the pretender can't be loved. Because the pretender is a lie. The true soul loves the truth. And when the true soul feels like this, it wants to kill the pretender. The love has turned into hate. Then you become dangerous. A killer. You have to kill the deceiver."

"Does this happen to everybody?"

The doctor answered simply, "Yes, to everybody. Of course, for simplification purposes, I have spoken of the soul; it isn't a scientific term, but it helps you to understand it. Whenever the slayer slays, he wants to slay the soul in him which has gypped and deceived him. Who is his enemy? Him. And his lover? Also. Therefore, all suicide is murder, and all murder is suicide. It's the one and identical phenomenon. Biologically, the pretender soul takes away the energy of the true soul and makes it feeble, like a parasite. It happens unconsciously, unawaringly, in the depths of the organism. Ever take up parasitology?"

"No, it's my dad who's the doctor."

"You should read a book about it."

Wilhelm said, "But this means that the world is full of murderers. So it's not the world. It's a kind of hell."

"Sure," the doctor said. "At least a kind of purgatory. You walk on the bodies. They are all around. I can hear them cry *de profundis*[35] and wring their hands. I hear them, poor human beasts. I can't help hearing. And my eyes are open to it. I have to cry, too. This is the human tragedy-comedy."

Wilhelm tried to capture his vision. And again the doctor looked untrustworthy to him, and he doubted him. "Well," he said, "there are also kind, ordinary, helpful people. They're—out in the country. All over. What kind of morbid stuff do you read anyway?" The doctor's room was full of books.

"I read the best literature, science and philosophy," Dr. Tamkin said. Wilhelm had observed that in his room even the TV aerial was set upon a pile of volumes. "Korzybski,[36] Aristotle, Freud, W. H. Sheldon, and all the great poets. You answer me like a layman. You haven't applied your mind strictly to this."

"Very interesting,"said Wilhelm. He was aware that he hadn't applied his mind strictly to anything. "You don't have to think I'm a dummy, though. I have ideas, too." A glance at the clock told him that the market would soon open. They could spare a few minutes yet. There were still more things he wanted to hear from Tamkin. He realized that Tamkin spoke faultily, but then scientific men were not always strictly literate. It was the description of the two souls that had awed him. In Tommy he saw the pretender and even Wilky might not be himself. Might the name of his true soul be the one by which his old grandfather had called him— Velvel? The name of a soul, however, must be only that—soul. What did it look like? Does my soul look like me? Is there a soul that looks like Dad? Like Tamkin? Where does the true soul get its strength? Why does it have to love truth? Wilhelm was tormented, but he tried to be oblivious to his torment. Secretly, he prayed the doctor would give him some useful advice and transform his life. "Yes, I understand you," he said. "It isn't lost on me."

"I never said you weren't intelligent, but only you just haven't made a study of it all. As a matter of fact you're a profound personality with very profound creative capacities but also disturbances. I've been concerned with you, and for some time I've been treating you."

"Without my knowing it? I haven't felt you doing anything. What do you

---

[35] "From the depths" (Latin), the beginning of Psalm 130.

[36] Alfred Korzybski (1879–1950), a Polish-American scientist and writer; William Herbert Sheldon (1898–1977), a psychologist and medical researcher.

mean? I don't think I like being treated without my knowledge. I'm of two minds. What's the matter, don't you think I'm normal?" And he really was divided in mind. That the doctor cared about him pleased him. This was what he craved, that someone should care about him, wish him well. Kindness, mercy, he wanted. But—and here he retracted his heavy shoulders in his peculiar way, drawing his hands up into his sleeves; his feet moved uneasily under the table—but he was worried, too, and even somewhat indignant. For what right had Tamkin to meddle without being asked? What kind of privileged life did this man lead? He took other people's money and speculated with it. Everybody came under his care. No one could have secrets from him.

The doctor looked at him with his deadly brown, heavy, impenetrable eyes, his naked shining head, his red hanging underlip, and said, "You have lots of guilt in you."

Wilhelm helplessly admitted, as he felt the heat rise to his wide face, "Yes, I think so too. But personally," he added, "I don't feel like a murderer. I always try to lay off. It's the others who get me. You know—make me feel oppressed. And if you don't mind, and it's all the same to you, I would rather know it when you start to treat me. And now, Tamkin, for Christ's sake, they're putting out the lunch menus already. Will you sign the check, and let's go!"

Tamkin did as he asked, and they rose. They were passing the bookkeeper's desk when he took out a substantial bundle of onionskin papers and said, "These are receipts of the transactions. Duplicates. You'd better keep them as the account is in your name and you'll need them for income taxes. And here is a copy of a poem I wrote yesterday."

"I have to leave something at the desk for my father," Wilhelm said, and he put his hotel bill in an envelope with a note. *Dear Dad, Please carry me this month, Yours, W.* He watched the clerk with his sullen pug's profile and his stiffnecked look push the envelope into his father's box.

"May I ask you really why you and your dad had words?" said Dr. Tamkin, who had hung back, waiting.

"It was about my future," said Wilhelm. He hurried down the stairs with swift steps, like a tower in motion, his hands in his trousers pockets. He was ashamed to discuss the matter. "He says there's a reason why I can't go back to my old territory, and there is. I told everybody I was going to be an officer of the corporation. And I was supposed to. It was promised. But then they welshed because of the son-in-law. I bragged and made myself look big."

"If you was humble enough, you could go back. But it doesn't make much difference. We'll make you a good living on the market."

They came into the sunshine of upper Broadway, not clear but throbbing through the dust and fumes, a false air of gas visible at eye-level as it spurted from the bursting buses. From old habit, Wilhelm turned up the collar of his jacket.

"Just a technical question," Wilhelm said. "What happens if your losses are bigger than your deposit?"

"Don't worry. They have ultra-modern electronic bookkeeping machinery, and it won't let you get in debt. It puts you out automatically. But I want you to read this poem. You haven't read it yet."

Light as a locust, a helicopter bringing mail from Newark Airport to La Guardia sprang over the city in a long leap.

The paper Wilhelm unfolded had ruled borders in red ink. He read:

MECHANISM VS FUNCTIONALISM
ISM VS HISM

If thee thyself couldst only see
Thy greatness that is and yet to be,
Thou would feel joy-beauty-what ecstasy.
They are at thy feet, earth-moon-sea, the trinity.

Why-forth then dost thou tarry
And partake thee only of the crust
And skim the earth's surface narry
When all creations art thy just?

Seek ye then that which art not there
In thine own glory let thyself rest.
Witness. Thy power is not bare.
Thou art King. Thou art at thy best.

Look then right before thee.
Open thine eyes and see.
At the foot of Mt. Serenity
Is thy cradle to eternity.

Utterly confused, Wilhelm said to himself explosively, What kind of mish-mash, claptrap is this! What does he want from me? Damn him to hell, he might as well hit me on the head, and lay me out, kill me. What does he give me this for? What's the purpose? Is it a deliberate test? Does he want to mix me up? He's already got me mixed up completely. I was never good at riddles. Kiss those seven hundred bucks good-by, and call it one more mistake in a long line of mistakes— Oh, Mama, what a line! He stood near the shining window of a fancy fruit store, holding Tamkin's paper, rather dazed, as though a charge of photographer's flash powder had gone up in his eyes.

But he's waiting for my reaction. I have to say something to him about his poem. It really is no joke. What will I tell him? Who is this King? The poem is written *to* someone. But who? I can't even bring myself to talk. I feel too choked and strangled. With all the books he reads, how come the guy is so illiterate? And why do people just naturally assume that you'll know what they're talking about? No. I don't know, and nobody knows. The planets don't, the stars don't, infinite space doesn't. It doesn't square with Planck's Constant[37] or anything else. So what's the good of it? Where's the need of it? What does he mean here by Mount Serenity? Could it be a figure of speech for Mount Everest? As he says people are all committing suicide, maybe those guys who climbed Everest[38] were only trying to kill themselves, and if we want peace we should stay at the foot of the mountain. In the here-and-now. But it's also here-and-now on the slope, and on the top,

[37] A universal constant number of physics, determined by the German physicist Max Planck (1858–1947); an integral part of quantum theory.
[38] Sir Edmond Hillary and Tensing Norgay, who reached the summit of Mt. Everest on May 28, 1953.

where they climbed to seize the day. Surface narry is something he can't mean, I don't believe. I'm about to start foaming at the mouth. "Thy cradle . . ." *Who* is resting in his cradle—in his glory? My thoughts are at an end. I feel the wall. No more. So ——k it all! The money and everything. Take it away! When I have the money they eat me alive, like those piranha fish in the movie about the Brazilian jungle. It was hideous when they ate up that Brahma bull in the river. He turned pale, just like clay, and in five minutes nothing was left except the skeleton still in one piece, floating away. When I haven't got it any more, at least they'll let me alone.

"Well, what do you think of this?" said Dr. Tamkin. He gave a special sort of wise smile, as though Wilhelm must now see what kind of man he was dealing with.

"Nice. Very nice. Have you been writing long?"

"I've been developing this line of thought for years and years. You follow it all the way?"

"I'm trying to figure out who this Thou is."

"Thou? Thou is you."

"Me! Why? This applies to *me?*"

"Why shouldn't it apply to you. You were in my mind when I composed it. Of course, the hero of the poem is sick humanity. If it would open its eyes it would be great."

"Yes, but how do I get into this?"

"The main idea of the poem is *con*struct or *de*struct. There is no ground in between. Mechanism is *de*struct. Money of course is *de*struct. When the last grave is dug, the gravedigger will have to be paid. If you could have confidence in nature you would not have to fear. It would keep you up. Creative is nature. Rapid. Lavish. Inspirational. It shapes leaves. It rolls the waters of the earth. Man is the chief of this. All creations are his just inheritance. You don't know what you've got within you. A person either creates or he destroys. There is no neutrality . . ."

"I realized you were no beginner," said Wilhelm with propriety. "I have only one criticism to make. I think 'why-forth' is wrong. You should write 'Wherefore then dost thou . . .'" And he reflected, So? I took a gamble. It'll have to be a miracle, though, to save me. My money will be gone, then it won't be able to destruct me. He can't just take and lose it, though. He's in it, too. I think he's in a bad way himself. He must be. I'm sure because, come to think of it, he sweated blood when he signed that check. But what have I let myself in for? The waters of the earth are going to roll over me.

V

Patiently, in the window of the fruit store, a man with a scoop spread crushed ice between his rows of vegetables. There were also Persian melons, lilacs, tulips with radiant black at the middle. The many street noises came back after a little while from the caves of the sky. Crossing the tide of Broadway traffic, Wilhelm was saying to himself, The reason Tamkin lectures me is that somebody has lectured him, and the reason for the poem is that he wants to give me good advice. Everybody seems to know something. Even fellows like Tamkin. Many people know what to do, but how many can do it?

He believed that he must, that he could and would recover the good things, the happy things, the easy tranquil things of life. He had made mistakes, but he could overlook these. He had been a fool, but that could be forgiven. The time wasted—must be relinquished. What else could one do about it? Things were too complex, but they might be reduced to simplicity again. Recovery was possible. First he had to get out of the city. No, first he had to pull out his money. . . .

From the carnival of the street—pushcarts, accordion and fiddle, shoeshine, begging, the dust going round like a woman on stilts—they entered the narrow crowded theater of the brokerage office. From front to back it was filled with the Broadway crowd. But how was lard doing this morning? From the rear of the hall Wilhelm tried to read the tiny figures. The German manager was looking through his binoculars. Tamkin placed himself on Wilhelm's left and covered his conspicuous bald head. "The guy'll ask me about the margin," he muttered. They passed, however, unobserved. "Look, the lard has held its place," he said.

Tamkin's eyes must be very sharp to read the figures over so many heads and at this distance—another respect in which he was unusual.

The room was always crowded. Everyone talked. Only at the front could you hear the flutter of the wheels within the board. Teletyped news items crossed the illuminated screen above.

"Lard. Now what about rye?" said Tamkin, rising on his toes. Here he was a different man, active and impatient. He parted people who stood in his way. His face turned resolute, and on either side of his mouth odd bulges formed under his mustache. Already he was pointing out to Wilhelm the appearance of a new pattern on the board. "There's something up today," he said.

"Then why'd you take so long with breakfast?" said Wilhelm.

There were no reserved seats in the room, only customary ones. Tamkin always sat in the second row, on the commodities side of the aisle. Some of his acquaintances kept their hats on the chairs for him.

"Thanks. Thanks," said Tamkin, and he told Wilhelm, "I fixed it up yesterday."

"That was a smart thought," said Wilhelm. They sat down.

With folded hands, by the wall, sat an old Chinese businessman in a seersucker coat. Smooth and fat, he wore a white Vandyke.[39] One day Wilhelm had seen him on Riverside Drive pushing two little girls along in a baby carriage—his grandchildren. Then there were two women in their fifties, supposed to be sisters, shrewd and able money-makers, according to Tamkin. They had never a word to say to Wilhelm. But they would chat with Tamkin. Tamkin talked to everyone.

Wilhelm sat between Mr. Rowland, who was elderly, and Mr. Rappaport, who was very old. Yesterday Rowland had told him that in the year 1908, when he was a junior at Harvard, his mother had given him twenty shares of steel for his birthday, and then he had started to read the financial news and had never practiced law but instead followed the market for the rest of his life. Now he speculated only in soy beans, of which he had made a specialty. By his conservative method, said Tamkin, he cleared two hundred a week. Small potatoes, but then he was a bachelor, retired, and didn't need money.

"Without dependents," said Tamkin. "He doesn't have the problems that you and I do."

---

[39] A closely trimmed, pointed beard.

Did Tamkin have dependents? He had everything that it was possible for man to have—science, Greek, chemistry, poetry, and now dependents too. That beautiful girl with epilepsy, perhaps. He often said that she was a pure, marvelous, spiritual child who had no knowledge of the world. He protected her, and, if he was not lying, adored her. And if you encouraged Tamkin by believing him, or even if you refrained from questioning him, his hints became more daring. Sometimes he said that he paid for her music lessons. Sometimes he seemed to have footed the bill for the brother's camera expedition to Brazil. And he spoke of paying for the support of the orphaned child of a dead sweetheart. These hints, made dully as asides, grew by repetition into sensational claims.

"For myself, I don't need much," said Tamkin. "But a man can't live for himself and I need the money for certain important things. What do you figure you have to have, to get by?"

"Not less than fifteen grand, after taxes. That's for my wife and the two boys."

"Isn't there anybody else?" said Tamkin with a shrewdness almost cruel. But his look grew more sympathetic as Wilhelm stumbled, not willing to recall another grief.

"Well—there was. But it wasn't a money matter."

"I should hope!" said Tamkin. "If love is love, it's free. Fifteen grand, though, isn't too much for a man of your intelligence to ask out of life. Fools, hard-hearted criminals, and murderers have millions to squander. They burn up the world—oil, coal, wood, metal, and soil, and suck even the air and the sky. They consume, and they give back no benefit. A man like you, humble for life, who wants to feel and live, has trouble—not wanting," said Tamkin in his parenthetical fashion, "to exchange an ounce of soul for a pound of social power—he'll never make it without help in a world like this. But don't you worry." Wilhelm grasped at this assurance. "Just you never mind. We'll go easily beyond your figure."

Dr. Tamkin gave Wilhelm comfort. He often said that he had made as much as a thousand a week in commodities. Wilhelm had examined the receipts, but until this moment it had never occurred to him that there must be debit slips too; he had been shown only the credits.

"But fifteen grand is not an ambitious figure," Tamkin was telling him. "For that you don't have to wear yourself out on the road, dealing with narrow-minded people. A lot of them don't like Jews, either, I suppose?"

"I can't afford to notice. I'm lucky when I have my occupation. Tamkin, do you mean you can save our money?"

"Oh, did I forget to mention what I did before closing yesterday? You see, I closed out one of the lard contracts and bought a hedge of December rye. The rye is up three points already and takes some of the sting out. But lard will go up, too."

"Where? God, yes, you're right," said Wilhelm, eager, and got to his feet to look. New hope freshened his heart. "Why didn't you tell me before?"

And Tamkin, smiling like a benevolent magician, said, "You must learn to have trust. The slump in lard can't last. And just take a look at eggs. Didn't I predict they couldn't go any lower? They're rising and rising. If we had taken eggs we'd be far ahead."

"Then why didn't we take them?"

"We were just about to. I had a buying order in at .24, but the tide turned at .26^{1}/4 and we barely missed. Never mind. Lard will go back to last year's levels."

Maybe. But when? Wilhelm could not allow his hopes to grow too strong.

However, for a little while he could breathe more easily. Late-morning trading was getting active. The shining numbers whirred on the board, which sounded like a huge cage of artificial birds. Lard fluctuated between two points, but rye slowly climbed.

He closed his strained, greatly earnest eyes briefly and nodded his Buddha's head, too large to suffer such uncertainties. For several moments of peace he was removed to his small yard in Roxbury.

He breathed in the sugar of the pure morning.

He heard the long phrases of the birds.

No enemy wanted his life.

Wilhelm thought, I will get out of here. I don't belong in New York any more. And he sighed like a sleeper.

Tamkin said, "Excuse me," and left his seat. He could not sit still in the room but passed back and forth between the stocks and commodities sections. He knew dozens of people and was continually engaging in discussions. Was he giving advice, gathering information, or giving it, or practicing—whatever mysterious profession he practiced? Hypnotism? Perhaps he could put people in a trance while he talked to them. What a rare, peculiar bird he was, with those pointed shoulders, that bare head, his loose nails, almost claws, and those brown, soft, deadly, heavy eyes.

He spoke of things that mattered, and as very few people did this he could take you by surprise, excite you, move you. Maybe he wished to do good, maybe give himself a lift to a higher level, maybe believe his own prophecies, maybe touch his own heart. Who could tell? He had picked up a lot of strange ideas; Wilhelm could only suspect, he could not say with certainty, that Tamkin hadn't made them his own.

Now Tamkin and he were equal partners, but Tamkin had put up only three hundred dollars. Suppose he did this not only once but five times; then an investment of fifteen hundred dollars gave him five thousand to speculate with. If he had power of attorney in every case, he could shift the money from one account to another. No, the German probably kept an eye on him. Nevertheless it was possible. Calculations like this made Wilhelm feel ill. Obviously Tamkin was a plunger. But how did he get by? He must be in his fifties. How did he support himself? Five years in Egypt; Hollywood before that; Michigan; Ohio; Chicago. A man of fifty has supported himself for at least thirty years. You could be sure that Tamkin had never worked in a factory or in an office. How did he make it? His taste in clothes was horrible, but he didn't buy cheap things. He wore corduroy or velvet shirts from Clyde's, painted neckties, striped socks. There was a slightly acid or pasty smell about his person; for a doctor, he didn't bathe much. Also, Dr. Tamkin had a good room at the Gloriana and had had it for about a year. But so was Wilhelm himself a guest, with an unpaid bill at present in his father's box. Did the beautiful girl with the skirts and belts pay him? Was he defrauding his so-called patients? So many questions impossible to answer could not be asked about an honest man. Nor perhaps about a sane man. Was Tamkin a lunatic, then? That sick Mr. Perls at breakfast had said that there was no easy way to tell the sane from the mad, and he was right about that in any big city and especially in New York—the end of the world, with its complexity and machinery, bricks and tubes, wires and stones, holes and heights. And was everybody crazy here? What sort of people did you see? Every other man spoke a language entirely his own, which he had figured out by private thinking; he had his own ideas and peculiar ways. If you wanted to talk about a glass of water, you had to start back with God creating the heavens and earth; the apple; Abraham; Moses and Jesus; Rome; the Middle Ages; gunpowder; the Revolution; back to Newton; up to Einstein; then war and Lenin and Hitler. After reviewing this and getting it all straight again you could proceed to talk about a glass of water. "I'm fainting, please get me a little water." You were lucky even then to make yourself understood. And this happened over and over and over with everyone you met. You had to translate and translate, explain and explain, back and forth, and it was the punishment of hell itself not to understand or be understood, not to know the crazy from the sane, the wise from the fools, the young from the old or the sick from the well. The fathers were no fathers and the sons no sons. You had to talk with yourself in the daytime and reason with yourself at night. Who else was there to talk to in a city like New York?

A queer look came over Wilhelm's face with its eyes turned up and his silent mouth with its hugh upper lip. He went several degrees further—when you are like this, dreaming that everybody is outcast, you realize that this must be one of the small matters. There is a larger body, and from this you cannot be separated. The glass of water fades out. You do not go from simple *a* and simple *b* to the great *x* and *y*, nor does it matter whether you agree about the glass but, far beneath such details, what Tamkin would call the real soul says plain and understandable things to everyone. There sons and fathers are themselves, and a glass of water is only an ornament; it makes a hoop of brightness on the cloth; it is an angel's mouth. There truth for everybody may be found, and confusion is only—only temporary, thought Wilhelm.

The idea of this larger body had been planted in him a few days ago beneath Times Square, when he had gone downtown to pick up tickets for the baseball game on Saturday (a double-header at the Polo Grounds[40]). He was going through an underground corridor, a place he had always hated and hated more than ever now. On the walls between the advertisements were words in chalk: "Sin No More," and "Do Not Eat the Pig,"[41] he had particularly noticed. And in the dark tunnel, in the haste, heat, and darkness which disfigure and make freaks and fragments of nose and eyes and teeth, all of a sudden, unsought, a general love for all these imperfect and lurid-looking people burst out in Wilhelm's breast. He loved them. One and all, he passionately loved them. They were his brothers and his sisters. He was imperfect and disfigured himself, but what difference did that make if he was united with them by this blaze of love? And as he walked he began to say, "Oh my brothers—my brothers and my sisters," blessing them all as well as himself.

So what did it matter how many languages there were, or how hard it was to describe a glass of water? Or matter that a few minutes later he didn't feel anything like a brother toward the man who sold him the tickets?

On that very same afternoon he didn't hold so high an opinion of this same onrush of loving kindness. What did it come to? As they had the capacity and must use it once in a while, people were bound to have such involuntary feelings. It was only another one of those subway things. Like having a hard-on at random. But today, his day of reckoning, he consulted his memory again and thought, I

[40] The home field of the New York Giants baseball team until it was razed in the 1960s; built in the 1880s as a polo field.

[41] Eating pork is forbidden by Jewish dietary laws.

must go back to that. That's the right clue and may do me the most good. Something very big. Truth, like.

The old fellow on the right, Mr. Rappaport, was nearly blind and kept asking Wilhelm, "What's the new figure on November wheat? Give me July soy beans too." When you told him he didn't say thank you. He said, "Okay," instead, or, "Check," and turned away until he needed you again. He was very old, older even than Dr. Adler, and if you believed Tamkin he had once been the Rockefeller of the chicken business and had retired with a large fortune.

Wilhelm had a queer feeling about the chicken industry, that it was sinister. On the road, he frequently passed chicken farms. Those big, rambling, wooden buildings out in the neglected fields; they were like prisons. The lights burned all night in them to cheat the poor hens into laying. Then the slaughter. Pile all the coops of the slaughtered on end, and in one week they'd go higher than Mount Everest or Mount Serenity. The blood filling the Gulf of Mexico. The chicken shit, acid, burning the earth.

How old—old this Mr. Rappaport was! Purple stains were buried in the flesh of his nose, and the cartilage of his ear was twisted like a cabbage heart. Beyond remedy by glasses, his eyes were smoky and faded.

"Read me that soy-bean figure now, boy," he said, and Wilhelm did. He thought perhaps the old man might give him a tip, or some useful advice or information about Tamkin. But no. He only wrote memoranda on a pad, and put the pad in his pocket. He let no one see what he had written. And Wilhelm thought this was the way a man who had grown rich by the murder of millions af animals, little chickens, would act. If there was a life to come he might have to answer for the killing of all those chickens. What if they all were waiting? But if there was a life to come, everybody would have to answer. But if there was a life to come, the chickens themselves would be all right.

Well! What stupid ideas he was having this morning. Phooey!

Finally old Rappaport did address a few remarks to Wilhelm. He asked him whether he had reserved his seat in the synagogue for Yom Kippur.[42]

"No," said Wilhelm.

"Well, you better hurry up if you expect to say *Yiskor*[43] for your parents. I never miss."

And Wilhelm thought, Yes, I suppose I should say a prayer for Mother once in a while. His mother had belonged to the Reform congregation. His father had no religion. At the cemetery Wilhelm had paid a man to say a prayer for her. He was among the tombs and he wanted to be tipped for the *El molai rachamin*. "Thou God of Mercy," Wilhelm thought that meant. *B' gan Aden*—"in Paradise." Singing, they drew it out. *B' gan Ay-den*. The broken bench beside the grave made him wish to do something. Wilhelm often prayed in his own manner. He did not go to the synagogue but he would occasionally perform certain devotions, according to his feelings. Now he reflected, In Dad's eyes I am the wrong kind of Jew. He doesn't like the way I act. Only he is the right kind of Jew. Whatever you are, it always turns out to be the wrong kind.

Mr. Rappaport grumbled and whiffed at his long cigar, and the board, like a swarm of electrical bees, whirred.

---

[42] "Day of Atonement" (Hebrew), the most solemn Jewish religious holiday of the year; a day of fasting.

[43] A Jewish prayer service for the dead.

"Since you were in the chicken business, I thought you'd speculate in eggs, Mr. Rappaport." Wilhelm, with his warm, panting laugh, sought to charm the old man.

"Oh. Yeah. Loyalty, hey?" said old Rappaport. "I should stick to them. I spent a lot of time amongst chickens. I got to be an expert chicken-sexer. When the chick hatches you have to tell the boys from the girls. It's not easy. You need long, long experience. What do you think, it's a joke? A whole industry depends on it. Yes, now and then I buy a contract eggs. What have you got today?"

Wilhelm said anxiously, "Lard. Rye."

"Buy? Sell?"

"Bought."

"Uh," said the old man. Wilhelm could not determine what he meant by this. But of course you couldn't expect him to make himself any clearer. It was not in the code to give information to anyone. Sick with desire, Wilhelm waited for Mr. Rappaport to make an exception in his case. Just this once! Because it was critical. Silently, by a sort of telepathic concentration, he begged the old man to speak the single word that would save him, give him the merest sign. "Oh, please—please help," he nearly said. If Rappaport would close one eye, or lay his head to one side, or raise his finger and point to a column in the paper or to a figure on his pad. A hint! A hint!

A long perfect ash formed on the end of the cigar, the white ghost of the leaf with all its veins and its fainter pungency. It was ignored, in its beauty, by the old man. For it was beautiful. Wilhelm he ignored as well.

Then Tamkin said to him, "Wilhelm, look at the jump our rye just took."

December rye climbed three points as they tensely watched; the tumblers raced and the machine's lights buzzed.

"A point and a half more, and we can cover the lard losses," said Tamkin. He showed him his calculations on the margin of the *Times*.

"I think you should put in the selling order now. Let's get out with a small loss."

"Get out now? Nothing doing."

"Why not? Why should we wait?"

"Because," said Tamkin with a smiling, almost openly scoffing look, "you've got to keep your nerve when the market starts to go places. Now's when you can make something."

"I'd get out while the getting's good."

"No, you shouldn't lose your head like this. It's obvious to me what the mechanism is, back in the Chicago market. There's a short supply of December rye. Look, it's just gone up another quarter. We should ride it."

"I'm losing my taste for the gamble," said Wilhelm. "You can't feel safe when it goes up so fast. It's liable to come down just as quick."

Dryly, as though he were dealing with a child, Tamkin told him in a tone of tiring patience, "Now listen, Tommy. I have it diagnosed right. If you wish I should sell I can give the sell order. But this is the difference between healthiness and pathology. One is objective, doesn't change his mind every minute, enjoys the risk element. But that's not the neurotic character. The neurotic character—"

"Damn it, Tamkin!" said Wilhelm roughly. "Cut that out. I don't like it. Leave my character out of consideration. Don't pull any more of that stuff on me. I tell you I don't like it."

Tamkin therefore went no further; he backed down. "I meant," he said, softer, "that as a salesman you are basically an artist type. The seller is in the visionary sphere of the business function. And then you're an actor, too."

"No matter what type I am—" An angry and yet weak sweetness rose into Wilhelm's throat. He coughed as though he had the flu. It was twenty years since he had appeared on the screen as an extra. He blew the bagpipes in a film called *Annie Laurie*.[44] Annie had come to warn the young Laird; he would not believe her and called the bagpipers to drown her out. He made fun of her while she wrung her hands. Wilhelm, in a kilt, barelegged, blew and blew and blew and not a sound came out. Of course all the music was recorded. He fell sick with the flu after that and still suffered sometimes from chest weakness.

"Something stuck in your throat?" said Tamkin. "I think maybe you are too disturbed to think clearly. You should try some of my 'here-and-now' mental exercises. It stops you from thinking so much about the future and the past and cuts down confusion."

"Yes, yes, yes, yes," said Wilhelm, his eyes fixed on December rye.

"Nature only knows one thing, and that's the present. Present, present, eternal present, like a big, huge, giant wave—colossal, bright and beautiful, full of life and death, climbing into the sky, standing in the seas. You must go along with the actual, the Here-and-Now, the glory—"

. . . chest weakness, Wilhelm's recollection went on. Margaret nursed him. They had had two rooms of furniture, which was later seized. She sat on the bed and read to him. He made her read for days, and she read stories, poetry, everything in the house. He felt dizzy, stifled when he tried to smoke. They had him wear a flannel vest.

> Come then, Sorrow!
> Sweetest Sorrow!
> Like an own babe I nurse thee on my breast![45]

Why did he remember that? Why?

"You have to pick out something that's in the actual, immediate present moment," said Tamkin. "And say to yourself here-and-now, here-and-now, here-and-now. 'Where am I?' 'Here.' 'When is it?' 'Now.' Take an object or a person. Anybody. 'Here and now I see a person.' 'Here and now I see a man.' 'Here and now I see a man sitting on a chair.' Take me, for instance. Don't let your mind wander. 'Here and now I see a man in a brown suit. Here and now I see a corduroy shirt.' You have to narrow it down, one item at a time, and not let your imagination shoot ahead. Be in the present. Grasp the hour, the moment, the instant."

Is he trying to hypnotize or con me? Wilhelm wondered. To take my mind off selling? But even if I'm back at seven hundred bucks, then where am I?

As if in prayer, his lids coming down with raised veins, frayed out, on his significant eyes. Tamkin said, "'Here and now I see a button. Here and now I see the thread that sews the button. Here and now I see the green thread.'" Inch by

---

[44] After a song written in 1824 by the Scottish poet William Douglas of Kirkcudbright (1672?–1748).

[45] From *Endymion* (1818), by the English poet John Keats (1795–1821); these lines and those below comprise lines 279–284 of Bk. IV.

inch he contemplated himself in order to show Wilhelm how calm it would make him. But Wilhelm was hearing Margaret's voice as she read, somewhat unwillingly,

> Come then, Sorrow!
>
> .   .   .   .
>
> I thought to leave thee,
> And deceive thee,
> But now of all the world I love thee best.

Then Mr. Rappaport's old hand pressed his thigh, and he said, "What's my wheat? Those damn guys are blocking the way. I can't see."

VI

Rye was still ahead when they went out to lunch, and lard was holding its own.

They ate in the cafeteria with the gilded front. There was the same art inside as outside. The food looked sumptuous. Whole fishes were framed like pictures with carrots, and the salads were like terraced landscapes or like Mexican pyramids; slices of lemon and onion and radishes were like sun and moon and stars; the cream pies were about a foot thick and the cakes swollen as if sleepers had baked them in their dreams.

"What'll you have?" said Tamkin.

"Not much. I ate a big breakfast. I'll find a table. Bring me some yogurt and crackers and a cup of tea. I don't want to spend much time over lunch."

Tamkin said, "You've got to eat."

Finding an empty place at this hour was not easy. The old people idled and gossiped over their coffee. The elderly ladies were rouged and mascaraed and hennaed and used blue hair rinse and eye shadow and wore costume jewelry, and many of them were proud and stared at you with expressions that did not belong to their age. Were there no longer any respectable old ladies who knitted and cooked and looked after their grandchildren? Wilhelm's grandmother had dressed him in a sailor suit and danced him on her knee, blew on the porridge for him and said, "Admiral, you must eat." But what was the use of remembering this so late in the day?

He managed to find a table, and Dr. Tamkin came along with a tray piled with plates and cups. He had Yankee pot roast, purple cabbage, potatoes, a big slice of watermelon, and two cups of coffee. Wilhelm could not even swallow his yogurt. His chest pained him still.

At once Tamkin involved him in a lengthy discussion. Did he do it to stall Wilhelm and prevent him from selling out the rye—or to recover the ground lost when he had made Wilhelm angry by hints about the neurotic character? Or did he have no purpose except to talk?

"I think you worry a lot too much about what your wife and your father will say. Do they matter so much?"

Wilhelm replied, "A person can become tired of looking himself over and trying to fix himself up. You can spend the entire second half of your life recovering from the mistakes of the first half."

"I believe your dad told me he had some money to leave you."

"He probably does have something."

"A lot?"

"Who can tell," said Wilhelm guardedly.

"You ought to think over what you'll do with it."

"I may be too feeble to do anything by the time I get it. If I get anything."

"A thing like this you ought to plan out carefully. Invest it properly." He began to unfold schemes whereby you bought bonds, and used the bonds as security to buy something else and thereby earned twelve per cent safely on your money. Wilhelm failed to follow the details. Tamkin said, "If he made you a gift now, you wouldn't have to pay the inheritance taxes."

Bitterly, Wilhelm told him, "My father's death blots out all other considerations from his mind. He forces me to think about it, too. Then he hates me because he succeeds. When I get desperate—of course I think about money. But I don't want anything to happen to him. I certainly don't want him to die." Tamkins' brown eyes glittered shrewdly at him. "You don't believe it. Maybe it's not psychological. But on my word of honor. A joke is a joke, but I don't want to joke about stuff like this. When he dies, I'll be robbed, like. I'll have no more father."

"You love your old man?"

Wilhelm grasped at this. "Of course, of course I love him. My father. My mother—" As he said this there was a great pull at the very center of his soul. When a fish strikes the line you feel the live force in your hand. A mysterious being beneath the water, driven by hunger, has taken the hook and rushes away and fights, writhing. Wilhelm never identified what struck within him. It did not reveal itself. It got away.

And Tamkin, the confuser of the imagination, began to tell, or to fabricate, the strange history of *his* father. "He was a great singer," he said. "He left us five kids because he fell in love with an opera soprano. I never held it against him, but admired the way he followed the life-principle. I wanted to do the same. Because of unhappiness, at a certain age, the brain starts to die back." (True, true! thought Wilhelm) "Twenty years later I was doing experiments in Eastman Kodak, Rochester, and I found the old fellow. He had five more children." (False, false!) "He wept; he was ashamed. I had nothing against him. I naturally felt strange."

"My dad is something of a stranger to me, too," said Wilhelm, and he began to muse. Where is the familiar person he used to be? Or I used to be? Catherine—she won't even talk to me any more, my own sister. It may not be so much my trouble that Papa turns his back on as my confusion. It's too much. The ruins of life, and on top of that confusion—chaos and old night. Is it an easier farewell for Dad if we don't part friends? He should maybe do it angrily— "Blast you with my curse!" And why, Wilhelm further asked, should he or anybody else pity me; or why should I be pitied sooner than another fellow? It is my childish mind that thinks people are ready to give it just because you need it.

Then Wilhelm began to think about his own two sons and to wonder how he appeared to them, and what they would think of him. Right now he had an advantage through baseball. When he went to fetch them, to go to Ebbets Field, though, he was not himself. He put on a front but he felt as if he had swallowed a fistful of sand. The strange, familiar house, horribly awkward; the dog, Scissors, rolled over on his back and barked and whined. Wilhelm acted as if there were nothing irregular, but a weary heaviness came over him. On the way to Flatbush he would think up anecdotes about old Pigtown and Charlie Ebbets[46] for the boys and reminiscences of the old stars, but it was very heavy going. They did not know how much he cared for them. No. It hurt him greatly and he blamed Margaret for turning them against him. She wanted to ruin him, while she wore the mask of kindness. Up in Roxbury he had to go and explain to the priest, who was not sympathetic. They don't care about individuals, their rules come first. Olive said she would marry him outside the Church when he was divorced. But Margaret would not let go. Olive's father was a pretty decent old guy, an osteopath, and he understood what it was all about. Finally he said, "See here, I have to advise Olive. She is asking me. I am mostly a freethinker myself, but the girl has to live in this town." And by now Wilhelm and Olive had had a great many troubles and she was beginning to dread his days in Roxbury, she said. He trembled at offending this small, pretty, dark girl whom he adored. When she would get up late on Sunday morning she would wake him almost in tears at being late for Mass. He would try to help her hitch her garters and smooth out her slip and dress and even put on her hat with shaky hands; then he would rush her to church and drive in second gear in his forgetful way, trying to apologize and to calm her. She got out a block from church to avoid gossip. Even so she loved him, and she would have married him if he had obtained the divorce. But Margaret must have sensed this. Margaret would tell him he did not really want a divorce; he was afraid of it. He cried, "Take everything I've got, Margaret. Let me go to Reno. Don't you want to marry again?" No. She went out with other men, but took his money. She lived in order to punish him.

Dr. Tamkin told Wilhelm, "Your dad is jealous of you."

Wilhelm smiled. "Of *me?* That's rich."

"Sure. People are always jealous of a man who leaves his wife."

"Oh," said Wilhelm scornfully. "When it comes to wives he wouldn't have to envy me."

"Yes, and your wife envies you, too. She thinks, He's free and goes with young women. Is she getting old?"

"Not exactly old," said Wilhelm, whom the mention of his wife made sad. Twenty years ago, in a neat blue wool suit, in a soft hat made of the same cloth—he could plainly see her. He stooped his yellow head and looked under the hat at her clear, simple face, her living eyes moving, her straight small nose, her jaw beautifully, painfully clear in its form. It was a cool day, but he smelled the odor of pines in the sun, in the granite canyon. Just south of Santa Barbara, this was.

"She's forty-some years old," he said.

"I was married to a lush," said Tamkin. "A painful alcoholic. I couldn't take her out to dinner because she'd say she was going to the ladies' toilet and disappear into the bar. I'd ask the bartenders they shouldn't serve her. But I loved her deeply. She was the most spiritual woman of my entire experience."

"Where is she now?"

"Drowned," said Tamkin. "At Provincetown, Cape Cod. It must have been a suicide. She was that way—suicidal. I tried everything in my power to cure her. Because," said Tamkin, "my real calling is to be a healer. I get wounded. I suffer

---

[46] The slum area in Brooklyn where Ebbets Field stood; Charles Ebbets owned the Brooklyn Dodgers.

from it. I would like to escape from the sicknesses of others, but I can't. I am only on loan to myself, so to speak. I belong to humanity."

Liar! Wilhelm inwardly called him. Nasty lies. He invented a woman and killed her off and then called himself a healer, and made himself so earnest he looked like a bad-natured sheep. He's a puffed-up little bogus and humbug with smelly feet. A doctor! A doctor would wash himself. He believes he's making a terrific impression, and he practically invites you to take off your hat when he talks about himself; and he thinks he has an imagination, but he hasn't, neither is he smart.

Then what am I doing with him here, and why did I give him the seven hundred dollars? thought Wilhelm.

Oh, this was a day of reckoning. It was a day, he thought, on which, willing or not, he would take a good close look at the truth. He breathed hard and his misshapen hat came low upon his congested dark blond face. A rude look. Tamkin was a charlatan, and furthermore he was desperate. And furthermore, Wilhelm had always known this about him. But he appeared to have worked it out at the back of his mind that Tamkin for thirty or forty years had gotten through many a tight place, that he would get through this crisis too and bring him, Wilhelm, to safety also. And Wilhelm realized that he was on Tamkin's back. It made him feel that he had virtually left the ground and was riding upon the other man. He was in the air. It was for Tamkin to take the steps.

The doctor, if he was a doctor, did not look anxious. But then his face did not have much variety. Talking always about spontaneous emotion and open receptors and free impulses, he was about as expressive as a pincushion. When his hypnotic spell failed, his big underlip made him look weak-minded. Fear stared from his eyes, sometimes, so humble as to make you sorry for him. Once or twice Wilhelm had seen that look. Like a dog, he thought. Perhaps he didn't look it now, but he was very nervous. Wilhelm knew, but he could not afford to recognize this too openly. The doctor needed a little room, a little time. He should not be pressed now. So Tamkin went on, telling his tales.

Wilhelm said to himself, I am on his back—his back. I gambled seven hundred bucks, so I must take this ride. I have to go along with him. It's too late. I can't get off.

"You know," Tamkin said, "that blind old man Rappaport—he's pretty close to totally blind—is one of the most interesting personalities around here. If you could only get him to tell his true story. It's fascinating. This is what he told me. You often hear about bigamists with a secret life. But this old man never hid anything from anybody. He's a regular patriarch. Now, I'll tell you what he did. He had two whole families, separate and apart, one in Williamsburg[47] and the other in the Bronx. The two wives knew about each other. The wife in the Bronx was younger; she's close to seventy now. When he got sore at one wife he went to live with the other one. Meanwhile he ran his chicken business in New Jersey. By one wife he had four kids, and by the other six. They're all grown, but they never have met their half-brothers and sisters and don't want to. The whole bunch of them are listed in the telephone book."

"I can't believe it," said Wilhelm.

"He told me this himself. And do you know what else? While he had his eye-

---

[47] A section of Brooklyn.

sight he used to read a lot, but the only books he would read were by Theodore Roosevelt.[48] He had a set in each of the places where he lived, and he brought his kids up on those books."

"Please," said Wilhelm, "don't feed me any more of this stuff, will you? Kindly do not—"

"In telling you this," said Tamkin with one of his hypnotic subtleties, "I do not have a motive. I want you to see how some people free themselves from morbid guilt feelings and follow their instincts. Innately, the female knows how to cripple by sickening a man with guilt. It is a very special *de*struct, and she sends her curse to make a fellow impotent. As if she says, 'Unless I allow it, you will never more be a man.' But men like my old dad or Mr. Rappaport answer, 'Woman, what art thou to me?' You can't do that yet. You're a halfway case. You want to follow your instinct, but you're too worried still. For instance, about your kids—"

"Now look here," said Wilhelm, stamping his feet. "One thing! Don't bring up my boys. Just lay off."

"I was only going to say that they are better off than with conflicts in the home."

"I'm deprived of my children." Wilhelm bit his lip. It was too late to turn away. The anguish struck him. "I pay and pay. I never see them. They grow up without me. She makes them like herself. She'll bring them up to be my enemies. Please let's not talk about this."

But Tamkin said, "Why do you let her make you suffer so? It defeats the original object in leaving her. Don't play her game. Now, Wilhelm, I'm trying to do you some good. I want to tell you, don't marry suffering. Some people do. They get married to it, and sleep and eat together, just as husband and wife. If they go with joy they think it's adultery."

When Wilhelm heard this he had, in spite of himself, to admit that there was a great deal in Tamkin's words. Yes, thought Wilhelm, suffering is the only kind of life they are sure they can have, and if they quit suffering they're afraid they'll have nothing. He knows it. This time the faker knows what he's talking about.

Looking at Tamkin he believed he saw all this confessed from his usually barren face. Yes, yes, he too. One hundred falsehoods, but at last one truth. Howling like a wolf from the city window. No one can bear it any more. Everyone is so full of it that at last everybody must proclaim it. It! It!

Then suddenly Wilhelm rose and said, "That's enough of this. Tamkin, let's go back to the market."

"I haven't finished my melon."

"Never mind that. You've had enough to eat. I want to go back."

Dr. Tamkin slid the two checks across the table. "Who paid yesterday? It's your turn, I think."

It was not until they were leaving the cafeteria that Wilhelm remembered definitely that he had paid yesterday too. But it wasn't worth arguing about.

Tamkin kept repeating as they walked down the street that there were many who were dedicated to suffering. But he told Wilhelm, "I'm optimistic in your case, and I have seen a world of maladjustment. There's hope for you. You don't really want to destroy yourself. You're trying hard to keep your feelings open, Wilhelm. I can see it. Seven per cent of this country is committing suicide by

---

[48] Roosevelt (1858–1919), twenty-sixth U.S. president (1901–1909), wrote books on such topics as history and hunting.

alcohol. Another three, maybe, narcotics. Another sixty just fading away into dust by boredom. Twenty more who have sold their souls to the Devil. Then there's a small percentage of those who want to live. That's the only significant thing in the whole world of today. Those are the only two classes of people there are. Some want to live, but the great majority don't." This fantastic Tamkin began to surpass himself. "They don't. Or else, why these wars? I'll tell you more," he said. "The love of the dying amounts to one thing; they want you to die with them. It's because they love you. Make no mistake."

True, true! thought Wilhelm, profoundly moved by these revelations. How does he know these things? How can he be such a jerk, and even perhaps an operator, a swindler, and understand so well what gives? I believe what he says. It simplifies much—everything. People are dropping like flies. I am trying to stay alive and work too hard at it. That's what's turning my brains. This working hard defeats its own end. At what point should I start over? Let me go back a ways and try once more.

Only a few hundred yards separated the cafeteria from the broker's, and within that short space Wilhelm turned again, in measurable degrees, from these wide considerations to the problems of the moment. The closer he approached to the market, the more Wilhelm had to think about money.

They passed the newsreel theater where the ragged shoeshine kids called after them. The same old bearded man with his bandaged beggar face and his tiny ragged feet and the old press clipping on his fiddle case to prove he had once been a concert violinist, pointed his bow at Wilhelm, saying, "You!" Wilhelm went by with worried eyes, bent on crossing Seventy-second Street. In full tumult the great afternoon current raced for Columbus Circle, where the mouth of midtown stood open and the skyscrapers gave back the yellow fire of the sun.

As they approached the polished stone front of the new office building, Dr. Tamkin said, "Well, isn't that old Rappaport by the door? I think he should carry a white cane, but he will never admit there's a single thing the matter with his eyes."

Mr. Rappaport did not stand well; his knees were sunk, while his pelvis only half filled his trousers. His suspenders held them, gaping.

He stopped Wilhelm with an extended hand, having somehow recognized him. In his deep voice he commanded him, "Take me to the cigar store."

"You want me—? Tamkin!" Wilhelm whispered, "You take him."

Tamkin shook his head. "He wants you. Don't refuse the old gentleman." Significantly he said in a lower voice. "This minute is another instance of the 'here-and-now.' You have to live in this very minute, and you don't want to. A man asks you for help. Don't think of the market. It won't run away. Show your respect to the old boy. Go ahead. That may be more valuable."

"Take me," said the old chicken merchant again.

Greatly annoyed, Wilhelm wrinkled his face at Tamkin. He took the old man's big but light elbow at the bone. "Well, let's step on it," he said. "Or wait—I want to have a look at the board first to see how we're doing."

But Tamkin had already started Mr. Rappaport forward. He was walking, and he scolded Wilhelm, saying, "Don't leave me standing in the middle of the sidewalk. I'm afraid to get knocked over."

"Let's get a move on. Come." Wilhelm urged him as Tamkin went into the broker's.

The traffic seemed to come down Broadway out of the sky, where the hot spokes of the sun rolled from the south. Hot, stony odors rose from the subway grating in the street.

"These teen-age hoodlums worry me. I'm ascared of these Puerto Rican kids, and these young characters who take dope," said Mr. Rappaport. "They go around all hopped up."

"Hoodlums?" said Wilhelm. "I went to the cemetery and my mother's stone bench was split. I could have broken somebody's neck for that. Which store do you go to?"

"Across Broadway. That La Magnita sign next door to the Automat."

"What's the matter with this store here on this side?"

"They don't carry my brand, that's what's the matter."

Wilhelm cursed, but checked the words.

"What are you talking?"

"Those damn taxis," said Wilhelm. "They want to run everybody down."

They entered the cool, odorous shop. Mr. Rappaport put away his large cigars with great care in various pockets while Wilhelm muttered, "Come on, you old creeper. What a poky old character! The whole world waits on him." Rappaport did not offer Wilhelm a cigar, but, holding one up, he asked, "What do you say at the size of these, huh? They're Churchill-type cigars."[49]

He barely crawls along, thought Wilhelm. His pants are dropping off because he hasn't got enough flesh for them to stick to. He's almost blind, and covered with spots, but this old man still makes money in the market. Is loaded with dough, probably. And I bet he doesn't give his children any. Some of them must be in their fifties. This is what keeps middle-aged men as children. He's master over the dough. Think—just think! Who controls everything? Old men of this type. Without needs. They don't need therefore they have. I need, therefore I don't have. That would be too easy.

"I'm older even than Churchill," said Rappaport.

Now he wanted to talk! But if you asked him a question in the market, he couldn't be bothered to answer.

"I bet you are," said Wilhelm. "Come, let's get going."

"I was a fighter, too, like Churchill," said the old man. "When we licked Spain[50] I went into the Navy. Yes, I was a gob that time. What did I have to lose? Nothing. After the battle of San Juan Hill,[51] Teddy Roosevelt kicked me off the beach."

"Come, watch the curb," said Wilhelm.

"I was curious and wanted to see what went on. I didn't have no business there, but I took a boat and rowed myself to the beach. Two of our guys was dead, layin' under the American flag to keep the flies off. So I says to the guy on duty, there, who was the sentry, 'Let's have a look at these guys. I want to see what went on here,' and he says, 'Naw,' but I talked him into it. So he took off the flag and there were these two tall guys, both gentlemen, lying in their boots. They was very tall. The two of them had long mustaches. They were high-society boys. I think one of them was called Fish,[52] from up the Hudson, a big-shot family. When I looked up, there was Teddy Roosevelt, with his hat off, and he was looking at

---

[49] Large cigars, the type smoked by the British prime minister Winston Churchill (1874–1965).
[50] In the Spanish-American War (1898); "gob" is slang for "sailor."
[51] Roosevelt emerged a hero from the Battle of San Juan Hill, in June 1898 in Cuba.
[52] A family prominent in New York politics.

these fellows, the only ones who got killed there. Then he says to me, 'What's the Navy want here? Have you got orders?' 'No, sir,' I says to him. 'Well, get the hell off the beach, then.'"

Old Rappaport was very proud of this memory. "Everything he said had such snap, such class. Man! I love that Teddy Roosevelt," he said, "I love him!"

Ah, what people are! He is almost not with us, and his life is nearly gone, but T. R. once yelled at him, so he loves him. I guess it is love, too. Wilhelm smiled. So maybe the rest of Tamkin's story was true, about the ten children and the wives and the telephone directory.

He said, "Come on, come on, Mr. Rappaport," and hurried the old man back by the large hollow elbow; he gripped it through the thin cotton cloth. Re-entering the brokerage office where under the lights the tumblers[53] were speeding with the clack of drumsticks upon wooden blocks, more than ever resembling a Chinese theater, Wilhelm strained his eyes to see the board.

The lard figures were unfamiliar. That amount couldn't be lard! They must have put the figures in the wrong slot. He traced the line back to the margin. It was down to .19, and had dropped twenty points since noon. And what about the contract of rye? It had sunk back to its earlier position, and they had lost their chance to sell.

Old Mr. Rappaport said to Wilhelm, "Read me my wheat figure."

"Oh, leave me alone for a minute," he said, and positively hid his face from the old man behind one hand. He looked for Tamkin, Tamkin's bald head, or Tamkin with his gray straw and the cocoa-colored band. He couldn't see him. Where was he? The seats next to Rowland were taken by strangers. He thrust himself over the one on the aisle, Mr. Rappaport's former place, and pushed at the back of the chair until the new occupant, a red-headed man with a thin, determined face, leaned forward to get out of his way but would not surrender the seat. "Where's Tamkin?" Wilhelm asked Rowland.

"Gee, I don't know. Is anything wrong?"

"You must have seen him. He came in a while back."

"No, but I didn't."

Wilhelm fumbled out a pencil from the top pocket of his coat and began to make calculations. His very fingers were numb, and in his agitation he was afraid he made mistakes with the decimal points and went over the subtraction and multiplication like a schoolboy at an exam. His heart, accustomed to many sorts of crisis, was now in a new panic. And, as he had dreaded, he was wiped out. It was unnecessary to ask the German manager. He could see for himself that the electronic bookkeeping device must have closed him out. The manager probably had known that Tamkin wasn't to be trusted, and on that first day he might have warned him. But you couldn't expect him to interfere.

"You get hit?" said Mr. Rowland.

And Wilhelm, quite cooly, said, "Oh, it could have been worse, I guess." He put the piece of paper into his pocket with its cigarette butts and packets of pills. The lie helped him out—although, for a moment, he was afraid he would cry. But he hardened himself. The hardening effort made a violent, vertical pain go through his chest, like that caused by a pocket of air under the collar bones. To the old chicken millionaire, who by this time had become acquainted with the drop in rye and lard, he also denied that anything serious had happened. "It's just one of

[53] Revolving numbers used to display stock-market prices.

those temporary slumps. Nothing to be scared about," he said, and remained in possession of himself. His need to cry, like someone in a crowd, pushed and jostled and abused him from behind, and Wilhelm did not dare turn. He said to himself, I will not cry in front of these people. I'll be damned if I'll break down in front of them like a kid, even though I never expect to see them again. No! No! And yet his unshed tears rose and rose and he looked like a man about to drown. But when they talked to him, he answered very distinctly. He tried to speak proudly.

" . . . going away?" he heard Rowland ask.

"What?"

"I thought you might be going away too. Tamkin said he was going to Maine this summer for his vacation."

"Oh, going away?"

Wilhelm broke off and went to look for Tamkin in the men's toilet. Across the corridor was the room where the machinery of the board was housed. It hummed and whirred like mechanical birds, and the tubes glittered in the dark. A couple of businessmen with cigarettes in their fingers were having a conversation in the lavatory. At the top of the closet door sat a gray straw hat with a cocoa-colored band. "Tamkin," said Wilhelm. He tried to identify the feet below the door. "Are you in there, Doctor Tamkin?" he said with stifled anger. "Answer me. It's Wilhelm."

The hat was taken down, the latch lifted, and a stranger came out who looked at him with annoyance.

"You waiting?" said one of the businessmen. He was warning Wilhelm that he was out of turn.

"Me? Not me," said Wilhelm. "I'm looking for a fellow."

Bitterly angry, he said to himself that Tamkin would pay him the two hundred dollars at least, his share of the original deposit. "And before he takes the train to Maine, too. Before he spends a penny on vacation—that liar! We went into this as equal partners."

VII

I was the man beneath; Tamkin was on my back, and I thought I was on his. He made me carry him, too, besides Margaret. Like this they ride on me with hoofs and claws. Tear me to pieces, stamp on me and break my bones.

Once more the hoary old fiddler pointed his bow at Wilhelm as he hurried by. Wilhelm rejected his begging and denied the omen. He dodged heavily through traffic and with his quick, small steps ran up the lower stairway of the Gloriana Hotel with its dark-tinted mirrors, kind to people's defects. From the lobby he phoned Tamkin's room, and when no one answered he took the elevator up. A rouged woman in her fifties with a mink stole led three tiny dogs on a leash, high-strung creatures with prominent black eyes, like dwarf deer, and legs like twigs. This was the eccentric Estonian lady who had been moved with her pets to the twelfth floor.

She identified Wilhelm. "You are Doctor Adler's son," she said.

Formally, he nodded.

"I am a dear friend of your father."

He stood in the corner and would not meet her glance, and she thought he was snubbing her and made a mental note to speak of it to the doctor.

The linen-wagon stood at Tamkin's door, and the chambermaid's key with its big brass tongue was in the lock.

"Has Doctor Tamkin been here?" he asked her.

"No, I haven't seen him."

Wilhelm came in, however, to look around. He examined the photos on the desk, trying to connect the faces with the strange people in Tamkin's stories. Big, heavy volumes were stacked under the double-pronged TV aerial. *Science and Sanity*,[54] he read, and there were several books of poetry. The *Wall Street Journal* hung in separate sheets from the bed-table under the weight of the silver water jug. A bathrobe with lightning streaks of red and white was laid across the foot of the bed with a pair of expensive batik pajamas. It was a box of a room, but from the windows you saw the river as far uptown as the bridge, as far downtown as Hoboken. What lay between was deep, azure, dirty, complex, crystal, rusty, with the red bones of new apartments rising on the bluffs of New Jersey, and huge liners in their berths, the tugs with matted beards of cordage. Even the brackish tidal river smell rose this high, like the smell of mop water. From every side he heard pianos, and the voices of men and women singing scales and opera, all mixed, and the sounds of pigeons on the ledges.

Again Wilhelm took the phone. "Can you locate Doctor Tamkin in the lobby for me?" he asked. And when the operator reported that she could not, Wilhelm gave the number of his father's room, but Dr. Adler was not in either. "Well, please give me the masseur. I say the massage room. Don't you undertand me? The men's health club. Yes, Max Schilper's—how am I supposed to know the name of it?"

There a strange voice said, "Toktor Adler?" It was the old Czech prizefighter with the deformed nose and ears who was attendant down there and gave out soap, sheets, and sandals. He went away. A hollow endless silence followed. Wilhelm flickered the receiver with his nails, whistled into it, but could not summon either the attendant or the operator.

The maid saw him examining the bottles of pills on Tamkin's table and seemed suspicious of him. He was running low on Phenaphen pills and was looking for something else. But he swallowed one of his own tablets and went out and rang again for the elevator. He went down to the health club. Through the steamy windows, when he emerged, he saw the reflection of the swimming pool swirling green at the bottom of the lowest stairway. He went through the locker-room curtains. Two men wrapped in towels were playing Ping-pong. They were awkward and the ball bounded high. The Negro in the toilet was shining shoes. He did not know Dr. Adler by name, and Wilhelm descended to the massage room. On the tables naked men were lying. It was not a brightly lighted place, and it was very hot, and under the white faint moons of the ceiling shone pale skins. Calendar pictures of pretty girls dressed in tiny fringes were pinned on the wall. On the first table, eyes deeply shut in heavy silent luxury lay a man with a full square beard and short legs, stocky and black-haired. He might have been an orthodox Russian. Wrapped in a sheet, waiting, the man beside him was newly shaved and red from the steambath. He had a big happy face and was dreaming. And after him was an

---

[54] A 1933 book by Korzybski.

athlete, strikingly muscled, powerful and young, with a strong white curve to his genital and a half-angry smile on his mouth. Dr. Adler was on the fourth table, and Wilhelm stood over his father's pale, slight body. His ribs were narrow and small, his belly round, white, and high. It had its own being, like something separate. His thighs were weak, the muscles of his arms had fallen, his throat was creased.

The masseur in his undershirt bent and whispered in his ear, "It's your son," and Dr. Adler opened his eyes into Wilhelm's face. At once he saw the trouble in it, and by an instantaneous reflex he removed himself from the danger of contagion, and he said serenely, "Well, have you taken my advice, Wilky?"

"Oh, Dad," said Wilhelm.

"To take a swim and get a massage?"

"Did you get my note?" said Wilhelm.

"Yes, but I'm afraid you'll have to ask somebody else, because I can't. I had no idea you were so low on funds. How did you let it happen? Didn't you lay anything aside?"

"Oh, please, Dad," said Wilhelm, almost bringing his hands together in a clasp.

"I'm sorry," said the doctor. "I really am. But I have set up a rule. I've thought about it, I believe it is a good rule, and I don't want to change it. You haven't acted wisely. What's the matter?"

"Everything. Just everything. What isn't? I did have a little, but I haven't been very smart."

"You took some gamble? You lost it? Was it Tamkin? I told you, Wilky, not to build on that Tamkin. Did you? I suspect—"

"Yes, Dad, I'm afraid I trusted him."

Dr. Adler surrendered his arm to the masseur, who was using wintergreen oil.

"Trusted! And got taken?"

"I'm afraid I kind of—" Wilhelm glanced at the masseur but he was absorbed in his work. He probably did not listen to conversations. "I did. I might as well say it. I should have listened to you."

"Well, I won't remind you how often I warned you. It must be very painful."

"Yes, Father, it is."

"I don't know how many times you have to be burned in order to learn something. The same mistakes, over and over."

"I couldn't agree with you more," said Wilhelm with a face of despair. "You're so right, Father. It's the same mistakes, and I get burned again and again. I can't seem to—I'm stupid, Dad, I just can't breathe. My chest is all up—I feel choked. I just simply can't catch my breath."

He stared at his father's nakedness. Presently he became aware that Dr. Adler was making an effort to keep his temper. He was on the verge of an explosion. Wilhelm hung his face and said, "Nobody likes bad luck, eh Dad?"

"So! It's bad luck, now. A minute ago it was stupidity."

"It is stupidity—it's some of both. It's true that I can't learn. But I—"

"I don't want to listen to the details," said his father. "And I want you to understand that I'm too old to take on new burdens. I'm just too old to do it. And people who will just wait for help—must *wait* for help. They have got to stop waiting."

"It isn't all a question of money—there are other things a father can give to a son." He lifted up his gray eyes and his nostrils grew wide with a look of suffering appeal that stirred his father even more deeply against him.

He warningly said to him, "Look out, Wilky, you're tiring my patience very much."

"I try not to. But one word from you, just a word, would go a long way. I've never asked you for very much. But you are not a kind man, Father. You don't give the little bit I beg you for."

He recognized that his father was now furiously angry. Dr. Adler started to say something, and then raised himself and gathered the sheet over him as he did so. His mouth opened, wide, dark, twisted, and he said to Wilhelm, "You want to make yourself into my cross. But I am not going to pick up a cross. I'll see you dead, Wilky, by Christ, before I let you do that to me."

"Father, listen! Listen!"

"Go away from me now. It's torture for me to look at you, you slob!" cried Dr. Adler.

Wilhelm's blood rose up madly, in anger equal to his father's, but then it sank down and left him helplessly captive to misery. He said stiffly, and with a strange sort of formality, "Okay, Dad. That'll be enough. That's about all we should say." And he stalked out heavily by the door adjacent to the swimming pool and the steam room, and labored up two long flights from the basement. Once more he took the elevator to the lobby on the mezzanine.

He inquired at the desk for Dr. Tamkin.

The clerk said, "No, I haven't seen him. But I think there's something in the box for you."

"Me? Give it here," said Wilhelm and opened a telephone message from his wife. It read, "Please phone Mrs. Wilhelm on return. Urgent."

Whenever he received an urgent message from his wife he was always thrown into a great fear for the children. He ran to the phone booth, spilled out the change from his pockets onto the little curved steel shelf under the telephone, and dialed the Digby number.

"Yes?" said his wife. Scissors barked in the parlor.

"Margaret?"

"Yes, hello." They never exchanged any other greeting. She instantly knew his voice.

"The boys all right?"

"They're out on their bicycles. Why shouldn't they be all right? Scissors, quiet!"

"Your message scared me," he said. "I wish you wouldn't make 'urgent' so common."

"I had something to tell you."

Her familiar unbending voice awakened in him a kind of hungry longing, not for Margaret but for the peace he had once known.

"You sent me a postdated check," she said. "I can't allow that. It's already five days past the first. You dated your check for the twelfth."

"Well, I have no money. I haven't got it. You can't send me to prison for that. I'll be lucky if I can raise it by the twelfth."

She answered, "You better get it, Tommy."

"Yes? What for?" he said. "Tell me. For the sake of what? To tell lies about me to everyone? You—"

She cut him off. "You know what for. I've got the boys to bring up."

Wilhelm in the narrow booth broke into a heavy sweat. He dropped his head and shrugged while with his fingers he arranged nickels, dimes and quarters in rows. "I'm doing my best," he said. "I've had some bad luck. As a matter of fact, it's been so bad that I don't know where I am. I couldn't tell you what day of the week this is. I can't think straight. I'd better not even try. This has been one of those days, Margaret. May I never live to go through another like it. I mean that with all my heart. So I'm not going to try to do any thinking today. Tomorrow I'm going to see some guys. One is a sales manager. The other is in television. But not to act," he hastily added. "On the business end."

"That's just some more of your talk, Tommy," she said. "You ought to patch things up with Rojax Corporation. They'd take you back. You've got to stop thinking like a youngster."

"What do you mean?"

"Well," she said, measured and unbending, remorselessly unbending, "you still think like a youngster. But you can't do that any more. Every other day you want to make a new start. But in eighteen years you'll be eligible for retirement. No-body wants to hire a new man of your age."

"I know. But listen, you don't have to sound so hard. I can't get on my knees to them. And really you don't have to sound so hard. I haven't done you so much harm."

"Tommy, I have to chase you and ask you for money that you owe us, and I hate it."

She hated also to be told that her voice was hard.

"I'm making an effort to control myself," she told him.

He could picture her, her graying bangs cut with strict fixity above her pretty, decisive face. She prided herself on being fair-minded. We could not bear, he thought, to know what we do. Even though blood is spilled. Even though the breath of life is taken from someone's nostrils. This is the way of the weak; quiet and fair. And then smash! They smash!

"Rojax take me back? I'd have to crawl back. They don't need me. After so many years I should have got stock in the firm. How can I support the three of you, and live myself, on half the territory? And why should I even try when you won't lift a finger to help? I sent you back to school, didn't I? At that time you said—"

His voice was rising. She did not like that and intercepted him. "You misunderstood me," she said.

"You must realize you're killing me. You can't be as blind as all that. Thou shalt not kill! Don't you remember that?"

She said, "You're just raving now. When you calm down it'll be different. I have great confidence in your earning ability."

"Margaret, you don't grasp the situation. You'll have to get a job."

"Absolutely not. I'm not going to have two young children running loose."

"They're not babies," Wilhelm said. "Tommy is fourteen. Paulie is going to be ten."

"Look," Margaret said in her deliberate manner. "We can't continue this conversation if you're going to yell so, Tommy. They're at a dangerous age. There are teen-aged gangs—the parents working, or the families broken up."

Once again she was reminding him that it was he who had left her. She had the bringing up of the children as her burden, while he must expect to pay the price of his freedom.

Freedom! he thought with consuming bitterness. Ashes in his mouth, not freedom. Give me my children. For they are mine too.

Can you be the woman I lived with? he started to say. Have you forgotten that we slept so long together? Must you now deal with me like this, and have no mercy?

He would be better off with Margaret again than he was today. This was what she wanted to make him feel, and she drove it home. "Are you in misery?" she was saying. "But you have deserved it." And he could not return to her any more than he could beg Rojax to take him back. If it cost him his life, he could not. Margaret had ruined him with Olive. She hit him and hit him, beat him, battered him, wanted to beat the very life out of him.

"Margaret, I want you please to reconsider about work. You have that degree now. Why did I pay your tuition?"

"Because it seemed practical. But it isn't. Growing boys need parental authority and a home."

He begged her, "Margaret, go easy on me. You ought to. I'm at the end of my rope and feel that I'm suffocating. You don't want to be responsible for a person's destruction. You've got to let up. I feel I'm about to burst." His face had expanded. He struck a blow upon the tin and wood and nails of the wall of the booth. "You've got to let me breathe. If I should keel over, what then? And it's something I can never understand about you. How you can treat someone like this whom you lived with so long. Who gave you the best of himself. Who tried. Who loved you." Merely to pronounce the word "love" made him tremble.

"Ah," she said with a sharp breath. "Now we're coming to it. How did you imagine it was going to be—big shot? Everything made smooth for you? I thought you were leading up to this."

She had not, perhaps, intended to reply as harshly as she did, but she brooded a great deal and now she could not forbear to punish him and make him feel pains like those she had to undergo.

He struck the wall again, this time with his knuckles, and he had scarcely enough air in his lungs to speak in a whisper, because his heart pushed upward with a frightful pressure. He got up and stamped his feet in the narrow enclosure.

"Haven't I always done my best?" he yelled, though his voice sounded weak and thin to his own ears. "Everything comes from me and nothing back again to me. There's no law that'll punish this, but you are committing a crime against me. Before God—and that's no joke. I mean that. Before God! Sooner or later the boys will know it."

In a firm tone, levelly, Margaret said to him, "I won't stand to be howled at. When you can speak normally and have something sensible to say I'll listen. But not to this." She hung up.

Wilhelm tried to tear the apparatus from the wall. He ground his teeth and seized the black box with insane digging fingers and made a stifled cry and pulled. Then he saw an elderly lady staring through the glass door, utterly appalled by him, and he ran from the booth, leaving a large amount of change on the shelf. He hurried down the stairs and into the street.

On Broadway it was still bright afternoon and the gassy air was almost motionless under the leaden spokes of sunlight, and sawdust footprints lay about the doorways of butcher shops and fruit stores. And the great, great crowd, the inexhaustible current of millions of every race and kind pouring out, pressing round, of every age, of every genius, possessors of every human secret, antique and future, in every face the refinement of one particular motive or essence—*I labor, I spend, I strive, I design, I love, I cling, I uphold, I give away, I envy, I long, I scorn, I die, I hide, I want*. Faster, much faster than any man could make the tally. The sidewalks were wider than any causeway; the street itself was immense, and it quaked and gleamed and it seemed to Wilhelm to throb at the last limit of endurance. And although the sunlight appeared like a broad tissue, its actual weight made him feel like a drunkard.

"I'll get a divorce if it's the last thing I do," he swore. "As for Dad— As for Dad— I'll have to sell the car for junk and pay the hotel. I'll have to go on my knees to Olive and say, 'Stand by me awhile. Don't let her win. Olive!'" And he thought, I'll try to start again with Olive. In fact, I must. Olive loves me. Olive—

Beside a row of limousines near the curb he thought he saw Dr. Tamkin. Of course he had been mistaken before about the hat with the cocoa-colored band and didn't want to make the same mistake twice. But wasn't that Tamkin who was speaking so earnestly, with pointed shoulders, to someone under the canopy of the funeral parlor? For this was a huge funeral. He looked for the singular face under the dark gray, fashionable hatbrim. There were two open cars filled with flowers, and a policeman tried to keep a path open to pedestrians. Right at the canopy-pole, now wasn't that that damned Tamkin talking away with a solemn face, gesticulating with an open hand?

"Tamkin!" shouted Wilhelm, going forward. But he was pushed to the side by a policeman clutching his nightstick at both end, like a rolling pin. Wilhelm was even farther from Tamkin now, and swore under his breath at the cop who continued to press him back, back, belly and ribs, saying, "Keep it moving there, please," his face red with impatient sweat, his brows like red fur. Wilhelm said to him haughtily, "You shouldn't push people like this."

The policemen, however, was not really to blame. He had been ordered to keep a way clear. Wilhelm was moved forward by the pressure of the crowd.

He cried, "Tamkin!"

But Tamkin was gone. Or rather, it was he himself who was carried from the street into the chapel. The pressure ended inside, where it was dark and cool. The flow of fan-driven air dried his face, which he wiped hard with his handkerchief to stop the slight salt itch. He gave a sigh when he heard the organ notes that stirred and breathed from the pipes and he saw people in the pews. Men in formal clothes and black homburgs[55] strode softly back and forth on the cork floor, up and down the center aisle. The white of the stained glass was like mother-of-pearl, the blue of the Star of David like velvet ribbon.

Well, thought Wilhelm, if that was Tamkin outside I might as well wait for him here where it's cool. Funny, he never mentioned he had a funeral to go to today. But that's just like the guy.

But within a few minutes he had forgotten Tamkin. He stood along the wall with others and looked toward the coffin and the slow line that was moving past it, gazing at the face of the dead. Presently he too was in this line, and slowly, slowly, foot by foot, the beating of his heart anxious, thick, frightening, but somehow also rich, he neared the coffin and paused for his turn, and gazed down. He caught his breath when he looked at the corpse, and his face swelled, his eyes shone hugely with instant tears.

The dead man was gray-haired. He had two large waves of gray hair at the front. But he was not old. His face was long, and he had a bony nose, slightly, delicately twisted. His brows were raised as though he had sunk into the final thought. Now at last he was with it, after the end of all distractions, and when his flesh was no longer flesh. And by this meditative look Wilhelm was so struck that he could not go away. In spite of the tinge of horror, and then the splash of

---

[55] Men's felt hats with the crown dented front to back.

heartsickness that he felt, he could not go. He stepped out of line and remained beside the coffin; his eyes filled silently and through his still tears he studied the man as the line of visitors moved with veiled looks past the satin coffin toward the standing bank of lilies, lilacs, roses. With great stifling sorrow, almost admiration, Wilhelm nodded and nodded. On the surface, the dead man with his formal shirt and his tie and silk lapels and his powdered skin looked so proper; only a little beneath so—black, Wilhelm thought, so fallen in the eyes.

Standing a little apart, Wilhelm began to cry. He cried at first softly and from sentiment, but soon from deeper feeling. He sobbed loudly and his face grew distorted and hot, and the tears stung his skin. A man—another human creature, was what first went through his thoughts, but other and different things were torn from him. What'll I do? I'm stripped and kicked out. . . . Oh, Father, what do I ask of you? What'll I do about the kids—Tommy, Paul? My children. And Olive? My dear! Why, why, why—you must protect me against that devil who wants my life. If you want it, then kill me. Take, take it, take it from me."

Soon he was past words, past reason, coherence. He could not stop. The source of all tears had suddenly sprung open within him, black, deep, and hot, and they were pouring out and convulsed his body, bending his stubborn head, bowing his shoulders, twisting his face, crippling the very hands with which he held the handkerchief. His efforts to collect himself were useless. The great knot of ill and grief in his throat swelled upward and he gave in utterly and held his face and wept. He cried with all his heart.

He, alone of all the people in the chapel, was sobbing. No one knew who he was.

One woman said, "Is that perhaps the cousin from New Orleans they were expecting?"

"It must be somebody real close to carry on so."

"Oh my, oh my! To be mourned like that," said one man and looked at Wilhelm's heavy shaken shoulders, his clutched face and whitened fair hair, with wide, glinting, jealous eyes.

"The man's brother, maybe?"

"Oh, I doubt that very much," said another bystander. "They're not alike at all. Night and day."

The flowers and lights fused ecstatically in Wilhelm's blind, wet eyes; the heavy sea-like music came up to his ears. It poured into him where he had hidden himself in the center of a crowd by the great and happy oblivion of tears. He heard it and sank deeper than sorrow, through torn sobs and cries toward the consummation of his heart's ultimate need.

1956

Norman Mailer
(1923–   )

Norman Mailer "has exhibited a literary ambition that can best be called imperialistic," writes the critic Richard Poirier in *Norman Mailer* (1972), adding that "he has wanted to translate his life into a literary career and then to translate that literary career into history." Mailer would perhaps concur. In his novel/biography *Marilyn* (1973) Mailer suggests that Marilyn Monroe was unable to find a sense of identity beneath her movie roles because identity is found within those roles. Although Mailer's own role-playing and self-formation have sometimes distracted readers from his formidable literary talents, the relationship between roles and identity concerns both Mailer the writer and Mailer the "figure." His bid for the mayoralty of New York City, his political activism, his countless battles with feminists, and his numerous, embattled marriages have made more people aware of Mailer the man than of Mailer the artist. The drama of being Norman Mailer may well be inseparable from the writings of Norman Mailer. "Till people see where their ideas lead," Mailer says in *Advertisements for Myself* (1959), "they know nothing."

Born in 1923 in Long Branch, New Jersey, Mailer grew up in Brooklyn, New York, and entered Harvard University when he was sixteen. It was at Harvard that Mailer vowed to become a major American novelist, studying the examples of Thomas Wolfe, Ernest Hemingway, William Faulkner, John Dos Passos, and John Steinbeck. Mailer was inducted into the army in 1944, and, eager for experience, volunteered as a rifleman with a unit fighting in the Philippines, where he took part in the World War II invasion of Luzon. He transformed his wartime experience into his first novel, *The Naked and the Dead* (1948), which won instant acclaim.

The success of that novel, coupled with his move to New York City's Greenwich Village in 1951, allowed Mailer to pursue perhaps the most enduring of his public roles—that of the rebellious "hipster." In *The White Negro: Superficial Reflections on the Hipster* (1957), Mailer explains that the hipster is an American existentialist who chooses "to accept the terms of death, to live with death as immediate danger, to divorce [himself] from society, to exist without roots, to set out on that uncharted journey into the rebellious imperatives of the self." A psychopath who opposes conformity and forms of totalitarianism in search of the ultimate, apocalyptic orgasm, the hipster runs wild in Mailer's work, from Stephen Rojack, the fictional hero in Mailer's *An American Dream* (1964), to his own novelized persona in *The Armies of the Night: History as a Novel, The Novel as History* (1968), to his chilling portrayal of convicted murderer Gary Gilmore in *The Executioner's Song* (1979). Mailer's historical novel *Ancient Evenings* (1983) locates the hipster in ancient Egypt, mixing magic with metaphysics to form a vitalistic religion that continues Mailer's grappling with his American transcendentalist predecessors.

Mailer promises in *Advertisements for Myself* to "settle for nothing else than making a revolution in the consciousness of our times." Whether or not he has succeeded may be less important than the ways in which he has embodied a revolutionary time that is somehow uniquely American. Twice a recipient of a Pulitzer Prize (in 1969 for *The Armies of the Night* and in 1980 for *The Executioner's Song*), co-founder of the *Village Voice,* part Ralph Waldo Emerson and part Muhammed Ali, Mailer remains a forceful presence in American literature.

Suggested Readings: *Barbary Shore,* 1951. *The Deer Park,* 1955. *The White Negro: Superficial Reflections on the Hipster,* 1957. *Advertisements for Myself,* 1959. *Cannibals and Christians,* 1966. *The Executioner's Song,* 1979. *The Naked and the Dead,* 1984. *Tough Guys Don't Dance,* 1984. L. Braudy, ed., *Norman Mailer: A Collection of Critical Essays,* 1972. R. Poirier, *Norman Mailer,* 1972. R. Solotaroff, *Down Mailer's Way,* 1974. W. S. Weatherby, *Squaring Off: Mailer vs. Baldwin,* 1976. P. Manso, *Mailer: His Life and Times,* 1985.

Text Used: *The Armies of the Night,* 1968.

from   THE ARMIES OF THE NIGHT*

5: TOWARD A THEATER OF IDEAS

The guests were beginning to leave the party for the Ambassador, which was two blocks away. Mailer did not know this yet, but the audience there had been waiting almost an hour. They were being entertained by an electronic folk rock guitar group, so presumably the young were more or less happy, and the middle-aged dim. Mailer was feeling the high sense of clarity which accompanies the light show of the aurora borealis when it is projected upon the inner universe of the chest, the lungs, and the heart. He was happy. On leaving, he had appropriated a coffee mug and filled it with bourbon. The fresh air illumined the bourbon, gave it a cerebrative edge; words entered his brain with the agreeable authority of fresh minted coins. Like all good professionals, he was stimulated by the chance to try a new if related line of work. Just as professional football players love sex because it it so close to football, so he was fond of speaking in public because it was thus near to writing. An extravagant analogy? Consider that a good half of writing consists of being sufficiently sensitive to the moment to reach for the next promise which is usually hidden in some word or phrase just a shift to the side of one's conscious intent. (Consciousness, that blunt tool, bucks in the general direction of the truth: instinct plucks the feather. Cheers!) Where public speaking is an exercise from prepared texts to demonstrate how successfully a low order of consciousness can beat upon the back of a collective flesh, public speaking being, therefore, a sullen expression of human possibility metaphorically equal to a bugger on his victim, speaking-in-public (as Mailer liked to describe any speech which was more or less improvised, impromptu, or dangerously written) was an activity like writing; one had to trick or seize or submit to the grace of each moment, which, except for those unexpected and sometimes well-deserved moments when consciousness and grace came together (and one felt on the consequence, heroic) were usually occasions of some mystery. The pleasure of speaking in public was the sensitivity it offered: with every phrase one was better or worse, close or less close to the existential promise of truth, *it feels true*, which hovers on good occasions like a presence between speaker and audience. Sometimes one was better, and worse, at the same moment; so strategic choices on the continuation of the attack would soon have to be decided, a moment to know the blood of the gambler in oneself.

Intimations of this approaching experience, obviously one of Mailer's preferred pleasures in life, at least when he did it well, were now connected to the professional sense of intrigue at the new task: tonight he would be both speaker and master of ceremonies. The two would conflict, but interestingly. Already he was looking in his mind for kind even celebrative remarks about Paul Goodman[1] which would not violate every reservation he had about Goodman's dank glory. But he had it. It would be possible with no violation of truth to begin by saying

---

* An account of the march to the Pentagon in protest against the Vietnam War in October 1967; when referring to himself, Mailer uses the third person. The ellipses and asterisks are Mailer's.

[1] Goodman (1911–1972) was a poet and cultural critic who wrote *Growing Up Absurd* (1963), an influential study of youth and delinquency.

that the first speaker looked very much like Nelson Algren,[2] because in fact the first speaker was Paul Goodman, and both Nelson Algren and Paul Goodman looked like old cons. Ladies and Gentlemen, without further ado let me introduce one of young America's favorite old cons, Paul Goodman! (It would not be necessary to add that where Nelson Algren looked like the sort of skinny old con who was in on every make in the joint, and would sign away Grandma's farm to stay in the game, Goodman looked like the sort of old con who had first gotten into trouble in the YMCA, and hadn't spoken to anyone since.)

All this while, Mailer had in clutch *Why Are We In Vietnam?*[3] He had neglected to bring his own copy to Washington and so had borrowed the book from his hostess on the promise he would inscribe it. (Later he was actually to lose it— working apparently on the principle that if you cannot make a hostess happy, the next best charity is to be so evil that the hostess may dine out on tales of your misconduct.) But the copy of the book is now noted because Mailer, holding it in one hand and the mug of whisky in the other, was obliged to notice on entering the Ambassador Theater that he has an overwhelming urge to micturate. The impulse to pass urine, being for some reason more difficult to restrain when both hands are occupied, there was no thought in the Master of Ceremonies' mind about the alternatives—he would have to find The Room before he went on stage.

That was not so immediately simple as one would have thought. The twenty guests from the party, looking a fair piece subdued under the fluorescent lights, had therefore the not unhaggard look of people who have arrived an hour late at the theater. No matter that the theater was by every evidence sleazy (for neighborhood movie houses built on the dream of the owner that some day Garbo or Harlow or Lombard[4] would give a look in, aged immediately they were not used for movies anymore) no matter, the guests had the uneasiness of very late arrivals. Apologetic, they were therefore in haste for the speakers to begin.

Mailer did not know this. He was off already in search of The Room, which, it developed was up on the balcony floor. Imbued with the importance of his first gig as Master of Ceremonies, he felt such incandescence of purpose that he could not quite conceive it necessary to notify de Grazia[5] he would be gone for a minute. Incandescence is the *satori*[6] of the Romantic spirit which spirit would insist—this is the essence of the Romantic—on accelerating time. The greater the power of any subjective state, the more total is a Romantic's assumption that everyone understands exactly what he is about to do, therefore waste not a moment by stopping to tell them.

Flush with his incandescence, happy in all the anticipation of liberty which this Götterdämmerung[7] of a urination was soon to provide, Mailer did not know, but he had already and unwitting to himself metamorphosed into the Beast. Wait and see!

He was met on the stairs by a young man from *Time* magazine, a stringer presumably, for the young man lacked that I-am-damned look in the eye and rep

---

[2] Algren (1908–1981) was a novelist who wrote *The Man With the Golden Arm* (1949).

[3] A 1967 novel by Mailer.

[4] The film stars Greta Garbo (1905–1990), Jean Harlow (1911–1937), and Carol Lombard (1909–1942).

[5] Ed de Grazia (1927–   ), a lawyer and author who was one of the organizers of the march against the Pentagon.

[6] Spiritual enlightenment; a term used in Zen Buddhism.

[7] "The twilight of the gods" (German); the title of an 1874 opera by Richard Wagner (1813–1883).

tie of those whose work for *Time* has become a life addiction. The young man had a somewhat ill-dressed look, a map showed on his skin of an old adolescent acne, and he gave off the unhappy furtive presence of a fraternity member on probation for the wrong thing, some grievous mis-deposit of vomit, some hanky panky with frat-house tickets.

But the Beast was in a great good mood. He was soon to speak; that was food for all. So the Beast greeted the *Time* man with the geniality of a surrogate Hemingway unbending for the Luce-ites[8] (Loo-sights was the pun) made some genial cryptic remark or two about finding Herr John, said cheerfully in answer to why he was in Washington that he had come to protest the war in Vietnam, and taking a sip of bourbon from the mug he kept to keep all fires idling right, stepped off into the darkness of the top balcony floor, went through a door into a pitch-black men's room, and was alone with his need. No chance to find the light switch for he had no matches, he did not smoke. It was therefore a matter of locating what's what with the probing of his toes. He found something finally which seemed appropriate, and pleased with the precision of these generally unused senses in his feet, took aim between them at a point twelve inches ahead, and heard in the darkness the sound of his water striking the floor. Some damn mistake had been made, an assault from the side doubtless instead of the front, the bowl was relocated now, and Master of Ceremonies breathed deep of the great reveries of this utterly non-Sisyphian[9] release—at last!!—and thoroughly enjoyed the next forty-five seconds, being left on the aftermath not a note depressed by the condition of the premises. No, he was off on the Romantic's great military dream, which is: seize defeat, convert it to triumph. Of course, pissing on the floor was bad; very bad; the attendant would probably gossip to the police (if the *Time* man did not sniff it out first) and The Uniformed in turn would report it to The Press who were sure to write about the scandalous condition in which this meeting had left the toilets. And all of this contretemps[10] merely because the management, bitter with their lost dream of Garbo and Harlow and Lombard, were now so pocked and stingy they doused the lights. (Out of such stuff is a novelist's brain.)

Well, he could convert this deficiency to an asset. From gap to gain is very American. He would confess straight out to all aloud that he was the one who wet the floor in the men's room, he alone! While the audience was recovering from the existential anxiety of encountering an orator who confessed to such a crime, he would be able—their attention now riveted—to bring them up to a contemplation of deeper problems, of, indeed, the deepest problems, the most chilling alternatives, and would from there seek to bring them back to a restorative view of man. Man might be a fool who peed in the wrong pot, man was also a scrupulous servant of the self-damaging admission; man was therefore a philosopher who possessed the magic stone; he could turn loss to philosophical gain, and so illumine the deeps, find the poles, and eventually learn to cultivate his most special fool's garden: *satori,* incandescence, and the hard gem-like flame of bourbon burning in the furnaces of metabolism.

Thus composed, illumined by these first stages of Emersonian transcendence,

---

[8] Employees of Henry Luce (1898–1967), the owner of Time-Life publications; "loo" is British slang for "toilet."

[9] According to Greek myth, Sisyphus was condemned to push an enormous boulder up a hill without relief—unlike Mailer.

[10] Awkward mishaps (French).

Mailer left the men's room, descended the stairs, entered the back of the orchestra, all opening remarks held close file in his mind like troops ranked in order before the parade, and then suddenly, most suddenly saw, with a cancerous swoop of albatross wings, that de Grazia was on the stage, was acting as M.C.,[11] was—no calling it back—launched into the conclusion of a gentle stammering stumbling—small orator, de Grazia!—introduction of Paul Goodman. All lost! The magnificent opening remarks about the forces gathered here to assemble on Saturday before the Pentagon, this historic occasion, let us hold it in our mind and focus on a puddle of passed water on the floor above and see if we assembled here can as leftists and proud dissenters contain within our minds the grandeur of the two—all lost!—no chance to do more than pick up later—later! after de Grazia and Goodman had finished dead-assing the crowd. Traitor de Grazia! Sicilian de Grazia!

As Mailer picked his way between people sitting on the stone floor (orchestra seats had been removed—the movie house was a dance hall now with a stage) he made a considerable stir in the orchestra. Mailer had been entering theaters for years, mounting stages—now that he had put on weight, it would probably have been fair to say that he came to the rostrum like a poor man's version of Orson Welles,[12] some minor note of the same contemplative presence. A titter and rise of expectation followed him. He could not resist its appeal. As he passed de Grazia, he scowled, threw a look from Lower Shakesperia "Et tu Bruté,"[13] and proceeded to slap the back of his hand against de Grazia's solar plexus. It was not a heavy blow, but then de Grazia was not a heavy man; he wilted some hint of an inch. And the audience pinched off a howl, squeaked on their squeal. It was not certain to them what had taken place.

Picture the scene two minutes later from the orchestra floor. Paul Goodman, now up at the microphone with no podium or rostrum, is reading the following lines:

> . . . these days my contempt
> for the misrulers of my country
> is icy and my indignation raucous.

It is impossible to tell what he is reading. Off at the wing of the stage where the others are collected—stout Macdonald, noble Lowell,[14] beleaguered de Grazia, and Mailer, Prince of Bourbon, the acoustics are atrocious. One cannot hear a word the speaker is saying. Nor are there enough seats. If de Grazia and Macdonald are sitting in folding chairs, Mailer is squatting on his haunches, or kneeling on one knee like a player about to go back into the ball game. Lowell has the expression on his face of a dues payer who is just about keeping up with the interest on some enormous debt. As he sits on the floor with his long arms clasped mournfully about his long Yankee legs, "I am here," says his expression, "but I do not have to pretend I like what I see." The hollows in his cheeks give a hint of the hanging judge. Lowell is of a good weight, not too heavy, not too light, but

---

[11] Emcee.

[12] The director and actor Welles (1915–1985) was a large, heavyset man.

[13] From Shakespeare's *Julius Caesar* (III.i.78), asked by the dying Caesar on realizing that Cassius is one of his assassins.

[14] Dwight Macdonald (1906–1982), a critic and journalist; the poet Robert Lowell (1917–1977), a descendant of early Puritan settlers in America.

the hollows speak of the great Puritan gloom in which the country was founded—man was simply not good enough for God.

At this moment, it is hard not to agree with Lowell. The cavern of the theater seems to resonate behind the glare of the footlights, but this is no resonance of a fine bass voice—it is rather electronics on the march. The public address system hisses, then rings in a random chorus of electronic music, sound of a cerebral mastication from some horror machine of Outer Space (where all that electricity doubtless comes from, child!) then a hum like the squeak in the hinges of the gates of Hell—we are in the penumbra[15] of psychedelic netherlands, ghost-odysseys from the dead brain cells of adolescent trysts with LSD, some ultrapurple spotlight from the balcony (not ultraviolet—ultrapurple, deepest purple one could conceive) there out in the dark like some neon eye of the night, the media is the message, and the message is purple, speaks of the monarchies of Heaven, madnesses of God, and clam-vaults of people on a stone floor. Mailer's senses are now tuned to absolute pitch or sheer error—he marks a ballot for absolute pitch—he is certain there is a profound pall in the audience. Yes, they sit there, stricken, inert, in terror of what Saturday will bring, and so are unable to rise to a word the speaker is offering them. It will take dynamite to bring life. The shroud of burned-out psychedelic dreams is in this audience, Cancer Gulch with open maw—and Mailer thinks of the vigor and the light (from marijuana?) in the eyes of those American soldiers in Vietnam who have been picked by the newsreel cameras to say their piece, and the happy healthy never unintelligent faces of all those professional football players he studies so assiduously on television come Sunday (he has neglected to put his bets in this week) and wonders how they would poll out on sentiment for the war.

HAWKS 95   DOVES 6

NFL Footballers Approve Vietnam War

Doubtless. All the healthy Marines, state troopers, professional athletes, movie stars, rednecks, sensuous life-loving Mafia, cops, mill workers, city officials, nice healthy-looking easy-grafting politicians full of the light (from marijuana?) in their eye of a life they enjoy—yes, they would be for the war in Vietnam. Arrayed against them as hard-core troops: an elite! the Freud-ridden embers of Marxism, good old American anxiety strata—the urban middle-class with their proliferated monumental adenoidal resentments, their secret slavish love for the oncoming hegemony of the computer and the suburb, yes, they and their children, by the sheer ironies, the sheer ineptitude, the *kinks* of history, were now being compressed into more and more militant stands, their resistance to the war some hopeless melange, somehow firmed, of Pacifism and closet Communism. And their children—on a freakout from the suburbs to a love-in on the Pentagon wall.

It was the children in whom Mailer had some hope, a gloomy hope. These mad middle-class children with their lobotomies from sin, their nihilistic embezzlement of all middle-class moral funds, their innocence, their lust for apocalypse, their unbelievable indifference to waste: twenty generations of buried hopes perhaps engraved in their chromosomes, and now conceivably burning like faggots in the secret inquisitional fires of LSD. It was a devil's drug—designed by the Devil to

---

[15] The partly lighted area surrounding the complete shadow of a body, like an eclipse.

consume the love of the best, and leave them liver-wasted, weeds of the big city. If there had been a player piano, Mailer might have put in a quarter to hear "In the Heart of the City Which Has No Heart."

Yes, these were the troops: middle-class cancer-pushers and drug-gutted flower children. And Paul Goodman to lead them. Was he now reading this?

> Once American faces
> were beautiful to me
> but now they look cruel
> and as if they had narrow thoughts.

Not much poetry, but well put prose. And yet there was always Goodman's damnable tolerance for all the varieties of sex. Did he know nothing of evil or entropy?[16] Sex was the superhighway to your own soul's entropy if it was used without a constant sharpening of the taste. And orgies? What did Goodman know of orgies, real ones, not lib-lab college orgies to carry out the higher program of the Great Society,[17] but real ones with murder in the air, and witches on the shoulder. The collected Tory[18] in Mailer came roaring to the surface like a docked hat in a royal coach.

"When Goodman finishes, I'm going to take over as M.C.," he whispered to de Grazia. (The revery we have just attended took no more in fact that a second. Mailer's melancholy assessment of the forces now mounting in America took place between two consecutive lines of Goodman's poem—not because Mailer cerebrated that instantly, but because he had had the revery many a time before— he had to do no more than sense the audience, whisper Cancer Gulch to himself and the revery went by with a mental ch-ch-ch Click! reviewed again.) In truth, Mailer was now in a state. He had been prepared to open the evening with apocalyptic salvos to announce the real gravity of the situation, and the intensely peculiar American aspect of it—which is that the urban and suburban middle class were to be offered on Saturday an opportunity for glory—what other nation could boast of such option for its middle class? Instead—lost! The benignity and good humor of his planned opening remarks now subjugated to the electronic hawking and squabbling *hum* of the P.A.,[19] the maniacal necessity to *wait* was on this hiatus transformed into a violent concentration of purpose, all intentions reversed. He glared at de Grazia. "How could you do this?" he whispered to his ear.

De Grazia looked somewhat confused at the intensity. Meetings to de Grazia were obviously just meetings, assemblages of people who coughed up for large admissions or kicked in for the pitch; at best, some meetings were less boring than others. De Grazia was much too wise and guilty-spirited to brood on apocalypse. "I couldn't find you," he whispered back.

"You didn't trust me long enough to wait one minute?"

"We were over an hour late," de Grazia whispered again. "We had to begin."

Mailer was all for having the conversation right then on stage: to hell with reciprocal rights and polite incline of the ear to the speaker. The Beast was ready to grapple with the world. "Did you think I wouldn't show up?" he asked de Grazia.

---

[16] Disorder.
[17] The ambitious social-welfare program carried out by Lyndon Baines Johnson (1908–1973), thirty-sixth U.S. president (1963–1968).
[18] Reactionary.   [19] Public Address system.

"Well, I was wondering."

In what sort of mumbo-jumbo of promise and betrayal did de Grazia live? How could de Grazia ever suppose he would not show up? He had spent his life showing up at the most boring and onerous places. He gave a blast of his eyes to de Grazia. But Macdonald gave a look at Mailer, as if to say, "You're creating disturbance."

Now Goodman was done.

Mailer walked to the stage. He did not have any idea any longer of what he would say, his mind was empty, but in a fine calm, taking for these five instants a total rest. While there was no danger of Mailer ever becoming a demagogue since if the first idea he offered could appeal to a mob, the second in compensation would be sure to enrage them, he might, nonetheless have made a fair country orator, for he loved to speak, he loved in fact to holler, and liked to hear a crowd holler back. (Of how many New York intellectuals may that be said?)

"I'm here as your original M.C., temporarily displaced owing to a contretemps"—which was pronounced purposefully as contretempse—"in the men's room," he said into the microphone for opening, but the gentle highstrung beast of a device pushed into a panic by the electric presence of a real Beast, let loose a squeal which shook the welds in the old foundation of the Ambassador. Mailer immediately decided he had had enough of public address systems, electronic fields of phase, impedance, and spooks in the circuitry. A hex on collaborating with Cancer Gulch. He pushed the microphone away, squared off before the audience. "Can you hear me?" he bellowed.

"Yes."

"Can you hear me in the balcony?"

"Yes."

"Then let's do away with electronics," he called out.

Cries of laughter came back. A very small pattern of applause. (Not too many on his side for electrocuting the public address system, or so his orator's ear recorded the vote.)

"Now I missed the beginning of this occasion, or I would have been here to introduce Paul Goodman, for which we're all sorry, right?"

Confused titters. Small reaction.

"What are you, dead-heads?" he bellowed at the audience. "Or are you all"—here he put on his false Irish accent—"in the nature of becoming dead ahsses?" Small laughs. A whistle or two. "No," he said, replying to the whistles, "I invoke these dead asses as part of the gravity of the occasion. The middle class plus one hippie surrealistic symbolic absolutely insane March on the Pentagon, bless us all," beginning of a big applause which offended Mailer for it came on "bless" and that was too cheap a way to win votes, "bless us all—shit!" he shouted, "I'm trying to say the middle class plus shit, I mean plus revolution is equal to one big collective dead ass." Some yells of approval, but much shocked curious rather stricken silence. He had broken the shank of his oratorical charge. Now he would have to sweep the audience together again. (Perhaps he felt like a surgeon delivering a difficult breech—nothing to do but plunge to the elbows again.)

"To resume our exposition," a good warm titter, then a ripple of laughter, not unsympathetic to his ear; the humor had been unwitting, but what was the life of an orator without some bonus? "To resume this orderly marshalling of concepts"—a conscious attempt at humor which worked less well; he was beginning to recognize for the first time that bellowing with a mike demanded a more forthright style—"I shall now *engage* in confession." More Irish accent. (He blessed

Brendan Behan[20] for what he had learned from him.) "A public speaker may offer you two opportunities. Instruction or confession." Laughter now. "Well, you're all college heads, so my instruction would be as pearls before—I dare not say it." Laughs. Boos. A voice from the balcony: "Come on, Norman, say something!"

"Is there a black man in the house?" asked Mailer. He strode up and down the stage pretending to peer at the audience. But in fact they were illumined just well enough to emphasize one sad discovery—if black faces there were they were certainly not in plenty. "Well, ah'll just have to be the *impromptu* Black Power for tonight. Woo-eeeeee! Woo-eeeeee! HMmmmmmmm." He grunted with some partial success, showing hints of Cassius Clay.[21] "Get your white butts moving."

"The confession. The confession!" screamed some adolescents from up front.

He came to a stop, shifted his voice. Now he spoke in a relaxed tone. "The confession, yeah!" Well, at least the audience was awake. He felt as if he had driven away some sepulchral phantoms of a variety which inhabited the profound middle-class schist. Now to charge the center of vested spookery.

"Say," he called out into the semidarkness with the ultrapurple light coming off the psychedelic lamp on the rail of the balcony, and the spotlights blaring against his eyes, "say," all happiness again, "I think of Saturday, and that March and do you know, fellow carriers of the holy unendurable grail, for the first time in my life I don't know whether I have the piss or the shit scared out of me most." It was an interesting concept, thought Mailer, for there was a difference between the two kinds of fear—pursue the thought, he would, in quieter times—"we are up, face this, all of you against an existential situation—we do not know how it is going to turn out, and what is even more inspiring of dread is that the government doesn't know either."

Beginning of a real hand, a couple of rebel yells. "We're going to try to stick it up the government's ass," he shouted, "right into the sphincter of the Pentagon." Wild yells and chills of silence from different reaches of the crowd. Yeah, he was cooking now. "Will reporters please get every word accurately," he called out dryly to warm the chill.

But humor may have been too late. *The New Yorker* did not have strictures against the use of sh*t for nothing; nor did Dwight Macdonald love *The New Yorker* for nothing, he also had strictures against sh*t's metaphorical associations. Mailer looked to his right to see Macdonald approaching, a book in his hands, arms at his side, a sorrowing look of concern in his face. "Norman," said Macdonald quietly, "I can't possibly follow you after all this. Please introduce me, and get it over with."

Mailer was near to stricken. On the one hand interrupted on a flight; on the other, he had fulfilled no duty whatsoever as M.C. He threw a look at Macdonald which said: give me this. I'll owe you one.

But de Grazia was there as well. "Norman, let me be M.C. now," he said.

They were being monstrous unfair, thought Mailer. They didn't understand what he had been doing, how good he had been, what he would do next. Fatal to walk off now—the verdict would claim he was unbalanced. Still, he could not hold the stage by force. That was unthinkably worse.

For the virtuous, however, deliverance (like buttercups) pops up everywhere.

---

[20] Behan (1925–1964) was a boisterous Irish playwright and performer.
[21] The heavyweight champion Muhammad Ali (1942–   ), who was stripped of his boxing title in 1967 for refusing to join the army on religious grounds.

Mailer now took the microphone and turned to the audience. He was careful to speak in a relaxed voice. "We are having a disagreement about the value of the proceedings. Some think de Grazia should resume his post as Master of Ceremonies. I would like to keep the position. It is an existential moment. We do not know how it will turn out. So let us vote on it." Happy laughter from the audience at these comic effects. Actually Mailer did not believe it was an existential situation any longer. He reckoned the vote would be well in his favor. "Will those," he asked, "who are in favor of Mr. de Grazia succeeding me as Master of Ceremonies please say aye."

A good sound number said aye.

Now for the ovation. "Will those opposed to this, please say no." The no's to Mailer's lack of pleasure were no greater in volume. "It seems the ayes and no's are about equal," said Mailer. (He was thinking to himself that he had posed the issue all wrong—the ayes should have been reserved for those who would keep him in office.) "Under the circumstances," he announced, "I will keep the chair." Laughter at this easy cheek. He stepped into the middle of such laughter. "You have all just learned an invaluable political lesson." He waved the microphone at the audience. "In the absence of a definitive vote, the man who holds the power, keeps it."

"Hey, de Grazia," someone yelled from the audience, "why do you let him have it?"

Mailer extended the microphone to de Grazia who smiled sweetly into it. "Because if I don't," he said in a gentle voice, "he'll beat the shit out of me." The dread word had been used again.

"Please, Norman," said Macdonald retreating.

So Mailer gave his introduction to Macdonald. It was less than he would have attempted if the flight had not been grounded, but it was certainly respectable. Under the military circumstances, it was a decent cleanup operation. For about a minute he proceeded to introduce Macdonald as a man with whom one might seldom agree, but could never disrespect because he always told the truth as he saw the truth, a man therefore of the most incorruptible integrity. "Pray heaven, I am right," said Mailer to himself, and walked past Macdonald who was on his way to the mike. Both men nodded coolly to each other.

In the wing, visible to the audience, Paul Goodman sat on a chair clearly avoiding any contaminatory encounter with The Existentialist. De Grazia gave his "It's tough all over" smile. Lowell sat in a mournful hunch on the floor, his eyes peering over his glasses to scrutinize the metaphysical substance of his boot, now hide? now machine? now, where the joining and to what? foot to foot, boot to earth—cease all speculations as to what was in Lowell's head. "The one mind a novelist cannot enter is the mind of a novelist superior to himself," said once to Mailer by Jean Malaquais.[22] So, by corollary, the one mind a minor poet may not enter . . .

Lowell looked most unhappy. Mailer, minor poet, had often observed that Lowell had the most disconcerting mixture of strength and weakness in his presence, a blending so dramatic in its visible sign of conflict that one had to assume he would be sensationally attractive to women. He had something untouchable, all insane in its force; one felt immediately there were any number of causes for which the man would be ready to die, and for some he would fight, with an axe in

[22] Malaquais (1908–   ) is a French novelist whose *Reflections on the Hip* was admired by Mailer.

his hand and a Cromwellian[23] light in his eye. It was even possible that physically he was very strong—one couldn't tell at all—he might be fragile, he might have the sort of farm mechanic's strength which could manhandle the rear axle and differential off a car and into the back of a pickup. But physical strength or no, his nerves were all too apparently delicate. Obviously spoiled by everyone for years, he seemed nonetheless to need the spoiling. These nerves—the nerves of a consummate poet—were not tuned to any battering. The squalls of the mike, now riding up a storm on the erratic piping breath of Macdonald's voice, seemed to tear along Lowell's back like a gale. He detested tumult—obviously. And therefore saw everything which was hopeless in a rife situation: the dank middle-class depths of the audience, the strident squalor of the mike, the absurdity of talent gathered to raise money—for what, dear God? who could finally know what this March might convey, or worse, purvey, and worst of all—to be associated now with Mailer's butcher boy attack. Lowell's eyes looked up from the shoe, and passed one withering glance by the novelist, saying much, saying, "Every single bad thing I have ever heard about you is not exaggerated."

Mailer, looking back, thought bitter words he would not say: "You, Lowell, beloved poet of many, what do you know of the dirt and the dark deliveries of the necessary? What do you know of dignity hard-achieved, and dignity lost through innocence, and dignity lost by sacrifice for a cause one cannot name. What do you know about getting fat against your will, and turning into a clown of an arriviste[24] baron when you would rather be an eagle or a count, or rarest of all, some natural aristocrat from these damned democratic states. No, the only subject we share, you and I, is that species of perception which shows that if we are not very loyal to our unendurable and most exigent inner light, then some day we may burn. How dare you condemn me! You know the diseases which inhabit the audience in this accursed psychedelic house. How dare you scorn the explosive I employ?"

And Lowell with a look of the greatest sorrow as if all this *mess* were finally too shapeless for the hard Protestant smith of his own brain, which would indeed burst if it could not forge his experience into the iron edge of the very best words and the most unsinkable relation of words, now threw up his eyes like an epileptic as if turned out of orbit by a turn of the vision—and fell backward, his head striking the floor with no last instant hesitation to cushion the blow, but like a baby, downright sudden, savagely to himself, as if from the height of a foot he had taken a pumpkin and dropped it splat on the floor. "There, much-regarded, much-protected brain, you have finally taken a blow," Lowell might have said to himself, for he proceeded to lie there, resting quietly, while Macdonald went on reading from "The White Man's Burden,"[25] Lowell seeming as content as if he had just tested the back of his cranium against a policeman's club. What a royal head they had all to lose!

6: A Transfer of Power

The evening went on. It was in fact far from climax. Lowell, resting in the wing on the floor of the stage, Lowell recuperating from the crack he had given his

---

[23] Like the British general and statesman Oliver Cromwell (1599–1658), the lord protector of England (1653—1658).

[24] A person who has recently gained power, wealth, and success and is regarded as an upstart (French).

[25] An 1899 poem, an homage to imperalism, by the English author Rudyard Kipling (1865–1936).

head, was a dreamy figure of peace in the corner of the proscenium, a reclining shepherd comtemplating his flute, although a Washington newspaper was to condemn him on Saturday in company with Mailer for "slobbish behavior" at this unseemly lounging.

Now Macdonald finished. What with the delays, the unmanageable public address system, and the choppy waters of the audience at his commencement, for Mailer had obviously done him no good, Macdonald had been somewhat less impressive than ever. A few people had shown audible boredom with him. (Old-line Communists perhaps. Dwight was now one of the oldest anti-Communists in America.)

> Take up the White Man's burden—
>   Ye dare not stoop to less—
> Nor call too loud on Freedom
>   To cloak your weariness;
> By all ye cry or whisper,
>   By all ye leave or do,
> The silent, sullen peoples
>   Shall weigh your Gods and you.[26]

read Macdonald from Kipling's poem, and the wit was in the selection, never the presentation.

He was done. He walked back to the wings with an air of no great satisfaction in himself, at most the sense of an obligation accomplished. Lowell's turn had arrived. Mailer stood up to introduce him.

The novelist gave a fulsome welcome to the poet. He did not speak of his poetry (with which he was not conspicuously familiar) nor of his prose which he thought excellent—Mailer told instead of why he had respect for Lowell as a man. A couple of years ago, the poet had refused an invitation from President Johnson to attend a garden party for artists and intellectuals, and it had attracted much attention at the time for it was one of the first dramatic acts of protest against the war in Vietnam, and Lowell was the only invited artist of first rank who had refused. Saul Bellow, for example, had attended the garden party. Lowell's refusal could not have been easy, the novelist suggested, because artists were attracted to formal afternoons of such elevated kind since that kind of experience was often stimulating to new perception and new work. So, an honorific occasion in full panoply was not easy for the mature artist to eschew. Capital! Lowell had therefore bypassed the most direct sort of literary capital. Ergo, Mailer respected him—he could not be certain he would have done the same himself, although, of course, he assured the audience he would not probably have ever had the opportunity to refuse. (Hints of merriment in the crowd at the thought of Mailer on the White House lawn.)

If the presentation had been formal up to here, it has also been somewhat graceless. On the consequence, our audience's amusement tipped the slumbering Beast. Mailer now cranked up a vaudeville clown for finale to Lowell's introduction. "Ladies and gentlemen, if novelists come from the middle class, poets tend to derive from the bottom and the top. We all know good poets at the bot'—ladies and gentlemen, here is a poet from the top, Mr. Robert Lowell." A large and

---

[26] The penultimate stanza of "The White Man's Burden."

vigorous hand of applause, genuine enthusiasm for Lowell, some standing ovation.

But Mailer was depressed. He had betrayed himself again. The end of the introduction belonged in a burlesque house—he worked his own worst veins, like a
man on the edge of bankruptcy trying to collect hopeless debts. He was fatally
vulgar! Lowell passing him on the stage had recovered sufficiently to cast him a
nullifying look. At this moment, they were obviously far from friends.

Lowell's shoulders had a slump, his modest stomach was pushed forward a
hint, his chin was dropped to his chest as he stood at the microphone, pondering
for a moment. One did not achieve the languid grandeurs of that slouch in one
generation—the grandsons of the first sons had best go through the best troughs in
the best eating clubs at Harvard before anyone in the family could try for such
elegant note. It was now apparent to Mailer that Lowell would move by instinct,
ability, and certainly by choice, in the direction most opposite from himself.

"Well," said Lowell, softly to the audience, his voice dry and gentle as any
New England executioner might ever hope to be, "this has been a zany evening."
Laughter came back, perhaps a little too much. It was as if Lowell wished to
reprove Mailer, not humiliate him. So he shifted, and talked a bit uneasily for
perhaps a minute about very little. Perhaps it was too little. Some of the audience,
encouraged by earlier examples, now whistled. "We can't hear you," they
shouted, "speak louder."

Lowell was annoyed. "I'll bellow," he said, "but it won't do any good." His
firmness, his distate for the occasion, communicated some subtle but impressive
sense of his superiority. Audiences are moved by many cues but the most satisfactory of them is probably the voice of their abdomen. There are speakers who give
a sense of security to the abdomen, and they always elicit the warmest kind of
applause. Mailer was not this sort of speaker; Lowell was. The hand of applause
which followed this remark was fortifying. Lowell now proceeded to read some
poetry.

He was not a splendid reader, merely decent to his own lines, and he read from
that slouch, that personification of ivy climbing a column, he was even diffident,
he looked a trifle helpless under the lights. Still, he made no effort to win the
audience, seduce them, dominate them, bully them, amuse them, no, they were
there for him, to please *him,* a sounding board for the plucked string of his poetic
line, and so he endeared himself to them. They adored him—for his talent, his
modesty, his superiority, his melancholy, his petulance, his weakness, his painful, almost stammering shyness, his noble strength—*there* was the string behind
other strings.

> O to break loose, like the chinook
> salmon jumping and falling back,
> nosing up to the impossible
> stone and bone-crushing waterfall—
> raw-jawed, weak-fleshed there, stopped by ten
> steps of the roaring ladder, and then
> to clear the top on the last try,
> alive enough to spawn and die.[27]

[27] The opening stanza of Lowell's poem "Waking Early Sunday Morning" (1967).

Mailer discovered he was jealous. Not of the talent. Lowell's talent was very large, but then Mailer was a bulldog about the value of his own talent. No, Mailer was jealous because he had worked for this audience, and Lowell without effort seemed to have stolen them: Mailer did not know if he was contemptuous of Lowell for playing *grand maître*,[28] or admiring of his ability to do it. Mailer knew his own version of *grand maître* did not compare. Of course no one would be there to accept his version either. The pain of bad reviews was not in the sting, but in the subsequent pressure which, like water on a joint, collected over the decade. People who had not read your books in fifteen years were certain they were missing nothing of merit. A buried sorrow, not very attractive, (for bile was in it and the bitterness of unrequited literary injustice) released itself from some ducts of the heart, and Mailer felt hot anger at how Lowell was loved and he was not, a pure and surprising recognition of how much emotion, how much simple and childlike bitter sorrowing emotion had been concealed from himself for years under the manhole cover of his contempt for bad reviews.

> Pity the planet, all joy gone
> from this sweet volcanic cone;
> peace to our children when they fall
> in small war on the heels of small
> war—until the end of time
> to police the earth, a ghost
> orbiting forever lost
> in our monotonous sublime.[29]

They gave Lowell a good standing ovation, much heartiness in it, much obvious pleasure that they were there on a night in Washington when Robert Lowell had read from his work—it was as nice as that—and then Lowell walked back to the wings, and Mailer walked forward. Lowell did not seem particularly triumphant. He looked still modest, still depressed, as if he had been applauded too much for too little and so the reservoir of guilt was still untapped.

Nonetheless, to Mailer it was now *mano a mano*.[30] Once, on a vastly larger scale of applause, perhaps people had reacted to Manolete[31] not unlike the way they reacted to Lowell, so stirred by the deeps of sorrow in the man, that the smallest move produced the largest emotion. If there was any value to the comparison then Mailer was kin to the young Dominguin, taking raucous chances, spitting in the eye of the bull, an excess of variety in his passes. But probably there was no parallel at all. He may have felt like a matador in the flush of full competition, going out to do his work after the other torero[32] has had a triumph, but for fact he was probably less close in essence now to the bullfighter than the bull. We must not forget the Beast. He had been sipping the last of the bourbon out of the mug. He had been delayed, piqued, twisted from his purpose and without anything to eat in close to ten hours. He was on the hunt. For what, he hardly knew. It is possible the hunt existed long before the victim was ever conceived.

---

[28] "Grand master" (French).   [29] The closing stanza of "Waking Early Sunday Morning."

[30] "Hand to hand" (Spanish); man to man.

[31] Manuel Rodríguez Sánchez (1917–1947), a celebrated Spanish matador, as is Dominguin (1926–   ).

[32] "Bullfighter" (Spanish).

"Now, you may wonder who I am," he said to the audience, or bellowed to them, for again he was not using the mike, "and you may wonder why I'm talking in a Southern accent which is phony"—the Southern accent as it sounded to him in his throat, was actually not too bad at this moment—"and the reason is that I want to make a presentation to you." He did not have a notion of what he would say next, but it never occurred to him something would not come. His impatience, his sorrow, his jealousy were gone, he just wanted to live on the edge of that rhetorical sword he would soon try to run through the heart of the audience. "We are gathered here"—shades of Lincoln in hippieland—"to make a move on Saturday to invest the Pentagon and halt and slow down its workings, and this will be at once a symbolic act and a real act"—he was roaring—"for real heads may possibly get hurt, and soldiers will be there to hold us back, and some of us may be arrested"—how, wondered the wise voice at the rear of this roaring voice, could one ever leave Washington now without going to jail?—"some blood conceivably will be shed. If I were the man in the government responsible for controlling this March, I would not know what to do." Sonorously—"I would not wish to arrest too many or hurt anyone for fear the repercussions in the world would be too large for my bureaucrat's heart to bear—it's so full of shit." Roars and chills from the audience again. He was off into obscenity. It gave a heartiness like the blood of beef tea to his associations. There was no villainy in obscenity for him, just—paradoxically, characteristically—his love for America: he had first come to love America when he served in the U.S. Army, not the America of course of the flag, the patriotic unendurable fix of the television programs and the newspapers, no, long before he was ever aware of the institutional oleo of the most suffocating American ideas he had come to love what editorial writers were fond of calling the democratic principle with its faith in the common man. He found that principle and that man in the Army, but what none of the editorial writers ever mentioned was that that noble common man was obscene as an old goat, and his obscenity was what saved him. The sanity of said common democratic man was in his humor, his humor was in his obscenity. And his philosophy as well—a reductive philosophy which looked to restore the hard edge of proportion to the overblown values overhanging each small military existence—viz: being forced to salute an overconscientious officer with your back stiffened into an exaggerated posture. "That Lieutenant is chicken-shit," would be the platoon verdict, and a blow had somehow been struck for democracy and the sanity of good temper. Mailer once heard a private end an argument about the merits of a general by saying, "his spit don't smell like ice cream either," only the private was not speaking of spit. Mailer thought enough of the line to put it into *The Naked and the Dead,*[33] along with a good many other such lines the characters in his mind and his memory of the Army had begun to offer him. The common discovery of America was probably that Americans were the first people on earth to live for their humor; nothing was so important to Americans as humor. In Brooklyn, he had taken this for granted, at Harvard he had thought it was a by-product of being at Harvard, but in the Army he discovered that the humor was probably in the veins and the roots of the local history of every state and county in America—the truth of the way it really felt over the years passed on a river of obscenity from small-town storyteller to storyteller there down below the bankers and the books and the educators and

---

[33] Mailer's 1948 novel that established his reputation.

the legislators—so Mailer never felt more like an American than when he was naturally obscene—all the gifts of the American language came out in the happy play of obscenity upon concept, which enabled one to go back to concept again. What was magnificent about the word shit is that it enabled you to use the word noble: a skinny Southern cracker with a beatific smile on his face saying in the dawn in a Filipino rice paddy, "Man, I just managed to take me a noble shit." Yeah, that was Mailer's America. If he was going to love something in the country, he would love that. So after years of keeping obscene language off to one corner of his work, as if to prove after *The Naked and the Dead* that he had many an arrow in his literary quiver, he had come back to obscenity again in the last year—he had kicked goodbye in his novel "Why Are We In Vietnam?" to the old literary corset of good taste, letting his sense of language play on obscenity as freely as it wished, so discovering that everything he knew about the American language (with its incommensurable resources) went flying in and out of the line of his prose with the happiest beating of wings—it was the first time his style seemed at once very American to him and very literary in the best way, at least as he saw the best way. But the reception of the book had been disappointing. Not because many of the reviews were bad (he had learned, despite all sudden discoveries of sorrow, to live with that as one lived with smog) no, what was disappointing was the crankiness across the country. Where fusty conservative old critics had once defended the obscenity in *The Naked and the Dead,* they, or their sons, now condemned it in the new book, and that *was* disappointing. The country was not growing up so much as getting a premature case of arthritis.

At any rate, he had come to the point where he liked to use a little obscenity in his public speaking. Once people got over the shock, they were sometimes able to discover that the humor it provided was not less powerful than the damage of the pain. Of course he did not do it often and he tried not to do it unless he was in good voice—Mailer was under no illusion that public speaking was equal to candid conversation; an obscenity uttered in a voice too weak for its freight was obscene, since obscenity probably resides in the quick conversion of excitement to nausea—which is why Lyndon's Johnson's speeches are called obscene by some. The excitement of listening to the American President alters abruptly into the nausea of wandering down the blind alleys of his voice.

This has been a considerable defense of the point, but then the point was at the center of his argument and it could be put thus: the American corporation executive, who was after all the foremost representative of Man in the world today, was perfectly capable of burning unseen women and children in the Vietnamese jungles, yet felt a large displeasure and fairly final disapproval at the generous use of obscenity in literature and in public.

The apology may now be well taken, but what in fact did Mailer say on the stage of the Ambassador before the evening was out? Well, not so very much, just about enough to be the stuff of which footnotes are made, for he did his best to imitate a most high and executive voice.

"I had an experience as I came to the theater to speak to all of you, which is that before appearing on this stage I went upstairs to the men's room as a prelude to beginning this oratory so beneficial to all"—laughs and catcalls—"and it was dark, so—ahem—I missed the bowl—all men will know what I mean. Forgiveness might reign. But tomorrow, they will blame that puddle of water on Communists which is the way we do things here in Amurrica, anyone of you pinko poos want to object, lemme tell ya, the reason nobody was in the men's room, and it so dark, is that if there been a light they'd had to put a CIA man in there and the hippies would grope him silly, see here, you know who I am, why it just came to me, ah'm so phony, I'm as full of shit as Lyndon Johnson. Why, man, I'm nothing but his little old alter ego. That's what you got right here working for you, Lyndon Johnson's little old *dwarf* alter ego. How you like him? How you like him?" (Shades of Cassius Clay again.)

And in the privacy of his brain, quiet in the glare of all that sound and spotlight, Mailer thought quietly, "My God, that is probably exactly what you are at this moment, Lyndon Johnson with all his sores, sorrows, and vanity, squeezed down to five foot eight," and Mailer felt for the instant possessed, as if he had seized some of the President's secret soul, or the President seized some of his— the bourbon was as luminous as moonshine to the spores of insanity in the flesh of his brain, a smoke of menace swished in the air, and something felt real, almost as if he had caught Lyndon Johnson by the toe and now indeed, bugger the rhyme, should never let him go.

"Publicity hound," shouted someone from the upper balcony.

"Fuck you," cried Mailer back with absolute delight, all the force of the Texas presidency in his being. Or was it Lucifer's fire? But let us use asterisks for these obscenities to emphasize how happily he used the words, they went off like fireworks in his orator's heart and asterisks look like rocket-bursts and the orbs from Roman candles ***. F*ck you he said to the heckler but with such gusto the vowel was doubled. F*-*ck you! was more like it. So, doubtless, had the President disposed of all opposition in private session. Well, Mailer was here to bring the presidency to the public.

"This yere dwarf alter ego has been telling you about his imbroglio with the p*ssarooney up on the top floor, and will all the reporters please note that I did not talk about defecation commonly known as sheeee-it!"—full imitation of LBJ was attempted there—"but to the contrary, speak of you-rye-nation! I p*ssed on the floor. Hoo-ee! Hoo-ee! How's that for Black Power full of white p*ss? You just know all those reporters are going to say it was sh*t tomorrow. F*ck them. F*ck all of them. Reporters, will you stand up and be counted?"

A wail of delight from the students in the audience. What would the reporters do? Would they stand?

One lone figure arose.

"Where are *you* from?" asked Mailer.

"Washington *Free Press*." A roar of delight from the crowd. It was obviously some student or hippie paper.

"Ah want *The Washington Post*," said Mailer in his best Texas tones, "and the *Star*. Ah know there's a *Time* magazine man here for one, and twenty more like him no doubt." But no one stood. So Mailer went into a diatribe. "Yeah, people," he said, "watch the reporting which follows. Yeah, these reporters will kiss Lyndon Johnson's *ss and Dean Rusk's *ss and Man Mountain McNamara's[34] *ss, they will rush to kiss it, but will they stand up in public? No! Because they

---

[34] Dean Rusk (1909–   ), the secretary of State (1961–1969), and Robert McNamara (1916–   ), the secretary of Defense (1961–1968): the cabinet members held most responsible for the Vietnam War during the Kennedy (1961–1963) and Johnson administrations.

are the silent assassins of the Republic. They alone have done more to destroy this nation than any force in it." They will certainly destroy me in the morning, he was thinking. But it was for this moment worth it, as if two very different rivers, one external, one subjective, had come together; the frustrated bile, piss, pus, and poison he had felt at the progressive contamination of all American life in the abscess of Vietnam, all of that, all heaped in lighted coals of brimstone on the press' collective ear, represented one river, and the other was the frustrated actor in Mailer—ever since seeing *All the King's Men*[35] years ago he had wanted to come on in public as a Southern demagogue.

The speech went on, and a few fine things possibly were said next to a few equally obscene words, and then Mailer thought in passing of reading a passage from *Why Are We In Vietnam?* but the passage was full of plays of repetition on the most famous four-letter word of them all, and Mailer thought that was conceivably redundant now and so he ended modestly with a final, "See you on Saturday!"

The applause was fair. Not weak, but empty of large demonstration. No standing ovation for certain. He felt cool, and in a quiet, pleasant, slightly depressed mood. Since there was not much conversation between Macdonald, Lowell, and himself, he turned after a moment, left the stage, and walked along the floor where the audience had sat. A few people gathered about him, thanked him, shook his hand. He was quiet and reserved now, with genial slightly muted attempts to be cordial. He had noticed this shift in mood before, even after readings or lectures which had been less eventful. There was a mutual embarrassment between speaker and audience once the speaker had left the stage and walked through the crowd. It was due no doubt to the intimacy—that most special intimacy—which can live between a speaker and the people he has addressed, yes they had been so intimate then, that the encounter now, afterward, was like the eye-to-the-side maneuvers of client and whore once the act is over and dressing is done.

Mailer went on from there to a party of more liberal academics, and drank a good bit more and joked with Macdonald about the superiority of the introduction he had given to Lowell over the introduction Dwight had received.

"Next time don't interrupt me," he teased Macdonald, "and I'll give you a better introduction."

"Goodness, I couldn't hear a word you said," said Macdonald, "you just sounded awful. Do you know, Norman, the acoustics were terrible on the wing. I don't think any of us heard anything anyone else said."

Some time in the early morning, or not so early, Mailer got to bed at the Hay-Adams and fell asleep to dream no doubt of fancy parties in Georgetown when the Federal period in architecture[36] was young. Of course if this were a novel, Mailer would spend the rest of the night with a lady. But it is history, and so the Novelist is for once blissfully removed from any description of the hump-your-backs of sex. Rather he can leave such matters to the happy or unhappy imagination of the reader.

1968

---

[35] A 1948 movie based on the 1946 novel by Robert Penn Warren (1905–1990).
[36] The period following the American Revolution and up to the Classic Revival in America.

Flannery O'Connor
(1925–1964)

To Flannery O'Connor the basis for art was truth, and religion was the truth. Her Catholic views, such as a belief in the Fall, Redemption, and Judgment, infused her two novels and thirty-one short stories with a moral structure and sensibility. She created characters who must face evil as well as grace, the certainty and mystery of which are behind every word she wrote. O'Connor comments in perhaps her most well-known essay, "The Fiction Writer & His Country," found in her volume of critical writing, *Mystery and Manners* (1969), that people always point out to her that life in Georgia is not at all how she depicts it. Nonetheless, her aim was to write "realistic" fiction. She states in another essay that she is "more interested in possibility than in probability." Her moral vision demands that her "real" and "possible" worlds be grounded in truth.

O'Connor's vision is distinguished from that of most other writers by her profound belief in the existence of evil. She complained that most people have a "diluted" sense of evil, without which Redemption would be meaningless. Her characters commit suicide, drown, suffer heart attacks, are gored or shot to death, or have their wooden legs stolen. Seductions backfire, love betrays, and families fail. Violence, she felt, brought her characters back to reality and made them ready to accept their "moment of grace."

This remarkable woman whose considerably small body of work has generated an enormous response—at least twenty-five books and countless articles and dissertations have been written about O'Connor—spent most of her life in Georgia. She was born Mary Flannery O'Connor in 1925 in Savannah. After earning her undergraduate degree at Georgia State College for Women, she attended the University of Iowa, where she earned a master of fine arts degree in 1947. O'Connor's stories and sections from her first novel, *Wise Blood* (1952), then began to appear in magazines. After briefly residing at the writer's colony Yaddo in Saratoga Springs, New York, she moved to New York City in 1949 and to Connecticut later that year. There she lived with the writers Robert and Sally Fitzgerald (who subsequently edited O'Connor's work), writing and helping to look after the children. O'Connor was forced to leave a year later when, at age twenty-five, she was struck with a form of lupus, the same inflammatory disease that claimed her father's life. After a long hospital stay and many blood transfusions, she returned to her mother's home on a farm near Milledgeville, Georgia. Except for short lecture trips and readings, she remained there the rest of her life.

New medication controlled the disease enough so that O'Connor was able to write. *Wise Blood* was published to rather curious critical acclaim. Who was this woman, people wondered, who had written such a disturbing and shocking novel? The story of Hazel Motes, a religious fanatic who wants to convert people to the "Church without Christ," *Wise Blood* nonetheless established O'Connor's literary career. A Kenyon Fellowship followed the novel, the cash award helping with medical costs and allowing her to continue to write. Several subsequent O'Connor stories won O'Henry Prizes, and in 1955 her first short-story collection, *A Good Man Is Hard to Find*, was published. In 1956 she began

Flannery O'Connor's mother was once directed to a house billed as easy to find: the only one in town with an "artificial nigger." O'Connor used that phrase, "a terrible symbol of what the South has done to itself," as the basis for "The Artificial Nigger."

lecture trips to colleges. The following year she traveled with her mother to Lourdes, France, and then to Rome for an audience with the Pope, although by then she was re-stricted to crutches. Her second novel, *The Violent Bear It Away* (1960), is the story of the education of her character Francis Tarwater, first by a religious zealot and then by a scien-tific rationalist. After O'Connor's death at age thirty-nine in 1964, a second volume of short stories, *Everything That Rises Must Converge* (1965), appeared. Six years later *The Complete Stories of Flannery O'Connor*, which includes the two earlier collections plus twelve additional stories, was published.

Two subsequent collections—one volume of prose written for special occasions and another of selected correspondence—were greeted with as much interest as her stories were. The essays in *Mystery and Manners* explore what O'Connor perceived to be the peculiar problem of the short-story writer: revealing in the action "as much of the mystery of existence as possible." There she writes in plain language about why she writes the way she writes and opens the volume with an essay on peacocks, which she raised in great numbers. *The Habit of Being* (1979), a selection of her letters from 1948 until her death, has gained extraordinary attention. Increasingly restricted by lupus, O'Connor depended heavily on her correspondence for social interaction. Her letters reveal the same searching mind and dark wit that is evident throughout her fiction. In them she comments on her fiction and her faith, wrestling with the profound questions of each.

Her fiction has commonly been termed grotesque, a description she disliked (preferring "realistic" or "literal") but acknowledged as appropriate. She explains in "The Fiction Writer & His Country" that her characters are deliberately distorted and act in unexpected ways because "to the hard of hearing you shout, and for the almost-blind you draw large and startling figures." O'Connor believed that most people are too accustomed to the world's evil to notice it; hence she imagined her audience to be partly deaf and blind.

O'Connor's style is consequently direct, deliberate, and relentless. Critics have long praised her carefully crafted fiction, generally preferring the short stories to the novels. Again and again her writing is called "precise" and "unsentimental." Her keen ear for dialogue and her unsettling humor are deservedly singled out. Although O'Connor's stories tend to elicit discomfort, even shock, they also penetrate the mystery of the "real" and the "possible."

Suggested Readings: *Wise Blood*, 1952. *The Violent Bear It Away*, 1960. *Mystery and Manners: Occasional Prose*, ed. R. Fitzgerald and S. Fitzgerald, 1969. *The Complete Stories of Flannery O'Connor*, 1971. *The Habit of Being*, ed. S. Fitzgerald, 1979. *Conversations With Flannery O'Connor*, ed. R. Magee, 1987. Georgia College, *The Flannery O'Connor Bulletin*, 1972– . M. Stephens, *The Question of Flannery O'Connor*, 1973. D. Walters, *Flannery O'Connor*, 1973. R. Coles, *Flannery O'Connor's South*, 1980. M. Friedman and B. L. Clark, eds., *Critical Essays on Flannery O'Connor*, 1985. H. Bloom, ed., *Flannery O'Connor*, 1986.

Text Used: *Collected Works*, ed. S. Fitzgerald, 1988.

A GOOD MAN IS HARD TO FIND*

The grandmother didn't want to go to Florida. She wanted to visit some of her connections in east Tennessee and she was seizing at every chance to change Bailey's mind. Bailey was the son she lived with, her only boy. He was sitting on the edge of his chair at the table, bent over the orange sports section of the *Journal.* "Now look here, Bailey," she said, "see here, read this," and she stood with one hand on her thin hip and the other rattling the newspaper at his bald head. "Here this fellow that calls himself The Misfit is aloose from the Federal Pen and headed toward Florida and you read here what it says he did to these people. Just you read it. I wouldn't take my children in any direction with a criminal like that aloose in it. I couldn't answer to my conscience if I did."

Bailey didn't look up from his reading so she wheeled around then and faced the children's mother, a young woman in slacks, whose face was as broad and innocent as a cabbage and was tied around with a green head-kerchief that had two points on the top like rabbit's ears. She was sitting on the sofa, feeding the baby his apricots out of a jar. "The children have been to Florida before," the old lady said. "You all ought to take them somewhere else for a change so they would see different parts of the world and be broad. They never have been to east Tennessee."

The children's mother didn't seem to hear her but the eight-year-old boy, John Wesley, a stocky child with glasses, said, "If you don't want to go to Florida, why dontcha stay at home?" He and the little girl, June Star, were reading the funny papers on the floor.

"She wouldn't stay at home to be queen for a day," June Star said without raising her yellow head.

"Yes and what would you do if this fellow, The Misfit, caught you?" the grandmother asked.

"I'd smack his face," John Wesley said.

---

* The title story of O'Connor's 1955 collection and the title of a 1918 blues song by Eddie Green.

"She wouldn't stay at home for a million bucks," June Star said. "Afraid she'd miss something. She has to go everywhere we go."

"All right, Miss," the grandmother said. "Just remember that the next time you want me to curl your hair."

June Star said her hair was naturally curly.

The next morning the grandmother was the first one in the car, ready to go. She had her big black valise that looked like the head of a hippopotamus in one corner, and underneath it she was hiding a basket with Pitty Sing,[1] the cat, in it. She didn't intend for the cat to be left alone in the house for three days because he would miss her too much and she was afraid he might brush against one of the gas burners and accidentally asphyxiate himself. Her son, Bailey, didn't like to arrive at a motel with a cat.

She sat in the middle of the back seat with John Wesley and June Star on either side of her. Bailey and the children's mother and the baby sat in front and they left Atlanta at eight forty-five with the mileage on the car at 55890. The grandmother wrote this down because she thought it would be interesting to say how many miles they had been when they got back. It took them twenty minutes to reach the outskirts of the city.

The old lady settled herself comfortably, removing her white cotton gloves and putting them up with her purse on the shelf in front of the back window. The children's mother still had on slacks and still had her head tied up in a green kerchief, but the grandmother had on a navy blue straw sailor hat with a bunch of white violets on the brim and a navy blue dress with a small white dot in the print. Her collars and cuffs were white organdy trimmed with lace and at her neckline she had pinned a purple spray of cloth violets containing a sachet. In case of an accident, anyone seeing her dead on the highway would know at once that she was a lady.

She said she thought it was going to be a good day for driving, neither too hot nor too cold, and she cautioned Bailey that the speed limit was fifty-five miles an hour and that the patrolmen hid themselves behind billboards and small clumps of trees and sped out after you before you had a chance to slow down. She pointed out interesting details of the scenery: Stone Mountain; the blue granite that in some places came up to both sides of the highway; the brilliant red clay banks slightly streaked with purple; and the various crops that made rows of green lacework on the ground. The trees were full of silver-white sunlight and the meanest of them sparkled. The children were reading comic magazines and their mother had gone back to sleep.

"Let's go through Georgia fast so we won't have to look at it much," John Wesley said.

"If I were a little boy," said the grandmother, "I wouldn't talk about my native state that way. Tennessee has the mountains and Georgia has the hills."

"Tennessee is just a hillbilly dumping ground," John Wesley said, "and Georgia is a lousy state too."

"You said it," June Star said.

"In my time," said the grandmother, folding her thin veined fingers, "children were more respectful of their native states and their parents and everything else.

---

[1] After Pitti-Sing, a character in the comic opera *The Mikado* (1885), by Sir William S. Gilbert (1836–1911) and Sir Arthur Sullivan (1842–1900).

People did right then. Oh look at the cute little pickaninny!" she said and pointed to a Negro child standing in the door of a shack. "Wouldn't that make a picture, now?" she asked and they all turned and looked at the little Negro out of the back window. He waved.

"He didn't have any britches on," June Star said.

"He probably didn't have any," the grandmother explained. "Little niggers in the country don't have things like we do. If I could paint, I'd paint that picture," she said.

The children exchanged comic books.

The grandmother offered to hold the baby and the children's mother passed him over the front seat to her. She set him on her knee and bounced him and told him about the things they were passing. She rolled her eyes and screwed up her mouth and stuck her leathery thin face into his smooth bland one. Occasionally he gave her a faraway smile. They passed a large cotton field with five or six graves fenced in the middle of it, like a small island. "Look at the graveyard!" the grandmother said, pointing it out. "That was the old family burying ground. That belonged to the plantation."

"Where's the plantation?" John Wesley asked.

"Gone With the Wind," said the grandmother. "Ha. Ha."

When the children finished all the comic books they had brought, they opened the lunch and ate it. The grandmother ate a peanut butter sandwich and an olive and would not let the children throw the box and the paper napkins out the window. When there was nothing else to do they played a game by choosing a cloud and making the other two guess what shape it suggested. John Wesley took one the shape of a cow and June Star guessed a cow and John Wesley said, no, an automobile, and June Star said he didn't play fair, and they began to slap each other over the grandmother.

The grandmother said she would tell them a story if they would keep quiet. When she told a story, she rolled her eyes and waved her head and was very dramatic. She said once when she was a maiden lady she had been courted by a Mr. Edgar Atkins Teagarden from Jasper, Georgia. She said he was a very good-looking man and a gentleman and that he brought her a watermelon every Saturday afternoon with his initials cut in it, E. A. T. Well, one Saturday, she said, Mr. Teagarden brought the watermelon and there was nobody at home and he left it on the front porch and returned in his buggy to Jasper, but she never got the watermelon, she said, because a nigger boy ate it when he saw the initials, E. A. T.! This story tickled John Wesley's funny bone and he giggled and giggled but June Star didn't think it was any good. She said she wouldn't marry a man that just brought her a watermelon on Saturday. The grandmother said she would have done well to marry Mr. Teagarden because he was a gentleman and had bought Coca-Cola stock when it first came out and that he had died only a few years ago, a very wealthy man.

They stopped at The Tower for barbecued sandwiches. The Tower was a part stucco and part wood filling station and dance hall set in a clearing outside of Timothy. A fat man named Red Sammy Butts ran it and there were signs stuck here and there on the building and for miles up and down the highway saying, TRY RED SAMMY'S FAMOUS BARBECUE. NONE LIKE FAMOUS RED SAMMY'S! RED SAM! THE FAT BOY WITH THE HAPPY LAUGH. A VETERAN! RED SAMMY'S YOUR MAN!

Red Sammy was lying on the bare ground outside The Tower with his head under a truck while a gray monkey about a foot high, chained to a small china-berry tree, chattered nearby. The monkey sprang back into the tree and got on the highest limb as soon as he saw the children jump out of the car and run toward him.

Inside, The Tower was a long dark room with a counter at one end and tables at the other and dancing space in the middle. They all sat down at a board table next to the nickelodeon and Red Sam's wife, a tall burnt-brown woman with hair and eyes lighter than her skin, came and took their order. The children's mother put a dime in the machine and played "The Tennessee Waltz,"[2] and the grandmother said that tune always made her want to dance. She asked Bailey if he would like to dance but he only glared at her. He didn't have a naturally sunny disposition like she did and trips made him nervous. The grandmother's brown eyes were very bright. She swayed her head from side to side and pretended she was dancing in her chair. June Star said play something she could tap to so the children's mother put in another dime and played a fast number and June Star stepped out onto the dance floor and did her tap routine.

"Ain't she cute?" Red Sam's wife said, leaning over the counter. "Would you like to come be my little girl?"

"No, I certainly wouldn't," June Star said. "I wouldn't live in a broken-down place like this for a million bucks!" and she ran back to the table.

"Ain't she cute?" the woman repeated, stretching her mouth politely.

"Arn't you ashamed?" hissed the grandmother.

Red Sam came in and told his wife to quit lounging on the counter and hurry up with these people's order. His khaki trousers reached just to his hip bones and his stomach hung over them like a sack of meal swaying under his shirt. He came over and sat down at a table nearby and let out a combination sigh and yodel. "You can't win," he said. "You can't win," and he wiped his sweating red face off with a gray handkerchief. "These days you don't know who to trust," he said. "Ain't that the truth?"

"People are certainly not nice like they used to be," said the grandmother.

"Two fellers come in here last week," Red Sammy said, "driving a Chrysler. It was a old beat-up car but it was a good one and these boys looked all right to me. Said they worked at the mill and you know I let them fellers charge the gas they bought? Now why did I do that?"

"Because you're a good man!" the grandmother said at once.

"Yes'm, I suppose so," Red Sam said as if he were struck with the answer.

His wife brought the orders, carrying the five plates all at once without a tray, two in each hand and one balanced on her arm. "It isn't a soul in this green world of God's that you can trust," she said. "And I don't count nobody out of that, not nobody," she repeated, looking at Red Sammy.

"Did you read about that criminal, The Misfit, that's escaped?" asked the grandmother.

"I wouldn't be a bit surprised if he didn't attact this place right here," said the woman. "If he hears about it being here, I wouldn't be none surprised to see him. If he hears it's two cent in the cash register, I wouldn't be a tall surprised if he . . ."

"That'll do," Red Sam said. "Go bring these people their Co'-Colas," and the woman went off to get the rest of the order.

---

[2] A popular 1948 song by Redd Steward and Pee Wee King.

"A good man is hard to find," Red Sammy said. "Everything is getting terrible. I remember the day you could go off and leave your screen door unlatched. Not no more."

He and the grandmother discussed better times. The old lady said that in her opinion Europe was entirely to blame for the way things were now. She said the way Europe acted you would think we were made of money and Red Sam said it was no use talking about it, she was exactly right. The children ran outside into the white sunlight and looked at the monkey in the lacy chinaberry tree. He was busy catching fleas on himself and biting each one carefully between his teeth as if it were a delicacy.

They drove off again into the hot afternoon. The grandmother took cat naps and woke up every few minutes with her own snoring. Outside of Toombsboro she woke up and recalled an old plantation that she had visited in this neighborhood once when she was a young lady. She said the house had six white columns across the front and that there was an avenue of oaks leading up to it and two little wooden trellis arbors on either side in front where you sat down with your suitor after a stroll in the garden. She recalled exactly which road to turn off to get to it. She knew that Bailey would not be willing to lose any time looking at an old house, but the more she talked about it, the more she wanted to see it once again and find out if the little twin arbors were still standing. "There was a secret panel in this house," she said craftily, not telling the truth but wishing that she were, "and the story went that all the family silver was hidden in it when Sherman[3] came through but it was never found . . ."

"Hey!" John Wesley said. "Let's go see it! We'll find it! We'll poke all the woodwork and find it! Who lives there? Where do you turn off at? Hey Pop, can't we turn off there?"

"We never have seen a house with a secret panel!" June Star shrieked. "Let's go to the house with the secret panel! Hey Pop, can't we go see the house with the secret panel!"

"It's not far from here, I know," the grandmother said. "It wouldn't take over twenty minutes."

Bailey was looking straight ahead. His jaw was as rigid as a horseshoe. "No," he said.

The children began to yell and scream that they wanted to see the house with the secret panel. John Wesley kicked the back of the front seat and June Star hung over her mother's shoulder and whined desperately into her ear that they never had any fun even on their vacation, that they could never do what THEY wanted to do. The baby began to scream and John Wesley kicked the back of the seat so hard that his father could feel the blows in his kidney.

"All right!" he shouted and drew the car to a stop at the side of the road. "Will you all shut up? Will you all just shut up for one second? If you don't shut up, we won't go anywhere."

"It would be very educational for them," the grandmother murmured.

"All right," Bailey said, "but get this: this is the only time we're going to stop for anything like this. This is the one and only time."

"The dirt road that you have to turn down is about a mile back," the grandmother directed. "I marked it when we passed."

---

[3] William Tecumseh Sherman (1820–1891), the Union Civil War general known for his "March to the Sea," a campaign of destruction from Chattanooga (May 1864) to Savannah (December 1864).

"A dirt road," Bailey groaned.

After they had turned around and were headed toward the dirt road, the grandmother recalled other points about the house, the beautiful glass over the front doorway and the candle-lamp in the hall. John Wesley said that the secret panel was probably in the fireplace.

"You can't go inside this house," Bailey said. "You don't know who lives there."

"While you all talk to the people in front, I'll run around behind and get in a window," John Wesley suggested.

"We'll all stay in the car," his mother said.

They turned onto the dirt road and the car raced roughly along in a swirl of pink dust. The grandmother recalled the times when there were no paved roads and thirty miles was a day's journey. The dirt road was hilly and there were sudden washes in it and sharp curves on dangerous embankments. All at once they would be on a hill, looking down over the blue tops of trees for miles around, then the next minute, they would be in a red depression with the dust-coated trees looking down on them.

"This place had better turn up in a minute," Bailey said, "or I'm going to turn around."

The road looked as if no one had traveled on it in months.

"It's not much farther," the grandmother said and just as she said it, a horrible thought came to her. The thought was so embarrassing that she turned red in the face and her eyes dilated and her feet jumped up, upsetting her valise in the corner. The instant the valise moved, the newspaper top she had over the basket under it rose with a snarl and Pitty Sing, the cat, sprang onto Bailey's shoulder.

The children were thrown to the floor and their mother, clutching the baby, was thrown out the door onto the ground; the old lady was thrown into the front seat. The car turned over once and landed right-side-up in a gulch off the side of the road. Bailey remained in the driver's seat with the cat—gray-striped with a broad white face and an orange nose—clinging to his neck like a caterpillar.

As soon as the children saw they could move their arms and legs, they scrambled out of the car, shouting, "We've had an ACCIDENT!" The grandmother was curled up under the dashboard, hoping she was injured so that Bailey's wrath would not come down on her all at once. The horrible thought she had had before the accident was that the house she had remembered so vividly was not in Georgia but in Tennessee.

Bailey removed the cat from his neck with both hands and flung it out the window against the side of a pine tree. Then he got out of the car and started looking for the children's mother. She was sitting against the side of the red gutted ditch, holding the screaming baby, but she only had a cut down her face and a broken shoulder. "We've had an ACCIDENT!" the children screamed in a frenzy of delight.

"But nobody's killed," June Star said with disappointment as the grandmother limped out of the car, her hat still pinned to her head but the broken front brim standing up at a jaunty angle and the violet spray hanging off the side. They all sat down in the ditch, except the children, to recover from the shock. They were all shaking.

"Maybe a car will come along," said the children's mother hoarsely.

"I believe I have injured an organ," said the grandmother, pressing her side, but no one answered her. Bailey's teeth were clattering. He had on a yellow sport shirt with bright blue parrots designed in it and his face was as yellow as the shirt. The grandmother decided that she would not mention that the house was in Tennessee.

The road was about ten feet above and they could see only the tops of the trees on the other side of it. Behind the ditch they were sitting in there were more woods, tall and dark and deep. In a few minutes they saw a car some distance away on top of a hill, coming slowly as if the occupants were watching them. The grandmother stood up and waved both arms dramatically to attract their attention. The car continued to come on slowly, disappeared around a bend and appeared again, moving even slower, on top of the hill they had gone over. It was a big black battered hearse-like automobile. There were three men in it.

It came to a stop just over them and for some minutes, the driver looked down with a steady expressionless gaze to where they were sitting, and didn't speak. Then he turned his head and muttered something to the other two and they got out. One was a fat boy in black trousers and a red sweat shirt with a silver stallion embossed on the front of it. He moved around on the right side of them and stood staring, his mouth partly open in a kind of loose grin. The other had on khaki pants and a blue striped coat and a gray hat pulled down very low, hiding most of his face. He came around slowly on the left side. Neither spoke.

The driver got out of the car and stood by the side of it, looking down at them. He was an older man than the other two. His hair was just beginning to gray and he wore silver-rimmed spectacles that gave him a scholarly look. He had a long creased face and didn't have on any shirt or undershirt. He had on blue jeans that were too tight for him and was holding a black hat and a gun. The two boys also had guns.

"We've had an ACCIDENT!" the children screamed.

The grandmother had the peculiar feeling that the bespectacled man was someone she knew. His face was as familiar to her as if she had known him all her life but she could not recall who he was. He moved away from the car and began to come down the embankment, placing his feet carefully so that he wouldn't slip. He had on tan and white shoes and no socks, and his ankles were red and thin. "Good afternoon," he said. "I see you all had you a little spill."

"We turned over twice!" said the grandmother.

"Oncet," he corrected. "We seen it happen. Try their car and see will it run, Hiram," he said quietly to the boy with the gray hat.

"What you got that gun for?" John Wesley asked. "Whatcha gonna do with that gun?"

"Lady," the man said to the children's mother, "would you mind calling them children to sit down by you? Children make me nervous. I want all you all to sit down right together there where you're at."

"What are you telling US what to do for?" June Star asked.

Behind them the line of woods gaped like a dark open mouth. "Come here," said their mother.

"Look here now," Bailey began suddenly, "we're in a predicament! We're in . . ."

The grandmother shrieked. She scrambled to her feet and stood staring. "You're The Misfit!" she said. "I recognized you at once!"

"Yes'm," the man said, smiling slightly as if he were pleased in spite of himself to be known, "but it would have been better for all of you, lady, if you hadn't of reckernized me."

Baily turned his head sharply and said something to his mother that shocked even the children. The old lady began to cry and The Misfit reddened.

"Lady," he said, "don't you get upset. Sometimes a man says things he don't mean. I don't reckon he meant to talk to you thataway."

"You wouldn't shoot a lady, would you?" the grandmother said and removed a clean handkerchief from her cuff and began to slap at her eyes with it.

The Misfit pointed the toe of his shoe into the ground and made a little hole and then covered it up again. "I would hate to have to," he said.

"Listen," the grandmother almost screamed, "I know you're a good man. You don't look a bit like you have common blood. I know you must come from nice people!"

"Yes mam," he said, "finest people in the world." When he smiled he showed a row of strong white teeth. "God never made a finer woman than my mother and my daddy's heart was pure gold," he said. The boy with the red sweat shirt had come around behind them and was standing with his gun at his hip. The Misfit squatted down on the ground. "Watch them children, Bobby Lee," he said. "You know they make me nervous." He looked at the six of them huddled together in front of him and he seemed to be embarrassed as if he couldn't think of anything to say. "Ain't a cloud in the sky," he remarked, looking up at it. "Don't see no sun but don't see no cloud neither."

"Yes, it's a beautiful day," said the grandmother. "Listen," she said, "you shouldn't call yourself The Misfit because I know you're a good man at heart. I can just look at you and tell."

"Hush!" Bailey yelled. "Hush! Everybody shut up and let me handle this!" He was squatting in the position of a runner about to sprint forward but he didn't move.

"I pre-chate that, lady," The Misfit said and drew a little circle in the ground with the butt of his gun.

"It'll take a half a hour to fix this here car," Hiram called, looking over the raised hood of it.

"Well, first you and Bobby Lee get him and that little boy to step over yonder with you," The Misfit said, pointing to Bailey and John Wesley. "The boys want to ast you something," he said to Bailey. "Would you mind stepping back in them woods there with them?"

"Listen," Bailey began, "we're in a terrible predicament! Nobody realizes what this is," and his voice cracked. His eyes were as blue and intense as the parrots in his shirt and he remained perfectly still.

The grandmother reached up to adjust her hat brim as if she were going to the woods with him but it came off in her hand. She stood staring at it and after a second she let it fall on the ground. Hiram pulled Bailey up by the arm as if he were assisting an old man. John Wesley caught hold of his father's hand and Bobby Lee followed. They went off toward the woods and just as they reached the dark edge, Bailey turned and supporting himself against a gray naked pine trunk, he shouted, "I'll be back in a minute, Mamma, wait on me!"

"Come back this instant!" his mother shrilled but they all disappeared into the woods.

"Bailey Boy!" the grandmother called in a tragic voice but she found she was looking at The Misfit squatting on the ground in front of her. "I just know you're a good man," she said desperately. "You're not a bit common!"

"Nome, I ain't a good man," The Misfit said after a second as if he had considered her statement carefully, "but I ain't the worst in the world neither. My daddy said I was a different breed of dog from my brothers and sisters. 'You know,' Daddy said, 'it's some that can live their whole life out without asking about it and it's others has to know why it is, and this boy is one of the latters. He's going to be into everything!' " He put on his black hat and looked up suddenly and then away deep into the woods as if he were embarrassed again. "I'm sorry I don't have on a shirt before you ladies," he said, hunching his shoulders slightly. "We buried our clothes that we had on when we escaped and we're just making do until we can get better. We borrowed these from some folks we met," he explained.

"That's perfectly all right," the grandmother said. "Maybe Bailey has an extra shirt in his suitcase."

"I'll look and see terrectly," The Misfit said.

"Where are they taking him?" the children's mother screamed.

"Daddy was a card himself," The Misfit said. "You couldn't put anything over on him. He never got in trouble with the Authorities though. Just had the knack of handling them."

"You could be honest too if you'd only try," said the grandmother. "Think how wonderful it would be to settle down and live a comfortable life and not have to think about somebody chasing you all the time."

The Misfit kept scratching in the ground with the butt of his gun as if he were thinking about it. "Yes'm, somebody is always after you," he murmured.

The grandmother noticed how thin his shoulder blades were just behind his hat because she was standing up looking down on him. "Do you ever pray?" she asked.

He shook his head. All she saw was the black hat wiggle between his shoulder blades. "Nome," he said.

There was a pistol shot from the woods, followed closely by another. Then silence. The old lady's head jerked around. She could hear the wind move through the tree tops like a long satisfied insuck of breath. "Bailey Boy!" she called.

"I was a gospel singer for a while," The Misfit said. "I been most everything. Been in the arm service, both land and sea, at home and abroad, been twict married, been an undertaker, been with the railroads, plowed Mother Earth, been in a tornado, seen a man burnt alive oncet," and he looked up at the children's mother and the little girl who were sitting close together, their faces white and their eyes glassy; "I even seen a woman flogged," he said.

"Pray, pray," the grandmother began, "pray, pray . . ."

"I never was a bad boy that I remember of," The Misfit said in an almost dreamy voice, "but somewheres along the line I done something wrong and got sent to the penitentiary. I was buried alive," and he looked up and held her attention to him by a steady stare.

"That's when you should have started to pray," she said. "What did you do to get sent to the penitentiary that first time?"

"Turn to the right, it was a wall," The Misfit said, looking up again at the cloudless sky. "Turn to the left, it was a wall. Look up it was a ceiling, look down it was a floor. I forget what I done, lady. I set there and set there, trying to remember what it was I done and I ain't recalled it to this day. Oncet in a while, I would think it was coming to me, but it never come."

"Maybe they put you in by mistake," the old lady said vaguely.

"Nome," he said. "It wasn't no mistake. They had the papers on me."

"You must have stolen something," she said.

The Misfit sneered slightly. "Nobody had nothing I wanted," he said. "It was a head-doctor at the penitentiary said what I had done was kill my daddy but I known that for a lie. My daddy died in nineteen ought nineteen of the epidemic flu[4] and I never had a thing to do with it. He was buried in the Mount Hopewell Baptist churchyard and you can go there and see for yourself."

"If you would pray, the old lady said, "Jesus would help you."

"That's right," The Misfit said.

"Well then, why don't you pray?" she asked trembling with delight suddenly.

"I don't want no hep," he said. "I'm doing all right by myself."

Bobby Lee and Hiram came ambling back from the woods. Bobby Lee was dragging a yellow shirt with bright blue parrots in it.

"Throw me that shirt, Bobby Lee," The Misfit said. The shirt came flying at him and landed on his shoulder and he put it on. The grandmother couldn't name what the shirt reminded her of. "No, lady," The Misfit said while he was buttoning it up, "I found out the crime don't matter. You can do one thing or you can do another, kill a man or take a tire off his car, because sooner or later you're going to forget what it was you done and just be punished for it."

The children's mother had begun to make heaving noises as if she couldn't get her breath. "Lady," he asked, "would you and that little girl like to step off yonder with Bobby Lee and Hiram and join your husband?"

"Yes, thank you," the mother said faintly. Her left arm dangled helplessly and she was holding the baby, who had gone to sleep, in the other. "Hep that lady up, Hiram," The Misfit said as she struggled to climb out of the ditch, "and Bobby Lee, you hold onto that little girl's hand."

"I don't want to hold hands with him," June Star said. "He reminds me of a pig."

The fat boy blushed and laughed and caught her by the arm and pulled her off into the woods after Hiram and her mother.

Alone with the Misfit, the grandmother found that she had lost her voice. There was not a cloud in the sky nor any sun. There was nothing around her but woods. She wanted to tell him that he must pray. She opened and closed her mouth several times before anything came out. Finally she found herself saying, "Jesus, Jesus," meaning, Jesus will help you, but the way she was saying it, it sounded as if she might be cursing.

"Yes'm" The Misfit said as if he agreed. "Jesus thown everything off balance. It was the same case with Him as with me except He hadn't committed any crime and they could prove I had committed one because they had the papers on me. Of course," he said, "they never shown me my papers. That's why I sign myself now. I said long ago, you get you a signature and sign everything you do and keep a copy of it. Then you'll know what you done and you can hold up the crime to the punishment and see do they match and in the end you'll have something to prove you ain't been treated right. I call myself The Misfit," he said, "because I can't make what all I done wrong fit what all I gone through in punishment."

There was a piercing scream from the woods, followed closely by a pistol report. "Does it seem right to you, lady, that one is punished a heap and another ain't punished at all?"

"Jesus!" the old lady cried. "You've got good blood! I know you wouldn't

---

[4] The worldwide flu epidemic of 1918 to 1919, which killed 500,000 in the United States alone.

shoot a lady! I know you come from nice people! Pray! Jesus, you ought not to shoot a lady. I'll give you all the money I've got!"

"Lady," The Misfit said, looking beyond her far into the woods, "there never was a body that give the undertaker a tip."

There were two more pistol reports and the grandmother raised her head like a parched old turkey hen crying for water and called, "Bailey Boy, Bailey Boy!" as if her heart would break.

"Jesus was the only One that ever raised the dead,"[5] The Misfit continued, "and He shouldn't have done it. He thown everything off balance. If He did what He said, then it's nothing for you to do but thow away everything and follow Him, and if He didn't, then it's nothing for you to do but enjoy the few minutes you got left the best way you can—by killing somebody or burning down his house or doing some other meanness to him. No pleasure but meanness," he said and his voice had become almost a snarl.

"Maybe He didn't raise the dead," the old lady mumbled, not knowing what she was saying and feeling so dizzy that she sank down in the ditch with her legs twisted under her.

"I wasn't there so I can't say He didn't," The Misfit said. "I wisht I had of been there," he said, hitting the ground with his fist. "It ain't right I wasn't there because if I had of been there I would of known. Listen lady," he said in a high voice, "if I had of been there I would of known and I wouldn't be like I am now." His voice seemed about to crack and the grandmother's head cleared for an instant. She saw the man's face twisted close to her own as if he were going to cry and she murmured, "Why you're one of my babies. You're one of my own children!" She reached out and touched him on the shoulder. The Misfit sprang back as if a snake had bitten him and shot her three times through the chest. Then he put his gun down on the ground and took off his glasses and began to clean them.

Hiram and Bobby Lee returned from the woods and stood over the ditch, looking down at the grandmother who half sat and half lay in a puddle of blood with her legs crossed under her like a child's and her face smiling up at the cloudless sky.

Without his glasses, The Misfit's eyes were red-rimmed and pale and defenseless-looking. "Take her off and thow her where you thown the others," he said, picking up the cat that was rubbing itself against his leg.

"She was a talker, wasn't she?" Bobby Lee said, sliding down the ditch with a yodel.

"She would of been a good woman," The Misfit said, "if it had been somebody there to shoot her every minute of her life."

"Some fun!" Bobby Lee said.

"Shut up, Bobby Lee," The Misfit said. "It's no real pleasure in life."

1955

THE ARTIFICIAL NIGGER

Mr. Head awakened to discover that the room was full of moonlight. He sat up and stared at the floor boards—the color of silver—and then at the ticking on his pillow, which might have been brocade, and after a second, he saw half of the

---

[5] In John 11 Jesus brought Lazarus, the brother of Mary, back from the dead.

moon five feet away in his shaving mirror, paused as if it were waiting for his permission to enter. It rolled forward and cast a dignifying light on everything. The straight chair against the wall looked stiff and attentive as if it were awaiting an order and Mr. Head's trousers, hanging to the back of it, had an almost noble air, like the garment some great man had just flung to his servant; but the face on the moon was a grave one. It gazed across the room and out the window where it floated over the horse stall and appeared to contemplate itself with the look of a young man who sees his old age before him.

Mr. Head could have said to it that age was a choice blessing and that only with years does a man enter into that calm understanding of life that makes him a suitable guide for the young. This, at least, had been his own experience.

He sat up and grasped the iron posts at the foot of his bed and raised himself until he could see the face on the alarm clock which sat on an overturned bucket beside the chair. The hour was two in the morning. The alarm on the clock did not work but he was not dependent on any mechanical means to awaken him. Sixty years had not dulled his responses; his physical reactions, like his moral ones, were guided by his will and strong character, and these could be seen plainly in his features. He had a long tube-like face with a long rounded open jaw and a long depressed nose. His eyes were alert but quiet, and in the miraculous moonlight they had a look of composure and of ancient wisdom as if they belonged to one of the great guides of men. He might have been Vergil summoned in the middle of the night to go to Dante, or better, Raphael, awakened by a blast of God's light to fly to the side of Tobias.[1] The only dark spot in the room was Nelson's pallet,[2] underneath the shadow of the window.

Nelson was hunched over on his side, his knees under his chin and his heels under his bottom. His new suit and hat were in the boxes that they had been sent in and these were on the floor at the foot of the pallet where he could get his hands on them as soon as he woke up. The slop jar, out of the shadow and made snow-white in the moonlight, appeared to stand guard over him like a small personal angel. Mr. Head lay back down, feeling entirely confident that he could carry out the moral mission of the coming day. He meant to be up before Nelson and to have the breakfast cooking by the time he awakened. The boy was always irked when Mr. Head was the first up. They would have to leave the house at four to get to the railroad junction by five-thirty. The train was to stop for them at five forty-five and they had to be there on time for this train was stopping merely to accommodate them.

This would be the boy's first trip to the city though he claimed it would be his second because he had been born there. Mr. Head had tried to point out to him that when he was born he didn't have the intelligence to determine his whereabouts but this had made no impression on the child at all and he continued to insist that this was to be his second trip. It would be Mr. Head's third trip. Nelson had said, "I will've already been there twict and I ain't but ten."

Mr. Head had contradicted him.

"If you ain't been there in fifteen years, how you know you'll be able to find your way about?" Nelson had asked. "How you know it hasn't changed some?"

"Have you ever," Mr. Head had asked, "seen me lost?"

---

[1] Virgil, or Publius Vergilius Maro (70–19 B.C.), the Roman poet who wrote the *Aeneid;* Dante Alighieri (1265–1321), the Italian poet who wrote *The Divine Comedy;* Raffaelo Sanzio (1483–1520), an Italian painter and architect, master of the Italian High Renaissance; Tobit, a Hebrew captive in Ninevah whose story is told in a book of the Apocrypha.

[2] A small bed or pad filled with straw, used on the floor.

Nelson certainly had not but he was a child who was never satisfied until he had given an impudent answer and he replied, "It's nowhere around here to get lost at."

"The day is going to come," Mr. Head prophesied, "when you'll find you ain't as smart as you think you are." He had been thinking about this trip for several months but it was for the most part in moral terms that he conceived it. It was to be a lesson that the boy would never forget. He was to find out from it that he had no cause for pride merely because he had been born in a city. He was to find out that the city is not a great place. Mr. Head meant him to see everything there is to see in a city so that he would be content to stay at home for the rest of his life. He fell asleep thinking how the boy would at last find out that he was not as smart as he thought he was.

He was awakened at three-thirty by the smell of fatback frying and he leaped off his cot. The pallet was empty and the clothes boxes had been thrown open. He put on his trousers and ran into the other room. The boy had a corn pone[3] on cooking and had fried the meat. He was sitting in the half-dark at the table, drinking cold coffee out of a can. He had on his new suit and his new gray hat pulled low over his eyes. It was too big for him but they had ordered it a size large because they expected his head to grow. He didn't say anything but his entire figure suggested satisfaction at having arisen before Mr. Head.

Mr. Head went to the stove and brought the meat to the table in the skillet. "It's no hurry," he said. "You'll get there soon enough and it's no guarantee you'll like it when you do neither," and he sat down across from the boy whose hat teetered back slowly to reveal a fiercely expressionless face, very much the same shape as the old man's. They were grandfather and grandson but they looked enough alike to be brothers and brothers not too far apart in age, for Mr. Head had a youthful expression by daylight, while the boy's look was ancient, as if he knew everything already and would be pleased to forget it.

Mr. Head had once had a wife and daughter and when the wife died, the daughter ran away and returned after an interval with Nelson. Then one morning, without getting out of bed, she died and left Mr. Head with sole care of the year-old child. He had made the mistake of telling Nelson that he had been born in Atlanta. If he hadn't told him that, Nelson couldn't have insisted that this was going to be his second trip.

"You may not like it a bit," Mr. Head continued. "It'll be full of niggers."

The boy made a face as if he could handle a nigger.

"All right," Mr. Head said. "You ain't ever seen a nigger."

"You wasn't up very early," Nelson said.

"You ain't ever seen a nigger," Mr. Head repeated. "There hasn't been a nigger in this county since we run that one out twelve years ago and that was before you were born." He looked at the boy as if he were daring him to say he had ever seen a Negro.

"How you know I never saw a nigger when I lived there before?" Nelson asked. "I probably saw a lot of niggers."

"If you seen one you didn't know what he was," Mr. Head said, completely exasperated. "A six-month-old child don't know a nigger from anybody else."

"I reckon I'll know a nigger if I see one," the boy said and got up and straightened his slick sharply creased gray hat and went outside to the privy.

---

[3] Bread or cake in small, oval loaves; of southern origin.

They reached the junction some time before the train was due to arrive and stood about two feet from the first set of tracks. Mr. Head carried a paper sack with some biscuits and a can of sardines in it for their lunch. A coarse-looking orange-colored sun coming up behind the east range of mountains was making the sky a dull red behind them, but in front of them it was still gray and they faced a gray transparent moon, hardly stronger than a thumbprint and completely without light. A small tin switch box and a black fuel tank were all there was to mark the place as a junction; the tracks were double and did not converge again until they were hidden behind the bends at either end of the clearing. Trains passing appeared to emerge from a tunnel of trees and, hit for a second by the cold sky, vanish terrified into the woods again. Mr. Head had had to make special arrangements with the ticket agent to have this train stop and he was secretly afraid it would not, in which case, he knew Nelson would say, "I never thought no train was going to stop for you." Under the useless morning moon the tracks looked white and fragile. Both the old man and the child stared ahead as if they were awaiting an apparition.

Then suddenly, before Mr. Head could make up his mind to turn back, there was a deep warning bleat and the train appeared, gliding very slowly, almost silently around the bend of trees about two hundred yards down the track, with one yellow front light shining. Mr. Head was still not certain it would stop and he felt it would make an even bigger idiot of him if it went by slowly. Both he and Nelson, however, were prepared to ignore the train if it passed them.

The engine charged by, filling their noses with the smell of hot metal and then the second coach came to a stop exactly where they were standing. A conductor with the face of an ancient bloated bulldog was on the step as if he expected them, though he did not look as if it mattered one way or the other to him if they got on or not. "To the right," he said.

Their entry took only a fraction of a second and the train was already speeding on as they entered the quiet car. Most of the travelers were still sleeping, some with their heads hanging off the chair arms, some stretched across two seats, and some sprawled out with their feet in the aisle. Mr. Head saw two unoccupied seats and pushed Nelson toward them. "Get in there by the winder," he said in his normal voice which was very loud at this hour of the morning. "Nobody cares if you sit there because it's nobody in it. Sit right there."

"I heard you," the boy muttered. "It's no use in you yelling," and he sat down and turned his head to the glass. There he saw a pale ghost-like face scowling at him beneath the brim of a pale ghost-like hat. His grandfather, looking quickly too, saw a different ghost, pale but grinning, under a black hat.

Mr. Head sat down and settled himself and took out his ticket and started reading aloud everything that was printed on it. People began to stir. Several woke up and stared at him. "Take off your hat," he said to Nelson and took off his own and put it on his knee. He had a small amount of white hair that had turned tobacco-colored over the years and this lay flat across the back of his head. The front of his head was bald and creased. Nelson took off his hat and put it on his knee and they waited for the conductor to come ask for their tickets.

The man across the aisle from them was spread out over two seats, his feet propped on the window and his head jutting into the aisle. He had on a light blue suit and a yellow shirt unbuttoned at the neck. His eyes had just opened and Mr. Head was ready to introduce himself when the conductor came up from behind and growled, "Tickets."

When the conductor had gone, Mr. Head gave Nelson the return half of his ticket and said, "Now put that in your pocket and don't lose it or you'll have to stay in the city."

"Maybe I will," Nelson said as if this were a reasonable suggestion.

Mr. Head ignored him. "First time this boy has ever been on a train," he explained to the man across the aisle, who was sitting up now on the edge of his seat with both feet on the floor.

Nelson jerked his hat on again and turned angrily to the window.

"He's never seen anything before," Mr. Head continued. "Ignorant as the day he was born, but I mean for him to get his fill once and for all."

The boy leaned forward, across his grandfather and toward the stranger. "I was born in the city," he said. "I was born there. This is my second trip." He said it in a high positive voice but the man across the aisle didn't look as if he understood. There were heavy purple circles under his eyes.

Mr. Head reached across the aisle and tapped him on the arm. "The thing to do with a boy," he said sagely, "is to show him all it is to show. Don't hold nothing back."

"Yeah," the man said. He gazed down at his swollen feet and lifted the left one about ten inches from the floor. After a minute he put it down and lifted the other. All through the car people began to get up and move about and yawn and stretch. Separate voices could be heard here and there and then a general hum. Suddenly Mr. Head's serene expression changed. His mouth almost closed and a light, fierce and cautious both, came into his eyes. He was looking down the length of the car. Without turning, he caught Nelson by the arm and pulled him forward. "Look," he said.

A hugh coffee-colored man was coming slowly forward. He had on a light suit and a yellow satin tie with a ruby pin in it. One of his hands rested on his stomach which rode majestically under his buttoned coat, and in the other he held the head of a black walking stick that he picked up and set down with a deliberate outward motion each time he took a step. He was proceeding very slowly, his large brown eyes gazing over the heads of the passengers. He had a small white mustache and white crinkly hair. Behind him there were two young women, both coffee-colored, one in a yellow dress and one in a green. Their progress was kept at the rate of his and they chatted in low throaty voices as they followed him.

Mr. Head's grip was tightening insistently on Nelson's arm. As the procession passed them, the light from a sapphire ring on the brown hand that picked up the cane reflected in Mr. Head's eye, but he did not look up nor did the tremendous man look at him. The group proceeded up the rest of the aisle and out of the car. Mr. Head's grip on Nelson's arm loosened. "What was that?" he asked.

"A man," the boy said and gave him an indignant look as if he were tired of having his intelligence insulted.

"What kind of a man?" Mr. Head persisted, his voice expressionless.

"A fat man," Nelson said. He was beginning to feel that he had better be cautious.

"You don't know what kind?" Mr. Head said in a final tone.

"An old man," the boy said and had a sudden foreboding that he was not going to enjoy the day.

"That was a nigger," Mr. Head said and sat back.

Nelson jumped up on the seat and stood looking backward to the end of the car but the Negro had gone.

"I'd of thought you'd know a nigger since you seen so many when you was in the city on your first visit," Mr. Head continued. "That's his first nigger," he said to the man across the aisle.

The boy slid down into the seat. "You said they were black," he said in an angry voice. "You never said they were tan. How do you expect me to know anything when you don't tell me right?"

"You're just ignorant is all," Mr. Head said and he got up and moved over in the vacant seat by the man across the aisle.

Nelson turned backward again and looked where the Negro had disappeared. He felt that the Negro had deliberately walked down the aisle in order to make a fool of him and he hated him with a fierce raw fresh hate; and also, he understood now why his grandfather disliked them. He looked toward the window and the face there seemed to suggest that he might be inadequate to the day's exactions. He wondered if he would even recognize the city when they came to it.

After he had told several stories, Mr. Head realized that the man he was talking to was asleep and he got up and suggested to Nelson that they walk over the train and see the parts of it. He particularly wanted the boy to see the toilet so they went first to the men's room and examined the plumbing. Mr. Head demonstrated the ice-water cooler as if he had invented it and showed Nelson the bowl with the single spigot where the travelers brushed their teeth. They went through several cars and came to the diner.

This was the most elegant car in the train. It was painted a rich egg-yellow and had a wine-colored carpet on the floor. There were wide windows over the tables and great spaces of the rolling view were caught in miniature in the sides of the coffee pots and in the glasses. Three very black Negroes in white suits and aprons were running up and down the aisle, swinging trays and bowing and bending over the travelers eating breakfast. One of them rushed up to Mr. Head and Nelson and said, holding up two fingers, "Space for two!" but Mr. Head replied in a loud voice, "We eaten before we left!"

The waiter wore large brown spectacles that increased the size of his eye whites. "Stan' aside then please," he said with an airy wave of the arm as if he were brushing aside flies.

Neither Nelson nor Mr. Head moved a fraction of an inch. "Look," Mr. Head said.

The near corner of the diner, containing two tables, was set off from the rest by a saffron-colored curtain. One table was set but empty but at the other, facing them, his back to the drape, sat the tremendous Negro. He was speaking in a soft voice to the two women while he buttered a muffin. He had a heavy sad face and his neck bulged over his white collar on either side. "They rope them off," Mr. Head explained. Then he said, "Let's go see the kitchen," and they walked the length of the diner but the black waiter was coming fast behind them.

"Passengers are not allowed in the kitchen!" he said in a haughty voice. "Passengers are NOT allowed in the kitchen!"

Mr. Head stopped where he was and turned. "And there's good reason for that," he shouted into the Negro's chest, "because the cockroaches would run the passengers out!"

All the travelers laughed and Mr. Head and Nelson walked out, grinning. Mr. Head was known at home for his quick wit and Nelson felt a sudden keen pride in him. He realized the old man would be his only support in the strange place they were approaching. He would be entirely alone in the world if he were ever lost from his grandfather. A terrible excitement shook him and he wanted to take hold of Mr. Head's coat and hold on like a child.

As they went back to their seats they could see through the passing windows that the countryside was becoming speckled with small houses and shacks and that a highway ran alongside the train. Cars sped by on it, very small and fast. Nelson felt that there was less breath in the air than there had been thirty minutes ago. The man across the aisle had left and there was no one near for Mr. Head to hold a conversation with so he looked out the window, through his own reflection, and read aloud the names of the buildings they were passing. "The Dixie Chemical Corp!" he announced. "Southern Maid Flour! Dixie Doors! Southern Belle Cotton Products! Patty's Peanut Butter! Southern Mammy Cane Syrup!"

"Hush up!" Nelson hissed.

All over the car people were beginning to get up and take their luggage off the overhead racks. Women were putting on their coats and hats. The conductor stuck his head in the car and snarled, "Firstoppppmry," and Nelson lunged out of his sitting position, trembling. Mr. Head pushed him down by the shoulder.

"Keep your seat," he said in dignified tones. "The first stop is on the edge of town. The second stop is at the main railroad station." He had come by this knowledge on his first trip when he had got off at the first stop and had had to pay a man fifteen cents to take him into the heart of town. Nelson sat back down, very pale. For the first time in his life, he understood that his grandfather was indispensable to him.

The train stopped and let off a few passengers and glided on as if it had never ceased moving. Outside, behind rows of brown rickety houses, a line of blue buildings stood up, and beyond them a pale rose-gray sky faded away to nothing. The train moved into the railroad yard. Looking down, Nelson saw lines and lines of silver tracks multiplying and criss-crossing. Then before he could start counting them, the face in the window started out at him, gray but distinct, and he looked the other way. The train was in the station. Both he and Mr. Head jumped up and ran to the door. Neither noticed that they had left the paper sack with the lunch in it on the seat.

They walked stiffly through the small station and came out of a heavy door into the squall of traffic. Crowds were hurrying to work. Nelson didn't know where to look. Mr. Head leaned against the side of the building and glared in front of him.

Finally Nelson said, "Well, how do you see what all it is to see?"

Mr. Head didn't answer. Then as if the sight of people passing had given him the clue, he said, "You walk" and started off down the street. Nelson followed, steadying his hat. So many sights and sounds were flooding in on him that for the first block he hardly knew what he was seeing. At the second corner, Mr. Head turned and looked behind him at the station they had left, a putty-colored terminal with a concrete dome on top. He thought that if he could keep the dome always in sight, he would be able to get back in the afternoon to catch the train again.

As they walked along, Nelson began to distinguish details and take note of the store windows, jammed with every kind of equipment—hardware, drygoods, chicken feed, liquor. They passed one that Mr. Head called his particular attention to where you walked in and sat on a chair with your feet upon two rests and let a Negro polish your shoes. They walked slowly and stopped and stood at the entrances so he could see what went on in each place but they did not go into any of them. Mr. Head was determined not to go into any city store because on his first trip here, he had got lost in a large one and had found his way out only after many people had insulted him.

They came in the middle of the next block to a store that had a weighing machine in front of it and they both in turn stepped up on it and put in a penny and received a ticket. Mr. Head's ticket said "You weigh 120 pounds. You are upright and brave and all your friends admire you." He put the ticket in his pocket, surprised that the machine should have got his character correct but his weight wrong, for he had weighed on a grain scale not long before and knew he weighed 110. Nelson's ticket said, "You weigh 98 pounds. You have a great destiny ahead of you but beware of dark women." Nelson did not know any women and he weighed only 68 pounds but Mr. Head pointed out that the machine had probably printed the number upsidedown, meaning the 9 for a 6.

They walked on and at the end of five blocks the dome of the terminal sank out of sight and Mr. Head turned to the left. Nelson could have stood in front of every store window for an hour if there had not been another more interesting one next to it. Suddenly he said, "I was born here!" Mr. Head turned and looked at him with horror. There was a sweaty brightness about his face. "This is where I come from!" he said.

Mr. Head was appalled. He saw the moment had come for drastic action. "Lemme show you one thing you ain't seen yet," he said and took him to the corner where there was a sewer entrance. "Squat down," he said, "and stick your head in there," and he held the back of the boy's coat while he got down and put his head in the sewer. He drew it back quickly, hearing a gurgling in the depths under the sidewalk. Then Mr. Head explained the sewer system, how the entire city was underlined with it, how it contained all the drainage and was full of rats and how a man could slide into it and be sucked along down endless pitchblack tunnels. At any minute any man in the city might be sucked into the sewer and never heard from again. He described it so well that Nelson was for some seconds shaken. He connected the sewer passages with the entrance to hell and understood for the first time how the world was put together in its lower parts. He drew away from the curb.

Then he said, "Yes, but you can stay away from the holes," and his face took on that stubborn look that was so exasperating to his grandfather. "This is where I come from!" he said.

Mr. Head was dismayed but he only muttered, "You'll get your fill," and they walked on. At the end of two more blocks he turned to the left, feeling that he was circling the dome; and he was correct for in a half-hour they passed in front of the railroad station again. At first Nelson did not notice that he was seeing the same stores twice but when they passed the one where you put your feet on the rests while the Negro polished your shoes, he perceived that they were walking in a circle.

"We done been here!" he shouted. "I don't believe you know where you're at!"

"The direction just slipped my mind for a minute," Mr. Head said and they turned down a different street. He still did not intend to let the dome get too far away and after two blocks in their new direction, he turned to the left. This street contained two- and three-story wooden dwellings. Anyone passing on the sidewalk could see into the rooms and Mr. Head, glancing through one window, saw a woman lying on an iron bed, looking out, with a sheet pulled over her. Her knowing expression shook him. A fierce-looking boy on a bicycle came driving down out of nowhere and he had to jump to the side to keep from being hit. "It's nothing to them if they knock you down," he said. "You better keep closer to me."

They walked on for some time on streets like this before he remembered to turn again. The houses they were passing now were all unpainted and the wood in them looked rotten; the street between was narrower. Nelson saw a colored man. Then another. Then another. "Niggers live in these houses," he observed.

"Well come on and we'll go somewheres else," Mr. Head said. "We didn't come to look at niggers," and they turned down another street but they continued to see Negroes everywhere. Nelson's skin began to prickle and they stepped along at a faster pace in order to leave the neighborhood as soon as possible. There were colored men in their undershirts standing in the doors and colored women rocking on the sagging porches. Colored children played in the gutters and stopped what they were doing to look at them. Before long they began to pass rows of stores with colored customers in them but they didn't pause at the entrances of these. Black eyes in black faces were watching them from every direction. "Yes," Mr. Head said, "this is where you were born—right here with all these niggers."

Nelson scowled. "I think you done got us lost," he said.

Mr. Head swung around sharply and looked for the dome. It was nowhere in sight. "I ain't got us lost either," he said. "You're just tired of walking."

"I ain't tired, I'm hungry," Nelson said. "Give me a biscuit."

They discovered then that they had lost the lunch.

"You were the one holding the sack," Nelson said. "I would have kepaholt of it."

"If you want to direct this trip, I'll go on by myself and leave you right here," Mr. Head said and was pleased to see the boy turn white. However, he realized they were lost and drifting farther every minute from the station. He was hungry himself and beginning to be thirsty and since they had been in the colored neighborhood, they had both begun to sweat. Nelson had on his shoes and he was unaccustomed to them. The concrete sidewalks were very hard. They both wanted to find a place to sit down but this was impossible and they kept on walking, the boy muttering under his breath, "First you lost the sack and then you lost the way," and Mr. Head growling from time to time, "Anybody wants to be from this nigger heaven can be from it!"

By now the sun was well forward in the sky. The odor of dinners cooking drifted out to them. The Negroes were all at their doors to see them pass. "Whyn't you ast one of these niggers the way?" Nelson said. "You got us lost."

"This is where you were born," Mr. Head said. "You can ast one yourself if you want to."

Nelson was afraid of the colored men and he didn't want to be laughed at by the colored children. Up ahead he saw a large colored woman leaning in a doorway that opened onto the sidewalk. Her hair stood straight out from her head for about four inches all around and she was resting on bare brown feet that turned pink at the sides. She had on a pink dress that showed her exact shape. As they came abreast of her, she lazily lifted one hand to her head and her fingers disappeared into her hair.

Nelson stopped. He felt his breath drawn up by the woman's dark eyes. "How do you get back to town?" he said in a voice that did not sound like his own.

After a minute she said, "You in town now," in a rich low tone that made Nelson feel as if a cool spray had been turned on him.

"How do you get back to the train?" he said in the same reed-like voice.

"You can catch you a car," she said.

He understood she was making fun of him but he was too paralyzed even to scowl. He stood drinking in every detail of her. His eyes traveled up from her great knees to her forehead and then made a triangular path from the glistening sweat on her neck down and across her tremendous bosom and over her bare arm back to where her fingers lay hidden in her hair. He suddenly wanted her to reach down and pick him up and draw him against her and then he wanted to feel her breath on his face. He wanted to look down and down into her eyes while she held him tighter and tighter. He had never had such a feeling before. He felt as if he were reeling down through a pitchblack tunnel.

"You can go a block down yonder and catch you a car take you to the railroad station, Sugarpie," she said.

Nelson would have collapsed at her feet if Mr. Head had not pulled him roughly away. "You act like you don't have any sense!" the old man growled.

They hurried down the street and Nelson did not look back at the woman. He pushed his hat sharply forward over his face which was already burning with shame. The sneering ghost he had seen in the train window and all the foreboding feelings he had on the way returned to him and he remembered that his ticket from the scale had said to beware of dark women and that his grandfather's had said he was upright and brave. He took hold of the old man's hand, a sign of dependence that he seldom showed.

They headed down the street toward the car tracks where a long yellow rattling trolley was coming. Mr. Head had never boarded a streetcar and he let that one pass. Nelson was silent. From time to time his mouth trembled slightly but his grandfather, occupied with his own problems, paid him no attention. They stood on the corner and neither looked at the Negroes who were passing, going about their business just as if they had been white, except that most of them stopped and eyed Mr. Head and Nelson. It occurred to Mr. Head that since the streetcar ran on tracks, they could simply follow the tracks. He gave Nelson a slight push and explained that they would follow the tracks on into the railroad station, walking, and they set off.

Presently to their great relief they began to see white people again and Nelson sat down on the sidewalk against the wall of a building. "I got to rest myself some," he said. "You lost the sack and the direction. You can just wait on me to rest myself."

"There's the tracks in front of us," Mr. Head said. "All we got to do is keep them in sight and you could have remembered the sack as good as me. This is where you were born. This is your old home town. This is your second trip. You ought to know how to do," and he squatted down and continued in this vein but the boy, easing his burning feet out of his shoes, did not answer.

"And standing there grinning like a chim-pan-zee while a nigger woman gives you directions. Great Gawd!" Mr. Head said.

"I never said I was nothing but born here," the boy said in a shaky voice. "I never said I would or wouldn't like it. I never said I wanted to come. I only said I was born here and I never had nothing to do with that. I want to go home. I never wanted to come in the first place. It was all your big idea. How you know you ain't following the tracks in the wrong direction?"

This last had occurred to Mr. Head too. "All these people are white," he said.

"We ain't passed here before," Nelson said. This was a neighborhood of brick buildings that might have been lived in or might not. A few empty automobiles were parked along the curb and there was an occasional passerby. The heat of the pavement came up through Nelson's thin suit. His eyelids began to droop, and after a few minutes his head tilted forward. His shoulders twitched once or twice and then he fell over on his side and lay sprawled in an exhausted fit of sleep.

Mr. Head watched him silently. He was very tired himself but they could not both sleep at the same time and he could not have slept anyway because he did not know where he was. In a few minutes Nelson would wake up, refreshed by his sleep and very cocky, and would begin complaining that he had lost the sack and the way. You'd have a mighty sorry time if I wasn't here, Mr. Head thought; and then another idea occurred to him. He looked at the sprawled figure for several minutes; presently he stood up. He justified what he was going to do on the grounds that it is sometimes necessary to teach a child a lesson he won't forget, particularly when the child is always reasserting his position with some new impudence. He walked without a sound to the corner about twenty feet away and sat down on a covered garbage can in the alley where he could look out and watch Nelson wake up alone.

The boy was dozing fitfully, half conscious of vague noises and black forms moving up from some dark part of him into the light. His face worked in his sleep and he had pulled his knees up under his chin. The sun shed a dull dry light on the narrow street; everything looked like exactly what it was. After a while Mr. Head, hunched like an old monkey on the garbage can lid, decided that if Nelson didn't wake up soon, he would make a loud noise by bamming his foot against the can. He looked at his watch and discovered that it was two o'clock. Their train left at six and the possibility of missing it was too awful for him to think of. He kicked his foot backwards on the can and a hollow boom reverberated in the alley.

Nelson shot up onto his feet with a shout. He looked where his grandfather should have been and stared. He seemed to whirl several times and then, picking up his feet and throwing his head back, he dashed down the street like a wild maddened pony. Mr. Head jumped off the can and galloped after but the child was almost out of sight. He saw a streak of gray disappearing diagonally a block ahead. He ran as fast as he could, looking both ways down every intersection, but without sight of him again. Then as he passed the third intersection, completely winded, he saw about half a block down the street a scene that stopped him altogether. He crouched behind a trash box to watch and get his bearings.

Nelson was sitting with both legs spread out and by his side lay an elderly woman, screaming. Groceries were scattered about the sidewalk. A crowd of women had already gathered to see justice done and Mr. Head distinctly heard the old woman on the pavement shout, "You've broken my ankle and your daddy'll pay for it! Every nickel! Police! Police!" Several of the women were plucking at Nelson's shoulder but the boy seemed too dazed to get up.

Something forced Mr. Head from behind the trash box and forward, but only at a creeping pace. He had never in his life been accosted by a policeman. The women were milling around Nelson as if they might suddenly all dive on him at once and tear him to pieces, and the old woman continued to scream that her ankle was broken and to call for an officer. Mr. Head came on so slowly that he could have been taking a backward step after each forward one, but when he was about ten feet away, Nelson saw him and sprang. The child caught him around the hips and clung panting against him.

The women all turned on Mr. Head. The injured one sat up and shouted, "You sir! You'll pay every penny of my doctor's bill that your boy caused. He's a juve-nile delinquent! Where is an officer? Somebody take this man's name and address!"

Mr. Head was trying to detach Nelson's fingers from the flesh in the back of his legs. The old man's head had lowered itself into his collar like a turtle's; his eyes were glazed with fear and caution.

"Your boy has broken my ankle!" the old woman shouted. "Police!"

Mr. Head sensed the approach of the policeman from behind. He stared straight ahead at the women who were massed in their fury like a solid wall to block his escape. "This is not my boy," he said. "I never seen him before."

He felt Nelson's fingers fall out of his flesh.

The women dropped back, staring at him with horror, as if they were so repulsed by a man who would deny his own image and likeness that they could not bear to lay hands on him. Mr. Head walked on, through a space they silently cleared, and left Nelson behind. Ahead of him he saw nothing but a hollow tunnel that had once been the street.

The boy remained standing where he was, his neck craned forward and his hands hanging by his sides. His hat was jammed on his head so that there were no longer any creases in it. The injured woman got up and shook her fist at him and the others gave him pitying looks, but he didn't notice any of them. There was no policeman in sight.

In a minute he began to move mechanically, making no effort to catch up with his grandfather but merely following at about twenty paces. They walked on for five blocks in this way. Mr. Head's shoulders were sagging and his neck hung forward at such an angle that it was not visible from behind. He was afraid to turn his head. Finally he cut a short hopeful glance over his shoulder. Twenty feet behind him, he saw two small eyes piercing into his back like pitchfork prongs.

The boy was not of a forgiving nature but this was the first time he had ever had anything to forgive. Mr. Head had never disgraced himself before. After two more blocks, he turned and called over his shoulder in a high desperately gay voice, "Let's us go get us a Co' Cola somewheres!"

Nelson, with a dignity he had never shown before, turned and stood with his back to his grandfather.

Mr. Head began to feel the depth of his denial. His face as they walked on became all hollows and bare ridges. He saw nothing they were passing but he perceived that they had lost the car tracks. There was no dome to be seen anywhere and the afternoon was advancing. He knew that if dark overtook them in the city, they would be beaten and robbed. The speed of God's justice was only what he expected for himself, but he could not stand to think that his sins would be visited upon Nelson and that even now, he was leading the boy to his doom.

They continued to walk on block after block through an endless section of small brick houses until Mr. Head almost fell over a water spigot sticking up about six inches off the edge of a grass plot. He had not had a drink of water since early morning but he felt he did not deserve it now. Then he thought that Nelson would be thirsty and they would both drink and be brought together. He squatted down and put his mouth to the nozzle and turned a cold stream of water into his throat. Then he called out in the high desperate voice, "Come on and getcher some water!"

This time the child stared through him for nearly sixty seconds. Mr. Head got up and walked on as if he had drunk poison. Nelson, though he had not had water since some he had drunk out of a paper cup on the train, passed by the spigot, disdaining to drink where his grandfather had. When Mr. Head realized this, he lost all hope. His face in the waning afternoon light looked ravaged and abandoned. He could feel the boy's steady hate, traveling at an even pace behind him and he knew that (if by some miracle they escaped being murdered in the city) it would continue just that way for the rest of his life. He knew that now he was wandering into a black strange place where nothing was like it had ever been before, a long old age without respect and an end that would be welcome because it would be the end.

As for Nelson, his mind had frozen around his grandfather's treachery as if he were trying to preserve it intact to present at the final judgment. He walked without looking to one side or the other, but every now and then his mouth would twitch and this was when he felt, from some remote place inside himself, a black mysterious form reach up as if it would melt his frozen vision in one hot grasp.

The sun dropped down behind a row of houses and hardly noticing, they passed into an elegant suburban section where mansions were set back from the road by lawns with birdbaths on them. Here everything was entirely deserted. For blocks they didn't pass even a dog. The big white houses were like partially submerged icebergs in the distance. There were no sidewalks, only drives, and these wound around and around in endless ridiculous circles. Nelson made no move to come nearer to Mr. Head. The old man felt that if he saw a sewer entrance he would drop down into it and let himself be carried away; and he could imagine the boy standing by, watching with only a slight interest, while he disappeared.

A loud bark jarred him to attention and he looked up to see a fat man approaching with two bulldogs. He waved both arms like someone shipwrecked on a desert island. "I'm lost!" he called, "I'm lost and can't find my way and me and this boy have got to catch this train and I can't find the station. Oh Gawd I'm lost! Oh hep me Gawd I'm lost!"

The man, who was bald-headed and had on golf knickers, asked him what train he was trying to catch and Mr. Head began to get out his tickets, trembling so violently he could hardly hold them. Nelson had come up to within fifteen feet and stood watching.

"Well," the fat man said, giving him back the tickets, "you won't have time to get back to town to make this but you can catch it at the suburb stop. That's three blocks from here," and he began explaining how to get there.

Mr. Head stared as if he were slowly returning from the dead and when the man had finished and gone off with the dogs jumping at his heels, he turned to Nelson and said breathlessly, "We're going to get home!"

The child was standing about ten feet away, his face bloodless under the gray hat. His eyes were triumphantly cold. There was no light in them, no feeling, no interest. He was merely there, a small figure, waiting. Home was nothing to him.

Mr. Head turned slowly. He felt he knew now what time would be like without seasons and what heat would be like without light and what man would be like without salvation. He didn't care if he never made the train and if it had not been for what suddenly caught his attention, like a cry out of the gathering dusk, he might have forgotten there was a station to go to.

He had not walked five hundred yards down the road when he saw, within reach of him, the plaster figure of a Negro sitting bent over on a low yellow brick fence that curved around a wide lawn. The Negro was about Nelson's size and he was pitched forward at an unsteady angle because the putty that held him to the wall had cracked. One of his eyes was entirely white and he held a piece of brown watermelon.

Mr. Head stood looking at him silently until Nelson stopped at a little distance. Then as the two of them stood there, Mr. Head breathed, "An artificial nigger!"

It was not possible to tell if the artificial Negro were meant to be young or old;

he looked too miserable to be either. He was meant to look happy because his mouth was stretched up at the corners but the chipped eye and the angle he was cocked at gave him a wild look of misery instead.

"An artificial nigger!" Nelson repeated in Mr. Head's exact tone.

The two of them stood there with their necks forward at almost the same angle and their shoulders curved in almost exactly the same way and their hands trembling identically in their pockets. Mr. Head looked like an ancient child and Nelson like a miniature old man. They stood gazing at the artificial Negro as if they were faced with some great mystery, some monument to another's victory that brought them together in their common defeat. They could both feel it dissolving their differences like an action of mercy. Mr. Head had never known before what mercy felt like because he had been too good to deserve any, but he felt he knew now. He looked at Nelson and understood that he must say something to the child to show that he was still wise and in the look the boy returned he saw a hungry need for that assurance. Nelson's eyes seemed to implore him to explain once and for all the mystery of existence.

Mr. Head opened his lips to make a lofty statement and heard himself say, "They ain't got enough real ones here. They got to have an artificial one."

After a second, the boy nodded with a strange shivering about his mouth, and said, "Let's go home before we get ourselves lost again."

Their train glided into the suburb stop just as they reached the station and they boarded it together, and ten minutes before it was due to arrive at the junction, they went to the door and stood ready to jump off if it did not stop; but it did, just as the moon, restored to its full splendor, sprang from a cloud and flooded the clearing with light. As they stepped off, the sage grass was shivering gently in shades of silver and the clinkers under their feet glittered with a fresh black light. The treetops, fencing the junction like the protecting walls of a garden, were darker than the sky which was hung with gigantic white clouds illuminated like lanterns.

Mr. Head stood very still and felt the action of mercy touch him again but this time he knew that there were no words in the world that could name it. He understood that it grew out of agony, which is not denied to any man and which is given in strange ways to children. He understood it was all a man could carry into death to give his Maker and he suddenly burned with shame that he had so little of it to take with him. He stood appalled, judging himself with the thoroughness of God, while the action of mercy covered his pride like a flame and consumed it. He had never thought himself a great sinner before but he saw now that his true depravity had been hidden from him lest it cause him despair. He realized that he was forgiven for sins from the beginning of time, when he had conceived in his own heart the sin of Adam,[4] until the present, when he had denied poor Nelson. He saw that no sin was too monstrous for him to claim as his own, and since God loved in proportion as He forgave, he felt ready at that instant to enter Paradise.

Nelson, composing his expression under the shadow of his hat brim, watched him with a mixture of fatigue and suspicion, but as the train glided past them and disappeared like a frightened serpent into the woods, even his face lightened and he muttered, "I'm glad I've went once, but I'll never go back again!"

1955

---

[4] Original Sin, the sin of disobedience (see Genesis 3).

Jazz is a major American cultural contribution. Here, two jazz greats, Charlie "Bird" Parker (on saxophone) and Miles Davis (on trumpet), perform in 1947. The writing styles of authors such as Ralph Ellison and James Baldwin have been influenced by jazz.

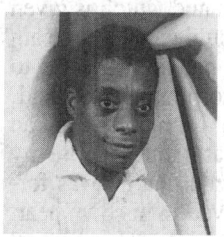

James Baldwin
(1924–1987)

James Baldwin, born in Harlem in 1924, was the illegitimate child of a domestic worker who later married a sternly moralistic storefront preacher. In his first novel, *Go Tell It on the Mountain* (1953), Baldwin drew upon memories of his difficult relationship with his stepfather. Like Baldwin, the protagonist of that novel undergoes a conversion experience as an adolescent and becomes an evangelist. At age fourteen Baldwin converted to the Pentecostal faith and preached weekly until he left home in 1942 to become a railroad worker in New Jersey. In Harlem Baldwin had enjoyed the intellectually nurturing influence of Countee Cullen, the advisor to Baldwin's high school literary club, and had been somewhat sheltered from racism. After two years' exposure to blatant racist abuses in New Jersey, he settled in New York City's Greenwich Village in 1944. There he met other writers who were enthusiastic about his work, including Richard Wright, who helped Baldwin obtain fellowship funding for his early writing efforts.

African-American writers such as Richard Wright and Chester Himes moved to Europe after World War II. Baldwin left for Paris in 1948 and spent most of his life in Europe and the Middle East, while his books became bestsellers in America. Other African-American writers criticized this self-imposed exile—most notably Eldridge Cleaver, who scathingly and scatologically denounced Baldwin's homosexuality as well as his absence from many 1960s civil rights demonstrations. But Baldwin was not uninvolved in the protest movement: he will be remembered as much for his essays chronicling the civil rights movement—*The Fire Next Time* (1963) and *No Name in the Street* (1972)—as for his fiction. As the radicalism of the 1960s disappointingly sputtered in the early 1970s, Baldwin grew increasingly militant, condoning the violence of the Black Panthers and even, in 1972, accepting Cleaver's viciously personal criticism as a "necessary warning."

Autobiographical elements are common in Baldwin's work. His characters are typically lonely men, some alienated by homosexuality (as in *Giovanni's Room* [1956] and *Just Above My Head* [1979]) as well as by race. He viewed the concepts of "Negro" and "homosexual" as categorical ghettos invented by mainstream culture: "People invent categories to feel safe. White people invented black people to give white people identity." Many of his black characters are entertainers—such as jazz musicians Rufus of *Another Country* (1962) and Sonny of "Sonny's Blues" (1957)—who have taken the invented identity thrust upon them and made it their livelihood. They feel trapped within artificial personae that paradoxically shield them, whether in a theater or a police lineup, as they desperately struggle to anticipate the demands of their audiences. "How," one of Baldwin's narrators asks, "can one be prepared for the spittle in the face, all the tireless ingenuity which goes into the spite and fear of small, unutterably miserable people whose . . . joy, whose safety, is entirely dependent on the humiliation and anguish of others?"

Baldwin's most tragic characters are those who, unable to discard the masks they hope will win the love or at least the tolerance of white society, find themselves estranged from their family and friends. Many of these characters turn to musical forms of communication or, like Baldwin himself, turn their gazes inward—a tendency Eldridge Cleaver considered a form of internal expatriation, a culpably irresponsible elopement with the self. Throughout Baldwin's career he insisted that the artist's private and public responsibilities are inextricably involved; he wanted to be a man who was both honest and a good writer and did not feel he could be one without being the other. By the time of his death in 1987, he had more than accomplished at least the latter goal.

Suggested Readings: *Go Tell It on the Mountain*, 1953. *The Amen Corner*, 1954. *Notes of a Native Son*, 1955. *Giovanni's Room*, 1956. *Nobody Knows My Name*, 1961. *Another Country*, 1962. *The Fire Next Time*, 1963. *The Blues for Mr. Charlie*, 1964. *Tell Me How Long the Train's Been Gone*, 1968. *No Name in the Street*, 1972. *If Beale Street Could Talk*, 1974. *Just Above My Head*, 1979. *The Evidence of Things Not Seen*, 1985. *Jimmy's Blues: Selected Poems*, 1985. *The Price of the Ticket: Collected Nonfiction*, 1985. *Harlem Quartet*, 1987. F. M. Eckman, *The Furious Passage of James Baldwin*, 1966. K. Kinnamon, ed., *James Baldwin: A Collection of Critical Essays*, 1974. H. Bloom, ed., *Modern Critical Views: James Baldwin*, 1986.

Text Used: *Going to Meet the Man*, 1965.

SONNY'S BLUES*

I read about it in the paper, in the subway, on my way to work. I read it, and I couldn't believe it, and I read it again. Then perhaps I just stared at it, at the newsprint spelling out his name, spelling out the story. I stared at it in the swinging lights of the subway car, and in the faces and bodies of the people, and in my own face, trapped in the darkness which roared outside.

It was not to be believed and I kept telling myself that, as I walked from the subway station to the high school. And at the same time I couldn't doubt it. I was scared, scared for Sonny. He became real to me again. A great block of ice got settled in my belly and kept melting there slowly all day long, while I taught my classes algebra. It was a special kind of ice. It kept melting, sending trickles of ice water all up and down my veins, but it never got less. Sometimes it hardened and seemed to expand until I felt my guts were going to come spilling out or that I was going to choke or scream. This would always be at a moment when I was remembering some specific thing Sonny had once said or done.

When he was about as old as the boys in my classes his face had been bright and open, there was a lot of copper in it; and he'd had wonderfully direct brown eyes, and great gentleness and privacy. I wondered what he looked like now. He had been picked up, the evening before, in a raid on an apartment downtown, for peddling and using heroin.

I couldn't believe it: but what I mean by that is that I couldn't find any room for it anywhere inside me. I had kept it outside me for a long time. I hadn't wanted to know. I had had suspicions, but I didn't name them, I kept putting them away. I told myself that Sonny was wild, but he wasn't crazy. And he'd always been a good boy, he hadn't ever turned hard or evil or disrespectful, the way kids can, so quick, so quick, especially in Harlem. I didn't want to believe that I'd ever see my brother going down, coming to nothing, all that light in his face gone out, in the condition I'd already seen so many others. Yet it had happened and here I was, talking about algebra to a lot of boys who might, every one of them for all I knew, be popping off needles every time they went to the head. Maybe it did more for them than algebra could.

I was sure that the first time Sonny had ever had horse,[1] he couldn't have been much older than these boys were now. These boys, now, were living as we'd been living then, they were growing up with a rush and their heads bumped abruptly against the low ceiling of their actual possibilities. They were filled with rage. All they really knew were two darknesses, the darkness of their lives, which was now closing in on them, and the darkness of the movies, which had blinded them to that other darkness, and in which they now vindictively, dreamed, at once more together than they were at any other time, and more alone.

When the last bell rang, the last class ended, I let out my breath. It seemed I'd been holding it for all that time. My clothes were wet—I may have looked as though I'd been sitting in a steam bath, all dressed up, all afternoon. I sat alone in the classroom a long time. I listened to the boys outside, downstairs, shouting and cursing and laughing. Their laughter struck me for perhaps the first time. It was

---

* First published in the *Partisan Review* of summer 1957 and collected in *Going to Meet the Man* (1965).

[1] Heroin.

not the joyous laughter which —God knows why—one associates with children. It was mocking and insular, its intent was to denigrate. It was disenchanted, and in this, also, lay the authority of their curses. Perhaps I was listening to them because I was thinking about my brother and in them I heard my brother. And myself.

One boy was whistling a tune, at once very complicated and very simple, it seemed to be pouring out of him as though he were a bird, and it sounded very cool and moving through all that harsh, bright air, only just holding its own through all those other sounds.

I stood up and walked over to the window and looked down into the courtyard. It was the beginning of the spring and the sap was rising in the boys. A teacher passed through them every now and again, quickly, as though he or she couldn't wait to get out of that courtyard, to get those boys out of their sight and off their minds. I started collecting my stuff. I thought I'd better get home and talk to Isabel.

The courtyard was almost deserted by the time I got downstairs. I saw this boy standing in the shadow of a doorway, looking just like Sonny. I almost called his name. Then I saw that it wasn't Sonny, but somebody we used to know, a boy from around our block. He'd been Sonny's friend. He'd never been mine, having been too young for me, and, anyway, I'd never liked him. And now, even though he was a grown-up man, he still hung around that block, still spent hours on the street corners, was always high and raggy. I used to run into him from time to time and he'd often work around to asking me for a quarter or fifty cents. He always had some real good excuse, too, and I always gave it to him, I don't know why.

But now, abruptly, I hated him. I couldn't stand the way he looked at me, partly like a dog, partly like a cunning child. I wanted to ask him what the hell he was doing in the school courtyard.

He sort of shuffled over to me, and he said, "I see you got the papers. So you already know about it."

"You mean about Sonny? Yes, I already know about it. How come they didn't get you?"

He grinned. It made him repulsive and it also brought to mind what he'd looked like as a kid. "I wasn't there. I stay away from them people."

"Good for you." I offered him a cigarette and I watched him through the smoke. "You come all the way down here just to tell me about Sonny?"

"That's right." He was sort of shaking his head and his eyes looked strange, as though they were about to cross. The bright sun deadened his damp dark brown skin and it made his eyes look yellow and showed up the dirt in his kinked hair. He smelled funky. I moved a little away from him and I said, "Well, thanks. But I already know about it and I got to get home."

"I'll walk you a little ways," he said. We started walking. There were a couple of kids still loitering in the courtyard and one of them said goodnight to me and looked strangely at the boy beside me.

"What're you going to do?" he asked me. "I mean, about Sonny?"

"Look. I haven't seen Sonny for over a year, I'm not sure I'm going to do anything. Anyway, what the hell *can* I do?"

"That's right," he said quickly, "ain't nothing you can do. Can't much help old Sonny no more, I guess."

It was what I was thinking and so it seemed to me he had no right to say it.

"I'm surprised at Sonny, though," he went on—he had a funny way of talking, he looked straight ahead as though he were talking to himself—"I thought Sonny was a smart boy, I thought he was too smart to get hung."

"I guess he thought so too," I said sharply, "and that's how he got hung. And now about you? You're pretty goddamn smart, I bet."

Then he looked directly at me, just for a minute. "I ain't smart," he said. "If I was smart, I'd have reached for a pistol a long time ago."

"Look. Don't tell *me* your sad story, if it was up to me, I'd give you one." Then I felt guilty—guilty, probably, for never having supposed that the poor bastard *had* a story of his own, much less a sad one, and I asked, quickly, "What's going to happen to him now?"

He didn't answer this. He was off by himself some place. "Funny thing," he said, and from his tone we might have been discussing the quickest way to get to Brooklyn, "when I saw the papers this morning, the first thing I asked myself was if I had anything to do with it. I felt sort of responsible."

I began to listen more carefully. The subway station was on the corner, just before us, and I stopped. He stopped, too. We were in front of a bar and he ducked slightly, peering in, but whoever he was looking for didn't seem to be there. The juke box was blasting away with something black and bouncy and I half watched the barmaid as she danced her way from the juke box to her place behind the bar. And I watched her face as she laughingly responded to something someone said to her, still keeping time to the music. When she smiled one saw the little girl, one sensed the doomed, still-struggling woman beneath the battered face of the semi-whore.

"I never *give* Sonny nothing," the boy said finally, "but a long time ago I come to school high and Sonny asked me how it felt." He paused, I couldn't bear to watch him, I watched the barmaid, and I listened to the music which seemed to be causing the pavement to shake. "I told him it felt great." The music stopped, the barmaid paused and watched the juke box until the music began again. "It did."

All this was carrying me some place I didn't want to go. I certainly didn't want to know how it felt. It filled everything, the people, the houses, the music, the dark, quicksilver barmaid, with menace; and this menace was their reality.

"What's going to happen to him now?" I asked again.

"They'll send him away some place and they'll try to cure him." He shook his head. "Maybe he'll even think he's kicked the habit. Then they'll let him loose"— he gestured, throwing his cigarette into the gutter. "That's all."

"What do you mean, that's *all?*"

But I knew what he meant.

"I *mean,* that's all." He turned his head and looked at me, pulling down the corners of his mouth. "Don't you know what I mean?" he asked, softly.

"How the hell *would* I know what you mean?" I almost whispered it, I don't know why.

"That's right," he said to the air, "how would *he* know what I mean?" He turned toward me again, patient and calm, and yet I somehow felt him shaking, shaking as though he were going to fall apart. I felt that ice in my guts again, the dread I'd felt all afternoon; and again I watched the barmaid, moving about the bar, washing glasses, and singing. "Listen. They'll let him out and then it'll just start all over again. That's what I mean."

"You mean—they'll let him out. And then he'll just start working his way back in again. You mean he'll never kick the habit. Is that what you mean?"

"That's right," he said, cheerfully. "*You* see what I mean."

"Tell me," I said at last, "why does he want to die? He must want to die, he's killing himself, why does he want to die?"

He looked at me in surprise. He licked his lips. "He don't want to die. He wants to live. Don't nobody want to die, ever."

Then I wanted to ask him—too many things. He could not have answered, or if he had, I could not have borne the answers. I started walking. "Well, I guess it's none of my business."

"It's going to be rough on old Sonny," he said. We reached the subway station. "This is your station?" he asked. I nodded. I took one step down. "Damn!" he said, suddenly. I looked up at him. He grinned again. "Damn it if I didn't leave all my money home. You ain't got a dollar on you, have you? Just for a couple of days, is all."

All at once something inside gave and threatened to come pouring out of me. I didn't hate him any more. I felt that in another moment I'd start crying like a child.

"Sure," I said. "Don't sweat." I looked in my wallet and didn't have a dollar, I only had a five. "Here," I said. "That hold you?"

He didn't look at it—he didn't want to look at it. A terrible, closed look came over his face, as though he were keeping the number on the bill a secret from him and me. "Thanks," he said, and now he was dying to see me go. "Don't worry about Sonny. Maybe I'll write him or something."

"Sure," I said. "You do that. So long."

"Be seeing you," he said. I went on down the steps.

And I didn't write Sonny or send him anything for a long time. When I finally did, it was just after my little girl died, he wrote me back a letter which made me feel like a bastard.

Here's what he said:

Dear brother,

You don't know how much I needed to hear from you. I wanted to write you many a time but I dug how much I must have hurt you and so I didn't write. But now I feel like a man who's been trying to climb up out of some deep, real deep and funky hole and just saw the sun up there, outside. I got to get outside.

I can't tell you much about how I got here. I mean I don't know how to tell you. I guess I was afraid of something or I was trying to escape from something and you know I have never been very strong in the head (smile). I'm glad Mama and Daddy are dead and can't see what's happened to their son and I swear if I'd known what I was doing I would never have hurt you so, you and a lot of other fine people who were nice to me and who believed in me.

I don't want you to think it had anything to do with me being a musician. It's more than that. Or maybe less than that. I can't get anything straight in my head down here and I try not to think about what's going to happen to me when I get outside again. Sometime I think I'm going to flip and *never* get outside and sometime I think I'll come straight back. I tell you one thing, though, I'd rather blow my brains out than go through this again. But that's what they all say, so they tell me. If I tell you when I'm coming to New York and if you could meet me, I sure would appreciate it. Give my love to Isabel and the kids and I was sure sorry to hear about little Gracie. I wish I could be like Mama and say the Lord's will be done, but I don't know it seems to me that trouble is the one thing that never does get stopped and I don't know what good it does to blame it on the Lord. But maybe it does some good if you believe it.

Your brother,
Sonny

Then I kept in constant touch with him and I sent him whatever I could and I went to meet him when he came back to New York. When I saw him many things I thought I had forgotten came flooding back to me. This was because I had begun, finally, to wonder about Sonny, about the life that Sonny lived inside. This life, whatever it was, had made him older and thinner and it had deepened the distant stillness in which he had always moved. He looked very unlike my baby brother. Yet, when he smiled, when we shook hands, the baby brother I'd never known looked out from the depths of his private life, like an animal waiting to be coaxed into the light.

"How you been keeping?" he asked me.

"All right. And you?"

"Just fine." He was smiling all over his face. "It's good to see you again."

"It's good to see you."

The seven years' difference in our ages lay between us like a chasm: I wondered if these years would ever operate between us as a bridge. I was remembering, and it made it hard to catch my breath, that I had been there when he was born; and I had heard the first words he had ever spoken. When he started to walk, he walked from our mother straight to me. I caught him just before he fell when he took the first steps he ever took in this world.

"How's Isabel?"

"Just fine. She's dying to see you."

"And the boys?"

"They're fine, too. They're anxious to see their uncle."

"Oh, come on. You know they don't remember me."

"Are you kidding? Of course they remember you."

He grinned again. We got into a taxi. We had a lot to say to each other, far too much to know how to begin.

As the taxi began to move, I asked, "You still want to go to India?"

He laughed. "You still remember that. Hell, no. This place is Indian enough for me."

"It used to belong to them," I said.

And he laughed again. "They damn sure knew what they were doing when they got rid of it."

Years ago, when he was around fourteen, he'd been all hipped on the idea of going to India. He read books about people sitting on rocks, naked, in all kinds of weather, but mostly bad, naturally, and walking barefoot through hot coals and arriving at wisdom. I used to say that it sounded to me as though they were getting away from wisdom as fast as they could. I think he sort of looked down on me for that.

"Do you mind," he asked, "if we have the driver drive alongside the park? On the west side—I haven't seen the city in so long."

"Of course not," I said. I was afraid that I might sound as though I were humoring him, but I hoped he wouldn't take it that way.

So we drove along, between the green of the park and the stony, lifeless elegance of hotels and apartment buildings, toward the vivid, killing streets of our childhood. These streets hadn't changed, though housing projects jutted up out of them now like rocks in the middle of a boiling sea. Most of the houses in which we had grown up had vanished, as had the stores from which we had stolen, the basements in which we had first tried sex, the rooftops from which we had hurled tin cans and bricks. But houses exactly like the houses of our past yet dominated the landscape, boys exactly like the boys we once had been found themselves smothering in these houses, came down into the streets for light and air and found themselves encircled by disaster. Some escaped the trap, most didn't. Those who got out always left something of themselves behind, as some animals amputate a leg and leave it in the trap. It might be said, perhaps, that I had escaped, after all, I was a school teacher; or that Sonny had, he hadn't lived in Harlem for years. Yet, as the cab moved uptown through streets which seemed, with a rush, to darken with dark people, and as I covertly studied Sonny's face, it came to me that what we both were seeking through our separate cab windows was that part of ourselves which had been left behind. It's always at the hour of trouble and confrontation that the missing member aches.

We hit 110th Street and started rolling up Lenox Avenue.² And I'd known this avenue all my life, but it seemed to me again, as it had seemed on the day I'd first heard about Sonny's trouble, filled with a hidden menace which was its very breath of life.

"We almost there," said Sonny.

"Almost." We were both too nervous to say anything more.

We live in a housing project. It hasn't been up long. A few days after it was up it seemed uninhabitably new, now, of course, it's already rundown. It looks like a parody of the good, clean, faceless life—God knows the people who live in it do their best to make it a parody. The beat-looking grass lying around isn't enough to make their lives green, the hedges will never hold out the streets, and they know it. The big windows fool no one, they aren't big enough to make space out of no space. They don't bother with the windows, they watch the TV screen instead. The playground is most popular with the children who don't play at jacks, or skip rope, or roller skate, or swing, and they can be found in it after dark. We moved in partly because it's not too far from where I teach, and partly for the kids; but it's really just like the houses in which Sonny and I grew up. The same things happen, they'll have the same things to remember. The moment Sonny and I started into the house I had the feeling that I was simply bringing him back into the danger he had almost died trying to escape.

Sonny has never been talkative. So I don't know why I was sure he'd be dying to talk to me when supper was over the first night. Everything went fine, the oldest boy remembered him, and the youngest boy liked him, and Sonny had remembered to bring something for each of them; and Isabel, who is really much nicer than I am, more open and giving, had gone to a lot of trouble about dinner and was genuinely glad to see him. And she's always been able to tease Sonny in a way that I haven't. It was nice to see her face so vivid again and to hear her laugh and watch her make Sonny laugh. She wasn't, or, anyway, she didn't seem to be, at all uneasy or embarrassed. She chatted as though there were no subject which had to be avoided and she got Sonny past his first, faint stiffness. And thank God she was there, for I was filled with that icy dread again. Everything I

---

² In central Manhattan; heading toward Harlem.

did seemed awkward to me, and everything I said sounded freighted with hidden meaning. I was trying to remember everything I'd heard about dope addiction and I couldn't help watching Sonny for signs. I wasn't doing it out of malice. I was trying to find out something about my brother. I was dying to hear him tell me he was safe.

"Safe!" my father grunted, whenever Mama suggested trying to move to a neighborhood which might be safer for children. "Safe, hell! Ain't no place safe for kids, nor nobody."

He always went on like this, but he wasn't, ever, really as bad as he sounded, not even on weekends, when he got drunk. As a matter of fact, he was always on the lookout for "something a little better," but he died before he found it. He died suddenly, during a drunken weekend in the middle of the war, when Sonny was fifteen. He and Sonny hadn't ever got on too well. And this was partly because Sonny was the apple of his father's eye. It was because he loved Sonny so much and was frightened for him, that he was always fighting with him. It doesn't do any good to fight with Sonny. Sonny just moves back, inside himself, where he can't be reached. But the principal reason that they never hit it off is that they were so much alike. Daddy was big and rough and loud-talking, just the opposite of Sonny, but they both had—that same privacy.

Mama tried to tell me something about this, just after Daddy died. I was home on leave from the army.

This was the last time I ever saw my mother alive. Just the same, this picture gets all mixed up in my mind with pictures I had of her when she was younger. The way I always see her is the way she used to be on a Sunday afternoon, say, when the old folks were talking after the big Sunday dinner. I always see her wearing pale blue. She'd be sitting on the sofa. And my father would be sitting in the easy chair, not far from her. And the living room would be full of church folks and relatives. There they sit, in chairs all around the living room, and the night is creeping up outside, but nobody knows it yet. You can see the darkness growing against the windowpanes and you hear the street noises every now and again, or maybe the jangling beat of a tambourine from one of the churches close by, but it's real quiet in the room. For a moment nobody's talking, but every face looks darkening, like the sky outside. And my mother rocks a little from the waist, and my father's eyes are closed. Everyone is looking at something a child can't see. For a minute they've forgotten the children. Maybe a kid is lying on the rug, half asleep. Maybe somebody's got a kid in his lap and is absent-mindedly stroking the kid's head. Maybe there's a kid, quiet and big-eyed, curled up in a big chair in the corner. The silence, the darkness coming, and the darkness in the faces frightens the child obscurely. He hopes that the hand which strokes his forehead will never stop—will never die. He hopes that there will never come a time when the old folks won't be sitting around the living room, talking about where they've come from, and what they've seen, and what's happened to them and their kinfolk.

But something deep and watchful in the child knows that this is bound to end, is already ending. In a moment someone will get up and turn on the light. Then the old folks will remember the children and they won't talk any more that day. And when light fills the room, the child is filled with darkness. He knows that every time this happens he's moved just a little closer to that darkness outside. The darkness outside is what the old folks have been talking about. It's what they've come from. It's what they endure. The child knows that they won't talk any more because if he knows too much about what's happened to *them*, he'll know too much too soon, about what's going to happen to *him*.

The last time I talked to my mother, I remember I was restless. I wanted to get out and see Isabel. We weren't married then and we had a lot to straighten out between us.

There Mama sat, in black, by the window. She was humming an old church song, *Lord, you brought me from a long ways off.* Sonny was out somewhere. Mama kept watching the streets.

"I don't know," she said, "if I'll ever see you again, after you go off from here. But I hope you'll remember the things I tried to teach you."

"Don't talk like that," I said, and smiled. "You'll be here a long time yet."

She smiled, too, but she said nothing. She was quiet for a long time. And I said, "Mama, don't you worry about nothing. I'll be writing all the time, and you be getting the checks. . . ."

"I want to talk to you about your brother," she said, suddenly. "If anything happens to me he ain't going to have nobody to look out for him."

"Mama," I said, "ain't nothing going to happen to you *or* Sonny. Sonny's all right. He's a good boy and he's got good sense."

"It ain't a question of his being a good boy," Mama said, "nor of his having good sense. It ain't only the bad ones, nor yet the dumb ones that gets sucked under." She stopped, looking at me. "Your Daddy once had a brother," she said, and she smiled in a way that made me feel she was in pain. "You didn't never know that, did you?"

"No," I said, "I never knew that," and I watched her face.

"Oh, yes," she said, "your Daddy had a brother." She looked out of the window again. "I know you never saw your Daddy cry. But *I* did—many a time, through all these years."

I asked her, "What happened to his brother? How come nobody's ever talked about him?"

This was the first time I ever saw my mother look old.

"His brother got killed," she said, "when he was just a little younger than you are now. I knew him. He was a fine boy. He was maybe a little full of the devil, but he didn't mean nobody no harm."

Then she stopped and the room was silent, exactly as it had sometimes been on those Sunday afternoons. Mama kept looking out into the streets.

"He used to have a job in the mill," she said, "and, like all young folks, he just liked to perform on Saturday nights. Saturday nights, him and your father would drift around to different places, go to dances and things like that, or just sit around with people they knew, and your father's brother would sing, he had a fine voice, and play along with himself on his guitar. Well, this particular Saturday night, him and your father was coming home from some place, and they were both a little drunk and there was a moon that night, it was bright like day. Your father's brother was feeling kind of good, and he was whistling to himself, and he had his guitar slung over his shoulder. They was coming down a hill and beneath them was a road that turned off from the highway. Well, your father's brother, being always kind of frisky, decided to run down this hill, and he did, with that guitar banging and clanging behind him, and he ran across the road, and he was making water behind a tree. And your father was sort of amused at him and he was still coming down the hill, kind of slow. Then he heard a car motor and that same minute his brother stepped from behind the tree, into the road, in the moonlight. And he started to cross the road. And your father started to run down the hill, he says he don't know why. This car was full of white men. They was all drunk, and when they seen your father's brother they let out a great whoop and holler and they aimed the car straight at him. They was having fun, they just wanted to scare him, the way they do sometimes, you know. But they was drunk. And I guess the boy, being drunk, too, and scared, kind of lost his head. By the time he jumped it was too late. Your father says he heard his brother scream when the car rolled over him, and he heard the wood of that guitar when it give, and he heard them strings go flying, and he heard them white men shouting, and the car kept on a-going and it ain't stopped till this day. And, time your father got down the hill, his brother weren't nothing but blood and pulp."

Tears were gleaming on my mother's face. There wasn't anything I could say.

"He never mentioned it," she said, "because I never let him mention it before you children. Your Daddy was like a crazy man that night and for many a night thereafter. He says he never in his life seen anything as dark as that road after the lights of that car had gone away. Weren't nothing, weren't nobody on that road, just your Daddy and his brother and that busted guitar. Oh, yes. Your Daddy never did really get right again. Till the day he died he weren't sure but that every white man he saw was the man that killed his brother."

She stopped and took out her handkerchief and dried her eyes and looked at me.

"I ain't telling you all this," she said, "to make you scared or bitter or to make you hate nobody. I'm telling you this because you got a brother. And the world ain't changed."

I guess I didn't want to believe this. I guess she saw this in my face. She turned away from me, toward the window again, searching those streets.

"But I praise my Redeemer," she said at last, "that He called your Daddy home before me. I ain't saying it to throw no flowers at myself, but, I declare, it keeps me from feeling too cast down to know I helped your father get safely through this world. Your father always acted like he was the roughest, strongest man on earth. And everybody took him to be like that. But if he hadn't had *me* there—to see his tears!"

She was crying again. Still, I couldn't move. I said, "Lord, Lord, Mama, I didn't know it was like that."

"Oh, honey," she said, "there's a lot that you don't know. But you are going to find it out." She stood up from the window and came over to me. "You got to hold on to your brother," she said, "and don't let him fall, no matter what it looks like is happening to him and no matter how evil you gets with him. You going to be evil with him many a time. But don't you forget what I told you, you hear?"

"I won't forget," I said. "Don't you worry, I won't forget. I won't let nothing happen to Sonny."

My mother smiled as though she were amused at something she saw in my face. Then, "You may not be able to stop nothing from happening. But you got to let him know you's *there*."

Two days later I was married, and then I was gone. And I had a lot of things on my mind and I pretty well forgot my promise to Mama until I got shipped home on a special furlough for her funeral.

And, after the funeral, with just Sonny and me alone in the empty kitchen, I tried to find out something about him.

"What do you want to do?" I asked him.

"I'm going to be a musician," he said.

For he had graduated, in the time I had been away, from dancing to the juke box to finding out who was playing what, and what they were doing with it, and he had bought himself a set of drums.

"You mean, you want to be a drummer?" I somehow had the feeling that being a drummer might be all right for other people but not for my brother Sonny.

"I don't think," he said, looking at me very gravely, "that I'll ever be a good drummer. But I think I can play a piano."

I frowned. I'd never played the role of the older brother quite so seriously before, had scarcely ever, in fact, *asked* Sonny a damn thing. I sensed myself in the presence of something I didn't really know how to handle, didn't understand. So I made my frown a little deeper as I asked: "What kind of musician do you want to be?"

He grinned. "How many kinds do you think there are?"

"Be *serious*," I said.

He laughed, throwing his head back, and then looked at me. "I *am* serious."

"Well, then, for Christ's sake, stop kidding around and answer a serious question. I mean, do you want to be a concert pianist, you want to play classical music and all that, or—or what?" Long before I finished he was laughing again. "For Christ's *sake*, Sonny!"

He sobered, but with difficulty. "I'm sorry. But you sound so—*scared!*" and he was off again.

"Well, you may think it's funny now, baby, but it's not going to be so funny when you have to make your living at it, let me tell you *that*." I was furious because I knew he was laughing at me and I didn't know why.

"No," he said, very sober now, and afraid, perhaps, that he'd hurt me, "I don't want to be a classical pianist. That isn't what interests me. I mean"—he paused, looking hard at me, as though his eyes would help me to understand, and then gestured helplessly, as though perhaps his hand would help—"I mean, I'll have a lot of studying to do, and I'll have to study *everything*, but, I mean, I want to play *with*—jazz musicians." He stopped. "I want to play jazz," he said.

Well, the word had never before sounded as heavy, as real, as it sounded that afternoon in Sonny's mouth. I just looked at him and I was probably frowning a real frown by this time. I simply couldn't see why on earth he'd want to spend his time hanging around nightclubs, clowning around on bandstands, while people pushed each other around a dance floor. It seemed—beneath him, somehow. I had never though about it before, had never been forced to, but I suppose I had always put jazz musicians in a class with what Daddy called "good-time people."

"Are you *serious?*"

"Hell, *yes*, I'm serious."

He looked more helpless than ever, and annoyed, and deeply hurt.

I suggested, helpfully: "You mean—like Louis Armstrong?"[3]

His face closed as though I'd struck him. "No. I'm not talking about none of that old-time, down home crap."

"Well, look, Sonny, I'm sorry, don't get mad. I just don't altogether get it, that's all. Name somebody—you know, a jazz musician you admire."

"Bird."

"Who?"

---

[3] Armstrong (1900–1971), called Satchmo, was a jazz trumpet virtuoso who invented the "scat" singing style.

"Bird! Charlie Parker![4] Don't they teach you nothing in the goddamn army?"

I lit a cigarette. I was surprised and then a little amused to discover that I was trembling. "I've been out of touch," I said. "You'll have to be patient with me. Now. Who's this Parker character?"

"He's just one of the greatest jazz musicians alive," said Sonny, sullenly, his hands in his pockets, his back to me. "Maybe *the* greatest," he added, bitterly, "that's probably why *you* never heard of him."

"All right," I said, "I'm ignorant. I'm sorry. I'll go out and buy all the cat's records right away, all right?"

"It don't," said Sonny, with dignity, "make any difference to me. I don't care what you listen to. Don't do me no favors."

I was beginning to realize that I'd never seen him so upset before. With another part of my mind I was thinking that this would probably turn out to be one of those things kids go through and that I shouldn't make it seem important by pushing it too hard. Still, I didn't think it would do any harm to ask: "Doesn't all this take a lot of time? Can you make a living at it?"

He turned back to me and half leaned, half sat, on the kitchen table. "Everything takes time," he said, "and—well, yes, sure, I can make a living at it. But what I don't seem to be able to make you understand is that it's the only thing I want to do."

"Well, Sonny," I said, gently, "you know people can't always do exactly what they *want* to do—"

"*No,* I don't know that," said Sonny, surprising me. "I think people *ought* to do what they want to do, what else are they alive for?"

"You getting to be a big boy," I said desperately, "it's time you started thinking about your future."

"I'm thinking about my future," said Sonny, grimly. "I think about it all the time."

I gave up. I decided, if he didn't change his mind, that we could always talk about it later. "In the meantime," I said, "you got to finish school." We had already decided that he'd have to move in with Isabel and her folks. I knew this wasn't the ideal arrangement because Isabel's folks are inclined to be dicty[5] and they hadn't especially wanted Isabel to marry me. But I didn't know what else to do. "And we have to get you fixed up at Isabel's."

There was a long silence. He moved from the kitchen table to the window. "That's a terrible idea. You know it yourself."

"Do you have a *better* idea?"

He just walked up and down the kitchen for a minute. He was as tall as I was. He had started to shave. I suddenly had the feeling that I didn't know him at all.

He stopped at the kitchen table and picked up my cigarettes. Looking at me with a kind of mocking, amused defiance, he put one between his lips. "You mind?"

"You smoking already?"

He lit the cigarette and nodded, watching me through the smoke. "I just wanted to see if I'd have the courage to smoke in front of you." He grinned and blew a great cloud of smoke to the ceiling. "It was easy." He looked at my face. "Come on, now. I bet you was smoking at my age, tell the truth."

---

[4] Charles Christopher Parker, Jr. (1920–1955), or Bird; a great jazz saxophonist who promoted bebop.
[5] Snobby.

I didn't say anything but the truth was on my face, and he laughed. But now there was something very strained in his laugh. "Sure. And I bet that ain't all you was doing."

He was frightening me a little. "Cut the crap," I said. "We already decided that you was going to go and live at Isabel's. Now what's got into you all of a sudden?"

"*You* decided it," he pointed out. "*I* didn't decide nothing." He stopped in front of me, leaning against the stove, arms loosely folded. "Look, brother. I don't want to stay in Harlem no more, I really don't." He was very earnest. He looked at me, then over toward the kitchen window. There was something in his eyes I'd never seen before, some thoughtfulness, some worry all his own. He rubbed the muscle of one arm. "It's time I was getting out of here."

"Where do you want to *go*, Sonny?"

"I want to join the army. Or the navy, I don't care. If I say I'm old enough, they'll believe me."

Then I got mad. It was because I was so scared. "You must be crazy. You goddamn fool, what the hell do you want to go and join the *army* for?"

"I just told you. To get out of Harlem."

"Sonny, you haven't even finished *school*. And if your really want to be a musician, how do you expect to study if you're in the *army?*"

He looked at me, trapped, and in anguish. "There's ways. I might be able to work out some kind of deal. Anyway, I'll have the G.I. Bill when I come out."

"*If* you come out." We stared at each other. "Sonny, please. Be reasonable. I know the setup is far from perfect. But we got to do the best we can."

"I ain't learning nothing in school," he said. "Even when I go." He turned away from me and opened the window and threw his cigarette out into the narrow alley. I watched his back. "At least, I ain't learning nothing you'd want me to learn." He slammed the window so hard I thought the glass would fly out, and turned back to me. "And I'm sick of the stink of these garbage cans!"

"Sonny," I said, "I know how you feel. But if you don't finish school now, you're going to be sorry later that you didn't." I grabbed him by the shoulders. "And you only got another year. It ain't so bad. And I'll come back and I swear I'll help you do *whatever* you want to do. Just try to put up with it till I come back. Will you please do that? For me?"

He didn't answer and he wouldn't look at me.

"Sonny. You hear me?"

He pulled away. "I hear you. But you never hear anything *I* say."

I didn't know what to say to that. He looked out of the window and then back at me. "OK," he said, and sighed. "I'll try."

Then I said, trying to cheer him up a little, "They got a piano at Isabel's. You can practice on it."

And as a matter of fact, it did cheer him up for a minute. "That's right," he said to himself. "I forgot that." His face relaxed a little. But the worry, the thoughtfulness, played on it still, the way shadows play on a face which is staring into the fire.

But I thought I'd never hear the end of that piano. At first, Isabel would write me, saying how nice it was that Sonny was so serious about his music and how, as soon as he came in from school, or wherever he had been when he was supposed to be at school, he went straight to that piano and stayed there until suppertime. And, after supper, he went back to that piano and stayed there until everybody went to bed. He was at the piano all day Saturday and all day Sunday. Then he bought a record player and started playing records. He'd play one record over and over again, all day long sometimes, and he'd improvise along with it on the piano. Or he'd play one section of the record, one chord, one change, one progression, then he'd do it on the piano. Then back to the record. Then back to the piano.

Well, I really don't know how they stood it. Isabel finally confessed that it wasn't like living with a person at all, it was like living with sound. And the sound didn't make any sense to her, didn't make any sense to any of them—naturally. They began, in a way, to be afflicted by this presence that was living in their home. It was as though Sonny were some sort of god, or monster. He moved in an atmosphere which wasn't like theirs at all. They fed him and he ate, he washed himself, he walked in and out of their door; he certainly wasn't nasty or unpleasant or rude, Sonny isn't any of those things; but it was as though he were all wrapped up in some cloud, some fire, some vision all his own; and there wasn't any way to reach him.

At the same time, he wasn't really a man yet, he was still a child, and they had to watch out for him in all kinds of ways. They certainly couldn't throw him out. Neither did they dare to make a great scene about that piano because even they dimly sensed, as I sensed, from so many thousands of miles away, that Sonny was at that piano playing for his life.

But he hadn't been going to school. One day a letter came from the school board and Isabel's mother got it—there had, apparently, been other letters but Sonny had torn them up. This day, when Sonny came in, Isabel's mother showed him the letter and asked where he'd been spending his time. And she finally got it out of him that he'd been down in Greenwich Village, with musicians and other characters, in a white girl's apartment. And this scared her and she started to scream at him and what came up, once she began—though she denies it to this day—was what sacrifices they were making to give Sonny a decent home and how little he appreciated it.

Sonny didn't play the piano that day. By evening, Isabel's mother had calmed down but then there was the old man to deal with, and Isabel herself. Isabel says she did her best to be calm but she broke down and started crying. She says she just watched Sonny's face. She could tell, by watching him, what was happening with him. And what was happening was that they penetrated his cloud, they had reached him. Even if their fingers had been a thousand times more gentle than human fingers ever are, he could hardly help feeling that they had stripped him naked and were spitting on that nakedness. For he also had to see that his presence, that music, which was life or death to him, had been torture for them and that they had endured it, not at all for his sake, but only for mine. And Sonny couldn't take that. He can take it a little better today than he could then but he's still not very good at it and, frankly, I don't know anybody who is.

The silence of the next few days must have been louder than the sound of all the music ever played since time began. One morning, before she went to work, Isabel was in his room for something and she suddenly realized that all of his records were gone. And she knew for certain that he was gone. And he was. He went as far as the navy would carry him. He finally sent me a postcard from some place in Greece and that was the first I knew that Sonny was still alive. I didn't see him any more until we were both back in New York and the war had long been over.

He was a man by then, of course, but I wasn't willing to see it. He came by the house from time to time, but we fought almost every time we met. I didn't like the way he carried himself, loose and dreamlike all the time, and I didn't like his friends, and his music seemed to be merely an excuse for the life he led. It sounded just that weird and disordered.

Then we had a fight, a pretty awful fight, and I didn't see him for months. By and by I looked him up, where he was living, in a furnished room in the Village, and I tried to make it up. But there were lots of people in the room and Sonny just lay on his bed, and he wouldn't come downstairs with me, and he treated these other people as though they were his family and I weren't. So I got mad and then he got mad, and then I told him that he might just as well be dead as live the way he was living. Then he stood up and he told me not to worry about him any more in life, that he *was* dead as far as I was concerned. Then he pushed me to the door and the other people looked on as though nothing were happening, and he slammed the door behind me. I stood in the hallway, staring at the door. I heard somebody laugh in the room and then the tears came to my eyes. I started down the steps, whistling to keep from crying, I kept whistling to myself, *You going to need me, baby, one of these cold, rainy days.*

I read about Sonny's trouble in the spring. Little Grace died in the fall. She was a beautiful little girl. But she only lived a little over two years. She died of polio and she suffered. She had a slight fever for a couple of days, but it didn't seem like anything and we just kept her in bed. And we would certainly have called the doctor, but the fever dropped, she seemed to be all right. So we thought it had just been a cold. Then, one day, she was up, playing, Isabel was in the kitchen fixing lunch for the two boys when they'd come in from school, and she heard Grace fall down in the living room. When you have a lot of children you don't always start running when one of them falls, unless they start screaming or something. And, this time, Grace was quiet. Yet, Isabel says that when she heard that *thump* and then that silence, something happened in her to make her afraid. And she ran to the living room and there was little Grace on the floor, all twisted up, and the reason she hadn't screamed was that she couldn't get her breath. And when she did scream, it was the worst sound, Isabel says, that she'd ever heard in all her life, and she still hears it sometimes in her dreams. Isabel will sometimes wake me up with a low, moaning, strangled sound and I have to be quick to awaken her and hold her to me and where Isabel is weeping against me seems a mortal wound.

I think I may have written Sonny the very day that little Grace was buried. I was sitting in the living room in the dark, by myself, and I suddenly thought of Sonny. My trouble made his real.

One Saturday afternoon, when Sonny had been living with us, or, anyway, been in our house, for nearly two weeks, I found myself wandering aimlessly about the living room, drinking from a can of beer, and trying to work up the courage to search Sonny's room. He was out, he was usually out whenever I was home, and Isabel had taken the children to see their grandparents. Suddenly I was standing still in front of the living room window, watching Seventh Avenue. The idea of searching Sonny's room made me still. I scarcely dared to admit to myself what I'd be searching for. I didn't know what I'd do if I found it. Or if I didn't.

On the sidewalk across from me, near the entrance to a barbecue joint, some people were holding an old-fashioned revival meeting. The barbecue cook, wearing a dirty white apron, his conked[6] hair reddish and metallic in the pale sun, and

---

[6] Chemically straightened and smoothed down.

a cigarette between his lips, stood in the doorway, watching them. Kids and older people paused in their errands and stood there, along with some older men and a couple of very tough-looking women who watched everything that happened on the avenue, as though they owned it, or were maybe owned by it. Well, they were watching this, too. The revival was being carried on by three sisters in black, and a brother. All they had were their voices and their Bibles and a tambourine. The brother was testifying and while he testified two of the sisters stood together, seeming to say, amen, and the third sister walked around with the tambourine outstretched and a couple of people dropped coins into it. Then the brother's testimony ended and the sister who had been taking up the collection dumped the coins into her palm and transferred them to the pocket of her long black robe. Then she raised both hands, striking the tambourine against the air, and then against one hand, and she started to sing. And the two other sisters and the brother joined in.

It was strange, suddenly, to watch, though I had been seeing these street meetings all my life. So, of course, had everybody else down there. Yet, they paused and watched and listened and I stood still at the window. *"Tis the old ship of Zion,"* they sang, and the sister with the tambourine kept a steady, jangling beat, *"it has rescued many a thousand!"* Not a soul under the sound of their voices was hearing this song for the first time, not one of them had been rescued. Nor had they seen much in the way of rescue work being done around them. Neither did they especially believe in the holiness of the three sisters and the brother, they knew too much about them, knew where they lived, and how. The woman with the tambourine, whose voice dominated the air, whose face was bright with joy, was divided by very little from the woman who stood watching her, a cigarette between her heavy, chapped lips, her hair a cuckoo's nest, her face scarred and swollen from many beatings, and her black eyes glittering like coal. Perhaps they both knew this, which was why, when, as rarely, they addressed each other, they addressed each other as Sister. As the singing filled the air the watching, listening faces underwent a change, the eyes focusing on something within; the music seemed to soothe a poison out of them; and time seemed, nearly, to fall away from the sullen, belligerent, battered faces, as though they were fleeing back to their first condition, while dreaming of their last. The barbecue cook half shook his head and smiled, and dropped his cigarette and disappeared into his joint. A man fumbled in his pockets for change and stood holding it in his hand impatiently, as though he had just remembered a pressing appointment further up the avenue. He looked furious. Then I saw Sonny, standing on the edge of the crowd. He was carrying a wide, flat notebook with a green cover, and it made him look, from where I was standing, almost like a schoolboy. The coppery sun brought out the copper in his skin, he was very faintly smiling, standing very still. Then the singing stopped, the tambourine turned into a collection plate again. The furious man dropped in his coins and vanished, so did a couple of the women, and Sonny dropped some change in the plate, looking directly at the woman with a little smile. He started across the avenue, toward the house. He has a slow, loping walk, something like the way Harlem hipsters walk, only he's imposed on this his own half-beat. I had never really noticed it before.

I stayed at the window, both relieved and apprehensive. As Sonny disappeared from my sight, they began singing again. And they were still singing when his key turned in the lock.

"Hey," he said.

"Hey, yourself. You want some beer?"

"No. Well, maybe." But he came up to the window and stood beside me, looking out. "What a warm voice," he said.

They were singing *If I could only hear my mother pray again!*

"Yes," I said, "and she can sure beat that tambourine."

"But what a terrible song," he said, and laughed. He dropped his notebook on the sofa and disappeared into the kitchen. "Where's Isabel and the kids?"

"I think they went to see their grandparents. You hungry?"

"No." He came back into the living room with his can of beer. "You want to come some place with me tonight?"

I sensed, I don't know how, that I couldn't possibly say no. "Sure. Where?"

He sat down on the sofa and picked up his notebook and started leafing through it. "I'm going to sit in with some fellows in a joint in the Village."

"You mean, you're going to play, tonight?"

"That's right." He took a swallow of his beer and moved back to the window. He gave me a sidelong look. "If you can stand it."

"I'll try," I said.

He smiled to himself and we both watched as the meeting across the way broke up. The three sisters and the brother, heads bowed, were singing *God be with you till we meet again.* The faces around them were very quiet. Then the song ended. The small crowd dispersed. We watched the three women and the lone man walk slowly up the avenue.

"When she was singing before," said Sonny, abruptly, "her voice reminded me for a minute of what heroin feels like sometimes—when it's in your veins. It makes you feel sort of warm and cool at the same time. And distant. And—and sure." He sipped his beer, very deliberately not looking at me. I watched his face. "It makes you feel—in control. Sometimes you've got to have that feeling."

"Do you?" I sat slowly in the easy chair.

"Sometimes." He went to the sofa and picked up his notebook again. "Some people do."

"In order," I asked, "to play?" And my voice was very ugly, full of contempt and anger.

"Well"—he looked at me with great, troubled eyes, as though, in fact, he hoped his eyes would tell me things he could never otherwise say—"they *think* so. And *if* they think so—!"

"And what do *you* think?" I asked.

He sat on the sofa and put his can of beer on the floor. "I don't know," he said, and I couldn't be sure if he were answering my question or pursuing his thoughts. His face didn't tell me. "It's not so much to *play.* It's to *stand* it, to be able to make it at all. On any level." He frowned and smiled: "In order to keep from shaking to pieces."

"But these friends of yours," I said, "they seem to shake themselves to pieces pretty goddamn fast."

"Maybe." He played with the notebook. And something told me that I should curb my tongue, that Sonny was doing his best to talk, that I should listen. "But of course you only know the ones that've gone to pieces. Some don't—or at least they haven't *yet* and that's just about all *any* of us can say." He paused. "And then there are some who just live, really, in hell, and they know it and they see what's happening and they go right on. I don't know." He sighed, dropped the notebook, folded his arms. "Some guys, you can tell from the way they play, they on something *all* the time. And you can see that, well, it makes something real for them. But of course," he picked up his beer from the floor and sipped it and put the can down again, "they *want* to, too, you've got to see that. Even some of them that say they don't—*some, not all.*"

"And what about you?" I asked—I couldn't help it. "What about you? Do *you* want to?"

He stood up and walked to the window and remained silent for a long time. Then he sighed. "Me," he said. Then: "While I was downstairs before, on my way here, listening to that woman sing, it struck me all of a sudden how much suffering she must have had to go through—to sing like that. It's *repulsive* to think you have to suffer that much."

I said: "But there's no way not to suffer—is there, Sonny?"

"I believe not," he said and smiled, "but that's never stopped anyone from trying." He looked at me. "Has it?" I realized, with this mocking look, that there stood between us, forever, beyond the power of time or forgiveness, the fact that I had held silence—so long!—when he had needed human speech to help him. He turned back to the window. "No, there's no way not to suffer. But you try all kinds of ways to keep from drowning in it, to keep on top of it, and to make it seem—well, like *you*. Like you did something, all right, and now you're suffering for it. You know?" I said nothing. "Well you know," he said, impatiently, "why *do* people suffer? Maybe it's better to do something to give it a reason, *any* reason."

" But we just agreed," I said, "that there's no way not to suffer. Isn't it better, then, just to—take it?"

"But nobody just takes it," Sonny cried, "that's what I'm telling you! *Everybody* tries not to. You're just hung up on the *way* some people try—it's not *your* way!"

The hair on my face began to itch, my face felt wet. "That's not true," I said, "that's not true. I don't give a damn what other people do, I don't even care how they suffer. I just care how *you* suffer." And he looked at me. "Please believe me," I said, "I don't want to see you—die—trying not to suffer."

"I won't," he said, flatly, "die trying not to suffer. At least, not any faster than anybody else."

"But there's no need," I said, trying to laugh, "is there? in killing yourself."

I wanted to say more, but I couldn't. I wanted to talk about will power and how life could be—well, beautiful. I wanted to say that it was all within; but was it? or, rather, wasn't that exactly the trouble? And I wanted to promise that I would never fail him again. But it would all have sounded—empty words and lies.

So I made the promise to myself and prayed that I would keep it.

"It's terrible sometimes, inside," he said, "that's what's the trouble. You walk these streets, black and funky and cold, and there's not really a living ass to talk to, and there's nothing shaking, and there's no way of getting it out—that storm inside. You can't talk it and can't make love with it, and when you finally try to get with it and play it, you realize *nobody's* listening. So *you've* got to listen. You got to find a way to listen."

And then he walked away from the window and sat on the sofa again, as though all the wind had suddenly been knocked out of him. "Sometimes you'll do *anything* to play, even cut your mother's throat." He laughed and looked at me. "Or your brother's." Then he sobered. "Or your own." Then: "Don't worry. I'm all right now and I think I'll *be* all right. But I can't forget—where I've been. I don't mean just the physical place I've been, I mean where I've *been*. And *what* I've been."

"What have you been, Sonny?" I asked.

He smiled—but sat sideways on the sofa, his elbow resting on the back, his fingers playing with his mouth and chin, not looking at me. "I've been something I didn't recognize, didn't know I could be. Didn't know anybody could be." He stopped, looking inward, looking helplessly young, looking old. "I'm not talking about it now because I feel *guilty* or anything like that—maybe it would be better if I did, I don't know. Anyway, I can't really talk about it. Not to you, not to anybody," and now he turned and faced me. "Sometimes, you know, and it was actually when I was most *out* of the world, I felt that I was in it, that I was *with* it, really, and I could play or I didn't really have to *play*, it just came out of me, it was there. And I don't know how I played, thinking about it now, but I know I did awful things, those times, sometimes, to people. Or it wasn't that I *did* anything to them—it was that they weren't real." He picked up the beer can; it was empty; he rolled it between his palms: "And other times—well, I needed a fix, I needed to find a place to lean, I needed to clear a space to *listen*—and I couldn't find it, and I—went crazy, I did terrible things to *me*, I was terrible *for* me." He began pressing the beer can between his hands, I watched the metal begin to give. It glittered, as he played with it, like a knife, and I was afraid he would cut himself, but I said nothing. "Oh well. I can never tell you. I was all by myself at the bottom of something, stinking and sweating and crying and shaking, and I smelled it, you know? *my* stink, and I thought I'd die if I couldn't get away from it and yet, all the same, I knew that everything I was doing was just locking me in with it. And I didn't know," he paused, still flattening the beer can, "I didn't know, I still *don't* know, something kept telling me that maybe it was good to smell your own stink, but I didn't think that *that* was what I'd been trying to do—and—who can stand it?" and he abruptly dropped the ruined beer can, looking at me with a small, still smile, and then rose, walking to the window as though it were the lodestone rock. I watched his face, he watched the avenue. "I couldn't tell you when Mama died—but the reason I wanted to leave Harlem so bad was to get away from drugs. And then, when I ran away, that's what I was running from—really. When I came back, nothing had changed, *I* hadn't changed, I was just—older." And he stopped, drumming with his fingers on the windowpane. The sun had vanished, soon darkness would fall. I watched his face. "It can come again," he said, almost as though speaking to himself. Then he turned to me. "It can come again," he repeated. "I just want you to know that."

"All right," I said, at last. "So it can come again. All right."

He smiled, but the smile was sorrowful. "I had to try to tell you," he said.

"Yes," I said, "I understand that."

"You're my brother," he said, looking straight at me, and not smiling at all.

"Yes," I repeated, "yes. I understand that."

He turned back to the window, looking out. "All that hatred down there," he said, "all that hatred and misery and love. It's a wonder it doesn't blow the avenue apart."

We went to the only nightclub on a short, dark street, downtown. We squeezed through the narrow, chattering, jampacked bar to the entrance of the big room, where the bandstand was. And we stood there for a moment, for the lights were very dim in this room and we couldn't see. Then, "Hello, boy," said a voice and an enormous black man, much older than Sonny or myself, erupted out of all that atmospheric lighting and put an arm around Sonny's shoulder. "I been sitting right here," he said, "waiting for you."

He had a big voice, too, and heads in the darkness turned toward us.

Sonny grinned and pulled a little away, and said, "Creole, this is my brother. I told you about him."

Creole shook my hand. "I'm glad to meet you, son," he said, and it was clear that he was glad to meet me *there,* for Sonny's sake. And he smiled, "You got a real musician in *your* family," and he took his arm from Sonny's shoulder and slapped him, lightly, affectionately, with the back of his hand.

"Well. Now I've heard it all," said a voice behind us. This was another musician, and a friend of Sonny's, a coal-black, cheerful-looking man, built close to the ground. He immediately began confiding to me, at the top of his lungs, the most terrible things about Sonny, his teeth gleaming like a lighthouse and his laugh coming up out of him like the beginning of an earthquake. And it turned out that everyone at the bar knew Sonny, or almost everyone; some were musicians, working there, or nearby, or not working, some were simply hangers-on, and some were there to hear Sonny play. I was introduced to all of them and they were all very polite to me. Yet, it was clear that, for them, I was only Sonny's brother. Here, I was in Sonny's world. Or, rather: his kingdom. Here, it was not even a question that his veins bore royal blood.

They were going to play soon and Creole installed me, by myself, at a table in a dark corner. Then I watched them, Creole, and the little black man, and Sonny, and the others, while they horsed around, standing just below the bandstand. The light from the bandstand spilled just a little short of them and, watching them laughing and gesturing and moving about, I had the feeling that they, nevertheless, were being most careful not to step into that circle of light too suddenly: that if they moved into the light too suddenly, without thinking, they would perish in flame. Then, while I watched, one of them, the small, black man, moved into the light and crossed the bandstand and started fooling around with his drums. Then—being funny and being, also, extremely ceremonious—Creole took Sonny by the arm and led him to the piano. A woman's voice called Sonny's name and a few hands started clapping. And Sonny, also being funny and being ceremonious, and so touched, I think, that he could have cried, but neither hiding it nor showing it, riding it like a man, grinned, and put both hands to his heart and bowed from the waist.

Creole then went to the bass fiddle and a lean, very bright-skinned brown man jumped up on the bandstand and picked up his horn. So there they were, and the atmosphere on the bandstand and in the room began to change and tighten. Someone stepped up to the microphone and announced them. Then there were all kinds of murmurs. Some people at the bar shushed others. The waitress ran around, frantically getting in the last orders, guys and chicks got closer to each other, and the lights on the bandstand, on the quartet, turned to a kind of indigo. Then they all looked different there. Creole looked about him for the last time, as though he were making certain that all his chickens were in the coop, and then he—jumped and struck the fiddle. And there they were.

All I know about music is that not many people ever really hear it. And even then, on the rare occasions when something opens within, and the music enters, what we mainly hear, or hear corroborated, are personal, private, vanishing evocations. But the man who creates the music is hearing something else, is dealing with the roar rising from the void and imposing order on it as it hits the air. What is evoked in him, then, is of another order, more terrible because it has no words, and triumphant, too, for that same reason. And his triumph, when he triumphs, is ours. I just watched Sonny's face. His face was troubled, he was working hard, but he wasn't with it. And I had the feeling that, in a way, everyone on the bandstand was waiting for him, both waiting for him and pushing him along. But as I began to watch Creole, I realized that it was Creole who held them all back. He had them on a short rein. Up there, keeping the beat with his whole body, wailing on the fiddle, with his eyes half closed, he was listening to everything, but he was listening to Sonny. He was having a dialogue with Sonny. He wanted Sonny to leave the shoreline and strike out for the deep water. He was Sonny's witness that deep water and drowning were not the same thing—he had been there, and he knew. And he wanted Sonny to know. He was waiting for Sonny to do the things on the keys which would let Creole know that Sonny was in the water.

And, while Creole listened, Sonny moved, deep within, exactly like someone in torment. I had never before thought of how awful the relationship must be between the musician and his instrument. He has to fill it, this instrument, with the breath of life, his own. He has to make it do what he wants it to do. And a piano is just a piano. It's made out of so much wood and wires and little hammers and big ones, and ivory. While there's only so much you can do with it, the only way to find this out is to try; to try and make it do everything.

And Sonny hadn't been near a piano for over a year. And he wasn't on much better terms with his life, not the life that stretched before him now. He and the piano stammered, started one way, got scared, stopped; started another way, panicked, marked time, started again; then seemed to have found a direction, panicked again, got stuck. And the face I saw on Sonny I'd never seen before. Everything had been burned out of it, and, at the same time, things usually hidden were being burned in, by the fire and fury of the battle which was occurring in him up there.

Yet, watching Creole's face as they neared the end of the first set, I had the feeling that something had happened, something I hadn't heard. Then they finished, there was scattered applause, and then, without an instant's warning, Creole started into something else, it was almost sardonic, it was *Am I Blue*.[7] And, as though he commanded, Sonny began to play. Something began to happen. And Creole let out the reins. The dry, low, black man said something awful on the drums, Creole answered, and the drums talked back. Then the horn insisted, sweet and high, slightly detached perhaps, and Creole listened, commenting now and then, dry, and driving, beautiful and calm and old. Then they all came together again, and Sonny was part of the family again. I could tell this from his face. He seemed to have found, right there beneath his fingers, a damn brand-new piano. It seemed that he couldn't get over it. Then, for awhile, just being happy

---

[7] A 1929 song by Grant Clarke and Harry Akst.

with Sonny, they seemed to be agreeing with him that brand-new pianos certainly were a gas.

Then Creole stepped forward to remind them that what they were playing was the blues. He hit something in all of them, he hit something in me, myself, and the music tightened and deepened, apprehension began to beat the air. Creole began to tell us what the blues were all about. They were not about anything very new. He and his boys up there were keeping it new, at the risk of ruin, destruction, madness, and death, in order to find new ways to make us listen. For, while the tale of how we suffer, and how we are delighted, and how we may triumph is never new, it always must be heard. There isn't any other tale to tell, it's the only light we've got in all this darkness.

And this tale, according to that face, that body, those strong hands on those strings, has another aspect in every country, and a new depth in every generation. Listen, Creole seemed to by saying, listen. Now these are Sonny's blues. He made the little black man on the drums know it, and the bright, brown man on the horn. Creole wasn't trying any longer to get Sonny in the water. He was wishing him Godspeed. Then he stepped back, very slowly, filling the air with the immense suggestion that Sonny speak for himself.

Then they all gathered around Sonny and Sonny played. Every now and again one of them seemed to say, amen. Sonny's fingers filled the air with life, his life. But that life contained so many others. And Sonny went all the way back, he really began with the spare, flat statement of the opening phrase of the song. Then he began to make it his. It was very beautiful because it wasn't hurried and it was no longer a lament. I seemed to hear with what burning he had made it his, with what burning we had yet to make it ours, how we could cease lamenting. Freedom lurked around us and I understood, at last, that he could help us to be free if we would listen, that he would never be free until we did. Yet, there was no battle in his face now. I heard what he had gone through, and would continue to go through until he came to rest in earth. He had made it his: that long line, of which we knew only Mama and Daddy. And he was giving it back, as everything must be given back, so that, passing through death, it can live forever. I saw my mother's face again, and felt, for the first time, how the stones of the road she had walked on must have bruised her feet. I saw the moonlit road where my father's brother died. And it brought something else back to me, and carried me past it, I saw my little girl again and felt Isabel's tears again, and I felt my own tears begin to rise. And I was yet aware that this was only a moment, that the world waited outside, as hungry as a tiger, and that trouble stretched above us, longer than the sky.

Then it was over. Creole and Sonny let out their breath, both soaking wet, and grinning. There was a lot of applause and some of it was real. In the dark, the girl came by and I asked her to take drinks to the bandstand. There was a long pause, while they talked up there in the indigo light and after awhile I saw the girl put a Scotch and milk on top of the piano for Sonny. He didn't seem to notice it, but just before they started playing again, he sipped from it and looked toward me, and nodded. Then he put it back on top of the piano. For me, then, as they began to play again, it glowed and shook above my brother's head like the very cup of trembling.[8]

1957

---

[8] "Thou hast drunken the dregs of the cup of trembling," from Isaiah 51:17.

William Gass
(1924–   )

"My fictions are, by and large, experimental constructions; that is, I try to make things out of words the way a sculptor might make a statue out of stone," comments William Gass in a 1986 interview with Chester Eisinger. "Readers will find very little in the way of character or story in my stories." His writing is an experience offered to the reader through words, a fiction that strives to be more than fiction. Particularly attentive to style, Gass's strategies in writing fiction are patterned after those of epic poetry.

Born William Howard Gass in 1924 in Fargo, North Dakota, Gass was educated at Kenyon College in Ohio and at Ohio Wesleyan University. After spending three years as an ensign in the U.S. Navy, he went on to earn a Ph.D. in philosophy in 1954 from Cornell University. Gass, who then taught at colleges in the Midwest, was named Distinguished University Professor in the Humanities at Washington University in St. Louis. His published fiction includes the novel *Omensetter's Luck* (1966) and *Willie Masters' Lonesome Wife* (1971)—a novella that serves as Gass's commentary on art—and the short-story collections *In the Heart of the Heart of the Country and Other Stories* (1968) and *The First Winter of My Married Life* (1979). His nonfiction essays appear in *Fiction and the Figures of Life* (1970); *On Being Blue* (1973), about the significance of the color blue; *The World Within the Word: Essays* (1978); and *Habitations of the Word: Essays* (1985), which won the National Book Critics' Circle Award for 1986.

Most of Gass's fiction is more experimental than is his short story "In the Heart of the Heart of the Country," based on the author's exploration of his relationship to the collection of people and artifacts that make up twentieth-century life in a small midwestern town. As the story's narrator muses about politics, the weather, business, education, and local people, the reader becomes more and more drawn into the life of the region. The narrator seems to ramble without pattern, but through sudden breaks in the narrative a hidden text surfaces. That text can be pieced together to tell the story of the author's childhood, his idiosyncratic personality, and his recently broken heart. In a deep sense the Midwest is the protagonist of the story, for everything that occurs seems to be a phenomenon of the story's singular but typically American geographic setting.

The structure of "In the Heart of the Heart of the Country," which is divided into short sections concerning specific topics, reinforces the way in which the story tends toward music as well as poetry. Gass attempts to break down the reader's preconceived notions about fiction. Gass believes that words exist for their own sake, not as agents to instruct or direct, and that the reader must be kept imprisoned in the novelist's language through linguistic events staged by metaphor. Yet, as Gass observes in *Contemporary Authors* (1987), "paradoxically, every loving act of definition reverses the retreat of attention to the word and returns it to the world."

Suggested Readings: *Omensetter's Luck,* 1967. *Fiction and the Figures of Life,* 1970. *Willie Masters' Lonesome Wife,* 1971. *On Being Blue,* 1976. *The World Within the Word: Essays,* 1978. *The First Winter of My Married Life,* 1979. *Habitations of the Word: Essays,* 1985. T. Tanner, *City of Words,* 1971. E. Shorris, "The Well-Spoken Passions of William Gass," in *Harper's,* (May) 1972. E. W. Burss, *Beautiful Theories: The Spectacle of Discourse in Contemporary Criticism,* 1982. L. McCaffery, *The Metafictional Muse: The Works of Robert Coover, Donald Barthelme, and William H. Gass,* 1982.

Text Used: *In the Heart of the Heart of the Country and Other Stories,* 1968.

IN THE HEART OF THE HEART OF THE COUNTRY*

A Place

So I have sailed the seas and come . . .
                        to B . . .¹
a small town fastened to a field in Indiana. Twice there have been twelve hundred people here to answer to the census. The town is outstandingly neat and shady, and always puts its best side to the highway. On one lawn there's even a wood or plastic iron deer.

You can reach us by crossing a creek. In the spring the lawns are green, the forsythia is singing, and even the railroad that guts the town has straight bright rails which hum when the train is coming, and the train itself has a welcome horning sound.

Down the back streets the asphalt crumbles into gravel. There's Westbrook's, with the geraniums, Horsefall's, Mott's. The sidewalk shatters. Gravel dust rises like breath behind the wagons. And I am in retirement from love.

Weather

In the Midwest, around the lower Lakes, the sky in the winter is heavy and close, and it is a rare day, a day to remark on, when the sky lifts and allows the heart up. I am keeping count, and as I write this page, it is eleven days since I have seen the sun.

My House

There's a row of headless maples behind my house, cut to free the passage of electric wires. High stumps, ten feet tall, remain, and I climb these like a boy to watch the country sail away from me. They are ordinary fields, a little more uneven than they should be, since in the spring they puddle. The topsoil's thin, but only moderately stony. Corn is grown one year, soybeans another. At dusk starlings darken the single tree—a larch—which stands in the middle. When the sky moves, fields move under it. I feel, on my perch, that I've lost my years. It's as though I were living at last in my eyes, as I have always dreamed of doing, and I think then I know why I've come here: to see, and so to go out against new things—oh god how easily—like air in a breeze. It's true there are moments—foolish moments, ecstasy on a tree stump—when I'm all but gone, scattered I like to think like seed, for I'm the sort now in the fool's position of having love left over which I'd like to lose; what good is it now to me, candy ungiven after Halloween?

---

* First appeared in the *New American Review* and was then revised as the title story of Gass's 1968 collection. The ellipses are Gass's.

¹ An archetypal statement of the homecoming hero, after "And therefore I have sailed the seas and come / To the holy city of Byzantium," from lines 15–16 of "Sailing to Byzantium" (1928), by William Butler Yeats (1865–1939).

A PERSON

There are vacant lots on either side of Billy Holsclaw's house. As the weather improves, they fill with hollyhocks. From spring through fall, Billy collects coal and wood and puts the lumps and pieces in piles near his door, for keeping warm is his one work. I see him most often on mild days sitting on his doorsill in the sun. I notice he's squinting a little, which is perhaps the reason he doesn't cackle as I pass. His house is the size of a single garage, and very old. It shed its paint with its youth, and its boards are a warped and weathered gray. So is Billy. He wears a short lumpy faded black coat when it's cold, otherwise he always goes about in the same loose, grease-spotted shirt and trousers. I suspect his galluses[2] were yellow once, when they were new.

WIRES

These wires offend me. Three trees were maimed on their account, and now these wires deface the sky. They cross like a fence in front of me, enclosing the crows with the clouds. I can't reach in, but like a stick, I throw my feelings over. What is it that offends me? I am on my stump, I've built a platform there and the wires prevent my going out. The cut trees, the black wires, all the beyond birds therefore anger me. When I've wormed through a fence to reach a meadow, do I ever feel the same about the field?

THE CHURCH

The church has a steeple like the hat of a witch, and five birds, all doves, perch in its gutters.

MY HOUSE

Leaves move in the windows. I cannot tell you yet how beautiful it is, what it means. But they do move. They move in the glass.

POLITICS

. . . for all those not in love.

I've heard Batista[3] described as a Mason. A farmer who'd seen him in Miami made this claim. He's as nice a fellow as you'd ever want to meet. Of Castro, of course, no one speaks.

For all those not in love there's law: to rule . . . to regulate . . . to rectify. I

---

[2] Galoshes.

[3] Fulgencio Batista (1901–), president of Cuba (1940–1944, 1952–1958) until he was ousted by Fidel Castro's revolution and fled to the Dominican Republic in January 1959; member of the Free and Accepted Masons, an international secret fraternity stressing brotherliness and charity.

cannot write the poetry of such proposals, the poetry of politics, though some-times—often—always now—I am in that uneasy peace of equal powers which makes a State; then I communicate by passing papers, proclamations, orders, through my bowels. Yet I was not a State with you, nor were we both together any Indiana. A squad of Pershing Rifles[4] at the moment, I make myself Right Face! Legislation packs the screw of my intestines. Well, king of the classroom's king of the hill. You used to waddle when you walked because my sperm between your legs was draining to a towel. Teacher, poet, folded lover—like the politician, like those drunkards, ill, or those who faucet-off while pissing heartily to preach upon the force and fullness of that stream, or pause from vomiting to praise the purity and passion of their puke—I chant, I beg, I orate, I command, I sing—

> Come back to Indiana—not too late!
>   (Or will you be a ranger to the end?)
> Good-bye . . . Good-bye . . . oh, I shall always wait
>   You, Larry, traveler—
>   stranger,
>   son,
>   —my friend—

my little girl, my poem by heart, my self, my childhood.

But I've heard Batista described as a Mason. That dries up my pity, melts my hate. Back from the garage where I have overheard it, I slap the mended fender of my car to laugh, and listen to the metal stinging tartly in my hand.

PEOPLE

Their hair in curlers and their heads wrapped in loud scarves, young mothers, fattish in trousers, lounge about in the speedwash,[5] smoking cigarettes, eating candy, drinking pop, thumbing magazines, and screaming at their children above the whir and rumble of the machines.

At the bank a young man freshly pressed is letting himself in with a key. Along the street, delicately teetering, many grandfathers move in a dream. During the murderous heat of summer, they perch on window ledges, their feet dangling just inside the narrow shelf of shade the store has made, staring steadily into the street. Where their consciousness has gone I can't say. It's not in the eyes. Perhaps it's diffuse, all temperature and skin, like an infant's, though more mild. Near the corner there are several large overalled men employed in standing. A truck turns to be weighed on the scales at the Feed and Grain. Images drift on the drugstore window. The wind has blown the smell of cattle into town. Our eyes have been driven in like the eyes of the old men. And there's no one to have mercy on us.

---

[4] Rifle-carrying soldiers in the American Expeditionary Force in World War I (1914–1918) under the command of General John "Black Jack" Pershing (1860–1948).
[5] A coin-operated laundry.

VITAL DATA

There are two restaurants here and a tearoom. two bars. one bank, three barbers, one with a green shade with which he blinds his window. two groceries. a dealer in Fords. one drug, one hardware, and one appliance store. several that sell feed, grain, and farm equipment. an antique shop. a poolroom. a laundromat. three doctors. a dentist. a plumber. a vet. a funeral home in elegant repair the color of a buttercup. numerous beauty parlors which open and shut like night-blooming plants. a tiny dime and department store of no width but several floors. a hutch, homemade, where you can order, after lying down or squirming in, furniture that's been fashioned from bent lengths of stainless tubing, glowing plastic, metallic thread, and clear shellac. an American Legion Post and a root beer stand. little agencies for this and that: cosmetics, brushes, insurance, greeting cards, and garden produce—anything—sample shoes—which do their business out of hats and satchels, over coffee cups and dissolving sugar. a factory for making paper sacks and pasteboard boxes that's lodged in an old brick building bearing the legend OPERA HOUSE, still faintly golden, on its roof. a library given by Carnegie.[6] a post office. a school. a railroad station. fire station. lumberyard. telephone company. welding shop. garage . . . and spotted through the town from one end to the other in a line along the highway, gas stations to the number five.

EDUCATION

In 1833, Colin Goodykoontz, an itinerant preacher with a name from a fairytale, summed up the situation in one Indiana town this way:

> Ignorance and her squalid brood. A universal dearth of intellect. Total abstinence from literature is very generally practiced. . . . There is not a scholar in grammar or geography, or a *teacher capable of instructing* in them, to my knowledge. . . . Others are supplied a few months of the year with the most antiquated & unreasonable forms of teaching reading, writing & cyphering. . . . Need I stop to remind you of the host of loathsome reptiles such a stagnant pool is fitted to breed! Croaking jealousy; bloated bigotry; coiling suspicion; wormish blindness; crocodile malice!

Things have changed since then, but in none of the respects mentioned.

BUSINESS

One side section of street is blocked off with sawhorses. Hard, thin, bitter men in blue jeans, cowboy boots and hats, untruck a dinky carnival. The merchants are promoting themselves. There will be free rides, raucous music, parades and coneys,[7] pop, popcorn, candy, cones, awards and drawings, with all you can endure

---

[6] Andrew Carnegie (1835–1919), an industrialist and philanthropist whose benefactions include New York City's Carnegie Hall and over 2,800 public libraries.

[7] Coney Island, a once-flourishing amusement park in Brooklyn.

of pinch, push, bawl, shove, shout, scream, shriek, and bellow. Children pedal past on decorated bicycles, their wheels a blur of color, streaming crinkled paper and excited dogs. A little later there's a pet show for a prize—dogs, cats, birds, sheep, ponies, goats—none of which wins. The whirlabouts whirl about. The Ferris wheel climbs dizzily into the sky as far as a tall man on tiptoe might be persuaded to reach, and the irritated operators measure the height and weight of every child with sour eyes to see if they are safe for the machines. An electrical megaphone repeatedly trumpets the names of the generous sponsors. The following day they do not allow the refuse to remain long in the street.

My House, This Place and Body

I have met with some mischance, wings withering, as Plato[8] says obscurely, and across the breadth of Ohio, like heaven on a table, I've fallen as far as the poet, to the sixth sort of body, this house in B, in Indiana, with its blue and gray bewitching windows, holy magical insides. Great thick evergreens protect its entry. And I live *in*.

Lost in the corn rows, I remember feeling just another stalk, and thus this country takes me over in the way I occupy myself when I am well . . . completely—to the edge of both my house and body. No one notices, when they walk by, that I am brimming in the doorways. My house, this place and body, I've come in mourning to be born in. To anybody else it's pretty silly: love. Why should I feel a loss? How am I bereft? She was never mine; she was a fiction, always a golden tomgirl, barefoot, with adolescent's slouch and a boy's taste for sports and fishing, a figure out of Twain, or worse, in Riley.[9] Age cannot be kind.

There's little hand-in-hand here . . . not in B. No one touches except in rage. Occasionally girls will twine their arms about each other and lurch along, school out, toward home and play. I dreamed my lips would drift down your back like a skiff on a river. I'd follow a vein with the point of my finger, hold your bare feet in my naked hands.

The Same Person

Billy Holsclaw lives alone—how alone it is impossible to fathom. In the post office he talks greedily to me about the weather. His head bobs on a wild flood of words, and I take this violence to be a measure of his eagerness for speech. He badly needs a shave, coal dust has layered his face, he spits when he speaks, and his fingers pick at his tatters. He wobbles out in the wind when I leave him, a paper sack mashed in the fold of his arm, the leaves blowing past him, and our encounter drives me sadly home to poetry—where there's no answer. Billy closes his door and carries coal or wood to his fire and closes his eyes, and there's simply no way of knowing how lonely and empty he is or whether he's as vacant and barren and loveless as the rest of us are—here in the heart of the country.

[8] The Greek philosopher Plato (427?–347? B.C.), known for his theories of idealism.
[9] Mark Twain, Samuel Clemens (1835–1910); the poet James Whitcomb Riley (1849–1916).

WEATHER

For we're always out of luck here. That's just how it is—for instance in the winter. The sides of the buildings, the roofs, the limbs of the trees are gray. Streets, sidewalks, faces, feelings—they are gray. Speech is gray, and the grass where it shows. Every flank and front, each top is gray. Everything is gray: hair, eyes, window glass, the hawkers' bills and touters' posters, lips, teeth, poles and metal signs—they're gray, quite gray. Cars are gray. Boots, shoes, suits, hats, gloves are gray. Horses, sheep, and cows, cats killed in the road, squirrels in the same way, sparrows, doves, and pigeons, all are gray, everything is gray, and everyone is out of luck who lives here.

A similar haze turns the summer sky milky, and the air muffles your head and shoulders like a sweater you've got caught in. In the summer light, too, the sky darkens a moment when you open your eyes. The heat is pure distraction. Steeped in our fluids, miserable in the folds of our bodies, we can scarcely think of anything but our sticky parts. Hot cyclonic winds and storms of dust crisscross the country. In many places, given an indifferent push, the wind will still coast for miles, gathering resource and edge as it goes, cunning and force. According to the season, paper, leaves, field litter, seeds, snow, fill up the fences. Sometimes I think the land is flat because the winds have leveled it, they blow so constantly. In any case, a gale can grow in a field of corn that's as hot as a draft from hell, and to receive it is one of the most dismaying experiences of this life, though the smart of the same wind in winter is more humiliating, and in that sense even worse. But in the spring it rains as well, and the trees fill with ice.

PLACE

Many small Midwestern towns are nothing more than rural slums, and this community could easily become one. Principally during the first decade of the century, though there were many earlier instances, well-to-do farmers moved to town and built fine homes to contain them in their retirement. Others desired a more social life, and so lived in, driving to their fields like storekeepers to their businesses. These houses are now dying like the bereaved who inhabit them; they are slowly losing their senses—deafness, blindness, forgetfulness, mumbling, an insecure gait, an uncontrollable trembling has overcome them. Some kind of Northern Snopes[10] will occupy them next: large-familied, Catholic, Democratic, scrambling, vigorous, poor; and since the parents will work in larger, nearby towns, the children will be loosed upon themselves and upon the hapless neighbors much as the fabulous Khan[11] loosed his legendary horde. These Snopes will undertake makeshift repairs with materials that other people have thrown away; paint halfway round their house, then quit; almost certainly maintain an ugly loud cantankerous dog and underfeed a pair of cats to keep the rodents down. They will collect piles of possibly useful junk in the back yard, park their cars in the front,

[10] The amoral, materialistic, and depraved Snopes family of Southerners, in many of the novels of William Faulkner (1897–1962).

[11] The ruthless Mongolian conqueror Genghis Khan (1162–1217).

live largely leaning over engines, give not a hoot for the land, the old community, the hallowed ways, the established clans. Weakening widow ladies have already begun to hire large rude youths from families such as these to rake and mow and tidy the grounds they will inherit.

PEOPLE

In the cinders at the station boys sit smoking steadily in darkened cars, their arms bent out the windows, white shirts glowing behind the glass. Nine o'clock is the best time. They sit in a line facing the highway—two or three or four of them—idling their engines. As you walk by a machine may growl at you or a pair of headlights flare up briefly. In a moment one will pull out, spinning cinders behind it, to stalk impatiently up and down the dark streets or roar half a mile into the country before returning to its place in line and pulling up.

MY HOUSE, MY CAT, MY COMPANY

I must organize myself. I must, as they say, pull myself together, dump this cat from my lap, stir—yes, resolve, move, do. But do what? My will is like the rosy dustlike light in this room: soft, diffuse, and gently comforting. It lets me do . . . anything . . . nothing. My ears hear what they happen to; I eat what's put before me; my eyes see what blunders into them; my thoughts are not thoughts, they are dreams. I'm empty or I'm full . . . depending; and I cannot choose. I sink my claws in Tick's fur and scratch the bones of his back until his rear rises amorously. Mr. Tick, I murmur, I must organize myself. I must pull myself together. And Mr. Tick rolls over on his belly, all ooze.

I spill Mr. Tick when I've rubbed his stomach. Shoo. He steps away slowly, his long tail rhyming with his paws. How beautifully he moves, I think; how beautifully, like you, he commands his loving, how beautifully he accepts. So I rise and wander from room to room, up and down, gazing through most of my forty-one windows. How well this house receives its loving too. Let out like Mr. Tick, my eyes sink in the shrubbery. I am not here; I've passed the glass, passed second-story spaces, flown by branches, brilliant berries, to the ground, grass high in seed and leafage every season; and it is the same as when I passed above you in my aged, ardent body; it's, in short, a kind of love; and I am learning to restore myself, my house, my body, by paying court to gardens, cats, and running water, and with neighbors keeping company.

Mrs. Desmond is my right-hand friend; she's eighty-five. A thin white mist of hair, fine and tangled, manifests the climate of her mind. She is habitually suspicious, fretful, nervous. Burglars break in at noon. Children trespass. Even now they are shaking the pear tree, stealing rhubarb, denting lawn. Flies caught in the screens and numbed by frost awake in the heat to buzz and scrape the metal cloth and frighten her, though she is deaf to me, and consequently cannot hear them. Boards creak, the wind whistles across the chimney mouth, drafts cruise like fish through the hollow rooms. It is herself she hears, her own flesh failing, for only death will preserve her from those daily chores she climbs like stairs, and all that anxious waiting. It is now, she wonders. No? Then: it is now?

We do not converse. She visits me to talk. My task to murmur. She talks about her grandsons, her daughter who lives in Delphi,[12] her sister or her husband—both gone—obscure friends—dead—obscurer aunts and uncles—lost—ancient neighbors, members of her church or of her clubs—passed or passing on; and in this way she brings the ends of her life together with a terrifying rush: she is a girl, a wife, a mother, widow, all at once. All at once—appalling—but I believe it; I wince in expectation of the clap. Her talk's a fence—a shade drawn, window fastened, door that's locked—for no one dies taking tea in a kitchen; and as her years compress and begin to jumble, I really believe in the brevity of life; I sweat in my wonder; death is the dog down the street, the angry gander, bedroom spider, goblin who's come to get her; and it occurs to me that in my listening posture I'm the boy who suffered the winds of my grandfather with an exactly similar politeness, that I am, right now, all my ages, out in elbows, as angular as badly stacked cards. Thus was I, when I loved you, every man I could be, youth and child—far from enough—and you, so strangely ambiguous a being, met me, heart for spade, play after play, the whole run of our suits.

Mr. Tick, you do me honor. You not only lie in my lap, but you remain alive there, coiled like a fetus. Through your deep nap, I feel you hum. You are, and are not, a machine. You are alive, alive exactly, and it means nothing to you—much to me. You are a cat—you cannot understand—you are a cat so easily. Your nature is not something you must rise to. You, not I, live in: in house, in skin, in shrubbery. Yes. I think I shall hat my head with a steeple; turn church; devour people. Mr. Tick, though, has a tail he can twitch, he need not fly his Fancy. Claws, not metrical schema, poetry his paws; while smoothing . . . smoothing . . . smoothing roughly, his tongue laps its neatness. O Mr. Tick, I know you; you are an electrical penis. Go on now, shoo. Mrs. Desmond doesn't like you. She thinks you will tangle yourself in her legs and she will fall. You murder her birds, she knows, and walk upon her roof with death in your jaws. I must gather myself together for a bound. What age is it I'm at right now, I wonder. The heart, don't they always say, keeps the true time. Mrs. Desmond is knocking. Faintly, you'd think, but she pounds. She's brought me a cucumber. I believe she believes I'm a woman. Come in, Mrs. Desmond, thank you, be my company, it looks lovely, and have tea. I'll slice it, crisp, with cream, for luncheon, each slice as thin as me.

POLITICS

O all ye isolate and separate powers, Sing! Sing, and sing in such a way that from a distance it will seem a harmony, a Strindberg[13] play, a friendship ring . . . so happy—happy, happy, happy—as here we go hand in handling, up and down. Our union was a singing, though we were silent in the songs we sang like single notes are silent in a symphony. In no sense sober, we barbershopped together and never heard the discords in our music or saw ourselves as dirty, cheap, or silly.

---

[12] Probably the town in northern Indiana by that name.
[13] The Swedish dramatist, novelist, and short-story writer August Strindberg (1849–1912); much of his writing concerns his unhappy life and three disastrous marriages.

Yet cats have worn out better shoes than those thrown through our love songs at us. Hush. Be patient—prudent—politic. Still, Cleveland killed you, Mr. Crane.[14] Were you not politic enough and fond of being beaten? Like a piece of sewage, the city shat you from its stern three hundred miles from history—beyond the loving reach of sailors. Well, I'm not a poet who puts Paris to his temple in his youth to blow himself from Idaho, or—fancy that—Missouri. My god, I said, this is my country, but must my country go so far as Terre Haute or Whiting, go so far as Gary?[15]

When the Russians first announced the launching of their satellite, many people naturally refused to believe them. Later others were outraged that they had sent a dog around the earth. I wouldn't want to take that mutt from out that metal flying thing if he's still living when he lands, our own dog catcher said; anybody knows you shut a dog up by himself to toss around the first thing he'll be setting on to do you let him out is bite somebody.

This Midwest. A dissonance of parts and people, we are a consonance of Towns. Like a man grown fat in everything but heart, we overlabor; our outlook never really urban, never rural either, we enlarge and linger at the same time, as Alice both changed and remained in her story.[16] You are blond. I put my hand upon your belly; feel it tremble from my trembling. We always drive large cars in my section of the country. How could you be a comfort to me now?

More Vital Data

The town is exactly fifty houses, trailers, stores, and miscellaneous buildings long, but in places no streets deep. It takes on width as you drive south, always adding to the east. Most of the dwellings are fairly spacious farm houses in the customary white, with wide wraparound porches and tall narrow windows, though there are many of the grander kind—fretted, scalloped, turreted, and decorated with clapboards set at angles or on end, with stained-glass windows at the stair landings and lots of wrought iron full of fancy curls—and a few of these look like castles in their rarer brick. Old stables serve as garages now, and the lots are large to contain them and the vegetable and flower gardens which, ultimately, widows plant and weed and then entirely disappear in. The shade is ample, the grass is good, the sky a glorious fall violet; the apple trees are heavy and red, the roads are calm and empty; corn has sifted from the chains of tractored wagons to speckle the streets with gold and with the russet fragments of the cob, and a man would be a fool who wanted, blessed with this, to live anywhere else in the world.

Education

Buses like great orange animals move through the early light to school. There the children will be taught to read and warned against Communism. By Miss Janet

---

[14] The poet Hart Crane (1899–1932), who was born in Ohio and committed suicide by jumping from a steamer in the Caribbean.

[15] Cities in Indiana.

[16] In the fantasy *Alice in Wonderland* (1865), by Lewis Carroll (1832–1898), Alice alternately shrinks and grows during the course of her adventures.

Jakes. That's not her name. Her name is Helen something—Scott or James. A teacher twenty years. She's now worn fine and smooth, and has a face, Wilfred says, like a mail-order ax. Her voice is hoarse, and she has a cough. For she screams abuse. The children stare, their faces blank. This is the thirteenth week. They are used to it. You will all, she shouts, you will all draw pictures of me. No. She is a Mrs.—someone's missus. And in silence they set to work while Miss Jakes jabs hairpins in her hair. Wilfred says an ax, but she has those rimless tinted glasses, graying hair, an almost dimpled chin. I must concentrate. I must stop making up things. I must give myself to life; let it mold me: that's what they say in *Wisdom's Monthly Digest* every day. Enough, enough—you've been at it long enough; and the children rise formally a row at a time to present their work to her desk. No, she wears rims; it's her chin that's dimpleless. Well, it will take more than a tablespoon of features to sweeten that face. So she grimly shuffles their sheets, examines her reflection crayoned on them. I would not dare . . . allow a child . . . to put a line around me. Though now and then she smiles like a nick in the blade, in the end these drawings depress her. I could not bear it—how can she ask?—that anyone . . . draw me. Her anger's lit. That's why she does it: flame. There go her eyes; the pink in her glasses brightens, dims. She is a pumpkin, and her rage is breathing like the candle in. No, she shouts, no—the cartoon trembling—no, John Mauck, John Stewart Mauck, this will not do. The picture flutters from her fingers. You've made me too muscular.

I work on my poetry. I remember my friends, associates, my students, by their names.[17] Their names are Maypop, Dormouse, Upsydaisy. Their names are Gladiolus, Callow Bladder, Prince and Princess Oleo, Hieronymus, Cardinal Mummum, Mr. Fitchew, The Silken Howdah, Spot. Sometimes you're Tom Sawyer, Huckleberry Finn; it is perpetually summer; your buttocks are my pillow; we are adrift on a raft; your back is our river. Sometimes you are Major Barbara,[18] sometimes a goddess who kills men in battle, sometimes you are soft like a shower of water; you are bread in my mouth.

I do not work on my poetry. I forget my friends, associates, my students, and their names: Gramophone, Blowgun, Pickle, Serenade . . . Marge the Barge, Arena, Uberhaupt . . . Doctor Dildoe, The Fog Machine. For I am now in B, in Indiana: out of job and out of patience, out of love and time and money, out of bread and out of body, in a temper, Mrs. Desmond, out of tea. So shut your fist up, bitch, you bag of death; go bang another door; go die, my dearie. Die, life-deaf old lady. Spill your breath. Fall over like a frozen board. Gray hair grows from the nose of your mind. You are a skull already—*memento mori*[19]—the foreskin retracts from your teeth. Will your plastic gums last longer than your bones, and color their grinning? And is your twot still hazel-hairy, or are you bald as a ditch? . . . bitch . . . . . . bitch . . . . bitch. I wanted to be famous, but you bring me age—my emptiness. Was it *that* which I thought would balloon me above the rest? Love? where are you? . . . love me. I want to rise so high, I said, that when I shit I won't miss anybody.

---

[17] The narrator's two lists of friends, students, and associates is a playful composite of horticultural, literary, and fancifully incongrous allusions suggesting the shifting nature of his experience.

[18] The title character of a 1905 play by George Bernard Shaw (1856–1950).

[19] "Remember that you must die" (Latin); any reminder of death.

Business

For most people, business is poor. Nearby cities have siphoned off all but a neighborhood trade. Except for feed and grain and farm supplies, you stand a chance to sell only what one runs out to buy. Chevrolet has quit, and Frigidaire. A locker plant has left its afterimage. The lumberyard has been, so far, six months about its going. Gas stations change hands clumsily, a restaurant becomes available, a grocery closes. One day they came and knocked the cornices from the watch repair and pasted campaign posters on the windows. Torn across, by now, by boys, they urge you still to vote for half an orange beblazoned man who as a whole one failed two years ago to win at his election. Everywhere, in this manner, the past speaks, and it mostly speaks of failure. The empty stores, the old signs and dusty fixtures, the debris in alleys, the flaking paint and rusty gutters, the heavy locks and sagging boards: they say the same disagreeable things. What do the sightless windows see, I wonder, when the sun throws a passerby against them? Here a stair unfolds toward the street—dark, rickety, and treacherous—and I always feel, as I pass it, that if I just went carefully up and turned the corner at the landing, I would find myself out of the world. But I've never had the courage.

That Same Person

The weeds catch up with Billy. In pursuit of the hollyhocks, they rise in coarse clumps all around the front of his house. Billy has to stamp down a circle by his door like a dog or cat does turning round to nest up, they're so thick. What particularly troubles me is that winter will find the weeds still standing stiff and tindery to take the sparks which Billy's little mortarless chimney spouts. It's true that fires are fun here. The town whistle, which otherwise only blows for noon (and there's no noon on Sunday), signals the direction of the fire by the length and number of its blasts, the volunteer firemen rush past in their cars and trucks, houses empty their owners along the street every time like an illustration in a children's book. There are many bikes, too, and barking dogs, and sometimes—halleluiah—the fire's right here in town—a vacant lot of weeds and stubble flaming up. But I'd rather it weren't Billy or Billy's lot or house. Quite selfishly I want him to remain the way he is—counting his sticks and logs, sitting on his sill in the soft early sun—though I'm not sure what his presence means to me . . . or to anyone. Nevertheless, I keep wondering whether, given time, I might not someday find a figure in our language which would serve him faithfully, and furnish his poverty and loneliness richly out.

Wires

Where sparrows sit like fists. Doves fly the steeple. In mist the wires change perspective, rise and twist. If they led to you, I would know what they were. Thoughts passing often, like the starlings who flock these fields at evening to sleep in the trees beyond, would form a family of paths like this; they'd foot down the natural height of air to just about a bird's perch. But they do not lead to you.

> Of whose beauty it was sung
> She shall make the old man young.[20]

They fasten me.

If I walked straight on, in my present mood, I would reach the Wabash.[21] It's not a mood in which I'd choose to conjure you. Similes dangle like baubles from me. This time of year the river is slow and shallow, the clay banks crack in the sun, weeds surprise the sandbars. The air is moist and I am sweating. It's impossible to rhyme in this dust. Everything—sky, the cornfield, stump, wild daisies, my old clothes and pressless feelings—seem fabricated for installment purchase. Yes. Christ. I am suffering a summer Christmas; and I cannot walk under the wires. The sparrows scatter like handfuls of gravel. Really, wires are voices in thin strips. They are words wound in cables. Bars of connection.

WEATHER

I would rather it were the weather that was to blame for what I am and what my friends and neighbors are—we who live here in the heart of the country. Better the weather, the wind, the pale dying snow . . . the snow—why not the snow? There's never much really, not around the lower Lakes anyway, not enough to boast about, not enough to be useful. My father tells how the snow in the Dakotas would sweep to the roofs of the barns in the old days, and he and his friends could sled on the crust that would form because the snow was so fiercely driven. In Bemidji[22] trees have been known to explode. That would be something—if the trees in Davenport or Francisville or Carbondale or Niles[23] were to go blam some winter—blam! blam! blam! all the way down the gray, cindery, snow-sick streets.

A cold fall rain is blackening the trees or the air is like lilac and full of parachuting seeds. Who cares to live in any season but his own? Still I suspect the secret's in this snow, the secret of our sickness, if we could only diagnose it, for we are all dying like the elms in Urbana.[24] This snow—like our skin it covers the country. Later dust will do it. Right now—snow. Mud presently. But it is snow without any laughter in it, a pale gray pudding thinly spread on stiff toast, and if that seems a strange description, it's accurate all the same. Of course soot blackens everything, but apart from that, we are never sufficiently cold here. The flakes as they come, alive and burning, we cannot retain, for if our temperatures fall, they rise promptly again, just as, in the summer, they bob about in the same feckless way. Suppose though . . . suppose they were to rise some August, climb and rise, and then hang in the hundreds like a hawk through December, what a desert we could make of ourselves—from Chicago to Cairo, from Hammond to Columbus—what beautiful Death Valleys.[25]

---

[20] After *Don Juan* (1819–1824), by George Gordon (1788–1824), Lord Byron: "Her beauty of that overpowering kind, / Whose force description only would abate; / I'd rather leave it much to your own mind, / Than lessen it by what I could relate / Of forms and features; it would strike you blind" (V.97. 2–6), according to Gass.

[21] A river in Indiana and Ohio, flowing into the Ohio River.   [22] A town in northern Minnesota.

[23] Cities in Iowa, Indiana, Illinois, and Illinois, respectively.

[24] Victims of the incurable Dutch Elm disease in Urbana, Illinois.

[25] Cities in Illinois, Indiana, and Ohio; desert basin in eastern California and western Nevada.

PLACE

I would rather it were the weather. It drives us in upon ourselves—an unlucky fate. Of course there is enough to stir our wonder anywhere; there's enough to love, anywhere, if one is strong enough, if one is diligent enough, if one is perceptive, patient, kind enough—whatever it takes; and surely it's better to live in the country, to live on a prairie by a drawing of rivers, in Iowa or Illinois or Indiana, say, than in any city, in any stinking fog of human beings, in any blooming orchard of machines. It ought to be. The cities are swollen and poisonous with people. It ought to be better. Man has never been a fit environment for man—for rats, maybe, rats do nicely, or for dogs or cats and the household beetle.

And how long the street is, nowadays. These endless walls are fallen to keep back the tides of earth. Brick could be beautiful but we have covered it gradually with gray industrial vomits. Age does not make concrete genial, and asphalt is always—like America—twenty-one, until it breaks up in crumbs like stale cake. The brick, the asphalt, the concrete, the dancing signs and garish posters, the feed and excrement of the automobile, the litter of its inhabitants: they compose, they decorate, they line our streets, and there is nowhere, nowadays, our streets can't reach.

A man in the city has no natural thing by which to measure himself. His parks are potted plants. Nothing can live and remain free where he resides but the pigeon, starling, sparrow, spider, cockroach, mouse, moth, fly and weed, and he laments the existence of even these and makes his plans to poison them. The zoo? There *is* the zoo. Through its bars the city man stares at the great cats and dully sucks his ice. Living, alas, among men and their marvels, the city man supposes that his happiness depends on establishing, somehow, a special kind of harmonious accord with others. The novelists of the city, of slums and crowds, they call it love—and break their pens.

Wordsworth[26] feared the accumulation of men in cities. He foresaw their "degrading thirst after outrageous stimulation," and some of their hunger for love. Living in a city, among so many, dwelling in the heat and tumult of incessant movement, a man's affairs are touch and go—that's all. It's not surprising that the novelists of the slums, the cities, and the crowds, should find that sex is but a scratch to ease a tickle, that we're most human when we're sitting on the john, and that the justest image of our life is in full passage through the plumbing.

> That man, immur'd in cities, still retains
> His inborn inextinguishable thirst
> Of rural scenes, compensating his loss
> By supplemental shifts, the best he may.[27]

Come into the country, then. The air nimbly and sweetly recommends itself unto our gentle senses.[28] Here, growling tractors tear the earth. Dust roils up behind them. Drivers sit jouncing under bright umbrellas. They wear refrigerated hats and steer by looking at the tracks they've cut behind them, their transistors

---

[26] The English romantic poet William Wordsworth (1770–1850).
[27] From Bk. IV (767–770) of *The Task* (1785), by William Cowper (1731–1800).
[28] From Shakespeare's *Macbeth* (I. vi. 1–3).

blaring. Close to the land, are they? good companions to the soil? Tell me: do they live in harmony with the alternating seasons?

It's a lie of old poetry. The modern husbandman uses chemicals from cylinders and sacks, spike-ball-and-claw machines, metal sheds, and cost accounting. Nature in the old sense does not matter. It does not exist. Our farmer's only mystical attachment is to parity.[29] And if he does not realize that cows and corn are simply different kinds of chemical engine, he cannot expect to make a go of it.

It isn't necessary to suppose our cows have feelings; our neighbor hasn't as many as he used to have either; but think of it this way a moment, you can correct for the human imputations later: how would it feel to nurse those strange tentacled calves with their rubber, glass, and metal lips, their stainless eyes?[30]

PEOPLE

Aunt Pet's still able to drive her car—a high square Ford—even though she walks with difficulty and a stout stick. She has a watery gaze, a smooth plump face despite her age, and jet black hair in a bun. She has the slowest smile of anyone I ever saw, but she hates dogs, and not very long ago cracked the back of one she cornered in her garden. To prove her vigor she will tell you this, her smile breaking gently while she raises the knob of her stick to the level of your eyes.

HOUSE, MY BREATH AND WINDOW

My window is a grave, and all that lies within it's dead. No snow is falling. There's no haze. It is not still, not silent. Its images are not an animal that waits, for movement is no demonstration. I have seen the sea slack, life bubble through a body without a trace, its spheres impervious as soda's. Downwound, the whore at wagtag clicks and clacks. Leaves wiggle. Grass sways. A bird chirps, pecks the ground. An auto wheel in penning circles keeps its rigid spokes. These images are stones; they are memorials. Beneath this sea lies sea: god rest it . . . rest the world beyond my window, me in front of my reflection, above this page, my shade. Death is not so still, so silent, since silence implies a falling quiet, stillness a stopping, containing, holding in; for death is time in a clock, like Mr. Tick, electric . . . like wind through a windup poet. And my blear floats out to visible against the glass, befog its country and bespill myself. The mist lifts slowly from the fields in the morning. No one now would say: the Earth throws back its covers; it is rising from sleep. Why is the feeling foolish? The image is too Greek. I used to gaze at you so wantonly your body blushed. Imagine: wonder: that my eyes could cause such flowering. Ah, my friend, your face is pale, the weather cloudy; a street has been felled through your chin, bare trees do nothing, houses take root in their rectangles, a steeple stands up in your head. You speak of loving; then give me a kiss. The pane is cold. On icy mornings the fog rises to greet me (as you always did); the barns and other buildings, rather than ghostly, seem all the more substantial for looming, as if they grew in themselves while I watched (as you always did). Oh my approach, I suppose, was like breath in a rubber

---

[29] A price for farm products, maintained by government support.   [30] On electric milking machines.

monkey. Nevertheless, on the road along the Wabash in the morning, though the trees are sometimes obscured by fog, their reflection floats serenely on the river, reasoning the banks, the sycamores in French rows. Magically, the world tips. I'm led to think that only those who grow down live (which will scarcely win me twenty-five from *Wisdom's Monthly Digest*), but I find I write that only those who live down grow; and what I write, I hold, whatever I really know. My every word's inverted, or reversed—or I am. I held you, too, that way. You were so utterly provisional, subject to my change. I could inflate your bosom with a kiss, disperse your skin with gentleness, enter your vagina from within, and make my love emerge like a fresh sex. The pane is cold. Honesty is cold, my inside lover. The sun looks, through the mist, like a plum on the tree of heaven, or a bruise on the slope of your belly. Which? The grass crawls with frost. We meet on this window, the world and I, inelegantly, swimmers of the glass; and swung wrong way round to one another, the world seems in. The world—how grand, how monumental, grave and deadly, that word is: the world, my house and poetry. All poets have their inside lovers. Wee penis does not belong to me, or any of this foggery. It is *his* property which he's thrust through what's womanly of me to set down this. These wooden houses in their squares, gray streets and fallen sidewalks, standing trees, your name I've written sentimentally across my breath into the whitening air, pale birds: they exist in me now because of him. I gazed with what intensity . . . A bush in the excitement of its roses could not have bloomed so beautifully as you did then. It was a look I'd like to give this page. For that is poetry: to bring within about, to change.

POLITICS

Sports, politics, and religion are the three passions of the badly educated. They are the Midwest's open sores. Ugly to see, a source of constant discontent, they sap the body's strength. Appalling quantities of money, time, and energy are wasted on them. The rural mind is narrow, passionate, and reckless on these matters. Greed, however shortsighted and direct, will not alone account for it. I have known men, for instance, who for years have voted squarely against their interests. Nor have I ever noticed that their surly Christian views prevented them from urging forward the smithereening, say, of Russia, China, Cuba, or Korea. And they tend to back their country like they back their local team: they have a fanatical desire to win; yelling is their forte; and if things go badly, they are inclined to sack the coach. All in all, then, Birch[31] is a good name. It stands for the bigot's stick, the wild-child-tamer's cane.

Forgetfulness—is that their object?

Oh, I was new, I thought. A fresh start: new cunt, new climate, and new country—there you were, and I was pioneer, and had no history. That language hurts me, too, my dear. You'll never hear it.

FINAL VITAL DATA

The Modern Homemakers' Demonstration Club. The Prairie Home Demonstration Club. The Night-outers' Home Demonstration Club. The IOOF, FFF, VFW,

---

[31] The John Birch Society, an ultraconservative, anticommunist organization established in 1958.

WCTU, WSCS, 4-H, 40 and 8, Psi Iota Chi, and PTA. The Boy and Girl Scouts, Rainbows, Masons, Indians and Rebekah Lodge. Also the Past Noble Grand Club of the Rebekah Lodge. As well as the Moose and the Ladies of the Moose. The Elks, the Eagles, the Jaynettes and the Eastern Star. The Women's Literary Club, the Hobby Club, the Art Club, the Sunshine Society, the Dorcas Society, the Pythian Sisters, the Pilgrim Youth Fellowship, the American Legion, the American Legion Auxiliary, the American Legion Junior Auxiliary, the Garden Club, the Bridge for Fun Club, the What-can-you-do? Club, the Get Together Club, the Coterie Club, the Worthwhile Club, the Let's Help Our Town Club, the No Name Club, the Forget-me-not Club, the Merry-go-round Club . . . [32]

EDUCATION

Has a quarter disappeared from Paula Frosty's pocket book? Imagine the landscape of that face: no crayon could engender it; soft wax is wrong; thin wire in trifling snips might do the trick. Paula Frosty and Christopher Roger accuse the pale and splotchy Cheryl Pipes. But Miss Jakes, I *saw* her. Miss Jakes is so extremely vexed she snaps her pencil. What else is missing? I appoint you a detective, John: search her desk. Gum, candy, paper, pencils, marble, round eraser—whose? A thief. I can't watch her all the time, I'm here to teach. Poor pale fossetted Cheryl, it's determined, can't return the money because she took it home and spent it. Cindy, Janice, John, and Pete—you four who sit around her—you will be detectives this whole term to watch her. A thief. In all my time. Miss Jakes turns, unfists, and turns again. I'll handle you, she cries. To think. A thief. In all my years. Then she writes on the blackboard the name of Cheryl Pipes and beneath that the figure twenty-five with a large sign for cents. Now Cheryl, she says, this won't be taken off until you bring that money out of home, out of home straight up to here, Miss Jakes says, tapping her desk.

Which is three days.

ANOTHER PERSON

I was raking leaves when Uncle Halley introduced himself to me. He said his name came from the comet,[33] and that his mother had borne him prematurely in her fright of it. I thought of Hobbes,[34] whom fear of the Spanish Armada had hurried into birth, and so I believed Uncle Halley to honor the philosopher, though Uncle Halley is a liar, and neither the one hundred twenty-nine nor the fifty-three he ought to be. That fall the leaves had burned themselves out on the trees, the leaf lobes had curled, and now they flocked noisily down the street and were broken in the wires of my rake. Uncle Halley was himself (like Mrs. Desmond and history generally) both deaf and implacable, and he shooed me down his basement stairs to a room set aside there for stacks of newspapers reaching to the ceiling, boxes of leaflets and letters and programs, racks of photo albums, scrapbooks, bundles of rolled-up posters and maps, flags and pennants and

---

[32] This list of organizations contains some bona fide clubs and some that are obviously made up.

[33] Halley's comet, discovered by Edmund Halley (1656–1742).

[34] Thomas Hobbes (1588–1679), an English philosopher whose theory of rationalist materialism offended the religious.

slanting piles of dusty magazines devoted mostly to motoring and the Christian ethic. I saw a bird cage, a tray of butterflies, a bugle, a stiff straw boater, and all kinds of tassels tied to a coat tree. He still possessed and had on display the steering lever from his first car, a linen duster, driving gloves and goggles, photographs along the wall of himself, his friends, and his various machines, a shell from the first war, a record of "Ramona"[35] nailed through its hole to a post, walking sticks and fanciful umbrellas, shoes of all sorts (his baby shoes, their counters broken, were held in sorrow beneath my nose—they had not been bronzed, but he might have them done someday before he died, he said), countless boxes of medals, pins, beads, trinkets, toys, and keys (I scarcely saw—they flowed like jewels from his palms), pictures of downtown when it was only a path by the railroad station, a brightly colored globe of the world with a dent in Poland, antique guns, belt buckles, buttons, souvenir plates and cups and saucers (I can't remember all of it—I won't), but I recall how shamefully, how rudely, how abruptly, I fled, a good story in my mouth but death in my nostrils; and how afterward I busily, righteously, burned my leaves as if I were purging the world of its years. I still wonder if this town—its life, and mine now—isn't really a record like the one of "Ramona" that I used to crank around on my grandmother's mahogany Victrola[36] through lonely rainy days as a kid.

THE FIRST PERSON

Billy's like the coal he's found: spilled, mislaid, discarded. The sky's no comfort. His house and his body are dying together. His windows are boarded. And now he's reduced to his hands. I suspect he has glaucoma. At any rate he can scarcely see, and weeds his yard of rubble on his hands and knees. Perhaps he's a surgeon cleansing a wound or an ardent and tactile lover. I watch, I must say, apprehensively. Like mine-war detectors, his hands graze in circles ahead of him. Your nipples were the color of your eyes. Pebble. Snarl of paper. Length of twine. He leans down closely, picks up something silvery, holds it near his nose. Foil? cap? coin? He has within him—what, I wonder? Does he know more now because he fingers everything and has to sniff to see? It would be romantic cruelty to think so. He bends the down on your arms like a breeze. You wrote me: something is strange when we don't understand. I write in return: I think when I loved you I fell to my death.

Billy, I could read to you from Beddoes;[37] he's your man perhaps; he held with dying, freed his blood of its arteries; and he said that there were many wretched love-ill fools like me lying alongside the last bone of their former selves, as full of spirit and speech, nonetheless, as Mrs. Desmond, Uncle Halley and the Ferris wheel, Aunt Pet, Miss Jakes, Ramona or the megaphone; yet I reverse him finally, Billy, on no evidence but braggadocio, and I declare that though my inner organs were devoured long ago, the worm which swallowed down my parts still throbs and glows like a crystal palace.[38]

[35] A popular song from the 1940s.

[36] The brand name of one of the earliest and most popular phonograph record players.

[37] Thomas Lovell Beddoes (1803–1849), an English poet and playwright in whose work the grotesque is contrasted with lyric beauty.

[38] The Crystal Palace, a building erected in Hyde Park, London, for the Great Exhibition in 1851; it was almost completely destroyed by fire in 1936.

Yes, you were younger. I was Uncle Halley, the museum man and infrequent meteor. Here is my first piece of ass. They weren't so flat in those days, had more round, more juice. And over here's the sperm I've spilled, nicely jarred and clearly labeled. Look at this tape like lengths of intestine where I've stored my spew, the endless worm of words I've written, a hundred million emissions or more: oh I was quite a man right from the start; even when unconscious in my cradle, from crotch to cranium, I was erectile tissue; though mostly, after the manner approved by Plato, I had intercourse by eye. Never mind, old Holsclaw, you are blind. We pull down darkness when we go to bed; put out like Oedipus[39] the actually offending organ, and train our touch to lies. All cats are gray, says Mr. Tick; so under cover of glaucoma you are sack gray too, and cannot be distinguished from a stallion.

I must pull myself together, get a grip, just as they say, but I feel spilled, bewildered, quite mislaid. I did not restore my house to its youth, but to its age. Hunting, you hitch through the hollyhocks. I'm inclined to say you aren't half the cripple I am, for there is nothing left of me but mouth. However, I resist the impulse. It is another lie of poetry. My organs are all there, though it's there where I fail—at the roots of my experience. Poet of the spiritual, Rilke,[40] weren't you? yet that's what you said. Poetry, like love, is—in and out—a physical caress. I can't tolerate any more of my sophistries about spirit, mind, and breath. Body equals being, and if your weight goes down, you are the less.

HOUSEHOLD APPLES

I knew nothing about apples. Why should I? My country came in my childhood, and I dreamed of sitting among the blooms like the bees. I failed to spray the pear tree too. I doubled up under them at first, admiring the sturdy low branches I should have pruned, and later I acclaimed the blossoms. Shortly after the fruit formed there were falls—not many—apples the size of goodish stones which made me wobble on my ankles when I walked about the yard. Sometimes a piece crushed by a heel would cling on the shoe to track the house. I gathered a few and heaved them over the wires. A slingshot would have been splendid. Hard, an unattractive green, the worms had them. Before long I realized the worms had them all. Even as the apples reddened, lit their tree, they were being swallowed. The birds preferred the pears, which were small—sugar pears I think they're called—with thick skins of graying green that ripen on toward violet. So the fruit fell, and once I made some applesauce by quartering and paring hundreds; but mostly I did nothing, left them, until suddenly, overnight it seemed, in that ugly late September heat we often have in Indiana, my problem was upon me.

My childhood came in the country. I remember, now, the flies on our snowy luncheon table. As we cleared away they would settle, fastidiously scrub themselves and stroll to the crumbs to feed where I would kill them in crowds with a swatter. It was quite a game to catch them taking off. I struck heavily since I didn't mind a few stains; they'd wash. The swatter was a square of screen bound down in red cloth. It drove no air ahead of it to give them warning. They might

---

[39] According to Greek myth, Oedipus unknowingly kills his father and marries his mother; he blinds himself upon discovering what he has done.

[40] Ranier Maria Rilke (1875–1926), a German lyric poet who blended impressionism and mysticism.

have thought they'd flown headlong into a summered window. The faint pink dot where they had died did not rub out as I'd supposed, and after years of use our luncheon linen would faintly, pinkly, speckle.

The country became my childhood. Flies braided themselves on the flypaper in my grandmother's house. I can smell the bakery and the grocery and the stables and the dairy in that small Dakota town I knew as a kid; knew as I dreamed I'd know your body, as I've known nothing, before or since; knew as the flies knew, in the honest, unchaste sense: the burned house, hose-wet, which drew a mist of insects like the blue smoke of it smolder, and gangs of boys, moist-lipped, destructive as its burning. Flies have always impressed me; they are so persistently alive. Now they were coating the ground beneath my trees. Some were ordinary flies; there were the large blue-green ones; there were swarms of fruit flies too, and the red-spotted scavenger beetle; there were a few wasps, several sorts of bees and butterflies—checkers, sulphurs, monarchs, commas, question marks—and delicate dragonflies . . . but principally houseflies and horseflies and bottleflies, flies and more flies in clusters around the rotting fruit. They loved the pears. Inside, they fed. If you picked up a pear, they flew, and the pear became skin and stem. They were everywhere the fruit was: in the tree still—apples like a hive for them—or where the fruit littered the ground, squashing itself as you stepped . . . there was no help for it. The flies droned, feasting on the sweet juice. No one could go near the trees; I could not climb; so I determined at last to labor like Hercules.[41] There were fruit baskets in the barn. Collecting them and kneeling under the branches, I began to gather remains. Deep in the strong rich smell of the fruit, I began to hum myself. The fruit caved in at the touch. Glistening red apples, my lifting disclosed, had families of beetles, flies, and bugs, devouring their rotten undersides. There were streams of flies; there were lakes and cataracts and rivers of flies, seas and oceans. The hum was heavier, higher, than the hum of the bees when they came to the blooms in the spring, though the bees were there, among the flies, ignoring me—ignoring everyone. As my work went on and juice covered my hands and arms, they would form a sleeve, black and moving, like knotty wool. No caress could have been more indifferently complete. Still I rose fearfully, ramming my head in the branches, apples bumping against me before falling, bursting with bugs. I'd snap my hand sharply but the flies would cling to the sweet. I could toss a whole cluster into a basket from several feet. As the pear or apple lit, they would explosively rise, like monads[42] for a moment, windowless, certainly, with respect to one another, sugar their harmony. I had to admit, though, despite my distaste, that my arm had never been more alive, oftener or more gently kissed. Those hundreds of feet were light. In washing them off, I pretended the hose was a pump. What have I missed? Childhood is a lie of poetry.

The Church

Friday night. Girls in dark skirts and white blouses sit in ranks and scream in concert. They carry funnels loosely stuffed with orange and black paper which

---

[41] According to classical myth, Hercules, the son of the supreme god, Zeus, and the mortal Alcmene, was renowned for his strength and for completing twelve labors imposed on him.

[42] Gottfried Wilhelm Leibniz (1646–1716), a German baron, philosopher, and mathematician, believed that the universe is made of an infinite number of units of spiritual force or matter, which he called monads; he considered God to be the supreme monad.

they shake wildly, and small megaphones through which, as drilled, they direct and magnify their shouting. Their leaders, barely pubescent girls, prance and shake and whirl their skirts above their bloomers. The young men, leaping, extend their arms and race through puddles of amber light, their bodies glistening. In a lull, though it rarely occurs, you can hear the squeak of tennis shoes against the floor. Then the yelling begins again, and then continues; fathers, mothers, neighbors joining in to form a single pulsing ululation—a cry of the whole community—for in this gymnasium each body becomes the bodies beside it, pressed as they are together, thigh to thigh, and the same shudder runs through all of them, and runs toward the same release. Only the ball moves serenely through this dazzling din. Obedient to law it scarcely speaks but caroms quietly and lives at peace.

BUSINESS

It is the week of Christmas and the stores, to accommodate the rush they hope for, are remaining open in the evening. You can see snow falling in the cones of the street lamps. The roads are filling—undisturbed. Strings of red and green lights droop over the principal highway, and the water tower wears a star. The windows of the stores have been bedizened. Shamelessly they beckon. But I am alone, leaning against a pole—no . . . there is no one in sight. They're all at home, perhaps by their instruments, tuning in on their evenings, and like Ramona, tirelessly playing and replaying themselves. There's a speaker perched in the tower, and through the boughs of falling snow and over the vacant streets, it drapes the twisted and metallic strains of a tune that can barely be distinguished—yes, I believe it's one of the jolly ones, it's "Joy to the World." There's no one to hear the music but myself, and though I'm listening, I'm no longer certain. Perhaps the record's playing something else.

1967?, 1968

Maya Angelou
(1928–   )

The first volume of Maya Angelou's autobiography, *I Know Why the Caged Bird Sings* (1970), begins "If growing up is painful for the Southern black girl, being aware of her displacement is the rust on the razor that threatens the throat." Despite the pain and humiliation Angelou suffered as a child, and despite her raw perceptions of her childhood, her story remains one of survival. Mere survival, however, does not interest her; she aims for "survival with some style, some faith," as she explained in a 1973 interview with Jeffrey Elliot.

Born Marguerite Johnson in St. Louis in 1928, to Vivian Baxter and Bailey Johnson, Angelou was renamed "Maya" by her beloved brother, Bailey. (She took the surname Angelou when, in her early twenties, she made her debut as a dancer, at the Purple Onion Cabaret.) The bestseller *I Know Why the Caged Bird Sings* is the story of her life until her pregnancy when she was sixteen. When her parents divorced, Maya, age three, and Bailey were sent to live with their grandmother in Stamps, Arkansas. There Maya learned to fear disapproval, laugh uncontrollably, read Shakespeare in secret, and sing gospel hymns, and she worked in her grandmother's store. After a brief stay with her mother in California, Maya was raped by her mother's boyfriend, who was later murdered. At age eight she returned to Stamps, mute. For years she did not talk. An older woman, the town aristocrat, brought her to speak by encouraging her to read novels and poetry aloud. Maya and Bailey returned to California to live with their mother, who was then a professional gambler. In high school the girl took dance and drama lessons and became the first African-American female street conductor in San Francisco. This segment of her life, marked by shame and innocence, ends with the birth of her son.

Angelou's tale continues in five subsequent autobiographical volumes with the themes of innocence and survival. *Gather Together in My Name* (1974) describes the experience of raising her son alone while she worked as a waitress, madame, prostitute, and maid. In *Singin' and Swingin' and Gettin' Merry Like Christmas* (1976) she chronicles her first marriage and her early career in dancing and theater with a European tour of *Porgy and Bess*. *Heart of a Woman* (1981), which has won much favorable critical notice, pairs Angelou's growth in the late 1950s and early 1960s with that of the civil rights movement. She recounts her experiences with the Harlem Writers Guild and the Southern Christian Leadership Conference and her travels in Egypt and Ghana, the first place she says she felt at home. In her books she presents the story of various romantic adventures. Her latest installment, *All God's Children Need Traveling Shoes* (1986), narrates Angelou's quest for identity in the strong metaphors, idiomatic and poetic diction, and passionate rhythms that characterize her work. Angelou, though best known for her autobiographical prose, has published several volumes of poetry, including *And I Still Rise* (1978); taught and lectured in various colleges; received honorary degrees from such schools as Smith College and Lawrence University; written screenplays; directed films; acted on Broadway; and given unforgettable performances of her work. She has clearly done much more than just survive.

Suggested Readings: *Gather Together in My Name*, 1974. *Singin' and Swingin' and Gettin' Merry Like Christmas*, 1976. *And Still I Rise*, 1978. *The Heart of a Woman*, 1981. *Shaker, Why Don't You Sing?*, 1983. *All God's Children Need Traveling Shoes*, 1986. *Conversations With Maya Angelou*, ed. J. Elliot, 1989. G. E. Kent, "Maya Angelou's *I Know Why the Caged Bird Sings* and Black Autobiographical Tradition," *Kansas Quarterly*, 7 (Summer): 72–78, 1975. C. Tate, ed., *Black Women Writers at Work*, 1983.

Text Used: *I Know Why the Caged Bird Sings*, 1970.

from   I KNOW WHY THE CAGED BIRD SINGS*

4

What sets one Southern town apart from another, or from a Northern town or hamlet, or city high-rise? The answer must be the experience shared between the unknowing majority (it) and the knowing minority (you). All of childhood's unanswered questions must finally be passed back to the town and answered there.

---

* The title is from the poem "Sympathy" (1899), by Paul Laurence Dunbar (1872–1906)

Heroes and bogey men, values and dislikes, are first encountered and labeled in that early environment. In later years they change faces, places, and maybe races, tactics, intensities and goals, but beneath those penetrable masks they wear forever the stocking-capped faces of childhood.

Mr. McElroy, who lived in the big rambling house next to the Store, was very tall and broad, and although the years had eaten away the flesh from his shoulders, they had not, at the time of my knowing him, gotten to his high stomach, or his hands or feet.

He was the only Negro I knew, except for the school principal and the visiting teachers, who wore matching pants and jackets. When I learned that men's clothes were sold like that and called suits, I remember thinking that somebody had been very bright, for it made men look less manly, less threatening and a little more like women.

Mr. McElroy never laughed, and seldom smiled, and to his credit was the fact that he liked to talk to Uncle Willie. He never went to church, which Bailey and I thought also proved he was a very courageous person. How great it would be to grow up like that, to be able to stare religion down, especially living next door to a woman like Momma.

I watched him with the excitement of expecting him to do anything at any time. I never tired of this, or became disappointed or disenchanted with him, although from the perch of age, I see him now as a very simple and uninteresting man who sold patent medicine and tonics to the less sophisticated people in towns (villages) surrounding the metropolis of Stamps.[1]

There seemed to be an understanding between Mr. McElroy and Grandmother. This was obvious to us because he never chased us off his land. In summer's late sunshine I often sat under the chinaberry tree in his yard, surrounded by the bitter aroma of its fruit and lulled by the drone of flies that fed on the berries. He sat in a slotted swing on his porch, rocking in his brown three-piece, his wide Panama nodding in time with the whir of insects.

One greeting a day was all that could be expected from Mr. McElroy. After his "Good morning, child," or "Good afternoon, child," he never said a word, even if I met him again on the road in front of his house or down by the well, or ran into him behind the house escaping in a game of hide-and-seek.

He remained a mystery in my childhood. A man who owned his land and the big many-windowed house with a porch that clung to its sides all around the house. An independent Black man. A near anachronism in Stamps.

Bailey was the greatest person in my world. And the fact that he was my brother, my only brother, and I had no sisters to share him with, was such good fortune that it made me want to live a Christian life just to show God that I was grateful. Where I was big, elbowy and grating, he was small, graceful and smooth. When I was described by our playmates as being shit color, he was lauded for his velvet-black skin. His hair fell down in black curls, and my head was covered with black steel wool. And yet he loved me.

When our elders said unkind things about my features (my family was handsome to a point of pain for me), Bailey would wink at me from across the room, and I knew that it was a matter of time before he would take revenge. He would allow the old ladies to finish wondering how on earth I came about, then he would ask, in a voice like cooling bacon grease, "Oh Mizeriz Coleman, how is your son? I saw him the other day, and he looked sick enough to die."

---

[1] The Arkansas town where Angelou spent most of her youth.

Aghast, the ladies would ask, "Die? From what? He ain't sick."

And in a voice oilier than the one before, he'd answer with a straight face, "From the Uglies."

I would hold my laugh, bite my tongue, grit my teeth and very seriously erase even the touch of a smile from my face. Later, behind the house by the black-walnut tree, we'd laugh and laugh and howl.

Bailey could count on very few punishments for his consistently outrageous behavior, for he was the pride of the Henderson/Johnson family.

His movements, as he was later to describe those of an acquaintance, were activated with oiled precision. He was also able to find more hours in the day than I thought existed. He finished chores, homework, read more books than I and played the group games on the side of the hill with the best of them. He could even pray out loud in church, and was apt at stealing pickles from the barrel that sat under the fruit counter and Uncle Willie's nose.

Once when the Store was full of lunchtime customers, he dipped the strainer, which we also used to sift weevils from meal and flour, into the barrel and fished for two fat pickles. He caught them and hooked the strainer onto the side of the barrel where they dripped until he was ready for them. When the last school bell rang, he picked the nearly dry pickles out of the strainer, jammed them into his pockets and threw the strainer behind the oranges. We ran out of the Store. It was summer and his pants were short, so the pickle juice made clean streams down his ashy legs, and he jumped with his pockets full of loot and his eyes laughing a "How about that?" He smelled like a vinegar barrel or a sour angel.

After our early chores were done, while Uncle Willie or Momma minded the Store, we were free to play the children's games as long as we stayed within yelling distance. Playing hide-and-seek, his voice was easily identified, singing, "Last night, night before, twenty-four robbers at my door. Who all is hid? Ask me to let them in, hit 'em in the head with a rolling pin. Who all is hid?" In follow the leader, naturally he was the one who created the most daring and interesting things to do. And when he was on the tail of the pop the whip, he would twirl off the end like a top, spinning, falling, laughing, finally stopping just before my heart beat its last, and then he was back in the game, still laughing.

Of all the needs (there are none imaginary) a lonely child has, the one that must be satisfied, if there is going to be hope and a hope of wholeness, is the unshaking need for an unshakable God. My pretty Black brother was my Kingdom Come.

In Stamps the custom was to can everything that could possibly be preserved. During the killing season, after the first frost, all neighbors helped each other to slaughter hogs and even the quiet, big-eyed cows if they had stopped giving milk.

The missionary ladies of the Christian Methodist Episcopal Church helped Momma prepare the pork for sausage. They squeezed their fat arms elbow deep in the ground meat, mixed it with gray nose-opening sage, pepper and salt, and made tasty little samples for all obedient children who brought wood for the slick black stove. The men chopped off the larger pieces of meat and laid them in the smoke-house to begin the curing process. They opened the knuckle of the hams with their deadly-looking knives, took out a certain round harmless bone ("it could make the meat go bad") and rubbed salt, coarse brown salt that looked like fine gravel, into the flesh, and the blood popped to the surface.

Throughout the year, until the next frost, we took our meals from the smoke-house, the little garden that lay cousin-close to the Store and from the shelves of canned foods. There were choices on the shelves that could set a hungry child's mouth to watering. Green beans, snapped always the right length, collards, cabbage, juicy red tomato preserves that came into their own on steaming buttered biscuits, and sausage, beets, berries and every fruit grown in Arkansas.

But at least twice yearly Momma would feel that as children we should have fresh meat included in our diets. We were then given money—pennies, nickels, and dimes entrusted to Bailey—and sent to town to buy liver. Since the whites had refrigerators, their butchers bought the meat from commercial slaughterhouses in Texarkana[2] and sold it to the wealthy even in the peak of summer.

Crossing the Black area of Stamps which in childhood's narrow measure seemed a whole world, we were obliged by custom to stop and speak to every person we met, and Bailey felt constrained to spend a few minutes playing with each friend. There was a joy in going to town with money in our pockets (Bailey's pockets were as good as my own) and time on our hands. But the pleasure fled when we reached the white part of town. After we left Mr. Willie Williams' Do Drop Inn, the last stop before whitefolksville, we had to cross the pond and adventure the railroad tracks. We were explorers walking without weapons into man-eating animals' territory.

In Stamps the segregation was so complete that most Black children didn't really, absolutely know what whites looked like. Other than that they were different, to be dreaded, and in that dread was included the hostility of the powerless against the powerful, the poor against the rich, the worker against the worked for and the ragged against the well dressed.

I remember never believing that whites were really real.

Many women who worked in their kitchens traded at our Store, and when they carried their finished laundry back to town they often set the big baskets down on our front porch to pull a singular piece from the starched collection and show either how graceful was their ironing hand or how rich and opulent was the property of their employers.

I looked at the items that weren't on display. I knew, for instance, that white men wore shorts, as Uncle Willie did, and that they had an opening for taking out their "things" and peeing, and that white women's breasts weren't built into their dresses, as some people said, because I saw their brassieres in the baskets. But I couldn't force myself to think of them as people. People were Mrs. LaGrone, Mrs. Hendricks, Momma, Reverend Sneed, Lillie B, and Louise and Rex. Whitefolks couldn't be people because their feet were too small, their skin too white and see-throughy, and they didn't walk on the balls of their feet the way people did—they walked on their heels like horses.

People were those who lived on my side of town. I didn't like them all, or, in fact, any of them very much, but they were people. These others, the strange pale creatures that lived in their alien unlife, weren't considered folks. They were whitefolks.

5

"Thou shalt not be dirty" and "Thou shall not be impudent" were the two commandments of Grandmother Henderson upon which hung our total salvation.

---

[2] A city on the southwestern border of Arkansas and the northwestern border of Texas.

Each night in the bitterest winter we were forced to wash faces, arms, necks, legs and feet before going to bed. She used to add, with a smirk that unprofane people can't control when venturing into profanity, "and wash as far as possible, then wash possible."

We would go to the well and wash in the ice-cold, clear water, grease our legs with the equally cold stiff Vaseline, then tiptoe into the house. We wiped the dust from our toes and settled down for schoolwork, cornbread, clabbered milk, prayers and bed, always in that order. Momma was famous for pulling the quilts off after we had fallen asleep to examine our feet. If they weren't clean enough for her, she took the switch (she kept one behind the bedroom door for emergencies) and woke up the offender with a few aptly placed burning reminders.

The area around the well at night was dark and slick, and boys told about how snakes love water, so that anyone who had to draw water at night and then stand there alone and wash knew that moccasins and rattlers, puff adders and boa constrictors were winding their way to the well and would arrive just as the person washing got soap in her eyes. But Momma convinced us that not only was cleanliness next to Godliness, dirtiness was the inventor of misery.

The impudent child was detested by God and a shame to its parents and could bring destruction to its house and line. All adults had to be addressed as Mister, Missus, Miss, Auntie, Cousin, Unk, Uncle, Buhbah, Sister, Brother and a thousand other appellations indicating familial relationship and the lowliness of the addressor.

Everyone I knew respected these customary laws, except for the powhitetrash children.

Some families of powhitetrash lived on Momma's farm land behind the school. Sometimes a gaggle of them came to the Store, filling the whole room, chasing out the air and even changing the well-known scents. The children crawled over the shelves and into the potato and onion bins, twanging all the time in their sharp voices like cigar-box guitars. They took liberties in my Store that I would never dare. Since Momma told us that the less you say to whitefolks (or even powhitetrash) the better, Bailey and I would stand, solemn, quiet, and in the displaced air. But if one of the playful apparitions got close to us, I pinched it. Partly out of angry frustration and partly because I didn't believe in its flesh reality.

They called my uncle by his first name and ordered him around the Store. He, to my crying shame, obeyed them in his limping dip-straight-dip fashion.

My grandmother, too, followed their orders, except that she didn't seem to be servile because she anticipated their needs.

"Here's sugar, Miz Potter, and here's baking powder. You didn't buy soda last month, you'll probably be needing some."

Momma always directed her statements to the adults, but sometimes, Oh painful sometimes, the grimy, snotty-nosed girls would answer her.

"Naw, Annie . . . "—to Momma? Who owned the land they lived on? Who forgot more than they would ever learn? If there was any justice in the world, God should strike them dumb at once!—"Just give us some extry sody crackers, and some more mackerel."

At least they never looked in her face, or I never caught them doing so. Nobody with a smidgen of training, not even the worst roustabout, would look right in a grown person's face. It meant the person was trying to take the words out before they were formed. The dirty little children didn't do that, but they threw their orders around the Store like lashes from a cat-o'-nine-tails.

When I was around ten years old, those scruffy children caused me the most painful and confusing experience I had ever had with my grandmother.

One summer morning, after I had swept the dirt yard of leaves, spearmint-gum wrappers and Vienna-sausage labels, I raked the yellow-red dirt, and made half-moons carefully, so that the design stood out clearly and mask-like. I put the rake behind the Store and came through the back of the house to find Grandmother on the front porch in her big, wide white apron. The apron was so stiff by virtue of the starch that it could have stood alone. Momma was admiring the yard, so I joined her. It truly looked like a flat redhead that had been raked with a big-toothed comb. Momma didn't say anything but I knew she liked it. She looked over toward the school principal's house and to the right at Mr. McElroy's. She was hoping one of those community pillars would see the design before the day's business wiped it out. Then she looked upward to the school. My head had swung with her, so at just about the same time we saw a troop of the powhitetrash kids marching over the hill and down by the side of the school.

I looked to Momma for direction. She did an excellent job of sagging from her waist down, but from the waist up she seemed to be pulling for the top of the oak tree across the road. Then she began to moan a hymn. Maybe not to moan, but the tune was so slow and the meter so strange that she could have been moaning. She didn't look at me again. When the children reached halfway down the hill, half-way to the Store, she said without turning, "Sister, go on inside."

I wanted to beg her, "Momma, don't wait for them. Come on inside with me. If they come in the Store, you go to the bedroom and let me wait on them. They only frighten me if you're around. Alone I know how to handle them." But of course I couldn't say anything, so I went in and stood behind the screen door.

Before the girls got to the porch I heard their laughter crackling and popping like pine logs in a cooking stove. I suppose my lifelong paranoia was born in those cold, molasses-slow minutes. They came finally to stand on the ground in front of Momma. At first they pretended seriousness. Then one of them wrapped her right arm in the crook of her left, pushed out her mouth and started to hum. I realized that she was aping my grandmother. Another said, "Naw, Helen, you ain't stand-ing like her. This here's it." Then she lifted her chest, folded her arms and mocked that strange carriage that was Annie Henderson. Another laughed, "Naw, you can't do it. Your mouth ain't pooched out enough. It's like this."

I thought about the rifle behind the door, but I knew I'd never be able to hold it straight, and the .410, our sawed-off shotgun, which stayed loaded and was fired every New Year's night, was locked in the trunk and Uncle Willie had the key on his chain. Through the fly-specked screen-door, I could see that the arms of Momma's apron jiggled from the vibrations of her humming. But her knees seemed to have locked as if they would never bend again.

She sang on. No louder than before, but no softer either. No slower or faster.

The dirt of the girls' cotton dresses continued on their legs, feet, arms and faces to make them all of a piece. Their greasy uncolored hair hung down, uncombed, with a grim finality. I knelt to see them better, to remember them for all time. The tears that had slipped down my dress left unsurprising dark spots, and made the front yard blurry and even more unreal. The world had taken a deep breath and was having doubts about continuing to revolve.

The girls had tired of mocking Momma and turned to other means of agitation. One crossed her eyes, stuck her thumbs in both sides of her mouth and said, "Look here, Annie." Grandmother hummed on and the apron strings trembled. I wanted to throw a handful of black pepper in their faces, to throw lye on them, to scream that they were dirty, scummy peckerwoods,[3] but I knew I was as clearly imprisoned behind the scence as the actors outside were confined to their roles.

One of the smaller girls did a kind of puppet dance while her fellow clowns laughed at her. But the tall one, who was almost a woman, said something very quietly, which I couldn't hear. They all moved backward from the porch, still watching Momma. For an awful second I thought they were going to throw a rock at Momma, who seemed (except for the apron strings) to have turned into stone herself. But the big girl turned her back, bent down and put her hands flat on the ground—she didn't pick up anything. She simply shifted her weight and did a hand stand.

Her dirty bare feet and long legs went straight for the sky. Her dress fell down around her shoulders, and she had on no drawers. The slick pubic hair made a brown triangle where her legs came together. She hung in the vacuum of that lifeless morning for only a few seconds, then wavered and tumbled. The other girls clapped her on the back and slapped their hands.

Momma changed her song to "Bread of Heaven, bread of Heaven, feed me till I want no more."

I found that I was praying too. How long could Momma hold out? What new indignity would they think of to subject her to? Would I be able to stay out of it? What would Momma really like me to do?

Then they were moving out of the yard, on their way to town. They bobbed their heads and shook their slack behinds and turned, one at a time:

"'Bye, Annie."

"'Bye, Annie."

"'Bye, Annie."

Momma never turned her head or unfolded her arms, but she stopped singing and said, "'Bye, Miz Helen, 'bye Miz Ruth, 'bye, Miz Eloise."

I burst. A firecracker July-the-Fourth burst. How could Momma call them Miz? The mean nasty things. Why couldn't she have come inside the sweet, cool store when we saw them breasting the hill? What did she prove? And then if they were dirty, mean and impudent, why did Momma have to call them Miz?

She stood another whole song through and then opened the screen door to look down on me crying in rage. She looked until I looked up. Her face was a brown moon that shone on me. She was beautiful. Something had happened out there, which I couldn't completely understand, but I could see that she was happy. Then she bent down and touched me as mothers of the church "lay hands on the sick and afflicted" and I quieted.

"Go wash your face, Sister." And she went behind the candy counter and hummed, "Glory, glory hallelujah, when I lay my burden down."

I threw the well water on my face and used the weekday handkerchief to blow my nose. Whatever the contest had been out front, I knew Momma had won.

I took the rake back to the front yard. The smudged footprints were easy to erase. I worked for a long time on my new design and laid the rake behind the wash pot. When I came back in the Store, I took Momma's hand and we both walked outside to look at the pattern.

It was a large heart with lots of hearts growing smaller inside, and piercing

---

[3] Poor whites: derogatory.

from the outside rim to the smallest heart was an arrow. Momma said, "Sister, that's right pretty." Then she turned back to the Store and resumed, "Glory, glory, hallelujah, when I lay my burden down."

* * *

16

Recently a white woman from Texas, who would quickly describe herself as a liberal, asked me about my hometown. When I told her that in Stamps my grandmother had owned the only Negro general merchandise store since the turn of the century, she exclaimed, "Why, you were a debutante." Ridiculous and even ludicrous. But Negro girls in small Southern towns, whether poverty-stricken or just munching along on a few of life's necessities, were given as extensive and irrelevant preparations for adulthood as rich white girls shown in magazines. Admittedly the training was not the same. While white girls learned to waltz and sit gracefully with a tea cup balanced on their knees, we were lagging behind, learning the mid-Victorian values with very little money to indulge them. (Come and see Edna Lomax spending the money she made picking cotton on five balls of ecru tatting[4] thread. Her fingers are bound to snag the work and she'll have to repeat the stitches time and time again. But she knows that when she buys the thread.)

We were required to embroider and I had trunkfuls of colorful dishtowels, pillowcases, runners and handkerchiefs to my credit. I mastered the art of crocheting and tatting, and there was a lifetime's supply of dainty doilies that would never be used in sacheted dresser drawers. It went without saying that all girls could iron and wash, but the finer touches around the home, like setting a table with real silver, baking roasts and cooking vegetables without meat, had to be learned elsewhere. Usually at the source of those habits. During my tenth year, a white woman's kitchen became my finishing school.

Mrs. Viola Cullinan was a plump woman who lived in a three-bedroom house somewhere behind the post office. She was singularly unattractive until she smiled, and then the lines around her eyes and mouth which made her look perpetually dirty disappeared, and her face looked like the mask of an impish elf. She usually rested her smile until late afternoon when her women friends dropped in and Miss Glory, the cook, served them cold drinks on the closed-in porch.

The exactness of her house was inhuman. This glass went here and only here. That cup had its place and it was an act of impudent rebellion to place it anywhere else. At twelve o'clock the table was set. At 12:15 Mrs. Cullinan sat down to dinner (whether her husband had arrived or not). At 12:16 Miss Glory brought out the food.

It took me a week to learn the difference between a salad plate, a bread plate and a dessert plate.

Mrs. Cullinan kept up the tradition of her wealthy parents. She was from Virginia. Miss Glory, who was a descendant of slaves that had worked for the Cullinans, told me her history. She had married beneath her (according to Miss Glory).

[4] Beige lace-making.

Her husband's family hadn't had their money very long and what they had "didn't 'mount to much."

As ugly as she was, I thought privately, she was lucky to get a husband above or beneath her station. But Miss Glory wouldn't let me say a thing against her mistress. She was very patient with me, however, over the housework. She explained the dishware, silverware and servants' bells.

The large round bowl in which soup was served wasn't a soup bowl, it was a tureen. There were goblets, sherbet glasses, ice-cream glasses, wine glasses, green glass coffee cups with matching saucers, and water glasses. I had a glass to drink from, and it sat with Miss Glory's on a separate shelf from the others. Soup spoons, gravy boat, butter knives, salad forks and carving platter were additions to my vocabulary and in fact almost represented a new language. I was fascinated with the novelty, with the fluttering Mrs. Cullinan and her Alice-in-Wonderland house.

Her husband remains, in my memory, undefined. I lumped him with all the other white men that I had ever seen and tried not to see.

On our way home one evening, Miss Glory told me that Mrs. Cullinan couldn't have children. She said that she was too delicate-boned. It was hard to imagine bones at all under those layers of fat. Miss Glory went on to say that the doctor had taken out all her lady organs. I reasoned that a pig's organs included the lungs, heart and liver, so if Mrs. Cullinan was walking around without those essentials, it explained why she drank alcohol out of unmarked bottles. She was keeping herself embalmed.

When I spoke to Bailey about it, he agreed that I was right, but he also informed me that Mr. Cullinan had two daughters by a colored lady and that I knew them very well. He added that the girls were the spitting image of their father. I was unable to remember what he looked like, although I had just left him a few hours before, but I thought of the Coleman girls. They were very light-skinned and certainly didn't look very much like their mother (no one ever mentioned Mr. Coleman).

My pity for Mrs. Cullinan preceded me the next morning like the Cheshire cat's smile. Those girls, who could have been her daughters, were beautiful. They didn't have to straighten their hair. Even when they were caught in the rain, their braids still hung down straight like tamed snakes. Their mouths were pouty little cupid's bows. Mrs. Cullinan didn't know what she missed. Or maybe she did. Poor Mrs. Cullinan.

For weeks after, I arrived early, left late and tried very hard to make up for her barrenness. If she had had her own children, she wouldn't have had to ask me to run a thousand errands from her back door to the back door of her friends. Poor old Mrs. Cullinan.

Then one evening Miss Glory told me to serve the ladies on the porch. After I set the tray down and turned toward the kitchen, one of the women asked, "What's your name, girl?" It was the speckled-faced one. Mrs. Cullinan said, "She doesn't talk much. Her name's Margaret."

"Is she dumb?"

"No. As I understand it, she can talk when she wants to but she's usually quiet as a mouse. Aren't you, Margaret?"

I smiled at her. Poor thing. No organs and couldn't even pronounce my name correctly.

"She's a sweet little thing, though."

"Well, that may be, but the name's too long. I'd never bother myself. I'd call her Mary if I was you."

I fumed into the kitchen. That horrible woman would never have a chance to call me Mary because if I was starving I'd never work for her. I decided I wouldn't pee on her if her heart was on fire. Giggles drifted in off the porch and into Miss Glory's pots. I wondered what they could be laughing about.

Whitefolks were so strange. Could they be talking about me? Everybody knew that they stuck together better than the Negroes did. It was possible that Mrs. Cullinan had friends in St. Louis who heard about a girl from Stamps being in court and wrote to tell her. Maybe she knew about Mr. Freeman.

My lunch was in my mouth a second time and I went outside and relieved myself on the bed of four-o'clocks. Miss Glory thought I might be coming down with something and told me to go on home, that Momma would give me some herb tea, and she'd explain to her mistress.

I realized how foolish I was being before I reached the pond. Of course Mrs. Cullinan didn't know. Otherwise she wouldn't have given me the two nice dresses that Momma cut down, and she certainly wouldn't have called me a "sweet little thing." My stomach felt fine, and I didn't mention anything to Momma.

That evening I decided to write a poem on being white, fat, old and without children. It was going to be a tragic ballad. I would have to watch her carefully to capture the essence of her loneliness and pain.

The very next day, she called me by the wrong name. Miss Glory and I were washing up the lunch dishes when Mrs. Cullinan came to the doorway. "Mary?"

Miss Glory asked, "Who?"

Mrs. Cullinan, sagging a little, knew and I knew. "I want Mary to go down to Mrs. Randall's and take her some soup. She's not been feeling well for a few days."

Miss Glory's face was a wonder to see. "You mean Margaret, ma'am. Her name's Margaret."

"That's too long. She's Mary from now on. Heat that soup from last night and put it in the china tureen and, Mary, I want you to carry it carefully."

Every person I knew had a hellish horror of being "called out of his name." It was a dangerous practice to call a Negro anything that could be loosely construed as insulting because of the centuries of their having been called niggers, jigs, dinges, blackbirds, crows, boots and spooks.

Miss Glory had a fleeting second of feeling sorry for me. Then as she handed me the hot tureen[5] she said, "Don't mind, don't pay that no mind. Sticks and stones may break your bones, but words . . . You know, I been working for her for twenty years."

She held the back door open for me. "Twenty years. I wasn't much older than you. My name used to be Hallelujah. That's what Ma named me, but my mistress give me 'Glory,' and it stuck. I likes it better too."

I was in the little path that ran behind the houses when Miss Glory shouted, "It's shorter too."

For a few seconds it was a tossup over whether I would laugh (imagine being

---

[5] A large, deep, lidded serving dish.

named Hallelujah) or cry (imagine letting some white woman rename you for her convenience). My anger saved me from either outburst. I had to quit the job, but the problem was going to be how to do it. Momma wouldn't allow me to quit for just any reason.

"She's a peach. That woman is a real peach." Mrs. Randall's maid was talking as she took the soup from me, and I wondered what her name used to be and what she answered to now.

For a week I looked into Mrs. Cullinan's face as she called me Mary. She ignored my coming late and leaving early. Miss Glory was a little annoyed because I had begun to leave egg yolk on the dishes and wasn't putting much heart in polishing the silver. I hoped she would complain to our boss, but she didn't.

Then Bailey solved my dilemma. He had me describe the contents of the cupboard and the particular plates she like best. Her favorite piece was a casserole shaped like a fish and the green glass coffee cups. I kept his instructions in mind, so on the next day when Miss Glory was hanging out clothes and I had again been told to serve the old biddies on the porch, I dropped the empty serving tray. When I heard Mrs. Cullinan scream, "Mary!" I picked up the casserole and two of the green glass cups in readiness. As she rounded the kitchen door I let them fall on the tiled floor.

I could never absolutely describe to Bailey what happened next, because each time I got to the part where she fell on the floor and screwed up her ugly face to cry, we burst out laughing. She actually wobbled around on the floor and picked up shards of the cups and cried, "Oh, Momma. Oh, dear Gawd. It's Momma's china from Virginia. Oh, Momma, I sorry."

Miss Glory came running in from the yard and the women from the porch crowded around. Miss Glory was almost as broken up as her mistress. "You mean to say she broke our Virginia dishes? What we gone do?"

Mrs. Cullinan cried louder, "That clumsy nigger. Clumsy little black nigger."

Old speckled-face leaned down and asked, "Who did it, Viola? Was it Mary? Who did it?"

Everything was happening so fast I can't remember whether her action preceded her words, but I know that Mrs. Cullinan said, "Her name's Margaret, god-damn it, her name's Margaret!" And she threw a wedge of the broken plate at me. It could have been the hysteria which put her aim off, but the flying crockery caught Miss Glory right over her ear and she started screaming.

I left the front door wide open so all the neighbors could hear.

Mrs. Cullinan was right about one thing. My name wasn't Mary.

* * *

23

The children in Stamps trembled visibly with anticipation. Some adults were excited too, but to be certain the whole young population had come down with graduation epidemic. Large classes were graduating from both the grammar school and the high school. Even those who were years removed from their own day of glorious release were anxious to help with preparations as a kind of dry run. The junior students who were moving into the vacating classes' chairs were tradition-bound to show their talents for leadership and management. They strutted through the school and around the campus exerting pressure on the lower grades. Their authority was so new that occasionally if they pressed a little too hard it had to be overlooked. After all, next term was coming, and it never hurt a sixth grader to have a play sister in the eighth grade, or a tenth-year student to be able to call a twelfth grader Bubba. So all was endured in a spirit of shared understanding. But the graduating classes themselves were the nobility. Like travelers with exotic destinations on their minds, the graduates were remarkably forgetful. They came to school without their books, or tablets or even pencils. Volunteers fell over themselves to secure replacements for the missing equipment. When accepted, the willing workers might or might not be thanked, and it was of no importance to the pregraduation rites. Even teachers were respectful of the now quiet and aging seniors, and tended to speak to them if not as equals, as beings only slightly lower than themselves. After tests were returned and grades given, the student body, which acted like an extended family, knew who did well, who excelled, and what piteous ones had failed.

Unlike the white high school, Lafayette County Training School distinguished itself by having neither lawn, nor hedges, nor tennis court, nor climbing ivy. Its two buildings (main classrooms, the grade school and home economics) were set on a dirt hill with no fence to limit either its boundaries or those of bordering farms. There was a large expanse to the left of the school which was used alternately as a baseball diamond or a basketball court. Rusty hoops on the swaying poles represented the permanent recreational equipment, although bats and balls could be borrowed from the P. E. teacher if the borrower was qualified and if the diamond wasn't occupied.

Over this rocky area relieved by a few shady tall persimmon trees the graduating class walked. The girls often held hands and no longer bothered to speak to the lower students. There was a sadness about them, as if this old world was not their home and they were bound for higher ground. The boys, on the other hand, had become more friendly, more outgoing. A decided change from the closed attitude they projected while studying for finals. Now they seemed not ready to give up the old school, the familiar paths and classrooms. Only a small percentage would be continuing on to college—one of the South's A & M (agricultural and mechanical) schools, which trained Negro youths to be carpenters, farmers, handymen, masons, maids, cooks and baby nurses. Their future rode heavily on their shoulders, and blinded them to the collective joy that had pervaded the lives of the boys and girls in the grammar school graduating class.

Parents who could afford it had ordered new shoes and ready-made clothes for themselves from Sears and Roebuck or Montgomery Ward. They also engaged in the best seamstresses to make the floating graduating dresses and to cut down secondhand pants which would be pressed to a military slickness for the important event.

Oh, it was important, all right. Whitefolks would attend the ceremony, and two or three would speak of God and home, and the Southern way of life, and Mrs. Parsons, the principal's wife, would play the graduation march while the lower-grade graduates paraded down the aisles and took their seats below the platform. The high school seniors would wait in empty classrooms to make their dramatic entrance.

In the Store I was the person of the moment. The birthday girl. The center. Bailey had graduated the year before, although to do so he had had to forfeit all pleasures to make up for his time lost in Baton Rouge.

My class was wearing butter-yellow piqué[6] dresses, and Momma launched out on mine. She smocked the yoke into tiny crisscrossing puckers, then shirred the rest of the bodice. Her dark fingers ducked in and out of the lemony cloth as she embroidered raised daisies around the hem. Before she considered herself finished she had added a crocheted cuff on the puff sleeves, and a pointy crocheted collar.

I was going to be lovely. A walking model of all the various styles of fine hand sewing and it didn't worry me that I was only twelve years old and merely graduating from the eighth grade. Besides, many teachers in Arkansas Negro schools had only that diploma and were licensed to impart wisdom.

The days had become longer and more noticeable. The faded beige of former times had been replaced with strong and sure colors. I began to see my classmates' clothes, their skin tones, and the dust that waved off pussy willows. Clouds that lazed across the sky were objects of great concern to me. Their shiftier shapes might have held a message that in my new happiness and with a little bit of time I'd soon decipher. During that period I looked at the arch of heaven so religiously my neck kept a steady ache. I had taken to smiling more often, and my jaws hurt from the unaccustomed activity. Between the two physical sore spots, I suppose I could have been uncomfortable, but that was not the case. As a member of the winning team (the graduating class of 1940) I had outdistanced unpleasant sensations by miles. I was headed for the freedom of open fields.

Youth and social approval allied themselves with me and we trammeled memories of slights and insults. The wind of our swift passage remodeled my features. Lost tears were pounded to mud and then to dust. Years of withdrawal were brushed aside and left behind, as hanging ropes of parasitic moss.

My work alone had awarded me a top place and I was going to be one of the first called in the graduating ceremonies. On the classroom blackboard, as well as on the bulletin board in the auditorium, there were blue stars and white stars and red stars. No absences, no tardiness, and my academic work was among the best of the year. I could say the preamble to the Constitution even faster than Bailey. We timed ourselves often: "WethepeopleoftheUnitedStatesinordertoformamoreperfectunion . . . " I had memorized the Presidents of the United States from Washington to Roosevelt in chronological as well as alphabetical order.

My hair pleased me too. Gradually the black mass had lengthened and thickened, so that it kept at last to its braided pattern, and I didn't have to yank my scalp off when I tried to comb it.

Louise and I had rehearsed the exercises until we tired out ourselves. Henry Reed was class valedictorian. He was a small, very black boy with hooded eyes, a long, broad nose and an oddly shaped head. I had admired him for years because each term he and I vied for the best grades in our class. Most often he bested me, but instead of being disappointed I was pleased that we shared top places between us. Like many Southern Black children, he lived with his grandmother, who was as strict as Momma and as kind as she knew how to be. He was courteous, respectful and soft-spoken to elders, but on the playground he chose to play the

---

[6] A firmly woven cotton fabric.

roughest games. I admired him. Anyone, I reckoned, sufficiently afraid or sufficiently dull could be polite. But to be able to operate at a top level with both adults and children was admirable.

His valedictory speech was entitled "To Be or Not to Be." The rigid tenth-grade teacher had helped him write it. He'd been working on the dramatic stresses for months.

The weeks until graduation were filled with heady activities. A group of small children were to be presented in a play about buttercups and daisies and bunny rabbits. They could be heard throughout the building practicing their hops and their little songs that sounded like silver bells. The older girls (nongraduates, of course) were assigned the task of making refreshments for the night's festivities. A tangy scent of ginger, cinnamon, nutmeg and chocolate wafted around the home economics building as the budding cooks made samples for themselves and their teachers.

In every corner of the workshop, axes and saws split fresh timber as the wood-shop boys made sets and stage scenery. Only the graduates were left out of the general bustle. We were free to sit in the library at the back of the building or look in quite detachedly, naturally, on the measures being taken for our event.

Even the minister preached on graduation the Sunday before. His subject was, "Let your light so shine that men will see your good works and praise your Father, Who is in Heaven." Although the sermon was purported to be addressed to us, he used the occasion to speak to backsliders, gamblers and general ne'er-do-wells. But since he had called our names at the beginning of the service we were mollified.

Among Negroes the tradition was to give presents to children going only from one grade to another. How much more important this was when the person was graduating at the top of the class. Uncle Willie and Momma had sent away for a Mickey Mouse watch like Bailey's. Louise gave me four embroidered handkerchiefs. (I gave her three crocheted doilies.) Mrs. Sneed, the minister's wife, made me an underskirt to wear for graduation, and nearly every customer gave me a nickel or maybe even a dime with the instruction "Keep on moving to higher ground," or some such encouragement.

Amazingly the great day finally dawned and I was out of bed before I knew it. I threw open the back door to see it more clearly, but Momma said, "Sister, come away from that door and put your robe on."

I hoped the memory of that morning would never leave me. Sunlight was itself still young, and the day had none of the insistence maturity would bring it in a few hours. In my robe and barefoot in the backyard, under cover of going to see about my new beans, I gave myself up to the gentle warmth and thanked God that no matter what evil I had done in my life He had allowed me to live to see this day. Somewhere in my fatalism I had expected to die, accidentally, and never had the chance to walk up the stairs in the auditorium and gracefully receive my hard-earned diploma. Out of God's merciful bosom I had won reprieve.

Bailey came out in his robe and gave me a box wrapped in Christmas paper. He said he had saved his money for months to pay for it. It felt like a box of chocolates, but I knew Baily wouldn't save money to buy candy when we had all we could want under our noses.

He was as proud of the gift as I. It was a soft-leather-bound copy of a collection of poems by Edgar Allan Poe, or, as Bailey and I called him, "Eap." I turned to "Annabel Lee"[7] and we walked up and down the garden rows, the cool dirt between our toes, reciting the beautifully sad lines.

Momma made a Sunday breakfast although it was only Friday. After we finished the blessing, I opened my eyes to find the watch on my plate. It was a dream of a day. Everything went smoothly and to my credit. I didn't have to be reminded or scolded for anything. Near evening I was too jittery to attend to chores, so Bailey volunteered to do all before his bath.

Days before, we had made a sign for the Store, and as we turned out the lights Momma hung the cardboard over the doorknob. It read clearly: CLOSED, GRADUATION.

My dress fitted perfectly and everyone said that I looked like a sunbeam in it. On the hill, going toward the school, Bailey walked behind with Uncle Willie, who muttered, "Go on, Ju." He wanted him to walk ahead with us because it embarrassed him to have to walk so slowly. Bailey said he'd let the ladies walk together, and the men would bring up the rear. We all laughed, nicely.

Little children dashed by out of the dark like fireflies. Their crepe-paper dresses and butterfly wings were not made for running and we heard more than one rip, dryly, and the regretful "uh uh" that followed.

The school blazed without gaiety. The windows seemed cold and unfriendly from the lower hill. A sense of ill-fated timing crept over me, and if Momma hadn't reached for my hand I would have drifted back to Bailey and Uncle Willie, and possibly beyond. She made a few slow jokes about my feet getting cold, and tugged me along to the now-strange building.

Around the front steps, assurance came back. There were my fellow "greats," the graduating class. Hair brushed back, legs oiled, new dresses and pressed pleats, fresh pocket handkerchiefs and little handbags, all homesewn. Oh, we were up to snuff, all right. I joined my comrades and didn't even see my family go in to find seats in the crowded auditorium.

The school band struck up a march and all classes filed in as had been rehearsed. We stood in front of our seats, as assigned, and on a signal from the choir director, we sat. No sooner had this been accomplished than the band started to play the national anthem. We rose again and sang the song, after which we recited the pledge of allegiance. We remained standing for a brief minute before the choir director and the principal signaled to us, rather desperately I thought, to take our seats. The command was so unusual that our carefully rehearsed and smooth-running machine was thrown off. For a full minute we fumbled for our chairs and bumped into each other awkwardly. Habits change or solidify under pressure, so in our state of nervous tension we had been ready to follow our usual assembly pattern: the American national anthem, then the pledge of allegiance, then the song every Black person I knew called the Negro National Anthem. All done in the same key, with the same passion and most often standing on the same foot.

Finding my seat at last, I was overcome with a presentiment of worse things to come. Something unrehearsed, unplanned, was going to happen, and we were going to be made to look bad. I distinctly remember being explicit in the choice of pronoun. It was "we," the graduating class, the unit, that concerned me then.

[7] A lyrical ballad by Poe (1809–1849), published posthumously in 1849.

The principal welcomed "parents and friends" and asked the Baptist minister to lead us in prayer. His invocation was brief and punchy, and for a second I thought we were getting back on the high road to right action. When the principal came back to the dais, however, his voice had changed. Sounds always affected me profoundly and the principal's voice was one of my favorites. During assembly it melted and lowed weakly into the audience. It had not been in my plan to listen to him, but my curiosity was piqued and I straighted up to give him my attention.

He was talking about Booker T. Washington,[8] our "late great leader," who said we can be as close as the fingers on the hand, etc. . . . . Then he said a few vague things about friendship and the friendship of kindly people to those less fortunate than themselves. With that his voice nearly faded, thin, away. Like a river diminishing to a stream and then to a trickle. But he cleared his throat and said, "Our speaker tonight, who is also our friend, came from Texarkana to deliver the commencement address, but due to the irregularity of the train schedule, he's going to, as they say, 'speak and run.'" He said that we understood and wanted the man to know that we were most grateful for the time he was able to give us and then something about how we were willing always to adjust to another's program, and without more ado—"I give you Mr. Edward Donleavy."

Not one but two white men came through the door offstage. The shorter one walked to the speaker's platform, and the tall one moved over to the center seat and sat down. But that was our principal's seat, and already occupied. The dislodged gentleman bounced around for a long breath or two before the Baptist minister gave him his chair, then with more dignity than the situation deserved, the minister walked off the stage.

Donleavy looked at the audience once (on reflection, I'm sure that he wanted only to reassure himself that we were really there), adjusted his glasses and began to read from a sheaf of papers.

He was glad "to be here and to see the work going on just as it was in the other schools."

At the first "Amen" from the audience I willed the offender to immediate death by choking on the word. But Amen and yes, sir's began to fall around the room like rain through a ragged umbrella.

He told us of the wonderful changes we children in Stamps had in store. The Central School (naturally, the white school was Central) had already been granted improvements that would be in use in the fall. A well-known artist was coming from Little Rock to teach art to them. They were going to have the newest microscopes and chemistry equipment for their laboratory. Mr. Donleavy didn't leave us long in the dark over who made these improvements available to Central High. Nor were we to be ignored in the general betterment scheme he had in mind.

He said that he had pointed out to people at a very high level that one of the first-line football tacklers at Arkansas Agricultural and Mechanical College had graduated from good old Lafayette County Training School. Here fewer Amen's were heard. Those few that did break through lay dully in the air with the heaviness of habit.

He went on to praise us. He went on to say how he had bragged that "one of the

---

[8] The famous African-American educator Washington (1856–1915), author of the autobiography *Up From Slavery* (1901).

best basketball players at Fisk sank his first ball right here at Lafayette County Training School."

The white kids were going to have a chance to become Galileos and Madame Curies and Edisons and Gauguins, and our boys (the girls weren't even in on it) would try to be Jesse Owenses and Joe Louises.[9]

Owens and the Brown Bomber were great heroes in our world, but what school official in the white-goddom of Little Rock had the right to decide that those two men must be our only heroes? Who decided that for Henry Reed to become a scientist he had to work like George Washington Carver,[10] as a bootblack, to buy a lousy microscope? Bailey was obviously always going to be too small to be an athlete, so which concrete angel glued to what country seat had decided that if my brother wanted to become a lawyer he had to first pay penance for his kin by picking cotton and hoeing corn and studying correspondence books at night for twenty years?

The man's dead words fell like bricks around the auditorium and too many settled in my belly. Constrained by hard-learned manners I couldn't look behind me, but to my left and right the proud graduating class of 1940 had dropped their heads. Every girl in my row had found something new to do with her handkerchief. Some folded the tiny squares into love knots, some into triangles, but most were wadding them, then pressing them flat on their yellow laps.

On the dais, the ancient tragedy was being replayed. Professor Parsons sat, a sculptor's reject, rigid. His large, heavy body seemed devoid of will or willingness, and his eyes said he was no longer with us. The other teachers examined the flag (which was draped stage right) or their notes, or the windows which opened on our now-famous playing diamond.

Graduation, the hush-hush magic time of frills and gifts and congratulations and diplomas, was finished for me before my name was called. The accomplishment was nothing. The meticulous maps, drawn in three colors of ink, learning and spelling decasyllabic words, memorizing the whole of *The Rape of Lucrece*[11]—it was for nothing. Donleavy had exposed us.

We were maids and farmers, handymen and washerwomen, and anything higher that we aspired to was farcical and presumptuous.

Then I wished that Gabriel Prosser and Nat Turner[12] had killed all whitefolks in their beds and that Abraham Lincoln had been assassinated before the signing of the Emancipation Proclamation, and that Harriet Tubman had been killed by that blow on her head and Christopher Columbus had drowned in the *Santa Maria*.[13]

[9] The Italian astronomer and physicist Galileo Galilei (1564–1642); the Polish-born physical chemist Marie Curie (1867–1934); the inventor Thomas Alva Edison (1847–1931); the French painter Paul Gauguin (1848–1903); Owens, (1913–1980), an African-American athlete, won four gold medals in track and field in the 1936 Olympics; Louis (1914–1981), an African-American boxer known as the Brown Bomber, was heavyweight champion of the world (1937–1949).

[10] Carver (1864?–1943), the son of slaves, worked his way up to become a renowned botanist and director of agriculture at Tuskegee Institute.

[11] A 1594 Shakespeare poem.

[12] Slaves who led unsuccessful slave revolts: Prosser (1776?–1800) in 1800 and Turner (1800–1831) in 1831; both were captured and hanged.

[13] Lincoln (1809–1865), the sixteenth U.S. president (1861–1865), signed the Emancipation Proclamation, freeing all slaves, in 1863; Tubman (1820?–1913), an escaped slave, was a leading abolitionist active in the Underground Railroad, helping others escape; the *Santa María* was one of the three ships in which Columbus (1451–1506) and his men sailed to America.

It was awful to be Negro and have no control over my life. It was brutal to be young and already trained to sit quietly and listen to charges brought against my color with no chance of defense. We should all be dead. I thought I should like to see us all dead, one on top of the other. A pyramid of flesh with the whitefolks on the bottom, as the bread base, then the Indians with their silly tomahawks and teepees and wigwams and treaties, the Negroes with their mops and recipes and cotton sacks and spirituals sticking out of their mouths. The Dutch children should all stumble in their wooden shoes and break their necks. The French should choke to death on the Louisiana Purchase (1803)[14] while silkworms ate all the Chinese with their stupid pigtails. As a species, we were an abomination. All of us.

Donleavy was running for election, and assured our parents that if he won we could count on having the only colored paved playing field in that part of Arkansas. Also—he never looked up to acknowledge the grunts of acceptance—also, we were bound to get some new equipment for the home economics building and the workshop.

He finished, and since there was no need to give any more than the most perfunctory thank-you's, he nodded to the men on the stage, and the tall white man who was never introduced joined him at the door. They left with the attitude that now they were off to something really important. (The graduation ceremonies at Lafayette County Training School had been a mere preliminary.)

The ugliness they left was palpable. An uninvited guest who wouldn't leave. The choir was summoned and sang a modern arrangement of "Onward, Christian Soldiers," with new words pertaining to graduates seeking their place in the world. But it didn't work. Elouise, the daughter of the Baptist minister, recited "Invictus," and I could have cried at the impertinence of "I am the master of my fate, I am the captain of my soul."

My name had lost its ring of familiarity and I had to be nudged to go and receive my diploma. All my preparations had fled. I neither marched up to the stage like a conquering Amazon, nor did I look in the audience for Bailey's nod of approval. Marguerite Johnson, I heard the name again, my honors were read, there were noises in the audience of appreciation, and I took my place on the stage as rehearsed.

I thought about colors I hated: ecru, puce, lavender, beige and black.

There was shuffling and rustling around me, then Henry Reed was giving his valedictory address, "To Be or Not to Be." Hadn't he heard the whitefolks? We couldn't *be*, so the question was a waste of time. Henry's voice came out clear and strong. I feared to look at him. Hadn't he got the message? There was no "nobler in the mind" for Negroes because the world didn't think we had minds, and they let us know it. "Outrageous fortune"? Now, that was a joke. When the ceremony was over I had to tell Henry Reed some things. That is, if I still cared. Not "rub," Henry, "erase." "Ah, there's the erase." Us.

Henry had been a good student in elocution. His voice rose on tides of promise and fell on waves of warnings. The English teacher had helped him to create a sermon winging through Hamlet's soliloquy. To be a man, a doer, a builder, a leader, or to be a tool, an unfunny joke, a crusher of funky toadstools. I marveled that Henry could go through with the speech as if we had a choice.

[14] The agreement by which the United States bought land from France for $15 million and doubled its area.

I had been listening and silently rebutting each sentence with my eyes closed; then there was a hush, which in an audience warns that something unplanned is happening. I looked up and saw Henry Reed, the conservative, the proper, the A student, turn his back to the audience and turn to us (the proud graduating class of 1940) and sing, nearly speaking,

> "Lift ev'ry voice and sing
> Till earth and heaven ring
> Ring with the harmonies of Liberty . . . "

It was the poem written by James Weldon Johnson.[15] It was the music composed by J. Rosamond Johnson. It was the Negro national anthem. Out of habit we were singing it.

Our mothers and fathers stood in the dark hall and joined the hymn of encouragement. A kindergarten teacher led the small children onto the stage and the buttercups and daisies and bunny rabbits marked time and tried to follow:

> "Stony the road we trod
> Bitter the chastening rod
> Felt in the days when hope, unborn, had died.
> Yet with a steady beat
> Have not our weary feet
> Come to the place for which our fathers sighed?"

Every child I knew had learned that song with his ABC's and along with "Jesus Loves Me This I Know." But I personally had never heard it before. Never heard the words, despite the thousands of times I had sung them. Never thought they had anything to do with me.

On the other hand, the words of Patrick Henry[16] had made such an impression on me that I had been able to stretch myself tall and trembling and say, "I know not what course others may take, but as for me, give me liberty or give me death."

And now I heard, really for the first time:

> "We have come over a way that with tears
> has been watered,
> We have come, treading our path through
> the blood of the slaughtered."

While echoes of the song shivered in the air, Henry Reed bowed his head, said "Thank you," and returned to his place in the line. The tears that slipped down many faces were not wiped away in shame.

We were on top again. As always, again. We survived. The depths had been icy and dark, but now a bright sun spoke to our souls. I was no longer simply a

---

[15] Johnson (1871–1938), an African-American lawyer and author, composed "Lift Every Voice and Sing" (1899) with his brother, John Rosamond Johnson (1873–1954).

[16] The American statesman and orator Henry (1736–1799); from his famous speech given in Richmond, Virginia, on March 23, 1775.

member of the proud graduating class of 1940; I was a proud member of the wonderful, beautiful Negro race.

Oh, Black known and unknown poets, how often have your auctioned pains sustained us? Who will compute the lonely nights made less lonely by your songs, or by the empty pots made less tragic by your tales?

If we were a people much given to revealing secrets, we might raise monuments and sacrifice to the memories of our poets, but slavery cured us of that weakness. It may be enough, however, to have it said that we survive in exact relationship to the dedication of our poets (include preachers, musicians and blues singers).

1970

Toni Morrison
(1931–   )

Toni Morrison contends that writing " . . . should have something in it that enlightens; something in it that opens the door and points the way. Something in it that suggests what the conflicts are, what the problems are. But it need not solve those problems because it is not a case study, it is not a recipe" (*Black Women Writers*, Mari Evans, 1984). True to her word, she does not hand her readers answers but envelops them in a cultural richness in which growth and transformation are possible, even when painful.

Born Chloe Anthony Wofford in 1931, she grew up in Lorain, Ohio. The setting of four of her five novels, the Midwest has offered her a way out of the settings stereotypical of African Americans. After completing her undergraduate studies at Howard University in 1953, Wofford attended Cornell University, where she earned an M.A. in 1955. Since then she has taught at such distinguished institutions as Howard and Princeton University. During her second stay at Howard, she married Harold Morrison, an architect; they have since divorced. As a senior editor at a leading publisher in New York City, Morrison promoted the work of other African-American writers, including the novelists Toni Cade Bambara and Gayl Jones.

As Morrison notes in *Conversations With American Writers* (Charles Ruas, 1984), she wrote her first novel, *The Bluest Eye* (1970), because she "wanted to read it." Her novels explore the tremendous power and danger inherent in growing up black and female in America. *Sula* (1973), the story of the friendship of two African-American girls, was nominated for a National Book Award. Her third novel, *Song of Solomon* (1977), won the National Book Critics' Circle Award, and *Tar Baby* (1981), which examines the complex relationship of race, gender, and class as played out on a Caribbean island, was also well received. *Beloved* (1987), winner of the Pulitzer Prize for fiction, takes place in Ohio during Reconstruction and concerns the lives of newly freed African Americans who are literally haunted by the legacy of slavery.

When Robert Smith promises to "fly from Mercy" on the opening page of *Song of Solomon*, it is but the first of the novel's many allusions to an empowering African-American folktale as old as the African presence in the Americas. Wherever Africans were transported into slavery there are stories of slaves who returned to Africa. This "old folks' lie" is one of the keys to the past that animates the quest of the novel's hero, Macon Dead, to reclaim a heritage far more precious than the gold he sets off to find. Like all Morrison's novels, *Song of Solomon* asserts the life-giving qualities of African-American folk culture, which is under siege not only from the old enemies of poverty and racism, but from modern materialism as well.

Morrison's elegant prose and vivid imagery define a style that counters reductive conceptions of African-American language, like those of Mark Twain and Joel Chandler Harris, based primarily on transcribing dialect pronunciation. She seeks the true African-American voice, "its syntax, its metaphors, and its music." In *Song of Solomon* Macon Dead wishes for an ancestor "whose name was not a joke," but in jokes such as the ironic renaming of "Not Doctor Street" and "No Mercy Hospital," history and identity are preserved through passionate uses of language. The name "Macon Dead" itself is in one sense a cruel reminder of the careless power of whites to define African Americans, but as passed down from father to son it also testifies to the persistence of African-American identity.

Suggested Readings: *The Bluest Eye,* 1970. *Sula,* 1973. *Tar Baby,* 1981. *Beloved,* 1987. R. Stepto, "Intimate Things in Place: A Conversation With Toni Morrison," in *Massachusetts Review,* 18, 1977. J. Bakerman, "The Seams Can't Show," in *Black American Literature Forum,* 12, 1978. B. Parker, "Complexity: Toni Morrison's Women: An Interview Essay," in *Sturdy Black Bridges: Visions of Black Women in Literature,* eds. R. Bell, B. Parker, and B. Guy-Sheftall, 1979. J. Bakerman, "Failures of Love: Female Initiation in the Novels of Toni Morrison," in *American Literature,* 52:4, 1981. S. Willis, "Eruptions of Funk: Historicizing Toni Morrison," in *Black American Literature Forum,* 16:1, 1982. M. Evans, ed., *Women Writers (1950–1980),* 1984. S. Willis, " 'The Sweet Life' in Toni Morrison's Fiction," in *American Literature,* 56:2, 1984. N. Y. McKay, ed., *Critical Essays on Toni Morrison,* 1988.

Text Used: *Song of Solomon,* 1977.

from   SONG OF SOLOMON*

CHAPTER 1

The North Carolina Mutual Life Insurance[1] agent promised to fly from Mercy to the other side of Lake Superior at three o'clock. Two days before the event was to take place he tacked a note on the door of his little yellow house:

> At 3:00 P. M. on Wednesday the 18th of February, 1931, I will take off from Mercy and fly away on my own wings. Please forgive me. I loved you all.
>
> (signed) Robert Smith,
> Ins. agent

Mr. Smith didn't draw as big a crowd as Lindbergh[2] had four years earlier— not more than forty or fifty people showed up—because it was already eleven

---

* Named for the biblical book consisting of the dramatic, lyrical love poem attributed to Solomon, a wise king of Israel.

[1] An African-American insurance company that catered exclusively to African Americans.

[2] Charles A. Lindbergh (1908–1981), the aviator who earned instant fame by making the first non-stop solo flight across the Atlantic Ocean, from New York to Paris, in 1927.

o'clock in the morning, on the very Wednesday he had chosen for his flight, before anybody read the note. At that time of day, during the middle of the week, word-of-mouth news just lumbered along. Children were in school; men were at work; and most of the women were fastening their corsets and getting ready to go see what tails or entrails the butcher might be giving away. Only the unemployed, the self-employed, and the very young were available—deliberately available because they'd heard about it, or accidentally available because they happened to be walking at that exact moment in the shore end of Not Doctor Street, a name the post office did not recognize. Town maps registered the street as Mains Avenue, but the only colored doctor in the city had lived and died on that street, and when he moved there in 1896 his patients took to calling the street, which none of them lived in or near, Doctor Street. Later, when other Negroes moved there, and when the postal service became a popular means of transferring messages among them, envelopes from Louisiana, Virginia, Alabama, and Georgia began to arrive addressed to people at house numbers on Doctor Street. The post office workers returned these envelopes or passed them on to the Dead Letter Office. Then in 1918, when colored men were being drafted, a few gave their address at the recruitment office as Doctor Street. In that way, the name acquired a quasi-official status. But not for long. Some of the city legislators, whose concern for appropriate names and the maintenance of the city's landmarks was the principal part of their political life, saw to it that "Doctor Street" was never used in any official capacity. And since they knew that only Southside residents kept it up, they had notices posted in the stores, barbershops, and restaurants in that part of the city saying that the avenue running northerly and southerly from Shore Road fronting the lake to the junction of routes 6 and 2 leading to Pennsylvania, and also running parallel to and between Rutherford Avenue and Broadway, had always been and would always be known as Mains Avenue and not Doctor Street.

It was a genuinely clarifying public notice because it gave Southside residents a way to keep their memories alive and please the city legislators as well. They called it Not Doctor Street, and were inclined to call the charity hospital at its northern end No Mercy Hospital since it was 1931, on the day following Mr. Smith's leap from its cupola, before the first colored expectant mother was allowed to give birth inside its wards and not on its steps. The reason for the hospital's generosity to that particular woman was not the fact that she was the only child of this Negro doctor, for during his entire professional life he had never been granted hospital privileges and only two of his patients were ever admitted to Mercy, both white. Besides, the doctor had been dead a long time by 1931. It must have been Mr. Smith's leap from the roof over their heads that made them admit her. In any case, whether or not the little insurance agent's conviction that he could fly contributed to the place of her delivery, it certainly contributed to its time.

When the dead doctor's daughter saw Mr. Smith emerge as promptly as he had promised from behind the cupola, his wide blue silk wings curved forward around his chest, she dropped her covered peck basket,[3] spilling red velvet rose petals. The wind blew them about, up, down, and into small mounds of snow. Her half-grown daughters scrambled about trying to catch them, while their mother moaned and held the underside of her stomach. The rose-petal scramble got a lot of attention, but the pregnant lady's moans did not. Everyone knew the girls had spent

---

[3] A basket with the capacity of one peck, or eight quarts.

hour after hour tracing, cutting, and stitching the costly velvet, and that Gerhardt's Department Store would be quick to reject any that were soiled.

It was nice and gay there for a while. The men joined in trying to collect the scraps before the snow soaked through them—snatching them from a gust of wind or plucking them delicately from the snow. And the very young children couldn't make up their minds whether to watch the man circled in blue on the roof or the bits of red flashing around on the ground. Their dilemma was solved when a woman suddenly burst into song. The singer, standing at the back of the crowd, was as poorly dressed as the doctor's daughter was well dressed. The latter had on a neat gray coat with the traditional pregnant-woman bow at her navel, a black cloche,[4] and a pair of four-button ladies' galoshes. The singing woman wore a knitted navy cap pulled far down over her forehead. She had wrapped herself up in an old quilt instead of a winter coat. Her head cocked to one side, her eyes fixed on Mr. Robert Smith, she sang in a powerful contralto:

> O Sugarman done fly away
> Sugarman done gone
> Sugarman cut across the sky
> Sugarman gone home. . . .

A few of the half a hundred or so people gathered there nudged each other and sniggered. Others listened as though it were the helpful and defining piano music in a silent movie. They stood this way for some time, none of them crying out to Mr. Smith, all of them preoccupied with one or the other of the minor events about them, until the hospital people came.

They had been watching from the windows—at first with mild curiosity, then, as the crowd seemed to swell to the very walls of the hospital, they watched with apprehension. They wondered if one of those things that racial-uplift groups were always organizing was taking place. But when they saw neither placards nor speakers, they ventured outside into the cold: white-coated surgeons, dark-jacketed business and personnel clerks, and three nurses in starched jumpers.

The sight of Mr. Smith and his wide blue wings transfixed them for a few seconds, as did the woman's singing and the roses strewn about. Some of them thought briefly that this was probably some form of worship. Philadelphia, where Father Divine[5] reigned, wasn't all that far away. Perhaps the young girls holding baskets of flowers were two of his virgins. But the laughter of a gold-toothed man brought them back to their senses. They stopped daydreaming and swiftly got down to business, giving orders. Their shouts and bustling caused great confusion where before there had been only a few men and some girls playing with pieces of velvet and a woman singing.

One of the nurses, hoping to bring some efficiency into the disorder, searched the faces around her until she saw a stout woman who looked as though she might move the earth if she wanted to.

"You," she said, moving toward the stout woman. "Are these your children?"

The stout woman turned her head slowly, her eyebrows lifted at the carelessness of the address. Then, seeing where the voice came from, she lowered her brows and veiled her eyes.

---

[4] A closefitting women's hat.
[5] George Baker (1877–1965), an African-American religious leader who founded the Peace Mission (1919), a communal religious society.

"Ma'am?"

"Send one around-back to the emergency office. Tell him to tell the guard to get over here quick. That boy there can go. That one." She pointed to a cat-eyed boy about five or six years old.

The stout woman slid her eyes down the nurse's finger and looked at the child she was pointing to.

"Guitar, ma'am."

"What?"

"Guitar."

The nurse gazed at the stout woman as though she had spoken Welsh. Then she closed her mouth, looked again at the cat-eyed boy, and lacing her fingers, spoke her next words very slowly to him.

"Listen. Go around to the back of the hospital to the guard's office. It will say 'Emergency Admissions' on the door. A-D-M-I-S-I-O-N-S. But the guard will be there. Tell him to get over here—on the double. Move now. Move!" She unlaced her fingers and made scooping motions with her hands, the palms pushing against the wintry air.

A man in a brown suit came toward her, puffing little white clouds of breath. "Fire truck's on its way. Get back inside. You'll freeze to death."

The nurse nodded.

"You left out a *s,* ma'am," the boy said. The North was new to him and he had just begun to learn he could speak up to white people. But she'd already gone, rubbing her arms against the cold.

"Granny, she left out a *s.*"

"And a 'please.'"

"You reckon he'll jump?"

"A nutwagon do anything."

"Who is he?"

"Collects insurance. A nutwagon."

"Who is that lady singing?"

"That, baby, is the very last thing in pea-time." But she smiled when she looked at the singing woman, so the cat-eyed boy listened to the musical performance with at least as much interest as he devoted to the man flapping his wings on top of the hospital.

The crowd was beginning to be a little nervous now that the law was being called in. They each knew Mr. Smith. He came to their houses twice a month to collect one dollar and sixty-eight cents and write down on a little yellow card both the date and their eighty-four cents a week payment. They were always half a month or so behind, and talked endlessly to him about paying ahead—after they had a preliminary discussion about what he was doing back so soon anyway.

"You back in here already? Look like I just got rid of you."

"I'm tired of seeing your face. Really tired."

"I knew it. Soon's I get two dimes back to back, here you come. More regular than the reaper. Do Hoover[6] know about you?"

They kidded him, abused him, told their children to tell him they were out sick or gone to Pittsburgh. But they held on to those little yellow cards as though they meant something—laid them gently in the shoe box along with the rent receipts, marriage licenses, and expired factory identification badges. Mr. Smith smiled through it all, managing to keep his eyes focused almost the whole time on his

---

[6] J. Edgar Hoover (1895–1972), director of the FBI from 1924 to 1972.

customers' feet. He wore a business suit for his work, but his house was not better than theirs. He never had a woman that any of them knew about and said nothing in church but an occasional "Amen." He never beat anybody up and he wasn't seen after dark, so they thought he was probably a nice man. But he was heavily associated with illness and death, neither of which was distinguishable from the brown picture of the North Carolina Mutual Life Building on the back of their yellow cards. Jumping from the roof on Mercy was the most interesting thing he had done. None of them had suspected he had it in him. Just goes to show, they murmured to each other, you never really do know about people.

The singing woman quieted down and, humming the tune, walked through the crowd toward the rose-petal lady, who was still cradling her stomach.

"You should make yourself warm," she whispered to her, touching her lightly on the elbow. "A little bird'll be here with the morning."

"Oh?" said the rose-petal lady. "Tomorrow morning?"

"That's the only morning coming."

"It can't be," the rose-petal lady said. "It's too soon."

"No it ain't. Right on time."

The women were looking deep into each other's eyes when a loud roar went up from the crowd—a kind of wavy *oo* sound. Mr. Smith had lost his balance for a second, and was trying gallantly to hold on to a triangle of wood that jutted from the cupola. Immediately the singing woman began again:

> O Sugarman done fly
> O Sugarman done gone . . .

Downtown the firemen pulled on their greatcoats, but when they arrived at Mercy, Mr. Smith had seen the rose petals, heard the music, and leaped on into the air.

The next day a colored baby was born inside Mercy for the first time. Mr. Smith's blue silk wings must have left their mark, because when the little boy discovered, at four, the same thing Mr. Smith had learned earlier—that only birds and airplanes could fly—he lost all interest in himself. To have to live without that single gift saddened him and left his imagination so bereft that he appeared dull even to the women who did not hate his mother. The ones who did, who accepted her invitations to tea and envied the doctor's big dark house of twelve rooms and the green sedan, called him "peculiar." The others, who knew that the house was more prison than palace, and that the Dodge sedan was for Sunday drives only, felt sorry for Ruth Foster and her dry daughters, and called her son "deep." Even mysterious.

"Did he come with a caul?"

"You should have dried it and made him some tea from it to drink. If you don't he'll see ghosts."

"You believe that?"

"I don't, but that's what the old people say."

"Well, he's a deep one anyway. Look at his eyes."

And they pried pieces of baked-too-fast sunshine cake from the roofs of their mouths and looked once more into the boy's eyes. He met their gaze as best he could until, after a pleading glance toward his mother, he was allowed to leave the room.

It took some planning to walk out of the parlor, his back washed with the hum of their voices, open the heavy double doors leading to the dining room, slip up the stairs past all those bedrooms, and not arouse the attention of Lena and Corinthians sitting like big baby dolls before a table heaped with scraps of red velvet. His sisters made roses in the afternoon. Bright, lifeless roses that lay in peck baskets for months until the specialty buyer at Gerhardt's sent Freddie the janitor over to tell the girls that they could use another gross. If he did manage to slip by his sisters and avoid their casual malice, he knelt in his room at the window sill and wondered again and again why he had to stay level on the ground. The quiet that suffused the doctor's house then, broken only by the murmur of the women eating sunshine cake, was only that: quiet. It was not peaceful, for it was preceded by and would soon be termintaed by the presence of Macon Dead.

Solid, rumbling, likely to erupt without prior notice, Macon kept each member of his family awkward with fear. His hatred of his wife glittered and sparked in every word he spoke to her. The disappointment he felt in his daughters sifted down on them like ash, dulling their buttery complexions and choking the lilt out of what should have been girlish voices. Under the frozen heat of his glance they tripped over doorsills and dropped the salt cellar into the yolks of their poached eggs. The way he mangled their grace, wit, and self-esteem was the single excitement of their days. Without the tension and drama he ignited, they might not have known what to do with themselves. In his absence his daughters bent their necks over blood-red squares of velvet and waited eagerly for any hint of him, and his wife, Ruth, began her days stunned into stillness by her husband's contempt and ended them wholly animated by it.

When she closed the door behind her afternoon guests, and let the quiet smile die from her lips, she began the preparation of food her husband found impossible to eat. She did not try to make her meals nauseating; she simply didn't know how not to. She would notice that the sunshine cake was too haggled to put before him and decide on a rennet[7] dessert. But the grinding of the veal and beef for a meat loaf took so long she not only forgot the pork, settling for bacon drippings poured over the meat, she had no time to make a dessert at all. Hurriedly, then, she began to set the table. As she unfolded the white linen and let it billow over the fine mahogany table, she would look once more at the large water mark. She never set the table or passed through the dining room without looking at it. Like a lighthouse keeper drawn to his window to gaze once again at the sea, or a prisoner automatically searching out the sun as he steps into the yard for his hour of exercise, Ruth looked for the water mark several times during the day. She knew it was there, would always be there, but she needed to confirm its presence. Like the keeper of the lighthouse and the prisoner, she regarded it as a mooring, a checkpoint, some stable visual object that assured her that the world was still there; that this was life and not a dream. That she was alive somewhere, inside, which she acknowledged to be true only because a thing she knew intimately was out there, outside herself.

Even in the cave of sleep, without dreaming of it or thinking of it all, she felt its presence. Oh, she talked endlessly to her daughters and her guests about how to get rid of it—what might hide this single flaw on the splendid wood: Vaseline, tobacco juice, iodine, sanding followed by linseed oil. She had tried them all. But her glance was nutritious; the spot became, if anything, more pronounced as the years passed.

---

[7] A junket, or custardlike dessert made from curdled milk.

The cloudy gray circle identified the place where the bowl filled every day during the doctor's life with fresh flowers had stood. Every day. And when there were no flowers, it held a leaf arrangement, a gathering of twigs, and berries, pussy willow, Scotch pine. . . . But always something to grace the dinner table in the evening.

It was for her father a touch that distinguished his own family from the people among whom they lived. For Ruth it was the summation of the affectionate elegance with which she believed her childhood had been surrounded. When Macon married her and moved into Doctor's house, she kept up the centerpiece-arranging. Then came the time she walked down to the shore through the roughest part of the city to get some driftwood. She had seen an arrangement of driftwood and dried seaweed in the homemakers section of the newspaper. It was a damp November day, and Doctor was paralyzed even then and taking liquid food in his bedroom. The wind had lifted her skirt from around her ankles and cut through her laced shoes. She'd had to rub her feet down with warm olive oil when she got back. At dinner, where just the two of them sat, she turned toward her husband and asked him how he liked the centerpiece. "Most people overlook things like that. They see it, but they don't see anything beautiful in it. They don't see that nature has already made it as perfect as it can be. Look at it from the side. It is pretty, isn't it?"

Her husband looked at the driftwood with its lacy beige seaweed, and without moving his head, said, "Your chicken is red at the bone. And there is probably a potato dish that is supposed to have lumps in it. Mashed ain't the dish."

Ruth let the seaweed disintegrate, and later, when its veins and stems dropped and curled into brown scabs on the table, she removed the bowl and brushed away the scabs. But the water mark, hidden by the bowl all these years, was exposed. And once exposed, it behaved as though it were itself a plant and flourished into a huge suede-gray flower that throbbed like fever, and sighed like the shift of sand dunes. But it could also be still. Patient, restful, and still.

But there was nothing you could do with a mooring—except acknowledge it, use it for the verification of some idea you wanted to keep alive. Something else is needed to get from sunup to sundown: a balm, a gentle touch or nuzzling of some sort. So Ruth rose up and out of her guileless inefficiency to claim her bit of balm right after the preparation of dinner and just before the return of her husband from his office. It was one of her two secret indulgences—the one that involved her son—and part of the pleasure it gave her came from the room in which she did it. A damp greenness lived there, made by the evergreen that pressed against the window and filtered the light. It was just a little room that Doctor had called a study, and aside from a sewing machine that stood in the corner along with a dress form, there was only a rocker and tiny footstool. She sat in this room holding her son on her lap, staring at his closed eyelids and listening to the sound of his sucking. Staring not so much from maternal joy as from a wish to avoid seeing his legs dangling almost to the floor.

In late afternoon, before her husband closed his office and came home, she called her son to her. When he came into the little room she unbuttoned her blouse and smiled. He was too young to be dazzled by her nipples, but he was old enough to be bored by the flat taste of mother's milk, so he came reluctantly, as to a chore, and lay as he had at least once each day of his life in his mother's arms, and tried to pull the thin faintly sweet milk from her flesh without hurting her with his teeth.

She felt him. His restraint, his courtesy, his indifference, all of which pushed her into fantasy. She had the distinct impression that his lips were pulling from her a thread of light. It was though she were a cauldron issuing spinning gold. Like the miller's daughter—the one who sat at night in a straw-filled room, thrilled with the secret power Rumpelstiltskin had given her: to see golden thread stream from her very own shuttle. And that was the other part of her pleasure, a pleasure she hated to give up. So when Freddie the janitor, who liked to pretend he was a friend of the family and not just their flunky as well as their tenant, brought his rent to the doctor's house late one day and looked in the window past the evergreen, the terror sprang to Ruth's eyes came from the quick realization that she was to lose fully half of what made her daily life bearable. Freddie, however, interpreted her look as simple shame, but that didn't stop him from grinning.

"Have mercy. I be damn."

He fought the evergreen for a better look, hampered more by his laughter than by the branches. Ruth jumped up as quickly as she could and covered her breast, dropping her son on the floor and confirming for him what he had begun to suspect—that these afternoons were strange and wrong.

Before either mother or son could speak, rearrange themselves properly, or even exchange looks, Freddie had run around the house, climbed the porch steps, and was calling them between gulps of laughter.

"Miss Rufie. Miss Rufie. Where you? Where you all at?" He opened the door to the green room as though it were his now.

"I be damn, Miss Rufie. When the last time I seen that? I don't even know the last time I seen that. I mean, ain't nothing wrong with it. I mean, old folks swear by it. It's just, you know, you don't see it up here much. . . . " But his eyes were on the boy. Appreciative eyes that communicated some complicity she was excluded from. Freddie looked the boy up and down, taking in the steady but secretive eyes and the startling contrast between Ruth's lemony skin and the boy's black skin. "Used to be a lot of womenfolk nurse they kids a long time down South. Lot of 'em. But you don't see it much no more. I knew a family—the mother wasn't too quick, though—nursed hers till the boy, I reckon, was near 'bout thirteen. But that's a bit much, ain't it?" All the time he chattered, he rubbed his chin and looked at the boy. Finally he stopped, and gave a long low chuckle. He'd found the phrase he'd been searching for. "A milkman. That's what you got here, Miss Rufie. A natural milkman if ever I seen one. Look out, womens. Here he come. Huh!"

Freddie carried his discovery not only into the homes of Ruth's neighborhood, but to Southside, where he lived and where Macon Dead owned rent houses. So Ruth kept close to home and had no afternoon guests for the better part of two months, to keep from hearing that her son had been rechristened with a name he was never able to shake and that did nothing to improve either one's relationship with his father.

Macon Dead never knew how it came about—how his only son acquired the nickname that stuck in spite of his own refusal to use it or acknowledge it. It was a matter that concerned him a good deal, for the giving of names in his family was always surrounded by what he believed to be monumental foolishness. No one mentioned to him the incident out of which the nickname grew because he was a difficult man to approach—a hard man, with a manner so cool it discouraged casual or spontaneous conversation. Only Freddie the janitor took liberties with

Macon Dead, liberties he purchased with the services he rendered, and Freddie was the last person on earth to tell him. So Macon Dead neither heard of nor visualized Ruth's sudden terror, her awkward jump from the rocking chair, the boy's fall broken by the tiny footstool, or Freddie's amused, admiring summation of the situation.

Without knowing any of the details, however, he guessed, with the accuracy of a mind sharpened by hatred, that the name he heard schoolchildren call his son, the name he overheard the ragman use when he paid the boy three cents for a bundle of old clothes—he guessed that this name was not clean. Milkman. It certainly didn't sound like the honest job of a dairyman, or bring to his mind cold bright cans standing on the back porch, glittering like captains on guard. It sounded dirty, intimate, and hot. He knew that wherever the name came from, it had something to do with his wife and was, like the emotion he always felt when thinking of her, coated with disgust.

This disgust and the uneasiness with which he regarded his son affected everything he did in that city. If he could have felt sad, simply sad, it would have relieved him. Fifteen years of regret at not having a son had become the bitterness of finally having one in the most revolting circumstances.

There had been a time when he had a head full of hair and when Ruth wore lovely complicated underwear that deliberately took a long time to undo. When all of his foreplay was untying, unclasping, unbuckling the snaps and strings of what must have been the most beautiful, the most delicate, the whitest and softest underwear on earth. Each eye of her corset he toyed with (and there were forty—twenty on each side); each grosgrain ribbon that threaded its pale-blue way through the snowy top of her bodice he unlaced. He not only undid the blue bow; he pulled it all the way out of the hem, so she had to rethread it afterward with a safety pin. The elastic bands that connected her perspiration shields to her slip he unsnapped and snapped again, teasing her and himself with the sound of the snaps and the thrill of his fingertips on her shoulders. They never spoke during these undressings. But they giggled occasionally, and as when children play "doctor," undresssing of course was the best part.

When Ruth was naked and lying there moist and crumbly as unbleached sugar, he bent to unlace her shoes. That was the final delight, for once he had undressed her feet, he peeled her stockings down over her ankles and toes, he entered her and ejaculated quickly. She liked it that way. So did he. And in almost twenty years during which he had not laid eyes on her naked feet, he missed only the underwear.

Once he believed that the sight of her mouth on the dead man's fingers would be the thing he would remember always. He was wrong. Little by little he remembered fewer and fewer of the details, until finally he had to imagine them, even fabricate them, guess what they must have been. The image left him, but the odiousness never did. For the nourishment of his outrage he depended on the memory of her underwear; those round, innocent corset eyes now lost to him forever.

So if the people were calling his son Milkman, and if she was lowering her eyelids and dabbing at the sweat on her top lip when she heard it, there was definitely some filthy connection and it did not matter at all to Macon Dead whether anyone gave him the details or not.

And they didn't. Nobody dared enough and cared enough to tell him. The ones who cared enough, Lena and Corinthians, the living proof of those years of undressing his wife, did not dare. And the one person who dared to but didn't care to was the one person in the world he hated more than his wife in spite of the fact that she was his sister. He had not crossed the tracks to see her since his son was born and he had no intention of renewing their relationship now.

Macon Dead dug in his pocket for his keys, and curled his fingers around them, letting their bunchy solidity calm him. They were the keys to all the doors of his houses (only four true houses; the rest were really shacks), and he fondled them from time to time as he walked down Not Doctor Street to his office. At least he thought of it as his office, had even painted the word OFFICE on the door. But the plate-glass window contradicted him. In peeling gold letters arranged in a semicircle, his business establishment was declared to be Sonny's Shop. Scraping the previous owner's name off was hardly worth the trouble since he couldn't scrape it from anybody's mind. His storefront office was never called anything but Sonny's Shop, although nobody now could remember thirty years back, when, presumably, Sonny did something or other there.

He walked there now—strutted is the better word, for he had a high behind and an athlete's stride—thinking of names. Surely, he thought, he and his sister had some ancestor, some lithe young man with onyx skin and legs as straight as cane stalks, who had a name that was real. A name given to him at birth with love and seriousness. A name that was not a joke, nor a disguise, nor a brand name. But who this lithe young man was, and where his cane-stalk legs carried him from or to, could never be known. No. Nor his name. His own parents, in some mood of perverseness of resignation, had agreed to abide by a naming done to them by somebody who couldn't have cared less. Agreed to take and pass on to all their issue this heavy name scrawled in perfect thoughtlessness by a drunken Yankee in the Union Army. A literal slip of the pen handed to his father on a piece of paper and which he handed on to his only son, and his son likewise handed on to his; Macon Dead who begat a second Macon Dead who married Ruth Foster (Dead) and begat Magdalene called Lena Dead and First Corinthians Dead and (when he least expected it) another Macon Dead, now known to the part of the world that mattered as Milkman Dead. And as if that were not enough, a sister named Pilate Dead, who would never mention to her brother the circumstances of the details of this foolish misnaming of his son because the whole thing would have delighted her. She would savor it, maybe fold it too in a brass box and hang it from her other ear.

He had cooperated as a young father with the blind selection of names from the Bible for every child other than the first male. And abided by whatever the finger pointed to, for he knew every configuration of the naming of his sister. How his father, confused and melancholy over his wife's death in childbirth, had thumbed through the Bible, and since he could not read a word, chose a group of letters that seemed to him strong and handsome; saw in them a large figure that looked like a tree hanging in some princely but protective way over a row of smaller trees. How he had copied the group of letters out on a piece of brown paper; copied, as illiterate people do, every curlicue, arch, and bend in the letters, and presented it to the midwife.

"That's the baby's name."

"You want this for the baby's name?"

"I want that for the baby's name. Say it."

"You can't name the baby this."

"Say it."

"It's a man's name."

"Say it."

"Pilate."

"What?"

"Pilate. You wrote down Pilate."

"Like a riverboat pilot?"

"No. Not like no riverboat pilot. Like a Christ-killing Pilate.[8] You can't get much worse than that for a name. And a baby girl at that."

"That's where my finger went down at."

"Well, your brain ain't got to follow it. You don't want to give this motherless child the name of the man that killed Jesus, do you?"

"I asked Jesus to save my wife."

"Careful, Macon."

"I asked him all night long."

"He give you your baby."

"Yes. He did. Baby name Pilate."

"Jesus, have mercy."

"Where you going with that piece of paper?"

"It's going back where it came from. Right in the Devil's flames."

"Give it here. It come from the Bible. It stays in the Bible."

And it did stay there, until the baby girl turned twelve and took it out, folded it up into a tiny knot and put it in a little brass box, and strung the entire contraption through her left earlobe. Fluky about her own name at twelve, how much more fluky she'd become since then Macon could only guess. But he knew for certain that she would treat the naming of the third Macon Dead with the same respect and awe she had treated the boy's birth.

Macon Dead remembered when his son was born, how she seemed to be more interested in this first nephew of hers than she was in her own daughter, and even that daughter's daughter. Long after Ruth was up and about, as capable as she ever would be—and that wasn't much—of running the house again, Pilate continued to visit, her shoelaces undone, a knitted cap pulled down over her forehead, bringing her foolish earring and sickening smell into the kitchen. He had not seen her since he was sixteen years old, until a year before the birth of his son, when she appeared in his city. Now she was acting like an in-law, like an aunt, dabbling at helping Ruth and the girls, but having no interest in or knowledge of decent housekeeping, she got in the way. Finally she just sat in a chair near the crib, singing to the baby. That wasn't so bad, but what Macon Dead remembered most was the expression on her face. Surprise, it looked like, and eagerness. But so intense it made him uneasy. Or perhaps it was more than that. Perhaps it was seeing her all those years after they had separated outside that cave, and remembering his anger and her betrayal. How far down she had slid since then. She had cut the last thread of propriety. At one time she had been the dearest thing in the world to him. Now she was odd, murky, and worst of all, unkempt. A regular source of embarrassment, if he would allow it. But he would not allow it.

Finally he had told her not to come again until she could show some respect for herself. Could get a real job instead of running a wine house.

---

[8] Pontius Pilate (1st century A. D.), the Roman official who tried Jesus and condemned him to crucifixion.

"Why can't you dress like a woman?" He was standing by the stove. "What's that sailor's cap doing on your head? Don't you have stockings? What are you trying to make me look like in this town?" He trembled with the thought of the white men in the bank—the men who helped him buy and mortgage houses—discovering that this raggedy bootlegger was his sister. That the propertied Negro who handled his business so well and who lived in the big house on Not Doctor Street had a sister who had a daughter but no husband, and that daughter had a daughter but no husband. A collection of lunatics who made wine and sang in the streets "like common street women! Just like common street women!"

Pilate had sat there listening to him, her wondering eyes resting on his face. Then she said, "I been worried sick about you too, Macon."

Exasperated, he had gone to the kitchen door. "Go 'head, Pilate. Go on now. I'm on the thin side of evil and trying not to break through."

Pilate stood up, wrapped her quilt around her, and with a last fond look at the baby, left through the kitchen door. She never came back.

When Macon Dead got to the front door of his office he saw a stout woman and two young boys standing a few feet away. Macon unlocked his door, walked over to his desk, and settled himself behind it. As he was thumbing through his accounts book, the stout woman entered, alone.

"Afternoon Mr. Dead, sir. I'm Mrs. Bains. Live over at number three on Fifteenth Street."

Macon Dead remembered—not the woman, but the circumstances at number three. His tenant's grandmother or aunt or something had moved in there and the rent was long overdue.

"Yes, Mrs. Bains, You got something for me?"

"Well, that's what I come to talk to you about. You know Cency left all them babies with me. And my relief check ain't no more'n it take to keep a well-grown yard dog alive—half alive, I should say."

"Your rent is four dollars a month, Mrs. Bains. You two months behind already."

"I do know that, Mr. Dead, sir, but babies can't make it with nothing to put in they stomach."

Their voices were low, polite, without any hint of conflict.

"Can they make it in the street, Mrs. Bains? That's where they gonna be if you don't figure out some way to get me my money."

"No sir. They can't make it in the street. We need both, I reckon. Same as yours does."

"Then you better rustle it up, Mrs. Bains. You got till"—he swiveled around to consult the calendar on the wall—"till Saturday coming. Saturday, Mrs. Bains. Not Sunday. Not Monday. Saturday."

If she had been younger and had more juice, the glitter in her eyes would have washed down onto her cheeks. Now, at her time of life, it simply gleamed. She pressed the flat of her hand on Macon Dead's desk and, holding the gleam steady in her eyes, pushed herself up from the chair. She turned her head a little to look out the plate-glass window; and then back at him.

"What's it gonna profit you, Mr. Dead, sir, to put me and them children out?"

"Saturday, Mrs. Bains."

Lowering her head, Mrs. Bains whispered something and walked slowly and heavily from the office. As she closed the door to Sonny's Shop, her grandchildren moved out of the sunlight into the shadow where she stood.

"What he say, Granny?"

Mrs. Bains put a hand on the taller boy's hair and fingered it lightly, absently searching with her nails for tetter spots.[9]

"He must've told her no," said the other boy.

"Do we got to move?" The tall boy tossed his head free of her fingers and looked at her sideways. His cat eyes were gashes of gold.

Mrs. Bains let her hand fall to her side. "A nigger in business is a terrible thing to see. A terrible, terrible thing to see."

The boys looked at each other and back at their grandmother. Their lips were parted as though they had heard something important.

When Mrs. Bains closed the door, Macon Dead went back to the pages of his accounts book, running his fingertips over the figures and thinking with the unoccupied part of his mind about the first time he called on Ruth Foster's father. He had only two keys in his pocket then, and if he had let people like the woman who just left have their way, he wouldn't have had any keys at all. It was because of those keys that he could dare walk over to that part of Not Doctor Street (it was still Doctor Street then) and approach the most important Negro in the city. To lift the lion's paw knocker, to entertain thoughts of marrying the doctor's daughter was possible because each key represented a house which he owned at the time. Without those keys he would have floated away at the doctor's first word: "Yes?" Or he would have melted like new wax under the heat of that pale eye. Instead he was able to say that he had been introduced to his daughter, Miss Ruth Foster, and would appreciate having the doctor's permission to keep her company now and then. That his intentions were honorable and that he himself was certainly worthy of the doctor's consideration as a gentleman friend for Miss Foster since, at twenty-five, he was already a colored man of property.

"I don't know anything about you," the doctor said, "other than your name, which I don't like, but I will abide by my daughter's preference."

In fact the doctor knew a good deal about him and was more grateful to this tall young man than he ever allowed himself to show. Fond as he was of his only child, useful as she was in his house since his wife had died, lately he had begun to chafe under her devotion. Her steady beam of love was unsettling, and she had never dropped those expressions of affection that had been so lovable in her childhood. The good-night kiss was itself a masterpiece of slow-wittedness on her part and discomfort on his. At sixteen, she still insisted on having him come to her at night, sit on her bed, exchange a few pleasantries, and plant a kiss on her lips. Perhaps it was the loud silence of his dead wife, perhaps it was Ruth's disturbing resemblance to her mother. More probably it was the ecstasy that always seemed to be shining in Ruth's face when he bent to kiss her—an ecstasy he felt inappropriate to the occasion.

None of that, of course, did he describe to the young man who came to call. Which is why Macon Dead still believed the magic had lain in the two keys.

In the middle of his reverie, Macon was interrupted by rapid tapping on the window. He looked up, saw Freddie peeping through the gold lettering, and nodded for him to enter. A gold-toothed bantamweight, Freddie was as much of a town crier as Southside had. It was this same rapid tapping on the windowpane,

---

[9] Evidence of a skin disease such as eczema.

the same flash-of-gold smile that had preceded his now-famous scream to Macon: "Mr. Smith went splat!" It was obvious to Macon that Freddie now had news of another calamity.

"Porter gone crazy drunk again! Got his shotgun!"

"Who's he out for?" Macon began closing books and opening desk drawers. Porter was a tenant and tomorrow was collection day.

"Ain't out for nobody in particular. Just perched himself up in the attic window and commenced to waving a shotgun. Say he gotta kill him somebody before morning."

"He go to work today?"

"Yep. Caught the eagle too."

"Drunk it all up?"

"Not all of it. He only got one bottle, and he still got a fist fulla money."

"Who's crazy enough to sell him any liquor?"

Freddie showed a few gold teeth but said nothing, so Macon knew it was Pilate. He locked all his drawers save one—the one he unlocked and took a small .32 from.

"Police warn every bootlegger in the county, and he still gets it somehow." Macon went on with the charade, pretending he didn't know his sister was the one Porter and anybody else—adult, child, or beast—could buy wine from. He thought for the hundredth time that she needed to be in jail and that he would be willing to put her there if he could be sure she wouldn't loudmouth him and make him seem trashy in the eyes of the law—and the banks.

"You know how to use that thing, Mr. Dead, sir?"

"I know how."

"Porter's crazy when he drunk."

"I know what he is."

"How you aiming to get him down?"

"I ain't aiming to get him down. I'm aiming to get my money down. He can go on and die up there if he wants to. But if he don't toss me my rent, I'm going to blow him out of that window."

Freddie's giggle was soft, but his teeth strengthened its impact. A born flunky, he loved gossip and the telling of it. He was the ear that heard every murmur of complaint, every namecalling; and his was the eye that saw everything: the secret loving glances, the fights, the new dresses.

Macon knew Freddie as a fool and a liar, but a reliable liar. He was always right about his facts and always wrong about the motives that produced the facts. Just as now he was right about Porter having a shotgun, being in the attic window, and being drunk. But Porter was not waiting to kill somebody, meaning anybody, before morning. In fact he was very specific about whom he wanted to kill—himself. However, he did have a precondition which he shouted down, loud and clear, from the attic. "I want to fuck! Send me up somebody to fuck! Hear me? Send me up somebody, I tell ya, or I'ma blow my brains out!"

As Macon and Freddie approached the yard, the women from the rooming house were hollering answers to Porter's plea.

"What kinda bargain is that?"

"Kill yourself first and then we'll send you somebody."

"Do it have to be a woman?"

"Do it got to be human?"

"Do it got to be alive?"

"Can it be a piece of liver?"

"Put that thing down and throw me my goddam money!" Macon's voice cut through the women's fun. "Float those dollars down here, nigger, then blow yourself up!"

Porter turned and aimed his shotgun at Macon.

"If you pull that trigger," shouted Macon, "you better not miss. If you take a shot you better make sure I'm dead, cause if you don't I'm gonna shoot your balls up in your throat!" He pulled out his own weapon. "Now get the hell outta that window!"

Porter hesistated for only a second, before turning the barrel of the shotgun toward himself—or trying to. Its length made it difficult; his drunkenness made it impossible. Struggling to get the right angle, he was suddenly distracted. He leaned his shotgun on the window sill, pulled out his penis and in a high arc, peed over the heads of the women, making them scream and run in a panic that the shotgun had not been able to create. Macon rubbed the back of his head while Freddie bent double with laughter.

For more than an hour Porter held them at bay: cowering, screaming, threatening, urinating, and interspersing all of it with pleas for a woman.

He would cry great shoulder-heaving sobs, followed by more screams.

"I love ya! I love ya all. Don't act like that. You women. Stop it. Don't act like that. Don't you see I love ya? I'd die for ya, kill for ya. I'm saying I love ya. I'm telling ya. Oh, God have mercy. What I'm gonna do? What in this fuckin world am I gonna dooooo?"

Tears streamed down his face and he cradled the barrel of the shotgun in his arms as though it were the woman he had been begging for, searching for, all his life. "Gimme hate, Lord," he whimpered. "I'll take hate any day. But don't give me love. I can't take no more love, Lord. I can't carry it. Just like Mr. Smith. He couldn't carry it. It's too heavy. Jesus, *you* know. You know all about it. Ain't it heavy? Jesus? Ain't love heavy? Don't you see, Lord? You own son couldn't carry it. If it killed Him, what You think it's gonna do to me? Huh? Huh?" He was getting angry again.

"Come down outta there, nigger!" Macon's voice was still loud, but it was getting weary.

"An you, you baby-dicked baboon"—he tried to point at Macon—"you the worst. You need killin, you really *need* killin. You know why? Well, I'm gonna tell you why. I *know* why. Everybody . . . "

Porter slumped down in the window, muttering, "Everybody know why," and fell fast asleep. As he sank deeper into it, the shotgun slipped from his hand, rattled down the roof, and hit the ground with a loud explosion. The shot zipped past a by-stander's shoe and blew a hole in the tire of a stripped Dodge parked in the road.

"Go get my money," Macon said.

"Me?" Freddie asked. "Suppose he . . . "

"Go get me my money."

Porter was snoring. Through the blast of the gun and the picking of his pocket he slept like a baby.

When Macon walked out of the yard, the sun had disappeared behind the bread company. Tired, irritable, he walked down Fifteenth Street, glancing up as he passed one of his other houses, its silhouette melting in the light that trembled between dusk and twilight. Scattered here and there, his houses stretched up beyond him like squat ghosts with hooded eyes. He didn't like to look at them in this light. During the day they were reassuring to see; now they did not seem to belong to him at all—in fact he felt as though the houses were in league with one another to make him feel like the outsider, the propertyless, landless wanderer. It was this feeling of loneliness that made him decide to take a shortcut back to Not Doctor Street, even though to do so would lead him past his sister's house. In the gathering darkness, he was sure his passing would be unnoticed by her. He crossed a yard and followed a fence that led into Darling Street where Pilate lived in a narrow single-story house whose basement seemed to be rising from rather than settling into the ground. She had no electricity because she would not pay for the service. Nor for gas. At night she and her daughter lit the house with candles and kerosene lamps; they warmed themselves and cooked with wood and coal, pumped kitchen water into a dry sink through a pipeline from a well and lived pretty much as though progress was a word that meant walking a little farther on down the road.

Her house sat eighty feet from the sidewalk and was backed by four huge pine trees, from which she got the needles she stuck into her mattress. Seeing the pine trees started him thinking about her mouth; how she loved, as a girl, to chew pine needles and as a result smelled even then like a forest. For a dozen years she had been like his own child. After their mother died, she had come struggling out of the womb without help from throbbing muscles or the pressure of swift womb water. As a result, for all the years he knew her, her stomach was as smooth and sturdy as her back, at no place interrupted by a navel. It was the absence of a navel that convinced people that she had not come into this world through normal channels; had never lain, floated, or grown in some warn and liquid place connected by a tissue-thin tube to a reliable source of human nourishment. Macon knew otherwise, because he was there and had seen the eyes of the midwife as his mother's legs collapsed. And heard as well her shouts when the baby, who they had believed was dead also, inched its way headfirst out of a still, silent, and indifferent cave of flesh, dragging her own cord and her own afterbirth behind her. But the rest was true. Once the new baby's lifeline was cut, the cord stump shriveled, fell off, and left no trace of having ever existed, which, as a young boy taking care of his baby sister, he thought no more strange than a bald head. He was seventeen years old, irreparably separated from her and already pressing forward in his drive for wealth, when he learned that there was probably not another stomach like hers on earth.

Now, nearing her yard, he trusted that the dark would keep anyone in her house from seeing him. He did not even look to his left as he walked by it. But then he heard the music. They were singing. All of them. Pilate, Reba, and Reba's daughter, Hagar. There was no one on the street that he could see; people were at supper, licking their fingers, blowing into saucers of coffee, and no doubt chattering about Porter's escapade and Macon's fearless confrontation of the wild man in the attic. There were no street lights in this part of town; only the moon directed the way of a pedestrian. Macon walked on, resisting as best he could the sound of the voices that followed him. He was rapidly approaching a part of the road where the music could not follow, when he saw, like a scene on the back of a postcard, a picture of where he was headed—his own home; his wife's narrow unyielding back; his daughters, boiled dry from years of yearning; his son, to whom he could speak only if his words held some command or—criticism. "Hello, Daddy." "Hello, son, tuck your shirt in." "I found a dead bird, Daddy." "Don't bring that mess in this house. . . . " There was no music there, and tonight he wanted just a bit of music—from the person who had been his first caring for.

He turned back and walked slowly toward Pilate's house. They were singing some melody that Pilate was leading. A phrase that the other two were taking up and building on. Her powerful contralto, Reba's piercing soprano in counterpoint, and the soft voice of the girl, Hagar, who must be about ten or eleven now, pulled him like a carpet tack under the influence of a magnet.

Surrendering to the sound, Macon moved closer. He wanted no conversation, no witness, only to listen and perhaps to see the three of them, the source of that music that made him think of fields and wild turkey and calico. Treading as lightly as he could, he crept up to the side window where the candlelight flickered lowest, and peeped in. Reba was cutting her toenails with a kitchen knife or a switchblade, her long neck bent almost to her knees. The girl, Hagar, was braiding her hair, while Pilate, whose face he could not see because her back was to the window, was stirring something in a pot. Wine pulp, perhaps. Macon knew it was not food she was stirring, for she and her daughters ate like children. Whatever they had a taste for. No meal was ever planned or balanced or served. Nor was there any gathering at the table. Pilate might bake hot bread and each one of them would eat it with butter whenever she felt like it. Or there might be grapes, left over from the winemaking, or peaches for days on end. If one of them bought a gallon of milk they drank it until it was gone. If another got a half bushel of tomatoes or a dozen ears of corn, they ate them until they were gone too. They ate what they had or came across or had a craving for. Profits from their wine-selling evaporated like sea water in a hot wind—going for junk jewelry for Hagar, Reba's gifts to men, and he didn't know what all.

Near the window, hidden by the dark, he felt the irritability of the day drain from him and relished the effortless beauty of the women singing in the candlelight. Reba's soft profile, Hagar's hands moving, moving in her heavy hair, and Pilate. He knew her face better than he knew his own. Singing now, her face would be a mask; all emotion and passion would have left her features and entered her voice. But he knew that when she was neither singing nor talking, her face was animated by her constantly moving lips. She chewed things. As a baby, as a very young girl, she kept things in her mouth—straw from brooms, gristle, buttons, seeds, leaves, string, and her favorite, when he could find some for her, rubber bands and India rubber erasers. Her lips were alive with small movements. If you were close to her, you wondered if she was about to smile or was she merely shifting a straw from the baseline of her gums to her tongue. Perhaps she was dislodging a curl of rubber band from inside her cheek, or was she really smiling? From a distance she appeared to be whispering to herself, when she was only nibbling or splitting tiny seeds with her front teeth. Her lips were darker than her skin, wine-stained, blueberry-dyed, so her face had a cosmetic look—as though she had applied a very dark lipstick neatly and blotted away its shine on a scrap of newspaper.

As Macon felt himself softening under the weight of memory and music, the song died down. The air was quiet and yet Macon Dead could not leave. He liked looking at them freely this way. They didn't move. They simply stopped singing and Reba went on paring her toenails, Hagar threaded and unthreaded her hair, and Pilate swayed like a willow over her stirring.

1977

John Updike
(1932–   )

In a 1973 interview with Wilford Sheed, John Updike joked that his "true and passionate ambition . . . was to be a cartoonist, first for Walt Disney, then for the syndicates, lastly for the *New Yorker*. What I have become is a sorry shadow of those high hopes." What Updike has in fact become one of the premier men of letters in America today. He has won a Guggenheim Fellowship and the Rosenthal Award of the National Institute of Arts and Letters in 1959, the National Book Award for fiction in 1964, and the O. Henry Prize in 1967 and 1968. In 1981 he was awarded a Pulitzer Prize, the National Book Critics' Circle Award, and an American Book Award for his novel *Rabbit Is Rich*. Born in 1932 in Reading, Pennsylvania, and raised nearby in the small town of Shillington, Updike graduated summa cum laude from Harvard University in 1954. While at Harvard he majored in English and honed his skillful caricatures into characterizations as a contributor and editor of the *Harvard Lampoon*. After graduating he studied at the Ruskin School of Drawing and Fine Art in Oxford, England, and joined the *New Yorker* staff upon returning to New York in 1955. Much of Updike's early fame was the result of the stories he had written for the *New Yorker* and later collected in *The Same Door* (1959) and *Pigeon Feathers* (1962), including his "Olinger" stories about small-town life in Pennsylvania.

Like his contemporary John Cheever, Updike chronicles the behavior of New York and New England suburbia and life among the small-town folk of his boyhood home. But Updike has always scrutinized the effects of secular materialism, with an eye toward contemporary religious thought. An early advocate of the theologians Karl Barth and Reinhold Neibuhr, Updike has also been influenced by the more liberal theology of Paul Tillich, with whom he shares a belief in the spiritual having a counterpart in the material world. As a result, Updike's fiction searches the waste and sterility of modern society for those moments of spiritual fulfillment that it affords, documenting along the way the morals and manners of middle America from the 1960s to the 1980s. Two characters in particular—Harry "Rabbit" Angstrom and Henry Bech—have stayed with Updike in this search, serving as fictional alter egos who reflect the bewildering changes from the empty material security of the 1950s to the social upheaval and material exhaustion of the 1970s.

Rabbit, Run (1960), *Rabbit Redux* (1971), *Rabbit Is Rich* (1981), and *Rabbit at Rest* (1990) each capture the feelings of a decade as Rabbit chases the American dream, only to find it fade at the onslaught of middle age and beyond and the growing youth rebellion. At home more in his nostalgic reminiscences of his high school basketball career, Rabbit ultimately trades in spiritual transcedence for a Caribbean vacation and a successful Toyota dealership. Bech is Updike's parody of the successful American writer, more famous for being famous than he is for producing great works. First Appearing in *Bech: A Book* (1970), Bech is the recipient of the "Melville Award" in *Bech Is Back* (1982), an award given "every five years to that American author who has maintained the most meaningful silence." Suffering from writer's block and disgusted with the hucksterism that surrounds modern writing, Bech gives in to the call for fame, changing the title of his work in progress from "Think Big" to "Easy Money." Updike once published fictional interviews between Bech and himself in the *New York Times*. The wry distance that Updike maintains between his own fictional temptations and the surety of his ever-growing craft perhaps best sums up his own lasting spiritual faith amid the confusions and joys of modern society.

Suggested Readings: *The Poorhouse Fair*, 1958. *Rabbit, Run*, 1960. *The Centaur*, 1963. *Of the Farm*, 1965. *Couples*, 1968. *Bech: A Book*, 1970. *Rabbit Redux*, 1971. *A Month of Sundays*, 1975. *Problems and Other Stories*, 1979. *Rabbit Is Rich*, 1981. *Bech Is Back*, 1982. *The Witches of Eastwick*, 1985. *Roger's Version*, 1986. *A Soft Night in Shillington*, 1986. *Trust Me*, 1987. *Self-Consciousness: Memoirs*, 1989. *Rabbit at Rest*, 1990. T. Tanner, *City of Words*, 1971. R. Detweiler, *John Updike*, 1972. G. Hicks, *Literary Horizons*, 1973. A. Kazin, *Bright Book of Life*, 1973. D. J. Grenier, *John Updike's Novels*, 1984. G. J. Searles, *The Fiction of Philip Roth and John Updike*, 1985.

Text Used: *Pigeon Feathers and Other Stories*, 1962.

A & P*

In walks these three girls in nothing but bathing suits. I'm in the third checkout slot, with my back to the door, so I don't see them until they're over by the bread. The one that caught my eye first was the one in the plaid green two-piece. She was a chunky kid, with a good tan and a sweet broad soft-looking can with those two crescents of white just under it, where the sun never seems to hit, at the top of the backs of her legs. I stood there with my hand on a box of HiHo crackers trying to remember if I rang it up or not. I ring it up again and the customer starts giving me hell. She's one of these cash-register-watchers, a witch about fifty with rouge on her cheekbones and no eyebrows, and I know it made her day to trip me up. She'd been watching cash registers for fifty years and probably never seen a mistake before.

By the time I got her feathers smoothed and her goodies into a bag—she gives me a little snort in passing, if she'd been born at the right time they would have burned her over in Salem[1]—by the time I get her on her way the girls had circled around the bread and were coming back, without a pushcart, back my way along the counters, in the aisle between the checkouts and the Special bins. They didn't even have shoes on. There was this chunky one, with the two-piece—it was bright green and the seams on the bra were still sharp and her belly was still pretty pale so I guessed she just got it (the suit)—there was this one, with one of those chubby berry-faces, the lips all bunched together under her nose, this one, and a tall one, with black hair that hadn't quite frizzed right, and one of these sunburns

---

* The Great Atlantic and Pacific Tea Company, a widespread grocery chain. First published in the *New Yorker*.

[1] Salem, Massachusetts, site of the witchcraft trials of 1692, in which hundreds were accused of practicing witchcraft and nineteen people were executed.

right across under the eyes, and a chin that was too long—you know, the kind of girl other girls think is very "striking" and "attractive" but never quite makes it, as they very well know, which is why they like her so much—and then the third one, that wasn't quite so tall. She was the queen. She kind of led them, the other two peeking around and making their shoulders round. She didn't look around, not this queen, she just walked straight on slowly, on these long white prima-donna legs. She came down a little hard on her heels, as if she didn't walk in her bare feet that much, putting down her heels and then letting the weight move along to her toes as if she was testing the floor with every step, putting a little deliberate extra action into it. You never know for sure how girls' minds work (do you really think it's a mind in there or just a little buzz like a bee in a glass jar?) but you got the idea she had talked the other two into coming in here with her, and now she was showing them how to do it, walk slow and hold yourself straight.

She had on a kind of dirty-pink—beige maybe, I don't know—bathing suit with a little nubble all over it and, what got me, the straps were down. They were off her shoulders looped loose around the cool tops of her arms, and I guess as a result the suit had slipped a little on her, so all around the top of the cloth there was this shining rim. If it hadn't been there you wouldn't have known there could have been anything whiter than those shoulders. With the straps pushed off, there was nothing between the top of the suit and the top of her head except just *her,* this clean bare plane of the top of her chest down from the shoulder bones like a dented sheet of metal tilted in the light. I mean, it was more than pretty.

She had sort of oaky hair that the sun and salt had bleached, done up in a bun that was unravelling, and a kind of prim face. Walking into the A & P with your straps down, I suppose it's the only kind of face you *can* have. She held her head so high her neck, coming up out of those white shoulders, looked kind of stretched, but I didn't mind. The longer her neck was, the more of her there was.

She must have felt in the corner of her eye me and over my shoulder Stokesie in the second slot watching, but she didn't tip. Not this queen. She kept her eyes moving across the racks, and stopped, and turned so slow it made my stomach rub the inside of my apron, and buzzed to the other two, who kind of huddled against her for relief, and then they all three of them went up the cat-and-dog-food-break-fast-cereal-macaroni-rice-raisins-seasonings-spreads-spaghetti-soft-drinks-crack-ers-and-cookies aisle. From the third slot I look straight up this aisle to the meat counter, and I watched them all the way. The fat one with the tan sort of fumbled with the cookies, but on second thought she put the package back. The sheep pushing their carts down the aisle—the girls were walking against the usual traffic (not that we have one-way signs or anything)—were pretty hilarious. You could see them, when Queenie's white shoulders dawned on them, kind of jerk, or hop, or hiccup, but their eyes snapped back to their own baskets and on they pushed. I bet you could set off dynamite in an A & P and the people would by and large keep reaching and checking oatmeal off their lists and muttering "Let me see, there was a third thing, began with A, asparagus, no, ah, yes, applesauce!" or whatever it is they do mutter. But there was no doubt, this jiggled them. A few houseslaves in pin curlers even looked around after pushing their carts past to make sure what they had seen was correct.

You know, it's one thing to have a girl in a bathing suit down on the beach, where what with the glare nobody can look at each other much anyway, and an-other thing in the cool of the A & P, under the fluorescent lights, against all those stacked packages, with her feet paddling along naked over our checkerboard green-and-cream rubber-tile floor.

"Oh Daddy," Stokesie said beside me, "I feel so faint."

"Darling," I said. "Hold me tight." Stokesie's married, with two babies chalked up on his fuselage already, but as far as I can tell that's the only difference. He's twenty-two, and I was nineteen this April.

"Is it done?" he asks, the responsible married man finding his voice. I forgot to say he thinks he's going to be manager some sunny day, maybe in 1990 when it's called the Great Alexandrov and Petrooshki Tea Company[2] or something.

What he meant was, our town is five miles from a beach, with a big summer colony out on the Point, but we're right in the middle of town, and the women generally put on a shirt or shorts or something before they get out of the car into the street. And anyway these are usually women with six children and varicose veins mapping their legs and nobody, including them, could care less. As I say, we're right in the middle of town, and if you stand at our front doors you can see two banks and the Congregational church and the newspaper store and three real-estate offices and about twenty-seven old freeloaders tearing up Central Street because the sewer broke again. It's not as if we're on the Cape;[3] we're north of Boston and there's people in this town haven't seen the ocean for twenty years.

The girls had reached the meat counter and were asking McMahon something. He pointed, they pointed, and they shuffled out of sight behind a pyramid of Diet Delight peaches. All that was left for us to see was old McMahon patting his mouth and looking after them sizing up their joints. Poor kids, I began to feel sorry for them, they couldn't help it.

Now here comes the sad part of the story, at least my family says it's sad, but I don't think it's so sad myself. The store's pretty empty, it being Thurdsay afternoon, so there was nothing much to do except lean on the register and wait for the girls to show up again. The whole store was like a pinball machine and I didn't know which tunnel they'd come out of. After a while they come around out of the far aisle, around the light bulbs, records at discount of the Caribbean Six or Tony Martin Sings[4] or some such gunk you wonder they waste the wax on, sixpacks of candy bars, and plastic toys done up in cellophane that fall apart when a kid looks at them anyway. Around they come, Queenie still leading the way, and holding a little gray jar in her hand. Slots Three through Seven are unmanned and I could see her wondering between Stokes and me, but Stokesie with his usual luck draws an old party in baggy gray pants who stumbles up with four giant cans of pineapple juice (what do these bums *do* with all that pineapple juice? I've often asked myself) so the girls come to me. Queenie puts down the jar and I take it into my fingers icy cold. Kingfish Fancy Herring Snacks in Pure Sour Cream: 49¢. Now her hands are empty, not a ring or a bracelet, bare as God made them, and I wonder where the money's coming from. Still with that prim look she lifts a folded dollar bill out of the hollow at the center of her nubble pink top. The jar went heavy in my hand. Really, I thought that was so cute.

Then everybody's luck begins to run out. Lengel comes in from haggling with a truck full of cabbages on the lot and is about to scuttle into that door marked MANAGER behind which he hides all day when the girls touch his eye. Lengel's pretty dreary, teaches Sunday school and the rest, but he doesn't miss that much. He comes over and says, "Girls, this isn't the beach."

---

[2] When the Russians will supposedly run the United States.
[3] Cape Cod, Massachusetts.
[4] Popular singing groups of the late 1950s.

Queenie blushes, though maybe it's just a brush of sunburn I was noticing for the first time, now that she was so close. "My mother asked me to pick up a jar of herring snacks." Her voice kind of startled me, the way voices do when you see the people first, coming out so flat and dumb yet kind of tony, too, the way it ticked over "pick up" and "snacks." All of a sudden I slid right down her voice into her living room. Her father and the other men were standing around in ice-cream coats and bow ties and the women were in sandals picking up herring snacks on toothpicks off a big glass plate and they were all holding drinks the color of water with olives and sprigs of mint in them. When my parents have somebody over they get lemonade and if it's a real racy affair Schlitz in tall glasses with "They'll Do It Every Time"[5] cartoons stencilled on.

"That's all right," Lengel said. "But this isn't the beach." His repeating this struck me as funny, as if it had just occurred to him, and he had been thinking all these years the A & P was a great big dune and he was the head lifeguard. He didn't like my smiling—as I say he doesn't miss much—but he concentrates on giving the girls that sad Sunday-school-superintendent stare.

Queenie's blush is no sunburn now, and the plump one in plaid, that I liked better from the back—a really sweet can—pipes up. "We weren't doing any shopping. We just came in for the one thing."

"That makes no difference," Lengel tells her, and I could see from the way his eyes went that he hadn't noticed she was wearing a two-piece before. "We want you decently dressed when you come in here."

"We *are* decent," Queenie says suddenly, her lower lip pushing, getting sore now that she remembers her place, a place from which the crowd that runs the A & P must look pretty crummy. Fancy Herring Snacks flashed in her very blue eyes.

"Girls, I don't want to argue with you. After this come in here with your shoulders covered. It's our policy." He turns his back. That's policy for you. Policy is what the kingpins want. What the others want is juvenile delinquency.

All this while, the customers had been showing up with their carts but, you know, sheep, seeing a scene, they had all bunched up on Stokesie, who shook open a paper bag as gently as peeling a peach, not wanting to miss a word. I could feel in the silence everybody getting nervous, most of all Lengel, who asks me, "Sammy, have you rung up their purchase?"

I thought and said "No" but it wasn't about that I was thinking. I go through the punches, 4, 9, GROC, TOT—it's more complicated than you think, and after you do it often enough, it begins to make a little song, that you heard words to, in my case "Hello (*bing*) there, you (*gung*) hap-py pee-pul (*splat*)!"—the *splat* being the drawer flying out. I uncrease the bill, tenderly as you may imagine, it just having come from between the two smoothest scoops of vanilla I had ever known were there, and pass a half and a penny into her narrow pink palm, and nestle the herrings in a bag and twist its neck and hand it over, all the time thinking.

The girls, and who'd blame them, are in a hurry to get out, so I say "I quit" to Lengel quick enough for them to hear, hoping they'll stop and watch me, their unsuspected hero. They keep right on going, into the electric eye; the door flies open and they flicker across the lot to their car, Queenie and Plaid and Big Tall Goony-Goony (not that as raw material she was so bad), leaving me with Lengel and a kink in his eyebrow.

"Did you say something, Sammy?"

---

[5] A syndicated cartoon series created in 1928 by James Hatlo (1898–1963).

"I said I quit."

"I thought you did."

"You didn't have to embarrass them."

"It was they who were embarrassing us."

I started to say something that came out "Fiddle-de-doo." It's a saying of my grandmother's, and I know she would have been pleased.

"I don't think you know what you're saying," Lengel said.

"I know you don't," I said. "But I do." I pull the bow at the back of my apron and start shrugging it off my shoulders. A couple customers that had been heading for my slot begin to knock against each other, like scared pigs in a chute.

Lengel sighs and begins to look very patient and old and gray. He's been a friend of my parents for years. "Sammy, you don't want to do this to your Mom and Dad," he tells me. It's true, I don't. But it seems to me that once you begin a gesture it's fatal not to go through with it. I fold the apron, "Sammy" stitched in red on the pocket, and put it on the counter, and drop the bow tie on top of it. The bow tie is theirs, if you've ever wondered. "You'll feel this for the rest of your life," Lengel says, and I know that's true, too, but remembering how he made that pretty girl blush makes me so scrunchy inside I punch the No Sale tab and the machine whirs "pee-pul" and the drawer splats out. One advantage to this scene taking place in summer, I can follow this up with a clean exit, there's no fumbling around getting your coat and galoshes, I just saunter into the electric eye in my white shirt that my mother ironed the night before, and the door heaves itself open, and outside the sunshine is skating around on the asphalt.

I look around for my girls, but they're gone, of course. There wasn't anybody but some young married screaming with her children about some candy they didn't get by the door of a powder-blue Falcon station wagon. Looking back in the big windows, over the bags of peat moss and aluminum lawn furniture stacked on the pavement, I could see Lengel in my place in the slot, checking the sheep through. His face was dark gray and his back stiff, as if he'd just had an injection of iron, and my stomach kind of fell as I felt how hard the world was going to be to me hereafter.

1961

Philip Roth
(1933–   )

Like Quentin Compson in William Faulkner's *Absalom, Absalom!* (1936), Philip Roth has often had to defend his relationship to his heritage. His short-story collection *Goodbye, Columbus* (1959), which includes "Defender of the Faith," won a National Book Award but opened a floodgate of criticism about Roth's portrayal of his lower middle-class Jewish roots in Newark, New Jersey. Roth was born in Newark in 1933 and studied at the Newark campus of Rutgers University from 1950 to 1951. He completed his undergraduate work at Bucknell University in 1954. After receiving an M. A. in English from the University of Chicago in 1955, he joined the army but was discharged after suffering a back injury in basic training. Roth continued graduate studies at Chicago until 1957.

Philip Roth's Goodbye, Columbus *was made into a 1969 motion picture starring Ali McGraw and Richard Benjamin.*

Roth's first two novels, *Letting Go* (1962) and *When She Was Good* (1967), demonstrate his ability to extend beyond the somewhat narrow range of *Goodbye, Columbus*. The novels explore Jewish-Gentile relations and examine love, family, sex, and marriage in university and midwestern settings. With *Portnoy's Complaint* (1969) Roth returned to his New Jersey boyhood to recall old radio shows, softball games, and lusting after girls; the narrative's sometimes crude humor and scenes of masturbation earned Roth widespread notoriety as the author of a "dirty" book. It was followed by *Our Gang* (1970), *The Breast* (1971), and *The Great American Novel* (1973)—three uneven works struggling to get out from under their initial conceits of social and political fantasy. But with *My Life as a Man* (1974) and *The Professor of Desire* (1977), Roth returned to the kind of social analysis and examination of relationships between individuals and their cultures that moves beyond what it means to be a Jew in America to explore more universal forms of discontent and dislocation.

Throughout Roth's career his endless self-examination has threatened to turn into self-absorption and parody, and yet his novels consistently transform private reflection into public revelation. His ironic humor and ruthless social scrutiny have often been perceived as the pursuit of a cheap joke in the creation of ethnic caricatures. But Roth's later work, particularly *Zuckerman Bound* (1985) and *The Counterlife* (1986), has transcended this criticism to fulfill the promise of his early work. In *Zuckerman Bound*, consisting of the novels *The Ghost Writer* (1979), *Zuckerman Unbound* (1981), and *The Anatomy Lesson* (1983) and the story "The Prague Orgy," Roth charts the ways in which the works of Nathan Zuckerman intersect the lives of his family, literary fathers, and an odd assortment of characters—from a woman Zuckerman imagines is Anne Frank to an alter ego modeled after a 1950s quiz-show champion. *Portnoy's Complaint,* now called *Carnovsky,* haunts these works and their author nearly as persistently as do questions of Judaism and of the boundaries between fiction and reality. In the novel *The Counterlife* (1986) Roth turns these questions into a powerful narrative technique, as Zuckerman and his brother, Henry, suffer from impotence brought on by medication. The story ends with Zuckerman's lover writing a letter to say that she is "leaving the novel before anything dreadful happens." Here, questions of Judaism intersect with questions of Zionism, and the relationships between self and culture stretch from America to England and Israel.

Roth has been a faculty member at such colleges as the University of Iowa, Princeton University (as writer in residence), and the University of Pennsylvania. His wife since 1959, Margaret Martinson, died in 1968. Roth has isolated himself from the literary community, maintaining residences in Connecticut and London with the British actress Claire Bloom; the couple married in 1990. And while isolated he continues to write; his *Deceptions* (1990) and *Patrimony* (1991) are both semi-autobiographical novels.

Suggested Readings: *When She Was Good,* 1967. *Portnoy's Complaint,* 1969. *Our Gang,* 1970. *The Great American Novel,* 1973. *My Life As a Man,* 1974. *Reading Myself and Others,* 1975. *The Professor of Desire,* 1977. *Zuckerman Bound,* 1985. *The Counterlife,* 1986. *The Facts: A Novelist's Autobiography,* 1988. A. Kazin, *Contemporaries,* 1962. A. Guttman, *The Jewish Writer in America,* 1971. T. Tanner, *City of Words: American Fiction 1950–1970,* 1971. R. Wisse, *The Schlemiel as Modern Hero,* 1971. I. Howe, "Philip Roth Reconsidered," in *Commentary,* 54, (December) 1972. B. F. Rodgers, *Philip Roth,* 1978. H. Lee, *Philip Roth,* 1982. G. J. Searles, *The Fiction of John Updike and Philip Roth,* 1985.

Text Used: *Goodbye, Columbus,* 1959.

from   **GOODBYE, COLUMBUS**

DEFENDER OF THE FAITH*

In May of 1945, only a few weeks after the fighting had ended in Europe,[1] I was rotated back to the States, where I spent the remainder of the war with a training company at Camp Crowder, Missouri. Along with the rest of the Ninth Army, I had been racing across Germany so swiftly during the late winter and spring that when I boarded the plane, I couldn't believe its destination lay to the west. My mind might inform me otherwise, but there was the inertia of the spirit that told me we were flying to a new front, where we would disembark and continue our push eastward—eastward until we'd circled the globe, marching through villages along whose twisting, cobbled streets crowds of the enemy would watch us take

---

* First published in the *New Yorker* in 1959 and collected in *Goodbye, Columbus* later that year.
[1] World War II ended in Europe when Germany surrendered on May 7, 1945; it ended in the Pacific when Japan surrendered on September 2, 1945.

possession of what, up till then, they'd considered their own. I had changed enough in two years not to mind the trembling of the old people, the crying of the very young, the uncertainty and fear in the eyes of the once arrogant. I had been fortunate enough to develop an infantryman's heart, which, like his feet, at first aches and swells but finally grows horny enough for him to travel the weirdest paths without feeling a thing.

Captain Paul Barrett was my C. O. in Camp Crowder. The day I reported for duty, he came out of his office to shake my hand. He was short, gruff, and fiery, and—indoors or out—he wore his polished helmet liner pulled down to his little eyes. In Europe, he had received a battlefield commission and a serious chest wound, and he'd been returned to the States only a few months before. He spoke easily to me, and at the evening formation he introduced me to the troops. "Gentlemen," he said, "Sergeant Thurston, as you know, is no longer with this company. Your new first sergeant is Sergeant Nathan Marx, here. He is a veteran of the European theater, and consequently will expect to find a company of soldiers here, and not a company of *boys*."

I sat up late in the orderly room that evening, trying half-heartedly to solve the riddle of duty rosters, personnel forms, and morning reports. The Charge of Quarters[2] slept with his mouth open on a mattress on the floor. A trainee stood reading the next day's duty roster, which was posted on the bulletin board just inside the screen door. It was a warm evening, and I could hear radios playing dance music over in the barracks. The trainee, who had been staring at me whenever he thought I wouldn't notice, finally took a step in my direction.

"Hey, Sarge—we having a G. I. party tomorrow night?" he asked. A G. I. party is a barracks cleaning.

"You usually have them on Friday nights?" I asked him.

"Yes," he said, and then he added, mysteriously, "that's the whole thing."

"Then you'll have a G. I. party."

He turned away, and I heard him mumbling. His shoulders were moving, and I wondered if he was crying.

"What's your name, soldier?" I asked.

He turned, not crying at all. Instead, his green-speckled eyes, long and narrow, flashed like fish in the sun. He walked over to me and sat on the edge of my desk. He reached out a hand. "Sheldon," he said.

"Stand on your feet, Sheldon."

Getting off the desk, he said, "Sheldon Grossbart." He smiled at the familiarity into which he'd led me.

"You against cleaning the barracks Friday night, Grossbart?" I said. "Maybe we shouldn't have G. I. parties. Maybe we should get a maid." My tone startled me. I felt I sounded like every top sergeant I had ever known.

"No, Sergeant." He grew serious, but with a seriousness that seemed to be only the stifling of a smile. "It's just—G. I. parties on Friday night, of all nights."

He slipped up onto the corner of the desk again—not quite sitting, but not quite standing, either. He looked at me with those speckled eyes flashing, and then made a gesture with his hand. It was very slight—no more than a movement back and forth of the wrist—and yet it managed to exclude from our affairs everything else in the orderly room, to make the two of us the center of the world. It seemed, in fact, to exclude everything even about the two of us except our hearts.

---

[2] The noncommissioned officer in charge of the barracks on weekends and at night; C. Q.

"Sergeant Thurston was one thing," he whispered, glancing at the sleeping C. Q., "but we thought that with you here things might be a little different."

"We?"

"The Jewish personnel."

"Why?" I asked, harshly. "What's on your mind?" Whether I was still angry at the "Sheldon" business, or now at something else, I hadn't time to tell, but clearly I was angry.

"We thought you–Marx, you know, like Karl Marx. The Marx Brothers. Those guys are all—M-a-r-x. Isn't that how *you* spell it, Sergeant?"

"M-a-r-x."

"Fishbein said—" He stopped. "What I mean to say, Sergeant—" His face and neck were red, and his mouth moved but no words came out. In a moment, he raised himself to attention, gazing down at me. It was as though he had suddenly decided he could expect no more sympathy from me than from Thurston, the reason being that I was of Thurston's faith, and not his. The young man had managed to confuse himself as to what my faith really was, but I felt no desire to straighten him out. Very simply, I didn't like him.

When I did nothing but return his gaze, he spoke, in an altered tone. "You see, Sergeant," he explained to me, "Friday nights, Jews are supposed to go to services."

"Did Sergeant Thurston tell you you couldn't go to them when there was a G. I. party?"

"No."

"Did he say you had to stay and scrub the floors?"

"No, Sergeant."

"Did the Captain say you had to stay and scrub the floors?"

"That isn't it, Sergeant. It's the other guys in the barracks." He leaned toward me. "They think we're goofing off. But we're not. That's when Jews go to services, Friday night. We have to."

"Then go."

"But the other guys make accusations. They have no right."

"That's not the Army's problem, Grossbart. It's a personal problem you'll have to work out yourself."

"But it's un*fair*."

I got up to leave. "There's nothing I can do about it," I said.

Grossbart stiffened and stood infront of me. "But this is a matter of *religion*, sir."

"Sergeant," I said.

"I mean 'Sergeant,'" he said, almost snarling.

"Look, go see the chaplain. You want to see Captain Barrett, I'll arrange an appointment."

"No, no. I don't want to make trouble, Sergeant. That's the first thing they throw up to you. I just want my rights!"

"Damn it, Grossbart, stop whining. You have your rights. You can stay and scrub floors or you can go to shul[3]—"

The smile swam in again. Spittle gleamed at the corners of his mouth. "You mean church, Sergeant."

"I mean shul, Grossbart!"

---

[3] "Synagogue" (Yiddish).

I walked past him and went outside. Near me, I heard the scrunching of a guard's boots on gravel. Beyond the lighted windows of the barracks, young men in T shirts and fatigue pants were sitting on their bunks, polishing their rifles. Suddenly there was a light rustling behind me. I turned and saw Grossbart's dark frame fleeing back to the barracks, racing to tell his Jewish friends that they were right—that, like Karl and Harpo,[4] I was one of them.

The next morning, while chatting with Captain Barrett, I recounted the incident of the previous evening. Somehow, in the telling, it must have seemed to the Captain that I was not so much explaining Grossbart's position as defending it. "Marx, I'd fight side by side with a nigger if the fella proved to me he was a man. I pride myself," he said, looking out the window, "that I've got an open mind. Consequently, Sergeant, nobody gets special treatment here, for the good *or* the bad. All a man's got to do is prove himself. A man fires well on the range, I give him a weekend pass. He scores high in P. T.,[5] he gets a weekend pass. He *earns* it." He turned from the window and pointed a finger at me. "You're a Jewish fella, am I right, Marx?"

"Yes, sir."

"And I admire you. I admire you because of the ribbons on your chest. I judge a man by what he shows me on the field of battle, Sergeant. It's what he's got *here*," he said, and then, though I expected he would point to his heart, he jerked a thumb toward the buttons straining to hold his blouse across his belly. "Guts," he said.

"O. K., sir. I only wanted to pass on to you how the men felt."

"Mr. Marx, you're going to be old before your time if you worry about how the men feel. Leave that stuff to the chaplain—that's his business, not yours. Let's us train these fellas to shoot straight. If the Jewish personnel feels the other men are accusing them of goldbricking—well, I just don't know. Seems awful funny that suddenly the Lord is calling so loud in Private Grossman's ear he's just got to run to church."

"Synagogue," I said.

"Synagogue is right, Sergeant. I'll write that down for handy reference. Thank you for stopping by."

That evening, a few minutes before the company gathered outside the orderly room for the chow formation, I called the C. Q., Corporal Robert LaHill, in to see me. LaHill was a dark, burly fellow whose hair curled out of his clothes wherever it could. He had a glaze in his eyes that made one think of caves and dinosaurs. "LaHill," I said, "when you take the formation, remind the men that they're free to attend church services *whenever* they are held, provided they report to the orderly room before they leave the area."

LaHill scratched his wrist, but gave no indicaton that he'd heard or understood.

"LaHill," I said, "*church.* You remember? Church, priest, Mass, confession."

He curled one lip into a kind of smile; I took it for a signal that for a second he had flickered back up into the human race.

"Jewish personnel who want to attend services this evening are to fall out in front of the orderly room at 1900," I said. Then, as an afterthought, I added, "By order of Captain Barrett."

---

[4] Harpo Marx (1893–1964), the silent Marx brother.   [5] Physical training.

A little while later, as the day's last light—softer than any I had seen that year—began to drop over Camp Crowder, I heard LaHill's thick, inflectionless voice outside my window: "Give me your ears, troopers. Toppie says for me to tell you that at 1900 hours all Jewish personnel is to fall out in front, here, if they want to attend the Jewish Mass."

At seven o'clock, I looked out the orderly-room window and saw three soldiers in starched khakis standing on the dusty quadrangle. They looked at their watches and fidgeted while they whispered back and forth. It was getting dimmer, and, alone on the otherwise deserted field, they looked tiny. When I opened the door, I heard the noises of the G. I. party coming from the surrounding barracks—bunks being pushed to the walls, faucets pounding water into buckets, brooms whisking at the wooden floors, cleaning the dirt away for Saturday's inspection. Big puffs of cloth moved round and round on the windowpanes. I walked outside, and the moment my foot hit the ground I thought I heard Grossbart call to the others, "'Ten-*hut!*" Or maybe, when they all three jumped to attention, I imagined I heard the command.

Grossbart stepped forward. "Thank you, sir," he said.

"'Sergeant,' Grossbart," I reminded him. "You call officers 'sir.' I'm not an officer. You've been in the Army three weeks—you know that."

He turned his palms out at his sides to indicate that, in truth, he and I lived beyond convention. "Thank you, anyway," he said.

"Yes," a tall boy behind him said. "Thanks a lot."

And the third boy whispered, "Thank you," but his mouth barely fluttered, so that he did not alter by more than a lip's movement his posture of attention.

"For what?" I asked.

Grossbart snorted happily. "For the announcement. The Corporal's announcement. It helped. It made it—"

"Fancier." The tall boy finished Grossbart's sentence.

Grossbart smiled. "He means formal, sir. Public," he said to me. "Now it won't seem as though we're just taking off—goldbricking because the work has begun."

"It was by order of Captain Barrett," I said.

"Aaah, but you pull a little weight," Grossbart said. "So we thank you." Then he turned to his companions. "Sergeant Marx, I want you to meet Larry Fishbein."

The tall boy stepped forward and extended his hand. I shook it. "You from New York?" he asked.

"Yes."

"Me, too." He had a cadaverous face that collapsed inward from his cheekbone to his jaw, and when he smiled—as he did at the news of our communal attachment—revealed a mouthful of bad teeth. He was blinking his eyes a good deal, as though he were fighting back tears. "What borough?" he asked.

I turned to Grossbart. "It's five after seven. What time are services?"

"Shul," he said, smiling, "is in ten minutes. I want you to meet Mickey Halpern. This is Nathan Marx, our sergeant."

The third boy hopped forward. "Private Michael Halpern." He saluted.

"Salute officers, Halpern," I said. The boy dropped his hand, and, on its way down, in his nervousness, checked to see if his shirt pockets were buttoned.

"Shall I march them over, sir?" Grossbart asked. "Or are you coming along?"

From behind Grossbart, Fishbein piped up. "Afterward, they're having refreshments. A ladies' auxiliary from St. Louis, the rabbi told us last week."

"The chaplain," Halpern whispered.

"You're welcome to come along," Grossbart said.

To avoid his plea, I looked away, and saw, in the windows of the barracks, a cloud of faces staring out at the four of us. "Hurry along, Grossbart," I said.

"O. K., then," he said. He turned to the others. "Double time, *march!*"

They started off, but ten feet away Grossbart spun around and, running backward, called to me, "Good *shabbus,[6]* sir!" And then the three of them were swallowed into the alien Missouri dusk.

Even after they had disappeared over the parade ground, whose green was now a deep blue, I could hear Grossbart singing the double-time cadence, and as it grew dimmer and dimmer, it suddenly touched a deep memory—as did the slant of the light—and I was remembering the shrill sounds of the Bronx playground where, years ago, beside the Grand Concourse,[7] I had played on long spring evenings such as this. It was a pleasant memory for a young man so far from peace and home, and it brought so many recollections with it that I began to grow exceedingly tender about myself. In fact, I indulged myself in a reverie so strong that I felt as though a hand were reaching down inside me. It had to reach so very far to touch me! It had to reach past those days in the forests of Belgium, and past the dying I'd refused to weep over; past the nights in German farmhouses whose books we'd burned to warm us; past endless stretches when I had shut off all softness I might feel for my fellows, and had managed even to deny myself the posture of a conqueror—the swagger that I, as a Jew, might well have worn as my boots whacked against the rubble of Wesel, Münster, and Braunschweig.

But now one night noise, one rumor of home and time past, and memory plunged down through all I had anesthetized, and came to what I suddenly remembered was myself. So it was not altogether curious that, in search of more of me, I found myself following Grossbart's tracks to Chapel No. 3, where the Jewish services were being held.

I took a seat in the last row, which was empty. Two rows in front of me sat Grossbart, Fishbein, and Halpern, holding little white Dixie cups. Each row of seats was raised higher than the one in front of it, and I could see clearly what was going on. Fishbein was pouring the contents of his cup into Grossbart's, and Grossbart looked mirthful as the liquid made a purple arc between Fishbein's hand and his. In the glaring yellow light, I saw the chaplain standing on the platform at the front; he was chanting the first line of the responsive reading. Grossbart's prayer book remained closed on his lap; he was swishing the cup around. Only Halpern responded to the chant by praying. The fingers of his right hand were spread wide across the cover of his open book. His cap was pulled down low onto his brow, which made it round, like a yarmulke.[8] From time to time, Grossbart wet his lips at the cup's edge; Fishbein, his long yellow face a dying light bulb, looked from here to there, craning forward to catch sight of the faces down the row, then of those in front of him, then behind. He saw me, and his eyelids beat a tattoo. His elbow slid into Grossbart's side, his neck inclined toward his friend, he whispered something, and then, when the congregation next responded to the

---

[6] "Sabbath" (Yiddish).
[7] A boulevard in the Bronx; the surrounding neighborhood was then mainly middle-class Jewish.
[8] "Skullcap" (Yiddish).

chant, Grossbart's voice was among the others. Fishbein looked into his book now, too; his lips, however, didn't move.

Finally, it was time to drink the wine. The chaplain smiled down at them as Grossbart swigged his in one long gulp, Halpern sipped, meditating, and Fishbein faked devotion with an empty cup. "As I look down amongst the congregation"— the chaplain grinned at the word—"this night, I see many new faces, and I want to welcome you to Friday-night services here at Camp Crowder. I am Major Leo Ben Ezra, your chaplain." Though an American, the chaplain spoke deliberately— syllable by syllable, almost—as though to communicate, above all, with the lip readers in his audience. "I have only a few words to say before we adjourn to the refreshment room, where the kind ladies of the Temple Sinai, St. Louis, Missouri, have a nice setting for you."

Applause and whistling broke out. After another momentary grin, the chaplain raised his hands, palms out, his eyes flicking upward a moment, as if to remind the troops where they were and Who Else might be in attendance. In the sudden silence that followed I thought I heard Grossbart cackle, "Let the goyim[9] clean the floors!" Were those the words? I wasn't sure, but Fishbein, grinning, nudged Halpern. Halpern looked dumbly at him, then went back to his prayer book, which had been occupying him all through the rabbi's talk. One hand tugged at the black kinky hair that stuck out under his cap. His lips moved.

The rabbi continued. "It is about the food that I want to speak to you for a moment. I know, I know, I know," he intoned, wearily, "how in the mouths of most of you the *trafe*[10] food tastes like ashes. I know how you gag, some of you, and how your parents suffer to think of their children eating foods unclean and offensive to the palate. What can I tell you? I can only say, close your eyes and swallow as best you can. Eat what you must to live, and throw away the rest. I wish I could help more. For those of you who find this impossible, may I ask that you try and try, but then come to see me in private. If your revulsion is so great, we will have to seek aid from those higher up."

A round of chatter rose and subsided. Then everyone sang "Ain Kelohainu";[11] after all those years, I discovered I still knew the words. Then, suddenly, the service over, Grossbart was upon me. "Higher up? He means the General?"

"Hey, Shelly," Fishbein said, "he means God." He smacked his face and looked at Halpern. "How high can you go!"

"Sh-h-h!" Grossbart said. "What do you think, Sergeant?"

"I don't know," I said. "You better ask the chaplain."

"I'm going to. I'm making an appointment to see him in private. So is Mickey."

Halpern shook his head. "No, no, Sheldon—"

"You have rights, Mickey," Grossbart said. "They can't push us around."

"It's O. K.," said Halpern. "It bothers my mother, not me."

Grossbart looked at me. "Yesterday he threw up. From the hash. It was all ham and God knows what else."

"I have a cold—that was why," Halpern said. He pushed his yarmulke back into a cap.

"What about you, Fishbein?" I asked. "You kosher, too?"

He flushed. "A little. But I'll let it ride. I have a very strong stomach, and I

---

[9] "Gentiles" (Yiddish); the singular is "*goy*."   [10] "Nonkosher" (Yiddish).
[11] "None Like Our God" (Hebrew).

don't eat a lot anyway." I continued to look at him, and he held up his wrist to reinforce what he'd just said; his watch strap was tightened to the last hole, and he pointed that out to me.

"But services are important to you?" I asked him.

He looked at Grossbart. "Sure, sir."

"'Sergeant.'"

"Not so much at home," said Grossbart, stepping between us, "but away from home it gives one a sense of his Jewishness."

"We have to stick together," Fishbein said.

I started to walk toward the door; Halpern stepped back to make way for me.

"That's what happened in Germany," Grossbart was saying, loud enough for me to hear. "They didn't stick together. They let themselves get pushed around."

I turned. "Look, Grossbart. This is the Army, not summer camp."

He smiled. "So?"

Halpern tried to sneak off, but Grossbart held his arm.

"Grossbart, how old are you?" I asked.

"Nineteen."

"And you?" I said to Fishbein.

"The same. The same month, even."

"And what about him?" I pointed to Halpern, who had by now made it safely to the door.

"Eighteen," Grossbart whispered. "But like he can't tie his shoes or brush his teeth himself. I feel sorry for him."

"I feel sorry for all of us, Grossbart," I said, "but just act like a man. Just don't overdo it."

"Overdo what, sir?"

"The 'sir' business, for one thing. Don't overdo that," I said.

I left him standing there. I passed by Halpern, but he did not look at me. Then I was outside, but, behind, I heard Grossbart call, "Hey, Mickey, my *leben*,[12] come on back. Refreshments!"

"*Leben!*" My grandmother's word for me!

One morning a week later, while I was working at my desk, Captain Barrett shouted for me to come into his office. When I entered, he had his helmet liner squashed down so far on his head that I couldn't even see his eyes. He was on the phone, and when he spoke to me, he cupped one hand over the mouthpiece. "Who the hell is Grossbart?"

"Third platoon, Captain," I said. "A trainee."

"What's all this stink about food? His mother called a goddam congressman about the food." He uncovered the mouthpiece and slid his helmet up until I could see his bottom eyelashes. "Yes, sir," he said into the phone. "Yes, sir. I'm still here, sir. I'm asking Marx, here, right now—"

He covered the mouthpiece again and turned his head back toward me. "Lightfoot Harry's on the phone," he said, between his teeth. "This congressman calls General Lyman, who calls Colonel Sousa, who calls the Major, who calls me. They're just dying to stick this thing on me. Whatsa matter?" He shook the phone at me. "I don't feed the troops? What the hell is this?"

"Sir, Grossbart is strange—" Barrett greeted that with a mockingly indulgent

---

[12] "Life" (Yiddish): a term of great affection.

smile. I altered my approach. "Captain, he's a very othodox Jew, and so he's only allowed to eat certain foods."

"He throws up, the congressman said. Every time he eats something, his mother says, he throws up!"

"He's accustomed to observing the dietary laws, Captain."

"So why's his old lady have to call the White House?"

"Jewish parents, sir—they're apt to be more protective than you expect. I mean, Jews have a very close family life. A boy goes away from home, sometimes the mother is liable to get very upset. Probably the boy mentioned something in a letter, and his mother misinterpreted."

"I'd like to punch him one right in the mouth," the Captain said. "There's a goddam war on, and he wants a silver platter!"

"I don't think the boy's to blame, sir. I'm sure we can straighten it out by just asking him. Jewish parents worry—"

"*All* parents worry, for Christ's sake. But they don't get on their high horse and start pulling strings—"

I interrupted, my voice higher, tighter than before. "The home life, Captain, is very important—but you're right, it may sometimes get out of hand. It's a very wonderful thing, Captain, but because it's so close, this kind of thing . . . "

He didn't listen any longer to my attempt to present both myself and Lightfoot Harry with an explanation for the letter. He turned back to the phone. "Sir?" he said. "Sir—Marx, here, tells me Jews have a tendency to be pushy. He says he thinks we can settle it right here in the company. . . . Yes, sir. . . . I *will* call back, sir, soon as I can." He hung up. "Where are the men, Sergeant?"

"On the range."

With a whack on the top of his helmet, he crushed it down over his eyes again, and charged out of his chair. "We're going for a ride," he said.

The Captain drove, and I sat beside him. It was a hot spring day, and under my newly starched fatigues I felt as though my armpits were melting down onto my sides and chest. The roads were dry, and by the time we reached the firing range, my teeth felt gritty with dust, though my mouth had been shut the whole trip. The Captain slammed the brakes on and told me to get the hell out and find Grossbart.

I found him on his belly, firing wildly at the five-hundred-feet target. Waiting their turns behind him were Halpern and Fishbein. Fishbein, wearing a pair of steel-rimmed G. I. glasses I hadn't seen on him before, had the appearance of an old peddler who would gladly have sold you his rifle and the cartridges that were slung all over him. I stood back by the ammo boxes, waiting for Grossbart to finish spraying the distant targets. Fishbein straggled back to stand near me.

"Hello, Sergeant Marx," he said.

"How are you?" I mumbled.

"Fine, thank you. Sheldon's really a good shot."

"I didn't notice."

"I'm not so good, but I think I'm getting the hang of it now. Sergeant, I don't mean to, you know, ask what I shouldn't—" The boy stopped. He was trying to speak intimately, but the noise of the shooting forced him to shout at me.

"What is it?" I asked. Down the range, I saw Captain Barrett standing up in the jeep, scanning the line for me and Grossbart.

"My parents keep asking and asking where we're going," Fishbein said. "Everybody says the Pacific. I don't care, but my parents— If I could relieve their minds, I think I could concentrate more on my shooting."

"I don't know where, Fishbein. Try to concentrate anyway."

"Sheldon says you might be able to find out."

"I don't know a thing, Fishbein. You just take it easy, and don't let Sheldon—"

"*I'm* taking it easy, Sergeant. It's at home—"

Grossbart had finished on the line, and was dusting his fatigues with one hand. I called to him. "Grossbart, the Captain wants to see you."

He came toward us. His eyes blazed and twinkled. "Hi!"

"Don't point that goddam rifle!" I said.

"I wouldn't shoot you, Sarge." He gave me a smile as wide as a pumpkin, and turned the barrel aside.

"Damn you, Grossbart, this is no joke! Follow me."

I walked ahead of him, and had the awful suspicion that, behind me, Grossbart was *marching,* his rifle on his shoulder, as though he were a one-man detachment. At the jeep, he gave the Captain a rifle salute. "Private Sheldon Grossbart, sir."

"At ease, Grossman." The Captain sat down, slid over into the empty seat, and, crooking a finger, invited Grossbart closer.

"Bart, sir. Sheldon Gross*bart.* It's a common error." Grossbart nodded at me; *I* understood, he indicated. I looked away just as the mess truck pulled up to the range, disgorging a half-dozen K. P.s with rolled-up sleeves. The mess sergeant screamed at them while they set up the chow-line equipment.

"Grossbart, your mama wrote some congressman that we don't feed you right. Do you know that?" the Captain said.

"It was my father, sir. He wrote to Representative Franconi that my religion forbids me to eat certain foods."

"What religion is that, Grossbart?"

"Jewish."

"'Jewish, *sir,*'" I said to Grossbart.

"Excuse me, sir. Jewish, sir."

"What have you been living on?" the Captain asked. You've been in the Army a month already. You don't look to me like you're falling to pieces."

"I eat because I have to, sir. But Sergeant Marx will testify to the fact that I don't eat one mouthful more than I need to in order to survive."

"Is that so, Marx?" Barrett asked.

"I've never seen Grossbart eat, sir," I said.

"But you heard the rabbi," Grossbart said. "He told us what to do, and I listened."

The Captain looked at me. "Well, Marx?"

"I still don't know what he eats and doesn't eat, sir."

Grossbart raised his arms to plead with me, and it looked for a moment as though he were going to hand me his weapon to hold. "But, Sergeant—"

"Look, Grossbart, just answer the Captain's questions," I said sharply.

Barrett smiled at me, and I resented it. "All right, Grossbart," he said. "What is it you want? The little piece of paper? You want out?"

"No, sir. Only to be allowed to live as a Jew. And for the others, too."

"What others?"

"Fishbein, sir, and Halpern."

"They don't like the way we serve, either?"

"Halpern throws up, sir. I've seen it."

"I thought *you* throw up."

"Just once, sir. I didn't know the sausage was sausage."

"We'll give menus, Grossbart. We'll show training films about the food, so you can identify when we're trying to poison you."

Grossbart did not answer. The men had been organized into two long chow lines. At the tail end of one, I spotted Fishbein—or, rather, his glasses spotted me. They winked sunlight back at me. Halpern stood next to him, patting the inside of his collar with a khaki handkerchief. They moved with the line as it began to edge up toward the food. The mess sergeant was still screaming at the K. P.s For a moment, I was actually terrified by the thought that somehow the mess sergeant was going to become involved in Grossbart's problem.

"Marx," the Captain said, "you're a Jewish fella—am I right?"

I played straight man. "Yes, sir."

"How long you been in the Army? Tell this boy."

"Three years and two months."

"A year in combat, Grossbart. Twelve goddam months in combat all through Europe. I admire this man." The Captain snapped a wrist against my chest. "Do you hear him peeping about the food? Do you? I want an answer, Grossbart. Yes or no."

"No, sir."

"And why not? He's a Jewish fella."

"Some things are more important to some Jews than other things to other Jews."

Barrett blew up. "Look, Grossbart. Marx, here, is a good man—a goddam hero. When you were in high school, Sergeant Marx was killing Germans. Who does more for the Jews—you, by throwing up over a lousy piece of sausage, a piece of first-cut meat, or Marx, by killing those Nazi bastards? If I was a Jew, Grossbart, I'd kiss this man's feet. He's a goddam hero, and *he* eats what we give him. Why do you have to cause trouble is what I want to know! What is it you're buckin' for—a discharge?"

"No, sir."

"I'm talking to a wall! Sergeant, get him out of my way." Barrett swung himself back into the driver's seat. "I'm going to see the chaplain." The engine roared, the jeep spun around in a whirl of dust, and the Captain was headed back to camp.

For a moment, Grossbart and I stood side by side, watching the jeep. Then he looked at me and said, "I don't want to start trouble. That's the first thing they toss up to us."

When he spoke, I saw that his teeth were white and straight, and the sight of them suddenly made me understand that Grossbart actually did have parents—that once upon a time someone had taken little Sheldon to the dentist. He was their son. Despite all the talk about his parents, it was hard to believe in Grossbart as a child, an heir—as related by blood to anyone, mother, father, or, above all, to me. This realization led me to another.

"What does your father do, Grossbart?" I asked as we started to walk back toward the chow line.

"He's a tailor."

"An American?"

"Now, yes. A son in the Army," he said, jokingly.

"And your mother?" I asked.

He winked. "A *ballabusta*.[13] She practically sleeps with a dustcloth in her hand."

---

[13] "Good housekeeper" (Yiddish).

"She's also an immigrant?"

"All she talks is Yiddish, still."

"And your father, too?"

"A little English. 'Clean,' 'Press,' 'Take the pants in.' That's the extent of it. But they're good to me."

"Then, Grossbart—" I reached out and stopped him. He turned toward me, and when our eyes met, his seemed to jump back, to shiver in their sockets. "Grossbart—you were the one who wrote that letter, weren't you?"

It took only a second or two for his eyes to flash happy again. "Yes." He walked on, and I kept pace. "It's what my father *would* have written if he had known how. It was his name, though. *He* signed it. He even mailed it. I sent it home. For the New York postmark."

I was astonished, and he saw it. With complete seriousness, he thrust his right arm in front of me. "Blood is blood, Sergeant," he said, pinching the blue vein in his wrist.

"What the hell *are* you trying to do, Grossbart?" I asked. "I've seen you eat. Do you know that? I told the Captain I don't know what you eat, but I've seen you eat like a hound at chow."

"We work hard, Sergeant. We're in training. For a furnace to work, you've got to feed it coal."

"Why did you say in the letter that you threw up all the time?"

"I was really talking about Mickey there. I was talking *for* him. He would never write, Sergeant, though I pleaded with him. He'll waste away to nothing if I don't help. Sergeant, I used my name—my father's name—but it's Mickey, and Fishbein, too, I'm watching out for."

"You're a regular Messiah, aren't you?"

We were at the chow line now.

"That's a good one, Sergeant," he said, smiling. "But who knows? Who can tell? Maybe you're the Messiah—a little bit. What Mickey says is the Messiah is a collective idea. He went to Yeshiva,[14] Mickey, for a while. He says *together* we're the Messiah. Me a little bit, you a little bit. You should hear that kid talk, Sergeant, when he gets going."

"Me a little bit, you a little bit," I said. "You'd like to believe that, wouldn't you, Grossbart? That would make everything so clean for you."

"It doesn't seem too bad a thing to believe, Sergeant. It only means we should all *give* a little, is all."

I walked off to eat my rations with the other noncoms.

Two days later, a letter addressed to Captain Barrett passed over my desk. It had come through the chain of command—from the office of Congressman Franconi, where it had been received, to General Lyman, to Colonel Sousa, to Major Lamont, now to Captain Barrett. I read it over twice. It was dated May 14, the day Barrett had spoken with Grossbart on the rifle range.

Dear Congressman:

First let me thank you for your interest in behalf of my son, Private Sheldon Grossbart. Fortunately, I was able to speak with Sheldon on the phone the other night, and I think I've been able to solve our problem. He is, as I mentioned in my

[14] A Jewish seminary.

last letter, a very religious boy, and it was only with the greatest difficulty that I could persuade him that the religious thing to do—what God Himself would want Sheldon to do—would be to suffer the pangs of religious remorse for the good of his country and all mankind. It took some doing, Congressman, but finally he saw the light. In fact, what he said (and I wrote down the words on a scratch pad so as never to forget), what he said was "I guess you're right, Dad. So many millions of my fellow-Jews gave up their lives to the enemy, the least I can do is live for a while minus a bit of my heritage so as to help end this struggle and regain for all the children of God dignity and humanity." That, Congressman, would make any father proud.

By the way, Sheldon wanted me to know—and to pass on to you—the name of a soldier who helped him reach this decision: SERGEANT NATHAN MARX. Sergeant Marx is a combat veteran who is Sheldon's first sergeant. This man has helped Sheldon over some of the first hurdles he's had to face in the Army, and is in part responsible for Sheldon's changing his mind about the dietary laws. I know Sheldon would appreciate any recognition Marx could receive.

Thank you and good luck. I look forward to seeing your name on the next election ballot.

> *Respectfully,*
> *Samuel E. Grossbart*

Attached to the Grossbart communiqué was another, addressed to General Marshall Lyman, the post commander, and signed by Representative Charles E. Franconi, of the House of Representatives. The communiqué informed General Lyman that Sergeant Nathan Marx was a credit to the U. S. Army and the Jewish people.

What was Grossbart's motive in recanting? Did he feel he'd gone too far? Was the letter a strategic retreat—a crafty attempt to strengthen what he considered our alliance? Or had he actually changed his mind, via an imaginary dialogue between Grossbart *pére* and Grossbart *fils?* I was puzzled, but only for a few days—that is, only until I realized that, whatever his reasons, he had actually decided to disappear from my life; he was going to allow himself to become just another trainee. I saw him at inspection, but he never winked; at chow formations, but he never flashed me a sign. On Sundays, with the other trainees, he would sit around watching the noncoms' softball team, for which I pitched, but not once did he speak an unnecessary word to me. Fishbein and Halpern retreated, too—at Grossbart's command, I was sure. Apparently he had seen that wisdom lay in turning back before he plunged over into the ugliness of privilege undeserved. Our separation allowed me to forgive him our past encounters, and, finally, to admire him for his good sense.

Meanwhile, free of Grossbart, I grew used to my job and my administrative tasks. I stepped on a scale one day, and discovered I had truly become a noncombatant; I had gained seven pounds. I found patience to get past the first three pages of a book. I thought about the future more and more, and wrote letters to girls I'd known before the war. I even got a few answers. I sent away to Columbia for a Law School catalogue. I continued to follow the war in the Pacific, but it was not my war. I thought I could see the end, and sometimes, at night, I dreamed that I was walking on the streets of Manhattan—Broadway, Third Avenue, 116th Street, where I had lived the three years I attended Columbia. I curled myself around these dreams and I began to be happy.

And then, one Saturday, when everybody was away and I was alone in the orderly room reading a month-old copy of the *Sporting News,* Grossbart reappeared.

"You a baseball fan, Sergeant?"

I looked up. "How are you?"

"Fine," Grossbart said. "They're making a soldier out of me."

"How are Fishbein and Halpern?"

"Coming along," he said. "We've got no training this afternoon. They're at the movies."

"How come you're not with them?"

"I wanted to come over and say hello."

He smiled—a shy, regular-guy smile, as though he and I well knew that our friendship drew its sustenance from unexpected visits, remembered birthdays, and borrowed lawnmowers. At first it offended me, and then the feeling was swallowed by the general uneasiness I felt at the thought that everyone on the post was locked away in a dark movie theater and I was here alone with Grossbart. I folded up my paper.

"Sergeant," he said, "I'd like to ask a favor. It is a favor, and I'm making no bones about it."

He stopped, allowing me to refuse him a hearing—which, of course, forced me into a courtesy I did not intend. "Go ahead."

"Well, actually it's two favors."

I said nothing.

"The first one's about these rumors. Everybody says we're going to the Pacific."

"As I told your friend Fishbein, I don't know." I said. "You'll just have to wait to find out. Like everybody else."

"You think there's a chance of any of us going East?"

"Germany?" I said. "Maybe."

"I meant New York."

"I don't think so, Grossbart. Offhand."

"Thanks for the information, Sergeant," he said.

"It's not information, Grossbart. Just what I surmise."

"It certainly would be good to be near home. My parents—you know." He took a step toward the door and then turned back. "Oh, the other thing. May I ask the other?"

"What is it?"

"The other thing is—I've got relatives in St. Louis, and they say they'll give me a whole Passover dinner if I can get down there. God, Sergeant, that'd mean an awful lot to me."

I stood up. "No passes during basic, Grossbart."

"But we're off from now till Monday morning, Sergeant. I could leave the post and no one would even know."

"I'd know. You'd know."

"But that's all. Just the two of us. Last night, I called my aunt, and you should have heard her. 'Come—come,' she said. 'I got gefilte fish, *chrain*[15]—the works!' Just a day, Sergeant. I'd take the blame if anything happened."

"The Captain isn't here to sign a pass."

[15] "Horseradish" (Yiddish).

"You could sign."

"Look, Grossbart—"

"Sergeant, for two months, practically, I've been eating *trafe* till I want to die."

"I thought you'd made up your mind to live with it. To be minus a little bit of heritage."

He pointed a finger at me. "You!" he said. "That wasn't for you to read."

"I read it. So what?"

"That letter was addressed to a congressman."

"Grossbart, don't feed me any baloney. You *wanted* me to read it."

"Why are you persecuting me, Sergeant?"

"Are you kidding!"

"I've run into this before," he said, "but never from my own!"

"Get out of here, Grossbart! Get the hell out of my sight!"

He did not move. "Ashamed, that's what you are," he said. "So you take it out on the rest of us. They say Hitler himself was half a Jew. Hearing you, I wouldn't doubt it."

"What are you trying to do with me, Grossbart?" I asked him. "What are you after? You want me to give you special privileges, to change the food, to find out about your orders, to give you weekend passes."

"You even talk like a goy!" Grossbart shook his fist. "Is this just a weekend pass I'm asking for? Is a Seder[16] sacred or not?"

Seder! It suddenly occurred to me that Passover had been celebrated weeks before. I said so.

"That's right," he replied. "Who says no? A month ago—and I was in the field eating hash! And now all I ask is a simple favor. A Jewish boy I thought would understand. My aunt's willing to go out of her way—to make a Seder a month later. . . . " He turned to go, mumbling.

"Come back here!" I called. He stopped and looked at me. "Grossbart, why can't you be like the rest? Why do you have to stick out like a sore thumb?"

"Because I'm a Jew, Sergeant. I *am* different. Better, maybe not. But different."

"This is a war, Grossbart. For the time being *be* the same."

"I refuse."

"What?"

"I refuse. I can't stop being me, that's all there is to it." Tears came to his eyes. "It's a hard thing to be a Jew. But now I understand what Mickey says—it's a harder thing to stay one." He raised a hand sadly toward me. "Look at *you*."

"Stop crying!"

"Stop this, stop that, stop the other thing! *You* stop, Sergeant. Stop closing your heart to your own!" And, wiping his face with his sleeve, he ran out the door. "The least we can do for one another—the least . . . "

An hour later, looking out of the window, I saw Grossbart headed across the field. He wore a pair of starched khakis and carried a little leather ditty bag. I went out into the heat of the day. It was quiet; not a soul was in sight except, over by the mess hall, four K. P.s sitting around a pan, sloped forward from their waists, gabbing and peeling potatoes in the sun.

"Grossbart!" I called.

---

[16] A ceremonial dinner during Passover, a holiday commemorating the Israelites' escape from bondage in Egypt.

He looked toward me and continued walking.

"Grossbart, get over here!"

He turned and came across the field. Finally, he stood before me.

"Where are you going?" I asked.

"St. Louis. I don't care."

"You'll get caught without a pass."

"So I'll get caught without a pass."

"You'll go to the stockade."

"I'm *in* the stockade." He made an about-face and headed off.

I let him go only a step or two. "Come back here," I said, and he followed me into the office, where I typed out a pass and signed the Captain's name, and my own initials after it.

He took the pass and then, a moment later, reached out and grabbed my hand. "Sergeant, you don't know how much this means to me."

"O. K., " I said. "Don't get in any trouble."

"I wish I could show you how much this means to me."

"Don't do me any favors. Don't write any more congressmen for citations."

He smiled. "You're right. I won't. But let me do something."

"Bring me a piece of that gefilte fish. Just get out of here."

"I will!" he said. "With a slice of carrot and a little horseradish. I won't forget."

"All right. Just show your pass at the gate. And don't tell *anybody*."

"I won't. It's a month late, but a good Yom Tov[17] to you."

"Good Yom Tov, Grossbart," I said.

"You're a good Jew, Sergeant. You like to think you have a hard heart, but underneath you're a fine, decent man. I mean that."

Those last three words touched me more than any words from Grossbart's mouth had the right to. "All right, Grossbart," I said. "Now call me 'sir,' and get the hell out of here."

He ran out the door and was gone. I felt very pleased with myself; it was a great relief to stop fighting Grossbart, and it had cost me nothing. Barrett would never find out, and if he did, I could manage to invent some excuse. For a while, I sat at my desk, comfortable in my decision. Then the screen door flew back and Grossbart burst in again. "Sergeant!" he said. Behind him I saw Fishbein and Halpern, both in starched khakis, both carrying ditty bags like Grossbart's.

"Sergeant, I caught Mickey and Larry coming out of the movies. I almost missed them."

"Grossbart—did I say tell no one?" I said.

"But my aunt said I could bring friends. That I should, in fact."

"*I'm* the Sergeant, Grossbart—not your aunt!"

Grossbart looked at me in disbelief. He pulled Halpern up by his sleeve. "Mickey, tell the Sergeant what this would mean to you."

Halpern looked at me and, shrugging, said. "A lot."

Fishbein stepped forward without prompting. "This would mean a great deal to me and my parents, Sergeant Marx."

"No!" I shouted.

Grossbart was shaking his head. "Sergeant, I could see you denying me, but how you can deny Mickey, a Yeshiva boy—that's beyond me."

---

[17] "Praise the day" (Yiddish): good holiday.

"I'm not denying Mickey anything," I said. "You just pushed a little too hard, Grossbart. *You* denied him."

"I'll give him my pass, then," Grossbart said. "I'll give him my aunt's address and a little note. At least let him go."

In a second, he had crammed the pass into Halpern's pants pocket. Halpern looked at me, and so did Fishbein. Grossbart was at the door, pushing it open. "Mickey, bring me a piece of gefilte fish, at least," he said, and then he was outside again.

The three of us looked at one another, and then I said, "Halpern, hand that pass over."

He took it from his pocket and gave it to me. Fishbein had now moved to the doorway, where he lingered. He stood there for a moment with his mouth slightly open, and then he pointed to himself. "And me?" he asked.

His utter ridiculousness exhausted me. I slumped down in my seat and felt pulses knocking at the back of my eyes. "Fishbein," I said, "you understand I'm not trying to deny you anything, don't you? If it was my Army, I'd serve gefilte fish in the mess hall. I'd sell *kugel* in the PX,[18] honest to God."

Halpern smiled.

"You understand, don't you Halpern?"

"Yes, Sergeant."

"And you, Fishbein? I don't want enemies. I'm just like you—I want to serve my time and go home. I miss the same things you miss."

"Then, Sergeant," Fishbein said, "why don't you come, too?"

"Where?"

"To St. Louis. To Shelly's aunt. We'll have a regular Seder. Play hide-the matzoh."[19] He gave me a broad, black-toothed smile.

I saw Grossbart again, on the other side of the screen.

"Pst!" He waved a piece of paper. "Mickey, here's the address. Tell her I couldn't get away."

Halpern did not move. He looked at me, and I saw the shrug moving up his arms into his shoulders again. I took the cover off my typewriter and made out passes for him and Fishbein. "Go," I said. "The three of you."

I thought Halpern was going to kiss my hand.

That afternoon, in a bar in Joplin, I drank beer and listened with half an ear to the Cardinal game. I tried to look squarely at what I'd become involved in, and began to wonder if perhaps the struggle with Grossbart wasn't as much my fault as his. What was I that I had to *muster* generous feelings? Who was I to have been feeling so grudging, so tight-hearted? After all, I wasn't being asked to move the world. Had I a right, then, or a reason, to clamp down on Grossbart, when that meant clamping down on Halpern, too? And Fishbein—that ugly, agreeable soul? Out of the many recollections of my childhood that had tumbled over me these past few days I heard my grandmother's voice: "What are you making a *tsimmes?*"[20] It was what she would ask my mother when, say, I had cut myself while doing something I shouldn't have done, and her daughter was busy bawling me out. I needed a hug and a kiss, and my mother would moralize. But my grandmother knew—mercy overrides justice. I should have known it, too. Who was

---

[18] Baked noodle or potato pudding in the post exchange, or the military-run store.

[19] Unleavened bread; a Seder ritual involves hiding a piece of matzoh and sending the children to find it.

[20] A carrot stew; also, a fuss (Yiddish).

Nathan Marx to be such a penny pincher with kindness? Surely, I thought, the Messiah himself—if He should ever come—won't niggle over nickels and dimes. God willing, he'll hug and kiss.

The next day, while I was playing softball over on the parade ground, I decided to ask Bob Wright, who was non-com in charge of Classification and Assignment, where he thought our trainees would be sent when their cycle ended, in two weeks. I asked casually, between innings, and he said, "They're pushing them all into the Pacific. Shulman cut the orders on your boys the other day."

The news shocked me, as though I were the father of Halpern, Fishbein, and Grossbart.

That night, I was just sliding into sleep when someone tapped on my door. "Who is it?" I asked.

"Sheldon."

He opened the door and came in. For a moment, I felt his presence without being able to see him. "How was it?" I asked.

He popped into sight in the near-darkness before me. "Great, Sergeant." Then he was sitting on the edge of the bed. I sat up.

"How about you?" he asked. "Have a nice weekend?"

"Yes."

"The others went to sleep." He took a deep, paternal breath. We sat silent for a while, and a homey feeling invaded my ugly little cubicle; the door was locked, the cat was out, the children were safely in bed.

"Sergeant, can I tell you something? Personal?"

I did not answer, and he seemed to know why. "Not about me. About Mickey. Sergeant, I never felt for anybody like I feel for him. Last night I heard Mickey in the bed next to me. He was crying so, it could have broken you heart. Real sobs."

"I'm sorry to hear that."

"I had to talk to him to stop him. He held my hand, Sergeant—he wouldn't let it go. He was almost hysterical. He kept saying if he only knew where we were going. Even if he knew it *was* the Pacific, that would be better than nothing. Just to know."

Long ago, someone had taught Grossbart the sad rule that only lies can get the truth. Not that I couldn't believe in the fact of Halpern's crying; his eyes *always* seemed red-rimmed. But, fact or not, it became a lie when Grossbart uttered it. He was entirely strategic. But then—it came with the force of indictment—so was I! There are strategies of aggression, but there are strategies of retreat as well. And so, recognizing that I myself had not been without craft and guile, I told him what I knew. "It is the Pacific."

He let out a small gasp, which was not a lie. "I'll tell him. I wish it was otherwise."

"So do I."

He jumped on my words. "You mean you think you could do something? A change, maybe?"

"No, I couldn't do a thing."

"Don't you know anybody over at C. and A.?"

"Grossbart, there's nothing I can do," I said. "If your orders are for the Pacific, then it's the Pacific."

"But Mickey—"

"Mickey, you, me—everybody, Grossbart. There's nothing to be done. Maybe the war'll end before you go. Pray for a miracle."

"But—"

"Good night, Grossbart." I settled back, and was relieved to feel the springs unbend as Grossbart rose to leave. I could see him clearly now; his jaw had dropped, and he looked like a dazed prizefighter. I noticed for the first time a little paper bag in his hand.

"Grossbart." I smiled. "My gift?"

"Oh, yes, Sergeant. Here—from all of us." He handed me the bag. "It's egg roll."

"Egg roll?" I accepted the bag and felt a damp grease spot on the bottom. I opened it, sure that Grossbart was joking.

"We thought you'd probably like it. You know—Chinese egg roll. We thought you'd probably have a taste for—"

"Your aunt served egg roll?"

"She wasn't home."

"Grossbart, she invited you. You told me she invited you and your friends."

"I know," he said. "I just reread the letter. *Next* week."

I got out of bed and walked to the window. "Grossbart," I said. But I was not calling to him.

"What?"

"What are you, Grossbart? Honest to God, what are you?"

I think it was the first time I'd asked him a question for which he didn't have an immediate answer.

"How can you do this to people?" I went on.

"Sergeant, the day away did us all a world of good. Fishbein, you should see him, he *loves* Chinese food."

"But the Seder," I said.

"We took second best, Sergeant."

Rage came charging at me. I didn't sidestep. "Grossbart, you're a liar!" I said. "You're a schemer and a crook. You've got no respect for anything. Nothing at all. Not for me, for the truth—not even for poor Halpern! You use us all—"

"Sergeant, Sergeant, I feel for Mickey. Honest to God, I do. I *love* Mickey. I try—"

"You try! You feel!" I lurched toward him and grabbed his shirt front. I shook him furiously. "Grossbart, get out! Get out and stay the hell away from me. Because if I see you, I'll make your life miserable. *You understand that?*"

"Yes."

I let him free, and when he walked from the room, I wanted to spit on the floor where he had stood. I couldn't stop the fury. It engulfed me, owned me, till it seemed I could only rid myself of it with tears or an act of violence. I snatched from the bed the bag Grossbart had given me and, with all my strength, threw it out the window. And the next morning, as the men policed the area around the barracks, I heard a great cry go up from one of the trainees, who had been anticipating only his morning handful of cigarette butts and candy wrappers. "Egg roll!" he shouted. "Holy Christ, Chinese goddam egg roll!"

A week later, when I read the orders that had come down from C. and A., I couldn't believe my eyes. Every single trainee was to be shipped to Camp Stoneman, California, and from there to the Pacific—every trainee but one. Private Sheldon Grossbart. He was to be sent to Fort Monmouth, New Jersey. I read the mimeographed sheet several times. Dee, Farrell, Fishbein, Fuselli, Fylypowycz, Glinicki, Gromke, Gucwa, Halpern, Hardy, Helbrandt, right down to Anton

Zygadlo—all were to be headed West before the month was out. All except Grossbart. He had pulled a string, and I wasn't it.

I lifted the phone and called C. and A.

The voice on the other end said smartly, "Corporal Shulman, sir."

"Let me speak to Sergeant Wright."

"Who is this calling, sir?"

"Sergeant Marx."

And, to my surprise, the voice said, *"Oh!"* Then, "Just a minute, Sergeant."

Shulman's *"Oh!"* stayed with me while I waited for Wright to come to the phone. Why *"Oh!"* Who was Shulman? And then, so simply, I knew I'd discovered the string that Grossbart had pulled. In fact, I could hear Grossbart the day he'd discovered Shulman in the PX, or in the bowling alley, or maybe even at services. "Glad to meet you. Where you from? Bronx? Me, too. Do you know So-and-So? And So-and-So? Me, too! You work at C. and A.? Really? Hey, how's chances of getting East? Could you do something? Change something? Swindle, cheat, lie? We gotta help each other, you know. If the Jews in Germany . . ."

Bob Wright answered the phone. "How are you, Nate? How's the pitching arm?"

"Good. Bob, I wonder if you could do me a favor." I heard clearly my own words, and they so reminded me of Grossbart that I dropped more easily than I could have imagined into what I had planned. "This may sound crazy, Bob, but I got a kid here on order to Monmouth who wants them changed. He had a brother killed in Europe, and he's hot to go to the Pacific. Says he'd feel like a coward if he wound up Stateside. I don't know, Bob—can anything be done? Put somebody else in the Monmouth slot?"

"Who?" he asked cagily.

"Anybody. First guy in the alphabet. I don't care. The kid just asked if something could be done."

"What's his name?"

"Grossbart, Sheldon."

Wright didn't answer.

"Yeah," I said. "He's a Jewish kid, so he thought I could help him out. You know."

"I guess I can do something," he finally said. "The Major hasn't been around here for weeks. Temporary duty to the golf course. I'll try, Nate, that's all I can say."

"I'd appreciate it, Bob. See you Sunday." And I hung up, perspiring.

"The following day, the corrected orders appeared: Fishbein, Fuselli, Fylypowycz, Glinicki, Gromke, Grossbart, Gucwa, Halpern, Hardy . . . Lucky Private Harley Alton was to go to Fort Monmouth, New Jersey, where, for some reason or other, they wanted an enlisted man with infantry training.

After chow that night, I stopped back at the orderly room to straighten out the guard-duty roster. Grossbart was waiting for me. He spoke first.

"You son of a bitch!"

I sat down at my desk, and while he glared at me, I began to make the necessary alterations in the duty roster.

"What do you have against me?" he cried. "Against my family? Would it kill you for me to be near my father, God knows how many months he has left to him?"

"Why so?"

"His heart," Grossbart said. "He hasn't had enough troubles in a lifetime, you've got to add to them. I curse the day I ever met you, Marx! Shulman told me what happened over there. There's no limit to your anti-Semitism, is there? The damage you've done here isn't enough. You have to make a special phone call! You really want me dead!"

I made the last few notations in the duty roster and got up to leave. "Good night, Grossbart."

"You owe me an explanation!" He stood in my path.

"Sheldon, you're the one who owes explanations."

He scowled, "To *you?*"

"To me, I think so—yes. Mostly to Fishbein and Halpern."

"That's right, twist things around. I owe nobody nothing, I've done all I could do for them. Now I think I've got the right to watch out for myself."

"For each other we have to learn to watch out, Sheldon. You told me yourself."

"You call this watching out for me—what you did?"

"No. For all of us."

I pushed him aside and started for the door. I heard his furious breathing behind me, and it sounded like steam rushing from an engine of terrible strength.

"*You'll* be all right," I said from the door. And, I thought, so would Fishbein and Halpern be all right, even in the Pacific, if only Grossbart continued to see— in the obsequiousness of the one, the soft spirituality of the other—some profit for himself.

I stood outside the orderly room, and I heard Grossbart weeping behind me. Over in the barracks, in the lighted windows, I could see the boys in their T shirts sitting on their bunks talking about their orders, as they'd been doing for the past two days. With a kind of quiet nervousness, they polished shoes, shined belt buckles, squared away underwear, trying as best they could to accept their fate. Behind me, Grossbart swallowed hard, accepting his. And then, resisting with all my will an impulse to turn and seek pardon for my vindictiveness, I accepted my own.

1959

Joan Didion
(1934–   )

In her fiction Joan Didion employs forms and techniques from popular culture, presented with irony. She executes soap-opera-like plots in a fragmented, cinematic style that she feels represents modern life more faithfully than the traditional narrative does. Born in Sacramento in 1934, she is a fifth-generation Californian. Didion graduated from the University of California at Berkeley in 1956, the same year she won a writing contest sponsored by *Vogue* magazine. After moving to New York City, she worked as an associate feature editor at *Vogue* until 1963, when her first novel, *River Run,* was published. The following year she married the writer John Gregory Dunne. The couple then moved to Los Angeles, where they collaborated on magazine columns and on screenplays for such movies as *The Panic in Needle Park* (1971) and *A Star Is Born* (1976).

Didion's second and third novels, *Play It as It Lays* (1970) and *A Book of Common Prayer* (1977), were great commercial successes. Her essays, however, collected in *Slouching Towards Bethlehem* (1968) and in *The White Album* (1979), attracted greater critical acclaim. The themes characteristic of Didion's fiction—the loss of a sense of history and entrapment in an alien culture—are also central to her cultural criticism. *Slouching Towards Bethlehem* warily examines the celebrities and life styles of California in the 1960s. "The future always looks good in the golden land," she writes in that collection, "because no one remembers the past." *The White Album* essays record Didion's personal anguish at the social upheaval of the late 1960s and the early 1970s. The book's title refers to the 1968 album by the Beatles, an album that Didion found "ominous and disturbing" because it came to be associated with the murders of actress Sharon Tate and six others by Charles Manson and his cult followers. The title essay alternates between accounts of the public crises of 1968—the assassinations of Martin Luther King, Jr., and Robert Kennedy, the violence that tore apart the Democratic National Convention in Chicago, student strikes, the imprisonment of black activists—and the author's own emotional breakdown.

In the 1980s Didion continued to deal with the connections between the personal and the political. The essays collected in *Salvador* (1983), based on her 1982 visit with Dunne to El Salvador, rage against the language politicians use to obscure the violence in such countries. And, although the heroines of all her novels are upper middle-class women caught up in male violence, the critique of American culture in the novel *Democracy* (1984) is more specifically feminist. Abandonment and incomplete efforts at independence and enpowerment are, she suggests, womens' rituals in a male-dominated society. In *Democracy* Didion stylistically undercuts the authority of the narrator by switching points of view and by interrupting to mention a work that she never completed.

Suggested Readings: *Slouching Towards Bethlehem*, 1968. *Play It As It Lays*, 1970. *A Book of Common Prayer*, 1977. *The White Album*, 1979. *Salvador*, 1983. *Democracy*, 1984. *Miami*, 1988. A. Kazin, "Joan Didion: Portrait of a Professional," in *Harper's Magazine*, 243 (December): 112–122, 1971. F. R. Jacobs, *Joan Didion—A Bibliography*, 1977. B. G. Harrison, "Joan Didion: The Courage of Her Afflictions," in *Nation*, 229 (26 September): 277–286, 1979. M. R. Winchell, *Joan Didion*, 1980. K. U. Henderson, *Joan Didion*, 1981. E. Friedman, ed., *Essays and Conversations*, 1984.

Text Used: *Telling Stories*, 1978.

WHEN DID MUSIC COME THIS WAY?
CHILDREN DEAR, WAS IT YESTERDAY?*

I am now at that age, as is Cary, when two drinks before lunch can blur my looks. In fact I am careful about it: a Bloody Mary, I say, because I dislike tomato juice, or bouillon-and-vodka, because bouillon nourishes; I have watched too many women bungle an excess of nonchalance about one more vodka martini. Although there are afternoons (today was one) when I would myself prefer to have several vodka martinis and go home to bed, I remember in time that it is not much my style.

But I digress. I meant only to suggest that I am no longer so very young. You might say that thirty-three is not yet so very old, either, but it is old enough so that

---

* First published in the *Denver Quarterly*.

I will never now be photographed for the New York Sunday newspapers wearing a discotheque dress, old enough so that I no longer think optimistically about "changes." I could start over, but never fresh. Divorce would mean sadness. "Sadness" is a word I did not understand until recently.

I want to tell you about a Christmas. I wish that memory made no connections, for I would like to tell you about it straight, would like you to see it as finished and as self-contained as a painting on a gallery wall; would like *you* to interpret it to *me*. Here is the way I would like you to see it: *Christmas Day. 1945. A family gathers*. There's Cary, the snow princess by the Christmas tree, and there I am, a year younger, no snow princess but the homely cousin (in plainness lay all virtue, they hinted as solace, but perhaps I was not quite plain enough), and wasn't Aunt Inez the great beauty she was said to be and didn't we all live happily ever after? But nothing is ever finished, nothing self-contained. And because I am corrupt in the ways of making connections, you must walk through this gallery with an annotated catalogue.

The snow reminds me. It has been snowing here for three days now. My husband woke me at four this morning by throwing snow on the bed, and this afternoon I took the children to Carl Schurz Park[1] to make angel wings in the drifted snow. That was a happy thing to do. In fact I did not want to leave the park, but a man came to lock the gate, and it was dark, and the children were hungry. Now. Just as it is snowing here tonight (drifting in the air shaft, sifting through the skylights, reminding me that the dining room window sash has been broken since summer and that the radiators need draining and that if I do not soon make the necessary telephone calls, the required small arrangements, our precarious shelter against the city will be lost), so it was snowing on that Christmas Day in 1945. Although Reno stands several thousand feet above sea level (4,490 feet, should you want the exact figure, and I will tell you right now that I am more and more interested in exact figures) we did not always have December snow; more often the dry wind would blow in from the desert and the Chamber of Commerce decorations along Virginia Street would tangle and whine with it and my mother would get sick headache from it and the boys in from the ranches would turn up the collars of their denim jackets and shove their knuckles deep into the pockets where the silver dollars were. They would hitch rides into town the afternoon before Christmas to buy presents and shoot craps and find some illuminated refuge from the wind.

Obiter dictum:[2] It occurs to me that refuge was simpler then, to find and to maintain. Mere colored lights could do it. Last night I turned on all the lights still left on the Christmas tree they tell me has become a fire hazard, but nothing happened, except that more needles fell; in fact they have almost all fallen, and many of the ornaments are broken. I looked steadily at the lights and tried very hard to hold on, just as I am trying tonight, but nothing happened. Nothing warm. Instead I thought again of the jet that fell into the East River on a night very like this one the winter we bought this apartment; I think more and more about that jet, as well as about what would happen should a crack develop in the Queens-Midtown Tunnel.[3] I mean exactly what would happen, precisely what volume of water would be involved, the actual facts. I have never seen a study on this, but think of it frequently; last night I thought of it until I had to lie down, on the floor in the children's room to be near something warm.

---

[1] Near the East River in New York City.   [2] An incidental remark or opinion (Latin).
[3] A tunnel linking the boroughs of Queens and Manhattan.

In any case. On that Christmas in 1945 we had not wind but snow, a dense fall of powder snow, so much snow that everyone who came to our house for dinner would have to stay the night. There was Cary, who arrived with snow on the shoulders of her new polo coat (we each had one, every Christmas, identical polo coats from our grandmother in San Francisco), with snow on her pale blonde hair and snow on the shopping bag of presents she thrust toward me when I opened the door. There was Aunt Inez, looking as she always looked, as if she were on the verge of something theatrical, some marriage or divorce or near-fatal accident. Whenever Aunt Inez took Cary and me to lunch at the Riverside Hotel, men would look up from the crap tables and stare as we walked through the lobby; I think now that they stared less because of her beauty (other people were beautiful, my own mother was beautiful, even I am not as homely as I once was, but men do not stare at me) than because of that air of moment, of imminent disaster. Men stared at Aunt Inez as we all stare at airplanes in flight.

And there was Ward. I try now to think of Ward and can call up only cartoon characters: Smilin' Jack, Steve Canyon, the nameless fliers in love with Lace. All I can say is that Ward was handsome, had flown a B-29, and did not, I think, like any of us. Presumably he liked Aunt Inez, since he had married her, but he did not like the rest of us. I do not mean that he disliked us; we simply failed to touch him. Very little touched him. Aunt Inez apparently had, and airplanes did, and there you were. Once, when my father observed that it was uncharacteristic of Aunt Inez to marry someone like Ward, who would have been a gas station attendant all his life had the war not happily intervened, my mother said sharply that it was quite in character. "She doesn't marry men," my mother added. "She marries problems. All some problem has to do is come along and look at Inez as if to die, and Inez marries it."

I see that I have said "and there was Ward." That is inaccurate, an example of how we remember what should have been instead of what was. For the salient fact of the afternoon was that Ward did not come. When I asked where he was, Aunt Inez seemed startled, as if she had not before noticed his absence. "Ward?" she repeated after me. "Oh. *Ward.* He'll be along. He'll be along a little later. He's out at the airfield. That's *very* probably where he is."

We did, that afternoon, what we always did. We exchanged presents, a silver music box from Cary to me, an ivory bracelet from me to Cary; we lighted the Christmas candles and sang songs around the piano, and the snow fell outside and it seemed that we were safe and warm inside. Ward, Aunt Inez said a number of times, would be along any minute. Only when dessert was served did she stop saying it. "I can't understand what's keeping Ward," she said then, and in the silence which followed, Cary pushed back her chair and ran from the table. "Cary, for *heaven*'s sake," Aunt Inez murmured helplessly, and then she followed Cary into the kitchen. When they reappeared Aunt Inez had two extra champagne glasses, one for me and one for Cary. We were both, she declared, old enough for a glass of champagne at Christmas; this moodiness, this downright *rude*ness of Cary's was just one more symptom of that. But all that was over now. We would toast our growing up.

"Never," Cary whispered later, sitting crosslegged on the floor while she wound long strands of hair around her finger and skewered each strand with a bobby pin. "I would *never* the longest day I ever lived marry somebody like Ward."

I sat up in bed. "How would you know?"

"How would I know what?"

"Know whether somebody was like Ward."

"I'd know," Cary said. "You can tell."

I lay back, and wondered what it was you could tell.

"Listen," Cary said, dipping her comb in a glass of water. "I'd have known before he even proposed. I'd have known that very first night he came to the house. You know what he did that night? He sat in front of the fire and drank an entire bottle of Jack Daniels bourbon. He sat there all night drinking Jack Daniels bourbon and when I came down for breakfast he was still there, just sitting there staring at Mama, and Mama staring at him."

"As if to die," I whispered.

"What's that supposed to mean?"

"Nothing."

"Jack Daniels is very expensive bourbon," she added. "Jack Daniels is one of *the* most expensive bourbons in the entire world. Bayard gave me a sip of it once and told me that. He used to buy it by the case."

"Bayard who?"

"You know perfectly well *Bayard who*. You're just trying to be smart and catty."

In fact I had forgotten Bayard, although I remembered as soon as I asked: He was married to Aunt Inez between Cary's father and Ward. It was difficult to keep Bayard in mind because he had spent only one Christmas with us. The rest of the time they were at Pensacola.[4] All I remember of that Christmas was that Bayard had taken a car into town on Christmas Eve and cracked it up.

"Anyway," Cary continued, "Bayard's not the point. Bayard was and is a *hero*. He was awarded the Purple Heart. He was wounded."

"In the Officers' Club at Pensacola." I had heard my father say it.

"All right. Just keep it up. You're not going to be the least bit popular, you keep on that way. Nobody likes a cat. *Any*way. The point is, I would never make the mistake of marrying somebody like *Ward*."

I watched Cary pinning up the last strands of her hair, and wished again that I had hair like hers. "Who you *plan*ning on marrying then?" I asked after a while. "Frank Sinatra? Audie Murphy? Dr. Albert Schweitzer?"[5]

"Never you mind. He won't stay away three days at a time on *Christ*mas, you can be sure. I guess I can call that tune."

I cannot now tell you why I turned on Cary, for I loved her. Did we not share a grandmother, wear identical polo coats? Had we not spent Christmas together always? How could I have not loved her? In any case what I did was stupid, blunted, vicious only in tone. It is the kind of thing I still do. I did something very like it this morning, when Charlie came in and threw the snow on the bed. As he pointed out before he left, I did not even get her name right. I said everything that was ugly and nothing that hit the mark.

So it was with Cary. *You guess you can call that tune*, I chanted, *what tune is that, Cary, is this the tune?* And while I chanted I grabbed up the silver music box she had given me, wound it, jammed it against her ear. Frightened, she wrenched it from me and dropped it; neither of us moved as the box cracked and the works shattered and shot across the floor, under the dressing table, under the bed, into

---

[4] A port city in Florida.

[5] Murphy (1924–1971) was the most decorated American soldier in World War II; he went on to star in movies in the 1950s and 1960s. Schweitzer (1875–1965) was a French theologian, philosopher, physician, and music scholar, best known as a medical missionary to Africa.

the open closet. Cary leaned back against the mirror then, sobbing, crying *I broke your present, I broke it, I picked it out myself and Mama said it was exactly right and now it's gone.*

"Never mind," I said. "It was my fault. We can have it fixed. You and I can take it into town and have. . . ."

"Don't you even care? Didn't you even care about it?"

"It was my fault. We can get it fixed."

"Oh sweet God," Cary sobbed. "Sometimes I wish I could jump in the Truckee River."[6]

"Why don't you," I whispered, but happily she had already run into the bathroom and locked the door—"happily" because what I had said was not in the spirit of Christmas, none of it was, and as my mother so often said, if we don't have our families, then who do we have—we have no one, no one at all.

It was not until it became clear that Cary would stay in the bathroom until I left that I went downstairs. And then it was not until I had been lying a long time on the sofa behind the Christmas tree, watching the shadows that the tree lights and dying fire threw on the ceiling, that I saw Aunt Inez and Ward. I could see them through the branches of the tree. Aunt Inez was wearing a robe of my mother's, but her hair was still up in a French twist, and she still wore her gold earrings and bracelets. Ward was slumped in a chair across from her, his arctic parka and a bottle of bourbon on the floor beside him. For a long time they said nothing, but finally they began talking. I do not remember all they said, not only because I was half asleep but because they repeated the same things over and over, words that meant nothing to me, fragments of sentences they seemed to have begun so many times before that there was no need to finish them. All I remember is that both their voices sounded sad, and wounded, and that every time Aunt Inez said that she could not go on, that she could not be made to look a fool up and down the state of Nevada, Ward would repeat *it has nothing to do with you, nothing, you're the one who's making a fool of yourself.* It has everything to do with me, she would say again. It has nothing, he would repeat.

I next remember Aunt Inez crying, and Ward leaning very close to her and saying: "Tell me, Inez. Tell me how much. Tell me what you'd do."

"Anything." Aunt Inez said again and again. "You know what I'd do. Anything."

"Tell me what you'd do for it."

"Don't. It's Christmas. Please."

"Say it."

"I'd do anything," she repeated.

"Say it out loud. Who would you betray."

"I can't tonight."

"*Say* it."

There was silence, and then Aunt Inez said, as if by rote, "I would betray my mother. I would betray my sister. I would betray Cary."

"OK," Ward said softly then, and sat back. "OK."

They said nothing for a long time, and when I woke there was a comforter over me and the lights were off and it was December 26, another Christmas gone, and when Cary came downstairs I could not look at her.

There it is. I have been trying hard tonight to remember exactly what Aunt Inez said, her precise words, not that it matters. We all say the same things. Here are

---

[6] A river flowing between California and Nevada, through Reno.

some facts. Ward died in 1949, in an aerial show in South Dakota. Aunt Inez did not marry again, and is now on a cruise of the Balkans;[7] I received a card today. "Happy landings," it closed. Cary has married, twice, and I saw her for lunch during the World's Fair. She had five vodka martinis, one in lieu of dessert. I see my mother and father once a year, in July, when I take the children out. They seem older, and to prefer talking to the children than to me. Charlie called a few hours ago to say that if the Christmas tree was not down by the time he came home he would call the Fire Department, that it would ignite one night soon and burn us in our beds. I pointed out that in any case it was unlikely to catch him. Those are the only facts. Now I have some questions. Was Aunt Inez as cold that night as I am tonight? When did Cary find out that she could not after all call the tune? Do we all marry Wards? If we are lucky? Was that Christmas warm only for me? How exactly did we get from there to here? As I told you, I am trying very hard tonight to hold on.

1967

=CONTEXTS=

Interpretation

In the essay "Against Interpretation" (1964) Susan Sontag (1933–   ) reacts against elitism and sexism in modern literary criticism by suggesting new, more socially enlightened methods of interpretation. She sees the traditional forms of hermeneutics, or literary interpretation, as acts of violence against works of literature, as attempts to impose the will of the critic on the meaning of the work of art:

Against Interpretation

The modern style of interpretation excavates, and as it excavates, destroys; it digs "behind" the text, to find a sub-text which is the true one. The most celebrated and influential modern doctrines, those of Marx and Freud, actually amount to elaborate systems of hermeneutics, aggressive and impious theories of interpretation. . . . Today is such a time, when the project of interpretation is largely reactionary, stifling. Like the fumes of the automobile and of heavy industry which befoul the urban atmosphere, the effusion of interpretations of art today poisons our sensibilities. In a culture whose already classical dilemma is the hypertrophy of the intellect at the expense of energy and sensual capability, interpretation is the revenge of the intellect upon art.

In place of the "brutality" of literary interpretation Sontag postulates a more "sensuous" approach to art and literature:

What is important now is to recover our senses. We must learn to *see* more, to *hear* more, to *feel* more.

Our task is not to find the maximum amount of content in a work of art, much less to squeeze more content out of the work than is already there. Our task is to cut back content so that we can see the thing at all.

In place of a hermeneutics we need an erotics of art.

Susan Sontag, 1964

---

[7] The countries of the Balkan Peninsula, including Greece and Yugoslavia.

N. Scott Momaday
(1934–   )

Navarre Scott Momaday was born in 1934 in Kiowa Indian country in southwestern Oklahoma. His parents, both teachers, raised him in Native-American and non-Native-American communities in Oklahoma, in Arizona, and in New Mexico, including Jemez Pueblo, New Mexico. Momaday earned a B.A. from the University of New Mexico in 1958, an M.A. from Stanford University in 1960, and a Ph.D. from Stanford in 1963. During the 1960s he received a Guggenheim Fellowship to study New England poets and edited *The Complete Poems of Frederick Goddard Tuckerman* (1965). In 1968 Momaday's Pulitzer Prize-winning novel, *House Made of Dawn*, was published. Abel, the protagonist, comes from Jemez Pueblo. He experiences a homeland obscured by a vague ancestry and painful encounters with World War II and with post war Los Angeles. He returns to Jemez, filled with harsh memories but also with hints of a renewed sense of place and of the power of sacred words.

The narrative *The Way to Rainy Mountain* (1969) grew out of *The Journey of Tai-me* (1967), Momaday's collection of Kiowa and family stories. *Rainy Mountain* celebrates the tribe's story in myth, history, and personal memory. Momaday knows that the golden years of the Kiowa culture—the Sun Dance, the buffalo herds, the glorious horsemen— are gone forever. And yet, his commitment to memories of oral traditions and to the power of imagination enables him to make the past a vital part of the present and to fix it at the center of a complex chronology of myth, fact, and recollection. In *Rainy Mountain* Momaday preserves the timeless moments of the Kiowas in a three-voice narrative. Each of its twenty-four sections contains a story, a history, and a lyric remembrance, each set in a different typeface.

Momaday is able to preserve these moments successfully because of his reverence for the power of language—a reverence he fears is declining in the modern "white" world. For Momaday, as he explains in *Rainy Mountain*, "a word has power in and of itself. It comes from nothing into sound and meaning; it gives origin to all things. By means of words can a man deal with the world on equal terms. And the word is sacred."

Momaday has traveled throughout the world lecturing and reading from his works. He has taught at the University of California at Berkeley, Stanford University, and the University of Arizona as well as in Germany and the Soviet Union. An autobiography of his early years, *The Names*, was published in a complex memoir form in 1976. He based his second novel, *The Ancient Child* (1989), on a Kiowa story about a man transformed into a bear. And Momaday has written two books of poetry, *Angle of Geese* (1974) and *The Gourd Dancer* (1976). Like his father, Al Momaday, he is also an artist, and his paintings and drawings have been displayed in Germany and Switzerland.

Suggested Readings: *The Journey of Tai-me*, 1967. *House Made of Dawn*, 1968. *Colorado: Summer, Fall, Winter, Spring*, 1973. *Angle of Geese*, 1974. *The Gourd Dancer*, 1976. *The Names: A Memoir*, 1976. *The Ancient Child*, 1989. M. S. Trimble, *N. Scott Momaday*, 1973. H. A. Baker, Jr., ed., *Three American Literatures: Essays in Chicano, Native American, Asian-American Literature for Teachers of American Literature*, 1982. A. R. Velie, *Four American Indian Literary Masters*, 1982. M. Schubnell, *N. Scott Momaday*, 1985. K. M. Roemer, ed., *Approaches to Teaching Momaday's The Way to Rainy Mountain*, 1988.

Text Used: *The Way to Rainy Mountain*, 1969.

America's first literary expressions appear in ancient cave paintings by Native Americans of the Southwest. N. Scott Momaday retains the tradition of the visual narrative in The Way to Rainy Mountain *with this drawing of a buffalo hunter by his father, Al Momaday.*

THE WAY TO RAINY MOUNTAIN*

HEADWATERS

Noon in the intermountain plain:
There is scant telling of the marsh—
A log, hollow and weather-stained,
An insect at the mouth, and moss—
Yet waters against the roots,

---

* In the Wichita Mountain Range of southwestern Oklahoma. The narrative's introduction first appeared in *The Reporter* on January 26, 1967. Momaday's note: "I wish to acknowledge my own book, *The Journey of Tai-me*, which is in a special sense the archetype of the present volume."

Stand brimming to the stalks. What moves?
What moves on this archaic force
Was wild and welling at the source.

PROLOGUE

The journey began one day long ago on the edge of the northern Plains. It was carried on over a course of many generations and many hundreds of miles. In the end there were many things to remember, to dwell upon and talk about.

"You know, everything had to begin. . . . " For the Kiowas[1] the beginning was a struggle for existence in the bleak northern mountains. It was there, they say, that they entered the world through a hollow log. The end, too, was a struggle, and it was lost. The young Plains culture of the Kiowas withered and died like grass that is burned in the prairie wind. There came a day like destiny; in every direction, as far as the eye could see, carrion lay out in the land. The buffalo was the animal representation of the sun, the essential and sacrificial victim of the Sun Dance. When the wild herds were destroyed, so too was the will of the Kiowa people; there was nothing to sustain them in spirit. But these are idle recollections, the mean and ordinary agonies of human history. The interim was a time of great adventure and nobility and fulfillment.

Tai-me came to the Kiowas in a vision born of suffering and despair. "Take me with you," Tai-me said, "and I will give you whatever you want." And it was so. The great adventure of the Kiowas was a going forth into the heart of the continent. They began a long migration from the headwaters of the Yellowstone River eastward to the Black Hills and south to the Wichita Mountains.[2] Along the way they acquired horses, the religion of the Plains, a love and possession of the open land. Their nomadic soul was set free. In alliance with the Comanches they held dominion in the southern Plains for a hundred years. In the course of that long migration they had come of age as a people. They had conceived a good idea of themselves; they had dared to imagine and determine who they were.

In one sense, then, the way to Rainy Mountain is preeminently the history of an idea, man's idea of himself, and it has old and essential being in language. The verbal tradition by which it has been preserved has suffered a deterioration in time. What remains is fragmentary: mythology, legend, lore, and hearsay—and of course the idea itself, as crucial and completed as it ever was. That is the miracle.

The journey herein recalled continues to be made anew each time the miracle comes to mind, for that is peculiarly the right and responsibility of the imagination. It is a whole journey, intricate with motion and meaning; and it is made with the whole memory, that experience of the mind which is legendary as well as historical, personal as well as cultural. And the journey is an evocation of three things in particular: a landscape that is incomparable, a time that is gone forever, and the human spirit, which endures. The imaginative experience and the historical express equally the traditions of man's reality. Finally, then, the journey recalled is among other things the revelation of one way in which these traditions are conceived, developed, and interfused in the human mind. There are on the way to

---

[1] The tribes mentioned throughout are those of the Plains Indians.

[2] A river flowing through Wyoming and Montana; mountains in South Dakota; a mountain range in Oklahoma.

Rainy Mountain many landmarks, many journeys in the one. From the beginning the migration of the Kiowas was an expression of the human spirit, and that expression is most truly made in terms of wonder and delight: "There were many people, and oh, it was beautiful. That was the beginning of the Sun Dance.[3] It was all for Tai-me, you know, and it was a long time ago."

INTRODUCTION

A single knoll rises out of the plain in Oklahoma, north and west of the Wichita Range. For my people, the Kiowas, it is an old landmark, and they gave it the name Rainy Mountain. The hardest weather in the world is there. Winter brings blizzards, hot tornadic winds arise in the spring, and in summer the prairie is an anvil's edge. The grass turns brittle and brown, and it cracks beneath your feet. There are green belts along the rivers and creeks, linear groves of hickory and pecan, willow and witch hazel. At a distance in July or August the steaming foliage seems almost to writhe in fire. Great green and yellow grasshoppers are everywhere in the tall grass, popping up like corn to sting the flesh, and tortoises crawl about on the red earth, going nowhere in the plenty of time. Loneliness is an aspect of the land. All things in the plain are isolate; there is no confusion of objects in the eye, but *one* hill or *one* tree or *one* man. To look upon that landscape in the early morning, with the sun at your back, is to lose the sense of proportion. Your imagination comes to life, and this, you think, is where Creation was begun.

I returned to Rainy Mountain in July. My grandmother had died in the spring, and I wanted to be at her grave. She had lived to be very old and at last infirm. Her only living daughter was with her when she died, and I was told that in death her face was that of a child.

I like to think of her as a child. When she was born, the Kiowas were living that last great moment of their history. For more than a hundred years they had controlled the open range from the Smoky Hill River to the Red, from the headwaters of the Canadian to the fork of the Arkansas and Cimarron.[4] In alliance with the Comanches, they had ruled the whole of the sourthern Plains. War was their sacred business, and they were among the finest horsemen the world has ever known. But warfare for the Kiowas was preeminently a matter of disposition rather than of survival, and they never understood the grim, unrelenting advance of the U.S. Cavalry. When at last, divided and ill-provisioned, they were driven onto the Staked Plains[5] in the cold rains of autumn, they fell into panic. In Palo Duro Canyon[6] they abandoned their crucial stores to pillage and had nothing then but their lives. In order to save themselves, they surrendered to the soldiers at Fort Sill[7] and were imprisoned in the old stone corral that now stands as a military museum. My grandmother was spared the humiliation of those high gray walls by eight or ten years, but she must have known from birth the affliction of defeat, the dark brooding of old warriors.

---

[3] A sacred ceremony of the Plains Indians, lasting eight days.

[4] From central Kansas to the Red River of the North, which crosses the Canadian border between North Dakota and Minnesota; to the fork of the Arkansas River (which flows through Oklahoma, Arkansas, and Mississippi) and the Cimarron River (which flows through New Mexico, Oklahoma, and Arkansas) at eastern Oklahoma.

[5] A large plateau extending over parts of New Mexico, Texas, and Oklahoma.

[6] A canyon in Texas.   [7] A military reserve outside Lawton, Oklahoma.

Her name was Aho, and she belonged to the last culture to evolve in North America. Her forebears came down from the high country in western Montana nearly three centuries ago. They were a mountain people, a mysterious tribe of hunters whose language has never been positively classified in any major group. In the late seventeenth century they began a long migration to the south and east. It was a journey toward the dawn, and it led to a golden age. Along the way the Kiowas were befriended by the Crows, who gave them the culture and religion of the Plains. They acquired horses, and their ancient nomadic spirit was suddenly free of the ground. They acquired Tai-me, the sacred Sun Dance doll, from that moment the object and symbol of their worship, and so shared in the divinity of the sun. Not least, they acquired the sense of destiny, therefore courage and pride. When they entered upon the southern Plains they had been transformed. No longer were they slaves to the simple necessity of survival; they were a lordly and dangerous society of fighters and thieves, hunters and priests of the sun. According to their origin myth, they entered the world through a hollow log. From one point of view, their migration was the fruit of an old prophecy, for indeed they emerged from a sunless world.

Although my grandmother lived out her long life in the shadow of Rainy Mountain, the immense landscape of the continental interior lay like memory in her blood. She could tell of the Crows, whom she had never seen, and of the Black Hills, where she had never been. I wanted to see in reality what she had seen more perfectly in the mind's eye, and traveled fifteen hundred miles to begin my pilgrimage.

Yellowstone, it seemed to me, was the top of the world, a region of deep lakes and dark timber, canyons and waterfalls. But, beautiful as it is, one might have the sense of confinement there. The skyline in all directions is close at hand, the high wall of the woods and deep cleavages of shade. There is a perfect freedom in the mountains, but it belongs to the eagle and the elk, the badger and the bear. The Kiowas reckoned their stature by the distance they could see, and they were bent and blind in the wilderness.

Descending eastward, the highland meadows are a stairway to the plain. In July the inland slope of the Rockies is luxuriant with flax and buckwheat, stonecrop and larkspur. The earth unfolds and the limit of the land recedes. Clusters of trees, and animals grazing far in the distance, cause the vision to reach away and wonder to build upon the mind. The sun follows a longer course in the day, and the sky is immense beyond all comparison. The great billowing clouds that sail upon it are shadows that move upon the grain like water, dividing light. Farther down, in the land of the Crows and Blackfeet, the plain is yellow. Sweet clover takes hold of the hills and bends upon itself to cover and seal the soil. There the Kiowas paused on their way; they had come to the place where they must change their lives. The sun is at home on the plains. Precisely there does it have the certain character of a god. When the Kiowas came to the land of the Crows, they could see the dark lees of the hills at dawn across the Bighorn River,[8] the profusion of light on the grain shelves, the oldest deity ranging after the solstices. Not yet would they veer southward to the caldron of the land that lay below; they must wean their blood from the northern winter and hold the mountains a while longer in their view. They bore Tai-me in procession to the east.

A dark mist lay over the Black Hills, and the land was like iron. At the top of a

---

[8] A river flowing from Wyoming through Montana.

ridge I caught sight of Devil's Tower[9] upthrust against the gray sky as if in the birth of time the core of the earth had broken through its crust and the motion of the world was begun. There are things in nature that engender an awful quiet in the heart of man; Devil's Tower is one of them. Two centuries ago, because they could not do otherwise, the Kiowas made a legend at the base of the rock. My grandmother said:

> *Eight children were there at play, seven sisters and their brother. Suddenly the boy was struck dumb; he trembled and began to run upon his hands and feet. His fingers became claws, and his body was covered with fur. Directly there was a bear where the boy had been. The sisters were terrified; they ran, and the bear after them. They came to the stump of a great tree, and the tree spoke to them. It bade them climb upon it, and as they did so it began to rise into the air. The bear came to kill them, but they were just beyond its reach. It reared against the tree and scored the bark all around with its claws. The seven sisters were borne into the sky, and they became the stars of the Big Dipper.*[10]

From that moment, and so long as the legend lives, the Kiowas have kinsmen in the night sky. Whatever they were in the mountains, they could be no more. However tenuous their well-being, however much they had suffered and would suffer again, they had found a way out of the wilderness.

My grandmother had a reverence for the sun, a holy regard that now is all but gone out of mankind. There was a wariness in her, and an ancient awe. She was a Christian in her later years, but she had come a long way about, and she never forgot her birthright. As a child she had been to the Sun Dances; she had taken part in those annual rites, and by them she had learned the restoration of her people in the presence of Tai-me. She was about seven when the last Kiowa Sun Dance was held in 1887 on the Washita River[11] above Rainy Mountain Creek. The buffalo were gone. In order to consummate the ancient sacrifice—to impale the head of a buffalo bull upon the medicine tree—a delegation of old men journeyed into Texas, there to beg and barter for an animal from the Goodnight herd. She was ten when the Kiowas came together for the last time as a living Sun Dance culture. They could find no buffalo; they had to hang an old hide from the sacred tree. Before the dance could begin, a company of soldiers rode out from Fort Sill under orders to disperse the tribe. Forbidden without cause the essential act of their faith, having seen the wild herds slaughtered and left to rot upon the ground, the Kiowas backed away forever from the medicine tree. That was July 20, 1890, at the great bend of the Washita. My grandmother was there. Without bitterness, and for as long as she lived, she bore a vision of deicide.

Now that I can have her only in memory, I see my grandmother in the several postures that were peculiar to her: standing at the wood stove on a winter morning and turning meat in a great iron skillet; sitting at the south window, bent above her beadwork, and afterwards, when her vision failed, looking down for a long time into the folds of her hands; going out upon a cane, very slowly as she did when the weight of age came upon her; praying. I remember her most often at prayer. She

---

[9] An 865-foot-high rock tower of volcanic origin in the Black Hills of Wyoming; established as a national monument in 1906.

[10] The seven principal stars of the constellation Ursa Major, arranged in a form resembling a dipper.

[11] A river in Oklahoma.

made long, rambling prayers out of suffering and hope, having seen many things. I was never sure that I had the right to hear, so exclusive were they of all mere custom and company. The last time I saw her she prayed standing by the side of her bed at night, naked to the waist, the light of a kerosene lamp moving upon her dark skin. Her long, black hair, always drawn and braided in the day, lay upon her shoulders and against her breasts like a shawl. I do not speak Kiowa, and I never understood her prayers, but there was something inherently sad in the sound, some merest hesitation upon the syllables of sorrow. She began in a high and descending pitch, exhausting her breath to silence; then again and again—and always the same intensity of effort, of something that is, and is not, like urgency in the human voice. Transported so in the dancing light among the shadows of her room, she seemed beyond the reach of time. But that was illusion; I think I knew then that I should not see her again.

Houses are like sentinels in the plain, old keepers of the weather watch. There, in a very little while, wood takes on the appearance of great age. All colors wear soon away in the wind and rain, and then the wood is burned gray and the grain appears and the nails turn red with rust. The windowpanes are black and opaque; you imagine there is nothing within, and indeed there are many ghosts, bones given up to the land. They stand here and there against the sky, and you approach them for a longer time than you expect. They belong in the distance; it is their domain.

Once there was a lot of sound in my grandmother's house, a lot of coming and going, feasting and talk. The summers there were full of excitement and reunion. The Kiowas are a summer people; they abide the cold and keep to themselves, but when the season turns and the land becomes warm and vital they cannot hold still; an old love of going returns upon them. The aged visitors who came to my grandmother's house when I was a child were made of lean and leather, and they bore themselves upright. They wore great black hats and bright ample shirts that shook in the wind. They rubbed fat upon their hair and wound their braids with strips of colored cloth. Some of them painted their faces and carried the scars of old and cherished enmities. They were an old council of warlords, come to remind and be reminded of who they were. Their wives and daughters served them well. The women might indulge themselves; gossip was at once the mark and compensation of their servitude. They made loud and elaborate talk among themselves, full of jest and gesture, fright and false alarm. They went abroad in fringed and flowered shawls, bright beadwork and German silver. They were at home in the kitchen, and they prepared meals that were banquets.

There were frequent prayer meetings, and great nocturnal feasts. When I was a child I played with my cousins outside, where the lamplight fell upon the ground and the singing of the old people rose up around us and carried away into the darkness. There were a lot of good things to eat, a lot of laughter and surprise. And afterwards, when the quiet returned, I lay down with my grandmother and could hear the frogs away by the river and feel the motion of the air.

Now there is a funeral silence in the rooms, the endless wake of some final word. The walls have closed in upon my grandmother's house. When I returned to it in mourning, I saw for the first time in my life how small it was. It was late at night, and there was a white moon, nearly full. I sat for a long time on the stone steps by the kitchen door. From there I could see out across the land; I could see the long row of trees by the creek, the low light upon the rolling plains, and the stars of the Big Dipper. Once I looked at the moon and caught sight of a strange thing. A cricket had perched upon the handrail, only a few inches away from me. My line of vision was such that the creature filled the moon like a fossil. It had gone there, I thought, to live and die, for there, of all places, was its small definition made whole and eternal. A warm wind rose up and purled like the longing within me.

The next morning I awoke at dawn and went out on the dirt road to Rainy Mountain. It was already hot, and the grasshoppers began to fill the air. Still, it was early in the morning, and the birds sang out of the shadows. The long yellow grass on the mountain shone in the bright light, and a scissortail hied above the land. There, where it ought to be, at the end of a long and legendary way, was my grandmother's grave. Here and there on the dark stones were ancestral names. Looking back once, I saw the mountain and came away.

The Setting Out

I

You know, everything had to begin, and this is how it was: the Kiowas came one by one into the world through a hollow log. They were many more than now, but not all of them got out. There was a woman whose body was swollen up with child, and she got stuck in the log. After that, no one could get through, and that is why the Kiowas are a small tribe in number. They looked all around and saw the world. It made them glad to see so many things. They called themselves *Kwuda*, "coming out."

They called themselves *Kwuda* and later *Tepda*, both of which mean "coming out." And later still they took the name *Gaigwu*, a name which can be taken to indicate something of which the two halves differ from each other in appearance. It was once a custom among Kiowa warriors that they cut their hair on the right side of the head only and on a line level with the lobe of the ear, while on the left they let the hair grow long and wore it in a thick braid wrapped in otter skin. "Kiowa" is indicated in sign language by holding the hand palm up and slightly cupped to the right side of the head and rotating it back and forth from the wrist. "Kiowa" is thought to derive from the softened Comanche form of *Gaigwu*.

I remember coming out upon the northern Great Plains in the late spring. There were meadows of blue and yellow wildflowers on the slopes, and I could see the still, sunlit plain below, reaching away out of sight. At first there is no discrimination in the eye, nothing but the land itself, whole and impenetrable. But then smallest things begin to stand out of the depths—herds and rivers and groves— and each of these has perfect being in terms of distance and of silence and of age. Yes, I thought, now I see the earth as it really is; never again will I see things as I saw them yesterday or the day before.

II

They were going along, and some were hunting, An antelope was killed and quartered in the meadow. Well, one of the big chiefs came up and took the udders of that animal for himself, but another big chief wanted those udders also, and there was a great quarrel between them. Then, in anger, one of these chiefs gathered all of his followers together and went away. They are called *Azatanhop,* "the udder-angry travelers off." No one knows where they went or what happened to them.

This is one of the oldest memories of the tribe. There have been reports of a people in the Northwest who speak a language that is similar to Kiowa.

In the winter of 1848–49, the buffalo ranged away from easy reach, and food was scarce. There was an antelope drive in the vicinity of Bent's Fort, Colorado. According to ancient custom, antelope medicine was made, and the Kiowas set out on foot and on horseback—men, women, and children—after game. They formed a great circle, inclosing a large area of the plain, and began to converge upon the center. By this means antelope and other animals were trapped and killed, often with clubs and even with the bare hands. By necessity were the Kiowas reminded of their ancient ways.

One morning on the high plains of Wyoming I saw several pronghorns in the distance. They were moving very slowly at an angle away from me, and they were almost invisible in the tall brown and yellow grass. They ambled along in their own wilderness dimension of time, as if no notion of flight could ever come upon them. But I remembered once having seen a frightened buck on the run, how the white rosette of its rump seemed to hang for the smallest fraction of time at the top of each frantic bound—like a succession of sunbursts against the purple hills.

III

Before there were horses the Kiowas had need of dogs. That was a long time ago, when dogs could talk. There was a man who lived alone; he had been thrown away, and he made his camp here and there on the high ground. Now it was dangerous to be alone, for there were enemies all around. The man spent his arrows hunting food. He had one arrow left, and he shot a bear; but the bear was only wounded and it ran away. The man wondered what to do. Then a dog came up to him and said that many enemies were coming; they were close by and all around. The man could think of no way to save himself. But the dog said: "You know, I have puppies. They are young and weak and they have nothing to eat. If you will take care of my puppies, I will show you how to get away." The dog led the man here and there, around and around, and they came to safety.

A hundred years ago the Comanche Ten Bears remarked upon the great number of horses which the Kiowas owned. "When we first knew you," he said, "you had nothing but dogs and sleds." It was so; the dog is primordial. Perhaps it was dreamed into being.

The principal warrior society of the Kiowas was the Ka-itsenko, "Real Dogs," and it was made up of ten men only, the ten most brave. Each of these men wore a long ceremonial sash and carried a sacred arrow. In time of battle he must by means of this arrow impale the end of his sash to the earth and stand his ground to the death. Tradition has it that the founder of the Ka-itsenko had a dream in which he saw a band of warriors, outfitted after the fashion of the society, being led by a dog. The dog sang the song of the Ka-itsenko, then said to the dreamer: "You are a dog; make a noise like a dog and sing a dog song."

There were always dogs about my grandmother's house. Some of them were nameless and lived a life of their own. They belonged there in a sense that the word "ownership" does not include. The old people paid them scarcely any attention, but they should have been sad, I think, to see them go.

IV

They lived at first in the mountains. They did not yet know of Tai-me, but this is what they knew: There was a man and his wife. They had a beautiful child, a little girl whom they would not allow to go out of their sight. But one day a friend of the family came and asked if she might take the child outside to play. The mother guessed that would be all right, but she told the friend to leave the child in its cradle and to place the cradle in a tree. While the child was in the tree, a redbird came among the branches. It was not like any bird that you have seen; it was very beautiful, and it did not fly away. It kept still upon a limb, close to the child. After a while the child got out of its cradle and began to climb after the redbird. And at the same time the tree began to grow taller, and the child was borne up into the sky. She was then a woman, and she found herself in a strange place. Instead of a redbird, there was a young man standing before her. The man spoke to her and said: "I have been watching you for a long time, and I knew that I would find a way to bring you here. I have brought you here to be my wife." The woman looked all around; she saw that he was the only living man there. She saw that he was the sun.

There the land itself ascends into the sky. These mountains lie at the top of the continent, and they cast a long rain shadow on the sea of grasses to the east. They arise out of the last North American wilderness, and they have wilderness names: Wasatch, Bitterroot, Bighorn, Wind River.[12]

I have walked in a mountain meadow bright with Indian paintbrush, lupine, and wild buckwheat, and I have seen high in the branches of a lodgepole pine the male pine grosbeak, round and rose-colored, its dark, striped wings nearly invisible in the soft, mottled light. And the uppermost branches of the tree seemed very slowly to ride across the blue sky.

V

After that the woman grew lonely. She thought about her people, and she wondered how they were getting on. One day she had a quarrel with the sun, and the sun went away. In her anger she dug up the root of a bush which the sun had warned her never to go near. A piece of earth fell from the root, and she could see her people far below. By that time she had given birth; she had a child—a boy by the sun. She made a rope out of sinew and took her child upon her back; she climbed down upon the rope, but when she came to the end, her people were still a long way off, and there she waited with her child on her back. It was evening;

---

[12] A mountain range extending through parts of Idaho and Utah; a Rocky mountain range on the Idaho-Montana boundary; mountains in northern Wyoming; a mountain range in central Wyoming.

the sun came home and found his woman gone. At once he thought of the bush and went to the place where it had grown. There he saw the woman and the child, hanging by the rope half way down to the earth. He was very angry, and he took up a ring, a gaming wheel, in his hand. He told the ring to follow the rope and strike the woman dead. Then he threw the ring and it did what he told it to do; it struck the woman and killed her, and then the sun's child was all alone.

The plant is said to have been the *pomme blanche,* or *pomme de prairie,* of the voyageurs, whose chronicles refer time and again to its use by the Indians. It grows on the high plains and has a farinaceous root that is turnip-like in taste and in shape. This root is a healthful food, and attempts have been made to cultivate the plant as a substitute for the potato.

The anthropologist Mooney[13] wrote in 1896: "Unlike the neighboring Cheyenne and Arapaho, who yet remember that they once lived east of the Missouri and cultivated corn, the Kiowa have no tradition of ever having been an agriculture people or anything but a tribe of hunters."

Even now they are meateaters; I think it is not in them to be farmers. My grandfather, Mammedaty, worked hard to make wheat and cotton grow on his land, but it came to very little in the end. Once when I was a small boy I went across the creek to the house where the old woman Keahdinekeah lived. Some men and boys came in from the pasture, where a calf had just been killed and butchered. One of the boys held the calf's liver—still warm and wet with life—in his hand, eating of it with great relish. I have heard that the old hunters of the Plains prized the raw liver and tongue of the buffalo above all other delicacies.

VI

The sun's child was big enough to walk around on the earth, and he saw a camp nearby. He made his way to it and saw that a great spider—that which is called a grandmother—lived there. The spider spoke to the sun's child, and the child was afraid. The grandmother was full of resentment; she was jealous, you see, for the child had not yet been weaned from its mother's breasts. She wondered whether the child were a boy or a girl, and therefore she made two things, a pretty ball and a bow and arrows. These things she left alone with the child all the next day. When she returned, she saw that the ball was full of arrows, and she knew then that the child was a boy and that he would be hard to raise. Time and again the grandmother tried to capture the boy, but he always ran away. Then one day she made a snare out of rope. The boy was caught up in the snare, and he cried and cried, but the grandmother sang to him and at last he fell asleep.

> Go to sleep and do not cry.
> Your mother is dead, and still you feed
>   upon her breasts.
> Oo-oo-la-la-la-la, oo-oo.

---

[13] James A. Mooney (1861–1921), an ethnologist, in *The Ghost Dance Religion and the Sioux Outbreak of 1890* (1896).

In the autumn of 1874, the Kiowas were driven southward towards the Staked Plains. Columns of troops were converging upon them from all sides, and they were bone-weary and afraid. They camped on Elk Creek,[14] and the next day it began to rain. It rained hard all that day, and the Kiowas waited on horseback for the weather to clear. Then, as evening came on, the earth was suddenly crawling with spiders, great black tarantulas, swarming on the flood.

I know of spiders. There are dirt roads in the Plains. You see them, and you wonder where and how far they go. They seem very old and untraveled, as if they all led away to deserted houses. But creatures cross these roads: dung beetles and grasshoppers, sidewinders and tortoises. Now and then there comes a tarantula, at evening, always larger than you imagine, dull and dark brown, covered with long, dusty hairs. There is something crochety about them; they stop and go and angle away.

VII

The years went by, and the boy still had the ring which killed his mother. The grandmother spider told him never to throw the ring into the sky, but one day he threw it up, and it fell squarely on top of his head and cut him in two. He looked around, and there was another boy, just like himself, his twin. The two of them laughed and laughed, and then they went to the grandmother spider. She nearly cried aloud when she saw them, for it had been hard enough to raise the one. Even so, she cared for them well and made them fine clothes to wear.

Mammedaty owned horses. And he could remember that it was essentially good to own horses, that it was hard to be without horses. There was a day: Mammedaty got down from a horse for the last time. Of all the tribes of the Plains, the Kiowas owned the greatest number of horses per person.

On summer afternoons, I went swimming in the Washita River. The current was slow, and the warm, brown water seemed to be standing still. It was a secret place. There in the deep shade, inclosed in the dense, overhanging growth of the banks, my mind fixed on the wings of a dragonfly or the flitting motion of a water strider, the great open land beyond was all but impossible to imagine. But it was there, a stone's throw away. Once, from the limb of a tree, I saw myself in the brown water; then a frog leaped from the bank, breaking the image apart.

VIII

Now each of the twins had a ring, and the grandmother spider told them never to throw the rings into the sky. But one day they threw them up into the high wind. The rings rolled over a hill, and the twins ran after them. They ran beyond the top of the hill and fell down into the mouth of a cave. There lived a giant and his wife. The giant had killed a lot of people in the past by building fires and filling the cave with smoke, so that the people could not breathe. Then the twins remembered

---

[14] In western Oklahoma, just west of the Wichita Mountains.

something that the grandmother spider had told them: "If ever you get caught in the cave, say to yourselves the word *thain-mom*, 'above my eyes.'" When the giant began to set fires around, the twins repeated the word *thain-mom* over and over to themselves, and the smoke remained above their eyes. When the giant had made three great clouds of smoke, his wife saw that the twins sat without coughing or crying, and she became frightened. "Let them go," she said, "or something bad will happen to us." The twins took up their rings and returned to the grandmother spider. She was glad to see them.

A word has power in and of itself. It comes from nothing into sound and meaning; it gives origin to all things. By means of words can a man deal with the world on equal terms. And the word is sacred. A man's name is his own; he can keep it or give it away as he likes. Until recent times, the Kiowas would not speak the name of a dead man. To do so would have been disrespectful and dishonest. The dead take their names with them out of the world.

When Aho saw or heard or thought of something bad, she said the word zei-dl-bei, *"frightful." It was the one word with which she confronted evil and the incomprehensible. I liked her to say it, for she screwed up her face in a wonderful look of displeasure and clicked her tongue. It was not an exclamation so much, I think, as it was a warding off, an exertion of language upon ignorance and disorder.*

IX

The next thing that happened to the twins was this: They killed a great snake which they found in their tipi. When they told the grandmother spider what they had done, she cried and cried. They had killed their grandfather, she said. And after that the grandmother spider died. The twins wrapped her in a hide and covered her with leaves by the water. The twins lived on for a long time, and they were greatly honored among the Kiowas.

In another and perhaps older version of the story, it is a porcupine and not a redbird that is the representation of the sun. In that version, too, one of the twins is said to have walked into the waters of a lake and disappeared forever, while the other at last transformed himself into ten portions of "medicine," thereby giving of his own body in eucharistic form to the Kiowas. The ten bundles of the talyi-da-i, "boy medicine" are, like Tai-me, chief objects of religious veneration.

When he was a boy, my father went with his grandmother, Keahdinekeah, to the shrine of one of the talyi-da-i. The old woman made an offering of bright cloth, and she prayed. The shrine was a small, specially-made tipi; inside, suspended from the lashing of the poles, was the medicine itself. My father knew that it was very powerful, and the very sight of it filled him with wonder and regard. The holiness of such a thing can be imparted to the human spirit, I believe, for I remember that it shone in the sightless eyes of Keahdinekeah. Once I was taken to see her at the old house on the other side of Rainy Mountain Creek. The room was dark, and her old age filled it like a substance. She was white-haired and blind, and, in that strange reversion that comes upon the very old, her skin was as soft as the skin of a baby. I remember the sound of her glad weeping and the water-like touch of her hand.

X

Long ago there were bad times. The Kiowas were hungry and there was no food. There was a man who heard his children cry from hunger, and he went out to look for food. He walked four days and became very weak. On the fourth day he came to a great canyon. Suddenly there was thunder and lightning. A voice spoke to him and said, "Why are you following me? What do you want?" The man was afraid. The thing standing before him had the feet of a deer, and its body was covered with feathers. The man answered that the Kiowas were hungry. "Take me with you," the voice said, "and I will give you whatever you want." From that day Tai-me has belonged to the Kiowas.

The great central figure of the *kado*, or Sun Dance, ceremony is the *taime*. This is a small image, less than 2 feet in length, representing a human figure dressed in a robe of white feathers, with a headdress consisting of a single upright feather and pendants of ermine skin, with numerous strands of blue beads around its neck, and painted upon the face, breast, and back with designs symbolic of the sun and moon. The image itself is of dark-green stone, in form rudely resembling a human head and bust, probably shaped by art like the stone fetishes of the Pueblo tribes. It is preserved in a rawhide box in charge of the hereditary keeper, and is never under any circumstances exposed to view except at the annual Sun Dance, when it is fastened to a short upright stick planted within the medicine lodge, near the western side. It was last exposed in 1888.—Mooney

Once I went with my father and grandmother to see the Tai-me bundle. It was suspended by means of a strip of ticking from the fork of a small ceremonial tree. I made an offering of bright red cloth, and my grandmother prayed aloud. It seemed a long time we were there. I had never come into the presence of Tai-me before—nor have I since. There was a great holiness all about in the room, as if an old person had died there or a child had been born.

XI

A long time ago there were two brothers. It was winter, and the buffalo had wandered far away. Food was very scarce. The two brothers were hungry, and they wondered what to do. One of them got up in the early morning and went out, and he found a lot of fresh meat there on the ground in front of the tipi. He was very happy, and he called his brother outside. "Look," he said. "Something very good has happened, and we have plenty of food." But his brother was afraid and said: "This is too strange a thing. I believe that we had better not eat that meat." But the first brother scolded him and said that he was foolish. Then he went ahead and ate of the meat all by himself. In a little while something awful happened to him; he began to change. When it was all over, he was no longer a man; he was some kind of water beast with little short legs and a long, heavy tail. Then he spoke to his brother and said: "You were right, and you must not eat of that meat. Now I must go and live in the water, but we are brothers, and you ought to come and see me now and then." After that the man went down to the water's edge, sometimes, and called his brother out. He told him how things were with the Kiowas.

During the peyote[15] ritual a fire is kept burning in the center of the tipi, inclosed within a crescent-shaped altar. On top of the altar there is a single, sacred peyote. After the chief priest utters the opening prayer, four peyotes are given to each celebrant, who eats them one after another. Then, in turn, each man sings four sacred songs, and all the while there is the sound of the rattle and the drum—and the fitful, many-colored glare of the fire. The songs go on all through the night, broken only by intervals of prayer, additional distributions of peyote, and, at midnight, a peculiar baptismal ceremony.

Mammedaty was a peyote man, and he was therefore distinguished by these things: a necklace of beans, a beaded staff and rattle, an eagle-bone whistle, and a fan made from the feathers of a water bird. He saw things that other men do not see. Once a heavy rain caused the Washita River to overflow and Rainy Mountain Creek to swell and "back up." Mammedaty went to the creek, near the crossing, to swim. And while he was there, the water began strangely to move against him, slowly at first, then fast, in high, hard waves. There was some awful commotion beneath the surface, and Mammedaty got out of the water and ran away. Later he went back to that place. There was a wide swath in the brush of the bank and the tracks of a huge animal, leading down to the water's edge.

THE GOING ON

XII

An old man there was who lived with his wife and child. One night the woman was pounding meat, and her little son wanted to taste it. She gave him a ball of meat and he went outside to eat it. Then he returned and wanted more. She gave him another ball of meat, and again he went outside. A third time he came and asked for meat. The old man began to be afraid. He told his wife to give the child a large ball of meat and to act as if these things were all right. When the little boy came in again, there was an enemy with him. The enemy said: "There are many of us and we are all around. We came to kill you, but your son has given me food. If you will feed us all, we will not harm you." But the old man did not believe his enemy, and while his wife cooked fat upon the fire he crept out and led their horses upstream. When he was well away, he called out in the voice of a bird. Then the woman knew that it was time to go. She set fire to the fat and threw it all around upon the enemies, who were sitting there; then she took up the little boy in her arms and ran upstream. That is how the old man and the woman and their child got away. From a safe distance they could see the fire and hear the screams of their enemies.

In the winter of 1872–73, a fine heraldic tipi was accidentally destroyed by fire. Known as the *Do-giagya guat,* "tipi with battle pictures," it was ornamented with fine pictures of fighting men and arms on one side and wide, horizontal bands of black and yellow on the other. The *Do-giagya guat* belonged to the family of the

[15] A stimulant drug derived from buttonlike tops of the mescal cactus, chewed by some Mexican Indians and Native Americans during religious ceremonies.

great chief Dohasan and occupied the second place in the tribal circle on ceremonial occasions.

There are meadowlarks and quail in the open land. One day late in the afternoon I walked about among the headstones at Rainy Mountain Cemetery. The shadows were very long; there was a deep blush on the sky, and the dark red earth seemed to glow with the setting sun. For a few moments, at that particular time of the day, there is deep silence. Nothing moves, and it does not occur to you to make any sound. Something is going on there in the shadows. Everything has slowed to a stop in order that the sun might take leave of the land. And then there is the sudden, piercing call of a bobwhite. The whole world is startled by it.

XIII

If an arrow is well made, it will have tooth marks upon it. That is how you know. The Kiowas made fine arrows and straightened them in their teeth. Then they drew them to the bow to see if they were straight. Once there was a man and his wife. They were alone at night in their tipi. By the light of the fire the man was making arrows. After a while he caught sight of something. There was a small opening in the tipi where two hides were sewn together. Someone was there on the outside, looking in. The man went on with his work, but he said to his wife: "Someone is standing outside. Do not be afraid. Let us talk easily, as of ordinary things." He took up an arrow and straightened it in his teeth; then, as it was right for him to do, he drew it to the bow and took aim, first in this direction and then in that. And all the while he was talking, as if to his wife. But this is how he spoke: "I know that you are there on the outside, for I can feel your eyes upon me. If you are a Kiowa, you will understand what I am saying, and you will speak your name." But there was no answer, and the man went on in the same way, pointing the arrow all around. At last his aim fell upon the place where his enemy stood, and he let go of the string. The arrow went straight to the enemy's heart.

The old men were the best arrowmakers, for they could bring time and patience to their craft. The young men—the fighters and hunters—were willing to pay a high price for arrows that were well made.

When my father was a boy, an old man used to come to Mammedaty's house and pay his respects. He was a lean old man in braids and was impressive in his age and bearing. His name was Cheney, and he was an arrowmaker. Every morning, my father tells me, Cheney would paint his wrinkled face, go out, and pray aloud to the rising sun. In my mind I can see that man as if he were there now. I like to watch him as he makes his prayer. I know where he stands and where his voice goes on the rolling grasses and where the sun comes up on the land. There, at dawn, you can feel the silence. It is cold and clear and deep like water. It takes hold of you and will not let you go.

XIV

The Kiowa language is hard to understand, but, you know, the storm spirit understands it. This is how it was: Long ago the Kiowas decided to make a horse; they decided to make it out of clay, and so they began to shape the clay with their hands. Well, the horse began to be. But it was a terrible, terrible thing. It began to writhe, slowly at first, then faster and faster until there was a great commotion everywhere. The wind grew up and carried everything away; great trees were uprooted, and even the buffalo were thrown up into the sky. The Kiowas were afraid of that awful thing, and they went running about, talking to it. And at last it was calm. Even now, when they see the storm clouds gathering, the Kiowas know what it is: that a strange wild animal roams on the sky. It has the head of a horse and the tail of a great fish. Lightning comes from its mouth, and the tail, whipping and thrashing on the air, makes the high, hot wind of the tornado. But they speak to it, saying "Pass over me." They are not afraid of *Man-ka-ih,* for it understands their language.

At times the plains are bright and calm and quiet; at times they are black with the sudden violence of weather. Always there are winds.

A few feet from the southwest corner of my grandmother's house, there is a storm cellar. It will be there, I think, when the house and the arbor and the barn have disappeared. There are many of those crude shelters in that part of the world. They conform to the shape of the land and are scarcely remarkable: low earthen mounds with heavy wooden trapdoors that appear to open upon the underworld. I have seen the wind drive the rain so hard that a grown man could not open the door against it, and once, descending into that place, I saw the whole land at night become visible and blue and phosphorescent in the flash of lightning.

XV

Quoetotai was a good-looking young man and a great warrior besides. One of Many Bears' wives fell in love with him, and they carried on. After that, Quoetotai went out one day. As he was crossing the river, Many Bears came out of a hiding place on the bank and shot him with an arrow; then he ran away. Quoetotai went back to the camp and someone pulled the arrow out of him. He was very sick, and he had lost a lot of blood. The medicine man worked over him for a long time, and the next day Quoetotai was all right. You know, he made up his mind to take Many Bears' wife away. After that, some of the men wanted to raid in Mexico. It was the custom to have a dance on the night before the men went away. There was a lot of singing, and now and then someone got up to say brave things. Many Bears' wife got up and called attention to herself. She said: "All of you, listen to my song. Something will happen tonight." Then she sang, and, you know, the old people still remember her song.

> I am going to leave my belongings,
> I am going to leave my home.
> Again I say it, I am going to leave my son.

Quoetotai took that woman away, and they roamed with the Comanches for fifteen years. When at last they returned to their own people, Many Bears was the first man to welcome them. "Quoetotai," he said, "from this time on you and I will be brothers. Now I give you six horses."

The artist George Catlin[16] traveled among the Kiowas in 1834. He observes that they are superior to the Comanches and Wichitas in appearance. They are tall and straight, relaxed and graceful. They have fine, classical features, and in this respect they resemble more closely the tribes of the north than those of the south.

Catlin's portrait of Kotsatoah is the striking figure of a man, tall and lean, yet powerful and fully developed. He is lithe, and he knows beyond any doubt of his great strength and vigor. He stands perfectly at ease, the long drape of his robe flowing with the lines of his body. His left hand rests upon his shield and holds a bow and arrows. His head is set firmly, and there is a look of bemused and infinite tolerance in his eyes. He is said to have been nearly seven feet tall and able to run down and kill a buffalo on foot. I should like to have seen that man, as Catlin saw him, walking toward me, or away in the distance, perhaps, alone and against the sky.

XVI

There was a strange thing, a buffalo with horns of steel. One day a man came upon it in the plain, just there where once upon a time four trees stood close together. The man and the buffalo began to fight. The man's hunting horse was killed right away, and the man climbed one of the trees. The great bull lowered its head and began to strike the tree with its black metal horns, and soon the tree fell. But the man was quick, and he leaped to the safety of the second tree. Again the bull struck with its unnatural horns, and the tree soon splintered and fell. The man leaped to the third tree and all the while he shot arrows at the beast; but the arrows glanced away like sparks from its dark hide. At last there remained only one tree and the man had only one arrow. He believed then that he would surely die. But something spoke to him and said: "Each time the buffalo prepares to charge, it spreads its cloven hooves and strikes the ground. Only there in the cleft of the hoof is it vulnerable; it is there you must aim." The buffalo went away and turned, spreading its hooves, and the man drew the arrow to his bow. His aim was true and the arrow struck deep into the soft flesh of the hoof. The great bull shuddered and fell, and its steel horns flashed once in the sun.

Forty years ago the townspeople of Carnegie, Oklahoma, gathered about two old Kiowa men who were mounted on work horses and armed with bows and arrows. Someone had got a buffalo, a poor broken beast in which there was no trace left of the wild strain. The old men waited silently amid the laughter and talk; then, at a signal, the buffalo was let go. It balked at first, more confused, perhaps, than afraid, and the horses had to be urged and then brought up short. The people shouted, and at last the buffalo wheeled and ran. The old men gave chase, and in the distance they were lost to view in a great, red cloud of dust. But they ran that animal down and killed it with arrows.

One morning my father and I walked in Medicine Park, on the edge of a small herd of buffalo. It was late in the spring, and many of the cows had newborn calves. Nearby a calf lay in the tall grass; it was red-orange in color, delicately

---

[16] Catlin (1796–1872) was an author and painter who depicted Plains Indians.

beautiful with new life. We approached, but suddenly the cow was there in our way, her great dark head low and fearful-looking. Then she came at us, and we turned and ran as hard as we could. She gave up after a short run, and I think we had not been in any real danger. But the spring morning was deep and beautiful and our hearts were beating fast and we knew just then what it was to be alive.

XVII

Bad women are thrown away. Once there was a handsome young man. He was wild and reckless, and the chief talked to the wind about him. After that, the man went hunting. A great whirlwind passed by, and he was blind. The Kiowas have no need of a blind man; they left him alone with his wife and child. The winter was coming on and food was scarce. In four days the man's wife grew tired of caring for him. A herd of buffalo came near, and the man knew the sound. He asked his wife to hand him a bow and an arrow. "You must tell me," he said, "when the buffalo are directly in front of me." And in that way he killed a bull, but his wife said that he had missed. He asked for another arrow and killed another bull, but again his wife said that he had missed. Now the man was a hunter, and he knew the sound an arrow makes when it strikes home, but he said nothing. Then his wife helped herself to the meat and ran away with her child. The man was blind; he ate grass and kept himself alive. In seven days a band of Kiowas found him and took him to their camp. There in the firelight a woman was telling a story. She told of how her husband had been killed by enemy warriors. The blind man listened, and he knew her voice. That was a bad woman. At sunrise they threw her away.

In the Kiowa calendars[17] there is graphic proof that the lives of women were hard, whether they were "bad women" or not. Only the captives, who were slaves, held lower status. During the Sun Dance of 1843, a man stabbed his wife in the breast because she accepted Chief Dohasan's invitation to ride with him in the ceremonial procession. And in the winter of 1851–52, Big Bow stole the wife of a man who was away on a raiding expedition. He brought her to his father's camp and made her wait outside in the bitter cold while he went in to collect his things. But his father knew what was going on, and he held Big Bow and would not let him go. The woman was made to wait in the snow until her feet were frozen.

Mammedaty's grandmother, Kau-au-ointy, was a Mexican captive, taken from her homeland when she was a child of eight or ten years. I never knew her, but I have been to her grave at Rainy Mountain.

KAU-AU-OINTY
BORN 1834
DIED 1929
AT REST

She raised a lot of eyebrows, they say, for she would not play the part of a Kiowa woman. From slavery she rose up to become a figure in the tribe. She owned a great herd of cattle, and she could ride as well as any man. She had blue eyes.

---

[17] Pictorial calendars of Kiowa history, as seen in Mooney's *Calendar History of the Kiowa Indians* (1898).

XVIII

You know, the Kiowas are a summer people. Once upon a time a group of young men sat down in a circle and spoke of mighty things. This is what they said: "When the fall of the year comes around, where does the summer go? Where does it live?" They decided to follow the sun southward to its home, and so they set out on horseback. They rode for days and weeks and months, farther to the south than any Kiowa had ever gone before, and they saw many strange and wonderful things. At last they came to the place where they saw the strangest thing of all. Night was coming on, and they were very tired of riding; they made camp in a great thicket. All but one of them went right to sleep. He was a good hunter, and he could see well in the moonlight. He caught sight of something: men were all about in the trees, moving silently from limb to limb. They darted across the face of the full moon, and he saw that they were small and had tails! He could not believe his eyes, but the next morning he told the others of what he had seen. They only laughed at him and told him not to eat such a large supper again. But later, as they were breaking camp, a certain feeling came over them all at once: they felt that they were being watched. And when they looked up, the small men with tails began to race about in the limbs overhead. That is when the Kiowas turned around and came away; they had had quite enough of that place. They had found the sun's home after all, they reasoned, and they were hungry for the good buffalo meat of their homeland.

It is unnecessary to dilate on the revolution made in the life of the Indian by the possession of the horse. Without it he was a half-starved skulker in the timber, creeping up on foot toward the unwary deer or building a brush corral with infinite labor to surround a herd of antelope, and seldom venturing more than a few days' journey from home. With the horse he was transformed into the daring buffalo hunter, able to procure in a single day enough food to supply his family for a year, leaving him free then to sweep the plains with his war parties along a range of a thousand miles.—Mooney

Some of my earliest memories are of the summers on Rainy Mountain Creek, when we lived in the arbor, on the north side of my grandmother's house. From there you could see downhill to the pecan grove, the dense, dark growth along the water, and beyond, the long sweep of the earth itself, curving out on the sky. The arbor was open on all sides to the light and the air and the sounds of the land. You could see far and wide even at night, by the light of the moon; there was nothing to stand in your way. And when the season turned and it was necessary to move back into the house, there was a sense of confinement and depression for a time. Now and then in winter, when I passed by the arbor on my way to draw water at the well, I looked inside and thought of the summer. The hard dirt floor was dark red in color—the color of pipestone.

THE CLOSING IN

XIX

On a raid against the Utes, one of two brothers was captured. The other, alone and of his own will, stole into the Ute camp and tried to set his brother free, but he too was captured. The chief of the Utes had respect for the man's bravery, and he made a bargain with him. If he could carry his brother on his back and walk upon a row of greased buffalo heads without falling to the ground, both brothers would be given horses and allowed to return in safety to their home. The man bore his brother on his back and walked upon the heads of the buffalo and kept his footing. The Ute chief was true to his word, and the brothers returned to their own people on horseback.

After the fight at Palo Duro Canyon, the Kiowas came in, a few at a time, to surrender at Fort Sill. Their horses and weapons were confiscated, and they were imprisoned. In a field just west of the post, the Indian ponies were destroyed. Nearly *800* horses were killed outright; two thousand more were sold, stolen, given away.

SUMMER 1879

Tsen-pia Kado, "Horse-eating sun dance." It is indicated on the Set-tan calendar by the figure of a horse's head above the medicine lodge. This dance was held on Elm Fork of Red River, and was so called because the buffalo had now become so scarce that the Kiowa, who had gone on their regular hunt the preceding winter, had found so few that they were obliged to kill and eat their ponies during the summer to save themselves from starving. This may be recorded as the date of the disappearance of the buffalo from the Kiowa country. Thenceforth the appearance of even a single animal was a rare event.—Mooney

In New Mexico the land is made of many colors. When I was a boy I rode out over the red and yellow and purple earth to the west of Jemez Pueblo. My horse was a small red roan, fast and easy-riding. I rode among the dunes, along the bases of mesas and cliffs, into canyons and arroyos. I came to know that country, not in the way a traveler knows the landmarks he sees in the distance, but more truly and intimately, in every season, from a thousand points of view. I know the living motion of a horse and the sound of hooves. I know what it is, on a hot day in August or September, to ride into a bank of cold, fresh rain.

XX

Once there was a man who owned a fine hunting horse. It was black and fast and afraid of nothing. When it was turned upon an enemy it charged in a straight line and struck at full speed; the man need have no hand upon the rein. But, you know, that man knew fear. Once during a charge he turned that animal from its course. That was a bad thing. The hunting horse died of shame.

In 1861 a Sun Dance was held near the Arkansas River in Kansas. As an offering to Tai-me, a spotted horse was left tied to a pole in the medicine lodge, where it starved to death. Later in that year an epidemic of smallpox broke out in the tribe, and the old man Gaapiatan sacrificed one of his best horses, a fine black-eared animal, that he and his family might be spared.

I like to think of old man Gaapiatan and his horse. I think I know how much he loved that animal; I think I know what was going on in his mind: If you will give me my life and the lives of my family, I will give you the life of this black-eared horse.

XXI

Mammedaty was the grandson of Guipahgo, and he was well-known on that account. Now and then Mammedaty drove a team and wagon out over the plain. Once, in the early morning, he was on the way to Rainy Mountain. It was summer and the grass was high and meadowlarks were calling all around. You know, the top of the plain is smooth and you can see a long way. There was nothing but the early morning and the land around. Then Mammedaty heard something. Someone whistled to him. He looked up and saw the head of a little boy nearby above the grass. He stopped the horses and got down from the wagon and went to see who was there. There was no one; there was nothing there. He looked for a long time, but there was nothing there.

There is a single photograph of Mammedaty. He is looking past the camera and a little to one side. In his face there is calm and good will, strength and intelligence. His hair is drawn close to the scalp, and his braids are long and wrapped with fur. He wears a kilt, fringed leggings, and beaded moccasins. In his right hand there is a peyote fan. A family characteristic: the veins stand out in his hands, and his hands are small and rather long.

Mammedaty saw four things that were truly remarkable. This head of the child was one, and the tracks of the water beast another. Once, when he walked near the pecan grove, he saw three small alligators on a log. No one had ever seen them before and no one ever saw them again. Finally, there was this: something had always bothered Mammedaty, a small aggravation that was never quite out of mind, like a name on the tip of the tongue. He had always wondered how it is that the mound of earth which a mole makes around the opening of its burrow is so fine. It is nearly as fine as powder, and it seems almost to have been sifted. One day Mammedaty was sitting quietly when a mole came out of the earth. Its cheeks were puffed out as if it had been a squirrel packing nuts. It looked all around for a moment, then blew the fine dark earth out of its mouth. And this it did again and again, until there was a ring of black, powdery earth on the ground. That was a strange and meaningful thing to see. It meant that Mammedaty had got possession of a powerful medicine.

XXII

Mammedaty was the grandson of Guipahgo, and he got on well most of the time. But, you know, one time he lost his temper. This is how it was: There were several horses in a pasture, and Mammedaty wanted to get them out. A fence ran all the way around and there was just one gate. There was a lot of ground inside. He could not get those horses out. One of them led the others; every time they were driven up to the gate, that one wheeled and ran as fast as it could to the other side. Well, that went on for a long time, and Mammedaty burned up. He ran to the house and got his bow and arrows. The horses were running in single file, and he shot at the one that was causing all the trouble. He missed, though, and the arrow went deep into the neck of the second horse.

In the winter of 1852–53, a Pawnee boy who had been held as a captive among the Kiowas succeeded in running away. He took with him an especially fine hunting horse, known far and wide as *Guadal-tseyu,* "Little Red." That was the most important event of the winter. The loss of that horse was a hard thing to bear.

Years ago there was a box of bones in the barn, and I used to go there to look at them. Later someone stole them, I believe. They were the bones of a horse which Mammedaty called by the name "Little Red." It was a small bay, nothing much to look at, I have heard, but it was the fastest runner in that whole corner of the world. White men and Indians alike came from far and near to match their best animals against it, but it never lost a race. I have often thought about that red horse. There have been times when I thought I understood how it was that a man might be moved to preserve the bones of a horse—and another to steal them away.

XXIII

Aho remembered something, a strange thing. This is how it was: You know, the Tai-me bundle is not very big, but it is full of power. Once Aho went to see the Tai-me keeper's wife. The two of them were sitting together, passing the time of day, when they heard an awful noise, as if a tree or some other very heavy object had fallen down. It frightened them, and they went to see what on earth it was. It was Tai-me—Tai-me had fallen to the floor. No one knows how it was that Tai-me fell; nothing caused it, as far as anyone could see.

For a time Mammedaty wore one of the grandmother bundles. This he did for his mother Keahdinekeah; he wore it on a string tied around his neck. Aho remembered this: that if anyone who wore a medicine bundle failed to show it the proper respect, it grew extremely heavy around his neck.

There was a great iron kettle which stood outside of my grandmother's house next to the south porch. It was huge and immovable, or so I thought when I was a child; I could not imagine that anyone had strength enough to lift it up. I don't know where it came from; it was always there. It rang like a bell when you struck it, and with the tips of your fingers you could feel the black metal sing for a long time afterward. It was used to catch the rainwater with which we washed our hair.

XXIV

East of my grandmother's house, south of the pecan grove, there is buried a woman in a beautiful dress. Mammedaty used to know where she is buried, but now no one knows. If you stand on the front porch of the house and look eastward towards Carnegie, you know that the woman is buried somewhere within the range of your vision. But her grave is unmarked. She was buried in a cabinet, and she wore a beautiful dress. How beautiful it was! It was one of those fine buckskin dresses, and it was decorated with elk's teeth and beadwork. That dress is still there, under the ground.

Aho's high moccasins are made of softest, cream-colored skins. On each instep there is a bright disc of beadwork—an eight-pointed star, red and pale blue on a white field—and there are bands of beadwork at the soles and ankles. The flaps of the leggings are wide and richly ornamented with blue and red and green and white and lavender beads.

East of my grandmother's house the sun rises out of the plain. Once in his life a man ought to concentrate his mind upon the remembered earth, I believe. He ought to give himself up to a particular landscape in his experience, to look at it from as many angles as he can, to wonder about it, to dwell upon it. He ought to imagine that he touches it with his hands at every season and listens to the sounds that are made upon it. He ought to imagine the creatures there and all the faintest motions of the wind. He ought to recollect the glare of noon and all the colors of the dawn and dusk.

Epilogue

During the first hours after midnight on the morning of November 13, 1833, it seemed that the world was coming to an end. Suddenly the stillness of the night was broken; there were brilliant flashes of light in the sky, light of such intensity that people were awakened by it. With the speed and density of a driving rain, stars were falling in the universe. Some were brighter than Venus; one was said to be as large as the moon.

That most brilliant shower of Leonid[18] meteors has a special place in the memory of the Kiowa people. It is among the earliest entries in the Kiowa calendars, and it marks the beginning as it were of the historical period in the tribal mind. In the preceding year Tai-me had been stolen by a band of Osages, and although it was later returned, the loss was an almost unimaginable tragedy; and in 1837 the Kiowas made the first of their treaties with the United States. The falling stars seemed to image the sudden and violent disintegration of an old order.

But indeed the golden age of the Kiowas had been short-lived, ninety or a hundred years, say, from about 1740. The culture would persist for a while in decline, until about 1875, but then it would be gone, and there would be very little material evidence that it had ever been. Yet it is within the reach of memory still, though tenuously now, and moreover it is even defined in a remarkaby rich and living verbal tradition which demands to be preserved for its own sake. The living memory and the verbal tradition which transcends it were brought together for me once and for all in the person of Ko-sahn.

A hundred-year-old woman came to my grandmother's house one afternoon in July. Aho was dead; Mammedaty had died before I was born. There were very

---

[18] One of the shooting stars constituting the meteor shower that occurs around November 15, appearing to radiate from the constellation Leo.

few Kiowas left who could remember the Sun Dances; Ko-sahn was one of them; she was a grown woman when my grandparents came into the world. Her body was twisted and her face deeply lined with age. Her thin white hair was held in place by a cap of black netting, though she wore braids as well, and she had but one eye. She was dressed in the manner of a Kiowa matron, a dark, full-cut dress that reached nearly to the ankles, full, flowing sleeves, and a wide, apron-like sash. She sat on a bench in the arbor so concentrated in her great age that she seemed extraordinarily small. She was quiet for a time—she might almost have been asleep—and then she began to speak and to sing. She spoke of many things, and once she spoke of the Sun Dance:

My sisters and I were very young; that was a long time ago. Early one morning they came to wake us up. They had brought a great buffalo in from the plain. Everyone went out to see and to pray. We heard a great many voices. One man said that the lodge was almost ready. We were told to go there, and someone gave me a piece of cloth. It was very beautiful. Then I asked what I ought to do with it, and they said that I must tie it to the Tai-me tree. There were other pieces of cloth on the tree, and so I put mine there as well.
When the lodge frame was finished, a woman—sometimes a man—began to sing. It was like this:

> *Everything is ready.*
> *Now the four societies must go out.*
> *They must go out and get the leaves,*
>   *the branches for the lodge.*

And when the branches were tied in place, again there was singing:

> *Let the boys go out.*
> *Come on, boys, now we must get the earth.*

The boys began to shout. Now they were not just ordinary boys, not all of them; they were those for whom prayers had been made, and they were dressed in different ways. There was an old, old woman. She had something on her back. The boys went out to see. The old woman had a bag full of earth on her back. It was a certain kind of sandy earth. That is what they must have in the lodge. The dancers must dance upon the sandy earth. The old woman held a digging tool in her hand. She turned towards the south and pointed with her lips. It was like a kiss, and she began to sing:

> *We have brought the earth.*
> *Now it is time to play;*
> *As old as I am, I still have the feeling of play.*

That was the beginning of the Sun Dance. The dancers treated themselves with buffalo medicine, and slowly they began to take their steps . . . And all the people were around, and they wore splendid things—beautiful buckskin and beads. The chiefs wore necklaces, and their pendants shone like the sun. There were many people, and oh, it was beautiful! That was the beginning of the Sun Dance. It was all for Tai-me, you know, and it was a long time ago.

It was—all of this and more—a quest, a going forth upon the way to Rainy Mountain. Probably Ko-sahn too is dead now. At times, in the quiet of evening, I think she must have wondered, dreaming, who she was. Was she become in her sleep that old purveyor of the sacred earth, perhaps, that ancient one who, old as she was, still had the feeling of play? And in her mind, at times, did she see the falling stars?

RAINY MOUNTAIN CEMETERY

Most is your name the name of this dark stone.
Deranged in death, the mind to be inheres
Forever in the nominal unknown,
The wake of nothing audible he hears
Who listens here and now to hear your name.

The early sun, red as a hunter's moon,
Runs in the plain. The mountain burns and shines;
And silence is the long approach of noon
Upon the shadow that your name defines—
And death this cold, black density of stone.

1967–1968, 1969

Tomás Rivera
(1935–1984)

The author of a novel, a book of poems, short stories, and many essays, Tomás Rivera was
born in 1935 in Crystal City, Texas. His parents, Florencio Rivera and Josefa Hernándes,
arrived in Texas from Mexico in the 1920s. As a boy Rivera traveled North yearly, as far
as Minnesota and Michigan, with his family and other Mexican migrant farm workers.
Even though his own work in the fields interrupted his education, Rivera graduated from
high school and in 1958 earned a B.A. in English from Southwest Texas State University.
Also in 1958 he married Concepción Garza. Continuing his education, he earned an M.A.
in English and administration at Southwest Texas State and a Ph.D. in Spanish literature at
the University of Oklahoma in 1969.

After teaching high school and college English for a few years, Rivera became the
vice-chancellor of administration at the University of Texas at San Antonio in 1976. He
was later named executive vice-chancellor at the University of Texas, El Paso. His concern for the educational problems of Chicano students earned him several honors, and
beginning in 1976 he was a member of the board of the National Chicano Council on
Higher Education. In 1979 he was appointed chancellor of the University of California at
Riverside, a position he held until his death in 1984.

In 1971 his novel . . . *y No Se Lo Tragó la Tierra* (". . . *and the Earth Did Not Devour Him"*) won the prestigious Quinto Sol Prize for Chicano literature. Rivera wrote the
novel in Spanish from somewhat fictionalized personal experiences; it was later translated
into English. His theme is one of social protest. Unlike earlier "realist" novelists, he incorporates the modernist fragmented structure and a stream-of-consciousness style of narrative. The novel reports the events occurring in one year through the eyes of a migrant farm
worker child, in a documentary, rather than expository, mode of narration. The twelve
sections of the novel are linked by the boy narrator, although he does not dominate all
sections. The lives of Chicano migrant farm workers during the 1940s are depicted through

the remembrances of this young narrator, who is seeking to understand the meaning of what he observes and to find an authentic sense of identity. Rivera has instilled his novel with a sense of tragedy and political urgency. He uses stylistic innovations in his attempt to expose and reform social injustice. Rivera has also written essays, published in various reviews and anthologies; a collection of short stories, *La Cosecha*, or *"The Harvest"* (1988); and a poetry collection, *Always and Other Poems* (1973).

Suggested Readings: "Into the Labyrinth: The Chicano in Literature," in *New Voices in Literature: The Mexican-American*, ed. E. Simmen, 1971. "On the Road to Texas: Pete Fonseca," in *Aztlan: An Anthology of Mexican American Literature*, eds. L. Valdez and S. Steiner, 1972. "Perspectives on Chicano Literature," in *Sociological Abstracts*, Special Issue, Spring, 1972. *Always and Other Poems*, 1973. "On Chicano Literature," in *Texas Books in Review*, I (1), 1977. *This Migrant Earth*, trans. R. Hinojosa, 1986. *The Harvest: Short Stories*, trans. J. Oliveras, 1988. J. Oliveras, ed., *International Studies in Honor of Tomás Rivera*, 1985. R. Saldívar, "A Dialectic of Difference: Toward a Theory in the Chicano Novel," in *Contemporary Chicano Fiction*, ed. V. E. Lattin, 1986. V. E. Lattin et al., eds., *Tomás Rivera: The Man and His Work*, 1988. C. R. Shirley and P. W. Shirley, *Understanding Chicano Literature*, 1988.

Text Used: . . . *y No Se Lo Tragó la Tierra*, 1987.

from   . . . Y NO SE LO TRAGÓ LA TIERRA*
(. . . AND THE EARTH DID NOT DEVOUR HIM)

THE CHILDREN COULDN'T WAIT

The heat had set in with severity. This was unusual because it was only the beginning of April and this kind of heat was not expected until the end of the month. It was so hot that the bucket of water the boss brought them was not enough. He would come only two times for the midday and sometimes they couldn't hold out. That was why they took to drinking water from a tank at the edge of the furrow. The boss had it there for the cattle and when he caught them drinking water there he got angry. He didn't much like the idea of their losing time going to drink water because they weren't on contract, but by the hour. He told them that if he caught them there again he was going to fire them and not pay them. The children were the ones who couldn't wait.

"I'm very thirsty, Dad. Is the boss gonna be here soon?"

"I think so. You can't wait any longer?"

"Well, I don't know. My throat already feels real dry. Do you think he's almost gonna be here? Should I go to the tank?"

"No, wait just a little longer. You already heard what he said."

"I know, that he'll fire us if he catches us there, but I can't wait."

"Come on now, come on, work. He'll be here real soon."

"Well . . . I'll try to wait. Why doesn't this one let us bring water? Up north . . . "

"Because he's no good, that's why."

"But we could hide it under the seat, couldn't we? It was always better up north . . . And what if I make like I'm gonna go relieve myself by the tank?"

* The ellipses are Rivera's.

And this was what they started doing that afternoon. They pretended they were going to relieve themselves and they would go on to the edge of the tank. The boss became aware of this almost right away. But he didn't let on. He wanted to catch a bunch of them and that way he could pay fewer of them and only after they had done more work. He noticed that one of the children kept going to drink water every little while and he became more and more furious. He thought then of giving him a scare and he crawled on the ground to get his rifle.

What he set out to do and what he did were two different things. He shot at him once to scare him but when he pulled the trigger he saw the boy with a hole in his head. And the child didn't even jump like a deer does. He just stayed in the water like a dirty rag and the water began to turn bloody . . .

"They say that the old man almost went crazy."

"You think so?"

"Yes, he's already lost the ranch. He hit the bottle pretty hard. And then after they tried him and he got off free, they say he jumped off a tree 'cause he wanted to kill himself."

"But he didn't kill himself, did he?"

"Well, no."

"Well, there you have it."

"Well, I'll tell you, compadre, I think he did go crazy. You've seen the likes of him nowadays. He looks like a beggar."

"Sure, but that's 'cause he doesn't have any more money."

"Well . . . that's true."

She had fallen asleep right away and everyone, very mindful of not crossing their arms and their legs nor their hands, watched her intensely. The spirit was already present in her body.

"Let's see, how may I help you this evening, brothers and sisters?"

"Well, you see, I haven't heard from my boy in two months. Yesterday a letter from the government arrived telling me that he's lost in action. I'd like to know whether or not he's alive. I feel like I'm losing my mind just thinking and thinking about it."

"Have no fear, sister. Julianito is fine. He's just fine. Don't worry about him anymore. Very soon he'll be in your arms. He'll be returning already next month."

"Thank you, thank you."

* * *

It's That It Hurts

It hurts a lot. That's why I hit him. And now, what do I do? Maybe they didn't expel me from school. Maybe it ain't so, after all. Maybe it's not. *Sure it is!* It is so, they did expel me. And now, what do I do?

I think it all started when I got so embarrassed and angry at the same time. I dread getting home. What am I going to tell Mother? And then when Dad gets home from the fields? They'll whip me for sure. But it's embarrassing and angering. It's always the same in these schools in the north. Everybody just stares at you up and down. And then they make fun of you and the teacher with her popsicle stick, poking your head for lice. It's embarrassing. And then when they turn up their noses. It makes you angry. I think it's better staying out here on the ranch, here in the quiet of this knoll, with its chicken coops, or out in the fields where you at least feel more free, more at ease.

"Come on, son, we're almost there."

"You gonna take me to the principal?"

"Of course not. Don't tell me you don't know how to speak English yet. Look, that's the entrance over there. Just ask if you don't know where to go. Don't be shy, ask someone. Don't be afraid."

"Why can't you go with me?"

"Don't tell me you're scared. Look, that's probably the entrance there. Here comes someone. Now, you behave, you hear me?"

"But why don't you help me?"

"No. You'll do just fine, don't be afraid."

It's always the same. They take you to the nurse and the first thing she does is check you for lice. And, too, those ladies are to blame. On Sundays they sit out in front of the chicken coops picking lice from each other's heads. And the gringos, passing by in their cars, looking and pointing at them. Dad is right when he says that they look like monkeys in the zoo. But it's not all that bad.

"Mother, you won't believe this. Do you know that I no sooner walked into the room, when they put me in a room with a nurse all dressed in white. And they made me take off my clothes and they even examined my behind. But where they took the longest was on my head. I had washed it, right? Well, the nurse brought out a jar of, like vaseline, it smelled like worm-killer, do I still smell? And she smeared it all over my head. It itched. And then she started parting my hair with a pencil. After a while they let me go but I was so ashamed because I had to take off my pants, even my underwear, in front of the nurse."

But now what do I tell them? That they threw me out of school? But it wasn't my fault. I didn't like that gringo,[1] right off. This one didn't laugh at me. He'd just stare and when they put me in the corner apart from everyone he kept turning to look at me, and then he'd make a gesture with his finger. I was mad but mostly I felt embarrassed because I was sitting away from everyone where they could see me better. Then when it was my turn to read, I couldn't. I could hear myself. And I could hear that no words were coming out . . . This cemetery isn't scarey at all. That's what I like best about the walk to school and back. The greenness! And everything so even. The roads all paved. It even looks like where they play golf. Today I won't have time to run up the hills and slide down tumbling. Nor to lie down on the grass and try to hear all the sounds. Last time I counted to 26 . . . If I hurry maybe I can go to the dump with Doña[2] Cuquita. She heads out about this time when the sun's not so hot.

---

[1] "White man" (Spanish); the male equivalent of "gringa."

[2] A title of respect, used before a woman's Christian name (Spanish); the female equivalent of "Don."

"Careful, children. Just be careful and don't step where there's fire burning underneath. Wherever you see smoke coming out, there's coals underneath. I know what I'm telling you, I once got a bad burn and I still have the scar . . . Look, each of you get a long stick and just turn the trash over briskly. If the dump man comes to see what we're doing, tell him we came to throw away some stuff. He's a kind man, but he likes to keep those little books with nasty pictures that people sometimes throw away . . . watch out for the train as you cross that bridge. It ran over a man last year . . . caught him right in middle of the bridge and he wasn't able to make it to the other side . . . Did they give you permission to come with me? . . . Don't eat anything until after you've washed it."

But if I go with her without permission they'll whip me even more. What am I going to tell them? Maybe they didn't expel me. *Sure, they did!* Maybe not. *Yeah, they did!* What am I going to tell them? But it wasn't all my fault. I couldn't wait anymore. While I was standing there in the restroom he's the one that started picking on me.

"Hey, Mex . . . I don't like Mexicans because they steal. You hear me?"
"Yes."
"I don't like Mexicans. You hear, Mex?"
"Yes."
"I don't like Mexicans because they steal. You hear me?"
"Yes."

I remember the first fight I had at school, I got real scared because everything happened so slow. There wasn't any reason, it's just that some of the older boys, who already had mustaches and who were still in the second grade, started pushing us against each other. And they kept it up until we started fighting, I think, 'cause we were plain scared. It was about a block from school, I remember, when they started pushing me towards Ramiro. Then we began to scuffle and hit at each other. Some ladies came out and broke us up. Since then I got to feeling bigger. But all it was, up until I fought, was plain fear.

This time it was different. He didn't warn me. I just felt a real hard blow on my ear and I heard something like when you put a conch to your ear at the beach. I don't remember anymore how or when I hit him but I know I did because someone told the principal that we were fighting in the restroom. Maybe they didn't throw me out? *Sure they did!* And then, I wonder who called the principal? And the janitor all scared and with his broom up in the air, ready to swat me if I tried to leave.

"The Mexican kid got into a fight and beat up a couple of our boys . . . No, not bad . . . but what do I do?"
" . . . . "
"No, I guess not, they could care less if I expel him . . . They need him in the fields."
" . . . . "
"Well, I just hope our boys don't make too much out about it to their parents. I guess I'll just throw him out."
" . . . . "

"Yeah, I guess you're right."

". . . . ."

"I know you warned me, I know, I know . . . but . . . yeah, okay."

But how could I even think of leaving knowing that everyone at home wanted me to go to school. Anyways, the janitor stood with his broom up in the air, ready for anything . . . And then they just told me to leave.

I'm halfway home. This cemetery is real pretty. It doesn't look anything like the one in Texas. That one *is* scarey, I don't like it at all. What scares me the most is when we're leaving after a burial and I look up and I read the letters on the arch over the gate that say, *Don't forget me*. It's like I can hear all the dead people buried there saying these words and then the sound of these words stays in my mind and sometimes even if I don't look up when I pass through the gate, I see them. But not this one, this one is real pretty. Just lots of soft grass and trees, I guess that's why here when people bury somebody they don't even cry. I like playing here. If only they would let us fish in the little creek that runs through here, there's lots of fish. But no, you even need a license to fish and then they don't even sell us one 'cause we're from out of state.

I won't be able to go to school anymore. What am I going to tell them? They've told me over and over that our teachers are like our second parents . . . and now? And when we get back to Texas everyone will find out too. Mother and Dad will be angry; I might get more than just a whipping. And then my Uncle will find out and Grandpa. Maybe they might even send me to a reform school like the ones I've heard them talk about. There they turn you into a good person if you're bad. They're real hard on you. They leave you soft as a glove. But maybe they didn't expel me, *sure they did,* maybe not, *sure they did.* I could make like I'm going to school and stay here in the cemetery. That would be better. But then what? I could tell them that I lost my report card. And then what if I stay in the same grade? What hurts me the most is that now I won't be able to be a telephone operator like Dad wants me to. You need to finish school for that.

"Vieja, call m'ijó[3] out here . . . look, compadre, ask your godson what he wants to be when he grows up and finishes school."

"What will you be, godson?"

"I don't know."

"Tell him! Don't be embarrassed. He's your godfather."

"What will you be, son?"

"A telephone operator."

"Is that so?"

"Yes, compadre, he's very determined, you know that? Every time we ask him he says he wants to be an operator. I think they pay well. I told the boss the other day and he laughed. I don't think he believes that my son can do it, but that's 'cause he doesn't know him. He's smarter than anything. I just pray God helps him finish school so he can become an operator."

That movie was good. The operator was the most important one. Ever since then I suppose that's why Dad has wanted me to study for that after I finish school. But . . . maybe they didn't throw me out. What if it's not true? Maybe

---

[3] "Old woman, call my son" (Spanish); the female equivalent of "viejo." "Compadre" means "pal."

not. *Sure, it is.* What do I tell them? What do I do? Now they won't be able to ask me what I'm going to be when I grow up. Maybe not. *No, yeah.* What do I do? It's that it hurts and it's embarrassing at the same time. I better just stay here. No, but then Mother will get scared like she does when there's lightning and thunder. I've gotta tell them. And when my padrino comes to visit us I'll just hide. No need for him to find out. Nor for me to read to him like Dad has me do every time he comes to visit us. What I'll do when he comes is hide behind the chest or under the bed. That way Dad and Mother won't feel embarrassed. And what if I really wasn't expelled? Maybe I wasn't? *No, yeah.*

"Why do y'all go to school so much?"

"My Dad says it's to prepare us. He says that if someday there's an opportunity, maybe they'll give it to us."

"Sure! If I were you I wouldn't worry about that. The poor can't get poorer. We can't get worst off than we already are. That's why I don't worry. The ones who have to be on their toes are the ones who are higher up. They've got something to lose. They can end up where we're at. But for us, what does it matter?"

* * *

The Night Before Christmas

Christmas Eve was approaching and the barrage of commercials, music and Christmas cheer over the radio and the blare of announcements over the loud speakers on top of the stationwagon advertising movies at the Teatro Ideal resounded and seemed to draw it closer. It was three days before Christmas when Doña María decided to buy something for her children. This was the first time she would buy them toys. Every year she intended to do it but she always ended up facing up to the fact that, no, they couldn't afford it. She knew that her husband would be bringing each of the children candies and nuts anyway and so she would rationalize that they didn't need to get them anything else. Nevertheless, every Christmas the children asked for toys. She always appeased them with the same promise. She would tell them to wait until the sixth of January, the day of the Magi, and by the time that day arrived the children had already forgotten all about it. But now she was noticing that each year the children seemed less and less taken with Don Chon's visit on Christmas Eve when he came bearing a sack of oranges and nuts.

"But why doesn't Santa Claus bring us anything?"

"What do you mean? What about the oranges and nuts he brings you?"

"No, that's Don Chon."

"No, I'm talking about what you always find under the sewing machine."

"What, Dad's the one who brings that, don't think we don't know that. Aren't we good like the other kids?"

"Of course, you're good children. Why don't you wait until the day of the Reyes Magos.[4] That's when toys and gifts really arrive. In Mexico, it's not Santa Claus who brings gifts, but the Three Wisemen. And they don't come until the sixth of January. That's the real date."

"Yeah, but they always forget. They've never brought us anything, not on Christmas Eve, not on the day of the Three Kings."

---

[4] "Wise Men" (Spanish): the three Magi.

"Well, maybe this time they will."

"Yeah, well, I sure hope so."

That was why she made up her mind to buy them something. But they didn't have the money to spend on toys. Her husband worked almost eighteen hours a day washing dishes and cooking at a restaurant. He didn't have time to go downtown and buy toys. Besides, they had to save money every week to pay for the trip up north. Now they even charged for children too, even if they rode standing up the whole way to Iowa. So it cost them a lot to make the trip. In any case, that night when her husband arrived, tired from work, she talked to him about getting something for the children.

"Look, viejo, the children want something for Christmas."

"What about the oranges and nuts I bring them."

"Well, they want toys. They're not content anymore with just fruits and nuts. They're a little older now and more aware of things."

"They don't need anything."

"Now, you can't tell me you didn't have toys when you were a kid."

"I used to *make* my own toys, out of clay . . . little horses and little soldiers . . ."

"Yes, but it's different here. They see so many things . . . come on, let's go get them something . . . I'll go to Kress[5] myself."

"You?"

"Yes, me."

"Aren't you afraid to go downtown? You remember that time in Wilmar, out in Minnesota, how you got lost downtown. Are you sure you're not afraid?"

"Yes, yes, I remember, but I'll just have to get up my courage. I've thought about it all day long and I've set my mind to it. I'm sure I won't get lost here. Look, I go out to the street. From here you can see the ice house. It's only four blocks away, so Doña Regina tells me. When I get to the ice house I turn to the right and go two blocks and there's downtown. Kress is right there. Then, I come out of Kress, walk back towards the ice house and turn back on this street, and here I am."

"I guess it really won't be difficult. Yeah. Fine. I'll leave you some money on top of the table when I go to work in the morning. But be careful, vieja, there's a lot of people downtown these days."

The fact was that Doña María very rarely left the house. The only time she did was when she visited her father and her sister who lived on the next block. And she only went to church whenever someone died and, occasionally, when there was a wedding. But she went with her husband, so she never took notice of where she was going. And her husband always brought her everything. He was the one who bought the groceries and clothing. In reality she was unfamiliar with downtown even though it was only six blocks away. The cemetery was on the other side of downtown and the church was also in that direction. The only time that they passed through downtown was whenever they were on their way to San Antonio or whenever they were returning from up north. And this would usually be during the wee hours of the morning or at night. But that day she was determined and she started making preparations.

[5] A "five-and-ten," or discount department store.

The next day she got up early as usual, and after seeing her husband and children off, she took the money from the table and began getting ready to go downtown. This didn't take her long.

"My god, I don't know why I'm so fearful. Why, downtown is only six blocks from here. I just go straight and then after I cross the tracks turn right. Then go two blocks and there's Kress. On the way back, I walk two blocks back and then I turn to the left and keep walking until I'm home again. God willing, there won't be any dogs on the way. And I just pray that the train doesn't come while I'm crossing the tracks and catches me right in the middle . . . I just hope there's no dogs . . . I hope there's no train coming down the tracks."

She walked the distance from the house to the railroad tracks rapidly. She walked down the middle of the street all the way. She was afraid to walk on the sidewalk. She feared she might get bitten by a dog or that someone might grab her. In actuality there was only one dog along the entire stretch and most of the people didn't even notice her walking toward downtown. She nevertheless kept walking down the middle of the street and, luckily, not a single car passed by, otherwise she would not have known what to do. Upon arriving at the crossing she was suddenly struck by intense fear. She could hear the sound of moving trains and their whistles blowing and this was unnerving her. She was too scared to cross. Each time she mustered enough courage to cross she heard the whistle of the train and, frightened, she retreated and ended up at the same place. Finally, overcoming her fear, she shut her eyes and crossed the tracks. Once she got past the tracks, her fear began to subside. She got to the corner and turned to the right.

The sidewalks were crowded with people and her ears started to fill up with a ringing sound, the kind that once it starts it doesn't cease. She didn't recognize any of the people around her. She wanted to turn back but she was caught in the flow of the crowd which shoved her onward toward downtown and the sound kept ringing louder and louder in her ears. She became frightened and more and more she was finding herself unable to remember why she was there among the crowd of people. She stopped in an alley way between two stores to regain her composure a bit. She stood there for a while watching the passing crowd.

"My god, what is happening to me? I'm starting to feel the same way I did in Wilmar. I hope I don't get worse. Let me see . . . the ice house is in that direction—no it's that way. No, my god, what's happening to me? Let me see . . . I came from over there to here. So it's in that direction. I should have just stayed home. Uh, can you tell me where Kress is, please? . . . Thank you."

She walked to where they had pointed and entered the store. The noise and pushing of the crowd was worse inside. Her anxiety soared. All she wanted was to leave the store but she couldn't find the doors anywhere, only stacks and stacks of merchandise and people crowded against one another. She even started hearing voices coming from the merchandise. For a while she stood, gazing blankly at what was in front of her. She couldn't even remember the names of the objects. Some people stared at her for a few seconds, others just pushed her aside. She remained in this state for a while, then she started walking again. She finally made out some toys and put them in her bag. Then she saw a wallet and also put that in her bag. Suddenly she no longer heard the noise of the crowd. She only saw the people moving about—their legs, their arms, their mouths, their eyes. She finally asked where the door, the exit was. They told her and she started in that direction. She pressed through the crowd, pushing her way until she pushed open the door and exited.

She had been standing on the sidewalk for only a few seconds, trying to figure out where she was, when she felt someone grab her roughly by the arm. She was grabbed so tightly that she gave out a cry.

"Here she is . . . these damn people, always stealing something, stealing. I've been watching you all along. Let's have that bag."
"But . . . "

Then she heard nothing for a long time. All she saw was the pavement moving swiftly toward her face and a small pebble that bounced into her eye and was hurting a lot. She felt someone pulling her arms and when they turned her, face up, all she saw were faces far away. Then she spotted a security guard with a gun in his holster and she became terrified. In that instant she thought about her children and her eyes filled with tears. She started crying. Then she lost consciousness of what was happening around her, only feeling herself drifting in a sea of people, their arms brushing against her like waves.

"It's a good thing my compadre happened to be there. He's the one who ran to the restaurant to tell me. How do you feel?"
"I think I must be insane, viejo."
"That's why I asked you if you weren't afraid you might get sick like in Wilmar."
"What will become of my children with a mother who's insane? A crazy woman who can't even talk, can't even go downtown."
"Anyway, I went and got the notary public. He's the one who went with me to the jail. He explained everything to the official. That you got dizzy and that you get nervous attacks whenever you're in a crowd of people."
"And if they send me to the insane asylum? I don't want to leave my children. Please, viejo, don't let them take me, don't let them. I shouldn't have gone downtown."
"Just stay here inside the house and don't leave the yard. There's no need for it anyway. I'll bring you everything you need. Look, don't cry anymore, don't cry. No, go ahead and cry, it'll make you feel better. I'm gonna talk to the kids and tell them to stop bothering you about Santa Claus. I'm gonna tell them there's no Santa Claus, that way they won't trouble you with that anymore."
"No, viejo, don't be mean. Tell them that if he doesn't bring them anything on Christmas Eve, it's because the Reyes Magos will be bringing them something."
"But . . . well, all right, whatever you say. I suppose it's always best to have hope."

The children, who were hiding behind the door, heard everything, but they didn't quite understand it all. They awaited the day of the Reyes Magos as they did every year. When that day came and went with no arrival of gifts, they didn't ask for explanations.

Before people left for up north the priest would bless their cars and trucks at five dollars each. One time he made enough money to take a trip to Barcelona, in

Spain, to visit his parents and friends. He brought back words of gratitude from his family and some postcards of a very modern church. These he placed by the entrance of the church for the people to see, that they might desire a church such as that one. It wasn't long before words began to appear on the cards, then crosses, lines, and con safos[6] symbols, just as had happened to the new church pews. The priest was never able to understand the sacrilege.

* * *

When We Arrive

At about four o'clock in the morning the truck broke down. All night they stood hypnotized by the high-pitched whir of the tires turning against the pavement. When the truck stopped they awakened. The silence alone told them something was wrong. All along the way the truck had been overheating and then when they stopped and checked the motor they saw that it had practically burned up. It just wouldn't go anymore. They would have to wait there until daybreak and then ask for a lift to the next town. Inside the trailer the people awakened and then struck up several conversations. Then, in the darkness, their eyes had gradually begun to close and all became so silent that all that could be heard was the chirping of the crickets. Some were sleeping, others were thinking.

"Good thing the truck stopped here. My stomach's been hurting a lot for some time but I would've had to wake up a lot of people to get to the window and ask them to stop. But you still can't hardly see anything. Well, I'm getting off, see if I can find a field or a ditch. Must've been that chile I ate, it was so hot but I hated to let it go to waste. I hope my vieja is doing all right in there, carrying the baby and all."

"This driver that we have this year is a good one. He keeps on going. He doesn't stop for anything. Just gases up and let's go. We've been on the road over twenty-four hours. We should be close to Des Moines. Sure wish I could sit down for just a little while at least. I'd get out and lie down on the side of the road but there's no telling if there's snakes or some other kind of animal. Just before I fell asleep on my feet it felt like my knees were going to buckle. But, I guess your body gets used to it right away 'cause it doesn't seem so hard anymore. But the kids must feel real tired standing like this all the way and with nothing to hold on to. Us grownups can at least hold on to this center bar that supports the canvas. And to think we're not as crowded as other times. I think there must be forty of us at the most. I remember that one time I traveled with that bunch of wetbacks, there were more than sixty of us. We couldn't even smoke."

"What a stupid woman! How could she be so dumb as to throw that diaper out the front of the truck. It came sliding along the canvas and good thing I had my glasses on or else I would've gotten my eyes full of shit too! What a stupid woman! How could she do that? She should've known that crap would be blown towards

---

[6] Graffiti (Spanish).

*all of us standing up back here. Why the hell couldn't she just wait until we got to
a gas station and dump the shit there!"*

"That Negrito's[7] eyes just about popped out when I ordered those fifty-four
hamburgers. At two o'clock in the morning . . . And since I walked into the restaurant alone and I'm sure he didn't see the truck pull up loaded with people. His
eyes just popped wide open . . . 'at two o'clock in the morning, hamburgers?
Fifty-four of them? Man, you must eat one hell of a lot.' It's that the people hadn't
eaten and the driver asked for just one of us to get out and order for everyone.
That Negrito was astounded. He couldn't believe what I ordered, that I wanted
fifty-four hamburgers. At two o'clock in the morning you can eat that many hamburgers very easily, especially when you're starving."

"This is the last fuckin' year I come out here. As soon as we get to the farm I'm
getting the hell out. I'll go look for a job in Minneapolis. I'll be damned if I go
back to Texas. Out here you can at least make a living at a decent job. I'll look for
my uncle, see if he can find me a job at the hotel where he works as a bellboy.
Who knows, maybe they'll give me a break there or at some other hotel. And then
the gringas, that's just a matter of finding them."

"If things go well this year maybe we'll buy us a car so we won't have to travel
this way, like cattle. The girls are pretty big now and I know they feel embarrassed. Sometimes they have some good buys at the gas stations out there. I'll talk
to my compadre, he knows some of the car salesmen. I'll get one I like, even if it's
old. I'm tired of coming out here in a truck like this. My compadre drove back a
good little car last year. If we do well with the onion crop, I'll buy me one that's
at least half-way decent. I'll teach my boy how to drive and he can take it all the
way to Texas. As long as he doesn't get lost like my nephew. They didn't stop to
ask for directions and ended up in New Mexico instead of Texas. Or I'll get
Mundo to drive it and I won't charge him for gas. I'll see if he wants to."

"With the money Mr. Thompson loaned me we have enough to buy food for at
least two months. By then we should have the money from the beet crop. Just hope
we don't get too much in debt. He loaned me two-hundred dollars but by the time
you pay for the trip practically half of it is gone, and now that they've started
charging me half-fare for the children . . . And then when we return, I have to
pay him back double. Four-hundred dollars. That's too much interest, but what
can you do? When you need it, you need it. Some people have told me to report
him because that's way too much interest, but now he's even got the deed to the
house. I'm just hoping that things go okay for us with the beet crop or else we'll
be left to the wind, homeless. We have to save enough to pay him back the four-
hundred. And then we'll see if we have something left. And these kids, they need
to start going to school. I don't know. I hope it goes okay for us, if not I don't
know how we're going to do it. I just pray to God that there's work."

"Fuckin' life, this goddamn fuckin' life! This fuckin' sonofabitchin' life for
being dumb! dumb! dumb! We're nothing but a bunch of goddam assholes! To hell

---

[7] "Negro boy's" (Spanish).

*with this goddamn motherfuckin' life! This is the last time I go through this, stand-
ing up all the way like a goddamn animal. As soon as we get there I'm headed for
Minneapolis. Somehow I'll find me something to do where I don't have to work
like a fuckin' mule. Fuckin' life! One of these days they'll fuckin' pay for this.
Sonofabitch! For being such a goddam asshole!"*

*"Poor viejo. He must be real tired now, standing up the whole trip. I saw him
nodding off a little while ago. And with no way to help him, what with these two in
my arms. How I wish we were there already so we could lie down, even if it's on
the hard floor. These children are nothing but trouble. I hope I'll be able to help
him out in the fields, but I'm afraid that this year, what with these kids, I won't be
able to do anything. I have to breastfeed them every little while and then they're
still so little. If only they were just a bit older. I'm still going to try my best to help
him out. At least along his row so he won't feel so overworked. Even if it's just for
short whiles. My poor viejo . . . the children are still so little and already he
wishes they could start school. I just hope I'll be able to help him. God willing,
I'll be able to help him."*

*"What a great view of the stars from here! It looks like they're coming down
and touching the tarp of the truck. It's almost like there aren't any people inside.
There's hardly any traffic at this hour. Every now and then a trailer passes by.
The silence of the morning twilight makes everything look like it's made of satin.
And now, what do I wipe myself with? Why couldn't it always be early dawn like
this? We're going to be here till midday for sure. By the time they find help in the
town and then by the time they fix the motor . . . If only it could stay like early
dawn, then nobody would complain. I'm going to keep my eyes on the stars till the
last one disappears. I wonder how many more people are watching the same star?
And how many more might there be wondering how many are looking at the same
star? It's so silent it looks like it's the stars the crickets are calling to."*

*"Goddam truck. It's nothing but trouble. When we get there everybody will just
have to look out for themselves. All I'm doing is dropping them off with the grow-
ers and I'm getting the hell out. Besides, we don't have a contract. They'll find
themselves somebody to take them back to Texas. Somebody's bound to come by
and pick them up. You can't make money off beets anymore. My best bet is to head
back to Texas just as soon as I drop these people off and then see how things go
hauling watermelons. The melon season's almost here. All I need now is for there
not to be anyone in this goddam town who can fix the truck. What the hell will I do
then? So long as the cops don't come by and start hassling me about moving the
truck from here. Boy, that town had to be the worst. We didn't even stop and still
the cop caught up with us just to tell us that he didn't want us staying there. I
guess he just wanted to show off in front of the town people. But we didn't even
stop in their goddam town. When we get there, as soon as I drop them off, I'll turn
back. Each one to fend for himself."*

*"When we get there I'm gonna see about getting a good bed for my vieja. Her
kidneys are really bothering her a lot nowadays. Just hope we don't end up in a
chicken coop like last year, with that cement floor. Even though you cover it with
straw, once the cold season sets in, you just can't stand it. That was why my
rheumatism got so bad, I'm sure of that."*

"When we arrive, when we arrive, the real truth is that I'm tired of arriving. Arriving and leaving, it's the same thing because we no sooner arrive and. . . the real truth of the matter . . . I'm tired of arriving. I really should say when we don't arrive because that's the real truth. We never arrive."

"When we arrive, when we arrive . . . "

Little by little the crickets ceased their chirping. It seemed as though they were becoming tired and the dawn gradually affirmed the presence of objects, ever so carefully and very slowly, so that no one would take notice of what was happening. And the people were becoming people. They began getting out of the trailer and they huddled around and commenced to talk about what they would do when they arrived.

1971

Joyce Carol Oates
(1938–   )

Born in the town of Lockport, New York, in 1938, Joyce Carol Oates was raised Roman Catholic in a working-class family. She received her early education in a rural one-room schoolhouse and went on to graduate as class valedictorian from Syracuse University in 1960. Oates earned an M.A. in English from the University of Wisconsin in 1961 and began an academic career that has included teaching positions at the University of Detroit, the University of Windsor, Ontario, and New York University, and in 1978 she became a member of the creative writing department of Princeton University. One of the most prolific and celebrated writers in America today, Oates has contributed novels, short stories, plays, volumes of poetry, books of critical essays, and scholarly studies as well as the book-length essay *On Boxing* (1987). Oates's first published story, "In the Old World," won the college fiction prize offered by *Mademoiselle* magazine in 1959, and she has since won such honors as the Rosenthal Foundation Award, a National Book Award (for the novel *them* [1969]), a Guggenheim Fellowship, the Rea Award for short stories, and the O. Henry Prize for Continuing Achievement.

In its various forms Oates's fiction offers a vision of contemporary America, ranging from portraits of suburban affluent society to experimental Gothic romances. But her intention is always to locate a moral center among even the most grotesque and violent occurrences. Beginning with her first novel, *With Shuddering Fall* (1964), and continuing through her most recent work, Oates commonly uses the shock of the macabre to recreate the mental equivalent of her characters' experiences within the mind of the reader. To Oates art is didactic—illustrative, moral, educational. This instruction is typically achieved through the accumulated detail of her rich, imaginary worlds and the cathartic release that accompanies the often unsettling violence of her plots. Another thread that runs throughout Oates's work is the exploration of social and economic histories as revealed through personal narratives. From her early trilogy of novels—*A Garden of Earthly*

Delights (1967), *Expensive People* (1968), and *them* (1969)—to *The Assignation* (1988) and *Because It Is Bitter and Because It Is My Heart* (1990), Oates has combined a keen, naturalistic attention to minute particulars with a fascination for psychological drama to create a social history that defies easy categorization, providing imaginative insight into the problems of "ordinary people." Equally at home in the fantasy world of *Bellefleur* (1980), the mythical/historical realm of *Angel of Light* (1981), and the gritty realism of *You Must Remember This* (1987), Oates's distinctive moral vision remains the one constant throughout her wide variety of formal and generic experiments.

Suggested Readings: *Marya: A Sweeping Flood and Other Stories*, 1966. *A Garden of Earthly Delights*, 1967. *them*, 1969. *The Goddess and Other Women*, 1974. *The Assassins*, 1975. *Bellefleur*, 1980. *Angel of Light*, 1981. *Contraries*, 1981. *The Profane Art: Essays and Reviews*, 1983. *Mysteries of Winterthurn*, 1985. *Raven's Wing*, 1986. *You Must Remember This*, 1987. *The Assignation*, 1988. *Woman Writer: Occasions and Opportunities*, 1988. *The Time Traveler: Poems 1983–1989*, 1989. M. K. Grant, *The Tragic Vision of Joyce Carol Oates*, 1978. J. V. Creighton, *Joyce Carol Oates*, 1979. L. W. Wagner, ed., *Critical Essays on Joyce Carol Oates*, 1979. K. Bastion, *Joyce Carol Oates's Short Stories: Between Tradition and Innovation*, 1983. G. Johnson, *Understanding Joyce Carol Oates*, 1987.

Text Used: *The Wheel of Love and Other Stories*, 1970.

WHERE ARE YOU GOING, WHERE HAVE YOU BEEN?*

For Bob Dylan

Her name was Connie. She was fifteen and she had a quick, nervous giggling habit of craning her neck to glance into mirrors or checking other people's faces to make sure her own was all right. Her mother, who noticed everything and knew everything and who hadn't much reason any longer to look at her own face, always scolded Connie about it. "Stop gawking at yourself. Who are you? You think you're so pretty?" she would say. Connie would raise her eyebrows at these familiar old complaints and look right through her mother, into a shadowy vision of herself as she was right at that moment: she knew she was pretty and that was everything. Her mother had been pretty once too, if you could believe those old snapshots in the album, but now her looks were gone and that was why she was always after Connie.

"Why don't you keep your room clean like your sister? How've you got your hair fixed—what the hell stinks? Hair spray? You don't see your sister using that junk."

Her sister June was twenty-four and still lived at home. She was a secretary in the high school Connie attended, and if that wasn't bad enough—with her in the same building—she was so plain and chunky and steady that Connie had to hear her praised all the time by her mother and her mother's sisters. June did this, June did that, she saved money and helped clean the house and cooked and Connie couldn't do a thing, her mind was all filled with trashy daydreams. Their father was away at work most of the time and when he came home he wanted supper and

* First published in *Epoch* in autumn 1966 and later collected in *The Wheel of Love and Other Stories* (1970).

he read the newspaper at supper and after supper he went to bed. He didn't bother talking much to them, but around his bent head Connie's mother kept picking at her until Connie wished her mother was dead and she herself was dead and it was all over. "She makes me want to throw up sometimes," she complained to her friends. She had a high, breathless, amused voice that made everything she said sound a little forced, whether it was sincere or not.

There was one good thing: June went places with girl friends of hers, girls who were just as plain and steady as she, and so when Connie wanted to do that her mother had no objections. The father of Connie's best girl friend drove the girls the three miles to town and left them at a shopping plaza so they could walk through the stores or go to a movie, and when he came to pick them up again at eleven he never bothered to ask what they had done.

They must have been familiar sights, walking around the shopping plaza in their shorts and flat ballerina slippers that always scuffed the sidewalk, with charm bracelets jingling on their thin wrists; they would lean together to whisper and laugh secretly if someone passed who amused or interested them. Connie had long dark blond hair that drew anyone's eye to it, and she wore part of it pulled up on her head and puffed out and the rest of it she let fall down her back. She wore a pull-over jersey blouse that looked one way when she was at home and another way when she was away from home. Everything about her had two sides to it, one for home and one for anywhere that was not home: her walk, which could be childlike and bobbing, or languid enough to make anyone think she was hearing music in her head; her mouth, which was pale and smirking most of the time, but bright and pink on these evenings out; her laugh, which was cynical and drawling at home—"Ha, ha, very funny,"—but high-pitched and nervous anywhere else, like the jingling of the charms on her bracelet.

Sometimes they did go shopping or to a movie, but sometimes they went across the highway, ducking fast across the busy road, to a drive-in restaurant where older kids hung out. The restaurant was shaped like a big bottle, though squatter than a real bottle, and on its cap was a revolving figure of a grinning boy holding a hamburger aloft. One night in midsummer they ran across, breathless with daring, and right away someone leaned out a car window and invited them over, but it was just a boy from high school they didn't like. It made them feel good to be able to ignore him. They went up through the maze of parked and cruising cars to the bright-lit, fly-infested restaurant, their faces pleased and expectant as if they were entering a sacred building that loomed up out of the night to give them what haven and blessing they yearned for. They sat at the counter and crossed their legs at the ankles, their thin shoulders rigid with excitement, and listened to the music that made everything so good: the music was always in the background, like music at a church service; it was something to depend upon.

A boy named Eddie came in to talk with them. He sat backwards on his stool, turning himself jerkily around in semicircles and then stopping and turning back again, and after a while he asked Connie if she would like something to eat. She said she would and so she tapped her friend's arm on her way out—her friend pulled her face up into a brave, droll look—and Connie said she would meet her at eleven, across the way. "I just hate to leave her like that," Connie said earnestly, but the boy said that she wouldn't be alone for long. So they went out to his car, and on the way Connie couldn't help but let her eyes wander over the windshields and faces all around her, her face gleaming with a joy that had nothing to do with Eddie or even this place; it might have been the music. She drew her shoulders up and sucked in her breath with the pure pleasure of being alive, and just at that moment she happened to glance at a face just a few feet from hers. It was a boy with shaggy black hair, in a convertible jalopy painted gold. He stared at her and then his lips widened into a grin. Connie slit her eyes at him and turned away, but she couldn't help glancing back and there he was, still watching her. He wagged a finger and laughed and said, "Gonna get you, baby," and Connie turned away again without Eddie noticing anything.

She spent three hours with him, at the restaurant where they ate hamburgers and drank Cokes in wax cups that were always sweating, and then down an alley a mile or so away, and when he left her off at five to eleven only the movie house was still open at the plaza. Her girl friend was there, talking with a boy. When Connie came up, the two girls smiled at each other and Connie said, "How was the movie?" and the girl said, "*You* should know." They rode off with the girl's father, sleepy and pleased, and Connie couldn't help but look back at the darkened shopping plaza with its big empty parking lot and its signs that were faded and ghostly now, and over at the drive-in restaurant where cars were still circling tirelessly. She couldn't hear the music at this distance.

Next morning June asked her how the movie was and Connie said, "So-so."

She and that girl and occasionally another girl went out several times a week, and the rest of the time Connie spent around the house—it was summer vacation—getting in her mother's way and thinking, dreaming about the boys she met. But all the boys fell back and dissolved into a single face that was not even a face but an idea, a feeling, mixed up with the urgent insistent pounding of the music and the humid night air of July. Connie's mother kept dragging her back to the daylight by finding things for her to do or saying suddenly, "What's this about the Pettinger girl?"

And Connie would say nervously, "Oh, her. That dope." She always drew thick clear lines between herself and such girls, and her mother was simple and kind enough to believe it. Her mother was so simple, Connie thought, that it was maybe cruel to fool her so much. Her mother went scuffling around the house in old bedroom slippers and complained over the telephone to one sister about the other, then the other called up and the two of them complained about the third one. If June's name was mentioned her mother's tone was approving, and if Connie's name was mentioned it was disapproving. This did not really mean she disliked Connie, and actually Connie thought that her mother preferred her to June just because she was prettier, but the two of them kept up a pretense of exasperation, a sense that they were tugging and struggling over something of little value to either of them. Sometimes, over coffee, they were almost friends, but something would come up—some vexation that was like a fly buzzing suddenly around their heads—and their faces went hard with contempt.

One Sunday Connie got up at eleven—none of them bothered with church—and washed her hair so that it could dry all day long in the sun. Her parents and sister were going to a barbecue at an aunt's house and Connie said no, she wasn't interested, rolling her eyes to let her mother know just what she thought of it. "Stay home alone then," her mother said sharply. Connie sat out back in a lawn chair and watched them drive away, her father quiet and bald, hunched around so that he could back the car out, her mother with a look that was still angry and not at all softened through the windshield, and in the back seat poor old June, all dressed up as if she didn't know what a barbecue was, with all the running yelling kids and the flies. Connie sat with her eyes closed in the sun, dreaming and dazed with the warmth about her as if this were a kind of love, the caresses of love, and her mind slipped over onto thoughts of the boy she had been with the night before and how nice he had been, how sweet it always was, not the way someone like June would suppose but sweet, gentle, the way it was in movies and promised in songs; and when she opened her eyes she hardly knew where she was, the back yard ran off into weeds and a fence-like line of trees and behind it the sky was perfectly blue and still. The asbestos "ranch house" that was now three years old startled her—it looked small. She shook her head as if to get awake.

It was too hot. She went inside the house and turned on the radio to drown out the quiet. She sat on the edge of her bed, barefoot, and listened for an hour and a half to a program called XYZ Sunday Jamboree, record after record of hard, fast, shrieking songs she sang along with, interspersed by exclamations from "Bobby King": "An' look here, you girls at Napolean's—Son and Charley want you to pay real close attention to this song coming up!"

And Connie paid close attention herself, bathed in a glow of slow-pulsed joy that seemed to rise mysteriously out of the music itself and lay languidly about the airless little room, breathed in and breathed out with each gentle rise and fall of her chest.

After a while she heard a car coming up the drive. She sat up at once, startled, because it couldn't be her father so soon. The gravel kept crunching all the way in from the road—the driveway was long—and Connie ran to the window. It was a car she didn't know. It was an open jalopy, painted a bright gold that caught the sunlight opaquely. Her heart began to pound and her fingers snatched at her hair, checking it, and she whispered, "Christ. Christ," wondering how bad she looked. The car came to a stop at the side door and then the horn sounded four short taps, as if this were a signal Connie knew.

She went into the kitchen and approached the door slowly, then hung out the screen door, her bare toes curling down off the step. There were two boys in the car and now she recognized the driver: he had shaggy, shabby black hair that looked crazy as a wig and he was grinning at her.

"I ain't late, am I?" he said.

"Who the hell do you think you are?" Connie said.

"Toldja I'd be out, didn't I?"

"I don't even know who you are."

She spoke sullenly, careful to show no interest or pleasure, and he spoke in a fast, bright monotone. Connie looked past him to the other boy, taking her time. He had fair brown hair, with a lock that fell onto his forehead. His sideburns gave him a fierce, embarrassed look, but so far he hadn't even bothered to glance at her. Both boys wore sunglasses. The driver's glasses were metallic and mirrored everything in miniature.

"You wanta come for a ride?" he said.

Connie smirked and let her hair fall loose over one shoulder.

"Don'tcha like my car? New paint job," he said. "Hey."

"What?"

"You're cute."

She pretended to fidget, chasing flies away from the door.

"Don'tcha believe me, or what?" he said.

"Look, I don't even know who you are," Connie said in disgust.

"Hey, Ellie's got a radio, see. Mine broke down." He lifted his friend's arm and showed her the little transistor radio the boy was holding, and now Connie began to hear the music. It was the same program that was playing inside the house.

"Bobby King?" she said.

"I listen to him all the time. I think he's great."

"He's kind of great," Connie said reluctantly.

"Listen, that guy's *great*. He knows where the action is."

Connie blushed a little, because the glasses made it impossible for her to see just what this boy was looking at. She couldn't decide if she liked him or if he was just a jerk, and so she dawdled in the doorway and wouldn't come down or go back inside. She said, "What's all that stuff painted on your car?"

"Can'tcha read it?" He opened the door very carefully, as if he were afraid it might fall off. He slid out just as carefully, planting his feet firmly on the ground, the tiny metallic world in his glasses slowing down like gelatine hardening, and in the midst of it Connie's bright green blouse. "This here is my name, to begin with," he said. ARNOLD FRIEND was written in tarlike black letters on the side, with a drawing of a round, grinning face that reminded Connie of a pumpkin, except it wore sunglasses. "I wanta introduce myself, I'm Arnold Friend and that's my real name and I'm gonna be your friend, honey, and inside the car's Ellie Oscar, he's kinda shy." Ellie brought his transistor radio up to his shoulder and balanced it there. "Now, these numbers are a secret code, honey," Arnold Friend explained. He read off the numbers 33, 19, 17 and raised his eyebrows at her to see what she thought of that, but she didn't think much of it. The left rear fender had been smashed and around it was written, on the gleaming gold background: DONE BY CRAZY WOMAN DRIVER. Connie had to laugh at that. Arnold Friend was pleased at her laughter and looked up at her. "Around the other side's a lot more—you wanta come and see them?"

"No."

"Why not?"

"Why should I?"

"Don'tcha wanta see what's on the car? Don'tcha wanta go for a ride?"

"I don't know."

"Why not?"

"I got things to do."

"Like what?"

"Things."

He laughed as if she had said something funny. He slapped his thighs. He was standing in a strange way, leaning back against the car as if he were balancing himself. He wasn't tall, only an inch or so taller than she would be if she came down to him. Connie liked the way he was dressed, which was the way all of them dressed: tight faded jeans stuffed into black, scuffed boots, a belt that pulled his waist in and showed how lean he was, and a white pull-over shirt that was a little soiled and showed the hard small muscles of his arms and shoulders. He looked as if he probably did hard work, lifting and carrying things. Even his neck looked muscular. And his face was a familiar face, somehow: the jaw and chin and cheeks slightly darkened because he hadn't shaved for a day or two, and the nose long and hawklike, sniffing as if she were a treat he was going to gobble up and it was all a joke.

"Connie, you ain't telling the truth. This is your day set aside for a ride with me and you know it," he said, still laughing. The way he straightened and recovered from his fit of laughing showed that it had been all fake.

"How do you know what my name is?" she said suspiciously.

"It's Connie."

"Maybe and maybe not."

"I know my Connie," he said, wagging his finger. Now she remembered him even better, back at the restaurant, and her cheeks warmed at the thought of how she had sucked in her breath just at the moment she passed him—how she must have looked to him. And he had remembered her. "Ellie and I come out here especially for you," he said. "Ellie can sit in back. How about it?"

"Where?"

"Where what?"

"Where're we going?"

He looked at her. He took off the sunglasses and she saw how pale the skin around his eyes was, like holes that were not in shadow but instead in light. His eyes were like chips of broken glass that catch the light in an amiable way. He smiled. It was as if the idea of going for a ride somewhere, to someplace, was a new idea to him.

"Just for a ride, Connie sweetheart."

"I never said my name was Connie," she said.

"But I know what it is. I know your name and all about you, lots of things," Arnold Friend said. He had not moved yet but stood still leaning back against the side of his jalopy. "I took a special interest in you, such a pretty girl, and found out all about you—like I know your parents and sister are gone somewheres and I know where and how long they're going to be gone, and I know who you were with last night, and your best girl friend's name is Betty. Right?"

He spoke in a simple lilting voice, exactly as if were reciting the words to a song. His smile assured her that everything was fine. In the car Ellie turned up the volume on his radio and did not bother to look around at them.

"Ellie can sit in the back seat," Arnold Friend said. He indicated his friend with a casual jerk of his chin, as if Ellie did not count and she should not bother with him.

"How'd you find out all that stuff?" Connie said.

"Listen: Betty Schultz and Tony Fitch and Jimmy Pettinger and Nancy Pettinger," he said in a chant. "Raymond Stanley and Bob Hutter—"

"Do you know all those kids?"

"I know everybody."

"Look, you're kidding. You're not from around here."

"Sure."

"But—how come we never saw you before?"

"Sure you saw me before," he said. He looked down at his boots, as if he were a little offended. "You just don't remember."

"I guess I'd remember you," Connie said.

"Yeah?" He looked up at this, beaming. He was pleased. He began to mark time with the music from Ellie's radio, tapping his fists lightly together. Connie looked away from his smile to the car, which was painted so bright it almost hurt her eyes to look at it. She looked at that name, ARNOLD FRIEND. And up at the front fender was an expression that was familiar—MAN THE FLYING SAUCERS. It was an expression kids had used the year before but didn't use this year. She looked at it for a while as if the words meant something to her that she did not yet know.

"What're you thinking about? Huh?" Arnold Friend demanded. "Not worried about your hair blowing around in the car, are you?"

"No."

"Think I maybe can't drive good?"

"How do I know?"

"You're a hard girl to handle. How come?" he said. "Don't you know I'm your friend? Didn't you see me put my sign in the air when you walked by?"

"What sign?"

"My sign." And he drew an X in the air, leaning out toward her. They were maybe ten feet apart. After his hand fell back to his side the X was still in the air, almost visible. Connie let the screen door close and stood perfectly still inside it, listening to the music from her radio and the boy's blend together. She stared at Arnold Friend. He stood there so stiffly relaxed, pretending to be relaxed, with one hand idly on the door handle as if he were keeping himself up that way and had no intention of ever moving again. She recognized most things about him, the tight jeans that showed his thighs and buttocks and the greasy leather boots and the tight shirt, and even that slippery friendly smile of his, that sleepy dreamy smile that all the boys used to get across ideas they didn't want to put into words. She recognized all this and also the singsong way he talked, slightly mocking, kidding, but serious and a little melancholy, and she recognized the way he tapped one fist against the other in homage to the perpetual music behind him. But all these things did not come together.

She said suddenly, "Hey, how old are you?"

His smile faded. She could see then that he wasn't a kid, he was much older—thirty, maybe more. At this knowledge her heart began to pound faster.

"That's a crazy thing to ask. Can'tcha see I'm your own age?"

"Like hell you are."

"Or maybe a coupla years older. I'm eighteen."

"Eighteen?" she said doubtfully.

He grinned to reassure her and lines appeared at the corners of his mouth. His teeth were big and white. He grinned so broadly his eyes became slits and she saw how thick the lashes were, thick and black as if painted with a black tarlike material. Then, abruptly, he seemed to become embarrassed and looked over his shoulder at Ellie. "*Him,* he's crazy," he said. "Ain't he a riot? He's a nut, a real character." Ellie was still listening to the music. His sunglasses told nothing about what he was thinking. He wore a bright orange shirt unbuttoned halfway to show his chest, which was a pale, bluish chest and not muscular like Arnold Friend's. His shirt collar was turned up all around and the very tips of the collar pointed out past his chin as if they were protecting him. He was pressing the transistor radio up against his ear and sat there in a kind of daze, right in the sun.

"He's kinda strange," Connie said.

"Hey, she says you're kinda strange! Kinda strange!" Arnold Friend cried. He pounded on the car to get Ellie's attention. Ellie turned for the first time and Connie saw with shock that he wasn't a kid either—he had a fair, hairless face, cheeks reddened slightly as if the veins grew too close to the surface of his skin, the face of a forty-year-old baby. Connie felt a wave of dizziness rise in her at this sight and she stared at him as if waiting for something to change the shock of the moment, make it all right again. Ellie's lips kept shaping words, mumbling along with the words blasting in his ear.

"Maybe you two better go away," Connie said faintly.

"What? How come?" Arnold Friend cried. "We come out here to take you for a ride. It's Sunday." He had the voice of the man on the radio now. It was the same voice, Connie thought. "Don'tcha know it's Sunday all day? And honey, no matter who you were with last night, today you're with Arnold Friend and don't you forget it! Maybe you better step out here," he said, and this last was in a different voice. It was a little flatter, as if the heat was finally getting to him.

"No. I got things to do."

"Hey."

"You two better leave."

"We ain't leaving until you come with us."

"Like hell I am—"

"Connie, don't fool around with me. I mean—I mean, don't fool *around*," he said, shaking his head. He laughed incredulously. He placed his sunglasses on top of his head, carefully, as if he were indeed wearing a wig, and brought the stems down behind his ears. Connie stared at him, another wave of dizziness and fear rising in her so that for a moment he wasn't even in focus but was just a blur standing there against his gold car, and she had the idea that he had driven up the driveway all right but had come from nowhere before that and belonged nowhere and that everything about him and even about the music that was so familiar to her was only half real.

"If my father comes and sees you—"

"He ain't coming. He's at a barbecue."

"How do you know that?"

"Aunt Tillie's. Right now they're—uh—they're drinking. Sitting around," he said vaguely, squinting as if he were staring all the way to town and over to Aunt Tillie's back yard. Then the vision seemed to get clear and he nodded energetically. "Yeah. Sitting around. There's your sister in a blue dress, huh? And high heels, the poor sad bitch—nothing like you, sweetheart! And your mother's helping some fat woman with the corn, they're cleaning the corn—husking the corn—"

"What fat woman?" Connie cried.

"How do I know what fat woman, I don't know every goddamn fat woman in the world!" Arnold Friend laughed.

"Oh, that's Mrs. Hornsby. . . . Who invited her?" Connie said. She felt a little lightheaded. Her breath was coming quickly.

"She's too fat. I don't like them fat. I like them the way you are, honey," he said, smiling sleepily at her. They stared at each other for a while through the screen door. He said softly, "Now what you're going to do is this: you're going to come out that door. You're going to sit up front with me and Ellie's going to sit in the back, the hell with Ellie, right? This isn't Ellie's date. You're my date. I'm your lover, honey."

"What? You're crazy—"

"Yes, I'm your lover. You don't know what that is but you will," he said. "I know that too. I know all about you. But look: it's real nice and you couldn't ask for nobody better than me, or more polite. I always keep my word. I'll tell you how it is, I'm always nice at first, the first time. I'll hold you so tight you won't think you have to try to get away or pretend anything because you'll know you can't. And I'll come inside you where it's all secret and you'll give in to me and you'll love me—"

"Shut-up! You're crazy!" Connie said. She backed away from the door. She put her hands up against her ears as if she'd heard something terrible, something not meant for her. "People don't talk like that, you're crazy," she muttered. Her heart was almost too big now for her chest and its pumping made sweat break out all over her. She looked out to see Arnold Friend pause and then take a step toward the porch, lurching. He almost fell. But, like clever drunken man, he managed to catch his balance. He wobbled in his high boots and grabbed hold of one of the porch posts.

"Honey?" he said. "You still listening?"

"Get the hell out of here!"

"Be nice, honey. Listen."

"I'm going to call the police—"

He wobbled again and out of the side of his mouth came a fast spat curse, an aside not meant for her to hear. But even this "Christ!" sounded forced. Then he began to smile again. She watched this smile come, awkward as if he were smiling from inside a mask. His whole face was a mask, she thought wildly, tanned down to his throat but then running out as if he had plastered make-up on his face but had forgotten about his throat.

"Honey—? Listen, here's how it is. I always tell the truth and I promise you this: I ain't coming in that house after you."

"You better not! I'm going to call the police if you—if you don't—"

"Honey," he said, talking right through her voice, "honey, I'm not coming in there but you are coming out here. You know why?"

She was panting. The kitchen looked like a place she had never seen before, some room she had run inside but that wasn't good enough, wasn't going to help her. The kitchen window had never had a curtain, after three years, and there were dishes in the sink for her to do—probably—and if you ran your hand across the table you'd probably feel something sticky there.

"You listening, honey? Hey?"

"—going to call the police—"

"Soon as you touch the phone I don't need to keep my promise and can come inside. You won't want that."

She rushed forward and tried to lock the door. Her fingers were shaking. "But why lock it," Arnold Friend said gently, talking right into her face. "It's just a screen door. It's just nothing." One of his boots was at a strange angle, as if his foot wasn't in it. It pointed out to the left, bent at the ankle. "I mean, anybody can break through a screen door and glass and wood and iron or anything else if he needs to, anybody at all, and specially Arnold Friend. If the place got lit up with a fire, honey, you'd come runnin' out into my arms, right into my arms an' safe at home—like you knew I was your lover and'd stopped fooling around. I don't mind a nice shy girl but I don't like no fooling around." Part of those words were spoken with a slight rhythmic lilt, and Connie somehow recognized them—the echo of a song from last year, about a girl rushing into her boy friend's arms and coming home again—

Connie stood barefoot on the linoleum floor, staring at him. "What do you want?" she whispered.

"I want you," he said.

"What?"

"Seen you that night and thought, that's the one, yes sir. I never needed to look anymore."

"But my father's coming back. He's coming to get me. I had to wash my hair first—" She spoke in a dry, rapid voice, hardly raising it for him to hear.

"No, your daddy is not coming and yes, you had to wash your hair and you washed it for me. It's nice and shining and all for me. I thank you sweetheart," he said with a mock bow, but again he almost lost his balance. He had to bend and adjust his boots. Evidently his feet did not go all the way down; the boots must have been stuffed with something so that he would seem taller. Connie stared out at him and behind him at Ellie in the car, who seemed to be looking off toward Connie's right, into nothing. This Ellie said, pulling the words out of the air one after another as if he were just discovering them, "You want me to pull out the phone?"

"Shut your mouth and keep it shut," Arnold Friend said, his face red from bending over or maybe from embarrassment because Connie had seen his boots. "This ain't none of your business."

"What—what are you doing? What do you want?" Connie said. "If I call the police they'll get you, they'll arrest you—"

"Promise was not to come in unless you touch that phone, and I'll keep that promise," he said. He resumed his erect position and tried to force his shoulders back. He sounded like a hero in a movie, declaring something important. But he spoke too loudly and it was as if he were speaking to someone behind Connie. "I ain't made plans for coming in that house where I don't belong but just for you to come out to me, the way you should. Don't you know who I am?"

"You're crazy," she whispered. She backed away from the door but did not want to go into another part of the house, as if this would give him permission to come through the door. "What do you . . . you're crazy, you. . . . "

"Huh? What're you saying, honey?"

Her eyes darted everywhere in the kitchen. She could not remember what it was, this room.

"This is how it is, honey: you come out and we'll drive away, have a nice ride. But if you don't come out we're gonna wait till your people come home and then they're all going to get it."

"You want that telephone pulled out?" Ellie said. He held the radio away from his ear and grimaced, as if without the radio the air was too much for him.

"I toldja shut up, Ellie," Arnold Friend said, "you're deaf, get a hearing aid, right? Fix yourself up. This little girl's no trouble and's gonna be nice to me, so Ellie keep to yourself, this ain't your date—right? Don't hem in on me, don't hog, don't crush, don't bird dog, don't trail me," he said in a rapid, meaningless voice, as if he were running through all the expressions he'd learned but was no longer sure which of them was in style, then rushing on to new ones, making them up with his eyes closed. "Don't crawl under my fence, don't squeeze in my chipmunk hole, don't sniff my glue, suck my popsicle, keep your own greasy fingers on yourself!" He shaded his eyes and peered in at Connie, who was backed against the kitchen table. "Don't mind him, honey, he's just a creep. He's a dope. Right? I'm the boy for you and like I said, you come out here nice like a lady and give me your hand, and nobody else gets hurt, I mean, your nice old bald-headed daddy and your mummy and your sister in her high heels. Because listen: why bring them in this?"

"Leave me alone," Connie whispered.

"Hey, you know that old woman down the road, the one with the chickens and stuff—you know her?"

"She's dead!"

"Dead? What? You know her?" Arnold Friend said.

"She's dead—"

"Don't you like her?"

"She's dead—she's—she isn't here any more—"

"But don't you like her, I mean, you got something against her? Some grudge or something?" Then his voice dipped as if he were conscious of a rudeness. He touched the sunglasses perched up on top of his head as if to make sure they were still there. "Now, you be a good girl."

"What are you going to do?"

"Just two things, or maybe three," Arnold Friend said. "But I promise it won't last long and you'll like me the way you get to like people you're close to. You will. It's all over for you here, so come on out. You don't want your people in any trouble, do you?"

She turned and bumped against a chair or something, hurting her leg, but she ran into the back room and picked up the telephone. Something roared in her ear, a tiny roaring, and she was so sick with fear that she could do nothing but listen to it—the telephone was clammy and very heavy and her fingers groped down to the dial but were too weak to touch it. She began to scream into the phone, into the roaring. She cried out, she cried for her mother, she felt her breath start jerking back and forth in her lungs as if it were something Arnold Friend was stabbing her with again and again with no tenderness. A noisy sorrowful wailing rose all about her and she was locked inside it the way she was locked inside this house.

After a while she could hear again. She was sitting on the floor with her wet back against the wall.

Arnold Friend was saying from the door, "That's a good girl. Put the phone back."

She kicked the phone away from her.

"No, honey. Pick it up. Put it back right."

She picked it up and put it back. The dial tone stopped.

"That's a good girl. Now, you come outside."

She was hollow with what had been fear but what was now just an emptiness. All that screaming had blasted it out of her. She sat, one leg cramped under her, and deep inside her brain was something like a pinpoint of light that kept going and would not let her relax. She thought, I'm not going to see my mother again. She thought, I'm not going to sleep in my bed again. Her bright green blouse was all wet.

Arnold Friend said, in a gentle-loud voice that was like a stage voice, "The place where you came from ain't there any more, and where you had in mind to go is cancelled out. This place you are now—inside your daddy's house—is nothing but a cardboard box I can knock down any time. You know that and always did know it. You hear me?"

She thought, I have got to think. I have got to know what to do.

"We'll go out to a nice field, out in the country here where it smells so nice and it's sunny," Arnold Friend said. "I'll have my arms tight around you so you won't need to try to get away and I'll show you what love is like, what it does. The hell with this house! It looks solid all right," he said. He ran a fingernail down the screen and the noise did not make Connie shiver, as it would have the day before. "Now, put your hand on your heart, honey. Feel that? That feels solid too but we know better. Be nice to me, be sweet like you can because what else is there for a girl like you but to be sweet and pretty and give in?—and get away before her people come back?"

She felt her pounding heart. Her hand seemed to enclose it. She thought for the first time in her life that it was nothing that was hers, that belonged to her, but just a pounding, living thing inside this body that wasn't really hers either.

"You don't want them to get hurt," Arnold Friend went on. "Now, get up, honey. Get up all by yourself."

She stood.

"Now, turn this way. That's right. Come over here to me.—Ellie, put that away, didn't I tell you? You dope. You miserable creepy dope," Arnold Friend said. His words were not angry but only part of an incantation. The incantation was kindly. "Now, come out through the kitchen to me, honey, and let's see a smile, try it, you're a brave, sweet little girl and now they're eating corn and hot dogs cooked to bursting over an outdoor fire, and they don't know one thing about you and never did and honey, you're better than them because not a one of them would have done this for you."

Connie felt the linoleum under her feet; it was cool. She brushed her hair back out of her eyes. Arnold Friend let go of the post tentatively and opened his arms for her, his elbows pointing in toward each other and his wrists limp, to show that this was an embarrassed embrace and a little mocking, he didn't want to make her self-conscious.

1966

Raymond Carver
(1938–1988)

"I like it when there is some feeling of threat or a sense of menace in short stories," declares Raymond Carver in the essay "On Writing" in *Fires* (1983). "What creates tension in a piece of fiction is partly . . . the things that are left out, that are implied, the landscape just under the smooth (but sometimes broken and unsettled) surface of things." This sense of menace, or "dis-ease," gnaws at both character and reader. Sometimes what happens is that nothing happens: a chance is missed, a word is left unsaid, and the characters remain in their very ordinary lives. In Carver's later fiction, including the story "Cathedral" (1981), more often something extremely unusual happens to a character who, though still stuck in an ordinary life, has somehow been changed.

Born in 1938 in Clatskanie, Oregon, Carver was raised in Yakima, Washington, and married at age eighteen. His two children greatly influenced his life as a writer—in fact, the responsibility and distraction of fatherhood are the reasons he wrote short stories and poems and nothing lengthier. While he snatched moments to write and to complete his B.A. at Chico State College in Chico, California, he and his wife worked odd jobs. At Chico State he studied with writer/professor John Gardner, who taught Carver about the accuracy of every word.

In the early 1960s Carver wrote a few plays and continued his writing apprenticeship at the Iowa Writers Workshop until funds ran out. During the late 1960s he wrote little, although the story "Will You Please Be Quiet, Please?" was included in the anthology *Best American Short Stories, 1967*. That same year he accepted his first white-collar job, editing textbooks; the following year his first poetry collection, *Near Klamuth*, was published. Carver was fired from his job in 1970 but received a fellowship and for the first time had months to devote to writing. He began to publish his work in national magazines and was then offered lectureships at several universities. Writing steadily, Carver was also drinking heavily, was hospitalized several times, and went bankrupt twice before he stopped drinking in 1977. Substantial fellowships awarded after the publication of *What We Talk About When We Talk About Love* (1981), the short-story collection that made him famous, allowed him once again to write fulltime. Carver married the writer Tess Gallagher a few months before his death in 1988. After he was diagnosed and treated for lung cancer, Carver and Gallagher went to Alaska for an extended fishing trip. Soon after their return Carver died at age fifty.

"Cathedral" has been called a transitional story for Carver because it, and the stories that followed, are more "generous" than the stories in *What We Talk About* that made his reputation. Because of those stories Carver's work is generally called minimalist or precisionist. His spare, nonlyrical, restrained style consists of short declarative sentences and brief dialogue spoken by the married, middle-class American. His characters tend not to reflect on the meanings of their lives and try, more or less, just to get by. "It's important to be reminded that we are human," Carver said in a June 1984 *New York Times Magazine* interview. He gives us that—uncomfortable glimpses into the lives of people we might recognize.

Suggested Readings: *Winter Insomnia*, 1970. *At Night the Salmon Move*, 1976. *Will You Please Be Quiet, Please?*, 1976. *Furious Seasons and Other Stories*, 1977. *What We Talk About When We Talk About Love*, 1981. *Fires: Essays, Poems, Stories*, 1983. *Where I'm Calling From*, 1988. M. Gorra, "Laughter and Bloodshed," in *Hudson Review*, 37 (Spring): 151–164, 1984. J. C. Robison, "1969–1980: Experiment and Tradition," in *The American Short Story 1945–1980*, ed. G. Weaver, 1983. M. Simpson, "The Art of Fiction LXXVI," in *Paris Review*, 25 (88, Summer): 192–221, 1983. A. M. Saltzman, *Understanding Raymond Carver*, 1988.

Text Used: *Cathedral*, 1984.

CATHEDRAL

This blind man, an old friend of my wife's, he was on his way to spend the night. His wife had died. So he was visiting the dead wife's relatives in Connecticut. He called my wife from his in-laws'. Arrangements were made. He would come by train, a five-hour trip, and my wife would meet him at the station. She hadn't seen him since she worked for him one summer in Seattle ten years ago. But she and the blind man had kept in touch. They made tapes and mailed them back and forth. I wasn't enthusiastic about his visit. He was no one I knew. And his being blind bothered me. My idea of blindness came from the movies. In the movies, the blind moved slowly and never laughed. Sometimes they were led by seeing-eye dogs. A blind man in my house was not something I looked forward to.

That summer in Seattle she had needed a job. She didn't have any money. The man she was going to marry at the end of the summer was in officers' training school. He didn't have any money, either. But she was in love with the guy, and he was in love with her, etc. She'd seen something in the paper: HELP WANTED—

Reading to Blind Man, and a telephone number. She phoned and went over, was hired on the spot. She'd worked with this blind man all summer. She read stuff to him, case studies, reports, that sort of thing. She helped him organize his little office in the county social-service department. They'd become good friends, my wife and the blind man. How do I know these things? She told me. And she told me something else. On her last day in the office, the blind man asked if he could touch her face. She agreed to this. She told me he touched his fingers to every part of her face, her nose—even her neck! She never forgot it. She even tried to write a poem about it. She was always trying to write a poem. She wrote a poem or two every year, usually after something really important had happened to her.

[handwritten margin note: How would that feel? What made it important?]

When we first started going out together, she showed me the poem. In the poem, she recalled his fingers and the way they had moved around over her face. In the poem, she talked about what she had felt at the time, about what went through her mind when the blind man touched her nose and lips. I can remember I didn't think much of the poem. Of course, I didn't tell her that. Maybe I just don't understand poetry. I admit it's not the first thing I reach for when I pick up something to read.

Anyway, this man who'd first enjoyed her favors, the officer-to-be, he'd been her childhood sweetheart. So okay. I'm saying that at the end of the summer she let the blind man run his hands over her face, said goodbye to him, married her childhood etc., who was now a commissioned officer, and she moved away from Seattle. But they'd kept in touch, she and the blind man. She made the first contact after a year or so. She called him up one night from an Air Force base in Alabama. She wanted to talk. They talked. He asked her to send him a tape and tell him about her life. She did this. She sent the tape. On the tape, she told the blind man about her husband and about their life together in the military. She told the blind man she loved her husband but she didn't like it where they lived and she didn't like it that he was a part of the military-industrial thing. She told the blind man she'd written a poem and he was in it. She told him that she was writing a poem about what it was like to be an Air Force officer's wife. The poem wasn't finished yet. She was still writing it. The blind man made a tape. He sent her the tape. She made a tape. This went on for years. My wife's officer was posted to one base and then another. She sent tapes from Moody AFB,[1] McGuire, McConnell, and finally, Travis, near Sacramento, where one night she got to feeling lonely and cut off from people she kept losing in that moving-around life. She got to feeling she couldn't go it another step. She went in and swallowed all the pills and capsules in the medicine chest and washed them down with a bottle of gin. Then she got into a hot bath and passed out.

But instead of dying, she got sick. She threw up. Her officer—why should he have a name? he was the childhood sweetheart, and what more does he want?—came home from somewhere, found her, and called the ambulance. In time, she put it all on a tape and sent the tape to the blind man. Over the years, she put all kinds of stuff on tapes and sent the tapes off lickety-split. Next to writing a poem every year, I think it was her chief means of recreation. On one tape, she told the blind man she'd decided to live away from her officer for a time. On another tape, she told him about her divorce. She and I began going out, and of course she told her blind man about it. She told him everything, or so it seemed to me. Once she

---

[1] Air Force Base.

asked me if I'd like to hear the latest tape from the blind man. This was a year
ago. I was on the tape, she said. So I said okay, I'd listen to it. I got us drinks and
we settled down in the living room. We made ready to listen. First she inserted
the tape into the player and adjusted a couple of dials. Then she pushed a lever.
The tape squeaked and someone began to talk in this loud voice. She lowered the
volume. After a few minutes of harmless chitchat, I heard my own name in the
mouth of this stranger, this blind man I didn't even know! And then this: "From
all you've said about him, I can only conclude—" But we were interrupted, a
knock at the door, something, and we didn't ever get back to the tape. Maybe it
was just as well. I'd heard all I wanted to.

Now this same blind man was coming to sleep in my house.

"Maybe I could take him bowling," I said to my wife. She was at the draining
board doing scalloped potatoes. She put down the knife she was using and turned
around.

"If you love me," she said, "you can do this for me. If you don't love me,
okay. But if you had a friend, any friend, and the friend came to visit, I'd make
him feel comfortable." She wiped her hands with the dish towel.

"I don't have any blind friends," I said.

"You don't have *any* friends," she said. "Period. Besides," she said, "goddamn
it, his wife's just died! Don't you understand that? The man's lost his wife!"

I didn't answer. She'd told me a little about the blind man's wife. Her name
was Beulah. Beulah! That's a name for a colored woman.

"Was his wife a Negro?" I asked.

"Are you crazy?" my wife said. "Have you just flipped or something?" She
picked up a potato. I saw it hit the floor, then roll under the stove. "What's wrong
with you?" she said. "Are you drunk?"

"I'm just asking," I said.

Right then my wife filled me in with more detail than I cared to know. I made a
drink and sat at the kitchen table to listen. Pieces of the story began to fall into
place.

Beulah had gone to work for the blind man the summer after my wife had
stopped working for him. Pretty soon Beulah and the blind man had themselves a
church wedding. It was a little wedding—who'd want to go to such a wedding in
the first place?—just the two of them, plus the minister and the minister's wife.
But it was a church wedding just the same. It was what Beulah had wanted, he'd
said. But even then Beulah must have been carrying the cancer in her glands.
After they had been inseparable for eight years—my wife's word, *inseparable*—
Beulah's health went into a rapid decline. She died in a Seattle hospital room, the
blind man sitting beside the bed and holding on to her hand. They'd married, lived
and worked together, slept together—had sex, sure—and then the blind man had
to bury her. All this without his having ever seen what the goddamned woman
looked like. It was beyond my understanding. Hearing this, I felt sorry for the
blind man for a little bit. And then I found myself thinking what a pitiful life this
woman must have led. Imagine a woman who could never see herself as she was
seen in the eyes of her loved one. A woman who could go on day after day and
never receive the smallest compliment from her beloved. A woman whose husband could never read the expression on her face, be it misery or something better. Someone who could wear makeup or not—what difference to him? She could,
if she wanted, wear green eye-shadow around one eye, a straight pin in her nos-
tril, yellow slacks and purple shoes, no matter. And then to slip off into death, the

blind man's hand on her hand, his blind eyes streaming tears—I'm imagining now—her last thought maybe this: that he never even knew what she looked like, and she on an express to the grave. Robert was left with a small insurance policy and half of a twenty-peso Mexican coin. The other half of the coin went into the box with her. Pathetic. *[handwritten: What's so great about his life?]*

So when the time rolled around, my wife went to the depot to pick him up. With nothing to do but wait—sure, I blamed him for that—I was having a drink and watching TV when I heard the car pull into the drive. I got up from the sofa with my drink and went to the window to have a look.

I saw my wife laughing as she parked the car. I saw her get out of the car and shut the door. She was still wearing a smile. Just amazing. She went around to the other side of the car to where the blind man was already starting to get out. This blind man, feature this, he was wearing a full beard! A beard on a blind man! Too much, I say. The blind man reached into the back seat and dragged out a suitcase. My wife took his arm, shut the car door, and, talking all the way, moved him down the drive and then up the steps to the front porch. I turned off the TV. I finished my drink, rinsed the glass, dried my hands. Then I went to the door.

My wife said, "I want you to meet Robert. Robert, this is my husband. I've told you all about him." She was beaming. She had this blind man by his coat sleeve.

The blind man let go of his suitcase and up came his hand.

I took it. He squeezed hard, held my hand, and then he let it go.

"I feel like we've already met," he boomed.

"Likewise," I said. I didn't know what else to say. Then I said, "Welcome. I've heard a lot about you." We began to move then, a little group, from the porch into the living room, my wife guiding him by the arm. The blind man was carrying his suitcase in his other hand. My wife said things like, "To your left here, Robert. That's right. Now watch it, there's a chair. That's it. Sit down right here. This is the sofa. We just bought this sofa two weeks ago."

I started to say something about the old sofa. I'd liked that old sofa. But I didn't say anything. Then I wanted to say something else, small-talk, about the scenic ride along the Hudson. How going *to* New York, you should sit on the right-hand side of the train, and coming *from* New York, the left-hand side. *[handwritten: Still dope.]*

"Did you have a good train ride?" I said. "Which side of the train did you sit on, by the way?"

"What a question, which side!" my wife said. "What's it matter which side?" she said.

"I just asked," I said.

"Right side," the blind man said. "I hadn't been on a train in nearly forty years. Not since I was a kid. With my folks. That's been a long time. I'd nearly forgotten the sensation. I have winter in my beard now," he said. "So I've been told, anyway. Do I look distinguished, my dear?" the blind man said to my wife.

"You look distinguished, Robert," she said. "Robert," she said. "Robert, it's just so good to see you." *[handwritten: moral message]*

My wife finally took her eyes off the blind man and looked at me. I had the feeling she didn't like what she saw. I shrugged.

I've never met, or personally known, anyone who was blind. This blind man was late forties, a heavy-set, balding man with stooped shoulders, as if he carried a great weight there. He wore brown slacks, brown shoes, a light-brown shirt, a tie, a sports coat. Spiffy. He also had this full beard. But he didn't use a cane and

stereotype

he didn't wear dark glasses. I'd always thought dark glasses were a must for the blind. Fact was, I wished he had a pair. At first glance, his eyes looked like anyone else's eyes. But if you looked close, there was something different about them. Too much white in the iris, for one thing, and the pupils seemed to move around in the sockets without his knowing it or being able to stop it. Creepy. As I stared at his face, I saw the left pupil turn in toward his nose while the other made an effort to keep in one place. But it was only an effort, for that eye was on the roam without his knowing it or wanting it to be.

I said, "Let me get you a drink. What's your pleasure? We have a little of everything. It's one of our pastimes."

"Bub, I'm a Scotch man myself," he said fast enough in this big voice.

"Right," I said. Bub! "Sure you are. I knew it."

He let his fingers touch his suitcase, which was sitting alongside the sofa. He was taking his bearings. I didn't blame him for that.

"I'll move that up to your room," my wife said.

"No, that's fine," the blind man said loudly. "It can go up when I go up."

"A little water with the Scotch?" I said.

"Very little," he said.

"I knew it," I said.

He said, "Just a tad. The Irish actor, Barry Fitzgerald?[2] I'm like that fellow. When I drink water, Fitzgerald said, I drink water. When I drink whiskey, I drink whiskey." My wife laughed. The blind man brought his hand up under his beard. He lifted his beard slowly and let it drop.

I did the drinks, three big glasses of Scotch with a splash of water in each. Then we made ourselves comfortable and talked about Robert's travels. First the long flight from the West Coast to Connecticut, we covered that. Then from Connecticut up here by train. We had another drink concerning that leg of the trip.

I remembered having read somewhere that the blind didn't smoke because, as speculation had it, they couldn't see the smoke they exhaled. I thought I knew that much and that much only about blind people. But this blind man smoked his cigarette down to the nubbin and then lit another one. This blind man filled his ashtray and my wife emptied it.

When we sat down at the table for dinner, we had another drink. My wife heaped Robert's plate with cube steak, scalloped potatoes, green beans. I buttered him up two slices of bread. I said, "Here's bread and butter for you." I swallowed some of my drink. "Now let us pray," I said, and the blind man lowered his head. My wife looked at me, her mouth agape. "Pray the phone won't ring and the food doesn't get cold," I said.

We dug in. We ate everything there was to eat on the table. We ate like there was no tomorrow. We didn't talk. We ate. We scarfed. We grazed that table. We were into serious eating. The blind man had right away located his foods, he knew just where everything was on his plate. I watched with admiration as he used his knife and fork on the meat. He'd cut two pieces of meat, fork the meat into his mouth, and then go all out for the scalloped potatoes, the beans next, and then he'd tear off a hunk of buttered bread and eat that. He'd follow this up with a big drink of milk. It didn't seem to bother him to use his fingers once in a while, either. *who doesn't?*

We finished everything, including half a strawberry pie. For a few moments,

---

[2] Fitzgerald, originally William Joseph Shields (1888–1961), was a stage and film actor who won an Academy Award for his role in *Going My Way* (1944).

we sat as if stunned. Sweat beaded on our faces. Finally, we got up from the table and left the dirty plates. We didn't look back. We took ourselves into the living room and sank into our places again. Robert and my wife sat on the sofa. I took the big chair. We had us two or three more drinks while they talked about the major things that had come to pass for them in the past ten years. For the most part, I just listened. Now and then I joined in. I didn't want him to think I'd left the room, and I didn't want her to think I was feeling left out. They talked of things that had happened to them—to them!—these past ten years. I waited in vain to hear my name on my wife's sweet lips: "And then my dear husband came into my life"—something like that. But I heard nothing of the sort. More talk of Robert. Robert had done a little of everything, it seemed, a regular blind jack-of-all-trades. But most recently he and his wife had had an Amway distributorship, from which, I gathered, they'd earned their living, such as it was. The blind man was also a ham radio operator. He talked in his loud voice about conversations he'd had with fellow operators in Guam, in the Philippines, in Alaska, and even in Tahiti. He said he'd have a lot of friends there if he ever wanted to go visit those places. From time to time, he'd turn his blind face toward me, put his hand under his beard, ask me something. How long had I been in my present position? (Three years.) Did I like my work? (I didn't.) Was I going to stay with it? (What were the options?) Finally, when I thought he was beginning to run down, I got up and turned on the TV.

My wife looked at me with irritation. She was heading toward a boil. Then she looked at the blind man and said, "Robert, do you have a TV?"

The blind man said, "My dear, I have two TVs. I have a color set and a black-and-white thing, an old relic. It's funny, but if I turn the TV on, and I'm always turning it on, I turn on the color set. It's funny, don't you think?"

I didn't know what to say to that. I had absolutely nothing to say to that. No opinion. So I watched the news program and tried to listen to what the announcer was saying.

"This is a color TV," the blind man said. "Don't ask me how, but I can tell."

"We traded up a while ago," I said.

The blind man had another taste of his drink. He lifted his beard, sniffed it, and let it fall. He leaned forward on the sofa. He positioned his ashtray on the coffee table, then put the lighter to his cigarette. He leaned back on the sofa and crossed his legs at the ankles.

My wife covered her mouth, and then she yawned. She stretched. She said, "I think I'll go upstairs and put on my robe. I think I'll change into something else. Robert, you make yourself comfortable," she said.

"I'm comfortable," the blind man said.

"I want you to feel comfortable in this house," she said.

"I am comfortable," the blind man said.

After she'd left the room, he and I listened to the weather report and then to the sports roundup. By that time, she'd been gone so long I didn't know if she was going to come back. I thought she might have gone to bed. I wished she'd come back downstairs. I didn't want to be left alone with a blind man. I asked him if he wanted another drink, and he said sure. Then I asked if he wanted to smoke some dope with me. I said I'd just rolled a number. I hadn't, but I planned to do so in about two shakes.

"I'll try some with you," he said.

"Damn right," I said. "That's the stuff."

I got our drinks and sat down on the sofa with him. Then I rolled us two fat numbers. I lit one and passed it. I brought it to his fingers. He took it and inhaled.

"Hold it as long as you can," I said. I could tell he didn't know the first thing.

My wife came back downstairs wearing her pink robe and her pink slippers.

"What do I smell?" she said.

"We thought we'd have us some cannabis," I said.

My wife gave me a savage look. Then she looked at the blind man and said, "Robert, I didn't know you smoked."

He said, "I do now, my dear. There's a first time for everything. But I don't feel anything yet."

"This stuff is pretty mellow," I said. "This stuff is mild. It's dope you can reason with," I said. "It doesn't mess you up."

"Not much it doesn't, bub," he said, and laughed.

My wife sat on the sofa between the blind man and me. I passed her the number. She took it and toked and then passed it back to me. "Which way is this going?" she said. Then she said, "I shouldn't be smoking this. I can hardly keep my eyes open as it is. That dinner did me in. I shouldn't have eaten so much."

"It was the strawberry pie," the blind man said. "That's what did it," he said, and he laughed his big laugh. Then he shook his head.

"There's more strawberry pie," I said.

"Do you want some more, Robert?" my wife said.

"Maybe in a little while," he said.

We gave our attention to the TV. My wife yawned again. She said, "Your bed is made up when you feel like going to bed, Robert. I know you must have had a long day. When you're ready to go to bed, say so." She pulled his arm. "Robert?"

He came to and said, "I've had a real nice time. This beats tapes, doesn't it?"

I said, "Coming at you," and I put the number between his fingers. He inhaled, held the smoke, and then let it go. It was like he'd been doing it since he was nine years old.

"Thanks, bub," he said. "But I think this is all for me. I think I'm beginning to feel it," he said. He held the burning roach out for my wife.

"Same here," she said. "Ditto. Me, too." She took the roach and passed it to me. "I may just sit here for a while between you two guys with my eyes closed. But don't let me bother you, okay? Either one of you. If it bothers you, say so. Otherwise, I may just sit here with my eyes closed until you're ready to go to bed," she said. "Your bed's made up, Robert, when you're ready. It's right next to our room at the top of the stairs. We'll show you up when you're ready. You wake me up now, you guys, if I fall asleep." She said that and then she closed her eyes and went to sleep.

The news program ended. I got up and changed the channel. I sat back down on the sofa. I wished my wife hadn't pooped out. Her head lay across the back of the sofa, her mouth open. She'd turned so that her robe had slipped away from her legs, exposing a juicy thigh. I reached to draw her robe back over her, and it was then that I glanced at the blind man. What the hell! I flipped the robe open again.

"You say when you want some strawberry pie," I said.

"I will," he said.

I said, "Are you tired? Do you want me to take you up to your bed? Are you ready to hit the hay?"

"Not yet," he said. "No, I'll stay up with you, bub. If that's all right. I'll stay up until you're ready to turn in. We haven't had a chance to talk. Know what I mean? I feel like me and her monopolized the evening." He lifted his beard and he let it fall. He picked up his cigarettes and his lighter.

"That's all right," I said. Then I said, "I'm glad for the company."

And I guess I was. Every night I smoked dope and stayed up as long as I could before I fell asleep. My wife and I hardly ever went to bed at the same time. When I did go to sleep, I had these dreams. Sometimes I'd wake up from one of them, my heart going crazy.

Something about the church and the Middle Ages was on the TV. Not your run-of-the-mill TV fare. I wanted to watch something else. I turned to the other channels. But there was nothing on them, either. So I turned back to the first channel and apologized.

"Bub, it's all right," the blind man said. "It's fine with me. Whatever you want to watch is okay. I'm always learning something. Learning never ends. It won't hurt me to learn something tonight. I got ears," he said.

We didn't say anything for a time. He was leaning forward with his head turned at me, his right ear aimed in the direction of the set. Very disconcerting. Now and then his eyelids drooped and then they snapped open again. Now and then he put his fingers into his beard and tugged, like he was thinking about something he was hearing on the television.

On the screen, a group of men wearing cowls was being set upon and tormented by men dressed in skeleton costumes and men dressed as devils. The men dressed as devils wore devil masks, horns, and long tails. This pageant was part of a procession. The Englishman who was narrating the thing said it took place in Spain once a year. I tried to explain to the blind man what was happening. *helping*

"Skeletons," he said. "I know about skeletons," he said, and he nodded.

The TV showed this one cathedral. Then there was a long, slow look at another one. Finally, the picture switched to the famous one in Paris, with its flying buttresses and its spires reaching up to the clouds. The camera pulled away to show the whole of the cathedral rising above the skyline.

There were times when the Englishman who was telling the thing would shut up, would simply let the camera move around over the cathedrals. Or else the camera would tour the countryside, men in fields walking behind oxen. I waited as long as I could. Then I felt I had to say something. I said, "They're showing the outside of this cathedral now. Gargoyles. Little statues carved to look like monsters. Now I guess they're in Italy. Yeah, they're in Italy. There's paintings on the walls of this one church."

"Are those fresco paintings, bub?" he asked, and he sipped from his drink.

I reached for my glass. But it was empty. I tried to remember what I could remember. "You're asking me are those frescoes?" I said. "That's a good question. I don't know."

The camera moved to a cathedral outside Lisbon. The differences in the Portuguese cathedral compared with the French and Italian were not that great. But they were there. Mostly the interior stuff. Then something occurred to me, and I said, "Something has occurred to me. Do you have any idea what a cathedral is? What they look like, that is? Do you follow me? If somebody says cathedral to you, do you have any notion what they're talking about? Do you know the difference between that and a Baptist church, say?" *Begins to be real.*

He let the smoke dribble from his mouth. "I know they took hundreds of workers fifty or a hundred years to build," he said. "I just heard the man say that, of course. I know generations of the same families worked on a cathedral. I heard him say that, too. The men who began their life's work on them, they never lived to see the completion of their work. In that wise, bub, they're no different from the rest of us, right?" He laughed. Then his eyelids drooped again. His head nodded. He seemed to be snoozing. Maybe he was imagining himself in Portugal. The TV was showing another cathedral now. This one was in Germany. The Englishman's voice droned on. "Cathedrals," the blind man said. He sat up and rolled his head back and forth. "If you want the truth, bub, that's about all I know. What I just said. What I heard him say. But maybe you could describe one to me? I wish you'd do it. I'd like that. If you want to know, I really don't have a good idea."

I stared hard at the shot of the cathedral on the TV. How could I even begin to describe it? But say my life depended on it. Say my life was being threatened by an insane guy who said I had to do it or else.

I stared some more at the cathedral before the picture flipped off into the countryside. There was no use. I turned to the blind man and said, "To begin with, they're very tall." I was looking around the room for clues. "They reach way up. Up and up. Toward the sky. They're so big, some of them, they have to have these supports. To help hold them up, so to speak. These supports are called buttresses. They remind me of viaducts, for some reason. But maybe you don't know viaducts, either? Sometimes the cathedrals have devils and such carved into the front. Sometimes lords and ladies. Don't ask me why this is," I said.

He was nodding. The whole upper part of his body seemed to be moving back and forth.

"I'm not doing so good, am I?" I said.

He stopped nodding and leaned forward on the edge of the sofa. As he listened to me, he was running his fingers through his beard. I wasn't getting through to him, I could see that. But he waited for me to go on just the same. He nodded, like he was trying to encourage me. I tried to think what else to say. "They're really big," I said. "They're massive. They're built of stone. Marble, too, sometimes. In those olden days, when they built cathedrals, men wanted to be close to God. In those olden days, God was an important part of everyone's life. You could tell this from their cathedral-building. I'm sorry," I said, "but it looks like that's the best I can do for you. I'm just no good at it."

"That's all right, bub," the blind man said. "Hey, listen. I hope you don't mind my asking you. Can I ask you something? Let me ask you a simple question, yes or no. I'm just curious and there's no offense. You're my host. But let me ask if you are in any way religious? You don't mind my asking?"

I shook my head. He couldn't see that, though. A wink is the same as a nod to a blind man. "I guess I don't believe in it. In anything. Sometimes it's hard. You know what I'm saying?"

"Sure, I do," he said.

"Right," I said.

The Englishman was still holding forth. My wife sighed in her sleep. She drew a long breath and went on with her sleeping.

"You'll have to forgive me," I said. "But I can't tell you what a cathedral looks like. It just isn't in me to do it. I can't do any more than I've done."

The blind man sat very still, his head down, as he listened to me.

I said, "The truth is, cathedrals don't mean anything special to me. Nothing. Cathedrals. They're something to look at on late-night TV. That's all they are."

It was then that the blind man cleared his throat. He brought something up. He took a handkerchief from his back pocket. Then he said, "I get it, bub. It's okay. It happens. Don't worry about it," he said. "Hey, listen to me. Will you do me a favor? I got an idea. Why don't you find us some heavy paper? And a pen. We'll do something. We'll draw one together. Get us a pen and some heavy paper. Go on, bub, get the stuff," he said.

So I went upstairs. My legs felt like they didn't have any strength in them. They felt like they did after I'd done some running. In my wife's room, I looked around. I found some ballpoints in a little basket on her table. And then I tried to think where to look for the kind of paper he was talking about.

Downstairs, in the kitchen, I found a shopping bag with onion skins in the bottom of the bag. I emptied the bag and shook it. I brought it into the living room and sat down with it near his legs. I moved some things, smoothed the wrinkles from the bag, spread it out on the coffee table.

The blind man got down from the sofa and sat next to me on the carpet.

He ran his fingers over the paper. He went up and down the sides of the paper. The edges, even the edges. He fingered the corners.

"All right," he said. "All right, let's do her."

He found my hand, the hand with the pen. He closed his hand over my hand. "Go ahead, bub, draw," he said. "Draw. You'll see. I'll follow along with you. It'll be okay. Just begin now like I'm telling you. You'll see. Draw," the blind man said.

So I began. First I drew a box that looked like a house. It could have been the house I lived in. Then I put a roof on it. At either end of the roof, I drew spires. Crazy. *Who's doing the learning?*

"Swell," he said. "Terrific. You're doing fine," he said. "Never thought anything like this could happen in your lifetime, did you, bub? Well, it's a strange life, we all know that. Go on now. Keep it up."

I put in windows with arches. I drew flying buttresses. I hung great doors. I couldn't stop. The TV station went off the air. I put down the pen and closed and opened my fingers. The blind man felt around over the paper. He moved the tips of his fingers over the paper, all over what I had drawn, and he nodded.

"Doing fine," the blind man said.

I took up the pen again, and he found my hand. I kept at it. I'm no artist. But I kept drawing just the same.

My wife opened up her eyes and gazed at us. She sat up on the sofa, her robe hanging open. She said, "What are you doing? Tell me, I want to know."

I didn't answer her.

The blind man said, "We're drawing a cathedral. Me and him are working on it. Press hard," he said to me. "That's right. That's good," he said. "Sure. You got it, bub. I can tell. You didn't think you could. But you can, can't you? You're cooking with gas now. You know what I'm saying? We're going to really have us something here in a minute. How's the old arm?" he said. "Put some people in there now. What's a cathedral without people?" *(He knows.)*

My wife said, "What's going on? Robert, what are you doing? What's going on?"

"It's all right," he said to her. "Close your eyes now," the blind man said to me.

I did it. I closed them just like he said.

"Are they closed?" he said. "Don't fudge."

"They're closed," I said.

"Keep them that way," he said. He said, "Don't stop now. Draw."

So we kept on with it. His fingers rode my fingers as my hand went over the paper. It was like nothing else in my life up to now.

Then he said, "I think that's it. I think you got it," he said. "Take a look. What do you think?"

But I had my eyes closed. I thought I'd keep them that way for a little longer. I thought it was something I ought to do.

"Well?" he said. "Are you looking?"

My eyes were still closed. I was in my house. I knew that. But I didn't feel like I was inside anything.

"It's really something," I said.

1981

Maxine Hong Kingston
(1940–   )

The eldest daughter of the Chinese immigrants Ying Lan Chew and Tom Hong, Maxine (Ting Ting) Hong was born in 1940 in Stockton, California. In 1962 she earned a B.A. from the University of California at Berkeley and married the actor Earll Kingston. She is the mother of a son and has taught English at both the high school and university levels in California and in Hawaii.

Perhaps the most widely recognized Asian-American writer today, Kingston has garnered attention and praise from the media as well as from scholars. Her first two books, *The Woman Warrior: Memoirs of a Girlhood Among Ghosts* (1976) and *China Men* (1980), are classified as nonfiction, yet Kingston's unique blend of history, autobiography, myth, and legend place them in a genre that transcends the traditional boundaries between fiction and nonfiction. In 1976 *The Woman Warrior* won the National Book Critics' Circle Award for nonfiction, and *Time* magazine later called it one of the ten best books of the decade. Two years later Kingston won the Anisfield Wolf Race Relation Award; in 1981 *China Men* won the American Book Award for general nonfiction, and Kingston was granted a Guggenheim Fellowship. In writing her first novel, *Tripmaster Monkey* (1989), Kingston again merged the world of Chinese myth with that of American reality to produce the story of a 1960s Berkeley playwright. Kingston has also contributed articles and stories to periodicals, including the *New Yorker,* the *Washington Post,* and *Ms.*

Like much of Kingston's work, *The Woman Warrior* explores aspects of the Asian-American experience. The book is set in a laundry in California; Kingston's parents both worked in such a laundry. Within this memoir she attempts to reconcile the complexities of her American and Chinese female identities by reshaping incidents in her own girlhood and the stories her mother told her as "lessons 'to grow up on.' " In writing "those of us in the first American generations have had to figure out how the invisible world the emigrants built around our childhoods fits in solid America," she points to the difficulties she and other first-generation Chinese Americans have in determining cultural identity. By embracing and reworking the stories her mother told her, Kingston is able to find and assert her own past and voice and ultimately her own identity in writing this memoir. By pointing to misogynistic acts such as the killing of female infants, the binding of girls' feet, and the selling of young females as slaves, she is also able to expose and protest the sexism in traditional Chinese culture and its carryover into Chinese-American culture. Countering these images of female powerlessness are powerful images of legendary Chinese warrior women. As a girl Kingston fantasized of becoming an avenger like the legendary Chinese female warrior Fa Mu Lan. As an adult writer Kingston recreates this warrior as the appealing image of a woman comfortable with herself in the role of woman and the role of warrior.

Suggested Readings: *China Men,* 1980. *Tripmaster Monkey,* 1989. P. L. Blinde, "Icicle in the Desert: Perspective and Form in the Works of Two Chinese American Women Writers," in *MELUS,* 6(3): 51–71, 1979. M. Gordon, "Mythic History," in *The New York Times Book Review,* (June 15): 24–25, 1980. T. Pfaff, "Talk With Mrs. Kingston," in *The New York Times Book Review,* (June 15): 1, 1980. A. Ling, "Thematic Threads in Maxine Hong Kingston's *The Woman Warrior,*" in *Tamkang Review,* 14: 155–164, 1983–1984.

Text Used: *The Woman Warrior: Memoirs of a Girlhood Among Ghosts,* 1976.

from   THE WOMAN WARRIOR

NO NAME WOMAN*

"You must not tell anyone," my mother said, "what I am about to tell you. In China your father had a sister who killed herself. She jumped into the family well. We say that your father has all brothers because it is as if she had never been born.

"In 1924 just a few days after our village celebrated seventeen hurry-up weddings—to make sure that every young man who went 'out on the road' would responsibly come home—your father and his brothers and your grandfather and his brothers and your aunt's new husband sailed for America, the Gold Mountain. It was your grandfather's last trip. Those lucky enough to get contracts waved good-bye from the decks. They fed and guarded the stowaways and helped them off in Cuba, New York, Bali, Hawaii. 'We'll meet in California next year,' they said. All of them sent money home.

"I remember looking at your aunt one day when she and I were dressing; I had not noticed before that she had a protruding melon of a stomach. But I did not think, 'She's pregnant,' until she began to look like other pregnant women, her shirt pulling and the white tops of her black pants showing. She could not have been pregnant, you see, because her husband had been gone for years. No one said anything. We did not discuss it. In early summer she was ready to have the child, long after the time when it could have been possible.

"The village had also been counting. On the night the baby was to be born the villagers raided our house. Some were crying. Like a great saw, teeth strung with lights, files of people walked zigzag across our land, tearing the rice. Their lan-

---

* First published in *Viva* in January 1975; revised slightly and collected in *The Woman Warrior* (1976).

terns doubled in the disturbed black water, which drained away through the broken bunds. As the villagers closed in, we could see that some of them, probably men and women we knew well, wore white masks. The people with long hair hung it over their faces. Women with short hair made it stand up on end. Some had tied white bands around their foreheads, arms, and legs.

"At first they threw mud and rocks at the house. Then they threw eggs and began slaughtering our stock. We could hear the animals scream their deaths—the roosters, the pigs, a last great roar from the ox. Familiar wild heads flared in our night windows; the villagers encircled us. Some of the faces stopped to peer at us, their eyes rushing like searchlights. The hands flattened against the panes, framed heads, and left red prints.

"The villagers broke in the front and the back doors at the same time, even though we had not locked the doors against them. Their knives dripped with the blood of our animals. They smeared blood on the doors and walls. One woman swung a chicken, whose throat she had slit, splattering blood in red arcs about her. We stood together in the middle of our house, in the family hall with the pictures and tables of the ancestors around us, and looked straight ahead.

"At that time the house had only two wings. When the men came back, we would build two more to enclose our courtyard and a third one to begin a second courtyard. The villagers pushed through both wings, even your grandparents' rooms, to find your aunt's, which was also mine until the men returned. From this room a new wing for one of the younger families would grow. They ripped up her clothes and shoes and broke her combs, grinding them underfoot. They tore her work from the loom. They scattered the cooking fire and rolled the new weaving in it. We could hear them in the kitchen breaking our bowls and banging the pots. They overturned the great waist-high earthenware jugs; duck eggs, pickled fruits, vegetables burst out and mixed in acrid torrents. The old woman from the next field swept a broom through the air and loosed the spirits-of-the-broom over our heads. 'Pig.' 'Ghost.' 'Pig,' they sobbed and scolded while they ruined our house.

"When they left, they took sugar and oranges to bless themselves. They cut pieces from the dead animals. Some of them took bowls that were not broken and clothes that were not torn. Afterward we swept up the rice and sewed it back up into sacks. But the smells from the spilled preserves lasted. Your aunt gave birth in the pigsty that night. The next morning when I went for the water, I found her and the baby plugging up the family well.

"Don't let your father know that I told you. He denies her. Now that you have started to menstruate, what happened to her could happen to you. Don't humiliate us. You wouldn't like to be forgotten as if you had never been born. The villagers are watchful."

Whenever she had to warn us about life, my mother told stories that ran like this one, a story to grow up on. She tested our strength to establish realities. Those in the emigrant generations who could not reassert brute survival died young and far from home. Those of us in the first American generations have had to figure out how the invisible world the emigrants built around our childhoods fits in solid America.

The emigrants confused the gods by diverting their curses, misleading them with crooked streets and false names. They must try to confuse their offspring as well, who I suppose, threaten them in similar ways—always trying to get things straight, always trying to name the unspeakable. The Chinese I know hide their names; sojourners take new names when their lives change and guard their real names with silence.

Chinese-Americans, when you try to understand what things in you are Chinese, how do you separate what is peculiar to childhood, to poverty, insanities, one family, your mother who marked your growing with stories, from what is Chinese? What is Chinese tradition and what is the movies?

If I want to learn what clothes my aunt wore, whether flashy or ordinary, I would have to begin, "Remember Father's drowned-in-the-well sister?" I cannot ask that. My mother has told me once and for all the useful parts. She will add nothing unless powered by Necessity, a riverbank that guides her life. She plants vegetable gardens rather than lawns; she carries the odd-shaped tomatoes home from the fields and eats food left for the gods.

Whenever we did frivolous things, we used up energy; we flew high kites. We children came up off the ground over the melting cones our parents brought home from work and the American movie on New Year's Day—*Oh, You Beautiful Doll* with Betty Grable one year, and *She Wore a Yellow Ribbon*[1] with John Wayne another year. After the one carnival ride each, we paid in guilt; our tired father counted his change on the dark walk home.

Adultery is extravagance. Could people who hatch their own chicks and eat the embryos and the heads for delicacies and boil the feet in vinegar for party food, leaving only the gravel, eating even the gizzard lining—could such people engender a prodigal aunt? To be a woman, to have a daughter in starvation time was a waste enough. My aunt could not have been the lone romantic who gave up everything for sex. Women in the old China did not choose. Some man had commanded her to lie with him and be his secret evil. I wonder whether he masked himself when he joined the raid on her family.

Perhaps she had encountered him in the fields or on the mountain where the daughters-in-law collected fuel. Or perhaps he first noticed her in the marketplace. He was not a stranger because the village housed no strangers. She had to have dealings with him other than sex. Perhaps he worked an adjoining field, or he sold her the cloth for the dress she sewed and wore. His demand must have surprised, then terrified her. She obeyed him; she always did as she was told.

When the family found a young man in the next village to be her husband, she had stood tractably beside the best rooster, his proxy, and promised before they met that she would be his forever. She was lucky that he was her age and she would be the first wife, an advantage secure now. The night she first saw him, he had sex with her. Then he left for America. She had almost forgotten what he looked like. When she tried to envision him, she only saw the black and white face in the group photograph the men had had taken before leaving.

The other man was not, after all, much different from her husband. They both gave orders: she followed. "If you tell your family, I'll beat you. I'll kill you. Be here again next week." No one talked sex, ever. And she might have separated the rapes from the rest of living if only she did not have to buy her oil from him or gather wood in the same forest. I want her fear to have lasted just as long as rape lasted so that the fear could have been contained. No drawn-out fear. But women at sex hazarded birth and hence lifetimes. The fear did not stop but permeated everywhere. She told the man, "I think I'm pregnant." He organized the raid against her.

---

[1] Both movies appeared in 1949; *Oh, You Beautiful Doll* starred June Haver, not Betty Grable.

On nights when my mother and father talked about their life back home, sometimes they mentioned an "outcast table" whose business they still seemed to be
settling, their voices tight. In a commensal[2] tradition, where food is precious, the
powerful older people made wrongdoers eat alone. Instead of letting them start
separate new lives like the Japanese, who could become samurais and geishas,[3]
the Chinese family, faces averted but eyes glowering sideways, hung on to the
offenders and fed them leftovers. My aunt must have lived in the same house as
my parents and eaten at an outcast table. My mother spoke about the raid as if she
had seen it, when she and my aunt, a daughter-in-law to a different household,
should not have been living together at all. Daughters-in-law lived with their husbands' parents, not their own; a synonym for marriage in Chinese is "taking a
daughter-in-law." Her husband's parents could have sold her, mortgaged her,
stoned her. But they had sent her back to her own mother and father, a mysterious
act hinting at disgraces not told me. Perhaps they had thrown her out to deflect the
avengers.

She was the only daughter; her four brothers went with her father, husband,
and uncles "out on the road" and for some years became western men. When the
goods were divided among the family, three of the brothers took land, and the
youngest, my father, chose an education. After my grandparents gave their daughter away to her husband's family, they had dispensed all the adventure and all the
property. They expected her alone to keep the traditional ways, which her brothers, now among the barbarians, could fumble without detection. The heavy, deep-
rooted women were to maintain the past against the flood, safe for returning. But
the rare urge west had fixed upon our family, and so my aunt crossed boundaries
not delineated in space.

The work of preservation demands that the feelings playing about in one's guts
not be turned into action. Just watch their passing like cherry blossoms. But perhaps my aunt, my forerunner, caught in a slow life, let dreams grow and fade and
after some months or years went toward what persisted. Fear at the enormities of
the forbidden kept her desires delicate, wire and bone. She looked at a man because she liked the way the hair was tucked behind his ears, or she liked the
question-mark line of a long torso curving at the shoulder and straight at the hip.
For warm eyes or a soft voice or a slow walk—that's all—a few hairs, a line, a
brightness, a sound, a pace, she gave up family. She offered us up for a charm
that vanished with tiredness, a pigtail that didn't toss when the wind died. Why,
the wrong lighting could erase the dearest thing about him.

It could very well have been, however, that my aunt did not take subtle enjoyment of her friend, but, a wild woman, kept rollicking company. Imagining her
free with sex doesn't fit, though. I don't know any women like that, or men either. Unless I see her life branching into mine, she gives me no ancestral help.

To sustain her being in love, she often worked at herself in the mirror, guessing
at the colors and shapes that would interest him, changing them frequently in
order to hit on the right combination. She wanted him to look back.

On a farm near the sea, a woman who tended her appearance reaped a reputation for eccentricity. All the married women blunt-cut their hair in flaps about
their ears or pulled it back in tight buns. No nonsense. Neither style blew easily

---

[2] Companionable; here, in which all family members eat together.
[3] Men who are Japanese army officers and girls trained in singing, dancing, and conversation to act as
companions to men.

into heart-catching tangles. And at their weddings they displayed themselves in their long hair for the last time. "It brushed the backs of my knees," my mother tells me. "It was braided, and even so, it brushed the backs of my knees."

At the mirror my aunt combed individuality into her bob. A bun could have been contrived to escape into black streamers blowing in the wind or in quiet wisps about her face, but only the older women in our picture album wear buns. She brushed her hair back from her forehead, tucking the flaps behind her ears. She looped a piece of thread, knotted into a circle between her index fingers and thumbs, and ran the double strand across her forehead. When she closed her fingers as if she were making a pair of shadow geese bite, the string twisted together catching the little hairs. Then she pulled the thread away from her skin, ripping the hairs out neatly, her eyes watering from the needles of pain. Opening her fingers, she cleaned the thread, then rolled it along her hairline and the tops of her eyebrows. My mother did the same to me and my sisters and herself. I used to believe that the expression "caught by the short hairs" meant a captive held with a depilatory string. It especially hurt at the temples, but my mother said we were lucky we didn't have to have our feet bound when we were seven. Sisters used to sit on their beds and cry together, she said, as their mothers or their slave removed the bandages for a few minutes each night and let the blood gush back into their veins. I hope that the man my aunt loved appreciated a smooth brow, that he wasn't just a tits-and-ass man.

Once my aunt found a freckle on her chin, at a spot that the almanac said predestined her for unhappiness. She dug it out with a hot needle and washed the wound with peroxide.

More attention to her looks than these pullings of hairs and pickings at spots would have caused gossip among the villagers. They owned work clothes and good clothes, and they wore good clothes for feasting the new seasons. But since a woman combing her hair hexes beginnings, my aunt rarely found an occasion to look her best. Women looked like great sea snails—the corded wood, babies, and laundry they carried were the whorls on their backs. The Chinese did not admire a bent back; goddesses and warriors stood straight. Still there must have been a marvelous freeing of beauty when a worker laid down her burden and stretched and arched.

Such commonplace loveliness, however, was not enough for my aunt. She dreamed of a lover for the fifteen days of New Year's, the time for families to exchange visits, money, and food. She plied her secret comb. And sure enough she cursed the year, the family, the village, and herself.

Even as her hair lured her imminent lover, many other men looked at her. Uncles, cousins, nephews, brothers would have looked, too, had they been home between journeys. Perhaps they had already been restraining their curiosity, and they left, fearful that their glances, like a field of nesting birds, might be startled and caught. Poverty hurt, and that was their first reason for leaving. But another, final reason for leaving the crowded house was the never-said.

She may have been unusually beloved, the precious only daughter, spoiled and mirror gazing because of the affection the family lavished on her. When her husband left, they welcomed the chance to take her back from the in-laws; she could live like the little daughter for just a while longer. There are stories that my grandfather was different from other people, "crazy ever since the little Jap bayoneted him in the head." He used to put his naked penis on the dinner table, laughing. And one day he brought home a baby girl, wrapped up inside his brown western-style greatcoat. He had traded one of his sons, probably my father, the youngest, for her. My grandmother made him trade back. When he finally got a daughter of his own, he doted on her. They must have all loved her, except perhaps my father, the only brother who never went back to China, having once been traded for a girl.

Brothers and sisters, newly men and women, had to efface their sexual color and present plain miens. Disturbing hair and eyes, a smile like no other, threatened the ideal of five generations living under one roof. To focus blurs, people shouted face to face and yelled from room to room. The immigrants I know have loud voices, unmodulated to American tones even after years away from the village where they called their friendships out across the fields. I have not been able to stop my mother's screams in public libraries or over telephones. Walking erect (knees straight, toes pointed forward, not pigeon-toed, which is Chinese-feminine) and speaking in an inaudible voice, I have tried to turn myself American-feminine. Chinese communication was loud, public. Only sick people had to whisper. But at the dinner table, where the family members came nearest one another, no one could talk, not the outcasts nor any eaters. Every word that falls from the mouth is a coin lost. Silently they gave and accepted food with both hands. A preoccupied child who took his bowl with one hand got a sideways glare. A complete moment of total attention is due everyone alike. Children and lovers have no singularity here, but my aunt used a secret voice, a separate attentiveness.

She kept the man's name to herself throughout her labor and dying; she did not accuse him that he be punished with her. To save her inseminator's name she gave silent birth.

He may have been somebody in her own household, but intercourse with a man outside the family would have been no less abhorrent. All the village were kinsmen, and the titles shouted in loud country voices never let kinship be forgotten. Any man within visiting distance would have been neutralized as a lover—"brother," "younger brother," "older brother"—one hundred and fifteen relationship titles. Parents researched birth charts probably not so much to assure good fortune as to circumvent incest in a population that has but one hundred surnames. Everybody has eight million relatives. How useless then sexual mannerisms, how dangerous.

As if it came from an atavism[4] deeper than fear, I used to add "brother" silently to boys' names. It hexed the boys, who would or would not ask me to dance, and made them less scary and as familiar and deserving of benevolence as girls.

But, of course, I hexed myself also—no dates. I should have stood up, both arms waving, and shouted out across libraries, "Hey, you! Love me back." I had no idea, though, how to make attraction selective, how to control its direction and magnitude. If I made myself American-pretty so that the five or six Chinese boys in the class fell in love with me, everyone else—the Caucasian, Negro, and Japanese boys—would too. Sisterliness, dignified and honorable, made much more sense.

Attraction eludes control so stubbornly that whole societies designed to organize relationships among people cannot keep order, not even when they bind people to one another from childhood and raise them together. Among the very poor

---

[4] The appearance in an individual of a characteristic found in a remote ancestor but not in close ancestors.

and the wealthy, brothers married their adopted sisters, like doves. Our family allowed some romance, paying adult brides' prices and providing dowries so that their sons and daughters could marry strangers. Marriage promises to turn strangers into friendly relatives—a nation of siblings.

In the village structure, spirits shimmered among the live creatures, balanced and held in equilibrium by time and land. But one human being flaring up into violence could open up a black hole, a maelstrom that pulled in the sky. The frightened villagers, who depended on one another to maintain the real, went to my aunt to show her a personal, physical representation of the break she had made in the "roundness." Misallying couples snapped off the future, which was to be embodied in true offspring. The villagers punished her for acting as if she could have a private life, secret and apart from them.

If my aunt had betrayed the family at a time of large grain yields and peace, when many boys were born, and wings were being built on many houses, perhaps she might have escaped such severe punishment. But the men—hungry, greedy, tired of planting in dry soil—and had been forced to leave the village in order to send food-money home. There were ghost plagues, bandit plagues, wars with the Japanese, floods. My Chinese brother and sister had died of an unknown sickness. Adultery, perhaps only a mistake during good times, became a crime when the village needed food.

The round moon cakes and round doorways, the round tables of graduated size that fit one roundness inside another, round windows and rice bowls—these talismans had lost their power to warn this family of the law: a family must be whole, faithfully keeping the descent line by having sons to feed the old and the dead, who in turn look after the family. The villagers came to show my aunt and her lover-in-hiding a broken house. The villagers were speeding up the circling of events because she was too shortsighted to see that her infidelity had already harmed the village, that waves of consequences would return unpredictably, sometimes in disguise, as now, to hurt her. This roundness had to be made coin-sized so that she would see its circumference: punish her at the birth of her baby. Awaken her to the inexorable. People who refused fatalism because they could invent small resources insisted on culpability. Deny accidents and wrest fault from the stars.

After the villagers left, their lanterns now scattering in various directions toward home, the family broke their silence and cursed her. "Aiaa, we're going to die. Death is coming. Death is coming. Look what you've done. You've killed us. Ghost! Dead ghost! Ghost! You've never been born." She ran out into the fields, far enough from the house so that she could no longer hear their voices, and pressed herself against the earth, her own land no more. When she felt the birth coming, she thought that she had been hurt. Her body seized together. "They've hurt me too much," she thought. "This is gall, and it will kill me." With forehead and knees against the earth, her body convulsed and then relaxed. She turned on her back, lay on the ground. The black well of sky and stars went out and out and out forever; her body and her complexity seemed to disappear. She was one of the stars, a bright dot in blackness, without home, without a companion, in eternal cold and silence. An agoraphobia rose in her, speeding higher and higher, bigger and bigger; she would not be able to contain it; there would be no end to fear.

Flayed, unprotected against space, she felt pain return, focusing her body. This pain chilled her—a cold, steady kind of surface pain. Inside, spasmodically, the other pain, the pain of the child, heated her. For hours she lay on the ground, alternately body and space. Sometimes a vision of normal comfort obliterated reality: she saw the family in the evening gambling at the dinner table, the young people massaging their elders' backs. She saw them congratulating one another, high joy on the mornings the rice shoots came up. When these pictures burst, the stars drew yet further apart. Black space opened.

She got to her feet to fight better and remembered that old-fashioned women gave birth in their pigsties to fool the jealous, pain-dealing gods, who do not snatch piglets. Before the next spasms could stop her, she ran to the pigsty, each step a rushing out into emptiness. She climbed over the fence and knelt in the dirt. It was good to have a fence enclosing her, a tribal person alone.

Laboring, this woman who had carried her child as a foreign growth that sickened her every day, expelled it at last. She reached down to touch the hot, wet, moving mass, surely smaller than anything human, and could feel that it was human after all—fingers, toes, nails, nose. She pulled it up on to her belly, and it lay curled there, butt in the air, feet precisely tucked one under the other. She opened her loose shirt and buttoned the child inside. After resting, it squirmed and thrashed and she pushed it up to her breast. It turned its head this way and that until it found her nipple. There, it made little snuffling noises. She clenched her teeth at its preciousness, lovely as a young calf, a piglet, a little dog.

She may have gone to the pigsty as a last act of responsibility: she would protect this child as she had protected its father. It would look after her soul, leaving supplies on her grave. But how would this tiny child without family find her grave when there would be no marker for her anywhere, neither in the earth nor the family hall? No one would give her a family hall name. She had taken the child with her into the wastes. At its birth the two of them had felt the same raw pain of separation, a wound that only the family pressing tight could close. A child with no descent line would not soften her life but only trail after her, ghostlike, begging her to give it purpose. At dawn the villagers on their way to the fields would stand around the fence and look.

Full of milk, the little ghost slept. When it awoke, she hardened her breasts against the milk that crying loosens. Toward morning she picked up the baby and walked to the well.

Carrying the baby to the well shows loving. Otherwise abandon it. Turn its face into the mud. Mothers who love their children take them along. It was probably a girl; there is some hope of forgiveness for boys.

"Don't tell anyone you had an aunt. Your father does not want to hear her name. She has never been born." I have believed that sex was unspeakable and words so strong and fathers so frail that "aunt" would do my father mysterious harm. I have thought that my family, having settled among immigrants who had also been their neighbors in the ancestral land, needed to clean their name, and a wrong word would incite the kinspeople even here. But there is more to this silence: they want me to participate in her punishment. And I have.

In the twenty years since I heard this story I have not asked for details nor said my aunt's name; I do not know it. People who can comfort the dead can also chase after them to hurt them further—a reverse ancestor worship. The real punishment was not the raid swiftly inflicted by the villagers, but the family's deliberately forgetting her. Her betrayal so maddened them, they saw to it that she would suffer forever, even after death. Always hungry, always needing, she would have to beg food from other ghosts, snatch and steal it from those whose living descendants give them gifts. She would have to fight the ghosts massed at crossroads for the buns a few thoughtful citizens leave to decoy her away from village and home so that the ancestral spirits could feast unharassed. At peace, they could act like gods, not ghosts, their descent lines providing them with paper suits and dresses, spirit money, paper houses, paper automobiles, chicken, meat, and rice into eternity—essences delivered up in smoke and flames, steam and incense rising from each rice bowl. In an attempt to make the Chinese care for people outside the family, Chairman Mao[5] encourages us now to give our paper replicas to the spirits of outstanding soldiers and workers, no matter whose ancestors they may be. My aunt remains forever hungry. Goods are not distributed evenly among the dead.

My aunt haunts me—her ghost drawn to me because now, after fifty years of neglect, I alone devote pages of paper to her, though not origamied[6] into houses and clothes. I do not think she always means me well. I am telling on her, and she was a spite suicide, drowning herself in the drinking water. The Chinese are always very frightened of the drowned one, whose weeping ghost, wet hair hanging and skin bloated, waits silently by the water to pull down a substitute.

1975

Alice Walker
(1944–   )

In a 1970 interview in *Library Journal,* Alice Walker described her writing about the relationship between forms of racism and the African-American family structure: "I was curious to know why people in families (specifically black families) are often cruel to each other and how much of this cruelty is caused by outside forces such as various social injustices, segregation, unemployment, etc." This fascination with violence and family gives Walker's work an added urgency in that forms of art—from quilting and sewing to the act of writing itself—become her characters' only means of finding spirituality and continuity in a deeply divided culture. As she writes in the essay "In Search of Our Mother's Gardens" (1983) of her mother's love of gardening, "her face, as she prepares the Art that is her gift, is a legacy of respect she leaves to me, for all that illuminates and cherishes life. She has handed down respect for the possibilities—and the will to grasp them."

Walker's own possibilities must have seemed particularly limited: born in 1944, she was the eighth and youngest child of Minnie Lou Grant and Willie Lee Walker, sharecroppers in Eatonton, Georgia. When Walker was eight, one of her brothers shot her with a BB gun, leaving her blind in one eye and feeling ugly and outcast, until the eye was healed in an operation when she was fourteen. Walker found her own ways to heal her spirit, writing poetry and keeping a private notebook as well as discovering an alternative world in the books her teachers lent her. She was awarded a "rehabilitation scholarship" from Georgia and attended Spelman College in Atlanta and Sarah Lawrence College in Bronxville, New

---

[5] Mao Tse-tung (1893–1976), the chairman of the Communist party and of the People's Republic of China (1949–1959).

[6] Folded, after origami, the Japanese art of paper folding.

York, in the 1960s during the height of the civil rights movement—a frightening but vital time that Walker celebrates in her early poems, her short stories, and her second novel, *Meridian* (1976). While at Sarah Lawrence, Walker became pregnant and grew increasingly suicidal, finding herself, as she said in an interview, "at the mercy of everything, including my body." Her rescue came in the release she found in her writing and in the community of women, from writers such as Virginia Woolf and Zora Neale Hurston to friends such as Muriel Rukeyser, a poet who shared Walker's horror at the restrictions that limited the lives of all women. Shortly after her graduation from Sarah Lawrence in 1965, Walker began to publish stories and poems. Marrying the civil rights attorney Melvyn Leventhal in 1967, she was faced with a new challenge: the harrassment she and her husband endured as an interracial couple in their new home, Mississippi.

Delineating the effects of racial and sexual restrictions led Walker to write what she has termed "womanist" works. Such works focus on the shared dangers of racism and sexism in the hope of going beyond the boundaries imposed on literature termed "feminist" or "African American" and of expressing the plight of a larger, more international community. From her first novel, *The Third Life of Grange Copeland* (1970), to her collections of short stories and poems, to her most recent successes—*The Color Purple* (1982), which won a Pulitzer Prize and an American Book Award, and the counter-myth *The Temple of My Familiar* (1989)—Walker's work explores the racial and sexual violence that combine to destroy the sense of self and traces networks of matriarchal and familial love, even self-love, that restore a sense of identity. Walker has also sought to restore and reshape our sense of a literary heritage, writing the biography *Langston Hughes, American Poet* (1974) and editing an anthology of Zora Neale Hurston's works, *I Love Myself When I Am Laughing* (1979). Remaining an active supporter for civil rights and speaking for such causes as the Woman's Party for Survival against nuclear weapons, Walker told an audience in 1982 that "only justice can stop a curse," and her writing actively seeks those forms of justice that can defeat the destructive curses of our society.

Suggested Readings: *The Third Life of Grange Copeland,* 1970. *Revolutionary Petunias & Other Poems,* 1973. *Meridian,* 1976. *The Color Purple,* 1982. *You Can't Keep a Good Woman Down,* 1982. *In Search of Our Mother's Gardens: Womanist Prose,* 1983. *Horses Make a Landscape Look More Beautiful: Poems,* 1986. *To Hell With Dying,* 1988. *The Temple of My Familiar,* 1989. T. Harris, "Folklore in the Fiction of Alice Walker," in *Black American Literature Forum,* 11, 1977. C. J. Fantenot, "Alice Walker, 'The Diary of an African Nun' and Du Bois' Double Consciousness," in *Sturdy Black Bridges: Visions of Black Women in Literature,* eds. R. Bell, B. Parker, and B. G. Sheftall, 1979. M. H. Washington, "An Essay on Alice Walker," in *Sturdy Black Bridges: Visions of Black Women in Literature,* eds. R. Bell, B. Parker, and B. G. Sheftall, 1979. D. McDowell, "The Self in Bloom: Alice Walker's *Meridian*," in *College Language Association Journal,* 24, 1981. T. Harris, "Tiptoeing Through Taboo: Incest in 'The Child Who Favored Daughter,'" in *Modern Fiction Studies,* 28, (Autumn) 1982. B. Christian, "Alice Walker," in *Black Women Writers (1950–1980),* ed. M. Evans, 1984.

Text Used: *In Love & Trouble: Stories of Black Women,* 1973.

EVERYDAY USE

for your grandmama

I will wait for her in the yard that Maggie and I made so clean and wavy yesterday afternoon. A yard like this is more comfortable than most people know. It is not just a yard. It is like an extended living room. When the hard clay is swept clean as a floor and the fine sand around the edges lined with tiny, irregular grooves, anyone can come and sit and look up into the elm tree and wait for the breezes that never come inside the house.

Maggie will be nervous until after her sister goes: she will stand hopelessly in corners, homely and ashamed of the burn scars down her arms and legs, eying her sister with a mixture of envy and awe. She thinks her sister has held life always in the palm of one hand, that "no" is a word the world never learned to say to her.

You've no doubt seen those TV shows[1] where the child who has "made it" is confronted, as a surprise, by her own mother and father, tottering in weakly from backstage. (A pleasant surprise, of course: What would they do if parent and child came on the show only to curse out and insult each other?) On TV mother and child embrace and smile into each other's faces. Sometimes the mother and father weep, the child wraps them in her arms and leans across the table to tell how she would not have made it without their help. I have seen these programs.

Sometimes I dream a dream in which Dee and I are suddenly brought together on a TV program of this sort. Out of a dark and soft-seated limousine I am ushered into a bright room filled with many people. There I meet a smiling, gray, sporty man like Johnny Carson who shakes my hand and tells me what a fine girl I have. Then we are on the stage and Dee is embracing me with tears in her eyes. She pins on my dress a large orchid, even though she has told me once that she thinks orchids are tacky flowers.

In real life I am a large, big-boned woman with rough, man-working hands. In the winter I wear flannel nightgowns to bed and overalls during the day. I can kill and clean a hog as mercilessly as a man. My fat keeps me hot in zero weather. I can work outside all day, breaking ice to get water for washing; I can eat pork liver cooked over the open fire minutes after it comes steaming from the hog. One winter I knocked a bull calf straight in the brain between the eyes with a sledge hammer and had the meat hung up to chill before nightfall. But of course all this does not show on television. I am the way my daughter would want me to be: a hundred pounds lighter, my skin like an uncooked barley pancake. My hair glistens in the hot bright lights. Johnny Carson has much to do to keep up with my quick and witty tongue.

But that is a mistake. I know even before I wake up. Who ever knew a Johnson with a quick tongue? Who can even imagine me looking a strange white man in the eye? It seems to me I have talked to them always with one foot raised in flight, with my head turned in whichever way is farthest from them. Dee, though. She would always look anyone in the eye. Hesitation was no part of her nature.

"How do I look, Mama?" Maggie says, showing just enough of her thin body enveloped in pink skirt and red blouse for me to know she's there, almost hidden by the door.

"Come out into the yard," I say.

Have you ever seen a lame animal, perhaps a dog run over by some careless person rich enough to own a car, sidle up to someone who is ignorant enough to be kind to him? That is the way my Maggie walks. She has been like this, chin on chest, eyes on ground, feet in shuffle, ever since the fire that burned the other house to the ground.

Dee is lighter than Maggie, with nicer hair and a fuller figure. She's a woman

---

[1] *This Is Your Life*, hosted by Ralph Edwards, reunited friends, relatives, and people who influenced the guest star; it ran from 1952 to 1961 and 1970 to 1973.

now, though sometimes I forget. How long ago was it that the other house burned? Ten, twelve years? Sometimes I can still hear the flames and feel Maggie's arms sticking to me, her hair smoking and her dress falling off her in little black papery flakes. Her eyes seemed stretched open, blazed open by the flames reflected in them. And Dee. I see her standing off under the sweet gum tree she used to dig gum out of; a look of concentration on her face as she watched the last dingy gray board of the house fall in toward the red-hot brick chimney. Why don't you do a dance around the ashes? I'd wanted to ask her. She had hated the house that much.

I used to think she hated Maggie, too. But that was before we raised the money, the church and me, to send her to Augusta[2] to school. She used to read to us without pity; forcing words, lies, other folks' habits, whole lives upon us two, sitting trapped and ignorant underneath her voice. She washed us in a river of make-believe, burned us with a lot of knowledge we didn't necessarily need to know. Pressed us to her with the serious way she read, to shove us away at just the moment, like dimwits, we seemed about to understand.

Dee wanted nice things. A yellow organdy dress to wear to her graduation from high school; black pumps to match a green suit she'd made from an old suit somebody gave me. She was determined to stare down any disaster in her efforts. Her eyelids would not flicker for minutes at a time. Often I fought off the temptation to shake her. At sixteen she had a style of her own: and knew what style was.

I never had an education myself. After second grade the school was closed down. Don't ask me why: in 1927 colored asked fewer questions than they do now. Sometimes Maggie reads to me. She stumbles along good-naturedly but can't see well. She knows she is not bright. Like good looks and money, quickness passed her by. She will marry John Thomas (who has mossy teeth in an earnest face) and then I'll be free to sit here and I guess just sing church songs to myself. Although I never was a good singer. Never could carry a tune. I was always better at a man's job. I used to love to milk till I was hooked[3] in the side in '49. Cows are soothing and slow and don't bother you, unless you try to milk them the wrong way.

I have deliberately turned my back on the house. It is three rooms, just like the one that burned, except the roof is tin; they don't make shingle roofs any more. There are no real windows, just some holes cut in the sides, like the portholes in a ship, but not round and not square, with rawhide holding the shutters up on the outside. This house is in a pasture, too, like the other one. No doubt when Dee sees it she will want to tear it down. She wrote me once that no matter where we "choose" to live, she will manage to come see us. But she will never bring her friends. Maggie and I thought about this and Maggie asked me, "Mama, when did Dee ever *have* any friends?"

She had a few. Furtive boys in pink shirts hanging about on washday after school. Nervous girls who never laughed. Impressed with her they worshiped the well-turned phrase, the cute shape, the scalding humor that erupted like bubbles in lye. She read to them.

When she was courting Jimmy T she didn't have much time to pay to us, but turned all her faultfinding power on him. He *flew* to marry a cheap city girl from a family of ignorant flashy people. She hardly had time to recompose herself.

When she comes I will meet—but there they are!

---

[2] Augusta, Georgia, where Paine College is located.   [3] Kicked.

Maggie attempts to make a dash for the house, in her shuffling way, but I stay her with my hand. "Come back here," I say. And she stops and tries to dig a well in the sand with her toe.

It is hard to see them clearly through the strong sun. But even the first glimpse of leg out of the car tells me it is Dee. Her feet were always neat-looking, as if God himself had shaped them with a certain style. From the other side of the car comes a short, stocky man. Hair is all over his head a foot long and hanging from his chin like a kinky mule tail. I hear Maggie suck in her breath. "Uhnnnh," is what it sounds like. Like when you see the wriggling end of a snake just in front of your foot on the road. "Uhnnnh."

Dee next. A dress down to the ground, in this hot weather. A dress so loud it hurts my eyes. There are yellows and oranges enough to throw back the light of the sun. I feel my whole face warming from the heat waves it throws out. Earrings gold, too, and hanging down to her shoulders. Bracelets dangling and making noises when she moves her arm up to shake the folds of the dress out of her armpits. The dress is loose and flows, and as she walks closer, I like it. I hear Maggie go "Uhnnnh" again. It is her sister's hair. It stands straight up like the wool on a sheep. It is black as night and around the edges are two long pigtails that rope about like small lizards disappearing behind her ears.

"Wa-su-zo-Tean-o!"[4] she says, coming on in that gliding way the dress makes her move. The short stocky fellow with the hair to his navel is all grinning and he follows up with "Asalamalakim,[5] my mother and sister!" He moves to hug Maggie but she falls back, right up against the back of my chair. I feel her trembling there and when I look up I see the perspiration falling off her chin.

"Don't get up," says Dee. Since I am stout it takes something of a push. You can see me trying to move a second or two before I make it. She turns, showing white heels through her sandals, and goes back to the car. Out she peeks next with a Polaroid. She stoops down quickly and lines up picture after picture of me sitting there in front of the house with Maggie cowering behind me. She never takes a shot without making sure the house is included. When a cow comes nibbling around the edge of the yard she snaps it and me and Maggie *and* the house. Then she puts the Polaroid in the back seat of the car, and comes up and kisses me on the forehead.

Meanwhile Asalamalakim is going through motions with Maggie's hand. Maggie's hand is as limp as a fish, and probably as cold, despite the sweat, and she keeps trying to pull it back. It looks like Asalamalakim wants to shake hands but wants to do it fancy. Or maybe he don't know how people shake hands. Anyhow, he soon gives up on Maggie.

"Well," I say. "Dee."

"No, Mama," she says. "Not 'Dee,' Wangero Leewanika Kemanjo!"

"What happened to 'Dee'?" I wanted to know.

"She's dead," Wangero said. "I couldn't bear it any longer, being named after the people who oppress me."

"You know as well as me you was named after your aunt Dicie," I said. Dicie is my sister. She named Dee. We called her "Big Dee" after Dee was born.

"But who was *she* named after?" asked Wangero.

"I guess after Grandma Dee," I said.

"And who was she named after?" asked Wangero.

"Her mother," I said, and saw Wangero was getting tired. "That's about as far

---

[4] A Swahili greeting, used by Black Muslims.   [5] "Peace be with you" (Arabic).

back as I can trace it," I said. Though, in fact, I probably could have carried it back beyond the Civil War through the branches.

"Well," said Asalamalakim, "there you are."

"Uhnnnh," I heard Maggie say.

"There I was not," I said, "before 'Dicie' cropped up in our family, so why should I try to trace it that far back?"

He just stood there grinning, looking down on me like somebody inspecting a Model A car.[6] Every once in a while he and Wangero sent eye signals over my head.

"How do you pronounce this name?" I asked.

"You don't have to call me by it if you don't want to," said Wangero.

"Why shouldn't I?" I asked. "If that's what you want us to call you, we'll call you."

"I know it might sound awkward at first," said Wangero.

"I'll get used to it," I said. "Ream it out again."

Well, soon we got the name out of the way. Asalamalakim had a name twice as long and three times as hard. After I tripped over it two or three times he told me to just call him Hakim-a-barber. I wanted to ask him was he a barber, but I didn't really think he was, so I didn't ask.

"You must belong to those beef-cattle peoples down the road," I said. They said "Asalamalakim" when they met you, too, but they didn't shake hands. Always too busy: feeding the cattle, fixing the fences, putting up salt-lick shelters,[7] throwing down hay. When the white folks poisoned some of the herd the men stayed up all night with rifles in their hands. I walked a mile and a half just to see the sight.

Hakim-a-barber said, "I accept some of their doctrines, but farming and raising cattle is not my style." (They didn't tell me, and I didn't ask, whether Wangero (Dee) had really gone and married him.)

We sat down to eat and right away he said he didn't eat collards and pork was unclean. Wangero, though, went on through the chitlins and corn bread, the greens and everything else. She talked a blue streak over the sweet potatoes. Everything delighted her. Even the fact that we still used the benches her daddy made for the table when we couldn't afford to buy chairs.

"Oh, Mama!" she cried. Then turned to Hakim-a-barber. "I never knew how lovely these benches are. You can feel the rump prints," she said, running her hands underneath her and along the bench. Then she gave a sigh and her hand closed over Grandma Dee's butter dish. "That's it!" she said. "I knew there was something I wanted to ask you if I could have." She jumped up from the table and went over in the corner where the churn stood, the milk in it clabber[8] by now. She looked at the churn and looked at it.

"This churn top is what I need," she said. "Didn't Uncle Buddy whittle it out of a tree you all used to have?"

"Yes," I said.

"Uh huh," she said happily. "And I want the dasher, too."

"Uncle Buddy whittle that, too?" asked the barber.

Dee (Wangero) looked up at me.

---

[6] A low-priced, durable car introduced by the Ford Motor Company in 1927; it replaced the Model T.
[7] Shelters to keep salt blocks, given to cattle in hot weather, from dissolving in rain.
[8] Sour, curdled.

"Aunt Dee's first husband whittled the dash," said Maggie so low you almost couldn't hear her. "His name was Henry, but they called him Stash."

"Maggie's brain is like an elephant's," Wangero said, laughing. "I can use the churn top as a centerpiece for the alcove table," she said, sliding a plate over the churn, "and I'll think of something artistic to do with the dasher."[9]

When she finished wrapping the dasher the handle stuck out. I took it for a moment in my hands. You didn't even have to look close to see where hands pushing the dasher up and down to make butter had left a kind of sink in the wood. In fact, there were a lot of small sinks; you could see where thumbs and fingers had sunk into the wood. It was beautiful light yellow wood, from a tree that grew in the yard where Big Dee and Stash had lived.

After dinner Dee (Wangero) went to the trunk at the foot of my bed and started rifling through it. Maggie hung back in the kitchen over the dishpan. Out came Wangero with two quilts. They had been pieced by Grandma Dee and then Big Dee and me had hung them on the quilt frames on the front porch and quilted them. One was in the Lone Star pattern. The other was Walk Around the Mountain. In both of them were scraps of dresses Grandma Dee had worn fifty and more years ago. Bits and pieces of Grandpa Jarrell's Paisley shirts. And one teeny faded blue piece, about the size of a penny matchbox, that was from Great Grandpa Ezra's uniform that he wore in the Civil War.

"Mama," Wangero said sweet as a bird. "Can I have these old quilts?"

I heard something fall in the kitchen, and a minute later the kitchen door slammed.

"Why don't you take one or two of the others?" I asked. "These old things was just done by me and Big Dee from some tops your grandma pieced before she died."

"No," said Wangero. "I don't want those. They are stitched around the borders by machine."

"That'll make them last better," I said.

"That's not the point," said Wangero. "These are all pieces of dresses Grandma used to wear. She did all this stitching by hand. Imagine!" She held the quilts securely in her arms, stroking them.

"Some of the pieces, like those lavender ones, come from old clothes her mother handed down to her," I said, moving up to touch the quilts. Dee (Wangero) moved back just enough so that I couldn't reach the quilts. They already belonged to her.

"Imagine!" she breathed again, clutching them closely to her bosom.

"The truth is," I said, "I promised to give them quilts to Maggie, for when she marries John Thomas."

She gasped like a bee had stung her.

"Maggie can't appreciate these quilts!" she said. "She'd probably be backward enough to put them to everyday use."

"I reckon she would," I said. "God knows I been saving 'em for long enough with nobody using 'em. I hope she will!" I didn't want to bring up how I had offered Dee (Wangero) a quilt when she went away to college. Then she had told me they were old-fashioned, out of style.

"But they're *priceless!*" she was saying now, furiously; for she has a temper. "Maggie would put them on the bed and in five years they'd be in rags. Less than that!"

---

[9] The part of the churn that agitates.

"She can always make some more," I said. "Maggie knows how to quilt."

Dee (Wangero) looked at me with hatred. "You just will not understand. The point is these quilts, *these* quilts!"

"Well," I said, stumped. "What would *you* do with them?"

"Hang them," she said. As if that was the only thing you *could* do with quilts.

Maggie by now was standing in the door. I could almost hear the sound her feet made as they scraped over each other.

"She can have them, Mama," she said, like somebody used to never winning anything, or having anything reserved for her. "I can 'member Grandma Dee without the quilts."

I looked at her hard. She had filled her bottom lip with checkerberry[10] snuff and it gave her face a kind of dopey, hangdog look. It was Grandma Dee and Big Dee who taught her how to quilt herself. She stood there with her scarred hands hidden in the folds of her skirt. She looked at her sister with something like fear but she wasn't mad at her. This was Maggie's portion. This was the way she knew God to work.

When I looked at her like that something hit me in the top of my head and ran down to the soles of my feet. Just like when I'm in church and the spirit of God touches me and I get happy and shout. I did something I never had done before: hugged Maggie to me, then dragged her on into the room, snatched the quilts out of Miss Wangero's hands and dumped them into Maggie's lap. Maggie just sat there on my bed with her mouth open.

"Take one or two of the others," I said to Dee.

But she turned without a word and went out to Hakim-a-barber.

"You just don't understand," she said, as Maggie and I came out to the car.

"What don't I understand?" I wanted to know.

"Your heritage," she said. And then she turned to Maggie, kissed her, and said, "You ought to try to make something of yourself, too, Maggie. It's really a new day for us. But from the way you and Mama still live you'd never know it."

She put on some sunglasses that hid everything above the tip of her nose and her chin.

Maggie smiled; maybe at the sunglasses. But a real smile, not scared. After we watched the car dust settle I asked Maggie to bring me a dip of snuff. And then the two of us sat there just enjoying, until it was time to go in the house and go to bed.

1973

Leslie Marmon Silko
(1948–   )

Leslie Marmon was raised in the Native-American settlement of Laguna Pueblo, New Mexico, near Albuquerque, where she was born in 1948. She has sought to capture in her work the stories and traditions that bind a people into a community. Of mixed Native-American, Mexican, and Caucasian origin, she attended Bureau of Indian Affairs Schools

---

[10] From the wintergreen bush.

and married John Silko, an attorney. In 1969 she graduated *magna cum laude* from the University of New Mexico. Silko spent more than a year in law school before she decided to obtain a graduate degree in English and to pursue a career as a writer. She has taught at Navajo Community College in Arizona, and the universities of Washington and New Mexico. She is the recipient of a National Endowment for the Humanities Award and a MacArthur Foundation Fellowship. Now divorced from her husband, Silko is the mother of two sons.

Silko published a volume of poetry, *Laguna Woman,* in 1974 but first came to national attention when her short story "Lullaby" was included in *The Best Short Stories of 1975*. Typical of her fiction, "Lullaby" mixes prose and poetry, traditional Navajo myth, and the all-too-real modern conditions of Native Americans. The story explores the ways in which a community and its attendant legends can empower the dispossessed. In the narrative *Ceremony* (1977) her protagonist, Tayo, escapes madness and death through a healing ceremony taught to him by an old medicine man and a young Laguna woman. Tayo, a half-breed Laguna Indian, returns home from World War II shattered by his experience as a Japanese prisoner of war and alienated from his family and from the white world of his soldiering. Only by embracing the traditional widsom of his tribe and learning to live with "great patience and love" does Tayo come to feel himself at one with the elements of his world and with the members of his tribe.

Storyteller (1981) combines narrative with verse and includes twenty-six photographs from Silko's father's and grandfather's lifetime collections. As Silko explains in the book, the photographs are "part of many of the stories, and . . . many of the stories can be traced in the photographs." Mixing traditional legends with stories of modern Native Americans, *Storyteller* charts the movement of stories and storytelling across generations and among Native-American and Anglo cultures. The book juxtaposes the myths of Corn Woman and Buffalo Man with the history of Silko's Grandpa Hank. As always, the strength of Silko's communities is found in the power of her stories.

Suggested Readings: *Laguna Woman,* 1974. *Ceremony,* 1977. *The Delicacy and Strength of Lace,* ed. A. Wright, 1986. E. Bicksilver, "Traditionalism vs. Modernity: Leslie Silko on American Indian Women," in *Southwest Review,* 64:2, 1979. A. L. Ruoff, "Ritual and Renewal: Keres Traditions in the Short Fiction of Leslie Silko," in *MELUS,* 5, 1979. D. Fisher, "Stories and Their Tellers—A Conversation With Leslie Marmon Silko," in *The Third Woman: Minority Women Writers of the United States,* 1980. P. Seyersted, *Leslie Marmon Silko,* 1980. J. Ruppert, "Story Telling: The Fiction of Leslie Silko," in *The Journal of Ethnic Studies,* 9:1, 1981.

Text Used: *Storyteller,* 1981.

STORYTELLER

Every day the sun came up a little lower on the horizon, moving more slowly until one day she got excited and started calling the jailer. She realized she had been sitting there for many hours, yet the sun had not moved from the center of the sky. The color of the sky had not been good lately; it had been pale blue, almost white, even when there were no clouds. She told herself it wasn't a good sign for the sky to be indistinguishable from the river ice, frozen solid and white against the earth. The tundra rose up behind the river but all the boundaries between the river and hills and sky were lost in the density of the pale ice.

She yelled again, this time some English words which came randomly into her mouth, probably swear words she'd heard from the oil drilling crews last winter.

The jailer was an Eskimo, but he would not speak Yupik[1] to her. She had watched people in other cells, when they spoke to him in Yupik he ignored them until they spoke English.

He came and stared at her. She didn't know if he understood what she was telling him until he glanced behind her at the small high window. He looked at the sun, and turned and walked away. She could hear the buckles on his heavy snow-mobile boots jingle as he walked to the front ot the building.

It was like the other buildings that white people, the Gussucks, brought with them: BIA[2] and school buildings, portable buildings that arrived sliced in halves, on barges coming up the river. Squares of metal panelling bulged out with the layers of insulation stuffed inside. She had asked once what it was and someone told her it was to keep out the cold. She had not laughed then, but she did now. She walked over to the small double-pane window and she laughed out loud. They thought they could keep out the cold with stringy yellow wadding. Look at the sun. It wasn't moving; it was frozen, caught in the middle of the sky. Look at the sky, solid as the river with ice which had trapped the sun. It had not moved for a long time; in a few more hours it would be weak, and heavy frost would begin to appear on the edges and spread across the face of the sun like a mask. Its light was pale yellow, worn thin by the winter.

She could see people walking down the snow-packed roads, their breath steaming out from their parka hoods, faces hidden and protected by deep ruffs of fur. There were no cars or snowmobiles that day; the cold had silenced their machines. The metal froze; it split and shattered. Oil hardened and moving parts jammed solidly. She had seen it happen to their big yellow machines and the giant drill last winter when they came to drill their test holes. The cold stopped them, and they were helpless against it.

Her village was many miles upriver from this town, but in her mind she could see it clearly. Their house was not near the village houses. It stood alone on the bank upriver from the village. Snow had drifted to the eaves of the roof on the north side, but on the west side, by the door, the path was almost clear. She had nailed scraps of red tin over the logs last summer. She had done it for the bright red color, not for added warmth the way the village people had done. This final winter had been coming even then; there had been signs of its approach for many years.

She went because she was curious about the big school where the Government sent all the other girls and boys. She had not played much with the village children while she was growing up because they were afraid of the old man, and they ran when her grandmother came. She went because she was tired of being alone with the old woman whose body had been stiffening for as long as the girl could re-member. Her knees and knuckles were swollen grotesquely, and the pain had squeezed the brown skin of her face tight against the bones; it left her eyes hard like river stone. The girl asked once what it was that did this to her body, and the old woman had raised up from sewing a sealskin boot, and stared at her.

"The joints," the old woman said in a low voice, whispering like wind across the roof, "the joints are swollen with anger."

Sometimes she did not answer and only stared at the girl. Each year she spoke less and less, but the old man talked more—all night sometimes, not to anyone but

---

[1] An Eskimo-Aleut language used throughout arctic America from western Alaska to Greenland.
[2] The Bureau of Indian Affairs.

himself; in a soft deliberate voice, he told stories, moving his smooth brown hands above the blankets. He had not fished or hunted with the other men for many years, although he was not crippled or sick. He stayed in his bed, smelling like dry fish and urine, telling stories all winter; and when warm weather came, he went to his place on the river bank. He sat with a willow stick, poking at the smoldering moss he burned against the insects while he continued with the stories.

The trouble was that she had not recognized the warnings in time. She did not see what the Gussuck school would do to her until she walked into the dormitory and realized that the old man had not been lying about the place. She thought he had been trying to scare her as he used to when she was very small and her grandmother was outside cutting up fish. She hadn't believed what he told her about the school because she knew he wanted to keep her there in the log house with him. She knew what he wanted.

The dormitory matron pulled down her underpants and whipped her with a leather belt because she refused to speak English.

"Those backwards village people," the matron said, because she was an Eskimo who had worked for the BIA a long time, "they kept this one until she was too big to learn." The other girls whispered in English. They knew how to work the showers, and they washed and curled their hair at night. They ate Gussuck food. She lay on her bed and imagined what her grandmother might be sewing, and what the old man was eating in his bed. When summer came, they sent her home.

The way her grandmother had hugged her before she left for school had been a warning too, because the old woman had not hugged or touched her for many years. Not like the old man, whose hands were always hunting, like ravens circling lazily in the sky, ready to touch her. She was not surprised when the priest and the old man met her at the landing strip, to say that the old lady was gone. The priest asked her where she would like to stay. He referred to the old man as her grandfather, but she did not bother to correct him. She had already been thinking about it; if she went with the priest, he would send her away to a school. But the old man was different. She knew he wouldn't send her back to school. She knew he wanted to keep her.

He told her one time, that she would get too old for him faster than he got too old for her; but again she had not believed him because sometimes he lied. He had lied about what he would do with her if she came into his bed. But as the years passed, she realized what he said was true. She was restless and strong. She had no patience with the old man who had never changed his slow smooth motions under the blankets.

The old man was in his bed for the winter; he did not leave it except to use the slop bucket in the corner. He was dozing with his mouth open slightly; his lips quivered and sometimes they moved like he was telling a story even while he dreamed. She pulled on the sealskin boots, the mukluks with the bright red flannel linings her grandmother had sewn for her, and she tied the braided red yarn tassels around her ankles over the gray wool pants. She zipped the wolfskin parka. Her grandmother had worn it for many years, but the old man said that before she died, she instructed him to bury her in an old black sweater, and to give the parka to the girl. The wolf pelts were creamy colored and silver, almost white in some places, and when the old lady had walked across the tundra in the winter, she was invisible in the snow.

She walked toward the village, breaking her own path through the deep snow.

A team of sled dogs tied outside a house at the edge of the village leaped against their chains to bark at her. She kept walking, watching the dusky sky for the first evening stars. It was warm and the dogs were alert. When it got cold again, the dogs would lie curled and still, too drowsy from the cold to bark or pull at the chains. She laughed loudly because it made them howl and snarl. Once the old man had seen her tease the dogs and he shook his head. "So that's the kind of woman you are," he said, "in the wintertime the two of us are no different from those dogs. We wait in the cold for someone to bring us a few dry fish."

She laughed out loud again, and kept walking. She was thinking about the Gussuck oil drillers. They were strange; they watched her when she walked near their machines. She wondered what they looked like underneath their quilted goosedown trousers; she wanted to know how they moved. They would be something different from the old man.

The old man screamed at her. He shook her shoulders so violently that her head bumped against the log wall. "I smelled it!" he yelled, "as soon as I woke up! I am sure of it now. You can't fool me!" His thin legs were shaking inside the baggy wool trousers; he stumbled over her boots in his bare feet. His toenails were long and yellow like bird claws; she had seen a gray crane last summer fighting another in the shallow water on the edge of the river. She laughed out loud and pulled her shoulder out of his grip. He stood in front of her. He was breathing hard and shaking; he looked weak. He would probably die next winter.

"I'm warning you," he said, "I'm warning you." He crawled back into his bunk then, and reached under the old soiled feather pillow for a piece of dry fish. He lay back on the pillow, staring at the ceiling and chewed dry stips of salmon. "I don't know what the old woman told you," he said, "but there will be trouble." He looked over to see if she was listening. His face suddenly relaxed into a smile, his dark slanty eyes were lost in wrinkles of brown skin. "I could tell you, but you are too good for warnings now. I can smell what you did all night with the Gussucks."

She did not understand why they came there, because the village was small and so far upriver that even some Eskimos who had been away to school did not want to come back. They stayed downriver in the town. They said the village was too quiet. They were used to the town where the boarding school was located, with electric lights and running water. After all those years away at school, they had forgotten how to set nets in the river and where to hunt seals in the fall. When she asked the old man why the Gussucks bothered to come to the village, his narrow eyes got bright with excitement.

"They only come when there is something to steal. The fur animals are too difficult for them to get now, and the seals and fish are hard to find. Now they come for oil deep in the earth. But this is the last time for them." His breathing was wheezy and fast; his hands gestured in the sky. "It is approaching. As it comes, ice will push across the sky." His eyes were open wide and he stared at the low ceiling rafters for hours without blinking. She remembered all this clearly because he began the story that day, the story he told from that time on. It began with a giant bear which he described muscle by muscle, from the curve of the ivory claws to the whorls of hair at the top of the massive skull. And for eight days he did not sleep, but talked continuously of the giant bear whose color was pale blue glacier ice.

The snow was dirty and worn down in a path to the door. On either side of the path, the snow was higher than her head. In front of the door there were jagged yellow stains melted into the snow where men had urinated. She stopped in the entry way and kicked the snow off her boots. The room was dim; a kerosene lantern by the cash register was burning low. The long wooden shelves were jammed with cans of beans and potted meats. On the bottom shelf a jar of mayonnaise was broken open, leaking oily white clots on the floor. There was no one in the room except the yellowish dog sleeping in front of the long glass display case. A reflection made it appear to be lying on the knives and ammunition inside the case. Gussucks kept dogs inside their houses with them; they did not seem to mind the odors which seeped out of the dogs. "They tell us we are dirty for the food we eat—raw fish and fermented meat. But we do not live with dogs," the old man once said. She heard voices in the back room, and the sound of bottles set down hard on the tables.

They were always confident. The first year they waited for the ice to break up on the river, and then they brought their big yellow machines up river on barges. They planned to drill their test holes during the summer to avoid the freezing. But the imprints and graves of their machines were still there, on the edge of the tundra above the river, where the summer mud had swallowed them before they ever left sight of the river. The village people had gathered to watch the white men, and to laugh as they drove the giant machines, one by one, off the steel ramp into the bogs; as if sheer numbers of vehicles would somehow make the tundra solid. But the old man said they behaved like desperate people, and they would come back again. When the tundra was frozen solid, they returned.

Village women did not even look through the door to the back room. The priest had warned them. The storeman was watching her because he didn't let Eskimos or Indians sit down at the tables in the back room. But she knew he couldn't throw her out if one of the Gussuck customers invited her to sit with him. She walked across the room. They stared at her, but she had the feeling she was walking for someone else, not herself, so their eyes did not matter. The red-haired man pulled out a chair and motioned for her to sit down. She looked back at the storeman while the red-haired man poured her a glass of red sweet wine. She wanted to laugh at the storeman the way she laughed at the dogs, straining against the chains, howling at her.

The red-haired man kept talking to the other Gussucks sitting around the table, but he slid one hand off the top of the table to her thighs. She looked over at the storeman to see if he was still watching her. She laughed out loud at him and the red-haired man stopped talking and turned to her. He asked if she wanted to go. She nodded and stood up.

Someone in the village had been telling him things about her, he said as they walked down the road to his trailer. She understood that much of what he was saying, but the rest she did not hear. The whine of the big generators at the construction camp sucked away the sound of his words. But English was of no concern to her anymore, and neither was anything the Christians in the village might say about her or the old man. She smiled at the effect of the subzero air on the electric lights around the trailers; they did not shine. They left only flat yellow holes in the darkness.

It took him a long time to get ready, even after she had undressed for him. She waited in the bed with the blankets pulled close, watching him. He adjusted the thermostat and lit candles in the room, turning out the electric lights. He searched through a stack of record albums until he found the right one. She was not sure about the last thing he did: he taped something on the wall behind the bed where he could see it while he lay on top of her. He was shriveled and white from the cold; he pushed against her body for warmth. He guided her hands to his thighs; he was shivering.

She had returned a last time because she wanted to know what it was he stuck on the wall above the bed. After he finished each time, he reached up and pulled it loose, folding it carefully so that she could not see it. But this time she was ready; she waited for his fast breathing and sudden collapse on top of her. She slid out from under him and stood up beside the bed. She looked at the picture while she got dressed. He did not raise his face from the pillow, and she thought she heard teeth rattling together as she left the room.

She heard the old man move when she came in. After the Gussuck's trailer, the log house felt cool. It smelled like dry fish and cured meat. The room was dark except for the blinking yellow flame in the mica[3] window of the oil stove. She squatted in front of the stove and watched the flames for a long time before she walked to the bed where her grandmother had slept. The bed was covered with a mound of rags and fur scraps the old woman had saved. She reached into the mound until she felt something cold and solid wrapped in a wool blanket. She pushed her fingers around it until she felt smooth stone. Long ago, before the Gussucks came, they had burned whale oil in the big stone lamp which made light and heat as well. The old woman had saved everything they would need when the time came.

In the morning, the old man pulled a piece of dry caribou meat from under the blankets and offered it to her. While she was gone, men from the village had brought a bundle of dry meat. She chewed it slowly, thinking about the way they still came from the village to take care of the old man and his stories. But she had a story now, about the red-haired Gussuck. The old man knew what she was thinking, and his smile made his face seem more round than it was.

"Well," he said, "what was it?"

"A woman with a big dog on top of her."

He laughed softly to himself and walked over to the water barrel. He dipped the tin cup into the water.

"It doesn't surprise me," he said.

"Grandma," she said, "there was something red in the grass that morning. I remember." She had not asked about her parents before. The old woman stopped splitting the fish bellies open for the willow drying racks. Her jaw muscles pulled so tightly against her skull, the girl thought the old woman would not be able to speak.

"They bought a tin can full of it from the storeman. Late at night. He told them it was alcohol safe to drink. They traded a rifle for it." The old woman's voice sounded like each word stole strength from her. "It made no difference about the rifle. That year the Gussuck boats had come, firing big guns at the walrus and seals. There was nothing left to hunt after that anyway. So," the old lady said, in a low soft voice the girl had not heard for a long time, "I didn't say anything to them when they left that night."

---

[3] A mineral that crystallizes into thin, transparent sheets.

"Right over there," she said, pointing at the fallen poles, half buried in the river sand and tall grass, "in the summer shelter. The sun was high half the night then. Early in the morning when it was still low, the policeman came around. I told the interpreter to tell him that the storeman had poisoned them." She made outlines in the air in front of her, showing how their bodies lay twisted on the sand; telling the story was like laboring to walk through deep snow; sweat shone in the white hair around her forehead. "I told the priest too, after he came. I told him the storeman lied." She turned away from the girl. She held her mouth even tighter, set solidly, not in sorrow or anger, but against the pain, which was all that remained. "I never believed," she said, "not much anyway. I wasn't surprised when the priest did nothing."

The wind came off the river and folded the tall grass into itself like river waves. She could feel the silence the story left, and she wanted to have the old woman go on.

"I heard sounds that night, grandma. Sounds like someone was singing. It was light outside. I could see something red on the ground." The old woman did not answer her; she moved to the tub full of fish on the ground beside the workbench. She stabbed her knife into the belly of a whitefish and lifted it onto the bench. "The Gussuck storeman left the village right after that," the old woman said as she pulled the entrails from the fish, "otherwise, I could tell you more." The old woman's voice flowed with the wind blowing off the river; they never spoke of it again.

When the willows got their leaves and the grass grew tall along the river banks and around the sloughs, she walked early in the morning. While the sun was still low on the horizon, she listened to the wind off the river; its sound was like the voice that day long ago. In the distance, she could hear the engines of the machinery the oil drillers had left the winter before, but she did not go near the village or the store. The sun never left the sky and the summer became the same long day, with only the winds to fan the sun into brightness or allow it to slip into twilight.

She sat beside the old man at his place on the river bank. She poked the smoky fire for him, and felt herself growing wide and thin in the sun as if she had been split from belly to throat and strung on the willow pole in preparation for the winter to come. The old man did not speak anymore. When men from the village brought him fresh fish he hid them deep in the river grass where it was cool. After he went inside, she split the fish open and spread them to dry on the willow frame the way the old woman had done. Inside, he dozed and talked to himself. He had talked all winter, softly and incessantly, about the giant polar bear stalking a lone hunter across Bering Sea ice. After all the months the old man had been telling the story, the bear was within a hundred feet of the man; but the ice fog had closed in on them now and the man could only smell the sharp ammonia odor of the bear, and hear the edge of the snow crust crack under the giant paws.

One night she listened to the old man tell the story all night in his sleep, describing each crystal of ice and the slightly different sounds they made under each paw; first the left and then the right paw, then the hind feet. Her grandmother was there suddenly, a shadow around the stove. She spoke in her low wind voice and the girl was afraid to sit up to hear more clearly. Maybe what she said had been to the old man because he stopped telling the story and began to snore softly the way he had long ago when the old woman had scolded him for telling his stories while others in the house were trying to sleep. But the last words she heard clearly: "It will take a long time, but the story must be told. There must not be any lies." She pulled the blankets up around her chin, slowly, so that her movements would not be seen. She thought her grandmother was talking about the old man's bear story; she did not know about the other story then.

She left the old man wheezing and snoring in his bed. She walked through river grass glistening with frost; the bright green summer color was already fading. She watched the sun move across the sky, already lower on the horizon, already moving away from the village. She stopped by the fallen poles of the summer shelter where her parents had died. Frost glittered on the river sand too; in a few more weeks there would be snow. The predawn light would be the color of an old woman. An old woman sky full of snow. There had been something red lying on the ground the morning they died. She looked for it again, pushing aside the grass with her foot. She knelt in the sand and looked under the fallen structure for some trace of it. When she found it, she would know what the old woman had never told her. She squatted down close to the gray poles and leaned her back against them. The wind made her shiver.

The summer rain had washed the mud from between the logs; the sod blocks stacked as high as her belly next to the log walls had lost their square-cut shape and had grown into soft mounds of tundra moss and stiff-bladed grass bending with clusters of seed bristles. She looked at the northwest, in the direction of the Bering Sea. The cold would come down from there to find narrow slits in the mud, rainwater holes in the outer layer of sod which protected the log house. The dark green tundra stretched away flat and continuous. Somewhere the sea and the land met; she knew by their dark green colors there were no boundaries between them. That was how the cold would come: when the boundaries were gone the polar ice would range across the land into the sky. She watched the horizon for a long time. She would stand in that place on the north side of the house and she would keep watch on the northwest horizon, and eventually she would see it come. She would watch for its approach in the stars, and hear it come with the wind. These preparations were unfamiliar, but gradually she recognized them as she did her own footprints in the snow.

She emptied the slop jar beside his bed twice a day and kept the barrel full of water melted from river ice. He did not recognize her anymore, and when he spoke to her, he called her by her grandmother's name and talked about people and events from long ago, before he went back to telling the story. The giant bear was creeping across the new snow on its belly, close enough now that the man could hear the rasp of its breathing. On and on in a soft singing voice, the old man caressed the story, repeating the words again and again like gentle strokes.

The sky was gray like a river crane's egg; its density curved into the thin crust of frost already covering the land. She looked at the bright red color of the tin against the ground and the sky and she told the village men to bring the pieces for the old man and her. To drill the test holes in the tundra, the Gussucks had used hundreds of barrels of fuel. The village people split open the empty barrels that were abandoned on the river bank, and pounded the red tin into flat sheets. The village people were using the strips of tin to mend walls and roofs for winter. But she nailed it on the log walls for its color. When she finished, she walked away with the hammer in her hand, not turning around until she was far away, on the ridge above the river banks, and then she looked back. She felt a chill when she saw how the sky and the land were already losing their boundaries, already becoming lost in each other. But the red tin penetrated the thick white color of earth and sky; it defined the boundaries like a wound revealing the ribs and heart of a great caribou about to bolt and be lost to the hunter forever. That night the wind howled and when she scratched a hole through the heavy frost on the inside of the window, she could see nothing but the impenetrable white; whether it was blowing snow or snow that had drifted as high as the house, she did not know.

It had come down suddenly, and she stood with her back to the wind looking at the river, its smoky water clotted with ice. The wind had blown the snow over the frozen river, hiding thin blue streaks where fast water ran under ice translucent and fragile as memory. But she could see shadows of boundaries, outlines of paths which were slender branches of solidity reaching out from the earth. She spent days walking on the river, watching the colors of ice that would safely hold her, kicking the heel of her boot into the snow crust, listening for a solid sound. When she could feel the paths through the soles of her feet, she went to the middle of the river where the fast gray water churned under a thin pane of ice. She looked back. On the river bank in the distance she could see the red tin nailed to the log house, something not swallowed up by the heavy white belly of the sky or caught in the folds of the frozen earth. It was time.

The wolverine fur around the hood of her parka was white with the frost from her breathing. The warmth inside the store melted it, and she felt tiny drops of water on her face. The storeman came in from the back room. She unzipped the parka and stood by the oil stove. She didn't look at him, but stared instead at the yellowish dog, covered with scabs of matted hair, sleeping in front of the stove. She thought of the Gussuck's picture, taped on the wall above the bed and she laughed out loud. The sound of her laughter was piercing; the yellow dog jumped to its feet and the hair bristled down its back. The storeman was watching her. She wanted to laugh again because he didn't know about the ice. He did not know that it was prowling the earth, or that it had already pushed its way into the sky to seize the sun. She sat down in the chair by the stove and shook her long hair loose. He was like a dog tied up all winter, watching while the others got fed. He remembered how she had gone with the oil drillers, and his blue eyes moved like flies crawling over her body. He held his thin pale lips like he wanted to spit on her. He hated the people because they had something of value, the old man said, something which the Gussucks could never have. They thought they could take it, suck it out of the earth or cut it from the mountains; but they were fools.

There was a matted hunk of dog hair on the floor by her foot. She thought of the yellow insulation coming unstuffed: their defense against the freezing going to pieces as it advanced on them. The ice was crouching on the northwest horizon like the old man's bear. She laughed out loud again. The sun would be down now; it was time.

The first time he spoke to her, she did not hear what he said, so she did not answer or even look up at him. He spoke to her again but his words were only noises coming from his pale mouth, trembling now as his anger began to unravel. He jerked her up and the chair fell over behind her. His arms were shaking and she could feel his hands tense up, pulling the edges of the parka tighter. He raised his fist to hit her, his thin body quivering with rage; but the fist collapsed with the desire he had for the valuable things, which, the old man had rightly said, was the only reason they came. She could hear his heart pounding as he held her close and arched his hips against her, groaning and breathing in spasms. She twisted away from him and ducked under his arms.

She ran with a mitten over her mouth, breathing through the fur to protect her lungs from the freezing air. She could hear him running behind her, his heavy breathing, the occasional sound of metal jingling against metal. But he ran without his parka or mittens, breathing the frozen air; its fire squeezed the lungs against the ribs and it was enough that he could not catch her near his store. On the river bank he realized how far he was from his stove, and the wads of yellow stuffing that held off the cold. But the girl was not able to run very fast through the deep drifts at the edge of the river. The twilight was luminous and he could still see clearly for a long distance; he knew he could catch her so he kept running.

When she neared the middle of the river she looked over her shoulder. He was not following her tracks; he went straight across the ice, running the shortest distance to reach her. He was close then; his face was twisted and scarlet from the exertion and the cold. There was satisfaction in his eyes; he was sure he could outrun her.

She was familiar with the river, down to the instant ice flexed into hairline fractures, and the cracking bone-sliver sounds gathered momentum with the opening ice until the churning gray water was set free. She stopped and turned to the sound of the river and the rattle of swirling ice fragments where he fell through. She pulled off a mitten and zipped the parka to her throat. She was conscious then of her own rapid breathing.

She moved slowly, kicking the ice ahead with the heel of her boot, feeling for sinews of ice to hold her. She looked ahead and all around herself; in the twilight, the dense white sky had merged into the flat snow-covered tundra. In the frantic running she had lost her place on the river. She stood still. The east bank of the river was lost in the sky; the boundaries had been swallowed by the freezing white. But then, in the distance, she saw something red, and suddenly it was as she had remembered all those years.

She sat on her bed and while she waited, she listened to the old man. The hunter had found a small jagged knoll on the ice. He pulled his beaver fur cap off his head; the fur inside it steamed with his body heat and sweat. He left it upside down on the ice for the great bear to stalk, and he waited downwind on top of the ice knoll; he was holding the jade knife.

She thought she could see the end of his story in the way he wheezed out the words; but still he reached into his cache of dry fish and dribbled water into his mouth from the tin cup. All night she listened to him describe each breath the man took, each motion of the bear's head as it tried to catch the sound of the man's breathing, and tested the wind for his scent.

The state trooper asked her questions, and the woman who cleaned house for the priest translated them into Yupik. They wanted to know what happened to the storeman, the Gussuck who had been seen running after her down the road onto the river late last evening. He had not come back, and the Gussuck boss in Anchorage was concerned about him. She did not answer for a long time because the old man suddenly sat up in his bed and began to talk excitedly, looking at all of them—the trooper in his dark glasses and the housekeeper in her corduroy parka. He kept saying, "The story! The story! Eh-ya! The great bear! The hunter!"

They asked her again, what happened to the man from the Northern Commercial store. "He lied to them. He told them it was safe to drink. But I will not lie." She stood up and put on the gray wolfskin parka. "I killed him," she said, "but I don't lie."

The attorney came back again, and the jailer slid open the steel doors and opened the cell to let him in. He motioned for the jailer to stay to translate for him. She laughed when she saw how the jailer would be forced by this Gussuck to speak Yupik to her. She liked the Gussuck attorney for that, and for the thinning hair on his head. He was very tall, and she liked to think about the exposure of his head to the freezing; she wondered if he would feel the ice descending from the sky before the others did. He wanted to know why she told the state trooper she had killed the storeman. Some village children had seen it happen, he said, and it was an accident. "That's all you have to say to the judge: it was an accident." He kept repeating it over and over again to her, slowly in a loud but gentle voice: "It was an accident. He was running after you and he fell through the ice. That's all you have to say in court. That's all. And they will let you go home. Back to your village." The jailer translated the words sullenly, staring down at the floor. She shook her head. "I will not change the story, not even to escape this place and go home. I intended that he die. The story must be told as it is." The attorney exhaled loudly; his eyes looked tired. "Tell her that she could not have killed him that way. He was a white man. He ran after her without a parka or mittens. She could not have planned that." He paused and turned toward the cell door. "Tell her I will do all I can for her. I will explain to the judge that her mind is confused." She laughed out loud when the jailer translated what the attorney said. The Gussucks did not understand the story; they could not see the way it must be told, year after year as the old man had done, without lapse or silence.

She looked out the window at the frozen white sky. The sun had finally broken loose from the ice but it moved like a wounded caribou running on strength which only dying animals find, leaping and running on bullet-shattered lungs. Its light was weak and pale; it pushed dimly through the clouds. She turned and faced the Gussuck attorney.

"It began a long time ago," she intoned steadily, "in the summertime. Early in the morning, I remember, something red in the tall river grass. . . . "

The day after the old man died, men from the village came. She was sitting on the edge of her bed, across from the woman the trooper hired to watch her. They came into the room slowly and listened to her. At the foot of her bed they left a king salmon that had been slit open wide and dried last summer. But she did not pause or hesitate; she went on with the story, and she never stopped, not even when the woman got up to close the door behind the village men.

The old man would not change the story even when he knew the end was approaching. Lies could not stop what was coming. He thrashed around on the bed, pulling the blankets loose, knocking bundles of dried fish and meat on the floor. The hunter had been on the ice for many hours. The freezing winds on the ice knoll had numbed his hands in the mittens, and the cold had exhausted him. He felt a single muscle tremor in his hand that he could not stop, and the jade knife fell; it shattered on the ice, and the blue glacier bear turned slowly to face him.

1981

~~~~~~

Writing About Literature

To read literature is to enter a conversation—a dialogue, really—with the author and other readers, to respond to their interpretations of the human situation with comments of your own. Writing about great literature may at first be intimidating—you may think "I can't say anything *new* about Mark Twain" or "I don't know as much about Black America as James Baldwin does." But if literature *doesn't* provoke you to respond, then the author hasn't done the job.

To provoke a response is why your instructor asks you to write about the works you read: to make you think, to make you take part in the conversation, even if your thoughts, discoveries, and "lines" in the dialogue have all been uttered before. You, too, have a right to take part in the ongoing discussion about American literature and to convey your response to your readers.

The nature of that response will vary from reader to reader and from situation to situation. You may react to a work differently in a short-answer exam question than you would in a ten-page paper, or differently if you particularly like a work than if you are particularly offended by it. Some readers are fascinated by works about the areas where they grew up, whereas others prefer the lure of faraway places and exotic situations. But all readers will create their interpretations based on several similar principles: the nature of their own readers, the kind of response for which they are asked, and the angle of their approach.

In literature classes you may be asked to construct your interpretation of a particular text, based only on the materials in this book and on your class discussions. Or your instructor may send you to outside sources to give you other perspectives as a way of shaping your response. We will discuss the procedures and pitfalls of both methods. But first we need to make some important observations about reading literature.

READING LITERATURE TO WRITE ABOUT IT

You can read a work of literature in two ways: *precritically* and *critically*. A *precritical reading* is a surface reading: you read to find out what goes on where, what happens, who says what about whatever. You do not look very deeply; you just go from the first line to the last. The dangers of such reading to writing about the work are many: you can write only about the obvious things. You can recount the plot and explain the obvious symbols and devices the author uses, but not in any great depth. The only audiences interested in this kind of writing are people who have not read the work—and your instructor does not fit into this group. A surface reading alone generally guarantees a disastrous paper.

A *critical reading* involves slow, careful, close reading and *rereading* of the text. You read "between the lines," trying to figure out what is really going on, what the author expects of you. You should take notes; ask questions; jot down your ideas, responses, perplexities. This careful process of reading and rereading will help you unfold a text's possibilities. You will write about *how* things happen in the work; you can assume that your readers already know what happens in the work and are interested in exploring beneath the surface with you.

FINDING A SUBJECT: THINKING ABOUT YOUR READERS

You need to remember a special factor of taking part in the conversation about literature: the readers with whom you are conversing. You must consciously imagine *someone* reading your paper. Generally, your reader will be your instructor, who will have special expectations regarding your response. Your instructor will want to see how clear an understanding of the work you have developed, how well you can express your response, and how strong a case you can make. The instructor typically does not want you to recount the plot in great detail: he or she has also read the work! (Think of conversations you have had in which someone repeated a story everyone else in the group already knew well. How interested were you in hearing that story?)

You do not want your readers to say "So what?" about your paper. You do not want to bore them with vague, uninteresting statements. A thesis like "There are many references to homemade items in 'Everyday Use'" will probably elicit the "so what?" response; who cares? But saying "Alice Walker uses domestic objects to emphasize values that readers might not consider otherwise" makes readers say "Really? Tell me how." That is the response you want.

USING ONLY A PRIMARY SOURCE

When you start to write about a work of literature, first ask yourself "What in this work might catch my readers' interest?" Some elements are so obvious that most readers understand their use the first time they read a work; these probably are not good elements to discuss. Go back to the notes you made in your critical reading. Look for an element that you had to think about for a while before you really understood it. Chances are that such an element will lead you to an interesting paper. These interesting elements tend to fall into three categories—*construction, language,* and *context*—within which you can usually find an angle of attack for your paper.

Writing About Construction

If you are writing about a work without referring to secondary sources such as journal articles or critical books, the work's construction is one of the best places to start: its plot (what happens), setting (when and where it happens), and its characters (to whom it happens, or who makes it happen). Each of these building blocks contributes to the overall structure of the work. The following list of questions can help you think about these elements. Not all the questions will apply to all works, but some will certainly apply to the work you are studying.

Plot. Does the work have a plot? (Some poems, for instance, do not.) What is the sequence of events? Did the author put them in chronological order or not, and why? Are key events omitted or just hinted at and why? Does the work have a particular pace or rhythm? Does the action seem to speed up or slow down? Where does the action happen, and why? Does the story seem to reach a climax, and where does that occur?

Setting. When and where does the work take place? In what ways would the work be different if it took place somewhere else? Does the choice of setting influence the action in different ways? (For instance, if the work were set upon a ship rather than in a large city, what would have to be left out of the plot?) How are the people and events in the work influenced by the setting?

Characters. Who are they? Do they actually appear in the work? (For instance, Miss Emily's father and fianceé are dead before William Faulkner's "A Rose for Emily" begins.) What sorts of elements in the work tell us about the characters: what they do, what they say, how they dress, what other people say about them, etc.? Who tells us about these characters: themselves, other characters, a narrator? Do the characters seem real (traditionally called "round" characters), or do they seem more like cartoon stereotypes ("flat" characters)?

Writing About Language

Few words in a work of literature are there accidentally; authors choose each word for precise reasons. Paying attention to what things are called, how they are described, and what those words bring to mind may lead to interesting angles for your "conversation" about the work. Here are some suggestions you can use to focus your attention on literary language.

Metaphor is a general term for language that has enriched meanings and a specific term for literary comparison. In general, metaphoric language is loaded with multiple meanings and connotations. In particular, a metaphor is an equation of two unlike objects:

> My life had stood — a Loaded Gun —
> In Corners —   (Emily Dickinson)

In this equation, the abstract concept "life" suddenly becomes the physical object "a Loaded Gun—In Corners." The comparison surprises us: women do not typically compare themselves to "masculine" items such as guns or see themselves as weapons to guard their homes and loved ones. Dickinson challenges her readers to see the implications of this comparison. The more oblique and nonstereotyped the comparison of objects being equated, the better—the deeper readers must explore to see the ramifications, and the richer the possibilities for writing.

Simile is a type of metaphorical language that compares two unrelated concepts, using the words "like" or "as" to emphasize the relationships. Unlike metaphor, which says one thing *is* another, simile suggests comparisons less forcefully:

> Like travelers with exotic destinations on their minds, the graduates were remarkably forgetful.   (Maya Angelou)

This example compares eighth-graders contemplating high school to travelers about to undertake some extraordinary journey; a little humor is implied in the comparison. Examining similes allows you to write about some of the most subtle effects an author creates.

Symbols are images that have literal as well as deeper meanings. By recognizing a symbol, readers can understand some of a work's deep implications. Some symbols have generalized meanings: a cross calls up Christian images; the American flag, patriotic images; a pillared mansion, images of the South and the Civil War. Other symbols have particular meanings in the work where they appear: Faith's pink hair ribbons in Nathaniel Hawthorne's "Young Goodman Brown," the quilts in "Everyday Use," the Mississippi River in Mark Twain's *Huckleberry Finn*. Writing about a symbol or set of symbols allows you to show your readers another level of meaning in the works you examine.

Tone is the author's attitude to the people and events described in a work: comic, ironic, satiric, sentimental, and so forth. Many things contribute to tone, including the narrator's point of view, the way things are described (for instance, journalistically, overstatedly, understatedly), the reactions of other characters in the work, and the types of sentences and vocabulary the author uses. Tone is sometimes hard to pin down, but writing about it is typically rewarding for both you and your readers because it requires you to look at how many elements work together to create an overall effect.

Writing About Context

Literature does not just happen in a vacuum. Writers are part of their times and part of literary history. When they create a work of literature, they draw on what they know of their own and of past times, the ideas and controversies that were important in their world, as well as the many things they have read. Examining one of these elements may give you an angle from which to approach your paper.

The writer's biography can play an important part in your discussion. The headnotes and introductions in this anthology may help you to understand what a writer has experienced in creating a particular work; for instance, knowing about

Anne Bradstreet's family tragedies may give you insight into some of her poems, and knowing about life in New Orleans can help you better understand Kate Chopin's stories. Knowing about Whitman's service as a nurse to wounded Civil War soldiers and his devotion to Abraham Lincoln lets you see new depths in "When Lilacs Last in the Dooryard Bloom'd." Knowing about Adrienne Rich's involvement in feminism helps you interpret "Snapshots of a Daughter-in-Law." Be careful, though, not to force correspondences: an author cannot control history but *does* control how history enters a particular work. The fickle women in Ernest Hemingway's war novels are not the actual nurse who jilted him, though that experience probably contributed to his development of those female characters.

Political and philosophical movements also contribute greatly to works. The introductions and nonfiction prose selections in this anthology show you how much literature is influenced by the ideas to which authors are exposed. Benjamin Franklin, Thomas Jefferson, John Adams, Thomas Paine, Alexander Hamilton, and James Madison, for instance, wrote in an era when revolution, democracy, and representative government were being widely discussed. Middle nineteenth-century writers were heavily influenced by the emancipation and women's rights movements. Late twentieth-century writers react to the civil rights movement, feminism, and the Vietnam War. A literary work interpreted in light of these movements can yield an interesting paper.

Allusion allows a writer to connect his or her work to other works of literature. In "The Jolly Corner" when Henry James refers to Penelope and Ulysses, James is suggesting that readers connect the long separation of his heroine and protagonist with those figures from Homer's *Odyssey*. In "The Jacob's Ladder" Denise Lever-tov is referring to a familiar episode in the Old Testament. The challenge in writing about allusions is for you to show readers *how* thinking about these suggested comparisons expands your understanding of the work in which they occur.

USING SECONDARY SOURCES

When your instructor asks you to use secondary sources, such as books and journal articles to help you write about literature, you are *not* being asked to summarize what everyone else thinks about a work, but to support *your* interpretation of a work with what other people have written. You are like a lawyer presenting a case: you make the arguments to the jury and call witnesses (the secondary sources) to provide evidence for your case. You have three tasks when you use secondary sources in writing a paper. First, you must find an angle of attack, just as you do when you write from a primary source only. Second, you must find supporting evidence in the works of other writers. And third, you must present that supporting evidence in correct fashion. We have already reviewed the first task, so let us look at what the other two involve.

Finding Secondary Sources

Libraries are full of secondary sources: biographies, collections of letters and diaries, critical interpretations, collections, and the like. You may wish to begin by looking in the card catalog and scanning the shelves for books that may apply. Skim the introductions, conclusions, tables of contents, and indexes to see if the work you are studying is covered in those books. You can use reference books and computer sources such as *Book Review Digest* or the *MLA International Bibliography* to find articles and reviews. (You can also check the suggested readings and texts used in this anthology). The sources you choose will depend on the author you are studying and your angle of approach.

Citing Sources in Your Paper

Every discipline has its own conventions for format and citing secondary sources. In literature those conventions are established by the Modern Language Association and set out in two books: the *MLA Handbook for Writers of Research Papers* (1988) and *the MLA Style Manual* (1985). These books cover in great detail the fine points we will summarize here; your instructor or reference librarian can help you find the books if you have questions not answered here.

Paper Format

In general, put your name and identification number, instructor's name, course name, and date in the top left corner of the first page, with a one-inch margin all around. Doublespace down and input the title, underlining only the names of complete works (see below). Put your last name and the page number in the upper right corner of every page after the first, and staple or clip the pages together firmly in the upper left corner. *Doublespace* the entire paper, including quotations and your list of Works Cited. Do not use a separate cover page or folder unless your instructor calls for it.

Working Quotations Into Your Text

Cite sources within your text through parenthetical references to sources you quote, paraphrase, or summarize. If the material you quote, paraphrase, or summarize takes up less than four typed lines, place a page reference in parentheses *after* the quotation marks and *before* the next major punctuation mark:

```
M. Wynn Thomas calls this lecture "astonishing" (243).
```
OR:
```
Richard F. Adams has found seven of the traditional seventeen

elements of pastoral elegy in "When Lilacs Last in the

Dooryard Bloom'd" (479-487).
```

(The end punctuation goes inside the quotation marks only when the line ends with a question mark or exclamation point, or when there is no parenthetical reference.) Drama is cited by act, scene, and line number rather than page number: (3.1.74). When making a first reference to a text not named in your introduction to the quote, briefly identify it with the parenthetical page reference: (Wright 564) or ("Lilacs" 23).

If a direct quote consists of more than four typed lines of prose or dialogue or more than two typed lines of poetry, end the introductory material with whatever punctuation mark is appropriate (or none, if none is required). Then doublespace, indent ten spaces from the left margin, and doublespace the long quotation (with no opening quotation marks, unless they appear in the original text). End the quote with the punctuation the original text uses, move two spaces to the right, and put the quote's page numbers in parentheses. No punctuation follows the parentheses. Then doublespace and return to your text. If continuing the same paragraph, return to the left margin; if starting a new paragraph, indent the usual five spaces.

Fine Points. If the original text has unusual spelling, punctuation, capitalization, or spacing, do your best to reproduce it on your page. If you begin quoting from poetry in the middle of a line, indent that line the number of spaces missing to indicate this positioning. Underline only the titles of complete works (such as novels, plays, long poems, and collections); names of newspapers, journals, magazines, movies, TV programs, records, and works of art; and unfamiliar foreign words and phrases. Use quotation marks around the titles of poems, articles in journals or magazines, and essays, introductions, forewords, and the like not published separately. (Follow these rules in the text, your title, and your list of Works Cited.)

If you leave words or sentences out of a quotation in your paper, use ellipsis marks, the spaced sets of three or four dots, to show readers where you have trimmed the original text. Three spaced dots indicate words or phrases are omitted; four spaced dots indicate that the omission includes the end of one or more sentences. (Omissions of one or more paragraphs may be indicated by three spaced asterisks.) If you need to tailor a quote to match your sentence grammar, include your alterations in square brackets to show your editorial changes. If there is a mistake, such as a typographical error, in your source, copy the mistake exactly and follow it with the Latin term "*sic*" in square brackets to tell your readers you recognize the mistake. To call attention to particular words, underline them to italicize them. (If you underline words in a direct quote, add the phrase *emphasis mine* to the cited page numbers to point out the change.)

Citing Sources at the End of Your Text

A bibliography, called a list of Works Cited, starts on a new page following your paper, with the title *Works Cited* centered one inch from the top of the page. Works you quoted, summarized, or paraphrased in your essay are listed here in alphabetical order by author. If a source has no author, list it alphabetically by the first word of its title (excepting "a," "an," and "the").

In accordance with recently adopted MLA guidelines, for every work cited give (1) the author's name (if applicable), last name first; (2) the full title (underlined or in quotations; use single quotation marks for a quotation within a quotation), followed by the edition number, if any; (3) the source in which the work appears (if appropriate), underlined; (4) the city (and state, if the city is not well known) of publication, followed by a colon; (5) the publisher (abbreviating "University" to "U" and "Press" to "P"), followed by a comma; and (6) the year or years published. For sources that appear in other bound volumes (such as articles in a journal or essays in a collection), include (7) the beginning and ending page numbers. Each of these seven elements, except for the place of publication and publisher, is separated from the others by a period and two spaces. Begin each reference at the left margin and indent continuation lines five spaces.

Works Cited entries can take hundreds of forms. Here are examples of the most common; you can find examples of other forms in the *MLA Handbook*.

A BOOK

Thomas, M. Wynn. The Lunar Light of Whitman's Poetry. Cambridge:

Harvard UP, 1987.

A LITERARY WORK IN A BOOK

Adams, Richard P. " 'Lilacs' as Pastoral Elegy." Critics on

Walt Whitman: Readings in Literary Criticism. Ed. Richard

H. Rupp. Coral Gables: U Miami P, 1972. 69-76.

AN EDITED TEXT

This form draws attention to the author:

Whitman, Walt. "When Lilacs Last in the Dooryard Bloom'd."

Leaves of Grass: A Textual Variorum of the Printed Poems.

Ed. Sculley Bradley, Harold W. Blodgett, Arthur Golden, and

William White. New York: New York UP, 1980. 2:529-539.

This form draws attention to the editors:

Bradley, Sculley, Harold W. Blodgett, Arthur Golden, and William

White, eds. "When Lilacs Last in the Dooryard Bloom'd."

By Walt Whitman. Leaves of Grass: A Textual Variorum of

the Printed Poems. New York: New York UP, 1980. 2:529-539.

AN ARTICLE APPEARING IN A JOURNAL

Wright, George T. "The Lyric Present: Simple Present Verbs in

English Poems." PMLA 89 (1974): 563-579.

A BOOK REVIEW

Kakutani, Michiko. Rev. of Sweet Desserts, by Lucy Ellmann.

New York Times 6 June 1989: B6.

Avoiding Plagiarism

Plagiarism is one of the worst of scholarly crimes. When you plagiarize, you present another writer's thoughts or words or concepts as if they were yours. Plagiarism not only denies writers true credit for their work, but it blurs the distinctions between your own arguments and the supporting evidence. You can suffer many penalties for plagiarism: an "F" on the paper or in the course, probation, suspension, even expulsion. It is important to indicate which ideas in your paper are yours and which come from your sources, in order to avoid committing this serious offense.

To avoid plagiarism, follow four simple rules. One, *keep accurate notes*. When making notes from a book or journal, use quotations marks to indicate words you have copied directly from your sources. Use underlining or highlighting pen to indicate information and ideas you have paraphrased or summarized. Anything that comes from your source must be documented in your paper.

Two, *provide an introduction* to all source material you use in your paper. This attribution can be as simple as "According to Gay Wilson Allen," "Feidelson argues that," or "Critics such as Allen (1970) and Thomas (1987) suggest." By introducing your sources, you signal to your reader that secondary material follows; you are providing expert evidence to back up your contentions, showing your audience that other readers agree with your interpretations. Attributions make your paper seem better integrated, not just a collection of notecards and photocopies cut and pasted together to form an essay.

Three, *include parenthetical references* to the sources of your evidence. These page or line references tell your readers specifically where you got your evidence, so that they can find it easily if they become interested in further exploring your topic. The sample student paper below shows you several skillful ways of incorporating these references to give the information without interrupting the prose.

Four, *provide a list of Works Cited*. This bibliography helps the interested reader find the sources of your evidence. It also provides continuity to the "conversation" by showing where in the discussion of a particular work you place yourself in that conversation. If you provide all four of these elements, you should produce a carefully documented paper that lets your readers easily see what your arguments are and how the evidence in secondary sources supports your positions.

Sample Student Paper

On the following pages you will find a sample student paper based on a student's reading of Whitman's poem "When Lilacs Last in the Dooryard Bloom'd." We point out her thesis and supporting arguments to show how she constructed her paper; we also provide annotations to show you some of the technical aspects of presentation. Following the paper is a paragraph from another paper on "Lilacs," this one using secondary sources to support the argument. These examples should help you see how a written response to literature is assembled.

1

    Susanna Jones (8583432)

    Dr. Tarvers

    Principles of Literary Study

    October 14, 19--

                    A Time to Mourn

        Funerals and memorial services are for the living,

    the cliché goes. They are an organized way to express

    grief and put it behind us, a way to stop thinking

    about the past ("Remember when . . .?") and the future

    ("She could have been . . . .") and return to the

2   present in which we must live. In "When Lilacs Last

    in the Dooryard Bloom'd," Walt Whitman conducts such

    a memorial service, forcing both himself and his

    readers to cease grieving for Abraham Lincoln and to

    move toward a future worthy of Lincoln's efforts, as

    a way of keeping Lincoln's memory perpetually present.

    Whitman reinforces this determination to leave the past

3   behind by repeatedly manipulating verb tenses through-

    out the poem.

---

1. Leave one-inch margins all around.
2. Titles of works not published are placed separately in quotation marks.
3. Thesis of the student's paper.

> Jones 2   **4**
>
> The poem begins in the sad past of 1865, when
>
> lilacs "bloom'd," Venus "droop'd," and the narrator
>
> "mourn'd" for the fallen president ("Lilacs" 1-3).   **5, 6**
>
> Immediately Whitman uses tense to force his readers to
>
> leave the past behind by reminding us that "Ever-
>
> returning spring" brings a "trinity sure" to mind: the   **7**
>
> lilac, the star, and the memory of Lincoln. Moreover,
>
> like the Holy Trinity of Christian symbolism, this
>
> trinity exists in the present, always the same, always
>
> true, always with us. The symbol representing the truth
>
> is described in the present tense: ". . . near the   **8**
>
> white-wash'd palings, / Stands the lilac-bush" (12-13;   **9**
>
> emphasis mine). And, in affirmation of the present,   **10**
>
> the narrator tells us that "a sprig with its flower
>
> I break" (17) at the same time that the hidden hermit
>
> thrush "sings by himself a song" (22). In choosing
>
> the present tense to describe these eternal symbols,
>
> Whitman reminds us that truth and love are timeless.

4. From page 2 on, put your last name and the page number in the right corner, one-half inch from the top.

5. Use a short title for the first citation of the work.

6. Indicate line numbers without using the abbreviation *ll.*

7. One of the student's supporting arguments.

8. Ellipsis marks show the omission of words.

9. Poetry quotes of fewer than three lines are run into the text, separated by a slash with one space on either side.

10. "Emphasis mine" shows that underlining was added by the student.

Jones 3

    The lilac and birdsong prompt the narrator to
remember Lincoln's funeral procession, with a grief
so real that past events seem to become real in the
present. Amid positive images of birth-budding
violets, sprouting grain, and blooming trees, "night
and day journeys a coffin" (32). The narrator's
present-tense report makes this stark contrast
seem as if he had just now observed it: the coffin
"passes," it "journey[s]," and he "give[s]" it the
spray of lilac (Stanza 6). His memory keeps these
past actions alive.

    Again the narrator gathers his composure and
forces his attention back to the present by choosing
the present tense. He assures us that he does not
mourn for Lincoln alone but for everyone who has died
in the past: "Blossoms and branches green to all coffins
I bring" (47); ". . . I cover you with roses and early
lilies, / ... I break the sprigs from the bushes"
(50, 52). But his grasp on the present is still weak,
and his memories again draw him back, as he turns to
address the evening star: "Now I know what you must

\) 7

11

11. The student's editorial changes for smooth grammar are enclosed in brackets.

Jones 4

have meant as a month since I walk'd" (56). He tells

the thrush "I hear, I come presently . . ." (68), "But

a moment I linger, for the lustrous star has detain'd

me" (69). Memories of the fallen president, "the dead

one there I loved" (71), make the future without

Lincoln seem overwhelming; the poet shifts into the

future tense as he wrestles with the impossibility of

finding a suitable way to mourn his lost leader

(Stanza 10).

    Whitman's solution to this dilemma is to escape

out of time entirely. He poses the question "how

shall I warble for the dead one there I loved?" (71)   7

and answers in phrases without verb tense--fragments

that use present participles to construct a timeless

picture of the vital, growing America that was Lincoln's

dream and will be his best monument: "growing spring

and farms and homes," "the fresh sweet herbage under

foot," and, above all,

12

          the city at hand with dwellings so

      dense, and stacks of chimneys,

    And all the scenes of life and the workshops,

    and the workmen homeward returning. . . .

    12. Poetry quotes of three lines or more are treated as excerpts, indented ten spaces, and doublespaced. Extra indention of the first line shows that this quote begins in mid-line. Turnovers (continuation lines) are also indented.

Jones 5

The varied and ample land, the South and the

North in the light, Ohio's shores and

flashing Missouri . . . .

The miracle spreading bathing all, the

fulfill'd noon,

The coming eve delicious, the welcome night

and the stars,

Over my cities shining all, enveloping man

and land. (87-98)   13

7   To celebrate this escape out of time, the poet

returns to the present tense and encourages the thrush

to sing on. The thrush's carol uses present tense to

remind us that death is always with us, just as are

life and joy, the objects of human curiosity, day and

night. But the song's calm acceptance of death sends

Whitman's memory back to the past one last time, to a

month before Lincoln's death and a night when Whitman

found himself at the edge of a marsh, listening to

another thrush, smelling lilacs, and watching the

evening star. That night Whitman had thought the

thrush "sang the carol of death, and a verse for him I

love" (128) in memory of the soldiers who died during

the Civil War--the men whom Whitman had nursed and whose

sufferings he describes so graphically (171-184).   14

13. Line reference numbers follow the punctuation in the last line of the excerpt.
14. Reference to summarized material.

Jones 6

This memory, underscored by the thrush's song,
"sadly sinking and fainting . . . and yet again
bursting with joy" (190), is transformed, just as
Whitman would later claim Lincoln's death had been,
into one of "those climax moments on the stage of
universal Time . . . suddenly ringing down the curtain"
15 (Prose 2:508). At last, through the agency of the
thrush's carol, Whitman passes from the grief of the   **7**
past into the determination of the present and future:

> As that powerful psalm in the night I <u>heard</u>
>> from recesses,
>
> Passing, I <u>leave</u> thee lilac with heart-shaped
>> leaves,
>
> I <u>leave</u> thee there in the dooryard, blooming,
>> returning with spring. (192-194, emphasis
>>> mine)   **10**

His grief has been mastered. From here on, he will
live and write about Lincoln in the present tense, and,
in doing so, will keep the memories of Lincoln, his
fallen soldiers, the lilac, the star, and the thrush
ever alive, ever well, ever present. The funeral is
over; life can go on.

15. Reference to another work by Whitman; the reference indicates Volume 2,
followed by a colon and the page number.

Jones 7   **16**

Works Cited

Whitman, Walt. "When Lilacs Last in the Dooryard

Bloom'd." American Literature: A Prentice Hall

Anthology. Ed. Emory Elliott, Linda Kerber,

A. Walton Litz, and Terence Martin. Englewood

Cliffs: Prentice Hall, 1991. 1:2014-2020.

——————————. "The Death of Abraham Lincoln." Prose   **17**

Works. Ed. Floyd Stovall. New York: New York U,

1963-1964. 2:497-509.

Sample Paragraph From a Paper With Secondary Sources

Although critics such as Feidelson (1956), Adams

(1957), Allen (1970), and Thomas (1987) have explored   **18**

the classical elements of mourning in this poem, few

other than George T. Wright have given weight to the

Christian religious imagery Whitman incorporates into

his elegy. This incorporation is subtle, handled mostly

through vocabulary and grammar. Every action is consid-

ered carefully, performed deliberately, and reinforced

by the poet's choice of the present tense, as in a

religious service. Wright (1974) calls this tense the   **19**

16. The Works Cited list begins on a new page.
17. Reference to a second work by the same author is indicated by typing ten hyphens followed by a period.
18. Attribution to secondary sources: author's last name and date.
19. First reference to an article: author's last name and date.

"lyric present," and notes that it "characteristically convey[s] a sense of elevation and, often, of solemnity which seems appropriate to visionary experience." Citing Whitman's "here, coffin, that slowly passes, / I <u>give</u> you my sprig of lilac" (emphasis his), Wright argues that the poet is acting as if he were the minister conducting Lincoln's funeral (568). This impression is reinforced by Whitman's references to the "trinity" of symbols and by his descriptions of dirges, processions, chants, miracles, souls, and powerful psalms in the poem.

20

21

20. Shows that the emphasis was added by the source, not the student.

21. Placing the parenthetical reference at the end of several sentences with attribution shows that everything between the first attribution and this reference comes from the same source.

Glossary

Allegory: a narrative in which the persons, things, concepts, or events signify a hidden or symbolic meaning; an extension of **metaphor.**

Alliteration: the repetition of a (generally initial) consonant sound within a line or phrase.

Allusion: an explicit or indirect reference in a work to something outside the work itself.

Apron: in theater, the part of the stage in front of the **proscenium arch.**

Archetype: themes, images, character types, or narrative designs that seem to be identifiable in a wide array of literature as well as in myths and dreams. Examples of archetypes are death and rebirth and Paradise versus Hell.

Assonance: the repetition of a vowel sound within a line, stanza, or sentence.

Ballad: a narrative poem, originally of folk origin and meant to be sung, that tends to focus upon a climactic episode and is told without comment.

Beat poetics: an often impassioned poetry of the 1950s and 1960s distinguished by its celebration of freedom, rejection of social mores, and frequent use of colloquial language, as exemplified by the work of such poets as Allen Ginsberg, Lawrence Ferlinghetti, and Leonard Cohen. "Beat" suggests the beat of the bongo drum, which often accompanied readings of beat poetry, as well as "beatniks," with whom the beat poets were associated.

Bildungsroman: a German term for a novel of development, which recounts a protagonist's life experience and typically involves a crisis of conscience.

Blank verse: lines of unrhymed iambic pentameter (see **meter**) in verse paragraphs rather than stanzas.

Burlesque: a form of satire that attempts to ridicule a serious literary work by means of an amusing imitation. Two classes of burlesque are *parody,* which imitates the serious materials and style of a work and applies them to a lowly subject, and *travesty,* which mocks a work by treating its lofty subject in a jocular and undignified manner.

Canto: a major division of a long poem; originally a singing or chanting section of a poem.

Closed form: a form of poetry in which the thought and grammar are complete within a couplet.

Dénouement: a French term for the final outcome or unraveling of a plot.

Deus ex machina: a Latin term (meaning "god from a machine") for any unlikely plot contrivance.

Didactic: intended to be instructive, educational, or moralistic.

Dramatic irony: an ironic situation in which a reader or the audience is aware of things of which a character is not, or in which a character's speech and actions reveal that character to differ from his or her self-image.

Elegy: a poem lamenting the death of a particular person, or a meditative poem concerning mortality.

Epic: a long narrative poem of elevated diction, typically recounting history, legend, or the deeds of a national hero.

Epistolary: written in, or conducted by, letters.

Foot: the basic metrical unit in poetry, generally containing one stressed syllable and one or two unstressed syllables.

Free verse: poetry free of traditional metrical, rhyming, and stanzaic patterns, although not necessarily free of a patterning device such as **alliteration** or a visual repetition of line length.

Genre: a French term for a literary form, such as **epic** poem, captivity narrative, or western novel.

Heroic couplet: a rhyming couplet of lines of ten syllables, so called because it was originally used for heroic, or **epic** poetry.

Homiletic: like a homily, or sermon.

Hudibrastic: in the style of Samuel Butler's *Hudibras* (1663–1678), a **mock-epic** satirical poem that ridiculed the Puritans.

Hyperbole: an overstatement or exaggeration.

Idiom: the language or dialect of a group or class, or a language unit of a group or class that differs from the norm in syntax or meaning.

Imagism: a poetic movement that flourished in England and America between about 1909 and 1917 as a reaction to **romanticism** and called for poetry that renders the poet's response to a visual object or scene as exactly and tersely as possible without abstraction. Influenced by T. E. Hulme's aesthetic philosophy and by the Japanese haiku, the movement's leaders included Ezra Pound, Amy Lowell, and Hilda Doolittle.

Irony: an expression in which the intended meaning is different from, or opposite to, the literal meaning.

"Little" magazine: a literary magazine, commonly avant-garde, with a small readership and generally a small page size.

Local color: writing that emphasizes the setting, dialect, ways of thinking and feeling, dress, and custom characteristic of a specific region; used most often in connection with the local-color movement in American literature from 1870 to 1890.

Lyric poetry: originally, ancient Greek poetry accompanied by a lyre; now, a relatively short nonnarrative poem expressing the poet's thoughts or feelings.

Masque: a short, elaborately staged court drama with actors and dancers usually masked.

Melodrama: a form of drama, especially popular in the nineteenth century, full of tragic elements but with a happy ending; the characters are flat types: the hero and heroine epitomize virtue, and the villain is Satan incarnate.

Metaphor: a figure of speech in which one thing is equated to another, normally unrelated thing, without the use of a word of comparison, such as "like" or "as"; for example, "Her wrinkles are love's graves."

Meter: a measure of poetic rhythm, determined by the type and number of **feet** in a **poetic line.** The four standard meters of verse in English are *iambic* (an unstressed syllable followed by a stressed), *anapestic* (two unstressed syllables followed by a stressed), *trochaic* (a stressed syllable followed by an unstressed), and *dactylic* (a stressed syllable followed by two unstressed). The number of feet in a line determines the type of verse: trimeter for a line with three feet, tetrameter for four feet, pentameter for five feet, and so on.

Metonymy: a figure of speech in which a closely related term is substituted for what is actually meant: for example, "the White House denies any wrongdoing" for "the president denies any wrongdoing."

Mock epic: a poem in **epic** form and manner, ludicrously elevating some trivial subject to epic grandeur (also known as mock heroic).

Modernism: a trend in literature of the first half of the twentieth century toward radical experimentation, such as the use of **stream-of-consciousness** narration and of **myth** as a structural principle. Cultural relativism, discontinuity, and alienation are the driving forces behind much modernist literature, which was promoted by such writers as T. S. Eliot, Ezra Pound, James Joyce, Virginia Woolf, and William Faulkner.

Motif: a frequently recurring literary element, such as a word, an image, or a symbol. A *leitmotif* is a recurrent element in a single work or in the work of a single author.

Myth: an ancient story dealing with fabulous deeds of gods or heroes, or an imaginary world in which fictitious characters and events are faithful to moral, philosophical, and/or aesthetic "truths" rather than to scientific truths.

Naturalism: a literary philosophy by which human beings are seen as part of the natural order, unconnected to a spiritual world outside nature, and as such are victims of blind external or biological forces. It evolved in the nineteenth century from **realism** and was influenced by the evolutionary principles of Charles Darwin and by scientific determinism.

Neoclassicism: an artistic and literary movement that began around 1660 in France and lasted until the age of **romanticism,** at the end of the eighteenth century. Neoclassicist writers, such as John Dryden and Alexander Pope, are distinguished by their interest in order, decorum, dialectical reasoning, and a return to classical aesthetic principles.

New Criticism: a methodology for interpreting literature, made popular in America by the work of Cleanth Brooks and Robert Penn Warren, which predominated in the 1940s and 1950s. New Critics are concerned with the autonomous nature of a text and with the interplay of meaning and structure rather than with biographical or historical considerations.

Ode: a serious poem on an exalted subject, generally in an elevated style.

Onomatopoeia: words that sound like their meaning, such as "buzz," "bark," and "hiss." Sound patterns that reinforce meaning over one or more lines may also be onomatopoeic.

Open form: a form of poetry in which the sense of the second line of a couplet is completed in the next couplet.

Organic form: the way in which structure may seem to develop inherently within a text as it unifies and stabilizes the work as a whole.

Oxymoron: the juxtaposition of terms or ideas that are literally contradictory, such as "living death," "howling stillness."

Paradox: a statement that seems self-contradictory but is somehow true.

Persona: a Latin term for "mask"; the projected speaker or narrator of a text, a mask for the author.

Personification: the attribution of human qualities to nature, animals, or objects.

Picaresque: a type of fiction, generally satiric, that deals with the adventures of a roguish hero.

Poetic line: a structural unit of measurement in verse; unlike a line of prose, a poetic line need not make sense as a unit. In *metrical verse,* the length of a line is determined by the number of **feet** it contains and by the **meter** used; in *accentual verse,* by the number of accented syllables; in *syllabic verse,* by a syllable count; and in **free verse,** by units of conversational rhythm, of syntax, of breath, or of thought, or by rhetorical units.

Point of view: the perspective through which a literary work is given. With a *first-person* point of view, the narrator identifies himself or herself as "I" and is commonly the main character. With a *third-person* point of view, the narrator is outside the story and refers to characters as "he," "she," and "they." With an *omniscient* point of view, the third-person narrator knows all, can be everywhere, and can enter characters' minds.

Postmodernism: a literary and artistic philosophy that rejects all formal constraints, following the **modernism** of the early twentieth century. The postmodern artist tends to accept the world as fragmented and incoherent and to represent those characteristics in art, typically in a comic and self-reflexive style.

Proscenium arch: an arch over the front of a stage. The arch, from which a curtain typically is hung, separates the audience from the action.

Prosody: the analysis of versification, including description of **meters** and of **stanzaic forms.**

Quatrain: a stanza consisting of four lines with some pattern of rhyme; it is the most common **stanzaic form** in English.

Realism: a nineteenth-century literary philosophy that attempted to represent "real life" faithfully as the common reader might know it, partly in reaction to **romanticism.** Realism also refers to a recurrent style of writing typified by the nineteenth-century realists.

Romanticism: a wide-ranging artistic and literary movement inspired politically, by the revolutions in America and in France, and intellectually, as a reaction to the Enlightenment. Romantic works are known for their rejection of classical models, the privileging of individual experience, the celebration of imagination, and a marked interest in the artist as a hero and prophet aspiring beyond human limitation.

Satire: literature that ridicules social institutions or vices and follies.

Sestina: a complicated verse form, invented by twelfth-century French troubadours, that consists of six stanzas of six lines each and a concluding tercet, or grouping of three lines. The terminal words of the first stanza are repeated as terminal words in the succeeding stanzas, as in the tercets, in a strict but varying order.

Socratic irony: an ironic situation in which a character feigns ignorance and a desire to be enlightened by opinions that turn out to be erroneous.

Soliloquy: in drama, a speech given by a character generally alone on stage, expressing thoughts aloud.

Sonnet: a poem of fourteen lines in *iambic pentameter* (see **meter**) with a rhyme scheme.

Stanzaic form: in poetry, a structure consisting of stanzas (groupings of verse/lines), generally marked by a recurrent rhyme scheme. Typical stanzaic forms are the *couplet,* a pair of rhymed lines; the *tercet,* or *triplet,* three lines with a single rhyme; and the **quatrain,** a four-line stanza.

Stream of consciousness: a narrative technique that attempts to reproduce the uninterrupted flow of a character's mental processes; ideas and sense impressions may intermingle without logical progression.

Synecdoche: a figure of speech in which a part is substituted for the whole, or vice-versa, such as "wheels" for "car" or "copper" for "penny."

Synesthesia: the description of one type of sensory experience in terms of another: for example, sound might be described in terms of color, as in "the trumpet's red blare."

Tone: the author's attitude—playful, serious, somber, ironic, and so on—revealed through language, atmosphere, and mood.

Transcendentalism: in American literature, a nonsystematic nineteenth-century philosophy that holds that all of creation is spiritual in nature and is best known through the intuitive rather than the rational mind. Largely developed by Ralph Waldo Emerson and derived from the work of Immanuel Kant and of Thomas Carlyle, among others, it was seen by many as a threat to traditional Christianity because of its pantheistic strain.

Unity: the sense that the aspects of a play form a unified entity: the *"three unities,"* as defined by Aristotle, are *unity of time* (the play's action occurring in one day), *unity of place* (in one setting), and *unity of action* (in an orderly manner leading toward the plot's resolution).

Vorticism: an artistic movement, begun in the early twentieth century, that relates art forms to the machine and to modern industrial civilization. Regarding lifelike representation as unnecessary, it insists upon an imaginative reconstruction of nature in mechanistic designs, aligning it with cubism and futurism.

Acknowledgments

Edward Albee. *The Zoo Story* by Edward Albee, copyright © 1960 by Edward Albee is reprinted by permission of The Putnam Publishing Group. *The Zoo Story* is the sole property of the author and is fully protected by copyright. It may not be acted either by professionals or amateurs without written consent. Public readings, radio and television broadcasts likewise are forbidden. All enquiries concerning these rights should be addressed to the William Morris Agency, 1350 Avenue of the Americas, New York, NY 10019.

Paula Gunn Allen. "C'Koy'u, Old Woman," "Pocahontas to Her English Husband, John Rolfe," "Coyote Jungle," "Weed," "Myth/Telling—Dream/Showing" from *Skins and Bones* by Paula Gunn Allen. West End Press, Inc., 1988.

A. R. Ammons. "So I Said I Am Ezra," "Apologia Pro Vita Sua," "Coon Song," "Laser," "He Held Radical Light," "Winter Saint" reprinted from *Collected Poems, 1951–1971*, by A. R. Ammons, by permission of W. W. Norton & Company, Inc. Copyright © 1972 by A. R. Ammons.

Sherwood Anderson. "Adventure" from *Winesburg, Ohio* by Sherwood Anderson. Copyright 1919 by B. W. Huebsch. Copyright renewed 1947 by Eleanor Copenhaver Anderson. Reprinted by permission of Viking Penguin, a division of Penguin Books USA Inc. "Death in the Woods" from *Death in the Woods and Other Stories*. Reprinted by permission of Harold Ober Associates Incorporated. Copyright 1926 by The American Mercury Inc. Copyright renewed 1953 by Eleanor Copenhaver Anderson.

Maya Angelou. From *I Know Why The Caged Bird Sings*. Copyright © 1969 by Maya Angelou. Reprinted by permission of Random House, Inc.

John Ashbery. "Some Trees," "The Painter," "Rivers and Mountains," "For John Clare," "Farm Implements and Rutabagas in a Landscape," "Scheherazade," "Wet Casements," "The Ice-Cream Wars," "My Erotic Double," "Some Old Tires" from *Selected Poems* by John Ashbery. Copyright © 1985 by John Ashbery. "Forgotten Sex," "Someone You Have," "Frost" from *April Galleons* by John Ashbery. Copyright © 1984, 1985, 1986, 1987 by John Ashbery. Reprinted by permission of the publisher, Viking Penguin, a division of Penguin Books USA Inc.

James Baldwin. "Sonny's Blues" from *Going to Meet the Man* by James Baldwin. Copyright © 1957 by James Baldwin. Reprinted with permission of Doubleday, a division of Bantam, Doubleday, Dell Publishing Company, Inc.

Amiri Baraka. "I Substitute for the Dead Lecturer" and "Political Poem" from *The Dead Lecturer* by Amiri Baraka. Copyright © 1964 by Amiri Baraka. Reprinted by permission of Sterling Lord Literistic, Inc. "Evil Nigger" and "Legacy" from *Black Magic: 1961–1967* by Amiri Baraka. Copyright © 1969 by Amiri Baraka. Reprinted by permission of Sterling Lord Literistic, Inc. "In Memory of Radio," "A Poem for Black Hearts," "A Poem for Speculative Hipsters," "Preface to a Twenty Volume Suicide Note" from *Selected Poetry of Amiri Baraka/LeRoi Jones* by Amiri Baraka. Copyright © 1979 by Amiri Baraka. Reprinted by permission of William Morrow & Co.

Saul Bellow. *Seize the Day* by Saul Bellow. Copyright © 1956, renewed 1984 by Saul Bellow. Reprinted by permission of the publisher, Viking Penguin, a division of Penguin Books USA Inc.

John Berryman. "The Statue," "The Ball Poem," "The Song of the Tortured Girl" from *Short Poems* by John Berryman. Copyright 1948 by John Berryman, renewal copyright © 1972 by Kate Berryman. Poems 1, 14, 18, 29, 40, 76, 77, 127, 153, 157, 187, 366 from *The Dream Songs* by John Berryman. Copyright © 1959, 1962, 1963, 1964, 1965, 1966, 1967, 1968, 1969 by John Berryman. "Henry's Understanding" from *Delusions, Etc.*, by John Berryman. Copyright © 1969, 1971 by John Berryman. "I didn't. And I didn't" from *Henry's Fate* by John Berryman. Copyright © 1975, 1976, 1977 by Kate Berryman. Reprinted by permission of Farrar, Straus & Giroux, Inc.

Elizabeth Bishop. "The Map," "The Imaginary Iceberg," "The Bight," "The Shampoo," "Questions of Travel," "Sestina," "Poem," "In the Waiting Room," "The Moose," "One Art" from *The Complete Poems, 1927–1979* by Elizabeth Bishop. Copyright 1935, 1936, 1949, © 1956, 1963, 1964, 1971, 1972, 1976, 1978 by Elizabeth Bishop. Copyright © 1979, 1983 by Alice Helen Methfessel. Reprinted by permission of Farrar, Straus & Giroux, Inc.

Louise Bogan. "Women," "Cassandra," "For a Marriage," "Sonnet," "Single Sonnet," "Italian Morning," "The Sleeping Fury," "Evening in the Sanitarium," "Song for the Last Act," "The Dragonfly," "Night" from *The Blue Estuaries* by Louise Bogan. Copyright 1923, 1929, 1930, 1931, 1933, 1934, 1935, 1936, 1937, 1938, 1941, 1949, 1951, 1952, 1954, © 1957, 1958, 1962, 1963, 1964, 1965, 1966, 1967, 1968 by Louise Bogan. Reprinted by permission of Farrar, Straus & Giroux, Inc.

Gwendolyn Brooks. "Southeast Corner," "The Mother," "A Song in the Front Yard," "Sadie and Maud," "Of DeWitt Williams on His Way to Lincoln Cemetery," "The Bean Eaters," "We Real Cool," "The Lovers of the Poor" from *Blacks* by Gwendolyn Brooks. Copyright © 1987 by The David Company, Chicago. Published by The David Company.

Raymond Carver. "Cathedral" from *Cathedral* by Raymond Carver. Copyright © 1981 by Raymond Carver. Reprinted by permission of Alfred A. Knopf, Inc.

Willa Cather. From *My Antonia* by Willa Cather. Copyright 1918 by Willa Sibert Cather, renewed 1946 by Willa Sibert Cather. Copyright 1926 by Willa Sibert Cather, renewed 1954 by Edith Lewis. Copyright 1949 by Houghton Mifflin Company. Copyright © renewed 1977 by Bertha Handlan. Reprinted by permission of Houghton Mifflin Company. "Peter" reprinted from *Willa Cather's Collected Short Fiction, 1892–1912*, edited by Virginia Faulkner, Introduction by Mildred R. Bennett, by permission of University of Nebraska Press. Copyright © 1965, 1970 by the University of Nebraska Press.

Raymond Chandler. "Red Wind" from *The Midnight Raymond Chandler* by Raymond Chandler. Copyright © 1971 by Helga Greene, Executrix. Copyright 1933, 1937, 1939, 1949, 1950, © 1959 by Raymond Chandler. Copyright in "Red Wind" renewed 1965 by Popular Publications. Reprinted by permission of Houghton Mifflin Company.

John Cheever. "The Enormous Radio" from *The Stories of John Cheever*. Copyright 1947 by John Cheever. Reprinted by permission of Alfred A. Knopf, Inc.

Charles W. Chesnutt. "Sis' Becky's Pickaninny" from *The Conjure Woman* by Charles W. Chesnutt. Ann Arbor, Mich.: The University of Michigan Press, 1969, pp. 132–61. Reprinted by permission.

Kate Chopin. "The Storm" from *The Complete Works of Kate Chopin*, edited by Per Seyersted. Copyright © 1969 by Louisiana State University Press. Reprinted by permission of Louisiana State University Press.

Hart Crane. "Legend," "Emblems of Conduct," "My Grandmother's Love Letters," "Chaplinesque," "Passage," "At Melville's Tomb," "Voyages," "To Brooklyn Bridge," "The River," "The Tunnel," "The Broken Tower" from *The Poems of Hart Crane*, edited by Marc Simon. Copyright © 1986 by Marc Simon. Reprinted by permission of Liveright Publishing Corporation.

Stephen Crane. From *The Works of Stephen Crane*, edited by Fredson Bowers and published by the University Press of Virginia: "Maggie" in *Bowery Tales*, Vol. I, 1969. "The Open Boat" and "The Bride Comes to Yellow Sky" in *Tales of Adventure*, Vol. V, 1970. "Stephen Crane's Own Story" in *Reports of War*, Vol. IX, No. 17, 1971. "An Illusion in Red and White" in *Tales, Sketches, and Reports*, Vol. VIII, No. 36, 1973. Poems 1, 9, 14, 24, 30, 31, 35, 46 in *The Black Riders and Other Lines*, Vol. X, 1975. Poems 69, 81, 89 in *War Is Kind Poems and Literary Remains*, Vol. X, 1975.

Countee Cullen. "Heritage" (excerpts) from *On These I Stand* by Countee Cullen. Copyright 1925 by Harper & Brothers; renewed 1953 by Ida M. Cullen. Reprinted by permission of GRM Associates, Inc., Agents for the Estate of Ida M. Cullen.

E. E. Cummings. "my love"; "All in green went my love riding"; "Buffalo Bill's"; "Spring is like a perhaps hand" Reprinted from *Tulips & Chimneys* by E. E. Cummings, Edited by George James Firmage, by permission of Liveright Publishing Corporation. Copyright 1923, 1925, and renewed 1951, 1953 by E. E. Cummings. Copyright © 1973, 1976 by the Trustees for the E. E. Cummings Trust. Copyright © 1973, 1976 by George James Firmage. "Anyone lived in a pretty how town"; "these children singing in stone a"; "as freedom is a breakfastfood" Reprinted from *Complete Poems, 1913–1962* by E. E. Cummings, by permission of Liveright Publishing Corporation. Copyright 1923, 1925, 1931, 1935, 1938, 1939, 1940, 1944, 1945, 1946, 1947, 1948, 1949, 1950, 1951, 1952, 1953, 1954, 1955, 1956, 1957, 1958, 1959, 1960, 1961, 1962 by the Trustees for the E.E. Cummings Trust. Copyright © 1961, 1963, 1968 by Marion Morehouse Cummings. "somewhere i have never travelled,gladly beyond" is reprinted from *ViVa*, poems by E. E. Cummings, Edited by George James Firmage, by permission of Liveright Publishing Corporation. Copyright 1931, 1959 by E. E. Cummings. Copyright © 1979, 1973, by the Trustees for the E. E. Cummings Trust. Copyright © 1979, 1973 by George James Firmage. "next to of course god america i" is reprinted from *IS 5* poems by E. E. Cummings, Edited by George James Firmage, by permission of Liveright Publishing Corporation. Copyright © 1985 by E. E. Cummings Trust. Copyright 1926 by Horace Liveright. Copyright © 1954 by E. E. Cummings. Copyright © 1985 by George James Firmage.

Emily Dickinson. Letters reprinted by permission of the publishers from *The Letters of Emily Dickinson,* edited by Thomas H. Johnson, Cambridge, Mass.: The Belknap Press of Harvard University Press. Copyright © 1958, 1986 by the President and Fellows of Harvard College. Poems reprinted by permission of the publishers and the Trustees of Amherst College from *The Poems of Emily Dickinson,* edited by Thomas H. Johnson, Cambridge, Mass.: The Belknap Press of Harvard University Press. Copyright 1951, © 1955, 1979, 1983 by the President and Fellows of Harvard College.

Joan Didion. "When Did Music Come This Way?" from *Telling Stories* by Joan Didion. Copyright © 1967 by Joan Didion. Reprinted by permission of the Wallace Literary Agency, Inc.

Hilda Doolittle (H.D.). "Pear Tree," "At Baia," "Evadne," "Helen," "Fragment Sixty-Eight," "Stars Wheel in Purple," "If You Take the Moon in Your Hands," "The Mysteries Remain" from *H.D.: The Collected Poems, 1912–1944.* Copyright © 1982 by The Estate of Hilda Doolittle. Reprinted by permission of New Directions Publishing Corporation.

John Dos Passos. From *The Big Money,* with permission of Elizabeth H. Dos Passos, co-executor, Estate of John Dos Passos.

Theodore Dreiser. "The Second Choice" from *Free and Other Stories* by Theodore Dreiser. Reprinted by permission of The Dreiser Trust, 1918.

T. S. Eliot. "The Love Song of J. Alfred Prufrock," "Cousin Nancy," "La Figlia Che Piange," "Sweeney Among the Nightingales," "The Waste Land," "Journey of the Magi," "Marina" from *Collected Poems 1909–1962* by T. S. Eliot, copyright 1936 by Harcourt Brace Jovanovich, Inc., copyright © 1964, 1963 by T. S. Eliot, reprinted by permission of the publisher. Reprinted by permission of Faber and Faber Ltd. "East Coker," from *Four Quartets,* copyright 1943 by T. S. Eliot and renewed © 1971 by Esme Valerie Eliot, reprinted by permission of Harcourt Brace Jovanovich, Inc. Reprinted by permission of Faber and Faber Ltd.

Ralph Ellison. From *Invisible Man* by Ralph Ellison. Copyright 1952 by Ralph Ellison. Reprinted by permission of Random House, Inc.

Louise Erdrich. From *Jacklight* by Louise Erdrich. Copyright © 1984 by Louise Erdrich. Reprinted by permission of Henry Holt and Company, Inc.

William Faulkner. "A Rose for Emily" and "That Evening Sun" from *Collected Stories of William Faulkner* by William Faulkner. Copyright 1950 by Random House, Inc. Reprinted by permission of Random House, Inc.

F. Scott Fitzgerald. "Babylon Revisited" from *Taps At Reveille* by F. Scott Fitzgerald. Copyright 1931 by The Curtis Publishing Company; renewal copyright © 1959 by Frances Scott Fitzgerald Lanahan. Reprinted with permission of Charles Scribner's Sons, an imprint of Macmillan Publishing Company.

Robert Frost. "The Pasture," "Mowing," "Mending Wall," "Home Burial," "After Apple-Picking," "The Wood-Pile," "An Old Man's Winter Night," "The Oven Bird," "Birches," "Putting in the Seed," "Locked Out," " 'Out,Out—'," "Dust of Snow," "Nothing Gold Can Stay," "For Once, Then Something," "Stopping By Woods on a Snowy Evening," "The Need of Being Versed in Country Things," "Spring Pools," "Fireflies in the Garden," "Once by the Pacific," "Acquainted With the Night," "What Fifty Said," "The Bear," "Desert Places," "Design," "Provide, Provide," "The Silken Tent," "Come In," "Never Again Would Birds' Song Be the Same," "Directive" from *The Poetry of Robert Frost,* edited by Edward Connery Lathem. Copyright 1916, 1923, 1928, 1930, 1934, 1939, 1947, © 1967, 1969 by Holt, Rinehart and Winston. Copyright 1936, 1942, 1944, 1951, © 1956, 1958, 1962 by Robert Frost. Copyright © 1964, 1967, 1970, 1975 by Lesley Frost Ballantine. "The Road Not Taken" from *The Poetry of Robert Frost,* edited by Edward Connery Lathem. Copyright 1930, 1939, © 1969 by Holt, Rinehart and Winston. Copyright © 1967 by Lesley Frost Ballantine. Copyright © 1958 by Robert Frost. All reprinted by permission of Henry Holt and Company, Inc.

William Gass. *In the Heart of the Heart of the Country* by William Gass. Copyright © 1967 by William Gass. Reprinted by permission of International Creative Management, Inc.

Allen Ginsberg. "Howl," "Footnote to Howl," "A Supermarket in California," "America," "Ode to Failure" from *Collected Poems 1947–1980* by Allen Ginsberg. Copyright © 1955, 1956, 1959, 1984 by Allen Ginsberg. Reprinted by permission of Harper & Row, Publishers, Inc.

Louise Glück. "Cottonmouth Country" from *Firstborn* by Louise Glück, first published by The Ecco Press in 1983. Copyright © 1968 by Louise Glück. "All Hallows" and "Gretel in Darkness" from *The House on Marshland* by Louise Glück, first published by The Ecco Press in 1975. Copyright © 1971, 1972, 1973, 1974, 1975 by Louise Glück. "Dedication to Hunger," "The Drowned Children," "Palais des Arts" from *Descending Figure* by Louise Glück, first published by The Ecco Press in 1980. Copyright © 1976, 1977, 1978, 1979, 1980 by Louise Glück. "Elms," "Horse," "Mythic Fragment" from *The Triumph of Achilles* by Louise Glück, first published by The Ecco Press in 1985. Copyright © 1985 by Louise Glück. All reprinted by permission of The Ecco Press.

Lorraine Hansberry. *A Raisin In the Sun* by Lorraine Hansberry. Copyright © 1958 by Robert

Nemiroff, as an unpublished work. Copyright © 1959, 1966, 1984 by Robert Nemiroff. Reprinted by permission of Random House, Inc.

Robert Hass. "Song" from *Field Guide* by Robert Hass. Copyright © 1973 by Robert Hass. Reprinted by permission of Yale University Press. "Meditation at Lagunitas," "Heroic Simile," "Sunrise," "The Yellow Bicycle" from *Praise* by Robert Hass, first published by The Ecco Press in 1979. Copyright © 1974, 1975, 1976, 1977, 1978, 1979 by Robert Hass. Reprinted by permission. "Spring Drawing" from *Human Wishes* by Robert Hass, first published by The Ecco Press in 1989. Copyright © 1989 by Robert Hass. Reprinted by permission.

Robert Hayden. "Those Winter Nights," " 'Mystery Boy' Looks for Kin," "Runagate Runagate," "A Road in Kentucky" from *Angle of Ascent* by Robert Hayden, by permission of Liveright Publishing Corporation. Copyright © 1975, 1972, 1970, 1966 by Robert Hayden. "Frederick Douglass" and "Bone-Flower Elegy" from *Collected Poems of Robert Hayden,* edited by Frederick Glaysher, by permission of Liveright Publishing Corporation. Copyright © 1985 by Erma Hayden.

Ernest Hemingway. "Big Two-Hearted River" from *In Our Time* by Ernest Hemingway. Copyright 1925 by Charles Scribner's Sons, renewal copyright 1953 by Ernest Hemingway. Reprinted with permission of Charles Scribner's Sons, an imprint of Macmillan Publishing Company.

William Dean Howells. Excerpts from *Literary Friends and Acquaintance,* Copyright © 1968 by W. D. Howells. Reprinted by permission of the Indiana University Press.

Langston Hughes. From *Selected Poems of Langston Hughes:* "The Negro Speaks of Rivers," "The Weary Blues," "Dream Variations," "Epilogue" Copyright 1926 by Alfred A. Knopf, Inc. and renewed 1954 by Langston Hughes. "Fire" Copyright 1927 by Alfred A. Knopf, Inc. and renewed 1955 by Langston Hughes. "Sylvester's Dying Bed" Copyright 1942 by Alfred A. Knopf, Inc. "Madam's Past History" and "Madam and the Minister" Copyright 1948 by Alfred A. Knopf, Inc. "Trumpet Player" Copyright 1947 by Langston Hughes. "Afro-American Fragment" Copyright 1959 by Langston Hughes. All reprinted by permission of Alfred A. Knopf, Inc. "Theme for English B," "Dream Boogie," "Sister" Copyright 1951 by Langston Hughes. Copyright renewed © 1979 by George Houston Bass. Reprinted by permission of Harold Ober Associates Inc. "Harlem" from *The Panther and the Lash* by Langston Hughes. Copyright 1951 by Langston Hughes. Reprinted by permission of Alfred A. Knopf, Inc. "Thank You, M'am" from *The Langston Hughes Reader.* Copyright © 1958 by Langston Hughes. Copyright renewed © 1986 by George Houston Bass. Reprinted by permission of Harold Ober Associates Inc. "Feet Live Their Own Life" from *The Best of Simple* by Langston Hughes. Copyright © 1961 by Langston Hughes. Reprinted by permission of Hill and Wang, a division of Farrar, Straus & Giroux, Inc.

Zora Neale Hurston. "The Gilded Six-Bits" from *Spunk: The Selected Stories of Zora Neale Hurston.* Reprinted with permission of Turtle Island Foundation, 1985. "How It Feels to Be Colored Me" from *I Love Myself—A Zora Neale Hurston Reader,* edited by Alice Walker. Reprinted with permission of Clifford Hurston, 1985.

Lawson Inada. "From Our Album," "In a Storm," "Utica, North Platte," "Wintersong" from *Before the War* by Lawson Inada. Copyright © 1971 by Lawson Inada. Reprinted by permission of William Morrow & Co.

Randall Jarrell. "The Death of the Ball Turret Gunner" and "90 North" from *The Complete Poems* by Randall Jarrell. Copyright 1941, 1945 and renewal copyright © 1968, 1972 by Mrs. Randall Jarrell. Reprinted by permission of Farrar, Straus & Giroux, Inc. "Bats" from *The Bat-Poet* by Randall Jarrell. Copyright © 1963, 1964 by Macmillan Publishing Company. Reprinted with permission of Macmillan Publishing Company. "Next Day" from *The Lost World* by Randall Jarrell. Copyright © 1963, 1965 by Randall Jarrell. Reprinted with permission of Macmillan Publishing Company. Originally appeared in *The New Yorker.* "Well Water" From *The Lost World* by Randall Jarrell. Copyright © 1965 by Randall Jarrell. Reprinted with permission of Macmillan Publishing Company. "The Woman at the Washington Zoo" reprinted by permission of Mary Jarrell for the Estate of Randall Jarrell, 1969.

Martin Luther King, Jr. Excerpts from *I Have a Dream . . . The Life and Times of Martin Luther King, Jr.,* by Lenwood G. Davis. Copyright © 1969 by Lenwood G. Davis.

Maxine Hong Kingston. "No Name Woman" from *The Woman Warrior: Memoirs of a Girlhood Among Ghosts* by Maxine Hong Kingston. Copyright © 1975, 1976 by Maxine Hong Kingston. Reprinted by permission of Alfred A. Knopf, Inc.

Galway Kinnell. "The Bear" from *Body Rags* by Galway Kinnell. Copyright © 1965, 1966, 1967 by Galway Kinnell. "Little Sleep's Head Sprouting Hair in the Moonlight" from *The Book of Nightmares* by Galway Kinnell. Copyright © 1971 by Galway Kinnell. "Daybreak" and "St. Francis and the Sow" from *Mortal Acts, Mortal Words* by Galway Kinnell. Copyright © 1980 by Galway Kinnell. All reprinted by permission of Houghton Mifflin Company.

Maxine Kumin. "Woodchucks," "The Longing to Be Saved," "The Envelope," "How It Is," "The Grace of Geldings in Ripe Pastures," "Family Reunion," "Morning Swim" from *Our Ground*

Time Here Will Be Brief by Maxine Kumin. Copyright © 1965, 1971, 1975, 1976, 1977, 1981 by Maxine Kumin. "How It Is" and "The Longing to Be Saved" originally appeared in *The New Yorker*. Reprinted by permission of Viking Penguin, a division of Penguin Books USA Inc.

Stanley Kunitz. "The Abduction" and "Passing Through" from *Next-to-Last Things* by Stanley Kunitz. Copyright © 1985 by Stanley Kunitz. Used by permission of Atlantic Monthly Press. "How Long Is the Night" and "Father and Son" from *Selected Poems 1928–1958* by Stanley Kunitz. Copyright 1929, 1930, 1936, 1944, 1951, 1953, 1954, © 1957, 1958 by Stanley Kunitz. By permission of Little, Brown and Company. "Portrait," "The Quarrel," "An Old Cracked Tune," "Quinnapoxet," "The Testing Tree" from *The Poems of Stanley Kunitz 1928–1978* by Stanley Kunitz. Copyright 1930, 1944, © 1958, 1971, 1973, 1974, 1976, 1978, 1979 by Stanley Kunitz. By permission of Little, Brown and Company.

Denise Levertov. "The Jacob's Ladder," "Matins," "The Ache of Marriage" from *Poems 1960–1967* by Denise Levertov. Copyright © 1961, 1964 by Denise Levertov Goodman. "O Taste and See" from *O Taste and See* by Denise Levertov. Copyright © 1964 by Denise Levertov Goodman. "Intrusion" from *Poems 1968–1972* by Denise Levertov. Copyright © 1972 by Denise Levertov Goodman. "Ways of Conquest" from *The Freeing of the Dust* by Denise Levertov. Copyright © 1975 by Denise Levertov. "Gathered at the River" from *Oblique Prayers* by Denise Levertov. Copyright © 1984 by Denise Levertov. All reprinted by permission of New Directions Publishing Corporation.

Robert Lowell. "Beyond the Alps," "My Last Afternoon With Uncle Devereux Winslow," "Waking in the Blue," "Memories of West Street and Lepke," "Man and Wife," "Skunk Hour," "The Mouth of the Hudson," "Eye and Tooth," "The Neo-Classical Urn," "For the Union Dead," "Reading Myself," "Dolphin" from *Selected Poems* by Robert Lowell. Copyright 1944, 1946, 1947, 1950, 1951, © 1956, 1960, 1961, 1962, 1963, 1964, 1965, 1966, 1967, 1968, 1969, 1970, 1973, 1976 by Robert Lowell. Renewal copyright 1972, 1974, 1975 by Robert Lowell. "Water 1948" from *Notebook, Revised and Expanded Edition* by Robert Lowell. Copyright © 1967, 1968, 1969, 1970 by Robert Lowell. "Epilogue" from *Day by Day* by Robert Lowell. Copyright © 1977 by Robert Lowell. Reprinted by permission of Farrar, Straus & Giroux, Inc. "The Quaker Graveyard in Nantucket" and "Mr. Edwards and the Spider" from *Lord Weary's Castle* by Robert Lowell. Copyright 1946 and renewed © 1974 by Robert Lowell. Reprinted by permission of Harcourt Brace Jovanovich, Inc.

Norman Mailer. From *The Armies of the Night* by Norman Mailer. Copyright © 1968 by Norman Mailer. Reprinted by permission of the publisher, New American Library, a division of Penguin Books USA Inc.

Bernard Malamud. From *The Magic Barrel* by Bernard Malamud. Copyright 1954 and renewal copyright © 1982 by Bernard Malamud. Reprinted by permission of Farrar, Straus & Giroux, Inc.

James Merrill. "Charles on Fire" from *Nights and Days* by James Merrill. Copyright © 1960, 1961, 1962, 1963, 1964, 1965, 1966 by James Merrill. "The Broken Home" from *Nights and Days* by James Merrill. Copyright © 1965, 1966. Originally appeared in *The New Yorker*. "The Victor Dog" from *Braving the Elements* by James Merrill. Copyright © 1969, 1970, 1971, 1972 by James Merrill. All reprinted with permission of Atheneum Publishers, an imprint of Macmillan Publishing Company. "Farewell Performance" from *The Inner Room* by James Merrill. Copyright © 1988 by James Merrill. Reprinted by permission of Alfred A. Knopf, Inc.

W. S. Merwin. "Ballad of John Cable and Three Gentlemen" from *A Mask for Janus* by W. S. Merwin. Copyright 1952, © 1956, 1957, 1958, 1959, 1960, 1963, 1967. "The Drunk in the Furnace," "Grandmother Dying," "One-Eye" from *The Drunk in the Furnace* by W. S. Merwin. Copyright 1952, © 1956, 1957, 1958, 1959, 1960, 1963, 1967. Reprinted by permission of Georges Borchardt Inc. and the author. "The Animals," "The Dry Stone Mason," "For the Anniversary of My Death" from *The Lice* by W. S. Merwin. Copyright 1952, © 1956, 1957, 1958, 1959, 1960, 1963, 1967. Reprinted by permission of Georges Borchardt Inc. "The Judgment of Paris" from *The Carrier of Ladders* by W. S. Merwin. Copyright © 1970 by W. S. Merwin. Originally appeared in *The New Yorker*. "Flies" from *Writings to an Unfinished Accompaniment* by W. S. Merwin. Copyright © 1969, 1970, 1971, 1972, 1973 by W. S. Merwin. "A Contemporary" from *The Compass Flower* by W. S. Merwin. Copyright © 1977 by W. S. Merwin. "Berryman" from *Opening the Hand* by W. S. Merwin. Copyright © 1983 by W. S. Merwin. All reprinted with permission of Atheneum Publishers, an imprint of Macmillan Publishing Company. "Thanks" and "Travelling Together" from *The Rain in the Trees* by W. S. Merwin. Copyright © 1988 by W. S. Merwin. Reprinted by permission of Alfred A. Knopf, Inc.

Arthur Miller. *Death of a Salesman* Copyright 1949 by Arthur Miller. Reprinted by permission of International Creative Management, Inc.

N. Scott Momaday. *The Way to Rainy Mountain* by N. Scott Momaday. Copyright © 1969, The University of New Mexico Press. Reprinted with permission.

Marianne Moore. "Bowls," "A Grave," "In the Days of Prismatic Color," "Nine Nectarines,"

"Poetry," "Silence," "When I Buy Pictures" from *Collected Poems* by Marianne Moore. Copyright 1935 by Marianne Moore, renewed © 1963 by Marianne Moore and T. S. Eliot. Reprinted with permission of Macmillan Publishing Company. "The Paper Nautilus" and "What Are Years?" from *Collected Poems* by Marianne Moore. Copyright 1941, and renewed © 1969 by Marianne Moore. Reprinted with permission of Macmillan Publishing Company. "The Animals Sick of the Plague," "A Jelly-Fish," "Baseball and Writing," "The Steeple-Jack" from *The Complete Poems of Marianne Moore.* Copyright © 1959 and 1961 by Marianne Moore. Reprinted by permission of the publisher, Viking Penguin, a division of Penguin Books USA Inc.

Toni Morrison. From *Song of Solomon* by Toni Morrison. Copyright © 1977 by Toni Morrison. Reprinted by permission of Alfred A. Knopf, Inc.

Joyce Carol Oates. "Where Are You Going, Where Have You Been?" from *Wheel of Love and Other Stories* by Joyce Carol Oates. Copyright © 1965 by Joyce Carol Oates. Reprinted by permission of John Hawkins & Associates, Inc.

Flannery O'Connor. "A Good Man Is Hard to Find" and "The Artificial Nigger" from *A Good Man Is Hard to Find and Other Stories.* Copyright 1953, © 1955 by Flannery O'Connor and renewed 1981, 1983 by Regina O'Connor. Reprinted by permission of Harcourt Brace Jovanovich, Inc.

Eugene O'Neill. *Desire Under the Elms* from *The Plays of Eugene O'Neill.* Copyright 1924 and renewed 1952 by Eugene O'Neill. Reprinted by permission of Random House, Inc.

Simon J. Ortiz. "Grief" and "The Sky Is Brilliant" from *From Sand Creek* by Simon J. Ortiz. Copyright © 1981 by Simon J. Ortiz. Used by permission of the publisher, Thunder's Mouth Press. "Dry Root in a Wash," "A Story of How a Wall Stands," "Wind and Glacier Voices," "The Creation, According to Coyote" from *Going for the Rain,* 1976 by Simon J. Ortiz. Reprinted by permission of the author.

Robert Pinsky. "The Unseen," "The Volume," "The Living," "The Changes," "The Saving" from *History of My Heart* by Robert Pinsky. Copyright © 1984 by Robert Pinsky. First published by The Ecco Press in 1984. Reprinted by permission.

Sylvia Plath. "You're," "The Hanging Man," "Tulips," "Blackberrying," "The Moon and the Yew Tree," "The Bee Meeting," "Daddy," "Lady Lazarus," "Ariel," "Nick and the Candlestick," "Edge" from *The Collected Poems of Sylvia Plath,* edited by Ted Hughes. Copyright © 1960, 1962, 1963, 1965, 1966 by Ted Hughes. Reprinted by permission of Harper & Row, Publishers, Inc. Published by Faber & Faber, London. Copyright © Ted Hughes 1965 and 1981, by permission of Olwyn Hughes.

Katherine Anne Porter. "Flowering Judas" from *Flowering Judas and Other Stories* by Katherine Ann Porter. Copyright 1930 and renewed © 1958 by Katherine Ann Porter. Reprinted by permission of Harcourt Brace Jovanovich, Inc.

Ezra Pound. "The Tree," "Sestina: Altaforte," "Portrait d'une Femme," "The Seafarer," "The Return," "Tenzone," "The Garden," "Les Millwin," "Liu Ch'e," "In a Station of the Metro," "The River Merchant's Wife: A Letter," "Lament of the Frontier Guard," "Hugh Selwyn Mauberley" from *Personae* by Ezra Pound. Copyright 1926 by Ezra Pound. Cantos I, IV, LXXI from *The Cantos of Ezra Pound.* Copyright 1934, 1948 by Ezra Pound. All reprinted by permission of New Directions Publishing Corporation.

John Crowe Ransom. "Vision by Sweetwater" from *Selected Poems, Third Edition, Revised and Enlarged* by John Crowe Ransom. Copyright 1927 by Alfred A. Knopf Inc. and renewed 1955 by John Crowe Ransom. Reprinted by permission of the publisher.

Adrienne Rich. "Toward the Solstice" from *The Dream of a Common Language, Poems 1974–1977* by Adrienne Rich. Copyright © 1978 by W. W. Norton & Company, Inc. "Living in Sin," "The Diamond Cutters," "Snapshots of a Daughter-in-Law," "Face to Face," "I Dream I'm the Death of Orpheus," "Orion," "A Valediction Forbidding Mourning," "From a Survivor" from *The Fact of a Doorframe, Poems Selected and New, 1950–1984* by Adrienne Rich. Copyright © 1984 by Adrienne Rich. Copyright © 1975, 1978 by W. W. Norton & Company, Inc. Copyright © 1981 by Adrienne Rich. "In Memorium: D. K." from *Time's Power, Poems 1985–1988* by Adrienne Rich. Copyright © 1989 by Adrienne Rich. All reprinted by permission of W. W. Norton & Company, Inc.

Alberto Ríos. From *Whispering to Fool the Wind* by Alberto Ríos. Copyright © 1982 by Alberto Ríos. Reprinted by permission of the author.

Tomás Rivera. Excerpts from *. . . y no se lo trago la tierra/[and the earth did not devour him]* by Tomás Rivera, trans. by Evangelina Vigil-Pinon. Houston: Arte Publico Press, University of Houston, 1987. Reprinted with permission of the Press.

Edwin Arlington Robinson. From *Collected Poems* by Edwin Arlington Robinson: "Veteran Sirens" Copyright 1916, by Edwin Arlington Robinson, renewed 1944, by Ruth Nivison. "Mr. Flood's Party" copyright 1921 by Edwin Arlington Robinson, renewed 1949 by Ruth Nivison. "Why He Was There" Copyright 1925 by Edwin Arlington Robinson, renewed 1953 by Ruth Nivison and Barbara R. Holt. All reprinted with permission of Macmillan Publishing Company.

Theodore Roethke. *From The Collected Poems of Theodore Roethke:* "The Waking," "Elegy for Jane," "Night Journey," "I Knew a Woman," "The Lost Son," "The Open House," "My Papa's Waltz," "Myrtle" Copyright 1940, 1941, 1942, 1947, 1950, 1952, 1953, 1954 by Theodore Roethke. "Root Cellar" Copyright 1943 by Modern Poetry Association, Inc. "In a Dark Time" Copyright © 1960 by Beatrice Roethke, Administratrix of the Estate of Theodore Roethke. "The Kitty-Cat Bird" Copyright © 1966 by Beatrice Roethke. All poems used by permission of Doubleday, a division of Bantam, Doubleday, Dell Publishing Groups, Inc.

Philip Roth. From *Goodbye Columbus* by Philip Roth. Copyright © 1959 by Philip Roth. Reprinted by permission of Houghton Mifflin Company.

Carl Sandburg. "Chicago" from *Chicago Poems* by Carl Sandburg. Copyright 1916 by Holt, Rinehart & Winston, Inc. and renewed 1944 by Carl Sandburg. Reprinted by permission of Harcourt Brace Jovanovich, Inc. "Cool Tombs," "River Roads," "Grass," "Gargoyle" from *Cornhuskers* by Carl Sandburg. Copyright 1918 by Holt, Rinehart & Winston, Inc. and renewed 1946 by Carl Sandburg. Reprinted by permission of Harcourt Brace Jovanovich, Inc. "Prayer After World War," "Aprons of Silence," "They All Want to Play Hamlet" from *Smoke And Steel* by Carl Sandburg. Copyright 1920 by Harcourt Brace Jovanovich, Inc. and renewed 1948 by Carl Sandburg. Reprinted by permission of the publisher. "Love in Labrador" from *Good Morning, America* by Carl Sandburg. Copyright 1928 and renewed © 1956 by Carl Sandburg. Reprinted by permission of Harcourt Brace Jovanovich, Inc.

Anne Sexton. "Kind Sir: These Woods," and "Her Kind" from *To Bedlam and Part Way Back* by Anne Sexton. Copyright © 1960 by Anne Sexton. "All My Pretty Ones" and "The Truth the Dead Know" from *All My Pretty Ones* by Anne Sexton. Copyright © 1962 by Anne Sexton. "Us" and "For My Lover, Returning to His Wife" from *Love Poems* by Anne Sexton. Copyright © 1967, 1968, 1969 by Anne Sexton. "The Fury of Beautiful Bones" from *Death Notebooks* by Anne Sexton. Copyright © 1974 by Anne Sexton. All reprinted by permission of Houghton Mifflin Company.

Leslie Marmon Silko. From *Storyteller* by Leslie Marmon Silko. Copyright © 1981 by Leslie Marmon Silko. Reprinted by permission of Seaver Books, New York, New York.

Susan Sontag. Excerpts from *Against Interpretation* by Susan Sontag. Copyright © 1966 by Susan Sontag. Reprinted by permission of Farrar, Straus & Giroux, Inc.

William Stafford. From *Stories That Could Be True* by William Stafford: "Traveling Through the Dark," "A Lecture on the Elegy," "Accountability," "The Farm on the Great Plains," "The Burning House," "A Ritual to Read to Each Other," "At the Bomb Testing Sight," "The Epitaph Ending in And" Copyright © 1960, 1965, 1973, 1976, 1977 by William Stafford. "After Arguing Against the Contention . . ." from *A Glass Face in the Rain* by William Stafford. Copyright © 1978 by William Stafford. "An Oregon Message" from *An Oregon Message* by William Stafford Copyright © 1987 by William Stafford. All reprinted by permission of Harper & Row, Publisher, Inc.

Gertrude Stein. "The Gentle Lena" and excerpt from *Tender Buttons* are from *Selected Writings of Gertrude Stein*, edited, with an Introduction and Notes, by Carl Van Vechten. Copyright 1946 by Random House, Inc. Reprinted by permission of Random House, Inc.

John Steinbeck. "Flight" from *The Long Valley* by John Steinbeck. Copyright 1938, renewed © 1966 by John Steinbeck. Reprinted by permission of Viking Penguin, a division of Penguin Books USA Inc.

Wallace Stevens. Reprinted from *The Collected Poems of Wallace Stevens* by permission of Alfred A. Knopf, Inc. "Sunday Morning," "Disillusionment of Ten O'Clock," "Thirteen Ways of Looking at a Blackbird," "Nuances of a Theme by Williams," "Anecdote of the Jar," "The Snow Man," "Tea at the Palaz of Hoon," "The Emperor of Ice-Cream" copyright 1923 and renewed 1951 by Wallace Stevens. "The Idea of Order at Key West," "Mozart, 1935," "Anglais Mort à Florence," "A Postcard From the Volcano" copyright 1936 by Wallace Stevens and renewed 1964 by Holly Stevens. Excerpt from "The Man With the Blue Guitar," "Study of Two Pears," "Of Hartford in a Purple Light," "Of Modern Poetry," "Mrs. Alfred Uruguay," "Asides on the Oboe" copyright 1942 by Wallace Stevens. "The River of Rivers in Connecticut," "So-and-So Reclining on Her Couch," and excerpts from "Notes Toward a Supreme Fiction" copyright 1954 by Wallace Stevens. "Large Red Man Reading," "This Solitude of Cataracts," "Angel Surrounded by Paysans" copyright 1950 by Wallace Stevens. "To an Old Philosopher in Rome" copyright 1952 by Wallace Stevens. "The Course of a Particular," "First Warmth," "As You Leave the Room," "A Clear Day and No Memories," and "Of Mere Being" copyright © 1957 by Elsie Stevens and Holly Stevens.

Allen Tate. "Mr. Pope," "Ode to the Confederate Dead," "The Oath," "The Mediterranean," "Shadow and Shade," "Sonnets at Christmas" from *Collected Poems, 1919–1976* by Allen Tate. Copyright 1952, 1953, © 1970, 1977 by Allen Tate. Reprinted by permission of Farrar, Straus & Giroux, Inc.

Jean Toomer. Excerpts from *Cane* by Jean Toomer. Reprinted by permission of Liveright Publishing Corporation. Copyright 1923 by Boni & Liveright. Copyright renewed 1951 by Jean Toomer.

John Updike. "A & P" reprinted from *Pigeon Feathers and Other Stories* by John Updike. Copyright © 1962 by John Updike. By permission of Alfred A. Knopf, Inc. Originally appeared in *The New Yorker*.

Alice Walker. "Everyday Use" from *In Love & Trouble* by Alice Walker. Copyright © 1973 by Alice Walker. Reprinted by permission of Harcourt Brace Jovanovich, Inc.

Eudora Welty. "Petrified Man" from *A Curtain of Green and Other Stories by Eudora Welty*. Copyright 1939 and renewed © 1967 by Eudora Welty. Reprinted by permission of Harcourt Brace Jovanovich, Inc.

Walt Whitman. Reprinted by permission of New York University Press from *Walt Whitman: Leaves of Grass, Reader's Comprehensive Edition*, edited by Harold W. Blodgett and Sculley Bradley. Copyright © 1965 by New York University.

Richard Wilbur. "Bell Speech" from *The Beautiful Changes* by Richard Wilbur. Copyright 1947 and renewed © 1975 by Richard Wilbur. "The Pardon" from *Ceremony* by Richard Wilbur. Copyright 1950 and renewed © 1978 by Richard Wilbur. "Love Calls Us to the Things of This World" from *Things Of This World* by Richard Wilbur. Copyright © 1956 and renewed 1984 by Richard Wilbur. "For Dudley" from *Walking to Sleep* by Richard Wilbur. Copyright © 1969 by Richard Wilbur. "The Writer" and "To the Etruscan Poets" from *The Mind Reader* by Richard Wilbur. Copyright © 1971, 1975 by Richard Wilbur. "Lying" from *New and Collected Poems* by Richard Wilbur. Copyright © 1987 by Richard Wilbur. All reprinted by permission of Harcourt Brace Jovanovich, Inc.

Tennessee Williams. *The Glass Menagerie* by Tennessee Williams. Copyright 1945 by Tennessee Williams and Edwina D. Williams and renewed © 1973 by Tennessee Williams. Reprinted by permission of Random House, Inc.

William Carlos Williams. "Postlude," "The Young Housewife," "Tract," "El Hombre," "Portrait of a Lady," "The Late Singer," "Overture to a Dance of Locomotives," "Spring and All," "The Pot of Flowers," "The Red Wheelbarrow," "The Wildflower," "The Attic Which Is Desire," "This Is Just to Say," "The Locust Tree in Flower" (first and second versions), "Proletarian Portrait," "The Yachts," "Fine Work With Pitch and Copper," "Classic Scene," "The Last Words of My English Grandmother" from *Collected Poems, Volume I, 1909–1939* by William Carlos Williams. Copyright 1938 by New Directions Publishing Corporation. "The Dance," "Burning the Christmas Greens," "Landscape With the Fall of Icarus" from *Collected Poems, Volume II, 1939–1962* by William Carlos Williams. Copyright 1944, 1948, © 1962 by William Carlos Williams. Excerpt from *Paterson* by William Carlos Williams. Copyright 1948 by William Carlos Williams. All reprinted by permission of New Directions Publishing Corporation.

Edmund Wilson. Excerpts from *The Triple Thinkers* by Edmund Wilson. Copyright 1938, 1948 by Edmund Wilson. Renewal copyright © 1956, 1971 by Edmund Wilson and © 1976 by Elena Wilson. Reprinted by permission of Farrar, Straus & Giroux, Inc.

Yvor Winters. "The Rows of Cold Trees" and "The Slow Pacific Swell" from *The Collected Poems of Yvor Winters*. Reprinted with the permission of The Ohio University Press, Athens, 1978. "Orpheus," "On Teaching the Young," "The Manzanita," "Sir Gawaine and the Green Knight," "An Elegy," "Time and the Garden" from *The Collected Poems of Yvor Winters*. Copyright 1943 by New Directions Publishing Corporation. Reprinted by permission of New Directions Publishing Corporation.

James Wright. "Saint Judas," "All the Beautiful Are Blameless," "Arrangements With Earth," "The Angel," "Having Lost My Sons," "A Blessing," "Lying in a Hammock," "Autumn Begins in Martins Ferry," "In Response to a Rumor," "Small Frogs Killed on the Highway" from *Collected Poems* by James Wright. Copyright © 1958, 1961, 1962, 1966, 1969, 1971 by James Wright. Reprinted by permission of University Press of New England. "Wherever Home Is" from *This Journey* by James Wright. Copyright © 1982 by Anne Wright, Executrix of the Estate of James Wright. Reprinted by permission of Random House, Inc.

Richard Wright. From *Uncle Tom's Children* by Richard Wright. Copyright 1936 by Richard Wright, renewed © 1964 by Ellen Wright. Reprinted by permission of Harper & Row, Publishers, Inc.

PHOTOS AND ILLUSTRATIONS

Amistad Research Center Collection: p. 1167. AP/Wide World Photos: pp. 1014, 1120, 1338, 2146. Courtesy of The Art Institute of Chicago, Helen Birch Bartlett Memorial Collection: p. 961. Brian J. Berman: p. 2325. The Bettman Archive: pp. 16, 150, 210, 665, 811, 930, 990, 1061, 1062, 1141, 1195, 1198, 1236, 1248, 1291, 1301, 1338, 1360, 1448, 1450, 1564, 1664, 1665, 1713, 1798, 1870, 2172, 2280. Courtesy of the Chicago Historical Society: p. 8. Nancy Crampton: 1854, 2018, 2345. Culver Pictures: pp. 652, 1023. Giraudon/Art Resource: p. 1080. Eugene Gordon: p. 1397. The Henry E. Huntington Library and Art Gallery: p. 959. The Jones Library, Incorporated, Amherst, MA: p. 151. Paul Briol/Kenyon College: p. 1649. Library of Congress: pp. 4, 9, 14, 231, 251, 1275, 1319, 1320, 1714, 1992, 2172. W. E. Smith/*Life* Magazine © Time Inc.: p. 1497. Robert Capa/Magnum Photos: p. 1362. Elliott Erwitt/Magnum Photos: pp. 1402, 2258. Burt Glinn/ Magnum Photos: p. 1652. Courtesy of Masco Corporation: p. 207. Rollie McKenna: pp. 1748, 1756, 1871. Photo by Barbara McKenzie, University of Georgia Press, Athens, GA; Reproduced with permission: p. 2147. Gerard Melanga: p. 1930. Metropolitan Arts Commission, Portland, OR: p. 1924. The Metropolitan Museum of Art, Bequest of Gertrude Stein, 1946: p. 1250. Mississippi Department of Archives and History, Eudora Welty Collection: p. 2019. Missouri Historical Society: pp. 529, 531. Movie Still Archives: pp. 1993, 2259. © Maria Mulas: p. 2235. Museum of the City of New York: pp. 13, 200. NASA: p. 1399. National Archives: pp. 909, 915, 1954. National Gallery of Art, Ailsa Melon Bruce Fund 1976: p. 1846. National Portrait Gallery, Smithsonian Institution: pp. 254, 1022. Nebraska State Historical Society: p. 1237. New York Public Library: pp. 632, 668, 1340. Theatre Collection, New York Public Library at Lincoln Center; Astor, Lenox and Tilden Foundations: p. 1408. Philadelphia Museum of Art, Louise and Walter Arensberg Collection: p. 917. Roger-Viollet, Paris: p. 212. Smith College Library, Rare Book Room: p. 1872. Sterling Memorial Library, Yale University: p. 813. Courtesy of the University of New Mexico Press: p. 2288. Van Pelt Library, University of Pennsylvania, Special Collections: p. 1277. Collection of Mr. and Mrs. William Carlos Williams, Rutherford, NJ: p. 991.

Index